2020–2021
FORTY-THIRD EDITION

Illinois School Directory

A State Guide to K-12 Districts, Dioceses, and Schools...

Powered by MDR's ConnectED Cloud

Key Features In This Edition
- Charter Management Organization Index
- Facebook and Twitter Indicators
- Email Address Availability Highlighted
- Detailed School and District Listings
- Names and Job Titles of Key Personnel
- New Schools and Personnel Index

MDR
A Dun & Bradstreet Division

Copyright 2020 Market Data Retrieval | 6 Armstrong Road, Shelton, CT 06484

Copyright 2020 Market Data Retrieval, a D&B Company. All Rights Reserved. No information furnished hereby may be reproduced or transmitted in any form or by any means, electronic or mechanical, including photocopying and recording, or by any information storage or retrieval system, except as may be expressly permitted by MDR, 6 Armstrong Road, Shelton, CT 06484.

The information in this directory is licensed with the express understanding and agreement that the information will be solely for internal use and will not be used for the creation and/or updating of databases, electronic or otherwise, that are sold or provided to any third party without the express written permission of MDR.

51-Volume National Set   ISBN# 978-1-57953-640-4

Individual Bound State Editions

	ISSN#	ISBN#		ISSN#	ISBN#
Alabama	1077-7393	978-1-951295-52-3	Montana	1077-7652	978-1-57953-608-4
Alaska	1077-7407	978-1-57953-332-8	Nebraska	1077-7660	978-1-57953-609-1
Arizona	1077-7415	978-1-57953-343-4	Nevada	1077-7679	978-1-57953-610-7
Arkansas	1077-7423	978-1-57953-353-3	New Hampshire	1077-7687	978-1-57953-612-1
California	1077-7431	978-1-57953-355-7	New Jersey	1077-7695	978-1-57953-613-8
Colorado	1077-744X	978-1-57953-374-8	New Mexico	1077-7709	978-1-57953-614-5
Connecticut	1077-7458	978-1-57953-376-2	New York	1077-7717	978-1-57953-615-2
Delaware	1077-7466	978-1-57953-430-1	North Carolina	1077-7725	978-1-57953-616-9
District of Columbia	1077-7474	978-1-57953-484-4	North Dakota	1077-7733	978-1-57953-617-6
Florida	1077-7482	978-1-57953-538-4	Ohio	1077-7741	978-1-57953-618-3
Georgia	1077-7490	978-1-57953-592-6	Oklahoma	1077-775X	978-1-57953-619-0
Hawaii	1077-7504	978-1-57953-593-3	Oregon	1077-7768	978-1-57953-620-6
Idaho	1077-7512	978-1-57953-594-0	Pennsylvania	1077-7776	978-1-57953-621-3
Illinois	1077-7520	978-1-57953-595-7	Rhode Island	1077-7784	978-1-57953-622-0
Indiana	1077-7539	978-1-57953-596-4	South Carolina	1077-7792	978-1-57953-624-4
Iowa	1077-7547	978-1-57953-597-1	South Dakota	1077-7806	978-1-57953-626-8
Kansas	1077-7555	978-1-57953-598-8	Tennessee	1077-7814	978-1-57953-627-5
Kentucky	1077-7563	978-1-57953-599-5	Texas	1077-7822	978-1-57953-629-9
Louisiana	1077-7571	978-1-57953-600-8	Utah	1077-7830	978-1-57953-630-5
Maine	1077-758X	978-1-57953-601-5	Vermont	1077-7849	978-1-57953-632-9
Maryland	1077-7598	978-1-57953-602-2	Virginia	1077-7857	978-1-57953-633-6
Massachusetts	1077-7601	978-1-57953-603-9	Washington	1077-7865	978-1-57953-634-3
Michigan	1077-761X	978-1-57953-604-6	West Virginia	1077-7873	978-1-57953-635-0
Minnesota	1077-7628	978-1-57953-605-3	Wisconsin	1077-7881	978-1-57953-637-4
Mississippi	1077-7636	978-1-57953-606-0	Wyoming	1077-789X	978-1-57953-638-1
Missouri	1077-7644	978-1-57953-607-7	Sales Manager's Guide	2150-2021	978-1-57953-639-8

If you have any questions or comments concerning this directory, please write to MDR, 6 Armstrong Road, Shelton, CT 06484, or call us toll-free at 800-333-8802 or collect at 203-926-4800.

MDR's School Directory

TABLE OF CONTENTS

Sample Directory Listings iv
- A complete listing of codes, definitions and data elements used throughout this directory.

Directory Statistics (Yellow Section)

State Statistics A1
- An overview of state statistics showing the distribution of districts, schools and personnel by key indicators.

County Statistics B1
- A county-by-county census of districts and schools and their enrollments.

District Buying Power Index C1
- A complete listing of counties and districts ranked by the amount of money they spend on instructional materials.

New Public Schools and Key Personnel Index (Cream Section) NEW1
- A summary of new public schools that have opened for the current school year, plus Superintendents and Principals who are new to their institution.

District and School Listings (White Section) 1
- Complete information provided for each district and school in the state, organized alphabetically by county.
- Listings within each county are in the following order: County Centers and Schools, Public School Districts and Schools, Catholic Diocesan Offices and/or Schools, Other Private Schools and Regional Centers.

Directory Indices

District Index (Ivory Section) Q1
- A complete listing of districts in alphabetical order for each district type: Public School Districts, Catholic Dioceses, County Centers and Regional Centers.
- Includes number of schools, enrollment, county location and page number.

County Index (Tan Section) R1
- A complete alphabetical listing by county of Public School Districts, Catholic Dioceses, County Centers and Regional Centers.

Supervisory Union Index (Gold Section) S1
- Included for the states of Maine, Massachusetts, New Hampshire and Vermont, where several local school districts are administered by the same administrative personnel located at a Supervisory Union office. The index lists each Supervisory Union followed by their local school districts.

District Personnel Index (Gray Section) T1
- A complete listing, in last name sequence, of all district personnel.

Principal Index (Green Section) U1
- A complete listing, in last name sequence, of all school principals.

District and School Telephone Index (Blue Section) V1
- A complete listing of all districts and schools in the state with their telephone and PID numbers.

District URL Index (Salmon Section) W1
- A listing of districts that have URL addresses.

Charter Management Organization (CMO) Index (Orchid Section) CMO1
- An alphabetical listing, by state-CMO sequence, of Charter Management Organizations.
- Includes CMO number, PID, full address and phone number.

Directory Code Reference Guide located on the bottom of each page.

Sample Directory Listings

MDR's School Directories are your complete reference source, providing comprehensive data on public school districts and schools, Catholic and other independent schools, and regional and county centers in all 50 states and the District of Columbia. Every public school district and school entry in MDR's School Directories is updated each year through telephone interviews conducted with school district personnel. These interviews take place from July to September, capturing the most current school year data available. In addition, information obtained from state, district and school directories is used to verify information contained in MDR's School Directories.

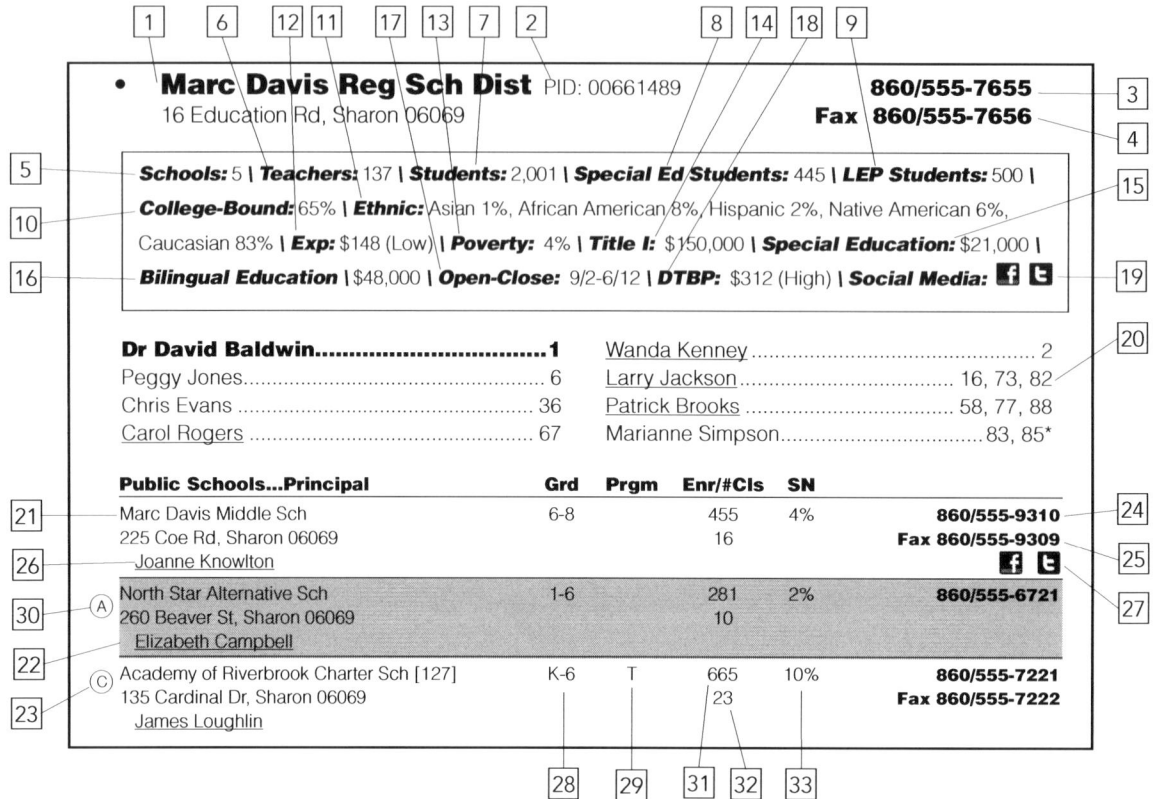

Each directory listing is uniformly organized to reflect the following data as applicable.

Definitions of Codes and Data:

DISTRICT DATA

1 District Name and Address
The physical location address for the superintendent's office is listed. MDR also maintains the mailing address, if different, for each district office. For this alternative mailing address, contact MDR directly at 800-333-8802.

2 District PID Number
Personal Identification Number of the district. Helps identify specific institutions when speaking to an MDR Representative or searching in Education MarketView.

3 Telephone Number
The telephone number of the district's central administration office.

4 Fax Number
The fax number of the district's central administration office. Please use the fax numbers in the directory appropriately.

> The FCC prohibits the use of a telephone facsimile machine to send unsolicited advertisements. If you need further clarification of the laws that exist, you can contact the FCC directly at 888-225-5322, or you can visit their website at http://www.fcc.gov.

5 Number of Schools
The number of schools reporting directly to the district. In the case of decentralized large districts (such as Chicago Public Schools), the number of schools reflects those reporting directly to the central school district in addition to those administered directly by each of the subdistrict offices.

6 Number of Teachers
The number of full-time equivalent teachers throughout the district as reported by the U.S. Department of Education.

7 District Enrollment
The projected number of students enrolled in the district for fall 2020.

8 Special Ed Students
The number of students having a written Individualized Education Plan (IEP) indicating their participation in a Special Education Program.

9 LEP Students
The number of Limited-English Proficient students being served in appropriate programs of language assistance (i.e., English as a second language, high-intensity language training, bilingual education).

10 College-Bound Students
The percentage of the district's 12th grade enrollment planning to attend two- or four-year colleges.

11 Student Ethnic Percentages
The student enrollment percentage by ethnic group: Asian, African American, Hispanic, Native American and Caucasian. This information is reported annually by the U.S. Department of Education. Due to rounding, the percentages may not add up to 100%.

12 District Expenditure
The district's expenditure per student for instructional materials. In addition to the actual dollar amount, a level of expenditure is provided as follows:
- High = $300+
- Med = $200-299
- Low = Under $200

13 Poverty Level
This census data reflects the percentage of school-age children in the district from families below the poverty line. Poverty levels are as follows:
- Low = 0-5%
- Med-Low = 6-15%
- Med-High = 16-29%
- High = 30%+

14 Title I
The district's Title I dollar allocation is for the 2019 fiscal year. Funding levels are as follows:
- Highest = $2.5 Million+
- High = $500,000-2.49 Million
- Medium = $150,000-499,999
- Low = Under $150,000

15 Special Education
The sum of federal and state dollars earmarked for special education programs in the district.

16 Bilingual Education
The sum of federal and state dollars earmarked for English Language Acquisition programs in the district.

17 District Opening/Closing Dates
The month and day of the official opening and closing dates of the school district.

18 District Tech Budget Per Pupil
The district's total IT technology budget dollars per pupil. DTBP levels are as follows:
- High = $100+
- Med = $80-99
- Low = $1-79

19 Social Media
The use of Facebook and/or Twitter for information communication, messaging and other content.

20 District-Level Administrators and Job Title Codes
The names of administrative staff with district-wide responsibilities are listed, followed by numeric codes representing their specific areas of responsibility. A full list of job title codes and their descriptions can be found on the bottom of the directory pages.

The names are listed, from left to right, in numeric job title sequence to facilitate identification of individuals responsible for specific administrative areas. In cases where an individual has multiple responsibilities, the job title with the lowest code number is used for sequencing.

An asterisk (*) denotes district administrators who maintain offices at one of the schools in the district rather than at the district office.

Superintendents who are new to the district are printed in **bold** type. Also see our index of new personnel on page NEW1.

An underscore of a district-level administrator indicates an email address at that institution in our database and in Education MarketView.

SCHOOL DATA

21 School Name and Address
The physical location address of the school is listed. MDR also maintains the mailing address, if different, for every school. For this alternative address, contact MDR directly at 800-333-8802.

22 New Schools
The listings of public schools opening for the first time during this school year are shaded for easy identification. Also see our index of new public schools on page NEW1.

23 Charter Management Organization (CMO)
Indicates the CMO number from the CMO Index to which this school reports.

24 Telephone Number
The telephone number of the school's central administration office. Note that in some cases a school district may require that all calls to schools must first go through a central switchboard to be routed to individual schools. In these cases, the central switchboard number is given for all schools affected.

25 Fax Number
The fax number of the school's administration office. Please use the fax numbers in the directory appropriately.

> The FCC prohibits the use of a telephone facsimile machine to send unsolicited advertisements. If you need further clarification of the laws that exist, you can contact the FCC directly at 888-225-5322, or you can visit their website at http://www.fcc.gov.

26 Principal Name
The name of the school principal. When a school has both an elementary and secondary principal, both names are given. The elementary principal is listed first, with the secondary principal listed below.

Principals who are new to their public school are printed in **bold** type. Also see our index of new personnel on page NEW1.

All principals printed with an underscore have an email address at that institution in our database and in Education MarketView.

27 Social Media
The use of Facebook and/or Twitter for information communication, messaging and other content.

28 School Grade Span/Voc, Special, Adult Schools
The lowest and highest grades taught in the school. Schools with dedicated programs in the areas of vocational, special and adult education are designated as Voc, Spec and Adult, respectively.

29 School Program Codes
In addition to the grades taught within the school, schools that have special curriculum programs are indicated with these codes following the school grade span.

- A = Alternative Program: Identifies traditional schools that also provide a special setting/curriculum for students who do not function well in traditional classroom settings.
- G = Adult Classes: Identifies schools that offer adult education classes.
- M = Magnet Program: Identifies traditional schools that also offer an enriched curricula in a special subject area to qualified students.
- T = Title I Schoolwide: Identifies public schools that have a Title I Schoolwide program, allowing greater spending flexibility.
- V = Career & Technical Education Programs: Identifies schools that offer Career & Technical Education programs.

30 Other School Types
Schools that are unique in the curriculum they offer or in the way they operate are indicated to the left of the school name.

- Ⓐ = Alternative School: Identifies schools that provide instruction exclusively for students who do not function well in traditional classroom settings.
- Ⓒ = Charter School: Public schools that have certain freedoms from state and local regulations and policies, having more administrative independence.
- Ⓜ = Magnet School: Identifies schools where all students are offered enriched curricula. Students qualify for admission by competitive exams.
- Ⓨ = Year-Round School: Schools that operate 12 months a year.

31 Student Enrollment
The projected number of students enrolled for fall 2020.

32 Number of Classrooms
The number of classrooms within a school. The number of classrooms prints below student enrollment when known.

33 Student Need
Percentage of students eligible for the free and reduced-price lunch program at the school.

Illinois

A Dun & Bradstreet Division

STATE STATISTICS

DISTRICT PERSONNEL BY JOB FUNCTION

Job Code	Job Description	Total	Under 2,500	Enrollment 2,500-9,000	10,000+
1	SUPERINTENDENT	1,002	676	145	23
2	BUS/FINANCE/PURCHASING	800	496	203	46
3	BUILDINGS AND GROUNDS	664	443	170	47
4	FOOD SERVICE	403	290	92	17
5	TRANSPORTATION	414	272	112	25
6	ATHLETIC	476	385	78	12
7	HEALTH SERVICES	217	134	66	12
8	CURRIC/INSTRUCT K-12	239	129	63	33
9	CURRIC/INSTRUCT ELEM	305	185	91	29
10	CURRIC/INSTRUCT SEC	155	82	50	23
11	FEDERAL PROGRAM	731	558	123	18
12	TITLE I	226	184	36	6
13	TITLE V	29	17	11	1
15	ASST SUPERINTENDENT	524	105	239	79
16	INSTRUCTIONAL MEDIA SERVICES	388	292	86	6
17	CHIEF OPERATIONS OFFICER	29	10	14	4
18	CHIEF ACADEMIC OFFICER	27	8	12	5
19	CHIEF FINANCIAL OFFICER	83	40	35	7
20	ART K-12	8	0	3	4
21	ART ELEM	5	1	1	3
22	ART SEC	5	1	4	0
23	MUSIC K-12	14	3	5	5
24	MUSIC ELEM	8	0	5	3
25	MUSIC SEC	8	1	7	0
26	BUSINESS EDUCATION	6	4	1	0
27	CAREER & TECH ED	88	42	32	9
28	TECHNOLOGY EDUCATION	14	4	8	0
29	FAMILY/CONSUMER SCIENCE	7	4	3	0
30	ADULT EDUCATION	18	4	9	2
31	CAREER/SCH-TO-WORK K-12	56	41	10	2
32	CAREER/SCH-TO-WORK ELEM	0	0	0	0
33	CAREER/SCH-TO-WORK SEC	18	15	3	0
34	EARLY CHILDHOOD ED	137	60	45	17
35	HEALTH/PHYS EDUCATION	72	42	22	7
36	GUIDANCE SERVICES K-12	96	78	11	6
37	GUIDANCE SERVICES ELEM	36	28	8	0
38	GUIDANCE SERVICES SEC	79	69	10	0
39	SOCIAL STUDIES K-12	7	0	2	4
40	SOCIAL STUDIES ELEM	5	0	3	2
41	SOCIAL STUDIES SEC	8	3	3	2
42	SCIENCE K-12	6	0	2	4
43	SCIENCE ELEM	13	5	4	4
44	SCIENCE SEC	8	1	5	2
45	MATH K-12	8	0	2	5
46	MATH ELEM	16	4	8	4
47	MATH SEC	8	1	6	1
48	ENGLISH/LANG ARTS K-12	7	2	3	2
49	ENGLISH/LANG ARTS ELEM	10	1	7	2
50	ENGLISH/LANG ARTS SEC	9	2	6	1
51	READING K-12	13	6	6	1
52	READING ELEM	8	5	0	3
53	READING SEC	3	1	2	0
54	REMEDIAL READING K-12	18	15	3	0
55	REMEDIAL READING ELEM	6	5	0	1
56	REMEDIAL READING SEC	3	3	0	0
57	BILINGUAL/ELL	337	200	112	23
58	SPECIAL EDUCATION K-12	274	160	64	32
59	SPECIAL EDUCATION ELEM	235	157	68	9
60	SPECIAL EDUCATION SEC	92	49	37	6
61	FOREIGN/WORLD LANG K-12	6	1	2	3
62	FOREIGN/WORLD LANG ELEM	2	0	2	0
63	FOREIGN/WORLD LANG SEC	6	2	4	0
64	RELIGIOUS EDUCATION K-12	3	0	0	0
65	RELIGIOUS EDUCATION ELEM	0	0	0	0
66	RELIGIOUS EDUCATION SEC	0	0	0	0
67	SCHOOL BOARD PRESIDENT	853	679	145	23
68	TEACHER PERSONNEL	273	65	150	40
69	ACADEMIC ASSESSMENT	382	261	92	23
70	RESEARCH/DEVELOPMENT	22	4	12	5
71	PUBLIC INFORMATION	146	40	73	26
72	SUMMER SCHOOL	37	16	18	3
73	INSTRUCTIONAL TECH	776	565	154	32
74	INSERVICE TRAINING	117	37	48	17
75	MARKETING/DISTRIBUTIVE	7	2	4	0
76	INFO SYSTEMS	292	150	102	27
77	PSYCHOLOGICAL ASSESSMENT	76	41	28	6
78	AFFIRMATIVE ACTION	31	3	19	9
79	STUDENT PERSONNEL	262	112	113	35
80	DRIVER ED/SAFETY	30	12	14	4
81	GIFTED/TALENTED	41	14	16	9
82	VIDEO SERVICES	90	71	17	2
83	SUBSTANCE ABUSE PREVENTION	417	349	60	6
84	ERATE	192	138	41	11
85	AIDS EDUCATION	95	80	14	1
88	ALTERNATIVE/AT RISK	252	174	60	11
89	MULTI-CULTURAL CURRICULUM	7	0	4	2
90	SOCIAL WORK	78	39	33	6
91	SAFETY/SECURITY	155	57	76	20
92	MAGNET SCHOOL	4	2	1	0
93	PARENTAL INVOLVEMENT	34	16	8	8
95	TECH PREP PROGRAM	27	7	19	0
97	CHIEF INFORMATION OFFICER	13	4	5	3
98	CHIEF TECHNOLOGY OFFICER	40	21	16	2
270	CHARACTER EDUCATION	99	84	13	2
271	MIGRANT EDUCATION	71	48	17	3
273	TEACHER MENTOR	152	96	49	6
274	BEFORE/AFTER SCH	71	52	15	4
275	RESPONSE TO INTERVENTION	155	108	35	6
277	REMEDIAL MATH K-12	5	2	2	1
280	LITERACY COACH	75	33	31	10
285	STEM	102	60	35	6
286	DIGITAL LEARNING	181	127	44	9
288	COMMON CORE STANDARDS	315	223	80	12
294	ACCOUNTABILITY	82	34	31	15
295	NETWORK SYSTEM	378	217	125	28
296	TITLE II PROGRAMS	187	121	61	5
297	WEBMASTER	95	50	37	6
298	GRANT WRITER/PTNRSHIPS	206	117	70	14
750	CHIEF INNOVATION OFFICER	4	0	2	1
751	CHIEF OF STAFF	13	4	6	2
752	SOCIAL EMOTIONAL LEARNING	89	55	25	8

DISTRICTS BY EXPENDITURE AND ENROLLMENT

Expenditure	Total	Under 2500	2500-9999	10,000+
Low (Under $200)	233	187	40	6
Medium ($200 - 299)	311	251	52	8
High ($300+)	306	241	55	10
TOTAL DISTRICTS	850	679	147	24

SCHOOLS BY LEVEL AND TYPE

School Level	Total	Public	Private	Catholic
Elementary	3,098	2,462	287	349
Middle/Junior	608	599	7	2
Senior	821	717	46	58
K-12 (Combined)	247	102	143	2
Adult/Special/Voc Ed	195	105	90	0
TOTAL SCHOOLS	4,969	3,985	573	411

Illinois School Directory — COUNTY STATISTICS

School Year 2020-2021

COUNTY		DISTRICTS	SCHOOLS	ELEM ENROLL[1]	MIDDLE/JHS ENROLL[2]	SENIOR ENROLL[3]	TOTAL ENROLL[4]	% OF STATE	K-5[5]	K-6	K-8	SCHOOLS BY GRADE SPAN 5-8[6]	7-9[7]	7-12[8]	K-12[9]	OTHER[10]
ADAMS	PUBLIC	5	22	4,285	2,000	2,625	9,427		9	1	0	0	0	5	2	2
	NONPUBLIC	0	9	1,335	0	472	1,807		0	0	5	3	0	1	1	2
	TOTAL	5	31	5,620	2,000	3,097	11,234	0.5	9	1	5	3	0	6	3	4
ALEXANDER	PUBLIC	2	4	470	0	241	715		0	1	0	0	0	1	1	1
	NONPUBLIC	0	1	8	0	4	12		0	0	0	0	0	0	1	0
	TOTAL	2	5	478	0	245	727		0	1	0	0	0	1	2	1
BOND	PUBLIC	2	9	1,219	392	660	2,150		3	0	2	2	0	2	0	0
	NONPUBLIC	0	0	0	0	0	0		0	0	0	0	0	0	0	0
	TOTAL	2	9	1,219	392	660	2,150	0.1	3	0	2	2	0	2	0	0
BOONE	PUBLIC	2	16	4,239	2,078	3,126	10,100		8	1	1	2	1	3	0	0
	NONPUBLIC	0	2	375	0	0	375		0	0	2	0	0	0	0	0
	TOTAL	2	18	4,614	2,078	3,126	10,475	0.5	8	1	3	2	1	3	0	0
BROWN	PUBLIC	1	3	312	196	201	750		1	0	0	1	0	1	0	0
	NONPUBLIC	0	1	80	0	0	80		0	0	1	0	0	0	0	0
	TOTAL	1	4	392	196	201	830		1	0	1	1	0	1	0	0
BUREAU	PUBLIC	12	20	2,857	553	1,514	4,913		6	0	6	2	0	5	1	0
	NONPUBLIC	0	0	0	0	0	0		0	0	0	0	0	0	0	0
	TOTAL	12	20	2,857	553	1,514	4,913	0.2	6	0	6	2	0	5	1	0
CALHOUN	PUBLIC	2	4	401	0	205	590		0	1	1	0	0	2	0	0
	NONPUBLIC	0	2	113	0	0	113		0	0	2	0	0	0	0	0
	TOTAL	2	6	514	0	205	703		0	1	3	0	0	2	0	0
CARROLL	PUBLIC	3	7	963	674	589	2,154		2	0	0	2	0	1	2	0
	NONPUBLIC	0	0	0	0	0	0		0	0	0	0	0	0	0	0
	TOTAL	3	7	963	674	589	2,154	0.1	2	0	0	2	0	1	2	0
CASS	PUBLIC	3	6	1,071	571	662	2,299		3	0	0	1	0	0	3	0
	NONPUBLIC	0	2	173	0	0	173		0	1	1	0	0	0	0	0
	TOTAL	3	8	1,244	571	662	2,472	0.1	3	1	1	1	0	0	3	0
CHAMPAIGN	PUBLIC	14	57	12,547	5,145	6,966	24,613		30	2	4	8	1	11	0	1
	NONPUBLIC	0	19	2,325	0	1,004	3,329		2	0	7	1	0	2	4	3
	TOTAL	14	76	14,872	5,145	7,970	27,942	1.3	32	2	11	9	1	13	4	4
CHRISTIAN	PUBLIC	6	18	2,392	1,293	1,651	5,356		7	1	0	3	0	4	0	0
	NONPUBLIC	0	5	531	0	26	557		0	1	2	0	0	0	2	0
	TOTAL	6	23	2,923	1,293	1,677	5,913	0.3	7	2	2	3	0	4	2	0

[1] **Elem Enroll** is the school by school total of enrollments in K-4, K-5, K-6, K-8 schools, elementary and middle/JHS students in K-12 schools and students in special ed schools. Public enrollments include public and county-operated schools.
[2] **Middle/JHS Enroll** is the school by school total of enrollments in 5-8 and 7-9 public schools. Public enrollments include public and county-operated schools. Private middle/JHS enrollments are included in Senior Enroll.
[3] **Senior Enroll** is the school by school total of enrollments in 7-12 and 9-12 schools, the secondary students in K-12 schools, students in vocational ed schools. Public enrollments include public and county-operated schools. For private schools, Senior Enroll includes middle/JHS enrollment plus senior enrollment.
[4] **Public Total Enroll** columns are not the sum of school building enrollments. They are projected district-wide Fall enrollments provided to MDR by each school district office, plus county-operated school enrollments.
[5] K-5 includes pre-kindergarten, kindergarten, K-3, K-4, K-5 schools.
[6] 5-8 includes schools with low grades of 4, 5, 6 and high grades of 7, 8, 9 (e.g., 4-8, 5-8, 6-8, 6-9).
[7] 7-9 includes schools with low grades of 7, 8 and high grades of 7, 8, 9 (e.g., 7-7, 7-8, 7-9, 8-9).
[8] 7-12 includes 7-12, 8-12, 9-12, 10-12, etc.
[9] K-12 includes schools with both elementary and secondary grades.
[10] **Other** includes special ed, vocational ed and adult schools.

***Public State Totals** for all columns can exceed the sum of the counties because state totals include state-operated schools and their enrollments.

COUNTY STATISTICS — Market Data Retrieval

COUNTY		DISTRICTS	SCHOOLS	ELEM ENROLL[1]	MIDDLE/JHS ENROLL[2]	SENIOR ENROLL[3]	TOTAL ENROLL[4]	% OF STATE	K-5[5]	K-6	K-8	5-8[6]	7-9[7]	7-12[8]	K-12[9]	OTHER[10]
CLARK	PUBLIC	3	8	1,465	201	836	2,525		1	3	0	0	1	3	0	0
	NONPUBLIC	0	0	0	0	0	0		0	0	0	0	0	0	0	0
	TOTAL	3	8	1,465	201	836	2,525	0.1	1	3	0	0	1	3	0	0
CLAY	PUBLIC	3	8	1,377	383	594	2,364		2	0	1	2	0	3	0	0
	NONPUBLIC	0	0	0	0	0	0		0	0	0	0	0	0	0	0
	TOTAL	3	8	1,377	383	594	2,364	0.1	2	0	1	2	0	3	0	0
CLINTON	PUBLIC	12	18	3,049	816	1,303	5,201		5	0	8	2	0	3	0	0
	NONPUBLIC	0	3	504	0	514	1,018		0	0	2	0	0	1	0	0
	TOTAL	12	21	3,553	816	1,817	6,219	0.3	5	0	10	2	0	4	0	0
COLES	PUBLIC	3	16	3,188	1,127	1,841	5,932		6	1	1	1	1	3	0	3
	NONPUBLIC	0	1	223	0	0	223		0	0	1	0	0	0	0	0
	TOTAL	3	17	3,411	1,127	1,841	6,155	0.3	6	1	2	1	1	3	0	3
COOK	PUBLIC	144	1,322	405,168	81,137	223,281	730,139		337	106	452	117	26	233	12	39
	NONPUBLIC	0	406	83,777	0	31,488	117,349		13	5	255	6	1	49	34	43
	TOTAL	144	1,728	488,945	81,137	254,769	847,438	38.6	350	111	707	123	27	282	46	82
CRAWFORD	PUBLIC	4	10	1,657	427	821	2,830		3	0	2	1	0	3	1	0
	NONPUBLIC	0	1	120	0	0	120		0	0	1	0	0	0	0	0
	TOTAL	4	11	1,777	427	821	3,000	0.1	3	0	3	1	0	3	1	0
CUMBERLAND	PUBLIC	2	5	663	321	615	1,535		2	0	0	1	0	2	0	0
	NONPUBLIC	0	0	0	0	0	0		0	0	0	0	0	0	0	0
	TOTAL	2	5	663	321	615	1,535	0.1	2	0	0	1	0	2	0	0
DE KALB	PUBLIC	8	41	7,730	3,705	5,145	16,786		23	0	1	8	0	8	0	1
	NONPUBLIC	0	5	888	0	21	909		0	0	3	0	0	0	1	1
	TOTAL	8	46	8,618	3,705	5,166	17,695	0.8	23	0	4	8	0	8	1	2
DEWITT	PUBLIC	2	8	1,123	605	797	2,500		4	0	0	2	0	2	0	0
	NONPUBLIC	0	0	0	0	0	0		0	0	0	0	0	0	0	0
	TOTAL	2	8	1,123	605	797	2,500	0.1	4	0	0	2	0	2	0	0
DOUGLAS	PUBLIC	4	12	1,960	406	1,134	3,508		1	2	3	1	1	4	0	0
	NONPUBLIC	0	1	86	0	34	120		0	0	0	0	0	0	1	0
	TOTAL	4	13	2,046	406	1,168	3,628	0.2	1	2	3	1	1	4	1	0
DU PAGE	PUBLIC	42	250	68,177	33,610	50,197	151,377		148	18	1	50	3	26	1	3
	NONPUBLIC	0	75	16,111	0	5,495	21,606		2	2	42	0	0	11	9	9
	TOTAL	42	325	84,288	33,610	55,692	172,983	7.9	150	20	43	50	3	37	10	12
EDGAR	PUBLIC	5	11	1,658	350	831	2,909		3	0	1	2	0	2	2	0
	NONPUBLIC	0	0	0	0	0	0		0	0	0	0	0	0	0	1
	TOTAL	5	11	1,658	350	831	2,909	0.1	3	0	1	2	0	2	2	1

[1] **Elem Enroll** is the school by school total of enrollments in K-4, K-5, K-6, K-8 schools, elementary and middle/JHS students in K-12 schools and students in special ed schools. Public enrollments include public and county-operated schools.

[2] **Middle/JHS Enroll** is the school by school total of the schools in 5-8 and 7-9 public schools. Public enrollments include public and county-operated schools. Private middle/JHS enrollments are included in Senior Enroll.

[3] **Senior Enroll** is the school by school total of enrollments in 7-12 and 9-12 schools, the secondary students in K-12 schools and students in vocational ed schools. Public enrollments include public and county-operated schools. For private schools, Senior Enroll includes middle/JHS enrollment plus senior enrollment.

[4] **Public Total Enroll** columns are not the sum of school building enrollments. They are projected district-wide Fall enrollments provided to MDR by each school district office, plus county-operated school enrollments.

[5] **K-5** includes pre-kindergarten, kindergarten, K-3, K-4, K-5 schools.
[6] **5-8** includes schools with low grades of 4, 5, 6 and high grades of 7, 8, 9 (e.g., 4-8, 5-8, 6-8, 6-9).
[7] **7-9** includes schools with low grades of 7, 8 and high grades of 7, 8, 9 (e.g., 7-7, 7-8, 7-9, 8-9).
[8] **7-12** includes 7-12, 8-12, 9-12, 10-12, etc.
[9] **K-12** includes schools with both elementary and secondary grades.
[10] **Other** includes special ed, vocational ed and adult schools.

***Public State Totals** for all columns can exceed the sum of the counties because state totals include state-operated schools and their enrollments.

School Year 2020-2021

Illinois School Directory — COUNTY STATISTICS

COUNTY		DISTRICTS	SCHOOLS	ELEM ENROLL[1]	MIDDLE/JHS ENROLL[2]	SENIOR ENROLL[3]	TOTAL ENROLL[4]	% OF STATE	K-5[5]	K-6	K-8	5-8[6]	7-9[7]	7-12[8]	K-12[9]	OTHER[10]
EDWARDS	PUBLIC	1	3	598	0	298	896		0	0	2	0	0	1	0	0
	NONPUBLIC	0	0	0	0	0	0		0	0	0	0	0	0	0	0
	TOTAL	1	3	598	0	298	896		0	0	2	0	0	1	0	0
EFFINGHAM	PUBLIC	5	15	2,679	815	1,570	5,013		4	2	1	1	0	5	1	1
	NONPUBLIC	0	4	719	0	214	933		0	0	3	0	1	1	0	0
	TOTAL	5	19	3,398	815	1,784	5,946	0.3	4	2	4	1	1	6	1	1
FAYETTE	PUBLIC	4	11	1,158	580	759	2,800		2	2	0	1	0	4	1	0
	NONPUBLIC	0	2	142	0	0	142		0	0	2	0	0	0	0	1
	TOTAL	4	13	1,300	580	759	2,942	0.1	2	2	2	1	0	4	1	1
FORD	PUBLIC	2	6	1,055	539	763	2,300		2	2	0	2	0	2	0	0
	NONPUBLIC	0	0	0	0	0	0		0	0	0	0	0	0	0	0
	TOTAL	2	6	1,055	539	763	2,300	0.1	2	2	0	2	0	2	0	0
FRANKLIN	PUBLIC	9	18	3,451	909	1,738	5,708		3	1	5	2	1	6	1	0
	NONPUBLIC	0	2	69	0	3	72		0	0	1	0	0	0	0	0
	TOTAL	9	20	3,520	909	1,741	5,780	0.3	3	1	6	2	1	6	1	0
FULTON	PUBLIC	6	17	2,039	1,039	1,426	4,552		6	2	2	2	0	4	3	0
	NONPUBLIC	0	1	20	0	8	28		0	0	0	0	0	0	1	0
	TOTAL	6	18	2,059	1,039	1,434	4,580	0.2	6	2	2	2	0	4	4	0
GALLATIN	PUBLIC	1	1	536	0	214	750		0	0	0	0	0	0	1	0
	NONPUBLIC	0	1	28	0	11	39		0	0	0	0	0	0	1	0
	TOTAL	1	2	564	0	225	789	0.1	0	0	0	0	0	0	2	0
GREENE	PUBLIC	3	6	1,141	0	703	1,919		0	1	2	0	0	3	0	0
	NONPUBLIC	0	1	130	0	0	130		0	0	1	0	0	0	0	0
	TOTAL	3	7	1,271	0	703	2,049	0.1	0	1	3	0	0	3	0	0
GRUNDY	PUBLIC	11	24	7,026	1,654	1,775	10,462		9	1	6	2	1	3	1	0
	NONPUBLIC	0	1	218	0	0	218		0	0	1	0	0	0	0	1
	TOTAL	11	25	7,244	1,654	1,775	10,680	0.5	9	1	7	2	1	3	1	1
HAMILTON	PUBLIC	1	4	644	0	555	1,199		1	2	0	0	0	1	0	0
	NONPUBLIC	0	0	0	0	0	0		0	0	0	0	0	0	0	0
	TOTAL	1	4	644	0	555	1,199	0.1	1	2	0	0	0	1	0	0
HANCOCK	PUBLIC	8	12	1,753	176	1,001	2,890		1	3	3	1	0	4	0	0
	NONPUBLIC	0	1	61	0	0	61		0	1	0	0	0	0	0	0
	TOTAL	8	13	1,814	176	1,001	2,951	0.1	1	4	3	1	0	4	0	0
HARDIN	PUBLIC	1	2	253	54	72	500		1	0	0	0	0	0	1	0
	NONPUBLIC	0	0	0	0	0	0		0	0	0	0	0	0	0	0
	TOTAL	1	2	253	54	72	500		1	0	0	0	0	0	1	0

[1] **Elem Enroll** is the school by school total of enrollments in K-4, K-5, K-6, K-8 schools, elementary and middle/JHS students in K-12 schools and students in special ed schools. Public enrollments include public and county-operated schools.
[2] **Middle/JHS Enroll** is the school by school total of enrollments in 5-8 and 7-9 public schools. Public enrollments include public and county-operated schools. Private middle/JHS enrollments are included in Senior Enroll.
[3] **Senior Enroll** is the school by school total of enrollments in 7-12 and 9-12 schools, the secondary students in K-12 schools and students in vocational ed schools. Public enrollments include public and county-operated schools. For private schools, Senior Enroll includes middle/JHS enrollment plus senior enrollment.
[4] **Public Total Enroll** columns are not the sum of school building enrollments. They are projected district-wide Fall enrollments provided to MDR by each school district office, plus county-operated school enrollments.
[5] **K-5** includes pre-kindergarten, kindergarten, K-3, K-4, K-5 schools.
[6] **5-8** includes schools with low grades of 4, 5, 6 and high grades of 7, 8, 9 (e.g., 4-8, 5-8, 6-8, 6-9).
[7] **7-9** includes schools with low grades of 7, 8 and high grades of 7, 8, 9 (e.g., 7-7, 7-8, 7-9, 8-9).
[8] **7-12** includes 7-12, 8-12, 9-12, 10-12, etc.
[9] **K-12** includes schools with both elementary and secondary grades.
[10] **Other** includes special ed, vocational ed and adult schools.
Public State Totals for all columns can exceed the sum of the counties because state totals include state-operated schools and their enrollments.

COUNTY STATISTICS — Market Data Retrieval

COUNTY		DISTRICTS	SCHOOLS	ELEM ENROLL[1]	MIDDLE/JHS ENROLL[2]	SENIOR ENROLL[3]	TOTAL ENROLL[4]	% OF STATE	K-5[5]	K-6	K-8	5-8[6]	7-9[7]	7-12[8]	K-12[9]	OTHER[10]
HENDERSON	PUBLIC	1	3	326	152	232	820		1	0	0	1	0	1	0	0
	NONPUBLIC	0	0	0	0	0	0		0	0	0	0	0	0	0	0
	TOTAL	1	3	326	152	232	820		1	0	0	1	0	1	0	0
HENRY	PUBLIC	9	25	4,054	1,825	2,352	7,642		8	3	3	3	0	6	2	0
	NONPUBLIC	0	2	216	0	0	216		0	1	1	0	0	0	0	0
	TOTAL	9	27	4,270	1,825	2,352	7,858	0.4	8	4	4	3	0	6	2	0
IROQUOIS	PUBLIC	7	21	1,907	822	1,302	4,427		8	0	2	3	0	4	3	1
	NONPUBLIC	0	3	226	0	13	239		0	0	2	0	0	1	0	0
	TOTAL	7	24	2,133	822	1,315	4,666	0.2	8	0	4	3	0	5	3	1
JACKSON	PUBLIC	8	20	3,594	1,181	2,013	6,698		8	0	3	4	0	4	0	1
	NONPUBLIC	0	6	441	0	43	484		0	0	3	1	0	0	1	1
	TOTAL	8	26	4,035	1,181	2,056	7,182	0.3	8	0	6	5	0	4	1	2
JASPER	PUBLIC	1	4	645	180	453	1,278		1	1	0	0	1	1	0	0
	NONPUBLIC	0	1	135	0	0	135		0	0	1	0	0	0	0	0
	TOTAL	1	5	780	180	453	1,413	0.1	1	1	1	0	1	1	0	0
JEFFERSON	PUBLIC	14	20	3,734	525	1,644	5,840		4	0	10	2	0	3	1	0
	NONPUBLIC	0	4	216	0	17	233		0	0	2	0	0	0	2	0
	TOTAL	14	24	3,950	525	1,661	6,073	0.3	4	0	12	2	0	3	3	0
JERSEY	PUBLIC	1	5	1,046	519	996	2,647		3	0	0	1	0	1	0	0
	NONPUBLIC	0	1	452	0	0	452		0	0	1	0	0	0	0	0
	TOTAL	1	6	1,498	519	996	3,099	0.1	3	0	1	1	0	1	0	0
JO DAVIESS	PUBLIC	6	17	1,480	684	1,051	3,270		5	1	0	4	0	5	1	1
	NONPUBLIC	0	1	51	0	0	51		0	0	1	0	0	0	0	0
	TOTAL	6	18	1,531	684	1,051	3,321	0.2	5	1	1	4	0	5	1	1
JOHNSON	PUBLIC	6	6	1,194	0	521	1,715		0	0	4	0	0	1	1	0
	NONPUBLIC	0	0	0	0	0	0		0	0	0	0	0	0	0	0
	TOTAL	6	6	1,194	0	521	1,715	0.1	0	0	4	0	0	1	1	0
KANE	PUBLIC	8	145	46,606	19,199	30,687	96,738		61	40	1	14	9	15	2	3
	NONPUBLIC	0	43	7,375	0	2,578	9,953		2	1	24	0	0	3	10	3
	TOTAL	8	188	53,981	19,199	33,265	106,691	4.9	63	41	25	14	9	18	12	6
KANKAKEE	PUBLIC	12	40	8,868	3,344	5,279	17,786		15	3	4	5	2	7	2	2
	NONPUBLIC	0	9	1,160	0	595	1,755		0	2	2	0	0	1	2	2
	TOTAL	12	49	10,028	3,344	5,874	19,541	0.9	15	5	6	5	2	8	4	4
KENDALL	PUBLIC	6	40	12,983	5,759	8,044	26,365		20	5	1	6	2	6	0	0
	NONPUBLIC	0	5	1,058	0	91	1,149		0	0	4	0	0	0	1	0
	TOTAL	6	45	14,041	5,759	8,135	27,514	1.3	20	5	5	6	2	6	1	0

[1] **Elem Enroll** is the school by school total of enrollments in K-4, K-5, K-6, K-8 schools, elementary and middle/JHS students in K-12 schools and students in special ed schools. Public enrollments include public and county-operated schools.
[2] **Middle/JHS Enroll** is the school by school total of enrollments in 5-8 and 7-9 public schools. Public enrollments include public and county-operated schools. Private middle/JHS enrollments are included in Senior Enroll.
[3] **Senior Enroll** is the school by school total of enrollments in 7-12 and 9-12 schools, the secondary students in K-12 schools and students in vocational ed schools. Public enrollments include public and county-operated schools. For private schools, Senior Enroll includes middle/JHS enrollment plus senior enrollment.
[4] **Public Total Enroll** columns are not the sum of school building enrollments. They are projected district-wide Fall enrollments provided to MDR by each school district office, plus county-operated school enrollments.
[5] **K-5** includes pre-kindergarten, kindergarten, K-3, K-4, K-5 schools.
[6] **5-8** includes schools with low grades of 4, 5, 6 and high grades of 7, 8, 9 (e.g., 4-8, 5-8, 6-8, 6-9).
[7] **7-9** includes schools with low grades of 7, 8 and high grades of 7, 8, 9 (e.g., 7-7, 7-8, 7-9, 8-9).
[8] **7-12** includes 7-12, 8-12, 9-12, 10-12, etc.
[9] **K-12** includes schools with both elementary and secondary grades.
[10] **Other** includes special ed, vocational and adult schools.
Public State Totals for all columns can exceed the sum of the counties because state totals include state-operated schools and their enrollments.

Illinois School Directory — COUNTY STATISTICS

COUNTY		DISTRICTS	SCHOOLS	ELEM ENROLL[1]	MIDDLE/JHS ENROLL[2]	SENIOR ENROLL[3]	TOTAL ENROLL[4]	% OF STATE	K-5[5]	K-6	K-8	5-8[6]	7-9[7]	7-12[8]	K-12[9]	OTHER[10]
KNOX	PUBLIC	5	19	3,182	1,018	2,348	7,333		7	2	0	2	1	5	2	0
	NONPUBLIC	0	2	513	0	55	568		0	0	1	2	1	0	1	0
	TOTAL	5	21	3,695	1,018	2,403	7,901	0.4	7	2	1	2	1	5	3	0
LA SALLE	PUBLIC	26	44	7,778	2,864	4,878	15,573		13	1	11	7	1	6	3	2
	NONPUBLIC	0	11	1,208	0	548	1,756		0	0	7	0	0	2	1	1
	TOTAL	26	55	8,986	2,864	5,426	17,329	0.8	13	1	18	7	1	8	4	3
LAKE	PUBLIC	45	205	59,622	28,361	44,008	134,636		113	11	8	38	4	25	1	5
	NONPUBLIC	0	48	7,908	0	2,945	10,853		3	5	24	0	0	6	8	2
	TOTAL	45	253	67,530	28,361	46,953	145,489	6.6	116	16	32	38	4	31	9	7
LAWRENCE	PUBLIC	2	6	1,118	259	728	2,102		2	1	0	1	0	2	0	0
	NONPUBLIC	0	0	0	0	0	0		0	0	0	0	0	0	0	0
	TOTAL	2	6	1,118	259	728	2,102	0.1	2	1	0	1	0	2	0	0
LEE	PUBLIC	5	12	2,045	844	1,239	3,883		4	1	2	2	0	3	0	0
	NONPUBLIC	0	4	370	0	122	492		0	0	2	0	0	1	0	1
	TOTAL	5	16	2,415	844	1,361	4,375	0.2	4	1	4	2	0	4	0	1
LIVINGSTON	PUBLIC	12	25	3,242	817	1,715	6,402		7	1	6	2	0	6	1	1
	NONPUBLIC	0	6	404	0	23	427		0	0	4	0	1	1	0	0
	TOTAL	12	31	3,646	817	1,738	6,829	0.3	7	1	10	2	1	7	2	1
LOGAN	PUBLIC	7	13	1,807	426	1,028	3,351		5	0	4	1	0	2	1	0
	NONPUBLIC	0	3	333	0	0	333		0	0	3	0	0	0	0	0
	TOTAL	7	16	2,140	426	1,028	3,684	0.2	5	0	7	1	0	2	1	0
MACON	PUBLIC	7	43	8,810	1,807	4,324	16,288		9	10	4	5	2	10	1	2
	NONPUBLIC	0	6	1,117	0	455	1,572		0	0	3	0	0	1	2	0
	TOTAL	7	49	9,927	1,807	4,779	17,860	0.8	9	10	7	5	2	11	3	2
MACOUPIN	PUBLIC	8	24	4,524	1,226	2,540	7,708		6	2	4	3	1	8	0	0
	NONPUBLIC	0	1	140	0	0	140		0	0	1	0	0	0	0	0
	TOTAL	8	25	4,664	1,226	2,540	7,848	0.4	6	2	5	3	1	8	0	0
MADISON	PUBLIC	13	82	19,691	8,091	12,149	38,665		49	2	1	9	2	12	2	5
	NONPUBLIC	0	36	5,129	0	710	5,839		1	1	20	0	0	3	9	2
	TOTAL	13	118	24,820	8,091	12,859	44,504	2.0	50	3	21	9	2	15	11	7
MARION	PUBLIC	13	21	3,103	1,226	2,085	6,638		5	1	6	3	0	5	1	0
	NONPUBLIC	0	4	343	0	123	466		0	0	3	0	0	1	0	0
	TOTAL	13	25	3,446	1,226	2,208	7,104	0.3	5	1	9	3	0	6	1	0
MARSHALL	PUBLIC	2	5	674	212	349	1,300		1	1	0	1	0	2	0	0
	NONPUBLIC	0	0	0	0	0	0		0	0	0	0	0	0	0	0
	TOTAL	2	5	674	212	349	1,300	0.1	1	1	1	1	0	2	0	0

[1] **Elem Enroll** is the school by school total of enrollments in K-4, K-5, K-6, K-8 schools, elementary and middle/JHS students in K-12 schools and students in special ed schools. Public enrollments include public and county-operated schools.

[2] **Middle/JHS Enroll** is the school by school total of enrollments in 5-8 and 7-9 public schools. Public enrollments include public and county-operated schools. Private middle/JHS enrollments are included in Senior Enroll.

[3] **Senior Enroll** is the school by school total of enrollments in 7-12 and 9-12 schools, the secondary students in K-12 schools and students in vocational ed schools. Public enrollments include public and county-operated schools. For private schools, Senior Enroll includes middle/JHS enrollment plus senior enrollment.

[4] **Public Total Enroll** columns are not the sum of school building enrollments. They are projected district-wide Fall enrollments provided to MDR by each school district office, plus county-operated school enrollments.

[5] **K-5** includes pre-kindergarten, kindergarten, K-3, K-4, K-5 schools.

[6] **5-8** includes schools with low grades of 4, 5, 6 and high grades of 7, 8, 9 (e.g., 4-8, 5-8, 6-9).

[7] **7-9** includes schools with low grades of 7, 8 and high grades of 7, 8, 9 (e.g., 7-7, 7-8, 7-9, 8-9).

[8] **7-12** includes 7-12, 8-12, 9-12, 10-12, etc.

[9] **K-12** includes schools with both elementary and secondary grades.

[10] **Other** includes special ed, vocational and adult schools.

*****Public State Totals** for all columns can exceed the sum of the counties because state totals include state-operated schools and their enrollments.

School Year 2020-2021 — 800-333-8802 — IL—B5

COUNTY STATISTICS — Market Data Retrieval

COUNTY		DISTRICTS	SCHOOLS	ELEM ENROLL[1]	MIDDLE/JHS ENROLL[2]	SENIOR ENROLL[3]	TOTAL ENROLL[4]	% OF STATE	K-5[5]	K-6	K-8	5-8[6]	7-9[7]	7-12[8]	K-12[9]	OTHER[10]
MASON	PUBLIC	3	10	1,053	641	764	2,563		4	0	0	3	0	3	0	0
	NONPUBLIC	0	0	0	0	0	0		0	0	0	0	0	0	0	0
	TOTAL	3	10	1,053	641	764	2,563	0.1	4	0	0	3	0	3	0	0
MASSAC	PUBLIC	2	9	1,348	315	655	2,330		0	5	1	0	1	2	0	0
	NONPUBLIC	0	0	0	0	0	0		0	0	0	0	0	0	0	0
	TOTAL	2	9	1,348	315	655	2,330	0.1	0	5	1	0	1	2	0	0
MCDONOUGH	PUBLIC	3	12	1,704	343	1,051	3,264		5	1	0	2	0	3	1	0
	NONPUBLIC	0	1	127	0	0	127		0	1	0	0	0	0	0	0
	TOTAL	3	13	1,831	343	1,051	3,391	0.2	5	2	0	2	0	3	1	0
MCHENRY	PUBLIC	19	104	32,413	13,976	22,319	69,640		61	0	4	19	0	17	3	0
	NONPUBLIC	0	14	2,779	0	750	3,529		0	0	10	0	0	1	1	2
	TOTAL	19	118	35,192	13,976	23,069	73,169	3.3	61	0	14	19	0	18	4	2
MCLEAN	PUBLIC	8	52	11,567	5,213	7,150	24,586		29	3	0	7	1	10	1	1
	NONPUBLIC	0	9	2,242	0	621	2,863		1	0	4	0	0	1	2	1
	TOTAL	8	61	13,809	5,213	7,771	27,449	1.3	30	3	4	7	1	11	3	2
MENARD	PUBLIC	3	8	1,276	177	855	2,320		2	2	0	0	1	2	1	0
	NONPUBLIC	0	0	0	0	0	0		0	0	0	0	0	0	0	0
	TOTAL	3	8	1,276	177	855	2,320	0.1	2	2	0	0	1	2	1	0
MERCER	PUBLIC	2	9	1,491	199	1,018	2,700		4	2	0	0	1	2	0	0
	NONPUBLIC	0	1	278	0	123	401		0	0	0	0	0	0	1	0
	TOTAL	2	10	1,769	199	1,141	3,101	0.1	4	2	0	0	1	2	1	0
MONROE	PUBLIC	3	10	2,231	1,236	1,554	5,169		5	0	0	2	0	2	0	0
	NONPUBLIC	0	3	624	0	247	871		0	0	2	0	0	1	1	0
	TOTAL	3	13	2,855	1,236	1,801	6,040	0.3	5	0	2	2	0	3	1	0
MONTGOMERY	PUBLIC	4	16	2,038	925	1,229	4,313		9	0	0	2	0	2	3	0
	NONPUBLIC	0	3	317	0	0	317		0	0	2	0	0	0	0	1
	TOTAL	4	19	2,355	925	1,229	4,630	0.2	9	0	2	2	0	2	3	1
MORGAN	PUBLIC	5	18	2,525	578	1,456	4,513		3	8	0	0	1	3	2	1
	NONPUBLIC	0	4	449	0	154	603		0	0	2	0	0	1	1	0
	TOTAL	5	22	2,974	578	1,610	5,116	0.2	3	8	2	0	1	4	3	1
MOULTRIE	PUBLIC	2	6	721	411	461	1,575		2	0	0	2	0	2	0	0
	NONPUBLIC	0	0	0	0	0	0		0	0	0	0	0	0	0	0
	TOTAL	2	6	721	411	461	1,575	0.1	2	0	0	2	0	2	0	0
OGLE	PUBLIC	10	25	4,311	1,782	2,747	8,697		10	1	3	4	1	5	1	0
	NONPUBLIC	0	1	164	0	0	164		0	0	1	0	0	0	0	0
	TOTAL	10	26	4,475	1,782	2,747	8,861	0.4	10	1	4	4	1	5	1	0

[1] **Elem Enroll** is the school by school total of enrollments in K-4, K-5, K-6, K-8 schools, elementary and middle/JHS students in K-12 schools and students in special ed schools. Public enrollments include public and county-operated schools.

[2] **Middle/JHS Enroll** is the school by school total of enrollments in 5-8 and 7-9 public schools. Public enrollments include public and county-operated schools. Private middle/JHS enrollments are included in Senior Enroll.

[3] **Senior Enroll** is the school by school total of enrollments in 7-12 and 9-12 schools, the secondary students in K-12 schools and students in vocational ed schools. Public enrollments include public and county-operated schools. For private schools, Senior Enroll includes middle/JHS enrollment plus senior enrollment.

[4] **Public Total Enroll** columns are not the sum of school building enrollments. They are projected district-wide Fall enrollments provided to MDR by each school district office, plus county-operated school enrollments.

[5] **K-5** includes pre-kindergarten, kindergarten, K-3, K-4, K-5 schools.
[6] **5-8** includes schools with low grades of 4, 5, 6 and high grades of 7, 8, 9 (e.g., 4-8, 5-8, 6-8, 6-9).
[7] **7-9** includes schools with low grades of 7, 8 and high grades of 7, 8, 9 (e.g., 7-7, 7-8, 7-9, 8-9).
[8] **7-12** includes 7-12, 8-12, 9-12, 10-12, etc.
[9] **K-12** includes schools with both elementary and secondary grades.
[10] **Other** includes special ed, vocational ed and adult schools.

__Public State Totals__ for all columns can exceed the sum of the counties because state totals include state-operated schools and their enrollments

Illinois School Directory — COUNTY STATISTICS

COUNTY		DISTRICTS	SCHOOLS	ELEM ENROLL[1]	MIDDLE/JHS ENROLL[2]	SENIOR ENROLL[3]	TOTAL ENROLL[4]	% OF STATE	K-5[5]	K-6	K-8	SCHOOLS BY GRADE SPAN 5-8[6]	7-9[7]	7-12[8]	K-12[9]	OTHER[10]
PEORIA	PUBLIC	18	69	15,082	5,002	8,364	27,639		19	3	13	14	0	13	4	3
	NONPUBLIC	0	21	3,236	0	1,098	4,334		1	1	13	0	0	1	4	1
	TOTAL	18	90	18,318	5,002	9,462	31,973	1.5	20	4	26	14	0	14	8	4
PERRY	PUBLIC	5	9	1,012	677	865	2,637		2	0	2	2	0	2	0	1
	NONPUBLIC	0	2	182	0	17	199		0	0	1	0	0	0	1	0
	TOTAL	5	11	1,194	677	882	2,836	0.1	2	0	3	2	0	2	1	1
PIATT	PUBLIC	4	12	1,189	427	920	2,588		4	1	1	2	0	4	0	0
	NONPUBLIC	0	0	0	0	0	0		0	0	0	0	0	0	0	0
	TOTAL	4	12	1,189	427	920	2,588	0.1	4	1	1	2	0	4	0	0
PIKE	PUBLIC	4	11	1,482	261	621	2,421		3	0	2	2	0	4	0	0
	NONPUBLIC	0	0	0	0	0	0		0	0	0	0	0	0	0	0
	TOTAL	4	11	1,482	261	621	2,421	0.1	3	0	2	2	0	4	0	0
POPE	PUBLIC	1	2	349	0	153	530		0	0	1	0	0	1	0	0
	NONPUBLIC	0	0	0	0	0	0		0	0	0	0	0	0	0	0
	TOTAL	1	2	349	0	153	530		0	0	1	0	0	1	0	0
PULASKI	PUBLIC	2	4	450	135	181	819		2	0	0	0	0	0	2	0
	NONPUBLIC	0	1	21	0	9	30		0	0	0	0	0	0	1	0
	TOTAL	2	5	471	135	190	849	0.2	2	0	0	0	0	0	3	0
PUTNAM	PUBLIC	1	4	401	186	266	853		2	0	0	0	0	1	0	0
	NONPUBLIC	0	0	0	0	0	0		0	0	0	1	0	1	0	0
	TOTAL	1	4	401	186	266	853	0.1	2	0	0	1	0	1	0	0
RANDOLPH	PUBLIC	6	14	2,723	13	1,277	4,153		2	0	6	0	0	4	2	2
	NONPUBLIC	0	7	653	0	20	673		0	0	6	0	0	1	0	0
	TOTAL	6	21	3,376	13	1,297	4,826	0.2	2	0	12	0	0	5	2	2
RICHLAND	PUBLIC	1	3	1,138	486	725	2,500		1	0	0	1	0	1	0	0
	NONPUBLIC	0	1	170	0	0	170		0	0	1	0	0	0	0	0
	TOTAL	1	4	1,308	486	725	2,670	0.1	1	0	1	1	0	1	0	0
ROCK ISLAND	PUBLIC	9	49	10,616	4,403	6,143	20,842		21	9	2	6	2	6	0	3
	NONPUBLIC	0	10	1,764	0	599	2,363		0	2	4	0	0	1	3	0
	TOTAL	9	59	12,380	4,403	6,742	23,205	1.1	21	11	6	6	2	7	3	3
SALINE	PUBLIC	4	11	2,012	662	1,173	3,893		3	1	1	0	0	4	0	0
	NONPUBLIC	0	1	9	0	4	13		0	0	0	0	0	0	1	0
	TOTAL	4	12	2,021	662	1,177	3,906	0.2	3	1	1	2	0	4	1	0
SANGAMON	PUBLIC	10	65	14,283	5,624	8,505	27,395		33	3	2	10	2	12	2	1
	NONPUBLIC	0	19	3,285	0	1,017	4,302		3	1	9	0	0	2	2	2
	TOTAL	10	84	17,568	5,624	9,522	31,697	1.4	36	4	11	10	2	14	4	3

[1] **Elem Enroll** is the school by school total of enrollments in K-4, K-5, K-6, K-8 schools, elementary and middle/JHS students in K-12 schools and students in special ed schools. Public enrollments include public and county-operated schools.
[2] **Middle/JHS Enroll** is the school by school total of enrollments in 5-8 and 7-9 public schools. Public enrollments include public and county-operated schools. Private middle/JHS enrollments are included in Senior Enroll.
[3] **Senior Enroll** is the school by school total of enrollments in 7-12 and 9-12 schools, the secondary students in K-12 schools and students in vocational ed schools. Public enrollments include public and county-operated schools. For private schools, Senior Enroll includes middle/JHS enrollment plus senior enrollment.
[4] **Public Total Enroll** columns are not the sum of school building enrollments. They are projected district-wide Fall enrollments provided to MDR by each school district office, plus county-operated school enrollments.

[5] **K-5** includes pre-kindergarten, kindergarten, K-3, K-4, K-5 schools.
[6] **5-8** includes schools with low grades of 4, 5, 6 and high grades of 7, 8, 9 (e.g., 4-8, 5-8, 6-8, 6-9).
[7] **7-9** includes schools with low grades of 7, 8 and high grades of 7, 8, 9 (e.g., 7-7, 7-8, 7-9, 8-9).
[8] **7-12** includes 7-12, 8-12, 9-12, 10-12, etc.
[9] **K-12** includes schools with both elementary and secondary grades.
[10] **Other** includes special ed, vocational ed and adult schools.
*Public State Totals for all columns can exceed the sum of the counties because state totals include state-operated schools and their enrollments.

School Year 2020-2021   800-333-8802   IL–B7

COUNTY STATISTICS — Market Data Retrieval

COUNTY		DISTRICTS	SCHOOLS	ELEM ENROLL[1]	MIDDLE/JHS ENROLL[2]	SENIOR ENROLL[3]	TOTAL ENROLL[4]	% OF STATE	K-5[5]	K-6	K-8	5-8[6]	7-9[7]	7-12[8]	K-12[9]	OTHER[10]
SCHUYLER	PUBLIC	1	4	418	309	354	1,100		2	0	0	0	0	1	0	0
	NONPUBLIC	0	0	0	0	0	0		0	0	0	1	0	0	0	0
	TOTAL	1	4	418	309	354	1,100	0.1	2	0	0	1	0	1	0	0
SCOTT	PUBLIC	2	3	604	0	248	9-1		0	0	1	0	0	1	1	0
	NONPUBLIC	0	0	0	0	0	9-1		0	0	0	0	0	0	0	0
	TOTAL	2	3	604	0	248	911	0.1	0	0	1	0	0	1	1	0
SHELBY	PUBLIC	4	9	973	538	694	2,304		2	1	1	1	0	3	1	1
	NONPUBLIC	0	3	252	0	12	264		0	0	2	0	0	0	1	6
	TOTAL	4	12	1,225	538	706	2,568	0.1	2	1	3	1	0	3	2	7
ST CLAIR	PUBLIC	27	84	20,879	7,030	12,515	40,319		30	12	8	11	5	13	4	0
	NONPUBLIC	0	31	3,547	0	607	4,154		2	0	14	0	0	2	7	0
	TOTAL	27	115	24,426	7,030	13,122	44,473	2.0	32	12	22	11	5	15	11	0
STARK	PUBLIC	2	4	467	156	214	837		1	0	1	1	0	1	0	0
	NONPUBLIC	0	0	0	0	0	0		0	0	0	0	0	0	0	0
	TOTAL	2	4	467	156	214	837	0.1	1	0	1	1	0	1	0	0
STEPHENSON	PUBLIC	5	17	2,960	1,345	2,015	6,411		7	1	0	3	0	4	2	0
	NONPUBLIC	0	6	492	0	158	650		0	1	2	0	0	1	1	1
	TOTAL	5	23	3,452	1,345	2,173	7,061	0.3	7	2	2	3	0	5	3	1
TAZEWELL	PUBLIC	18	52	9,476	4,161	6,072	19,858		20	9	4	7	3	7	1	0
	NONPUBLIC	0	10	1,679	0	73	1,752		1	1	5	0	0	0	3	1
	TOTAL	18	62	11,155	4,161	6,145	21,610	1.0	21	10	9	7	3	7	4	1
UNION	PUBLIC	7	12	1,490	513	865	2,889		4	0	2	1	0	1	3	1
	NONPUBLIC	0	1	19	0	8	27		0	0	0	0	0	0	1	0
	TOTAL	7	13	1,509	513	873	2,916	0.1	4	0	2	1	0	1	4	1
VERMILION	PUBLIC	11	34	7,098	1,792	3,442	12,345		12	3	4	3	3	9	0	0
	NONPUBLIC	0	7	727	0	334	1,061		0	0	1	0	0	1	5	0
	TOTAL	11	41	7,825	1,792	3,776	13,406	0.6	12	3	5	3	3	10	5	0
WABASH	PUBLIC	2	5	905	234	482	1,580		1	1	1	0	1	1	0	0
	NONPUBLIC	0	1	126	0	0	126		0	0	1	0	0	0	0	0
	TOTAL	2	6	1,031	234	482	1,706	0.1	1	1	2	0	1	1	0	0
WARREN	PUBLIC	2	9	1,410	415	758	2,636		4	1	0	1	1	2	0	0
	NONPUBLIC	0	1	133	0	0	133		0	0	1	0	0	0	0	0
	TOTAL	2	10	1,543	415	758	2,769	0.1	4	1	1	1	1	2	0	0
WASHINGTON	PUBLIC	6	8	1,122	0	676	1,836		0	1	4	0	0	2	0	0
	NONPUBLIC	0	4	350	0	0	350		0	0	4	0	0	0	0	1
	TOTAL	6	12	1,472	0	676	2,186	0.1	0	1	8	0	0	2	0	1

[1] **Elem Enroll** is the school by school total of enrollments in K-4, K-5, K-6, K-8 schools, elementary and middle/JHS students in K-12 schools and students in special ed schools. Public enrollments include public and county-operated schools.

[2] **Middle/JHS Enroll** is the school by school total of enrollments in 5-8 and 7-9 public schools. Public enrollments include public and county-operated schools. Private middle/JHS enrollments are included in Senior Enroll.

[3] **Senior Enroll** is the school by school total of enrollments in 7-12 and 9-12 schools, the secondary students in K-12 schools and students in vocational ed schools. Public enrollments include public and county-operated schools. For private schools, Senior Enroll includes middle/JHS enrollment plus senior enrollment.

[4] **Public Total Enroll** columns are not the sum of school building enrollments. They are projected district-wide Fall enrollments provided to MDR by each school district office, plus county-operated school enrollments.

[5] **K-5** includes pre-kindergarten, kindergarten, K-3, K-4, K-5 schools.

[6] **5-8** includes schools with low grades of 4, 5, 6 and high grades of 7, 8, 9 (e.g., 4-8, 5-8, 6-8, 6-9).

[7] **7-9** includes schools with low grades of 7, 8 and high grades of 7, 8, 9 (e.g., 7-7, 7-8, 7-9, 8-9).

[8] **7-12** includes 7-12, 8-12, 9-12, 10-12, etc.

[9] **K-12** includes schools with both elementary and secondary grades.

[10] **Other** includes special ed, vocational ed and adult schools.

***Public State Totals** for all columns can exceed the sum of the counties because state totals include state-operated schools and their enrollments.

School Year 2020-2021

Illinois School Directory — COUNTY STATISTICS

COUNTY		DISTRICTS	SCHOOLS	ELEM ENROLL[1]	MIDDLE/JHS ENROLL[2]	SENIOR ENROLL[3]	TOTAL ENROLL[4]	% OF STATE	K-5[5]	K-6	SCHOOLS BY GRADE SPAN K-8[6]	5-8[6]	7-9[7]	7-12[8]	K-12[9]	OTHER[10]
WAYNE	PUBLIC	7	12	1,335	431	692	2,500		3	0	4	2	0	3	0	0
	NONPUBLIC	0	1	60	0	15	75		0	0	0	0	0	0	0	0
	TOTAL	7	13	1,395	431	707	2,575	0.1	3	0	4	2	0	3	0	0
WHITE	PUBLIC	3	11	1,533	187	681	2,355		2	2	2	0	1	3	0	1
	NONPUBLIC	0	1	10	0	4	14		0	0	0	0	0	0	0	0
	TOTAL	3	12	1,543	187	685	2,369	0.1	2	2	2	0	1	3	1	1
WHITESIDE	PUBLIC	9	29	4,326	1,831	2,609	9,038		14	0	2	6	0	6	0	1
	NONPUBLIC	0	6	779	0	305	1,084		0	0	4	0	0	1	1	0
	TOTAL	9	35	5,105	1,831	2,914	10,122	0.5	14	0	6	6	0	7	1	1
WILL	PUBLIC	30	167	51,128	23,159	39,144	113,812		89	9	9	26	6	21	3	4
	NONPUBLIC	0	38	5,956	0	2,356	8,312		2	2	24	0	0	3	4	3
	TOTAL	30	205	57,084	23,159	41,500	122,124	5.6	91	11	33	26	6	24	7	7
WILLIAMSON	PUBLIC	5	22	5,043	2,012	2,955	10,233		9	1	1	3	1	5	1	1
	NONPUBLIC	0	4	517	0	79	596		0	0	3	0	0	1	0	0
	TOTAL	5	26	5,560	2,012	3,034	10,829	0.5	9	1	4	3	1	6	1	1
WINNEBAGO	PUBLIC	11	85	22,590	8,741	12,266	44,875		41	9	4	12	3	13	2	1
	NONPUBLIC	0	27	4,075	0	3,110	7,185		4	1	10	0	0	1	8	3
	TOTAL	11	112	26,665	8,741	15,376	52,060	2.4	45	10	14	12	3	14	10	4
WOODFORD	PUBLIC	9	24	3,362	1,639	2,443	7,478		10	1	2	5	0	6	0	0
	NONPUBLIC	0	3	284	0	30	314		0	0	2	0	0	0	1	0
	TOTAL	9	27	3,646	1,639	2,473	7,792	0.4	10	1	4	5	0	6	1	0
STATE TOTAL	PUBLIC*	850	3,985	1,002,871	321,262	608,251	1,966,398		1,463	326	666	502	97	707	101	100
	NONPUBLIC	0	984	172,137	0	59,362	233,583		37	30	569	8	1	104	145	90
	TOTAL	850	4,969	1,175,008	321,262	667,613	2,199,981		1,500	356	1,235	510	98	811	246	190

[1] **Elem Enroll** is the school by school total of enrollments in K-4, K-5, K-6, K-8 schools, elementary and middle/JHS students in K-12 schools and students in special ed schools. Public enrollments include public and county-operated schools.
[2] **Middle/JHS Enroll** is the school by school total of enrollments in 5-8 and 7-9 public schools. Public enrollments include public and county-operated schools. Private middle/JHS enrollments are included in Senior Enroll.
[3] **Senior Enroll** is the school by school total of enrollments in 7-12 and 9-12 schools, the secondary students in K-12 schools and students in vocational ed schools. Public enrollments include public and county-operated schools. For private schools, Senior Enroll includes middle/JHS enrollment plus senior enrollment.
[4] **Public Total Enroll** columns are not the sum of school building enrollments. They are projected district-wide Fall enrollments provided to MDR by each school district office, plus county-operated school enrollments.
[5] **K-5** includes pre-kindergarten, kindergarten, K-3, K-4, K-5 schools.
[6] **5-8** includes schools with low grades of 4, 5, 6 and high grades of 7, 8, 9 (e.g., 4-8, 5-8, 6-8, 6-9).
[7] **7-9** includes schools with low grades of 7, 8 and high grades of 7, 8, 9 (e.g., 7-7, 7-8, 7-9, 8-9).
[8] **7-12** includes 7-12, 8-12, 9-12, 10-12, etc.
[9] **K-12** includes schools with both elementary and secondary grades.
[10] **Other** includes special ed, vocational ed and adult schools.
***Public State Totals** for all columns can exceed the sum of the counties because state totals include state-operated schools and their enrollments

School Year 2020-2021 800-333-8802 IL—B9

Illinois School Directory

DISTRICT BUYING POWER INDEX

DISTRICT BUYING POWER INDEX
COUNTIES RANKED BY PERCENTAGE OF STATE SPENDING

COUNTY / DISTRICT	PID	COUNTY % OF STATE	DISTRICT % OF COUNTY	DISTRICT % OF STATE	NUMBER OF SCHOOLS	ENROLL	EXP	POV
COOK		36.33						
Chicago Public School Dist 299	00274914		37.95	13.79	666	355,156	LOW	MED-HIGH
Township High School Dist 214	00271649		3.50	1.27	10	12,000	HIGH	MED-LOW
Schaumburg Cmty Cons SD 54	00273843		2.53	0.92	28	15,296	HIGH	MED-LOW
Maine Twp High Sch Dist 207	00271039		2.34	0.85	3	6,322	HIGH	MED-LOW
J Sterling Morton HSD 201	00270451		1.81	0.66	4	8,600	HIGH	MED-HIGH
Community Cons School Dist 15	00272514		1.74	0.63	20	12,000	MED	MED-LOW
Cicero School District 99	00268563		1.68	0.61	17	12,418	MED	MED-HIGH
Township High School Dist 211	00272722		1.44	0.52	7	12,490	MED	MED-LOW
Bremen Cmty High SD 228	00268070		1.40	0.51	5	4,800	HIGH	MED-LOW
Arlington Hts School Dist 25	00267002		1.32	0.48	9	5,550	HIGH	LOW
Niles Twp High School Dist 219	00271792		1.03	0.37	3	4,555	HIGH	MED-LOW
Community Cons School Dist 59	00267193		1.00	0.36	15	6,000	MED	MED-LOW
Thornton Twp High Sch Dist 205	00274756		1.00	0.36	4	4,524	HIGH	MED-HIGH
East Maine School District 63	00269098		0.99	0.36	6	3,500	HIGH	MED-LOW
Maywood-Melrose Brdview SD 89	00271338		0.99	0.36	9	4,300	HIGH	MED-HIGH
Evanston-Skokie Cmty CSD 65	00269282		0.93	0.34	18	8,030	MED	MED-LOW
Community High School Dist 218	00282313		0.81	0.29	5	5,400	HIGH	MED-LOW
Wheeling Cmty Cons Sch Dist 21	00281371		0.81	0.29	13	6,058	MED	MED-LOW
Consolidated High Sch Dist 230	00272904		0.75	0.27	3	7,308	LOW	MED-LOW
Glenview Cmty Cons Sch Dist 34	00269921		0.75	0.27	8	4,900	MED	MED-LOW
Oak Park & River Forest SD 200	00272435		0.72	0.26	1	3,468	HIGH	LOW
Park Ridge Niles CMCSD 64	00273051		0.71	0.26	8	4,500	MED	LOW
Flossmoor School District 161	00269608		0.71	0.26	5	2,374	HIGH	MED-LOW
New Trier Twp HS District 203	00271730		0.65	0.24	2	3,978	HIGH	LOW
Chicago Heights Elem SD 170	00268381		0.64	0.23	10	3,100	HIGH	HIGH
Cmty Cons Sch Dist 146	00274823		0.59	0.21	5	2,500	HIGH	MED-LOW
Mannheim School District 83	00271089		0.59	0.21	6	2,800	HIGH	MED-LOW
Lyons Twp HS District 204	00271003		0.58	0.21	2	4,200	MED	LOW
Kirby School District 140	00270504		0.57	0.21	7	3,500	HIGH	MED-LOW
Northbrook Elem School Dist 27	00271924		0.56	0.20	3	1,237	HIGH	LOW
Orland School District 135	00272459		0.56	0.21	10	5,201	MED	MED-LOW
Glenbrook High Sch Dist 225	00269842		0.55	0.20	2	5,102	MED	LOW
Homewood Flossmoor CHSD 233	00270396		0.54	0.20	1	2,897	HIGH	MED-LOW
Leyden Cmty High Sch Dist 212	00270827		0.54	0.20	2	3,420	MED	MED-LOW
Cook County School Dist 130	00267961		0.54	0.20	11	4,000	MED	MED-HIGH
Des Plaines Cmty Cons SD 62	00268733		0.54	0.20	11	4,800	MED	MED-LOW
South Holland School Dist 151	00274421		0.54	0.20	4	1,753	HIGH	MED-HIGH
Burbank School District 111	00274471		0.53	0.19	8	3,400	HIGH	MED-HIGH
Thornton Fractnl Twp HSD 215	00274794		0.52	0.19	4	3,177	HIGH	MED-HIGH
Riverside Public Sch Dist 96	00273673		0.52	0.19	5	1,686	HIGH	MED-LOW
Bloom Twp High Sch Dist 206	00267935		0.51	0.19	3	3,558	HIGH	MED-HIGH
Oak Park Elem School Dist 97	00272318		0.50	0.18	10	6,000	LOW	LOW
Lyons Elem School Dist 103	00270920		0.47	0.17	6	2,612	HIGH	MED-LOW
Evanston Twp High SD 202	00269505		0.47	0.17	1	3,800	MED	MED-LOW
Rich Twp High School Dist 227	00273453		0.46	0.17	2	2,800	HIGH	MED-LOW
Proviso Twp High Sch Dist 209	00273386		0.45	0.16	3	4,339	LOW	MED-LOW
Ridgeland School District 122	00272124		0.45	0.16	5	2,300	HIGH	MED-HIGH
Bellwood School District 88	00267600		0.45	0.16	7	2,425	MED	MED-HIGH
Forest Ridge Sch Dist 142	00269737		0.42	0.15	4	1,650	HIGH	MED-LOW
Homewood School Dist 153	00270334		0.41	0.15	3	2,000	HIGH	MED-LOW
Berkeley School Dist 87	00267698		0.41	0.15	6	2,600	MED	MED-HIGH
Berwyn South School Dist 100	00267856		0.40	0.15	8	3,700	MED	MED-LOW
Alsip-Hazelgrn-Oaklawn SD 126	00266876		0.40	0.14	5	1,580	HIGH	MED-LOW
Indian Springs Sch Dist 109	00268123		0.40	0.15	6	2,764	MED	MED-HIGH
Harvey Public School Dist 152	00270126		0.37	0.14	6	2,264	HIGH	HIGH
Oak Lawn Cmty High SD 229	00272186		0.37	0.14	1	1,850	HIGH	MED-LOW
Berwyn North School Dist 98	00267806		0.37	0.13	4	2,600	MED	MED-HIGH
Lansing School Dist 158	00270700		0.36	0.13	5	2,500	MED	MED-HIGH
Park Forest Chicago Hgt SD 163	00272930		0.35	0.13	6	2,000	HIGH	MED-HIGH
River Forest Sch Dist 90	00273518		0.34	0.12	3	1,400	HIGH	LOW
West Harvey-Dixmoor Pub SD 147	00270059		0.34	0.12	3	1,000	HIGH	HIGH
Dolton-Riverdale Sch Dist 148	00268874		0.33	0.12	10	2,183	MED	HIGH
Palos Cmty Cons Sch Dist 118	00272784		0.33	0.12	3	2,050	HIGH	MED-LOW
Prairie Hills Elem SD 144	00271144		0.32	0.12	8	3,000	MED	HIGH
La Grange Elem Sch Dist 102	00270566		0.32	0.12	6	3,100	LOW	LOW
Cook County School Dist 104	00274641		0.32	0.12	5	1,800	HIGH	MED-HIGH
Argo Cmty High School Dist 217	00266981		0.31	0.11	1	2,100	HIGH	MED-HIGH
Arbor Park School District 145	00266931		0.30	0.11	4	1,350	HIGH	MED-LOW
La Grange Cmty School Dist 105	00270645		0.30	0.11	5	1,300	HIGH	MED-LOW
Lincolnwood Sch Dist 74	00270853		0.30	0.11	3	1,200	HIGH	MED-LOW
Forest Park School District 91	00269684		0.30	0.11	5	861	HIGH	MED-LOW
Northbrook School District 28	00271986		0.29	0.11	4	1,870	MED	LOW

DISTRICT BUYING POWER INDEX

Market Data Retrieval

DISTRICT BUYING POWER INDEX
COUNTIES RANKED BY PERCENTAGE OF STATE SPENDING

COUNTY / DISTRICT	PID	COUNTY % OF STATE	DISTRICT % OF COUNTY	DISTRICT % OF STATES	NUMBER OF SCHOOLS	ENROLL	EXP	POV
Posen-Robbins Sch Dist 143-5	00273245		0.28	0.10	5	1,452	HIGH	MED-HIGH
Wilmette Public School Dist 39	00281577		0.28	0.10	6	3,563	LOW	LOW
Sunnybrook School District 171	00274691		0.27	0.10	2	1,012	HIGH	MED-HIGH
Skokie School District 68	00274196		0.27	0.10	5	1,700	MED	MED-HIGH
Riverside-Brookfld Twp SD 208	00273738		0.27	0.10	1	1,630	HIGH	MED-LOW
Prospect Hts School Dist 23	00273324		0.27	0.10	4	1,500	HIGH	MED-LOW
Lemont High Sch Dist 210	00270803		0.27	0.10	1	1,400	HIGH	MED-LOW
Glencoe Sch District 35	00269878		0.26	0.10	3	1,200	HIGH	LOW
Franklin Park Pub Sch Dist 84	00269787		0.26	0.10	4	1,400	HIGH	MED-LOW
Kenilworth School District 38	00270487		0.25	0.09	1	425	HIGH	MED-LOW
North Palos School Dist 117	00271869		0.25	0.09	5	3,402	LOW	MED-HIGH
Steger School Dist 194	00274586		0.25	0.09	3	1,500	HIGH	MED-HIGH
Chicago Ridge Sch Dist 127-5	00268513		0.25	0.09	3	1,476	HIGH	HIGH
Evergreen Park Elem SD 124	00269529		0.24	0.09	5	1,900	MED	MED-LOW
Rhodes School District 84 1/2	00273439		0.24	0.09	1	637	HIGH	MED-HIGH
Matteson Elem SD 162	00271247		0.24	0.09	7	2,700	LOW	MED-HIGH
Midlothian School District 143	00271467		0.24	0.09	4	1,800	MED	MED-HIGH
Hazel Crest School Dist 152-5	00270217		0.23	0.09	2	1,000	HIGH	HIGH
Reavis Twp HSD 220	00273415		0.23	0.09	1	1,800	MED	MED-HIGH
Dolton School District 149	00268977		0.23	0.08	8	2,600	LOW	MED-HIGH
River Trails Sch Dist 26	00273594		0.21	0.08	4	1,600	MED	MED-LOW
West Northfield Sch Dist 31	00281228		0.21	0.07	2	880	HIGH	MED-LOW
Westchester Public SD 92 1/2	00281254		0.21	0.07	3	1,250	HIGH	MED-LOW
Northbrook-Glenview SD 30	00272057		0.21	0.08	3	1,195	HIGH	LOW
Oak Lawn-Hometown Sch Dist 123	00272203		0.20	0.07	6	3,000	LOW	MED-LOW
Lemont-Bromberek Sch Dist 113A	00270774		0.20	0.07	3	2,300	LOW	MED-LOW
Elementary School District 159	00274158		0.20	0.07	5	1,700	LOW	MED-HIGH
Norridge School Dist 80	00271833		0.18	0.07	2	1,000	HIGH	MED-LOW
E F Lindop Elem Sch Dist 92	00270906		0.17	0.06	1	480	HIGH	MED-HIGH
Elmwood Park Cmty Unit SD 401	00269232		0.17	0.06	5	2,800	LOW	MED-LOW
Winnetka School Dist 36	00281917		0.16	0.06	5	1,100	LOW	LOW
Ridgewood Cmty HSD 234	00273491		0.16	0.06	1	900	HIGH	MED-LOW
Skokie School District 69	00274251		0.16	0.06	3	1,700	LOW	MED-HIGH
Avoca School District 37	00267454		0.15	0.06	2	750	HIGH	LOW
Brookwood School District 167	00268226		0.15	0.05	4	1,200	MED	MED-HIGH
Niles Elem School District 71	00271766		0.15	0.05	1	600	HIGH	MED-LOW
Mt Prospect School Dist 57	00271560		0.15	0.05	4	2,222	LOW	LOW
Ford Heights School Dist 169	00269050		0.14	0.05	2	455	HIGH	HIGH
Atwood Heights SD 125	00267404		0.14	0.05	3	620	HIGH	MED-LOW
Calumet Public School Dist 132	00268331		0.14	0.05	3	1,200	MED	MED-HIGH
Evergreen Park Cmty HSD 231	00269581		0.14	0.05	1	850	HIGH	MED-LOW
Skokie School District 73 1/2	00274304		0.14	0.05	3	1,118	MED	MED-LOW
Schiller Park School Dist 81	00274110		0.14	0.05	3	1,500	LOW	MED-HIGH
South Holland School Dist 150	00274378		0.14	0.05	3	1,000	MED	MED-HIGH
Sunset Ridge Sch Dist 29	00272095		0.14	0.05	2	480	HIGH	MED-LOW
River Grove School Dist 85-5	00273570		0.13	0.05	1	750	HIGH	MED-HIGH
Calumet City School Dist 155	00268288		0.13	0.05	3	1,026	MED	MED-HIGH
Community Cons School Dist 168	00273790		0.12	0.04	3	1,287	LOW	HIGH
Fairview South School Dist 72	00274342		0.12	0.05	1	722	HIGH	MED-LOW
Brookfield-LaGrange Park SD 95	00268197		0.11	0.04	2	1,257	LOW	MED-LOW
La Grange-Highlands SD 106	00270279		0.11	0.04	2	850	MED	LOW
Lincoln Elem School Dist 156	00268317		0.11	0.04	1	950	MED	HIGH
Pleasantdale School Dist 107	00273219		0.11	0.04	2	845	MED	LOW
Union Ridge School Dist 86	00274897		0.10	0.04	1	675	MED	MED-LOW
Worth School District 127	00282246		0.09	0.03	4	1,087	LOW	MED-HIGH
Country Club Hills SD 160	00268680		0.09	0.03	3	1,221	LOW	MED-HIGH
Hoover-Schrum Sch Dist 157	00270413		0.09	0.03	2	850	MED	MED-HIGH
Komarek School District 94	00270542		0.08	0.03	1	580	HIGH	MED-LOW
Morton Grove School Dist 70	00271510		0.08	0.03	1	900	LOW	MED-LOW
Western Springs Sch Dist 101	00281307		0.08	0.03	4	1,435	LOW	LOW
Rosemont Elem Sch Dist 78	00273752		0.07	0.03	1	220	HIGH	MED-LOW
Cook County School Dist 154	00274720		0.07	0.02	1	225	HIGH	MED-HIGH
East Prairie School Dist 73	00269218		0.07	0.03	1	505	MED	MED-LOW
Willow Springs School Dist 108	00281553		0.06	0.02	1	359	MED	MED-HIGH
Palos Heights School Dist 128	00272837		0.06	0.02	4	700	LOW	MED-LOW
General George S Patton SD 133	00273178		0.06	0.02	1	268	HIGH	HIGH
Hillside School District 93	00270310		0.05	0.02	1	410	MED	MED-LOW
Golf School District 67	00270011		0.05	0.02	2	725	LOW	MED-LOW
Pennoyer School District 79	00273192		0.05	0.02	1	444	MED	MED-LOW
Central Stickney Sch Dist 110	00268367		0.04	0.01	1	384	LOW	MED-HIGH
Burnham School District 1545	00268264		0.02	0.01	1	180	LOW	MED-HIGH
Sandridge Sch Dist 172	00273776		0.02	0.01	1	350	LOW	MED-HIGH
DU PAGE		8.80						
Naperville Cmty Unit SD 203	00290700		13.47	1.19	22	17,000	HIGH	LOW

Illinois School Directory
DISTRICT BUYING POWER INDEX

DISTRICT BUYING POWER INDEX
COUNTIES RANKED BY PERCENTAGE OF STATE SPENDING

COUNTY / DISTRICT	PID	COUNTY % OF STATE	DISTRICT % OF COUNTY	DISTRICT % OF STATES	NUMBER OF SCHOOLS	ENROLL	EXP	POV
Indian Prairie Sch Dist 204	00290205		11.23	0.99	34	27,400	LOW	LOW
West Chicago Elementary SD 33	00291479		7.07	0.62	8	4,300	HIGH	MED-LOW
Community Unit School Dist 200	00290877		6.05	0.53	20	12,000	MED	MED-LOW
Elmhurst Cmty Unit SD 205	00289488		4.85	0.43	13	8,499	MED	LOW
Dupage High School Dist 88	00289684		4.54	0.40	2	3,929	HIGH	MED-LOW
Downers Grove School Dist 58	01844562		4.03	0.35	13	5,000	HIGH	LOW
Glenbard Twp High Sch Dist 87	00289907		3.75	0.33	4	7,500	MED	MED-LOW
Marquardt School District 15	00290580		3.36	0.30	5	2,491	HIGH	MED-HIGH
Community Cons School Dist 181	00290061		3.10	0.27	9	3,800	HIGH	LOW
Community High School Dist 99	00289323		2.99	0.26	2	5,015	MED	LOW
Woodridge Elem Sch District 68	00289957		2.71	0.24	7	2,950	HIGH	MED-LOW
Community Cons School Dist 93	00289141		2.68	0.24	9	3,200	HIGH	MED-LOW
Hinsdale Twp High Sch Dist 86	00290176		2.64	0.23	2	4,000	MED	LOW
Addison School District 4	00288850		2.20	0.19	9	4,000	MED	MED-LOW
Bensenville Elem Sch Dist 2	00288989		2.02	0.18	3	2,350	HIGH	MED-LOW
Lake Park Cmty High SD 108	00290322		1.95	0.17	2	2,500	HIGH	MED-LOW
Lombard Elem SD 44	00290413		1.68	0.15	8	3,100	MED	MED-LOW
Community Cons School Dist 89	00289830		1.66	0.15	5	2,300	HIGH	MED-LOW
Maercker School District 60	00290554		1.65	0.15	3	1,401	HIGH	MED-LOW
School Dist 45 Dupage Co	00291261		1.56	0.14	8	3,410	MED	MED-LOW
Itasca School District 10	00290255		1.53	0.13	3	1,033	HIGH	LOW
Lisle Cmty Unit Sch Dist 202	00290346		1.28	0.11	3	1,450	HIGH	MED-LOW
Fenton Cmty High Sch Dist 100	00289713		1.28	0.11	1	1,433	HIGH	LOW
Glen Ellyn School District 41	00289737		1.26	0.11	5	3,549	LOW	MED-LOW
Community Unit School Dist 201	00291429		0.92	0.08	5	1,365	HIGH	MED-LOW
Community High School Dist 94	00291546		0.90	0.08	1	2,006	MED	MED-LOW
Benjamin Sch District 25	00288965		0.89	0.08	2	650	HIGH	LOW
Center Cass Sch Dist 66	00289220		0.69	0.06	3	1,100	MED	LOW
Gower School District 62	00290035		0.63	0.06	2	900	HIGH	MED-LOW
Salt Creek School District 48	00291223		0.63	0.06	3	550	HIGH	MED-LOW
Medinah Elementary SD 11	00290669		0.62	0.05	3	700	HIGH	MED-LOW
Community Cons School Dist 180	00290841		0.62	0.05	2	630	HIGH	HIGH
Wood Dale School Dist 7	00291625		0.59	0.05	4	1,082	MED	MED-LOW
Keeneyville Elem Sch Dist 20	00290293		0.48	0.04	3	1,597	LOW	MED-LOW
Darien Public Sch Dist 61	00289268		0.48	0.04	3	1,400	LOW	MED-LOW
Bloomingdale School Dist 13	00289050		0.48	0.04	3	1,390	LOW	LOW
Butler School District 53	00289115		0.42	0.04	2	518	HIGH	LOW
Cass School District 63	00289191		0.42	0.04	2	766	MED	MED-LOW
Queen Bee School District 16	00291120		0.33	0.03	4	1,900	LOW	MED-LOW
Winfield School District 34	00291584		0.18	0.02	2	275	MED	LOW
Roselle School District 12	00291170		0.18	0.02	2	700	LOW	LOW
LAKE		8.05						
Waukegan Cmty Unit SD 60	00302080		13.58	1.09	24	17,000	HIGH	MED-HIGH
Barrington Cmty Unit SD 220	00267492		6.89	0.56	12	9,000	HIGH	MED-LOW
North Chicago Cmty Unit SD 187	00301725		6.12	0.49	8	3,900	HIGH	MED-HIGH
Warren Twp High Sch Dist 121	00301995		4.47	0.36	2	4,049	HIGH	MED-LOW
Community High School Dist 128	00301517		3.92	0.32	2	3,397	HIGH	LOW
Woodland School District 50	00302420		3.85	0.31	5	5,700	MED	MED-LOW
Wauconda Cmty Unit SD 118	00302016		3.57	0.29	6	4,500	HIGH	MED-LOW
Round Lake Area Co Dist 116	00301878		3.50	0.28	10	7,300	MED	MED-HIGH
Adlai E Stevenson HSD 125	00300355		3.34	0.27	1	4,337	HIGH	LOW
Lake Zurich Cmty Sch Dist 95	00301385		3.29	0.26	8	5,516	MED	LOW
Zion Public School District 6	00302468		3.02	0.24	7	2,700	HIGH	MED-HIGH
North Shore School Dist 112	00300991		2.35	0.19	10	3,800	MED	MED-LOW
Deerfield Public SD 109	00300587		2.18	0.18	6	3,400	HIGH	LOW
Hawthorn Cmty Cons Sch Dist 73	00300939		2.14	0.17	7	4,300	MED	MED-LOW
Mundelein Cons High SD 120	00301684		2.02	0.16	1	2,026	HIGH	MED-LOW
Mundelein Elem School Dist 75	00301622		2.01	0.16	4	1,586	HIGH	MED-LOW
Grayslake Cmty HS District 127	00300886		2.01	0.16	2	3,000	HIGH	LOW
Lake Villa Cmty Cons SD 41	00301335		1.94	0.16	4	2,700	HIGH	LOW
Zion-Benton Twp High SD 126	00302547		1.83	0.15	2	2,100	MED	MED-LOW
Aptakisic-Tripp Sch Dist 102	00300446		1.82	0.15	4	2,400	HIGH	LOW
Big Hollow School District 38	00300551		1.75	0.14	3	1,800	HIGH	MED-LOW
Community High School Dist 117	00300422		1.74	0.14	2	2,677	MED	LOW
Lake Forest School District 67	00301244		1.72	0.14	5	1,660	HIGH	LOW
Township High School Dist 113	00301098		1.70	0.14	2	3,616	LOW	LOW
Lake Forest Cmty HSD 115	00301309		1.59	0.13	1	1,600	HIGH	LOW
Kildeer Countryside CCSD 96	00301165		1.53	0.12	7	3,213	LOW	LOW
Antioch Cmty Cons Sch Dist 34	00300379		1.42	0.11	6	2,775	MED	MED-LOW
Grant Cmty High Sch Dist 124	00300800		1.42	0.11	1	1,850	HIGH	MED-LOW
Community Cons School Dist 46	00300848		1.41	0.11	8	3,800	LOW	LOW
Fremont School District 79	00300745		1.39	0.11	3	2,200	MED	LOW
Lincolnshre-Prairieview SD 103	00301543		1.30	0.10	3	1,832	MED	LOW
Beach Park Cmty Cons SD 3	00300501		1.30	0.10	5	2,106	MED	MED-LOW

School Year 2020-2021

DISTRICT BUYING POWER INDEX

Market Data Retrieval

DISTRICT BUYING POWER INDEX
COUNTIES RANKED BY PERCENTAGE OF STATE SPENDING

COUNTY / DISTRICT	PID	COUNTY % OF STATE	DISTRICT % OF COUNTY	DISTRICT % OF STATES	NUMBER OF SCHOOLS	ENROLL	EXP	POV
Libertyville Pub Sch Dist 70	00301440		1.05	0.08	5	2,258	LOW	LOW
Lake Bluff Elem Sch Dist 65	00301191		1.04	0.08	2	880	HIGH	LOW
Oak Grove School District 68	00301854		0.89	0.07	1	900	HIGH	LOW
Diamond Lake School Dist 76	00300654		0.85	0.07	3	900	HIGH	MED-LOW
Fox Lake School Dist 114	00300719		0.85	0.07	2	741	HIGH	MED-LOW
Gurnee School District 56	00300903		0.64	0.05	4	2,083	LOW	MED-LOW
Gavin School District 37	00300769		0.57	0.05	2	850	MED	MED-LOW
Millburn Cmty Cons Sch Dist 24	00301608		0.55	0.04	2	1,150	LOW	LOW
Winthrop Harbor School Dist 1	00302377		0.39	0.03	2	542	HIGH	MED-LOW
Emmons School District 33	00300692		0.34	0.03	1	300	HIGH	MED-LOW
Bannockburn Sch Dist 106	00300484		0.28	0.02	1	155	HIGH	MED-LOW
Rondout School District 72	00301945		0.22	0.02	1	140	HIGH	LOW
Grass Lake School District 36	00300824		0.21	0.02	1	190	HIGH	MED-HIGH
KANE		5.70						
Elgin School District U-46	00298154		33.94	1.94	58	38,000	MED	MED-LOW
East Aurora School Dist 131	00297497		19.83	1.13	20	14,000	HIGH	MED-HIGH
Community Unit School Dist 303	00298740		16.96	0.97	16	12,262	HIGH	LOW
West Aurora School Dist 129	00297643		11.75	0.67	18	12,000	MED	MED-LOW
Central Cmty Unit SD 301	00297904		6.54	0.37	7	4,500	HIGH	LOW
Batavia Unit School Dist 101	00297837		5.96	0.34	8	5,518	HIGH	LOW
Geneva CUSD 304	00298594		2.73	0.16	10	5,808	LOW	LOW
Kaneland Cmty Unit SD 302	00298661		2.29	0.13	7	4,560	LOW	LOW
WILL		5.60						
Joliet Public School Dist 86	00324856		18.64	1.04	21	12,000	HIGH	MED-HIGH
Plainfield Cons Sch Dist 202	00325525		13.97	0.78	30	25,000	LOW	LOW
Valley View Cmty SD 365-U	00325587		7.41	0.41	20	18,000	LOW	MED-LOW
Crete-Monee Cmty SD 201-U	00324636		6.36	0.36	9	5,000	HIGH	MED-LOW
Laraway Cmty Cons SD 70-C	00325161		6.30	0.35	1	427	HIGH	MED-HIGH
Lincoln-Way Cmty HS Dist 210	00325197		5.08	0.28	3	6,811	MED	LOW
New Lenox School District 122	00325379		4.91	0.27	12	5,300	MED	LOW
Homer Cmty Cons Sch Dist 33C	00324832		4.11	0.23	6	3,800	HIGH	LOW
Lockport Twp High Sch Dist 205	00325214		3.82	0.21	2	3,890	MED	LOW
Joliet Twp High Sch Dist 204	00325123		3.69	0.21	3	6,589	LOW	MED-LOW
Frankfort School Dist 157-C	00324806		3.60	0.20	3	2,521	HIGH	LOW
Troy Cmty Cons SD 30-C	00325824		2.78	0.16	7	4,100	LOW	MED-LOW
Minooka Cmty High Sch Dist 111	00294201		2.49	0.14	2	2,800	MED	LOW
Summit Hill School Dist 161	00325769		1.99	0.11	6	2,800	LOW	LOW
Mokena Public School Dist 159	00325331		1.83	0.10	3	1,500	HIGH	LOW
Wilmington Cmty Unit SD 209-U	00325886		1.80	0.10	4	1,400	HIGH	MED-LOW
Will Co School District 92	00325240		1.71	0.10	4	1,550	HIGH	LOW
Reed-Custer Cmty Unit SD 255-U	00324569		1.61	0.09	3	1,476	HIGH	MED-LOW
Milne-Kelvin Grove District 91	00325305		1.21	0.07	2	550	HIGH	MED-LOW
Channahon School District 17	00324612		1.12	0.06	4	1,234	MED	MED-LOW
Richland School Dist 88A	00325721		0.90	0.05	1	923	MED	MED-LOW
Manhattan School Dist 114	00325288		0.87	0.05	3	1,540	LOW	LOW
Beecher Cmty Sch Dist 200-U	00324533		0.86	0.05	3	1,100	MED	MED-LOW
Peotone Cmty Unit SD 207-U	00325460		0.83	0.05	5	1,453	MED	LOW
Chaney-Monge School Dist 88	00324583		0.55	0.03	1	500	HIGH	MED-HIGH
Fairmont School District 89	00324765		0.51	0.03	1	350	HIGH	MED-HIGH
Elwood Cmty Cons SD 203	00324741		0.32	0.02	1	318	MED	MED-LOW
Union School District 81	00325862		0.28	0.02	1	105	HIGH	MED-LOW
Taft School District 90	00325800		0.23	0.01	1	300	MED	MED-LOW
Rockdale School District 84	00325745		0.19	0.01	1	275	LOW	MED-HIGH
MCHENRY		3.17						
Community Unit School Dist 300	00297966		25.79	0.82	27	20,985	MED	MED-LOW
Huntley Cmty School Dist 158	00305616		12.74	0.40	8	9,606	MED	LOW
Community High School Dist 155	00305458		12.52	0.40	5	5,800	HIGH	LOW
Crystal Lake Elem Distict 47	00305355		8.22	0.26	12	7,500	LOW	MED-LOW
McHenry Cmty Cons Sch Dist 15	00305745		7.97	0.25	8	4,300	HIGH	MED-LOW
Cary Cmty Cons Sch Dist 26	00305305		5.79	0.18	5	2,426	HIGH	MED-LOW
Woodstock Cmty Unit SD 200	00305991		4.91	0.16	12	6,600	LOW	MED-LOW
Harvard Cmty Unit Sch Dist 50	00305537		4.82	0.15	5	2,633	MED	MED-LOW
McHenry Cmty High Sch Dist 156	00305812		3.60	0.11	2	2,143	MED	MED-LOW
Marengo Cmty High Sch Dist 154	00305721		2.91	0.09	1	700	HIGH	MED-LOW
Richmond-Burton Cmty HSD 157	00305903		2.08	0.07	1	636	HIGH	MED-LOW
Johnsburg Cmty School Dist 12	00305642		1.93	0.06	4	1,800	LOW	LOW
Prairie Grove Cons SD 46	00305848		1.25	0.04	2	720	HIGH	LOW
Nippersink School District 2	00305886		1.14	0.04	3	1,100	LOW	MED-LOW
Marengo Union Elem Cons SD 165	00305692		1.07	0.03	3	1,200	LOW	MED-LOW
Harrison School Dist 36	00305513		1.04	0.03	1	404	HIGH	MED-LOW
Alden-Hebron School Dist 19	00305276		0.96	0.03	2	430	HIGH	MED-HIGH
Riley Cmty Cons Sch Dist 18	00305927		0.74	0.02	1	267	HIGH	MED-LOW

Illinois School Directory

DISTRICT BUYING POWER INDEX

DISTRICT BUYING POWER INDEX

COUNTIES RANKED BY PERCENTAGE OF STATE SPENDING

COUNTY / DISTRICT	PID	COUNTY % OF STATE	DISTRICT % OF COUNTY	DISTRICT % OF STATES	NUMBER OF SCHOOLS	ENROLL	EXP	POV
Fox River Grove Cons SD 3	00305484		0.51	0.02	2	390	MED	LOW
WINNEBAGO		2.98						
Rockford School District 205	00327406		73.21	2.18	46	28,940	HIGH	HIGH
Harlem Unit Sch District 122	00327121		12.61	0.38	11	6,300	HIGH	MED-HIGH
Hononegah Cmty High SD 207	00327274		3.22	0.10	1	1,500	MED	LOW
Kinnikinnick Cmty Cons SD 131	00327298		2.54	0.08	4	1,750	MED	MED-LOW
Winnebago Cmty Unit SD 323	00328254		2.09	0.06	4	1,330	MED	MED-HIGH
Rockton School District 140	00328151		1.76	0.05	3	1,600	LOW	MED-LOW
South Beloit Cmty Sch Dist 320	00328199		1.19	0.04	5	960	LOW	MED-HIGH
Durand Cmty Sch Dist 322	00327092		1.13	0.03	4	565	HIGH	MED-LOW
Prairie Hill Cmty Cons SD 133	00327389		1.12	0.03	2	743	MED	MED-LOW
Pecatonica Cmty Unit SD 321	00327315		0.79	0.02	3	950	LOW	MED-LOW
Shirland Cmty Cons SD 134	00328175		0.34	0.01	1	111	HIGH	MED-LOW
ST CLAIR		1.88						
East St Louis Sch Dist 189	00316639		19.49	0.37	11	5,200	HIGH	HIGH
Belleville Public Sch Dist 118	00316237		12.39	0.23	11	4,500	HIGH	MED-HIGH
Belleville Township HSD 201	00316366		10.62	0.20	3	4,500	MED	MED-LOW
Mascoutah Cmty Sch Dist 19	00317308		10.60	0.20	5	4,000	MED	LOW
Cahokia Unit Sch Dist 187	00316419		8.79	0.16	10	3,400	MED	HIGH
O'Fallon Twp School Dist 203	00317475		5.97	0.11	2	2,400	MED	MED-LOW
O'Fallon Cmty Cons Sch Dist 90	00317425		5.15	0.10	7	3,761	LOW	MED-LOW
Belle Valley School Dist 119	00316201		2.67	0.05	1	1,038	MED	MED-HIGH
High Mount Sch Dist 116	00317205		2.54	0.05	1	475	HIGH	MED-HIGH
Dupo Cmty School District 196	00316574		2.49	0.05	2	985	MED	MED-HIGH
Harmony-Emge School Dist 175	00317164		2.13	0.04	3	800	MED	MED-HIGH
Whiteside School District 115	00317619		1.91	0.04	2	1,036	LOW	MED-LOW
Signal Hill Sch Dist 181	00317542		1.80	0.03	1	330	HIGH	MED-HIGH
Grant Cmty Cons Sch Dist 110	00317102		1.49	0.03	2	600	MED	MED-HIGH
Pontiac-Wm Holliday SD 105	00317499		1.43	0.03	2	500	LOW	MED-LOW
Central School District 104	00316550		1.25	0.02	2	700	LOW	MED-LOW
Brooklyn School District 188	00316392		1.23	0.02	1	161	HIGH	HIGH
New Athens CUSD 60	00317396		1.21	0.02	1	500	MED	MED-LOW
Wolf Branch School Dist 113	00317645		1.18	0.02	2	720	LOW	MED-LOW
Lebanon Cmty Unit Sch Dist 9	00317229		1.11	0.02	2	540	LOW	MED-HIGH
Millstadt Cmty Cons SD 160	00317360		1.09	0.02	2	800	LOW	MED-LOW
Marissa Cmty Unit Sch Dist 40	00317267		1.02	0.02	2	550	LOW	MED-HIGH
Freeburg Cmty High Sch Dist 77	00317085		0.96	0.02	1	675	LOW	LOW
Freeburg Cmty Cons SD 70	00317061		0.56	0.01	2	780	LOW	MED-LOW
Smithton Cmty Cons SD 130	00317566		0.43	0.01	1	568	LOW	LOW
Shiloh Village Sch Dist 85	00317528		0.36	0.01	2	571	LOW	MED-LOW
St Libory Cons Sch District 30	00317592		0.13	0.00	1	53	MED	MED-LOW
PEORIA		1.65						
Peoria Public Sch Dist 150	00312683		64.87	1.07	30	12,531	HIGH	HIGH
Dunlap Cmty Unit Sch Dist 323	00312322		7.92	0.13	8	4,500	LOW	MED-LOW
Illinois Vly Ctl Sch Dist 321	00312504		5.60	0.09	5	2,173	MED	MED-LOW
Limestone Cmty High SD 310	00312578		4.08	0.07	2	1,000	HIGH	MED-LOW
Princeville Cmty Unit SD 326	00313259		3.20	0.05	2	761	HIGH	MED-LOW
Illini Bluffs Cmty Unit SD 327	00312425		2.40	0.04	3	909	MED	MED-LOW
Peoria Heights Cmty SD 325	00313156		2.34	0.04	2	720	MED	MED-HIGH
Farmington Ctl Cmty SD 265	00293568		1.56	0.03	3	1,425	LOW	MED-LOW
Brimfield Cmty Unit SD 309	00312293		1.33	0.02	2	680	LOW	LOW
Pleasant Valley Sch Dist 62	00313223		1.24	0.02	2	363	MED	MED-LOW
Oak Grove School District 68	00312657		0.94	0.02	1	250	MED	MED-LOW
Monroe School District 70	00312619		0.92	0.02	1	287	MED	MED-LOW
Elmwood Cmty Unit Sch Dist 322	00312360		0.89	0.01	2	700	LOW	MED-LOW
Norwood Sch Dist 63	00312633		0.88	0.01	2	475	MED	MED-HIGH
Bartonville School District 66	00312243		0.77	0.01	1	300	MED	MED-HIGH
Pleasant Hill School Dist 69	00313209		0.40	0.01	1	230	LOW	MED-HIGH
Limestone Walters CCSD 316	00312592		0.35	0.01	1	200	LOW	LOW
Hollis Cons School Dist 328	00312401		0.30	0.00	1	135	LOW	MED-LOW
MADISON		1.49						
Edwardsville Cmty Unit SD 7	00308606		24.11	0.36	15	7,500	MED	MED-LOW
Granite City Cmty Unit SD 9	00308682		17.11	0.25	8	5,764	MED	MED-HIGH
Collinsville Cmty Sch Dist 10	00308333		14.24	0.21	13	5,000	LOW	MED-HIGH
Alton Cmty School District 11	00308010		8.83	0.13	12	6,000	LOW	MED-HIGH
Triad Cmty School District 2	00309155		8.23	0.12	6	4,000	LOW	LOW
Highland Cmty Sch District 5	00308917		6.21	0.09	6	3,000	LOW	MED-LOW
Roxana Cmty Unit Sch Dist 1	00309088		5.60	0.08	4	2,000	MED	MED-HIGH
Bethalto Cmty Unit SD 8	00308242		4.37	0.07	5	2,500	LOW	MED-HIGH
East Alton-Wood River SD 14	00309337		3.53	0.05	1	556	HIGH	MED-HIGH
East Alton Elementary SD 13	00308539		2.77	0.04	3	800	MED	MED-HIGH
Madison Cmty Unit Sch Dist 12	00309014		2.49	0.04	3	700	MED	HIGH

DISTRICT BUYING POWER INDEX

COUNTIES RANKED BY PERCENTAGE OF STATE SPENDING

COUNTY / DISTRICT	PID	COUNTY % OF STATE	DISTRICT % OF COUNTY	DISTRICT % OF STATES	NUMBER OF SCHOOLS	ENROLL	EXP	POV
Wood River-Hartford Elem SD 15	00309272		1.99	0.03	3	706	MED	MED-HIGH
Venice Cmty Unit School Dist 3	00309222		0.52	0.01	1	80	HIGH	MED-HIGH
SANGAMON		1.37						
Springfield Pub Sch Dist 186	00318883		58.91	0.80	33	13,000	HIGH	MED-HIGH
Ball Chatham Cmty Unit SD 5	00318560		11.28	0.15	6	4,500	LOW	LOW
Riverton Cmty Unit SD 14	00318728		5.64	0.08	3	1,443	MED	MED-HIGH
Community Unit School Dist 16	00318675		5.05	0.07	3	939	HIGH	MED-LOW
Rochester Cmty Unit SD 3-A	00318845		4.14	0.06	5	2,215	LOW	LOW
Pleasant Plains Cmty Unit SD 8	00318792		3.95	0.05	3	1,271	MED	MED-LOW
Auburn Cmty Unit Sch Dist 10	00318522		3.90	0.05	4	1,317	MED	MED-LOW
Williamsville Cmty Unit SD 15	00319291		2.83	0.04	4	1,540	LOW	LOW
Tri-City Cmty Unit Sch Dist 1	00319277		2.19	0.03	1	570	MED	MED-LOW
Pawnee Cmty Unit Sch Dist 11	00318766		2.12	0.03	2	550	MED	MED-LOW
CHAMPAIGN		1.27						
Champaign Cmty Unit Sch Dist 4	00264713		41.12	0.52	19	10,179	MED	MED-HIGH
Urbana School District 116	00265406		14.33	0.18	10	4,175	MED	MED-HIGH
Mahomet-Seymour Cmty SD 3	00265016		10.37	0.13	4	3,170	MED	MED-LOW
Rantoul City School Dist 137	00265119		9.75	0.12	5	1,750	HIGH	MED-HIGH
Tolono Cmty Unit Sch Dist 7	00265327		7.17	0.09	4	1,615	MED	MED-LOW
Rantoul Twp High Sch Dist 193	00265195		3.66	0.05	2	765	HIGH	MED-HIGH
Heritage Cmty Unit Sch Dist 8	00264971		3.55	0.04	2	421	HIGH	MED-LOW
Fisher Cmty Unit School Dist 1	00264907		3.27	0.04	2	601	HIGH	MED-LOW
St Joseph Cmty Cons SD 169	00265236		1.90	0.02	2	850	LOW	MED-LOW
St Joseph-Ogden Cmty HSD 305	00265250		1.44	0.02	1	450	MED	LOW
Thomasboro Cmty Cons SD 130	00265303		1.02	0.01	1	150	HIGH	MED-HIGH
Gifford Cmty Cons SD 188	00264957		0.94	0.01	1	183	HIGH	MED-LOW
Prairieview-Ogden Sch Dist 197	00265212		0.84	0.01	3	247	MED	MED-LOW
Ludlow Cons Cmty Sch Dist 142	00264995		0.64	0.01	1	57	HIGH	MED-HIGH
KENDALL		1.21						
Community Unit School Dist 308	00299689		56.90	0.69	21	17,250	LOW	LOW
Yorkville Cmty Unit SD 115	00299809		29.76	0.36	10	6,200	HIGH	LOW
Plano Cmty Unit Sch Dist 88	00299744		10.76	0.13	5	2,400	MED	MED-LOW
Newark Cmty High Sch Dist 18	00299641		1.38	0.02	1	170	HIGH	LOW
Newark Cmty Cons Sch Dist 66	00299665		0.69	0.01	2	239	LOW	LOW
Lisbon Cmty Cons Sch Dist 90	00299627		0.51	0.01	1	106	MED	LOW
ROCK ISLAND		1.08						
Rock Island-Milan Sch Dist 41	00315831		41.84	0.45	14	5,800	HIGH	MED-HIGH
Moline-Coal Valley SD No 40	00315491		27.63	0.30	15	7,182	MED	MED-HIGH
East Moline Public Sch Dist 37	00315386		8.01	0.09	5	2,650	LOW	MED-HIGH
United Twp High Sch Dist 30	00316146		7.24	0.08	2	1,678	MED	MED-HIGH
Riverdale Cmty Unit SD 100	00315752		4.73	0.05	3	1,160	MED	MED-LOW
Rockridge Cmty Unit SD 300	00316031		4.61	0.05	5	1,097	MED	MED-LOW
Silvis School District 34	00316110		3.22	0.03	2	648	MED	MED-HIGH
Carbon Cliff Barstow SD 36	00315350		1.83	0.02	1	270	HIGH	HIGH
Hampton School District 29	00315477		0.88	0.01	1	210	MED	MED-LOW
TAZEWELL		0.97						
Morton Cmty Unit Sch Dist 709	00321311		16.64	0.16	7	3,060	MED	LOW
Pekin Cmty High Sch Dist 303	00321579		16.46	0.16	1	1,821	HIGH	MED-LOW
East Peoria Elem Sch Dist 86	00321141		12.30	0.12	7	1,500	HIGH	MED-LOW
Pekin Public School Dist 108	00321426		11.64	0.11	11	3,650	LOW	MED-HIGH
East Peoria Cmty HS Dist 309	00321256		9.64	0.09	1	1,000	HIGH	MED-LOW
Washington Cmty HS Dist 308	00321816		5.63	0.05	1	1,406	MED	LOW
Rankin Cmty School Dist 98	00321634		3.74	0.04	1	250	HIGH	MED-LOW
Delavan Cmty Unit Sch Dist 703	00321115		3.51	0.03	2	480	HIGH	MED-LOW
District 50 Schools	00321713		3.46	0.03	2	700	MED	MED-LOW
Central Sch Dist 51	00320991		3.36	0.03	2	1,400	LOW	LOW
Deer Creek-Mackinaw CUSD 701	00321074		3.36	0.03	3	1,040	LOW	LOW
Tremont Cmty Unit SD 702	00321751		2.31	0.02	3	1,000	LOW	LOW
Washington School Dist 52	00321787		2.16	0.02	2	930	LOW	LOW
Creve Coeur Sch Dist 76	00321012		1.85	0.02	2	600	LOW	MED-HIGH
N Pekin-Marquette Hts SD 102	00321385		1.85	0.02	3	512	LOW	MED-LOW
South Pekin Grade Sch Dist 137	00321672		1.20	0.01	1	200	MED	MED-LOW
Robein Cmty School District 85	00321658		0.55	0.01	1	175	LOW	MED-LOW
Spring Lake Elem SD 606	00321696		0.35	0.00	1	60	HIGH	MED-HIGH
MACON		0.91						
Decatur Public Schools 61	00306921		67.71	0.62	18	8,700	HIGH	HIGH
Mt Zion Cmty Unit Sch Dist 3	00307406		10.06	0.09	5	2,400	LOW	MED-LOW
Maroa Forsyth CU Sch Dist 2	00307353		5.59	0.05	3	1,215	MED	
Sangamon Valley Cmty Unit SD 9	00307482		5.08	0.05	4	687	HIGH	MED-LOW
Warrensburg-Latham CU SD 11	00307523		4.30	0.04	3	1,200	MED	MED-LOW
Argenta Oreana Cmty Unit SD 1	00306828		4.27	0.04	3	800	MED	MED-LOW

Illinois School Directory
DISTRICT BUYING POWER INDEX

DISTRICT BUYING POWER INDEX
COUNTIES RANKED BY PERCENTAGE OF STATE SPENDING

COUNTY / DISTRICT	PID	COUNTY % OF STATE	DISTRICT % OF COUNTY	DISTRICT % OF STATES	NUMBER OF SCHOOLS	ENROLL	EXP	POV
Meridian Cmty Unit Sch Dist 15	00306880		3.00	0.03	3	1,065	LOW	MED-LOW
MCLEAN		0.88						
McLean Co Unit District 5	00306490		38.66	0.34	23	13,346	LOW	MED-LOW
Bloomington School District 87	00306141		35.88	0.32	10	5,200	HIGH	MED-LOW
Olympia Cmty Unit Sch Dist 16	00306634		7.93	0.07	5	1,900	LOW	MED-LOW
Tri-Valley Cmty School Dist 3	00306775		4.81	0.04	3	1,150	LOW	LOW
Heyworth Cmty Sch District 4	00306385		3.76	0.03	2	975	LOW	MED-LOW
Le Roy Cmty Unit SD 2	00306426		3.62	0.03	3	775	MED	MED-LOW
Ridgeview Cmty Unit SD 19	00306323		3.35	0.03	2	600	MED	MED-LOW
Lexington Cmty Sch Dist 7	00306464		1.99	0.02	3	490	LOW	MED-LOW
LA SALLE		0.83						
Streator Twp High Sch Dist 40	00303412		9.27	0.08	1	844	HIGH	MED-HIGH
La Salle Elem SD 122	00302767		7.86	0.07	2	900	HIGH	HIGH
Mendota Cmty School Dist 289	00303008		7.62	0.06	3	1,200	MED	MED-HIGH
Streator Elem School Dist 44	00303436		6.63	0.05	3	1,540	LOW	MED-HIGH
Ottawa Elementary Sch Dist 141	00303149		6.48	0.05	5	1,950	LOW	MED-HIGH
LaSalle Peru Twp HSD 120	00302834		6.11	0.05	1	1,200	MED	MED-LOW
Marseilles Elem Sch Dist 150	00302925		6.04	0.05	1	550	HIGH	MED-HIGH
Seneca Twp High Sch Dist 160	00303333		5.41	0.04	1	430	HIGH	MED-LOW
Serena Cmty Unit School Dist 2	01559236		5.21	0.04	4	665	HIGH	MED-HIGH
Oglesby Public Sch Dist 125	00303072		5.19	0.04	2	529	HIGH	MED-LOW
Earlville Cmty Unit Sch Dist 9	00302664		4.83	0.04	1	430	HIGH	MED-HIGH
Ottawa Twp High Sch Dist 140	00303125		4.29	0.04	1	1,450	LOW	MED-LOW
Seneca Cmty Cons Sch Dist 170	01557848		3.78	0.03	2	503	HIGH	MED-LOW
Peru Elem Sch Dist 124	00303266		3.50	0.03	2	970	LOW	MED-HIGH
Mendota Twp High Sch Dist 280	00302987		3.34	0.03	1	541	MED	MED-LOW
Wallace Cmty Cons Sch Dist 195	00303565		3.01	0.02	1	410	HIGH	MED-LOW
Miller Cmty Cons Sch Dist 210	00303058		1.86	0.02	1	158	HIGH	MED-LOW
Leland Cmty Unit Sch Dist 1	00302860		1.44	0.01	1	260	MED	MED-LOW
Dimmick Cmty School Dist 175	00302626		1.43	0.01	1	160	HIGH	MED-LOW
Grand Ridge CCSD 95	00302729		1.35	0.01	1	189	HIGH	MED-LOW
Tonica Cmty Cons Sch Dist 79	00303515		1.18	0.01	1	159	HIGH	MED-LOW
Waltham Elementary SD 185	00303589		1.03	0.01	1	200	MED	MED-LOW
Allen-Otter Creek CCSD 65	00302585		1.01	0.01	1	70	HIGH	MED-LOW
Deer Park Cmty Cons SD 82	00302602		0.89	0.01	1	75	HIGH	MED-LOW
Rutland Cmty Cons SD 230	00303319		0.70	0.01	1	75	HIGH	MED-LOW
Lostant Cmty Unit Sch Dist 425	00302896		0.53	0.00	1	55	HIGH	MED-LOW
KANKAKEE		0.82						
Kankakee School District 111	00299160		23.46	0.19	11	5,200	LOW	MED-HIGH
Bradley Elem School Dist 61	00298996		14.81	0.12	3	1,500	HIGH	MED-HIGH
Bourbonnais Elem Sch Dist 53	00298958		14.29	0.12	5	2,400	MED	MED-LOW
Herscher Cmty School Dist 2	00299108		11.52	0.09	4	1,650	MED	MED-LOW
Manteno Cmty Unit Sch Dist 5	00299316		9.61	0.08	3	2,100	MED	MED-LOW
Bradley-Bourbonnais CHSD 307	00299031		9.09	0.07	1	2,100	LOW	MED-LOW
Momence Cmty Unit Sch Dist 1	00299366		4.63	0.04	3	1,100	LOW	MED-HIGH
Pembroke Cmty Cons SD 259	00299419		4.20	0.03	1	200	HIGH	HIGH
St George School District 258	00299550		2.46	0.02	1	431	MED	MED-LOW
Grant Park Cmty Unit SD 6	00299067		2.07	0.02	3	475	LOW	MED-LOW
St Anne Cmty HSD 302	00299536		1.96	0.02	1	210	HIGH	MED-HIGH
St Anne Cmty Cons Sch Dist 256	00299512		1.90	0.02	1	351	MED	MED-LOW
DE KALB		0.74						
DeKalb Cmty Unit SD 428	00287959		33.20	0.25	12	6,600	LOW	MED-HIGH
Sycamore Cmty Unit SD 427	00288379		24.78	0.18	7	3,800	MED	MED-LOW
Sandwich Cmty Unit SD 430	00288214		14.60	0.11	6	2,000	MED	MED-LOW
Genoa-Kingston Cmty SD 424	00288068		12.25	0.09	4	1,700	MED	MED-LOW
Somonauk Cmty Unit SD 432	00288331		5.32	0.04	3	800	MED	MED-LOW
Indian Creek Cmty Unit SD 425	00288288		4.83	0.04	3	740	MED	MED-LOW
Hinckley-Big Rock Cmty SD 429	00288147		3.18	0.02	3	696	LOW	MED-LOW
Hiawatha Cmty Unit SD 426	00288111		1.83	0.01	2	450	LOW	MED-HIGH
VERMILION		0.65						
Danville School District 118	00322212		38.52	0.25	11	5,505	MED	HIGH
Hoopeston Area Cmty Unit SD 11	00322509		16.62	0.11	4	1,100	HIGH	MED-HIGH
Oakwood Cmty Unit Sch Dist 76	00322638		10.96	0.07	3	1,000	HIGH	MED-HIGH
Westville Cmty Unit Sch Dist 2	00322834		7.46	0.05	3	1,306	LOW	MED-HIGH
Bismarck-Henning Cmty SD 1	00322119		7.28	0.05	3	859	MED	MED-HIGH
Rossville-Alvin Cmty Unit SD 7	00322755		6.62	0.04	1	300	HIGH	MED-HIGH
Georgetown-Ridge Farm CUSD 4	00322444		4.86	0.03	3	1,010	LOW	MED-HIGH
Salt Fork Cmty Unit SD 512	00322781		4.16	0.03	3	900	LOW	MED-LOW
Armstrong Ellis SD 61	00322066		1.35	0.01	1	80	HIGH	MED-HIGH
Potomac Cmty Unit Sch Dist 10	00322652		1.25	0.01	1	145	MED	MED-HIGH
Armstrong Twp High SD 225	00322092		0.92	0.01	1	140	MED	MED-LOW

School Year 2020-2021

DISTRICT BUYING POWER INDEX

Market Data Retrieval

DISTRICT BUYING POWER INDEX
COUNTIES RANKED BY PERCENTAGE OF STATE SPENDING

COUNTY / DISTRICT	PID	COUNTY % OF STATE	DISTRICT % OF COUNTY	DISTRICT % OF STATES	NUMBER OF SCHOOLS	ENROLL	EXP	POV
STEPHENSON		0.55						
Freeport School District 145	00320745		76.95	0.42	10	4,000	HIGH	MED-HIGH
Dakota Cmty Unit Sch Dist 201	00320707		10.31	0.06	2	750	HIGH	MED-LOW
Lena-Winslow Cmty Unit SD 202	00320874		6.00	0.03	3	850	MED	MED-LOW
Pearl City Cmty Unit SD 200	00320953		4.09	0.02	1	431	MED	MED-LOW
Orangeville Cmty Unit SD 203	00320927		2.65	0.01	1	380	LOW	MED-LOW
WILLIAMSON		0.47						
Marion Cmty School Dist 2	00326983		44.22	0.21	7	3,914	MED	MED-HIGH
Johnston City Cmty Unit SD 1	00326933		18.66	0.09	4	1,100	HIGH	MED-HIGH
Carterville Cmty Unit SD 5	00326749		16.76	0.08	4	2,400	LOW	MED-LOW
Herrin Cmty School District 4	00326842		15.70	0.07	4	2,300	LOW	MED-HIGH
Crab Orchard Cmty Sch Dist 3	00326804		4.66	0.02	1	497	MED	MED-LOW
WHITESIDE		0.44						
Sterling Cmty Unit Sch Dist 5	00323929		43.16	0.19	6	3,500	MED	MED-HIGH
Erie Cmty School District 1	00324105		13.65	0.06	3	650	HIGH	MED-LOW
Rock Falls Elem Sch Dist 13	00324416		11.81	0.05	4	1,050	MED	MED-HIGH
Prophetstown-Lyndon-Tampico 3	00324260		7.48	0.03	4	800	LOW	MED-LOW
Rock Falls Twp High SD 301	00324466		7.08	0.03	1	630	MED	MED-HIGH
River Bend Cmty School Dist 2	00324337		6.16	0.03	4	900	LOW	MED-LOW
Morrison Cmty Unit Sch Dist 6	00324181		5.62	0.02	4	1,033	LOW	MED-LOW
East Coloma-Nelson Cesd 20	00324088		3.92	0.02	1	245	HIGH	MED-LOW
Montmorency Cmty Cons SD 145	00324167		1.11	0.00	1	230	LOW	MED-LOW
BOONE		0.40						
Belvidere Cmty Unit SD 100	00263422		76.88	0.31	10	8,500	LOW	MED-LOW
North Boone Cmty Unit SD 200	00263513		23.12	0.09	6	1,600	MED	MED-LOW
ADAMS		0.38						
Quincy School District 172	00263032		79.53	0.31	10	6,700	MED	MED-LOW
Liberty Cmty Unit Sch Dist 2	00262911		8.52	0.03	1	650	MED	MED-LOW
Central School District 3	00262856		4.53	0.02	4	837	LOW	MED-LOW
Payson Cmty Unit School Dist 1	00263006		3.88	0.01	2	550	LOW	MED-LOW
Mendon Cmty Unit School Dist 4	00262947		3.55	0.01	3	670	LOW	MED-LOW
LIVINGSTON		0.37						
Prairie Central Cmty USD 8	00304181		23.76	0.09	6	2,150	MED	MED-LOW
Pontiac Cmty Cons Sch Dist 429	00304387		14.06	0.05	4	1,300	MED	MED-HIGH
Dwight Twp High Sch Dist 230	00304155		11.67	0.04	1	221	HIGH	MED-LOW
Saunemin Cmty Cons SD 438	00304480		10.50	0.04	1	115	HIGH	MED-LOW
Dwight Common Elem SD 232	01557850		8.18	0.03	1	450	HIGH	MED-LOW
Pontiac Twp High Sch Dist 90	00304351		8.17	0.03	2	700	MED	MED-LOW
Tri-Point Cmty Unit SD 6J	00304571		7.15	0.03	3	395	HIGH	MED-HIGH
Flanagan-Cornell Unit 74 SD	00304222		6.20	0.02	1	195	HIGH	MED-LOW
Woodland Cmty Unit Sch Dist 5	00304519		5.47	0.02	2	540	MED	MED-LOW
Odell Cmty Cons Sch Dist 435	00304313		3.49	0.01	1	150	HIGH	MED-LOW
Cornell Cmty Cons Sch Dist 426	00304131		1.17	0.00	1	110	LOW	MED-HIGH
Rooks Creek Cmty Cons SD 425	00304466		0.17	0.00	1	50	LOW	LOW
OGLE		0.37						
Byron Cmty Unit SD 226	00311768		32.43	0.12	3	1,523	HIGH	LOW
Meridian Cmty Unit SD 223	00311940		17.13	0.06	4	1,614	MED	MED-LOW
Rochelle Cmty Cons SD 231	00312176		12.58	0.05	5	1,600	LOW	MED-LOW
Forrestville Valley CUSD 221	00311859		10.47	0.04	3	750	MED	MED-LOW
Rochelle Twp High Sch Dist 212	00312152		9.50	0.04	1	900	MED	MED-LOW
Oregon Cmty Unit Sch Dist 220	00312035		8.72	0.03	3	1,461	LOW	MED-LOW
Polo Cmty Unit Sch Dist 222	00312102		6.03	0.02	3	603	LOW	MED-LOW
Eswood Cmty Cons SD 269	00311823		1.23	0.00	1	68	HIGH	MED-LOW
Kings Cons School District 144	00311902		1.07	0.00	1	90	MED	MED-LOW
Creston Cmty Cons Sch Dist 161	00311809		0.83	0.00	1	88	LOW	LOW
HENRY		0.36						
Geneseo Cmty Unit Sch Dist 228	00295279		29.44	0.11	5	2,000	MED	MED-LOW
Kewanee Cmty Unit Sch Dist 229	00295346		24.87	0.09	6	2,000	MED	MED-HIGH
Orion Cmty Unit Sch Dist 223	00295425		8.98	0.03	3	990	LOW	LOW
Wethersfield Cmty Unit SD 230	00295463		8.30	0.03	2	580	MED	MED-LOW
Galva Cmty Unit Sch Dist 224	00295229		7.71	0.03	2	525	MED	MED-HIGH
Cambridge Cmty Unit SD 227	00295176		7.08	0.03	2	432	HIGH	MED-LOW
Annawan Cmty Unit SD 226	00295102		4.93	0.02	2	330	MED	MED-LOW
Colona Cmty School Dist 190	00295205		4.66	0.02	1	400	LOW	MED-HIGH
Alwood Cmty Unit Sch Dist 225	00295061		4.03	0.01	2	385	MED	MED-LOW
MACOUPIN		0.36						
Carlinville Cmty Unit SD 1	00307626		21.06	0.08	4	1,400	MED	MED-HIGH
Southwestern Cmty Unit SD 9	00307860		16.79	0.06	5	1,300	MED	MED-LOW
North Mac Cmty Unit SD 34	00307743		16.45	0.06	3	1,150	MED	MED-HIGH

School Year 2020-2021

Illinois School Directory

DISTRICT BUYING POWER INDEX

DISTRICT BUYING POWER INDEX
COUNTIES RANKED BY PERCENTAGE OF STATE SPENDING

COUNTY / DISTRICT	PID	COUNTY % OF STATE	DISTRICT % OF COUNTY	DISTRICT % OF STATES	NUMBER OF SCHOOLS	ENROLL	EXP	POV
Community Unit School Dist 7	00307690		13.19	0.05	3	1,250	LOW	MED-HIGH
Staunton Cmty Unit Sch Dist 6	00307925		11.29	0.04	3	1,200	LOW	MED-LOW
Mt Olive Cmty Unit Sch Dist 5	00307781		8.36	0.03	2	452	HIGH	MED-LOW
Bunker Hill Cmty Unit SD 8	00307585		8.31	0.03	2	600	MED	MED-HIGH
Northwestern CUSD 2	00307834		4.56	0.02	2	356	MED	MED-HIGH
GRUNDY		0.35						
Coal City Cmty Unit Sch Dist 1	00294055		28.02	0.10	5	2,151	MED	MED-LOW
Minooka Cmty Cons Sch Dist 201	00294225		21.96	0.08	7	4,400	LOW	LOW
Morris Elem School Dist 54	00294251		14.70	0.05	1	1,200	MED	MED-LOW
Morris Cmty High Sch Dist 101	00294316		11.94	0.04	1	867	MED	MED-LOW
Saratoga Cmty Cons SD 60C	00294378		8.93	0.03	1	799	MED	MED-LOW
Gardner Cmty Cons SD 72-C	00294093		3.69	0.01	1	152	HIGH	MED-LOW
Mazon-Verona-Kinsman ESD 2-C	00294158		3.68	0.01	2	325	MED	MED-LOW
Gardner S Wilmington HSD 73	00294110		3.54	0.01	1	200	MED	LOW
Braceville Elem School Dist 75	00294031		1.52	0.01	1	112	MED	MED-LOW
Nettle Creek Cmty SD 24-C	00294342		1.30	0.00	1	91	MED	LOW
S Wilmington Cons Elem SD 74	00294392		0.72	0.00	1	85	LOW	MED-LOW
MARION		0.35						
Sandoval Cmty Unit SD 501	00309818		24.87	0.09	2	504	HIGH	HIGH
Salem Elem Sch District 111	00309741		14.81	0.05	2	1,000	MED	MED-HIGH
South Central Cmty Unit SD 401	00309636		11.35	0.04	3	650	HIGH	MED-HIGH
Salem Cmty High Sch Dist 600	00309791		10.44	0.04	1	650	MED	MED-HIGH
Centralia High School Dist 200	00309571		9.70	0.03	1	900	MED	MED-HIGH
Centralia City Sch Dist 135	00309466		7.02	0.02	4	1,250	LOW	HIGH
Central City School Dist 133	00309442		4.89	0.02	1	349	MED	MED-HIGH
Patoka Cmty Unit SD 100	00309703		3.94	0.01	1	260	MED	MED-HIGH
Selmaville Cmty Cons SD 10	00309844		3.70	0.01	1	260	MED	MED-HIGH
Odin Public School Dist 722	00309674		2.93	0.01	2	250	MED	HIGH
Raccoon Cons School Dist 1	00309727		2.66	0.01	1	240	LOW	MED-HIGH
Iuka Community Cons Sch Dist 7	00309595		2.08	0.01	1	225	LOW	MED-HIGH
Kell Cons School District 2	00309612		1.61	0.01	1	100	HIGH	MED-HIGH
JACKSON		0.34						
Murphysboro Cmty Unit SD 186	00296261		43.62	0.15	4	1,800	HIGH	MED-HIGH
Carbondale Cmty HSD 165	00296089		15.71	0.05	1	1,000	MED	HIGH
Carbondale Elem School Dist 95	00295994		12.82	0.04	4	1,560	LOW	HIGH
Trico Cmty Unit Sch Dist 176	00296364		12.77	0.04	3	850	MED	MED-HIGH
Elverado Cmty Unit SD 196	00296144		7.32	0.02	4	420	HIGH	MED-HIGH
Unity Point Cmty Cons SD 140	00296429		3.11	0.01	1	610	LOW	MED-HIGH
DeSoto Grade School Dist 86	00296120		2.63	0.01	1	203	MED	MED-HIGH
Giant City Cmty Cons SD 130	00296194		2.02	0.01	1	210	LOW	MED-HIGH
CHRISTIAN		0.32						
Taylorville Cmty Unit SD 3	00265793		39.51	0.13	4	2,480	MED	MED-LOW
Central A&M Cmty Unit SD 21	00265535		25.20	0.08	5	670	HIGH	MED-LOW
Pana Cmty Unit School Dist 8	00265676		22.89	0.07	4	1,347	MED	MED-HIGH
South Fork School Dist 14	00265755		4.66	0.01	2	319	MED	MED-LOW
Morrisonville Cmty Unit SD 1	00265614		4.01	0.01	2	250	MED	MED-LOW
Edinburg Cmty Unit Sch Dist 4	00265561		3.73	0.01	1	290	MED	MED-LOW
MORGAN		0.31						
Jacksonville School Dist 117	00311407		75.21	0.23	9	3,200	HIGH	MED-HIGH
Franklin Cmty Unit SD 1	00311366		8.60	0.03	3	290	HIGH	MED-HIGH
Triopia Cmty Unit Sch Dist 27	00311574		6.43	0.02	2	382	MED	MED-LOW
Waverly Cmty Unit SD 6	00311615		5.61	0.02	2	369	WAVERLY	MED-HIGH
Meredosia-Chambersburg SD 11	00311548		4.16	0.01	1	195	HIGH	
FRANKLIN		0.28						
Frankfort Cmty Unit SD 168	00293207		19.91	0.06	4	1,650	LOW	MED-HIGH
Christopher Unit Sch Dist 99	00292980		16.82	0.05	2	702	MED	MED-HIGH
Benton Cons High Sch Dist 103	00292966		14.80	0.04	1	561	HIGH	MED-HIGH
Benton Cmty Cons Sch Dist 47	00292899		13.28	0.04	2	1,150	LOW	MED-HIGH
Zeigler Royalton CUSD 188	00293257		12.17	0.03	2	370	MED	MED-HIGH
Thompsonville Cmty USD 174	00293166		7.92	0.02	2	285	HIGH	MED-HIGH
Sesser-Valier Cmty Unit SD 196	00293104		7.57	0.02	3	700	LOW	MED-LOW
Akin Elem School District 91	00292875		4.55	0.01	1	80	HIGH	MED-HIGH
Ewing Northern Cmty SD 115	00293025		2.98	0.01	1	210	MED	MED-HIGH
JEFFERSON		0.28						
Mt Vernon City Sch Dist 80	00296766		29.93	0.08	4	1,700	MED	HIGH
Mt Vernon Twp HS District 201	00296845		22.53	0.06	1	1,250	MED	MED-HIGH
Woodlawn Unit School Dist 209	00296986		8.07	0.02	1	503	MED	MED-LOW
Waltonville Cmty Unit SD 1	00296936		7.52	0.02	2	325	HIGH	MED-LOW
Summersville Sch Dist 79	00296912		5.94	0.02	1	245	HIGH	MED-HIGH
Opdyke-Belle Rive Cmty CSSD 5	00296572		5.07	0.01	1	140	HIGH	MED-HIGH

DISTRICT BUYING POWER INDEX

Market Data Retrieval

DISTRICT BUYING POWER INDEX
COUNTIES RANKED BY PERCENTAGE OF STATE SPENDING

COUNTY / DISTRICT	PID	COUNTY % OF STATE	DISTRICT % OF COUNTY	DISTRICT % OF STATES	NUMBER OF SCHOOLS	ENROLL	EXP	POV
Field Cmty Cons Sch Dist 3	00296687		4.53	0.01	1	275	MED	MED-LOW
Rome Cmty Cons Sch Dist 2	00296895		4.30	0.01	1	450	LOW	MED-LOW
Bluford Unit School Dist 318	00296625		3.74	0.01	1	350	LOW	MED-HIGH
Bethel School District 82	00296601		3.69	0.01	1	170	MED	HIGH
Grand Prairie Cmty Cons SD 6	00296704		1.67	0.00	1	80	HIGH	MED-HIGH
Spring Garden Cmty CSD 178	00296649		1.51	0.00	2	249	LOW	MED-HIGH
Farrington Cmty Cons SD 99	00296663		0.81	0.00	1	58	MED	MED-LOW
McClellan Cons SD 12	00296742		0.71	0.00	1	45	LOW	MED-LOW
WOODFORD		0.28						
Eureka Cmty Unit Sch Dist 140	00328993		20.24	0.06	5	1,567	LOW	MED-LOW
El Paso-Gridley CUSD 11	00328955		17.74	0.05	4	1,200	MED	MED-LOW
Metamora Twp HS Dist 122	00329090		17.28	0.05	1	970	MED	LOW
Germantown Hills SD 69	00329052		12.90	0.04	2	900	MED	LOW
Metamora Cmty Cons Sch Dist 1	00329076		11.14	0.03	1	875	LOW	MED-LOW
Roanoke-Benson Cmty Unit SD 60	00329179		7.16	0.02	3	500	MED	MED-LOW
Fieldcrest Cmty School Dist 6	00329117		5.00	0.01	4	909	LOW	MED-LOW
Lowpoint-Washburn CUSD 21	00329210		4.63	0.01	3	325	LOW	MED-LOW
Riverview Cmty Cons Sch Dist 2	00329155		3.91	0.01	1	232	MED	MED-LOW
COLES		0.27						
Mattoon Cmty Unit Sch Dist 2	00266682		76.69	0.21	5	2,500	HIGH	MED-HIGH
Charleston Cmty Unit SD 1	00266589		18.03	0.05	6	2,500	LOW	MED-HIGH
Oakland Cmty Unit Sch Dist 5	00266840		5.28	0.01	2	245	MED	MED-HIGH
CLINTON		0.26						
Wesclin Cmty Unit Sch Dist 3	00266474		28.98	0.07	4	1,375	MED	MED-LOW
Central Cmty High Sch Dist 71	00266395		19.17	0.05	1	615	HIGH	MED-LOW
Carlyle Cmty Unit Sch Dist 1	00266333		16.99	0.04	3	1,006	MED	MED-LOW
Aviston Elem School Dist 21	00266266		10.01	0.03	1	390	HIGH	LOW
Breese Elementary SD 12	00266307		6.55	0.02	2	630	LOW	MED-LOW
Albers Elem School District 63	00266242		4.59	0.01	1	200	HIGH	MED-LOW
North Wamac School Dist 186	00266539		4.33	0.01	1	120	HIGH	HIGH
St Rose School District 14-15	00266450		2.87	0.01	1	207	MED	MED-LOW
Willow Grove School Dist 46	00266553		2.09	0.01	1	165	LOW	HIGH
Bartelso School District 57	00266280		1.62	0.00	1	158	LOW	LOW
Germantown Elem Sch Dist 60	00266436		1.50	0.00	1	250	LOW	LOW
Damiansville School Dist 62	00266412		1.29	0.00	1	85	LOW	MED-LOW
KNOX		0.26						
Galesburg Cmty Unit SD 205	00299926		43.99	0.12	8	4,500	LOW	MED-HIGH
Knoxville Cmty Unit SD 202	00300173		19.30	0.05	3	1,068	MED	MED-LOW
Abingdon-Avon Cmty Unit SD 276	00299873		16.37	0.04	4	877	MED	MED-HIGH
Rowva Cmty School Dist 208	00300240		10.57	0.03	2	600	MED	MED-LOW
Williamsfield Cmty Unit SD 210	00300305		9.76	0.03	1	275	HIGH	MED-HIGH
SALINE		0.26						
Harrisburg Cmty Unit SD 3	00318443		57.70	0.15	4	1,879	HIGH	MED-HIGH
Eldorado Cmty Unit Sch Dist 4	00318340		24.48	0.06	3	1,200	MED	HIGH
Carrier Mills-Stonefort SD 2	00318302		11.24	0.03	2	450	HIGH	HIGH
Galatia Cmty Unit Sch Dist 1	00318417		6.59	0.02	2	364	MED	MED-HIGH
BUREAU		0.25						
Bureau Valley Cmty Unit 340	00263874		23.16	0.06	4	1,082	MED	MED-LOW
Princeton Elem Sch Dist 115	00263953		21.12	0.05	4	1,156	MED	MED-LOW
Spring Valley Cmty Cons SD 99	00264036		12.88	0.03	1	633	MED	MED-HIGH
DePue Unit Sch Dist 103	00263692		10.09	0.03	1	390	HIGH	MED-LOW
Princeton Twp HSD 500	00264012		9.60	0.02	1	550	MED	MED-LOW
Hall Twp High School Dist 502	00263719		9.12	0.02	1	405	MED	MED-HIGH
La Moille Cmty Unit SD 303	00263757		4.63	0.01	3	205	MED	MED-LOW
Ladd Cmty Cons Sch Dist 94	00263800		4.04	0.01	1	190	MED	MED-HIGH
Malden Cmty Cons SD 84	00263848		2.90	0.01	1	100	HIGH	MED-LOW
Dalzell Elem School Dist 98	00263678		1.63	0.00	1	56	HIGH	MED-LOW
Ohio Cmty Cons School Dist 17	00263927		0.48	0.00	1	113	LOW	MED-HIGH
Ohio Cmty High School Dist 505	01843829		0.34	0.00	1	33	LOW	MED-LOW
EFFINGHAM		0.23						
Effingham Cmty Sch Dist 40	00292265		44.71	0.10	5	2,400	MED	MED-LOW
Teutopolis Cmty Unit SD 50	00292370		19.44	0.04	3	1,000	MED	LOW
Altamont Cmty Unit SD 10	00292148		14.90	0.03	2	700	MED	MED-LOW
Dieterich Community Unit SD 30	00292215		13.72	0.03	2	550	HIGH	MED-LOW
Beecher City Cmty Unit SD 20	00292174		7.24	0.02	2	333	MED	MED-LOW
MONTGOMERY		0.22						
Litchfield Cmty Unit SD 12	00311108		44.02	0.10	6	1,450	HIGH	MED-HIGH
Hillsboro Cmty Unit Sch Dist 3	00310996		29.60	0.07	4	1,700	LOW	MED-LOW
Nokomis Cmty Unit Sch Dist 22	00311196		15.24	0.03	2	630	MED	MED-HIGH

Illinois School Directory

DISTRICT BUYING POWER INDEX

DISTRICT BUYING POWER INDEX
COUNTIES RANKED BY PERCENTAGE OF STATE SPENDING

COUNTY / DISTRICT	PID	COUNTY % OF STATE	DISTRICT % OF COUNTY	DISTRICT % OF STATES	NUMBER OF SCHOOLS	ENROLL	EXP	POV
Panhandle Cmty Unit SD 2	00311251		11.14	0.02	3	520	MED	MED-LOW
FULTON		0.19						
Canton Union School Dist 66	00293350		38.29	0.07	5	2,490	LOW	MED-HIGH
Lewistown Community Unit SD 97	00293635		22.60	0.04	2	620	HIGH	MED-LOW
Fulton Co Cmty Unit Sch Dist 3	00293477		13.41	0.03	2	400	HIGH	MED-HIGH
Spoon River Valley Cmty SD 4	00293532		12.76	0.02	2	320	HIGH	MED-LOW
Vit Cmty Unit School Dist 2	00293740		8.43	0.02	2	370	MED	MED-HIGH
Astoria Cmty Unit Sch Dist 1	00293295		4.50	0.01	3	320	LOW	MED-HIGH
HANCOCK		0.19						
Hamilton Cmty Cons SD 328	00294603		21.51	0.04	2	600	HIGH	MED-LOW
Nauvoo-Colusa CUSD 325	00294718		12.53	0.02	1	244	HIGH	MED-LOW
Warsaw Cmty Unit Sch Dist 316	00294823		12.49	0.02	2	444	HIGH	MED-LOW
Southeastern Cmty Unit SD 337	00294770		12.13	0.02	2	450	MED	MED-HIGH
Dallas Elem Sch Dist 327	00294562		11.01	0.02	1	193	HIGH	MED-HIGH
Carthage Elementary SD 317	00294483		10.61	0.02	2	400	MED	MED-LOW
Illini West High Sch Dist 307	10915928		9.88	0.02	1	350	HIGH	MED-LOW
La Harpe Cmty Sch Dist 347	00294653		9.84	0.02	1	209	HIGH	MED-HIGH
IROQUOIS		0.19						
Iroquois West Cmty Unit SD 10	00295700		24.83	0.05	5	980	MED	MED-LOW
Central Cmty Unit SD 4	00295554		19.67	0.04	4	1,100	LOW	MED-LOW
Iroquois Co Cmty Unit SD 9	00295748		18.17	0.03	4	1,000	LOW	MED-HIGH
Milford Area Public SD 124	00295839		17.56	0.03	2	610	HIGH	MED-HIGH
Donovan Cmty Unit Sch Dist 3	00295671		8.73	0.02	2	290	MED	MED-LOW
Cissna Park Cmty Unit SD 6	00295619		8.32	0.02	1	294	MED	MED-LOW
Crescent Iroquois Cmty SD 249	00295645		2.72	0.01	1	70	HIGH	MED-LOW
DOUGLAS		0.17						
Arcola Cmty Unit Sch Dist 306	00288666		57.09	0.09	2	717	HIGH	MED-LOW
Tuscola Cmty Unit SD 301	00288783		17.68	0.03	3	1,000	LOW	MED-LOW
Arthur CUSD 305	00288707		12.79	0.02	4	1,140	LOW	MED-LOW
Villa Grove Cmty Unit SD 302	00288836		12.45	0.02	3	651	LOW	MED-LOW
MONROE		0.17						
Columbia Cmty Unit SD 4	00310867		48.35	0.08	4	2,000	MED	LOW
Waterloo Cmty Unit Sch Dist 5	00310934		42.34	0.07	5	2,739	LOW	LOW
Valmeyer Cmty School Dist 3	00310908		9.32	0.02	1	430	LOW	LOW
DEWITT		0.16						
Clinton Cmty Unit Sch Dist 15	00288484		61.57	0.10	5	1,800	MED	MED-LOW
Blue Ridge Cmty SD 18	00288563		38.43	0.06	3	700	HIGH	MED-LOW
CRAWFORD		0.15						
Robinson Cmty Unit Sch Dist 2	00287820		44.15	0.06	4	1,616	MED	MED-LOW
Oblong Cmty Unit Sch Dist 4	00287741		32.02	0.05	2	565	HIGH	MED-HIGH
Palestine Cmty Unit SD 3	00287791		16.35	0.02	2	375	HIGH	MED-HIGH
Hutsonville Cmty Unit SD 1	00287715		7.48	0.01	2	324	LOW	MED-HIGH
FAYETTE		0.15						
Vandalia Cmty Unit SD 203	00292590		50.37	0.07	4	1,490	MED	MED-HIGH
St Elmo Cmty Unit Sch Dist 202	00292552		19.01	0.03	2	440	HIGH	MED-HIGH
Brownstown Cmty Unit SD 201	00292459		17.55	0.03	2	380	HIGH	MED-HIGH
Ramsey Cmty Unit Sch Dist 204	00292526		13.07	0.02	2	450	MED	MED-HIGH
MCDONOUGH		0.15						
Macomb Cmty Unit Sch Dist 185	00305111		62.15	0.09	4	2,000	MED	MED-HIGH
Bushnell Prairie Cmty USD 170	00305006		23.63	0.03	3	630	MED	MED-HIGH
West Prairie Cmty Sch Dist 103	00305068		14.21	0.02	4	600	LOW	MED-HIGH
MERCER		0.14						
Sherrard Cmty Sch Dist 200	00310702		65.86	0.09	4	1,400	HIGH	MED-LOW
Mercer County SD 404	00310635		34.14	0.05	5	1,300	LOW	MED-LOW
RANDOLPH		0.14						
Sparta Cmty School Dist 140	00315063		31.40	0.04	3	1,213	LOW	MED-HIGH
Chester Cmty Unit Sch Dist 139	00314966		26.10	0.04	2	950	LOW	MED-HIGH
Red Bud Cmty Unit Sch Dist 132	00315037		25.12	0.04	2	1,000	LOW	MED-LOW
Steeleville Cmty Sch Dist 138	00315130		8.87	0.01	2	425	LOW	MED-LOW
Coulterville Unit Sch Dist 1	00314992		5.84	0.01	1	196	MED	MED-LOW
Prairie Du Rocher CCSD 134	00315013		2.68	0.00	1	152	LOW	MED-LOW
WARREN		0.14						
Monmouth-Roseville CUSD 238	00323058		76.28	0.10	5	1,686	HIGH	MED-HIGH
United Cmty Unit Sch Dist 304	00323151		23.72	0.03	4	950	LOW	MED-LOW
WHITE		0.14						
Carmi-White Co School Dist 5	00323682		49.93	0.07	6	1,400	MED	MED-HIGH

DISTRICT BUYING POWER INDEX

Market Data Retrieval

DISTRICT BUYING POWER INDEX
COUNTIES RANKED BY PERCENTAGE OF STATE SPENDING

COUNTY / DISTRICT	PID	COUNTY % OF STATE	DISTRICT % OF COUNTY	DISTRICT % OF STATES	NUMBER OF SCHOOLS	ENROLL	EXP	POV
Norris City-Omaha-Enfield SD 3	00323890		35.04	0.05	3	675	HIGH	MED-HIGH
Grayville Cmty Unit Sch Dist 1	00323814		15.03	0.02	2	280	HIGH	MED-HIGH
CLARK		0.13						
Marshall Cmty Sch Dist C-2	00265937		60.09	0.08	4	1,250	HIGH	MED-LOW
Casey-Westfield Cmty USD C-4	00265896		22.83	0.03	2	875	LOW	MED-LOW
Martinsville Cmty Unit SD C-3	00265999		17.08	0.02	2	400	MED	MED-HIGH
JO DAVIESS		0.13						
East Dubuque Unit SD 119	00297124		25.48	0.03	2	672	MED	MED-LOW
Galena Unit School Dist 120	00297174		22.39	0.03	3	830	LOW	MED-LOW
Stockton Cmty Unit SD 206	00297265		20.91	0.03	3	603	MED	MED-LOW
Scales Mound Cmty Unit SD 211	00297241		12.05	0.02	3	265	HIGH	MED-LOW
Warren Community Unit SD 205	00297306		10.60	0.01	2	400	LOW	MED-LOW
River Ridge Cmty Unit SD 210	00297150		8.58	0.01	3	500	LOW	MED-LOW
PERRY		0.13						
Du Quoin Cmty Unit SD 300	00314033		45.57	0.06	3	1,420	MED	MED-HIGH
Pinckneyville Sch Dist 50	00314100		34.34	0.05	2	504	HIGH	MED-HIGH
Pinckneyville Cmty High SD 101	00314148		13.68	0.02	1	415	MED	MED-HIGH
Tamaroa Elem School Dist 5	00314203		3.97	0.01	1	82	HIGH	MED-LOW
Community Cons School Dist 204	00314162		2.44	0.00	1	156	LOW	MED-LOW
WAYNE		0.13						
Fairfield Pub Sch District 112	00323486		29.32	0.04	2	700	HIGH	HIGH
Wayne City Cmty Unit SD 100	00323618		16.90	0.02	2	530	MED	MED-HIGH
North Wayne Cmty Unit SD 200	00323436		16.72	0.02	4	383	HIGH	MED-LOW
Fairfield Cmty High SD 225	00323515		16.61	0.02	1	430	MED	MED-HIGH
Jasper Cmty Cons Sch Dist 17	00323553		9.36	0.01	1	185	HIGH	MED-HIGH
New Hope Cmty Cons Sch Dist 6	00323591		7.33	0.01	1	180	MED	MED-LOW
Geff Cmty Cons School Dist 14	00323539		3.75	0.00	1	92	MED	MED-HIGH
EDGAR		0.12						
Paris Union School District 95	00292021		48.06	0.06	4	1,452	MED	MED-HIGH
Shiloh School District 1	00291948		19.39	0.02	1	380	HIGH	MED-HIGH
Paris Cmty Unit Sch Dist 4	00292007		14.41	0.02	1	480	LOW	MED-LOW
Edgar Co Cmty Sch Dist 6	00291900		12.64	0.02	3	307	MED	MED-LOW
Kansas Cmty School District 3	00291974		5.49	0.01	1	205	LOW	MED-LOW
FORD		0.12						
Gibson Cty-Melvin-Sibley CUSD5	00292708		51.37	0.06	3	1,000	HIGH	MED-LOW
Paxton-Buckley-Loda CUSD 10	00292784		48.63	0.06	3	1,300	MED	MED-LOW
LAWRENCE		0.12						
Lawrence Co Cmty Sch Dist 20	00303620		68.18	0.08	3	1,125	HIGH	MED-HIGH
Red Hill Cmty School Dist 10	00303723		31.82	0.04	3	977	LOW	MED-HIGH
LOGAN		0.12						
Lincoln Elem School Dist 27	00304789		31.50	0.04	5	1,200	LOW	MED-HIGH
Mt Pulaski Cmty Unit SD 23	00304911		19.90	0.02	2	530	MED	MED-LOW
Lincoln Cmty High Sch Dist 404	00304868		17.89	0.02	1	811	LOW	MED-LOW
Hartsburg Emden School Dist 21	00304741		9.00	0.01	2	200	MED	MED-LOW
West Lincoln-Broadwell ESD 92	00304973		8.35	0.01	1	220	MED	MED-LOW
Chester-E Lincoln Cmty SD 61	00304686		6.69	0.01	1	300	LOW	MED-LOW
New Holland Middletown ESD 88	00304935		6.67	0.01	1	90	HIGH	MED-LOW
PIKE		0.12						
Pikeland Cmty Sch Dist 10	00314576		41.90	0.05	3	1,200	MED	MED-HIGH
Pleasant Hill CUSD 3	00314667		20.90	0.02	2	311	HIGH	MED-HIGH
Griggsville-Perry Cmty SD 4	00314502		20.64	0.02	3	340	HIGH	MED-HIGH
Western CUSD 12	00314693		16.56	0.02	3	570	LOW	MED-HIGH
UNION		0.12						
Cobden Cmty Unit Sch Dist 17	00321892		23.89	0.03	2	526	MED	MED-HIGH
Shawnee Cmty Unit Sch Dist 84	00322004		21.94	0.03	2	300	HIGH	MED-HIGH
Anna-Jonesboro Cmty HSD 81	00321878		21.78	0.03	1	530	MED	MED-HIGH
Anna Cmty Cons Sch Dist 37	00321830		12.00	0.01	3	695	LOW	MED-HIGH
Jonesboro Cmty Cons SD 43	00321969		10.10	0.01	1	370	LOW	MED-HIGH
Dongola Unit School Dist 66	00321933		8.10	0.01	1	286	LOW	MED-HIGH
Lick Creek School Dist 16	00321983		2.20	0.00	1	150	LOW	MED-LOW
BOND		0.11						
Bond Co Cmty Unit Sch Dist 2	00263329		91.41	0.10	6	1,750	MED	MED-LOW
Mulberry Grove Cmty Sch Dist 1	00263381		8.59	0.01	3	400	LOW	MED-HIGH
CASS		0.11						
Beardstown Cmty Sch Dist 15	00264505		74.74	0.08	3	1,560	MED	MED-LOW
A-C Central Cmty Unit SD 262	00264488		16.62	0.02	2	419	MED	MED-LOW
Virginia Cmty Unit Sch Dist 64	00264608		8.64	0.01	1	320	LOW	MED-LOW

Illinois School Directory

DISTRICT BUYING POWER INDEX

DISTRICT BUYING POWER INDEX
COUNTIES RANKED BY PERCENTAGE OF STATE SPENDING

COUNTY / DISTRICT	PID	COUNTY % OF STATE	DISTRICT % OF COUNTY	DISTRICT % OF STATES	NUMBER OF SCHOOLS	ENROLL	EXP	POV
CLAY		0.11						
Flora Cmty Unit School Dist 35	00266163		60.76	0.06	3	1,396	MED	MED-HIGH
North Clay Cmty Unit SD 25	00266072		28.85	0.03	2	618	MED	MED-HIGH
Clay City Cmty Unit SD 10	00266137		10.39	0.01	3	350	LOW	MED-LOW
CUMBERLAND		0.11						
Cumberland Cmty Unit SD 77	00287882		73.33	0.08	3	1,000	HIGH	MED-LOW
Neoga Cmty Unit School Dist 3	00287911		26.67	0.03	2	535	MED	MED-LOW
GREENE		0.11						
North Greene Unit Dist 3	00293960		39.21	0.04	2	875	MED	MED-HIGH
Carrollton Cmty Unit SD 1	00293881		38.07	0.04	2	600	HIGH	MED-LOW
Greenfield Cmty Unit SD 10	00293922		22.72	0.03	2	444	MED	MED-HIGH
PIATT		0.11						
Monticello Cmty Unit SD 25	00314411		44.03	0.05	5	1,600	LOW	MED-LOW
Bement Cmty Unit Sch Dist 5	00314306		24.27	0.03	3	298	HIGH	MED-LOW
Deland-Weldon Cmty Unit SD 57	00314382		17.18	0.02	2	200	HIGH	MED-HIGH
Cerro Gordo Cmty Unit SD 100	00314332		14.52	0.02	2	490	LOW	MED-LOW
SHELBY		0.11						
Shelbyville Cmty Sch Dist 4	00320381		41.82	0.05	3	1,250	MED	MED-LOW
Windsor Cmty Unit SD 1	00320501		26.09	0.03	2	300	HIGH	MED-HIGH
Stewardson-Strasburg SD 5-A	00320446		19.81	0.02	2	374	HIGH	MED-LOW
Cowden Herrick CUSD 3A	00320288		12.28	0.01	2	380	LOW	MED-HIGH
CARROLL		0.09						
Eastland Cmty Unit SD 308	00264294		45.96	0.04	2	650	HIGH	MED-LOW
West Carroll CUSD 314	00264464		41.69	0.04	3	1,054	LOW	MED-HIGH
Chadwick Milledgevill CUSD 399	00264323		12.35	0.01	2	450	LOW	MED-LOW
MENARD		0.09						
Athens Cmty Unit Sch Dist 213	00310506		51.39	0.04	4	1,100	MED	MED-LOW
Porta Cmty Unit Sch Dist 202	00310570		45.16	0.04	3	1,009	LOW	MED-LOW
Greenview Cmty Unit SD 200	00310556		3.46	0.00	1	211	LOW	MED-LOW
JERSEY		0.08						
Jersey Cmty Sch Dist 100	00297021		100.00	0.08	5	2,647	LOW	MED-LOW
JOHNSON		0.08						
Goreville Cmty Unit SD 1	00297394		32.19	0.03	1	565	MED	MED-LOW
Vienna High School Dist 13-3	00297473		23.95	0.02	1	360	MED	MED-LOW
New Simpson Hill Cons SD 32	00297423		15.24	0.01	1	200	MED	MED-HIGH
Vienna Public School Dist 55	00297459		12.23	0.01	1	410	LOW	MED-HIGH
Buncombe Cons School Dist 43	00297356		8.24	0.01	1	60	HIGH	MED-HIGH
Cypress School District 64	00297370		8.15	0.01	1	120	MED	MED-HIGH
LEE		0.08						
Dixon Cmty Unit Sch Dist 170	00303905		34.50	0.03	5	2,432	LOW	MED-LOW
Amboy Cmty Unit Sch Dist 272	00303797		29.54	0.02	3	720	LOW	MED-LOW
Ashton-Franklin Center SD 275	00303864		17.98	0.01	2	560	LOW	MED-LOW
Paw Paw Cmty Unit SD 271	00303981		13.64	0.01	1	120	HIGH	MED-LOW
Steward Elem School Dist 220	00304064		4.34	0.00	1	51	MED	MED-LOW
MARSHALL		0.08						
Henry Senachwine CUSD 5	00309909		60.91	0.05	2	580	HIGH	MED-LOW
Midland Cmty Unit Sch Dist 7	00309923		39.09	0.03	3	720	MED	MED-LOW
MASON		0.08						
Illini Central CUSD 189	00310219		45.78	0.04	4	663	MED	MED-HIGH
Havana Cmty Sch District 126	00310154		34.83	0.03	3	1,000	LOW	MED-HIGH
Midwest Ctl Cmty Unit SD 191	00310116		19.39	0.02	3	900	LOW	MED-LOW
PULASKI		0.08						
Meridian Cmty School Dist 101	00314796		73.77	0.06	2	450	HIGH	HIGH
Century Cmty Unit SD 100	00314760		26.23	0.02	2	369	MED	HIGH
PUTNAM		0.08						
Putnam Co Cmty Unit SD 535	00314851		100.00	0.08	4	853	HIGH	MED-LOW
RICHLAND		0.08						
Richland Co Cmty Unit SD 1	00315219		100.00	0.08	3	2,500	LOW	MED-HIGH
EDWARDS		0.07						
Edwards Co Cmty Unit SD 1	00292095		100.00	0.07	3	896	HIGH	MED-LOW
MOULTRIE		0.07						
Sullivan Cmty Unit SD 300	00311718		59.11	0.04	3	1,100	LOW	MED-LOW
Okaw Valley Cmty Unit SD 302	00311653		40.89	0.03	3	475	MED	MED-LOW

DISTRICT BUYING POWER INDEX

COUNTIES RANKED BY PERCENTAGE OF STATE SPENDING

COUNTY / DISTRICT	PID	COUNTY % OF STATE	DISTRICT % OF COUNTY	DISTRICT % OF STATES	NUMBER OF SCHOOLS	ENROLL	EXP	POV
WASHINGTON		0.07						
Nashville Cmty Cons SD 49	00323292		32.28	0.02	1	585	MED	MED-LOW
Nashville Cmty HSD 99	00323319		28.98	0.02	1	410	MED	MED-LOW
West Washington Co Cmty SD 10	00323357		25.63	0.02	2	544	LOW	MED-LOW
Ashley Cmty Cons SD 15	00323230		6.79	0.01	1	130	LOW	MED-LOW
Irvington Cmty Cons SD 11	00323278		4.24	0.00	1	60	MED	MED-LOW
Oakdale Cmty Cons Sch Dist 1	00323333		2.08	0.00	1	69	LOW	MED-LOW
ALEXANDER		0.05						
Egyptian Cmty Unit Sch Dist 5	00263290		77.45	0.04	1	400	HIGH	HIGH
Cairo School District 1	00263238		22.55	0.01	2	315	LOW	HIGH
CALHOUN		0.05						
Calhoun Cmty Unit Sch Dist 40	00264232		76.82	0.04	2	484	HIGH	MED-LOW
Brussels Cmty Unit Sch Dist 42	00264206		23.18	0.01	2	106	HIGH	MED-LOW
JASPER		0.05						
Jasper Co Cmty Unit SD 1	00296479		100.00	0.05	4	1,278	MED	MED-LOW
MASSAC		0.05						
Massac Unit School District 1	00310398		89.21	0.04	7	2,100	LOW	MED-HIGH
Joppa-Maple Grove Unit SD 38	00310350		10.79	0.01	2	230	LOW	MED-HIGH
STARK		0.05						
Stark Co Cmty Unit SD 100	00320616		62.36	0.03	3	692	MED	MED-LOW
Bradford Cmty Unit Sch Dist 1	00320563		37.64	0.02	1	145	HIGH	MED-HIGH
WABASH		0.05						
Wabash Cmty Unit Sch Dist 348	00322949		84.05	0.04	4	1,450	LOW	MED-HIGH
Allendale Cmty Cons SD 17	00322925		15.95	0.01	1	130	MED	MED-HIGH
GALLATIN		0.04						
Gallatin Cmty Unit Sch Dist 7	00293855		100.00	0.04	1	750	MED	MED-HIGH
HAMILTON		0.04						
Hamilton Co Cmty Unit SD 10	00294419		100.00	0.04	4	1,199	LOW	MED-HIGH
HENDERSON		0.04						
West Central Cmty Unit SD 235	00295009		100.00	0.04	3	820	HIGH	MED-LOW
SCOTT		0.04						
Winchester Cmty Unit SD 1	00320238		80.05	0.03	2	680	MED	MED-LOW
Scott Morgan Cmty Unit SD 2	00320214		19.95	0.01	1	231	LOW	MED-HIGH
BROWN		0.03						
Brown Co Cmty Unit Sch Dist 1	00263575		100.00	0.03	3	750	LOW	MED-LOW
SCHUYLER		0.03						
Schuyler-Industry CUSD 5	00320135		100.00	0.03	4	1,100	LOW	MED-LOW
HARDIN		0.02						
Hardin Co Cmty Unit Sch Dist 1	00294914		100.00	0.02	2	500	LOW	MED-HIGH
POPE		0.02						
Pope Co Cmty Unit Sch Dist 1	00314734		100.00	0.02	2	530	MED	MED-HIGH

Illinois School Directory

NEW PUBLIC SCHOOLS AND KEY PERSONNEL

NEW PRINCIPALS

SCHOOL	PRINCIPAL	GRADES	ENROLLMENT	COUNTY	PAGE
Seymour Jr Sr High Sch	Nelson, Ashli	7-12	239	Adams	2
Unity Middle Sch	Arnsman, Josh	4-8	252	Adams	2
Greenville High Sch	Harris, Kara	9-12	539	Bond	4
Belvidere North High Sch	Friesema, James	9-12	1,433	Boone	4
Washington Academy	Walocha, Christopher	PK-8	825	Boone	4
Depute Unit Sch	Jansen, Tari	PK-12	390	Bureau	6
West Carroll High Sch	Hansen, Joe	9-12	311	Carroll	9
West Carroll High Sch	Asche, Ben	9-12	311	Carroll	9
Fisher Grade Sch	Palmer, Jake	K-6	328	Champaign	10
Prairieview-Ogden South ES	Heuer, Carl	1-6	123	Champaign	11
Yankee Ridge Elem Sch	Jackson, Mykah, Dr	K-5	345	Champaign	13
Arland D Williams Elem Sch	Schaefer, McLain	PK-5	659	Coles	19
Ashmore Elem Sch	Brown, Kristen	PK-4	100	Coles	19
Carl Sandburg Elem Sch	Williams, Eddie	1-3	503	Coles	19
Charleston High Sch	Lock, Aaron	9-12	811	Coles	19
Charleston Middle Sch	Lynn, Robert	7-8	380	Coles	19
Academy for Global Citizenship	Rangel, Berenice	K-8	466	Cook	38
Acero CS-Sandra Cisneros ES [156]	Keller, Jill	K-8	520	Cook	38
Algonquin Middle Sch	Jones, Donald	6-8	662	Cook	46
Anne Fox Elem Sch	Buchanan, Priscilla	K-6	374	Cook	66
Argo Cmty High Sch	Cotter, Brandon, Dr	9-12	2,100	Cook	21
Betsy Ross Elem Sch	Huff, Tinisa	K-2	137	Cook	50
Brook Park Elem Sch	King, Kelly	K-5	831	Cook	23
Campanelli Elem Sch	Houlihan, Amy, Dr	K-6	557	Cook	66
Carleton W Washburne Sch	Horwitz, Benjamin	7-8	394	Cook	72
Chicago Academy Elem Sch	Pae, Joyce	PK-8	514	Cook	25
Chicago HS for the Arts	Milsap, Teresa	9-12	611	Cook	39
Chippewa Middle Sch	Blakley, Kermit	6-8	666	Cook	46
Churchill Elem Sch	Schnoor, Sara	3-5	656	Cook	52
CICS-West Belden	Collins, S	K-8	530	Cook	39
Cottage Grove Upper Grade Ctr	Jones, Chantel	5-8	165	Cook	49
Crow Island Sch	Joynt, Lawrence	PK-4	309	Cook	72
District 54 Early Learning Ctr	Azab, Carrie	PK-PK	675	Cook	66
Edward J Tobin Elem Sch	Schmitz, Stephanie	PK-6	363	Cook	24
Elm Middle Sch	Groeneveld, Ashley	7-8	423	Cook	48
Eugene Field Elem Sch	Goodman, Courtney	K-5	650	Cook	62
Evergreen Academy Middle Sch	Marian, Strok	6-8	268	Cook	32
Forest Park Middle Sch	Brunson, Tiffany	6-8	193	Cook	50
Frank A Brodnicki Elem Sch	Touch, Kelly	K-6	691	Cook	53
Franklin Fine Arts Center	Booker-Thomas, Joyce, Dr	K-8	359	Cook	27
Fredrick Nerge Elem Sch	Frederick, Karolyn	K-6	675	Cook	66
Freedom Middle Sch	Brodeur, Tim	6-8	659	Cook	23
George Washington Middle Sch	Baker, Carol	6-8	735	Cook	56
Glenbrook North High Sch	Kirch, Karin	9-12	2,023	Cook	51
Glenbrook North High Sch	Woods, Deborah	9-12	2,023	Cook	51
Glenbrook North High Sch	Pehlke, Robin	9-12	2,023	Cook	51
Glenbrook North High Sch	Panzer, Jodie	9-12	2,023	Cook	51
Grant Primary Sch	DelGado, Carlos	K-K	76	Cook	22
Hanover Highlands Elem Sch	Thompson, Amy	K-6	517	Cook	66
Haven Middle Sch	Latting, Chris	6-8	836	Cook	48
Highlands Elem Sch	Montgomery, Ms	K-5	312	Cook	63
Hoffman Estates High Sch	Alther, Michael	9-12	1,959	Cook	69
Hoover Math & Science Academy	Zingler, Cassie	K-6	702	Cook	66
Horace Mann Elem Sch	Ali, Hussain	K-5	490	Cook	61
Jack London Middle Sch	Netzel, Anastasia	6-8	668	Cook	71
James Hart Sch	Johnson, Kimberly	6-8	702	Cook	52
Jensen Scholastic Acad	Jordan, Beverly, Dr	PK-8	360	Cook	31
John Fiske Elem Sch	Underwood, Kenya	PK-8	395	Cook	33
John Middleton Elem Sch	Berger, Erica, Dr	1-5	537	Cook	67
John V Leigh Elem Sch	Palmer, S	PK-8	494	Cook	59
Joseph Sears Sch	Helfand, Stephanie	PK-8	425	Cook	53
Kimball Hill Elem Sch	LaCamera, Michelle	PK-6	584	Cook	43
Komarek Elem Sch	Dilallo, Caitlin	PK-8	580	Cook	54
Komarek Elem Sch	Gold, Jason, Dr	PK-8	580	Cook	54
Komensky Elem Sch	Valadez, Leticia	PK-5	388	Cook	23
Liberty Junior High Sch	Abousweilem, Shwkar, Dr	7-8	811	Cook	24
Little Black Pearl Art Acad	Giggers, Donika	9-12	109	Cook	40
Luther Burbank Elem Sch	Martin, Tom	PK-6	507	Cook	24
MacArthur Middle Sch	Grochowski, Kevin	6-8	390	Cook	22
Maple Sch	Kurtz, Sam	6-8	384	Cook	60
Margaret Mead Jr High Sch	Ross, Scott	7-8	652	Cook	66
Maria Saucedo Scholastic Acad	Hitlz, Virginia	PK-8	917	Cook	32

School Year 2020-2021 800-333-8802

NEW PUBLIC SCHOOLS AND KEY PERSONNEL

Market Data Retrieval

School	Contact	Grades	Enrollment	County	Code
Mark Twain Elem Sch	Shlensky, Alyssa	PK-5	471	Cook	71
McKinley Educational Center	Salto, Luis	5-8	200	Cook	42
Melrose Park Elem Sch	Rodriguez, Sherri	K-8	930	Cook	57
Melzer Elem Sch	Maki, Angela	K-5	506	Cook	47
Middlefork Primary Sch	Kiedaisch, Jennifer	PK-3	197	Cook	68
Morton Sch of Excellence	Wise, Peggie, Dr	PK-8	202	Cook	26
Navajo Heights Elem Sch	Curran, Kaitlin	4-5	147	Cook	62
Nettelhorst Elem Sch	Muhammad, Yasmeen	PK-8	730	Cook	30
Newcomer Center	Rogers, Keir	9-12	51	Cook	70
Nob Hill Elem Sch	Smith, Ms	PK-5	193	Cook	63
Northeast Elem Sch	Berry, Carrie	PK-5	314	Cook	49
Oakwood Elem Sch	Kwasny, Kate	PK-2	761	Cook	55
Ogden International HS-West	Herrick, Devon	9-12	649	Cook	37
Pennoyer Sch	Ibrahim, Aliaa	PK-8	444	Cook	62
Percy Julian Middle Sch	Christian, Jeremy	6-8	1,043	Cook	61
Perspectives lit Math-Sci Acad [166]	Banks, Tyneisha	7-12	462	Cook	41
Pilsen Community Academy	Juarez, Jasmine	PK-8	252	Cook	32
Prosser Career Academy	Shimon, Sandra	Voc	1,236	Cook	37
Proviso West High Sch	Kosina, Joe	9-12	1,853	Cook	64
Ray Elem Sch	Neely, Gayle	PK-8	569	Cook	33
Reilly Elem Sch	Costilla, Marcelo	PK-8	677	Cook	31
Richard E Byrd Elem Sch	Faust, Michaela	K-6	298	Cook	24
Ridgewood High Sch	Castellano, Gina	9-12	900	Cook	64
River Trails ELC at Parkview	Veytsman, Amy	PK-PK	77	Cook	65
Robert Frost Elem Sch	Prikkel, Tim	PK-5	504	Cook	71
Ronald McNair Elem Sch	Lucas, Benetrice	PK-8	346	Cook	26
Roosevelt Middle Sch	Durry, Adrian	7-8	750	Cook	22
Salt Creek Elem Sch	Humboldt, Sarah	K-5	435	Cook	44
Sauk Elem Sch	Morgan, Richard, Dr	4-6	365	Cook	57
Schaumburg High Sch	Harlan, Brian	9-12	2,095	Cook	69
Scott Elem Sch	Schaffer, Lisa	K-5	424	Cook	57
Sherlock Elem Sch	Lago, Joanna	PK-6	401	Cook	42
Southwest Elem Sch	Liska, Scott	K-6	298	Cook	49
Southwood Middle Sch	Richardson, Brenda	6-8	444	Cook	45
Steger Primary Center	Leoni, Patricia	PK-1	316	Cook	68
Steger Primary Center	Smith, Venus	PK-1	316	Cook	68
Thornridge High Sch	Moore, Justin	9-12	1,093	Cook	69
Virginia Lake Elem Sch	Daly, Stephanie	K-6	745	Cook	43
Walsh Elem Sch	Smith, Christine	K-4	353	Cook	45
Walt Whitman Elem Sch	Almodovar, Jorge	PK-5	481	Cook	71
Washington High Sch	San-Roman, Barbara	9-12	1,484	Cook	38
Westchester Primary Sch	Lafin, Lora	PK-2	391	Cook	70
Westgate Elem Sch	Buch, Ann	K-5	568	Cook	21
William Beye Elem Sch	Schemidt, Jennifer	K-5	367	Cook	61
Wilmette Junior High Sch	Dominique, Kate	7-8	892	Cook	72
Worth Elem Sch	Eichstaedt, Maureen	PK-5	402	Cook	72
Zenon Sykuta Elem Sch	Stewart, Leatha	PK-2	354	Cook	45
Neoga Elem Sch	Helmers, Denise	K-5	224	Cumberland	84
Genoa-Kingston High Sch	Cascio, Matthew	9-12	562	De Kalb	85
Gwendolyn Brooks Elem Sch	Sago, Melissa	K-5	315	De Kalb	84
Indian Creek High Sch	McCarty, K	9-12	198	De Kalb	85
Prairie View Sch	Ryan, Garrett	K-3	213	De Kalb	86
East Prairie Junior High Sch	Vanausdoll, Jared	5-8	300	Douglas	88
Brookdale Elem Sch	Schmid, Keeley	K-5	508	Du Page	95
Carl Sandburg Elem Sch	Bailey, Stacey	K-5	380	Du Page	92
Elmwood Elem Sch	Langes, Matt	K-5	668	Du Page	98
Gary Elem Sch	Kassir, Mary	K-5	551	Du Page	99
Glenbard East High Sch	Anderson, Antoine	9-12	2,244	Du Page	94
Indian Trail Elem Sch	Nicasio, Mariana	PK-6	375	Du Page	93
Lake Park High Sch-East Campus	Brode-Rico, Amanda	9-10	1,360	Du Page	96
Mary Lou Cowlishaw Elem Sch	Azcoitia, Carlos	K-5	697	Du Page	95
Monroe Elem Sch	Reingruber, Kristin	K-5	346	Du Page	91
Owen Elem Sch	Bonomo, Ken	K-5	579	Du Page	95
Pierce Downer Elem Sch	Wagner, Leland	K-6	341	Du Page	93
Roy Deshane Elem Sch	Gray, Amy	K-5	266	Du Page	90
Turner Elem Sch	McDavid, Maurice	K-5	376	Du Page	100
Waterbury Elem Sch	Pokora, Jon, Dr	K-5	453	Du Page	96
Westfield Elem Sch	McDonald, Matt	PK-5	343	Du Page	90
Wheaton-Warrenville South HS	McDermott, Scott	9-12	1,936	Du Page	92
White Eagle Elem Sch	Howicz, Mary	K-5	562	Du Page	96
York Community High Sch	Bagdasarian, Shahe, Dr	9-12	2,829	Du Page	94
Paris Co-op High Sch	Cox, Mark	9-12	559	Edgar	103
Beecher City Jr Sr High Sch	Hanfland, Karen	6-12	157	Effingham	104
Teutopolis Grade Sch	Harmon, Sherry	PK-6	561	Effingham	105
Thompsonville High Sch	Chiaventone, Jamie	9-12	107	Franklin	108
Zeigler Royalton High Sch	Morgan, Matt	9-12	179	Franklin	108

Illinois School Directory — NEW PUBLIC SCHOOLS AND KEY PERSONNEL

School	Contact	Grades	Enrollment	County	Page
Canton High Sch	Valencia, Jay	9-12	680	Fulton	109
Cuba Elem Sch	Braun, Jeff	PK-5	178	Fulton	109
Lewistown Central Elem Sch	McLaughlin, Joey	PK-6	367	Fulton	110
Lewistown Central Elem Sch	Well, Richard	PK-6	367	Fulton	110
Westview Elem Sch	Gardner, Eleanor	PK-4	429	Fulton	109
North Greene Elem Sch	Kuchy, Jackie	PK-6	493	Greene	111
Walnut Trails Elem Sch	Monroe, Sarah	K-4	568	Grundy	112
Carthage Middle Sch	Nason, Ryanne	5-8	176	Hancock	114
La Harpe Elem Sch	Ryner, Sara	PK-8	209	Hancock	115
Iroquois West High Sch	Smith, Erin	9-12	306	Iroquois	119
Wanda Kendall Elem Sch	Heldt, Jessica	2-3	138	Iroquois	119
General Logan Attendance Ctr	Finke, Stephanie	K-2	406	Jackson	121
Waltonville Grade Sch	Dagner, Andrew	PK-8	240	Jefferson	124
Abbott Middle Sch	Zugel, Christine	7-8	690	Kane	130
Clinton Elem Sch	Miquelon, Jonathon	K-6	454	Kane	130
Creekside Elem Sch	Pollack, Joel	K-6	555	Kane	130
Fox Meadow Elem Sch	Gold, Jason	K-6	550	Kane	130
Fred Rodgers Magnet Academy	Skelly, Lisa	3-8	441	Kane	129
G N Dieterich Elem Sch	Holland, Lauren	PK-5	486	Kane	129
Geneva Middle School North	Westerhoff, Brenna	6-8	647	Kane	131
Geneva Middle School South	Bidlack, Lawrence	6-8	656	Kane	131
Goodwin Elem Sch	Hetrick, Jeff	PK-5	367	Kane	132
Greenman Elem Sch	Papp, Kelly	PK-5	589	Kane	132
H C Storm Elem Sch	Milka, Chris	K-5	392	Kane	128
Hill Elem Sch	Smith, Elizabeth	PK-5	623	Kane	132
John Stewart Elem Sch	Aversa, Samantha	PK-5	426	Kane	132
K D Waldo Middle Sch	Hills, Kelly	6-8	952	Kane	129
Kaneland Harter Middle Sch	Schmitt, Nathan	6-8	1,100	Kane	132
L D Brady Elem Sch	Vivanco, Elizabeth	K-5	336	Kane	129
Larkin High Sch	Bush, Krystal	9-12	2,045	Kane	130
Lowrie Elem Sch	Robinson, Tiffany	K-6	394	Kane	131
Nicholson Elem Sch	Bernal, Jen	K-5	286	Kane	132
Rose E Krug Elem Sch	Conrad, Sheila	PK-5	293	Kane	129
Rotolo Middle School-Batavia	Karnick, Kelley	6-8	1,307	Kane	128
South Elgin High Sch	Johansen, Kurt, Dr	9-12	2,666	Kane	131
South Elgin High Sch	Moran, Brian	9-12	2,666	Kane	131
Streamwood High Sch	Vandeusen, Jennifer, Dr	9-12	1,937	Kane	131
Wasco Elem Sch	Brennan, Stephanie	K-5	404	Kane	129
Wild Rose Elem Sch	Solomon, Theresa	K-5	478	Kane	129
Shabbona Elem Sch	Tingley, Jackie	1-4	314	Kankakee	134
Steuben Elem Sch	Newsome, Anna	PK-3	272	Kankakee	135
Emily G Johns Elem Sch	Baughman, Lucas	4-6	530	Kendall	138
Fox Chase Elem Sch	Haddock, Patrick	K-5	577	Kendall	137
Hunt Club Elem Sch	Stoffers, Elisabeth	K-5	707	Kendall	137
Murphy Junior High Sch	Bingham, Laura	6-8	773	Kendall	137
King Elem Sch	Hawkins, Valerie	K-4	355	Knox	140
Kimes Elem Sch	Ketcham, Heather	PK-1	387	La Salle	144
LaSalle Peru Twp High Sch	Cushing, Ingrid	9-12	1,200	La Salle	142
B J Hooper Elem Sch	Feldman, Steve	K-6	689	Lake	152
Barrington MS-Station Campus	Aalfs, Jim	6-8	991	Lake	147
Central Elem Sch	Coats, Carrie	PK-4	486	Lake	150
Clearview Elem Sch	Johnson, Sandi	K-5	515	Lake	156
Hawthorn Elem School South	Hunter, Christy	K-5	717	Lake	151
Hawthorn Sch of Dual Language	Fabrizio, S	K-5	407	Lake	151
Hawthorn Sch of Dual Language	Gordon, A, Dr	K-5	407	Lake	151
Hough St Elem Sch	Ernst, Zach	PK-5	294	Lake	147
Howe Elem Sch	Mekky, Nashwa	K-5	365	Lake	147
Jack Benny Middle Sch	Kirkwood, Issac	6-8	589	Lake	156
Kipling Elem Sch	Elbert, Andy	K-5	469	Lake	149
Lake Bluff Elem Sch	Bae, Kellie	PK-5	576	Lake	151
Lake Zurich High Sch	Deluga, Erin	9-12	1,819	Lake	152
Newport Elem Sch	Anderson, Chris	K-5	267	Lake	147
Oak Crest Elem Sch	Convey, Jennifer	PK-5	302	Lake	147
Oakland Elem Sch	Adams, Rebecca	2-5	365	Lake	146
Preschool at Early Educ Ctr	Metzger, Jeanette	PK-PK	192	Lake	155
Raymond Ellis Elem Sch	Kubelka, Scott	1-5	593	Lake	155
Rockland Elem Sch	Cieciwa, Jim	K-5	276	Lake	153
William L Thompson Elem Sch	Crowley, Lauren	PK-6	624	Lake	152
Woodland Elem Sch East	Wollberg, Ryan	1-3	1,445	Lake	157
Reagan Middle Sch	Magnafici, Matthew	6-8	628	Lee	160
Dwight High Sch	Pittenger, Andrew	9-12	221	Livingston	161
Mt Pulaski Grade Sch	Lora, Danielle	PK-8	357	Logan	164
Hope Academy Magnet Sch	Spencer-Burks, Tasia	K-8	491	Macon	165
McGaughey Elem Sch	Ethel, Heather	PK-1	371	Macon	166
Michael E Baum Elem Sch	Brady, Mary	K-6	316	Macon	165
Mt Zion High Sch	Johnson, Justin	9-12	757	Macon	166

School Year 2020-2021   800-333-8802   IL-NEW3

NEW PUBLIC SCHOOLS AND KEY PERSONNEL

Market Data Retrieval

School	Contact	Grades	Enrollment	County	Code
Sangamon Valley Intermed Sch	Sommer, Kristina	3-5	168	Macon	166
Sangamon Valley Middle Sch	Kelly, Brandi	6-8	144	Macon	166
South Shores Elem Sch	Shores, South	K-6	279	Macon	165
South Shores Elem Sch	Fraas, Matt	K-6	279	Macon	165
Stevenson Elem Sch	Galligan, Ms	K-6	256	Macon	165
Gillespie High Sch	Rosentreter, Jill	9-12	364	Macoupin	167
Gillespie Middle Sch	Cooper, Tara	6-8	280	Macoupin	167
Staunton Elem Sch	Allen, Brett	PK-8	939	Macoupin	168
Staunton Junior High Sch	McGowen, Ryan	6-7	401	Macoupin	168
Albert Cassens Elem Sch	Montgomery, Tiana	3-5	505	Madison	171
Collinsville Middle Sch	Snow, Brad	7-8	951	Madison	170
Edwardsville High Sch	Stuart, Steve, Dr	9-12	2,359	Madison	171
Glen Carbon Elem Sch	Robbins, Mandy	K-2	333	Madison	171
Grantfork Elem Sch	Hickey, Anne	4-5	53	Madison	171
Liberty Middle Sch	Duncan, Allen	6-8	954	Madison	171
Lincoln Middle Sch	Morgan, Jennifer	6-8	803	Madison	171
Prather Elem Sch	Bratten, Genie	PK-K	650	Madison	171
Venice Elem Sch	Ferrell, Ronald, Dr	PK-8	80	Madison	172
Webster Elem Sch	Schumacher, Alison	PK-4	359	Madison	170
Woodland Elem Sch	Converse, Susan	3-5	483	Madison	171
Centralia High Sch	Lane, Chuck	9-12	900	Marion	174
Midland Elem Sch	Sams, Jesse	PK-4	291	Marshall	176
Midland High Sch	Hoffmann, Ann	9-12	195	Marshall	176
Harvard Junior High Sch	Cardamone, Tom	6-8	590	McHenry	181
Heineman Middle Sch	Faulkner, Brian	6-8	859	McHenry	182
Husmann Elem Sch	Sromek, Guy	K-5	471	McHenry	181
North Elem Sch	Barrett, Michelle	K-5	696	McHenry	181
Olson Elem Sch	Watson, Stephanie	1-5	441	McHenry	184
Richmond Burton Cmty High Sch	Baird, Michael	9-12	636	McHenry	184
Bent Elem Sch	DelGado, Guillermina	K-5	360	Mclean	185
Sarah Raymond Early Chldhd Ctr	Dobbs, Jeffrey	PK-PK	274	Mclean	185
Sheridan Elem Sch	Harr, Danel	K-5	374	Mclean	185
Stevenson Elem Sch	Shook, Lynn	K-5	397	Mclean	185
Tri-Valley Elem Sch	Swearingen, Tyler	PK-3	359	Mclean	187
Tri-Valley Middle Sch	Burnett, Sara	4-8	390	Mclean	187
Sherrard Elem Sch	Wyant, Casey	PK-4	262	Mercer	189
Parkview Elem Sch	Dugan, Bobby	2-4	398	Monroe	190
Farmersville Grade Sch	Masten, Jana	PK-1	96	Montgomery	191
Raymond Grade Sch	Schuster, Ken	2-5	138	Montgomery	191
Jacksonville High Sch	Dion, Joey	9-12	971	Morgan	192
Jacksonville Middle Sch	Barlow, Gary	7-8	515	Morgan	192
Triopia Jr Sr High Sch	Sorrells, Josh	7-12	180	Morgan	192
Monroe Center Elem Sch	Simpson, Deana	3-5	319	Ogle	195
Oregon High Sch	Deininger, Heidi	9-12	398	Ogle	195
Brimfield High Sch	Robison, Mr	9-12	232	Peoria	196
Calvin Coolidge Middle Sch	Swanson, Mervyn	5-8	352	Peoria	199
Dr Maude A Sanders Primary Sch	Hiles, Dan	K-4	396	Peoria	199
Franklin Primary Sch	Mastin, Emily	K-5	483	Peoria	199
Glen Oak Cmty Learning Center	Suggs, Ilethea	K-6	836	Peoria	199
Hines Primary Sch	Lough, Marcia	PK-4	479	Peoria	199
Kellar Primary Sch	Baron, Heidi	K-4	361	Peoria	199
Mark Bills Middle Sch	Padilla, Krystle	5-8	227	Peoria	199
Oak Grove Elem Middle Sch	Baughman, Rachel	K-8	250	Peoria	198
Peoria Heights Grade Sch	Tallon, Ellen	PK-8	537	Peoria	198
Pleasant Valley Elem Sch	Galyean, Kelly	K-4	288	Peoria	199
Pleasant Valley Middle Sch	Wall, Jacob	5-8	184	Peoria	199
Richwoods High Sch	Emken, Carly	9-12	1,270	Peoria	199
Roosevelt Magnet Sch	Rodgers, Laura	K-8	668	Peoria	199
Von Steuben Middle Sch	Cruz, Michelle	5-8	337	Peoria	199
Tamaroa Elem Sch	Opp, Cynthia	PK-8	82	Perry	201
Monticello Middle Sch	Hughes, Mark	6-8	363	Piatt	202
Pope Co High Sch	Graves, Seth	9-12	153	Pope	204
Meridian Jr Sr High Sch	Boren, Maryann	6-12	110	Pulaski	204
Putnam Co Primary Center	Huffaker, Chawn	PK-2	243	Putnam	204
Red Bud High Sch	Guehne, Alan	9-12	391	Randolph	205
Sparta Lincoln Sch	Laramore, Amy	PK-8	760	Randolph	205
George Washington Elem Sch	Price, Brian	K-5	271	Rock Island	208
Riverdale Elem Sch	Lofgren, Mark	PK-5	562	Rock Island	208
Taylor Ridge Elem Sch	Emery, Jenna	PK-2	163	Rock Island	209
Thomas Jefferson Elem Sch	Maag, Dorian, Dr	PK-6	370	Rock Island	208
Thomas Jefferson Elem Sch	Nitzel, Mike	PK-6	370	Rock Island	208
East Side Intermediate Sch	McCollum, Eric	3-5	409	Saline	211
Washington Elem Sch	Willis, Noah	PK-1	202	Schuyler	215
Webster Elem Sch	Willis, Noah	2-4	216	Schuyler	215
Dupo Jr Sr High Sch	Brown, Stevie	7-12	413	St Clair	218
Lebanon Elem Sch	Foster, Jasen	PK-5	281	St Clair	220

Illinois School Directory

NEW PUBLIC SCHOOLS AND KEY PERSONNEL

School	Principal	Grades	Enrollment	County	Page
Lebanon High Sch	Teasley, Jeff	6-12	274	St Clair	220
Marissa Jr Sr High Sch	Mueller, Dawn	7-12	250	St Clair	220
Pearl City Sch	Asche, Ben	K-12	431	Stephenson	225
Parkview Middle Sch	Bevard, Dustin	5-8	260	Tazewell	226
Tremont High Sch	Uhlman, Jill	9-12	336	Tazewell	228
Garfield Elem Sch	Sollars, Stacie	K-5	300	Vermilion	232
South View Upper Elem Sch	Prunkard, Lindsey	5-6	701	Vermilion	232
Central Intermediate Sch	Hutton, Becky	4-6	341	Warren	234
Grayville Jr Sr High Sch	Harrelson, Julie	7-12	141	White	238
Montmorency Elem Sch	Dillon, Megan	PK-8	230	Whiteside	239
Elwood Cmty Cons Sch	Rekruciak, Ryan	PK-8	318	Will	242
Heritage Grove Middle Sch	Cournaya, Danielle	6-8	951	Will	246
Hickory Creek Middle Sch	Dotson, Tricia	6-8	901	Will	242
Hilda Walker Interm Sch	Carroll, Maura	5-6	685	Will	247
Issac Singleton Elem Sch	Hodge, Laura	K-5	580	Will	243
Monee Elem Sch	Vaughn, Amos	K-5	435	Will	242
N B Galloway Elem Sch	Cobarrubias, Dacia	PK-2	396	Will	241
Oak Prairie Junior High Sch	Forcash, Sue	6-8	565	Will	249
Pioneer Path	Dooley, Erin	3-4	241	Will	241
Plainfield Central High Sch	Chlebek, Chris	9-12	2,070	Will	246
Summit Hill Junior High Sch	Goebel, Laura	7-8	732	Will	247
Taft Elem Sch	Henderson, Doriane	K-5	416	Will	243
Thomas Jefferson Elem Sch	Ramirez, Consuelo	K-5	452	Will	243
Thomas Jefferson Elem Sch	Foster, Vicky	K-5	639	Will	246
Three Rivers Sch	DuBois, Laura	5-6	295	Will	241
Herrin Cmty Elem Sch	Heuring, Bobbi	2-5	696	Williamson	251
Johnston City High Sch	Pietrantoni, Josh	9-12	358	Williamson	251
Washington Elem Mid Sch	Pietrantoni, Josh	5-8	318	Williamson	251
Dorothy Simon Elem Sch	Baker, Heather	PK-2	307	Winnebago	255
Riverview Elem Sch	Doherty, Tim	2-4	236	Winnebago	255
West Middle Sch	Goodrich, Larry	6-8	930	Winnebago	255
Metamora High Sch	Kiesewetter, Ron	9-12	970	Woodford	258

NEW SUPERINTENDENTS

DISTRICT	SUPERINTENDENT	GRADES	ENROLLMENT	COUNTY	PAGE
Cairo School District 1	Rice, Patrick, Dr	PK-12	315	Alexander	3
Mulberry Grove Cmty Sch Dist 1	Koontz, Robert	PK-12	400	Bond	4
Calhoun Cmty Unit Sch Dist 40	Lee, Andrea	PK-12	484	Calhoun	8
Gifford Cmty Cons SD 188	Smith, Jay	K-8	183	Champaign	10
Prairieview-Ogden Sch Dist 197	Isenhower, Jeffery	K-8	247	Champaign	11
Carlyle Cmty Unit Sch Dist 1	Gray, Annie	K-12	1,006	Clinton	17
Mattoon Cmty Unit Sch Dist 2	Condron, Tim	PK-12	2,500	Coles	19
Argo Cmty High School Dist 217	Toulious, William	9-12	2,100	Cook	21
Central Stickney Sch Dist 110	Hackett, Erin	PK-8	384	Cook	25
Country Club Hills SD 160	Meighan, Duane, Dr	K-8	1,221	Cook	45
East Prairie School Dist 73	Goldberg, Paul, Dr	PK-8	505	Cook	47
Elmwood Park Cmty Unit SD 401	Gauthier, Leah, Dr	PK-12	2,800	Cook	47
Evergreen Park Elem SD 124	Longo, Margret, Dr	PK-8	1,900	Cook	49
Hazel Crest School Dist 152-5	Stales, Kenneth	PK-8	1,000	Cook	52
Komarek School District 94	Fitzgerrald, Todd, Dr	PK-8	580	Cook	54
La Grange Cmty School Dist 105	Ganan, Brian, Dr	PK-8	1,300	Cook	54
Lemont-Bromberek Sch Dist 113A	McConnell, Anthony	K-8	2,300	Cook	55
Lincoln Elem School Dist 156	Rice, Anita	PK-8	950	Cook	55
Norridge School Dist 80	Palmer, Stephanie	K-8	1,000	Cook	59
Proviso Twp High Sch Dist 209	Henderson, James, Dr	9-12	4,339	Cook	63
Sandridge Sch Dist 172	Sutton, Nicholas	K-8	350	Cook	66
Sunnybrook School District 171	Pettis, Erika, Dr	K-8	1,012	Cook	68
Thornton Fractnl Twp HSD 215	Jones-Raymond, Shophia, Dr	9-12	3,177	Cook	69
Palestine Cmty Unit SD 3	Sisil, Jessica	PK-12	375	Crawford	83
DeKalb Cmty Unit SD 428	Lechner, Ray	PK-12	6,600	De Kalb	84
Sycamore Cmty Unit SD 427	Wilder, Steve	K-12	3,800	De Kalb	86
Blue Ridge Cmty SD 18	Stanifer, Hillary	PK-12	700	Dewitt	87
Cass School District 63	Cross, Mark	PK-8	766	Du Page	89
Center Cass Sch Dist 66	Wise, Andrew, Dr	K-8	1,100	Du Page	90
Darien Public Sch Dist 61	Langman, Robert, Dr	K-8	1,400	Du Page	92
Indian Prairie Sch Dist 204	Talley, Adrian, Dr	PK-12	27,400	Du Page	95
Lake Park Cmty High SD 108	Feucht, Jeffrey, Dr	9-12	2,500	Du Page	96
Teutopolis Cmty Unit SD 50	Sturgeon, Matthew	PK-12	1,000	Effingham	105
Benton Cons High Sch Dist 103	Johnson, Benjamin	9-12	561	Franklin	107
Morris Cmty High Sch Dist 101	Ortiz, Craig	9-12	867	Grundy	113
Iroquois Co Cmty Unit SD 9	Andriano, David, Dr	PK-12	1,000	Iroquois	119
Iroquois West Cmty Unit SD 10	Lekkas, Angelo	PK-12	980	Iroquois	119
Murphysboro Cmty Unit SD 186	Evers, Andrea, Dr	K-12	1,800	Jackson	121
McClellan Cons SD 12	Milt, Terry	K-8	45	Jefferson	123

School Year 2020-2021   800-333-8802   IL-NEW5

NEW PUBLIC SCHOOLS AND KEY PERSONNEL

Market Data Retrieval

District	Contact	Grades	Enrollment	County	Page
Mt Vernon Twp HS District 201	Andrews, Melanie	9-12	1,250	Jefferson	123
Rome Cmty Cons Sch Dist 2	Phillips, Steven	PK-8	450	Jefferson	123
Woodlawn Unit School Dist 209	Helbig, Eric	K-12	503	Jefferson	124
Galena Unit School Dist 120	Vincent, Tim	PK-12	830	Jo Daviess	125
Bourbonnais Elem Sch Dist 53	Ehrman, Adam, Dr	PK-8	2,400	Kankakee	134
Knoxville Cmty Unit SD 202	Burgess, Joe	PK-12	1,068	Knox	140
Peru Elem Sch Dist 124	Craven, Jamie	PK-8	970	La Salle	143
Antioch Cmty Cons Sch Dist 34	Hubbard, Bradford, Dr	PK-8	2,775	Lake	146
Deerfield Public SD 109	Westerhold, Jane, Dr	PK-8	3,400	Lake	149
Lake Bluff Elem Sch Dist 65	Leali, Lisa, Dr	PK-8	880	Lake	151
Mundelein Elem School Dist 75	Myers, Kevin	K-8	1,586	Lake	153
Oak Grove School District 68	Sherman, Allison	K-8	900	Lake	154
Woodland School District 50	Casey, Lori	PK-8	5,700	Lake	156
Zion-Benton Twp High SD 126	Rodgreguez, Jesse, Dr	9-12	2,100	Lake	157
Ashton-Franklin Center SD 275	Lindy, Michael	PK-12	560	Lee	159
Lincoln Cmty High Sch Dist 404	Stricklin, Dwight	9-12	811	Logan	163
New Holland Middletown ESD 88	Bruley, Brandi	K-8	90	Logan	164
Meridian Cmty Unit Sch Dist 15	Pygott, Andy	PK-12	1,065	Macon	166
Warrensburg-Latham CU SD 11	Warner, Cheryl	PK-12	1,200	Macon	166
Community Unit School Dist 7	Owsley, Shane	PK-12	1,250	Macoupin	167
Staunton Cmty Unit Sch Dist 6	Tolbert, Cynthia	PK-12	1,200	Macoupin	168
Alton Cmty School District 11	Baumgartner, Kristie	PK-12	6,000	Madison	169
Granite City Cmty Unit SD 9	Cann, Stephanie	PK-12	5,764	Madison	171
Venice Cmty Unit School Dist 3	Ferrell, Ronald, Dr	K-8	80	Madison	172
Kell Cons School District 2	Consolino, John	K-8	100	Marion	174
Raccoon Cons School Dist 1	Johaness, Misty	PK-8	240	Marion	175
West Prairie Cmty Sch Dist 103	Gradert, Guy	PK-12	600	McDonough	178
McLean Co Unit District 5	Weikle, Kristen	PK-12	13,346	Mclean	186
Olympia Cmty Unit Sch Dist 16	O'Donnell, Laura	PK-12	1,900	Mclean	187
Columbia Cmty Unit SD 4	Grode, Christopher	K-12	2,000	Monroe	189
Litchfield Cmty Unit SD 12	Fuerstenau, Greggory, Dr	PK-12	1,450	Montgomery	191
Franklin Cmty Unit SD 1	Simonson, Curt, Dr	K-12	290	Morgan	192
Kings Cons School District 144	Lamb, Matt	K-8	90	Ogle	194
Polo Cmty Unit Sch Dist 222	Mandrell, Kelly, Dr	PK-12	603	Ogle	195
Brimfield Cmty Unit SD 309	Shinall, Tony	PK-12	680	Peoria	196
Tamaroa Elem School Dist 5	Brink, Brian	K-8	82	Perry	201
Pikeland Cmty Sch Dist 10	Kilver, Carol, Dr	PK-12	1,200	Pike	203
Pope Co Cmty Unit Sch Dist 1	Fritch, Ryan	PK-12	530	Pope	204
Prairie Du Rocher CCSD 134	Pipher, Rob	PK-8	152	Randolph	205
Riverdale Cmty Unit SD 100	Temple, Joshua	PK-12	1,160	Rock Island	208
Rochester Cmty Unit SD 3-A	Cox, Dan	PK-12	2,215	Sangamon	212
Tri-City Cmty Unit Sch Dist 1	Colmone, Chad	PK-12	570	Sangamon	214
Belleville Township HSD 201	Mentzer, Brian	9-12	4,500	St Clair	217
Stark Co Cmty Unit SD 100	Elliott, Brett	PK-12	692	Stark	223
Creve Coeur Sch Dist 76	Johnson, Steve	PK-8	600	Tazewell	226
Tremont Cmty Unit SD 702	Barry, Sean	PK-12	1,000	Tazewell	228
Jasper Cmty Cons Sch Dist 17	Berger, Shari	K-8	185	Wayne	237
Grayville Cmty Unit Sch Dist 1	Harlson, Julie	PK-12	280	White	238
Prophetstown-Lyndon-Tampico 3	Petzke, John	PK-12	800	Whiteside	239
Joliet Twp High Sch Dist 204	Guseman, Karla	9-12	6,589	Will	243
Lockport Twp High Sch Dist 205	McBride, Robert, Dr	9-12	3,890	Will	244
Mokena Public School Dist 159	Cohen, Mark, Dr	K-8	1,500	Will	245
New Lenox School District 122	Motsch, Lori	PK-8	5,300	Will	245
Valley View Cmty SD 365-U	Kinder, Rachel	PK-12	18,000	Will	248
Fieldcrest Cmty School Dist 6	Rockwell, Kari, Dr	PK-12	909	Woodford	257

Illinois School Directory

Adams County

ILLINOIS

- **Illinois Dept of Education** PID: 00262844 — 217/782-4321
  100 N 1st St Ste 1, Springfield 62702 — Fax 217/782-3097

Schools: 23

Dr Carmen Ayala	1	Robert Wolfe	2
Mark Haller	4	Dr Jason Helfer	8,15
Dr Annie Brooks	11	Matthew Ulmer	11,298
Carol Brooks	26,31,75	Marci Johnson	31,81
Carisa Hurley	34	Cara Wiley	35
Samuel Aguirre	57	Heather Calomese	58
Darren Reisberg	67	Miguel Calderon	68
Annie Rae Clementz	69,294	Jackie Matthews	71
John Shake	76		

STATE-OPERATED SCHOOLS

State Schs..Principal	Grd	Prgm	Enr/#Cls	SN		
ⓒ Ace Amandla Charter Sch 6820 S Washtenaw Ave, Chicago 60629 Turon Ivy	9-12	T	250		85%	773/535-7150 Fax 773/535-7151
ⓒ Horizon Sci Acad-Belmont [161] 1336 Basswood Rd Ste 702, Schaumburg 60173 Serdar Kartal	K-8		550			773/237-2702 Fax 773/237-2726
ⓒ Horizon Sci Acad-McKinley Park [161] 2245 W Pershing Rd, Chicago 60609 Cafer Cengiz	K-12	T	830		76%	773/247-8400 Fax 773/247-8401
Illinois Center for Rehab & Ed 1950 W Roosevelt Rd, Chicago 60608 Letitia Doe	Spec		60 9		56%	312/433-3125 Fax 312/433-3254
Illinois Math & Science Acad 1500 Sullivan Rd, Aurora 60506 Comfort Anderson	10-12	V	562			630/907-5000 Fax 630/907-5976
Illinois Sch-Visually Impaired 658 E State St, Jacksonville 62650 Aimee Veith	Spec		51 40		47%	217/479-4436 Fax 217/479-4433
Illinois School for the Deaf 125 S Webster Ave, Jacksonville 62650 Angela Kuhn \ Allison Fraas	Spec	V	157 52		56%	217/479-4200 Fax 217/479-4209
ⓐ Illinois Youth Center 1201 W Poplar St, Harrisburg 62946 Michael Butler	7-12	GV	332 20		88%	618/252-8681 Fax 618/253-7538
ⓐ Illinois Youth Detention Ctr 30W200 Ferry Rd, Naperville 60563 Dr Joyce Nelson	8-12	GV	23 8			630/983-6231 Fax 630/983-6213
ⓐ Illinois Youth-St Charles Ctr 3825 Campton Hills Dr, Saint Charles 60175 Mike Zarco	8-12	GV	68 19		82%	630/584-0506
ⓐ Iyc Pere Marquette 17808 State Highway 100 W, Grafton 62037 Cynthia Houston	8-12		24 3		87%	618/786-2371 Fax 618/786-2381
John C Dunham STEM Sch 405 S Gladstone Ave, Aurora 60506 Arin Carter	3-8		198		16%	630/947-1240
ⓒ Learn 9 Chtr Sch-Waukegan [164] 1200 W Glen Flora Ave, Waukegan 60085 Dr Cassandra Brooks	K-3	T	192		90%	847/377-0690 Fax 847/249-3315
Philip J Rock Sch 818 Du Page Blvd, Glen Ellyn 60137 Diane Finn	Spec		10			630/790-2474 Fax 630/790-4893
ⓒ Prairie Crossing Charter Sch 1531 Jones Point Rd, Grayslake 60030 Geoff Deigan	K-8		431 10		4%	847/543-9722 Fax 847/543-9744
Rosecrance Sch-G Williamson 1601 University Dr, Rockford 61107 Cyndie Kelly	Spec		78 6			844/711-5106 Fax 815/387-2590
ⓒ Shabazz CS-Sizemore Acad [158] 6547 S Stewart Ave, Chicago 60621 Jocelyn Mills	K-8		245 15		96%	773/651-1661 Fax 773/651-4125
ⓒ Shabazz CS-Betty Shabbazz Acd [158] 7823 S Ellis Ave, Chicago 60619 Shannon Mason	K-8	T	322 11		97%	773/651-1221 Fax 773/651-0302
ⓒ Southland College Prep Chtr HS 4601 Sauk Trl, Richton Park 60471 Dr Bryan Hale	9-12		555		55%	708/748-8105 Fax 708/833-4298
Thomas Metcalf Sch 107 University St, Normal 61790 Dr Amy Fritson	PK-8		400 25		7%	309/438-7621 Fax 309/438-2580
University High Sch 601 Gregory St, Normal 61761 Andrea Markert	9-12	V	615 35		2%	309/438-8346 Fax 309/438-5198
University Laboratory High Sch 1212 Springfield Ave, Urbana 61801 Dr Elizabeth Majerus	8-12		319		6%	217/333-2870 Fax 217/333-4064
ⓐ Youthbuild McLean Co CS ⓒ 360 Wylie Dr, Normal 61761 Tracey Poalson	9-12	V	52		62%	309/454-3898 Fax 309/454-3913

ADAMS COUNTY

ADAMS COUNTY SCHOOLS

County Schs..Principal	Grd	Prgm	Enr/#Cls	SN		
Adams Co Juv Det Center Sch 200 N 52nd St, Quincy 62305 Marcy Wells	5-12	A	20 3		60%	217/228-0026 Fax 217/228-8770
Quincy Area Voc Tech Center 219 Baldwin Dr, Quincy 62301 Mark Pfleiger	Voc	A	500 30			217/224-3775 Fax 217/221-4800

ADAMS PUBLIC SCHOOLS

- **Central School District 3** PID: 00262856 — 217/593-7116
  2110 Highway 94 N, Camp Point 62320 — Fax 217/593-7026

Schools: 4 \ **Students:** 837 \ **College-Bound:** 73% \ **Ethnic:** Caucasian 99% \ **Exp:** $107 (Low) \ **Poverty:** 13% \ **Title I:** $191,702 \ **Special Education:** $315,000 \ **Open-Close:** 08/20 - 05/21 \ **DTBP:** $185 (High)

Erica Smith	1,11	Theresa Piehler	2
Mick Gooding	3	Rick Boss	5
Matt Long	6	Jennifer Hetzler	7*
Chevi Ingalls	8	Bobbi Salmons	12
Kristen Kamprath	58*	Chris Marlow	67
Shelly Cramer	73		

Public Schs..Principal	Grd	Prgm	Enr/#Cls	SN		
Central Elem Sch 109 W School St, Camp Point 62320 Eric Stotts	PK-2	T	195 13		43%	217/593-7795 Fax 217/593-6514
Central Junior High Sch 2110 Highway 94 N, Camp Point 62320 Erica Smith	5-8	T	281		44%	217/593-7741 Fax 217/593-7028
Central Middle Sch 301 Hanna St, Golden 62339 Chevi Ingalls	3-4	AT	124 8		44%	217/696-4652 Fax 217/696-4385
Central Senior High Sch 2110 Highway 94 N, Camp Point 62320 Marty Cook	9-12	ATV	237 30		42%	217/593-7731 Fax 217/593-7025

Adams County

Market Data Retrieval

- **Liberty Cmty Unit Sch Dist 2** PID: 00262911 217/645-3433
  505 N Park St, Liberty 62347 Fax 217/645-3241

  Schools: 1 \ **Teachers:** 54 \ **Students:** 650 \ **Special Ed Students:** 101 \ **College-Bound:** 58% \ **Ethnic:** Caucasian 100% \ **Exp:** $266 (Med) \ **Poverty:** 6% \ **Title I:** $56,789 \ **Special Education:** $385,000 \ **Open-Close:** 08/20 - 05/28 \ **DTBP:** $175 (High)

Kelle Bunch 1,11,83	Allen Flynn 3*
Wes Gerzi 5	Jody Obert 12*
Krista Tenhouse 59*	Thera Green 60*
Rod Barry 67	Michael Smith 76,295*

Public Schs..Principal	Grd	Prgm	Enr/#Cls	SN	
Liberty Sch 505 N Park St, Liberty 62347 Jody Obert \ Justin Edgar	PK-12	V	650 60	20%	217/645-3433

- **Mendon Cmty Unit School Dist 4** PID: 00262947 217/936-2111
  453 W Collins St, Mendon 62351 Fax 217/936-2643

  Schools: 3 \ **Teachers:** 49 \ **Students:** 670 \ **Special Ed Students:** 138 \ **LEP Students:** 8 \ **Ethnic:** African American 1%, Hispanic 2%, Caucasian 97% \ **Exp:** $102 (Low) \ **Poverty:** 8% \ **Title I:** $93,296 \ **Special Education:** $290,000 \ **Open-Close:** 08/31 - 05/26 \ **DTBP:** $174 (High)

Scott Riddle 1	Gina Whelan 2,84
Jim Farmer 67	Seth Klusmeyer 73
Shelby Maas 83*	

Public Schs..Principal	Grd	Prgm	Enr/#Cls	SN	
Unity Elem Sch 136 W Washington St, Mendon 62351 Jerry Ellerman	PK-3	T	236 5	44%	217/936-2512 Fax 217/936-2124
Unity High Sch 453 W Collins St, Mendon 62351 Bill Dorethy	9-12	GV	201 30	34%	217/936-2116 Fax 217/936-2117
Unity Middle Sch 453 W Collins St, Mendon 62351 Josh Arnsman	4-8	T	252 12	38%	217/936-2111 Fax 217/936-2730

- **Payson Cmty Unit School Dist 1** PID: 00263006 217/656-3323
  406 W State St, Payson 62360 Fax 217/656-4042

  Schools: 2 \ **Teachers:** 39 \ **Students:** 550 \ **Special Ed Students:** 101 \ **LEP Students:** 5 \ **College-Bound:** 68% \ **Ethnic:** Asian 1%, Caucasian 99% \ **Exp:** $139 (Low) \ **Poverty:** 12% \ **Title I:** $108,779 \ **Special Education:** $205,000 \ **Open-Close:** 08/19 - 05/25

Dr Donna Veile 1,11	Don Koetters 3
Brian Rea 6*	Karrie Wolf 58*
Lisa Schwartz 67	Barb Speckhart 73*

Public Schs..Principal	Grd	Prgm	Enr/#Cls	SN	
Seymour Elem Sch 404 W State St, Payson 62360 Julie Phelan	PK-6	T	316 19	52%	217/656-3439 Fax 217/656-4034
Seymour Jr Sr High Sch 420 W Brainard St, Payson 62360 Ashli Nelson	7-12	T	239 20	46%	217/656-3355 Fax 217/656-3584

- **Quincy School District 172** PID: 00263032 217/223-8700
  1416 Maine St, Quincy 62301 Fax 217/228-7162

  Schools: 10 \ **Teachers:** 389 \ **Students:** 6,700 \ **Special Ed Students:** 1,327 \ **LEP Students:** 16 \ **Ethnic:** Asian 1%, African American 10%, Hispanic 4%, Caucasian 85% \ **Exp:** $236 (Med) \ **Poverty:** 15% \ **Title I:** $2,266,153 \ **Special Education:** $3,297,000 \ **Open-Close:** 08/20 - 05/28 \ **DTBP:** $192 (High)

Roy Webb 1	Ryan Whicker 2,3,17
Tracey Dance 2	Shane Bartley 3
Jean Kinder 4	Shane Barnes 5
Scott Douglas 6*	Jody Steinke 8*
Michaela Fray 8,69	Kim Dinkheller 9,11,69,73,275,286,298*
Kim Mast 51	Eryn Beswick 58
Sayeed Ali 67	Lisa Otten 68
Dan Ware 73	Robin Walters 76
Carol Frericks 79	Lori Miles 88*
Dan Arns 91	Marilyn Smith 273*

Public Schs..Principal	Grd	Prgm	Enr/#Cls	SN	
ABC Academy 1416 Maine St, Quincy 62301 Lori Miles	Spec		30	84%	217/228-7175 Fax 217/222-2794
Ⓐ Adams Co Regional Safe Sch 1416 Maine St, Quincy 62301 Lori Miles	7-12		25	88%	217/223-8700
Baldwin Elem Sch 3001 Maine St, Quincy 62301 Jim Sohn	K-5	T	291 13	62%	217/223-0003 Fax 217/228-7148
Col Isles Elem Sch 3111 N 12th St, Quincy 62305 Brad Funkenbusch	K-5	T	475 23	68%	217/222-4059 Fax 217/222-8077
Denman Elem Sch 4100 Harrison St, Quincy 62305 Chrissy Cox	K-5		580 20		217/222-2530 Fax 217/221-3461
Lincoln-Douglas Elem Sch 3211 Payson Rd, Quincy 62305 Brian Trowbridge	K-5	T	572 14		217/223-8871 Fax 217/228-7188
Quincy Early Childhood 401 S 8th St, Quincy 62301 Julie Schuckman	PK-PK		526 24	78%	217/228-7121 Fax 217/221-3476
Quincy Junior High Sch 100 S 14th St, Quincy 62301 Daniel Sparrow	6-8	T	1,457 100	58%	217/222-3073 Fax 217/228-7185
Quincy Senior High Sch 3322 Maine St, Quincy 62301 Jody Steinke	9-12	AGTV	1,752 30	49%	217/224-3770 Fax 217/228-7149
Rooney Elem Sch 4900 Columbus Rd, Quincy 62305 Melanie Schrand	K-5	T	476 25	63%	217/228-7117 Fax 217/221-3462

ADAMS CATHOLIC SCHOOLS

- **Diocese of Springfield Ed Off** PID: 00319394
  Listing includes only schools located in this county. See District Index for location of Diocesan Offices.

Catholic Schs..Principal	Grd	Prgm	Enr/#Cls	SN	
Blessed Sacrament Catholic Sch 1115 S 7th St, Quincy 62301 Christie Bliven	PK-8		177 10		217/228-1477 Fax 217/222-6463

1 Superintendent	8 Curric/Instruct K-12	19 Chief Financial Officer	29 Family/Consumer Science	39 Social Studies K-12	49 English/Lang Arts Elem	59 Special Education Elem	69 Academic Assessment
2 Bus/Finance/Purchasing	9 Curric/Instruct Elem	20 Art K-12	30 Adult Education	40 Social Studies Elem	50 English/Lang Arts Sec	60 Special Education Sec	70 Research/Development
3 Buildings And Grounds	10 Curric/Instruct Sec	21 Art Elem	31 Career/Sch-to-Work K-12	41 Social Studies Sec	51 Reading K-12	61 Foreign/World Lang K-12	71 Public Information
4 Food Service	11 Federal Program	22 Art Sec	32 Career/Sch-to-Work Elem	42 Science K-12	52 Reading Elem	62 Foreign/World Lang Elem	72 Summer School
5 Transportation	12 Title I	23 Music K-12	33 Career/Sch-to-Work Sec	43 Science Elem	53 Reading Sec	63 Foreign/World Lang Sec	73 Instructional Tech
6 Athletic	13 Title V	24 Music Elem	34 Early Childhood Ed	44 Science Sec	54 Remedial Reading K-12	64 Religious Education K-12	74 Inservice Training
7 Health Services	15 Asst Superintendent	25 Music Sec	35 Health/Phys Education	45 Math K-12	55 Remedial Reading Elem	65 Religious Education Elem	75 Marketing/Distributive
	16 Instructional Media Svcs	26 Business Education	36 Guidance Services K-12	46 Math Elem	56 Remedial Reading Sec	66 Religious Education Sec	76 Info Systems
	17 Chief Operations Officer	27 Career & Tech Ed	37 Guidance Services Elem	47 Math Sec	57 Bilingual/ELL	67 School Board President	77 Psychological Assess
	18 Chief Academic Officer	28 Technology Education	38 Guidance Services Sec	48 English/Lang Arts K-12	58 Special Education K-12	68 Teacher Personnel	78 Affirmative Action

Illinois School Directory — Alexander County

Quincy Notre Dame High Sch 1400 S 11th St, Quincy 62301 Mark McDowell	9-12	V	461 32	217/223-2479 Fax 217/223-0023
St Dominic Sch 4100 Columbus Rd, Quincy 62305 Carol Frericks	PK-8		178 10	217/224-0041 Fax 217/224-0042
St Francis Solanus Sch 1720 College Ave, Quincy 62301 Lori Shepard	PK-8		313 15	217/222-4077 Fax 217/222-5049
St Peter Sch 2500 Maine St, Quincy 62301 Cindy Venvertloh	PK-8		409 18	217/223-1120 Fax 217/223-1173

ADAMS PRIVATE SCHOOLS

Private Schs..Principal	Grd	Prgm	Enr/#Cls	SN	
Chaddock Sch 205 S 24th St, Quincy 62301 Cory Powell	Spec	V	70 10		217/222-0034 Fax 217/592-0391
Quincy Area Christian Sch 1236 N 10th St, Quincy 62301 Susan Hill	PK-12		38 7		217/223-5698 Fax 217/223-5724
St James Lutheran Sch 900 S 17th St, Quincy 62301 Nathan Landskroener	PK-8		140 15		217/222-8267 Fax 217/222-3415
Transitions Sch 732 Hampshire St, Quincy 62301 Kelly Schlueter	Spec		21 4		217/223-9694 Fax 217/221-9430

ADAMS REGIONAL CENTERS

- **Adams Co Special Ed Co-op** PID: 02184171   217/223-8700
  1416 Maine St, Quincy 62301   Fax 217/228-7162

Eryn Beswick 58

ALEXANDER COUNTY

ALEXANDER COUNTY SCHOOLS

County Schs..Principal	Grd	Prgm	Enr/#Cls	SN	
Five Co Reg Voc System Sch 130 Washington Ave, Tamms 62988 Patrick Harner	Voc	A	55 4		618/747-2703 Fax 618/747-2872

ALEXANDER PUBLIC SCHOOLS

- **Cairo School District 1** PID: 00263238   618/734-4102
  4201 Sycamore St, Cairo 62914   Fax 618/734-4047

> **Schools:** 2 \ **Teachers:** 25 \ **Students:** 315 \ **Special Ed Students:** 64 \ **College-Bound:** 57% \ **Ethnic:** African American 87%, Hispanic 1%, Caucasian 12% \ **Exp:** $199 (Low) \ **Poverty:** 46% \ **Title I:** $626,417 \ **Special Education:** $142,000 \ **Open-Close:** 08/11 - 05/28 \ **DTBP:** $169 (High)

Dr Patrick Rice 1,11,83   Janice Blake 2,19
Sheila Nelson 67

Public Schs..Principal	Grd	Prgm	Enr/#Cls	SN	
Cairo Elem Sch 3101 Elm St, Cairo 62914 Regina Brown	PK-6	T	184 14	99%	618/734-1027 Fax 618/734-1806
Cairo Jr Sr High Sch 4201 Sycamore St, Cairo 62914 Dr Lisa Thomas	7-12	ATV	127 20	99%	618/734-2187 Fax 618/734-2189

- **Egyptian Cmty Unit Sch Dist 5** PID: 00263290   618/776-5251
  20023 Diswood Rd, Tamms 62988   Fax 618/776-5122

> **Schools:** 1 \ **Teachers:** 36 \ **Students:** 400 \ **Special Ed Students:** 69 \ **College-Bound:** 44% \ **Ethnic:** African American 22%, Hispanic 1%, Caucasian 77% \ **Exp:** $426 (High) \ **Poverty:** 34% \ **Title I:** $384,286 \ **Special Education:** $102,000 \ **Open-Close:** 08/10 - 05/28 \ **DTBP:** $197 (High)

Brad Misner 1   Lisa Essex 2
Richard Kee .... 3*   Delinda Juneker 4*
David Newell 5   Alan Pearman 6*
Linda Davis .... 11,88,274,296*   Linda Davis 11,69
Carie Arbuckle .... 58,275,288*   Jeremy Greenley 67
Leslie Thompson 73,295   Amy Sitton 79,270

Public Schs..Principal	Grd	Prgm	Enr/#Cls	SN	
Egyptian Sch 20023 Diswood Rd, Tamms 62988 Bret Gowin	PK-12	TV	400 40	98%	618/776-5251

ALEXANDER PRIVATE SCHOOLS

Private Schs..Principal	Grd	Prgm	Enr/#Cls	SN	
Olive Branch Christian Academy 22461 Railroad St, Olive Branch 62969 Paula Alderson	K-12		12 3		618/776-6082 Fax 618/776-5452

ALEXANDER REGIONAL CENTERS

- **Five Co Reg EFE System** PID: 04177760   618/747-2703
  130 Washington Ave, Tamms 62988   Fax 618/747-2872

Patrick Harner 1,11

---

79 Student Personnel	91 Safety/Security	275 Response To Intervention	298 Grant Writer/Ptnrships	**School Programs**	**Social Media**	
80 Driver Ed/Safety	92 Magnet School	277 Remedial Math K-12	750 Chief Innovation Officer	A = Alternative Program		
81 Gifted/Talented	93 Parental Involvement	280 Literacy Coach	751 Chief of Staff	G = Adult Classes	= Facebook	
82 Video Services	95 Tech Prep Program	285 STEM	752 Social Emotional Learning	M = Magnet Program		
83 Substance Abuse Prev	97 Chief Infomation Officer	286 Digital Learning		T = Title I Schoolwide	= Twitter	
84 Erate	98 Chief Technology Officer	288 Common Core Standards	**Other School Types**	V = Career & Tech Ed Programs		
85 AIDS Education	270 Character Education	294 Accountability	Ⓐ = Alternative School			
88 Alternative/At Risk	271 Migrant Education	295 Network System	Ⓒ = Charter School	New Schools are shaded		
89 Multi-Cultural Curriculum	273 Teacher Mentor	296 Title II Programs	Ⓜ = Magnet School	New Superintendents and Principals are bold		
90 Social Work	274 Before/After Sch	297 Webmaster	Ⓨ = Year-Round School	Personnel with email addresses are underscored		

Bond County

BOND COUNTY

BOND PUBLIC SCHOOLS

- **Bond Co Cmty Unit Sch Dist 2** PID: 00263329   618/664-0170
  1008 N Hena St, Greenville 62246   Fax 618/664-5000

Schools: 6 \ Teachers: 123 \ Students: 1,750 \ Special Ed Students: 390 \ LEP Students: 3 \ College-Bound: 69% \ Ethnic: Asian 1%, African American 3%, Hispanic 3%, Caucasian 94% \ Exp: $279 (Med) \ Poverty: 14% \ Title I: $445,399 \ Special Education: $981,000 \ Open-Close: 08/18 - 06/01 \ DTBP: $233 (High) \

Name	Code
Wesley Olson	1
Adam Doll	3
Teresa Tompkins	4
Joe Alstat	6
Scott Pasely	58,88
Charles Meyer	73
Dena Petroline	2
Mike Wilhite	3
Sean Traylor	5
Meg File	8,11,57,73,286,296
Edmar Schreiber	67
Elizabeth Finn	270,288*

Public Schs..Principal	Grd	Prgm	Enr/#Cls	SN	
Early Childhood Center 1318 E State Route 140, Greenville 62246 Meg File	PK-PK		40		618/664-5009
Greenville Elem Sch 800 N Dewey St, Greenville 62246 Eric Swingler	PK-5	T	640 27	54%	618/664-3117 Fax 618/664-5014
Greenville High Sch 1000 E State Route 140, Greenville 62246 **Kara Harris**	9-12	AV	539 60	36%	618/664-1370 Fax 618/664-4786
Greenville Junior High Sch 1200 Jr High Dr, Greenville 62246 Gary Brauns	6-8	AT	294 12	41%	618/664-1226 Fax 618/664-5071
Pocahontas Elem Sch 4 E State St, Pocahontas 62275 Jason Rakers	PK-8	T	205 9	52%	618/669-2296 Fax 618/669-2627
Sorento Elem Sch 510 S Main St, Sorento 62086 Amy Jackson	PK-8	T	134 12	53%	217/272-4111 Fax 217/272-4591

- **Mulberry Grove Cmty Sch Dist 1** PID: 00263381   618/326-8812
  801 W Wall St, Mulberry GRV 62262   Fax 618/326-8482

Schools: 3 \ Teachers: 32 \ Students: 400 \ Special Ed Students: 66 \ College-Bound: 60% \ Ethnic: African American 1%, Hispanic 2%, Caucasian 97% \ Exp: $113 (Low) \ Poverty: 20% \ Title I: $140,520 \ Special Education: $181,000 \ Open-Close: 08/20 - 05/20 \ DTBP: $172 (High)

Name	Code
Robert Koontz	1
Marcy Mollett	11*
Kasie Bowman	2,16,296
Nathan Mollett	67

Public Schs..Principal	Grd	Prgm	Enr/#Cls	SN	
Mulberry Grove Elem Sch 801 W Wall St, Mulberry GRV 62262 Casie Bowman	PK-5	TV	200 23	57%	618/326-8811 Fax 618/326-8884
Mulberry Grove High Sch 801 W Wall St, Mulberry GRV 62262 Robert Koontz	9-12	T	121	42%	618/326-8221 Fax 618/326-7504
Mulberry Grove Jr High Sch 801 W Wall St, Mulberry GRV 62262 Brad Turner	6-8	T	98	60%	618/326-8221 Fax 618/326-7504

BOONE COUNTY

BOONE PUBLIC SCHOOLS

- **Belvidere Cmty Unit SD 100** PID: 00263422   815/544-0301
  1201 5th Ave, Belvidere 61008   Fax 815/544-4260

Schools: 10 \ Teachers: 530 \ Students: 8,500 \ Special Ed Students: 1,294 \ LEP Students: 1,247 \ College-Bound: 63% \ Ethnic: Asian 1%, African American 4%, Hispanic 40%, Native American: 1%, Caucasian 55% \ Exp: $192 (Low) \ Poverty: 11% \ Title I: $1,432,166 \ Special Education: $4,741,000 \ Bilingual Education: $178,000 \ Open-Close: 08/24 - 05/21 \

Name	Code	Name	Code
Dr Daniel Woestman	1	Greg Brown	2,3,17
Larry Bone	3,91	Teresa Tice	4*
Ladel Cass	5	Kelli Billesbach	7
Billy Lewis	8,11,36,69,78,79,298*	Joy Bauman	8
Megan Johnson	8,12,15,18,69,296	David Carson	15
William Ady	15,68	T Hill	23
Phil Bermillion	25*	Theresa Owen	30,58,77,88,752
Rene Mandujano	57	Karla Maville	67
Mike Lascola	69,79	Christine Morgan	73
Dena Karlson	76	Kara Graves	76
Tyler Bell	76,95,98,295	Christopher Walocha	285
Sarah Brenner	285*	David Kenny	295

Public Schs..Principal	Grd	Prgm	Enr/#Cls	SN	
Belvidere Central Middle Sch 8787 Beloit Rd, Belvidere 61008 Brett McPherson	6-8		974 50	40%	815/544-0190 Fax 815/544-1128
Belvidere High Sch 1500 East Ave, Belvidere 61008 Billy Lewis	9-12	AV	1,214 60	58%	815/547-6345 Fax 815/547-7304
Belvidere North High Sch 9393 Beloit Rd, Belvidere 61008 **James Friesema**	9-12		1,433	35%	815/547-2636 Fax 815/547-2916
Belvidere South Middle Sch 919 E 6th St, Belvidere 61008 Ben Commare	6-8	T	837 70	58%	815/544-3175 Fax 815/544-2780
Caledonia Elem Sch 2311 Randolph St, Caledonia 61011 Kelly Cotter	PK-5		398 35	35%	815/547-1977 Fax 815/547-3566
Lincoln Elem Sch 1011 Bonus Ave, Belvidere 61008 Elizabeth Marchini	PK-5	T	597 35	50%	815/544-2671 Fax 815/544-4222
Meehan Elem Sch 1401 E 6th St, Belvidere 61008 Jennifer Seykora	K-5	T	609 28	54%	815/547-3546 Fax 815/547-3946
Perry Elem Sch 633 W Perry St, Belvidere 61008 Frank Mandera	K-5	T	277 12	62%	815/544-9274 Fax 815/544-1459
Seth Whitman Elem Sch 8989 Beloit Rd, Belvidere 61008 Theresa Lozdoski	PK-5		669	37%	815/544-3357 Fax 815/547-7258
ⓜ Washington Academy 1031 5th Ave, Belvidere 61008 **Christopher Walocha**	PK-8	T	825 42	62%	815/544-3124 Fax 815/544-4182

1	Superintendent	8	Curric/Instruct K-12	19	Chief Financial Officer	29	Family/Consumer Science	39	Social Studies K-12	49	English/Lang Arts Elem	59	Special Education Elem	69	Academic Assessment
2	Bus/Finance/Purchasing	9	Curric/Instruct Elem	20	Art K-12	30	Adult Education	40	Social Studies Elem	50	English/Lang Arts Sec	60	Special Education Sec	70	Research/Development
3	Buildings And Grounds	10	Curric/Instruct Sec	21	Art Elem	31	Career/Sch-to-Work K-12	41	Social Studies Sec	51	Reading K-12	61	Foreign/World Lang K-12	71	Public Information
4	Food Service	11	Federal Program	22	Art Sec	32	Career/Sch-to-Work Elem	42	Science K-12	52	Reading Elem	62	Foreign/World Lang Elem	72	Summer School
5	Transportation	12	Title I	23	Music K-12	33	Career/Sch-to-Work Sec	43	Science Elem	53	Reading Sec	63	Foreign/World Lang Sec	73	Instructional Tech
6	Athletic	13	Title V	24	Music Elem	34	Early Childhood Ed	44	Science Sec	54	Remedial Reading K-12	64	Religious Education K-12	74	Inservice Training
7	Health Services	14	Asst Superintendent	25	Music Sec	35	Health/Phys Education	45	Math K-12	55	Remedial Reading Elem	65	Religious Education Elem	75	Marketing/Distributive
		15	Instructional Media Svcs	26	Business Education	36	Guidance Services K-12	46	Math Elem	56	Remedial Reading Sec	66	Religious Education Sec	76	Info Systems
		16	Chief Operations Officer	27	Career & Tech Ed	37	Guidance Services Elem	47	Math Sec	57	Bilingual/ELL	67	School Board President	77	Psychological Assess
		17	Chief Academic Officer	28	Technology Education	38	Guidance Services Sec	48	English/Lang Arts K-12	58	Special Education K-12	68	Teacher Personnel	78	Affirmative Action

Illinois School Directory — Brown County

- **North Boone Cmty Unit SD 200** PID: 00263513   815/765-3322
  6248 N Boone School Rd, Poplar Grove 61065   Fax 815/765-2053

Schools: 6 \ **Teachers:** 114 \ **Students:** 1,600 \ **Special Ed Students:** 233 \ **LEP Students:** 148 \ **College-Bound:** 61% \ **Ethnic:** African American 2%, Hispanic 27%, Caucasian 71% \ **Exp:** $285 (Med) \ **Poverty:** 12% \ **Title I:** $286,650 \ **Special Education:** $1,031,000 \ **Bilingual Education:** $29,000 \ **Open-Close:** 09/08 - 06/04 \ **DTBP:** $175 (High) \ f t

Mike Greenlee	1,11	Melissa Geyman	2,5
Jim Nolen	3,91	Janice Burmeister	4*
Aaron Sullivan	6*	Barb Sager	7*
Allison Lois	12,298	Jarrod Peterson	16,286
Ashley Doetch	58*	Joe Haverly	67
Jerry Rudolph	73	Elizabeth Saveley	273*
Molly Lilja	288*	Randy Porter	295

Public Schs..Principal	Grd	Prgm	Enr/#Cls	SN	
Capron Elem Sch 200 N Wooster St, Capron 61012 Nicole Difford	PK-4	T	185 16	54%	815/569-2314 Fax 815/569-2633 f t
Manchester Elem Sch 3501 Blaine Rd, Poplar Grove 61065 Molly Lilja	K-4	T	161 10	47%	815/765-2826 Fax 815/292-3334 f t
North Boone High Sch 17823 Poplar Grove Rd, Poplar Grove 61065 Jacob Hubert	9-12	T	479 30	42%	815/765-3311 Fax 815/765-3316 f t
North Boone Middle Sch 17641 Poplar Grove Rd, Poplar Grove 61065 Allison Louis	7-8	T	267 24	55%	815/765-9274 Fax 815/765-9275
North Boone Upper Elem Sch 6200 N Boone School Rd, Poplar Grove 61065 Jarrod Peterson	5-6	T	243 18	48%	815/765-9006 Fax 815/765-2496
Poplar Grove Elem Sch 208 N State St, Poplar Grove 61065 Heather Walsh	K-4	T	275 14	34%	815/765-3113 Fax 815/765-1604 f t

BOONE CATHOLIC SCHOOLS

- **Diocese of Rockford Ed Office** PID: 00328345
  Listing includes only schools located in this county. See District Index for location of Diocesan Offices.

Catholic Schs..Principal	Grd	Prgm	Enr/#Cls	SN	
St James Catholic Sch 320 Logan Ave, Belvidere 61008 Dr Kathleen Miller	PK-8		125 10		815/547-7633 Fax 815/544-2294 f t

BOONE PRIVATE SCHOOLS

Private Schs..Principal	Grd	Prgm	Enr/#Cls	SN	
Immanuel Lutheran Sch 1225 E 2nd St, Belvidere 61008 Judy Schaefer	PK-8		250 16		815/547-5346 Fax 815/544-5704

BOONE REGIONAL CENTERS

- **Boone Co Special Ed Co-op** PID: 02182305   815/544-9851
  1201 5th Ave, Belvidere 61008   Fax 815/544-4260

Dr Daniel Woestman	1	Megan Zanocco	34
Theresa Owen	58	Karla Maville	67

BROWN COUNTY

BROWN PUBLIC SCHOOLS

- **Brown Co Cmty Unit Sch Dist 1** PID: 00263575   217/773-3359
  503 NW Cross St, Mt Sterling 62353   Fax 217/773-7409

Schools: 3 \ **Teachers:** 61 \ **Students:** 750 \ **Special Ed Students:** 126 \ **College-Bound:** 83% \ **Ethnic:** African American 1%, Hispanic 2%, Caucasian 97% \ **Exp:** $191 (Low) \ **Poverty:** 13% \ **Title I:** $157,427 \ **Special Education:** $153,000 \ **Open-Close:** 08/19 - 05/28

Vicki Phillips	1	Tracy Conley	2
James McKay	3	Dave Phelps	6
Sandy Prather	12*	Chris McCaskill	16,82
Philip Krupps	67	Kris Gallaher	73,76,84

Public Schs..Principal	Grd	Prgm	Enr/#Cls	SN	
Brown Co Elem Sch 501 NW Cross St, Mt Sterling 62353 Shelly Sheffler	PK-4	T	312 15	50%	217/773-7500 Fax 217/773-7509
Brown Co High Sch 500 E Main St, Mt Sterling 62353 Pollee Craven	9-12	TV	201 24	39%	217/773-7500 Fax 217/773-7709
Brown County Middle Sch 504 E Main St, Mt Sterling 62353 Karen Jirjis	5-8	T	196 12	46%	217/773-7500 Fax 217/773-7609

BROWN CATHOLIC SCHOOLS

- **Diocese of Springfield Ed Off** PID: 00319394
  Listing includes only schools located in this county. See District Index for location of Diocesan Offices.

Catholic Schs..Principal	Grd	Prgm	Enr/#Cls	SN	
St Mary Sch 408 W Washington St, Mt Sterling 62353 Melissa Obert	PK-8		80 7		217/773-2825 Fax 217/773-2399

---

79 Student Personnel	91 Safety/Security	275 Response To Intervention	298 Grant Writer/Ptnrships	**School Programs**	**Social Media**
80 Driver Ed/Safety	92 Magnet School	277 Remedial Math K-12	750 Chief Innovation Officer	A = Alternative Program	f = Facebook
81 Gifted/Talented	93 Parental Involvement	280 Literacy Coach	751 Chief of Staff	G = Adult Classes	t = Twitter
82 Video Services	95 Tech Prep Program	285 STEM	752 Social Emotional Learning	M = Magnet Program	
83 Substance Abuse Prev	97 Chief Infomation Officer	286 Digital Learning		T = Title I Schoolwide	
84 Erate	98 Chief Technology Officer	288 Common Core Standards	**Other School Types**	V = Career & Tech Ed Programs	
85 AIDS Education	270 Character Education	294 Accountability	Ⓐ = Alternative School		
88 Alternative/At Risk	271 Migrant Education	295 Network System	Ⓒ = Charter School	New Schools are shaded	
89 Multi-Cultural Curriculum	273 Teacher Mentor	296 Title II Programs	Ⓜ = Magnet School	New Superintendents and Principals are bold	
90 Social Work	274 Before/After Sch	297 Webmaster	Ⓨ = Year-Round School	Personnel with email addresses are underscored	

Bureau County

Market Data Retrieval

BUREAU COUNTY

BUREAU PUBLIC SCHOOLS

- **Bureau Valley Cmty Unit 340** PID: 00263874   815/445-3101
  9068 2125 North Ave, Manlius 61338   Fax 815/445-2802

Schools: 4 \ Teachers: 87 \ Students: 1,082 \ Special Ed Students: 227 \ LEP Students: 3 \ College-Bound: 61% \ Ethnic: Hispanic 4%, Caucasian 95% \ Exp: $280 (Med) \ Poverty: 14% \ Title I: $256,017 \ Special Education: $354,000 \ Open-Close: 08/17 - 05/21 \ DTBP: $165 (High)

Jason Stabler	1	Rita Hanna	2
Glenda Klingenburg	5	Sheri Litherland	8,285*
Amber Harper	11,298	Mary Heing	16*
Aimee Stoller	38*	Justin Yepsen	67
Marilyn Jensen	72,83,296*	Joshua Bell	73,84
Ryan Carlson	73		

Public Schs..Principal	Grd	Prgm	Enr/#Cls	SN	
Bureau Valley High Sch 9154 2125 North Ave, Manlius 61338 Duane Price	9-12	T	341 25	43%	815/445-4004 Fax 815/445-3017
Bureau Valley Jr High Elem Sch 9080 2125 North Ave, Manlius 61338 Julie Decker-Platz	3-8		225 18		815/445-2121
Bureau Valley Walnut Elem Sch 323 S Main St, Walnut 61376 Kristy Cady	PK-5	T	376 35	42%	815/379-2900 Fax 815/379-9285
Bureau Valley Wyanet Elem Sch 109 W 4th St, Wyanet 61379 Kristie Cady	PK-2	T	128 8	66%	815/699-2251 Fax 815/699-7046

- **Dalzell Elem School Dist 98** PID: 00263678   815/663-8821
  307 Chestnut St, Dalzell 61320   Fax 815/664-4515

Schools: 1 \ Teachers: 7 \ Students: 56 \ Special Ed Students: 7 \ Ethnic: Asian 2%, Hispanic 10%, Caucasian 88% \ Exp: $375 (High) \ Poverty: 13% \ Title I: $18,538 \ Special Education: $21,000 \ Open-Close: 08/20 - 05/28

| Dr Bruce Bauer | 1,83 | Jyll Pozzi | 2 |
| Luke Simpson | 67 | | |

Public Schs..Principal	Grd	Prgm	Enr/#Cls	SN	
Dalzell Grade Sch 307 Chestnut St, Dalzell 61320 Dr Bruce Bauer	K-8		56 5	13%	815/663-8821

- **DePue Unit Sch Dist 103** PID: 00263692   815/447-2121
  204 Pleasant St, Depue 61322   Fax 815/447-2067

Schools: 1 \ Teachers: 32 \ Students: 390 \ Special Ed Students: 64 \ LEP Students: 128 \ College-Bound: 86% \ Ethnic: Asian 2%, Hispanic 84%, Caucasian 15% \ Exp: $335 (High) \ Poverty: 15% \ Title I: $99,841 \ Special Education: $137,000 \ Bilingual Education: $25,000 \ Open-Close: 08/17 - 05/27 \ DTBP: $167 (High)

Brad Kenser	1,11,288	Vickie Gilbert	2
Roberta Fox	6*	Susan Bruner	8*
Deeanne Dudley	58*	Jason Hayes	67
Dave Gilbert	73*		

Public Schs..Principal	Grd	Prgm	Enr/#Cls	SN	
Depute Unit Sch 204 Pleasant St, Depue 61322 Susan Bruner | Tari Jansen	PK-12	T	390 50	80%	815/447-2121 Fax 815/447-2610

- **Hall Twp High School Dist 502** PID: 00263719   815/664-2100
  800 W Erie St, Spring Valley 61362   Fax 815/664-2300

Schools: 1 \ Teachers: 31 \ Students: 405 \ Special Ed Students: 69 \ LEP Students: 21 \ College-Bound: 71% \ Ethnic: Asian 1%, African American 1%, Hispanic 26%, Caucasian 71% \ Exp: $259 (Med) \ Poverty: 17% \ Title I: $145,140 \ Special Education: $178,000 \ Open-Close: 08/13 - 05/20 \ 📘 🄴

Jesse Brandt	1,11,83	Nicole Pellegrini	2
Mark Scheri	3*	Eric Bryant	6*
Joanna McConville	10,60,271,273*	Susan Lucas	38,69,88*
John Piccatto	67	Jim Van Fleet	73

Public Schs..Principal	Grd	Prgm	Enr/#Cls	SN	
Hall High Sch 800 W Erie St, Spring Valley 61362 Adam Meyer	9-12		405 25	49%	815/664-2100

- **La Moille Cmty Unit SD 303** PID: 00263757   815/638-2018
  801 S Main St, La Moille 61330   Fax 815/638-2186

Schools: 3 \ Teachers: 25 \ Students: 205 \ Special Ed Students: 49 \ College-Bound: 93% \ Ethnic: African American 1%, Hispanic 6%, Caucasian 92% \ Exp: $281 (Med) \ Poverty: 10% \ Title I: $41,570 \ Special Education: $100,000 \ Open-Close: 08/14 - 05/28 \ DTBP: $184 (High)

| Jay McCracken | 1,11,73,83 | Jeff Pinter | 67 |

Public Schs..Principal	Grd	Prgm	Enr/#Cls	SN	
Allen Junior High Sch 301 Main St, La Moille 61330 Chawn Huffaker	4-8		89 5	47%	815/638-2233 Fax 815/638-2392
La Moille High Sch 801 S Main St, La Moille 61330 Brent Ziegler	9-12	T	74 12	35%	815/638-2052 Fax 815/638-2392
Van Orin Grade Sch 25890-2790 North Ave, Van Orin 61374 Chawn Huffaker	PK-3		50 9	40%	815/638-3141 Fax 815/638-2392

- **Ladd Cmty Cons Sch Dist 94** PID: 00263800   815/894-2363
  232 E Cleveland St, Ladd 61329   Fax 815/894-2364

Schools: 1 \ Teachers: 15 \ Students: 190 \ Special Ed Students: 27 \ LEP Students: 3 \ Ethnic: Hispanic 15%, Caucasian 85% \ Exp: $267 (Med) \ Poverty: 16% \ Title I: $62,801 \ Special Education: $49,000 \ Open-Close: 08/17 - 05/27

Michelle Zeko	1,83	Leona Hall	6*
Dana Dawson	16*	Katy DeRubeis	59*
Marie Giordano	67		

#	Code	#	Code	#	Code	#	Code	#	Code	#	Code	#	Code	#	Code
1	Superintendent	8	Curric/Instruct K-12	19	Chief Financial Officer	29	Family/Consumer Science	39	Social Studies K-12	49	English/Lang Arts Elem	59	Special Education Elem	69	Academic Assessment
2	Bus/Finance/Purchasing	9	Curric/Instruct Elem	20	Art K-12	30	Adult Education	40	Social Studies Elem	50	English/Lang Arts Sec	60	Special Education Sec	70	Research/Development
3	Buildings And Grounds	10	Curric/Instruct Sec	21	Art Elem	31	Career/Sch-to-Work K-12	41	Social Studies Sec	51	Reading K-12	61	Foreign/World Lang K-12	71	Public Information
4	Food Service	11	Federal Program	22	Art Sec	32	Career/Sch-to-Work Elem	42	Science K-12	52	Reading Elem	62	Foreign/World Lang Elem	72	Summer School
5	Transportation	12	Title I	23	Music K-12	33	Career/Sch-to-Work Sec	43	Science Elem	53	Reading Sec	63	Foreign/World Lang Sec	73	Instructional Tech
6	Athletic	13	Title V	24	Music Elem	34	Early Childhood Ed	44	Science Sec	54	Remedial Reading K-12	64	Religious Education K-12	74	Inservice Training
7	Health Services	15	Asst Superintendent	25	Music Sec	35	Health/Phys Education	45	Math K-12	55	Remedial Reading Elem	65	Religious Education Elem	75	Marketing/Distributive
		16	Instructional Media Svcs	26	Business Education	36	Guidance Services K-12	46	Math Elem	56	Remedial Reading Sec	66	Religious Education Sec	76	Info Systems
		17	Chief Operations Officer	27	Career & Tech Ed	37	Guidance Services Elem	47	Math Sec	57	Bilingual/ELL	67	School Board President	77	Psychological Assess
		18	Chief Academic Officer	28	Technology Education	38	Guidance Services Sec	48	English/Lang Arts K-12	58	Special Education K-12	68	Teacher Personnel	78	Affirmative Action

Illinois School Directory

Bureau County

Public Schs..Principal	Grd	Prgm	Enr/#Cls	SN	
Ladd Cmty Consolidated Sch 232 E Cleveland St, Ladd 61329 Dana Dawson	PK-8		190 10	51%	815/894-2363

● **Malden Cmty Cons SD 84** PID: 00263848 815/643-2436
350 East St, Malden 61337 Fax 815/643-2132

Schools: 1 \ **Teachers:** 8 \ **Students:** 100 \ **Special Ed Students:** 16 \
Ethnic: African American 3%, Hispanic 5%, Caucasian 92% \ **Exp:** $371
(High) \ **Poverty:** 14% \ **Title I:** $16,974 \ **Special Education:** $50,000 \
Open-Close: 08/18 - 05/27 \ **DTBP:** $174 (High)

Michael Patterson ....1,11 Jeremey Mount 67

Public Schs..Principal	Grd	Prgm	Enr/#Cls	SN	
Malden Elem Sch 216 S East St, Malden 61337 Michael Patterson	PK-8		100 11	47%	815/643-2436

● **Ohio Cmty Cons School Dist 17** PID: 00263927 815/376-4414
103 S Memorial St, Ohio 61349 Fax 815/376-2102

Schools: 1 \ **Teachers:** 12 \ **Students:** 113 \ **Special Ed Students:** 21
\ **Ethnic:** African American 3%, Hispanic 8%, Caucasian 89% \ **Exp:** $82
(Low) \ **Poverty:** 16% \ **Title I:** $25,298 \ **Special Education:** $39,000 \
Open-Close: 08/17 - 05/19

Jennifer Hamilton ....1,11 Sharon Kania 4
Robb Kleist ....5 Sue Cater 7*
Joann Bowman ....16* Rachael Fitzpatrick 67
Jason Wilt 69,288

Public Schs..Principal	Grd	Prgm	Enr/#Cls	SN	
Ohio Community Grade Sch 103 S Memorial St, Ohio 61349 Jason Wilt	K-8	T	113 15	45%	815/376-2934

● **Ohio Cmty High School Dist 505** PID: 01843829 815/376-2934
103 S Memorial St, Ohio 61349 Fax 815/376-2102

Schools: 1 \ **Teachers:** 7 \ **Students:** 33 \ **Special Ed Students:** 3 \
College-Bound: 30% \ **Ethnic:** Caucasian 100% \ **Exp:** $151 (Low) \
Poverty: 8% \ **Special Education:** $5,000 \ **Open-Close:** 08/17 - 05/20

Jennifer Hamilton ....1,11 Sharon Kania 4
Robb Kleist ....5 Harold Albrecht 67
Lisa Wilt ....73 Amy Fleck 83
Jason Wilt 288

Public Schs..Principal	Grd	Prgm	Enr/#Cls	SN	
Ohio Cmty High Sch 103 S Memorial St, Ohio 61349 Jason Wilt	9-12	T	33 10	31%	815/376-4414

● **Princeton Elem Sch Dist 115** PID: 00263953 815/875-3162
506 E Dover Rd, Princeton 61356 Fax 815/875-3101

Schools: 4 \ **Teachers:** 79 \ **Students:** 1,156 \ **Special Ed Students:** 191
\ **LEP Students:** 3 \ **Ethnic:** Asian 1%, African American 1%, Hispanic 7%,
Caucasian 91% \ **Exp:** $236 (Med) \ **Poverty:** 14% \ **Title I:** $321,684 \
Special Education: $445,000 \ **Open-Close:** 08/14 - 05/21 \ **DTBP:** $197
(High)

Tim Smith ....1 Wayne Barr 3,5,91*
Sue Cater ....7* Bob Bima 12
Amy Haring ....16* Steve Bouslog 67

Public Schs..Principal	Grd	Prgm	Enr/#Cls	SN	
Douglas Elem Sch 220 E LaSalle St, Princeton 61356 Lynette Bima	PK-K		266 5	47%	815/875-6075 Fax 815/872-0756
Jefferson Elem Sch 725 W Putnam St, Princeton 61356 J Orwig	1-2		222 11	50%	815/875-4417 Fax 815/872-0620
Lincoln Elem Sch 501 S Euclid Ave, Princeton 61356 Kylee Gutshall	3-4		219 12	44%	815/875-1164 Fax 815/872-0801
Logan Junior High Sch 302 W Central Ave, Princeton 61356 Amanda Carr	5-8		464 35	37%	815/875-6415 Fax 815/872-0034

● **Princeton Twp HSD 500** PID: 00264012 815/875-3308
103 S Euclid Ave, Princeton 61356 Fax 815/875-8525

Schools: 1 \ **Teachers:** 33 \ **Students:** 550 \ **Special Ed Students:** 101 \
College-Bound: 65% \ **Ethnic:** Asian 1%, African American 1%, Hispanic
4%, Caucasian 94% \ **Exp:** $223 (Med) \ **Poverty:** 13% \ **Title I:** $112,226 \
Special Education: $211,000 \ **Open-Close:** 08/18 - 05/28

Kirk Haring ....1 Laurie Ciesielski 2
Steven Gray ....3,5* Shawn Lewis 4*
Jeff Ohlson ....6,60* Susan Cater 7,85*
Andy Berlinski ....10,11,69,74* Renee Kozeal 16*
Steve Morton ....16,73,286,295,297* Tameran Polowy 38,88*
Colleen Sailor 67

Public Schs..Principal	Grd	Prgm	Enr/#Cls	SN	
Princeton High Sch 103 S Euclid Ave, Princeton 61356 Andy Berlinski	9-12	T	550 50	35%	815/875-3308

● **Spring Valley Cmty Cons SD 99** PID: 00264036 815/664-4242
999 N Strong Ave, Spring Valley 61362 Fax 815/664-2205

Schools: 1 \ **Teachers:** 46 \ **Students:** 633 \ **Special Ed Students:** 118
\ **LEP Students:** 64 \ **Ethnic:** African American 1%, Hispanic 37%,
Caucasian 62% \ **Exp:** $263 (Med) \ **Poverty:** 18% \ **Title I:** $204,468
\ **Special Education:** $190,000 \ **Bilingual Education:** $21,000 \
Open-Close: 08/18 - 05/26

James Hermes ....1 Ryan Geisd 6
Shelly Nauman ....9,59* Raymond Nolasco 67
Greg Walder ....73 Shelley Nauman 270,273

Public Schs..Principal	Grd	Prgm	Enr/#Cls	SN	
John F Kennedy Sch 800 N Richards St, Spring Valley 61362 Shelly Nauman	PK-8	T	633 30	64%	815/664-4601 Fax 815/664-4213

BUREAU REGIONAL CENTERS

● **BMP Spec Ed Co-op** PID: 02183907 815/646-8031
400 N Galena St, Tiskilwa 61368 Fax 815/646-8087

Gwen Garver 1

---

79 Student Personnel
80 Driver Ed/Safety
81 Gifted/Talented
82 Video Services
83 Substance Abuse Prev
84 Erate
85 AIDS Education
88 Alternative/At Risk
89 Multi-Cultural Curriculum
90 Social Work

91 Safety/Security
92 Magnet School
93 Parental Involvement
95 Tech Prep Program
97 Chief Infomation Officer
98 Chief Technology Officer
270 Character Education
271 Migrant Education
273 Teacher Mentor
274 Before/After Sch

275 Response To Intervention
277 Remedial Math K-12
280 Literacy Coach
285 STEM
286 Digital Learning
288 Common Core Standards
294 Accountability
295 Network System
296 Title II Programs
297 Webmaster

298 Grant Writer/Ptnrships
750 Chief Innovation Officer
751 Chief of Staff
752 Social Emotional Learning

Other School Types
Ⓐ = Alternative School
Ⓒ = Charter School
Ⓜ = Magnet School
Ⓨ = Year-Round School

School Programs
A = Alternative Program
G = Adult Classes
M = Magnet Program
T = Title I Schoolwide
V = Career & Tech Ed Programs

New Schools are shaded
New Superintendents and Principals are bold
Personnel with email addresses are underscored

Social Media
 = Facebook
 = Twitter

IL-7

Calhoun County

CALHOUN COUNTY

CALHOUN PUBLIC SCHOOLS

- **Brussels Cmty Unit Sch Dist 42** PID: 00264206   618/883-2131
128 School Street, Brussels 62013   Fax 618/883-2514

Schools: 2 \ Teachers: 14 \ Students: 106 \ Special Ed Students: 22 \ College-Bound: 111% \ Ethnic: African American 2%, Hispanic 3%, Caucasian 95% \ **Exp:** $461 (High) \ **Poverty:** 7% \ **Title I:** $20,282 \ **Special Education:** $46,000 \ **Open-Close:** 08/14 - 05/14

Dr Mark Martin 1,11   Keishia Hartle 6
Megan Steward 12   Amanda Brodback 67

Public Schs..Principal	Grd	Prgm	Enr/#Cls	SN	
Brussels Grade Sch 128 School Street, Brussels 62013 Mark Martin	K-6		45 5	44%	618/883-2131
Brussels High Sch 128 School Street, Brussels 62013 Andy Stumps	7-12	V	77 6	39%	618/883-2131

- **Calhoun Cmty Unit Sch Dist 40** PID: 00264232   618/576-2722
101 Calhoun Ave, Hardin 62047   Fax 618/576-2641

Schools: 2 \ Teachers: 41 \ Students: 484 \ Special Ed Students: 101 \ LEP Students: 3 \ College-Bound: 78% \ Ethnic: Asian 1%, Hispanic 1%, Caucasian 99% \ **Exp:** $398 (High) \ **Poverty:** 15% \ **Title I:** $124,887 \ **Special Education:** $122,000 \ **Open-Close:** 08/17 - 05/28 \ **DTBP:** $195 (High)

Andrea Lee 1   Dianne Dick 4
Jody Heidenreich 5   Ryan Graner 6*
Christie Lorsbach .... 11,88,275,288,296*   Dylan Ranghausen 36,69*
Luke Fraley 67   Nathan Bloodworth 73*
Dr Kate Sievers 83   Lisa Kallal 273*
Bill Henke 295

Public Schs..Principal	Grd	Prgm	Enr/#Cls	SN	
Calhoun Elem Sch 52 Poor Farm Hollow Rd, Hardin 62047 Christie Lorsbach	PK-8	T	356 15	39%	618/576-2341 Fax 618/576-2787
Calhoun High Sch 102 Calhoun Ave, Hardin 62047 Cheri Burris	9-12	T	128 15	31%	618/576-2229 Fax 618/576-8031

CALHOUN CATHOLIC SCHOOLS

- **Diocese of Springfield Ed Off** PID: 00319394
Listing includes only schools located in this county. See District Index for location of Diocesan Offices.

Catholic Schs..Principal	Grd	Prgm	Enr/#Cls	SN	
St Mary's Sch Main St, Brussels 62013 Becky Lorts	1-8		58 4		618/883-2124 Fax 618/883-2511

St Norbert Sch 401 Vineyard St, Hardin 62047 Angie Goode	K-8		55 5		618/576-2514 Fax 618/576-8074

CARROLL COUNTY

CARROLL PUBLIC SCHOOLS

- **Chadwick Milledgevill CUSD 399** PID: 00264323   815/684-5191
19 School St, Chadwick 61014   Fax 815/684-5241

Schools: 2 \ Teachers: 40 \ Students: 450 \ Special Ed Students: 71 \ LEP Students: 3 \ College-Bound: 65% \ Ethnic: Hispanic 2%, Caucasian 98% \ **Exp:** $120 (Low) \ **Poverty:** 11% \ **Title I:** $71,411 \ **Special Education:** $81,000 \ **Open-Close:** 08/21 - 05/24 \ **DTBP:** $193 (High) \ 📘

Tim Schurman 1,11   Sandra Baylor-Schmidt 67
Eric Hernandez 295*

Public Schs..Principal	Grd	Prgm	Enr/#Cls	SN	
Chadwick Elem Jr High Sch 19 School St, Chadwick 61014 Tim Schurman	4-8	T	220 20	41%	815/684-5191 📘
Milledgeville Sch 100 E 8th St, Milledgeville 61051 Brian Maloy	K-12	V	308 17	22%	815/225-7141 📘

- **Eastland Cmty Unit SD 308** PID: 00264294   815/493-6301
500 S School Dr, Lanark 61046   Fax 815/493-6343

Schools: 2 \ Teachers: 43 \ Students: 650 \ Special Ed Students: 81 \ Ethnic: Hispanic 4%, Caucasian 95% \ **Exp:** $328 (High) \ **Poverty:** 12% \ **Title I:** $119,979 \ **Special Education:** $104,000 \ **Open-Close:** 08/19 - 06/04 \ **DTBP:** $179 (High)

Alex Kashner 1,11,73,83   Scott Hartman 6*
Erin Paulsen .... 8*   Steven Snider 67
Eric Haan 95,295*

Public Schs..Principal	Grd	Prgm	Enr/#Cls	SN	
Eastland Elemenary Sch 601 S Chestnut St, Shannon 61078 Angela Mahoney	PK-5		310 13	44%	815/864-2300 Fax 815/864-2281
Eastland Jr Sr High Sch 500 S School Dr, Lanark 61046 Monica Burkholder	6-12	V	321 15	33%	815/493-6341

- **West Carroll CUSD 314** PID: 00264464   815/734-3374
642 S East St, Mount Carroll 61053   Fax 815/244-0211

Schools: 3 \ Teachers: 67 \ Students: 1,054 \ Special Ed Students: 202 \ LEP Students: 19 \ College-Bound: 51% \ Ethnic: African American 1%, Hispanic 10%, Native American: 1%, Caucasian 88% \ **Exp:** $176 (Low) \ **Poverty:** 17% \ **Title I:** $333,510 \ **Special Education:** $533,000 \ **Open-Close:** 08/19 - 05/24

Julie Katzenberger 1,11   Claudine Guenzler 2
Kurt Beck 3   Sherry Falls 4

1	Superintendent	8	Curric/Instruct K-12	19	Chief Financial Officer	29	Family/Consumer Science	39	Social Studies K-12	49	English/Lang Arts Elem	59	Special Education Elem	69	Academic Assessment
2	Bus/Finance/Purchasing	9	Curric/Instruct Elem	20	Art K-12	30	Adult Education	40	Social Studies Elem	50	English/Lang Arts Sec	60	Special Education Sec	70	Research/Development
3	Buildings And Grounds	10	Curric/Instruct Sec	21	Art Elem	31	Career/Sch-to-Work K-12	41	Social Studies Sec	51	Reading K-12	61	Foreign/World Lang K-12	71	Public Information
4	Food Service	11	Federal Program	22	Art Sec	32	Career/Sch-to-Work Elem	42	Science K-12	52	Reading Elem	62	Foreign/World Lang Elem	72	Summer School
5	Transportation	12	Title I	23	Music K-12	33	Career/Sch-to-Work Sec	43	Science Elem	53	Reading Sec	63	Foreign/World Lang Sec	73	Instructional Tech
6	Athletic	13	Title V	24	Music Elem	34	Early Childhood Ed	44	Science Sec	54	Remedial Reading K-12	64	Religious Education K-12	74	Inservice Training
7	Health Services	14	Asst Superintendent	25	Music Sec	35	Health/Phys Education	45	Math K-12	55	Remedial Reading Elem	65	Religious Education Elem	75	Marketing/Distributive
		15	Instructional Media Svcs	26	Business Education	36	Guidance Services K-12	46	Math Elem	56	Remedial Reading Sec	66	Religious Education Sec	76	Info Systems
		16	Chief Operations Officer	27	Career & Tech Ed	37	Guidance Services Elem	47	Math Sec	57	Bilingual/ELL	67	School Board President	77	Psychological Assess
		17	Chief Academic Officer	28	Technology Education	38	Guidance Services Sec	48	English/Lang Arts K-12	58	Special Education K-12	68	Teacher Personnel	78	Affirmative Action

Illinois School Directory — Cass County

Bob Nolan 5	Tracy Rein 9
Tracy Rein 9*	Ben Ashy 10,38
Ben Ashy 10,38*	Brady Knop 10*
Mike Noble 58	John McIntyre 67
Joe Michels 73,295	

Public Schs..Principal	Grd	Prgm	Enr/#Cls	SN	
West Carroll High Sch	9-12	AV	311	48%	815/273-7715
500 Cragmoor St, Savanna 61074			30		Fax 815/273-7819
Joe Hansen \ Ben Asche					
West Carroll Middle Sch	5-8	A	316	48%	815/244-2002
633 S East St, Mount Carroll 61053			25		Fax 815/244-1051
Brady Knop					
West Carroll Primary Sch	PK-4		440	52%	815/273-7747
2215 Wacker Rd, Savanna 61074			17		Fax 815/273-3846
Andrew Jordon					

CASS COUNTY

CASS PUBLIC SCHOOLS

• **A-C Central Cmty Unit SD 262** PID: 00264488 217/476-8112
501 W Buchanan St, Ashland 62612 Fax 217/476-8100

Schools: 2 \ **Teachers:** 33 \ **Students:** 419 \ **Special Ed Students:** 71 \ **LEP Students:** 3 \ **College-Bound:** 56% \ **Ethnic:** African American 2%, Hispanic 3%, Caucasian 95% \ **Exp:** $222 (Med) \ **Poverty:** 13% \ **Title I:** $70,310 \ **Special Education:** $110,000 \ **Open-Close:** 08/19 - 05/21 \ **DTBP:** $174 (High) \ 🅕 🅣

Timothy Page 1,11	Raven McBurney 5
Colin Arthalony 6*	Candy Schaver 8,69,83,85,88,273
Lisa Doyle 12,275*	Diane Hatcher 16*
Brittany Kirchner 34	Todd Jokisch 67
Brendon Dejaynes 73*	

Public Schs..Principal	Grd	Prgm	Enr/#Cls	SN	
A-C Central Elem Sch	PK-4		167	48%	217/458-2224
191 S Bluff St, Chandlerville 62627			20		Fax 217/458-2223
Deb Rogers					
A-C Central Middle High Sch	5-12	T	246	41%	217/476-3313
601 W Buchanan St, Ashland 62612			18		Fax 217/476-3730
Steve Groll					

• **Beardstown Cmty Sch Dist 15** PID: 00264505 217/323-3099
500 E 15th St, Beardstown 62618 Fax 217/323-5190

Schools: 3 \ **Teachers:** 95 \ **Students:** 1,560 \ **Special Ed Students:** 260 \ **LEP Students:** 609 \ **Ethnic:** Asian 1%, African American 12%, Hispanic 52%, Native American: 1%, Caucasian 35% \ **Exp:** $265 (Med) \ **Poverty:** 15% \ **Title I:** $377,708 \ **Special Education:** $477,000 \ **Bilingual Education:** $170,000 \ **Open-Close:** 08/24 - 05/27 \ **DTBP:** $183 (High) \ 🅕 🅣

Ronald Gilbert 1	Kelly Herter 2,19
Jim Childers 3,17*	Julie Towery 4*
Lori Young 12,296*	Darcie Barker 16
Patrick Wildman 36	Tammy Peterson 57,271
Mike Seaman 67	Ashley Eckert 69,83
Wendy McClenning 73,76,286*	

Public Schs..Principal	Grd	Prgm	Enr/#Cls	SN	
Beardstown Middle High Sch	5-12	TV	896	78%	217/323-3665
500 E 15th St, Beardstown 62618			60		Fax 217/323-3667
Bill Myers					
Gard Elem Sch	K-4	T	490	79%	217/323-1364
400 E 15th St, Beardstown 62618			20		Fax 217/323-4307
Lori Young					
Grand Avenue Sch	PK-PK	T	185	45%	217/323-1510
1301 Grand Ave, Beardstown 62618			6		Fax 217/323-5984
Lori Young					

• **Virginia Cmty Unit Sch Dist 64** PID: 00264608 217/452-3085
651 S Morgan St, Virginia 62691 Fax 217/452-3088

Schools: 1 \ **Teachers:** 27 \ **Students:** 320 \ **Special Ed Students:** 69 \ **LEP Students:** 5 \ **Ethnic:** African American 2%, Hispanic 3%, Native American: 1%, Caucasian 94% \ **Exp:** $155 (Low) \ **Poverty:** 13% \ **Title I:** $60,845 \ **Special Education:** $30,000 \ **Open-Close:** 08/19 - 05/28

Gary Depatis 1,11,83	Brittnie Morrell 2,298
Mekelle Neathery 8,11,285,288,296*	Casey French 67
Tina McQuill 90*	

Public Schs..Principal	Grd	Prgm	Enr/#Cls	SN	
Virginia Cmty Unit 64 Sch	PK-12	TV	320	56%	217/452-3085
651 S Morgan St, Virginia 62691					
Mekelle Neathery					

CASS PRIVATE SCHOOLS

Private Schs..Principal	Grd	Prgm	Enr/#Cls	SN	
Beardstown Christian Academy	K-9		130		217/323-1685
1421 Beard St, Beardstown 62618			8		Fax 217/323-1421
Jeremy Norton					
Trinity Lutheran Sch	PK-6		43		217/997-5535
201 Frederick Street, Arenzville 62611			5		
Breanna Winkelman					

CASS REGIONAL CENTERS

• **Two Rivers Voc Ed System** PID: 04177930 217/452-7239
651 S Morgan St Rm 119, Virginia 62691 Fax 217/323-4712

Reggie Clinton 1   Sarah Graham 15

---

79 Student Personnel	91 Safety/Security	275 Response To Intervention	298 Grant Writer/Ptnrships	**School Programs**	**Social Media**
80 Driver Ed/Safety	92 Magnet School	277 Remedial Math K-12	750 Chief Innovation Officer	A = Alternative Program	
81 Gifted/Talented	93 Parental Involvement	280 Literacy Coach	751 Chief of Staff	G = Adult Classes	🅕 = Facebook
82 Video Services	95 Tech Prep Program	285 STEM	752 Social Emotional Learning	M = Magnet Program	
83 Substance Abuse Prev	97 Chief Information Officer	286 Digital Learning		T = Title I Schoolwide	🅣 = Twitter
84 Erate	98 Chief Technology Officer	288 Common Core Standards	**Other School Types**	V = Career & Tech Ed Programs	
85 AIDS Education	270 Character Education	294 Accountability	Ⓐ = Alternative School		
88 Alternative/At Risk	271 Migrant Education	295 Network System	Ⓒ = Charter School	New Schools are shaded	
89 Multi-Cultural Curriculum	273 Teacher Mentor	296 Title II Programs	Ⓜ = Magnet School	New Superintendents and Principals are bold	
90 Social Work	274 Before/After Sch	297 Webmaster	Ⓨ = Year-Round School	Personnel with email addresses are underscored	

Champaign County

CHAMPAIGN COUNTY

CHAMPAIGN PUBLIC SCHOOLS

- **Champaign Cmty Unit Sch Dist 4** PID: 00264713   217/351-3800
  502 W Windsor Rd, Champaign 61820   Fax 217/351-3871

Schools: 19 \ Teachers: 766 \ Students: 10,179 \
Special Ed Students: 1,470 \ LEP Students: 1,196 \ College-Bound: 74%
\ Ethnic: Asian 10%, African American 38%, Hispanic 13%, Caucasian
39% \ Exp: $265 (Med) \ Poverty: 17% \ Title I: $3,799,670 \
Special Education: $9,111,000 \ Bilingual Education: $260,000 \
Open-Close: 08/20 - 05/21 \ DTBP: $225 (High) \ f

Dr Susan Zola 1
Thomas Lockman 2,19
Laura Dees 4
Orlando Thomas 6,79,88,91,270,275
Jamie Roundtree 9,12
Mike Lehr 10,288
Angela Ward 15,36,69,74,78,81
Andrew O'Neil 58
Daniel Casillas 68
John Lyday 71
Katina Wilcher 93
Lori Scott 298

Paul Douglas 2
David Lund 3
Amy Magrini 5*
Angelica Franklin 8
Rhonda Thornton 9,12,69,76,286
Dr Laura Taylor 11,15,35,83
Viodelda Judkins 57,271
Amy Armstrong 67
Ken Kleber 68,74,273
John Gutzmer 73,76,84,295
Danielle Cook 274*

Public Schs..Principal	Grd	Prgm	Enr/#Cls	SN		
B T Washington STEM Acad 606 E Grove St, Champaign 61820 Jaime Roundtree	K-5	T	423 14	63%	217/351-3901 Fax 217/373-7350	
Bottenfield Elem Sch 1801 S Prospect Ave, Champaign 61820 Jason Pope	K-5	T	453 18	43%	217/351-3807 Fax 217/355-2582	
Carrie Busey Elem Sch 304 Prairie Rose Ln, Savoy 61874 Craig Keer	K-5	T	476 18	31%	217/351-3811 Fax 217/355-6458	
Centennial High Sch 913 Crescent Dr, Champaign 61821 Charles Neitzel	9-12	V	1,396 100	56%	217/351-3951 Fax 217/351-3730	
Central High Sch 610 W University Ave, Champaign 61820 Joe Williams	9-12	V	1,218	48%	217/351-3911 Fax 217/351-3740	
Champaign Early Childhood Ctr 809 N Neil St, Champaign 61820 Cheryl Dearing	PK-PK	T	317 10	72%	217/351-3881 Fax 217/351-3883	
Dr Howard Elem Sch 103 N Neil St, Champaign 61820 Jeffrey Dobbs	K-5	T	312 20	59%	217/351-3866 Fax 217/359-7036	
Edison Middle Sch 306 W Green St, Champaign 61820 Angela Schoonover	6-8	V	727	56%	217/351-3771 Fax 217/355-2564	
Franklin Middle Sch 817 N Harris Ave, Champaign 61820 Sara Sanders	6-8	V	663 35	61%	217/351-3819 Fax 217/351-3729	
Garden Hills Elem Sch 2001 Garden Hills Dr, Champaign 61821 Elizabeth Ladd	K-5	T	425 22	87%	217/351-3872 Fax 217/355-8180	
International Prep Academy 1605 W Kirby Ave, Champaign 61821 Jonathan Kosovski	K-5	T	336	68%	217/351-3995 Fax 217/351-3939	
Jefferson Middle Sch 1115 Crescent Dr, Champaign 61821 Jesse Guzman	6-8	V	717 61	59%	217/351-3790 Fax 217/351-3754	
Ⓨ Kenwood Elem Sch 1001 Stratford Dr, Champaign 61821 Trevor Nadrozny	K-5	MT	357 18	59%	217/351-3815 Fax 217/355-4944	
Ⓐ Novak Academy 815 N Randolph St, Champaign 61820 Danielle Cook	9-12		42	79%	217/352-4328 Fax 217/352-7292	
Robeson Elem Sch 2501 Southmoor Dr, Champaign 61821 Jessica Pitcher	K-5	T	415 22	48%	217/351-3884 Fax 217/351-3751	
South Side Elem Sch 715 S New St, Champaign 61820 Christian Mahone	K-5	T	287 12	34%	217/351-3890 Fax 217/373-7318	
Stratton Elem Sch 902 N Randolph St, Champaign 61820 Stephanie Eckels	K-5	T	474 21	69%	217/373-7330 Fax 217/373-7337	
Ⓨ Vernon L Barkstall Elem Sch 2201 Hallbeck Dr, Champaign 61822 Jessica Bradford	K-5	MT	445 20	39%	217/373-5580 Fax 217/373-5587	f
Westview Elem Sch 703 S Russell St, Champaign 61821 Nick Swords	K-5	T	436 18	52%	217/351-3905 Fax 217/352-7290	

- **Fisher Cmty Unit School Dist 1** PID: 00264907   217/897-6125
  801 S 5th St, Fisher 61843   Fax 217/897-6676

Schools: 2 \ Teachers: 47 \ Students: 601 \ Special Ed Students: 77
\ LEP Students: 3 \ College-Bound: 67% \ Ethnic: Asian 1%, African
American 1%, Hispanic 2%, Caucasian 96% \ Exp: $353 (High) \
Poverty: 10% \ Title I: $101,647 \ Special Education: $177,000 \
Open-Close: 08/17 - 05/21 \ DTBP: $175 (High)

Barbara Thompson 1,11,83
Sandy Moore 5
Leonard DeLaney 67

Mark Varner 3
Jake Palmer 6*
Scott Williams 73,76*

Public Schs..Principal	Grd	Prgm	Enr/#Cls	SN	
Fisher Grade Sch 801 S 5th St, Fisher 61843 Jake Palmer	K-6		328 25	34%	217/897-1133
Fisher Jr Sr High Sch 211 W Division St, Fisher 61843 Jon Kelly	7-12	V	281 30	37%	217/897-1225

- **Gifford Cmty Cons SD 188** PID: 00264957   217/568-7733
  406 S Main St, Gifford 61847   Fax 217/568-7228

Schools: 1 \ Teachers: 15 \ Students: 183 \ Special Ed Students: 22
\ Ethnic: African American 1%, Caucasian 99% \ Exp: $338 (High)
\ Poverty: 8% \ Title I: $25,690 \ Special Education: $33,000 \
Open-Close: 08/14 - 05/21 \ DTBP: $168 (High)

Jay Smith 1
Jay Smith 11,76,88,288*
Tammy Pollard 73*

Diane Baker 2
Travis Huls 67
Rod Grimsley 83

Public Schs..Principal	Grd	Prgm	Enr/#Cls	SN	
Gifford Grade Sch 406 S Main St, Gifford 61847 Jay Smith	K-8		183 16	31%	217/568-7733 t

---

1	Superintendent	8	Curric/Instruct K-12	19	Chief Financial Officer	29	Family/Consumer Science	39	Social Studies K-12	49	English/Lang Arts Elem	59	Special Education Elem	69	Academic Assessment
2	Bus/Finance/Purchasing	9	Curric/Instruct Elem	20	Art K-12	30	Adult Education	40	Social Studies Elem	50	English/Lang Arts Sec	60	Special Education Sec	70	Research/Development
3	Buildings And Grounds	10	Curric/Instruct Sec	21	Art Elem	31	Career/Sch-to-Work K-12	41	Social Studies Sec	51	Reading K-12	61	Foreign/World Lang K-12	71	Public Information
4	Food Service	11	Federal Program	22	Art Sec	32	Career/Sch-to-Work Elem	42	Science K-12	52	Reading Elem	62	Foreign/World Lang Elem	72	Summer School
5	Transportation	12	Title I	23	Music K-12	33	Career/Sch-to-Work Sec	43	Science Elem	53	Reading Sec	63	Foreign/World Lang Sec	73	Instructional Tech
6	Athletic	13	Title V	24	Music Elem	34	Early Childhood Ed	44	Science Sec	54	Remedial Reading K-12	64	Religious Education K-12	74	Inservice Training
7	Health Services	15	Asst Superintendent	25	Music Sec	35	Health/Phys Education	45	Math K-12	55	Remedial Reading Elem	65	Religious Education Elem	75	Marketing/Distributive
		16	Instructional Media Svcs	26	Business Education	36	Guidance Services K-12	46	Math Elem	56	Remedial Reading Sec	66	Religious Education Sec	76	Info Systems
		17	Chief Operations Officer	27	Career & Tech Ed	37	Guidance Services Elem	47	Math Sec	57	Bilingual/ELL	67	School Board President	77	Psychological Assess
		18	Chief Academic Officer	28	Technology Education	38	Guidance Services Sec	48	English/Lang Arts K-12	58	Special Education K-12	68	Teacher Personnel	78	Affirmative Action

Illinois School Directory — Champaign County

- **Heritage Cmty Unit Sch Dist 8** PID: 00264971   217/834-3393
  512 W 1st St, Homer 61849   Fax 217/896-2338

> **Schools:** 2 \ **Teachers:** 35 \ **Students:** 421 \ **Special Ed Students:** 57 \
> **College-Bound:** 61% \ **Ethnic:** Asian 1%, African American 1%, Hispanic 1%, Caucasian 97% \ **Exp:** $554 (High) \ **Poverty:** 10% \ **Title I:** $112,936 \
> **Special Education:** $114,000 \ **Open-Close:** 08/17 - 05/21

Thomas Davis 1,11,73   Deana Wolf 2
Shelley Fitzgerald 5   Lori Archer 6*
Patti Knott .... 31*   Mary Kay Anderson 58,88*
John Lannon 67   Jane Cramer 83*
Cami White 288*

Public Schs..Principal	Grd	Prgm	Enr/#Cls	SN	
Heritage Elem Sch 512 W 1st St, Homer 61849 Kristi Sanders	K-8		262 28	45%	217/896-2421 Fax 217/896-2715
Heritage High Sch 206 E Diller St, Broadlands 61816 Corey White	9-12	V	159 16	33%	217/834-3392 Fax 217/834-3016

- **Ludlow Cons Cmty Sch Dist 142** PID: 00264995   217/396-5261
  245 S Orange St, Ludlow 60949   Fax 217/396-8858

> **Schools:** 1 \ **Teachers:** 8 \ **Students:** 57 \ **Special Ed Students:** 14 \
> **LEP Students:** 9 \ **Ethnic:** Hispanic 25%, Caucasian 75% \ **Exp:** $799 (High) \ **Poverty:** 25% \ **Title I:** $56,795 \ **Special Education:** $17,000 \
> **Open-Close:** 08/14 - 05/21

Jeff Graham 1,83   Tharla Plumbo 67
Mike Brehm .... 73*   Linda Bergman 84

Public Schs..Principal	Grd	Prgm	Enr/#Cls	SN	
Ludlow Elem Sch 245 S Orange St, Ludlow 60949 Tanya Turner	K-8	T	57 12	100%	217/396-5261

- **Mahomet-Seymour Cmty SD 3** PID: 00265016   217/586-4995
  1301 S Bulldog Dr, Mahomet 61853   Fax 217/586-7591

> **Schools:** 4 \ **Teachers:** 178 \ **Students:** 3,170 \ **Special Ed Students:** 303 \ **LEP Students:** 31 \ **College-Bound:** 75% \ **Ethnic:** Asian 2%, African American 1%, Hispanic 5%, Caucasian 92% \ **Exp:** $215 (Med) \ **Poverty:** 7% \ **Title I:** $298,819 \ **Special Education:** $1,627,000 \ **Open-Close:** 08/19 - 05/25 \ **DTBP:** $189 (High)

Dr Lindsey Hall 1   Trent Nuxoll 2
Shane Truitt 3   Jeremy Roark 5
Matt Hensley .... 6*   Nita Bachman 7,85*
Dr Nicole Rummel 8,12   Lauren Ochs 16*
Neal Garrison .... 36*   Christine Northrup 58*
Max McComb 67   Jared Lynn 84

Public Schs..Principal	Grd	Prgm	Enr/#Cls	SN	
Lincoln Trail Elem Sch 102 E State St, Mahomet 61853 Megan Hunter	3-5	T	717 26	22%	217/586-2811 Fax 217/586-5072
Mahomet-Seymour High Sch 302 W State St, Mahomet 61853 Chad Benedict	9-12	AV	937 35	18%	217/586-4962 Fax 217/586-6844
Mahomet-Seymour Jr High Sch 201 W State St, Mahomet 61853 Nathan Mills	6-8		751 40	21%	217/586-4415 Fax 217/586-5869 ▮

| Middletown Prairie Elem Sch
1301 S Bulldog Dr, Mahomet 61853
Ryan Martin | PK-2 | T | 765
16 | 23% | 217/586-5833
Fax 217/586-8919 |

- **Prairieview-Ogden Sch Dist 197** PID: 00265212   217/583-3300
  106 N Vine St, Royal 61871   Fax 217/583-3391

> **Schools:** 3 \ **Teachers:** 21 \ **Students:** 247 \ **Special Ed Students:** 27 \
> **Ethnic:** Hispanic 1%, Caucasian 99% \ **Exp:** $213 (Med) \ **Poverty:** 7% \
> **Title I:** $27,042 \ **Special Education:** $39,000 \ **Open-Close:** 08/14 - 05/26

Jeffery Isenhower 1   Darrell Lee 3
Tim Frerichs 5   Carl Heuer 6*
Jeffrey Isenhower .... 8,11,16,69,73,74,288*   Dirk Harms 67

Public Schs..Principal	Grd	Prgm	Enr/#Cls	SN	
Prairieview-Ogden Jr High Sch 2499 County Road 2100 E, Thomasboro 61878 Carl Heuer	7-8		49 5	16%	217/694-4122 Fax 217/694-4123
Prairieview-Ogden North ES 106 N Vine St, Royal 61871 Jeff Isenhower	K-4		89 5	12%	217/583-3300
Prairieview-Ogden South ES 304 N Market St, Ogden 61859 Carl Heuer	1-6		123 7	30%	217/582-2725 Fax 217/582-2509

- **Rantoul City School Dist 137** PID: 00265119   217/893-5400
  400 E Wabash Ave, Rantoul 61866   Fax 217/892-4313

> **Schools:** 5 \ **Teachers:** 159 \ **Students:** 1,750 \ **Special Ed Students:** 328 \ **LEP Students:** 339 \ **Ethnic:** Asian 1%, African American 31%, Hispanic 33%, Caucasian 34% \ **Exp:** $377 (High) \ **Poverty:** 29% \ **Title I:** $955,049 \ **Special Education:** $1,057,000 \ **Bilingual Education:** $82,000 \
> **Open-Close:** 08/17 - 05/21 \ **DTBP:** $61 (Low)

Michelle Ramage 1,11   Kendra Good 2
Shannon Clark 3   Debby Wilcoxon 4
Jane Jordahl .... 6*   Jennifer Frerichs 15
Dr Scott Woods 57   Allison Didier 58*
Bill Sweat 67   Tara Minion 68,71
Nakia Benson 73,76,84

Public Schs..Principal	Grd	Prgm	Enr/#Cls	SN	
Broadmeadow Grade Level Sch 500 Sunview Rd, Rantoul 61866 Tom Magers	PK-5	T	306 12	82%	217/893-5405 Fax 217/892-2382
Eastlawn Elem Sch 650 N Maplewood Dr, Rantoul 61866 Chris Forman	PK-5	T	282 22	87%	217/893-5404 Fax 217/893-1442
J W Eater Junior High Sch 400 E Wabash Ave, Rantoul 61866 Dr Scott Woods	6-8	T	503 40	76%	217/893-5401 Fax 217/893-3426
Northview Elem Sch 400 N Sheldon St, Rantoul 61866 Kelly Mahoney	PK-5	T	350 15	72%	217/893-5403 Fax 217/893-1335
Pleasant Acres Elem Sch 1625 Short St, Rantoul 61866 Wendy Starwalt	PK-5	T	269 12	86%	217/893-5402 Fax 217/893-0328

---

79   Student Personnel
80   Driver Ed/Safety
81   Gifted/Talented
82   Video Services
83   Substance Abuse Prev
84   Erate
85   AIDS Education
88   Alternative/At Risk
89   Multi-Cultural Curriculum
90   Social Work

91   Safety/Security
92   Magnet School
93   Parental Involvement
95   Tech Prep Program
97   Chief Information Officer
98   Chief Technology Officer
270   Character Education
271   Migrant Education
273   Teacher Mentor
274   Before/After Sch

275   Response To Intervention
277   Remedial Math K-12
280   Literacy Coach
285   STEM
286   Digital Learning
288   Common Core Standards
294   Accountability
295   Network System
296   Title II Programs
297   Webmaster

298   Grant Writer/Ptnrships
750   Chief Innovation Officer
751   Chief of Staff
752   Social Emotional Learning

Other School Types
Ⓐ = Alternative School
Ⓒ = Charter School
Ⓜ = Magnet School
Ⓨ = Year-Round School

School Programs
A = Alternative Program
G = Adult Classes
M = Magnet Program
T = Title I Schoolwide
V = Career & Tech Ed Programs

Social Media
▮ = Facebook
▮ = Twitter

New Schools are shaded
New Superintendents and Principals are bold
Personnel with email addresses are underscored

Champaign County

Market Data Retrieval

- **Rantoul Twp High Sch Dist 193** PID: 00265195   217/892-2151
  200 S Sheldon St, Rantoul 61866   Fax 217/892-4442

Schools: 2 \ Teachers: 59 \ Students: 765 \ Special Ed Students: 137 \ LEP Students: 91 \ College-Bound: 53% \ Ethnic: Asian 1%, African American 30%, Hispanic 25%, Caucasian 44% \ Exp: $326 (High) \ Poverty: 18% \ Title I: $376,366 \ Special Education: $415,000 \ Open-Close: 08/20 - 05/26 \ DTBP: $239 (High)

Scott Amerio 1
Tony Worthington 3,5
Travis Flesner 6*
Toyna Turner 10,60
Holly Regan 16*
Hannah Yean 57*
Todd Wilson 69,288*
Angela Krickovich 2
Luana Donald 4*
April Jones 7*
Megan Anderson 11,83,88,275,296,298*
Bud Root 27
Anne Reale 67
Greg VanHorn 73,76,286

Public Schs..Principal	Grd	Prgm	Enr/#Cls	SN	
ⓐ Eagle Academy 205 W Borman Dr, Rantoul 61866 Megan Anderson	9-12		40		217/926-6002
Rantoul Twp High Sch 200 S Sheldon St, Rantoul 61866 Todd Wilson	9-12	TV	738	71%	217/892-2151

- **St Joseph Cmty Cons SD 169** PID: 00265236   217/469-2291
  404 S 5th St, Saint Joseph 61873   Fax 217/469-8906

Schools: 2 \ Teachers: 55 \ Students: 850 \ Special Ed Students: 88 \ LEP Students: 3 \ College-Bound: 86% \ Ethnic: Asian 1%, African American 1%, Hispanic 1%, Caucasian 96% \ Exp: $146 (Low) \ Poverty: 7% \ Title I: $89,240 \ Special Education: $172,000 \ Open-Close: 08/14 - 05/25

Todd Pence 1,11,83,288
Brian Hawkins 3
Mr Downes 5
Michael Sennert 9,16,73,82*
Marsha Robbins 2
Brenda Collenberger 4*
Chris Graham 6*
Lois Hewervine 67

Public Schs..Principal	Grd	Prgm	Enr/#Cls	SN	
St Joseph Grade Sch 404 S 5th St, Saint Joseph 61873 Michelle Wagner	PK-4		499	18%	217/469-2291
St Joseph Middle Sch 606 E Peters Dr, Saint Joseph 61873 Chris Graham	5-8		369 23	14%	217/469-2334 Fax 217/469-2537

- **St Joseph-Ogden Cmty HSD 305** PID: 00265250   217/469-2586
  301 N Main St, Saint Joseph 61873   Fax 217/469-2478

Schools: 1 \ Teachers: 30 \ Students: 450 \ Special Ed Students: 37 \ College-Bound: 90% \ Ethnic: Asian 1%, African American 1%, Hispanic 1%, Caucasian 96% \ Exp: $208 (Med) \ Poverty: 3% \ Title I: $17,752 \ Special Education: $70,000 \ Open-Close: 08/17 - 05/28 \ DTBP: $233 (High)

Brian Brooks 1,11
Gary Page 57,83,273,275,294*
Terri Rein 69*
Marshal Schacht 88*
Justin Franzen 6*
James Rein 67
Josh Halls 76,295
Veronica Harbaugh 297*

Public Schs..Principal	Grd	Prgm	Enr/#Cls	SN	
St Joseph-Ogden High Sch 301 N Main St, Saint Joseph 61873 Gary Page	9-12	V	450 35	5%	217/469-2332 Fax 217/469-8290

- **Thomasboro Cmty Cons SD 130** PID: 00265303   217/643-3275
  201 N Phillips St, Thomasboro 61878   Fax 217/643-2022

Schools: 1 \ Teachers: 15 \ Students: 150 \ Special Ed Students: 32 \ LEP Students: 13 \ Ethnic: Asian 1%, African American 2%, Hispanic 13%, Caucasian 83% \ Exp: $382 (High) \ Poverty: 28% \ Title I: $153,927 \ Special Education: $44,000 \ Open-Close: 08/10 - 05/24

Bonnie McArthur 1,84
Elizebeth Acton 752
William Wilken 67

Public Schs..Principal	Grd	Prgm	Enr/#Cls	SN	
Thomasboro Grade Sch 201 N Phillips St, Thomasboro 61878 Elizabeth Acton	PK-8	T	150 16	65%	217/643-3275

- **Tolono Cmty Unit Sch Dist 7** PID: 00265327   217/485-6510
  1121 County Road 800 N, Tolono 61880   Fax 217/485-3091

Schools: 4 \ Teachers: 115 \ Students: 1,615 \ Special Ed Students: 222 \ LEP Students: 10 \ College-Bound: 69% \ Ethnic: Asian 1%, African American 2%, Hispanic 1%, Caucasian 96% \ Exp: $291 (Med) \ Poverty: 7% \ Title I: $193,315 \ Special Education: $620,000 \ Open-Close: 08/19 - 05/28 \ DTBP: $173 (High)

Andrew Larson 1,83
Josh Terven 3
Scott Hamilton 6*
Kris Graves 16*
Fred Koss 67
Paul Bierman 84,295
Deanna Wheeler 2
Denise Cloud 4
Laura Fitzgerald 8,11,69,296,298*
Janah Sudduth 58
Tim Gateley 73,286*

Public Schs..Principal	Grd	Prgm	Enr/#Cls	SN	
Unity East Elem Sch 1638 County Road 1000 N, Philo 61864 Jim Carver	PK-5		283 17	22%	217/684-5218 Fax 217/684-5220
Unity High Sch 1127 County Road 800 N, Tolono 61880 Phil Morrison	9-12	V	535 40	25%	217/485-6230 Fax 217/485-6220
Unity Junior High Sch 1121 County Road 800 N, Tolono 61880 Laura Fitzgerald	6-8		387 20	29%	217/485-6735 Fax 217/485-3218
Unity West Elem Sch 1035 County Road 600 N, Tolono 61880 Lanee Reichert	K-5		410 24	34%	217/485-3918 Fax 217/485-3451

- **Urbana School District 116** PID: 00265406   217/384-3600
  205 N Race St, Urbana 61801   Fax 217/337-4973

Schools: 10 \ Teachers: 362 \ Students: 4,175 \ Special Ed Students: 774 \ LEP Students: 749 \ College-Bound: 67% \ Ethnic: Asian 6%, African American 42%, Hispanic 17%, Native American: 1%, Caucasian 35% \ Exp: $209 (Med) \ Poverty: 23% \ Title I: $2,227,891 \ Special Education: $6,244,000 \ Bilingual Education: $273,000 \ Open-Close: 08/21 - 06/03 \ DTBP: $211 (High) \ 🅣

Jennifer Ivory-Tatum 1,84
Liz Walden 2
Steve Waller 6*
Yavonnda Smith 8*
Todd Taylor 15,54,58,79,275*
Crystal Vowels 34*
Jacinda Crawmer 68
M C Neal 73,76
Diann Richardson 79
Carol Baker 2,19
Randy Ashman 3,19,27
Andrea Jackson 8,93
Angi Franklin 15,68,74
Dionne Webster 31,93
John Dimit 67
Jessica Brown 68,74
Jennifer Eiron-Conway 76

1	Superintendent	8	Curric/Instruct K-12	19	Chief Financial Officer	29	Family/Consumer Science	39	Social Studies K-12	49	English/Lang Arts Elem	59	Special Education Elem	69	Academic Assessment
2	Bus/Finance/Purchasing	9	Curric/Instruct Elem	20	Art K-12	30	Adult Education	40	Social Studies Elem	50	English/Lang Arts Sec	60	Special Education Sec	70	Research/Development
3	Buildings And Grounds	10	Curric/Instruct Sec	21	Art Elem	31	Career/Sch-to-Work K-12	41	Social Studies Sec	51	Reading K-12	61	Foreign/World Lang K-12	71	Public Information
4	Food Service	11	Federal Program	22	Art Sec	32	Career/Sch-to-Work Elem	42	Science K-12	52	Reading Elem	62	Foreign/World Lang Elem	72	Summer School
5	Transportation	12	Title I	23	Music K-12	33	Career/Sch-to-Work Sec	43	Science Elem	53	Reading Sec	63	Foreign/World Lang Sec	73	Instructional Tech
6	Athletic	13	Title V	24	Music Elem	34	Early Childhood Ed	44	Science Sec	54	Remedial Reading K-12	64	Religious Education K-12	74	Inservice Training
7	Health Services	14	Asst Superintendent	25	Music Sec	35	Health/Phys Education	45	Math K-12	55	Remedial Reading Elem	65	Religious Education Elem	75	Marketing/Distributive
		15	Instructional Media Svcs	26	Business Education	36	Guidance Services K-12	46	Math Elem	56	Remedial Reading Sec	66	Religious Education Sec	76	Info Systems
		16	Chief Operations Officer	27	Career & Tech Ed	37	Guidance Services Elem	47	Math Sec	57	Bilingual/ELL	67	School Board President	77	Psychological Assess
		17	Chief Academic Officer	28	Technology Education	38	Guidance Services Sec	48	English/Lang Arts K-12	58	Special Education K-12	68	Teacher Personnel	78	Affirmative Action

Illinois School Directory — Champaign County

Public Schs..Principal	Grd	Prgm	Enr/#Cls	SN	
Dr Preston L Williams Elem Sch 2102 E Washington St, Urbana 61802 Danielle Jackson	K-5	T	462 17	88%	217/384-3628 Fax 217/384-3626 t
Flossie Wiley Elem Sch 1602 S Anderson St, Urbana 61801 Jennifer Heinhorst	K-5	T	232 16	78%	217/384-3670 Fax 217/384-3559 t
Leal Elem Sch 312 W Oregon St, Urbana 61801 Adriana Ochoa	K-5	T	396 19	58%	217/384-3618 Fax 217/384-3622 t
Martin Luther King Elem Sch 1108 Fairview Ave, Urbana 61801 Christina Lewandowski	K-5	T	307 35	85%	217/384-3675 Fax 217/344-5610
Thomas Paine Elem Sch 1801 James Cherry Dr, Urbana 61802 Delores Lloyd	K-5	T	293 18	75%	217/384-3602 Fax 217/384-1835
Urbana Adult Education Sch 211 N Race St, Urbana 61801 Samuel Byndon	Adult		250		217/384-3530 Fax 217/337-4987
Urbana Early Childhood Sch 2202 E Washington St, Urbana 61802 Cris Vowels	PK-PK		283 12	89%	217/843-3616 Fax 217/384-3615
Urbana High Sch 1002 S Race St, Urbana 61801 Dr Mitchell Berenson	9-12	T	1,210 80	65%	217/384-3505 Fax 217/384-3532
Urbana Middle Sch 1201 S Vine St, Urbana 61801 Dr Joseph Wiemelt	6-8	T	979 80	71%	217/384-3685 Fax 217/367-3156 t
Yankee Ridge Elem Sch 2102 S Anderson St, Urbana 61801 Dr Mykah Jackson	K-5	T	345 16	62%	217/384-3607 Fax 217/384-3611 t

CHAMPAIGN CATHOLIC SCHOOLS

• **Diocese of Peoria Ed Office** PID: 00313338
Listing includes only schools located in this county. See District Index for location of Diocesan Offices.

Catholic Schs..Principal	Grd	Prgm	Enr/#Cls	SN	
High School of St Thomas More 3901 N Mattis Ave, Champaign 61822 Sr M Bridget	9-12		360 14		217/352-7210 Fax 217/352-7213 f t
Holy Cross Sch 410 W White St, Champaign 61820 Greg Koerner	K-8		340 20		217/356-9521 Fax 217/356-1745
St Malachy Sch 340 E Belle Ave, Rantoul 61866 Dave Auth	PK-8		196 9		217/892-2011 Fax 217/892-5780
St Matthew Sch 1307 Lincolnshire Dr, Champaign 61821 Michelle Biggs	K-8		449 20		217/359-4114 Fax 217/359-8319
St Thomas Sch 311 E Madison St, Philo 61864 Lisa Doughan	K-8		83 10		217/684-2309 Fax 217/684-2217

CHAMPAIGN PRIVATE SCHOOLS

Private Schs..Principal	Grd	Prgm	Enr/#Cls	SN	
Academy High 2302 Fox Dr, Champaign 61820 Dr Darren Pascavage	9-10		401		217/239-6000
Calvary Baptist Christian Acad 2106 E Windsor Ln, Urbana 61802 Gary Gritton	K-12		43 5		217/367-2262
Campus Middle School for Girls 108 S Webber St, Urbana 61802 Tammy Adams	6-8		42 3		217/344-8279 Fax 217/344-6842
Canaan Academy 207 N Central Ave, Urbana 61801 Bryant Tatum	PK-5		60 5		217/367-6590 Fax 217/367-5130
Circle Academy 1303 N Cunningham Ave, Urbana 61802 Charles Hogue	K-12	A	75		217/367-6923 Fax 217/337-9391
Countryside Sch 4301 W Kirby Ave, Champaign 61822 Stephanie Harman \ Stacy Kirby \ Chris Antonsen	K-8		150 10		217/355-1253 Fax 217/355-7492
Judah Christian Sch 908 N Prospect Ave, Champaign 61820 Cheryl Black \ Taylor-Imani Gates	PK-12		534		217/359-1701 Fax 217/359-0214
Kingswood Sch 2111 N Willow Rd, Urbana 61801 Dr Marsh Jones	6-12		12 7		217/344-5540 Fax 217/344-5535
Next Generation Sch 2521 Galen Dr, Champaign 61821 Chris Woller	K-8		260 9		217/356-6995 Fax 217/356-6345
Pavilion Foundation Sch 810 W Church St, Champaign 61820 Mary Lanoue	Spec		60		217/373-1889 Fax 217/373-1786
St John Lutheran Sch 509 S Mattis Ave, Champaign 61821 Tim Gabbert	PK-8		148 11		217/359-1714 Fax 217/359-7972
Swann Sch 2418 W Springfield Ave, Champaign 61821 John Lawrence	Spec	G	20 5		217/398-9270
University Primary Sch 51 Gerty Dr, Champaign 61820 Ali Lewis	PK-5		51 2		217/333-3996
Winfred Gerber Sch 1301 N Cunningham Ave, Urbana 61802 Sharla Jolly	Spec		45 7		217/367-3728 Fax 217/367-2896

CHAMPAIGN REGIONAL CENTERS

• **EFE System 330** PID: 04180315   217/355-1382
2400 W Bradley Ave Rm A113, Champaign 61821   Fax 217/355-1396

Nick Elder 1   Shelly Dunn 2

• **Learning Tech Ctr of Illinois** PID: 04433150   217/893-3219
3358 Big Pine Trl, Champaign 61822

Tim McIlvain 1   Christina Ronquest 2,297
Brian Bates 73,286   Chris Wherley 76,295

• **Regional Office of Ed 9** PID: 02097530   217/893-3219
3358 Big Pine Trl Ste A, Champaign 61822   Fax 217/893-0024

Gary Lewis 1   Donna Kaufman 15

• **Rural Champaign Co Sp Ed Co-op** PID: 02182240   217/892-8877
807 N Mattis Ave, Champaign 61821   Fax 217/892-8627

Jennifer Armstrong 1   Jennifer Hastings 59

---

79 Student Personnel	91 Safety/Security	275 Response To Intervention	298 Grant Writer/Ptnrships	**School Programs**	**Social Media**	
80 Driver Ed/Safety	92 Magnet School	277 Remedial Math K-12	750 Chief Innovation Officer	A = Alternative Program		
81 Gifted/Talented	93 Parental Involvement	280 Literacy Coach	751 Chief of Staff	G = Adult Classes	f = Facebook	
82 Video Services	95 Tech Prep Program	285 STEM	752 Social Emotional Learning	M = Magnet Program		
83 Substance Abuse Prev	97 Chief Information Officer	286 Digital Learning		T = Title I Schoolwide	t = Twitter	
84 Erate	98 Chief Technology Officer	288 Common Core Standards	**Other School Types**	V = Career & Tech Ed Programs		
85 AIDS Education	270 Accountability	294 Accountability	Ⓐ = Alternative School			
88 Alternative/At Risk	271 Migrant Education	295 Network System	Ⓒ = Charter School	New Schools are shaded		
89 Multi-Cultural Curriculum	273 Teacher Mentor	296 Title II Programs	Ⓜ = Magnet School	New Superintendents and Principals are bold		
90 Social Work	274 Before/After Sch	297 Webmaster	Ⓨ = Year-Round School	Personnel with email addresses are underscored		

IL—13

Christian County

Market Data Retrieval

CHRISTIAN COUNTY

CHRISTIAN PUBLIC SCHOOLS

- **Central A&M Cmty Unit SD 21** PID: 00265535   217/226-4042
  406 E Colegrove St, Assumption 62510   Fax 217/226-4133

  Schools: 5 \ Teachers: 66 \ Students: 670 \
  Special Ed Students: 133 \ College-Bound: 79% \ Ethnic: African American 2%, Caucasian 98% \ Exp: $556 (High) \ Poverty: 9% \ Title I: $167,120 \
  Special Education: $616,000 \ Open-Close: 08/20 - 05/20 \ DTBP: $184 (High)

Dr Deann Heck	1,11,83	Rick Hauffe		2,84
Ray Odle	3*	Joan Mitsdarffer		5
Sean Hayes	6	Joanne Coady		58*
Josh Burgner	67	Dotty Simmons		69*
Jared Cook	286*			

Public Schs..Principal	Grd	Prgm	Enr/#Cls	SN	
Bond Elementary 404 Colegrove St Ste B, Assumption 62510 Courtney Hiler	PK-1	T	176 8	37%	217/226-4022
Central A & M High Sch 229 E Pine St, Moweaqua 62550 Charles Brown	9-12	TV	223 30	35%	217/768-3866 Fax 217/768-3797
Central A & M Middle Sch 404 Colegrove St Ste A, Assumption 62510 Courtney Hiler	6-8	T	162 16	39%	217/226-4241 Fax 217/226-4442
Gregory Intermediate Sch 221 E Pine St, Moweaqua 62550 Charles Brown	2-5	T	127 11	37%	217/768-3860 Fax 217/768-2130
Ⓐ Kemmerer Village Sch 941 N 2500 East Rd, Assumption 62510 Joanne Coady	6-12		37 8	77%	217/226-2139 Fax 217/226-2170

- **Edinburg Cmty Unit Sch Dist 4** PID: 00265561   217/623-5733
  100 E Martin St, Edinburg 62531   Fax 217/623-5604

  Schools: 1 \ Teachers: 23 \ Students: 290 \ Special Ed Students: 46 \
  College-Bound: 71% \ Ethnic: Hispanic 3%, Caucasian 97% \ Exp: $213 (Med) \ Poverty: 14% \ Title I: $70,637 \ Special Education: $69,000 \
  Open-Close: 08/20 - 05/21

Ben Theiland	1,288	Adam Feld		6*
Michelle Reiss	8,69*	Jennifer Tracy		12*
Adam Swinger	67			

Public Schs..Principal	Grd	Prgm	Enr/#Cls	SN	
Edinburg Cmty Unit Sch 100 E Martin St, Edinburg 62531 Michelle Reiss	PK-12	AV	290 40	39%	217/623-5603

- **Morrisonville Cmty Unit SD 1** PID: 00265614   217/526-4431
  301 School St, Morrisonville 62546   Fax 217/526-4433

  Schools: 2 \ Teachers: 26 \ Students: 250 \ Special Ed Students: 60 \
  College-Bound: 40% \ Ethnic: Hispanic 2%, Caucasian 98% \ Exp: $265 (Med) \ Poverty: 10% \ Title I: $45,972 \ Special Education: $115,000 \
  Open-Close: 08/17 - 05/21 \ DTBP: $185 (High) \ 🇪

Dave Meister	1,73	Lela Ferill		2,19
Jim Kelmel	3*	Paul Stutz		6
Megan Hanlon	11	Amy Schmedeke		58*
Ed Goebel	67	Kylie Halbrook		273

Public Schs..Principal	Grd	Prgm	Enr/#Cls	SN	
Morrisonville Elem Sch 301 School St, Morrisonville 62546 Christy Willman	PK-6		172 9	36%	217/526-4441
Morrisonville Jr Sr High Sch 204 N Perrine St, Morrisonville 62546 Ann Little	7-12	V	89 18	26%	217/526-4432 Fax 217/526-4452

- **Pana Cmty Unit School Dist 8** PID: 00265676   217/562-1500
  14 Main St, Pana 62557   Fax 217/562-1501

  Schools: 4 \ Teachers: 83 \ Students: 1,347 \ Special Ed Students: 204 \ LEP Students: 4 \ College-Bound: 56% \ Ethnic: African American 1%, Hispanic 1%, Caucasian 98% \ Exp: $296 (Med) \ Poverty: 18% \
  Title I: $478,811 \ Special Education: $529,000 \ Open-Close: 08/18 - 05/21 \ DTBP: $192 (High) \ 🇫 🇪

Jason Bauer	1	Heather Phillips		2
Jeff Stauder	3,5	Amy Christian		4
Gary Ade	6*	Paul Donahue		8,58
Juletta Ellis	10,69*	Cheri Wysong		11*
Dr Wilfred Beyers	67	Scott Savage		73,295
Amanda Skinner	286	Amber Daniels		752

Public Schs..Principal	Grd	Prgm	Enr/#Cls	SN	
Lincoln Elem Sch 614 E 2nd St, Pana 62557 Kelly Millburg	3-5	T	277 14	70%	217/562-8500 Fax 217/562-9259 🇫 🇪
Pana Junior High Sch 203 W 8th St, Pana 62557 Juletta Ellis	6-8	T	297 14	65%	217/562-6500 Fax 217/562-6712
Pana Senior High Sch 201 W 8th St, Pana 62557 Casey Adam	9-12	TV	394 40	56%	217/562-6600 Fax 217/562-6714
Washington Elem Sch 200 Sherman St, Pana 62557 Cheri Wysong	PK-2	T	312 23	67%	217/562-7500 Fax 217/562-9262

- **South Fork School Dist 14** PID: 00265755   217/237-4333
  612 Dial St, Kincaid 62540   Fax 217/237-2245

  Schools: 2 \ Teachers: 24 \ Students: 319 \ Special Ed Students: 69 \ LEP Students: 3 \ College-Bound: 52% \ Ethnic: Hispanic 3%, Caucasian 97% \ Exp: $241 (Med) \ Poverty: 11% \ Title I: $94,010 \
  Special Education: $118,000 \ Open-Close: 08/17 - 05/21 \ DTBP: $184 (High)

Chris Clark	1	Wendy Dulakis		2*
Chris Clark	3,10,15,275,288*	Megan Nunn		4
Michelle Rogers	8*	Theresa Ess		11,286,296*
Jack Hanlon	67	Dee Ford		69,88*
Jesse Foiles	73,295*	Lindsey Pembrook		83,294*

---

1 Superintendent	8 Curric/Instruct K-12	19 Chief Financial Officer	29 Family/Consumer Science	39 Social Studies K-12	49 English/Lang Arts Elem	59 Special Education Elem	69 Academic Assessment
2 Bus/Finance/Purchasing	9 Curric/Instruct Elem	20 Art K-12	30 Adult Education	40 Social Studies Elem	50 English/Lang Arts Sec	60 Special Education Sec	70 Research/Development
3 Buildings And Grounds	10 Curric/Instruct Sec	21 Art Elem	31 Career/Sch-to-Work K-12	41 Social Studies Sec	51 Reading K-12	61 Foreign/World Lang K-12	71 Public Information
4 Food Service	11 Federal Program	22 Art Sec	32 Career/Sch-to-Work Elem	42 Science K-12	52 Reading Elem	62 Foreign/World Lang Elem	72 Summer School
5 Transportation	12 Title I	23 Music K-12	33 Career/Sch-to-Work Sec	43 Science Elem	53 Reading Sec	63 Foreign/World Lang Sec	73 Instructional Tech
6 Athletic	13 Title V	24 Music Elem	34 Early Childhood Ed	44 Science Sec	54 Remedial Reading K-12	64 Religious Education K-12	74 Inservice Training
7 Health Services	15 Asst Superintendent	25 Music Sec	35 Health/Phys Education	45 Math K-12	55 Remedial Reading Elem	65 Religious Education Elem	75 Marketing/Distributive
	16 Instructional Media Svcs	26 Business Education	36 Guidance Services K-12	46 Math Elem	56 Remedial Reading Sec	66 Religious Education Sec	76 Info Systems
	17 Chief Operations Officer	27 Career & Tech Ed	37 Guidance Services Elem	47 Math Sec	57 Bilingual/ELL	67 School Board President	77 Psychological Assess
	18 Chief Academic Officer	28 Technology Education	38 Guidance Services Sec	48 English/Lang Arts K-12	58 Special Education K-12	68 Teacher Personnel	78 Affirmative Action

Illinois School Directory — Clark County

Public Schs..Principal	Grd	Prgm	Enr/#Cls	SN	
South Fork Elem Sch 550 Prairie St, Kincaid 62540 Michelle Rogers	PK-5	T	168 6	61%	217/237-4331
South Fork Jr Sr High Sch 612 Dial St, Kincaid 62540 Stephen Groll	6-12	TV	151 20	58%	217/237-4333 Fax 217/237-4370

• **Taylorville Cmty Unit SD 3** PID: 00265793   217/824-4951
512 W Spresser St, Taylorville 62568   Fax 217/824-5157

Schools: 4 \ **Teachers:** 151 \ **Students:** 2,480 \ **Special Ed Students:** 461 \ **LEP Students:** 4 \ **College-Bound:** 64% \ **Ethnic:** Asian 1%, African American 1%, Hispanic 2%, Caucasian 96% \ **Exp:** $263 (Med) \ **Poverty:** 14% \ **Title I:** $611,609 \ **Special Education:** $888,000 \ **Open-Close:** 08/18 - 06/02 \ **DTBP:** $192 (High)

Dr Chris Dougherty 1		Wendy Duklias 2	
Chris Westrick 3		Steve Walters 3	
Megan Nunn 4		Jason Hadley 6	
Anita Brown 8,11,296		Kelly Suey 58	
Michael Edwards 58		Stephen Turner 67	
Chris Kuntzman 73,285,295			

Public Schs..Principal	Grd	Prgm	Enr/#Cls	SN	
Memorial Elem Sch 101 E Adams St, Taylorville 62568 Nancy Ganci	3-4		307 14	54%	217/287-7929 Fax 217/287-7696
North Elem Sch 805 N Cherokee St, Taylorville 62568 Anita Brown	PK-2		646 8	58%	217/824-3315 Fax 217/824-5949
Taylorville High Sch 815 W Springfield Rd, Taylorville 62568 Mathew Hutchison	9-12	TV	755 60	44%	217/824-2268 Fax 217/824-3352
Taylorville Junior High Sch 120 E Bidwell St, Taylorville 62568 K Kettelkamp	5-8	T	753 30	48%	217/824-4924 Fax 217/824-7180

CHRISTIAN CATHOLIC SCHOOLS

• **Diocese of Springfield Ed Off** PID: 00319394
Listing includes only schools located in this county. See District Index for location of Diocesan Offices.

Catholic Schs..Principal	Grd	Prgm	Enr/#Cls	SN	
Sacred Heart Sch 3 E 4th St, Pana 62557 Ms Zueck	PK-8		145 9		217/562-2425 Fax 217/562-2942
St Mary Sch 422 S Washington St, Taylorville 62568 Cathy Robertson	K-6		105 7		217/824-6501 Fax 217/824-2803

CHRISTIAN PRIVATE SCHOOLS

Private Schs..Principal	Grd	Prgm	Enr/#Cls	SN	
Faith Bible Christian Acad 301 Mary St, Rosamond 62083 Caleb Wheeler	PK-12		80 11		217/562-5054
Pana Christian Academy 409 W Orange St, Pana 62557 Jonathan Blake	K-12		11 2		217/562-5893

Vision Way Christian Sch 1124 N Webster St, Taylorville 62568 Glenna Tolliver	PK-8		216 14		217/824-6722 Fax 217/824-6622

CHRISTIAN REGIONAL CENTERS

• **Mid-State Special Education** PID: 02183919   217/526-8121
202 Prairie St, Morrisonville 62546   Fax 217/526-8205

Angela Armour 1

• **Montgomery-Carlinville Reg SE** PID: 10776710   217/526-8121
202 Prairie St, Morrisonville 62546   Fax 217/526-8205

Angela Armour 1   Lyn Becker 15

CLARK COUNTY

CLARK PUBLIC SCHOOLS

• **Casey-Westfield Cmty USD C-4** PID: 00265896   217/932-2184
502 E Delaware Ave, Casey 62420   Fax 217/932-5553

Schools: 2 \ **Teachers:** 59 \ **Students:** 875 \ **Special Ed Students:** 138 \ **LEP Students:** 4 \ **College-Bound:** 58% \ **Ethnic:** Asian 1%, African American 1%, Hispanic 2%, Caucasian 96% \ **Exp:** $183 (Low) \ **Poverty:** 14% \ **Title I:** $234,162 \ **Special Education:** $305,000 \ **Open-Close:** 08/19 - 05/27

Dee Scott 1,11   Casey Overbeck 67
Gail Grissom .... 73*   Diane Bolin 83,93*

Public Schs..Principal	Grd	Prgm	Enr/#Cls	SN	
Casey-Westfield Jr Sr High Sch 306 E Edgar Ave, Casey 62420 Jim Sullivan	7-12	ATV	290 25	51%	217/932-2175 Fax 217/932-2986
Monroe Elem Sch 301 E Monroe Ave, Casey 62420 Linda Campbell	PK-6	T	522 25		833/888-8101 Fax 217/932-2816

• **Marshall Cmty Sch Dist C-2** PID: 00265937   217/826-5912
503 Pine St, Marshall 62441   Fax 217/826-5170

Schools: 4 \ **Teachers:** 94 \ **Students:** 1,250 \ **Special Ed Students:** 278 \ **LEP Students:** 7 \ **Ethnic:** Hispanic 1%, Caucasian 98% \ **Exp:** $323 (High) \ **Poverty:** 14% \ **Title I:** $320,022 \ **Special Education:** $600,000 \ **Open-Close:** 08/18 - 05/28 \ **DTBP:** $179 (High)

Kevin Ross 1,11,83	Molly Richardson 2
Garry Engerski 3,5	Teresa Wright 4*
Kevin Keown 6	John Ritchey 8*
Tamara Fraiely 8,36,69	Beth Grooms 12*
Katie Dailey 16,82*	Lauretta Morris 27,84
Katie Williams 58	David Macke 67
Darin Hostetter 73	

79	Student Personnel	91	Safety/Security	275	Response To Intervention	298	Grant Writer/Ptnrships
80	Driver Ed/Safety	92	Magnet School	277	Remedial Math K-12	750	Chief Innovation Officer
81	Gifted/Talented	93	Parental Involvement	280	Literacy Coach	751	Chief of Staff
82	Video Services	95	Tech Prep Program	285	STEM	752	Social Emotional Learning
83	Substance Abuse Prev	97	Chief Information Officer	286	Digital Learning		
84	Erate	98	Chief Technology Officer	288	Common Core Standards		**Other School Types**
85	AIDS Education	270	Character Education	294	Accountability	Ⓐ	= Alternative School
88	Alternative/At Risk	271	Migrant Education	295	Network System	Ⓒ	= Charter School
89	Multi-Cultural Curriculum	273	Teacher Mentor	296	Title II Programs	Ⓜ	= Magnet School
90	Social Work	274	Before/After Sch	297	Webmaster	Ⓨ	= Year-Round School

School Programs
A = Alternative Program
G = Adult Classes
M = Magnet Program
T = Title I Schoolwide
V = Career & Tech Ed Programs

Social Media
= Facebook
= Twitter

New Schools are shaded
New Superintendents and Principals are bold
Personnel with email addresses are underscored

Clay County

Public Schs..Principal	Grd	Prgm	Enr/#Cls	SN	
Marshall High Sch 806 N 6th St, Marshall 62441 John Ritchey	9-12	V	379 35	30%	217/826-2395 Fax 217/826-5511
Marshall Junior High Sch 806 N 6th St, Marshall 62441 Tony Graham	7-8		201 13	34%	217/826-2812 Fax 217/826-6065
North Elem Sch 1001 N 6th St, Marshall 62441 Clare Beaven	3-6	T	394 22	39%	217/826-2355 Fax 217/826-6127
South Elem Sch 805 S 6th St, Marshall 62441 Connie Morgan	PK-2	T	311	44%	217/826-5411 Fax 217/826-5822

- **Martinsville Cmty Unit SD C-3** PID: 00265999 217/382-4321
  255 W Cumberland St, Martinsville 62442 Fax 217/382-4183

Schools: 2 \ **Teachers:** 30 \ **Students:** 400 \ **Special Ed Students:** 75 \ **Ethnic:** Hispanic 2%, Caucasian 98% \ **Exp:** $291 (Med) \ **Poverty:** 19% \ **Title I:** $121,778 \ **Special Education:** $113,000 \ **Open-Close:** 08/24 - 05/28 \ **DTBP:** $186 (High)

Jill Rogers .... 1,11,83 Sherri Strange 6
Rachel Johnson .... 12* Jennifer Williams 16,73*
Lisa Parker .... 31,36,69* Michale Connelly 67

Public Schs..Principal	Grd	Prgm	Enr/#Cls	SN	
Martinsville Elem Sch 410 E Kendall St, Martinsville 62442 Victoria Norton	PK-6	T	238 9	60%	217/382-4116 Fax 217/382-5219
Martinsville Jr Sr High Sch 300 W Cumberland St, Martinsville 62442 Jeff Thompson	7-12	TV	167 18	57%	217/382-4132 Fax 217/382-4761

CLAY COUNTY

CLAY PUBLIC SCHOOLS

- **Clay City Cmty Unit SD 10** PID: 00266137 618/676-1431
  607 S Walnut St SE, Clay City 62824 Fax 618/676-1430

Schools: 3 \ **Teachers:** 26 \ **Students:** 350 \ **Special Ed Students:** 49 \ **College-Bound:** 95% \ **Ethnic:** African American 1%, Hispanic 1%, Caucasian 98% \ **Exp:** $191 (Low) \ **Poverty:** 13% \ **Title I:** $70,469 \ **Special Education:** $56,000 \ **Open-Close:** 08/17 - 05/27 \ **DTBP:** $197 (High)

Cathy Croy .... 1 Beth Hance 2
Matt Lindeman .... 3,5* Leslie Keller 12*
David Rauch .... 67 Taylor Strom 69

Public Schs..Principal	Grd	Prgm	Enr/#Cls	SN	
Clay City Elem Sch 607 S Walnut St SE, Clay City 62824 Cathy Croy	PK-5	T	204 21	65%	618/676-1431 Fax 618/676-1537
Clay City High Sch 607 S Walnut St SE, Clay City 62824 Ben Borries	9-12	TV	51 10	59%	618/676-1522 Fax 618/676-1481
Clay City Junior High Sch 607 S Walnut St SE, Clay City 62824 Ben Borries	6-8	T	85	64%	618/676-1522 Fax 618/676-1481

- **Flora Cmty Unit School Dist 35** PID: 00266163 618/662-2412
  630 Vincennes Ave, Flora 62839 Fax 618/662-7522

Schools: 3 \ **Teachers:** 86 \ **Students:** 1,396 \ **Special Ed Students:** 237 \ **LEP Students:** 3 \ **Ethnic:** Asian 1%, Hispanic 1%, Caucasian 97% \ **Exp:** $240 (Med) \ **Poverty:** 17% \ **Title I:** $410,450 \ **Special Education:** $250,000 \ **Open-Close:** 08/17 - 05/20 \ **DTBP:** $156 (High)

Joel Hackney .... 1,11,83 Hollie Brooks 2
Bob Johnson .... 3 Frank Lusk 5
Bobby McNeely .... 6 Paige Earleywine 7
Kelli Massie .... 27,31 Tonya Behnke 58
Joe McCoy .... 67 Heather Durre 73,84

Public Schs..Principal	Grd	Prgm	Enr/#Cls	SN	
Flora Elem Sch 445 Emory St, Flora 62839 Julie Pearce	PK-5	T	746 13	58%	618/662-2014 Fax 618/662-8393
Flora High Sch 600 S Locust St, Flora 62839 Toby Pearce	9-12	T	352 42	40%	618/662-8316 Fax 618/662-2725
Floyd Henson Jr High Sch 609 N Stanford Rd, Flora 62839 Amy Leonard	6-8	AGT	298 18	58%	618/662-8394 Fax 618/662-8395

- **North Clay Cmty Unit SD 25** PID: 00266072 618/665-3358
  953 Kinmundy Rd, Louisville 62858 Fax 618/665-3893

Schools: 2 \ **Teachers:** 48 \ **Students:** 618 \ **Special Ed Students:** 116 \ **College-Bound:** 54% \ **Ethnic:** Hispanic 2%, Caucasian 98% \ **Exp:** $257 (Med) \ **Poverty:** 17% \ **Title I:** $193,803 \ **Special Education:** $131,000 \ **Open-Close:** 08/14 - 05/19

Travis Wyatt .... 1,11,83 Roy Taylor 6
Kim Briggs .... 58 Barry Adair 67
Chad Traub 73

Public Schs..Principal	Grd	Prgm	Enr/#Cls	SN	
North Clay Cmty High Sch 500 S Route 45, Louisville 62858 Keith Price	9-12	TV	191 17	41%	618/665-3394 Fax 618/665-4803
North Clay Elem Jr High Sch 550 Route 45 N, Louisville 62858 Aron Spicer	PK-8	T	427 25	54%	618/665-3393 Fax 618/665-4803

CLAY REGIONAL CENTERS

- **Clay-Jaspr-Richlnd-N Wayne EFE** PID: 04184397 618/662-4059
  600 S Locust St, Flora 62839 Fax 618/662-8942

Kelli Massie 1

1	Superintendent	8	Curric/Instruct K-12	19	Chief Financial Officer	29	Family/Consumer Science	39	Social Studies K-12	49	English/Lang Arts Elem	59	Special Education Elem	69	Academic Assessment
2	Bus/Finance/Purchasing	9	Curric/Instruct Elem	20	Art K-12	30	Adult Education	40	Social Studies Elem	50	English/Lang Arts Sec	60	Special Education Sec	70	Research/Development
3	Buildings And Grounds	10	Curric/Instruct Sec	21	Art Elem	31	Career/Sch-to-Work K-12	41	Social Studies Sec	51	Reading K-12	61	Foreign/World Lang K-12	71	Public Information
4	Food Service	11	Federal Program	22	Art Sec	32	Career/Sch-to-Work Elem	42	Science K-12	52	Reading Elem	62	Foreign/World Lang Elem	72	Summer School
5	Transportation	12	Title I	23	Music K-12	33	Career/Sch-to-Work Sec	43	Science Elem	53	Reading Sec	63	Foreign/World Lang Sec	73	Instructional Tech
6	Athletic	13	Title V	24	Music Elem	34	Early Childhood Ed	44	Science Sec	54	Remedial Reading K-12	64	Religious Education K-12	74	Inservice Training
7	Health Services	14	Asst Superintendent	25	Music Sec	35	Health/Phys Education	45	Math K-12	55	Remedial Reading Elem	65	Religious Education Elem	75	Marketing/Distributive
		15	Instructional Media Svcs	26	Business Education	36	Guidance Services K-12	46	Math Elem	56	Remedial Reading Sec	66	Religious Education Sec	76	Info Systems
		16	Chief Operations Officer	27	Career & Tech Ed	37	Guidance Services Elem	47	Math Sec	57	Bilingual/ELL	67	School Board President	77	Psychological Assess
		17	Chief Academic Officer	28	Technology Education	38	Guidance Services Sec	48	English/Lang Arts K-12	58	Special Education K-12	68	Teacher Personnel	78	Affirmative Action

Illinois School Directory

Clinton County

CLINTON COUNTY

CLINTON PUBLIC SCHOOLS

- **Albers Elem School District 63** PID: 00266242   618/248-5146
  206 N Broadway, Albers 62215   Fax 618/248-5659

  Schools: 1 \ Teachers: 14 \ Students: 200 \ Special Ed Students: 36 \ LEP Students: 3 \ Ethnic: Hispanic 9%, Caucasian 91% \ Exp: $300 (High) \ Poverty: 8% \ Title I: $20,282 \ Special Education: $30,000 \ Open-Close: 08/17 - 05/21 \ DTBP: $140 (High)

  Mike Toeben 1,11,57,73,83,288   Joe Glynn 6
  Kurt Rickhoff 67

Public Schs..Principal	Grd	Prgm	Enr/#Cls	SN	
Albers Elem Sch 206 N Broadway, Albers 62215 Michael Toeben	PK-8		200 12	20%	618/248-5146

- **Aviston Elem School Dist 21** PID: 00266266   618/228-7245
  350 S Hull St, Aviston 62216   Fax 618/228-7121

  Schools: 1 \ Teachers: 24 \ Students: 390 \ Special Ed Students: 64 \ Ethnic: Hispanic 1%, Caucasian 99% \ Exp: $349 (High) \ Poverty: 3% \ Title I: $8,453 \ Special Education: $67,000 \ Open-Close: 08/17 - 06/02

  Phillip Hamil 1,11,83   Brad Eversgerd 67
  Lisa Niemeyer 273*

Public Schs..Principal	Grd	Prgm	Enr/#Cls	SN	
ⓎAviston Elem Sch 350 S Hull St, Aviston 62216 Dr Tami Kampwerth	PK-8	M	390 20	8%	618/228-7245

- **Bartelso School District 57** PID: 00266280   618/765-2164
  306 S Washington St, Bartelso 62218   Fax 618/765-2712

  Schools: 1 \ Teachers: 13 \ Students: 158 \ Special Ed Students: 26 \ Ethnic: Caucasian 100% \ Exp: $125 (Low) \ Poverty: 5% \ Special Education: $24,000 \ Open-Close: 08/17 - 06/02

  Tom Siegler 1,83,84   Jill Tasker 12*
  John Feldman .... 28,73*   Jill Daugherty 67

Public Schs..Principal	Grd	Prgm	Enr/#Cls	SN	
Bartelso Elem Sch 306 S Washington St, Bartelso 62218 Rdeane Gale	PK-8		158 15	10%	618/765-2164

- **Breese Elementary SD 12** PID: 00266307   618/526-7128
  777 Memorial Dr, Breese 62230   Fax 618/526-2787

  Schools: 2 \ Teachers: 34 \ Students: 630 \ Special Ed Students: 145 \ LEP Students: 33 \ Ethnic: Hispanic 9%, Caucasian 90% \ Exp: $144 (Low) \ Poverty: 8% \ Title I: $90,592 \ Special Education: $182,000 \ Open-Close: 08/17 - 05/21 \ DTBP: $173 (High)

  Joe Novsek 1   Jennie Santel 2
  Sandy Johnson 5   Jamie Toeben 67

Public Schs..Principal	Grd	Prgm	Enr/#Cls	SN	
Beckemeyer Elem Sch 110 E 4th St, Beckemeyer 62219 Kerrick Rahm	2-4	T	188 9	34%	618/227-8242 Fax 618/227-8587
Breese Elem Sch 777 Memorial Dr, Breese 62230 Travis Schmale	PK-1	T	420 30	34%	618/526-7128

- **Carlyle Cmty Unit Sch Dist 1** PID: 00266333   618/594-8283
  1400 13th St, Carlyle 62231   Fax 618/594-8285

  Schools: 3 \ Teachers: 73 \ Students: 1,006 \ Special Ed Students: 199 \ LEP Students: 3 \ College-Bound: 73% \ Ethnic: Asian 1%, African American 2%, Hispanic 1%, Caucasian 96% \ Exp: $226 (Med) \ Poverty: 12% \ Title I: $238,184 \ Special Education: $407,000 \ Open-Close: 08/17 - 05/14 \ DTBP: $233 (High)

  Annie Gray 1   Linda Scott 2,68
  Connie Geoffray 4   Kevin Stanowski 5
  Darin Smith 6   Lualice Campwerth 16,273
  Teresa Linton .... 58*   Keith Rensing 67
  Marc Smith 73,295*

Public Schs..Principal	Grd	Prgm	Enr/#Cls	SN	
Carlyle Grade Sch 951 6th St, Carlyle 62231 Kerrick Rahm	PK-4	T	374 23	53%	618/594-3766 Fax 618/594-8110
Carlyle High Sch 1461 12th St, Carlyle 62231 Jered Weh	9-12	TV	309 30	39%	618/594-2453 Fax 618/594-8286
Carlyle Junior High Sch 1631 12th St, Carlyle 62231 Bryan Rainey	5-8	T	323 32	46%	618/594-8292 Fax 618/594-8294

- **Central Cmty High Sch Dist 71** PID: 00266395   618/526-4578
  7740 Old US Highway 50, Breese 62230   Fax 618/526-7647

  Schools: 1 \ Teachers: 38 \ Students: 615 \ Special Ed Students: 91 \ LEP Students: 4 \ College-Bound: 77% \ Ethnic: Hispanic 2%, Caucasian 98% \ Exp: $422 (High) \ Poverty: 6% \ Title I: $77,071 \ Special Education: $156,000 \ Open-Close: 08/17 - 05/27 \ DTBP: $176 (High)

  Dr Dustin Foutch 1,11,83   Becky Boeschen 2
  Joe Lampe 3   Neil Hamon 6*
  Ami Shanafelt .... 12*   Britney Hogg 13,16,82*
  Trisha Lowman 57,288   Michael Netemeier 67
  Anthony Rancilio .... 73*   Ryan Ketchum 296

Public Schs..Principal	Grd	Prgm	Enr/#Cls	SN	
Central Community High Sch 7740 Old US Highway 50, Breese 62230 Ryan Ketchum	9-12	V	615 33	19%	618/526-4578

- **Damiansville School Dist 62** PID: 00266412   618/248-5188
  101 E Main St, Damiansville 62215   Fax 618/248-5910

  Schools: 1 \ Teachers: 10 \ Students: 85 \ Special Ed Students: 5 \ LEP Students: 3 \ Ethnic: Hispanic 13%, Caucasian 87% \ Exp: $158 (Low) \ Poverty: 8% \ Special Education: $15,000 \ Open-Close: 08/17 - 05/21 \ DTBP: $172 (High)

---

79 Student Personnel	91 Safety/Security	275 Response To Intervention	298 Grant Writer/Ptnrships	School Programs	Social Media	
80 Driver Ed/Safety	92 Magnet School	277 Remedial Math K-12	750 Chief Innovation Officer	A = Alternative Program		
81 Gifted/Talented	93 Parental Involvement	280 Literacy Coach	751 Chief of Staff	G = Adult Classes	= Facebook	
82 Video Services	95 Tech Prep Program	285 STEM	752 Social Emotional Learning	M = Magnet Program		
83 Substance Abuse Prev	97 Chief Infomation Officer	286 Digital Learning		T = Title I Schoolwide	= Twitter	
84 Erate	98 Chief Technology Officer	288 Common Core Standards	Other School Types	V = Career & Tech Ed Programs		
85 AIDS Education	270 Character Education	294 Accountability	Ⓐ = Alternative School			
88 Alternative/At Risk	271 Migrant Education	295 Network System	Ⓒ = Charter School	New Schools are shaded		
89 Multi-Cultural Curriculum	273 Teacher Mentor	296 Title II Programs	Ⓜ = Magnet School	New Superintendents and Principals are bold		
90 Social Work	274 Before/After Sch	297 Webmaster	Ⓨ = Year-Round School	Personnel with email addresses are underscored		

IL—17

Clinton County
Market Data Retrieval

Dustin Nail 1,11,288
Mike Caraker 67,73,286,295
Erin Korte 2

Public Schs..Principal	Grd	Prgm	Enr/#Cls	SN	
Damiansville Elem Sch 101 E Main St, Damiansville 62215 Dustin Nail	PK-8		85 9	28%	618/248-5188

• **Germantown Elem Sch Dist 60** PID: 00266436   618/523-4253
401 Walnut St, Germantown 62245   Fax 618/523-7879

> Schools: 1 \ Teachers: 18 \ Students: 250 \ Special Ed Students: 39
> \ LEP Students: 6 \ Ethnic: Hispanic 3%, Caucasian 97% \ Exp: $79
> (Low) \ Poverty: 5% \ Title I: $16,225 \ Special Education: $56,000 \
> Open-Close: 08/17 - 05/19 \ DTBP: $223 (High) \ 🅕 🅣

Robin Becker 1,11,83
Matt Korte 67
Leig-Ann Arentsen 2

Public Schs..Principal	Grd	Prgm	Enr/#Cls	SN	
Germantown Elem Sch 401 Walnut St, Germantown 62245 Robin Becker	PK-8		250 18	22%	618/523-4253 🅕

• **North Wamac School Dist 186** PID: 00266539   618/532-1826
1500 Case St, Centralia 62801   Fax 618/532-8250

> Schools: 1 \ Teachers: 10 \ Students: 120 \ Special Ed Students: 38
> \ LEP Students: 3 \ Ethnic: African American 4%, Hispanic 5%,
> Caucasian 90% \ Exp: $483 (High) \ Poverty: 31% \ Title I: $74,437 \
> Special Education: $52,000 \ Open-Close: 08/17 - 06/04

Brad Morris 1,11,83,84,288
John Pomlianovich 73
Norman Faulkner 67

Public Schs..Principal	Grd	Prgm	Enr/#Cls	SN	
North Wamac Grade Sch 1500 Case St, Centralia 62801 Brad Morris	K-8	T	120 13	91%	618/532-1826

• **St Rose School District 14-15** PID: 00266450   618/526-7484
18004 Saint Rose Rd, Saint Rose 62230   Fax 618/526-7168

> Schools: 1 \ Teachers: 13 \ Students: 207 \ Special Ed Students: 22 \
> Ethnic: Hispanic 4%, Caucasian 96% \ Exp: $209 (Med) \ Poverty: 6% \
> Title I: $13,521 \ Special Education: $28,000 \ Open-Close: 08/17 - 05/21
> \ 🅕

Dr Erick Baer 1,11,73,83,84,288
Emily Henrichs 67

Public Schs..Principal	Grd	Prgm	Enr/#Cls	SN	
St Rose Elem Sch 18004 Saint Rose Rd, Saint Rose 62230 Dr Erick Baer	PK-8		207 10	21%	618/526-7484

• **Wesclin Cmty Unit Sch Dist 3** PID: 00266474   618/224-7583
699 Wesclin Rd, Trenton 62293   Fax 618/588-9106

> Schools: 4 \ Teachers: 86 \ Students: 1,375 \ Special Ed Students: 241
> \ LEP Students: 34 \ College-Bound: 80% \ Ethnic: Asian 1%, African
> American 1%, Hispanic 7%, Caucasian 91% \ Exp: $284 (Med) \ Poverty: 8%
> \ Title I: $160,902 \ Special Education: $553,000 \ Open-Close: 08/13 -
> 05/20 \ DTBP: $233 (High)

Jennifer Filyaw 1,11
Ray Kauling 6*
Roger Freeze 10,69,83,285*
Kristen Oster 16,82*
Jamie Peince 58*
K Kunz 73,295*
Angie Woll 88
Tom Krumsieg 3,4,5*
Rita Wuebbels 7,85*
James Rahm 12*
Katrina Hanke 36,79
Aaron Hoerchler 67
Kelly Kunz 73,84,98,295
Cathy Powers 90,271,752*

Public Schs..Principal	Grd	Prgm	Enr/#Cls	SN	
New Baden Elem Sch 700 Marilyn Dr, New Baden 62265 James Rahm	PK-3	T	231 12	40%	618/588-3535 Fax 618/588-4364
Trenton Elem Sch 308 N Washington St, Trenton 62293 Angela Woll	PK-3		261 10	39%	618/224-9411 Fax 618/224-9417
Wesclin Middle Sch 10003 State Route 160, Trenton 62293 Roger Freeze	4-8	T	493 13	39%	618/224-7355 Fax 618/224-7085
Wesclin Senior High Sch 699 Wesclin Rd, Trenton 62293 John Isenhower	9-12	V	379 11	25%	618/224-7341

• **Willow Grove School Dist 46** PID: 00266553   618/532-3313
815 W 7th St, Centralia 62801   Fax 618/532-5638

> Schools: 1 \ Teachers: 16 \ Students: 165 \ Special Ed Students: 56 \
> Ethnic: African American 3%, Hispanic 5%, Caucasian 92% \ Exp: $152
> (Low) \ Poverty: 34% \ Title I: $120,104 \ Special Education: $57,000 \
> Open-Close: 08/18 - 05/21

Dave Fults 1,11
Clay Beaver 67
Tricia Timmons 2

Public Schs..Principal	Grd	Prgm	Enr/#Cls	SN	
Willow Grove Elem Sch 815 W 7th St, Centralia 62801 Dave Fults	PK-8	T	165 10	59%	618/532-3313

CLINTON CATHOLIC SCHOOLS

• **Diocese of Belleville Ed Off** PID: 00317671
Listing includes only schools located in this county. See District Index for
location of Diocesan Offices.

Catholic Schs..Principal	Grd	Prgm	Enr/#Cls	SN	
All Saints Academy 295 N Clinton St, Breese 62230 Dr Robin Booth	PK-8		425 20		618/526-4323 Fax 618/526-2547
Mater Dei High Sch 900 Mater Dei Dr, Breese 62230 Dennis Litteken	9-12	V	514 34		618/526-7216 Fax 618/526-8310 🅕

CLINTON PRIVATE SCHOOLS

Private Schs..Principal	Grd	Prgm	Enr/#Cls	SN	
Trinity Lutheran Sch 8701 Huey Rd, Hoffman 62250 Beth Boester	PK-8		79 6		618/495-2246 Fax 618/495-2692

---

1 Superintendent	8 Curric/Instruct K-12	19 Chief Financial Officer	29 Family/Consumer Science	39 Social Studies K-12	49 English/Lang Arts Elem	59 Special Education Elem	69 Academic Assessment
2 Bus/Finance/Purchasing	9 Curric/Instruct Elem	20 Art K-12	30 Adult Education	40 Social Studies Elem	50 English/Lang Arts Sec	60 Special Education Sec	70 Research/Development
3 Buildings And Grounds	10 Curric/Instruct Sec	21 Art Elem	31 Career/Sch-to-Work K-12	41 Social Studies Sec	51 Reading K-12	61 Foreign/World Lang K-12	71 Public Information
4 Food Service	11 Federal Program	22 Art Sec	32 Career/Sch-to-Work Elem	42 Science K-12	52 Reading Elem	62 Foreign/World Lang Elem	72 Summer School
5 Transportation	12 Title I	23 Music K-12	33 Career/Sch-to-Work Sec	43 Science Elem	53 Reading Sec	63 Foreign/World Lang Sec	73 Instructional Tech
6 Athletic	13 Title V	24 Music Elem	34 Early Childhood Ed	44 Science Sec	54 Remedial Reading K-12	64 Religious Education K-12	74 Inservice Training
7 Health Services	15 Asst Superintendent	25 Music Sec	35 Health/Phys Education	45 Math K-12	55 Remedial Reading Elem	65 Religious Education Elem	75 Marketing/Distributive
	16 Instructional Media Svcs	26 Business Education	36 Guidance Services K-12	46 Math Elem	56 Remedial Reading Sec	66 Religious Education Sec	76 Info Systems
	17 Chief Operations Officer	27 Career & Tech Ed	37 Guidance Services Elem	47 Math Sec	57 Bilingual/ELL	67 School Board President	77 Psychological Assess
	18 Chief Academic Officer	28 Technology Education	38 Guidance Services Sec	48 English/Lang Arts K-12	58 Special Education K-12	68 Teacher Personnel	78 Affirmative Action

Illinois School Directory

Coles County

CLINTON REGIONAL CENTERS

- **Regional Office of Ed 13** PID: 02097578   618/594-2432
  930 Fairfax St Ste B, Carlyle 62231   Fax 618/594-7192

Ron Daniels 1,83   Don Griffin 8,16,73
Melanie Andrews 15,58   Dr Dwain Baldridge 27

COLES COUNTY

COLES COUNTY SCHOOLS

County Schs..Principal	Grd	Prgm	Enr/#Cls	SN	
Humboldt Treatment & Lrng Ctr 306 Adams St, Humboldt 61931 **David Logston**	Spec		65 8	78%	217/856-2223 Fax 217/856-2234
Project Help-Arcola 5837 Park Dr, Charleston 61920 **Laura Shull**	Spec		550 2		217/345-9119 Fax 217/348-7640
Student Life Academy 2405 Champaign Ave, Mattoon 61938 **Jennifer Weber**	Spec		72 8	63%	217/258-5286 Fax 217/235-4332

COLES PUBLIC SCHOOLS

- **Charleston Cmty Unit SD 1** PID: 00266589   217/639-1000
  410 W Polk Ave, Charleston 61920   Fax 217/639-1005

Schools: 6 \ **Teachers:** 158 \ **Students:** 2,500 \ **Special Ed Students:** 526 \ **LEP Students:** 23 \ **College-Bound:** 74% \ **Ethnic:** Asian 1%, African American 5%, Hispanic 5%, Caucasian 89% \ **Exp:** $94 (Low) \ **Poverty:** 18% \ **Title I:** $907,611 \ **Special Education:** $782,000 \ **Open-Close:** 08/11 - 05/20 \ **DTBP:** $203 (High)

Todd Vilardo 1,11,57,83   Alyssa Matar 2
Chad Burgett 2,8,15,88,294   Jim Kuykendall 3,91
Derrick Zerrusen 6   Amanda Lock 7
Kristen Holly 15,79,298   Aaron Taylor 16,76*
Kirstin Runyon 16,82   Kristen Brown 58
Jason Coe 67   Kim Fergeson 68

Public Schs..Principal	Grd	Prgm	Enr/#Cls	SN	
Ashmore Elem Sch 313 S Ohio St, Ashmore 61912 **Kristen Brown**	PK-4		100 5	49%	217/349-3000 Fax 217/349-3005
Carl Sandburg Elem Sch 1924 Reynolds Dr, Charleston 61920 **Eddie Williams**	1-3		503 25	55%	217/639-4000 Fax 217/639-4005
Charleston High Sch 1615 Lincoln Ave, Charleston 61920 **Aaron Lock**	9-12	V	811 45	40%	217/639-5000 Fax 217/639-5005
Charleston Middle Sch 920 Smith Dr, Charleston 61920 **Robert Lynn**	7-8		380 35	49%	217/639-6000 Fax 217/639-6005
Jefferson Elem Sch 801 Jefferson Ave, Charleston 61920 **Rob Ulm**	4-6		615 23	53%	217/639-7000 Fax 217/639-7005
Mark Twain Elem Sch 1021 13th St, Charleston 61920 **Denise Titus**	PK-K		240 11	57%	217/639-8000 Fax 217/639-8005

- **Mattoon Cmty Unit Sch Dist 2** PID: 00266682   217/238-8850
  1701 Charleston Ave, Mattoon 61938   Fax 217/238-8878

Schools: 5 \ **Teachers:** 199 \ **Students:** 2,500 \ **Special Ed Students:** 564 \ **LEP Students:** 6 \ **College-Bound:** 70% \ **Ethnic:** Asian 1%, African American 4%, Hispanic 4%, Caucasian 91% \ **Exp:** $335 (High) \ **Poverty:** 20% \ **Title I:** $1,383,184 \ **Special Education:** $1,054,000 \ **Open-Close:** 08/17 - 05/21 \ **DTBP:** $96 (Med) \ 🇫 🇹

Tim Condron 1   Tom Sherman 2,15
Kent Metzger 3,91   Mark Nelson 5
David Vieth .... 6*   Vicky Wright 7
Richard Stuart .... 8,72*   Christy Hild 9,12,69,79,275,285,288,752
Dave Skocy 11,15,27,57,68,273,296,298   Katrina Farris 34*
Jame Hilt 58   Michelle Skinlo 67
Chris Roberts 73,76,84,295

Public Schs..Principal	Grd	Prgm	Enr/#Cls	SN	
Arland D Williams Elem Sch 1709 S 9th St, Mattoon 61938 **McLain Schaefer**	PK-5		659 18	66%	217/238-2800 Fax 217/238-2805
Franklin Preschool 1201 S 6th St, Mattoon 61938 **Jayme Holt**	PK-PK		141	46%	217/238-8800 Fax 217/238-8805
Mattoon High Sch 2521 Walnut Ave, Mattoon 61938 **Richard Stuart**	9-12	V	955 80	47%	217/238-7800 Fax 217/238-7905
Mattoon Middle Sch 1200 S 9th St, Mattoon 61938 **Nathan Pugh**	6-8		747 50	54%	217/238-5800 Fax 217/238-5805 🇫 🇹
Riddle Elem Sch 4201 Western Ave, Mattoon 61938 **Christy Hild**	K-5		744 37	61%	217/238-3800 Fax 217/238-3805

- **Oakland Cmty Unit Sch Dist 5** PID: 00266840   217/346-2555
  310 Teeter St, Oakland 61943   Fax 217/346-2267

Schools: 2 \ **Teachers:** 27 \ **Students:** 245 \ **Special Ed Students:** 31 \ **College-Bound:** 24% \ **Ethnic:** African American 1%, Hispanic 3%, Caucasian 96% \ **Exp:** $286 (Med) \ **Poverty:** 17% \ **Title I:** $90,761 \ **Special Education:** $50,000 \ **Open-Close:** 08/17 - 05/20 \ **DTBP:** $193 (High)

Lance Landeck 1,73   Luanne Centers 4*
Jennifer Kapraun -Veach 6   Patty Stark 8,11,35,69,79,83*
Julie Findley .... 16*   Andrew Dowden 67
Tedra Nelk 90,752*

Public Schs..Principal	Grd	Prgm	Enr/#Cls	SN	
Lake Crest Elem Sch 310 Teeter St, Oakland 61943 **Adam Clapp**	PK-8		186 20	49%	217/346-2166
Oakland High Sch 310 Teeter St, Oakland 61943 **Adam Clapp**	9-12	TV	75 12	42%	217/346-2118

---

79 Student Personnel	91 Safety/Security	275 Response To Intervention	298 Grant Writer/Ptnrships	**School Programs**	**Social Media**	
80 Driver Ed/Safety	92 Magnet School	277 Remedial Math K-12	750 Chief Innovation Officer	A = Alternative Program		
81 Gifted/Talented	93 Parental Involvement	280 Literacy Coach	751 Chief of Staff	G = Adult Classes	🇫 = Facebook	
82 Video Services	95 Tech Prep Program	285 STEM	752 Social Emotional Learning	M = Magnet Program		
83 Substance Abuse Prev	97 Chief Infomation Officer	286 Digital Learning		T = Title I Schoolwide	🇹 = Twitter	
84 Erate	98 Chief Technology Officer	288 Common Core Standards	**Other School Types**	V = Career & Tech Ed Programs		
85 AIDS Education	270 Accountability	294 Character Education	Ⓐ = Alternative School			
88 Alternative/At Risk	271 Migrant Education	295 Network System	Ⓒ = Charter School	New Schools are shaded		
89 Multi-Cultural Curriculum	273 Teacher Mentor	296 Title II Programs	Ⓜ = Magnet School	New Superintendents and Principals are bold		
90 Social Work	274 Before/After Sch	297 Webmaster	Ⓨ = Year-Round School	Personnel with email addresses are underscored		

IL—19

Cook County

COLES PRIVATE SCHOOLS

Private Schs..Principal	Grd	Prgm	Enr/#Cls	SN	
St Johns Lutheran Sch 100 Broadway Ave, Mattoon 61938 Trent Duckett	PK-8		223		217/234-4911 Fax 217/234-4925

COLES REGIONAL CENTERS

- **Eastern Illinois Area of Sp Ed** PID: 02183921   217/348-7700
  5837 Park Dr, Charleston 61920   Fax 217/348-7704

  Tony Reeley ....1 Rachel Beever 2
  April Fox .... 15,271 Matt Ogle 73

- **Eastern Illinois EFE System** PID: 04177837   217/258-6283
  1617 Lake Land Blvd, Mattoon 61938   Fax 217/258-6284

  Laura Sullivan 1

- **Regional Office of Ed 11** PID: 02097580   217/348-0151
  730 7th St, Charleston 61920   Fax 217/348-0171

  Kyle Thompson ....1 Zakry Standerder 15

COOK COUNTY

COOK COUNTY SCHOOLS

County Schs..Principal	Grd	Prgm	Enr/#Cls	SN	
Aero Special Education Center 7600 Mason Ave, Burbank 60459 Jean Piet	Spec		130 15	45%	708/496-3330 Fax 708/496-3920
Benjamin Braun Educational Ctr 6020 151st St, Oak Forest 60452 Kristine Jones	Spec		90 7	60%	708/687-4971 Fax 708/687-6495
Britten Sch 10110 Gladstone St Lowr 1, Westchester 60154 Michele Hixon	Spec		80 8		708/343-7500 Fax 708/343-0363
Echo Sch 350 W 154th St, South Holland 60473 Jennifer Cowan	Spec		150 17	83%	708/596-3200 Fax 708/333-0352
Harbor Academy 605 N Hillside Ave, Hillside 60162 Tammy Raffen	9-12		16	31%	708/236-3250
Independence Elem Sch 1125 Division St, Chicago HTS 60411 Amina Payne	Spec	A	100 7	70%	708/481-6103 Fax 708/503-4104
Independence High Sch 1125 Division St, Chicago HTS 60411 Linda Wilson	Spec	AV	120 10	79%	708/481-6103 Fax 708/503-4104
Julia S Molloy Ed Center 8701 Menard Ave, Morton Grove 60053 Christine Perry	Spec		186 30	39%	847/966-8600 Fax 847/965-9760
Kirk Sch 520 S Plum Grove Rd, Palatine 60067 Catherine Ivack	Spec		174 27	28%	847/463-8500 Fax 847/485-2623
MacArthur/Echo Sch 640 E 168th Pl, South Holland 60473 Melissa Mendoza	Spec		129 12	75%	708/333-7812 Fax 708/333-7819
Miner Sch 1101 E Miner St, Arlington HTS 60004 Erik Brekke	Spec	V	91 12	26%	847/463-8400 Fax 847/463-8415
North Shore Academy 255 Revere Dr, Northbrook 60062 Dr Doug Bolton	K-5		85 4	17%	847/291-7905 Fax 847/291-9641
Paec Elem Sch 1636 S 10th Ave, Maywood 60153 Roshune Pechacek	Spec	A	130 7	81%	708/338-3250 Fax 708/338-3253
Paec High Sch 1636 S 10th Ave, Maywood 60153 Shaylon Walker	Spec	A	65 9	38%	708/450-1515 Fax 708/450-1818
Program for Adaptive Lrng Sch 1125 Division St, Chicago HTS 60411 April Brown	Spec	G	190 27	60%	708/481-6102 Fax 708/481-7728
Project Challenge 6020 151st St, Oak Forest 60452 Kristine Jones	Spec	A	29 1	46%	708/687-4971 Fax 708/687-6495
Proviso Area Excptnl Chldrn 1000 Van Buren St, Maywood 60153 Kim Baratta	Spec		203 16	52%	708/450-2129 Fax 708/450-1116
Timber Ridge Sch 201 S Evanston Ave, Arlington HTS 60004 Michael Wagrowski	Spec		85 10	51%	847/463-8300 Fax 847/463-8304
West 40 Regional Safe Sch MS 605 N Hillside Ave, Hillside 60162 Karen Tiemann	6-8		28		708/236-3250 Fax 708/236-3251

COOK PUBLIC SCHOOLS

- **Alsip-Hazelgrn-Oaklawn SD 126** PID: 00266876   708/389-1900
  11900 S Kostner Ave, Alsip 60803   Fax 708/396-3793

  Schools: 5 \ **Teachers:** 108 \ **Students:** 1,580 \ **Special Ed Students:** 259 \ **LEP Students:** 233 \ **Ethnic:** Asian 2%, African American 19%, Hispanic 38%, Caucasian 41% \ **Exp:** $475 (High) \ **Poverty:** 15% \ **Title I:** $422,955 \ **Special Education:** $734,000 \ **Bilingual Education:** $58,000 \ **Open-Close:** 08/24 - 06/04 \ **DTBP:** $227 (High)

  Craig Gwaltney ....1 Steve Gress 2,15
  Joann Potsic .... 3* Joe Rizzo 5*
  Lori Connolly ....9 Kelly Rank 59*
  Robert Condon .... 59 Marigrace Sinnott-Snooks 67
  Gina Fiske .... 73 John Chapman 73,76

Public Schs..Principal	Grd	Prgm	Enr/#Cls	SN	
Early Childhood Center 12250 S Orchard Ave, Alsip 60803 Gina Fiske	PK-PK	T	110	85%	708/631-0490 Fax 708/575-9434
Hazelgreen Elem Sch 11751 S Lawler Ave, Alsip 60803 Leah Humphrey	PK-6	T	298 15	60%	708/371-5351 Fax 708/396-3754
Lane Elem Sch 4600 W 123rd St, Alsip 60803 Patti Egan	PK-6	T	240 16	66%	708/371-0720 Fax 708/396-3753
Prairie Junior High Sch 11910 S Kostner Ave, Alsip 60803 Maureen Paulmeyer	7-8	T	373 20	54%	708/371-3080 Fax 708/396-3798
Stony Creek Elem Sch 11700 S Kolin Ave, Alsip 60803 Nicole Leggett-Gallus	PK-6	T	669	53%	708/371-0220 Fax 708/396-3755

#		#		#		#		#		#		#	
1	Superintendent	8	Curric/Instruct K-12	19	Chief Financial Officer	29	Family/Consumer Science	39	Social Studies K-12	49	English/Lang Arts Elem	59	Special Education Elem	69	Academic Assessment
2	Bus/Finance/Purchasing	9	Curric/Instruct Elem	20	Art K-12	30	Adult Education	40	Social Studies Elem	50	English/Lang Arts Sec	60	Special Education Sec	70	Research/Development
3	Buildings And Grounds	10	Curric/Instruct Sec	21	Art Elem	31	Career/Sch-to-Work K-12	41	Social Studies Sec	51	Reading K-12	61	Foreign/World Lang K-12	71	Public Information
4	Food Service	11	Federal Program	22	Art Sec	32	Career/Sch-to-Work Elem	42	Science K-12	52	Reading Elem	62	Foreign/World Lang Elem	72	Summer School
5	Transportation	12	Title I	23	Music K-12	33	Career/Sch-to-Work Sec	43	Science Elem	53	Reading Sec	63	Foreign/World Lang Sec	73	Instructional Tech
6	Athletic	13	Title V	24	Music Elem	34	Early Childhood Ed	44	Science Sec	54	Remedial Reading K-12	64	Religious Education K-12	74	Inservice Training
7	Health Services	14	Asst Superintendent	25	Music Sec	35	Health/Phys Education	45	Math K-12	55	Remedial Reading Elem	65	Religious Education Elem	75	Marketing/Distributive
		15	Instructional Media Svcs	26	Business Education	36	Guidance Services K-12	46	Math Elem	56	Remedial Reading Sec	66	Religious Education Sec	76	Info Systems
		16	Chief Operations Officer	27	Career & Tech Ed	37	Guidance Services Elem	47	Math Sec	57	Bilingual/ELL	67	School Board President	77	Psychological Assess
		17	Chief Academic Officer	28	Technology Education	38	Guidance Services Sec	48	English/Lang Arts K-12	58	Special Education K-12	68	Teacher Personnel	78	Affirmative Action

Illinois School Directory

Cook County

• Arbor Park School District 145 PID: 00266931   708/687-8040
17301 Central Ave, Oak Forest 60452   Fax 708/687-9498

Schools: 4 \ **Teachers:** 93 \ **Students:** 1,350 \ **Special Ed Students:** 160 \ **LEP Students:** 197 \ **Ethnic:** Asian 10%, African American 15%, Hispanic 25%, Caucasian 51% \ **Exp:** $421 (High) \ **Poverty:** 14% \ **Title I:** $296,824 \ **Special Education:** $806,000 \ **Bilingual Education:** $74,000 \ **Open-Close:** 08/19 - 06/07 \ **DTBP:** $241 (High)

Dr Andrea Sala	1,83	Brian O'Keeffe	2,3,5,11,15
Allen Slager	3	Kristine Fransen	5
Camille Hogan	9,12,275*	Eliza Lopez	57*
Gina Dioguardi	59	Tina Moslander	67
David Termunde	73,98		

Public Schs..Principal	Grd	Prgm	Enr/#Cls	SN	
Arbor Park Middle Sch 17303 Central Ave, Oak Forest 60452 Dave Evans	5-8	T	647 45	40%	708/687-5330 Fax 708/535-4527
Kimberly Heights Elem Sch 6141 Kimberly Dr, Tinley Park 60477 Eliza Lopez	PK-K		172 10	14%	708/532-6434 Fax 708/532-4495
Morton Gingerwood Elem Sch 16936 Forest Ave, Oak Forest 60452 Tom Flynn	1-2		227 13	39%	708/560-0092 Fax 708/535-5071
Scarlet Oak Elem Sch 5731 Albert Dr, Oak Forest 60452 Scot Pierce	3-4		260 12	38%	708/687-5822 Fax 708/687-4292

• Argo Cmty High School Dist 217 PID: 00266981   708/728-3200
7329 W 63rd St, Summit 60501   Fax 708/728-3155

Schools: 1 \ **Teachers:** 124 \ **Students:** 2,100 \ **Special Ed Students:** 250 \ **LEP Students:** 209 \ **College-Bound:** 67% \ **Ethnic:** Asian 2%, African American 12%, Hispanic 49%, Caucasian 36% \ **Exp:** $304 (High) \ **Poverty:** 19% \ **Title I:** $650,244 \ **Special Education:** $1,221,000 \ **Bilingual Education:** $25,000 \ **Open-Close:** 08/14 - 05/21 \ **DTBP:** $239 (High)

William Toulious	1,11,288	Joseph Murphy	2
Gary Nochnagel	3	Branden Cotters	10,12
John Bagares	10	Sinead Blake	15
Jon Leonard	16*	Dan McCarthy	38
Tom Jankowicz	57,271*	Bijal Phell	60
Dr Daniel Kozal	67	Brett Lettiere	72*
Nick Simov	73,76,295,297*	Allison Bean	83*

Public Schs..Principal	Grd	Prgm	Enr/#Cls	SN	
Argo Cmty High Sch 7329 W 63rd St, Summit 60501 **Dr Brandon Cotter**	9-12	AT	2,100 75	64%	708/728-3200

• Arlington Hts School Dist 25 PID: 00267002   847/758-4900
1200 S Dunton Ave Ste 2, Arlington HTS 60005   Fax 847/758-4907

Schools: 9 \ **Teachers:** 390 \ **Students:** 5,550 \ **Special Ed Students:** 699 \ **LEP Students:** 625 \ **Ethnic:** Asian 15%, African American 1%, Hispanic 8%, Caucasian 75% \ **Exp:** $452 (High) \ **Poverty:** 3% \ **Title I:** $146,683 \ **Special Education:** $3,892,000 \ **Bilingual Education:** $104,000 \ **Open-Close:** 08/20 - 06/04 \ **DTBP:** $223 (High) \ f t

Lori Bein	1	Stacey Mallek	2,15
Daniel Mendoza	3	Ryan Schulz	3,5,91
Coletta Hines-Newell	4	Peg Lasiewicki	7,34,37,57,79,90,271,275
Becky Fitzpatrick	11,16,27,69,73,285	Brian Kaye	15,68*
Ellie Chin	16	Melanie Zenisek	40,43
Kristin Williams	46,69	Shab Poloz	49,62
Brian Cerniglia	67	Adam Harris	71,297
Chris Fahnoe	73,295	Diane Kaffka	79
Kellie Klasen	79	Lindsay Anastacio	79
Lisa Kramp	79		

Public Schs..Principal	Grd	Prgm	Enr/#Cls	SN	
Dryden Elem Sch 722 S Dryden Pl, Arlington HTS 60005 Akemi Sessler	K-5		502 24	7%	847/398-4280 Fax 847/394-6946
Greenbrier Elem Sch 2330 N Verde Dr, Arlington HTS 60004 Donna Bingaman	PK-5		404 13	5%	847/398-4272 Fax 847/394-6291
Ivy Hill Elem Sch 2211 N Burke Dr, Arlington HTS 60004 Scott Kaese	K-5		610 24	4%	847/398-4275 Fax 847/394-6556
Olive-Mary Stitt Sch 303 E Olive St, Arlington HTS 60004 Erin Davis	K-5		585 22	3%	847/398-4282 Fax 847/394-6935
Patton Elem Sch 1616 N Patton Ave, Arlington HTS 60004 Eric Larson	K-5		434 22	5%	847/398-4288 Fax 847/394-6618
South Middle Sch 400 S Highland Ave, Arlington HTS 60005 Dr Jim Morrison	6-8		879 30	11%	847/398-4250 Fax 847/394-6260
Thomas Middle Sch 1430 N Belmont Ave, Arlington HTS 60004 Lori Naumowicz	6-8		928 40	9%	847/398-4260 Fax 847/394-6843
Westgate Elem Sch 500 S Dwyer Ave, Arlington HTS 60005 **Ann Buch**	K-5		568 21	7%	847/398-4292 Fax 847/394-6191 t
Windsor Elem Sch 1315 E Miner St, Arlington HTS 60004 Piper Boston	K-5		524 26	9%	847/398-4297 Fax 847/394-6611

• Atwood Heights SD 125 PID: 00267404   708/371-0080
12150 S Hamlin Ave, Alsip 60803   Fax 708/371-7847

Schools: 3 \ **Teachers:** 52 \ **Students:** 620 \ **Special Ed Students:** 157 \ **LEP Students:** 45 \ **Ethnic:** Asian 3%, African American 14%, Hispanic 48%, Caucasian 36% \ **Exp:** $431 (High) \ **Poverty:** 13% \ **Title I:** $160,435 \ **Special Education:** $627,000 \ **Bilingual Education:** $1,000 \ **Open-Close:** 08/21 - 06/04

Dr Thomas Livingston	1	Lisa Doig	11*
Michelle Tosch	34	Margarita Medina	57*
Anne Krause	59	Chris Lantz	67

Public Schs..Principal	Grd	Prgm	Enr/#Cls	SN	
Hamlin Upper Grade Center 12150 S Hamlin Ave, Alsip 60803 Lisa Doig	6-8		215 9	46%	708/597-1550 Fax 708/396-0515
Lawn Manor Sch 4300 W 108th Pl, Oak Lawn 60453 Heather Wills	PK-2		225 12	64%	708/423-3078 Fax 708/423-9331
Meadow Lane Sch 11800 S Meadow Lane Dr, Merrionett Pk 60803 Laura Gray	3-5		181 10	50%	708/388-6958 Fax 708/388-6983

79	Student Personnel	91	Safety/Security	275	Response To Intervention
80	Driver Ed/Safety	92	Magnet School	277	Remedial Math K-12
81	Gifted/Talented	93	Parental Involvement	280	Literacy Coach
82	Video Services	95	Tech Prep Program	285	STEM
83	Substance Abuse Prev	97	Chief Information Officer	286	Digital Learning
84	Erate	98	Chief Technology Officer	288	Common Core Standards
85	AIDS Education	270	Character Education	294	Accountability
88	Alternative/At Risk	271	Migrant Education	295	Network System
89	Multi-Cultural Curriculum	273	Teacher Mentor	296	Title II Programs
90	Social Work	274	Before/After Sch	297	Webmaster

298	Grant Writer/Ptnrships		
750	Chief Innovation Officer		
751	Chief of Staff		
752	Social Emotional Learning		

Other School Types
- Ⓐ = Alternative School
- Ⓒ = Charter School
- Ⓜ = Magnet School
- Ⓨ = Year-Round School

School Programs
- A = Alternative Program
- G = Adult Classes
- M = Magnet Program
- T = Title I Schoolwide
- V = Career & Tech Ed Programs

Social Media
- f = Facebook
- t = Twitter

New Schools are shaded
New Superintendents and Principals are bold
Personnel with email addresses are underscored

IL—21

Cook County　　　　　　　　　　　　　　　　　　　　　　　　　　　　　Market Data Retrieval

• Avoca School District 37 PID: 00267454   847/251-3587
2921 Illinois Rd, Wilmette 60091   Fax 847/251-7742

Schools: 2 \ **Teachers:** 72 \ **Students:** 750 \ **Special Ed Students:** 81 \ **LEP Students:** 77 \ **Ethnic:** Asian 27%, African American 1%, Hispanic 9%, Caucasian 63% \ **Exp:** $380 (High) \ **Poverty:** 5% \ **Title I:** $51,587 \ **Special Education:** $413,000 \ **Bilingual Education:** $33,000 \ **Open-Close:** 08/26 - 06/10 \ **DTBP:** $247 (High)

Kaine Osburn 1	Beth Dever 2,3,4,5,79,84,91
Chad Henley 6*	Jessica Hutchison 9*
Matthew Palcer 11*	Patricia Patrick 12*
Beth Haugeberg 16,73,295,297*	Christina Isherwood 57
Kristen Moore 59,69,83,88,270,275,752	Rick Zelinsky 67
Carrie Stotz 73	Susan Geidner 73

Public Schs..Principal	Grd	Prgm	Enr/#Cls	SN	
Avoca West Elem Sch 235 Beech Dr, Glenview 60025 Jessica Hutchison	K-5		447 24	6%	847/724-6800 Fax 847/724-7323
Marie Murphy Middle Sch 2921 Illinois Rd, Wilmette 60091 Matthew Palcer	6-8		254 16	5%	847/251-3617 Fax 847/251-4179

• Bellwood School District 88 PID: 00267600   708/344-9344
640 Eastern Ave, Bellwood 60104   Fax 708/493-0390

Schools: 7 \ **Teachers:** 177 \ **Students:** 2,425 \ **Special Ed Students:** 361 \ **LEP Students:** 680 \ **College-Bound:** 75% \ **Ethnic:** Asian 1%, African American 46%, Hispanic 52%, Caucasian 1% \ **Exp:** $266 (Med) \ **Poverty:** 23% \ **Title I:** $1,147,358 \ **Special Education:** $742,000 \ **Bilingual Education:** $150,000 \ **Open-Close:** 08/19 - 05/28 \ **DTBP:** $216 (High)

Mark Holder 1,11	Jan Baptist 2
Joseph Burdi 3	Gladys Robinson 4*
Tyreese Stafford 5	Victoria Hansen 9,12,285,298
Karen Mitchell 15	Ignacio Garza 57
Charlotte Larson 59	Sondra McClendon 67
Jeninne Hixson-Rusike 68	Harold Daniels 73,286,295

Public Schs..Principal	Grd	Prgm	Enr/#Cls	SN	
Grant Elem Sch 1300 N 34th Ave, Melrose Park 60160 Robyn Lee-Diaz	1-5		398 25	99%	708/343-0410 Fax 708/345-2515
Grant Primary Sch 1801 N 36th Ave, Stone Park 60165 Carlos DelGado	K-K		76	100%	708/345-3625 Fax 708/544-0062
Lincoln Elem Sch 3420 Jackson St, Bellwood 60104 Rosalind Banks	K-5		359 25	99%	708/410-3100 Fax 708/544-0112
Lincoln Primary EC Center 3519 Wilcox Ave, Bellwood 60104 Tequila Stamps	PK-PK		222	99%	708/544-2815 Fax 708/544-1757
McKinley Elem Sch 3317 Butterfield Rd, Bellwood 60104 Sarah Kilgore	K-6		370 20	99%	708/410-3600 Fax 708/544-0134
Roosevelt Middle Sch 2500 Oak St, Bellwood 60104 Adrian Durry	7-8		750 70	99%	708/410-3906 Fax 708/544-0192
Thurgood Marshall Elem Sch 2501 Oak St, Bellwood 60104 Paul Glover	K-6		316 23	100%	708/544-6995 Fax 708/544-3338

• Berkeley School Dist 87 PID: 00267698   708/449-3350
1200 N Wolf Rd, Berkeley 60163   Fax 708/547-3341

Schools: 6 \ **Teachers:** 179 \ **Students:** 2,600 \ **Special Ed Students:** 485 \ **LEP Students:** 860 \ **Ethnic:** Asian 1%, African American 21%, Hispanic 73%, Caucasian 4% \ **Exp:** $295 (Med) \ **Poverty:** 18% \ **Title I:** $818,240 \ **Special Education:** $975,000 \ **Bilingual Education:** $272,000 \ **Open-Close:** 08/19 - 06/04 \ **DTBP:** $197 (High)

Terri Bresnahan 1	Irene Daciuk 2
Pawel Pytel 2	Dale White 3,5
Kathleen Kuceba 4	Marcus Shelton 4
Dr Margaret Sickele 9,15,83	Dr Dan Sullivan 11,15,59,285,294,296,298
Latesh Travis 15,68	Laura Vince 15,84
Monica Mahaffey 16	Joseph Byrne 28,73,76
Eulalia Valdez 57	Nicole Spataforie 59
Peg O'Connell 67	Chris Weber 295

Public Schs..Principal	Grd	Prgm	Enr/#Cls	SN	
J W Riley Elem Sch 123 S Wolf Rd, Northlake 60164 Eve Munoz	K-5	T	347 24	89%	708/449-3180 Fax 708/547-2541
MacArthur Middle Sch 1310 N Wolf Rd, Berkeley 60163 Kevin Grochowski	6-8	T	390 22	81%	708/449-3185 Fax 708/649-3780
Northlake Middle Sch 202 S Lakewood Ave, Northlake 60164 Dr Sunilkumar Mody	6-8	T	465 22	90%	708/449-3195 Fax 708/547-2548
Sunnyside Elem Sch 5412 Saint Charles Rd, Berkeley 60163 Kevin Grochowski	K-5	T	443 21	83%	708/449-3170 Fax 708/547-3770
Thomas Jefferson Elem Sch 225 46th Ave, Bellwood 60104 Nancy Tortora	PK-5	I	398 22	79%	708/449-3165 Fax 708/649-3046
Whittier Elem Sch 338 Whitehall Ave, Northlake 60164 Tracy Bodenstab	PK-5	T	521 23	84%	708/449-3175 Fax 708/547-3313

• Berwyn North School Dist 98 PID: 00267806   708/484-6200
6633 16th St, Berwyn 60402   Fax 708/795-2482

Schools: 4 \ **Teachers:** 194 \ **Students:** 2,600 \ **Special Ed Students:** 532 \ **LEP Students:** 855 \ **Ethnic:** Asian 1%, African American 12%, Hispanic 82%, Caucasian 5% \ **Exp:** $241 (Med) \ **Poverty:** 19% \ **Title I:** $1,075,780 \ **Special Education:** $2,071,000 \ **Bilingual Education:** $306,000 \ **Open-Close:** 08/19 - 05/28 \ **DTBP:** $191 (High)

Michelle Smith 1	Regina Johnson 2
Scott Vieu 3	Dr Robert Hubbirt 15
Francela Lopez 49,57	Maria McCarthy 59
Adam Mounce 67	Gary Eshenk 73

Public Schs..Principal	Grd	Prgm	Enr/#Cls	SN	
Karel Havlicek Elem Sch 6401 15th St, Berwyn 60402 Jessica Hartless	PK-5	T	530 32	92%	708/795-2451 Fax 708/795-0386
Lincoln Middle Sch 6432 16th St, Berwyn 60402 Dena Thill	6-8	T	969 100	89%	708/795-2475 Fax 708/795-2880
Prairie Oak Elem Sch 1427 Oak Park Ave, Berwyn 60402 Venus Smith	PK-5	T	783 40	89%	708/795-2442 Fax 708/795-2443
Thomas Jefferson Elem Sch 7035 16th St, Berwyn 60402 Stephanie Mitchell	PK-5	T	580 27	83%	708/795-2454 Fax 708/795-2465

1	Superintendent	8	Curric/Instruct K-12	19	Chief Financial Officer	29	Family/Consumer Science	39	Social Studies K-12	49	English/Lang Arts Elem	59	Special Education Elem	69	Academic Assessment
2	Bus/Finance/Purchasing	9	Curric/Instruct Elem	20	Art K-12	30	Adult Education	40	Social Studies Elem	50	English/Lang Arts Sec	60	Special Education Sec	70	Research/Development
3	Buildings And Grounds	10	Curric/Instruct Sec	21	Art Elem	31	Career/Sch-to-Work K-12	41	Social Studies Sec	51	Reading K-12	61	Foreign/World Lang K-12	71	Public Information
4	Food Service	11	Federal Program	22	Art Sec	32	Career/Sch-to-Work Elem	42	Science K-12	52	Reading Elem	62	Foreign/World Lang Elem	72	Summer School
5	Transportation	12	Title I	23	Music K-12	33	Career/Sch-to-Work Sec	43	Science Elem	53	Reading Sec	63	Foreign/World Lang Sec	73	Instructional Tech
6	Athletic	13	Title V	24	Music Elem	34	Early Childhood Ed	44	Science Sec	54	Remedial Reading K-12	64	Religious Education K-12	74	Inservice Training
7	Health Services	15	Asst Superintendent	25	Music Sec	35	Health/Phys Education	45	Math K-12	55	Remedial Reading Elem	65	Religious Education Elem	75	Marketing/Distributive
		16	Instructional Media Svcs	26	Business Education	36	Guidance Services K-12	46	Math Elem	56	Remedial Reading Sec	66	Religious Education Sec	76	Info Systems
		17	Chief Operations Officer	27	Career & Tech Ed	37	Guidance Services Elem	47	Math Sec	57	Bilingual/ELL	67	School Board President	77	Psychological Assess
		18	Chief Academic Officer	28	Technology Education	38	Guidance Services Sec	48	English/Lang Arts K-12	58	Special Education K-12	68	Teacher Personnel	78	Affirmative Action

Illinois School Directory — Cook County

Berwyn South School Dist 100 PID: 00267856   708/795-2300
3401 Gunderson Ave, Berwyn 60402   Fax 708/795-2317

Schools: 8 \ **Teachers:** 277 \ **Students:** 3,700 \ **Special Ed Students:** 542 \ **LEP Students:** 956 \ **Ethnic:** Asian 1%, African American 3%, Hispanic 86%, Caucasian 10% \ **Exp:** $208 (Med) \ **Poverty:** 15% \ **Title I:** $951,657 \ **Special Education:** $3,042,000 \ **Bilingual Education:** $251,000 \ **Open-Close:** 08/24 - 05/28 \ **DTBP:** $195 (High)

Dr Mary Havis 1	Jennifer Hosty 2,5
George Lambesis 3	Toni LeGare 4
Victor Tello 5	Beatriz Maldonado .7,9,11,15,90,285,286,288
Amanda Thompson 34	Jeanette Briseno 57
Deanna Durica 67	David Bruno 68,69,79,88,275,294,752
Jim Kloss 73,76,295,297	Samantha Shuman 81*
Jane Coughlin 93	

Public Schs..Principal	Grd	Prgm	Enr/#Cls	SN	
Emerson Elem Sch 6850 31st St, Berwyn 60402 Jean Suchy	K-5	T	364 10	75%	708/795-2322 Fax 708/749-6124
Freedom Middle Sch 3016 Ridgeland Ave, Berwyn 60402 James Clarke \ **Tim Brodeur**	6-8	T	659 42	79%	708/795-5800 Fax 708/795-5806
Heritage Middle Sch 6850 31st St, Berwyn 60402 Allison Boutet	6-8	T	597	77%	708/749-6110 Fax 708/749-6124
Hiawatha Elem Sch 6539 26th St, Berwyn 60402 Jodi Meyer	PK-5	T	410 19	86%	708/795-2327 Fax 708/795-1270
Irving Elem Sch 3501 Clinton Ave, Berwyn 60402 Marty Stachura	PK-5	T	457 22	79%	708/795-2334 Fax 708/795-2336
Komensky Elem Sch 2515 Cuyler Ave, Berwyn 60402 **Leticia Valadez**	PK-5	T	388 20	92%	708/795-2342 Fax 708/795-1254
Pershing Elem Sch 6537 37th St, Berwyn 60402 Diona Iacobazzi	PK-5	T	480 18	81%	708/795-2349 Fax 708/795-1277
Piper Elem Sch 2435 Kenilworth Ave, Berwyn 60402 Samantha Shuman	K-5	T	292 14	76%	708/795-2364 Fax 708/795-0140

Bloom Twp High Sch Dist 206 PID: 00267935   708/755-7010
100 W 10th St, Chicago HTS 60411   Fax 708/755-6859

Schools: 3 \ **Teachers:** 175 \ **Students:** 3,558 \ **Special Ed Students:** 591 \ **LEP Students:** 472 \ **College-Bound:** 49% \ **Ethnic:** African American 50%, Hispanic 42%, Caucasian 8% \ **Exp:** $332 (High) \ **Poverty:** 25% \ **Title I:** $1,927,633 \ **Special Education:** $1,629,000 \ **Bilingual Education:** $23,000 \ **Open-Close:** 08/20 - 06/04 \ **DTBP:** $187 (High)

Dr Lenell Navarre 1,11	Richard Amadio 3
Tim Debartalo 4	Renea Amos 5
Joe Reda 6,80*	Cynthia Berg 7*
Doriph Johnson 10,12,15,296,298	Carole Burns 13,60,77,90
Latunja Williams 15,68,79	Andrew Schmidt 16,73,84,95,295
Marilyn Bittner 27*	Kimberly Kimbrough 44
Michael Camp 57	Henry Drake 67
Mariba Woods 83	Michael Campbell 88*

Public Schs..Principal	Grd	Prgm	Enr/#Cls	SN	
Bloom High Sch 101 W 10th St, Chicago HTS 60411 Dr Kenyatta Starks	9-12	TV	1,642	86%	708/755-1122 Fax 708/709-7192
Bloom Trail High Sch 22331 Cottage Grove Ave, Chicago HTS 60411 Glynis Keene	9-12	TV	1,225 130	78%	708/758-7000 Fax 708/758-8372
ⓐ Bloom Twp Alternative High Sch 100 W 10th St, Chicago HTS 60411 Michael Campbell	9-12		40 6	88%	708/754-4095 Fax 708/754-4099

Bremen Cmty High SD 228 PID: 00268070   708/389-1175
15233 Pulaski Rd, Midlothian 60445   Fax 708/389-2552

Schools: 5 \ **Teachers:** 308 \ **Students:** 4,800 \ **Special Ed Students:** 802 \ **LEP Students:** 264 \ **College-Bound:** 67% \ **Ethnic:** Asian 2%, African American 38%, Hispanic 29%, Caucasian 30% \ **Exp:** $539 (High) \ **Poverty:** 14% \ **Title I:** $1,301,492 \ **Special Education:** $2,891,000 \ **Bilingual Education:** $38,000 \ **Open-Close:** 08/17 - 05/27 \ **DTBP:** $193 (High)

Dr Bill Kendall 1	Brittany Morrison 2
Terry Masterson 3,5,91	Eric Washington 6*
Lisa Wunar 6*	Michael Mongon 6*
Ron Towner 6*	Dr Corinne Williams 10,11,15,69,74,270,273,288
Dr Corinne Williams 12*	Maurice Young 13*
Dan Goggins 15,68,79,83	Jim Boswell 16,71,73,95,97,98*
Jenny Reid 22,25*	April Nykasa 27,29*
Colin Milton 41	Vivian Turek 44
Kelli Lattyak 47	Tom O'Shea 50,53*
Maureen Miller 57,63*	Lisa Giglio-Byczek 60,88*
Kristine Resler 67	Edwin Lipowski 72*
Jeff Staley 76	Miche'Le Rita 295

Public Schs..Principal	Grd	Prgm	Enr/#Cls	SN	
Bremen High Sch 15203 Pulaski Rd, Midlothian 60445 David Kibelkis	9-12	AV	1,417 47	37%	708/371-3600 Fax 708/371-7194
ⓐ Delta Academy 15233 Pulaski Rd, Midlothian 60445 Otis Lane	9-12		50		708/389-1175
Hillcrest High Sch 17401 Crawford Ave, Cntry CLB Hls 60478 Renee Simms	9-12	TV	1,147	56%	708/799-7000 Fax 708/799-0402
Oak Forest High Sch 15201 Central Ave, Oak Forest 60452 Brad Sikora	9-12	V	1,363 100	28%	708/687-0500 Fax 708/687-0594
Tinley Park High Sch 6111 175th St, Tinley Park 60477 Dr Theresa Nolan	9-12	AV	970	29%	708/532-1900 Fax 708/532-4332

Brookfield-LaGrange Park SD 95 PID: 00268197   708/485-0606
3724 Prairie Ave, Brookfield 60513   Fax 708/485-8066

Schools: 2 \ **Teachers:** 85 \ **Students:** 1,257 \ **Special Ed Students:** 142 \ **LEP Students:** 39 \ **Ethnic:** Asian 1%, African American 2%, Hispanic 33%, Caucasian 64% \ **Exp:** $167 (Low) \ **Poverty:** 9% \ **Title I:** $153,599 \ **Special Education:** $548,000 \ **Bilingual Education:** $10,000 \ **Open-Close:** 08/26 - 06/04 \ **DTBP:** $233 (High)

Dr Mark Kuzniewski 1	Rich Batka 3
Cathy Cannon 9,74,273,288,296*	Nora Skentzos 9,15,79
Scott Encher 67	Amanda Pelsor 73
Ryan Evans 83	Jeff Turntane 275*

Public Schs..Principal	Grd	Prgm	Enr/#Cls	SN	
Brook Park Elem Sch 1214 Raymond Ave, La Grange Pk 60526 **Kelly King**	K-5		831 29	18%	708/354-3740 Fax 708/354-3146

---

79 Student Personnel	91 Safety/Security	275 Response To Intervention	298 Grant Writer/Ptnrships	**School Programs**	**Social Media**
80 Driver Ed/Safety	92 Magnet School	277 Remedial Math K-12	750 Chief Innovation Officer	A = Alternative Program	
81 Gifted/Talented	93 Parental Involvement	280 Literacy Coach	751 Chief of Staff	G = Adult Classes	🄵 = Facebook
82 Video Services	95 Tech Prep Program	285 STEM	752 Social Emotional Learning	M = Magnet Program	
83 Substance Abuse Prev	97 Chief Information Officer	286 Digital Learning		T = Title I Schoolwide	🅃 = Twitter
84 Erate	98 Chief Technology Officer	288 Common Core Standards	**Other School Types**	V = Career & Tech Ed Programs	
85 AIDS Education	270 Character Education	294 Accountability	ⓐ = Alternative School		
88 Alternative/At Risk	271 Migrant Education	295 Network System	ⓒ = Charter School	New Schools are shaded	
89 Multi-Cultural Curriculum	273 Teacher Mentor	296 Title II Programs	ⓜ = Magnet School	New Superintendents and Principals are bold	
90 Social Work	274 Before/After Sch	297 Webmaster	ⓨ = Year-Round School	Personnel with email addresses are underscored	

Cook County — Market Data Retrieval

SE Gross Middle Sch	6-8		426	19%	708/485-0600
3524 Maple Ave, Brookfield 60513			30		Fax 708/485-0638
Ryan Evans					

• Brookwood School District 167 PID: 00268226
201 E Glenwood Dyer Rd, Glenwood 60425
708/758-5190
Fax 708/757-2104

Schools: 4 \ Teachers: 85 \ Students: 1,200 \ Special Ed Students: 134 \ LEP Students: 112 \ Ethnic: African American 77%, Hispanic 18%, Caucasian 5% \ Exp: $253 (Med) \ Poverty: 25% \ Title I: $599,211 \ Special Education: $638,000 \ Bilingual Education: $40,000 \ Open-Close: 08/25 - 06/04 \ DTBP: $228 (High) \

Bethany Lindsey 1,11
Michael McDaniel 3*
Kathy Hatczel 9,73
Doreen Davis 67
Debra Sudd 2,11
Jan Machnikowski 4
Lena Martinez 15,59
Jill Larson 72*

Public Schs..Principal	Grd	Prgm	Enr/#Cls	SN	
Brookwood Junior High Sch	7-8	T	268	58%	708/758-5252
201 E Glenwood Lansing Rd, Glenwood 60425			22		Fax 708/758-3954
Jill Larson					
Brookwood Middle Sch	5-6	T	250	54%	708/758-5350
200 E Glenwood Lansing Rd, Glenwood 60425			12		Fax 708/757-4528
Onquanette Pierce					
Hickory Bend Elem Sch	K-4	T	257	54%	708/758-4520
600 E 191st Pl, Glenwood 60425			15		Fax 708/758-0364
Shawn Jackson					
Longwood Elem Sch	PK-4	T	351	61%	708/757-2100
441 N Longwood Dr, Glenwood 60425			19		Fax 708/756-2504
Reginald Patterson					

• Burbank School District 111 PID: 00274471
7600 Central Ave, Burbank 60459
708/496-0500
Fax 708/496-0510

Schools: 8 \ Teachers: 230 \ Students: 3,400 \ Special Ed Students: 593 \ LEP Students: 1,211 \ Ethnic: Asian 2%, African American 2%, Hispanic 53%, Caucasian 43% \ Exp: $300 (High) \ Poverty: 21% \ Title I: $1,206,150 \ Special Education: $901,000 \ Bilingual Education: $232,000 \ Open-Close: 08/25 - 06/04 \ DTBP: $190 (High)

Dr Franzy Fleck 1
Joseph Ficker 3
Denise Flavin 9,69,83,286,288
Pamela Lindenann 15,68,74,91,273,275
Sandra Hock 37,59,77,79,81,90
Carleen Skowronski 67
Robert McCartney 73,95,295,297
Dr Ana Ochoa 2,4,5
Shannon Schroeder 7
Kristi Mueller 11,296,298
Ian Chafee 16,73*
Kristen Welsh 57
Grace Votteler 73

Public Schs..Principal	Grd	Prgm	Enr/#Cls	SN	
Edward J Tobin Elem Sch	PK-6	T	363	28%	708/599-6655
8501 Narragansett Ave, Burbank 60459			13		Fax 708/233-9014
Stephanie Schmitz					
Frances B McCord Elem Sch	K-6	T	281	49%	708/599-4411
8450 Nashville Ave, Burbank 60459			18		Fax 708/233-9104
Sharon Walker-Hood					
Harry E Fry Elem Sch	K-6	T	416	58%	708/599-5554
7805 Mobile Ave, Burbank 60459					Fax 708/599-1348
Mary Rein					
Jacqueline B Kennedy Elem Sch	K-6	T	370	72%	708/496-0563
7644 Central Ave, Burbank 60459			18		Fax 708/496-8365
John Entsminger					
Liberty Junior High Sch	7-8	T	811	59%	708/952-3255
5900 W 81st St, Burbank 60459					Fax 708/229-0659
Dr Shwkar Abousweilem					

Luther Burbank Elem Sch	PK-6	T	507	32%	708/499-0838
8235 Linder Ave, Burbank 60459			32		Fax 708/952-9518
Tom Martin					
Richard E Byrd Elem Sch	K-6	T	298	58%	708/499-3049
8259 Lavergne Ave, Burbank 60459			14		Fax 708/499-1002
Michaela Faust					
Rosa G Maddock Elem Sch	PK-6	T	425	53%	708/598-0515
8258 Sayre Ave, Burbank 60459			21		Fax 708/233-6401
Patricia Gonzalez					

• Burnham School District 1545 PID: 00268264
13945 S Green Bay Ave, Burnham 60633
708/862-8636
Fax 708/862-8638

Schools: 1 \ Teachers: 12 \ Students: 180 \ Special Ed Students: 21 \ LEP Students: 46 \ Ethnic: African American 44%, Hispanic 53%, Caucasian 3% \ Exp: $178 (Low) \ Poverty: 29% \ Title I: $115,062 \ Special Education: $121,000 \ Open-Close: 08/24 - 05/27 \ DTBP: $116 (High)

Stephen Geraci 1,11,83,84
Jim Drombrowski 3
Richard Stephens 67
Denise Cundiff 2,79*
Denise Cundiff 4,5

Public Schs..Principal	Grd	Prgm	Enr/#Cls	SN	
Burnham Elem Sch	PK-8	T	180	98%	708/862-8636
13945 S Green Bay Ave, Burnham 60633			9		
Stephen Geraci					

• Calumet City School Dist 155 PID: 00268288
540 Superior Ave Frnt, Calumet City 60409
708/862-7665
Fax 708/868-7555

Schools: 3 \ Teachers: 84 \ Students: 1,026 \ Special Ed Students: 188 \ LEP Students: 222 \ Ethnic: African American 61%, Hispanic 36%, Native American: 1%, Caucasian 2% \ Exp: $246 (Med) \ Poverty: 24% \ Title I: $667,228 \ Special Education: $707,000 \ Bilingual Education: $2,000 \ Open-Close: 08/20 - 05/28 \ DTBP: $217 (High)

Joe Zotto 1,11
Mary Valle 3
Tonya Davis 67
Judy Caban 2
Michelle Hassler 59
Tara Lawrence 296

Public Schs..Principal	Grd	Prgm	Enr/#Cls	SN	
Wentworth Intermediate Sch	3-5	T	364	94%	708/868-7926
530 Superior Ave, Calumet City 60409			21		Fax 708/868-7671
Julie Hassel					
Wentworth Junior High Sch	6-8	T	370	92%	708/862-0750
560 Superior Ave, Calumet City 60409			22		Fax 708/862-1194
Andrew Morgan					
Woodrow Wilson Elem Sch	PK-2	T	301	88%	708/862-5166
560 Wentworth Ave, Calumet City 60409			30		Fax 708/868-7086
Deborah Smith					

• Calumet Public School Dist 132 PID: 00268331
1440 W Vermont Ave, Calumet Park 60827
708/388-8920
Fax 708/388-8950

Schools: 3 \ Teachers: 65 \ Students: 1,200 \ Special Ed Students: 135 \ LEP Students: 104 \ Ethnic: Asian 1%, African American 76%, Hispanic 22%, Native American: 1%, Caucasian 1% \ Exp: $260 (Med) \ Poverty: 28% \ Title I: $676,669 \ Special Education: $623,000 \ Bilingual Education: $21,000 \ Open-Close: 08/24 - 06/07 \ DTBP: $253 (High)

Dr Elizabeth Reynolds 1
Yvonne Redmond 2
Julie Stearns 2,294
Adrienne Saverson 11,57,74,83,280,288,296

1	Superintendent	8	Curric/Instruct K-12	19	Chief Financial Officer	29	Family/Consumer Science	39	Social Studies K-12	49	English/Lang Arts K-12	59	Special Education Elem	69	Academic Assessment
2	Bus/Finance/Purchasing	9	Curric/Instruct Elem	20	Art K-12	30	Adult Education	40	Social Studies Elem	50	English/Lang Arts Sec	60	Special Education Sec	70	Research/Development
3	Buildings And Grounds	10	Curric/Instruct Sec	21	Art Elem	31	Career/Sch-to-Work K-12	41	Social Studies Sec	51	Reading K-12	61	Foreign/World Lang K-12	71	Public Information
4	Food Service	11	Federal Program	22	Art Sec	32	Career/Sch-to-Work Elem	42	Science K-12	52	Reading Elem	62	Foreign/World Lang Elem	72	Summer School
5	Transportation	12	Title I	23	Music K-12	33	Career/Sch-to-Work Sec	43	Science Elem	53	Reading Sec	63	Foreign/World Lang Sec	73	Instructional Tech
6	Athletic	13	Title V	24	Music Elem	34	Early Childhood Ed	44	Science Sec	54	Remedial Reading K-12	64	Religious Education K-12	74	Inservice Training
7	Health Services	14	Asst Superintendent	25	Music Sec	35	Health/Phys Education	45	Math K-12	55	Remedial Reading Elem	65	Religious Education Elem	75	Marketing/Distributive
		15	Instructional Media Svcs	26	Business Education	36	Guidance Services K-12	46	Math Elem	56	Remedial Reading Sec	66	Religious Education Sec	76	Info Systems
		16	Chief Operations Officer	27	Career & Tech Ed	37	Guidance Services Elem	47	Math Sec	57	Bilingual/ELL	67	School Board President	77	Psychological Assess
		17	Chief Academic Officer	28	Technology Education	38	Guidance Services Sec	48	English/Lang Arts K-12	58	Special Education K-12	68	Teacher Personnel	78	Affirmative Action

Illinois School Directory

Cook County

Andrea DeLaney 59*
Nancy Munoz 68
Karen Ivey 67
Echelle Mohen 73,285,286

Public Schs..Principal	Grd	Prgm	Enr/#Cls	SN		
Burr Oak Academy 1441 W 124th St, Calumet Park 60827 Dalyn Drown	PK-2	T	338 25		52%	708/824-3090 Fax 708/388-1211
Burr Oak Elem Sch 1441 W 124th St, Calumet Park 60827 Dalyn Drown	3-5	T	330 31		62%	708/388-8010 Fax 708/389-5835
Calumet Elem Sch 1440 W Vermont Ave, Calumet Park 60827 Andrea DeLaney	6-8	T	347 43		72%	708/388-8820 Fax 708/388-8557

- **Central Stickney Sch Dist 110** PID: 00268367   708/458-1152
  5001 S Long Ave, Chicago 60638   Fax 708/458-1168

Schools: 1 \ **Teachers:** 30 \ **Students:** 384 \ **Special Ed Students:** 61
\ **LEP Students:** 156 \ **Ethnic:** Asian 1%, African American 1%, Hispanic 81%, Caucasian 16% \ **Exp:** $188 (Low) \ **Poverty:** 16% \ **Title I:** $104,244
\ **Special Education:** $100,000 \ **Bilingual Education:** $31,000 \
Open-Close: 08/21 - 06/01

Erin Hackett 1
Cheryl Valek 9,83,85,270*
Jacqueline Basa 67
George Zapata 3
Dr Christina Leahy 11
Jennifer Toschi 69,73,288,295*

Public Schs..Principal	Grd	Prgm	Enr/#Cls	SN		
Charles J Sahs Elem Sch 5001 S Long Ave, Chicago 60638 Jennifer Toschi	PK-8	T	384 19		64%	708/458-1152

- **Chicago Heights Elem SD 170** PID: 00268381   708/756-4165
  30 W 16th St, Chicago HTS 60411   Fax 708/755-3536

Schools: 10 \ **Teachers:** 240 \ **Students:** 3,100 \ **Special Ed Students:** 468
\ **LEP Students:** 867 \ **Ethnic:** African American 33%, Hispanic 63%, Caucasian 3% \ **Exp:** $375 (High) \ **Poverty:** 32% \ **Title I:** $2,545,805
\ **Special Education:** $1,964,000 \ **Bilingual Education:** $147,000 \
Open-Close: 09/08 - 06/03 \ **DTBP:** $212 (High) \ 🇫 🇹

Tom Amadio 1
Laretta Adams 2
Marty Riley 4,5
Mary Entsminger .. 9,11,69,72,83,280,296,298
Phil Leli 16,73*
Sam Costello 67
Anthony Leli 2,19
Ron Mascitti 3,91
Nick Pezzuto 6,68,285
Jill Raymond 15,59,752
Shannon Vera 57*

Public Schs..Principal	Grd	Prgm	Enr/#Cls	SN		
Garfield Elem Sch 140 E 23rd St, Chicago HTS 60411 Maricela Ruiz	K-8	T	305 23		100%	708/756-4150 Fax 708/314-7493
Grant Elem Sch 2712 Miller Ave, S Chicago HTS 60411 Marco Pellillo	K-8	T	308 15		99%	708/756-4156 Fax 708/300-1089
Greenbriar Elem Sch 101 W Greenbriar Ave, Chicago HTS 60411 Joe Taylor	K-8	T	273 13		100%	708/756-4159 Fax 708/300-1046
Highland Prekindergarten 828 Willow Dr, Chicago HTS 60411 Brandi Robinson	PK-PK		214 5		100%	708/756-0008 Fax 708/754-1532
Jefferson Elem Sch 176 E 11th St, Chicago HTS 60411 Dr Terry Brink	K-8	T	293 18		98%	708/756-4162 Fax 708/756-0132
Kennedy Elem Sch 1013 Division St, Chicago HTS 60411 Artis McCann	K-8	T	237 12		100%	708/756-4830 Fax 708/748-9964
Lincoln-Gavin Elem Sch 1520 Center Ave, Chicago HTS 60411 Cara Pastere	K-8	T	111 11		100%	708/756-4833 Fax 708/314-7494
Roosevelt Elem Sch 1345 Sunnyside Ave, Chicago HTS 60411 Erin Salamon	K-8	T	483 20		100%	708/756-4836 Fax 708/314-7497
Washington McKinley Elem Sch 25 W 16th Pl, Chicago HTS 60411 Gretchen Southerland	K-8	T	589 35		99%	708/756-4841 Fax 708/756-1008
Wilson Elem Sch 422 W 16th Pl, Chicago HTS 60411 Tony Banks	K-8	T	275 16		96%	708/283-4839 Fax 708/283-0411

- **Chicago Public School Dist 299** PID: 00274914   773/553-1000
  42 W Madison St, Chicago 60602   Fax 773/553-1501

Schools: 666 \ **Teachers:** 21,809 \ **Students:** 355,156 \
Special Ed Students: 51,114 \ **LEP Students:** 65,398 \ **College-Bound:** 67%
\ **Ethnic:** Asian 4%, African American 37%, Hispanic 48%, Caucasian 11% \ **Exp:** $198 (Low) \ **Poverty:** 23% \ **Title I:** $273,462,474 \
Special Education: $93,096,000 \ **Bilingual Education:** $21,610,000 \
Open-Close: 09/08 - 06/22 \ **DTBP:** $257 (High) \ 🇫 🇹

Dr Janice Jackson 1
Miroslava Mejiakrag 2,19
Clarence Carson 3
Karl Kemp 6
Latanya McDade 8,18
Lisa Perez 16
Dr Michael Deuser 23
Bryon Stokes 34
Lizzie McDermott 45
Dr Elizabeth Keenan 58
Matt Lyons 67
Sam Mathias 70,750
Phillip DiBartolo 71,97
Jadine Chou 91
Herald Johnson 93
Jessica Mahon 285
Jon Maples 298
Melinda Gildart 2
Arnie Rivera 3,17
Paul Osland 5
Dr Kenneth Fox 7
Pedro Soto 15,751
Evan Plummer 20,27
Alan Mather 27,36
Jessica Marshal 39
Jorge Macias 57,89,271
Miguel DelValle 67
Peter Leonard 69
Michael Passman 71
Dr Veronica Nash 81,92
Frank Bilecki 93
Jane Fleming 280
Rochelle Washington 294
Erica Faulkner 752

- **Chicago PSD-Ausl** PID: 11931248   773/534-0129
  3400 N Austin Ave, Chicago 60634

Jarvis Sanford 15

Public Schs..Principal	Grd	Prgm	Enr/#Cls	SN		
Ⓨ Chalmers Elem Sch 2745 W Roosevelt Rd, Chicago 60608 Romian Crockett	PK-8	MT	251 20		98%	773/534-1720 Fax 773/534-1718 🇫 🇹
Chicago Academy Elem Sch 3400 N Austin Ave, Chicago 60634 Joyce Pae	PK-8	T	514 19		73%	773/534-3885 Fax 773/534-0109 🇫 🇹
Chicago Academy High Sch 3400 N Austin Ave, Chicago 60634 Lydia Menzer	9-12	T	574		80%	773/534-0146 Fax 773/534-0192 🇫 🇹
Collins Academy 1313 S Sacramento Dr, Chicago 60623 Lekenya Sharpe	9-12	T	243		97%	773/534-1840 Fax 773/542-6471
Curtis Sch of Excellence 32 E 115th St, Chicago 60628 Laquita Louie	PK-8	T	425 25		96%	773/535-5050 Fax 773/535-5044
Ⓨ Deneen Sch of Excellence 7240 S Wabash Ave, Chicago 60619 Karla Kemp	PK-8	MT	403 43		97%	773/535-3035 Fax 773/535-3247

---

79 Student Personnel	91 Safety/Security	275 Response To Intervention	298 Grant Writer/Ptnrships	**School Programs**	**Social Media**
80 Driver Ed/Safety	92 Magnet School	277 Remedial Math K-12	750 Chief Innovation Officer	A = Alternative Program	
81 Gifted/Talented	93 Parental Involvement	280 Literacy Coach	751 Chief of Staff	G = Adult Classes	🇫 = Facebook
82 Video Services	95 Tech Prep Program	285 STEM	752 Social Emotional Learning	M = Magnet Program	
83 Substance Abuse Prev	97 Chief Information Officer	286 Digital Learning		T = Title I Schoolwide	🇹 = Twitter
84 Erate	98 Chief Technology Officer	288 Common Core Standards	**Other School Types**	V = Career & Tech Ed Programs	
85 AIDS Education	270 Character Education	294 Accountability	Ⓐ = Alternative School		
88 Alternative/At Risk	271 Migrant Education	295 Network System	Ⓒ = Charter School	New Schools are shaded	
89 Multi-Cultural Curriculum	273 Teacher Mentor	296 Title II Programs	Ⓜ = Magnet School	New Superintendents and Principals are bold	
90 Social Work	274 Before/After Sch	297 Webmaster	Ⓨ = Year-Round School	Personnel with email addresses are underscored	

IL—25

Cook County

Market Data Retrieval

School	Grd	Prgm	Enr/#Cls	SN	Phone
Dewey Elem Acad of Fine Arts 5415 S Union Ave, Chicago 60609 Valencia Koker	1-8	T	267	17	97% 773/535-1666 Fax 773/535-1802
Ⓜ Dvorak Tech Academy ES 3615 W 16th St, Chicago 60623 Terrie Rayburn	PK-8	T	341	27	98% 773/534-1690 Fax 773/534-1676
Eric Solorio Academy HS 5400 S Saint Louis Ave, Chicago 60632 Victor Iturralde	9-12	T	1,294		93% 773/535-9070 Fax 773/535-9073
Ⓨ Fuller Elem Sch 4214 S Saint Lawrence Ave, Chicago 60653 Marilyn McCottrell	PK-8	MT	347		95% 773/535-1687 Fax 773/535-1689
Gresham Elem Sch 8524 S Green St, Chicago 60620 Steve Fisher	PK-8	T	356	34	97% 773/535-3350 Fax 773/535-3563
Ⓨ Harvard Elem Sch 7525 S Harvard Ave, Chicago 60620 Aisha McCarthy	PK-8	MT	360	31	96% 773/535-3045 Fax 773/535-3332
Ⓨ Herzl Elem Sch 3711 W Douglas Blvd, Chicago 60623 Tamara Davis	PK-8	MT	459	25	97% 773/534-1480 Fax 773/534-1486
Ⓨ Howe School of Excellence 720 N Lorel Ave, Chicago 60644 Daphne Sherrod	PK-8	MT	375	35	96% 773/534-6060 Fax 773/534-6080
John Foster Dulles Elem Sch 6311 S Calumet Ave, Chicago 60637 Toyia Pullum	PK-8	T	739	23	90% 773/535-0690 Fax 773/535-0689
Johnson Elem Sch 1420 S Albany Ave, Chicago 60623 Takia Foster	PK-8	T	368	15	99% 773/534-1829 Fax 773/534-1355
Leslie Lewis Elem Sch 1431 N Leamington Ave, Chicago 60651 Aquabah Gonney	PK-8	T	452	26	91% 773/534-3060 Fax 773/534-3010
Marquette Elem Sch 6550 S Richmond St, Chicago 60629 Rovel Pollock	PK-8	T	934		96% 773/535-9260 Fax 773/535-9266
Ⓨ Morton Sch of Excellence 431 N Troy St, Chicago 60612 **Dr Peggie Wise**	PK-8	MT	202		98% 773/534-6791 Fax 773/534-6790
Ⓨ National Teachers Academy 55 W Cermak Rd, Chicago 60616 Isaac Castelaz	PK-8	MT	746		71% 773/534-9970 Fax 773/534-9971
Ⓜ O'Keeffe Elem Sch 6940 S Merrill Ave, Chicago 60649 Tabitha White	PK-8	T	553	30	91% 773/535-0600 Fax 773/535-0611
Orr Academy High Sch 730 N Pulaski Rd, Chicago 60624 Shanele Andrews	9-12	TV	257		93% 773/534-6500 Fax 773/534-6504
• Pablo Casals Elem Sch 3501 W Potomac Ave, Chicago 60651 Kristie Langbehn	PK-8	MT	325	28	96% 773/534-4444 Fax 773/534-4559
Ⓨ Piccolo Sch of Excellence 1040 N Keeler Ave Ste 1, Chicago 60651 Heather Pusatcioglu	PK-8	MT	462	51	95% 773/534-4425 Fax 773/534-4248
Ⓨ Ronald McNair Elem Sch 4820 W Walton St, Chicago 60651 **Benetrice Lucas**	PK-8	MT	346	28	99% 773/534-8980 Fax 773/534-0668
Ⓨ Sherman Elem Sch 1000 W 52nd St, Chicago 60609 Regina Roberts	PK-8	MT	237	25	100% 773/535-1757 Fax 773/535-0343
Stagg Elem Sch 7424 S Morgan St, Chicago 60621 Miyoshi Knox	PK-8	T	424	25	89% 773/535-3565 Fax 773/535-3564
Tarkington Sch of Excellence 3330 W 71st St, Chicago 60629 Jessica Reisner	PK-8	T	871	20	92% 773/535-4700 Fax 773/535-4713
Wendell Phillips Academy HS 244 E Pershing Rd, Chicago 60653 Matthew Sullivan	9-12	AGT	707	10	94% 773/535-1603 Fax 773/535-1605
William Carter Elem Sch 5740 S Michigan Ave, Chicago 60637 Carmel Perkins	PK-8	T	310	15	95% 773/535-0860 Fax 773/535-0698

• **Chicago PSD-Isp** PID: 12232681 773/553-2568
42 W Madison St, Chicago 60602

Zipporah Hightower 15

Public Schs..Principal	Grd	Prgm	Enr/#Cls	SN	Phone
Agassiz Elem Sch 2851 N Seminary Ave Ste 1, Chicago 60657 Mira Weber	PK-8		464	15	34% 773/534-5725 Fax 773/534-5784
Ⓨ Alfred Nobel Elem Sch 4127 W Hirsch St, Chicago 60651 Manuel Adrianzen	PK-8	MT	647	27	85% 773/534-4365 Fax 773/534-4369
Amundsen High Sch 5110 N Damen Ave, Chicago 60625 Anna Pavichevich	9-12	T	1,504	45	75% 773/534-2320 Fax 773/534-2330
Ⓨ Avalon Park Elem Sch 8045 S Kenwood Ave, Chicago 60619 Takeshi White-James	PK-8	MT	243	25	95% 773/535-6615 Fax 773/535-6660
Back of the Yards IB High Sch 2111 W 47th St, Chicago 60609 Patricia Brekke	9-12	T	1,090		93% 773/535-7320 Fax 773/535-6880
Barry Elem Sch 2828 N Kilbourn Ave, Chicago 60641 Estuardo Mazin	PK-8	T	469	35	88% 773/534-3455 Fax 773/534-3489
Ⓨ Belmont-Cragin Elem Sch 5252 W Palmer St, Chicago 60639 Stacy Stewart	PK-8	MT	394	9	773/534-2900 Fax 773/534-2907
Benito Juarez Cmty Academy 1450 W Cermak Rd 1510, Chicago 60608 Juan Ocon	9-12	GTV	1,843	105	72% 773/534-7030 Fax 773/534-7058
Bradwell School of Excellence 7736 S Burnham Ave, Chicago 60649 Tyese Sims	PK-8	T	480	40	98% 773/535-6600 Fax 773/535-6612
Budlong Elem Sch 2701 W Foster Ave, Chicago 60625 Naomi Nakayama	PK-8	T	595	35	80% 773/534-2591 Fax 773/534-2544
Burley Elem Sch 1630 W Barry Ave, Chicago 60657 Catherine Plocher	PK-8		537	15	14% 773/534-5475 Fax 773/534-5786
Ⓨ Burroughs Elem Sch 3542 S Washtenaw Ave, Chicago 60632 Donald Morris	PK-8	MT	398	23	90% 773/535-7226 Fax 773/535-7126
Ⓨ Caldwell Elem Acad of Math-Sci 8546 S Cregier Ave, Chicago 60617 Danielle Porch	PK-8	MT	266	9	84% 773/535-6300 Fax 773/535-6611
Cameron Elem Sch 1234 N Monticello Ave, Chicago 60651 Stephen Harden	PK-8	T	652	51	98% 773/534-4290 Fax 773/534-0405
Cardenas Elem Sch 2345 S Millard Ave, Chicago 60623 Jeremy Feiwell	PK-8	T	930	26	97% 773/534-1465 Fax 773/534-1512
Carl Von Linne Elem Sch 3221 N Sacramento Ave, Chicago 60618 Renee Mackin	PK-8	T	621	28	80% 773/534-5262 Fax 773/534-5287
Carnegie Elem Sch 1414 E 61st Pl, Chicago 60637 Docilla Pollard	PK-8	T	556	25	79% 773/535-0530 Fax 773/535-0525
Cassell Elem Sch 11314 S Spaulding Ave, Chicago 60655 Eileen Scanlan	K-8		381	18	20% 773/535-2640 Fax 773/535-2667

---

1 Superintendent	8 Curric/Instruct K-12	19 Chief Financial Officer	29 Family/Consumer Science	39 Social Studies K-12	49 English/Lang Arts Elem	59 Special Education Elem	69 Academic Assessment
2 Bus/Finance/Purchasing	9 Curric/Instruct Elem	20 Art K-12	30 Adult Education	40 Social Studies Elem	50 English/Lang Arts Sec	60 Special Education Sec	70 Research/Development
3 Buildings And Grounds	10 Curric/Instruct Sec	21 Art Elem	31 Career/Sch-to-Work K-12	41 Social Studies Sec	51 Reading K-12	61 Foreign/World Lang K-12	71 Public Information
4 Food Service	11 Federal Program	22 Art Sec	32 Career/Sch-to-Work Elem	42 Science K-12	52 Reading Elem	62 Foreign/World Lang Elem	72 Summer School
5 Transportation	12 Title I	23 Music K-12	33 Career/Sch-to-Work Sec	43 Science Elem	53 Reading Sec	63 Foreign/World Lang Sec	73 Instructional Tech
6 Athletic	13 Title V	24 Music Elem	34 Early Childhood Ed	44 Science Sec	54 Remedial Reading K-12	64 Religious Education K-12	74 Inservice Training
7 Health Services	15 Asst Superintendent	25 Music Sec	35 Health/Phys Education	45 Math K-12	55 Remedial Reading Elem	65 Religious Education Elem	75 Marketing/Distributive
	16 Instructional Media Svcs	26 Business Education	36 Guidance Services K-12	46 Math Elem	56 Remedial Reading Sec	66 Religious Education Sec	76 Info Systems
	17 Chief Operations Officer	27 Career & Tech Ed	37 Guidance Services Elem	47 Math Sec	57 Bilingual/ELL	67 School Board President	77 Psychological Assess
	18 Chief Academic Officer	28 Technology Education	38 Guidance Services Sec	48 English/Lang Arts K-12	58 Special Education K-12	68 Teacher Personnel	78 Affirmative Action

Illinois School Directory — Cook County

School	Grades	Type	Enroll	%	Phone
Chappell Elem Sch 2135 W Foster Ave, Chicago 60625 Joseph Peila	PK-8	T	548 30	64%	773/534-2390 Fax 773/534-2638
ⓨ Chavez Elem Multicultural Acad 4747 S Marshfield Ave, Chicago 60609 Barton Dassinger	PK-8	MT	786 23	99%	773/535-4600 Fax 773/535-4603
Chicago HS-Agricultural Sci 3857 W 111th St, Chicago 60655 William Hook	9-12	V	845 30	40%	773/535-2500 Fax 773/535-2507
Columbus Elem Sch 1003 N Leavitt St, Chicago 60622 Wendy Oleksy	PK-8	T	240 11	71%	773/534-4350 Fax 773/534-4362
Corkery Elem Sch 2510 S Kildare Ave, Chicago 60623 Carol Devens-Falk	PK-8	T	405 33	94%	773/534-1650 Fax 773/534-1674
ⓜ Devry Univ Advantage Acad HS 3300 N Campbell Ave, Chicago 60618 Anna Ruiz-Villa	9-12	T	150 8		773/697-2216 Fax 773/327-4262
Dyett Arts High Sch 555 E 51st St, Chicago 60615 Cortez McCoy	9-12	TV	592 40	85%	773/535-1825 Fax 773/535-1037
Eberhart Elem Sch 3400 W 65th Pl, Chicago 60629 Nneka Gunn	K-8	T	1,104 69	95%	773/535-9190 Fax 773/535-9494
Ebinger Elem Sch 7350 W Pratt Ave, Chicago 60631 Serena Klosa	K-8		845 23	13%	773/534-1070 Fax 773/534-1088
ⓨ Edwards Elem Sch 4815 S Karlov Ave, Chicago 60632 Judith Sauri	PK-8	MT	1,242 54	87%	773/534-4875 Fax 773/535-4470
Federico G Lorca Elem Sch 3231 N Springfield Ave, Chicago 60618 Erleah Cyrwus	PK-8	T	659	91%	773/534-0950 Fax 773/534-0953
ⓜ Franklin Fine Arts Center 225 W Evergreen Ave, Chicago 60610 **Dr Joyce Booker-Thomas**	K-8		359 22	41%	773/534-8510 Fax 773/534-8022
ⓨ G Rogers Clark Elem Sch 1045 S Monitor Ave, Chicago 60644 Natasha Buckner	PK-8	MT	190 16	92%	773/534-6225 Fax 773/534-6278
ⓜ Gillespie Tech Mag Cluster Sch 9301 S State St, Chicago 60619 Dr Michelle Willis	PK-8	T	466 28	81%	773/535-5065 Fax 773/535-3971
Goudy Elem Sch 5120 N Winthrop Ave, Chicago 60640 Pamela Brandt	PK-8	T	586 30	88%	773/534-2480 Fax 773/534-2588
Grissom Elem Sch 12810 S Escanaba Ave, Chicago 60633 Dr Dennis Sweeney	PK-8	T	269 10	63%	773/535-5380 Fax 773/535-5362
ⓜ Gunsaulus Scholastic Academy 4420 S Sacramento Ave, Chicago 60632 Kiltae Kim	PK-8	T	688 23	88%	773/535-7215 Fax 773/535-7222
ⓨ Hefferan Elem Sch 4409 W Wilcox St, Chicago 60624 Jacqueline Hearns	PK-8	MT	274 25	97%	773/534-6192 Fax 773/534-6190
Holden Elem Sch 1104 W 31st St, Chicago 60608 Konstantinos Patsiopoulos	PK-8	T	274 21	86%	773/535-7200 Fax 773/535-7113
Infinity Math Sci & Tech HS 3120 S Kostner Ave, Chicago 60623 Charles Smith	9-12	T	409 16	96%	773/535-4225 Fax 773/535-4270
J Ward Elem Sch 2701 S Shields Ave, Chicago 60616 Karen Anderson	PK-8	GT	550 20	81%	773/534-9050 Fax 773/534-9044
Jane Addams Elem Sch 10810 S Avenue H, Chicago 60617 Ruth Walsh	PK-8	T	620 37	88%	773/535-6210 Fax 773/535-6292
Jones College Prep Sch 700 S State St, Chicago 60605 Dr Joseph Powers	9-12		1,989 35	37%	773/534-8600 Fax 773/534-8625
Jungman Elem Sch 1746 S Miller St, Chicago 60608 Suzanne Mazenis-Luzzi	PK-8	T	237 14	90%	773/534-7375 Fax 773/534-7383
Kinzie Elem Sch 5625 S Mobile Ave Ste 1, Chicago 60638 Dawn Caetta	PK-8	T	646 43	57%	773/535-2425 Fax 773/535-2086
Kipling Elem Sch 9351 S Lowe Ave, Chicago 60620 Lawanda Bishop	PK-8	T	253 22	83%	773/535-3151 Fax 773/535-3187
ⓜ LaSalle II Magnet Elem Sch 1148 N Honore St, Chicago 60622 Lauren Albani	PK-8		524 26	35%	773/534-0490 Fax 773/534-0491
ⓨ Lee Elem Sch 6448 S Tripp Ave, Chicago 60629 Lisa Epstein	PK-8	MT	708 30	92%	773/535-2255 Fax 773/535-2287
Lincoln Elem Sch 615 W Kemper Pl, Chicago 60614 Mark Armendariz	K-8		936 25	13%	773/534-5720 Fax 773/534-5778
Lincoln Park High Sch 2001 N Orchard St, Chicago 60614 John Thuet	9-12		2,147 70	47%	773/534-8130 Fax 773/534-8218
ⓨ Little Village Academy 2620 S Lawndale Ave, Chicago 60623 Lillian Lazu	PK-8	MT	635 32	97%	773/534-1880 Fax 773/534-1893
ⓨ Lloyd Elem Sch 2103 N Lamon Ave, Chicago 60639 Jay Thompson	PK-5	MT	823 28	95%	773/534-3070 Fax 773/534-3388
ⓨ Mariano Azuela Elem Sch 4707 W Marquette Rd, Chicago 60629 Carmen Navarro	PK-8	MT	785	84%	773/535-7395 Fax 773/535-7397
Marine Leadership Acad at Ames 1920 N Hamlin Ave, Chicago 60647 Erin Galfer	7-12	T	830	98%	773/534-4970 Fax 773/534-4975
Mark T Skinner West Elem Sch 111 S Throop St, Chicago 60607 Deborah Clark	PK-8		1,106 15	18%	773/534-7790 Fax 773/534-7879
McClellan Elem Sch 3527 S Wallace St, Chicago 60609 Kiersten Nanavati	PK-8	T	327 10	87%	773/535-1732 Fax 773/535-1940
McDowell Sch 1419 E 89th St, Chicago 60619 Dr Jo Hood	PK-5	T	140 9	91%	773/535-6404 Fax 773/535-6434
Moos Elem Sch 1711 N California Ave, Chicago 60647 Lauren Degiulio	PK-8	T	406 17	91%	773/534-4340 Fax 773/534-4778
Mt Greenwood Elem Sch 10841 S Homan Ave, Chicago 60655 Catherine Reidy	K-8		1,244 31	14%	773/535-2786 Fax 773/535-2743
Northside College Prep HS 5501 N Kedzie Ave, Chicago 60625 Kelly Mest	9-12		1,074 52	44%	773/534-3954 Fax 773/534-3964
ⓜ O A Thorp Scholastic Academy 6024 W Warwick Ave, Chicago 60634 Efren Toledo	K-8		837 34	46%	773/534-3640 Fax 773/534-3639
ⓨ Pasteur Elem Sch 5825 S Kostner Ave, Chicago 60629 Gerardo Trujillo	PK-4	MT	507 36	91%	773/535-2270 Fax 773/535-2235
ⓐ Peace & Educ Coalition HS ⓨ 4946 S Paulina St, Chicago 60609 Brigitte Swenson	10-12	MT	79 7	87%	773/535-9023 Fax 773/535-9477
ⓨ Peck Elem Sch 3826 W 58th St, Chicago 60629 Okab Hassan	PK-4	MT	852 42	95%	773/535-2450 Fax 773/535-2228

79	Student Personnel	91	Safety/Security	275	Response To Intervention	298	Grant Writer/Ptnrships
80	Driver Ed/Safety	92	Magnet School	277	Remedial Math K-12	750	Chief Innovation Officer
81	Gifted/Talented	93	Parental Involvement	280	Literacy Coach	751	Chief of Staff
82	Video Services	95	Tech Prep Program	285	STEM	752	Social Emotional Learning
83	Substance Abuse Prev	97	Chief Information Officer	286	Digital Learning		
84	Erate	98	Chief Technology Officer	288	Common Core Standards		
85	AIDS Education	270	Character Education	294	Accountability		
88	Alternative/At Risk	271	Migrant Education	295	Network System		
89	Multi-Cultural Curriculum	273	Teacher Mentor	296	Title II Programs		
90	Social Work	274	Before/After Sch	297	Webmaster		

School Programs
A = Alternative Program
G = Adult Classes
M = Magnet Program
T = Title I Schoolwide
V = Career & Tech Ed Programs

Other School Types
ⓐ = Alternative School
ⓒ = Charter School
ⓜ = Magnet School
ⓨ = Year-Round School

New Schools are shaded
New Superintendents and Principals are bold
Personnel with email addresses are underscored

Social Media
[f] = Facebook
[t] = Twitter

IL—27

Cook County

Market Data Retrieval

School	Grd	Prgm	Enr/#Cls	SN	Phone
Phoenix Military Academy 145 S Campbell Ave, Chicago 60612 Ferdinand Wipachit	9-12	AT	587 30	89%	773/534-7275 Fax 773/534-7273
Pickard Elem Sch 2301 W 21st Pl, Chicago 60608 Rigo Hernandez	PK-8	T	358 20	97%	773/535-7280 Fax 773/535-7199
Rachel Carson Elem Sch 5516 S Maplewood Ave, Chicago 60629 Javier Arriola-Lopez	PK-8	T	863 46	96%	773/535-9222 Fax 773/535-9552
Ravenswood Elem Sch 4332 N Paulina St, Chicago 60613 Patrina Singleton	PK-8		526 28	35%	773/534-5525 Fax 773/534-5775
Rickover Naval Academy 5700 W Berteau Ave, Chicago 60634 Michael Biela	9-12	T	457 20	86%	773/534-2890 Fax 773/534-2895
Rogers Elem Sch 7345 N Washtenaw Ave, Chicago 60645 Christine Jabbari	PK-8	T	661 25	72%	773/534-2125 Fax 773/534-2193
Ruben Salazar Bilingual Center 160 W Wendell St Ste 1, Chicago 60610 Lourdes Jimenez	PK-8	T	301 16	85%	773/534-8310 Fax 773/534-8313
Sauganash Elem Sch 6040 N Kilpatrick Ave, Chicago 60646 Christine Munns	K-8		637 17	24%	773/534-3470 Fax 773/534-3707
Ⓜ Sheridan Math & Science Acad 533 W 27th St, Chicago 60616 John O'Connell	K-8		542 18	47%	773/534-9120 Fax 773/534-9124
Sherwood Elem Sch 245 W 57th St, Chicago 60621 Alice Buzanis	PK-8	T	257 35	100%	773/535-0829 Fax 773/535-0872
Smyser Elem Sch 4310 N Melvina Ave, Chicago 60634 Jerry Travlos	PK 8	T	782 36	67%	773/534 3711 Fax 773/534-3555
South Loop Elem Sch 1212 S Plymouth Ct, Chicago 60605 Tara Shelton	K-8		764 26	28%	773/534-8690 Fax 773/534-8689
Southside Occupational Academy 7342 S Hoyne Ave, Chicago 60636 Joshua Long	Spec	T	289 25	91%	773/535-9100 Fax 773/535-9110
Ⓜ STEM Magnet Academy 1522 W Fillmore St, Chicago 60607 Maria McManus	K-8		426	39%	773/534-7300 Fax 773/534-7302
Talcott Fine Arts Museum Acad 1840 W Ohio St, Chicago 60622 Olimpia Bahena	PK-8	T	435 36	78%	773/534-7130 Fax 773/534-7126
Talman Elem Sch 5450 S Talman Ave, Chicago 60632 Jacqueline Medina	PK-8	T	337 10	92%	773/535-7850 Fax 773/535-7857
Ted Lenart Regional Gifted Ctr 8101 S La Salle St, Chicago 60620 Angela Sims	PK-8		250 10	30%	773/535-0040 Fax 773/535-0048
Ⓨ Tonti Elem Sch 5815 S Homan Ave, Chicago 60629 Gerardo Arriaga	PK-5	MT	789 29	91%	773/535-9280 Fax 773/535-0470
Velma Thomas Early Chldhd Ctr 3625 S Hoyne Ave, Chicago 60609 Mary Richardson	PK-PK		84 6	73%	773/535-4088 Fax 773/535-4085
Wacker Elem Sch 9746 S Morgan St, Chicago 60643 Ekaterini Panagakis	PK-8	T	229 10	86%	773/535-2821 Fax 773/535-2829
Wadsworth Elem Sch 6650 S Ellis Ave, Chicago 60637 Rashid Shabazz	PK-8	T	479 20	90%	773/535-0730 Fax 773/535-0743
Ⓜ Walt Disney Magnet Sch 4140 N Marine Dr, Chicago 60613 Dr Kathleen Hagstrom	PK-8	T	1,620 60	61%	773/534-5840 Fax 773/534-5714
Walter Payton College Prep HS 1034 N Wells St, Chicago 60610 Tim DeVine	9-12		1,139 55	31%	773/534-0034 Fax 773/534-0035
West Ridge Elem Sch 6700 N Whipple St, Chicago 60645 Antigoni Sofios	PK-8	T	672	87%	773/534-8250 Fax 773/534-8251
Ⓜ Whitney Young Magnet High Sch 211 S Laflin St, Chicago 60607 Dr Joyce Kenner	7-12		2,122	38%	773/534-7500 Fax 773/534-7261
Ⓨ Zapata Academy 2728 S Kostner Ave, Chicago 60623 Ruth Garcia	PK-8	MT	579 35	95%	773/534-1390 Fax 773/534-1398

● **Chicago PSD-Network 1** PID: 11931080   773/534-1038
6323 N Avondale Ave, Chicago 60631

Julie McGlade 15

Public Schs..Principal	Grd	Prgm	Enr/#Cls	SN	Phone
Albany Park Multicultural Acad 4929 N Sawyer Ave, Chicago 60625 Marie Hammerlund	7-8	T	245 10	93%	773/534-5108 Fax 773/534-5178
Ⓨ Alessandro Volta Elem Sch 4950 N Avers Ave, Chicago 60625 Emily Mariano	PK-8	MT	828 45	90%	773/534-5080 Fax 773/534-5280
Beard Elem Sch 6445 W Strong St, Chicago 60656 Manda Lukic	Spec	T	114 18	62%	773/534-1228 Fax 773/534-1247
Beaubien Elem Sch 5025 N Laramie Ave, Chicago 60630 Michelle Ludford	PK-8		996 37	44%	773/534-3500 Fax 773/534-3517
Belding Elem Sch 4257 N Tripp Ave, Chicago 60641 Heather Yutzy	PK-8	T	535 21	57%	773/534-3590 Fax 773/534-3598
Bridge Elem Sch 3800 N New England Ave, Chicago 60634 Rita Ortiz	PK-8	T	1,020 24	65%	773/534-3718 Fax 773/534-3612
Canty Elem Sch 3740 N Panama Ave, Chicago 60634 Jennifer Rath	PK-8		730 26	48%	773/534-1238 Fax 773/534-1236
Cleveland Elem Sch 3121 W Byron St, Chicago 60618 Debora Ward	PK-8	T	485 40	81%	773/534-5130 Fax 773/534-5266
Dever Elem Sch 3436 N Osceola Ave, Chicago 60634 Jason Major	PK-8	T	664 35	56%	773/534-3090 Fax 773/534-3337
Ⓨ Dirksen Elem Sch 8601 W Foster Ave, Chicago 60656 Daniel Lucas	PK-8	MT	875 26	70%	773/534-1090 Fax 773/534-1065
Edgebrook Elem Sch 6525 N Hiawatha Ave, Chicago 60646 Camille Unger	K-8		466 17	14%	773/534-1194 Fax 773/534-1170
Edison Park Elem Sch 6220 N Olcott Ave, Chicago 60631 John Finelli	K-8		511	16%	773/534-0960 Fax 773/534-0969
Edison Regional Gifted Center 4929 N Sawyer Ave, Chicago 60625 Karen Valentine	K-8		242 9	8%	773/534-0540 Fax 773/534-0539
Farnsworth Elem Sch 5414 N Linder Ave, Chicago 60630 Barbara Oken	PK-8	T	573 22	61%	773/534-3535 Fax 773/534-3515
Garvy Elem Sch 5225 N Oak Park Ave, Chicago 60656 Heather Chron-Bernard	K-8		749 30	36%	773/534-1185 Fax 773/534-1124
Gray Elem Sch 3730 N Laramie Ave, Chicago 60641 Susan Gross	PK-8	T	1,009	85%	773/534-3520 Fax 773/534-3613

1 Superintendent	8 Curric/Instruct K-12	19 Chief Financial Officer	29 Family/Consumer Science	39 Social Studies K-12	49 English/Lang Arts Elem	59 Special Education Elem	69 Academic Assessment
2 Bus/Finance/Purchasing	9 Curric/Instruct Elem	20 Art K-12	30 Adult Education	40 Social Studies Elem	50 English/Lang Arts Sec	60 Special Education Sec	70 Research/Development
3 Buildings And Grounds	10 Curric/Instruct Sec	21 Art Elem	31 Career/Sch-to-Work K-12	41 Social Studies Sec	51 Reading K-12	61 Foreign/World Lang K-12	71 Public Information
4 Food Service	11 Federal Program	22 Art Sec	32 Career/Sch-to-Work Elem	42 Science K-12	52 Reading Elem	62 Foreign/World Lang Elem	72 Summer School
5 Transportation	12 Title I	23 Music K-12	33 Career/Sch-to-Work Sec	43 Science Elem	53 Reading Sec	63 Foreign/World Lang Sec	73 Instructional Tech
6 Athletic	13 Title V	24 Music Elem	34 Early Childhood Ed	44 Science Sec	54 Remedial Reading K-12	64 Religious Education K-12	74 Inservice Training
7 Health Services	15 Asst Superintendent	25 Music Sec	35 Health/Phys Education	45 Math K-12	55 Remedial Reading Elem	65 Religious Education Elem	75 Marketing/Distributive
	16 Instructional Media Svcs	26 Business Education	36 Guidance Services K-12	46 Math Elem	56 Remedial Reading Sec	66 Religious Education Sec	76 Info Systems
	17 Chief Operations Officer	27 Career & Tech Ed	37 Guidance Services Elem	47 Math Sec	57 Bilingual/ELL	67 School Board President	77 Psychological Assess
	18 Chief Academic Officer	28 Technology Education	38 Guidance Services Sec	48 English/Lang Arts K-12	58 Special Education K-12	68 Teacher Personnel	78 Affirmative Action

Illinois School Directory — Cook County

School	Grd	Prgm	Enr/#Cls	SN	Phone
Haugan Elem Sch 4540 N Hamlin Ave, Chicago 60625 Rosa Valdez	PK-6	T	905 61	96%	773/534-5040 Fax 773/534-5045
Hibbard Elem Sch 3244 W Ainslie St, Chicago 60625 Scott Ahlman	PK-6	T	778 50	91%	773/534-5191 Fax 773/534-5208 [f][t]
Hitch Elem Sch 5625 N McVicker Ave, Chicago 60646 Adam Stich	PK-8	T	510 25	54%	773/534-1189 Fax 773/534-1176 [f]
John Murphy Elem Sch 3539 W Grace St, Chicago 60618 Christine Zelenka	PK-8	T	543 25	71%	773/534-5223 Fax 773/534-5212 [f][t]
Newton Bateman Elem Sch 4220 N Richmond St, Chicago 60618 Georgia Davos	PK-8	T	848	78%	773/534-5055 Fax 773/534-5052 [f][t]
North River Elem Sch 4416 N Troy St, Chicago 60625 Jaime Sanchez	PK-8	T	245 13	87%	773/534-0590 Fax 773/534-0597
Norwood Park Elem Sch 5900 N Nina Ave, Chicago 60631 Ryan Coors	PK-8		412 15	15%	773/534-1198 Fax 773/534-1178 [f][t]
Onahan Elem Sch 6634 W Raven St, Chicago 60631 Marianne Patten	PK-8		622 28	31%	773/534-1180 Fax 773/534-1163
Oriole Park Elem Sch 5424 N Oketo Ave, Chicago 60656 Tim Riff	PK-8		691 21	25%	773/534-1201 Fax 773/534-1066
Palmer Elem Sch 5051 N Kenneth Ave, Chicago 60630 Jennifer Dixon	PK-8	T	655 40	77%	773/534-3704 Fax 773/534-3771 [f][t]
Patrick Henry Elem Sch 4250 N Saint Louis Ave, Chicago 60618 Juan Gutierrez	PK-6	T	511 28	93%	773/534-5060 Fax 773/534-5042
Peterson Elem Sch 5510 N Christiana Ave, Chicago 60625 Elsie Kane	PK-8	T	848 26	69%	773/534-5070 Fax 773/534-5077 [f][t]
Portage Park Elem Sch 5330 W Berteau Ave, Chicago 60641 Maureen Wood	PK-8	T	831 47	71%	773/534-3576 Fax 773/534-3558 [f][t]
Prussing Elem Sch 4650 N Menard Ave, Chicago 60630 Dr George Chipain	K-8	T	695	69%	773/534-3460 Fax 773/534-3530 [f]
Reinberg Elem Sch 3425 N Major Ave, Chicago 60634 Edwin Loch	PK-8	T	710 33	81%	773/534-3465 Fax 773/534-3798
Ⓨ Scammon Elem Sch 4201 W Henderson St, Chicago 60641 Christos Liberos	PK-8	MT	640 39	93%	773/534-3475 Fax 773/534-3516
Solomon Elem Sch 6206 N Hamlin Ave, Chicago 60659 Chris Gamble	PK-8		321 14	53%	773/534-5226 Fax 773/534-5167 [f][t]
Stock Sch 7507 W Birchwood Ave, Chicago 60631 Ann McNally	Spec		130 7	17%	773/534-1215 Fax 773/534-1221
Ⓜ Wildwood IB World Magnet Sch 6950 N Hiawatha Ave, Chicago 60646 Lissette Rua	K-8		427 13	12%	773/534-1188 Fax 773/534-1144 [f][t]
Boone Elem Sch 6710 N Washtenaw Ave, Chicago 60645 Jaclyn DeLaney	PK-8	T	771 40	92%	773/534-2160 Fax 773/534-2190
Brennemann Elem Sch 4251 N Clarendon Ave, Chicago 60613 Sakinah Abdal-Saboor	PK-8	T	379 26	77%	773/534-5766 Fax 773/534-5787
Coonley Elem Sch 4046 N Leavitt St, Chicago 60618 Gregory Zurawski	K-8		1,013 19	15%	773/534-5140 Fax 773/534-5213
Courtenay Language Arts Acad 4420 N Beacon St, Chicago 60640 MacQuline King	PK-8	T	295 14	73%	773/534-5790 Fax 773/534-5799
Decatur Classical Sch 7030 N Sacramento Ave, Chicago 60645 Yolanda Luna-Mroz	K-6		285 10	15%	773/534-2200 Fax 773/534-2191
DeWitt Clinton Elem Sch 6110 N Fairfield Ave Ste 1, Chicago 60659 Maureen DelGado	PK-8	T	1,152	93%	773/534-2025 Fax 773/534-2069
Eugene Field Elem Sch 7019 N Ashland Blvd, Chicago 60626 Adrian Dobbins	4-8	T	159 70	71%	773/534-2030 Fax 773/534-2189
G B Swift Elem Specialty Sch 5900 N Winthrop Ave, Chicago 60660 Sal Cannella	PK-8	T	699 40		773/534-2695 Fax 773/534-2575 [f][t]
Gale Math & Science Academy 1631 W Jonquil Ter, Chicago 60626 Francisco Leal	PK-8	T	256 28	92%	773/534-2100 Fax 773/534-2188
Hayt Elem Sch 1518 W Granville Ave, Chicago 60660 Daniel Gomez	PK-8	T	807 42	86%	773/534-2040 Fax 773/534-2187
Jamieson Elem Sch 5650 N Mozart St, Chicago 60659 Robert Baughman	PK-8	T	820 35	69%	773/534-2395 Fax 773/534-2579 [f][t]
Jordan Community Sch 7414 N Wolcott Ave, Chicago 60626 Gilberto Piedrahita	PK-8	T	477 34	94%	773/534-2220 Fax 773/534-2231
Kilmer Elem Sch 6700 N Greenview Ave, Chicago 60626 Jean Papagianis	PK-8	T	732 48	93%	773/534-2115 Fax 773/534-2186
McCutcheon Elem Sch 4865 N Sheridan Rd, Chicago 60640 Mary Theodosopoulos	PK-8	T	315 22	86%	773/534-2680 Fax 773/534-2578
McPherson Elem Sch 4728 N Wolcott Ave, Chicago 60640 Debbie Nikokavouras	PK-8	T	612 40	72%	773/534-2625 Fax 773/534-2637 [f][t]
New Field Primary Sch 1707 W Morse Ave, Chicago 60626 Conrey Callahan	PK-4	T	512 30	84%	773/534-2760 Fax 773/534-2773
Peirce Int'l Studies ES 1423 W Bryn Mawr Ave, Chicago 60660 Lorianne Zaimi	PK-8	T	955 36	52%	773/534-2440 Fax 773/534-2577
Ⓜ Stone Scholastic Academy 6239 N Leavitt St, Chicago 60659 James Brandon	K-8		570 24	51%	773/534-2045 Fax 773/534-2092
Thomas J Waters Elem Sch 4540 N Campbell Ave, Chicago 60625 Titia Kipp	K-8		606 23	29%	773/534-5090 Fax 773/534-5087

● **Chicago PSD-Network 2** PID: 11931092   773/534-1100
6323 N Avondale Ave, Chicago 60631

Mauricio Segovia 15

Public Schs..Principal	Grd	Prgm	Enr/#Cls	SN	Phone
Armstrong Int'l Studies ES 2110 W Greenleaf Ave, Chicago 60645 Otis Dunson	PK-8	T	1,163 40	90%	773/534-2150 Fax 773/534-2192

● **Chicago PSD-Network 3** PID: 11931107   773/534-6520
5101 W Harrison St, Chicago 60644

Jennifer Rottman 15

Public Schs..Principal	Grd	Prgm	Enr/#Cls	SN	Phone
Ⓨ Brunson Math & Sci Sch 932 N Central Ave, Chicago 60651 Dr Carol Wilson	PK-8	MT	400 40	92%	773/534-6025 Fax 773/534-6031

---

79 Student Personnel	91 Safety/Security	275 Response To Intervention	298 Grant Writer/Ptnrships	**School Programs**	**Social Media**
80 Driver Ed/Safety	92 Magnet School	277 Remedial Math K-12	750 Chief Innovation Officer	A = Alternative Program	[f] = Facebook
81 Gifted/Talented	93 Parental Involvement	280 Literacy Coach	751 Chief of Staff	G = Adult Classes	[t] = Twitter
82 Video Services	95 Tech Prep Program	285 STEM	752 Social Emotional Learning	M = Magnet Program	
83 Substance Abuse Prev	97 Chief Infomation Officer	286 Digital Learning		T = Title I Schoolwide	
84 Erate	98 Chief Technology Officer	288 Common Core Standards	**Other School Types**	V = Career & Tech Ed Programs	
85 AIDS Education	270 Character Education	294 Accountability	Ⓐ = Alternative School		
88 Alternative/At Risk	271 Migrant Education	295 Network System	Ⓒ = Charter School	New Schools are shaded	
89 Multi-Cultural Curriculum	273 Teacher Mentor	296 Title II Programs	Ⓜ = Magnet School	New Superintendents and Principals are bold	
90 Social Work	274 Before/After Sch	297 Webmaster	Ⓨ = Year-Round School	Personnel with email addresses are underscored	

Cook County   Market Data Retrieval

School	Grd	Prgm	Enr	#Cls	SN	Phone
ⓨ DePriest Elem Sch 139 S Parkside Ave, Chicago 60644 Latasha Geverola	PK-8	MT	484	31	93%	773/534-6800 Fax 773/534-6799
Dr J Prieto Math & Sci Academy 2231 N Central Ave, Chicago 60639 Amy Narea	PK-8	T	948		89%	773/534-0210 Fax 773/534-0211
Edward Ellington Elem Sch 243 N Parkside Ave, Chicago 60644 Shirley Scott	PK-8	T	443	19	98%	773/534-6361 Fax 773/534-6374
ⓨ Ella Flagg Young Elem Sch 1434 N Parkside Ave, Chicago 60651 Crystal Bell	PK-8	MT	715	68	96%	773/534-6200 Fax 773/534-6203
Falconer Elem Sch 3020 N Lamon Ave, Chicago 60641 James Cosme	PK-6	T	1,002	52	93%	773/534-3560 Fax 773/534-3636
George Leland Elem Sch 512 S Lavergne Ave, Chicago 60644 Jamikka Nelson	PK-8	T	372	9	95%	773/534-6340 Fax 773/534-6040
Hanson Park Elem Sch 5411 W Fullerton Ave, Chicago 60639 David Belanger	PK-8	T	1,262	48	93%	773/534-3100 Fax 773/534-3374
ⓨ John Hay Community Academy 1018 N Laramie Ave, Chicago 60651 Latrese Mathis	PK-8	GMT	293	26	96%	773/534-6000 Fax 773/534-6035
Locke Elem Sch 2828 N Oak Park Ave, Chicago 60634 John Fitzpatrick	PK-8	T	1,114	44	92%	773/534-3300 Fax 773/534-3168
ⓨ Lovett Elem Sch 6333 W Bloomingdale Ave, Chicago 60639 Tara Cain	PK-8	MT	329	27	90%	773/534-3130 Fax 773/534-3384
Luther Burbank Elem Sch 2035 N Mobile Ave, Chicago 60639 Hiram Broyls	PK 8	T	887	43	93%	773/534-3000 Fax 773/534-3338
Marvin Camras Elem Sch 3000 N Mango Ave, Chicago 60634 Clariza Dominicci	PK-8	T	850		85%	773/534-2960 Fax 773/534-2963
Mary Lyon Sch 2941 N McVicker Ave, Chicago 60634 Clifford Gabor	K-8	T	1,153	50	93%	773/534-3120 Fax 773/534-3375
ⓨ Nash Elem Sch 4837 W Erie St, Chicago 60644 Marcie Byrd	PK-8	MT	229	25	95%	773/534-6125 Fax 773/534-6105
Northwest Middle Sch 5252 W Palmer St, Chicago 60639 Margaret Byrne	6-8	T	531	35	95%	773/534-3250 Fax 773/534-3251
Ⓜ Sayre Language Academy 1850 N Newland Ave, Chicago 60707 Folasade Adekunle	PK-8	T	418	19	68%	773/534-3351 Fax 773/534-3394
ⓨ Schubert Elem Sch 2727 N Long Ave, Chicago 60639 Anita Hernandez	PK-5	MT	564	39	91%	773/534-3080 Fax 773/534-3079
Spencer Tech Academy 214 N Lavergne Ave, Chicago 60644 Frances Thibodeaux-Fox	PK-8	T	480	70	97%	773/534-6150 Fax 773/534-6239

• **Chicago PSD-Network 4** PID: 11931119   773/534-1035
  6323 N Avondale Ave, Chicago 60631

William Klee 15

Public Schs..Principal	Grd	Prgm	Enr/#Cls	SN	Phone
Alcott College Prep West 2957 N Hoyne Ave, Chicago 60618 Grace Moody	9-12		336	75%	773/534-5970 Fax 773/534-5789
Alcott Elem Sch 2625 N Orchard St, Chicago 60614 Elias Estrada	PK-8		680 21	13%	773/534-5460 Fax 773/534-5789
Audubon Elem Sch 3500 N Hoyne Ave, Chicago 60618 Meghan Duffy	PK-8		526 30	15%	773/534-5470 Fax 773/534-5785
Avondale-Logandale Sch 3212 W George St, Chicago 60618 Evelyn Roman	PK-8		549 28		773/534-5350 Fax 773/534-5349
Bell Elem Sch 3730 N Oakley Ave, Chicago 60618 Kathleen Miller	PK-8		983 46	12%	773/534-5150 Fax 773/534-5163
Brentano Math & Science Acad 2723 N Fairfield Ave, Chicago 60647 Seth LaVin	PK-8	T	576 36	59%	773/534-4100 Fax 773/534-4508
Chase Elem Sch 2021 N Point St, Chicago 60647 Raquel Saucedo	PK-8	T	373 40	87%	773/534-4185 Fax 773/534-4727
Darwin Elem Sch 3116 W Belden Ave, Chicago 60647 Daniel De Los Reyes	PK-8	T	517 28	90%	773/534-4110 Fax 773/534-4323
ⓨ Funston Elem Sch 2010 N Central Park Ave, Chicago 60647 Julie Hallums	PK-8	MT	404 31	95%	773/534-4125 Fax 773/534-4551
Goethe Elem Sch 2236 N Rockwell St, Chicago 60647 Barbara Kargas	PK-8	T	703 30	43%	773/534-4135 Fax 773/534-4138
Hamilton Elem Sch 1650 W Cornelia Ave, Chicago 60657 Amy Vondra	PK-8		473 20	13%	773/534-5484 Fax 773/534-5782
Ⓜ Hawthorne Scholastic Academy 3319 N Clifton Ave, Chicago 60657 Patricia Davlantes	K-8		533 18	19%	773/534-5550 Fax 773/534-5781
Horace Greeley Elem Sch 832 W Sheridan Rd, Chicago 60613 Raquel Gonzalez	PK-8	T	425 22	81%	773/534-5800 Fax 773/534-5783
Ⓜ Inter-American Magnet Sch 851 W Waveland Ave, Chicago 60613 Daniela Bylaitis	PK-8	T	726 30	53%	773/534-5490 Fax 773/534-5483
Jahn Elem Sch 3149 N Wolcott Ave, Chicago 60657 Michael Herring	PK-8	T	331 35	51%	773/534-5500 Fax 773/534-5533
James G Blaine Elem Sch 1420 W Grace Ave, Chicago 60613 Angela Brito	PK-8		821 25	15%	773/534-5750 Fax 773/534-5748
Ⓜ LaSalle Language Academy 1734 N Orleans St, Chicago 60614 Christopher Graves	K-8		495 18	31%	773/534-8470 Fax 773/534-8021
Manierre Elem Sch 1420 N Hudson Ave, Chicago 60610 Tinishi Davis	PK-8	T	282 17	94%	773/534-8456 Fax 773/534-8020
McAuliffe Elem Sch 1841 N Springfield Ave, Chicago 60647 Ryan Belville	PK-8		620 45	95%	773/534-4400 Fax 773/534-4744
Monroe Elem Sch 3651 W Schubert Ave, Chicago 60647 Bryan Quinlan	PK-8	T	692 46	96%	773/534-4155 Fax 773/534-4593
Mozart Elem Sch 2200 N Hamlin Ave, Chicago 60647 Rachel Mota	PK-8	T	498 30	98%	773/534-4160 Fax 773/534-4588
Nettelhorst Elem Sch 3252 N Broadway St, Chicago 60657 **Yasmeen Muhammad**	PK-8		730 29	22%	773/534-5810 Fax 773/534-5776
Ⓜ Newberry Math & Science Acad 700 W Willow St, Chicago 60614 Linda Foley-Acevedo	PK-8	T	398 27	62%	773/534-8000 Fax 773/534-8018
Nixon Elem Sch 2121 N Keeler Ave, Chicago 60639 Diana Rodriguez	PK-6	T	638 37	96%	773/534-4375 Fax 773/534-4539

1 Superintendent	8 Curric/Instruct K-12	19 Chief Financial Officer	29 Family/Consumer Science	39 Social Studies K-12	49 English/Lang Arts Elem	59 Special Education Elem	69 Academic Assessment
2 Bus/Finance/Purchasing	9 Curric/Instruct Elem	20 Art K-12	30 Adult Education	40 Social Studies Elem	50 English/Lang Arts Sec	60 Special Education Sec	70 Research/Development
3 Buildings And Grounds	10 Curric/Instruct Sec	21 Art Elem	31 Career/Sch-to-Work K-12	41 Social Studies Sec	51 Reading K-12	61 Foreign/World Lang K-12	71 Public Information
4 Food Service	11 Federal Program	22 Art Sec	32 Career/Sch-to-Work Elem	42 Science K-12	52 Reading Elem	62 Foreign/World Lang Elem	72 Summer School
5 Transportation	12 Title I	23 Music K-12	33 Career/Sch-to-Work Sec	43 Science Elem	53 Reading Sec	63 Foreign/World Lang Sec	73 Instructional Tech
6 Athletic	13 Title V	24 Music Elem	34 Early Childhood Ed	44 Science Sec	54 Remedial Reading K-12	64 Religious Education K-12	74 Inservice Training
7 Health Services	15 Asst Superintendent	25 Music Sec	35 Health/Phys Education	45 Math K-12	55 Remedial Reading Elem	65 Religious Education Elem	75 Marketing/Distributive
	16 Instructional Media Svcs	26 Business Education	36 Guidance Services K-12	46 Math Elem	56 Remedial Reading Sec	66 Religious Education Sec	76 Info Systems
	17 Chief Operations Officer	27 Career & Tech Ed	37 Guidance Services Elem	47 Math Sec	57 Bilingual/ELL	67 School Board President	77 Psychological Assess
	18 Chief Academic Officer	28 Technology Education	38 Guidance Services Sec	48 English/Lang Arts K-12	58 Special Education K-12	68 Teacher Personnel	78 Affirmative Action

Illinois School Directory — Cook County

School	Grd	Prgm	Enr/#Cls	SN	Phone
Oscar Mayer Elem Sch 2250 N Clifton Ave, Chicago 60614 Danielle Drayton	PK-8		759 27	11%	773/534-5535 Fax 773/534-5777
ⓨ Prescott Elem Sch 1632 W Wrightwood Ave, Chicago 60614 Erin Roche	K-8	M	463 10	38%	773/534-5505 Fax 773/534-5542 [f]
Reilly Elem Sch 3650 W School St, Chicago 60618 **Marcelo Costilla**	PK-8	T	677 60	86%	773/534-5250 Fax 773/534-5169
Skinner North Classical Sch 640 W Scott St Ste 1, Chicago 60610 Katie Magnuson	K-8		486	11%	773/534-8500 Fax 773/534-8502

● **Chicago PSD-Network 5** PID: 11931121 773/534-6544
2935 W Polk St, Chicago 60612
Shontae Higginbottom 15

Public Schs..Principal	Grd	Prgm	Enr/#Cls	SN	Phone
Chopin Elem Sch 2450 W Rice St, Chicago 60622 Frederick Williams	PK-8	T	308 12	95%	773/534-4080 Fax 773/534-4163
ⓨ Crown Community Academy 2128 S Saint Louis Ave, Chicago 60623 Zarree Walker	PK-8	MT	184 20	97%	773/534-1680 Fax 773/534-1677
ⓨ Daniel Webster Elem Sch 4055 W Arthington St, Chicago 60624 Khalid Oluewu	PK-8	MT	275 20	83%	773/534-6925 Fax 773/534-6949
De Diego Community Academy 1313 N Claremont Ave, Chicago 60622 Jacqueline Menoni	PK-8	T	587 85	89%	773/534-4451 Fax 773/534-4696 [t]
ⓨ Faraday Elem Sch 3250 W Monroe St, Chicago 60624 Dr Tawana Williams	PK-8	MT	210 10	100%	773/534-6670 Fax 773/534-6659 [f][t]
Ⓜ Frazier Prospective Mag Sch ⓨ 4027 W Grenshaw St, Chicago 60624 Charlette Broxton	K-8	MT	178	89%	773/534-6880 Fax 773/534-6616 [f][t]
George W Tilton Elem Sch 223 N Keeler Ave, Chicago 60624 Sylvia Hodge	PK-8	T	305 17	98%	773/534-6746 Fax 773/826-1915
Gregory Elem Sch 3715 W Polk St, Chicago 60624 Donella Carter	PK-8	MT	330 26	99%	773/534-6820 Fax 773/534-6484 [f][t]
Harriet Beecher Stowe Elem Sch 3444 W Wabansia Ave, Chicago 60647 Jimmy Lugo	PK-8	T	634 72	96%	773/534-4175 Fax 773/534-4167
Hughes Elem Sch 4247 W 15th St, Chicago 60623 Lucille Howard	PK-8	MT	252 28	99%	773/534-1762 Fax 773/534-1715
Jacob Beidler Elem Sch 3151 W Walnut St, Chicago 60612 Ursula Hoskins	PK-8	MT	396 22	93%	773/534-6811 Fax 773/534-6817 [f][t]
Ⓜ Jensen Scholastic Acad ⓨ 3030 W Harrison St, Chicago 60612 **Dr Beverly Jordan**	PK-8	MT	360 25	99%	773/534-6840 Fax 773/534-6722
ⓨ Joseph Kellman Corporate ES 3030 W Arthington St, Chicago 60612 Sherisse Freeney	PK-8	MT	218 11	97%	773/534-6602 Fax 773/534-6601
ⓨ Laura Ward Elem Sch 646 N Lawndale Ave, Chicago 60624 Rhea Bush	PK-8	MT	396 25	98%	773/534-6440 Fax 773/534-6718 [f][t]
ⓨ Lawndale Community Academy 3500 W Douglas Blvd, Chicago 60623 Natasha Jones	PK-8	MT	226 31	100%	773/534-1635 Fax 773/534-1644
Ⓜ Leif Ericson Scholastic Acad 3600 W 5th Ave, Chicago 60624 Leavelle Abram	PK-8	T	494 35	96%	773/534-6660 Fax 773/534-6636
ⓨ Lowell Elem Sch 3320 W Hirsch St, Chicago 60651 Gladys Rivera	PK-8	MT	319 38	98%	773/534-4300 Fax 773/534-4306
ⓨ Melody Elem Sch 3937 W Wilcox St, Chicago 60624 Tiffany Tillman	PK-8	MT	359 25	97%	773/534-6850 Fax 773/534-6614
Mitchell Elem Sch 2233 W Ohio St, Chicago 60612 Katherine Welsh	PK-8	T	359 10	45%	773/534-7655 Fax 773/534-7633 [f][t]
ⓨ Penn Elem Sch 1616 S Avers Ave, Chicago 60623 Sherryl Moore-Ollie	PK-8	MT	277 13	100%	773/534-1665 Fax 773/534-1673 [f]
ⓨ Plamondon Elem Sch 2642 W 15th Pl, Chicago 60608 Althea Hammond	K-8	MT	130 15	92%	773/534-1789 Fax 773/534-1858
ⓨ Roswell Mason Elem Sch 4217 W 18th St, Chicago 60623 Tonya Tolbert	PK-8	MT	357	98%	773/534-1530 Fax 773/534-1544 [f][t]
Sumner Math & Science Academy 4320 W 5th Ave, Chicago 60624 Fatima Cooke		T	224 30	94%	773/534-6730 Fax 773/534-6736
West Park Academy 1425 N Tripp Ave, Chicago 60651 Karime Asaf		T	453 30	93%	773/534-4940 Fax 773/534-4945
ⓨ Willa Cather Elem Sch 2908 W Washington Blvd, Chicago 60612 Wanda Carey	PK-8	MT	367 10	92%	773/534-6780 Fax 773/534-6727
Yates Elem Sch 1839 N Richmond St, Chicago 60647 Israel Perez	PK-8	T	323 39	83%	773/534-4550 Fax 773/534-4517

● **Chicago PSD-Network 6** PID: 11931133 773/534-7565
2245 W Jackson Blvd, Chicago 60612
Nicole Milberg 15

Public Schs..Principal	Grd	Prgm	Enr/#Cls	SN	Phone
Ⓜ Albert Sabin Magnet Sch 2216 W Hirsch St, Chicago 60622 Gwen Kasper-Couty	PK-8	T	433 26	81%	773/534-4490 Fax 773/534-4511
Ⓜ Andrew Jackson Language Acad 1340 W Harrison St, Chicago 60607 Marilou Rebolledo	K-8	G	471 33	41%	773/534-7000 Fax 773/534-9338
Armour Elem Sch 950 W 33rd Pl, Chicago 60608 Katherine Cheng	PK-8	T	234 29	79%	773/535-4530 Fax 773/535-4501
Burr Elem Sch 1621 W Wabansia Ave, Chicago 60622 Amy Klimowski	PK-8		446 10	32%	773/534-4090 Fax 773/534-4718 [f][t]
Ⓜ Drummond Elem Sch ⓨ 1845 W Cortland St, Chicago 60622 Erica Kittle	PK-8	M	342 12	22%	773/534-4120 Fax 773/534-4199 [f][t]
Ⓜ Galileo Scholastic Academy 820 S Carpenter St, Chicago 60607 Meredith Bawden	K-8	T	577 32	51%	773/534-7070 Fax 773/534-7109 [f][t]
Graham Elem Sch 4436 S Union Ave, Chicago 60609 John Nichols	PK-8	T	351 25	91%	773/535-1308 Fax 773/535-1424
Haines Elem Sch 247 W 23rd Pl, Chicago 60616 Catherine Moy	PK-8	T	546 30	86%	773/534-9200 Fax 773/534-9209
Healy Elem Sch 3010 S Parnell Ave, Chicago 60616 Elizabeth Nessner	K-8	T	1,309 45	82%	773/534-9190 Fax 773/534-9182 [f][t]
James Otis Elem Sch 525 N Armour St, Chicago 60642 Nancy Mendez	PK-8	T	342 23	81%	773/534-7665 Fax 773/534-7673

---

79 Student Personnel
80 Driver Ed/Safety
81 Gifted/Talented
82 Video Services
83 Substance Abuse Prev
84 Erate
85 AIDS Education
88 Alternative/At Risk
89 Multi-Cultural Curriculum
90 Social Work
91 Safety/Security
92 Magnet School
93 Parental Involvement
95 Tech Prep Program
97 Chief Infomation Officer
98 Chief Technology Officer
270 Accountability
271 Migrant Education
273 Teacher Mentor
274 Before/After Sch
275 Response To Intervention
277 Remedial Math K-12
280 Literacy Coach
285 STEM
286 Digital Learning
288 Common Core Standards
294 Accountability
295 Network System
296 Title II Programs
297 Webmaster
298 Grant Writer/Ptnrships
750 Chief Innovation Officer
751 Chief of Staff
752 Social Emotional Learning

Other School Types
Ⓐ = Alternative Program
Ⓒ = Charter School
Ⓜ = Magnet School
ⓨ = Year-Round School

School Programs
A = Alternative Program
G = Adult Classes
M = Magnet Program
T = Title I Schoolwide
V = Career & Tech Ed Programs

New Schools are shaded
New Superintendents and Principals are bold
Personnel with email addresses are underscored

Social Media
[f] = Facebook
[t] = Twitter

IL—31

Cook County

ⓨ Jenner Academy of the Arts Sch | PK-8 | M | 226 | | 773/534-8440
1119 N Cleveland Ave, Chicago 60610 | | | 21 | | Fax 773/534-8188
Robert Croston

Ⓜ John N Smyth Magnet Sch | PK-8 | MT | 435 | 74% | 773/534-7180
ⓨ 1059 W 13th St, Chicago 60608 | | | 16 | | Fax 773/534-7127
Dana Turner

Lozano Bilingual Sch | PK-8 | T | 191 | 91% | 773/534-4750
1501 N Greenview Ave, Chicago 60642 | | | 16 | | Fax 773/534-4740
Dr Terri Campos

Pritzker Sch | PK-8 | | 721 | 41% | 773/534-4415
2009 W Schiller St, Chicago 60622 | | | 30 | | Fax 773/534-4634
Dr Joenile Albert-Reese

Pulaski Int'l Sch of Chicago | PK-8 | T | 840 | 57% | 773/534-4391
2230 W McLean Ave, Chicago 60647 | | | | | Fax 773/534-4392
Diana Racasi

ⓨ Robert Nathaniel Dett Elem Sch | PK-8 | MT | 307 | 95% | 773/534-7160
2131 W Monroe St, Chicago 60612 | | | 14 | | Fax 773/534-7291
Heather Hampton

Ⓜ Suder Montessori Magnet Sch | PK-8 | T | 437 | 51% | 773/534-7685
2022 W Washington Blvd, Chicago 60612 | | | 3 | | Fax 773/534-7933
Bosede Bada

ⓨ Washington Irving Elem Sch | PK-8 | MT | 386 | 90% | 773/534-7295
749 S Oakley Blvd, Chicago 60612 | | | 19 | | Fax 773/534-7289
Narineh Gharashor

William H Brown Elem Sch | PK-8 | T | 225 | 80% | 773/534-7250
54 N Hermitage Ave, Chicago 60612 | | | 14 | | Fax 773/534-7323
Latoya Lyons

ⓨ Wilma G Rudolph Learning Ctr | Spec | MT | 68 | 85% | 773/534-7460
110 N Paulina St, Chicago 60612 | | | 10 | | Fax 773/534-7466
Holly Dacres

● **Chicago PSD-Network 7** PID: 11931145 — 773/535-7101
4655 S Dearborn St, Chicago 60609

Minerva Garcia-Sanchez 15

Public Schs..Principal	Grd	Prgm	Enr/#Cls	SN	
Cooper Dual Language Academy 1624 W 19th St, Chicago 60608 Martha Alba	PK-5	T	434 32	95%	773/534-7205 Fax 773/534-7245
Eli Whitney Elem Sch 2815 S Komensky Ave, Chicago 60623 Evelia Diaz	PK-8	T	715 49	96%	773/534-1560 Fax 773/534-1567
Gary Elem Sch 3740 W 31st St, Chicago 60623 Alberto Juarez	PK-8	T	958	95%	773/534-1455 Fax 773/534-1435
ⓨ Hammond Elem Sch 2819 W 21st Pl, Chicago 60623 Anamaria Orbe-Lugo	PK-8	MT	309 25	96%	773/535-4580 Fax 773/535-4579
John Spry Elem Sch 2400 S Marshall Blvd, Chicago 60623 Elvia Garcia-Graham	PK-8	T	367 31	98%	773/534-1700 Fax 773/534-1688
Josefa Ortiz De Dominguez ES 3000 S Lawndale Ave, Chicago 60623 Angelica Herrera-Vest	PK-2	T	376 23	96%	773/534-1600 Fax 773/534-1415
Ⓜ Kanoon Magnet Sch 2233 S Kedzie Ave, Chicago 60623 Dr Marin Gonzalez	PK-8	T	484 36	97%	773/534-1736 Fax 773/534-1740
ⓨ Madero Middle Sch 3202 W 28th St, Chicago 60623 Hamed Flores	6-8	MT	302 22	97%	773/535-4466 Fax 773/535-4469
ⓨ Manuel Perez Elem Sch 1241 W 19th St, Chicago 60608 Jessica Johnson	PK-8	MT	288 23	93%	773/534-7650 Fax 773/534-7621
Ⓜ Maria Saucedo Scholastic Acad 2850 W 24th Blvd, Chicago 60623 **Virginia Hitlz**	PK-8	GT	917 50	94%	773/534-1770 Fax 773/534-1356

ⓨ McCormick Elem Sch | PK-5 | MT | 523 | 89% | 773/535-7252
2712 S Sawyer Ave, Chicago 60623 | | | 47 | | Fax 773/535-7347
Denise Makowski

Orozco Fine Arts & Sciences ES | PK-8 | T | 363 | 94% | 773/534-7215
1940 W 18th St, Chicago 60608 | | | 29 | | Fax 773/534-7329
Efrain Martinez

Pilsen Community Academy | PK-8 | T | 252 | 90% | 773/534-7675
1420 W 17th St, Chicago 60608 | | | 35 | | Fax 773/534-7797
Jasmine Juarez

Ruiz Elem Sch | PK-8 | T | 527 | 93% | 773/535-4825
2410 S Leavitt St, Chicago 60608 | | | 36 | | Fax 773/535-4618
Marla Elitzer

Telpochcalli Elem Sch | PK-8 | T | 224 | 88% | 773/534-1402
2832 W 24th Blvd, Chicago 60623 | | | 11 | | Fax 773/534-1404
Tamara Witzl

ⓨ Walsh Elem Sch | PK-8 | MT | 286 | 77% | 773/534-7950
2015 S Peoria St, Chicago 60608 | | | 25 | | Fax 773/534-7168
Patricia Reynolds

Whittier Elem Sch | PK-8 | T | 173 | 89% | 773/535-4590
1900 W 23rd St, Chicago 60608 | | | 16 | | Fax 773/535-4818
Antonio Acevedo

ⓨ William F Finkl Academy | PK-8 | MT | 245 | 96% | 773/535-5850
2332 S Western Ave, Chicago 60608 | | | 23 | | Fax 773/535-4409
Denise Lynch

● **Chicago PSD-Network 8** PID: 11931157 — 773/535-8211
4655 S Dearborn St, Chicago 60609

Elizabeth Alvarez 15

Public Schs..Principal	Grd	Prgm	Enr/#Cls	SN	
Augustin Lara Elem Acad 4619 S Wolcott Ave, Chicago 60609 Paul Schissler	PK-8	T	355 24	96%	773/535-4389 Fax 773/535-4471
Brighton Park Elem Sch 3825 S Washtenaw Ave, Chicago 60632 Sara Haas	PK-8	T	334 35	96%	773/535-7237 Fax 773/535-7198
Calmeca Academy 3456 W 38th St, Chicago 60632 Nancy Paulette	PK-8	T	675 10	89%	773/535-7000 Fax 773/535-7010
ⓨ Columbia Explorers Academy 4520 S Kedzie Ave, Chicago 60632 Eileen Considine	PK-8	MT	766 37	94%	773/535-4050 Fax 773/535-4083
ⓨ Daley Academy 5024 S Wolcott Ave, Chicago 60609 Kamilah Hampton	PK-8	MT	528 40	100%	773/535-9091 Fax 773/535-0407
ⓨ Everett Elem Sch 3419 S Bell Ave, Chicago 60608 Rodolfo Rojas	PK-5	MT	122 15	91%	773/535-4550 Fax 773/535-4615
ⓨ Evergreen Academy Middle Sch 3537 S Paulina St, Chicago 60609 **Strok Marian**	6-8	AMT	268 16	94%	773/535-4836 Fax 773/535-4853
Greene Elem Sch 3525 S Honore St, Chicago 60609 Shelley Cordova	PK-5	T	338 27	95%	773/535-4560 Fax 773/535-4617
Hamline Elem Sch 4747 S Bishop St, Chicago 60609 Erik Olson	PK-8	T	530 17	92%	773/535-4565 Fax 773/535-4546
ⓨ Hedges Elem Sch 4747 S Winchester Ave, Chicago 60609 Jose Jimenez	PK-8	MT	512 40	96%	773/535-7360 Fax 773/535-4178
ⓨ Irene Hernandez Middle Sch 3510 W 55th St, Chicago 60632 Luis Tellez	6-8	MT	1,017	97%	773/535-8850 Fax 773/535-8851
James Shields Elem Sch 4250 S Rockwell St, Chicago 60632 Michael Pacourek	PK-4	T	497 60	98%	773/535-7286 Fax 773/535-7129

1	Superintendent	8	Curric/Instruct K-12	19	Chief Financial Officer	29	Family/Consumer Science	39	Social Studies K-12	49	English/Lang Arts Elem	59	Special Education Elem	69	Academic Assessment
2	Bus/Finance/Purchasing	9	Curric/Instruct Elem	20	Art K-12	30	Adult Education	40	Social Studies Elem	50	English/Lang Arts Sec	60	Special Education Sec	70	Research/Development
3	Buildings And Grounds	10	Curric/Instruct Sec	21	Art Elem	31	Career/Sch-to-Work K-12	41	Social Studies Sec	51	Reading K-12	61	Foreign/World Lang K-12	71	Public Information
4	Food Service	11	Federal Program	22	Art Sec	32	Career/Sch-to-Work Elem	42	Science K-12	52	Reading Elem	62	Foreign/World Lang Elem	72	Summer School
5	Transportation	12	Title I	23	Music K-12	33	Career/Sch-to-Work Sec	43	Science Elem	53	Reading Sec	63	Foreign/World Lang Sec	73	Instructional Tech
6	Athletic	13	Title V	24	Music Elem	34	Early Childhood Ed	44	Science Sec	54	Remedial Reading K-12	64	Religious Education K-12	74	Inservice Training
7	Health Services	15	Asst Superintendent	25	Music Sec	35	Health/Phys Education	45	Math K-12	55	Remedial Reading Elem	65	Religious Education Elem	75	Marketing/Distributive
		16	Instructional Media Svcs	26	Business Education	36	Guidance Services K-12	46	Math Elem	56	Remedial Reading Sec	66	Religious Education Sec	76	Info Systems
		17	Chief Operations Officer	27	Career & Tech Ed	37	Guidance Services Elem	47	Math Sec	57	Bilingual/ELL	67	School Board President	77	Psychological Assess
		18	Chief Academic Officer	28	Technology Education	38	Guidance Services Sec	48	English/Lang Arts K-12	58	Special Education K-12	68	Teacher Personnel	78	Affirmative Action

Illinois School Directory — Cook County

School	Grd	Prgm	Enr/#Cls	SN	Phone
James Shields Middle Sch 2611 W 48th St, Chicago 60632 Debra Fritz-Fanning	5-8	T	591	95%	773/535-7115 Fax 773/535-7296
Nathan S Davis Elem Sch 3014 W 39th Pl, Chicago 60632 Rocio Rosales	PK-8	T	571 60	99%	773/535-4540 Fax 773/535-4510
Ⓨ Nightingale Elem Sch 5250 S Rockwell St, Chicago 60632 Adriana Arias	PK-8	MT	1,031 51	74%	773/535-9270 Fax 773/535-0430
Ⓨ Sandoval Elem Sch 5534 S Saint Louis Ave, Chicago 60629 Wilma David	PK-5	MT	763 48	96%	773/535-0457 Fax 773/535-0467
Sawyer Elem Sch 5248 S Sawyer Ave, Chicago 60632 Nelly Robles	PK-8	T	1,156 50	96%	773/535-9275 Fax 773/535-9216
Seward Communctn Arts Acad 4600 S Hermitage Ave, Chicago 60609 Nora Cadenas	PK-8	T	539 35	100%	773/535-4890 Fax 773/535-4884
Sor Juana Elem Sch 4120 W 57th St, Chicago 60629 Megan Kehr	PK-3		224	48%	773/535-8280 Fax 773/535-7596
W S Christopher Elem Sch 5042 S Artesian Ave, Chicago 60632 Katherine Gallagher	Spec	T	347 30	91%	773/535-9375 Fax 773/535-9567

● **Chicago PSD-Network 9** PID: 11931169   773/535-8955
4655 S Dearborn St, Chicago 60609

Tiffany Sanders 15

Public Schs..Principal	Grd	Prgm	Enr/#Cls	SN	Phone
Ariel Community Academy 1119 E 46th St, Chicago 60653 Dr Lennette Coleman	PK-8	T	420 25	83%	773/535-1996 Fax 773/535-1931
Ⓜ Beasley Elem Mgnt Academic Ctr 5255 S State St, Chicago 60609 Donnell Rader	PK-8	T	1,116 40	87%	773/535-1230 Fax 773/535-1248
Ⓨ Beethoven Elem Sch 25 W 47th St, Chicago 60609 Mellodie Brown	PK-8	MT	259 14	86%	773/535-1480 Fax 773/535-1478
Bret Harte Elem Sch 1556 E 56th St, Chicago 60637 Charles Bright	PK-8	T	385 8	74%	773/535-0870 Fax 773/535-0666
Bronzeville Classical Elem Sch 8 W Root St, Chicago 60609 Nicole Spicer	K-2		89	27%	773/535-8085 Fax 773/535-8686
Ⓨ Burke Elem Sch 5356 S King Dr, Chicago 60615 Lauren Norwood	PK-8	MT	306 9		773/535-1325 Fax 773/535-1913
Ⓐ Doolittle East Elem Sch Ⓨ 535 E 35th St, Chicago 60616 Iysha Jones	PK-8	MT	243 18	99%	773/535-1040 Fax 773/535-1034
Ⓨ Emmett Till Math & Sci Academy 6543 S Champlain Ave, Chicago 60637 Terea Peoples-Brown	PK-8	MT	308 25	98%	773/535-0570 Fax 773/535-0598
Hendricks Elem Cmty Acad 4316 S Princeton Ave, Chicago 60609 Sandee McDonald	PK-8	T	189 12	97%	773/535-1696 Fax 773/535-1700
Jackie Robinson Elem Sch 4225 S Lake Park Ave, Chicago 60653 Gretta Ellis	PK-3	T	139 8	92%	773/535-1777 Fax 773/535-1727
Ⓨ John B Drake Elem Sch 2710 S Dearborn St Ste 3, Chicago 60616 Sydney Golliday	PK-8	MT	266 12	89%	773/534-9129 Fax 773/534-9133
Ⓨ John Fiske Elem Sch 6020 S Langley Ave, Chicago 60637 Kenya Underwood	PK-8	MT	395 20	97%	773/535-0990 Fax 773/535-0580
Ⓨ Kozminski Cmty Academy 936 E 54th St, Chicago 60615 Bernadette Glover	PK-8	MT	239 20	74%	773/535-0980 Fax 773/535-0982
Mollison Elem Sch 4415 S King Dr, Chicago 60653 Valencia Hudson-Barnes	PK-8	MT	243 9	98%	773/535-1804 Fax 773/535-1803
Ⓜ Murray Language Academy 5335 S Kenwood Ave, Chicago 60615 Gregory Mason	K-8	T	488 20	62%	773/535-0585 Fax 773/535-0590
Ⓜ Pershing Humanities Mag Sch 3200 S Calumet Ave, Chicago 60616 Dr Safurat Giwa	PK-8	T	527 9	78%	773/534-9272 Fax 773/534-9277
Ray Elem Sch 5631 S Kimbark Ave, Chicago 60637 **Gayle Neely**	PK-8		569 35	42%	773/535-0970 Fax 773/535-0842
Reavis Math & Sci Elem Sch 834 E 50th St, Chicago 60615 Gail King	PK-8	T	248 16	89%	773/535-1060 Fax 773/535-1032
Shoesmith Elem Sch 1330 E 50th St, Chicago 60615 Sabrina Gates	K-6	T	350 16	73%	773/535-1765 Fax 773/535-1877
Wells Preparatory Elem Acad 249 E 37th St, Chicago 60653 Jeffery White	PK-8	T	324 9	91%	773/535-1204 Fax 773/535-1267
Woodlawn Community Sch 6657 S Kimbark Ave Ste 1, Chicago 60637 Lawanda Bell	PK-6	T	179 7	94%	773/535-0801 Fax 773/535-0773
Ⓨ Woodson Elem Sch 4414 S Evans Ave, Chicago 60653 Tamara Littlejohn	PK-8	MT	308 27	83%	773/535-1280 Fax 773/535-1390

● **Chicago PSD-Network 10** PID: 11931171   773/535-7543
11424 S Western Ave, Chicago 60643

Alfonso Carmona 15

Public Schs..Principal	Grd	Prgm	Enr/#Cls	SN	Phone
Ashburn Elem Sch 8300 S Saint Louis Ave Ste 1, Chicago 60652 Jewel Diaz	PK-8	T	389 20	82%	773/535-7860 Fax 773/535-7867
Barbara Vick Early Chld Center 2554 W 113th St, Chicago 60655 Amy O'Connor	PK-PK		203 7	52%	773/535-2671 Fax 773/535-2783
Ⓨ Barnard Elem Comp Math & Sci 10354 S Charles St, Chicago 60643 Kathleen Valente	PK-8	MT	246 12	84%	773/535-2625 Fax 773/535-2629
Blair Early Childhood Center 6751 W 63rd Pl, Chicago 60638 Elizabeth Hendry	Spec	T	171 27	62%	773/535-2076 Fax 773/535-2362
Byrne Elem Sch 5329 S Oak Park Ave, Chicago 60638 Elizabeth Gallo	K-8	T	593 25	53%	773/535-2170 Fax 773/229-0281
Ⓨ Carroll-Rosenwald Elem Sch 2929 W 83rd St, Chicago 60652 Adell Brock	PK-8	MT	411 9	88%	773/535-9414 Fax 773/535-9568
Claremont Academy Elem Sch 2300 W 64th St, Chicago 60636 Mary Beth Zonca	PK-8	T	401 40	95%	773/535-8110 Fax 773/535-8108
Clissold Elem Sch 2350 W 110th Pl Ste 1, Chicago 60643 Jamonica Marion	PK-8		427 40	38%	773/535-2560 Fax 773/535-2556
Dawes Elem Sch 3810 W 81st Pl, Chicago 60652 Mary Dixon	PK-8	T	941 45	96%	773/535-2350 Fax 773/535-2367
Dore Elem Sch 7134 W 65th St, Chicago 60638 Tai Basurto	PK-8		703 24	49%	773/535-2080 Fax 773/535-2084

79 Student Personnel	91 Safety/Security	275 Response To Intervention	298 Grant Writer/Ptnrships	**School Programs**	**Social Media**
80 Driver Ed/Safety	92 Magnet School	277 Remedial Math K-12	750 Chief Innovation Officer	A = Alternative Program	= Facebook
81 Gifted/Talented	93 Parental Involvement	280 Literacy Coach	751 Chief of Staff	G = Adult Classes	
82 Video Services	95 Tech Prep Program	285 STEM	752 Social Emotional Learning	M = Magnet Program	= Twitter
83 Substance Abuse Prev	97 Chief Information Officer	286 Digital Learning		T = Title I Schoolwide	
84 Erate	98 Chief Technology Officer	288 Common Core Standards	**Other School Types**	V = Career & Tech Ed Programs	
85 AIDS Education	270 Character Education	294 Accountability	Ⓐ = Alternative School		
88 Alternative/At Risk	271 Migrant Education	295 Network System	Ⓒ = Charter School	New Schools are shaded	
89 Multi-Cultural Curriculum	273 Teacher Mentor	296 Title II Programs	Ⓜ = Magnet School	New Superintendents and Principals are bold	
90 Social Work	274 Before/After Sch	297 Webmaster	Ⓨ = Year-Round School	Personnel with email addresses are underscored	

IL—33

Cook County

Public Schs..Principal	Grd	Prgm	Enr/#Cls	SN		
Durkin Park Elem Sch 8445 S Kolin Ave, Chicago 60652 Daniel Redmond	PK-8	T	627 20	83%	773/535-2322 Fax 773/535-2299	
Ⓨ Esmond Elem Sch 1865 W Montvale Ave, Chicago 60643 Angela Tucker	PK-8	MT	242 10	96%	773/535-2650 Fax 773/535-2676	
Fairfield Academy 6201 S Fairfield Ave, Chicago 60629 Claudia Lopez	PK-8	T	498	98%	773/535-9500 Fax 773/535-0438	
Grimes Elem Sch 5450 W 64th Pl Ste 1, Chicago 60638 Judith Carlson	PK-8	T	418 18	80%	773/535-2364 Fax 773/535-2366	
Hale Elem Sch 6140 S Melvina Ave Ste 1, Chicago 60638 Dawn Iles-Gomez	K-8	T	799 28	68%	773/535-2265 Fax 773/535-2275	
Ⓨ Hampton Arts Sch 3434 W 77th St, Chicago 60652 Zaneta Abdul-Ahad	K-8	MT	434	92%	773/535-4030 Fax 773/535-4031	
Ⓨ Hearst Elem Sch 4640 S Lamon Ave Ste 1, Chicago 60638 Teresa Chrobak-Prince	PK-8	MT	330 37	89%	773/535-2376 Fax 773/535-2341	
Ⓨ Hurley Elem Sch 3849 W 69th Pl, Chicago 60629 Angel Aguirre	PK-8	MT	739 40	89%	773/535-2068 Fax 773/535-2059	
Keller Regional Gifted Center 3020 W 108th St, Chicago 60655 Chalese Dunbar	1-8		218 8	24%	773/535-2636 Fax 773/535-2635	
Kellogg Elem Sch 9241 S Leavitt St, Chicago 60643 Cory Overstreet	K-8		258 9	36%	773/535-2590 Fax 773/535-2596	
Mark Twain Elem Sch 5134 S Lotus Ave, Chicago 60638 Laura Paull	PK 8	T	957 45	80%	773/535-2290 Fax 773/535-2248	
Ⓨ McKay Elem Sch 6938 S Washtenaw Ave, Chicago 60629 Dawn Hawk	PK-8	MT	696 43	95%	773/535-9340 Fax 773/535-9443	
Ⓨ Morrill MA & SC Speciality Sch 6011 S Rockwell St, Chicago 60629 Dawn Sydnor	PK-8	MT	561 40	97%	773/535-9288 Fax 773/535-9214	
Ⓜ Owen Scholastic Academy 8247 S Christiana Ave, Chicago 60652 Sheila Morris	K-8	T	255 10	54%	773/535-9330 Fax 773/535-9496	
Richardson Middle Sch 6018 S Karlov Ave, Chicago 60629 Marie Clouston	5-8	T	1,001	96%	773/535-8640 Fax 773/535-8010	
Stevenson Elem Sch 8010 S Kostner Ave, Chicago 60652 Paul O'Toole	PK-8	T	1,071 47	88%	773/535-2280 Fax 773/535-2339	
Sutherland Elem Sch 10015 S Leavitt St, Chicago 60643 Margaret Burns	K-8		659 28	33%	773/535-2580 Fax 773/535-2621	
Ⓜ Vanderpoel Magnet Elem Sch 9510 S Prospect Ave, Chicago 60643 Kia Banks	K-8	T	218 11	65%	773/535-2690 Fax 773/535-2677	

- **Chicago PSD-Network 11** PID: 11931183 773/535-7267
  4655 S Dearborn St, Chicago 60609

Julious Lawson 15

Public Schs..Principal	Grd	Prgm	Enr/#Cls	SN		
Barton Elem Sch 7650 S Wolcott Ave, Chicago 60620 Augusta Smith	PK-8	T	337 25	92%	773/535-3260 Fax 773/535-3271	
Ⓨ Bass Elem Sch 1140 W 66th St, Chicago 60621 Carolyn Jones	PK-8	MT	394 15	95%	773/535-3275 Fax 773/535-3330	
Ⓨ Benjamin Mays Academy 6656 S Normal Blvd, Chicago 60621 Tanyelle Hannah-Reed	PK-8	MT	342 18	74%	773/535-3892 Fax 773/535-3895	
Bond Elem Sch 7050 S May St, Chicago 60621 Valesta Cobbs	PK-8	AMT	240 24	98%	773/535-3480 Fax 773/535-3433	
Cook Elem Sch 8150 S Bishop St, Chicago 60620 El Roy Estes	PK-8	MT	348 23	73%	773/535-3315 Fax 773/535-3383	
Cuffe Math Science Tech Acad 8324 S Racine Ave, Chicago 60620 Lakita Reed	PK-8	MT	222 26	92%	773/535-8250 Fax 773/535-3497	
Earle Elem Sch 2040 W 62nd St, Chicago 60636 Cederrall Petties	PK-8	MT	298 12	96%	773/535-9130 Fax 773/535-9140	
Foster Park Elem Sch 8530 S Wood St, Chicago 60620 Kimberly Harper-Young	PK-8	T	330 25	85%	773/535-2725 Fax 773/535-2740	
Ft Dearborn Elem Sch 9025 S Throop St, Chicago 60620 Vernita Sims	PK-8	T	347 18	100%	773/535-2680 Fax 773/535-2891	
Ⓨ Fulton Elem Sch 5300 S Hermitage Ave, Chicago 60609 Vasiliki Kleros	PK-8	MT	352 29	96%	773/535-9000 Fax 773/535-9464	
Ⓨ Henderson Elem Academy 5650 S Wolcott Ave, Chicago 60636 Marvis Jackson-Ivy	PK-8	MT	225 28	95%	773/535-9080 Fax 773/535-9548	
Holmes Elem Sch 955 W Garfield Blvd, Chicago 60621 Diedre Coleman	PK-8	T	128 25	96%	773/535-9025 Fax 773/535-9127	
Ⓨ Joplin Elem Sch 7931 S Honore St, Chicago 60620 Alene Mason	PK-8	MT	382 25	96%	773/535-3425 Fax 773/535-3442	
Ⓜ Kershaw Elem Sch Ⓨ 6450 S Lowe Ave, Chicago 60621 Tanya Fields	PK-8	MT	238	88%	773/535-3050 Fax 773/535-3677	
Ⓨ King School of Social Justice 644 W 71st St, Chicago 60621 Jasmine Thurmond	PK-8	MT	214 30	100%	773/535-3875 Fax 773/535-3885	
Ⓨ Langford Academy 6010 S Throop St, Chicago 60636 Linda Woods	PK-8	MT	213 22	97%	773/535-9180 Fax 773/535-9428	
Ⓨ Libby Elem Sch 5300 S Loomis Blvd, Chicago 60609 Rochonda Knox	K-8	MT	284 25	89%	773/535-9050 Fax 773/535-9383	
Ⓨ Mahalia Jackson Elem Sch 917 W 88th St, Chicago 60620 Teresa Nagy	PK-8	MT	346 18	82%	773/535-3341 Fax 773/535-3453	
Medgar Evers Elem Sch 9811 S Lowe Ave, Chicago 60628 Caroline Ellis	PK-8	T	218 13	85%	773/535-2565 Fax 773/535-2570	
Nicholson Tech Academy 6006 S Peoria St, Chicago 60621 Mark Carson	PK-8	MT	467 45	97%	773/535-3285 Fax 773/535-3443	
Ⓨ O'Toole Elem Sch 6550 S Seeley Ave, Chicago 60636 King Hall	PK-8	MT	366 30	98%	773/535-9040 Fax 773/535-9093	
Ⓨ Oglesby Elem Sch 7646 S Green St, Chicago 60620 Patricia Miller	PK-8	GMT	362 25	98%	773/535-3390	
Parker Child Parent Center 328 W 69th St, Chicago 60621 Rufina Brown	PK-PK		122 6		773/535-3853	
Parker Community Academy 6800 S Stewart Ave, Chicago 60621 Rufina Brown	PK-8	T	402 36	89%	773/535-3375 Fax 773/535-3336	

1	Superintendent	8	Curric/Instruct K-12	19	Chief Financial Officer	29	Family/Consumer Science
2	Bus/Finance/Purchasing	9	Curric/Instruct Elem	20	Art K-12	30	Adult Education
3	Buildings And Grounds	10	Curric/Instruct Sec	21	Art Elem	31	Career/Sch-to-Work K-12
4	Food Service	11	Federal Program	22	Art Sec	32	Career/Sch-to-Work Elem
5	Transportation	12	Title I	23	Music K-12	33	Career/Sch-to-Work Sec
6	Athletic	13	Title V	24	Music Elem	34	Early Childhood Ed
7	Health Services	14	Asst Superintendent	25	Music Sec	35	Health/Phys Education
		15	Instructional Media Svcs	26	Business Education	36	Guidance Services K-12
		16	Chief Operations Officer	27	Career & Tech Ed	37	Guidance Services Elem
		18	Chief Academic Officer	28	Technology Education	38	Guidance Services Sec

39	Social Studies K-12	49	English/Lang Arts Elem	59	Special Education Elem	69	Academic Assessment
40	Social Studies Sec	50	English/Lang Arts Sec	60	Special Education Sec	70	Research/Development
41	Social Studies Sec	51	Reading K-12	61	Foreign/World Lang K-12	71	Public Information
42	Science K-12	52	Reading Elem	62	Foreign/World Lang Elem	72	Summer School
43	Science Elem	53	Reading Sec	63	Foreign/World Lang Sec	73	Instructional Tech
44	Science Sec	54	Remedial Reading K-12	64	Religious Education K-12	74	Inservice Training
45	Math K-12	55	Remedial Reading Elem	65	Religious Education Elem	75	Marketing/Distributive
46	Math Elem	56	Remedial Reading Sec	66	Religious Education Sec	76	Info Systems
47	Math Sec	57	Bilingual/ELL	67	School Board President	77	Psychological Assess
48	English/Lang Arts K-12	58	Special Education K-12	68	Teacher Personnel	78	Affirmative Action

IL—34

Illinois School Directory — Cook County

School	Grd	Prgm	Enr/#Cls	SN	Phone
ⓜ Randolph Magnet Sch 7316 S Hoyne Ave, Chicago 60636 Elizabeth Meyers	PK-8	MT	397 60	97%	773/535-9015 Fax 773/535-9455
ⓨ Ryder Math & Sci Elem Sch 8716 S Wallace St, Chicago 60620 Aaron Rucker	PK-8	MT	371 30	86%	773/535-3843 Fax 773/535-3883
ⓜ Sir Miles Davis Magnet Academy 6740 S Paulina St, Chicago 60636 Cheryl Armstrong-Belt	K-8	T	152 13	95%	773/535-9120 Fax 773/535-9129
ⓜ Turner-Drew Language Academy 9300 S Princeton Ave, Chicago 60620 Dr Sabrina Jackson	K-8	T	201 18	72%	773/535-5720 Fax 773/535-5203
ⓜ Wendell E Green Elem Sch 1150 W 96th St, Chicago 60643 Tyrone Dowdell	PK-8	T	291 9	86%	773/535-2575 Fax 773/535-2742
ⓨ Wentworth Elem Sch 1340 W 71st St, Chicago 60636 Janelle Thompson	PK-8	MT	389 26	94%	773/535-3394 Fax 773/535-3434
ⓨ Westcott Elem Sch 409 W 80th St, Chicago 60620 Monique Dockery	PK-8	MT	394 23	95%	773/535-3090 Fax 773/535-3099

● **Chicago PSD-Network 12** PID: 11931195   773/535-8975
4655 S Dearborn St, Chicago 60609

Shenthe Parks 15

Public Schs..Principal	Grd	Prgm	Enr/#Cls	SN	Phone
ⓨ Arnold Mireles Academy 9000 S Exchange Ave, Chicago 60617 Evelyn Randle-Robbins	PK-8	MT	440 70	97%	773/535-6360 Fax 773/535-6303
ⓨ Arthur Ashe Elem Sch 8505 S Ingleside Ave, Chicago 60619 Clyde King	PK-8	MT	323 35	92%	773/535-3550 Fax 773/535-3362
ⓨ Brownell Elem Sch 6741 S Michigan Ave, Chicago 60637 Latrice Flowers	PK-6	MT	189 13	99%	773/535-3030 Fax 773/535-3413
ⓜ Burnside Scholastic Academy 650 E 91st Pl, Chicago 60619 Kelly Thigpen	PK-8	T	362	80%	773/535-3300 Fax 773/535-3230
Coles Elem Sch 8441 S Yates Blvd, Chicago 60617 Charlie McSpadden	PK-8	T	348 26	93%	773/535-6550 Fax 773/535-6570
ⓨ Dixon Elem Sch 8306 S Saint Lawrence Ave, Chicago 60619 Terrycita Perry	PK-8	MT	506 35	78%	773/535-3834 Fax 773/535-3811
E A Bouchet Math & Sci Acad 7355 S Jeffery Blvd, Chicago 60649 David Young	PK-8	T	594 68	96%	773/535-0501 Fax 773/535-0559
ⓨ Earhart Elem Opt for Knwl Sch 1710 E 93rd St, Chicago 60617 Dr Brenda Demar-Williams	K-8	MT	186 12	68%	773/535-6416 Fax 773/535-6077
Harold Washington Elem Sch 9130 S University Ave, Chicago 60619 Sherri Walker	PK-8	T	264 25	99%	773/535-6225 Fax 773/535-6277
ⓨ Hoyne Elem Sch 8905 S Crandon Ave, Chicago 60617 Michael Hinton	K-8	MT	198 15	76%	773/535-6425 Fax 773/535-6076
J N Thorp Elem Sch 8914 S Buffalo Ave, Chicago 60617 Sharrone Travis	PK-8	T	296 33	99%	773/535-6250 Fax 773/535-6582
Madison Elem Sch 7433 S Dorchester Ave, Chicago 60619 Allania Moore	PK-8	T	203 26	98%	773/535-0551 Fax 773/535-0582
ⓨ Mann Elem Sch 8050 S Chappel Ave, Chicago 60617 Jeffrey Porter	PK-8	MT	346 27	93%	773/535-6640 Fax 773/535-6664
McDade Classical Sch 8801 S Indiana Ave, Chicago 60619 Stacy Gray	K-6		169 7	27%	773/535-3669 Fax 773/535-3667
Neil Elem Sch 8555 S Michigan Ave, Chicago 60619 Tawane Knox	Spec	T	256 26	90%	773/535-3000 Fax 773/535-3010
New Sullivan Elem Sch 8331 S Mackinaw Ave, Chicago 60617 Kathy McCoy	PK-8	T	394 37	97%	773/535-6585 Fax 773/535-6561
ⓨ Ninos Heroes Community Academy 8344 S Commercial Ave, Chicago 60617 Kimberly Denton	PK-8	MT	320	93%	773/535-6694 Fax 773/535-6673
ⓨ Park Manor Elem Sch 7037 S Rhodes Ave, Chicago 60637 Lashae Merrell	PK-8	MT	249 25	100%	773/535-3070 Fax 773/535-3273
ⓨ Parkside Community Academy 6938 S East End Ave, Chicago 60649 Tori Williams	PK-8	MT	248 13	96%	773/535-0940 Fax 773/535-0966
ⓨ Pirie Elem Fine Arts & Acadmcs 650 E 85th St, Chicago 60619 Senalda Grady	PK-6	MT	238 18	91%	773/535-3435 Fax 773/535-3405
ⓨ Powell Elem Paideia Comm Acad 7511 S South Shore Dr, Chicago 60649 Sheila Barlow	K-8	MT	479 24	95%	773/535-6650 Fax 773/535-6602
ⓨ Revere Elem Sch 1010 E 72nd St, Chicago 60619 Veronica Thompson	PK-8	MT	210 23	98%	773/535-0618 Fax 773/535-0614
ⓜ Robert A Black Magnet Sch 9101 S Euclid Ave, Chicago 60617 Rhonda Butler	K-8	T	427 17	78%	773/535-6390 Fax 773/535-6047
Ruggles Elem Sch 7831 S Prairie Ave, Chicago 60619 Tonya Weatherly	PK-8	T	350 20	82%	773/535-3085 Fax 773/535-3129
Schmid Elem Sch 9755 S Greenwood Ave, Chicago 60628 Andrea Black	PK-8	T	183 10	97%	773/535-6235 Fax 773/535-6092
South Shore Fine Arts Academy 1415 E 70th St, Chicago 60637 Vicki Brown	PK-8	T	354 8	86%	773/535-8340 Fax 773/535-8341
Tanner Elem Sch 7350 S Evans Ave, Chicago 60619 Nicole White	PK-8	T	343 24	97%	773/535-3870 Fax 773/535-3874
Warren Elem Sch 9239 S Jeffery Ave, Chicago 60617 Shontell Smith	PK-8	T	209 13	92%	773/535-6625 Fax 773/535-6698

● **Chicago PSD-Network 13** PID: 11931200   773/535-7525
11424 S Western Ave, Chicago 60643

Daniel Perry 15

Public Schs..Principal	Grd	Prgm	Enr/#Cls	SN	Phone
Aldridge Elem Sch 630 E 131st St, Chicago 60827 Cynthia Treadwell	PK-8	T	199 25	94%	773/535-5614 Fax 773/535-5613
Alex Haley Academy 11411 S Eggleston Ave, Chicago 60628 Sherry Pirtle	PK-8	T	496 19	96%	773/535-5340 Fax 773/535-5782
Bennett Elem Sch 10115 S Prairie Ave, Chicago 60628 Teresa Huggins	PK-8	T	293 39	95%	773/535-5460 Fax 773/535-5577
Bright Sch 10740 S Calhoun Ave, Chicago 60617 Alicia Lewis	PK-8	T	270 30	94%	773/535-6215 Fax 773/535-6373
Burnham Math & Sci Academy 9928 S Crandon Ave, Chicago 60617 Sheryl Freeman	PK-8	T	447 6	95%	773/535-6530 Fax 773/535-6515

Legend:

79 Student Personnel
80 Driver Ed/Safety
81 Gifted/Talented
82 Video Services
83 Substance Abuse Prev
84 Erate
85 AIDS Education
88 Alternative/At Risk
89 Multi-Cultural Curriculum
90 Social Work
91 Safety/Security
92 Magnet School
93 Parental Involvement
95 Tech Prep Program
97 Chief Infomation Officer
98 Chief Technology Officer
270 Character Education
271 Migrant Education
273 Teacher Mentor
274 Before/After Sch
275 Response To Intervention
277 Remedial Math K-12
280 Literacy Coach
285 STEM
286 Digital Learning
288 Common Core Standards
294 Accountability
295 Network System
296 Title II Programs
297 Webmaster
298 Grant Writer/Ptnrships
750 Chief Innovation Officer
751 Chief of Staff
752 Social Emotional Learning

Other School Types
Ⓐ = Alternative School
Ⓒ = Charter School
Ⓜ = Magnet School
Ⓨ = Year-Round School

School Programs
A = Alternative Program
G = Adult Classes
M = Magnet Program
T = Title I Schoolwide
V = Career & Tech Ed Programs

Social Media
🅕 = Facebook
🆃 = Twitter

New Schools are shaded
New Superintendents and Principals are bold
Personnel with email addresses are underscored

Cook County

School	Grd	Prgm	Enr/#Cls	SN	Phone
ⓨ Carver Elem Sch 901 E 133rd Pl, Chicago 60827 Martell Hines	PK-8	MT	402 16	99%	773/535-5674 Fax 773/535-5455
ⓨ Cullen Elem Sch 10650 S Eberhart Ave, Chicago 60628 Bud Bryant	K-8	MT	193 20	92%	773/535-5375 Fax 773/535-5366
ⓨ DuBois Elem Sch 330 E 133rd St, Chicago 60827 Vanessa Johnson	PK-8	MT	200 15	97%	773/535-5582 Fax 773/535-5587
ⓨ Dunne Tech Academy 10845 S Union Ave, Chicago 60628 Chandra Byrd-Wright	PK-8	MT	199 22		773/535-5517 Fax 773/535-5018
ⓨ Ed White Elem Career Academy 1136 W 122nd St, Chicago 60643 Maya Sadder	PK-8	MT	157 5	92%	773/535-5672 Fax 773/535-5644
Edward E Sadlowski Elem Sch 3930 E 105th St, Chicago 60617 Kenya Underwood	PK-8	T	572	86%	773/535-8040 Fax 773/535-8020
ⓨ Fernwood Elem Sch 10041 S Union Ave, Chicago 60628 Robert Towner	PK-8	MT	259 23	92%	773/535-2700 Fax 773/535-2711
ⓜ Gallistel Language Academy 10347 S Ewing Ave, Chicago 60617 Kimberly Nelson	PK-8	T	587 37	93%	773/535-6540 Fax 773/535-6569
George Pullman Elem Sch 11311 S Forrestville Ave, Chicago 60628 Romeldia Salter	PK-8	T	310 30	93%	773/535-5395 Fax 773/535-5393
George Washington Elem Sch 3611 E 114th St, Chicago 60617 Sergio Ramirez	PK-8	T	663 31	70%	773/535-5010 Fax 773/535-5098
Henry Clay Elem Sch 13231 S Burley Ave, Chicago 60633 Jennifer Laurincik	PK-8	T	522 25	92%	773/535-5600 Fax 773/535-5606
ⓨ Higgins Community Academy 11710 S Morgan St, Chicago 60643 Crystal Dorsey	PK-8	MT	257 19	89%	773/535-5625 Fax 773/535-5623
Jesse Owens Community Academy 12302 S State St, Chicago 60628 Katina Stovail-Brown	PK-8	T	360 18	94%	773/535-5475 Fax 773/535-5483
John L Marsh Elem Sch 9822 S Exchange Ave, Chicago 60617 Jose Torres	PK-8	T	699 25	87%	773/535-6430 Fax 773/535-6446
ⓨ Johnnie Colemon Academy 1441 W 119th St, Chicago 60643 Paulette Williams	PK-8	MT	189 26	82%	773/535-3975 Fax 773/535-3979
Langston Hughes Elem Sch 240 W 104th St, Chicago 60628 Kimbreana Taylor-Goode	PK-8	T	434 28	83%	773/535-5075 Fax 773/535-5082
ⓨ Lavizzo Elem Sch 138 W 109th St, Chicago 60628 Tracey Stelly	PK-8	MT	393 15	97%	773/535-5300 Fax 773/535-5313
ⓨ Marcus Garvey Elem Sch 10309 S Morgan St Ste 1, Chicago 60643 Sabrina Anderson	PK-8	MT	233 25	98%	773/535-2763 Fax 773/535-2761
ⓨ Metcalfe Community Academy 12339 S Normal Ave, Chicago 60628 Stephen Fabiyi	PK-8	MTV	309 32	98%	773/535-5590 Fax 773/535-5758
ⓨ Mt Vernon Elem Sch 10540 S Morgan St, Chicago 60643 Raquel Davis	PK-8	MT	224 17	96%	773/535-2825 Fax 773/535-2827
Poe Classical Sch 10538 S Langley Ave, Chicago 60628 Eric Dockery	K-6		194 7	37%	773/535-5525 Fax 773/535-5213
ⓨ R Brown Academy 12607 S Union Ave, Chicago 60628 Steven Askew	PK-8	MT	295 16	90%	773/535-5385 Fax 773/535-5359
ⓨ Shoop Math-Sci Tech Elem Acad 11140 S Bishop St, Chicago 60643 Natasha Topps	PK-8	MT	440 34	97%	773/535-2715 Fax 773/535-2714
ⓨ Smith Elem Sch 744 E 103rd St, Chicago 60628 Tiffany Brown	PK-8	MT	306 20	96%	773/535-5689 Fax 773/535-8550
Taylor Elem Sch 9912 S Avenue H, Chicago 60617 Dawn Hill	PK-8	T	359 40	97%	773/535-6240 Fax 773/535-6232
ⓨ Whistler Elem Sch 11533 S Ada St Ste 1, Chicago 60643 Katina Manuel	PK-8	MT	319 35	90%	773/535-5560 Fax 773/535-5589

● **Chicago PSD-Network 14** PID: 12313247   773/535-8193
110 N Paulina St, Chicago 60612

Laura Lemone 15

Public Schs..Principal	Grd	Prgm	Enr/#Cls	SN	Phone
ⓜ Disney II Mag Sch-Kedvale 3815 N Kedvale Ave, Chicago 60641 Kathleen Speth	PK-6		380	33%	773/534-3750 Fax 773/534-3757
ⓜ Disney II Mag Sch-Lawndale 3900 N Lawndale Ave, Chicago 60618 Kathleen Speth	7-12		820	48%	773/534-5010 Fax 773/534-5199
Foreman College & Career Acad 3235 N Leclaire Ave, Chicago 60641 Anthony Escamilla	9-12	AGT	629 45	94%	773/534-3400 Fax 773/534-3684
Kelvyn Park High Sch 4343 W Wrightwood Ave, Chicago 60639 Keith Adams	7-12	AGT	435	97%	773/534-4200 Fax 773/534-4507
Lake View High Sch 4015 N Ashland Ave, Chicago 60613 Paul Karafiol	9-12	T	1,369 60	72%	773/534-5440 Fax 773/534-5908
Lane Technical College Prep HS 2501 W Addison St, Chicago 60618 Brian Tennison	7-12		4,488 200	44%	773/534-5400 Fax 773/534-5544
Mather High Sch 5835 N Lincoln Ave, Chicago 60659 Peter Auffant	9-12	TV	1,649 70	86%	773/534-2350 Fax 773/534-2424
Nicholas Senn High Sch 5900 N Glenwood Ave, Chicago 60660 Mary Beck	9-12	T	1,597	80%	773/534-2365 Fax 773/534-2369
Northside Learning Center 3730 W Bryn Mawr Ave, Chicago 60659 Karren Ray	Spec	T	237 35	85%	773/534-5180 Fax 773/534-5188
Ray Graham Training Center 2347 S Wabash Ave, Chicago 60616 Kusan Thomas	Spec	TV	201 14	92%	773/534-9257 Fax 773/534-9247
Roosevelt High Sch 3436 W Wilson Ave, Chicago 60625 Daniel Kramer	9-12	T	1,058	94%	773/534-5000 Fax 773/534-5044
Schurz High Sch 3601 N Milwaukee Ave, Chicago 60641 Anthony Rodriguez	9-12	TV	1,553 108	89%	773/534-3420 Fax 773/534-3573
Steinmetz Academic Center 3030 N Mobile Ave, Chicago 60634 Jaime Jaramillo	9-12	TV	1,159 75	83%	773/534-3030 Fax 773/534-3151
Sullivan High Sch 6631 N Bosworth Ave, Chicago 60626 Chad Thomas	9-12	T	631 40	88%	773/534-2000 Fax 773/534-2141
Taft High Sch 6530 W Bryn Mawr Ave, Chicago 60631 Mark Grishaber	7-12	V	3,881	47%	773/534-1000 Fax 773/534-1027
Uplift Community High Sch 900 W Wilson Ave, Chicago 60640 Tyrese Graham	9-12	T	106 42	91%	773/534-2875 Fax 773/534-2876

1	Superintendent	8	Curric/Instruct K-12	19	Chief Financial Officer	29	Family/Consumer Science	39	Social Studies K-12
2	Bus/Finance/Purchasing	9	Curric/Instruct Elem	20	Art K-12	30	Adult Education	40	Social Studies Elem
3	Buildings And Grounds	10	Curric/Instruct Sec	21	Art Elem	31	Career/Sch-to-Work K-12	41	Social Studies Sec
4	Food Service	11	Federal Program	22	Art Sec	32	Career/Sch-to-Work Elem	42	Science K-12
5	Transportation	12	Title I	23	Music K-12	33	Career/Sch-to-Work Sec	43	Science Elem
6	Athletic	13	Title V	24	Music Elem	34	Early Childhood Ed	44	Science Sec
7	Health Services	15	Asst Superintendent	25	Music Sec	35	Health/Phys Education	45	Math K-12
		16	Instructional Media Svcs	26	Business Education	36	Guidance Services K-12	46	Math Elem
		17	Chief Operations Officer	27	Career & Tech Ed	37	Guidance Services Elem	47	Math Sec
		18	Chief Academic Officer	28	Technology Education	38	Guidance Services Sec	48	English/Lang Arts K-12

49	English/Lang Arts Elem	59	Special Education Elem	69	Academic Assessment
50	English/Lang Arts Sec	60	Special Education Sec	70	Research/Development
51	Reading K-12	61	Foreign/World Lang K-12	71	Public Information
52	Reading Elem	62	Foreign/World Lang Elem	72	Summer School
53	Reading Sec	63	Foreign/World Lang Sec	73	Instructional Tech
54	Remedial Reading K-12	64	Religious Education K-12	74	Inservice Training
55	Remedial Reading Elem	65	Religious Education Elem	75	Marketing/Distributive
56	Remedial Reading Sec	66	Religious Education Sec	76	Info Systems
57	Bilingual/ELL	67	School Board President	77	Psychological Assess
58	Special Education K-12	68	Teacher Personnel	78	Affirmative Action

Illinois School Directory — Cook County

School	Grd	Prgm	Enr/#Cls	SN	Phone
Vaughn Occupational High Sch 4355 N Linder Ave, Chicago 60641 Noel McNally	Spec	T	229 20	73%	773/534-3600 Fax 773/534-3631
ⓜ Von Steuben Metro Science Ctr 5039 N Kimball Ave, Chicago 60625 Jennifer Sutton	9-12	T	1,707 50	66%	773/534-5100 Fax 773/534-5210

● Chicago PSD-Network 15 PID: 12313259   773/535-8232
110 N Paulina St, Chicago 60612

Michael Boraz 15

Public Schs..Principal	Grd	Prgm	Enr/#Cls	SN	Phone
AL Raby High Sch 3545 W Fulton Blvd, Chicago 60624 Michelle Harrell	9-12	T	254 45	94%	773/534-6755 Fax 773/534-6938
Austin College & Career Acad 231 N Pine Ave, Chicago 60644 Simone Griffin	9-12	T	227	94%	773/534-0660 Fax 773/534-6046
Clemente Cmty Academy 1147 N Western Ave, Chicago 60622 Fernando Mojica	9-12	TV	688	88%	773/534-4000 Fax 773/534-4003
ⓜ Curie Metropolitan High Sch 4959 S Archer Ave, Chicago 60632 Allison Tingwall	9-12	TV	3,062	88%	773/535-2100 Fax 773/535-2049
Douglass Academy High Sch 543 N Waller Ave, Chicago 60644 Abdul Muhammad	9-12	TV	48 40	85%	773/534-6176 Fax 773/534-6172
Grtr Lawndale Social Justice 3120 S Kostner Ave, Chicago 60623 Omar Chilous	9-12	T	225	95%	773/535-4300 Fax 773/535-4271
Hancock College Prep HS 4034 W 56th St, Chicago 60629 Devon Herrick	9-12	T	1,032 45	82%	773/535-2410 Fax 773/535-2434
John Marshall Metro High Sch 3250 W Adams St, Chicago 60624 Jammie Poole	9-12	TV	258 66	97%	773/534-6455 Fax 773/534-6409
ⓜ M Clark Academy Prep Magnet HS 5101 W Harrison St, Chicago 60644 Charles Anderson	9-12	GTV	536 41	76%	773/534-6250 Fax 773/534-6292
Manley Career Academy 2935 W Polk St, Chicago 60612 Trista Harper	Voc	T	172 60	85%	773/534-6900 Fax 773/534-6924
Multicultural Acad Scholarship 3120 S Kostner Ave, Chicago 60623 Maria Amador	9-12	T	221	95%	773/535-4242 Fax 773/535-4273
North Grand High Sch 4338 W Wabansia Ave, Chicago 60639 Emily Feltes	9-12	TV	1,052	89%	773/534-8520 Fax 773/534-8535
Ogden Elem Sch 24 W Walton St, Chicago 60610 David Domovic	K-4		1,014 25		773/534-8110 Fax 773/534-8017
Ogden International HS-West 1250 W Erie St, Chicago 60642 **Devon Herrick**	9-12		649 36	64%	773/534-0866 Fax 773/534-0869
Prosser Career Academy 2148 N Long Ave, Chicago 60639 **Sandra Shimon**	Voc	AT	1,236 48	89%	773/534-3200 Fax 773/534-3382
Richard T Crane Med Prep HS 2245 W Jackson Blvd, Chicago 60612 Fareeda Shabazz	9-11	T	422	87%	773/534-7600 Fax 773/534-7612
ⓐ Simpson Acad for Young Women 1321 S Paulina St, Chicago 60608 Sherita Carter-King	6-12	GTV	23 13	97%	773/534-7812 Fax 773/534-7819
Wells Community Academy HS 936 N Ashland Ave, Chicago 60622 Michael Stosek	9-12	GTV	351 40	90%	773/534-7010 Fax 773/534-7078
Westinghouse College Prep 3223 W Franklin Blvd, Chicago 60624 Kerry Leuschel	9-12	TV	1,302 40	77%	773/534-6400 Fax 773/534-6422
World Language Academy 3120 S Kostner Ave, Chicago 60623 Brian Rogers	9-12	T	358	97%	773/535-4334 Fax 773/254-8470

● Chicago PSD-Network 16 PID: 12313261   773/535-8240
110 N Paulina St, Chicago 60612

Megan Hougard 15

Public Schs..Principal	Grd	Prgm	Enr/#Cls	SN	Phone
Air Force Academy High Sch 3630 S Wells St, Chicago 60609 Yashika Eggleston	9-10	T	190 22	87%	773/535-1590 Fax 773/535-1847
Bogan Computer Tech High Sch 3939 W 79th St, Chicago 60652 Alahrie Aziz-Sims	Voc	T	751 100	90%	773/535-2180 Fax 773/535-2165
ⓐ Consuela B York Alt High Sch ⓨ 2700 S California Ave, Chicago 60608 Sharnette Sims	9-12	MT	106 35	98%	773/535-7021 Fax 773/535-7109
Englewood STEM High Sch 6835 S Normal Blvd, Chicago 60621 Conrad Timbers-Ausar	9-9		695		773/535-3685 Fax 773/535-3680
Farragut Career Academy 2345 S Christiana Ave, Chicago 60623 Tonya Hammaker	9-12	AGTV	563 92	97%	773/534-1300 Fax 773/534-1336
Gage Park High Sch 5630 S Rockwell St, Chicago 60629 Tamika Ball	9-12	TV	354 60	97%	773/535-9230 Fax 773/535-9411
Harper High Sch 6520 S Wood St, Chicago 60636 Leonetta Sanders	9-12	TV	21 70	91%	773/535-9150 Fax 773/535-9090
Hubbard High Sch 6200 S Hamlin Ave, Chicago 60629 Angelica Altamirano	9-12	T	1,724 55	96%	773/535-2200 Fax 773/535-2218
John Hope College Prep HS 5515 S Lowe Ave, Chicago 60621 Michael Durr	10-12	T	23 45	87%	773/535-3160 Fax 773/535-3444
Kennedy High Sch 6325 W 56th St, Chicago 60638 George Szkapiak	9-12	TV	1,491 50	66%	773/535-2325 Fax 773/535-2485
Lindblom Math Science Academy 6130 S Wolcott Ave, Chicago 60636 Wayne Bevis	7-12	T	1,416 33	64%	773/535-9300 Fax 773/535-9314
Morgan Park High Sch 1744 W Pryor Ave, Chicago 60643 Femi Skanes	7-12	T	1,094	86%	773/535-2550 Fax 773/535-2706
ⓐ Nancy B Jefferson Alt High Sch ⓨ 1100 S Hamilton Ave, Chicago 60612 Leonard Harris	5-12	MT	122 40	79%	312/433-7110 Fax 312/433-4442
Percy L Julian High Sch 10330 S Elizabeth St, Chicago 60643 Myron Hester	9-12	TV	371 60	86%	773/535-5170 Fax 773/535-5230
Richards Career Academy 5009 S Laflin St, Chicago 60609 Ellen Kennedy	Voc	T	244 38	99%	773/535-4945 Fax 773/535-4883
Sarah E Goode STEM Academy 7651 S Homan Ave, Chicago 60652 Armando Rodriguez	9-12	T	956	86%	773/535-7875 Fax 773/535-7877
ⓨ Spry Community Links High Sch 2400 S Marshall Blvd, Chicago 60623 Francisco Borras	9-12	MT	113 12	93%	773/534-1997 Fax 773/534-0354
Team Englewood Cmty Academy HS 6201 S Stewart Ave, Chicago 60621 Michelle Russell	9-12	T	180		773/535-3530 Fax 773/535-3586

---

79 Student Personnel
80 Driver Ed/Safety
81 Gifted/Talented
82 Video Services
83 Substance Abuse Prev
84 Erate
85 AIDS Education
88 Alternative/At Risk
89 Multi-Cultural Curriculum
90 Social Work

91 Safety/Security
92 Magnet School
93 Parental Involvement
95 Tech Prep Program
97 Chief Infomation Officer
98 Chief Technology Officer
270 Character Education
271 Migrant Education
273 Teacher Mentor
274 Before/After Sch

275 Response To Intervention
277 Remedial Math K-12
280 Literacy Coach
285 STEM
286 Digital Learning
288 Common Core Standards
294 Accountability
295 Network System
296 Title II Programs
297 Webmaster

298 Grant Writer/Ptnrships
750 Chief Innovation Officer
751 Chief of Staff
752 Social Emotional Learning

Other School Types
ⓐ = Alternative School
ⓒ = Charter School
ⓜ = Magnet School
ⓨ = Year-Round School

School Programs
A = Alternative Program
G = Adult Classes
M = Magnet Program
T = Title I Schoolwide
V = Career & Tech Ed Programs

Social Media
🅕 = Facebook
🅣 = Twitter

New Schools are shaded
New Superintendents and Principals are bold
Personnel with email addresses are underscored

IL—37

Cook County   Market Data Retrieval

ⓨ Thomas Kelly College Prep 9-12 GMTV 1,832 94% 773/535-4900
4136 S California Ave, Chicago 60632   80   Fax 773/535-4841
Raul Magdaleno

Tilden Career Community Acad 9-12 TV 205 93% 773/535-1625
4747 S Union Ave, Chicago 60609   Fax 773/535-4651
Dawn Ramos

• **Chicago PSD-Network 17** PID: 12313273   773/535-8520
110 N Paulina St, Chicago 60612

Lauryn Fullerton 15

Public Schs..Principal	Grd	Prgm	Enr/#Cls	SN	
Bronzeville Scholastic Inst 4934 S Wabash Ave, Chicago 60615 Dr Demetra Starks	9-12	T	83 30	72%	773/535-1150 Fax 773/535-1228
Carver Military Academy 13100 S Doty Ave, Chicago 60827 Steven Rouse	9-12	T	451 60	85%	773/535-5250 Fax 773/535-5037
Chicago Military Academy 3519 S Giles Ave, Chicago 60653 Octavio Casas	9-12	T	287 55	74%	773/534-9750 Fax 773/534-9760
Chicago Vocational Career Acad 2100 E 87th St, Chicago 60617 Douglas MacLin	Voc	GT	840	93%	773/535-7990 Fax 773/535-7993
Christian Fenger Academy HS 11220 S Wallace St, Chicago 60628 Richard Smith	8-12	GTV	245 88	93%	773/535-5430 Fax 773/535-5444
Corliss Early College STEM HS 821 E 103rd St, Chicago 60628 Ali Muhammad	9-12	T	302 84	91%	773/535-5115 Fax 773/535-5511
D H Williams Medical Prep HS 4934 S Wabash Ave, Chicago 60615 Jullanar Naselli	9-12	TV	113 20	94%	773/535-1120 Fax 773/535-1004
Dunbar Voc Career Academy 3000 S King Dr, Chicago 60616 Gerald Morrow	Voc	GT	412	96%	773/534-9000 Fax 773/534-9250
Gwendolyn Brooks Coll Prep Aca 250 E 111th St, Chicago 60628 Shannae Jackson	9-12	TV	1,001 55	68%	773/535-9930 Fax 773/535-9939
Harlan Community Academy HS 9652 S Michigan Ave, Chicago 60628 Ramona Outlaw	9-12	TV	285 30	95%	773/535-5400 Fax 773/535-5061
Hirsch Metro High Sch 7740 S Ingleside Ave, Chicago 60619 David Narain	9-12	TV	176 40	99%	773/535-3100 Fax 773/535-3240
Hyde Park Academy High Sch 6220 S Stony Island Ave, Chicago 60637 Antonio Ross	9-12	GTV	785 87	97%	773/535-0880 Fax 773/535-0633
James H Bowen Sch 2710 E 89th St Ste 1, Chicago 60617 Priscilla Horton	9-12	T	220 25	86%	773/535-7650 Fax 773/535-6489
Kenwood Academy 5015 S Blackstone Ave, Chicago 60615 Karen Calloway	7-12	TV	2,080 110	57%	773/535-1350 Fax 773/535-1408
Martin L King College Prep HS 4445 S Drexel Blvd, Chicago 60653 Brian Kelly	9-12	TV	459 80	79%	773/535-1180 Fax 773/535-1658
Simeon Career Academy 8147 S Vincennes Ave, Chicago 60620 Dr Trista Harper	Voc	T	1,423 200	89%	773/535-3200 Fax 773/535-3465
South Shore Intl Clg High Sch 1955 E 75th St, Chicago 60649 Towanna Butler	9-12	T	582	82%	773/535-8350
Washington High Sch 3535 E 114th St Ste 1, Chicago 60617 Barbara San-Roman	9-12	TV	1,484	86%	773/535-5725 Fax 773/535-5038

• **Chicago PSD-Options** PID: 11559424   773/553-1530
42 W Madison St Fl 3, Chicago 60602

Zabrina Evans 15

Public Schs..Principal	Grd	Prgm	Enr/#Cls	SN	
ⓒ Academy for Global Citizenship 4647 W 47th St, Chicago 60632 Saskia Rombouts \ **Berenice Rangel**	K-8	T	466	71%	773/582-1100 Fax 773/582-1101
ⓒ Acero CS-Bart De Las Casas ES [156] 1641 W 16th St, Chicago 60608 Marissa Akason	K-8		265 9	88%	312/432-3224 Fax 312/432-1066
ⓒ Acero CS-Brighton Park ES [156] 4420 S Fairfield Ave, Chicago 60632 Laura Castle	K-8		450	95%	312/455-5434
ⓒ Acero CS-Carlos Fuentes ES [156] 2845 W Barry Ave, Chicago 60618 Joanne Tanner	K-8		540	91%	773/279-9826 Fax 773/279-9852
ⓒ Acero CS-Esmeralda Santiago ES [156] 2510 W Cortez St, Chicago 60622 Melissa Sweazy	K-8		275	95%	312/455-5410 Fax 312/455-5411
ⓒ Acero CS-Ines De La Cruz [156] 7416 N Ridge Blvd, Chicago 60645 Molly Robinson	K-12		657	93%	312/455-5440 Fax 312/455-5441
ⓒ Acero CS-Jovita Idar Elem Sch [156] 5050 S Homan Ave, Chicago 60632 Melinda Jean-Baptiste	K-8		561	92%	312/455-5450 Fax 312/455-5451
ⓒ Acero CS-Major Garcia HS [156] 4248 W 47th St 3rd Fl, Chicago 60632 Brian Chelmecki	9-12		618	93%	773/579-3480 Fax 773/376-5785
ⓒ Acero CS-Marquez ES [156] 2916 W 47th St, Chicago 60632 Allison Hansen	K-8	G	570	92%	773/321-2200 Fax 773/321-2250
ⓒ Acero CS-Octavio Paz ES [156] 2651 W 23rd St, Chicago 60608 Karem Gomez	K-8		319 15	97%	773/890-1054 Fax 773/890-1069
ⓒ Acero CS-Omar Torres ES [156] 4248 W 47th St, Chicago 60632 Jill Bousson	K-8		608	88%	773/579-3475 Fax 773/376-5645
ⓒ Acero CS-Roberto Clemente ES [156] 2050 N Natchez Ave, Chicago 60707 Christina Laino	K-8		534	88%	312/455-5425 Fax 312/455-5456
ⓒ Acero CS-Rufino Tamayo ES [156] 5135 S California Ave, Chicago 60632 Matthew Katz	K-8		288 9	92%	773/434-6355 Fax 773/434-5036
ⓒ Acero CS-Sandra Cisneros ES [156] 2744 W Pershing Rd, Chicago 60632 **Jill Keller**	K-8		520	95%	773/376-8830 Fax 773/376-8825
ⓒ Acero CS-Victoria Soto HS [156] 5025 S Saint Louis Ave, Chicago 60632 Kelly Smith	9-12		541	90%	312/455-5446 Fax 312/455-5447
ⓒ Acero CS-Zizumbo ES [156] 4248 W 47th St 1st Fl, Chicago 60632 Christopher Allen	K-8		626	88%	773/579-3470 Fax 773/376-5605
ⓒ Ahs-Passages Charter Sch 1643 W Bryn Mawr Ave, Chicago 60660 Maritza Torres	PK-8	T	423 22	84%	773/433-3530 Fax 773/769-3229
ⓒ Alain Locke Charter Academy ⓨ 3141 W Jackson Blvd, Chicago 60612 Patrick Love	PK-8	MT	470 12	87%	773/265-7232 Fax 773/265-7258
ⓒ Art In Motion 7415 S East End Ave, Chicago 60649 Kara Bickman May	7-8		195		773/820-9426
ⓒ Aspira Business & Finance HS [130] 2989 N Milwaukee Ave, Chicago 60618 Raul Guerra	9-9		50	66%	773/303-3559

1	Superintendent	8	Curric/Instruct K-12	19	Chief Financial Officer	29	Family/Consumer Science	39	Social Studies K-12	49	English/Lang Arts Elem	59	Special Education Elem	69	Academic Assessment
2	Bus/Finance/Purchasing	9	Curric/Instruct Elem	20	Art K-12	30	Adult Education	40	Social Studies Elem	50	English/Lang Arts Sec	60	Special Education Sec	70	Research/Development
3	Buildings And Grounds	10	Curric/Instruct Sec	21	Art Elem	31	Career/Sch-to-Work K-12	41	Social Studies Sec	51	Reading K-12	61	Foreign/World Lang K-12	71	Public Information
4	Food Service	11	Federal Program	22	Art Sec	32	Career/Sch-to-Work Elem	42	Science K-12	52	Reading Elem	62	Foreign/World Lang Elem	72	Summer School
5	Transportation	12	Title I	23	Music K-12	33	Career/Sch-to-Work Sec	43	Science Elem	53	Reading Sec	63	Foreign/World Lang Sec	73	Instructional Tech
6	Athletic	13	Title V	24	Music Elem	34	Early Childhood Ed	44	Science Sec	54	Remedial Reading K-12	64	Religious Education K-12	74	Inservice Training
7	Health Services	15	Asst Superintendent	25	Music Sec	35	Health/Phys Education	45	Math K-12	55	Remedial Reading Elem	65	Religious Education Elem	75	Marketing/Distributive
		16	Instructional Media Svcs	26	Business Education	36	Guidance Services K-12	46	Math Elem	56	Remedial Reading Sec	66	Religious Education Sec	76	Info Systems
		17	Chief Operations Officer	27	Career & Tech Ed	37	Guidance Services Elem	47	Math Sec	57	Bilingual/ELL	67	School Board President	77	Psychological Assess
		18	Chief Academic Officer	28	Technology Education	38	Guidance Services Sec	48	English/Lang Arts K-12	58	Special Education K-12	68	Teacher Personnel	78	Affirmative Action

Illinois School Directory — Cook County

School	Grades	Type	Enroll	%	Phone
© Aspira Chtr-Early College HS [130] 3119 N Pulaski Rd, Chicago 60641 Brenda Stolle	9-12		328		773/243-1626 Fax 773/289-0427
© Aspira Haugan Middle Sch [130] Ⓨ 3729 W Leland Ave, Chicago 60625 Erica Pacheco	6-8	M	306	95%	773/303-3549 Fax 773/267-3568
© Bronzeville Academy CS 4930 S Cottage Grove Ave, Chicago 60615 Leticia Lichipin	K-8	T	197	99%	773/285-8040
Ⓐ Camelot Safe ES & HS 7877 S Coles Ave, Chicago 60649 Joe Haley	4-12	T	26		773/902-2487 Fax 773/902-7961
Ⓐ Camelot-Chicago Excel Roseland 1257 W 111th St, Chicago 60643 Glenda Forbes	9-12	T	294	85%	773/629-8379
© Camelot-Excel Englewood HS 7141 S Morgan St, Chicago 60621 Kevin Sweetland	9-12	T	265	91%	773/675-6654 Fax 773/675-6358
© Camelot-Excel Southshore HS 7530 S South Shore Dr, Chicago 60649 Anthony Haley	9-12	T	145	75%	773/902-7800 Fax 773/902-7615
© Camelot-Excel Southwest HS 7050 S Washtenaw Ave, Chicago 60629 Lisa Sykes	9-12	T	89	85%	773/424-0721 Fax 773/424-0746
© Catalyst CS-Circle Rock [159] 5608 W Washington Blvd, Chicago 60644 Elizabeth Dunn	K-8	T	519	81%	773/945-5025 Fax 312/626-2345
© Catalyst CS-Maria [159] 6727 S California Ave, Chicago 60629 Dawn Sandoval	K-12	T	1,095	93%	773/993-1770 Fax 773/993-1771
© Chicago Collegiate Charter Sch 11816 S Indiana Ave, Chicago 60628 Tracie Sanlin	4-9	T	374	84%	773/536-9098 Fax 773/264-5792
© Chicago HS for the Arts 2714 W Augusta Blvd, Chicago 60622 **Teresa Milsap**	9-12		611	37%	773/534-9710 Fax 773/534-4022
© Chicago Math & Sci Academy [161] 7212 N Clark St, Chicago 60626 Aydin Kara	6-12	T	604	91%	773/761-8960 Fax 773/761-8961
Chicago Tech Academy HS 1301 W 14th St, Chicago 60608 Keith Palz	9-12	T	272	89%	773/534-7755 Fax 773/534-7757
© Chicago Virtual Charter Sch [336] 38 S Peoria St, Chicago 60607 Erik Toman \ Rebecca Davis-Dobson	K-12	T	673 8	64%	773/535-6100 Fax 773/535-6633
© Christopher House Charter Sch 5235 W Belden St, Chicago 60639 Kristin Novy	K-3	T	222	83%	773/922-7500 Fax 773/922-7559
© CICS-Avalon/S Shore [167] 1501 E 83rd Pl, Chicago 60619 Marquis Washington \ Mary Griffin	K-8		448 17	90%	773/721-0858 Fax 773/731-0142
© CICS-Basil [167] 1816 W Garfield Blvd, Chicago 60609 Dayna Sanders \ Michelle Mathews-Ndely	K-8		709	96%	773/778-9455 Fax 773/778-9456
© CICS-Bucktown 2235 N Hamilton Ave, Chicago 60647 Ms O'Connell	K-8		676 24	75%	773/645-3321 Fax 773/645-3323
© CICS-Chicago Quest [160] 1443 N Ogden Ave, Chicago 60610 Zataya Shackelford	9-12		258	92%	773/565-2100 Fax 312/951-2906
© CICS-Irving Park 3820 N Spaulding Ave, Chicago 60618 Karin Breo	K-8		557 18	59%	773/433-5000 Fax 773/433-5009
© CICS-Lloyd Bond 13300 S Langley Ave, Chicago 60827 Tyson Daniel	K-6		338	98%	773/468-1300 Fax 773/253-0988
© CICS-Loomis Longwood Mid HS 1309 W 95th St, Chicago 60643 Lindsey Girard \ Jill Cannon \ Maria Freeman	K-12		1,285 63	88%	773/238-5330 Fax 773/238-5350
© CICS-Loomis Primary 9535 S Loomis Ave, Chicago 60643 Lindsey Girard	K-2		546 30	91%	773/429-8955 Fax 773/429-8441
© CICS-Northtown Academy [160] 3900 W Peterson Ave Ste 1, Chicago 60659 Torry Bennett	9-12		920	77%	773/478-3655 Fax 773/478-6029
© CICS-Prairie 11530 S Prairie Ave, Chicago 60628 Ms Barrera	K-8		426 15	95%	773/928-0480 Fax 773/928-6971
© CICS-Ralph Ellison [160] 1817 W 80th St, Chicago 60620 Taquia Hylton	9-12		346 15	92%	773/478-4434 Fax 773/224-2594
© CICS-Washington Park ES [167] 110 E 61st St, Chicago 60637 Alysson Malgieri \ Shaymora Banks	K-8		474 17	93%	773/324-3300 Fax 773/324-3302
© CICS-West Belden 2245 N McVicker Ave Ste 1, Chicago 60639 **S Collins**	K-8		530 18	86%	773/637-9430 Fax 773/637-9791
© CICS-Wrightwood [160] 8130 S California Ave, Chicago 60652 Derrick Orr	K-8		750 24	88%	773/434-4575 Fax 773/471-6178
© Epic Academy 8255 S Houston Ave, Chicago 60617 Andromeda Bellamy	9-12	T	545	96%	773/535-7930 Fax 773/535-7934
© Erie Elem Charter Sch 1405 N Washtenaw Ave, Chicago 60622 Kim Kays	K-8	T	413	78%	773/486-7161 Fax 773/486-7234
© Foundations College Prep CS 1233 W 109th Pl, Chicago 60643 Jillian Carew	6-12		110	95%	773/298-5800
© Frazier Preparatory Academy [126] 3711 W Douglas Blvd Ste 309, Chicago 60623 Donald Gordon	PK-8	T	320 18	97%	773/521-1303 Fax 773/521-1365
© Great Lakes Acad Charter Sch 8401 S Saginaw Ave, Chicago 60617 Katherine Myers	K-2	T	125	86%	773/530-3040 Fax 773/530-3039
© Hope Institute Learning Acad 1628 W Washington Blvd, Chicago 60612 Michael Jakubowski	K-5	T	331	88%	773/534-7405 Fax 773/534-7623
© Horizon Sci Acad SW Chicago [161] 5401 S Western Blvd, Chicago 60609 Matt Yildiz	K-12		736	95%	773/498-3355 Fax 773/498-4984
© Instituto Hlth Sci Career Acad 2520 S Western Ave Ste 201, Chicago 60608 Elias Alonzo	9-12	T	741	95%	773/890-8020 Fax 773/376-8573
Ⓐ Instituto Justice Ldrshp Acad © 2570 S Blue Island Ave, Chicago 60608 Helen Sennhoplz	9-12	TV	165	97%	773/890-0055 Fax 773/890-1537
© Instituto-Lozano High Sch 2570 S Blue Island Ave, Chicago 60608 Christine Diaz	9-12		99		773/890-8060 Fax 773/890-1537
© Instituto-Lozano Mastery HS 2570 S Blue Island Ave, Chicago 60608 Stephanie Vazquez	9-12		38		773/890-8060 Fax 773/890-1537
© Intrinsic School-Belmont 4540 W Belmont Ave, Chicago 60641 Michelle Trojan	7-12	T	1,009	84%	708/887-2735 Fax 708/887-2812
© Intrinsic School-Downtown 79 W Monroe St Ste 400, Chicago 60603 Tim Ligue	9-9		100		708/887-2810
© KIPP Acad Chicago Austin Area [163] 4818 W Ohio St, Chicago 60644 Kate Mazurek	5-8		381	94%	773/938-8553 Fax 773/287-4548

---

79 Student Personnel
80 Driver Ed/Safety
81 Gifted/Talented
82 Video Services
83 Substance Abuse Prev
84 Erate
85 AIDS Education
88 Alternative/At Risk
89 Multi-Cultural Curriculum
90 Social Work
91 Safety/Security
92 Magnet School
93 Parental Involvement
95 Tech Prep Program
97 Chief Information Officer
98 Chief Technology Officer
270 Character Education
271 Migrant Education
273 Teacher Mentor
274 Before/After Sch
275 Response To Intervention
277 Remedial Math K-12
280 Literacy Coach
285 STEM
286 Digital Learning
288 Common Core Standards
294 Accountability
295 Network System
296 Title II Programs
297 Webmaster
298 Grant Writer/Ptnrships
750 Chief Innovation Officer
751 Chief of Staff
752 Social Emotional Learning

Other School Types
Ⓐ = Alternative School
© = Charter School
Ⓜ = Magnet School
Ⓨ = Year-Round School

School Programs
A = Alternative Program
G = Adult Classes
M = Magnet Program
T = Title I Schoolwide
V = Career & Tech Ed Programs

Social Media
◼ = Facebook
◼ = Twitter

New Schools are shaded
New Superintendents and Principals are bold
Personnel with email addresses are underscored

IL—39

Cook County

School	Grades		Enroll		Phone
© KIPP Ascend MS [163] 1616 S Avers Ave, Chicago 60623 Lauren Henley	5-8		724 20		773/521-4399 Fax 773/521-4766
© KIPP Ascend Primary [163] 1440 S Christiana Ave, Chicago 60623 Ellen Bhattacharyya	K-5		554	95%	773/522-1261 Fax 773/522-1185
© KIPP Bloom College Prep [163] 5515 S Lowe Ave, Chicago 60621 Ellen Sale	5-8		353	94%	773/938-8565 Fax 773/783-6910
© KIPP Bloom Primary Sch [163] 5515 S Lowe Ave, Chicago 60621	K-1		116		773/938-8567
© KIPP One Academy [163] 730 N Pulaski Rd, Chicago 60624 Kenneth Lee	5-8		303		773/938-8578 Fax 773/589-4442
© KIPP One Primary [163] 730 N Pulaski Rd, Chicago 60624 Rashid Bell	K-3		225	97%	773/938-8578 Fax 773/589-4442
© Latino Youth High Sch 2001 S California Ave, Chicago 60608 Leticia Fernandez	9-12	G	321 9	85%	773/648-2130 Fax 773/648-2098
© Learn 7 Chtr Sch-ES [164] 3021 W Carroll Ave, Chicago 60612 Tamikka Sykes	K-5		213	92%	773/584-4350
© Learn 8 Chtr Sch-MS [164] 3021 W Carroll Ave, Chicago 60612 Jessica Beasley	6-8		271	77%	773/584-4300
© Learn Chtr Sch-Campbell [164] Ⓨ 212 S Francisco Ave, Chicago 60612 Karin McGuire	K-6	M	402	97%	773/826-0370 Fax 773/826-0109
© Learn Chtr Sch-Excel [164] 3021 W Carroll Ave, Chicago 60612 Shaunda Deron	K-6		450	88%	773/584-4399 Fax 773/826-0266
© Learn Chtr Sch-Hunter Perkins [164] 1700 W 83rd St, Chicago 60620 Jon Bennett	K-8		322	85%	773/488-1634 Fax 773/488-1753
© Learn Chtr Sch-Romano Butler [164] 1132 S Homan Ave, Chicago 60624 Robin Johnson	K-8		554 21	93%	773/772-0200 Fax 773/826-0015
© Learn Chtr Sch-South Chicago [164] 8914 S Buffalo Ave, Chicago 60617 Tina Walker	K-8		420	96%	773/722-8577
© Legacy Charter Sch 3318 W Ogden Ave, Chicago 60623 Elizabeth Goss	K-8	T	471 12	90%	773/542-1640 Fax 773/542-1699
© Legal Prep Charter Academy 4319 W Washington Blvd, Chicago 60624 Samuel Finkelstein	9-12	T	346	95%	773/922-7800 Fax 312/386-5796
© Little Black Pearl Art Acad 1060 E 47th St, Chicago 60653 Donika Giggers	9-12	T	109	89%	773/285-1211 Fax 773/285-1633
© Montessori Sch of Englewood 6936 S Hermitage Ave, Chicago 60636 Rita Nolan	PK-8	T	216	98%	773/535-9255 Fax 312/756-7087
© Moving Everest Charter Sch 416 N Laramie Ave, Chicago 60644 Larita Henry	K-5	T	445	90%	312/683-9695 Fax 312/674-7221
© N Lawndale Chtr-Christiana 1615 S Christiana Ave, Chicago 60623 Senita Murphy	9-12		353 25	97%	773/542-1490 Fax 773/542-1492
© Namaste Charter Sch 3737 S Paulina St, Chicago 60609 Rocio Tovar	K-8	T	480 12	75%	773/715-9558 Fax 773/376-6495
© Noble CS-Baker Clg Prep [165] 2710 E 89th St, Chicago 60617 Mary Arrigo	9-12		230	96%	773/535-6460 Fax 773/913-0346
© Noble CS-Butler Clg Prep [165] 821 E 103rd St, Chicago 60628 Christopher Goins	9-12		647	89%	773/535-5490 Fax 773/442-0343
© Noble CS-Chicago Bulls Clg Prp [165] 2040 W Adams St, Chicago 60612 Mark Hamstra	9-12		1,138	90%	773/534-7599 Fax 312/850-0192
© Noble CS-Comer Clg Prep HS [165] 7131 S South Chicago Ave, Chicago 60619 Estee Kelly	9-12		755	84%	773/729-3969 Fax 773/729-3960
© Noble CS-Comer Middle Sch [165] 1010 E 72nd St, Chicago 60619 Trent Epley	6-8		225		773/535-0755 Fax 773/439-2169
© Noble CS-Drw Clg Prep [165] 931 S Homan Ave, Chicago 60624 Matthew Kelley	9-12		355	94%	773/893-4500 Fax 773/893-4501
© Noble CS-Golder Clg Prep [165] 1454 W Superior St, Chicago 60642 Vincent Gay	9-12		666 29	89%	312/265-9925 Fax 312/243-8402
© Noble CS-Hansberry Clg Prep [165] 8748 S Aberdeen St, Chicago 60620 Kashawndra Wilson	9-12		554	80%	773/729-3400 Fax 773/304-1995
© Noble CS-Itw David Speer Acad [165] 5321 W Grand Ave, Chicago 60639 Jordan Kruger	9-12		1,008	89%	773/622-7484 Fax 773/304-2700
© Noble CS-Johnson Clg Prep [165] 6350 S Stewart Ave, Chicago 60621 Matthew Brown	9-12		780	92%	312/348-1888 Fax 312/278-0449
© Noble CS-Mansueto High Sch [165] 2911 W 47th St, Chicago 60632 Darko Simunovic	9-12		173	91%	773/349-8200 Fax 773/409-0440
© Noble CS-Muchin Clg Prep [165] 1 N State St, Chicago 60602 Emily Mason	9-12		973 33	85%	312/445-4680 Fax 312/332-0058
© Noble CS-Noble Academy [165] 1443 N Ogden Ave, Chicago 60610 Lauren Boros	9-12		444	82%	312/574-1527 Fax 708/575-4217
© Noble CS-Noble Street Clg Prep [165] 1010 N Noble St, Chicago 60642 Ben Gunty	9-12		668 25	83%	773/862-1449 Fax 773/289-0468
© Noble CS-Pritzker Clg Prep [165] 4131 W Cortland St, Chicago 60639 Carrie Spitz	9-12		974	96%	773/394-2848 Fax 773/394-2931
© Noble CS-Rauner Clg Prep [165] 1337 W Ohio St, Chicago 60642 Brendan Bedell	9-12		620	84%	312/226-5345 Fax 312/226-3552
© Noble CS-Rowe Clark Math & Sci [165] 3645 W Chicago Ave, Chicago 60651 Brenda Cora	9-12		461	95%	773/242-2212 Fax 773/826-6936
© Noble CS-UIC Clg Prep [165] 1231 S Damen Ave, Chicago 60608 Audrey Borling	9-12		934	85%	312/768-4858 Fax 773/496-7149
© North Lawndale HS-Collins 1313 S Sacramento Dr, Chicago 60623 Senita Murphy	9-12		387	94%	773/542-6766 Fax 773/542-6995
Ⓐ Ombudsman No 1 High School NW 7500 N Harlem Ave, Chicago 60631 Moses Tighil	9-12		198	81%	708/669-7828
© Ombudsman-Chicago Roseland CSA 10928 S Halsted St, Chicago 60628 Robert Tuner	9-12		76		773/941-6674
Ⓐ Ombudsman-South High Sch 6057 S Western Ave, Chicago 60636 Audry Blinstrup	9-12		400	91%	773/498-5085 Fax 773/424-7291
Ⓐ Ombudsman-West High Sch 2401 W Congress Pkwy, Chicago 60612 Lyntina Lampley	9-12		263		312/243-1550 Fax 312/243-1562

1	Superintendent	8	Curric/Instruct K-12	19	Chief Financial Officer	29	Family/Consumer Science	39	Social Studies K-12
2	Bus/Finance/Purchasing	9	Curric/Instruct Elem	20	Art K-12	30	Adult Education	40	Social Studies Elem
3	Buildings And Grounds	10	Curric/Instruct Sec	21	Art Elem	31	Career/Sch-to-Work K-12	41	Social Studies Sec
4	Food Service	11	Federal Program	22	Art Sec	32	Career/Sch-to-Work Elem	42	Science K-12
5	Transportation	12	Title I	23	Music K-12	33	Career/Sch-to-Work Sec	43	Science Elem
6	Athletic	13	Title V	24	Music Elem	34	Early Childhood Ed	44	Science Sec
7	Health Services	15	Asst Superintendent	25	Music Sec	35	Health/Phys Education	45	Math K-12
		16	Instructional Media Svcs	26	Business Education	36	Guidance Services K-12	46	Math Elem
		17	Chief Operations Officer	27	Career & Tech Ed	37	Guidance Services Elem	47	Math Sec
		18	Chief Academic Officer	28	Technology Education	38	Guidance Services Sec	48	English/Lang Arts K-12

49	English/Lang Arts Elem	59	Special Education Elem	69	Academic Assessment
50	English/Lang Arts Sec	60	Special Education Sec	70	Research/Development
51	Reading K-12	61	Foreign/World Lang K-12	71	Public Information
52	Reading Elem	62	Foreign/World Lang Elem	72	Summer School
53	Reading Sec	63	Foreign/World Lang Sec	73	Instructional Tech
54	Remedial Reading K-12	64	Religious Education K-12	74	Inservice Training
55	Remedial Reading Elem	65	Religious Education Elem	75	Marketing/Distributive
56	Remedial Reading Sec	66	Religious Education Sec	76	Info Systems
57	Bilingual/ELL	67	School Board President	77	Psychological Assess
58	Special Education K-12	68	Teacher Personnel	78	Affirmative Action

Illinois School Directory — Cook County

School	Grades	Prog	Enroll	%	Phone
Pathways In Educ-Brighton Park 3124 W 47th St, Chicago 60632 Nicholas Perez	9-12		365	80%	773/579-1220 Fax 773/579-1224
ⓒ Pathways In Educ-Humboldt Park 2421 W Division St, Chicago 60622 Nicholas Perez	9-12		27	90%	773/804-8866
Ⓐ Pathways In Education-Ashburn ⓒ 3284 W 87th St, Chicago 60652 Andrew Morgan	9-12		885	91%	773/434-6300 Fax 773/434-6301
Ⓐ Pathways In Education-Avondale ⓒ 3100 W Belmont Ave, Chicago 60618 Andrew Morgan	9-12		300	82%	773/588-5007 Fax 773/588-5009
ⓒ Perspectives CS-HS of Tech [166] 8522 S Lafayette Ave, Chicago 60620 Eron Powell	9-12		317	92%	773/358-6120 Fax 773/358-6129
ⓒ Perspectives CS-Joslin [166] 1930 S Archer Ave, Chicago 60616 Sauda Porter	6-12		383 8	85%	312/225-7400 Fax 312/225-7411
ⓒ Perspectives CS-Ldrship Acad [166] 8522 S Lafayette Ave, Chicago 60620 Eron Powell	9-12		675 32	92%	773/358-6100 Fax 773/358-6199
ⓒ Perspectives CS-Mid Acad [166] 8522 S Lafayette Ave, Chicago 60620 Victoria Jackson	6-8		380		773/358-6300 Fax 773/358-6399
ⓒ Perspectives lit Math-Sci Acad [166] 3663 S Wabash Ave, Chicago 60653 Tyneisha Banks	7-12		462	91%	773/358-6800 Fax 773/358-6055
ⓒ Plato Lrg Academy Primary [157] 5545 W Harrison St, Chicago 60644 Christopher Austria	K-8	T	446	89%	773/413-3090 Fax 773/413-3095
ⓒ Polaris Charter Academy 620 N Sawyer Ave, Chicago 60624 Michelle Navarre	K-8	T	438	88%	773/534-0820 Fax 773/534-6645
ⓒ Providence Englewood CS 6515 S Ashland Ave, Chicago 60636 Angela Williams	K-8	T	464	90%	773/434-0202 Fax 773/434-0196
ⓒ Rowe Elem Charter Sch 1424 N Cleaver St, Chicago 60642 Tony Sutton	K-5	T	694	85%	312/445-5870 Fax 312/445-5875
ⓒ Univ of Chicago CS-Donoghue 707 E 37th St, Chicago 60653 Erin Gilmore	PK-5		539	77%	773/285-5301 Fax 773/268-2088
ⓒ Univ of Chicago CS-Nko 1119 E 46th St, Chicago 60653 Aneesa Sergeant	PK-5		348 13	66%	773/536-2399 Fax 773/536-2435
ⓒ Univ of Chicago CS-Woodlawn 6300 S University Ave, Chicago 60637 Donald Gordon \ Daena Adams	6-12		621	78%	773/752-8101 Fax 773/324-0653
ⓒ Urban Prep CS-Bronzeville 521 E 35th St, Chicago 60616 Conrad Timbers-Auser	9-12	T	332	80%	773/624-3444 Fax 773/624-3405
ⓒ Urban Prep CS-Englewood 6201 S Stewart Ave, Chicago 60621 Joseph Mason	9-12	T	259	86%	773/535-9724 Fax 773/535-0012
ⓒ Urban Prep CS-West 1900 W Jackson Blvd Ste 203, Chicago 60612 Cory Cain	9-12		100		773/534-8860 Fax 773/534-1050
Ⓐ YCCS-Aspira Antonia Pantoja HS [130] ⓒ 3121 N Pulaski Rd, Chicago 60641 Nestor Corona	9-12		89	83%	773/486-6303 Fax 773/427-0872
ⓒ YCCS-Assoc House 1116 N Kedzie Ave, Chicago 60651 David Piper	9-12		96	93%	773/772-7170 Fax 773/772-8617
Ⓐ YCCS-Austin Career 5352 W Chicago Ave, Chicago 60651 Anne Gottlieb	10-12		106 8	92%	773/626-6988 Fax 773/626-2641
Ⓐ YCCS-Chatham Acad HS ⓒ 9035 S Langley Ave, Chicago 60619 Tony Lyons	10-12		174	94%	773/651-1500 Fax 773/651-1523
ⓒ YCCS-Community Chrn Alt Acad 1231 S Pulaski Rd, Chicago 60623 Nahid Zahedi	9-12	G	172 9	96%	773/762-2272 Fax 773/762-2065
ⓒ YCCS-Dr Pedro Albizu Campos HS 2739 W Division St 41, Chicago 60622 Melissa Lewis	9-12	AG	200 10	92%	773/342-8022 Fax 773/342-6609
Ⓐ YCCS-Innovations HS ⓒ 2911 W 47th St, Chicago 60632 Melissa Cotirla	9-12		290 12		312/999-9360 Fax 312/999-9361
Ⓐ YCCS-Jane Addams Alt HS ⓒ 1814 S Union Ave, Chicago 60616 Theresa Comparini	9-12		200 8	72%	312/563-1746 Fax 312/563-1756
Ⓐ YCCS-McKinley-Lakeside HS ⓒ 2920 S Wabash Ave, Chicago 60616 Y Pamela Kennedy	10-12	M	50 9	96%	312/949-5010 Fax 312/949-5015
Ⓐ YCCS-Olive Harvey Mid Clg HS 10001 S Woodlawn Ave, Chicago 60628 Devon Morales	10-12		102	89%	773/291-6518 Fax 773/291-6131
ⓒ YCCS-Progressive Leadership 7847 S Jeffery Blvd, Chicago 60649 Kim Ellison	9-12		164	80%	773/723-9631
ⓒ YCCS-Scholastic Achievement 4651 W Madison St, Chicago 60644 Nicole Simpson	10-12	AV	170 10	88%	773/921-1315 Fax 773/921-1121
ⓒ YCCS-Sullivan House Alt HS 8164 S South Chicago Ave, Chicago 60617 Dr Thomas Gattuso	9-12	AV	304 30	98%	773/978-8680 Fax 773/375-1482
Ⓐ YCCS-Truman Middle Clg HS ⓒ 1145 W Wilson Ave Rm 173, Chicago 60640 Michelle Yoo	10-12		218	78%	773/907-4840 Fax 773/907-4844
ⓒ YCCS-Virtual High Sch 1900 W Van Buren St, Chicago 60612 Mary Bradley	10-12		200		312/429-0027 Fax 312/243-5733
Ⓐ YCCS-West 4909 W Division St, Chicago 60651 Mr King	10-12		155	92%	773/261-0994 Fax 773/261-1029
Ⓐ YCCS-West Town Acad Alt HS 534 N Sacramento Blvd, Chicago 60612 Dr Kent Nolen	9-12		160 14	84%	312/563-9044 Fax 312/563-9672
ⓒ YCCS-Youth Connection Ldrshp 3424 S State St, Chicago 60616 Sheila Venson	9-12		219	83%	312/225-4668 Fax 312/225-4862
ⓒ YCCS-Youth Dev Inst HS 7836 S Union Ave, Chicago 60620 Aaron Royster	10-12		137	98%	773/224-2273 Fax 773/224-2214

● **Chicago Ridge Sch Dist 127-5** PID: 00268513   708/636-2000
6135 108th St, Chicago Ridge 60415   Fax 708/636-0916

> **Schools:** 3 \ **Teachers:** 106 \ **Students:** 1,476 \ **Special Ed Students:** 236 \ **LEP Students:** 442 \ **Ethnic:** Asian 2%, African American 9%, Hispanic 21%, Caucasian 68% \ **Exp:** $314 (High) \ **Poverty:** 31% \ **Title I:** $819,158 \ **Special Education:** $788,000 \ **Bilingual Education:** $108,000 \ **Open-Close:** 08/21 - 06/02 \ **DTBP:** $207 (High)

Dr Adam Thorns	1	Katheryn Picciolini	2
Wesley Smith	3	Cassie Picciolini	4
Geoffrey Youngberg	5*	Kathleen Lambrecht	7,83,85*
Fran Setaro	9,12,27,88*	Cary Hillegonds	11,34,59,69,271*
Brittany Yelnick	37*	Nancy Salzer	67
Gino Fricano	73,295		

79	Student Personnel	91	Safety/Security	275	Response To Intervention
80	Driver Ed/Safety	92	Magnet School	277	Remedial Math K-12
81	Gifted/Talented	93	Parental Involvement	280	Literacy Coach
82	Video Services	95	Tech Prep Program	285	STEM
83	Substance Abuse Prev	97	Chief Information Officer	286	Digital Learning
84	Erate	98	Chief Technology Officer	288	Common Core Standards
85	AIDS Education	270	Accountability	294	Alternative Education
88	Alternative/At Risk	271	Migrant Education	295	Network System
89	Multi-Cultural Curriculum	273	Teacher Mentor	296	Title II Programs
90	Social Work	274	Before/After Sch	297	Webmaster

298	Grant Writer/Ptnrships	
750	Chief Innovation Officer	
751	Chief of Staff	
752	Social Emotional Learning	

Other School Types
Ⓐ = Alternative School
ⓒ = Charter School
Ⓜ = Magnet School
Ⓨ = Year-Round School

School Programs
A = Alternative Program
G = Adult Classes
M = Magnet Program
T = Title I Schoolwide
V = Career & Tech Ed Programs

Social Media
🅕 = Facebook
🅣 = Twitter

New Schools are shaded
New Superintendents and Principals are bold
Personnel with email addresses are underscored

IL—41

Cook County
Market Data Retrieval

Public Schs..Principal	Grd	Prgm	Enr/#Cls	SN		
Elden D Finley Jr High Sch 10835 Lombard Ave, Chicago Ridge 60415 Geoffrey Youngberg	6-8	T	435 30	56%	708/636-2005 Fax 708/636-0045	
Ridge Central Elem Sch 10800 Lyman Ave, Chicago Ridge 60415 Megan Nothnagel	PK-5	T	511 26	51%	708/636-2001 Fax 708/636-0361	
Ridge Lawn Elem Sch 5757 105th St, Chicago Ridge 60415 Fran Setaro	PK-5	T	530 19	76%	708/636-2002 Fax 708/636-1062	

● **Cicero School District 99** PID: 00268563
5110 W 24th St, Cicero 60804
708/863-4856
Fax 708/652-8105

Schools: 17 \ **Teachers:** 743 \ **Students:** 12,418 \
Special Ed Students: 1,578 \ **LEP Students:** 6,076 \ **Ethnic:** African American 2%, Hispanic 96%, Caucasian 1% \ **Exp:** $253 (Med) \
Poverty: 21% \ **Title I:** $5,244,506 \ **Special Education:** $6,869,000 \
Bilingual Education: $2,084,000 \ **Open-Close:** 08/24 - 06/11 \ **DTBP:** $205 (High)

Rudolfo Hernandez 1
Brian Dominick 3
Michael Wolff 5
Susan Kleinmeyer 6,21,40,81*
Joyce Hodan 9,15
Monique Abbatte 9*
Elisabeth Nealon 15,79
Tom Gerardi 34
Denise Thul 49,52
Becky Caruso 59
Thomas Tomschin 67
Rita Tarullo 68
Jacqueline Glosniak 71
Fernando Ruiz 91

Dorene Cherry 2
Janice Wolff 4*
Sonia Abad 5
Colleen Arriola 7,40,43
Maria Burgos 9
Nancy Oesterreich 11,52,294
Cao Mac 16,71,84,97,295
Mary Mycyk 46*
Araceli Medina 57
Sergio Rodriguez 59
Marybeth King 68*
Leticia Brandt 69,76
Bryan Snyder 73
Melissa Sanchez 298

Public Schs..Principal	Grd	Prgm	Enr/#Cls	SN		
Cicero Early Childhood Center 5330 W 35th St, Cicero 60804 Thomas Geraghty	PK-PK		118		708/982-4500	
Cicero East Elem Sch 3003 50th Ct, Cicero 60804 Jill Miller	5-6		753 36	99%	708/652-9440 Fax 708/780-4444	
Cicero West Elem Sch 4937 W 23rd St, Cicero 60804 Veronica Morales	PK-4		918 45	93%	708/780-4487 Fax 708/656-2937	
Columbus East Sch 3100 S 54th Ave, Cicero 60804 Donata Heppner	4-6		346 28	97%	708/652-6085 Fax 708/780-4446	
Columbus West Sch 5425 W 31st St, Cicero 60804 Heriberto Garcia	PK-4		657 50	93%	708/780-4482 Fax 708/780-0735	
Daniel Burnham Elem Sch 1630 S 59th Ave, Cicero 60804 Jennifer Evans	K-6		868 45	97%	708/652-9577 Fax 708/780-4441	
Drexel Elem Sch 5407 W 36th St, Cicero 60804 Luis Illa	K-6		515 34	95%	708/652-5532 Fax 708/780-4449	
Goodwin Elem Sch 2625 S Austin Blvd, Cicero 60804 Alberto Molina	PK-6		652 34	95%	708/652-5500 Fax 708/780-4452	
Liberty Elem Sch 4946 W 13th St, Cicero 60804 Robert Mensch	K-3		531 38	93%	708/780-4475 Fax 708/780-7062	
Lincoln Elem Sch 3545 S 61st Ave, Cicero 60804 Gretchen Gorgal	PK-6		887 26	93%	708/652-8889 Fax 708/780-4454	
Ⓐ McKinley Educational Center 5900 W 14th St, Cicero 60804 Luis Salto	5-8		200		708/652-8890	
Sherlock Elem Sch 5347 W 22nd Pl, Cicero 60804 Joanna Lago	PK-6		401		708/652-8885	
Theodore Roosevelt Elem Sch 1500 S 50th Ave, Cicero 60804 Nichole Gross	3-6		629 37	99%	708/652-7833 Fax 708/780-4461	
Unity Junior High Sch 2115 S 54th Ave, Cicero 60804 Aldo Calderin	7-8		2,555	98%	708/863-8229 Fax 708/656-5652	
Warren Park Elem Sch 1225 S 60th Ct, Cicero 60804 Raquel Jenke	PK-6		635	93%	708/780-2299 Fax 708/780-4466	
Woodbine Elem Sch 3003 S 50th Ct, Cicero 60804 Kate Lyman	K-2		223 18	99%	708/652-8884 Fax 708/780-4470	
Woodrow Wilson Elem Sch 2310 S 57th Ave, Cicero 60804 Kate Lyman	K-6		729	93%	708/652-2552 Fax 708/780-4468	

● **Cmty Cons Sch Dist 146** PID: 00274823
6611 171st St, Tinley Park 60477
708/614-4500
Fax 708/614-8992

Schools: 5 \ **Teachers:** 192 \ **Students:** 2,500 \ **Special Ed Students:** 464 \ **LEP Students:** 273 \ **Ethnic:** Asian 3%, African American 7%, Hispanic 19%, Caucasian 72% \ **Exp:** $442 (High) \ **Poverty:** 12% \ **Title I:** $445,265 \ **Special Education:** $1,582,000 \ **Bilingual Education:** $114,000 \
Open-Close: 08/24 - 06/04 \ **DTBP:** $227 (High)

Dr Jeff Stawick 1
Matt Shannahan 3,91
Marian Betley 7
Vern Bettis 28,73,76,286
Keegan Kociss 71,97

Jeff Charleston 2,5,19
Cheryl Witas 4
Wendy Wolgan 9,11,68,69,270,273,285
John Malloy 67
Kelly Voliva 79,83,88,298,752

Public Schs..Principal	Grd	Prgm	Enr/#Cls	SN		
Arnold W Kruse Ed Center 7617 Hemlock Dr, Orland Park 60462 Carey Radke	PK-5		405 18	38%	708/614-4530 Fax 708/614-7602	
Bert H Fulton Elem Sch 6601 171st St, Tinley Park 60477 Megan Mitera	PK-5	T	530 20	34%	708/614-4525 Fax 708/614-7442	
Central Middle Sch 18146 Oak Park Ave, Tinley Park 60477 Randy Fortin	6-8	T	810 54	37%	708/614-4510 Fax 708/614-7271	
Memorial Elem Sch 6701 179th St, Tinley Park 60477 Joe Trsar	PK-5		368 15	29%	708/614-4535 Fax 708/614-7501	
Walter F Fierke Ed Center 6535 Victoria Dr, Oak Forest 60452 Damien Aherne	PK-5		383 14	25%	708/614-4520 Fax 708/535-0841	

● **Community Cons School Dist 15** PID: 00272514
580 N 1st Bank Dr, Palatine 60067
847/963-3000
Fax 847/963-3200

Schools: 20 \ **Teachers:** 751 \ **Students:** 12,000 \
Special Ed Students: 1,399 \ **LEP Students:** 3,345 \ **Ethnic:** Asian 19%, African American 4%, Hispanic 37%, Caucasian 40% \ **Exp:** $260 (Med) \ **Poverty:** 9% \ **Title I:** $1,812,775 \ **Special Education:** $8,472,000 \
Bilingual Education: $1,331,000 \ **Open-Close:** 08/19 - 06/04 \ **DTBP:** $202 (High)

Dr Laurie Heinz 1
Dianna McCluskey 2

Danielle Cockrum 2
Joshua Schott 2

1 Superintendent	8 Curric/Instruct K-12	19 Chief Financial Officer	29 Family/Consumer Science	39 Social Studies K-12	49 English/Lang Arts Elem	59 Special Education Elem	69 Academic Assessment
2 Bus/Finance/Purchasing	9 Curric/Instruct Elem	20 Art K-12	30 Adult Education	40 Social Studies Elem	50 English/Lang Arts Sec	60 Special Education Sec	70 Research/Development
3 Buildings And Grounds	10 Curric/Instruct Sec	21 Art Elem	31 Career/Sch-to-Work K-12	41 Social Studies Sec	51 Reading K-12	61 Foreign/World Lang K-12	71 Public Information
4 Food Service	11 Federal Program	22 Art Sec	32 Career/Sch-to-Work Elem	42 Science K-12	52 Reading Elem	62 Foreign/World Lang Elem	72 Summer School
5 Transportation	12 Title I	23 Music K-12	33 Career/Sch-to-Work Sec	43 Science Elem	53 Reading Sec	63 Foreign/World Lang Sec	73 Instructional Tech
6 Athletic	13 Title V	24 Music Elem	34 Early Childhood Ed	44 Science Sec	54 Remedial Reading K-12	64 Religious Education K-12	74 Inservice Training
7 Health Services	15 Asst Superintendent	25 Music Sec	35 Health/Phys Education	45 Math K-12	55 Remedial Reading Elem	65 Religious Education Elem	75 Marketing/Distributive
	16 Instructional Media Svcs	26 Business Education	36 Guidance Services K-12	46 Math Elem	56 Remedial Reading Sec	66 Religious Education Sec	76 Info Systems
	17 Chief Operations Officer	27 Career & Tech Ed	37 Guidance Services Elem	47 Math Sec	57 Bilingual/ELL	67 School Board President	77 Psychological Assess
	18 Chief Academic Officer	28 Technology Education	38 Guidance Services Sec	48 English/Lang Arts K-12	58 Special Education K-12	68 Teacher Personnel	78 Affirmative Action

Illinois School Directory — Cook County

Name	Page
Andy Tholm	3
Kristin Voigts	4
Tom Bramley	5
Karen Flor	7
Dr Tom Edgar	9,15,69,294
Ann Skully	15,79,83,275
Lisa Nuss	15,68
Matthew Warren	34,88*
Renee Urbanski	57,89
Tracey Wrobel	59
Joanna Shostachuk	68,273*
Laura Swanlund	70,76,77
Colleen Seick	73
Robyn Cook	73
Tim Woomert	76
Paul Budin	90*
Cathi Fabjance	274
Kelly Olivero	280
Sandy Cramer	297
Ernie Baez	3
Judith Bramer	5
Reisa Cohen	6,21,24,43,46
Dr Meg Schnoor	9,11,15,288
Colleen Mullins	12,49,52,55,280,298
Claire Kowalczyk	15
Dave Kuechenberg	16,73,295
Angelica Brifcani	57
Ann Cygnar	59
Lisa Szczupaj	67
Philip Georgia	68
Morgan Delack	71
Emily McFadden	73
Mary Zarr	74
Alicia Corrigan	79
James Kaplanes	91
Heather Trausch	280
Sara Rossi	280

Public Schs..Principal	Grd	Prgm	Enr/#Cls	SN		
Carl Sandburg Jr High Sch 2600 Martin Ln, Rolling MDWS 60008 Doug Harter	7-8	T	508 60		46%	847/963-7800 Fax 847/963-7806
Central Road Elem Sch 3800 Central Rd, Rolling MDWS 60008 Patti VanWinkle	PK-6	T	541 23		38%	847/963-5100 Fax 847/963-5106
Frank C Whiteley Elem Sch 4335 Haman Ave, Hoffman Est 60192 Faith Rivera	K-6		594 31		14%	847/963-7200 Fax 847/963-7206
Gray M Sanborn Elem Sch 101 N Oak St, Palatine 60067 Erika Johansen	PK-6	T	607 25		59%	847/963-7000 Fax 847/963-7006
Hunting Ridge Elem Sch 1105 W Illinois Ave, Palatine 60067 Christine Ortlund	PK-6		724 34		14%	847/963-5300 Fax 847/963-5306
Jane Addams Elem Sch 1020 E Sayles Dr, Palatine 60074 Amy Molinsky	K-6	T	579 27		66%	847/963-5000 Fax 847/963-5006
John G Conyers Learning Acad 2800 Central Rd, Rolling MDWS 60008 Matthew Warren	Spec	A	28 19		35%	847/963-3400 Fax 847/963-3406
Kimball Hill Elem Sch 2905 Meadow Dr, Rolling MDWS 60008 **Michelle LaCamera** \ Natalie Milo-Nicolasin	PK-6	T	584 24		52%	847/963-5200 Fax 847/963-5206
Lake Louise Elem Sch 500 N Jonathan Dr, Palatine 60074 Jennifer Seoane	PK-6	T	761 32		56%	847/963-5600 Fax 847/963-5606
Lincoln Elem Sch 1021 N Ridgewood Ln, Palatine 60067 Mary Beth Knoeppel	K-6	T	755 38		47%	847/963-5700 Fax 847/963-5706
Marion Jordan Elem Sch 100 N Harrison Ave, Palatine 60067 Jennifer Grosch	K-6		480 22		9%	847/963-5500 Fax 847/963-5506
Pleasant Hill Elem Sch 434 W Illinois Ave, Palatine 60067 David Morris	PK-6		649 35		5%	847/963-5900 Fax 847/963-5906
Plum Grove Junior High Sch 2600 Plum Grove Rd, Rolling MDWS 60008 Dr Kerry Wilson	7-8	V	814 30		13%	847/963-7600 Fax 847/963-7606 t
Stuart R Paddock Sch 225 W Washington St, Palatine 60067 Rachel Bland	K-6	T	703 30		42%	847/963-5800 Fax 847/963-5806 t
Thomas Jefferson Elem Sch 3805 Winston Dr, Hoffman Est 60192 Larry Sasso	K-6	T	448 30		36%	847/963-5400 Fax 847/963-5406
Virginia Lake Elem Sch 925 N Glenn Dr, Palatine 60074 **Stephanie Daly**	K-6		745 50		64%	847/963-7100 Fax 847/963-7106
Walter Sundling Jr High Sch 1100 N Smith St, Palatine 60067 Jason Dietz	7-8	V	634 45		31%	847/963-3700 Fax 847/963-3706 t
Willow Bend Elem Sch 4700 Barker Ave, Rolling MDWS 60008 Robert Harris	K-6		631 19		18%	847/963-7300 Fax 847/963-7306
Winston Campus Elem Sch 900 E Palatine Rd, Palatine 60074 Marilynn Smith	PK-6	TV	465 20		41%	847/963-7500 Fax 847/963-7406
Winston Campus Junior High Sch 120 N Babcock Dr, Palatine 60074 Martin Da Costa	7-8	T	845		65%	847/963-7400 Fax 847/963-7508

• **Community Cons School Dist 59** PID: 00267193 847/593-4300
  1001 Leicester Rd, Elk Grove Vlg 60007 Fax 847/593-4409

> **Schools:** 15 \ **Teachers:** 437 \ **Students:** 6,000 \ **Special Ed Students:** 990 \ **LEP Students:** 2,625 \ **Ethnic:** Asian 12%, African American 4%, Hispanic 45%, Native American: 2%, Caucasian 38% \ **Exp:** $278 (Med) \ **Poverty:** 12% \ **Title I:** $1,174,484 \ **Special Education:** $3,954,000 \ **Bilingual Education:** $578,000 \ **Open-Close:** 08/12 - 06/03 \ **DTBP:** $217 (High)

Name	Page	Name	Page
Dr Arthur Fessler	1	Janet Russo	2
Vickie Nissen	2,15	Andy Skic	3,91
Eric Swanson	3	Maribel Gonzalez	5
Denise Webster	7	Jennifer Chiappetta	9,270
Linda Buniak	9	Maureen McAbee	9,15,57,288
Natalie Amato-Zech	9,59	Thomas Luedloff	9,15
Ben Grey	15,286	Melissa Ward	34*
Ashley Robertson	37	Mary Niles	46
Karen Starr	59	Janice Krinsky	67
Cynthia Pullen	68	Ross Vittore	68
Carolyn Whitson	71	Justin Sampson	71
Eduardo Barrios	73	Cathy Savage	76,295
Corey King	76	Katie Ahsell	78,88,296
Griselda Pirtle	89	Travis Hodges	297

Public Schs..Principal	Grd	Prgm	Enr/#Cls	SN		
Adm Richard E Byrd Elem Sch 265 Wellington Ave, Elk Grove Vlg 60007 Mary Esser	K-5	T	364 18		67%	847/593-4388 Fax 847/593-7188 f
Brentwood Elem Sch 260 Dulles Rd, Des Plaines 60016 Kimberly Barrett	K-5	T	481 17		51%	847/593-4401 Fax 847/593-7184
Clearmont Elem Sch 280 Clearmont Dr, Elk Grove Vlg 60007 Monika Farfan	K-5	T	411 15		41%	847/593-4372 Fax 847/593-7194
Devonshire Elem Sch 1401 Pennsylvania Ave, Des Plaines 60018 Randy Steinkamp	K-5	T	449 22		55%	847/593-4398 Fax 847/593-7183 f t
Early Learning Center 1900 W Lonnquist Blvd, Mt Prospect 60056 Michele Ramsey	PK-PK		328		46%	847/593-4306 Fax 847/593-7199
Forest View Elem Sch 1901 W Estates Dr, Mt Prospect 60056 Michael Wall	K-5	T	396 22		40%	847/593-4359 Fax 847/593-4360
Friendship Junior High Sch 550 Elizabeth Ln, Des Plaines 60018 William Timmins	6-8	T	674 40		52%	847/593-4350 Fax 847/593-7182
Grove Junior High Sch 777 W Elk Grove Blvd, Elk Grove Vlg 60007 John Harrington	6-8	T	945 75		56%	847/593-4367 Fax 847/472-3001
Holmes Junior High Sch 1900 W Lonnquist Blvd, Mt Prospect 60056 Mark Rasar	6-8	T	526 30		60%	847/593-4390 Fax 847/593-7386

79 Student Personnel	91 Safety/Security	275 Response To Intervention	298 Grant Writer/Ptnrships	**School Programs**	**Social Media**
80 Driver Ed/Safety	92 Magnet School	277 Remedial Math K-12	750 Chief Innovation Officer	**A** = Alternative Program	
81 Gifted/Talented	93 Parental Involvement	280 Literacy Coach	751 Chief of Staff	**G** = Adult Classes	f = Facebook
82 Video Services	95 Tech Prep Program	285 STEM	752 Social Emotional Learning	**M** = Magnet Program	
83 Substance Abuse Prev	97 Chief Information Officer	286 Digital Learning		**T** = Title I Schoolwide	t = Twitter
84 Erate	98 Chief Technology Officer	288 Common Core Standards	**Other School Types**	**V** = Career & Tech Ed Programs	
85 AIDS Education	270 Character Education	294 Accountability	Ⓐ = Alternative School		
88 Alternative/At Risk	271 Migrant Education	295 Network System	Ⓒ = Charter School	New Schools are shaded	
89 Multi-Cultural Curriculum	273 Teacher Mentor	296 Title II Programs	Ⓜ = Magnet School	New Superintendents and Principals are bold	
90 Social Work	274 Before/After Sch	297 Webmaster	Ⓨ = Year-Round School	Personnel with email addresses are underscored	

IL—43

Cook County　　　　　　　　　　　　　　　　　　　　　　　　　　　　　　Market Data Retrieval

John Jay Elem Sch 1835 W Pheasant Trl, Mt Prospect 60056 Joshua Segura	K-5	T	337 20	74%	847/593-4385 Fax 847/593-8656
Juliette Low Elem Sch 1530 S Highland Ave, Arlington HTS 60005 Susan Ejma	K-5	T	368 21	65%	847/593-4383 Fax 847/593-7291
ⓐ Ridge Family Center for Lrng ⓨ 650 Ridge Ave, Elk Grove Vlg 60007 Dr Rob Bohanek	K-5	M	268 17	31%	847/593-4070 Fax 847/593-4075
Robert Frost Elem Sch 1308 S Cypress Dr, Mt Prospect 60056 Susan Savage	K-5	T	323 20	64%	847/593-4378 Fax 847/593-4365
Rupley Elem Sch 305 Oakton St, Elk Grove Vlg 60007 Diana Odonnell	K-5	T	374 23	71%	847/593-4353 Fax 847/593-4405
Salt Creek Elem Sch 65 Jf Kennedy Blvd, Elk Grove Vlg 60007 Sarah Humboldt	K-5	T	435 26	62%	847/593-4375 Fax 847/593-7390

• **Community Cons School Dist 168** PID: 00273790　　708/758-1610
  21899 Torrence Ave, Sauk Village 60411　　　　　　　Fax 708/758-5929

Schools: 3 \ Teachers: 112 \ Students: 1,287 \ Special Ed Students: 207 \ LEP Students: 69 \ Ethnic: African American 81%, Hispanic 15%, Caucasian 4% \ Exp: $176 (Low) \ Poverty: 30% \ Title I: $976,477 \ Special Education: $872,000 \ Open-Close: 08/14 - 05/25 \ DTBP: $207 (High)

Dr Donna Leak 1	Sharlyne Williams 2,4,294	
Dave Rana 3,91	Myra Patterson .... ,, 9,11,84,88,288	
Tricia Walpon 34	Dr Jeremiah Johnson 59,77	
Tammy Jones 67	Karen Harris 68	
Monica Miller 72,76		

Public Schs..Principal	Grd	Prgm	Enr/#Cls	SN	
Rickover Junior High Sch 22151 Torrence Ave, Sauk Village 60411 Chantel Bullock	6-8	T	416 40	57%	708/758-1900 Fax 708/758-1601
Strassburg Elem Sch 2002 223rd St, Sauk Village 60411 Dr Jennifer Camilleri	3-5	T	428 32	88%	708/758-4754 Fax 708/758-2202
Wagoner Elem Sch 1831 215th Pl, Sauk Village 60411 Sharon Paver-Nepote	PK-2	T	493 22	63%	708/758-3322 Fax 708/758-0801

• **Community High School Dist 218** PID: 00282313　　708/424-2000
  10701 Kilpatrick Ave, Oak Lawn 60453　　　　　　　Fax 708/424-6191

Schools: 5 \ Teachers: 378 \ Students: 5,400 \ Special Ed Students: 919 \ LEP Students: 409 \ College-Bound: 70% \ Ethnic: Asian 1%, African American 28%, Hispanic 39%, Caucasian 32% \ Exp: $305 (High) \ Poverty: 15% \ Title I: $1,628,242 \ Special Education: $3,395,000 \ Bilingual Education: $77,000 \ Open-Close: 08/17 - 05/28 \ DTBP: $196 (High) \

Dr Ty Harting 1	Ilsa Richardella 2
Lisa Krueger 3	Mike Ryan 3,15,68
Rodger Ford 3	John Hallberg 5,11,286,296,298
Jeannine Prucha 10,47	Josh Barron 15
Sue Feeney 15,60,752	Raymond Stadt 22,25,44
Jacqueline Johnson 25	Frank Lamantia 26,27,29
Audra Van Raiden 35,80	Sean McSwenney 41
Karen Krueger 50,63	Ronell Whitaker 50
Kerri Piscitelli 60	Thomas Kosowski 67
Anthony Corsi 69	Bob McParland 71
Timothy Prost 73,76	Judith Keigher 84

Public Schs..Principal	Grd	Prgm	Enr/#Cls	SN	
Alan B Shepard High Sch 13049 S Ridgeland Ave, Palos Heights 60463 Gregory Walder	9-12	TV	1,755 66	63%	708/371-1111 Fax 708/371-7688
ⓐ Delta Learning Center 3940 W 137th St, Crestwood 60418 Joe Fowler	9-12	T	184	88%	708/371-1880 Fax 708/371-4782
Eisenhower Campus High Sch 12700 Sacramento Ave, Blue Island 60406 Erik Briseno	9-12	TV	1,811 59	84%	708/597-6300 Fax 708/597-7291
H L Richards High Sch 10601 Central Ave, Oak Lawn 60453 Mike Jacobson	9-12	TV	1,643 75	63%	708/499-2550 Fax 708/499-5463
Summit Learning Center 3940 W 137th St, Crestwood 60418 Joe Fowler	Spec	A	99 7		708/371-1986 Fax 708/371-6427

• **Consolidated High Sch Dist 230** PID: 00272904　　708/745-5203
  15100 S 94th Ave, Orland Park 60462　　　　　　　Fax 708/737-7711

Schools: 3 \ Teachers: 483 \ Students: 7,308 \ Special Ed Students: 990 \ LEP Students: 347 \ College-Bound: 87% \ Ethnic: Asian 5%, African American 5%, Hispanic 13%, Caucasian 76% \ Exp: $193 (Low) \ Poverty: 12% \ Title I: $1,602,080 \ Special Education: $4,331,000 \ Bilingual Education: $50,000 \ Open-Close: 08/17 - 05/27 \ DTBP: $192 (High) \

Dr James Gay 1	John LaVelle 2,15
Tera Wagner 2	Bob Hughes 3,91
Mary Morgan 4	Ed Langevin 5
Michael Dwyer 6,35*	Terry Treasure 6*
Stacey Gonzales 10	Dr Kim Dryier 11,16,27,57,88,275,294,298
Julia Wheaton 15,68,74,273	Tony Serratore 67
Dawn Rueterocox 69,76	Carla Erdey 71
John Connolly 73,98	Lisa Shulman 79
Mike Caruso 295	Scott Anthony 297

Public Schs..Principal	Grd	Prgm	Enr/#Cls	SN	
Amos Alonzo Stagg High Sch 8015 W 111th St, Palos Hills 60465 Eric Olsen	9-12	ATV	2,276 120	33%	708/974-7400 Fax 708/737-7716
Carl Sandburg High Sch 13300 S La Grange Rd, Orland Park 60462 Jennifer Tyrrell	9-12	V	2,818 100	12%	708/671-3100 Fax 708/737-7720
Victor J Andrew High Sch 9001 171st St, Tinley Park 60487 Robert Nolting	9-12	AV	2,214 100	18%	708/342-5800 Fax 708/737-7724

• **Cook County School Dist 104** PID: 00274641　　708/458-0505
  6021 S 74th Ave, Summit 60501　　　　　　　　　Fax 708/458-0532

Schools: 5 \ Teachers: 118 \ Students: 1,800 \ Special Ed Students: 200 \ LEP Students: 738 \ Ethnic: Asian 1%, African American 5%, Hispanic 85%, Caucasian 9% \ Exp: $336 (High) \ Poverty: 23% \ Title I: $680,583 \ Special Education: $756,000 \ Bilingual Education: $310,000 \ Open-Close: 08/24 - 05/28 \ DTBP: $220 (High)

Dr Troy Whalen 1,11	Kathleen Dunn 2,88,752
Jeff Moore 5	Scott Forman 6,27*
Jon Baricovich 9,57,76,79,270,288,296	Tim Willis 16,73,286,297*
Kathleen Johnson 59*	William Green 67
Christine Smith 69	Don Dames 91*
Barb Horazdovsky 294	

1 Superintendent	8 Curric/Instruct K-12	19 Chief Financial Officer	29 Family/Consumer Science	39 Social Studies K-12	49 English/Lang Arts Elem	59 Special Education Elem	69 Academic Assessment
2 Bus/Finance/Purchasing	9 Curric/Instruct Elem	20 Art K-12	30 Adult Education	40 Social Studies Elem	50 English/Lang Arts Sec	60 Special Education Sec	70 Research/Development
3 Buildings And Grounds	10 Curric/Instruct Sec	21 Art Elem	31 Career/Sch-to-Work K-12	41 Social Studies Sec	51 Reading K-12	61 Foreign/World Lang K-12	71 Public Information
4 Food Service	11 Federal Program	22 Art Sec	32 Career/Sch-to-Work Elem	42 Science K-12	52 Reading Elem	62 Foreign/World Lang Elem	72 Summer School
5 Transportation	12 Title I	23 Music K-12	33 Career/Sch-to-Work Sec	43 Science Elem	53 Reading Sec	63 Foreign/World Lang Sec	73 Instructional Tech
6 Athletic	13 Title V	24 Music Elem	34 Early Childhood Ed	44 Science Sec	54 Remedial Reading K-12	64 Religious Education K-12	74 Inservice Training
7 Health Services	15 Asst Superintendent	25 Music Sec	35 Health/Phys Education	45 Math K-12	55 Remedial Reading Elem	65 Religious Education Elem	75 Marketing/Distributive
	16 Instructional Media Svcs	26 Business Education	36 Guidance Services K-12	46 Math Elem	56 Remedial Reading Sec	66 Religious Education Sec	76 Info Systems
	17 Chief Operations Officer	27 Career & Tech Ed	37 Guidance Services Elem	47 Math Sec	57 Bilingual/ELL	67 School Board President	77 Psychological Assess
	18 Chief Academic Officer	28 Technology Education	38 Guidance Services Sec	48 English/Lang Arts K-12	58 Special Education K-12	68 Teacher Personnel	78 Affirmative Action

Illinois School Directory Cook County

Public Schs..Principal	Grd	Prgm	Enr/#Cls	SN		
Heritage Middle Sch 6021 S 74th Ave, Summit 60501 Robert Bassett	6-8	T	564 24		87%	708/458-7590 Fax 708/728-3111
Otis P Graves Elem Sch 6021 S 74th Ave, Summit 60501 Guillermina Arteaga	PK-4	T	492 27		89%	708/458-7260 Fax 708/728-3111
W W Walker Elem Sch 7735 W 66th Pl, Bedford Park 60501 Amanda Deaton	K-4	T	205 10		69%	708/458-7150 Fax 708/458-8466
Walsh Elem Sch 5640 S 75th Ave, Summit 60501 Christine Smith	K-4	T	353 18		83%	708/458-7165 Fax 708/458-7532
Wharton Fifth Grade Center 7555 W 64th St, Summit 60501 Carol Brackins	5-5	T	205 6		89%	708/458-0640 Fax 708/458-8467

- **Cook County School Dist 130** PID: 00267961 708/385-6800
  12300 Greenwood Ave, Blue Island 60406 Fax 708/385-8467

Schools: 11 \ Teachers: 258 \ Students: 4,000 \ Special Ed Students: 599 \ LEP Students: 846 \ Ethnic: African American 23%, Hispanic 60%, Caucasian 16% \ Exp: $276 (Med) \ Poverty: 19% \ Title I: $1,189,470 \ Special Education: $1,751,000 \ Bilingual Education: $274,000 \ Open-Close: 08/19 - 05/28 \ DTBP: $203 (High)

Dr Colleen McKay 1,11		Lucero Moreno 2,4,15		
Daniel Grand 3		Maria Montemayor 5		
Carrie Tisch 9,15*		Graig Mason 9		
Stephanie DelGrosso 9		Enid Alvarez 12,49,81		
John Dudzik 15,68		Alma Cano 34*		
Catherine Rotimi 57		Ernest Cherullo 59,79		
Gail Rubio 59,79		Jason Slattery 67		
Ernesto Santacruz 73,286				

Public Schs..Principal	Grd	Prgm	Enr/#Cls	SN		
E F Kerr Middle Sch 12915 Maple Ave, Blue Island 60406 Carl Gmazel	6-8	T	311 23		88%	708/385-5959 Fax 708/489-3582
George Washington Elem Sch 12545 S Homan Ave, Alsip 60803 Bridgette McNeal	K-5	T	268 14		84%	708/489-3523 Fax 708/371-3580
Horace Mann Sch 2975 W Broadway St, Blue Island 60406 Gerri Latting	PK-PK	T	259 10		16%	708/385-2450 Fax 708/293-4083
Lincoln Elem Sch 2140 Broadway St, Blue Island 60406 Terese Maurer	K-3	T	371 27		87%	708/385-5370 Fax 708/597-3405
Nathan Hale Intermediate Sch 5324 135th St Ste 2, Crestwood 60418 Churchill Daniels	4-5	T	211 10		72%	708/385-4690 Fax 708/293-4087
Nathan Hale Middle Sch 5220 135th St, Crestwood 60418 Kiwana Sanders	6-8	T	440 27		72%	708/385-6690 Fax 708/385-2417
Nathan Hale Primary Sch 5324 135th St, Crestwood 60418 Alicia Smith	PK-5	T	564 21		70%	708/385-4690 Fax 708/293-4087
Paul Revere Intermediate Sch 12331 Gregory St, Blue Island 60406 Connie Grason	4-5	T	224 13		88%	708/385-4450 Fax 708/489-3576
Paul Revere Primary Sch 2300 123rd Pl, Blue Island 60406 Darren Jones	K-3	T	385 25		86%	708/489-3533 Fax 708/385-3546
Veterans Memorial Middle Sch 12320 Greenwood Ave, Blue Island 60406 Michael Steele	6-8	T	377 20		89%	708/385-6630 Fax 708/489-3522

Public Schs..Principal	Grd	Prgm	Enr/#Cls	SN		
Whittier Sch 13043 Maple Ave, Blue Island 60406 Danielle Graber	4-5	T	189 12		89%	708/385-6170 Fax 708/389-4569

- **Cook County School Dist 154** PID: 00274720 708/877-5160
  200 N Wolcott St, Thornton 60476 Fax 708/877-2537

Schools: 1 \ Teachers: 22 \ Students: 225 \ Special Ed Students: 29 \ LEP Students: 39 \ Ethnic: African American 33%, Hispanic 37%, Caucasian 30% \ Exp: $513 (High) \ Poverty: 16% \ Title I: $74,546 \ Special Education: $234,000 \ Bilingual Education: $4,000 \ Open-Close: 08/24 - 06/04 \ f t

Dr Thomas Hurlburt 1	Danielle Byrd 2,73
Peter Frezza 3*	Megan Drangsholt 12,59,88,298
Marg Schweitzer 67	

Public Schs..Principal	Grd	Prgm	Enr/#Cls	SN		
Wolcott Sch 200 N Wolcott St, Thornton 60476 Dr Thomas Hurlburt	PK-8		225 18		54%	708/877-2526

- **Country Club Hills SD 160** PID: 00268680 708/957-6200
  4411 185th St, Cntry CLB Hls 60478 Fax 708/957-8686

Schools: 3 \ Teachers: 80 \ Students: 1,221 \ Special Ed Students: 220 \ LEP Students: 28 \ Ethnic: Asian 1%, African American 93%, Hispanic 4%, Caucasian 2% \ Exp: $131 (Low) \ Poverty: 25% \ Title I: $753,634 \ Special Education: $1,125,000 \ Bilingual Education: $2,000 \ Open-Close: 08/17 - 05/28 \ DTBP: $241 (High)

Dr Duane Meighan 1	Kenya Austin 2
Brenda Richardson 9	Dr Tawanda Lawrence 9,11,73,288,296
Dr Sandra Thomas 11,57,83	Sheleah Blissett 59,79,275
Jacqueline Doss 67	Dr Tracy Lett-Foreman 68,71,298
Millicent Griffin 76	Rebecca Dixon 79

Public Schs..Principal	Grd	Prgm	Enr/#Cls	SN		
Meadowview Intermediate Sch 4701 179th St, Cntry CLB Hls 60478 Dr Sonya Hubbard-Green	3-5	T	423 23		75%	708/957-6220 Fax 708/922-2673
Southwood Middle Sch 18635 Lee St, Cntry CLB Hls 60478 Brenda Richardson	6-8	T	444 26		75%	708/957-6230 Fax 708/799-4033
Zenon Sykuta Elem Sch 4301 180th St, Cntry CLB Hls 60478 Brenda Richardson \ **Leatha Stewart**	PK-2	T	354 22		64%	708/957-6210 Fax 708/799-2053

- **Des Plaines Cmty Cons SD 62** PID: 00268733 847/824-1136
  777 E Algonquin Rd, Des Plaines 60016 Fax 847/824-0612

Schools: 11 \ Teachers: 398 \ Students: 4,800 \ Special Ed Students: 777 \ LEP Students: 1,375 \ Ethnic: Asian 12%, African American 4%, Hispanic 44%, Caucasian 40% \ Exp: $211 (Med) \ Poverty: 12% \ Title I: $956,690 \ Special Education: $2,894,000 \ Bilingual Education: $359,000 \ Open-Close: 08/17 - 06/04 \ DTBP: $222 (High) \ f t

Paul Hertel 1	Mark Bertolozzi 2,4,15
Michael Vilendrer 3,5	Mark Moser 6,35
Laura Sangroula 9,15	Adam Denenberg 12,17,19,73,76,98,288,296
Dr Ellen Swanson 15	Michael Amadei 15,68
Christy Bowman 29,43,46	Margarite Beniaris 34,79,274
Carlos Rojas 57	Erica Tae 57
Libby Juskiewicz 57	Milagros Bravo 57,89,271
Jennifer Bova 71	Ejaz Syed 297

79 Student Personnel	91 Safety/Security	275 Response To Intervention	298 Grant Writer/Ptnrships	**School Programs**	**Social Media**	
80 Driver Ed/Safety	92 Magnet School	277 Remedial Math K-12	750 Chief Innovation Officer	A = Alternative Program		
81 Gifted/Talented	93 Parental Involvement	280 Literacy Coach	751 Chief of Staff	G = Adult Classes	f = Facebook	
82 Video Services	95 Tech Prep Program	285 STEM	752 Social Emotional Learning	M = Magnet Program		
83 Substance Abuse Prev	97 Chief Information Officer	286 Digital Learning		T = Title I Schoolwide	t = Twitter	
84 Erate	98 Chief Technology Officer	288 Common Core Standards	**Other School Types**	V = Career & Tech Ed Programs		
85 AIDS Education	270 Accountability	294 Accountability	Ⓐ = Alternative School			
88 Alternative/At Risk	271 Migrant Education	295 Network System	Ⓒ = Charter School	New Schools are shaded		
89 Multi-Cultural Curriculum	273 Teacher Mentor	296 Title II Programs	Ⓜ = Magnet School	New Superintendents and Principals are bold		
90 Social Work	274 Before/After Sch	297 Webmaster	Ⓨ = Year-Round School	Personnel with email addresses are underscored		

IL—45

Cook County

Market Data Retrieval

Public Schs..Principal	Grd	Prgm	Enr/#Cls	SN	
Algonquin Middle Sch 767 E Algonquin Rd, Des Plaines 60016 **Donald Jones**	6-8	TV	662 40	56%	847/824-1205 Fax 847/824-1270
Central Elem Sch 1526 E Thacker St, Des Plaines 60016 Erica Cupuro	K-5	T	259 14	36%	847/824-1575 Fax 847/824-1656
Chippewa Middle Sch 123 N 8th Ave, Des Plaines 60016 **Kermit Blakley**	6-8	T	666 65	50%	847/824-1503 Fax 847/824-1514
Cumberland Elem Sch 700 E Golf Rd, Des Plaines 60016 Colleen White	K-5	T	294 22	37%	847/824-1451 Fax 847/824-0724
Forest Elem Sch 1375 S 5th Ave, Des Plaines 60018 Ania Figueroa	PK-5	T	622 22	45%	847/824-1380 Fax 847/824-1732
Iroquois Community Sch 1836 E Touhy Ave, Des Plaines 60018 Kelly Krueger	K-8	M	474 17	23%	847/824-1308 Fax 847/824-1310
North Elem Sch 1789 Rand Rd, Des Plaines 60016 Dr Margo Giannoulis	K-5	T	456 29	61%	847/824-1399 Fax 847/824-1768
Orchard Place Elem Sch 2727 Maple St, Des Plaines 60018 Jennifer Bautista	K-5	T	271 18	59%	847/824-1255 Fax 847/824-1752
Plainfield Elem Sch 1850 Plainfield Dr, Des Plaines 60018 Lisa Carlos	K-5	T	304 17	59%	847/824-1301 Fax 847/824-1547
South Elem Sch 1535 Everett Ave, Des Plaines 60018 Kristin Jares	K-5	T	238 20	55%	847/824-1566 Fax 847/824-1759
Terrace Elem Sch 735 S Westgate Rd, Des Plaines 60016 Bradley Stein	K-5	T	216 11	39%	847/824-1501 Fax 847/824-1764

● **Dolton School District 149** PID: 00268977
292 Torrence Ave, Calumet City 60409
708/868-8300
Fax 708/868-9412

Schools: 8 \ **Teachers:** 136 \ **Students:** 2,600 \ **Special Ed Students:** 362 \ **LEP Students:** 101 \ **Ethnic:** African American 96%, Hispanic 3%, Caucasian 1% \ **Exp:** $191 (Low) \ **Poverty:** 28% \ **Title I:** $1,902,904 \ **Special Education:** $1,342,000 \ **Bilingual Education:** $11,000 \ **Open-Close:** 08/24 - 06/02 \ **DTBP:** $165 (High)

Dr Shelly Davis-Jones 1
Akil Khalfani 3
April Davis 34*
Darlene Gray-Everett 67
Cedric Lewis 2,73,84
Twyla Harris 15
Vedia Page 59

Public Schs..Principal	Grd	Prgm	Enr/#Cls	SN	
Berger-Vandenberg Elem Sch 14833 Avalon Ave, Dolton 60419 Taquia Hylton	K-5	T	370 15	100%	708/841-3606 Fax 708/201-4725
Carol Mosley Braun Elem Sch 1655 153rd St, Calumet City 60409 Jamie Hayes	1-5	T	320 17	100%	708/868-9470 Fax 708/868-9466
Caroline Sibley Elem Sch 1550 Sibley Blvd, Calumet City 60409 Carolyn Franklin	K-6	T	603 36	100%	708/868-1870 Fax 708/868-7591
Creative Communications Acad 1650 Pulaski Rd, Calumet City 60409 Gerald Scott	6-8	T	210	99%	708/868-7585 Fax 708/868-1246
Diekman Elem Sch 15121 Dorchester Ave, Dolton 60419 April Davis	PK-6	T	360 16	100%	708/841-3838 Fax 708/201-4719
New Beginnings Learning Acad 15703 Clyde Ave, South Holland 60473 Karen Slate	K-6	T	402 18	99%	708/768-5200 Fax 708/768-5209
School of Fine Arts 1650 Pulaski Rd, Calumet City 60409 Dellnora Winters	7-8	T	188	99%	708/868-7565 Fax 708/868-7589
STEM Academy 1650 Pulaski Rd, Calumet City 60409 Michael Steele	6-8	T	207	98%	708/868-7595 Fax 708/868-7562

● **Dolton-Riverdale Sch Dist 148** PID: 00268874
114 W 144th St, Riverdale 60827
708/841-2290
Fax 708/841-5048

Schools: 10 \ **Teachers:** 191 \ **Students:** 2,183 \ **Special Ed Students:** 314 \ **LEP Students:** 83 \ **Ethnic:** African American 96%, Hispanic 4%, \ **Exp:** $287 (Med) \ **Poverty:** 32% \ **Title I:** $1,946,146 \ **Special Education:** $827,000 \ **Open-Close:** 08/21 - 06/01 \ **DTBP:** $233 (High)

Dr Kevin Nohelty 1
Jason Cooley 3
Dr Sonya Whittaker ... 6,15,68,69,288,296,298
Lisa Davis-Smith 11
Larry Lawrence 67
Karen Marshall 71,73,76,286,294,295*
Torie Navarre 275
Kevin Reese 2,3
Michelle O'Malley 4
Shinora Montgomery 9,93*
Melanie Llanes 59
John Donermeyer 70*
Mike Hurst 273*

Public Schs..Principal	Grd	Prgm	Enr/#Cls	SN	
Early Childhood Center 333 E 142nd St, Dolton 60419 Shinora Montgomery	PK-PK		110 5		708/841-2602 Fax 708/201-2082
Franklin Elem Sch 14701 Martin Luther King Jr Dr, Dolton 60419 Martez James	K-6	T	251 15	97%	708/201-2083 Fax 708/201-2084
Lincoln Elem Sch 14151 Lincoln Ave, Dolton 60419 Byron Stingily	K-6	T	333 39	86%	708/201-2075 Fax 708/849-3758
Lincoln Junior High Sch 14151 Lincoln Ave, Dolton 60419 Byron Stingily	7-8	T	181	75%	708/201-2075 Fax 708/849-3758
Park Sch 14200 S Wentworth Ave, Riverdale 60827 Dione Wilson	K-6	T	207 16	98%	708/849-9440 Fax 708/201-2144
Riverdale Sch 325 W 142nd St, Riverdale 60827 Shinora Montgomery	K-4	T	151 6	86%	708/849-7153 Fax 708/201-2145
Roosevelt Elem Sch 111 W 146th St, Dolton 60419 Kim Brasfield	K-5	T	377 16	94%	708/201-2070 Fax 708/849-7880
Roosevelt Junior High Sch 111 W 146th St, Dolton 60419 Kim Brasfield	6-8	T	200	88%	708/201-2071 Fax 708/849-1285
Washington Elem Sch 13900 S School St, Riverdale 60827 Dornetta Walker	K-5	T	300 19	95%	708/201-2078 Fax 708/201-2148
Washington Junior High Sch 13900 S School St, Riverdale 60827 Dornetta Walker	6-8	T	200	98%	708/201-2078 Fax 708/201-2148

1	Superintendent	8	Curric/Instruct K-12	19	Chief Financial Officer	29	Family/Consumer Science	39	Social Studies K-12	49	English/Lang Arts Elem	59	Special Education Elem	69	Academic Assessment
2	Bus/Finance/Purchasing	9	Curric/Instruct Elem	20	Art K-12	30	Adult Education	40	Social Studies Elem	50	English/Lang Arts Sec	60	Special Education Sec	70	Research/Development
3	Buildings And Grounds	10	Curric/Instruct Sec	21	Art Elem	31	Career/Sch-to-Work K-12	41	Social Studies Sec	51	Reading K-12	61	Foreign/World Lang K-12	71	Public Information
4	Food Service	11	Federal Program	22	Art Sec	32	Career/Sch-to-Work Elem	42	Science K-12	52	Reading Elem	62	Foreign/World Lang Elem	72	Summer School
5	Transportation	12	Title I	23	Music K-12	33	Career/Sch-to-Work Sec	43	Science Elem	53	Reading Sec	63	Foreign/World Lang Sec	73	Instructional Tech
6	Athletic	13	Title V	24	Music Elem	34	Early Childhood Ed	44	Science Sec	54	Remedial Reading K-12	64	Religious Education K-12	74	Inservice Training
7	Health Services	15	Asst Superintendent	25	Music Sec	35	Health/Phys Education	45	Math K-12	55	Remedial Reading Elem	65	Religious Education Elem	75	Marketing/Distributive
		16	Instructional Media Svcs	26	Business Education	36	Guidance Services K-12	46	Math Elem	56	Remedial Reading Sec	66	Religious Education Sec	76	Info Systems
		17	Chief Operations Officer	27	Career & Tech Ed	37	Guidance Services Elem	47	Math Sec	57	Bilingual/ELL	67	School Board President	77	Psychological Assess
		18	Chief Academic Officer	28	Technology Education	38	Guidance Services Sec	48	English/Lang Arts K-12	58	Special Education K-12	68	Teacher Personnel	78	Affirmative Action

Illinois School Directory   Cook County

● E F Lindop Elem Sch Dist 92 PID: 00270906   708/345-8834
2400 S 18th Ave, Broadview 60155   Fax 708/345-8569

Schools: 1 \ **Teachers:** 32 \ **Students:** 480 \ **Special Ed Students:** 70 \ **LEP Students:** 28 \ **Ethnic:** African American 82%, Hispanic 16%, Caucasian 2% \ **Exp:** $725 (High) \ **Poverty:** 18% \ **Title I:** $142,701 \ **Special Education:** $189,000 \ **Open-Close:** 08/14 - 05/26 \ **DTBP:** $212 (High)

Dr Janiece Jackson 1,11	Dajuan Ballentine 3
Scott Beranek 4,294	Dr Emily Betz 9,285
Dr Sonya Spaulding 12,275,288*	Evan Whitehead ...18,19,57,76,83,88,296,298
Carla Joiner-Herrod 67	Dr Erison Betz 69,79,280
Joshua Eliscu 73,84,286,295*	John Kanobe 270

Public Schs..Principal	Grd	Prgm	Enr/#Cls	SN	
E F Lindop Elem Sch 2400 S 18th Ave, Broadview 60155 Dr Sonya Spaulding	PK-8		480 28	46%	708/345-3110

● East Maine School District 63 PID: 00269098   847/299-1900
10150 Dee Rd, Des Plaines 60016   Fax 847/299-9963

Schools: 6 \ **Teachers:** 256 \ **Students:** 3,500 \ **Special Ed Students:** 496 \ **LEP Students:** 1,184 \ **Ethnic:** Asian 31%, African American 4%, Hispanic 28%, Caucasian 37% \ **Exp:** $533 (High) \ **Poverty:** 15% \ **Title I:** $911,831 \ **Special Education:** $1,815,000 \ **Bilingual Education:** $290,000 \ **Open-Close:** 08/17 - 06/01 \ **DTBP:** $223 (High) \ f t

Dr Scott Clay 1	Jordi Camps 2,4
Dan Barrie 3,91	Leslie White 7,35,85*
Aaron Roberson 9,11,16,69,74,83,273,296	Keith Shaffer 13,27,73,95,295,297
Dr Shawn Schleizer 15,68,79	Erin Sterling 57
Vasiliki Frake 59	Alexandra Brook 67
Jacqueline Loera 68	Janet Bishop 71
Angelica Schab 274	Abin Koshy 295

Public Schs..Principal	Grd	Prgm	Enr/#Cls	SN	
Apollo Elem Sch 10100 Dee Rd, Des Plaines 60016 Cassandra Schwartz	K-5	T	595 25	59%	847/827-6231 Fax 847/827-1785
Gemini Middle Sch 8955 N Greenwood Ave, Niles 60714 Lewis Roberts	6-8	T	694 70	51%	847/827-1181 Fax 847/827-3499
Mark Twain Elem Sch 9401 N Hamlin Ave, Niles 60714 Howard Sussman	K-5	T	307 18	59%	847/296-5341 Fax 847/296-5345
Melzer Elem Sch 9400 Oriole Ave, Morton Grove 60053 **Angela Maki**	K-5		506 21	37%	847/965-7474 Fax 847/965-0539
V H Nelson Elem Sch 8901 N Ozanam Ave, Niles 60714 Lauren Leitao	K-6	T	572 20	52%	847/965-0050 Fax 847/965-7630
Washington Elem Sch 2701 Golf Rd, Glenview 60025 Kate Anderson	K-5	T	305 13	46%	847/965-4780 Fax 847/965-4807

● East Prairie School Dist 73 PID: 00269218   847/673-1141
7616 E Prairie Rd, Skokie 60076   Fax 847/673-1186

Schools: 1 \ **Teachers:** 42 \ **Students:** 505 \ **Special Ed Students:** 70 \ **LEP Students:** 101 \ **Ethnic:** Asian 36%, African American 5%, Hispanic 17%, Native American: 1%, Caucasian 42% \ **Exp:** $274 (Med) \ **Poverty:** 12% \ **Title I:** $84,950 \ **Special Education:** $138,000 \ **Bilingual Education:** $31,000 \ **Open-Close:** 08/24 - 06/02 \ **DTBP:** $119 (High)

Dr Paul Goldberg 1	Cyndi Cohen 2
Mark Kierznowski 2,3	Theresa Alberico-Madl 11,83,288
Carolyn Mertz 35,85*	Debra Yasutake 59
Atanu Das 67	Jordan Stephen 70*
Rich Chiuppi 73	

Public Schs..Principal	Grd	Prgm	Enr/#Cls	SN	
East Prairie Elem Sch 7616 E Prairie Rd, Skokie 60076 Hal Schmeisser	PK-8		505 22	28%	847/673-1141

● Elementary School District 159 PID: 00274158   708/720-1300
6202 Vollmer Rd, Matteson 60443   Fax 708/720-3218

Schools: 5 \ **Teachers:** 146 \ **Students:** 1,700 \ **Special Ed Students:** 219 \ **LEP Students:** 83 \ **Ethnic:** African American 87%, Hispanic 10%, Caucasian 2% \ **Exp:** $193 (Low) \ **Poverty:** 20% \ **Title I:** $725,159 \ **Special Education:** $1,202,000 \ **Bilingual Education:** $17,000 \ **Open-Close:** 08/24 - 05/31 \ **DTBP:** $233 (High)

Dr Mable Alfred 1	Demetria Brown 2
Dwight Major 3	Dr Denean Adams 9,15,288
Lisa Odonvan 43	Miriam McCoy 57
Dr William McClinton 67	Ed Short 73
Shelia Friday 298	

Public Schs..Principal	Grd	Prgm	Enr/#Cls	SN	
Colin Powell Middle Sch 20600 Matteson Ave, Matteson 60443 Vincent Payne	6-8		660	70%	708/283-9600 Fax 708/283-0718
Marya Yates Elem Sch 6131 Allemong Dr, Matteson 60443 Lawanda Gordon	K-5		347 35	75%	708/720-1800 Fax 708/720-0199
Neil Armstrong Elem Sch 5030 Imperial Dr, Richton Park 60471 Shahran Etherly	K-5		333 26	68%	708/481-7424 Fax 708/481-7476
Sieden Prairie Elem Sch 725 Notre Dame Dr, Matteson 60443 Latonya McCaskill	K-5		248 24	81%	708/720-2626 Fax 708/720-4640
Woodgate Elem Sch 101 Central Ave, Matteson 60443 Antonia Hill	PK-5		322 35	73%	708/720-1107 Fax 708/720-3225

● Elmwood Park Cmty Unit SD 401 PID: 00269232   708/452-7292
8201 W Fullerton Ave, Elmwood Park 60707   Fax 708/452-9504

Schools: 5 \ **Teachers:** 191 \ **Students:** 2,800 \ **Special Ed Students:** 502 \ **LEP Students:** 523 \ **College-Bound:** 76% \ **Ethnic:** Asian 2%, African American 2%, Hispanic 55%, Caucasian 40% \ **Exp:** $115 (Low) \ **Poverty:** 12% \ **Title I:** $648,456 \ **Special Education:** $1,770,000 \ **Bilingual Education:** $174,000 \ **Open-Close:** 08/31 - 06/09 \ **DTBP:** $191 (High)

Dr Leah Gauthier 1	James Jennings 2,15*
Joseph Sierra 3	Douglas Noyes 6,35,80,85
Barbara Meilinger 7*	Lia Gauthier 8,11,78,90,298*

---

79 Student Personnel	91 Safety/Security	275 Response To Intervention	298 Grant Writer/Ptnrships	**School Programs**	**Social Media**
80 Driver Ed/Safety	92 Magnet School	277 Remedial Math K-12	750 Chief Innovation Officer	A = Alternative Program	f = Facebook
81 Gifted/Talented	93 Parental Involvement	280 Literacy Coach	751 Chief of Staff	G = Adult Classes	
82 Video Services	95 Tech Prep Program	285 STEM	752 Social Emotional Learning	M = Magnet Program	t = Twitter
83 Substance Abuse Prev	97 Chief Information Officer	286 Digital Learning		T = Title I Schoolwide	
84 Erate	98 Chief Technology Officer	288 Common Core Standards	**Other School Types**	V = Career & Tech Ed Programs	
85 AIDS Education	270 Accountability	294 Character Education	Ⓐ = Alternative School		
88 Alternative/At Risk	271 Migrant Education	295 Network System	Ⓒ = Charter School	New Schools are shaded	
89 Multi-Cultural Curriculum	273 Teacher Mentor	296 Title II Programs	Ⓜ = Magnet School	New Superintendents and Principals are bold	
90 Social Work	274 Before/After Sch	297 Webmaster	Ⓨ = Year-Round School	Personnel with email addresses are underscored	IL—47

Cook County — Market Data Retrieval

Paige Cozyra 36	Pamela Stutzman 58
Sara Barrick 58	Mary Bruscato 67
Jessica Iovinelli 73	Tom Kinane 73
Dr Kari Smith 79	Barbara Bocka 88*
Douglas Selix 295	Quirino Carlin 295

Public Schs..Principal	Grd	Prgm	Enr/#Cls	SN	
Elm Middle Sch 7607 W Cortland St, Elmwood Park 60707 **Ashley Groeneveld**	7-8	TV	423 31	50%	708/452-3550 Fax 708/452-0662
Elmwood Elem Sch 2319 N 76th Ave, Elmwood Park 60707 Matthew Lerner	1-6	T	585 22	44%	708/452-3558 Fax 708/452-5567
Elmwood Park Early Chldhd Ctr 4 W Conti Pkwy, Elmwood Park 60707 Kevin Seibel	PK-K	AT	214 14	48%	708/583-5860 Fax 708/583-5899
Elmwood Park High Sch 8201 W Fullerton Ave, Elmwood Park 60707 Douglas Wildes	9-12	GTV	952 40	46%	708/452-7272 Fax 708/452-0732
John Mills Elem Sch 2824 N 76th Ave, Elmwood Park 60707 Frank Kuzniewski	1-6	T	610 26	55%	708/452-3560 Fax 708/452-0349

• **Evanston Twp High SD 202** PID: 00269505 847/424-7000
1600 Dodge Ave, Evanston 60201 Fax 847/492-3872

Schools: 1 \ **Teachers:** 263 \ **Students:** 3,800 \ **Special Ed Students:** 485 \ **LEP Students:** 191 \ **College-Bound:** 78% \ **Ethnic:** Asian 6%, African American 28%, Hispanic 19%, Caucasian 47% \ **Exp:** $254 (Med) \ **Poverty:** 7% \ **Title I:** $325,861 \ **Special Education:** $3,393,000 \ **Bilingual Education:** $43,000 \ **Open-Close:** 08/17 - 05/28 \ **DTBP:** $231 (High)

Dr Eric Witherspoon 1	Mary Rodino 2,11,19
Clarance Gregory 3	Kim Minestra 4*
Chris Livatino 6	Jeanette Cruz 7
Peter Bavis 10,288*	Robert Brown 12,17*
Marcus Campbell 15,296*	David Chan 16
Mike Corcoran 16,73,82,98*	Shelley Gates 27*
Beth Arey 33*	Dale Leibforth 47*
Jenny Neal 57	Rachel Gressel 57*
Pat Savage-William 67	Toya Campbell 68,751
Carrie Levy 69	Anya Pierce 70
Takumi Iseda 71	Dondelayo White 79*
Anna Landmeier 83*	Matthew Driscoll 91*
Scott Bramley 280*	Fdavid Chan 286
Joanne Bertsche 298	

Public Schs..Principal	Grd	Prgm	Enr/#Cls	SN	
Evanston Twp High Sch 1600 Dodge Ave, Evanston 60201 Marcus Campbell	9-12	AGV	3,800	36%	847/424-7000 Fax 847/429-3879

• **Evanston-Skokie Cmty CSD 65** PID: 00269282 847/859-8000
1500 McDaniel Ave, Evanston 60201 Fax 847/866-7265

Schools: 18 \ **Teachers:** 644 \ **Students:** 8,030 \ **Special Ed Students:** 1,036 \ **LEP Students:** 1,030 \ **Ethnic:** Asian 5%, African American 25%, Hispanic 23%, Caucasian 47% \ **Exp:** $217 (Med) \ **Poverty:** 9% \ **Title I:** $1,007,379 \ **Special Education:** $6,238,000 \ **Bilingual Education:** $307,000 \ **Open-Close:** 08/24 - 06/01 \ **DTBP:** $216 (High)

Cheryl Geary 2	Raphael Obafemi 2,3,17,19,298
Don Stevenson 3	Kathryn Mason-Schultz 4*
Lou Gatta 5	James McHolland 6,35*
Mary Larson 7	Stacy Beardsley 9,15,288
Elizabeth Cardenas-Lopez 12,280	Andalib Khelghati 15*

Beatrice Davis 15,68	Romona DeCristosaro 15,34,59
Angela Johnson 30,93	Sharon Sprague 34
Amy Correa 57*	Sunith Kartha 67
Melissa Messinger 71	Joe Caravello 73,82
Leo Ruiz 76	Charlotte Carter 274*
David Wartowski 285	Kylie Klein 294
Mark Annerud 295	Joaquim Stephenson 752

Public Schs..Principal	Grd	Prgm	Enr/#Cls	SN	
Chute Middle Sch 1400 Oakton St, Evanston 60202 James McHolland	6-8	T	611 30	55%	847/859-8600 Fax 847/492-7956
Dawes Elem Sch 440 Dodge Ave, Evanston 60202 Marlene Aponte	K-5	T	369 17	59%	847/905-3400 Fax 847/492-9841
Dewey Elem Sch 1551 Wesley Ave, Evanston 60201 Donna Sokolowski	K-5		484 16	29%	847/859-8140 Fax 847/492-7994
Dr MLK Jr Sch-Lit/Fine Arts 2424 Lake St, Evanston 60201 Dr Jeff Brown	K-8	T	560 30	45%	847/859-8500 Fax 847/492-1413
Francis Willard Elem Sch 2700 Hurd Ave, Evanston 60201 Jerry Michel	K-5		501 16	25%	847/905-3600 Fax 847/733-2100
Haven Middle Sch 2417 Prairie Ave, Evanston 60201 Chris Latting	6-8	V	836 40	27%	847/859-8200 Fax 847/492-9983
Joseph E Hill Education Center 1500 McDaniel Ave, Evanston 60201 Amy Small	PK-PK		327	53%	847/859-8300 Fax 847/866-7259
Kingsley Elem Sch 2300 Green Bay Rd, Evanston 60201 David Davis	K-5		398 19	31%	847/859-8400 Fax 847/492-5868
Lincoln Elem Sch 910 Forest Ave, Evanston 60202 Michelle Cooney	K-5		518 18	27%	847/905-3500 Fax 847/492-1870
Lincolnwood Elem Sch 2600 Colfax St, Evanston 60201 Max Weinberg	K-5		390 19	28%	847/859-8880 Fax 847/492-7958
Nichols Middle Sch 800 Greenleaf St, Evanston 60202 Adrian Harries	6-8	V	780 25	30%	847/859-8660 Fax 847/492-7880
Oakton Elem Sch 436 Ridge Ave, Evanston 60202 Michael Allen	K-5	T	375 27	67%	847/859-8800 Fax 847/492-7960
Orrington Elem Sch 2636 Orrington Ave, Evanston 60201 Jessica Plaza	K-5		378 22	16%	847/859-8780 Fax 847/492-9003
Park Sch 828 Main St, Evanston 60202 Jillian Anderson	Spec		61 10	60%	847/424-2300 Fax 847/492-7962
Rhodes Sch of Global Studies 3701 Davis St, Skokie 60076 Keri Mendez	K-8		270 18	45%	847/859-8440 Fax 847/674-3926
Rice Education Center 1101 Washington St, Evanston 60202 John Mitchell	Spec		46 7	91%	847/424-2450
Walker Elem Sch 3601 Church St, Evanston 60203 James Gray	K-5	T	387 15	42%	847/859-8330 Fax 847/674-7004
Washington Elem Sch 914 Ashland Ave, Evanston 60202 Kate Ellison	K-5	T	536 24	41%	847/905-4900 Fax 847/492-8433

1 Superintendent	8 Curric/Instruct K-12	19 Chief Financial Officer	29 Family/Consumer Science	39 Social Studies K-12	49 English/Lang Arts Elem	59 Special Education Elem	69 Academic Assessment
2 Bus/Finance/Purchasing	9 Curric/Instruct Elem	20 Art K-12	30 Adult Education	40 Social Studies Elem	50 English/Lang Arts Sec	60 Special Education Sec	70 Research/Development
3 Buildings And Grounds	10 Curric/Instruct Sec	21 Art Elem	31 Career/Sch-to-Work K-12	41 Social Studies Sec	51 Reading K-12	61 Foreign/World Lang K-12	71 Public Information
4 Food Service	11 Federal Program	22 Art Sec	32 Career/Sch-to-Work Elem	42 Science K-12	52 Reading Elem	62 Foreign/World Lang Elem	72 Summer School
5 Transportation	12 Title I	23 Music K-12	33 Career/Sch-to-Work Sec	43 Science Elem	53 Reading Sec	63 Foreign/World Lang Sec	73 Instructional Tech
6 Athletic	13 Title V	24 Music Elem	34 Early Childhood Ed	44 Science Sec	54 Remedial Reading K-12	64 Religious Education K-12	74 Inservice Training
7 Health Services	14 Instructional Media Svcs	25 Music Sec	35 Health/Phys Education	45 Math K-12	55 Remedial Reading Elem	65 Religious Education Elem	75 Marketing/Distributive
	15 Asst Superintendent	26 Business Education	36 Guidance Services K-12	46 Math Elem	56 Remedial Reading Sec	66 Religious Education Sec	76 Info Systems
	16 Chief Operations Officer	27 Career & Tech Ed	37 Guidance Services Elem	47 Math Sec	57 Bilingual/ELL	67 School Board President	77 Psychological Assess
	17 Chief Academic Officer	28 Technology Education	38 Guidance Services Sec	48 English/Lang Arts K-12	58 Special Education K-12	68 Teacher Personnel	78 Affirmative Action

Illinois School Directory — Cook County

● Evergreen Park Cmty HSD 231 PID: 00269581 708/424-7400
9901 S Kedzie Ave, Evergreen Pk 60805 Fax 708/424-7497

Schools: 1 \ **Teachers:** 58 \ **Students:** 850 \ **Special Ed Students:** 114 \ **LEP Students:** 22 \ **Ethnic:** Asian 1%, African American 35%, Hispanic 22%, Caucasian 42% \ **Exp:** $320 (High) \ **Poverty:** 6% \ **Title I:** $147,130 \ **Special Education:** $780,000 \ **Open-Close:** 08/19 - 06/04 \ **DTBP:** $254 (High) \ f

Tom Omalley	1	Terry Masterson	3	
Jim Soldan	6*	Debbie Schillo	10,74,273,288*	
Deborah Schillo	10,11	William Sanderson	15,69,79,93*	
Tina Ward	16*	Larry Symanski	67	
Jim Smith	73,286	Jim Donato	76	
Shaunita Bowen	83,88*			

Public Schs..Principal	Grd	Prgm	Enr/#Cls	SN	
Evergreen Park Cmty High Sch 9901 S Kedzie Ave, Evergreen Pk 60805 William Sanderson	9-12	V	850	32%	708/424-7400 f

● Evergreen Park Elem SD 124 PID: 00269529 708/423-0950
2929 W 87th St, Evergreen Pk 60805 Fax 708/423-4292

Schools: 5 \ **Teachers:** 161 \ **Students:** 1,900 \ **Special Ed Students:** 326 \ **LEP Students:** 157 \ **Ethnic:** Asian 1%, African American 27%, Hispanic 28%, Caucasian 43% \ **Exp:** $235 (Med) \ **Poverty:** 10% \ **Title I:** $317,748 \ **Special Education:** $1,196,000 \ **Bilingual Education:** $49,000 \ **Open-Close:** 08/24 - 06/04 \ **DTBP:** $230 (High)

Dr Margret Longo	1	Tim Kostecki	2
James Hennessy	3	Deborah Michicich	4
Veda Newman	7,57,77,79	Kathleen Prabo	9,11,69,74,288
Matt Kellett	16,73,76,297	Emory Burdette	46
Jennifer Gervase	52,280	Kim Leonard	67
Alex Mayster	71	Janet Fettig	76
Denise McField	79	Patrice Boswell	274
Michael Freewalt	295		

Public Schs..Principal	Grd	Prgm	Enr/#Cls	SN	
Central Middle Sch 9400 S Sawyer Ave, Evergreen Pk 60805 Kathleen Prado	7-8	T	547 28	44%	708/424-0148 Fax 708/229-8406
Northeast Elem Sch 9058 S California Ave, Evergreen Pk 60805 Jackie Janicke \ **Carrie Berry**	PK-5	T	314 18	62%	708/422-6501 Fax 708/229-8410
Northwest Elem Sch 3630 W 92nd St, Evergreen Pk 60805 Dr Matthew Banach	PK-6	T	326 18	42%	708/425-9473 Fax 708/229-8407
Southeast Elem Sch 9800 S Francisco Ave, Evergreen Pk 60805 Timothy Sheldon	K-5	T	306 20	48%	708/422-1021 Fax 708/229-8413
Southwest Elem Sch 9900 S Central Park Ave, Evergreen Pk 60805 Scott Liska	K-6	T	298 15	19%	708/424-2444 Fax 708/229-8416

● Fairview South School Dist 72 PID: 00274342 847/929-1048
7040 Laramie Ave, Skokie 60077 Fax 847/929-1058

Schools: 1 \ **Teachers:** 68 \ **Students:** 722 \ **Special Ed Students:** 135 \ **LEP Students:** 67 \ **Ethnic:** Asian 33%, African American 2%, Hispanic 14%, Caucasian 51% \ **Exp:** $331 (High) \ **Poverty:** 9% \ **Title I:** $136,435 \ **Special Education:** $235,000 \ **Bilingual Education:** $7,000 \ **Open-Close:** 08/25 - 06/09 \ **DTBP:** $105 (High)

Dr Cindy Whittaker	1,11,83,288	Jeff Feyerer	2
Cassio DaSilva	3*	Kristen Godfrey	16,82*
Mary Brown	67	Gloria Meske	68
Mark Fidor	73,286	Carly Gross	79

Public Schs..Principal	Grd	Prgm	Enr/#Cls	SN	
Fairview South Elem Sch 7040 Laramie Ave, Skokie 60077 Athanasia Albans \ Mike Lopatka	PK-8		722 48	26%	847/929-1048

● Flossmoor School District 161 PID: 00269608 708/647-7000
41 E Elmwood Dr, Chicago HTS 60411 Fax 708/754-2153

Schools: 5 \ **Teachers:** 163 \ **Students:** 2,374 \ **Special Ed Students:** 332 \ **LEP Students:** 111 \ **Ethnic:** Asian 1%, African American 67%, Hispanic 17%, Caucasian 15% \ **Exp:** $586 (High) \ **Poverty:** 11% \ **Title I:** $388,059 \ **Special Education:** $1,152,000 \ **Bilingual Education:** $25,000 \ **Open-Close:** 08/14 - 05/27 \ **DTBP:** $227 (High) \ f

Dr Dana Smith	1	Frances LaBella	2,15
Scott Stachacz	3	Kathy Knawa	7
Carol Humm	9,18,296	Sarah Rudenga	16*
Jacqueline Renko	57	Robin Latman	59
Michele Hoereth	67	Terri Statler	68
Lennard Razor	73,76,286,295		

Public Schs..Principal	Grd	Prgm	Enr/#Cls	SN	
Flossmoor Hills Elem Sch 3721 Beech St, Flossmoor 60422 Haley Marti	PK-5		331 17	53%	708/647-7100 Fax 708/798-8324 f t
Heather Hill Elem Sch 1439 Lawrence Cres, Flossmoor 60422 Ashley Holland	PK-5		260 17	44%	708/647-7200 Fax 708/206-2749 f t
Parker Junior High Sch 2810 School St, Flossmoor 60422 Amabel Crawford	6-8		910 80	42%	708/647-5400 Fax 708/799-9207 t
Serena Hills Elem Sch 255 Pleasant Dr, Chicago HTS 60411 Elizabeth Reich	PK-5		327 20	69%	708/647-7300 Fax 708/756-4465 f t
Western Ave Elem Sch 940 Western Ave, Flossmoor 60422 Gina Isabelli	PK-5		446 25	19%	708/647-7400 Fax 708/206-2350 f t

● Ford Heights School Dist 169 PID: 00269050 708/758-1370
910 Woodlawn Ave, Ford Heights 60411 Fax 708/758-1372

Schools: 2 \ **Teachers:** 31 \ **Students:** 455 \ **Special Ed Students:** 54 \ **Ethnic:** African American 95%, Hispanic 5%, \ **Exp:** $566 (High) \ **Poverty:** 38% \ **Title I:** $617,981 \ **Special Education:** $288,000 \ **Open-Close:** 08/19 - 05/21 \ **DTBP:** $251 (High)

Dr Gregory Jackson	1	Coretta Jackson	2,3,5,15,84
Curta Jackson	4*	Timothy Williams	6
Marilyn Barnes	9,11	Mark Mitchell	67
Jason Scott	73		

Public Schs..Principal	Grd	Prgm	Enr/#Cls	SN	
Cottage Grove Upper Grade Ctr 800 E 14th St, Ford Heights 60411 Chantel Jones	5-8	T	165 14	90%	708/758-1400 Fax 708/758-0711
Medgar Evers Primary Sch 1101 E 10th St, Ford Heights 60411 Monique Johnson-Bibbs	PK-4	T	290 25	97%	708/758-2520 Fax 708/758-2474

79	Student Personnel	91	Safety/Security	275	Response To Intervention	298	Grant Writer/Ptnrships
80	Driver Ed/Safety	92	Magnet School	277	Remedial Math K-12	750	Chief Innovation Officer
81	Gifted/Talented	93	Parental Involvement	280	Literacy Coach	751	Chief of Staff
82	Video Services	95	Tech Prep Program	285	STEM	752	Social Emotional Learning
83	Substance Abuse Prev	97	Chief Information Officer	286	Digital Learning		
84	Erate	98	Chief Technology Officer	288	Common Core Standards		
85	AIDS Education	270	Character Education	294	Accountability		
88	Alternative/At Risk	271	Migrant Education	295	Network System		
89	Multi-Cultural Curriculum	273	Teacher Mentor	296	Title II Programs		
90	Social Work	274	Before/After Sch	297	Webmaster		

School Programs
A = Alternative Program
G = Adult Classes
M = Magnet Program
T = Title I Schoolwide
V = Career & Tech Ed Programs

Other School Types
Ⓐ = Alternative School
Ⓒ = Charter School
Ⓜ = Magnet School
Ⓨ = Year-Round School

Social Media
f = Facebook
t = Twitter

New Schools are shaded
New Superintendents and Principals are bold
Personnel with email addresses are underscored

Cook County

Market Data Retrieval

- **Forest Park School District 91** PID: 00269684   708/366-5700
  424 Des Plaines Ave, Forest Park 60130   Fax 708/366-5761

Schools: 5 \ Teachers: 86 \ Students: 861 \ Special Ed Students: 159 \ LEP Students: 50 \ Ethnic: Asian 4%, African American 51%, Hispanic 15%, Caucasian 29% \ Exp: $745 (High) \ Poverty: 14% \ Title I: $215,466 \ Special Education: $839,000 \ Open-Close: 08/21 - 06/03 \ DTBP: $233 (High) \ 🅕 🅣

Dr Louis Cavallo	1,11,83,288	Bonnie Doolin	2,12
Laura Dickinson	2	Edward Brophy	3,15,69
Paula Atherton	5	Michelle Bernero	7
James Edler	9	Kyra Tyler	67
Scott Dunnell	71	Michelle Hopper	79*
Jacqueline Luehrs	90*	Zack Frangidakis	295

Public Schs..Principal	Grd	Prgm	Enr/#Cls	SN	
Betsy Ross Elem Sch 1315 Marengo Ave, Forest Park 60130 Tinisa Huff	K-2		137 9	39%	708/366-7498 Fax 708/771-4232 🅕 🅣
Field-Stevenson Elem Sch 925 Beloit Ave, Forest Park 60130 Dr Tiffany Brunson	3-5		144 20	60%	708/366-5703 Fax 708/366-2091
Forest Park Middle Sch 925 Beloit Ave, Forest Park 60130 Joe Pisano \ Tiffany Brunson	6-8		193 26	70%	708/366-5742 Fax 708/366-2091
Garfield Elem Sch 543 Hannah Ave, Forest Park 60130 Mary Stauder	PK-2		193 11	25%	708/366-6945 Fax 708/366-8044 🅕 🅣
Grant-White Elem Sch 147 Circle Ave, Forest Park 60130 Roger Beauford	3-5		98 7	59%	708/366-5704 Fax 708/771-1649 🅕 🅣

- **Forest Ridge Sch Dist 142** PID: 00269737   708/687-3334
  15000 Laramie Ave, Oak Forest 60452   Fax 708/687-8887

Schools: 4 \ Teachers: 105 \ Students: 1,650 \ Special Ed Students: 265 \ LEP Students: 156 \ Ethnic: Asian 3%, African American 9%, Hispanic 24%, Caucasian 64% \ Exp: $474 (High) \ Poverty: 12% \ Title I: $332,780 \ Special Education: $875,000 \ Bilingual Education: $31,000 \ Open-Close: 08/28 - 06/09 \ DTBP: $230 (High)

Dr Paul McDermott	1	Heather Rose	2
Tom Beaver	3	Rose Eichorst	7*
Elizabeth Ehrhart	9,11,57,273,285,288,296	Dr Lori Leppert	34,59,69,79
Nancy Kukulka	37*	Mary Derman	67
Brian Skibinski	71,73,97		

Public Schs..Principal	Grd	Prgm	Enr/#Cls	SN	
G Kerkstra Elem Sch 14950 Laramie Ave, Oak Forest 60452 Jeff Kulik	1-5	T	440 16	36%	708/687-2860 Fax 708/687-0571
Jack Hille Middle Sch 5800 151st St, Oak Forest 60452 John Orth	6-8	T	581 40	34%	708/687-5550 Fax 708/687-8569
Lee R Foster Elem Sch 5931 School St, Oak Forest 60452 Curt Beringer	1-5	T	402 20	42%	708/687-4763 Fax 708/687-2659
Ridge Early Childhood Center 5151 149th St, Oak Forest 60452 Kathrina Davis	PK-K	T	233 14	36%	708/687-2964 Fax 708/687-8458

- **Franklin Park Pub Sch Dist 84** PID: 00269787   847/455-4230
  2915 Maple St Ste 1, Franklin Park 60131   Fax 847/455-9094

Schools: 4 \ Teachers: 104 \ Students: 1,400 \ Special Ed Students: 198 \ LEP Students: 331 \ Ethnic: Asian 3%, African American 1%, Hispanic 67%, Caucasian 29% \ Exp: $351 (High) \ Poverty: 11% \ Title I: $220,432 \ Special Education: $586,000 \ Bilingual Education: $122,000 \ Open-Close: 08/17 - 05/26 \ DTBP: $242 (High)

David Katzin	1,11,83	John Barry	2
Ray Heyer	3,5	Daniel Locascio	67
Teri Radziejewski	68	Taneesha Thomas	73,286,295

Public Schs..Principal	Grd	Prgm	Enr/#Cls	SN	
Hester Junior High Sch 2836 Gustav St, Franklin Park 60131 Giffen Trotter	6-8	T	463	62%	847/455-2150 Fax 847/455-0945
North Elem Sch 9500 Gage Ave, Franklin Park 60131 Cody Huisman	PK-5	T	239 14	46%	847/678-7962 Fax 847/678-3616
Passow Elem Sch 2838 Calwagner St, Franklin Park 60131 Judy Martin	PK-5	T	426 18	59%	847/455-6781 Fax 847/455-1465
Pietrini Elem Sch 9750 Fullerton Ave, Franklin Park 60131 Melissa Llano	PK-5	T	280 10	64%	847/455-7960 Fax 847/455-1809

- **General George S Patton SD 133** PID: 00273178   708/841-3955
  150 W 137th St, Riverdale 60827   Fax 708/841-5911

Schools: 1 \ Teachers: 21 \ Students: 268 \ Special Ed Students: 41 \ LEP Students: 3 \ Ethnic: African American 95%, Hispanic 5%, \ Exp: $401 (High) \ Poverty: 30% \ Title I: $277,766 \ Special Education: $247,000 \ Open-Close: 08/27 - 05/28

Dr Carol Kunst	1,11	Lynette Hutcherson	2*
Jeanine Rogers	9,69,288*	David Brown	12,15,298
Latroy Robinson	67	Paula Brown	69*
Harold Milner	73,76,286*		

Public Schs..Principal	Grd	Prgm	Enr/#Cls	SN	
General George Patton Elem Sch 13700 S Stewart Ave, Riverdale 60827 Jeanine Rogers	PK-8	T	268 26	37%	708/841-2420 Fax 708/201-3682

- **Glenbrook High Sch Dist 225** PID: 00269842   847/998-6100
  3801 W Lake Ave, Glenview 60026   Fax 847/486-4733

Schools: 2 \ Teachers: 398 \ Students: 5,102 \ Special Ed Students: 692 \ LEP Students: 155 \ College-Bound: 98% \ Exp: $203 (Med) \ Poverty: 4% \ Title I: $178,362 \ Special Education: $3,771,000 \ Bilingual Education: $63,000 \ Open-Close: 08/19 - 06/03 \ DTBP: $189 (High)

Dr Charles Johns	1	Dr Kim Ptak	2,3,4
Dr R Gravel	2,15,16,73,76,295	Vicki Tarver	2
Lisa Wall	5	Steve Rockrohr	6*
Julie Haenisch	7*	Ryan Bretag	10,70
Dr Roseanne Williamson	11,69,74,83,88,275,296,298 15,68,78	Brad Swanson	
Karen Geddeis	16,71	Dawn Hall	27,95
Mina Moon	57*	Jennifer Pearson	60
Bruce Doughty	67	Alice Raflores	68
Josh Koo	72		

1	Superintendent	8	Curric/Instruct K-12	19	Chief Financial Officer	29	Family/Consumer Science	39	Social Studies K-12	49	English/Lang Arts Elem	59	Special Education Elem	69	Academic Assessment
2	Bus/Finance/Purchasing	9	Curric/Instruct Elem	20	Art K-12	30	Adult Education	40	Social Studies Elem	50	English/Lang Arts Sec	60	Special Education Sec	70	Research/Development
3	Buildings And Grounds	10	Curric/Instruct Sec	21	Art Elem	31	Career/Sch-to-Work K-12	41	Social Studies Sec	51	Reading K-12	61	Foreign/World Lang K-12	71	Public Information
4	Food Service	11	Federal Program	22	Art Sec	32	Career/Sch-to-Work Elem	42	Science K-12	52	Reading Elem	62	Foreign/World Lang Elem	72	Summer School
5	Transportation	12	Title I	23	Music K-12	33	Career/Sch-to-Work Sec	43	Science Elem	53	Reading Sec	63	Foreign/World Lang Sec	73	Instructional Tech
6	Athletic	13	Title V	24	Music Elem	34	Early Childhood Ed	44	Science Sec	54	Remedial Reading K-12	64	Religious Education K-12	74	Inservice Training
7	Health Services	15	Asst Superintendent	25	Music Sec	35	Health/Phys Education	45	Math K-12	55	Remedial Reading Elem	65	Religious Education Elem	75	Marketing/Distributive
		16	Instructional Media Svcs	26	Business Education	36	Guidance Services K-12	46	Math Elem	56	Remedial Reading Sec	66	Religious Education Sec	76	Info Systems
		17	Chief Operations Officer	27	Career & Tech Ed	37	Guidance Services Elem	47	Math Sec	57	Bilingual/ELL	67	School Board President	77	Psychological Assess
		18	Chief Academic Officer	28	Technology Education	38	Guidance Services Sec	48	English/Lang Arts K-12	58	Special Education K-12	68	Teacher Personnel	78	Affirmative Action

Illinois School Directory — Cook County

Public Schs..Principal	Grd	Prgm	Enr/#Cls	SN
Glenbrook North High Sch 2300 Shermer Rd, Northbrook 60062 Scott Williams \ Edward Solis \ John Finan \ Karin Kirch \ Deborah Woods \ Robin Pehlke \ Jodie Panzer	9-12	GV	2,023	5% 847/272-6400 Fax 847/509-2411
Glenbrook South High Sch 4000 W Lake Ave, Glenview 60026 Dr Lauren Fagel	9-12	AGV	3,078 80	18% 847/729-2000 Fax 847/486-4462

- **Glencoe Sch District 35** PID: 00269878   847/835-7800
  620 Greenwood Ave, Glencoe 60022   Fax 847/835-7805

Schools: 3 \ **Teachers:** 97 \ **Students:** 1,200 \ **Special Ed Students:** 143 \ **LEP Students:** 24 \ **Ethnic:** Asian 6%, Hispanic 6%, Caucasian 87% \ **Exp:** $423 (High) \ **Poverty:** 4% \ **Title I:** $55,791 \ **Special Education:** $694,000 \ **Open-Close:** 08/27 - 06/08 \ **DTBP:** $259 (High)

Dr Catherine Wang 1,73	Jason Edelheit 2,3,11,17,19,294,296,298
Amy Holaday 9,57,69,74,270,273,275	Valerie Lamberti 11,34,37,55,59,79
Julia Eidelman 16*	Mary Kelly 16,82*
Matthew Smolka 16*	Kelly Glauberman 67
Randy Saeks 76,295*	Ben Baird 79

Public Schs..Principal	Grd	Prgm	Enr/#Cls	SN
Central Sch 620 Greenwood Ave, Glencoe 60022 Dr Ryan Mollet	5-8		530 70	847/835-7600 Fax 847/835-7605
South Sch 266 Linden Ave, Glencoe 60022 Kelly Zonghetti	PK-2		400 18	847/835-6400 Fax 847/835-6405
West Sch 1010 Forestway Dr, Glencoe 60022 David Rongey	3-4		244 14	847/835-6600 Fax 847/835-6605

- **Glenview Cmty Cons Sch Dist 34** PID: 00269921   847/998-5000
  1401 Greenwood Rd, Glenview 60026   Fax 847/998-5094

Schools: 8 \ **Teachers:** 348 \ **Students:** 4,900 \ **Special Ed Students:** 620 \ **LEP Students:** 729 \ **Ethnic:** Asian 20%, African American 2%, Hispanic 14%, Caucasian 64% \ **Exp:** $289 (Med) \ **Poverty:** 6% \ **Title I:** $436,735 \ **Special Education:** $2,954,000 \ **Bilingual Education:** $217,000 \ **Open-Close:** 08/21 - 06/04 \ **DTBP:** $184 (High)

Dr Dane Delli 1	Eric Miller 2,15
Mark Hoversen 2	Steve Ruelli 3,91
Kimberly Cleveland 4*	Rob Conner 5
Matt Silverman 9,11,69,74,83,271,288,296	Brian Engle 16,28,73,286
Mary Geraghty 59,79,752	Natalie Jachtorowycz 67
Dr Heather Hopkins 68	Cathy Kedjidjian 71
Kelly Conwell 295	

Public Schs..Principal	Grd	Prgm	Enr/#Cls	SN
Glen Grove Elem Sch 3900 Glenview Rd, Glenview 60025 Helena Vena	3-5		477 21	27% 847/998-5030 Fax 847/998-5101
Henking Primary Sch 2941 Linneman St, Glenview 60025 Patricia Puetz	PK-2		456 25	29% 847/998-5035 Fax 847/998-9938
Hoffman Elem Sch 2000 Harrison St, Glenview 60025 Selene Stewart	3-5		533 25	30% 847/998-5040 Fax 847/998-6840
Lyon Elem Sch 1335 Waukegan Rd, Glenview 60025 Kevin Dorken	PK-2		463 17	15% 847/998-5045 Fax 847/998-9701
Pleasant Ridge Elem Sch 1730 Sunset Ridge Rd, Glenview 60025 Erik Friedman	3-5		560 22	14% 847/998-5050 Fax 847/998-5532
Springman Middle Sch 2701 Central Rd, Glenview 60025 Jason Kaiz	6-8	V	857 6	27% 847/998-5020 Fax 847/998-4032
Westbrook Primary Sch 1333 Greenwood Rd, Glenview 60026 Jeannie Sung	PK-2		510 30	32% 847/998-5055 Fax 847/998-1872
William J Attea Middle Sch 2500 Chestnut Ave, Glenview 60026 Mark Richter	6-8		863	19% 847/486-7700 Fax 847/729-6251

- **Golf School District 67** PID: 00270011   847/966-8200
  9401 Waukegan Rd, Morton Grove 60053   Fax 847/966-8290

Schools: 2 \ **Teachers:** 43 \ **Students:** 725 \ **Special Ed Students:** 79 \ **LEP Students:** 118 \ **Ethnic:** Asian 38%, African American 2%, Hispanic 9%, Caucasian 50% \ **Exp:** $123 (Low) \ **Poverty:** 8% \ **Title I:** $62,198 \ **Special Education:** $167,000 \ **Bilingual Education:** $12,000 \ **Open-Close:** 08/26 - 06/04

Dr Beth Flores 1	Edie Riportella 2
Richard Searl 3	Faisal Baig 16,73,76*
Amy Feinstein 57*	Nada Ardeleanu 67
Lynn Kurokawa 79	Jenni Orsello 90*

Public Schs..Principal	Grd	Prgm	Enr/#Cls	SN
Golf Middle Sch 9401 Waukegan Rd, Morton Grove 60053 Karen Chvojka	5-8		313 15	30% 847/965-3740 Fax 847/966-9493
Hynes Elem Sch 9000 Belleforte Ave, Morton Grove 60053 Carol Westley	PK-4		412 15	26% 847/965-4500 Fax 847/965-4565

- **Harvey Public School Dist 152** PID: 00270126   708/333-0300
  16001 Lincoln Ave, Harvey 60426   Fax 708/333-0349

Schools: 6 \ **Teachers:** 110 \ **Students:** 2,264 \ **Special Ed Students:** 208 \ **LEP Students:** 345 \ **Ethnic:** Asian 2%, African American 67%, Hispanic 31%, \ **Exp:** $310 (High) \ **Poverty:** 36% \ **Title I:** $1,971,333 \ **Special Education:** $940,000 \ **Open-Close:** 08/17 - 06/01 \ **DTBP:** $191 (High)

John Thomas 1	Cassandra Watkins 2,19
Alfred Daniels 3	Lynette Lane 4
Chandra Williams 7*	Dana Nichols 9,68,285,288
Derrika Williams 11	Arlethea Bolton 30
Gabriela DelGado 57	Dana Ash 59
Janet Rogers 67	Oscar Herrera 73,84
Carmen Armstrong 91	Sherly Fowlkes 298

Public Schs..Principal	Grd	Prgm	Enr/#Cls	SN
Brooks Middle Sch 14741 Wallace St, Harvey 60426 Dr Stacey Hunt	7-8	AT	407 45	99% 708/333-6390 Fax 708/333-3177
Bryant Elem Sch 14730 Main St, Harvey 60426 Durrell Anderson	K-6	AT	362 19	100% 708/331-1390 Fax 708/225-9510
Holmes Elem Sch 16000 Carse Ave, Harvey 60426 Doelynn Strong	K-6	AT	339 17	99% 708/333-0440 Fax 708/225-9511
Maya Angelou Elem Sch 15748 Page Ave, Harvey 60426 Iretha Brown	K-6	AT	294 15	99% 708/333-0740 Fax 708/333-9216

79 Student Personnel	91 Safety/Security	275 Response To Intervention	298 Grant Writer/Ptnrships	**School Programs**	**Social Media**
80 Driver Ed/Safety	92 Magnet School	277 Remedial Math K-12	750 Chief Innovation Officer	A = Alternative Program	
81 Gifted/Talented	93 Parental Involvement	280 Literacy Coach	751 Chief of Staff	G = Adult Classes	= Facebook
82 Video Services	95 Tech Prep Program	285 STEM	752 Social Emotional Learning	M = Magnet Program	
83 Substance Abuse Prev	97 Chief Information Officer	286 Digital Learning		T = Title I Schoolwide	= Twitter
84 Erate	98 Chief Technology Officer	288 Common Core Standards	**Other School Types**	V = Career & Tech Ed Programs	
85 AIDS Education	270 Character Education	294 Accountability	Ⓐ = Alternative School		
88 Alternative/At Risk	271 Migrant Education	295 Network System	Ⓒ = Charter School	New Schools are shaded	
89 Multi-Cultural Curriculum	273 Teacher Mentor	296 Title II Programs	Ⓜ = Magnet School	New Superintendents and Principals are bold	
90 Social Work	274 Before/After Sch	297 Webmaster	Ⓨ = Year-Round School	Personnel with email addresses are underscored	

Cook County

Riley Early Childhood Center PK-PK 149 98% 708/210-3960
16001 Lincoln Ave, Harvey 60426   6 Fax 708/210-2218
Deborah Hill

Whittier Elem Sch K-6 AT 257 100% 708/331-1130
71 E 152nd St, Harvey 60426   16 Fax 708/333-9162
Roxie Thomas

• Hazel Crest School Dist 152-5 PID: 00270217
1910 170th St, Hazel Crest 60429
708/335-0790
Fax 708/335-3520

Schools: 2 \ Teachers: 64 \ Students: 1,000 \
Special Ed Students: 133 \ LEP Students: 34 \ Ethnic: African American 88%, Hispanic 12%, \ Exp: $449 (High) \ Poverty: 33% \ Title I: $814,513 \ Special Education: $440,000 \ Open-Close: 08/24 - 05/27 \ DTBP: $200 (High)

Kenneth Stales 1
William Hulett 3
Yolanda Payne 59,275
Vincent Rucker 73
Nicole Terrell-Smith 2,15,84
Dr Linda McClinton 9
Dean Barnett 67

Public Schs..Principal	Grd	Prgm	Enr/#Cls	SN		
Barack Obama Learning Academy 16448 Park Ave, Markham 60428 Carole Davis	PK-8	T	475	99%	708/825-2400	
Jesse White Learning Academy 16910 Western Ave, Hazel Crest 60429 Dr Cynthia Levy	PK-8	T	506	99%	708/825-2190	

• Hillside School District 93 PID: 00270310
4804 Harrison St, Hillside 60162
708/449-7280
Fax 708/449-5056

Schools: 1 \ Teachers: 44 \ Students: 410 \ Special Ed Students: 70 \ LEP Students: 107 \ Ethnic: Asian 2%, African American 44%, Hispanic 51%, Native American: 1%, Caucasian 3% \ Exp: $240 (Med) \ Poverty: 13% \ Title I: $106,393 \ Special Education: $149,000 \ Open-Close: 08/21 - 06/04 \ DTBP: $244 (High) \

Dr Kevin Suchinski 1,11
Jacqui Oddo 4
Kreg Kemper 6,35*
Bridget Gainer 12,57,59,83,273,275*
Sharon Venchus 16,82*
Daryl Richardson 67
Kenya Dockens 88,90*
Sarah Johnson-Millon 2,15
Jennifer McGuire 5,7,270*
Cynthia Wagner 9,69,288*
Robert Gilmore 16,76,295,297*
Gerald Erjavec 43*
Carlos Nunez 73

Public Schs..Principal	Grd	Prgm	Enr/#Cls	SN		
Hillside Elem Sch 4804 Harrison St, Hillside 60162 Bridget Gainer	PK-8	T	410 60	63%	708/449-6490 Fax 708/449-1644	

• Homewood Flossmoor CHSD 233 PID: 00270396
999 Kedzie Ave, Flossmoor 60422
708/799-3000
Fax 708/799-8552

Schools: 1 \ Teachers: 182 \ Students: 2,897 \ Special Ed Students: 358 \ LEP Students: 23 \ Ethnic: Asian 1%, African American 73%, Hispanic 8%, Caucasian 19% \ Exp: $368 (High) \ Poverty: 6% \ Title I: $248,790 \ Special Education: $1,748,000 \ Open-Close: 08/17 - 05/28 \ DTBP: $178 (High) \

Dr Von Mansfield 1
Tom Wagner 3
Jane Harper 16,82,286*
Angela Taylor 57,60,88*
Jodi Bryant 68,71
Paula Crawford 80*
Dr Lawrence Cook 2
Gary Posing 16,73,295*
Kevin Thomas 27*
Steve Anderson 67
James Schmidt 77*
Marina Brennan 275*

David Kush 294*
Jenn Odin 752

Public Schs..Principal	Grd	Prgm	Enr/#Cls	SN		
Homewood Flossmoor High Sch 999 Kedzie Ave, Flossmoor 60422 Dr Jerry Anderson	9-12		2,897	20%	708/799-3000	

• Homewood School Dist 153 PID: 00270334
18205 Aberdeen St, Homewood 60430
708/799-8721
Fax 708/799-1377

Schools: 3 \ Teachers: 156 \ Students: 2,000 \ Special Ed Students: 307 \ LEP Students: 68 \ Ethnic: African American 54%, Hispanic 15%, Caucasian 30% \ Exp: $388 (High) \ Poverty: 10% \ Title I: $265,016 \ Special Education: $1,126,000 \ Bilingual Education: $2,000 \ Open-Close: 08/21 - 06/04 \ DTBP: $260 (High)

Dr Dale Mitchell 1
Kevin Keane 3
Melanie Mandisodza 11,59,69,79*
Shelley Peck 71*
John Gibson 2
Kathy Schaeflein 9*
Shelly Marks 67
Beth White 73,295*

Public Schs..Principal	Grd	Prgm	Enr/#Cls	SN		
Churchill Elem Sch 1300 190th St, Homewood 60430 Sara Schnoor	3-5	T	656 19	33%	708/798-3424 Fax 708/798-0417	
James Hart Sch 18220 Morgan St, Homewood 60430 Kimberly Johnson	6-8	T	702 29	31%	708/799-5544 Fax 708/799-8360	
Willow Elem Sch 1804 Willow Rd, Homewood 60430 Melissa Lawson	PK-2	T	615 27	30%	708/798-3720 Fax 708/798-4336	

• Hoover-Schrum Sch Dist 157 PID: 00270413
1255 Superior Ave, Calumet City 60409
708/868-7500
Fax 708/868-7511

Schools: 2 \ Teachers: 67 \ Students: 850 \ Special Ed Students: 135 \ LEP Students: 99 \ Ethnic: African American 74%, Hispanic 23%, Caucasian 1% \ Exp: $207 (Med) \ Poverty: 27% \ Title I: $516,670 \ Special Education: $711,000 \ Open-Close: 08/19 - 06/02 \ DTBP: $228 (High)

Dr Dawayne Evans 1
Erin Byrns 3*
Miguel Rosales 16,73,76,84
Charles Garcia 67
Kimberly Lewis-Williams ...2,11,294,296,298*
Jill Uher 9
Kizwanda Ololee 57,59,271*
Cynthia Young 83,88,275*

Public Schs..Principal	Grd	Prgm	Enr/#Cls	SN		
Hoover Elem Sch 1260 Superior Ave, Calumet City 60409 Semaj Coleman	PK-5	T	570 32	95%	708/862-4230 Fax 708/832-3713	
Schrum Memorial Sch 485 165th St, Calumet City 60409 Dr Shernita Mays	6-8	T	299 28	95%	708/862-4236 Fax 708/832-3739	

• Indian Springs Sch Dist 109 PID: 00268123
7540 S 86th Ave, Justice 60458
708/496-8700
Fax 708/496-8641

Schools: 6 \ Teachers: 206 \ Students: 2,764 \ Special Ed Students: 382 \ LEP Students: 715 \ Ethnic: Asian 1%, African American 16%, Hispanic 23%, Caucasian 60% \ Exp: $275 (Med) \ Poverty: 25% \ Title I: $1,296,602 \ Special Education: $1,842,000 \ Bilingual Education: $257,000 \ Open-Close: 08/19 - 05/31 \ DTBP: $185 (High)

Dr Blair Noccio 1,83
Tom Zolecki 3
Linda Jeffers 2,13,84,288,296,298,752
Linda Neumann 4

1	Superintendent	8	Curric/Instruct K-12	19	Chief Financial Officer	29	Family/Consumer Science	39	Social Studies K-12	49	English/Lang Arts Elem	59	Special Education Elem	69	Academic Assessment
2	Bus/Finance/Purchasing	9	Curric/Instruct Elem	20	Art K-12	30	Adult Education	40	Social Studies Elem	50	English/Lang Arts Sec	60	Special Education Sec	70	Research/Development
3	Buildings And Grounds	10	Curric/Instruct Sec	21	Art Elem	31	Career/Sch-to-Work K-12	41	Social Studies Sec	51	Reading K-12	61	Foreign/World Lang K-12	71	Public Information
4	Food Service	11	Federal Program	22	Art Sec	32	Career/Sch-to-Work Elem	42	Science K-12	52	Reading Elem	62	Foreign/World Lang Elem	72	Summer School
5	Transportation	12	Title I	23	Music K-12	33	Career/Sch-to-Work Sec	43	Science Elem	53	Reading Sec	63	Foreign/World Lang Sec	73	Instructional Tech
6	Athletic	13	Title V	24	Music Elem	34	Early Childhood Ed	44	Science Sec	54	Remedial Reading K-12	64	Religious Education K-12	74	Inservice Training
7	Health Services	15	Asst Superintendent	25	Music Sec	35	Health/Phys Education	45	Math K-12	55	Remedial Reading Elem	65	Religious Education Elem	75	Marketing/Distributive
		16	Instructional Media Svcs	26	Business Education	36	Guidance Services K-12	46	Math Elem	56	Remedial Reading Sec	66	Religious Education Sec	76	Info Systems
		17	Chief Operations Officer	27	Career & Tech Ed	37	Guidance Services Elem	47	Math Sec	57	Bilingual/ELL	67	School Board President	77	Psychological Assess
		18	Chief Academic Officer	28	Technology Education	38	Guidance Services Sec	48	English/Lang Arts K-12	58	Special Education K-12	68	Teacher Personnel	78	Affirmative Action

Illinois School Directory | Cook County

Sandy Zagorski 7*
Christine Baldwin 11,74,88,273,285*
Sue Almendarez 34,274*
Ruba Aqel 57
John Janisch 73,295

Christine Baldwin 9,11,73,74,88,273,285
Crystal Skoczylas 15
Heath Brosseau 37,59,77,85,90,275,294
Johnny Smith 67

Public Schs..Principal	Grd	Prgm	Enr/#Cls	SN	
Bridgeview Elem Sch 7800 S Thomas Ave, Bridgeview 60455 Candice Del Prete	K-6		410 20	69%	708/496-8713 Fax 708/496-1142
Frank A Brodnicki Elem Sch 8641 W 75th St, Justice 60458 **Kelly Touch**	K-6		691 32	66%	708/496-8716 Fax 708/496-8173
George T Wilkins Elem Sch 8001 S 82nd Ave, Justice 60458 Robert Serdar	K-5		509 40	80%	708/496-8708 Fax 708/728-3114
George T Wilkins Jr High Sch 8001 S 82nd Ave, Justice 60458 Joseph Porrey	5-8		550	70%	708/496-8708 Fax 708/728-3114
Player Early Childhood Center 8600 S Roberts Rd, Justice 60458 Sue Almendarez	PK-PK		186 5		708/430-8191 Fax 708/430-8295
Robina Lyle Elem Sch 7801 W 75th St, Bridgeview 60455 Nuray Kavustuk	K-6		417 18	69%	708/496-8722 Fax 708/728-3120

● **J Sterling Morton HSD 201** PID: 00270451   708/780-2800
5801 W Cermak Rd, Cicero 60804   Fax 708/780-2111

Schools: 4 \ **Teachers:** 397 \ **Students:** 8,600 \ **Special Ed Students:** 1,062 \ **LEP Students:** 1,560 \ **College-Bound:** 63% \ **Ethnic:** Asian 1%, African American 4%, Hispanic 90%, Caucasian 5% \ **Exp:** $410 (High) \ **Poverty:** 16% \ **Title I:** $2,673,886 \ **Special Education:** $4,851,000 \ **Bilingual Education:** $166,000 \ **Open-Close:** 08/17 - 05/25 \ **DTBP:** $199 (High) \ 📘 🇹

Timothy Truesdale 1
James Zundell 3
Joshua McMahon 11,15,74,83,271,273,275
James Monaco 16,50
Eric Mastey 27
Anne Semenske 44
Melody Becker 57
Jeffry Pesek 67
Matsa Felda 69,294
Robert Niedermeyer 73

Mike Pustelnik 2
Nicole Ebson 6*
Joe Gunty 12
Ricardo Garcia 22,25
Joseph Collins 35,80
Mary O'Sullivan 47
Dr Ramona Stravos 60
Kathleen Colgan 68
Darrielle McCorde 71
Samantha Skubal 73,286

Public Schs..Principal	Grd	Prgm	Enr/#Cls	SN	
Ⓐ J Sterling Morton Alt Sch 1874 S 54th Ave, Cicero 60804 Erin Kelly	9-12	TV	22 7	86%	708/222-3080 Fax 708/780-2309 📘 🇹
J Sterling Morton East HS 2423 S Austin Blvd, Cicero 60804 Jose Gamboa	10-12	TV	3,476	91%	708/780-4000 Fax 708/222-3090 📘 🇹
J Sterling Morton West HS 2400 Home Ave, Berwyn 60402 Josh McMahon	9-12	TV	3,573	80%	708/780-4100 Fax 708/222-5903 📘 🇹
Morton Freshman Campus 1801 S 55th Ave, Cicero 60804 Wendy Mullen	9-9	T	1,242	94%	708/863-7900 Fax 708/780-2886

● **Kenilworth School District 38** PID: 00270487   847/256-5006
542 Abbotsford Rd, Kenilworth 60043   Fax 847/256-4418

Schools: 1 \ **Teachers:** 57 \ **Students:** 425 \ **Special Ed Students:** 56 \ **LEP Students:** 12 \ **Ethnic:** Asian 3%, African American 1%, Hispanic 4%, Caucasian 93% \ **Exp:** $987 (High) \ **Poverty:** 7% \ **Title I:** $50,028 \ **Special Education:** $221,000 \ **Open-Close:** 08/26 - 06/08 \ **DTBP:** $236 (High)

Dr Chrystal Leroy 1
Natalie McLemore 6*
Evan Lukasik 67
Nancy Economou 83*
Terry Oquendo 85

Moris Quijada 3*
Lisa Leali 9,18
Elizabeth Lebris 73,297*
Janet Brothers 85*

Public Schs..Principal	Grd	Prgm	Enr/#Cls	SN	
Joseph Sears Sch 542 Abbotsford Rd, Kenilworth 60043 Roger Prosise \ **Stephanie Helfand**	PK-8		425 35		847/256-5006

● **Kirby School District 140** PID: 00270504   708/532-6462
16931 Grissom Dr, Tinley Park 60477   Fax 708/532-1512

Schools: 7 \ **Teachers:** 260 \ **Students:** 3,500 \ **Special Ed Students:** 666 \ **LEP Students:** 131 \ **Ethnic:** Asian 5%, African American 3%, Hispanic 9%, Caucasian 83% \ **Exp:** $307 (High) \ **Poverty:** 9% \ **Title I:** $471,890 \ **Special Education:** $2,655,000 \ **Bilingual Education:** $36,000 \ **Open-Close:** 08/26 - 06/11 \ **DTBP:** $201 (High)

Dr Shawn Olson 1
Robert Prost 3
Dr Kristine Roth 9,12,288
Thomas Martelli 67
Susan Haynie 297

Michael Andreshak 2,84
Rosanne Ballard 5
Mary Dwyer 59
Brian Nemeth 73,98

Public Schs..Principal	Grd	Prgm	Enr/#Cls	SN	
Christa McAuliffe Sch 8944 174th St, Tinley Park 60487 Annette Szczasny	PK-5		545 25	14%	708/429-4565 Fax 708/532-8533
Fernway Park Elem Sch 16600 S 88th Ave, Orland Park 60462 Sandy Hutchinson	PK-5		410 32	21%	708/349-3810 Fax 708/349-9463
Helen Keller Elem Sch 7846 163rd St, Tinley Park 60477 Joann Greene	PK-5		359 17	16%	708/532-2144 Fax 708/532-8531
John A Bannes Elem Sch 16835 Odell Ave, Tinley Park 60477 Daniel Callaghan	PK-5		444 22	10%	708/532-6466 Fax 708/532-8530
Millennium Elem Sch 17830 84th Ave, Tinley Park 60487 Julianne Cosentino	PK-5		566 25	8%	708/532-3150 Fax 708/614-2376
Prairie View Middle Sch 8500 175th St, Tinley Park 60487 Meghan Maurer	6-8		632 50	11%	708/532-8540 Fax 708/532-8544
Virgil Grissom Middle Sch 17000 80th Ave, Tinley Park 60477 Deborah Broadwell	6-8		606 40	15%	708/429-3030 Fax 708/532-8529 🇹

---

79 Student Personnel	91 Safety/Security	275 Response To Intervention	298 Grant Writer/Ptnrships	**School Programs**	**Social Media**
80 Driver Ed/Safety	92 Magnet School	277 Remedial Math K-12	750 Chief Innovation Officer	A = Alternative Program	📘 = Facebook
81 Gifted/Talented	93 Parental Involvement	280 Literacy Coach	751 Chief of Staff	G = Adult Classes	🇹 = Twitter
82 Video Services	95 Tech Prep Program	285 STEM	752 Social Emotional Learning	M = Magnet Program	
83 Substance Abuse Prev	97 Chief Infomation Officer	286 Digital Learning		T = Title I Schoolwide	
84 Erate	98 Chief Technology Officer	288 Common Core Standards	**Other School Types**	V = Career & Tech Ed Programs	
85 AIDS Education	270 Character Education	294 Accountability	Ⓐ = Alternative School		
88 Alternative/At Risk	271 Migrant Education	295 Network System	Ⓒ = Charter School	New Schools are shaded	
89 Multi-Cultural Curriculum	273 Teacher Mentor	296 Title II Programs	Ⓜ = Magnet School	New Superintendents and Principals are bold	
90 Social Work	274 Before/After Sch	297 Webmaster	Ⓨ = Year-Round School	Personnel with email addresses are underscored	IL—53

Cook County   Market Data Retrieval

- **Komarek School District 94** PID: 00270542   708/447-8030
  8940 W 24th St, N Riverside 60546   Fax 708/447-9546

Schools: 1 \ **Teachers:** 44 \ **Students:** 580 \ **Special Ed Students:** 102 \ **LEP Students:** 55 \ **Ethnic:** Asian 4%, African American 14%, Hispanic 47%, Caucasian 35% \ **Exp:** $303 (High) \ **Poverty:** 10% \ **Title I:** $70,310 \ **Special Education:** $220,000 \ **Bilingual Education:** $1,000 \ **Open-Close:** 08/19 - 06/01 \ **DTBP:** $233 (High)

Dr Todd Fitzgerrald	1,11	Kathy Gibson	2
Elio Anfuso	3	Leslie Banas	6
Diane Michelini	9,69,288	Danea Rodea	57
Caitlin Dilallo	59,79,85,88,275	Christopher Waas	67
Jovaughn Fairman	73	Ashley Sapada	274*

Public Schs..Principal	Grd	Prgm	Enr/#Cls	SN	
Komarek Elem Sch 8940 W 24th St, N Riverside 60546 **Caitlin Dilallo** \ Dr Jason Gold	PK-8	T	580 40	40%	708/447-8030

- **La Grange Cmty School Dist 105** PID: 00270645   708/482-2700
  701 7th Ave, La Grange 60525   Fax 708/482-2727

Schools: 5 \ **Teachers:** 119 \ **Students:** 1,300 \ **Special Ed Students:** 218 \ **LEP Students:** 215 \ **Ethnic:** Asian 1%, African American 3%, Hispanic 41%, Caucasian 55% \ **Exp:** $417 (High) \ **Poverty:** 9% \ **Title I:** $204,556 \ **Special Education:** $707,000 \ **Bilingual Education:** $111,000 \ **Open-Close:** 08/19 - 05/28 \ **DTBP:** $235 (High)

Dr Brian Ganan	1	Dr George Tolczyk	2,11
Eric Bryant	3	Kathryn Heeke	9,280,285,288
Trish Murphy	16,73	Marcela Ortiz	57
Coleen Winterfield	59,83,752	David Herndon	67

Public Schs..Principal	Grd	Prgm	Enr/#Cls	SN	
Gurrie Middle Sch 1001 S Spring Ave, La Grange 60525 Edmund Hood	7-8		305 30	38%	708/482-2720 Fax 708/482-2724
Hodgkins Elem Sch 6516 Kane Ave, Hodgkins 60525 John Signatur	PK-6	T	178 11	70%	708/482-2740 Fax 708/482-2728
Ideal Elem Sch 9901 W 58th St, Countryside 60525 Timothy Sheldon	PK-6	T	292 17	72%	708/482-2750 Fax 708/482-2729
Seventh Ave Elem Sch 701 7th Ave, La Grange 60525 Erin Hall	PK-6		251 13	28%	708/482-2730 Fax 708/482-2726
Spring Ave Elem Sch 1001 S Spring Ave, La Grange 60525 Brian Lawson	K-6		313 16	4%	708/482-2710 Fax 708/482-2725

- **La Grange Elem Sch Dist 102** PID: 00270566   708/482-2400
  333 N Park Rd, La Grange Pk 60526   Fax 708/482-2402

Schools: 6 \ **Teachers:** 224 \ **Students:** 3,100 \ **Special Ed Students:** 472 \ **LEP Students:** 149 \ **Ethnic:** Asian 2%, African American 6%, Hispanic 19%, Caucasian 73% \ **Exp:** $197 (Low) \ **Poverty:** 4% \ **Title I:** $131,584 \ **Special Education:** $1,869,000 \ **Bilingual Education:** $56,000 \ **Open-Close:** 08/24 - 06/02 \ **DTBP:** $175 (High)

Dr Kyle Schumacher	1	Deborah Handke	2
Tonisha Sibley	2,4,5,15,91	Mark Pavljasevic	3
Christopher Finch	9,11,15	Terry Sofianos	15,59
Jessica Greenberg	16	Lynn Lawrence	37,273
Traci Milledge	59	Brian Anderson	67
David Holt	68,71	Linda McShane	69

| Juan Lyle | 73,297 | Randy Lange | 74 |

Public Schs..Principal	Grd	Prgm	Enr/#Cls	SN	
Barnsdale Road Sch 920 Barnsdale Rd, La Grange Pk 60526 Kathy Boxell	PK-K		298 13	17%	708/482-3003 Fax 708/482-1425
Congress Park Elem Sch 9311 Shields Ave, Brookfield 60513 James Robinette	K-6	T	445 22	38%	708/482-2430 Fax 708/482-2437
Cossitt Elem Sch 115 W Cossitt Ave, La Grange 60525 Mike Michowski	K-6		540 35	6%	708/482-2450 Fax 708/482-2734
Forest Road Elem Sch 901 Forest Rd, La Grange Pk 60526 Jeffrey Bergholtz	1-6		539 21	22%	708/482-2525 Fax 708/352-4573
Ogden Avenue Elem Sch 501 W Ogden Ave, La Grange 60525 Joe McCauley	K-6		578 28	3%	708/482-2480 Fax 708/482-2488
Park Junior High Sch 333 N Park Rd, La Grange Pk 60526 Philip Abraham	7-8		675 38	16%	708/482-2500 Fax 708/352-1170

- **La Grange-Highlands SD 106** PID: 00270279   708/246-3085
  1750 W Plainfield Rd, La Grange 60525   Fax 708/246-0220

Schools: 2 \ **Teachers:** 69 \ **Students:** 850 \ **Special Ed Students:** 104 \ **LEP Students:** 50 \ **Ethnic:** Asian 4%, African American 1%, Hispanic 13%, Caucasian 82% \ **Exp:** $235 (Med) \ **Poverty:** 3% \ **Title I:** $31,495 \ **Special Education:** $426,000 \ **Open-Close:** 08/19 - 05/03 \ **DTBP:** $233 (High)

Dr Amy Warke	1,11	Michael Duback	2
Kent Hoefling	3	Karen Lippold	7*
Ali Beiermeister	9	Carly Cappuli	37*
Amy Laskowski	59,79*	John Corcoran	67
Eric Callis	73,76*		

Public Schs..Principal	Grd	Prgm	Enr/#Cls	SN	
Highlands Elem Sch 5850 Laurel Ave, La Grange 60525 Laura Magruder	PK-5		515 24	5%	708/579-6886 Fax 708/485-3611
Highlands Middle Sch 1850 W Plainfield Rd, La Grange 60525 Michael Papierski	6-8		290 20	4%	708/579-6890 Fax 708/485-3593

- **Lansing School Dist 158** PID: 00270700   708/474-6700
  18300 Greenbay Ave, Lansing 60438   Fax 708/474-9976

Schools: 5 \ **Teachers:** 153 \ **Students:** 2,500 \ **Special Ed Students:** 516 \ **LEP Students:** 145 \ **Ethnic:** Asian 1%, African American 58%, Hispanic 26%, Caucasian 15% \ **Exp:** $270 (Med) \ **Poverty:** 21% \ **Title I:** $987,176 \ **Special Education:** $1,104,000 \ **Open-Close:** 08/19 - 06/04 \ **DTBP:** $253 (High)

Nathon Schilling	1	Mark Crotty	2,4,5,73
Ryan Fortin	3,91	Shirley Bragg	11,69,83,88,288,294,298
Robert Wood	67	David Lesak	73,295*
Dr Tanya Carter	79	Valerie Kooy	81*

Public Schs..Principal	Grd	Prgm	Enr/#Cls	SN	
Coolidge Elem Sch 17845 Henry St, Lansing 60438 Pam Hodgson	K-5	T	565 32	68%	708/474-4320 Fax 708/474-8466
Lester Crawl Primary Center 18300 Greenbay Ave, Lansing 60438 Dr Kim Morley-Hogan	PK-K	T	30 3	17%	708/474-4868 Fax 708/474-0149

1 Superintendent	8 Curric/Instruct K-12	19 Chief Financial Officer	29 Family/Consumer Science	39 Social Studies K-12	49 English/Lang Arts Elem	59 Special Education Elem	69 Academic Assessment
2 Bus/Finance/Purchasing	9 Curric/Instruct Elem	20 Art K-12	30 Adult Education	40 Social Studies Elem	50 English/Lang Arts Sec	60 Special Education Sec	70 Research/Development
3 Buildings And Grounds	10 Curric/Instruct Sec	21 Art Elem	31 Career/Sch-to-Work K-12	41 Social Studies Sec	51 Reading K-12	61 Foreign/World Lang K-12	71 Public Information
4 Food Service	11 Federal Program	22 Art Sec	32 Career/Sch-to-Work Elem	42 Science K-12	52 Reading Elem	62 Foreign/World Lang Elem	72 Summer School
5 Transportation	12 Title I	23 Music K-12	33 Career/Sch-to-Work Sec	43 Science Elem	53 Reading Sec	63 Foreign/World Lang Sec	73 Instructional Tech
6 Athletic	13 Title V	24 Music Elem	34 Early Childhood Ed	44 Science Sec	54 Remedial Reading K-12	64 Religious Education K-12	74 Inservice Training
7 Health Services	15 Asst Superintendent	25 Music Sec	35 Health/Phys Education	45 Math K-12	55 Remedial Reading Elem	65 Religious Education Elem	75 Marketing/Distributive
	16 Instructional Media Svcs	26 Business Education	36 Guidance Services K-12	46 Math Elem	56 Remedial Reading Sec	66 Religious Education Sec	76 Info Systems
	17 Chief Operations Officer	27 Career & Tech Ed	37 Guidance Services Elem	47 Math Sec	57 Bilingual/ELL	67 School Board President	77 Psychological Assess
	18 Chief Academic Officer	28 Technology Education	38 Guidance Services Sec	48 English/Lang Arts K-12	58 Special Education K-12	68 Teacher Personnel	78 Affirmative Action

Illinois School Directory — Cook County

Memorial Junior High Sch	6-8	T	921	66%	708/474-2383
2721 Ridge Rd, Lansing 60438			43		Fax 708/474-8463
Keli Ross					
Oak Glen Elem Sch	K-5	T	523	76%	708/474-1714
2101 182nd St, Lansing 60438			21		Fax 708/474-8461
Mike Earnshaw					
Reavis Elem Sch	K-5	T	450	78%	708/474-8523
17121 Roy St, Lansing 60438			14		Fax 708/474-3071
David Kostopouos					

● **Lemont High Sch Dist 210** PID: 00270803   630/257-5838
800 Porter St, Lemont 60439   Fax 630/243-0310

Schools: 1 \ **Teachers:** 95 \ **Students:** 1,400 \ **Special Ed Students:** 122 \ **LEP Students:** 37 \ **Ethnic:** Asian 5%, African American 1%, Hispanic 11%, Caucasian 83% \ **Exp:** $369 (High) \ **Poverty:** 7% \ **Title I:** $158,198 \ **Special Education:** $635,000 \ **Open-Close:** 08/24 - 05/26 \ **DTBP:** $233 (High)

Mary Ticknor ...1		Cheryl Roy ...2,3,91	
Judy Morton ...2		Ken Parchem ...2	
Tina Mehta ...4*		John Young ...6*	
John St Clair ...6		Katie Dulle ...7	
Tina Malak ...10,11,69,88,270,288*		Dana Browne ...38	
Christine Flores ...60*		Pam Drescoll ...67	
Margaret Jazdzewski ...68		Tony Hamilton ...71*	
Donna Wall ...73,295		Helga Schlinger ...76	
John Conestent ...80		Kelsey Pellus ...90*	

Public Schs..Principal	Grd	Prgm	Enr/#Cls	SN	
Lemont High Sch	9-12	V	1,400	12%	630/257-5838
800 Porter St, Lemont 60439			60		
Eric Michaelsen					

● **Lemont-Bromberek Sch Dist 113A** PID: 00270774   630/257-2286
16100 W 127th St, Lemont 60439   Fax 630/243-3005

Schools: 3 \ **Teachers:** 129 \ **Students:** 2,300 \ **Special Ed Students:** 295 \ **LEP Students:** 182 \ **Ethnic:** Asian 5%, African American 1%, Hispanic 8%, Caucasian 86% \ **Exp:** $175 (Low) \ **Poverty:** 8% \ **Title I:** $356,960 \ **Special Education:** $1,303,000 \ **Bilingual Education:** $52,000 \ **Open-Close:** 08/14 - 05/28 \ **DTBP:** $239 (High)

Anthony McConnell ...1		Pat Crean ...2,3,5
Barbra Germany ...4		Daniella Fountain ...11,68,69,275,288,294,296,298
Susan Wulczyn ...34,37,57,77,79,83,88,271		Damon Ascolani ...67
Stephen Davis ...73,76,295,297		Tracy Simon ...286*

Public Schs..Principal	Grd	Prgm	Enr/#Cls	SN	
Oakwood Elem Sch	PK-2		761	12%	630/257-2286
1130 Kim Pl, Lemont 60439			35		
Kate Kwasny					
Old Quarry Middle Sch	5-8		819	14%	630/257-2286
16100 W 127th St, Lemont 60439			35		Fax 630/243-3004
Joe Sweeney					
River Valley Sch	3-4		745	17%	630/257-2286
15425 E 127th St, Lemont 60439			40		Fax 630/243-3007
Debbie Lynch					

● **Leyden Cmty High Sch Dist 212** PID: 00270827   847/451-3000
3400 Rose St, Franklin Park 60131   Fax 847/451-3644

Schools: 2 \ **Teachers:** 227 \ **Students:** 3,420 \ **Special Ed Students:** 492 \ **LEP Students:** 420 \ **College-Bound:** 73% \ **Ethnic:** Asian 3%, African American 2%, Hispanic 66%, Native American: 1%, Caucasian 29% \ **Exp:** $298 (Med) \ **Poverty:** 12% \ **Title I:** $615,398 \ **Special Education:** $2,153,000 \ **Bilingual Education:** $48,000 \ **Open-Close:** 08/13 - 05/21 \ **DTBP:** $193 (High)

Dr Nick Polyak ...1		Patrick Hatfield ...2
Dr Beth Concannon ...3,15,68		Kenneth Reyes ...3
Elizabeth Kujawa ...4		Kim Cropper ...5
Sandra Rosas ...5		Randy Conrad ...6
Dr Micheal Manderino ...10,11,69,72,288,296		Dr Tatiana Bonuma ...15
Janine Asmus ...16,81,82*		Thomas Janeteas ...19
Frank Holthouse ...27		Chris Cook ...35
Kato Gupta ...38*		Lisa Baran Janco ...57*
Amy Ramsay ...60*		Greg Ignoffo ...67
Bryan Weinert ...73,76		Todd Beltman ...74,95
Joe Hamilton ...80*		Michele Ratini ...90*
Michael Grosch ...91*		

Public Schs..Principal	Grd	Prgm	Enr/#Cls	SN	
East Leyden High Sch	9-12	AGV	1,813	54%	847/451-3000
3400 Rose St, Franklin Park 60131			110		
Jason Markey					
West Leyden High Sch	9-12	AGV	1,607	61%	847/451-3122
1000 N Wolf Rd, Northlake 60164					Fax 847/451-3180
Patricia Makishima					

● **Lincoln Elem School Dist 156** PID: 00268317   708/862-6625
410 157th St, Calumet City 60409   Fax 708/862-1227

Schools: 1 \ **Teachers:** 52 \ **Students:** 950 \ **Special Ed Students:** 132 \ **LEP Students:** 132 \ **Ethnic:** African American 53%, Hispanic 46%, Caucasian 1% \ **Exp:** $227 (Med) \ **Poverty:** 33% \ **Title I:** $731,201 \ **Special Education:** $550,000 \ **Bilingual Education:** $40,000 \ **Open-Close:** 08/21 - 06/01 \ **DTBP:** $230 (High)

Anita Rice ...1		Gerald Lesczynski ...3,91*
Dr Darryl Taylor ...11		Anita Rice ...58,288*
Valencia Ross ...67		

Public Schs..Principal	Grd	Prgm	Enr/#Cls	SN	
Lincoln Elem Sch	PK-8	T	950	84%	708/862-6620
410 157th St, Calumet City 60409					Fax 708/862-1510
Robert Hubbird					

● **Lincolnwood Sch Dist 74** PID: 00270853   847/675-8234
6950 N East Prairie Rd, Lincolnwood 60712   Fax 847/675-4207

Schools: 3 \ **Teachers:** 103 \ **Students:** 1,200 \ **Special Ed Students:** 175 \ **LEP Students:** 225 \ **Ethnic:** Asian 39%, African American 3%, Hispanic 6%, Native American: 1%, Caucasian 52% \ **Exp:** $451 (High) \ **Poverty:** 12% \ **Title I:** $236,595 \ **Special Education:** $422,000 \ **Bilingual Education:** $86,000 \ **Open-Close:** 08/25 - 06/09 \ **DTBP:** $224 (High)

Dr Kim Nasshan ...1		Courtney Whited ...2
Jim Caldwell ...3		Angie Schmidt ...4*
Mark Raciti ...6*		David Russo ...9,12,15
Elena Menicocci ...16*		Jennifer Ruttkay ...59
Scott Anderson ...67		Chris Barnabas ...68
Christina Audisho ...71		Christopher Edman ...73,76,84
Sylvia Hernandez ...294		George Hu ...295

---

79 Student Personnel	91 Safety/Security	275 Response To Intervention	298 Grant Writer/Ptnrships	**School Programs**	**Social Media**		
80 Driver Ed/Safety	92 Magnet School	277 Remedial Math K-12	750 Chief Innovation Officer	A = Alternative Program			
81 Gifted/Talented	93 Parental Involvement	280 Literacy Coach	751 Chief of Staff	G = Adult Classes	= Facebook		
82 Video Services	95 Tech Prep Program	285 STEM	752 Social Emotional Learning	M = Magnet Program			
83 Substance Abuse Prev	97 Chief Information Officer	286 Digital Learning		T = Title I Schoolwide	= Twitter		
84 Erate	98 Chief Technology Officer	288 Common Core Standards	**Other School Types**	V = Career & Tech Ed Programs			
85 AIDS Education	270 Character Education	294 Accountability	Ⓐ = Alternative School				
88 Alternative/At Risk	271 Migrant School	295 Network System	Ⓒ = Charter School	New Schools are shaded			
89 Multi-Cultural Curriculum	273 Teacher Mentor	296 Title II Programs	Ⓜ = Magnet School	New Superintendents and Principals are bold			
90 Social Work	274 Before/After Sch	297 Webmaster	Ⓨ = Year-Round School	Personnel with email addresses are underscored			

IL—55

Cook County — Market Data Retrieval

Public Schs..Principal	Grd	Prgm	Enr/#Cls	SN	
Lincoln Hall Middle Sch 6855 N Crawford Ave, Lincolnwood 60712 Dominick Lupo	6-8		435 30	19%	847/675-8240 Fax 847/675-8124
Rutledge Hall Elem Sch 6850 N East Prairie Rd Ste 1, Lincolnwood 60712 Erin Curry	3-5		381 19	20%	847/675-8236 Fax 847/675-9320 t
Todd Hall Elem Sch 3925 W Lunt Ave Ste 2, Lincolnwood 60712 Christopher Harmon	PK-2		427 45	10%	847/675-8235 Fax 847/675-9378 t

- **Lyons Elem School Dist 103** PID: 00270920 — 708/783-4100
  4100 Joliet Ave, Lyons 60534 — Fax 708/780-9725

Schools: 6 \ Teachers: 208 \ Students: 2,612 \ Special Ed Students: 472 \ LEP Students: 697 \ Ethnic: Asian 1%, African American 5%, Hispanic 73%, Caucasian 21% \ Exp: $338 (High) \ Poverty: 15% \ Title I: $605,747 \ Special Education: $1,349,000 \ Bilingual Education: $195,000 \ Open-Close: 08/28 - 06/04 \ DTBP: $233 (High)

Kristopher Rivera 1		Martin McConahay 2	
Mark Galba 3		Julie Turrubiates 7	
Darek Naglak 9		Kyle Hastings 15	
Jorge Torres 67		Brian Towne 68	
John Williamsen 73*		Colleen Bergren 79	
Christine Newell 88*		Jason Gold 273*	

Public Schs..Principal	Grd	Prgm	Enr/#Cls	SN	
Costello Sch 4632 Clyde Ave, Lyons 60534 Mark Antkiewicz	PK-5	T	302 14	76%	708/783-4300 Fax 708/442-8859
Edison Elem Sch 4100 Scoville Ave, Stickney 60402 Janice Bernard	PK-5	T	289 14	73%	708/783-4400 Fax 708/780-0035 t
George Washington Middle Sch 8101 Ogden Ave, Lyons 60534 Don Jones \ **Carol Baker**	6-8	T	735 38	75%	708/783-4200 Fax 708/780-9757
Home Elem Sch 4400 Home Ave, Stickney 60402 Kristen Smith	PK-5	T	291 12	73%	708/783-4500 Fax 708/780-0041
J W Robinson Elem Sch 4431 Gage Ave, Lyons 60534 Garrett Lefferson	K-5	T	273 14	81%	708/783-4700 Fax 708/780-0172
Lincoln Elem Sch 4300 Grove Ave, Brookfield 60513 Theresa Silva	PK-5	T	523 21	70%	708/783-4600 Fax 708/387-2103

- **Lyons Twp HS District 204** PID: 00271003 — 708/579-6300
  100 S Brainard Ave, La Grange 60525 — Fax 708/579-6768

Schools: 2 \ Teachers: 251 \ Students: 4,200 \ Special Ed Students: 488 \ LEP Students: 85 \ College-Bound: 86% \ Ethnic: Asian 2%, African American 4%, Hispanic 21%, Caucasian 73% \ Exp: $272 (Med) \ Poverty: 4% \ Title I: $156,384 \ Special Education: $2,017,000 \ Open-Close: 08/20 - 06/02 \ DTBP: $189 (High)

Dr Timothy Kilrea 1	Brian Stachacz 2
Ed Drake 3	Marcy Lingo 4
Shanna Lewis 5	John Grundke 6*
Scott Eggerding 10,11,74,273,288,296,298*	Leslie Owens 38,79,88,275
Dr Melissa Boore 60	Tom Cushing 67
Ed Piotrowski 68	Katherine Smith 69,70*
Jennifer Bialobok 71	Ed Tennant 73,76*
William Allan 82*	Nadia Malik 83

Public Schs..Principal	Grd	Prgm	Enr/#Cls	SN	
Lyons Twp High School North 100 S Brainard Ave, La Grange 60525 Dr Brian Waterman	11-12	AGV	2,000	12%	708/579-6300 Fax 708/579-3187
Lyons Twp High School South 4900 Willow Springs Rd, Western Sprgs 60558 Dr Brian Waterman	9-10	AGV	2,000 118		708/579-6500 Fax 708/588-7473

- **Maine Twp High Sch Dist 207** PID: 00271039 — 847/696-3600
  1177 S Dee Rd, Park Ridge 60068 — Fax 847/696-3254

Schools: 3 \ Teachers: 403 \ Students: 6,322 \ Special Ed Students: 886 \ LEP Students: 512 \ College-Bound: 84% \ Ethnic: Asian 15%, African American 3%, Hispanic 23%, Caucasian 59% \ Exp: $697 (High) \ Poverty: 8% \ Title I: $792,343 \ Special Education: $3,270,000 \ Bilingual Education: $51,000 \ Open-Close: 08/17 - 05/28 \ DTBP: $275 (High) \ t

Dr Kenneth Wallace 1	Karen McGovern 2
Mary Kalou 2,13,15	Mary Phillips 2
David Ulm 3,91	Andrew Turner 6*
Jarrett Kirshner 6*	Shawn Messmer 10,15,280,288*
Dr Don Marzolf 11,69,280,298	Greg Dietz 15,68,70,78,273
Mark Ordenez 16,73,76,98,286,295,297	Jill Geocaris 30
Alan Matan 57*	Deb Larsen 60,79
Paula Besler 67	Debra Michalik 68
Brett Clark 71	Dave Beery 71
Natalya Trach 76	

Public Schs..Principal	Grd	Prgm	Enr/#Cls	SN	
Maine East High Sch 2601 Dempster St, Park Ridge 60068 Dr Michael Pressler	9-12	TV	1,853	42%	847/825-4484 Fax 847/692-8260
Maine South High Sch 1111 S Dee Rd, Park Ridge 60068 Ben Collins	9-12	AV	2,391	6%	847/825-7711 Fax 847/692-8210
Maine West High Sch 1755 S Wolf Rd, Des Plaines 60018 Dr Eileen McMahon	9-12	TV	2,078	32%	847/827-6176 Fax 847/296-4916

- **Mannheim School District 83** PID: 00271089 — 847/455-4413
  10401 Grand Ave, Franklin Park 60131 — Fax 847/451-2703

Schools: 6 \ Teachers: 211 \ Students: 2,800 \ Special Ed Students: 390 \ LEP Students: 939 \ Ethnic: Asian 2%, African American 1%, Hispanic 84%, Caucasian 12% \ Exp: $427 (High) \ Poverty: 15% \ Title I: $617,800 \ Special Education: $1,444,000 \ Bilingual Education: $430,000 \ Open-Close: 08/14 - 05/21 \ DTBP: $194 (High)

Kimberly Petrasek 1	Alicia Cieszykowski 2,4,19,37,76,83
Ronald Carleton 3,5,91	Jacklyn Gaffney 7
Michael Corrington 9,12,69,81,280,288,296,298	Dr Michael Dzaillo 11,68,79,294
Theresa Clupimski 16,286*	Dr Piedad Kaye 57
Danielle Welch 59	Marianne Anderson 67
Robert Junna 73,84	Jay Duff 295

Public Schs..Principal	Grd	Prgm	Enr/#Cls	SN	
Enger Sch 10401 Grand Ave, Franklin Park 60131 Erica Granada	Spec	T	57 12	63%	847/455-5299 Fax 847/455-2092
Mannheim Early Childhood Ctr 101 W Diversey Ave, Northlake 60164 Shannon Cribaroo	PK-K	T	199	28%	847/455-3611 Fax 847/455-0143
Mannheim Middle Sch 2600 Hyde Park Ave, Melrose Park 60164 Tim Daley	6-8	T	940	64%	847/455-5020 Fax 847/455-2038

---

1 Superintendent	8 Curric/Instruct K-12	19 Chief Financial Officer	29 Family/Consumer Science	39 Social Studies K-12	49 English/Lang Arts Elem	59 Special Education Elem	69 Academic Assessment
2 Bus/Finance/Purchasing	9 Curric/Instruct Elem	20 Art K-12	30 Adult Education	40 Social Studies Elem	50 English/Lang Arts Sec	60 Special Education Sec	70 Research/Development
3 Buildings And Grounds	10 Curric/Instruct Sec	21 Art Elem	31 Career/Sch-to-Work K-12	41 Social Studies Sec	51 Reading K-12	61 Foreign/World Lang K-12	71 Public Information
4 Food Service	11 Federal Program	22 Art Sec	32 Career/Sch-to-Work Elem	42 Science K-12	52 Reading Elem	62 Foreign/World Lang Elem	72 Summer School
5 Transportation	12 Title I	23 Music K-12	33 Career/Sch-to-Work Sec	43 Science Elem	53 Reading Sec	63 Foreign/World Lang Sec	73 Instructional Tech
6 Athletic	13 Title V	24 Music Elem	34 Early Childhood Ed	44 Science Sec	54 Remedial Reading K-12	64 Religious Education K-12	74 Inservice Training
7 Health Services	15 Asst Superintendent	25 Music Sec	35 Health/Phys Education	45 Math K-12	55 Remedial Reading Elem	65 Religious Education Elem	75 Marketing/Distributive
	16 Instructional Media Svcs	26 Business Education	36 Guidance Services K-12	46 Math Elem	56 Remedial Reading Sec	66 Religious Education Sec	76 Info Systems
	17 Chief Operations Officer	27 Career & Tech Ed	37 Guidance Services Elem	47 Math Sec	57 Bilingual/ELL	67 School Board President	77 Psychological Assess
	18 Chief Academic Officer	28 Technology Education	38 Guidance Services Sec	48 English/Lang Arts K-12	58 Special Education K-12	68 Teacher Personnel	78 Affirmative Action

Illinois School Directory — Cook County

Roy Elem Sch	K-5	T	594	59%	847/451-2700
533 N Roy Ave, Northlake 60164			26		Fax 708/562-9819
Joseph Stanislao					
Scott Elem Sch	K-5	T	424	65%	847/455-4818
2250 Scott St, Melrose Park 60164			50		Fax 847/455-2039
Lisa Schaffer					
Westdale Elem Sch	K-5	T	505	65%	847/455-4060
99 W Diversey Ave, Northlake 60164			80		Fax 847/455-2050
Tara Kjome					f

- **Matteson Elem SD 162** PID: 00271247 — 708/748-0100
  4601 Sauk Trl, Richton Park 60471 — Fax 708/748-7302

Schools: 7 \ **Teachers:** 199 \ **Students:** 2,700 \ **Special Ed Students:** 467 \ **LEP Students:** 27 \ **Ethnic:** Asian 1%, African American 93%, Hispanic 5%, Caucasian 2% \ **Exp:** $165 (Low) \ **Poverty:** 18% \ **Title I:** $983,459 \ **Special Education:** $2,130,000 \ **Open-Close:** 08/25 - 06/03 \ **DTBP:** $186 (High) \ f t

Dr Blondean Davis 1	Craig Englert 2,15
Mark Walczak 3	Susan Friedericks 4
Debbie Szczecina 5	Lee Stanton 11,15,57,288
Dr Doug Hamilton 15	Earnestine Foster 15
Daniel Evans 16,73,295	Dr Latunja Williams 46
Deborah Duskey 59	Rebecca Akridge-Dixon 59
Sheloanda Porche-Box 59	Yvonne Williams 59
Alicia McCray 67	Melissa Renz 68

Public Schs..Principal	Grd	Prgm	Enr/#Cls	SN	
Arcadia Elem Sch	K-3	T	452	78%	708/747-3535
20519 Arcadian Dr, Olympia FLDS 60461			28		Fax 708/503-0961
Stephanie Healy					
Illinois Elem Sch	K-8	T	353	75%	708/747-0301
210 Illinois St Ste 1, Park Forest 60466			25		Fax 708/503-2241
Karen Clay					
Indiana Elem Sch	4-6	T	339	81%	708/747-5300
165 Indiana St, Park Forest 60466			25		Fax 708/503-1012
William Howard					
Matteson Elem Sch	K-3	T	406	93%	708/748-0480
21245 Main St, Matteson 60443			23		Fax 708/503-0812
Gregory Huelsman					
O W Huth Middle Sch	7-8	AT	525	78%	708/748-0470
3718 213th Pl, Matteson 60443			50		Fax 708/503-1119
Robert Tomic					
Richton Square Sch	PK-K	T	260	66%	708/283-2706
22700 Richton Square Rd, Richton Park 60471					Fax 708/283-8594
Pamela Powell					
Sauk Elem Sch	4-6	T	365	89%	708/747-2660
4435 S Churchill Dr, Richton Park 60471			30		Fax 708/503-1335
Dr Richard Morgan					

- **Maywood-Melrose Brdview SD 89** PID: 00271338 — 708/450-2460
  906 Walton St, Melrose Park 60160 — Fax 708/450-2461

Schools: 9 \ **Teachers:** 315 \ **Students:** 4,300 \ **Special Ed Students:** 535 \ **LEP Students:** 1,431 \ **Ethnic:** African American 34%, Hispanic 64%, Caucasian 2% \ **Exp:** $433 (High) \ **Poverty:** 23% \ **Title I:** $2,335,689 \ **Special Education:** $2,881,000 \ **Bilingual Education:** $598,000 \ **Open-Close:** 08/27 - 06/04 \ **DTBP:** $191 (High) \ t

David Negron 1,11	Janet Moreno 2
Dr Raymond Lauk 2,4,5,294	Clarence Thomas 3,91
Frank Pochop 3	Marisa Raymond 4
Barbra Dahly 9,15	David Brusak 15,68
Lauren Pace 34	Scott Wold 46
Maribell Taboda 57*	Anna Candelario 59
Caroline Pate-Hefty 59,79,90	Gwaine Williams 67
Luisa Berardi 71	Micah Miner 73
Mary Carbonari 79	David DelGado 84
Brandy Bolden 280	Jill Deets 280
Joshua Habel 295	Valerie Watkins 298

Public Schs..Principal	Grd	Prgm	Enr/#Cls	SN	
Emerson Elem Sch	PK-5	T	407	29%	708/450-2002
311 Washington Blvd, Maywood 60153			21		Fax 708/338-3495
Tyrone Smith					
Garfield Elem Sch	PK-5	T	454	28%	708/450-2009
1514 S 9th Ave, Maywood 60153			21		Fax 708/344-0593
Marsha Alexander					
Irving Middle Sch	6-8		619	66%	708/450-2015
805 S 17th Ave, Maywood 60153			30		Fax 708/343-0762
Keith Mahone					
Jane Addams Elem Sch	PK-5	T	435	27%	708/450-2023
910 Division St, Melrose Park 60160			18		Fax 708/344-0982
Scott Wold					
Lincoln Elem Sch	PK-5	T	603	29%	708/450-2036
811 Chicago Ave, Maywood 60153			25		Fax 708/344-0986
Yadira Gomez-Munoz					
Melrose Park Elem Sch	K-8	T	930	31%	708/450-2042
1715 W Lake St, Melrose Park 60160			35		Fax 708/344-1162
Leticia Valadez \ **Sherri Rodriguez**					t
Roosevelt Elem Sch	PK-5	T	341	28%	708/450-2047
1927 S 15th Ave, Broadview 60155			10		Fax 708/344-1179
Kimberly Wright					t
Stevenson Middle Sch	6-8	T	915	77%	708/450-2053
1630 N 20th Ave, Melrose Park 60160			35		Fax 708/344-1356
James Parker					
Washington Dual Language Acad	PK-1	T	160	29%	708/450-2065
1111 Washington Blvd, Maywood 60153					Fax 708/344-1185
Lourdes Perez					

- **Midlothian School District 143** PID: 00271467 — 708/388-6450
  14959 Pulaski Rd, Midlothian 60445 — Fax 708/388-4793

Schools: 4 \ **Teachers:** 115 \ **Students:** 1,800 \ **Special Ed Students:** 305 \ **LEP Students:** 321 \ **Ethnic:** Asian 1%, African American 26%, Hispanic 41%, Native American: 2%, Caucasian 30% \ **Exp:** $254 (Med) \ **Poverty:** 21% \ **Title I:** $664,596 \ **Special Education:** $777,000 \ **Open-Close:** 08/28 - 06/04 \ **DTBP:** $232 (High)

Michael Hollingsworth 1	Dr Angela Crotty 2,5,84,298
Mike Galvin 3,91	Mary Ericksen 7
Dr Carrie Cahill 9,11,27,57,74,273,285,288	Anthony Burbatt 16,73,76,286,295*
Cheryl Vacca 34,69,270*	Kelly Burle 34,37,59,77,79,83
Joanne Keilman 67	

Public Schs..Principal	Grd	Prgm	Enr/#Cls	SN	
Central Park Elem Sch	PK-8	T	744	66%	708/385-0045
3621 151st St, Midlothian 60445					Fax 708/385-7063
Colandra Hamilton					
Kolmar Elem Sch	K-8	T	574	56%	708/385-6747
4500 143rd St, Crestwood 60418			34		Fax 708/385-8243
Kelly Andruch					
Spaulding Sch	PK-3	T	91	46%	708/385-4546
14811 Turner Ave, Midlothian 60445			5		Fax 708/385-7406
Cheryl Vacca					
Springfield Elem Sch	PK-6	T	345	63%	708/388-4121
14620 Springfield Ave, Midlothian 60445			22		Fax 708/388-3307
Amanda Brown					

79 Student Personnel	91 Safety/Security	275 Response To Intervention	298 Grant Writer/Ptnrships	**School Programs**	**Social Media**
80 Driver Ed/Safety	92 Magnet School	277 Remedial Math K-12	750 Chief Innovation Officer	A = Alternative Program	
81 Gifted/Talented	93 Parental Involvement	280 Literacy Coach	751 Chief of Staff	G = Adult Classes	f = Facebook
82 Video Services	95 Tech Prep Program	285 STEM	752 Social Emotional Learning	M = Magnet Program	
83 Substance Abuse Prev	97 Chief Information Officer	286 Digital Learning		T = Title I Schoolwide	t = Twitter
84 Erate	98 Chief Technology Officer	288 Common Core Standards	**Other School Types**	V = Career & Tech Ed Programs	
85 AIDS Education	270 Character Education	294 Accountability	Ⓐ = Alternative School		
88 Alternative/At Risk	271 Migrant Education	295 Network System	Ⓒ = Charter School	New Schools are shaded	
89 Multi-Cultural Curriculum	273 Teacher Mentor	296 Title II Programs	Ⓜ = Magnet School	New Superintendents and Principals are bold	
90 Social Work	274 Before/After Sch	297 Webmaster	Ⓨ = Year-Round School	Personnel with email addresses are underscored	

IL—57

Cook County
Market Data Retrieval

- **Morton Grove School Dist 70** PID: 00271510   847/965-6200
  6200 Lake St, Morton Grove 60053   Fax 847/965-6234

Schools: 1 \ **Teachers:** 63 \ **Students:** 900 \ **Special Ed Students:** 130 \ **LEP Students:** 169 \ **Ethnic:** Asian 32%, African American 2%, Hispanic 17%, Caucasian 49% \ **Exp:** $166 (Low) \ **Poverty:** 9% \ **Title I:** $108,170 \ **Special Education:** $222,000 \ **Bilingual Education:** $57,000 \ **Open-Close:** 08/24 - 06/02

Brad Voehringer	1
Jim Johnson	3*
Matt Condon	6,9,11,83,271*
Jessica Matis	16
Brian Galuski	73,286*
Katie Douglas	79
Erin Majchrowski	2
Georiga Senensky	4*
Matt Meyer	11,15,57,288,296,298
Paul McGivern	67
Alana McCloskey	76

Public Schs..Principal	Grd	Prgm	Enr/#Cls	SN	
Park View Sch 6200 Lake St, Morton Grove 60053 Matt Condon	PK-8	T	900 34	28%	847/965-6200

- **Mt Prospect School Dist 57** PID: 00271560   847/394-7300
  701 W Gregory St, Mt Prospect 60056   Fax 847/394-7311

Schools: 4 \ **Teachers:** 148 \ **Students:** 2,222 \ **Special Ed Students:** 289 \ **LEP Students:** 170 \ **Ethnic:** Asian 8%, African American 1%, Hispanic 7%, Caucasian 84% \ **Exp:** $121 (Low) \ **Poverty:** 4% \ **Title I:** $79,460 \ **Special Education:** $1,336,000 \ **Bilingual Education:** $40,000 \ **Open-Close:** 08/20 - 06/01 \ **DTBP:** $233 (High) \ 🅕 🅣

Dr Elaine Aumiller	1
David Obrill	3
Eileen Kowalczyk	67
Maria Potratz	73
Sara Tyburski	79,296,298,752
Adam Parisi	2,3,5,15,19
Dr Mary Gorr	7,11,16,57,77,83,88,288
Thomas O'Rourke	68
Allie Oyman	76

Public Schs..Principal	Grd	Prgm	Enr/#Cls	SN	
Fairview Elem Sch 300 N Fairview Ave, Mt Prospect 60056 Daniel Ophus	2-5		564 26	10%	847/394-7320 Fax 847/394-7328 🅣
Lincoln Middle Sch 700 W Lincoln St, Mt Prospect 60056 Paul Suminski	6-8	V	767 40	10%	847/394-7350 Fax 847/394-7358 🅕 🅣
Lions Park Sch 300 E Council Trl, Mt Prospect 60056 Katherine Kelly	2-5		480 25	8%	847/394-7330 Fax 847/394-7338 🅕 🅣
Westbrook Sch 103 S Busse Rd, Mt Prospect 60056 Kristin Vonder Haar	PK-1		513 5	1%	847/394-7340 Fax 847/394-7349

- **New Trier Twp HS District 203** PID: 00271730   847/446-7000
  7 Happ Rd, Northfield 60093   Fax 847/784-7500

Schools: 2 \ **Teachers:** 343 \ **Students:** 3,978 \ **Special Ed Students:** 648 \ **LEP Students:** 26 \ **College-Bound:** 90% \ **Ethnic:** Asian 10%, African American 1%, Hispanic 5%, Caucasian 84% \ **Exp:** $309 (High) \ **Poverty:** 2% \ **Title I:** $108,201 \ **Special Education:** $3,798,000 \ **Bilingual Education:** $1,000 \ **Open-Close:** 08/26 - 06/10 \ **DTBP:** $189 (High) \ 🅕 🅣

Dr Paul Sally	1
Myron Spiwak	2
Rebecca Cohen	4*
Augustino Fonpanetta	6*
Peter Tragos	8,15,74,273*
Joann Panopoulos	15,58*
Christopher Johnson	2,3,11,15
Daftan Blair	3
Frank Lamerti	5
Colleen Sheridan	7,85*
Mike Lee	12*
Timothy Hayes	15,79

Pamela Strom	16*
John Gilchrist	35*
Kurt Weiler	57,271*
Cathleen Albrecht	67
Renee Zoladz	68
Nicole Dizon	71
Richard Williams	73
George Sanders	78
Christine Bell	91*
Boris Spektor	297*
Stephanie Helfand	16,76,98*
James Conroy	38,270*
Laurel Burman	60*
Kimberly McDermott	68
Linda Knier	69,93*
Athena Arvanitis	72*
Tiffany Myers	77,90*
Christine Schmitt	83
Michael Valadez	295

Public Schs..Principal	Grd	Prgm	Enr/#Cls	SN	
New Trier HS-Freshman Camp 7 Happ Rd, Northfield 60093 Paul Waechtler	9-9	G	1,015 8	3%	847/446-7000 Fax 847/446-7500
New Trier Township High Sch 385 Winnetka Ave, Winnetka 60093 Denise Dubravec	10-12		2,963	4%	847/446-7000 Fax 847/835-9851 🅕 🅣

- **Niles Elem School District 71** PID: 00271766   847/966-9280
  6901 W Oakton St, Niles 60714   Fax 847/966-1478

Schools: 1 \ **Teachers:** 54 \ **Students:** 600 \ **Special Ed Students:** 69 \ **LEP Students:** 60 \ **Ethnic:** Asian 19%, African American 2%, Hispanic 20%, Caucasian 59% \ **Exp:** $471 (High) \ **Poverty:** 13% \ **Title I:** $144,197 \ **Special Education:** $235,000 \ **Bilingual Education:** $35,000 \ **Open-Close:** 08/28 - 06/09 \ **DTBP:** $252 (High)

John Kosirog	1
Laura Guarraci	11,79,296*
Mary Ellen Mueller	57*
Liz Lawrence	69,77,88*
Dr Erica Smolinski	288
Ken Juris	3*
Maria Glaser	16*
Matt Holbrook	67
Ken Kaufhold	73*

Public Schs..Principal	Grd	Prgm	Enr/#Cls	SN	
Clarence E Culver Sch 6901 W Oakton St, Niles 60714 Dr Erica Smolinski	PK-8		600 32	48%	847/966-9280

- **Niles Twp High School Dist 219** PID: 00271792   847/626-3000
  7700 Gross Point Rd, Skokie 60077   Fax 847/626-3090

Schools: 3 \ **Teachers:** 330 \ **Students:** 4,555 \ **Special Ed Students:** 546 \ **LEP Students:** 377 \ **College-Bound:** 86% \ **Ethnic:** Asian 36%, African American 7%, Hispanic 15%, Caucasian 42% \ **Exp:** $426 (High) \ **Poverty:** 10% \ **Title I:** $704,455 \ **Special Education:** $3,196,000 \ **Bilingual Education:** $102,000 \ **Open-Close:** 08/12 - 05/19 \ **DTBP:** $222 (High)

Steven Isoye	1
Dr Sheila Johnson	2
Dr Sandra Arreguin	10,15
Jim Szczepaniak	16,71*
Dr David Ko	67
La Wanna Wells	68,78
Becky Lothian	76
Al Lopez	91*
Dr Eric Trimberger	2,3,5,15
Dr Anne Roloff	10,11,57,69
Tom Kim	15,68
Bridget Connolly	60,79
Jean Moy	68
Oyindamola Idowu	73,98
Marcelo Sanz	76
Steve Shadel	285*

Public Schs..Principal	Grd	Prgm	Enr/#Cls	SN	
Ⓐ Niles Central High Sch 7700 Gross Point Rd, Skokie 60077 Anne Hellmer	9-12	V	23	35%	847/626-3121 Fax 847/626-3080
Niles North High Sch 9800 Lawler Ave, Skokie 60077 James Edwards	9-12	V	2,068 225	32%	847/626-2000 Fax 847/626-3340

1	Superintendent	8	Curric/Instruct K-12	19	Chief Financial Officer	29	Family/Consumer Science	39	Social Studies K-12	49	English/Lang Arts Elem	59	Special Education Elem	69	Academic Assessment
2	Bus/Finance/Purchasing	9	Curric/Instruct Elem	20	Art K-12	30	Adult Education	40	Social Studies Elem	50	English/Lang Arts Sec	60	Special Education Sec	70	Research/Development
3	Buildings And Grounds	10	Curric/Instruct Sec	21	Art Elem	31	Career/Sch-to-Work K-12	41	Social Studies Sec	51	Reading K-12	61	Foreign/World Lang K-12	71	Public Information
4	Food Service	11	Federal Program	22	Art Sec	32	Career/Sch-to-Work Elem	42	Science K-12	52	Reading Elem	62	Foreign/World Lang Elem	72	Summer School
5	Transportation	12	Title I	23	Music K-12	33	Career/Sch-to-Work Sec	43	Science Elem	53	Reading Sec	63	Foreign/World Lang Sec	73	Instructional Tech
6	Athletic	13	Title V	24	Music Elem	34	Early Childhood Ed	44	Science Sec	54	Remedial Reading K-12	64	Religious Education K-12	74	Inservice Training
7	Health Services	15	Asst Superintendent	25	Music Sec	35	Health/Phys Education	45	Math K-12	55	Remedial Reading Elem	65	Religious Education Elem	75	Marketing/Distributive
		16	Instructional Media Svcs	26	Business Education	36	Guidance Services K-12	46	Math Elem	56	Remedial Reading Sec	66	Religious Education Sec	76	Info Systems
		17	Chief Operations Officer	27	Career & Tech Ed	37	Guidance Services Elem	47	Math Sec	57	Bilingual/ELL	67	School Board President	77	Psychological Assess
		18	Chief Academic Officer	28	Technology Education	38	Guidance Services Sec	48	English/Lang Arts K-12	50	Special Education K-12	68	Teacher Personnel	78	Affirmative Action

Illinois School Directory — Cook County

Niles West High Sch		9-12	V	2,464	30%	847/626-2500
5701 Oakton St, Skokie 60077				125		Fax 847/626-3700
Karen Ritter						

● **Norridge School Dist 80** PID: 00271833 — 708/583-2068
8151 W Lawrence Ave, Norridge 60706 — Fax 708/583-2072

Schools: 2 \ **Teachers:** 60 \ **Students:** 1,000 \ **Special Ed Students:** 123 \ **LEP Students:** 183 \ **Ethnic:** Asian 7%, Hispanic 16%, Caucasian 76% \ **Exp:** $302 (High) \ **Poverty:** 10% \ **Title I:** $143,325 \ **Special Education:** $606,000 \ **Bilingual Education:** $1,000 \ **Open-Close:** 08/24 - 06/04 \ **DTBP:** $233 (High) \ [f]

Stephanie Palmer 1		Michele Guzik 9,15*	
Sam Palazzo 67			

Public Schs..Principal	Grd	Prgm	Enr/#Cls	SN	
James Giles Sch	PK-8		622	32%	708/453-4847
4251 N Oriole Ave, Norridge 60706			30		Fax 708/456-0798
Stephanie Palmer					
John V Leigh Elem Sch	PK-8	T	494	31%	708/456-8848
8151 W Lawrence Ave, Norridge 60706			30		Fax 708/583-2053
Michele Guzik \ S Palmer					[f][t]

● **North Palos School Dist 117** PID: 00271869 — 708/598-5500
7825 W 103rd St Ste 2, Palos Hills 60465 — Fax 708/598-5539

Schools: 5 \ **Teachers:** 201 \ **Students:** 3,402 \ **Special Ed Students:** 424 \ **LEP Students:** 1,124 \ **Ethnic:** Asian 3%, African American 5%, Hispanic 16%, Native American: 1%, Caucasian 76% \ **Exp:** $140 (Low) \ **Poverty:** 22% \ **Title I:** $1,078,976 \ **Special Education:** $1,494,000 \ **Bilingual Education:** $357,000 \ **Open-Close:** 08/19 - 06/02 \ **DTBP:** $193 (High)

Dr Jeannie Stachowiak 1	James Bunn 2,11,15,76,286	
Dan Ford 3,91	Shelly Marr 5	
Cynthia Grochocinski 7,35,85*	Christine Dobra 9,13,27,69,74,83,273,288	
Melissa Murphy 9,13,16,69,74,83,273,288	Carrie Stacy 11,15,27,59,83,90,296	
Kara Smit 28	Shadia Salem 57,89	
Dr Tom Kostes 67	Jim Hook 71	
Sean Joyce 73,295	Marilyn Marino 273	

Public Schs..Principal	Grd	Prgm	Enr/#Cls	SN	
Dorn Elem Sch	PK-1	T	459	65%	708/598-5509
7840 W 92nd St, Hickory Hills 60457			23		Fax 708/430-6649
Eileen McCaffrey					[f]
Glen Oaks Elem Sch	2-5	T	707	70%	708/598-5711
9045 S 88th Ave, Hickory Hills 60457			40		Fax 708/430-6636
Kristin Reingruber					
H H Conrady Junior High Sch	6-8	T	1,100	59%	708/598-5721
7950 W 97th St, Hickory Hills 60457			45		Fax 708/430-8964
Adrienne Pavek					[f]
Oak Ridge Elem Sch	2-5	T	734	60%	708/598-5713
8791 W 103rd St, Palos Hills 60465			25		Fax 708/430-8648
Kevin Buscemi					
Sorrick Sch	PK-1	T	402	58%	708/233-8200
7825 W 103rd St Ste 2, Palos Hills 60465			14		Fax 708/599-7763
Natalie Profita					

● **Northbrook Elem School Dist 27** PID: 00271924 — 847/498-2610
1250 Sanders Rd, Northbrook 60062 — Fax 847/498-5916

Schools: 3 \ **Teachers:** 108 \ **Students:** 1,237 \ **Special Ed Students:** 193 \ **LEP Students:** 63 \ **Ethnic:** Asian 19%, African American 1%, Hispanic 5%, Caucasian 75% \ **Exp:** $848 (High) \ **Poverty:** 3% \ **Title I:** $37,768 \ **Special Education:** $750,000 \ **Bilingual Education:** $14,000 \ **Open-Close:** 08/20 - 06/08 \ **DTBP:** $245 (High) \ [f]

Dr David Kroeze 1	Kimberly Arakelian 2,3,15
Douglas Heurich 3	Karen Kornick 7
Dr Katharine Olson 9,15,69	Dr Theresa Fournier 15,68,79,273
Laura Singer 49,52	Julie Revello 59
Mitch Singer 59	Helen Melnick 67
Gail Kahover 71	Reggie Ryan 73,295
James Phillips 76*	James Phillips 76
Helene Spak 274	

Public Schs..Principal	Grd	Prgm	Enr/#Cls	SN	
Hickory Point Elem Sch	PK-2		378	3%	847/498-3830
500 Laburnum Dr, Northbrook 60062			12		Fax 847/480-4837
Maureen Deely					[f]
Shabonee Sch	3-5		420	4%	847/498-4970
1000 Pfingsten Rd, Northbrook 60062			16		Fax 847/480-4836
John Panozzo					
Wood Oaks Junior High Sch	6-8	V	441	2%	847/272-1900
1250 Sanders Rd, Northbrook 60062			20		Fax 847/480-4834
Robert McElligott					

● **Northbrook School District 28** PID: 00271986 — 847/498-7900
1475 Maple Ave, Northbrook 60062 — Fax 847/498-7970

Schools: 4 \ **Teachers:** 181 \ **Students:** 1,870 \ **Special Ed Students:** 245 \ **LEP Students:** 140 \ **Ethnic:** Asian 14%, African American 1%, Hispanic 5%, Caucasian 81% \ **Exp:** $297 (Med) \ **Poverty:** 3% \ **Title I:** $50,719 \ **Special Education:** $1,017,000 \ **Bilingual Education:** $33,000 \ **Open-Close:** 08/24 - 06/02 \ **DTBP:** $237 (High)

Dr Larry Hewitt 1	Jessica Donato 2,4,7,275
Joel Gillegos 3,5,91	Kristin Raitzer 9,11,16,69,280,288,296,298
Wendy Conklin 35	Kelly Sculles 57,752
Tracy Muhl 67	Terry Ryan 71,76
Judi Epcke 73,98	Heather Schultz 79
Jenna Duffy 79	Becky Heller 81
Jessica Mann 81	Michelle Jackson 81
Rachael Weeks 81	Sarah Wippman 81
Scott Meek 273*	Mary Berger 274

Public Schs..Principal	Grd	Prgm	Enr/#Cls	SN	
Greenbriar Elem Sch	K-5		390	2%	847/498-7950
2195 Cherry Ln, Northbrook 60062			17		Fax 847/504-3710
Ginny Hiltz					
Meadowbrook Elem Sch	K-5		419	2%	847/498-7940
1600 Walters Ave, Northbrook 60062			26		Fax 847/504-3610
Patrick Tohme					
Northbrook Junior High Sch	6-8		591	3%	847/498-7920
1475 Maple Ave, Northbrook 60062			40		Fax 847/656-1712
Scott Meek					
Westmoor Elem Sch	PK-5		434	2%	847/498-7960
2500 Cherry Ln, Northbrook 60062			18		Fax 847/504-3810
Mary Sturgill					

---

79 Student Personnel	91 Safety/Security	275 Response To Intervention	296 Grant Writer/Ptnrships	**School Programs**	**Social Media**
80 Driver Ed/Safety	92 Magnet School	277 Remedial Math K-12	750 Chief Innovation Officer	A = Alternative Program	
81 Gifted/Talented	93 Parental Involvement	280 Literacy Coach	751 Chief of Staff	G = Adult Classes	[f] = Facebook
82 Video Services	95 Tech Prep Program	285 STEM	752 Social Emotional Learning	M = Magnet Program	
83 Substance Abuse Prev	97 Chief Information Officer	286 Digital Learning		T = Title I Schoolwide	[t] = Twitter
84 Erate	98 Chief Technology Officer	288 Common Core Standards	**Other School Types**	V = Career & Tech Ed Programs	
85 AIDS Education	270 Character Education	294 Accountability	Ⓐ = Alternative School		
87 Character Education	271 Migrant Education	295 Network System	Ⓒ = Charter School	New Schools are shaded	
88 Alternative/At Risk	273 Teacher Mentor	296 Title II Programs	Ⓜ = Magnet School	New Superintendents and Principals are bold	
89 Multi-Cultural Curriculum	274 Before/After Sch	297 Webmaster	Ⓨ = Year-Round School	Personnel with email addresses are underscored	
90 Social Work					

Cook County

- **Northbrook-Glenview SD 30** PID: 00272057   847/498-4190
  2374 Shermer Rd, Northbrook 60062   Fax 847/498-8981

  Schools: 3 \ **Teachers:** 107 \ **Students:** 1,195 \ **Special Ed Students:** 148 \ **LEP Students:** 116 \ **Ethnic:** Asian 39%, African American 1%, Hispanic 3%, Caucasian 57% \ **Exp:** $344 (High) \ **Poverty:** 4% \ **Title I:** $50,690 \ **Special Education:** $606,000 \ **Bilingual Education:** $21,000 \ **Open-Close:** 08/20 - 06/02 \ **DTBP:** $273 (High) \

Dr Brian Wegley 1	Dale Falk 2,3,15
Don Zabski 3,91	Dr Melissa Hirsch 11,16,57,275,288,294,296,298
Lauren Schulman 59,69,79,83,88,270,280	Ursula Sedlak 67
Beth Preis 71	Andrew Kohl 73,285,286,295
Jeff Loppnow 76	Michele Pollina 752

Public Schs..Principal	Grd	Prgm	Enr/#Cls	SN	
Maple Sch 2370 Shermer Rd, Northbrook 60062 Sam Kurtz	6-8		384 33	2%	847/400-8900 Fax 847/272-0979
Wescott Elem Sch 1820 Western Ave, Northbrook 60062 Christopher Brown	1-5		414 20	2%	847/272-4660 Fax 847/205-5241
Willowbrook Elem Sch 2500 Happy Hollow Rd, Glenview 60026 Scott Carlson	PK-5		397 17	1%	847/498-1090 Fax 847/272-0893

- **Oak Lawn Cmty High SD 229** PID: 00272186   708/424-5200
  9400 Southwest Hwy, Oak Lawn 60453   Fax 708/424-5263

  Schools: 1 \ **Teachers:** 102 \ **Students:** 1,850 \ **Special Ed Students:** 281 \ **LEP Students:** 142 \ **College-Bound:** 75% \ **Ethnic:** Asian 1%, African American 7%, Hispanic 32%, Native American: 1%, Caucasian 59% \ **Exp:** $383 (High) \ **Poverty:** 15% \ **Title I:** $509,480 \ **Special Education:** $737,000 \ **Bilingual Education:** $16,000 \ **Open-Close:** 08/19 - 05/28 \ **DTBP:** $227 (High)

Dr Michael Riordan 1	Jean Paluszkiewicz 2
Joseph Giglio 3*	Joseph McCurdy 4*
Joseph McCurdy 5,15	Jeremy Cryan 6*
Amy Tucker 7,85*	Mike Sunquist 10,11,33,60,273*
Lauren May 16*	Robert Loehr 67
Marcus Wargin 69,71,72*	Thomas Magdziasz 73*

Public Schs..Principal	Grd	Prgm	Enr/#Cls	SN	
Oak Lawn Cmty High Sch 9400 Southwest Hwy, Oak Lawn 60453 Jeana Lietz	9-12	T	1,850 90	40%	708/424-5200

- **Oak Lawn-Hometown Sch Dist 123** PID: 00272203 708/423-0150
  4201 W 93rd St Ste 1, Oak Lawn 60453   Fax 708/423-0160

  Schools: 6 \ **Teachers:** 226 \ **Students:** 3,000 \ **Special Ed Students:** 525 \ **LEP Students:** 500 \ **Ethnic:** Asian 2%, African American 7%, Hispanic 38%, Caucasian 53% \ **Exp:** $125 (Low) \ **Poverty:** 12% \ **Title I:** $621,473 \ **Special Education:** $1,966,000 \ **Bilingual Education:** $56,000 \ **Open-Close:** 08/21 - 06/04 \ **DTBP:** $196 (High) \

Paul Enderle 1	Michael Loftin 2,4,15
Leo Cassidy 3,91	Dr Kathleen Gavin 15,285,288,298
Joseph MacChia 16,73,286,295	Angela Goetz 57
Cynthia Riha 59,275	Brian Nichols 67
Natalie Vitale 71	Tammie Lagioia 76
Dennis Stellern 295	

Public Schs..Principal	Grd	Prgm	Enr/#Cls	SN	
Hannum Elem Sch 9800 S Tripp Ave, Oak Lawn 60453 Anne McGovern	PK-5	T	415 16	49%	708/423-1690 Fax 708/499-7676
Hometown Elem Sch 8870 S Duffy Ave, Hometown 60456 Kathleen Spreitzer	PK-5	T	387 21	64%	708/423-7360 Fax 708/499-7679
J Covington Elem Sch 9130 S 52nd Ave, Oak Lawn 60453 John Wawczak	PK-5	T	457 18	46%	708/423-1530 Fax 708/499-7674
Kolmar Ave Elem Sch 10425 S Kolmar Ave, Oak Lawn 60453 David Creech	PK-5	T	438 17	35%	708/422-1800 Fax 708/499-7681
Oak Lawn Hometown Middle Sch 5345 W 99th St, Oak Lawn 60453 Sean McNichols	6-8	T	1,092 40	44%	708/499-6400 Fax 708/499-7684
Sward Elem Sch 9830 Brandt Ave, Oak Lawn 60453 Candice Kramer	PK-5	T	516 21	33%	708/423-7820 Fax 708/499-7684

- **Oak Park & River Forest SD 200** PID: 00272435 708/383-0700
  201 N Scoville Ave, Oak Park 60302   Fax 708/434-3910

  Schools: 1 \ **Teachers:** 242 \ **Students:** 3,468 \ **Special Ed Students:** 594 \ **LEP Students:** 20 \ **College-Bound:** 85% \ **Ethnic:** Asian 4%, African American 22%, Hispanic 13%, Caucasian 61% \ **Exp:** $398 (High) \ **Poverty:** 3% \ **Title I:** $116,271 \ **Special Education:** $3,534,000 \ **Open-Close:** 08/17 - 05/27 \ **DTBP:** $190 (High) \

Joylynn Pruitt-Adam 1	Cyndi Sidor 2
Fred Preuss 3	Jeff Bergmann 3
Mike Carioscio 3,17,71,97,295,297	Micheline Piekarski 4*
Carolyn Gust 5	John Stelzer 6*
Gregory Johnson 10,15	Janel Bishop 35,80,83,85*
Lynda Parker 38*	Gwendolyne Walker-Qualls 60*
Dr Jackie Moore 67	Roxana Sanders 68
Krystal Jones 69*	Christopher Thieme 73*
Christopher Thieme 84	Alisa Walton 275
Brian Beyers 275	Jonathan Weintraub 275
Jonathan Silver 275	

Public Schs..Principal	Grd	Prgm	Enr/#Cls	SN	
Oak Park & River Forest HS 201 N Scoville Ave, Oak Park 60302 Nathaniel Rouse	9-12	AV	3,468	19%	708/383-0700 Fax 708/383-3910

- **Oak Park Elem School Dist 97** PID: 00272318   708/524-3000
  260 Madison St, Oak Park 60302   Fax 708/524-3019

  Schools: 10 \ **Teachers:** 446 \ **Students:** 6,000 \ **Special Ed Students:** 860 \ **LEP Students:** 159 \ **Ethnic:** Asian 4%, African American 20%, Hispanic 14%, Caucasian 61% \ **Exp:** $154 (Low) \ **Poverty:** 5% \ **Title I:** $442,143 \ **Special Education:** $5,331,000 \ **Open-Close:** 08/24 - 06/04 \ **DTBP:** $210 (High) \

Dr Carol Kelley 1	Latoya Champ 2
Mark Sheehan 2,3,4,5,15	Jeanne Keane 3
Carla Ellis 4	Donna Middleton 7,13,34,37,59,77,88,752
Eboney Lofton 9,18,69,294	Emily Fenske 9
Dr Felicia Starks-Turner 9,11,19,79,288,296,298 9,69	Dr Tawanda Lawrence
Gina Herrmann 15,68,74	Mike Arensdorff 16,73,84
Michele Suedbeck 34	Tracy Hamm 59
Keecia Broy 67	Siania Obidi 68
Tulicia Edwards 68	Amanda Siegfried 71
Kristin Imberger 76	Liz Battaglia 76
Dr Carrie Kamm 78	Adam Domchymski 295

1	Superintendent	8	Curric/Instruct K-12	19	Chief Financial Officer	29	Family/Consumer Science	39	Social Studies K-12	49	English/Lang Arts Elem	59	Special Education Elem	69	Academic Assessment
2	Bus/Finance/Purchasing	9	Curric/Instruct Elem	20	Art K-12	30	Adult Education	40	Social Studies Elem	50	English/Lang Arts Sec	60	Special Education Sec	70	Research/Development
3	Buildings And Grounds	10	Curric/Instruct Sec	21	Art Elem	31	Career/Sch-to-Work K-12	41	Social Studies Sec	51	Reading K-12	61	Foreign/World Lang K-12	71	Public Information
4	Food Service	11	Federal Program	22	Art Sec	32	Career/Sch-to-Work Elem	42	Science K-12	52	Reading Elem	62	Foreign/World Lang Elem	72	Summer School
5	Transportation	12	Title I	23	Music K-12	33	Career/Sch-to-Work Sec	43	Science Elem	53	Reading Sec	63	Foreign/World Lang Sec	73	Instructional Tech
6	Athletic	13	Title V	24	Music Elem	34	Early Childhood Ed	44	Science Sec	54	Remedial Reading K-12	64	Religious Education K-12	74	Inservice Training
7	Health Services	15	Asst Superintendent	25	Music Sec	35	Health/Phys Education	45	Math K-12	55	Remedial Reading Elem	65	Religious Education Elem	75	Marketing/Distributive
		16	Instructional Media Svcs	26	Business Education	36	Guidance Services K-12	46	Math Elem	56	Remedial Reading Sec	66	Religious Education Sec	76	Info Systems
		17	Chief Operations Officer	27	Career & Tech Ed	37	Guidance Services Elem	47	Math Sec	57	Bilingual/ELL	67	School Board President	77	Psychological Assess
		18	Chief Academic Officer	28	Technology Education	38	Guidance Services Sec	48	English/Lang Arts K-12	58	Special Education K-12	68	Teacher Personnel	78	Affirmative Action

Illinois School Directory — Cook County

Will Brackett 295

Public Schs..Principal	Grd	Prgm	Enr/#Cls	SN	
Abraham Lincoln Elem Sch 1111 S Grove Ave, Oak Park 60304 Laura Zaniolo	K-5		685 27	17%	708/524-3110 Fax 708/524-3124 t
Gwendolyn Brooks Middle Sch 325 S Kenilworth Ave, Oak Park 60302 April Capuder	6-8	A	906 75	16%	708/524-3050 Fax 708/524-3036
Horace Mann Elem Sch 921 N Kenilworth Ave, Oak Park 60302 **Hussain Ali**	K-5		490 25	6%	708/524-3085 Fax 708/524-3049
Irving Elem Sch 1125 S Cuyler Ave, Oak Park 60304 John Hodge	K-5	T	483 21	18%	708/524-3090 Fax 708/524-3056
Longfellow Elem Sch 715 Highland Ave, Oak Park 60304 Amy Jefferson	PK-5	T	703 16	19%	708/524-3060 Fax 708/524-3037
Oliver Wendell Holmes Elem Sch 508 N Kenilworth Ave, Oak Park 60302 Dr Christine Zelaya	K-5	T	571 30	19%	708/524-3100 Fax 708/524-7622
Percy Julian Middle Sch 416 S Ridgeland Ave, Oak Park 60302 Jeremy Christian	6-8	A	1,043	19%	708/524-3040 Fax 708/524-3035
Whittier Elem Sch 715 N Harvey Ave, Oak Park 60302 Patrick Robinson	PK-5	T	448 40	20%	708/524-3080 Fax 708/524-3047 t
William Beye Elem Sch 230 N Cuyler Ave, Oak Park 60302 Jennifer Schemidt	K-5	T	367 20	19%	708/524-3070 Fax 708/524-3069 t
William Hatch Elem Sch 1000 N Ridgeland Ave, Oak Park 60302 Sarah Mendez	PK-5		379 13	14%	708/524-3095 Fax 708/524-3139 t

● **Orland School District 135** PID: 00272459 708/364-3300
15100 S 94th Ave, Orland Park 60462 Fax 708/349-5707

Schools: 10 \ **Teachers:** 360 \ **Students:** 5,201 \ **Special Ed Students:** 880 \ **LEP Students:** 672 \ **Ethnic:** Asian 6%, African American 5%, Hispanic 15%, Caucasian 74% \ **Exp:** $212 (Med) \ **Poverty:** 8% \ **Title I:** $678,765 \ **Special Education:** $3,297,000 \ **Bilingual Education:** $97,000 \ **Open-Close:** 08/26 - 06/08 \ **DTBP:** $198 (High)

Rick Hanson .... 3 Dr Dave Snyder 9,273
Dr Lynn Zeder .... 9,11,15,57,59,69 Karen Janettas 34,59,77,88,90,275
Linda Peckham-Dodge .... 67 June DeSimone 68
Suzanne Owens .... 68 Chris Bohula 84
Jerry Hughes .... 91 Eric Simms 295

Public Schs..Principal	Grd	Prgm	Enr/#Cls	SN	
Centennial Elem Sch 14101 Creek Crossing Dr, Orland Park 60467 Beth Hayden	PK-3		493 25	10%	708/364-3444 Fax 708/873-6450
Center Sch 9407 W 151st St, Orland Park 60462 Courtney Milligan	PK-2		353 22	16%	708/364-3242 Fax 708/873-6453
Century Junior High Sch 10801 W 159th St, Orland Park 60467 Brian Horn	6-8		671 35	13%	708/364-3500 Fax 708/873-6423
High Point Elem Sch 14825 West Ave, Orland Park 60462 Colleen Joyce	3-5		447 20	16%	708/364-4400 Fax 708/460-5970
Jerling Junior High Sch 8851 W 151st St, Orland Park 60462 Kevin Brown	6-8		622 30	19%	708/364-3700 Fax 708/873-6457
Liberty Elem Sch 8801 W 151st St, Orland Park 60462 Daniel Prorok	3-5		548 22	23%	708/364-3800 Fax 708/873-1103
Meadow Ridge Elem Sch 10959 W 159th St, Orland Park 60467 Dana Karczewski	3-5		564 50	16%	708/364-3600 Fax 708/873-6461
Orland Junior High Sch 14855 West Ave, Orland Park 60462 Edward Boswell	6-8		566 35	16%	708/364-4200 Fax 708/349-5843
Park Sch 9960 W 143rd St, Orland Park 60462 Brian Fogarty	PK-2		387 19	21%	708/364-3900 Fax 708/460-6139
Prairie Sch 14200 S 82nd Ave, Orland Park 60462 Jeffrey Nightingale	PK-3		514 22	20%	708/364-4840 Fax 708/873-6451

● **Palos Cmty Cons Sch Dist 118** PID: 00272784 708/448-4800
8800 W 119th St, Palos Park 60464 Fax 708/448-4880

Schools: 3 \ **Teachers:** 133 \ **Students:** 2,050 \ **Special Ed Students:** 385 \ **LEP Students:** 230 \ **Ethnic:** Asian 3%, African American 2%, Hispanic 14%, Caucasian 82% \ **Exp:** $309 (High) \ **Poverty:** 8% \ **Title I:** $219,044 \ **Special Education:** $1,307,000 \ **Bilingual Education:** $31,000 \ **Open-Close:** 08/26 - 06/09 \ **DTBP:** $236 (High)

Dr Anthony Scarsella .... 1 Justin Veihman 2
Kathy Pagoria .... 4 Mary Meyer 5
Carolyn Shaver .... 6 Dr Ron Cozza 9,15,288
Nadine Scodro .... 67 Deborah Balayti 73,286
Scott Fox .... 76,295* Erin Deval 79,88

Public Schs..Principal	Grd	Prgm	Enr/#Cls	SN	
Palos East Elem Sch 7700 W 127th St, Palos Heights 60463 Robert Szklanecki	PK-5		647 29	30%	708/448-1084 Fax 708/923-7077
Palos South Middle Sch 13100 S 82nd Ave, Palos Park 60464 Stuart Wrzesinski	6-8		708 35	27%	708/448-5971 Fax 708/448-0754
Palos West Elem Sch 12700 S 104th Ave, Palos Park 60464 Jennifer Peloquin	PK-5		643 40	26%	708/448-6888 Fax 708/923-7064 f

● **Palos Heights School Dist 128** PID: 00272837 708/597-9040
12809 S McVickers Ave, Palos Heights 60463 Fax 708/597-9089

Schools: 4 \ **Teachers:** 55 \ **Students:** 700 \ **Special Ed Students:** 132 \ **LEP Students:** 32 \ **Ethnic:** Asian 2%, African American 3%, Hispanic 15%, Caucasian 80% \ **Exp:** $171 (Low) \ **Poverty:** 12% \ **Title I:** $135,212 \ **Special Education:** $423,000 \ **Bilingual Education:** $6,000 \ **Open-Close:** 08/21 - 06/02 \ **DTBP:** $235 (High)

Dr Merryl Brownlow .... 1 Jason Smitt 16,28,73
William Grady .... 67 Cathy Leslie 79

Public Schs..Principal	Grd	Prgm	Enr/#Cls	SN	
Chippewa Elem Sch 12425 S Austin Ave, Palos Heights 60463 Mary Duffy	1-3		189 12	6%	708/388-7260 Fax 708/388-2761
Independence Jr High Sch 6610 W Highland Dr, Palos Heights 60463 Kevin Kirk	6-8	A	236 30	11%	708/448-0737 Fax 708/448-0179
Indian Hill Sch 12800 S Austin Ave, Palos Heights 60463 Mary Duffy	PK-K	A	139 5	3%	708/597-1285 Fax 708/597-4230

---

79 Student Personnel
80 Driver Ed/Safety
81 Gifted/Talented
82 Video Services
83 Substance Abuse Prev
84 Erate
85 AIDS Education
88 Alternative/At Risk
89 Multi-Cultural Curriculum
90 Social Work
91 Safety/Security
92 Magnet School
93 Parental Involvement
95 Tech Prep Program
97 Chief Information Officer
98 Chief Technology Officer
270 Character Education
271 Migrant Education
273 Teacher Mentor
274 Before/After Sch
275 Response To Intervention
277 Remedial Math K-12
280 Literacy Coach
285 STEM
286 Digital Learning
288 Common Core Standards
294 Accountability
295 Network System
296 Title II Programs
297 Webmaster
298 Grant Writer/Ptnrships
750 Chief Innovation Officer
751 Chief of Staff
752 Social Emotional Learning

Other School Types
Ⓐ = Alternative School
Ⓒ = Charter School
Ⓜ = Magnet School
Ⓨ = Year-Round School

School Programs
A = Alternative Program
G = Adult Classes
M = Magnet Program
T = Title I Schoolwide
V = Career & Tech Ed Programs

Social Media
f = Facebook
t = Twitter

New Schools are shaded
New Superintendents and Principals are bold
Personnel with email addresses are underscored

Cook County — Market Data Retrieval

Navajo Heights Elem Sch 4-5 147 18% 708/385-3269
12401 S Oak Park Ave, Palos Heights 60463   6   Fax 708/385-0429
Kaitlin Curran

- **Park Forest Chicago Hgt SD 163** PID: 00272930 708/668-9400
  242 S Orchard Dr, Park Forest 60466   Fax 708/844-0288

> Schools: 6 \ Teachers: 130 \ Students: 2,000 \ Special Ed Students: 317 \ LEP Students: 44 \ Ethnic: African American 88%, Hispanic 9%, Caucasian 3% \ Exp: $332 (High) \ Poverty: 29% \ Title I: $1,016,210 \ Special Education: $1,274,000 \ Open-Close: 08/27 - 06/08 \ DTBP: $233 (High)

David Ricker 2,3
Brenda Porter 7
Dr Cheryl Muench 9,74*
Regina Nottke 15,59*
Lance Jefferson 67
Heather Cullen 76
Sandi Gordon 4,5
Caletha White 9,11,296,298*
Dr Ericka Patterson 15,68*
Valerie Valente 46
Susan Klimczak 73,295
Mo Awad 76

Public Schs..Principal	Grd	Prgm	Enr/#Cls	SN	
21st Century Primary Center 240 S Orchard Dr, University Pk 60466 Chrishawn Chinn	K-3	T	185 11	84%	708/668-9490 Fax 708/747-0261
Algonquin Pre-Kindergarten Ctr 170 Algonquin St, Park Forest 60466 Lori Colbert	PK-PK	T	156 9	72%	708/668-9202 Fax 708/395-2512
Barack Obama Leadership & STEM 401 Concord Dr, Chicago HTS 60411 Khari Grant	4-8	T	500	83%	708/668-9100 Fax 708/283-2358
Blackhawk Primary Center 130 Blackhawk Dr, Park Forest 60466 Dr Felix Anderson	K-3	T	221 11	81%	708/668-9500 Fax 708/481-0917
Michelle Obama Sch Tech & Arts 530 Lakewood Blvd, Park Forest 60466 Dr Cheryl Muench	4-8	T	536	87%	708/668-9600 Fax 708/395-2516
Mohawk Primary Center 301 Mohawk St, Park Forest 60466 Chrishawn Chinn	K-3	T	265 15	86%	708/668-9300 Fax 708/395-2513

- **Park Ridge Niles CMCSD 64** PID: 00273051 847/318-4300
  164 S Prospect Ave, Park Ridge 60068   Fax 847/318-4351

> Schools: 8 \ Teachers: 352 \ Students: 4,500 \ Special Ed Students: 651 \ LEP Students: 343 \ Ethnic: Asian 6%, African American 1%, Hispanic 8%, Caucasian 85% \ Exp: $299 (Med) \ Poverty: 4% \ Title I: $192,733 \ Special Education: $2,701,000 \ Open-Close: 08/27 - 06/11 \ DTBP: $198 (High) \ f t

Dr Eric Olson 1
Ron De George 3,5
Dr Lori Lopez 9,15
Dr Joel Martin 15,68,273
Tony Galan 59
Mary Jane Warden 73
Dr Lea Frost 79
Lisa Halverson 274*
Gorman Christian 295
Luann Kolstad 2
Dr Lori Hinton Lopez 9,15,69,74,288,296
Leeann Frost 11,59,83,88,90,270,271
Shannon Rodriguez 57*
Susan Dilillo 68
Angela Phillips 79
Tracie Thomas 81*
Dina Pappas 285

Public Schs..Principal	Grd	Prgm	Enr/#Cls	SN	
Benjamin Franklin Elem Sch 2401 Manor Ln, Park Ridge 60068 Dr Marybeth Delamar	K-5		531 25	6%	847/318-4390 Fax 847/318-4203
Emerson Middle Sch 8101 N Cumberland Ave, Niles 60714 Samantha Alaimo	6-8		875 45	4%	847/318-8110 Fax 847/318-8701
Eugene Field Elem Sch 707 Wisner St, Park Ridge 60068 Courtney Goodman	K-5		650 27	5%	847/318-4385 Fax 847/318-4202
George B Carpenter Elem Sch 300 N Hamlin Ave, Park Ridge 60068 Brett Balduf	K-5		461 21	2%	847/318-4370 Fax 847/318-4201
George Washington Elem Sch 1500 Stewart Ave, Park Ridge 60068 Angela Brito	K-5		653 27	3%	847/318-4360 Fax 847/318-4247
Jefferson Sch 8200 W Greendale Ave Ste 1, Niles 60714 Lisa Halverson	PK-PK		137 5	2%	847/318-5360 Fax 847/318-5442
Lincoln Middle Sch 200 S Lincoln Ave, Park Ridge 60068 David Szwed	6-8		724 30	4%	847/318-4215 Fax 847/318-4210
Roosevelt Elem Sch 1001 S Fairview Ave, Park Ridge 60068 Dr Kevin Dwyer	K-5		647 28	1%	847/318-4235 Fax 847/318-4205

- **Pennoyer School District 79** PID: 00273192 708/456-9094
  5200 N Cumberland Ave, Norridge 60706   Fax 708/456-9098

> Schools: 1 \ Teachers: 29 \ Students: 444 \ Special Ed Students: 39 \ LEP Students: 89 \ Ethnic: Asian 9%, Hispanic 14%, Caucasian 77% \ Exp: $225 (Med) \ Poverty: 14% \ Title I: $79,775 \ Special Education: $130,000 \ Bilingual Education: $3,000 \ Open-Close: 08/24 - 06/03 \ DTBP: $233 (High) \ f t

Dr Kristen Kopta 1,11
James Nelsen 6,35*
William Madueno 43*
Kay Malusa 59*
Rachel Michaels 69*
Gina Sierra 288,296,298*
Dawn Wallace 2
Molissa Tronco 12*
Tom Pazden 57*
Michael Malusa 67
Patrick Christl 73*

Public Schs..Principal	Grd	Prgm	Enr/#Cls	SN	
Pennoyer Sch 5200 N Cumberland Ave, Norridge 60706 Aliaa Ibrahim	PK-8	T	444 22	35%	708/456-9094 f t

- **Pleasantdale School Dist 107** PID: 00273219 708/784-2013
  7450 Wolf Rd, Burr Ridge 60527   Fax 708/246-0161

> Schools: 2 \ Teachers: 65 \ Students: 845 \ Special Ed Students: 92 \ LEP Students: 92 \ Ethnic: Asian 8%, African American 1%, Hispanic 15%, Caucasian 76% \ Exp: $259 (Med) \ Poverty: 5% \ Title I: $54,085 \ Special Education: $393,000 \ Bilingual Education: $1,000 \ Open-Close: 08/19 - 06/03 \ DTBP: $232 (High)

Dr Dave Palzet 1
Debbie Lubeck 9,11,57,59
John McAtee 16,98
Frank Adams 2,3,11,84,85
Dr Jennifer Ban 9,15,298
Kristin Violante 67

Public Schs..Principal	Grd	Prgm	Enr/#Cls	SN	
Pleasantdale Elem Sch 8100 School St, La Grange 60525 Kathleen Tomei	PK-4		440 24	8%	708/246-4700 Fax 708/246-4625
Pleasantdale Middle Sch 7450 Wolf Rd, Burr Ridge 60527 Griffin Sonntag	5-8		388 20	12%	708/246-3210 Fax 708/352-0092

1 Superintendent	8 Curric/Instruct K-12	19 Chief Financial Officer	29 Family/Consumer Science	39 Social Studies K-12	49 English/Lang Arts Elem	59 Special Education Elem	69 Academic Assessment
2 Bus/Finance/Purchasing	9 Curric/Instruct Elem	20 Art K-12	30 Adult Education	40 Social Studies Elem	50 English/Lang Arts Sec	60 Special Education Sec	70 Research/Development
3 Buildings And Grounds	10 Curric/Instruct Sec	21 Art Elem	31 Career/Sch-to-Work K-12	41 Social Studies Sec	51 Reading K-12	61 Foreign/World Lang K-12	71 Public Information
4 Food Service	11 Federal Program	22 Art Sec	32 Career/Sch-to-Work Elem	42 Science K-12	52 Reading Elem	62 Foreign/World Lang Elem	72 Summer School
5 Transportation	12 Title I	23 Music K-12	33 Career/Sch-to-Work Sec	43 Science Elem	53 Reading Sec	63 Foreign/World Lang Sec	73 Instructional Tech
6 Athletic	13 Title V	24 Music Elem	34 Early Childhood Ed	44 Science Sec	54 Remedial Reading K-12	64 Religious Education K-12	74 Inservice Training
7 Health Services	15 Asst Superintendent	25 Music Sec	35 Health/Phys Education	45 Math K-12	55 Remedial Reading Elem	65 Religious Education Elem	75 Marketing/Distributive
	16 Instructional Media Svcs	26 Business Education	36 Guidance Services K-12	46 Math Elem	56 Remedial Reading Sec	66 Religious Education Sec	76 Info Systems
	17 Chief Operations Officer	27 Career & Tech Ed	37 Guidance Services Elem	47 Math Sec	57 Bilingual/ELL	67 School Board President	77 Psychological Assess
	18 Chief Academic Officer	28 Technology Education	38 Guidance Services Sec	48 English/Lang Arts K-12	58 Special Education K-12	68 Teacher Personnel	78 Affirmative Action

Illinois School Directory — Cook County

- **Posen-Robbins Sch Dist 143-5** PID: 00273245   708/388-7200
  14025 S Harrison Ave, Posen 60469   Fax 708/388-3868

Schools: 5 \ **Teachers:** 104 \ **Students:** 1,452 \ **Special Ed Students:** 158 \ **LEP Students:** 448 \ **Ethnic:** Asian 1%, African American 34%, Hispanic 62%, Caucasian 2% \ **Exp:** $366 (High) \ **Poverty:** 24% \ **Title I:** $780,722 \ **Special Education:** $456,000 \ **Bilingual Education:** $124,000 \ **Open-Close:** 08/26 - 06/11 \ **DTBP:** $235 (High)

Dr Anthony Edison 1
Devetta Foster 3*
Dr Evisha Ford-Sills 15,59,79,83,90
Fran Bryant 67
Bridgette Simmons 71
Vanessa Hallom 79
Aaron Bell 295
Demicka Oray 295,297
Dr Michael Moore 2,16
Dr Tracy Olawumi 9,11,15,16,72
Ernst Jourdain 57
Toni Grayer 68
Jacob Cooper 73,84
Arleta Bazile 274*
Charo Thomas 295

Public Schs..Principal	Grd	Prgm	Enr/#Cls	SN	
Childs Elem Sch 14123 S Lydia Ave, Robbins 60472 Tarita Lowery	K-3	T	145 9	82%	708/388-7203 Fax 708/489-4368
Gordon Sch 14100 S Harrison Ave, Posen 60469 Andrea McKinney	K-3	T	322 26	81%	708/388-7202 Fax 708/388-6891
Kellar Middle Sch 14123 S Lydia Ave, Robbins 60472 Dr Monica Spence	6-8	T	519 23	87%	708/388-7201 Fax 708/388-6177
Posen Intermediate Sch 14545 S California Ave, Posen 60469 Dr Don Parker	4-5	T	316 18	86%	708/388-7204 Fax 708/489-4375
Turner Elem Sch 3847 W 135th St, Crestwood 60418 Angela Craig	PK-K	T	150 7	98%	708/388-7205 Fax 708/489-4376

- **Prairie Hills Elem SD 144** PID: 00271144   708/210-2888
  3015 W 163rd St, Markham 60428   Fax 708/210-9925

Schools: 8 \ **Teachers:** 136 \ **Students:** 3,000 \ **Special Ed Students:** 365 \ **LEP Students:** 128 \ **Ethnic:** Asian 1%, African American 85%, Hispanic 11%, Caucasian 2% \ **Exp:** $203 (Med) \ **Poverty:** 31% \ **Title I:** $1,730,075 \ **Special Education:** $1,083,000 \ **Bilingual Education:** $18,000 \ **Open-Close:** 08/21 - 06/01 \ **DTBP:** $204 (High) \ f t

Dr Kimako Patterson 1,83
Foy Bryant 3
Rhonda Jones 4*
Timothy Heard 6
Juanita McWilliams 16,76,286,297
Lisa Adrianven 57
Sharron Davis 67
Paul Huffaker 69,74,285
Deborah Clayton 2
Teddy Young 3
Carrie Ablin 5,7,34,59,77,79,88
Julia Veazey ..11,73,280,288,294,296,298
Codjhia Shelton 46
Michelle Hardmon 59,79*
Dr Kenneth Scott 68
June Yang 295

Public Schs..Principal	Grd	Prgm	Enr/#Cls	SN	
Chateaux Sch 3600 Chambord Ln, Hazel Crest 60429 Glenn Greene	K-5	T	335	97%	708/335-9776 Fax 708/957-6090 f t
Fieldcrest Elem Sch 4100 Wagman St, Oak Forest 60452 Kimberly Cook	K-5	T	293 20	88%	708/210-2872 Fax 708/535-0224 f t
Highlands Elem Sch 3420 Laurel Ln, Hazel Crest 60429 Ms Montgomery	K-5	T	312 17	91%	708/335-9773 Fax 708/335-4650 f t
Mae Jemison Elem Sch 3450 W 177th St, Hazel Crest 60429 Kevin Johns	PK-5	T	418 23	98%	708/225-3636 Fax 708/799-8363

Markham Park Elem Sch 16239 Lawndale Ave, Markham 60428 Tiffany Rucker	PK-5	T	313	96%	708/210-2869 Fax 708/210-9201 f t
Nob Hill Elem Sch 3701 168th St, Cntry CLB Hls 60478 Ms Smith	PK-5	T	193 12	99%	708/335-9770 Fax 708/957-6092
Prairie Hills Jr High Sch 16315 Richmond St, Markham 60428 Kenndell Smith	6-8	T	938 30	96%	708/210-2860 Fax 708/331-7367
Primary Learning Center 3215 W 162nd St, Markham 60428 Michelle Hardmon	PK-PK		60		708/331-3364

- **Prospect Hts School Dist 23** PID: 00273324   847/870-3850
  700 N Schoenbeck Rd, Prospect HTS 60070   Fax 847/870-3896

Schools: 4 \ **Teachers:** 101 \ **Students:** 1,500 \ **Special Ed Students:** 199 \ **LEP Students:** 382 \ **Ethnic:** Asian 11%, African American 2%, Hispanic 20%, Caucasian 68% \ **Exp:** $328 (High) \ **Poverty:** 7% \ **Title I:** $143,325 \ **Special Education:** $755,000 \ **Bilingual Education:** $93,000 \ **Open-Close:** 08/19 - 06/04 \ **DTBP:** $239 (High)

Dr Don Angelaccio 1,11
Brian Rominski 3
Dr Amy Zaher 9,11,15,57,81,273,288,298
Jim Bednar 67
Maria Stavropoulos 73,286
Kris Lebrecht 274
Amy McPartlin 2,3,4,5,19
Mark Coleman 3
Dr Chrys Sroka 59,79,88,275
Carrie Vergil 68
Deborah Pitts 76
Justin Heller 295

Public Schs..Principal	Grd	Prgm	Enr/#Cls	SN	
Anne Sullivan Elem Sch 700 N Schoenbeck Rd, Prospect HTS 60070 Traci Meziere	4-5		354 13	39%	847/870-3865 Fax 847/870-8113
Betsy Ross Elem Sch 700 N Schoenbeck Rd, Prospect HTS 60070 Craig Curtis	2-3		318 25	33%	847/870-3868 Fax 847/870-3898
Eisenhower Elem Sch 1 N Schoenbeck Rd, Prospect HTS 60070 Dr Luke Lambatos	PK-1		347 16	33%	847/870-3875 Fax 847/870-3877
MacArthur Middle Sch 700 N Schoenbeck Rd, Prospect HTS 60070 Camron Nystrom	6-8		513 42	34%	847/870-3879 Fax 847/870-3881

- **Proviso Twp High Sch Dist 209** PID: 00273386   708/338-5900
  8601 Roosevelt Rd, Forest Park 60130   Fax 708/338-5999

Schools: 3 \ **Teachers:** 236 \ **Students:** 4,339 \ **Special Ed Students:** 790 \ **LEP Students:** 543 \ **College-Bound:** 60% \ **Ethnic:** Asian 1%, African American 39%, Hispanic 57%, Native American: 1%, Caucasian 2% \ **Exp:** $195 (Low) \ **Poverty:** 15% \ **Title I:** $1,746,545 \ **Special Education:** $2,433,000 \ **Bilingual Education:** $136,000 \ **Open-Close:** 08/17 - 05/27 \ **DTBP:** $176 (High)

Dr James Henderson 1
Paul Starck-King 2,15,19
L Taylor 3
Dr Nicole Howard 10,15,69,79
Rodney Alexander 67
Cesar Rodriguez 71
Julie Suva 76
James Krolik 295
Arlene Sabado 2
Rachel Rivera 2
Gwendolyn Williams 4
Dr Jeremy Burnham 57,63
Greta Williams 69
Tracy Avant-Bey 73,75,84,95,297
Vanessa Schmitt 79
Dr Bessie Karvelas 750

Public Schs..Principal	Grd	Prgm	Enr/#Cls	SN	
Proviso East High Sch 807 S 1st Ave, Maywood 60153 Dr Patrick Hardy	9-12	ATV	1,664	46%	708/344-7000 Fax 708/344-5942

---

79 Student Personnel	91 Safety/Security	275 Response To Intervention	298 Grant Writer/Ptnrships
80 Driver Ed/Safety	92 Magnet School	277 Remedial Math K-12	750 Chief Innovation Officer
81 Gifted/Talented	93 Parental Involvement	280 Literacy Coach	751 Chief of Staff
82 Video Services	95 Tech Prep Program	285 STEM	752 Social Emotional Learning
83 Substance Abuse Prev	97 Chief Information Officer	286 Digital Learning	
84 Erate	98 Chief Technology Officer	288 Common Core Standards	**Other School Types**
85 AIDS Education	270 Character Education	294 Accountability	Ⓐ = Alternative School
88 Alternative/At Risk	271 Migrant Education	295 Network System	Ⓒ = Charter School
89 Multi-Cultural Curriculum	273 Teacher Mentor	296 Title II Programs	Ⓜ = Magnet School
90 Social Work	274 Before/After Sch	297 Webmaster	Ⓨ = Year-Round School

School Programs
A = Alternative Program
G = Adult Classes
M = Magnet Program
T = Title I Schoolwide
V = Career & Tech Ed Programs

Social Media
f = Facebook
t = Twitter

New Schools are shaded
New Superintendents and Principals are bold
Personnel with email addresses are underscored

Cook County   Market Data Retrieval

Ⓜ Proviso Math & Science Academy 9-12 T 822 31% 708/338-4100
8601 Roosevelt Rd, Forest Park 60130   Fax 708/338-4199
Dr Bessie Karvales

Proviso West High Sch 9-12 AGTV 1,853 25% 708/449-6400
4701 Harrison St, Hillside 60162   124   Fax 708/449-3636
Joe Kosina

• **Reavis Twp HSD 220** PID: 00273415   708/599-7200
6034 W 77th St, Burbank 60459   Fax 708/599-8751

Schools: 1 \ **Teachers:** 108 \ **Students:** 1,800 \ **Special Ed Students:** 240 \ **LEP Students:** 274 \ **College-Bound:** 70% \ **Ethnic:** Asian 3%, African American 2%, Hispanic 38%, Caucasian 58% \ **Exp:** $246 (Med) \ **Poverty:** 16% \ **Title I:** $517,129 \ **Special Education:** $284,000 \ **Bilingual Education:** $22,000 \ **Open-Close:** 08/11 - 05/26 \ **DTBP:** $235 (High) \ 🅵 🅴

Dr Daniel Riordan	1	Eric Novak	2,4,11
Mark Appleby	3	Michael Hock	5
Robert Morack	6*	Maureen Carey	7*
Dr Heather McCurdy	10,12,298*	Jim Ward	11*
Erika Banick	41*	Krystyna Nasinska	57*
Leslie Schall	60*	Russell McKinley	67
Tom Witting	71,83,270*	Don Erickson	73*
Don Erickson	73		

Public Schs..Principal	Grd	Prgm	Enr/#Cls	SN
Reavis High Sch	9-12	ATV	1,800	41% 708/599-7200
6034 W 77th St, Burbank 60459			96	
Julie Schultz				🅵 🅴

• **Rhodes School District 84 1/2** PID: 00273439   708/453-1266
8931 Fullerton Ave, River Grove 60171   Fax 708/453-0817

Schools: 1 \ **Teachers:** 61 \ **Students:** 637 \ **Special Ed Students:** 82 \ **LEP Students:** 256 \ **Ethnic:** Asian 1%, African American 7%, Hispanic 76%, Caucasian 16% \ **Exp:** $697 (High) \ **Poverty:** 23% \ **Title I:** $244,942 \ **Special Education:** $290,000 \ **Bilingual Education:** $28,000 \ **Open-Close:** 08/13 - 05/21 \ **DTBP:** $312 (High)

James Prather	1,11	John Barry	2
Don Palmer	3*	Laurie Hedlund	3,16
Cynthia Darre	4*	Pam Card	5
Sean Sheridan	6,35*	Lisa Lonigro	7*
Brian McConnell	9,69,74,83,88,285,294*	Chrystal Lis	12
Sandra Adamski	57	Nicole Newsome	59
Janice Roeder	67	Debbie Polen	71
John Mertes	73,295,297*	Maggie Valek	93
Rhonda Schiess	274*		

Public Schs..Principal	Grd	Prgm	Enr/#Cls	SN
Rhodes Elem Sch	PK-8	AGT	637	76% 708/453-6813
8931 Fullerton Ave, River Grove 60171			27	Fax 708/452-6324
Brian McConnell				

• **Rich Twp High School Dist 227** PID: 00273453   708/679-5800
20550 S Cicero Ave, Matteson 60443   Fax 708/679-5733

Schools: 2 \ **Teachers:** 223 \ **Students:** 2,800 \ **Special Ed Students:** 554 \ **LEP Students:** 58 \ **College-Bound:** 90% \ **Ethnic:** African American 92%, Hispanic 6%, Caucasian 2% \ **Exp:** $302 (High) \ **Poverty:** 14% \ **Title I:** $1,046,847 \ **Special Education:** $2,424,000 \ **Bilingual Education:** $65,000 \ **Open-Close:** 08/17 - 06/03 \ **DTBP:** $198 (High) \ 🅵 🅴

Dr Johnnie Thomas 1   Dr Alicia Evans 2,3,5,15,91

Kevin Baffoe 3
Jacalyn Bailey 7,60
Dr Stephen Bournes 10,11,15,83,288,296
Andrea Bonds 67
Aaron Atchison 71
Roosevelt Louissaint 295

Betsy Williams 4
Jeff Bonomo 10,69,76
Hope Stovall 27
Dr Kim Echols 68,74,78,273
Ted Koutavas 73,95

Public Schs..Principal	Grd	Prgm	Enr/#Cls	SN
Rich Twp High Sch STEM	9-12	ATV	1,500	74% 708/679-5600
3600 W 203rd St, Olympia FLDS 60461				Fax 708/679-5632
Dr Leviis Haney				
Rich Twp HS Fine Arts Com	9-12	ATV	1,300	80% 708/679-3000
5000 Sauk Trl, Richton Park 60471			63	Fax 708/679-3168
Larry Varn				

• **Ridgeland School District 122** PID: 00272124   708/599-5550
6500 W 95th St, Oak Lawn 60453   Fax 708/599-5626

Schools: 5 \ **Teachers:** 162 \ **Students:** 2,300 \ **Special Ed Students:** 373 \ **LEP Students:** 761 \ **Ethnic:** Asian 2%, African American 5%, Hispanic 28%, Caucasian 65% \ **Exp:** $343 (High) \ **Poverty:** 24% \ **Title I:** $1,022,234 \ **Special Education:** $1,128,000 \ **Bilingual Education:** $100,000 \ **Open-Close:** 08/20 - 06/02 \ **DTBP:** $224 (High)

Joseph Matise	1	Douglas Ogarek	2,3,15
Sheri Maher	9,12*	Lorenzo Nevarez	57
Catherine Lattz	59,79,88	Timothy Beemsterboer	59,79
David Lis	67	Ashish Gandhi	73*
Jean Sommerseld	77*		

Public Schs..Principal	Grd	Prgm	Enr/#Cls	SN
Columbus Manor Elem Sch	PK-5		402	58% 708/424-3481
9700 Mayfield Ave, Oak Lawn 60453			20	Fax 708/424-9412
Meghan Dougherty				
George W Lieb Elem Sch	K-5		365	67% 708/599-1050
9101 Pembroke Ln, Bridgeview 60455			25	Fax 708/599-8189
Rhonda Kulig				
Harnew Elem Sch	PK-5		588	64% 708/599-7070
9101 Meade Ave, Oak Lawn 60453			55	Fax 708/599-9636
Anthony Gill				
Kolb Elem Sch	K-5		311	68% 708/598-8090
9620 Normandy Ave, Oak Lawn 60453			12	Fax 708/598-6445
Dan McDermott				
Simmons Middle Sch	6-8		784	61% 708/599-8540
6450 W 95th St, Oak Lawn 60453			48	Fax 708/599-8015
Tracy Flood				

• **Ridgewood Cmty HSD 234** PID: 00273491   708/456-4242
7500 W Montrose Ave, Norridge 60706   Fax 708/456-0342

Schools: 1 \ **Teachers:** 56 \ **Students:** 900 \ **Special Ed Students:** 97 \ **LEP Students:** 70 \ **College-Bound:** 90% \ **Ethnic:** Asian 7%, Hispanic 24%, Caucasian 69% \ **Exp:** $360 (High) \ **Poverty:** 9% \ **Title I:** $118,987 \ **Special Education:** $409,000 \ **Bilingual Education:** $1,000 \ **Open-Close:** 08/17 - 05/28 \ **DTBP:** $800 (High)

Dr Jennifer Kelsall	1	Tom Parrillo	2,11
Pat Rossi	3*	Robert St John	6*
Jennette Gonzalez	16*	Paul Draniczarek	67
Jennifer Snyder	69,83,271,273	Carl Schorsch	73,295

Public Schs..Principal	Grd	Prgm	Enr/#Cls	SN
Ridgewood High Sch	9-12	ATV	900	30% 708/456-4242
7500 W Montrose Ave, Norridge 60706			55	
Gina Castellano				

1 Superintendent	8 Curric/Instruct K-12	19 Chief Financial Officer	29 Family/Consumer Science	39 Social Studies K-12	49 English/Lang Arts Elem	59 Special Education Elem	69 Academic Assessment
2 Bus/Finance/Purchasing	9 Curric/Instruct Elem	20 Art K-12	30 Adult Education	40 Social Studies Elem	50 English/Lang Arts Sec	60 Special Education Sec	70 Research/Development
3 Buildings And Grounds	10 Curric/Instruct Sec	21 Art Elem	31 Career/Sch-to-Work K-12	41 Social Studies Sec	51 Reading K-12	61 Foreign/World Lang K-12	71 Public Information
4 Food Service	11 Federal Program	22 Art Sec	32 Career/Sch-to-Work Elem	42 Science K-12	52 Reading Elem	62 Foreign/World Lang Elem	72 Summer School
5 Transportation	12 Title V	23 Music K-12	33 Career/Sch-to-Work Sec	43 Science Elem	53 Reading Sec	63 Foreign/World Lang Sec	73 Instructional Tech
6 Athletic	13 Title V	24 Music Elem	34 Early Childhood Ed	44 Science Sec	54 Remedial Reading K-12	64 Religious Education K-12	74 Inservice Training
7 Health Services	15 Asst Superintendent	25 Music Sec	35 Health/Phys Education	45 Math K-12	55 Remedial Reading Elem	65 Religious Education Elem	75 Marketing/Distributive
	16 Instructional Media Svcs	26 Business Education	36 Guidance Services K-12	46 Math Elem	56 Remedial Reading Sec	66 Religious Education Sec	76 Info Systems
	17 Chief Operations Officer	27 Career & Tech Ed	37 Guidance Services Elem	47 Math Sec	57 Bilingual/ELL	67 School Board President	77 Psychological Assess
	18 Chief Academic Officer	28 Technology Education	38 Guidance Services Sec	48 English/Lang Arts K-12	58 Special Education K-12	68 Teacher Personnel	78 Affirmative Action

Illinois School Directory — Cook County

• River Forest Sch Dist 90 PID: 00273518   708/771-8282
7776 Lake St, River Forest 60305

Schools: 3 \ **Teachers:** 115 \ **Students:** 1,400 \ **Special Ed Students:** 221 \ **LEP Students:** 33 \ **Ethnic:** Asian 7%, African American 7%, Hispanic 12%, Caucasian 75% \ **Exp:** $437 (High) \ **Poverty:** 5% \ **Title I:** $100,057 \ **Special Education:** $1,285,000 \ **Bilingual Education:** $4,000 \ **Open-Close:** 08/26 - 06/18 \ **DTBP:** $234 (High) \ f t

Dr Edward Condon	1	Anthony Cozzi	2,3,91
Dr Alison Hawley	9,11,79,288	Kevin Martin	16,73,76,295
Denise Matthews	59	Rich Moore	67
Dawn Simmons	71		

Public Schs..Principal	Grd	Prgm	Enr/#Cls	SN	
Lincoln Elem Sch 511 Park Ave, River Forest 60305 Casey Godfrey	K-4		411 20	4%	708/366-7340 Fax 708/771-3956
Roosevelt Middle Sch 7560 Oak Ave, River Forest 60305 Larry Garstki	5-8		665 27	6%	708/366-9230
Willard Elem Sch 1250 Ashland Ave, River Forest 60305 Diane Wood	PK-4		390 18	4%	708/366-6740 Fax 708/366-1416

• River Grove School Dist 85-5 PID: 00273570   708/453-6172
2650 Thatcher Ave, River Grove 60171   Fax 708/453-6186

Schools: 1 \ **Teachers:** 45 \ **Students:** 750 \ **Special Ed Students:** 90 \ **LEP Students:** 177 \ **Ethnic:** Asian 2%, African American 1%, Hispanic 52%, Caucasian 45% \ **Exp:** $334 (High) \ **Poverty:** 17% \ **Title I:** $183,331 \ **Special Education:** $355,000 \ **Bilingual Education:** $6,000 \ **Open-Close:** 08/19 - 05/28 \ f t

Dr Jan Rashid	1,11	Nino Makula	3*
Mary Suba	4*	Jenny Turocy	6*
Shannon Bono	12*	Romana Klimek-Gagor	57*
Marlene Flahaven	67	Denise Nero	79
Adam Cohla	84,286	Cameron Wiley	288

Public Schs..Principal	Grd	Prgm	Enr/#Cls	SN	
River Grove Elem Sch 2650 Thatcher Ave, River Grove 60171 Cameron Wiley	PK-8	T	750 30	69%	708/453-6172

• River Trails Sch Dist 26 PID: 00273594   847/297-4120
1900 E Kensington Rd, Mt Prospect 60056   Fax 847/297-4124

Schools: 4 \ **Teachers:** 120 \ **Students:** 1,600 \ **Special Ed Students:** 187 \ **LEP Students:** 339 \ **Ethnic:** Asian 20%, African American 2%, Hispanic 21%, Native American: 1%, Caucasian 56% \ **Exp:** $253 (Med) \ **Poverty:** 6% \ **Title I:** $144,529 \ **Special Education:** $1,004,000 \ **Bilingual Education:** $53,000 \ **Open-Close:** 08/21 - 05/28 \ **DTBP:** $231 (High)

Nancy Wagner	1	Dr Lyndl Schuster	2,15
Daniel Whisler	3,91	Coletta Hines-Newell	4
Eileen Ackermann	4	Sue Grimm	4*
Jane Holtz	5	Kristine Seifert	9,11,59,69,74,285,286,288
Karen Daly	12,57	Karen Daly	12,57
Jodi Megerle	13,15,34,59,78,83,88,275	Sue Hankey	16*
Frank Fiarito	67	Erin Stein	68
Susan Hoffman	73,295,297	John Dunleavy	76
Tracy Hillman	298		

Public Schs..Principal	Grd	Prgm	Enr/#Cls	SN	
Euclid Elem Sch 1211 N Wheeling Rd, Mt Prospect 60056 Karen Daly	K-5	T	468 26	42%	847/259-3303 Fax 847/259-3395
Indian Grove Elem Sch 1340 N Burning Bush Ln, Mt Prospect 60056 Lynn Fisher	K-5		535	11%	847/298-1976 Fax 847/298-3495
River Trails ELC at Parkview 805 N Burning Bush Ln, Mt Prospect 60056 Amy Veytsman	PK-PK		77	64%	224/612-7800 Fax 847/635-0408
River Trails Middle Sch 1000 N Wolf Rd, Mt Prospect 60056 Keir Rogers	6-8	T	506 55	32%	847/298-1750 Fax 847/298-2639

• Riverside Public Sch Dist 96 PID: 00273673   708/447-5007
3340 Harlem Ave, Riverside 60546   Fax 708/447-3252

Schools: 5 \ **Teachers:** 129 \ **Students:** 1,686 \ **Special Ed Students:** 247 \ **LEP Students:** 86 \ **Ethnic:** Asian 2%, African American 3%, Hispanic 35%, Caucasian 60% \ **Exp:** $585 (High) \ **Poverty:** 8% \ **Title I:** $196,057 \ **Special Education:** $938,000 \ **Bilingual Education:** $20,000 \ **Open-Close:** 08/31 - 06/10

Martha Ryan-Toye	1	James Fitton	2,3
Bill Radtke	3	Judy Steinke	4
Angela Dolezal	9,11,57,69,288	Donald Tufano	16,73
Pamela Shaw	59	Dan Hunt	67

Public Schs..Principal	Grd	Prgm	Enr/#Cls	SN	
Albert F Ames Elem Sch 86 Southcote Rd, Riverside 60546 Todd Gierman	PK-5		360	21%	708/447-0759 Fax 708/447-6904
Blythe Park Elem Sch 735 Leesley Rd, Riverside 60546 Casimira Gorman	PK-5		195 9	14%	708/447-2168 Fax 708/447-1703 f
Central Elem Sch 61 Woodside Rd, Riverside 60546 Peter Gatz	PK-5		397 20	24%	708/447-1106 Fax 708/447-5030
Hollywood Elem Sch 3423 Hollywood Ave, Brookfield 60513 Kimberly Hefner	K-5		157 6	13%	708/485-7630 Fax 708/485-7925 f
L J Hauser Junior High Sch 65 Woodside Rd, Riverside 60546 April Mahy	6-8		577 35	25%	708/447-3896 Fax 708/447-5180

• Riverside-Brookfld Twp SD 208 PID: 00273738   708/442-7500
160 Ridgewood Rd, Riverside 60546   Fax 708/447-5570

Schools: 1 \ **Teachers:** 96 \ **Students:** 1,630 \ **Special Ed Students:** 210 \ **LEP Students:** 84 \ **College-Bound:** 76% \ **Ethnic:** Asian 2%, African American 5%, Hispanic 38%, Caucasian 55% \ **Exp:** $310 (High) \ **Poverty:** 7% \ **Title I:** $148,733 \ **Special Education:** $883,000 \ **Bilingual Education:** $5,000 \ **Open-Close:** 08/14 - 05/21 \ **DTBP:** $235 (High) \ f t

Dr Kevin Skinkis	1	Kristen Smetana	2,15,19,298*
Joel Hatje	3*	Beth Augustine	38*
Jill McGrath	63*	William Smithing	67
Mike Connors	73*		

Public Schs..Principal	Grd	Prgm	Enr/#Cls	SN	
Riverside-Brookfield Twp HS 160 Ridgewood Rd, Riverside 60546 Hctor Freytas	9-12		1,630 96	12%	708/442-7500

---

79 Student Personnel	91 Safety/Security	275 Response To Intervention	298 Grant Writer/Ptnrships	**School Programs**	**Social Media**
80 Driver Ed/Safety	92 Magnet School	277 Remedial Math K-12	750 Chief Innovation Officer	A = Alternative Program	f = Facebook
81 Gifted/Talented	93 Parental Involvement	280 Literacy Coach	751 Chief of Staff	G = Adult Classes	t = Twitter
82 Video Services	95 Tech Prep Program	285 STEM	752 Social Emotional Learning	M = Magnet Program	
83 Substance Abuse Prev	97 Chief Information Officer	286 Digital Learning		T = Title I Schoolwide	
84 Erate	98 Chief Technology Officer	288 Common Core Standards	**Other School Types**	V = Career & Tech Ed Programs	
85 AIDS Education	270 Character Education	294 Accountability	Ⓐ = Alternative School		
88 Alternative/At Risk	271 Migrant Education	295 Network System	Ⓒ = Charter School	New Schools are shaded	
89 Multi-Cultural Curriculum	273 Teacher Mentor	296 Title II Programs	Ⓜ = Magnet School	New Superintendents and Principals are bold	
90 Social Work	274 Before/After Sch	297 Webmaster	Ⓨ = Year-Round School	Personnel with email addresses are underscored	

IL—65

Cook County

Market Data Retrieval

- **Rosemont Elem Sch Dist 78** PID: 00273752   847/825-0144
  6101 Ruby St, Rosemont 60018   Fax 847/825-9704

Schools: 1 \ **Teachers:** 24 \ **Students:** 220 \ **Special Ed Students:** 33 \
LEP Students: 24 \ **Ethnic:** Asian 3%, African American 1%, Hispanic 36%,
Caucasian 60% \ **Exp:** $624 (High) \ **Poverty:** 13% \ **Title I:** $55,003 \
Special Education: $109,000 \ **Open-Close:** 08/18 - 05/28 \ **DTBP:** $119
(High)

Kevin Anderson 1
Kathlene Gilhooly 12
Cam Stevens 35,85*
Christopher Stephens 67
Julie Cullerton 2
Lourene Solarz 16,82*
Diana Martinez 57*
Ray Baghdassarian 73,286

Public Schs..Principal	Grd	Prgm	Enr/#Cls	SN	
Rosemont Elem Sch 6101 Ruby St, Rosemont 60018 Laurie Kovalcik	PK-8		220 18	26%	847/825-0144

- **Sandridge Sch Dist 172** PID: 00273776   708/895-8339
  2950 Glenwood Dyer Rd, Chicago HTS 60411   Fax 708/895-2451

Schools: 1 \ **Teachers:** 22 \ **Students:** 350 \ **Special Ed Students:** 85
\ **LEP Students:** 25 \ **Ethnic:** African American 66%, Hispanic 19%,
Caucasian 15% \ **Exp:** $135 (Low) \ **Poverty:** 25% \ **Title I:** $196,065
\ **Special Education:** $202,000 \ **Bilingual Education:** $5,000 \
Open-Close: 08/26 - 06/09 \ **DTBP:** $238 (High)

Nicholas Sutton 1
Carol Mazurkiewicz 4*
Jan Debruin 59,270,752*
Jack McCleverty 3*
Kelly Marotz 9,69,74*
Roger Sons 67

Public Schs..Principal	Grd	Prgm	Enr/#Cls	SN	
Sandridge Elem Sch 2950 Glenwood Dyer Rd, Chicago HTS 60411 Kelly Marotz	PK-8	T	350 40	74%	708/895-2450

- **Schaumburg Cmty Cons SD 54** PID: 00273843   847/357-5000
  524 E Schaumburg Rd, Schaumburg 60194   Fax 847/357-5006

Schools: 28 \ **Teachers:** 1,199 \ **Students:** 15,296 \
Special Ed Students: 1,753 \ **LEP Students:** 2,975 \ **Ethnic:** Asian 26%,
African American 6%, Hispanic 25%, Caucasian 43% \ **Exp:** $317 (High)
\ **Poverty:** 8% \ **Title I:** $1,771,995 \ **Special Education:** $8,438,000 \
Bilingual Education: $940,000 \ **Open-Close:** 08/24 - 05/28 \ **DTBP:** $214
(High) \

Andrew Duross 1
Michael Mostacci 3
Julie Gorvett 9,15,35
Colette Bell 15,21,24,35,74
Dr Erin Knoll 15,288,752
Carrie Azab 34*
Jennifer Naddeu 59
Terri McHugh 71
Joe Tomchuk 76
Habib Behrouzi 286
Ric King 2,15
Nanette Sykes 5
Cassandra Williams 15,59
Danette Meyer 15,68
Dr Nick Myers 15
Cynthia Gordon 59,81
Bob Kaplan 67
John Wilms 73,295
Michelle Burke 285

Public Schs..Principal	Grd	Prgm	Enr/#Cls	SN	
Adlai Stevenson Elem Sch 1414 Armstrong Ln, Elk Grove Vlg 60007 Kenneth Haase	K-6		498 20	29%	847/357-5200 Fax 847/357-5201
Adolph Link Elem Sch 900 W Glenn Trl, Elk Grove Vlg 60007 Quinn Wulbecker	K-6		628 19	8%	847/357-5300 Fax 847/357-5301
Albert Einstein Elem Sch 1100 Laurie Ln, Hanover Park 60133 Julie Tarasiuk	K-6		525 25	27%	630/736-2500 Fax 630/736-2501
Anne Fox Elem Sch 1035 Parkview Dr, Hanover Park 60133 Priscilla Buchanan	K-6		374 23	36%	630/736-3500 Fax 630/736-3501
Campanelli Elem Sch 310 S Springinsguth Rd, Schaumburg 60193 Dr Amy Houlihan	K-6		557 45	8%	847/357-5333 Fax 847/357-5334
District 54 Early Learning Ctr 520 E Schaumburg Rd, Schaumburg 60194 Carrie Azab	PK-PK		675	27%	847/230-1700 Fax 847/230-1701
Edwin Aldrin Elem Sch 617 Boxwood Dr, Schaumburg 60193 Dr Mary Botterman	K-6		526 30	22%	847/357-5400 Fax 847/357-5401
Eisenhower Junior High Sch 800 Hassell Rd, Hoffman Est 60169 Heather Wilson	7-8	V	564 32	26%	847/357-5500 Fax 847/357-5501
Elizabeth Blackwell Elem Sch 345 N Walnut Ln, Schaumburg 60194 Jillian Sagan	K-6		493 20	22%	847/357-5555 Fax 847/357-5556
Enders-Salk Elem Sch 345 N Salem Dr, Schaumburg 60194 Mike Henry	K-6		406	27%	847/357-6400 Fax 847/357-6401
Everett Dirksen Elem Sch 116 W Beech Dr, Schaumburg 60193 Joanne Kort	K-6		523 19	10%	847/357-5600 Fax 847/357-5601
Fairview Elem Sch 375 Arizona Blvd, Hoffman Est 60169 Megan Ankrom	K-6		550 23	8%	847/357-5700 Fax 847/357-5701
Fredrick Nerge Elem Sch 660 Woodfield Trl, Roselle 60172 Karolyn Frederick	K-6		675 29	11%	847/357-5777 Fax 847/357-5778
Hanover Highlands Elem Sch 1451 Cypress Ave, Hanover Park 60133 Amy Thompson	K-6		517 26	26%	630/736-4230 Fax 630/736-4231
Helen Keller Jr High Sch 820 Bode Rd, Schaumburg 60194 Thomas Barbini	7-8	V	545 30	20%	847/357-6500 Fax 847/357-6501
Hoover Math & Science Academy 315 N Springinsguth Rd, Schaumburg 60194 Cassie Zingler	K-6		702 24	12%	847/357-5800 Fax 847/357-5801
Jane Addams Junior High Sch 700 S Springinsguth Rd, Schaumburg 60193 Chris Bingen	7-8	V	686 60	17%	847/357-5900 Fax 847/357-5901
John Muir Literacy Academy 1973 Kensington Ln, Hoffman Est 60169 Carolyn Allar	K-6		423 30	34%	847/357-6444 Fax 847/357-6445
Lakeview Elem Sch 615 Lakeview Ln, Hoffman Est 60169 Beth Erbach	K-6		493 30	36%	847/357-6600 Fax 847/357-6601
Lincoln Prairie Sch 500 Hillcrest Blvd, Hoffman Est 60169 Amanda Stochl	K-8		410 20	5%	847/357-5955 Fax 847/357-5956
MacArthur Int'l Spanish Acad 1800 Chippendale Rd, Hoffman Est 60169 Sonia Esquivel	K-6		436 23	25%	847/357-6650 Fax 847/357-6651
Margaret Mead Jr High Sch 1765 Biesterfield Rd, Elk Grove Vlg 60007 Scott Ross	7-8	V	652 80	12%	847/357-6000 Fax 847/357-6001
Michael Collins Elem Sch 407 Summit Dr, Schaumburg 60193 Nell Haack	K-6		777	8%	847/357-6100 Fax 847/357-6101
Nathan Hale Elem Sch 1300 W Wise Rd, Schaumburg 60193 Brian Kaszewicz	K-6		485 24	12%	847/357-6200 Fax 847/357-6201

1	Superintendent	8	Curric/Instruct K-12	19	Chief Financial Officer	29	Family/Consumer Science	
2	Bus/Finance/Purchasing	9	Curric/Instruct Elem	20	Art K-12	30	Adult Education	
3	Buildings And Grounds	10	Curric/Instruct Sec	21	Art Elem	31	Career/Sch-to-Work K-12	
4	Food Service	11	Federal Program	22	Art Sec	32	Career/Sch-to-Work Elem	
5	Transportation	12	Title I	23	Music K-12	33	Career/Sch-to-Work Sec	
6	Athletic	13	Title V	24	Music Elem	34	Early Childhood Ed	
7	Health Services	15	Asst Superintendent	25	Music Sec	35	Health/Phys Education	
		16	Instructional Media Svcs	26	Business Education	36	Guidance Services K-12	
		17	Chief Operations Officer	27	Career & Tech Ed	37	Guidance Services Elem	
		18	Chief Academic Officer	28	Technology Education	38	Guidance Services Sec	
39	Social Studies K-12	49	English/Lang Arts Elem	59	Special Education Elem	69	Academic Assessment	
40	Social Studies Elem	50	English/Lang Arts Sec	60	Special Education Sec	70	Research/Development	
41	Social Studies Sec	51	Reading K-12	61	Foreign/World Lang K-12	71	Public Information	
42	Science K-12	52	Reading Elem	62	Foreign/World Lang Elem	72	Summer School	
43	Science Elem	53	Reading Sec	63	Foreign/World Lang Sec	73	Instructional Tech	
44	Science Sec	54	Remedial Reading K-12	64	Religious Education K-12	74	Inservice Training	
45	Math K-12	55	Remedial Reading Elem	65	Religious Education Elem	75	Marketing/Distributive	
46	Math Elem	56	Remedial Reading Sec	66	Religious Education Sec	76	Info Systems	
47	Math Sec	57	Bilingual/ELL	67	School Board President	77	Psychological Assess	
48	English/Lang Arts K-12	58	Special Education K-12	68	Teacher Personnel	78	Affirmative Action	

Illinois School Directory — Cook County

Neil Armstrong Elem Sch 1320 Kingsdale Rd, Hoffman Est 60169 Diana Lipman	K-6		459 27	30% 847/357-6700 Fax 847/357-6701
Robert Frost Jr High Sch 320 W Wise Rd, Schaumburg 60193 Cj Schmid	7-8	V	655 30	15% 847/357-6800 Fax 847/357-6801
Thomas Dooley Elem Sch 622 Norwood Ln, Schaumburg 60193 Holly Schlicher	K-6		483 22	5% 847/357-6250 Fax 847/357-6251
Winston Churchill Elem Sch 1520 Jones Rd, Schaumburg 60195 Steve Kern	K-6		579 19	5% 847/357-6300 Fax 847/357-6301

● **Schiller Park School Dist 81** PID: 00274110 847/671-1816
9760 Soreng Ave, Schiller Park 60176 Fax 847/671-1872

Schools: 3 \ Teachers: 115 \ Students: 1,500 \ Special Ed Students: 193 \ LEP Students: 365 \ Ethnic: Asian 7%, African American 1%, Hispanic 42%, Native American: 2%, Caucasian 48% \ Exp: $184 (Low) \ Poverty: 17% \ Title I: $331,041 \ Special Education: $1,040,000 \ Bilingual Education: $103,000 \ Open-Close: 08/17 - 05/21 \ DTBP: $183 (High)

Dr Kimberly Boryszewski 1   Pasquale Maranto 2
Michael Deany 3,5   Nancy Myszka 4*
Kathy Brant ....9,11,71,298*   Susan Piltaver 59
Mary Ann Desecki 67   Eric Humbels 73

Public Schs..Principal	Grd	Prgm	Enr/#Cls	SN
George Washington Elem Sch 4835 Michigan Ave, Schiller Park 60176 Tiffany Leiva	4-5	T	306 12	69% 847/671-1922 Fax 847/671-1972
John F Kennedy Elem Sch 3945 Wehrman Ave, Schiller Park 60176 Melissa Kartsimans	PK-3	T	678 29	58% 847/671-0250 Fax 847/671-0256
Lincoln Middle Sch 9750 Soreng Ave, Schiller Park 60176 Constance Stavrou	6-8	T	411 24	61% 847/678-2916 Fax 847/678-4059

● **Skokie School District 68** PID: 00274196 847/676-9000
9440 Kenton Ave, Skokie 60076 Fax 847/676-9232

Schools: 5 \ Teachers: 141 \ Students: 1,700 \ Special Ed Students: 281 \ LEP Students: 425 \ Ethnic: Asian 34%, African American 9%, Hispanic 18%, Caucasian 39% \ Exp: $284 (Med) \ Poverty: 16% \ Title I: $507,130 \ Special Education: $651,000 \ Bilingual Education: $69,000 \ Open-Close: 08/27 - 06/02 \ DTBP: $100 (High)

Dr James Garwood 1   Ryan Berry 2,15,19
Ernie Nelson 3,5   Dr Christie Samojedny ....
9,11,83,273,275,285,288,298
Derek Senn 16,73,286,295   Dr Barbara Marler 57,271
Crissy Mombela 59,77,296,752   Una McGeough 67
Phyllis Carlstrom 68,71

Public Schs..Principal	Grd	Prgm	Enr/#Cls	SN
Devonshire Elem Sch 9040 Kostner Ave, Skokie 60076 Dr Daniel Schuth	K-5	T	317 19	54% 847/568-4901 Fax 847/568-4999
Early Childhood Center 9300 Kenton Ave, Skokie 60076 Jac McBride	PK-PK		73 4	847/677-4560 Fax 847/677-5124
Highland Elem Sch 9700 Crawford Ave, Skokie 60076 Karen Bradley	K-5	T	402 25	51% 847/676-5001 Fax 847/676-4048
Jane Stenson Elem Sch 9201 Lockwood Ave, Skokie 60077 Robyn Huemmer	K-5	T	339 20	45% 847/676-7301 Fax 847/967-9386
Old Orchard Junior High Sch 9310 Kenton Ave, Skokie 60076 Greg Hanson	6-8	T	637 36	50% 847/568-7501 Fax 847/676-3827

● **Skokie School District 69** PID: 00274251 847/675-7666
5050 Madison St, Skokie 60077 Fax 847/675-7675

Schools: 3 \ Teachers: 127 \ Students: 1,700 \ Special Ed Students: 228 \ LEP Students: 501 \ Ethnic: Asian 32%, African American 11%, Hispanic 19%, Caucasian 38% \ Exp: $179 (Low) \ Poverty: 19% \ Title I: $547,474 \ Special Education: $924,000 \ Bilingual Education: $132,000 \ Open-Close: 08/28 - 06/09 \ DTBP: $99 (Med) \

Margaret Clauson 1   Justin Attaway 2,3,4,5
Rita Gorguis 2   John Tinetti 3
Bryan Kelly ....9*   Katie Sullivan 9
Mark Rasar ....9*   Dr Megan Aseltine 9,15
Chris Miller 16,73,297   Terry Stroh 43
Steven Shadel 46,280,285   Sarah Aseltine 57
Joaquin Schubert 59   Kristine Joaquin-Schube 59
Steve Dembo 67   Nick Korzenlowski 76,295
Jennifer Laughlin 280

Public Schs..Principal	Grd	Prgm	Enr/#Cls	SN
Lincoln Junior High Sch 7839 Lincoln Ave, Skokie 60077 Lorenzo Cervantes	6-8	T	508 30	50% 847/676-3545 Fax 847/676-3595
Madison Elem Sch 5100 Madison St, Skokie 60077 Kristen Ulery	PK-2	T	532 25	52% 847/675-3048 Fax 847/675-1691
Thomas Edison Elem Sch 8200 Gross Point Rd, Morton Grove 60053 Andy Carpenter	3-5	T	541 24	52% 847/966-6210 Fax 847/966-6236

● **Skokie School District 73 1/2** PID: 00274304 847/324-0509
8000 E Prairie Rd, Skokie 60076 Fax 847/673-1282

Schools: 3 \ Teachers: 87 \ Students: 1,118 \ Special Ed Students: 154 \ LEP Students: 180 \ Ethnic: Asian 36%, African American 8%, Hispanic 14%, Caucasian 41% \ Exp: $241 (Med) \ Poverty: 11% \ Title I: $189,083 \ Special Education: $535,000 \ Bilingual Education: $92,000 \ Open-Close: 08/26 - 06/02 \ DTBP: $103 (High)

Kate Donegan 1   Dr Ann Williams 2,19
Cyndi Cohen 2   Michael Torres 3
Thomas Berkson ....4*   Becky Fischer 9*
Becky Mathison 9,69   Kristen Moore 59*
Nicholas Weth 67   Bob Hanrahan 73*
Robert Hanrahan 73   Dr Eden Olson 76
Amber Brydon 77   Annie Monak 82*

Public Schs..Principal	Grd	Prgm	Enr/#Cls	SN
Elizabeth Meyer Sch 8100 Tripp Ave, Skokie 60076 Dr Helen Wei	PK-K		216 8	25% 847/673-1223 Fax 847/933-4382
John Middleton Elem Sch 8300 Saint Louis Ave, Skokie 60076 **Dr Erica Berger**	1-5		537 25	34% 847/673-1222 Fax 847/673-1256
Oliver McCracken Middle Sch 8000 E Prairie Rd, Skokie 60076 Nancy Ariola	6-8		365 30	37% 847/673-1220 Fax 847/673-1565

---

79 Student Personnel	91 Safety/Security	275 Response To Intervention	296 Grant Writer/Ptnrships	School Programs	Social Media
80 Driver Ed/Safety	92 Magnet School	277 Remedial Math K-12	750 Chief Innovation Officer	A = Alternative Program	
81 Gifted/Talented	93 Parental Involvement	280 Literacy Coach	751 Chief of Staff	G = Adult Classes	= Facebook
82 Video Services	95 Tech Prep Program	285 STEM	752 Social Emotional Learning	M = Magnet Program	
83 Substance Abuse Prev	97 Chief Information Officer	286 Digital Learning		T = Title I Schoolwide	= Twitter
84 Erate	98 Chief Technology Officer	288 Common Core Standards	Other School Types	V = Career & Tech Ed Programs	
85 AIDS Education	270 Accountability	294 Accountability	Ⓐ = Alternative School		
88 Alternative/At Risk	271 Migrant Education	295 Network System	Ⓒ = Charter School	New Schools are shaded	
89 Multi-Cultural Curriculum	273 Teacher Mentor	296 Title II Programs	Ⓜ = Magnet School	New Superintendents and Principals are bold	
90 Social Work	274 Before/After Sch	297 Webmaster	Ⓨ = Year-Round School	Personnel with email addresses are underscored	

IL—67

Cook County

Market Data Retrieval

- **South Holland School Dist 150** PID: 00274378 708/339-4240
  848 E 170th St, South Holland 60473 Fax 708/339-4244

  Schools: 3 \ **Teachers:** 46 \ **Students:** 1,000 \ **Special Ed Students:** 110 \ **LEP Students:** 14 \ **Ethnic:** African American 93%, Hispanic 7%, \ **Exp:** $269 (Med) \ **Poverty:** 18% \ **Title I:** $363,315 \ **Special Education:** $412,000 \ **Open-Close:** 08/24 - 06/07 \ **DTBP:** $222 (High)

Dr Denise Julius	1	Gerardo Lopez	3
Joseph Ingram	6*	Tiffany Webb	9,11,15,16,69,84,288
Sherie Nunnally	67	Myra Lolkema	73,286,295

Public Schs..Principal	Grd	Prgm	Enr/#Cls	SN	
Greenwood Elem Sch 16800 Greenwood Ave, South Holland 60473 Carla Cunningham	PK-3	T	386 19	66%	708/339-4433 Fax 708/339-3942
McKinley Elem Jr High Sch 16949 Cottage Grove Ave, South Holland 60473 Jerome Ferrell	6-8	T	603 35	74%	708/339-8500 Fax 708/331-5805
McKinley Elem Sch 16949 Cottage Grove Ave, South Holland 60473 Jerome Ferrell	4-5	T	204 10	80%	708/339-8500 Fax 708/331-5805

- **South Holland School Dist 151** PID: 00274421 708/339-1516
  525 E 162nd St, South Holland 60473 Fax 708/331-7600

  Schools: 4 \ **Teachers:** 121 \ **Students:** 1,753 \ **Special Ed Students:** 283 \ **LEP Students:** 301 \ **Ethnic:** African American 66%, Hispanic 33%, Caucasian 1% \ **Exp:** $613 (High) \ **Poverty:** 25% \ **Title I:** $816,240 \ **Special Education:** $857,000 \ **Bilingual Education:** $95,000 \ **Open-Close:** 08/07 - 06/11 \ **DTBP:** $254 (High)

Dr Teresa Hill	1,11	Paul Woehlke	2,3,5,15
Warren Chestang	3,91	Kathryn Varner	9,69,74,270,271,273,288
Anthony Palomo	57*	Julieta Monterroso	59
Lanell Gilbert	67	Vanessa Bradley	71
Kyle Alston	73,295	Airielle Franklin	76

Public Schs..Principal	Grd	Prgm	Enr/#Cls	SN	
Coolidge Middle Sch 15500 7th Ave, Phoenix 60426 Patricia Payne	6-8	T	591 21	100%	708/339-5300 Fax 708/339-5327
Eisenhower Sch 16001 Minerva Ave, South Holland 60473 Peter Kolinski	2-3	T	326 12	100%	708/339-5900 Fax 708/210-3252
Madison Sch 15700 Orchid Dr, South Holland 60473 Jerald McNair	4-5	T	336 12	100%	708/339-2117 Fax 708/210-3250
Taft Elem Sch 393 E 163rd St, Harvey 60426 Christine Wilson	PK-1	T	396 25	99%	708/339-2710 Fax 708/210-3254

- **Steger School Dist 194** PID: 00274586 708/753-4300
  3753 Park Ave, Steger 60475 Fax 708/755-9512

  Schools: 3 \ **Teachers:** 111 \ **Students:** 1,500 \ **Special Ed Students:** 185 \ **LEP Students:** 159 \ **Ethnic:** Asian 1%, African American 29%, Hispanic 38%, Caucasian 32% \ **Exp:** $320 (High) \ **Poverty:** 18% \ **Title I:** $475,478 \ **Special Education:** $746,000 \ **Bilingual Education:** $32,000 \ **Open-Close:** 08/31 - 06/08 \ **DTBP:** $238 (High)

Dr David Frusher	1	Eric Diehl	2
Anthony Graziani	3	Rachael Diehl	4
Jan Lerci	9,57,69	Morgan Sharp	37
Kim Mahoney	59	Michele Helsel	67

Teri St Pierre	68	Tim Tufts 73,84,295

Public Schs..Principal	Grd	Prgm	Enr/#Cls	SN	
Columbia Central Sch 94 Richton Rd, Steger 60475 Bruce Nieminski	5-8	T	644 22	76%	708/753-4700 Fax 708/755-1877
Steger Intermediate Center 3411 Hopkins St, Steger 60475 Janet Inglese	2-4	T	471 22	79%	708/753-4200 Fax 708/755-1884
Steger Primary Center 3341 Miller Ave, S Chicago HTS 60411 Patricia Leoni \ **Venus Smith**	PK-1	T	316 27	73%	708/753-4100 Fax 708/755-1921

- **Sunnybrook School District 171** PID: 00274691 708/895-0750
  19266 Burnham Ave, Lansing 60438 Fax 708/895-8580

  Schools: 2 \ **Teachers:** 66 \ **Students:** 1,012 \ **Special Ed Students:** 162 \ **LEP Students:** 124 \ **Ethnic:** Asian 1%, African American 79%, Hispanic 17%, Caucasian 3% \ **Exp:** $507 (High) \ **Poverty:** 18% \ **Title I:** $377,807 \ **Special Education:** $563,000 \ **Bilingual Education:** $2,000 \ **Open-Close:** 08/21 - 05/28

Dr Erika Pettis	1	David Shrader	2,3,4,5,91
Andrea Warner	7	Dr Erika Millhouse	15,34,59,69,77*
Lori Cuevas	37	Timothy Terrell	67
Michael McGowan	73,295,297*	Rick Zalud	76
Debra Guzak	88*	Marianne Wysocki	286*
Diana Salgado	752*		

Public Schs..Principal	Grd	Prgm	Enr/#Cls	SN	
Heritage Middle Sch 19250 Burnham Ave, Lansing 60438 Joseph Kent	5-8	AT	519 27	72%	708/895-0790 Fax 708/895-6840
Nathan Hale Elem Sch 19055 Burnham Ave, Lansing 60438 Shannon Shockley	PK-4	T	506 40	73%	708/895-3030 Fax 708/895-2290

- **Sunset Ridge Sch Dist 29** PID: 00272095 847/881-9400
  525 Sunset Ridge Rd, Northfield 60093 Fax 847/446-6388

  Schools: 2 \ **Teachers:** 52 \ **Students:** 480 \ **Special Ed Students:** 83 \ **LEP Students:** 17 \ **Ethnic:** Asian 8%, Hispanic 3%, Caucasian 89% \ **Exp:** $546 (High) \ **Poverty:** 12% \ **Title I:** $79,775 \ **Special Education:** $403,000 \ **Open-Close:** 08/27 - 06/08 \ **DTBP:** $233 (High)

Dr Edward Stange	1,11,83	Thomas Beerheide	2
Corey Dreher	3	Emily Dunham	12,79
Lauren Gray	16*	Sheri Styczen	16,73,295
Neha Varughese	57*	Adelcert Spaan	67
Jennifer Kiedaisch	288		

Public Schs..Principal	Grd	Prgm	Enr/#Cls	SN	
Middlefork Primary Sch 405 Wagner Rd, Northfield 60093 Jennifer Kiedaisch	PK-3		197 12	2%	847/881-9500 Fax 847/446-6221
Sunset Ridge Elem Sch 525 Sunset Ridge Rd, Northfield 60093 Ivy Sukenik	4-8		273 24	1%	847/881-9400

---

1 Superintendent	8 Curric/Instruct K-12	19 Chief Financial Officer	29 Family/Consumer Science	39 Social Studies K-12	49 English/Lang Arts Elem	59 Special Education Elem	69 Academic Assessment
2 Bus/Finance/Purchasing	9 Curric/Instruct Elem	20 Art K-12	30 Adult Education	40 Social Studies Elem	50 English/Lang Arts Sec	60 Special Education Sec	70 Research/Development
3 Buildings And Grounds	10 Curric/Instruct Sec	21 Art Elem	31 Career/Sch-to-Work K-12	41 Social Studies Sec	51 Reading K-12	61 Foreign/World Lang K-12	71 Public Information
4 Food Service	11 Federal Program	22 Art Sec	32 Career/Sch-to-Work Elem	42 Science K-12	52 Reading Elem	62 Foreign/World Lang Elem	72 Summer School
5 Transportation	12 Title I	23 Music K-12	33 Career/Sch-to-Work Sec	43 Science Elem	53 Reading Sec	63 Foreign/World Lang Sec	73 Instructional Tech
6 Athletic	13 Title V	24 Music Elem	34 Early Childhood Ed	44 Science Sec	54 Remedial Reading K-12	64 Religious Education K-12	74 Inservice Training
7 Health Services	15 Asst Superintendent	25 Music Sec	35 Health/Phys Education	45 Math K-12	55 Remedial Reading Elem	65 Religious Education Elem	75 Marketing/Distributive
	16 Instructional Media Svcs	26 Business Education	36 Guidance Services K-12	46 Math Elem	56 Remedial Reading Sec	66 Religious Education Sec	76 Info Systems
	17 Chief Operations Officer	27 Career & Tech Ed	37 Guidance Services Elem	47 Math Sec	57 Bilingual/ELL	67 School Board President	77 Psychological Assess
	18 Chief Academic Officer	28 Technology Education	38 Guidance Services Sec	48 English/Lang Arts K-12	58 Special Education K-12	68 Teacher Personnel	78 Affirmative Action

Illinois School Directory — Cook County

• Thornton Fractnl Twp HSD 215 PID: 00274794 708/585-2300
18601 Torrence Ave, Lansing 60438 Fax 708/585-2317

Schools: 4 \ **Teachers:** 196 \ **Students:** 3,177 \ **Special Ed Students:** 550 \ **LEP Students:** 205 \ **College-Bound:** 63% \ **Ethnic:** African American 66%, Hispanic 26%, Caucasian 7% \ **Exp:** $309 (High) \ **Poverty:** 16% \ **Title I:** $1,204,366 \ **Special Education:** $1,278,000 \ **Bilingual Education:** $1,000 \ **Open-Close:** 08/21 - 06/01 \ **DTBP:** $174 (High)

Dr Shophia Jones-Raymond 1
Peggy Banks 4*
Michael Fies 11,16,69,280,288,294,298
Rich Dust 67
Melanie Mulheron 68
Brandie Edwards 73,76,286
Kelly Hasse 79
Dr Dwayne Evans 93*
Charles DiMartino 2
Rene Whitten 7,57,60,77,79,81,83,88
John Robinzine 27*
April Jerger 68
Kent Farlow 72*
Brian Bergthold 79
Tashara Tate 79
Miguel Gutierrez 295

Public Schs..Principal	Grd	Prgm	Enr/#Cls	SN	
Center for Academics & Tech 1605 Wentworth Ave, Calumet City 60409 John Robinzine	Voc		1,000 5	74%	708/585-2353 Fax 708/585-2356
Ⓐ Center for Alternative Lrng 1601 Wentworth Ave, Calumet City 60409 Rena Whitten	9-12		41	71%	708/585-9401
Thornton Fractional North HS 755 Pulaski Rd, Calumet City 60409 Brian Rucinski	9-12	T	1,312 81	71%	708/585-1000 Fax 708/585-1010
Thornton Fractional South HS 18500 Burnham Ave, Lansing 60438 Jacob Gourley	9-12	T	1,824 78	65%	708/585-2000 Fax 708/585-2009

• Thornton Twp High Sch Dist 205 PID: 00274756 708/225-4000
465 E 170th St, South Holland 60473 Fax 708/225-4004

Schools: 4 \ **Teachers:** 385 \ **Students:** 4,524 \ **Special Ed Students:** 794 \ **LEP Students:** 309 \ **College-Bound:** 62% \ **Ethnic:** African American 84%, Hispanic 15%, Caucasian 1% \ **Exp:** $416 (High) \ **Poverty:** 20% \ **Title I:** $2,927,664 \ **Special Education:** $2,702,000 \ **Bilingual Education:** $21,000 \ **Open-Close:** 08/17 - 05/28 \ **DTBP:** $210 (High) \

Nathaniel Cunningham 1
Torano Horton 2,15
Dr Elbert Holmes 12
John Arrington 27
Nina Graham 67
Robert Penman 69,70,294
Rakyah Merriweather 297
Amy Jacobs 2
Brett Fickes 10
Jerry Doss 15,68
Thomas Porter 60,79*
Rosaura Duran 68
Vincent Jones 84,295
Sarit Hampton 298

Public Schs..Principal	Grd	Prgm	Enr/#Cls	SN	
Ⓐ Peace Center 306 W 144th St, Dolton 60419 Tyran Cox-Bey	10-12		39	92%	708/985-3525
Thornridge High Sch 15000 Cottage Grove Ave, Dolton 60419 **Justin Moore**	9-12	TV	1,093 200	97%	708/271-4411 Fax 708/271-5020
Thornton Township High Sch 15001 Broadway Ave, Harvey 60426 Tony Ratliff	9-12	TV	1,650	64%	708/225-4109 Fax 708/225-5014
Thornwood High Sch 17101 S Park Ave, South Holland 60473 Don Holmes	9-12	TV	1,781 180	99%	708/339-7800 Fax 708/225-5033

• Township High School Dist 211 PID: 00272722 847/755-6600
1750 S Roselle Rd, Palatine 60067 Fax 847/755-6810

Schools: 7 \ **Teachers:** 784 \ **Students:** 12,490 \ **Special Ed Students:** 1,256 \ **LEP Students:** 781 \ **College-Bound:** 85% \ **Ethnic:** Asian 21%, African American 6%, Hispanic 27%, Caucasian 46% \ **Exp:** $217 (Med) \ **Poverty:** 7% \ **Title I:** $1,265,649 \ **Special Education:** $7,623,000 \ **Bilingual Education:** $121,000 \ **Open-Close:** 08/13 - 05/28 \ **DTBP:** $205 (High)

Dr Daniel Cates 1
David Grelyak 3
Stacy Lenihan 4*
Eric Wenckowski 6,80
Lisa Small 10,11,15,57,60,288
Mark Kovack 15,79
Kara Prusko 60
Renee Erickson 60
James Britton 68
Gary Gorson 73,76,98
Karen Lasher 2
Lauren Hummel 3,17
Diana Mikelski 5
Danielle Hauser 10,11,69,74,296
Jacquese Gilbert 12,72
Scott Weidig 16,73*
Mary Krones 60
Robert LeFevre 67
Thomas Petersen 71,298

Public Schs..Principal	Grd	Prgm	Enr/#Cls	SN	
Ⓐ Academy South 1030 W Higgins Rd Ste 106, Hoffman Est 60169 Jessica Orstead	9-12		117 4		847/755-6640
Hoffman Estates High Sch 1100 W Higgins Rd, Hoffman Est 60169 Michael Alther	9-12	GTV	1,959 180	51%	847/755-5600 Fax 847/755-5759
James B Conant High Sch 700 E Cougar Trl, Hoffman Est 60169 Julie Nowak	9-12	GV	2,334 90	28%	847/755-3600 Fax 847/755-3904
Ⓐ North Campus Alt Lrng Acad 335 E Illinois Ave, Palatine 60067 Dane Henning	9-12	T	50	78%	847/755-6700
Palatine High Sch 1111 N Rohlwing Rd, Palatine 60074 Tony Medina	9-12	AGTV	2,567 65	55%	847/755-1600 Fax 847/755-1623
Schaumburg High Sch 1100 W Schaumburg Rd, Schaumburg 60194 Brian Harlan	9-12	GV	2,095 105	33%	847/755-4600
William Fremd High Sch 1000 S Quentin Rd, Palatine 60067 Kurt Tenopir	9-12	GV	2,577 100	15%	847/755-2600 Fax 847/755-2623

• Township High School Dist 214 PID: 00271649 847/718-7600
2121 S Goebbert Rd, Arlington HTS 60005 Fax 847/718-7609

Schools: 10 \ **Teachers:** 708 \ **Students:** 12,000 \ **Special Ed Students:** 1,433 \ **LEP Students:** 1,000 \ **Ethnic:** Asian 8%, African American 2%, Hispanic 34%, Caucasian 56% \ **Exp:** $558 (High) \ **Poverty:** 6% \ **Title I:** $1,185,789 \ **Special Education:** $5,826,000 \ **Bilingual Education:** $178,000 \ **Open-Close:** 08/17 - 05/28 \ **DTBP:** $250 (High)

Dr David Schuler 1
Cathy Johnson 2,15
Ken Roland 3
Chris Yule 6,68,91
Marcella Zipp 11
Kara Kendrick 15*
Patrick Mogge 30,71
Ann Petro 67
Jeffrey Smith 70
Gabriella Stetz-Jackson 74
Lyn Comer-Jaworski 81*
Nick Mazza 295
Bonnie Boll 2
Sherry Koerner 2
Christine Frole 4
Dr LaZaro Lopez 10,15,16,57,72,277,294,296
Marni Johnson 13,15,77,78,90,271,275,294
Meghan Knight 27,285,752
Lisa Cooley 60
Julie Kim 69
Matt Liberatore 73,79
Tony Sclulorffton 76
Keir Rodgers 88
Maureen Stabile 298

---

79 Student Personnel
80 Driver Ed/Safety
81 Gifted/Talented
82 Video Services
83 Substance Abuse Prev
84 Erate
88 AIDS Education
88 Alternative/At Risk
89 Multi-Cultural Curriculum
90 Social Work
91 Safety/Security
92 Magnet School
93 Parental Involvement
95 Tech Prep Program
97 Chief Infomation Officer
98 Chief Technology Officer
270 Character Education
271 Migrant Education
273 Teacher Mentor
274 Before/After Sch
275 Response To Intervention
277 Remedial Math K-12
280 Literacy Coach
285 STEM
288 Common Core Standards
294 Accountability
295 Network System
296 Title II Programs
297 Webmaster
298 Grant Writer/Ptnrships
750 Chief Innovation Officer
751 Chief of Staff
752 Social Emotional Learning

Other School Types
Ⓐ = Alternative School
Ⓒ = Charter School
Ⓜ = Magnet School
Ⓨ = Year-Round School

School Programs
A = Alternative Program
G = Adult Classes
M = Magnet Program
T = Title I Schoolwide
V = Career & Tech Ed Programs

Social Media
 = Facebook
 = Twitter

New Schools are shaded
New Superintendents and Principals are bold
Personnel with email addresses are underscored

IL—69

Cook County — Market Data Retrieval

Public Schs..Principal	Grd	Prgm	Enr/#Cls	SN	
Buffalo Grove High Sch 1100 W Dundee Rd, Buffalo Grove 60089 Jeff Wardle	9-12	GV	1,981	16%	847/718-4000 Fax 847/718-4122
Elk Grove High Sch 500 W Elk Grove Blvd, Elk Grove Vlg 60007 Paul Kelly	9-12	GTV	1,944 95	29%	847/718-4400 Fax 847/718-4417
John Hersey High Sch 1900 E Thomas St, Arlington HTS 60004 Gordon Sisson	9-12	GV	1,898 82	12%	847/718-4800 Fax 847/718-4817
Newcomer Center 2121 S Goebbert Rd Bldg A, Arlington HTS 60005 Keir Rogers	9-12		51	67%	847/718-7937 Fax 847/718-7956
Prospect High Sch 801 W Kensington Rd, Mt Prospect 60056 Gregory Minter	9-12	GV	2,133 60	7%	847/718-5200 Fax 847/718-5216
Rolling Meadows High Sch 2901 Central Rd, Rolling MDWS 60008 Eileen Hart	9-12	GTV	1,863 75	21%	847/718-5600 Fax 847/718-5617
ⓐ The Academy at Forest View 2121 S Goebbert Rd, Arlington HTS 60005 Kara Kendrick	9-12	V	162 7	37%	847/718-7772 Fax 847/718-7773
ⓐ Vanguard Sch 2121 S Goebbert Rd, Arlington HTS 60005 Carmel Kraft	10-12	V	77 6	44%	847/718-7870 Fax 847/718-7869
Wheeling High Sch 900 S Elmhurst Rd, Wheeling 60090 Jerry Cook	9-12	GTV	1,739 74	37%	847/718-7000 Fax 847/718-7007
ⓐ Young Adult Alternative Ctr 2121 S Goebbert Rd, Arlington HTS 60005 Dan Williams	11-12	G	34	25%	847/718-7877 Fax 847/718-7908

- **Union Ridge School Dist 86** PID: 00274897   708/867-5822
  4600 N Oak Park Ave, Harwood HTS 60706   Fax 708/867-5826

Schools: 1 \ **Teachers:** 46 \ **Students:** 675 \ **Special Ed Students:** 87 \ **LEP Students:** 189 \ **Ethnic:** Asian 6%, Hispanic 23%, Caucasian 70% \ **Exp:** $276 (Med) \ **Poverty:** 15% \ **Title I:** $114,622 \ **Special Education:** $194,000 \ **Bilingual Education:** $21,000 \ **Open-Close:** 08/21 - 06/02 \ **DTBP:** $218 (High)

Michael MaGuire 1,11
Tom Simmons 3
Jolanta Kloptowski 67
Daniel Chambers 79*
Linda Bergstrom 273
Margaret Kyne 2
Timothy Corrigan 9
Rodney Bien-Aime 73,84*
Joseph Kerke 83*

Public Schs..Principal	Grd	Prgm	Enr/#Cls	SN	
Union Ridge Elem Sch 4600 N Oak Park Ave, Harwood HTS 60706 Julie Borner	PK-8	A	675 35	37%	708/867-5822

- **West Harvey-Dixmoor Pub SD 147** PID: 00270059   708/339-9500
  191 W 155th Pl, Harvey 60426   Fax 708/596-7020

Schools: 3 \ **Teachers:** 62 \ **Students:** 1,000 \ **Special Ed Students:** 165 \ **LEP Students:** 258 \ **Ethnic:** African American 61%, Hispanic 38%, Caucasian 1% \ **Exp:** $567 (High) \ **Poverty:** 43% \ **Title I:** $1,659,177 \ **Special Education:** $872,000 \ **Bilingual Education:** $100,000 \ **Open-Close:** 08/26 - 06/11

Johnnetta Miller 1
Tonisha Sibley 2,4,294
Mildred Clark 3
Frank Williams 6*
Dr David Lopez 11,59,79*
Gary Ofisher 2,84
Eric Lee 3,91
Lorraine Porter 4
Paul Sanchez 9
Dr Deborah Watson-Hill 15

Alicia LeMore 16
Alecia Lamar 73
Bonnie Rateree 67
Daniel Richmond 79

Public Schs..Principal	Grd	Prgm	Enr/#Cls	SN	
Lincoln Elem Sch 14100 Honore Ave, Dixmoor 60426 Rese Neal	PK-K	T	73 17	99%	708/597-4160 Fax 708/385-2859
Martin L King Elem Sch 14535 Seeley Ave, Dixmoor 60426 Dr Ayana Whaley	1-4	T	380 19	99%	708/385-5400 Fax 708/293-1748
Rosa L Parks Middle Sch 14700 Robey Ave, Dixmoor 60426 Taiyuan Tillmon	5-8	T	391 40	99%	708/371-9575 Fax 708/371-1412

- **West Northfield Sch Dist 31** PID: 00281228   847/272-6880
  3131 Techny Rd, Northbrook 60062   Fax 847/272-4818

Schools: 2 \ **Teachers:** 89 \ **Students:** 880 \ **Special Ed Students:** 118 \ **LEP Students:** 163 \ **Ethnic:** Asian 40%, African American 2%, Hispanic 11%, Caucasian 46% \ **Exp:** $450 (High) \ **Poverty:** 11% \ **Title I:** $164,445 \ **Special Education:** $555,000 \ **Bilingual Education:** $51,000 \ **Open-Close:** 08/20 - 06/08 \ **DTBP:** $226 (High)

Dr Erin Murphy 1
Ed Blankenheim 3
Janine Gruhn 11,59,79,88,296
Susan Harrison 71,295
David Kondela 285,298*
Catherine Lauria 2,3,15
Jennie Winters 9
Melissa Valentinas 67
Dave Delboccio 73,98,295

Public Schs..Principal	Grd	Prgm	Enr/#Cls	SN	
Field Middle Sch 2055 Landwehr Rd, Northbrook 60062 April Miller	6-8		272 36	23%	847/272-6884 Fax 847/272-1050
Henry Winkelman Elem Sch 1919 Landwehr Rd, Glenview 60026 Erica Berger	PK-5		586 29	19%	847/729-5650 Fax 847/729-5654

- **Westchester Public SD 92 1/2** PID: 00281254   708/450-2700
  9981 Canterbury St, Westchester 60154   Fax 708/450-2718

Schools: 3 \ **Teachers:** 79 \ **Students:** 1,250 \ **Special Ed Students:** 213 \ **LEP Students:** 124 \ **Ethnic:** Asian 2%, African American 27%, Hispanic 38%, Native American: 1%, Caucasian 33% \ **Exp:** $336 (High) \ **Poverty:** 9% \ **Title I:** $177,128 \ **Special Education:** $593,000 \ **Bilingual Education:** $27,000 \ **Open-Close:** 08/21 - 06/09 \ **DTBP:** $236 (High)

Philip Salemi 1
Shirlee Kribbs 5
Beth Malinski 59,88
Jakub Banbor 73,84,285
Dennis Gress 2,3,4,5,19,84
Kelly Bass 9,11,15,280,288,296,298
Donald Slager 67

Public Schs..Principal	Grd	Prgm	Enr/#Cls	SN	
Westchester Intermediate Sch 10900 Canterbury St, Westchester 60154 Shawn Barrett	3-5	T	394 18	39%	708/562-1011 Fax 708/562-0299
Westchester Middle Sch 1620 Norfolk Ave, Westchester 60154 Greg Leban	6-8	T	375 30	37%	708/450-2735 Fax 708/450-2752
Westchester Primary Sch 2400 Downing Ave, Westchester 60154 Lora Lafin	PK-2	T	391 16	36%	708/562-1509 Fax 708/562-1547

---

1 Superintendent	8 Curric/Instruct K-12	19 Chief Financial Officer	29 Family/Consumer Science	39 Social Studies K-12	49 English/Lang Arts Elem	59 Special Education Elem	69 Academic Assessment
2 Bus/Finance/Purchasing	9 Curric/Instruct Elem	20 Art K-12	30 Adult Education	40 Social Studies Elem	50 English/Lang Arts Sec	60 Special Education Sec	70 Research/Development
3 Buildings And Grounds	10 Curric/Instruct Sec	21 Art Elem	31 Career/Sch-to-Work K-12	41 Social Studies Sec	51 Reading K-12	61 Foreign/World Lang K-12	71 Public Information
4 Food Service	11 Federal Program	22 Art Sec	32 Career/Sch-to-Work Elem	42 Science K-12	52 Reading Elem	62 Foreign/World Lang Elem	72 Summer School
5 Transportation	12 Title I	23 Music K-12	33 Career/Sch-to-Work Sec	43 Science Elem	53 Reading Sec	63 Foreign/World Lang Sec	73 Instructional Tech
6 Athletic	13 Title V	24 Music Elem	34 Early Childhood Ed	44 Science Sec	54 Remedial Reading K-12	64 Religious Education K-12	74 Inservice Training
7 Health Services	14 Asst Superintendent	25 Music Sec	35 Health/Phys Education	45 Math K-12	55 Remedial Reading Elem	65 Religious Education Elem	75 Marketing/Distributive
	15 Instructional Media Svcs	26 Business Education	36 Guidance Services K-12	46 Math Elem	56 Remedial Reading Sec	66 Religious Education Sec	76 Info Systems
	16 Chief Operations Officer	27 Career & Tech Ed	37 Guidance Services Elem	47 Math Sec	57 Bilingual/ELL	67 School Board President	77 Psychological Assess
	18 Chief Academic Officer	28 Technology Education	38 Guidance Services Sec	48 English/Lang Arts K-12	58 Special Education K-12	68 Teacher Personnel	78 Affirmative Action

Illinois School Directory — Cook County

• Western Springs Sch Dist 101 PID: 00281307   708/246-3700
4225 Wolf Rd, Western Sprgs 60558   Fax 708/246-4280

Schools: 4 \ **Teachers:** 120 \ **Students:** 1,435 \ **Special Ed Students:** 153 \ **Ethnic:** Asian 2%, African American 1%, Hispanic 3%, Caucasian 94% \ **Exp:** $104 (Low) \ **Poverty:** 5% \ **Title I:** $120,339 \ **Special Education:** $604,000 \ **Open-Close:** 08/26 - 06/04 \ **DTBP:** $234 (High)

Dr Brian Barnhart	1	Adny Brown	3
Joan Kirlic	7,83,88	Dr Sarah Coffey	9,15,69,273,288
Maureen Moran	59	Virginia Sulek	59
Julie O'Connor	67	Matt Ryan	73

Public Schs..Principal	Grd	Prgm	Enr/#Cls	SN	
Field Park Elem Sch 4335 Howard Ave, Western Sprgs 60558 Ashley Burger	K-5		267 13		708/246-7675 Fax 708/482-2582
Forest Hills Elem Sch 5020 Central Ave, Western Sprgs 60558 Rachel Corrough	PK-5		271 12	1%	708/246-7678 Fax 708/482-2589
John Laidlaw Elem Sch 4072 Forest Ave, Western Sprgs 60558 Erin Debartlo	PK-5		407 17		708/246-7673 Fax 708/482-2496
McClure Junior High Sch 4225 Wolf Rd, Western Sprgs 60558 Dan Chick	6-8		490 40		708/246-7590 Fax 708/246-4370

• Wheeling Cmty Cons Sch Dist 21 PID: 00281371   847/537-8270
999 W Dundee Rd, Wheeling 60090   Fax 847/520-2710

Schools: 13 \ **Teachers:** 429 \ **Students:** 6,058 \ **Special Ed Students:** 829 \ **LEP Students:** 2,753 \ **Ethnic:** Asian 9%, African American 2%, Hispanic 56%, Native American: 1%, Caucasian 33% \ **Exp:** $245 (Med) \ **Poverty:** 12% \ **Title I:** $1,239,436 \ **Special Education:** $3,189,000 \ **Bilingual Education:** $672,000 \ **Open-Close:** 08/20 - 05/27 \ **DTBP:** $191 (High)

Dr Michael Connelly	1	Melisa Morgese	2
Micheal Debartolo	2,15,19	Bill Weiss	3
Glen Michelini	3	Rosemarie Meyer	9,15
Brigid Ohlwein	11	Kim Cline	15
Robert Gurney	15,68	Carolyn Droll	21,35,46
Amy Breiler	24,49	Lynne Duffy	34
Chris Lapetino	40,43	Noreen Segal	57
Phil Pritzker	67	Kara Beach	71
Mike Frantini	73,98,295	Alicia Duell	76

Public Schs..Principal	Grd	Prgm	Enr/#Cls	SN	
Booth Tarkington Elem Sch 310 Scott St, Wheeling 60090 Joe Arduino	PK-5	T	427 19	34%	847/520-2775 Fax 847/419-3074
Cooper Middle Sch 1050 Plum Grove Cir, Buffalo Grove 60089 Dave DeMuth	6-8		662 50	37%	847/520-2750 Fax 847/419-3071
Edgar Allan Poe Elem Sch 2800 N Highland Ave, Arlington HTS 60004 Christy Campbell	K-5		351 30	32%	847/670-3200 Fax 847/670-3216
Eugene Field Elem Sch 51 Saint Armand Ln, Wheeling 60090 Luis Bonilla	K-5	T	541 25	68%	847/520-2780 Fax 847/419-3077
Hawthorn Early Childhood Ctr 200 Glendale St, Wheeling 60090 Holly Harperkelly	PK-PK		173 8	48%	847/465-7290 Fax 847/465-7296
Henry Longfellow Elem Sch 501 S Arlington Heights Rd, Buffalo Grove 60089 Michelle Friedman	K-5		409 17	13%	847/520-2755 Fax 847/419-3078
J W Riley Sch 1209 E Burr Oak Dr, Arlington HTS 60004 Kevin Olsen	K-5		278 20	24%	847/670-3400 Fax 847/670-3418
Jack London Middle Sch 1001 W Dundee Rd, Wheeling 60090 Anastasia Netzel	6-8	T	668 28	44%	847/520-2745 Fax 847/520-2842
Joyce Kilmer Elem Sch 655 Golfview Ter, Buffalo Grove 60089 Matthew Lombardo	K-5	T	506 19	51%	847/520-2760 Fax 847/520-2601
Mark Twain Elem Sch 515 E Merle Ln, Wheeling 60090 Alyssa Shlensky	PK-5	T	471 24	59%	847/520-2785 Fax 847/419-3080
O W Holmes Middle Sch 221 S Wolf Rd, Wheeling 60090 Martin Hopkins	6-8	T	725 50	59%	847/520-2790 Fax 847/419-3073
Robert Frost Elem Sch 1805 N Aspen Dr, Mt Prospect 60056 Tim Prikkel	PK-5	T	504 25	53%	847/803-4815 Fax 847/803-4855
Walt Whitman Elem Sch 133 Wille Ave, Wheeling 60090 Jorge Almodovar	PK-5	T	481 22	72%	847/520-2795 Fax 847/520-2607

• Willow Springs School Dist 108 PID: 00281553   708/839-6828
8345 Archer Ave, Willow Spgs 60480   Fax 708/839-8399

Schools: 1 \ **Teachers:** 33 \ **Students:** 359 \ **Special Ed Students:** 88 \ **LEP Students:** 58 \ **Ethnic:** Asian 1%, African American 6%, Hispanic 39%, Caucasian 54% \ **Exp:** $299 (Med) \ **Poverty:** 19% \ **Title I:** $120,661 \ **Special Education:** $174,000 \ **Open-Close:** 08/19 - 05/26 \ **DTBP:** $226 (High)

Frank Patrick	1,73,288	Dan Dickman	3
Cindy Layer	6*	Karen Triezenberg	9,83,93,270,271,274*
Linda Szejcar	11,275	Carol Graf	59*
Mary Weeg	67		

Public Schs..Principal	Grd	Prgm	Enr/#Cls	SN	
Willow Springs Elem Sch 8345 Archer Ave, Willow Spgs 60480 Lori Smuda	PK-8		359 19	66%	708/839-6828

• Wilmette Public School Dist 39 PID: 00281577   847/256-2450
615 Locust Rd, Wilmette 60091   Fax 847/256-1920

Schools: 6 \ **Teachers:** 284 \ **Students:** 3,563 \ **Special Ed Students:** 549 \ **LEP Students:** 145 \ **Ethnic:** Asian 12%, African American 1%, Hispanic 6%, Caucasian 81% \ **Exp:** $147 (Low) \ **Poverty:** 2% \ **Title I:** $98,902 \ **Special Education:** $2,736,000 \ **Bilingual Education:** $38,000 \ **Open-Close:** 08/26 - 06/09 \ **DTBP:** $191 (High)

Kari Cremascoli	1	Corey Bultemeier	2
Stan Stankiewicz	3	Dan Lambert	4
Katie Lee	9,11,57,69,270,273,288,298	Kristin Swanson	13,59,79,83,88,298
Tony Demonte	16,73	Lisa Fabes	67
Heather Glowacki	68	Debbie Cooper	72
Maryann Esler	274		

Public Schs..Principal	Grd	Prgm	Enr/#Cls	SN	
Central Elem Sch 910 Central Ave, Wilmette 60091 Rebecca Littmann	K-4		452 28	2%	847/512-6100 Fax 847/251-4086
Harper Elem Sch 1101 Dartmouth St, Wilmette 60091 Dr Susan Kick	K-4		434 18	2%	847/512-6200 Fax 847/251-4176

---

79 Student Personnel	91 Safety/Security	275 Response To Intervention	298 Grant Writer/Ptnrships	**School Programs**
80 Driver Ed/Safety	92 Magnet School	277 Remedial Math K-12	750 Chief Innovation Officer	A = Alternative Program
81 Gifted/Talented	93 Parental Involvement	280 Literacy Coach	751 Chief of Staff	G = Adult Classes
82 Video Services	95 Tech Prep Program	285 STEM	752 Social Emotional Learning	M = Magnet Program
83 Substance Abuse Prev	97 Chief Infomation Officer	286 Digital Learning		T = Title I Schoolwide
84 Erate	98 Chief Technology Officer	288 Common Core Standards	**Other School Types**	V = Career & Tech Ed Programs
85 AIDS Education	270 Accountability	294 Accountability	Ⓐ = Alternative School	
88 Alternative/At Risk	271 Migrant Education	295 Network System	Ⓒ = Charter School	**Social Media**
89 Multi-Cultural Curriculum	273 Teacher Mentor	296 Title II Programs	Ⓜ = Magnet School	▢ = Facebook
90 Social Work	274 Before/After Sch	297 Webmaster	Ⓨ = Year-Round School	▢ = Twitter

New Schools are shaded
New Superintendents and Principals are bold
Personnel with email addresses are underscored

Cook County
Market Data Retrieval

Highcrest Middle Sch 569 Hunter Rd, Wilmette 60091 Kelly Jackson	5-6	811 50	3%	847/512-6500 Fax 847/256-0083
McKenzie Elem Sch 649 Prairie Ave, Wilmette 60091 Dana Nasiakos	K-4	430 23	3%	847/512-6300 Fax 847/251-4067
Romona Elem Sch 600 Romona Rd, Wilmette 60091 Cindy Anderson	PK-4	545 25	4%	847/512-6400 Fax 847/251-4153
Wilmette Junior High Sch 620 Locust Rd, Wilmette 60091 **Kate Dominique**	7-8	892 35	3%	847/512-6600 Fax 847/256-0204

● **Winnetka School Dist 36** PID: 00281917 847/446-9400
1235 Oak St, Winnetka 60093 Fax 847/446-9408

Schools: 5 \ **Teachers:** 163 \ **Students:** 1,100 \
Special Ed Students: 364 \ **LEP Students:** 19 \ **Ethnic:** Asian 3%, Hispanic 3%, Caucasian 94% \ **Exp:** $184 (Low) \ **Poverty:** 4% \ **Title I:** $86,223 \
Special Education: $1,269,000 \ **Open-Close:** 08/24 - 06/03 \ **DTBP:** $254 (High)

Trisha Kocanda 1,83
Adam Rappaport 3
Beth Martin 11,37,59,77,79
Maureen Miller 16,73,84
Katharine Hughes 71
Anne Lascelles 274
Jennifer Marshall 295
Lance Gilchrist 297
Brad Goldstein 2,3,4,5,19
Barry Rodgers 9,70
Kelly Tess 15,74
Dawn Livingston 67
Elizabeth Migalla 76
Jen Sieghan 280
Robert Repp 295

Public Schs..Principal	Grd	Prgm	Enr/#Cls	SN	
Carleton W Washburne Sch 515 Hibbard Rd, Winnetka 60093 **Benjamin Horwitz** \ Andrew Fenton	7-8		394 35	1%	847/446-5892 Fax 847/446-1380
Crow Island Sch 1112 Willow Rd, Winnetka 60093 Julie Pfeffer \ **Lawrence Joynt**	PK-4		309 18		847/446-0353 Fax 847/446-9021
Greeley Elem Sch 275 Fairview Ave, Winnetka 60093 Joshua Swanner	PK-4		276 15		847/446-6060 Fax 847/501-5737
Hubbard Woods Elem Sch 1110 Chatfield Rd, Winnetka 60093 Beth Carmody	PK-4		301 20	1%	847/446-0920 Fax 847/501-6124
Skokie Sch 520 Glendale Ave, Winnetka 60093 Betty Weir	5-6		352 45	1%	847/441-1750 Fax 847/441-2193

● **Worth School District 127** PID: 00282246 708/448-2800
11218 S Ridgeland Ave Ste A, Worth 60482 Fax 708/448-6215

Schools: 4 \ **Teachers:** 75 \ **Students:** 1,087 \ **Special Ed Students:** 211 \ **LEP Students:** 206 \ **Ethnic:** Asian 2%, African American 3%, Hispanic 17%, Caucasian 78% \ **Exp:** $158 (Low) \ **Poverty:** 22% \ **Title I:** $417,533 \ **Special Education:** $504,000 \ **Bilingual Education:** $46,000 \
Open-Close: 08/24 - 06/01 \ **DTBP:** $223 (High)

Dr Mark Fleming 1,11
Scott Tamkus 3
Robert Jeffers 16,73,295*
Donna Weinert 68
Joe Zampillo 85*
Cindy Dykas 2,4
Sinead Chambers 9,57,59,88,275
Drew Sernus 67
Linda Esposito 83*

Public Schs..Principal	Grd	Prgm	Enr/#Cls	SN	
Worth Elem Sch 11158 S Oak Park Ave, Worth 60482 **Maureen Eichstaedt**	PK-5		402 25	55%	708/448-2801 Fax 708/448-6023
Worth Junior High Sch 11151 S New England Ave, Worth 60482 Joe Zampillo	6-8		355 25	54%	708/448-2803 Fax 708/448-6155
Worthridge Elem Sch 11218 S Ridgeland Ave, Worth 60482 Dr Rita Wojtylewski	PK-PK		45	67%	708/448-2800
Worthwoods Elem Sch 11000 S Oketo Ave, Worth 60482 Linda Esposito	K-5		284 12	63%	708/448-2802 Fax 708/448-5623

COOK CATHOLIC SCHOOLS

● **Archdiocese of Chicago Ed Off** PID: 00282923 312/534-5200
835 N Rush St, Chicago 60611 Fax 312/534-5295

Schools: 198 \ **Students:** 75,039 \ **Open-Close:** 08/23 - 06/03

Listing includes only schools located in this county. See District Index for location of Diocesan Offices.

Dr Jim Rigg 1
Miriam Shabo 2
Katrina McDermott 11
Jerry Spapara 15
Julie Ramski 34
Elise Matson-Dite 68
Anne Maselli 71
Matt Walter 2
Paula DeLuca 4
Bridgett Delapena 15
Phyllis Cavallore 18
Kate McOnnell 58
Hedi Belkaoui 69

Catholic Schs..Principal	Grd	Prgm	Enr/#Cls	SN	
Acad St Benedict-the African 6020 S Laflin St, Chicago 60636 Patricia Murphy	PK-8		250 18		773/776-3316 Fax 773/776-3715
Alphonsus Academy 1439 W Wellington Ave, Chicago 60657 Gerit McAllister	PK-8		507 15		773/348-4629 Fax 773/348-4829
Annunciata Elem Sch 3750 E 112th St, Chicago 60617 Edward Renas	PK-8		180 10		773/375-5711 Fax 773/375-5704
Ascension Sch 601 Van Buren St, Oak Park 60304 Maryanne Polega	PK-8		450 20		708/386-7282 Fax 708/524-4796
Augustus Tolton Academy 7120 S Calumet Ave, Chicago 60619 Philip Bazile	PK-8		109		773/224-3811
Bridgeport Catholic Academy 3700 S Lowe Ave, Chicago 60609 Daniel Flaherty	PK-8		305 11		773/376-6223 Fax 773/376-3864
Brother Rice High Sch 10001 S Pulaski Rd, Chicago 60655 Robert Alberts	9-12		1,200 60		773/429-4300 Fax 773/779-5239
Cardinal Bernardin Mont Acad 1651 W Diversey Pkwy, Chicago 60614 Barbara Labotka	PK-6		150 7		773/975-6330 Fax 773/975-6339
Cardinal Joseph Bernardin ES 9250 W 167th St, Orland Hills 60487 Kelly Bourrell	PK-8		720		708/403-6525 Fax 708/403-8621
Children of Peace Sch 1900 W Taylor St, Chicago 60612 Lida Nantwi	PK-8		220 17		312/243-8186 Fax 312/243-8479

1 Superintendent	8 Curric/Instruct K-12	19 Chief Financial Officer	29 Family/Consumer Science	39 Social Studies K-12	49 English/Lang Arts Elem	59 Special Education Elem	69 Academic Assessment
2 Bus/Finance/Purchasing	9 Curric/Instruct Elem	20 Art K-12	30 Adult Education	40 Social Studies Elem	50 English/Lang Arts Sec	60 Special Education Sec	70 Research/Development
3 Buildings And Grounds	10 Curric/Instruct Sec	21 Art Elem	31 Career/Sch-to-Work K-12	41 Social Studies Sec	51 Reading K-12	61 Foreign/World Lang K-12	71 Public Information
4 Food Service	11 Federal Program	22 Art Sec	32 Career/Sch-to-Work Elem	42 Science K-12	52 Reading Elem	62 Foreign/World Lang Elem	72 Summer School
5 Transportation	12 Title I	23 Music K-12	33 Career/Sch-to-Work Sec	43 Science Elem	53 Reading Sec	63 Foreign/World Lang Sec	73 Instructional Tech
6 Athletic	13 Title V	24 Music Elem	34 Early Childhood Ed	44 Science Sec	54 Remedial Reading K-12	64 Religious Education K-12	74 Inservice Training
7 Health Services	15 Asst Superintendent	25 Music Sec	35 Health/Phys Education	45 Math K-12	55 Remedial Reading Elem	65 Religious Education Elem	75 Marketing/Distributive
	16 Instructional Media Svcs	26 Business Education	36 Guidance Services K-12	46 Math Elem	56 Remedial Reading Sec	66 Religious Education Sec	76 Info Systems
	17 Chief Operations Officer	27 Career & Tech Ed	37 Guidance Services Elem	47 Math Sec	57 Bilingual/ELL	67 School Board President	77 Psychological Assess
	18 Chief Academic Officer	28 Technology Education	38 Guidance Services Sec	48 English/Lang Arts K-12	58 Special Education K-12	68 Teacher Personnel	78 Affirmative Action

Illinois School Directory — Cook County

School	Grades	Prog	Enroll	Phone
Christ Our Savior Sch 900 E 154th St, South Holland 60473 Karen Brodzik	PK-8		380	708/333-8173 Fax 708/333-3247
Christ the King Sch 9240 S Hoyne Ave, Chicago 60643 Dr Ann Riordan	PK-8		318 19	773/779-3329 Fax 773/779-3390 f t
De La Salle Institute 3434 S Michigan Ave, Chicago 60616 Thomas Schergen	9-12	V	760 50	312/842-7355 Fax 312/842-5640 f t
DePaul Clg Prep-Gordon Campus 3633 N California Ave, Chicago 60618 Dr Megan Anderson	9-12	GV	647 35	773/539-3600 Fax 773/539-9158 f t
Divine Providence Sch 2500 Mayfair Ave, Westchester 60154 Lynn Letourneau	PK-8		205 10	708/562-2258 Fax 708/562-9171
Epiphany Sch 4223 W 25th St, Chicago 60623 Scott Ernst	PK-8		184 10	773/762-1542 Fax 773/762-2247 f t
Fenwick High Sch 505 Washington Blvd, Oak Park 60302 Peter Groom	9-12		1,050 48	708/386-0127 Fax 708/386-3052
Guerin College Prep Sch 8001 Belmont Ave, River Grove 60171 Karen Booth	9-12		620 47	708/453-6233 Fax 708/453-6296 f t
Hales Franciscan High Sch 4930 S Cottage Grove Ave, Chicago 60615 Nichole Jackson	9-12		300 35	773/285-8400 Fax 773/285-7025 f t
Holy Angels Sch 750 E 40th St, Chicago 60653 Nicole Merz	PK-8	G	214 11	773/624-0727 Fax 773/538-9683 f t
Holy Family Catholic Academy 2515 Palatine Rd, Inverness 60067 Kate O'Brien	PK-8		500 7	847/907-3452 Fax 847/705-7646 f
Holy Trinity High Sch 1443 W Division St, Chicago 60642 Quincy Paden	9-12		420 35	773/278-4212 Fax 773/278-0144 f
Immaculate Cncptn St Joseph 1431 N North Park Ave, Chicago 60610 Katie Sullivan \ Maria Hill	PK-8		456 1	312/944-0304 Fax 312/944-0695
Immaculate Cncpton-St Joseph 363 W Hill St, Chicago 60610 Maria Hill	4-8		174	312/944-0304 Fax 312/291-8520
Immaculate Conception Elem Sch 8739 S Exchange Ave, Chicago 60617 Sr Katia Alcantar	K-8		170	773/375-4674 Fax 773/375-3526
Immaculate Conception Sch 7263 W Talcott Ave, Chicago 60631 Susan Canzoneri	PK-8		516 27	773/775-0545 Fax 773/775-3822
Infant Jesus of Prague Sch 1101 Douglas Ave, Flossmoor 60422 Charlotte Kelly	PK-8		260 24	708/799-5200 Fax 708/799-5293 f t
Josephinum Academy 1501 N Oakley Blvd, Chicago 60622 Colleen Schrantz	6-12		120 20	773/276-1261 Fax 773/292-3963 f t
Leo High Sch 7901 S Sangamon St, Chicago 60620 Shaka Rawls	9-12		300 20	773/224-9600 Fax 773/224-3856
Loyola Academy 1100 Laramie Ave, Wilmette 60091 Charles Heintz	9-12		2,000 60	847/256-1100 Fax 847/853-4512
Marian Catholic High Sch 700 Ashland Ave, Chicago HTS 60411 Steven Tortorello	9-12		1,500 54	708/755-7565 Fax 708/756-9758 f
Marist High Sch 4200 W 115th St, Chicago 60655 Dr Kathryn Baal	9-12		1,797 63	773/881-5300 Fax 773/881-0595
Mary Seat of Wisdom Sch 1352 S Cumberland Ave, Park Ridge 60068 Julie Due	PK-8		457 28	847/825-2500 Fax 847/825-1943 f t
Maternity BVM Sch 1537 N Lawndale Ave, Chicago 60651 Christine Molina	PK-8		248	773/227-1140 Fax 773/227-2939 f t
Most Holy Redeemer Sch 9536 S Millard Ave, Evergreen Pk 60805	PK-8		340 24	708/422-8280 Fax 708/422-4193 f t
Mother McAuley Lib Arts HS 3737 W 99th St, Chicago 60655 Eileen O'Reilly	9-12		1,709 65	773/881-6500 Fax 773/881-6562
Mt Carmel High Sch 6410 S Dante Ave, Chicago 60637 Scott Tabernacki	9-12		760 36	773/324-1020 Fax 773/324-9235
Nativity BVM Sch 6820 S Washtenaw Ave, Chicago 60629 Robert Gawlik	PK-8		220 10	773/476-0571 Fax 773/476-0065 f t
Nazareth Academy 1209 W Ogden Ave, La Grange Pk 60526 Therese Hawkins	9-12		763	708/354-0061 Fax 708/354-0109
Northside Cath Acad-Primary 6216 N Glenwood Ave, Chicago 60660 Christine Huzenis	PK-4		320 16	773/743-6277 Fax 773/743-6174
Northside Cath Academy Mid Sch 7318 N Oakley Ave, Chicago 60645 Christine Huzenis	5-8		200 6	773/271-2008 Fax 773/764-1095
Notre Dame College Prep HS 7655 W Dempster St, Niles 60714 Daniel Tully	9-12		800 55	847/965-2900 Fax 847/965-2975
Old St Mary's Sch 1474 S Michigan Ave, Chicago 60605 Diana Smith	PK-8		360	312/386-1560 Fax 312/386-1578 f
Our Lady of Charity Sch 3620 S 57th Ct, Cicero 60804 Dr Frank Zarate	PK-8		250 10	708/652-0262 Fax 708/652-0601 f
Our Lady of Grace Sch 2446 N Ridgeway Ave, Chicago 60647 Kaitlin Reichart	PK-8		148 11	773/342-0170 Fax 773/342-5305
Our Lady of Guadalupe Sch 9050 S Burley Ave, Chicago 60617 Bonnie Hall	PK-8		142 11	773/768-0999 Fax 773/768-0529 f t
Our Lady of Mt Carmel Acad 720 W Belmont Ave, Chicago 60657 Shane Staszcuk	PK-8		269 13	773/525-8779 Fax 773/525-7810 f
Our Lady of Perpetual Help Sch 1123 Church St, Glenview 60025 Dr Amy Mills	PK-8		825 50	847/724-6990 Fax 847/724-7025
Our Lady of Tepeyac Elem Sch 2235 S Albany Ave, Chicago 60623 Patricia Krielaart	PK-8		227 10	773/522-0024 Fax 773/522-4577
Our Lady of Tepeyac High Sch 2228 S Whipple St, Chicago 60623 Kathy Ingram	9-12		185 15	773/522-0023 Fax 773/522-0508
Our Lady of the Snows Sch 4810 S Leamington Ave, Chicago 60638 Eileen Sheedy	PK-8		225 10	773/735-4810 Fax 773/582-3363 f
Our Lady of the Wayside Sch 432 S Mitchell Ave, Arlington HTS 60005 David Wood	PK-8		653 32	847/255-0050 Fax 847/253-0543
Pope John Paul II Sch 4325 S Richmond St, Chicago 60632 Dr Lisa Griffiths	PK-8		138 16	773/523-6161 f
Pope John XXIII Sch 1120 Washington St, Evanston 60202 Dr Molly Cinnamon	PK-8		316 28	847/475-5678 Fax 847/475-5683

79 Student Personnel
80 Driver Ed/Safety
81 Gifted/Talented
82 Video Services
83 Substance Abuse Prev
84 Erate
85 AIDS Education
88 Alternative/At Risk
89 Multi-Cultural Curriculum
90 Social Work
91 Safety/Security
92 Magnet School
93 Parental Involvement
95 Tech Prep Program
97 Chief Information Officer
98 Chief Technology Officer
270 Character Education
271 Migrant Education
273 Teacher Mentor
274 Before/After Sch
275 Response To Intervention
277 Remedial Math K-12
280 Literacy Coach
285 STEM
286 Digital Learning
288 Common Core Standards
294 Accountability
295 Network System
296 Title II Programs
297 Webmaster
298 Grant Writer/Ptnrships
750 Chief Innovation Officer
751 Chief of Staff
752 Social Emotional Learning

School Programs
A = Alternative Program
G = Adult Classes
M = Magnet Program
T = Title I Schoolwide
V = Career & Tech Ed Programs

Other School Types
A = Alternative School
C = Charter School
M = Magnet School
Y = Year-Round School

Social Media
f = Facebook
t = Twitter

New Schools are shaded
New Superintendents and Principals are bold
Personnel with email addresses are underscored

IL–73

Cook County

School	Grade	Enrollment	Phone
Queen of All Saints Sch 6230 N Lemont Ave, Chicago 60646 Emily Carlson	PK-8	700 28	773/736-0567 Fax 773/736-7142
Queen of Angels Sch 4520 N Western Ave, Chicago 60625 Rana Brizgys	PK-8	380 20	773/769-4211 Fax 773/769-4289
Queen of Martyrs Sch 3550 W 103rd St, Chicago 60805 Doc Mathius	PK-8	470 22	708/422-1540 Fax 708/422-1811
Queen of the Rosary Sch 690 W Elk Grove Blvd, Elk Grove Vlg 60007 Kathy McGinn	PK-8	285 17	847/437-3322 Fax 847/437-3290
Queen of the Universe Sch 7130 S Hamlin Ave, Chicago 60629 Linda Kelly	PK-8	180 12	773/582-4266 Fax 773/585-7254
Regina Dominican High Sch 701 Locust Rd, Wilmette 60091 Kathleen Porreca	9-12	300 39	847/256-7660 Fax 847/256-3726
Resurrection College Prep HS 7500 W Talcott Ave, Chicago 60631 Richard Piwowarski	9-12 G	920 45	773/775-6616 Fax 773/775-0611
Sacred Heart Sch 1095 Gage St, Winnetka 60093 Kristen Fink	PK-8	200 18	847/446-0005 Fax 847/446-4961
Sacred Heart Sch 815 N 16th Ave, Melrose Park 60160 Barbara Ciconte	PK-8	130 10	708/681-0240 Fax 708/681-0454
Sacred Heart Sch 2926 E 96th St, Chicago 60617 Kathleen Tomaszewski	PK-8	170 9	773/768-3728 Fax 773/768-5034
Saint Andrew Sch 1710 W Addison St, Chicago 60613 Allen Ackerman	PK-8	500 20	773/248-2500 Fax 773/248-2709
Santa Lucia Grammar Sch 3017 S Wells St, Chicago 60616 Eileen Sheedy	PK-8	81 9	312/326-1839 Fax 312/326-1945
SS Alphonsus & Patrick Sch 20W145 Davey Rd, Lemont 60439 Jackie Chiaramonte	PK-8	243 10	630/783-2220 Fax 630/783-2230
SS Catherine of Siena-Lucy Sch 27 Washington Blvd, Oak Park 60302 Sharon Leamy	PK-8	330 9	708/386-5286 Fax 708/386-7328
SS Cyril & Methodius Sch 607 Sobieski St, Lemont 60439 Shirley Tkachuk	PK-8	375 18	630/257-6488 Fax 630/257-6465
SS Faith Hope & Charity Sch 180 Ridge Ave, Winnetka 60093 Dr Tom Meagher	PK-8	360 20	847/446-0031 Fax 847/446-9064
St Agnes Sch 1501 Chicago Rd, Chicago HTS 60411 Matthew Lungaro	PK-8	200 14	708/756-2333 Fax 708/709-2693
St Agnes School Bohemia 2643 S Central Park Ave, Chicago 60623 Bill Taylor	PK-8	465 20	773/522-0143 Fax 773/522-0132
St Ailbe Sch 9037 S Harper Ave, Chicago 60619 Alyssa Mostyn	PK-8	151 10	773/734-1386 Fax 773/734-1440
St Albert the Great Sch 5535 State Rd, Burbank 60459 Mrs McLawhorn	PK-8	410	708/424-7757
St Alexander Sch 7025 W 126th St, Palos Heights 60463 Sharon O'Toole	PK-8	300 12	708/448-0408 Fax 708/448-5947
St Alphonsus Ligouri Sch 411 N Wheeling Rd Frnt 1, Prospect HTS 60070 Janice Divincenzo	PK-8	200 17	847/255-5538
St Angela Sch 1332 N Massasoit Ave, Chicago 60651 Bruce Schooler	PK-8	252 10	773/626-2655 Fax 773/626-8156
St Ann Grade Sch 2211 W 18th Pl, Chicago 60608 McKenna Corrigan	PK-8	200 10	312/829-4153 Fax 312/829-4155
St Ann Sch 3014 Ridge Rd, Lansing 60438 Eliza Gonzalez	K-8	300 26	708/895-1661 Fax 708/895-6923
St Athanasius Sch 2510 Ashland Ave, Evanston 60201 Carol McClay	PK-8	320 18	847/864-2650 Fax 847/475-7385
St Barbara Elem Sch 2867 S Throop St, Chicago 60608 Nicole Nolazco	PK-8	220 10	312/326-6243 Fax 312/842-7960
St Barnabas Sch 10121 S Longwood Dr, Chicago 60643 Elaine Gaffney	PK-8	426 24	773/445-7711 Fax 773/445-9815
St Bartholomew Sch 4941 W Patterson Ave, Chicago 60641 Nilma Osiecki	PK-8	250 11	773/282-9373 Fax 773/282-4757
St Bede the Venerable Sch 4440 W 83rd St, Chicago 60652 Sherry Stewart	PK-8	728 28	773/884-2020 Fax 773/582-3366
St Benedict Prep Elem Sch 3920 N Leavitt St, Chicago 60618 Mary Deletioglu \ Rachel Waldron	PK-8	300 20	773/463-6797 Fax 773/463-0782
St Benedict Sch 2324 New St, Blue Island 60406 Dr Emily Namlon	PK-8	180 10	708/385-2016 Fax 708/385-4490
St Bruno Sch 4839 S Harding Ave, Chicago 60632 Carla Sever	PK-8	250 13	773/847-0697 Fax 773/847-1620
St Cajetan Sch 2447 W 112th St, Chicago 60655 Michelle Nitsche	PK-8	398	773/233-8844 Fax 773/474-7821
St Catherine Laboure Sch 3425 Thornwood Ave, Glenview 60026 Jodi Reuter	PK-8	310 20	847/724-2240 Fax 847/724-5805
St Catherine of Alexandria Sch 10621 Kedvale Ave, Oak Lawn 60453 Kristine Owens	PK-8	484 22	708/425-5547 Fax 708/425-3701
St Celestine Sch 3017 N 77th Ave, Elmwood Park 60707 Sheila Klich	PK-8	530 19	708/453-8234 Fax 708/452-0237
St Christina Sch 3333 W 110th St, Chicago 60655 Mary Stokes	PK-8	450 27	773/445-2969 Fax 773/445-0444
St Christopher Sch 14611 Keeler Ave, Midlothian 60445 Dr Michelle Walthers	PK-8	210 15	708/385-8776 Fax 708/385-8102
St Clement Sch 2524 N Orchard St, Chicago 60614 Mari Hanson	PK-8	292	773/348-8212 Fax 773/348-4712
St Cletus Sch 700 W 55th St, La Grange 60525 Greg Porod	PK-8	444 23	708/352-4820 Fax 708/352-0788
St Constance Sch 5841 W Strong St, Chicago 60630 Eva Panczyk	PK-8	129 10	773/283-2311 Fax 773/283-3515
St Damian Sch 5300 155th St, Oak Forest 60452 Jennifer Miller	K-8	663 25	708/687-4230 Fax 708/687-8347
St Daniel the Prophet Sch 5337 S Natoma Ave, Chicago 60638 Cynthia Zabilka	PK-8	680	773/586-1225 Fax 773/586-1232

1. Superintendent
2. Bus/Finance/Purchasing
3. Buildings And Grounds
4. Food Service
5. Transportation
6. Athletic
7. Health Services
8. Curric/Instruct K-12
9. Curric/Instruct Elem
10. Curric/Instruct Sec
11. Federal Program
12. Title I
13. Title V
15. Asst Superintendent
16. Instructional Media Svcs
17. Chief Operations Officer
18. Chief Academic Officer
19. Chief Financial Officer
20. Art K-12
21. Art Elem
22. Art Sec
23. Music K-12
24. Music Elem
25. Music Sec
26. Business Education
27. Career & Tech Ed
28. Technology Education
29. Family/Consumer Science
30. Adult Education
31. Career/Sch-to-Work K-12
32. Career/Sch-to-Work Elem
33. Career/Sch-to-Work Sec
34. Early Childhood Ed
35. Health/Phys Education
36. Guidance Services K-12
37. Guidance Services Elem
38. Guidance Services Sec
39. Social Studies K-12
40. Social Studies Elem
41. Social Studies Sec
42. Science K-12
43. Science Elem
44. Science Sec
45. Math K-12
46. Math Elem
47. Math Sec
48. English/Lang Arts K-12
49. English/Lang Arts Elem
50. English/Lang Arts Sec
51. Reading K-12
52. Reading Elem
53. Reading Sec
54. Remedial Reading K-12
55. Remedial Reading Elem
56. Remedial Reading Sec
57. Bilingual/ELL
58. Special Education K-12
59. Special Education Elem
60. Special Education Sec
61. Foreign/World Lang K-12
62. Foreign/World Lang Elem
63. Foreign/World Lang Sec
64. Religious Education K-12
65. Religious Education Elem
66. Religious Education Sec
67. School Board President
68. Teacher Personnel
69. Academic Assessment
70. Research/Development
71. Public Information
72. Summer School
73. Instructional Tech
74. Inservice Training
75. Marketing/Distributive
76. Info Systems
77. Psychological Assess
78. Affirmative Action

Illinois School Directory — Cook County

School	Grades	Enrollment / Staff	Phone / Fax
St Edward Sch 4343 W Sunnyside Ave, Chicago 60630 Sara Lasica	PK-8	346 25	773/736-9133 Fax 773/736-9280
St Elizabeth of the Trinity 6040 W Ardmore Ave, Chicago 60646 Dr Kristine Hillman	PK-8	411 20	773/763-7080 Fax 773/775-3893
St Elizabeth Trinity Sch 6040 W Ardmore Ave, Chicago 60646 Dr Kristine Hillman	PK-8	401	773/763-7080 Fax 773/775-3893
St Emily Sch 1400 E Central Rd, Mt Prospect 60056 Karen Booth	PK-8	600 30	847/296-3490 Fax 847/296-1155
St Ethelreda Sch 8734 S Paulina St, Chicago 60620 Denise Spells	PK-8	200 16	773/238-1757 Fax 773/238-6059
St Eugene Sch 7930 W Foster Ave, Chicago 60656 Margaret Kinel	PK-8	210 14	773/763-2235 Fax 773/763-2775
St Ferdinand Sch 3131 N Mason Ave, Chicago 60634 Erin Folino	PK-8	178 13	773/622-3022 Fax 773/622-2807
St Frances of Rome Sch 1401 S Austin Blvd, Cicero 60804 Dr Anthony Clishem	PK-8	250 11	708/652-2277 Fax 708/780-6360
St Francis Borgia Sch 3535 N Panama Ave, Chicago 60634 Susan Betzolt	PK-8	513 20	773/589-1000 Fax 773/589-0781
St Francis De Sales High Sch 10155 S Ewing Ave, Chicago 60617 Roni-Nicole Facen	9-12	285 30	773/731-7272 Fax 773/731-7888
St Francis Xavier Sch 145 N Waiola Ave, La Grange 60525 Sharon Garcia	PK-8	490 24	708/352-2175 Fax 708/352-2057
St Francis Xavier Sch 808 Linden Ave, Wilmette 60091 Colleen Barrett	PK-8	450	847/256-0644 Fax 847/256-0753
St Gabriel Sch 4500 S Wallace St, Chicago 60609 Steve Adams	PK-8	270 11	773/268-6636 Fax 773/268-2501
St Gall Sch 5515 S Sawyer Ave, Chicago 60629 Caitlin Lee	PK-8	275 10	773/737-3454 Fax 773/737-5592
St Genevieve Sch 4854 W Montana St, Chicago 60639 Amanda Parker	PK-8	290 10	773/237-7131 Fax 773/237-7265
St George Sch 6700 176th St, Tinley Park 60477 Charlotte Pratl	K-8	541 19	708/532-2626 Fax 708/532-2025
St Gerald Sch 9320 S 55th Ct, Oak Lawn 60453 Al Theis	PK-8	370 27	708/422-0121 Fax 708/422-9216
St Germaine Sch 9735 S Kolin Ave, Oak Lawn 60453 Kevin Reedy	PK-8	300 15	708/425-6063 Fax 708/425-7463
St Giles Sch 1034 Linden Ave, Oak Park 60302 Meg Bigane	PK-8	479	708/383-6279 Fax 708/383-9952
St Helen Sch 2347 W Augusta Blvd, Chicago 60622 Dana Vance	PK-8	315 12	773/486-1055
St Hilary Sch 5614 N Fairfield Ave, Chicago 60659 Kathie Donovan	PK-8	221 21	773/561-5885 Fax 773/561-6409
St Hubert Sch 255 Flagstaff Ln, Hoffman Est 60169 Kelly Bourrell	PK-8	480 27	847/885-7702 Fax 847/885-0604
St Ignatius College Prep Sch 1076 W Roosevelt Rd Ste 1, Chicago 60608 Brianna Latko	9-12	1,345 53	312/421-5900 Fax 312/421-7124
St James Sch 820 N Arlington Heights Rd, Arlington HTS 60004 Mike Kendrick	PK-8	497 25	224/345-7145 Fax 224/345-7220
St Jerome Sch 2801 S Princeton Ave, Chicago 60616 Elisabeth Dworak	PK-8	211 9	312/842-7668
St Joan of Arc Sch 9245 Lawndale Ave, Evanston 60203 Dr Marcia Tornatore	PK-8	250 14	847/679-0660 Fax 847/679-0689
St John Berchmans Sch 2511 W Logan Blvd, Chicago 60647 Margaret Roketenetz	PK-8	250 12	773/486-1334 Fax 773/486-1782
St John Brebeuf Sch 8301 N Harlem Ave, Niles 60714 Dr Mary Maloney	PK-8	300 30	847/966-3266 Fax 847/966-5351
St John De LaSalle Academy 10212 S Vernon Ave, Chicago 60628 Sally Santellano	PK-8	145 11	773/785-2331 Fax 773/785-3630
St John Fisher Sch 10200 S Washtenaw Ave, Chicago 60655 Maura Nash	PK-8	710	773/445-4737 Fax 773/233-3012
St John of the Cross Sch 708 51st St, Western Sprgs 60558 Kathleen Gorman	PK-8	684 28	708/246-4454 Fax 708/246-9010
St John the Evangelist Sch 513 Parkside Cir, Streamwood 60107 Beth Wennerstrom	PK-8	200 9	630/289-3040 Fax 630/289-3026
St John Vianney Sch 27 N Lavergne Ave, Northlake 60164 Heidi Reith	PK-8	180 11	708/562-1466 Fax 708/562-0142
St Josaphat Sch 2245 N Southport Ave, Chicago 60614 Nel Mullens	PK-8	378 18	773/549-0909 Fax 773/549-3127
St Joseph High Sch 10900 W Cermak Rd, Westchester 60154 David Hotek	9-12	400 29	708/562-4433 Fax 708/562-4459
St Joseph Sch 5641 S 73rd Ave, Summit Argo 60501 Claudia Mendez	PK-8	236 12	708/458-2927 Fax 708/458-9750
St Joseph Sch 1740 Lake Ave, Wilmette 60091 Colleen Barrett	PK-8	270 16	847/256-7870 Fax 847/256-9514
St Juliana Sch 7400 W Touhy Ave, Chicago 60631 Catherine Scotkovsky	PK-8	500 24	773/631-2256 Fax 773/631-1125
St Laurence High Sch 5556 W 77th St, Burbank 60459 James Muting	9-12 GV	650 44	708/458-6900 Fax 708/458-6908
St Leonard Sch 3322 Clarence Ave, Berwyn 60402 Scott Decaluwe	PK-8	215	708/749-3666 Fax 708/749-7981
St Linus Sch 10400 Lawler Ave, Oak Lawn 60453 Margaret Hayes	PK-8	379 18	708/425-1656 Fax 708/499-4492
St Luke Sch 519 Ashland Ave, River Forest 60305 Andrew DiMarco	PK-8	380 20	708/366-8587
St Malachy Sch 2252 W Washington Blvd, Chicago 60612 Patrick Dwyer	PK-8	250 12	312/733-2252 Fax 312/733-5703
St Margaret of Scotland Sch 9833 S Throop St, Chicago 60643 Shauntae Davis	PK-8	205 37	773/238-1088 Fax 773/238-1049

79 Student Personnel
80 Driver Ed/Safety
81 Gifted/Talented
82 Video Services
83 Substance Abuse Prev
84 Erate
85 AIDS Education
88 Alternative/At Risk
89 Multi-Cultural Curriculum
90 Social Work
91 Safety/Security
92 Magnet School
93 Parental Involvement
95 Tech Prep Program
97 Chief Information Officer
98 Chief Technology Officer
270 Character Education
271 Migrant Education
273 Teacher Mentor
274 Before/After Sch
275 Response To Intervention
277 Remedial Math K-12
280 Literacy Coach
285 STEM
286 Digital Learning
288 Common Core Standards
294 Accountability
295 Network System
296 Title II Programs
297 Webmaster
298 Grant Writer/Ptnrships
750 Chief Innovation Officer
751 Chief of Staff
752 Social Emotional Learning

Other School Types
Ⓐ = Alternative School
Ⓒ = Charter School
Ⓜ = Magnet School
Ⓨ = Year-Round School

School Programs
A = Alternative Program
G = Adult Classes
M = Magnet Program
T = Title I Schoolwide
V = Career & Tech Ed Programs

Social Media
= Facebook
= Twitter

New Schools are shaded
New Superintendents and Principals are bold
Personnel with email addresses are underscored

Cook County — Market Data Retrieval

School	Grd	Enr/#Cls	Phone/Fax
St Mary of the Angels Sch 1810 N Hermitage Ave, Chicago 60622 Beth Dolack	PK-8	256 9	773/486-0119 Fax 773/486-0996
St Mary of the Lake Sch 1026 W Buena Ave, Chicago 60613 Christine Boyd	PK-8	260 12	773/281-0018 Fax 773/281-0112
St Mary of the Woods Sch 6959 N Hiawatha Ave, Chicago 60646 Geralyn Lawler	PK-8	360 18	773/763-7577 Fax 773/763-4293
St Mary Sch 97 Herrick Rd, Riverside 60546 Nicole Nolazco	PK-8	473	708/442-5747 Fax 708/442-0125
St Mary Star of the Sea Sch 6424 S Kenneth Ave, Chicago 60629 Candice Usauskas	PK-8	571 22	773/767-6160 Fax 773/767-7077
St Matthias Elem Sch 4910 N Claremont Ave, Chicago 60625 Kathleen Carden	PK-8	299 13	773/784-0999 Fax 773/784-3601
St Michael Sch 14355 Highland Ave, Orland Park 60462 Paul Smith	PK-8	620 26	708/349-0068 Fax 708/349-2658
St Monica Academy 5115 N Mont Clare Ave, Chicago 60656 Ray Coleman	PK-8	380 13	773/631-7880 Fax 773/631-3266
St Nicholas Cathedral Sch 2200 W Rice St, Chicago 60622 Anna Cirilli	PK-8	159 10	773/384-7243
St Nicholas of Tolentine Sch 3741 W 62nd St, Chicago 60629 Dr Mari Agnes Menden	PK-8	375 10	773/735-0772 Fax 773/735-5414
St Norbert Sch 1817 Walters Ave, Northbrook 60062 Stephen Schacherer	PK-8	335 18	847/272-0051 Fax 847/272-5274
St Odilo Sch 6617 23rd St, Berwyn 60402 William Donegan	PK-8	225 18	708/484-0755 Fax 708/484-3088
St Patricia Sch 9000 S 86th Ave, Hickory Hills 60457 Jamie Nowinski	PK-8	200 16	708/598-8200 Fax 708/598-8233
St Patrick High Sch 5900 W Belmont Ave, Chicago 60634 Jon Baffico	9-12	968 41	773/282-8844 Fax 773/282-2361
St Paul of the Cross Sch 140 S Northwest Hwy, Park Ridge 60068 Dr Erika Mickelburgh	PK-8	620 40	847/825-6366 Fax 847/825-2466
St Philip Neri Sch 2110 E 72nd St, Chicago 60649 Ken Koll	PK-8	267 10	773/288-1138 Fax 773/288-8252
St Pius V Sch 1919 S Ashland Ave, Chicago 60608 Nancy Nasko	PK-8	210 10	312/226-1590 Fax 312/226-7265
St Procopius Sch 1625 S Allport St, Chicago 60608 Griselda Ferguson	PK-8	230 11	312/421-5135 Fax 312/492-7688
St Raymond Sch 300 S Elmhurst Ave, Mt Prospect 60056 Mary Eileen Ward	PK-8	500 23	847/253-8555 Fax 847/253-8939
St Richard Sch 5025 S Kenneth Ave, Chicago 60632 Michelle Napier	PK-8	330 20	773/582-8083 Fax 773/582-8330
St Rita of Cascia High Sch 7740 S Western Ave, Chicago 60620 Sante Iacovelli	9-12	850 20	773/925-6600 Fax 773/925-2451
St Robert Bellarmine Sch 6036 W Eastwood Ave, Chicago 60630 Cattie Tenzillo	PK-8	285 20	773/725-5133 Fax 773/725-7611
St Sabina Academy 7801 S Throop St, Chicago 60620 Janice Wells	PK-8	220 16	773/483-5000 Fax 773/483-0305
St Stanislaus Kostka Sch 1255 N Noble St, Chicago 60642 Michele Alday	PK-8	175 10	773/278-4560 Fax 773/278-9097
St Sylvester Sch 3027 W Palmer Blvd, Chicago 60647 Allyn Doyle	PK-8	318 12	773/772-5222 Fax 773/772-0352
St Symphorosa Sch 6125 S Austin Ave, Chicago 60638 Kathy Berry	PK-8	250 16	773/585-6888 Fax 773/585-8411
St Theresa Sch 445 N Benton St, Palatine 60067 Mary Keenley	PK-8	500 28	847/359-1820 Fax 847/705-2084
St Therese Sch 247 W 23rd St, Chicago 60616 Lisa Oi	PK-8	300 10	312/326-2837 Fax 312/326-6068
St Thomas of Canterbury Sch 4827 N Kenmore Ave, Chicago 60640 Christine Boyd	PK-8	200 10	773/271-8655 Fax 773/271-1624
St Thomas of Villanova Sch 1141 E Anderson Dr, Palatine 60074 Mary Brinkman	PK-8	170 11	847/358-2110 Fax 847/776-1435
St Thomas the Apostle Sch 5467 S Woodlawn Ave, Chicago 60615 Erin Monahan	PK-8	225 20	773/667-1142 Fax 773/891-0602
St Viator High Sch 1213 E Oakton St, Arlington HTS 60004 Karen Love	9-12	1,030	847/392-4050 Fax 847/392-4101
St Viator Sch 4140 W Addison St, Chicago 60641 Lisa Rieger	PK-8	222	773/545-2173 Fax 773/794-1697
St Vincent Ferrer Sch 1515 Lathrop Ave, River Forest 60305 Katie Cahill	PK-8	275 20	708/771-5905 Fax 708/771-7114
St Walter Sch 11741 S Western Ave, Chicago 60643 Sharon O'Toole	PK-8	217 10	773/445-8850 Fax 773/445-0277
St William Sch 2559 N Sayre Ave, Chicago 60707 Nancy Zver	PK-8	190 10	773/637-5130 Fax 773/745-4208
St Zachary Sch 567 W Algonquin Rd, Des Plaines 60016 Darlene Potenza	PK-8	174 10	847/437-4022 Fax 847/758-1064
Trinity High Sch 7574 Division St, River Forest 60305 Amy Gallie	9-12	546 45	708/771-8383 Fax 708/488-2014
Visitation Sch 900 W Garfield Blvd, Chicago 60609 Jennifer Markoff	PK-8	160 11	773/373-5200 Fax 773/373-5201

COOK PRIVATE SCHOOLS

Private Schs..Principal	Grd	Prgm	Enr/#Cls	SN
A-Karrasel Sch 5510 W Fullerton Ave, Chicago 60639 Anthony Morelli	PK-K		80 3	773/637-1220 Fax 708/452-0049
Achievement Ctrs-Acacia Acad 6425 Willow Springs Rd, La Grange 60525 Kathie Fouks	1-12	G	110 12	708/579-9040 Fax 708/579-5872
Akiba Schechter Day Sch 5235 S Cornell Ave, Chicago 60615 Miriam Kass	PK-8		250 20	773/493-8880 Fax 773/493-9377

1	Superintendent	8	Curric/Instruct K-12	19	Chief Financial Officer	29	Family/Consumer Science	39	Social Studies K-12	49	English/Lang Arts Elem	59	Special Education Elem	69	Academic Assessment
2	Bus/Finance/Purchasing	9	Curric/Instruct Elem	20	Art K-12	30	Adult Education	40	Social Studies Elem	50	English/Lang Arts Sec	60	Special Education Sec	70	Research/Development
3	Buildings And Grounds	10	Curric/Instruct Sec	21	Art Elem	31	Career/Sch-to-Work K-12	41	Social Studies Sec	51	Reading K-12	61	Foreign/World Lang K-12	71	Public Information
4	Food Service	11	Federal Program	22	Art Sec	32	Career/Sch-to-Work Elem	42	Science K-12	52	Reading Elem	62	Foreign/World Lang Elem	72	Summer School
5	Transportation	12	Title I	23	Music K-12	33	Career/Sch-to-Work Sec	43	Science Elem	53	Reading Sec	63	Foreign/World Lang Sec	73	Instructional Tech
6	Athletic	13	Title V	24	Music Elem	34	Early Childhood Ed	44	Science Sec	54	Remedial Reading K-12	64	Religious Education K-12	74	Inservice Training
7	Health Services	14	Asst Superintendent	25	Music Sec	35	Health/Phys Education	45	Math K-12	55	Remedial Reading Elem	65	Religious Education Elem	75	Marketing/Distributive
		15	Instructional Media Svcs	26	Business Education	36	Guidance Services K-12	46	Math Elem	56	Remedial Reading Sec	66	Religious Education Sec	76	Info Systems
		16	Chief Operations Officer	27	Career & Tech Ed	37	Guidance Services Elem	47	Math Sec	57	Bilingual/ELL	67	School Board President	77	Psychological Assess
		17	Chief Academic Officer	28	Technology Education	38	Guidance Services Sec	48	English/Lang Arts K-12	58	Special Education K-12	68	Teacher Personnel	78	Affirmative Action

Illinois School Directory — Cook County

School	Grades	Enroll/Staff	Phone
Albert J Shegog Christian Acad 440 Sibley Blvd, Calumet City 60409	PK-8	35	708/574-7553
Alcuin Montessori Sch 324 N Oak Park Ave, Oak Park 60302 Gina Gleason	PK-8	150 8	708/366-1882 Fax 708/386-1892
Alexander Graham Bell Mont Sch 9300 Capitol Dr, Wheeling 60090 Dr Debra Trude-Suter	PK-6	80 10	847/850-5490
Ancona Sch 4770 S Dorchester Ave, Chicago 60615 Nancy Nassr	PK-8	271 10	773/924-2356 Fax 773/924-8905
Aqsa Sch 7361 W 92nd St, Bridgeview 60455 Tammie Ismail	PK-12	250 16	708/598-2700 Fax 708/598-2731
Arie Crown Hebrew Day Sch 4600 Main St, Skokie 60076 Eli Samber	PK-8	790	847/982-9191 Fax 847/982-9525
Att-Ptach Special Ed Program 4600 Main St, Skokie 60076 Susan Feuer	Spec	25 2	847/675-1670
Bais Yaakov High Sch 5800 N Kimball Ave, Chicago 60659 Sara Neuman	9-12	171 10	773/267-1494
Baker Demonstration Sch 201 Sheridan Rd, Wilmette 60091 Carly Andrews	PK-8	218 18	847/425-5800 Fax 847/425-5801
Beacon Academy 1574 Sherman Ave, Evanston 60201 Jeff Bell	9-12	129	224/999-1177
Bennett Day School-Flagship 955 W Grand Ave, Chicago 60642 Kate Cicchelli	K-9	100	312/236-6388
Bernard Zell Anshe Emet Sch 3751 N Broadway St, Chicago 60613 Karen Leavitt	PK-8	514 32	773/281-1858 Fax 773/281-4709
Bethel Academy 35 E North Ave, Northlake 60164 Louisa Feldman	K-12	85 7	708/865-2855 Fax 708/865-2870
Bethesda Lutheran Sch 6803 N Campbell Ave, Chicago 60645 Joseph Dembowski	PK-8	63 8	773/743-0800 Fax 773/743-4415
Beverly Hills Elem Sch 9356 S Justine St, Chicago 60620 Dahne Foster	K-8	7 2	773/779-5158
Brentwood Bapt Christian Acad 588 Dara James Rd, Des Plaines 60016 Daryl York	K-12	19 12	847/298-3399 Fax 847/298-3408
Brickton Montessori Sch 8622 W Catalpa Ave, Chicago 60656 Cheryl Lacost	PK-8	133 11	773/714-0646 Fax 773/714-9361
Bridge View Extended Day Sch 6935 W Touhy Ave, Niles 60714 Christopher Raspante	Spec	52	847/588-2038 Fax 847/588-2084
British Int'l Chicago-S Loop 161 W 9th St, Chicago 60605 Michael Henderson	PK-12	550	773/998-2472
British School of Chicago 814 W Eastman St, Chicago 60642 Ed Pearce	PK-12	800 20	773/506-2097 Fax 773/506-4805
Calvary Academy 16300 State St, South Holland 60473 Mathew James	K-8	315 18	708/333-5471 Fax 708/333-5771
Calvin Christian Sch 528 E 161st Pl, South Holland 60473 Randy Moes	PK-8	230 12	708/331-5027 Fax 708/331-8728
Cambridge Sch 1014 E 47th St, Chicago 60653 Derek Barber	PK-8	110	773/924-1200
Camelot Theraputic Day Sch 580 Slawin Ct, Mt Prospect 60056 Karen Fletcher	Spec	71 7	224/612-8338 Fax 224/612-8321
Catherine Cook Sch 226 W Schiller St, Chicago 60610 Sunni Kitson \ Cory Stutts	PK-8	500	312/266-3381 Fax 312/266-3616
Centerview Therapeutic Sch 3444 Dundee Rd, Northbrook 60062 April Hutchens	Spec G	18 4	847/559-0110 Fax 847/559-8199
Challenger Day Sch 6935 W Touhy Ave, Niles 60714 Christopher Raspante	Spec	52	847/588-2038 Fax 847/588-2084
Chedar Lubavitch Girls Sch 2809 W Jarvis Ave, Chicago 60645 Leah Pearlstein	K-8	125 8	773/465-0863
Chiaravalle Montessori Sch 425 Dempster St, Evanston 60201 Robyn Springer	PK-8	400 20	847/864-2190 Fax 847/864-2206
Chicago Academy for the Arts 1010 W Chicago Ave, Chicago 60642 Jason Patera	9-12	142 30	312/421-0202 Fax 312/421-3816
Chicago Christian High Sch 12001 S Oak Park Ave, Palos Heights 60463 Mike Drury	9-12 V	320 24	708/388-7650 Fax 708/388-0154
Chicago City Day Sch 541 W Hawthorne Pl, Chicago 60657 Galeta Clayton	PK-8	250 10	773/327-0900 Fax 773/327-6381
Chicago Futabakai Japan Sch 2550 N Arlington Heights Rd, Arlington HTS 60004 Iowa Cuada	PK-9	60 25	847/590-5700 Fax 847/590-9759
Chicago Grammar Sch 900 N Franklin St Ste 102, Chicago 60610 Phillip Jackson	PK-8	90	312/944-5600
Chicago Hope Academy 2189 W Bowler St, Chicago 60612 Ike Muzikowski	9-12	238	312/491-1600 Fax 312/491-1616
Chicago Jesuit Academy 5058 W Jackson Blvd, Chicago 60644 Thomas Beckley	5-8	93 6	773/638-6103 Fax 773/638-6107
Chicago Jewish Day Sch 3730 N California Ave, Chicago 60618 Judy Taff	PK-8	196 8	773/271-2700 Fax 773/271-2570
Chicago Lighthouse Dev Center 1850 W Roosevelt Rd, Chicago 60608 Lee Burklund	Spec	18 4	312/666-1331 Fax 312/243-8539
Chicago SDA Elementary 7008 S Michigan Ave, Chicago 60637 Terrilyn Jemison	PK-8	38 8	773/873-3005 Fax 773/873-6953
Chicago Waldorf Sch 5200 N Ashland Ave, Chicago 60640 Luke Goodwin	PK-12	348	773/465-2662 Fax 773/465-6648
Childbridge Ctr for Education 1760 W Algonquin Rd, Palatine 60067 Karoline Dean	Spec	25	847/221-7752
Christ the King Jesuit Prep 5088 W Jackson Blvd, Chicago 60644 Temple Payne	9-12	365	773/261-7505 Fax 773/261-7507
Christ the King Luth Sch 3701 S Lake Park Ave, Chicago 60653 Geraldine Brazeal	PK-8	30 4	773/536-1984
Christian Heritage Academy 315 Waukegan Rd, Northfield 60093 Joan Okamoto	PK-12	450 22	847/446-5252 Fax 847/446-5267

Code	Category	Code	Category	Code	Category
79	Student Personnel	91	Safety/Security	275	Response To Intervention
80	Driver Ed/Safety	92	Magnet School	277	Remedial Math K-12
81	Gifted/Talented	93	Parental Involvement	280	Literacy Coach
82	Video Services	95	Tech Prep Program	285	STEM
83	Substance Abuse Prev	97	Chief Information Officer	286	Digital Learning
84	Erate	98	Chief Technology Officer	288	Common Core Standards
85	AIDS Education	270	Character Education	294	Accountability
88	Alternative/At Risk	271	Migrant Education	295	Network System
89	Multi-Cultural Curriculum	273	Teacher Mentor	296	Title II Programs
90	Social Work	274	Before/After Sch	297	Webmaster
298	Grant Writer/Ptnrships				
750	Chief Innovation Officer				
751	Chief of Staff				
752	Social Emotional Learning				

School Programs
A = Alternative Program
G = Adult Classes
M = Magnet Program
T = Title I Schoolwide
V = Career & Tech Ed Programs

Other School Types
Ⓐ = Alternative School
Ⓒ = Charter School
Ⓜ = Magnet School
Ⓨ = Year-Round School

Social Media
= Facebook
= Twitter

New Schools are shaded
New Superintendents and Principals are bold
Personnel with email addresses are underscored

IL—77

Cook County — Market Data Retrieval

School	Level		Enroll	Phone
Christian Hill Church Sch 9001 159th St, Tinley Park 60487 Gayle Bergstrand	PK-8		170 20	708/349-7166 Fax 708/349-9665
Christian Liberty Academy 502 W Euclid Ave, Arlington HTS 60004 Thad Bennett	PK-12		603 30	847/259-4444 Fax 847/259-9972
Community Christian Academy 3400 W 111th St 304, Chicago 60655 Nahid Zahedi	PK-8		60	773/289-0796
Cornerstone Academy 1111 N Wells St Ste 403, Chicago 60610 Jim Wilkes	9-12		30 3	312/573-8854 Fax 312/573-8850
Cornerstone Christian Sch 2926 Commercial Ave, Chicago HTS 60412 Alison Donald	PK-8		150 23	708/756-3566 Fax 708/756-3678
Council Oak Montessori Sch 2521 Grove St, Blue Island 60406 Lila Jokanovic	PK-8		60 3	708/926-9720
Country Club Hills Tech&Trade 4187 183rd St, Cntry CLB Hls 60478 Shawanda Barga	Spec	V	150	708/798-9542 Fax 708/798-9756
Countryside Montessori Sch 1985 Pfingsten Rd, Northbrook 60062 Wendy Calise	PK-8		180 6	847/498-1105
Cove Sch 350 Lee Rd, Northbrook 60062 Regina Aniolowski \ Alexander Laube	Spec		142	847/562-2100 Fax 847/562-2112
Cristo Rey Jesuit High Sch 1852 W 22nd Pl, Chicago 60608 Lucas Schroeder	9-12		550 21	773/890-6800 Fax 773/890-6801
CS Academy Campus I 6014 S Racine Ave, Chicago 60636 Teresa Diegler-Mosley	PK-8		56	773/778-0818
CS Academy Campus II 1443 W 63rd St, Chicago 60636 Teresa Diegler-Mosley	PK-8		15	312/675-8691
DayStar Sch 1550 S State St Ste 100, Chicago 60605 Tami Doig	PK-9		350 9	312/791-0001 Fax 312/791-0002
Deer Creek Christian Sch 330 W Highland Dr, Chicago HTS 60411 Dr Monica Cole-Jackson	PK-8		125 18	708/672-6200 Fax 708/672-6226
Eagle Academy Christian Sch 2750 Glenwood Lansing Rd, Lansing 60438 Medina Bailey	PK-7		110	708/418-3000
Easterseals Academy-Chicago 1939 W 13th St, Chicago 60608 Rose Decanniore	Spec		60	312/491-4110
Easterseals Academy-Tinley PK 17300 Ozark Ave, Tinley Park 60477 Maryellen Bucci	Spec		60	708/802-9050 Fax 708/802-9898
Elim Christian Sch 13020 S Central Ave, Crestwood 60418 Mike Otte	Spec	G	275 34	708/389-0555 Fax 708/389-0671
Embers Elem Sch 8340 N Greenwood Ave, Niles 60714 Lisa Hanretty	PK-5		149	847/518-1185 Fax 847/518-9625
Esperanza Sch 520 N Marshfield Ave, Chicago 60622 Anne Hellmer	Spec	G	250 6	312/243-6097 Fax 312/243-2076
Everest Academy 11550 Bell Rd, Lemont 60439 Mary DeRoche	PK-8		210	630/243-1995 Fax 630/243-1988
Frances X Warde Sch-Holy Name 751 N State St, Chicago 60654 Michael Kennedy	4-8		435 27	312/466-0700 Fax 312/337-7180
Frances X Warde Sch-St Patrick 120 S Desplaines St, Chicago 60661 Erin Horne	PK-3		500	312/466-0700 Fax 312/466-0711
Francis W Parker Sch 330 W Webster Ave, Chicago 60614 Dr Daniel Frank	PK-12		940	773/353-3000
Fusion Academy-Evanston 847 Chicago Ave Ste 200, Evanston 60202 Chrissy Dale	6-12		50	847/868-8693
Fusion Academy-Lincoln Park 1440 N Dayton St Ste 104, Chicago 60642 Natalia Bondy	6-12		50	312/763-6990
Gateway to Learning Sch 4925 N Lincoln Ave, Chicago 60625 Ms LaVin	Spec	G	100 5	773/784-3200 Fax 773/784-7229
Gems World Academy 350 E South Water St, Chicago 60601 Cindy Rigling \ Tracey Wood	PK-12		130	312/809-8941
German Int'l School Chicago 1726 W Berteau Ave, Chicago 60613 Petra Obritzberger	PK-8		150	773/880-8812
Glenview New Church Sch 74 Park Dr, Glenview 60025 Philip Parker	PK-8		60 4	847/724-0057 Fax 847/724-3042
Glenwood Academy 500 W 187th St, Glenwood 60425 Anne Budicin	2-8		150 20	708/754-0175 Fax 708/754-7834
Glenwood Sch 500 W 187th St, Glenwood 60425 Anne Budicin	4-8		72 7	847/464-8200 Fax 847/464-8201
Global Citizenship Exp Sch 1535 N Dayton St, Chicago 60642 Cabell King	9-12		100	312/643-0991 Fax 312/643-0975
Good Shepherd Center 17314 Kedzie Ave, Hazel Crest 60429 Brendan McCormick	Spec		60 6	708/957-2600 Fax 708/957-5739
Good Shepherd Christian Acad 3740 W Belden Ave, Chicago 60647 Jo Ellen Hoffmann	PK-8		30 6	773/342-5854 Fax 773/342-6048
Grace Christian Academy 4106 W 28th St, Chicago 60623 Carlo Giannotta	PK-8		78 6	773/762-1234 Fax 773/762-4476
Grace Lutheran Sch 7300 Division St, River Forest 60305 Bill Koehne	PK-8		205 12	708/366-6901 Fax 708/366-0966
Grace Lutheran Sch 2725 N Laramie Ave, Chicago 60639 Douglas Markworth	PK-8		25 4	773/637-2250 Fax 773/637-1188
Guardian Angel Orthodox Sch 2350 E Dempster St, Des Plaines 60016 Irene Robaidek	PK-6		180	847/827-5510 Fax 847/824-3455
Hadi School of Excellence 375 S Roselle Rd Frnt 1, Schaumburg 60193 Azra Naqvi	PK-5		175	847/891-4440 Fax 847/805-4445
Hanna Sacks Bais Yaakov HS 3021 W Devon Ave, Chicago 60659 Tobie Teller	9-12		126 15	773/338-9222 Fax 773/338-2405
Hartgrove Academy 5730 W Roosevelt Rd, Chicago 60644 Tom Pusateri	Spec		100	773/413-1700 Fax 773/413-1875
Hillel Torah N Sub Day Sch 7120 Laramie Ave, Skokie 60077 Menachem Linzer	PK-8		430 36	847/674-6533 Fax 847/674-8313
Holy Family Lutheran Sch 3415 W Arthington St, Chicago 60624 Dr Candice Smith	PK-8		288 9	773/265-0550 Fax 773/265-0508

#	Title	#	Title	#	Title	#	Title	#	Title	#	Title	#	Title
1	Superintendent	8	Curric/Instruct K-12	19	Chief Financial Officer	29	Family/Consumer Science	39	Social Studies K-12	49	English/Lang Arts Elem	59	Special Education Elem	69	Academic Assessment
2	Bus/Finance/Purchasing	9	Curric/Instruct Elem	20	Art K-12	30	Adult Education	40	Social Studies Elem	50	English/Lang Arts Sec	60	Special Education Sec	70	Research/Development
3	Buildings And Grounds	10	Curric/Instruct Sec	21	Art Elem	31	Career/Sch-to-Work K-12	41	Social Studies Sec	51	Reading K-12	61	Foreign/World Lang K-12	71	Public Information
4	Food Service	11	Federal Program	22	Art Sec	32	Career/Sch-to-Work Elem	42	Science K-12	52	Reading Elem	62	Foreign/World Lang Elem	72	Summer School
5	Transportation	12	Title I	23	Music K-12	33	Career/Sch-to-Work Sec	43	Science Elem	53	Reading Sec	63	Foreign/World Lang Sec	73	Instructional Tech
6	Athletic	13	Title V	24	Music Elem	34	Early Childhood Ed	44	Science Sec	54	Remedial Reading K-12	64	Religious Education K-12	74	Inservice Training
7	Health Services	14	Asst Superintendent	25	Music Sec	35	Health/Phys Education	45	Math K-12	55	Remedial Reading Elem	65	Religious Education Elem	75	Marketing/Distributive
		15	Instructional Media Svcs	26	Business Education	36	Guidance Services K-12	46	Math Elem	56	Remedial Reading Sec	66	Religious Education Sec	76	Info Systems
		16	Chief Operations Officer	27	Career & Tech Ed	37	Guidance Services Elem	47	Math Sec	57	Bilingual/ELL	67	School Board President	77	Psychological Assess
		17	Chief Academic Officer	28	Technology Education	38	Guidance Services Sec	48	English/Lang Arts K-12	58	Special Education K-12	68	Teacher Personnel	78	Affirmative Action

Illinois School Directory — Cook County

School	Grades		Enrollment	Phone
Hyde Park Day Sch 6254 S Ellis Ave, Chicago 60637 Evan Hammontree	Spec		61 4	773/834-5080 Fax 773/834-5079
Hyde Park Day Sch 1980 Old Willow Rd, Northfield 60093 Melanie Mitra	Spec		65	847/446-4152 Fax 847/446-7026 [f]
Icc Elem Sch 3333 W Peterson Ave, Chicago 60659 Ather Sultana	PK-8		115	773/267-6167
Icci Academy 6435 W Belmont Ave, Chicago 60634 Sawsan Alsawi	PK-8		95	773/637-3755 Fax 773/836-2961
Ida Crown Jewish Academy 8233 Central Park Ave, Skokie 60076 Leonard Matanky	9-12		300 25	773/973-1450 Fax 773/973-6131
Immanuel Christian Academy 2329 S Wolf Rd, Hillside 60162 Valerie Winston	PK-8		65 6	708/562-5580 Fax 708/562-6085
Immanuel Lutheran Sch 200 N Plum Grove Rd, Palatine 60067 Dr Joy Mullaney	PK-8		270 15	847/359-1936 Fax 847/359-1583 [f][t]
Irving A Hokin Keshet High Sch 8111 Saint Louis Ave, Skokie 60076 Abbie Weisberg	Spec		500	773/508-5778
Jeanine Schultz Mem Sch 2101 Oakton St, Park Ridge 60068 Jody Rubin	Spec		65 3	847/696-3315 Fax 847/696-3330
Jerusalem Ev Luth Sch 6218 Capulina Ave, Morton Grove 60053 Duane Vance	K-8		80 6	847/965-4750
Jfh Educational Academy 1001 Oak Ave, Prospect HTS 60070 Marianne Thein	K-6		50	847/541-5577 [f][t]
Jfh Educational Academy West 1001 Oak Ave, Prospect HTS 60070 Amber Grafman	K-6		100	847/541-5577 Fax 847/541-3834 [f][t]
Joan Dachs Bais Yaakov ES 3200 W Peterson Ave, Chicago 60659 Rana Wechesler	PK-8		429 22	773/583-5329 Fax 773/583-6530
Joseph Academy-Des Plaines 1101 Gregory St, Des Plaines 60016 Bob Malek	Spec	V	55 6	847/803-1930 Fax 847/803-8669
Joseph Academy-Melrose Park 1100 N 22nd Ave, Melrose Park 60160 Diane Schorr	Spec		46	708/345-4500 Fax 708/345-4516
Keystone Montessori Sch 7415 North Ave, River Forest 60305 Victoria Shea	PK-8		150 13	708/366-1080 Fax 708/366-1083
Knapp School and Yeshiva 3145 W Pratt Blvd, Chicago 60645 Sandra Spicher	Spec		150 12	773/467-3900 Fax 773/467-3999
Koraes Sch 11025 S Roberts Rd 45, Palos Hills 60465 Beth Lind	PK-8		179 10	708/974-3402 Fax 708/974-0179
Lake Shore Schools 6759 N Greenview Ave, Chicago 60626 Farah Essa	PK-K		346 19	773/561-6707 Fax 773/271-4564
Lakeview Learning Center 3310 N Clark St, Chicago 60657 Armondo Mata	Adult		2,000 15	773/907-4400 Fax 773/907-4413
Lansing Christian Sch 3660 Randolph St, Lansing 60438 John Postma	PK-8		230 17	708/474-1700 Fax 708/474-1746
Latin School of Chicago 59 W North Blvd, Chicago 60610 Randall Dunn	PK-12	G	1,150	312/582-6000 Fax 312/582-6061
Lawrence Hall Youth Services 4833 N Francisco Ave, Chicago 60625 Victoria Hicks	Adult	V	69 8	773/769-3500 Fax 773/769-0106
Learning House 5110 Capitol Dr, Wheeling 60090 Mark Fisher	7-12		40	847/459-8330
Logos Christian Academy 7280 N Caldwell Ave, Niles 60714 Larry Murg	K-12		250	847/647-9456 Fax 847/892-0491
Lubavitch Girls HS of Chicago 6350 N Whipple St, Chicago 60659 Esther Moscowitz	9-12	G	90 5	773/743-7716 Fax 773/743-7735
Lycee Francais De Chicago 1929 W Wilson Ave, Chicago 60640 Severine Fougerol	PK-12		450	773/665-0066 Fax 773/665-1725
Maryville Jen Sch 1150 N River Rd, Des Plaines 60016 Anne Craig	Spec		53	847/390-3020 Fax 847/294-1738
Masters Academy 6620 S King Dr, Chicago 60637 Delilah Brooks	PK-8		50	773/643-6620 Fax 773/326-4202
Mcc Acad-Morton Grove Campus 8601 Menard Ave, Morton Grove 60053 Habeeb Quadri	PK-8		600 10	847/470-8801 Fax 847/470-8873 [f]
Mcc Academy-Skokie Campus 9301 Gross Point Rd, Skokie 60076 Habeeb Quadri	K-5		401	224/534-7638 Fax 847/423-2182
Meca Christian Elem Sch 425 Bohland Ave, Bellwood 60104 Glennetta Crowder	PK-8		150	708/547-9980 Fax 708/547-8715
Menta Academy Chicago West 3049 W Harrison St, Chicago 60612 Adrienne Porter	Spec		95	773/533-9605 Fax 773/638-6235
Menta Academy Hillside 4100 Warren Ave Ste G, Hillside 60162 Cheryl Frederickson	Spec		190	630/449-1310 Fax 708/449-0474
Metropolitan Preparatory Sch 2525 E Oakton St, Arlington HTS 60005 Kate Dunlap	K-12		69	847/956-7912 Fax 847/956-7930
Midwestern Christian Academy 3465 N Cicero Ave, Chicago 60641 Ralph Saunders	PK-8		200 10	773/685-1106 Fax 773/685-6541
Misericordia Heart of Mercy 6300 N Ridge Ave, Chicago 60660 Deborah Hays	Spec	V	7 8	773/973-6300 Fax 773/973-4292
Montessori Foundations Chicago 2239 W 35th St, Chicago 60609 Beata Skorusa	PK-4		401	773/254-5437
Montessori School of Lemont 16427 135th St, Lemont 60439 Therese Colby	PK-8		150	815/834-0607
Morgan Park Academy 2153 W 111th St, Chicago 60643 Heather Kurut \ Thomas Drahozal	PK-12		450 40	773/881-6700 Fax 773/326-0630 [f][t]
Muhammad Univ of Islam 7351 S Stony Island Ave, Chicago 60649 Jason Karriem	K-12		172	773/643-0700 Fax 773/643-0384
Nautilus Sch 1917 W 93rd St, Chicago 60643 Milissa McClaire-Gary	PK-3		15	773/462-4223
Near North Montessori Sch 1434 W Division St, Chicago 60642 Audrey Perrott	PK-8		585 20	773/384-1434 Fax 773/384-2711
New Covenent Christian Academy 15213 5th Ave, Phoenix 60426 Richard McCreary	PK-8		47 13	708/331-3661 Fax 708/331-2459

---

79 Student Personnel
80 Driver Ed/Safety
81 Gifted/Talented
82 Video Services
83 Substance Abuse Prev
84 Erate
85 AIDS Education
88 Alternative/At Risk
89 Multi-Cultural Curriculum
90 Social Work

91 Safety/Security
92 Magnet School
93 Parental Involvement
95 Tech Prep Program
97 Chief Information Officer
98 Chief Technology Officer
270 Character Education
271 Migrant Education
273 Teacher Mentor
274 Before/After Sch

275 Response To Intervention
277 Remedial Math K-12
280 Literacy Coach
285 STEM
286 Digital Learning
288 Common Core Standards
294 Accountability
295 Network System
296 Title II Programs
297 Webmaster

298 Grant Writer/Ptnrships
750 Chief Innovation Officer
751 Chief of Staff
752 Social Emotional Learning

Other School Types
Ⓐ = Alternative School
Ⓒ = Charter School
Ⓜ = Magnet School
Ⓨ = Year-Round School

School Programs
A = Alternative Program
G = Adult Classes
M = Magnet Program
T = Title I Schoolwide
V = Career & Tech Ed Programs

Social Media
[f] = Facebook
[t] = Twitter

New Schools are shaded
New Superintendents and Principals are bold
Personnel with email addresses are underscored

Cook County — Market Data Retrieval

School	Grades		Enroll	Phone
New Hope Academy 3250 N Arlington Heights Rd, Arlington HTS 60004 Rebecca McClaney	Spec		80 4	847/588-0463 Fax 847/588-0464
New Horizon Center 6737 W Forest Preserve Ave, Chicago 60634 Edward O'Neill	Spec	G	60	773/286-6226 Fax 773/286-7674
New Life Celebration Chrn Acad 14243 Dante Ave, Dolton 60419 Michael Reynolds	PK-8		50	708/849-3635
New Life Christian Sch 5133 W Fullerton Ave, Chicago 60639 Erma Quintana	PK-12		28 6	773/637-7442 Fax 773/637-7629
North Ctr-Handicap Children 5104 W Belmont Ave, Chicago 60641 Lucia Alexandru	Spec	G	24 4	773/777-4111 Fax 773/777-6390
North Park Elem Sch 2017 W Montrose Ave, Chicago 60618 Dr Randy Needlman	PK-8		230 9	773/327-3144 Fax 773/327-0331
North Shore Adventist Academy 5220 N California Ave, Chicago 60625 Walter Turner	K-8		70 7	773/769-0733 Fax 773/769-0928
North Shore Country Day Sch 310 Green Bay Rd, Winnetka 60093 Tom Flemma	PK-12		540	847/446-0674 Fax 847/446-0675
Northridge Prep Sch 8320 W Ballard Rd, Niles 60714 Niall Fagan \ Joseph Rhee \ Peter Fletcher	6-12		300 19	847/375-0600 Fax 847/375-0606
Northwest Institute 5108 W Division St, Chicago 60651 Shirley Allison	PK-8		75 8	773/921-2800 Fax 773/854-2304
Oakdale Christian Academy 9440 S Vincennes Ave, Chicago 60620 Dr Wytress Richardson	PK-8		200	773/779-9440 Fax 773/779-9531
Ombudsman School-Crestwood 14162 Cicero Ave, Crestwood 60418 Denise Mulcurnt	6-12		32 1	708/489-2215 Fax 708/239-0137
Our Lady Immaculate Academy 410 Washington Blvd, Oak Park 60302 Charles Ward	K-8		20	708/524-2408 Fax 708/524-0753
Pactt Learning Center 7101 N Greenview Ave, Chicago 60626 Paula Jablonski	Spec		20 4	773/338-9102 Fax 773/338-9103
Parkview Baptist Academy 70 Golfview Dr, Northlake 60164 Todd Morrissey	K-12		58 8	708/562-2351 Fax 708/562-3041
Peckwas Preparatory Academy 5714 S Harlem Ave, Summit Argo 60501 Kim Stazelczyk	PK-8		65 6	708/594-6857
Pilgrim Lutheran Sch 4300 N Winchester Ave, Chicago 60613 Chris Comella	PK-8		168 7	773/477-4824 Fax 773/477-8996
Prairie Lake Sch 404 E Devon Ave, Elk Grove Vlg 60007 Amanda Lishamer	3-12		30	847/593-4120 Fax 847/593-4863
Promise Christian Academy 13560 S Indiana Ave, Riverdale 60827 Margaret White	PK-8		140 7	708/201-9088 Fax 708/799-8895
Providence St Mel Sch 119 S Central Park Blvd, Chicago 60624 Jeanette Butala	PK-12		400	773/722-4600 Fax 773/722-9004
Pui Tak Christian Sch 2301 S Wentworth Ave, Chicago 60616 Bonnie Ho	PK-8		150	312/842-8546
Quest Academy 500 N Benton St, Palatine 60067 Jacquelyn Negus	PK-8		250 17	847/202-8035 Fax 847/202-8085
Rabbi Oscar Fasman Yeshiva HS 7135 Carpenter Rd, Skokie 60077 Dovid Kupchick	9-12	G	150	847/982-2500 Fax 847/674-6381
Ravenswood Bapt Christian Sch 4437 N Seeley Ave, Chicago 60625 Dustin Moore	PK-12		75 12	773/561-6576 Fax 773/561-3080
Ridge Academy 2501 W 103rd St, Chicago 60655 Kenneth Koll	1-8		37 4	773/233-0033 Fax 773/233-0037
Rogers Park Montessori Sch 1800 W Balmoral Ave, Chicago 60640 Debra Langford	PK-8		350 16	773/271-1700 Fax 773/271-0771
Roycemore Sch 1200 Davis St, Evanston 60201 Darcy Aksamitowski \ Adrienne Floro \ Stefanie Rivera	PK-12		300	847/866-6055 Fax 847/866-6545
Rush Day Sch 2150 W Harrison St, Chicago 60612 Jean Heideman	Spec		31 4	312/942-6627
Ryan Banks Academy 6620 S Martin Luther King Dr, Chicago 60637 Audrey Bland-Hampston	7-7		40	312/585-5883
Sacred Heart Sch 6250 N Sheridan Rd, Chicago 60660 Mary Ann Ligon \ Dan Gargano	K-8		670 32	773/262-4446 Fax 773/262-6178
Sager Solomon Schechter Sch 3210 Dundee Rd, Northbrook 60062 Dr Lena Kushnir	K-8		326	847/498-2100 Fax 847/498-5837
Salem Christian Sch 2018 N Richmond St, Chicago 60647 Hector Quintana	PK-8		171 10	773/227-5580 Fax 773/227-8592
San Miguel Sch-Back Yard 1954 W 48th St, Chicago 60609 Br Mark Snodgrass	6-8	G	90 3	773/890-1481
Sanders Academy of Excellence 11515 S Prairie Ave, Chicago 60628 Tonisia Reid	PK-8		30	773/568-7240
Sanders Academy-Excellence 11515 S Prairie Ave, Chicago 60628 Tonisia Reid	K-8		40	773/568-7240 Fax 773/568-7290
Schaumburg Christian Sch 200 N Roselle Rd, Schaumburg 60194 Jim Toth \ Jay Cummins \ Mark McVey	PK-12		1,100 42	847/885-3230 Fax 847/885-3354
Science & Arts Academy 1825 Miner St, Des Plaines 60016 Timothy Costello	PK-8		240 40	847/827-7880 Fax 847/827-7716
Science Academy of Chicago 501 Midway Dr Ste 101, Mt Prospect 60056 Brianna Bartucci	PK-8		70	847/258-5254 Fax 847/378-8242
Scuola Italiana Enrico Fermi 1510 N Claremont Ave, Chicago 60622 Anna Maria Fantuzzi	PK-K		401	312/971-8064
Sol Sch 4014 W Chicago Ave, Chicago 60651 Kathy Englesman	Spec		40 4	773/252-3320 Fax 773/252-3323
Solace Academy 721 N La Salle Dr, Chicago 60654 Rick Erdman	9-12		40 6	312/655-7000 Fax 773/476-4272
Sonia Shankman Orthogenic Sch 6245 S Ingleside Ave, Chicago 60637 Jerry Martin	Spec		70 7	773/420-2900 Fax 773/420-2805
South Central Cmty Service 7550 S Phillips Ave, Chicago 60649 Geneva Reynolds	Spec		15 7	773/374-2223 Fax 773/374-8590
South Suburban SDA Chrn Sch 119 Chestnut St, Park Forest 60466 Alexandria Miller	PK-8		24 10	708/481-8909 Fax 708/481-0918

#	Title	#	Title	#	Title	#	Title	#	Title	#	Title	#	Title
1	Superintendent	8	Curric/Instruct K-12	19	Chief Financial Officer	29	Family/Consumer Science	39	Social Studies K-12	49	English/Lang Arts Elem	59	Special Education Elem	69	Academic Assessment
2	Bus/Finance/Purchasing	9	Curric/Instruct Elem	20	Art K-12	30	Adult Education	40	Social Studies Elem	50	English/Lang Arts Sec	60	Special Education Sec	70	Research/Development
3	Buildings And Grounds	10	Curric/Instruct Sec	21	Art Elem	31	Career/Sch-to-Work K-12	41	Social Studies Sec	51	Reading K-12	61	Foreign/World Lang K-12	71	Public Information
4	Food Service	11	Federal Program	22	Art Sec	32	Career/Sch-to-Work Elem	42	Science K-12	52	Reading Elem	62	Foreign/World Lang Elem	72	Summer School
5	Transportation	12	Title I	23	Music K-12	33	Career/Sch-to-Work Sec	43	Science Elem	53	Reading Sec	63	Foreign/World Lang Sec	73	Instructional Tech
6	Athletic	13	Title V	24	Music Elem	34	Early Childhood Ed	44	Science Sec	54	Remedial Reading K-12	64	Religious Education K-12	74	Inservice Training
7	Health Services	15	Asst Superintendent	25	Music Sec	35	Health/Phys Education	45	Math K-12	55	Remedial Reading Elem	65	Religious Education Elem	75	Marketing/Distributive
		16	Instructional Media Svcs	26	Business Education	36	Guidance Services K-12	46	Math Elem	56	Remedial Reading Sec	66	Religious Education Sec	76	Info Systems
		17	Chief Operations Officer	27	Career & Tech Ed	37	Guidance Services Elem	47	Math Sec	57	Bilingual/ELL	67	School Board President	77	Psychological Assess
		18	Chief Academic Officer	28	Technology Education	38	Guidance Services Sec	48	English/Lang Arts K-12	58	Special Education K-12	68	Teacher Personnel	78	Affirmative Action

Illinois School Directory — Cook County

School	Grades		Enrollment / Staff	Phone / Fax
Southwest Chicago Chrn Sch 17171 84th Ave, Tinley Park 60477 Phil Sierner	PK-8		300 18	708/429-7171 Fax 708/429-7210
Southwest Chicago Chrn Sch 5665 W 100 First St, Oak Lawn 60453 Nate Pettinga	PK-8		225 11	708/636-8550 Fax 708/636-0175
St Andrew's Lutheran Sch 260 N Northwest Hwy, Park Ridge 60068 Laura Boggs	PK-8		195 11	847/823-9308 Fax 847/823-1196
St Coletta of Illinois 18350 Crossing Dr, Tinley Park 60487 Cynthia James	Spec		36	708/342-5200 Fax 708/429-3467
St James Lutheran Sch 2101 N Fremont St, Chicago 60614 Sheri Meyer	PK-8		210 11	773/525-4990 Fax 773/326-3645 f t
St John Lutheran Sch 4231 183rd St, Cntry CLB Hls 60478 Matthew Kamien	PK-8		170 9	708/799-7491 Fax 708/798-4193 f
St John Lutheran Sch 18100 Wentworth Ave, Lansing 60438 Allison Clous	PK-8		100 12	708/895-9280 Fax 708/895-9303 f t
St John's Lutheran Sch 505 S Park Rd, La Grange 60525 Terri Mannes	PK-8		150 11	708/354-1690 Fax 708/354-4910
St John's Lutheran Sch 4939 W Montrose Ave, Chicago 60641 Dan Green	PK-8		175 13	773/736-1196 Fax 773/736-3614
St Luke Academy 1500 W Belmont Ave, Chicago 60657 Donna Beck	PK-8		60 9	773/472-3837 Fax 773/929-3910
St Paul Early Childhood Ctr 5650 N Canfield Ave, Chicago 60631 Jenna Scifo	PK-2		25	708/867-5044 Fax 708/867-0083
St Paul Evanglical Luth Sch 7621 S Dorchester Ave, Chicago 60619 Dr Robin Dubose	PK-8		65 5	773/721-1438
St Paul Lutheran Sch 846 N Menard Ave, Chicago 60651 Mark Bersie	K-8		60 5	773/378-6644 Fax 773/378-7442
St Paul Lutheran Sch 18 S School St, Mt Prospect 60056 Julia Heinz	PK-8		255 16	847/255-6733 Fax 847/255-6834
St Paul Lutheran Sch 9035 Grant Ave, Brookfield 60513 Ben Fluga	K-8		26 5	708/485-0650
St Peter Lutheran Sch 111 W Olive St, Arlington HTS 60004 Jonathan Heinemann	PK-8		502 16	847/253-6638 Fax 847/259-4185
St Peter Lutheran Sch 208 E Schaumburg Rd, Schaumburg 60194 Steve Zielke	PK-8		275 15	847/885-7636 Fax 847/882-9157 f t
St Philip Lutheran Sch 2500 W Bryn Mawr Ave, Chicago 60659 Donna Tennis	PK-8		40 14	773/561-9830 Fax 773/561-9831
St Sava Academy 5701 N Redwood Dr, Chicago 60631 Protinica Jannakos	PK-8		100	773/714-0299 Fax 773/693-7615
Stuart G Ferst Sch 6050 N California Ave, Chicago 60659 Mo Buty	Spec		20	773/761-4651 Fax 773/761-0669
Tabernacle Christian Academy 1233 W 109th Pl, Chicago 60643 Muriel Williams	PK-8		110 8	773/445-3007 Fax 773/881-1255 f
Telshe Yeshiva Boys Sch 3535 W Foster Ave, Chicago 60625 Aaron Cohen	9-12		100 8	773/463-7738 Fax 773/463-2849
The Children's Sch 200 S Oak Park Ave, Oak Park 60302 Christina Martin	K-8		150	708/484-8033
The Field Sch 931 Lake St, Oak Park 60301 Jeremy Mann	PK-3		117	708/434-5811
Thresholds Young Adult Program 4219 N Lincoln Ave, Chicago 60618 Thomas Moore	Adult	V	15 4	773/537-3280 Fax 773/472-2696
Trinity Lutheran Sch 6850 159th St Ste 1, Tinley Park 60477 Gerald Gliege	PK-8	G	260 13	708/532-3529 Fax 708/532-0799 f t
Trusting Hearts Pre-Sch & Kdgn 12424 S 71st Ct, Palos Heights 60463 Kiara Potempa	PK-K		37 2	708/448-2260
Ucan Academy 3605 W Fillmore St, Chicago 60624 Cheralyn Thomas	Spec		100 16	773/588-0180 Fax 773/826-3620
United Ed Cultural Acad 1236 W 103rd St 42, Chicago 60643 Dr Barbara Standberry	PK-8		100	773/238-2707 Fax 773/238-4259
Unity Christian Academy 16341 S Park Ave Ste A, South Holland 60473 Loukisha Smart-Pennix	9-9		21	708/980-1040 Fax 708/980-0980
Univ of Chicago Lab Sch 1362 E 59th St, Chicago 60637 Daniel Ryan \ Ryan Allen \ Sylvie Anglin \ Sandra Bixby \ Paul Beekmeyer	PK-12		1,600	773/702-9450 Fax 773/702-7455
Universal Sch 7350 W 93rd St, Bridgeview 60455 Hanan Abdallah	PK-12		650 60	708/599-4100 Fax 708/599-1588
Valeo Academy 2500 Beverly Rd, Hoffman Est 60192 Grace Dickow	K-12		105	847/645-9300
Village Leadership Academy 800 S Wells St Ste 90, Chicago 60607 Dayo Harris	K-8		200	312/675-0056 Fax 312/675-0069
Virginia Frank Child Dev Ctr 6639 N Kedzie Ave, Chicago 60645 Linnet Nendez	Spec		8 1	773/765-3100
Walther Lutheran High Sch 900 Chicago Ave, Melrose Park 60160 Tim Bouman	9-12		350 25	708/344-0404 Fax 708/344-0525
West Side Christian Sch 1240 S Pulaski Rd, Chicago 60623 Jeralyn Harris	PK-8		180 9	773/542-0663 Fax 773/542-0664
Willows Academy 1015 Rose Ave, Des Plaines 60016 Dr Jamie Vasquez	6-12		225	847/824-6900 Fax 847/824-7089
Ⓐ Winnie Mandela Alt HS 7847 S Jeffery Blvd, Chicago 60649 Jamillah Kareem	9-12		250	773/375-0529 Fax 773/375-0610
Winston Knolls Sch 2353 Hassell Rd Ste 110, Hoffman Est 60169 Robert Lee	Spec	A	401	630/283-3221
Wolcott Sch 524 N Wolcott Ave, Chicago 60622 Dr Mariam Pike	9-12		160	312/610-4900 Fax 312/610-4950
Yeshiva Eitz Chaim 6045 N Keystone Ave, Chicago 60646 Yitzchak Lurie	9-9		401	773/455-1001
Yeshiva Meor Hatorah-Boys HS 3635 W Devon Ave, Chicago 60659 Steven Kurtz	9-12		42	773/465-0419 Fax 773/465-0520
Yeshiva Ohr Boruch 2828 W Pratt Blvd, Chicago 60645 Hallel Mandel	K-8		165 9	773/262-0885 Fax 773/262-2016

---

79 Student Personnel	91 Safety/Security	275 Response To Intervention	298 Grant Writer/Ptnrships	**School Programs**	**Social Media**	
80 Driver Ed/Safety	92 Magnet School	277 Remedial Math K-12	750 Chief Innovation Officer	A = Alternative Program		
81 Gifted/Talented	93 Parental Involvement	280 Literacy Coach	751 Chief of Staff	G = Adult Classes	f = Facebook	
82 Video Services	95 Tech Prep Program	285 STEM	752 Social Emotional Learning	M = Magnet Program		
83 Substance Abuse Prev	97 Chief Infomation Officer	286 Digital Learning		T = Title I Schoolwide	t = Twitter	
84 Erate	98 Chief Technology Officer	288 Common Core Standards	**Other School Types**	V = Career & Tech Ed Programs		
85 AIDS Education	270 Character Education	294 Accountability	Ⓐ = Alternative School			
88 Alternative/At Risk	271 Migrant Education	295 Network System	Ⓒ = Charter School	New Schools are shaded		
89 Multi-Cultural Curriculum	273 Teacher Mentor	296 Title II Programs	Ⓜ = Magnet School	New Superintendents and Principals are bold		
90 Social Work	274 Before/After Sch	297 Webmaster	Ⓨ = Year-Round School	Personnel with email addresses are underscored		

IL—81

Cook County

Yeshivas Brisk Academy 12-12 G 15 773/274-1177
3000 W Devon Ave, Chicago 60659 6
Asher Krupnack

Yeshivas Tiferes Tzvi Academy PK-8 350 773/973-6150
6317 N California Ave, Chicago 60659
Nosson Muller

COOK REGIONAL CENTERS

- **Aero Special Ed Co-op** PID: 03032662 708/496-3330
  7600 Mason Ave, Burbank 60459 Fax 708/496-3920

Dr James Gunnell 1	Margaret Lesniak 2,11
Maggie Sheldon 8,15	Christine Putlak 15
Lisa Poe 34	Janell Babulic 68
Jason Wiegel 73,76,295	Mary Meehan 88

- **Career Development System** PID: 04177966 708/225-6021
  16333 Kilbourne Ave, Oak Forest 60452 Fax 708/225-6025

  Carol Brooks 1

- **Career Preparation Network** PID: 04180509 708/709-7903
  202 S Halsted St, Chicago HTS 60411

  Janice Stoettner 1,11

- **Des Plaines Valley EFE System** PID: 04182600 708/779-4786
  2000 5th Ave Ste M103, River Grove 60171 Fax 708/779-4627

  Dr Anne Cothran 1

- **Echo Joint Agreement** PID: 03032674 708/333-7880
  350 W 154th St, South Holland 60473 Fax 708/333-9561

Dr Sandra Thomas 1	Tarra Batts 2
Cindy Arresola 15,68	Calvin Harding 73

- **Eisenhower Cooperative** PID: 02097657 708/389-7580
  5318 135th St, Crestwood 60418 Fax 708/389-7584

  Angela Zajac 1,11

- **La Grange Area Dept of Spec Ed** PID: 02183531 708/354-5730
  1301 W Cossitt Ave, La Grange 60525 Fax 708/354-0733

Ellie Ambuehl 1	Suzanne Soluri 15
Carol Byron 58	

- **Leyden Area Spec Ed Co-op** PID: 03032650 847/455-3143
  10401 Grand Ave, Franklin Park 60131 Fax 847/451-4892

Dr Danielle Welch 1	Cinda Pembroke 2
Jaime Cerda 5	Monica Potempa 15
Paul Thompson 76	

- **Maine Twp Spec Ed Program** PID: 03032698 847/696-3600
  1177 S Dee Rd, Park Ridge 60068 Fax 847/696-8007

Dr Kenneth Wallace 1	Mary Kalou 2,15
David Ulm 3	Shawn Messmer 8,15
Greg Dietz 15,68	Jill Geocaris 30
Anna Hamilton 58	Brett Clark 71
Mark Ordonez 73,98	

Market Data Retrieval

- **Moraine Area Career System** PID: 04177992 708/422-6230
  4625 W 107th St, Oak Lawn 60453 Fax 708/422-6710

Debbie Canna 1	Suzanne Kendryna 15,95
Michelle Cognetti 73	

- **Niles Twp Dept of Spec Ed #807** PID: 05026621 847/965-9040
  8701 Menard Ave, Morton Grove 60053 Fax 847/965-0003

Tarin Kendrick 1	Kathy Gavin 2,11
Candice Hartranft 15,58	Francesca Pilati 34
Ryan Mayhall 76,295	

- **North Cook Interm Svc Center** PID: 03064689 847/824-8300
  1001 E Touhy Ave Ste 200, Des Plaines 60018 Fax 847/824-1033

Dr Bruce Brown 1	Terrie Simmons 2
Margot Fennelly 7	Dr Diane Betts 15

- **North Suburban Ed Reg for Voc** PID: 04184452 847/692-8023
  1131 S Dee Rd, Park Ridge 60068 Fax 847/692-8055

  Martha Eldridge-Stark 1,11

- **Northwest Suburban Sp Ed Org** PID: 02183555 847/463-8100
  799 W Kensington Rd, Mt Prospect 60056 Fax 847/463-8114

Dr Judith Hackett 1	Julie Jilek 2
Marcia Guiffre 15	

- **NW Ed Council Stdnt Success** PID: 04182155 847/718-6800
  2121 S Goebbert Rd, Arlington HTS 60005 Fax 847/718-6805

  Nancy Awdziejczyk 1

- **South Cook Interm Svc Center** PID: 03064718 708/754-6600
  253 W Joe Orr Rd, Chicago HTS 60411 Fax 708/754-8687

Dr Vanessa Kinder 1	Anthony Marinello 8,79
Dr Kathleen Doyle 15	

- **Southwest Cook Co Assc Spec Ed** PID: 02183608 708/687-0900
  6020 151st St, Oak Forest 60452 Fax 708/687-5695

Dr Gineen O'Neil 1	Tage Shumway 2,11

- **Speed Seja 802** PID: 03266502 708/481-6100
  1125 Division St, Chicago HTS 60411 Fax 708/481-5713

Dr Tina Halliman 1	Brenda Murillo 2
Joe Kekelik 3	Toia Keith 4
Linda Wilson 34	Ron Bean 67
Vanessa Duffin 68	Greg Furgason 73,76

- **West 40 Interm Serv Center 2** PID: 03064691 708/449-4284
  4413 Roosevelt Rd Ste 104, Hillside 60162 Fax 708/449-4288

Dr Mark Klaisner 1	Dr Mike Popp 15
Angela Mooney 71	Josh Boies 73,76
Tammy Marrero 88	

1	Superintendent	8	Curric/Instruct K-12	19	Chief Financial Officer	29	Family/Consumer Science	39 Social Studies K-12	49 English/Lang Arts Elem	59 Special Education Elem	69 Academic Assessment
2	Bus/Finance/Purchasing	9	Curric/Instruct Elem	20	Art K-12	30	Adult Education	40 Social Studies Elem	50 English/Lang Arts Sec	60 Special Education Sec	70 Research/Development
3	Buildings And Grounds	10	Curric/Instruct Sec	21	Art Elem	31	Career/Sch-to-Work K-12	41 Social Studies Sec	51 Reading K-12	61 Foreign/World Lang K-12	71 Public Information
4	Food Service	11	Federal Program	22	Art Sec	32	Career/Sch-to-Work Elem	42 Science K-12	52 Reading Elem	62 Foreign/World Lang Elem	72 Summer School
5	Transportation	12	Title I	23	Music K-12	33	Career/Sch-to-Work Sec	43 Science Elem	53 Reading Sec	63 Foreign/World Lang Sec	73 Instructional Tech
6	Athletic	13	Title V	24	Music Elem	34	Early Childhood Ed	44 Science Sec	54 Remedial Reading K-12	64 Religious Education K-12	74 Inservice Training
7	Health Services	15	Asst Superintendent	25	Music Sec	35	Health/Phys Education	45 Math K-12	55 Remedial Reading Elem	65 Religious Education Elem	75 Marketing/Distributive
		16	Instructional Media Svcs	26	Business Education	36	Guidance Services K-12	46 Math Elem	56 Remedial Reading Sec	66 Religious Education Sec	76 Info Systems
		17	Chief Operations Officer	27	Career & Tech Ed	37	Guidance Services Elem	47 Math Sec	57 Bilingual/ELL	67 School Board President	77 Psychological Assess
		18	Chief Academic Officer	28	Technology Education	38	Guidance Services Sec	48 English/Lang Arts K-12	58 Special Education K-12	68 Teacher Personnel	78 Affirmative Action

Illinois School Directory

Crawford County

CRAWFORD COUNTY

CRAWFORD PUBLIC SCHOOLS

- **Hutsonville Cmty Unit SD 1** PID: 00287715   618/563-4912
  500 W Clover St, Hutsonville 62433   Fax 618/563-9122

Schools: 2 \ Teachers: 29 \ Students: 324 \ Special Ed Students: 58 \ College-Bound: 45% \ Ethnic: Hispanic 1%, Caucasian 99% \ Exp: $176 (Low) \ Poverty: 17% \ Title I: $99,119 \ Special Education: $59,000 \ Open-Close: 08/24 - 06/02 \ DTBP: $172 (High)

Julie Kraemer 1,84
Diana Stephens 11,54,296*
Jill Weens 58
Lori Crumrin 2
Michelle Goodwine 16,82*
Tina Callaway 67

Public Schs..Principal	Grd	Prgm	Enr/#Cls	SN	
Hutsonville Grade Sch 500 W Clover St, Hutsonville 62433 Guy Rumler	PK-5	T	220 8	51%	618/563-4812 Fax 618/563-4602
Hutsonville High Sch 500 W Clover St, Hutsonville 62433 Travis Titsworth	6-12	TV	180 10	47%	618/563-4913

- **Oblong Cmty Unit Sch Dist 4** PID: 00287741   618/592-3933
  600 W Main St, Oblong 62449   Fax 618/592-3427

Schools: 2 \ Teachers: 45 \ Students: 565 \ Special Ed Students: 107 \ College-Bound: 75% \ Ethnic: Asian 1%, African American 1%, Hispanic 2%, Caucasian 97% \ Exp: $399 (High) \ Poverty: 18% \ Title I: $188,246 \ Special Education: $129,000 \ Open-Close: 08/21 - 05/24

Jeffery Patchett 1,11,83
Jeff Allen 3*
Mary Patchett 6*
Kendra Ridlen 58,69,752*
John Ireland 73,286*
Susan Madlem 2
Jason Blankenbaker 6
Michelle Meese 9,15,288*
Rod Sparks 67

Public Schs..Principal	Grd	Prgm	Enr/#Cls	SN	
Oblong Elem Sch 600 W Main St, Oblong 62449 Dave Parker	PK-8		434 20	48%	618/592-4225 Fax 618/592-4299
Oblong High Sch 700 S Range St, Oblong 62449 Jeff Patchett	9-12	V	173 25	40%	618/592-4235 Fax 618/592-3540

- **Palestine Cmty Unit SD 3** PID: 00287791   618/586-2713
  100 S Main St, Palestine 62451   Fax 618/586-2905

Schools: 2 \ Teachers: 28 \ Students: 375 \ Special Ed Students: 52 \ College-Bound: 83% \ Ethnic: African American 1%, Caucasian 99% \ Exp: $405 (High) \ Poverty: 17% \ Title I: $152,943 \ Special Education: $63,000 \ Open-Close: 08/21 - 06/04 \ DTBP: $152 (High)

Jessica Sisil 1,11,73,288
Marcy Adams 16
Sharon Schackmann 58
Travis Blank 6*
Jana Banye 51,54
Corie Biggs 67

Public Schs..Principal	Grd	Prgm	Enr/#Cls	SN	
Palestine Grade Sch 205 S Washington St, Palestine 62451 Jessica Sisil	PK-8	T	220 18	43%	618/586-2711 Fax 618/586-5126
Palestine High Sch 102 N Main St, Palestine 62451 Tangie Waldrop	9-12		85 15	40%	618/586-2712 Fax 618/586-5328

- **Robinson Cmty Unit Sch Dist 2** PID: 00287820   618/544-7511
  1301 N Allen St, Robinson 62454   Fax 618/544-9284

Schools: 4 \ Teachers: 105 \ Students: 1,616 \ Special Ed Students: 333 \ LEP Students: 3 \ College-Bound: 77% \ Ethnic: African American 1%, Hispanic 3%, Caucasian 96% \ Exp: $208 (Med) \ Poverty: 14% \ Title I: $368,415 \ Special Education: $518,000 \ Open-Close: 08/24 - 05/18

Joshua Quick 1,11
Angela Langley 5
Jamie Rains 58
Eric Schmidt 83
Susan Trimble 2
Janet Jenkins 16,82*
Bill Sandiford 67

Public Schs..Principal	Grd	Prgm	Enr/#Cls	SN	
Lincoln Grade Sch 301 E Poplar St, Robinson 62454 Kathy Bemont	3-5	T	360 15	47%	618/544-3315 Fax 618/544-4136
Nuttall Middle Sch 400 W Rustic St, Robinson 62454 Craig Beals	6-8	AT	350 25	44%	618/544-8618 Fax 618/544-5304
Robinson High Sch 2000 N Cross St, Robinson 62454 Victoria McDonald	9-12	AV	460 40	38%	618/544-9510 Fax 618/544-7921
Washington Elem Sch 507 W Condit St, Robinson 62454 Jason Stark	PK-2	T	423 24	45%	618/544-2233 Fax 618/544-5502

CRAWFORD PRIVATE SCHOOLS

Private Schs..Principal	Grd	Prgm	Enr/#Cls	SN	
New Hebron Christian Sch 10755 E 700th Ave, Robinson 62454 Susan Wassel	PK-8		120 9		618/544-7619 Fax 618/544-4493

CRAWFORD REGIONAL CENTERS

- **Area 6 Learning Technology Ctr** PID: 04433203   618/544-2719
  300 W Main St Ste 307, Robinson 62454

Monty Hewlin 1
Eddie Chapa 295

- **Twin Rivers Career & Tech Ed** PID: 04184335   618/544-8664
  301 S Cross St Ste 235, Robinson 62454   Fax 618/544-7712

Richard Johnson 1

Cumberland County

CUMBERLAND COUNTY

CUMBERLAND PUBLIC SCHOOLS

- **Cumberland Cmty Unit SD 77** PID: 00287882   217/923-3132
  1496 Illinois Route 121, Toledo 62468

Schools: 3 \ Teachers: 64 \ Students: 1,000 \ Special Ed Students: 139 \ LEP Students: 3 \ College-Bound: 62% \ Ethnic: Caucasian 99% \ Exp: $390 (High) \ Poverty: 13% \ Title I: $200,246 \ Special Education: $297,000 \ Open-Close: 08/17 - 05/20 \ DTBP: $165 (High)

Name	Code
Todd Butler	1,11
George Hensley	3,91
Stacy Keyser	6*
Kevin Maynard	10,27*
Megan Walk	16,82
Sheila Plummer	37,83*
Mallory Foster	58,294
Kathy Darling	2
Justin Roedl	6*
Katherine Wetherell	7
Debbie Clark	12,54,275*
Steve Wheeler	16,73,95,295*
Janet Blade	57*
Robert Blade	67

Public Schs..Principal	Grd	Prgm	Enr/#Cls	SN	
Cumberland Elem Sch 1496 Illinois Route 121, Toledo 62468 Daniel Huffman	PK-4	A	439 35	38%	217/923-3132 Fax 217/923-5449
Cumberland High Sch 1496 Illinois Route 121, Toledo 62468 Kevin Maynard	9-12	AV	269 25	39%	217/923-3132 Fax 217/923-5514
Cumberland Middle Sch 1496 Illinois Route 121, Toledo 62468 Stacy Keyser	5-8	A	321	37%	217/923-3132 Fax 217/923-5449

- **Neoga Cmty Unit School Dist 3** PID: 00287911   217/895-2201
  790 E 7th St, Neoga 62447   Fax 217/895-3476

Schools: 2 \ Teachers: 39 \ Students: 535 \ Special Ed Students: 121 \ LEP Students: 3 \ College-Bound: 81% \ Ethnic: Asian 1%, African American 1%, Hispanic 2%, Caucasian 96% \ Exp: $258 (Med) \ Poverty: 11% \ Title I: $151,525 \ Special Education: $153,000 \ Open-Close: 08/18 - 05/20 \ DTBP: $167 (High)

Name	Code
Bill Fritcher	1
Angela Eden	4
Mike Taylor	6*
Seth James	58*
Kim Weaver	2
Troy Vaughn	5
Kirby Davis	36*
Chuck Campbell	67

Public Schs..Principal	Grd	Prgm	Enr/#Cls	SN	
Neoga Elem Sch 850 E 7th St, Neoga 62447 **Denise Helmers**	K-5	T	224 12	2%	217/895-2200 Fax 217/895-2974
Neoga Jr Sr High Sch 790 E 7th St, Neoga 62447 Kevin Haarman	7-12	TV	346 32	4%	217/775-6049 Fax 217/895-3957

DE KALB COUNTY

DE KALB COUNTY SCHOOLS

County Schs..Principal	Grd	Prgm	Enr/#Cls	SN	
Indian Valley Vocational Ctr 600 Lions Rd, Sandwich 60548 Joe Barbic	Voc		475 17		815/786-9873 Fax 815/786-6928

DE KALB PUBLIC SCHOOLS

- **DeKalb Cmty Unit SD 428** PID: 00287959   815/754-2350
  901 S 4th St, Dekalb 60115   Fax 815/758-6933

Schools: 12 \ Teachers: 400 \ Students: 6,600 \ Special Ed Students: 1,084 \ LEP Students: 939 \ College-Bound: 67% \ Ethnic: Asian 2%, African American 22%, Hispanic 30%, Caucasian 46% \ Exp: $197 (Low) \ Poverty: 17% \ Title I: $1,946,897 \ Special Education: $4,993,000 \ Bilingual Education: $170,000 \ Open-Close: 08/24 - 05/27 \ DTBP: $203 (High) \

Name	Code
Ray Lechner	1
Cindy Carpenter	2,84
Peter Goff	6*
Kim Lyle	8,11,288,296
Amy Crook	13,57
Steve Lundeen	25*
Sarah Moses	67
Amy Luckner	69,70*
Kyle Gerdes	79
Armir Doka	2
Tammy Carson	3
Nicole Huber	7*
Billy Hueramo	9
Jill McCormick	24*
Lisa Gorchels	34*
Deetra Sallis	68
Ben Bayle	73,76,98,297
Denise Flemming	286*

Public Schs..Principal	Grd	Prgm	Enr/#Cls	SN	
Clinton Rosette Middle Sch 650 N 1st St, Dekalb 60115 Tim Vincent	6-8		547 32	65%	815/754-2226 Fax 815/758-1097
Cortland Elem Sch 370 E Lexington Ave, Cortland 60112 Jennifer Hilliard	K-5	T	508 20	58%	815/754-2360 Fax 815/756-8426
DeKalb Early Learning Dev Ctr 1515 S 4th St, Dekalb 60115 Lisa Gorchels	PK-PK	T	253	55%	815/754-2999 Fax 815/754-2998
DeKalb High Sch 501 W Dresser Rd, Dekalb 60115 James Horne	9-12	AT	1,774 110	51%	815/754-2100 Fax 815/754-2156
Founders Elem Sch 821 S 7th St, Dekalb 60115 Connie Rohlman	K-5	T	590 12	77%	815/754-3800 Fax 815/754-2249
Gwendolyn Brooks Elem Sch 3225 Sangamon Dr, Dekalb 60115 **Melissa Sago**	K-5	T	315 16	68%	815/754-9936 Fax 815/754-1345
Huntley Middle Sch 1515 S 4th St, Dekalb 60115 Amonaquenette Parker	6-8	T	850 28	57%	815/754-2241 Fax 815/758-6062
Jefferson Elem Sch 211 McCormick Dr, Dekalb 60115 Melanie Bickley	K-5	T	315 13	53%	815/754-2263 Fax 815/758-1206
Lincoln Elem Sch 220 E Sunset Pl, Dekalb 60115 Jennifer Tallitsch	K-5	T	292 12	58%	815/754-2212 Fax 815/758-1279

#		#		#		#		#		#		#	
1	Superintendent	8	Curric/Instruct K-12	19	Chief Financial Officer	29	Family/Consumer Science	39	Social Studies K-12	49	English/Lang Arts Elem	59	Special Education Elem	69	Academic Assessment
2	Bus/Finance/Purchasing	9	Curric/Instruct Elem	20	Art K-12	30	Adult Education	40	Social Studies Elem	50	English/Lang Arts Sec	60	Special Education Sec	70	Research/Development
3	Buildings And Grounds	10	Curric/Instruct Sec	21	Art Elem	31	Career/Sch-to-Work K-12	41	Social Studies Sec	51	Reading K-12	61	Foreign/World Lang K-12	71	Public Information
4	Food Service	11	Federal Program	22	Art Sec	32	Career/Sch-to-Work Elem	42	Science K-12	52	Reading Elem	62	Foreign/World Lang Elem	72	Summer School
5	Transportation	12	Title I	23	Music K-12	33	Career/Sch-to-Work Sec	43	Science Elem	53	Reading Sec	63	Foreign/World Lang Sec	73	Instructional Tech
6	Athletic	13	Title V	24	Music Elem	34	Early Childhood Ed	44	Science Sec	54	Remedial Reading K-12	64	Religious Education K-12	74	Inservice Training
7	Health Services	15	Asst Superintendent	25	Music Sec	35	Health/Phys Education	45	Math K-12	55	Remedial Reading Elem	65	Religious Education Elem	75	Marketing/Distributive
		16	Instructional Media Svcs	26	Business Education	36	Guidance Services K-12	46	Math Elem	56	Remedial Reading Sec	66	Religious Education Sec	76	Info Systems
		17	Chief Operations Officer	27	Career & Tech Ed	37	Guidance Services Elem	47	Math Sec	57	Bilingual/ELL	67	School Board President	77	Psychological Assess
		18	Chief Academic Officer	28	Technology Education	38	Guidance Services Sec	48	English/Lang Arts K-12	58	Special Education K-12	68	Teacher Personnel	78	Affirmative Action

Illinois School Directory — De Kalb County

Little John Elem Sch		K-5	T	434	76%	815/754-2258
1121 School St, Dekalb 60115				19		Fax 815/758-1065
Billy Hueramo						
Malta Elem Sch		K-5	T	322	56%	815/754-2970
5068 Il Route 38, Malta 60150				12		Fax 815/754-2973
Kristi Baccheschi						f t
Tyler Elem Sch		K-5	T	258	71%	815/754-2389
1021 Alden Cir, Dekalb 60115				15		Fax 815/754-1331
Timmerman Robyn						

● **Genoa-Kingston Cmty SD 424** PID: 00288068   815/784-6222
980 Park Ave, Genoa 60135   Fax 815/784-6059

Schools: 4 \ **Teachers:** 108 \ **Students:** 1,700 \ **Special Ed Students:** 192 \ **LEP Students:** 131 \ **College-Bound:** 74% \ **Ethnic:** Asian 1%, African American 2%, Hispanic 19%, Caucasian 78% \ **Exp:** $289 (Med) \ **Poverty:** 6% \ **Title I:** $187,945 \ **Special Education:** $929,000 \ **Bilingual Education:** $15,000 \ **Open-Close:** 08/17 - 05/26 \ **DTBP:** $235 (High)

Brent O'Daniell 1
Joe Ratliff 3,36
Phil Jerbi 6*
Tara Wilkins 16,82*
Kristen Andrews 67
Karen Simmons 79
Brad Shortridge 2,15
Cam Fradkin 5
Stefanie Hill 8,285,288*
Christy Fraticola 38*
Scott Herrig 73,98

Public Schs..Principal	Grd	Prgm	Enr/#Cls	SN	
Genoa Elem Sch	3-5		323	37%	815/784-3742
602 E Hill St, Genoa 60135			22		Fax 815/784-3731
John Francis					
Genoa-Kingston High Sch	9-12	V	562	31%	815/784-5111
980 Park Ave, Genoa 60135			24		Fax 815/784-3124
Matthew Cascio					
Genoa-Kingston Middle Sch	6-8		396	38%	815/784-5222
941 W Main St, Genoa 60135			14		Fax 815/784-4323
Craig Butcher					
Kingston Elem Sch	PK-2		354	40%	815/784-5246
100 School St, Kingston 60145			15		Fax 815/784-9049
Stefanie Hill					

● **Hiawatha Cmty Unit SD 426** PID: 00288111   815/522-6676
410 1st St, Kirkland 60146   Fax 815/522-6619

Schools: 2 \ **Teachers:** 39 \ **Students:** 450 \ **Special Ed Students:** 79 \ **LEP Students:** 9 \ **College-Bound:** 66% \ **Ethnic:** Hispanic 14%, Caucasian 86% \ **Exp:** $141 (Low) \ **Poverty:** 16% \ **Title I:** $157,694 \ **Special Education:** $310,000 \ **Bilingual Education:** $1,000 \ **Open-Close:** 08/17 - 05/26

Jared Poynter 1,11
Cindy Lauritzen 4
Malloy Faivre 6
Caitlin Benes 57
Tim Hall 67
Angela Messenger 286
Dave Huntsman 3
Carolyn Amerman 5
Connie Wood 12*
Craig Pate 58,79,296,298
Cody Sauber 73,295
Haley Caron 752

Public Schs..Principal	Grd	Prgm	Enr/#Cls	SN	
Hiawatha Elem Sch	PK-8		308	40%	815/522-3336
410 1st St, Kirkland 60146			35		Fax 815/522-3185
Caitlin Benes					
Hiawatha High Sch	9-12		265	43%	815/522-3335
410 1st St, Kirkland 60146			35		Fax 815/522-9918
Mark Zych					

● **Hinckley-Big Rock Cmty SD 429** PID: 00288147   815/286-7578
700 E Lincoln Ave, Hinckley 60520   Fax 815/286-7577

Schools: 3 \ **Teachers:** 56 \ **Students:** 696 \ **Special Ed Students:** 110 \ **LEP Students:** 3 \ **College-Bound:** 71% \ **Ethnic:** Asian 1%, African American 1%, Hispanic 9%, Caucasian 90% \ **Exp:** $176 (Low) \ **Poverty:** 6% \ **Title I:** $109,227 \ **Special Education:** $382,000 \ **Open-Close:** 08/17 - 05/26 \ **DTBP:** $230 (High)

Travis McGuire 1,288
Kim Halverson 6*
Sandy Madden 12,54*
Jessica Sonntag 58
Jeff Woo 73*
Susan Dell 2
Jay Brickman 8,73*
Gina Tauer 27,83*
Eric Wackerlin 67
Jeff Strouss 81*

Public Schs..Principal	Grd	Prgm	Enr/#Cls	SN	
Hinckley Big Rock Middle Sch	6-8		165	13%	630/556-4180
47 W 984 Route 30, Big Rock 60511			16		Fax 815/286-7584
Jeff Strouss					
Hinckley-Big Rock Elem Sch	PK-5		320	1%	815/286-3400
600 W Lincoln Hwy, Hinckley 60520			19		Fax 815/286-3401
Julie Melnyk					
Hinckley-Big Rock High Sch	9-12	V	211	6%	815/286-7501
700 E Lincoln Ave, Hinckley 60520			30		Fax 815/286-7505
Jay Brickman					

● **Indian Creek Cmty Unit SD 425** PID: 00288288   815/824-2197
506 S Shabbona Rd, Shabbona 60550   Fax 815/824-2199

Schools: 3 \ **Teachers:** 63 \ **Students:** 740 \ **Special Ed Students:** 97 \ **LEP Students:** 14 \ **College-Bound:** 74% \ **Ethnic:** African American 1%, Hispanic 7%, Caucasian 91% \ **Exp:** $272 (Med) \ **Poverty:** 9% \ **Title I:** $136,141 \ **Special Education:** $480,000 \ **Open-Close:** 08/14 - 05/20 \ **DTBP:** $185 (High)

Chad Willis 1
Pete Post 3
Nic Gaston 5
Paula Kennedy 8,12*
Jennifer Darlinger 58*
Keenan Moen 73,84
Sherri Gavin 2
Cheri Ballard 4
Ehren Mertz 6*
Alyx Bickle 36
Vaughn Boehne 67
Duane Farnsworth 83*

Public Schs..Principal	Grd	Prgm	Enr/#Cls	SN	
Indian Creek Elem Sch	PK-4		278	24%	815/824-2122
301 W Cherokee Ave, Shabbona 60550			18		Fax 815/824-8130
Dave Mantzke					
Indian Creek High Sch	9-12	AV	198	22%	815/824-2197
506 S Shabbona Rd, Shabbona 60550			24		
K McCarty					
Indian Creek Middle Sch	5-8	A	208	30%	815/264-3351
335 E Garfield St, Waterman 60556			19		Fax 815/264-7826
Steve Simpson					

● **Sandwich Cmty Unit SD 430** PID: 00288214   815/786-2187
720 S Wells St, Sandwich 60548   Fax 815/786-6229

Schools: 6 \ **Teachers:** 141 \ **Students:** 2,000 \ **Special Ed Students:** 322 \ **LEP Students:** 84 \ **College-Bound:** 66% \ **Ethnic:** Asian 1%, Hispanic 18%, Caucasian 81% \ **Exp:** $268 (Med) \ **Poverty:** 9% \ **Title I:** $309,636 \ **Special Education:** $1,546,000 \ **Bilingual Education:** $1,000 \ **Open-Close:** 08/20 - 05/28 \ **DTBP:** $199 (High)

Rick Schmit 1,11
Susan Graham 5
Wally Marquardt 8,12,288
Crystal Swan-Grazett 58
Dan Ford 3
Tim Gipe 6*
Marta Dunne 57
David Stahl 67

79	Student Personnel	91	Safety/Security	275	Response To Intervention	298	Grant Writer/Ptnrships	
80	Driver Ed/Safety	92	Magnet School	277	Remedial Math K-12	750	Chief Innovation Officer	
81	Gifted/Talented	93	Parental Involvement	280	Literacy Coach	751	Chief of Staff	
82	Video Services	95	Tech Prep Program	285	STEM	752	Social Emotional Learning	
83	Substance Abuse Prev	97	Chief Information Officer	286	Digital Learning			
84	Erate	98	Chief Technology Officer	288	Common Core Standards			
85	AIDS Education	270	Accountability	294	Accountability			
88	Alternative/At Risk	271	Migrant Education	295	Network System			
89	Multi-Cultural Curriculum	273	Teacher Mentor	296	Title II Programs			
90	Social Work	274	Before/After Sch	297	Webmaster			

School Programs
A = Alternative Program
G = Adult Classes
M = Magnet Program
T = Title I Schoolwide
V = Career & Tech Ed Programs

Other School Types
Ⓐ = Alternative School
Ⓒ = Charter School
Ⓜ = Magnet School
Ⓨ = Year-Round School

Social Media
f = Facebook
t = Twitter

New Schools are shaded
New Superintendents and Principals are bold
Personnel with email addresses are underscored

De Kalb County

Glen Bloemker 73,76,295
Tom Sodaro 91
Dawn Greenacre 88

Public Schs..Principal	Grd	Prgm	Enr/#Cls	SN
Herman E Dummer Elem Sch 422 S Wells St, Sandwich 60548 Lynette Ford	4-5	T	249 16	45% 815/786-8498 Fax 815/786-1920
Lynn G Haskin Elem Sch 720 S Wells St, Sandwich 60548 Dawn Greenacre	PK-3	T	269 12	35% 815/786-8812 Fax 815/786-8986
Prairie View Sch 1201 Castle St, Sandwich 60548 Garrett Ryan	K-3		213 18	32% 815/786-8811 Fax 815/786-2691
Sandwich Cmty High Sch 515 Lions Rd, Sandwich 60548 Tom Sodaro	9-12		643 53	34% 815/786-2157 Fax 815/786-2632
Sandwich Middle Sch 600 S Wells St, Sandwich 60548 Andy Heilemeier	6-8		453 20	40% 815/786-2138 Fax 815/786-6606
W W Woodbury Sch 322 E 3rd St, Sandwich 60548 Jennifer Kern	K-3	T	166 9	43% 815/786-6316 Fax 815/786-2691

- **Somonauk Cmty Unit SD 432** PID: 00288331 815/498-2315
  501 W Market St, Somonauk 60552 Fax 815/498-9523

Schools: 3 \ **Teachers:** 55 \ **Students:** 800 \ **Special Ed Students:** 130 \ **LEP Students:** 3 \ **College-Bound:** 82% \ **Ethnic:** Asian 1%, African American 1%, Hispanic 11%, Caucasian 87% \ **Exp:** $250 (Med) \ **Poverty:** 7% \ **Title I:** $93,296 \ **Special Education:** $430,000 \ **Open-Close:** 08/18 - 05/25

Jay Streicher 1,84
Jan Adams 5
Kathleen Weeks 12*
Angie Koontz 36,83
Michael Short 67
Alex Marshall 3,91*
Elizabeth Ness 6*
Angie Koontz 36,83*
Tim Ulrich 58,79*
Brian Maxwell 73,76*

Public Schs..Principal	Grd	Prgm	Enr/#Cls	SN
James R Wood Elem Sch 320 Maple St, Somonauk 60552 Christine Pruski	PK-4	T	296 19	34% 815/498-2338 Fax 815/498-9361
Somonauk High Sch 500 W LaSalle St, Somonauk 60552 Eric Benson	9-12	V	278 30	26% 815/498-2314 Fax 815/498-9841
Somonauk Middle Sch 510 W LaSalle St, Somonauk 60552 Justin Snider	5-8		246 16	28% 815/498-1866 Fax 815/498-1647

- **Sycamore Cmty Unit SD 427** PID: 00288379 815/899-8100
  245 W Exchange St, Sycamore 60178 Fax 815/899-8110

Schools: 7 \ **Teachers:** 241 \ **Students:** 3,800 \ **Special Ed Students:** 548 \ **LEP Students:** 90 \ **Ethnic:** Asian 2%, African American 3%, Hispanic 9%, Caucasian 85% \ **Exp:** $256 (Med) \ **Poverty:** 6% \ **Title I:** $382,650 \ **Special Education:** $2,154,000 \ **Bilingual Education:** $15,000 \ **Open-Close:** 08/19 - 05/28 \ **DTBP:** $196 (High)

Steve Wilder 1
Chauncey Carrick 6,83,85,270*
Roxanne Horton 16,73,295
Jim Dombek 67
Courtney Dennison 88,274*
Nicole Stuckert 2,19
Dr Kris Webster 8,288
Lynn Reilley 34,58,90
David Olson 71

Public Schs..Principal	Grd	Prgm	Enr/#Cls	SN
North Elem Sch 1680 Brickville Rd, Sycamore 60178 Thomas Franks	K-5		288 15	12% 815/899-8209 Fax 815/899-8213
North Grove Elem Sch 850 Republic Ave, Sycamore 60178 Ryan Janisch	K-5		484	15% 815/899-8124 Fax 815/899-8114
South Prairie Elem Sch 820 Borden Ave, Sycamore 60178 Kreg Wesley	PK-5		272 13	26% 815/899-8299 Fax 815/899-8292
Southeast Elem Sch 718 S Locust St, Sycamore 60178 Kristi Crawford	K-5		351 15	26% 815/899-8219 Fax 815/899-8221
Sycamore High Sch 427 Spartan Trl, Sycamore 60178 Tim Carlson	9-12	V	1,214	19% 815/899-8160 Fax 815/899-8166
Sycamore Middle Sch 150 Maplewood Dr, Sycamore 60178 Jim Cleven	6-8		840 60	25% 815/899-8170 Fax 815/899-8177
West Elem Sch 240 Fair St, Sycamore 60178 Ryan Schrader	K-5		272 16	47% 815/899-8199 Fax 815/899-8195

DE KALB CATHOLIC SCHOOLS

- **Diocese of Rockford Ed Office** PID: 00328345
  Listing includes only schools located in this county. See District Index for location of Diocesan Offices.

Catholic Schs..Principal	Grd	Prgm	Enr/#Cls	SN
St Mary Sch 210 Gurler Rd, Dekalb 60115 Ashley Davis	PK-8		242 11	815/756-7905 Fax 815/758-1459
St Mary Sch 222 Waterman St, Sycamore 60178 Patricia Strang	PK-8		235 12	815/895-5215 Fax 815/895-5295

DE KALB PRIVATE SCHOOLS

Private Schs..Principal	Grd	Prgm	Enr/#Cls	SN
Camelot School-DeKalb Campus 123 W 1st St, Genoa 60135 Jennifer Johnson	Spec		90 6	815/787-4144 Fax 815/758-3538
Cornerstone Christian Academy 355 N Cross St, Sycamore 60178 Dr Collette House	PK-8		270 25	815/895-8522 Fax 815/895-8717
Somonauk Christian Sch 315 E North St, Somonauk 60552 Dennis Keith	PK-12		72 8	815/498-2312 Fax 815/498-2019

DE KALB REGIONAL CENTERS

- **Indian Valley Voc Ed System** PID: 04338615 815/786-9873
  600 Lions Rd, Sandwich 60548 Fax 815/786-6928

Joe Barbic 1
Laura Edwards 15

#		#		#		#		#		#		#	
1	Superintendent	8	Curric/Instruct K-12	19	Chief Financial Officer	29	Family/Consumer Science	39	Social Studies K-12	49	English/Lang Arts Elem	59	Special Education Elem	69	Academic Assessment
2	Bus/Finance/Purchasing	9	Curric/Instruct Elem	20	Art K-12	30	Adult Education	40	Social Studies Elem	50	English/Lang Arts Sec	60	Special Education Sec	70	Research/Development
3	Buildings And Grounds	10	Curric/Instruct Sec	21	Art Elem	31	Career/Sch-to-Work K-12	41	Social Studies Sec	51	Reading K-12	61	Foreign/World Lang K-12	71	Public Information
4	Food Service	11	Federal Program	22	Art Sec	32	Career/Sch-to-Work Elem	42	Science K-12	52	Reading Elem	62	Foreign/World Lang Elem	72	Summer School
5	Transportation	12	Title I	23	Music K-12	33	Career/Sch-to-Work Sec	43	Science Elem	53	Reading Sec	63	Foreign/World Lang Sec	73	Instructional Tech
6	Athletic	13	Title V	24	Music Elem	34	Early Childhood Ed	44	Science Sec	54	Remedial Reading K-12	64	Religious Education K-12	74	Inservice Training
7	Health Services	14	Asst Superintendent	25	Music Sec	35	Health/Phys Education	45	Math K-12	55	Remedial Reading Elem	65	Religious Education Elem	75	Marketing/Distributive
		15	Instructional Media Svcs	26	Business Education	36	Guidance Services K-12	46	Math Elem	56	Remedial Reading Sec	66	Religious Education Sec	76	Info Systems
		16	Chief Operations Officer	27	Career & Tech Ed	37	Guidance Services Elem	47	Math Sec	57	Bilingual/ELL	67	School Board President	77	Psychological Assess
		17	Chief Academic Officer	28	Technology Education	38	Guidance Services Sec	48	English/Lang Arts K-12	58	Special Education K-12	68	Teacher Personnel	78	Affirmative Action

Illinois School Directory

Douglas County

- **Kishwaukee Ed Consortium** PID: 04178257   815/825-2000
  21255 Malta Rd, Malta 60150   Fax 815/825-2582
  Tom Crouch 1   Margaret Delano 2
  Dave Wessel 73

- **Northwestern IL Association** PID: 02182094   815/895-9227
  245 W Exchange St Ste 4, Sycamore 60178   Fax 815/895-2971
  John Malone 1,11   Cynthia Vogeler 2,298
  Rebecca Moody 8   Jean Tritle 68
  Tiffany Agustin 76

- **Regional Office of Ed 16** PID: 02097695   815/217-0460
  2500 N Annie Glidden Rd Ste C, Dekalb 60115   Fax 815/217-0467
  Amanda Christensen 1   Jeff Smith 5,15

Public Schs..Principal	Grd	Prgm	Enr/#Cls	SN
Clinton Elem Sch 680 Illini Dr, Clinton 61727 Sacha Young	2-5		516 16	50% 217/935-6772 Fax 217/935-8215
Clinton High Sch 1200 State Route 54 W, Clinton 61727 Jerome Wayne	9-12	ATV	565 40	43% 217/935-8337 Fax 217/935-8847
Clinton Junior High Sch 701 Illini Dr, Clinton 61727 Josh Maxwell	6-8	TV	364 40	53% 217/935-2103 Fax 217/937-1918
Douglas Elem Sch 905 E Main St, Clinton 61727 Beth Wickenhauser	PK-1		183 12	64% 217/935-2987 Fax 217/935-2525
Lincoln Elem Sch 407 S Jackson St, Clinton 61727 Beth Wickenhauser	PK-1		180 11	48% 217/935-6383 Fax 217/935-3713

DEWITT COUNTY

DEWITT PUBLIC SCHOOLS

- **Blue Ridge Cmty SD 18** PID: 00288563   309/928-9141
  411 N John St, Farmer City 61842   Fax 309/928-5478

  Schools: 3 \ **Teachers:** 58 \ **Students:** 700 \ **Special Ed Students:** 111 \ **LEP Students:** 3 \ **College-Bound:** 65% \ **Ethnic:** African American 1%, Hispanic 3%, Caucasian 96% \ **Exp:** $446 (High) \ **Poverty:** 11% \ **Title I:** $124,463 \ **Special Education:** $421,000 \ **Open-Close:** 08/19 - 05/26 \ **DTBP:** $197 (High)

  Hillary Stanifer 1,83   Tonya Evans 4
  Debra Field 5   Evan Miles 6*
  Paige Trimble 8   Leslie Whitehouse 33,38,69*
  Silvia Allen ....35*   Dale Schneman 67
  Dave Kramer 73

Public Schs..Principal	Grd	Prgm	Enr/#Cls	SN
Blue Ridge High Sch 411 N John St, Farmer City 61842 John Lawrence	9-12	TV	232 20	41% 309/928-2622 Fax 309/928-5301
Blue Ridge Interm Jr High Sch 107 South McKinley, Mansfield 61854 Katie Nichols	4-8	T	241 8	45% 217/489-5201 Fax 217/489-9051
Ruth M Schneider Elem Sch 309 N John St, Farmer City 61842 Ryan Peyton	PK-3	T	244 11	42% 309/928-2611 Fax 309/928-2195

- **Clinton Cmty Unit Sch Dist 15** PID: 00288484   217/935-8321
  1210 State Route 54 W, Clinton 61727   Fax 217/935-2300

  Schools: 5 \ **Teachers:** 136 \ **Students:** 1,800 \ **Special Ed Students:** 338 \ **LEP Students:** 28 \ **College-Bound:** 55% \ **Ethnic:** African American 1%, Hispanic 7%, Caucasian 92% \ **Exp:** $284 (Med) \ **Poverty:** 13% \ **Title I:** $407,971 \ **Special Education:** $1,101,000 \ **Open-Close:** 08/19 - 06/03 \ **DTBP:** $178 (High)

  Curt Nettles 1   Drew Goebel 2,5,11
  Steve Hamilton ....4*   Matt Koepell 6*
  Eric Barringer ....16,73,295*   Kari Veldman 58
  Dan Matthews 67

DOUGLAS COUNTY

DOUGLAS PUBLIC SCHOOLS

- **Arcola Cmty Unit Sch Dist 306** PID: 00288666   217/268-4963
  351 W Washington St, Arcola 61910   Fax 217/268-3809

  Schools: 2 \ **Teachers:** 60 \ **Students:** 717 \ **Special Ed Students:** 88 \ **LEP Students:** 85 \ **College-Bound:** 67% \ **Ethnic:** African American 1%, Hispanic 44%, Caucasian 54% \ **Exp:** $683 (High) \ **Poverty:** 10% \ **Title I:** $163,528 \ **Special Education:** $242,000 \ **Bilingual Education:** $23,000 \ **Open-Close:** 08/19 - 05/27 \ **DTBP:** $177 (High)

  Thomas Mulligan 1,11   Jenny Frichtl 2
  Lynn Klopfleisch ....16*   Cathy Brimner 58
  Chad Strader 67   Jill Hohlbauch 73

Public Schs..Principal	Grd	Prgm	Enr/#Cls	SN
Arcola Elem Sch 351 W Washington St, Arcola 61910 Angela Gentry	PK-6	T	385 21	48% 217/268-4961 Fax 217/268-4719
Arcola Jr Sr High Sch 351 W Washington St, Arcola 61910 Lisa Sigrist	7-12	TV	332	47% 217/268-4962 Fax 217/268-4483

- **Arthur CUSD 305** PID: 00288707   217/543-2511
  301 E Columbia St, Arthur 61911   Fax 217/543-2210

  Schools: 4 \ **Teachers:** 95 \ **Students:** 1,140 \ **Special Ed Students:** 200 \ **LEP Students:** 30 \ **College-Bound:** 44% \ **Ethnic:** African American 1%, Hispanic 3%, Caucasian 96% \ **Exp:** $93 (Low) \ **Poverty:** 11% \ **Title I:** $340,152 \ **Special Education:** $306,000 \ **Open-Close:** 08/17 - 05/26 \ **DTBP:** $154 (High) \ t

  Shannon Cheek 1   Haley McGrath 2
  Jann Harris ....11*   Renee Brown 16,82*
  Jessica Clarkson 58   Beth Wiley 67
  Mark Smith 286*

---

79 Student Personnel	91 Safety/Security	275 Response To Intervention	298 Grant Writer/Ptnrships	**School Programs**	**Social Media**	
80 Driver Ed/Safety	92 Magnet School	277 Remedial Math K-12	750 Chief Innovation Officer	A = Alternative Program		
81 Gifted/Talented	93 Parental Involvement	280 Literacy Coach	751 Chief of Staff	G = Adult Classes	f = Facebook	
82 Video Services	95 Tech Prep Program	285 STEM	752 Social Emotional Learning	M = Magnet Program		
83 Substance Abuse Prev	97 Chief Information Officer	286 Digital Learning		T = Title I Schoolwide	t = Twitter	
84 Erate	98 Chief Technology Officer	288 Common Core Standards	**Other School Types**	V = Career & Tech Ed Programs		
85 AIDS Education	270 Character Education	294 Accountability	A = Alternative School			
88 Alternative/At Risk	271 Migrant Education	295 Network System	C = Charter School	New Schools are shaded		
89 Multi-Cultural Curriculum	273 Teacher Mentor	296 Title II Programs	M = Magnet School	New Superintendents and Principals are bold		
90 Social Work	274 Before/After Sch	297 Webmaster	Y = Year-Round School	Personnel with email addresses are underscored		

IL—87

Du Page County

Market Data Retrieval

Public Schs..Principal	Grd	Prgm	Enr/#Cls	SN
Arthur Grade Sch 126 E Lincoln St, Arthur 61911 Sage Hale	PK-8	T	392 16	41% 217/543-2109 Fax 217/543-2308
Arthur Lovington High Sch 301 E Columbia St, Arthur 61911 Steffanie Seegmiller	9-12	T	322	39% 217/543-2146 Fax 217/543-2174
Atwood-Hammond Grade Sch 316 N Illinois St, Atwood 61913 Kristin Nall	PK-8	T	270 20	43% 217/578-2229 Fax 217/578-3314
Lovington Grade Sch 330 S High St, Lovington 61937 Brandon Stone	PK-8	AT	196 25	57% 217/873-4318 Fax 217/873-6120

• **Tuscola Cmty Unit SD 301** PID: 00288783 217/253-4241
409 S Prairie St, Tuscola 61953 Fax 217/253-3236

Schools: 3 \ **Teachers:** 67 \ **Students:** 1,000 \ **Special Ed Students:** 126 \ **LEP Students:** 14 \ **College-Bound:** 67% \ **Ethnic:** Asian 1%, African American 1%, Hispanic 4%, Caucasian 94% \ **Exp:** $160 (Low) \ **Poverty:** 14% \ **Title I:** $194,705 \ **Special Education:** $256,000 \ **Open-Close:** 08/20 - 05/21 \

Gary Alexander 1
Jason Wallace 11,296*
Justin Bozarth 38,69*
Shannon Smith 73
Dr Kay Dorner 275
Ryan Hornaday 6*
Steven Fiscus 27,60
Cathy Mannen 67
Katie Hatfield 83,88*

Public Schs..Principal	Grd	Prgm	Enr/#Cls	SN
East Prairie Junior High Sch 409 S Prairie St, Tuscola 61953 Jared Vanausdoll	5-8		300 20	38% 217/253-2828 Fax 217/253-3226
North Ward Elem Sch 1201 N Prairie St, Tuscola 61953 R Jason Wallace	PK-4	T	365 24	41% 217/253-2712 Fax 217/253-4851
Tuscola High Sch 500 S Prairie St, Tuscola 61953 Steve Fiscus	9-12	V	287 35	34% 217/253-2377 Fax 217/253-4861

• **Villa Grove Cmty Unit SD 302** PID: 00288836 217/832-2261
400 N Sycamore St, Villa Grove 61956 Fax 217/832-8615

Schools: 3 \ **Teachers:** 47 \ **Students:** 651 \ **Special Ed Students:** 128 \ **LEP Students:** 8 \ **College-Bound:** 70% \ **Ethnic:** African American 1%, Hispanic 2%, Caucasian 97% \ **Exp:** $164 (Low) \ **Poverty:** 10% \ **Title I:** $102,761 \ **Special Education:** $200,000 \ **Open-Close:** 08/20 - 05/21 \ **DTBP:** $93 (Med)

Norm Tracy 1
Jack Clapp 3
Steve Vandeventer 5
Angela Coady 12*
Jim Clark 67
Shirley Badman 2,68,84
Cathy Raymer 4
Bobby Beck 9,73,76,79*
Eric Rittman 16*

Public Schs..Principal	Grd	Prgm	Enr/#Cls	SN
Villa Grove Elem Sch 400 N Sycamore St, Villa Grove 61956 Bobby Beck \ Sara Jones	PK-6	A	352 25	53% 217/832-2261
Villa Grove High Sch 400 N Sycamore St, Villa Grove 61956 S Jones	9-12		193	35% 217/832-2321 Fax 217/832-8689
Villa Grove Junior High Sch 400 N Sycamore St, Villa Grove 61956 Stephen Killion	7-8	T	106	50% 217/832-2261

DOUGLAS PRIVATE SCHOOLS

Private Schs..Principal	Grd	Prgm	Enr/#Cls	SN
Arthur Christian Sch 1637 State Highway 133, Arthur 61911 Greg Mast	PK-12		120 5	217/543-2397 Fax 217/543-3781

DU PAGE COUNTY

DU PAGE COUNTY SCHOOLS

County Schs..Principal	Grd	Prgm	Enr/#Cls	SN
Lincoln Academy 320 Lincoln St, Roselle 60172 William Grotthuss	Spec	V	66 6	53% 630/529-4050 Fax 630/529-3472
Mark Lund Day Sch 164 S Prairie Ave, Bloomingdale 60108 Paula Bodzioch	Spec	G	72 4	630/307-1882 Fax 630/397-5624
Ⓐ Southeast Alternative Sch 6S331 Cornwall Rd, Naperville 60540 Andy Hubble	K-12	V	100 17	51% 630/778-4510 Fax 630/778-0503
Technology Center of Dupage 301 S Swift Rd Ste B, Addison 60101 Jason Hlavacs	Voc		825 15	630/620-8770 Fax 630/691-7592

DU PAGE PUBLIC SCHOOLS

• **Addison School District 4** PID: 00288850 630/458-2500
222 N Jf Kennedy Dr Rear 2, Addison 60101 Fax 630/628-8829

Schools: 9 \ **Teachers:** 288 \ **Students:** 4,000 \ **Special Ed Students:** 669 \ **LEP Students:** 1,506 \ **Ethnic:** Asian 4%, African American 2%, Hispanic 64%, Native American: 3%, Caucasian 26% \ **Exp:** $245 (Med) \ **Poverty:** 12% \ **Title I:** $810,797 \ **Special Education:** $3,118,000 \ **Bilingual Education:** $236,000 \ **Open-Close:** 09/01 - 06/10 \ **DTBP:** $188 (High)

John Langton 1
Keri Karpman 59,296
Mike Kucko 76
Tim Keeley 2,3,17,19
Dave Williams 67
Janet Diaz 274*

Public Schs..Principal	Grd	Prgm	Enr/#Cls	SN
Addison Early Learning Center 650 S Ardmore Ave, Addison 60101 Erin Alexander	PK-PK	T	170	59% 630/458-3095 Fax 630/834-0905
Ardmore Elem Sch 644 S Ardmore Ave, Addison 60101 Kara Dohman	K-5	T	254 15	62% 630/458-2900 Fax 630/833-3572
Army Trail Elem Sch 346 W Army Trail Blvd, Addison 60101 Rob Tucker	PK-5	T	394 20	84% 630/458-2502 Fax 630/628-2516
Fullerton Elem Sch 400 S Michigan Ave, Addison 60101 Craig Bennett	K-5	T	528 26	68% 630/458-2950 Fax 630/833-3949
Indian Trail Jr High Sch 222 N Jf Kennedy Dr, Addison 60101 Kathleen Purse	6-8	T	1,290 70	60% 630/458-2600 Fax 630/628-2841

1 Superintendent	8 Curric/Instruct K-12	19 Chief Financial Officer	29 Family/Consumer Science	39 Social Studies K-12	49 English/Lang Arts Elem	59 Special Education Elem	69 Academic Assessment
2 Bus/Finance/Purchasing	9 Curric/Instruct Elem	20 Art K-12	30 Adult Education	40 Social Studies Elem	50 English/Lang Arts Sec	60 Special Education Sec	70 Research/Development
3 Buildings And Grounds	10 Curric/Instruct Sec	21 Art Elem	31 Career/Sch-to-Work K-12	41 Social Studies Sec	51 Reading K-12	61 Foreign/World Lang K-12	71 Public Information
4 Food Service	11 Federal Program	22 Art Sec	32 Career/Sch-to-Work Elem	42 Science K-12	52 Reading Elem	62 Foreign/World Lang Elem	72 Summer School
5 Transportation	12 Title I	23 Music K-12	33 Career/Sch-to-Work Sec	43 Science Elem	53 Reading Sec	63 Foreign/World Lang Sec	73 Instructional Tech
6 Athletic	13 Title V	24 Music Elem	34 Early Childhood Ed	44 Science Sec	54 Remedial Reading K-12	64 Religious Education K-12	74 Inservice Training
7 Health Services	15 Asst Superintendent	25 Music Sec	35 Health/Phys Education	45 Math K-12	55 Remedial Reading Elem	65 Religious Education Elem	75 Marketing/Distributive
	16 Instructional Media Svcs	26 Business Education	36 Guidance Services K-12	46 Math Elem	56 Remedial Reading Sec	66 Religious Education Sec	76 Info Systems
	17 Chief Operations Officer	27 Career & Tech Ed	37 Guidance Services Elem	47 Math Sec	57 Bilingual/ELL	67 School Board President	77 Psychological Assess
	18 Chief Academic Officer	28 Technology Education	38 Guidance Services Sec	48 English/Lang Arts K-12	58 Special Education K-12	68 Teacher Personnel	78 Affirmative Action

Illinois School Directory — Du Page County

Lake Park Elem Sch 330 W Lake Park Dr, Addison 60101 Dave Smogor	K-5	T	276 16	77%	630/458-3010 Fax 630/628-2526
Lincoln Elem Sch 720 N Lincoln Ave, Addison 60101 Karla Kelly	K-5	T	340 20	86%	630/458-3040 Fax 630/628-2524
Stone Elem Sch 1404 W Stone Ave, Addison 60101 Cristina Villalobos	K-5		456 22	31%	630/628-4020 Fax 630/628-2546
Wesley Elem Sch 1111 W Westwood Trl, Addison 60101 Kathryn Ahart	K-5	T	231 13	52%	630/628-4060 Fax 630/628-2536

● **Benjamin Sch District 25** PID: 00288965   630/876-7800
28W250 Saint Charles Rd, West Chicago 60185   Fax 630/876-3325

> **Schools:** 2 \ **Teachers:** 54 \ **Students:** 650 \ **Special Ed Students:** 88 \ **LEP Students:** 54 \ **Ethnic:** Asian 9%, African American 2%, Hispanic 19%, Caucasian 70% \ **Exp:** $625 (High) \ **Poverty:** 4% \ **Title I:** $32,122 \ **Special Education:** $258,000 \ **Open-Close:** 08/26 - 06/02 \ **DTBP:** $221 (High)

Dr Jim Woell 1   Cheryl Witham 2
Tim Kazmierczak 3   Dr Debra LeBlanc 9,11,57,69,88,270,296
Vince Enstrom 67   Greg Martin 73,76
Dr Todd Huenecke .... 77,83*   Janice Youngith 298

Public Schs..Principal	Grd	Prgm	Enr/#Cls	SN	
Benjamin Middle Sch 28W300 Saint Charles Rd, West Chicago 60185 Michael Fitzgerald	5-8		272 20	8%	630/876-7820 Fax 630/231-3886
Evergreen Elem Sch 1041 Evergreen Dr, Carol Stream 60188 Laura Pfanenstiel	PK-4		315 27	6%	630/876-7810 Fax 630/231-4292

● **Bensenville Elem Sch Dist 2** PID: 00288989   630/766-5940
210 S Church Rd, Bensenville 60106   Fax 630/766-6099

> **Schools:** 3 \ **Teachers:** 160 \ **Students:** 2,350 \ **Special Ed Students:** 328 \ **LEP Students:** 903 \ **Ethnic:** Asian 4%, African American 3%, Hispanic 70%, Caucasian 22% \ **Exp:** $417 (High) \ **Poverty:** 12% \ **Title I:** $367,608 \ **Special Education:** $1,595,000 \ **Bilingual Education:** $273,000 \ **Open-Close:** 08/12 - 05/21 \ **DTBP:** $229 (High) \ f t

James Stelter 1   Paul Novack 2,19
Greg Jones 3   Tanya Barrett 4*
Claire Cooper 5   Dr Kathleen Dugan 11,69,74,83,280,288,296,298
Mary Anderson .... 16,73*   Edgar Palacios 57
Juliann Greene .... 59*   Robert Laudadio 67
Tammy Hoeflinger 68   Tim Waldore 71,297
Keith Lippoldt 295

Public Schs..Principal	Grd	Prgm	Enr/#Cls	SN	
Blackhawk Middle Sch 250 S Church Rd, Bensenville 60106 Perry Finch	6-8	T	744 40	64%	630/766-2601 Fax 630/766-7612
Tioga Elem Sch 212 W Memorial Rd, Bensenville 60106	PK-5	T	805 25	60%	630/766-2602 Fax 630/766-4114
W A Johnson Elem Sch 252 Ridgewood Ave, Bensenville 60106 Carlos Patino	PK-5	T	657 15	64%	630/766-2605 Fax 630/595-3609

● **Bloomingdale School Dist 13** PID: 00289050   630/893-9590
164 Euclid Ave, Bloomingdale 60108   Fax 630/893-1818

> **Schools:** 3 \ **Teachers:** 97 \ **Students:** 1,390 \ **Special Ed Students:** 184 \ **LEP Students:** 39 \ **Ethnic:** Asian 18%, African American 1%, Hispanic 11%, Caucasian 70% \ **Exp:** $160 (Low) \ **Poverty:** 5% \ **Title I:** $90,592 \ **Special Education:** $619,000 \ **Bilingual Education:** $4,000 \ **Open-Close:** 08/26 - 06/08 \ **DTBP:** $233 (High)

Dr Jon Bartelt 1   John Reiniche 2,296
Greg Leyden 3   Dr Evonne Waugh ... 9,11,15,69,74,83,294,298
Kristin Novotny .... 16*   Samia Hefferan 34,59,271,275*
Angel Frattinger .... 57*   Cary Moreth 67
Kelly Ordoqui 73,76,286,295

Public Schs..Principal	Grd	Prgm	Enr/#Cls	SN	
Du Jardin Elem Sch 166 Euclid Ave, Bloomingdale 60108 Mark Dwyer	PK-5		400 16	10%	630/894-9200 Fax 630/894-9545
Erickson Elem Sch 277 Springfield Dr, Bloomingdale 60108 Patrick Haugens	PK-5		515 19	4%	630/529-2223 Fax 630/893-9849
Westfield Middle Sch 149 Fairfield Way, Bloomingdale 60108 Stefan Larsson	6-8		483	6%	630/529-6211 Fax 630/893-9336

● **Butler School District 53** PID: 00289115   630/573-2887
2801 York Rd, Oak Brook 60523   Fax 630/573-5374

> **Schools:** 2 \ **Teachers:** 46 \ **Students:** 518 \ **Special Ed Students:** 68 \ **LEP Students:** 21 \ **Ethnic:** Asian 53%, African American 1%, Hispanic 3%, Caucasian 43% \ **Exp:** $368 (High) \ **Poverty:** 3% \ **Title I:** $14,646 \ **Special Education:** $225,000 \ **Open-Close:** 08/14 - 05/28 \ **DTBP:** $235 (High)

Dr Paul Omalley 1,11   Sandi Moore 2*
Dr Sandra Martin 2   Bob Jakupi 3,4
Mike Finke .... 6*   Terry Hillen 7*
Gena Considine 12   Kim Bayer 13,37,69,77,83*
Farheen Beg 16,73,76,84,295   Christopher Edmonds 67
Nick Wlodarczyk 73   Andrea Prola 79

Public Schs..Principal	Grd	Prgm	Enr/#Cls	SN	
Brook Forest Elem Sch 60 Regent Dr, Oak Brook 60523 Chad Prosen	K-5		306 15	1%	630/325-6888 Fax 630/325-8452
Butler Junior High Sch 2801 York Rd, Oak Brook 60523 Andrea Prola	6-8		212 20	2%	630/573-2760 Fax 630/573-1725 t

● **Cass School District 63** PID: 00289191   630/985-2000
8502 Bailey Rd, Darien 60561   Fax 630/985-0225

> **Schools:** 2 \ **Teachers:** 52 \ **Students:** 766 \ **Special Ed Students:** 89 \ **LEP Students:** 73 \ **Ethnic:** Asian 16%, African American 5%, Hispanic 10%, Caucasian 69% \ **Exp:** $247 (Med) \ **Poverty:** 6% \ **Title I:** $67,606 \ **Special Education:** $308,000 \ **Open-Close:** 08/17 - 06/02 \ **DTBP:** $230 (High) \ f t

Mark Cross 1   Debbie Dolehide 2
Robert Strande 2   Wayne Ostrowski 3
Kevin Carver 5   Dr Kerry Foderaro 11,57
Theresa Murphy .... 59*   Shelly Camden 67
Christine Marcinkewicz .... 73*   Pamela Worth 88,93*
Matt Etherington 297*

79	Student Personnel	91	Safety/Security	275	Response To Intervention	298	Grant Writer/Ptnrships
80	Driver Ed/Safety	92	Magnet School	277	Remedial Math K-12	750	Chief Innovation Officer
81	Gifted/Talented	93	Parental Involvement	280	Literacy Coach	751	Chief of Staff
82	Video Services	95	Tech Prep Program	285	STEM	752	Social Emotional Learning
83	Substance Abuse Prev	97	Chief Information Officer	286	Digital Learning		
84	Erate	98	Chief Technology Officer	288	Common Core Standards		
85	AIDS Education	270	Accountability	294	Network System		
88	Alternative/At Risk	271	Migrant Education	295	Network System		
89	Multi-Cultural Curriculum	273	Teacher Mentor	296	Title II Programs		
90	Social Work	274	Before/After Sch	297	Webmaster		

Other School Types
Ⓐ = Alternative School
Ⓒ = Charter School
Ⓜ = Magnet School
Ⓨ = Year-Round School

School Programs
A = Alternative Program
G = Adult Classes
M = Magnet Program
T = Title I Schoolwide
V = Career & Tech Ed Programs

Social Media
f = Facebook
t = Twitter

New Schools are shaded
New Superintendents and Principals are bold
Personnel with email addresses are underscored

Du Page County　　　　　　　　　　　　　　　　　　　　　　　　　　　　　　Market Data Retrieval

Public Schs..Principal	Grd	Prgm	Enr/#Cls	SN	
Cass Junior High Sch 8502 Bailey Rd, Darien 60561 Christine Marcinkewicz	5-8	V	293 20	22%	331/481-4020 Fax 331/481-4001
Concord Elem Sch 1019 Concord Pl, Darien 60561 Dr Laura Anderson	PK-4		473 22	15%	331/481-4010 Fax 331/481-4011

● **Center Cass Sch Dist 66** PID: 00289220　　　630/783-5000
699 Plainfield Rd, Downers Grove 60516　　　　　Fax 630/910-0980

Schools: 3 \ **Teachers:** 74 \ **Students:** 1,100 \ **Special Ed Students:** 126 \ **LEP Students:** 80 \ **Ethnic:** Asian 11%, African American 4%, Hispanic 11%, Caucasian 74% \ **Exp:** $298 (Med) \ **Poverty:** 4% \ **Title I:** $44,802 \ **Special Education:** $587,000 \ **Bilingual Education:** $9,000 \ **Open-Close:** 08/20 - 05/27 \ **DTBP:** $241 (High)

Dr Andrew Wise 1	Carol Tedeschi 2,19
Tom Tiede 5	Beth Nyhlen 6*
Deb Doyle 9	Kim Liles 12,58,79,83,752*
Shannon Haye 16,82*	Liane Raso 67
Cheryl Novotny 274	

Public Schs..Principal	Grd	Prgm	Enr/#Cls	SN	
Elizabeth Ide Elem Sch 2000 Manning Rd, Darien 60561 Sean Rhoads	K-2		346 13	6%	630/783-5200 Fax 630/971-3367
Lakeview Junior High Sch 701 Plainfield Rd, Downers Grove 60516 Paul Windsor	6-8		356 20	16%	630/985-2700 Fax 630/985-1545
Prairieview Elem Sch 699 Plainfield Rd, Downers Grove 60516 Mark Pagel	3-5		309 17	11%	630/783-5100 Fax 630/910-0803

● **Community Cons School Dist 89** PID: 00289830　　630/469-8900
22W600 Butterfield Rd, Glen Ellyn 60137　　　　　　　Fax 630/469-8936

Schools: 5 \ **Teachers:** 142 \ **Students:** 2,300 \ **Special Ed Students:** 295 \ **LEP Students:** 213 \ **Ethnic:** Asian 18%, African American 7%, Hispanic 13%, Caucasian 63% \ **Exp:** $335 (High) \ **Poverty:** 6% \ **Title I:** $182,536 \ **Special Education:** $837,000 \ **Bilingual Education:** $35,000 \ **Open-Close:** 08/24 - 05/25 \ **DTBP:** $237 (High)

Dr Emily Tammaru 1	Maureen Jones 2,15,17
Tim Tomazin 3,91	Sandy Lawinger 7
Dr Jill Kingsfield 9,11,15,57,296,298	Katie Kreller 59,79,90
Beth Powers 67	Courtney Magliano 68
Matt Hanley 71	Jeff Romani 73,76,295,297*

Public Schs..Principal	Grd	Prgm	Enr/#Cls	SN	
Arbor View Elem Sch 22W430 Ironwood Dr, Glen Ellyn 60137 Emily Burnett	PK-5		298 18	20%	630/469-5505 Fax 630/790-6073
Briar Glen Elem Sch 1800 Briarcliffe Blvd, Wheaton 60189 Mitch Dubinsky	PK-5		472 15	20%	630/545-3300 Fax 630/665-2847
Glen Crest Middle Sch 725 Sheehan Ave, Glen Ellyn 60137 Kim Price	6-8		684 50	18%	630/469-5220 Fax 630/469-5250
Park View Elem Sch 250 S Park Blvd, Glen Ellyn 60137 Kristie Mate	K-5		462 18	22%	630/858-1600 Fax 630/858-1634
Westfield Elem Sch 2S125 Mayfield Ln, Glen Ellyn 60137 Matt McDonald	PK-5		343 20	16%	630/858-2770 Fax 630/858-3618

● **Community Cons School Dist 93** PID: 00289141　　630/893-9393
230 Covington Dr, Bloomingdale 60108　　　　　　　　Fax 630/539-3450

Schools: 9 \ **Teachers:** 310 \ **Students:** 3,200 \ **Special Ed Students:** 556 \ **LEP Students:** 726 \ **Ethnic:** Asian 21%, African American 7%, Hispanic 26%, Caucasian 46% \ **Exp:** $325 (High) \ **Poverty:** 9% \ **Title I:** $471,890 \ **Special Education:** $1,820,000 \ **Bilingual Education:** $151,000 \ **Open-Close:** 08/20 - 06/02 \ **DTBP:** $170 (High)

David Hill 1,11	John Bendetti 2,15
Sean Gordon 3,91	Susan Grady 9,288,296,298
Crysta Morrissey 15,79,752	Mireya Sanchez 57,89
Keith Briggs 67	Julie Tobin 68,273
Karen Landorf 70,73	Ryan McPherrin 71
Cathy Drobysh 76	Julie Augustyn 83,88
Tim Musa 295	Kevin Casella 297
Kevin Kinsall 297	

Public Schs..Principal	Grd	Prgm	Enr/#Cls	SN	
Carol Stream Elem Sch 422 Sioux Ln, Carol Stream 60188 Steven Kyle	K-5		307 14	39%	630/588-5400 Fax 630/588-5499
Cloverdale Elem Sch 1182 Merbach Dr, Carol Stream 60188 Korrie McCarry	K-5		566 28	30%	630/588-5300 Fax 630/588-5399
Early Childhood Center 280 Old Gary Ave, Bloomingdale 60108 Rosary Horne	PK-PK		238	33%	630/307-3750 Fax 630/307-3845
Elsie Johnson Elem Sch 1380 Nautilus Ln, Hanover Park 60133 Rosanne Sikich	PK-5		317 24	48%	630/671-8800 Fax 630/671-8899
Heritage Lakes Elem Sch 925 Woodhill Dr, Carol Stream 60188 Bob Yelaska	K-5		368 25	21%	630/588-6200 Fax 630/588-6299
Jay Stream Middle Sch 283 El Paso Ln, Carol Stream 60188 Christopher Pietroski	6-8	T	648 36	39%	630/588-5200 Fax 630/588-5299
Roy Deshane Elem Sch 475 Chippewa Trl, Carol Stream 60188 Amy Gray	K-5	T	266 12	40%	630/588-6300 Fax 630/588-6399
Stratford Middle Sch 251 Butterfield Dr, Bloomingdale 60108 Patrick Dawson	6-8		584 51	33%	630/671-4300 Fax 630/671-4399
Western Trails Elem Sch 860 Idaho St, Carol Stream 60188 Joylynn Sebastian	K-5		335 24	46%	630/588-6400 Fax 630/588-6499

● **Community Cons School Dist 180** PID: 00290841　　630/734-6600
15W451 91st St, Burr Ridge 60527　　　　　　　　　　　Fax 630/325-6450

Schools: 2 \ **Teachers:** 51 \ **Students:** 630 \ **Special Ed Students:** 105 \ **LEP Students:** 36 \ **Ethnic:** Asian 5%, African American 73%, Hispanic 7%, Caucasian 15% \ **Exp:** $473 (High) \ **Poverty:** 34% \ **Title I:** $574,499 \ **Special Education:** $699,000 \ **Open-Close:** 08/20 - 05/25 \ **DTBP:** $250 (High)

Dr Thomas Schneider 1	Dr Ben Nowakowski 2,11
Jim Borchert 3	Ashay Wilks 4
Jan Schlemmer 7*	Tenika Pickens 59,79*
Paula DuPont 67	Rene DeGuzman 73,76,286,295
Meghan Radtke 83,270*	

Public Schs..Principal	Grd	Prgm	Enr/#Cls	SN	
Anne M Jeans Elem Sch 16W631 91st St, Willowbrook 60527 Tracy Ritchey	PK-4	T	347 24	79%	630/325-8186 Fax 630/325-9576

---

1 Superintendent	8 Curric/Instruct K-12	19 Chief Financial Officer	29 Family/Consumer Science	39 Social Studies K-12	49 English/Lang Arts Elem	59 Special Education Elem	69 Academic Assessment
2 Bus/Finance/Purchasing	9 Curric/Instruct Elem	20 Art K-12	30 Adult Education	40 Social Studies Elem	50 English/Lang Arts Sec	60 Special Education Sec	70 Research/Development
3 Buildings And Grounds	10 Curric/Instruct Sec	21 Art Elem	31 Career/Sch-to-Work K-12	41 Social Studies Sec	51 Reading K-12	61 Foreign/World Lang K-12	71 Public Information
4 Food Service	11 Federal Program	22 Art Sec	32 Career/Sch-to-Work Elem	42 Science K-12	52 Reading Elem	62 Foreign/World Lang Elem	72 Summer School
5 Transportation	12 Title I	23 Music K-12	33 Career/Sch-to-Work Sec	43 Science Elem	53 Reading Sec	63 Foreign/World Lang Sec	73 Instructional Tech
6 Athletic	13 Title V	24 Music Elem	34 Early Childhood Ed	44 Science Sec	54 Remedial Reading K-12	64 Religious Education K-12	74 Inservice Training
7 Health Services	15 Asst Superintendent	25 Music Sec	35 Health/Phys Education	45 Math K-12	55 Remedial Reading Elem	65 Religious Education Elem	75 Marketing/Distributive
	16 Instructional Media Svcs	26 Business Education	36 Guidance Services K-12	46 Math Elem	56 Remedial Reading Sec	66 Religious Education Sec	76 Info Systems
	17 Chief Operations Officer	27 Career & Tech Ed	37 Guidance Services Elem	47 Math Sec	57 Bilingual/ELL	67 School Board President	77 Psychological Assess
	18 Chief Academic Officer	28 Technology Education	38 Guidance Services Sec	48 English/Lang Arts K-12	58 Special Education K-12	68 Teacher Personnel	78 Affirmative Action

Illinois School Directory — Du Page County

Burr Ridge Middle Sch   5-8   T   253   89%   630/325-5454
15W451 91st St, Burr Ridge 60527   20
Julie Bartell

- **Community Cons School Dist 181**   PID: 00290061   630/861-4900
115 55th St, Clarendon Hls 60514   Fax 630/887-1079

Schools: 9 \ **Teachers:** 303 \ **Students:** 3,800 \ **Special Ed Students:** 495 \ **LEP Students:** 125 \ **Ethnic:** Asian 16%, African American 1%, Hispanic 7%, Caucasian 75% \ **Exp:** $382 (High) \ **Poverty:** 2% \ **Title I:** $101,438 \ **Special Education:** $1,643,000 \ **Bilingual Education:** $23,000 \ **Open-Close:** 08/24 - 06/02 \ **DTBP:** $191 (High)

Dr Hector Garcia	1	Joshua Schoot	2
Moshin Dada	2,5,19,91	Patricia O'Connor	2
Debbie Prasch	3	Jim LaBorn	3
Mike Duggan	3	Dr Kathleen Robinson	9,11,15,57,69,81
Dana Bergthold	11,59,79	John Munch	15,68
Matt Kunesh	16,73,286	Tracey Miller	18,69,294
Margaret Kleber	67	Angela Rangel	68
Jamie LaVigueur	71	Stephanie Gardner	76

Public Schs..Principal	Grd	Prgm	Enr/#Cls	SN		
Clarendon Hills Middle Sch	6-8		584	3%	630/861-4800	
301 Chicago Ave, Clarendon Hls 60514					Fax 630/887-4267	
Levi Brown						
Elm Elem Sch	K-5		286	3%	630/861-4000	
15W201 60th St, Burr Ridge 60527			25		Fax 630/655-9734	
Sara Olson						
Hinsdale Middle Sch	6-8		722	6%	630/861-4700	
100 S Garfield Ave, Hinsdale 60521			30		Fax 630/861-4086	
Ruben Pena						
Lane Elem Sch	K-5		316	4%	630/861-4500	
500 N Elm St, Hinsdale 60521			14		Fax 630/655-9735	
Brandon Todd						
Madison Elem Sch	K-5		465	2%	630/861-4100	
611 S Madison St, Hinsdale 60521			19		Fax 630/655-9742	
Kimberley Rutan						
Monroe Elem Sch	K-5		346	2%	630/861-4200	
210 N Madison St, Hinsdale 60521			21		Fax 630/655-9716	
Kristin Reingruber						
Oak Elem Sch	PK-5		350	1%	630/861-4300	
950 S Oak St, Hinsdale 60521			16		Fax 630/887-0240	
Martha Henrikson						
Prospect Elem Sch	K-5		406	6%	630/861-4400	
100 N Prospect Ave, Clarendon Hls 60514			19		Fax 630/655-9721	
Kristin Cummings						
Walker Elem Sch	K-5		286	3%	630/861-4600	
120 Walker Ave, Clarendon Hls 60514					Fax 630/887-0387	
Eric Chisausky						

- **Community High School Dist 94**   PID: 00291546   630/876-6200
157 W Washington St, West Chicago 60185   Fax 630/876-6217

Schools: 1 \ **Teachers:** 125 \ **Students:** 2,006 \ **Special Ed Students:** 311 \ **LEP Students:** 409 \ **College-Bound:** 64% \ **Ethnic:** Asian 4%, African American 2%, Hispanic 67%, Caucasian 27% \ **Exp:** $205 (Med) \ **Poverty:** 10% \ **Title I:** $371,241 \ **Special Education:** $1,140,000 \ **Bilingual Education:** $58,000 \ **Open-Close:** 09/10 - 06/11 \ **DTBP:** $232 (High) \ t

Dr Douglas Domeracki	1	Dan Oberg	2
David Blatchley	3*	Doug Mullaney	6
Peter Martino	11,72,83,296,298*	Jennifer Brady	16*
Marc Wolfe	27*	Donald Zabelin	30*
Danielle Welch	60*	Leslie Springer	60

Sandy Pampuch	60	Veronica Jimenez	61*
Gary Saake	67	Cheryl Moore	68
Becky Koltz	71	Bob Schmidt	73
Dr Moses Cheng	74,294*	Beth Schuck	76
Len Egan	79	Allister Scott	273,288*
David Pater	275*	Joe Neilon	286,297*
Steven Korpal	295		

Public Schs..Principal	Grd	Prgm	Enr/#Cls	SN		
Community High Sch	9-12	AGV	2,006	36%	630/876-6200	
326 Joliet St, West Chicago 60185					Fax 630/867-6241	
Dr Moses Cheng						

- **Community High School Dist 99**   PID: 00289323   630/795-7100
6301 Springside Ave, Downers Grove 60516   Fax 630/795-7199

Schools: 2 \ **Teachers:** 328 \ **Students:** 5,015 \ **Special Ed Students:** 670 \ **LEP Students:** 162 \ **Ethnic:** Asian 7%, African American 9%, Hispanic 17%, Caucasian 67% \ **Exp:** $277 (Med) \ **Poverty:** 5% \ **Title I:** $404,284 \ **Special Education:** $3,414,000 \ **Bilingual Education:** $44,000 \ **Open-Close:** 08/17 - 05/21 \ **DTBP:** $189 (High) \ f t

Dr Henry Thiele	1	Mark Staehlin	2,4,5,11
Jim Kolodziej	3,91	Randy Konstans	6*
Gina Ziccardi	10,15,57,298	Dr Robert Lang	15,68,74,273,296
Scott Wuggazer	15,79	Lisa Bollow	60
Dr Nancy Kupka	67	Jill Browning	71,297
Rod Russeau	73,76,84,286,295	Diana Benoist	83*
Keith Bullock	83*	Colleen Davoren	295
Tony Dotts	295		

Public Schs..Principal	Grd	Prgm	Enr/#Cls	SN		
North High Sch	9-12	AV	2,150	14%	630/795-8400	
4436 Main St, Downers Grove 60515			100		Fax 630/795-8499	
Janice Schwarze						
South High Sch	9-12	AV	2,766	28%	630/795-8500	
1436 Norfolk St, Downers Grove 60516					Fax 630/795-8599	
Edward Schwartz						

- **Community Unit School Dist 200**   PID: 00290877   630/682-2000
130 W Park Ave, Wheaton 60189   Fax 630/682-2227

Schools: 20 \ **Teachers:** 862 \ **Students:** 12,000 \ **Special Ed Students:** 1,932 \ **LEP Students:** 1,276 \ **College-Bound:** 82% \ **Ethnic:** Asian 8%, African American 7%, Hispanic 18%, Caucasian 67% \ **Exp:** $214 (Med) \ **Poverty:** 6% \ **Title I:** $1,289,437 \ **Special Education:** $10,197,000 \ **Bilingual Education:** $417,000 \ **Open-Close:** 09/01 - 05/27 \ **DTBP:** $205 (High) \ f t

Dr Jeff Schuler	1	Kim Funkhouser	2
Lisa Maher	2	Roxanne Mildice	2
William Farley	2,5,15,80,91	Colin Wilkie	3
John Robinson	3	Matthew Duhig	3
Michael Duhig	3	Mike Healy	6*
Cindy Reuter	8	Melissa Murphy	8,11,15
Matt Jewell	9	Lee Cook	10,73,286
Dr Charles Kyle	15	Chris Silagi	15,34,36,77,79,83,88,90*
Limaris Pueyo	51,57	Bridget Dickinson	58
Dan Cochrane	58	Erica Ekstrom	58
Megan Burress	58	Brad Paulsen	67
Catia Capiga	68	Jana Gorman	68
Jenny Schon	68	Kristy Kuntz	68
Erica Loiacono	71	Rodney Mack	73,76,297
B Gray	295	Lesley Boyum	295

79	Student Personnel	91	Safety/Security	275	Response To Intervention
80	Driver Ed/Safety	92	Magnet School	277	Remedial Math K-12
81	Gifted/Talented	93	Parental Involvement	280	Literacy Coach
82	Video Services	95	Tech Prep Program	285	STEM
83	Substance Abuse Prev	97	Chief Information Officer	286	Digital Learning
84	Erate	98	Chief Technology Officer	288	Common Core Standards
85	AIDS Education	270	Accountability	294	Alternative Education
88	Alternative/At Risk	271	Migrant Education	295	Network System
89	Multi-Cultural Curriculum	273	Teacher Mentor	296	Title II Programs
90	Social Work	274	Before/After Sch	297	Webmaster

298	Grant Writer/Ptnrships	750	Chief Innovation Officer
751	Chief of Staff	752	Social Emotional Learning

Other School Types
- Ⓐ = Alternative School
- Ⓒ = Charter School
- Ⓜ = Magnet School
- Ⓨ = Year-Round School

School Programs
- A = Alternative Program
- G = Adult Classes
- M = Magnet Program
- T = Title I Schoolwide
- V = Career & Tech Ed Programs

Social Media
- f = Facebook
- t = Twitter

New Schools are shaded
New Superintendents and Principals are bold
Personnel with email addresses are underscored

Du Page County

Public Schs..Principal	Grd	Prgm	Enr/#Cls	SN	
Bower Elem Sch 4S241 River Rd, Warrenville 60555 Bridget Moore	K-5		449 28	27%	630/393-9413 Fax 630/393-9403
Carl Sandburg Elem Sch 1345 Jewell Rd, Wheaton 60187 Stacey Bailey	K-5	T	380 18	33%	630/682-2105 Fax 630/682-2350
Clifford A Johnson Elem Sch 2S700 Continental Dr, Warrenville 60555 Derick Edwards	K-5	T	455 26	59%	630/393-1787 Fax 630/393-7064
Edison Middle Sch 1125 S Wheaton Ave, Wheaton 60189 Rachel Bednar	6-8		628	18%	630/682-2050 Fax 630/682-2337
Emerson Elem Sch 119 S Woodlawn St, Wheaton 60187 Debra Klein	K-5		298 15	18%	630/682-2055 Fax 630/682-2372
Franklin Middle Sch 211 E Franklin St, Wheaton 60187 David Bendis	6-8		690 46	24%	630/682-2060 Fax 630/682-2340
Hawthorne Elem Sch 334 Wakeman Ave, Wheaton 60187 Danielle Moran	K-5	T	229 13	42%	630/682-2065 Fax 630/682-2392
Hubble Middle Sch 3S600 Herrick Rd, Warrenville 60555 Jon Pilkington	6-8	G	723 70	34%	630/821-7900 Fax 630/821-7901
Jefferson Early Chldhd Center 130 N Hazelton Ave, Wheaton 60187 Stephanie Farrelly	PK-PK		182 12	28%	630/682-2474 Fax 630/462-1914
Lincoln Elem Sch 630 Dawes Ave, Wheaton 60189 Jeff Mitchem	K-5	T	480 26	31%	630/682-2075 Fax 630/682-2367
Longfellow Elem Sch 311 W Seminary Ave, Wheaton 60187 Sean Walsh	K-5		368 20	17%	630/682-2080 Fax 630/682-2342
Lowell Elem Sch 312 S President St, Wheaton 60187 Jacqueline Rodriguez	K-5		357 22	31%	630/682-2085 Fax 630/682-2245
Madison Elem Sch 1620 Mayo Ave, Wheaton 60189 Tim Callahan	PK-5		480 21	24%	630/682-2095 Fax 630/682-2435
Monroe Middle Sch 1855 Manchester Rd, Wheaton 60189 Bryan Buck	6-8		778 50	31%	630/682-2285 Fax 630/682-2331
Pleasant Hill Elem Sch 1N220 Pleasant Hill Rd, Winfield 60190 Christine Frederick	K-5	T	646 27	35%	630/682-2100 Fax 630/682-2366
Washington Elem Sch 911 Bridle Ln, Wheaton 60187 Jennifer Craig	K-5	T	402	32%	630/682-2222 Fax 630/682-2333
Wheaton North High Sch 701 W Thomas Rd, Wheaton 60187 Mathew Biscan	9-12	AGV	2,067 225	24%	630/784-7300 Fax 630/682-2158
Wheaton-Warrenville South HS 1920 S Wiesbrook Rd, Wheaton 60189 Scott McDermott	9-12	AGV	1,936	24%	630/784-7200 Fax 630/682-2042
Whittier Elem Sch 218 W Park Ave, Wheaton 60189 Kathryn Schafermeyer	K-5		450 22	12%	630/682-2185 Fax 630/682-2409
Wiesbrook Elem Sch 2160 Durfee Rd, Wheaton 60189 Dr Brian Turyna	K-5		481 22	10%	630/682-2190 Fax 630/682-2339

Market Data Retrieval

• **Community Unit School Dist 201** PID: 00291429 630/468-8000
133 S Grant St, Westmont 60559 Fax 630/969-9022

Schools: 5 \ **Teachers:** 110 \ **Students:** 1,365 \ **Special Ed Students:** 262 \ **LEP Students:** 107 \ **College-Bound:** 73% \ **Ethnic:** Asian 5%, African American 7%, Hispanic 23%, Caucasian 65% \ **Exp:** $330 (High) \ **Poverty:** 7% \ **Title I:** $178,480 \ **Special Education:** $996,000 \ **Bilingual Education:** $39,000 \ **Open-Close:** 08/19 - 05/26 \ **DTBP:** $237 (High)

Kevin Carey 1,83
Mike Mayoros 3
Francesca Canzoneri 4*
Sue Pacelli 7,85*
Linda Klawitter 11,34,58,79,88,275*
Joel Price 67
Kimberly Anderson 2,5,11,296,298
Scott Russo 3
Dan McCulloch 6
Nadine Norris 8,16,73,76,286,288,295
Tim Wyller 57*
James Carrera 84,295

Public Schs..Principal	Grd	Prgm	Enr/#Cls	SN	
C E Miller Elem Sch 125 W Traube Ave, Westmont 60559 Tim Wyller	K-5	T	251 11	41%	630/468-8300 Fax 630/969-5401
Manning Elem Sch 200 N Linden Ave, Westmont 60559 Lindsay Pietrzak	K-5		333 21	26%	630/468-8050 Fax 630/969-2492
South Early Childhood Center 133 S Grant St, Westmont 60559 Linda Klawitter	PK-PK		52	54%	630/468-8015
Westmont High Sch 909 Oakwood Dr, Westmont 60559 Jack Baldermann	9-12	T	365 45	31%	630/468-8100 Fax 630/654-2758
Westmont Junior High Sch 944 Oakwood Dr, Westmont 60559 John Jonak	6-8	T	273 25	36%	630/468-8200 Fax 630/654-2203

• **Darien Public Sch Dist 61** PID: 00289268 630/968-7505
7414 Cass Ave, Darien 60561 Fax 630/968-0872

Schools: 3 \ **Teachers:** 110 \ **Students:** 1,400 \ **Special Ed Students:** 212 \ **LEP Students:** 194 \ **Ethnic:** Asian 7%, African American 14%, Hispanic 20%, Caucasian 59% \ **Exp:** $150 (Low) \ **Poverty:** 9% \ **Title I:** $213,635 \ **Special Education:** $835,000 \ **Bilingual Education:** $46,000 \ **Open-Close:** 08/19 - 05/27 \ **DTBP:** $219 (High)

Dr Robert Langman 1
Kurt Stadtler 3,5
Jennifer Pena 16,73*
Keith Roberts 73,98,295
Michele Goshko 297*
Dennis Forst 2,11,19
Lillie Lillie 4*
Janine Kiwiet 67
Mary Andersen 274*
Katirie Quinonez 752

Public Schs..Principal	Grd	Prgm	Enr/#Cls	SN	
Eisenhower Junior High Sch 1410 75th St, Darien 60561 Jacob Buck	6-8		488 36	36%	630/964-5200 Fax 630/968-8002
Lace Elem Sch 7414 Cass Ave, Darien 60561 Erin Dwyer	3-5		467 19	39%	630/968-2589 Fax 630/968-5920
Mark Delay Sch 6801 Wilmette Ave, Darien 60561 Lisa Kompare	PK-2		505 15	38%	630/852-0200 Fax 630/968-7506

1	Superintendent	8	Curric/Instruct K-12	19	Chief Financial Officer	29	Family/Consumer Science	39	Social Studies K-12	49	English/Lang Arts Elem	59	Special Education Elem	69	Academic Assessment
2	Bus/Finance/Purchasing	9	Curric/Instruct Elem	20	Art K-12	30	Adult Education	40	Social Studies Elem	50	English/Lang Arts Sec	60	Special Education Sec	70	Research/Development
3	Buildings And Grounds	10	Curric/Instruct Sec	21	Art Elem	31	Career/Sch-to-Work K-12	41	Social Studies Sec	51	Reading K-12	61	Foreign/World Lang K-12	71	Public Information
4	Food Service	11	Federal Program	22	Art Sec	32	Career/Sch-to-Work Elem	42	Science K-12	52	Reading Elem	62	Foreign/World Lang Elem	72	Summer School
5	Transportation	12	Title I	23	Music K-12	33	Career/Sch-to-Work Sec	43	Science Elem	53	Reading Sec	63	Foreign/World Lang Sec	73	Instructional Tech
6	Athletic	13	Title V	24	Music Elem	34	Early Childhood Ed	44	Science Sec	54	Remedial Reading K-12	64	Religious Education K-12	74	Inservice Training
7	Health Services	14	Asst Superintendent	25	Music Sec	35	Health/Phys Education	45	Math K-12	55	Remedial Reading Elem	65	Religious Education Elem	75	Marketing/Distributive
		15	Instructional Media Svcs	26	Business Education	36	Guidance Services K-12	46	Math Elem	56	Remedial Reading Sec	66	Religious Education Sec	76	Info Systems
		16	Chief Operations Officer	27	Career & Tech Ed	37	Guidance Services Elem	47	Math Sec	57	Bilingual/ELL	67	School Board President	77	Psychological Assess
		17	Chief Academic Officer	28	Technology Education	38	Guidance Services Sec	48	English/Lang Arts K-12	58	Special Education K-12	68	Teacher Personnel	78	Affirmative Action

Illinois School Directory — Du Page County

• Downers Grove School Dist 58 PID: 01844562   630/719-5800
1860 63rd St, Downers Grove 60516   Fax 630/719-9857

Schools: 13 \ **Teachers:** 300 \ **Students:** 5,000 \ **Special Ed Students:** 716 \ **LEP Students:** 265 \ **Ethnic:** Asian 5%, African American 4%, Hispanic 11%, Caucasian 80% \ **Exp:** $369 (High) \ **Poverty:** 4% \ **Title I:** $204,567 \ **Special Education:** $3,853,000 \ **Bilingual Education:** $41,000 \ **Open-Close:** 08/27 - 06/07 \ **DTBP:** $190 (High) \ f t

Name	Ref	Name	Ref
Kevin Russell	1	Catherine Hannigan	2,4,5
Todd Drafall	2	Kevin Barto	3,91
Jessica Stewart	7,35,57,77,83,88,90,271	Dr Jayne Yudzentis	15,68,74,273,751
Justin Sisul	16,73,277,280	Todd Cherney	17
Jackelyn Cadard	34	Darren Hughes	67
Megan Hewitt	71	James Eichmiller	73,286,297
Maria Velez	76	Rod Novotny	295

Public Schs..Principal	Grd	Prgm	Enr/#Cls	SN	
Belle Aire Elem Sch 3935 Belle Aire Ln, Downers Grove 60515 Brent Borchelt	K-6		241 12	6%	630/719-5820 Fax 630/719-9311 f
El Sierra Elem Sch 6835 Fairmount Ave, Downers Grove 60516 Jason Lynde	K-6		213 13	15%	630/719-5825 Fax 630/719-9281
Fairmount Elem Sch 6036 Blodgett Ave, Downers Grove 60516 Lisa Niforatos	K-6		337 13	7%	630/719-5830 Fax 630/719-1161
Henry Puffer Sch 2220 Haddow Ave, Downers Grove 60515 Britta Waszak	PK-6		400 30	18%	630/968-0294 Fax 630/968-4061
Herrick Middle Sch 4335 Middaugh Ave, Downers Grove 60515 Amy Read	7-8		656 32	8%	630/719-5810 Fax 630/719-1628 f
Highland Elem Sch 3935 Highland Ave, Downers Grove 60515 Zachary Craft	PK-6		396 14	6%	630/719-5835 Fax 630/719-0150
Hillcrest Elem Sch 1435 Jefferson Ave, Downers Grove 60516 Michelle Rzepka	K-6		384 20	7%	630/719-5840 Fax 630/719-0122 f
Indian Trail Elem Sch 6235 Stonewall Ave, Downers Grove 60516 Mariana Nicasio	PK-6		375 21	9%	630/719-5845 Fax 630/719-1275
Kingsley Elem Sch 6509 Powell St, Downers Grove 60516 Melissa Sawisch	K-6		431 17	11%	630/719-5850 Fax 630/719-0982
Lester Elem Sch 236 Indianapolis Ave, Downers Grove 60515 Carin Novak	PK-6		525 21	6%	630/719-5855 Fax 630/719-0053 f t
O'Neill Middle Sch 635 59th St, Downers Grove 60516 Matthew Durbala	7-8		437 45	19%	630/719-5815 Fax 630/719-1436 f
Pierce Downer Elem Sch 1436 Grant St, Downers Grove 60515 Leland Wagner	K-6		341 16	1%	630/719-5860 Fax 630/719-1176
Whittier Elem Sch 536 Hill St, Downers Grove 60515 Michael Krugman	K-6		322 11	5%	630/719-5865 Fax 630/719-1105 f

• Dupage High School Dist 88 PID: 00289684   630/530-3981
2 Friendship Plz, Addison 60101   Fax 630/832-0198

Schools: 2 \ **Teachers:** 243 \ **Students:** 3,929 \ **Special Ed Students:** 574 \ **LEP Students:** 351 \ **College-Bound:** 71% \ **Ethnic:** Asian 7%, African American 6%, Hispanic 48%, Native American: 1%, Caucasian 38% \ **Exp:** $527 (High) \ **Poverty:** 9% \ **Title I:** $538,144 \ **Special Education:** $2,613,000 \ **Bilingual Education:** $69,000 \ **Open-Close:** 08/19 - 05/28 \ **DTBP:** $191 (High) \ f

Name	Ref	Name	Ref
Dr Scott Helton	1	Ryan Domeracki	2,4,5,91
Tom Manka	3*	Brandon Murphy	6*
Aaron Lenaghan	10,73	Yvonne Tsagalis	10,15
Jean Barbanente	12,88	Edward Hoster	19
Kevin Redding	38*	Donna Cain	67
Danielle Brink	71	Chris Grice	79
Jorge De Leon	90*	Jian Zhang	295

Public Schs..Principal	Grd	Prgm	Enr/#Cls	SN	
Addison Trail High Sch 213 N Lombard Rd, Addison 60101 Michael Bolden	9-12	TV	1,999	54%	630/628-3300 Fax 630/628-0177
Willowbrook High Sch 1250 S Ardmore Ave, Villa Park 60181 Dan Krause	9-12	TV	1,930 60	44%	630/530-3400 Fax 630/530-3401

• Elmhurst Cmty Unit SD 205 PID: 00289488   630/834-4530
162 S York St, Elmhurst 60126   Fax 630/617-2345

Schools: 13 \ **Teachers:** 590 \ **Students:** 8,499 \ **Special Ed Students:** 1,273 \ **LEP Students:** 678 \ **Ethnic:** Asian 6%, African American 2%, Hispanic 17%, Caucasian 74% \ **Exp:** $260 (Med) \ **Poverty:** 3% \ **Title I:** $282,337 \ **Special Education:** $4,430,000 \ **Bilingual Education:** $343,000 \ **Open-Close:** 08/24 - 06/04 \ **DTBP:** $191 (High) \ t

Name	Ref	Name	Ref
Dr David Moyer	1	Adrian Gaerlan	2
Chris Whelton	2,3,5,15	Nikki Tammaro	3,8,11,27,69,280,294,298
Todd Schmidt	3	Cheryl Spencer	4*
Jennifer Conwell	7	Leslie Weber	8
Kevin Rubenstein	15,79,83	Luke Pavone	15,68
Ariana Leonard	57	Brigid Peterson	59
Kim James	59	Jason Vanderplow	60
Kara Caforio	67	Helen Romios	68
Mariann Lemke	70	Bev Redmonte	71
Kate Sampson	71	Robert Bialk	73,76,295
David Beedy	285	Sami Mohmmad	295

Public Schs..Principal	Grd	Prgm	Enr/#Cls	SN	
Bryan Middle Sch 111 W Butterfield Rd, Elmhurst 60126 Jacquelyn Discipio	6-8		711 35	6%	630/617-2350 Fax 630/617-2232
Churchville Middle Sch 155 E Victory Pkwy, Elmhurst 60126 Gina Reeder	6-8	V	524 40	36%	630/832-8682 Fax 630/617-2387
Conrad Fischer Elem Sch 888 N Wilson St, Elmhurst 60126 Irene Villa	K-5	T	464 35	63%	630/832-8601 Fax 630/532-5910
Edison Elem Sch 246 S Fair Ave, Elmhurst 60126 James Pluskota	K-5		295 15	5%	630/834-4272 Fax 630/617-8333
Emerson Elem Sch 400 N West Ave, Elmhurst 60126 Sheleen Delockery	K-5		442 24	12%	630/834-5562 Fax 630/993-8883
Field Elem Sch 295 N Emroy Ave, Elmhurst 60126 Heidi Thomas	K-5		405 19	8%	630/834-5313 Fax 630/993-8896

---

79 Student Personnel
80 Driver Ed/Safety
81 Gifted/Talented
82 Video Services
83 Substance Abuse Prev
84 Erate
85 AIDS Education
88 Alternative/At Risk
89 Multi-Cultural Curriculum
90 Social Work

91 Safety/Security
92 Magnet School
93 Parental Involvement
95 Tech Prep Program
97 Chief Information Officer
98 Chief Technology Officer
270 Character Education
271 Migrant Education
273 Teacher Mentor
274 Before/After Sch

275 Response To Intervention
277 Remedial Math K-12
280 Literacy Coach
285 STEM
286 Digital Learning
288 Common Core Standards
294 Accountability
295 Network System
296 Title II Programs
297 Webmaster

298 Grant Writer/Ptnrships
750 Chief Innovation Officer
751 Chief of Staff
752 Social Emotional Learning

Other School Types
Ⓐ = Alternative School
Ⓒ = Charter School
Ⓜ = Magnet School
Ⓨ = Year-Round School

School Programs
A = Alternative Program
G = Adult Classes
M = Magnet Program
T = Title I Schoolwide
V = Career & Tech Ed Programs

New Schools are shaded
New Superintendents and Principals are bold
Personnel with email addresses are underscored

Social Media
f = Facebook
t = Twitter

IL—93

Du Page County

Market Data Retrieval

School	Grade	Prgm	Enr/#Cls	SN	Phone
Hawthorne Elem Sch 145 W Arthur St, Elmhurst 60126 Timothy Riordan	K-5		495 26	5%	630/834-4541 Fax 630/993-8886
Jackson Elem Sch 925 S Swain Ave, Elmhurst 60126 Christine Trendel	K-5		458 22	9%	630/834-4544 Fax 630/993-8897
Jefferson Elem Sch 360 E Crescent Ave, Elmhurst 60126 Christina Podraza	K-5		382 20	3%	630/834-6261 Fax 630/993-8888
Lincoln Elem Sch 565 S Fairfield Ave, Elmhurst 60126 Jennifer Barnabee	K-5		540 20	2%	630/834-4548 Fax 630/532-5911
Madison Early Childhood Edu CT 130 W Madison St, Elmhurst 60126 Susan Kondrat	PK-PK		302	25%	630/617-2385 Fax 630/617-8212
Sandburg Middle Sch 345 E Saint Charles Rd, Elmhurst 60126 Linda Fehrenbacher	6-8	V	670 60	8%	630/834-4534 Fax 630/617-8293
York Community High Sch 355 W Saint Charles Rd, Elmhurst 60126 Dr Shahe Bagdasarian	9-12	V	2,829 100	16%	630/617-2400 Fax 630/617-2399

● **Fenton Cmty High Sch Dist 100** PID: 00289713   630/766-2500
1000 W Green St, Bensenville 60106   Fax 630/766-3178

Schools: 1 \ **Teachers:** 96 \ **Students:** 1,433 \ **Special Ed Students:** 193 \ **LEP Students:** 197 \ **College-Bound:** 73% \ **Ethnic:** Asian 3%, African American 2%, Hispanic 66%, Caucasian 29% \ **Exp:** $406 (High) \ **Poverty:** 9% \ **Title I:** $224,193 \ **Special Education:** $647,000 \ **Bilingual Education:** $4,000 \ **Open-Close:** 08/20 - 05/25 \ **DTBP:** $225 (High)

James Ongtengco 1
Blake Brodie 3,5*
Tom Kobel 3,5
Jill Wisnewski 7,85*
Jovan Lazarevic 15*
Nancy Coleman 33,60*
Michele Rodriguez 57,271*
Rick Kambic 71
Mike Feeley 73
Mary Thomas 2
Sammuel Bentsen 3,15,68
Todd Becker 6,35,72*
Michelle Papanicolaou 10,11,69,74,273,296,298*
Angela Nelson 33*
Sarah McDougal 38*
Paul Wedemann 67
James Batson 73*
Peggy Mellenthin 90*

Public Schs..Principal	Grd	Prgm	Enr/#Cls	SN	
Fenton High Sch 1000 W Green St, Bensenville 60106 Jovan Lazarevic	9-12	AGTV	1,433 85	53%	630/766-2500 Fax 630/860-8627

● **Glen Ellyn School District 41** PID: 00289737   630/790-6400
793 N Main St, Glen Ellyn 60137   Fax 630/790-1867

Schools: 5 \ **Teachers:** 232 \ **Students:** 3,549 \ **Special Ed Students:** 435 \ **LEP Students:** 425 \ **Ethnic:** Asian 14%, African American 3%, Hispanic 14%, Native American: 1%, Caucasian 69% \ **Exp:** $162 (Low) \ **Poverty:** 6% \ **Title I:** $358,312 \ **Special Education:** $1,621,000 \ **Bilingual Education:** $125,000 \ **Open-Close:** 08/19 - 05/27 \ **DTBP:** $231 (High)

Dr Paul Gordon 1
Eric Deporter 2,3,4,5,15
Katherine Schillinger 5
Marci Conlin 15,68
Robert Bruno 67
Michael Wood 73,84
Laurel O'Brien 79
Anthony Ruelli 2
Dave Scarmardo 3
Katie McClusky 9,15,294
Theresa Ulrich 62
Erica Krehbiel 71
Gail Minkus 76
Ken Harbauer 297

Public Schs..Principal	Grd	Prgm	Enr/#Cls	SN	
Abraham Lincoln Elem Sch 380 Greenfield Ave, Glen Ellyn 60137 Sarah Rodriguez	K-5		543 30	10%	630/790-6475 Fax 630/790-6404
Benjamin Franklin Elem Sch 350 Bryant Ave, Glen Ellyn 60137 Jeff Burke	K-5		518 28	11%	630/790-6480 Fax 630/790-6403
Churchill Elem Sch 23W240 Geneva Rd, Glen Ellyn 60137 Rachel Solomon	K-5	T	673 28	45%	630/790-6485 Fax 630/790-6498
Forest Glen Elem Sch 561 Elm St, Glen Ellyn 60137 Scott Klespitz	PK-5		656 12	21%	630/790-6490 Fax 630/790-6468
W M Hadley Junior High Sch 240 Hawthorne Blvd, Glen Ellyn 60137 Steven Diveley	6-8		1,159 45	23%	630/790-6450 Fax 630/790-6469

● **Glenbard Twp High Sch Dist 87** PID: 00289907   630/469-9100
596 Crescent Blvd, Glen Ellyn 60137   Fax 630/469-9107

Schools: 4 \ **Teachers:** 479 \ **Students:** 7,500 \ **Special Ed Students:** 1,023 \ **LEP Students:** 513 \ **Ethnic:** Asian 17%, African American 8%, Hispanic 24%, Caucasian 51% \ **Exp:** $214 (Med) \ **Poverty:** 7% \ **Title I:** $892,400 \ **Special Education:** $3,671,000 \ **Bilingual Education:** $95,000 \ **Open-Close:** 08/17 - 05/21 \ **DTBP:** $191 (High)

Dr David Larson 1
Patrick McGill 10,15,285,286,288
Janet Cook 15,60,79,752
Tina Saviano 60
Marcia Sommerfeld 68
Anna Strati 70
Nate Dhameres 76
Robert Verisario 2,3,5,15,91
Susanna Malone 12,57
Josh Chambers 15,68,79
Judith Weinstock 67
Tori Johnson 68
Mellisa Creech 73
Gilda Ross 83,88

Public Schs..Principal	Grd	Prgm	Enr/#Cls	SN	
Glenbard East High Sch 1014 S Main St, Lombard 60148 Shahe Bagdasarian \ **Antoine Anderson**	9-12	ATV	2,244	42%	630/627-9250 Fax 630/627-9264
Glenbard North High Sch 990 Kuhn Rd, Carol Stream 60188 Dr John Mensik	9-12	AV	2,236	33%	630/653-7000 Fax 630/653-7259
Glenbard South High Sch 23W200 Butterfield Rd, Glen Ellyn 60137 Sandra Coughlin	9-12	AV	1,164 32	26%	630/469-6500 Fax 630/469-6572
Glenbard West High Sch 670 Crescent Blvd, Glen Ellyn 60137 Peter Monaghan	9-12	V	2,344 80	23%	630/469-8600 Fax 630/942-7559

● **Gower School District 62** PID: 00290035   630/986-5383
7700 Clarendon Hills Rd, Willowbrook 60527   Fax 630/323-3074

Schools: 2 \ **Teachers:** 63 \ **Students:** 900 \ **Special Ed Students:** 132 \ **LEP Students:** 69 \ **Ethnic:** Asian 18%, African American 5%, Hispanic 10%, Native American: 1%, Caucasian 67% \ **Exp:** $331 (High) \ **Poverty:** 7% \ **Title I:** $91,944 \ **Special Education:** $241,000 \ **Bilingual Education:** $14,000 \ **Open-Close:** 08/21 - 05/28 \ **DTBP:** $257 (High)

Dr Victor Simon 1
Vesna Nikolic 2,19*
Tricia Tokash 57,271*
Rebecca Laratta 286,298*
Vesna Nikolic 2,19
Rebecca Laratta 9,13,69,73,79,83,88,286
Ryan Asmus 67

1	Superintendent	8	Curric/Instruct K-12	19	Chief Financial Officer	29	Family/Consumer Science	39	Social Studies K-12	49	English/Lang Arts Elem	59	Special Education Elem	69	Academic Assessment
2	Bus/Finance/Purchasing	9	Curric/Instruct Elem	20	Art K-12	30	Adult Education	40	Social Studies Elem	50	English/Lang Arts Sec	60	Special Education Sec	70	Research/Development
3	Buildings And Grounds	10	Curric/Instruct Sec	21	Art Elem	31	Career/Sch-to-Work K-12	41	Social Studies Sec	51	Reading K-12	61	Foreign/World Lang K-12	71	Public Information
4	Food Service	11	Federal Program	22	Art Sec	32	Career/Sch-to-Work Elem	42	Science K-12	52	Reading Elem	62	Foreign/World Lang Elem	72	Summer School
5	Transportation	12	Title I	23	Music K-12	33	Career/Sch-to-Work Sec	43	Science Elem	53	Reading Sec	63	Foreign/World Lang Sec	73	Instructional Tech
6	Athletic	13	Title V	24	Music Elem	34	Early Childhood Ed	44	Science Sec	54	Remedial Reading K-12	64	Religious Education K-12	74	Inservice Training
7	Health Services	15	Asst Superintendent	25	Music Sec	35	Health/Phys Education	45	Math K-12	55	Remedial Reading Elem	65	Religious Education Elem	75	Marketing/Distributive
		16	Instructional Media Svcs	26	Business Education	36	Guidance Services K-12	46	Math Elem	56	Remedial Reading Sec	66	Religious Education Sec	76	Info Systems
		17	Chief Operations Officer	27	Career & Tech Ed	37	Guidance Services Elem	47	Math Sec	57	Bilingual/ELL	67	School Board President	77	Psychological Assess
		18	Chief Academic Officer	28	Technology Education	38	Guidance Services Sec	48	English/Lang Arts K-12	58	Special Education K-12	68	Teacher Personnel	78	Affirmative Action

Illinois School Directory — Du Page County

Public Schs..Principal	Grd	Prgm	Enr/#Cls	SN	
Gower Middle Sch 7941 S Madison St, Burr Ridge 60527 Tracy Murphy	5-8		370 31	12%	630/323-8275 Fax 630/323-2055
Gower West Elem Sch 7650 Clarendon Hills Rd, Willowbrook 60527 Gina Rodewald	PK-4		499 20	9%	630/323-6446 Fax 630/323-6494

- **Hinsdale Twp High Sch Dist 86** PID: 00290176   630/655-6100
  5500 S Grant St, Hinsdale 60521   Fax 630/325-9153

Schools: 2 \ **Teachers:** 335 \ **Students:** 4,000 \ **Special Ed Students:** 517 \ **LEP Students:** 75 \ **College-Bound:** 98% \ **Ethnic:** Asian 16%, African American 8%, Hispanic 10%, Caucasian 66% \ **Exp:** $289 (Med) \ **Poverty:** 4% \ **Title I:** $186,816 \ **Special Education:** $2,709,000 \ **Bilingual Education:** $25,000 \ **Open-Close:** 08/17 - 05/28 \ **DTBP:** $410 (High)

Tammy Prentiss 1	Josh Stephenson 2,3,4,5,19
Mark Gillono 2	Jessica Orama 3
Dan Jones 6	Karen Banks 7*
Missy Geibel 7*	Chris Cavino 10,11,15,18,288,296,298
Bradley Verthein 15,79,275,752	Jennifer Regnier 38,69,90*
Kelly Sarrels 57*	Kevin Camden 67
Domenico Maniscalco 68,78	Christopher Koutavas 71
Christopher Jasculca 71	Susan Grady 72
Keith Bockwoldt 73,76,84,97,98,295	Kevin Simpson 91
William Walsh 270*	Debra Kedrowski 751

Public Schs..Principal	Grd	Prgm	Enr/#Cls	SN	
Hinsdale Central High Sch 550 S Grant St, Hinsdale 60521 William Walsh	9-12		2,728	6%	630/570-8000 Fax 630/887-1362
Hinsdale South High Sch 7401 Clarendon Hills Rd, Darien 60561 Arwen Pokorny Lyp	9-12		1,421 50	27%	630/468-4000 Fax 630/920-8649

- **Indian Prairie Sch Dist 204** PID: 00290205   630/375-3000
  780 Shoreline Dr, Aurora 60504   Fax 630/375-3001

Schools: 34 \ **Teachers:** 1,765 \ **Students:** 27,400 \ **Special Ed Students:** 3,339 \ **LEP Students:** 2,620 \ **College-Bound:** 85% \ **Ethnic:** Asian 34%, African American 9%, Hispanic 13%, Caucasian 44% \ **Exp:** $183 (Low) \ **Poverty:** 4% \ **Title I:** $966,201 \ **Special Education:** $17,865,000 \ **Bilingual Education:** $457,000 \ **Open-Close:** 09/03 - 06/04 \ **DTBP:** $206 (High) \

Dr Adrian Talley 1	Jay Strang 2
Todd DePaul 3	Jill Ghosn 4
Dr Christina Sepiol 7,15,58,79	Grant Sahr 8
Joan Peterson 9	Laura Rosenblum 9,15
Brad Hillman 10,15	Linda Rakestraw 10,15
Michael Purcell 10	Tarah Fowler 10
Doug Eccarius 15	Louis Lee 15,68
Rafael Segarra 57	Michael Raczak 67
Charles Sprandel 69,70	Brian Giovanini 70
Janet Buglio 71	Adam Smeets 73,84,98
Candy Michelli 74*	Jennifer Rowe 78
Elizabeth Jansen 79	Kimberly Miller 79
Michelle Gallo 79	Laura Nylen 286
Kent Vanderploeg 295*	Greg Gibson 297

Public Schs..Principal	Grd	Prgm	Enr/#Cls	SN	
Arlene Welch Elem Sch 2620 Leverenz Rd, Naperville 60564 Sarah Nowak	K-5		624 33	19%	630/428-7200 Fax 630/428-7201
Brookdale Elem Sch 1200 Redfield Rd, Naperville 60563 **Keeley Schmid**	K-5		508 21	24%	630/428-6800 Fax 630/428-6801
Clifford Crone Middle Sch 4020 111th St, Naperville 60564 Melissa Couch	6-8	V	872 50	5%	630/428-5600 Fax 630/428-5601
Fischer Middle Sch 1305 Long Grove Dr, Aurora 60504 Jennifer Nonnemacher	6-8		882	33%	630/375-3100 Fax 630/375-3101
Francis Granger Middle Sch 2721 Stonebridge Blvd, Aurora 60502 Allan Davenport	6-8	V	1,015 42	19%	630/375-1010 Fax 630/375-1110
Fry Elem Sch 3204 Tall Grass Dr, Naperville 60564 Laurie Hillman	K-5		617 22	5%	630/428-7400 Fax 630/428-7401
Georgetown Elem Sch 995 Long Grove Dr, Aurora 60504 Janan Szurek	K-5	T	495 26	60%	630/375-3456 Fax 630/375-3461
Gordon Gregory Middle Sch 2621 Springdale Cir, Naperville 60564 Leslie Mitchell	6-8	V	851 41	8%	630/428-6300 Fax 630/428-6301
Gwendolyn Brooks Elem Sch 2700 Stonebridge Blvd, Aurora 60502 Terri Russell	K-5		642 26	9%	630/375-3200 Fax 630/375-3201
Longwood Elem Sch 30W240 Bruce Ln, Naperville 60563 Tracey Ratner	K-5	T	408 19	43%	630/428-6789 Fax 630/428-6761
Mary Lou Cowlishaw Elem Sch 1212 Sanctuary Ln, Naperville 60540 **Carlos Azcoitia**	K-5	T	697 25	27%	630/428-6100 Fax 630/428-6101
May Watts Elem Sch 800 S Whispering Hills Dr, Naperville 60540 Brian Lecrone	K-5		629 23	6%	630/428-6700 Fax 630/428-6701
McCarty Elem Sch 3000 Village Green Dr, Aurora 60504 Kevin Schnable	K-5	T	527 28	33%	630/375-3400 Fax 630/375-3401
Metea Valley High Sch 1801 N Eola Rd, Aurora 60502 Dr Darrell Echols	9-12		2,928	20%	630/375-5900 Fax 630/375-5901
Nancy Young Elem Sch 800 Asbury Dr, Aurora 60502 Adrienne Morgan	K-5		657 30	17%	630/375-3800 Fax 630/375-3801
Neuqua Valley High Sch 2360 95th St, Naperville 60564 Lance Fuhrer	10-12	V	3,568 120	9%	630/428-6000 Fax 630/428-6001
Nvhs Kathryn J Birkett Center 3220 Cedar Glade Dr, Naperville 60564 Dr Lance Fuhrer	9-9	V	1,000		630/428-6000 Fax 630/428-6401
Oliver Julian Kendall Elem Sch 2408 Meadow Lake Dr, Naperville 60564 Breah Jerger	K-5		355 27	6%	630/428-7100 Fax 630/428-7101
Owen Elem Sch 1560 Westglen Dr, Naperville 60565 **Ken Bonomo**	K-5		579 24	16%	630/428-7300 Fax 630/428-7301
Patterson Elem Sch 3731 Lawrence Dr, Naperville 60564 Michele Frost	K-5		497 35	4%	630/428-6500 Fax 630/428-6501
Peter M Gombert Elem Sch 2707 Ridge Rd, Aurora 60504 Jeremy Ricken	K-5	T	377 18	37%	630/375-3700 Fax 630/375-3701
Peterson Elem Sch 4008 Chinaberry Ln, Naperville 60564 Allison Landstrom	K-5		684 16	5%	630/428-5678 Fax 630/428-6181
Prairie Children Pre-Sch 780 Shoreline Dr, Aurora 60504 Sally Osborne	PK-PK		663 31	19%	630/375-3030 Fax 630/375-3029

79 Student Personnel	91 Safety/Security	275 Response To Intervention	298 Grant Writer/Ptnrships	**School Programs**
80 Driver Ed/Safety	92 Magnet School	277 Remedial Math K-12	750 Chief Innovation Officer	A = Alternative Program
81 Gifted/Talented	93 Parental Involvement	280 Literacy Coach	751 Chief of Staff	G = Adult Classes
82 Video Services	95 Tech Prep Program	285 STEM	752 Social Emotional Learning	M = Magnet Program
83 Substance Abuse Prev	97 Chief Information Officer	286 Digital Learning		T = Title I Schoolwide
84 Erate	98 Chief Technology Officer	288 Common Core Standards	**Other School Types**	V = Career & Tech Ed Programs
85 AIDS Education	270 Accountability	294 Accountability	Ⓐ = Alternative School	
88 Alternative/At Risk	271 Migrant Education	295 Network System	Ⓒ = Charter School	**Social Media**
89 Multi-Cultural Curriculum	273 Teacher Mentor	296 Title II Programs	Ⓜ = Magnet School	= Facebook
90 Social Work	274 Before/After Sch	297 Webmaster	Ⓨ = Year-Round School	= Twitter

New Schools are shaded
New Superintendents and Principals are bold
Personnel with email addresses are underscored

Du Page County — Market Data Retrieval

Reba O Steck Elem Sch 460 Inverness Dr, Aurora 60504 Elizabeth Pohlmann	K-5		633 28	9%	630/375-3500 Fax 630/375-3501
Robert E Clow Elem Sch 1301 Springdale Cir, Naperville 60564 Katie Bennett	K-5		368 25	13%	630/428-6060 Fax 630/428-6061
Scullen Middle Sch 2815 Mistflower Ln, Naperville 60564 Scott Loughrige	6-8		1,045 50	11%	630/428-7000 Fax 630/428-7001
Spring Brook Elem Sch 2700 Seiler Dr, Naperville 60565 David Worst	K-5		595 32	4%	630/428-6600 Fax 630/428-6601
Still Middle Sch 787 Meadowridge Dr, Aurora 60504 Kimberly Cornish	6-8	V	782	17%	630/375-3900 Fax 630/375-3901
Thayer J Hill Middle Sch 1836 Brookdale Rd, Naperville 60563 Mike Dutdut	6-8	V	881 60	20%	630/428-6200 Fax 630/428-6201
V Blanche Graham Elem Sch 2315 High Meadow Rd, Naperville 60564 Claudette Walton	K-5		328 27	7%	630/428-6900 Fax 630/428-6901
Waubonsie Valley High Sch 2590 Ogden Ave, Aurora 60504 Jason Stipp	9-12	V	2,596	21%	630/375-3300 Fax 630/375-3301
Wayne Builta Elem Sch 1835 Apple Valley Rd, Bolingbrook 60490 Kim Stevens	K-5		343	14%	630/226-4400 Fax 630/226-4401
ⓐ Wheatland Academy 3003 103rd St, Naperville 60564 Cecelia Tobin	9-12		150 12		630/375-3375 Fax 630/375-3361
White Eagle Elem Sch 1585 White Eagle Dr, Naperville 60564 **Mary Howicz**	K-5		562 27	11%	630/375-3600 Fax 630/375-3601

• **Itasca School District 10** PID: 00290255 630/773-1232
200 N Maple St, Itasca 60143 Fax 630/773-1342

Schools: 3 \ **Teachers:** 70 \ **Students:** 1,033 \ **Special Ed Students:** 147 \ **LEP Students:** 100 \ **Ethnic:** Asian 9%, African American 1%, Hispanic 17%, Caucasian 73% \ **Exp:** $676 (High) \ **Poverty:** 4% \ **Title I:** $39,730 \ **Special Education:** $418,000 \ **Bilingual Education:** $2,000 \ **Open-Close:** 08/20 - 06/02 \ **DTBP:** $221 (High) \ 🅵 🆃

Craig Benes 1,11	Brian Weintraub 2,3*	
Doug Anderson 6*	Marty Lundeen 67	
Steve Schmidt 73,295*		

Public Schs..Principal	Grd	Prgm	Enr/#Cls	SN	
E H Franzen Intermediate Sch 730 Catalpa Ave, Itasca 60143 Jason Taylor	3-5		354 12	8%	630/773-0100 Fax 630/285-7468
F E Peacock Middle Sch 301 E North St, Itasca 60143 Heidi Weeks	6-8		360 25	9%	630/773-0335 Fax 630/285-7460
Raymond Benson Primary Sch 301 E Washington St, Itasca 60143 Jason Taylor	PK-2		319 14	3%	630/773-0554 Fax 630/285-7474

• **Keeneyville Elem Sch Dist 20** PID: 00290293 630/894-2250
5540 Arlington Dr E, Hanover Park 60133 Fax 630/894-9661

Schools: 3 \ **Teachers:** 119 \ **Students:** 1,597 \ **Special Ed Students:** 224 \ **LEP Students:** 289 \ **Ethnic:** Asian 8%, African American 18%, Hispanic 32%, Native American: 2%, Caucasian 40% \ **Exp:** $138 (Low) \ **Poverty:** 11% \ **Title I:** $270,424 \ **Special Education:** $627,000 \ **Bilingual Education:** $110,000 \ **Open-Close:** 08/20 - 06/01 \ **DTBP:** $237 (High)

Dr Omar Castillo 1	Wendy Flaherty 2,3,5
Emmie Pawlak 9,11,69,288,296,298	Kim Cline 59
Heather Weishaar 67	Arthur Andersen 73
Holly Kaye 76	Donna Rivard 79

Public Schs..Principal	Grd	Prgm	Enr/#Cls	SN	
Greenbrook Elem Sch 5208 Arlington Cir, Hanover Park 60133 John Gustafson	PK-5	T	544 24	69%	630/894-4544 Fax 630/289-6183
Spring Wood Middle Sch 5540 Arlington Dr E, Hanover Park 60133 Jamison Pearce	6-8	T	534 30	57%	630/893-8900 Fax 630/894-9658
Waterbury Elem Sch 355 Rodenburg Rd, Roselle 60172 **Dr Jon Pokora**	K-5	T	453 29	36%	630/893-8180 Fax 630/539-2316

• **Lake Park Cmty High SD 108** PID: 00290322 630/529-4500
590 Medinah Rd, Roselle 60172 Fax 630/295-5414

Schools: 2 \ **Teachers:** 157 \ **Students:** 2,500 \ **Special Ed Students:** 234 \ **LEP Students:** 73 \ **Ethnic:** Asian 9%, African American 6%, Hispanic 20%, Caucasian 65% \ **Exp:** $356 (High) \ **Poverty:** 6% \ **Title I:** $220,396 \ **Special Education:** $1,472,000 \ **Open-Close:** 08/12 - 05/25 \ **DTBP:** $179 (High)

Dr Jeffrey Feucht 1	Dr Jeff O'Connell 2,3,5,15,91*
Peter Schauer 6*	Mike Wojtowicz 10,15,73
James Roberts 11,288*	Jim Roberts 15,69
Amy Allison 16,76*	Kevin Jones 27*
Kimberly Murphy 60,88*	Barbara Layer 67
Sherri Anderson 71	Ebony Baker 77,79,90
Tim Richmond 97,295*	Tim Roberts 298

Public Schs..Principal	Grd	Prgm	Enr/#Cls	SN	
Lake Park High Sch-East Campus 600 Medinah Rd, Roselle 60172 **Amanda Brode-Rico**	9-10	V	1,360		630/529-4500 Fax 630/529-1056
Lake Park High Sch-West Campus 500 W Bryn Mawr Ave, Roselle 60172 John Gouriotis	11-12	AV	1,241 60	15%	630/529-4500 Fax 630/351-0710

• **Lisle Cmty Unit Sch Dist 202** PID: 00290346 630/493-8000
5211 Center Ave, Lisle 60532 Fax 630/971-4054

Schools: 3 \ **Teachers:** 116 \ **Students:** 1,450 \ **Special Ed Students:** 259 \ **LEP Students:** 69 \ **College-Bound:** 85% \ **Ethnic:** Asian 8%, African American 8%, Hispanic 13%, Caucasian 70% \ **Exp:** $403 (High) \ **Poverty:** 6% \ **Title I:** $158,198 \ **Special Education:** $1,370,000 \ **Open-Close:** 08/19 - 06/04 \ **DTBP:** $224 (High)

Keith Filipiak 1	David Wilkinson 2
John Posego 3	Dr Linda Kotalik 8,12,15,73*
Jennifer Law 11,34,57,58,79,88	Meg Sima 67

---

1 Superintendent	19 Chief Financial Officer	39 Social Studies K-12	59 Special Education Elem	69 Academic Assessment
2 Bus/Finance/Purchasing	20 Art K-12	40 Social Studies Elem	60 Special Education Sec	70 Research/Development
3 Buildings And Grounds	21 Art Elem	41 Social Studies Sec	61 Foreign/World Lang K-12	71 Public Information
4 Food Service	22 Art Sec	42 Science K-12	62 Foreign/World Lang Elem	72 Summer School
5 Transportation	23 Music K-12	43 Science Elem	63 Foreign/World Lang Sec	73 Instructional Tech
6 Athletic	24 Music Elem	44 Science Sec	64 Religious Education K-12	74 Inservice Training
7 Health Services	25 Music Sec	45 Math K-12	65 Religious Education Elem	75 Marketing/Distributive
8 Curric/Instruct K-12	26 Business Education	46 Math Elem	66 Religious Education Sec	76 Info Systems
9 Curric/Instruct Elem	27 Career & Tech Ed	47 Math Sec	67 School Board President	77 Psychological Assess
10 Curric/Instruct Sec	28 Technology Education	48 English/Lang Arts K-12	68 Teacher Personnel	78 Affirmative Action
11 Federal Program	29 Family/Consumer Science	49 English/Lang Arts Elem		
12 Title I	30 Adult Education	50 English/Lang Arts Sec		
13 Title V	31 Career/Sch-to-Work K-12	51 Reading K-12		
14 Early Childhood Ed	32 Career/Sch-to-Work Elem	52 Reading Elem		
15 Asst Superintendent	33 Career/Sch-to-Work Sec	53 Reading Sec		
16 Instructional Media Svcs	34 Early Childhood Ed	54 Remedial Reading K-12		
17 Chief Operations Officer	35 Health/Phys Education	55 Remedial Reading Elem		
18 Chief Academic Officer	36 Guidance Services K-12	56 Remedial Reading Sec		
	37 Guidance Services Elem	57 Bilingual/ELL		
	38 Guidance Services Sec	58 Special Education K-12		

Illinois School Directory — Du Page County

Public Schs..Principal	Grd	Prgm	Enr/#Cls	SN	
Lisle Elem Sch 5801 Westview Ln, Lisle 60532 Wesley Gosselink \ Melissa Payne	PK-5		650 21		630/493-8100 Fax 630/963-8843
Lisle High Sch 1800 Short St, Lisle 60532 Jeff Howard	9-12	V	462 40	27%	630/493-8300 Fax 630/971-1234
Lisle Junior High Sch 5207 Center Ave, Lisle 60532 David Kearney	6-8		291 30	34%	630/493-8200 Fax 630/493-8209

• Lombard Elem SD 44 PID: 00290413
150 W Madison St, Lombard 60148
630/827-4400 Fax 630/620-3798

Schools: 8 \ **Teachers:** 244 \ **Students:** 3,100 \ **Special Ed Students:** 483 \ **LEP Students:** 446 \ **Ethnic:** Asian 14%, African American 6%, Hispanic 18%, Caucasian 62% \ **Exp:** $247 (Med) \ **Poverty:** 7% \ **Title I:** $352,903 \ **Special Education:** $1,760,000 \ **Bilingual Education:** $65,000 \ **Open-Close:** 08/19 - 06/01 \ **DTBP:** $187 (High)

Ted Stec 1		Neal Perry 2,15,17,19,73,98,751	
Pam Hernandez 2,4		Phil McEntee 2	
Brett Sharkey 9,18		Annetta Spychalski 11,280,298	
Catharine Angelos 34*		Maria Martin 49,57	
Clodagh McCall 59,79,275*		Courtney Long 67	
Rebecca Harris 68		Tod Altenburg 68	
Jennifer Nimke 71		Bonnie Schwieterman 297	

Public Schs..Principal	Grd	Prgm	Enr/#Cls	SN	
Butterfield Elem Sch 2S500 Gray Ave, Lombard 60148 Maura Burns	K-5	T	288 11	28%	630/827-4000 Fax 630/889-7960
Glenn Westlake Middle Sch 1514 S Main St, Lombard 60148 Mike Fumagalli	6-8		1,001	33%	630/827-4500 Fax 630/620-3791
John Schroder ECC 1519 S Grace St, Lombard 60148 Catharine Angelos	PK-PK		150	38%	630/827-4265 Fax 630/216-8412
Madison Elem Sch 150 W Madison St, Lombard 60148 Yesenia Vasquez	K-5	T	521 44	50%	630/827-4100 Fax 630/620-3769
Manor Hill Elem Sch 1464 S Main St, Lombard 60148 Eric Haren	PK-5	T	266 18	33%	630/827-4300 Fax 630/889-7964
Park View Elem Sch 341 N Elizabeth St, Lombard 60148 Roberta Wallerstedt	K-5		239 12	23%	630/827-4040 Fax 630/620-3749
Pleasant Lane Elem Sch 401 N Main St, Lombard 60148 Stephanie Loth	K-5		281 16	21%	630/827-4640 Fax 630/620-3760
William Hammerschmidt Elem Sch 617 Hammerschmidt Ave, Lombard 60148 David Danielski	K-5		424 18	11%	630/827-4200 Fax 630/620-3733

• Maercker School District 60 PID: 00290554
1 S Cass Ave Ste 202, Westmont 60559
630/515-4840 Fax 630/515-4845

Schools: 3 \ **Teachers:** 95 \ **Students:** 1,401 \ **Special Ed Students:** 143 \ **LEP Students:** 285 \ **Ethnic:** Asian 25%, African American 8%, Hispanic 19%, Native American: 1%, Caucasian 48% \ **Exp:** $538 (High) \ **Poverty:** 9% \ **Title I:** $186,593 \ **Special Education:** $687,000 \ **Bilingual Education:** $74,000 \ **Open-Close:** 08/31 - 06/04 \ **DTBP:** $240 (High)

Sean Nugent 1,83	Susan Caddy 2,3,4,5,91
Catherine Fisher 11,57,88,285,286,288,296,298	Sherry Hackney 55*
Mary Satchwell 67	Mike Ryan 73

Public Schs..Principal	Grd	Prgm	Enr/#Cls	SN	
Holmes Elem Sch 5800 Holmes Ave, Clarendon Hls 60514 Laura Gilmartin	PK-2		500 24	32%	630/515-4810 Fax 630/515-4815
Maercker Intermediate Sch 5827 S Cass Ave, Westmont 60559 Dominic Sepich	3-5	T	467 21	38%	630/515-4820 Fax 630/515-4825
Westview Hills Middle Sch 630 65th St, Willowbrook 60527 Amber Quirk	6-8		474 35	36%	630/515-4830 Fax 630/515-4835

• Marquardt School District 15 PID: 00290580
1860 Glen Ellyn Rd, Glendale HTS 60139
630/469-7615 Fax 630/790-1650

Schools: 5 \ **Teachers:** 193 \ **Students:** 2,491 \ **Special Ed Students:** 357 \ **LEP Students:** 754 \ **Ethnic:** Asian 14%, African American 13%, Hispanic 53%, Native American: 1%, Caucasian 20% \ **Exp:** $615 (High) \ **Poverty:** 18% \ **Title I:** $941,834 \ **Special Education:** $878,000 \ **Bilingual Education:** $148,000 \ **Open-Close:** 08/19 - 05/28 \ **DTBP:** $191 (High)

Dr Jerome O'Shea 1	Armand Gasbarro 2,5,15,91
Sandy Voss 4	Stefanie Giannini 4
Lisa Pickering 7*	Jill Meciej 9
Marie Cimaglia 15,68	Judith Smith 16*
Amie Kaczmarek 34,59	Jean Randazzo 67
Rebecca Bald 71	Cindy Darling 73,76
Kerry Westra 77	Tomasz Krupinski 295

Public Schs..Principal	Grd	Prgm	Enr/#Cls	SN	
Blackhawk Elem Sch 2101 Gladstone Dr, Glendale HTS 60139 Kim Roberts	K-5	T	488 21	92%	630/893-5750 Fax 630/307-6525
G Stanley Hall Elem Sch 1447 Wayne Ave, Glendale HTS 60139 Karen Marino	PK-5	T	373 21	87%	630/469-7720 Fax 630/790-5040
Marquardt Middle Sch 1912 Glen Ellyn Rd, Glendale HTS 60139 Meredith Haugens	6-8	T	792	95%	630/858-3850 Fax 630/790-5042
Reskin Elem Sch 1555 Ardmore Ave, Glendale HTS 60139 David Rojas	PK-5	T	428 25	94%	630/469-0612 Fax 630/790-5041
Winnebago Elem Sch 195 Greenway Dr, Bloomingdale 60108 Shari Lazor	PK-5	T	410 28	80%	630/351-3416 Fax 630/307-6524

• Medinah Elementary SD 11 PID: 00290669
700 E Granville Ave, Roselle 60172
630/893-3737 Fax 630/893-4947

Schools: 3 \ **Teachers:** 47 \ **Students:** 700 \ **Special Ed Students:** 105 \ **LEP Students:** 128 \ **Ethnic:** Asian 7%, African American 6%, Hispanic 22%, Caucasian 65% \ **Exp:** $427 (High) \ **Poverty:** 7% \ **Title I:** $75,719 \ **Special Education:** $390,000 \ **Bilingual Education:** $14,000 \ **Open-Close:** 08/21 - 06/04 \ **DTBP:** $218 (High)

Dr John Butts 1	Kathy Kaminski 2
Mark Rajcevich 3	Steve Olson 6
Susan Redell 11,73,83,88,286,288,296,298	James Mallory 67
Connor Beard 76,295	

Public Schs..Principal	Grd	Prgm	Enr/#Cls	SN	
Medinah Intermediate Sch 7N330 Medinah Rd, Medinah 60157 Natalie Czarnecki	3-5		208 11	33%	630/529-6105 Fax 630/539-3812

---

79 Student Personnel	91 Safety/Security	275 Response To Intervention	298 Grant Writer/Ptnrships	**School Programs**	**Social Media**
80 Driver Ed/Safety	92 Magnet School	277 Remedial Math K-12	750 Chief Innovation Officer	A = Alternative Program	
81 Gifted/Talented	93 Parental Involvement	280 Literacy Coach	751 Chief of Staff	G = Adult Classes	= Facebook
82 Video Services	95 Tech Prep Program	285 STEM	752 Social Emotional Learning	M = Magnet Program	
83 Substance Abuse Prev	97 Chief Information Officer	286 Digital Learning		T = Title I Schoolwide	= Twitter
84 Erate	98 Chief Technology Officer	288 Common Core Standards	**Other School Types**	V = Career & Tech Ed Programs	
85 AIDS Education	270 Accountability	294 Accountability	Ⓐ = Alternative School		
88 Alternative/At Risk	271 Migrant Education	295 Network System	Ⓒ = Charter School	New Schools are shaded	
89 Multi-Cultural Curriculum	273 Teacher Mentor	296 Title II Programs	Ⓜ = Magnet School	New Superintendents and Principals are bold	
90 Social Work	274 Before/After Sch	297 Webmaster	Ⓨ = Year-Round School	Personnel with email addresses are underscored	

Du Page County   Market Data Retrieval

Medinah Middle Sch 700 E Granville Ave, Roselle 60172 George Gouriotis	6-8	T	213 15	53%	630/893-3838 Fax 630/893-5198
Medinah Primary Sch 22W300 Sunnyside Rd, Medinah 60157 Melissa Langietti	PK-2		242 10	37%	630/529-9788 Fax 630/529-6304

• **Naperville Cmty Unit SD 203** PID: 00290700   630/420-6300
  203 W Hillside Rd, Naperville 60540   Fax 630/420-1066

Schools: 22 \ **Teachers:** 1,104 \
Students: 17,000 \ **Special Ed Students:** 1,920 \ **LEP Students:** 1,048 \
College-Bound: 85% \ **Ethnic:** Asian 18%, African American 5%, Hispanic 11%, Caucasian 66% \ **Exp:** $361 (High) \ **Poverty:** 4% \ **Title I:** $697,389
\ **Special Education:** $9,858,000 \ **Bilingual Education:** $142,000 \
Open-Close: 09/01 - 06/10 \ **DTBP:** $241 (High)

Dan Bridges 1	Melanie Brown 2,79
Tracy Oliver 2	Bob Ross 3,17,68
Patrick Dolan 3	Paul Benetazzo 3
Tanera Winters 4	Cindy La Born 5
Jeanette Harris 7*	Holly Bontkowski 8
Janet Sommerville 8	Jayne Willard 8,15
Dr Jennifer Schalk 8,18	Jennifer Donatelli 8
Kelly Talaga 8	Trish Sniadecki 8
Veronica Zamora 8	Chuck Freundt 9,15
Colleen Cannon-Ruffo 9*	Nancy Voise 10,15
Dr Christine Igoe 15,58,79	Patrick Nolten 15,294
Nancy Havenaar 20*	Marion Frebus-Flaman 34,48,89
Gabriela Velazquez 57	Kristin Fitzgerald 67
Gretchen Gallois 68	Alex Gervacio 69
Kristine Zieman 69	Roger Brunelle 71,97
Sinikka Mondini 71	Jill Hlavacek 73
Sophia Lewis 73	Kenneth Wilson 76
Elizabeth Kanne 79	Lisa Xagas 79
Sue Striedl 81	Chris Kunzer 84
Stacy Colgan 90	Lou Cammiso 91
Jeff Petrick 295	Joe Jaruseski 295

Public Schs..Principal	Grd	Prgm	Enr/#Cls	SN	
Ann Reid Early Childhood Ctr 1011 S Naper Blvd, Naperville 60540 Andrew McCree	PK-PK		327	31%	630/420-6899 Fax 630/637-4033
Beebe Elem Sch 110 E 11th Ave, Naperville 60563 Christine O'Neil	K-5		559 34	23%	630/420-6332 Fax 630/420-6962
Ellsworth Elem Sch 145 N Sleight St, Naperville 60540 Cheryl Degan	K-5		255 12	15%	630/420-6338 Fax 630/637-7321
Elmwood Elem Sch 1024 Magnolia Ln, Naperville 60540 **Matt Langes**	K-5		668 31	17%	630/420-6341 Fax 630/637-7348
Highlands Elem Sch 525 S Brainard St, Naperville 60540 Laura Noon	PK-5		510 26	4%	630/420-6335 Fax 630/420-6957
Jefferson Junior High Sch 1525 N Loomis St, Naperville 60563 Megan Ptak	6-8	V	848 46	25%	630/420-6363 Fax 630/420-6930
Kennedy Junior High Sch 2929 Green Trails Dr, Lisle 60532 Dr Anthony Murray	6-8		961 46	8%	630/420-3220 Fax 630/420-6960
Kingsley Elem Sch 2403 Kingsley Dr, Naperville 60565 Erin Marker	PK-5		450 29	13%	630/420-3208 Fax 630/420-3213
Lincoln Junior High Sch 1320 Olympus Dr, Naperville 60565 Patrick Gaskin	6-8	V	797 50	14%	630/420-6370 Fax 630/637-4582
Madison Junior High Sch 1000 River Oak Dr, Naperville 60565 Erin Anderson	6-8		583 42	13%	630/420-6400 Fax 630/420-6402
Maplebrook Elem Sch 1630 Warbler Dr, Naperville 60565 Araceli Ordaz	PK-5		505 24	13%	630/420-6381 Fax 630/420-6638
Meadow Glens Elem Sch 1150 Muirhead Ave, Naperville 60565 Katy Lynch	K-5		475 21	7%	630/420-3200 Fax 630/420-6897
Mill Street Elem Sch 1300 N Mill St, Naperville 60563 Suzanne Salness	PK-5		645 31	26%	630/420-6353 Fax 630/637-4680
Naper Elem Sch 39 S Eagle St, Naperville 60540 Tracy Dvorchak	K-5		295 11	15%	630/420-6345 Fax 630/637-7328
Naperville Central High Sch 440 Aurora Ave, Naperville 60540 William Wiesbrook	9-12	AGV	2,718 150	13%	630/420-6420 Fax 630/369-6247
Naperville North High Sch 899 N Mill St, Naperville 60563 Stephanie Posey	9-12	AGV	2,675 125	15%	630/420-6480 Fax 630/420-4255
Prairie Elem Sch 500 S Charles Ave, Naperville 60540 Brian Zallis	PK-5		535 28	7%	630/420-6348 Fax 630/717-0801
Ranch View Elem Sch 1651 Ranchview Dr, Naperville 60565 Angela Stallion	K-5		540 24	10%	630/420-6575 Fax 630/420-0915
River Woods Elem Sch 2607 River Woods Dr, Naperville 60565 Gina Baumgartner	K-5		508 25	8%	630/420-6630 Fax 630/420-6961
Scott Elem Sch 500 Warwick Dr, Naperville 60565 Hugh Boger	PK-5		445 24	30%	630/420-6477 Fax 630/420-6471
Steeple Run Elem Sch 6S151 Steeple Run Dr, Naperville 60540 Joshua Louis	K-5		595 25	19%	630/420-6385 Fax 630/420-6935
Washington Junior High Sch 201 N Washington St, Naperville 60540 Jon Vogel	6-8	V	621 20	13%	630/420-6390 Fax 630/420-6474

• **Queen Bee School District 16** PID: 00291120   630/260-6100
  1560 Bloomingdale Rd, Glendale HTS 60139   Fax 630/260-6103

Schools: 4 \ **Teachers:** 124 \ **Students:** 1,900 \ **Special Ed Students:** 272
\ **LEP Students:** 644 \ **Ethnic:** Asian 25%, African American 6%, Hispanic 50%, Caucasian 19% \ **Exp:** $78 (Low) \ **Poverty:** 11% \ **Title I:** $338,770
\ **Special Education:** $856,000 \ **Bilingual Education:** $242,000 \
Open-Close: 08/25 - 06/10 \ **DTBP:** $225 (High) \

Dr Joseph Williams 1,11,73	Kevin Hooper 2
Scott Tamcus 3	Deborah Kamperman 4
Sandy Voss 4	Lonna Hancock 9,285
Michelle Bonham 9,59,88	Annel Justiniano 57*
Michael Summerville 67	Said Mendoza 76
Astrid Rodiguez 83	

Public Schs..Principal	Grd	Prgm	Enr/#Cls	SN	
Americana Elem Sch 1629 President St, Glendale HTS 60139 Astrid Rodrigues	K-4	T	490 22	43%	630/260-6135 Fax 630/510-8570
Glen Hill Elem Sch 1324 Bloomingdale Rd, Glendale HTS 60139 Jennifer Jonas	K-4	T	450 23	41%	630/260-6141 Fax 630/510-8566
Glenside Middle Sch 1560 Bloomingdale Rd, Glendale HTS 60139 Edward Garza	5-8	T	680 50	39%	630/260-6112 Fax 630/510-8568

1	Superintendent	8	Curric/Instruct K-12	19	Chief Financial Officer	29	Family/Consumer Science	39	Social Studies K-12	49	English/Lang Arts Elem	59	Special Education Elem	69	Academic Assessment
2	Bus/Finance/Purchasing	9	Curric/Instruct Elem	20	Art K-12	30	Adult Education	40	Social Studies Elem	50	English/Lang Arts Sec	60	Special Education Sec	70	Research/Development
3	Buildings And Grounds	10	Curric/Instruct Sec	21	Art Elem	31	Career/Sch-to-Work K-12	41	Social Studies Sec	51	Reading K-12	61	Foreign/World Lang K-12	71	Public Information
4	Food Service	11	Federal Program	22	Art Sec	32	Career/Sch-to-Work Elem	42	Science K-12	52	Reading Elem	62	Foreign/World Lang Elem	72	Summer School
5	Transportation	12	Title I	23	Music K-12	33	Career/Sch-to-Work Sec	43	Science Elem	53	Reading Sec	63	Foreign/World Lang Sec	73	Instructional Tech
6	Athletic	13	Title V	24	Music Elem	34	Early Childhood Ed	44	Science Sec	54	Remedial Reading K-12	64	Religious Education K-12	74	Inservice Training
7	Health Services	14	Instructional Media Svcs	25	Music Sec	35	Health/Phys Education	45	Math K-12	55	Remedial Reading Elem	65	Religious Education Elem	75	Marketing/Distributive
		15	Asst Superintendent	26	Business Education	36	Guidance Services K-12	46	Math Elem	56	Remedial Reading Sec	66	Religious Education Sec	76	Info Systems
		16	Chief Operations Officer	27	Career & Tech Ed	37	Guidance Services Elem	47	Math Sec	57	Bilingual/ELL	67	School Board President	77	Psychological Assess
		17	Chief Academic Officer	28	Technology Education	38	Guidance Services Sec	48	English/Lang Arts K-12	58	Special Education K-12	68	Teacher Personnel	78	Affirmative Action

Illinois School Directory — Du Page County

Queen Bee Early Childhood Ctr PK-PK 40 53% 630/344-5600
1525 Bloomingdale Rd, Glendale HTS 60139 Fax 630/510-8578
Christine Wagner

• Roselle School District 12 PID: 00291170 630/529-2091
100 E Walnut St, Roselle 60172 Fax 630/529-2467

Schools: 2 \ Teachers: 47 \ Students: 700 \ Special Ed Students: 105 \ LEP Students: 96 \ Ethnic: Asian 7%, African American 2%, Hispanic 12%, Caucasian 79% \ Exp: $114 (Low) \ Poverty: 5% \ Title I: $52,733 \ Special Education: $426,000 \ Bilingual Education: $33,000 \ Open-Close: 08/19 - 05/27 \ DTBP: $178 (High)

Dr Mary Henderson 1,11   Anthony Arbogast 2,3,15
Jeff Fontanetta ....6*   Kelly Lynne 9
Kelly Lynn 9,15   Blythe Cammy 67
Pam David 73   Dr Tiffanie Jeffrey 79
Georgina Meyer 83,90*

Public Schs..Principal	Grd	Prgm	Enr/#Cls	SN	
Roselle Middle Sch 500 S Park St, Roselle 60172 Anthony Bradburn	6-8		230 12	19%	630/529-1600 Fax 630/529-1882
Spring Hills Elem Sch 560 Pinecroft Dr, Roselle 60172 Lew Girmscheid	PK-5		470 19	22%	630/529-1883 Fax 630/529-1948

• Salt Creek School District 48 PID: 00291223 630/279-8400
1110 S Villa Ave, Villa Park 60181 Fax 630/279-6167

Schools: 3 \ Teachers: 35 \ Students: 550 \ Special Ed Students: 79 \ LEP Students: 49 \ Ethnic: Asian 12%, African American 9%, Hispanic 19%, Caucasian 59% \ Exp: $523 (High) \ Poverty: 9% \ Title I: $72,659 \ Special Education: $271,000 \ Open-Close: 08/25 - 06/04 \ DTBP: $232 (High)

Dr Jake Chung 1,84   Dr Frank Evans 2,11
Juan Godinez 3   Angeline Ross 9
Dane Cuny 67   Nancy Fryzlewicz 68
Jennifer Sabourin 79   Angie Russ 288*

Public Schs..Principal	Grd	Prgm	Enr/#Cls	SN	
John E Albright Middle Sch 1110 S Villa Ave, Villa Park 60181 Gerrie Aulisa	5-8		194 8	43%	630/279-6160 Fax 630/279-1614
Salt Creek Primary Sch 980 S Riverside Dr, Elmhurst 60126 Sarah Smith	PK-1	T	137 6	33%	630/832-6122 Fax 630/617-2658
Stella May Swartz Elem Sch 17W160 16th St, Oakbrook Ter 60181 Sarah Smith	2-4		161 10	43%	630/834-9256 Fax 630/617-2643

• School Dist 45 Dupage Co PID: 00291261 630/516-7700
255 W Vermont St, Villa Park 60181 Fax 630/530-1624

Schools: 8 \ Teachers: 221 \ Students: 3,410 \ Special Ed Students: 680 \ LEP Students: 736 \ Ethnic: Asian 9%, African American 7%, Hispanic 38%, Caucasian 46% \ Exp: $208 (Med) \ Poverty: 11% \ Title I: $664,982 \ Special Education: $2,704,000 \ Bilingual Education: $353,000 \ Open-Close: 08/19 - 05/27 \ DTBP: $194 (High)

Dr Anthony Palmisano 1,11   Patti Volling 2,15
Robert Cline 2   John Wilson 3
Karen Simko 7   Brunella Greco-Lenzey 9,69*
Christoher Collins 9,11,15   Scott Morris 9

Nancy Munoz Breto 15,68,78,273   Kelly Nettleton 34*
Lisa Speakman 57   Judy Degnan 67
Jean Hockensmith 71   Beth Slusher 73,286*
Mike Pinney 76,295   Diana Brown 79

Public Schs..Principal	Grd	Prgm	Enr/#Cls	SN	
Ardmore Elem Sch 225 S Harvard Ave, Villa Park 60181 Kristin Simpkins	PK-5	T	538 22	25%	630/516-7370 Fax 630/530-3660
Jackson Middle Sch 301 W Jackson St, Villa Park 60181 Jill Amrhein	6-8	T	716 45	37%	630/516-7600 Fax 630/530-6271
Jefferson Middle Sch 255 W Vermont St, Villa Park 60181 Raul Gaston	6-8	T	407 30	61%	630/516-7800 Fax 630/993-6348
North Elem Sch 150 W Sunset Ave, Villa Park 60181 Fred Leinweber	PK-5	T	398 20	64%	630/516-7790 Fax 630/530-1385
Schafer Elem Sch 700 E Pleasant Ln, Lombard 60148 Edith Rivera	PK-5	T	449 26	63%	630/516-6500 Fax 630/932-6471
Stevenson Elem Sch 18W331 15th St, Lombard 60148 Kelly Nettleton	PK-2	T	230 12	61%	630/516-7780 Fax 630/889-7923
Westmore Elem Sch 340 S School St, Lombard 60148 Scott Dart	PK-5	T	387 23	25%	630/516-7500 Fax 630/932-6492
York Center Elem Sch 895 E 14th St, Lombard 60148 Andrea Derdenger	3-5	T	207 9	69%	630/516-6540 Fax 630/932-6543

• West Chicago Elementary SD 33 PID: 00291479 630/293-6000
312 E Forest Ave, West Chicago 60185 Fax 630/231-3472

Schools: 8 \ Teachers: 312 \ Students: 4,300 \ Special Ed Students: 720 \ LEP Students: 2,156 \ Ethnic: Asian 3%, African American 3%, Hispanic 81%, Caucasian 13% \ Exp: $782 (High) \ Poverty: 14% \ Title I: $931,966 \ Special Education: $2,647,000 \ Bilingual Education: $771,000 \ Open-Close: 09/02 - 06/10 \ DTBP: $179 (High)

Kristina Davis 1   John Haffner 2
Fred Cadena 3   Gloria Trejo 9,280,285,288,296
Lea DeLuca 9   Sandra Warner 34*
Maddie Vazquez 57   Gil Wagner 67
Angelica Romano 68   Beth Walrath 69,294
Dave Venchus 73   Suzanne Nissen 79
Marjory Lewe-Brady 91

Public Schs..Principal	Grd	Prgm	Enr/#Cls	SN	
Currier Elem Sch 800 Garys Mill Rd, West Chicago 60185 Mark Truckenbrod	K-5	T	420 22	56%	630/293-6600 Fax 630/562-2579
Early Learning Center 300 E Forest Ave, West Chicago 60185 Sandra Warner	PK-PK		120 9	35%	630/293-6000 Fax 630/231-7605
Gary Elem Sch 130 E Forest Ave, West Chicago 60185 **Mary Kassir**	K-5	T	551 24	51%	630/293-6010 Fax 630/562-2583
Indian Knoll Elem Sch 0n645 Indian Knoll Rd, West Chicago 60185 Jackie Campos	K-5	T	344 23	46%	630/293-6020 Fax 630/562-2584
Leman Middle Sch 238 E Hazel St, West Chicago 60185 Lea DeLuca	6-8	T	1,336 50	52%	630/293-6060 Fax 630/562-2586
Pioneer Elem Sch 615 Kenwood Ave, West Chicago 60185 Lissette Jacobson	K-6	T	424 25	61%	630/293-6040 Fax 630/562-2587

79	Student Personnel	91	Safety/Security	275	Response To Intervention	298	Grant Writer/Ptnrships	**School Programs**
80	Driver Ed/Safety	92	Magnet School	277	Remedial Math K-12	750	Chief Innovation Officer	A = Alternative Program
81	Gifted/Talented	93	Parental Involvement	280	Literacy Coach	751	Chief of Staff	G = Adult Classes
82	Video Education	95	Tech Prep Program	285	STEM	752	Social Emotional Learning	M = Magnet Program
83	Substance Abuse Prev	97	Chief Infomation Officer	286	Digital Learning			T = Title I Schoolwide
84	Erate	98	Chief Technology Officer	288	Common Core Standards		**Other School Types**	V = Career & Tech Ed Programs
85	AIDS Education	270	Accountability	294	Character Education	Ⓐ	= Alternative School	
88	Alternative/At Risk	271	Migrant Education	295	Network System	Ⓒ	= Charter School	**Social Media**
89	Multi-Cultural Curriculum	273	Teacher Mentor	296	Title II Programs	Ⓜ	= Magnet School	= Facebook
90	Social Work	274	Before/After Sch	297	Webmaster	Ⓨ	= Year-Round School	= Twitter

New Schools are shaded
New Superintendents and Principals are bold
Personnel with email addresses are underscored

Du Page County

Market Data Retrieval

Turner Elem Sch	K-5	T	376	58%	630/293-6050
750 Ingalton Ave, West Chicago 60185			30		Fax 630/562-2589
Maurice McDavid					
Wegner Elem Sch	K-5	T	382	53%	630/293-6400
1180 Marcella Ln, West Chicago 60185			25		Fax 630/562-2590
Karen Apostoli					

- **Winfield School District 34** PID: 00291584   630/909-4900
  0S150 Winfield Rd, Winfield 60190   Fax 630/260-2382

Schools: 2 \ **Teachers:** 27 \ **Students:** 275 \ **Special Ed Students:** 43 \ **LEP Students:** 15 \ **Ethnic:** Asian 1%, African American 3%, Hispanic 15%, Caucasian 80% \ **Exp:** $274 (Med) \ **Poverty:** 5% \ **Title I:** $31,099 \ **Special Education:** $219,000 \ **Bilingual Education:** $4,000 \ **Open-Close:** 08/20 - 06/02 \ **DTBP:** $242 (High)

Dr Matt Rich 1,11		Doug Gallois 2	
Antwan Blake 3		Jess Honaker 6*	
Trisha Martinez 7*		Dawn Reinke 9,12,57,69,288,294,298*	
Laura Bothwell 16,82,83,270		Melissa Doucet 52,73,280,285,286,288*	
Elizabeth Lee 67		Jessica Peters 77	
Dawn Winkelman 79,88,296		Shona Dave 83,270*	

Public Schs..Principal	Grd	Prgm	Enr/#Cls	SN	
Winfield Central Sch	3-8		183	18%	630/909-4960
0S150 Park St, Winfield 60190			12		Fax 630/933-9236
Dawn Reinke					
Winfield Primary Sch	K-2		88	9%	630/909-4900
0S150 Winfield Rd, Winfield 60190			8		
Dawn Reinke					

- **Wood Dale School Dist 7** PID: 00291625   630/595-9510
  543 N Wood Dale Rd, Wood Dale 60191   Fax 630/595-5625

Schools: 4 \ **Teachers:** 80 \ **Students:** 1,082 \ **Special Ed Students:** 133 \ **Ethnic:** Asian 5%, African American 3%, Hispanic 52%, Caucasian 40% \ **Exp:** $250 (Med) \ **Poverty:** 11% \ **Title I:** $194,416 \ **Special Education:** $813,000 \ **Bilingual Education:** $90,000 \ **Open-Close:** 08/17 - 05/28 \ **DTBP:** $239 (High) \ f t

Dr John Corbett 1		Steve Wilt 2,11,84,298	
Gus Gonzalez 3		Pam Wawczak 5	
Su Malec 7		Dr Merri Beth Kudrna 9,69	
Carol Skog 57*		Kelly Gould 59	
Joe Petrella 67		Joshua Halverson 73,76,286,295*	

Public Schs..Principal	Grd	Prgm	Enr/#Cls	SN	
Early Childhood Ed Center	PK-PK	T	111	55%	630/694-1174
543 N Wood Dale Rd, Wood Dale 60191			5		Fax 630/694-4922
Elvia Villalobos					
Oakbrook Elem Sch	K-2	T	282	62%	630/766-6336
170 S Wood Dale Rd, Wood Dale 60191			17		Fax 630/766-6337
Timothy Shermak					
Westview Elem Sch	3-5	T	354	57%	630/766-8040
200 N Addison Rd, Wood Dale 60191			18		Fax 630/766-8041
Alan Buttimer					f t
Wood Dale Junior High Sch	6-8	T	325	58%	630/766-6210
6N655 Wood Dale Rd, Wood Dale 60191			33		Fax 630/766-6211
Shelly Skarzynski					

- **Woodridge Elem Sch District 68** PID: 00289957   217/795-6800
  7925 Janes Ave, Woodridge 60517   Fax 217/853-2935

Schools: 7 \ **Teachers:** 208 \ **Students:** 2,950 \ **Special Ed Students:** 534 \ **LEP Students:** 509 \ **Ethnic:** Asian 8%, African American 16%, Hispanic 30%, Caucasian 46% \ **Exp:** $402 (High) \ **Poverty:** 10% \ **Title I:** $424,566 \ **Special Education:** $2,047,000 \ **Bilingual Education:** $64,000 \ **Open-Close:** 08/20 - 05/27 \ **DTBP:** $183 (High) \ f

Dr Patrick Broncato 1		Curtis Saindon 2,5,15	
Alex Gliwa 3,91		Cindy Dore 7,11,35,59,77,88	
Greg Wolcott 11,57,69,83,275,288,296,298		Dr William Schmidt 15,68,78,79,273	
Yadi Alfaro 57		Steven Gustis 67	
Amy Melinder 71		Scott Dixon 73,76,295	
Dr Anne Bowers 90			

Public Schs..Principal	Grd	Prgm	Enr/#Cls	SN	
Edgewood Elem Sch	PK-6	T	429	56%	630/795-6000
7900 Woodridge Dr, Woodridge 60517			25		Fax 844/380-4147
Tanya Hughes					
Goodrich Elem Sch	PK-6	T	413	29%	630/795-6100
3450 Hobson Rd, Woodridge 60517			16		Fax 844/380-4148
Paul Scaletta					
John L Sipley Elem Sch	PK-6	T	394	52%	630/795-6300
2806 83rd St, Woodridge 60517			17		Fax 844/380-4152
Don Mrozik					
Meadowview Elem Sch	PK-6	T	385	43%	630/795-6400
2525 Mitchell Dr, Woodridge 60517			18		Fax 844/380-4150
Kelly Neylon					
Thomas Jefferson Jr High Sch	7-8	T	687	42%	630/795-6700
7200 Janes Ave, Woodridge 60517			45		Fax 844/380-4149
Justin Warnke					
William F Murphy Elem Sch	PK-6	T	384	45%	630/795-6500
7700 Larchwood Ln, Woodridge 60517			23		Fax 844/380-4151
Jacob Engler					
Willow Creek Elem Sch	PK-6	T	355	39%	630/795-6600
2901 Jackson Dr, Woodridge 60517			21		Fax 844/380-4153
Kurt Kramer					t

DU PAGE CATHOLIC SCHOOLS

- **Diocese of Joliet Ed Office** PID: 00325965
  Listing includes only schools located in this county. See District Index for location of Diocesan Offices.

Catholic Schs..Principal	Grd	Prgm	Enr/#Cls	SN	
All Saints Catholic Academy	PK-8		445		630/961-6125
1155 Aurora Ave, Naperville 60540					
Melissa Santos					
Benet Academy	9-12		1,313		630/969-6550
2200 Maple Ave, Lisle 60532			65		Fax 630/719-2849
Stephen Marth					
Holy Trinity Catholic Sch	PK-8		214		630/971-0184
108 S Linden Ave, Westmont 60559			12		Fax 630/971-1175
Dr Pamela Simon					
IC Catholic Prep	9-12		253		630/530-3460
217 S Cottage Hill Ave, Elmhurst 60126			20		Fax 630/530-2290
Stephen Davidson					
Immaculate Conception Sch	PK-8		570		630/530-3490
132 W Arthur St, Elmhurst 60126			18		Fax 630/530-9787
Cathy Linley					

1	Superintendent	8	Curric/Instruct K-12	19	Chief Financial Officer	29	Family/Consumer Science	39	Social Studies K-12	49	English/Lang Arts Elem	59	Special Education Elem	69	Academic Assessment
2	Bus/Finance/Purchasing	9	Curric/Instruct Elem	20	Art K-12	30	Adult Education	40	Social Studies Elem	50	English/Lang Arts Sec	60	Special Education Sec	70	Research/Development
3	Buildings And Grounds	10	Curric/Instruct Sec	21	Art Elem	31	Career/Sch-to-Work K-12	41	Social Studies Sec	51	Reading K-12	61	Foreign/World Lang K-12	71	Public Information
4	Food Service	11	Federal Program	22	Art Sec	32	Career/Sch-to-Work Elem	42	Science K-12	52	Reading Elem	62	Foreign/World Lang Elem	72	Summer School
5	Transportation	12	Title I	23	Music K-12	33	Career/Sch-to-Work Sec	43	Science Elem	53	Reading Sec	63	Foreign/World Lang Sec	73	Instructional Tech
6	Athletic	13	Title V	24	Music Elem	34	Early Childhood Ed	44	Science Sec	54	Remedial Reading K-12	64	Religious Education K-12	74	Inservice Training
7	Health Services	14	Asst Superintendent	25	Music Sec	35	Health/Phys Education	45	Math K-12	55	Remedial Reading Elem	65	Religious Education Elem	75	Marketing/Distributive
		15	Instructional Media Svcs	26	Business Education	36	Guidance Services K-12	46	Math Elem	56	Remedial Reading Sec	66	Religious Education Sec	76	Info Systems
		16	Chief Operations Officer	27	Career & Tech Ed	37	Guidance Services Elem	47	Math Sec	57	Bilingual/ELL	67	School Board President	77	Psychological Assess
		18	Chief Academic Officer	28	Technology Education	38	Guidance Services Sec	48	English/Lang Arts K-12	58	Special Education K-12	68	Teacher Personnel	78	Affirmative Action

Illinois School Directory — Du Page County

School	Grd	Enr/#Cls	Phone/Fax
Mary Queen of Heaven Pre-Sch 426 N West Ave, Elmhurst 60126 Elizabeth Lowery	PK-PK	95	630/833-9500
Montini Catholic High Sch 19W070 16th St, Lombard 60148 Kevin Beirne	9-12	700 32	630/627-6930 Fax 630/627-0537
Notre Dame Sch 66 Norfolk Ave, Clarendon Hls 60514 Tom Smyth	PK-8	210 16	630/323-1642 Fax 630/654-3255
Our Lady of Peace Sch 709 Plainfield Rd, Darien 60561 Dr J Chavez	K-8	508	630/325-9220 Fax 630/325-1995
Sacred Heart Sch 322 W Maple St, Lombard 60148 Maureen Nielsen	PK-8	276 10	630/629-0536 Fax 630/629-4752
SS Peter & Paul Sch 201 E Franklin Ave, Naperville 60540 Frank Glowaty	K-8	380 25	630/355-0113 Fax 630/355-9803
St Francis High Sch 2130 W Roosevelt Rd, Wheaton 60187 Raeann Huhn	9-12	724 40	630/668-5800 Fax 630/668-5893
St Irene Catholic Sch 3S601 Warren Ave, Warrenville 60555 Margaret Detwiler	PK-8	152 10	630/393-9303 Fax 630/393-7009
St Isaac Jogues Sch 421 S Clay St, Hinsdale 60521 Carol Burlinski	K-8	559 25	630/323-3244 Fax 630/655-6676
St Isidore Sch 431 W Army Trail Rd, Bloomingdale 60108 Corie Alimento	PK-8	351 10	630/529-9323 Fax 630/529-8882
St James the Apostle Sch 490 S Park Blvd, Glen Ellyn 60137 Paul Kirk	PK-8	265 11	630/469-8060 Fax 630/469-1107
St Joan of Arc Sch 4913 Columbia Ave, Lisle 60532 Michelle Picchione	PK-8	640 23	630/969-1732 Fax 630/353-4590
St John the Baptist Sch 259 Church St, Winfield 60190 Joanne Policht	PK-8	361 11	630/668-2625 Fax 630/668-7176
St Joseph Sch 4832 Highland Ave, Downers Grove 60515 Rita Stasi	K-8	461	630/969-4306 Fax 630/969-3946
St Mary of Gostyn Sch 440 Prairie Ave, Downers Grove 60515 Chris Tiritilli	PK-8	549 20	630/968-6155 Fax 630/968-6208
St Matthew Sch 1555 Glen Ellyn Rd, Glendale HTS 60139 Regina Pestrak	PK-8	177 21	630/858-3112
St Michael Sch 314 W Willow Ave, Wheaton 60187 Adam Ferguson	PK-8	607 18	630/665-1454 Fax 630/665-1491
St Petronille Sch 425 Prospect Ave Ste 100, Glen Ellyn 60137 Maureen Aspell	K-8	548 20	630/469-5041 Fax 630/469-5071
St Philip the Apostle Sch 1233 W Holtz Ave, Addison 60101 Julie Noonan	PK-8	328 12	630/543-4130 Fax 630/458-8750
St Pius X Sch 601 Westmore Meyers Rd, Lombard 60148 Toni Miller	PK-8	406	630/627-2353 Fax 630/627-1810
St Raphael Sch 1215 Modaff Rd, Naperville 60540 Mavis Demar	K-8	310 16	630/355-1880 Fax 630/428-4974
St Scholastica Sch 7720 Janes Ave, Woodridge 60517 Elizabeth Driscoll	K-8	273 11	630/985-2515 Fax 630/985-2395
St Walter Sch 201 W Maple Ave, Roselle 60172 Mrs Warco	PK-8	691 20	630/529-1721 Fax 630/529-9290
Visitation Sch 851 S York St, Elmhurst 60126 Carrie Mijal	PK-8	500 70	630/834-4931 Fax 630/834-4936
Marmion Academy 1000 Butterfield Rd, Aurora 60502 Anthony Tinerella	9-12	525 25	630/897-6936 Fax 630/897-7086

• **Diocese of Rockford Ed Office** PID: 00328345
Listing includes only schools located in this county. See District Index for location of Diocesan Offices.

DU PAGE PRIVATE SCHOOLS

Private Schs..Principal	Grd	Prgm	Enr/#Cls	SN
Avery Coonley Sch 1400 Maple Ave, Downers Grove 60515 Paul Druzinsky	PK-8		337 31	630/969-0800 Fax 630/969-0131
Bethany Lutheran Sch 1550 Modaff Rd, Naperville 60565 Erin Dunwell	PK-8		275 10	630/355-6607 Fax 630/355-2216
Bridge High Sch 2318 Wisconsin Ave, Downers Grove 60515 Camille Smith	Spec		25 4	630/355-6533 Fax 630/964-5308
Camelot Tds of Naperville 1220 Bond St Ste 136, Naperville 60563 Michael Gurley	Spec		89 10	630/355-0200 Fax 630/357-7903
Carmel Montessori Academy 3S238 State Route 59, Warrenville 60555 Carmen Lafranzo	PK-12	G	40 4	630/393-2995
Chesterbrook Academy 1571 Oswego Rd, Naperville 60540 Jenae Kleifges	K-7		90	630/527-0833 Fax 630/527-1204
Chesterton Academy-Holy Family 5205 Kingston Ave, Lisle 60532 Julie Bowles	9-12		90	630/442-1424
Clare Woods Academy 125 E Seminary Ave, Wheaton 60187 John Utterback	Spec		100 13	630/289-4221 Fax 630/289-4390
College Prep School-America 331 W Madison St, Lombard 60148 Dr Mohammed Taher	PK-12		443 25	630/889-8000 Fax 630/889-8012
Concord Lutheran Sch 865 S Church Rd, Bensenville 60106 Matt Tuomi	PK-8		92 11	630/766-0228 Fax 630/766-3902
Cosmic Montessori Sch 4100 Westbrook Dr, Aurora 60504 Slyvia Dei Rossi	PK-5		170	630/585-8881
Downers Grove Adventist Sch 5524 Lee Ave, Downers Grove 60515 Patricia Williams	PK-8		40 5	630/968-8848
Downers Grove Christian Sch 929 Maple Ave, Downers Grove 60515 Shari Peterson	PK-8		150 12	630/852-0832 Fax 630/852-0880
Dupage Montessori Sch 1111 E Warrenville Rd, Naperville 60563	PK-8		204	630/369-6899 Fax 630/369-7306
Four Winds Sch 30W160 Calumet Ave W, Warrenville 60555 Jocelyne Roy	PK-8		150 10	630/836-9400

---

79 Student Personnel	91 Safety/Security	275 Response To Intervention	298 Grant Writer/Ptnrships
80 Driver Ed/Safety	92 Magnet School	277 Remedial Math K-12	750 Chief Innovation Officer
81 Gifted/Talented	93 Parental Involvement	280 Literacy Coach	751 Chief of Staff
82 Video Services	95 Tech Prep Program	285 STEM	752 Social Emotional Learning
83 Substance Abuse Prev	97 Chief Information Officer	286 Digital Learning	
84 Erate	98 Chief Technology Officer	288 Common Core Standards	**Other School Types**
85 AIDS Accountability	270 Character Education	294 Accountability	Ⓐ = Alternative School
88 Alternative/At Risk	271 Migrant Education	295 Network System	Ⓒ = Charter School
89 Multi-Cultural Curriculum	273 Teacher Mentor	296 Title II Programs	Ⓜ = Magnet School
90 Social Work	274 Before/After Sch	297 Webmaster	Ⓨ = Year-Round School

School Programs
A = Alternative Program
G = Adult Classes
M = Magnet Program
T = Title I Schoolwide
V = Career & Tech Ed Programs

Social Media
= Facebook
= Twitter

New Schools are shaded
New Superintendents and Principals are bold
Personnel with email addresses are underscored

Du Page County

School	Grades		Enroll	Phone
Fusion Academy-Oak Brook 3041 Butterfield Rd Ste 200, Oak Brook 60523 Michael Wang	6-12		60	630/368-0824 Fax 630/574-2327
Giant Steps 2500 Cabot Dr, Lisle 60532 Slyvia Smith	Spec		401	630/864-3800 Fax 630/864-3820
Glen Oaks Therapeutic Day Sch 1N450 Main St, Glen Ellyn 60137 Lisa Grigsby	Spec		45	630/469-3602 Fax 630/469-3897
Good Shepherd Lutheran Sch 525 63rd St, Downers Grove 60516 David Roekle	K-8		70 7	630/852-5081 Fax 630/852-1532
Hinsdale Adventist Academy 631 E Hickory St, Hinsdale 60521 Fawn Scherencel	PK-12		200 18	630/323-9211 Fax 630/323-9237
Immanuel Lutheran Sch 148 E 3rd St, Elmhurst 60126 Angela Schlie	PK-8		240 13	630/832-9302 Fax 630/832-8307
Islamic Foundation Sch 300 W Highridge Rd, Villa Park 60181 Khalida Baste	PK-12		631 33	630/941-8800 Fax 630/941-0114
Kindi Mont Academy 8161 Cass Ave, Darien 60561 Hatem Elagha	PK-8		140	630/560-4900 Fax 630/914-6969
Kingswood Academy 133 Plainfield Rd, Darien 60561 Glenn Purpura	PK-8		75 10	630/887-1411 Fax 630/887-1424
Krejci Academy 619 E Franklin Ave, Naperville 60540 Lori Deichstetter	Spec		96 19	630/355-6870 Fax 630/281-6937
Mansion Private Sch 126 N Wright St, Naperville 60540 Camille Smith	Spec		25 3	630/357-1226 Fax 630/961-9932
Marquette Manor Baptist Acad 333 75th St, Downers Grove 60516 Donald Sherwin	PK-12		161 15	630/964-5363 Fax 630/964-5385
Naperville Christian Academy 1451 Raymond Dr Ste 200, Naperville 60563 Kim MacIntyre \ Ann Nikchevich	PK-12		112 10	630/637-9622
Ombudsman Sch-Downers Grove 2777 Finley Rd, Downers Grove 60515 David Bagger	7-12		39 1	630/629-1414 Fax 630/629-3654
Ombudsman Sch-Naperville 1815 W Diehl Rd Ste 400, Naperville 60563 Holly McLaughlin	7-12		40 1	630/428-9667 Fax 630/717-0587
Ombudsman Sch 148 S Bloomingdale Rd Ste 106, Bloomingdale 60108 Dee Elehrman	7-12		35 1	630/351-9153 Fax 630/351-3794
Parkland Preparatory Academy 2220 Southwind Blvd, Bartlett 60103 Jillian Barker	Spec		300	630/823-8323 Fax 630/855-3697
Pythagoras Childrens Academy 893 N Church Rd, Elmhurst 60126 Christina Brales	PK-6		100	630/834-0477
Sch Exp Arts & Lrng-Lombard 240 E Progress Rd, Lombard 60148 Matt Stary	Spec		25	630/953-1222
Seton Academy 350 N Westmore Ave, Villa Park 60181 Mary Thornton	PK-6		35 2	630/279-4101
St John Lutheran Sch 220 S Lincoln Ave, Lombard 60148 Aaron Landgrave	PK-8		260 11	630/629-2515 Fax 630/932-4016
St Luke Lutheran Sch 410 S Rush St, Itasca 60143 Patti Fagalde	PK-8		120 10	630/773-0509 Fax 630/773-0786
Timothy Christian High Sch 1061 S Prospect Ave, Elmhurst 60126 Brad Mitchell	9-12		380 16	630/833-7575 Fax 630/833-9821
Timothy Christian Sch 188 W Butterfield Rd, Elmhurst 60126 Justin Horne \ Brad Mitchell	K-12		700 30	630/833-4717 Fax 630/833-9828
Trinity Lutheran Sch 11503 German Church Rd, Burr Ridge 60527 Andy DeWitt	PK-8		100 9	708/839-1444 Fax 708/839-8503
Trinity Lutheran Sch 1165 Westmore Meyers Rd, Lombard 60148 Julie Messina	PK-8		70 6	630/627-5601 Fax 630/627-5676
Trinity Lutheran Sch 405 Rush St, Roselle 60172 Dawn Koenig	PK-8		250 12	630/894-3263 Fax 630/894-1430
Vine Academy 6880 N Frontage Rd Ste 400, Burr Ridge 60527 Amanda Vogel	K-12		60	630/423-5916
Wheaton Academy 900 Prince Crossing Rd, West Chicago 60185 Kori Hockett	9-12	V	650 36	630/562-7500 Fax 630/231-0842
Wheaton Christian Grammar Sch 1N350 Taylor Dr, Winfield 60190 Marc Painter	K-8		500 23	630/668-1385 Fax 630/668-2475

DU PAGE REGIONAL CENTERS

- **Cooperative Assn for Spec Ed** PID: 02182018 630/942-5600
  22W600 Butterfield Rd, Glen Ellyn 60137 Fax 630/942-5601

  Dr Mary Furbush 1   Jerry Brendel 2
  Cindy D'Ambrosio 15,74   Emily Shields 79
  Mindy Long 271

- **Dupage Area Occupational Sys** PID: 04189402 630/620-8770
  301 S Swift Rd, Addison 60101 Fax 630/691-7592

  Sonia Martinez 2

- **Dupage Reg Office of Ed 19** PID: 02097724 630/407-5800
  421 N County Farm Rd, Wheaton 60187 Fax 630/407-5802

  Dr Darlene Ruscitti 1   Jeremy Dotson 2

- **North Dupage Spec Ed Co-op** PID: 10031596 630/894-0490
  132 E Pine Ave, Roselle 60172 Fax 630/894-5960

  Jim Nelson 1   Reiley Straub 2
  Dr Todd Putnam 15,58,74,275

- **Philip J Rock Center & School** PID: 03266540 630/790-2474
  818 Du Page Blvd, Glen Ellyn 60137 Fax 630/790-4893

  Bonnie Jordan 1

- **School Assoc for Sp Ed-Dupage** PID: 02097736 630/778-4500
  2900 Ogden Ave, Lisle 60532 Fax 630/778-0196

  Dr Mindy McGuffin 1   Sam Cannata 2
  Christine Martin 8,15,69   Nan Diamond 58
  Lynn Schroeder 68   Elliot May 73

---

1 Superintendent	8 Curric/Instruct K-12	19 Chief Financial Officer	29 Family/Consumer Science	39 Social Studies K-12	49 English/Lang Arts Elem	59 Special Education Elem	69 Academic Assessment
2 Bus/Finance/Purchasing	9 Curric/Instruct Elem	20 Art K-12	30 Adult Education	40 Social Studies Elem	50 English/Lang Arts Sec	60 Special Education Sec	70 Research/Development
3 Buildings And Grounds	10 Curric/Instruct Sec	21 Art Elem	31 Career/Sch-to-Work K-12	41 Social Studies Sec	51 Reading K-12	61 Foreign/World Lang K-12	71 Public Information
4 Food Service	11 Federal Program	22 Art Sec	32 Career/Sch-to-Work Elem	42 Science K-12	52 Reading Elem	62 Foreign/World Lang Elem	72 Summer School
5 Transportation	12 Title I	23 Music K-12	33 Career/Sch-to-Work Sec	43 Science Elem	53 Reading Sec	63 Foreign/World Lang Sec	73 Instructional Tech
6 Athletic	13 Title V	24 Music Elem	34 Early Childhood Ed	44 Science Sec	54 Remedial Reading K-12	64 Religious Education K-12	74 Inservice Training
7 Health Services	15 Asst Superintendent	25 Music Sec	35 Health/Phys Education	45 Math K-12	55 Remedial Reading Elem	65 Religious Education Elem	75 Marketing/Distributive
	16 Instructional Media Svcs	26 Business Education	36 Guidance Services K-12	46 Math Elem	56 Remedial Reading Sec	66 Religious Education Sec	76 Info Systems
	17 Chief Operations Officer	27 Career & Tech Ed	37 Guidance Services Elem	47 Math Sec	57 Bilingual/ELL	67 School Board President	77 Psychological Assess
	18 Chief Academic Officer	28 Technology Education	38 Guidance Services Sec	48 English/Lang Arts K-12	58 Special Education K-12	68 Teacher Personnel	78 Affirmative Action

Illinois School Directory — Edgar County

EDGAR COUNTY

EDGAR COUNTY SCHOOLS

County Schs..Principal	Grd	Prgm	Enr/#Cls	SN	
Kansas Treatment & Lrng Center 201 Catherine St, Kansas 61933 Jane Gregory	Spec		85 8	82%	217/948-5751 Fax 217/948-5752

EDGAR PUBLIC SCHOOLS

• **Edgar Co Cmty Sch Dist 6** PID: 00291900   217/269-2513
23231 Il Highway 1, Chrisman 61924   Fax 217/269-3231

Schools: 3 \ **Teachers:** 28 \ **Students:** 307 \ **Special Ed Students:** 90 \ **College-Bound:** 62% \ **Ethnic:** Asian 1%, African American 1%, Hispanic 1%, Caucasian 98% \ **Exp:** $249 (Med) \ **Poverty:** 13% \ **Title I:** $65,253 \ **Special Education:** $111,000 \ **Open-Close:** 08/19 - 05/19 \ **DTBP:** $169 (High)

Jim Acklin 1   Sunny Hughes 2
Rachel Swinderman .... 11,54* Jody Kirby 16
McKenzie Vilerdal 31,73   Kate Pillen 36
Leslie Henry 67   Cole Huber 273

Public Schs..Principal	Grd	Prgm	Enr/#Cls	SN	
Chrisman Elem Sch 111 N Pennsylvania St, Chrisman 61924 Kelly Schluter	PK-5	T	147 9	43%	217/269-2022 Fax 217/269-3222
Chrisman High Sch 23231 Il Highway 1, Chrisman 61924 Cole Huber	9-12		100 15	38%	217/269-2823 Fax 217/269-2329
Chrisman-Scottland Jr High Sch 23231 Il Highway 1, Chrisman 61924 Cole Huber	6-8	T	75 12	48%	217/269-3980

• **Kansas Cmty School District 3** PID: 00291974   217/948-5174
310 S Front St, Kansas 61933   Fax 217/948-5134

Schools: 1 \ **Teachers:** 20 \ **Students:** 205 \ **Special Ed Students:** 36 \ **College-Bound:** 66% \ **Ethnic:** Hispanic 1%, Caucasian 99% \ **Exp:** $176 (Low) \ **Poverty:** 12% \ **Title I:** $43,998 \ **Special Education:** $91,000 \ **Open-Close:** 08/17 - 05/21 \ **DTBP:** $189 (High)

John Hasten 1,11,288   Ann Motley 2*
Jenni Veach 6   Cindy Spencer 8,12,298*
Marc Eskew 67   Joe Morrisey 80,85
Michael Lowery 273*

Public Schs..Principal	Grd	Prgm	Enr/#Cls	SN	
Kansas Sch 310 S Front St, Kansas 61933 Cindy Spencer	K-12	TV	205 25	48%	217/948-5175

• **Paris Cmty Unit Sch Dist 4** PID: 00292007   217/465-5391
15601 US Highway 150, Paris 61944   Fax 217/466-1225

Schools: 1 \ **Teachers:** 28 \ **Students:** 480 \ **Special Ed Students:** 90 \ **LEP Students:** 3 \ **College-Bound:** 68% \ **Ethnic:** Asian 2%, Hispanic 1%, Caucasian 97% \ **Exp:** $187 (Low) \ **Poverty:** 10% \ **Title I:** $105,465 \ **Special Education:** $165,000 \ **Open-Close:** 08/12 - 05/21

Danette Young 1,11   Josh McCarty 3
Shelley East .... 12*   Jim Blue 67
Megan Damler .... 69,88*   Jim Pattenaude 295*

Public Schs..Principal	Grd	Prgm	Enr/#Cls	SN	
Crestwood Sch 15601 US Highway 150, Paris 61944 Dan Lynch	PK-8	T	480 44	33%	217/465-5391

• **Paris Union School District 95** PID: 00292021   217/465-8448
300 E Wood St, Paris 61944   Fax 217/463-2243

Schools: 4 \ **Teachers:** 65 \ **Students:** 1,452 \ **Special Ed Students:** 259 \ **College-Bound:** 68% \ **Ethnic:** Hispanic 1%, Caucasian 99% \ **Exp:** $209 (Med) \ **Poverty:** 22% \ **Title I:** $481,876 \ **Special Education:** $459,000 \ **Open-Close:** 08/17 - 05/19

Dr Jeremy Larson 1   Sally Keller 2
Jerry Thurman 3   Gary Doughan 5*
Mick Roberts .... 6*   Dr Jeremy Larson 11*
Jeff Barnes .... 36*   Kevin Knoepfel 67
Nathan Bell 73

Public Schs..Principal	Grd	Prgm	Enr/#Cls	SN	
Carolyn Wenz Elem Sch 437 W Washington St, Paris 61944 Megan Carroll	3-5	T	302 15	65%	217/466-3140 Fax 217/466-6718
Mayo Middle Sch 300 E Wood St, Paris 61944 Kyle Shay	6-8	T	275 20	64%	217/466-3050 Fax 217/466-3905
Memorial Elem Sch 509 E Newton St, Paris 61944 Dr Jeremy Larson	PK-2	T	316 18	58%	217/466-6170 Fax 217/466-5586
Paris Co-op High Sch 14040 E 1200th Rd, Paris 61944 Mark Cox	9-12	V	559		217/466-1175 Fax 217/466-1903

• **Shiloh School District 1** PID: 00291948   217/887-2364
21751 N 575th St, Hume 61932   Fax 217/887-2448

Schools: 1 \ **Teachers:** 31 \ **Students:** 380 \ **Special Ed Students:** 66 \ **College-Bound:** 55% \ **Ethnic:** Caucasian 100% \ **Exp:** $339 (High) \ **Poverty:** 19% \ **Title I:** $126,471 \ **Special Education:** $87,000 \ **Open-Close:** 08/17 - 05/18

Allen Hall 1   Elizabeth Harbaugh ... 2,8,11,88,273,274,296*
Dick Waggoner .... 3,5*   Richard Kinosky 6
Glenda Milam .... 16,82*   David Smith 67
Aly Barry 73

Public Schs..Principal	Grd	Prgm	Enr/#Cls	SN	
Shiloh Community Sch 21751 N 575th St, Hume 61932 Elizabeth Harbaugh	PK-12	V	380 40	47%	217/887-2364

---

79 Student Personnel
80 Driver Ed/Safety
81 Gifted/Talented
82 Video Services
83 Substance Abuse Prev
84 Erate
85 AIDS Education
88 Alternative/At Risk
89 Multi-Cultural Curriculum
90 Social Work
91 Safety/Security
92 Magnet School
93 Parental Involvement
95 Tech Prep Program
97 Chief Infomation Officer
98 Chief Technology Officer
270 Character Education
271 Migrant Education
273 Teacher Mentor
274 Before/After Sch
275 Response To Intervention
277 Remedial Math K-12
280 Literacy Coach
285 STEM
286 Digital Learning
288 Common Core Standards
294 Accountability
295 Network System
296 Title II Programs
297 Webmaster
298 Grant Writer/Ptnrships
750 Chief Innovation Officer
751 Chief of Staff
752 Social Emotional Learning

Other School Types
Ⓐ = Alternative School
Ⓒ = Charter School
Ⓜ = Magnet School
Ⓨ = Year-Round School

School Programs
A = Alternative Program
G = Adult Classes
M = Magnet Program
T = Title I Schoolwide
V = Career & Tech Ed Programs

Social Media
 = Facebook
 = Twitter

New Schools are shaded
New Superintendents and Principals are bold
Personnel with email addresses are underscored

Edwards County

Market Data Retrieval

EDWARDS COUNTY

EDWARDS PUBLIC SCHOOLS

• **Edwards Co Cmty Unit SD 1** PID: 00292095   618/445-2814
361 W Main St Ste 100, Albion 62806   Fax 618/445-2272

Schools: 3 \ Teachers: 64 \ Students: 896 \ Special Ed Students: 185 \ LEP Students: 4 \ College-Bound: 77% \ Ethnic: Hispanic 1%, Caucasian 98% \ Exp: $398 (High) \ Poverty: 12% \ Title I: $198,576 \ Special Education: $212,000 \ Open-Close: 08/13 - 05/26 \ DTBP: $178 (High)

David Cowger	1,83	Sherry Giese	2
Jim Ballard	3	Melissa Fisher	4
Aline Berjer	5	Kris Duncan	6
Preston Nelson	8,288*	Shane Carter	8,11,34,57,58,74,273
Dale Schmittler	13,93*	Tambree Krouse	16,82*
Kelley Biggs	36,69*	Dale Woods	67
Dustin Leek	73	Jon Julius	79*
Erica Anderson	85*		

Public Schs..Principal	Grd	Prgm	Enr/#Cls	SN	
Albion Grade Sch 361 W Main St, Albion 62806 Preston Nelson	PK-8		449 24	39%	618/445-2327 Fax 618/445-2672
Edwards Co High Sch 361 W Main St, Albion 62806 Preston Nelson	9-12		298 35	32%	618/445-2327 Fax 618/445-3154
West Salem Elem Sch 105 E School St, West Salem 62476 Dale Schmittler	PK-8		149 12	50%	618/456-8881 Fax 618/456-3510

EFFINGHAM COUNTY

EFFINGHAM COUNTY SCHOOLS

County Schs..Principal	Grd	Prgm	Enr/#Cls	SN	
Ⓐ Aspire Alternative High Sch 900 W Edgar Ave, Effingham 62401 Amber Kidd	9-12		30	47%	217/342-2865 Fax 217/342-9840

EFFINGHAM PUBLIC SCHOOLS

• **Altamont Cmty Unit SD 10** PID: 00292148   618/483-6195
7 S Ewing St, Altamont 62411   Fax 618/483-6303

Schools: 2 \ Teachers: 55 \ Students: 700 \ Special Ed Students: 127 \ LEP Students: 3 \ College-Bound: 59% \ Ethnic: African American 1%, Hispanic 1%, Caucasian 98% \ Exp: $262 (Med) \ Poverty: 13% \ Title I: $188,161 \ Special Education: $243,000 \ Open-Close: 08/13 - 05/27 \ DTBP: $186 (High)

Dr Steven Mayerhofer	1,11,83	Mark Holland	5
Jerry Tkachuk	8*	Doug Hill	12*
Ross Cornett	16,73,286,295	Kathy Clausius	58,88*
Shelly Kuhns	67		

Public Schs..Principal	Grd	Prgm	Enr/#Cls	SN	
Altamont Grade Sch 407 S Edwards St, Altamont 62411 Doug Hill	PK-8	T	439 55	63%	618/483-5171 Fax 618/483-6793 f
Altamont High Sch 7 S Ewing St, Altamont 62411 Jerry Tkachuk	9-12	V	234 26	38%	618/483-6193 Fax 618/483-5399

• **Beecher City Cmty Unit SD 20** PID: 00292174   618/487-5100
438 E State Highway 33, Beecher City 62414   Fax 618/487-5242

Schools: 2 \ Teachers: 27 \ Students: 333 \ Special Ed Students: 61 \ College-Bound: 76% \ Ethnic: Asian 2%, African American 1%, Hispanic 1%, Caucasian 96% \ Exp: $258 (Med) \ Poverty: 13% \ Title I: $85,223 \ Special Education: $80,000 \ Open-Close: 08/14 - 05/18 \ DTBP: $154 (High)

Philip Lark	1,11	Kim Miller	2
Bill Hammer	16*	Lee Road-Armel	67
Bryan Deadman	69*		

Public Schs..Principal	Grd	Prgm	Enr/#Cls	SN	
Beecher City Grade Sch 306 E Vine St, Beecher City 62414 Rosa Milleville	PK-5		170 9	41%	618/487-5108 Fax 618/487-5126
Beecher City Jr Sr High Sch 438 E State Highway 33, Beecher City 62414 Karen Hanfland \ Bryan Deadman	6-12	V	157 12	41%	618/487-5117

• **Dieterich Community Unit SD 30** PID: 00292215   217/925-5247
205 S Pine St, Dieterich 62424   Fax 217/925-5447

Schools: 2 \ Teachers: 36 \ Students: 550 \ Special Ed Students: 69 \ College-Bound: 75% \ Ethnic: Hispanic 2%, Caucasian 98% \ Exp: $308 (High) \ Poverty: 14% \ Title I: $108,551 \ Special Education: $114,000 \ Open-Close: 08/18 - 05/25 \ DTBP: $166 (High)

Cary Jackson	1,73	Charles Fritcher	3,91*
Donetta Ohnesorge	6*	Joshua Benesiel	9,11,58,88,288,296*
Cory Niebrugge	67	Ashley Kreke	69,83*

Public Schs..Principal	Grd	Prgm	Enr/#Cls	SN	
Dieterich Elem Sch 205 S Pine St, Dieterich 62424 Josh Benefiel	PK-6		326 13	23%	217/925-5248
Dieterich Jr Sr High Sch 108 W Church St, Dieterich 62424 Scott Kocher	7-12		194 25	21%	217/925-5247

• **Effingham Cmty Sch Dist 40** PID: 00292265   217/540-1500
2803 S Banker St, Effingham 62401   Fax 217/540-1510

Schools: 5 \ Teachers: 160 \ Students: 2,400 \ Special Ed Students: 500 \ LEP Students: 64 \ College-Bound: 70% \ Ethnic: Asian 1%, African American 2%, Hispanic 4%, Caucasian 93% \ Exp: $209 (Med) \ Poverty: 13% \ Title I: $673,915 \ Special Education: $958,000 \ Open-Close: 08/26 - 05/31 \ DTBP: $207 (High)

Mark Doan	1	Jason Fox	2,3,15,73,76,91
Denise Anderson	4	Kristen Harvey	5

Illinois School Directory

Fayette County

Dave Woltman 6*
Michelle Beck 8,11,57,83,285,288,296,298
Jennifer Seachrist 58,88
Kevin McKenna 84
Donna Pierson 7
Jennifer Fox 34*
Angie Byers 67

Public Schs..Principal	Grd	Prgm	Enr/#Cls	SN	
Central Grade Sch 10421 N US Highway 45, Effingham 62401 Amy Niebrugge	2-5	T	704 24	50%	217/540-1400 Fax 217/540-1454
Early Learning Center 3224 S Banker St, Effingham 62401 Jennifer Fox	PK-K	T	185 10	50%	217/540-1460 Fax 217/540-1484
Effingham High Sch 1301 W Grove Ave, Effingham 62401 Kurt Roberts	9-12	V	718 60	33%	217/540-1100 Fax 217/540-1102
Effingham Junior High Sch 600 S Henrietta St, Effingham 62401 Cody Lewis	6-8	T	594 40	50%	217/540-1300 Fax 217/540-1362
South Side Elem Sch 211 W Douglas Ave, Effingham 62401 Cheri Marten	1-2	T	294 19	53%	217/540-1530 Fax 217/540-1559

- **Teutopolis Cmty Unit SD 50** PID: 00292370   217/857-3535
  801 W Main St, Teutopolis 62467   Fax 217/857-6265

Schools: 3 \ **Teachers:** 66 \ **Students:** 1,000 \
Special Ed Students: 157 \ **LEP Students:** 3 \ **College-Bound:** 74% \
Ethnic: Caucasian 99% \ **Exp:** $216 (Med) \ **Poverty:** 4% \ **Title I:** $79,775 \
Special Education: $525,000 \ **Open-Close:** 08/14 - 05/18

Matthew Sturgeon 1
Norma Koester 4
Amy Nice 16*
Bradley Koester 67
Greg Beck 83,288*
Brian Keoster 2,5
Mary Bushue 11*
Kyla Hall 36,69
Doug Runde 73,76,295*
Jessica Bierman 88*

Public Schs..Principal	Grd	Prgm	Enr/#Cls	SN	
Teutopolis Grade Sch 309 E Main St, Teutopolis 62467 Sherry Harmon	PK-6		561 23	1%	217/857-3232 Fax 217/857-6609
Teutopolis High Sch 801 W Main St, Teutopolis 62467 Greg Beck	9-12	V	334 40	2%	217/857-3139 Fax 217/857-3473
Teutopolis Junior High Sch 904 W Water St, Teutopolis 62467 Patrick Drees	7-8		154 11	2%	217/857-6678 Fax 217/857-6051

EFFINGHAM CATHOLIC SCHOOLS

- **Diocese of Springfield Ed Off** PID: 00319394
  Listing includes only schools located in this county. See District Index for location of Diocesan Offices.

Catholic Schs..Principal	Grd	Prgm	Enr/#Cls	SN	
Sacred Heart Sch 407 S Henrietta St, Effingham 62401 Vicki Wenthe	PK-8		219 15		217/342-4060 Fax 217/342-9251
St Anthony of Padua High Sch 304 E Roadway Ave, Effingham 62401 Greg Fearday	9-12	GV	214 26		217/342-6969 Fax 217/342-6997
St Anthony of Padua Sch 405 N 2nd St, Effingham 62401 Cody Rincker	K-8		329 22		217/347-0419 Fax 217/347-2749

EFFINGHAM PRIVATE SCHOOLS

Private Schs..Principal	Grd	Prgm	Enr/#Cls	SN	
Altamont Lutheran Sch 7 S Edwards St, Altamont 62411 Robinette Flach	K-8		171 13		618/483-6428 Fax 618/483-6296

FAYETTE COUNTY

FAYETTE COUNTY SCHOOLS

County Schs..Principal	Grd	Prgm	Enr/#Cls	SN	
Ⓐ New Approach Alt High Sch 1500 W Jefferson St, Vandalia 62471 Laura Benhoff	9-12		40	79%	618/283-9311 Fax 618/283-9339

FAYETTE PUBLIC SCHOOLS

- **Brownstown Cmty Unit SD 201** PID: 00292459   618/427-3355
  421 S College Ave, Brownstown 62418   Fax 618/427-3704

Schools: 2 \ **Teachers:** 28 \ **Students:** 380 \ **Special Ed Students:** 63 \
Ethnic: Hispanic 1%, Caucasian 99% \ **Exp:** $379 (High) \ **Poverty:** 21% \
Title I: $143,468 \ **Special Education:** $85,000 \ **Open-Close:** 08/20 - 05/20
\ **DTBP:** $192 (High) \ 🇫 🇹

Mike Shackelford 1,11,73
Martin Son 12,296
Jessica Sefton 35,85*
Vince Rohr 6*
Shannon Claycomb 16,82*
Don Bloemker 67

Public Schs..Principal	Grd	Prgm	Enr/#Cls	SN	
Brownstown Elem Sch 460 W South St, Brownstown 62418 Sherry Harmon	PK-6	T	250 11	49%	618/427-3368 Fax 618/427-5247
Brownstown Jr Sr High Sch 421 S College Ave, Brownstown 62418 Jeff Wooters	7-12	ATV	103 15	59%	618/427-3839

- **Ramsey Cmty Unit Sch Dist 204** PID: 00292526 618/423-2335
  702 W 6th St, Ramsey 62080   Fax 618/423-2314

Schools: 2 \ **Teachers:** 33 \ **Students:** 450 \ **Special Ed Students:** 85 \
College-Bound: 54% \ **Ethnic:** Hispanic 1%, Caucasian 99% \ **Exp:** $240
(Med) \ **Poverty:** 18% \ **Title I:** $166,382 \ **Special Education:** $199,000 \
Open-Close: 08/17 - 06/01 \ **DTBP:** $94 (Med)

Melissa Ritter 1,84
Felechia Williams 4
Bill Eddy 6*
Ginger Edwards 8,60,88,92*
Mike Reiss 16,73,76
Shane Hadley 67
Andy Carter 3
Bryan Kimbro 5
Jennifer Ruhl 7*
Travis Portz 8,11,54,58,296,298*
Whitney Hill 25

---

79 Student Personnel	91 Safety/Security	275 Response To Intervention	298 Grant Writer/Ptnrships	**School Programs**
80 Driver Ed/Safety	92 Magnet School	277 Remedial Math K-12	750 Chief Innovation Officer	A = Alternative Program
81 Gifted/Talented	93 Parental Involvement	280 Literacy Coach	751 Chief of Staff	G = Adult Classes
82 Video Services	95 Tech Prep Program	285 STEM	752 Social Emotional Learning	M = Magnet Program
83 Substance Abuse Prev	97 Chief Infomation Officer	286 Digital Learning		T = Title I Schoolwide
84 Erate	98 Chief Technology Officer	288 Common Core Standards	**Other School Types**	V = Career & Tech Ed Programs
85 AIDS Education	270 Accountability	294 Accountability	Ⓐ = Alternative School	
88 Alternative/At Risk	271 Migrant Education	295 Network System	Ⓒ = Charter School	**Social Media**
89 Multi-Cultural Curriculum	273 Teacher Mentor	296 Title II Programs	Ⓜ = Magnet School	🇫 = Facebook
90 Social Work	274 Before/After Sch	297 Webmaster	Ⓨ = Year-Round School	🇹 = Twitter

New Schools are shaded
New Superintendents and Principals are bold
Personnel with email addresses are underscored

Ford County

Market Data Retrieval

Public Schs..Principal	Grd	Prgm	Enr/#Cls	SN	
Ramsey Grade Sch 516 W 6th St, Ramsey 62080 Travis Portz	PK-5	TV	175 24	63%	618/423-2010
Ramsey High Sch 702 W 6th St, Ramsey 62080 Ginger Edwards	6-12	ATV	125 14	55%	618/423-2333 Fax 618/423-1275

- **St Elmo Cmty Unit Sch Dist 202** PID: 00292552   618/829-3264
  1200 N Walnut St, Saint Elmo 62458   Fax 618/829-5161

Schools: 2 \ Teachers: 32 \ Students: 440 \ Special Ed Students: 77 \ College-Bound: 45% \ Ethnic: African American 1%, Hispanic 1%, Caucasian 99% \ Exp: $341 (High) \ Poverty: 18% \ Title I: $181,404 \ Special Education: $155,000 \ Open-Close: 08/17 - 05/27 \ DTBP: $177 (High)

Julie Healy 1		Ashley Towler 2	
Roger Mitchell 3,5		Ryan Beccue 6	
Sean Hannagan 9,12*		Brian Garrard 10*	
Kevin Maxey 67			

Public Schs..Principal	Grd	Prgm	Enr/#Cls	SN	
St Elmo Elem Sch 519 W 2nd St, Saint Elmo 62458 Sean Hannagan	PK-6	AT	243	56%	618/829-3263 Fax 618/829-5723
St Elmo Jr Sr High Sch 300 W 12th St, Saint Elmo 62458 Brian Garrard	7-12	ATV	178 25	46%	618/829-3227 Fax 618/829-3814

- **Vandalia Cmty Unit SD 203** PID: 00292590   618/283-4525
  1109 N 8th St, Vandalia 62471   Fax 618/283-4107

Schools: 4 \ Teachers: 100 \ Students: 1,490 \ Special Ed Students: 229 \ College-Bound: 55% \ Ethnic: Hispanic 2%, Caucasian 97% \ Exp: $267 (Med) \ Poverty: 19% \ Title I: $517,159 \ Special Education: $714,000 \ Open-Close: 08/14 - 05/28 \ DTBP: $174 (High)

Dr Jennifer Garrison 1	Hailey McGinnis 2
Josh Bogart 3	Colleen Reams 4
Whitney Smith 5	Jason Clay 6*
Dana Bivens 58	Joe Lawson 67
Cj Schmidt 73	

Public Schs..Principal	Grd	Prgm	Enr/#Cls	SN	
Okaw Area Vocational Center 1109 N 8th St, Vandalia 62471 Nick Casey	Voc		300 14		618/283-5150 Fax 618/283-2014
Vandalia Cmty High Sch 1109 N 8th St, Vandalia 62471 Randy Protz	9-12	T	407 40	50%	618/283-5155 Fax 618/283-9855
Vandalia Elem Sch 1017 W Fletcher St, Vandalia 62471 Stacy Mesnard	PK-3	T	490 25	60%	618/283-5166 Fax 618/283-9479
Vandalia Junior High Sch 1011 W Fletcher St, Vandalia 62471 Brian Kern	4-8	T	526 32	60%	618/283-5151 Fax 618/283-8165

FAYETTE PRIVATE SCHOOLS

Private Schs..Principal	Grd	Prgm	Enr/#Cls	SN	
St Peter Lutheran Sch 701 E 3rd St, Saint Peter 62880 Brian Mann	PK-8		82 6		618/349-8888
Vandalia Christian Academy 201 S 6th St, Vandalia 62471 Terri Sutton	PK-8		60 4		618/283-9901 Fax 618/669-4380

FAYETTE REGIONAL CENTERS

- **Regional Office of Ed 3** PID: 02097750   618/283-5011
  1500 W Jefferson St, Vandalia 62471   Fax 618/283-5013

Julie Wollerman 1   Annette Hartlieb 11,15,74

- **Regional Office of Education 3** PID: 04177693   618/283-5011
  1500 W Jefferson St, Vandalia 62471   Fax 618/283-5013

Julie Wollerman 1   Angela Reeter 8
Annette Hartlieb 15

FORD COUNTY

FORD PUBLIC SCHOOLS

- **Gibson Cty-Melvin-Sibley CUSD5** PID: 00292708   217/784-8296
  307 N Sangamon Ave, Gibson City 60936   Fax 217/784-8558

Schools: 3 \ Teachers: 82 \ Students: 1,000 \ Special Ed Students: 162 \ LEP Students: 16 \ Ethnic: Asian 1%, Hispanic 4%, Caucasian 95% \ Exp: $323 (High) \ Poverty: 14% \ Title I: $228,057 \ Special Education: $489,000 \ Open-Close: 08/19 - 05/27 \ DTBP: $243 (High) \ ▪

Jeremy Darnell 1	Doris Defries 2
Rich Doman 3	Raymond Gowen 4*
Mike Allen 6*	Erin Nuss 11,57,69,79,285,288,296,298*
Jessica Titus 16	Josh Carter 27,31,36
Jennifer Jamison 31,36*	Jesse McFarling 58*
Josh Johnson 67	Lori Christianson 68
Donald Worthington 73,76*	Cathy Walker 83,88
Staci Lindeloof 273*	

Public Schs..Principal	Grd	Prgm	Enr/#Cls	SN	
Gibson City-Melvin-Sibley ES 902 N Church St, Gibson City 60936 Justin Kean	PK-5	T	475 26	40%	217/784-4278 Fax 217/784-4782
Gibson City-Melvin-Sibley HS 815 N Church St, Gibson City 60936 Christopher Garard	9-12	TV	301 30	32%	217/784-4292 Fax 217/784-8293
Gibson City-Melvin-Sibley MS 316 E 19th St, Gibson City 60936 Kyle Bielfeldt	6-8	T	230 29	42%	217/784-8731 Fax 217/784-8726

---

1 Superintendent	8 Curric/Instruct K-12	19 Chief Financial Officer	29 Family/Consumer Science	39 Social Studies K-12	49 English/Lang Arts Elem	59 Special Education Elem	69 Academic Assessment
2 Bus/Finance/Purchasing	9 Curric/Instruct Elem	20 Art K-12	30 Adult Education	40 Social Studies Elem	50 English/Lang Arts Sec	60 Special Education Sec	70 Research/Development
3 Buildings And Grounds	10 Curric/Instruct Sec	21 Art Elem	31 Career/Sch-to-Work K-12	41 Social Studies Sec	51 Reading K-12	61 Foreign/World Lang K-12	71 Public Information
4 Food Service	11 Federal Program	22 Art Sec	32 Career/Sch-to-Work Elem	42 Science K-12	52 Reading Elem	62 Foreign/World Lang Elem	72 Summer School
5 Transportation	12 Title I	23 Music K-12	33 Career/Sch-to-Work Sec	43 Science Elem	53 Reading Sec	63 Foreign/World Lang Sec	73 Instructional Tech
6 Athletic	13 Title V	24 Music Elem	34 Early Childhood Ed	44 Science Sec	54 Remedial Reading K-12	64 Religious Education K-12	74 Inservice Training
7 Health Services	14 Asst Superintendent	25 Music Sec	35 Health/Phys Education	45 Math K-12	55 Remedial Reading Elem	65 Religious Education Elem	75 Marketing/Distributive
	15 Instructional Media Svcs	26 Business Education	36 Guidance Services K-12	46 Math Elem	56 Remedial Reading Sec	66 Religious Education Sec	76 Info Systems
	16 Chief Operations Officer	27 Career & Tech Ed	37 Guidance Services Elem	47 Math Sec	57 Bilingual/ELL	67 School Board President	77 Psychological Assess
	18 Chief Academic Officer	28 Technology Education	38 Guidance Services Sec	48 English/Lang Arts K-12	58 Special Education K-12	68 Teacher Personnel	78 Affirmative Action

Illinois School Directory | Franklin County

- **Paxton-Buckley-Loda CUSD 10** PID: 00292784   217/379-3314
  700 Panther Way, Paxton 60957   Fax 217/379-2862

Schools: 3 \ **Teachers:** 104 \ **Students:** 1,300 \ **Special Ed Students:** 226 \ **LEP Students:** 24 \ **College-Bound:** 59% \ **Ethnic:** Asian 1%, African American 2%, Hispanic 5%, Caucasian 92% \ **Exp:** $234 (Med) \ **Poverty:** 13% \ **Title I:** $290,931 \ **Special Education:** $875,000 \ **Open-Close:** 08/19 - 05/28

Clifford McClure 1
Sherrie Elliott 4
Brock Neibuhr 6
Tara Chandler 8,16,69,74,273,288
Jesse McFarland 58
Dave Bachtold 3
Molly Steiger 5
Kelli Vaughn 6
Dustin Franky 11,73,295,298
Dawn Bachtold 67

Public Schs..Principal	Grd	Prgm	Enr/#Cls	SN	
Clara Peterson Elem Sch 580 E Franklin St, Paxton 60957 Amanda Wetherell	PK-5	T	580 16	55%	217/379-2531 Fax 217/379-9781
Paxton-Buckley-Loda High Sch 700 Panther Way, Paxton 60957 Travis Duley	9-12	V	462 40	39%	217/379-4331 Fax 217/379-2491
Paxton-Buckley-Loda Jr HS 700 W Center St, Paxton 60957 Josh Didier	6-8	T	309 20	53%	217/379-9202 Fax 217/379-9169

FORD REGIONAL CENTERS

- **Ford Co Spec Ed Co-op** PID: 10031601   217/784-5470
  815 N Church St, Gibson City 60936   Fax 217/784-5458

Jesse McFarling 1

FRANKLIN COUNTY

FRANKLIN PUBLIC SCHOOLS

- **Akin Elem School District 91** PID: 00292875   618/627-2180
  21962 Akin Blacktop, Akin 62890   Fax 618/627-2119

Schools: 1 \ **Teachers:** 10 \ **Students:** 80 \ **Special Ed Students:** 20 \ **Ethnic:** Caucasian 100% \ **Exp:** $694 (High) \ **Poverty:** 18% \ **Title I:** $35,056 \ **Special Education:** $32,000 \ **Open-Close:** 08/10 - 05/18 \ **DTBP:** $209 (High)

Tammy McCollumn 1,11,73,288
Alisha Lindhorst 34*
Rosetta Thomason 2
Jeff Wilderson 67

Public Schs..Principal	Grd	Prgm	Enr/#Cls	SN	
Akin Cmty Cons Elem Sch 21962 Akin Blacktop, Akin 62890 Tammy McCollumn	PK-8	T	80 10	47%	618/627-2180

- **Benton Cmty Cons Sch Dist 47** PID: 00292899   618/439-3136
  1000 Forrest St, Benton 62812   Fax 618/435-4840

Schools: 2 \ **Teachers:** 67 \ **Students:** 1,150 \ **Special Ed Students:** 230 \ **LEP Students:** 9 \ **Ethnic:** Hispanic 1%, Caucasian 98% \ **Exp:** $167 (Low) \ **Poverty:** 25% \ **Title I:** $463,352 \ **Special Education:** $445,000 \ **Open-Close:** 08/10 - 05/21 \ **DTBP:** $166 (High)

Stephen Smith 1
Justin Wyant 3
Doug Jones 6
Debra Blakey 9*
Sarah VanHorn 34*
Wayne Williford 73,295*
Justin Miller 2,11
Mary Poole 4
Angela Rock 7,83*
Ellen Gibbs 12
Brad Wilson 67
Carla Barnes 84

Public Schs..Principal	Grd	Prgm	Enr/#Cls	SN	
Benton Grade School 5-8 1000 Forrest St, Benton 62812 Ellen Gibbs	5-8	T	480 40	53%	618/438-4011 Fax 618/435-2152
Benton Grade School K-4 1000 E McKenzie St, Benton 62812 Ellen Gibbs	PK-4	T	659 24	57%	618/438-7181 Fax 618/439-6112

- **Benton Cons High Sch Dist 103** PID: 00292966   618/439-3103
  511 E Main St, Benton 62812   Fax 618/438-2915

Schools: 1 \ **Teachers:** 37 \ **Students:** 561 \ **Special Ed Students:** 74 \ **LEP Students:** 3 \ **College-Bound:** 30% \ **Ethnic:** Hispanic 2%, Caucasian 97% \ **Exp:** $378 (High) \ **Poverty:** 19% \ **Title I:** $235,356 \ **Special Education:** $185,000 \ **Open-Close:** 08/11 - 05/28 \ **DTBP:** $168 (High) \ 🇫 🇹

Benjamin Johnson 1
Tim Montgomery 3*
Heather Mitchell 10,73,84
MacKenzie Martin 38
Mark Minor 67
Jeremy Jackson 295*
Ronda Suver 2
Ryan Miller 6*
Marla Harp 10,11,288,298*
Kathy Shurtz 60,88*
Tristan House 76
Gayla McLeeren 297*

Public Schs..Principal	Grd	Prgm	Enr/#Cls	SN	
Benton Cons Dist 103 High Sch 511 E Main St, Benton 62812 Wade Thomas	9-12	AGTV	561 42	56%	618/439-3103

- **Christopher Unit Sch Dist 99** PID: 00292980   618/724-9461
  1 Bearcat Dr, Christopher 62822   Fax 618/724-2586

Schools: 2 \ **Teachers:** 52 \ **Students:** 702 \ **Special Ed Students:** 162 \ **LEP Students:** 3 \ **College-Bound:** 78% \ **Ethnic:** Caucasian 100% \ **Exp:** $299 (Med) \ **Poverty:** 26% \ **Title I:** $427,779 \ **Special Education:** $341,000 \ **Open-Close:** 08/12 - 05/21 \ **DTBP:** $179 (High) \ 🇫

Richard Towers 1,11
Ron Little 3
Josh McCurren 6
Tiffany Hobbs 12,16,82*
Gary Anderton 67
Sandra Zawaske 83
Carla Hammond 2
Trish Calloni 4
Tammy Valette 7*
Sammy Stanton 34
Tom Harrison 73,295,297

Public Schs..Principal	Grd	Prgm	Enr/#Cls	SN	
Christopher Cmty High Sch 1 Bearcat Dr, Christopher 62822 Gabe Sveda	9-12	TV	252 22	61%	618/724-9461 Fax 618/724-9400

---

79 Student Personnel
80 Driver Ed/Safety
81 Gifted/Talented
82 Video Services
83 Substance Abuse Prev
84 Erate
85 AIDS Education
88 Alternative/At Risk
89 Multi-Cultural Curriculum
90 Social Work
91 Safety/Security
92 Magnet School
93 Parental Involvement
95 Tech Prep Program
97 Chief Information Officer
98 Chief Technology Officer
270 Character Education
271 Migrant Education
273 Teacher Mentor
274 Before/After Sch
275 Response To Intervention
277 Remedial Math K-12
280 Literacy Coach
285 STEM
286 Digital Learning
288 Common Core Standards
294 Accountability
295 Network System
296 Title II Programs
297 Webmaster
298 Grant Writer/Ptnrships
750 Chief Innovation Officer
751 Chief of Staff
752 Social Emotional Learning

Other School Types
Ⓐ = Alternative School
Ⓒ = Charter School
Ⓜ = Magnet School
Ⓨ = Year-Round School

School Programs
A = Alternative Program
G = Adult Classes
M = Magnet Program
T = Title I Schoolwide
V = Career & Tech Ed Programs

Social Media
🇫 = Facebook
🇹 = Twitter

New Schools are shaded
New Superintendents and Principals are bold
Personnel with email addresses are underscored

Franklin County

Market Data Retrieval

Christopher Elem Sch — PK-8 T 553 67% 618/724-2631
501 S Snider St, Christopher 62822 — 29 — Fax 618/724-4324
Roy Kirkpatrick

- **Ewing Northern Cmty SD 115** PID: 00293025 — 618/629-2181
  51 N Main St, Ewing 62836 — Fax 618/629-2510

  Schools: 1 \ **Teachers:** 17 \ **Students:** 210 \ **Special Ed Students:** 28 \
  Ethnic: Hispanic 1%, Native American: 1%, Caucasian 98% \ **Exp:** $206 (Med) \ **Poverty:** 16% \ **Title I:** $63,743 \ **Special Education:** $68,000 \
  Open-Close: 08/14 - 05/21

  Kristin Ing 1,11,84
  Tammy Cripps 12*
  Andrea Dungy 2*
  Adam Allsopp 67

Public Schs..Principal	Grd	Prgm	Enr/#Cls	SN	
Ewing Northern Elem Sch 51 N Main St, Ewing 62836 Kristin Ing	PK-8	T	210 12	50%	618/629-2181

- **Frankfort Cmty Unit SD 168** PID: 00293207 — 618/937-2421
  900 N Cherry St, W Frankfort 62896 — Fax 618/932-2025

  Schools: 4 \ **Teachers:** 108 \ **Students:** 1,650 \ **Special Ed Students:** 305 \ **LEP Students:** 3 \ **Ethnic:** Asian 1%, African American 1%, Hispanic 3%, Caucasian 96% \ **Exp:** $168 (Low) \ **Poverty:** 26% \ **Title I:** $939,109 \ **Special Education:** $1,055,000 \ **Open-Close:** 08/14 - 05/28 \ **DTBP:** $174 (High) \

  R Matthew Donkin 1,11
  Chad Stence 3
  Angie Jilek 6
  Amy Bates 8,36,69,88*
  Melanie Hamilton 34
  Elizabeth Robinson 57*
  Joe Smith 85*
  Keri White 2
  Tara Sullivan 4,9,288,298
  Jodi Dejarnett 7,58,275
  Doug Corzine 10,12,294,296*
  Pete Gordon 35
  John Alexander 67
  Jessica O Daniel 93*

Public Schs..Principal	Grd	Prgm	Enr/#Cls	SN	
Central Junior High Sch 1500 E 9th St, W Frankfort 62896 Charlie Cass	7-8	T	285 20	58%	618/937-2444 Fax 618/937-2445
Denning Elem Sch 1401 W 6th St, W Frankfort 62896 Susan Glodich	PK-2	T	488 24	53%	618/937-2464 Fax 618/937-2465
Frankfort Community High Sch 601 E Main St, W Frankfort 62896 Jory Dial	9-12	TV	466 45	43%	618/932-3126 Fax 618/932-6515
Frankfort Intermediate Sch 800 N Cherry St, W Frankfort 62896 Doug Corzine	3-6	T	496 24	52%	618/937-1412 Fax 618/937-4912

- **Sesser-Valier Cmty Unit SD 196** PID: 00293104 — 618/625-5105
  4626 State Highway 154, Sesser 62884 — Fax 618/625-6696

  Schools: 3 \ **Teachers:** 44 \ **Students:** 700 \ **Special Ed Students:** 98 \ **LEP Students:** 3 \ **College-Bound:** 72% \ **Ethnic:** Hispanic 3%, Caucasian 96% \ **Exp:** $173 (Low) \ **Poverty:** 15% \ **Title I:** $180,545 \ **Special Education:** $235,000 \ **Open-Close:** 08/18 - 06/02 \ **DTBP:** $171 (High)

  Dr Jason Henry 1,11
  Brandon Dilliner 3
  Michael Sample 8,31,73*
  Kerri Henry 36*
  Teresa Stacey 67
  Vera Malinee 2,71
  Chip Basso 6*
  Tracy Masters 12,31*
  Mary Lynn Berthoux 58*
  Keith Jones 83,85,88,270,296*

Public Schs..Principal	Grd	Prgm	Enr/#Cls	SN	
Sesser-Valier Elem Sch 4626 State Highway 154, Sesser 62884 Keith Jones	PK-5	T	310 30	53%	618/625-5105 Fax 618/625-3040
Sesser-Valier High Sch 4626 State Highway 154, Sesser 62884 Natalie Page	9-12	T	173 75	42%	618/625-5105
Sesser-Valier Jr High Sch 4626 State Highway 154, Sesser 62884 Keith Jones	6-8	T	144 15	42%	618/625-5105 Fax 618/625-3040

- **Thompsonville Cmty USD 174** PID: 00293166 — 618/627-2301
  21191 Shawneetown Rd, Thompsonville 62890 — Fax 618/627-2302

  Schools: 2 \ **Teachers:** 23 \ **Students:** 285 \ **Special Ed Students:** 50 \ **College-Bound:** 90% \ **Ethnic:** Caucasian 100% \ **Exp:** $323 (High) \ **Poverty:** 19% \ **Title I:** $114,491 \ **Special Education:** $80,000 \ **Open-Close:** 08/12 - 06/01 \ **DTBP:** $209 (High)

  Brock Harris 1,11
  Miranda Wissinger 6*
  Kevin Smith 67
  Robin Culbreth 296
  Kelly Darnell 2
  Jamie Chiaventone 36,79
  Jamie Sheventon 83*

Public Schs..Principal	Grd	Prgm	Enr/#Cls	SN	
Thompsonville Grade Sch 21165 Shawneetown Rd, Thompsonville 62890 Jamie Chiaventone	PK-8	T	245	49%	618/627-2511
Thompsonville High Sch 21135 Shawneetown Rd, Thompsonville 62890 Jamie Chiaventone	9-12	TV	107 12	41%	618/627-2301

- **Zeigler Royalton CUSD 188** PID: 00293257 — 618/596-5841
  4989 State Highway 148, Mulkeytown 62865 — Fax 618/596-2075

  Schools: 2 \ **Teachers:** 43 \ **Students:** 370 \ **Special Ed Students:** 110 \ **College-Bound:** 65% \ **Ethnic:** African American 2%, Hispanic 3%, Caucasian 95% \ **Exp:** $296 (Med) \ **Poverty:** 23% \ **Title I:** $274,641 \ **Special Education:** $303,000 \ **Open-Close:** 08/10 - 05/27 \ **DTBP:** $1/1 (High)

  Quint Hamilton 1,11
  Joe Hargraves 3
  Jeremy May 6*
  Jimmy Stevens 36,69,79,83,85*
  Andy Odle 73,76,84
  Sharon Vaughn 2*
  Phil Hicks 5*
  Sarah Geiger 8
  Randy Dominick 67

Public Schs..Principal	Grd	Prgm	Enr/#Cls	SN	
Zeigler Royalton Elem Jr HS 4877 State Highway 148, Mulkeytown 62865 Leighanne Bailey	PK-8	T	410 25	67%	618/596-2121
Zeigler Royalton High Sch 4989 State Highway 148, Mulkeytown 62865 Matt Morgan	9-12	TV	179 25	55%	618/596-5841 Fax 618/596-6789

FRANKLIN CATHOLIC SCHOOLS

- **Diocese of Belleville Ed Off** PID: 00317671
  Listing includes only schools located in this county. See District Index for location of Diocesan Offices.

1	Superintendent	8	Curric/Instruct K-12	19	Chief Financial Officer	29	Family/Consumer Science	39	Social Studies K-12	49	English/Lang Arts Elem	59	Special Education Elem	69	Academic Assessment
2	Bus/Finance/Purchasing	9	Curric/Instruct Elem	20	Art K-12	30	Adult Education	40	Social Studies Elem	50	English/Lang Arts Sec	60	Special Education Sec	70	Research/Development
3	Buildings And Grounds	10	Curric/Instruct Sec	21	Art Elem	31	Career/Sch-to-Work K-12	41	Social Studies Sec	51	Reading K-12	61	Foreign/World Lang K-12	71	Public Information
4	Food Service	11	Federal Program	22	Art Sec	32	Career/Sch-to-Work Elem	42	Science K-12	52	Reading Elem	62	Foreign/World Lang Elem	72	Summer School
5	Transportation	12	Title I	23	Music K-12	33	Career/Sch-to-Work Sec	43	Science Elem	53	Reading Sec	63	Foreign/World Lang Sec	73	Instructional Tech
6	Athletic	13	Title V	24	Music Elem	34	Early Childhood Ed	44	Science Sec	54	Remedial Reading K-12	64	Religious Education K-12	74	Inservice Training
7	Health Services	15	Asst Superintendent	25	Music Sec	35	Health/Phys Education	45	Math K-12	55	Remedial Reading Elem	65	Religious Education Elem	75	Marketing/Distributive
		16	Instructional Media Svcs	26	Business Education	36	Guidance Services K-12	46	Math Elem	56	Remedial Reading Sec	66	Religious Education Sec	76	Info Systems
		17	Chief Operations Officer	27	Career & Tech Ed	37	Guidance Services Elem	47	Math Sec	57	Bilingual/ELL	67	School Board President	77	Psychological Assess
		18	Chief Academic Officer	28	Technology Education	38	Guidance Services Sec	48	English/Lang Arts K-12	58	Special Education K-12	68	Teacher Personnel	78	Affirmative Action

Illinois School Directory

Fulton County

Catholic Schs..Principal	Grd	Prgm	Enr/#Cls	SN
St John the Baptist Sch 702 E Poplar St, W Frankfort 62896 Debbie Powell	PK-8		56 8	618/937-2017 Fax 618/937-2287 🅕 🅣

FRANKLIN PRIVATE SCHOOLS

Private Schs..Principal	Grd	Prgm	Enr/#Cls	SN
Thompsonville Christian Sch 3608 Angel Ln, Thompsonville 62890 Evelyn Hainey	1-10		16	618/627-2065

FRANKLIN REGIONAL CENTERS

• **Franklin-Jefferson Sp Ed Co-op** PID: 02182317 618/439-7231
409 E Park St, Benton 62812 Fax 618/438-2210

Jera Pieper .... 1 Laurie McNeal 2

• **Regional Office of Ed 21** PID: 02097774 618/438-9711
901 Public Sq, Benton 62812 Fax 618/435-2861

Lorie Lequatte .... 1 Johna Schullian 2,11
Mandy Horn .... 8 Char Melborne 73,74
Mickey Sullivan 275

FULTON COUNTY

FULTON COUNTY SCHOOLS

County Schs..Principal	Grd	Prgm	Enr/#Cls	SN
Ⓐ New Horizons Alternative Sch 315 S Illinois St, Lewistown 61542 Melissa Robinson	6-12		32 5	82% 309/547-7323 Fax 309/547-7335

FULTON PUBLIC SCHOOLS

• **Astoria Cmty Unit Sch Dist 1** PID: 00293295 309/329-2156
402 N Jefferson St, Astoria 61501 Fax 309/329-2246

Schools: 3 \ Teachers: 32 \ Students: 320 \ Special Ed Students: 56 \ LEP Students: 3 \ College-Bound: 40% \ Ethnic: Hispanic 1%, Caucasian 99% \ Exp: $134 (Low) \ Poverty: 18% \ Title I: $104,677 \ Special Education: $92,000 \ Open-Close: 08/19 - 05/25 \ DTBP: $194 (High)

Don Willett .... 1,57 Tammie McCormick 2
Jared Trone .... 3 Tammy Stambaugh 4
David Crouse .... 5,9* Lindy Schenk 11,296*
Chris Shaw .... 67 Bobette Massaglia 73,76,84,286,295
Catharine Reavley 83*

Public Schs..Principal	Grd	Prgm	Enr/#Cls	SN
Astoria Grade Sch 402 N Jefferson St, Astoria 61501 David Crouse	PK-5		154 9	56% 309/329-2158 Fax 309/329-2963
Astoria High Sch 402 N Jefferson St, Astoria 61501 Don Willett	9-12	TV	100 10	54% 309/329-2156
Astoria Junior High Sch 402 N Jefferson St, Astoria 61501 David Crouse	6-8	TV	73 8	37% 309/329-2156 Fax 309/329-2963

• **Canton Union School Dist 66** PID: 00293350 309/647-9411
20 W Walnut St, Canton 61520 Fax 309/649-5036

Schools: 5 \ Teachers: 158 \ Students: 2,490 \ Special Ed Students: 462 \ LEP Students: 16 \ College-Bound: 66% \ Ethnic: African American 2%, Hispanic 1%, Caucasian 96% \ Exp: $154 (Low) \ Poverty: 20% \ Title I: $835,711 \ Special Education: $1,223,000 \ Open-Close: 08/13 - 05/20 \ DTBP: $191 (High)

Rolf Sivertsen .... 1 Rodney Harris 3,91
Kyle Nelson .... 4 Ryan Gilles 5
Brad Hulet .... 6 Jason Parsons 8,11,57,69,88,271,273
Tad Derenzy .... 15 Christy Semande 16,82*
Jennifer Watts .... 31* Cheley Martin 37,58,77,79
Leonard Barnard .... 67 Don Howell 73*
Justin Miller 80*

Public Schs..Principal	Grd	Prgm	Enr/#Cls	SN
Canton High Sch 1001 N Main St, Canton 61520 Jay Valencia	9-12	TV	680 55	41% 309/647-1820 Fax 309/649-5039
Eastview Elem Sch 1490 E Myrtle St, Canton 61520 Christopher Piper	PK-4	T	307 20	59% 309/647-0136 Fax 309/647-3430
Ingersoll Middle Sch 1605 E Ash St, Canton 61520 Wayne Krus	5-8	T	780 50	54% 309/647-6951 Fax 309/647-6959 🅕
Lincoln Elem Sch 20 Lincoln Rd, Canton 61520 Kilee Lidwell	K-4	T	214 10	52% 309/647-7594 Fax 309/647-2043 🅕
Westview Elem Sch 700 Old West Vine St, Canton 61520 Eleanor Gardner	PK-4	T	429 20	63% 309/647-2111 Fax 309/647-2047 🅕

• **Fulton Co Cmty Unit Sch Dist 3** PID: 00293477 309/785-5021
652 E Main St, Cuba 61427 Fax 309/785-5432

Schools: 2 \ Teachers: 35 \ Students: 400 \ Special Ed Students: 84 \ College-Bound: 52% \ Ethnic: African American 1%, Caucasian 98% \ Exp: $322 (High) \ Poverty: 17% \ Title I: $151,361 \ Special Education: $143,000 \ Open-Close: 08/17 - 05/18

Angela Simmons .... 1 Nicky Ledbetter 2
Mark Mathis .... 3* Logan Link 38
Bridgett Dennis .... 58 Sue McCance 67
Mark Thompson 73*

Public Schs..Principal	Grd	Prgm	Enr/#Cls	SN
Cuba Elem Sch 652 E Main St, Cuba 61427 Angela Simmons-Kenser \ Jeff Braun	PK-5	T	178 16	48% 309/785-8054 Fax 309/785-5238
Cuba Middle High Sch 20325 N State Route 97, Cuba 61427 Jeff Braun	6-12	T	240 25	47% 309/785-5023 Fax 309/785-5233

---

79 Student Personnel	91 Safety/Security	275 Response To Intervention	298 Grant Writer/Ptnrships	**School Programs**	**Social Media**	
80 Driver Ed/Safety	92 Magnet School	277 Remedial Math K-12	750 Chief Innovation Officer	A = Alternative Program		
81 Gifted/Talented	93 Parental Involvement	280 Literacy Coach	751 Chief of Staff	G = Adult Classes	🅕 = Facebook	
82 Video Services	95 Tech Prep Program	285 STEM	752 Social Emotional Learning	M = Magnet Program		
83 Substance Abuse Prev	97 Chief Information Officer	286 Digital Learning		T = Title I Schoolwide	🅣 = Twitter	
84 Erate	98 Chief Technology Officer	288 Common Core Standards	**Other School Types**	V = Career & Tech Ed Programs		
85 AIDS Education	270 Accountability	294 Accountability	Ⓐ = Alternative School			
88 Alternative/At Risk	271 Migrant Education	295 Network System	Ⓒ = Charter School	New Schools are shaded		
89 Multi-Cultural Curriculum	273 Teacher Mentor	296 Title II Programs	Ⓜ = Magnet School	New Superintendents and Principals are bold		
90 Social Work	274 Before/After Sch	297 Webmaster	Ⓨ = Year-Round School	Personnel with email addresses are underscored		

IL-109

Gallatin County
Market Data Retrieval

- **Lewistown Community Unit SD 97** PID: 00293635   309/547-5826
  15501 E Avenue L, Lewistown 61542   Fax 309/547-5235

  Schools: 2 \ **Teachers:** 46 \ **Students:** 620 \ **Special Ed Students:** 111 \ **LEP Students:** 3 \ **College-Bound:** 67% \ **Ethnic:** Hispanic 1%, Caucasian 99% \ **Exp:** $352 (High) \ **Poverty:** 12% \ **Title I:** $134,835 \ **Special Education:** $193,000 \ **Open-Close:** 08/17 - 05/19 \ **DTBP:** $147 (High)

  Jeanne Davis 1,83
  Deb Grosclaude 2
  Jan Braun 8,11,57,58,69,88*
  Dale Shaeffer 67
  Deb Grosclaude 2*
  Greg Bennett 6*
  Richard Well 15
  Chad Bent 73,76

Public Schs..Principal	Grd	Prgm	Enr/#Cls	SN	
Lewistown Central Elem Sch 15501 E Avenue L, Lewistown 61542 **Joey McLaughlin** \ **Richard Well**	PK-6	T	367 43	58%	309/547-2240
Lewistown Jr Senior High Sch 15205 N State 100 Hwy, Lewistown 61542 **Clay Ginglen**	7-12	TV	279 24	43%	309/547-2288 Fax 309/547-9870

- **Spoon River Valley Cmty SD 4** PID: 00293532   309/778-2204
  35265 N Il Hwy 97, London Mills 61544   Fax 309/778-2655

  Schools: 2 \ **Teachers:** 28 \ **Students:** 320 \ **Special Ed Students:** 62 \ **College-Bound:** 64% \ **Ethnic:** African American 2%, Hispanic 1%, Caucasian 96% \ **Exp:** $383 (High) \ **Poverty:** 10% \ **Title I:** $66,824 \ **Special Education:** $93,000 \ **Open-Close:** 08/20 - 06/01

  Chris Janssen 1,84
  Matt Harrison 5
  Jody Collier 8,11*
  Joanne Nell 58*
  Jason Kepple 295
  Christy Bull 4*
  David Freeman 6*
  Jeff Taylor 16,82*
  Gary Tompkins 67

Public Schs..Principal	Grd	Prgm	Enr/#Cls	SN	
Spoon River Valley Elem Sch 35265 N Il Route 97, London Mills 61544 **Jody Collier**	PK-6	T	176 14	49%	309/778-2207 Fax 309/778-2707
Spoon River Vly Jr Sr High Sch 35265 N Il Hwy 97, London Mills 61544 **Jody Collier**	7-12	T	120 19	39%	309/778-2201

- **Vit Cmty Unit School Dist 2** PID: 00293740   309/758-5138
  1502 E US Highway 136, Table Grove 61482   Fax 309/758-5298

  Schools: 2 \ **Teachers:** 31 \ **Students:** 370 \ **Special Ed Students:** 54 \ **College-Bound:** 85% \ **Ethnic:** Hispanic 3%, Caucasian 97% \ **Exp:** $212 (Med) \ **Poverty:** 20% \ **Title I:** $115,887 \ **Special Education:** $82,000 \ **Open-Close:** 08/12 - 05/20 \ **DTBP:** $199 (High)

  Matt Klaska 1,11,83
  Charles Lascelles 3*
  Paula Churchill 16,82
  Bob Lascelles 67
  Erin Bucher 76
  Travis Snowden 2,19,84
  Mark Darr 6,10,27,31,95
  Lacey Remington 58,69,77
  Aaron Bucher 73,98
  Laura Holmes 88*

Public Schs..Principal	Grd	Prgm	Enr/#Cls	SN	
Vit Elem Sch 1502 E US Highway 136, Table Grove 61482 **Matt Klaska**	PK-5	T	214 14	46%	309/758-5138
Vit Jr Sr High Sch 1500 E US Highway 136, Table Grove 61482 **Mark Darr**	6-12	T	161 25	37%	309/758-5136 Fax 309/758-5126

FULTON PRIVATE SCHOOLS

Private Schs..Principal	Grd	Prgm	Enr/#Cls	SN	
Calvary Baptist Academy 20 N Avenue I, Canton 61520 Greg Ogle	PK-12		28 3		309/647-3444 Fax 309/647-3312

FULTON REGIONAL CENTERS

- **Western Area Career System** PID: 04180274   309/575-3230
  1 College Pkwy, Canton 61520

  David Messersmith 1

GALLATIN COUNTY

GALLATIN PUBLIC SCHOOLS

- **Gallatin Cmty Unit Sch Dist 7** PID: 00293855   618/272-3821
  5175 Highway 13, Junction 62954   Fax 618/272-4101

  Schools: 1 \ **Teachers:** 58 \ **Students:** 750 \ **Special Ed Students:** 166 \ **LEP Students:** 6 \ **College-Bound:** 62% \ **Ethnic:** Hispanic 1%, Caucasian 99% \ **Exp:** $242 (Med) \ **Poverty:** 26% \ **Title I:** $360,143 \ **Special Education:** $175,000 \ **Open-Close:** 08/17 - 05/21 \ **DTBP:** $197 (High)

  Judy Kaeji 1,11
  Mike Crayne 3
  Mariah Dennison 6
  David Cruson 38*
  Steve Galt 67
  Denise Luckett 2
  Jamie Rider 4
  Rob Holloway 16,27,73,76,295*
  Keri Koester 58*

Public Schs..Principal	Grd	Prgm	Enr/#Cls	SN	
Gallatin Cmty Unit Dist 7 Sch 5175 Highway 13, Junction 62954 **Chris Fromm** \ **Jara Mitchell**	PK-12	TV	750 45	51%	618/272-3821

GALLATIN PRIVATE SCHOOLS

Private Schs..Principal	Grd	Prgm	Enr/#Cls	SN	
Equality Christian Center 519 N McHenry St, Equality 62934 Fred Stacy	PK-12		39 8		618/276-4236 Fax 618/276-4239

#		#		#		#		#		#		#	
1	Superintendent	8	Curric/Instruct K-12	19	Chief Financial Officer	29	Family/Consumer Science	39	Social Studies K-12	49	English/Lang Arts Elem	59	Special Education Elem	69	Academic Assessment
2	Bus/Finance/Purchasing	9	Curric/Instruct Elem	20	Art K-12	30	Adult Education	40	Social Studies Elem	50	English/Lang Arts Sec	60	Special Education Sec	70	Research/Development
3	Buildings And Grounds	10	Curric/Instruct Sec	21	Art Elem	31	Career/Sch-to-Work K-12	41	Social Studies Sec	51	Reading K-12	61	Foreign/World Lang K-12	71	Public Information
4	Food Service	11	Federal Program	22	Art Sec	32	Career/Sch-to-Work Elem	42	Science K-12	52	Reading Elem	62	Foreign/World Lang Elem	72	Summer School
5	Transportation	12	Title I	23	Music K-12	33	Career/Sch-to-Work Sec	43	Science Elem	53	Reading Sec	63	Foreign/World Lang Sec	73	Instructional Tech
6	Athletic	13	Title V	24	Music Elem	34	Early Childhood Ed	44	Science Sec	54	Remedial Reading K-12	64	Religious Education K-12	74	Inservice Training
7	Health Services	15	Asst Superintendent	25	Music Sec	35	Health/Phys Education	45	Math K-12	55	Remedial Reading Elem	65	Religious Education Elem	75	Marketing/Distributive
		16	Instructional Media Svcs	26	Business Education	36	Guidance Services K-12	46	Math Elem	56	Remedial Reading Sec	66	Religious Education Sec	76	Info Systems
		17	Chief Operations Officer	27	Career & Tech Ed	37	Guidance Services Elem	47	Math Sec	57	Bilingual/ELL	67	School Board President	77	Psychological Assess
		18	Chief Academic Officer	28	Technology Education	38	Guidance Services Sec	48	English/Lang Arts K-12	58	Special Education K-12	68	Teacher Personnel	78	Affirmative Action

Illinois School Directory — Grundy County

GREENE COUNTY

GREENE PUBLIC SCHOOLS

- **Carrollton Cmty Unit SD 1** PID: 00293881 217/942-5314
  950A 3rd St, Carrollton 62016 Fax 217/942-9259

Schools: 2 \ **Teachers:** 46 \ **Students:** 600 \ **Special Ed Students:** 97 \ **College-Bound:** 65% \ **Ethnic:** Hispanic 3%, Caucasian 97% \ **Exp:** $415 (High) \ **Poverty:** 12% \ **Title I:** $129,130 \ **Special Education:** $141,000 \ **Open-Close:** 08/20 - 05/24 \ **DTBP:** $176 (High)

Mark Halwaphca	1,11	Nancy Waters	2,298
Jack Staples	3,5	Kyle Smith	6
Becky Haugland	7	Ronda Smith	8
Andrew Thomas	27,73,76,286,295*	Sarah Schmidt	34
Rodney Reif	67	Becky Howard	68
Leslee Frazier	69,273*	Jeri Rothe	93

Public Schs..Principal	Grd	Prgm	Enr/#Cls	SN	
Carrollton Grade Sch 721 4th St, Carrollton 62016 Ronda Smith	PK-8	T	334 20	66%	217/942-6831 Fax 217/942-6053
Carrollton High Sch 950 3rd St, Carrollton 62016 Leslee Frazier	9-12	TV	201 30	49%	217/942-6913 Fax 217/942-6835

- **Greenfield Cmty Unit SD 10** PID: 00293922 217/368-2447
  311 Mulberry St, Greenfield 62044 Fax 217/368-2724

Schools: 2 \ **Teachers:** 40 \ **Students:** 444 \ **Special Ed Students:** 56 \ **College-Bound:** 51% \ **Ethnic:** Caucasian 100% \ **Exp:** $299 (Med) \ **Poverty:** 18% \ **Title I:** $139,780 \ **Special Education:** $90,000 \ **Open-Close:** 08/20 - 05/27 \ **DTBP:** $150 (High)

Kevin Bowman	1	Joe Pembrook	6*
Pam Armold	12*	Elaine Willis	16,82*
Melissa Struif	36,69*	Rodney Knittel	67
Rebecca McClelland	84		

Public Schs..Principal	Grd	Prgm	Enr/#Cls	SN	
Greenfield Elem Sch 115 Prairie St, Greenfield 62044 Jeremy Lansaw	PK-8	V	314 24	47%	217/368-2551 Fax 217/368-2232
Greenfield High Sch 502 East St, Greenfield 62044 Beth Bettis	9-12	TV	130 14	39%	217/368-2219 Fax 217/368-2230

- **North Greene Unit Dist 3** PID: 00293960 217/374-2842
  250 E Sherman St, White Hall 62092 Fax 217/374-2849

Schools: 2 \ **Teachers:** 63 \ **Students:** 875 \ **Special Ed Students:** 206 \ **College-Bound:** 62% \ **Ethnic:** Caucasian 99% \ **Exp:** $264 (Med) \ **Poverty:** 23% \ **Title I:** $398,955 \ **Special Education:** $416,000 \ **Open-Close:** 08/12 - 05/21 \ **DTBP:** $188 (High)

Mark Scott	1	Tiffany Mumford	2
Vance Dirkmeyer	3	John Davidson	5
Brett Berry	6	Melissa Killam	58
Stacy Schutz	67	Susan Williams	83,85,90

Public Schs..Principal	Grd	Prgm	Enr/#Cls	SN	
North Greene Elem Sch 403 W North St, Roodhouse 62082 Jackie Kuchy	PK-6	T	493 17	69%	217/589-4623 Fax 217/589-4028
North Greene Jr Sr High Sch 546 N Main St, White Hall 62092 Amanda Macias	7-12	TV	372 30	64%	217/374-2131 Fax 217/374-2132

GREENE CATHOLIC SCHOOLS

- **Diocese of Springfield Ed Off** PID: 00319394
  Listing includes only schools located in this county. See District Index for location of Diocesan Offices.

Catholic Schs..Principal	Grd	Prgm	Enr/#Cls	SN	
St John the Evangelist Sch 426 3rd St, Carrollton 62016 Julie Lake	PK-8		130 10		217/942-6814 Fax 217/942-9797

GRUNDY COUNTY

GRUNDY COUNTY SCHOOLS

County Schs..Principal	Grd	Prgm	Enr/#Cls	SN	
Grundy Area Voc Center 1002 Union St, Morris 60450 Lance Copes	Voc	A	550 10		815/942-4390 Fax 815/942-6650
Ⓐ Premier Academy 7700 Ashley Rd, Morris 60450 Meghan Martin	6-12		80 4	38%	815/416-0377 Fax 815/828-0639

GRUNDY PUBLIC SCHOOLS

- **Braceville Elem School Dist 75** PID: 00294031 815/237-8040
  209 N Mitchell St, Braceville 60407 Fax 815/237-8044

Schools: 1 \ **Teachers:** 12 \ **Students:** 112 \ **Special Ed Students:** 23 \ **Ethnic:** Hispanic 8%, Caucasian 92% \ **Exp:** $283 (Med) \ **Poverty:** 13% \ **Title I:** $37,801 \ **Special Education:** $63,000 \ **Open-Close:** 08/13 - 05/21 \ **DTBP:** $157 (High)

Josh DeLong	1	Sherry Garrett	2
Michael Demarah	3	Burgandy Johnson	4*
Sue Avery	11,16,69,273,286,288*	Adriana Howe	12
Kailey Brandt	57,88,271,294*	Jennifer Williams	67
John Williamson	73	John Williamson	73*

Public Schs..Principal	Grd	Prgm	Enr/#Cls	SN	
Braceville Elem Sch 209 N Mitchell St, Braceville 60407 Nicole Black	K-8	T	112 14	55%	815/237-8040

79	Student Personnel	91	Safety/Security	275	Response To Intervention	298	Grant Writer/Ptnrships
80	Driver Ed/Safety	92	Magnet School	277	Remedial Math K-12	750	Chief Innovation Officer
81	Gifted/Talented	93	Parental Involvement	280	Literacy Coach	751	Chief of Staff
82	Video Services	95	Tech Prep Program	285	STEM	752	Social Emotional Learning
83	Substance Abuse Prev	97	Chief Infomation Officer	286	Digital Learning		
84	Erate	98	Chief Technology Officer	288	Common Core Standards		
85	AIDS Education	270	Character Education	294	Accountability		
88	Alternative/At Risk	271	Migrant Education	295	Network System		
89	Multi-Cultural Curriculum	273	Teacher Mentor	296	Title II Programs		
90	Social Work	274	Before/After Sch	297	Webmaster		

School Programs
A = Alternative Program
G = Adult Classes
M = Magnet Program
T = Title I Schoolwide
V = Career & Tech Ed Programs

Other School Types
Ⓐ = Alternative School
Ⓒ = Charter School
Ⓜ = Magnet School
Ⓨ = Year-Round School

Social Media
 = Facebook
 = Twitter

New Schools are shaded
New Superintendents and Principals are bold
Personnel with email addresses are underscored

Grundy County

Market Data Retrieval

• **Coal City Cmty Unit Sch Dist 1** PID: 00294055   815/634-2287
550 S Carbon Hill Rd, Coal City 60416   Fax 815/770-2088

Schools: 5 \ **Teachers:** 151 \ **Students:** 2,151 \ **Special Ed Students:** 297 \ **LEP Students:** 19 \ **Ethnic:** African American 1%, Hispanic 9%, Caucasian 90% \ **Exp:** $244 (Med) \ **Poverty:** 7% \ **Title I:** $202,818 \ **Special Education:** $712,000 \ **Open-Close:** 08/17 - 06/08 \ **DTBP:** $237 (High) \

Dr Kent Bugg	1	Jason Smith	2
Danny Hutchings	6	Tammy Elledge	8,69,73,297*
Jennifer Kenney	12*	Allison Peterson	16*
Sandy Rakes	58	Kenneth Miller	67
Leah Hajdu	76		

Public Schs..Principal	Grd	Prgm	Enr/#Cls	SN	
Coal City Early Chldhd Center 755 S Carbon Hill Rd, Coal City 60416 Amanda Davidson	PK-1	T	404	33%	815/634-5042 Fax 815/634-0669
Coal City Elem Sch 300 N Broadway St, Coal City 60416 Jennifer Kenney	2-3	T	302	33%	815/634-2334 Fax 815/634-5036
Coal City High Sch 655 W Division St, Coal City 60416 Chris Spencer	9-12	TV	662 50	24%	815/634-2396 Fax 815/634-2313
Coal City Intermediate Sch 305 E Division St, Coal City 60416 Tracy Carlson	4-5	T	300 12	27%	815/634-2182 Fax 815/770-5818
Coal City Middle Sch 500 S Carbon Hill Rd, Coal City 60416 Travis Johnson	6-8	T	500 38	26%	815/634-5039 Fax 815/634-5049

• **Gardner Cmty Cons SD 72-C** PID: 00294093   815/237-2313
598 N Elm St, Gardner 60424   Fax 815/237-2114

Schools: 1 \ **Teachers:** 16 \ **Students:** 152 \ **Special Ed Students:** 35 \ **LEP Students:** 3 \ **Ethnic:** Hispanic 6%, Caucasian 94% \ **Exp:** $380 (High) \ **Poverty:** 7% \ **Title I:** $21,634 \ **Special Education:** $125,000 \ **Open-Close:** 08/17 - 05/24 \ **DTBP:** $191 (High)

Dr Michael Merritt	1	Mike Cornale	2,3*
Katie Johnson	12*	Lauren Walsh	16,73*
Denny Christensen	67		

Public Schs..Principal	Grd	Prgm	Enr/#Cls	SN	
Gardner Grade Sch 598 N Elm St, Gardner 60424 Ron Harris	PK-8		152 10	33%	815/237-2313

• **Gardner S Wilmington HSD 73** PID: 00294110   815/237-2176
500 E Main St, Gardner 60424   Fax 815/237-2842

Schools: 1 \ **Teachers:** 19 \ **Students:** 200 \ **Special Ed Students:** 32 \ **LEP Students:** 3 \ **College-Bound:** 66% \ **Ethnic:** African American 1%, Hispanic 4%, Caucasian 95% \ **Exp:** $285 (Med) \ **Poverty:** 5% \ **Title I:** $17,578 \ **Special Education:** $160,000 \ **Open-Close:** 08/17 - 05/21 \ **DTBP:** $209 (High) \

Josh DeLong	1	Sherri Garrett	2
Wally Debelak	3	John Engelman	6,10,88*
Angelena Dallio	11,288*	Jennifer Kilmer	38,69,270*
Marsha Ortega	57*	Pam Brooks	67
Jillian Wills	69,752*	John Williamson	73,76*
Jillian Wills	83,752		

Public Schs..Principal	Grd	Prgm	Enr/#Cls	SN	
Gardner S Wilmington High Sch 500 E Main St, Gardner 60424 John Engelman	9-12	AV	200 18	20%	815/237-2176

• **Mazon-Verona-Kinsman ESD 2-C** PID: 00294158   815/448-2200
1013 North St, Mazon 60444   Fax 815/448-3005

Schools: 2 \ **Teachers:** 25 \ **Students:** 325 \ **Special Ed Students:** 64 \ **LEP Students:** 3 \ **Ethnic:** Hispanic 6%, Caucasian 94% \ **Exp:** $217 (Med) \ **Poverty:** 8% \ **Title I:** $44,620 \ **Special Education:** $90,000 \ **Open-Close:** 08/21 - 05/28

| Nancy Dillow | 1,11,83 | Tony DiNello | 6 |
| Shane Gilbertson | 67 | Ralph Rowe | 73* |

Public Schs..Principal	Grd	Prgm	Enr/#Cls	SN	
Mazon Verona Kinsman Mid Sch 1013 North St, Mazon 60444 Tony DiNello	5-8	T	138 8	41%	815/448-2127
Mazon-Verona-Kinsman Elem Sch 513 8th St, Mazon 60444 Melanie Elias	PK-4	T	169 15	35%	815/448-2471 Fax 815/448-2056

• **Minooka Cmty Cons Sch Dist 201** PID: 00294225   815/467-6121
305 W Church St, Minooka 60447   Fax 815/467-9544

Schools: 7 \ **Teachers:** 279 \ **Students:** 4,400 \ **Special Ed Students:** 638 \ **LEP Students:** 136 \ **Ethnic:** Asian 1%, African American 5%, Hispanic 21%, Caucasian 72% \ **Exp:** $90 (Low) \ **Poverty:** 4% \ **Title I:** $155,539 \ **Special Education:** $1,298,000 \ **Bilingual Education:** $11,000 \ **Open-Close:** 08/19 - 05/27 \ **DTBP:** $167 (High)

Dr Kris Monn	1	Colleen Bogart	2
Kevin Smith	3	Cathy Haase	5
Erin Witcofski	7*	Dr Joshua Ruland	9,11,15,57,69,88,288,296
Jill Lustik	59	Tiffany Staab	59
James Satorius	67	Aaron Souza	73,76,295
Atrim Bakii	295		

Public Schs..Principal	Grd	Prgm	Enr/#Cls	SN	
Aux Sable Elem Sch 1004 Misty Creek Dr, Minooka 60447 Ciara Manno	1-4		684 21	19%	815/467-5301 Fax 815/467-2166
Jones Elem Sch 800 Barberry Way, Joliet 60431 Dr Rodney Hiser	K-4		640	21%	815/290-7100 Fax 815/290-7120
Minooka Elem Sch 400 W Coady Dr, Minooka 60447 Natalie Baxter	K-4		578 32	29%	815/467-2261 Fax 815/467-4423
Minooka Intermediate Sch 321 W McEvilly Rd, Minooka 60447 Jeana Pekol	5-6		936 53	24%	815/467-4692 Fax 815/467-3121
Minooka Junior High Sch 333 W McEvilly Rd, Minooka 60447 Sarah Massey	7-8		982 45	23%	815/467-2136 Fax 815/467-5087
Minooka Primary Center 305 W Church St, Minooka 60447 Teresa Miller	PK-K		6	15%	815/467-3167 Fax 815/467-3168
Walnut Trails Elem Sch 301 Wynstone Dr, Shorewood 60404 Kathleen Cheshareck \ Sarah Monroe	K-4		568 36	11%	815/290-7400 Fax 815/290-7420

1	Superintendent	8	Curric/Instruct K-12	19	Chief Financial Officer	29	Family/Consumer Science	39	Social Studies K-12	49	English/Lang Arts Elem	59	Special Education Elem	69	Academic Assessment
2	Bus/Finance/Purchasing	9	Curric/Instruct Elem	20	Art K-12	30	Adult Education	40	Social Studies Elem	50	English/Lang Arts Sec	60	Special Education Sec	70	Research/Development
3	Buildings And Grounds	10	Curric/Instruct Sec	21	Art Elem	31	Career/Sch-to-Work K-12	41	Social Studies Sec	51	Reading K-12	61	Foreign/World Lang K-12	71	Public Information
4	Food Service	11	Federal Program	22	Art Sec	32	Career/Sch-to-Work Elem	42	Science K-12	52	Reading Elem	62	Foreign/World Lang Elem	72	Summer School
5	Transportation	12	Title I	23	Music K-12	33	Career/Sch-to-Work Sec	43	Science Elem	53	Reading Sec	63	Foreign/World Lang Sec	73	Instructional Tech
6	Athletic	13	Title V	24	Music Elem	34	Early Childhood Ed	44	Science Sec	54	Remedial Reading K-12	64	Religious Education K-12	74	Inservice Training
7	Health Services	14	Asst Superintendent	25	Music Sec	35	Health/Phys Education	45	Math K-12	55	Remedial Reading Elem	65	Religious Education Elem	75	Marketing/Distributive
		15	Instructional Media Svcs	26	Business Education	36	Guidance Services K-12	46	Math Elem	56	Remedial Reading Sec	66	Religious Education Sec	76	Info Systems
		16	Chief Operations Officer	27	Career & Tech Ed	37	Guidance Services Elem	47	Math Sec	57	Bilingual/ELL	67	School Board President	77	Psychological Assess
		17	Chief Academic Officer	28	Technology Education	38	Guidance Services Sec	48	English/Lang Arts K-12	58	Special Education K-12	68	Teacher Personnel	78	Affirmative Action

IL—112

Illinois School Directory

Grundy County

- **Morris Cmty High Sch Dist 101** PID: 00294316   815/942-1294
  1000 Union St, Morris 60450   Fax 815/941-5407

Schools: 1 \ **Teachers:** 50 \ **Students:** 867 \ **Special Ed Students:** 124 \ **LEP Students:** 17 \ **College-Bound:** 67% \ **Ethnic:** Asian 2%, African American 1%, Hispanic 18%, Caucasian 79% \ **Exp:** $249 (Med) \ **Poverty:** 7% \ **Title I:** $105,465 \ **Special Education:** $486,000 \ **Open-Close:** 08/14 - 05/25 \ **DTBP:** $176 (High) \

Craig Ortiz	1	Mark Walker	3
Jeffrey Johnson	6	Kelli Simpson	16,82*
Eva Schutter	57*	Lori Dite	60
Scot Hastings	67	JD Morrison	73,286*
Elizabeth Lee	83*	Michael Gourley	273

Public Schs..Principal	Grd	Prgm	Enr/#Cls	SN	
Morris Cmty High Sch 1000 Union St, Morris 60450 Michael Gourley	9-12	AV	867 50	18%	815/942-1294 Fax 815/941-5405

- **Morris Elem School Dist 54** PID: 00294251   815/942-0056
  2001 Dupont Ave, Morris 60450   Fax 815/942-0240

Schools: 1 \ **Teachers:** 78 \ **Students:** 1,200 \ **Special Ed Students:** 216 \ **LEP Students:** 83 \ **Ethnic:** Asian 1%, African American 2%, Hispanic 21%, Caucasian 77% \ **Exp:** $222 (Med) \ **Poverty:** 10% \ **Title I:** $185,241 \ **Special Education:** $558,000 \ **Bilingual Education:** $7,000 \ **Open-Close:** 08/24 - 06/03 \ **DTBP:** $183 (High) \

Dr Shannon Dudek	1	Jill Mills	2
Don Tondini	3	Chris Lines	4
Keith Anderson	6	Gina VanCleave	7
Marie Stover	34,59,79,88,275,285,752	Jerald White	67
Greg Mann	73,84,295	Dr Melissa Terry	77

Public Schs..Principal	Grd	Prgm	Enr/#Cls	SN	
Morris Grade Sch 2001 Dupont Ave, Morris 60450 David Raffel	PK-8	T	1,200	41%	815/942-0056 Fax 815/318-6900

- **Nettle Creek Cmty SD 24-C** PID: 00294342   815/942-0511
  8820 Scott School Rd, Morris 60450   Fax 815/942-9124

Schools: 1 \ **Teachers:** 10 \ **Students:** 91 \ **Special Ed Students:** 14 \ **LEP Students:** 4 \ **Ethnic:** Asian 1%, African American 2%, Hispanic 13%, Caucasian 83% \ **Exp:** $258 (Med) \ **Poverty:** 3% \ **Special Education:** $15,000 \ **Open-Close:** 08/14 - 05/21 \ **DTBP:** $174 (High)

| Al Gegenheimer | 1 | Jackie Nusbaumer | 67 |

Public Schs..Principal	Grd	Prgm	Enr/#Cls	SN	
Nettle Creek Elem Sch 8820 Scott School Rd, Morris 60450 Marissa Darlington	K-8		91 10	9%	815/942-0511

- **S Wilmington Cons Elem SD 74** PID: 00294392   815/237-2281
  375 Fifth Ave, S Wilmington 60474   Fax 815/237-2713

Schools: 1 \ **Teachers:** 8 \ **Students:** 85 \ **Special Ed Students:** 20 \ **Ethnic:** Hispanic 1%, Caucasian 99% \ **Exp:** $174 (Low) \ **Poverty:** 7% \ **Special Education:** $22,000 \ **Open-Close:** 08/17 - 05/21 \ **DTBP:** $174 (High)

| Cynthia Christensen | 1,11 | Christopher Jett | 67 |
| John Williamsen | 73,295 | | |

Public Schs..Principal	Grd	Prgm	Enr/#Cls	SN	
S Wilmington Grade Sch 375 Fifth Ave, S Wilmington 60474 Cynthia Christensen	PK-8		85 8	15%	815/237-2281

- **Saratoga Cmty Cons SD 60C** PID: 00294378   815/942-2128
  4040 N Division St, Morris 60450   Fax 815/942-0301

Schools: 1 \ **Teachers:** 55 \ **Students:** 799 \ **Special Ed Students:** 142 \ **LEP Students:** 38 \ **Ethnic:** Asian 1%, African American 4%, Hispanic 14%, Caucasian 80% \ **Exp:** $204 (Med) \ **Poverty:** 12% \ **Title I:** $131,156 \ **Special Education:** $284,000 \ **Bilingual Education:** $2,000 \ **Open-Close:** 08/24 - 06/02 \ **DTBP:** $182 (High) \

Kathy Perry	1,11	Marsha Henne	2
Vince Zomboracz	6*	Debi Schultz	7*
Kelli Simpson	16*	Joe Zweeres	18
Luz Carmona Colon	57	Anne McDonnell	67
Tyler DeMoraes	73,76,286,295*	Jennifer Gromm	83*
Sandy Krugel	280,285,288,752	Amy Shannon	295*
Mary Kelly	298		

Public Schs..Principal	Grd	Prgm	Enr/#Cls	SN	
Saratoga Elem Sch 4040 N Division St, Morris 60450 Joe Zweeres	PK-8		799 60	28%	815/942-2128

GRUNDY CATHOLIC SCHOOLS

- **Diocese of Joliet Ed Office** PID: 00325965
  Listing includes only schools located in this county. See District Index for location of Diocesan Offices.

Catholic Schs..Principal	Grd	Prgm	Enr/#Cls	SN	
Immaculate Conception Sch 505 E North St, Morris 60450 Stacey Swanson	PK-8		218 12		815/942-4111 Fax 815/942-5094

GRUNDY REGIONAL CENTERS

- **Grundy Area Voc Ed System** PID: 04338603   815/942-4390
  1002 Union St, Morris 60450   Fax 815/942-6650

| Lance Copes | 1 | Jeanne Skube | 15 |

- **Grundy Co Special Ed Co-op** PID: 02183969   815/942-5780
  725 School St, Morris 60450   Fax 815/942-5782

| Neil Sanburg | 1,11 | Carol Senica | 15 |

- **Regional Office of Ed 24** PID: 02097815   815/941-3247
  1320 Union St, Morris 60450   Fax 815/942-5384

| Christopher Mehochko | 1 | Michelle Senffner | 15 |

---

79 Student Personnel	91 Safety/Security	275 Response To Intervention	298 Grant Writer/Ptnrships	**School Programs**	**Social Media**
80 Driver Ed/Safety	92 Magnet School	277 Remedial Math K-12	750 Chief Innovation Officer	A = Alternative Program	= Facebook
81 Gifted/Talented	93 Parental Involvement	280 Literacy Coach	751 Chief of Staff	G = Adult Classes	
82 Video Services	95 Tech Prep Program	285 STEM	752 Social Emotional Learning	M = Magnet Program	= Twitter
83 Substance Abuse Prev	97 Chief Information Officer	286 Digital Learning		T = Title I Schoolwide	
84 Erate	98 Chief Technology Officer	288 Common Core Standards	**Other School Types**	V = Career & Tech Ed Programs	
85 AIDS Education	270 Character Education	294 Accountability	Ⓐ = Alternative School		
88 Alternative/At Risk	271 Migrant Education	295 Network System	Ⓒ = Charter School	New Schools are shaded	
89 Multi-Cultural Curriculum	273 Teacher Mentor	296 Title II Programs	Ⓜ = Magnet School	New Superintendents and Principals are bold	
90 Social Work	274 Before/After Sch	297 Webmaster	Ⓨ = Year-Round School	Personnel with email addresses are underscored	

IL–113

Hamilton County

Market Data Retrieval

HAMILTON COUNTY

HAMILTON PUBLIC SCHOOLS

- **Hamilton Co Cmty Unit SD 10** PID: 00294419   618/643-2328
  804 Golf Course Rd, Mc Leansboro 62859   Fax 618/643-2015

  Schools: 4 \ Teachers: 75 \ Students: 1,199 \ Special Ed Students: 265 \ LEP Students: 3 \ Ethnic: African American 1%, Hispanic 2%, Caucasian 97% \ Exp: $176 (Low) \ Poverty: 17% \ Title I: $369,848 \ Special Education: $295,000 \ Open-Close: 08/18 - 05/25 \ DTBP: $90 (Med)

  Jeff Fetcho 1,11
  John Biggerstaff 3
  Clint Winemiller 6*
  Connie Lueke 38*
  Christina Epperson 58,69*
  Brian Warren 73,76,98,286,295*
  Shawna Scott 2,19
  Jay Lentz 4*
  Amanda Woodrow 16*
  Lisa Fetcho 38*
  Dennis Lynch 67

Public Schs..Principal	Grd	Prgm	Enr/#Cls	SN	
Dahlgren Elem Sch 5th and Dale St, Dahlgren 62828 Jay Lentz	K-6	T	140 9	46%	618/736-2316 Fax 618/736-2057
East Side Elem Sch 405 E Randolph St, Mc Leansboro 62859 Stephine Lasswell	K-6	T	424 21	57%	618/643-2328 Fax 618/643-2070
Hamilton Co Jr Sr High Sch 1 Fox Ln, Mc Leansboro 62859 Travis McCollum	7-12	ATV	555 40	49%	618/643-2328 Fax 618/643-2307
Hamilton Co Pre-School Center 210 S Pearl St, Mc Leansboro 62859 Christina Epperson	PK-PK	T	80 5	54%	618/643-2328 Fax 618/643-2307

HANCOCK COUNTY

HANCOCK PUBLIC SCHOOLS

- **Carthage Elementary SD 317** PID: 00294483   217/357-3922
  210 S Adams St, Carthage 62321   Fax 217/357-6793

  Schools: 2 \ Teachers: 26 \ Students: 400 \ Special Ed Students: 44 \ LEP Students: 4 \ Ethnic: Asian 1%, Hispanic 1%, Caucasian 98% \ Exp: $231 (Med) \ Poverty: 12% \ Title I: $90,851 \ Special Education: $100,000 \ Open-Close: 08/14 - 05/21 \ DTBP: $164 (High)

  Vicki Hardy 1,11
  Jerry Butcher 15
  Brent Ufkes 67
  Lyle Klein 270
  Shannon Twaddle 2,5
  Lori Christner 59*
  Rose Fisher 88*

Public Schs..Principal	Grd	Prgm	Enr/#Cls	SN	
Carthage Middle Sch 600 Buchanan, Carthage 62321 Ryanne Nason	5-8	T	176 15	51%	217/357-3914 Fax 217/357-3755
Carthage Primary Sch 600 Miller St, Carthage 62321 Mike Snowden	PK-4	T	296 12	47%	217/357-9202 Fax 217/357-0585

- **Dallas Elem Sch Dist 327** PID: 00294562   217/852-3201
  921 Creamery Hill Rd, Dallas City 62330   Fax 217/852-3203

  Schools: 1 \ Teachers: 19 \ Students: 193 \ Special Ed Students: 31 \ Ethnic: Asian 1%, Hispanic 1%, Caucasian 98% \ Exp: $586 (High) \ Poverty: 27% \ Title I: $101,702 \ Special Education: $52,000 \ Open-Close: 08/20 - 05/25 \ DTBP: $174 (High)

  Michelle Lee 1
  Alissa Tucker 9,11,16,69,88,270,298*
  Robert Castillo 67
  Becky Thompson 2
  Rebecca Walker 12*

Public Schs..Principal	Grd	Prgm	Enr/#Cls	SN	
Dallas Elem Sch 921 Creamery Hill Rd, Dallas City 62330 Alissa Tucker	PK-8	T	193 15	72%	217/852-3201

- **Hamilton Cmty Cons SD 328** PID: 00294603   866/332-3880
  270 N 10th St, Hamilton 62341   Fax 217/847-3915

  Schools: 2 \ Teachers: 46 \ Students: 600 \ Special Ed Students: 93 \ LEP Students: 3 \ College-Bound: 75% \ Ethnic: Asian 1%, African American 1%, Caucasian 98% \ Exp: $368 (High) \ Poverty: 14% \ Title I: $184,206 \ Special Education: $138,000 \ Open-Close: 08/19 - 05/25 \ DTBP: $160 (High)

  Joe Yurko 1,11,57,73
  Brittany Bavery 4*
  Donna Rodeffer 7*
  Michelle Aurand 31,36,69,83
  Tricia Kinnamon 58
  Michael Coultas 76*
  Kiersti Lock 2
  Travis Cook 6*
  Eric Bryan 9,11,88,275*
  Kim Martin 34*
  Matthew Star 67

Public Schs..Principal	Grd	Prgm	Enr/#Cls	SN	
Hamilton Elem Sch 1830 Broadway St, Hamilton 62341 Eric Bryan	PK-6		345 20	48%	866/332-3880 Fax 217/847-2337
Hamilton Jr Sr High Sch 1100 Keokuk St, Hamilton 62341 Shellie Jennings	7-12	AGTV	242 20	42%	866/332-3880 Fax 217/847-3474

- **Illini West High Sch Dist 307** PID: 10915928   217/357-9607
  600 Miller St, Carthage 62321   Fax 217/357-9609

  Schools: 1 \ Teachers: 26 \ Students: 350 \ Special Ed Students: 46 \ LEP Students: 3 \ College-Bound: 54% \ Ethnic: Caucasian 100% \ Exp: $300 (High) \ Poverty: 11% \ Title I: $84,321 \ Special Education: $71,000 \ Open-Close: 08/17 - 05/20 \ 🅕 🅣

  Kim Schilson 1,11
  Shari Shupe 12*
  John Huston 67
  Shannon Short 2
  Scott Schneider 16,57,69,74,83,271,273
  Chris Greenhalge 73*

Public Schs..Principal	Grd	Prgm	Enr/#Cls	SN	
Illini West High Sch 600 Miller St, Carthage 62321 Scott Schneider	9-12	TV	350 20	13%	217/357-2136 Fax 217/357-3569 🅕 🅣

1	Superintendent	8	Curric/Instruct K-12	19	Chief Financial Officer	29	Family/Consumer Science	39	Social Studies K-12	49	English/Lang Arts Elem	59	Special Education Elem	69	Academic Assessment
2	Bus/Finance/Purchasing	9	Curric/Instruct Elem	20	Art K-12	30	Adult Education	40	Social Studies Elem	50	English/Lang Arts Sec	60	Special Education Sec	70	Research/Development
3	Buildings And Grounds	10	Curric/Instruct Sec	21	Art Elem	31	Career/Sch-to-Work K-12	41	Social Studies Sec	51	Reading K-12	61	Foreign/World Lang K-12	71	Public Information
4	Food Service	11	Federal Program	22	Art Sec	32	Career/Sch-to-Work Elem	42	Science K-12	52	Reading Elem	62	Foreign/World Lang Elem	72	Summer School
5	Transportation	12	Title I	23	Music K-12	33	Career/Sch-to-Work Sec	43	Science Elem	53	Reading Sec	63	Foreign/World Lang Sec	73	Instructional Tech
6	Athletic	13	Title V	24	Music Elem	34	Early Childhood Ed	44	Science Sec	54	Remedial Reading K-12	64	Religious Education K-12	74	Inservice Training
7	Health Services	14	Instructional Media Svcs	25	Music Sec	35	Health/Phys Education	45	Math K-12	55	Remedial Reading Elem	65	Religious Education Elem	75	Marketing/Distributive
		15	Asst Superintendent	26	Business Education	36	Guidance Services K-12	46	Math Elem	56	Remedial Reading Sec	66	Religious Education Sec	76	Info Systems
		16	Instructional Media Svcs	27	Career & Tech Ed	37	Guidance Services Elem	47	Math Sec	57	Bilingual/ELL	67	School Board President	77	Psychological Assess
		17	Chief Operations Officer	28	Technology Education	38	Guidance Services Sec	48	English/Lang Arts K-12	58	Special Education K-12	68	Teacher Personnel	78	Affirmative Action

Illinois School Directory — Hardin County

- **La Harpe Cmty Sch Dist 347** PID: 00294653 217/659-7739
  404 W Main St, La Harpe 61450 Fax 217/659-7730

Schools: 1 \ **Teachers:** 19 \ **Students:** 209 \ **Special Ed Students:** 39 \
Ethnic: African American 1%, Hispanic 1%, Caucasian 97% \ **Exp:** $484
(High) \ **Poverty:** 16% \ **Title I:** $73,334 \ **Special Education:** $69,000 \
Open-Close: 08/17 - 05/28 \ **DTBP:** $211 (High) \ [f] [t]

Dr Michelle Lee	1,11,83	Laura Claassen	2
Grant James	3*	Jeanne Clayton	5
Susan Bray	12*	Erin Neff	16*
Sara Ryner	57,58,69,270,273,288,294*	Bobi James	67
Joanna Sholl	73,286,297*		

Public Schs..Principal	Grd	Prgm	Enr/#Cls	SN	
La Harpe Elem Sch 404 W Main St, La Harpe 61450 Sara Ryner	PK-8	T	209 11	67%	217/659-3713

- **Nauvoo-Colusa CUSD 325** PID: 00294718 217/453-6639
  2461 N State Highway 96, Nauvoo 62354 Fax 217/453-6395

Schools: 1 \ **Teachers:** 21 \ **Students:** 244 \ **Special Ed Students:** 35 \
Ethnic: Hispanic 3%, Caucasian 97% \ **Exp:** $522 (High) \ **Poverty:** 8% \
Title I: $41,916 \ **Special Education:** $60,000 \ **Open-Close:** 08/17 - 05/19 \
DTBP: $168 (High) \ [f]

Dr Kent Young	1,11	Trevor Knipe	2
Jeff McCarty	3*	Kerry Jenkins	4
Dan Ayer	9,59,88,273*	Tina Elschlager	16,57*
Michael Siegfried	67	Michael Coultas	73*

Public Schs..Principal	Grd	Prgm	Enr/#Cls	SN	
Nauvoo-Colusa Elem Sch 2461 N State Highway 96, Nauvoo 62354 Dan Ayer	PK-8	AT	244 9	54%	217/453-2231

- **Southeastern Cmty Unit SD 337** PID: 00294770 217/392-2172
  90 W Green St, Augusta 62311 Fax 217/392-2174

Schools: 2 \ **Teachers:** 32 \ **Students:** 450 \ **Special Ed Students:** 96
\ **College-Bound:** 65% \ **Ethnic:** African American 1%, Hispanic 2%,
Caucasian 98% \ **Exp:** $257 (Med) \ **Poverty:** 23% \ **Title I:** $237,680 \
Special Education: $135,000 \ **Open-Close:** 08/19 - 05/24 \ **DTBP:** $172
(High)

D Todd Fox	1,83	Lisa Knorr	2,84
Cyle Rigg	6*	Tim Kerr	8,58,69,286*
John Eilers	67	Tecia Lantz	270,295*

Public Schs..Principal	Grd	Prgm	Enr/#Cls	SN	
Southeastern Elem Sch 607 N Worrell St, Bowen 62316 Tecia Lantz	PK-6	T	256 12	67%	217/842-5236 Fax 217/842-5248
Southeastern Jr Sr High Sch 90 W Green St, Augusta 62311 Tim Kerr	7-12	TV	217 20	60%	217/392-2125 Fax 217/392-2229

- **Warsaw Cmty Unit Sch Dist 316** PID: 00294823 217/256-4282
  340 S 11th St, Warsaw 62379 Fax 217/256-4283

Schools: 2 \ **Teachers:** 32 \ **Students:** 444 \ **Special Ed Students:** 46
\ **Ethnic:** Asian 1%, Hispanic 1%, Caucasian 97% \ **Exp:** $312 (High)
\ **Poverty:** 11% \ **Title I:** $80,090 \ **Special Education:** $243,000 \
Open-Close: 08/17 - 05/19 \ **DTBP:** $174 (High)

Robert Gound	1,84	Ellie Froman	2
Coy Dorothy	6	Jennifer Lucie	11,296
Paul O'Day	36,69,83*	Stephanie Froman	58
Scott Baumann	67		

Public Schs..Principal	Grd	Prgm	Enr/#Cls	SN	
Warsaw Elem Sch 220 Underwood St, Warsaw 62379 Bill Knowles	PK-6		210 14	39%	217/256-4614 Fax 217/256-3106
Warsaw High Sch 340 S 11th St, Warsaw 62379 Brad Froman	9-12		192 30	18%	217/256-4281

HANCOCK CATHOLIC SCHOOLS

- **Diocese of Peoria Ed Office** PID: 00313338
  Listing includes only schools located in this county. See District Index for
  location of Diocesan Offices.

Catholic Schs..Principal	Grd	Prgm	Enr/#Cls	SN	
SS Peter & Paul Sch 1115 Young St, Nauvoo 62354 Lisa Gray	PK-6		61 5		217/453-2511 Fax 217/453-2015 [f] [t]

HARDIN COUNTY

HARDIN PUBLIC SCHOOLS

- **Hardin Co Cmty Unit Sch Dist 1** PID: 00294914 618/287-2411
  4 School Rd, Elizabethtown 62931 Fax 618/287-2421

Schools: 2 \ **Teachers:** 36 \ **Students:** 500 \ **Special Ed Students:** 122
\ **College-Bound:** 63% \ **Ethnic:** Caucasian 100% \ **Exp:** $189 (Low)
\ **Poverty:** 27% \ **Title I:** $297,092 \ **Special Education:** $121,000 \
Open-Close: 08/10 - 05/18 \ **DTBP:** $174 (High)

Andy Edmondson	1	Jessica Daymon	2
Keith Willax	3	Susan Armstrong	8,57,288
Wendell Robinson	11,83,274,296,298	Nick McDowell	67
Larry Degrave	73,76,286*	Ira Couson	83

Public Schs..Principal	Grd	Prgm	Enr/#Cls	SN	
Hardin Co Elem Sch RR 2, Elizabethtown 62931	PK-5	T	253 18	72%	618/287-7601 Fax 618/287-6091
Hardin Co Jr Sr High Sch 4 School Rd, Elizabethtown 62931	6-12	T	126 40	70%	618/287-2141

79	Student Personnel	91	Safety/Security	275	Response To Intervention	298	Grant Writer/Ptnrships
80	Driver Ed/Safety	92	Magnet School	277	Remedial Math K-12	750	Chief Innovation Officer
81	Gifted/Talented	93	Parental Involvement	280	Literacy Coach	751	Chief of Staff
82	Video Services	95	Tech Prep Program	285	STEM	752	Social Emotional Learning
83	Substance Abuse Prev	97	Chief Infomation Officer	286	Digital Learning		
84	Erate	98	Chief Technology Officer	288	Common Core Standards		
85	AIDS Education	270	Character Education	294	Accountability		
88	Alternative/At Risk	271	Migrant Education	295	Network System		
89	Multi-Cultural Curriculum	273	Teacher Mentor	296	Title II Programs		
90	Social Work	274	Before/After Sch	297	Webmaster		

Other School Types
- Ⓐ = Alternative School
- Ⓒ = Charter School
- Ⓜ = Magnet School
- Ⓨ = Year-Round School

School Programs
- A = Alternative Program
- G = Adult Classes
- M = Magnet Program
- T = Title I Schoolwide
- V = Career & Tech Ed Programs

Social Media
- [f] = Facebook
- [t] = Twitter

New Schools are shaded
New Superintendents and Principals are bold
Personnel with email addresses are underscored

IL—115

Henderson County

HENDERSON COUNTY

HENDERSON PUBLIC SCHOOLS

- **West Central Cmty Unit SD 235** PID: 00295009   309/627-2371
  1514 Old US Route 34, Biggsville 61418   Fax 309/627-2453

  Schools: 3 \ **Teachers:** 66 \ **Students:** 820 \ **Special Ed Students:** 107 \ **LEP Students:** 3 \ **Ethnic:** Hispanic 2%, Caucasian 97% \ **Exp:** $305 (High) \ **Poverty:** 11% \ **Title I:** $172,958 \ **Special Education:** $177,000 \ **Open-Close:** 08/17 - 05/28 \ **DTBP:** $180 (High) \

  Paula Markey 1,11,83
  Rose Garner 4
  Jason Kirby 10,69*
  Renee Russell 16,82*
  Jodi Arnold 67
  Barry Cisna 295
  Nancy Clark 2
  Shane Tucker 6
  Julie Ricketts 12,286,296*
  Shaila Ayer 57,58,275
  Melinda Frakes 73,97,297*

Public Schs..Principal	Grd	Prgm	Enr/#Cls	SN	
West Central Elem Sch 1514 Old US Route 34, Biggsville 61418 Kathy Lafary	K-5		326 20	60%	309/627-2339 Fax 309/627-9919
West Central High Sch 1514 Old US Route 34, Biggsville 61418 Jason Kirby	9-12		232 25	50%	309/627-2377 Fax 309/627-2120
West Central Middle Sch 215 W South St, Stronghurst 61480 Joe Peters	6-8		152	61%	309/924-1681 Fax 309/924-1122

HENRY COUNTY

HENRY PUBLIC SCHOOLS

- **Alwood Cmty Unit Sch Dist 225** PID: 00295061   309/334-2719
  301 E 5th Ave, Woodhull 61490   Fax 309/334-2925

  Schools: 2 \ **Teachers:** 36 \ **Students:** 385 \ **Special Ed Students:** 73 \ **College-Bound:** 83% \ **Ethnic:** Hispanic 1%, Caucasian 99% \ **Exp:** $210 (Med) \ **Poverty:** 11% \ **Title I:** $56,789 \ **Special Education:** $163,000 \ **Open-Close:** 08/18 - 06/03 \ **DTBP:** $174 (High)

  Shannon Bumann 1,11
  Ron Hoburg 3*
  Benjamin Rees 6,27,57,69,83*
  Maggie Hyde 12*
  Melissa Brown 67
  Hannah Garrett 2,84
  Benjamin Rees 6,27,57,69,83
  Catherine Staker 8,37*
  Toni Litton 58,275*
  Robert Hull 73,76,286*

Public Schs..Principal	Grd	Prgm	Enr/#Cls	SN	
Alwood Elem Sch 101 E A St, Alpha 61413 Reggie Larson	PK-6		162 21	48%	309/629-5011 Fax 309/629-4023
Alwood Jr Sr High Sch 301 E 5th Ave, Woodhull 61490 Ben Rees	7-12	TV	199 20	41%	309/334-2102 Fax 309/334-2632

- **Annawan Cmty Unit SD 226** PID: 00295102   309/935-6781
  501 W South St, Annawan 61234   Fax 309/935-6065

  Schools: 2 \ **Teachers:** 30 \ **Students:** 330 \ **Special Ed Students:** 39 \ **LEP Students:** 3 \ **Ethnic:** Asian 2%, Hispanic 2%, Caucasian 96% \ **Exp:** $259 (Med) \ **Poverty:** 11% \ **Title I:** $59,844 \ **Special Education:** $60,000 \ **Open-Close:** 08/18 - 05/27 \ **DTBP:** $203 (High)

  Matt Nordstrom 1
  Alta Courter 16,82
  Jason Burkiewicz 80*
  Lana Wolf 10,57,83,85,288*
  Dwaine Shaw 67

Public Schs..Principal	Grd	Prgm	Enr/#Cls	SN	
Annawan Grade Sch 503 W South St, Annawan 61234 Dawn Heitzler	PK-8		257 20	32%	309/935-6623 Fax 309/935-6894
Annawan High Sch 501 W South St, Annawan 61234 Matt Nordstrom	9-12		102 16	33%	309/935-6781

- **Cambridge Cmty Unit SD 227** PID: 00295176   309/937-2144
  300 S West St, Cambridge 61238   Fax 309/937-5128

  Schools: 2 \ **Teachers:** 40 \ **Students:** 432 \ **Special Ed Students:** 69 \ **College-Bound:** 69% \ **Ethnic:** African American 2%, Hispanic 2%, Caucasian 96% \ **Exp:** $309 (High) \ **Poverty:** 14% \ **Title I:** $93,296 \ **Special Education:** $100,000 \ **Open-Close:** 08/14 - 05/21 \ **DTBP:** $177 (High) \

  Thomas Akers 1
  Shelly Capps 9,11,54,274,275,298*
  Lisa Miller 36,69,83,85*
  Alan Steider 73,295*
  Sunny Letterle 280*
  Jeff Hannam 6,273*
  Robert Reagan 10*
  Chad Humphry 67
  Anne Wood 83,85*

Public Schs..Principal	Grd	Prgm	Enr/#Cls	SN	
Cambridge Cmty Elem Sch 312 S West St, Cambridge 61238 Shelly Capps	PK-5		225 16	39%	309/937-2028 Fax 309/937-5219
Cambridge Cmty Jr Sr High Sch 300 S West St, Cambridge 61238 Robert Reagan	6-12	GV	207 25	46%	309/937-2051 Fax 309/937-5788

- **Colona Cmty School Dist 190** PID: 00295205   309/792-1232
  700 1st St, Colona 61241   Fax 309/792-2249

  Schools: 1 \ **Teachers:** 30 \ **Students:** 400 \ **Special Ed Students:** 82 \ **LEP Students:** 3 \ **Ethnic:** African American 1%, Hispanic 10%, Caucasian 89% \ **Exp:** $195 (Low) \ **Poverty:** 17% \ **Title I:** $116,597 \ **Special Education:** $195,000 \ **Open-Close:** 08/06 - 05/28 \ **DTBP:** $221 (High)

  Carl Johnson 1,11,288
  Ian Malmstrom 6*
  Mike Carlson 13,280,285,298,752
  Kyle Taylor 73*
  Crissy Winters 2
  Michael Carlson 11,57,69,275,298,752*
  Julie Wittenauer 67

Public Schs..Principal	Grd	Prgm	Enr/#Cls	SN	
Colona Grade Sch 700 1st St, Colona 61241 Michael Carlson	PK-8	MT	400 40	65%	309/792-1232

1	Superintendent	8	Curric/Instruct K-12	19	Chief Financial Officer	29	Family/Consumer Science	39	Social Studies K-12	49	English/Lang Arts Elem	59	Special Education Elem	69	Academic Assessment
2	Bus/Finance/Purchasing	9	Curric/Instruct Elem	20	Art K-12	30	Adult Education	40	Social Studies Elem	50	English/Lang Arts Sec	60	Special Education Sec	70	Research/Development
3	Buildings And Grounds	10	Curric/Instruct Sec	21	Art Elem	31	Career/Sch-to-Work K-12	41	Social Studies Sec	51	Reading K-12	61	Foreign/World Lang K-12	71	Public Information
4	Food Service	11	Federal Program	22	Art Sec	32	Career/Sch-to-Work Elem	42	Science K-12	52	Reading Elem	62	Foreign/World Lang Elem	72	Summer School
5	Transportation	12	Title I	23	Music K-12	33	Career/Sch-to-Work Sec	43	Science Elem	53	Reading Sec	63	Foreign/World Lang Sec	73	Instructional Tech
6	Athletic	13	Title V	24	Music Elem	34	Early Childhood Ed	44	Science Sec	54	Remedial Reading K-12	64	Religious Education K-12	74	Inservice Training
7	Health Services	15	Asst Superintendent	25	Music Sec	35	Health/Phys Education	45	Math K-12	55	Remedial Reading Elem	65	Religious Education Elem	75	Marketing/Distributive
		16	Instructional Media Svcs	26	Business Education	36	Guidance Services K-12	46	Math Elem	56	Remedial Reading Sec	66	Religious Education Sec	76	Info Systems
		17	Chief Operations Officer	27	Career & Tech Ed	37	Guidance Services Elem	47	Math Sec	57	Bilingual/ELL	67	School Board President	77	Psychological Assess
		18	Chief Academic Officer	28	Technology Education	38	Guidance Services Sec	48	English/Lang Arts K-12	58	Special Education K-12	68	Teacher Personnel	78	Affirmative Action

Illinois School Directory — Henry County

- **Galva Cmty Unit Sch Dist 224** PID: 00295229   309/932-2108
  224 Morgan Rd, Galva 61434   Fax 309/932-8326

Schools: 2 \ **Teachers:** 37 \ **Students:** 525 \ **Special Ed Students:** 90 \ **College-Bound:** 80% \ **Ethnic:** African American 1%, Hispanic 3%, Caucasian 95% \ **Exp:** $295 (Med) \ **Poverty:** 17% \ **Title I:** $160,695 \ **Special Education:** $80,000 \ **Open-Close:** 08/14 - 05/28

Doug O'Riley 1,11
Amanda Norway 16,73,76,82*
Greg Wertheim 58,77
Jerry Becker 10,93,273*
Vicki Conner 38,69,83*
John Vandevelde 67

Public Schs..Principal	Grd	Prgm	Enr/#Cls	SN	
Galva Elem Sch 224 Morgan Rd, Galva 61434 Mary Kelly	PK-6		281 25	55%	309/932-2420 Fax 309/932-8716
Galva Jr Sr High Sch 1020 N Center Ave, Galva 61434 Jerry Becker	7-12	TV	200 23	45%	309/932-2151 Fax 309/932-2152

- **Geneseo Cmty Unit Sch Dist 228** PID: 00295279   309/945-0450
  648 N Chicago St, Geneseo 61254   Fax 309/945-0445

Schools: 5 \ **Teachers:** 156 \ **Students:** 2,000 \ **Special Ed Students:** 289 \ **LEP Students:** 7 \ **College-Bound:** 75% \ **Ethnic:** Asian 1%, African American 1%, Hispanic 4%, Caucasian 94% \ **Exp:** $213 (Med) \ **Poverty:** 8% \ **Title I:** $292,058 \ **Special Education:** $433,000 \ **Open-Close:** 08/13 - 05/21 🇫

Dr Adam Brumball 1,11
Randy Boreman 3
Joseph Nichols 6*
Cassie Hanson 58
James Roodhouse 73,76
Nathan O'Dell 83,273*
Megan Lundeen 274*
Tim Gronski 2,5,12,91
Michelle Hepner 4
Deb Rokis 7*
Barry Snodgrass 67
Jon Murray 80
Linda Vanderleest 270*

Public Schs..Principal	Grd	Prgm	Enr/#Cls	SN	
Geneseo High Sch 700 N State St, Geneseo 61254 Travis Mackey	9-12	AV	828 50	20%	309/945-0399 Fax 309/945-0374 🇫🇹
Geneseo Middle Sch 333 E Ogden Ave, Geneseo 61254 Nathan O'Dell	6-8	A	650 35	21%	309/945-0599 Fax 309/945-0580 🇫
Millikin Elem Sch 920 S Congress St, Geneseo 61254 Sarah Boone	K-5		408 18	23%	309/945-0475 Fax 309/945-0480
Northside Elem Sch 415 N Russell Ave, Geneseo 61254 J Mowen	PK-5		346 14	33%	309/945-0625 Fax 309/945-0620
Southwest Elem Sch 715 S Center St, Geneseo 61254 Brian Hofer	K-5		368 16	28%	309/945-0699 Fax 309/945-0670 🇫

- **Kewanee Cmty Unit Sch Dist 229** PID: 00295346   309/853-3341
  1001 N Main St, Kewanee 61443   Fax 309/852-5504

Schools: 6 \ **Teachers:** 129 \ **Students:** 2,000 \ **Special Ed Students:** 368 \ **LEP Students:** 123 \ **College-Bound:** 63% \ **Ethnic:** African American 9%, Hispanic 20%, Caucasian 71% \ **Exp:** $247 (Med) \ **Poverty:** 28% \ **Title I:** $1,069,768 \ **Special Education:** $713,000 \ **Bilingual Education:** $38,000 \ **Open-Close:** 08/18 - 05/28

Dr Chris Sullens 1
Rebecca Baney 8
Tim Atwell 6
Rebecca Baney 8*

Jamie Bryan 10,83,270,273
Katie Wager 38
Jeff Johnson 67
Dena Hodge- Bates 11,296,298
Tammy Brown 57,271
Michael Perva 73,286

Public Schs..Principal	Grd	Prgm	Enr/#Cls	SN	
Belle Alexander Elem Sch 1401 Lake St, Kewanee 61443 Rebecca Baney	K-1		253 12	83%	309/852-2449 Fax 309/852-0279
Central Elem & Jr High Sch 215 E Central Blvd, Kewanee 61443 Jason Anderson	4-8		639 35	74%	309/853-4290 Fax 309/853-3195
Irving Elem Sch 609 W Central Blvd, Kewanee 61443 Tammy Brown	2-3		239 13	82%	309/853-3013 Fax 309/852-0094
Kewanee High Sch 1211 E 3rd St, Kewanee 61443 Jamie Bryan	6-12		532 40	73%	309/853-3328 Fax 309/854-0210
Lyle Sch 920 N Burr St, Kewanee 61443 Kelly Walters	PK-PK		206 7	78%	309/853-2741 Fax 309/852-0179
Neponset Grade Sch 201 W Main St, Neponset 61345 Dena Hodge	PK-8		115 11	70%	309/594-2306 Fax 309/853-3820

- **Orion Cmty Unit Sch Dist 223** PID: 00295425   309/526-3388
  1002 11th Ave, Orion 61273   Fax 309/526-3711

Schools: 3 \ **Teachers:** 68 \ **Students:** 990 \ **Special Ed Students:** 141 \ **College-Bound:** 66% \ **Ethnic:** Hispanic 3%, Caucasian 97% \ **Exp:** $163 (Low) \ **Poverty:** 5% \ **Title I:** $79,775 \ **Special Education:** $438,000 \ **Open-Close:** 08/17 - 05/24 \ **DTBP:** $173 (High) 🇫🇹

Joseph Blessman 1,11
Tom Hamerlinck 3
Ashlee Amador 6
Cassie Kingsford 27
Kyle Taylor 73,76
Denise Jacobsen 2
Julie Lough 5
RC Lowe 12,296*
Peter Nedved 67
Calvin Kruse 295

Public Schs..Principal	Grd	Prgm	Enr/#Cls	SN	
C R Hanna Elem Sch 900 14th Ave, Orion 61273 RC Lowe	PK-5		461 23	20%	309/526-3386 Fax 309/526-3864
Orion High Sch 1100 13th St, Orion 61273 Nathan Debaillie	9-12	V	354 25	20%	309/526-3361 Fax 309/526-3854 🇫🇹
Orion Middle Sch 800 12th Ave, Orion 61273 Laura Nelson	6-8		219 20	19%	309/526-3392 Fax 309/526-3872

- **Wethersfield Cmty Unit SD 230** PID: 00295463   309/853-4860
  439 Willard St, Kewanee 61443   Fax 309/856-7976

Schools: 2 \ **Teachers:** 42 \ **Students:** 580 \ **Special Ed Students:** 68 \ **LEP Students:** 7 \ **College-Bound:** 67% \ **Ethnic:** Asian 2%, African American 3%, Hispanic 16%, Caucasian 80% \ **Exp:** $270 (Med) \ **Poverty:** 14% \ **Title I:** $134,977 \ **Special Education:** $104,000 \ **Open-Close:** 08/17 - 05/21 \ **DTBP:** $219 (High)

Shane Kazubowski 1,73,83
Dan Bryan 67
Jeff Parson 6*
Regina Walk 90

Public Schs..Principal	Grd	Prgm	Enr/#Cls	SN	
Wethersfield Elem Sch 439 Willard St, Kewanee 61443 Gus Elliott	PK-6	T	333 13	50%	309/853-4800

---

79 Student Personnel
80 Driver Ed/Safety
81 Gifted/Talented
82 Video Services
83 Substance Abuse Prev
84 Erate
85 AIDS Education
88 Alternative/At Risk
89 Multi-Cultural Curriculum
90 Social Work

91 Safety/Security
92 Magnet School
93 Parental Involvement
95 Tech Prep Program
97 Chief Information Officer
98 Chief Technology Officer
270 Character Education
271 Migrant Education
273 Teacher Mentor
274 Before/After Sch

275 Response To Intervention
277 Remedial Math K-12
280 Literacy Coach
285 STEM
286 Digital Learning
288 Common Core Standards
294 Accountability
295 Network System
296 Title II Programs
297 Webmaster

298 Grant Writer/Ptnrships
750 Chief Innovation Officer
751 Chief of Staff
752 Social Emotional Learning

Other School Types
Ⓐ = Alternative School
Ⓒ = Charter School
Ⓜ = Magnet School
Ⓨ = Year-Round School

School Programs
A = Alternative Program
G = Adult Classes
M = Magnet Program
T = Title I Schoolwide
V = Career & Tech Ed Programs

Social Media
🇫 = Facebook
🇹 = Twitter

New Schools are shaded
New Superintendents and Principals are bold
Personnel with email addresses are underscored

Iroquois County — Market Data Retrieval

	Grd	Prgm	Enr/#Cls	SN	
Wethersfield Jr Sr High Sch 439 Willard St, Kewanee 61443 Carrie Griffith	7-12	TV	247 30	39%	309/853-4205 Fax 309/856-7800

HENRY CATHOLIC SCHOOLS

- **Diocese of Peoria Ed Office** PID: 00313338
  Listing includes only schools located in this county. See District Index for location of Diocesan Offices.

Catholic Schs..Principal	Grd	Prgm	Enr/#Cls	SN	
St Malachy Sch 595 E Ogden Ave, Geneseo 61254 Heather Francque	K-6		106 7		309/944-3230 Fax 309/944-5319
Visitation Catholic Sch 101 S Lexington Ave, Kewanee 61443 Wayne Brau	PK-8		110 12		309/856-7451 Fax 309/852-4259

HENRY REGIONAL CENTERS

- **Henry-Stark Co Sp Ed Dist 801** PID: 02182044   309/852-5696
  1318 W 6th St, Kewanee 61443   Fax 309/853-4398

T Greg Wertheim 1,11   Candace Wexell 68
Kelly Miller 76

- **Regional Office of Ed 28** PID: 02097839   309/936-7890
  107 S State St, Atkinson 61235   Fax 309/936-1111

Angie Zarvell 1   Kathy Marshall 15

IROQUOIS COUNTY

IROQUOIS COUNTY SCHOOLS

County Schs..Principal	Grd	Prgm	Enr/#Cls	SN	
Ⓐ Bryce-Ash Grove Ed Center 1101 N 1800 East Rd, Milford 60953 Trent Eshleman	3-12		19 3	80%	815/889-4120 Fax 815/889-5206
Onarga Academy Grand Prairie 300 E Seminary Ave, Onarga 60955 Tare Lemenager	Spec		64 10		815/268-4001 Fax 815/268-7439

IROQUOIS PUBLIC SCHOOLS

- **Central Cmty Unit SD 4** PID: 00295554   815/698-2212
  203 N Third St, Ashkum 60911   Fax 815/698-2575

Schools: 4 \ **Teachers:** 70 \ **Students:** 1,100 \ **Special Ed Students:** 169 \ **LEP Students:** 3 \ **Ethnic:** African American 1%, Hispanic 8%, Caucasian 91% \ **Exp:** $175 (Low) \ **Poverty:** 12% \ **Title I:** $167,663 \ **Special Education:** $501,000 \ **Open-Close:** 08/20 - 06/03 \ **DTBP:** $180 (High) \ 🅕 🆃

Tonya Evans 1,83   Ryan Busick 2,19
Dan Fry 3   Jeff Fenton 6*
Dee Christensen .... 11*   Gina Siore 36
Dawn Oltmanns .... 58*   Paul Swanson 67
Tim Saathoff 73,286

Public Schs..Principal	Grd	Prgm	Enr/#Cls	SN	
Ashkum Early Literacy Center 203 N Third St, Ashkum 60911 Andrea Lemenager	PK-PK	T	59 5	41%	815/698-2212
Central High Sch 1134 E 3100 North Rd Ste A, Clifton 60927 Marc Shaner	9-12	AV	354 35	35%	815/694-2321 Fax 815/694-2709 🅕 🆃
Chebanse Elem Sch 475 School St, Chebanse 60922 Andrea Lemenager	K-4	V	362 18	41%	815/697-2642 Fax 815/697-2448
John L Nash Middle Sch 1134 E 3100 North Rd Ste B, Clifton 60927 Brandon Burke	5-8	TV	303 14	40%	815/694-2323 Fax 815/694-2830 🅕 🆃

- **Cissna Park Cmty Unit SD 6** PID: 00295619   815/457-2171
  511 N 2nd St, Cissna Park 60924   Fax 815/457-3033

Schools: 1 \ **Teachers:** 23 \ **Students:** 294 \ **Special Ed Students:** 40 \ **LEP Students:** 3 \ **College-Bound:** 66% \ **Ethnic:** Hispanic 9%, Caucasian 91% \ **Exp:** $271 (Med) \ **Poverty:** 12% \ **Title I:** $45,243 \ **Special Education:** $30,000 \ **Open-Close:** 08/24 - 05/28

Dr Daniel Hylbert 1,11,83   Bud Petry 67

Public Schs..Principal	Grd	Prgm	Enr/#Cls	SN	
Cissna Park Sch 511 N 2nd St Ste 1, Cissna Park 60924 Bethanie Marshall \ Mark Portwood	K-12		294 40	31%	815/457-2171

- **Crescent Iroquois Cmty SD 249** PID: 00295645   815/683-2141
  600 South St, Crescent City 60928   Fax 815/683-2219

Schools: 1 \ **Teachers:** 8 \ **Students:** 70 \ **Special Ed Students:** 19 \ **Ethnic:** Hispanic 3%, Caucasian 97% \ **Exp:** $353 (High) \ **Poverty:** 14% \ **Title I:** $29,512 \ **Special Education:** $14,000 \ **Open-Close:** 08/18 - 05/21

Dr Rodney Grimsley 1,11   Victoria Legan 2,83
Jessica Rabe 4   James Demay 6
Steve Massey 67   Walter Hawkins 73
Heather Johnson .... 273*   Liz Martin 280*

Public Schs..Principal	Grd	Prgm	Enr/#Cls	SN	
Crescent City Grade Sch 600 South St, Crescent City 60928 Dr Jeffery Olstock	K-8		70 9	27%	815/683-2141

---

1 Superintendent	8 Curric/Instruct K-12	19 Chief Financial Officer	29 Family/Consumer Science	39 Social Studies K-12	49 English/Lang Arts Elem	59 Special Education Elem	69 Academic Assessment
2 Bus/Finance/Purchasing	9 Curric/Instruct Elem	20 Art K-12	30 Adult Education	40 Social Studies Elem	50 English/Lang Arts Sec	60 Special Education Sec	70 Research/Development
3 Buildings And Grounds	10 Curric/Instruct Sec	21 Art Elem	31 Career/Sch-to-Work K-12	41 Social Studies Sec	51 Reading K-12	61 Foreign/World Lang K-12	71 Public Information
4 Food Service	11 Federal Program	22 Art Sec	32 Career/Sch-to-Work Elem	42 Science K-12	52 Reading Elem	62 Foreign/World Lang Elem	72 Summer School
5 Transportation	12 Title I	23 Music K-12	33 Career/Sch-to-Work Sec	43 Science Elem	53 Reading Sec	63 Foreign/World Lang Sec	73 Instructional Tech
6 Athletic	13 Title V	24 Music Elem	34 Early Childhood Ed	44 Science Sec	54 Remedial Reading K-12	64 Religious Education K-12	74 Inservice Training
7 Health Services	15 Asst Superintendent	25 Music Sec	35 Health/Phys Education	45 Math K-12	55 Remedial Reading Elem	65 Religious Education Elem	75 Marketing/Distributive
	16 Instructional Media Svcs	26 Business Education	36 Guidance Services K-12	46 Math Elem	56 Remedial Reading Sec	66 Religious Education Sec	76 Info Systems
	17 Chief Operations Officer	27 Career & Tech Ed	37 Guidance Services Elem	47 Math Sec	57 Bilingual/ELL	67 School Board President	77 Psychological Assess
	18 Chief Academic Officer	28 Technology Education	38 Guidance Services Sec	48 English/Lang Arts K-12	58 Special Education K-12	68 Teacher Personnel	78 Affirmative Action

Illinois School Directory — Iroquois County

Donovan Cmty Unit Sch Dist 3 PID: 00295671
600 North St, Donovan 60931
815/486-7398
Fax 815/486-7030

Schools: 2 \ **Teachers:** 25 \ **Students:** 290 \ **Special Ed Students:** 47 \ **LEP Students:** 3 \ **College-Bound:** 59% \ **Ethnic:** Asian 1%, African American 3%, Hispanic 7%, Caucasian 90% \ **Exp:** $295 (Med) \ **Poverty:** 14% \ **Title I:** $78,628 \ **Special Education:** $34,000 \ **Open-Close:** 08/21 - 05/26 \ **DTBP:** $174 (High)

Toby Coates 1,11
Justin LaReau 3*
Holly Robinson 8,37,69,83
Megan Parks 16
Andrew Jordan 58
Jewel Legan 73
Julie Shortsleeve 2
Emily Snyder 6
Mandi Askew 12*
Kevin Venner 35,85
Joe Schultz 67
Kelly Fiedentop 273*

Public Schs..Principal	Grd	Prgm	Enr/#Cls	SN	
Donovan Elem Sch 2561 E US Highway 52, Donovan 60931 Toby Coates	PK-5	T	128 12	59%	815/486-7321 Fax 815/486-7445
Donovan Jr Sr High Sch 600 North St, Donovan 60931 Scott Vogel	6-12	V	156 15	54%	815/486-7395 Fax 815/486-7038

Iroquois Co Cmty Unit SD 9 PID: 00295748
1411 W Lafayette St, Watseka 60970
815/432-4931
Fax 815/432-6889

Schools: 4 \ **Teachers:** 74 \ **Students:** 1,000 \ **Special Ed Students:** 186 \ **LEP Students:** 21 \ **College-Bound:** 50% \ **Ethnic:** Asian 1%, African American 1%, Hispanic 12%, Caucasian 86% \ **Exp:** $174 (Low) \ **Poverty:** 17% \ **Title I:** $332,779 \ **Special Education:** $182,000 \ **Open-Close:** 08/19 - 05/26

Dr David Andriano 1,11,83
Janine Clifton 4*
Barry Bauer 6*
Julie Dunn 16*
James Bruns 67
Dale Verkler 3
Kris Miller 5
Heather Gerth 12,51,54,57,72,298*
Lakeshia Dillard 38
Joe Schall 73,76

Public Schs..Principal	Grd	Prgm	Enr/#Cls	SN	
Glenn Raymond Sch 101 W Mulberry St, Watseka 60970 James Bunting	6-8	T	241 21	60%	815/432-2115 Fax 815/432-6896
Nettie Davis Elem Sch 495 N 4th St, Watseka 60970 Heather Gerth	PK-1	T	132 10	59%	815/432-2112 Fax 815/432-7292
Wanda Kendall Elem Sch 535 E Porter Ave, Watseka 60970 Jessica Heldt	2-3	T	138 9	64%	815/432-4581
Watseka Cmty High Sch 138 S Belmont Ave, Watseka 60970 Carolyn Short	9-12	AGTV	290 22	54%	815/432-2486 Fax 815/432-5578

Iroquois West Cmty Unit SD 10 PID: 00295700
529 E 2nd St, Gilman 60938
815/265-4642
Fax 815/265-7008

Schools: 5 \ **Teachers:** 70 \ **Students:** 980 \ **Special Ed Students:** 212 \ **LEP Students:** 57 \ **College-Bound:** 63% \ **Ethnic:** Hispanic 34%, Caucasian 65% \ **Exp:** $238 (Med) \ **Poverty:** 14% \ **Title I:** $182,119 \ **Special Education:** $1,194,000 \ **Bilingual Education:** $14,000 \ **Open-Close:** 08/21 - 05/28 \ **DTBP:** $169 (High)

Angelo Lekkas 1
Kristy Arie 6*
Katie Redwitz 31*
Dave Haase 67
Cameron Stone 6*
Ashley Carlson 9,298*
Erami Izquierdo 57,271*
Brian Eggemeyer 73,295,297*

Public Schs..Principal	Grd	Prgm	Enr/#Cls	SN	
Iroquois West ES-Danforth 101 E Locust St, Danforth 60930 Ashley Carlson	PK-K	T	120 3	36%	815/269-2230 Fax 815/269-2205
Iroquois West ES-Gilman 529 E 2nd St, Gilman 60938 Jim Harkins	1-3	T	197 10	53%	815/265-7631 Fax 815/265-7693
Iroquois West High Sch 529 E 2nd St, Gilman 60938 **Erin Smith**	9-12	T	306 26	52%	815/265-4229 Fax 815/265-8108
Iroquois West Middle Sch 303 N Evergreen St, Onarga 60955 Duane Ehmen	6-8	T	211 20	59%	815/268-4355 Fax 815/268-7608
Iroquois West Upper Elem Sch 106 W County Rd, Thawville 60968 Christina Duncan	4-5	T	114 9	61%	217/387-2291 Fax 217/387-2205

Milford Area Public SD 124 PID: 00295839
208 S Chicago St, Milford 60953
815/889-5176
Fax 815/889-5221

Schools: 2 \ **Teachers:** 51 \ **Students:** 610 \ **Special Ed Students:** 66 \ **LEP Students:** 3 \ **College-Bound:** 60% \ **Ethnic:** Asian 1%, African American 1%, Hispanic 3%, Caucasian 95% \ **Exp:** $313 (High) \ **Poverty:** 18% \ **Title I:** $206,263 \ **Special Education:** $101,000 \ **Open-Close:** 08/21 - 06/01

Dr Michele Lindenmeyer 1
Steve Totheroh 10,270*
Jill Brown 37*
Kena Clark 73*
Deb Longis 7*
Sarah Swartzentruber 36,69,88*
Mary Ronna 67
Michelle Schoolman 273*

Public Schs..Principal	Grd	Prgm	Enr/#Cls	SN	
Milford Grade Sch 100 S Chicago St, Milford 60953 Michelle Sobkoviak	PK-8	T	372 19	52%	815/889-4174 Fax 815/889-5503
Milford High Sch 200 S Chicago St, Milford 60953 Steve Totheroh	9-12	T	165 25	44%	815/889-4184 Fax 815/889-4871

IROQUOIS PRIVATE SCHOOLS

Private Schs..Principal	Grd	Prgm	Enr/#Cls	SN	
Christ Lutheran High Sch 201 W Lincoln St, Buckley 60918 Sandy Spitz	9-12	V	13 6		217/394-2547 Fax 217/394-2097
St John's Lutheran Sch 206 E Main St, Buckley 60918 John Britton	PK-8		112 8		217/394-2422
St Paul's Lutheran Sch 108 W Woodworth Rd, Milford 60953 Holly Rice	PK-8		114 7		815/889-4209 Fax 815/889-4364

IROQUOIS REGIONAL CENTERS

Iroquois Spec Educ Association PID: 02097762
106 E Front St, Gilman 60938
815/683-2662
Fax 815/683-9913

Nicole Bullington 1
Lynn Canady 2
Cindy Johnson 2

---

79 Student Personnel
80 Driver Ed/Safety
81 Gifted/Talented
82 Video Services
83 Substance Abuse Prev
84 Erate
85 AIDS Education
88 Alternative/At Risk
89 Multi-Cultural Curriculum
90 Social Work
91 Safety/Security
92 Magnet School
93 Parental Involvement
95 Tech Prep Program
97 Chief Information Officer
98 Chief Technology Officer
270 Character Education
271 Migrant Education
273 Teacher Mentor
274 Before/After Sch
275 Response To Intervention
277 Remedial Math K-12
280 Literacy Coach
285 STEM
286 Digital Learning
288 Common Core Standards
294 Accountability
295 Network System
296 Title II Programs
297 Webmaster
298 Grant Writer/Ptnrships
750 Chief Innovation Officer
751 Chief of Staff
752 Social Emotional Learning

Other School Types
Ⓐ = Alternative School
Ⓒ = Charter School
Ⓜ = Magnet School
Ⓨ = Year-Round School

School Programs
A = Alternative Program
G = Adult Classes
M = Magnet Program
T = Title I Schoolwide
V = Career & Tech Ed Programs

Social Media
= Facebook
= Twitter

New Schools are shaded
New Superintendents and Principals are bold
Personnel with email addresses are underscored

Jackson County

Market Data Retrieval

JACKSON COUNTY

JACKSON COUNTY SCHOOLS

County Schs..Principal	Grd	Prgm	Enr/#Cls	SN		
Tri-Co Special Ed Sch 1725 Shomaker Dr, Murphysboro 62966 Zeppelyn Brewer	Spec		45 7		86%	618/684-2109 Fax 618/687-1638

JACKSON PUBLIC SCHOOLS

- **Carbondale Cmty HSD 165** PID: 00296089   618/457-3371
  1301 E Walnut St, Carbondale 62901   Fax 618/549-1686

Schools: 1 \ **Teachers:** 75 \ **Students:** 1,000 \ **Special Ed Students:** 149 \ **LEP Students:** 40 \ **College-Bound:** 66% \ **Ethnic:** Asian 4%, African American 29%, Hispanic 11%, Caucasian 55% \ **Exp:** $276 (Med) \ **Poverty:** 30% \ **Title I:** $733,134 \ **Special Education:** $378,000 \ **Open-Close:** 08/17 - 05/28 \ **DTBP:** $182 (High)

Steve Murphy 1	Donna Fager 2,4,5,11,19,296*		
Don Biggs 3*	Mark Albertini 6*		
Brian Thomas 7,18,68,79,273,275,751	Ethan Graham 10,73,286,295*		
Theresa Goodin 12,298*	Dawn Taylor 16		
Dallas Terry 26,27,28,29,95	Sandra Snowden 30,88*		
Michelle Thomas 35	Lori Koester 38,81*		
Arnold Taylor 57*	Mandy McKee 60,280		
Dr Brian Woodward 67	Erinn Murphy 69,288*		
Gwen Poore 72	Easton Graham 74		
Matt Young 76,82,84,98,297	Terica Doyle 78,80		
Amy Prudencio 83,90,93*	Kyle Povolish 85		
Stephanie Dillow 91*	Benda Berg 277		

Public Schs..Principal	Grd	Prgm	Enr/#Cls	SN		
Carbondale Cmty High Sch 1301 E Walnut St, Carbondale 62901 Ryan Thomas	9-12	AGTV	1,000 55		61%	618/457-3371

- **Carbondale Elem School Dist 95** PID: 00295994   618/457-3591
  925 S Giant City Rd, Carbondale 62902   Fax 618/457-2043

Schools: 4 \ **Teachers:** 110 \ **Students:** 1,560 \ **Special Ed Students:** 236 \ **LEP Students:** 133 \ **Ethnic:** Asian 4%, African American 53%, Hispanic 13%, Caucasian 31% \ **Exp:** $149 (Low) \ **Poverty:** 36% \ **Title I:** $1,162,953 \ **Special Education:** $572,000 \ **Bilingual Education:** $57,000 \ **Open-Close:** 08/19 - 05/21 \ **DTBP:** $186 (High)

Daniel Booth 1	Eric Trimberger 2,15
Aaron Dixon 3	Zena Madison 6
Janice Pavelonis 9,11,57,88,288,298	Seren Connor 16
John Major 67	Stephanie Esters 71
Melody Spaulding 73	Latasha Schraeder 79
Yoko Kawazoe 274*	

Public Schs..Principal	Grd	Prgm	Enr/#Cls	SN		
Carbondale Middle Sch 1150 E Grand Ave, Carbondale 62901 Dr Carmen Williams-Bonds	6-8	TV	424 56		61%	618/457-2174 Fax 618/457-2176

	Grd	Prgm	Enr/#Cls	SN		
Lewis Elem Sch 801 S Lewis Ln, Carbondale 62901 Marilynn Ross	4-5	T	318 12		70%	618/457-2632 Fax 618/351-9816
Parrish Elem Sch 121 N Parrish Ln, Carbondale 62901 Jerrah Henson	PK-1	T	461 20		66%	618/457-5781 Fax 618/457-4661
Thomas Elem Sch 1025 N Wall St, Carbondale 62901 Kris Uffelman	2-3	T	321 18		69%	618/457-6226 Fax 618/457-5636

- **DeSoto Grade School Dist 86** PID: 00296120   618/867-2317
  311 Hurst Rd, De Soto 62924   Fax 618/867-3233

Schools: 1 \ **Teachers:** 17 \ **Students:** 203 \ **Special Ed Students:** 34 \ **Ethnic:** African American 2%, Hispanic 1%, Caucasian 97% \ **Exp:** $225 (Med) \ **Poverty:** 16% \ **Title I:** $144,438 \ **Special Education:** $75,000 \ **Open-Close:** 08/10 - 05/25

Nathaniel Wilson 1,11	Lauren Clough 6,73
Patty Rosenberger 12,288*	Karen Hicks 16,286*
Lisa Fisher 59*	Paul Copeland 67
Erin Tarrantes 84	

Public Schs..Principal	Grd	Prgm	Enr/#Cls	SN		
DeSoto Grade Sch 311 Hurst Rd, De Soto 62924 Nathaniel Wilson \ Michele Baird	PK-8	T	203 15		57%	618/867-2317

- **Elverado Cmty Unit SD 196** PID: 00296144   618/568-1321
  514 S 6th St, Elkville 62932   Fax 618/568-2015

Schools: 4 \ **Teachers:** 37 \ **Students:** 420 \ **Special Ed Students:** 96 \ **College-Bound:** 85% \ **Ethnic:** African American 3%, Hispanic 1%, Caucasian 96% \ **Exp:** $319 (High) \ **Poverty:** 20% \ **Title I:** $195,927 \ **Special Education:** $161,000 \ **Open-Close:** 08/18 - 05/19 \ **DTBP:** $179 (High)

Kevin Spain 1	Alyssa Guethle 4
Belinda Connor 8,11,288	Belinda Conner 11,58,288,298*
Kenton Schafer 67	Adam Lewis 73,76,84,286,752
Max Schnider 91	

Public Schs..Principal	Grd	Prgm	Enr/#Cls	SN		
Elverado High Sch 514 S 6th St, Elkville 62932 Neil Hargis	9-12	ATV	116 14		52%	618/568-1104 Fax 618/568-1551
Elverado Intermediate Sch 190 Harrison St, Vergennes 62994 Connie Clendenin	3-5	T	75		72%	618/684-3527 Fax 618/687-3363
Elverado Junior High Sch 190 Harrison St, Vergennes 62994 Connie Clendenin	6-8	T	95 10		62%	618/684-3527 Fax 618/687-3363
Elverado Primary Sch 114 S 8th St, Elkville 62932 Kevin Spain	PK-2	T	114 10		76%	618/568-1321

- **Giant City Cmty Cons SD 130** PID: 00296194   618/457-5391
  1062 Boskydell Rd, Carbondale 62902   Fax 618/549-5060

Schools: 1 \ **Teachers:** 16 \ **Students:** 210 \ **Special Ed Students:** 30 \ **LEP Students:** 3 \ **Ethnic:** Asian 2%, African American 9%, Hispanic 2%, Caucasian 87% \ **Exp:** $150 (Low) \ **Poverty:** 20% \ **Title I:** $105,689 \ **Special Education:** $52,000 \ **Open-Close:** 08/12 - 05/21 \ **DTBP:** $160 (High)

---

1 Superintendent	8 Curric/Instruct K-12	19 Chief Financial Officer	29 Family/Consumer Science	39 Social Studies K-12	49 English/Lang Arts Elem	59 Special Education Elem	69 Academic Assessment
2 Bus/Finance/Purchasing	9 Curric/Instruct Elem	20 Art K-12	30 Adult Education	40 Social Studies Elem	50 English/Lang Arts Sec	60 Special Education Sec	70 Research/Development
3 Buildings And Grounds	10 Curric/Instruct Sec	21 Art Elem	31 Career/Sch-to-Work K-12	41 Social Studies Sec	51 Reading K-12	61 Foreign/World Lang K-12	71 Public Information
4 Food Service	11 Federal Program	22 Art Sec	32 Career/Sch-to-Work Elem	42 Science K-12	52 Reading Elem	62 Foreign/World Lang Elem	72 Summer School
5 Transportation	12 Title I	23 Music K-12	33 Career/Sch-to-Work Sec	43 Science Elem	53 Reading Sec	63 Foreign/World Lang Sec	73 Instructional Tech
6 Athletic	13 Title V	24 Music Elem	34 Early Childhood Ed	44 Science Sec	54 Remedial Reading K-12	64 Religious Education K-12	74 Inservice Training
7 Health Services	14 Instructional Media Svcs	25 Music Sec	35 Health/Phys Education	45 Math K-12	55 Remedial Reading Elem	65 Religious Education Elem	75 Marketing/Distributive
	15 Asst Superintendent	26 Business Education	36 Guidance Services K-12	46 Math Elem	56 Remedial Reading Sec	66 Religious Education Sec	76 Info Systems
	16 Chief Operations Officer	27 Career & Tech Ed	37 Guidance Services Elem	47 Math Sec	57 Bilingual/ELL	67 School Board President	77 Psychological Assess
	17 Chief Academic Officer	28 Technology Education	38 Guidance Services Sec	48 English/Lang Arts K-12	58 Special Education K-12	68 Teacher Personnel	78 Affirmative Action

Illinois School Directory — Jackson County

Belinda Hill 1	Ray Toliver 2
Keith Joiner 3	David Wright 4
Rebecca Abcar 12,280	Nikki Burrows 59*
Lori Martin 67	Jessica Carsrud 76,82
Sarah Honza 85*	

Public Schs..Principal	Grd	Prgm	Enr/#Cls	SN	
Giant City Elem Sch 1062 Boskydell Rd, Carbondale 62902 Belinda Hill	PK-8	T	210 13	37%	618/457-5391

● **Murphysboro Cmty Unit SD 186** PID: 00296261   618/684-3781
593 Ava Rd, Murphysboro 62966   Fax 618/684-2465

> **Schools:** 4 \ **Teachers:** 145 \ **Students:** 1,800 \ **Special Ed Students:** 432
> \ **LEP Students:** 50 \ **Ethnic:** African American 18%, Hispanic 7%,
> Caucasian 75% \ **Exp:** $362 (High) \ **Poverty:** 26% \ **Title I:** $1,161,775 \
> **Special Education:** $789,000 \ **Open-Close:** 08/17 - 05/21 \ **DTBP:** $194
> (High)

Dr Andrea Evers 1	Janet Bush 2,11,19
Len Novara 6*	Charlene Mileur 7*
Cody Elimire 8,85	Jeff White 16*
Darren Ripley 17	Lisa Brown 34
Katie Hickaman 38	Rick Runge 67
Steve Carrington 71,84,97	Kevin Haldeman 73*

Public Schs..Principal	Grd	Prgm	Enr/#Cls	SN	
Carruthers Elem Sch 80 Candy Ln, Murphysboro 62966 Matthew Todd	3-5	T	442 21	98%	618/687-3231 Fax 618/687-2811
General Logan Attendance Ctr 320 Watson Rd, Murphysboro 62966 Stephanie Finke	K-2	T	406 18	98%	618/684-6061 Fax 618/565-8119
Murphysboro High Sch 50 Blackwood Dr, Murphysboro 62966 Cody Ellermeyer	9-12	T	589 55	99%	618/687-2336 Fax 618/687-3532
Murphysboro Middle Sch 2125 Spruce St, Murphysboro 62966 Jeffery Keener	6-8	T	454 24	98%	618/684-3041 Fax 618/687-1042 f t

● **Trico Cmty Unit Sch Dist 176** PID: 00296364   618/426-1111
16411 Highway 4, Campbell Hill 62916   Fax 618/426-3625

> **Schools:** 3 \ **Teachers:** 58 \ **Students:** 850 \ **Special Ed Students:** 171
> \ **LEP Students:** 47 \ **Ethnic:** African American 1%, Hispanic 10%,
> Caucasian 89% \ **Exp:** $247 (Med) \ **Poverty:** 19% \ **Title I:** $370,883 \
> **Special Education:** $224,000 \ **Open-Close:** 08/20 - 06/01

Larry Lovel 1	Ken King 3*
Susan Moore 4*	Cheryl Lodge 6
Amy Vogt 11*	Jessica Fisher 16*
Lois Jones 67	Casey Hawkins 69*
Justin Morgan 73,295*	

Public Schs..Principal	Grd	Prgm	Enr/#Cls	SN	
Trico Elem Sch 16343 Highway 4, Campbell Hill 62916 Jenny Wilson	PK-5	T	434 20	64%	618/426-1111 Fax 618/426-3988
Trico High Sch 16533 Highway 4, Campbell Hill 62916 Mark Rielly	9-12	TV	308 18	53%	618/426-1111 Fax 618/426-3712
Trico Junior High Sch 16533 Highway 4, Campbell Hill 62916 Ron Coleman	6-8	T	208 12	55%	618/426-1111 Fax 618/426-3712

● **Unity Point Cmty Cons SD 140** PID: 00296429   618/529-4151
4033 S Illinois Ave, Carbondale 62903   Fax 618/529-4154

> **Schools:** 1 \ **Teachers:** 55 \ **Students:** 610 \ **Special Ed Students:** 111
> \ **LEP Students:** 99 \ **Ethnic:** Asian 12%, African American 14%,
> Hispanic 7%, Native American: 2%, Caucasian 66% \ **Exp:** $80 (Low)
> \ **Poverty:** 18% \ **Title I:** $203,897 \ **Special Education:** $157,000 \
> **Bilingual Education:** $31,000 \ **Open-Close:** 08/17 - 06/02 \ **DTBP:** $176
> (High)

Dr Lori James-Gross 1	Michelle Brown 2
Ulli Tragoudas 4*	Mary Beth Goff 12*
Leslie Barble 13,288,296	Tabatha Noland 16,82*
Michelle Pritchard 34*	Colleen Doyle-Perritt 57,271*
D Presley 67	Chris Rogers 73,76,286,295,297*
Ron Rogers 83,85	Crystal Phillips 274*

Public Schs..Principal	Grd	Prgm	Enr/#Cls	SN	
Unity Point Elem Sch 4033 S Illinois Ave, Carbondale 62903 Leslie Varble	PK-8	AT	610 48	62%	618/529-4151

JACKSON CATHOLIC SCHOOLS

● **Diocese of Belleville Ed Off** PID: 00317671
Listing includes only schools located in this county. See District Index for location of Diocesan Offices.

Catholic Schs..Principal	Grd	Prgm	Enr/#Cls	SN	
St Andrew Sch 723 Mulberry St, Murphysboro 62966 Jenny Martin	PK-8		158 10		618/687-2013 Fax 618/684-4969

JACKSON PRIVATE SCHOOLS

Private Schs..Principal	Grd	Prgm	Enr/#Cls	SN	
Brehm Preparatory Sch 950 S Brehm Ln, Carbondale 62901	Spec		55 23		618/457-0371 Fax 618/529-1248
Carbondale New Sch 1302 E Pleasant Hill Rd, Carbondale 62902 Kathy Compton	PK-8		52 5		618/457-4765 Fax 618/551-7655
Christ Lutheran Sch 146 W Jacob Rd, Jacob 62950 Karen Hall	5-8		9 5		618/763-4664 Fax 618/763-4363
Immanuel Lutheran Sch 1915 Pine St, Murphysboro 62966 Veronica Manwaring	PK-8		90 6		618/684-3012 Fax 618/684-5115
Trinity Christian Sch 1218 W Freeman St, Carbondale 62901 Phil Bankester	PK-12		120 15		618/529-3733 Fax 618/549-8252

JACKSON REGIONAL CENTERS

● **Regional Office of Ed 30** PID: 02097853   618/687-7290
1001 Walnut St, Murphysboro 62966   Fax 618/687-7296

Cheryl Graff 1	Dr Ronda Dunn 8
Karen Wolfe 15	Megan Wece 15
Sheila Frampton 76	

79	Student Personnel	91	Safety/Security	275	Response To Intervention	298	Grant Writer/Ptnrships	**School Programs**
80	Driver Ed/Safety	92	Magnet School	277	Remedial Math K-12	750	Chief Innovation Officer	A = Alternative Program
81	Gifted/Talented	93	Parental Involvement	280	Literacy Coach	751	Chief of Staff	G = Adult Classes
82	Video Services	95	Tech Prep Program	285	STEM	752	Social Emotional Learning	M = Magnet Program
83	Substance Abuse Prev	97	Chief Information Officer	286	Digital Learning			T = Title I Schoolwide
84	Erate	98	Chief Technology Officer	288	Common Core Standards	**Other School Types**		V = Career & Tech Ed Programs
85	AIDS Education	270	Character Education	294	Accountability	Ⓐ = Alternative School		
88	Alternative/At Risk	271	Migrant Education	295	Network System	Ⓒ = Charter School		New Schools are shaded
89	Multi-Cultural Curriculum	273	Teacher Mentor	296	Title II Programs	Ⓜ = Magnet School		New Superintendents and Principals are bold
90	Social Work	274	Before/After Sch	297	Webmaster	Ⓨ = Year-Round School		Personnel with email addresses are underscored

Social Media: f = Facebook, t = Twitter

Jasper County

- **Tri-Co Special Ed JT Agreement** PID: 02184016 618/684-2109
  1335 Cedar Ct, Carbondale 62901 Fax 618/708-3403

Jan Pearcy .... 1 Renee Evans 2
Shannon Owings 68

JASPER COUNTY

JASPER PUBLIC SCHOOLS

- **Jasper Co Cmty Unit SD 1** PID: 00296479 618/783-8459
  609 S Lafayette St, Newton 62448 Fax 618/783-3679

Schools: 4 \ **Teachers:** 73 \ **Students:** 1,278 \ **Special Ed Students:** 189 \ **LEP Students:** 3 \ **College-Bound:** 75% \ **Ethnic:** Hispanic 2%, Caucasian 98% \ **Exp:** $216 (Med) \ **Poverty:** 14% \ **Title I:** $362,182 \ **Special Education:** $971,000 \ **Open-Close:** 08/14 - 05/21 \ **DTBP:** $111 (High) \

Andrew Johnson .... 1 Misty Heath 2
Chris Parr .... 3,5 Craig Carr 6*
Kathy Johnson .... 8,11,57,69,275,288,298* Beth Probst 27*
Jennifer Bales .... 58 Gordan Yager 67
Aaron Kurtz 73*

Public Schs..Principal	Grd	Prgm	Enr/#Cls	SN	
Jasper Co Junior High Sch 1104 W Jourdan St, Newton 62448 Beth Probst	7-8	T	180	43%	618/783-4202 Fax 618/783-4257
Newton Cmty High Sch 201 West End Ave, Newton 62448 Beth Probst	9-12	TV	453 40	37%	618/783-2303 Fax 618/783-3783
Newton Elem Sch 100 Maxwell St, Newton 62448 Jessica Guzman	1-6	T	524 26	41%	618/783-8464 Fax 618/783-4106
Sainte Marie Elem Sch 311 Franklin St, Sainte Marie 62459 Kathy Johnson	PK-K	T	121 7	33%	618/455-3219 Fax 618/455-3223

JASPER CATHOLIC SCHOOLS

- **Diocese of Springfield Ed Off** PID: 00319394
  Listing includes only schools located in this county. See District Index for location of Diocesan Offices.

Catholic Schs..Principal	Grd	Prgm	Enr/#Cls	SN	
St Thomas the Apostle Sch 306 W Jourdan St, Newton 62448 Jill Bierman	K-8		135 9		618/783-3517 Fax 618/783-2224

JASPER REGIONAL CENTERS

- **South Eastern Special Ed Dist** PID: 02182123 618/455-3396
  111 W Mound St, Sainte Marie 62459 Fax 618/455-3134

Kim Kessler .... 1 Joyce Reis 2

JEFFERSON COUNTY

JEFFERSON PUBLIC SCHOOLS

- **Bethel School District 82** PID: 00296601 618/244-8095
  1201 Bethel Rd, Mount Vernon 62864 Fax 618/244-8096

Schools: 1 \ **Teachers:** 13 \ **Students:** 170 \ **Special Ed Students:** 35 \ **Ethnic:** African American 11%, Hispanic 5%, Caucasian 83% \ **Exp:** $291 (Med) \ **Poverty:** 38% \ **Title I:** $123,446 \ **Special Education:** $91,000 \ **Open-Close:** 08/14 - 05/28

Craig Kujawa .... 1 Kristin Tate 9*
Rodney McCoy .... 67 Rachel Wagner 73,295*

Public Schs..Principal	Grd	Prgm	Enr/#Cls	SN	
Bethel Grade Sch 1201 Bethel Rd, Mount Vernon 62864 Craig Kujawa	PK-8	T	170 8	78%	618/244-8095

- **Bluford Unit School Dist 318** PID: 00296625 618/732-8242
  901 6th St, Bluford 62814 Fax 618/732-6114

Schools: 1 \ **Teachers:** 25 \ **Students:** 350 \ **Special Ed Students:** 63 \ **College-Bound:** 66% \ **Ethnic:** Hispanic 1%, Caucasian 98% \ **Exp:** $143 (Low) \ **Poverty:** 17% \ **Title I:** $139,241 \ **Special Education:** $84,000 \ **Open-Close:** 08/17 - 05/20 \ **DTBP:** $178 (High)

Shane Gordon .... 1,11 Kim McCormick 2*
Jeff Dunaway .... 3* Katelynn Phelps 4*
Steve Tate .... 67 Ramona Eyre 275*

Public Schs..Principal	Grd	Prgm	Enr/#Cls	SN	
Bluford Sch 901 6th St, Bluford 62814 Kevin Westall	K-12	T	350 30	44%	618/732-8242

- **Farrington Cmty Cons SD 99** PID: 00296663 618/755-4414
  20941 E Divide Rd, Bluford 62814 Fax 618/755-4461

Schools: 1 \ **Teachers:** 4 \ **Students:** 58 \ **Special Ed Students:** 14 \ **Ethnic:** Asian 4%, Caucasian 96% \ **Exp:** $201 (Med) \ **Poverty:** 11% \ **Title I:** $1,723 \ **Special Education:** $21,000 \ **Open-Close:** 08/10 - 05/14 \ **DTBP:** $174 (High)

Sandra Kabat .... 1,73 Jessica Dolener 4
Michelle Middendorf .... 59,88* Kent Donono 67

Public Schs..Principal	Grd	Prgm	Enr/#Cls	SN	
Farrington Elem Sch 20941 E Divide Rd, Bluford 62814 Sandra Kabat	K-8	T	58 5	38%	618/755-4414

1 Superintendent	8 Curric/Instruct K-12	19 Chief Financial Officer	29 Family/Consumer Science	39 Social Studies K-12	49 English/Lang Arts Elem	59 Special Education Elem	69 Academic Assessment
2 Bus/Finance/Purchasing	9 Curric/Instruct Elem	20 Art K-12	30 Adult Education	40 Social Studies Elem	50 English/Lang Arts Sec	60 Special Education Sec	70 Research/Development
3 Buildings And Grounds	10 Curric/Instruct Sec	21 Art Elem	31 Career/Sch-to-Work K-12	41 Social Studies Sec	51 Reading K-12	61 Foreign/World Lang K-12	71 Public Information
4 Food Service	11 Federal Program	22 Art Sec	32 Career/Sch-to-Work Elem	42 Science K-12	52 Reading Elem	62 Foreign/World Lang Elem	72 Summer School
5 Transportation	12 Title I	23 Music K-12	33 Career/Sch-to-Work Sec	43 Science Elem	53 Reading Sec	63 Foreign/World Lang Sec	73 Instructional Tech
6 Athletic	13 Title V	24 Music Elem	34 Early Childhood Ed	44 Science Sec	54 Remedial Reading K-12	64 Religious Education K-12	74 Inservice Training
7 Health Services	14 Asst Superintendent	25 Music Sec	35 Health/Phys Education	45 Math K-12	55 Remedial Reading Elem	65 Religious Education Elem	75 Marketing/Distributive
	15 Instructional Media Svcs	26 Business Education	36 Guidance Services K-12	46 Math Elem	56 Remedial Reading Sec	66 Religious Education Sec	76 Info Systems
	16 Chief Operations Officer	27 Career & Tech Ed	37 Guidance Services Elem	47 Math Sec	57 Bilingual/ELL	67 School Board President	77 Psychological Assess
	17 Chief Academic Officer	28 Technology Education	38 Guidance Services Sec	48 English/Lang Arts K-12	58 Special Education K-12	68 Teacher Personnel	78 Affirmative Action

Illinois School Directory — Jefferson County

• **Field Cmty Cons Sch Dist 3** PID: 00296687 618/755-4611
21075 N Hails Ln, Texico 62889 Fax 618/755-9701

Schools: 1 \ **Teachers:** 20 \ **Students:** 275 \ **Special Ed Students:** 38 \ **Ethnic:** African American 1%, Caucasian 99% \ **Exp:** $260 (Med) \ **Poverty:** 12% \ **Title I:** $49,299 \ **Special Education:** $75,000 \ **Open-Close:** 08/12 - 05/14 \ **DTBP:** $174 (High)

Wayne Stone ....1,11 Rob Hulbert 16,73,84,295
Christine Hayes 67

Public Schs..Principal	Grd	Prgm	Enr/#Cls	SN	
Field Elem Sch
21075 N Hails Ln, Texico 62889
Jennifer Arnold	PK-8	T	275
15	44%	618/755-4611

• **Grand Prairie Cmty Cons SD 6** PID: 00296704 618/249-6289
21462 N Richview Ln, Centralia 62801 Fax 618/249-8477

Schools: 1 \ **Teachers:** 6 \ **Students:** 80 \ **Special Ed Students:** 14 \ **Ethnic:** African American 7%, Hispanic 3%, Caucasian 91% \ **Exp:** $318 (High) \ **Poverty:** 21% \ **Title I:** $37,924 \ **Special Education:** $24,000 \ **Open-Close:** 08/12 - 05/21 \ **DTBP:** $232 (High)

Stuart Parks ....1,11,73,288 Ron Jourgen 67

Public Schs..Principal	Grd	Prgm	Enr/#Cls	SN	
Grand Prairie Elem Sch
21462 N Richview Ln, Centralia 62801
Ryan Robinson	K-8	T	80
6	99%	618/249-6289

• **McClellan Cons SD 12** PID: 00296742 618/244-8072
9475 N Il Highway 148, Mount Vernon 62864 Fax 618/244-8129

Schools: 1 \ **Teachers:** 7 \ **Students:** 45 \ **Special Ed Students:** 11 \ **Ethnic:** Caucasian 100% \ **Exp:** $178 (Low) \ **Poverty:** 12% \ **Special Education:** $12,000 \ **Open-Close:** 08/17 - 05/19 \ **DTBP:** $174 (High)

Terry Milt ....1 Dolores McGehee 4*
Jessica Stout ....59 Eddie Vaughn 67
Shelly McDowell 288

Public Schs..Principal	Grd	Prgm	Enr/#Cls	SN	
McClellan Elem Sch
9475 N Il Highway 148, Mount Vernon 62864
Tammy Beckham	K-8		45
7	55%	618/244-8072

• **Mt Vernon City Sch Dist 80** PID: 00296766 618/244-8080
2710 North St, Mount Vernon 62864 Fax 618/244-8082

Schools: 4 \ **Teachers:** 108 \ **Students:** 1,700 \ **Special Ed Students:** 325 \ **LEP Students:** 42 \ **Ethnic:** Asian 2%, African American 30%, Hispanic 4%, Caucasian 63% \ **Exp:** $255 (Med) \ **Poverty:** 33% \ **Title I:** $1,113,350 \ **Special Education:** $794,000 \ **Open-Close:** 08/19 - 05/26 \ **DTBP:** $155 (High)

Aletta Lawrence ....1 Amy Spotanski 2
John Burkett ....3 Sarah Kluck 4
Scott Williams ....6 Shannon Myers 7
Mary McGreer ....9,57,69,270,280,285,288 Lori Given 11,296,298*
Ryan Swan ....15,752 Alicia Snyder 59
Jodi Cooper ....59 Matt Reynolds 67
Terry Knowles 73,84,295

Public Schs..Principal	Grd	Prgm	Enr/#Cls	SN	
Dr Andy Hall Early Chldhd Ctr
301 S 17th St, Mount Vernon 62864
Lori Given	PK-PK	T	320
12	94%	618/244-8087
Fax 618/244-8088
Dr Nick Osborne Primary Center
401 N 30th St, Mount Vernon 62864
Mr Alvis	K-3	T	700
30	84%	618/244-8068
Fax 618/244-8075
J L Buford Intermediate Ed Ctr
623 S 34th St, Mount Vernon 62864
Mr Alvis	4-5	T	301
22	86%	618/244-8064
Fax 618/244-8103
Zadok Casey Middle Sch
1829 Broadway St, Mount Vernon 62864
Mr McGreer	6-8	T	416
38	79%	618/244-8060
Fax 618/244-8104

• **Mt Vernon Twp HS District 201** PID: 00296845 618/244-3700
11101 N Wells Bypass Rd, Mount Vernon 62864 Fax 618/246-1762

Schools: 1 \ **Teachers:** 80 \ **Students:** 1,250 \ **Special Ed Students:** 209 \ **LEP Students:** 6 \ **College-Bound:** 58% \ **Ethnic:** Asian 1%, African American 13%, Hispanic 4%, Caucasian 81% \ **Exp:** $281 (Med) \ **Poverty:** 18% \ **Title I:** $489,549 \ **Special Education:** $1,030,000 \ **Open-Close:** 08/13 - 05/21 \ **DTBP:** $174 (High) \ 🇫 🇹

Melanie Andrews ....1 Taylor Evans 2,19
Brian Rightnowar ....3,17* Emily York 4
Abby Greg ....7 Sean Docherty 10,11,296,298*
Ann Garrett ....16,57,82* Julie Littlefair 18
Crystal Michels ....22* Kara Andrews 27
Lamanda Brookman ....57,83,275,286,294* Megan Clodi 60,77*
Matthew Flanigan .... 67 Michael Koehnke 69,79,88,91,288
Gina Williamson .... 73,76,84,98,286,295 Rowdy Fatheree 751

Public Schs..Principal	Grd	Prgm	Enr/#Cls	SN	
Mt Vernon High Sch
11101 N Wells Bypass Rd, Mount Vernon 62864
Rowdy Fatheree	9-12	ATV	1,250	56%	618/244-3700

• **Opdyke-Belle Rive Cmty CSSD 5** PID: 00296572 618/756-2492
19380 E 4th St, Opdyke 62872 Fax 618/756-2792

Schools: 1 \ **Teachers:** 14 \ **Students:** 140 \ **Special Ed Students:** 30 \ **Ethnic:** Asian 2%, Hispanic 2%, Caucasian 97% \ **Exp:** $540 (High) \ **Poverty:** 24% \ **Title I:** $124,793 \ **Special Education:** $68,000 \ **Open-Close:** 08/14 - 05/21 \ **DTBP:** $162 (High) \ 🇹

Mark Miller ....1,11,73,83 Elizabeth Bernard 2
Jason Moore ....6* Anna Jukes 12,76*
Janet Dickey ....59* Henry Leeck 67

Public Schs..Principal	Grd	Prgm	Enr/#Cls	SN	
Opdyke Attendance Center
19380 E 4th St, Opdyke 62872	PK-8	T	140
4	61%	618/756-2492

• **Rome Cmty Cons Sch Dist 2** PID: 00296895 618/266-7214
233 W South St, Dix 62830 Fax 618/266-7902

Schools: 1 \ **Teachers:** 25 \ **Students:** 450 \ **Special Ed Students:** 67 \ **Ethnic:** Asian 1%, African American 1%, Hispanic 1%, Caucasian 97% \ **Exp:** $156 (Low) \ **Poverty:** 12% \ **Title I:** $59,730 \ **Special Education:** $103,000 \ **Open-Close:** 08/17 - 05/26

Steven Phillips ....1,11,73,83 Debbie Simmons 16*
Michelle Taylor ....55* Amanda McKee 67

---

79 Student Personnel	91 Safety/Security	275 Response To Intervention	298 Grant Writer/Ptnrships	**School Programs**	**Social Media**
80 Driver Ed/Safety	92 Magnet School	277 Remedial Math K-12	750 Chief Innovation Officer	A = Alternative Program	
81 Gifted/Talented	93 Parental Involvement	280 Literacy Coach	751 Chief of Staff	G = Adult Classes	🇫 = Facebook
82 Video Services	95 Tech Prep Program	285 STEM	752 Social Emotional Learning	M = Magnet Program	
83 Substance Abuse Prev	97 Chief Information Officer	286 Digital Learning		T = Title I Schoolwide	🇹 = Twitter
84 Erate	98 Chief Technology Officer	288 Common Core Standards	**Other School Types**	V = Career & Tech Ed Programs	
85 AIDS Education	270 Accountability	294 Accountability	Ⓐ = Alternative School		
88 Alternative/At Risk	271 Migrant Education	295 Network System	Ⓒ = Charter School	New Schools are shaded	
89 Multi-Cultural Curriculum	273 Teacher Mentor	296 Title II Programs	Ⓜ = Magnet School	New Superintendents and Principals are bold	
90 Social Work	274 Before/After Sch	297 Webmaster	Ⓨ = Year-Round School	Personnel with email addresses are underscored	**IL—123**

Jefferson County
Market Data Retrieval

Public Schs..Principal	Grd	Prgm	Enr/#Cls	SN	
Rome Elem Sch 233 W South St, Dix 62830 Sarah Mellott	PK-8	T	450 20	46%	618/266-7214

● **Spring Garden Cmty CSD 178** PID: 00296649 — 618/244-8070 — Fax 618/244-8071
14975 E Bakerville Rd, Mount Vernon 62864

Schools: 2 \ **Teachers:** 17 \ **Students:** 249 \ **Special Ed Students:** 45 \ **Ethnic:** African American 1%, Hispanic 1%, Caucasian 98% \ **Exp:** $87 (Low) \ **Poverty:** 23% \ **Title I:** $112,790 \ **Special Education:** $84,000 \ **Open-Close:** 08/13 - 05/27 \ **DTBP:** $197 (High)

Tammy Beckham 1,11
Traven Watts 67
Tommi Jo Ryan 6

Public Schs..Principal	Grd	Prgm	Enr/#Cls	SN	
Spring Garden Elem Sch 14975 E Bakerville Rd, Mount Vernon 62864 Tammy Beckham	K-4	T	140 12	52%	618/244-8070
Spring Garden Middle Sch 511 S Elm St, Ina 62846 Tommi Ryan	5-8	T	109	100%	618/437-5361 Fax 618/437-5333

● **Summersville Sch Dist 79** PID: 00296912 — 618/244-8079 — Fax 618/244-8078
1118 Fairfield Rd, Mount Vernon 62864

Schools: 1 \ **Teachers:** 20 \ **Students:** 245 \ **Special Ed Students:** 38 \ **Ethnic:** Asian 1%, African American 2%, Hispanic 1%, Caucasian 95% \ **Exp:** $300 (High) \ **Poverty:** 18% \ **Title I:** $73,829 \ **Special Education:** $73,000 \ **Open-Close:** 08/13 - 05/28 \ **DTBP:** $181 (High) \

Michael DeNault 1
Rick Mitchell 3*
Monica Maxey 11,59,69,88,275*
Vicki Penrod 2
Amy Johnson 6*
Jay Tate 67

Public Schs..Principal	Grd	Prgm	Enr/#Cls	SN	
Summersville Grade Sch 1118 Fairfield Rd, Mount Vernon 62864 Mike DeNault	PK-8	T	245 16	46%	618/244-8079

● **Waltonville Cmty Unit SD 1** PID: 00296936 — 618/279-7211 — Fax 618/279-3291
804 W Knob St, Waltonville 62894

Schools: 2 \ **Teachers:** 30 \ **Students:** 325 \ **Special Ed Students:** 63 \ **College-Bound:** 44% \ **Ethnic:** African American 1%, Caucasian 98% \ **Exp:** $310 (High) \ **Poverty:** 14% \ **Title I:** $84,298 \ **Special Education:** $130,000 \ **Open-Close:** 08/19 - 05/21 \ **DTBP:** $185 (High) \

Dr Melanie Brink 1
Pam Kash 2
Sandy Frick 67
Angie Owens 2
Colene Stanley 12
Trisha Stanford 69*

Public Schs..Principal	Grd	Prgm	Enr/#Cls	SN	
Waltonville Grade Sch 804 W Knob St, Waltonville 62894 **Andrew Dagner**	PK-8	T	240 25	44%	618/279-7221 Fax 618/279-7771
Waltonville High Sch 804 W Knob St, Waltonville 62894 Melanie Brink	9-12	V	111 17	32%	618/279-7211

● **Woodlawn Unit School Dist 209** PID: 00296986 — 618/735-2661 — Fax 618/735-2288
301 S Central St, Woodlawn 62898

Schools: 2 \ **Teachers:** 39 \ **Students:** 503 \ **Special Ed Students:** 62 \ **College-Bound:** 75% \ **Ethnic:** Hispanic 1%, Caucasian 99% \ **Exp:** $232 (Med) \ **Poverty:** 13% \ **Title I:** $98,919 \ **Special Education:** $141,000 \ **Open-Close:** 08/14 - 05/24

Eric Helbig 1
Robert Schwarzlose 3*
Jan Peterson 6
Beck Web 7
Lois Herzing 12*
Scott Owens 67
Rick Skibinski 3*
Sheryl Skibinski 4
Shane Witzel 6*
Mark Richardson 8
Leslie Witzel 38,69,83,88*
David Larkin 271*

Public Schs..Principal	Grd	Prgm	Enr/#Cls	SN	
Woodlawn Grade Sch 301 S Central St, Woodlawn 62898 Sandra Kabat	PK-8	T	328 20	43%	618/735-2661
Woodlawn High Sch 300 N Central St, Woodlawn 62898 Eric Helbig	9-12	V	175 20	33%	618/735-2631 Fax 618/735-2032

JEFFERSON CATHOLIC SCHOOLS

● **Diocese of Belleville Ed Off** PID: 00317671
Listing includes only schools located in this county. See District Index for location of Diocesan Offices.

Catholic Schs..Principal	Grd	Prgm	Enr/#Cls	SN	
St Mary Sch 1416 Main St, Mount Vernon 62864 Brett Heinzman	PK-8		140 9		618/242-5353 Fax 618/242-5365

JEFFERSON PRIVATE SCHOOLS

Private Schs..Principal	Grd	Prgm	Enr/#Cls	SN	
Coram Deo Classical Sch 1600 Salem Rd, Mount Vernon 62864 Candace Polk	K-8		38		618/244-9338
Mt Vernon Christian Sch 817 Woodland Dr, Mount Vernon 62864 Tim Reynolds	PK-12		30 7		618/244-5404 Fax 618/244-5726
Victory Christian Academy 1719 Broadway St, Mount Vernon 62864 Bonnie Payne	K-12		25 3		618/214-1666 Fax 618/242-3489

1	Superintendent	8	Curric/Instruct K-12	19	Chief Financial Officer	29	Family/Consumer Science	39	Social Studies K-12	49	English/Lang Arts Elem
2	Bus/Finance/Purchasing	9	Curric/Instruct Elem	20	Art K-12	30	Adult Education	40	Social Studies Elem	50	English/Lang Arts Sec
3	Buildings And Grounds	10	Curric/Instruct Sec	21	Art Elem	31	Career/Sch-to-Work K-12	41	Social Studies Sec	51	Reading K-12
4	Food Service	11	Federal Program	22	Art Sec	32	Career/Sch-to-Work Elem	42	Science K-12	52	Reading Elem
5	Transportation	12	Title I	23	Music K-12	33	Career/Sch-to-Work Sec	43	Science Elem	53	Reading Sec
6	Athletic	13	Title V	24	Music Elem	34	Early Childhood Ed	44	Science Sec	54	Remedial Reading K-12
7	Health Services	14	Asst Superintendent	25	Music Sec	35	Health/Phys Education	45	Math K-12	55	Remedial Reading Elem
		15	Instructional Media Svcs	26	Business Education	36	Guidance Services K-12	46	Math Elem	56	Remedial Reading Sec
		16	Chief Operations Officer	27	Career & Tech Ed	37	Guidance Services Elem	47	Math Sec	57	Bilingual/ELL
		17	Chief Academic Officer	28	Technology Education	38	Guidance Services Sec	48	English/Lang Arts K-12	58	Special Education K-12

59	Special Education Elem	69	Academic Assessment
60	Special Education Sec	70	Research/Development
61	Foreign/World Lang K-12	71	Public Information
62	Foreign/World Lang Elem	72	Summer School
63	Foreign/World Lang Sec	73	Instructional Tech
64	Religious Education K-12	74	Inservice Training
65	Religious Education Elem	75	Marketing/Distributive
66	Religious Education Sec	76	Info Systems
67	School Board President	77	Psychological Assess
68	Teacher Personnel	78	Affirmative Action

Illinois School Directory — Jo Daviess County

JERSEY COUNTY

JERSEY PUBLIC SCHOOLS

- **Jersey Cmty Sch Dist 100** PID: 00297021 — 618/498-5561
  100 Lincoln Ave Ste A, Jerseyville 62052 — Fax 618/498-5265

  Schools: 5 \ **Teachers:** 134 \ **Students:** 2,647 \ **Special Ed Students:** 391 \ **LEP Students:** 7 \ **College-Bound:** 68% \ **Ethnic:** Asian 1%, African American 1%, Hispanic 2%, Caucasian 97% \ **Exp:** $160 (Low) \ **Poverty:** 12% \ **Title I:** $585,223 \ **Special Education:** $1,257,000 \ **Open-Close:** 08/14 - 05/28 \ **DTBP:** $193 (High)

Brad Tuttle	1,11	Lisa Schuenke	2,68
Alan Churchman	3,5,91	Michelle Brown	12,298*
Keri Lakin	34,58	Greg Brown	67
Keith Norman	73,295,297	Chris Griffin	295
Rusty Lee	295		

Public Schs..Principal	Grd	Prgm	Enr/#Cls	SN	
Grafton Elem Sch 1200 Grafton Hills Dr, Grafton 62037 Michelle Brown	PK-4	T	190 8	44%	618/786-3388 Fax 618/786-2180
Jersey Community High Sch 801 N State St, Jerseyville 62052 Cory Breden	8-12		996 72	37%	618/498-5521 Fax 618/498-5332
Jersey Community Middle Sch 1101 S Liberty St, Jerseyville 62052 Jason Brunaugh	5-7	T	519 50	48%	618/498-5527 Fax 618/498-7079
Jerseyville East Elem Sch 201 N Giddings Ave, Jerseyville 62052 Kim Anderson	2-4	T	435 12	53%	618/498-3814 Fax 618/498-6805
Jerseyville West Elem Sch 1010 W Carpenter St, Jerseyville 62052 Kristie Hurley	PK-1	T	421 16	52%	618/984-4313 Fax 618/498-9870

JERSEY CATHOLIC SCHOOLS

- **Diocese of Springfield Ed Off** PID: 00319394
  Listing includes only schools located in this county. See District Index for location of Diocesan Offices.

Catholic Schs..Principal	Grd	Prgm	Enr/#Cls		
St Francis-Holy Ghost Sch 412 S State St, Jerseyville 62052 Dr Dennis Cramsey	PK-8		452 19		618/498-4823 Fax 618/498-3827

JERSEY REGIONAL CENTERS

- **Central Illinois Rural Rvs** PID: 04184402 — 618/498-5541
  201 W Exchange St, Jerseyville 62052 — Fax 618/498-5543

  Kerry Lorton 1

JO DAVIESS COUNTY

JO DAVIESS COUNTY SCHOOLS

County Schs..Principal	Grd	Prgm	Enr/#Cls	SN	
Jo Davies-Carroll Cte Academy 950 US Highway 20 W, Elizabeth 61028 Kris Hall	Voc	G	300 8		815/858-2203 Fax 815/858-2316

JO DAVIESS PUBLIC SCHOOLS

- **East Dubuque Unit SD 119** PID: 00297124 — 815/747-2111
  100 N School Rd, East Dubuque 61025 — Fax 815/747-3201

  Schools: 2 \ **Teachers:** 48 \ **Students:** 672 \ **Special Ed Students:** 95 \ **LEP Students:** 5 \ **College-Bound:** 67% \ **Ethnic:** African American 1%, Hispanic 3%, Caucasian 95% \ **Exp:** $262 (Med) \ **Poverty:** 8% \ **Title I:** $85,184 \ **Special Education:** $370,000 \ **Open-Close:** 08/21 - 05/28 \ **DTBP:** $173 (High)

Tj Potts	1,11	Lisa Barklow	2
Grover Priebe	3	Jeff Weydert	5
Deb Borley	7*	Wes Heiar	9,34
Darren Sirianni	10,27,270,271,273*	Sandy Luchterhand	11*
Glen Foote	67	Wendy Woolf	69,83*

Public Schs..Principal	Grd	Prgm	Enr/#Cls	SN	
East Dubuque Elem Sch 100 N School Rd, East Dubuque 61025 Wesley Heiar	PK-6		357 19	28%	815/747-3188 Fax 815/747-3827
East Dubuque Junior Senior HS 200 Parklane Dr, East Dubuque 61025 Darren Sirianni	7-12	V	315 20	20%	815/747-3188 Fax 815/747-3516

- **Galena Unit School Dist 120** PID: 00297174 — 815/777-3086
  1206 Franklin St, Galena 61036 — Fax 815/777-0303

  Schools: 3 \ **Teachers:** 66 \ **Students:** 830 \ **Special Ed Students:** 110 \ **LEP Students:** 63 \ **College-Bound:** 80% \ **Ethnic:** Asian 2%, African American 1%, Hispanic 15%, Caucasian 81% \ **Exp:** $193 (Low) \ **Poverty:** 9% \ **Title I:** $105,465 \ **Special Education:** $560,000 \ **Bilingual Education:** $10,000 \ **Open-Close:** 08/19 - 05/24

Tim Vincent	1,11	Karen Marsden	2
David Phillips	3	Jamie Schubert	4*
Brett Noble	6*	Jill Muehleip	9,12*
Ben Soat	10,274*	Beth Murphy	10,16,27,81*
Brooke Deppe	38,69	Jorden Rijpma	57
Heide O'Shea	58*	Tom Long	67
Rich Rehfeldt	73,84,98	Lisa Breitsprecker	270*

Public Schs..Principal	Grd	Prgm	Enr/#Cls	SN	
Galena High Sch 1206 Franklin St, Galena 61036 Beth Murphy	9-12	V	236 25	29%	815/777-0917 Fax 815/777-2089
Galena Middle Sch 1230 Franklin St, Galena 61036 Ben Soat	5-8		249 20	29%	815/777-2413 Fax 815/777-4259

---

79 Student Personnel	91 Safety/Security	275 Response To Intervention	298 Grant Writer/Ptnrships	**School Programs**	**Social Media**
80 Driver Ed/Safety	92 Magnet School	277 Remedial Math K-12	750 Chief Innovation Officer	A = Alternative Program	= Facebook
81 Gifted/Talented	93 Parental Involvement	280 Literacy Coach	751 Chief of Staff	G = Adult Classes	
82 Video Services	95 Tech Prep Program	285 STEM	752 Social Emotional Learning	M = Magnet Program	= Twitter
83 Substance Abuse Prev	97 Chief Infomation Officer	286 Digital Learning		T = Title I Schoolwide	
84 Erate	98 Chief Technology Officer	288 Common Core Standards	**Other School Types**	V = Career & Tech Ed Programs	
85 AIDS Education	270 Character Education	294 Accountability	Ⓐ = Alternative School		
88 Alternative/At Risk	271 Migrant Education	295 Network System	Ⓒ = Charter School	New Schools are shaded	
89 Multi-Cultural Curriculum	273 Teacher Mentor	296 Title II Programs	Ⓜ = Magnet School	New Superintendents and Principals are bold	
90 Social Work	274 Before/After Sch	297 Webmaster	Ⓨ = Year-Round School	Personnel with email addresses are underscored	

IL—125

Jo Daviess County

Galena Primary Sch K-4 305 38% 815/777-2200
219 Kelly Ln, Galena 61036 17 Fax 815/777-4842
Jill Muehleip

- **River Ridge Cmty Unit SD 210** PID: 00297150 815/858-9005
  4141 Il Route 84 S, Hanover 61041 Fax 815/858-9006

Schools: 3 \ **Teachers:** 45 \ **Students:** 500 \ **Special Ed Students:** 88 \ **LEP Students:** 3 \ **College-Bound:** 66% \ **Ethnic:** African American 1%, Hispanic 7%, Caucasian 91% \ **Exp:** $116 (Low) \ **Poverty:** 11% \ **Title I:** $75,719 \ **Special Education:** $375,000 \ **Open-Close:** 08/18 - 06/02 \ **DTBP:** $171 (High)

Bradley Albrecht 1,11
Teri Potter 4
Shean Albrecht 6*
Beau Buchs 8,11,57,58,88,275,285*
Brenda Potter 69,83*
Brian Wurster 285*
Mike Smallwood 3
Lloyd Haas 5
Lisa Haas 7
Allen Crist 67
Doug Nicholas 73,295
Michael Foltz 288*

Public Schs..Principal	Grd	Prgm	Enr/#Cls	SN		
River Ridge Elem Sch 4141 Il Route 84 S, Hanover 61041 Beau Buchs	PK-5		243 60		45%	815/858-9005
River Ridge High Sch 4141 Il Route 84 S, Hanover 61041 Michael Foltz	9-12	TV	147		39%	815/858-9005
River Ridge Middle Sch 4141 Il Route 84 S, Hanover 61041 Michael Foltz	6-8		120		35%	815/858-9005

- **Scales Mound Cmty Unit SD 211** PID: 00297241 815/845-2215
  210 Main St, Scales Mound 61075 Fax 815/845-2238

Schools: 3 \ **Teachers:** 25 \ **Students:** 265 \ **Special Ed Students:** 30 \ **LEP Students:** 3 \ **College-Bound:** 64% \ **Ethnic:** Caucasian 99% \ **Exp:** $322 (High) \ **Poverty:** 9% \ **Title I:** $29,537 \ **Special Education:** $111,000 \ **Open-Close:** 08/17 - 06/01

Dr William Caron 1,11
Jeff Williams 4*
Dr Matthew Wiederholt 8,58,288*
Hannah Wiegel 16*
Paul Homb 67
David Hoftender 3
Dave Wiegel 6*
Jennifer Raab 12*
Susan Winter 31,36,69,83,752

Public Schs..Principal	Grd	Prgm	Enr/#Cls	SN		
Scales Mound Elem Sch 210 Main St, Scales Mound 61075 Dr William Caron \ Dr Matthew Wiederholt	PK-5		129 7		27%	815/845-2215 Fax 815/584-5223
Scales Mound High Sch 210 Main St, Scales Mound 61075 Dr Matthew Wiederholt	9-12	V	69		30%	815/845-2215
Scales Mound Junior High Sch 210 Main St, Scales Mound 61075 Dr Matthew Wiederholt	6-8		60		33%	815/845-2215

- **Stockton Cmty Unit SD 206** PID: 00297265 815/947-3391
  540 N Rush St, Stockton 61085 Fax 815/947-2673

Schools: 3 \ **Teachers:** 43 \ **Students:** 603 \ **Special Ed Students:** 89 \ **College-Bound:** 78% \ **Ethnic:** Hispanic 1%, Caucasian 99% \ **Exp:** $239 (Med) \ **Poverty:** 12% \ **Title I:** $98,883 \ **Special Education:** $272,000 \ **Open-Close:** 08/14 - 05/14

Colleen Fox 1
Deanna Smith 3
Barbara Schultz 4*
Jesse Snyder 6*
Krystal Posey 58*
Gary Baglin 73
Douglas Broshous 5
Jeni Pearce 12*
Neill Cahill 67

Public Schs..Principal	Grd	Prgm	Enr/#Cls	SN		
Stockton Elem Sch 236 N Pearl St, Stockton 61085 Colleen Fox	PK-4		253 15		42%	815/947-3321 Fax 815/947-3055
Stockton High Sch 540 N Rush St, Stockton 61085 Casey Downey	9-12	V	176 17		39%	815/947-3323
Stockton Middle Sch 500 N Rush St Ste A, Stockton 61085 Brad Fox	5-8		174 14		42%	815/947-3702 Fax 815/947-2114

- **Warren Community Unit SD 205** PID: 00297306 815/745-2653
  311 S Water St, Warren 61087 Fax 815/745-9333

Schools: 2 \ **Teachers:** 35 \ **Students:** 400 \ **Special Ed Students:** 65 \ **College-Bound:** 90% \ **Ethnic:** Caucasian 100% \ **Exp:** $191 (Low) \ **Poverty:** 11% \ **Title I:** $99,861 \ **Special Education:** $184,000 \ **Open-Close:** 08/20 - 05/20 \ **DTBP:** $196 (High)

Shawn Teske 1
Tammy Goken 4*
Joel Wild 6*
Deedee Calow 12*
Kip Sabinson 67
Sarah Janecke 88*
Ron Vick 3*
Gary Roberts 5
Josh Knuth 8*
Sarah Harbach 16*
Jason Bennett 73,286,295*

Public Schs..Principal	Grd	Prgm	Enr/#Cls	SN		
Warren Elem Sch 311 S Water St, Warren 61087 Shawn Teske	PK-5		193 10		27%	815/745-2653
Warren Jr Sr High Sch 311 S Water St, Warren 61087 Josh Knuth	6-12	V	189 20		28%	815/745-2641

JO DAVIESS CATHOLIC SCHOOLS

- **Diocese of Rockford Ed Office** PID: 00328345
  Listing includes only schools located in this county. See District Index for location of Diocesan Offices.

Catholic Schs..Principal	Grd	Prgm	Enr/#Cls	SN	
St Mary's Sch 701 Il Route 35 N, East Dubuque 61025 Angela Jones	PK-8		51 9		815/747-3010 Fax 815/747-6188

JO DAVIESS REGIONAL CENTERS

- **Northwest Special Ed District** PID: 02182082 815/599-1947
  310 N West St, Elizabeth 61028 Fax 815/858-2195

Tracy Dahl 1
Rebecca Hatfield 68
Carissa Bradt 2

1	Superintendent	8	Curric/Instruct K-12	19	Chief Financial Officer	29	Family/Consumer Science	39	Social Studies K-12	49	English/Lang Arts Elem	59	Special Education Elem	69	Academic Assessment
2	Bus/Finance/Purchasing	9	Curric/Instruct Elem	20	Art K-12	30	Adult Education	40	Social Studies Elem	50	English/Lang Arts Sec	60	Special Education Sec	70	Research/Development
3	Buildings And Grounds	10	Curric/Instruct Sec	21	Art Elem	31	Career/Sch-to-Work K-12	41	Social Studies Sec	51	Reading K-12	61	Foreign/World Lang K-12	71	Public Information
4	Food Service	11	Federal Program	22	Art Sec	32	Career/Sch-to-Work Elem	42	Science K-12	52	Reading Elem	62	Foreign/World Lang Elem	72	Summer School
5	Transportation	12	Title I	23	Music K-12	33	Career/Sch-to-Work Sec	43	Science Elem	53	Reading Sec	63	Foreign/World Lang Sec	73	Instructional Tech
6	Athletic	13	Title V	24	Music Elem	34	Early Childhood Ed	44	Science Sec	54	Remedial Reading K-12	64	Religious Education K-12	74	Inservice Training
7	Health Services	15	Asst Superintendent	25	Music Sec	35	Health/Phys Education	45	Math K-12	55	Remedial Reading Elem	65	Religious Education Elem	75	Marketing/Distributive
		16	Instructional Media Svcs	26	Business Education	36	Guidance Services K-12	46	Math Elem	56	Remedial Reading Sec	66	Religious Education Sec	76	Info Systems
		17	Chief Operations Officer	27	Career & Tech Ed	37	Guidance Services Elem	47	Math Sec	57	Bilingual/ELL	67	School Board President	77	Psychological Assess
		18	Chief Academic Officer	28	Technology Education	38	Guidance Services Sec	48	English/Lang Arts K-12	58	Special Education K-12	68	Teacher Personnel	78	Affirmative Action

Illinois School Directory — Johnson County

JOHNSON COUNTY

JOHNSON PUBLIC SCHOOLS

• **Buncombe Cons School Dist 43** PID: 00297356   618/658-8830
164 Main St, Buncombe 62912

> **Schools:** 1 \ **Teachers:** 6 \ **Students:** 60 \ **Special Ed Students:** 11 \
> **Ethnic:** Caucasian 100% \ **Exp:** $558 (High) \ **Poverty:** 16% \ **Title I:** $27,517 \ **Special Education:** $23,000 \ **Open-Close:** 08/13 - 05/21 \ **DTBP:** $181 (High) \ f t

Vicki Tripp 1   Julie Krawczyk 2*
Robby Trigg 67

Public Schs..Principal	Grd	Prgm	Enr/#Cls	SN	
Buncombe Consolidated Sch 164 Main St, Buncombe 62912 Vicki Tripp	PK-8	T	60 5	63%	618/658-8830

• **Cypress School District 64** PID: 00297370   618/657-2525
4580 Mount Pisgah Rd, Cypress 62923   Fax 618/657-2570

> **Schools:** 1 \ **Teachers:** 10 \ **Students:** 120 \ **Special Ed Students:** 21 \
> **Ethnic:** Caucasian 100% \ **Exp:** $274 (Med) \ **Poverty:** 17% \ **Title I:** $32,710 \ **Special Education:** $26,000 \ **Open-Close:** 08/13 - 05/25

Kimberly Shoemaker 1,11,83   Cindy Gholson 58*
Angela Rudluff 67   Ted Beggs 296

Public Schs..Principal	Grd	Prgm	Enr/#Cls	SN	
Cypress Elem Sch 4580 Mount Pisgah Rd, Cypress 62923 Kimberly Shoemaker	PK-8		120 11	63%	618/657-2525

• **Goreville Cmty Unit SD 1** PID: 00297394   618/995-2142
201 S Ferne Clyffe Rd, Goreville 62939   Fax 618/995-1188

> **Schools:** 1 \ **Teachers:** 39 \ **Students:** 565 \ **Special Ed Students:** 69 \
> **College-Bound:** 61% \ **Ethnic:** Hispanic 2%, Caucasian 98% \ **Exp:** $231 (Med) \ **Poverty:** 10% \ **Title I:** $81,127 \ **Special Education:** $132,000 \ **Open-Close:** 08/13 - 05/28 \ **DTBP:** $171 (High) \ f

Dr Steve Webb 1   Laura Hood 2
Danny White ....3*   Joni Foster 4*
Denny Parrish 5   Todd Tripp 6*
Treca McConnell ....7*   Jeri Miller 8*
Allison Robison ....16,82*   Anna Craig 36,69,79*
Christina King ....58*   Steve Benard 67
Mike Helton 73

Public Schs..Principal	Grd	Prgm	Enr/#Cls	SN	
Goreville Sch 201 S Ferne Clyffe Rd, Goreville 62939 Jeri Miller \ Christina King	PK-12	V	565 50	38%	618/995-2142

• **New Simpson Hill Cons SD 32** PID: 00297423   618/658-8536
95 Tunnel Hill Rd, Tunnel Hill 62972   Fax 618/658-4130

> **Schools:** 1 \ **Teachers:** 15 \ **Students:** 200 \ **Special Ed Students:** 38 \
> **Ethnic:** Caucasian 100% \ **Exp:** $243 (Med) \ **Poverty:** 18% \ **Title I:** $91,575 \ **Special Education:** $54,000 \ **Open-Close:** 08/13 - 05/21 \ **DTBP:** $179 (High)

Joe Nighswander 1,84   Racheal Huckelberry 2
Candace Armstrong ....8,38*   Kay Walker 11,296,298*
Breanna Bain 16,82,286   Patty McGinnis 59*
Vince Hoffard 67   Kim Hogan 76*
Sara Goddard 83,90*

Public Schs..Principal	Grd	Prgm	Enr/#Cls	SN	
New Simpson Hill Sch 95 Tunnel Hill Rd, Tunnel Hill 62972 Candace Armstrong	PK-8	T	200 13	51%	618/658-8536

• **Vienna High School Dist 13-3** PID: 00297473   618/658-4461
601 N 1st St, Vienna 62995   Fax 618/658-9727

> **Schools:** 1 \ **Teachers:** 23 \ **Students:** 360 \ **Special Ed Students:** 50 \ **LEP Students:** 3 \ **College-Bound:** 80% \ **Ethnic:** Asian 1%, African American 1%, Hispanic 2%, Caucasian 96% \ **Exp:** $252 (Med) \ **Poverty:** 15% \ **Title I:** $117,476 \ **Special Education:** $91,000 \ **Open-Close:** 08/13 - 05/21 \ **DTBP:** $184 (High)

Joshua Stafford 1,11   Cythia Webb 2*
Roy West ....3*   David Hill 6*
Joshua Stafford ....16*   Kathy Anderson 57,298
Kara Hight ....60,275*   John Summers 67
Rhiannon Slife 69,83,88,273*

Public Schs..Principal	Grd	Prgm	Enr/#Cls	SN	
Vienna High Sch 601 N 1st St, Vienna 62995 John Giffin	9-12	T	360 30	49%	618/658-4461 Fax 618/658-2122

• **Vienna Public School Dist 55** PID: 00297459   618/658-8286
310 N 3rd St, Vienna 62995   Fax 618/658-9036

> **Schools:** 1 \ **Teachers:** 29 \ **Students:** 410 \ **Special Ed Students:** 57 \ **LEP Students:** 7 \ **Ethnic:** Hispanic 2%, Caucasian 98% \ **Exp:** $124 (Low) \ **Poverty:** 17% \ **Title I:** $110,563 \ **Special Education:** $90,000 \ **Open-Close:** 08/13 - 06/01 \ **DTBP:** $170 (High)

Greg Frehner 1,11,83   Sheri Robinson 2
Heath Holloman ....3,5*   Jody Stafford 4*
Adam Hanks ....6,275*   Allyssa Tonner 16,82*
Nathan Corbit ....21*   Joseph McMahan 57
Joseph McMahan ....57*   Anna Eldridge 58*
Sherie Smith 67   Lorylee Hensley 73*
Deborah Wiley 83,88

Public Schs..Principal	Grd	Prgm	Enr/#Cls	SN	
Vienna Elem Sch 310 N 3rd St, Vienna 62995 Adam Hanks	PK-8	T	410 26	59%	618/658-8286

---

79 Student Personnel	91 Safety/Security	275 Response To Intervention	296 Grant Writer/Ptnrships	**School Programs**
80 Driver Ed/Safety	92 Magnet School	277 Remedial Math K-12	750 Chief Innovation Officer	A = Alternative Program
81 Gifted/Talented	93 Parental Involvement	280 Literacy Coach	751 Chief of Staff	G = Adult Classes
82 Video Services	95 Tech Prep Program	285 STEM	752 Social Emotional Learning	M = Magnet Program
83 Substance Abuse Prev	97 Chief Information Officer	286 Digital Learning		T = Title I Schoolwide
84 Erate	98 Chief Technology Officer	288 Common Core Standards	**Other School Types**	V = Career & Tech Ed Programs
85 AIDS Education	270 Character Education	294 Accountability	Ⓐ = Alternative School	
88 Alternative/At Risk	271 Migrant Education	295 Network System	Ⓒ = Charter School	**Social Media**
89 Multi-Cultural Curriculum	273 Teacher Mentor	296 Title II Programs	Ⓜ = Magnet School	f = Facebook
90 Social Work	274 Before/After Sch	297 Webmaster	Ⓨ = Year-Round School	t = Twitter

New Schools are shaded
New Superintendents and Principals are bold
Personnel with email addresses are underscored

Kane County

Market Data Retrieval

KANE COUNTY

KANE COUNTY SCHOOLS

County Schs..Principal	Grd	Prgm	Enr/#Cls	SN	
Mades-Johnstone Center 1304 Ronzheimer Ave, Saint Charles 60174 Christopher Payton	Spec		90	49%	630/377-4858 Fax 331/228-4874

KANE PUBLIC SCHOOLS

● **Batavia Unit School Dist 101** PID: 00297837   630/937-8800
335 W Wilson St, Batavia 60510   Fax 630/937-8801

Schools: 8 \ **Teachers:** 363 \ **Students:** 5,518 \ **Special Ed Students:** 820 \ **LEP Students:** 241 \ **College-Bound:** 83% \ **Ethnic:** Asian 3%, African American 4%, Hispanic 11%, Caucasian 82% \ **Exp:** $319 (High) \ **Poverty:** 3% \ **Title I:** $246,175 \ **Special Education:** $4,309,000 \ **Bilingual Education:** $55,000 \ **Open-Close:** 08/12 - 05/20 \ **DTBP:** $188 (High) \

Dr Lisa Hichins 1
Carol Feltgen 2
Mark Anderson 2,5,91
Dr Brad Newkirk 8,11,18,57,69,273,288
Steve Perce 15,68,751
Cara Heidgen 38*
Josh Bulak 72*
Kyle Freise 295
Anton Inglese 2,16,19,76,95
Lindsay Jannotta 2
Robert Schmidt 3
Anne Paonessa 12*
Kari Ruh 36,58,79
Cathy Dremel 67
Don Seawall 73,76*

Public Schs..Principal	Grd	Prgm	Enr/#Cls	SN	
Alice Gustafson Elem Sch 905 Carlisle Rd, Batavia 60510 Tim McDermott	PK-5		544 20	14%	630/937-8000 Fax 630/937-8001
Batavia High Sch 1201 Main St, Batavia 60510 Joanne Smith	9-12	GV	1,942 85	17%	630/937-8600 Fax 630/937-8601
H C Storm Elem Sch 305 N Van Nortwick Ave, Batavia 60510 Chris Milka	K-5		392 21	26%	630/937-8200 Fax 630/937-8201
Hoover Wood Elem Sch 1640 Wagner Rd, Batavia 60510 Gina Greenwald	K-5		348 21	25%	630/937-8300 Fax 630/937-8301
J B Nelson Elem Sch 334 William Wood Ln, Batavia 60510 Nicole Prentiss	PK-5		403 27	18%	630/937-8400 Fax 630/937-8401
Louise White Elem Sch 800 N Prairie St, Batavia 60510 Kevin Skomer	PK-5		359 25	20%	630/937-8500 Fax 630/937-8501
McWayne Elem Sch 3501 Hapner Way, Batavia 60510 Jeff Modaff	K-5		316 21	8%	630/937-8100 Fax 630/937-8101
Rotolo Middle School-Batavia 1501 S Raddant Rd, Batavia 60510 Kelley Karnick	6-8		1,307 105	18%	630/937-8700 Fax 630/937-8701

● **Central Cmty Unit SD 301** PID: 00297904   847/464-6005
275 South St, Burlington 60109   Fax 847/464-6021

Schools: 7 \ **Teachers:** 271 \ **Students:** 4,500 \ **Special Ed Students:** 518 \ **LEP Students:** 316 \ **College-Bound:** 81% \ **Ethnic:** Asian 12%, African American 2%, Hispanic 17%, Caucasian 68% \ **Exp:** $471 (High) \ **Poverty:** 5% \ **Title I:** $319,434 \ **Special Education:** $1,255,000 \ **Bilingual Education:** $47,000 \ **Open-Close:** 08/31 - 06/03 \ **DTBP:** $178 (High)

Dr Todd Stirn 1
Dan Polowy 3
Shayne Birkmeier 9,69
Brian Tobin 16,73,82,84,286,295
Sofia Mills 57
Jeff Gorman 67
Daina Pflug 2
Pam Mirenda 4
Dr Esther Mongan 11,15,68,69,88,273,288
Michelle Vaughn 34,79
Mike Potsic 58,79

Public Schs..Principal	Grd	Prgm	Enr/#Cls	SN	
Central High Sch 44W625 Plato Rd, Burlington 60109 Chris Testone	9-12	V	1,178 30	14%	847/464-6030 Fax 847/464-6039
Central Middle Sch 44W303 Plato Rd, Burlington 60109 Carie Walter	8-8		328 34	15%	847/464-6000 Fax 847/464-0233
Country Trails Elem Sch 3701 Highland Woods Blvd, Elgin 60124 Graydon Engle	PK-5		652 26	11%	847/717-8000 Fax 847/717-8006
Howard B Thomas Grade Sch 44W575 Plato Rd, Burlington 60109 Jeff Gerard	PK-5		600 21	12%	847/464-6008 Fax 847/464-6022
Lily Lake Grade Sch 5N720 Il Route 47, Maple Park 60151 Rebecca Jurs	PK-5		229 12	14%	847/464-6011 Fax 630/387-7912
Prairie Knolls Middle Sch 225 Nesler Rd, Elgin 60124 Matthew Haug	6-7		642	12%	847/717-8100 Fax 847/717-8105
Prairie View Grade Sch 10N630 Nesler Rd, Elgin 60124 Jill Schreiber	PK-5		660 22	8%	847/464-6014 Fax 847/464-6024

● **Community Unit School Dist 303** PID: 00298740   331/228-2000
201 S 7th St, Saint Charles 60174   Fax 331/228-2001

Schools: 16 \ **Teachers:** 814 \ **Students:** 12,262 \ **Special Ed Students:** 1,579 \ **LEP Students:** 677 \ **College-Bound:** 55% \ **Ethnic:** Asian 7%, African American 1%, Hispanic 13%, Caucasian 78% \ **Exp:** $386 (High) \ **Poverty:** 3% \ **Title I:** $476,295 \ **Special Education:** $7,225,000 \ **Bilingual Education:** $135,000 \ **Open-Close:** 08/19 - 05/28 \ **DTBP:** $207 (High)

Dr Jason Pearson 1
John Baird 3,4,5,15,91
Dr Cindy Ruesch 7,57,68,79,81,93
Jan Geier 9,15,34
Dr Denise Herrmann 15,18,74,294
Dr Melissa Byrne 27,36
Laurel Bergren 68
Carol Smith 71
Pamela Jensen 74
Mark Moore 2,10,15,68
Terry Primdahl 5
Dr Christine Warren 8
Patti Palagi 11,36,58,77,88,275,752
Seth Chapman 15,19
Nick Manheim 67
David Chiszar 69,294
Matt Smith 73,76,295

Public Schs..Principal	Grd	Prgm	Enr/#Cls	SN	
Anderson Elem Sch 35W071 Villa Maria Rd, Saint Charles 60174 Nathan Jarot	K-5	T	424 26	29%	331/228-3300 Fax 331/228-3301
Bell-Graham Elem Sch 4N505 Fox Mill Blvd, Saint Charles 60175 Amy Klueppel	K-5		434 24	9%	331/228-2100 Fax 331/228-2101

1	Superintendent	8	Curric/Instruct K-12	19	Chief Financial Officer	29	Family/Consumer Science	39	Social Studies K-12	49	English/Lang Arts Elem	59	Special Education Elem	69	Academic Assessment
2	Bus/Finance/Purchasing	9	Curric/Instruct Elem	20	Art K-12	30	Adult Education	40	Social Studies Elem	50	English/Lang Arts Sec	60	Special Education Sec	70	Research/Development
3	Buildings And Grounds	10	Curric/Instruct Sec	21	Art Elem	31	Career/Sch-to-Work K-12	41	Social Studies Sec	51	Reading K-12	61	Foreign/World Lang K-12	71	Public Information
4	Food Service	11	Federal Program	22	Art Sec	32	Career/Sch-to-Work Elem	42	Science K-12	52	Reading Elem	62	Foreign/World Lang Elem	72	Summer School
5	Transportation	12	Title I	23	Music K-12	33	Career/Sch-to-Work Sec	43	Science Elem	53	Reading Sec	63	Foreign/World Lang Sec	73	Instructional Tech
6	Athletic	13	Title V	24	Music Elem	34	Early Childhood Ed	44	Science Sec	54	Remedial Reading K-12	64	Religious Education K-12	74	Inservice Training
7	Health Services	15	Asst Superintendent	25	Music Sec	35	Health/Phys Education	45	Math K-12	55	Remedial Reading Elem	65	Religious Education Elem	75	Marketing/Distributive
		16	Instructional Media Svcs	26	Business Education	36	Guidance Services K-12	46	Math Elem	56	Remedial Reading Sec	66	Religious Education Sec	76	Info Systems
		17	Chief Operations Officer	27	Career & Tech Ed	37	Guidance Services Elem	47	Math Sec	57	Bilingual/ELL	67	School Board President	77	Psychological Assess
		18	Chief Academic Officer	28	Technology Education	38	Guidance Services Sec	48	English/Lang Arts K-12	58	Special Education K-12	68	Teacher Personnel	78	Affirmative Action

Illinois School Directory — Kane County

School	Grd	Prgm	Enr/#Cls	SN	Phone
Corron Elem Sch 455 Thornwood Way, South Elgin 60177 Christine Balaskovits	PK-5		512	7%	331/228-6900 Fax 331/228-6903
Davis Primary Sch 1125 S 7th St, Saint Charles 60174 Denise Liechty	K-2	T	375 29	38%	331/228-2200 Fax 331/228-2201
Ferson Creek Elem Sch 38W160 Bolcum Rd, Saint Charles 60175 Kristina McKnight	PK-5		531 20	6%	331/228-2300 Fax 331/228-2301
Fox Ridge Sch 1905 E Tyler Rd, Saint Charles 60174 Jennifer Mursu	PK-PK		193 22	24%	331/228-2400 Fax 331/228-2401
Lincoln Elem Sch 211 S 6th Ave, Saint Charles 60174 Michelle Woodring	K-5		188 11	13%	331/228-2500 Fax 331/228-2501
Munhall Elem Sch 1400 S 13th Ave, Saint Charles 60174 Jarrod Buxton	K-5		476 25	17%	331/228-2600 Fax 331/228-2601
Norton Creek Elem Sch 2033 Smith Rd, West Chicago 60185 Anthony White	K-5		478 25	10%	331/228-2700 Fax 331/228-2701
Richmond Intermediate Sch 300 S 12th St, Saint Charles 60174 Lisa Bulak	3-5	T	410	40%	331/228-2800 Fax 331/228-2801
St Charles East High Sch 1020 Dunham Rd, Saint Charles 60174 James Richter	9-12	V	2,448 250	18%	331/228-4000 Fax 630/513-5751
St Charles North High Sch 255 Red Gate Rd, Saint Charles 60175 Audra Christenson	9-12	V	1,999 100	7%	331/228-4400 Fax 630/443-2769 f t
Thompson Middle Sch 705 W Main St, Saint Charles 60174 Steve Morrill	6-8	V	1,453 60	16%	331/228-3100 Fax 331/228-3101
Wasco Elem Sch 4N782 School St, Wasco 60183 Stephanie Brennan	K-5		404 21	7%	331/228-2900 Fax 331/228-2901
Wild Rose Elem Sch 36W730 Red Haw Ln, Saint Charles 60174 Theresa Solomon	K-5		478 22	6%	331/228-3000 Fax 331/228-3001
Wredling Middle Sch 1200 Dunham Rd, Saint Charles 60174 Tim Loversky	6-8	V	1,386 60	15%	331/228-3700 Fax 331/228-3701

• **East Aurora School Dist 131** PID: 00297497 630/299-5550
417 5th St, Aurora 60505 Fax 630/299-5500

Schools: 20 \ **Teachers:** 836 \ **Students:** 14,000 \
Special Ed Students: 1,921 \ **LEP Students:** 5,506 \ **College-Bound:** 51%
\ **Ethnic:** Asian 1%, African American 8%, Hispanic 89%, Caucasian 3% \ **Exp:** $409 (High) \ **Poverty:** 17% \ **Title I:** $7,266,303 \
Special Education: $8,271,000 \ **Bilingual Education:** $829,000 \
Open-Close: 08/31 - 06/04 \ **DTBP:** $198 (High) \ f t

Name	Code	Name	Code
Dr Jennifer Norrell	1	Ann Williams	2,19
Jesse Vargas	3	Steve Megazzini	3,15
Lisa Dallacqua	8,74	Dr Lori Campbell	8,15
Paula Ek	9	Dr Glend Rosado	15,79
Kathleen Kogut	34*	Elizabeth Caparelli-Ruff	58,79
Annette Johnson	67	Caridad Garcia	68
Brittany Henning	69,294	Tom Jackson	71
Andrew Allen	73	Brandon Cochrane	79
Alfred Morales	93	Paula Cardona	295
Lisa Skelly	298		

Public Schs..Principal	Grd	Prgm	Enr/#Cls	SN	Phone
Benavides Steam Academy 250 E Indian Trl, Aurora 60505 Lisa Bulak	PK-K	T	420	67%	630/299-7560 Fax 630/299-7561
C F Simmons Middle Sch 1130 Sheffer Rd, Aurora 60505 Mechelle Patterson	6-8	TV	1,035	71%	630/299-4150 Fax 630/299-4151
C I Johnson Elem Sch 1934 Liberty St, Aurora 60502 Ines Sem	K-5	T	352 21	76%	630/299-5400 Fax 630/299-5401
C M Bardwell Elem Sch 550 S Lincoln Ave, Aurora 60505 Armando Rodriguez	PK-5	T	786 46	80%	630/299-5300 Fax 630/299-5302
East Aurora ECC 278 E Indian Trl, Aurora 60505 Susan Orozco	PK-PK	T	306	71%	630/299-7460 Fax 630/844-5236
ⓐ East Aurora Extension Center 1685 N Farnsworth Ave, Aurora 60505 Taveras Crump	6-12		70	81%	630/299-3084
East Aurora High Sch 500 Tomcat Ln, Aurora 60505 John Simpson	9-12	AGTV	3,972	64%	630/299-8000 Fax 630/299-8199
Edna M Rollins Elem Sch 950 Kane St, Aurora 60505 Laura Sandoval	K-5	T	443 21	81%	630/299-5480 Fax 630/299-5481
ⓐ Fred Rodgers Magnet Academy Ⓜ 157 N Root St, Aurora 60505 Lisa Skelly	3-8	T	441 8	56%	630/299-7175 Fax 630/978-9492
G N Dieterich Elem Sch 1141 Jackson St, Aurora 60505 Lauren Holland	PK-5	T	486 20	71%	630/299-8280 Fax 630/299-8281
Henry W Cowherd Middle Sch 441 N Farnsworth Ave, Aurora 60505 Jacqueline Gibson	6-8	TV	989 25	69%	630/299-5900 Fax 630/299-5901
John Gates Elem Sch 800 7th Ave, Aurora 60505 Stephanie Brennan	PK-5	T	503 30	70%	630/299-5600 Fax 630/299-5601
K D Waldo Middle Sch 56 Jackson St, Aurora 60505 Kelly Hills	6-8	TV	952 54	77%	630/299-8400 Fax 630/299-8401
L D Brady Elem Sch 600 Columbia St, Aurora 60505 Elizabeth Vivanco	K-5	T	336 22	82%	630/299-5425 Fax 630/299-5474
Mabel O'Donnell Elem Sch 1640 Reckinger Rd, Aurora 60505 Tonetta Davis	PK-5	T	406 19	75%	630/299-8300 Fax 630/299-8301
Nicholas A Hermes Elem Sch 1000 Jungles Ave, Aurora 60505 Timothy Cordina	PK-5	T	581 37	70%	630/299-8200 Fax 630/299-8201
Oak Park Elem Sch 1200 Front St, Aurora 60505 Annette McMahon	PK-5	T	484 30	69%	630/299-8250 Fax 630/299-8251
Olney C Allen Elem Sch 700 S Farnsworth Ave, Aurora 60505 Jalitza Martinez	PK-5	T	720 35	71%	630/299-5200 Fax 630/299-5201
Rose E Krug Elem Sch 240 Melrose Ave, Aurora 60505 Sheila Conrad	PK-5	T	293 20	75%	630/299-5280 Fax 630/299-5299
W S Beaupre Elem Sch 954 E Benton St, Aurora 60505 Amanda Clark	PK-5	T	178 17	74%	630/299-5390 Fax 630/299-5399

Code	Description	Code	Description	Code	Description
79	Student Personnel	91	Safety/Security	275	Response To Intervention
80	Driver Ed/Safety	92	Magnet School	277	Remedial Math K-12
81	Gifted/Talented	93	Parental Involvement	280	Literacy Coach
82	Video Services	95	Tech Prep Program	285	STEM
83	Substance Abuse Prev	97	Chief Infomation Officer	286	Digital Learning
84	Erate	98	Chief Technology Officer	288	Common Core Standards
85	AIDS Education	270	Accountability	294	Character Education
88	Alternative/At Risk	271	Migrant Education	295	Network System
89	Multi-Cultural Curriculum	273	Teacher Mentor	296	Title II Programs
90	Social Work	274	Before/After Sch	297	Webmaster

Code	Description
298	Grant Writer/Ptnrships
750	Chief Innovation Officer
751	Chief of Staff
752	Social Emotional Learning

Other School Types
ⓐ = Alternative School
Ⓒ = Charter School
Ⓜ = Magnet School
Ⓨ = Year-Round School

School Programs
A = Alternative Program
G = Adult Classes
M = Magnet Program
T = Title I Schoolwide
V = Career & Tech Ed Programs

Social Media
f = Facebook
t = Twitter

New Schools are shaded
New Superintendents and Principals are bold
Personnel with email addresses are underscored

Kane County

Market Data Retrieval

- **Elgin School District U-46** PID: 00298154 847/888-5000
  355 E Chicago St, Elgin 60120 Fax 847/608-4173

  Schools: 58 \ **Teachers:** 2,206 \ **Students:** 38,000 \
  Special Ed Students: 5,538 \ **LEP Students:** 12,235 \ **College-Bound:** 67%
  \ **Ethnic:** Asian 9%, African American 6%, Hispanic 57%, Native American:
  1%, Caucasian 27% \ **Exp:** $268 (Med) \ **Poverty:** 10% \ **Title I:** $9,030,799
  \ **Special Education:** $22,711,000 \ **Bilingual Education:** $2,445,000 \
  Open-Close: 08/24 - 06/02 \ **DTBP:** $257 (High) \

Tony Sanders	1	Bruce Phelps	2
Justin Farrell	2	Karan Bhatia	2
Bill Meyer	3	Dr Jeff King	3,15
Joseph Creadon	3	Josh Beu	3
Marcus LaPointe	3	Patricia Waldau	3
Shaun Terranova	3	Elena Hildreth	4
Jeffrey Prowell	5	Paul Pennington	6
Jeffrey Judge	7*	Dr Josh Carpenter	8,15
Dr Trisha Shrode	8,73	Steven Burger	9,15,78
Dr Ushma Shah	9,15,78	Lela Majstorovic	10,15,78
Marci Short	12,296	Ann Chan	15,68
Melanie Meidel	15	Laura Macias	16,73,76,82,295
Jaimie Abney-Giraldo	20,23,74*	Tracey Stewart	23,27
Peggy Ondera	34,274	Tracey Jakaitis	35
Jacob Vandemoortel	39,61	Deb McMullen	42
Amy Ingente	45	Dr Annette Acevedo	57
Mario Pestana	57	Sylvia Rodriguez	57
Dr Latrece Satterwhite	58,79	Sue Kerr	67
Beth Berg	68	Laura Hill	69,294
Mary Fergus	71	April Wells	81
Richard Ramos	84	Randal Ellison	88
John Heiderscheidt	91	Karla Jimenez	93
Judy Havemann	273	Celia Banks	280
Kathy Fitzpatrick	298		

Public Schs..Principal	Grd	Prgm	Enr/#Cls	SN		
Abbott Middle Sch 949 Van St, Elgin 60123 **Christine Zugel**	7-8	TV	690 30	79%	847/888-5160 Fax 847/608-2740	
Bartlett Elem Sch 111 E North Ave, Bartlett 60103 **John Signatur**	K-6		503 28	30%	630/213-5545 Fax 630/213-5544	
Bartlett High Sch 701 W Schick Rd, Bartlett 60103 Mike Demovsky	9-12	AV	2,417 120	38%	630/372-4700 Fax 630/372-4682	
Canton Middle Sch 1100 Sunset Cir, Streamwood 60107 Jeff Smith	7-8	TV	494 80	52%	630/213-5525 Fax 630/213-5709	
Centennial Elem Sch 234 E Stearns Rd, Bartlett 60103 Sarah Rabe	K-6		452 20	20%	630/213-5632 Fax 630/213-5630	
Central School Programs 355 E Chicago St, Elgin 60120 Tracy Morton	Spec		98 12	82%	847/888-5340 Fax 847/608-2783	
Century Oaks Elem Sch 1235 Braeburn Dr, Elgin 60123 Andrea Erickson	K-6	T	526 20	78%	847/888-5181 Fax 847/608-2741	
ⓨ Channing Elem Sch 63 S Channing St, Elgin 60120 Josefina Melendez	K-6	MT	437 24	89%	847/888-5185 Fax 847/888-7016	
Clinton Elem Sch 770 Mill St, South Elgin 60177 **Jonathon Miquelon**	K-6	T	454 20	40%	847/888-7045 Fax 847/608-2742	
Coleman Elem Sch 1220 Dundee Ave, Elgin 60120 **Brian Stark**	K-6	T	676 32	81%	847/888-5190 Fax 847/608-2743	
Creekside Elem Sch 655 N Airlite St, Elgin 60123 **Joel Pollack**	K-6	T	555 28	67%	847/289-6270 Fax 847/289-6040	
Ⓐ Dream Academy 46 S Gifford St, Elgin 60120 **Krystal Bush**	7-12	G	105 15		847/888-5000 Fax 847/888-5087	
Eastview Middle Sch 321 N Oak Ave, Bartlett 60103 Donald Donner	7-8		819 52	25%	630/213-5550 Fax 630/213-5563	
Elgin High Sch 1200 Maroon Dr, Elgin 60120 **Krystal Thomas**	9-12	AGTV	2,593 100	75%	847/888-5100 Fax 847/888-6997	
© Elgin Math and Science Academy 1600 Dundee Ave, Elgin 60120 Lezlie Fuhr	K-3	T	200	4%	630/883-5013	
Ellis Middle Sch 225 S Liberty St, Elgin 60120 Yvette Collins	7-8	TV	718 34	87%	847/888-5151 Fax 847/289-6610	
Fox Meadow Elem Sch 1275 Jenna Dr, South Elgin 60177 **Jason Gold**	K-6		550 25	36%	847/888-7182 Fax 847/888-7194	
ⓨ Garfield Elem Sch 420 May St, Elgin 60120 Kyle Bunker	K-6	MT	299 40	91%	847/888-5192 Fax 847/608-2745	
Glenbrook Elem Sch 315 Garden Cir, Streamwood 60107 Cheryl Deroo	K-6	T	493 18	57%	630/213-5555 Fax 630/213-5548	
Hanover Countryside Elem Sch 6 S Bartlett Rd, Streamwood 60107 Harold Shepherd	K-6	T	380 18	53%	630/213-5560 Fax 630/213-6133	
Harriet Gifford Elem Sch 240 S Clifton Ave, Elgin 60123 Joseph Corcoran	K-6	T	418 22	84%	847/888-5195 Fax 847/608-2763	
Hawk Hollow Elem Sch 235 Jacaranda Dr, Bartlett 60103 Noelle DuPuis	K-6		365 20	30%	630/540-7676 Fax 630/372-3365	
Heritage Elem Sch 507 Arnold Ave, Streamwood 60107 Catherine Fletcher	K-6	T	447 20	77%	630/213-5565 Fax 630/213-5549	
Highland Elem Sch 190 N Melrose Ave, Elgin 60123 Steve Johnson	K-6	T	616 26	88%	847/888-5280 Fax 847/608-2746	
Hillcrest Elem Sch 80 N Airlite St, Elgin 60123 Teresa Winters	K-6	T	492 36	82%	847/888-5282 Fax 847/742-3297	
Hilltop Elem Sch 1855 Rohrssen Rd, Elgin 60120 Dr Kyle Vonschnase	K-6	T	598 28	54%	847/289-6655 Fax 847/888-7199	
Horizon Elem Sch 1701 Greenbrook Blvd, Hanover Park 60133 Dr Jennifer Schwartz	PK-6	T	575 30	48%	630/213-5570 Fax 630/213-5564	
Huff Elem Sch 801 Hastings St, Elgin 60120 Dr Angelica Ernst	PK-6	T	595 22	88%	847/888-5285 Fax 847/608-2747	
Illinois Park Early Lrng Ctr 1350 Wing St, Elgin 60123 Apryl Lowe	PK-K		600	55%	847/289-6041 Fax 847/888-5332	
Independence Early Lrng Ctr 200 E Taylor Ave, Bartlett 60103 Lisa Bergbreiter	PK-PK	G	316 14	52%	630/213-5629 Fax 630/213-5584	
Kenyon Woods Middle Sch 1515 Raymond St, South Elgin 60177 Lisa Olsen	7-8		968	36%	847/289-6685 Fax 847/628-6166	
Kimball Middle Sch 451 N McLean Blvd, Elgin 60123 Charlotte Coleman	7-8	TV	611 46	76%	847/888-5290 Fax 847/608-2749	
Larkin High Sch 1475 Larkin Ave, Elgin 60123 **Krystal Bush**	9-12	GTV	2,045 105	75%	847/888-5200 Fax 847/888-6996	

1	Superintendent	8	Curric/Instruct K-12	19	Chief Financial Officer	29	Family/Consumer Science	39	Social Studies K-12
2	Bus/Finance/Purchasing	9	Curric/Instruct Elem	20	Art K-12	30	Adult Education	40	Social Studies Elem
3	Buildings And Grounds	10	Curric/Instruct Sec	21	Art Elem	31	Career/Sch-to-Work K-12	41	Social Studies Sec
4	Food Service	11	Federal Program	22	Art Sec	32	Career/Sch-to-Work Elem	42	Science K-12
5	Transportation	12	Title I	23	Music K-12	33	Career/Sch-to-Work Sec	43	Science Elem
6	Athletic	13	Title V	24	Music Elem	34	Early Childhood Ed	44	Science Sec
7	Health Services	14	Instructional Media Svcs	25	Music Sec	35	Health/Phys Education	45	Math K-12
		15	Asst Superintendent	26	Business Education	36	Guidance Services K-12	46	Math Elem
		16	Instructional Media Svcs	27	Career & Tech Ed	37	Guidance Services Elem	47	Math Sec
		17	Chief Operations Officer	28	Technology Education	38	Guidance Services Sec	48	English/Lang Arts K-12
		18	Chief Academic Officer						

49	English/Lang Arts Elem	59	Special Education Elem	69	Academic Assessment
50	English/Lang Arts Sec	60	Special Education Sec	70	Research/Development
51	Reading K-12	61	Foreign/World Lang K-12	71	Public Information
52	Reading Elem	62	Foreign/World Lang Elem	72	Summer School
53	Reading Sec	63	Foreign/World Lang Sec	73	Instructional Tech
54	Remedial Reading K-12	64	Religious Education K-12	74	Inservice Training
55	Remedial Reading Elem	65	Religious Education Elem	75	Marketing/Distributive
56	Remedial Reading Sec	66	Religious Education Sec	76	Info Systems
57	Bilingual/ELL	67	School Board President	77	Psychological Assess
58	Special Education K-12	68	Teacher Personnel	78	Affirmative Action

Illinois School Directory — Kane County

School	Grd	Prgm	Enr/#Cls	%	Phone
Larsen Middle Sch 665 Dundee Ave, Elgin 60120 Gina Crespo	7-8	TV	634 55	75%	847/888-5250 Fax 847/888-5053
Laurel Hill Elem Sch 1750 Laurel Ave, Hanover Park 60133 Maria Lopez	K-6	T	491 24	84%	630/213-5580 Fax 630/213-5569 f
Liberty Elem Sch 1375 W Bartlett Rd, Bartlett 60103 Stephanie Sylvester	PK-6	T	620 24	39%	630/540-7680 Fax 630/540-7666
Lincoln Elem Sch 1650 Maureen Dr, Hoffman Est 60192 Abbie Eklund	PK-6	T	413 26	63%	847/289-6639 Fax 847/888-7195
Lords Park Elem Sch 323 Waverly Dr, Elgin 60120 Noe Velazquez	PK-6	T	668 29	86%	847/888-5360 Fax 847/608-2750
Lowrie Elem Sch 264 Oak St, Elgin 60123 **Tiffany Robinson**	K-6	T	394 18	88%	847/888-5260 Fax 847/608-2751
McKinley Elem Sch 258 Lovell St, Elgin 60120 Juan Lira	K-6	T	387 21	87%	847/888-5262 Fax 847/608-2752 f
Nature Ridge Elem Sch 1899 Westridge Blvd, Bartlett 60103 Cyndi Aleman	K-6	T	596 32	42%	630/372-4647 Fax 630/372-4654
Ⓨ O'Neal Elem Sch 510 Franklin Blvd, Elgin 60120 Marcie Marzullo	K-6	MT	545 24	88%	847/888-5266 Fax 847/608-2753
Oakhill Elem Sch 502 S Oltendorf Rd, Streamwood 60107 Laura Alegria	K-6	T	424 23	74%	630/213-5585 Fax 630/213-5573
Ontarioville Elem Sch 2100 Elm Ave, Hanover Park 60133 Dr Elizabeth Ma	PK-6	T	550 27	90%	630/213-5590 Fax 630/213-5574 f t
Otter Creek Elem Sch 2701 Hopps Rd, Elgin 60124 David Aleman	K-6	T	676 31	57%	847/888-6995 Fax 847/888-7607
Parkwood Elem Sch 2150 Laurel Ave, Hanover Park 60133 Ana Arroyo	K-6	T	375 20	88%	630/213-5595 Fax 630/213-5579
Prairieview Elem Sch 285 Mayflower Ln, Bartlett 60103 Paul Flatley	K-6	T	342 21	23%	630/213-5603 Fax 630/213-5588
Ridge Circle Elem Sch 420 Ridge Cir, Streamwood 60107 Janelle Raine	K-6	T	522 24	66%	630/213-5600 Fax 630/213-9407 f t
South Elgin High Sch 760 E Main St, South Elgin 60177 **Dr Kurt Johansen** \ **Brian Moran**	9-12		2,666	33%	847/289-3760 Fax 847/888-7014
Spring Trail Elem Sch 1384 Spring Valley Dr, Carol Stream 60188 Amy Kendryna	K-6	T	347 20	40%	630/213-6230 Fax 630/213-6236
Streamwood High Sch 701 W Schaumburg Rd, Streamwood 60107 **Dr Jennifer Vandeusen**	9-12	AGTV	1,937 87	68%	630/213-5500 Fax 630/483-5909
Sunnydale Elem Sch 716 Sunnydale Blvd, Streamwood 60107 Dr Maria Bhatia	K-6	T	383 20	74%	630/213-5610 Fax 630/213-5594
Sycamore Trails Elem Sch 1025 Sycamore Ln, Bartlett 60103 Marcia Martino	PK-6		692 23	20%	630/213-5641 Fax 630/213-5599
Tefft Middle Sch 1100 Shirley Ave, Streamwood 60107 Luis De Leon	7-8	TV	914	78%	630/213-5535 Fax 630/213-5646
Timber Trails Elem Sch 1675 McDonough Rd, Hoffman Est 60192 Dawn Paquin	K-6	T	467	51%	847/289-6640 Fax 847/888-7011
Washington Elem Sch 819 W Chicago St, Elgin 60123 Lori Brandes	K-6	T	399 20	87%	847/888-5270 Fax 847/608-2754
Wayne Elem Sch 5N443 School St, Wayne 60184 Adam Zurko	K-6	T	369 23	21%	630/736-7100 Fax 630/443-2877 f t
Willard Elem Sch 370 W Spring St, South Elgin 60177 Dustin Covarrubias	K-6	T	318 17	59%	847/888-5275 Fax 847/608-2755

● **Geneva CUSD 304** PID: 00298594   630/463-3000
227 N 4th St, Geneva 60134   Fax 630/463-3009

Schools: 10 \ **Teachers:** 402 \ **Students:** 5,808 \ **Special Ed Students:** 741 \ **LEP Students:** 106 \ **College-Bound:** 90% \ **Ethnic:** Asian 5%, African American 1%, Hispanic 9%, Caucasian 86% \ **Exp:** $139 (Low) \ **Poverty:** 3% \ **Title I:** $257,760 \ **Special Education:** $2,746,000 \ **Bilingual Education:** $40,000 \ **Open-Close:** 08/19 - 05/26 \ **DTBP:** $191 (High)

Dr Kent Mutchler 1
Todd Latham 2
Mary Dunmead 5
Dr Andrew Barrett ...8,11,15,31,69,74,288,296
Adam Law 15,68,273
Jill Marsh 42
Taylor Egan 67
Michael Wilkes 73,84,295,297
Jamie Benavides 79
Victoria Fladung 295
Dean Romano 2,15
Scott Ney 3
David Carli 6*
Shonette Sims 8
Jennifer Seaton 34
Matthew Johnson 58
Laura Sprague 71
Anne Giarrante 79,88
Ray Adkins 91

Public Schs..Principal	Grd	Prgm	Enr/#Cls	SN	Phone
Early Learning Center 0S350 Grengs Ln, Geneva 60134 Stephanie Martin	PK-PK		75		630/444-8700 Fax 630/444-8709
Fabyan Elem Sch Os 350 Grengs La, Geneva 60134 Lauri Haugen	PK-5		252	2%	630/444-8600 Fax 630/444-8609
Geneva High Sch 416 McKinley Ave, Geneva 60134 Thomas Rogers	9-12	GV	1,889 125	5%	630/463-3800 Fax 630/463-3809
Geneva Middle School North 1357 Viking Dr, Geneva 60134 **Brenna Westerhoff**	6-8		647	6%	630/463-3700 Fax 630/463-3709
Geneva Middle School South 1415 Viking Dr, Geneva 60134 Terry Bleau \ **Lawrence Bidlack**	6-8		656	5%	630/463-3600 Fax 630/463-3609
Harrison Street Elem Sch 201 N Harrison St, Geneva 60134 Brenda Westerhoff	K-5		404 30	16%	630/463-3300 Fax 630/463-3309
Heartland Elem Sch 3300 Heartland Dr, Geneva 60134 Kimberly Hornberg	K-5		407 23	4%	630/463-3200 Fax 630/463-3209
Mill Creek Elem Sch 0N900 Brundige Dr, Geneva 60134 George Petmezas	K-5		403 22	2%	630/463-3400 Fax 630/463-3409
Western Ave Elem Sch 1500 Western Ave, Geneva 60134 Ronald Zeman	K-5		350 26	3%	630/463-3500 Fax 630/463-3509 t
Williamsburg Elem Sch 1812 Williamsburg Ave, Geneva 60134 Dr Julie Dye	K-5		505 26	4%	630/463-3100 Fax 630/463-3109

79 Student Personnel	91 Safety/Security	275 Response To Intervention	298 Grant Writer/Ptnrships	School Programs	Social Media
80 Driver Ed/Safety	92 Magnet School	277 Remedial Math K-12	750 Chief Innovation Officer	A = Alternative Program	
81 Gifted/Talented	93 Parental Involvement	280 Literacy Coach	751 Chief of Staff	G = Adult Classes	f = Facebook
82 Video Services	95 Tech Prep Program	285 STEM	752 Social Emotional Learning	M = Magnet Program	
83 Substance Abuse Prev	97 Chief Infomation Officer	286 Digital Learning		T = Title I Schoolwide	t = Twitter
84 Erate	98 Chief Technology Officer	288 Common Core Standards	Other School Types	V = Career & Tech Ed Programs	
85 AIDS Education	270 Character Education	294 Accountability	Ⓐ = Alternative School		
88 Alternative/At Risk	271 Migrant Education	295 Network System	Ⓒ = Charter School	New Schools are shaded	
89 Multi-Cultural Curriculum	273 Teacher Mentor	296 Title II Programs	Ⓜ = Magnet School	New Superintendents and Principals are bold	
90 Social Work	274 Before/After Sch	297 Webmaster	Ⓨ = Year-Round School	Personnel with email addresses are underscored	

IL—131

Kane County

Market Data Retrieval

- **Kaneland Cmty Unit SD 302** PID: 00298661 630/365-5111
  47W326 Keslinger Rd, Maple Park 60151 Fax 630/365-8421

Schools: 7 \ **Teachers:** 296 \ **Students:** 4,560 \ **Special Ed Students:** 613 \ **LEP Students:** 73 \ **College-Bound:** 77% \ **Ethnic:** Asian 2%, African American 2%, Hispanic 11%, Caucasian 84% \ **Exp:** $148 (Low) \ **Poverty:** 3% \ **Title I:** $158,969 \ **Special Education:** $3,107,000 \ **Bilingual Education:** $13,000 \ **Open-Close:** 08/12 - 05/18 \ **DTBP:** $194 (High) \

Dr Todd Leden 1	Jennifer Stambaugh 2
Dr Julie-Ann Fuchs 2,15	Mark Payton 3,91
Karen Smith 5	Louis Garcia 5
Peter Goff 6*	Dr Sarah Mumm 9,11,57,69,275,298*
Mike Rice 10*	Sophia Mills 57*
Fran Eggleston 58	Laura Frankiewicz 58
Tressa Matuszewski 58	Shana Sparber 67
Christopher Adkins 68	Tim Wolf 73,76*
Megan Pilip 77*	Erin Shore 83*
Jennifer Houdek 297*	

Public Schs..Principal	Grd	Prgm	Enr/#Cls	SN	
Blackberry Creek Elem Sch 1122 Anderson Rd, Elburn 60119 Martne McCoy	PK-5		506 21	8%	630/365-1122 Fax 630/365-3905
Fox Valley Career Center 47W326 Keslinger Rd, Maple Park 60151 Rick Burchell	11-12		503 10		630/365-5113 Fax 630/365-9088
John Shields Elem Sch 85 S Main St, Sugar Grove 60554 Shelley Hueber	PK-5		493 34	13%	630/466-8500 Fax 630/466-5320
John Stewart Elem Sch 817 Prairie Valley St, Elburn 60119 Samantha Aversa	PK-5		426 30	19%	630/365-8170 Fax 630/365-0651
Kaneland Harter Middle Sch 1601 N Esker Dr, Sugar Grove 60554 Nathan Schmitt	6-8		1,100 32	15%	630/466-8400 Fax 630/466-1999
Kaneland Senior High Sch 47W326 Keslinger Rd, Maple Park 60151 Jill Maras	9-12		1,288 51	15%	630/365-5100
McDole Elem Sch 2901 Foxmoor Dr, Montgomery 60538 Jake Countryman	PK-5		466	14%	630/897-1961 Fax 630/897-3229

- **West Aurora School Dist 129** PID: 00297643 630/301-5000
  1877 W Downer Pl Ste 100, Aurora 60506 Fax 630/897-1319

Schools: 18 \ **Teachers:** 765 \ **Students:** 12,000 \ **Special Ed Students:** 1,763 \ **LEP Students:** 2,780 \ **College-Bound:** 67% \ **Ethnic:** Asian 3%, African American 12%, Hispanic 60%, Caucasian 25% \ **Exp:** $275 (Med) \ **Poverty:** 12% \ **Title I:** $3,257,069 \ **Special Education:** $8,950,000 \ **Bilingual Education:** $319,000 \ **Open-Close:** 08/24 - 05/27 \ **DTBP:** $1,971 (High) \

Dr Jeff Craig 1	Ryan Abrahamson 2
Suzanne Fatout 2,298	Angela Smith 3,4,15
Jeff Schiller 3	Lynn Head 5
Dr Brent Raby 8,11,15	Sarah Waddell 9,285
Dr Jamie Max 10	Mike Smith 15,68
Maria Lozano 57	Jennifer Herman 58
Lisa Rausch 58	Rachel Naleway 58
Robert Gonzalez 67	Liz Wendel 69
Anna Gonzales 71,93	Anthony Reiskis 73,295
Michelle Jones 73,286	Sharon Thierfelder 76,295
Marti Neahring 79,91,752	Jeff Drenthe 295
Robert Halverson 298	

Public Schs..Principal	Grd	Prgm	Enr/#Cls	SN	
Fearn Elem Sch 1600 Hawksley Ln, North Aurora 60542 Dave Russell	K-5		542 28	24%	630/301-5001 Fax 630/907-2472
Frank Hall Elem Sch 2001 Heather Dr, Aurora 60506 Zak Fitzenreider	PK-5	T	555 26	57%	630/301-5005 Fax 630/844-4617
Freeman Elem Sch 153 S Randall Rd, Aurora 60506 Crystal Dvorak	PK-5	T	566 28	43%	630/301-5002 Fax 630/844-4527
Gary D Jewel Middle Sch 1501 Waterford Rd, North Aurora 60542 Michael Smith	6-8	T	686 40	44%	630/301-5010 Fax 630/907-3161
Goodwin Elem Sch 18 Poplar Pl, North Aurora 60542 Jeff Hetrick	PK-5	T	367 24	38%	630/301-5003 Fax 630/844-6959
Greenman Elem Sch 729 W Galena Blvd, Aurora 60506 Kelly Papp	PK-5	T	589 30	69%	630/301-5004 Fax 630/844-4618
Herget Middle Sch 1550 Deerpath Rd, Aurora 60506 Cindy Larry	6-8	T	703 35	51%	630/301-5006 Fax 630/907-3146
Hill Elem Sch 724 Pennsylvania Ave, Aurora 60506 Elizabeth Smith	PK-5	T	623 27	70%	630/301-5007 Fax 630/897-4289
Hope D Wall Sch 449 New Indian Trail Ct, Aurora 60506 Dr Terry Collette	Spec		157 18	61%	630/301-5008 Fax 630/844-4534
Jefferson Middle Sch 1151 Plum St, Aurora 60506 Shawn Munos	6-8	TV	715	62%	630/301-5009 Fax 630/844-5711
McCleery Elem Sch 1002 W Illinois Ave, Aurora 60506 Daniel Ulrich	PK-5	T	592	66%	630/301-5012 Fax 630/844-9491
Nicholson Elem Sch 649 N Main St, Montgomery 60538 Jen Bernal	K-5	T	286 16	60%	630/301-5013 Fax 630/844-4616
Schneider Elem Sch 304 Banbury Rd, North Aurora 60542 Olivia Smith	K-5	T	423 23	49%	630/301-5014 Fax 630/264-0591
Smith Elem Sch 1332 Robinwood Dr, Aurora 60506 Dr Pete Clabough	PK-5	T	455 26	62%	630/301-5015 Fax 630/896-9442
ⓐ Success Academy 1870 W Galena Blvd, Aurora 60506 Elroy Phillips	6-12		60	58%	630/301-5000 Fax 630/907-1063
Todd Early Childhood Center 1870 W Galena Blvd, Aurora 60506 Laurie Klomhaus	PK-PK	T	400 11	50%	630/301-5016 Fax 630/844-4522
Washington Middle Sch 231 S Constitution Dr, Aurora 60506 Tom Davidson	6-8	TV	722 37	50%	630/301-5017 Fax 630/844-5712
West Aurora High Sch 1201 W New York St, Aurora 60506 Charles Hiscock	9-12	GTV	3,665 120	48%	630/301-5600 Fax 630/844-4505

KANE CATHOLIC SCHOOLS

- **Diocese of Rockford Ed Office** PID: 00328345
  Listing includes only schools located in this county. See District Index for location of Diocesan Offices.

1	Superintendent	8	Curric/Instruct K-12	19	Chief Financial Officer	29	Family/Consumer Science	39	Social Studies K-12	49	English/Lang Arts Elem	59	Special Education Elem	69	Academic Assessment
2	Bus/Finance/Purchasing	9	Curric/Instruct Elem	20	Art K-12	30	Adult Education	40	Social Studies Elem	50	English/Lang Arts Sec	60	Special Education Sec	70	Research/Development
3	Buildings And Grounds	10	Curric/Instruct Sec	21	Art Elem	31	Career/Sch-to-Work K-12	41	Social Studies Sec	51	Reading K-12	61	Foreign/World Lang K-12	71	Public Information
4	Food Service	11	Federal Program	22	Art Sec	32	Career/Sch-to-Work Elem	42	Science K-12	52	Reading Elem	62	Foreign/World Lang Elem	72	Summer School
5	Transportation	12	Title I	23	Music K-12	33	Career/Sch-to-Work Sec	43	Science Elem	53	Reading Sec	63	Foreign/World Lang Sec	73	Instructional Tech
6	Athletic	13	Title V	24	Music Elem	34	Early Childhood Ed	44	Science Sec	54	Remedial Reading K-12	64	Religious Education K-12	74	Inservice Training
7	Health Services	15	Asst Superintendent	25	Music Sec	35	Health/Phys Education	45	Math K-12	55	Remedial Reading Elem	65	Religious Education Elem	75	Marketing/Distributive
		16	Instructional Media Svcs	26	Business Education	36	Guidance Services K-12	46	Math Elem	56	Remedial Reading Sec	66	Religious Education Sec	76	Info Systems
		17	Chief Operations Officer	27	Career & Tech Ed	37	Guidance Services Elem	47	Math Sec	57	Bilingual/ELL	67	School Board President	77	Psychological Assess
		18	Chief Academic Officer	28	Technology Education	38	Guidance Services Sec	48	English/Lang Arts K-12	58	Special Education K-12	68	Teacher Personnel	78	Affirmative Action

Illinois School Directory — Kane County

Catholic Schs..Principal	Grd	Prgm	Enr/#Cls	SN	
Annunciation BVM Sch 1840 Church Rd, Aurora 60505 Jennifer Wardynski	PK-8		250 10		630/851-4300 Fax 630/851-4316
Aurora Central Catholic HS 1255 N Edgelawn Dr, Aurora 60506 F Etheredge	9-12		650 27		630/907-0095 Fax 630/907-1076
Holy Angels Sch 720 Kensington Pl, Aurora 60506 Tonya Forbes	PK-8		475 22		630/897-3613 Fax 630/897-8233
Holy Cross Catholic Sch 2300 Main St, Batavia 60510 Mike Puttin	PK-8		420		630/593-5290 Fax 630/593-5289
Pope St John Paul 11 Academy S 601 Talma St, Aurora 60505 Sr Ann Brummel	PK-8		114 10		630/851-4400 Fax 630/851-8220
Pope St John Paul II Academy N 706 High St, Aurora 60505 Sr Ann Brummel	PK-8		250 15		630/844-3781 Fax 630/844-3656
Rosary High Sch 901 N Edgelawn Dr, Aurora 60506 Anthony Wilkinson	9-12		330 20		630/896-0831 Fax 630/896-8372
St Catherine of Siena Sch 845 W Main St, West Dundee 60118 Colleen Cannon	PK-8		263 10		847/426-4808 Fax 847/426-0437
St Charles Borromeo Sch 288 E Jefferson Ave, Hampshire 60140 Maureen Jackson	PK-8		190 10		847/683-3450 Fax 847/683-3209
St Edward High Sch 335 Locust St, Elgin 60123 Brian Tekampe	9-12		420 27		847/741-7535 Fax 847/741-8658
St Joseph Sch 274 Division St, Elgin 60120 Peter Trumblay	PK-8		125 10		847/931-2804 Fax 847/931-2811
St Laurence Sch 572 Standish St, Elgin 60123 Manuel Cantu	PK-8		181 10		847/468-6100 Fax 847/468-6104
St Mary Sch 103 S Gifford St, Elgin 60120 Michael Neis	K-8		210 9		847/695-6609 Fax 847/695-6623
St Patrick Catholic Sch 787 Crane Rd, Saint Charles 60175 Lisa Brown	K-8		580 21		630/338-8100 Fax 630/338-8108
St Peter Sch 1881 Kaneville Rd, Geneva 60134 Becky Ward	PK-8		547 21		630/232-0476 Fax 630/208-5681
St Peter Sch 915 Sard Ave, Aurora 60506 Mary Elliott	PK-8		110 9		630/892-1283 Fax 630/892-4836
St Rita of Cascia Sch 770 Old Indian Trl, Aurora 60506 Elizabeth Faxon	PK-8		260 16		630/892-0200 Fax 630/892-4236
St Thomas More Sch 1625 W Highland Ave, Elgin 60123 Sonja Keane	PK-8		271 10		847/742-3959 Fax 847/931-1066

KANE PRIVATE SCHOOLS

Private Schs..Principal	Grd	Prgm	Enr/#Cls	SN	
Aurora Christian Elem Sch 2255 Sullivan Rd, Aurora 60506 Mayra Johnson	PK-5		273 15		630/892-1551 Fax 630/892-1692
Aurora Chrn Middle High Sch 2255 Sullivan Rd, Aurora 60506 Stacy Beebe	6-12		500		630/892-1551 Fax 630/892-1692
Bible Baptist Chrn Academy 1701 Papoose Rd, Carpentersvle 60110 Diane Jacoby	K-12	V	3 2		847/428-0870
Children's House Mont Sch 417 W Main St, West Dundee 60118 Donna Butcher	PK-3		60		847/426-3570
Core Academy 801 W Illinois Ave, Aurora 60506 Elizabeth Martinez	Spec		130 10		630/906-7900 Fax 630/906-7950
Covenant Christian Sch 10 N Edgelawn Dr, Aurora 60506 Phil Lundquist	PK-8		105 8		630/801-7955 Fax 630/801-7904
Da Vinci Academy 2600 Hopps Rd, Elgin 60124 Raquel Anderson	PK-8		130 9		847/841-7532 Fax 847/841-7546
Einstein Academy 747 Davis Rd, Elgin 60123 Cathryn Ilani	PK-12		130 12		847/697-3836 Fax 847/697-6085
Elgin Academy 350 Park St, Elgin 60120 Seth Hanford	PK-12		320 50		847/695-0300 Fax 847/695-5017
Fox Tech Center 801 W Illinois Ave, Aurora 60506 Jason Kudelka	Voc		90		630/906-7900 Fax 630/906-7950
Fox Valley Montessori Sch 850 N Commonwealth Ave, Aurora 60506 Lynor Johnson	PK-6		110 7		630/896-7557 Fax 630/896-8104
Griffin Christian Sch 16N562 Vista Ln, Dundee 60118 Tammy Zilinski	PK-12		21		847/428-5413 Fax 847/851-1975
Hamilton Academy 180 S 8th St, West Dundee 60118 Barbara Hamilton	Spec		23 4		847/695-9732 Fax 847/551-3464
Harvest Christian Academy 1000 N Randall Rd, Elgin 60123 Bob Young \ Judy Bethge	PK-12		700		847/214-3500 Fax 847/214-3501
Highland Christian Academy 2250 W Highland Ave, Elgin 60123 Larry Sauter	PK-8		90 11		847/741-5530 Fax 847/741-6397
Immanuel Lutheran Sch 5 S Van Buren St, East Dundee 60118 Sue Domeier	PK-8		250 10		847/428-1010 Fax 847/836-6217
Immanuel Lutheran Sch 950 Hart Rd, Batavia 60510 Donna Laughlin	PK-8		193 10		630/406-0157 Fax 630/879-7614
Institute of Islamic Ed 1048 Bluff City Blvd, Elgin 60120 Ubaid Saleem	1-12		60 7		847/695-4685 Fax 847/695-4806
Mooseheart Sch 255 W James J Davis Dr, Mooseheart 60539 Jeffrey Szymczak	PK-12	V	174 35		847/906-3646 Fax 630/906-3617
North Aurora SDA Elem Sch 950 Mooseheart Rd, North Aurora 60542 Marjaine Drayson	K-8		25 2		630/896-5188 Fax 630/896-5189
Ombudsman School-Dundee 665 Tollgate Rd Ste A, Elgin 60123 Nowell Herr	6-12		40 1		847/622-0923 Fax 847/695-1804
Resurrection Lutheran Sch 2567 W Sullivan Rd, Aurora 60506 Brad Essig	PK-8		60 5		630/907-1313 Fax 630/907-1008
St John's Lutheran Sch 109 N Spring St, Elgin 60120 Steve Moeller	PK-8		150 10		847/741-7633 Fax 847/741-7687
St Paul Lutheran Sch 85 S Constitution Dr, Aurora 60506 Diane Katz	PK-8		170 8		630/896-3250

79 Student Personnel
80 Driver Ed/Safety
81 Gifted/Talented
82 Video Services
83 Substance Abuse Prev
84 Erate
85 AIDS Education
88 Alternative/At Risk
89 Multi-Cultural Curriculum
90 Social Work
91 Safety/Security
92 Magnet School
93 Parental Involvement
95 Tech Prep Program
97 Chief Infomation Officer
98 Chief Technology Officer
270 Character Education
271 Migrant Education
273 Teacher Mentor
274 Before/After Sch
275 Response To Intervention
277 Remedial Math K-12
280 Literacy Coach
285 STEM
286 Digital Learning
288 Common Core Standards
294 Accountability
295 Network System
296 Title II Programs
297 Webmaster
298 Grant Writer/Ptnrships
750 Chief Innovation Officer
751 Chief of Staff
752 Social Emotional Learning

Other School Types
Ⓐ = Alternative School
Ⓒ = Charter School
Ⓜ = Magnet School
Ⓨ = Year-Round School

School Programs
A = Alternative Program
G = Adult Classes
M = Magnet Program
T = Title I Schoolwide
V = Career & Tech Ed Programs

Social Media
= Facebook
= Twitter

New Schools are shaded
New Superintendents and Principals are bold
Personnel with email addresses are underscored

IL—133

Kankakee County

Market Data Retrieval

Westminster Christian Sch	PK-12	500	847/695-0310
2700 W Highland Ave, Elgin 60124		30	Fax 847/695-0135
Debbie Layne \ Erik Schwartz			

KANE REGIONAL CENTERS

- **Mid-Valley Special Ed Co-op** PID: 02184066   331/228-4873
  1304 Ronzheimer Ave, Saint Charles 60174   Fax 331/228-6003

  Lisa Palese 1

- **Northern Kane Co Reg Voc Sys** PID: 04178075   847/888-5000
  355 E Chicago St, Elgin 60120   Fax 847/608-2778

  Carol DePue 1   Pam Harris 58

- **Regional Office of Ed Kane Co** PID: 02097906   630/232-5955
  28 N 1st St, Geneva 60134   Fax 630/208-5115

  Patricia Dal Santo 1   Meg Fetzer 2
  Deanna Oliver 15,68,88   Molly McQueeny 71
  Phil Morris 73,76,295   Katie Algrim 74
  Josh Axelsen 88

- **Valley Ed for Employment Sys** PID: 04182284   630/466-5736
  Rt 47 Waubonsee Dr- Room 161, Sugar Grove 60554   Fax 630/466-9621

  Cassie Blickem 1

KANKAKEE COUNTY

KANKAKEE COUNTY SCHOOLS

County Schs..Principal	Grd	Prgm	Enr/#Cls	SN	
ⓐ I-Kan Reg Alt Attendance Ctr	6-12		60	77%	815/933-4918
50 W Industrial Dr, Kankakee 60901			6		Fax 815/933-1742
Justine Wills					
Kankakee Area Career Center	Voc	G	850		815/939-4971
4083 N 1000W Rd, Bourbonnais 60914			16		Fax 815/939-7598
Timothy Guerin					
Kankakee Area Co-op Day Sch	Spec		9		815/422-4151
650 W Guertin St, Saint Anne 60964			3		Fax 815/939-7236
Debora Quain					

KANKAKEE PUBLIC SCHOOLS

- **Bourbonnais Elem Sch Dist 53** PID: 00298958   815/929-5100
  281 W John Casey Rd, Bourbonnais 60914   Fax 815/939-0481

  Schools: 5 \ Teachers: 153 \ Students: 2,400 \ Special Ed Students: 391
  \ LEP Students: 86 \ Ethnic: Asian 2%, African American 12%, Hispanic
  13%, Caucasian 73% \ Exp: $269 (Med) \ Poverty: 14% \ Title I: $575,516
  \ Special Education: $1,675,000 \ Bilingual Education: $15,000 \
  Open-Close: 08/19 - 05/26 \ DTBP: $189 (High)

  Dr Adam Ehrman 1   Dennis Crawford 2,3,4,84,91
  Jackie Hazzard 5   Anitra Crockett 7,13,37,59,79,90

  Dr James Duggan 9,57,285,286,288,298   Roger Hale 16,73,76,295,297*
  Paiyuan Banks 34   Michelle Brosseau 52
  Robert Rodewald 67

Public Schs..Principal	Grd	Prgm	Enr/#Cls	SN	
Alan B Shepard Elem Sch	PK-4	T	601	49%	815/929-4600
325 N Convent St, Bourbonnais 60914					Fax 815/935-7834
Shirley Padera					
Bourbonnais Upper Grade Center	7-8	T	511	42%	815/929-5200
200 W John Casey Rd, Bourbonnais 60914			30		Fax 815/935-7849
Shannon Swilley					
Liberty Intermediate Sch	5-6	T	537	43%	815/929-5000
1690 Career Center Rd, Bourbonnais 60914			23		Fax 815/929-2467
Bret Pignatiello					
Noel LeVasseur Elem Sch	1-4	T	320	34%	815/929-4500
601 W Bethel Dr, Bourbonnais 60914			17		Fax 815/935-7856
Mary Bicknell					
Shabbona Elem Sch	1-4	T	314	55%	815/929-4700
321 N Convent St, Bourbonnais 60914			14		Fax 815/935-7846
Jackie Tingley					

- **Bradley Elem School Dist 61** PID: 00298996   815/933-3371
  111 N Crosswell Ave, Bradley 60915   Fax 815/939-6601

  Schools: 3 \ Teachers: 103 \ Students: 1,500 \ Special Ed Students: 262
  \ LEP Students: 78 \ Ethnic: Asian 1%, African American 12%, Hispanic
  18%, Caucasian 68% \ Exp: $418 (High) \ Poverty: 21% \ Title I: $469,839
  \ Special Education: $1,244,000 \ Bilingual Education: $31,000 \
  Open-Close: 08/19 - 05/26 \ DTBP: $113 (High) \

  Scott Goselin 1   Nicole McCarty 2,11
  Matt Memenga 3   Tammie Glidewell 4
  Anna Kirchner .... 5*   Jennifer Vaughn 7
  Rebecca Selk 9,273,275,285,294,296,298   Dave Andriano 15
  Dorothy Hamrick .... 34*   Lindsey Coffey 57,59,88
  Terrie Golwitzer 67   Michael Bland 73,295,297*
  Elizabeth Middlebrook 77*

Public Schs..Principal	Grd	Prgm	Enr/#Cls	SN	
Bradley Central Middle Sch	6-8	T	442	61%	815/939-3564
260 N Wabash Ave, Bradley 60915			30		Fax 815/939-6603
Mark Kohl					
Bradley East Elem Sch	PK-2	T	529	47%	815/933-2233
610 Liberty St, Bradley 60915			24		Fax 815/933-3810
Anna Kirchner					
Bradley West Elem Sch	3-5	T	473	66%	815/933-2216
200 W State St, Bradley 60915			21		Fax 815/933-2071
Trisha Anderson					

- **Bradley-Bourbonnais CHSD 307** PID: 00299031   815/937 3707
  700 W North St, Bradley 60915   Fax 815/937-0156

  Schools: 1 \ Teachers: 117 \ Students: 2,100 \ Special Ed Students: 329
  \ LEP Students: 51 \ College-Bound: 63% \ Ethnic: Asian 2%, African
  American 11%, Hispanic 14%, Caucasian 73% \ Exp: $196 (Low) \
  Poverty: 11% \ Title I: $333,974 \ Special Education: $1,125,000 \
  Bilingual Education: $1,000 \ Open-Close: 08/19 - 05/27 \ DTBP: $96 (Med)

  Dr Scott Wakeley 1   Christopher Hammond 2
  Ryan Friedricks .... 3*   Kim Abrassart 4*
  Michael Stone 5   Mike Kohl 6
  Amy Hagenow .... 7*   Tiffany Kohl 8,11,69,288*
  Candace Wells .... 11,33,60,88,271,296*   Michael Dorsam 16,82*
  Karla Breitenbucher .... 26,75*   Kevin Peterson 27*
  Kate Lippoldt 38   Justin Caldwell 67
  Andrew Ekhoff 73   Scott Bennett 76

1 Superintendent	8 Curric/Instruct K-12	19 Chief Financial Officer	29 Family/Consumer Science	39 Social Studies K-12	49 English/Lang Arts Elem	59 Special Education Elem	69 Academic Assessment
2 Bus/Finance/Purchasing	9 Curric/Instruct Elem	20 Art K-12	30 Adult Education	40 Social Studies Elem	50 English/Lang Arts Sec	60 Special Education Sec	70 Research/Development
3 Buildings And Grounds	10 Curric/Instruct Sec	21 Art Elem	31 Career/Sch-to-Work K-12	41 Social Studies Sec	51 Reading K-12	61 Foreign/World Lang K-12	71 Public Information
4 Food Service	11 Federal Program	22 Art Sec	32 Career/Sch-to-Work Elem	42 Science K-12	52 Reading Elem	62 Foreign/World Lang Elem	72 Summer School
5 Transportation	12 Title I	23 Music K-12	33 Career/Sch-to-Work Sec	43 Science Elem	53 Reading Sec	63 Foreign/World Lang Sec	73 Instructional Tech
6 Athletic	13 Title V	24 Music Elem	34 Early Childhood Ed	44 Science Sec	54 Remedial Reading K-12	64 Religious Education K-12	74 Inservice Training
7 Health Services	15 Asst Superintendent	25 Music Sec	35 Health/Phys Education	45 Math K-12	55 Remedial Reading Elem	65 Religious Education Elem	75 Marketing/Distributive
	16 Instructional Media Svcs	26 Business Education	36 Guidance Services K-12	46 Math Elem	56 Remedial Reading Sec	66 Religious Education Sec	76 Info Systems
	17 Chief Operations Officer	27 Career & Tech Ed	37 Guidance Services Elem	47 Math Sec	57 Bilingual/ELL	67 School Board President	77 Psychological Assess
	18 Chief Academic Officer	28 Technology Education	38 Guidance Services Sec	48 English/Lang Arts K-12	58 Special Education K-12	68 Teacher Personnel	78 Affirmative Action

Illinois School Directory — Kankakee County

Evan Tingley .... 79 Bryan Smith 83*

Public Schs..Principal	Grd	Prgm	Enr/#Cls	SN	
Bradley-Bourbonnais High Sch 700 W North St, Bradley 60915 Dr Brian Wright	9-12	ATV	2,100 91	42%	815/937-3707

• **Grant Park Cmty Unit SD 6** PID: 00299067   815/465-6013
421 Esson Farm Rd, Grant Park 60940   Fax 815/465-2505

Schools: 3 \ **Teachers:** 37 \ **Students:** 475 \ **Special Ed Students:** 63 \ **College-Bound:** 68% \ **Ethnic:** Hispanic 5%, Caucasian 95% \ **Exp:** $175 (Low) \ **Poverty:** 9% \ **Title I:** $75,719 \ **Special Education:** $184,000 \ **Open-Close:** 08/19 - 05/26 \ **DTBP:** $181 (High)

Dr John Palan 1,11	Sue Anderson 2
Mike Ewold 3	Deb Stanley 4,16*
Tracy Planeta 5,31*	Rob Bailey 6
Nicole Fosley 36,69,83,85,88	Krystal Johnson 58,273
Dave Dickson 67	Andy Dillman 73

Public Schs..Principal	Grd	Prgm	Enr/#Cls	SN	
Grant Park Elem Sch 421 W Taylor St, Grant Park 60940 Tracy Planeta	PK-5		221 15	34%	815/465-2183 Fax 815/465-2381
Grant Park High Sch 421 Esson Farm Rd, Grant Park 60940 Matt Maxwell	9-12	AV	161 20	35%	815/465-2181
Grant Park Middle Sch 421 Esson Farm Rd, Grant Park 60940 Matt Maxwell	6-8		135 12		815/465-2184 Fax 815/465-2099

• **Herscher Cmty School Dist 2** PID: 00299108   815/426-2162
501 N Main St, Herscher 60941   Fax 815/426-2872

Schools: 4 \ **Teachers:** 115 \ **Students:** 1,650 \ **Special Ed Students:** 255 \ **LEP Students:** 14 \ **College-Bound:** 71% \ **Ethnic:** African American 1%, Hispanic 2%, Caucasian 97% \ **Exp:** $279 (Med) \ **Poverty:** 7% \ **Title I:** $186,593 \ **Special Education:** $1,009,000 \ **Open-Close:** 08/20 - 05/27

Dr Richard Decman 1	Larry Houberg 2,3*
Michelle Armstrong 5,16	Todd Schwarzkopf 6
Pete Falk 8,11,273,288,296,298	Shelly Parsons 34,58,88
Sally Sullivan 67	Ben Seeman 76
Jill Fulton 275	

Public Schs..Principal	Grd	Prgm	Enr/#Cls	SN	
Bonfield Grade Sch 522 E Smith St, Bonfield 60913 Molly Wepprecht	PK-1	T	296 4	25%	815/933-6995 Fax 815/936-4125
Herscher High Sch 501 N Main St, Herscher 60941 Brad Elliot	9-12		515 65	23%	815/426-2103 Fax 815/426-2957
Herscher Intermediate Sch 391 N Main St, Herscher 60941 Brett Miller	2-4	T	400 38	30%	815/426-2242 Fax 815/426-6862
Limestone Middle Sch 963 N 5000W Rd, Kankakee 60901 Michelle Chavers	5-8		501 45	33%	815/933-2243 Fax 815/936-4123

• **Kankakee School District 111** PID: 00299160   815/802-7730
240 Warren Ave, Kankakee 60901   Fax 815/936-8949

Schools: 11 \ **Teachers:** 316 \ **Students:** 5,200 \ **Special Ed Students:** 648 \ **LEP Students:** 684 \ **College-Bound:** 48% \ **Ethnic:** African American 48%, Hispanic 31%, Caucasian 20% \ **Exp:** $171 (Low) \ **Poverty:** 28% \ **Title I:** $3,003,898 \ **Special Education:** $3,198,000 \ **Bilingual Education:** $161,000 \ **Open-Close:** 08/19 - 05/28 \ **DTBP:** $248 (High)

Dr Genevra Walters 1	Robert Grossi 2,5,15,16,76,80,82
Rich Stanevicius 3	Dawn Botensten 4
Ronnie Wilcox 6*	Rossy Williams 7,35
Felice Hybert 8,11,18,83,286,288,296,298	Kathleen O'Connor 15*
Elizabeth Gibson 34	Barbara Wells 67
Lynn Zugenbuehler 68	Michelle Mullin 68
Daniel Dannenberg 73,95	Joel Margliano 76
Benjamin Williams 79	Corey Zych 295

Public Schs..Principal	Grd	Prgm	Enr/#Cls	SN	
Ⓐ Avis Huff Impact 369 N 5th Ave, Kankakee 60901 Leah Carter	K-12		50	85%	815/802-4400 Fax 815/933-9220
Edison Primary Sch 1991 E Maple St, Kankakee 60901 Cheryl O'Leary	K-3	T	236 14	90%	815/932-0621 Fax 815/936-4096
Kankakee High Sch 1200 W Jeffery St, Kankakee 60901 Shari Demitrowicz	9-12	TV	1,261 60	77%	815/933-0740 Fax 815/933-9149
Kankakee Junior High Sch 2250 E Crestwood St, Kankakee 60901 George Harris	7-8	TV	700 65	82%	815/933-0730 Fax 815/935-7272
Kennedy Middle Grade Sch 1550 W Calista St, Kankakee 60901 Cynthia Veronda	4-6	T	610 32	84%	815/933-0760 Fax 815/928-7390
King Middle Grade Sch 1440 E Court St, Kankakee 60901 Shemeka Fountain	4-6	T	540 25	85%	815/933-0750 Fax 815/933-4548
Mark Twain Primary Sch 2250 E Court St, Kankakee 60901 Ericka Garza	PK-3	T	262 16	90%	815/933-0722 Fax 815/936-4099
Ⓜ Montessori Magnet Sch-Lincoln 240 Warren Ave, Kankakee 60901 Chuck Hensley	K-8	T	455 12	74%	815/933-0709 Fax 815/933-0710
Proegler Sch 710 N Chicago Ave, Kankakee 60901 Jennifer Hering	PK-PK		349 14	98%	815/933-0719 Fax 815/936-3310
Steuben Elem Sch 520 S Wildwood Ave, Kankakee 60901 Anna Newsome	PK-3		272 18	96%	815/802-4600 Fax 815/936-4093
Taft Primary Sch 1155 W Hawkins St, Kankakee 60901 Terrence Lee	K-3	T	405 20	88%	815/932-0811 Fax 815/933-0684

• **Manteno Cmty Unit Sch Dist 5** PID: 00299316   815/928-7000
84 N Oak St, Manteno 60950   Fax 815/468-6439

Schools: 3 \ **Teachers:** 131 \ **Students:** 2,100 \ **Special Ed Students:** 350 \ **LEP Students:** 31 \ **College-Bound:** 65% \ **Ethnic:** Asian 1%, African American 2%, Hispanic 9%, Caucasian 88% \ **Exp:** $205 (Med) \ **Poverty:** 10% \ **Title I:** $308,284 \ **Special Education:** $1,332,000 \ **Open-Close:** 08/19 - 06/02 \ **DTBP:** $230 (High) \ 📘

Lisa Harrod 1	Jake Emerson 2
John Depoister 3,91*	Lynn Davis 4*
Ryan Diedrich 5	Kim Couch 7*

79	Student Personnel	91	Safety/Security	275	Response To Intervention	298	Grant Writer/Ptnrships
80	Driver Ed/Safety	92	Magnet School	277	Remedial Math K-12	750	Chief Innovation Officer
81	Gifted/Talented	93	Parental Involvement	280	Literacy Coach	751	Chief of Staff
82	Video Services	95	Tech Prep Program	285	STEM	752	Social Emotional Learning
83	Substance Abuse Prev	97	Chief Information Officer	286	Digital Learning		
84	Erate	98	Chief Technology Officer	288	Common Core Standards		
85	AIDS Education	270	Character Education	294	Accountability		
88	Alternative/At Risk	271	Migrant Education	295	Network System		
89	Multi-Cultural Curriculum	273	Teacher Mentor	296	Title II Programs		
90	Social Work	274	Before/After Sch	297	Webmaster		

School Programs
A = Alternative Program
G = Adult Classes
M = Magnet Program
T = Title I Schoolwide
V = Career & Tech Ed Programs

Other School Types
Ⓐ = Alternative School
Ⓒ = Charter School
Ⓜ = Magnet School
Ⓨ = Year-Round School

Social Media
📘 = Facebook
🐦 = Twitter

New Schools are shaded
New Superintendents and Principals are bold
Personnel with email addresses are underscored

IL–135

Kankakee County

Cathy Creek 8,11,69,275,285,288,296,298
Erin Ruff 58,79
Nancy Kaufman 68
Andy Furbee 79*
Jaime Finkelstein 8,69
Mark Stauffenberg 67
Tom Steele 73,295*

Public Schs..Principal	Grd	Prgm	Enr/#Cls	SN		
Manteno Elem Sch & ECC 555 W Cook St, Manteno 60950 Matthew Glenn	PK-4	T	739 22	34%	815/928-7200 Fax 815/468-3030	
Manteno High Sch 443 N Maple St, Manteno 60950 Roger Schnitzler	9-12		660 42	31%	815/928-7100 Fax 815/468-2344	
Manteno Middle Sch 250 N Poplar St, Manteno 60950 Kyle Flanigan	5-8		579 35	32%	815/928-7150 Fax 815/468-8082	

- **Momence Cmty Unit Sch Dist 1** PID: 00299366   815/472-3501
  400 N Pine St, Momence 60954   Fax 815/472-3516

Schools: 3 \ **Teachers:** 72 \ **Students:** 1,100 \ **Special Ed Students:** 154 \ **LEP Students:** 96 \ **College-Bound:** 53% \ **Ethnic:** African American 17%, Hispanic 28%, Caucasian 55% \ **Exp:** $164 (Low) \ **Poverty:** 16% \ **Title I:** $327,298 \ **Special Education:** $951,000 \ **Bilingual Education:** $39,000 \ **Open-Close:** 08/17 - 05/21 \ **DTBP:** $229 (High)

Shannon Anderson 1
Terry Spencer 3,91
Tedd Rounds 6*
Dolores Potemp 58,79
Sharadi Kweli 73
Mary Jones 2
Marie Chico 4*
Lashawn Stewart 8,11*
Sandra Illum 67

Public Schs..Principal	Grd	Prgm	Enr/#Cls	SN	
Je-Neir Elem Sch 1001 W 2nd St, Momence 60954 Lashawn Stewart	K-4	T	327 16	68%	815/472-6646 Fax 815/472-9822
Momence High Sch 101 N Franklin St, Momence 60954 Steven Graham	9-12	ATV	338 26	66%	815/472-6477 Fax 815/472-2055
Momence Junior High Sch 801 W 2nd St, Momence 60954 Jack Richards	5-8	T	450 23	62%	815/472-4184 Fax 815/472-3517

- **Pembroke Cmty Cons SD 259** PID: 00299419   815/944-5448
  4120 S Wheeler Road, Hopkins Park 60944   Fax 815/944-9214

Schools: 1 \ **Teachers:** 14 \ **Students:** 200 \ **Special Ed Students:** 21 \ **LEP Students:** 7 \ **Ethnic:** African American 78%, Hispanic 19%, Caucasian 4% \ **Exp:** $871 (High) \ **Poverty:** 37% \ **Title I:** $300,987 \ **Special Education:** $175,000 \ **Open-Close:** 08/12 - 05/25 \ **DTBP:** $186 (High)

Dr Marcus Alexander 1
Angela Robins 4*
Ira Smeed 67
Royal Pope 3
Kevin Johns 9,15

Public Schs..Principal	Grd	Prgm	Enr/#Cls	SN	
Lorenzo R Smith Sust Tech Acad 4120 S Wheeler Rd, Hopkins Park 60944 Fenecia Toney	PK-8	T	200 25	44%	815/944-5448

- **St Anne Cmty Cons Sch Dist 256** PID: 00299512   815/422-5022
  333 S Saint Louis Ave, Saint Anne 60964   Fax 815/422-5023

Schools: 1 \ **Teachers:** 23 \ **Students:** 351 \ **Special Ed Students:** 54 \ **LEP Students:** 3 \ **Ethnic:** African American 2%, Hispanic 26%, Caucasian 71% \ **Exp:** $232 (Med) \ **Poverty:** 14% \ **Title I:** $69,856 \ **Special Education:** $182,000 \ **Open-Close:** 08/17 - 05/26 \ **DTBP:** $157 (High)

Charlie Stegall 1,11
Betsy Statler 4*
Scott Strong 9,12,57,69,79,271,273*
Seneca Popovich 16
Jedd Beaupre 67
Heather Girodano 752
Lisa Stalnecker 2*
Erin Galloway 6*
Jay Fruenot 16,73,76,286,295
Kelly Hesselberth 34,88*
Heather Oosterhoff 83,270

Public Schs..Principal	Grd	Prgm	Enr/#Cls	SN	
St Anne Elem Sch 333 S Saint Louis Ave, Saint Anne 60964 Scott Strong	PK-8	T	351 18	59%	815/427-8153 Fax 815/427-8186

- **St Anne Cmty HSD 302** PID: 00299536   815/422-5022
  650 W Guertin St, Saint Anne 60964   Fax 815/422-5023

Schools: 1 \ **Teachers:** 19 \ **Students:** 210 \ **Special Ed Students:** 30 \ **LEP Students:** 5 \ **College-Bound:** 56% \ **Ethnic:** Asian 1%, African American 34%, Hispanic 26%, Caucasian 39% \ **Exp:** $418 (High) \ **Poverty:** 17% \ **Title I:** $76,631 \ **Special Education:** $137,000 \ **Open-Close:** 08/17 - 05/21 \ **DTBP:** $162 (High)

Charlie Stegal 1
Betsy Statler 4*
Ramie Kolitwenzew 11,69,273,275,286,296,298*
Eric Bertram 73*
Heather Giordano 752
Tom Sparenberg 3,91*
Kathryn Shutter 6,60,85*
....Bill Jennings 67
Heather Oosterhoff 83

Public Schs..Principal	Grd	Prgm	Enr/#Cls	SN	
St Anne Cmty High Sch 650 W Guertin St, Saint Anne 60964 Ramie Kolitwenzew	9-12	T	210 19	81%	815/427-8141

- **St George School District 258** PID: 00299550   815/933-1503
  5200 E Center St, Bourbonnais 60914   Fax 815/933-1563

Schools: 1 \ **Teachers:** 28 \ **Students:** 431 \ **Special Ed Students:** 68 \ **LEP Students:** 14 \ **Ethnic:** Asian 1%, African American 11%, Hispanic 8%, Caucasian 79% \ **Exp:** $242 (Med) \ **Poverty:** 6% \ **Title I:** $45,972 \ **Special Education:** $274,000 \ **Bilingual Education:** $5,000 \ **Open-Close:** 08/17 - 05/21

Helen Boehrnsen 1
Tyson Clifton 3*
Crystal Johnson 59
Christine Johnston 69,74,273*
John Grill 2
Bryan Wells 6*
Darrell Pendleton 67
Timothy Koerner 297

Public Schs..Principal	Grd	Prgm	Enr/#Cls	SN	
St George Elem Sch 5200 E Center St, Bourbonnais 60914 Christine Johnston	PK-8	T	431 20	24%	815/933-1503 Fax 815/933-1562

1 Superintendent	8 Curric/Instruct K-12	19 Chief Financial Officer	29 Family/Consumer Science	39 Social Studies K-12	49 English/Lang Arts Elem	59 Special Education Elem	69 Academic Assessment
2 Bus/Finance/Purchasing	9 Curric/Instruct Elem	20 Art K-12	30 Adult Education	40 Social Studies Elem	50 English/Lang Arts Sec	60 Special Education Sec	70 Research/Development
3 Buildings And Grounds	10 Curric/Instruct Sec	21 Art Elem	31 Career/Sch-to-Work K-12	41 Social Studies Sec	51 Reading K-12	61 Foreign/World Lang K-12	71 Public Information
4 Food Service	11 Federal Program	22 Art Sec	32 Career/Sch-to-Work Elem	42 Science K-12	52 Reading Elem	62 Foreign/World Lang Elem	72 Summer School
5 Transportation	12 Title I	23 Music K-12	33 Career/Sch-to-Work Sec	43 Science Elem	53 Reading Sec	63 Foreign/World Lang Sec	73 Instructional Tech
6 Athletic	13 Title V	24 Music Elem	34 Early Childhood Ed	44 Science Sec	54 Remedial Reading K-12	64 Religious Education K-12	74 Inservice Training
7 Health Services	15 Asst Superintendent	25 Music Sec	35 Health/Phys Education	45 Math K-12	55 Remedial Reading Elem	65 Religious Education Elem	75 Marketing/Distributive
	16 Instructional Media Svcs	26 Business Education	36 Guidance Services K-12	46 Math Elem	56 Remedial Reading Sec	66 Religious Education Sec	76 Info Systems
	17 Chief Operations Officer	27 Career & Tech Ed	37 Guidance Services Elem	47 Math Sec	57 Bilingual/ELL	67 School Board President	77 Psychological Assess
	18 Chief Academic Officer	28 Technology Education	38 Guidance Services Sec	48 English/Lang Arts K-12	58 Special Education K-12	68 Teacher Personnel	78 Affirmative Action

Illinois School Directory — Kendall County

KANKAKEE CATHOLIC SCHOOLS

- **Diocese of Joliet Ed Office** PID: 00325965
  Listing includes only schools located in this county. See District Index for location of Diocesan Offices.

Catholic Schs..Principal	Grd	Prgm	Enr/#Cls	SN
Bishop McNamara Cath Sch 247 N Center Ave, Bradley 60915 Dana Berg	PK-6		181 12	815/933-8013
Bishop McNamara Catholic Sch 324 E Marsile St, Bourbonnais 60914 Nicole Gernon	PK-6		212 10	815/933-7758 Fax 815/933-1884
Bishop McNamara High Sch 550 W Brookmont Blvd, Kankakee 60901 Terry Granger	7-12	V	450 26	815/932-7413 Fax 815/932-0926 f t

KANKAKEE PRIVATE SCHOOLS

Private Schs..Principal	Grd	Prgm	Enr/#Cls	SN
Camelot Sch-Bourbonnais 650 N Convent St, Bourbonnais 60914 Nicole Davenport	Spec		100	815/602-8200
Grace Christian Academy 2499 Waldron Rd, Kankakee 60901 Aaron Most	PK-12		215 18	815/939-4579 Fax 815/939-1334
Indian Oaks Academy 101 N Bramble St, Manteno 60950 Dr John Werner	Spec		109 16	815/802-3700 Fax 815/468-0122
Kankakee Trinity Academy 1580 Butterfield Trl, Kankakee 60901 Brad Prairie	PK-12		293 14	815/935-8080 Fax 815/935-0280 f
St Paul's Lutheran Sch 1780 Career Center Rd, Bourbonnais 60914 James Krupski	PK-8		175 12	815/932-3241 Fax 815/932-7588
Unity Christian Sch 920 W 2nd St, Momence 60954 Elizabeth Porte	PK-8		20 4	815/472-3230

KANKAKEE REGIONAL CENTERS

- **Iroquois-Kankakee Reg Off Ed** PID: 02097918 815/937-2950
  1 Stuart Dr, Kankakee 60901 Fax 815/937-2921

Dr Gregg Murphy 1   Kay Williams 2
Frank Petkunas 15   Jeff Boudreau 73
Patty High 74

- **Kankakee Area Reg Voc Ed Sys** PID: 04178116 815/939-4971
  4083 N 1000W Rd, Bourbonnais 60914 Fax 815/939-7598

Matt Kelley 1,11   Daniel Gesell 2
Alice Argyelan 15,68

- **Kankakee Area Special Ed Co-op** PID: 02182070 815/422-4151
  650 W Guertin St, Saint Anne 60964 Fax 815/427-8409

Debra Quain 1,11

KENDALL COUNTY

KENDALL PUBLIC SCHOOLS

- **Community Unit School Dist 308** PID: 00299689 630/636-3080
  4175 State Route 71, Oswego 60543 Fax 630/636-3688

> **Schools:** 21 \ **Teachers:** 1,103 \
> **Students:** 17,250 \ **Special Ed Students:** 2,471 \ **LEP Students:** 1,220 \
> **College-Bound:** 78% \ **Ethnic:** Asian 8%, African American 9%, Hispanic 24%, Caucasian 59% \ **Exp:** $198 (Low) \ **Poverty:** 4% \ **Title I:** $662,731 \ **Special Education:** $8,785,000 \ **Bilingual Education:** $249,000 \
> **Open-Close:** 08/24 - 05/26 \ **DTBP:** $199 (High) \ f t

Dr John Sparlin 1,11   Christi Tyler 2,19
Eric Simon 3   Rob Allison 3
Dawn Simosky 5   Debbie Miller 7
Faith Dahlquist 8,15   Lindsay Allen 9,69,288
Heather Kincaid 10,69,288   Heather Kincaid 10,69,288*
Shannon Lueders 10,69,288   Shannon Lueders 10,69,288*
Andrea Wuiaduch 11,298   Renee Sartore 57
Dr Denise Hildebrand 58   Lauri Doyle 67
Ken Miller 68   Theresa Komitas 71
Kyle Olesen 73,295   Kim O'Hara 76
Valerie Patterson 79   Meredith Gerardot 88
John Sturk 295   Dr Heidi Podjasek 752

Public Schs..Principal	Grd	Prgm	Enr/#Cls	SN
Bednarcik Junior High Sch 3025 Heggs Rd, Aurora 60503 John Francis	6-8	V	699 45	19% 630/636-2500 Fax 630/636-2591
Boulder Hill Elem Sch 163 Boulder Hill Pass, Montgomery 60538 Toia Jones	K-5		607 27	47% 630/636-2900 Fax 630/636-2968 f t
Brokaw Early Learning Center 1000 5th St, Oswego 60543 Barbara Garrison	PK-PK		547	23% 630/551-9600 Fax 630/551-9619
Churchill Elem Sch 520 Secretariat Ln, Oswego 60543 Larry Piatek	K-5		553	14% 630/636-3800 Fax 630/636-3891
Fox Chase Elem Sch 260 Fox Chase Dr N, Oswego 60543 **Patrick Haddock**	K-5		577 31	31% 630/636-3000 Fax 630/636-3078
Grande Park Elem Sch 26933 W Grande Park Blvd, Plainfield 60585 Sean Smith	K-5		570 15	8% 630/551-9700 Fax 630/551-9719 f t
Homestead Elem Sch 2830 Hillsboro Blvd, Aurora 60503 Casey O'Connell	K-5		614 25	19% 630/636-3100 Fax 630/636-3168
Hunt Club Elem Sch 4001 Hunt Club Dr, Oswego 60543 **Elisabeth Stoffers**	K-5		707 31	24% 630/636-2800 Fax 630/636-2893
Lakewood Creek Elem Sch 2301 Lakewood Crk, Montgomery 60538 Kelley Budd	K-5		746	26% 630/636-3200 Fax 630/636-3291
Long Beach Elem Sch 67 Longbeach Rd, Montgomery 60538 Philip Murray	K-5		470 30	53% 630/636-3300 Fax 630/636-3391
Murphy Junior High Sch 26923 W Grande Park Blvd, Plainfield 60585 Brent Anderson \ **Laura Bingham**	6-8		773	14% 630/608-5100 Fax 630/608-5191 f t

---

79 Student Personnel	91 Safety/Security	275 Response To Intervention	298 Grant Writer/Ptnrships	**School Programs**	**Social Media**	
80 Driver Ed/Safety	92 Magnet School	277 Remedial Math K-12	750 Chief Innovation Officer	A = Alternative Program	f = Facebook	
81 Gifted/Talented	93 Parental Involvement	280 Literacy Coach	751 Chief of Staff	G = Adult Classes		
82 Video Services	95 Tech Prep Program	285 STEM	752 Social Emotional Learning	M = Magnet Program	t = Twitter	
83 Substance Abuse Prev	97 Chief Infomation Officer	286 Digital Learning		T = Title I Schoolwide		
84 Erate	98 Chief Technology Officer	288 Common Core Standards	**Other School Types**	V = Career & Tech Ed Programs		
85 AIDS Education	270 Accountability	294 Accountability	Ⓐ = Alternative School			
88 Alternative/At Risk	271 Migrant Education	295 Network System	Ⓒ = Charter School	New Schools are shaded		
89 Multi-Cultural Curriculum	273 Teacher Mentor	296 Title II Programs	Ⓜ = Magnet School	New Superintendents and Principals are bold		
90 Social Work	274 Before/After Sch	297 Webmaster	Ⓨ = Year-Round School	Personnel with email addresses are underscored		

Kendall County　　　　　　　　　　　　　　　　　　　　　　　　　　　　　Market Data Retrieval

Old Post Elem Sch 100 Old Post Rd, Oswego 60543 Michael Mitchinson	K-5		462 17	25%	630/636-3400 Fax 630/636-3491
Oswego East High Sch 1525 Harvey Rd, Oswego 60543 Laura Bankowski	9-12	V	2,717 203	22%	630/636-2200 Fax 630/636-2454
Oswego High Sch 4250 State Route 71, Oswego 60543 Michael Wayne	9-12	V	2,802 101	25%	630/636-2000 Fax 630/636-2199
Plank Junior High Sch 510 Secretariat Ln, Oswego 60543 Tyler Haymond	6-8		837	36%	630/551-9400 Fax 630/551-9691
Prairie Point Elem Sch 3650 Grove Rd, Oswego 60543 Dr Jennifer Groves	PK-5		472 28	12%	630/636-3600 Fax 630/636-3612
Southbury Elem Sch 820 Preston Ln, Oswego 60543 Samantha Sinovich	K-5		595	15%	630/551-9800 Fax 630/551-9819
Thompson Junior High Sch 440 Boulder Hill Pass, Oswego 60543 Anthony DeFeo	6-8	V	836 55	34%	630/636-2600 Fax 630/636-2691
Traughber Junior High Sch 570 Colchester Dr, Oswego 60543 Mindy Renier	6-8	V	1,151 60	22%	630/636-2700 Fax 630/636-2791
Wheatlands Elem Sch 2290 Barrington Dr, Aurora 60503 Tammie Harmon	K-5		602 36	19%	630/636-3500 Fax 630/636-3591
Wolfs Crossing Elem Sch 3015 Heggs Rd, Aurora 60503 Cortnye Russell	K-5		524	16%	630/636-3700 Fax 630/636-3791

- **Lisbon Cmty Cons Sch Dist 90** PID: 00299627　　　815/736-6324
  127 S Canal St, Newark 60541　　　　　　　　　　Fax 815/736-6326

Schools: 1 \ Teachers: 11 \ Students: 106 \ Special Ed Students: 10
\ Ethnic: African American 1%, Caucasian 99% \ Exp: $298 (Med) \
Poverty: 2% \ Special Education: $28,000 \ Open-Close: 08/21 - 05/28

Melanie Elias .... 1,83　Jason Carlson 67

Public Schs..Principal	Grd	Prgm	Enr/#Cls	SN	
Lisbon Grade Sch 127 S Canal St, Newark 60541 Melanie Elias	K-8		106 11	10%	815/736-6324

- **Newark Cmty Cons Sch Dist 66** PID: 00299665　　　815/695-5143
  503 Chicago Rd, Newark 60541　　　　　　　　　Fax 815/695-5776

Schools: 2 \ Teachers: 16 \ Students: 239 \ Special Ed Students: 30
\ LEP Students: 3 \ Ethnic: Hispanic 8%, Caucasian 92% \ Exp: $166
(Low) \ Poverty: 5% \ Title I: $24,338 \ Special Education: $55,000 \
Open-Close: 08/19 - 05/28 \ DTBP: $189 (High)

Demetra Turman .... 1,11,73　Delene Drew 2,19
Cynthia Oconnell .... 6　Pam Rowe 9,280,288
Liz Barajaz .... 59*　Matt Toftoy 67
Micah Bennett .... 83　Norman Lee 98,286,295*
Jessica Kokla 752

Public Schs..Principal	Grd	Prgm	Enr/#Cls	SN	
Millbrook Junior High Sch 8411 Fox River Rd, Millbrook 60536 Pam Rowe	5-8		116 8	22%	630/553-5435 Fax 630/553-1027

Newark Elem Sch 503 Chicago Rd, Newark 60541 Pam Rowe	PK-4		146 8	27%	815/695-5143

- **Newark Cmty High Sch Dist 18** PID: 00299641　　　815/695-5164
  413 Chicago Rd, Newark 60541　　　　　　　　　Fax 815/695-5752

Schools: 1 \ Teachers: 17 \ Students: 170 \ Special Ed Students: 23
\ LEP Students: 3 \ College-Bound: 68% \ Ethnic: African American
1%, Hispanic 6%, Caucasian 94% \ Exp: $538 (High) \ Poverty: 5% \
Title I: $21,634 \ Special Education: $47,000 \ Open-Close: 08/19 - 05/28 \
DTBP: $164 (High)

Amy Smith .... 1　Jennette Bulhe 2
Kirk English .... 3*　Kellie Turner 5
Josh Cooper .... 6　Mindi Chase 6
James Still .... 11,93,273*　Megan Pfister 57
Holly Larson .... 60,88*　Phillip Chapman 67
Michelle McAnally .... 69*　Tom Lesak 73*
Alyssa Olin .... 90,752　Lisa Woods 285*

Public Schs..Principal	Grd	Prgm	Enr/#Cls	SN	
Newark Cmty High Sch 413 Chicago Rd, Newark 60541 James Still	9-12	V	170 25	19%	815/695-5164

- **Plano Cmty Unit Sch Dist 88** PID: 00299744　　　630/552-8978
  800 S Hale St, Plano 60545　　　　　　　　　Fax 630/552-8548

Schools: 5 \ Teachers: 166 \ Students: 2,400 \ Special Ed Students: 371
\ LEP Students: 360 \ College-Bound: 75% \ Ethnic: Asian 1%,
African American 10%, Hispanic 50%, Caucasian 39% \ Exp: $289 (Med)
\ Poverty: 9% \ Title I: $344,791 \ Special Education: $466,000 \
Bilingual Education: $97,000 \ Open-Close: 08/25 - 06/01

Tony Baker .... 1　Bryan Appel 3
Becky Taylor .... 4　Gretchen Konczyk 5
Jim Schmidt .... 6　Dr Tracy Thurwanger 8,12,15,18
Jessica Dellorto .... 16,82　Abby Alvarez 57
Amy Lee .... 58　Tim Campbell 67
Gina Hubbard 73

Public Schs..Principal	Grd	Prgm	Enr/#Cls	SN	
Centennial Elem Sch 800 S West St, Plano 60545 Mike Zeman	2-3	T	305 15	59%	630/552-3234 Fax 630/552-0324
Emily G Johns Elem Sch 430 Mitchell Ct, Plano 60545 Lucas Baughman	4-6	T	530 23	56%	630/552-9182 Fax 630/552-9208
P H Miller Elem Sch 904 N Lew St, Plano 60545 Laurel Mateyka	PK-1	T	478 30	60%	630/552-8504 Fax 630/552-3089
Plano High Sch 704 W Abe St, Plano 60545 James Seput	9-12	ATV	717 110	53%	630/552-3178 Fax 630/552-8824
Plano Middle Sch 804 S Hale St, Plano 60545 Mark Heller	7-8	T	363 24	60%	630/552-3608 Fax 630/552-3802

1	Superintendent	8	Curric/Instruct K-12	19	Chief Financial Officer	29	Family/Consumer Science
2	Bus/Finance/Purchasing	9	Curric/Instruct Elem	20	Art K-12	30	Adult Education
3	Buildings And Grounds	10	Curric/Instruct Sec	21	Art Elem	31	Career/Sch-to-Work K-12
4	Food Service	11	Federal Program	22	Art Sec	32	Career/Sch-to-Work Elem
5	Transportation	12	Title I	23	Music K-12	33	Career/Sch-to-Work Sec
6	Athletic	13	Title V	24	Music Elem	34	Early Childhood Ed
7	Health Services	15	Asst Superintendent	25	Music Sec	35	Health/Phys Education
		16	Instructional Media Svcs	26	Business Education	36	Guidance Services K-12
		17	Chief Operations Officer	27	Career & Tech Ed	37	Guidance Services Elem
		18	Chief Academic Officer	28	Technology Education	38	Guidance Services Sec

39	Social Studies K-12	49	English/Lang Arts Elem	59	Special Education Elem	69	Academic Assessment
40	Social Studies Elem	50	English/Lang Arts Sec	60	Special Education Sec	70	Research/Development
41	Social Studies Sec	51	Reading K-12	61	Foreign/World Lang K-12	71	Public Information
42	Science K-12	52	Reading Elem	62	Foreign/World Lang Elem	72	Summer School
43	Science Elem	53	Reading Sec	63	Foreign/World Lang Sec	73	Instructional Tech
44	Science Sec	54	Remedial Reading K-12	64	Religious Education K-12	74	Inservice Training
45	Math K-12	55	Remedial Reading Elem	65	Religious Education Elem	75	Marketing/Distributive
46	Math Elem	56	Remedial Reading Sec	66	Religious Education Sec	76	Info Systems
47	Math Sec	57	Bilingual/ELL	67	School Board President	77	Psychological Assess
48	English/Lang Arts K-12	58	Special Education K-12	68	Teacher Personnel	78	Affirmative Action

Illinois School Directory — Knox County

- **Yorkville Cmty Unit SD 115** PID: 00299809   630/553-4382
  602 Center Pkwy Ste A, Yorkville 60560   Fax 630/553-4398

Schools: 10 \ **Teachers:** 412 \ **Students:** 6,200 \ **Special Ed Students:** 1,020 \ **LEP Students:** 312 \ **College-Bound:** 78% \ **Ethnic:** Asian 2%, African American 7%, Hispanic 19%, Caucasian 72% \ **Exp:** $302 (High) \ **Poverty:** 4% \ **Title I:** $230,772 \ **Special Education:** $2,575,000 \ **Bilingual Education:** $44,000 \ **Open-Close:** 08/18 - 05/26 \ **DTBP:** $171 (High) \ 🅵 🅣

Tim Shimp 1
Mindy Bradford 2,3,17
Nick Baughman 8,11,18,34,83,270,296,298
Ryan Adkins 16,73,295
Dr Lynn Burkes 67
Kristine Liptrot 71
Steve Reese 295
Carolyn Franck 2
Luke Englehart 6
Pete Marcelo 15,58,88
Jill Zapata 57
Troy Courtney 68
Melinda Lasky 79

Public Schs..Principal	Grd	Prgm	Enr/#Cls	SN	
Autumn Creek Elem Sch 2377 Autumn Creek Blvd, Yorkville 60560 Elisa Maldonado	K-6		673	22%	630/553-4048 Fax 630/553-4060
Bristol Bay Elem Sch 427 Bristol Bay Dr, Yorkville 60560 Katie Spallasso	K-6		576 25	16%	630/553-5121 Fax 630/882-6267
Bristol Grade Sch 23 Hunt St, Bristol 60512 Brett Kueker	PK-3		257 12	16%	630/553-4383 Fax 630/553-4459 🅵🅣
Circle Center Grade Sch 901 Mill St, Yorkville 60560 Shannon Hamm	PK-3		491 28	15%	630/553-4388 Fax 630/553-4456
Grande Reserve Elem Sch 3142 Grande Trl, Yorkville 60560 Robert Battey	K-6		544 26	13%	630/553-5513 Fax 630/553-5030
Yorkville Grade Sch 201 W Somonauk St, Yorkville 60560 Emily Lech	K-3		190 12	18%	630/553-4390 Fax 630/553-4450 🅵🅣
Yorkville High Sch 797 Game Farm Rd, Yorkville 60560 David Travis	10-12	AV	1,188 30	20%	630/553-4380 Fax 630/553-4397
Yorkville High School Academy 702 Game Farm Rd, Yorkville 60560 David Travis	9-9	A	450	43%	630/553-4385 Fax 630/553-4592
Yorkville Intermediate Sch 103 E Schoolhouse Rd, Yorkville 60560 Steve Bjork	4-6		641 30	22%	630/553-4594 Fax 630/553-4596 🅣
Yorkville Middle Sch 920 Prairie Crossing Dr, Yorkville 60560 Lisa Adler	7-8		984 60	22%	630/553-4544 Fax 630/553-5181

KENDALL CATHOLIC SCHOOLS

- **Diocese of Joliet Ed Office** PID: 00325965
  Listing includes only schools located in this county. See District Index for location of Diocesan Offices.

Catholic Schs..Principal	Grd	Prgm	Enr/#Cls	SN	
St Mary Sch 817 N Center St, Plano 60545 Joe Scarpino	K-8		189 9		630/552-3345 Fax 630/552-4385

KENDALL PRIVATE SCHOOLS

Private Schs..Principal	Grd	Prgm	Enr/#Cls	SN	
Cross Evang Lutheran Sch 8535 State Route 47, Yorkville 60560 Paul Goffron	PK-8		300 14		630/553-7861 Fax 630/553-2580
Parkview Christian Academy 201 W Center St, Yorkville 60560 Craig Rapinchuk \ John Gutman	PK-12		320 10		630/553-5158
Peaceful Pathways Mont Academy 8250 State Route 71, Yorkville 60560 Shawna Watkins	PK-9		125		630/553-4263
St Luke's Christian Academy 63 Fernwood Rd, Montgomery 60538 Mary Sotiroff	PK-8		215 11		630/892-0310 Fax 630/892-9320

KNOX COUNTY

KNOX COUNTY SCHOOLS

County Schs..Principal	Grd	Prgm	Enr/#Cls	SN	
Ⓐ Raes East 235 E Main St, Galesburg 61401 Nick Stoneking	6-12		13 2	67%	309/345-0101 Fax 309/345-0172

KNOX PUBLIC SCHOOLS

- **Abingdon-Avon Cmty Unit SD 276** PID: 00299873   309/462-2301
  507 N Monroe St Ste 3, Abingdon 61410   Fax 309/462-3870

Schools: 4 \ **Teachers:** 71 \ **Students:** 877 \ **Special Ed Students:** 142 \ **College-Bound:** 64% \ **Ethnic:** Hispanic 5%, Caucasian 95% \ **Exp:** $256 (Med) \ **Poverty:** 21% \ **Title I:** $374,553 \ **Special Education:** $149,000 \ **Open-Close:** 08/17 - 05/25 \ **DTBP:** $174 (High)

Mike Curry 1
Tina Stier 8*
Adam Powell 16*
Stacy Nagel 69*
Darla Admire 4*
Michelle Andrews 11,296*
Anthony Brooks 67
Mark Rogers 73,295*

Public Schs..Principal	Grd	Prgm	Enr/#Cls	SN	
Abingdon-Avon High Sch 600 W Martin St, Abingdon 61410 Brad Weedman	9-12	V	263 40	45%	309/462-2338 Fax 309/462-2492
Abingdon-Avon Middle Sch 320 E Woods St, Avon 61415 Kristi Anderson	6-8	TV	207 22	55%	309/465-3621 Fax 309/465-7194
Avon Elem Sch 400 E Woods St, Avon 61415 Kristi Anderson	PK-5	T	125 8	54%	309/465-3851 Fax 309/465-7194
Hedding Grade Sch 401 W Latimer St, Abingdon 61410 Michelle Andrews	PK-5	T	344 20	53%	309/462-2363 Fax 309/462-2105

---

79 Student Personnel
80 Driver Ed/Safety
81 Gifted/Talented
82 Video Services
83 Substance Abuse Prev
84 Erate
85 AIDS Education
88 Alternative/At Risk
89 Multi-Cultural Curriculum
90 Social Work
91 Safety/Security
92 Magnet School
93 Parental Involvement
95 Tech Prep Program
97 Chief Information Officer
98 Chief Technology Officer
270 Character Education
271 Migrant Education
273 Teacher Mentor
274 Before/After Sch
275 Response To Intervention
277 Remedial Math K-12
280 Literacy Coach
285 STEM
286 Digital Learning
288 Common Core Standards
294 Accountability
295 Network System
296 Title II Programs
297 Webmaster
298 Grant Writer/Ptnrships
750 Chief Innovation Officer
751 Chief of Staff
752 Social Emotional Learning

Other School Types
Ⓐ = Alternative School
Ⓒ = Charter School
Ⓜ = Magnet School
Ⓨ = Year-Round School

School Programs
A = Alternative Program
G = Adult Classes
M = Magnet Program
T = Title I Schoolwide
V = Career & Tech Ed Programs

Social Media
🅵 = Facebook
🅣 = Twitter

New Schools are shaded
New Superintendents and Principals are bold
Personnel with email addresses are underscored

Knox County

Market Data Retrieval

- **Galesburg Cmty Unit SD 205** PID: 00299926   309/973-2000
  932 Harrison St, Galesburg 61401   Fax 309/343-7757

Schools: 8 \ **Teachers:** 298 \ **Students:** 4,500 \ **Special Ed Students:** 672 \ **LEP Students:** 237 \ **College-Bound:** 80% \ **Ethnic:** Asian 1%, African American 17%, Hispanic 14%, Caucasian 68% \ **Exp:** $151 (Low) \ **Poverty:** 23% \ **Title I:** $1,852,296 \ **Special Education:** $788,000 \ **Bilingual Education:** $9,000 \ **Open-Close:** 08/31 - 05/28 \ **DTBP:** $195 (High)

Name	Ref	Name	Ref
Dr John Asplund	1	Donna Palmer	2
Jennifer Bloyd-Hamm	2,3,15	Matt Davis	4
Paulette Earp	5	Eric Matthews	6
Courtney Kunth	7	Mark Reed	8
Tiffany Springer	8,11,280,285,296*	Ross Robb	20,23
Dawn Michaud	58,77,90	Tianna Cervantes	67
Tammy Folger	71	Seth Wade	295
Mindy Ritchie	752		

Public Schs..Principal	Grd	Prgm	Enr/#Cls	SN	
Bright Futures Preschool 932 Harrison St Ste 1, Galesburg 61401 Ellen Spittell	PK-PK		199 6	65%	309/973-2031 Fax 309/342-7260
Churchill Junior High Sch 905 Maple Ave, Galesburg 61401 Tom Hawkins	7-8	TV	495 35	49%	309/973-2002 Fax 309/342-6384
Galesburg High Sch 1135 W Fremont St, Galesburg 61401 Jeff Houston	9-12	GTV	1,254 100	53%	309/973-2001 Fax 309/343-7122
Ⓐ Galesburg High School N 1135 W Fremont St, Galesburg 61401 Jason Spring	9-12		87		309/973-2003 Fax 309/343-1237
King Elem Sch 1018 S Farnham St, Galesburg 61401 **Valerie Hawkins**	K-4	T	355 19	66%	309/973-2012 Fax 309/343-2161
Lombard Middle Sch 1220 E Knox St, Galesburg 61401 Nick Young	5-6	TV	437 50	70%	309/973-2004 Fax 309/342-7135
Silas Willard Elem Sch 460 Fifer St, Galesburg 61401 Jonathan Bradburn	K-4	T	451 21	52%	309/973-2015 Fax 309/343-0569
Steele Elem Sch 1480 W Main St, Galesburg 61401 Jennifer Graves	K-4	T	364 20	71%	309/973-2016 Fax 309/343-1259

- **Knoxville Cmty Unit SD 202** PID: 00300173   309/289-2328
  809 E Main St, Knoxville 61448   Fax 309/289-9614

Schools: 3 \ **Teachers:** 73 \ **Students:** 1,068 \ **Special Ed Students:** 172 \ **College-Bound:** 66% \ **Ethnic:** Hispanic 4%, Caucasian 95% \ **Exp:** $248 (Med) \ **Poverty:** 11% \ **Title I:** $174,474 \ **Special Education:** $193,000 \ **Open-Close:** 08/19 - 05/26

Name	Ref	Name	Ref
Joe Burgess	1,11,288	Kevin Maurer	3
Diane Raterman	4	Chuck Hillary	5
Heather Smith	6*	Tara Bahnks	8
Tara Bahnks	12*	Zac Marquith	16,295*
Patrick Callahan	67		

Public Schs..Principal	Grd	Prgm	Enr/#Cls	SN	
Knoxville High Sch 600 E Main St, Knoxville 61448 Chad Bahnks	9-12	TV	370 33	40%	309/289-2324 Fax 309/289-9466
Knoxville Junior High Sch 701 E Mill St, Knoxville 61448 Matt Maaske	5-8	T	310 20	45%	309/289-4126 Fax 309/289-4128
Mable Woolsey Elem Sch 106 Pleasant Ave, Knoxville 61448 Tara Bahnks	PK-4	T	388 23	49%	309/289-4134 Fax 309/289-9300

- **Rowva Cmty School Dist 208** PID: 00300240   309/483-3711
  335 N Joy St, Oneida 61467   Fax 309/483-6123

Schools: 2 \ **Teachers:** 46 \ **Students:** 600 \ **Special Ed Students:** 81 \ **LEP Students:** 3 \ **College-Bound:** 71% \ **Ethnic:** Hispanic 5%, Caucasian 94% \ **Exp:** $242 (Med) \ **Poverty:** 9% \ **Title I:** $82,479 \ **Special Education:** $207,000 \ **Open-Close:** 08/18 - 05/26 \ **DTBP:** $178 (High)

Name	Ref	Name	Ref
Joe Sornberger	1	Julie Dorm	4
Adam Feaney	10	Kerry Danner	11,58,296*
Sarah Manecke	12*	James Haynes	67
Tim Reynolds	73	Dawn Pelyon	88

Public Schs..Principal	Grd	Prgm	Enr/#Cls	SN	
Rowva Central Elem Sch 333 E Holmes St, Oneida 61467 Kerry Danner	PK-6	T	323 10	41%	309/483-6376 Fax 309/483-6378
Rowva Jr Sr High Sch 346 E Rova Dr, Oneida 61467 Adam Seaney	7-12	T	288 26	41%	309/483-6371 Fax 309/483-8223

- **Williamsfield Cmty Unit SD 210** PID: 00300305   309/639-2219
  325 W Kentucky Ave, Williamsfield 61489

Schools: 1 \ **Teachers:** 27 \ **Students:** 275 \ **Special Ed Students:** 36 \ **College-Bound:** 55% \ **Ethnic:** African American 1%, Hispanic 2%, Caucasian 97% \ **Exp:** $487 (High) \ **Poverty:** 18% \ **Title I:** $70,053 \ **Special Education:** $43,000 \ **Open-Close:** 08/25 - 05/24 \ **DTBP:** $198 (High)

Name	Ref	Name	Ref
Tim Farquer	1,11	Adam Doubert	5
Zack Binder	36,69,79*	Teresa Stewart	67

Public Schs..Principal	Grd	Prgm	Enr/#Cls	SN	
Williamsfield Sch 325 W Kentucky Ave, Williamsfield 61489 Zack Binder	PK-12		275 18	35%	309/639-2216 Fax 309/639-2618

KNOX CATHOLIC SCHOOLS

- **Diocese of Peoria Ed Office** PID: 00313338
  Listing includes only schools located in this county. See District Index for location of Diocesan Offices.

Catholic Schs..Principal	Grd	Prgm	Enr/#Cls	SN	
Costa Catholic Academy 2726 Costa Dr, Galesburg 61401 Joe Buresh	PK-8		375 20		309/344-3151 Fax 309/344-1594

KNOX PRIVATE SCHOOLS

Private Schs..Principal	Grd	Prgm	Enr/#Cls	SN	
Galesburg Christian Sch 1881 E Fremont St, Galesburg 61401 Jeremiah Barker \ Kim Reynolds	PK-12		193 7		309/343-8008 Fax 309/343-8006

#		#		#		#		#		#	
1	Superintendent	8	Curric/Instruct K-12	19	Chief Financial Officer	29	Family/Consumer Science	39	Social Studies K-12	49	English/Lang Arts Elem	59	Special Education Elem	69	Academic Assessment
2	Bus/Finance/Purchasing	9	Curric/Instruct Elem	20	Art K-12	30	Adult Education	40	Social Studies Elem	50	English/Lang Arts Sec	60	Special Education Sec	70	Research/Development
3	Buildings And Grounds	10	Curric/Instruct Sec	21	Art Elem	31	Career/Sch-to-Work K-12	41	Social Studies Sec	51	Reading K-12	61	Foreign/World Lang K-12	71	Public Information
4	Food Service	11	Federal Program	22	Art Sec	32	Career/Sch-to-Work Elem	42	Science K-12	52	Reading Elem	62	Foreign/World Lang Elem	72	Summer School
5	Transportation	12	Title I	23	Music K-12	33	Career/Sch-to-Work Sec	43	Science Elem	53	Reading Sec	63	Foreign/World Lang Sec	73	Instructional Tech
6	Athletic	13	Title V	24	Music Elem	34	Early Childhood Ed	44	Science Sec	54	Remedial Reading K-12	64	Religious Education K-12	74	Inservice Training
7	Health Services	15	Asst Superintendent	25	Music Sec	35	Health/Phys Education	45	Math K-12	55	Remedial Reading Elem	65	Religious Education Elem	75	Marketing/Distributive
		16	Instructional Media Svcs	26	Business Education	36	Guidance Services K-12	46	Math Elem	56	Remedial Reading Sec	66	Religious Education Sec	76	Info Systems
		17	Chief Operations Officer	27	Career & Tech Ed	37	Guidance Services Elem	47	Math Sec	57	Bilingual/ELL	67	School Board President	77	Psychological Assess
		18	Chief Academic Officer	28	Technology Education	38	Guidance Services Sec	48	English/Lang Arts K-12	58	Special Education K-12	68	Teacher Personnel	78	Affirmative Action

Illinois School Directory

La Salle County

KNOX REGIONAL CENTERS

- **Knox-Warren Spec Ed District** PID: 02182238   309/351-7224
  311 E Main St Ste 632, Galesburg 61401   Fax 309/343-3116
  Zach Crowl 1   Lynn Burnham 2
  Sherry McIlravy 15

- **Regional Office of Ed 33** PID: 02097932   309/345-3828
  121 S Prairie St, Galesburg 61401   Fax 309/345-6735
  Jodi Scott 1   Lori Loving 15

LA SALLE COUNTY

LA SALLE COUNTY SCHOOLS

County Schs..Principal	Grd	Prgm	Enr/#Cls	SN	
Circuit Breaker Sch 2233 6th St Ste 1, Peru 61354 Jayme Salzar	Spec	A	60 5	73%	815/220-0740 Fax 815/220-0881
LaSalle-Peru Area Career Ctr 200 9th St, Peru 61354 Dwayne Mentgen	Voc		327 11		815/223-2454 Fax 815/223-1010
Ⓐ Regional Safe Sch 2233 6th St Ste 2, Peru 61354 Jennifer Ferguson	6-12		100		815/220-3560 Fax 815/220-3557

LA SALLE PUBLIC SCHOOLS

- **Allen-Otter Creek CCSD 65** PID: 00302585   815/586-4611
  400 S Lane St, Ransom 60470   Fax 815/586-4306

  Schools: 1 \ **Teachers:** 12 \ **Students:** 70 \
  Special Ed Students: 14 \ **Exp:** $647 (High) \ **Poverty:** 10% \ **Title I:** $16,225
  \ **Special Education:** $41,000 \ **Open-Close:** 08/19 - 05/24 \ **DTBP:** $182 (High)

  Mary Baima 1,11   Dratina Gagnon 59
  Diane Rzasa 67   Linda Plymire 71*
  Linda Plymire 71   Laura Mentgen 73,295*

Public Schs..Principal	Grd	Prgm	Enr/#Cls	SN	
Allen Otter Creek Sch 400 S Lane St, Ransom 60470 Mary Baima	K-8		70 10		815/586-4611

- **Deer Park Cmty Cons SD 82** PID: 00302602   815/434-6930
  2350 E 1025th Rd, Ottawa 61350   Fax 815/434-6942

  Schools: 1 \ **Students:** 75 \ **Special Ed Students:** 13 \
  LEP Students: 3 \ **Ethnic:** Asian 4%, African American 1%, Hispanic 7%, Caucasian 88% \ **Exp:** $503 (High) \ **Poverty:** 15% \ **Title I:** $17,279 \
  Special Education: $27,000 \ **Open-Close:** 08/19 - 05/28 \ **DTBP:** $174 (High)

  Michael Struna 1,11,84   Staci Horner 4*
  Sandy Harsted .... 6,35*   Bridgette Thomas 43,46,83,85*
  Troy Woods 67

Public Schs..Principal	Grd	Prgm	Enr/#Cls	SN	
Deer Park Elem Sch 2350 E 1025th Rd, Ottawa 61350 Michael Struna	PK-8		75 9	11%	815/434-6930

- **Dimmick Cmty School Dist 175** PID: 00302626   815/223-2933
  297 N 33rd Rd, La Salle 61301   Fax 815/223-0169

  Schools: 1 \ **Teachers:** 11 \ **Students:** 160 \
  Special Ed Students: 22 \ **LEP Students:** 11 \ **Ethnic:** Asian 1%, Hispanic 8%, Caucasian 91% \ **Exp:** $390 (High) \ **Poverty:** 14% \ **Title I:** $31,099
  \ **Special Education:** $36,000 \ **Open-Close:** 08/19 - 05/24 \ **DTBP:** $171 (High)

  Ryan Linnig 1,11   Joel Foster 35,83,85
  Teri Rossman 59,71,84   Debora Black 67
  Maggie Olderman 270   Ronda Ketner 270*

Public Schs..Principal	Grd	Prgm	Enr/#Cls	SN	
Dimmick Cmty Cons 175 Sch 297 N 33rd Rd, La Salle 61301 Teri Rossman	PK-8		160 9	20%	815/223-2933

- **Earlville Cmty Unit Sch Dist 9** PID: 00302664   815/246-8361
  415 W Union St, Earlville 60518   Fax 815/246-8371

  Schools: 1 \ **Teachers:** 34 \ **Students:** 430 \ **Special Ed Students:** 78
  \ **LEP Students:** 9 \ **College-Bound:** 59% \ **Ethnic:** Hispanic 16%, Caucasian 84% \ **Exp:** $505 (High) \ **Poverty:** 18% \ **Title I:** $130,239 \
  Special Education: $233,000 \ **Open-Close:** 08/19 - 05/27 \ **DTBP:** $170 (High)

  Rich Faivre 1   Melissa Aviles 2*
  Shawn Collins 6   Jenette Fruit 8*
  Becky Eager .... 11*   Amanda Ossmon 16,73*
  Pam Marks 27,36,69,83,270   Dyllon Reel 35,80,85*
  Barbara Meloy 67

Public Schs..Principal	Grd	Prgm	Enr/#Cls	SN	
Earlville Cmty Unit 9 Sch 415 W Union St, Earlville 60518 Jenette Fruit	PK-12	T	430	45%	815/246-8361 Fax 815/246-8672

- **Grand Ridge CCSD 95** PID: 00302729   815/249-6225
  400 W Main St, Grand Ridge 61325   Fax 815/249-5049

  Schools: 1 \ **Teachers:** 19 \ **Students:** 189 \
  Special Ed Students: 28 \ **Ethnic:** Asian 1%, African American 2%, Hispanic 4%, Caucasian 93% \ **Exp:** $307 (High) \ **Poverty:** 10% \ **Title I:** $49,633 \
  Special Education: $147,000 \ **Open-Close:** 08/20 - 05/28 \ **DTBP:** $178 (High)

  Ted Sanders 1   Richard Frye 67

Public Schs..Principal	Grd	Prgm	Enr/#Cls	SN	
Grand Ridge Cmty Cons Elem Sch 400 W Main St, Grand Ridge 61325 Terry Ahearn	PK-8		189 18	25%	815/249-6225

#	Label	#	Label	#	Label	#	Label
79	Student Personnel	91	Safety/Security	275	Response To Intervention	298	Grant Writer/Ptnrships
80	Driver Ed/Safety	92	Magnet School	277	Remedial Math K-12	750	Chief Innovation Officer
81	Gifted/Talented	93	Parental Involvement	280	Literacy Coach	751	Chief of Staff
82	Video Services	95	Tech Prep Program	285	STEM	752	Social Emotional Learning
83	Substance Abuse Prev	97	Chief Information Officer	286	Digital Learning		
84	Erate	98	Chief Technology Officer	288	Common Core Standards		
85	AIDS Education	270	Accountability	294	Accountability		
88	Alternative/At Risk	271	Migrant Education	295	Network System		
89	Multi-Cultural Curriculum	273	Teacher Mentor	296	Title II Programs		
90	Social Work	274	Before/After Sch	297	Webmaster		

Other School Types
- Ⓐ = Alternative School
- Ⓒ = Charter School
- Ⓜ = Magnet School
- Ⓨ = Year-Round School

School Programs
- A = Alternative Program
- G = Adult Classes
- M = Magnet Program
- T = Title I Schoolwide
- V = Career & Tech Ed Programs

Social Media
- 🅵 = Facebook
- 🆃 = Twitter

New Schools are shaded
New Superintendents and Principals are bold
Personnel with email addresses are underscored

La Salle County

Market Data Retrieval

- **La Salle Elem SD 122** PID: 00302767 — 815/223-0786
  1165 Saint Vincent Ave, La Salle 61301 — Fax 815/223-8740

  Schools: 2 \ Teachers: 64 \ Students: 900 \ Special Ed Students: 212 \ LEP Students: 118 \ Ethnic: African American 6%, Hispanic 35%, Caucasian 58% \ Exp: $337 (High) \ Poverty: 31% \ Title I: $604,372 \ Special Education: $489,000 \ Bilingual Education: $30,000 \ Open-Close: 08/17 - 05/21 \ DTBP: $177 (High)

Brian Debernardi	1	Diane Mertel 2
Mary Moss	4,57	Jon Fox 6
Maureen Hanson	7*	Derek Kilmartin 11,34,296,298*
Mary Mauck	59*	Charlie Faletti 67
Jan Krug	69,77,271*	Kirston McLendon 73,76,84
Sarah Morscheiser	83,90,270,273*	

Public Schs..Principal	Grd	Prgm	Enr/#Cls	SN	
Lincoln Junior High Sch 1165 Saint Vincent Ave, La Salle 61301 Jon Fox	6-8	T	289 15	76%	815/223-0786
Northwest Elem Sch 1735 Malcolm Ave, La Salle 61301 Julie Defore	PK-5	T	637 30	75%	815/223-0786 Fax 815/224-6961

- **LaSalle Peru Twp HSD 120** PID: 00302834 — 815/223-1721
  541 Chartres St, La Salle 61301 — Fax 815/223-3444

  Schools: 1 \ Teachers: 87 \ Students: 1,200 \ Special Ed Students: 176 \ LEP Students: 50 \ Ethnic: Asian 2%, African American 3%, Hispanic 19%, Caucasian 76% \ Exp: $211 (Med) \ Poverty: 15% \ Title I: $320,022 \ Special Education: $558,000 \ Bilingual Education: $5,000 \ Open-Close: 08/18 - 05/27

Dr Steven Wrobleski	1	Diane Bergogna 2
Ritchie Kowalczyk	3*	Marsha Anderson 4*
Dan Le	6	Ingred Cushing 11
Dave Kelty	16*	Emily Carney 33,38,69*
Tony Sparks	67	Matt Baker 71
Amy Williams	73,76,84,295*	Lisa Jones 752

Public Schs..Principal	Grd	Prgm	Enr/#Cls	SN	
LaSalle Peru Twp High Sch 541 Chartres St, La Salle 61301 Ingrid Cushing	9-12	V	1,200 100	41%	815/223-1721

- **Leland Cmty Unit Sch Dist 1** PID: 00302860 — 815/495-3231
  370 N Main St, Leland 60531 — Fax 815/495-4611

  Schools: 1 \ Teachers: 22 \ Students: 260 \ Special Ed Students: 58 \ LEP Students: 6 \ College-Bound: 50% \ Ethnic: Hispanic 18%, Caucasian 82% \ Exp: $242 (Med) \ Poverty: 10% \ Title I: $39,211 \ Special Education: $139,000 \ Open-Close: 08/10 - 06/04 \ DTBP: $174 (High)

Jodi Moore	1,11	Jason Zaleski 2,6
Chris Bickel	9,83,288*	Kelsey Stegman 16,82*
Victor Epperson	36*	Janet Plote 67
Chris Bland	73,76*	

Public Schs..Principal	Grd	Prgm	Enr/#Cls	SN	
Leland Community Sch 370 N Main St, Leland 60531 Chris Bickel	K-12	T	260 30	47%	815/495-3231

- **Lostant Cmty Unit Sch Dist 425** PID: 00302896 — 815/368-3392
  315 W 3rd St, Lostant 61334 — Fax 815/368-3132

  Schools: 1 \ Teachers: 7 \ Students: 55 \ Special Ed Students: 18 \ Ethnic: African American 3%, Caucasian 97% \ Exp: $364 (High) \ Poverty: 13% \ Title I: $27,957 \ Special Education: $69,000 \ Open-Close: 08/28 - 05/28 \ DTBP: $179 (High)

Sandra Malahy	1,11,73,83,84,288	Jessica Flaherty 2
Quillard Skinner	67	

Public Schs..Principal	Grd	Prgm	Enr/#Cls	SN	
Lostant Elem Sch 315 W 3rd St, Lostant 61334 Nick McLaughlin	PK-8	T	55 13	49%	815/368-3392

- **Marseilles Elem Sch Dist 150** PID: 00302925 — 815/795-2162
  201 Chicago St, Marseilles 61341 — Fax 815/795-3415

  Schools: 1 \ Teachers: 38 \ Students: 550 \ Special Ed Students: 117 \ LEP Students: 7 \ Ethnic: African American 2%, Hispanic 9%, Caucasian 88% \ Exp: $500 (High) \ Poverty: 28% \ Title I: $274,975 \ Special Education: $219,000 \ Open-Close: 08/19 - 06/07 \ DTBP: $177 (High) \ t

Brenda Donahue	1	Rachel Lauer 2,298
Terri Spicer	4*	Jeff Owens 6,9,69,288*
Julie Sesto	7*	Traci Grandgeorge 11,73,295*
Kristi Schmidt	12*	Jim Barnes 67
Missy Stortz	69,90,271,274,752*	

Public Schs..Principal	Grd	Prgm	Enr/#Cls	SN	
Marseilles Elem Sch 201 Chicago St, Marseilles 61341 Jeff Owens	PK-8	T	550 35	53%	815/795-2428

- **Mendota Cmty School Dist 289** PID: 00303008 — 815/539-7631
  1806 Guiles Ave, Mendota 61342 — Fax 815/538-2927

  Schools: 3 \ Teachers: 75 \ Students: 1,200 \ Special Ed Students: 236 \ LEP Students: 251 \ Ethnic: African American 2%, Hispanic 42%, Caucasian 56% \ Exp: $272 (Med) \ Poverty: 19% \ Title I: $381,266 \ Special Education: $683,000 \ Bilingual Education: $66,000 \ Open-Close: 08/20 - 05/21 \ f t

Dr Kristen School	1,11,83	Ed DeWitt 3*
Stacy Kelly	12*	Beth Wackerlin 16,288
Jodi Peterson	34,59,77	Sean Pappas 67
Jason March	73,295	

Public Schs..Principal	Grd	Prgm	Enr/#Cls	SN	
Blackstone Elem Sch 1309 Jefferson St, Mendota 61342 Stacy Kelly	K-1	T	214 12	59%	815/539-6888 Fax 815/539-2370 f t
Lincoln Elem Sch 805 4th Ave, Mendota 61342 David Lawrence	2-4	T	362 16	33%	815/538-6226 Fax 815/539-5757
Northbrook Sch 1804 Guiles Ave, Mendota 61342 Paula Daley	5-8	T	550 25	60%	815/539-6237 Fax 815/538-3090

---

1 Superintendent	8 Curric/Instruct K-12	19 Chief Financial Officer	29 Family/Consumer Science	39 Social Studies K-12	49 English/Lang Arts Elem	59 Special Education Elem	69 Academic Assessment
2 Bus/Finance/Purchasing	9 Curric/Instruct Elem	20 Art K-12	30 Adult Education	40 Social Studies Elem	50 English/Lang Arts Sec	60 Special Education Sec	70 Research/Development
3 Buildings And Grounds	10 Curric/Instruct Sec	21 Art Elem	31 Career/Sch-to-Work K-12	41 Social Studies Sec	51 Reading K-12	61 Foreign/World Lang K-12	71 Public Information
4 Food Service	11 Federal Program	22 Art Sec	32 Career/Sch-to-Work Elem	42 Science K-12	52 Reading Elem	62 Foreign/World Lang Elem	72 Summer School
5 Transportation	12 Title I	23 Music K-12	33 Career/Sch-to-Work Sec	43 Science Elem	53 Reading Sec	63 Foreign/World Lang Sec	73 Instructional Tech
6 Athletic	13 Title V	24 Music Elem	34 Early Childhood Ed	44 Science Sec	54 Remedial Reading K-12	64 Religious Education K-12	74 Inservice Training
7 Health Services	15 Asst Superintendent	25 Music Sec	35 Health/Phys Education	45 Math K-12	55 Remedial Reading Elem	65 Religious Education Elem	75 Marketing/Distributive
	16 Instructional Media Svcs	26 Business Education	36 Guidance Services K-12	46 Math Elem	56 Remedial Reading Sec	66 Religious Education Sec	76 Info Systems
	17 Chief Operations Officer	27 Career & Tech Ed	37 Guidance Services Elem	47 Math Sec	57 Bilingual/ELL	67 School Board President	77 Psychological Assess
	18 Chief Academic Officer	28 Technology Education	38 Guidance Services Sec	48 English/Lang Arts K-12	58 Special Education K-12	68 Teacher Personnel	78 Affirmative Action

Illinois School Directory — La Salle County

Mendota Twp High Sch Dist 280 PID: 00302987   815/539-7446
2300 W Main St, Mendota 61342   Fax 815/539-3103

Schools: 1 \ **Teachers:** 35 \ **Students:** 541 \
Special Ed Students: 85 \ **LEP Students:** 61 \ **College-Bound:** 67% \
Ethnic: African American 1%, Hispanic 40%, Caucasian 59% \ **Exp:** $258
(Med) \ **Poverty:** 15% \ **Title I:** $145,181 \ **Special Education:** $382,000 \
Bilingual Education: $2,000 \ **Open-Close:** 08/17 - 05/21 \ **DTBP:** $170
(High)

Jeff Prusator	1	Andy Knowlton	3*	
Gary Kettleborough	5	Steve Hanson	6,35*	
Denise Aughenbaugh	10,69,274,275*	Heath Raley	27,33,75	
Melissa Sallee	29*	Mitch Landgraf	38*	
Janice Campbell	57*	Jim Lauer	67	
Scott Siri	73,76,295*	David Boylan	77*	
Tammy Guerrero	83,88,90*	Joe Masini	273*	

Public Schs..Principal	Grd	Prgm	Enr/#Cls	SN	
Mendota Twp High Sch 2300 W Main St, Mendota 61342 Denise Aughenbaugh	9-12	ATV	541 42	48%	815/539-7446

Miller Cmty Cons Sch Dist 210 PID: 00303058   815/357-8151
3197 E 28th Rd, Marseilles 61341   Fax 815/357-8159

Schools: 1 \ **Teachers:** 13 \ **Students:** 158 \ **Special Ed Students:** 38
\ **LEP Students:** 3 \ **Ethnic:** African American 1%, Hispanic 1%,
Caucasian 98% \ **Exp:** $447 (High) \ **Poverty:** 10% \ **Title I:** $37,859 \
Special Education: $96,000 \ **Open-Close:** 08/20 - 05/28

David Hermann	1	Juanita Peterson	6*
Mark Giertz	11,57,74,83,271,275*	Michelle Thorson	12
Teresa Schaibley	16*	Dan Mitchell	67
Kayli O'Flanagan	73,295*		

Public Schs..Principal	Grd	Prgm	Enr/#Cls	SN	
Milton Pope Elem Sch 3197 E 28th Rd, Marseilles 61341 Mark Giertz	K-8		158 8	8%	815/357-8151

Oglesby Public Sch Dist 125 PID: 00303072   815/883-9297
755 Bennett Ave, Oglesby 61348   Fax 815/883-3568

Schools: 2 \ **Teachers:** 36 \ **Students:** 529 \ **Special Ed Students:** 99 \
LEP Students: 10 \ **Ethnic:** Asian 1%, African American 1%, Hispanic 17%,
Caucasian 81% \ **Exp:** $421 (High) \ **Poverty:** 13% \ **Title I:** $119,781 \
Special Education: $249,000 \ **Open-Close:** 08/20 - 05/26

Michael Pillion	1,11	Merritt Burns	16,69,85,270*
Doug Kramarsic	67	Glenda Valle	73*
Elizabeth Kutz	84	Michael Balestri	298*

Public Schs..Principal	Grd	Prgm	Enr/#Cls	SN	
Lincoln Elem Sch 755 Bennett Ave, Oglesby 61348 Michael Balestri	PK-5	T	368 14	50%	815/883-8932
Washington Junior High Sch 212 W Walnut St, Oglesby 61348 Merritt Burns	6-8	T	161 12	47%	815/883-3517 Fax 815/883-9282 f t

Ottawa Elementary Sch Dist 141 PID: 00303149   815/433-1133
320 W Main St, Ottawa 61350   Fax 815/433-1888

Schools: 5 \ **Teachers:** 134 \ **Students:** 1,950 \ **Special Ed Students:** 369
\ **LEP Students:** 108 \ **Ethnic:** Asian 1%, African American 4%, Hispanic
17%, Caucasian 78% \ **Exp:** $140 (Low) \ **Poverty:** 20% \ **Title I:** $705,183 \
Special Education: $1,135,000 \ **Open-Close:** 08/19 - 06/04 \ **DTBP:** $292
(High)

Carrie Price	6	Dr Jeremy Lambe	7,77,752
Christine Bucciarelli	35,277,280,285,296	Kerry Bryson	67
James Addis	73,295,297		

Public Schs..Principal	Grd	Prgm	Enr/#Cls	SN	
Central Intermediate Sch 711 E McKinley Rd, Ottawa 61350 Ryan Myers	5-6	T	440 17	57%	815/433-3761 Fax 815/433-9572
Jefferson Elem Sch 1709 Columbus St, Ottawa 61350 Nate Pinter	K-4	T	309 20	71%	815/434-0726 Fax 815/434-7451
Lincoln Elem Sch 1110 W Main St, Ottawa 61350 Melanie Conley	PK-4	T	491 30	62%	815/434-1250 Fax 815/434-2931
McKinley Elem Sch 1320 State St, Ottawa 61350 Moriah Mott	PK-4	T	373 22	40%	815/434-1907 Fax 815/434-9124
Shepherd Middle Sch 701 E McKinley Rd, Ottawa 61350 Gary Windy	7-8	AT	418 40	51%	815/434-7925 Fax 815/434-9447

Ottawa Twp High Sch Dist 140 PID: 00303125   815/433-1323
211 E Main St, Ottawa 61350   Fax 815/433-1338

Schools: 1 \ **Teachers:** 90 \ **Students:** 1,450 \ **Special Ed Students:** 196
\ **LEP Students:** 19 \ **College-Bound:** 65% \ **Ethnic:** Asian 1%,
African American 2%, Hispanic 12%, Caucasian 85% \ **Exp:** $141 (Low)
\ **Poverty:** 15% \ **Title I:** $348,121 \ **Special Education:** $788,000 \
Open-Close: 08/13 - 05/28 \ **DTBP:** $171 (High)

Dr Michael Cushing	1	Janet Pearson	2,11,19,88,296
Brad Johnson	3*	Jeff DeWalt	12*
Jen Jobst	57*	Dawn Roalson	58*
Donald Harris	67	Dr Kristin Heredia	73*
Richard Denk	76,295*	Kim Highland	752

Public Schs..Principal	Grd	Prgm	Enr/#Cls	SN	
Ottawa Township High Sch 211 E Main St, Ottawa 61350 Patrick Leonard	9-12	ATV	1,450 100	35%	815/433-1323

Peru Elem Sch Dist 124 PID: 00303266   815/223-0486
1800 Church St, Peru 61354   Fax 815/223-0490

Schools: 2 \ **Teachers:** 70 \ **Students:** 970 \ **Special Ed Students:** 144 \
LEP Students: 59 \ **Ethnic:** Asian 2%, African American 2%, Hispanic 17%,
Caucasian 79% \ **Exp:** $154 (Low) \ **Poverty:** 17% \ **Title I:** $280,470 \
Special Education: $364,000 \ **Open-Close:** 08/19 - 05/26 \ f

Jamie Craven	1,11,83	Brandi Anderson-Maier	9*
Mellisa Bosnich	16,73,285	Mark Lamboley	67
Sean Baron	76	Rita Strickler	84

79	Student Personnel	91	Safety/Security	275	Response To Intervention	298	Grant Writer/Ptnrships
80	Driver Ed/Safety	92	Magnet School	277	Remedial Math K-12	750	Chief Innovation Officer
81	Gifted/Talented	93	Parental Involvement	280	Literacy Coach	751	Chief of Staff
82	Video Services	95	Tech Prep Program	285	STEM	752	Social Emotional Learning
83	Substance Abuse Prev	97	Chief Infomation Officer	286	Digital Learning		
84	Erate	98	Chief Technology Officer	288	Common Core Standards		
85	AIDS Education	270	Accountability	294	Accountability		
88	Alternative/At Risk	271	Migrant Education	295	Network System		
89	Multi-Cultural Curriculum	273	Teacher Mentor	296	Title II Programs		
90	Social Work	274	Before/After Sch	297	Webmaster		

School Programs
A = Alternative Program
G = Adult Classes
M = Magnet Program
T = Title I Schoolwide
V = Career & Tech Ed Programs

Other School Types
Ⓐ = Alternative School
Ⓒ = Charter School
Ⓜ = Magnet School
Ⓨ = Year-Round School

Social Media
f = Facebook
t = Twitter

New Schools are shaded
New Superintendents and Principals are bold
Personnel with email addresses are underscored

La Salle County

Market Data Retrieval

Public Schs..Principal	Grd	Prgm	Enr/#Cls	SN	
Northview Elem Sch 2100 Plum St, Peru 61354 Sara McDonald	PK-4		577 17	6%	815/223-1111 Fax 815/223-0618
Parkside Middle Sch 1800 Church St, Peru 61354 Brandi Anderson-Maier	5-8	T	395 32	48%	815/223-1111 Fax 815/223-0285

• Rutland Cmty Cons SD 230 PID: 00303319
3231 N State Route 71, Ottawa 61350   815/433-2949   Fax 815/433-2322

Schools: 1 \ **Teachers:** 9 \ **Students:** 75 \ **Special Ed Students:** 13 \ **Ethnic:** Asian 2%, Hispanic 6%, Caucasian 92% \ **Exp:** $424 (High) \ **Poverty:** 13% \ **Title I:** $15,448 \ **Special Education:** $29,000 \ **Open-Close:** 08/18 - 05/28 \ **DTBP:** $174 (High) \

Michael Matteson 1,11,83
Dan Macias 3*
Amy Jimenez 67
Kathy Holtzman 271
Marline Rackos 2
Trudy Carretto 12,73,270,273,275,288*
Julie Defore 69,76,295*

Public Schs..Principal	Grd	Prgm	Enr/#Cls	SN	
Rutland Grade Sch 3231 N State Route 71, Ottawa 61350 Tom Jeppson	K-8		75 12	32%	815/433-2949

• Seneca Cmty Cons Sch Dist 170 PID: 01557848
174 Oak St, Seneca 61360   815/357-8744   Fax 815/357-1516

Schools: 2 \ **Teachers:** 45 \ **Students:** 503 \ **Special Ed Students:** 93 \ **Ethnic:** African American 1%, Hispanic 9%, Caucasian 89% \ **Exp:** $309 (High) \ **Poverty:** 13% \ **Title I:** $83,831 \ **Special Education:** $226,000 \ **Open-Close:** 08/19 - 05/25 \ **DTBP:** $181 (High)

Eric Misener 1,11
Wendy Condon 4
Lynn McGhee 9,57,69,271,273,288,294*
Katie Ranallo 59,77*
Brandon Gilbertson 73,295,297*
Hope Fabris 275*
John Vaughn 3
Justin Holman 6
Jamie Lain 16*
Ken Sangston 67
Jennifer Ceko 83,90

Public Schs..Principal	Grd	Prgm	Enr/#Cls	SN	
Seneca North Elem Sch 174 Oak St, Seneca 61360 Lynn McGhee	PK-4		308 20	30%	815/357-8744
Seneca South Elem Sch 174 Oak St, Seneca 61360 Shane Severson	5-8		217 14	36%	815/357-8744 Fax 815/357-1078

• Seneca Twp High Sch Dist 160 PID: 00303333
307 E Scott St, Seneca 61360   815/357-5000   Fax 815/357-5050

Schools: 1 \ **Teachers:** 37 \ **Students:** 430 \ **Special Ed Students:** 55 \ **LEP Students:** 3 \ **College-Bound:** 66% \ **Ethnic:** African American 1%, Hispanic 8%, Native American: 2%, Caucasian 89% \ **Exp:** $543 (High) \ **Poverty:** 12% \ **Title I:** $85,063 \ **Special Education:** $139,000 \ **Open-Close:** 08/17 - 05/21 \ **DTBP:** $193 (High) \

Dr Jim Carlson 1
Barry Buchanan 3,91*
Steve Haines 6*
Mike Coughlin 12,57,60,77,83,88,294*
Dan Baker 35*
Ron Frye 67
Lesley McGuan 2
Marty Voiles 4,10,93,273*
Dan Stecken 10,11,68
Marty Harig 16,73,76,286,295,297*
Chris Jackson 38,69,275*

Public Schs..Principal	Grd	Prgm	Enr/#Cls	SN	
Seneca Township High Sch 307 E Scott St, Seneca 61360 Marty Voiles	9-12	V	430 41	29%	815/357-5000

• Serena Cmty Unit School Dist 2 PID: 01559236
2283 N 3812th Rd, Serena 60549   815/496-2850   Fax 815/496-6630

Schools: 4 \ **Teachers:** 51 \ **Students:** 665 \ **Special Ed Students:** 92 \ **LEP Students:** 4 \ **College-Bound:** 55% \ **Ethnic:** African American 1%, Hispanic 8%, Native American: 1%, Caucasian 90% \ **Exp:** $341 (High) \ **Poverty:** 21% \ **Title I:** $293,691 \ **Special Education:** $471,000 \ **Open-Close:** 08/18 - 05/25

Spencer Byrd 1,83
Deb Fuchs 4
Dean Derango 6*
Andy Allen 16,73*
Paige Hammil 58
Andrew Allen 295*
Mike McCoy 3
Janice Jones 5
Angie Merboth 11
Jennifer Hoppis 38*
Renee Thompson 67

Public Schs..Principal	Grd	Prgm	Enr/#Cls	SN	
Harding Grade Sch 1643 N 40th Rd, Earlville 60518 Angie Merboth	K-4		102 13	41%	815/792-8216 Fax 815/792-0016
Serena High Sch 2283 N 3812th Rd, Serena 60549 Aaron Rios	9-12	V	210 25	29%	815/496-2361
Serena Middle Sch 2283 N 3812th Rd, Serena 60549 Aaron Rios	5-8		189 12	37%	815/496-9250 Fax 815/496-2987
Sheridan Grade Sch 115 E Si Johnson Ave, Sheridan 60551 Randall Goodbred	PK-4		154 9	44%	815/496-2002 Fax 815/496-6633

• Streator Elem School Dist 44 PID: 00303436
1520 N Bloomington St, Streator 61364   815/672-2926   Fax 815/673-2032

Schools: 3 \ **Teachers:** 94 \ **Students:** 1,540 \ **Special Ed Students:** 331 \ **LEP Students:** 129 \ **Ethnic:** Asian 1%, African American 6%, Hispanic 23%, Caucasian 70% \ **Exp:** $185 (Low) \ **Poverty:** 26% \ **Title I:** $888,648 \ **Special Education:** $718,000 \ **Bilingual Education:** $26,000 \ **Open-Close:** 08/17 - 06/04 \ **DTBP:** $172 (High)

Dr Lisa Parker 1
Kerry Jolly 4*
Robert Kechan 11
Anne McDonnell 57*
Bryan Venturi 73,295*
Beth Lawless 90*
Holly Creel 2,3,5,76,286,288,296,298
Diana Gatinski 7
Heidi Schultz 34,37,59,69,275
Barbara Ehling 67
Karie Benning 88

Public Schs..Principal	Grd	Prgm	Enr/#Cls	SN	
Centennial Elem Sch 614 Oakley Ave, Streator 61364 Anne McDonnell	2-4	T	468 20	59%	815/672-2747 Fax 815/672-0594
Kimes Elem Sch 1207 Reading St, Streator 61364 Heather Ketcham	PK-1	T	387 7	63%	815/672-2496 Fax 815/672-1344
Northlawn Junior High Sch 1520 N Bloomington St, Streator 61364 Gail Russell	5-8	T	645 40	57%	815/672-4558 Fax 815/672-8109

1	Superintendent	8	Curric/Instruct K-12	19	Chief Financial Officer	29	Family/Consumer Science	39	Social Studies K-12	49	English/Lang Arts Elem	59	Special Education Elem	69	Academic Assessment
2	Bus/Finance/Purchasing	9	Curric/Instruct Elem	20	Art K-12	30	Adult Education	40	Social Studies Elem	50	English/Lang Arts Sec	60	Special Education Sec	70	Research/Development
3	Buildings And Grounds	10	Curric/Instruct Sec	21	Art Elem	31	Career/Sch-to-Work K-12	41	Social Studies Sec	51	Reading K-12	61	Foreign/World Lang K-12	71	Public Information
4	Food Service	11	Federal Program	22	Art Sec	32	Career/Sch-to-Work Elem	42	Science K-12	52	Reading Elem	62	Foreign/World Lang Elem	72	Summer School
5	Transportation	12	Title I	23	Music K-12	33	Career/Sch-to-Work Sec	43	Science Elem	53	Reading Sec	63	Foreign/World Lang Sec	73	Instructional Tech
6	Athletic	13	Title V	24	Music Elem	34	Early Childhood Ed	44	Science Sec	54	Remedial Reading K-12	64	Religious Education K-12	74	Inservice Training
7	Health Services	15	Asst Superintendent	25	Music Sec	35	Health/Phys Education	45	Math K-12	55	Remedial Reading Elem	65	Religious Education Elem	75	Marketing/Distributive
		16	Instructional Media Svcs	26	Business Education	36	Guidance Services K-12	46	Math Elem	56	Remedial Reading Sec	66	Religious Education Sec	76	Info Systems
		17	Chief Operations Officer	27	Career & Tech Ed	37	Guidance Services Elem	47	Math Sec	57	Bilingual/ELL	67	School Board President	77	Psychological Assess
		18	Chief Academic Officer	28	Technology Education	38	Guidance Services Sec	48	English/Lang Arts K-12	58	Special Education K-12	68	Teacher Personnel	78	Affirmative Action

Illinois School Directory — La Salle County

- **Streator Twp High Sch Dist 40** PID: 00303412 815/672-0545
  202 W Lincoln Ave, Streator 61364 Fax 815/673-3637

Schools: 1 \ **Teachers:** 58 \ **Students:** 844 \ **Special Ed Students:** 159 \ **LEP Students:** 29 \ **College-Bound:** 53% \ **Ethnic:** Asian 1%, African American 4%, Hispanic 19%, Caucasian 75% \ **Exp:** $471 (High) \ **Poverty:** 21% \ **Title I:** $337,996 \ **Special Education:** $691,000 \ **Bilingual Education:** $2,000 \ **Open-Close:** 08/12 - 05/20 \ **DTBP:** $178 (High) \ t

Matthew Seaton	1	James Dennis		3*
Kevin Wargo	6*	Jayne Park		7*
Amy Jo Mascal	10,11*	Robert Beck		16,73,82,84*
Ana Hughes	57*	Nick McGurk		60*
Earl Woeltje	67	Brad Brittin		69,83

Public Schs..Principal	Grd	Prgm	Enr/#Cls	SN	
Streator Twp High Sch 202 W Lincoln Ave, Streator 61364 Amy Jo Mascal	9-12	ATV	844 80	48%	815/672-0545 t

- **Tonica Cmty Cons Sch Dist 79** PID: 00303515 815/442-3420
  535 N 1981st Rd, Tonica 61370 Fax 815/442-3111

Schools: 1 \ **Teachers:** 13 \ **Students:** 159 \ **Special Ed Students:** 30 \ **LEP Students:** 8 \ **Ethnic:** Hispanic 9%, Caucasian 91% \ **Exp:** $329 (High) \ **Poverty:** 8% \ **Title I:** $21,634 \ **Special Education:** $73,000 \ **Open-Close:** 08/18 - 05/21 \ **DTBP:** $170 (High) \ f

Chuck Schneider	1,11	Lori Zach		2
Dan Stoffle	3	Michelle Carmean		4*
Al Leffelman	67			

Public Schs..Principal	Grd	Prgm	Enr/#Cls	SN	
Tonica Grade Sch 535 N 1981st Rd, Tonica 61370 Chuck Schneider	PK-8	T	159 15	29%	815/442-3420

- **Wallace Cmty Cons Sch Dist 195** PID: 00303565 815/433-2986
  1463 N 33rd Rd, Ottawa 61350 Fax 815/433-2989

Schools: 1 \ **Teachers:** 27 \ **Students:** 410 \ **Special Ed Students:** 73 \ **LEP Students:** 5 \ **Ethnic:** Asian 2%, African American 4%, Hispanic 9%, Caucasian 85% \ **Exp:** $366 (High) \ **Poverty:** 9% \ **Title I:** $33,803 \ **Special Education:** $236,000 \ **Open-Close:** 08/17 - 06/02 \ **DTBP:** $182 (High)

Mike Matteson	1,11,73,83	Cathy Kain		2
Patrick Allen	6*	Toby Coates		59,69,88,270,271,273,274*
Bill Vogel	67			

Public Schs..Principal	Grd	Prgm	Enr/#Cls	SN	
Wallace Elem Sch 1463 N 33rd Rd, Ottawa 61350 Joe Landers	PK-8		410 20	26%	815/433-2986

- **Waltham Elementary SD 185** PID: 00303589 815/667-4417
  2902 N Il Route 178, Utica 61373 Fax 815/667-4462

Schools: 1 \ **Teachers:** 17 \ **Students:** 200 \ **Special Ed Students:** 19 \ **Ethnic:** Asian 2%, African American 1%, Hispanic 6%, Caucasian 92% \ **Exp:** $220 (Med) \ **Poverty:** 7% \ **Title I:** $27,042 \ **Special Education:** $73,000 \ **Open-Close:** 08/19 - 05/28

Kristine Eager	1	Shaun Defore		3*
Katye Alvarado	59*	Jim McCabe		67
Andrew Cawley	73	Melanie Lukascy		288*

Public Schs..Principal	Grd	Prgm	Enr/#Cls	SN	
Waltham Elem Sch 2902 N Il Route 178, Utica 61373 Melanie Lukascy	K-8		200 9	9%	815/667-4417

LA SALLE CATHOLIC SCHOOLS

- **Diocese of Peoria Ed Office** PID: 00313338
  Listing includes only schools located in this county. See District Index for location of Diocesan Offices.

Catholic Schs..Principal	Grd	Prgm	Enr/#Cls	SN	
Holy Cross Sch 1008 Jefferson St, Mendota 61342 Anita Kobilsek	PK-8		144 10		815/539-7003 Fax 815/539-9082 f
Holy Family Sch 336 Alice Ave, Oglesby 61348 Jyll Jasiek	PK-8		222 9		815/883-8916 Fax 815/883-8943 f
Marquette Academy-High Sch 1000 Paul St, Ottawa 61350 Brooke Rick	9-12		236 25		815/433-0125 Fax 815/433-2632 f
Marquette Academy-St Columba 1110 La Salle St, Ottawa 61350 Brooke Rick	PK-8		210 10		815/433-1199 Fax 815/433-1219 f
Peru Catholic Sch 2003 5th St, Peru 61354 Julie Schmitt	PK-8		227 9		815/224-1914 Fax 815/223-1354
St Michael the Archangel Sch 410 S Park St, Streator 61364 Emily Blumenshine	PK-8		189 11		815/672-3847 Fax 815/673-3590 f
Trinity Catholic Academy 650 4th St, La Salle 61301 Debbie Myers	PK-8		167 11		815/223-8523 Fax 815/223-7450

LA SALLE PRIVATE SCHOOLS

Private Schs..Principal	Grd	Prgm	Enr/#Cls	SN	
La Salle Peru Christian Sch 200 24th St, La Salle 61301	K-12		10 8		815/223-1037 Fax 815/223-1334
Lighted Way Assoc Sch 941 6th St, La Salle 61301 Jessica Kreiser	Spec		34 3		815/224-1345 Fax 815/224-4759
Seventh Day Adventist Sch 3904 E 2603rd Rd, Sheridan 60551 Laura Damon	1-8		8 1		815/496-2947
St Bede Academy 24 W US Highway 6, Peru 61354 Michelle Mershon	9-12	V	309 25		815/223-3140 Fax 815/223-8580

LA SALLE REGIONAL CENTERS

- **LaSalle-Putnam Sped Alliance** PID: 02184092 815/433-6433
  1009 Boyce Memorial Dr, Ottawa 61350 Fax 815/433-6164

Mary Jane Chapman 1,11

---

79 Student Personnel	91 Safety/Security	275 Response To Intervention	298 Grant Writer/Ptnrships	**School Programs**
80 Driver Ed/Safety	92 Magnet School	277 Remedial Math K-12	750 Chief Innovation Officer	A = Alternative Program
81 Gifted/Talented	93 Parental Involvement	280 Literacy Coach	751 Chief of Staff	G = Adult Classes
82 Video Services	95 Tech Prep Program	285 STEM	752 Social Emotional Learning	M = Magnet Program
83 Substance Abuse Prev	97 Chief Information Officer	286 Digital Learning		T = Title I Schoolwide
84 Erate	98 Chief Technology Officer	288 Common Core Standards	**Other School Types**	V = Career & Tech Ed Programs
85 AIDS Education	270 Character Education	294 Accountability	Ⓐ = Alternative School	
88 Alternative/At Risk	271 Migrant Education	295 Network System	Ⓒ = Charter School	New Schools are shaded
89 Multi-Cultural Curriculum	273 Teacher Mentor	296 Title II Programs	Ⓜ = Magnet School	New Superintendents and Principals are bold
90 Social Work	274 Before/After Sch	297 Webmaster	Ⓨ = Year-Round School	Personnel with email addresses are underscored

Social Media
f = Facebook
t = Twitter

Lake County

- **Regional Office of Ed 35** PID: 02098003   815/434-0780
  119 W Madison St Ste 102, Ottawa 61350   Fax 815/434-2453

  Christopher Dvorak 1   Jessica Haywood 4
  Matt Winchester 15

- **Starved Rock Assoc Voc Tech Ed** PID: 04180195   815/223-2454
  200 9th St, Peru 61354   Fax 815/223-1010

  DeWayne Mentgen 1   Chris Wickie 2

LAKE COUNTY

LAKE COUNTY SCHOOLS

County Schs..Principal	Grd	Prgm	Enr/#Cls	SN	
ⓐ Cyd Lash Academy 18042 W Gages Lake Rd, Gages Lake 60030 Michael O'Brien	8-12		111 18	63%	847/231-5570 Fax 847/231-5071
Gages Lake Sch 18180 W Gages Lake Rd, Gages Lake 60030 Kristina Bacci	Spec		20 10	64%	847/223-5586 Fax 847/223-5698
John Powers Center 201 W Hawthorn Pkwy, Vernon Hills 60061 Pamela Evans	Spec		50 15	47%	847/680-8320 Fax 847/680-8918
Lake Co High Sch Tech Campus 19525 W Washington St, Grayslake 60030 Derrick Burress	Voc		1,200 25		847/223-6681 Fax 847/223-7363
Lake Co Roe Alternative HS 1620 23rd St, Zion 60099 Michael Munda	6-12		31	64%	847/872-1900 Fax 847/905-7272
Laremont Sch 17934 W Gages Lake Rd, Gages Lake 60030 Tegan Dittmer	Spec		150 22	45%	847/223-8191 Fax 847/548-2508
North Shore Academy 760 Red Oak Ln, Highland Park 60035 Lara Levine	Spec	V	145 9	13%	847/831-0603 Fax 847/831-2289

LAKE PUBLIC SCHOOLS

- **Adlai E Stevenson HSD 125** PID: 00300355   847/415-4000
  2 Stevenson Dr, Lincolnshire 60069   Fax 847/634-0239

  > **Schools:** 1 \ **Teachers:** 279 \ **Students:** 4,337 \ **Special Ed Students:** 418 \ **LEP Students:** 106 \ **College-Bound:** 91% \ **Ethnic:** Asian 33%, African American 2%, Hispanic 8%, Caucasian 56% \ **Exp:** $327 (High) \ **Poverty:** 2% \ **Title I:** $97,212 \ **Special Education:** $2,133,000 \ **Bilingual Education:** $8,000 \ **Open-Close:** 08/13 - 05/24 \ **DTBP:** $196 (High) \

  Dr Eric Twadell 1   Melissa Mickey 2
  Tricia Betthauser .... 6*   Marla Israel 10
  Sean Carney 15   Jonathan Grice 22,25*
  Eric Ramos .... 35*   Brad Smith 41*
  Darshan Jain .... 47*   Justin Fisk 57*
  Jay Miller .... 60*   Steve Frost 67
  Dr Kimberly Chambers .... 68*   Anthony Reibel 69*
  Jim Conrey 71   Doug Kahler 76,295*
  Sarah Bowen .... 79*   Christina Cortesi 83*
  Molly Gosline 752

Public Schs..Principal	Grd	Prgm	Enr/#Cls	SN	
Adlai E Stevenson High Sch 1 Stevenson Dr, Lincolnshire 60069 Troy Gobble	9-12	GV	4,337	5%	847/415-4000 Fax 847/634-7309

- **Antioch Cmty Cons Sch Dist 34** PID: 00300379   847/838-8400
  964 Spafford St, Antioch 60002   Fax 847/838-8404

  > **Schools:** 6 \ **Teachers:** 190 \ **Students:** 2,775 \ **Special Ed Students:** 401 \ **LEP Students:** 115 \ **Ethnic:** Asian 3%, African American 4%, Hispanic 7%, Native American: 1%, Caucasian 85% \ **Exp:** $213 (Med) \ **Poverty:** 6% \ **Title I:** $266,368 \ **Special Education:** $1,261,000 \ **Open-Close:** 08/19 - 05/27 \ **DTBP:** $192 (High) \

  Dr Bradford Hubbard 1   Betty Ratzke 2
  Cheryl Wadsworth 2,3,4,5,19   Bill Schenk 3,91
  Julie Byczek 4   Mary Holfinger 5
  Ann Scully 7,34,57,59,79   Adam Sax 9,11,69,73,76,270,286,294
  Kristina Gunthorp 9,12,15,74,275,288,296   Sara Elfering 9
  Jennifer Dunne .... 59,77,79*   Marybeth Hulting 67
  Jason Feldman 68   Dan Ocenas 295

Public Schs..Principal	Grd	Prgm	Enr/#Cls	SN	
Antioch Elem Sch 817 Main St, Antioch 60002 David Shepherd	2-5		322 16	30%	847/838-8901 Fax 847/838-8904
Antioch Upper Grade Sch 800 Highview Dr, Antioch 60002 Joe Koeune	6-8		995 44	23%	847/838-8301 Fax 847/838-8304
Hillcrest Elem Sch 433 E Depot St, Antioch 60002 Dave Shepherd	PK-1	T	677 24	28%	847/838-8001 Fax 847/838-8004
Mary Kay McNeill ELC 817 Main St, Antioch 60002 Michele Barkley	PK-PK		401		847/838-8901 Fax 847/838-8904
Oakland Elem Sch 818 E Grass Lake Rd, Lake Villa 60046 **Rebecca Adams**	2-5		365 20	20%	847/838-8601 Fax 847/838-8604
W C Petty Elem Sch 850 Highview Dr, Antioch 60002 Joanna Gerritsen	2-5	T	416 19	28%	847/838-8101 Fax 847/838-8104

- **Aptakisic-Tripp Sch Dist 102** PID: 00300446   847/353-5650
  1351 Abbott Ct, Buffalo Grove 60089   Fax 847/634-5334

  > **Schools:** 4 \ **Teachers:** 179 \ **Students:** 2,400 \ **Special Ed Students:** 300 \ **LEP Students:** 578 \ **Ethnic:** Asian 51%, African American 1%, Hispanic 6%, Caucasian 42% \ **Exp:** $337 (High) \ **Poverty:** 4% \ **Title I:** $71,852 \ **Special Education:** $1,119,000 \ **Bilingual Education:** $189,000 \ **Open-Close:** 08/19 - 06/02 \ **DTBP:** $227 (High)

  Dr Lori Wilcox 1   Stacey Bachar 2,4,15,91
  Daniel Mortensen 3   Jeff Livingston 6*
  Patrick Hoover 9,57,273   Dr Robert Hudson 11,15,70,74
  Betsy Sostak 57   Ellyn Ross 67
  Susan Murtaugh 68   Vickie Walter 71
  Tom Donovan 73,98,295   Susan Byrne 76
  Eli Rogers 79   Mary Bhardwaj 79
  Evan Tiberi 295

Public Schs..Principal	Grd	Prgm	Enr/#Cls	SN	
Aptakisic Junior High Sch 1231 Weiland Rd, Buffalo Grove 60089 Dana Tarnez	6-8		755 30	8%	847/353-5500 Fax 847/353-5505

1	Superintendent	8	Curric/Instruct K-12	19	Chief Financial Officer	29	Family/Consumer Science	39	Social Studies K-12	49	English/Lang Arts Elem	59	Special Education Elem	69	Academic Assessment
2	Bus/Finance/Purchasing	9	Curric/Instruct Elem	20	Art K-12	30	Adult Education	40	Social Studies Elem	50	English/Lang Arts Sec	60	Special Education Sec	70	Research/Development
3	Buildings And Grounds	10	Curric/Instruct Sec	21	Art Elem	31	Career/Sch-to-Work K-12	41	Social Studies Sec	51	Reading K-12	61	Foreign/World Lang K-12	71	Public Information
4	Food Service	11	Federal Program	22	Art Sec	32	Career/Sch-to-Work Elem	42	Science K-12	52	Reading Elem	62	Foreign/World Lang Elem	72	Summer School
5	Transportation	12	Title I	23	Music K-12	33	Career/Sch-to-Work Sec	43	Science Elem	53	Reading Sec	63	Foreign/World Lang Sec	73	Instructional Tech
6	Athletic	13	Title V	24	Music Elem	34	Early Childhood Ed	44	Science Sec	54	Remedial Reading K-12	64	Religious Education K-12	74	Inservice Training
7	Health Services	15	Asst Superintendent	25	Music Sec	35	Health/Phys Education	45	Math K-12	55	Remedial Reading Elem	65	Religious Education Elem	75	Marketing/Distributive
		16	Instructional Media Svcs	26	Business Education	36	Guidance Services K-12	46	Math Elem	56	Remedial Reading Sec	66	Religious Education Sec	76	Info Systems
		17	Chief Operations Officer	27	Career & Tech Ed	37	Guidance Services Elem	47	Math Sec	57	Bilingual/ELL	67	School Board President	77	Psychological Assess
		18	Chief Academic Officer	28	Technology Education	38	Guidance Services Sec	48	English/Lang Arts K-12	58	Special Education K-12	68	Teacher Personnel	78	Affirmative Action

Illinois School Directory — Lake County

	Grd	Enr/#Cls	SN	
Meridian Sch	4-5	501 / 20	7%	847/955-3500 Fax 847/634-4229
2195 Brandywyn Ln, Buffalo Grove 60089 — Gregory Michels				
Pritchett Elem Sch	K-3	456 / 28	5%	847/353-5700 Fax 847/215-3259
200 Horatio Blvd, Buffalo Grove 60089 — Dr Matt Moreland				
Tripp Elem Sch	PK-3	554 / 27	7%	847/955-3600 Fax 847/215-3268 t
850 Highland Grove Dr, Buffalo Grove 60089 — Tina Schenk				

● **Bannockburn Sch Dist 106** PID: 00300484 847/945-5900
2165 Telegraph Rd, Bannockburn 60015 Fax 847/945-5909

Schools: 1 \ **Teachers:** 19 \ **Students:** 155 \ **Special Ed Students:** 17 \ **LEP Students:** 8 \ **Ethnic:** Asian 15%, African American 9%, Hispanic 2%, Caucasian 74% \ **Exp:** $780 (High) \ **Poverty:** 11% \ **Title I:** $29,747 \ **Special Education:** $98,000 \ **Open-Close:** 08/20 - 06/07 \ **DTBP:** $239 (High) \ f t

Dr Scott Herrmann 1,83
Whitman Williams 3
Adam Mihelbergel 9,11,27,88,275,288,298*
Dr Lucy Hammerberg 67
Liz Loghnane 73*
Kathy Garneau 285
Lisa Pease 2,79
Chad Vincent 6*
Dana Hughes 57*
Joan Lampert 69*
Kathy Feldheim 280*

Public Schs..Principal	Grd	Prgm	Enr/#Cls	SN	
Bannockburn Elem Sch	PK-8		155 / 20	17%	847/945-5900
2165 Telegraph Rd, Bannockburn 60015 — Adam Mihelbergel					

● **Barrington Cmty Unit SD 220** PID: 00267492 847/381-6300
515 W Main St, Barrington 60010 Fax 847/842-1344

Schools: 12 \ **Teachers:** 602 \ **Students:** 9,000 \ **Special Ed Students:** 1,586 \ **LEP Students:** 671 \ **College-Bound:** 98% \ **Ethnic:** Asian 16%, African American 1%, Hispanic 19%, Caucasian 63% \ **Exp:** $323 (High) \ **Poverty:** 6% \ **Title I:** $823,441 \ **Special Education:** $6,652,000 \ **Bilingual Education:** $157,000 \ **Open-Close:** 08/20 - 05/28 \ **DTBP:** $194 (High) \ f t

Dr Brian Harris 1
Dr Craig Winkelman 3,15
Mike Obsuszt 6*
John Bruesch 8,15
Kelly Hansen 10,288
Beth Jones 15,79
Teresa Reiche 15,68
Michelle Acosta 34
Laura Pawlak 59
Chelsea Gray 68
Samantha Ptashkin 71
Ty Gorman 73
Shannon O'Neill 74
Russ Vandermey 295
Dave Bein 2,15
Elliott Eckles 3
Eva Detloff 7
Becky Gill 9
Becky Wiegel 11,57,61,298
Matt Fuller 15,73
Brigid Tileston 20,23*
Sharon Jacobellis 38,60
Penny Kazmier 67
Ben Ditkowsky 69,76,294
Hector Ontiveros 73
Margo Schmitt 74,81,92,274
Phillip Hintz 76
Annie Loizzi 297

Public Schs..Principal	Grd	Prgm	Enr/#Cls	SN	
Arnett C Lines Elem Sch	K-5		451 / 26	16%	847/381-7850 Fax 847/304-3918
217 Eastern Ave, Barrington 60010 — Ken Hyllberg					
Barbara B Rose Elem Sch	K-5		454 / 24	3%	847/844-1200 Fax 847/844-1443 f t
61 W Penny Rd, S Barrington 60010 — Heather Schumacher					
Barrington Early Learning Ctr	PK-K		282 / 12	36%	224/770-4300 Fax 847/304-4392 f t
40 E Dundee Rd, Barrington 60010 — Barbara Romano					
Barrington High Sch	9-12	A	2,923 / 115	18%	847/381-1400 Fax 847/304-3937
616 W Main St, Barrington 60010 — Steve McWilliams					
Barrington MS-Prairie Campus	6-8		1,013 / 52	19%	847/304-3990 Fax 847/304-3986
40 E Dundee Rd, Barrington 60010 — Travis Lobbins					
Barrington MS-Station Campus	6-8		991	20%	847/756-6400 Fax 847/842-1343 f t
215 Eastern Ave, Barrington 60010 — Jim Aalfs					
Countryside Elem Sch	K-5		398 / 20	8%	847/381-1162 Fax 847/304-3927
205 W County Line Rd, Barrington 60010 — Dr Micah Korb					
Grove Ave Elem Sch	K-5		541 / 21	17%	847/381-1888 Fax 847/304-3922 f t
900 S Grove Ave, Barrington 60010 — Katie Matthews					
Hough St Elem Sch	PK-5		294	8%	847/381-1108 Fax 847/304-3919 f t
310 S Hough St, Barrington 60010 — Zach Ernst					
North Barrington Elem Sch	K-5		472 / 16	8%	847/381-4340 Fax 847/304-3924
24175 N Grandview Dr, Barrington 60010 — Austin Johnson					
Roslyn Road Elem Sch	K-5		433 / 19	11%	847/381-4148 Fax 847/304-3923 f t
224 Roslyn Rd, Barrington 60010 — Paul Kirk					
Sunny Hill Elem Sch	K-5	T	351 / 20	87%	847/426-4232 Fax 847/426-0896 t
2500 Helm Rd, Carpentersvle 60110 — Cynthia Maxwell					

● **Beach Park Cmty Cons SD 3** PID: 00300501 847/599-5005
11315 W Wadsworth Rd, Beach Park 60099 Fax 847/263-2133

Schools: 5 \ **Teachers:** 146 \ **Students:** 2,106 \ **Special Ed Students:** 371 \ **LEP Students:** 452 \ **Ethnic:** Asian 3%, African American 24%, Hispanic 54%, Caucasian 19% \ **Exp:** $257 (Med) \ **Poverty:** 14% \ **Title I:** $466,482 \ **Special Education:** $980,000 \ **Bilingual Education:** $78,000 \ **Open-Close:** 09/09 - 06/22 \ **DTBP:** $237 (High)

Dr Craig Doster 1
Jose Medina 3*
Teanna Hutson 5
Rosemary Betz 12,16,57,59
Charlie Ongena 73*
Jorge Seda 79
Terry O'Brien 2
Monika Jankovics 4
April Miller 9
Jeanette Coletta 67
Maureen Urban 76,295*
Marie Gehrig 81

Public Schs..Principal	Grd	Prgm	Enr/#Cls	SN	
Beach Park Middle Sch	6-8	T	782 / 30	46%	847/596-5860 Fax 847/731-2402
40667 N Green Bay Rd, Beach Park 60099 — John Fredrickson					
Howe Elem Sch	K-5	T	365 / 18	64%	847/599-5362 Fax 847/623-5286
10271 W Beach Rd, Beach Park 60087 — Nashwa Mekky					
Kenneth Murphy Elem Sch	K-5	T	390 / 16	46%	847/599-5052 Fax 847/360-8635
11315 W Wadsworth Rd, Beach Park 60099 — Gabe Cappozzo					
Newport Elem Sch	K-5	T	267 / 19	52%	847/599-5330 Fax 847/599-0893 f
15872 W 21st St, Wadsworth 60083 — Chris Anderson					
Oak Crest Elem Sch	PK-5	T	302 / 18	43%	847/599-5519 Fax 847/623-0560
38550 N Lewis Ave, Beach Park 60099 — Lisa Schaffer \ Jennifer Convey					

---

79 Student Personnel	91 Safety/Security	275 Response To Intervention	298 Grant Writer/Ptnrships	**School Programs**	**Social Media**
80 Driver Ed/Safety	92 Magnet School	277 Remedial Math K-12	750 Chief Innovation Officer	A = Alternative Program	f = Facebook
81 Gifted/Talented	93 Parental Involvement	280 Literacy Coach	751 Chief of Staff	G = Adult Classes	t = Twitter
82 Video Services	95 Tech Prep Program	285 STEM	752 Social Emotional Learning	M = Magnet Program	
83 Substance Abuse Prev	97 Chief Information Officer	286 Digital Learning		T = Title I Schoolwide	
84 Erate	98 Chief Technology Officer	288 Common Core Standards	**Other School Types**	V = Career & Tech Ed Programs	
85 AIDS Education	270 Character Education	294 Accountability	Ⓐ = Alternative School		
88 Alternative/At Risk	271 Migrant Education	295 Network System	Ⓒ = Charter School	New Schools are shaded	
89 Multi-Cultural Curriculum	273 Teacher Mentor	296 Title II Programs	Ⓜ = Magnet School	New Superintendents and Principals are bold	
90 Social Work	274 Before/After Sch	297 Webmaster	Ⓨ = Year-Round School	Personnel with email addresses are underscored	

Lake County

Big Hollow School District 38 PID: 00300551
26051 W Nippersink Rd, Ingleside 60041
847/740-1490
Fax 847/740-9172

Schools: 3 \ **Teachers:** 113 \ **Students:** 1,800 \ **Special Ed Students:** 240 \ **LEP Students:** 167 \ **Ethnic:** Asian 5%, African American 5%, Hispanic 25%, Caucasian 64% \ **Exp:** $405 (High) \ **Poverty:** 6% \ **Title I:** $154,142 \ **Special Education:** $641,000 \ **Bilingual Education:** $37,000 \ **Open-Close:** 08/19 - 06/04 \ **DTBP:** $233 (High)

Bob Gold 1
Barb Steinseifer 9
Erin Pittman 59
Sophia Rogalevich 68
Doug Westerman 5
Christine Arndt 12,15*
Kevin Lyons 67
Matt McCulley 73

Public Schs..Principal	Grd	Prgm	Enr/#Cls	SN
Big Hollow Elem Sch 33315 N Fish Lake Rd, Ingleside 60041 Michelle Hetrovicz	2-4		571	28% 847/740-5321 Fax 847/740-3795
Big Hollow Middle Sch 26051 W Nippersink Rd, Ingleside 60041 Scott Whipple	5-8		830 24	31% 847/740-5322 Fax 847/740-9021
Big Hollow Primary Sch 33335 N Fish Lake Rd, Ingleside 60041 Lenayn Janusz	PK-1		383 22	27% 847/740-5320 Fax 847/740-3490

Community Cons School Dist 46 PID: 00300848
565 Frederick Rd, Grayslake 60030
847/223-3650
Fax 847/223-3695

Schools: 8 \ **Teachers:** 258 \ **Students:** 3,800 \ **Special Ed Students:** 685 \ **LEP Students:** 577 \ **Ethnic:** Asian 6%, African American 5%, Hispanic 32%, Caucasian 57% \ **Exp:** $147 (Low) \ **Poverty:** 5% \ **Title I:** $324,509 \ **Special Education:** $1,942,000 \ **Bilingual Education:** $103,000 \ **Open-Close:** 08/20 - 06/01 \ **DTBP:** $189 (High) \ 🅕 🅣

Lynn Glickman 1
Mary Werling 2
Bambi Johnson 4,5*
Lori Isaacs 7
Paul Louis 9,15,79
Chris Vipond 16,73,76
Marcus Smith 37*
Jim Weidman 67
Heather Lorenzo 77,79*
Brian Kalisz 295
Leslie McLeod 297
Marko Matic 2
Adam Halperin 3
Elisa Bundy 7*
Amanda Woodruff 9,11,69,72,74,273,275,288
Barb Zarras 12,280
Jana Donahue 34
Dr Stephanie Diaz 57
Staci Parmer 68
Wendy Chiswick 79
Mark Zottmann 295

Public Schs..Principal	Grd	Prgm	Enr/#Cls	SN
Avon Center Elem Sch 1617 Il Route 83, Round Lk Bch 60073 Barbara Zarras	K-4	T	367 20	54% 847/223-3530 Fax 847/223-3532 🅕 🅣
Frederick Sch 595 Frederick Rd, Grayslake 60030 Eric Detweiler	5-6		654 30	30% 847/543-5300 Fax 847/548-7768
Grays Lake Early Childhood Ctr 103 E Belvidere Rd, Grayslake 60030 Heather Lorenzo	PK-PK		116	32% 847/543-6204 Fax 847/543-4132
Grayslake Middle Sch 440 Barron Blvd, Grayslake 60030 Marcus Smith	7-8		651 40	24% 847/223-3680
Meadowview Elem Sch 291 Lexington Ln, Grayslake 60030 Laura Morgan	K-4		324 23	14% 847/223-3656 Fax 847/223-3531
Park Sch 400 W Townline Rd, Round Lake 60073 Matthew Melamed	K-8		805 30	24% 847/201-7010 Fax 847/201-1971 🅕
Prairieview Elem Sch 103 E Belvidere Rd, Grayslake 60030 Vince Murra	K-4	T	350 27	28% 847/543-4230 Fax 847/543-4125
Woodview Sch 340 N Alleghany Rd, Grayslake 60030 Cathy Santelle	K-4		425 18	24% 847/223-3668 Fax 847/223-3525

Community High School Dist 117 PID: 00300422
1133 Main St, Antioch 60002
847/395-1421
Fax 847/395-7553

Schools: 2 \ **Teachers:** 172 \ **Students:** 2,677 \ **Special Ed Students:** 349 \ **LEP Students:** 29 \ **College-Bound:** 81% \ **Ethnic:** Asian 4%, African American 2%, Hispanic 13%, Caucasian 81% \ **Exp:** $271 (Med) \ **Poverty:** 4% \ **Title I:** $274,480 \ **Special Education:** $2,604,000 \ **Open-Close:** 08/14 - 05/21 \ **DTBP:** $191 (High)

James McKay 1,11
Ken Mlincsek 3
Curt Rowells 6
Bradford Hubbard 15
Susan Soukup 16*
Dr Brie Cederna 60
Wayne Sobczak 67
Aryan Haren 74,286*
Megan Bargar 79*
David Nikkila 295
Jennifer Nolde 2,15,298
Lisa Swiderek 4
Steve Schoenfelder 6*
Brie Serdar 15
Jori Bowen 33,74*
Sandra Jarrett 60
Ryan Miles 73,98
Nicholas Schock 76
Ben Tompkins 295

Public Schs..Principal	Grd	Prgm	Enr/#Cls	SN
Antioch Cmty High Sch 1133 Main St, Antioch 60002 Eric Hamilton	9-12	AV	1,339 70	17% 847/395-1421 Fax 847/395-2435 🅕
Lakes Community High Sch 1600 Eagle Way, Lake Villa 60046 Dave Newberry	9-12	A	1,338	12% 847/838-7100 Fax 847/838-3670

Community High School Dist 128 PID: 00301517
50 Lakeview Pkwy Ste 101, Vernon Hills 60061
847/247-4500
Fax 847/247-4543

Schools: 2 \ **Teachers:** 235 \ **Students:** 3,397 \ **Special Ed Students:** 368 \ **LEP Students:** 73 \ **College-Bound:** 91% \ **Ethnic:** Asian 15%, African American 2%, Hispanic 11%, Caucasian 73% \ **Exp:** $493 (High) \ **Poverty:** 2% \ **Title I:** $74,388 \ **Special Education:** $1,792,000 \ **Bilingual Education:** $11,000 \ **Open-Close:** 08/12 - 05/26 \ **DTBP:** $190 (High) \ 🅕 🅣

Dr Prentiss Lea 1
Mark Koopman 3
Briant Kelly 15,68,78,273
Debra Kellum 27,33,75*
Paul Reiff 57*
Kelli Hartweg 60
Mary Todoric 71
Mick Torres 73
Amy Dillon 83,88*
Daniel Stanley 2,5,15
Dr Rita Fischer 10,11,15,270,288,296,298
Mike Torres 16
Diane Phillips 30
Wendy Meister-Louria 57*
Patrick Groody 67
Stephan Korney 72*
Temple Murphy 73

Public Schs..Principal	Grd	Prgm	Enr/#Cls	SN
Libertyville High Sch 708 W Park Ave, Libertyville 60048 Thomas Koulentes	9-12	GV	1,859 200	5% 847/327-7000 Fax 847/327-7195 🅕 🅣
Vernon Hills High Sch 145 Lakeview Pkwy, Vernon Hills 60061 Jon Guillaume	9-12	GV	1,459	10% 847/932-2000 Fax 847/932-2049

1	Superintendent	8	Curric/Instruct K-12	19	Chief Financial Officer	29	Family/Consumer Science	39	Social Studies K-12	49	English/Lang Arts Elem	59	Special Education Elem	69	Academic Assessment
2	Bus/Finance/Purchasing	9	Curric/Instruct Elem	20	Art K-12	30	Adult Education	40	Social Studies Elem	50	English/Lang Arts Sec	60	Special Education Sec	70	Research/Development
3	Buildings And Grounds	10	Curric/Instruct Sec	21	Art Elem	31	Career/Sch-to-Work K-12	41	Social Studies Sec	51	Reading K-12	61	Foreign/World Lang K-12	71	Public Information
4	Food Service	11	Federal Program	22	Art Sec	32	Career/Sch-to-Work Elem	42	Science K-12	52	Reading Elem	62	Foreign/World Lang Elem	72	Summer School
5	Transportation	12	Title I	23	Music K-12	33	Career/Sch-to-Work Sec	43	Science Elem	53	Reading Sec	63	Foreign/World Lang	73	Instructional Tech
6	Athletic	13	Title V	24	Music Elem	34	Early Childhood Ed	44	Science Sec	54	Remedial Reading K-12	64	Religious Education K-12	74	Inservice Training
7	Health Services	15	Asst Superintendent	25	Music Sec	35	Health/Phys Education	45	Math K-12	55	Remedial Reading Elem	65	Religious Education Elem	75	Marketing/Distributive
		16	Instructional Media Svcs	26	Business Education	36	Guidance Services K-12	46	Math Elem	56	Remedial Reading Sec	66	Religious Education Sec	76	Info Systems
		17	Chief Operations Officer	27	Career & Tech Ed	37	Guidance Services Elem	47	Math Sec	57	Bilingual/ELL	67	School Board President	77	Psychological Assess
		18	Chief Academic Officer	28	Technology Education	38	Guidance Services Sec	48	English/Lang Arts K-12	58	Special Education K-12	68	Teacher Personnel	78	Affirmative Action

Illinois School Directory — Lake County

Deerfield Public SD 109 PID: 00300587
517 Deerfield Rd, Deerfield 60015
847/945-1844
Fax 847/945-1853

Schools: 6 \ **Teachers:** 249 \ **Students:** 3,400 \ **Special Ed Students:** 344 \ **LEP Students:** 104 \ **Ethnic:** Asian 6%, Hispanic 5%, Caucasian 88% \ **Exp:** $312 (High) \ **Poverty:** 2% \ **Title I:** $64,244 \ **Special Education:** $1,957,000 \ **Open-Close:** 08/19 - 06/04 \ **DTBP:** $190 (High)

Dr Jane Westerhold 1
Susan Monaghan 2
Dr Scott Schwartz 9,11,74,288
Joanna Ford 15,79
Eric Steckling 71
Sarah Rose 79
Greg Himebaugh 2,3,5,15
Danielle Arnold 9
Dr Dale Fisher 15,68
Nick Begley 67
Adam Levine-Stein 73,76,295

Public Schs..Principal	Grd	Prgm	Enr/#Cls	SN	
A B Shepard Middle Sch 440 Grove Ave, Deerfield 60015 Christopher Cybulski	6-8	A	497 30	1%	847/948-0620 Fax 847/948-8589
Charles J Caruso Middle Sch 1801 Montgomery Rd, Deerfield 60015 Megan Russell	6-8	A	484 50	1%	847/945-8430 Fax 847/945-1963
Kipling Elem Sch 700 Kipling Pl, Deerfield 60015 **Andy Elbert**	K-5		469 26	1%	847/948-5151 Fax 847/948-8264
South Park Elem Sch 1421 Hackberry Rd, Deerfield 60015 Dr David Sherman	PK-5		467 20	1%	847/945-5895 Fax 847/945-5291
Walden Elem Sch 630 Essex Ct, Deerfield 60015 Stephanie Strenger	K-5		480 20	2%	847/945-9660 Fax 847/945-0035
Wilmot Elem Sch 795 Wilmot Rd, Deerfield 60015 Eileen Brett	K-5		500 26	1%	847/945-1075 Fax 847/405-9736

Diamond Lake School Dist 76 PID: 00300654
26156 N Acorn Ln, Mundelein 60060
847/566-9221
Fax 847/566-5689

Schools: 3 \ **Teachers:** 91 \ **Students:** 900 \ **Special Ed Students:** 146 \ **LEP Students:** 349 \ **Ethnic:** Asian 6%, African American 5%, Hispanic 66%, Caucasian 23% \ **Exp:** $363 (High) \ **Poverty:** 13% \ **Title I:** $246,298 \ **Special Education:** $456,000 \ **Bilingual Education:** $70,000 \ **Open-Close:** 08/31 - 05/28 \ **DTBP:** $254 (High)

Dr Bhavna Sharma Lewis 1
Kurt Preble 3*
Joy Hail 67
Eric Hansen 73,76
Eric Rogers 2,3
Steve Juracka 9,11,15,57,68,288,296,298
Lake Dole 69,79

Public Schs..Principal	Grd	Prgm	Enr/#Cls	SN	
Diamond Lake Sch 25807 N Diamond Lake Rd, Mundelein 60060 Juliane Fredericks	PK-2	T	261 15	60%	847/566-6601 Fax 847/566-9851
West Oak Interm Sch 26235 N Acorn Ln, Mundelein 60060 Dr Juliane Fredericks	3-5		291 20		847/970-3544
West Oak Middle Sch 26235 N Acorn Ln, Mundelein 60060	6-8	T	423 54	60%	847/566-9220

Emmons School District 33 PID: 00300692
24226 W Beach Grove Rd, Antioch 60002
847/395-1105
Fax 847/395-1223

Schools: 1 \ **Teachers:** 27 \ **Students:** 300 \ **Special Ed Students:** 28 \ **LEP Students:** 4 \ **Ethnic:** African American 1%, Hispanic 7%, Caucasian 91% \ **Exp:** $434 (High) \ **Poverty:** 6% \ **Title I:** $27,042 \ **Special Education:** $111,000 \ **Open-Close:** 08/24 - 06/04 \ **DTBP:** $219 (High)

Janean Friedman 1,11,288
Liz McClary 16,73
Eileen Houston 275*
Lisa Lawler 2,3,298
Laurie Christophersen 67
Cheryl McCameron 286*

Public Schs..Principal	Grd	Prgm	Enr/#Cls	SN	
Emmons Elem Sch 24226 W Beach Grove Rd, Antioch 60002 Janean Friedman	PK-8		300 30	12%	847/395-1105

Fox Lake School Dist 114 PID: 00300719
29067 W Grass Lake Rd, Spring Grove 60081
847/973-4114
Fax 847/973-4110

Schools: 2 \ **Teachers:** 71 \ **Students:** 741 \ **Special Ed Students:** 127 \ **LEP Students:** 57 \ **Ethnic:** Asian 1%, African American 3%, Hispanic 24%, Caucasian 73% \ **Exp:** $480 (High) \ **Poverty:** 12% \ **Title I:** $142,158 \ **Special Education:** $544,000 \ **Open-Close:** 08/20 - 05/28 \ **DTBP:** $234 (High)

Heather Frizielle 1
Don Ukleja 3*
Rachelle Peters 6*
Natalie Udstuen 12,288*
Sandra Popp 68
Lynn Smolen 83*
Mary Taylor 2
Georgette Franco 4
Stacy Zagar 11
Matthew Dabrowski 67
Kim Vanhoorelbaeke 82*

Public Schs..Principal	Grd	Prgm	Enr/#Cls	SN	
Lotus Elem Sch 29067 W Grass Lake Rd, Spring Grove 60081 Matthew Peters	PK-4	T	420 28	55%	847/973-4100 Fax 847/973-4210
Stanton Middle Sch 101 Hawthorne Ln, Fox Lake 60020 Jeff Sefcik	5-8	T	321 20	56%	847/973-4200 Fax 847/973-4210

Fremont School District 79 PID: 00300745
28855 N Fremont Center Rd, Mundelein 60060
847/566-0169
Fax 847/566-7280

Schools: 3 \ **Teachers:** 134 \ **Students:** 2,200 \ **Special Ed Students:** 306 \ **LEP Students:** 261 \ **Ethnic:** Asian 10%, African American 2%, Hispanic 15%, Caucasian 73% \ **Exp:** $264 (Med) \ **Poverty:** 3% \ **Title I:** $77,822 \ **Special Education:** $1,001,000 \ **Bilingual Education:** $79,000 \ **Open-Close:** 08/19 - 06/02 \ **DTBP:** $234 (High) \ 🅕 🅣

Dr William Robertson 1
Mike Tanner 2,3,15
Adam Halperin 3
Barb Stout 4*
Keith Johnson 5
Carol Bennett 9,11*
Maureen Tedor 12,59,79
Pamela Motsenbocker 68
Cheri Conway 2
Nancy Lepinski 2
Dan Wagner 3
Jill Wetteland 5
Dr Brian Bullis 9,15
Elizabeth Freeman 9,88*
Jason Bonds 67
Nick Brilowski 71

Public Schs..Principal	Grd	Prgm	Enr/#Cls	SN	
Fremont Elem Sch 28908 N Fremont Center Rd, Mundelein 60060 Stefan Ladenburger	K-2		745 75	8%	847/837-0437 Fax 847/837-9540 🅕 🅣

---

79 Student Personnel
80 Driver Ed/Safety
81 Gifted/Talented
82 Video Services
83 Substance Abuse Prev
84 Erate
85 AIDS Education
88 Alternative/At Risk
89 Multi-Cultural Curriculum
90 Social Work
91 Safety/Security
92 Magnet School
93 Parental Involvement
95 Tech Prep Program
97 Chief Information Officer
98 Chief Technology Officer
270 Character Education
271 Migrant Education
273 Teacher Mentor
274 Before/After Sch
275 Response To Intervention
277 Remedial Math K-12
280 Literacy Coach
285 STEM
286 Digital Learning
288 Common Core Standards
294 Accountability
295 Network System
296 Title II Programs
297 Webmaster
298 Grant Writer/Ptnrships
750 Chief Innovation Officer
751 Chief of Staff
752 Social Emotional Learning

Other School Types
Ⓐ = Alternative School
Ⓒ = Charter School
Ⓜ = Magnet School
Ⓨ = Year-Round School

School Programs
A = Alternative Program
G = Adult Classes
M = Magnet Program
T = Title I Schoolwide
V = Career & Tech Ed Programs

Social Media
🅕 = Facebook
🅣 = Twitter

New Schools are shaded
New Superintendents and Principals are bold
Personnel with email addresses are underscored

IL—149

Lake County

Market Data Retrieval

Fremont Intermediate Sch 3-5 714 9% 847/388-3700
28754 N Fremont Center Rd, Mundelein 60060 31 Fax 847/388-6900
Stefan Ladenburger

Fremont Middle Sch 6-8 758 10% 847/566-9384
28871 N Fremont Center Rd, Mundelein 60060 65 Fax 847/566-7805
Krista Winkelman

● **Gavin School District 37** PID: 00300769 847/546-2916
25775 W Il Route 134, Ingleside 60041 Fax 847/546-9584

Schools: 2 \ Teachers: 52 \ Students: 850 \ Special Ed Students: 143
\ LEP Students: 80 \ Ethnic: African American 6%, Hispanic 27%, Native American: 1%, Caucasian 66% \ Exp: $275 (Med) \ Poverty: 13% \
Title I: $156,846 \ Special Education: $430,000 \ Open-Close: 08/26 - 06/04 \ DTBP: $233 (High) \

Dr Julie Brua	1	Becky Allard	2,3,4,5,12,73
Mary Lang	5	Sean Connelly	34,79*
Eric Bechelli	67	Caryn Redman	69,88
Alex Fernandez	295		

Public Schs..Principal	Grd	Prgm	Enr/#Cls	SN	
Central Elem Sch 36414 N Ridge Rd, Ingleside 60041 **Carrie Coats**	PK-4	T	486 25	63%	847/973-3280 Fax 847/973-3285
Gavin South Junior High Sch 25775 W Il Route 134, Ingleside 60041 Jason Jurgaitis	5-8	T	380 21	62%	847/546-9336 Fax 847/546-9338

● **Grant Cmty High Sch Dist 124** PID: 00300800 847/587-2561
285 E Grand Ave, Fox Lake 60020 Fax 847/587-2991

Schools: 1 \ Teachers: 106 \ Students: 1,850 \ Special Ed Students: 244
\ LEP Students: 52 \ College-Bound: 76% \ Ethnic: Asian 4%, African American 5%, Hispanic 26%, Caucasian 65% \ Exp: $327 (High) \
Poverty: 7% \ Title I: $177,128 \ Special Education: $1,024,000 \
Open-Close: 08/12 - 05/21 \ DTBP: $230 (High)

Dr Cristine Sefcik	1	Beth Reich	2*
Josh Staples	3*	Deb Carole	5
Tom Ross	6	Greg Urbaniak	10,286*
Jeremy Schmidt	13,69,270,271,273,296*	Blair Schoell	26,29,35,63
Eric Taubery	27,44,47*	Veronica Lukemeyer	41,50,57*
Tina Sonders	60*	Steve Hill	67
Tom Furlan	73*	Ryan Geist	83,752*
Karen Durlak	288		

Public Schs..Principal	Grd	Prgm	Enr/#Cls	SN	
Grant Cmty High Sch 285 E Grand Ave, Fox Lake 60020 Jeremy Schmidt	9-12		1,850 81	33%	847/587-2561

● **Grass Lake School District 36** PID: 00300824 847/395-1550
26177 W Grass Lake Rd, Antioch 60002 Fax 847/395-8632

Schools: 1 \ Teachers: 19 \ Students: 190 \
Special Ed Students: 38 \ LEP Students: 3 \ Ethnic: Asian 1%, Hispanic 16%, Caucasian 83% \ Exp: $508 (High) \ Poverty: 17% \ Title I: $76,449
\ Special Education: $88,000 \ Open-Close: 08/21 - 05/28 \ DTBP: $218 (High)

Dr William Newby	1	Kathy Mueller	2
Ivy Sitkowski	12*	Donna Plath	59,88,275*
John Frendreis	67	Trish Giombetti	73*
Susan Lee	77	Susan Potthast	90
Nancy Nava	91		

Public Schs..Principal	Grd	Prgm	Enr/#Cls	SN	
Grass Lake Elem Sch 26177 W Grass Lake Rd, Antioch 60002 Donna Plath	PK-8		190 12	24%	847/395-1550

● **Grayslake Cmty HS District 127** PID: 00300886 847/986-3400
400 N Lake St, Grayslake 60030 Fax 847/231-6827

Schools: 2 \ Teachers: 197 \ Students: 3,000 \ Special Ed Students: 422
\ LEP Students: 101 \ College-Bound: 84% \ Ethnic: Asian 8%, African American 4%, Hispanic 25%, Caucasian 63% \ Exp: $300 (High) \ Poverty: 5% \ Title I: $198,762 \ Special Education: $1,304,000 \
Bilingual Education: $8,000 \ Open-Close: 08/20 - 05/24 \ DTBP: $186 (High)

Dr Mikkel Storaasli	1	Abe Singh	2,4,5,11,15
Dan Gonzalez	3	Danielle Carter	10,15,68,288
Tracie Landry	10	Jessica Iovinelli	16,28,73,295
Mark Kettering	60	Kathleen Conlon-Wasik	67
Dan Landry	79*		

Public Schs..Principal	Grd	Prgm	Enr/#Cls	SN	
Grayslake Central High Sch 400 N Lake St, Grayslake 60030 Dan Landry	9-12		1,335 58	11%	847/986-3300 Fax 847/223-8690
Grayslake North High Sch 1925 N Il Route 83, Grayslake 60030 Dr Jim Roscoe	9-12		1,457	13%	847/986-3100 Fax 847/986-3020

● **Gurnee School District 56** PID: 00300903 847/336-0800
3706 Florida Ave, Gurnee 60031 Fax 847/336-1110

Schools: 4 \ Teachers: 153 \ Students: 2,083 \ Special Ed Students: 385
\ LEP Students: 399 \ Ethnic: Asian 7%, African American 22%, Hispanic 47%, Caucasian 24% \ Exp: $133 (Low) \ Poverty: 10% \ Title I: $296,114
\ Special Education: $905,000 \ Bilingual Education: $106,000 \
Open-Close: 08/19 - 06/02 \ DTBP: $233 (High)

Dr Colleen Pacatte	1	Mark Lindem	2,19
Sean Smith	3,91	Alex Stewart	5
Nicholas Streicher	6*	Tami Kroc	7,57,59,79,85,88,90,275
Pete Helfers	9,11,74,83,273,286,288,294	Kathy Kibitlewski	16*
Dr James Blockinger	67	Ryan Lazar	69
Phil Hintz	73,297	Dain Elman	285*

Public Schs..Principal	Grd	Prgm	Enr/#Cls	SN	
Prairie Trail Sch 13600 W Wadsworth Rd, Wadsworth 60083 Kevin Simmons	3-5		487 30	39%	847/623-4333 Fax 847/623-4456
River Trail Sch 333 N Oplaine Rd, Gurnee 60031 Jennifer Glickley	K-8		518 30	26%	847/249-6253 Fax 847/249-4662
Spaulding Sch 2000 Belle Plaine Ave, Gurnee 60031 Dr Ellen Mauer	PK-2		465 25	30%	847/662-3701 Fax 847/249-6262
Viking Middle Sch 4460 Old Grand Ave, Gurnee 60031 Patrick Jones	6-8		534 50	31%	847/336-2108 Fax 847/249-0719

1	Superintendent	8	Curric/Instruct K-12	19	Chief Financial Officer	29	Family/Consumer Science
2	Bus/Finance/Purchasing	9	Curric/Instruct Elem	20	Art K-12	30	Adult Education
3	Buildings And Grounds	10	Curric/Instruct Sec	21	Art Elem	31	Career/Sch-to-Work K-12
4	Food Service	11	Federal Program	22	Art Sec	32	Career/Sch-to-Work Elem
5	Transportation	12	Title I	23	Music K-12	33	Career/Sch-to-Work Sec
6	Athletic	13	Title V	24	Music Elem	34	Early Childhood Ed
7	Health Services	15	Asst Superintendent	25	Music Sec	35	Health/Phys Education
		16	Instructional Media Svcs	26	Business Education	36	Guidance Services K-12
		17	Chief Operations Officer	27	Career & Tech Ed	37	Guidance Services Elem
		18	Chief Academic Officer	28	Technology Education	38	Guidance Services Sec

39	Social Studies K-12	49	English/Lang Arts Elem	59	Special Education Elem	69	Academic Assessment
40	Social Studies Elem	50	English/Lang Arts Sec	60	Special Education Sec	70	Research/Development
41	Social Studies Sec	51	Reading K-12	61	Foreign/World Lang K-12	71	Public Information
42	Science K-12	52	Reading Elem	62	Foreign/World Lang Elem	72	Summer School
43	Science Elem	53	Reading Sec	63	Foreign/World Lang Sec	73	Instructional Tech
44	Science Sec	54	Remedial Reading K-12	64	Religious Education K-12	74	Inservice Training
45	Math K-12	55	Remedial Reading Elem	65	Religious Education Elem	75	Marketing/Distributive
46	Math Elem	56	Remedial Reading Sec	66	Religious Education Sec	76	Info Systems
47	Math Sec	57	Bilingual/ELL	67	School Board President	77	Psychological Assess
48	English/Lang Arts K-12	58	Special Education K-12	68	Teacher Personnel	78	Affirmative Action

Illinois School Directory — Lake County

• Hawthorn Cmty Cons Sch Dist 73   PID: 00300939   847/990-4200
841 W End Ct, Vernon Hills 60061   Fax 847/367-3290

Schools: 7 \ **Teachers:** 321 \ **Students:** 4,300 \ **Special Ed Students:** 572 \ **LEP Students:** 961 \ **Ethnic:** Asian 24%, African American 2%, Hispanic 26%, Caucasian 47% \ **Exp:** $216 (Med) \ **Poverty:** 6% \ **Title I:** $293,410 \ **Special Education:** $1,614,000 \ **Bilingual Education:** $199,000 \ **Open-Close:** 08/20 - 06/02 \ **DTBP:** $190 (High)

Dr Pete Hannigan 1	Abe Singh 2,4,5,15
Michael Christensen 3	Allison Stein 9,15,69,288
Renee Ullberg 11,59	Dr Art Abrego 57,296
Robin Cleek 67	Adam Palmer 68,273
Leslie Piotrowski 71	Dr Karen Maturo 74
Lisa Gosen 76	John Reid 84

Public Schs..Principal	Grd	Prgm	Enr/#Cls	SN	
Aspen Elem Sch 500 N Aspen Dr, Vernon Hills 60061 Bill Fredricksen	K-5		419 24	18%	847/990-4300 Fax 847/816-6931
Hawthorn Elem School North 301 W Hawthorn Pkwy, Vernon Hills 60061 Katie Waggoner	K-5		555 24	28%	847/990-4500 Fax 847/367-3297
Hawthorn Elem School South 430 N Aspen Dr, Vernon Hills 60061 Christy Hunter	K-5		717 22	18%	847/990-4800 Fax 847/918-9251
Hawthorn Middle School North 201 W Hawthorn Pkwy, Vernon Hills 60061 Robert Collins	6-8		687 26	29%	847/990-4400 Fax 847/367-8124
Hawthorn Middle School South 600 N Aspen Dr, Vernon Hills 60061 Robert Natale	6-8		724 40	26%	847/990-4100 Fax 847/816-9259
Hawthorn Sch of Dual Language 810 N Aspen Dr, Vernon Hills 60061 S Fabrizio \ Dr A Gordon	K-5	T	407	52%	847/990-4900 Fax 847/990-4999
Townline Elem Sch 810 N Aspen Dr, Vernon Hills 60061 J Haack	K-5		421 37	24%	847/990-4901 Fax 847/990-4999

• Kildeer Countryside CCSD 96   PID: 00301165   847/459-4260
1050 Ivy Hall Ln, Buffalo Grove 60089   Fax 847/459-2344

Schools: 7 \ **Teachers:** 265 \ **Students:** 3,213 \ **Special Ed Students:** 355 \ **LEP Students:** 543 \ **Ethnic:** Asian 36%, African American 2%, Hispanic 9%, Caucasian 52% \ **Exp:** $198 (Low) \ **Poverty:** 3% \ **Title I:** $88,759 \ **Special Education:** $1,504,000 \ **Bilingual Education:** $110,000 \ **Open-Close:** 08/24 - 06/02 \ **DTBP:** $159 (High)

Julie Schmidt 1	Jonathan Hitcho 2,4,15
Michelle Whitlow 2	Sam Miranda 3,5,91
Jason Keenon 9	Jeanne Spiller 9,15,273,288,296,298,752
Katie Sheridan 9,12,49,57,69,280	Amy Glauck 11,59,88,90,271*
Dr Beth Dalton 15,68,74,273,294	Marc Tepper 67
Betsy Fresen 71	Lucas Dowden 73,76,285,295

Public Schs..Principal	Grd	Prgm	Enr/#Cls	SN	
Country Meadows Elem Sch 6360 Gilmer Rd, Long Grove 60047 Meghan Bird	1-5		417 19	20%	847/353-8600 Fax 847/949-8233
Ivy Hall Elem Sch 1072 Ivy Hall Ln, Buffalo Grove 60089 Robert Hanrahan	1-5		459 20	5%	847/459-0022 Fax 847/229-9650
Kildeer Countryside Elem Sch 3100 Old McHenry Rd, Long Grove 60047 Vail Kieser	1-5		516 19	4%	847/634-3243 Fax 847/821-7570
Prairie Elem Sch 1530 Brandywyn Ln, Buffalo Grove 60089 Christine Pfaff	1-5		414 19	4%	847/634-3144 Fax 847/821-7571
Twin Groves Middle Sch 2600 N Buffalo Grove Rd, Buffalo Grove 60089 Jessica Barnes	6-8		594 60	3%	847/821-8946 Fax 847/821-8949
Willow Grove Kindergarten 777 Checker Dr, Buffalo Grove 60089 Jennifer Smith	PK-K		311 10	6%	847/541-3660 Fax 847/821-7572
Woodlawn Middle Sch 6362 Gilmer Rd, Long Grove 60047 Greg Grana	6-8		611 35	11%	847/353-8500 Fax 847/949-8237

• Lake Bluff Elem Sch Dist 65   PID: 00301191   847/234-9400
121 E Sheridan Pl, Lake Bluff 60044   Fax 847/234-9403

Schools: 2 \ **Teachers:** 83 \ **Students:** 880 \ **Special Ed Students:** 120 \ **LEP Students:** 61 \ **Ethnic:** Asian 4%, African American 2%, Hispanic 15%, Native American: 1%, Caucasian 78% \ **Exp:** $494 (High) \ **Poverty:** 4% \ **Title I:** $37,194 \ **Special Education:** $566,000 \ **Bilingual Education:** $10,000 \ **Open-Close:** 08/21 - 06/01 \ **DTBP:** $233 (High)

Dr Lisa Leali 1	Jay Kahn 2,5,298
Steve Miller 3*	Kellie Bae 9,288*
Dr Kevin Rubenstein 11,37,59,73,77,90,286	Mark Barry 67

Public Schs..Principal	Grd	Prgm	Enr/#Cls	SN	
Lake Bluff Elem Sch 350 W Washington Ave, Lake Bluff 60044 Kellie Bae	PK-5		576 18	10%	847/234-9405 Fax 847/234-4819
Lake Bluff Middle Sch 31 E Sheridan Pl, Lake Bluff 60044 Nathan Blackmer	6-8		304 31	10%	847/234-9407 Fax 847/615-9144

• Lake Forest Cmty HSD 115   PID: 00301309   847/234-3600
300 S Waukegan Rd, Lake Forest 60045   Fax 847/582-7797

Schools: 1 \ **Teachers:** 130 \ **Students:** 1,600 \ **Special Ed Students:** 204 \ **LEP Students:** 9 \ **College-Bound:** 87% \ **Ethnic:** Asian 4%, African American 1%, Hispanic 7%, Caucasian 88% \ **Exp:** $420 (High) \ **Poverty:** 2% \ **Title I:** $47,368 \ **Special Education:** $982,000 \ **Open-Close:** 08/24 - 06/10 \ **DTBP:** $236 (High)

Mike Simeck 1	Brittany Tjardes 2
Jennifer Hermes 2,3,4,5,11,15,17	Carol White 3
Anne Simons 4	Tim Burkhalter 6
Alan Wahlert 10,69*	Renee Fitzsimmons 10
Rebecca Jenkins 15,68	Jordan Salus 16,73*
David Lane 67	Allison Stempien 68
Jordan Salus 73,98	Jenny Sterpin 79
Donna Lavitola 298	

Public Schs..Principal	Grd	Prgm	Enr/#Cls	SN	
Lake Forest High Sch 1285 N McKinley Rd, Lake Forest 60045 Dr Chala Holland	9-12	V	1,600 89	1%	847/234-3600

---

79 Student Personnel	91 Safety/Security	275 Response To Intervention	298 Grant Writer/Ptnrships	**School Programs**	**Social Media**
80 Driver Ed/Safety	92 Magnet School	277 Remedial Math K-12	750 Chief Innovation Officer	A = Alternative Program	
81 Gifted/Talented	93 Parental Involvement	280 Literacy Coach	751 Chief of Staff	G = Adult Classes	= Facebook
82 Video Services	95 Tech Prep Program	285 STEM	752 Social Emotional Learning	M = Magnet Program	
83 Substance Abuse Prev	97 Chief Information Officer	286 Digital Learning		T = Title I Schoolwide	= Twitter
84 Erate	98 Chief Technology Officer	288 Common Core Standards	**Other School Types**	V = Career & Tech Ed Programs	
85 AIDS Education	270 Accountability	294 Alternative School	Ⓐ = Alternative School		
88 Alternative/At Risk	271 Migrant Education	295 Network System	Ⓒ = Charter School	New Schools are shaded	
89 Multi-Cultural Curriculum	273 Teacher Mentor	296 Title II Programs	Ⓜ = Magnet School	New Superintendents and Principals are bold	
90 Social Work	274 Before/After Sch	297 Webmaster	Ⓨ = Year-Round School	Personnel with email addresses are underscored	

IL—151

Lake County

Market Data Retrieval

- **Lake Forest School District 67** PID: 00301244   847/235-9657
  300 S Waukegan Rd, Lake Forest 60045   Fax 847/234-5132

Schools: 5 \ **Teachers:** 158 \ **Students:** 1,660 \ **Special Ed Students:** 234 \ **LEP Students:** 31 \ **Ethnic:** Asian 6%, Hispanic 3%, Native American: 1%, Caucasian 90% \ **Exp:** $434 (High) \ **Poverty:** 3% \ **Title I:** $73,315 \ **Special Education:** $1,134,000 \ **Open-Close:** 08/26 - 06/09 \ **DTBP:** $223 (High)

Name	Code
Michael Simeck	1,11
Katie Labuhn	2
Anne Simons	4
Tom Cardamone	7*
Rebecca Jenkins	9,15,16,68,81
Kate Cavanaugh	59
Allison Stempien	68
Anne Whipple	71
Julie Patrick	76
Janice Patterson	297
Jennifer Hermes	2,3,4,5,17,19
Carol White	3
Jim Troemel	6*
Jeff McHugh	9
Dr Michelle Shinn	34,83,91,275,296*
Justin Engelland	67
Shannon Weld	68
Jordan Salus	73,98,295,297
Lisa Gillespie	76

Public Schs..Principal	Grd	Prgm	Enr/#Cls	SN		
Cherokee Elem Sch 475 Cherokee Rd, Lake Forest 60045 Lucas Livingston	PK-4		310 19	1%	847/234-3805 Fax 847/615-4467
Deer Path Middle School-East 95 W Deerpath, Lake Forest 60045 Tom Cardamone	5-6		388	2%	847/615-4470 Fax 847/615-4464
Deer Path Middle School-West 155 W Deerpath, Lake Forest 60045 Renee Devre	7-8		459 24	2%	847/604-7400 Fax 847/234-2389
Everett Elem Sch 1111 Everett School Rd, Lake Forest 60045 Dr Angela Sopko	PK-4		292 22	2%	847/234-5713 Fax 847/615-4466
Sheridan Elem Sch 1360 N Sheridan Rd, Lake Forest 60045 Susan Milsk	PK-4		233 14	3%	847/234-1160 Fax 847/615-4465

- **Lake Villa Cmty Cons SD 41** PID: 00301335   847/356-2385
  131 McKinley Ave, Lake Villa 60046   Fax 847/356-2670

Schools: 4 \ **Teachers:** 159 \ **Students:** 2,700 \ **Special Ed Students:** 497 \ **LEP Students:** 279 \ **Ethnic:** Asian 3%, African American 3%, Hispanic 30%, Caucasian 64% \ **Exp:** $315 (High) \ **Poverty:** 5% \ **Title I:** $240,677 \ **Special Education:** $1,292,000 \ **Bilingual Education:** $25,000 \ **Open-Close:** 08/19 - 06/02 \ **DTBP:** $191 (High)

Name	Code
Dr Lynette Zimmer	1
Kevin Wisenberger	3
Dr Mary Conkling	59,83
Jonathan Chase	73,76,295
Anna Kasprzyk	2
Dr Alex Barbour	9,11,57,69,271,288,296,298
Michael Conway	67

Public Schs..Principal	Grd	Prgm	Enr/#Cls	SN		
B J Hooper Elem Sch 2400 E Sand Lake Rd, Lindenhurst 60046 Steve Feldman	K-6		689 28	32%	847/356-2151 Fax 847/356-0934
Olive C Martin Elem Sch 24750 W Dering Ln, Lake Villa 60046 Dr Scott Klene	PK-6		618 28	38%	847/245-3400 Fax 847/245-4521
Peter J Palombi Middle Sch 133 McKinley Ave, Lake Villa 60046 Vic Wight	7-8		635 54	30%	847/356-2118 Fax 847/356-0833
William L Thompson Elem Sch 515 Thompson Ln, Lake Villa 60046 Lauren Crowley	PK-6		624 30	22%	847/265-2488 Fax 847/265-2667

- **Lake Zurich Cmty Sch Dist 95** PID: 00301385   847/438-2831
  832 S Rand Rd, Lake Zurich 60047   Fax 847/438-6702

Schools: 8 \ **Teachers:** 398 \ **Students:** 5,516 \ **Special Ed Students:** 766 \ **LEP Students:** 477 \ **Ethnic:** Asian 10%, African American 1%, Hispanic 7%, Native American: 1%, Caucasian 81% \ **Exp:** $245 (Med) \ **Poverty:** 3% \ **Title I:** $184,280 \ **Special Education:** $3,681,000 \ **Bilingual Education:** $127,000 \ **Open-Close:** 08/19 - 05/28 \ **DTBP:** $200 (High)

Name	Code
Dr Kelley Gallt	1
Josie Morrisroe	2
Vicky Cullinan	2
Lyle Erstad	3
Leslie Lauritzen	5
Angela Stallion	8,11,15,271,288,296,298
Zach Gimm	10
Phil Howard	16,73,82,286,297
Lynn Owens	59
Scott McConnell	67
Jeff Bivin	69
Jean Malek	71
Christine Green	2
Terese Cowell	2
Greg Fleming	3
Kathy Taylor	4*
Joan Hyatt	7*
Stacey Noisey	8,34,57,273
Lauren McArdle	15,58
Todd Gregory	35,80*
Carie Cohen	60
Julia Becich	68
Joshua Minsley	69,76

Public Schs..Principal	Grd	Prgm	Enr/#Cls	SN		
Isaac Fox Elem Sch 395 W Cuba Rd, Lake Zurich 60047 Lisa Gregoire	K-5		579 28	6%	847/540-7020 Fax 847/540-7032
Lake Zurich High Sch 300 Church St, Lake Zurich 60047 **Erin Deluga**	9-12	V	1,819 72	11%	847/438-5155 Fax 847/438-5989
Lake Zurich Mid Sch N Campus 95 Hubbard Ln, Hawthorn WDS 60047 Todd Jakowitsch	6-8		699 80	15%	847/719-3600 Fax 847/719-3620
Lake Zurich Mid Sch S Campus 435 W Cuba Rd, Lake Zurich 60047 John Walsh	6-8		589 40	9%	847/540-7070 Fax 847/540-9438
May Whitney Elem Sch 100 Church St, Lake Zurich 60047 Amy Mahr	PK-5		581 30	20%	847/438-2351 Fax 847/438-2696
Sarah Adams Elem Sch 555 Old Mill Grove Rd, Lake Zurich 60047 Kathleen Culver	K-5		362 22	19%	847/438-5986 Fax 847/438-7740
Seth Paine Elem Sch 50 Miller Rd, Lake Zurich 60047 Marie Rothermel	K-5		381 21	23%	847/438-2163 Fax 847/438-2528
Spencer Loomis Elem Sch 1 Hubbard Ln, Hawthorn WDS 60047 Sandy Allen	K-5		563 23	9%	847/719-3300 Fax 847/719-3320

- **Libertyville Pub Sch Dist 70** PID: 00301440   847/362-9695
  1381 Lake St, Libertyville 60048   Fax 847/362-3003

Schools: 5 \ **Teachers:** 172 \ **Students:** 2,258 \ **Special Ed Students:** 196 \ **LEP Students:** 52 \ **Ethnic:** Asian 7%, African American 1%, Hispanic 7%, Caucasian 85% \ **Exp:** $196 (Low) \ **Poverty:** 2% \ **Title I:** $54,946 \ **Special Education:** $1,145,000 \ **Open-Close:** 08/20 - 06/04 \ **DTBP:** $80 (Med)

Name	Code
Matt Barbini	1
Dan Gilbert	3
Erik Youngman	9,11,57,69,83,270,285,288
Tom Vickers	67
Dimitri Andrievosky	73,84
John Herrin	2,15
Stephanie Cox	3
Dr Christian Otto	59,285
Dr Tom Bean	68

Legend

#		#		#		#		#		#		#	
1	Superintendent	8	Curric/Instruct K-12	19	Chief Financial Officer	29	Family/Consumer Science	39	Social Studies K-12	49	English/Lang Arts Elem	59	Special Education Elem	69	Academic Assessment
2	Bus/Finance/Purchasing	9	Curric/Instruct Elem	20	Art K-12	30	Adult Education	40	Social Studies Elem	50	English/Lang Arts Sec	60	Special Education Sec	70	Research/Development
3	Buildings And Grounds	10	Curric/Instruct Sec	21	Art Elem	31	Career/Sch-to-Work K-12	41	Social Studies Sec	51	Reading K-12	61	Foreign/World Lang K-12	71	Public Information
4	Food Service	11	Federal Program	22	Art Sec	32	Career/Sch-to-Work Elem	42	Science K-12	52	Reading Elem	62	Foreign/World Lang Elem	72	Summer School
5	Transportation	12	Title I	23	Music K-12	33	Career/Sch-to-Work Sec	43	Science Elem	53	Reading Sec	63	Foreign/World Lang Sec	73	Instructional Tech
6	Athletic	13	Title V	24	Music Elem	34	Early Childhood Ed	44	Science Sec	54	Remedial Reading K-12	64	Religious Education K-12	74	Inservice Training
7	Health Services	15	Asst Superintendent	25	Music Sec	35	Health/Phys Education	45	Math K-12	55	Remedial Reading Elem	65	Religious Education Elem	75	Marketing/Distributive
		16	Instructional Media Svcs	26	Business Education	36	Guidance Services K-12	46	Math Elem	56	Remedial Reading Sec	66	Religious Education Sec	76	Info Systems
		17	Chief Operations Officer	27	Career & Tech Ed	37	Guidance Services Elem	47	Math Sec	57	Bilingual/ELL	67	School Board President	77	Psychological Assess
		18	Chief Academic Officer	28	Technology Education	38	Guidance Services Sec	48	English/Lang Arts K-12	58	Special Education K-12	68	Teacher Personnel	78	Affirmative Action

Illinois School Directory — Lake County

Public Schs..Principal	Grd	Prgm	Enr/#Cls	SN	
Adler Park Elem Sch 1740 N Milwaukee Ave, Libertyville 60048 **Kerri Bongle**	K-5		247 13	8%	847/362-7275 Fax 847/362-8158
Butterfield Elem Sch 1441 Lake St, Libertyville 60048 **Candice Kehoe**	PK-5		486 27	4%	847/362-3120 Fax 847/816-5613
Copeland Manor Elem Sch 801 7th Ave, Libertyville 60048 **Lori Poelking**	K-5		359 19	1%	847/362-0240 Fax 847/247-8617
Highland Middle Sch 310 W Rockland Rd, Libertyville 60048 **Jon Hallmark**	6-8		873	5%	847/362-9020 Fax 847/362-0870
Rockland Elem Sch 160 N Rockland Rd, Libertyville 60048 **Jim Cieciwa**	K-5		276 17	9%	847/362-3134 Fax 847/247-8618

● Lincolnshire-Prairieview SD 103   PID: 00301543   847/295-4030
1370 N Riverwoods Rd, Lincolnshire 60069   Fax 847/295-9196

Schools: 3 \ **Teachers:** 146 \ **Students:** 1,832 \ **Special Ed Students:** 236 \ **LEP Students:** 178 \ **Ethnic:** Asian 48%, African American 1%, Hispanic 3%, Caucasian 48% \ **Exp:** $296 (Med) \ **Poverty:** 2% \ **Title I:** $27,050 \ **Special Education:** $773,000 \ **Bilingual Education:** $35,000 \ **Open-Close:** 08/25 - 06/04 \ **DTBP:** $233 (High)

Dr Scott Warren	1	Patrick Palbicke	2,15
Scott Gaunky	3	Anthony Mendoza	5
Katie Reynolds	9,11,15,16,57,273,288	Kendra Perri	9
Gina Finaldi	34,59,79	Anne Van Gerven	67
R Bialk	69,73,84,295,297	Margerat Vanduch	71

Public Schs..Principal	Grd	Prgm	Enr/#Cls	SN	
Daniel Wright Jr High Sch 1370 N Riverwoods Rd, Lincolnshire 60069 **Michelle Blackley**	6-8		669 50	2%	847/295-1560 Fax 847/295-7136
Half Day Sch 239 Olde Half Day Rd, Lincolnshire 60069 **Jill Mau**	3-5		624 16	2%	847/634-6463 Fax 847/634-1968
Laura B Sprague Sch 2425 Riverwoods Rd, Lincolnshire 60069 **Ann Hofmeier**	PK-2		539 35	1%	847/945-6665 Fax 847/945-6718

● Millburn Cmty Cons Sch Dist 24   PID: 00301608   847/356-8331
18550 W Millburn Rd, Wadsworth 60083   Fax 847/356-9722

Schools: 2 \ **Teachers:** 88 \ **Students:** 1,150 \ **Special Ed Students:** 159 \ **LEP Students:** 72 \ **Ethnic:** Asian 10%, African American 3%, Hispanic 11%, Caucasian 77% \ **Exp:** $187 (Low) \ **Poverty:** 2% \ **Title I:** $39,176 \ **Special Education:** $882,000 \ **Bilingual Education:** $16,000 \ **Open-Close:** 08/19 - 05/28 \ **DTBP:** $181 (High)

Jason Lind	1,11	Dr Stephen Johns	2,3,4
Laura Sikorski	5	Daniel Jazo	6*
Elizabeth Keefe	11,57,59,83	Carissa Latourette	67
Joanne Rathunde	73,76,295		

Public Schs..Principal	Grd	Prgm	Enr/#Cls	SN	
Millburn Elem Sch 18550 W Millburn Rd, Wadsworth 60083 **Ben Walshire**	PK-5		712 72	15%	847/356-8331
Millburn Middle Sch 640 Freedom Way, Lindenhurst 60046 **Jake Jorgenson**	6-8		452	15%	847/245-1600 Fax 847/265-8198

● Mundelein Cons High SD 120   PID: 00301684   847/949-2200
1350 W Hawley St, Mundelein 60060   Fax 847/949-4756

Schools: 1 \ **Teachers:** 131 \ **Students:** 2,026 \ **Special Ed Students:** 335 \ **LEP Students:** 155 \ **College-Bound:** 75% \ **Ethnic:** Asian 6%, African American 2%, Hispanic 48%, Caucasian 44% \ **Exp:** $416 (High) \ **Poverty:** 6% \ **Title I:** $205,522 \ **Special Education:** $1,320,000 \ **Bilingual Education:** $6,000 \ **Open-Close:** 08/12 - 05/21 \ **DTBP:** $249 (High)

Dr Kevin Myers	1	Andrew Searle	2,19
Kevin Quinn	3	Troy Parola	6
Stacey Gorman	10*	Jaime DeCarlo	15,60,79*
Rebecca Plaza	16,82*	Joan Hornby	30
Justin Hart	35	Tom Buenik	38*
Anthony Crespell	57	Laura Vogt	67
Shane McCreery	68	Dr Ron Girard	71
Dan Crowe	73,76*		

Public Schs..Principal	Grd	Prgm	Enr/#Cls	SN	
Mundelein Cons High Sch 1350 W Hawley St, Mundelein 60060 **Dr Anthony Kroll**	9-12	AGV	2,026 110	29%	847/949-2200

● Mundelein Elem School Dist 75   PID: 00301622   847/949-2700
470 N Lake St, Mundelein 60060   Fax 847/949-2727

Schools: 4 \ **Teachers:** 127 \ **Students:** 1,586 \ **Special Ed Students:** 306 \ **LEP Students:** 473 \ **Ethnic:** Asian 5%, African American 3%, Hispanic 53%, Caucasian 39% \ **Exp:** $528 (High) \ **Poverty:** 8% \ **Title I:** $194,705 \ **Special Education:** $765,000 \ **Bilingual Education:** $178,000 \ **Open-Close:** 08/12 - 05/25 \

Kevin Myers	1	Joanne Logan	2
T Ferrier	2	Dave Zarembsa	5
Mike Fansler	6*	Dan Swartz	9,280,285,288*
Dr Andy Henrikson	11	Dr Holly Colin	12,34,59,88,271
Kevin Holly	67	Dan Crowe	73

Public Schs..Principal	Grd	Prgm	Enr/#Cls	SN	
Carl Sandburg Middle Sch 855 W Hawley St, Mundelein 60060 **Mark Pilut**	6-8		553 60	40%	847/949-2707 Fax 847/949-2716
Lincoln Early Learning Center 200 W Maple Ave, Mundelein 60060 Carol Bennett	PK-PK		123	47%	847/949-2720 Fax 847/566-0123
Mechanics Grove Elem Sch 1200 N Midlothian Rd, Mundelein 60060 Tanya Fergus	3-5		541 20	37%	847/949-2712 Fax 847/949-2711
Washington Elem Sch 122 S Garfield Ave, Mundelein 60060 **Jim Kallieris**	K-2		521 18	37%	847/949-2714 Fax 847/949-2710

● North Chicago Cmty Unit SD 187   PID: 00301725   847/689-8150
2000 Lewis Ave, North Chicago 60064   Fax 847/689-0270

Schools: 8 \ **Teachers:** 215 \ **Students:** 3,900 \ **Special Ed Students:** 540 \ **LEP Students:** 1,003 \ **College-Bound:** 54% \ **Ethnic:** Asian 1%, African American 34%, Hispanic 59%, Caucasian 6% \ **Exp:** $655 (High) \ **Poverty:** 23% \ **Title I:** $1,565,406 \ **Special Education:** $2,596,000 \ **Bilingual Education:** $263,000 \ **Open-Close:** 08/17 - 05/27 \ **DTBP:** $178 (High)

John Price	1	Gregory Volan	3,5
Susan Oglesby	4	Kim Baumann	7*
Janina Hall	8	Yesenia Sanchez	8,18,36,79

---

79 Student Personnel	91 Safety/Security	275 Response To Intervention	298 Grant Writer/Ptnrships	**School Programs**	**Social Media**
80 Driver Ed/Safety	92 Magnet School	277 Remedial Math K-12	750 Chief Innovation Officer	A = Alternative Program	= Facebook
81 Gifted/Talented	93 Parental Involvement	280 Literacy Coach	751 Chief of Staff	G = Adult Classes	= Twitter
82 Video Services	95 Tech Prep Program	285 STEM	752 Social Emotional Learning	M = Magnet Program	
83 Substance Abuse Prev	97 Chief Information Officer	286 Digital Learning		T = Title I Schoolwide	
84 Erate	98 Chief Technology Officer	288 Common Core Standards	**Other School Types**	V = Career & Tech Ed Programs	
85 AIDS Education	270 Character Education	294 Accountability	Ⓐ = Alternative School		
88 Alternative/At Risk	271 Migrant Education	295 Network System	Ⓒ = Charter School	New Schools are shaded	
89 Multi-Cultural Curriculum	273 Teacher Mentor	296 Title II Programs	Ⓜ = Magnet School	New Superintendents and Principals are bold	
90 Social Work	274 Before/After Sch	297 Webmaster	Ⓨ = Year-Round School	Personnel with email addresses are underscored	

IL–153

Lake County — Market Data Retrieval

Oscar Hawthorne 11,15,16,69
Shalima Francois-Bulv 58
David Collins 73
Carol Du Clos 58
Dora King 67

Public Schs..Principal	Grd	Prgm	Enr/#Cls	SN	
A J Katzmaier Academy 1829 Kennedy Dr, North Chicago 60064 Michael Grenda	4-5		339 18	99% Fax	847/689-6330 847/689-2818
Forrestal Elem Sch 2833 E Washington Ave, Great Lakes 60088 Inez Mitchell	K-2		326 20	100% Fax	847/689-6310 847/689-3501
Green Bay Early Childhood Cent 2100 Green Bay Rd, North Chicago 60064 Nicole Johnson	PK-PK		239	68%	847/775-7100
© Learn 6 Chtr Sch-N Chicago [164] 3131 Sheridan Rd, Great Lakes 60088 Kelly Tyson	K-8		468	59% Fax	847/377-0600 847/473-2988
© Learn 10 CS North Chicago [164] 1811 Morrow Ave, North Chicago 60064 Chris Cigan	K-6		250	48% Fax	847/693-5021 847/473-9085
Neal Math & Science Academy 1905 Argonne Dr, North Chicago 60064 Wayne Williams	6-8		600	99% Fax	847/689-6313 847/689-6332
North Chicago High Sch 1717 17th St, North Chicago 60064 Lilith Warner	9-12	V	757	99% Fax	847/578-7400 847/689-7473
North Elem Sch 1210 Adams St, North Chicago 60064 Andres Orbe	K-2		290 21	99% Fax	847/689-7345 847/578-6018

• **North Shore School Dist 112** PID: 00300991
1936 Green Bay Rd, Highland Park 60035
224/765-3000
Fax 224/765-3082

Schools: 10 \ **Teachers:** 312 \ **Students:** 3,800 \ **Special Ed Students:** 615 \ **LEP Students:** 620 \ **Ethnic:** Asian 3%, African American 2%, Hispanic 26%, Caucasian 68% \ **Exp:** $258 (Med) \ **Poverty:** 6% \ **Title I:** $401,632 \ **Special Education:** $3,252,000 \ **Bilingual Education:** $226,000 \ **Open-Close:** 08/24 - 06/07 \ **DTBP:** $188 (High) \

Dr Michael Lubelfeld 1
Katie Herak 2
Kevin Liebe 3,5,91
Christopher Wildman 4,11,19
Stephanie Eriksen 7*
Dr Kevin Ryan 9,11,15,69,288
Holly Colin 15,59,79,83,88
John Petzke 16,88,98,295
Bennett Lasko 67
Nicholas Glenn 71
Tim Pflug 76
Becy Haney 2
Virginia Brown 2
Nancy Gallo 3
Susanna Rabin 5
Jason Williams 9
Dr Leah Kimmelman 9
Dr Monica Schroeder 15,68
Lindsey Rose 57
John Sprangers 68
Terrie Carpenter 76
Patty Samuelian 273

Public Schs..Principal	Grd	Prgm	Enr/#Cls	SN	
Braeside Elem Sch 150 Pierce Rd, Highland Park 60035 Joseph Hailpern	K-5		269 15	3% Fax	224/765-3400 224/765-3408
Edgewood Middle Sch 929 Edgewood Rd, Highland Park 60035 Samuel Kurtz	6-8	V	792 45	11% Fax	224/765-3200 224/765-3208
Green Bay Early Childhood Ctr 1936 Green Bay Rd, Highland Park 60035 Chelsey Maxwell	PK-PK	T	223 7	44% Fax	224/765-3060 224/765-3084
Indian Trail Elem Sch 2075 Saint Johns Ave, Highland Park 60035 Maria Grable	K-5		426 22	11% Fax	224/765-3500 224/765-3508
Northwood Junior High Sch 945 North Ave, Highland Park 60035 Joanne Dimitriou	6-8	TV	516 50	46% Fax	224/765-3600 224/765-3608
Oak Terrace Elem Sch 240 Prairie Ave, Highwood 60040 Amy Cengel	K-5	T	480 25	58% Fax	224/765-3100 224/765-3108
Ravinia Elem Sch 763 Dean Ave, Highland Park 60035 Courtney Nordstrom	K-5		226 15	5% Fax	224/765-3700 224/765-3708
Red Oak Elem Sch 530 Red Oak Ln, Highland Park 60035 Nicole Bellini	PK-5	T	251 18	45% Fax	224/765-3750 224/765-3758
Sherwood Elem Sch 1900 Stratford Rd, Highland Park 60035 Rachel Filippi	K-5		381 19	8% Fax	224/765-3800 224/765-1719
Wayne Thomas Elem Sch 2939 Summit Ave, Highland Park 60035 Michael Rodrigo	K-5		324 17	19% Fax	224/765-3900 224/765-3908

• **Oak Grove School District 68** PID: 00301854
1700 Oplaine Rd, Libertyville 60048
847/367-4120
Fax 847/367-7933

Schools: 1 \ **Teachers:** 74 \ **Students:** 900 \ **Special Ed Students:** 128 \ **LEP Students:** 75 \ **Ethnic:** Asian 25%, African American 3%, Hispanic 5%, Caucasian 68% \ **Exp:** $407 (High) \ **Poverty:** 2% \ **Special Education:** $345,000 \ **Open-Close:** 08/20 - 06/03 \ **DTBP:** $235 (High) \

Allison Sherman 1
Oswaldo Suarez 3,91
Lily Mulaned 34,59*
Scott Blumberg 73,84
Sarah Cacciatore 288*
Dr Kurt Valentin 2,12,298
Nick Heckel 5*
Anthony Giamis 67
Ryan Murray 83,88*

Public Schs..Principal	Grd	Prgm	Enr/#Cls	SN	
Oak Grove Sch 1700 Oplaine Rd, Libertyville 60048 Nick Heckel	K-8		900 54		847/367-4120

• **Rondout School District 72** PID: 00301945
28593 N Bradley Rd, Lake Forest 60045
847/362-2021
Fax 847/816-2067

Schools: 1 \ **Teachers:** 16 \ **Students:** 140 \ **Special Ed Students:** 39 \ **LEP Students:** 5 \ **Ethnic:** Asian 9%, Hispanic 8%, Caucasian 83% \ **Exp:** $670 (High) \ **Poverty:** 4% \ **Title I:** $8,453 \ **Special Education:** $88,000 \ **Open-Close:** 08/24 - 05/28 \ **DTBP:** $240 (High)

Dr Jenny Wojcik 1,11
Lora Kellie 7*
Judith Satkiewicz 73*
Bryan Albro 3*
Jennifer Koenig 67
Ilysa Grossman 90*

Public Schs..Principal	Grd	Prgm	Enr/#Cls	SN	
Rondout Elem Sch 28593 N Bradley Rd, Lake Forest 60045 David Nitka	PK-8		140 15	4%	847/362-2021

• **Round Lake Area Co Dist 116** PID: 00301878
884 W Nippersink Rd, Round Lake 60073
847/270-9000
Fax 847/201-2669

Schools: 10 \ **Teachers:** 502 \ **Students:** 7,300 \ **Special Ed Students:** 1,208 \ **LEP Students:** 2,131 \ **College-Bound:** 64% \ **Ethnic:** Asian 1%, African American 7%, Hispanic 78%, Native American: 1%, Caucasian 13% \ **Exp:** $200 (Med) \ **Poverty:** 17% \ **Title I:** $2,135,799 \ **Special Education:** $4,155,000 \ **Bilingual Education:** $893,000 \ **Open-Close:** 08/17 - 05/26 \ **DTBP:** $191 (High)

Dr Donn Mendoza 1
Bill Johnston 2,15,19

1	Superintendent	8	Curric/Instruct K-12	19	Chief Financial Officer	29	Family/Consumer Science	39	Social Studies K-12	49	English/Lang Arts K-12	59	Special Education Elem	69	Academic Assessment
2	Bus/Finance/Purchasing	9	Curric/Instruct Elem	20	Art K-12	30	Adult Education	40	Social Studies Elem	50	English/Lang Arts Sec	60	Special Education Sec	70	Research/Development
3	Buildings And Grounds	10	Curric/Instruct Sec	21	Art Elem	31	Career/Sch-to-Work K-12	41	Social Studies Sec	51	Reading K-12	61	Foreign/World Lang K-12	71	Public Information
4	Food Service	11	Federal Program	22	Art Sec	32	Career/Sch-to-Work Elem	42	Science K-12	52	Reading Elem	62	Foreign/World Lang Elem	72	Summer School
5	Transportation	12	Title I	23	Music K-12	33	Career/Sch-to-Work Sec	43	Science Elem	53	Reading Sec	63	Foreign/World Lang Sec	73	Instructional Tech
6	Athletic	13	Title V	24	Music Elem	34	Early Childhood Ed	44	Science Sec	54	Remedial Reading K-12	64	Religious Education K-12	74	Inservice Training
7	Health Services	15	Asst Superintendent	25	Music Sec	35	Health/Phys Education	45	Math K-12	55	Remedial Reading Elem	65	Religious Education Elem	75	Marketing/Distributive
		16	Instructional Media Svcs	26	Business Education	36	Guidance Services K-12	46	Math Elem	56	Remedial Reading Sec	66	Religious Education Sec	76	Info Systems
		17	Chief Operations Officer	27	Career & Tech Ed	37	Guidance Services Elem	47	Math Sec	57	Bilingual/ELL	67	School Board President	77	Psychological Assess
		18	Chief Academic Officer	28	Technology Education	38	Guidance Services Sec	48	English/Lang Arts K-12	58	Special Education K-12	68	Teacher Personnel	78	Affirmative Action

Illinois School Directory — Lake County

Name	Ref
Dr Mary Lamping	3,17
Becky Moran	6*
Dr Susan Center	8,18
Kurt Rohlwing	10
Daniel Nicholas	39
Sarah Fontana	48,280
Melanie Lanni	57
Lisa Mari	58
Kristie Belesiotis	68
Dejan Kozic	73,84
Elizabeth Dampf	74
Yesenia Jimenez Captai	79
Luis Garcia	5
Eric Apgar	8,15
Elizabeth Kiewicz	9
Christina Cacciatore	20,23
Christopher Haruska	45
Mariel Doty	57
Jane Wilson	58
Kevin Daniels	67
Heather Bennett	71
Cariee Gibson	74
Lori Hausherr	76
Jennifer Wells	752

Public Schs..Principal	Grd	Prgm	Enr/#Cls	SN	
Beach Elem Sch 1421 Ardmore Dr, Round Lake 60073 Trina Metz	1-5	T	464 26	77%	847/270-9930 Fax 847/270-3153 f
Indian Hill Elem Sch 1920 Lotus Dr, Round Lake 60073 Raymond Porten	1-5	T	472 23	74%	847/270-9970 Fax 847/270-3172
John T MaGee Middle Sch 500 N Cedar Lake Rd, Round Lake 60073 Dr Lisa Steffen	6-8	T	775	75%	847/270-9060 Fax 847/740-3836
Kindergarten at Pleviak 304 E Grand Ave, Lake Villa 60046 Dr Jeff King	K-K	T	448 22	76%	847/270-9490 Fax 847/740-5183
Preschool at Early Educ Ctr 882 W Nippersink Rd, Round Lake 60073 Jeanette Metzger	PK-PK		192		847/270-9920
Raymond Ellis Elem Sch 720 Central Park Dr, Round Lake 60073 Scott Kubelka	1-5	T	593 35	77%	847/270-9900 Fax 847/270-9905
Round Lake High Sch 800 High School Dr, Round Lake 60073 Michael Berrie	9-12	TV	2,219 45	71%	847/270-9300 Fax 847/270-9332
Round Lake Middle Sch 2000 Lotus Dr, Round Lake 60073 David Higgs	6-8	T	896 40	72%	847/270-9400 Fax 847/270-9419
Village Elem Sch 880 W Nippersink Rd, Round Lake 60073 Jason Smith	K-5	T	450 23	77%	847/270-9470 Fax 847/201-2661
W J Murphy Elem Sch 220 Greenwood Dr, Round Lake 60073 Dr Phillip Georgia	1-5	T	511 26	81%	847/270-9950 Fax 847/546-2394

- **Township High School Dist 113** PID: 00301098   224/765-1000
  1040 Park Ave W, Highland Park 60035   Fax 224/765-1061

Schools: 2 \ **Teachers:** 264 \ **Students:** 3,616 \ **Special Ed Students:** 543 \ **LEP Students:** 109 \ **College-Bound:** 80% \ **Ethnic:** Asian 3%, African American 2%, Hispanic 15%, Caucasian 80% \ **Exp:** $196 (Low) \ **Poverty:** 4% \ **Title I:** $125,107 \ **Special Education:** $2,594,000 \ **Bilingual Education:** $23,000 \ **Open-Close:** 08/17 - 05/28 \ **DTBP:** $191 (High)

Name	Ref
Bruce Law	1
John Sghrurjohn	3
Tom Kreger	15,68,78
Reni Mitkova	30,57
Elizabeth Garlovsky	67
Ali Menhanti	2,15
Michael Lach	10,11,15,27,69,74,81
Ronald Casbohm	16,73,295
Tiffany Chavez	60

Public Schs..Principal	Grd	Prgm	Enr/#Cls	SN	
Deerfield High Sch 1959 Waukegan Rd, Deerfield 60015 Kathryn Anderson	9-12	GV	1,635 90	4%	224/632-3000 Fax 224/632-3700 f t
Highland Park High Sch 433 Vine Ave, Highland Park 60035 Deborah Finn	9-12	GV	1,981 50	14%	224/765-2000 Fax 224/765-2700

- **Warren Twp High Sch Dist 121** PID: 00301995   847/662-1400
  34090 N Almond Rd, Gurnee 60031   Fax 847/548-0564

Schools: 2 \ **Teachers:** 236 \ **Students:** 4,049 \ **Special Ed Students:** 513 \ **LEP Students:** 207 \ **College-Bound:** 78% \ **Ethnic:** Asian 12%, African American 10%, Hispanic 35%, Caucasian 42% \ **Exp:** $461 (High) \ **Poverty:** 6% \ **Title I:** $369,129 \ **Special Education:** $2,677,000 \ **Bilingual Education:** $31,000 \ **Open-Close:** 08/13 - 05/28 \ **DTBP:** $204 (High) \ f t

Name	Ref	Name	Ref
Dr John Ahlgrim	1	Dollie Jacobson	2
Mike Engel	2,3,15	Jose Zires	3
Jeanne Turf	5,60	Becky Belmont	6
Chris Geocaris	10,15	Wileen Gehrig	10,68*
Patrick Keeley	15,79	Peg Merar	60*
Thomas Drake	67	Nate Karasek	72*
Rico D'Amore	73*		

Public Schs..Principal	Grd	Prgm	Enr/#Cls	SN	
Warren Twp HS-Almond Campus 34090 N Almond Rd, Gurnee 60031 Rob Parrott	11-12	GV	1,929	17%	847/662-1400 Fax 847/548-6444
Warren Twp HS-O'Plaine Campus 500 N Oplaine Rd, Gurnee 60031 Gregory Meyer	9-10	GV	1,916		847/662-1400 Fax 847/599-4848 f t

- **Wauconda Cmty Unit SD 118** PID: 00302016   847/526-7690
  555 N Main St, Wauconda 60084   Fax 847/526-1019

Schools: 6 \ **Teachers:** 300 \ **Students:** 4,500 \ **Special Ed Students:** 674 \ **LEP Students:** 589 \ **College-Bound:** 73% \ **Ethnic:** Asian 4%, African American 2%, Hispanic 31%, Caucasian 63% \ **Exp:** $314 (High) \ **Poverty:** 7% \ **Title I:** $435,383 \ **Special Education:** $2,025,000 \ **Bilingual Education:** $157,000 \ **Open-Close:** 08/17 - 05/27 \ **DTBP:** $190 (High)

Name	Ref	Name	Ref
Dr Daniel Coles	1	Adam Tjardes	3
Rick Strauss	5	Mark Ribbens	6*
Lisa Dewelde	7,15,68,74,85	Dr David Wilm	8,15
Dr Julia Nadler	15	Scott Cittadino	15,16,73,76,95,295*
Sandra Marian	57	Heather Fontanetta	58,79
Kelly Plunk	58	Stacy O'Dea	58
Kathy Bianco	67	William Stanton	69

Public Schs..Principal	Grd	Prgm	Enr/#Cls	SN	
Cotton Creek Elem Sch 545 Newport Ct, Island Lake 60042 Diane Kelly	PK-5	T	592 25	32%	847/526-4700 Fax 847/526-4725
Matthews Middle Sch 3500 Darrell Rd, Island Lake 60042 Bob Taterka	6-8		437	39%	847/526-6210 Fax 847/526-8918
Robert Crown Elem Sch 620 W Bonner Rd, Wauconda 60084 Karrie Diol	PK-5		926 37	19%	847/526-7100 Fax 847/487-3596
Wauconda Cmty High Sch 555 N Main St, Wauconda 60084 Daniel Klett	9-12	ATV	1,370 50	38%	847/526-6611 Fax 847/487-3595
Wauconda Grade Sch 225 Osage St, Wauconda 60084 Debra Monroe	PK-5	T	590 35	47%	847/526-6671 Fax 847/487-3598
Wauconda Middle Sch 217 Slocum Lake Rd, Wauconda 60084 Danny Stoller	6-8	T	636 30	39%	847/526-2122 Fax 847/487-3597

---

79 Student Personnel	91 Safety/Security	275 Response To Intervention	298 Grant Writer/Ptnrships	**School Programs** A = Alternative Program
80 Driver Ed/Safety	92 Magnet School	277 Remedial Math K-12	750 Chief Innovation Officer	G = Adult Classes
81 Gifted/Talented	93 Parental Involvement	280 Literacy Coach	751 Chief of Staff	M = Magnet Program
82 Video Services	95 Tech Prep Program	285 STEM	752 Social Emotional Learning	T = Title I Schoolwide
84 Substance Abuse Prev	97 Chief Information Officer	286 Digital Learning		V = Career & Tech Ed Programs
84 Erate	98 Chief Technology Officer	288 Common Core Standards	**Other School Types**	
85 AIDS Education	270 Character Education	294 Accountability	A = Alternative School	**Social Media** f = Facebook
88 Alternative/At Risk	271 Migrant Education	295 Network System	C = Charter School	t = Twitter
89 Multi-Cultural Curriculum	273 Teacher Mentor	296 Title II Programs	M = Magnet School	New Schools are shaded
90 Social Work	274 Before/After Sch	297 Webmaster	Y = Year-Round School	New Superintendents and Principals are bold Personnel with email addresses are underscored

Lake County

Market Data Retrieval

• **Waukegan Cmty Unit SD 60** PID: 00302080 224/303-1000
1201 N Sheridan Rd, Waukegan 60085 Fax 224/399-8581

Schools: 24 \ **Teachers:** 834 \ **Students:** 17,000 \
Special Ed Students: 2,225 \ **LEP Students:** 5,481 \ **College-Bound:** 60%
\ **Ethnic:** Asian 1%, African American 14%, Hispanic 80%, Native American: 1%, Caucasian 4% \ **Exp:** $328 (High) \ **Poverty:** 21% \ **Title I:** $6,520,913
\ **Special Education:** $9,545,000 \ **Bilingual Education:** $1,484,000 \
Open-Close: 08/17 - 05/27 \ **DTBP:** $73 (Low)

Theresa Plascencia	1	Brian Luosa	2
Gwen Polk	2,15	LeBaron Moten	3,17
Otis Hickman	3	Alicia Williams	4,5
Colette Erbach	6*	Eduardo Cesario	8,15,18
Dr Staci Stratigakes	10	Nicholas Chin	11*
Angel Figueroa	15,68	Josue Cuevas	15,76
Nicholas Alajakis	15,71,751	Rasoc Cretia	34
Mary Olson	35	Anne Zahn	43,81
Matthew Foster	46*	Elisabeth Ambroiggie	57
Lana Reiner	58	Brandon Ewing	67
Elisa Trevino	68	Tasia Fields	73
Eric Christianson	79	Dr Robert Lopez	91
Jason Nault	294		

Public Schs..Principal	Grd	Prgm	Enr/#Cls	SN		
Ⓐ Alternative Optional Ed Ctr 1020 Glen Rock Ave, Waukegan 60085 Kevin Turner	7-12		228 6		224/303-2860 Fax 224/399-8520	
Ⓜ Andrew Cooke Magnet Elem Sch 522 Belvidere Rd, Waukegan 60085 Stephanie Jensen	PK-5	T	472 22	52%	224/303-1700 Fax 224/399-8528	
Carman-Buckner Elem Sch 520 Helmholz Ave, Waukegan 60085 Roberto Silva	PK-5	T	553 36	85%	224/303-1500 Fax 224/399-8514	
Clearview Elem Sch 1700 Delaware Rd, Waukegan 60087 Sandi Johnson	K-5	T	515 30	77%	224/303-1600 Fax 224/399-8526	
Daniel Webster Middle Sch 930 New York St, Waukegan 60085 Yvonne Brown	6-8	T	693 50	71%	224/303-2760 Fax 224/399-8540	
Glen Flora Elem Sch 1110 Chestnut St, Waukegan 60085 Joel Ruiz	K-5	T	488 22	73%	224/303-1800 Fax 224/399-8532	
Glenwood Elem Sch 2500 Northmoor Ave, Waukegan 60085 Cabrina Leneau	K-5	T	697 20	72%	224/303-2010 Fax 224/399-8504	
Greenwood Elem Sch 1919 North Ave, Waukegan 60087 Joyce Meyer	PK-5	T	304 18	62%	224/303-2080 Fax 224/399-8534	
H R McCall Elem Sch 3215 N McAree Rd, Waukegan 60087 Carol May	PK-5	T	452 13	60%	224/303-1760 Fax 224/399-8502	
Hyde Park Elem Sch 1525 Hyde Park Ave, Waukegan 60085 Brian Carr	K-5	T	290 13	70%	224/303-1970 Fax 224/399-8500	
Jack Benny Middle Sch 1401 Montesano Ave, Waukegan 60087 Issac Kirkwood	6-8	T	589	54%	224/303-2460 Fax 224/399-8524	
John S Clark Elem Sch 601 Blanchard Rd, Waukegan 60085 Gladys Rodriguez	K-5	T	223 12	67%	224/303-1570 Fax 224/399-8522	
Little Fort Elem Sch 1775 Blanchard Rd, Waukegan 60087 Amy Grossman	K-5	T	488 29	64%	224/303-3700 Fax 224/399-8510	
Ⓜ Lyon Magnet Elem Sch 800 S Elmwood Ave, Waukegan 60085 Amanda Pryce	PK-5	T	495 25	63%	224/303-2300 Fax 224/399-8530	
Miguel Juarez Middle Sch 201 N Butrick St, Waukegan 60085 Nelson Campos	6-8	T	764 85	64%	224/303-2660 Fax 224/399-8506	
North Elem Sch 410 Franklin St, Waukegan 60085 Nicole Lemberger	PK-5	T	570 25	74%	224/303-2160 Fax 224/399-8518	
Oakdale Elem Sch 2230 N McAree Rd, Waukegan 60087 Catalina Nelson	PK-5	T	498 25	63%	224/303-1860 Fax 224/399-8508	
Robbie M Lightfoot ELC 1721 N McAree Rd, Waukegan 60085 Nicole Session	PK-PK		380		224/303-1400 Fax 224/399-8610	
Robert Abbott Middle Sch 1319 Washington St, Waukegan 60085 Carl Hagman	6-8	T	767 65	65%	224/303-2360 Fax 224/399-8512	
Thomas Jefferson Middle Sch 600 S Lewis Ave, Waukegan 60085 Clarence Berry	6-8	T	899 56	67%	224/303-2560 Fax 224/399-8516	
Washington Elem Sch 110 S Orchard Ave, Waukegan 60085 Jason Siegellak	K-5	T	529 24	68%	224/303-2220 Fax 224/399-8536	
Waukegan HS Brookside 2325 Brookside Ave, Waukegan 60085 Timothy Bryner	9-12	GTV	4,606 120	59%	224/303-3000 Fax 224/399-8542	
Waukegan HS-Washington 1011 Washington St, Waukegan 60085 Timothy Bryner	9-12		1,675 75		224/303-3301 Fax 224/399-8549	
Whittier Elem Sch 901 N Lewis Ave, Waukegan 60085 Jennifer De La Sanchez	K-5	GT	540 26	71%	224/303-1900 Fax 224/399-8538	

• **Winthrop Harbor School Dist 1** PID: 00302377 847/731-3085
500 North Ave, Winthrop HBR 60096 Fax 847/731-3156

Schools: 2 \ **Teachers:** 41 \ **Students:** 542 \ **Special Ed Students:** 82
\ **LEP Students:** 16 \ **Ethnic:** Asian 2%, African American 6%, Hispanic 27%, Caucasian 64% \ **Exp:** $302 (High) \ **Poverty:** 9% \ **Title I:** $83,831 \
Special Education: $210,000 \ **Open-Close:** 08/27 - 06/04 \ **DTBP:** $233 (High)

Jeffrey McCartney	1,11	Julie Lippeth	2
Traci Strieter	59	Rick Lambert	67
Phillip Traskaski	73		

Public Schs..Principal	Grd	Prgm	Enr/#Cls	SN	
North Prairie Junior High Sch 500 North Ave, Winthrop HBR 60096 Carrie Nottingham	5-8		240 20	42%	847/731-3089 Fax 847/731-3152
Westfield Sch 2309 9th St, Winthrop HBR 60096 Summer Poepping	PK-4		302 18	32%	847/872-5438 Fax 847/746-1477

• **Woodland School District 50** PID: 00302420 847/596-5600
1105 N Hunt Club Rd, Gurnee 60031 Fax 847/856-0311

Schools: 5 \ **Teachers:** 420 \ **Students:** 5,700 \ **Special Ed Students:** 695
\ **LEP Students:** 1,144 \ **Ethnic:** Asian 12%, African American 8%, Hispanic 35%, Native American: 1%, Caucasian 44% \ **Exp:** $282 (Med)
\ **Poverty:** 6% \ **Title I:** $612,511 \ **Special Education:** $3,460,000 \
Bilingual Education: $378,000 \ **Open-Close:** 08/26 - 06/11 \ **DTBP:** $198 (High) \ ✉

Lori Casey	1,83	Robert Leonard	2
Robert Burke	3	Walter Doughty	5
Steven Thomas	9,11,16,57,69,286,288,294	Christopher Bobek	15
Donna Vandenbroek	15,59,90	Elizabeth Szepesi	57

1	Superintendent	8	Curric/Instruct K-12	19	Chief Financial Officer	29	Family/Consumer Science	39	Social Studies K-12	49	English/Lang Arts Elem	59	Special Education Elem	69	Academic Assessment
2	Bus/Finance/Purchasing	9	Curric/Instruct Elem	20	Art K-12	30	Adult Education	40	Social Studies Elem	50	English/Lang Arts Sec	60	Special Education Sec	70	Research/Development
3	Buildings And Grounds	10	Curric/Instruct Sec	21	Art Elem	31	Career/Sch-to-Work K-12	41	Social Studies Sec	51	Reading K-12	61	Foreign/World Lang K-12	71	Public Information
4	Food Service	11	Federal Program	22	Art Sec	32	Career/Sch-to-Work Elem	42	Science K-12	52	Reading Elem	62	Foreign/World Lang Elem	72	Summer School
5	Transportation	12	Title I	23	Music K-12	33	Career/Sch-to-Work Sec	43	Science Elem	53	Reading Sec	63	Foreign/World Lang Sec	73	Instructional Tech
6	Athletic	13	Title V	24	Music Elem	34	Early Childhood Ed	44	Science Sec	54	Remedial Reading K-12	64	Religious Education K-12	74	Inservice Training
7	Health Services	14	Instructional Media Svcs	25	Music Sec	35	Health/Phys Education	45	Math K-12	55	Remedial Reading Elem	65	Religious Education Elem	75	Marketing/Distributive
		15	Asst Superintendent	26	Business Education	36	Guidance Services K-12	46	Math Elem	56	Remedial Reading Sec	66	Religious Education Sec	76	Info Systems
		16	Chief Operations Officer	27	Career & Tech Ed	37	Guidance Services Elem	47	Math Sec	57	Bilingual/ELL	67	School Board President	77	Psychological Assess
		17	Chief Academic Officer	28	Technology Education	38	Guidance Services Sec	48	English/Lang Arts K-12	58	Special Education K-12	68	Teacher Personnel	78	Affirmative Action

Illinois School Directory — Lake County

Valerie Morey 57	Dr Carla Little 67
Martha Gutierrez 68	Nancy Whittall 68
Sharon Cook 68	Carolyn Waller-Gordon 71
Dann Giesey 73,295	Steve Kohl 73

Public Schs..Principal	Grd	Prgm	Enr/#Cls	SN	
Woodland Elem Sch East 17261 W Gages Lake Rd, Gages Lake 60030 Lisa West \ Ryan Wollberg	1-3		1,445 52	32%	847/984-8800 Fax 847/549-9806
Woodland Elem Sch West 17371 W Gages Lake Rd, Gages Lake 60030 Ryan Wollberg	1-3		850 51		847/984-8900 Fax 847/816-0708 t
Woodland Intermediate Sch 1115 N Hunt Club Rd, Gurnee 60031 Derek Straight	4-5		1,230 70	38%	847/596-5900 Fax 847/855-9828 t
Woodland Middle Sch 7000 Washington St, Gurnee 60031 Tiffany Drake	6-8	A	1,935	34%	847/856-3400 Fax 847/856-1306
Woodland Primary Sch 17366 W Gages Lake Rd, Gages Lake 60030 Stacey Anderson	PK-K		620 33	35%	847/984-8700 Fax 847/816-4511

- **Zion Public School District 6**   PID: 00302468   847/872-5455
  2800 29th St, Zion 60099   Fax 847/505-0720

Schools: 7 \ **Teachers:** 221 \ **Students:** 2,700 \ **Special Ed Students:** 417 \ **LEP Students:** 600 \ **Ethnic:** African American 40%, Hispanic 54%, Caucasian 6% \ **Exp:** $464 (High) \ **Poverty:** 26% \ **Title I:** $1,202,056 \ **Special Education:** $1,291,000 \ **Bilingual Education:** $230,000 \ **Open-Close:** 08/27 - 06/04 \ **DTBP:** $193 (High) \ f t

Dr Keely Roberts 1	George Tolczyk 2,3,19,91
Wanda Warren 7*	Amy Gannon 9,11,280,285,288,296,298
Suzy Peterson 9	Donelle Staples 16,71,286,295
Amy Gannon 57*	Ruth Davis 67
Dr Sandra Stringer 68,78	Jeremy Wickham 73
Sean Connolly 79	Michael Scofield 84,295
Craig Kennedy 295	

Public Schs..Principal	Grd	Prgm	Enr/#Cls	SN	
Beulah Park Elem Sch 1910 Gilboa Ave, Zion 60099 Curtiss Tolefree	K-6	T	384 16	88%	847/746-1429 Fax 847/746-7803 f t
East Elem Sch 2913 Elim Ave, Zion 60099 Charmekia Edelstein	K-6	T	176 16	85%	847/872-5425 Fax 847/872-8130 f t
Elmwood Elem Sch 3025 Ezra St, Zion 60099 Deidre Garnett	K-6	T	295 16	88%	847/746-1491 Fax 847/746-0052 f t
Lakeview Sch 2200 Bethesda Blvd, Zion 60099 Cheryl Caesar	PK-PK		240 3	77%	847/872-0255 Fax 847/416-4840
Shiloh Park Elem Sch 2635 Gabriel Ave, Zion 60099 Robert Schulz	K-6	T	462 21	88%	847/746-8136 Fax 847/731-8453
West Elem Sch 2412 Jethro Ave, Zion 60099 Nicholas Heckel	K-6	T	459 23	88%	847/746-8222 Fax 847/731-8490 f t
Zion Central Middle Sch 1716 27th St, Zion 60099 Venus Shannon	7-8	TV	546 46	84%	847/746-1431 Fax 847/746-9750 f t

- **Zion-Benton Twp High SD 126**   PID: 00302547   847/731-9300
  3901 21st St, Zion 60099   Fax 847/731-4441

Schools: 2 \ **Teachers:** 171 \ **Students:** 2,100 \ **Special Ed Students:** 408 \ **LEP Students:** 188 \ **College-Bound:** 64% \ **Ethnic:** Asian 2%, African American 28%, Hispanic 49%, Caucasian 20% \ **Exp:** $299 (Med) \ **Poverty:** 15% \ **Title I:** $652,532 \ **Special Education:** $1,415,000 \ **Bilingual Education:** $30,000 \ **Open-Close:** 08/31 - 06/03 \ **DTBP:** $198 (High)

Dr Jesse Rodregruez 1	Matthew Wilkinson 2,11
Joshua Gehrig 3	Jason Ponivas 4
Rita Maki 5	Lonnie Bible 6
Melissa Digangi 10*	Deborah Will 16,82*
Jacey Kolarik 41	Michael Blades 50,53,56*
Dr Susan Barker 60*	Shawn White 67
Dalila Mondragon 68	Jake Carlson 69,79*
Ryan Faith 73,286	Bob Worthington 91
Robert Worthington 91*	Joe Fleming 295

Public Schs..Principal	Grd	Prgm	Enr/#Cls	SN	
New Tech High Zion-Benton East 1634 23rd St, Zion 60099 Christopher Kubic	9-12	T	350	47%	847/731-9800 Fax 847/746-5428 f t
Ⓐ Zion Benton Township High Sch 3901 21st St, Zion 60099 Chris Pawelczyk	9-12	TV	2,210	57%	847/731-9300

LAKE CATHOLIC SCHOOLS

- **Archdiocese of Chicago Ed Off**   PID: 00282923
  Listing includes only schools located in this county. See District Index for location of Diocesan Offices.

Catholic Schs..Principal	Grd	Prgm	Enr/#Cls	SN	
Carmel High Sch 1 Carmel Pkwy, Mundelein 60060 Jason Huther	9-12		1,360 58		847/566-3000 Fax 847/566-8465
East Lake Academy 13911 W Laurel Dr, Lake Forest 60045 Rosario Echavez	PK-8		80		847/247-0035 f t
Frassati Catholic Academy 22277 W Erhart Rd, Mundelein 60060 Tammy Kleckner	PK-5		155 12		847/223-4021 Fax 847/223-3489 f
Frassati Catholic Academy 316 W Mill St, Wauconda 60084 Tammy Kleckner	PK-8		200 11		847/526-6311 Fax 847/526-4637 f
Most Blessed Trinity Academy 510 Grand Ave, Waukegan 60085 Lynne Saccaro	PK-8		272 11		847/623-4110 Fax 847/599-0477
Our Lady of Humility Sch 10601 W Wadsworth Rd, Beach Park 60099 M Dolan	PK-8		285 15		847/746-3722 Fax 847/731-2870
Prince of Peace Sch 135 S Milwaukee Ave, Lake Villa 60046 Dr Stephanie Stoneberg	K-8		220 9		847/356-6111 Fax 847/356-6121
School of St Mary 185 E Illinois Rd, Lake Forest 60045 David Wieters	PK-8		544 31		847/234-0371 Fax 847/234-9593 f
St Anastasia Sch 629 W Glen Flora Ave, Waukegan 60085 Paula Dean	PK-8		240 18		847/623-8320 Fax 847/623-0556 f

79 Student Personnel	91 Safety/Security	275 Response To Intervention	298 Grant Writer/Ptnrships	**School Programs**
80 Driver Ed/Safety	92 Magnet School	277 Remedial Math K-12	750 Chief Innovation Officer	A = Alternative Program
81 Gifted/Talented	93 Parental Involvement	280 Literacy Coach	751 Chief of Staff	G = Adult Classes
82 Video Services	95 Tech Prep Program	285 STEM	752 Social Emotional Learning	M = Magnet Program
83 Substance Abuse Prev	97 Chief Infomation Officer	286 Digital Learning		T = Title I Schoolwide
84 Erate	98 Chief Technology Officer	288 Common Core Standards	**Other School Types**	V = Career & Tech Ed Programs
85 AIDS Education	270 Accountability	294 Accountability	Ⓐ = Alternative School	
88 Alternative/At Risk	271 Migrant Education	295 Network System	Ⓒ = Charter School	**Social Media**
89 Multi-Cultural Curriculum	273 Teacher Mentor	296 Title II Programs	Ⓜ = Magnet School	f = Facebook
90 Social Work	274 Before/After Sch	297 Webmaster	Ⓨ = Year-Round School	t = Twitter

New Schools are shaded
New Superintendents and Principals are bold
Personnel with email addresses are underscored

Lake County

St Anne Catholic Sch 319 Franklin St, Barrington 60010 Dawn Kapka	PK-8	470 24	847/381-0311 Fax 847/381-0384	
St Bede Sch 36399 N Wilson Rd, Ingleside 60041 Kari Rybarczyk	PK-8	200 14	847/587-5541 Fax 847/587-2713	f
St Francis De Sales Sch 11 S Buesching Rd, Lake Zurich 60047 Kyle Schmitt	PK-8	281 25	847/438-7921 Fax 847/438-7114	f
St Gilbert Sch 231 E Belvidere Rd, Grayslake 60030 Christine Buckley	PK-8	430 27	847/223-8600 Fax 847/223-8626	
St Joseph Sch 221 Park Pl, Libertyville 60048 Anne Phoenix	PK-8	515 19	847/362-0730 Fax 847/362-8130	f
St Mary Sch 50 N Buffalo Grove Rd, Buffalo Grove 60089 Kris Gritzmacher	PK-8	650 30	847/459-6270 Fax 847/537-2810	f
St Patrick Sch 15020 W Wadsworth Rd, Wadsworth 60083 Mary Vitulli	K-8	425 18	847/623-8446 Fax 847/623-3119	f
Woodlands Academy Sacred Heart 760 E Westleigh Rd, Lake Forest 60045 Rocco Gargiulo	9-12	165 15	847/234-4300 Fax 847/234-4348	

LAKE PRIVATE SCHOOLS

Private Schs..Principal	Grd	Prgm	Enr/#Cls SN		
Allendale Sch Route 132 & Offield Dr, Lake Villa 60046 Jennifer Stiemsma	Spec	V	180 20	847/245-6401 Fax 847/356-0455	
Arlyn Day Sch 2789 Oak St, Highland Park 60035 Judith Goldstein	6-12	V	36 5	847/256-7117 Fax 847/256-7188	
Calvary Christian Academy 134 Monaville Rd, Lake Villa 60046 Dirk Moore	PK-6		90 8	847/356-6198	f
Country Meadows Montessori Sch 6151 Washington St, Gurnee 60031 Mary O'Young	PK-8		130 9	847/244-9352 Fax 847/244-1068	
Cristo Rey St Martin Clg Prep 3106 Belvidere Rd, Waukegan 60085 Michael Odiotti	9-12		380	224/215-9400 Fax 224/219-9737	
DaVinci Waldorf Sch 150 W Bonner Rd, Wauconda 60084 Marrianne Fieber	PK-8		100	847/526-1372	
Faith Lutheran Sch 1275 Main St, Antioch 60002 Craig Breitkreutz	PK-8		181 10	847/395-1660 Fax 847/589-0519	
Fusion Academy-Lake Forest 840 S Waukegan Rd Ste 224, Lake Forest 60045 Cindi Di Iorio	6-12		70	847/295-4039 Fax 847/295-4116	
Gurnee Christian Academy 2190 Fuller Rd, Gurnee 60031 Katrina Baun	PK-12		110 5	847/623-7773 Fax 847/599-9114	
Hellenic American Acad 445 Pine St, Deerfield 60015 Christina Bennett	PK-8	G	160 12	847/317-1063 Fax 847/317-9653	
Immanuel Lutheran Sch 1310 N Frolic Ave, Waukegan 60085 Steven Rudunzel	PK-6		45 6	847/249-0011 Fax 847/739-7313	
Lake Co Baptist Sch 1550 W York House Rd, Waukegan 60087 Tim Kowach	PK-12		165 14	847/623-7600 Fax 847/623-2085	
Lake Forest Academy 1500 W Kennedy Rd, Lake Forest 60045 Jose De Jesus	9-12		300 30	847/234-3210 Fax 847/615-3202	
Lake Forest Country Day Sch 145 S Green Bay Rd, Lake Forest 60045 Pete Moore \ Andrew Sperling	PK-8		400 45	847/234-2350 Fax 847/234-2352	
Lake Shore Academy 621 Belvidere Rd, Waukegan 60085 Sheela Patel	Spec		85	847/599-1680 Fax 847/599-2475	
Life Pointe Christian Sch 5501 Stearns School Rd, Gurnee 60031 Jodi Abbott	PK-1		46	847/662-2335 Fax 847/662-2332	
Lions Math & Science Chrn Acad 1011 Porter St, Waukegan 60085 Dr Jean Swopes	PK-8		125	847/360-1054 Fax 847/782-9362	
Montessori Sch of Lake Forest 13700 W Laurel Dr, Lake Forest 60045 Ann Jordahl	PK-6	G	210 8	847/918-1000 Fax 847/918-1304	
Montessori School-Long Grove 1115 RFD, Long Grove 60047 Carol Martorano	PK-6		64 6	847/634-0430 Fax 847/726-7928	
Old School Montessori 144 Commerce Dr Ste E, Grayslake 60030 Cristina Youtsey	PK-6		100 7	847/223-9606	
Our Saviour's Lutheran Sch 1800 23rd St, Zion 60099 John Kujath	PK-8		68 5	847/872-5922 Fax 847/872-5539	
Quentin Road Christian Sch 24126 N Quentin Rd, Lake Zurich 60047 John Tanney	PK-12		160 20	847/438-4494 Fax 847/550-9967	
Rochelle Zell Jewish High Sch 1095 Lake Cook Rd, Deerfield 60015 Tony Frank	9-12		165	847/470-6700 Fax 847/324-3701	
Sabio Academy 830 S Buffalo Grove Rd Ste 115, Buffalo Grove 60089 James Choi	7-12		200	847/219-8817 Fax 866/214-4643	
Sheila Daniels Christian Acad 3601 N Lewis Ave, Waukegan 60087 Tynisha Gardner	PK-8		53 7	847/263-8147 Fax 847/263-8377	
St John Lutheran Sch 501 W Park Ave, Libertyville 60048 John Woldt	PK-8		90 8	847/367-1441	
St Matthew Lutheran Sch 24480 N Old McHenry Rd, Hawthorn WDS 60047 Doug Duval \ Timothy Kinne	PK-K		130 8	847/438-6103 Fax 847/438-0376	
Stepping Stone Sch 600 W Grand Ave, Lake Villa 60046 Jennifer Stayma	K-12		160	847/356-3334 Fax 847/356-0455	
Torah Academy 720 Armstrong Dr, Buffalo Grove 60089 Elisa Zehnwirth	PK-8		20	773/771-2613	
Westlake Christian Academy 275 S Lake St, Grayslake 60030 Laura Dereus	PK-12		186 15	847/548-6209 Fax 847/548-6481	f
Zion Christian Sch 1828 Hebron Ave, Zion 60099 Valerie Burnette	PK-12		152 5	847/872-4088 Fax 847/872-3028	

LAKE REGIONAL CENTERS

• **Lake County Regional of Ed** PID: 03062306   847/543-7833
   800 Lancer Ln Ste E128, Grayslake 60030   Fax 847/543-7832

Roycealee Wood 1,11   Mike Munda 15

---

1 Superintendent	8 Curric/Instruct K-12	19 Chief Financial Officer	29 Family/Consumer Science	39 Social Studies K-12	49 English/Lang Arts Elem	59 Special Education Elem	69 Academic Assessment
2 Bus/Finance/Purchasing	9 Curric/Instruct Elem	20 Art K-12	30 Adult Education	40 Social Studies Elem	50 English/Lang Arts Sec	60 Special Education Sec	70 Research/Development
3 Buildings And Grounds	10 Curric/Instruct Sec	21 Art Elem	31 Career/Sch-to-Work K-12	41 Social Studies Sec	51 Reading K-12	61 Foreign/World Lang K-12	71 Public Information
4 Food Service	11 Federal Program	22 Art Sec	32 Career/Sch-to-Work Elem	42 Science K-12	52 Reading Elem	62 Foreign/World Lang Elem	72 Summer School
5 Transportation	12 Title I	23 Music K-12	33 Career/Sch-to-Work Sec	43 Science Elem	53 Reading Sec	63 Foreign/World Lang Sec	73 Instructional Tech
6 Athletic	13 Title V	24 Music Elem	34 Early Childhood Ed	44 Science Soc	54 Remedial Reading K-12	64 Religious Education K-12	74 Inservice Training
7 Health Services	15 Asst Superintendent	25 Music Sec	35 Health/Phys Education	45 Math K-12	55 Remedial Reading Elem	65 Religious Education Elem	75 Marketing/Distributive
	16 Instructional Media Svcs	26 Business Education	36 Guidance Services K-12	46 Math Elem	56 Remedial Reading Sec	66 Religious Education Sec	76 Info Systems
	17 Chief Operations Officer	27 Career & Tech Ed	37 Guidance Services Elem	47 Math Sec	57 Bilingual/ELL	67 School Board President	77 Psychological Assess
	18 Chief Academic Officer	28 Technology Education	38 Guidance Services Sec	48 English/Lang Arts K-12	58 Special Education K-12	68 Teacher Personnel	78 Affirmative Action

Illinois School Directory

Lee County

- **Northern Suburban Spec Ed Dist** PID: 02123696   847/831-5100
  760 Red Oak Ln, Highland Park 60035   Fax 847/868-9580
  Dr Kurt Schnieder 1   Andy Piper 15,68,74

- **Special Education Dist Lake Co** PID: 02182006   847/548-8470
  18160 W Gages Lake Rd, Gages Lake 60030   Fax 847/548-8472
  Valerie Donnan 1   Susan Kruckman 7
  Dr Ann Gear 34

LAWRENCE COUNTY

LAWRENCE PUBLIC SCHOOLS

- **Lawrence Co Cmty Sch Dist 20** PID: 00303620   618/943-2326
  1802 Cedar St, Lawrenceville 62439   Fax 618/943-4092

Schools: 3 \ Teachers: 91 \ Students: 1,125 \ Special Ed Students: 168 \ LEP Students: 4 \ College-Bound: 67% \ Ethnic: African American 1%, Hispanic 3%, Caucasian 95% \ Exp: $356 (High) \ Poverty: 22% \ Title I: $514,895 \ Special Education: $319,000 \ Open-Close: 08/14 - 05/28 \ f t

Doug Daugherty 1,11   Terry Cochran 7,35,85*
Rose West .....12*   Kris Rhinehart 58*
Mike Seitzinger 67   Brandon Stewart 73*

Public Schs..Principal	Grd	Prgm	Enr/#Cls	SN	
Lawrenceville High Sch 2200 James St, Lawrenceville 62439 Paul Higginbotham	9-12	TV	319 45	48%	618/943-3389 Fax 618/943-4925
Parkside Elem Sch 1900 Cedar St, Lawrenceville 62439 Julie Hayes	PK-5	T	569 50	53%	618/943-3992 Fax 618/943-4591
Parkview Junior High Sch 1802 Cedar St, Lawrenceville 62439 Jeremy Brush	6-8	T	259 25	63%	618/943-2327

- **Red Hill Cmty School Dist 10** PID: 00303723   618/945-2061
  1250 Judy Ave, Bridgeport 62417   Fax 618/945-7607

Schools: 3 \ Teachers: 64 \ Students: 977 \ Special Ed Students: 121 \ LEP Students: 3 \ College-Bound: 69% \ Ethnic: Hispanic 1%, Caucasian 99% \ Exp: $199 (Low) \ Poverty: 16% \ Title I: $261,073 \ Special Education: $251,000 \ Open-Close: 08/17 - 05/21 \ DTBP: $167 (High)

Jakie Walker 1,11,83   Kim Aldrige 2
Jennifer Schilt .....4*   Tracy Grey 6*
Clarance Groves 11,296   Bob Christy 67
Tammy Parker .....73*   Clarence Gross 288*

Public Schs..Principal	Grd	Prgm	Enr/#Cls	SN	
Bridgeport Grade Sch 1300 N Main St, Bridgeport 62417 Tony Gaither	PK-3	T	366 19	63%	618/945-5721 Fax 618/945-7111
Red Hill Jr Sr High Sch 908 Church St, Bridgeport 62417 Clarence Gross	7-12	T	409 30	57%	618/945-2521 Fax 618/945-7151

Sumner Attendance Center   4-6   T   183   58%   618/936-2412
110 W Locust St, Sumner 62466   12   Fax 618/936-2742
Todd Tiffany

LEE COUNTY

LEE PUBLIC SCHOOLS

- **Amboy Cmty Unit Sch Dist 272** PID: 00303797   815/857-2164
  11 E Hawley St, Amboy 61310   Fax 815/857-4434

Schools: 3 \ Teachers: 58 \ Students: 720 \ Special Ed Students: 99 \ LEP Students: 3 \ College-Bound: 73% \ Ethnic: Hispanic 6%, Caucasian 93% \ Exp: $169 (Low) \ Poverty: 10% \ Title I: $120,339 \ Special Education: $224,000 \ Open-Close: 08/17 - 05/21 \ DTBP: $166 (High)

Joshua Nichols 1,11   Molly Noble 2
Ken Willey 3,91   Amy Wittenauer 4,68
Al Quest 5   George Schwamberger 6*
Joyce Schamberger .....12*   Mary Jo Zinke 16*
Nicole Jones 67   Arnie Wiseman 73,286*
Kelly Whitman 83*

Public Schs..Principal	Grd	Prgm	Enr/#Cls	SN	
Amboy Central Elem Sch 30 E Provost St, Amboy 61310 Joyce Schamberger	PK-4		296 15	41%	815/857-3619 Fax 815/857-9024
Amboy High Sch 11 E Hawley St, Amboy 61310 Janet Crownhart	9-12		207 25	40%	815/857-3632 Fax 815/857-3631
Amboy Junior High Sch 140 S Appleton Ave, Amboy 61310 Andrew Full	5-8		216 27	50%	815/857-3528 Fax 815/857-4603 f

- **Ashton-Franklin Center SD 275** PID: 00303864   815/453-7461
  611 Western Ave, Ashton 61006   Fax 815/453-7462

Schools: 2 \ Teachers: 37 \ Students: 560 \ Special Ed Students: 63 \ LEP Students: 3 \ College-Bound: 68% \ Ethnic: African American 1%, Hispanic 6%, Caucasian 93% \ Exp: $149 (Low) \ Poverty: 13% \ Title I: $116,282 \ Special Education: $113,000 \ Open-Close: 08/27 - 06/03

Michael Lindy 1   Traci Gittleson 6*
Jennifer Warrenfeltz .....9*   Kim Torman 10,16
John Zick 11   Amy Drew 36,69,83,88*
Jennifer Cissna .....58*   Chad Murphy 67
Joe Gleissner 73,98,286*

Public Schs..Principal	Grd	Prgm	Enr/#Cls	SN	
Ashton Franklin Ctr Elem Sch 217 S Elm St, Franklin GRV 61031 Jennifer Warrenfeltz	PK-6		266 10	45%	815/456-2325 Fax 815/456-2713
Ashton Franklin Jr Sr High 611 Western Ave, Ashton 61006 Trina Dillon	7-12	V	229 20	45%	815/453-7461

---

79 Student Personnel
80 Driver Ed/Safety
81 Gifted/Talented
82 Video Services
83 Substance Abuse Prev
84 Erate
85 AIDS Education
88 Alternative/At Risk
89 Multi-Cultural Curriculum
90 Social Work

91 Safety/Security
92 Magnet School
93 Parental Involvement
95 Tech Prep Program
97 Chief Infomation Officer
98 Chief Technology Officer
270 Character Education
271 Migrant Education
273 Teacher Mentor
274 Before/After Sch

275 Response To Intervention
277 Remedial Math K-12
280 Literacy Coach
285 STEM
286 Digital Learning
288 Common Core Standards
294 Accountability
295 Network System
296 Title II Programs
297 Webmaster

298 Grant Writer/Ptnrships
750 Chief Innovation Officer
751 Chief of Staff
752 Social Emotional Learning

Other School Types
Ⓐ = Alternative School
Ⓒ = Charter School
Ⓜ = Magnet School
Ⓨ = Year-Round School

School Programs
A = Alternative Program
G = Adult Classes
M = Magnet Program
T = Title I Schoolwide
V = Career & Tech Ed Programs

New Schools are shaded
New Superintendents and Principals are bold
Personnel with email addresses are underscored

Social Media
f = Facebook
t = Twitter

Livingston County

- **Dixon Cmty Unit Sch Dist 170** PID: 00303905   815/284-7722
  1335 Franklin Grove Rd, Dixon 61021   Fax 815/284-8576

Schools: 5 \ **Teachers:** 154 \ **Students:** 2,432 \ **Special Ed Students:** 454 \ **LEP Students:** 58 \ **College-Bound:** 59% \ **Ethnic:** Asian 1%, African American 2%, Hispanic 6%, Caucasian 90% \ **Exp:** $58 (Low) \ **Poverty:** 13% \ **Title I:** $610,137 \ **Special Education:** $1,118,000 \ **Open-Close:** 08/17 - 05/24 \ **DTBP:** $195 (High)

Margo Empen 1
Kevin Schultz 3
Sharon Hafer 7*
Corena Steinmeyer 58,88
Dianne Frye 68
David Blackburn 2,5,91
Jared Shaner 6,27*
Dan Rick 8,12,15
Linda Wegner 67
Jim Manley 73*

Public Schs..Principal	Grd	Prgm	Enr/#Cls	SN		
Dixon High Sch 300 Lincoln Statue Dr, Dixon 61021 Mike Grady	9-12		803 58	36%	815/453-4966 Fax 815/284-4297	
Jefferson Elem Sch 800 4th Ave, Dixon 61021 Crystal Thorpe	2-3		388 18	60%	815/934-9661 Fax 815/284-0435	
Madison Elem Sch 618 Division St, Dixon 61021 Joseph Sagel	4-5	T	390 25	56%	815/934-9662 Fax 815/284-1305	
Reagan Middle Sch 620 Division St, Dixon 61021 **Matthew Magnafici**	6-8	T	628 40	49%	815/253-4966 Fax 815/284-1711	
Washington Elem Sch 703 E Morgan St, Dixon 61021 Jeff Gould	PK-1		534 23	61%	815/934-9660 Fax 815/284-0440	

- **Paw Paw Cmty Unit SD 271** PID: 00303981   815/627-2841
  511 Chapman St, Paw Paw 61353   Fax 815/627-8481

Schools: 1 \ **Teachers:** 19 \ **Students:** 120 \ **Special Ed Students:** 31 \ **LEP Students:** 5 \ **College-Bound:** 80% \ **Ethnic:** African American 7%, Hispanic 11%, Caucasian 82% \ **Exp:** $312 (High) \ **Poverty:** 11% \ **Title I:** $48,165 \ **Special Education:** $44,000 \ **Open-Close:** 08/25 - 05/28

Stan Adcock 1,11,83
Jason Penman 67
Kristin Hall 296
Kellen Irving 6
Jeff Westbrook 73

Public Schs..Principal	Grd	Prgm	Enr/#Cls	SN	
Paw Paw Elem Sch 511 Chapman St, Paw Paw 61353 Stan Adcock	K-8	T	120 6	27%	815/627-2841

- **Steward Elem School Dist 220** PID: 00304064   815/396-2413
  602 Main St, Steward 60553   Fax 815/396-2407

Schools: 1 \ **Teachers:** 9 \ **Students:** 51 \ **Special Ed Students:** 14 \ **Ethnic:** African American 4%, Hispanic 6%, Caucasian 90% \ **Exp:** $263 (Med) \ **Poverty:** 9% \ **Title I:** $2,542 \ **Special Education:** $14,000 \ **Open-Close:** 08/17 - 05/24 \ **DTBP:** $196 (High)

Alyssia Benford 2
Chris Roberts 752
James Knetsch 67

Public Schs..Principal	Grd	Prgm	Enr/#Cls	SN	
Steward Elem Sch 602 Main St, Steward 60553 Lowell Taylor	K-8		51 11	19%	815/396-2413

LEE CATHOLIC SCHOOLS

- **Diocese of Rockford Ed Office** PID: 00328345
  Listing includes only schools located in this county. See District Index for location of Diocesan Offices.

Catholic Schs..Principal	Grd	Prgm	Enr/#Cls	SN	
St Anne Sch 1112 N Brinton Ave, Dixon 61021 Michael Armato	PK-8		100 11		815/288-5619 Fax 815/288-5820
St Mary-Dixon Sch 704 S Peoria Ave, Dixon 61021 Jean Spohn	PK-8		210 13		815/284-6986 Fax 815/284-6905

LEE PRIVATE SCHOOLS

Private Schs..Principal	Grd	Prgm	Enr/#Cls	SN	
Cdh Educational Center 501 S Lincoln Ave, Dixon 61021 Susan Johnson	Spec		60		815/255-8866 Fax 630/395-9198
Faith Christian Sch 7571 S Ridge Rd, Dixon 61021 Linda Foster \ Carrie Worrell	9-12		122 16		815/652-4806 Fax 815/652-4871

LEE REGIONAL CENTERS

- **Lee Co Spec Ed Association** PID: 02184119   815/284-6651
  1335 Franklin Grove Rd Ste B, Dixon 61021   Fax 815/284-9680

Robert Sondgeroth 1,11

LIVINGSTON COUNTY

LIVINGSTON COUNTY SCHOOLS

County Schs..Principal	Grd	Prgm	Enr/#Cls	SN	
Ⓐ Livingston Co Crossroads Acad 920 W Custer Ave, Pontiac 61764 Larry Piwnicki	7-12		26 3	87%	815/844-5749 Fax 815/842-3170

LIVINGSTON PUBLIC SCHOOLS

- **Cornell Cmty Cons Sch Dist 426** PID: 00304131   815/358-2216
  300 N 7th St, Cornell 61319   Fax 815/358-2217

Schools: 1 \ **Teachers:** 13 \ **Students:** 110 \ **Special Ed Students:** 19 \ **Ethnic:** African American 1%, Hispanic 8%, Caucasian 91% \ **Exp:** $194 (Low) \ **Poverty:** 20% \ **Title I:** $40,063 \ **Special Education:** $25,000 \ **Open-Close:** 08/20 - 05/28 \ **DTBP:** $193 (High)

Geoff Schoonover 1,11,73,83,288
Dan Leonard 3

1	Superintendent	8	Curric/Instruct K-12	19	Chief Financial Officer	29	Family/Consumer Science	39	Social Studies K-12	49	English/Lang Arts Elem	59	Special Education Elem	69	Academic Assessment
2	Bus/Finance/Purchasing	9	Curric/Instruct Elem	20	Art K-12	30	Adult Education	40	Social Studies Elem	50	English/Lang Arts Sec	60	Special Education Sec	70	Research/Development
3	Buildings And Grounds	10	Curric/Instruct Sec	21	Art Elem	31	Career/Sch-to-Work K-12	41	Social Studies Sec	51	Reading K-12	61	Foreign/World Lang K-12	71	Public Information
4	Food Service	11	Federal Program	22	Art Sec	32	Career/Sch-to-Work Elem	42	Science K-12	52	Reading Elem	62	Foreign/World Lang Elem	72	Summer School
5	Transportation	12	Title I	23	Music K-12	33	Career/Sch-to-Work Sec	43	Science Elem	53	Reading Sec	63	Foreign/World Lang Sec	73	Instructional Tech
6	Athletic	13	Title V	24	Music Elem	34	Early Childhood Ed	44	Science Sec	54	Remedial Reading K-12	64	Religious Education K-12	74	Inservice Training
7	Health Services	15	Asst Superintendent	25	Music Sec	35	Health/Phys Education	45	Math K-12	55	Remedial Reading Elem	65	Religious Education Elem	75	Marketing/Distributive
		16	Instructional Media Svcs	26	Business Education	36	Guidance Services K-12	46	Math Elem	56	Remedial Reading Sec	66	Religious Education Sec	76	Info Systems
		17	Chief Operations Officer	27	Career & Tech Ed	37	Guidance Services Elem	47	Math Sec	57	Bilingual/ELL	67	School Board President	77	Psychological Assess
		18	Chief Academic Officer	28	Technology Education	38	Guidance Services Sec	48	English/Lang Arts K-12	58	Special Education K-12	68	Teacher Personnel	78	Affirmative Action

Illinois School Directory — Livingston County

Amber Christenson 12
Todd Pinkerton 67
Susan Decker 16*

Public Schs..Principal	Grd	Prgm	Enr/#Cls	SN	
Cornell Grade Sch 300 N 7th St, Cornell 61319 Geoff Schoonover	K-8		110 9	49%	815/358-2216

• Dwight Common Elem SD 232   PID: 01557850
801 S Columbia St, Dwight 60420
815/584-6219
Fax 815/584-2950

Schools: 1 \ **Teachers:** 39 \ **Students:** 450 \ **Special Ed Students:** 87 \ **LEP Students:** 3 \ **Ethnic:** Asian 1%, African American 1%, Hispanic 8%, Caucasian 91% \ **Exp:** $350 (High) \ **Poverty:** 12% \ **Title I:** $220,042 \ **Special Education:** $141,000 \ **Open-Close:** 08/14 - 05/21 \ 🇫 🇹

Dr Richard Jancek 1
Barbara Szornik 11
Chuck Butterbrodt 73,286*
Debbie Conroy 2,19
Bo Partney 67

Public Schs..Principal	Grd	Prgm	Enr/#Cls	SN	
Dwight Grade Sch 801 S Columbia St, Dwight 60420 Brandon Owens	PK-8	T	450 40	40%	815/584-6220 Fax 815/584-3771

• Dwight Twp High Sch Dist 230   PID: 00304155
801 S Franklin St, Dwight 60420
815/584-6219
Fax 815/584-2950

Schools: 1 \ **Teachers:** 26 \ **Students:** 221 \ **Special Ed Students:** 36 \ **College-Bound:** 67% \ **Ethnic:** African American 1%, Hispanic 6%, Caucasian 93% \ **Exp:** $1,017 (High) \ **Poverty:** 12% \ **Title I:** $54,085 \ **Special Education:** $92,000 \ **Open-Close:** 08/14 - 05/21 \ **DTBP:** $174 (High) \ 🇫 🇹

Dr Richard Jancek 1,11,288
Brian Berta 3
Sharon Soto 4
Dan Kaiser 10,88*
Jackie Froelich 38*
Cathy Fatigante 60*
Coreen Pershnick 68*
Chuck Butterbrodt 76,95,295*
Deb Conroy 2,19
Jack Connor 3
Ryan Kemp 6*
Stephanie Flott 16,82*
Nicole Dunnill 57*
Brian Pershnick 67
Logan Murray 73
Eric Black 80

Public Schs..Principal	Grd	Prgm	Enr/#Cls	SN	
Dwight High Sch 801 S Franklin St, Dwight 60420 Andrew Pittenger	9-12	AT	221 28	31%	815/584-6200

• Flanagan-Cornell Unit 74 SD   PID: 00304222
202 E Falcon Hwy, Flanagan 61740
815/796-2233
Fax 815/796-2856

Schools: 1 \ **Teachers:** 33 \ **Students:** 195 \ **Special Ed Students:** 69 \ **College-Bound:** 70% \ **Ethnic:** Asian 1%, African American 2%, Hispanic 4%, Caucasian 92% \ **Exp:** $341 (High) \ **Poverty:** 12% \ **Title I:** $61,966 \ **Special Education:** $102,000 \ **Open-Close:** 08/19 - 05/25

Jerry Farris 1,11
Jerry Farris 8,58*
Heather Richards 59*
Brian Yoder 69*
Amanda Gordon 83*
Susan Ulrich 4
Merre Rogers 12*
Mark Harms 67
Dean Lankton 73*

Public Schs..Principal	Grd	Prgm	Enr/#Cls	SN	
Flanagan-Cornell Unit 74 Sch 202 E Falcon Hwy, Flanagan 61740 Brian Yoder \ Ryan Hansen	PK-12	V	195 20	42%	815/796-2233

• Odell Cmty Cons Sch Dist 435   PID: 00304313
203 N East St, Odell 60460
815/998-2272
Fax 815/998-2619

Schools: 1 \ **Teachers:** 16 \ **Students:** 150 \ **Special Ed Students:** 32 \ **Ethnic:** African American 1%, Hispanic 3%, Caucasian 96% \ **Exp:** $448 (High) \ **Poverty:** 11% \ **Title I:** $36,616 \ **Special Education:** $52,000 \ **Open-Close:** 08/14 - 05/21 \ **DTBP:** $199 (High) \ 🇫 🇹

Mark Hettmansberger 1,11,57
Sue Francis 2
Elizabeth Muller 12*
Jenna Schroen 34*
Emily Gall 67
Deb Zega 2
Steve Verdun 3
Amber Tarnowski 16*
Cheryl Crater 59*
Judy Adams 73,83*

Public Schs..Principal	Grd	Prgm	Enr/#Cls	SN	
ⓨ Odell Grade Sch 203 N East St, Odell 60460 Mark Hettmansberger	PK-8	M	150 15	30%	815/998-2272

• Pontiac Cmty Cons Sch Dist 429   PID: 00304387
600 N Morrow St, Pontiac 61764
815/842-1533
Fax 815/844-5773

Schools: 4 \ **Teachers:** 97 \ **Students:** 1,300 \ **Special Ed Students:** 359 \ **LEP Students:** 6 \ **Ethnic:** Asian 1%, African American 4%, Hispanic 13%, Caucasian 83% \ **Exp:** $216 (Med) \ **Poverty:** 20% \ **Title I:** $435,917 \ **Special Education:** $818,000 \ **Open-Close:** 08/12 - 05/26 \ **DTBP:** $172 (High) \ 🇫 🇹

Brian Dukes 1
Mary Schmidgall 4*
Matt Starker 6*
Mike Weaver 12*
Cheryl Dearing 59
Michael McCabe 73*
Jill Amm 2
Korrin Giovengo 5
Josh DeLong 9
Cheryl Corrigan 59,88
Stacey Shrewsbury 67

Public Schs..Principal	Grd	Prgm	Enr/#Cls	SN	
Central Elem Sch 117 W Livingston St, Pontiac 61764 Kel Krenz	PK-1	T	350 19	53%	815/844-3023 Fax 815/844-2583
Lincoln Elem Sch 514 S Main St, Pontiac 61764 Mike Weaver	2-3	T	229 12	51%	815/844-3924 Fax 815/844-4720
Pontiac Junior High Sch 600 N Morrow St, Pontiac 61764 Brian Hensley	6-8	T	350 20	44%	815/842-4343 Fax 815/844-6230
Washington Elem Sch 400 N Morrow St, Pontiac 61764 Brad Welch	4-5	T	260 13	49%	815/844-3687 Fax 815/844-2710

• Pontiac Twp High Sch Dist 90   PID: 00304351
1100 E Indiana Ave, Pontiac 61764
815/844-6113
Fax 815/844-6116

Schools: 2 \ **Teachers:** 50 \ **Students:** 700 \ **Special Ed Students:** 96 \ **LEP Students:** 3 \ **College-Bound:** 60% \ **Ethnic:** African American 3%, Hispanic 8%, Caucasian 88% \ **Exp:** $241 (Med) \ **Poverty:** 13% \ **Title I:** $167,888 \ **Special Education:** $200,000 \ **Open-Close:** 08/18 - 05/20 \ **DTBP:** $174 (High) \ 🇫 🇹

Jon Kilgore 1,11
Diana Dennis 4*
Gary Brunner 6*
Jennifer McCoy 10,56*
Nicole Hayner 35,83,85
Brian Blair 48*
Roger Corrigan 67
Nancy Fox 2*
Roger Henkel 4
Eric Bohm 10,12,13,88,273,288,296*
Amy Krause 16,73,84,286,295*
Lisa Meyer 38,57,69,270*
Angela Thomas 58,275*

---

79 Student Personnel	91 Safety/Security	275 Response To Intervention	298 Grant Writer/Ptnrships	**School Programs**	**Social Media**
80 Driver Ed/Safety	92 Magnet School	277 Remedial Math K-12	750 Chief Innovation Officer	**A** = Alternative Program	
81 Gifted/Talented	93 Parental Involvement	280 Literacy Coach	751 Chief of Staff	**G** = Adult Classes	🇫 = Facebook
82 Video Services	95 Tech Prep Program	285 STEM	752 Social Emotional Learning	**M** = Magnet Program	
83 Substance Abuse Prev	97 Chief Infomation Officer	286 Digital Learning		**T** = Title I Schoolwide	🇹 = Twitter
84 Erate	98 Chief Technology Officer	288 Common Core Standards	**Other School Types**	**V** = Career & Tech Ed Programs	
85 AIDS Education	270 Character Education	294 Accountability	Ⓐ = Alternative School		
88 Alternative/At Risk	271 Migrant Education	295 Network System	Ⓒ = Charter School	New Schools are shaded	
89 Multi-Cultural Curriculum	273 Teacher Mentor	296 Title II Programs	Ⓜ = Magnet School	New Superintendents and Principals are bold	
90 Social Work	274 Before/After Sch	297 Webmaster	Ⓨ = Year-Round School	Personnel with email addresses are underscored	

IL—161

Livingston County

Market Data Retrieval

Public Schs..Principal	Grd	Prgm	Enr/#Cls	SN	
Livingston Area Career Center 1100 E Indiana Ave, Pontiac 61764 Tara Grays	Voc		400 10	48%	815/842-2557 Fax 815/842-1005
Pontiac Township High Sch 1100 E Indiana Ave, Pontiac 61764 Eric Bohm	9-12	TV	651 70	37%	815/844-6113

• **Prairie Central Cmty USD 8** PID: 00304181 815/692-2504
605 N 7th St, Fairbury 61739 Fax 815/692-3195

Schools: 6 \ Teachers: 137 \ Students: 2,150 \ Special Ed Students: 333 \ LEP Students: 46 \ College-Bound: 59% \ Ethnic: Asian 1%, African American 1%, Hispanic 4%, Caucasian 94% \ Exp: $213 (Med) \ Poverty: 11% \ Title I: $298,819 \ Special Education: $1,078,000 \ Open-Close: 08/19 - 06/04

Paula Crane 1	Michael Scott 3,91
Joni Besgrove 4	Charisse Price 5
Brad Beyers 6*	Tonya Dieken 8
Stephanie Flott 16,82*	Lisa Bounds 58
Mark Slagel 67	Phil Tetley 73,84
Colin Duncan 76,295	

Public Schs..Principal	Grd	Prgm	Enr/#Cls	SN	
Paririe Central Primary West 700 S Division St, Chenoa 61726 Dan Groce	PK-1	T	218 9	42%	815/945-2971 Fax 815/945-2068
Prairie Central Elem Sch 600 S 1st St, Fairbury 61739 Codi Conway	2-4	T	352 24	46%	815/692-2623 Fax 815/692-3726
Prairie Central High Sch 411 N 7th St, Fairbury 61739 Brad Allen	9-12	GV	530 540	30%	815/692-2355 Fax 815/692-2438
Prairie Central Jr High Sch 800 N Wood St, Forrest 61741 Kristal Deming	7-8	TV	311 22	39%	815/657-8660 Fax 815/657-8677
Prairie Central Primary East 407 S 4th St, Chatsworth 60921 Shannon Fuhr	PK-1	T	95 8	58%	815/635-3561 Fax 815/635-3429
Prairie Central Upper Elem Sch 312 N Center St, Forrest 61741 Keri Jancek	5-6	T	267 14	40%	815/657-8238 Fax 815/657-8821

• **Rooks Creek Cmty Cons SD 425** PID: 00304466 815/743-5346
228 Lydia St, Graymont 61743 Fax 815/743-5394

Schools: 1 \ Teachers: 7 \ Students: 50 \ Special Ed Students: 7 \ Ethnic: African American 7%, Hispanic 2%, Caucasian 91% \ Exp: $71 (Low) \ Poverty: 5% \ Special Education: $5,000 \ Open-Close: 08/19 - 05/26

Todd Bean 1,11,73,83,84   Matt Dwaid 67

Public Schs..Principal	Grd	Prgm	Enr/#Cls	SN	
Graymont Elem Sch 228 Lydia St, Graymont 61743 William James	K-8		50 6	11%	815/743-5346

• **Saunemin Cmty Cons SD 438** PID: 00304480 815/832-4421
39 Main St, Saunemin 61769 Fax 815/832-4435

Schools: 1 \ Teachers: 15 \ Students: 115 \ Special Ed Students: 28 \ Ethnic: Hispanic 8%, Caucasian 92% \ Exp: $1,791 (High) \ Poverty: 12% \ Title I: $28,874 \ Special Education: $24,000 \ Open-Close: 08/19 - 05/26

Gary Doughan 1,11	Bailey Conroy 2
Lisa Heiser 34*	Eric Johnson 67
Cynthia Palen 88	

Public Schs..Principal	Grd	Prgm	Enr/#Cls	SN	
Saunemin Elem Sch 39 Main St, Saunemin 61769 Gary Doughan	PK-8	T	115 10	53%	815/832-4421

• **Tri-Point Cmty Unit SD 6J** PID: 00304571 815/253-6299
101 Main St, Kempton 60946 Fax 815/253-6298

Schools: 3 \ Teachers: 37 \ Students: 395 \ Special Ed Students: 84 \ LEP Students: 5 \ College-Bound: 73% \ Ethnic: African American 1%, Hispanic 9%, Caucasian 90% \ Exp: $349 (High) \ Poverty: 16% \ Title I: $119,701 \ Special Education: $115,000 \ Open-Close: 09/01 - 05/27 \ DTBP: $179 (High)

Jeff Bryan 1,11,83,84,288	Lynne Feldkamp 2
Don Emerson 36,69*	Cherie Smolkovich 67
Dan Andrews 73,286	

Public Schs..Principal	Grd	Prgm	Enr/#Cls	SN	
Kempton Elem Sch 101 Main St, Kempton 60946 Angela Winger-Bryan	PK-3	T	104 10	38%	815/253-6299
Tri-Point High Sch 100 E Vanaistyne St, Cullom 60929 Kellee Hill	9-12	TV	97 17	56%	815/689-2110 Fax 815/689-2377
Tri-Point Upper ES JHS 519 S Margaret Ave, Piper City 60959 Jay Bennett	4-8	T	156 20	58%	815/686-2247 Fax 815/686-2663

• **Woodland Cmty Unit Sch Dist 5** PID: 00304519 815/672-5974
5800 E 3000 North Rd, Streator 61364 Fax 815/673-1630

Schools: 2 \ Teachers: 38 \ Students: 540 \ Special Ed Students: 103 \ LEP Students: 3 \ College-Bound: 65% \ Ethnic: African American 1%, Hispanic 5%, Caucasian 94% \ Exp: $205 (Med) \ Poverty: 13% \ Title I: $94,458 \ Special Education: $178,000 \ Open-Close: 08/17 - 05/27

Ryan McGukin 1	Mike Hoekstra 3
Michelle Simpson 4*	Heather Perhach 16
Amy Lee 36,69,83,270*	Jeremy Adams 67
Dan Borio 73	Christine Brown 88*
Jacob Burcenski 285	

Public Schs..Principal	Grd	Prgm	Enr/#Cls	SN	
Woodland Elem Sch 5800 E 3000 North Rd, Streator 61364 Jodi Peterson	PK-8		353 60	45%	815/672-2909
Woodland High Sch 5800 E 3000 North Rd, Streator 61364 Jodi Peterson	9-12	TV	160 20	36%	815/672-2900

LIVINGSTON CATHOLIC SCHOOLS

• **Diocese of Peoria Ed Office** PID: 00313338
Listing includes only schools located in this county. See District Index for location of Diocesan Offices.

1	Superintendent	8	Curric/Instruct K-12	19	Chief Financial Officer	29	Family/Consumer Science	39	Social Studies K-12	49	English/Lang Arts Elem	59	Special Education Elem	69	Academic Assessment
2	Bus/Finance/Purchasing	9	Curric/Instruct Elem	20	Art K-12	30	Adult Education	40	Social Studies Elem	50	English/Lang Arts Sec	60	Special Education Sec	70	Research/Development
3	Buildings And Grounds	10	Curric/Instruct Sec	21	Art Elem	31	Career/Sch-to-Work K-12	41	Social Studies Sec	51	Reading K-12	61	Foreign/World Lang K-12	71	Public Information
4	Food Service	11	Federal Program	22	Art Sec	32	Career/Sch-to-Work Elem	42	Science K-12	52	Reading Elem	62	Foreign/World Lang Elem	72	Summer School
5	Transportation	12	Title I	23	Music K-12	33	Career/Sch-to-Work Sec	43	Science Elem	53	Reading Sec	63	Foreign/World Lang Sec	73	Instructional Tech
6	Athletic	13	Title V	24	Music Elem	34	Early Childhood Ed	44	Science Sec	54	Remedial Reading K-12	64	Religious Education K-12	74	Inservice Training
7	Health Services	14	Asst Superintendent	25	Music Sec	35	Health/Phys Education	45	Math K-12	55	Remedial Reading Elem	65	Religious Education Elem	75	Marketing/Distributive
		15	Instructional Media Svcs	26	Business Education	36	Guidance Services K-12	46	Math Elem	56	Remedial Reading Sec	66	Religious Education Sec	76	Info Systems
		16	Chief Operations Officer	27	Career & Tech Ed	37	Guidance Services Elem	47	Math Sec	57	Bilingual/ELL	67	School Board President	77	Psychological Assess
		17	Chief Academic Officer	28	Technology Education	38	Guidance Services Sec	48	English/Lang Arts K-12	58	Special Education K-12	68	Teacher Personnel	78	Affirmative Action

Illinois School Directory

Logan County

Catholic Schs..Principal	Grd	Prgm	Enr/#Cls SN	
St Mary's School-Pontiac	K-8		197	815/844-6585
414 N Main St, Pontiac 61764			9	Fax 815/844-6987
Karen Jones				
St Paul Sch	PK-8		76	815/998-2194
300 S West St, Odell 60460			5	Fax 815/998-1514
Richard Morehouse				

LIVINGSTON PRIVATE SCHOOLS

Private Schs..Principal	Grd	Prgm	Enr/#Cls SN	
Dwight Baptist Academy	K-12	V	36	815/584-3182
401 N Clinton St, Dwight 60420			4	Fax 815/584-1867
Eric Bryant				
Grace Christian Sch	PK-8		27	815/419-2030
1314 E Indiana Ave, Pontiac 61764				
Jennifer Morrison				
Pontiac Christian Sch	PK-8		79	815/842-1322
18034 N 2100 East Rd, Pontiac 61764			5	Fax 815/844-2033
Denise Plenert				
Ⓐ Salem4Youth Valor High Sch	7-12		12	815/796-4561
15161 N 400 East Rd, Flanagan 61740				Fax 815/796-4565
Terry Benge				

LIVINGSTON REGIONAL CENTERS

• **Livingston Area EFE System** PID: 04177863　　815/842-2557
1100 E Indiana Ave, Pontiac 61764　　Fax 815/842-1005

Tera Graves ....1,11　Amy Richardson 58

• **Livingston Co Spec Svc Unit** PID: 02184133　　815/844-7115
205 N Adams St, Flanagan 61740　　Fax 815/842-3170

Dr Joshua Olsen ....1　Christina Butterbrodt 15

LOGAN COUNTY

LOGAN PUBLIC SCHOOLS

• **Chester-E Lincoln Cmty SD 61** PID: 00304686　　217/732-4136
1300 1500th St, Lincoln 62656　　Fax 217/732-3265

Schools: 1 \ **Teachers:** 21 \ **Students:** 300 \
Special Ed Students: 38 \ **LEP Students:** 4 \ **Ethnic:** Asian 2%, African American 2%, Caucasian 96% \ **Exp:** $142 (Low) \ **Poverty:** 9% \
Title I: $43,268 \ **Special Education:** $162,000 \ **Open-Close:** 08/14 - 05/21 \ **DTBP:** $177 (High)

Laura Irwin .... 1,11,73,83　Colleen Jodlowski 2
Randy Ely .... 3　Mary-Beth Landstrom 4
Ashley Aper .... 59*　Jeff Brooks 67
Matt Grammer 73*

Public Schs..Principal	Grd	Prgm	Enr/#Cls SN	
Chester-East Lincoln Cmty ES	PK-8	T	300	39% 217/732-4136
1300 1500th St, Lincoln 62656			19	Fax 217/323-2651
Laura Irwin				

• **Hartsburg Emden School Dist 21** PID: 00304741　　217/642-5244
400 W Front St, Hartsburg 62643　　Fax 217/642-5333

Schools: 2 \ **Teachers:** 24 \ **Students:** 200 \ **Special Ed Students:** 25 \
College-Bound: 70% \ **Ethnic:** Hispanic 3%, Caucasian 97% \ **Exp:** $263 (Med) \ **Poverty:** 10% \ **Title I:** $36,497 \ **Special Education:** $77,000 \
Open-Close: 08/19 - 05/27 \ **DTBP:** $191 (High)

Terry Wisniewski .... 1,11　Laurie Lessen 2
Fred Wagner .... 3　Erin Eeten 4
Matt Stoltzenburg .... 6*　Amanda Feltes 10,36,69*
Greg Phillips .... 67　John Robinson 73,286*

Public Schs..Principal	Grd	Prgm	Enr/#Cls SN	
Emden Elem Sch	K-5		87	55% 217/376-3151
309 Market St, Emden 62635			5	
Jon Leslie				
Hartsburg Emden Jr Sr High Sch	5-12	V	121	47% 217/642-5244
400 W Front St, Hartsburg 62643			21	
Jon Leslie				

• **Lincoln Cmty High Sch Dist 404** PID: 00304868　　217/732-4131
1000 Railer Way, Lincoln 62656　　Fax 217/735-3963

Schools: 1 \ **Teachers:** 55 \ **Students:** 811 \ **Special Ed Students:** 87
\ **LEP Students:** 4 \ **College-Bound:** 61% \ **Ethnic:** Asian 1%, African American 3%, Hispanic 2%, Caucasian 94% \ **Exp:** $138 (Low) \ **Poverty:** 14%
\ **Title I:** $213,868 \ **Special Education:** $404,000 \ **Open-Close:** 08/17 - 05/21 \ **DTBP:** $174 (High) \

Dwight Stricklin .... 1　Lori Lawson 4*
Neil Alexander .... 6*　Todd Poelker 10,16,69,88,273*
Rhonda Hyde .... 11*　Matt Puckett 33*
Jacqueline Meyer .... 56*　Melissa Koning 57,60*
Susan Gleason .... 67　Robert Bagby 83

Public Schs..Principal	Grd	Prgm	Enr/#Cls SN	
Lincoln Cmty High Sch	9-12	AGV	811	43% 217/732-4131
1000 Railer Way, Lincoln 62656			80	Fax 217/732-3963
Todd Poelker				

• **Lincoln Elem School Dist 27** PID: 00304789　　217/732-2522
304 8th St, Lincoln 62656　　Fax 217/732-2198

Schools: 5 \ **Teachers:** 86 \ **Students:** 1,200 \ **Special Ed Students:** 225
\ **LEP Students:** 4 \ **Ethnic:** African American 4%, Hispanic 1%, Caucasian 94% \ **Exp:** $165 (Low) \ **Poverty:** 22% \ **Title I:** $563,884 \
Special Education: $711,000 \ **Open-Close:** 08/14 - 05/21 \ **DTBP:** $155 (High)

Kent Froebe .... 1,83　Colleen Jodlowski 2
Connie Crawley .... 4　Brent Bainter 6,72*
Jamie Fruge .... 7,275*　Ashley Phillips 9
Ginger Chaudoin .... 11,57,270,271,273*　Trent Kavelman 16,82
Stephen Rohrer .... 67　Barb Coffey 73,84,295,297

Public Schs..Principal	Grd	Prgm	Enr/#Cls SN	
Adams Elem Sch	PK-2	T	102	59% 217/732-3253
1311 Nicholson Rd, Lincoln 62656			6	Fax 217/732-8098
Christa Healy				

79	Student Personnel	91	Safety/Security	275	Response To Intervention	298	Grant Writer/Ptnrships	School Programs	Social Media
80	Driver Ed/Safety	92	Magnet School	277	Remedial Math K-12	750	Chief Innovation Officer	A = Alternative Program	
81	Gifted/Talented	93	Parental Involvement	280	Literacy Coach	751	Chief of Staff	G = Adult Classes	▯ = Facebook
82	Video Services	95	Tech Prep Program	285	STEM	752	Social Emotional Learning	M = Magnet Program	
83	Substance Abuse Prev	97	Chief Information Officer	286	Digital Learning			T = Title I Schoolwide	▯ = Twitter
84	Erate	98	Chief Technology Officer	288	Common Core Standards	Other School Types	V = Career & Tech Ed Programs	
85	AIDS Education	270	Accountability	294	Accountability	Ⓐ = Alternative School		
88	Alternative/At Risk	271	Migrant Education	295	Network System	Ⓒ = Charter School	New Schools are shaded	
89	Multi-Cultural Curriculum	273	Teacher Mentor	296	Title II Programs	Ⓜ = Magnet School	New Superintendents and Principals are bold	
90	Social Work	274	Before/After Sch	297	Webmaster	Ⓨ = Year-Round School	Personnel with email addresses are underscored	

IL—163

Macon County

Market Data Retrieval

Central Elem Sch 100 7th St, Lincoln 62656 Kelly Bogdanic	K-5	T	187 12	44%	217/732-3386 Fax 217/732-9532
Lincoln Junior High Sch 208 Broadway St, Lincoln 62656 Mike Workman	6-8		365 20	49%	217/732-3535 Fax 217/732-2685
Northwest Elem Sch 506 11th St, Lincoln 62656 Chris Allen	K-5	T	244 10	63%	217/732-6819 Fax 217/735-2172
Washington-Monroe Elem Sch 1002 Pekin St, Lincoln 62656 Ginger Chaudoin	PK-5	T	220 13	66%	217/732-4764 Fax 217/732-5913

- **Mt Pulaski Cmty Unit SD 23** PID: 00304911   217/792-7222
119 N Garden St, Mount Pulaski 62548   Fax 217/792-5551

Schools: 2 \ **Teachers:** 44 \ **Students:** 530 \ **Special Ed Students:** 73 \ **LEP Students:** 3 \ **College-Bound:** 65% \ **Ethnic:** African American 1%, Hispanic 2%, Caucasian 97% \ **Exp:** $243 (Med) \ **Poverty:** 8% \ **Title I:** $68,958 \ **Special Education:** $273,000 \ **Open-Close:** 09/08 - 06/03 \ **DTBP:** $184 (High)

Fred Lamkey 1,11,83		Kathy Tschantz 2	
Louis Volle 3		Gene Schoth 5	
Ryan McVickers 6		Danielle Lora 9,59,88,288	
Keri Elliott 12		Heather Fricke 16,73,286	
Eric Cowan 67		Melanie Hinson 273*	

Public Schs..Principal	Grd	Prgm	Enr/#Cls	SN	
Mt Pulaski Grade Sch 119 N Garden St, Mount Pulaski 62548 **Danielle Lora**	PK-8	T	357 28	38%	217/792-7220 Fax 217/792-7221
Mt Pulaski High Sch 206 S Spring St, Mount Pulaski 62548 Terry Morgan	9-12	TV	157 30	40%	217/792-3209 Fax 217/792-3248

- **New Holland Middletown ESD 88** PID: 00304935   217/445-2421
75 1250th St, Middletown 62666   Fax 217/445-2632

Schools: 1 \ **Teachers:** 12 \ **Students:** 90 \ **Special Ed Students:** 13 \ **Ethnic:** African American 1%, Hispanic 3%, Native American: 2%, Caucasian 94% \ **Exp:** $432 (High) \ **Poverty:** 12% \ **Title I:** $24,232 \ **Special Education:** $55,000 \ **Open-Close:** 08/14 - 05/28 \ **DTBP:** $176 (High)

Brandi Bruley 1,11		Rachel Stapleton 2	
Rick Deters 3*		Linda Harnacke 4*	
Diane Bicknell 12*		John Coers 67	

Public Schs..Principal	Grd	Prgm	Enr/#Cls	SN	
New Holland Middletown Sch 75 1250th St, Middletown 62666 Todd Dugan	K-8	T	90 8	63%	217/445-2421

- **West Lincoln-Broadwell ESD 92** PID: 00304973   217/732-2630
2695 Woodlawn Rd, Lincoln 62656   Fax 217/732-3623

Schools: 1 \ **Teachers:** 16 \ **Students:** 220 \ **Special Ed Students:** 31 \ **Ethnic:** Asian 1%, African American 2%, Hispanic 4%, Caucasian 93% \ **Exp:** $270 (Med) \ **Poverty:** 11% \ **Title I:** $25,690 \ **Special Education:** $148,000 \ **Open-Close:** 08/17 - 05/21

Heather Baker 1,11,57,73,288		Sarah Struebing 2	
Jackie Lessen 3,5*		Tom Kissel 67	
Kris Skold 83,85			

Public Schs..Principal	Grd	Prgm	Enr/#Cls	SN	
West Lincoln-Broadwell ES 2695 Woodlawn Rd, Lincoln 62656 Heather Baker	PK-8	T	220 12	35%	217/732-2630

LOGAN CATHOLIC SCHOOLS

- **Diocese of Peoria Ed Office** PID: 00313338
Listing includes only schools located in this county. See District Index for location of Diocesan Offices.

Catholic Schs..Principal	Grd	Prgm	Enr/#Cls	SN	
Carroll Catholic Sch 111 4th St, Lincoln 62656 David Welch	PK-8		120 14		217/732-7518

LOGAN PRIVATE SCHOOLS

Private Schs..Principal	Grd	Prgm	Enr/#Cls	SN	
Zion Lutheran Sch 1600 Woodlawn Rd, Lincoln 62656 Ben Barth	PK-8		88 10		217/732-3977 Fax 217/732-3398
Zion Lutheran Sch 203 S Vine St, Mount Pulaski 62548 Lori Allen	PK-8		125 5		217/792-5715 Fax 217/792-5915

MACON COUNTY

MACON COUNTY SCHOOLS

County Schs..Principal	Grd	Prgm	Enr/#Cls	SN	
Ⓐ Futures Unlimited Sch 300 E Eldorado St, Decatur 62523 Matt Snyder	9-12	V	170 11	29%	217/429-1054 Fax 217/429-3827
Heartland Tech Acad-Eldorado 1 College Park, Decatur 62521 Bret Hitchings	Voc	G	100 25		217/872-4050 Fax 217/876-0918
Heartland Tech Acad-Richland 1 College Park, Decatur 62521 Bret Hitchings	Voc		500		217/872-4050 Fax 217/876-0918
Milligan Academy Safe Sch 300 E Eldorado St, Decatur 62523 Brian Plummer	7-12		51	51%	217/424-3062 Fax 217/424-3074

1	Superintendent	8	Curric/Instruct K-12	19	Chief Financial Officer	29	Family/Consumer Science	39	Social Studies K-12	49	English/Lang Arts Elem	59	Special Education Elem	69	Academic Assessment
2	Bus/Finance/Purchasing	9	Curric/Instruct Elem	20	Art K-12	30	Adult Education	40	Social Studies Elem	50	English/Lang Arts Sec	60	Special Education Sec	70	Research/Development
3	Buildings And Grounds	10	Curric/Instruct Sec	21	Art Elem	31	Career/Sch-to-Work K-12	41	Social Studies Sec	51	Reading K-12	61	Foreign/World Lang K-12	71	Public Information
4	Food Service	11	Federal Program	22	Art Sec	32	Career/Sch-to-Work Elem	42	Science K-12	52	Reading Elem	62	Foreign/World Lang Elem	72	Summer School
5	Transportation	12	Title I	23	Music K-12	33	Career/Sch-to-Work Sec	43	Science Elem	53	Reading Sec	63	Foreign/World Lang Sec	73	Instructional Tech
6	Athletic	13	Title V	24	Music Elem	34	Early Childhood Ed	44	Science Sec	54	Remedial Reading K-12	64	Religious Education K-12	74	Inservice Training
7	Health Services	15	Asst Superintendent	25	Music Sec	35	Health/Phys Education	45	Math K-12	55	Remedial Reading Elem	65	Religious Education Elem	75	Marketing/Distributive
		16	Instructional Media Svcs	26	Business Education	36	Guidance Services K-12	46	Math Elem	56	Remedial Reading Sec	66	Religious Education Sec	76	Info Systems
		17	Chief Operations Officer	27	Career & Tech Ed	37	Guidance Services Elem	47	Math Sec	57	Bilingual/ELL	67	School Board President	77	Psychological Assess
		18	Chief Academic Officer	28	Technology Education	38	Guidance Services Sec	48	English/Lang Arts K-12	58	Special Education K-12	68	Teacher Personnel	78	Affirmative Action

Illinois School Directory — Macon County

MACON PUBLIC SCHOOLS

- **Argenta Oreana Cmty Unit SD 1** PID: 00306828   217/795-2313
  500 N Main St, Argenta 62501   Fax 217/795-2174

Schools: 3 \ **Teachers:** 67 \ **Students:** 800 \ **Special Ed Students:** 143 \ **LEP Students:** 7 \ **College-Bound:** 70% \ **Ethnic:** Asian 2%, African American 3%, Hispanic 4%, Caucasian 91% \ **Exp:** $209 (Med) \ **Poverty:** 14% \ **Title I:** $249,656 \ **Special Education:** $109,000 \ **Open-Close:** 08/20 - 05/24 \ [f] [t]

Damian Jones	1,11	Mark Daley	5
Mike Williams	6*	Denise Klover	16
Amanda Mendez	31	Todd Armstrong	67
Tom Altig	73	Kathleen Outven	752

Public Schs..Principal	Grd	Prgm	Enr/#Cls	SN		
Argenta Oreana Elem Sch 400 W South St, Oreana 62554 Amanda Ryder	PK-5		493 27	51%	217/468-2412 Fax 217/468-2403	
Argenta Oreana High Sch 500 N Main St, Argenta 62501 Sean German	9-12	TV	281 30	37%	217/795-4821 Fax 217/795-4550	[f]
Argenta Oreana Middle Sch 200 E East St, Argenta 62501 Patrick Blair	6-8	T	189 14	52%	217/795-2163 Fax 217/795-4502	

- **Decatur Public Schools 61** PID: 00306921   217/362-3000
  101 W Cerro Gordo St, Decatur 62523   Fax 217/424-3009

Schools: 18 \ **Teachers:** 483 \ **Students:** 8,700 \ **Special Ed Students:** 1,622 \ **LEP Students:** 172 \ **College-Bound:** 55% \ **Ethnic:** Asian 1%, African American 53%, Hispanic 5%, Caucasian 41% \ **Exp:** $361 (High) \ **Poverty:** 34% \ **Title I:** $7,477,532 \ **Special Education:** $1,413,000 \ **Bilingual Education:** $15,000 \ **Open-Close:** 08/17 - 05/21 \ **DTBP:** $223 (High)

Dr Paul Fregeau	1	Joanie Watson	2
Todd Covault	2,3,17	Steve Kline	3,91
Scott Gregory	4	Henry Walker	5,91
Angie Wetzel	7	Jeff Dase	8,15,79
Dr Judith Campbell	10,73,288	Ashley Grayned	11,70,74,750
Mary Ann Scheloz	11,296	Megan Flanigan	39,280
Kathleen Horath	58	Beth Nolan	67
Deanne Hillman	68,751	Denise Swarthout	71
Maria Robertson	71	Maurice Payne	73,76,297
Lawrence Trimble	79*		

Public Schs..Principal	Grd	Prgm	Enr/#Cls	SN		
Ⓐ Alt Educ Ctr-Harris 620 E Garfield Ave, Decatur 62526 Barb Morrow	4-12	T	28	72%	217/362-3360	
Benjamin Franklin Elem Sch 2440 N Summit Ave, Decatur 62526 Stephanie Strang	K-6	T	300 14	79%	217/362-3560	[f]
Dennis Lab Sch 1499 W Main St, Decatur 62522 Dan Lynch	K-6	T	457 12	58%	217/362-3510 Fax 217/424-3067	
Eisenhower High Sch 1200 S 16th St, Decatur 62521 Amy Zahm	9-12	ATV	990 85	68%	217/362-3100 Fax 217/362-3588	
French STEM Academy 520 W Wood St, Decatur 62522 Julie Fane	K-6	T	302 14	76%	217/362-3380 Fax 217/424-3134	
Ⓨ Hope Academy Magnet Sch 955 N Illinois St, Decatur 62521 Tasia Spencer-Burks	K-8	MT	491	86%	217/362-3280 Fax 217/424-3343	
Ⓜ Johns Hill Magnet Sch 1025 E Johns Ave, Decatur 62521 Robert Prange	K-8	T	462 30	45%	217/362-3350 Fax 217/424-3192	
MacArthur High Sch 1499 W Grand Ave, Decatur 62522 Cordell Ingram	9-12	ATV	1,120 62	59%	217/362-3150 Fax 217/362-3589	
Michael E Baum Elem Sch 801 S Lake Ridge Ave, Decatur 62521 **Mary Brady**	K-6	T	316 18	65%	217/362-3520 Fax 217/424-3024	
Ⓜ Montessori Academy of Peace 4735 E Cantrell St, Decatur 62521 Mary Anderson	PK-8	T	500 13	40%	217/362-3370 Fax 217/424-3148	
Muffley Elem Sch 88 S Country Club Rd, Decatur 62521 Carrie Hogue	K-6	T	393 18	73%	217/362-3340 Fax 217/424-3137	
Oak Grove Elem Sch 2160 W Center St, Decatur 62526 Diane Brandt	K-6	T	280 14	78%	217/362-3550 Fax 217/424-3138	
Parsons Accelerated Elem Sch 3591 N MacArthur Rd, Decatur 62526 Patricia Paulson	K-6	T	308 20	70%	217/362-3330 Fax 217/424-3139	
Pershing Early Learning Center 2912 N University Ave, Decatur 62526 Sarah Knuppel	PK-K		512 15	73%	217/362-3300 Fax 217/876-8322	
Ⓒ Robertson Charter Sch 2240 E Geddes Ave, Decatur 62526 Niki Fenderson	K-8	T	326 8	73%	217/428-7072 Fax 217/428-9214	[f]
South Shores Elem Sch 2500 S Franklin Street Rd, Decatur 62521 **South Shores \ Matt Fraas**	K-6	T	279 15	76%	217/362-3320 Fax 217/424-3176	
Stephen Decatur Middle Sch 1 N Educational Park Dr, Decatur 62526 **Matthew Fraas**	7-8	AT	345	68%	217/362-3250 Fax 217/876-8003	
Stevenson Elem Sch 3900 N Neely Ave, Decatur 62526 Ms Galligan	K-6	T	256 12	76%	217/362-3540 Fax 217/876-8753	

- **Maroa Forsyth CU Sch Dist 2** PID: 00307353   217/794-3488
  641 E Shafer St, Forsyth 62535

Schools: 3 \ **Students:** 1,215 \ **College-Bound:** 75% \ **Ethnic:** Asian 8%, African American 4%, Hispanic 1%, Caucasian 86% \ **Exp:** $221 (Med) \ **Title I:** $289,354 \ **Open-Close:** 08/19 - 05/21

Dr John Ahlemeyer	1	Leo Johnson	2
Sandy Cummins	2	Lisa Russell	4
Jody Luttrell	5	Phillip Applebee	6*
Stacy Goodwin	12*	Troy Holthaus	38,69,83*
Lindsey Wise	67	Leshelle Donoho	68
Jessica Hill	90		

Public Schs..Principal	Grd	Prgm	Enr/#Cls	SN		
Maroa Forsyth Grade Sch 641 E Shafer St, Forsyth 62535 Carrie Reynolds	PK-5		558 18		217/877-2023 Fax 217/877-6216	
Maroa Forsyth Middle Sch 101 S Cedar St, Maroa 61756 Kristopher Kahler	6-8		255 20	25%	217/794-5115 Fax 217/794-3351	
Maroa Forsyth Sr High Sch 610 W Washington St, Maroa 61756 Brice Stewart	9-12	V	379 21	18%	217/794-3463 Fax 217/794-5459	[f][t]

---

79 Student Personnel	91 Safety/Security	275 Response To Intervention	298 Grant Writer/Ptnrships	**School Programs**	**Social Media**	
80 Driver Ed/Safety	92 Magnet School	277 Remedial Math K-12	750 Chief Innovation Officer	A = Alternative Program		
81 Gifted/Talented	93 Parental Involvement	280 Literacy Coach	751 Chief of Staff	G = Adult Classes	[f] = Facebook	
82 Video Services	95 Tech Prep Program	285 STEM	752 Social Emotional Learning	M = Magnet Program		
83 Substance Abuse Prev	97 Chief Infomation Officer	286 Digital Learning		T = Title I Schoolwide	[t] = Twitter	
84 Erate	98 Chief Technology Officer	288 Common Core Standards	**Other School Types**	V = Career & Tech Ed Programs		
85 AIDS Education	270 Accountability	294 Accountability	Ⓐ = Alternative School			
88 Alternative/At Risk	271 Migrant Education	295 Network System	Ⓒ = Charter School	New Schools are shaded		
89 Multi-Cultural Curriculum	273 Teacher Mentor	296 Title II Programs	Ⓜ = Magnet School	New Superintendents and Principals are bold		
90 Social Work	274 Before/After Sch	297 Webmaster	Ⓨ = Year-Round School	Personnel with email addresses are underscored		

IL—165

Macon County

Market Data Retrieval

- **Meridian Cmty Unit Sch Dist 15** PID: 00306880   217/764-5269
  728 S Wall St, Macon 62544   Fax 217/764-5291

  Schools: 3 \ **Teachers:** 67 \ **Students:** 1,065 \ **Special Ed Students:** 116 \ **College-Bound:** 80% \ **Ethnic:** African American 1%, Hispanic 1%, Caucasian 97% \ **Exp:** $141 (Low) \ **Poverty:** 11% \ **Title I:** $166,311 \ **Special Education:** $120,000 \ **Open-Close:** 08/31 - 05/17

Andy Pygott 1,11,83	Paula Ray 5
Michelle McKinney 16*	Heather Johnson 36,69,72,88*
Chris Jones 67	Phil Stielow 73*

Public Schs..Principal	Grd	Prgm	Enr/#Cls	SN	
Meridian Elem Sch 509 S Lewis St, Blue Mound 62513 Lori Guebert	PK-5		486 9	39%	217/692-2535 Fax 217/692-2013
Meridian High Sch 728 S Wall St, Macon 62544 Eric Hurelbrink	9-12	V	259 28	27%	217/764-5233 Fax 217/764-5282
Meridian Middle Sch 728 S Wall St, Macon 62544 Mindy McGuire	6-8		253 20	36%	217/764-3367 Fax 217/764-3902

- **Mt Zion Cmty Unit Sch Dist 3** PID: 00307406   217/864-2366
  1595 W Main St, Mt Zion 62549

  Schools: 5 \ **Teachers:** 134 \ **Students:** 2,400 \ **Special Ed Students:** 280 \ **LEP Students:** 16 \ **Ethnic:** Asian 1%, African American 2%, Hispanic 2%, Caucasian 94% \ **Exp:** $198 (Low) \ **Poverty:** 9% \ **Title I:** $308,284 \ **Special Education:** $308,000 \ **Open-Close:** 08/18 - 06/04

Dr Travis Roundcount 1	Brian Rhoades 2,8,11,15,31,58,296,298
Steve Blickensdefer 3	Darcie Hayes 4
Mark Hogan 5	Theresa Lane 5
Ben Davis 6*	Jeanne Luckenbill 7*
Billy Rockey 10,73,285,286,295*	Michael Mose 10*
Valerie Brunner 16*	Todd Garner 67
Lori Rutherford 274*	Ina Brown 297*
Renea Smith 752	

Public Schs..Principal	Grd	Prgm	Enr/#Cls	SN	
McGaughey Elem Sch 1320 W Main St, Mt Zion 62549 Heather Ethel	PK-1		371 20	24%	217/864-2711 Fax 217/864-4126
Mt Zion Grade Sch 725 W Main St, Mt Zion 62549 Gary Gruen	2-3		360 17	21%	217/864-3631 Fax 217/864-6131
Mt Zion High Sch 305 S Henderson St, Mt Zion 62549 Justin Johnson	9-12	AV	757 50	16%	217/864-2363 Fax 217/864-5815
Mt Zion Intermediate Sch 310 S Henderson St, Mt Zion 62549 Randall Thacker	4-6		589 23	20%	217/864-2921 Fax 217/864-5175
Mt Zion Junior High Sch 315 S Henderson St, Mt Zion 62549 Julie Marquardt	7-8	A	389 35	21%	217/864-2369 Fax 217/864-6829

- **Sangamon Valley Cmty Unit SD 9** PID: 00307482   217/668-2338
  398 N Illinois St, Niantic 62551   Fax 217/668-2406

  Schools: 4 \ **Teachers:** 53 \ **Students:** 687 \ **Special Ed Students:** 121 \ **College-Bound:** 61% \ **Ethnic:** Asian 1%, African American 1%, Hispanic 2%, Native American: 1%, Caucasian 96% \ **Exp:** $348 (High) \ **Poverty:** 10% \ **Title I:** $113,578 \ **Special Education:** $113,000 \ **Open-Close:** 08/14 - 05/28 \ **DTBP:** $183 (High)

Robert Meadows 1,11	Carol Stacey 2
Bruce Stolz 3	Amy Day 4*
Ryan Slexter 5	Josh Myers 6*
Johnathon Field 8*	Valerie Janvrin 11,88,275,285,288*
Joe Scanavino 57*	Stephanie Guerrero 67
Jamie Antonacci 79,83*	

Public Schs..Principal	Grd	Prgm	Enr/#Cls	SN	
Sangamon Valley High Sch 398 N Illinois St, Niantic 62551 Johnathon Field	9-12	AV	217 35	35%	217/668-2392 Fax 217/668-2221
Sangamon Valley Intermed Sch 341 Matilda St, Illiopolis 62539 Kristina Sommer	3-5	T	168 10	63%	217/486-7521 Fax 217/486-5601
Sangamon Valley Middle Sch 341 Matilda St, Illiopolis 62539 Brandi Kelly	6-8	AT	144 15	47%	217/486-2241 Fax 217/486-6038
Sangamon Valley Primary Sch 1095 N Meridian St, Harristown 62537 Bethany Wellbaum	PK-2		158 11	50%	217/963-2621 Fax 217/963-2440

- **Warrensburg-Latham CU SD 11** PID: 00307523   217/672-3514
  430 W North St, Warrensburg 62573   Fax 217/672-8468

  Schools: 3 \ **Teachers:** 61 \ **Students:** 1,200 \ **Special Ed Students:** 117 \ **LEP Students:** 10 \ **College-Bound:** 90% \ **Ethnic:** Asian 1%, African American 2%, Hispanic 2%, Caucasian 94% \ **Exp:** $209 (Med) \ **Poverty:** 9% \ **Title I:** $140,476 \ **Special Education:** $143,000 \ **Open-Close:** 08/19 - 05/21

Cheryl Warner 1,11	Teresa Bailey 2,68
Keith Hackl 3,91	Leann Terneus 4,7*
Daniel Epperson 5	Bret Reedy 6
Jonathan Downing 10	Jody Dawson 12*
Dave Munson 67	Chris Reed 73*
Gretchen Underwood 88*	

Public Schs..Principal	Grd	Prgm	Enr/#Cls	SN	
Warrensburg-Latham Elem Sch 101 S West St, Warrensburg 62573 Laura Anderson	PK-5	T	445 30	47%	217/672-3612 Fax 217/672-8614
Warrensburg-Latham High Sch 427 W North St, Warrensburg 62573 Jonathan Downing	9-12	V	309 25	28%	217/672-3612 Fax 217/672-3261
Warrensburg-Latham Middle Sch 425 W North St, Warrensburg 62573 Paul Hoffman	6-8	T	216	36%	217/672-3321 Fax 217/672-3770

MACON CATHOLIC SCHOOLS

- **Diocese of Springfield Ed Off** PID: 00319394
  Listing includes only schools located in this county. See District Index for location of Diocesan Offices.

Catholic Schs..Principal	Grd	Prgm	Enr/#Cls	SN	
Holy Family Catholic Sch 2400 S Franklin Street Rd, Decatur 62521 Debbie Alexander	PK-8		249 16		217/423-7049 Fax 217/423-0137
Our Lady of Lourdes Sch 3950 Lourdes Dr, Decatur 62526 Theresa Bowser	PK-8		342 16		217/877-4408 Fax 217/872-3655
St Patrick Sch 412 N Jackson St, Decatur 62523 Nick Blackburn	PK-8		153 10		217/423-4351 Fax 217/423-7288

1	Superintendent	8	Curric/Instruct K-12	19	Chief Financial Officer	29	Family/Consumer Science	39	Social Studies K-12	49	English/Lang Arts Elem	59	Special Education Elem	69	Academic Assessment
2	Bus/Finance/Purchasing	9	Curric/Instruct Elem	20	Art K-12	30	Adult Education	40	Social Studies Elem	50	English/Lang Arts Sec	60	Special Education Sec	70	Research/Development
3	Buildings And Grounds	10	Curric/Instruct Sec	21	Art Elem	31	Career/Sch-to-Work K-12	41	Social Studies Sec	51	Reading K-12	61	Foreign/World Lang K-12	71	Public Information
4	Food Service	11	Federal Program	22	Art Sec	32	Career/Sch-to-Work Elem	42	Science K-12	52	Reading Elem	62	Foreign/World Lang Elem	72	Summer School
5	Transportation	12	Title I	23	Music K-12	33	Career/Sch-to-Work Sec	43	Science Elem	53	Reading Sec	63	Foreign/World Lang Sec	73	Instructional Tech
6	Athletic	13	Title V	24	Music Elem	34	Early Childhood Ed	44	Science Sec	54	Remedial Reading K-12	64	Religious Education K-12	74	Inservice Training
7	Health Services	15	Asst Superintendent	25	Music Sec	35	Health/Phys Education	45	Math K-12	55	Remedial Reading Elem	65	Religious Education Elem	75	Marketing/Distributive
		16	Instructional Media Svcs	26	Business Education	36	Guidance Services K-12	46	Math Elem	56	Remedial Reading Sec	66	Religious Education Sec	76	Info Systems
		17	Chief Operations Officer	27	Career & Tech Ed	37	Guidance Services Elem	47	Math Sec	57	Bilingual/ELL	67	School Board President	77	Psychological Assess
		18	Chief Academic Officer	28	Technology Education	38	Guidance Services Sec	48	English/Lang Arts K-12	58	Special Education K-12	68	Teacher Personnel	78	Affirmative Action

Illinois School Directory — **Macoupin County**

St Teresa High Sch	9-12	295	217/875-2431
2710 N Water St, Decatur 62526		30	Fax 217/875-2436
Larry Daly			🅕 🅣

MACON PRIVATE SCHOOLS

Private Schs..Principal	Grd	Prgm	Enr/#Cls	SN
Decatur Christian Sch	PK-12		190	217/877-5636
137 S Grant St, Forsyth 62535			14	Fax 217/877-7627
Amy Miller \ Stephen Hohm				
Lutheran Assoc Sch	K-12		343	217/233-2001
2001 E Mound Rd, Decatur 62526			11	Fax 217/233-2002
Joel Witt \ Allison Nolen				🅕

MACON REGIONAL CENTERS

- **Heartland Technical Academy** PID: 04184373 — 217/872-4050
  1 College Park, Decatur 62521 — Fax 217/876-0918

Bret Hitchings 1

- **Macon-Piatt Roe#39** PID: 02098089 — 217/872-3721
  1690 Huston Dr, Decatur 62526 — Fax 217/872-0240

Matthew Snyder 1,11   Mike Rogers 2
Jill Reedy 15

- **Macon-Piatt Spec Ed** PID: 02184169 — 217/424-3025
  335 E Cerro Gordo St, Decatur 62523 — Fax 217/424-3022

Kathy Horath 1   Travis Friedrich 15

MACOUPIN COUNTY

MACOUPIN PUBLIC SCHOOLS

- **Bunker Hill Cmty Unit SD 8** PID: 00307585 — 618/585-3116
  504 E Warren St, Bunker Hill 62014 — Fax 618/585-3212

Schools: 2 \ **Teachers:** 41 \ **Students:** 600 \ **Special Ed Students:** 109 \ **Ethnic:** African American 2%, Hispanic 1%, Caucasian 97% \ **Exp:** $256 (Med) \ **Poverty:** 16% \ **Title I:** $179,023 \ **Special Education:** $91,000 \ **Open-Close:** 08/14 - 05/19 \ **DTBP:** $177 (High)

Todd Dugan 1,11   Doug Dey 3,5,91*
Shelly Wuellner 4   Christy Scott 7,85*
Shonda Ronen 8   Lacy Wieseman 67

Public Schs..Principal	Grd	Prgm	Enr/#Cls	SN	
Bunker Hill High Sch	9-12	AV	189	43%	618/585-3232
314 S Meissner St, Bunker Hill 62014			20		Fax 618/585-3241
Matt Smith					
Wolf Ridge Elem Jr High Sch	PK-8	T	366	38%	618/585-4831
700 W Orange St, Bunker Hill 62014			16		Fax 618/585-3123
Shonda Ronen					

- **Carlinville Cmty Unit SD 1** PID: 00307626 — 217/854-9823
  829 W Main St, Carlinville 62626 — Fax 217/854-2777

Schools: 4 \ **Teachers:** 90 \ **Students:** 1,400 \ **Special Ed Students:** 285 \ **LEP Students:** 7 \ **College-Bound:** 68% \ **Ethnic:** Asian 1%, African American 1%, Hispanic 2%, Caucasian 96% \ **Exp:** $268 (Med) \ **Poverty:** 18% \ **Title I:** $435,969 \ **Special Education:** $400,000 \ **Open-Close:** 08/14 - 05/21 \ **DTBP:** $241 (High) \ 🅕 🅣

Dr Becky Schuchman 1   Heather Deneve 2
Jon Klaus .... 3*   Kim MaGuire 4
Jim Roth 5   Darrin Deneve 6*
Elise Schwartz .... 11,296*   Roy Kulenkamp 34*
Kathy Norris 67   Gayla Walters 73*
Dan Presley 295

Public Schs..Principal	Grd	Prgm	Enr/#Cls	SN	
Carlinville High Sch	9-12	TV	467	44%	217/854-3104
829 W Main St, Carlinville 62626			60		Fax 217/854-5260
Patrick Drew					
Carlinville Intermediate Sch	4-5	T	228	53%	217/854-9523
450 W Buchanan St, Carlinville 62626			9		Fax 217/854-3417
Dr Becky Schuchman					
Carlinville Middle Sch	6-8	T	331	49%	217/854-3106
110 Illinois Ave, Carlinville 62626			21		Fax 217/854-4503
Roy Kulenkamp					
Carlinville Primary Sch	K-3	T	363	50%	217/854-9849
18456 Shipman Rd, Carlinville 62626			16		Fax 217/854-7867
Elise Schwartz					

- **Community Unit School Dist 7** PID: 00307690 — 217/839-2464
  510 W Elm St, Gillespie 62033 — Fax 217/839-3353

Schools: 3 \ **Teachers:** 83 \ **Students:** 1,250 \ **Special Ed Students:** 233 \ **LEP Students:** 3 \ **Ethnic:** Hispanic 1%, Native American: 1%, Caucasian 98% \ **Exp:** $195 (Low) \ **Poverty:** 22% \ **Title I:** $514,958 \ **Special Education:** $489,000 \ **Open-Close:** 08/21 - 06/03 \ **DTBP:** $235 (High)

Shane Owsley 1   Rob Graham 3
Penny Seeley 4   Gary Niehaus 5
Mike Bertnagolli .... 6*   Angela Sandretto 11,34*
Mary Kirk .... 16*   Alison Storm 58,77*
Mark Hayes 67   Mark Carpani 73,295

Public Schs..Principal	Grd	Prgm	Enr/#Cls	SN	
Ben-Gld Elem Sch	PK-5	T	626	98%	217/839-4828
340 Kelly St, Gillespie 62033			34		Fax 217/839-3360
Angela Sandretto					
Gillespie High Sch	9-12	TV	364	54%	217/839-2114
612 Broadway St, Gillespie 62033			20		Fax 217/839-4302
Shane Owsley \ Jill Rosentreter					
Gillespie Middle Sch	6-8	T	280	59%	217/839-2116
412 Oregon St, Gillespie 62033			15		Fax 217/839-3104
Jill Rosentreter \ Tara Cooper					

- **Mt Olive Cmty Unit Sch Dist 5** PID: 00307781 — 217/999-7831
  804 W Main St, Mount Olive 62069 — Fax 217/999-2150

Schools: 2 \ **Teachers:** 39 \ **Students:** 452 \ **Special Ed Students:** 111 \ **College-Bound:** 67% \ **Ethnic:** Caucasian 100% \ **Exp:** $342 (High) \ **Poverty:** 14% \ **Title I:** $117,899 \ **Special Education:** $257,000 \ **Open-Close:** 08/21 - 06/04 \ **DTBP:** $180 (High) \ 🅕

Patrick Murphy 1   Joyce Bruch 2

---

79 Student Personnel	91 Safety/Security	275 Response To Intervention	298 Grant Writer/Ptnrships	**School Programs**
80 Driver Ed/Safety	92 Magnet School	277 Remedial Math K-12	750 Chief Innovation Officer	A = Alternative Program
81 Gifted/Talented	93 Parental Involvement	280 Literacy Coach	751 Chief of Staff	G = Adult Classes
82 Video Services	95 Tech Prep Program	285 STEM	752 Social Emotional Learning	M = Magnet Program
83 Substance Abuse Prev	97 Chief Information Officer	286 Digital Learning		T = Title I Schoolwide
84 Erate	98 Chief Technology Officer	288 Common Core Standards	**Other School Types**	V = Career & Tech Ed Programs
85 AIDS Education	270 Character Education	294 Accountability	Ⓐ = Alternative School	
88 Alternative/At Risk	271 Migrant Education	295 Network System	Ⓒ = Charter School	**Social Media**
89 Multi-Cultural Curriculum	273 Teacher Mentor	296 Title II Programs	Ⓜ = Magnet School	🅕 = Facebook
90 Social Work	274 Before/After Sch	297 Webmaster	Ⓨ = Year-Round School	🅣 = Twitter

New Schools are shaded
New Superintendents and Principals are bold
Personnel with email addresses are underscored

Macoupin County

Market Data Retrieval

Karrie Markovitch 6
Mary Gajewski 16
Alice Adden 73*
Kelly Titsworth 11,288*
David Brunnworth 67

Public Schs..Principal	Grd	Prgm	Enr/#Cls	SN	
Mt Olive Elem Jr HS 804 W Main St, Mount Olive 62069 Karrie Scheller	PK-8	T	326 25	51%	217/999-4241 Fax 217/999-4302
Mt Olive High Sch 804 W Main St, Mount Olive 62069 Jon Baumberger	9-12		126 14	45%	217/999-4231 Fax 217/999-4301

● **North Mac Cmty Unit SD 34** PID: 00307743   217/627-2915
525 N 3rd St, Girard 62640   Fax 217/627-3519

Schools: 3 \ Teachers: 91 \ Students: 1,150 \ Special Ed Students: 256 \ LEP Students: 3 \ College-Bound: 55% \ Ethnic: Asian 1%, African American 2%, Hispanic 2%, Caucasian 96% \ Exp: $232 (Med) \ Poverty: 16% \ Title I: $406,111 \ Special Education: $429,000 \ Open-Close: 08/20 - 05/20 \ DTBP: $174 (High)

Jay Goble 1,83
Michael Riffey 3*
Eric Lancaster 5
Robyn Hays 67
Pattie Fetter 2
Aprille Kuhar 4
Sarah Rynor 8,11
Jon Langellier 73

Public Schs..Principal	Grd	Prgm	Enr/#Cls	SN	
North Mac Elem Sch 755 W Fortune St, Virden 62690 Michele Cimarossa	PK-2	T	307 46	60%	217/965-5424 Fax 217/965-4342
North Mac High Sch 231 W Fortune St, Virden 62690 Robert Horn	9-12	ATV	402 19	54%	217/965-4127 Fax 217/965-4006
North Mac Interm Mid Sch 525 N 3rd St, Girard 62640 John Downs	3-8	TV	601 35	58%	217/627-2419 Fax 217/627-3409

● **Northwestern CUSD 2** PID: 00307834   217/436-2442
30953 Route 111, Palmyra 62674   Fax 217/436-2701

Schools: 2 \ Teachers: 35 \ Students: 356 \ Special Ed Students: 92 \ College-Bound: 55% \ Ethnic: African American 1%, Caucasian 99% \ Exp: $234 (Med) \ Poverty: 20% \ Title I: $115,731 \ Special Education: $304,000 \ Open-Close: 08/20 - 05/26 \ DTBP: $205 (High)

Kevin Bowman 1,11
Lindsey Bearidge 4
Debbie White 12,296*
Brock Campbell 67
Keppen Clanton 273
Brian Thibadeau 3,5
Rachel Kinser 6*
Matt Phillips 16,73,84
Denise Joiner 88

Public Schs..Principal	Grd	Prgm	Enr/#Cls	SN	
Northwestern Elem Sch 30953 Route 111, Palmyra 62674 Heather Haley	PK-6	T	213 10	58%	217/362-2210
Northwestern Jr Sr High Sch 30953 Route 111, Palmyra 62674 Keppen Clanton	7-12	TV	146 48	58%	217/362-2210 Fax 217/436-9112

● **Southwestern Cmty Unit SD 9** PID: 00307860   618/372-3813
201 E City Limits Rd, Brighton 62012   Fax 618/372-4681

Schools: 5 \ Teachers: 86 \ Students: 1,300 \ Special Ed Students: 191 \ LEP Students: 3 \ College-Bound: 66% \ Ethnic: African American 1%, Hispanic 1%, Caucasian 97% \ Exp: $207 (Med) \ Poverty: 11% \ Title I: $250,142 \ Special Education: $716,000 \ Open-Close: 08/18 - 05/26 \ DTBP: $174 (High)

Kyle Hacke 1
Bob Ruyle 3*
Kevin Means 5
Corey Pace 31
Andrew Bagley 67
Jason Blankenship 73,295
Anne Christopher 2,11,19,294
Cheryl Darr 4*
Steve Wooley 6*
Stephanie Renken 58*
Scott Hopkins 69*
Dan Mathis 83*

Public Schs..Principal	Grd	Prgm	Enr/#Cls	SN	
Brighton North Primary Sch 201 E City Limits Rd, Brighton 62012 Diane Milner	PK-2	T	299 18	42%	618/372-3813 Fax 618/372-4915
Medora Intermediate Sch 124 S Elm St, Medora 62063 Shannon Bowman	5-6	T	147 13	36%	618/372-3813 Fax 618/729-4531
Shipman Elem Sch 211 Dora Reno White St, Shipman 62685 Diane Milner	3-4	T	109 10	37%	618/372-3813 Fax 618/836-7014
Southwestern High Sch 8226 Route 111, Piasa 62079 Mark Bearley	9-12	V	471 30	36%	618/372-3813 Fax 618/729-4276
Southwestern Middle Sch 8226 Route 111, Piasa 62079 Virgil Moore	7-8	T	214 14	43%	618/729-3217 Fax 618/729-9231

● **Staunton Cmty Unit Sch Dist 6** PID: 00307925   618/635-2962
801 N Deneen St, Staunton 62088   Fax 618/635-2994

Schools: 3 \ Teachers: 73 \ Students: 1,200 \ Special Ed Students: 232 \ College-Bound: 65% \ Ethnic: Asian 1%, Hispanic 3%, Caucasian 96% \ Exp: $159 (Low) \ Poverty: 14% \ Title I: $265,735 \ Special Education: $503,000 \ Open-Close: 08/13 - 05/26 \ DTBP: $233 (High)

Cynthia Tolbert 1
Brian Dustman 3*
Brandon Ray 5
Alli Hughes 7
Tabatha Miller 16,82
Shannon Lickenbrock 38,69
Kimberly Peterson 67
Trisha Steelman 2
Angie Abernathy 4
Troy Redfern 6*
Nancy Werden 9,11,83,88*
Brett Allen 33*
Allison Storm 58
Brian Coalson 73*

Public Schs..Principal	Grd	Prgm	Enr/#Cls	SN	
Staunton Elem Sch 801 N Deneen St, Staunton 62088 **Brett Allen**	PK-8	T	939 65	42%	618/635-3831 Fax 618/635-4637
Staunton High Sch 801 N Deneen St, Staunton 62088 Brett Allen	9-12		375 36	31%	618/635-3838 Fax 618/635-2834
Staunton Junior High Sch 801 N Deneen St, Staunton 62088 **Ryan McGowen**	6-7		401		618/635-3831 Fax 618/635-4637

1 Superintendent	8 Curric/Instruct K-12	19 Chief Financial Officer	29 Family/Consumer Science	39 Social Studies K-12	49 English/Lang Arts Elem	59 Special Education Elem	69 Academic Assessment
2 Bus/Finance/Purchasing	9 Curric/Instruct Elem	20 Art K-12	30 Adult Education	40 Social Studies Elem	50 English/Lang Arts Sec	60 Special Education Sec	70 Research/Development
3 Buildings And Grounds	10 Curric/Instruct Sec	21 Art Elem	31 Career/Sch-to-Work K-12	41 Social Studies Sec	51 Reading K-12	61 Foreign/World Lang K-12	71 Public Information
4 Food Service	11 Federal Program	22 Art Sec	32 Career/Sch-to-Work Elem	42 Science K-12	52 Reading Elem	62 Foreign/World Lang Elem	72 Summer School
5 Transportation	12 Title I	23 Music K-12	33 Career/Sch-to-Work Sec	43 Science Elem	53 Reading Sec	63 Foreign/World Lang Sec	73 Instructional Tech
6 Athletic	13 Title V	24 Music Elem	34 Early Childhood Ed	44 Science Sec	54 Remedial Reading K-12	64 Religious Education K-12	74 Inservice Training
7 Health Services	14 Instructional Media Svcs	25 Music Sec	35 Health/Phys Education	45 Math K-12	55 Remedial Reading Elem	65 Religious Education Elem	75 Marketing/Distributive
	15 Asst Superintendent	26 Business Education	36 Guidance Services K-12	46 Math Elem	56 Remedial Reading Sec	66 Religious Education Sec	76 Info Systems
	16 Instructional Media Svcs	27 Career & Tech Ed	37 Guidance Services Elem	47 Math Sec	57 Bilingual/ELL	67 School Board President	77 Psychological Assess
	17 Chief Operations Officer	28 Technology Education	38 Guidance Services Sec	48 English/Lang Arts K-12	58 Special Education K-12	68 Teacher Personnel	78 Affirmative Action
	18 Chief Academic Officer						

Illinois School Directory — Madison County

MACOUPIN PRIVATE SCHOOLS

Private Schs..Principal	Grd	Prgm	Enr/#Cls	SN	
Zion Lutheran Sch 220 W Henry St, Staunton 62088 David Manning	PK-8		140 6		618/635-3060 Fax 618/635-3994

MACOUPIN REGIONAL CENTERS

- **Regional Office of Ed 40** PID: 02098091 — 217/854-4016
  225 E Nicholas St, Carlinville 62626 — Fax 217/854-2032

  Michelle Mueller 1   Chad Hoesman 15,74

MADISON COUNTY

MADISON COUNTY SCHOOLS

County Schs..Principal	Grd	Prgm	Enr/#Cls	SN	
Ⓐ Center Educational Opportunity 201 Staunton Rd, Troy 62294 Anthony Smith	9-12		100	65%	618/667-0633
Education Therapy Ctr-Madison 201 Staunton Rd, Troy 62294 Christie Johnson	Spec	A	59 6		618/667-0633 Fax 618/667-0670

MADISON PUBLIC SCHOOLS

- **Alton Cmty School District 11** PID: 00308010 — 618/474-2600
  550 Landmarks Blvd Ste A, Alton 62002 — Fax 618/463-2128

Schools: 12 \ **Teachers:** 409 \ **Students:** 6,000 \ **Special Ed Students:** 1,326 \ **LEP Students:** 42 \ **College-Bound:** 70% \ **Ethnic:** Asian 1%, African American 34%, Hispanic 3%, Caucasian 61% \ **Exp:** $113 (Low) \ **Poverty:** 23% \ **Title I:** $3,234,236 \ **Special Education:** $4,730,000 \ **Open-Close:** 08/20 - 05/21 \ **DTBP:** $209 (High) \ f

Kristie Baumgartner 1   Mary Schell 2,274
David McClintock 3,5,91   Keith Brueggemann 4
Chris Kusnerich 6   Cathy Elliott 7,58,90,752*
Renee Hart 8,16,51,57,69,280,285,288   Elaine Kane 12,15
Claire Clancy 16   Angie Kuchnicki 58
Karen Botterbush 60   David Fritz 67
Wendy Adams 68   Matt Derrick 73,76,84,286,295

Public Schs..Principal	Grd	Prgm	Enr/#Cls	SN	
Alton High Sch 4200 Humbert Rd, Alton 62002 Michael Bellm	9-12	TV	1,971	44%	618/474-2700 Fax 618/463-2092
Alton Middle Sch 2200 College Ave, Alton 62002 Cindy Inman	6-8	TV	1,401 40	57%	618/474-2200 Fax 618/463-2028
Ⓐ Alton Success Academy 4200 Humbert Rd, Alton 62002 Brian Johnson	9-12	G	100 20		618/474-2203 Fax 618/463-2121
Early Childhood Center 2400 Henry St, Alton 62002 Cynthia Schuenke	PK-PK		246 15	61%	618/463-2166 Fax 618/463-8253
East Elem Sch 1035 Washington Ave, Alton 62002 Lanea DeConcini	K-5	T	532 29	66%	618/463-2130 Fax 618/463-2132
Eunice Smith Elem Sch 2400 Henry St, Alton 62002 Jody Meggos	K-5	T	307 15	75%	618/463-2077 Fax 618/433-4973
Gilson Brown Elem Sch 1613 W Delmar Ave, Godfrey 62035 Joanne Curvey	K-5	T	290 14	63%	618/463-2175 Fax 618/433-4962
Lewis & Clark Elem Sch 6800 Humbert Rd, Godfrey 62035 Ms Flore-Porter	K-5	T	293 15	60%	618/463-2177 Fax 618/463-8293
Lovejoy Elem Sch 1043 Tremont St, Alton 62002 John Ducey	K-5	T	268 15	63%	618/463-2057 Fax 618/433-7440
Mark Twain Sch 907 Milton Rd, Alton 62002 Stacie Frankie	Spec		31 5	82%	618/463-2063 Fax 618/463-2004
North Elem Sch 5600 Godfrey Rd, Godfrey 62035 Heather Johnson	K-5	T	491 27	57%	618/463-2171 Fax 618/463-2143
West Elem Sch 1513 State St, Alton 62002 Brian Saenz	K-5	T	590 28	55%	618/463-2134 Fax 618/463-2144

- **Bethalto Cmty Unit SD 8** PID: 00308242 — 618/377-7200
  101 School St, Bethalto 62010 — Fax 618/551-7628

Schools: 5 \ **Teachers:** 164 \ **Students:** 2,500 \ **Special Ed Students:** 337 \ **LEP Students:** 22 \ **College-Bound:** 68% \ **Ethnic:** Asian 1%, African American 2%, Hispanic 2%, Caucasian 95% \ **Exp:** $139 (Low) \ **Poverty:** 14% \ **Title I:** $629,116 \ **Special Education:** $1,280,000 \ **Open-Close:** 08/19 - 05/25 \ **DTBP:** $165 (High) \ f

Dr Jill Griffin 1,11   Dr Barrett Deist 2,15
Bill Stratton 3,5,91   Gabrielle Rivera 4
Todd Hannaford ....6*   Sherri Verdun 7*
Amy Wysocki 8,54,57,69,277,285,288   Kim Wilks 10,30,35,273,280*
Christine Wright 31   Jennifer Weber 34,36,58,81,88,752*
Tom Beiermann 67   Dr Kelly McClain 68,79
Tyler Warren 73,76,95,286   Joe Griffin 296,298

Public Schs..Principal	Grd	Prgm	Enr/#Cls	SN	
Bethalto East Primary Sch 309 Albers Pl, Bethalto 62010 Racheal Leckrone	PK-1	T	410 24	54%	618/377-7250 Fax 618/551-8663
Civic Memorial High Sch 200 School St, Bethalto 62010 Justin Newell	9-12	GTV	754 41	37%	618/377-7230 Fax 618/551-7816
Meadowbrook Intermediate Sch 111 W Roosevelt Dr, Moro 62067 Kim Wilks	4-5	T	390 11	47%	618/377-7270 Fax 618/551-7741
Parkside Primary Sch 600 E Central St, Bethalto 62010 Aaron Kilpatrick	2-3	T	361 22	49%	618/377-4100 Fax 618/551-7791 f
Wilbur Trimpe Middle Sch 910 2nd St, Bethalto 62010 Adam Miller	6-8	T	511 40	45%	618/377-7240 Fax 618/377-7218

---

79 Student Personnel
80 Driver Ed/Safety
81 Gifted/Talented
82 Video Services
83 Substance Abuse Prev
84 Erate
85 AIDS Education
88 Alternative/At Risk
89 Multi-Cultural Curriculum
90 Social Work
91 Safety/Security
92 Magnet School
93 Parental Involvement
95 Tech Prep Program
97 Chief Information Officer
98 Chief Technology Officer
270 Character Education
271 Migrant Education
273 Teacher Mentor
274 Before/After Sch
275 Response To Intervention
277 Remedial Math K-12
280 Literacy Coach
285 STEM
286 Digital Learning
288 Common Core Standards
294 Accountability
295 Network System
296 Title II Programs
297 Webmaster
298 Grant Writer/Ptnrships
750 Chief Innovation Officer
751 Chief of Staff
752 Social Emotional Learning

Other School Types
Ⓐ = Alternative School
Ⓒ = Charter School
Ⓜ = Magnet School
Ⓨ = Year-Round School

School Programs
A = Alternative Program
G = Adult Classes
M = Magnet Program
T = Title I Schoolwide
V = Career & Tech Ed Programs

Social Media
f = Facebook
t = Twitter

New Schools are shaded
New Superintendents and Principals are bold
Personnel with email addresses are underscored

Madison County

Collinsville Cmty Sch Dist 10   PID: 00308333   618/346-6350
201 W Clay St, Collinsville 62234   Fax 618/346-6357

Schools: 13 \ **Teachers:** 412 \ **Students:** 5,000 \ **Special Ed Students:** 1,137 \ **LEP Students:** 714 \ **College-Bound:** 66% \ **Ethnic:** Asian 1%, African American 14%, Hispanic 25%, Caucasian 60% \ **Exp:** $161 (Low) \ **Poverty:** 16% \ **Title I:** $2,158,697 \ **Special Education:** $3,743,000 \ **Bilingual Education:** $140,000 \ **Open-Close:** 08/14 - 05/19 \ **DTBP:** $191 (High)

Dr Brad Skertich 1	Uta Robison 2
Josh Dewitte 3,91	Darin Lee 6*
Ali Underwood 7,34,58,77,90	Latoya Berry Coleman 8,11,288,296,298
Brad Hyre 15,79	Mike Kunz 16,28,82*
Tricia Blackard 27,72,75,95*	Carla Cruise 57*
Gary Peccola 67	Kevin Robinson 68
Derek Turner 73,95*	Derek Turner 73,84
Katie Miller 76*	Jason Watts 285
Eric Weiss 295*	

Public Schs..Principal	Grd	Prgm	Enr/#Cls	SN	
Caseyville Elem Sch 433 S 2nd St, Caseyville 62232 Chelsey Clark	K-4	T	361 17	84%	618/346-6205 Fax 618/343-6131
Collinsville Area Voc Center 2201 S Morrison Ave, Collinsville 62234 Tricia Blackard	Voc		450 20		618/343-6140 Fax 618/343-6121
Collinsville High Sch 2201 S Morrison Ave, Collinsville 62234 David Snider	9-12	GV	1,896	54%	618/346-6320 Fax 618/346-6341
Collinsville Middle Sch 9649 Collinsville Rd, Collinsville 62234 **Brad Snow**	7-8	T	951 55	61%	618/343-2100 Fax 618/343-2102
Dorris Intermediate Sch 1841 Vandalia St, Collinsville 62234 Kevin Stirnaman	5-6	T	952 44	63%	618/346-6311 Fax 618/343-2787
Hollywood Heights Sch 6 S Oakland Dr, Caseyville 62232 Dr Kari Karadis	Spec		10	84%	618/343-2740
Jefferson Elem Sch 152 Boskydells Dr, Collinsville 62234 Chelsea Clark	K-4	T	105 5	40%	618/346-6212 Fax 618/343-2747
Kreitner Elem Sch 9000 College St, Collinsville 62234 Dr Kari Karidis	PK-4	T	352 25	86%	618/346-6213 Fax 618/346-6375
Maryville Elem Sch 6900 W Main St, Maryville 62062 Carmen Loemker	K-4	T	351 23	31%	618/346-6262 Fax 618/343-2750
Renfro Elem Sch 311 Camelot Dr, Collinsville 62234 Laura Bauer	PK-4	T	579 35	58%	618/346-6265 Fax 618/346-6379
Summit Elem Sch 408 Willoughby Ln, Collinsville 62234 Stephanie Pulse	K-4	T	105 7	54%	618/346-6222 Fax 618/343-6133
Twin Echo Elem Sch 1937 S Morrison Ave, Collinsville 62234 Dr Julie Haake	K-4	T	224 12	60%	618/346-6227 Fax 618/346-6135
Webster Elem Sch 108 W Church St, Collinsville 62234 Alison Schumacher	PK-4	T	359 30	66%	618/346-6301 Fax 618/346-6368

East Alton Elementary SD 13   PID: 00308539   618/433-2051
210 E Saint Louis Ave, East Alton 62024   Fax 618/433-2096

Schools: 3 \ **Teachers:** 53 \ **Students:** 800 \ **Special Ed Students:** 164 \ **LEP Students:** 3 \ **Ethnic:** African American 9%, Hispanic 1%, Caucasian 90% \ **Exp:** $280 (Med) \ **Poverty:** 29% \ **Title I:** $437,671 \ **Special Education:** $587,000 \ **Open-Close:** 08/19 - 05/21 \ **DTBP:** $255 (High)

Emily Warnecke 1,11	Ricci Voorhees 2,17,19,298
Doug Bogert 5	Miranda Sellars 7,83
Alyssa Smith 9,12,288*	Stacey Egan 59*
Joan Mudge 67	Sean Skelton 73*

Public Schs..Principal	Grd	Prgm	Enr/#Cls	SN	
East Alton Middle Sch 1000 3rd St, East Alton 62024 Kelli Decker	6-8	T	217 15	65%	618/433-2201 Fax 618/433-2203
Eastwood Elem Sch 1030 3rd St, East Alton 62024 Matt Stimac	K-5	T	441 28	59%	618/433-2199 Fax 618/433-2181
Washington Early Childhood Ctr 210 E Saint Louis Ave, East Alton 62024 Stacey Egan	PK-PK	T	107 8	76%	618/433-2001

East Alton-Wood River SD 14   PID: 00309337   618/254-3151
777 N Wood River Ave, Wood River 62095   Fax 618/254-9113

Schools: 1 \ **Teachers:** 34 \ **Students:** 556 \ **Special Ed Students:** 132 \ **LEP Students:** 3 \ **College-Bound:** 59% \ **Ethnic:** African American 5%, Hispanic 4%, Caucasian 90% \ **Exp:** $495 (High) \ **Poverty:** 20% \ **Title I:** $226,868 \ **Special Education:** $311,000 \ **Open-Close:** 08/19 - 05/28 \ **DTBP:** $238 (High)

Dr John Pearson 1	Jeff Foxall 3,5
Shone Fry 4	Kevin Gockel 6
Kelly Naville 7,85*	Leigh Robinson 10,69,74,273*
Mary Budde 16*	Cari Mueller 57*
Patricia Scott 60*	Jennifer Murray 67
Gerry Mattix-Wand 73,295*	Susan Caraway 83*

Public Schs..Principal	Grd	Prgm	Enr/#Cls	SN	
East Alton-Wood River Cmty HS 777 N Wood River Ave, Wood River 62095 Leigh Robinson	9-12	TV	556 50	62%	618/254-3151

Edwardsville Cmty Unit SD 7   PID: 00308606   618/656-1182
708 Saint Louis St, Edwardsville 62025   Fax 618/692-7423

Schools: 15 \ **Teachers:** 420 \ **Students:** 7,500 \ **Special Ed Students:** 839 \ **LEP Students:** 71 \ **College-Bound:** 84% \ **Ethnic:** Asian 3%, African American 8%, Hispanic 4%, Caucasian 85% \ **Exp:** $245 (Med) \ **Poverty:** 6% \ **Title I:** $689,582 \ **Special Education:** $3,960,000 \ **Bilingual Education:** $3,000 \ **Open-Close:** 08/13 - 05/21 \ **DTBP:** $191 (High)

Dr Jason Henderson 1	David Courtney 2,15,91,294
Rich Fore 3	Breanna Gordon 4
Felicia Minor 4	Arlene Kyro 5
Alex Fox 6*	Christy Buie 7*
Catherine Wright 8,12,34,58	Nancy Spina 15,68
Bill Miener 16,73,76,82,295*	Adam Garrett 31,36,58,79,81
Jill Bertels 67	

1	Superintendent	8	Curric/Instruct K-12	19	Chief Financial Officer	29	Family/Consumer Science	39	Social Studies K-12	49	English/Lang Arts Elem	59	Special Education Elem	69	Academic Assessment
2	Bus/Finance/Purchasing	9	Curric/Instruct Elem	20	Art K-12	30	Adult Education	40	Social Studies Elem	50	English/Lang Arts Sec	60	Special Education Sec	70	Research/Development
3	Buildings And Grounds	10	Curric/Instruct Sec	21	Art Elem	31	Career/Sch-to-Work K-12	41	Social Studies Sec	51	Reading K-12	61	Foreign/World Lang K-12	71	Public Information
4	Food Service	11	Federal Program	22	Art Sec	32	Career/Sch-to-Work Elem	42	Science K-12	52	Reading Elem	62	Foreign/World Lang Elem	72	Summer School
5	Transportation	12	Title I	23	Music K-12	33	Career/Sch-to-Work Sec	43	Science Elem	53	Reading Sec	63	Foreign/World Lang Sec	73	Instructional Tech
6	Athletic	13	Title V	24	Music Elem	34	Early Childhood Ed	44	Science Sec	54	Remedial Reading K-12	64	Religious Education K-12	74	Inservice Training
7	Health Services	15	Asst Superintendent	25	Music Sec	35	Health/Phys Education	45	Math K-12	55	Remedial Reading Elem	65	Religious Education Elem	75	Marketing/Distributive
		16	Instructional Media Svcs	26	Business Education	36	Guidance Services K-12	46	Math Elem	56	Remedial Reading Sec	66	Religious Education Sec	76	Info Systems
		17	Chief Operations Officer	27	Career & Tech Ed	37	Guidance Services Elem	47	Math Sec	57	Bilingual/ELL	67	School Board President	77	Psychological Assess
		18	Chief Academic Officer	28	Technology Education	38	Guidance Services Sec	48	English/Lang Arts K-12	58	Special Education K-12	68	Teacher Personnel	78	Affirmative Action

Illinois School Directory — Madison County

Public Schs..Principal	Grd	Prgm	Enr/#Cls	SN	
Albert Cassens Elem Sch 1014 Glen Crossing Rd, Glen Carbon 62034 **Tiana Montgomery**	3-5		505 23	20%	618/655-6150 Fax 618/288-9630
Columbus Elem Sch 315 N Kansas St, Edwardsville 62025 **Julie Matarelli**	3-5	T	428 25	18%	618/656-5167 Fax 618/655-1099
Edwardsville High Sch 6161 Center Grove Rd, Edwardsville 62025 **Dr Steve Stuart**	9-12	GV	2,359	16%	618/656-7100 Fax 618/655-1037
Ⓐ Edwardsville High School-South 6148 Center Grove Rd, Edwardsville 62025 **Dr Dennis Cramsey**	9-12		50 4		618/692-7466 Fax 618/659-9648
Edwardsville HS-Nelson Campus 600 Troy Rd, Edwardsville 62025 **Dr Dennis Cramsey**	Voc		500		618/468-5801 Fax 618/656-4859
Glen Carbon Elem Sch 141 Birger Ave, Glen Carbon 62034 **Mandy Robbins**	K-2	V	333 15	14%	618/692-7460 Fax 618/288-1356
Goshen Elem Sch 101 District Dr, Edwardsville 62025 **Curt Schumacher**	PK-2		487 18	17%	618/655-6250 Fax 618/659-9960
Hamel Elem Sch 400 W State Route 140, Hamel 62046 **Matthew Sidarous**	K-2	T	110 8	29%	618/692-7444 Fax 618/633-1702
LeClaire Elem Sch 801 Franklin Ave, Edwardsville 62025 **Cornelia Smith**	K-2	T	318 20	21%	618/656-3825 Fax 618/655-1038
Liberty Middle Sch 1 District Dr, Edwardsville 62025 **Allen Duncan**	6-8		954	17%	618/655-6800 Fax 618/692-9264
Lincoln Middle Sch 145 West St, Edwardsville 62025 **Jennifer Morgan**	6-8	V	803 50	20%	618/656-0485 Fax 618/659-1268
Midway Elem Sch 6321 Midway Dr, Moro 62067 Matt Sidarous	PK-3		121 13	15%	618/692-7446 Fax 618/377-2577
N O Nelson Elem Sch 1225 W High St, Edwardsville 62025 **Andrew Gipson**	PK-2	T	326 22	29%	618/656-8480 Fax 618/655-1063
Woodland Elem Sch 59 S State Route 157, Edwardsville 62025 **Susan Converse**	3-5	T	483 30	20%	618/692-8790 Fax 618/692-7467
Worden Elem Sch 110 N Main St, Worden 62097 **Beth Renth**	3-5	T	250 12	23%	618/692-7442 Fax 618/459-2174 🅕

• **Granite City Cmty Unit SD 9** PID: 00308682   618/451-5800
   3200 Maryville Rd, Granite City 62040   Fax 618/452-7180

Schools: 8 \ **Teachers:** 318 \ **Students:** 5,764 \ **Special Ed Students:** 1,341 \ **LEP Students:** 224 \ **College-Bound:** 56% \ **Ethnic:** Asian 1%, African American 16%, Hispanic 11%, Native American: 1%, Caucasian 71% \ **Exp:** $229 (Med) \ **Poverty:** 22% \ **Title I:** $2,869,905 \ **Special Education:** $4,380,000 \ **Bilingual Education:** $2,000 \ **Open-Close:** 08/24 - 05/28 \ **DTBP:** $200 (High) \ 🅣

Stephanie Cann 1	Zack Suhre 2
Leroy Metgtzer 3,91	Chris McCullough 4
Donald Harris 5,57,69,71,79,275,294,298	John Moad 6,35*
Kristen Koberna 9,11	Dr David Keel 10,27,31,74,83,285
Tim Moran 27*	Jill Relleke 58,90
Mickiey Watkins 58,77,752	Stephanie Boyer 58
Matt Jones 67	Jim Parker 68,273
Brad Smith 73,84	Brad Ervay 76,295

Public Schs..Principal	Grd	Prgm	Enr/#Cls	SN	
Coolidge Junior High Sch 3231 Nameoki Rd, Granite City 62040 **Patrick Curry**	7-8	V	950 42	55%	618/451-5826 Fax 618/876-5154
Frohardt Elem Sch 2040 Johnson Rd, Granite City 62040 **Terry Mitchell**	3-4	T	420 18	62%	618/451-5821 Fax 618/877-5856
Granite City High Sch 3148 Fehling Rd, Granite City 62040 **Daren Depew**	9-12	ATV	1,806 110	47%	618/451-5808 Fax 618/451-6296
Grigsby Intermediate Sch 3801 Cargill Rd, Granite City 62040 **Donald Stratton**	5-6	T	876 35	59%	618/931-5544 Fax 618/931-5689
Maryville Elem Sch 4651 Maryville Rd, Granite City 62040 **Mark Lull**	1-2	T	371 18	59%	618/931-2044 Fax 618/931-6042
Mitchell Elem Sch 316 E Chain of Rocks Rd, Granite City 62040 **Lisa Yarbrough**	3-4	T	410 21	58%	618/931-0057 Fax 618/931-0059
Prather Elem Sch 2300 W 25th St, Granite City 62040 Dottie Falter \ **Genie Bratten**	PK-K	T	650 24	58%	618/451-5823 Fax 618/876-3843
Wilson Elem Sch 2400 Wilson Ave, Granite City 62040 **Jack Schooley**	1-2	T	473 18	67%	618/451-5817 Fax 618/451-6889

• **Highland Cmty Sch District 5** PID: 00308917   618/654-2106
   400 Broadway, Highland 62249   Fax 618/654-5424

Schools: 6 \ **Teachers:** 185 \ **Students:** 3,000 \ **Special Ed Students:** 587 \ **LEP Students:** 8 \ **College-Bound:** 82% \ **Ethnic:** Asian 1%, African American 1%, Hispanic 1%, Native American: 1%, Caucasian 97% \ **Exp:** $165 (Low) \ **Poverty:** 10% \ **Title I:** $495,123 \ **Special Education:** $1,990,000 \ **Open-Close:** 08/17 - 05/27 \ **DTBP:** $194 (High) \ 🅕 🅣

Michael Sutton 1	Tim Bair 2,5,84
Jeff Williams 3,91	Terry Plocher 4
Amy Boscolo 6*	Jae Kuberski 7*
Derek Hacke 8,11,57,83,88,288,296,298	Mary Beil 16,82
Mary Jackson 27,36*	Gayle Stirewalt 31*
Pamela Tyler 58	Aaron Schuster 67
Alicia Sarris 73	Jeff Kopsic 76
Wendy Phillips 270	Alicia Farris 286
Ryan Haselhorst 295	

Public Schs..Principal	Grd	Prgm	Enr/#Cls	SN	
Alhambra Primary Sch 302 W Main St, Alhambra 62001 Cindy Tolbert	PK-3		169 8	33%	618/488-2200 Fax 618/488-2201
Grantfork Elem Sch 206 N Mulberry St, Highland 62249 Cindy Tolbert \ **Anne Hickey**	4-5		53 8	21%	618/675-2200 Fax 618/675-2204
Highland Elem Sch 1600 Lindenthal Ave, Highland 62249 **Lori Miscik**	3-5		485 38	32%	618/654-2108 Fax 618/654-8767
Highland High Sch 12760 Troxler Ave, Highland 62249 **Chris Becker**	9-12	V	899 75	27%	618/654-7131 Fax 618/654-6548
Highland Middle Sch 2813 State Route 160, Highland 62249 **Liz Weder**	6-8		677 32	29%	618/651-8800 Fax 618/654-1551
Highland Primary Sch 1600 Lindenthal Ave, Highland 62249 **Julie Korte**	PK-2		582 31	34%	618/654-2107 Fax 618/654-1591

79 Student Personnel	91 Safety/Security	275 Response To Intervention	298 Grant Writer/Ptnrships	**School Programs**	**Social Media**
80 Driver Ed/Safety	92 Magnet School	277 Remedial Math K-12	750 Chief Innovation Officer	A = Alternative Program	🅕 = Facebook
81 Gifted/Talented	93 Parental Involvement	280 Literacy Coach	751 Chief of Staff	G = Adult Classes	🅣 = Twitter
82 Video Services	95 Tech Prep Program	285 STEM	752 Social Emotional Learning	M = Magnet Program	
83 Substance Abuse Prev	97 Chief Infomation Officer	286 Digital Learning		T = Title I Schoolwide	
84 Erate	98 Chief Technology Officer	288 Common Core Standards	**Other School Types**	V = Career & Tech Ed Programs	
85 AIDS Education	270 Accountability	294 Network System	Ⓐ = Alternative School		
88 Alternative/At Risk	271 Migrant Education	295 Network System	Ⓒ = Charter School	New Schools are shaded	
89 Multi-Cultural Curriculum	273 Teacher Mentor	296 Title II Programs	Ⓜ = Magnet School	New Superintendents and Principals are bold	
90 Social Work	274 Before/After Sch	297 Webmaster	Ⓨ = Year-Round School	Personnel with email addresses are underscored	

Madison County

Madison Cmty Unit Sch Dist 12 PID: 00309014
602 Farrish St, Madison 62060
618/877-1712
Fax 618/877-2690

Schools: 3 \ **Teachers:** 59 \ **Students:** 700 \ **Special Ed Students:** 117 \ **LEP Students:** 3 \ **College-Bound:** 41% \ **Ethnic:** African American 93%, Hispanic 4%, Native American: 1%, Caucasian 3% \ **Exp:** $240 (Med) \ **Poverty:** 32% \ **Title I:** $667,749 \ **Special Education:** $646,000 \ **Open-Close:** 08/12 - 05/21 \ **DTBP:** $267 (High)

Dr Andrew Reinking 1,11
Lucia Simms 4
Torri Jones 7
Raynard Nichols 73,84
Sharon Bailey 2
Michael Floore 5
Marie Nelson 67

Public Schs..Principal	Grd	Prgm	Enr/#Cls	SN	
Bernard Long Sch 1003 Farrish St, Madison 62060 Terrien Fennoy	PK-5	T	339 8	99%	618/877-1712 Fax 618/877-2696
Madison Jr Sr High Sch 600 Farrish St, Madison 62060 Juan Gardner	6-12	T	311 22	100%	618/877-1712 Fax 618/877-2694
Madison Student Support Center 1634 7th St, Madison 62060 Karen Missey	3-12	TV	18 4	83%	618/877-1712

Roxana Cmty Unit Sch Dist 1 PID: 00309088
401 Chaffer Ave, Roxana 62084
618/254-7544
Fax 618/254-7547

Schools: 4 \ **Teachers:** 115 \ **Students:** 2,000 \ **Special Ed Students:** 279 \ **LEP Students:** 4 \ **College-Bound:** 64% \ **Ethnic:** Asian 1%, African American 2%, Hispanic 3%, Caucasian 94% \ **Exp:** $236 (Med) \ **Poverty:** 20% \ **Title I:** $688,703 \ **Special Education:** $921,000 \ **Open-Close:** 08/14 - 05/28 \ **DTBP:** $238 (High)

Debra Kreutztrager 1
Tim Dyer 3,91
Angela Simms 5
Minette Wilson 7
Kristin Schrewe 16*
Denise Briggs 35
Butch McGill 67
Tammy Steckel 2,7
Mari-Anne Luckert 4
Mark Briggs 6
Stephen Oertle 8,11,15,83,88,285,288,296
Lesa Cope 34
Laura Ballard 57,58,77,275
Marcus Schaefer 73,76,295*

Public Schs..Principal	Grd	Prgm	Enr/#Cls	SN	
Central Intermediate Sch 601 Chaffer Ave, Roxana 62084 James Miller	3-5	T	463 24	53%	618/254-7594 Fax 618/254-7530
Roxana Junior High Sch 401 Chaffer Ave, Roxana 62084 Chad Ambuehl	6-8	T	420 40	48%	618/254-7561 Fax 618/254-8107
Roxana Senior High Sch 401 Chaffer Ave, Roxana 62084 Jason Dandurand	9-12	TV	536 48	51%	618/254-7551 Fax 618/254-7580
South Primary Sch 414 Indiana Ave, South Roxana 62087 Ryan Tusek	PK-2	T	504 23	54%	618/254-7591 Fax 618/254-7592

Triad Cmty School District 2 PID: 00309155
203 E Throp St, Troy 62294
618/667-8851
Fax 618/667-8854

Schools: 6 \ **Teachers:** 235 \ **Students:** 4,000 \ **Special Ed Students:** 606 \ **LEP Students:** 8 \ **College-Bound:** 80% \ **Ethnic:** Asian 1%, African American 2%, Hispanic 1%, Caucasian 96% \ **Exp:** $176 (Low) \ **Poverty:** 5% \ **Title I:** $309,636 \ **Special Education:** $2,107,000 \ **Open-Close:** 08/12 - 05/27 \ **DTBP:** $203 (High)

Leigh Lewis 1
Mike Raymond 2,296
Ruth Cunningham 4
Ken Deatherage 6*
Amy Van Hoose 8,12,51,288
Linda Kowalski 57,58
Mike Wielgus 73
Kennan Fagan 2,11,16,69,73,74,76,286
Lon Henke 3
Kevin McGraw 5
Rhonda Grammer 7*
Josh Ackerman 16,82
Jeff Hewitt 67
Michael Smargiassi 80*

Public Schs..Principal	Grd	Prgm	Enr/#Cls	SN	
C A Henning Elem Sch 520 E US Highway 40, Troy 62294 Kay Burrough	PK-5	T	764 29	27%	618/667-5401 Fax 618/667-5565
Marine Elem Sch 725 W Division St, Marine 62061 Michael Speer	PK-5	T	136 11	21%	618/667-5404 Fax 618/887-4092
Silver Creek Elem Sch 209 N Dewey St, Troy 62294 Sandy Padak	PK-5	T	696 27	21%	618/667-5403 Fax 618/667-3087
St Jacob Elem Sch 305 Jacob St, Saint Jacob 62281 Jay Simpson	PK-5		216 10	14%	618/644-2541 Fax 618/644-5474
Triad High Sch 703 E US Highway 40, Troy 62294 Rodney Winslow	9-12	V	1,137 50	18%	618/667-5409 Fax 618/667-8853
Triad Middle Sch 9539 US Highway 40, Saint Jacob 62281 Matt Noyes	6-8		845 31	21%	618/667-5406 Fax 618/644-9435

Venice Cmty Unit School Dist 3 PID: 00309222
300 4th St, Venice 62090
618/274-7953
Fax 618/274-7138

Schools: 1 \ **Teachers:** 12 \ **Students:** 80 \ **Special Ed Students:** 24 \ **Ethnic:** African American 97%, Caucasian 3% \ **Exp:** $499 (High) \ **Poverty:** 28% \ **Title I:** $129,053 \ **Special Education:** $100,000 \ **Open-Close:** 08/14 - 05/21 \ **DTBP:** $192 (High) \

Dr Ronald Ferrell 1
Tisha Glasper 67
Tamara Miller 2

Public Schs..Principal	Grd	Prgm	Enr/#Cls	SN	
Venice Elem Sch 300 4th St, Venice 62090 Dr Ronald Ferrell	PK-8	T	80 17	96%	618/274-7953

Wood River-Hartford Elem SD 15 PID: 00309272
501 E Lorena Ave, Wood River 62095
618/254-0607
Fax 618/254-9048

Schools: 3 \ **Teachers:** 45 \ **Students:** 706 \ **Special Ed Students:** 142 \ **LEP Students:** 3 \ **Ethnic:** African American 4%, Hispanic 3%, Caucasian 93% \ **Exp:** $218 (Med) \ **Poverty:** 23% \ **Title I:** $295,605 \ **Special Education:** $362,000 \ **Open-Close:** 08/21 - 05/21 \ **DTBP:** $213 (High)

Dr Patrick Anderson 1
Duane Amistadi 3,91
Mathew Herndon 6*
Kelly Bohnenstiehl 9*
Steven Scroggins 67
Chris Edwards 73,295,297*
Michelle Billingsley 2,11,68
Patty Redman 4*
Megan Henry 7,85
Cindy Barnhart 59*
Natalie Bouillon 69,273,275*
Susan Weshinskey 83,90*

Public Schs..Principal	Grd	Prgm	Enr/#Cls	SN	
Hartford Elem Sch 110 W 2nd St, Hartford 62048 Natalie Bouillon	PK-5	T	203 11	71%	618/254-9814 Fax 618/254-7602

1	Superintendent	8	Curric/Instruct K-12	19	Chief Financial Officer	29	Family/Consumer Science	39	Social Studies K-12	49	English/Lang Arts Elem	59	Special Education Elem	69	Academic Assessment
2	Bus/Finance/Purchasing	9	Curric/Instruct Elem	20	Art K-12	30	Adult Education	40	Social Studies Elem	50	English/Lang Arts Sec	60	Special Education Sec	70	Research/Development
3	Buildings And Grounds	10	Curric/Instruct Sec	21	Art Elem	31	Career/Sch-to-Work K-12	41	Social Studies Sec	51	Reading K-12	61	Foreign/World Lang K-12	71	Public Information
4	Food Service	11	Federal Program	22	Art Sec	32	Career/Sch-to-Work Elem	42	Science K-12	52	Reading Elem	62	Foreign/World Lang Elem	72	Summer School
5	Transportation	12	Title I	23	Music K-12	33	Career/Sch-to-Work Sec	43	Science Elem	53	Reading Sec	63	Foreign/World Lang Sec	73	Instructional Tech
6	Athletic	13	Title V	24	Music Elem	34	Early Childhood Ed	44	Science Soc	54	Remedial Reading K-12	64	Religious Education K-12	74	Inservice Training
7	Health Services	14	Asst Superintendent	25	Music Sec	35	Health/Phys Education	45	Math K-12	55	Remedial Reading Elem	65	Religious Education Elem	75	Marketing/Distributive
		15	Instructional Media Svcs	26	Business Education	36	Guidance Services K-12	46	Math Elem	56	Remedial Reading Sec	66	Religious Education Sec	76	Info Systems
		16	Chief Operations Officer	27	Career & Tech Ed	37	Guidance Services Elem	47	Math Sec	57	Bilingual/ELL	67	School Board President	77	Psychological Assess
		17	Chief Academic Officer	28	Technology Education	38	Guidance Services Sec	48	English/Lang Arts K-12	58	Special Education K-12	68	Teacher Personnel	78	Affirmative Action

Illinois School Directory — Madison County

School	Grd	Prgm	Enr/#Cls	SN	Phone
Lewis & Clark Elem Sch 501 E Lorena Ave, Wood River 62095 Jill Christeson	K-5	T	274 19	64%	618/254-4354 Fax 618/254-7601
Lewis & Clark Jr High Sch 501 E Lorena Ave, Wood River 62095 Radena Lemmon	6-8	T	229 18	70%	618/254-4355 Fax 618/254-7600

MADISON CATHOLIC SCHOOLS

- **Diocese of Springfield Ed Off** PID: 00319394
  Listing includes only schools located in this county. See District Index for location of Diocesan Offices.

Catholic Schs..Principal	Grd	Prgm	Enr/#Cls	SN	Phone
Father McGivney Catholic HS 7190 Bouse Rd, Glen Carbon 62034 Joseph Lombardi	9-9		60		618/855-9010
Holy Family Sch 1900 Saint Clair Ave, Granite City 62040 Margaret Pennell	PK-8		180 11		618/877-5500 Fax 618/877-5502
Marquette Catholic High Sch 219 E 4th St, Alton 62002 Michael Slaughter	9-12		264 23		618/463-0580 Fax 618/465-4029
Our Lady Queen of Peace Sch 618 N Prairie St, Bethalto 62010 Steve Menke	PK-8		125 10		618/377-6401 Fax 618/377-6146 f
SS Peter & Paul Sch 210 N Morrison Ave, Collinsville 62234 Julie Buehler	PK-8		238 10		618/344-5450 Fax 618/344-5536
St Ambrose Sch 822 W Homer M Adams Pkwy, Godfrey 62035 Robert Baird	K-8		250 12		618/466-4216 Fax 618/466-4575 f t
St Boniface Sch 128 N Buchanan St, Edwardsville 62025 Laura Kretzer	K-8		300 9		618/656-6917
St Elizabeth Sch 2300 Pontoon Rd, Granite City 62040 Michelle Williams	K-8		135 9		618/877-3348 Fax 618/877-3352
St John Neumann Sch 142 Wilma Dr, Maryville 62062 David Gregson	PK-8		357 13		618/345-7230 Fax 618/345-4350
St Mary Sch 1802 Madison Ave, Edwardsville 62025 Diane Wepking	PK-8		248 17		618/656-1230 Fax 618/656-1715 f t
St Mary Sch 536 E 3rd St, Alton 62002 Alex Pulido	PK-8		355 21		618/465-8523 Fax 618/465-4725
St Paul Catholic Sch 1416 Main St, Highland 62249 Haidee Todora	PK-8		305 18		618/654-7525 Fax 618/654-8795 f t

MADISON PRIVATE SCHOOLS

Private Schs..Principal	Grd	Prgm	Enr/#Cls	SN	Phone
Catholic Children's Home Sch 1400 State St, Alton 62002 Michael Shelton-Montez	Spec		105 90		618/465-3594 Fax 618/465-1083
Central Baptist Sch 3940 Highway 111, Granite City 62040 Wayne Musatics	K-12		20 1		618/931-0964 Fax 618/931-0990
Connect Christian Sch 1417 Herbert St, South Roxana 62087 Gregory Gomez	PK-12		105 12		618/254-0188 Fax 618/254-2647
Evangelical Elem Sch 1212 W Homer M Adams Pkwy, Godfrey 62035 Maria Baalman	PK-8		374 7		618/466-1599 Fax 618/466-9498
Faith Chrn Fellowship Academy 200 Sinclair Ave, South Roxana 62087 Arthur Hooper	1-12		5		618/254-9636
Faith Lutheran Sch 6809 Godfrey Rd, Godfrey 62035 Tracy Wiggenhorn	PK-PK		20 2		618/466-3833 Fax 618/466-3839
Gateway Legacy Christian Acad 97 Oaklawn Dr, Glen Carbon 62034 Melissa Morreson	PK-12		200		618/288-0452 Fax 618/288-0453
Good Shepherd Lutheran Sch 1300 Belt Line Rd, Collinsville 62234 Robert Mayhew	PK-8		310 27		618/344-3153 Fax 618/344-3156
Holy Cross Lutheran Sch 304 South St, Collinsville 62234 Darrin Houck	PK-8		163 19		618/344-0474 Fax 618/344-1222
Lahr-Well Academy 903 N 2nd St, Edwardsville 62025 Dr Almeda Lahr-Well	PK-12		15 4		618/288-8024 Fax 618/288-2440
Maryville Christian Sch 7110 State Route 162, Maryville 62062 Brian Kamadulski	PK-8		236		618/505-7000 Fax 618/667-0650
Metro East Lutheran High Sch 6305 Center Grove Rd, Edwardsville 62025 Dr Jay Krause	9-12		180 17		618/656-0043 Fax 618/656-3315 f
Metro East Montessori Sch 4405 State Route 162, Granite City 62040 Kyra Lakin	PK-6		64 5		618/931-2508 Fax 618/931-5816 f
Mississippi Valley Chrn Sch 2009 Seminary St, Alton 62002 Dave Schneider	PK-12		100 13		618/462-1071 Fax 618/462-9877
Montessori Children's House 5800 Godfrey Rd, Godfrey 62035 Roderick Connell	PK-8		106 5		618/467-2333 Fax 618/467-2332
Ⓐ River's Edge Sch 1611 W 3rd St, Granite City 62040	K-12		100		618/451-0552 Fax 618/451-1257
Rivers of Life Christian Sch 3201 E 23rd St, Granite City 62040 Antonette Encarnacion \ Dawn Artis	PK-12		125 6		618/797-7933
St Paul Lutheran Sch 112 N Border St, Troy 62294 Bruce McLaughlin	PK-8		106 7		618/667-6314 Fax 618/667-8098
St Paul Lutheran Sch 6961 W Frontage Rd, Worden 62097 Kate Thoelke	K-8		47 5		618/633-2202 Fax 618/633-1709
St Peter Lutheran Sch 7182 Renken Rd, Dorsey 62021 Melissa Burns	PK-8		36 3		618/888-2252
Trinity Lutheran Sch 600 Water St, Edwardsville 62025 Wes Jones	PK-8		240 12		618/656-7002 Fax 618/656-5941
William M Bedell-A R C Sch 400 S Main St, Wood River 62095 Kathy Germscheid	Spec		75 8		618/251-2175 Fax 618/251-6294
Word of Life Christian Sch 4870 Maryville Rd, Granite City 62040 Lisa Cochran	PK-12		40		618/931-3744
Zion Lutheran Sch 625 Church Dr, Bethalto 62010 Joseph Snyder	PK-8		250 14		618/377-5507 Fax 618/377-3630

---

79 Student Personnel	91 Safety/Security	275 Response To Intervention	298 Grant Writer/Ptnrships
80 Driver Ed/Safety	92 Magnet School	277 Remedial Math K-12	750 Chief Innovation Officer
81 Gifted/Talented	93 Parental Involvement	280 Literacy Coach	751 Chief of Staff
82 Video Services	95 Tech Prep Program	285 STEM	752 Social Emotional Learning
83 Substance Abuse Prev	97 Chief Information Officer	286 Digital Learning	
84 Erate	98 Chief Technology Officer	288 Common Core Standards	
85 AIDS Education	270 Character Education	294 Accountability	
88 Alternative/At Risk	271 Migrant Education	295 Network System	
89 Multi-Cultural Curriculum	273 Teacher Mentor	296 Title II Programs	
90 Social Work	274 Before/After Sch	297 Webmaster	

School Programs
A = Alternative Program
G = Adult Classes
M = Magnet Program
T = Title I Schoolwide
V = Career & Tech Ed Programs

Other School Types
Ⓐ = Alternative School
Ⓒ = Charter School
Ⓜ = Magnet School
Ⓨ = Year-Round School

Social Media
f = Facebook
t = Twitter

New Schools are shaded
New Superintendents and Principals are bold
Personnel with email addresses are underscored

Marion County

MADISON REGIONAL CENTERS

- **Area 5 Learning Technology Hub** PID: 04433186 217/646-0221
  200 Clay St, Edwardsville 62025 Fax 618/659-9338

  Marvin Warner 1   Mat Marietta 295

- **Madison Co Cte System** PID: 03032636 618/656-0415
  6161 Center Grove Rd, Edwardsville 62025 Fax 618/656-0514

  Kaleb Smith 1,11

- **Madison Co Reg 1 Spec Ed Co-op** PID: 02184030 618/451-5800
  3200 Maryville Rd, Granite City 62040 Fax 618/451-0398

  Paula Hubbard 1,11

- **Region 3 Spec Ed Co-op** PID: 02182068 618/462-1031
  1800 Storey Ln, Cottage Hills 62018 Fax 618/462-1035

  Messina Lenger 1

- **Regional Office of Ed 41** PID: 02098106 618/296-4530
  157 N Main St, Edwardsville 62025 Fax 618/692-7018

  Robert Werden 1   Dr Tricia Blackard 15,88

MARION COUNTY

MARION PUBLIC SCHOOLS

- **Central City School Dist 133** PID: 00309442 618/532-9521
  129 Douglas St, Centralia 62801 Fax 618/533-2219

  Schools: 1 \ **Teachers:** 22 \ **Students:** 349 \ **Special Ed Students:** 84 \
  Ethnic: African American 4%, Hispanic 2%, Caucasian 94% \ **Exp:** $255
  (Med) \ **Poverty:** 34% \ **Title I:** $174,605 \ **Special Education:** $106,000 \
  Open-Close: 08/17 - 05/18

  Tim Branon 1   Mike Sloat 6*
  Rick Starr 67   Julie Martin 275*

Public Schs..Principal	Grd	Prgm	Enr/#Cls	SN	
Central City Elem Sch	PK-8	T	349	81%	618/532-9521
129 Douglas St, Centralia 62801			15		
Tim Branon					

- **Centralia City Sch Dist 135** PID: 00309466 618/532-1907
  400 S Elm St, Centralia 62801 Fax 618/532-4986

  Schools: 4 \ **Teachers:** 93 \ **Students:** 1,250 \ **Special Ed Students:** 339
  \ **Ethnic:** African American 19%, Hispanic 5%, Caucasian 75% \ **Exp:** $102
  (Low) \ **Poverty:** 38% \ **Title I:** $1,219,951 \ **Special Education:** $645,000 \
  Open-Close: 08/17 - 05/21 \ **DTBP:** $175 (High)

  Craig Clark 1   Debbie Redfeairn 2,5
  Mike Hafeli 3   Susan Baum Gartener 4
  Sarah Epplin 59   Ron Johnson 67

  Don Ford 73,295

Public Schs..Principal	Grd	Prgm	Enr/#Cls	SN
Centralia Junior High Sch	4-8	T	523	100% 618/533-7130
900 S Pine St, Centralia 62801			50	Fax 618/533-7123
Tron Young				
Centralia Pre-Kindergarten Ctr	PK-PK		50	93% 618/533-7122
422 S Elm St, Centralia 62801				
Brenda Mulvany				
Jordan Elem Sch	K-3	T	300	100% 618/533-7145
311 Airport Rd, Centralia 62801			12	Fax 618/533-7146
Craig Bland				
Schiller Elem Sch	K-3	T	250	100% 618/533-7140
800 W 4th St, Centralia 62801			10	Fax 618/533-7141
Amanda Marshall				

- **Centralia High School Dist 200** PID: 00309571 618/532-7391
  2100 E Calumet St, Centralia 62801 Fax 618/532-8952

  Schools: 1 \ **Teachers:** 67 \ **Students:** 900 \ **Special Ed Students:** 183 \
  College-Bound: 62% \ **Ethnic:** Asian 1%, African American 10%, Hispanic
  6%, Caucasian 83% \ **Exp:** $200 (Med) \ **Poverty:** 25% \ **Title I:** $524,717 \
  Special Education: $1,093,000 \ **Open-Close:** 08/17 - 06/01

  Chuck Lane 1   Randy Redfeairn 3*
  Jason Pauley 4   Brad Boewey 6
  Lee Bennett .... 6*   Amy Brink 7*
  Reid Shipley .... 10,79*   Vicky Benjamin 16*
  Derek Harlan .... 38,69,83,88*   Lisa Griffin 38*
  Gaylin Mahle 67   John Tomlianovich 73*

Public Schs..Principal	Grd	Prgm	Enr/#Cls	SN
Centralia High Sch	9-12	ATV	900	60% 618/532-7391
2100 E Calumet St, Centralia 62801				
Chuck Lane				

- **Iuka Community Cons Sch Dist 7** PID: 00309595 618/323-6233
  405 S Main St, Iuka 62849 Fax 618/323-6932

  Schools: 1 \ **Teachers:** 16 \ **Students:** 225 \ **Special Ed Students:** 43 \
  Ethnic: Hispanic 1%, Caucasian 98% \ **Exp:** $175 (Low) \ **Poverty:** 23% \
  Title I: $103,181 \ **Special Education:** $103,000 \ **Open-Close:** 08/21 -
  05/20 \ **DTBP:** $167 (High) \ [f] [t]

  John Consolino 1,73,83   Barbi Cleary 2*
  Don Frech 6   Melissa Eddings 11,296
  Denise Phillips .... 37*   Kevin Cripps 67

Public Schs..Principal	Grd	Prgm	Enr/#Cls	SN
Iuka Grade Sch	PK-8	T	225	47% 618/323-6233
405 S Main St, Iuka 62849			12	Fax 618/323-6192
John Consolino				

- **Kell Cons School District 2** PID: 00309612 618/822-6234
  207 N Johnson St, Kell 62853 Fax 618/822-6733

  Schools: 1 \ **Teachers:** 11 \ **Students:** 100 \
  Special Ed Students: 24 \ **Ethnic:** Asian 1%, Hispanic 1%, Native American:
  1%, Caucasian 97% \ **Exp:** $309 (High) \ **Poverty:** 17% \ **Title I:** $34,298 \
  Special Education: $33,000 \ **Open-Close:** 08/17 - 05/21 \ **DTBP:** $62 (Low)

  John Consolino 1   Mariahh Green 2
  Jerod Kelly 3   Karen Collier 6
  Jennifer Hackney .... 12*   Lisa Sligar 16,59*
  Michelle Murphy .... 35*   Jennifer Timm 67

1	Superintendent	8	Curric/Instruct K-12	19	Chief Financial Officer	29	Family/Consumer Science	39	Social Studies K-12	49	English/Lang Arts Elem	59	Special Education Elem	69	Academic Assessment
2	Bus/Finance/Purchasing	9	Curric/Instruct Elem	20	Art K-12	30	Adult Education	40	Social Studies Elem	50	English/Lang Arts Sec	60	Special Education Sec	70	Research/Development
3	Buildings And Grounds	10	Curric/Instruct Sec	21	Art Elem	31	Career/Sch-to-Work K-12	41	Social Studies Sec	51	Reading K-12	61	Foreign/World Lang K-12	71	Public Information
4	Food Service	11	Federal Program	22	Art Sec	32	Career/Sch-to-Work Elem	42	Science K-12	52	Reading Elem	62	Foreign/World Lang Elem	72	Summer School
5	Transportation	12	Title I	23	Music K-12	33	Career/Sch-to-Work Sec	43	Science Elem	53	Reading Sec	63	Foreign/World Lang Sec	73	Instructional Tech
6	Athletic	13	Title V	24	Music Elem	34	Early Childhood Ed	44	Science Sec	54	Remedial Reading K-12	64	Religious Education K-12	74	Inservice Training
7	Health Services	15	Asst Superintendent	25	Music Sec	35	Health/Phys Education	45	Math K-12	55	Remedial Reading Elem	65	Religious Education Elem	75	Marketing/Distributive
		16	Instructional Media Svcs	26	Business Education	36	Guidance Services K-12	46	Math Elem	56	Remedial Reading Sec	66	Religious Education Sec	76	Info Systems
		17	Chief Operations Officer	27	Career & Tech Ed	37	Guidance Services Elem	47	Math Sec	57	Bilingual/ELL	67	School Board President	77	Psychological Assess
		18	Chief Academic Officer	28	Technology Education	38	Guidance Services Sec	48	English/Lang Arts K-12	58	Special Education K-12	68	Teacher Personnel	78	Affirmative Action

Illinois School Directory — Marion County

Hollie Arnold ....69* Sarah Ferrell 83

Public Schs..Principal	Grd	Prgm	Enr/#Cls	SN	
Kell Elem Sch 207 N Johnson St, Kell 62853 Christopher McCann	K-8	T	100 10	66%	618/822-6234

● **Odin Public School Dist 722** PID: 00309674 618/775-8266
102 S Merritt St, Odin 62870 Fax 618/775-8268

Schools: 2 \ **Teachers:** 23 \ **Students:** 250 \ **Special Ed Students:** 45 \ **Ethnic:** African American 3%, Hispanic 1%, Caucasian 95% \ **Exp:** $213 (Med) \ **Poverty:** 32% \ **Title I:** $193,321 \ **Special Education:** $61,000 \ **Open-Close:** 08/17 - 05/25 \ **DTBP:** $35 (Low)

Jeff Humes ....1,11 Lisa Telford 2
Mary Minor ....4* Kristin Reynold 7*
Sam Alli ....8 Amanda Coleman 38,83,88,270
Rod Hawley ....67 Sarah Loepker 83,85,90
Deborah Ellis 288

Public Schs..Principal	Grd	Prgm	Enr/#Cls	SN	
Odin Attendance Center 9-12 102 S Merritt St, Odin 62870 Sam Alli	9-12	TV	69 4	67%	618/775-8266 Fax 618/775-8262
Odin Attendance Center K-8 102 S Merritt St, Odin 62870 Sam Alli	PK-8	T	181 10	63%	618/775-8266 Fax 618/775-8262

● **Patoka Cmty Unit SD 100** PID: 00309703 618/432-5440
1220 Kinoka Rd, Patoka 62875 Fax 618/432-5306

Schools: 1 \ **Teachers:** 21 \ **Students:** 260 \ **Special Ed Students:** 45 \ **College-Bound:** 100% \ **Ethnic:** Caucasian 100% \ **Exp:** $283 (Med) \ **Poverty:** 17% \ **Title I:** $73,164 \ **Special Education:** $78,000 \ **Open-Close:** 08/27 - 05/18 \ **DTBP:** $188 (High)

David Rademaker ....1,11,288 Kim Hassell 2
Larry Landreth ....3* Tammy Adams 4*
Lora Lee Pierce ....6* Sarah Payne 7,59*
Justin Zenhaus ....8,74,273,274,275 Tracy Burkett 12*
Pat Torrence ....16* Chrisitne Meng 31,36,69*
Kurt Belcher ....67 Kim Willis 73,295*
Christine Meno 83

Public Schs..Principal	Grd	Prgm	Enr/#Cls	SN	
Patoka Cmty Sch 1220 Kinoka Rd, Patoka 62875 Ryan Robinson	K-12	T	260 18	50%	618/432-5643

● **Raccoon Cons School Dist 1** PID: 00309727 618/532-7329
3601 State Route 161, Centralia 62801 Fax 618/532-7336

Schools: 1 \ **Teachers:** 18 \ **Students:** 240 \ **Special Ed Students:** 57 \ **Ethnic:** Asian 1%, African American 2%, Hispanic 3%, Caucasian 94% \ **Exp:** $183 (Low) \ **Poverty:** 20% \ **Title I:** $80,658 \ **Special Education:** $86,000 \ **Open-Close:** 08/20 - 05/24 \ **DTBP:** $98 (Med)

Misty Johaness ....1,11,83 Stacy Dalton 2
Rick Meredith ....3 Valerie Sherman 6*
Kayla White ....67 Jill Dare 84,298

Public Schs..Principal	Grd	Prgm	Enr/#Cls	SN	
Raccoon Sch 3601 State Route 161, Centralia 62801 Matt Renaud	PK-8	T	240 12	52%	618/532-7329

● **Salem Cmty High Sch Dist 600** PID: 00309791 618/548-0727
1200 N Broadway Ave, Salem 62881 Fax 618/548-8021

Schools: 1 \ **Teachers:** 42 \ **Students:** 650 \ **Special Ed Students:** 95 \ **College-Bound:** 65% \ **Ethnic:** Asian 1%, Hispanic 1%, Caucasian 97% \ **Exp:** $294 (Med) \ **Poverty:** 16% \ **Title I:** $231,258 \ **Special Education:** $227,000 \ **Open-Close:** 08/20 - 05/27 \ **DTBP:** $178 (High) \ t

Dr Brad Detering ....1,11 Tom Thomason 3
Scott Steward ....6* Hope Nottmeyer 16,82*
Megan Kessler ....38,69,83,88 Eric Bandy 67
Zach Lamczyk 73,74,76,295*

Public Schs..Principal	Grd	Prgm	Enr/#Cls	SN	
Salem Cmty High Sch 1200 N Broadway Ave, Salem 62881 John Boles	9-12	ATV	650 100	47%	618/548-0727

● **Salem Elem Sch District 111** PID: 00309741 618/548-7702
1300 Bobcat Cir, Salem 62881 Fax 618/548-7714

Schools: 2 \ **Teachers:** 72 \ **Students:** 1,000 \ **Special Ed Students:** 216 \ **LEP Students:** 3 \ **Ethnic:** Asian 1%, African American 1%, Hispanic 1%, Caucasian 98% \ **Exp:** $269 (Med) \ **Poverty:** 29% \ **Title I:** $573,216 \ **Special Education:** $368,000 \ **Open-Close:** 08/14 - 05/21

Dr Leslie Foppe ....1,11 Mike Pugh 3,91*
Linda Hayes ....4* John Gaston 67
Jacob Burkett 73*

Public Schs..Principal	Grd	Prgm	Enr/#Cls	SN	
Franklin Park Middle Sch 1325 Bobcat Cir, Salem 62881 Tyler Lux	4-8	T	521 31	53%	618/548-7704 Fax 618/548-7712
Hawthorn Grade Sch 1300 Bobcat Cir, Salem 62881 Marty Adams	K-3	T	416 17	56%	618/548-7702 Fax 618/548-7712

● **Sandoval Cmty Unit SD 501** PID: 00309818 618/247-3233
859 W Missouri Ave, Sandoval 62882 Fax 618/247-3243

Schools: 2 \ **Teachers:** 34 \ **Students:** 504 \ **Special Ed Students:** 134 \ **LEP Students:** 3 \ **College-Bound:** 50% \ **Ethnic:** African American 1%, Hispanic 1%, Caucasian 98% \ **Exp:** $898 (High) \ **Poverty:** 31% \ **Title I:** $305,460 \ **Special Education:** $148,000 \ **Open-Close:** 08/21 - 06/08 \ **DTBP:** $174 (High)

Rob Miller ....1,11 Cara Garnar 2
Jered Gambill ....67 Jill Strole 69*
Stephen Raisley ....73* Rhonda Benjamin 275*

Public Schs..Principal	Grd	Prgm	Enr/#Cls	SN	
Sandoval Elem Sch 300 E Perry Ave, Sandoval 62882 Annie Gray	PK-6	T	326 21	70%	618/247-3450 Fax 618/247-3161
Sandoval Jr Sr High Sch 859 W Missouri Ave, Sandoval 62882 Matt Dannaman	7-12	TV	178 20	68%	618/247-3361 Fax 618/247-3235

---

79 Student Personnel	91 Safety/Security	275 Response To Intervention	296 Grant Writer/Ptnrships	**School Programs**
80 Driver Ed/Safety	92 Magnet School	277 Remedial Math K-12	750 Chief Innovation Officer	A = Alternative Program
81 Gifted/Talented	93 Parental Involvement	280 Literacy Coach	751 Chief of Staff	G = Adult Classes
82 Video Services	95 Tech Prep Program	285 STEM	752 Social Emotional Learning	M = Magnet Program
83 Substance Abuse Prev	97 Chief Infomation Officer	286 Digital Learning		T = Title I Schoolwide
84 Erate	98 Chief Technology Officer	288 Common Core Standards	**Other School Types**	V = Career & Tech Ed Programs
85 AIDS Education	270 Accountability	294 Accountability	Ⓐ = Alternative School	
88 Alternative/At Risk	271 Migrant Education	295 Network System	Ⓒ = Charter School	
89 Multi-Cultural Curriculum	273 Teacher Mentor	296 Title II Programs	Ⓜ = Magnet School	
90 Social Work	274 Before/After Sch	297 Webmaster	Ⓨ = Year-Round School	

Social Media
f = Facebook
t = Twitter

New Schools are shaded
New Superintendents and Principals are bold
Personnel with email addresses are underscored

Marshall County — Market Data Retrieval

- **Selmaville Cmty Cons SD 10** PID: 00309844   618/548-2416
  3185 Selmaville Rd, Salem 62881   Fax 618/548-6063

Schools: 1 \ **Teachers:** 19 \ **Students:** 260 \ **Special Ed Students:** 48 \
LEP Students: 3 \ **Ethnic:** Asian 1%, African American 2%, Hispanic 3%,
Caucasian 94% \ **Exp:** $240 (Med) \ **Poverty:** 17% \ **Title I:** $66,742 \
Special Education: $74,000 \ **Open-Close:** 08/18 - 05/19

Robin Brooks 1,11,73,83   Dale Helpingstine 67

Public Schs..Principal	Grd	Prgm	Enr/#Cls	SN	
Selmaville Elem Sch 3185 Selmaville Rd, Salem 62881 Robin Brooks	K-8	T	260 15	44%	618/548-2416

- **South Central Cmty Unit SD 401** PID: 00309636   618/547-3414
  501 S Madison St, Kinmundy 62854   Fax 618/547-7790

Schools: 3 \ **Teachers:** 52 \ **Students:** 650 \ **Special Ed Students:** 152
\ **College-Bound:** 58% \ **Ethnic:** African American 1%, Hispanic 1%,
Caucasian 99% \ **Exp:** $318 (High) \ **Poverty:** 19% \ **Title I:** $261,181 \
Special Education: $228,000 \ **Open-Close:** 08/14 - 06/04

Kerry Herdes 1,83   Blake During 6
Danielle Chastin 36,69,88   Mike Vandeveer 67

Public Schs..Principal	Grd	Prgm	Enr/#Cls	SN	
South Central Elem Sch 810 E 1st St, Kinmundy 62854 Sara Rose	PK-4	T	226 14	55%	618/547-7696 Fax 618/547-3144
South Central High Sch 800 W Washington St, Farina 62838 Jamie Vanscyoc	9-12		208 18	48%	618/245-2222 Fax 618/245-6165
South Central Middle Sch 503 S Madison St, Kinmundy 62854 Greg Grinestaff	5-8	T	182 16	50%	618/547-7734 Fax 618/547-7441

MARION CATHOLIC SCHOOLS

- **Diocese of Belleville Ed Off** PID: 00317671
  Listing includes only schools located in this county. See District Index for
  location of Diocesan Offices.

Catholic Schs..Principal	Grd	Prgm	Enr/#Cls	SN	
St Mary Sch 424 E Broadway, Centralia 62801 Steven Pautler	PK-8		72 7		618/532 3473 Fax 618/532-5180

MARION PRIVATE SCHOOLS

Private Schs..Principal	Grd	Prgm	Enr/#Cls	SN	
Christ Our Rock Lutheran HS 9545 Shattuc Rd, Centralia 62801 Don Duensing	9-12		123 3		618/226-3315 Fax 618/226-3312
New Horizon Christian Sch 12 Greenview Church Rd, Centralia 62801 Grace Malekovic	K-8		132 9		618/533-6910 Fax 618/533-6911
Trinity Lutheran Sch 203 S Pleasant Ave, Centralia 62801 Christina DeBoard	PK-8		139 9		618/532-2614 Fax 618/532-4277

MARION REGIONAL CENTERS

- **Kaskaskia Spec Ed District** PID: 02183933   618/532-4721
  224 S Locust St, Centralia 62801   Fax 618/532-0004

Cassie Clark 1   Terry Burgener 15

MARSHALL COUNTY

MARSHALL PUBLIC SCHOOLS

- **Henry Senachwine CUSD 5** PID: 00309909   309/364-3614
  1023 College St, Henry 61537   Fax 309/364-3217

Schools: 2 \ **Teachers:** 46 \ **Students:** 580 \ **Special Ed Students:** 105 \
Ethnic: Hispanic 1%, Caucasian 98% \ **Exp:** $454 (High) \ **Poverty:** 13% \
Title I: $128,437 \ **Special Education:** $185,000 \ **Open-Close:** 08/31 -
05/25 \ **DTBP:** $181 (High) \

Michael Miller 1,11   Stephanie Sannemin 2
Dan Smith .... 3*   Joel Anderson 3,5
Laurie Calrroll .... 4*   Matt Emmons 6
Jordan Krebs 36   Rita Self 38,83,88*
Debbie Pletctsch 55   Julie Nelson 58
Randy Witko 67   Karen Robertson 68
Demetrio Salazar 73,295*

Public Schs..Principal	Grd	Prgm	Enr/#Cls	SN	
Henry Senachwine Grade Sch 201 Richard St, Henry 61537 Julie Nelson	PK-8	A	383 25	48%	309/364-2531 Fax 309/364-2000
Henry Senachwine High Sch 1023 College St, Henry 61537 Jon Hill	9-12	V	154 25	49%	309/364-2829 Fax 309/364-2990

- **Midland Cmty Unit Sch Dist 7** PID: 00309923   309/469-2061
  901 Hilltop Dr, Sparland 61565   Fax 309/469-2063

Schools: 3 \ **Teachers:** 49 \ **Students:** 720 \ **Special Ed Students:** 102 \
College-Bound: 67% \ **Ethnic:** Hispanic 2%, Caucasian 97% \ **Exp:** $224
(Med) \ **Poverty:** 11% \ **Title I:** $131,913 \ **Special Education:** $220,000 \
Open-Close: 08/21 - 05/28 \ **DTBP:** $175 (High)

Bill Wrenn 1   Patty Kargol 2
Diane Wunder 4   Lynn Jason 5
Crystal Padilla .... 9,11,274*   Wylee Bickerman 12,296*
Gary Leato .... 16,27,73,76*   Jay Riddell 67

Public Schs..Principal	Grd	Prgm	Enr/#Cls	SN	
Midland Elem Sch 625 6th St, Lacon 61540 **Jesse Sams**	PK-4	T	291 25	42%	309/246-2775 Fax 309/246-2364
Midland High Sch 1830 State Route 17, Varna 61375 **Ann Hoffmann**	9-12	TV	195 25	31%	309/463-2095 Fax 309/463-2630
Midland Middle Sch 901 Hilltop Dr, Sparland 61565 **Adam Janssen**	5-8	T	212 25	47%	309/469-3131 Fax 309/469-5701

---

1 Superintendent	19 Chief Financial Officer	39 Social Studies K-12	59 Special Education Elem	69 Academic Assessment
2 Bus/Finance/Purchasing	20 Art K-12	40 Social Studies Elem	60 Special Education Sec	70 Research/Development
3 Buildings And Grounds	21 Art Elem	41 Social Studies Sec	61 Foreign/World Lang K-12	71 Public Information
4 Food Service	22 Art Sec	42 Science K-12	62 Foreign/World Lang Elem	72 Summer School
5 Transportation	23 Music K-12	43 Science Elem	63 Foreign/World Lang Sec	73 Instructional Tech
6 Athletic	24 Music Elem	44 Science Sec	64 Religious Education K-12	74 Inservice Training
7 Health Services	25 Music Sec	45 Math K-12	65 Religious Education Elem	75 Marketing/Distributive
8 Curric/Instruct K-12	26 Business Education	46 Math Elem	66 Religious Education Sec	76 Info Systems
9 Curric/Instruct Elem	27 Career & Tech Ed	47 Math Sec	67 School Board President	77 Psychological Assess
10 Curric/Instruct Sec	28 Technology Education	48 English/Lang Arts K-12	68 Teacher Personnel	78 Affirmative Action
11 Federal Program	29 Family/Consumer Science	49 English/Lang Arts Elem		
12 Title I	30 Adult Education	50 English/Lang Arts Sec		
13 Title V	31 Career/Sch-to-Work K-12	51 Reading K-12		
14 Asst Superintendent	32 Career/Sch-to-Work Elem	52 Reading Elem		
15 Instructional Media Svcs	33 Career/Sch-to-Work Sec	53 Reading Sec		
16 Chief Operations Officer	34 Early Childhood Ed	54 Remedial Reading K 12		
17 Chief Academic Officer	35 Health/Phys Education	55 Remedial Reading Elem		
	36 Guidance Services K-12	56 Remedial Reading Sec		
18 Chief Academic Officer	37 Guidance Services Elem	57 Bilingual/ELL		
	38 Guidance Services Sec	58 Special Education K-12		

Illinois School Directory | Massac County

MASON COUNTY

MASON PUBLIC SCHOOLS

- **Havana Cmty Sch District 126** PID: 00310154   309/543-3384
  501 S McKinley St, Havana 62644   Fax 309/543-3385

Schools: 3 \ **Teachers:** 64 \ **Students:** 1,000 \ **Special Ed Students:** 155 \ **College-Bound:** 69% \ **Ethnic:** Caucasian 99% \ **Exp:** $149 (Low) \ **Poverty:** 22% \ **Title I:** $379,560 \ **Special Education:** $415,000 \ **Open-Close:** 08/19 - 05/24

R Mathew Plater 1,11,83   Pete Brown 3*
Monica Smith 5   Rhonda Eckle 7
Rhonda Cameron .... 8,58*   Brian Ley 67
Lisa Kolves 68

Public Schs..Principal	Grd	Prgm	Enr/#Cls	SN	
Havana High Sch 501 S McKinley St, Havana 62644 Dave McKinney	9-12	GT	266 20	38%	309/543-3337 Fax 309/543-6721
Havana Junior High Sch 801 E Laurel Ave, Havana 62644 Chris Snider	5-8	T	292 25	57%	309/543-6677 Fax 309/543-6678
New Central Elem Sch 215 N Pearl St, Havana 62644 Randi Cowell	K-4	T	312 25	60%	309/543-2241 Fax 309/543-6259

- **Illini Central CUSD 189** PID: 00310219   217/482-5180
  208 N West Ave, Mason City 62664   Fax 217/482-3323

Schools: 4 \ **Teachers:** 62 \ **Students:** 663 \ **Special Ed Students:** 152 \ **College-Bound:** 56% \ **Ethnic:** Hispanic 2%, Caucasian 97% \ **Exp:** $262 (Med) \ **Poverty:** 20% \ **Title I:** $254,086 \ **Special Education:** $399,000 \ **Open-Close:** 08/25 - 05/31

Mike Ward 1,11   Alice Williams 2
Mike Strauman .... 3*   Jennifer Harrison 4*
Elliot Hernan 5,6   Tonya Harris 7
Julie Toland .... 16,82*   Laura Jasko 57*
Lori Sarff .... 58*   May Brooks 67
Anthony Wherley ...... 73,286,295*   Valerie Henning 88*
Colly Bonner 298

Public Schs..Principal	Grd	Prgm	Enr/#Cls	SN	
Illini Central Grade Sch 208 N West Ave, Mason City 62664 Michelle Hellman	K-5	T	289 19	30%	217/482-3269 Fax 217/482-3988
Illini Central High Sch 208 N West Ave, Mason City 62664 Jennifer Durbin	9-12	ATV	179 23	49%	217/482-3252
Illini Central Middle Sch 208 N West Ave, Mason City 62664 Jennifer Durbin	6-8	AT	154 10	49%	217/482-5180
West Campus Pre-Kindergarten 916 W Chestnut St, Mason City 62664 Michelle Hellman	PK-PK	T	31	4%	217/842-9846

- **Midwest Ctl Cmty Unit SD 191** PID: 00310116   309/968-6868
  1010 S Washington St, Manito 61546   Fax 309/968-7916

Schools: 3 \ **Teachers:** 71 \ **Students:** 900 \ **Special Ed Students:** 146 \ **College-Bound:** 81% \ **Ethnic:** African American 2%, Hispanic 2%, Caucasian 96% \ **Exp:** $89 (Low) \ **Poverty:** 13% \ **Title I:** $227,934 \ **Special Education:** $382,000 \ **Open-Close:** 08/19 - 06/07

Todd Hellrigel 1   Don Lazarz 6*
Amanda Shaffer .... 16*   Natalie Putney 31,38,69*
Ariane Taft 57,58,270,271   Mark Berg 67
Kyan Royalty 73*

Public Schs..Principal	Grd	Prgm	Enr/#Cls	SN	
Midwest Central High Sch 910 S Washington St, Manito 61546 Jay Blair	9-12	TV	319 30	48%	309/968-6766 Fax 309/968-6340
Midwest Central Middle Sch 121 N Church St, Green Valley 61534 Kyra Fancher	6-8	T	195 20	51%	309/352-2300 Fax 309/352-2903
Midwest Central Primary Sch 450 E Southmoor St, Manito 61546 Rodney Norris	PK-5	T	421 24	54%	309/968-6464 Fax 309/968-7652

MASSAC COUNTY

MASSAC PUBLIC SCHOOLS

- **Joppa-Maple Grove Unit SD 38** PID: 00310350   618/543-9023
  911 Joppa North Avenue, Joppa 62953   Fax 618/543-9264

Schools: 2 \ **Teachers:** 21 \ **Students:** 230 \ **Special Ed Students:** 25 \ **College-Bound:** 47% \ **Ethnic:** African American 2%, Hispanic 1%, Caucasian 97% \ **Exp:** $110 (Low) \ **Poverty:** 23% \ **Title I:** $121,785 \ **Special Education:** $59,000 \ **Open-Close:** 08/17 - 06/25

Dr Vickie Artman 1   Justin Miller 2
Kent Kester .... 3*   Hunter Kreuter 6
Dr Jeffery DuFour 8,13,58,69,288   Penny Bellamey 31,38*
Kathy Dunning .... 59*   Kevin Castleman 67
Craig McClellan 73   Chelsea McNickels 83,88

Public Schs..Principal	Grd	Prgm	Enr/#Cls	SN	
Joppa High Sch 911 North Ave, Joppa 62953 Terri Waddell	7-12	AT	104 15	55%	618/543-7589
Maple Grove Elem Sch 1698 Grand Chain Rd, Metropolis 62960 Landon Sommer	PK-6	T	143 15	91%	618/543-7434 Fax 618/543-7486

- **Massac Unit School District 1** PID: 00310398   618/524-9376
  401 Metropolis St, Metropolis 62960   Fax 618/524-4432

Schools: 7 \ **Teachers:** 137 \ **Students:** 2,100 \ **Special Ed Students:** 373 \ **Ethnic:** African American 6%, Hispanic 3%, Caucasian 90% \ **Exp:** $103 (Low) \ **Poverty:** 21% \ **Title I:** $802,423 \ **Special Education:** $1,081,000 \ **Open-Close:** 08/10 - 06/02 \ **DTBP:** $177 (High) \

Jason Hayes 1,11,83   Jamey Mitchell 2

---

79 Student Personnel	91 Safety/Security	275 Response To Intervention	298 Grant Writer/Ptnrships	**School Programs**	**Social Media**		
80 Driver Ed/Safety	92 Magnet School	277 Remedial Math K-12	750 Chief Innovation Officer	A = Alternative Program			
81 Gifted/Talented	93 Parental Involvement	280 Literacy Coach	751 Chief of Staff	G = Adult Classes	= Facebook		
82 Video Services	95 Tech Prep Program	285 STEM	752 Social Emotional Learning	M = Magnet Program			
83 Substance Abuse Prev	97 Chief Infomation Officer	286 Digital Learning		T = Title I Schoolwide	= Twitter		
84 Erate	98 Chief Technology Officer	288 Common Core Standards	**Other School Types**	V = Career & Tech Ed Programs			
85 AIDS Education	270 Accountability	294 Accountability	Ⓐ = Alternative School				
88 Alternative/At Risk	271 Migrant Education	295 Network System	Ⓒ = Charter School	New Schools are shaded			
89 Multi-Cultural Curriculum	273 Teacher Mentor	296 Title II Programs	Ⓜ = Magnet School	New Superintendents and Principals are bold			
90 Social Work	274 Before/After Sch	297 Webmaster	Ⓨ = Year-Round School	Personnel with email addresses are underscored			

IL—177

McDonough County

Market Data Retrieval

Marlene Clapp	4
Cynthia Jackson	58
Thomas Walker	73,84
Jill Shelton	16*
Mark Soulders	67

Public Schs..Principal	Grd	Prgm	Enr/#Cls	SN	
Brookport Elem Sch 319 Ferry St, Brookport 62910 Brooke Durham	PK-6	T	210 10	90%	618/564-2482 Fax 618/564-3509
Franklin Elem Sch 1006 Mount Mission Rd, Metropolis 62960 Rebecca West	K-6		181 8	40%	618/524-2243 Fax 618/524-2725
Jefferson Elem Sch 4915 Jefferson School Rd, Metropolis 62960 Rebecca West	K-8		135 9	34%	618/524-4390 Fax 618/524-3019
Massac Co High Sch 2841 Old Marion Rd, Metropolis 62960 Parker Windhorst	9-12	ATV	551 56	49%	618/524-3440 Fax 618/524-3131
Massac Junior High Sch 3028 Old Marion Rd, Metropolis 62960 Laura Hayes	7-8	T	315 25	62%	618/524-2645 Fax 618/524-2765
Metropolis Elem Sch 1015 Filmore St, Metropolis 62960 J Conkle	PK-6	T	529 23	98%	618/524-4821 Fax 618/524-2352
Unity Elem Sch 6846 Unity School Rd, Brookport 62910 Brooke Durham	K-6	T	150 9	49%	618/564-2582 Fax 618/564-2014

MCDONOUGH COUNTY

MCDONOUGH COUNTY SCHOOLS

County Schs..Principal	Grd	Prgm	Enr/#Cls	SN	
Ⓐ Project Insight Alt Sch 330 N McArthur St, Macomb 61455 Stephanie Winship	6-12	V	34 7	56%	309/837-5685 Fax 309/836-5030

MCDONOUGH PUBLIC SCHOOLS

● **Bushnell Prairie Cmty USD 170** PID: 00305006 309/772-9461
845 Walnut St, Bushnell 61422 Fax 309/772-9462

Schools: 3 \ Teachers: 57 \ Students: 630 \ Special Ed Students: 154
\ LEP Students: 3 \ College-Bound: 61% \ Ethnic: African American 1%, Hispanic 2%, Caucasian 97% \ Exp: $268 (Med) \ Poverty: 17% \ Title I: $237,901 \ Special Education: $283,000 \ Open-Close: 08/19 - 05/31 \ DTBP: $168 (High)

Kathy Dinger	1
Chad Sharp	3*
Jean Akers	4
Nate Zaehringer	6*
Staci Kramer	12,296*
Paul Zarello	58*
Amy Struhs	69,77
Marjorie Rhoades	79
Rose Pieper	2
Bertie Mahr	4
Kenneth Vantine	5
Kristi White	7
Lauren Settles	31,38,270*
John McCleery	67
Lisa Webb	73

Public Schs..Principal	Grd	Prgm	Enr/#Cls	SN	
Bushnell Prairie City Elem Sch 345 E Hess St, Bushnell 61422 Paul Zarello	PK-5	T	301 37	64%	309/772-9464 Fax 309/772-9466
Bushnell Prairie City High Sch 845 Walnut St, Bushnell 61422 Dawna Daily	9-12	ATV	203 22	43%	309/772-2113 Fax 309/772-2104
Bushnell Prairie City Jr HS 847 Walnut St, Bushnell 61422 Dawna Daily	6-8	T	167 16	52%	309/772-3123 Fax 309/772-2666

● **Macomb Cmty Unit Sch Dist 185** PID: 00305111 309/833-4161
323 W Washington St, Macomb 61455 Fax 309/836-2133

Schools: 4 \ Teachers: 139 \ Students: 2,000 \ Special Ed Students: 347 \ LEP Students: 57 \ College-Bound: 78% \ Ethnic: Asian 3%, African American 10%, Hispanic 5%, Native American: 1%, Caucasian 82% \ Exp: $236 (Med) \ Poverty: 20% \ Title I: $729,608 \ Special Education: $503,000 \ Open-Close: 08/24 - 05/27 \ DTBP: $165 (High)

Dr Patrick Twomey	1,11,83
Randall Smith	3
Deb Nelson	5
Dana Isackson	8
Kelly Carpenter	58*
Velvet Taflinger	68
Roberta Keck	77
Diane Hudgens	2
Kathy Brooks	4
Steve Horrell	6
Ed Fulkerson	12,91*
Jill Myers	67
Katie Hoge	73,84
Tim Suter	295*

Public Schs..Principal	Grd	Prgm	Enr/#Cls	SN	
Edison Elem Sch 521 S Pearl St, Macomb 61455 Kellee Sullivan	4-6		439 15	56%	309/837-3993 Fax 309/837-9992
Lincoln Elem Sch 315 N Bonham St, Macomb 61455 Kimberly Gillam	K-3	T	567 27	58%	309/833-2095 Fax 309/837-7802
MacArthur Early Childhood Ctr 235 W Grant St, Macomb 61455 Kelly Carpenter	PK-PK	T	124 7	73%	309/833-4273 Fax 309/833-5651
Macomb Jr Sr High Sch 1525 S Johnson St, Macomb 61455 Dana Isackson \ Scott Sullivan	7-12	AV	670 70	34%	309/833-2074 Fax 309/836-1034

● **West Prairie Cmty Sch Dist 103** PID: 00305068 309/776-3180
204 S Hun St, Colchester 62326 Fax 309/776-3194

Schools: 4 \ Teachers: 50 \ Students: 600 \ Special Ed Students: 117 \ LEP Students: 3 \ Ethnic: Asian 1%, Hispanic 1%, Caucasian 98% \ Exp: $180 (Low) \ Poverty: 22% \ Title I: $289,334 \ Special Education: $364,000 \ Open-Close: 08/19 - 05/25 \ DTBP: $48 (Low)

Guy Gradert	1,83
Kevin Klinedinst	3
Melissa Peterson	5
Kelley Coplan	7*
Lee Moore	67
Annette Lekrone	73,76,286,295*
Crista Rigg	2,11,88
Mandy Palmer	4
Caleb Hall	6*
Jennifer Edholm	11,296*
Jami Minter	69

Public Schs..Principal	Grd	Prgm	Enr/#Cls	SN	
West Prairie High Sch 18575 E 800th St, Sciota 61475 Chad Cox	9-12	TV	159 20	51%	309/456-3750 Fax 309/456-3997
West Prairie Middle Sch 600 S Hun St, Colchester 62326 Caitlien Watson	5-8	TV	161 20	50%	309/776-3220 Fax 309/776-3115

1	Superintendent	8	Curric/Instruct K-12	19	Chief Financial Officer	29	Family/Consumer Science	39	Social Studies K-12	49	English/Lang Arts Elem	59	Special Education Elem	69	Academic Assessment
2	Bus/Finance/Purchasing	9	Curric/Instruct Elem	20	Art K-12	30	Adult Education	40	Social Studies Elem	50	English/Lang Arts Sec	60	Special Education Sec	70	Research/Development
3	Buildings And Grounds	10	Curric/Instruct Sec	21	Art Elem	31	Career/Sch-to-Work K-12	41	Social Studies Sec	51	Reading K-12	61	Foreign/World Lang K-12	71	Public Information
4	Food Service	11	Federal Program	22	Art Sec	32	Career/Sch-to-Work Elem	42	Science K-12	52	Reading Elem	62	Foreign/World Lang Elem	72	Summer School
5	Transportation	12	Title I	23	Music K-12	33	Career/Sch-to-Work Sec	43	Science Elem	53	Reading Sec	63	Foreign/World Lang Sec	73	Instructional Tech
6	Athletic	13	Title V	24	Music Elem	34	Early Childhood Ed	44	Science Sec	54	Remedial Reading K-12	64	Religious Education K-12	74	Inservice Training
7	Health Services	15	Asst Superintendent	25	Music Sec	35	Health/Phys Education	45	Math K-12	55	Remedial Reading Elem	65	Religious Education Elem	75	Marketing/Distributive
		16	Instructional Media Svcs	26	Business Education	36	Guidance Services K-12	46	Math Elem	56	Remedial Reading Sec	66	Religious Education Sec	76	Info Systems
		17	Chief Operations Officer	27	Career & Tech Ed	37	Guidance Services Elem	47	Math Sec	57	Bilingual/ELL	67	School Board President	77	Psychological Assess
		18	Chief Academic Officer	28	Technology Education	38	Guidance Services Sec	48	English/Lang Arts K-12	58	Special Education K-12	68	Teacher Personnel	78	Affirmative Action

Illinois School Directory

McHenry County

West Prairie North Elem Sch 100 N Washington St, Good Hope 61438 Jennifer Edholm	PK-4	T	113 9	44%	309/456-3920 Fax 309/456-3936
West Prarie South Elem Sch 310 S Coal St, Colchester 62326 Jennifer Edholm	PK-4	T	160 25	56%	309/776-3790 Fax 309/776-4267 t

---

MCDONOUGH CATHOLIC SCHOOLS

- **Diocese of Peoria Ed Office** PID: 00313338
  Listing includes only schools located in this county. See District Index for location of Diocesan Offices.

Catholic Schs..Principal	Grd	Prgm	Enr/#Cls	SN	
St Paul Sch 322 W Washington St, Macomb 61455 Laura Cody	PK-6		127 8		309/833-2470

MCDONOUGH REGIONAL CENTERS

- **Regional Office of Ed 26** PID: 02098053   309/575-3226
  130 S Lafayette St Ste 200, Macomb 61455   Fax 309/837-2887

John Meixner 1   Deb Wright 2
Dave Demler 15   Danielle Lewis 16,297
Allyson Curry 68   Joni Deens 298

- **West Central IL Spec Ed Co-op** PID: 02182214   309/837-3911
  130 S Lafayette St Ste 201, Macomb 61455   Fax 309/833-2367

Leyona Wiley 1   Michelle Marky 2
Betsy Wujek 15,27,34,58,83,88

- **Western Area Career System** PID: 03266552   309/837-4821
  130 S Lafayette St Ste 200, Macomb 61455   Fax 309/837-2887

Dave Messersmith 1

MCHENRY COUNTY

MCHENRY PUBLIC SCHOOLS

- **Alden-Hebron School Dist 19** PID: 00305276   815/648-2442
  11915 Price Rd, Hebron 60034   Fax 815/648-2339

Schools: 2 \ **Teachers:** 40 \ **Students:** 430 \ **Special Ed Students:** 63 \ **LEP Students:** 33 \ **College-Bound:** 66% \ **Ethnic:** Asian 1%, Hispanic 22%, Caucasian 77% \ **Exp:** $377 (High) \ **Poverty:** 16% \ **Title I:** $124,667 \ **Special Education:** $253,000 \ **Bilingual Education:** $3,000 \ **Open-Close:** 08/14 - 05/25 \ **DTBP:** $200 (High)

Debbie Ehlenburg 1,11   Patricia Syens 2
Scott Redden .... 3*   Cyndie Erckfritz 5
John Lalor .... 6*   Davina Vanderpal 8,31,36,69,83,85*
Scott LeBaron .... 16,73,82*   Kristen Norton 57,271*
Mike Norton 67   Grace Eskridge 274*

Public Schs..Principal	Grd	Prgm	Enr/#Cls	SN	
Alden-Hebron Elem Sch 11915 Price Rd, Hebron 60034 Tiffany Elswick	PK-5	T	216 15	44%	815/648-2442
Alden-Hebron Middle High Sch 9604 Illinois St, Hebron 60034 Tim Hayunga	6-12	AV	204 20	29%	815/648-2442

- **Cary Cmty Cons Sch Dist 26** PID: 00305305   224/357-5100
  2115 Crystal Lake Rd, Cary 60013   Fax 847/639-3898

Schools: 5 \ **Teachers:** 168 \ **Students:** 2,426 \ **Special Ed Students:** 414 \ **LEP Students:** 244 \ **Ethnic:** Asian 2%, African American 1%, Hispanic 21%, Caucasian 76% \ **Exp:** $382 (High) \ **Poverty:** 7% \ **Title I:** $309,636 \ **Special Education:** $2,076,000 \ **Bilingual Education:** $62,000 \ **Open-Close:** 08/21 - 05/28 \ **DTBP:** $186 (High)

Brian Coleman 1   Maria Treto-French 2,3
Paulina MacHola 2   Steve Fields 3
Diane Verner 4   Donna Grap 5
Jennifer Thomas 7,59,83,88   Dawn Barrett 9
Valerie McCall 9,11,288   Tracy Kuhn 57
Linda Cruise 59   Robert Bridge 67
Caryn Sturz 68   Andrew Fitzsimons 73,76,295
Lynn Swanson 73

Public Schs..Principal	Grd	Prgm	Enr/#Cls	SN	
Briargate Elem Sch 100 S Wulff St, Cary 60013 Chad Nass	1-5		356 15	16%	224/357-5250 Fax 847/516-5516
Cary Junior High Sch 2109 Crystal Lake Rd, Cary 60013 Kim Qualls	6-8	V	843 40	21%	224/357-5150 Fax 847/516-5507
Deer Path Elem Sch 2211 Crystal Lake Rd, Cary 60013 Thom Gippert	K-5		464 22	19%	224/357-5350 Fax 847/516-6355
Oak Knoll Early Childhod Ctr 409 1st St, Cary 60013 Jenny Aherne	PK-K		349	26%	224/357-5550
Three Oaks Elem Sch 1514 3 Oaks Rd, Cary 60013 Andrew Gibbs	K-5		477 23	44%	224/357-5450 Fax 847/516-5514

- **Community High School Dist 155** PID: 00305458   815/455-8500
  1 Virginia Rd, Crystal Lake 60014   Fax 815/459-5022

Schools: 5 \ **Teachers:** 353 \ **Students:** 5,800 \ **Special Ed Students:** 772 \ **LEP Students:** 133 \ **College-Bound:** 100% \ **Ethnic:** Asian 2%, African American 2%, Hispanic 15%, Caucasian 82% \ **Exp:** $344 (High) \ **Poverty:** 4% \ **Title I:** $440,791 \ **Special Education:** $3,364,000 \ **Bilingual Education:** $13,000 \ **Open-Close:** 08/12 - 05/18 \ **DTBP:** $194 (High)

Steve Olson 1   Anne Robinson 2
Erica Bruso 2   Jeremy Davis 2,11,15,68,91
Dan Sandberg 3   Jim Podgorski 3
Troy Stinger 3   Penny Fleming 5
Matt Timmerman 10,27,69,74,273,286,288,296   Jay Sargeant 15,68*
Scott Shepard 15,79   Kim Dahlem 60,77,79,83,91
Jason Blake 67   Shanon Podzimek 71
George Divenere 73,76,84,295

Public Schs..Principal	Grd	Prgm	Enr/#Cls	SN	
Cary Grove Cmty High Sch 2208 3 Oaks Rd, Cary 60013 Neil Lesinski	9-12	AV	1,644 60	17%	847/639-3825 Fax 847/639-3873

---

79 Student Personnel	91 Safety/Security	275 Response To Intervention	298 Grant Writer/Ptnrships	**School Programs**	**Social Media**	
80 Driver Ed/Safety	92 Magnet School	277 Remedial Math K-12	750 Chief Innovation Officer	A = Alternative Program	f = Facebook	
81 Gifted/Talented	93 Parental Involvement	280 Literacy Coach	751 Chief of Staff	G = Adult Classes		
82 Video Services	95 Tech Prep Program	285 STEM	752 Social Emotional Learning	M = Magnet Program	t = Twitter	
83 Substance Abuse Prev	97 Chief Infomation Officer	286 Digital Learning		T = Title I Schoolwide		
84 Erate	98 Chief Technology Officer	288 Common Core Standards	**Other School Types**	V = Career & Tech Ed Programs		
85 AIDS Education	270 Character Education	294 Accountability	A = Alternative School			
88 Charter School	271 Migrant Education	295 Network System	C = Charter School	New Schools are shaded		
89 Multi-Cultural Curriculum	273 Teacher Mentor	296 Title II Programs	M = Magnet School	New Superintendents and Principals are bold		
90 Social Work	274 Before/After Sch	297 Webmaster	Y = Year-Round School	Personnel with email addresses are underscored		

IL-179

McHenry County

Market Data Retrieval

Crystal Lake Central High Sch — 9-12 AV 1,478 28% 815/459-2505
45 W Franklin Ave, Crystal Lake 60014 — Fax 815/459-2536
Eric Ernd

Crystal Lake South High Sch — 9-12 AV 1,483 23% 815/455-3860
1200 S McHenry Ave, Crystal Lake 60014 — Fax 815/455-5706
Joshua Nobilio

Ⓐ Haber Oaks Campus Sch — 9-12 20 815/893-5300
1200 S McHenry Ave, Crystal Lake 60014 — Fax 815/893-5310
Julie Duncan

Prairie Ridge High Sch — 9-12 AGV 1,373 11% 815/479-0404
6000 Dvorak Dr, Crystal Lake 60012 — 75 Fax 815/459-8993
Dr Steven Koch

● **Community Unit School Dist 300** PID: 00297966 — 847/551-8300
2550 Harnish Dr, Algonquin 60102 — Fax 847/551-8413

Schools: 27 \ **Teachers:** 1,410 \ **Students:** 20,985 \
Special Ed Students: 3,145 \ **LEP Students:** 3,357 \ **College-Bound:** 69%
\ **Ethnic:** Asian 6%, African American 5%, Hispanic 40%, Caucasian
49% \ **Exp:** $200 (Med) \ **Poverty:** 7% \ **Title I:** $2,809,141 \
Special Education: $12,956,000 \ **Bilingual Education:** $1,270,000 \
Open-Close: 08/13 - 05/20 \ **DTBP:** $205 (High) \ 🅕 🅣

Fred Heid	1	Diane White	2
Jennifer Porter	2	Michelle Kovar	2
Dan Opels	3	Susan Harkin	3,5,15,17,751
Donna Bordsen	5	Sherrie Schmidt	8
Basilio Salazar	8,752	Kara Vicente	8,18
Kara McMahon	8,18	Kristin Corriveau	8,15
Susan Rohlwing	8	Patricia Whitecotton	11,298
Lindsay Jonas	12	Shelley Nacke	15,58,83,85
Sheila Crotty-Kagan	20,23	Lindsay Sharp	27
Linda Breen	34*	Thomas Parisi	35,80
Mark Wetzel	39	Ami Engel	42
Jacquie Duginske	45	Joshua Perdomo	57,61
Anne Miller	67	Eberto Mora	68,78
Patricia Schmidt	69,294	Anthony McGinn	71
Jayce Bolhous	73,84	Joseph Ehrmann	73
Elizabeth Freeman	74	Jason Emricson	76,295
Daniel Palombit	79	Todd Rohlwing	91
Jacquelyn Johnson	280	Anne Pasco	286

Public Schs..Principal	Grd	Prgm	Enr/#Cls	SN		
Algonquin Lakes Elem Sch 1401 Compton Dr, Algonquin 60102 Christopher Columbaro	K-5		424 22	41%	847/532-7500 Fax 847/532-7515	
Algonquin Middle Sch 520 Longwood Dr, Algonquin 60102 Jason Lentz	6-8		462 40	41%	847/532-7100 Fax 847/658-2547	
© Cambridge Lakes Charter Sch 900 Wester Blvd, Pingree Grove 60140 Julie Skaggs \ Nicole Brady	K-8		868	23%	847/464-4300 Fax 847/464-0318	
Carpentersville Middle Sch 100 Cleveland Ave, Carpentersvle 60110 Martina Smith	6-8	TV	1,231 72	81%	224/484-2100 Fax 847/426-1404 🅕🅣	
De Lacey Family Education Ctr 50 Cleveland Ave, Carpentersvle 60110 Kelly Burke	PK-PK	T	350 20	50%	224/484-2300 Fax 224/484-2319	
Dundee Highlands Elem Sch 407 S 5th St, Dundee 60118 Karen Cumpata	PK-5		351 25	37%	224/484-4700 Fax 847/426-1935	
Dundee Middle Sch 4200 W Main St, Dundee 60118 Jeffrey Herb	6-8	V	874 50	33%	224/484-4500 Fax 847/426-4008 🅕🅣	
Dundee-Crown High Sch 1500 Kings Rd, Carpentersvle 60110 Katie Wetzel	9-12	AV	2,533 110	63%	224/484-5000 Fax 224/484-5098 🅕🅣	
Eastview Elem Sch 540 Longwood Dr, Algonquin 60102 James Zursin	PK-5	T	464 25	42%	847/532-7400 Fax 847/458-5509	
Gilberts Elem Sch 729 Paper Bark Ln, Gilberts 60136 Craig Zieleniewski	PK-5		773 25	19%	224/484-5900 Fax 224/484-5915	
Golfview Elem Sch 124 Golfview Ln, Carpentersvle 60110 Pamela Carlos	PK-4	T	612 31	86%	224/484-2800 Fax 224/484-2815	
Hampshire Elem Sch 321 Terwilliger Ave, Hampshire 60140 Lisa Van Wageningen	K-5		436 24	26%	847/792-3400 Fax 847/683-4806 🅕🅣	
Hampshire High Sch 1600 Big Timber Rd, Hampshire 60140 Brett Bending	9-12		1,738	24%	847/792-3500 Fax 847/792-3515	
Hampshire Middle Sch 560 S State St, Hampshire 60140 James Szymczak	6-8	AV	1,038 30	22%	847/792-3200 Fax 847/683-1030 🅕🅣	
Harry D Jacobs High Sch 2601 Bunker Hill Dr, Algonquin 60102 Barbara Valle	9-12	AV	2,090 70	23%	847/532-6100 Fax 847/532-6115 🅣	
Josephine Perry Elem Sch 251 Amarillo Dr, Carpentersvle 60110 Susan Rohlwing	PK-4	T	582 35	89%	224/484-5600 Fax 224/484-5615	
Kenneth E Neubert Elem Sch 1100 Huntington Dr, Algonquin 60102 Jennifer Breeze	K-5		450 24	28%	847/532-6800 Fax 847/658-9809 🅕🅣	
Lake In the Hills Elem Sch 519 Willow St, Lk In The Hls 60156 Michelle Smith	PK-5	T	553 26	41%	847/532-6900 Fax 847/532-6915 🅕🅣	
Lakewood Sch 1651 Ravine Ln, Carpentersvle 60110 Brittany Porsche	PK-5	T	634 38	81%	224/484-2600 Fax 224/484-2615	
Liberty Elem Sch 6500 Miller Rd, Carpentersvle 60110 Robert Chleboun	PK-5		757 30	31%	224/484-4800 Fax 224/484-4815	
Lincoln Prairie Elem Sch 500 Harvest Gate, Lk In The Hls 60156 Niki Burkey	K-5		431 19	32%	847/532-6600 Fax 847/532-6615	
Meadowdale Elem Sch 14 Ash St, Carpentersvle 60110 Jorge Almodovar	PK-4	T	422 22	79%	224/484-2900 Fax 224/484-2915	
Ⓐ Oak Ridge Sch 300 Cleveland Ave, Carpentersvle 60110 Stacy Wilkinson	6-12		20 6	75%	224/484-5800 Fax 847/426-4474	
Parkview Elem Sch 122 Carpenter Blvd, Carpentersvle 60110 Nancy Regul	K-4	T	521 18	63%	224/484-2500 Fax 847/426-2962	
Sleepy Hollow Elem Sch 898 Glen Oak Dr, Sleepy Hollow 60118 Angela Reincke	K-5		320 22	28%	224/484-4900 Fax 224/484-4915	
Westfield Community Sch 2100 Sleepy Hollow Rd, Algonquin 60102 Thomas Ruzinok	PK-8		1,373 100	26%	847/532-7800 Fax 847/532-7615	
Wright Elem Sch 1500 Ketchum Rd, Hampshire 60140 Melanie Gravel	K-5		787 18	23%	847/683-5700 Fax 847/683-5799	

1	Superintendent	8	Curric/Instruct K-12	19	Chief Financial Officer	29	Family/Consumer Science	39	Social Studies K-12
2	Bus/Finance/Purchasing	9	Curric/Instruct Elem	20	Art K-12	30	Adult Education	40	Social Studies Elem
3	Buildings And Grounds	10	Curric/Instruct Sec	21	Art Elem	31	Career/Sch-to-Work K-12	41	Social Studies Sec
4	Food Service	11	Federal Program	22	Art Sec	32	Career/Sch-to-Work Elem	42	Science K-12
5	Transportation	12	Title I	23	Music K-12	33	Career/Sch-to-Work Sec	43	Science Elem
6	Athletic	13	Title V	24	Music Elem	34	Early Childhood Ed	44	Science Sec
7	Health Services	15	Asst Superintendent	25	Music Sec	35	Health/Phys Education	45	Math K-12
		16	Instructional Media Svcs	26	Business Education	36	Religious Education K-12	46	Math Elem
		17	Chief Operations Officer	27	Career & Tech Ed	37	Guidance Services Elem	47	Math Sec
		18	Chief Academic Officer	28	Technology Education	38	Guidance Services Sec	48	English/Lang Arts K-12

49	English/Lang Arts Elem	59	Special Education Elem	69	Academic Assessment
50	English/Lang Arts Sec	60	Special Education Sec	70	Research/Development
51	Reading K-12	61	Foreign/World Lang K-12	71	Public Information
52	Reading Elem	62	Foreign/World Lang Elem	72	Summer School
53	Reading Sec	63	Foreign/World Lang Sec	73	Instructional Tech
54	Remedial Reading K-12	64	Religious Education K-12	74	Inservice Training
55	Remedial Reading Elem	65	Religious Education Elem	75	Marketing/Distributive
56	Remedial Reading Sec	66	Religious Education Sec	76	Info Systems
57	Bilingual/ELL	67	School Board President	77	Psychological Assess
58	Special Education K-12	68	Teacher Personnel	78	Affirmative Action

Illinois School Directory — McHenry County

- **Crystal Lake Elem Distict 47** PID: 00305355 815/788-5000
  300 Commerce Dr, Crystal Lake 60014 Fax 815/459-0263

Schools: 12 \ **Teachers:** 544 \ **Students:** 7,500 \ **Special Ed Students:** 1,107 \ **LEP Students:** 816 \ **Ethnic:** Asian 3%, African American 2%, Hispanic 24%, Caucasian 71% \ **Exp:** $180 (Low) \ **Poverty:** 6% \ **Title I:** $724,737 \ **Special Education:** $5,507,000 \ **Bilingual Education:** $168,000 \ **Open-Close:** 08/24 - 05/26 \ **DTBP:** $191 (High)

Dr Kathy Hinz 1	Catherine Nelson 2,15
Mary Ann Brown 2	Mark Herron 3
Penny Fleming 5	Amy Belrichard 7
Christina Moran 9,15	David Jenkins 15,73,295
Dr Greg Buchanan 15,68	Erin Anderson 40,280
Carolyn Stadlman 43,46,285	Sandra Adamski 57
Anthony Brooks 59	Rob Fetzner 67
Denise Barr 71	Stasia Gruper 74
Judy Shuh 76,79	Sandra Correa 76,295
Dave Schuh 91	Tommy Chanthasene 295

Public Schs..Principal	Grd	Prgm	Enr/#Cls	SN	
Canterbury Elem Sch 875 Canterbury Dr, Crystal Lake 60014 Stacy Graff	K-5	T	439 21	53%	815/788-5650 Fax 815/479-5117
Carl Wehde Early Chldhd Sp Ed 1120 Village Rd, Crystal Lake 60014 Pamela White	PK-PK		125		815/788-3100 Fax 815/477-5548
Coventry Elem Sch 820 Darlington Ln, Crystal Lake 60014 Matt Grubbs	K-5	T	583	45%	815/788-5500 Fax 815/479-5114
Glacier Ridge Elem Sch 1120 Village Rd, Crystal Lake 60014 John Jacobsen	PK-5		621 28	21%	815/444-4850 Fax 815/477-5547
Hannah Beardsley Middle Sch 515 E Crystal Lake Ave, Crystal Lake 60014 Cathy Alberth	6-8	T	1,014 50	32%	815/788-5750 Fax 815/479-5119
Husmann Elem Sch 131 W Paddock St, Crystal Lake 60014 **Guy Sromek**	K-5		471 23	20%	815/356-3400 Fax 815/479-5110
Indian Prairie Elem Sch 651 Village Rd, Crystal Lake 60014 Jodie Moss	K-5		506 26	29%	815/788-5700 Fax 815/479-5118
Lundahl Middle Sch 560 Nash Rd, Crystal Lake 60014 Angie Compere	6-8		755 50	26%	815/788-5450 Fax 815/479-5113
North Elem Sch 500 W Woodstock St, Crystal Lake 60014 **Michelle Barrett**	K-5	T	696 55	33%	815/356-3450 Fax 815/479-5111
South Elem Sch 601 Golf Rd, Crystal Lake 60014 Rachael Alt	K-5		374 22	23%	815/788-5400 Fax 815/479-5112
West Elem Sch 100 Briarwood Dr, Crystal Lake 60014 Beth Klinsky	K-5		512 28	21%	815/788-5550 Fax 815/479-5115
Woods Creek Elem Sch 1100 Alexandra Blvd, Crystal Lake 60014 Amy Marks	K-5		566 35	11%	815/444-4800 Fax 815/356-2729

- **Fox River Grove Cons SD 3** PID: 00305484 847/516-5100
  403 Orchard St, Fox River GRV 60021 Fax 847/516-9169

Schools: 2 \ **Teachers:** 32 \ **Students:** 390 \ **Special Ed Students:** 69 \ **LEP Students:** 14 \ **Ethnic:** Asian 2%, African American 1%, Hispanic 9%, Caucasian 89% \ **Exp:** $216 (Med) \ **Poverty:** 5% \ **Title I:** $37,859 \ **Special Education:** $246,000 \ **Bilingual Education:** $5,000 \ **Open-Close:** 08/26 - 06/04 \ **DTBP:** $233 (High)

Dr Tim Mahaffy 1,11	Rick Miller 3
Janet Mollet 4	Lisa Liparoto 7
Heather Trom 59,69,275*	Kristine Hester 67

Public Schs..Principal	Grd	Prgm	Enr/#Cls	SN	
Algonquin Road Elem Sch 975 Algonquin Rd, Fox River GRV 60021 Sandy Ozimek	PK-4		203 20	13%	847/516-5101 Fax 847/516-9058
Fox River Grove Middle Sch 401 Orchard St, Fox River GRV 60021 Jessica McKenzie	5-8		187 20	12%	847/516-5105 Fax 847/516-5104

- **Harrison School Dist 36** PID: 00305513 815/653-2311
  6809 McCullom Lake Rd, Wonder Lake 60097 Fax 815/653-1712

Schools: 1 \ **Teachers:** 31 \ **Students:** 404 \ **Special Ed Students:** 85 \ **LEP Students:** 24 \ **Ethnic:** African American 1%, Hispanic 21%, Caucasian 78% \ **Exp:** $421 (High) \ **Poverty:** 14% \ **Title I:** $93,018 \ **Special Education:** $207,000 \ **Open-Close:** 08/19 - 05/28 \ **DTBP:** $165 (High)

Susan Wings 1	Julie Franklin 2
Dale Point 3	Anne Huff 9,11,69,74,88,275,288*
Jennifer Lachel 16,73*	Karen Parks 67
Abbie Wertin 83*	Stefanie Rios 280*

Public Schs..Principal	Grd	Prgm	Enr/#Cls	SN	
Harrison Elem Sch 6809 McCullom Lake Rd, Wonder Lake 60097 Anne Huff	PK-8	T	404 30	68%	815/653-2311

- **Harvard Cmty Unit Sch Dist 50** PID: 00305537 815/943-4022
  401 N Division St, Harvard 60033 Fax 815/943-4282

Schools: 5 \ **Teachers:** 212 \ **Students:** 2,633 \ **Special Ed Students:** 352 \ **LEP Students:** 932 \ **College-Bound:** 54% \ **Ethnic:** African American 1%, Hispanic 69%, Caucasian 30% \ **Exp:** $293 (Med) \ **Poverty:** 15% \ **Title I:** $550,841 \ **Special Education:** $1,498,000 \ **Bilingual Education:** $277,000 \ **Open-Close:** 08/14 - 05/21 \ **DTBP:** $219 (High)

Dr Corey Tafoya 1	Michael Prombo 2,19
Steve Miller 3	Andrew Walters 6*
Margaret Segersten 8,69,296,298	Mary Cooke 12,51,280,288
Dr Victoria Larson 15	Maura Bridges 27
Amber Bowgren 57	Nara Mahone 58,79
Julie Lehmann 67	John Hummel 73,76,295*

Public Schs..Principal	Grd	Prgm	Enr/#Cls	SN	
Harvard High Sch 1103 N Jefferson St, Harvard 60033 Carl Hobbs	9-12	TV	740 30	43%	815/943-6461 Fax 815/943-8506
Harvard Junior High Sch 1301 Garfield St, Harvard 60033 **Tom Cardamone**	6-8	T	590 35	49%	815/943-6466 Fax 815/943-8521
Jefferson Elem Sch 1200 N Jefferson St, Harvard 60033 Judy Floeter	4-5	T	407 23	30%	815/943-6464 Fax 815/943-7495
Richard D Crosby Elem Sch 401 Hereley Dr, Harvard 60033 Kathleen Ferguson	K-3	T	801 7	50%	815/943-6125 Fax 815/943-4230
Washington Sch 305 S Hutchinson St, Harvard 60033 Nikki Gardner	PK-PK	T	164 4	56%	815/943-6367 Fax 815/943-0293

79 Student Personnel	91 Safety/Security	275 Response To Intervention	298 Grant Writer/Ptnrships
80 Driver Ed/Safety	92 Magnet School	277 Remedial Math K-12	750 Chief Innovation Officer
81 Gifted/Talented	93 Parental Involvement	280 Literacy Coach	751 Chief of Staff
82 Video Services	95 Tech Prep Program	285 STEM	752 Social Emotional Learning
83 Substance Abuse Prev	97 Chief Infomation Officer	286 Digital Learning	
84 Erate	98 Chief Technology Officer	288 Common Core Standards	**Other School Types**
85 AIDS Education	270 Character Education	294 Accountability	Ⓐ = Alternative School
88 Alternative/At Risk	271 Migrant Education	295 Network System	Ⓒ = Charter School
89 Multi-Cultural Curriculum	273 Teacher Mentor	296 Title II Programs	Ⓜ = Magnet School
90 Social Work	274 Before/After Sch	297 Webmaster	Ⓨ = Year-Round School

School Programs
A = Alternative Program
G = Adult Classes
M = Magnet Program
T = Title I Schoolwide
V = Career & Tech Ed Programs

Social Media
 = Facebook
 = Twitter

New Schools are shaded
New Superintendents and Principals are bold
Personnel with email addresses are underscored

McHenry County

• Huntley Cmty School Dist 158 PID: 00305616
650 Dr John Burkey Dr, Algonquin 60102
847/659-6158
Fax 847/659-6121

Schools: 8 \ **Teachers:** 590 \ **Students:** 9,606 \ **Special Ed Students:** 1,179 \ **LEP Students:** 382 \ **College-Bound:** 84% \ **Ethnic:** Asian 7%, African American 2%, Hispanic 13%, Caucasian 78% \ **Exp:** $209 (Med) \ **Poverty:** 3% \ **Title I:** $233,308 \ **Special Education:** $4,781,000 \ **Bilingual Education:** $61,000 \ **Open-Close:** 08/19 - 06/04 \ **DTBP:** $190 (High) \

Scott Rowe 1	Debbie Salm 2
Mark Altmayer 2,19	Doug Renkosik 3
Kevin Harris 4	Laura Hooper 5
Chris Rozanski 6*	Karen Rowe 7*
Amy Maccrindle 8,69	Erika Schlichter 8,15,16,70,285
Rocio Del Castillo 8,11,15,78	Sarah Anderson Wolf 8
Jessica Lombard 9,15	Julia Cloat 9
William Johnson 10	Adam Zehr 15,68
Caitlin Dilallo 58	Alicia Parker 59
Monica Furlong 59,88	Kevin Wolf 60,88
Anthony Quagliano 67	Dan Armstrong 71
Christopher Budzynski 73,76,98,295	Jacki Carrasco 81
Adam Dean 91	Greg Conrad 295

Public Schs..Principal	Grd	Prgm	Enr/#Cls	SN	
Chesak Elem Sch
10910 Reed Rd, Lk In The Hls 60156
Jennifer Zayas	PK-2		774
30	16%	847/659-5700
Fax 847/659-5720
Conley Elem Sch
750 Academic Dr, Algonquin 60102
Rhonda Maciejewski	3-5		675
30	13%	847/659-3700
Fax 847/659-3720
Hannah Martin Elem Sch
10920 Reed Rd, Lk In The Hls 60156
Michele Happold	3-5		887
42	14%	847/659-5300
Fax 847/659-5320
Heineman Middle Sch
725 Academic Dr, Algonquin 60102
James Litchfield \ **Brian Faulkner**	6-8		859	13%	847/659-4300
Fax 847/659-4320
Henry Marlowe Middle Sch
9625 Haligus Rd, Lk In The Hls 60156
Tony Venetico	6-8		1,372
70	14%	847/659-4700
Fax 847/659-4720
Huntley Senior High Sch
13719 Harmony Rd, Huntley 60142
Marcus Belin	9-12	GV	3,082
70	11%	847/659-6600
Fax 847/659-6628
Leggee Elem Sch
13723 Harmony Rd, Huntley 60142
Scott Iddings	K-5		882
46	12%	847/659-6200
Fax 847/659-6220
Mackeben Elem Sch
800 Academic Dr, Algonquin 60102
Anna Hoyou	K-2		614	12%	847/659-3400
Fax 847/659-3420

• Johnsburg Cmty School Dist 12 PID: 00305642
2222 Church St, Johnsburg 60051
815/385-6916
Fax 815/385-4715

Schools: 4 \ **Teachers:** 123 \ **Students:** 1,800 \ **Special Ed Students:** 300 \ **LEP Students:** 36 \ **College-Bound:** 76% \ **Ethnic:** Asian 1%, African American 1%, Hispanic 8%, Caucasian 90% \ **Exp:** $179 (Low) \ **Poverty:** 5% \ **Title I:** $174,424 \ **Special Education:** $1,304,000 \ **Bilingual Education:** $7,000 \ **Open-Close:** 08/25 - 06/03 \ **DTBP:** $235 (High)

Dan Johnson 1	Annie Mulvaney 2,11,19,84,751
Jane Hahn 2	Tom Schwartz 3,5
Ted Juske 6	Terie Engelbrecht 8,18,285,288
Fran Milewski 36,57,58,69,79,88	Tom Oeffling 67
Michael Cooper 73,76,286	

Public Schs..Principal	Grd	Prgm	Enr/#Cls	SN	
Johnsburg Elem Sch
2117 Church St, Johnsburg 60051
Dr Bridget Belcastro	3-4		300
15	30%	815/385-6210
Fax 815/344-7104
Johnsburg High Sch
2002 W Ringwood Rd, McHenry 60051
Kevin Shelton	9-12	V	594
50	22%	815/385-9233
Fax 815/344-0451
Johnsburg Junior High Sch
2220 Church St, Johnsburg 60051
Joshua Cornwell	5-8		642
64	25%	815/385-6210
Fax 815/344-7106
Ringwood School Primary Ctr
4700 School Rd, Ringwood 60072
Andy Elbert	PK-2		422
26	29%	815/728-0459
Fax 815/728-0690

• Marengo Cmty High Sch Dist 154 PID: 00305721
110 Franks Rd, Marengo 60152
815/568-6511
Fax 815/568-6510

Schools: 1 \ **Teachers:** 47 \ **Students:** 700 \ **Special Ed Students:** 63 \ **LEP Students:** 19 \ **College-Bound:** 74% \ **Ethnic:** Asian 1%, African American 1%, Hispanic 20%, Caucasian 78% \ **Exp:** $719 (High) \ **Poverty:** 7% \ **Title I:** $85,184 \ **Special Education:** $688,000 \ **Open-Close:** 08/13 - 05/20 \ **DTBP:** $189 (High) \

David Engelbrecht 1,73	Heather Shephard 2
Don Swanson 3	Elizabeth Molbeck 4*
Nathan Wright 6	Dr Angela Fink 10,93*
Julie Amendt 11,88,275*	Alicia Tippins 16,82*
Greg Halverson 35*	Nadia Moreno 57*
Linda Dujmovich 67	Natasha Schultz 69*
Kathleen Joyce 90*	Susan McGuire 297

Public Schs..Principal	Grd	Prgm	Enr/#Cls	SN	
Marengo Community High Sch
110 Franks Rd, Marengo 60152
Dr Angela Fink	9-12	V	700
50	28%	815/568-6511

• Marengo Union Elem Cons SD 165 PID: 00305692
816 E Grant Hwy, Marengo 60152
815/568-8323
Fax 815/568-8367

Schools: 3 \ **Teachers:** 70 \ **Students:** 1,200 \ **Special Ed Students:** 120 \ **LEP Students:** 91 \ **Ethnic:** African American 2%, Hispanic 26%, Caucasian 72% \ **Exp:** $145 (Low) \ **Poverty:** 10% \ **Title I:** $162,254 \ **Special Education:** $537,000 \ **Bilingual Education:** $14,000 \ **Open-Close:** 08/14 - 05/21 \ **DTBP:** $25 (Low)

Lea Damisch 1,11	Sue Rice-Maurer 2
Scott Fillmore 3	Dena Montgomery 5
Michele Frank 5	Jill Victora 37,83,85,270*
Cheryl Heinz 59,88*	Greg Wright 67
Alyssa Denison 73	

Public Schs..Principal	Grd	Prgm	Enr/#Cls	SN	
Grant Intermediate Sch
816 E Grant Hwy, Marengo 60152
Cheryl Heinz	4-5	T	223	46%	815/568-7427
Fax 815/568-8905
Locust Elem Sch
539 Locust St, Marengo 60152
Sue Ellen Lopez	PK-3	T	465
23	50%	815/568-7632
Fax 815/568-1830
Marengo Cmty Middle Sch
816 E Grant Hwy, Marengo 60152
Tracy Beam	6-8	T	341
30	39%	815/568-5720
Fax 815/568-7572

1	Superintendent	8	Curric/Instruct K-12	19	Chief Financial Officer	29	Family/Consumer Science	39	Social Studies K-12	49	English/Lang Arts Elem	59	Special Education Elem	69	Academic Assessment
2	Bus/Finance/Purchasing	9	Curric/Instruct Elem	20	Art K-12	30	Adult Education	40	Social Studies Elem	50	English/Lang Arts Sec	60	Special Education Sec	70	Research/Development
3	Buildings And Grounds	10	Curric/Instruct Sec	21	Art Elem	31	Career/Sch-to-Work K-12	41	Social Studies Sec	51	Reading K-12	61	Foreign/World Lang K-12	71	Public Information
4	Food Service	11	Federal Program	22	Art Sec	32	Career/Sch-to-Work Elem	42	Science K-12	52	Reading Elem	62	Foreign/World Lang Elem	72	Summer School
5	Transportation	12	Title I	23	Music K-12	33	Career/Sch-to-Work Sec	43	Science Elem	53	Reading Sec	63	Foreign/World Lang Sec	73	Instructional Tech
6	Athletic	13	Title V	24	Music Elem	34	Early Childhood Ed	44	Science Sec	54	Remedial Reading K-12	64	Religious Education K-12	74	Inservice Training
7	Health Services	14	Instructional Media Svcs	25	Music Sec	35	Health/Phys Education	45	Math K-12	55	Remedial Reading Elem	65	Religious Education Elem	75	Marketing/Distributive
		15	Asst Superintendent	26	Business Education	36	Guidance Services K-12	46	Math Elem	56	Remedial Reading Sec	66	Religious Education Sec	76	Info Systems
		16	Chief Operations Officer	27	Career & Tech Ed	37	Guidance Services Elem	47	Math Sec	57	Bilingual/ELL	67	School Board President	77	Psychological Assess
		18	Chief Academic Officer	28	Technology Education	38	Guidance Services Sec	48	English/Lang Arts K-12	58	Special Education K-12	68	Teacher Personnel	78	Affirmative Action

Illinois School Directory — McHenry County

McHenry Cmty Cons Sch Dist 15 PID: 00305745   779/244-1000
1011 N Green St, McHenry 60050   Fax 815/344-7121

Schools: 8 \ **Teachers:** 318 \ **Students:** 4,300 \ **Special Ed Students:** 869 \ **LEP Students:** 600 \ **Ethnic:** Asian 1%, African American 1%, Hispanic 24%, Caucasian 73% \ **Exp:** $327 (High) \ **Poverty:** 9% \ **Title I:** $624,680 \ **Special Education:** $2,879,000 \ **Bilingual Education:** $164,000 \ **Open-Close:** 08/24 - 05/25 \ **DTBP:** $189 (High) \ t

Dr R Alan Hoffman	1	Jeff Schubert	2
Kevin Harris	4	Kimberly Frost	5
Amelia Wuerger	7,35,85	Fred Laudadio	9,16,73,74,285,288,295,297
Josh Reitz	9,11,15,69,83,273,294,296	Kelli Katini	34,59,88,275
Juan Saurez	57	Maureen Cassidy	57
Matthew Stauner	67	Brian Kilinski	68
Kim Capranica	79	Andrew Lund	91
Andrew Dreher	295	Lois Zalewski	298

Public Schs..Principal	Grd	Prgm	Enr/#Cls	SN	
Chauncey H Duker Sch 3711 W Kane Ave, McHenry 60050 Alison Kos	4-5	T	476 18	44%	779/244-1100 Fax 815/363-5024
Edgebrook Elem Sch 701 N Green St, McHenry 60050 Michelle Reinhardt	PK-3	T	434 26	43%	779/244-1200 Fax 815/363-5025
Hilltop Elem Sch 2615 W Lincoln Rd, McHenry 60051 Christy Brown	K-3	T	441 25	45%	779/244-1300 Fax 815/363-5027
ⓨ Landmark Elem Sch 3614 Waukegan Rd, McHenry 60050 Margaret Carey	K-5	M	239 9	11%	779/244-1800 Fax 815/363-5026
McHenry Middle Sch 2120 W Lincoln Rd, McHenry 60051 Mike Glover	6-8		762 45	36%	779/244-1600 Fax 815/578-2101
Parkland Middle Sch 1802 N Ringwood Rd, McHenry 60050 Mike Adams	6-8		821 50	39%	779/244-1700 Fax 815/363-5023
Riverwood Elem Sch 300 S Driftwood Trl, McHenry 60050 Kristen Cannon	K-5	T	602 36	47%	779/244-1400 Fax 815/363-5021
Valley View Elem Sch 6515 W Il Route 120, McHenry 60050 Amanda Cohn	K-5	T	563 25	35%	779/244-1500 Fax 815/363-5022

McHenry Cmty High Sch Dist 156 PID: 00305812   815/385-7900
4716 W Crystal Lake Rd, McHenry 60050   Fax 815/344-7153

Schools: 2 \ **Teachers:** 142 \ **Students:** 2,143 \ **Special Ed Students:** 319 \ **LEP Students:** 89 \ **College-Bound:** 69% \ **Ethnic:** Asian 2%, African American 1%, Hispanic 23%, Caucasian 74% \ **Exp:** $275 (Med) \ **Poverty:** 8% \ **Title I:** $269,072 \ **Special Education:** $1,152,000 \ **Bilingual Education:** $7,000 \ **Open-Close:** 08/17 - 05/28 \ **DTBP:** $195 (High)

Dr Ryan McTague	1,11,83	David Lawson	2,3,4,11,19
Hugh Flack	3	Joann May	4
Barry Burmeister	6*	Carl Vallianatos	10,12,15
Vickie Piekarski	11,27,33,57,60,88,274	Angela Welch	16*
Becky Colvolt	60	Becky Covalt	60
Gary Kinshofer	67	Julia Pontarelli	68
Jim Popovich	69*	Paul Wilm	69
Doug Primus	73	Joseph Zelek	76*
Mike Kennedy	79		

Public Schs..Principal	Grd	Prgm	Enr/#Cls	SN	
McHenry East High Sch 1012 N Green St, McHenry 60050 Jeff Prickett	9-12		700 60	29%	815/385-1145 Fax 815/363-8435
McHenry West High Sch 4724 W Crystal Lake Rd, McHenry 60050 Marsha Potthoff	9-12		1,443 30	33%	815/385-7077 Fax 815/363-8651

Nippersink School District 2 PID: 00305886   815/678-4242
4213 US Highway 12, Richmond 60071   Fax 815/675-0413

Schools: 3 \ **Teachers:** 93 \ **Students:** 1,100 \ **Special Ed Students:** 187 \ **LEP Students:** 16 \ **Ethnic:** Asian 1%, African American 1%, Hispanic 10%, Caucasian 88% \ **Exp:** $165 (Low) \ **Poverty:** 6% \ **Title I:** $123,043 \ **Special Education:** $788,000 \ **Open-Close:** 08/19 - 05/26 \ **DTBP:** $239 (High)

Dr Thomas Lind	1	Denise Levendoski	2
Rick Cesario	3*	Belinda Veillon	9*
Paul Ciszek	16,295	Rose Richer	16*
Jackie Miller	59*	Bert Irslinger	67
Paul Fields	73	Kim Mantych	280*

Public Schs..Principal	Grd	Prgm	Enr/#Cls	SN	
Nippersink Middle Sch 10006 N Main St, Richmond 60071 Tim Molitor	6-8	A	409 25	20%	815/678-7129 Fax 815/678-7210
Richmond Grade Sch 5815 Broadway St, Richmond 60071 Lisa Kuhl	PK-5	A	428 28	20%	815/678-4717 Fax 815/678-2279
Spring Grove Elem Sch 2018 Main Street Rd, Spring Grove 60081 Chris Pittman	PK-5	A	298 26	16%	815/678-6750 Fax 815/678-6760

Prairie Grove Cons SD 46 PID: 00305848   815/459-3023
3223 Il Route 176, Crystal Lake 60014   Fax 815/356-0519

Schools: 2 \ **Teachers:** 62 \ **Students:** 720 \ **Special Ed Students:** 124 \ **LEP Students:** 35 \ **Ethnic:** Asian 1%, African American 1%, Hispanic 10%, Caucasian 87% \ **Exp:** $300 (High) \ **Poverty:** 5% \ **Title I:** $63,550 \ **Special Education:** $409,000 \ **Open-Close:** 08/17 - 05/21 \ **DTBP:** $220 (High) \ f t

Dr John Bute	1	Kevin Werner	2
Kim Boltz	5	Martha Maggiore	9,83*
Rachel Kessey	12,79	Mary O'Leary	16*
Scott Martin	16,73*	Khushali Shah	67

Public Schs..Principal	Grd	Prgm	Enr/#Cls	SN	
Prairie Grove Elem Sch 3223 Il Route 176, Crystal Lake 60014 Martha Maggiore	PK-5		454 35	19%	815/459-3023 f t
Prairie Grove Jr High Sch 3225 Il Route 176, Crystal Lake 60014 Martha Maggiore	6-8		232 21	22%	815/459-3557 Fax 815/459-3785

Richmond-Burton Cmty HSD 157 PID: 00305903   815/678-4242
4213 US Highway 12, Richmond 60071   Fax 815/675-0413

Schools: 1 \ **Teachers:** 47 \ **Students:** 636 \ **Special Ed Students:** 75 \ **LEP Students:** 4 \ **College-Bound:** 83% \ **Ethnic:** Asian 2%, African American 1%, Hispanic 8%, Caucasian 90% \ **Exp:** $536 (High) \ **Poverty:** 6% \ **Title I:** $63,550 \ **Special Education:** $396,000 \ **Open-Close:** 08/19 - 05/26 \ **DTBP:** $229 (High)

---

79 Student Personnel	91 Safety/Security	275 Response To Intervention	298 Grant Writer/Ptnrships	**School Programs**	**Social Media**
80 Driver Ed/Safety	92 Magnet School	277 Remedial Math K-12	750 Chief Innovation Officer	A = Alternative Program	f = Facebook
81 Gifted/Talented	93 Parental Involvement	280 Literacy Coach	751 Chief of Staff	G = Adult Classes	t = Twitter
82 Video Services	95 Tech Prep Program	285 STEM	752 Social Emotional Learning	M = Magnet Program	
83 Substance Abuse Prev	97 Chief Infomation Officer	286 Digital Learning		T = Title I Schoolwide	
84 Erate	98 Chief Technology Officer	288 Common Core Standards	**Other School Types**	V = Career & Tech Ed Programs	
85 AIDS Education	270 Accountability	294 Accountability	Ⓐ = Alternative School		
88 Alternative/At Risk	271 Migrant Education	295 Network System	Ⓒ = Charter School	New Schools are shaded	
89 Multi-Cultural Curriculum	273 Teacher Mentor	296 Title II Programs	Ⓜ = Magnet School	New Superintendents and Principals are bold	
90 Social Work	274 Before/After Sch	297 Webmaster	Ⓨ = Year-Round School	Personnel with email addresses are underscored	

McHenry County

Market Data Retrieval

Tom Lind 1	Denise Levendoski 2
Rich Holtz 3*	Cindy Donohue 4*
Mary Beth Tibbs 5*	Kristi Martin 6*
Lindsay McMillan 7*	Belinda Veillon 10*
Dr Jackie Miller 13,60,83*	Seth Herchenbach 16*
Rebecca Botts 27*	Brett Wojcik 35,85
Kelly Canavan 38,69,88,270*	Michelle Graham 67
Paul Fields 73,295*	

Public Schs..Principal	Grd	Prgm	Enr/#Cls	SN
Richmond Burton Cmty High Sch 8311 Illinois Route 21, Richmond 60071 **Michael Baird**	9-12		636 50	11% 815/678-4525 Fax 815/678-4324

- **Riley Cmty Cons Sch Dist 18** PID: 00305927   815/568-8637
  9406 Riley Rd, Marengo 60152   Fax 815/568-3709

Schools: 1 \ **Teachers:** 26 \ **Students:** 267 \ **Special Ed Students:** 48 \ **LEP Students:** 19 \ **Ethnic:** African American 1%, Hispanic 19%, Caucasian 81% \ **Exp:** $414 (High) \ **Poverty:** 9% \ **Title I:** $47,324 \ **Special Education:** $107,000 \ **Open-Close:** 08/26 - 06/01 \ **DTBP:** $179 (High) \ 📧

Christine Conkleign 1	Karen Schnable 2,5
Larry Greief 3*	Laurie King 4*
Frank Vichar 11,288	Kristina Paluch 12,52*
Kimberly O'Brien 13,57,59	Christine Moore 16,73,295,297*
Anita Mitchell 67	Brian Warren 83,85,285,286*
Lisa Gruber 88*	

Public Schs..Principal	Grd	Prgm	Enr/#Cls	SN
Riley Community Cons Sch 9406 Riley Rd, Marengo 60152 **Frank Vacarri**	K-8		267 18	23% 815/568-8637

- **Woodstock Cmty Unit SD 200** PID: 00305991   815/338-8200
  2990 Raffel Rd, Woodstock 60098   Fax 815/338-2005

Schools: 12 \ **Teachers:** 405 \ **Students:** 6,600 \ **Special Ed Students:** 857 \ **LEP Students:** 908 \ **College-Bound:** 70% \ **Ethnic:** Asian 2%, African American 3%, Hispanic 35%, Caucasian 60% \ **Exp:** $123 (Low) \ **Poverty:** 10% \ **Title I:** $846,428 \ **Special Education:** $3,817,000 \ **Bilingual Education:** $228,000 \ **Open-Close:** 08/17 - 05/21 \ **DTBP:** $191 (High)

Dr Michael Moan 1	Curt Johannsen 2
Elena Arains 2	Risa Hanson 2,19
Kenneth Roiland 3,91	Sue Malley 4
Diane Carter 5	Jerilyn Burkett 5
Chris Kirkpatrick 6*	Lisa Tate 7
Keely Krueger 8,11,15,57,61,275,296,298	Jacqueline Carrasco 9
George Oslovich 10,69,73,76,84,295	Brian McAdow 15,68
Julie Jennett 58	Kristy Mikol 58
Lisa Pearson 58	Carl Gilmore 67
Kevin Lyons 71	Debra Walsdorf 297

Public Schs..Principal	Grd	Prgm	Enr/#Cls	SN
Clay Academy 112 Grove St, Woodstock 60098 **Dawn Cook**	K-12	T	64 16	58% 815/337-2529 Fax 815/337-2140
Creekside Middle Sch 3201 Hercules Rd, Woodstock 60098 **Michael Wheatley**	6-8	T	808 43	44% 815/337-5200 Fax 815/206-0476
Dean St Elem Sch 600 Dean St, Woodstock 60098 **Ryan Doyle**	1-5	T	318 21	39% 815/338-1133 Fax 815/338-3089
Greenwood Elem Sch 4618 Greenwood Rd, Woodstock 60098 **Julie Smith**	1-5	T	348 14	32% 815/648-2606 Fax 815/648-4808
Mary Endres Elem Sch 2181 N Seminary Ave, Woodstock 60098 **Keri Pala**	1-5	T	466 24	45% 815/337-8177 Fax 815/337-5765
Northwood Middle Sch 2121 N Seminary Ave, Woodstock 60098 **Bethany Hall**	6-8	T	640 45	41% 815/338-4900 Fax 815/337-2150
Olson Elem Sch 720 W Judd St, Woodstock 60098 **Stephanie Watson**	1-5	T	441	46% 815/338-0473 Fax 815/338-8142
Prairiewood Elem Sch 3215 Hercules Rd, Woodstock 60098 **Jared Skorburg**	1-5	T	402	41% 815/337-5300 Fax 815/206-0479
Verda Dierzen Early Lrng Ctr 2045 N Seminary Ave, Woodstock 60098 **Tricia Bogott**	PK-K	T	761 30	49% 815/338-8883 Fax 815/337-5431
Westwood Elem Sch 14124 W South Street Rd, Woodstock 60098 **Ryan Hart**	1-5	T	347 27	50% 815/337-8173 Fax 815/337-8175
Woodstock High Sch 501 W South St, Woodstock 60098 **Arthur Vallicelli**	9-12	ATV	1,008	39% 815/338-4370 Fax 815/334-0811
Woodstock North High Sch 3000 Raffel Rd, Woodstock 60098 **Darlea Livengood**	9-12		929	33% 815/334-2100 Fax 815/334-2101

MCHENRY CATHOLIC SCHOOLS

- **Diocese of Rockford Ed Office** PID: 00328345
  Listing includes only schools located in this county. See District Index for location of Diocesan Offices.

Catholic Schs..Principal	Grd	Prgm	Enr/#Cls	SN
Marian Central Catholic HS 1001 McHenry Ave, Woodstock 60098 **Debra Novy**	9-12		689 37	815/338-4220 Fax 815/338-4253
Montini Catholic Sch 1405 N Richmond Rd, McHenry 60050 **Julie Stark**	PK-8		433 12	815/385-1022 Fax 815/363-7536
SS Peter & Paul Sch 416 1st St, Cary 60013 **Nick Satterlee**	K-8		400 18	847/639-3041 Fax 847/639-5329
St John the Baptist Sch 2304 Church St, Johnsburg 60051 **Brenda Baldassano**	PK-7		73 10	815/385-3959 Fax 815/363-3337
St Margaret Mary Sch 119 S Hubbard St, Algonquin 60102 **Brenna O'Hearn**	PK-8		300 12	847/658-5313 Fax 847/854-0501
St Mary Sch 313 N Tryon St, Woodstock 60098 **Vince Sossong**	PK-8		250 14	815/338-3598 Fax 815/338-3408
St Thomas the Apostle Sch 265 King St, Crystal Lake 60014 **Gina Houston**	PK-8		376 18	815/459-0496 Fax 815/459-0591

1	Superintendent	8	Curric/Instruct K-12	19	Chief Financial Officer	29	Family/Consumer Science	39	Social Studies K-12	49	English/Lang Arts Elem	59	Special Education Elem	69	Academic Assessment
2	Bus/Finance/Purchasing	9	Curric/Instruct Elem	20	Art K-12	30	Adult Education	40	Social Studies Elem	50	English/Lang Arts Sec	60	Special Education Sec	70	Research/Development
3	Buildings And Grounds	10	Curric/Instruct Sec	21	Art Elem	31	Career/Sch-to-Work K-12	41	Social Studies Sec	51	Reading K-12	61	Foreign/World Lang K-12	71	Public Information
4	Food Service	11	Federal Program	22	Art Sec	32	Career/Sch-to-Work Elem	42	Science K-12	52	Reading Elem	62	Foreign/World Lang Elem	72	Summer School
5	Transportation	12	Title I	23	Music K-12	33	Career/Sch-to-Work Sec	43	Science Elem	53	Reading Sec	63	Foreign/World Lang Sec	73	Instructional Tech
6	Athletic	13	Title V	24	Music Elem	34	Early Childhood Ed	44	Science Sec	54	Remedial Reading K-12	64	Religious Education K-12	74	Inservice Training
7	Health Services	14	Asst Superintendent	25	Music Sec	35	Health/Phys Education	45	Math K-12	55	Remedial Reading Elem	65	Religious Education Elem	75	Marketing/Distributive
		15	Instructional Media Svcs	26	Business Education	36	Guidance Services K-12	46	Math Elem	56	Remedial Reading Sec	66	Religious Education Sec	76	Info Systems
		16	Chief Operations Officer	27	Career & Tech Ed	37	Guidance Services Elem	47	Math Sec	57	Bilingual/ELL	67	School Board President	77	Psychological Assess
		17	Chief Academic Officer	28	Technology Education	38	Guidance Services Sec	48	English/Lang Arts K-12	58	Special Education K-12	68	Teacher Personnel	78	Affirmative Action

Illinois School Directory — Mclean County

MCHENRY PRIVATE SCHOOLS

Private Schs..Principal	Grd	Prgm	Enr/#Cls	SN
Alexander Leigh Center Autism 4100 Veterans Pkwy, McHenry 60050 Kelly Weaver	Spec		45	815/344-2522
Crystal Lake Montessori Sch 3013 S Country Club Rd, Woodstock 60098 Nancy Bauerband	PK-8		150 14	815/338-0013 Fax 815/338-8588
Immanuel Lutheran Sch 300 S Pathway Ct, Crystal Lake 60014 John Meulendyke	PK-8		200 9	815/459-1444 Fax 815/459-1462
Lord & Savior Evang Luth Sch 9300 Ridgefield Rd, Crystal Lake 60012 Michelle Behrens	PK-8		39 4	815/455-4175 Fax 815/455-9725
Sch Exp Arts & Lrng-Woodstock 1200 Claussen Dr, Woodstock 60098 Jessica Anello	Spec		60	815/337-2005 Fax 815/337-2040
Trinity Oaks Christian Academy 233 Trinity Oaks Way, Cary 60013 Dr Paul Wrobbel	PK-12		214 12	847/462-5971 Fax 847/462-5972
Zion Lutheran Sch 408 Jackson St, Marengo 60152 Dr Dan Bertrand	PK-8		300 22	815/568-5156 Fax 815/568-6345

MCHENRY REGIONAL CENTERS

- **McHenry Co Reg Office of Ed 44** PID: 02098065   815/334-4475
  2200 N Seminary Ave, Woodstock 60098   Fax 815/338-0475

Leslie Schermerhorn 1   Michael Freeman 15

- **McHenry Co Work Force Ctr** PID: 04178037   815/338-7100
  500 Russel Ct, Woodstock 60098   Fax 815/338-7125

Jeffery Poynter 1

- **Special Ed Dist of McHenry Co** PID: 02182252   815/338-3622
  1200 Claussen Dr, Woodstock 60098   Fax 815/338-7550

Dr Tim Burns 1,11   Kim Egerstaffer 2

MCLEAN COUNTY

MCLEAN COUNTY SCHOOLS

County Schs..Principal	Grd	Prgm	Enr/#Cls	SN
Regional Alternative Sch 408 W Washington St, Bloomington 61701 Bryan Kendall	9-12		150	56% 309/828-5807 Fax 309/828-8564

MCLEAN PUBLIC SCHOOLS

- **Bloomington School District 87** PID: 00306141   309/827-6031
  300 E Monroe St, Bloomington 61701   Fax 309/827-5717

Schools: 10 \ Teachers: 347 \ Students: 5,200 \ Special Ed Students: 895 \ LEP Students: 352 \ Ethnic: Asian 4%, African American 27%, Hispanic 16%, Caucasian 53% \ Exp: $314 (High) \ Poverty: 14% \ Title I: $1,844,173 \ Special Education: $2,926,000 \ Bilingual Education: $85,000 \ Open-Close: 08/24 - 05/27 \ DTBP: $227 (High)

Dr Barry Reilly 1   Colin Manahan 2,3,5,17,19,91
Caroline Bubulka 4   Anthony Bauman 6,35,80*
Leslie Hanson 7,11,36,58,77,83,90,275   Diane Wolf 8,11,88,285,286,288,296,298
Sherri Thomas 15,68   Tom Frazier 27,30,75*
Jeff Dobbs 34   Guille Delgato 57
Brigette Beasley 67   Suzanne Daniels 68
Jim Peterson 73,76,95,295   Brian Evans 91

Public Schs..Principal	Grd	Prgm	Enr/#Cls	SN
Bent Elem Sch 904 N Roosevelt Ave, Bloomington 61701 **Guillermina DelGado**	K-5	T	360 15	71% 309/828-4315 Fax 309/828-3587
Bloomington Area Voc Center 1202 E Locust St, Bloomington 61701 Tom Frazier	Voc	G	500 13	309/829-8671 Fax 309/828-3546
Bloomington High Sch 1202 E Locust St, Bloomington 61701 Tim Moore	9-12	T	1,491 50	55% 309/828-5201 Fax 309/829-0178
Bloomington Junior High Sch 901 Colton Ave, Bloomington 61701 Sherrilyn Thomas	6-8	T	1,219 68	61% 309/827-0086 Fax 309/829-0084
Irving Elem Sch 602 W Jackson St, Bloomington 61701 Messina Lambert	K-5	T	360 23	80% 309/827-8091 Fax 309/829-2295
Oakland Elem Sch 1605 E Oakland Ave, Bloomington 61701 David LaFrance	K-5	T	465 21	34% 309/662-4302 Fax 309/663-4385
Sarah Raymond Early Chldhd Ctr 1402 W Olive St, Bloomington 61701 Jeffrey Dobbs	PK-PK	T	274 10	76% 309/827-0308 Fax 309/829-2574
Sheridan Elem Sch 1403 W Walnut St, Bloomington 61701 **Danel Harr**	K-5	T	374 20	82% 309/828-2359 Fax 309/829-3209
Stevenson Elem Sch 2106 Arrowhead Dr, Bloomington 61704 Lynn Shook	K-5	T	397 25	54% 309/663-2351 Fax 309/827-3613
Washington Elem Sch 1201 E Washington St, Bloomington 61701 Jeff Lockenvitz	K-5	T	385 18	35% 309/829-7034 Fax 309/829-1207

- **Heyworth Cmty Sch District 4** PID: 00306385   309/473-3727
  522 E Main St, Heyworth 61745   Fax 309/473-2220

Schools: 2 \ Teachers: 59 \ Students: 975 \ Special Ed Students: 115 \ LEP Students: 9 \ College-Bound: 69% \ Ethnic: Hispanic 4%, Caucasian 95% \ Exp: $181 (Low) \ Poverty: 7% \ Title I: $132,368 \ Special Education: $596,000 \ Open-Close: 08/20 - 05/28

Lisa Taylor 1   Randy Richards 5
Lyndon Jason 6   Matt Andrews 9
April Hicklin .... 10,83,88*   Amanda Denning 12
Michelle Harris .... 16,82*   Rebbeca Stanton 36,69*
Chuck Brannock 67   Ryan Hahn 73,295

---

79 Student Personnel	91 Safety/Security	275 Response To Intervention	298 Grant Writer/Ptnrships	**School Programs**	**Social Media**	
80 Driver Ed/Safety	92 Magnet School	277 Remedial Math K-12	750 Chief Innovation Officer	A = Alternative Program	ⓕ = Facebook	
81 Gifted/Talented	93 Parental Involvement	280 Literacy Coach	751 Chief of Staff	G = Adult Classes		
82 Video Services	95 Tech Prep Program	285 STEM	752 Social Emotional Learning	M = Magnet Program	ⓣ = Twitter	
83 Substance Abuse Prev	97 Chief Infomation Officer	286 Digital Learning		T = Title I Schoolwide		
84 Erate	98 Chief Technology Officer	288 Common Core Standards	**Other School Types**	V = Career & Tech Ed Programs		
85 AIDS Education	270 Character Education	294 Accountability	Ⓐ = Alternative School			
88 Alternative/At Risk	271 Migrant Education	295 Network System	Ⓒ = Charter School	New Schools are shaded		
89 Multi-Cultural Curriculum	273 Teacher Mentor	296 Title II Programs	Ⓜ = Magnet School	New Superintendents and Principals are bold		
90 Social Work	274 Before/After Sch	297 Webmaster	Ⓨ = Year-Round School	Personnel with email addresses are underscored		

IL—185

Mclean County
Market Data Retrieval

Public Schs..Principal	Grd	Prgm	Enr/#Cls	SN		
Heyworth Elem Sch 100 S Joselyn St, Heyworth 61745 Matt Andrews	PK-6		549 28	28%	309/473-2822 Fax 309/857-0157	
Heyworth Jr Sr High Sch 308 W Cleveland St, Heyworth 61745 April Hicklin	7-12	V	398 40	26%	309/473-2322 Fax 309/213-9481	

- **Le Roy Cmty Unit SD 2** PID: 00306426   309/962-4211
107 W Cherry St, Le Roy 61752   Fax 309/962-9312

> **Schools:** 3 \ **Teachers:** 62 \ **Students:** 775 \ **Special Ed Students:** 97 \ **College-Bound:** 75% \ **Ethnic:** African American 1%, Hispanic 2%, Caucasian 97% \ **Exp:** $213 (Med) \ **Poverty:** 8% \ **Title I:** $89,240 \ **Special Education:** $401,000 \ **Open-Close:** 08/14 - 05/20 \ **DTBP:** $238 (High)

Gary Tipsord 1,11		Mark Edmundson 2		
Chip Warlow 3,5		Ed Underhill 3		
Monica Hankins 4*		Brian Zeleznik 6		
Steve Reschke 10*		Ashalie Marcy 16,82*		
Maggie Baughman 34*		Angie Elliott 35,83,85*		
Lisa Wiggins 54*		Kevin Daugherty 67		
Jeff Baughman 69*		Heath Henderson 73,295		
Katie Buckley 285*				

Public Schs..Principal	Grd	Prgm	Enr/#Cls	SN	
Le Roy Elem Sch 805 N Barnett St, Le Roy 61752 Erin Conn	PK-6		420 25	29%	309/962-4771 Fax 309/962-2893
Le Roy Jr Sr High Sch 505 E Center St, Le Roy 61752 Steve Reschke \ Jeff Baughman	7-12		355 60	21%	309/962-2911 Fax 309/962-8421
Ⓐ Le Roy Preparatory Academy 809 Century, Le Roy 61752 Steve Reschke	7-12		25		309/962-4303 Fax 309/962-4190

- **Lexington Cmty Sch Dist 7** PID: 00306464   309/365-4141
100 E Wall St, Lexington 61753   Fax 309/365-7381

> **Schools:** 3 \ **Teachers:** 40 \ **Students:** 490 \ **Special Ed Students:** 73 \ **College-Bound:** 80% \ **Ethnic:** African American 1%, Caucasian 98% \ **Exp:** $176 (Low) \ **Poverty:** 6% \ **Title I:** $50,028 \ **Special Education:** $272,000 \ **Open-Close:** 08/19 - 05/25 \ **DTBP:** $174 (High)

Paul Peters 1,11	Les Thomas 5*
Julie Strating 9,31,58,88*	Jason Thomas 67

Public Schs..Principal	Grd	Prgm	Enr/#Cls	SN	
Lexington Cmty Jr High Sch 100 E Wall St, Lexington 61753 Jennifer McCoy	7-8	V	72 20	25%	309/365-2711 Fax 309/365-5032
Lexington Grade Sch 100 E Wall St, Lexington 61753 Julie Strating	PK-6		261 14	30%	309/365-2741 Fax 309/365-8538
Lexington High Sch 100 E Wall St, Lexington 61753 Jennifer McCoy	9-12	V	129 12	30%	309/365-2711 Fax 309/365-5032

- **McLean Co Unit District 5** PID: 00306490   309/452-4476
1809 Hovey Ave, Normal 61761   Fax 309/557-4100

> **Schools:** 23 \ **Teachers:** 827 \ **Students:** 13,346 \ **Special Ed Students:** 2,223 \ **LEP Students:** 624 \ **College-Bound:** 82% \ **Ethnic:** Asian 9%, African American 13%, Hispanic 8%, Caucasian 69% \ **Exp:** $130 (Low) \ **Poverty:** 6% \ **Title I:** $1,879,466 \ **Special Education:** $7,813,000 \ **Bilingual Education:** $173,000 \ **Open-Close:** 08/19 - 06/03 \ **DTBP:** $232 (High) \ 📧

Kristen Weikle 1	Joe Adelman 2
Martin Hickman 2,295	Doug Johnson 3,91
Pat Powers 4	Ray Epperson 8,15
Maureen Backe 9	Daniel Lamboley 10*
Michelle Lamboley 34,58,77,90*	Leslie Romagnoli 57
Carrie Chapman 58	Jessica Alt 58
Melanie Aslinger 58	Nancy Braun 58
Amy Roser 67	Dr James Harden 68,79
Monica Wilks 68	Dayna Brown 71
Matt Harr 72,90*	David Schumer 73,84
Sean Mullins 286	Dusty Behrens 295

Public Schs..Principal	Grd	Prgm	Enr/#Cls	SN	
Benjamin Elem Sch 6006 Ireland Grove Rd, Bloomington 61705 Marlys Bennington	K-5		575	7%	309/557-4410 Fax 309/557-4511
Brigham Early Learning Ctr 201 Brigham School Rd, Bloomington 61704 Julia Knepler	PK-PK	T	182 18	63%	309/557-4411 Fax 309/557-4460
Carlock Elem Sch 301 W Washington St, Carlock 61725 Laura DelGado	K-5		113 6	24%	309/557-4412 Fax 309/557-4461
Cedar Ridge Elem Sch 2808 Breezewood Blvd, Bloomington 61704 Karrah Jensen	K-5	T	504	74%	309/557-4413 Fax 309/557-4462
Chiddix Junior High Sch 300 S Walnut St, Normal 61761 Jim Allen	6-8		699 60	27%	309/557-4405 Fax 309/557-4454
Colene Hoose Elem Sch 600 Grandview Dr, Normal 61761 Adam Zbrozek	K-5		466 25	26%	309/557-4414 Fax 309/557-4463
Evans Junior High Sch 2901 Morrissey Dr, Bloomington 61704 Chris McGraw	6-8		790	33%	309/557-4406 Fax 309/557-4455
Fairview Elem Sch 416 Fairview St, Normal 61761 G Tenuta	PK-5	T	284 16	48%	309/557-4415 Fax 309/557-4516 📧
Fox Creek Elem Sch 3910 Timberwolf Trl, Bloomington 61705 Leslie Davenport	K-5	T	284 19	63%	309/557-4416 Fax 309/557-4517
Glenn Elem Sch 306 Glenn Ave, Normal 61761 Cari Oester	K-5	T	256 13	39%	309/557-4418 Fax 309/557-4519 📧
Grove Elem Sch 1101 Airport Rd, Normal 61761 Sarah Edwards	K-5		593 28	13%	309/557-4417 Fax 309/557-4466
Hudson Elem Sch 205 S McLean St, Hudson 61748 Scott Myers	K-5		278 12	12%	309/557-4419 Fax 309/557-4468
Kingsley Junior High Sch 303 Kingsley St, Normal 61761 Stacie France	6-8		838 75	29%	309/557-4407 Fax 309/557-4456
Normal Cmty High Sch 3900 E Raab Rd, Normal 61761 Trevor Chapman	9-12	V	2,114 40	25%	309/557-4401 Fax 309/557-4450

1	Superintendent	8	Curric/Instruct K-12	19	Chief Financial Officer	29	Family/Consumer Science	39	Social Studies K-12	49	English/Lang Arts Elem	59	Special Education Elem	69	Academic Assessment
2	Bus/Finance/Purchasing	9	Curric/Instruct Elem	20	Art K-12	30	Adult Education	40	Social Studies Elem	50	English/Lang Arts Sec	60	Special Education Sec	70	Research/Development
3	Buildings And Grounds	10	Curric/Instruct Sec	21	Art Elem	31	Career/Sch-to-Work K-12	41	Social Studies Sec	51	Reading K-12	61	Foreign/World Lang K-12	71	Public Information
4	Food Service	11	Federal Program	22	Art Sec	32	Career/Sch-to-Work Elem	42	Science K-12	52	Reading Elem	62	Foreign/World Lang Elem	72	Summer School
5	Transportation	12	Title I	23	Music K-12	33	Career/Sch-to-Work Sec	43	Science Elem	53	Reading Sec	63	Foreign/World Lang Sec	73	Instructional Tech
6	Athletic	13	Title V	24	Music Elem	34	Early Childhood Ed	44	Science Sec	54	Remedial Reading K-12	64	Religious Education K-12	74	Inservice Training
7	Health Services	15	Asst Superintendent	25	Music Sec	35	Health/Phys Education	45	Math K-12	55	Remedial Reading Elem	65	Religious Education Elem	75	Marketing/Distributive
		16	Instructional Media Svcs	26	Business Education	36	Guidance Services K-12	46	Math Elem	56	Remedial Reading Sec	66	Religious Education Sec	76	Info Systems
		17	Chief Operations Officer	27	Career & Tech Ed	37	Guidance Services Elem	47	Math Sec	57	Bilingual/ELL	67	School Board President	77	Psychological Assess
		18	Chief Academic Officer	28	Technology Education	38	Guidance Services Sec	48	English/Lang Arts K-12	58	Special Education K-12	68	Teacher Personnel	78	Affirmative Action

Illinois School Directory — Mclean County

School	Grd	Prgm	Enr/#Cls	SN	Phone
Normal West High Sch 501 N Parkside Rd, Normal 61761 David Johnson	9-12	V	1,614 64	32%	309/557-4402 Fax 309/557-4503
NorthPoint Elem Sch 2602 E College Ave, Bloomington 61704 Matt Harr	K-5		502 31	8%	309/557-4420 Fax 309/557-4521
Oakdale Elem Sch 601 S Adelaide St, Normal 61761 Liz Holtz	K-5	T	375 18	67%	309/557-4421 Fax 309/557-4470
Parkside Elem Sch 1900 W College Ave, Normal 61761 Chris Elllis	PK-5	T	290 13	56%	309/557-4422 Fax 309/557-4523
Parkside Junior High Sch 101 N Parkside Rd, Normal 61761 Suzi Hesser	6-8		674 50	33%	309/557-4408 Fax 309/557-4457
Pepper Ridge Elem Sch 2602 Danbury Dr, Bloomington 61705 Tina Fogal	K-5	T	331 22	44%	309/557-4423 Fax 309/557-4472
Prairieland Elem Sch 1300 E Raab Rd, Normal 61761 Scott Peters	K-5		468 26	19%	309/557-4424 Fax 309/557-4473
Sugar Creek Elem Sch 200 N Towanda Ave, Normal 61761 Kristina Peifer	PK-5	T	485 16	56%	309/557-4425 Fax 309/557-4474
Towanda Elem Sch 304 S East St, Towanda 61776 Scott Vogel	K-5		188 7	7%	309/557-4426 Fax 309/557-4725

● **Olympia Cmty Unit Sch Dist 16** PID: 00306634 — 309/379-6011
903 E 800 North Rd, Stanford 61774 — Fax 309/379-2328

Schools: 5 \ **Teachers:** 117 \ **Students:** 1,900 \ **Special Ed Students:** 302 \ **LEP Students:** 3 \ **College-Bound:** 69% \ **Ethnic:** African American 1%, Hispanic 3%, Caucasian 96% \ **Exp:** $199 (Low) \ **Poverty:** 8% \ **Title I:** $244,734 \ **Special Education:** $1,155,000 \ **Open-Close:** 08/20 - 05/27 \ **DTBP:** $171 (High) \

Laura O'Donnell .... 1,288 Joe Gaither 3
Scott Thornton .... 3 Andy Walsh 4,5,79*
Mike Castleman .... 6* Kris Morgan 11,58,88,92,298
Kevin Frazier .... 67 Sean Mullins 73,286

Public Schs..Principal	Grd	Prgm	Enr/#Cls	SN	Phone
Olympia High Sch 7832 N 100 East Rd, Stanford 61774 Ed Jodlowski	9-12	AV	517 53	35%	309/379-5911 Fax 309/379-2583
Olympia Middle Sch 911 E 800 North Rd, Stanford 61774 Ben Lee	6-8	T	397 35	41%	309/379-5941 Fax 309/379-5411
Olympia North Elem Sch 205 N State St, Danvers 61732 Matt Hurley	PK-5		303 17	33%	309/963-4514 Fax 844/367-3062
Olympia South Elem Sch 103 NE 5th St, Atlanta 61723 Stacey Rogers	PK-5		331 16	53%	217/648-2302 Fax 217/648-5248
Olympia West Elem Sch 302 N School St, Minier 61759 Lisa Castleman	PK-5		269 12	33%	309/392-2671 Fax 309/392-2497

● **Ridgeview Cmty Unit SD 19** PID: 00306323 — 309/723-5111
300 S Harrison St, Colfax 61728

Schools: 2 \ **Teachers:** 44 \ **Students:** 600 \ **Special Ed Students:** 63 \ **LEP Students:** 3 \ **College-Bound:** 75% \ **Ethnic:** African American 1%, Hispanic 7%, Caucasian 92% \ **Exp:** $255 (Med) \ **Poverty:** 9% \ **Title I:** $102,338 \ **Special Education:** $249,000 \ **Open-Close:** 08/21 - 05/28 \

Erik Young .... 1 Jake Kennedy 6*
Alesha Kern .... 7 Jeffrey Harris 67

Public Schs..Principal	Grd	Prgm	Enr/#Cls	SN	Phone
Ridgeview Elem Sch 300 S Harrison St, Colfax 61728 Ben Hutley	PK-5		286	45%	309/723-6531 Fax 309/723-2019
Ridgeview Jr Sr High Sch 202 E Wood St, Colfax 61728 Brandon Burke	6-12	T	312 23	43%	309/723-2951 Fax 309/723-4851

● **Tri-Valley Cmty School Dist 3** PID: 00306775 — 309/378-2351
410 E Washington St, Downs 61736 — Fax 309/378-2223

Schools: 3 \ **Teachers:** 79 \ **Students:** 1,150 \ **Special Ed Students:** 168 \ **College-Bound:** 88% \ **Ethnic:** Asian 1%, African American 1%, Hispanic 2%, Caucasian 95% \ **Exp:** $198 (Low) \ **Poverty:** 1% \ **Special Education:** $419,000 \ **Open-Close:** 09/08 - 06/04 \ **DTBP:** $178 (High)

David Mouser .... 1,11 Cade Hasselbring 3,5
Julie Rogers .... 4 Josh Roop 6*
Sara Burnett .... 12,81,296* Aime Mouser 16*
Gail McCane .... 58* Carl Neubauer 67
Josh White .... 73,295,297* Pam Broadrick 275*

Public Schs..Principal	Grd	Prgm	Enr/#Cls	SN	Phone
Tri-Valley Elem Sch 409 E Washington St, Downs 61736 Sara Burnett \ **Tyler Swearingen**	PK-3		359 16	11%	309/378-2031 Fax 309/378-4578
Tri-Valley High Sch 503 E Washington St, Downs 61736 Ben Derges	9-12	V	354 30	10%	309/378-2911 Fax 309/378-3202
Tri-Valley Middle Sch 112 S Highway Ave, Downs 61736 Sara Burnett	4-8		390 19	11%	309/378-3414 Fax 309/378-3214

MCLEAN CATHOLIC SCHOOLS

● **Diocese of Peoria Ed Office** PID: 00313338
Listing includes only schools located in this county. See District Index for location of Diocesan Offices.

Catholic Schs..Principal	Grd	Prgm	Enr/#Cls	SN	Phone
Central Catholic High Sch 1201 Airport Rd, Bloomington 61704 Sean Foster	9-12		413 25		309/661-7000 Fax 309/661-7001
Corpus Christi Catholic Sch 1909 E Lincoln St, Bloomington 61701 Richard Pantges	PK-8		643 30		309/662-3712 Fax 309/829-2243
Epiphany Sch 1002 E College Ave, Normal 61761 Mike Lootens	PK-8		427 20		309/452-3268 Fax 309/454-8087

---

79 Student Personnel
80 Driver Ed/Safety
81 Gifted/Talented
82 Video Services
84 Substance Abuse Prev
85 Erate
86 AIDS Education
88 Alternative/At Risk
89 Multi-Cultural Curriculum
90 Social Work
91 Safety/Security
92 Magnet School
93 Parental Involvement
95 Tech Prep Program
97 Chief Infomation Officer
98 Chief Technology Officer
270 Character Education
271 Migrant Education
273 Teacher Mentor
274 Before/After Sch
275 Response To Intervention
277 Remedial Math K-12
280 Literacy Coach
285 STEM
286 Digital Learning
288 Common Core Standards
294 Accountability
295 Network System
296 Title II Programs
297 Webmaster
298 Grant Writer/Ptnrships
750 Chief Innovation Officer
751 Chief of Staff
752 Social Emotional Learning

Other School Types
Ⓐ = Alternative School
Ⓒ = Charter School
Ⓜ = Magnet School
Ⓨ = Year-Round School

School Programs
A = Alternative Program
G = Adult Classes
M = Magnet Program
T = Title I Schoolwide
V = Career & Tech Ed Programs

Social Media
= Facebook
= Twitter

New Schools are shaded
New Superintendents and Principals are bold
Personnel with email addresses are underscored

Menard County

Market Data Retrieval

St Mary's Sch		PK-8	176	309/828-5954
603 W Jackson St, Bloomington 61701			14	Fax 309/829-3061
Jamie Hartrich				

MCLEAN PRIVATE SCHOOLS

Private Schs..Principal	Grd	Prgm	Enr/#Cls	SN	
Calvary Christian Academy	PK-12		329		309/452-7912
1017 N School St, Normal 61761			17		Fax 309/451-0033
Dale Lempa					
Cornerstone Christian Academy	PK-12		400		309/662-9900
22017 E 1200 North Rd, Bloomington 61705					Fax 309/662-9904
Sue Chambers \ Nic Rassi					
Hammitt Sch at the Baby Fold	Spec		95		309/452-1170
108 E Willow St, Normal 61761			15		Fax 309/862-2902
Melody Donnelly					
Mulberry Sch	PK-3		55		309/862-0510
1101 Douglas St, Normal 61761			6		Fax 309/862-0582
Kim Walk					
Trinity Lutheran Sch	PK-8		325		309/829-7513
1102 W Hamilton Rd, Bloomington 61704			20		Fax 309/834-3237
Shawn Hoffman					

MCLEAN REGIONAL CENTERS

- **Mackinaw Valley Spec Ed Assoc** PID: 02183945   309/557-4439
  201 Brigham School Rd, Bloomington 61704   Fax 309/557-4535

  Michele Lamboley 1

- **McLean-DeWitt Reg Voc System** PID: 04177916   309/829-8671
  1202 E Locust St, Bloomington 61701   Fax 309/828-3546

  Tom Frazier 1   Peggy Arbuckle 275

- **Regional Office of Ed 17** PID: 02098077   309/888-5120
  200 W Front St Ste 500D, Bloomington 61701

  Mark Jontry 1   Angie Reithmaier 5
  Molly Allen 15   Victoria Padilla 15
  Kimberly Maddox-Reihl 275,298

- **Tri-Co Special Ed Association** PID: 02183957   309/828-5231
  105 E Hamilton Rd, Bloomington 61704   Fax 309/828-3013

  Scott Hogan 1   Kris Dean 15,58

MENARD COUNTY

MENARD PUBLIC SCHOOLS

- **Athens Cmty Unit Sch Dist 213** PID: 00310506   217/636-8761
  501 Warrior Way, Athens 62613   Fax 217/636-8851

  Schools: 4 \ **Teachers:** 69 \ **Students:** 1,100 \ **Special Ed Students:** 185 \ **LEP Students:** 3 \ **College-Bound:** 81% \ **Ethnic:** Asian 1%, African American 2%, Hispanic 1%, Caucasian 96% \ **Exp:** $204 (Med) \ **Poverty:** 11% \ **Title I:** $164,959 \ **Special Education:** $285,000 \ **Open-Close:** 08/24 - 06/03 \ **DTBP:** $174 (High)

  Scott Laird 1,11   Debbie Lott 2
  Terry Brown .... 3*   Amanda Nix 4
  Helen Wiedhuner .... 4*   Jerry Beiermann 5
  Ryan Knox 6   Stacey Binegar 8,288*
  Eric Szoke .... 12*   Amy Holtsclaw 16,82*
  Jen Rhoades .... 51*   Elizabeth Barrett 54*
  Elizabeth Barrett 54   Ashley Pasbrig 58
  Doug Penrod 67   Joann Benz 69,78,270*
  Amy Stickler .... 81*   Amy Stickler 81
  Christy Hibbs 294

Public Schs..Principal	Grd	Prgm	Enr/#Cls	SN	
Athens High Sch	9-12	V	321	25%	217/636-8314
501 Warrior Way, Athens 62613			25		
Bill Reed					
Athens Junior High Sch	7-8		177	34%	217/636-8380
501 Warrior Way, Athens 62613			20		
Matt Rhoades					
Cantrall Elem Sch	PK-3		375	37%	217/487-7312
1 Braves Ln, Cantrall 62625			18		Fax 217/487-7187
Eric Szoke					
Cantrall Intermediate Sch	4-6		237	36%	217/487-9082
155 Claypool St, Cantrall 62625			26		Fax 217/487-9104
Stacey Binegar					

- **Greenview Cmty Unit SD 200** PID: 00310556   217/968-2295
  147 E Palmer St, Greenview 62642   Fax 217/968-2297

  Schools: 1 \ **Teachers:** 26 \ **Students:** 211 \ **Special Ed Students:** 39 \ **College-Bound:** 67% \ **Ethnic:** Hispanic 1%, Caucasian 99% \ **Exp:** $72 (Low) \ **Poverty:** 12% \ **Title I:** $45,071 \ **Special Education:** $26,000 \ **Open-Close:** 08/20 - 05/28 \ **DTBP:** $174 (High)

  Ryan Heavner 1   Gary Gaut 5
  Zach Reid .... 31,69,83*   Rex Arkebauer 67
  Justin Kossak 73,295

Public Schs..Principal	Grd	Prgm	Enr/#Cls	SN	
Greenview Unit Sch	K-12	TV	211	41%	217/968-2295
147 E Palmer St, Greenview 62642			30		
Tim Turner					

---

1 Superintendent	8 Curric/Instruct K-12	19 Chief Financial Officer	29 Family/Consumer Science	39 Social Studies K-12	49 English/Lang Arts Elem	59 Special Education Elem	69 Academic Assessment
2 Bus/Finance/Purchasing	9 Curric/Instruct Elem	20 Art K-12	30 Adult Education	40 Social Studies Elem	50 English/Lang Arts Sec	60 Special Education Sec	70 Research/Development
3 Buildings And Grounds	10 Curric/Instruct Sec	21 Art Elem	31 Career/Sch-to-Work K-12	41 Social Studies Sec	51 Reading K-12	61 Foreign/World Lang K-12	71 Public Information
4 Food Service	11 Federal Program	22 Art Sec	32 Career/Sch-to-Work Elem	42 Science K-12	52 Reading Elem	62 Foreign/World Lang Elem	72 Summer School
5 Transportation	12 Title I	23 Music K-12	33 Career/Sch-to-Work Sec	43 Science Elem	53 Reading Sec	63 Foreign/World Lang Sec	73 Instructional Tech
6 Athletic	13 Title V	24 Music Elem	34 Early Childhood Ed	44 Science Sec	54 Remedial Reading K-12	64 Religious Education K-12	74 Inservice Training
7 Health Services	15 Asst Superintendent	25 Music Sec	35 Health/Phys Education	45 Math K-12	55 Remedial Reading Elem	65 Religious Education Elem	75 Marketing/Distributive
	16 Instructional Media Svcs	26 Business Education	36 Guidance Services K-12	46 Math Elem	56 Remedial Reading Sec	66 Religious Education Sec	76 Info Systems
	17 Chief Operations Officer	27 Career & Tech Ed	37 Guidance Services Elem	47 Math Sec	57 Bilingual/ELL	67 School Board President	77 Psychological Assess
	18 Chief Academic Officer	28 Technology Education	38 Guidance Services Sec	48 English/Lang Arts K-12	58 Special Education K-12	68 Teacher Personnel	78 Affirmative Action

Illinois School Directory — Monroe County

- **Porta Cmty Unit Sch Dist 202** PID: 00310570   217/632-3803
  17651 Bluejay Rd, Petersburg 62675   Fax 217/632-3221

Schools: 3 \ **Teachers:** 85 \ **Students:** 1,009 \ **Special Ed Students:** 243 \ **College-Bound:** 58% \ **Ethnic:** Asian 1%, African American 1%, Hispanic 1%, Caucasian 97% \ **Exp:** $194 (Low) \ **Poverty:** 14% \ **Title I:** $224,301 \ **Special Education:** $346,000 \ **Open-Close:** 08/24 - 05/21 \ **DTBP:** $235 (High)

Matt Brue	1,11	Kari Eddings	2
Rebecca King	2	Bob Wethington	3*
Laura Esslinger	5	Jeff Hill	6*
Brianna Todd	7,85*	Lonie McAnally	27*
Jill Hoke	34	Linnay Taylor	36*
Melissa Corey	58	Kevin Bettis	67
Kirtus French	73,295*	Hiedi Jacobus	83

Public Schs..Principal	Grd	Prgm	Enr/#Cls	SN	
Petersburg Elem Sch 514 W Monroe St, Petersburg 62675 Jeff Hill	PK-2	T	237 19	37%	217/632-7731 Fax 217/632-3551 f
Porta Central Sch 1500 Owen Ave, Petersburg 62675 Eric Kesler	3-6	T	281 14	45%	217/632-7781 Fax 217/632-5103 f t
Porta Jr Sr High Sch 17651 Bluejay Rd, Petersburg 62675 Amy McMahan	7-12	ATV	469 40	38%	217/632-3219 Fax 217/632-5448

MERCER COUNTY

MERCER PUBLIC SCHOOLS

- **Mercer County SD 404** PID: 00310635   309/582-2238
  1002 SW 6th St, Aledo 61231   Fax 309/582-7428

Schools: 5 \ **Teachers:** 100 \ **Students:** 1,300 \ **Special Ed Students:** 213 \ **LEP Students:** 3 \ **College-Bound:** 61% \ **Ethnic:** Asian 1%, Hispanic 2%, Caucasian 97% \ **Exp:** $192 (Low) \ **Poverty:** 13% \ **Title I:** $264,671 \ **Special Education:** $557,000 \ **Open-Close:** 08/17 - 05/28 \ **DTBP:** $174 (High)

Scott Petrie	1	Andrew Hofer	6*
Ryan Korsesko	12	Tammy Hainds	38*
Julie Wagner	67	Amber Norton	73
Geff Long	295		

Public Schs..Principal	Grd	Prgm	Enr/#Cls	SN	
Apollo Elem Sch 801 SW 9th St, Aledo 61231 William Fleuette	PK-4	T	342 20	36%	309/582-5350 Fax 309/582-3457
Mercer Co Intermediate Sch 1002 SW 6th St, Aledo 61231 Ryan Koresko	5-6	T	219 18	38%	309/582-2441 Fax 309/582-2440
Mercer County High Sch 1500 S College Ave, Aledo 61231 Stacey Day	9-12	V	368 25	35%	309/582-2223 Fax 309/582-5920
Mercer County Jr High Sch 203 N Washington St, Joy 61260 Tim Sedam	7-8	T	199 25	40%	309/584-4174 Fax 309/584-4257

New Boston Elem Sch 301 Jefferson St, New Boston 61272 Marcus Bush	PK-4	T	185 30	45%	309/587-8141 Fax 309/587-3349

- **Sherrard Cmty Sch Dist 200** PID: 00310702   309/593-4075
  507 3rd St, Sherrard 61281   Fax 309/593-4078

Schools: 4 \ **Teachers:** 103 \ **Students:** 1,400 \ **Special Ed Students:** 156 \ **LEP Students:** 4 \ **College-Bound:** 62% \ **Ethnic:** African American 1%, Hispanic 5%, Caucasian 94% \ **Exp:** $348 (High) \ **Poverty:** 11% \ **Title I:** $227,156 \ **Special Education:** $524,000 \ **Open-Close:** 08/17 - 05/25 \ **DTBP:** $191 (High)

Alan Boucher	1	Marla Miller	2,4
Jim Wheatley	3*	Becky Breiby	5
Michael Applegate	6	Polly Dahlstrom	8,11,58,273*
Jackie Kelly	12*	Jill Bennin	16*
Donna Lamb	17,83,88,270,275,288*	Victoria Connelly	57,296,298*
Rhyse Fullerlov	67	Tim Wernetas	69
Janette Finch	73	Jay Wyckoff	73
Brian Hutton	76	Steve Miller	286,751
Brian Hutton	295*		

Public Schs..Principal	Grd	Prgm	Enr/#Cls	SN	
ⓨ Matherville Intermediate Sch 1376 252nd St, Matherville 61263 Jeff Shillinger	5-6	M	225 10	35%	309/754-8244 Fax 309/754-8245
ⓨ Sherrard Elem Sch 209 1st St, Sherrard 61281 Casey Wyant	PK-4	M	262 15	30%	309/593-2917 Fax 309/593-2409
ⓨ Sherrard Jr Sr High Sch 4701 176th Ave, Sherrard 61281 Rick Basala | Tim Wernentin	7-12	MV	650 60	20%	309/593-2135 Fax 309/593-2143
ⓨ Winola Elem Sch 1804 17th Ave, Viola 61486 Kari Roberts	PK-4	MT	258 16	34%	309/596-2114 Fax 309/596-2979

MERCER PRIVATE SCHOOLS

Private Schs..Principal	Grd	Prgm	Enr/#Cls	SN	
L'Abris Academy 221 E Main St Ste 2, Aledo 61231 Lynn Pauley	K-12		401		309/331-3784

MONROE COUNTY

MONROE PUBLIC SCHOOLS

- **Columbia Cmty Unit SD 4** PID: 00310867   618/281-4772
  5 Veterans Pkwy, Columbia 62236   Fax 618/281-4570

Schools: 4 \ **Teachers:** 108 \ **Students:** 2,000 \ **Special Ed Students:** 240 \ **LEP Students:** 6 \ **College-Bound:** 86% \ **Ethnic:** Asian 1%, African American 1%, Hispanic 3%, Caucasian 96% \ **Exp:** $216 (Med) \ **Poverty:** 3% \ **Title I:** $67,626 \ **Special Education:** $905,000 \ **Open-Close:** 08/20 - 05/14

Christopher Grode	1	Lora Glowacki	4*

---

79 Student Personnel	91 Safety/Security	275 Response To Intervention	298 Grant Writer/Ptnrships	**School Programs**	**Social Media**	
80 Driver Ed/Safety	92 Magnet School	277 Remedial Math K-12	750 Chief Innovation Officer	A = Alternative Program		
81 Gifted/Talented	93 Parental Involvement	280 Literacy Coach	751 Chief of Staff	G = Adult Classes	f	= Facebook
82 Video Services	95 Tech Prep Program	285 STEM	752 Social Emotional Learning	M = Magnet Program		
83 Substance Abuse Prev	97 Chief Information Officer	286 Digital Learning		T = Title I Schoolwide	t	= Twitter
84 Erate	98 Chief Technology Officer	288 Common Core Standards	**Other School Types**	V = Career & Tech Ed Programs		
85 AIDS Education	270 Accountability	294 Accountability	Ⓐ = Alternative School			
88 Alternative/At Risk	271 Migrant Education	295 Network System	Ⓒ = Charter School	New Schools are shaded		
89 Multi-Cultural Curriculum	273 Teacher Mentor	296 Title II Programs	Ⓜ = Magnet School	New Superintendents and Principals are bold		
90 Social Work	274 Before/After Sch	297 Webmaster	Ⓨ = Year-Round School	Personnel with email addresses are underscored		IL—189

Montgomery County

Market Data Retrieval

April Becherer 5
Dr Courtney Castelli 9,15,285,298
Kathleen Kelley 36*
Scott Middelkamp 67
Jan Turley 85*
Scott Horner 6,35,80*
Krista Schoellhorn 16*
Jeanne Goacher 58*
Trent Mehaffey 84

Public Schs..Principal	Grd	Prgm	Enr/#Cls	SN
Columbia High Sch 77 Veterans Pkwy, Columbia 62236 Brian Reeves	9-12	V	629 37	10% 618/281-5001 Fax 618/281-8081
Columbia Middle Sch 100 Eagle Dr, Columbia 62236 Angela Huels	5-8		604 45	14% 618/281-4993 Fax 618/281-4964
Eagleveiw Elem Sch 113 S Rapp Ave, Columbia 62236 April Becherer	PK-1		293	13% 618/281-4995 Fax 618/281-4775
Parkview Elem Sch 1 Veterans Pkwy, Columbia 62236 Bobby Dugan	2-4		398 40	12% 618/281-4997 Fax 618/281-3605

- **Valmeyer Cmty School Dist 3** PID: 00310908   618/935-2100
  300 S Cedar Bluff Dr, Valmeyer 62295   Fax 618/935-2108

> **Schools:** 1 \ **Teachers:** 35 \ **Students:** 430 \ **Special Ed Students:** 54
> \ **College-Bound:** 72% \ **Ethnic:** African American 2%, Hispanic 1%,
> Caucasian 97% \ **Exp:** $192 (Low) \ **Poverty:** 2% \ **Title I:** $11,388 \
> **Special Education:** $144,000 \ **Open-Close:** 08/13 - 05/18 \ **DTBP:** $200
> (High)

Eric Frankford 1,11,73
Lori Brutton 11,16,82*
Rebecca Karsten 58,69*
Sheryl Gean 274*
Elise Rolfing 7,83,85*
Chris Harness 16,73,295*
Virginia Rusteberg 67
Teena Riechmann 275*

Public Schs..Principal	Grd	Prgm	Enr/#Cls	SN
Valmeyer Sch 300 S Cedar Bluff Dr, Valmeyer 62295 Teena Riechmann \ Eric Frankford	PK-12		430 30	17% 618/935-2100

- **Waterloo Cmty Unit Sch Dist 5** PID: 00310934   618/939-3453
  302 Bellefontaine Dr, Waterloo 62298   Fax 618/939-4578

> **Schools:** 5 \ **Teachers:** 158 \ **Students:** 2,739 \ **Special Ed Students:** 421
> \ **LEP Students:** 3 \ **College-Bound:** 76% \ **Ethnic:** Hispanic 1%,
> Caucasian 98% \ **Exp:** $140 (Low) \ **Poverty:** 4% \ **Title I:** $112,428 \
> **Special Education:** $1,034,000 \ **Open-Close:** 08/19 - 05/26 \ **DTBP:** $197
> (High)

Brian Charron 1
Will Hewitt 3
Brian Unger 6
John Schmieg 8,11,51,286,288,296
Andy Mayer 16
John Caupert 67
Marla Byrd 2
Ruth Mason 4
Carolyn Sabo 7*
Mary Gardner 9*
Julie Bender 34,58
Nick Hergenroeder 73*

Public Schs..Principal	Grd	Prgm	Enr/#Cls	SN
Gardner Elem Sch 1 Ed Gardner Pl, Waterloo 62298 Jessica Washausen	4-5	T	431	20% 618/939-3060 Fax 618/939-3065
Rogers Elem Sch 200 Rogers St, Waterloo 62298 Brian Smith	2-3	T	366 24	19% 618/939-3454 Fax 618/939-7980
W J Zahnow Elem Sch 301 Hamacher St, Waterloo 62298 Mary Gardner	PK-1	T	436 30	20% 618/939-3458 Fax 618/939-1377

	Grd	Prgm	Enr/#Cls	SN
Waterloo High Sch 505 E Bulldog, Waterloo 62298 Lori Costello	9-12	GV	802 50	17% 618/939-3455 Fax 618/939-1373
Waterloo Junior High Sch 200 Bellefontaine Dr, Waterloo 62298 Nicholas Schwartz	6-8		632 30	23% 618/939-3457 Fax 618/939-1383

MONROE CATHOLIC SCHOOLS

- **Diocese of Belleville Ed Off** PID: 00317671
  Listing includes only schools located in this county. See District Index for
  location of Diocesan Offices.

Catholic Schs..Principal	Grd	Prgm	Enr/#Cls	SN
Gibault Catholic High Sch 501 Columbia Ave, Waterloo 62298 Stephen Kidd	9-12		247 30	618/939-3883 Fax 618/939-7215
Immaculate Conception Sch 409 Palmer Rd, Columbia 62236 Michael Kish	K-8		292 23	618/281-5353 Fax 618/281-6044
SS Peter & Paul Sch 217 W 3rd St, Waterloo 62298 Lori Matzenbacher	PK-8		332 20	618/939-7217 Fax 618/939-5994

MONROE REGIONAL CENTERS

- **Monroe-Randolph Reg Off** PID: 02098170   618/939-5650
  107 E Mill St, Waterloo 62298   Fax 618/939-5332

Kelton Davis 1,73
Christopher Diddlebock 15
Tricia Bockhorn 2
Tom Springborn 27,30

MONTGOMERY COUNTY

MONTGOMERY COUNTY SCHOOLS

County Schs..Principal	Grd	Prgm	Enr/#Cls	SN
Ⓐ Cornerstone Academy/Christmont 316 E South St, Nokomis 62075 Casey Adam	K-12		13 3	82% 217/563-7600 Fax 217/563-7606

MONTGOMERY PUBLIC SCHOOLS

- **Hillsboro Cmty Unit Sch Dist 3** PID: 00310996   217/532-2942
  1311 Vandalia Rd, Hillsboro 62049   Fax 217/532-3137

> **Schools:** 4 \ **Teachers:** 106 \ **Students:** 1,700 \ **Special Ed Students:** 282
> \ **LEP Students:** 3 \ **Ethnic:** African American 1%, Hispanic 3%,
> Caucasian 96% \ **Exp:** $199 (Low) \ **Poverty:** 15% \ **Title I:** $435,221 \
> **Special Education:** $578,000 \ **Open-Close:** 08/17 - 05/28 \ **DTBP:** $186
> (High)

David Powell 1
Nancy McDowell 2

Illinois School Directory — Montgomery County

Fred Butler 3
Marcy Gutierrez 34,88*
Greg Bellaver 67
Shawn Perkins 73*
Bobbi Lowe 7,83,85
Tim Morford 38*
Laura Butler 68
Sheri Reynolds 274

Public Schs..Principal	Grd	Prgm	Enr/#Cls	SN	
Beckemeyer Elem Sch 1035 Seymour Ave, Hillsboro 62049 Zachary Frailey	K-5	T	560 26	53%	217/532-6994 Fax 217/532-5153
Coffeen Elem Sch 200 School St, Coffeen 62017 Marcy Gutierrez	PK-PK	T	220 10	62%	217/534-2314 Fax 217/534-6088
Hillsboro High Sch 522 E Tremont St, Hillsboro 62049 Patty Heyen	9-12	T	519 45	35%	217/532-2841 Fax 217/532-5142
Hillsboro Junior High Sch 909 Rountree St, Hillsboro 62049 Don Van Giesen	6-8	T	350 20	48%	217/532-3742 Fax 217/532-6211

- **Litchfield Cmty Unit SD 12** PID: 00311108
  1702 N State St, Litchfield 62056
  217/324-2157
  Fax 217/324-2158

Schools: 6 \ Teachers: 97 \ Students: 1,450 \ Special Ed Students: 287 \ LEP Students: 4 \ College-Bound: 61% \ Ethnic: Asian 1%, African American 1%, Hispanic 2%, Caucasian 96% \ Exp: $348 (High) \ Poverty: 19% \ Title I: $470,881 \ Special Education: $400,000 \ Open-Close: 08/14 - 05/21

Dr Greggory Fuerstenau 1
Brett Holliday 3,4
Jeniffer Thompson 8,11,57*
Julie Abel 67
Della Witter 2
Mark Hunt 5,79
Paula Dal Canton 36,88*

Public Schs..Principal	Grd	Prgm	Enr/#Cls	SN	
J D Colt Elem Sch 615 E Tyler Ave, Litchfield 62056 Jeremy Heigert	2-3	T	194 9	64%	217/324-3565 Fax 217/324-3703
Litchfield High Sch 1705 N State St, Litchfield 62056 Doug Hoster	9-12	TV	389 41	58%	217/324-3955 Fax 217/324-5851
Litchfield Middle Sch 1701 N State St, Litchfield 62056 Russ Tepen	6-8	TV	337 30	55%	217/324-4668 Fax 217/324-5693
Litchfield Pre-K at Sihler Sch 601 S State St, Litchfield 62056 Adam Favre	PK-PK	T	104 5	46%	217/324-3652 Fax 217/324-2129
Madison Park Elem Sch 800 N Chestnut St, Litchfield 62056 Adam Favre	K-1	T	198 10	65%	217/324-2851 Fax 217/324-5562
Russell Elem Sch 705 N Jefferson St, Litchfield 62056 Jeremy Heigert	4-5	T	199 10	57%	217/324-4034 Fax 217/324-3977

- **Nokomis Cmty Unit Sch Dist 22** PID: 00311196
  511 Oberle St, Nokomis 62075
  217/563-7311
  Fax 217/563-2549

Schools: 2 \ Teachers: 45 \ Students: 630 \ Special Ed Students: 106 \ College-Bound: 62% \ Ethnic: Hispanic 2%, Caucasian 98% \ Exp: $277 (Med) \ Poverty: 23% \ Title I: $335,863 \ Special Education: $174,000 \ Open-Close: 08/18 - 06/22

Dr Scott Doerr 1
Monte Epley 5
Mike Miller 2,73,84
Chad Ruppert 67

Public Schs..Principal	Grd	Prgm	Enr/#Cls	SN	
Nokomis Jr Sr High Sch 511 Oberle St, Nokomis 62075 Rachelle McDowell	6-12	ATV	301 30	41%	217/563-2014 Fax 217/563-2671
North Elem Sch 110 W Hamilton St, Nokomis 62075 Kevin Reedy	PK-5		320 11	44%	217/563-8521 Fax 217/563-2675

- **Panhandle Cmty Unit SD 2** PID: 00311251
  509 N Prairie St, Raymond 62560
  217/229-4215
  Fax 217/229-4216

Schools: 3 \ Teachers: 42 \ Students: 520 \ Special Ed Students: 101 \ College-Bound: 78% \ Ethnic: Hispanic 1%, Caucasian 99% \ Exp: $261 (Med) \ Poverty: 10% \ Title I: $128,999 \ Special Education: $176,000 \ Open-Close: 08/19 - 05/31 \ DTBP: $156 (High)

Aaron Hopper 1,11,83
Josh Stone 6
Robert Straub 73,84
Donna Lemon 2
Terri Payne 67

Public Schs..Principal	Grd	Prgm	Enr/#Cls	SN	
Farmersville Grade Sch 407 Sedentop St, Farmersville 62533 Jana Masten	PK-1	T	96 6	21%	217/227-3306 Fax 217/227-3246
Lincolnwood Jr Sr High Sch 507 N Prairie St, Raymond 62560 Ken Schuster	6-12	T	254 17	51%	217/229-4237 Fax 217/229-3005
Raymond Grade Sch 505 N Prairie St, Raymond 62560 Ken Schuster	2-5	T	138 7	51%	217/229-3124 Fax 217/229-3037

MONTGOMERY CATHOLIC SCHOOLS

- **Diocese of Springfield Ed Off** PID: 00319394
  Listing includes only schools located in this county. See District Index for location of Diocesan Offices.

Catholic Schs..Principal	Grd	Prgm	Enr/#Cls	SN	
St Louis Sch 509 E Union St, Nokomis 62075 Elaine Wagner	K-8		77 5		217/563-7445 Fax 217/563-7450

MONTGOMERY PRIVATE SCHOOLS

Private Schs..Principal	Grd	Prgm	Enr/#Cls	SN	
Cornerstone Academy 316 E South St, Nokomis 62075 Casey Adam	Spec		100		217/563-7600 Fax 217/563-7606
Zion Lutheran Sch 1301 N State St, Litchfield 62056 Mark Lofink	PK-8		140 8		217/324-3166

MONTGOMERY REGIONAL CENTERS

- **Christian-Montgomery EFE Sys** PID: 04184309
  203 S Main St, Hillsboro 62049
  217/532-9591
  Fax 217/532-5756

Julie Wollerman 1

---

79 Student Personnel	91 Safety/Security	275 Response To Intervention	298 Grant Writer/Ptnrships	**School Programs**	**Social Media**	
80 Driver Ed/Safety	92 Magnet School	277 Remedial Math K-12	750 Chief Innovation Officer	A = Alternative Program	= Facebook	
81 Gifted/Talented	93 Parental Involvement	280 Literacy Coach	751 Chief of Staff	G = Adult Classes		
82 Video Services	95 Tech Prep Program	285 STEM	752 Social Emotional Learning	M = Magnet Program	= Twitter	
83 Substance Abuse Prev	97 Chief Infomation Officer	286 Digital Learning		T = Title I Schoolwide		
84 Erate	98 Chief Technology Officer	288 Common Core Standards	**Other School Types**	V = Career & Tech Ed Programs		
85 AIDS Education	270 Character Education	294 Accountability	Ⓐ = Alternative School			
88 Alternative/At Risk	271 Migrant Education	295 Network System	Ⓒ = Charter School	New Schools are shaded		
89 Multi-Cultural Curriculum	273 Teacher Mentor	296 Title II Programs	Ⓜ = Magnet School	New Superintendents and Principals are bold		
90 Social Work	274 Before/After Sch	297 Webmaster	Ⓨ = Year-Round School	Personnel with email addresses are underscored		

Morgan County

MORGAN COUNTY

MORGAN COUNTY SCHOOLS

County Schs..Principal	Grd	Prgm	Enr/#Cls	SN	
Four Rivers Sp Ed Ctr-Garrison 936 W Michigan Ave, Jacksonville 62650 Rhonda Massey	Spec	A	77 9	72%	217/245-7174 Fax 217/245-5533

MORGAN PUBLIC SCHOOLS

- **Franklin Cmty Unit SD 1** PID: 00311366   217/675-2395
  110 State, Franklin 62638   Fax 217/675-2396

  Schools: 3 \ **Teachers:** 30 \ **Students:** 290 \ **Special Ed Students:** 44 \ **LEP Students:** 3 \ **College-Bound:** 48% \ **Ethnic:** Hispanic 1%, Native American: 2%, Caucasian 97% \ **Exp:** $470 (High) \ **Poverty:** 18% \ **Title I:** $181,566 \ **Open-Close:** 08/21 - 06/01 \ **DTBP:** $178 (High)

Dr Curt Simonson 1	Kim Allen 2		
Darin Seymour 3	Bill Wallbaum 5		
Rick Smith 6*	Melissa Gerard 11*		
Wesley Koehler 16,73,286*	Greg Tabeek 36*		
Curt Reznicek 67			

Public Schs..Principal	Grd	Prgm	Enr/#Cls	SN	
Franklin East Grade Sch 412 Wyatt St, Franklin 62638 Christy Willman	PK-2		87 4	33%	217/675-2334
Franklin Elem Sch 110 State, Franklin 62638 Christy Willman	3-5		74 8		217/675-2395
Franklin Jr Sr High Sch 110 State, Franklin 62638 Jeff Waggener	6-12	V	147 30	33%	217/675-2395

- **Jacksonville School Dist 117** PID: 00311407   217/243-9411
  211 W State St, Jacksonville 62650   Fax 217/243-6844

  Schools: 9 \ **Teachers:** 234 \ **Students:** 3,200 \ **Special Ed Students:** 757 \ **LEP Students:** 87 \ **College-Bound:** 58% \ **Ethnic:** Asian 1%, African American 11%, Hispanic 4%, Caucasian 84% \ **Exp:** $373 (High) \ **Poverty:** 20% \ **Title I:** $1,373,253 \ **Special Education:** $1,966,000 \ **Bilingual Education:** $15,000 \ **Open-Close:** 08/24 - 05/24 \ **DTBP:** $196 (High) \

Steve Ptacek 1	Jamie Hadjan 2,19
Craig Castleberry 3,11	Joyce Hiler 4*
Brent Dunn 5	Ryan Vanaken 6
Kelly Zoellner 8	Mike McGiles 15,17
Bill Poole 16,28,73,76,84	Barbie Davidsmeyer 57,58,79,271
Noel Beard 67	Tami Stice 68

Public Schs..Principal	Grd	Prgm	Enr/#Cls	SN	
Early Years Program 516 Jordan St, Jacksonville 62650 Sarah English	PK-PK	T	181	46%	217/243-2876 Fax 217/243-0602
Eisenhower Elem Sch 1901 W Lafayette Ave, Jacksonville 62650 Beth Brockschmidt	K-6	T	338 17	42%	217/245-5107 Fax 217/243-2433
Jacksonville High Sch 1211 N Diamond St, Jacksonville 62650 Joey Dion	9-12	TV	971 60	48%	217/243-4384 Fax 217/245-0445
Jacksonville Middle Sch 664 Lincoln Ave, Jacksonville 62650 Gary Barlow	7-8	TV	515 55	58%	217/243-3383 Fax 217/243-3459
Lincoln Elem Sch 320 W Independence Ave, Jacksonville 62650 Sue Lovdahl	K-6	T	288 12	86%	217/245-8720 Fax 217/243-2757
Murrayville Woodson Elem Sch 307 Masters St, Murrayville 62668 Emily English	K-6	T	166 8	56%	217/882-3121 Fax 217/882-2302
North Elem Sch 1626 State Highway 78 N, Jacksonville 62650 Bobbie Mills	K-6	T	216 15	56%	217/245-4084 Fax 217/243-2818
South Elem Sch 1700 S West St, Jacksonville 62650 Tim Chipman	K-6	T	329 15	46%	217/245-5514 Fax 217/245-2804
Washington Elem Sch 524 S Kosciusko St, Jacksonville 62650 Mary Camerer	K-6	T	301 13	71%	217/243-6711 Fax 217/243-3055

- **Meredosia-Chambersburg SD 11** PID: 00311548   217/584-1744
  830 Main St, Meredosia 62665   Fax 217/584-1129

  Schools: 1 \ **Teachers:** 24 \ **Students:** 195 \ **Special Ed Students:** 44 \ **College-Bound:** 64% \ **Ethnic:** Caucasian 100% \ **Exp:** $336 (High) \ **Poverty:** 16% \ **Title I:** $74,984 \ **Special Education:** $56,000 \ **Open-Close:** 08/14 - 05/21

Thad Walker 1	Jerry Phillips 3*
Debbie Gregory 4*	Rob Windell 5*
Kirk Graham 6*	Jeff Abell 8,288*
Sheryl Session 11*	Jason Morton 67

Public Schs..Principal	Grd	Prgm	Enr/#Cls	SN	
Meredosia-Chambersberg Sch 830 Main St, Meredosia 62665 Jeff Abell \ Thad Walker	PK-12		195 25	51%	217/584-1291 Fax 217/584-1741

- **Triopia Cmty Unit Sch Dist 27** PID: 00311574   217/457-2283
  2204 Concord Arenzville Rd, Concord 62631   Fax 217/457-2297

  Schools: 2 \ **Teachers:** 33 \ **Students:** 382 \ **Special Ed Students:** 46 \ **LEP Students:** 3 \ **College-Bound:** 70% \ **Ethnic:** Hispanic 2%, Caucasian 98% \ **Exp:** $267 (Med) \ **Poverty:** 11% \ **Title I:** $52,733 \ **Special Education:** $92,000 \ **Open-Close:** 08/14 - 05/21 \ **DTBP:** $176 (High) \

Adam Dean 1,11,83	Theresa Langly 2
Roger Graves 3	Jamie Hobrock 16,73*
Linda Wilson 35,85*	Amanda Surratt 36,270*
Tracie Sayre 67	

Public Schs..Principal	Grd	Prgm	Enr/#Cls	SN	
Triopia Grade Sch 2206 Concord Arenzville Rd, Concord 62631 Jamie Hobrock	PK-6		202 13	29%	217/457-2284
Triopia Jr Sr High Sch 2204 Concord Arenzville Rd, Concord 62631 Josh Sorrells	7-12	V	180 15	37%	217/457-2281 Fax 217/457-2277

---

1 Superintendent	8 Curric/Instruct K-12	19 Chief Financial Officer	29 Family/Consumer Science	39 Social Studies K-12	49 English/Lang Arts Elem	59 Special Education Elem	69 Academic Assessment
2 Bus/Finance/Purchasing	9 Curric/Instruct Elem	20 Art K-12	30 Adult Education	40 Social Studies Elem	50 English/Lang Arts Sec	60 Special Education Sec	70 Research/Development
3 Buildings And Grounds	10 Curric/Instruct Sec	21 Art Elem	31 Career/Sch-to-Work K-12	41 Social Studies Sec	51 Reading K-12	61 Foreign/World Lang K-12	71 Public Information
4 Food Service	11 Federal Program	22 Art Sec	32 Career/Sch-to-Work Elem	42 Science K-12	52 Reading Elem	62 Foreign/World Lang Elem	72 Summer School
5 Transportation	12 Title I	23 Music K-12	33 Career/Sch-to-Work Sec	43 Science Elem	53 Reading Sec	63 Foreign/World Lang Sec	73 Instructional Tech
6 Athletic	13 Title V	24 Music Elem	34 Early Childhood Ed	44 Science Sec	54 Remedial Reading K-12	64 Religious Education K-12	74 Inservice Training
7 Health Services	15 Asst Superintendent	25 Music Sec	35 Health/Phys Education	45 Math K-12	55 Remedial Reading Elem	65 Religious Education Elem	75 Marketing/Distributive
	16 Instructional Media Svcs	26 Business Education	36 Guidance Services K-12	46 Math Elem	56 Remedial Reading Sec	66 Religious Education Sec	76 Info Systems
	17 Chief Operations Officer	27 Career & Tech Ed	37 Guidance Services Elem	47 Math Sec	57 Bilingual/ELL	67 School Board President	77 Psychological Assess
	18 Chief Academic Officer	28 Technology Education	38 Guidance Services Sec	48 English/Lang Arts K-12	58 Special Education K-12	68 Teacher Personnel	78 Affirmative Action

Illinois School Directory — Moultrie County

- **Waverly Cmty Unit SD 6** PID: 00311615   217/435-8121
  201 N Miller St, Waverly 62692   Fax 217/435-3431

Schools: 2 \ **Teachers:** 30 \ **Students:** 369 \ **Special Ed Students:** 65 \ **LEP Students:** 4 \ **College-Bound:** 58% \ **Ethnic:** Asian 2%, African American 1%, Hispanic 1%, Caucasian 96% \ **Exp:** $241 (Med) \ **Poverty:** 22% \ **Title I:** $135,573 \ **Special Education:** $80,000 \ **Open-Close:** 08/20 - 05/21 \ **DTBP:** $165 (High)

Dustin Day 1,11
Angie Jennings 5
James Roeschley 8,36,69*
Michelle Wagner 16*
Greg Nelson 73,76,286*
Lisa Nevius 2
Scott Hendricks 6*
Christie Green 12*
Mike Keeton 67

Public Schs..Principal	Grd	Prgm	Enr/#Cls	SN	
Waverly Elem Sch 499 W Elm St, Waverly 62692 Tammy Hermes	PK-6	T	204 17	36%	217/435-2331 Fax 217/435-2321
Waverly High Sch 201 N Miller St, Waverly 62692 Brian Cook	7-12	V	165 11	38%	217/435-2211

MORGAN CATHOLIC SCHOOLS

- **Diocese of Springfield Ed Off** PID: 00319394
  Listing includes only schools located in this county. See District Index for location of Diocesan Offices.

Catholic Schs..Principal	Grd	Prgm	Enr/#Cls	SN	
Our Saviour Sch 455 E State St, Jacksonville 62650 Stevie Vandevelde	K-8		216 13		217/243-8621 Fax 217/245-9981
Routt Catholic High Sch 500 E College Ave, Jacksonville 62650 Nick Roscetti	9-12		125 18		217/243-8563 Fax 217/243-3138

MORGAN PRIVATE SCHOOLS

Private Schs..Principal	Grd	Prgm	Enr/#Cls	SN	
Salem Lutheran Sch 222 E Beecher Ave, Jacksonville 62650	PK-8		162 8		217/243-3419 Fax 217/245-0289
Westfair Christian Academy 14 Clarke Dr, Jacksonville 62650 Randy Cooper	PK-12		100 10		217/243-7100 Fax 217/243-2386

MORGAN REGIONAL CENTERS

- **Four Rivers Spec Ed District** PID: 02182056   217/245-7174
  936 W Michigan Ave, Jacksonville 62650   Fax 217/245-5533

Chris Pennell 1   Valerie Hasting 74,77

- **Regional Office of Ed 1** PID: 02097475   217/243-1804
  110 N West St, Jacksonville 62650   Fax 217/243-5354

Jill Reis 1
Julie Stratman 15
Jeff Stephens 7,91

MOULTRIE COUNTY

MOULTRIE PUBLIC SCHOOLS

- **Okaw Valley Cmty Unit SD 302** PID: 00311653   217/665-3232
  709 S Saint John St, Bethany 61914   Fax 217/665-3601

Schools: 3 \ **Teachers:** 41 \ **Students:** 475 \ **Special Ed Students:** 53 \ **College-Bound:** 88% \ **Ethnic:** Caucasian 100% \ **Exp:** $292 (Med) \ **Poverty:** 10% \ **Title I:** $89,240 \ **Special Education:** $140,000 \ **Open-Close:** 08/17 - 05/21 \ **DTBP:** $179 (High) \ [f]

Kent Stauder 1,11
Jason Fleshner 3,5
Lara Macklin 16,73*
Tim Rothrock 67
Cindy Hauck 2
Brooks Inman 6*
Jennifer Crowder 58

Public Schs..Principal	Grd	Prgm	Enr/#Cls	SN	
Okaw Valley Elem Sch 319 N Washington St, Bethany 61914 Heidi Vander Burgh	PK-4	T	190 11	41%	217/665-3541 Fax 217/665-3511
Okaw Valley High Sch 709 S Saint John St, Bethany 61914 Matthew Shoaff	9-12		157 15	43%	217/665-3631 Fax 217/665-3863
Okaw Valley Middle Sch 501 W Division St, Findlay 62534 Ross Forlines	5-8	T	161 33	48%	217/756-8521 Fax 217/756-8599

- **Sullivan Cmty Unit SD 300** PID: 00311718   217/728-8341
  725 N Main St, Sullivan 61951   Fax 217/728-4139

Schools: 3 \ **Teachers:** 68 \ **Students:** 1,100 \ **Special Ed Students:** 152 \ **College-Bound:** 72% \ **Ethnic:** Asian 1%, African American 1%, Hispanic 2%, Caucasian 96% \ **Exp:** $195 (Low) \ **Poverty:** 12% \ **Title I:** $258,555 \ **Special Education:** $276,000 \ **Open-Close:** 08/17 - 05/27 \ **DTBP:** $174 (High)

Ted Walk 1
Kevin Landris 3,5
Ryan Aikman 6*
Jessica Reeder 11,34,57,58,72,273
Jeff White 67
Valerie Kalagian 73*
Nathan Ogle 275*
Christy Molzen 2,19
Jessica Keith 4
Brenda Moore 7*
Jackie Collins 31,36,270*
Mark Waelde 73,76,295
Stefanie Keifer 90

Public Schs..Principal	Grd	Prgm	Enr/#Cls	SN	
Sullivan Elem Sch 910 N Graham St, Sullivan 61951 Heather Ethell	PK-5	T	531 24	44%	217/728-2321 Fax 217/728-4399
Sullivan High Sch 725 N Main St, Sullivan 61951 Daniel Allen	9-12	TV	304 40	39%	217/728-8311
Sullivan Middle Sch 713 N Main St, Sullivan 61951 Nathan Ogle	6-8	T	250 12	47%	217/728-8381 Fax 217/728-4296

---

79 Student Personnel
80 Driver Ed/Safety
81 Gifted/Talented
82 Video Services
83 Substance Abuse Prev
84 Erate
85 AIDS Education
88 Alternative/At Risk
89 Multi-Cultural Curriculum
90 Social Work
91 Safety/Security
92 Magnet School
93 Parental Involvement
95 Tech Prep Program
97 Chief Information Officer
98 Chief Technology Officer
270 Character Education
271 Migrant Education
273 Teacher Mentor
274 Before/After Sch
275 Response To Intervention
277 Remedial Math K-12
280 Literacy Coach
285 STEM
286 Digital Learning
288 Common Core Standards
294 Accountability
295 Network System
296 Title II Programs
297 Webmaster
298 Grant Writer/Ptnrships
750 Chief Innovation Officer
751 Chief of Staff
752 Social Emotional Learning

Other School Types
Ⓐ = Alternative School
Ⓒ = Charter School
Ⓜ = Magnet School
Ⓨ = Year-Round School

School Programs
A = Alternative Program
G = Adult Classes
M = Magnet Program
T = Title I Schoolwide
V = Career & Tech Ed Programs

Social Media
[f] = Facebook
[t] = Twitter

New Schools are shaded
New Superintendents and Principals are bold
Personnel with email addresses are underscored

Ogle County

Market Data Retrieval

OGLE COUNTY

OGLE PUBLIC SCHOOLS

- **Byron Cmty Unit SD 226** PID: 00311768
  696 N Colfax St, Byron 61010
  815/234-5491
  Fax 815/234-4106

  Schools: 3 \ Teachers: 116 \ Students: 1,523 \ Special Ed Students: 265 \ LEP Students: 8 \ College-Bound: 62% \ Ethnic: Asian 1%, African American 1%, Hispanic 7%, Caucasian 91% \ Exp: $413 (High) \ Poverty: 5% \ Title I: $112,226 \ Special Education: $744,000 \ Open-Close: 08/19 - 05/27 \ DTBP: $176 (High)

  Buster Barton 1,57
  Tania Vanbriesen 4
  Jim Kann 6*
  Janelle Smith 58*
  Amy Adkins 68
  Terry Wilken 73,76*
  Christian Kerr 2
  Steve Walters 5
  Jill Smith 16*
  Christine Lynde 67
  Jay Mullins 69,72,83*

Public Schs..Principal	Grd	Prgm	Enr/#Cls	SN		
Byron High Sch 696 N Colfax St, Byron 61010 Jay Mullins	9-12	V	465 48	27%	815/234-5491 Fax 815/234-2045	
Byron Middle Sch 850 N Colfax St, Byron 61010 Zack Ettelbrick	6-8		333 30	25%	815/234-5491 Fax 815/234-4225	📧
Mary Morgan Elem Sch 420 N Colfax St, Byron 61010 Steve Stewart	PK-5		725 32	22%	815/234-5491 Fax 815/234-4094	

- **Creston Cmty Cons Sch Dist 161** PID: 00311809
  202 W South St, Creston 60113
  815/384-3920
  Fax 815/384-3410

  Schools: 1 \ Teachers: 11 \ Students: 88 \ Special Ed Students: 12 \ Ethnic: African American 5%, Hispanic 20%, Caucasian 76% \ Exp: $190 (Low) \ Poverty: 5% \ Special Education: $23,000 \ Open-Close: 08/14 - 05/21 \ DTBP: $174 (High)

  Curt Rheingans 1,84
  Lisa Hohlfeld 59*
  Karen Collins 2
  Miriah Ranken 67

Public Schs..Principal	Grd	Prgm	Enr/#Cls	SN	
Creston Elem Sch 202 W South St, Creston 60113 Dr Bill Robertson	K-8	T	88 12	42%	815/384-3920 Fax 815/381-3410

- **Eswood Cmty Cons SD 269** PID: 00311823
  304 Main St, Lindenwood 61049
  815/393-4477
  Fax 815/393-4478

  Schools: 1 \ Teachers: 8 \ Students: 68 \ Special Ed Students: 17 \ LEP Students: 4 \ Ethnic: Hispanic 17%, Caucasian 83% \ Exp: $314 (High) \ Poverty: 13% \ Title I: $29,145 \ Special Education: $141,000 \ Open-Close: 08/14 - 05/21 \ DTBP: $214 (High)

  Joe Schwartz 1,11,83
  Christine Schweitzer 67
  Erin Whitehead 2

Public Schs..Principal	Grd	Prgm	Enr/#Cls	SN	
Eswood Cmty Cons Grade Sch 304 Main St, Lindenwood 61049 Joe Schwartz	PK-8		68 12	47%	815/393-4477

- **Forrestville Valley CUSD 221** PID: 00311859
  601 E Main St, Forreston 61030
  815/938-2036
  Fax 815/938-9028

  Schools: 3 \ Teachers: 52 \ Students: 750 \ Special Ed Students: 150 \ LEP Students: 3 \ College-Bound: 65% \ Ethnic: Asian 1%, African American 1%, Hispanic 3%, Caucasian 95% \ Exp: $226 (Med) \ Poverty: 9% \ Title I: $106,250 \ Special Education: $261,000 \ Open-Close: 08/19 - 05/25

  Sheri Smith 1,11
  Kyle Zick 6,8*
  Jonathan Schneiderman 8
  Kim Snider 16*
  Tom Hartman 73,84
  Linda Beetz 2
  Christy Garnhart 8
  Travis Heinzes 8
  John Reining 67
  Christine Bergin 79

Public Schs..Principal	Grd	Prgm	Enr/#Cls	SN	
Forreston Grade Sch 401 S 1st Ave, Forreston 61030 Jonathan Schneiderman	K-5		325 25	40%	815/938-2301 Fax 815/938-2471
Forreston Jr Sr High Sch 601 E Main St, Forreston 61030 Travis Heinz	6-12	V	430 25	32%	815/938-2175 Fax 815/938-2546
German Valley Grade Sch 200 N Rock City Rd, German Valley 61039 Jonathan Schneiderman	PK-1		142 8	20%	815/362-2279 Fax 815/362-2235

- **Kings Cons School District 144** PID: 00311902
  100 1st St, Kings 61068
  815/562-7191
  Fax 815/562-5405

  Schools: 1 \ Teachers: 12 \ Students: 90 \ Special Ed Students: 17 \ Ethnic: Hispanic 5%, Caucasian 95% \ Exp: $242 (Med) \ Poverty: 8% \ Title I: $3,341 \ Special Education: $21,000 \ Open-Close: 08/18 - 05/21

  Matt Lamb 1,11
  Rich Pelka 5,91
  Nicole Adamski 67
  Jodi Horn 2
  Kim Dewey 12
  Tammy Greene 270*

Public Schs..Principal	Grd	Prgm	Enr/#Cls	SN	
Kings Sch 100 1st St, Kings 61068 Matt Lamb	K-8		90 9	43%	815/562-7191

- **Meridian Cmty Unit SD 223** PID: 00311940
  207 W Main St, Stillman Vly 61084
  815/645-2230
  Fax 815/645-4325

  Schools: 4 \ Teachers: 103 \ Students: 1,614 \ Special Ed Students: 218 \ LEP Students: 52 \ College-Bound: 68% \ Ethnic: African American 1%, Hispanic 12%, Caucasian 87% \ Exp: $206 (Med) \ Poverty: 9% \ Title I: $229,448 \ Special Education: $452,000 \ Bilingual Education: $20,000 \ Open-Close: 08/18 - 05/20 \ DTBP: $166 (High)

  Dr Phillip Caposey 1
  Ken Lamer 3
  Jen Hagemann 5
  Kayla McKinney 7,83,85*
  Mary Ortgiesen 2
  Lisa Reber 4
  Perky Ruggeberg 5
  John Smith 67

1	Superintendent	8	Curric/Instruct K-12	19	Chief Financial Officer	29	Family/Consumer Science	39	Social Studies K-12	49	English/Lang Arts Elem	59	Special Education Elem	69	Academic Assessment
2	Bus/Finance/Purchasing	9	Curric/Instruct Elem	20	Art K-12	30	Adult Education	40	Social Studies Elem	50	English/Lang Arts Sec	60	Special Education Sec	70	Research/Development
3	Buildings And Grounds	10	Curric/Instruct Sec	21	Art Elem	31	Career/Sch-to-Work K-12	41	Social Studies Sec	51	Reading K-12	61	Foreign/World Lang K-12	71	Public Information
4	Food Service	11	Federal Program	22	Art Sec	32	Career/Sch-to-Work Elem	42	Science K-12	52	Reading Elem	62	Foreign/World Lang Elem	72	Summer School
5	Transportation	12	Title I	23	Music K-12	33	Career/Sch-to-Work Sec	43	Science Elem	53	Reading Sec	63	Foreign/World Lang Sec	73	Instructional Tech
6	Athletic	13	Title V	24	Music Elem	34	Early Childhood Ed	44	Science Sec	54	Remedial Reading K-12	64	Religious Education K-12	74	Inservice Training
7	Health Services	14	Instructional Media Svcs	25	Music Sec	35	Health/Phys Education	45	Math K-12	55	Remedial Reading Elem	65	Religious Education Elem	75	Marketing/Distributive
		15	Asst Superintendent	26	Business Education	36	Guidance Services K-12	46	Math Elem	56	Remedial Reading Sec	66	Religious Education Sec	76	Info Systems
		16	Chief Operations Officer	27	Career & Tech Ed	37	Guidance Services Elem	47	Math Sec	57	Bilingual/ELL	67	School Board President	77	Psychological Assess
		18	Chief Academic Officer	28	Technology Education	38	Guidance Services Sec	48	English/Lang Arts K-12	58	Special Education K-12	68	Teacher Personnel	78	Affirmative Action

Illinois School Directory — Ogle County

Public Schs..Principal	Grd	Prgm	Enr/#Cls	SN	
Highland Elem Sch 410 S Hickory St, Stillman Vly 61084 Joe Mullikin	PK-2	T	342 19	23%	815/645-8188 Fax 815/645-8200
Meridian Junior High Sch 207 W Main St, Stillman Vly 61084 Jill Davis	6-8		386 23	25%	815/645-2277 Fax 815/645-8181 f t
Monroe Center Elem Sch 17500 E Il Route 72, Monroe Center 61052 Deana Simpson	3-5	T	319 21	37%	815/393-4424 Fax 815/393-4530
Stillman Valley High Sch 425 S Pine St, Stillman Vly 61084 Leslie Showers	9-12	V	567 40	21%	815/645-2291 Fax 815/645-8145 f t

• **Oregon Cmty Unit Sch Dist 220** PID: 00312035
206 S 10th St, Oregon 61061
815/732-5300
Fax 815/732-2187

> **Schools:** 3 \ **Teachers:** 92 \ **Students:** 1,461 \ **Special Ed Students:** 205
> \ **LEP Students:** 17 \ **College-Bound:** 55% \ **Ethnic:** Asian 1%,
> African American 1%, Hispanic 11%, Caucasian 87% \ **Exp:** $115 (Low)
> \ **Poverty:** 12% \ **Title I:** $312,510 \ **Special Education:** $638,000 \
> **Open-Close:** 08/13 - 05/19 \ **DTBP:** $174 (High)

Dr Thomas Mahoney 1,11,83   Marty Boyd 4*
Adam Larsen .... 15*   Bryan Wills 67
Shawn Gadow 73,295

Public Schs..Principal	Grd	Prgm	Enr/#Cls	SN	
David L Rahn Junior High Sch 105 W Brayton Rd, Mount Morris 61054 Kip Crandall	7-8	T	208 25	40%	815/732-5300 Fax 815/732-7129
Oregon Elem Sch 1150 Jefferson St, Oregon 61061 Kelli Virgil	PK-6		792 19	46%	815/732-2181 Fax 815/732-6108
Oregon High Sch 210 S 10th St, Oregon 61061 Heidi Deininger	9-12	AV	398 50	39%	815/732-5300 Fax 815/732-3361

• **Polo Cmty Unit Sch Dist 222** PID: 00312102
100 S Union Ave, Polo 61064
815/946-3815
Fax 815/734-3636

> **Schools:** 3 \ **Teachers:** 47 \ **Students:** 603 \ **Special Ed Students:** 78
> \ **College-Bound:** 59% \ **Ethnic:** African American 1%, Hispanic 5%,
> Caucasian 94% \ **Exp:** $194 (Low) \ **Poverty:** 11% \ **Title I:** $128,904 \
> **Special Education:** $151,000 \ **Open-Close:** 08/21 - 06/03 \ **DTBP:** $174
> (High)

Dr Kelly Mandrell 1,11,83   Christina Kitson 2
Betty Miller .... 4*   Christine Shenefelt 4
Mark Downey .... 5*   Ted Alston 6*
Brenda Rhodes 7   Beth Wiegmann 8,273*
Melydi Huyett .... 11*   Jill Blake 16*
Angelia Faller 36,69   Yancy Webster 67
Dan Baker .... 73,295*   Leslie Butler 73
Nina Setchell 752

Public Schs..Principal	Grd	Prgm	Enr/#Cls	SN	
Aplington Middle Sch 610 E Mason St, Polo 61064 Mark Downey	6-8	T	141 13	46%	815/946-2519 Fax 815/734-3643
Centennial Elem Sch 308 S Pleasant Ave, Polo 61064 Melydi Huyett	PK-5		291 14	50%	815/946-3811 Fax 815/734-3707
Polo Cmty High Sch 100 S Union Ave, Polo 61064 Andy Faivre	9-12	T	171 35	43%	815/946-3314

• **Rochelle Cmty Cons SD 231** PID: 00312176
1401 Flagg Rd, Rochelle 61068
815/562-6363
Fax 815/562-6693

> **Schools:** 5 \ **Teachers:** 116 \ **Students:** 1,600 \ **Special Ed Students:** 273
> \ **LEP Students:** 342 \ **Ethnic:** Asian 1%, African American 2%, Hispanic
> 46%, Caucasian 51% \ **Exp:** $143 (Low) \ **Poverty:** 12% \ **Title I:** $310,399
> \ **Special Education:** $632,000 \ **Bilingual Education:** $80,000 \
> **Open-Close:** 08/24 - 05/27 \ **DTBP:** $170 (High)

Jason Harper 1   Kevin Bell 2
Lester Davis 3   Lora Matcalf 4
Rick Dornick 6   Tony Doyle 9,11,15,69,88,288,298
Celeste Canfield 57   Dave Casey 67
Mike Burchfield 73,76,297

Public Schs..Principal	Grd	Prgm	Enr/#Cls	SN	
Central Elem Sch 444 N 8th St, Rochelle 61068 Celeste Canfield	K-5	T	274 17	6%	815/562-8251 Fax 815/562-5993 f
Lincoln Elem Sch 1450 20th St, Rochelle 61068 Justin Adolph	PK-5	T	434 20	6%	815/562-4520 Fax 815/561-1005
May Elem Sch 1033 N 2nd St, Rochelle 61068 Becky Cox	K-5	T	202 15	9%	815/562-6331 Fax 815/562-2430
Rochelle Middle Sch 111 School Ave, Rochelle 61068 Jordan Young	6-8	T	530 36	8%	815/562-7997 Fax 815/562-8527
Tilton Elem Sch 1050 N 9th St, Rochelle 61068 Jennifer Derricks	K-5	T	219 12	8%	815/562-6665 Fax 815/562-2607

• **Rochelle Twp High Sch Dist 212** PID: 00312152
1401 Flagg Rd, Rochelle 61068
815/562-4161
Fax 815/562-6693

> **Schools:** 1 \ **Teachers:** 54 \ **Students:** 900 \ **Special Ed Students:** 145
> \ **LEP Students:** 79 \ **Ethnic:** African American 2%, Hispanic 35%,
> Caucasian 62% \ **Exp:** $215 (Med) \ **Poverty:** 9% \ **Title I:** $140,912 \
> **Special Education:** $270,000 \ **Bilingual Education:** $6,000 \
> **Open-Close:** 08/14 - 05/19 \ **DTBP:** $182 (High)

Jason Harper 1   Kevin Dale 2,11*
Mark Klouse .... 3*   Sherri Smith 5
Richard Harvey 6   Jacquline Johnson 7
Dr David Perrin 10,69,79,273,288   Danae White 12*
Ann Marie Jinkins .... 16*   Laurie Pillen 38,69*
Erin Bergeson 60   Thomas Huddleston 67
William Wise 73,76*

Public Schs..Principal	Grd	Prgm	Enr/#Cls	SN	
Rochelle Twp High Sch 1401 Flagg Rd, Rochelle 61068 Christopher Lewis	9-12	ATV	900 55	25%	815/562-4161

OGLE PRIVATE SCHOOLS

Private Schs..Principal	Grd	Prgm	Enr/#Cls	SN	
St Paul Lutheran Sch 1415 10th Ave, Rochelle 61068 Steve Hall	PK-8		164 10		815/562-6323 Fax 815/561-8074

---

79 Student Personnel
80 Driver Ed/Safety
81 Gifted/Talented
82 Video Services
83 Substance Abuse Prev
84 Erate
85 AIDS Education
88 Alternative/At Risk
89 Multi-Cultural Curriculum
90 Social Work

91 Safety/Security
92 Magnet School
93 Parental Involvement
95 Tech Prep Program
97 Chief Infomation Officer
98 Chief Technology Officer
270 Character Education
271 Migrant Education
273 Teacher Mentor
274 Before/After Sch

275 Response To Intervention
277 Remedial Math K-12
280 Literacy Coach
285 STEM
286 Digital Learning
288 Common Core Standards
294 Accountability
295 Network System
296 Title II Programs
297 Webmaster

298 Grant Writer/Ptnrships
750 Chief Innovation Officer
751 Chief of Staff
752 Social Emotional Learning

Other School Types
Ⓐ = Alternative School
Ⓒ = Charter School
Ⓜ = Magnet School
Ⓨ = Year-Round School

School Programs
A = Alternative Program
G = Adult Classes
M = Magnet Program
T = Title I Schoolwide
V = Career & Tech Ed Programs

New Schools are shaded
New Superintendents and Principals are bold
Personnel with email addresses are underscored

Social Media
f = Facebook
t = Twitter

Peoria County

Market Data Retrieval

OGLE REGIONAL CENTERS

- **Ogle Co Educational Co-op** PID: 02228997   815/234-2722
  417 N Colfax St, Byron 61010   Fax 815/234-2938
  Matt Zilm 1   Amy Henkel 15

PEORIA COUNTY

PEORIA PUBLIC SCHOOLS

- **Bartonville School District 66** PID: 00312243   309/697-3253
  6000 S Adams St, Bartonville 61607   Fax 309/697-3254

Schools: 1 \ **Teachers:** 22 \ **Students:** 300 \ **Special Ed Students:** 61 \ **LEP Students:** 3 \ **Ethnic:** Asian 1%, African American 10%, Hispanic 3%, Native American: 1%, Caucasian 85% \ **Exp:** $255 (Med) \ **Poverty:** 20% \ **Title I:** $76,104 \ **Special Education:** $54,000 \ **Open-Close:** 08/21 - 05/26

Dr Lan Eberle 1   Peggy Scidham 2
Gary Carr .... 3*   Lori Cowan 4*
Randy Westerdahl .... 6*   Wes McGownd 16*
Nick Hefkett 67

Public Schs..Principal	Grd	Prgm	Enr/#Cls	SN	
Bartonville Elem Sch 6000 S Adams St, Bartonville 61607 Brad Jockisch	PK-8	T	300 23	63%	309/697-3253

- **Brimfield Cmty Unit SD 309** PID: 00312293   309/446-3378
  323 E Clinton St, Brimfield 61517   Fax 309/446-9962

Schools: 2 \ **Teachers:** 47 \ **Students:** 680 \ **Special Ed Students:** 79 \ **College-Bound:** 77% \ **Ethnic:** Asian 1%, Hispanic 1%, Caucasian 98% \ **Exp:** $170 (Low) \ **Poverty:** 5% \ **Title I:** $60,845 \ **Special Education:** $145,000 \ **Open-Close:** 08/19 - 05/28

Tony Shinall 1   Kevin Kreiter 6*
Lonna Sumner .... 7*   Kelly Walker 12,73
John Thompson 67   Jamie Henson 76

Public Schs..Principal	Grd	Prgm	Enr/#Cls	SN	
Brimfield Grade Sch 216 E Clinton St, Brimfield 61517 Julie Albritton	PK-8		436 25	13%	309/446-3366 Fax 309/446-9500
Brimfield High Sch 323 E Clinton St, Brimfield 61517 Mr Robison	9-12	V	232 20	15%	309/446-3349 Fax 309/446-3716

- **Dunlap Cmty Unit Sch Dist 323** PID: 00312322   309/691-3955
  3020 W Willow Knolls Dr Ste 3, Peoria 61614   Fax 309/691-6764

Schools: 8 \ **Teachers:** 262 \ **Students:** 4,500 \ **Special Ed Students:** 563 \ **LEP Students:** 286 \ **College-Bound:** 87% \ **Ethnic:** Asian 23%, African American 7%, Hispanic 4%, Caucasian 66% \ **Exp:** $153 (Low) \ **Poverty:** 6% \ **Title I:** $384,002 \ **Special Education:** $1,166,000 \ **Bilingual Education:** $83,000 \ **Open-Close:** 08/17 - 05/28 \ **DTBP:** $206 (High) \

Dr Scott Dearman 1   Damon Hackett 2,11,15,19,68,83
Tom Grimm 3   Lisa Leitner 4*
James Barrett 5   Katie Cazalet 6*
Matthew Anderews 8,69,288   Kim Klokkenga 38*
Alyssa Hart 57,58,79,90   Dr Abby Humbles 67
Beatriz Leyva-Cutler 73   Jeremy Etnyre 88*

Public Schs..Principal	Grd	Prgm	Enr/#Cls	SN	
Banner Elem Sch 12610 N Allen Rd, Dunlap 61525 Greg Fairchild	PK-5		351 16	14%	309/243-7774 Fax 309/243-7775
Dunlap Grade Sch 301 S 1st St, Dunlap 61525 Mandy Ellis	PK-5		244 13	12%	309/243-7772 Fax 309/243-5267
Dunlap High Sch 5220 W Legion Hall Rd, Dunlap 61525 Scott Adreon	9-12	V	1,274 35	13%	309/243-7751 Fax 309/243-9565
Dunlap Middle Sch 5200 W Cedar Hills Dr, Dunlap 61525 Antonio Johnson	6-8		693 27	13%	309/243-7778 Fax 309/243-1136
Dunlap Valley Middle Sch 13120 N State Route 91, Dunlap 61525 Jason Holmes	6-8		378	18%	309/243-1034 Fax 309/243-5358
Hickory Grove Elem Sch 2514 W Hickory Grove Rd, Dunlap 61525 Jeremy Etnyre	PK-5		686	7%	309/243-8711 Fax 309/243-1075
Ridgeview Elem Sch 3903 W Ridgeview Dr, Peoria 61615 Todd Jefferson	PK-5	T	420 21	29%	309/243-7717 Fax 309/692-8357
Wilder-Waite Elem Sch 10021 N Pacific St, Peoria 61615 Stacy Berg	PK-5		368 15	20%	309/243-7728 Fax 309/243-5272

- **Elmwood Cmty Unit Sch Dist 322** PID: 00312360   309/742-8464
  301 W Butternut St, Elmwood 61529   Fax 309/742-8812

Schools: 2 \ **Teachers:** 46 \ **Students:** 700 \ **Special Ed Students:** 89 \ **College-Bound:** 85% \ **Ethnic:** African American 2%, Hispanic 3%, Caucasian 96% \ **Exp:** $111 (Low) \ **Poverty:** 8% \ **Title I:** $87,888 \ **Special Education:** $154,000 \ **Open-Close:** 08/18 - 05/26 \ **DTBP:** $193 (High) \

Dr Chad Wagner 1,11   Sherri Swindler 2
Joe Harkness 3   Shanna Swadinsky 4
Chuck Vermillion .... 6*   Tony McCoy 10,27,60,270,273*
Rusty Koll .... 12,88,296,298*   Dr Dean Cantu 67
Caleb Wadell .... 73,286*   Cheryl Whitehurst 274*
Sandi Cross 752

Public Schs..Principal	Grd	Prgm	Enr/#Cls	SN	
Elmwood Elem Sch 501 N Morgan St, Elmwood 61529 Dimitri Almasi	PK-6	T	377 23	24%	309/742-4261 Fax 309/742-8833
Elmwood Jr Sr High Sch 301 W Butternut St, Elmwood 61529 Tony McCoy	7-12	V	307 29	17%	309/742-2851 Fax 309/742-8350

1	Superintendent	8	Curric/Instruct K-12	19	Chief Financial Officer	29	Family/Consumer Science	39	Social Studies K-12	49	English/Lang Arts Elem	59	Special Education Elem	69	Academic Assessment
2	Bus/Finance/Purchasing	9	Curric/Instruct Elem	20	Art K-12	30	Adult Education	40	Social Studies Elem	50	English/Lang Arts Sec	60	Special Education Sec	70	Research/Development
3	Buildings And Grounds	10	Curric/Instruct Sec	21	Art Elem	31	Career/Sch-to-Work K-12	41	Social Studies Sec	51	Reading K-12	61	Foreign/World Lang K-12	71	Public Information
4	Food Service	11	Federal Program	22	Art Sec	32	Career/Sch-to-Work Elem	42	Science K-12	52	Reading Elem	62	Foreign/World Lang Elem	72	Summer School
5	Transportation	12	Title I	23	Music K-12	33	Career/Sch-to-Work Sec	43	Science Elem	53	Reading Sec	63	Foreign/World Lang Sec	73	Instructional Tech
6	Athletic	13	Title V	24	Music Elem	34	Early Childhood Ed	44	Science Sec	54	Remedial Reading K-12	64	Religious Education K-12	74	Inservice Training
7	Health Services	14	Asst Superintendent	25	Music Sec	35	Health/Phys Education	45	Math K-12	55	Remedial Reading Elem	65	Religious Education Elem	75	Marketing/Distributive
		15	Instructional Media Svcs	26	Business Education	36	Guidance Services K-12	46	Math Elem	56	Remedial Reading Sec	66	Religious Education Sec	76	Info Systems
		16	Chief Operations Officer	27	Career & Tech Ed	37	Guidance Services Elem	47	Math Sec	57	Bilingual/ELL	67	School Board President	77	Psychological Assess
		18	Chief Academic Officer	28	Technology Education	38	Guidance Services Sec	48	English/Lang Arts K-12	58	Special Education K-12	68	Teacher Personnel	78	Affirmative Action

Illinois School Directory — Peoria County

• **Farmington Ctl Cmty SD 265** PID: 00293568 309/245-1000
212 N Lightfoot Rd, Farmington 61531 Fax 309/245-9161

Schools: 3 \ **Teachers:** 92 \ **Students:** 1,425 \ **Special Ed Students:** 179 \ **College-Bound:** 83% \ **Ethnic:** Hispanic 2%, Caucasian 97% \ **Exp:** $98 (Low) \ **Poverty:** 10% \ **Title I:** $190,649 \ **Special Education:** $401,000 \ **Open-Close:** 08/14 - 05/21 \ **DTBP:** $233 (High)

Name	Codes
Zack Chaterton	1
Jeff Flater	6
Denise Strobe-Piper	11,296,298
Kerry Klesath	58
Clint Matthewson	73
Christy Garlish	2
Missy Ryba	8,11,57,58,294*
Ryan Lambert	16,286
Chad Johnson	67
Toby Vallace	288

Public Schs..Principal	Grd	Prgm	Enr/#Cls	SN	
Farmington Central Elem Sch 108 N Lightfoot Rd, Farmington 61531 Missy Ryba	PK-5	T	625 35	39%	309/245-1000 Fax 309/245-9165
Farmington Central High Sch 310 N Lightfoot Rd, Farmington 61531 Dennis McMillin	9-12	TV	419 31	39%	309/245-1000 Fax 309/245-9163
Farmington Central Jr High Sch 300 N Lightfoot Rd, Farmington 61531 Chris Uptmor	6-8	T	293	42%	309/245-1000 Fax 309/245-9162

• **Hollis Cons School Dist 328** PID: 00312401 309/697-1325
5613 W Tuscarora Rd, Peoria 61607 Fax 309/697-1334

Schools: 1 \ **Teachers:** 13 \ **Students:** 135 \ **Special Ed Students:** 17 \ **Ethnic:** Hispanic 2%, Native American: 2%, Caucasian 96% \ **Exp:** $170 (Low) \ **Poverty:** 8% \ **Special Education:** $17,000 \ **Open-Close:** 08/13 - 05/26 \ **DTBP:** $217 (High)

Name	Codes
Chad Jones	1,11
Rebecca Gall	12*
Shawn Lindsay	73
Tonya Kalister	274*
Diane Kirkley	2
Josh Sheckler	67
Alisha Schoedel	270*

Public Schs..Principal	Grd	Prgm	Enr/#Cls	SN	
Hollis Consolidated Grade Sch 5613 W Tuscarora Rd, Peoria 61607 Chad Jones	K-8		135 9	17%	309/697-1325

• **Illini Bluffs Cmty Unit SD 327** PID: 00312425 309/389-2231
9611 S Hanna City Glasford Rd, Glasford 61533 Fax 309/389-2251

Schools: 3 \ **Teachers:** 63 \ **Students:** 909 \ **Special Ed Students:** 141 \ **College-Bound:** 81% \ **Ethnic:** African American 1%, Hispanic 3%, Caucasian 96% \ **Exp:** $226 (Med) \ **Poverty:** 7% \ **Title I:** $104,113 \ **Special Education:** $222,000 \ **Open-Close:** 08/17 - 05/25

Name	Codes
Dr Roger Alvey	1
Jim Mohn	3,5
Steve Schafer	6*
Chris Coats	67
Melissa Brown	2
Trudy Heitzman	4*
Cody Martzluf	16,73,84
Courtney Klinedinst	69,83*

Public Schs..Principal	Grd	Prgm	Enr/#Cls	SN	
Illini Bluffs Elem Sch 9611 S Hanna City Glasford Rd, Glasford 61533 Janet Huene	PK-5		440 23	25%	309/389-5025 Fax 309/389-5027
Illini Bluffs High Sch 9611 S Hanna City Glasford Rd, Glasford 61533 Keith Brown	9-12	V	252 30	29%	309/389-5681 Fax 309/389-5682
Illini Bluffs Middle Sch 212 N Saylor St, Glasford 61533 Karen Peterson	6-8		217 8	29%	309/389-3451 Fax 309/389-3454

• **Illinois Vly Ctl Sch Dist 321** PID: 00312504 309/274-5418
1300 W Sycamore St, Chillicothe 61523 Fax 309/274-5046

Schools: 5 \ **Teachers:** 139 \ **Students:** 2,173 \ **Special Ed Students:** 364 \ **LEP Students:** 14 \ **College-Bound:** 78% \ **Ethnic:** Asian 1%, African American 2%, Hispanic 5%, Caucasian 93% \ **Exp:** $228 (Med) \ **Poverty:** 10% \ **Title I:** $333,974 \ **Special Education:** $799,000 \ **Open-Close:** 08/14 - 05/28 \ **DTBP:** $234 (High) \ t

Name	Codes
Chad Allison	1
Tim Dixon	3
Dan Camp	6
Jennifer Freeman	57,58
Nick McMillion	71
Adam Bussard	2,7,15,295
Bob Howell	5
Brooke Geltmaker	8,11,288,298
Michael Birch	67
Dawn Cohenour	73

Public Schs..Principal	Grd	Prgm	Enr/#Cls	SN	
Chillicothe Jr High & Elem Ctr 914 W Truitt Ave, Chillicothe 61523 Joe Gallo	4-8	T	438 25	41%	309/274-6266 Fax 309/274-2010
Illinois Valley Central HS 1300 W Sycamore St, Chillicothe 61523 Kenton Bergman	9-12	TV	598 50	31%	309/274-5481 Fax 309/274-8613 t
ⓐ Ivc Learning Center 1057 N 2nd St, Chillicothe 61523 Mr Auge	9-12	G	24	58%	309/274-0001
Mossville Jr High & Elem Sch 12207 N Galena Rd, Mossville 61552 Patrick Sell	PK-8	T	605 45	30%	309/579-2328 Fax 309/579-2168 t
South Elem Sch 616 W Hickory St, Chillicothe 61523 Shaun Grant	PK-3	T	432 16	46%	309/274-4841 Fax 309/274-9715 t

• **Limestone Cmty High SD 310** PID: 00312578 309/697-6271
4201 Airport Rd, Bartonville 61607 Fax 309/697-9635

Schools: 2 \ **Teachers:** 70 \ **Students:** 1,000 \ **Special Ed Students:** 171 \ **LEP Students:** 3 \ **College-Bound:** 75% \ **Ethnic:** Asian 1%, African American 12%, Hispanic 4%, Caucasian 83% \ **Exp:** $370 (High) \ **Poverty:** 13% \ **Title I:** $237,066 \ **Special Education:** $833,000 \ **Open-Close:** 08/13 - 05/21 \ **DTBP:** $219 (High)

Name	Codes
Allen Gresham	1
Laurie Fas	4*
Charlie Zimmerman	11,38,60,273*
Jennifer Campbell	16,82
Eugene Sanders	67
Rusty Russell	3
Brian Clausen	6*
Denise Ryder	12,15*
Jonathon Frederick	16,73*
Stephanie Decker	69*

Public Schs..Principal	Grd	Prgm	Enr/#Cls	SN	
Limestone Cmty High Sch 4201 Airport Rd, Bartonville 61607 Jerolee Look	9-12	AGTV	944 71	41%	309/697-6271 f
ⓐ Peoria Co Juvenile Det Center 223 N Maxwell Rd, Peoria 61604 Teresa Rusk	5-12		10 3		309/634-4200 Fax 309/634-4222

---

79 Student Personnel	91 Safety/Security	275 Response To Intervention	298 Grant Writer/Ptnrships	**School Programs**	**Social Media**
80 Driver Ed/Safety	92 Magnet School	277 Remedial Math K-12	750 Chief Innovation Officer	A = Alternative Program	f = Facebook
81 Gifted/Talented	93 Parental Involvement	280 Literacy Coach	751 Chief of Staff	G = Adult Classes	t = Twitter
82 Video Services	95 Tech Prep Program	285 STEM	752 Social Emotional Learning	M = Magnet Program	
83 Substance Abuse Prev	97 Chief Infomation Officer	286 Digital Learning		T = Title I Schoolwide	
84 Erate	98 Chief Technology Officer	288 Common Core Standards	**Other School Types**	V = Career & Tech Ed Programs	
85 AIDS Education	270 Character Education	294 Accountability	ⓐ = Alternative School		
88 Alternative/At Risk	271 Migrant Education	295 Network System	ⓒ = Charter School	New Schools are shaded	
89 Multi-Cultural Curriculum	273 Teacher Mentor	296 Title II Programs	ⓜ = Magnet School	New Superintendents and Principals are bold	
90 Social Work	274 Before/After Sch	297 Webmaster	ⓨ = Year-Round School	Personnel with email addresses are underscored	

Peoria County

Limestone Walters CCSD 316 PID: 00312592
8223 W Smithville Rd, Peoria 61607
309/697-3035
Fax 309/697-9466

Schools: 1 \ **Teachers:** 12 \ **Students:** 200 \ **Special Ed Students:** 22 \ **LEP Students:** 3 \ **College-Bound:** 76% \ **Ethnic:** African American 1%, Hispanic 3%, Caucasian 97% \ **Exp:** $161 (Low) \ **Poverty:** 5% \ **Title I:** $16,225 \ **Special Education:** $20,000 \ **Open-Close:** 08/21 - 05/27 \ **DTBP:** $240 (High)

Tim Dotson	1,11,73	Sherry Rose	2*
Chad Bentley	6,83,85*	Cody Martzluf	16*
Ken Herz	67		

Public Schs..Principal	Grd	Prgm	Enr/#Cls	SN	
Limestone Walters Elem Sch 8223 W Smithville Rd, Peoria 61607 Tim Dotson	PK-8		200 9	22%	309/697-3035

Monroe School District 70 PID: 00312619
5137 W Cisna Rd, Bartonville 61607
309/697-3120
Fax 309/697-3185

Schools: 1 \ **Teachers:** 20 \ **Students:** 287 \ **Special Ed Students:** 53 \ **Ethnic:** Asian 2%, African American 4%, Hispanic 3%, Native American: 1%, Caucasian 89% \ **Exp:** $250 (Med) \ **Poverty:** 6% \ **Title I:** $30,686 \ **Special Education:** $46,000 \ **Open-Close:** 08/14 - 05/21 \ **DTBP:** $256 (High)

Dr Darrick Reiley	1,11,73,83	Wendy Johnson	2
Marcella Kolowski	4*	Evan Haffner	6
Kendell Cranford	17	Shaun Karmenzind	67
Carrie Kleist	275,288*		

Public Schs..Principal	Grd	Prgm	Enr/#Cls	SN	
Monroe Elem Sch 5137 W Cisna Rd, Bartonville 61607 Carrie Kleist	PK-8	T	287 20	31%	309/697-3120

Norwood Sch Dist 63 PID: 00312633
6521 W Farmington Rd, Peoria 61604
309/676-3523
Fax 309/676-6099

Schools: 2 \ **Teachers:** 32 \ **Students:** 475 \ **Special Ed Students:** 93 \ **LEP Students:** 3 \ **Ethnic:** African American 3%, Hispanic 8%, Caucasian 88% \ **Exp:** $201 (Med) \ **Poverty:** 19% \ **Title I:** $136,078 \ **Special Education:** $188,000 \ **Open-Close:** 08/20 - 05/24 \ **DTBP:** $80 (Med)

David Black	1,73	Diana Bowcott	4
Sandy Linhart	11*	Jim Sanford	67
Anthony Almasi	83,85*		

Public Schs..Principal	Grd	Prgm	Enr/#Cls	SN	
Norwood Elem Sch 6521 W Farmington Rd, Peoria 61604 Jake Flowers	5-8	T	170 14	70%	309/676-3523
Norwood Primary Sch 200 S Main St, Peoria 61604 Sandy Linhart	PK-4	T	259 12	68%	309/697-6312 Fax 309/697-2235

Oak Grove School District 68 PID: 00312657
6018 W Lancaster Rd, Bartonville 61607
309/697-3367
Fax 309/633-2381

Schools: 1 \ **Teachers:** 24 \ **Students:** 250 \ **Special Ed Students:** 61 \ **Ethnic:** Asian 1%, African American 2%, Caucasian 96% \ **Exp:** $288 (Med) \ **Poverty:** 9% \ **Title I:** $82,790 \ **Special Education:** $100,000 \ **Open-Close:** 08/17 - 05/21 \ **DTBP:** $250 (High) \

Dr Loren Baele	1,83	Matt Bender	67
Lenora Bright	275		

Public Schs..Principal	Grd	Prgm	Enr/#Cls	SN	
Oak Grove Elem Middle Sch 6018 W Lancaster Rd, Bartonville 61607 Rachel Baughman	K-8	T	250 12	40%	309/697-0621 Fax 309/633-4523

Peoria Heights Cmty SD 325 PID: 00313156
500 E Glen Ave, Peoria HTS 61616
309/686-8800
Fax 309/686-8801

Schools: 2 \ **Teachers:** 56 \ **Students:** 720 \ **Special Ed Students:** 154 \ **LEP Students:** 3 \ **College-Bound:** 81% \ **Ethnic:** Asian 1%, African American 15%, Hispanic 6%, Caucasian 79% \ **Exp:** $269 (Med) \ **Poverty:** 22% \ **Title I:** $338,322 \ **Special Education:** $190,000 \ **Open-Close:** 08/18 - 05/26 \ **DTBP:** $189 (High) \

Eric Heath	1	Kim Surber	2
Jim Carter	3*	Michelle Barnes	6
Samantha Alvarado	8	Pam Kerr	38*
Don Gorman	67	Jennifer Reichert	73*
Erin Stout	88		

Public Schs..Principal	Grd	Prgm	Enr/#Cls	SN	
Peoria Heights Grade Sch 500 E Glen Ave Unit 1, Peoria HTS 61616 Ellen Tallon	PK-8	T	537 30	60%	309/686-8809 Fax 309/686-7272
Peoria Heights High Sch 508 E Glen Ave, Peoria HTS 61616 Dave Carroll	9-12	TV	208 24	56%	309/686-8803 Fax 309/686-8808

Peoria Public Sch Dist 150 PID: 00312683
3202 N Wisconsin Ave, Peoria 61603
309/672-6512
Fax 309/282-3080

Schools: 30 \ **Teachers:** 910 \ **Students:** 12,531 \ **Special Ed Students:** 2,283 \ **LEP Students:** 777 \ **Ethnic:** Asian 1%, African American 64%, Hispanic 12%, Caucasian 22% \ **Exp:** $403 (High) \ **Poverty:** 30% \ **Title I:** $10,296,010 \ **Special Education:** $11,574,000 \ **Bilingual Education:** $363,000 \ **Open-Close:** 08/24 - 05/28 \ **DTBP:** $240 (High)

Dr Sharon Kherat	1	Carla Eman	2
Michael McKenzie	2	Mick Willis	2,19
David Myers	3	Gabi Klein	4
Josh Collins	5	Lance Randle	5
Saskia Courtney	5	Arthur Guyton	6
Dr Sandra Wilson	8,15,288	Dr Nicole Wood	9
Dr Jerry Bell	10	Dr Alexander Ikejiaku	15,68
Katie Cobb-Powers	34*	Lisa Gifford	39,280
Tracy Donath	42,45,285	Anna Rose	57
Dr Ann Bond	58	Marci Hayes	59
Rachel Eveland	60	Doug Shaw	67
Geri Hammer	68	Barbara Pierce	71,297
Thomas Bruch	71,295	Michelle Siepel	73,84,295
Shannon Marlin	79,294	DeMario Boone	91*
DeMario Boone	91	Richard Gould	91
Dr Susan Grzanich	298,750	Derrick Booth	752

---

1 Superintendent	8 Curric/Instruct K-12	19 Chief Financial Officer	29 Family/Consumer Science	39 Social Studies K-12	49 English/Lang Arts Elem	59 Special Education Elem	69 Academic Assessment
2 Bus/Finance/Purchasing	9 Curric/Instruct Elem	20 Art K-12	30 Adult Education	40 Social Studies Elem	50 English/Lang Arts Sec	60 Special Education Sec	70 Research/Development
3 Buildings And Grounds	10 Curric/Instruct Sec	21 Art Elem	31 Career/Sch-to-Work K-12	41 Social Studies Sec	51 Reading K-12	61 Foreign/World Lang K-12	71 Public Information
4 Food Service	11 Federal Program	22 Art Sec	32 Career/Sch-to-Work Elem	42 Science K-12	52 Reading Elem	62 Foreign/World Lang Elem	72 Summer School
5 Transportation	12 Title I	23 Music K-12	33 Career/Sch-to-Work Sec	43 Science Elem	53 Reading Sec	63 Foreign/World Lang Sec	73 Instructional Tech
6 Athletic	13 Title V	24 Music Elem	34 Early Childhood Ed	44 Science Sec	54 Remedial Reading K-12	64 Religious Education K-12	74 Inservice Training
7 Health Services	15 Asst Superintendent	25 Music Sec	35 Health/Phys Education	45 Math K-12	55 Remedial Reading Elem	65 Religious Education Elem	75 Marketing/Distributive
	16 Instructional Media Svcs	26 Business Education	36 Guidance Services K-12	46 Math Elem	56 Remedial Reading Sec	66 Religious Education Sec	76 Info Systems
	17 Chief Operations Officer	27 Career & Tech Ed	37 Guidance Services Elem	47 Math Sec	57 Bilingual/ELL	67 School Board President	77 Psychological Assess
	18 Chief Academic Officer	28 Technology Education	38 Guidance Services Sec	48 English/Lang Arts K-12	58 Special Education K-12	68 Teacher Personnel	78 Affirmative Action

Illinois School Directory — Peoria County

Public Schs..Principal	Grd	Prgm	Enr/#Cls	SN	
Calvin Coolidge Middle Sch 2708 W Rohmann Ave, West Peoria 61604 **Mervyn Swanson**	5-8	T	352 20	79%	309/672-6506 Fax 309/673-7605
Charles A Lindbergh Middle Sch 6327 N Sheridan Rd, Peoria 61614 Sue Malahy	5-8	T	231 23	50%	309/693-4427 Fax 309/693-0499
Charter Oak Primary Sch 5221 W Timberedge Dr, Peoria 61615 Kathy Rodriguez	K-4	T	347 19	59%	309/693-4433 Fax 309/693-8701
Day Treatment 1419 S Folkers Ave, Peoria 61605 Darryies Johnson	Spec		38	84%	309/673-1898 Fax 309/673-4620
Dr Maude A Sanders Primary Sch 1907 W Forrest Hill Ave, Peoria 61604 **Dan Hiles**	K-4	T	396 27	78%	309/672-6571 Fax 309/688-0320
Franklin Primary Sch 807 W Columbia Ter, Peoria 61606 **Emily Mastin**	K-5	T	483 25	85%	309/682-2693 Fax 309/682-7283
Glen Oak Cmty Learning Center 2100 N Wisconsin Ave, Peoria 61603 Ilethea Suggs	K-6	T	836 26	82%	309/672-6518 Fax 309/686-2459
Harrison Cmty Learning Center 2727 W Krause Ave, Peoria 61605 Fabian Daniels	K-8	T	662 27	81%	309/672-6522 Fax 309/672-6523
Hines Primary Sch 4603 N Knoxville Ave, Peoria 61614 **Marcia Lough**	PK-4	T	479 24	69%	309/672-6525 Fax 309/672-6526
Kellar Primary Sch 6413 N Mount Hawley Rd, Peoria 61614 **Heidi Baron**	K-4	T	361 24	47%	309/693-4439 Fax 309/282-0974
Ⓐ Knoxvill Ctr-Student Success 2628 N Knoxville Ave, Peoria 61604 Eric Thomas	9-12		98	65%	309/439-0000 Fax 309/282-0007
Lincoln K-8 Sch 700 Mary St, Peoria 61603 Thomas Blumer	K-8	T	726 14	88%	309/672-6542 Fax 309/676-6615
Manual Academy 811 S Griswold St, Peoria 61605 Devon Hawks	7-12	TV	802 57	82%	309/672-6600 Fax 309/672-6607
Mark Bills Middle Sch 6001 N Frostwood Pkwy, Peoria 61615 **Krystle Padilla**	5-8	T	227 22	61%	309/693-4437 Fax 309/693-4438
Northmoor Primary Sch 1819 W Northmoor Rd, Peoria 61614 Angela Stockman	K-4	T	356 21	53%	309/692-9481 Fax 309/692-9738
Online Learning Academy 3202 N Wisconsin Ave, Peoria 61603 Susan Grzanich	PK-11		401		309/672-6790
Peoria High Sch 1615 N North St, Peoria 61604 Annette Coleman	9-12	ATV	1,230 80	73%	309/672-6630 Fax 309/672-6629
Ⓒ Quest Charter Academy 2503 N University St, Peoria 61604 Robyn McCracken	5-12	T	574	67%	309/402-0030 Fax 309/685-3001
Richwoods High Sch 6301 N University St, Peoria 61614 **Carly Emken**	9-12	TV	1,270 100	40%	309/693-4400 Fax 309/693-4414
Robert A Jamieson Sch 2721 W Richwoods Blvd, Peoria 61604 Erin Reid	Spec	T	63 10	77%	309/672-6594 Fax 309/672-6595
Rolling Acres Middle Sch 5617 N Merrimac Ave, Peoria 61614 Michael Barber	5-8	T	318 32	56%	309/689-1100 Fax 309/282-0020
Ⓜ Roosevelt Magnet Sch 1704 W Aiken Ave, Peoria 61605 **Laura Rodgers**	K-8	T	668	86%	309/672-6574 Fax 309/282-2631
Sterling Middle Sch 2315 N Sterling Ave, Peoria 61604 Lynn Lane	5-8	T	402 30	76%	309/672-6557 Fax 309/681-8286
Thomas Jefferson Primary Sch 918 W Florence Ave, Peoria 61604 Kary Boerger	PK-6	T	456 27	73%	309/672-6531 Fax 309/672-6527
Trewyn K-8 Sch 1419 S Folkers Ave, Peoria 61605 Renee Andrews	PK-8		292 28	92%	309/672-6500 Fax 309/673-6537
Valeska Hinton Early Ed Ctr 800 W Romeo B Garrett Ave, Peoria 61605 Katie Cobb-Powers	PK-1		514 21	88%	309/672-6810 Fax 309/676-9831
Von Steuben Middle Sch 801 E Forrest Hill Ave, Peoria 61603 **Michelle Cruz**	5-8	T	337 45	77%	309/672-6561 Fax 309/685-7631
Washington Gifted Sch 3706 N Grand Blvd, Peoria 61614 Susan Martin	5-8		302 15	22%	309/672-6563 Fax 309/672-6564
Whittier Primary Sch 1619 W Fredonia Ave, Peoria 61606 Julie Deignan	K-4	T	269 18	75%	309/672-6569 Fax 309/673-3349
Woodruff Career & Tech Center 1800 NE Perry Ave, Peoria 61603 Michael Kuhn	Voc	A	96		309/672-6665 Fax 309/282-5260

- **Pleasant Hill School Dist 69** PID: 00313209   309/637-6829
  3717 W Malone St, Peoria 61605   Fax 309/637-8612

Schools: 1 \ **Teachers:** 15 \ **Students:** 230 \ **Special Ed Students:** 65 \
LEP Students: 8 \ **Ethnic:** Asian 2%, African American 22%, Hispanic 12%,
Caucasian 65% \ **Exp:** $153 (Low) \ **Poverty:** 27% \ **Title I:** $130,591 \
Special Education: $70,000 \ **Open-Close:** 08/12 - 05/19

Lisa Weaver 1   Kitty Joos 2
Ann Kluesner ....12*   William Preston 67

Public Schs..Principal	Grd	Prgm	Enr/#Cls	SN	
Pleasant Hill Elem Sch 3717 W Malone St, Peoria 61605 Lisa Weaver	PK-8	T	230 13	99%	309/637-6829

- **Pleasant Valley Sch Dist 62** PID: 00313223   309/673-6750
  3314 W Richwoods Blvd, Peoria 61604   Fax 309/679-0652

Schools: 2 \ **Teachers:** 46 \ **Students:** 363 \ **Special Ed Students:** 93
\ **LEP Students:** 3 \ **Ethnic:** African American 61%, Hispanic 2%,
Caucasian 37% \ **Exp:** $292 (Med) \ **Poverty:** 36% \ **Title I:** $431,392 \
Special Education: $152,000 \ **Open-Close:** 08/21 - 05/28 \ **DTBP:** $233
(High)

Tracy Colwell-Forck 1   Rick Hart 11*
Cliff Quine 67

Public Schs..Principal	Grd	Prgm	Enr/#Cls	SN	
Pleasant Valley Elem Sch 4623 W Red Bud Dr, Peoria 61604 Angie Robertson \ **Kelly Galyean**	K-4	T	288 12	94%	309/673-6750 Fax 309/674-0165
Pleasant Valley Middle Sch 3314 W Richwoods Blvd, Peoria 61604 **Jacob Wall**	5-8		184 12	89%	309/679-0634

---

79 Student Personnel	91 Safety/Security	275 Response To Intervention	298 Grant Writer/Ptnrships	**School Programs**	**Social Media**
80 Driver Ed/Safety	92 Magnet School	277 Remedial Math K-12	750 Chief Innovation Officer	A = Alternative Program	
81 Gifted/Talented	93 Parental Involvement	280 Literacy Coach	751 Chief of Staff	G = Adult Classes	▮ = Facebook
82 Video Services	95 Tech Prep Program	285 STEM	752 Social Emotional Learning	M = Magnet Program	
83 Substance Abuse Prev	97 Chief Infomation Officer	286 Digital Learning		T = Title I Schoolwide	▮ = Twitter
84 Erate	98 Chief Technology Officer	288 Common Core Standards	**Other School Types**	V = Career & Tech Ed Programs	
85 AIDS Education	270 Character Education	294 Accountability	Ⓐ = Alternative School		
88 Alternative/At Risk	271 Migrant Education	295 Network System	Ⓒ = Charter School	New Schools are shaded	
89 Multi-Cultural Curriculum	273 Teacher Mentor	296 Title II Programs	Ⓜ = Magnet School	New Superintendents and Principals are bold	
90 Social Work	274 Before/After Sch	297 Webmaster	Ⓨ = Year-Round School	Personnel with email addresses are underscored	

Peoria County

Market Data Retrieval

- **Princeville Cmty Unit SD 326** PID: 00313259   309/385-2213
  909 N Town Ave, Princeville 61559   Fax 309/385-1823

> **Schools:** 2 \ **Teachers:** 53 \ **Students:** 761 \ **Special Ed Students:** 99
> \ **LEP Students:** 14 \ **College-Bound:** 77% \ **Ethnic:** Asian 1%,
> African American 2%, Hispanic 7%, Caucasian 89% \ **Exp:** $360 (High)
> \ **Poverty:** 12% \ **Title I:** $143,325 \ **Special Education:** $151,000 \
> **Bilingual Education:** $1,000 \ **Open-Close:** 08/14 - 05/21 \ **DTBP:** $168
> (High)

Name	#
Shannon Duling	1
Michele Boland	5
Julie Bayless	8,275*
Kathy Sullivan	16,82*
Lora Haas	58*
Kelly Jenkins	73,295*
Stefanie Baysinger	2
Jeff Kratzer	6*
Raquell Daniel	12
Scott Endress	57,271*
Michael Harmon	67
Ann Ladd	274

Public Schs..Principal	Grd	Prgm	Enr/#Cls	SN	
Princeville Elem Sch 602 N Town Ave, Princeville 61559 Julie Bayless	PK-5	T	357 29	26%	309/385-4994 Fax 309/385-2518
Princeville Jr Sr High Sch 302 Cordis Ave Ste 1, Princeville 61559 Rich Thole	6-12	V	404 38	32%	309/385-4660 Fax 309/385-1110

PEORIA CATHOLIC SCHOOLS

- **Diocese of Peoria Ed Office** PID: 00313338   309/671-1550
  419 NE Madison Ave, Peoria 61603   Fax 309/671-1579

> **Schools:** 43 \ **Students:** 11,872

Listing includes only schools located in this county. See District Index for location of Diocesan Offices.

Name	#
Dr Sharon Weiss	1
Dr Susan Stolt	15
Jerry Sanderson	15

Catholic Schs..Principal	Grd	Prgm	Enr/#Cls	SN	
Holy Family Parish Sch 2329 W Reservoir Blvd, Peoria 61615 Stacie Gianessi	PK-8		215 20		309/688-2931 Fax 309/681-5687
Peoria Notre Dame High Sch 5105 N Sheridan Rd, Peoria 61614 Sr Sara Kowal	9-12		889 43		309/691-8741 Fax 309/691-0875
St Edward Sch 1221 N 5th St, Chillicothe 61523 Mike Domico	PK-8		160 10		309/274-2994 Fax 309/274-4141
St Jude Sch 10811 N Knoxville Ave, Peoria 61615 Sr Maria Nelson	PK-4		110		309/243-2493
St Mark Sch 711 N Underhill St, Peoria 61606 Dr Noreen Dillon	PK-8		177 12		309/676-7131 Fax 309/677-8060
St Mary's of Kickapoo Sch 9910 W Knox St, Edwards 61528 Bill Lamb	PK-8		107 9		309/691-3015 Fax 309/691-2898
St Philomena Sch 3216 N Emery Ave, Peoria 61604 Jack Dippold	PK-8		390 13		309/685-1208 Fax 309/681-5676
St Thomas the Apostle Sch 4229 N Monroe Ave, Peoria HTS 61616 Maureen Bentley	PK-8		330 19		309/685-2533
St Vincent De Paul Sch 6001 N University St, Peoria 61614 Patsy Santen	PK-8		501 30		309/691-5012 Fax 309/683-1036

PEORIA PRIVATE SCHOOLS

Private Schs..Principal	Grd	Prgm	Enr/#Cls	SN
Calvary Baptist Academy 1028 W Cloverdale Rd, Chillicothe 61523 Curtis Cochran	PK-12		45 8	309/274-4343 Fax 309/274-5520
Christ Lutheran Sch 1311 S Faraday Ave, Peoria 61605 Terry Mooney	K-8		170 9	309/637-1512 Fax 309/637-7829
Concordia Lutheran Sch 2000 W Glen Ave, Peoria 61614 Paul Thompson	K-8		165 20	309/691-8921 Fax 309/691-2913
Daarul Uloom Islamic Sch 4125 W Charter Oak Rd, Peoria 61615 Burhan Hamdan	PK-12		129	309/691-9089 Fax 309/691-6970
El Vista Baptist Academy 6301 N Syler St, Peoria 61615 Joey Watt	K-8		23 5	309/692-8675
Kiefer Sch 404 NE Madison Ave, Peoria 61603 Dan Ramos	Spec		135 18	309/687-7779 Fax 309/687-7599
Light House Academy 2322 W Willow Knolls Dr, Peoria 61614 Dean Ramseyer	K-8		14 4	309/691-3242
Mont Sch of Peoria 4906 N Prospect Rd, Peoria HTS 61616 John Cox	PK-6		53 5	309/685-8995 Fax 309/685-5413
New Life Christian Academy 3510 W Malone St, Peoria 61605 Jonathan Lashley	1-12		15 1	309/637-8359 Fax 309/637-9284
Peoria Academy 2711 W Willow Knolls Dr, Peoria 61614 Jay Riven	PK-8		147	309/692-7570 Fax 309/692-7665
Peoria Christian Sch 3506 N California Ave, Peoria 61603 Sandy Wiele \ Ron Shobert \ Angie Lyons	PK-12		540	309/686-4500 Fax 309/686-2569
Peoria Hebrew Day Sch 5614 N University St, Peoria 61614 Tempest Henning	PK-8		19 5	309/692-2821

PEORIA REGIONAL CENTERS

- **Area 3 Learning Technology Ctr** PID: 04433198   309/680-5800
  10112 W Dubois Rd, Edwards 61528   Fax 309/680-5808

Name	#
John Closen	1
Scott Delawder	73,295

- **Peoria Co Special Ed Assoc** PID: 02184121   309/697-0880
  4812 Pfeiffer Rd, Bartonville 61607   Fax 309/697-0884

Name	#
Lora Haas	1
Jodie Vanderheydt	31
Karen Beverlin	2

- **Peoria Ed Reg Emp & Career** PID: 04177813   309/693-7373
  2000 W Pioneer Pkwy Ste 19C, Peoria 61615   Fax 309/693-7375

Chris Kendall 1

#	Role	#	Role	#	Role	#	Role	#	Role	#	Role	#	Role
1	Superintendent	8	Curric/Instruct K-12	19	Chief Financial Officer	29	Family/Consumer Science	39	Social Studies K-12	49	English/Lang Arts Elem	59	Special Education Elem	69	Academic Assessment
2	Bus/Finance/Purchasing	9	Curric/Instruct Elem	20	Art K-12	30	Adult Education	40	Social Studies Elem	50	English/Lang Arts Sec	60	Special Education Sec	70	Research/Development
3	Buildings And Grounds	10	Curric/Instruct Sec	21	Art Elem	31	Career/Sch-to-Work K-12	41	Social Studies Sec	51	Reading K-12	61	Foreign/World Lang K-12	71	Public Information
4	Food Service	11	Federal Program	22	Art Sec	32	Career/Sch-to-Work Elem	42	Science K-12	52	Reading Elem	62	Foreign/World Lang Elem	72	Summer School
5	Transportation	12	Title I	23	Music K-12	33	Career/Sch-to-Work Sec	43	Science Elem	53	Reading Sec	63	Foreign/World Lang Sec	73	Instructional Tech
6	Athletic	13	Title V	24	Music Elem	34	Early Childhood Ed	44	Science Sec	54	Remedial Reading K-12	64	Religious Education K-12	74	Inservice Training
7	Health Services	14	Asst Superintendent	25	Music Sec	35	Health/Phys Education	45	Math K-12	55	Remedial Reading Elem	65	Religious Education Elem	75	Marketing/Distributive
		15	Instructional Media Svcs	26	Business Education	36	Guidance Services K-12	46	Math Elem	56	Remedial Reading Sec	66	Religious Education Sec	76	Info Systems
		16	Chief Operations Officer	27	Career & Tech Ed	37	Guidance Services Elem	47	Math Sec	57	Bilingual/ELL	67	School Board President	77	Psychological Assess
		17	Chief Academic Officer	28	Technology Education	38	Guidance Services Sec	48	English/Lang Arts K-12	58	Special Education K-12	68	Teacher Personnel	78	Affirmative Action

Illinois School Directory — Perry County

- **Regional Office of Ed 48** PID: 02098211 — 309/672-6906
  324 Main St Ste 401, Peoria 61602 — Fax 309/672-6053

  Elizabeth Crider .... 1 Jennifer Yoder 2
  George McKenna .... 15 Oliver Mack 88

PERRY COUNTY

PERRY COUNTY SCHOOLS

County Schs..Principal	Grd	Prgm	Enr/#Cls	SN	
Tri-County at Ward Sch 200 N Division St, Du Quoin 62832 Staci Hood	Spec		60	86%	618/542-5954

PERRY PUBLIC SCHOOLS

- **Community Cons School Dist 204** PID: 00314162 — 618/357-2419
  6067 State Route 154, Pinckneyville 62274 — Fax 618/357-3016

  Schools: 1 \ **Teachers:** 12 \ **Students:** 156 \ **Special Ed Students:** 22 \ **Ethnic:** Asian 1%, Caucasian 99% \ **Exp:** $114 (Low) \ **Poverty:** 11% \ **Title I:** $27,042 \ **Special Education:** $27,000 \ **Open-Close:** 08/17 - 05/14 \ **DTBP:** $181 (High)

  Jerry Travelstead 1,11,57,288   Jenny Malanowski 2,84
  Heather Alvis 6,7   Tammy Epplin 59*
  Mary Jackson 67

Public Schs..Principal	Grd	Prgm	Enr/#Cls	SN	
Community Cons SD 204 Sch 6067 State Route 154, Pinckneyville 62274 Jerry Travelstead	PK-8		156 13	40%	618/357-2419

- **Du Quoin Cmty Unit SD 300** PID: 00314033 — 618/542-3856
  845 E Jackson St, Du Quoin 62832 — Fax 618/542-6614

  Schools: 3 \ **Teachers:** 102 \ **Students:** 1,420 \ **Special Ed Students:** 251 \ **College-Bound:** 79% \ **Ethnic:** Asian 1%, African American 5%, Hispanic 3%, Caucasian 92% \ **Exp:** $222 (Med) \ **Poverty:** 24% \ **Title I:** $632,503 \ **Special Education:** $512,000 \ **Open-Close:** 08/17 - 06/01 \ **DTBP:** $177 (High) \ f t

  Matt Hickam 1,11,57   Cory Robbins 2,3
  Donna Lively 4   Jeremy Cornett 6*
  Diana Rea .... 9*   Zach McPherson 67
  Mike Riggio .... 73,98,295*   Tim Craft 73*

Public Schs..Principal	Grd	Prgm	Enr/#Cls	SN	
Duquoin Elem Sch 845 E Jackson St, Du Quoin 62832 Diana Rea	PK-4	T	486 29	53%	618/542-2646 Fax 618/542-6291
Duquoin High Sch 500 E South St, Du Quoin 62832 Tim McChristian	9-12	TV	450 37	52%	618/542-4744 Fax 618/542-8822
Duquoin Middle Sch 845 E Jackson St, Du Quoin 62832 Aaron Hill	5-8	T	437 40	57%	618/542-2646 Fax 618/542-4373 f t

- **Pinckneyville Cmty High SD 101** PID: 00314148 — 618/357-5013
  600 E Water St, Pinckneyville 62274 — Fax 618/357-6045

  Schools: 1 \ **Teachers:** 27 \ **Students:** 415 \ **Special Ed Students:** 70 \ **College-Bound:** 67% \ **Ethnic:** African American 1%, Caucasian 99% \ **Exp:** $225 (Med) \ **Poverty:** 10% \ **Title I:** $66,254 \ **Special Education:** $129,000 \ **Open-Close:** 08/19 - 05/21 \ **DTBP:** $196 (High) \ t

  Keith Hagene 1   Kathryn Restoff 2
  Robert Waggoner .... 6*   Heather Genesio 33*
  Marilyn Smith .... 57*   Diane Plumlee 60*
  Greg Thompson 67   Cheryl Clark 73*
  Katie Smith 83,88*

Public Schs..Principal	Grd	Prgm	Enr/#Cls	SN	
Pinckneyville Community HS 600 E Water St, Pinckneyville 62274 Tony Wilson	9-12		415 42	35%	618/357-5013

- **Pinckneyville Sch Dist 50** PID: 00314100 — 618/357-2724
  301 W Mulberry St, Pinckneyville 62274 — Fax 618/357-8731

  Schools: 2 \ **Teachers:** 32 \ **Students:** 504 \ **Special Ed Students:** 88 \ **Ethnic:** Asian 1%, African American 1%, Hispanic 3%, Caucasian 96% \ **Exp:** $451 (High) \ **Poverty:** 19% \ **Title I:** $205,216 \ **Special Education:** $109,000 \ **Open-Close:** 08/19 - 06/03 \ **DTBP:** $170 (High)

  Scott Wagner 1,11,73,83,288   Larry Louis 3*
  Kyle Pursell 67

Public Schs..Principal	Grd	Prgm	Enr/#Cls	SN	
Pinckneyville Elem Sch 301 W Mulberry St, Pinckneyville 62274 Scott Wagner	PK-4	T	288 15	43%	618/357-5161 Fax 618/357-9431
Pinckneyville Jr High Sch 700 E Water St, Pinckneyville 62274 Mark Rohlfing	5-8	T	240 12	40%	618/357-2724 Fax 618/357-6314

- **Tamaroa Elem School Dist 5** PID: 00314203 — 618/496-5513
  200 W Main St, Tamaroa 62888 — Fax 618/496-3911

  Schools: 1 \ **Teachers:** 8 \ **Students:** 82 \ **Special Ed Students:** 27 \ **Ethnic:** Hispanic 1%, Caucasian 99% \ **Exp:** $335 (High) \ **Poverty:** 15% \ **Title I:** $31,744 \ **Special Education:** $26,000 \ **Open-Close:** 08/20 - 05/18 \ **DTBP:** $185 (High)

  Brian Brink 1   Rhonda Fleming 2*
  Phillip Hamil 11,83,288   Charles Stein 67
  Cynthia Opp 88*

Public Schs..Principal	Grd	Prgm	Enr/#Cls	SN	
Tamaroa Elem Sch 200 W Main St, Tamaroa 62888 Cynthia Opp	PK-8	T	82 8	82%	618/496-5513 Fax 618/498-3911

PERRY CATHOLIC SCHOOLS

- **Diocese of Belleville Ed Off** PID: 00317671
  Listing includes only schools located in this county. See District Index for location of Diocesan Offices.

							School Programs	Social Media
79	Student Personnel	91	Safety/Security	275	Response To Intervention	298 Grant Writer/Ptnrships	A = Alternative Program	f = Facebook
80	Driver Ed/Safety	92	Magnet School	277	Remedial Math K-12	750 Chief Innovation Officer	G = Adult Classes	t = Twitter
81	Gifted/Talented	93	Parental Involvement	280	Literacy Coach	751 Chief of Staff	M = Magnet Program	
82	Video Services	95	Tech Prep Program	285	STEM	752 Social Emotional Learning	T = Title I Schoolwide	
83	Substance Abuse Prev	97	Chief Infomation Officer	286	Digital Learning		V = Career & Tech Ed Programs	
84	Erate	98	Chief Technology Officer	288	Common Core Standards	Other School Types		
85	AIDS Education	270	Character Education	294	Accountability	A = Alternative School		
88	Alternative/At Risk	271	Migrant Education	295	Network System	C = Charter School	New Schools are shaded	
89	Multi-Cultural Curriculum	273	Teacher Mentor	296	Title II Programs	M = Magnet School	New Superintendents and Principals are bold	
90	Social Work	274	Before/After Sch	297	Webmaster	Y = Year-Round School	Personnel with email addresses are underscored	

IL—201

Piatt County

Catholic Schs..Principal	Grd	Prgm	Enr/#Cls	SN		
St Bruno Sch	PK-8		139			618/357-8276
210 N Gordon St, Pinckneyville 62274			9			Fax 618/357-6425
Brittany Goldman						

PERRY PRIVATE SCHOOLS

Private Schs..Principal	Grd	Prgm	Enr/#Cls	SN		
Christian Fellowship Sch	PK-12	G	60			618/542-6800
616 US Route 51, Du Quoin 62832			12			
Stuart Davis						

PIATT COUNTY

PIATT PUBLIC SCHOOLS

- **Bement Cmty Unit Sch Dist 5** PID: 00314306   217/678-4200
  201 S Champaign St, Bement 61813   Fax 217/678-4251

> **Schools:** 3 \ **Teachers:** 28 \ **Students:** 298 \ **Special Ed Students:** 64
> \ **Ethnic:** African American 2%, Hispanic 1%, Native American: 1%,
> Caucasian 96% \ **Exp:** $427 (High) \ **Poverty:** 8% \ **Title I:** $50,028 \
> **Special Education:** $37,000 \ **Open-Close:** 08/17 - 05/14

Sheila Greenwood 1,11   Steve Cline 6,8*
Doug Kepley .... 16*   Donna Sharp 38*
Todd Scott 67   Andrew Brown .... 73"
Linda Taylor 285

Public Schs..Principal	Grd	Prgm	Enr/#Cls	SN		
Bement Elem Sch	PK-5		145		45%	217/678-4200
201 S Champaign St, Bement 61813			12			
Dr Sheila Greenwood						
Bement High Sch	9-12	T	97		38%	217/678-4200
201 S Champaign St, Bement 61813			30			
Doug Kepley						
Bement Middle Sch	6-8		64		58%	217/678-4200
201 S Champaign St, Bement 61813			10			
Doug Kepley						

- **Cerro Gordo Cmty Unit SD 100** PID: 00314332   217/763-5221
  300 E Durfee St, Cerro Gordo 61818   Fax 217/763-6562

> **Schools:** 2 \ **Teachers:** 35 \ **Students:** 490 \ **Special Ed Students:** 51
> \ **College-Bound:** 63% \ **Ethnic:** African American 1%, Hispanic 1%,
> Caucasian 97% \ **Exp:** $164 (Low) \ **Poverty:** 13% \ **Title I:** $117,854 \
> **Special Education:** $123,000 \ **Open-Close:** 08/13 - 05/18

Brett Robinson 1,11   Jodi Neaveill 9,12,274*
Meredith Riddle 16   Tony Piraino 67
Brandon Willard .... 69,270*   Andrew Bahr 83,88*

Public Schs..Principal	Grd	Prgm	Enr/#Cls	SN		
Cerro Gordo Elem Sch	PK-6		262		37%	217/763-2551
209 S Monroe St, Cerro Gordo 61818			15			Fax 217/763-6560
Jodi Neaveill						
Cerro Gordo Jr Sr High Sch	7-12	V	222		39%	217/763-2711
300 E Durfee St, Cerro Gordo 61818			16			Fax 217/763-6287
Jeremy Rodebaugh						

- **Deland-Weldon Cmty Unit SD 57** PID: 00314382   217/736-2311
  304 E Il Route 10, De Land 61839   Fax 217/736-2654

> **Schools:** 2 \ **Teachers:** 21 \ **Students:** 200 \ **Special Ed Students:** 33 \
> **College-Bound:** 66% \ **Ethnic:** Hispanic 3%, Caucasian 97% \ **Exp:** $433
> (High) \ **Poverty:** 18% \ **Title I:** $64,163 \ **Special Education:** $27,000 \
> **Open-Close:** 08/14 - 05/19 \ **DTBP:** $182 (High) \

Amanda Geary 1,11   Cheryl Jones 2
Mike White .... 3*   Matt Goldman 5
Ryan Pray .... 6*   Christopher Hill 12,280*
Samantha Kirkton .... 57,69,83*   Ashley Hieronymus 58*
Jamie Dunn 67

Public Schs..Principal	Grd	Prgm	Enr/#Cls	SN		
Deland-Weldon Elem Jr High Sch	PK-8	T	150		54%	217/736-2401
2311 N 300 East Rd, Weldon 61882			12			Fax 217/736-2354
Amanda Geary \ Matt Goldman						
Deland-Weldon High Sch	9-12	T	67		55%	309/928-7691
304 E Il Route 10, De Land 61839			13			Fax 309/928-7695
Matt Goldman						

- **Monticello Cmty Unit SD 25** PID: 00314411   217/762-8511
  2 Sage Dr, Monticello 61856   Fax 217/762-8534

> **Schools:** 5 \ **Teachers:** 115 \ **Students:** 1,600 \ **Special Ed Students:** 246
> \ **LEP Students:** 10 \ **College-Bound:** 77% \ **Ethnic:** Asian 1%, African
> American 2%, Hispanic 1%, Caucasian 96% \ **Exp:** $160 (Low) \ **Poverty:** 6%
> \ **Title I:** $147,381 \ **Special Education:** $549,000 \ **Open-Close:** 09/02 -
> 05/28 \ **DTBP:** $235 (High)

Dr Victor Zimmerman 1,11   Nichole Boss 2
Michael Lane 3   Denise Troester 5*
Daniel Sheehan .... 6*   Amy Hoss 7,31*
Elizabeth Rost .... 27*   Mary Vogt 48,69*
Gary Huisinga 67   Jana McGiles 68
Windy Stokowski 73,84

Public Schs..Principal	Grd	Prgm	Enr/#Cls	SN		
Lincoln Elem Sch	PK-1	T	201		21%	217/762-8511
700 N Buchanan St, Monticello 61856			13			Fax 217/762-2733
Mary Vogt						
Monticello High Sch	9-12	V	534		23%	217/762-8511
1 Sage Dr, Monticello 61856			40			Fax 217/762-8505
Adam Clapp						
Monticello Middle Sch	6-8		363		26%	217/762-8511
2015 E Washington St, Monticello 61856			25			Fax 217/762-7765
Mark Hughes						
Washington Elem Sch	4-5	T	213		22%	217/762-8511
3 Sage Dr, Monticello 61856			11			Fax 217/762-8408
Nancy Rosenbery						
White Heath Elem Sch	2-3	T	218		23%	217/762-8511
300 W High St, White Heath 61884			12			Fax 217/762-8333
Emily Weidner						

1	Superintendent	8	Curric/Instruct K-12	19	Chief Financial Officer	29	Family/Consumer Science	39	Social Studies K-12	49	English/Lang Arts Elem	59	Special Education Elem	69	Academic Assessment
2	Bus/Finance/Purchasing	9	Curric/Instruct Elem	20	Art K-12	30	Adult Education	40	Social Studies Elem	50	English/Lang Arts Sec	60	Special Education Sec	70	Research/Development
3	Buildings And Grounds	10	Curric/Instruct Sec	21	Art Elem	31	Career/Sch-to-Work K-12	41	Social Studies Sec	51	Reading K-12	61	Foreign/World Lang K-12	71	Public Information
4	Food Service	11	Federal Program	22	Art Sec	32	Career/Sch-to-Work Elem	42	Science K-12	52	Reading Elem	62	Foreign/World Lang Elem	72	Summer School
5	Transportation	12	Title I	23	Music K-12	33	Career/Sch-to-Work Sec	43	Science Elem	53	Reading Sec	63	Foreign/World Lang Sec	73	Instructional Tech
6	Athletic	13	Title V	24	Music Elem	34	Early Childhood Ed	44	Science Sec	54	Remedial Reading K-12	64	Religious Education K-12	74	Inservice Training
7	Health Services	14	Asst Superintendent	25	Music Sec	35	Health/Phys Education	45	Math K-12	55	Remedial Reading Elem	65	Religious Education Elem	75	Marketing/Distributive
		15	Instructional Media Svcs	26	Business Education	36	Guidance Services K-12	46	Math Elem	56	Remedial Reading Sec	66	Religious Education Sec	76	Info Systems
		16	Chief Operations Officer	27	Career & Tech Ed	37	Guidance Services Elem	47	Math Sec	57	Bilingual/ELL	67	School Board President	77	Psychological Assess
		17	Chief Academic Officer	28	Technology Education	38	Guidance Services Sec	48	English/Lang Arts K-12	58	Special Education K-12	68	Teacher Personnel	78	Affirmative Action

Illinois School Directory

PIKE COUNTY

PIKE PUBLIC SCHOOLS

• **Griggsville-Perry Cmty SD 4** PID: 00314502 217/833-2352
202 N Stanford St, Griggsville 62340 Fax 217/833-2354

Schools: 3 \ **Teachers:** 37 \ **Students:** 340 \ **Special Ed Students:** 90 \ **LEP Students:** 3 \ **College-Bound:** 60% \ **Ethnic:** African American 2%, Caucasian 98% \ **Exp:** $354 (High) \ **Poverty:** 16% \ **Title I:** $115,526 \ **Special Education:** $117,000 \ **Open-Close:** 08/17 - 05/27 \ **DTBP:** $196 (High)

Kent Hawley 1,11   Doug Whitlock 3
Eric Cunzeman 67

Public Schs..Principal	Grd	Prgm	Enr/#Cls	SN	
Griggsville-Perry Elem Sch 202 N Stanford St, Griggsville 62340 Jillian Theis	PK-4		119 12	78%	217/833-2352
Griggsville-Perry High Sch 202 N Stanford St, Griggsville 62340 Jillian Theis	9-12	GV	84 12	100%	217/833-2352
Griggsville-Perry Middle Sch 201 E North St, Perry 62362 Jeff Bourne	5-8		122 14	98%	217/236-9161 Fax 217/236-7221

• **Pikeland Cmty Sch Dist 10** PID: 00314576 217/285-2147
512 S Madison St, Pittsfield 62363 Fax 217/285-5059

Schools: 3 \ **Teachers:** 91 \ **Students:** 1,200 \ **Special Ed Students:** 214 \ **LEP Students:** 3 \ **College-Bound:** 81% \ **Ethnic:** Hispanic 1%, Caucasian 98% \ **Exp:** $206 (Med) \ **Poverty:** 16% \ **Title I:** $408,354 \ **Special Education:** $353,000 \ **Open-Close:** 08/19 - 05/18 \ **DTBP:** $177 (High)

Dr Carol Kilver 1   Jim Shade 3
Susan Collins .... 4*   Matt Davidsmeyer 5
Jarred Heinz 6   Tasha Bartlett 7*
Angie Ruebush 11,15,74,275,296,298   Michelle Westbrook 11,36,69*
Kathy Hoover .... 16*   Becky Pepper 58*
Mike Gerard 67   Michael Smith 73*
Michael Smith 84,285   Gretchen Petty 93*
Kenny Smith 752

Public Schs..Principal	Grd	Prgm	Enr/#Cls	SN	
Pikeland Community Sch 601 Piper Ln, Pittsfield 62363 Jon Frieden \ Lisa Jockisch	3-8		560 35	48%	217/285-9462 Fax 217/285-9551
Pittsfield High Sch 201 E Higbee St, Pittsfield 62363 Angie Greger	9-12	TV	323 35	37%	217/285-6888 Fax 217/285-9583
Pittsfield South Elem Sch 655 Clarksville Rd, Pittsfield 62363 Doug Smith	PK-2		341 14	52%	217/285-2431 Fax 217/285-5479

Pope County

• **Pleasant Hill CUSD 3** PID: 00314667 217/734-2311
501 E Quincy St, Pleasant Hill 62366 Fax 217/734-2725

Schools: 2 \ **Teachers:** 23 \ **Students:** 311 \ **Special Ed Students:** 73 \ **College-Bound:** 50% \ **Ethnic:** African American 1%, Caucasian 99% \ **Exp:** $404 (High) \ **Poverty:** 20% \ **Title I:** $105,717 \ **Special Education:** $109,000 \ **Open-Close:** 08/21 - 05/25 \

Ron Edwards 1   Gina Lundrie 2
Jerry Hausmann .... 3,5*   Lisa Hannel 12*
Mike Peebles 67

Public Schs..Principal	Grd	Prgm	Enr/#Cls	SN	
Pleasant Hill Elem Sch 501 E Quincy St, Pleasant Hill 62366 Ryan Lowe	PK-8	T	237 20	58%	217/734-2311 Fax 217/134-2629
Pleasant Hill High Sch 501 E Quincy St, Pleasant Hill 62366 Ron Edwards	9-12	TV	74 15	61%	217/734-2311

• **Western CUSD 12** PID: 00314693 217/335-2323
401 McDonough St, Barry 62312 Fax 217/335-2211

Schools: 3 \ **Teachers:** 41 \ **Students:** 570 \ **Special Ed Students:** 104 \ **LEP Students:** 3 \ **College-Bound:** 48% \ **Ethnic:** Hispanic 3%, Caucasian 97% \ **Exp:** $175 (Low) \ **Poverty:** 25% \ **Title I:** $271,194 \ **Special Education:** $149,000 \ **Open-Close:** 08/17 - 05/18 \ **DTBP:** $174 (High)

Jessica Funk 1,288   Kelsi Neese 2
Jeremy Walston 5   Ellen Archinbel 11
Alicia Smith 16   Kathleen Schlueter 34*
Stefanie Rennecker .... 36,69*   Leslie Duncan 58*
Inky Shover 67   Justin Martin 73,286*

Public Schs..Principal	Grd	Prgm	Enr/#Cls	SN	
Western Barry Elem Sch 401 McDonough St, Barry 62312 Connie Thomas	K-5	T	225	65%	217/335-2323 Fax 217/335-2706
Western High Sch 401 McDonough St, Barry 62312 Connie Thomas	9-12	T	140	62%	217/335-2323
Western Junior High Sch 300 Chaney St, Kinderhook 62345 Brandi Pennock	5-8		139 10	52%	217/432-8324 Fax 217/432-8003

POPE COUNTY

POPE PUBLIC SCHOOLS

• **Pope Co Cmty Unit Sch Dist 1** PID: 00314734 618/683-2301
125 State Highway 146 W, Golconda 62938 Fax 618/683-5181

Schools: 2 \ **Teachers:** 39 \ **Students:** 530 \ **Special Ed Students:** 92 \ **College-Bound:** 45% \ **Ethnic:** African American 1%, Hispanic 1%, Native American: 1%, Caucasian 98% \ **Exp:** $225 (Med) \ **Poverty:** 24% \ **Title I:** $184,498 \ **Special Education:** $140,000 \ **Open-Close:** 08/14 - 05/21 \ **DTBP:** $172 (High)

---

79 Student Personnel	91 Safety/Security	275 Response To Intervention	298 Grant Writer/Ptnrships	**School Programs**	**Social Media**
80 Driver Ed/Safety	92 Magnet School	277 Remedial Math K-12	750 Chief Innovation Officer	A = Alternative Program	= Facebook
81 Gifted/Talented	93 Parental Involvement	280 Literacy Coach	751 Chief of Staff	G = Adult Classes	= Twitter
82 Video Services	95 Tech Prep Program	285 STEM	752 Social Emotional Learning	M = Magnet Program	
83 Substance Abuse Prev	97 Chief Information Officer	286 Digital Learning		T = Title I Schoolwide	
84 Erate	98 Chief Technology Officer	288 Common Core Standards	**Other School Types**	V = Career & Tech Ed Programs	
85 AIDS Education	270 Character Education	294 Accountability	Ⓐ = Alternative School		
88 Alternative/At Risk	271 Migrant Education	295 Network System	Ⓒ = Charter School	New Schools are shaded	
89 Multi-Cultural Curriculum	273 Teacher Mentor	296 Title II Programs	Ⓜ = Magnet School	New Superintendents and Principals are bold	
90 Social Work	274 Before/After Sch	297 Webmaster	Ⓨ = Year-Round School	Personnel with email addresses are underscored	

Pulaski County

Ryan Fritch 1,11
James Forthman 6*
Candace Potts 38,69,83*
Michael Henson 67
Margie Bowman 2
Lisa Reed 8,288,298*
Ed Blankenship 58*
Laura Hosfeldt 273*

Public Schs..Principal	Grd	Prgm	Enr/#Cls	SN		
Pope Co Elem Sch 125 State Highway 146 W, Golconda 62938 Ed Blankenship	PK-8	T	349 18	62%	618/683-4011 Fax 618/683-6022	
Pope Co High Sch 125 State Highway 146 W, Golconda 62938 Seth Graves	9-12	TV	153 15	59%	618/683-3071 Fax 618/683-9956	

PULASKI COUNTY

PULASKI PUBLIC SCHOOLS

• **Century Cmty Unit SD 100** PID: 00314760 618/845-3518
4721 Shawnee College Rd, Ullin 62992 Fax 618/845-3586

Schools: 2 \ **Teachers:** 29 \ **Students:** 369 \ **Special Ed Students:** 55 \ **College-Bound:** 64% \ **Ethnic:** Asian 1%, African American 12%, Hispanic 1%, Caucasian 86% \ **Exp:** $264 (Med) \ **Poverty:** 31% \ **Title I:** $270,857 \ **Special Education:** $78,000 \ **Open-Close:** 08/14 - 05/21 \ **DTBP:** $174 (High)

Brandon Sommer 1,11,288
Connie Duty 5
Ashley Dexter 8,12,69,83,85*
Dan Cook 16,31,73,76,295*
Vanessa Sickling 2
David Dexter 6*
Melinda Duke 9*
Wesley Anderson 67

Public Schs..Principal	Grd	Prgm	Enr/#Cls	SN	
Century Elem Sch 4819 Shawnee College Rd, Ullin 62992 Melinda Duke	PK-5	T	163 14	69%	618/845-3572
Century Jr Sr High Sch 4721 Shawnee College Rd, Ullin 62992 Landon Sommer	6-12	T	206 17	52%	618/845-3518

• **Meridian Cmty School Dist 101** PID: 00314796 618/342-6776
1401 Mounds Rd, Mounds 62964 Fax 618/342-6401

Schools: 2 \ **Teachers:** 27 \ **Students:** 450 \ **Special Ed Students:** 99 \ **Ethnic:** African American 61%, Hispanic 1%, Caucasian 38% \ **Exp:** $705 (High) \ **Poverty:** 32% \ **Title I:** $367,061 \ **Special Education:** $130,000 \ **Open-Close:** 08/12 - 05/21 \ **DTBP:** $174 (High)

Jonathan Green 1,11
Randy Gardner 3
Scotty Henry 67
Lori Crow 2
Sherri Calvin 4
Cara Smith 79

Public Schs..Principal	Grd	Prgm	Enr/#Cls	SN	
Meridian Elem Sch 1401 Mounds Rd, Mounds 62964 Novella Harris	PK-5	T	287 60	98%	618/426-6776 Fax 618/426-6401
Meridian Jr Sr High Sch 1401 Mounds Rd, Mounds 62964 Maryann Boren	6-12	T	110 31	100%	618/342-6778 Fax 618/426-6401

PULASKI PRIVATE SCHOOLS

Private Schs..Principal	Grd	Prgm	Enr/#Cls	SN	
Caledonia Christian Academy PO Box 86, Olmsted 62970 Jennifer Windings	K-12		30 3		618/742-8223 Fax 618/742-8224

PULASKI REGIONAL CENTERS

• **Jamp Special Ed Services** PID: 02183880 618/634-9800
251 W 2nd St, Grand Chain 62941 Fax 618/634-9864

Doug Edwards 1,11

PUTNAM COUNTY

PUTNAM PUBLIC SCHOOLS

• **Putnam Co Cmty Unit SD 535** PID: 00314851 815/882-2800
400 E Silverspoon Ave, Granville 61326 Fax 815/882-2802

Schools: 4 \ **Teachers:** 68 \ **Students:** 853 \ **Special Ed Students:** 130 \ **LEP Students:** 14 \ **College-Bound:** 73% \ **Ethnic:** Hispanic 13%, Caucasian 86% \ **Exp:** $508 (High) \ **Poverty:** 11% \ **Title I:** $123,043 \ **Special Education:** $505,000 \ **Open-Close:** 08/13 - 05/25

Carl Carlson 1
Dan Rimzz 28,73
Tyler Ellena 31,69*
Rollie Copeland 67
Kylie Judd 274
Ronda Cross 11*
Carolyn Whiteside 29*
Suan McNelis 58,77*
Ethan Sproul 76

Public Schs..Principal	Grd	Prgm	Enr/#Cls	SN	
Putnam Co Elem Sch 326 S 5th St, Hennepin 61327 Courtney Balestri	3-5	T	158 16	46%	815/882-2800 Fax 815/925-7435
Putnam Co High Sch 402 E Silverspoon Ave, Granville 61326 Clayton Theisinger	9-12	AT	266 20	39%	815/882-2800 Fax 815/339-2628
Putnam Co Junior High Sch 13183 N 350th Ave, Mc Nabb 61335 Mike Olson	6-8	T	186 18	36%	815/882-2800 Fax 815/882-2299
Putnam Co Primary Center 400 E Silverspoon Ave, Granville 61326 Chawn Huffaker	PK-2	T	243	28%	815/882-2800 Fax 815/882-2801

Illinois School Directory

Randolph County

RANDOLPH COUNTY

RANDOLPH COUNTY SCHOOLS

County Schs..Principal	Grd	Prgm	Enr/#Cls	SN	
Beck Area Career Center 6137 Beck Rd, Red Bud 62278 Stephanie Mohr	Voc	AG	120 19		618/473-2222 Fax 618/473-2292
Perandoe Ed Program Red Bud 500 W South 4th St, Red Bud 62278 Mary Jo Renzaglia-Weir	Spec	A	67 6		618/282-7228 Fax 618/282-0809
Ⓐ Red Brick Sch 6137 Beck Rd, Red Bud 62278 Jana Bollman Young	6-12		30 2	60%	618/473-2222 Fax 618/282-7723

RANDOLPH PUBLIC SCHOOLS

• **Chester Cmty Unit Sch Dist 139** PID: 00314966   618/826-4509
1940 Swanwick St, Chester 62233   Fax 618/826-4500

> **Schools:** 2 \ **Teachers:** 63 \ **Students:** 950 \ **Special Ed Students:** 208 \ **LEP Students:** 25 \ **College-Bound:** 62% \ **Ethnic:** African American 2%, Hispanic 8%, Caucasian 90% \ **Exp:** $191 (Low) \ **Poverty:** 16% \ **Title I:** $308,848 \ **Special Education:** $491,000 \ **Open-Close:** 08/14 - 05/14 \ **DTBP:** $174 (High)

Brian Pasero 1,11,84   Brian McMath 3*
Jeremy Blechle ....6*   Shirley Stegmann 8
Mitch Hammel 67   Jeannie Golding 294

Public Schs..Principal	Grd	Prgm	Enr/#Cls	SN	
Chester Grade Sch 650 Opdyke St, Chester 62233 William Grafton	PK-8	T	660 35	55%	618/826-2354 Fax 618/826-2805 ⓕ
Chester High Sch 1901 Swanwick St, Chester 62233 Missy Meyer	9-12	TV	332 40	39%	618/826-2302 Fax 618/826-3723 ⓕ

• **Coulterville Unit Sch Dist 1** PID: 00314992   618/758-2881
101 W Grant St, Coulterville 62237   Fax 618/758-2887

> **Schools:** 1 \ **Teachers:** 17 \ **Students:** 196 \ **Special Ed Students:** 39 \ **College-Bound:** 27% \ **Ethnic:** African American 8%, Caucasian 92% \ **Exp:** $216 (Med) \ **Poverty:** 15% \ **Title I:** $59,982 \ **Special Education:** $108,000 \ **Open-Close:** 08/17 - 05/07 \ **DTBP:** $172 (High)

Karen Albers 1,11,73,84   Karen Carter 12*
Susan Watt ....35,85*   Richard Wooten 67

Public Schs..Principal	Grd	Prgm	Enr/#Cls	SN	
Coulterville Unit Sch 101 W Grant St, Coulterville 62237 Brandon Taylor	PK-12	GTV	196 13	62%	618/758-2881

• **Prairie Du Rocher CCSD 134** PID: 00315013   618/284-3530
714 Middle St, Pr Du Rocher 62277   Fax 618/284-3444

> **Schools:** 1 \ **Teachers:** 15 \ **Students:** 152 \ **Special Ed Students:** 45 \ **Ethnic:** Caucasian 100% \ **Exp:** $137 (Low) \ **Poverty:** 11% \ **Title I:** $24,298 \ **Special Education:** $65,000 \ **Open-Close:** 08/20 - 05/21

Rob Pipher 1   Donnie Godier 3*
Amanda Mudd 4   Thomas Springborn 11,73,288*
Terra Barbeau ....12*   Jacob Ratz 35,85
Kim Deterding 67   Kim Harmsen 88,270*

Public Schs..Principal	Grd	Prgm	Enr/#Cls	SN	
Prairie Du Rocher Elem Sch 714 Middle St, Pr Du Rocher 62277 Thomas Springborn	PK-8		152 10	47%	618/284-3530

• **Red Bud Cmty Unit Sch Dist 132** PID: 00315037   618/282-3507
815 Locust St, Red Bud 62278   Fax 618/282-6151

> **Schools:** 2 \ **Teachers:** 71 \ **Students:** 1,000 \ **Special Ed Students:** 175 \ **LEP Students:** 5 \ **Ethnic:** Hispanic 2%, Caucasian 97% \ **Exp:** $180 (Low) \ **Poverty:** 10% \ **Title I:** $177,128 \ **Special Education:** $426,000 \ **Open-Close:** 08/17 - 05/17 \ **DTBP:** $171 (High)

Jonathan Tallman 1   Kim Schaefer 2
Gordon Doty ....3*   Cari Lucht 5
Kevin Cartee ....6*   Tammy Kueker 7,85*
Ryan McClelan 11,296,298   Amy Howell 59*
Victoria Mudd ....60*   Larry Gielow 67
Kent Logsdon 73*

Public Schs..Principal	Grd	Prgm	Enr/#Cls	SN	
Red Bud Elem Sch 200 W Field Dr, Red Bud 62278 Ryan McClellan	PK-8	T	621 34	44%	618/282-3858 Fax 618/282-3965
Red Bud High Sch 815 Locust St, Red Bud 62278 Alan Guehne	9-12		391 34	35%	618/282-3826 Fax 618/282-6828

• **Sparta Cmty School Dist 140** PID: 00315063   618/443-5331
203B Dean Ave, Sparta 62286   Fax 618/443-2023

> **Schools:** 3 \ **Teachers:** 87 \ **Students:** 1,213 \ **Special Ed Students:** 216 \ **College-Bound:** 54% \ **Ethnic:** African American 16%, Hispanic 3%, Caucasian 81% \ **Exp:** $188 (Low) \ **Poverty:** 20% \ **Title I:** $563,605 \ **Special Education:** $338,000 \ **Open-Close:** 08/12 - 05/17 \ **DTBP:** $182 (High)

Gabrielle Schwemmer 1,11,83   Tina Witherby 2
Linda McMaster 4   Staci Kramper 6*
Staci Kramper 6   Sheila Eaton 31*
Amy Laramore 58   Cory Rheinecker 67
Rick Oeth 73,76,98,286,295,297

Public Schs..Principal	Grd	Prgm	Enr/#Cls	SN	
Evansville Attendance Center 701 Oak St, Evansville 62242 Chris Miesner	K-8	T	120 9	33%	618/853-4411 Fax 618/853-2243
Sparta High Sch 205 W Hood St, Sparta 62286 Scott Beckley	9-12	TV	333 40	50%	618/443-4341 Fax 618/443-5059
Sparta Lincoln Sch 203A Dean Ave, Sparta 62286 **Amy Laramore**	PK-8	T	760 21	64%	618/443-5331 Fax 618/443-2892

---

79 Student Personnel	91 Safety/Security	275 Response To Intervention	298 Grant Writer/Ptnrships	**School Programs**	**Social Media**	
80 Driver Ed/Safety	92 Magnet School	277 Remedial Math K-12	750 Chief Innovation Officer	A = Alternative Program		
81 Gifted/Talented	93 Parental Involvement	280 Literacy Coach	751 Chief of Staff	G = Adult Classes	ⓕ = Facebook	
82 Video Services	95 Tech Prep Program	285 STEM	752 Social Emotional Learning	M = Magnet Program		
83 Substance Abuse Prev	97 Chief Infomation Officer	286 Digital Learning		T = Title I Schoolwide	ⓣ = Twitter	
84 Erate	98 Chief Technology Officer	288 Common Core Standards	**Other School Types**	V = Career & Tech Ed Programs		
85 AIDS Education	270 Accountability	294 Accountability	Ⓐ = Alternative School			
88 Alternative/At Risk	271 Migrant Education	295 Network System	Ⓒ = Charter School	New Schools are shaded		
89 Multi-Cultural Curriculum	273 Teacher Mentor	296 Title II Programs	Ⓜ = Magnet School	New Superintendents and Principals are bold		
90 Social Work	274 Before/After Sch	297 Webmaster	Ⓨ = Year-Round School	Personnel with email addresses are underscored		

IL—205

Richland County

Market Data Retrieval

- **Steeleville Cmty Sch Dist 138** PID: 00315130   618/965-3469
  609 S Sparta St, Steeleville 62288   Fax 618/965-3490

Schools: 2 \ **Teachers:** 32 \ **Students:** 425 \ **Special Ed Students:** 69 \ **LEP Students:** 3 \ **College-Bound:** 67% \ **Ethnic:** African American 1%, Caucasian 98% \ **Exp:** $154 (Low) \ **Poverty:** 9% \ **Title I:** $66,568 \ **Special Education:** $196,000 \ **Open-Close:** 08/17 - 06/11 \ **DTBP:** $174 (High)

Dr Stephanie Mulholland 1,11   Kylie Mueller 2
Jennifer Haertling 15   Michelle Hamilton 31,36,69,83,88*
Tim Mitchell 67   Kathryn Cole 274*

Public Schs..Principal	Grd	Prgm	Enr/#Cls	SN	
Steeleville Elem Sch 609 S Sparta St, Steeleville 62288 Stephanie Mulholland	PK-8		270 15	36%	618/965-3469 Fax 618/653-3490
Steeleville High Sch 701 S Sparta St, Steeleville 62288 Jennifer Haertling	9-12	V	148 18	28%	618/965-3432 Fax 618/965-3433

RANDOLPH CATHOLIC SCHOOLS

- **Diocese of Belleville Ed Off** PID: 00317671
  Listing includes only schools located in this county. See District Index for location of Diocesan Offices.

Catholic Schs..Principal	Grd	Prgm	Enr/#Cls	SN	
St John the Baptist Sch 519 Hazel St, Red Bud 62278 Kris Hill	PK-8		92 10		618/282-3215 Fax 618/282-6790
St Mary's Sch 835 Swanwick St, Chester 62233 Janelle Robinson	PK-8		70 10		618/826-3120 Fax 618/826-3486

RANDOLPH PRIVATE SCHOOLS

Private Schs..Principal	Grd	Prgm	Enr/#Cls	SN	
Christ Our Savior Lutheran HS 810 Soldiers Way, Evansville 62242 Matthew Foster	9-12		20 6		618/853-7300 Fax 618/853-7361
St John Lutheran Sch 302 W Holmes St, Chester 62233 Kaela Powley	PK-8		113 14		618/826-4345 Fax 618/826-4804
St John Lutheran Sch 808 S Main St, Red Bud 62278 Deitt Schneider	PK-8		193 15		618/282-3873 Fax 618/282-4087
St Mark's Lutheran Sch 504 N James St, Steeleville 62288 Tim Lochhead	PK-8		136 11		618/965-3838 Fax 618/965-3060
Trinity Lutheran Sch 10247 S Prairie Rd, Red Bud 62278 John Bione	PK-8		49 5		618/282-2881 Fax 618/282-4045

RANDOLPH REGIONAL CENTERS

- **Okaw Regional Voc System** PID: 04184426   618/826-5471
  1 Taylor St Rm 101, Chester 62233   Fax 618/826-5474

- **Perandoe Special Ed District** PID: 02182173   618/282-6251
  1525 Locust St, Red Bud 62278   Fax 618/282-6880

Kathleen Hopkins 1   Maryjo Weir 15

RICHLAND COUNTY

RICHLAND PUBLIC SCHOOLS

- **Richland Co Cmty Unit SD 1** PID: 00315219   618/395-2324
  1100 E Laurel St, Olney 62450   Fax 618/392-4147

Schools: 3 \ **Teachers:** 142 \ **Students:** 2,500 \ **Special Ed Students:** 320 \ **LEP Students:** 15 \ **College-Bound:** 74% \ **Ethnic:** Asian 1%, African American 1%, Hispanic 4%, Caucasian 95% \ **Exp:** $181 (Low) \ **Poverty:** 19% \ **Title I:** $892,624 \ **Special Education:** $827,000 \ **Open-Close:** 08/31 - 06/03 \ **DTBP:** $174 (High)

Chris Simpson 1,11   Rita Kman 2
John McSarland 4   Matt Music 6
Chad Lecrone 15   Beth Petty 16,73,295,297*
Denise Eagleson ....16*   Heather Lee 36
Mick Whittler ....57,58,275*   Jeff Wilson 67

Public Schs..Principal	Grd	Prgm	Enr/#Cls	SN	
Richland Co Elem Sch 1001 N Holly Rd, Olney 62450 Chris Edwards	PK-5	T	1,138 48	60%	618/395-8540 Fax 618/395-8672
Richland Co High Sch 1200 E Laurel St, Olney 62450 Andrew Thomann	9-12	TV	725 52	41%	618/393-2191 Fax 618/395-1256
Richland Co Middle Sch 1099 N Van St, Olney 62450 Darrell Houchin	6-8	T	486 35	48%	618/395-4372 Fax 618/392-3399

RICHLAND CATHOLIC SCHOOLS

- **Diocese of Belleville Ed Off** PID: 00317671
  Listing includes only schools located in this county. See District Index for location of Diocesan Offices.

Catholic Schs..Principal	Grd	Prgm	Enr/#Cls	SN	
St Joseph Sch 520 E Chestnut St, Olney 62450 Carol Potter	PK-8		170 11		618/395-3081 Fax 618/395-8500

1 Superintendent	8 Curric/Instruct K-12	19 Chief Financial Officer	29 Family/Consumer Science	39 Social Studies K-12	49 English/Lang Arts Elem	59 Special Education Elem	69 Academic Assessment
2 Bus/Finance/Purchasing	9 Curric/Instruct Elem	20 Art K-12	30 Adult Education	40 Social Studies Elem	50 English/Lang Arts Sec	60 Special Education Sec	70 Research/Development
3 Buildings And Grounds	10 Curric/Instruct Sec	21 Art Elem	31 Career/Sch-to-Work K-12	41 Social Studies Sec	51 Reading K-12	61 Foreign/World Lang K-12	71 Public Information
4 Food Service	11 Federal Program	22 Art Sec	32 Career/Sch-to-Work Elem	42 Science K-12	52 Reading Elem	62 Foreign/World Lang Elem	72 Summer School
5 Transportation	12 Title I	23 Music K-12	33 Career/Sch-to-Work Sec	43 Science Elem	53 Reading Sec	63 Foreign/World Lang Sec	73 Instructional Tech
6 Athletic	13 Title V	24 Music Elem	34 Early Childhood Ed	44 Science Sec	54 Remedial Reading K-12	64 Religious Education K-12	74 Inservice Training
7 Health Services	15 Asst Superintendent	25 Music Sec	35 Health/Phys Education	45 Math K-12	55 Remedial Reading Elem	65 Religious Education Elem	75 Marketing/Distributive
	16 Instructional Media Svcs	26 Business Education	36 Guidance Services K-12	46 Math Elem	56 Remedial Reading Sec	66 Religious Education Sec	76 Info Systems
	17 Chief Operations Officer	27 Career & Tech Ed	37 Guidance Services Elem	47 Math Sec	57 Bilingual/ELL	67 School Board President	77 Psychological Assess
	18 Chief Academic Officer	28 Technology Education	38 Guidance Services Sec	48 English/Lang Arts K-12	58 Special Education K-12	68 Teacher Personnel	78 Affirmative Action

Illinois School Directory — Rock Island County

RICHLAND REGIONAL CENTERS

- **Regional Office of Ed 12** PID: 02098297   618/392-4631
  103 W Main St, Olney 62450   Fax 618/392-3993
  Monte Newlin 1

ROCK ISLAND COUNTY

ROCK ISLAND COUNTY SCHOOLS

County Schs..Principal	Grd	Prgm	Enr/#Cls	SN	
Black Hawk Area Spec Ed Center 4670 11th St, East Moline 61244 Kristi Loy	Spec		147 18	58%	309/796-2500 Fax 309/796-2911

ROCK ISLAND PUBLIC SCHOOLS

- **Carbon Cliff Barstow SD 36** PID: 00315350   309/792-2002
  2002 Eagle Ridge Dr, Silvis 61282   Fax 309/792-2242

Schools: 1 \ **Teachers:** 31 \ **Students:** 270 \ **Special Ed Students:** 62 \ **LEP Students:** 25 \ **Ethnic:** African American 31%, Hispanic 10%, Caucasian 59% \ **Exp:** $373 (High) \ **Poverty:** 33% \ **Title I:** $188,322 \ **Special Education:** $144,000 \ **Open-Close:** 08/18 - 05/28 \ **DTBP:** $97 (Med)

Andy Richmond 1,11,83   Ryan Moore 3
Michelle Wirt .... 4*   Carol Nutt 7*
Heidi Lensing 16,73,275,286,288   Mira Raya 57
Lisa Cantrell 67   Barb Moller 285*

Public Schs..Principal	Grd	Prgm	Enr/#Cls	SN	
Eagle Ridge Elem Sch 2002 Eagle Ridge Dr, Silvis 61282 Heidi Lensing	PK-8	T	270 16	100%	309/792-2002 t

- **East Moline Public Sch Dist 37** PID: 00315386   309/792-2887
  3451 Morton Dr, East Moline 61244   Fax 309/792-6010

Schools: 5 \ **Teachers:** 180 \ **Students:** 2,650 \ **Special Ed Students:** 424 \ **LEP Students:** 584 \ **Ethnic:** Asian 5%, African American 26%, Hispanic 28%, Caucasian 42% \ **Exp:** $166 (Low) \ **Poverty:** 26% \ **Title I:** $1,338,264 \ **Special Education:** $1,286,000 \ **Bilingual Education:** $213,000 \ **Open-Close:** 08/17 - 05/27 \ **DTBP:** $211 (High)

Dr Kristin Humphries 1   Casey Kyser 2
Jim Franks 3   Colin Kave 4
Evelyn Gay 5   Jaylee Swanson 7,34,74,77,83,88,90,271
Sheri Coder 9,11,15,69,275,288,296,298   Branson Rasco 16,73,76,295,297
Paul Southwell 57   Kai Killam 67
Christine Mueller 68   Erik Tank 295
Alan Daso 752

Public Schs..Principal	Grd	Prgm	Enr/#Cls	SN	
Bowlesburg Elem Sch 2221 10th St, Silvis 61282 Jeff Fairweather	K-4	T	337 18	99%	309/792-2947 Fax 309/792-9658
Glenview Middle Sch 3100 7th St, East Moline 61244 Tracy Anderson	5-8	T	1,167 60	99%	309/755-1919 Fax 309/752-2564
Hillcrest Elem Sch 451 22nd Ave, East Moline 61244 Stephanie Christensen	K-4	T	338 17	99%	309/755-7621 Fax 309/752-2569
Ridgewood Elem Sch 814 30th Ave, East Moline 61244 Alexander Mayszak	K-4	T	413 21	100%	309/755-1585 Fax 309/752-2570
Wells Elem Sch 490 Avenue of the Cities, East Moline 61244 Kenneth Spranger	PK-4	T	437 20	99%	309/796-1251 Fax 309/796-1751 t

- **Hampton School District 29** PID: 00315477   309/755-0693
  206 5th St, Hampton 61256   Fax 309/755-0694

Schools: 1 \ **Teachers:** 16 \ **Students:** 210 \ **Special Ed Students:** 38 \ **Ethnic:** African American 5%, Hispanic 12%, Caucasian 83% \ **Exp:** $229 (Med) \ **Poverty:** 12% \ **Title I:** $47,773 \ **Special Education:** $39,000 \ **Open-Close:** 08/05 - 05/24 \ **DTBP:** $233 (High)

Scott McKissick 1,11,73,83   Bo Rigsby 3*
Chris Wils 6   Maureen Okeefe 7*
Teri DeCock 12   Jessica Thorpe 59*
Liz Bornhoeft 67

Public Schs..Principal	Grd	Prgm	Enr/#Cls	SN	
Hampton Elem Sch 206 5th St, Hampton 61256 Thomas Berg	PK-8		210 18	24%	309/755-0693

- **Moline-Coal Valley SD No 40** PID: 00315491   309/743-1600
  1619 11th Ave, Moline 61265   Fax 309/757-3476

Schools: 15 \ **Teachers:** 416 \ **Students:** 7,182 \ **Special Ed Students:** 997 \ **LEP Students:** 909 \ **College-Bound:** 59% \ **Ethnic:** Asian 3%, African American 10%, Hispanic 32%, Caucasian 55% \ **Exp:** $203 (Med) \ **Poverty:** 18% \ **Title I:** $2,511,697 \ **Special Education:** $4,428,000 \ **Bilingual Education:** $218,000 \ **Open-Close:** 08/18 - 05/28 \ **DTBP:** $230 (High)

Dr Rachel Savage 1   David McDermott 2,4,5,19,31
Dan Smith 3,91   Richard Knar 6
Kim Nelson .... 7,85*   Matt Debaene 8,15,16,273
Stephanee Jordan 8,11,57   Tom Ryerson 8
Todd Detaeye 12,15,68,69   Kristin Sanders 15,58,77,78,79,90
Jose Castro .... 63*   Sangeetha Rayapati 67
Craig Reid 73,76,84   Kevin Gorgal 80*
Rachel Fowler 88*

Public Schs..Principal	Grd	Prgm	Enr/#Cls	SN	
Benjamin Franklin Elem Sch 5312 11th Avenue C, Moline 61265 Michele Pittington	K-5	T	262 13	53%	309/743-1607 Fax 309/736-2231
Bicentennial Elem Sch 1004 1st St, Coal Valley 61240 Steven Etheridge	K-5		291 8	28%	309/431-1614 Fax 309/799-7789
Butterworth Elem Sch 4205 48th St, Moline 61265 Chris Lensing	PK-5	T	248 17	58%	309/743-1604 Fax 309/757-3503

---

79 Student Personnel	91 Safety/Security	275 Response To Intervention	298 Grant Writer/Ptnrships	**School Programs**	**Social Media**
80 Driver Ed/Safety	92 Magnet School	277 Remedial Math K-12	750 Chief Innovation Officer	A = Alternative Program	
81 Gifted/Talented	93 Parental Involvement	280 Literacy Coach	751 Chief of Staff	G = Adult Classes	f = Facebook
82 Video Services	95 Tech Prep Program	285 STEM	752 Social Emotional Learning	M = Magnet Program	
83 Substance Abuse Prev	97 Chief Infomation Officer	286 Digital Learning		T = Title I Schoolwide	t = Twitter
84 Erate	98 Chief Technology Officer	288 Common Core Standards	**Other School Types**	V = Career & Tech Ed Programs	
85 AIDS Education	270 Character Education	294 Accountability	A = Alternative School		
88 Alternative/At Risk	271 Migrant Education	295 Network System	C = Charter School	New Schools are shaded	
89 Multi-Cultural Curriculum	273 Teacher Mentor	296 Title II Programs	M = Magnet School	New Superintendents and Principals are bold	
90 Social Work	274 Before/After Sch	297 Webmaster	Y = Year-Round School	Personnel with email addresses are underscored	

Rock Island County

Market Data Retrieval

School	Grd	Prgm	Enr/#Cls	SN	Phone
George Washington Elem Sch 1550 41st St, Moline 61265 **Brian Price**	K-5	T	271 16	74%	309/743-1619 Fax 309/757-3665
Hamilton Elem Sch 700 32nd Ave, Moline 61265 Todd Williams	PK-5	T	579 6	54%	309/743-1610 Fax 309/757-3669
Jane Addams Elem Sch 3520 53rd St, Moline 61265 Teresa Landon	K-5	T	274 13	39%	309/743-1601 Fax 309/757-3580
Jefferson Early Childhood Ctr 3010 26th Ave, Moline 61265 Rachel Fowler	PK-PK	T	210 9	52%	309/743-1611 Fax 309/757-1895
John Deere Middle Sch 2035 11th St, Moline 61265 Dusti Adrian	6-8	TV	783 50	59%	309/743-1622 Fax 309/757-3668
Lincoln-Irving Elem Sch 1015 16th Ave, Moline 61265 Rosalva Portillo	PK-5	T	359 26	88%	309/743-1612 Fax 309/757-3584
Logan Elem Sch 1602 25th St, Moline 61265 Tom Ferguson	K-5	T	328 19	70%	309/743-1613 Fax 309/757-3583
Ⓐ Moline Alt-Coolidge Campus Ⓨ 3428 Avenue of the Cities, Moline 61265 Chad Davis	9-12	MTV	94 5	88%	309/743-8587 Fax 309/757-3522
Moline Senior High Sch 3600 Avenue of the Cities, Moline 61265 Trista Sanders	9-12	TV	2,082 100	47%	309/743-1624 Fax 309/757-3667
Roosevelt Elem Sch 3530 Avenue of the Cities, Moline 61265 Sharon Lanskey	PK-5	T	384 20	49%	309/743-1617 Fax 309/757-3521
Willard Elem Sch 1616 16th St, Moline 61265 Victoria Bohlman	K-5	T	218 10	80%	309/743-1620 Fax 309/736-2230
Woodrow Wilson Middle Sch 1301 48th St, Moline 61265 Robert Beem	6-8	TV	860 40	50%	309/743-1623 Fax 309/757-3586

• **Riverdale Cmty Unit SD 100** PID: 00315752 309/523-3184
9624 256th St N, Port Byron 61275 Fax 309/523-3550

Schools: 3 \ **Teachers:** 74 \ **Students:** 1,160 \ **Special Ed Students:** 148 \ **LEP Students:** 3 \ **College-Bound:** 72% \ **Ethnic:** Hispanic 4%, Caucasian 95% \ **Exp:** $228 (Med) \ **Poverty:** 13% \ **Title I:** $233,375 \ **Special Education:** $428,000 \ **Open-Close:** 08/17 - 05/20 \ **DTBP:** $172 (High)

Joshua Temple 1
Deb Beale 4
Guy Dierkx 6*
Lisa Petersen 37*
Brian Plumb 67
Ami Henricksen 76*
Jan Hamelin 3
Lori Ortiz 5
Richard Dwyer 10,27,57*
James Jennings 58*
Jason Dennhardt 73
Melissa Olson 85*

Public Schs..Principal	Grd	Prgm	Enr/#Cls	SN	Phone
Riverdale Elem Sch 9424 256th St N, Port Byron 61275 **Mark Lofgren**	PK-5		562 26	4%	309/523-3186 Fax 309/523-2870
Riverdale Middle Sch 9822 256th St N, Port Byron 61275 James Jennings	6-8	A	260 13		309/523-3131 Fax 309/523-3934
Riverdale Senior High Sch 9622 256th St N, Port Byron 61275 Richard Dwyer	9-12	AV	334 31		309/523-3181 Fax 309/523-2885

• **Rock Island-Milan Sch Dist 41** PID: 00315831 309/793-5900
2101 6th Ave, Rock Island 61201 Fax 309/793-5905

Schools: 14 \ **Teachers:** 379 \ **Students:** 5,800 \ **Special Ed Students:** 1,088 \ **LEP Students:** 673 \ **College-Bound:** 52% \ **Ethnic:** Asian 6%, African American 34%, Hispanic 14%, Caucasian 46% \ **Exp:** $410 (High) \ **Poverty:** 24% \ **Title I:** $3,059,959 \ **Special Education:** $3,394,000 \ **Bilingual Education:** $200,000 \ **Open-Close:** 08/06 - 05/28 \ **DTBP:** $218 (High)

Dr Reginald Lawrence 1
Dewinn Hume 3
Michelle Lillis 6
Kathryn Ruggeberg .8,11,15,285,286,288,298
Egan Colbrese 15,68,90,273
Peter Carlin 23*
Lashanta Williams 57
Patricia Walls 68
Melanie Lloyd 76
Bob Beckwith 2,298
Beth MacKenna 4
Alicia Sierra-Sanders 7,58,77,79,83,88
Ramona Dixson 11,31,51,54,69,72,294,298
Troy Bevans 16,73,76,82,295
Nicole Berry 34*
Gary Rowe 67
Holly Sparkman 71

Public Schs..Principal	Grd	Prgm	Enr/#Cls	SN	Phone
Denkmann Elem Sch 4101 22nd Ave, Rock Island 61201 John Frieden	K-6	T	411 20	50%	309/793-5922 Fax 309/793-5988
Earl Hanson Elem Sch 4000 9th St, Rock Island 61201 Daniel Coyne-Logan	PK-6	T	388 24	80%	309/793-5930 Fax 309/793-4195
Edison Junior High Sch 4141 9th St, Rock Island 61201 Christi Varnes	7-8	T	389 30	74%	309/793-5920 Fax 309/793-5919
Eugene Field Elem Sch 2900 31st Ave, Rock Island 61201 Dennis Weiss	K-6	T	389 11	40%	309/793-5935 Fax 309/793-5936
Frances Willard Elem Sch 2503 9th St, Rock Island 61201 Lance Clark	K-6	T	335 13	97%	309/793-5940 Fax 309/793-5941
Horace Mann Early Learning Ctr 3530 38th Ave, Rock Island 61201 Nicole Berry	PK-PK	T	158 7	55%	309/793-5928 Fax 309/793-5979
Longfellow Liberal Arts ES 4198 7th Ave, Rock Island 61201 Dave Knuckey	PK-6	T	287 9	70%	309/793-5975 Fax 309/793-5977
Ridgewood Elem Sch 9607 14th St W, Rock Island 61201 Joey Di Iulio	PK-6	T	279 14	75%	309/793-5980 Fax 309/793-5981
Rock Island Academy 930 14th St, Rock Island 61201 Thomas Ryan	PK-6	T	458 16	92%	309/793-5944 Fax 309/793-5909
Rock Island Ctr Math & Science 2101 16th Ave, Rock Island 61201 Amy Schelker	PK-6	T	535	61%	309/793-5995 Fax 309/793-5996
Rock Island High Sch 1400 25th Ave, Rock Island 61201 Jeff Whitaker	9-12	T	1,595 100	58%	309/793-5950 Fax 309/793-9866
Thomas Jefferson Elem Sch 1307 4th St W, Milan 61264 **Dr Dorian Maag** \ Mike Nitzel	PK-6	T	370 20	69%	309/793-5985 Fax 309/793-5986
Thurgood Marshall Lrng Center 600 11th Ave, Rock Island 61201 Phil Ambrose	Spec	T	105 10	55%	309/793-5924 Fax 309/793-5979
Washington Junior High Sch 3300 18th Ave, Rock Island 61201 Kristin Allen	7-8	T	500 40	62%	309/793-5915 Fax 309/793-5917

1 Superintendent	8 Curric/Instruct K-12	19 Chief Financial Officer	29 Family/Consumer Science	39 Social Studies K-12	49 English/Lang Arts Elem	59 Special Education Elem	69 Academic Assessment
2 Bus/Finance/Purchasing	9 Curric/Instruct Elem	20 Art K-12	30 Adult Education	40 Social Studies Elem	50 English/Lang Arts Sec	60 Special Education Sec	70 Research/Development
3 Buildings And Grounds	10 Curric/Instruct Sec	21 Art Elem	31 Career/Sch-to-Work K-12	41 Social Studies Sec	51 Reading K-12	61 Foreign/World Lang K-12	71 Public Information
4 Food Service	11 Federal Program	22 Art Sec	32 Career/Sch-to-Work Elem	42 Science K-12	52 Reading Elem	62 Foreign/World Lang Elem	72 Summer School
5 Transportation	12 Title I	23 Music K-12	33 Career/Sch-to-Work Sec	43 Science Elem	53 Reading Sec	63 Foreign/World Lang Sec	73 Instructional Tech
6 Athletic	13 Title V	24 Music Elem	34 Early Childhood Ed	44 Science Sec	54 Remedial Reading K-12	64 Religious Education K-12	74 Inservice Training
7 Health Services	15 Asst Superintendent	25 Music Sec	35 Health/Phys Education	45 Math K-12	55 Remedial Reading Elem	65 Religious Education Elem	75 Marketing/Distributive
	16 Instructional Media Svcs	26 Business Education	36 Guidance Services K-12	46 Math Elem	56 Remedial Reading Sec	66 Religious Education Sec	76 Info Systems
	17 Chief Operations Officer	27 Career & Tech Ed	37 Guidance Services Elem	47 Math Sec	57 Bilingual/ELL	67 School Board President	77 Psychological Assess
	18 Chief Academic Officer	28 Technology Education	38 Guidance Services Sec	48 English/Lang Arts K-12	58 Special Education K-12	68 Teacher Personnel	78 Affirmative Action

Illinois School Directory — Rock Island County

• **Rockridge Cmty Unit SD 300** PID: 00316031   309/793-8001
14110 134th Ave W, Taylor Ridge 61284   Fax 309/795-1719

Schools: 5 \ **Teachers:** 70 \ **Students:** 1,097 \ **Special Ed Students:** 126 \ **LEP Students:** 3 \ **College-Bound:** 73% \ **Ethnic:** Hispanic 2%, Caucasian 98% \ **Exp:** $239 (Med) \ **Poverty:** 9% \ **Title I:** $198,176 \ **Special Education:** $408,000 \ **Open-Close:** 08/17 - 05/28

Perry Miller 1	Jaymie Lum 2
Kelli Weeks 4*	Sarah Stropes 5
Scott Daly 6*	Sarah Leonard 11,296*
Jacque Peterson 16,82*	Anne Bohnsack 38,83*
Nathan Faith 67	Jon Lehtola 73,295*

Public Schs..Principal	Grd	Prgm	Enr/#Cls	SN		
Andalusia Elem Sch 112 7th Ave E, Andalusia 61232 Mike Ruff	3-5		225 15	19%	309/793-8080 Fax 309/798-9651	
Illinois City Elem Sch 24017 122nd Ave W, Illinois City 61259 Sarah Leonard	K-2		69 1	20%	309/793-8040 Fax 309/791-0710	
Rockridge High Sch 14110 134th Ave W, Taylor Ridge 61284 Katie Hasson	9-12	V	360 34	21%	309/793-8020 Fax 309/795-1763	
Rockridge Junior High Sch 14110 134th Ave W, Taylor Ridge 61284 Scott Daly	6-8		261 14	21%	309/793-8040 Fax 309/795-9823	
Taylor Ridge Elem Sch 13227 Turkey Hollow Rd, Taylor Ridge 61284 Jenna Emery	PK-2		163 7	9%	309/793-8070 Fax 309/798-5523	

• **Silvis School District 34** PID: 00316110   309/792-9325
4280 4th Ave, East Moline 61244   Fax 309/203-1322

Schools: 2 \ **Teachers:** 41 \ **Students:** 648 \ **Special Ed Students:** 102 \ **LEP Students:** 62 \ **Ethnic:** Asian 1%, African American 14%, Hispanic 26%, Caucasian 59% \ **Exp:** $283 (Med) \ **Poverty:** 22% \ **Title I:** $241,852 \ **Special Education:** $262,000 \ **Bilingual Education:** $12,000 \ **Open-Close:** 08/11 - 05/28 \ **DTBP:** $262 (High)

Dr Terri Vandewiele 1	Wendy Harrell 2,11,84,296
Jim Franks 3	Colin Kave 4
Amber Sensabaugh 5,16,280	Jim Widdop 5,88,271,275,285*
Valery Schneider 5	Ryan Lootens 6
America Bunker 7*	David Mills 9,11,288
Megan Terry 16	Gail Staples 34
Jennifer Caldwell 37,59,83,85,270,752	Paul Southwell 57
Kevin Rossmiller 67	John Wolfe 73,286,295
Dionne Sibley 280	

Public Schs..Principal	Grd	Prgm	Enr/#Cls	SN	
George O Barr Elem Sch 1305 5th Avenue, Silvis 61282 Michael Hughes	PK-5	T	453 35	59%	309/792-0639 Fax 309/792-8092
Northeast Jr High Sch 4280 4th Ave, East Moline 61244 Jim Widdop	6-8		183 10	54%	309/203-1300

• **United Twp High Sch Dist 30** PID: 00316146   309/752-1611
1275 Avenue of the Cities, East Moline 61244   Fax 309/752-1615

Schools: 2 \ **Teachers:** 92 \ **Students:** 1,678 \ **Special Ed Students:** 256 \ **LEP Students:** 122 \ **College-Bound:** 57% \ **Ethnic:** Asian 3%, African American 15%, Hispanic 26%, Caucasian 56% \ **Exp:** $241 (Med) \ **Poverty:** 18% \ **Title I:** $588,121 \ **Special Education:** $600,000 \ **Bilingual Education:** $18,000 \ **Open-Close:** 08/03 - 06/01 \ **DTBP:** $251 (High)

Dr Jay Morrow 1	Tracy Decleck 2
Scott Ringberg 4*	Pam Curless 5
Mark Pustelnik 6*	Sharon Morris 7*
Shannon Miller 10,11,15,69,296*	Deborah Holmes 33*
Erin Terstriep 60	Susan Koska 67

Public Schs..Principal	Grd	Prgm	Enr/#Cls	SN	
ⓨ United Township High Sch 1275 Avenue of the Cities, East Moline 61244 Mathew Wright	9-12	MT	1,678 120	60%	309/752-1633
ⓨ United Twp Area Career Center 1275 Avenue of the Cities, East Moline 61244 Larry Shimmin	Voc	M	200 15		309/752-1691 Fax 309/752-1692

ROCK ISLAND CATHOLIC SCHOOLS

• **Diocese of Peoria Ed Office** PID: 00313338
Listing includes only schools located in this county. See District Index for location of Diocesan Offices.

Catholic Schs..Principal	Grd	Prgm	Enr/#Cls	SN	
Alleman High Sch 1103 40th St, Rock Island 61201 Sara Stroud	9-12		465 35		309/786-7793 Fax 309/786-7834
Jordan Catholic Sch 2901 24th St, Rock Island 61201 Jacob Smithers	PK-8		475 20		309/793-7350 Fax 309/793-7361 f
Our Lady of Grace Cath Academy 602 17th Ave, East Moline 61244 Jim Caparula	PK-8		150 13		309/755-9771 Fax 309/755-7407
Seton Catholic Sch 1320 16th Ave, Moline 61265 Jane Barrett	PK-8		545 24		309/757-5500 Fax 309/762-0545

ROCK ISLAND PRIVATE SCHOOLS

Private Schs..Principal	Grd	Prgm	Enr/#Cls	SN	
Arrowhead Ranch Sch 12200 104th St, Coal Valley 61240 David Hobin	6-12	V	17 6		309/799-7044 Fax 309/799-7090
East Moline Christian Sch 900 46th Ave, East Moline 61244 Ron Patrick	PK-12		380		309/796-1485 Fax 309/796-1152
Riverside Christian Sch 309 3rd St E, Andalusia 61232 William Gluck	PK-12		29 2		309/798-2857
St Paul Lutheran Sch 153 19th Ave, Moline 61265 Robert Pagel	PK-8		62 3		309/762-4494

79 Student Personnel	91 Safety/Security	275 Response To Intervention	298 Grant Writer/Ptnrships	**School Programs**	**Social Media**
80 Driver Ed/Safety	92 Magnet School	277 Remedial Math K-12	750 Chief Innovation Officer	A = Alternative Program	f = Facebook
81 Gifted/Talented	93 Parental Involvement	280 Literacy Coach	751 Chief of Staff	G = Adult Classes	t = Twitter
82 Video Services	95 Tech Prep Program	285 STEM	752 Social Emotional Learning	M = Magnet Program	
83 Substance Abuse Prev	97 Chief Infomation Officer	286 Digital Learning	**Other School Types**	T = Title I Schoolwide	
84 Erate	98 Chief Technology Officer	288 Common Core Standards	Ⓐ = Alternative School	V = Career & Tech Ed Programs	
85 AIDS Education	270 Character Education	294 Accountability	Ⓒ = Charter School	New Schools are shaded	
88 Alternative/At Risk	271 Migrant Education	295 Network System	Ⓜ = Magnet School	New Superintendents and Principals are bold	
89 Multi-Cultural Curriculum	273 Teacher Mentor	296 Title II Programs	Ⓨ = Year-Round School	Personnel with email addresses are underscored	
90 Social Work	274 Before/After Sch	297 Webmaster			

Saline County   Market Data Retrieval

Temple Christian Academy 2305 7th Ave, Moline 61265 Laura Stout	PK-6	150 14	309/764-1302
Villa Montessori Sch 2100 48th St, Moline 61265 Renee Detloff	PK-6	90 5	309/764-7047 Fax 309/764-9925

ROCK ISLAND REGIONAL CENTERS

● **Black Hawk Area Spec Ed Dist** PID: 02182226 309/796-2500
4670 11th St, East Moline 61244 Fax 309/796-2911

Christan Schrader ....1,11 Carole Allert 58

● **Rock Island Reg Off of Ed 49** PID: 02098302 309/736-1111
3430 Avenue of the Cities, Moline 61265 Fax 309/736-1127

Tammy Muerhoff .... 1 Natalie Doyle 34
Molly Van 73,76

● **UT Area Career Center** PID: 04178219 309/752-1691
1275 Avenue of the Cities, East Moline 61244 Fax 309/752-1692

Larry Shimmin .... 1 Michael Legate 28

SALINE COUNTY

SALINE PUBLIC SCHOOLS

● **Carrier Mills-Stonefort SD 2** PID: 00318302 618/994-2392
7071 US 45 S, Carrier Mills 62917 Fax 618/994-2929

Schools: 2 \ **Teachers:** 31 \ **Students:** 450 \ **Special Ed Students:** 101 \ **College-Bound:** 70% \ **Ethnic:** African American 13%, Hispanic 1%, Caucasian 86% \ **Exp:** $339 (High) \ **Poverty:** 33% \ **Title I:** $294,883 \ **Special Education:** $115,000 \ **Open-Close:** 08/14 - 05/18

Bryce Jerrell ....1,288 Megan Cain 2
Melissa Kuhlmann ....8,57,58,83* Charles Parks 11*
Robert Manier ....16,73,286* Scott Fig 67
Bob Manter 298

Public Schs..Principal	Grd	Prgm	Enr/#Cls	SN	
Carrier Mills-Stonefort ES 213 W Furlong St, Carrier Mills 62917 Bryce Jerrell	PK-8	T	323 21	47%	618/994-2413 Fax 618/994-4141
Carrier Mills-Stonefort HS 7071 US 45 S, Carrier Mills 62917 Richard Morgan	9-12	T	127	48%	618/994-2392

● **Eldorado Cmty Unit Sch Dist 4** PID: 00318340 618/273-6394
2200 Illinois Ave, Eldorado 62930 Fax 618/273-9311

Schools: 3 \ **Teachers:** 79 \ **Students:** 1,200 \ **Special Ed Students:** 203 \ **College-Bound:** 69% \ **Ethnic:** African American 1%, Hispanic 1%, Caucasian 98% \ **Exp:** $288 (Med) \ **Poverty:** 30% \ **Title I:** $642,966 \ **Special Education:** $247,000 \ **Open-Close:** 08/14 - 06/01 \ **DTBP:** $168 (High)

Ryan Hobbs ....1,83 Michelle Bradley 2
Eric Cantrell .... 3* Robbie Spurlock 4*
Cody Cusic .... 5* Rick Cox 11,57,69,270,273,274,296
Rachel Anderson ....36* Tracy Stafford 58*
David Bartok .... 67 Tj Zurliene 73*

Public Schs..Principal	Grd	Prgm	Enr/#Cls	SN	
Eldorado Elem Sch 1100 Alexander St, Eldorado 62930 Blake Bradley	PK-5	T	570 28	59%	618/273-9324 Fax 618/273-9661
Eldorado High Sch 2200 Illinois Ave, Eldorado 62930 Cody Cusic	9-12	TV	353 25	61%	618/273-2881 Fax 618/273-8153
Eldorado Middle Sch 1907 1st St, Eldorado 62930 Billy Tippett	6-8	T	234 21	66%	618/273-8056 Fax 618/273-2943

● **Galatia Cmty Unit Sch Dist 1** PID: 00318417 618/297-4570
200 N Hickory St, Galatia 62935 Fax 618/268-4949

Schools: 2 \ **Teachers:** 34 \ **Students:** 364 \ **Special Ed Students:** 102 \ **College-Bound:** 82% \ **Ethnic:** Hispanic 1%, Native American: 1%, Caucasian 98% \ **Exp:** $246 (Med) \ **Poverty:** 22% \ **Title I:** $139,361 \ **Special Education:** $103,000 \ **Open-Close:** 08/17 - 05/18 \ **DTBP:** $174 (High)

Shain Crank .... 1 Starla Digg 4
Paula Allen .... 6 Tim Pribble 67
Cheryl Disney 73,295

Public Schs..Principal	Grd	Prgm	Enr/#Cls	SN	
Galatia Grade Sch 200 N Hickory St, Galatia 62935 Shain Crank	K-6		211 16	53%	618/268-6371
Galatia Jr Sr High Sch 200 N McKinley St, Galatia 62935 Ashley Lanius	7-12	ATV	150 20	41%	618/297-4571 Fax 618/297-4504

● **Harrisburg Cmty Unit SD 3** PID: 00318443 618/253-7637
411 W Poplar St, Harrisburg 62946 Fax 618/253-2095

Schools: 4 \ **Teachers:** 127 \ **Students:** 1,879 \ **Special Ed Students:** 384 \ **LEP Students:** 3 \ **College-Bound:** 63% \ **Ethnic:** Asian 2%, African American 4%, Hispanic 2%, Caucasian 92% \ **Exp:** $418 (High) \ **Poverty:** 27% \ **Title I:** $1,063,671 \ **Special Education:** $620,000 \ **Open-Close:** 08/24 - 05/20 \ **DTBP:** $172 (High)

Mike Gauch .... 1 Elizabeth Williams 2,19
Anthony Chrisman .... 3 Valerie Hodges 4
Randy Smith Peters .... 5 Greg Langley 6*
Natlie Fry ....8,57,298 Cindy Black 11,84
Sherri Fox ....16,73 Kim Williams 58,752*
Chris Penrod .... 67 Nikki Williams 73
Scott DeWar ....88* Stephanie Milligan 274

---

1 Superintendent	8 Curric/Instruct K-12	19 Chief Financial Officer	29 Family/Consumer Science	39 Social Studies K-12	49 English/Lang Arts Elem	59 Special Education Elem	69 Academic Assessment
2 Bus/Finance/Purchasing	9 Curric/Instruct Elem	20 Art K-12	30 Adult Education	40 Social Studies Elem	50 English/Lang Arts Sec	60 Special Education Sec	70 Research/Development
3 Buildings And Grounds	10 Curric/Instruct Sec	21 Art Elem	31 Career/Sch-to-Work K-12	41 Social Studies Sec	51 Reading K-12	61 Foreign/World Lang K-12	71 Public Information
4 Food Service	11 Federal Program	22 Art Sec	32 Career/Sch-to-Work Elem	42 Science K-12	52 Reading Elem	62 Foreign/World Lang Elem	72 Summer School
5 Transportation	12 Title I	23 Music K-12	33 Career/Sch-to-Work Sec	43 Science Elem	53 Reading Sec	63 Foreign/World Lang Sec	73 Instructional Tech
6 Athletic	13 Title V	24 Music Elem	34 Early Childhood Ed	44 Science Sec	54 Remedial Reading K-12	64 Religious Education K-12	74 Inservice Training
7 Health Services	15 Asst Superintendent	25 Music Sec	35 Health/Phys Education	45 Math K-12	55 Remedial Reading Elem	65 Religious Education Elem	75 Marketing/Distributive
	16 Instructional Media Svcs	26 Business Education	36 Guidance Services K-12	46 Math Elem	56 Remedial Reading Sec	66 Religious Education Sec	76 Info Systems
	17 Chief Operations Officer	27 Career & Tech Ed	37 Guidance Services Elem	47 Math Sec	57 Bilingual/ELL	67 School Board President	77 Psychological Assess
	18 Chief Academic Officer	28 Technology Education	38 Guidance Services Sec	48 English/Lang Arts K-12	58 Special Education K-12	68 Teacher Personnel	78 Affirmative Action

Illinois School Directory

Sangamon County

Public Schs..Principal	Grd	Prgm	Enr/#Cls	SN	
East Side Intermediate Sch 315 E Church St, Harrisburg 62946 Natalie Fry \ **Eric McCollum**	3-5	T	409 23	65% Fax	618/253-7637 618/253-2087
Harrisburg High Sch 333 W College St, Harrisburg 62946 Scott DeWar	9-12	TV	543 45	55% Fax	618/253-7637 618/252-0994
Harrisburg Middle Sch 312 Bulldog Blvd, Harrisburg 62946 Debbie McGowan	6-8	T	428 25	58% Fax	618/253-7637 618/253-2093
West Side Primary Sch 411 W Lincoln St, Harrisburg 62946 Eric Witges	PK-2	T	499 23	68% Fax	618/253-7637 618/253-2094

SALINE PRIVATE SCHOOLS

Private Schs..Principal	Grd	Prgm	Enr/#Cls	SN	
Lighthouse Baptist Sch 70 Lighthouse Rd, Harrisburg 62946 Loy Barger	PK-12		13 3		618/252-7579

SALINE REGIONAL CENTERS

- **Regional Office of Ed 20** PID: 02098338   618/253-5581
  512 N Main St, Harrisburg 62946   Fax 618/252-8472

Dr Beth Rister 1   Sarah Emery 15
Adam Morton 34

SANGAMON COUNTY

SANGAMON COUNTY SCHOOLS

County Schs..Principal	Grd	Prgm	Enr/#Cls	SN	
Sased Central Sch 2500 Taylor Ave, Springfield 62703 Liz Horn	Spec		50 10	64%	217/786-3250

SANGAMON PUBLIC SCHOOLS

- **Auburn Cmty Unit Sch Dist 10** PID: 00318522   217/438-6164
  606 W North St, Auburn 62615   Fax 217/438-6483

Schools: 4 \ **Teachers:** 86 \ **Students:** 1,317 \ **Special Ed Students:** 180 \ **College-Bound:** 65% \ **Ethnic:** African American 1%, Hispanic 2%, Caucasian 97% \ **Exp:** $209 (Med) \ **Poverty:** 10% \ **Title I:** $291,009 \ **Special Education:** $295,000 \ **Open-Close:** 08/19 - 05/24 \ **DTBP:** $266 (High) \ ◘ ◙

Darren Root 1   Gina Guile 2
Bob Oller 3,5   Dave Bates 6
Amy Donaldson ....11,296,298*   Christy Bailey 36,69*
Denise Meyers 58   Fred Jessep 67
Dave Scheuermann 73*

Public Schs..Principal	Grd	Prgm	Enr/#Cls	SN	
Auburn Elem Sch 445 N 5th St, Auburn 62615 Amy Donaldson	PK-2	T	344 30	32% Fax	217/438-6916 217/438-3912
Auburn High Sch 511 N 7th St, Auburn 62615 Nathan Essex	9-12		414 30	32% Fax	217/438-6817 217/438-6153 ◙
Auburn Junior High Sch 303 E Kenney St, Divernon 62530 Mark Dudley	6-8	T	296 29	40% Fax	217/628-3414 217/628-3814
Auburn Middle Sch 601 N 7th St, Auburn 62615 Matt Grimm	3-5	T	290 14	35% Fax	217/438-6919 217/438-3700 ◙

- **Ball Chatham Cmty Unit SD 5** PID: 00318560   217/483-2416
  201 W Mulberry St, Chatham 62629   Fax 217/483-2940

Schools: 6 \ **Teachers:** 255 \ **Students:** 4,500 \ **Special Ed Students:** 545 \ **LEP Students:** 122 \ **College-Bound:** 84% \ **Ethnic:** Asian 6%, African American 6%, Hispanic 4%, Caucasian 84% \ **Exp:** $170 (Low) \ **Poverty:** 5% \ **Title I:** $384,413 \ **Special Education:** $2,690,000 \ **Open-Close:** 08/17 - 05/27 \ **DTBP:** $195 (High)

Dr Douglas Wood 1   Charolette Montgomery 2,19,298
Michael Dobbs 3   Chad Martel 4
Jim Lovelace 5   Dusty Burk 6*
Jennifer Farnsworth 8,15,288   William Brewer 67
Ashley Romadka 68   Betsy Schroeder 71
Josh Mulvaney 73,76,295   Randy Allen 91*

Public Schs..Principal	Grd	Prgm	Enr/#Cls	SN	
Ball Elem Sch 1015 New City Rd, Chatham 62629 Trisha Burke	PK-4	T	660 28	22% Fax	217/483-2414 217/483-3968
Chatham Elem Sch 525 S College St, Chatham 62629 Cynthia Crow	K-4	T	581 45	23% Fax	217/483-2411 217/483-5270
Glenwood Elem Sch 1401 E Plummer Blvd, Chatham 62629 Chelsey Ziebler	K-4	T	667	25% Fax	217/483-6704 217/483-6904
Glenwood High Sch 1501 E Plummer Blvd, Chatham 62629 Doug Szcinski	9-12	V	1,400 78	19% Fax	217/483-2424 217/483-5402
Glenwood Intermediate Sch 465 Chatham Rd, Chatham 62629 Elizabeth Gregurich	5-6		726 26	21% Fax	217/483-1183 217/483-1254
Glenwood Middle Sch 595 Chatham Rd, Chatham 62629 Christine Lehnen	7-8		723 65	21% Fax	217/483-2481 217/483-4940

- **Community Unit School Dist 16** PID: 00318675   217/488-2040
  600 N Cedar St, New Berlin 62670   Fax 217/488-2043

Schools: 3 \ **Teachers:** 65 \ **Students:** 939 \ **Special Ed Students:** 121 \ **College-Bound:** 70% \ **Ethnic:** African American 1%, Hispanic 2%, Caucasian 97% \ **Exp:** $380 (High) \ **Poverty:** 9% \ **Title I:** $118,987 \ **Special Education:** $254,000 \ **Open-Close:** 08/17 - 05/21 \ **DTBP:** $196 (High) \ ◘

Adam Ehrman 1   Lori Niemeier 2,11,19,296,298
Matt Brown ....3*   Rich Clark 3*
Jay Ayers ....4*   John Finke 5
Blake Lucas 6   Casey Wills 9*
Kim Dykstra ....16*   Bill Alexander 67
Kevin Cummins 73*

---

79 Student Personnel	91 Safety/Security	275 Response To Intervention	298 Grant Writer/Ptnrships	**School Programs**	**Social Media**
80 Driver Ed/Safety	92 Magnet School	277 Remedial Math K-12	750 Chief Innovation Officer	A = Alternative Program	
81 Gifted/Talented	93 Parental Involvement	280 Literacy Coach	751 Chief of Staff	G = Adult Classes	◘ = Facebook
82 Video Services	95 Tech Prep Program	285 STEM	752 Social Emotional Learning	M = Magnet Program	
83 Substance Abuse Prev	97 Chief Information Officer	286 Digital Learning		T = Title I Schoolwide	◙ = Twitter
84 Erate	98 Chief Technology Officer	288 Common Core Standards	**Other School Types**	V = Career & Tech Ed Programs	
85 AIDS Education	270 Character Education	294 Accountability	Ⓐ = Alternative School		
88 Alternative/At Risk	271 Migrant Education	295 Network System	Ⓒ = Charter School	New Schools are shaded	
89 Multi-Cultural Curriculum	273 Teacher Mentor	296 Title II Programs	Ⓜ = Magnet School	New Superintendents and Principals are bold	
90 Social Work	274 Before/After Sch	297 Webmaster	Ⓨ = Year-Round School	Personnel with email addresses are underscored	IL–211

Sangamon County

Market Data Retrieval

Public Schs..Principal	Grd	Prgm	Enr/#Cls	SN	
New Berlin Elem Sch 600 N Cedar St, New Berlin 62670 Brian Bishop	PK-5	T	470 38	31%	217/488-6054 Fax 217/488-6039
New Berlin High Sch 300 E Ellis St, New Berlin 62670 Hattie Llewellyn	9-12	V	280 30	27%	217/488-6012 Fax 217/488-3207
New Berlin Junior High Sch 300 E Ellis St, New Berlin 62670 Megan Doerfler	6-8		196 7	30%	217/488-6012 Fax 217/488-3207

• Pawnee Cmty Unit Sch Dist 11 PID: 00318766   217/625-2471
810 4th St, Pawnee 62558   Fax 217/625-2251

Schools: 2 \ **Teachers:** 52 \ **Students:** 550 \ **Special Ed Students:** 123 \ **College-Bound:** 67% \ **Ethnic:** African American 1%, Caucasian 98% \ **Exp:** $250 (Med) \ **Poverty:** 12% \ **Title I:** $134,642 \ **Special Education:** $135,000 \ **Open-Close:** 08/24 - 05/21 \ **DTBP:** $23 (Low) \ f t

Scott Cameron	1,288	Jill Hamilton		2
Steve Kirby	6*	Chris Hinmen		9,11,83*
Tim Kratochvil	10*	Josh Ward		67
Bob Hagler	73*	Bob Hagler		73,98,286
Angie Hyde	79			

Public Schs..Principal	Grd	Prgm	Enr/#Cls	SN	
Pawnee Grade Sch 810 4th St, Pawnee 62558 W Christopher Hennemann	PK-6	T	345 17	29%	217/625-2231
Pawnee High Sch 810 4th St, Pawnee 62558 Tim Kratochvil	7-12	T	255 60	30%	217/625-2471

• Pleasant Plains Cmty Unit SD 8 PID: 00318792   217/626-1041
315 W Church St, Pleasant PLNS 62677   Fax 217/626-1082

Schools: 3 \ **Teachers:** 77 \ **Students:** 1,271 \ **Special Ed Students:** 136 \ **LEP Students:** 3 \ **College-Bound:** 73% \ **Ethnic:** Asian 1%, African American 1%, Hispanic 2%, Caucasian 95% \ **Exp:** $220 (Med) \ **Poverty:** 6% \ **Title I:** $132,508 \ **Special Education:** $176,000 \ **Open-Close:** 08/19 - 05/26

Matt Runge	1	Bill Dargert		2,3,19
Brent Grisham	6	Jill Fessler		8,11,58,288,752
Gregg Humphrey	67	John Langley		73
Mike Squires	73,295*	Kim Moore		88*

Public Schs..Principal	Grd	Prgm	Enr/#Cls	SN	
Farmingdale Elem Sch 2473 N Farmingdale Rd, Pleasant PLNS 62677 Jamie Yates	PK-4		477 35	14%	217/626-1221 Fax 217/626-1839
Pleasant Plains High Sch 500 N Cartwright Street, Pleasant PLNS 62677 Luke Brooks	9-12	V	420 25	13%	217/626-1044 Fax 217/626-1667
Pleasant Plains Middle Sch 2455 N Farmingdale Rd, Pleasant PLNS 62677 Heather Greer	5-8		374 30	11%	217/626-1061 Fax 217/626-2272

• Riverton Cmty Unit SD 14 PID: 00318728   217/629-6009
6425 Old Route 36, Riverton 62561   Fax 217/629-6008

Schools: 3 \ **Teachers:** 90 \ **Students:** 1,443 \ **Special Ed Students:** 309 \ **LEP Students:** 3 \ **College-Bound:** 58% \ **Ethnic:** Asian 1%, African American 5%, Hispanic 1%, Native American: 1%, Caucasian 93% \ **Exp:** $261 (Med) \ **Poverty:** 16% \ **Title I:** $386,853 \ **Special Education:** $916,000 \ **Open-Close:** 08/07 - 05/21 \ **DTBP:** $228 (High)

Bradley Polanin	1	Mike Gum		2,73,84
Doug Brown	3	Gary Lane		5
Tom Weir	6	Ashlee Bell		7*
Ashlee Schoby	7*	Nancy Penk		38*
Jenny Mendenhall	58*	Pam Cuffle		67

Public Schs..Principal	Grd	Prgm	Enr/#Cls	SN	
Riverton Elem Sch 209 N 7th St, Riverton 62561 Jacie Shoufer	PK-4	T	511 38	53%	217/629-6001 Fax 217/629-6023
Riverton High Sch 841 N 3rd St, Riverton 62561 Matt Moore	9-12	T	413 40	48%	217/629-6003 Fax 217/629-6020 f t
Riverton Middle Sch 1014 E Lincoln St, Riverton 62561 Megan Doerfler	5-8	T	430 24	58%	217/629-6002 Fax 217/629-6017

• Rochester Cmty Unit SD 3-A PID: 00318845   217/498-6210
4 Rocket Dr, Rochester 62563   Fax 217/498-8045

Schools: 5 \ **Teachers:** 125 \ **Students:** 2,215 \ **Special Ed Students:** 308 \ **LEP Students:** 17 \ **College-Bound:** 78% \ **Ethnic:** Asian 2%, African American 2%, Hispanic 1%, Caucasian 95% \ **Exp:** $132 (Low) \ **Poverty:** 3% \ **Title I:** $98,899 \ **Special Education:** $1,146,000 \ **Open-Close:** 08/13 - 05/19 \ **DTBP:** $229 (High) \ t

Dan Cox	1	Bob McDermott		2
Brad Alewelt	3*	Matt Hilsabeck		5
Jr Boudouris	6	Heather Arnold		7*
Suzanne Keller	8,11,286,294*	Rachel Fuller		16
Sandra Hendricks	27,31,36,69,79*	Meg Thurman		34,57,88,275
Marsha Marvel	54*	Jennifer Shaw		58
Dr Magoulias	67	Wilson Avedano		73,76,295

Public Schs..Principal	Grd	Prgm	Enr/#Cls	SN	
Rochester Elem Sch 2-3 456 Bertrand Dr, Rochester 62563 Jeff Reed	2-3		271	12%	217/498-6216 Fax 217/498-6217
Rochester Elem Sch EC-1 707 W Main St, Rochester 62563 Jeff Reed	PK-1		325 32	16%	217/498-9778 Fax 217/498-9160
Rochester High Sch 1 Rocket Dr, Rochester 62563 Brent Ashbaugh	9-12		801 54	11%	217/498-9761 Fax 217/498-9829
Rochester Intermediate Sch 900 Jack Taylor Dr, Rochester 62563 Cassy Carey	4-6		497 21	15%	217/498-6215 Fax 217/498-6218 t
Rochester Junior High Sch 3 Rocket Dr, Rochester 62563 Kim Poole	7-8		348 30	15%	217/498-9761 Fax 217/498-6204

1	Superintendent	8	Curric/Instruct K-12	19	Chief Financial Officer	29	Family/Consumer Science	39	Social Studies K-12	49	English/Lang Arts Elem	59	Special Education Elem	69	Academic Assessment
2	Bus/Finance/Purchasing	9	Curric/Instruct Elem	20	Art K-12	30	Adult Education	40	Social Studies Elem	50	English/Lang Arts Sec	60	Special Education Sec	70	Research/Development
3	Buildings And Grounds	10	Curric/Instruct Sec	21	Art Elem	31	Career/Sch-to-Work K-12	41	Social Studies Sec	51	Reading K-12	61	Foreign/World Lang K-12	71	Public Information
4	Food Service	11	Federal Program	22	Art Sec	32	Career/Sch-to-Work Elem	42	Science K-12	52	Reading Elem	62	Foreign/World Lang Elem	72	Summer School
5	Transportation	12	Title I	23	Music K-12	33	Career/Sch-to-Work Sec	43	Science Elem	53	Reading Sec	63	Foreign/World Lang Sec	73	Instructional Tech
6	Athletic	13	Title V	24	Music Elem	34	Early Childhood Ed	44	Science Sec	54	Remedial Reading K-12	64	Religious Education K-12	74	Inservice Training
7	Health Services	14	Asst Superintendent	25	Music Sec	35	Health/Phys Education	45	Math K-12	55	Remedial Reading Elem	65	Religious Education Elem	75	Marketing/Distributive
		15	Instructional Media Svcs	26	Business Education	36	Guidance Services K-12	46	Math Elem	56	Remedial Reading Sec	66	Religious Education Sec	76	Info Systems
		16	Chief Operations Officer	27	Career & Tech Ed	37	Guidance Services Elem	47	Math Sec	57	Bilingual/ELL	67	School Board President	77	Psychological Assess
		17	Chief Academic Officer	28	Technology Education	38	Guidance Services Sec	48	English/Lang Arts K-12	58	Special Education K-12	68	Teacher Personnel	78	Affirmative Action

Illinois School Directory — Sangamon County

- **Springfield Pub Sch Dist 186** PID: 00318883 217/525-3006
  1900 W Monroe St, Springfield 62704 Fax 217/525-3005

Schools: 33 \ **Teachers:** 1,013 \ **Students:** 13,000 \
Special Ed Students: 3,093 \ **LEP Students:** 153 \ **College-Bound:** 59%
\ **Ethnic:** Asian 3%, African American 47%, Hispanic 4%, Caucasian 47% \ **Exp:** $301 (High) \ **Poverty:** 25% \ **Title I:** $9,503,504 \
Special Education: $12,416,000 \ **Bilingual Education:** $46,000 \
Open-Close: 08/31 – 06/02 \ **DTBP:** $236 (High) \ 🅵 🅣

Jennifer Gill 1	Nate Fretz 2,84
Darrell Schaver 3,80	Cheryl McBride 4
Lance Thurman 5	Jason Wind 6,78,79*
Meg Phurman 7,57,58,271	Shila Boozer 8,15,288
Cherie Morrison 10,41,44,285	Larry McVey 11,296
Lynn Gilmore 23,48,61*	Kathi Lee Deassuncao 30*
Kate Dabbs 34*	Nalo Mitchell 36
Renee Johnson 45	Scott McFarland 67
Gina Schurman 68,79	Dr Nicole Gales 69
Bree Hankins 71	Stephen Minch 73,76,295*
Kelly Sholtis 83,88,270	William Taylor 91
Peggy Cormeny 93	Adrianne Ostermeier 273*
Queen Drake 274	

Public Schs..Principal	Grd	Prgm	Enr/#Cls	SN		
Benjamin Franklin Middle Sch 1200 Outer Park Dr, Springfield 62704 Tod Davis	6-8	T	803 50	48%	217/787-3006 Fax 217/787-3054	
Black Hawk Elem Sch 2500 S College St, Springfield 62704 Terrance Jordan	K-5	T	249 13	64%	217/525-3195 Fax 217/525-3168	
Butler Elem Sch 1701 S MacArthur Blvd, Springfield 62704 Tracy Gage	K-5	T	365 16	48%	217/787-3189 Fax 217/788-6250	
Ⓐ Douglas Prep Alternative Sch 444 W Reynolds St, Springfield 62702 Kari Borders	6-12		120 10	70%	217/525-4400 Fax 217/525-4401	
DuBois Elem Sch 120 S Lincoln Ave, Springfield 62704 Donna Jefferson	K-5	T	422 23	57%	217/787-3066 Fax 217/787-3078	
Early Learning Center 2501 S 1st St, Springfield 62704 Charlena Jackson	PK-PK	T	632 8	65%	217/525-3163	
Edwin A Lee Elem Sch 1201 Bunn Ave, Springfield 62703 Nathan Kochanowski	PK-5	T	192 19	82%	217/585-5828 Fax 217/535-2755	
Ⓨ Elizabeth Graham Elem Sch 900 W Edwards St, Springfield 62704 Steve Miller	K-5	MT	236 18	74%	217/525-3220 Fax 217/525-3348	
Enos Elem Sch 524 W Elliott Ave, Springfield 62702 Claudia Johnson	K-5	T	264 17	74%	217/525-3208 Fax 217/525-7498	
Fairview Elem Sch 2200 E Ridgely Ave, Springfield 62702 Patricia Nikson	K-5	T	265 14	61%	217/525-3211 Fax 217/525-3286	
Feitshans Elem Sch 1101 S 15th St, Springfield 62703 Keneisha Boozer	PK-5	T	359 13	76%	217/525-3030 Fax 217/525-3333	
Harvard Park Elem Sch 2501 S 11th St, Springfield 62703 James Hayes	PK-5	T	347 20	75%	217/525-3214 Fax 217/525-3280	
Hazel Dell Elem Sch 850 W Lake Shore Dr, Springfield 62712 Jamar Scott	K-5	T	164 11	60%	217/525-3223 Fax 217/525-3216	
Iles Sch 1700 S 15th St, Springfield 62703 Kenyatta Revelle	1-8		406 12	19%	217/525-3226 Fax 217/525-4408	
Jane Addams Elem Sch 10 Babiak Ln, Springfield 62702 Mike Grossen	K-5	T	251 13	65%	217/787-3144 Fax 217/787-3164	
Jefferson Middle Sch 3001 S Allis St, Springfield 62703 Karen Crump	6-8	T	541 60	73%	217/585-5810 Fax 217/525-3293	
Laketown Elem Sch 1825 Lee St, Springfield 62703 Renee Colwell-Roy	K-5	T	168 12	57%	217/585-5819 Fax 217/585-5820	
Lanphier High Sch 1300 N 11th St, Springfield 62702 Artie Doss	9-12	TV	1,134 70	63%	217/525-3080 Fax 217/525-3084	
Ⓜ Lincoln Magnet Sch 300 S 11th St, Springfield 62703 Nicole Heyen	6-8		311 20	32%	217/525-3236 Fax 217/525-3294	
Lindsay Elem Sch 3600 Fielding Dr, Springfield 62711 Jennifer Russel	K-5	T	455 30	36%	217/546-0200 Fax 217/747-5774	
Matheny-Withrow Elem Sch 1200 S Pope Ave, Springfield 62703 Kathy Hulcher	K-5	T	254 13	74%	217/525-3245	
McClernand Elem Sch 801 N 6th St, Springfield 62702 Michelle Robertson	K-5	T	224 13	78%	217/525-3247 Fax 217/525-7925	
Owen Marsh Elem Sch 1100 Avon Dr, Springfield 62704 Wendy Conaway	PK-5	T	295 14	39%	217/787-3173 Fax 217/787-3183	
Ridgely Elem Sch 2040 N 8th St, Springfield 62702 Kenneth Gilmore	PK-5	T	323 19	72%	217/525-3259 Fax 217/525-7932	
Sandburg Elem Sch 2051 Wabash Ave, Springfield 62704 Keith Kincaid	K-5	T	286 12	42%	217/787-3112 Fax 217/535-2759	
Ⓨ Southern View Elem Sch 3338 S 5th St, Springfield 62703 Alicia Miller	K-5	MT	202 11	62%	217/585-5837 Fax 217/585-5838	
Ⓒ Springfield Ball Charter Sch 2530 E Ash St, Springfield 62703 Tiffany Williams	K-8	T	397 19	44%	217/525-3275 Fax 217/525-3316	
Springfield High Sch 101 S Lewis St, Springfield 62704 Dr Lisa Leardi	9-12	V	1,478	32%	217/525-3100 Fax 217/525-3122	
Ⓐ Springfield Learning Center 101 E Laurel St, Springfield 62704 Reiko Hurd	9-12	GV	100 25	72%	217/525-3144 Fax 217/525-3090	
Springfield Southeast High Sch 2350 E Ash St, Springfield 62703 Cody Trigg	9-12	TV	1,231 72	56%	217/525-3130 Fax 217/525-3146	
Ulysses S Grant Middle Sch 1800 W Monroe St, Springfield 62704 Robert Schurman	6-8	T	569 50	61%	217/525-3170 Fax 217/525-3390	
Washington Middle Sch 2300 E Jackson St, Springfield 62703 Vincent Turner	6-8	T	638 47	74%	217/525-3182 Fax 217/525-3319	
Wilcox Elem Sch 2000 Hastings Rd, Springfield 62702 Erica Filipiak	K-5	T	257 14	56%	217/525-3281 Fax 217/525-3308	

79 Student Personnel	91 Safety/Security	275 Response To Intervention	298 Grant Writer/Ptnrships	**School Programs**	**Social Media**		
80 Driver Ed/Safety	92 Magnet School	277 Remedial Math K-12	750 Chief Innovation Officer	A = Alternative Program			
81 Gifted/Talented	93 Parental Involvement	280 Literacy Coach	751 Chief of Staff	G = Adult Classes	🅵 = Facebook		
82 Video Services	95 Tech Prep Program	285 STEM	752 Social Emotional Learning	M = Magnet Program			
83 Substance Abuse Prev	97 Chief Information Officer	286 Digital Learning		T = Title I Schoolwide	🅣 = Twitter		
84 Erate	98 Chief Technology Officer	288 Common Core Standards	**Other School Types**	V = Career & Tech Ed Programs			
85 AIDS Education	270 Accountability	294 Accountability	Ⓐ = Alternative School				
88 Alternative/At Risk	271 Migrant Education	295 Network System	Ⓒ = Charter School	New Schools are shaded			
89 Multi-Cultural Curriculum	273 Teacher Mentor	296 Title II Programs	Ⓜ = Magnet School	New Superintendents and Principals are bold			
90 Social Work	274 Before/After Sch	297 Webmaster	Ⓨ = Year-Round School	Personnel with email addresses are underscored			

Sangamon County

Market Data Retrieval

- **Tri-City Cmty Unit Sch Dist 1** PID: 00319277   217/364-4811
  324 W Charles St, Buffalo 62515   Fax 217/364-4896

Schools: 1 \ **Teachers:** 46 \ **Students:** 570 \ **Special Ed Students:** 115 \ **College-Bound:** 56% \ **Ethnic:** African American 2%, Hispanic 1%, Caucasian 97% \ **Exp:** $271 (Med) \ **Poverty:** 9% \ **Title I:** $75,719 \ **Special Education:** $139,000 \ **Open-Close:** 08/20 - 05/21 \ **DTBP:** $182 (High) \

Chad Colmone	1	Danielle Devos	2
Dan Rodden	5	Stanley Ellis Price	6*
Kathy Getz	7*	Kara Cummins	9,88,93*
Christy Kindel	10,11,73,74,288*	Sarah Heberling	31,36,57,69*
Travis Heck	67	Cathy Justice	83,270,271*
Carolyn Dee Ward	273*	Kathy Benton	280

Public Schs..Principal	Grd	Prgm	Enr/#Cls	SN	
Tri-City Sch 324 W Charles St, Buffalo 62515 Christy Kindel \ Kara Cummins	PK-12	AV	570 50	35%	217/364-4811

- **Williamsville Cmty Unit SD 15** PID: 00319291   217/566-2014
  800 S Walnut St, Williamsville 62693   Fax 217/566-3890

Schools: 4 \ **Teachers:** 92 \ **Students:** 1,540 \ **Special Ed Students:** 200 \ **LEP Students:** 5 \ **College-Bound:** 91% \ **Ethnic:** Asian 1%, African American 1%, Hispanic 1%, Caucasian 97% \ **Exp:** $130 (Low) \ **Poverty:** 5% \ **Title I:** $104,113 \ **Special Education:** $369,000 \ **Open-Close:** 08/18 - 05/24 \ **DTBP:** $173 (High)

Tip Reedy	1	Jennifer Brennan	2,68
Tricia Miller	2,5	Pauline Osman	4
Adam Eucker	6*	Adam Ibbotson	8,12,288
Cj Compardo	11,296,298	Shannon Swaney	16*
Ashley Pasbrig	58*	Matt Seman	67
Mitch Boston	73,295		

Public Schs..Principal	Grd	Prgm	Enr/#Cls	SN	
Sherman Elem Sch 312 South St, Sherman 62684 Adam Ibbotson	PK-4		571 29	2%	217/496-2021 Fax 217/496-2473
Williamsville High Sch 900 S Walnut St, Williamsville 62693 Doug Furlow	9-12		447 40	11%	217/566-3361 Fax 217/566-3792
Williamsville Junior High Sch 500 S Walnut St, Williamsville 62693 Clay Shoufler	6-8		344 28	11%	217/566-3600 Fax 217/566-2475
Williamsville Middle Sch 504 S Walnut St, Williamsville 62693 Clay Shoufler	5-5		128		217/566-4070 Fax 217/566-2183

SANGAMON CATHOLIC SCHOOLS

- **Diocese of Springfield Ed Off** PID: 00319394   217/698-8500
  1615 W Washington St, Springfield 62702   Fax 217/698-0802

Schools: 44 \ **Students:** 10,260

Listing includes only schools located in this county. See District Index for location of Diocesan Offices.

| Brandi Borries | 1 | Chris Sommer | 2 |

Catholic Schs..Principal	Grd	Prgm	Enr/#Cls	SN
Blessed Sacrament Sch 748 W Laurel St, Springfield 62704 Dawn Klinner	PK-8		438 20	217/522-7534
Christ the King Sch 1920 Barberry Dr, Springfield 62704 Pam Fahey	PK-8		432 18	217/546-2159 Fax 217/546-0291
Little Flower Catholic Sch 900 Adlai Stevenson Dr, Springfield 62703 Dr Bill Moredock	PK-8		304 20	217/529-4511 Fax 217/529-0405
Sacred Heart-Griffin High Sch 1200 W Washington St, Springfield 62702 Kara Rapacz	9-12		777 66	217/787-1595 Fax 217/787-9856
St Agnes Sch 251 N Amos Ave, Springfield 62702 Rachel Cunningham	K-8		440 24	217/793-1370 Fax 217/793-1238
St Aloysius Catholic Sch 2125 N 21st St, Springfield 62702 Denise Reavis	PK-8		198 17	217/544-4553 Fax 217/544-1680
St Joseph Pre-School 700 E Spruce St, Chatham 62629 John Nolan	PK-PK		38 1	217/483-3772 Fax 217/483-4581
St Patrick Sch 1800 South Grand Ave E, Springfield 62703 Jan Williams	PK-4		77 6	217/523-7670 Fax 217/523-0760

SANGAMON PRIVATE SCHOOLS

Private Schs..Principal	Grd	Prgm	Enr/#Cls	SN
Calvary Academy 1730 W Jefferson St, Springfield 62702 Dr Jay Hinckley	PK-12		300 23	217/546-5987 Fax 217/321-1063
Concordia Lutheran Sch 2300 E Wilshire Rd, Springfield 62703 Janet Burmeister	PK-8		58 8	217/529-3309 Fax 217/529-3096
Grace Baptist Academy 2812 S Walnut St, Springfield 62704 Dave Brady	1-12		12 1	217/522-2881
Hope Institute Sch 15 East Hazel Dell Ln, Springfield 62712 Jim Lee	Spec		126 22	217/953-0894 Fax 217/585-5205
Lutheran High Sch 3500 W Washington St, Springfield 62711 Glenn Rollins	9-12		150 16	217/546-6363 Fax 217/546-6489
Montessori Children's House 4147 Sandhill Rd, Springfield 62702 Suzanne Harris	PK-6		68 4	217/544-7702 Fax 217/544-5502
Montessori Schoolhouse 717 Rickard Rd, Springfield 62704 Nils Westholm	PK K		60 5	217/787-5505
Our Savior's Lutheran Sch 2645 Old Jacksonville Rd, Springfield 62704 Nancy Bray	PK-8		235 11	217/546-4531 Fax 217/546-0293
Springfield Christian Sch 2850 Cider Mill Ln, Springfield 62702 Sonya Sims	K-8		375 18	217/698-1933 Fax 217/698-1931
Springfield Developmental Ctr 4595 Laverna Rd, Springfield 62707 Cathi Clark	Spec	G	94 3	217/525-8271 Fax 217/525-5801
Trinity Lutheran Sch 515 S MacArthur Blvd, Springfield 62704 Zachary Klug	PK-8		120 12	217/787-2323 Fax 217/787-1145

1 Superintendent	8 Curric/Instruct K-12	19 Chief Financial Officer	29 Family/Consumer Science	39 Social Studies K-12	49 English/Lang Arts Elem	59 Special Education Elem	69 Academic Assessment
2 Bus/Finance/Purchasing	9 Curric/Instruct Elem	20 Art K-12	30 Adult Education	40 Social Studies Elem	50 English/Lang Arts Sec	60 Special Education Sec	70 Research/Development
3 Buildings And Grounds	10 Curric/Instruct Sec	21 Art Elem	31 Career/Sch-to-Work K-12	41 Social Studies Sec	51 Reading K-12	61 Foreign/World Lang K-12	71 Public Information
4 Food Service	11 Federal Program	22 Art Sec	32 Career/Sch-to-Work Elem	42 Science K-12	52 Reading Elem	62 Foreign/World Lang Elem	72 Summer School
5 Transportation	12 Title I	23 Music K-12	33 Career/Sch-to-Work Sec	43 Science Elem	53 Reading Sec	63 Foreign/World Lang Sec	73 Instructional Tech
6 Athletic	13 Title V	24 Music Elem	34 Early Childhood Ed	44 Science Sec	54 Remedial Reading K-12	64 Religious Education K-12	74 Inservice Training
7 Health Services	15 Asst Superintendent	25 Music Sec	35 Health/Phys Education	45 Math K-12	55 Remedial Reading Elem	65 Religious Education Elem	75 Marketing/Distributive
	16 Instructional Media Svcs	26 Business Education	36 Guidance Services K-12	46 Math Elem	56 Remedial Reading Sec	66 Religious Education Sec	76 Info Systems
	17 Chief Operations Officer	27 Career & Tech Ed	37 Guidance Services Elem	47 Math Sec	57 Bilingual/ELL	67 School Board President	77 Psychological Assess
	18 Chief Academic Officer	28 Technology Education	38 Guidance Services Sec	48 English/Lang Arts K-12	58 Special Education K-12	68 Teacher Personnel	78 Affirmative Action

Illinois School Directory — Scott County

SANGAMON REGIONAL CENTERS

- **Regional Office-Career Tech Ed** PID: 04180432   217/529-3716
  2450 Foundation Dr Ste 100, Springfield 62703   Fax 217/529-8361
  Mary Jo Wood 1

- **Sangamon Area Spec Ed District** PID: 02182147   217/786-3250
  2500 Taylor Ave, Springfield 62703   Fax 217/786-3652
  Mark Strawn 1,11   Gwen Williams 2
  Tony Grider 73

- **Sangamon-Menard Roe #51** PID: 02098352   217/753-6620
  2201 S Dirksen Pkwy, Springfield 62703   Fax 217/535-3166
  Jeff Vose 1   Angie Bentlinger 2
  Shannon Fehrholz 15

SCHUYLER COUNTY

SCHUYLER PUBLIC SCHOOLS

- **Schuyler-Industry CUSD 5** PID: 00320135   217/322-4311
  740 Maple Ave, Rushville 62681   Fax 217/322-4398

  Schools: 4 \ Teachers: 72 \ Students: 1,100 \ Special Ed Students: 178 \ LEP Students: 33 \ College-Bound: 57% \ Ethnic: African American 4%, Hispanic 1%, Caucasian 95% \ Exp: $177 (Low) \ Poverty: 13% \ Title I: $239,935 \ Special Education: $288,000 \ Open-Close: 08/19 - 05/21 \ DTBP: $198 (High)

  Dr Beau Fretueg 1,11   Terri Quillen 2
  Michael Trone 3   Kurt Trone 5
  Britney Trone 7   Emily Higgins 11
  Christy Glick 58,88   Brad Eskridge 67
  Jaimee Steele 69,77,83,752   Brian Hardy 73,84,286
  Linda Kennedy 84

Public Schs..Principal	Grd	Prgm	Enr/#Cls	SN	
Rushville-Industry High Sch 730 N Congress St, Rushville 62681 Brad Gooding	9-12	V	354 25	42%	217/322-4311 Fax 217/322-2844 t
Schuyler-Industry Middle Sch 750 N Congress St, Rushville 62681 Jim Shepherd	5-8		309 25	45%	217/322-4311 Fax 217/322-3938
Washington Elem Sch 100 Buchanan St, Rushville 62681 Noah Willis	PK-1	T	202 9	7%	217/322-4311 Fax 217/322-3195
Webster Elem Sch 310 N Monroe St, Rushville 62681 Noah Willis	2-4	T	216 11	47%	217/322-4311 Fax 217/322-2391

SCOTT COUNTY

SCOTT PUBLIC SCHOOLS

- **Scott Morgan Cmty Unit SD 2** PID: 00320214   217/754-3714
  100 W Rockwood St, Bluffs 62621   Fax 217/754-3908

  Schools: 1 \ Teachers: 21 \ Students: 231 \ Special Ed Students: 46 \ LEP Students: 3 \ College-Bound: 66% \ Ethnic: Hispanic 2%, Caucasian 98% \ Exp: $162 (Low) \ Poverty: 23% \ Title I: $90,024 \ Special Education: $46,000 \ Open-Close: 08/17 - 05/21 \ DTBP: $153 (High)

  Kevin Blankenship 1,11,288   Brenda Kaufmann 2
  Clint Coats .... 3,5*   Amy Gillis 4*
  Brian Bettis .... 6*   Sara Fry 12,280*
  Jodie DeGroot 31,36,69,83   Gary Westermeyer 67
  Grace Pinkerton .... 270*   Joseph Kuhlman 275*

Public Schs..Principal	Grd	Prgm	Enr/#Cls	SN	
Bluffs Cmty Unit Sch 100 W Rockwood St, Bluffs 62621 Mr Kuhlmann	PK-12	TV	231 26	52%	217/754-3815 Fax 217/754-3275

- **Winchester Cmty Unit SD 1** PID: 00320238   217/742-3175
  149 S Elm St, Winchester 62694

  Schools: 2 \ Teachers: 52 \ Students: 680 \ Special Ed Students: 116 \ College-Bound: 63% \ Ethnic: Hispanic 1%, Caucasian 99% \ Exp: $239 (Med) \ Poverty: 9% \ Title I: $85,829 \ Special Education: $209,000 \ Open-Close: 08/14 - 05/21

  Kevin Blankenship 1,83   Andy Ftumpf 9*
  Steve Moore 67

Public Schs..Principal	Grd	Prgm	Enr/#Cls	SN	
Winchester Elem Sch 283 S Elm St, Winchester 62694 Andy Stumpf	PK-8	T	439 20	49%	217/742-9551 Fax 217/742-0014
Winchester High Sch 200 W Cross St, Winchester 62694 Denny Vortman	9-12	V	182 22	37%	217/742-3151 Fax 217/742-0311

---

79 Student Personnel   91 Safety/Security   275 Response To Intervention   298 Grant Writer/Ptnrships   **School Programs**   **Social Media**
80 Driver Ed/Safety   92 Magnet School   277 Remedial Math K-12   750 Chief Innovation Officer   A = Alternative Program
81 Gifted/Talented   93 Parental Involvement   280 Literacy Coach   751 Chief of Staff   G = Adult Classes   = Facebook
82 Video Services   95 Tech Prep Program   285 STEM   752 Social Emotional Learning   M = Magnet Program
83 Substance Abuse Prev   97 Chief Infomation Officer   286 Digital Learning   T = Title I Schoolwide   t = Twitter
84 Erate   98 Chief Technology Officer   288 Common Core Standards   **Other School Types**   V = Career & Tech Ed Programs
85 AIDS Education   270 Character Education   294 Accountability   Ⓐ = Alternative School
88 Alternative/At Risk   271 Migrant Education   295 Network System   Ⓒ = Charter School   New Schools are shaded
89 Multi-Cultural Curriculum   273 Teacher Mentor   296 Title II Programs   Ⓜ = Magnet School   New Superintendents and Principals are bold
90 Social Work   274 Before/After Sch   297 Webmaster   Ⓨ = Year-Round School   Personnel with email addresses are underscored

Shelby County

SHELBY COUNTY

SHELBY PUBLIC SCHOOLS

- **Cowden Herrick CUSD 3A** PID: 00320288   217/783-2126
  633 County Highway 22, Cowden 62422   Fax 217/783-2713

Schools: 2 \ **Teachers:** 32 \ **Students:** 380 \ **Special Ed Students:** 44 \ **LEP Students:** 3 \ **College-Bound:** 63% \ **Ethnic:** Hispanic 1%, Caucasian 99% \ **Exp:** $188 (Low) \ **Poverty:** 19% \ **Title I:** $152,240 \ **Special Education:** $313,000 \ **Open-Close:** 08/14 - 05/18

Seth Schuler 1,11,73,83   Greg Jones 67
Britt Broehm 288*

Public Schs..Principal	Grd	Prgm	Enr/#Cls	SN	
Cowden Jr Sr High Sch 633 County Highway 22, Cowden 62422 Brett Boehm	6-12	T	222 13	64%	217/783-2137 Fax 217/783-2129
Herrick Elem Sch 301 N Broadway St, Herrick 62431 Tina Oldham	K-5	T	145 11	77%	618/428-5223 Fax 618/428-5222

- **Shelbyville Cmty Sch Dist 4** PID: 00320381   217/774-4626
  720 W Main St, Shelbyville 62565   Fax 217/774-2521

Schools: 3 \ **Teachers:** 88 \ **Students:** 1,250 \ **Special Ed Students:** 151 \ **College-Bound:** 73% \ **Ethnic:** Asian 1%, Hispanic 2%, Caucasian 96% \ **Exp:** $222 (Med) \ **Poverty:** 12% \ **Title I:** $201,466 \ **Special Education:** $349,000 \ **Open-Close:** 08/13 - 05/17

Shane Schuright 1,11   Scott Rader 3,91
Rich Vanetta 5   Nick Caldwell 38
Robert Bosgraas 67

Public Schs..Principal	Grd	Prgm	Enr/#Cls	SN	
Main Street Elem Sch 225 W Main St, Shelbyville 62565 Ryan Scott	PK-3	T	341 13	44%	217/774-4731 Fax 217/774-3016
Moulton Middle Sch 1101 W North 6th St, Shelbyville 62565 Russell Tomblin	4-8	T	443 35	42%	217/774-2169 Fax 217/774-3042
Shelbyville High Sch 1001 W North 6th St, Shelbyville 62565 Kyle Ladd	9-12	TV	312 45	42%	217/774-3926 Fax 217/774-5836

- **Stewardson-Strasburg SD 5-A** PID: 00320446   217/682-3355
  2806 E 600 North Rd, Strasburg 62465   Fax 217/682-3305

Schools: 2 \ **Teachers:** 27 \ **Students:** 374 \ **Special Ed Students:** 58 \ **LEP Students:** 3 \ **College-Bound:** 66% \ **Ethnic:** Hispanic 1%, Caucasian 99% \ **Exp:** $309 (High) \ **Poverty:** 11% \ **Title I:** $79,336 \ **Special Education:** $121,000 \ **Open-Close:** 08/17 - 05/20 \ **DTBP:** $185 (High)

Kenneth Schwengel 1   Michele Vonderheide 2
Nick Hartke 3   Robert Long 5
Shane Smith 6   Justin Deters 8,58,288
Dr Michele Lindenmeyer 11   Michelle Barnes 12,51,54*

Shara Johnson 16,73,82   Bob Schlechte 67

Public Schs..Principal	Grd	Prgm	Enr/#Cls	SN	
Stewardson-Strasburg Elem JHS South Rte 32, Strasburg 62465 Justin Deters	PK-8	T	264 21	34%	217/682-3621
Stewardson-Strasburg High Sch South Rte 32, Strasburg 62465 Cody McCollum	9-12	TV	110 20	29%	217/682-3355

- **Windsor Cmty Unit SD 1** PID: 00320501   217/459-2636
  1424 Minnesota Ave, Windsor 61957   Fax 217/459-2794

Schools: 2 \ **Teachers:** 30 \ **Students:** 300 \ **Special Ed Students:** 56 \ **College-Bound:** 85% \ **Ethnic:** Caucasian 100% \ **Exp:** $413 (High) \ **Poverty:** 16% \ **Title I:** $110,564 \ **Special Education:** $147,000 \ **Open-Close:** 08/19 - 05/20 \ **DTBP:** $177 (High)

Erik Vanhoveln 1,83   Rebecca McClain 2
Becky Sogarty 8,73,88   Erik Bannoveln 11,288
Ginger Handy .... 12*   Bruce Brewer 16*
April Drake 58   Matt Grule 67
Lndsey Sines 752

Public Schs..Principal	Grd	Prgm	Enr/#Cls	SN	
Windsor Elem Sch 808 Wisconsin Ave, Windsor 61957 April Drake	PK-6	T	223 7	49%	217/459-2447 Fax 217/459-2408
Windsor Jr Sr High Sch 1424 Minnesota Ave, Windsor 61957 Jennifer Bridges	7-12	T	145 22	40%	217/459-2636

SHELBY CATHOLIC SCHOOLS

- **Diocese of Springfield Ed Off** PID: 00319394
  Listing includes only schools located in this county. See District Index for location of Diocesan Offices.

Catholic Schs..Principal	Grd	Prgm	Enr/#Cls	SN	
St Michael the Archangel Sch 200 N Church St, Sigel 62462 Nick Niemerg	K-8		154 9		217/844-2231 Fax 217/844-2323

SHELBY PRIVATE SCHOOLS

Private Schs..Principal	Grd	Prgm	Enr/#Cls	SN	
Mid-America Preparatory Sch 10 N Myers St, Herrick 62431 Rick Allen	K-12		40		618/428-5620 Fax 618/428-5604
Trinity Lutheran Sch 318 E South 1st St, Stewardson 62463 Kent Rincker	PK-8		70 5		217/682-3881

---

1 Superintendent	8 Curric/Instruct K-12	19 Chief Financial Officer	29 Family/Consumer Science	39 Social Studies K-12	49 English/Lang Arts Elem	59 Special Education Elem	69 Academic Assessment
2 Bus/Finance/Purchasing	9 Curric/Instruct Elem	20 Art K-12	30 Adult Education	40 Social Studies Elem	50 English/Lang Arts Sec	60 Special Education Sec	70 Research/Development
3 Buildings And Grounds	10 Curric/Instruct Sec	21 Art Elem	31 Career/Sch-to-Work K-12	41 Social Studies Sec	51 Reading K-12	61 Foreign/World Lang K-12	71 Public Information
4 Food Service	11 Federal Program	22 Art Sec	32 Career/Sch-to-Work Elem	42 Science K-12	52 Reading Elem	62 Foreign/World Lang Elem	72 Summer School
5 Transportation	12 Title I	23 Music K-12	33 Career/Sch-to-Work Sec	43 Science Elem	53 Reading Sec	63 Foreign/World Lang Sec	73 Instructional Tech
6 Athletic	13 Title V	24 Music Elem	34 Early Childhood Ed	44 Science Sec	54 Remedial Reading K-12	64 Religious Education K-12	74 Inservice Training
7 Health Services	15 Asst Superintendent	25 Music Sec	35 Health/Phys Education	45 Math K-12	55 Remedial Reading Elem	65 Religious Education Elem	75 Marketing/Distributive
	16 Instructional Media Svcs	26 Business Education	36 Guidance Services K-12	46 Math Elem	56 Remedial Reading Sec	66 Religious Education Sec	76 Info Systems
	17 Chief Operations Officer	27 Career & Tech Ed	37 Guidance Services Elem	47 Math Sec	57 Bilingual/ELL	67 School Board President	77 Psychological Assess
	18 Chief Academic Officer	28 Technology Education	38 Guidance Services Sec	48 English/Lang Arts K-12	58 Special Education K-12	68 Teacher Personnel	78 Affirmative Action

Illinois School Directory — St Clair County

ST CLAIR COUNTY

ST CLAIR COUNTY SCHOOLS

County Schs..Principal	Grd	Prgm	Enr/#Cls	SN	
Pathways Sch 2411 Pathways Xing, Belleville 62221 Diane Warfield	Spec		135 13	45%	618/355-4410 Fax 618/355-4751
Ⓐ St Clair Co Alternative Ed Ctr 1722 W Main St, Belleville 62226 Stacy Louderman	6-12		41 7		618/233-6874 Fax 618/233-6982

ST CLAIR PUBLIC SCHOOLS

- **Belle Valley School Dist 119** PID: 00316201   618/236-5200
  2465 Amann Dr, Belleville 62220   Fax 618/236-4550

Schools: 1 \ **Teachers:** 71 \ **Students:** 1,038 \ **Special Ed Students:** 236 \ **LEP Students:** 5 \ **Ethnic:** Asian 2%, African American 65%, Hispanic 1%, Caucasian 32% \ **Exp:** $249 (Med) \ **Poverty:** 20% \ **Title I:** $306,758 \ **Special Education:** $499,000 \ **Open-Close:** 08/18 - 05/28 \ 🇫 🇹

R Dane Gale 1		Joan McKay 2		
Dave Grohmann 3		Danita Duecker 7*		
Cindy Callahan 9*		Krystina Kelley 16*		
Karen Kunz 67		Doug Sawyer 73,295*		
Marge Belt 83*				

Public Schs..Principal	Grd	Prgm	Enr/#Cls	SN	
Belle Valley Elem Sch 2465 Amann Dr, Belleville 62220 Cindy Callahan \ Dr Tammy Leib	PK-8	T	1,038 25	70%	618/236-5200 Fax 618/234-5938

- **Belleville Public Sch Dist 118** PID: 00316237   618/233-2830
  105 W A St, Belleville 62220   Fax 618/233-8355

Schools: 11 \ **Teachers:** 231 \ **Students:** 4,500 \ **Special Ed Students:** 908 \ **LEP Students:** 17 \ **Ethnic:** Asian 1%, African American 49%, Hispanic 5%, Caucasian 46% \ **Exp:** $326 (High) \ **Poverty:** 20% \ **Title I:** $1,355,871 \ **Special Education:** $2,330,000 \ **Open-Close:** 08/20 - 05/26 \ **DTBP:** $187 (High)

Dr Ryan Boike 1	Jon Boente 2,3,5*
Steve Ebbesmeyer 4	Susan Price 5,57,59,77,88,90,270*
Tracey Gray 11,83,280,285,288,296,298	Chris McMahon 16,73,76,286,295*
Judy Keplar 67	Barb Jenkins 274
Geoffrey Schwalenberg 274*	Geoss Schwalenberg 274

Public Schs..Principal	Grd	Prgm	Enr/#Cls	SN	
Abraham Lincoln Sch 820 Royal Heights Rd, Belleville 62226 Edmund Langen	K-6	T	555 20	79%	618/233-2414 Fax 618/236-2597
Central Junior High Sch 1801 Central School Rd, Belleville 62220 Rocky Horrighs	7-8	TV	412 24	67%	618/233-5377 Fax 618/233-5440
Douglas Sch 125 Carlyle Ave, Belleville 62220 Geoff Schwalenberg	1-6	T	289 15	64%	618/233-2417 Fax 618/236-0593
Franklin Sch 301 N 2nd St, Belleville 62220 Jon Boente	K-6	T	162 17	90%	618/233-2413 Fax 618/236-2704
Henry Raab Elem Sch 1120 Union Ave, Belleville 62220 Jamie Buss	K-6	T	164 7	86%	618/234-4330 Fax 618/236-2768
Jefferson Sch 1400 N Charles St, Belleville 62221 Jamey McCloskey	PK-6	T	399 19	70%	618/233-3798 Fax 618/236-2873
Roosevelt Sch 700 W Cleveland Ave, Belleville 62220 Craig Hayes	K-6	T	312 13	64%	618/233-1608 Fax 618/233-1757
Union Sch 20 S 27th St, Belleville 62226 Lori Taylor	K-6	T	430 16	78%	618/233-4132 Fax 618/236-2548
Washington Sch 400 S Charles St, Belleville 62220 Jamie Buss	PK-K		80 4	75%	618/277-2017 Fax 618/277-2504
West Junior High Sch 840 Royal Heights Rd, Belleville 62226 Gustavo Cotto	7-8	TV	429 25	75%	618/234-8200 Fax 618/234-8220
Westhaven Sch 118 Westhaven School Rd, Belleville 62220 Geoffrey Schwalenberg	K-6	T	457 30	67%	618/257-9201 Fax 618/257-9310

- **Belleville Township HSD 201** PID: 00316366   618/222-8241
  920 N Illinois St, Belleville 62220   Fax 618/233-7586

Schools: 3 \ **Teachers:** 273 \ **Students:** 4,500 \ **Special Ed Students:** 933 \ **LEP Students:** 17 \ **College-Bound:** 69% \ **Ethnic:** Asian 1%, African American 42%, Hispanic 5%, Caucasian 52% \ **Exp:** $227 (Med) \ **Poverty:** 12% \ **Title I:** $1,051,141 \ **Special Education:** $2,210,000 \ **Open-Close:** 08/14 - 05/27 \ **DTBP:** $196 (High)

Brian Mentzer 1,11	Holly Matzenbacker 4*
Lee Mayer 6	Mark Larsen 6*
Julie Blankenship 7,77*	Melissa Taylor 10,15,38,60,79,275,288
Ashley Cryder 12,69,90*	Tiffany Droege 16*
Zach Rogers 16,73,82*	Andrea Gannon 30,88*
Carol Eckert 67	Dr Marshaun Warren 68
Curtis McKay 295*	Jason Hoffmann 295

Public Schs..Principal	Grd	Prgm	Enr/#Cls	SN	
Ⓐ Belleville Alternative Sch 2555 West Blvd, Belleville 62221 Andrea Gannon	9-12		25		618/222-3723
Belleville High School-East 2555 West Blvd, Belleville 62221 Josh Lane	9-12	AT	2,393 124	45%	618/222-3700 Fax 618/222-3799
Belleville Twp High Sch-West 4063 Frank Scott Pkwy W, Belleville 62223 Rich Mertens	9-12	AT	2,159	49%	618/222-7500 Fax 618/235-2484

- **Brooklyn School District 188** PID: 00316392   618/271-1014
  800 Madison St, Lovejoy 62059   Fax 618/271-9108

Schools: 1 \ **Teachers:** 10 \ **Students:** 161 \ **Special Ed Students:** 10 \ **College-Bound:** 75% \ **Ethnic:** African American 100%, \ **Exp:** $744 (High) \ **Poverty:** 53% \ **Title I:** $233,515 \ **Special Education:** $15,000 \ **Open-Close:** 08/14 - 06/03 \ **DTBP:** $233 (High)

Dr Ronald Ferrell 1,11,57,83,288	Betrenna Caldwell 2,12*
Gary Webster 3,5*	Jaye Woolfork 16,73,84
Angela Cotton 67	Carlos Stanford 85

---

79 Student Personnel	91 Safety/Security	275 Response To Intervention	298 Grant Writer/Ptnrships	**School Programs**
80 Driver Ed/Safety	92 Magnet School	277 Remedial Math K-12	750 Chief Innovation Officer	A = Alternative Program
81 Gifted/Talented	93 Parental Involvement	280 Literacy Coach	751 Chief of Staff	G = Adult Classes
82 Video Services	95 Tech Prep Program	285 STEM	752 Social Emotional Learning	M = Magnet Program
83 Substance Abuse Prev	97 Chief Infomation Officer	286 Digital Learning		T = Title I Schoolwide
84 Erate	98 Chief Technology Officer	288 Common Core Standards	**Other School Types**	V = Career & Tech Ed Programs
85 AIDS Education	270 Accountability	294 Accountability	Ⓐ = Alternative School	
88 Alternative/At Risk	271 Migrant Education	295 Network System	Ⓒ = Charter School	**Social Media**
89 Multi-Cultural Curriculum	273 Teacher Mentor	296 Title II Programs	Ⓜ = Magnet School	🇫 = Facebook
90 Social Work	274 Before/After Sch	297 Webmaster	Ⓨ = Year-Round School	🇹 = Twitter

New Schools are shaded
New Superintendents and Principals are bold
Personnel with email addresses are underscored

St Clair County

Market Data Retrieval

Public Schs..Principal	Grd	Prgm	Enr/#Cls	SN
Lovejoy Academy 800 Madison St, Lovejoy 62059 Dr Ronald Ferrell	PK-12	T	161 15	100% 618/271-1014

● **Cahokia Unit Sch Dist 187** PID: 00316419   618/332-3700
1700 Jerome Ln, Cahokia 62206   Fax 618/332-3706

Schools: 10 \ **Teachers:** 207 \ **Students:** 3,400 \ **Special Ed Students:** 768 \ **LEP Students:** 19 \ **College-Bound:** 46% \ **Ethnic:** African American 93%, Hispanic 2%, Caucasian 6% \ **Exp:** $259 (Med) \ **Poverty:** 38% \ **Title I:** $3,942,254 \ **Special Education:** $3,315,000 \ **Open-Close:** 08/17 - 05/24 \ **DTBP:** $202 (High)

Arnett Harvey 1,11
Dave Augustine 3
Pam Russell 4
Leonard Manley 6
Tanya Mitchell 11,36,68,69,88,288,294,296
Quennetta Chambers 58
Larry Wynn 67
Tony Priest 91*
Stepahine Scual-Bet 298
Ciara Corley 2
Steve Crum 3
Cynthia Moore 5
Gegi RA-El 8,280
Jen Barr 16,73,286*
Vicki Breckel 58,77,275
Tiffany Pearce 68
Sandra Chisom 285

Public Schs..Principal	Grd	Prgm	Enr/#Cls	SN
Cahokia 7th Grade Center 1900 Mousette Ln, Cahokia 62206 John Dozier	7-7	T	208	96% 618/332-3722 Fax 618/332-3741
Cahokia 8th Grade Center 1900 Mousette Ln, Cahokia 62206 Felicia Rush-Taylor	8-8	T	190	94% 618/332-3722 Fax 618/332-3724
Cahokia High Sch 800 Range Ln, Cahokia 62206 Valeska Hill	9-12	TV	772 85	91% 618/332-3730 Fax 618/332-3747
Elizabeth Morris Elem Sch 1500 Andrews Dr, Cahokia 62206 Karen Thompson	K-2	T	242 15	92% 618/332-3718 Fax 618/332-3785
Estelle Sauget Sch of Choice 1700 Jerome Ln, Cahokia 62206 Dr Trenese Steel	PK-8	T	270	84% 618/332-3820 Fax 618/332-3824
Helen Huffman Elem Sch 600 Saint Robert Dr, Cahokia 62206 Alison Schumacher	3-5	T	300 14	92% 618/332-3720 Fax 618/332-3782
Lalumier Elem Sch 6702 Bond Ave, Centreville 62207 Cynthia Langston	PK-3	T	293 17	98% 618/332-3713 Fax 618/332-3811
Maplewood Elem Sch 600 Jerome Ln, Cahokia 62206 Kristi Schroeder	PK-2	T	340 18	93% 618/332-3709 Fax 618/332-3787
Oliver Parks 6th Grade Center 1900 Mousette Ln Rear, Cahokia 62206 Gloria Perry	6-6	T	244 46	96% 618/332-3722 Fax 618/332-3797
Penniman Elem Sch 1820 Jerome Ln, Cahokia 62206 Wendy Lange	3-5	T	325 16	95% 618/332-1915 Fax 618/332-1918

● **Central School District 104** PID: 00316550   618/632-6336
309 Hartman Ln, O Fallon 62269   Fax 618/632-0870

Schools: 2 \ **Teachers:** 46 \ **Students:** 700 \ **Special Ed Students:** 118 \ **LEP Students:** 14 \ **Ethnic:** Asian 3%, African American 39%, Hispanic 10%, Caucasian 48% \ **Exp:** $174 (Low) \ **Poverty:** 16% \ **Title I:** $168,090 \ **Special Education:** $280,000 \ **Open-Close:** 08/14 - 05/26 \ **DTBP:** $303 (High)

Dawn Elser 1,288
Jane Hamm 2,274

Derek Morgan 6*
Rebecca Watson 37,83,88*
Sarah Svoboda 67
Carol Davison 11,296*
Cassy Shelton 59*
Steven Guay 73,286*

Public Schs..Principal	Grd	Prgm	Enr/#Cls	SN
Central Elem Sch 309 Hartman Ln, O Fallon 62269 Jayson Baker	PK-4	T	384 18	54% 618/632-6336
Joseph Arthur Middle Sch 160 Saint Ellen Mine Rd, O Fallon 62269 Tron Young	5-8	T	253 20	57% 618/632-6336 Fax 618/622-8691

● **Dupo Cmty School District 196** PID: 00316574   618/286-3812
600 Louisa Ave, Dupo 62239   Fax 618/286-5554

Schools: 2 \ **Teachers:** 72 \ **Students:** 985 \ **Special Ed Students:** 178 \ **LEP Students:** 6 \ **College-Bound:** 57% \ **Ethnic:** African American 3%, Hispanic 4%, Caucasian 92% \ **Exp:** $246 (Med) \ **Poverty:** 17% \ **Title I:** $306,660 \ **Special Education:** $570,000 \ **Open-Close:** 08/14 - 05/25

Dr Kelly Carpenter 1,11,288
Jill Weier 6
Kelly Kloess 16*
Krystin Baker 31,36,83,85*
Kraig Roth 58*
Leonard Aldridge 73,84
Steve Duke 3,4
Victoria White 12*
William Harris 27,57*
Jessie Duke 34
Jaci Declue 67
Mike Treece 73*

Public Schs..Principal	Grd	Prgm	Enr/#Cls	SN
Bluffview Elem Sch 905 Bluffview Elementary Ln, Dupo 62239 Victoria White	PK-6	T	572 27	49% 618/286-3311 Fax 618/286-4092
Dupo Jr Sr High Sch 600 Louisa Ave, Dupo 62239 Stevie Brown	7-12	TV	413 40	52% 618/286-3214 Fax 618/286-5535

● **East St Louis Sch Dist 189** PID: 00316639   618/646-3000
1005 State St, E Saint Louis 62201   Fax 618/583-7186

Schools: 11 \ **Teachers:** 341 \ **Students:** 5,200 \ **Special Ed Students:** 798 \ **LEP Students:** 60 \ **College-Bound:** 51% \ **Ethnic:** African American 98%, Hispanic 1%, Caucasian 1% \ **Exp:** $316 (High) \ **Poverty:** 41% \ **Title I:** $7,892,349 \ **Special Education:** $5,681,000 \ **Bilingual Education:** $11,000 \ **Open-Close:** 08/17 - 05/26 \ **DTBP:** $191 (High)

Arthur Culver 1
Dr Sherry Whitaker 2,19
Norquise Cooper 5
Jennifer Brumback 10,18
Keisa Garrett 15
Dekietrich Lockett 27,31
Michelle Chism 34
Latonya Fulton 58
R C Clark 67
Lori Chalmers 68
Tiffany Gholson 79,93,752
Michael Hubbard 91
Sydney Stigge-Kaufman 298
Delfaye Jason 2
Alonzo Nelson 3
Antionette Johnson 8,57
Dr Teresa Williams 11
Abe Loveless 16,73,76,84
Melanie Hood 34*
Kimberly Hopkins 58
Robin Carey-Boyd 58
Latoya Greenwood 68
Tina Frye 68
Joseph Haskell 88
Zorina Brown 93

Public Schs..Principal	Grd	Prgm	Enr/#Cls	SN
Annette Harris Officer ES 558 N 27th St, E Saint Louis 62205 Lori Chalmers	K-4	T	422 18	95% 618/646-3970 Fax 618/646-3978
Dunbar Elem Sch 1835 Tudor Ave, E Saint Louis 62207 Carlynda Coleman	K-4	T	475 20	94% 618/646-3840 Fax 618/646-3848

1 Superintendent	8 Curric/Instruct K-12	19 Chief Financial Officer	29 Family/Consumer Science	39 Social Studies K-12	49 English/Lang Arts Elem	59 Special Education Elem	69 Academic Assessment
2 Bus/Finance/Purchasing	9 Curric/Instruct Elem	20 Art K-12	30 Adult Education	40 Social Studies Elem	50 English/Lang Arts Sec	60 Special Education Sec	70 Research/Development
3 Buildings And Grounds	10 Curric/Instruct Sec	21 Art Elem	31 Career/Sch-to-Work K-12	41 Social Studies Sec	51 Reading K-12	61 Foreign/World Lang K-12	71 Public Information
4 Food Service	11 Federal Program	22 Art Sec	32 Career/Sch-to-Work Elem	42 Science K-12	52 Reading Elem	62 Foreign/World Lang Elem	72 Summer School
5 Transportation	12 Title I	23 Music K-12	33 Career/Sch-to-Work Sec	43 Science Elem	53 Reading Sec	63 Foreign/World Lang Sec	73 Instructional Tech
6 Athletic	13 Title V	24 Music Elem	34 Early Childhood Ed	44 Science Sec	54 Remedial Reading K-12	64 Religious Education K-12	74 Inservice Training
7 Health Services	14 Instructional Media Svcs	25 Music Sec	35 Health/Phys Education	45 Math K-12	55 Remedial Reading Elem	65 Religious Education Elem	75 Marketing/Distributive
	15 Asst Superintendent	26 Business Education	36 Guidance Services K-12	46 Math Elem	56 Remedial Reading Sec	66 Religious Education Sec	76 Info Systems
	16 Chief Operations Officer	27 Career & Tech Ed	37 Guidance Services Elem	47 Math Sec	57 Bilingual/Fl I	67 School Board President	77 Psychological Assess
	17 Chief Academic Officer	28 Technology Education	38 Guidance Services Sec	48 English/Lang Arts K-12	58 Special Education K-12	68 Teacher Personnel	78 Affirmative Action

Illinois School Directory — St Clair County

East St Louis Sr High Sch 4901 State St, E Saint Louis 62205 Justin Moore	9-12	TV	1,090	97%	618/646-3700 Fax 618/646-3958
Gordon D Bush Elem Sch 1516 Gross Ave, E Saint Louis 62205 Brittany Green	K-5	T	461 21	96%	618/646-3930 Fax 618/646-3038
James Avant Elem Sch 1915 N 55th St, Washington Pk 62204 Charlotte Edwards	K-4	T	494 24	94%	618/646-3870 Fax 618/646-3878
Katie Harper-Wright Elem Sch 7710 State St, E Saint Louis 62203 Kiandra Smith	K-5	T	468 27	92%	618/646-3860 Fax 618/646-3868
Lincoln Middle Sch 12 S 10th St, E Saint Louis 62201 Maria Burton	5-8	TV	647	97%	618/646-3770 Fax 618/646-3778
Mason Clark Middle Sch 5510 State St, E Saint Louis 62203 Kim Jones-Riley	5-8	TV	749 32	99%	618/646-3750 Fax 618/646-3758
Ⓐ Siue East St Louis Charter Sch Ⓒ 601 James R Thompson Blvd, E Saint Louis 62201 Gina Jeffries	9-12	TV	113 15	97%	618/482-6912 Fax 618/482-8372
Vivian Adams Early Chldhd Ctr 501 Katherine Dunham Pl, E Saint Louis 62201 Melanie Hood	PK-PK	T	425 13	57%	618/646-3290 Fax 618/646-3298
Ⓐ Wyvetter Younge Alt Ctr for Ed 3939 Caseyville Ave, E Saint Louis 62204 Alonzo Nelson	9-12	GTV	115 14	97%	618/646-3760 Fax 618/646-3768

● **Freeburg Cmty Cons SD 70** PID: 00317061 618/539-3188
408 S Belleville St, Freeburg 62243 Fax 618/539-5795

Schools: 2 \ **Teachers:** 47 \ **Students:** 780 \ **Special Ed Students:** 116
\ **LEP Students:** 4 \ **Ethnic:** Hispanic 2%, Caucasian 97% \ **Exp:** $71
(Low) \ **Poverty:** 9% \ **Title I:** $93,296 \ **Special Education:** $288,000 \
Open-Close: 08/13 - 05/21 \ **DTBP:** $178 (High)

Tomi Diefenbach 1   Mark Janssen 2,11,15
Tim Havel ....3*   Abby Vosse 4
Fritz Holcomb 5   Mike Joseph 6*
Barb Bauman 67   Jeff Foster 73*
Theresa Goscinski 83*

Public Schs..Principal	Grd	Prgm	Enr/#Cls	SN	
Freeburg Elem Sch 408 S Belleville St, Freeburg 62243 Theresa Goscinski	3-8		500 45	6%	618/539-3188
Freeburg Primary Center 650 S State St, Freeburg 62243 Theresa Goscinski	PK-2		248 20	5%	618/539-3188 Fax 618/539-6008

● **Freeburg Cmty High Sch Dist 77** PID: 00317085 618/539-5533
401 S Monroe St, Freeburg 62243 Fax 618/539-4887

Schools: 1 \ **Teachers:** 39 \ **Students:** 675 \ **Special Ed Students:** 80
\ **LEP Students:** 3 \ **College-Bound:** 76% \ **Ethnic:** Hispanic 2%,
Caucasian 97% \ **Exp:** $143 (Low) \ **Poverty:** 5% \ **Title I:** $50,028 \
Special Education: $256,000 \ **Open-Close:** 08/17 - 06/01 \ **DTBP:** $180
(High)

Greg Frerking 1,11,83,288   Diane Schaefer 2
Doug Parrish 67   Jeff Alt 73,76,84
Tina Overbey 752

Public Schs..Principal	Grd	Prgm	Enr/#Cls	SN	
Freeburg Cmty High Sch 401 S Monroe St, Freeburg 62243 Jill Jung	9-12	V	675 55	14%	618/539-5533

● **Grant Cmty Cons Sch Dist 110** PID: 00317102 618/398-5577
10110 Old Lincoln Trl, Fairview HTS 62208 Fax 618/397-7809

Schools: 2 \ **Teachers:** 42 \ **Students:** 600 \ **Special Ed Students:** 139
\ **Ethnic:** Asian 1%, African American 41%, Hispanic 4%, Caucasian
54% \ **Exp:** $237 (Med) \ **Poverty:** 16% \ **Title I:** $211,732 \
Special Education: $364,000 \ **Open-Close:** 08/13 - 05/25 \ **DTBP:** $218
(High)

Matthew Stines 1   Glenna Creek 2
Jim Murphy ....6*   Carla Lasley 9,11,57,67,74,88,275,288
Stacey Schulte ....11*   Donna Brockmeyer 16*
Carla Lasley 58   Brien Bednara 73,295,297*
Tracie Boever ....83,270* Brien Bednara 84

Public Schs..Principal	Grd	Prgm	Enr/#Cls	SN	
Grant Middle Sch 10110 Old Lincoln Trl, Fairview HTS 62208 Carla Lasley	5-8	T	282 21	51%	618/397-2764
Illini Elem Sch 21 Circle Dr, Fairview HTS 62208 Travis Klein	PK-4	T	330 28	57%	618/398-5552 Fax 618/394-9801

● **Harmony-Emge School Dist 175** PID: 00317164 618/397-8444
7401 Westchester Dr, Belleville 62223 Fax 618/397-8446

Schools: 3 \ **Teachers:** 49 \ **Students:** 800 \ **Special Ed Students:** 109
\ **LEP Students:** 6 \ **Ethnic:** Asian 1%, African American 50%, Hispanic
4%, Caucasian 46% \ **Exp:** $267 (Med) \ **Poverty:** 16% \ **Title I:** $251,980
\ **Special Education:** $392,000 \ **Bilingual Education:** $3,000 \
Open-Close: 08/17 - 05/21

Dave Deets 1,11   Dennis O'Neill 2
Debbie Brem 4   Norman Mars 5
Mark Bower ....6*   Tessa Keys 67
Katherine Kaiser 274*

Public Schs..Principal	Grd	Prgm	Enr/#Cls	SN	
Ellis Elem Sch 250 Illini Dr, Belleville 62223 Terri Kraemer	PK-3	T	343 21	63%	618/538-6114 Fax 618/538-6118
Emge Junior High Sch 7401 Westchester Dr, Belleville 62223 David Deets	7-8	T	158 23	65%	618/397-6557 Fax 618/397-3011
Harmony Intermediate Sch 7401 Westchester Dr, Belleville 62223 Dave Deets	4-6	T	274	63%	618/397-3747 Fax 618/397-3011

● **High Mount Sch Dist 116** PID: 00317205 618/233-1054
1721 Boul Ave, Swansea 62226 Fax 618/233-1136

Schools: 1 \ **Teachers:** 29 \ **Students:** 475 \ **Special Ed Students:** 88
\ **LEP Students:** 7 \ **Ethnic:** African American 38%, Hispanic 12%,
Caucasian 50% \ **Exp:** $596 (High) \ **Poverty:** 19% \ **Title I:** $156,095 \
Special Education: $190,000 \ **Open-Close:** 08/14 - 05/21 \ **DTBP:** $234
(High)

Beth Horner 1,73   Marilyn Rossi 2
Gary Emmons ....3*   Jim Robbon 6*
Karen Hand ....12*   George Wilkerson 57,69,273*

---

79 Student Personnel
80 Driver Ed/Safety
81 Gifted/Talented
82 Video Services
83 Substance Abuse Prev
84 Erate
85 AIDS Education
88 Alternative/At Risk
89 Multi-Cultural Curriculum
90 Social Work

91 Safety/Security
92 Magnet School
93 Parental Involvement
95 Tech Prep Program
97 Chief Information Officer
98 Chief Technology Officer
270 Character Education
271 Migrant Education
273 Teacher Mentor
274 Before/After Sch

275 Response To Intervention
277 Remedial Math K-12
280 Literacy Coach
285 STEM
286 Digital Learning
288 Common Core Standards
294 Accountability
295 Network System
296 Title II Programs
297 Webmaster

298 Grant Writer/Ptnrships
750 Chief Innovation Officer
751 Chief of Staff
752 Social Emotional Learning

Other School Types
Ⓐ = Alternative School
Ⓒ = Charter School
Ⓜ = Magnet School
Ⓨ = Year-Round School

School Programs
A = Alternative Program
G = Adult Classes
M = Magnet Program
T = Title I Schoolwide
V = Career & Tech Ed Programs

Social Media
🅕 = Facebook
🅣 = Twitter

New Schools are shaded
New Superintendents and Principals are bold
Personnel with email addresses are underscored

St Clair County

Market Data Retrieval

Justin Chapman	67
Debra Bellm	83,90*
Dave Shevess	76,286
Julie Burns	274*

Public Schs..Principal	Grd	Prgm	Enr/#Cls	SN		
High Mount Elem Sch 1721 Boul Ave, Swansea 62226 George Wilkerson	PK-8	T	475 27	74%	618/233-1054	

• **Lebanon Cmty Unit Sch Dist 9** PID: 00317229 618/537-4611
200 W Schuetz St, Lebanon 62254 Fax 618/537-9588

Schools: 2 \ Teachers: 46 \ Students: 540 \ Special Ed Students: 123 \
LEP Students: 3 \ Ethnic: Asian 5%, African American 20%, Hispanic 2%,
Caucasian 73% \ Exp: $194 (Low) \ Poverty: 24% \ Title I: $311,623 \
Special Education: $288,000 \ Open-Close: 08/19 - 06/01 \ DTBP: $238
(High)

Patrick Keeney	1	Penni Liebig	2
Bryan Reifing	3	Karen Wehrle	5
Josiah Maunton	6	Tracie Mason	7*
Jeffrey Teasley	10,275*	Joanie Thole	11*
Brent Koenig	67	Jeannette Schorfheide	69,83,294*
Adam Richter	73,76,84,97,98,286,295		

Public Schs..Principal	Grd	Prgm	Enr/#Cls	SN		
Lebanon Elem Sch 408 Mary Jane St, Lebanon 62254 **Jasen Foster**	PK-5	T	281 21	42%	618/537-4553 Fax 618/537-2746	
Lebanon High Sch 200 W Schuetz St, Lebanon 62254 **Jeff Teasley**	6-12	AT	274 30	42%	618/537-4423	

• **Marissa Cmty Unit Sch Dist 40** PID: 00317267 618/295-2313
1 E Marissa St, Marissa 62257 Fax 618/295-2609

Schools: 2 \ Teachers: 46 \ Students: 550 \ Special Ed Students: 115
\ College-Bound: 61% \ Ethnic: African American 1%, Hispanic 1%,
Caucasian 98% \ Exp: $174 (Low) \ Poverty: 18% \ Title I: $170,179 \
Special Education: $265,000 \ Open-Close: 08/17 - 05/25

Jeff Strieker	1	Sandy Hahn	4
Russ Clark	5	Lori Selman	6*
James Heil	67	Angela Birch	69*
Gary Stewart	76,295*		

Public Schs..Principal	Grd	Prgm	Enr/#Cls	SN		
Marissa Elem Sch 206 E Fulton St, Marissa 62257 Lacey Schmersahl	PK-6	T	320 21	61%	618/295-2339 Fax 618/295-3673	
Marissa Jr Sr High Sch 300 School View Dr, Marissa 62257 **Dawn Mueller**	7-12	T	250 20	60%	618/295-2393 Fax 618/295-2276	

• **Mascoutah Cmty Sch Dist 19** PID: 00317308 618/566-7414
421 W Harnett St, Mascoutah 62258 Fax 618/448-0507

Schools: 5 \ Teachers: 239 \ Students: 4,000 \ Special Ed Students: 609
\ LEP Students: 40 \ College-Bound: 80% \ Ethnic: Asian 2%, African
American 11%, Hispanic 9%, Caucasian 77% \ Exp: $251 (Med) \
Poverty: 5% \ Title I: $238,535 \ Special Education: $1,373,000 \
Open-Close: 08/24 - 05/21 \ DTBP: $194 (High)

Dr Craig Fiegel	1	Frank Williams	2,91
Wayne Kunde	3	Susan Sommers	4
Kenneth Neuner	5	Scott Battaf	6*

Colleen Henson	7*
Laura Yarber	11,298
Mario Sherall	18,280
Jessica Seger	58
Tara Laidley	73,286
Cindi Presnell	8,11,57,69,81,88,273,288
Breanna Gober	16,82*
Nancy Seibert	34,58,77,90
Matthew Stukenberg	67
Scott Walthes	295

Public Schs..Principal	Grd	Prgm	Enr/#Cls	SN		
Mascoutah Elem Sch 533 N 6th St, Mascoutah 62258 **Kim Enriquez**	PK-5		856 40	27%	618/566-2152 Fax 618/566-8543	
Mascoutah High Sch 1313 W Main St, Mascoutah 62258 **Brandon Woodrome**	9-12	V	1,086 65	22%	618/566-8523 Fax 618/566-8693	
Mascoutah Middle Sch 846 N 6th St, Mascoutah 62258 **Paolo Dulcamara**	6-8	V	879	23%	618/566-2305 Fax 618/566-2307	
Scott Elem Sch 4732 Patriots Dr, Scott Afb 62225 **Susanne Riechmann**	PK-5	T	811 39	24%	618/746-4738 Fax 618/746-2186	
WinGate Elem Sch 150 Wingate Blvd, Belleville 62221 **Randy Blakely**	PK-5		420	18%	618/746-4802 Fax 618/235-4421	

• **Millstadt Cmty Cons SD 160** PID: 00317360 618/476-1803
211 W Mill St, Millstadt 62260 Fax 618/476-1893

Schools: 2 \ Teachers: 51 \ Students: 800 \
Special Ed Students: 156 \ Ethnic: Asian 1%, African American 3%, Hispanic
1%, Caucasian 95% \ Exp: $143 (Low) \ Poverty: 6% \ Title I: $77,071 \
Special Education: $212,000 \ Open-Close: 08/18 - 05/28 \ DTBP: $243
(High)

Dr Brad Landgraf	1	Julie Beine	2
Bryan Weaver	6	Kelly Snyder	16
Bob Dahm	67	Jennifer Missey	83,90,270*

Public Schs..Principal	Grd	Prgm	Enr/#Cls	SN		
Millstadt Cons Sch 211 W Mill St, Millstadt 62260 **Sandra Pegg**	3-8		562 38	15%	618/476-1681 Fax 618/476-3401	
Millstadt Primary Center 105 W Parkview Dr, Millstadt 62260 Sandra Pegg	PK-2		257 15	2%	618/476-7100 Fax 618/476-7182	

• **New Athens CUSD 60** PID: 00317396 618/475-2174
501 Hanft St, New Athens 62264 Fax 618/475-2176

Schools: 1 \ Teachers: 37 \ Students: 500 \ Special Ed Students: 81
\ LEP Students: 3 \ College-Bound: 76% \ Ethnic: African American
1%, Hispanic 1%, Native American: 1%, Caucasian 97% \ Exp: $231
(Med) \ Poverty: 9% \ Title I: $83,831 \ Special Education: $285,000 \
Open-Close: 08/13 - 05/19 \ DTBP: $172 (High)

Brian Karraker	1	Shelly Fizer	2
Amber Walsh	7,83,85*	Jim Marlow	8*
Roxanne Jenkins	57*	Terry Hamon	67
Conrad Widdersheim	273*		

Public Schs..Principal	Grd	Prgm	Enr/#Cls	SN		
New Athens Sch 501 Hanft St, New Athens 62264 Jim Marlow \ Dan Lehman	PK-12		500 24	30%	618/475-2172	

1	Superintendent	8	Curric/Instruct K-12	19	Chief Financial Officer	29	Family/Consumer Science	39	Social Studies K-12	49	English/Lang Arts Elem	59	Special Education Elem	69	Academic Assessment
2	Bus/Finance/Purchasing	9	Curric/Instruct Elem	20	Art K-12	30	Adult Education	40	Social Studies Elem	50	English/Lang Arts Sec	60	Special Education Sec	70	Research/Development
3	Buildings And Grounds	10	Curric/Instruct Sec	21	Art Elem	31	Career/Sch-to-Work K-12	41	Social Studies Sec	51	Reading K-12	61	Foreign/World Lang K-12	71	Public Information
4	Food Service	11	Federal Program	22	Art Sec	32	Career/Sch-to-Work Elem	42	Science K-12	52	Reading Elem	62	Foreign/World Lang Elem	72	Summer School
5	Transportation	12	Title I	23	Music K-12	33	Career/Sch-to-Work Sec	43	Science Elem	53	Reading Sec	63	Foreign/World Lang Sec	73	Instructional Media
6	Athletic	13	Title V	24	Music Elem	34	Early Childhood Ed	44	Science Sec	54	Remedial Reading K-12	64	Religious Education K-12	74	Inservice Training
7	Health Services	15	Asst Superintendent	25	Music Sec	35	Health/Phys Education	45	Math K-12	55	Remedial Reading Elem	65	Religious Education Elem	75	Marketing/Distributive
		16	Instructional Media Svcs	26	Business Education	36	Guidance Services K-12	46	Math Elem	56	Remedial Reading Sec	66	Religious Education Sec	76	Info Systems
		17	Chief Operations Officer	27	Career & Tech Ed	37	Guidance Services Elem	47	Math Sec	57	Bilingual/ELL	67	School Board President	77	Psychological Assess
		18	Chief Academic Officer	28	Technology Education	38	Guidance Services Sec	48	English/Lang Arts K-12	58	Special Education K-12	68	Teacher Personnel	78	Affirmative Action

Illinois School Directory — St Clair County

- **O'Fallon Cmty Cons Sch Dist 90** PID: 00317425   618/632-3666
  118 E Washington St, O Fallon 62269   Fax 618/632-7864

Schools: 7 \ **Teachers:** 195 \ **Students:** 3,761 \ **Special Ed Students:** 641 \ **LEP Students:** 12 \ **Ethnic:** Asian 2%, African American 18%, Hispanic 5%, Caucasian 74% \ **Exp:** $133 (Low) \ **Poverty:** 6% \ **Title I:** $324,081 \ **Special Education:** $1,522,000 \ **Open-Close:** 08/14 - 05/20 \ **DTBP:** $193 (High)

Carrie Hruby	1,11	Patty Cavins	2,12,296
Ed Smith	3	Tracy Lauderdale	6*
Jill Lyons	9	Beth Bendele	16*
Aaron Kennedy	24	Mark Donahue	24*
Mark Donahue	24	Laurin McWhorter	59
Tracie Bauer	59	John Wagnon	67
Grady Niles	73*	Grady Niles	84
Mark Berry	91*	Mark Berry	91
Gina Harding	274*	Mike Abell	295*

Public Schs..Principal	Grd	Prgm	Enr/#Cls	SN	
Amelia Carriel Junior High Sch 451 N 7 Hills Rd, O Fallon 62269 Ellen Hays	6-8		685	25%	618/622-2932 Fax 618/622-2940
Delores Moye Elem Sch 1010 Moye School Rd, O Fallon 62269 Becky Williams	PK-5		660 24	24%	618/206-2300 Fax 618/206-2260
Edward Fulton Jr High Sch 307 Kyle Rd, O Fallon 62269 Joi Wills	6-8		629 40	20%	618/628-0090 Fax 618/624-9390
Estelle Kampmeyer Elem Sch 707 N Smiley St, O Fallon 62269 Mark Dismukes	PK-5		409 19	22%	618/632-6391 Fax 618/632-7580
J E Hinchcliffe Elem Sch 1050 Ogle Rd, O Fallon 62269 Kristie Belobrajdic	PK-5		402 60	21%	618/632-8406 Fax 618/632-1774
Laverna Evans Elem Sch 802 Dartmouth Dr, O Fallon 62269 Ryan Keller	PK-5		357 19	32%	618/632-3335 Fax 618/632-1530
Marie Schaefer Elem Sch 505 S Cherry St, O Fallon 62269 Tracy Newton-Duggins	PK-5		587 27	21%	618/632-3621 Fax 618/632-9258

- **O'Fallon Twp School Dist 203** PID: 00317475   618/632-3507
  600 S Smiley St, O Fallon 62269   Fax 618/632-6484

Schools: 2 \ **Teachers:** 136 \ **Students:** 2,400 \ **Special Ed Students:** 333 \ **LEP Students:** 11 \ **College-Bound:** 80% \ **Ethnic:** Asian 2%, African American 21%, Hispanic 6%, Caucasian 71% \ **Exp:** $243 (Med) \ **Poverty:** 6% \ **Title I:** $221,077 \ **Special Education:** $1,197,000 \ **Open-Close:** 08/13 - 05/19 \ **DTBP:** $194 (High) \ f t

Dr Darcy Benway	1	Beth Shackelford	2*
Todd Moeller	6*	Tiffany Niedringhause	11,74
Jennifer Lara	16*	Tiffany Lugge	38*
Martha Blackburn	60,274*	Linda Couzad	67
Dan Howe	73*		

Public Schs..Principal	Grd	Prgm	Enr/#Cls	SN	
O'Fallon Twp High Sch 600 S Smiley St, O Fallon 62269 Rich Bickel	10-12	ATV	2,500 118	24%	618/632-3507
O'Fallon Twp HS-Milburn 650 Milburn School Rd, O Fallon 62269 Rich Bickel	9-9	AV	580		618/622-9647 Fax 618/622-9630

- **Pontiac-Wm Holliday SD 105** PID: 00317499   618/233-2320
  400 Ashland Ave, Fairview HTS 62208   Fax 618/233-0918

Schools: 2 \ **Teachers:** 46 \ **Students:** 500 \ **Special Ed Students:** 113 \ **LEP Students:** 15 \ **Ethnic:** Asian 2%, African American 49%, Hispanic 10%, Caucasian 38% \ **Exp:** $194 (Low) \ **Poverty:** 12% \ **Title I:** $133,179 \ **Special Education:** $318,000 \ **Open-Close:** 08/12 - 05/20 \ **DTBP:** $233 (High)

Dr Julie Brown	1,11	Rebecca Skillern	5*
Brad Gotshall	6,69,280,285,288*	Lori Flowers	7*
Dr Amy Seelman	9*	Joanna Luehmann	9*
Marcia Billhartz	12*	Chris McMahon	67
Eric Muckensturm	84	Shelia Wildermuth	274*

Public Schs..Principal	Grd	Prgm	Enr/#Cls	SN	
Pontiac Junior High Sch 400 Ashland Ave, Fairview HTS 62208 Joanna Luehmann	6-8	T	237 19	51%	618/233-6004
William Holliday Elem Sch 400 Joseph Dr, Fairview HTS 62208 Dr Amy Seelman	PK-5		476 25	53%	618/233-7588 Fax 618/233-1619

- **Shiloh Village Sch Dist 85** PID: 00317528   618/632-7434
  125 Diamond Ct, Shiloh 62269   Fax 618/632-8343

Schools: 2 \ **Teachers:** 37 \ **Students:** 571 \ **Special Ed Students:** 116 \ **LEP Students:** 3 \ **Ethnic:** Asian 5%, African American 21%, Hispanic 4%, Caucasian 70% \ **Exp:** $60 (Low) \ **Poverty:** 10% \ **Title I:** $79,775 \ **Special Education:** $215,000 \ **Open-Close:** 08/11 - 05/17 \ **DTBP:** $221 (High)

Dale Sauer	1	Michele Tiberend	2
Leslie Ecker	67	Bill Kampmeyer	73,76*
Wendy Kassing	275*		

Public Schs..Principal	Grd	Prgm	Enr/#Cls	SN	
Shiloh Middle Sch 1 Wildcat Xing, Shiloh 62269 Darin Loepker	5-8		250	38%	618/632-7434
Shiloh Village Elem Sch 125 Diamond Ct, Shiloh 62269 Tiana Montgomery	PK-3		245 23	37%	618/632-7448

- **Signal Hill Sch Dist 181** PID: 00317542   618/397-0325
  40 Signal Hill Pl, Belleville 62223   Fax 618/397-2828

Schools: 1 \ **Teachers:** 33 \ **Students:** 330 \ **Special Ed Students:** 77 \ **LEP Students:** 3 \ **Ethnic:** Asian 1%, African American 48%, Hispanic 2%, Native American: 1%, Caucasian 48% \ **Exp:** $514 (High) \ **Poverty:** 16% \ **Title I:** $115,761 \ **Special Education:** $109,000 \ **Open-Close:** 08/17 - 05/25

Kelly Bohnenstiehl	1,11	Jennifer Monroe	2
Corey Gabriel	3*	Kim Pryor	6*
Brooke Wiemers	9,16,73,83,95,270,273*	Sarah Goode	12*
Tara Poindexter	34	Paul Slocomb	67

Public Schs..Principal	Grd	Prgm	Enr/#Cls	SN	
Signal Hill Elem Sch 40 Signal Hill Pl, Belleville 62223 Brooke Wiemers	PK-8	T	330 28	55%	618/397-0325

---

79 Student Personnel	91 Safety/Security	275 Response To Intervention	298 Grant Writer/Ptnrships	**School Programs**	**Social Media**
80 Driver Ed/Safety	92 Magnet School	277 Remedial Math K-12	750 Chief Innovation Officer	A = Alternative Program	
81 Gifted/Talented	93 Parental Involvement	280 Literacy Coach	751 Chief of Staff	G = Adult Classes	f = Facebook
82 Video Services	95 Tech Prep Program	285 STEM	752 Social Emotional Learning	M = Magnet Program	
83 Substance Abuse Prev	97 Chief Infomation Officer	286 Digital Learning		T = Title I Schoolwide	t = Twitter
84 Erate	98 Chief Technology Officer	288 Common Core Standards	**Other School Types**	V = Career & Tech Ed Programs	
85 AIDS Education	270 Character Education	294 Accountability	A = Alternative School		
88 Alternative/At Risk	271 Migrant Education	295 Network System	C = Charter School	New Schools are shaded	
89 Multi-Cultural Curriculum	273 Teacher Mentor	296 Title II Programs	M = Magnet School	New Superintendents and Principals are bold	
90 Social Work	274 Before/After Sch	297 Webmaster	Y = Year-Round School	Personnel with email addresses are underscored	

St Clair County

- **Smithton Cmty Cons SD 130** PID: 00317566 618/233-6863
  316 S Hickory St, Smithton 62285 Fax 618/233-8413

  Schools: 1 \ **Teachers:** 35 \ **Students:** 568 \
  Special Ed Students: 75 \ **Ethnic:** Asian 1%, African American 1%, Hispanic 1%, Caucasian 97% \ **Exp:** $76 (Low) \ **Poverty:** 5% \ **Title I:** $47,040 \
  Special Education: $180,000 \ **Open-Close:** 08/13 - 05/21 \ **DTBP:** $179 (High)

  Dr Ryan Wamser 1,84
  Ray Lauer 3
  Tim Keefe 6
  Jennifer Hoover 12*
  Alex Amarsaglia 73,295
  Hiedi Etling 2
  Fritz Holcomb 5
  Vicki Norton 9,59,69,83,88,270*
  Dale Barschak 67
  Lori Rainbolt 90

Public Schs..Principal	Grd	Prgm	Enr/#Cls	SN	
Smithton Elem Sch 316 S Hickory St, Smithton 62285 Vicki Norton	PK-8		568 26	10%	618/233-6863

- **St Libory Cons Sch District 30** PID: 00317592 618/768-4923
  811 Darmstadt St, Saint Libory 62282 Fax 618/768-4518

  Schools: 1 \ **Teachers:** 7 \ **Students:** 53 \
  Special Ed Students: 9 \ **Ethnic:** Asian 2%, African American 3%, Hispanic 3%, Caucasian 92% \ **Exp:** $200 (Med) \ **Poverty:** 13% \ **Title I:** $18,282 \
  Special Education: $45,000 \ **Open-Close:** 08/13 - 05/21 \ **DTBP:** $50 (Low)

  Dr Thomas Rude 1,11,84
  Sarah Brandt 67
  Tim Lange 6
  Michelle Albrecht 275*

Public Schs..Principal	Grd	Prgm	Enr/#Cls	SN	
St Libory Elem Sch 811 Darmstadt St, Saint Libory 62282 Dr Thomas Rude	K-8		53 11	11%	618/768-4923

- **Whiteside School District 115** PID: 00317619 618/239-0000
  111 Warrior Way, Belleville 62221 Fax 618/239-9240

  Schools: 2 \ **Teachers:** 81 \ **Students:** 1,036 \ **Special Ed Students:** 287 \ **LEP Students:** 3 \ **Ethnic:** Asian 3%, African American 60%, Hispanic 3%, Caucasian 34% \ **Exp:** $168 (Low) \ **Poverty:** 13% \ **Title I:** $328,697 \
  Special Education: $712,000 \ **Open-Close:** 08/14 - 05/19 \ **DTBP:** $233 (High) \

  Mark Heuring 1
  Daniel Mattern 3
  Nathan Rakers 9*
  Cindy Doder 16
  Sean McKee 67
  Justin Ballou 73,286,295*
  Kristy Frazer 274
  Karma Falkenbury 2
  Shea Lodes 6*
  Dorothy Simpson 11,296*
  Christine Stinnett 59
  Monica Laurent 69*
  Terry Haas 91

Public Schs..Principal	Grd	Prgm	Enr/#Cls	SN	
Whiteside Elem Sch 2028 Lebanon Ave, Belleville 62221 Nathan Rakers	PK-4	T	630 45	58%	618/239-0000 Fax 618/233-7931
Whiteside Middle Sch 111 Warrior Way, Belleville 62221 Monica Laurent	5-8	T	537	53%	618/239-0000 Fax 618/233-7931

- **Wolf Branch School Dist 113** PID: 00317645 618/277-2100
  410 Huntwood Rd, Swansea 62226 Fax 618/235-2376

  Schools: 2 \ **Teachers:** 49 \ **Students:** 720 \ **Special Ed Students:** 107 \ **LEP Students:** 19 \ **Ethnic:** Asian 6%, African American 17%, Hispanic 5%, Caucasian 72% \ **Exp:** $151 (Low) \ **Poverty:** 6% \ **Title I:** $72,622 \ **Special Education:** $278,000 \ **Bilingual Education:** $1,000 \
  Open-Close: 08/14 - 05/20

  Scott Harres 1
  Bob Lonsdale 67
  Nicole Sanderson 9,288

Public Schs..Principal	Grd	Prgm	Enr/#Cls	SN	
Wolf Branch Elem Sch 125 Huntwood Rd, Swansea 62226 Madonna Harris	PK-4		412 27	22%	618/277-2100 Fax 618/277-9786
Wolf Branch Middle Sch 125 Huntwood Rd, Swansea 62226 Jennifer Poirot	5-8		350 13	15%	618/277-2100 Fax 618/277-9786

ST CLAIR CATHOLIC SCHOOLS

- **Diocese of Belleville Ed Off** PID: 00317671 618/235-9601
  2620 Lebanon Ave Bldg 6, Belleville 62221 Fax 618/235-7115

  Schools: 30 \ **Students:** 5,497

  Listing includes only schools located in this county. See District Index for location of Diocesan Offices.

  Jonathan Birdsong 1
  David Timmermann 15
  Michael Gibbons 2
  Jamie Gill 64

Catholic Schs..Principal	Grd	Prgm	Enr/#Cls	SN	
Althoff Catholic High Sch 5401 W Main St, Belleville 62226 Dr Sarah Gass	9-12		400		618/235-1100 Fax 618/235-9535
Blessed Sacrament Sch 8809 W Main St, Belleville 62223 Claire Hatch	PK-8		200 15		618/397-1111 Fax 618/397-8431
Holy Childhood Sch 215 N John St, Mascoutah 62258 Claudia Dougherty	K-8		153 9		618/566-2922 Fax 618/566-2720
Holy Trinity Catholic Sch 504 Fountains Pkwy, Fairview HTS 62208 Kristy Frawley	PK-8		260 12		618/628-7395 Fax 618/628-1570
Notre Dame Acad-St Augustine 1900 W Belle St, Belleville 62226 Linda Hobbs	PK-4		120 12		618/234-4958 Fax 618/234-3360
Notre Dame Academy-Cathedral 200 S 2nd St, Belleville 62220 Linda Hobbs	PK-8		74 17		618/233-6414 Fax 618/233-3587
Our Lady Queen of Peace Sch 5915 N Belt W, Belleville 62223 Michelle Tidwell	PK-8		245 15		618/234-1206 Fax 618/234-6123
Sr Thea Bowman Catholic Sch 8213 Church Ln, E Saint Louis 62203 Daniel Nickerson	K-8		137 11		618/397-0316 Fax 618/397-0337
St Agatha Sch 207 S Market St, New Athens 62264 Kelly Schaaf	K-8		52 5		618/475-2170 Fax 618/475-3177
St Clare Catholic Sch 214 W 3rd St, O Fallon 62269 Clarice McKay	PK-8		459 22		618/632-6327 Fax 618/632-5587

1 Superintendent	8 Curric/Instruct K-12	19 Chief Financial Officer	29 Family/Consumer Science	39 Social Studies K-12	49 English/Lang Arts Elem	59 Special Education Elem	69 Academic Assessment
2 Bus/Finance/Purchasing	9 Curric/Instruct Elem	20 Art K-12	30 Adult Education	40 Social Studies Elem	50 English/Lang Arts Sec	60 Special Education Sec	70 Research/Development
3 Buildings And Grounds	10 Curric/Instruct Sec	21 Art Elem	31 Career/Sch-to-Work K-12	41 Social Studies Sec	51 Reading K-12	61 Foreign/World Lang K-12	71 Public Information
4 Food Service	11 Federal Program	22 Art Sec	32 Career/Sch-to-Work Elem	42 Science K-12	52 Reading Elem	62 Foreign/World Lang Elem	72 Summer School
5 Transportation	12 Title I	23 Music K-12	33 Career/Sch-to-Work Sec	43 Science Elem	53 Reading Sec	63 Foreign/World Lang Sec	73 Instructional Tech
6 Athletic	13 Title V	24 Music Elem	34 Early Childhood Ed	44 Science Sec	54 Remedial Reading K-12	64 Religious Education K-12	74 Inservice Training
7 Health Services	14 Asst Superintendent	25 Music Sec	35 Health/Phys Education	45 Math K-12	55 Remedial Reading Elem	65 Religious Education Elem	75 Marketing/Distributive
	15 Instructional Media Svcs	26 Business Education	36 Guidance Services K-12	46 Math Elem	56 Remedial Reading Sec	66 Religious Education Sec	76 Info Systems
	16 Chief Operations Officer	27 Career & Tech Ed	37 Guidance Services Elem	47 Math Sec	57 Bilingual/ELL	67 School Board President	77 Psychological Assess
	17 Chief Academic Officer	28 Technology Education	38 Guidance Services Sec	48 English/Lang Arts K-12	58 Special Education K-12	68 Teacher Personnel	78 Affirmative Action

Illinois School Directory — Stark County

St James Sch 412 W Washington St, Millstadt 62260 Cyndi Hasenstab	K-8		105 9	618/476-3510
St John Baptist Catholic Sch 10 S Lincoln St, Smithton 62285 Sarah Lanham	PK-8		103 8	618/233-0581
St Joseph Sch PO Box 98, Freeburg 62243 John Correll	K-8		77 9	618/539-3930 Fax 618/539-0254
St Teresa Sch 1108 Lebanon Ave, Belleville 62221 Sandy Jouglard	PK-8		312 15	618/235-4066 Fax 618/235-7930

ST CLAIR PRIVATE SCHOOLS

Private Schs..Principal	Grd	Prgm	Enr/#Cls SN	
Berean Christian Sch 5100 N Illinois St, Fairview HTS 62208 William Root	PK-12		70 5	618/825-0609 Fax 618/825-0744
Calvary Baptist Academy 423 Lucinda Ave, Belleville 62221 Gary Huffman	PK-12		12 4	618/234-3620
Elite Scholars Steam Academy 4510 N Illinois St Ste 5, Swansea 62226 Anetrise Jones	PK-5		30	618/726-2022
Faith Baptist Sch 405 E Main St, Belleville 62220 Br Ewing	PK-12		43 6	618/236-1044
First Baptist Academy 1111 E Highway 50, O Fallon 62269 Jackye Biehl	K-12		270	618/632-6223 Fax 618/632-8029
Foundations Sch 1400 S Lincoln Ave Ste K, O Fallon 62269 Wendy Cantrell	Spec		13 2	618/975-0270
Gateway Christian Academy 1771 Camp Jackson Rd, Cahokia 62206 Tony Ye	K-12		25 2	618/337-1376
Hazel Bland Promise Center 2900 State St, E Saint Louis 62205 Joyce Williams	Spec		25 5	618/274-3500 Fax 618/274-3510
Illinois Center for Autism 548 S Ruby Ln, Fairview HTS 62208 Troy Metheney	Spec	G	126 23	618/398-7500 Fax 618/394-9869
Jtc Academy East 353 N 88th St, E Saint Louis 62203 Amy Polt	Spec		40	618/398-2524 Fax 618/398-2582
Jtc Academy West 4850 Market St, E Saint Louis 62207 Amy Polt	Spec		40	618/332-3630 Fax 618/332-3040
Legacy Christian Academy 111 S 2nd St, Caseyville 62232 Anita Gajewski	PK-10		44 5	618/345-9571 Fax 618/345-9756
Menta Academy Belleville 6400 W Main St Ste 30, Belleville 62223 Kaleb Rowe	Spec		35	618/230-6143
The Governor French Academy 219 W Main St, Belleville 62220 Kim Powers	PK-12		120 15	618/233-7542 Fax 618/233-0541
Unity Lutheran Chrn Elem Sch 1600 N 40th St, E Saint Louis 62204 Aaron Dickerson	PK-8		195 11	618/874-6605 Fax 618/874-2707
Ⓐ Vincent Gray Academy 1048 State St, E Saint Louis 62201 Lillian Grinston	9-12		40 5	618/875-7880 Fax 618/875-7887

Zion Lutheran Sch 1810 McClintock Ave, Belleville 62221 Ananda Baron	PK-8		329 16	618/234-0275 Fax 618/233-2972

ST CLAIR REGIONAL CENTERS

- **Belleville Area Sp Svc Co-op** PID: 02184078   618/355-4700
  2411 Pathways Xing, Belleville 62221   Fax 618/355-4415

  Dr Jeffrey Daugherty ....1 Brian Arteberry 2

- **E St Louis Area JT Agreement** PID: 02184042   618/646-3146
  1005 State St, E Saint Louis 62201   Fax 618/583-8295

  Kimberly Hopkins 1

- **East St Louis Reg Voc System** PID: 04176510   618/646-3000
  1005 State St, E Saint Louis 62201   Fax 618/583-8254

  Arthur Culver ....1 Abe Loveless 73

- **St Clair Co Regional Off of Ed** PID: 02098314   618/825-3900
  1000 S Illinois St, Belleville 62220   Fax 618/825-3999

  Susan Sarfaty ....1,11 Denise Henry 34,58
  Kelly West 74

STARK COUNTY

STARK PUBLIC SCHOOLS

- **Bradford Cmty Unit Sch Dist 1** PID: 00320563   309/897-2801
  115 High St, Bradford 61421   Fax 309/897-4451

  Schools: 1 \ **Teachers:** 14 \ **Students:** 145 \ **Special Ed Students:** 39
  \ **Ethnic:** African American 1%, Caucasian 99% \ **Exp:** $599 (High)
  \ **Poverty:** 17% \ **Title I:** $84,220 \ **Special Education:** $51,000 \
  Open-Close: 08/18 - 05/20

  Chad Gripp .... 1,11,73 Tanya Walker 67

Public Schs..Principal	Grd	Prgm	Enr/#Cls SN	
Bradford Grade Sch 345 Silver St, Bradford 61421 Chad Gripp	PK-8	T	145 12	57% 309/897-4611 Fax 309/897-8361

- **Stark Co Cmty Unit SD 100** PID: 00320616   309/695-6123
  300 W Van Buren St, Wyoming 61491   Fax 309/695-3062

  Schools: 3 \ **Teachers:** 59 \ **Students:** 692 \ **Special Ed Students:** 118
  \ **LEP Students:** 4 \ **College-Bound:** 73% \ **Ethnic:** Asian 1%, African
  American 1%, Hispanic 3%, Caucasian 95% \ **Exp:** $220 (Med) \
  Poverty: 14% \ **Title I:** $162,720 \ **Special Education:** $242,000 \
  Bilingual Education: $2,000 \ **Open-Close:** 08/17 - 05/27 \ **DTBP:** $177
  (High)

  Brett Elliott ....1,11 Michelle Morrissey 4
  Lonnie Dennison ....5 Scott Paxson 6*

---

79 Student Personnel	91 Safety/Security	275 Response To Intervention	298 Grant Writer/Ptnrships	School Programs	Social Media
80 Driver Ed/Safety	92 Magnet School	277 Remedial Math K-12	750 Chief Innovation Officer	A = Alternative Program	
81 Gifted/Talented	93 Parental Involvement	280 Literacy Coach	751 Chief of Staff	G = Adult Classes	▮ = Facebook
82 Video Services	95 Tech Prep Program	285 STEM	752 Social Emotional Learning	M = Magnet Program	
83 Substance Abuse Prev	97 Chief Infomation Officer	286 Digital Learning		T = Title I Schoolwide	▮ = Twitter
84 Erate	98 Chief Technology Officer	288 Common Core Standards	Other School Types	V = Career & Tech Ed Programs	
85 AIDS Education	270 Character Education	294 Accountability	Ⓐ = Alternative School		
88 Alternative/At Risk	271 Migrant Education	295 Network System	Ⓒ = Charter School	New Schools are shaded	
89 Multi-Cultural Curriculum	273 Teacher Mentor	296 Title II Programs	Ⓜ = Magnet School	New Superintendents and Principals are bold	
90 Social Work	274 Before/After Sch	297 Webmaster	Ⓨ = Year-Round School	Personnel with email addresses are underscored	

Stephenson County

Market Data Retrieval

Anne Snyder 8	Jeff Utsinger 10*
Mary Beth Kelley 16	Angela McGrath 36,69*
Ann Orwig 67	Dale Heinold 73,84

Public Schs..Principal	Grd	Prgm	Enr/#Cls	SN	
Stark Co Elem Sch 300 W Van Buren St, Wyoming 61491 Jenna Bibb	PK-5		322 23	53% Fax	309/695-5181 309/695-4302
Stark Co High Sch 418 S Franklin St, Toulon 61483 Jeff Utsinger	9-12		214 25	36% Fax	309/286-4451 309/286-3321
Stark Co Junior High Sch 402 S Franklin St, Toulon 61483 Jeff Utsinger	6-8	T	156 17	37% Fax	309/286-3451 309/286-7100

STEPHENSON COUNTY

STEPHENSON PUBLIC SCHOOLS

- **Dakota Cmty Unit Sch Dist 201** PID: 00320707 844/632-5682
  400 Campus Dr, Dakota 61018 Fax 815/449-2459

Schools: 2 \ **Teachers:** 58 \ **Students:** 750 \ **Special Ed Students:** 79 \ **College-Bound:** 69% \ **Ethnic:** Asian 1%, African American 1%, Hispanic 4%, Caucasian 94% \ **Exp:** $369 (High) \ **Poverty:** 11% \ **Title I:** $123,043 \ **Special Education:** $383,000 \ **Open-Close:** 08/20 - 05/21 \ **DTBP:** $194 (High)

Jason Grey 1	Brittney Kunz 2
David Hauger 3	Kathy Davis 4
Dallas Pieper 5	Chad Fergenson 6*
Diane Scaduto 7*	Michelle Shippy 16*
Karen Kleckner 67	Deanna Kraft 295

Public Schs..Principal	Grd	Prgm	Enr/#Cls	SN	
Dakota Elem Sch 400 Campus Dr, Dakota 61018 Jeff Milburn	PK-6		419 28	35% 	815/449-2852
Dakota Jr Sr High Sch 300 Campus Dr, Dakota 61018 Randy Bay	7-12		378 33	27% Fax	815/632-5682 815/449-2322

- **Freeport School District 145** PID: 00320745 815/232-0300
  501 E South St, Freeport 61032 Fax 815/235-4177

Schools: 10 \ **Teachers:** 291 \ **Students:** 4,000 \ **Special Ed Students:** 668 \ **LEP Students:** 183 \ **College-Bound:** 61% \ **Ethnic:** Asian 1%, African American 30%, Hispanic 13%, Caucasian 56% \ **Exp:** $536 (High) \ **Poverty:** 21% \ **Title I:** $2,032,414 \ **Special Education:** $2,745,000 \ **Bilingual Education:** $76,000 \ **Open-Close:** 08/24 - 06/09 \ **DTBP:** $198 (High)

Anna Alverado 1	Patrick McDermott 2,7,15
Greg Munda 3,91	Amanda Williams 4
Dallas Pieper 5	Jeff Fitzpatrick 6
Dwayne Meighan 8,12,15,16,31,57,285	Sandra Ehrat 11
Patricia Schneider 42,48	Tara Hersey 45
Jack Code 58,79,83,85,88,271	Janice Crutchfield 67
Chris Shockey 68,273	Jesse Johnson 71,298
Tim Mangan 73	Tom Elzen 73,84,295
Nita White 78	

Public Schs..Principal	Grd	Prgm	Enr/#Cls	SN	
Blackhawk Elem Sch 1401 S Blackhawk Ave, Freeport 61032 Stacey Kleindl	PK-4	T	268 15	74% Fax	815/232-0490 815/232-0578
Carl Sandburg Middle Sch 1717 W Eby St, Freeport 61032 Jennifer Macek	5-7	T	485 27	71% Fax	815/232-0340 815/232-1241
Center Elem Sch 718 E Illinois St, Freeport 61032 Danielle Summers	PK-4	T	316 15	66% Fax	815/232-0480 815/232-3247
Empire Elem Sch 1325 Empire Ct, Freeport 61032 Pamela Powell	PK-4	T	250 16	54% Fax	815/232-0380 815/232-0577
Ⓐ Freeport Alternative High Sch 1330 S Locust Ave, Freeport 61032 Beth Summers	11-12		40	72% Fax	815/233-0796 815/232-2311
Freeport High Sch 701 W Moseley St, Freeport 61032 Beth Summers	9-12	T	1,139	60% Fax	815/232-0400 815/232-0629
Freeport Middle Sch 701 W Empire St, Freeport 61032 Renee Coleman	5-8	T	678 50	67% Fax	815/232-0500 815/232-0536
Ⓜ Jones-Farrar IB World Sch 1386 Kiwanis Dr, Freeport 61032 Jennifer De Jong	K-4	T	279 17	49% Fax	815/232-0610 815/235-9220
Lincoln-Douglas Elem Sch 1700 W Laurel St, Freeport 61032 Matthew Bohrer	PK-4	T	230 15	60% Fax	815/232-0370 815/232-0379
Taylor Park Elem Sch 806 E Stephenson St, Freeport 61032 Brian Lamm	PK-4	T	229 15	69% Fax	815/232-0390 815/232-0399

- **Lena-Winslow Cmty Unit SD 202** PID: 00320874 815/369-2525
  401 Fremont St, Lena 61048 Fax 815/369-3102

Schools: 3 \ **Teachers:** 60 \ **Students:** 850 \ **Special Ed Students:** 97 \ **LEP Students:** 12 \ **College-Bound:** 66% \ **Ethnic:** African American 2%, Hispanic 4%, Caucasian 93% \ **Exp:** $204 (Med) \ **Poverty:** 9% \ **Title I:** $145,919 \ **Special Education:** $378,000 \ **Open-Close:** 08/19 - 05/21 \ **DTBP:** $182 (High)

Dr Thomas Chiles 1	Amy Lieb 2
Dough Wybourn 3	Duane Reed 5
Tom Smargiassi 6*	Anne Dezell 9,11,58,275
Heather Benson 16*	Katrina Linnemann 38,69,83,85,270*
John Leuenberger 67	Jordan Camerer 76
Bill Worst 83*	Darcy Schierloh 84
Westley Price 752	

Public Schs..Principal	Grd	Prgm	Enr/#Cls	SN	
Lena-Winslow Elem Sch 401 Fremont St, Lena 61048 Ann Dezell	PK-5	T	408 29	36% Fax	815/668-0809 815/369-3171
Lena-Winslow High Sch 516 Fremont St, Lena 61048 Mark Kuehl	9-12	V	248 22	34% Fax	815/668-0821 815/369-3165
Lena-Winslow Jr High Sch 517 Fremont St, Lena 61048 Andrew Lobdell	6-8	T	182 20	41% Fax	815/668-0818 815/369-3162

1 Superintendent	8 Curric/Instruct K-12	19 Chief Financial Officer	29 Family/Consumer Science	39 Social Studies K-12	49 English/Lang Arts Elem	59 Special Education Elem	69 Academic Assessment
2 Bus/Finance/Purchasing	9 Curric/Instruct Elem	20 Art K-12	30 Adult Education	40 Social Studies Elem	50 English/Lang Arts Sec	60 Special Education Sec	70 Research/Development
3 Buildings And Grounds	10 Curric/Instruct Sec	21 Art Elem	31 Career/Sch-to-Work K-12	41 Social Studies Sec	51 Reading K-12	61 Foreign/World Lang K-12	71 Public Information
4 Food Service	11 Federal Program	22 Art Sec	32 Career/Sch-to-Work Elem	42 Science K-12	52 Reading Elem	62 Foreign/World Lang Elem	72 Summer School
5 Transportation	12 Title I	23 Music K-12	33 Career/Sch-to-Work Sec	43 Science Elem	53 Reading Sec	63 Foreign/World Lang Sec	73 Instructional Tech
6 Athletic	13 Title V	24 Music Elem	34 Early Childhood Ed	44 Science Sec	54 Remedial Reading K-12	64 Religious Education K-12	74 Inservice Training
7 Health Services	15 Asst Superintendent	25 Music Sec	35 Health/Phys Education	45 Math K-12	55 Remedial Reading Elem	65 Religious Education Elem	75 Marketing/Distributive
	16 Instructional Media Svcs	26 Business Education	36 Guidance Services K-12	46 Math Elem	56 Remedial Reading Sec	66 Religious Education Sec	76 Info Systems
	17 Chief Operations Officer	27 Career & Tech Ed	37 Guidance Services Elem	47 Math Sec	57 Bilingual/ELL	67 School Board President	77 Psychological Assess
	18 Chief Academic Officer	28 Technology Education	38 Guidance Services Sec	48 English/Lang Arts K-12	58 Special Education K-12	68 Teacher Personnel	78 Affirmative Action

Illinois School Directory — Tazewell County

- **Orangeville Cmty Unit SD 203** PID: 00320927   815/789-4450
310 S East St, Orangeville 61060   Fax 815/789-4607

Schools: 1 \ **Teachers:** 27 \ **Students:** 380 \ **Special Ed Students:** 53 \ **College-Bound:** 73% \ **Ethnic:** Hispanic 1%, Caucasian 99% \ **Exp:** $199 (Low) \ **Poverty:** 9% \ **Title I:** $50,028 \ **Special Education:** $160,000 \ **Open-Close:** 09/03 - 06/15

Dr Douglas Deschepper 1,83   Amy Baker 67

Public Schs..Principal	Grd	Prgm	Enr/#Cls	SN		
Orangeville Sch 201 S Orange St, Orangeville 61060 Andrew Janecke	K-12		380 25	15%	815/789-4289 Fax 815/789-4709	

- **Pearl City Cmty Unit SD 200** PID: 00320953   815/443-2715
100 S Summit St, Pearl City 61062   Fax 815/443-2237

Schools: 1 \ **Teachers:** 35 \ **Students:** 431 \ **Special Ed Students:** 63 \ **LEP Students:** 8 \ **College-Bound:** 96% \ **Ethnic:** Asian 1%, Hispanic 3%, Caucasian 96% \ **Exp:** $268 (Med) \ **Poverty:** 13% \ **Title I:** $89,240 \ **Special Education:** $211,000 \ **Open-Close:** 08/21 - 06/11

Dr Mike Chiffman 1,11,73   Janice Sheffey 2
John Keltner .... 3*   Lori Boyer 4*
Brent Chrismen 9   Brent Chrisman 9,11,57,88,286,288,298*
Ben Asche 10   Shawna Enderess 12,280
Katelyn Pickard .... 59*   Chad Bremmer 67

Public Schs..Principal	Grd	Prgm	Enr/#Cls	SN	
Pearl City Sch 100 S Summit St, Pearl City 61062 Ben Asche \ Brent Chrisman	K-12	V	431 40	28%	815/443-2715

STEPHENSON CATHOLIC SCHOOLS

- **Diocese of Rockford Ed Office** PID: 00328345
Listing includes only schools located in this county. See District Index for location of Diocesan Offices.

Catholic Schs..Principal	Grd	Prgm	Enr/#Cls	SN	
Aquin Catholic Jr Sr High Sch 1419 S Galena Ave, Freeport 61032 Jeremy Keesee	7-12	V	140 19		815/235-3154 Fax 815/235-3185 [f]
Aquin Elementary 202 W Pleasant St, Freeport 61032 Jeremy Keesee	PK-6		120 8		815/232-6416 Fax 815/599-8526

STEPHENSON PRIVATE SCHOOLS

Private Schs..Principal	Grd	Prgm	Enr/#Cls	SN	
Freeport Christian Academy 2810 W Pearl City Rd, Freeport 61032 Richard Kolcharno	K-12		57 1		815/235-9840
Immanuel Lutheran Sch 1964 W Pearl City Rd, Freeport 61032 Nicholas Muench	PK-8		130 13		815/232-3511 Fax 815/233-9158 [f]
Tri-County Christian Sch 2900 Loras Dr, Freeport 61032 Wendy Schardet	PK-8		158 11		815/233-1876 Fax 815/233-4862 [f][t]

Willowglen Academy-Illinois   Spec   45   815/233-6162
701 W Lamm Rd, Freeport 61032   Fax 815/233-6167
Lee Genandt

STEPHENSON REGIONAL CENTERS

- **Career & Tech Ed Consortium** PID: 04180767   815/232-0709
2037 W Galena Ave Ste C, Freeport 61032   Fax 815/235-8050

Brian Greene 1   Jody Ackerman 2
Doug Meyers 28

- **Regional Office of Ed 8** PID: 01536650   815/599-1408
27 S State Ave Ste 101, Freeport 61032   Fax 815/297-9032

Aaron Mercier 1   Deb Endress 8
Jen Newendyke 15   Brent Chrisman 16
Casey Coon 68

TAZEWELL COUNTY

TAZEWELL COUNTY SCHOOLS

County Schs..Principal	Grd	Prgm	Enr/#Cls	SN	
Schramm Education Center 300 Cedar St Ste 1, Pekin 61554 Kristina Lazar	Spec		74 7	51%	309/346-1186 Fax 309/346-1297

TAZEWELL PUBLIC SCHOOLS

- **Central Sch Dist 51** PID: 00320991   309/444-3943
1301 Eagle Ave, Washington 61571   Fax 309/444-9898

Schools: 2 \ **Teachers:** 81 \ **Students:** 1,400 \ **Special Ed Students:** 178 \ **LEP Students:** 16 \ **Ethnic:** Asian 1%, African American 1%, Hispanic 4%, Caucasian 93% \ **Exp:** $121 (Low) \ **Poverty:** 4% \ **Title I:** $43,957 \ **Special Education:** $386,000 \ **Open-Close:** 09/08 - 06/09 \ **DTBP:** $222 (High) \ [t]

Dale Heidbreeder 1,83   Shannan Dobbelaire 2*
Mark Wertz .... 3*   Angie Tribbett 4*
Brandon Dash 5   Trent Halpin 9*
Brian Hoelescher ...... 11,57,69,274,275,288*   Annette Gresham 59
Amy Johnson 67   Dave Nason 73,76,295*
Amanda Lawry 285   Andrea Arms 752

Public Schs..Principal	Grd	Prgm	Enr/#Cls	SN	
Central Intermediate Sch 1301 Eagle Ave, Washington 61571 Brian Hoelescher	4-8		769 24	10%	309/444-3943 Fax 309/444-3414
Central Primary Sch 1400 Newcastle Rd, Washington 61571 John Cox	PK-3		628	10%	309/444-3580 Fax 309/444-3670 [f]

---

79 Student Personnel	91 Safety/Security	275 Response To Intervention	298 Grant Writer/Ptnrships
80 Driver Ed/Safety	92 Magnet School	277 Remedial Math K-12	750 Chief Innovation Officer
81 Gifted/Talented	93 Parental Involvement	280 Literacy Coach	751 Chief of Staff
82 Video Services	95 Tech Prep Program	285 STEM	752 Social Emotional Learning
83 Substance Abuse Prev	97 Chief Infomation Officer	286 Digital Learning	
84 Erate	98 Chief Technology Officer	288 Common Core Standards	**Other School Types**
85 AIDS Education	270 Character Education	294 Accountability	Ⓐ = Alternative School
88 Alternative/At Risk	271 Migrant Education	295 Network System	Ⓒ = Charter School
89 Multi-Cultural Curriculum	273 Teacher Mentor	296 Title II Programs	Ⓜ = Magnet School
90 Social Work	274 Before/After Sch	297 Webmaster	Ⓨ = Year-Round School

School Programs
A = Alternative Program
G = Adult Classes
M = Magnet Program
T = Title I Schoolwide
V = Career & Tech Ed Programs

Social Media
[f] = Facebook
[t] = Twitter

New Schools are shaded
New Superintendents and Principals are bold
Personnel with email addresses are underscored

IL—225

Tazewell County

Market Data Retrieval

- **Creve Coeur Sch Dist 76** PID: 00321012   309/698-3600
  400 N Highland St, Creve Coeur 61610   Fax 309/698-9827

  Schools: 2 \ **Teachers:** 44 \ **Students:** 600 \ **Special Ed Students:** 138 \ **LEP Students:** 3 \ **Ethnic:** African American 3%, Hispanic 4%, Caucasian 93% \ **Exp:** $148 (Low) \ **Poverty:** 21% \ **Title I:** $253,824 \ **Special Education:** $339,000 \ **Open-Close:** 08/19 - 05/28 \ **DTBP:** $204 (High)

Steve Johnson	1	Shelly Cornwell	2
Michelle Davis	4	Paul Nettles	6*
Dr Tatia Beckwith	9	Tony Whiston	11
Jay Wendelin	16,73,295*	David Roeharig	59
Linda Bailey	67	Amy Baird	83
Donna McCow	288		

Public Schs..Principal	Grd	Prgm	Enr/#Cls	SN		
LaSalle Elem Sch 300 N Highland St, Creve Coeur 61610 Dr Tatia Beckwith	PK-4	T	315 19	78%	309/698-3605 Fax 309/698-1499	
Parkview Middle Sch 800 Groveland St, Creve Coeur 61610 **Dustin Bevard**	5-8	T	260 12	77%	309/698-3610 Fax 309/698-3902	

- **Deer Creek-Mackinaw CUSD 701** PID: 00321074   309/359-8965
  401 E Fifth St, Mackinaw 61755   Fax 309/359-5291

  Schools: 3 \ **Teachers:** 71 \ **Students:** 1,040 \ **Special Ed Students:** 131 \ **College-Bound:** 80% \ **Ethnic:** Hispanic 2%, Caucasian 97% \ **Exp:** $163 (Low) \ **Poverty:** 5% \ **Title I:** $86,536 \ **Special Education:** $525,000 \ **Open-Close:** 08/17 - 05/27 \

Michele Jacobs	1,11	Brenda Seibert	2
Greg Guilliams	3	Patsy Davis	4*
Darren Adams	5	Mary Lanier	10,88*
James Lines	57,58,83,85,275,296	Steve Yarnall	67
John Embry	73,286,295*	Caroline McMahan	273*

Public Schs..Principal	Grd	Prgm	Enr/#Cls	SN		
Deer Creek-Mackinaw High Sch 401 E Fifth St, Mackinaw 61755 Mary Lanier	9-12	V	341 30	22%	309/359-4421 Fax 309/359-3125	
Deer Creek-Mackinaw Interm Sch 506 N Logan St, Deer Creek 61733 Lance Hawkins	4-6		224 14	29%	309/447-6226 Fax 309/447-5201	
Deer Creek-Mackinaw Prim JHS 102 E Fifth St, Mackinaw 61755 Teri Justus	PK-8		471 23	28%	309/359-4321 Fax 309/359-4015	

- **Delavan Cmty Unit Sch Dist 703** PID: 00321115   309/244-8283
  907 S Locust St, Delavan 61734   Fax 309/244-7301

  Schools: 2 \ **Teachers:** 45 \ **Students:** 480 \ **Special Ed Students:** 106 \ **LEP Students:** 3 \ **College-Bound:** 93% \ **Ethnic:** Asian 1%, African American 3%, Hispanic 1%, Caucasian 95% \ **Exp:** $370 (High) \ **Poverty:** 11% \ **Title I:** $85,341 \ **Special Education:** $480,000 \ **Open-Close:** 08/20 - 06/01 \ **DTBP:** $341 (High) \

Andrew Brooks	1,84	Jared Williams	3
Brenda Culp	2	Ryon Kramer	6
Amy Albers	8,11,58,69	Kathy Nelson	16*
Robin Bell	34*	Kevin Knaggs	38,83,88
Matthew Shippon	67	Mark Miller	73,295

- **District 50 Schools** PID: 00321713   309/745-8914
  304 E Almond Dr, Washington 61571   Fax 309/745-5417

Public Schs..Principal	Grd	Prgm	Enr/#Cls	SN		
Delavan Elem Sch 907 S Locust St, Delavan 61734 Staci Harper	PK-6	TV	278 30	40%	309/244-8283 Fax 309/244-8694	
Delavan Jr Sr High Sch 907 S Locust St, Delavan 61734 Staci Harper \ Amy Albers	7-12	V	202	26%	309/244-8285	

  Schools: 2 \ **Teachers:** 50 \ **Students:** 700 \ **Special Ed Students:** 147 \ **LEP Students:** 3 \ **Ethnic:** African American 2%, Hispanic 6%, Caucasian 92% \ **Exp:** $247 (Med) \ **Poverty:** 13% \ **Title I:** $185,289 \ **Special Education:** $438,000 \ **Open-Close:** 08/11 - 05/27 \ **DTBP:** $209 (High)

Dr Chad Allaman	1,11,83,84	Chase Wilson	2
Steve Sepich	3	Joan Wood	4*
Jennifer Miller	5,6	Cathy Trimble	9,69,298*
Missy Grescham	59	James Washburn	67
Tom Wilson	73,76,295*	Connie Wort	274*

Public Schs..Principal	Grd	Prgm	Enr/#Cls	SN		
Beverly Manor Sch 1014 School St, Washington 61571 Corey Sharp	4-8	T	397 35	58%	309/745-3921 Fax 309/745-1305	
John L Hensey Elem Sch 304 E Almond Dr, Washington 61571 Josh Zaiser	PK-3	T	310 40	61%	309/745-3625	

- **East Peoria Cmty HS Dist 309** PID: 00321256   309/694-8300
  1401 E Washington St, East Peoria 61611   Fax 309/694-8322

  Schools: 1 \ **Teachers:** 63 \ **Students:** 1,000 \ **Special Ed Students:** 171 \ **LEP Students:** 3 \ **College-Bound:** 76% \ **Ethnic:** Asian 1%, African American 3%, Hispanic 6%, Caucasian 90% \ **Exp:** $499 (High) \ **Poverty:** 11% \ **Title I:** $210,931 \ **Special Education:** $589,000 \ **Open-Close:** 08/20 - 05/28 \ **DTBP:** $254 (High)

Margorie Greuter	1,11	Mary Ann Day	2*
Jim Booth	3*	Mark Debons	4
Shawn Dasgupta	5	Jason Bowman	
Elisabeth Barclay	7,85*	Paul Stanford	16,73,76,295*
Julie Darko	38,69,79*	Jill Thornton	60,90*
Matt Eckberg	67	Brett Gonigam	80
Brooke Nelson	82*	Laura Weidner	90*
Mike Sergenti	91*		

Public Schs..Principal	Grd	Prgm	Enr/#Cls	SN	
East Peoria Cmty High Sch 1401 E Washington St, East Peoria 61611 Lori Laredo	9-12	T	1,000 80	49%	309/694-8300

- **East Peoria Elem Sch Dist 86** PID: 00321141   309/427-5100
  601 Taylor St, East Peoria 61611   Fax 309/698-1364

  Schools: 7 \ **Teachers:** 113 \ **Students:** 1,500 \ **Special Ed Students:** 328 \ **LEP Students:** 10 \ **Ethnic:** Asian 1%, African American 2%, Hispanic 5%, Caucasian 92% \ **Exp:** $388 (High) \ **Poverty:** 13% \ **Title I:** $400,694 \ **Special Education:** $820,000 \ **Open-Close:** 08/21 - 05/25 \ **DTBP:** $236 (High)

Tony Ingold	1,11	Jason Warner	2,15
Tom Sego	3	Cindy Gladwell	4

#		#		#		#		#		#		#	
1	Superintendent	8	Curric/Instruct K-12	19	Chief Financial Officer	29	Family/Consumer Science	39	Social Studies K-12	49	English/Lang Arts Elem	59	Special Education Elem	69	Academic Assessment
2	Bus/Finance/Purchasing	9	Curric/Instruct Elem	20	Art K-12	30	Adult Education	40	Social Studies Elem	50	English/Lang Arts Sec	60	Special Education Sec	70	Research/Development
3	Buildings And Grounds	10	Curric/Instruct Sec	21	Art Elem	31	Career/Sch-to-Work K-12	41	Social Studies Sec	51	Reading K-12	61	Foreign/World Lang K-12	71	Public Information
4	Food Service	11	Federal Program	22	Art Sec	32	Career/Sch-to-Work Elem	42	Science K-12	52	Reading Elem	62	Foreign/World Lang Elem	72	Summer School
5	Transportation	12	Title I	23	Music K-12	33	Career/Sch-to-Work Sec	43	Science Elem	53	Reading Sec	63	Foreign/World Lang Sec	73	Instructional Tech
6	Athletic	13	Title V	24	Music Elem	34	Early Childhood Ed	44	Science Sec	54	Remedial Reading K-12	64	Religious Education K-12	74	Inservice Training
7	Health Services	14	Instructional Media Svcs	25	Music Sec	35	Health/Phys Education	45	Math K-12	55	Remedial Reading Elem	65	Religious Education Elem	75	Marketing/Distributive
		15	Asst Superintendent	26	Business Education	36	Guidance Services K-12	46	Math Elem	56	Remedial Reading Sec	66	Religious Education Sec	76	Info Systems
		16	Chief Operations Officer	27	Career & Tech Ed	37	Guidance Services Elem	47	Math Sec	57	Bilingual/E.L.I.	67	School Board President	77	Psychological Assess
		17	Chief Academic Officer	28	Technology Education	38	Guidance Services Sec	48	English/Lang Arts K-12	58	Special Education K-12	68	Teacher Personnel	78	Affirmative Action

Illinois School Directory

Tazewell County

Mike Wallace 6*
Shanna Gerth 16*
Phil Seggebruch 35*
Christie Vescogni 59
Aaron Zuercher 73,295

Dr Scott Estes 7,12,68,79,280,286,288
Jason Gambill 34,57,59,77,90,271,273,275
Mara Miller 37
Eric Beckworth 67

Public Schs..Principal	Grd	Prgm	Enr/#Cls	SN	
Central Junior High Sch 601 Taylor St, East Peoria 61611 Dustin Schrank	6-8	T	553 25	52%	309/427-5200 Fax 309/306-7562
Don D Shute Elem Sch 300 Briarbrook Dr, East Peoria 61611 Brad Wood	PK-2	T	192 15	54%	309/427-5500 Fax 309/306-7565
Glendale Elem Sch 1000 Bloomington Rd, East Peoria 61611 Terrie Armstrong	3-5	T	143 12	55%	309/427-5400 Fax 309/306-7563
Lincoln Elem Sch 801 Springfield Rd, East Peoria 61611 Nikki Combs	3-5	T	148 11	64%	309/427-5450 Fax 309/306-7564
Neil A Armstrong Elem Sch 1848 Highview Rd, East Peoria 61611 Ashley Ricca	PK-2	T	171 11	36%	309/427-5300 Fax 309/306-7559
P L Bolin Elem Sch 428 Arnold Rd, East Peoria 61611 Chris Kolowski	3-5	T	178 9	43%	309/427-5350 Fax 309/306-7561
Woodrow Wilson Elem Sch 300 Oakwood Ave, East Peoria 61611 Derek Schulze	PK-2	T	165 9	61%	309/427-5550 Fax 309/306-7566

● Morton Cmty Unit Sch Dist 709 PID: 00321311
1050 S 4th Ave Ste 200, Morton 61550
309/263-2581
Fax 309/266-6320

Schools: 7 \ **Teachers:** 200 \ **Students:** 3,060 \ **Special Ed Students:** 505 \ **LEP Students:** 21 \ **College-Bound:** 89% \ **Ethnic:** Asian 2%, African American 2%, Hispanic 3%, Caucasian 93% \ **Exp:** $274 (Med) \ **Poverty:** 3% \ **Title I:** $121,726 \ **Special Education:** $1,432,000 \ **Open-Close:** 08/11 - 05/26 \ **DTBP:** $188 (High)

Dr Jeff Hill 1
Leonard Shumaker 3,91
Scott Jones 6*
Kate Wyman 12,16,74*
Dayrim Sheehan 57
Tom Neeley 67
Lindsay Franklin 79
Christian D'Alfonso 275

Lisa Kowalski 2,19
Julie Tharp 5
Troy Teater 8,11,73,286,288,294,295
Craig Smock 15
Amanda Rickenberg 58
Brenda Heppard 68
Daniel Rohman 83*
Michael Saunders 296*

Public Schs..Principal	Grd	Prgm	Enr/#Cls	SN	
Jefferson Elem Sch 220 E Jefferson St, Morton 61550 Kate Wyman	K-6		331 13	30%	309/263-2650 Fax 309/284-3025
Lettie Brown Elem Sch 2550 N Morton Ave, Morton 61550 Faith Waterfield	K-6		346 13	8%	309/266-5309 Fax 309/284-1015
Lincoln Elem Sch 100 S Nebraska Ave, Morton 61550 Julie Albers	K-6		520 22	10%	309/266-6989 Fax 309/284-4015
Morton Academy 260 E Queenwood Rd, Morton 61550 Kristina Peifer	3-12		14	67%	309/284-8033
Morton High Sch 350 N Illinois Ave, Morton 61550 Deidre Ripka	9-12		960 80	14%	309/266-7182 Fax 309/263-2168
Morton Junior High Sch 225 E Jackson St, Morton 61550 Lee Hoffman	7-8		476 25	15%	309/266-6522 Fax 309/284-5031

Public Schs..Principal	Grd	Prgm	Enr/#Cls	SN	
Ward Grundy Elem Sch 1100 S 4th Ave, Morton 61550 Michael Saunders	PK-6		426 20	16%	309/263-1421 Fax 309/284-2000

● N Pekin-Marquette Hts SD 102 PID: 00321385
51 Yates Rd, Marquette HTS 61554
309/382-2172
Fax 309/382-2122

Schools: 3 \ **Teachers:** 38 \ **Students:** 512 \ **Special Ed Students:** 90 \ **LEP Students:** 5 \ **Ethnic:** Asian 2%, African American 1%, Hispanic 4%, Caucasian 94% \ **Exp:** $162 (Low) \ **Poverty:** 11% \ **Title I:** $123,016 \ **Special Education:** $220,000 \ **Open-Close:** 08/19 - 05/27 \ **DTBP:** $146 (High)

Byron Sondgeroth 1
Justin Hoffman 3*
Jennifer Dietrich 9,11*
Jennifer Lindsay 59,69*

Cheryl Linton 2
Joann Covington 4
Jay Wendlin 16,73,295
Keith Knox 67

Public Schs..Principal	Grd	Prgm	Enr/#Cls	SN	
Georgetowne Middle Sch 51 Yates Rd, Pekin 61554 Tom Brown	6-8	T	188 14	48%	309/382-3456
Marquette Elem Sch 100 Joliet Rd, Pekin 61554 Jennifer Dietrich	PK-2	T	161 16	63%	309/382-3612
Rogers Elem Sch 109 Rogers Rd, Pekin 61554 Jennifer Lindsay	3-5	T	156 11	46%	309/382-3401

● Pekin Cmty High Sch Dist 303 PID: 00321579
320 Stadium Dr, Pekin 61554
309/347-4101
Fax 309/477-4376

Schools: 1 \ **Teachers:** 111 \ **Students:** 1,821 \ **Special Ed Students:** 267 \ **LEP Students:** 6 \ **College-Bound:** 78% \ **Ethnic:** Asian 1%, African American 1%, Hispanic 3%, Caucasian 95% \ **Exp:** $456 (High) \ **Poverty:** 12% \ **Title I:** $385,354 \ **Special Education:** $910,000 \ **Open-Close:** 08/14 - 05/24 \ **DTBP:** $233 (High)

Dr Danielle Owens 1
Tim Bonnette 3*
Sheila Martin 10,11,15,69,288,296,298
Cynthia Hinderliter 16,73,76,286*
Kristen Walraven 60*
Lisa Stolz 275

Carla Schaefer 2,5
Becky Lane 4*
Stephanie Bala 12
Doug Nutter 35,80
Ryan Wrigley 67
Eric Lynd 295*

Public Schs..Principal	Grd	Prgm	Enr/#Cls	SN	
Pekin Community High Sch 1903 Court St, Pekin 61554 Amy Hubner	9-12	ATV	1,821 85	45%	309/347-4101 Fax 309/477-4377

● Pekin Public School Dist 108 PID: 00321426
501 Washington St, Pekin 61554
309/477-4740
Fax 309/477-4701

Schools: 11 \ **Teachers:** 217 \ **Students:** 3,650 \ **Special Ed Students:** 794 \ **LEP Students:** 12 \ **Ethnic:** Asian 1%, African American 1%, Hispanic 3%, Caucasian 95% \ **Exp:** $161 (Low) \ **Poverty:** 16% \ **Title I:** $1,040,622 \ **Special Education:** $1,668,000 \ **Open-Close:** 08/20 - 05/28 \ **DTBP:** $190 (High)

Dr Bill Link 1
Leonard Ealey 9,11,57,83,88,271,274,288
Karla Kenney 34*
Karen Frazier 67
Sherry Harding 273*

Glayn Worrell 2,3,4,5,91
Angie Arnold 16,73,82,84
Julia Spanos 59
Joe Franklin 68,79
Lisa Applegate 295

---

79 Student Personnel
80 Driver Ed/Safety
81 Gifted/Talented
82 Video Services
83 Substance Abuse Prev
84 Erate
85 AIDS Education
88 Alternative/At Risk
89 Multi-Cultural Curriculum
90 Social Work

91 Safety/Security
92 Magnet School
93 Parental Involvement
95 Tech Prep Program
97 Chief Information Officer
98 Chief Technology Officer
270 Character Education
271 Migrant Education
273 Teacher Mentor
274 Before/After Sch

275 Response To Intervention
277 Remedial Math K-12
280 Literacy Coach
285 STEM
286 Digital Learning
288 Common Core Standards
294 Accountability
295 Network System
296 Title II Programs
297 Webmaster

298 Grant Writer/Ptnrships
750 Chief Innovation Officer
751 Chief of Staff
752 Social Emotional Learning

Other School Types
Ⓐ = Alternative School
Ⓒ = Charter School
Ⓜ = Magnet School
Ⓨ = Year-Round School

School Programs
A = Alternative Program
G = Adult Classes
M = Magnet Program
T = Title I Schoolwide
V = Career & Tech Ed Programs

New Schools are shaded
New Superintendents and Principals are bold
Personnel with email addresses are underscored

Social Media
= Facebook
= Twitter

Tazewell County

Public Schs..Principal	Grd	Prgm	Enr/#Cls	SN	
Broadmoor Junior High Sch 501 Maywood Ave, Pekin 61554 Ty Goss	7-8	T	400 40	52%	309/477-4731 Fax 309/477-4739
C B Smith Primary Sch 1314 Matilda St, Pekin 61554 A Schroff	K-3	T	288 13	62%	309/477-4713 Fax 309/477-4762
Dirksen Primary Sch 501 Maywood Ave, Pekin 61554 Melissa Lard	K-3	T	179 8	70%	309/477-4711 Fax 309/477-4760
Edison Junior High Sch 1400 Earl St, Pekin 61554 Bill Heisel	7-8	T	354 25	49%	309/477-4732 Fax 309/477-4738
Jefferson Primary Sch 900 S Capitol St, Pekin 61554 Luke Arnsman	K-3	T	332 15	63%	309/477-4712 Fax 309/477-4761
L E Starke Primary Sch 1610 Holiday Dr, Pekin 61554 Matt Green	K-3	T	199 11	42%	309/477-4714 Fax 309/477-4763
Perkin Pre-Sch Family Ed Ctr 1000 Koch St, Pekin 61554 Karla Kenney	PK-PK		233 10	60%	309/477-4730 Fax 309/477-4737
Scott Altman Primary Sch 1730 Highwood Ave, Pekin 61554 Lynn Brown	K-3	T	193 8	48%	309/477-4715 Fax 309/477-4764
Washington Intermediate Sch 501 Washington St, Pekin 61554 Marc Fogal	4-6	T	518 29	58%	309/477-4721 Fax 309/477-4729
Willow Elem Sch 1110 Veerman St, Pekin 61554 Vickie Armbrust	K-3	T	251 15	63%	309/477-4716 Fax 309/477-4765
Wilson Intermediate Sch 900 Koch St Bldg 1, Pekin 61554 Josh Norman	4-6	T	619 28	59%	309/477-4722 Fax 309/477-4728

- **Rankin Cmty School Dist 98** PID: 00321634   309/346-3182
  13716 5th St, Pekin 61554   Fax 309/346-7928

Schools: 1 \ **Teachers:** 18 \ **Students:** 250 \ **Special Ed Students:** 23 \ **LEP Students:** 6 \ **Ethnic:** Asian 2%, African American 2%, Hispanic 2%, Caucasian 94% \ **Exp:** $835 (High) \ **Poverty:** 10% \ **Title I:** $33,803 \ **Special Education:** $81,000 \ **Open-Close:** 08/19 - 05/27 \ **DTBP:** $232 (High) \

Dr Matt Gordan 1,73   Jessi Schneider 6*
Myra Larkin ....12* Debbie Lowman 67

Public Schs..Principal	Grd	Prgm	Enr/#Cls	SN	
Rankin Elem Sch 13716 5th St, Pekin 61554 April McLaughlin	K-8	T	250 14	26%	309/346-3182

- **Robein Cmty School District 85** PID: 00321658   309/694-1409
  200 Campus Ave, East Peoria 61611   Fax 309/694-1450

Schools: 1 \ **Teachers:** 13 \ **Students:** 175 \ **Special Ed Students:** 31 \ **LEP Students:** 3 \ **Ethnic:** Asian 1%, African American 3%, Hispanic 6%, Caucasian 90% \ **Exp:** $176 (Low) \ **Poverty:** 10% \ **Title I:** $33,803 \ **Special Education:** $59,000 \ **Open-Close:** 08/19 - 05/31 \ **DTBP:** $250 (High)

Brad Bennett 1,11,83   Terry Newlan 4
Michelle Girshan ....16,270* Ryan Snell 35*
Josh Eaker 67

Public Schs..Principal	Grd	Prgm	Enr/#Cls	SN	
Robein Grade Sch 200 Campus Ave, East Peoria 61611 Brad Bennett	K-8	T	175 10	40%	309/694-1409

- **South Pekin Grade Sch Dist 137** PID: 00321672   309/348-3695
  206 Main St, South Pekin 61564   Fax 309/348-3162

Schools: 1 \ **Teachers:** 17 \ **Students:** 200 \ **Special Ed Students:** 52 \ **Ethnic:** Caucasian 100% \ **Exp:** $285 (Med) \ **Poverty:** 10% \ **Title I:** $66,857 \ **Special Education:** $169,000 \ **Open-Close:** 08/13 - 05/25 \ **DTBP:** $238 (High)

Seth Mingus 1,83   Natalie Vohland 2
Charles Grogan ....3*   Angie Hoffman 4*
Tara Zaayenga 12   Tracy Canete 59
Dawn Chambers 67   Seth Mingus 298*

Public Schs..Principal	Grd	Prgm	Enr/#Cls	SN	
South Pekin Grade Sch 206 Main St, South Pekin 61564 Seth Mingus	PK-8	T	200 15	91%	309/348-3695

- **Spring Lake Elem SD 606** PID: 00321696   309/545-2241
  13650 N Manito Rd, Manito 61546   Fax 309/545-2695

Schools: 1 \ **Teachers:** 5 \ **Students:** 60 \ **Special Ed Students:** 16 \ **Ethnic:** Caucasian 100% \ **Exp:** $356 (High) \ **Poverty:** 20% \ **Title I:** $30,130 \ **Special Education:** $22,000 \ **Open-Close:** 08/19 - 06/04 \

Dr Charles Nagel 1,11   Gloria Lovelace 67

Public Schs..Principal	Grd	Prgm	Enr/#Cls	SN	
Spring Lake Elem Sch 13650 N Manito Rd, Manito 61546 Chuck Nagel	PK-6		60 5	27%	309/545-2241

- **Tremont Cmty Unit SD 702** PID: 00321751   309/925-3461
  400 W Pearl St, Tremont 61568   Fax 309/925-5817

Schools: 3 \ **Teachers:** 63 \ **Students:** 1,000 \ **Special Ed Students:** 140 \ **LEP Students:** 4 \ **College-Bound:** 85% \ **Ethnic:** Asian 1%, African American 2%, Hispanic 4%, Caucasian 94% \ **Exp:** $118 (Low) \ **Poverty:** 3% \ **Title I:** $29,586 \ **Special Education:** $327,000 \ **Open-Close:** 08/20 - 05/26

Sean Barry 1   Kim Wicks 2
Josh Weer 3   Vince Imig 3
Sonja Bolliger 4   Zach Zehr 6
Sean Berry ....10*   Becky Hansen 11*
Tracey Harrell ....12*   Michelle McKune 58*
Volkan Sumer 67   Kathy Genard 69*
Jamason Isenburg ....73,286* Laura Watts 76,297

Public Schs..Principal	Grd	Prgm	Enr/#Cls	SN	
Tremont Grade Sch 200 S James St, Tremont 61568 Becky Hansen	PK-4		364 17	10%	309/925-4841 Fax 309/925-3849
Tremont High Sch 400 W Pearl St, Tremont 61568 Jill Uhlman	9-12		336 30	13%	309/925-2051
Tremont Middle Sch 400 W Pearl St, Tremont 61568 Jeremy Garrett	5-8		289 12	13%	309/925-3823

1	Superintendent	8	Curric/Instruct K-12	19	Chief Financial Officer	29	Family/Consumer Science	39	Social Studies K-12	49	English/Lang Arts Elem	59	Special Education Elem	69	Academic Assessment
2	Bus/Finance/Purchasing	9	Curric/Instruct Elem	20	Art K-12	30	Adult Education	40	Social Studies Elem	50	English/Lang Arts Sec	60	Special Education Sec	70	Research/Development
3	Buildings And Grounds	10	Curric/Instruct Sec	21	Art Elem	31	Career/Sch-to-Work K-12	41	Social Studies Sec	51	Reading K-12	61	Foreign/World Lang K-12	71	Public Information
4	Food Service	11	Federal Program	22	Art Sec	32	Career/Sch-to-Work Elem	42	Science K-12	52	Reading Elem	62	Foreign/World Lang Elem	72	Summer School
5	Transportation	12	Title I	23	Music K-12	33	Career/Sch-to-Work Sec	43	Science Elem	53	Reading Sec	63	Foreign/World Lang Sec	73	Instructional Tech
6	Athletic	13	Title V	24	Music Elem	34	Early Childhood Ed	44	Science Sec	54	Remedial Reading K-12	64	Religious Education K-12	74	Inservice Training
7	Health Services	14	Instructional Media Svcs	25	Music Sec	35	Health/Phys Education	45	Math K-12	55	Remedial Reading Elem	65	Religious Education Elem	75	Marketing/Distributive
		15	Asst Superintendent	26	Business Education	36	Guidance Services K-12	46	Math Elem	56	Remedial Reading Sec	66	Religious Education Sec	76	Info Systems
		16	Chief Operations Officer	27	Career & Tech Ed	37	Guidance Services Elem	47	Math Sec	57	Bilingual/ELL	67	School Board President	77	Psychological Assess
		18	Chief Academic Officer	28	Technology Education	38	Guidance Services Sec	48	English/Lang Arts K-12	58	Special Education K-12	68	Teacher Personnel	78	Affirmative Action

Illinois School Directory

Union County

- **Washington Cmty HS Dist 308** PID: 00321816 309/444-3167
  115 Bondurant St, Washington 61571 Fax 309/444-5767

Schools: 1 \ Teachers: 81 \ Students: 1,406 \ Special Ed Students: 144 \ LEP Students: 4 \ College-Bound: 87% \ Ethnic: Asian 1%, African American 1%, Hispanic 4%, Caucasian 94% \ Exp: $207 (Med) \ Poverty: 5% \ Title I: $96,001 \ Special Education: $370,000 \ Open-Close: 08/18 - 05/25 \ DTBP: $243 (High)

Dr Kyle Freeman 1	Dr Joe Sander 2,15
Ryne Meardy 3*	Laura McCue-Newport 4
Laura McCue-Newport 4*	Herb Knoblauch 6
Carol Jordan 7,83,85	Carol Jordan 7,83,85*
Karen Stevens 11,69,273,288,298*	Annette Gresham 60*
Jennifer Essig 67	Adam Mangold 69
Holly Raubach-Davis 73,76,286*	

Public Schs..Principal	Grd	Prgm	Enr/#Cls	SN	
Washington High Sch 115 Bondurant St, Washington 61571 Karen Stevens	9-12	V	1,406 80	22%	309/444-3167

- **Washington School Dist 52** PID: 00321787 309/444-4182
  303 Jackson St, Washington 61571

Schools: 2 \ Teachers: 58 \ Students: 930 \ Special Ed Students: 133 \ LEP Students: 5 \ Ethnic: Asian 1%, African American 1%, Hispanic 3%, Caucasian 94% \ Exp: $118 (Low) \ Poverty: 4% \ Title I: $39,730 \ Special Education: $367,000 \ Open-Close: 08/20 - 05/26 \ DTBP: $204 (High)

Pat Minasian 1	Heather Bowman 9
Tara Scribner 16,82*	Charlie Zimmerman 67
Matt Jensen 73	Kathy Lee 274*

Public Schs..Principal	Grd	Prgm	Enr/#Cls	SN	
Lincoln Grade Sch 303 Jackson St, Washington 61571 Heather Bowman	PK-4		444 23	25%	309/444-2326
Washington Middle Sch 1100 N Main St, Washington 61571 Dan Foehrkolb	5-8		475 22	23%	309/444-3361 Fax 309/444-3941

TAZEWELL CATHOLIC SCHOOLS

- **Diocese of Peoria Ed Office** PID: 00313338
  Listing includes only schools located in this county. See District Index for location of Diocesan Offices.

Catholic Schs..Principal	Grd	Prgm	Enr/#Cls	SN	
Blessed Sacrament Sch 1018 S 1st Ave, Morton 61550 Mike Birdoes	PK-8		279 12		309/263-8442 Fax 309/263-8443
St Joseph Sch 300 S 6th St, Pekin 61554 Mary Sarff	PK-8		266 10		309/347-7194 Fax 309/347-7198
St Patrick Sch 100 Harvey St, Washington 61571 Doreen Shipman	PK-8		304 16		309/444-4345 Fax 309/444-7100

TAZEWELL PRIVATE SCHOOLS

Private Schs..Principal	Grd	Prgm	Enr/#Cls	SN	
Bethel Lutheran Sch 325 E Queenwood Rd, Morton 61550 John Jacob	PK-8		450 20		309/266-6592 Fax 309/266-8510
Childrens Center Tazwell Co 210 N Thorncrest Ave, Creve Coeur 61610 Sr Cora Marie	PK-5		5 2		309/699-6141 Fax 309/699-5147
Christian Life Academy 222 Tremont St, Hopedale 61747 Josh Horning	PK-12		70 2		309/449-3346
Faith Baptist Christian Sch 1501 Howard Ct, Pekin 61554 Tim Collard	PK-12		94 12		309/347-6178 Fax 309/347-8716
Good Shepherd Lutheran Sch 3201 Court St, Pekin 61554 Dan Rees	PK-8		185 19		309/347-2020 Fax 309/347-9099
Illinois Central Christian Sch 22648 Grosenbach Rd, Washington 61571 David Williams	K-12		85		309/698-2000 Fax 309/698-2065
Judah Prep Academy 31506 Fast Ave, Mackinaw 61755 Diann Stone	K-6		14 12		309/359-4673 Fax 309/359-4303

TAZEWELL REGIONAL CENTERS

- **Regional Office of Ed 53** PID: 02098390 309/477-2290
  414 Court St Ste 100, Pekin 61554 Fax 309/347-3735

Jeff Ekena 1	Jay Windel 73

- **Tazewell Co Area EFE #320** PID: 04177796 309/353-5011
  200 S 2nd St Ste 12, Pekin 61554 Fax 309/353-1350

Jill Warren 1	Cindy Gierch 58,275

- **Tazewell-Mason Sp Ed Assoc** PID: 02182159 309/347-5164
  300 Cedar St, Pekin 61554 Fax 309/346-0440

Kristina Neville 1	Zina Young 7
Amber Ealey 34	Todd Hellrigel 67

UNION COUNTY

UNION COUNTY SCHOOLS

County Schs..Principal	Grd	Prgm	Enr/#Cls	SN	
Tri-Co Education Center 1000 N Main St, Anna 62906 Gina Stokes	Spec	A	32 3	89%	618/833-4541 Fax 618/833-4833

Union County

UNION PUBLIC SCHOOLS

- **Anna Cmty Cons Sch Dist 37** PID: 00321830   618/833-6812
  301 S Green St, Anna 62906   Fax 618/833-3205

  Schools: 3 \ Teachers: 41 \ Students: 695 \ Special Ed Students: 171 \ LEP Students: 20 \ Ethnic: Asian 1%, African American 1%, Hispanic 6%, Caucasian 91% \ Exp: $108 (Low) \ Poverty: 29% \ Title I: $407,564 \ Special Education: $213,000 \ Open-Close: 08/20 - 06/02 \ DTBP: $167 (High)

  Julie Bullard 1,11
  John Kenne 37,69
  Karen Frick 73*
  Rob Lannom 6
  Grant Capel 67

Public Schs..Principal	Grd	Prgm	Enr/#Cls	SN	
Anna Junior High Sch 301 S Green St, Anna 62906 Mark Laster	5-8	T	303 18	60%	618/833-6415 Fax 618/833-6535
Davie Elem Sch 301 S Green St, Anna 62906 Mark Laster	3-4	T	142 5	65%	618/833-6415 Fax 618/833-6535
Lincoln Elem Sch 108 Warren St, Anna 62906 Mark Laster	PK-2	T	250 12	54%	618/833-6851 Fax 618/833-3262

- **Anna-Jonesboro Cmty HSD 81** PID: 00321878   618/833-8421
  608 Main St, Anna 62906   Fax 618/833-4239

  Schools: 1 \ Teachers: 31 \ Students: 530 \ Special Ed Students: 93 \ LEP Students: 3 \ College-Bound: 63% \ Ethnic: Asian 1%, African American 1%, Hispanic 5%, Caucasian 93% \ Exp: $263 (Med) \ Poverty: 20% \ Title I: $235,908 \ Special Education: $91,000 \ Open-Close: 08/17 - 05/21 \ DTBP: $174 (High) \

  Rob Wright 1,11,83
  Alecia Pitts 4*
  Amy Wilson 12,60*
  Dr April Teske 67
  Brett Detering 288
  Brian Moore 3*
  Scott Finders 10,752
  Brian Meyer 16,73,76,286*
  Natalie McLean Miller 83,273*

Public Schs..Principal	Grd	Prgm	Enr/#Cls	SN	
ⓥ Anna-Jonesboro High Sch 608 S Main St, Anna 62906 Brett Detering	9-12	MT	530 40	40%	618/833-8421

- **Cobden Cmty Unit Sch Dist 17** PID: 00321892   618/893-2313
  413 N Appleknocker St, Cobden 62920   Fax 618/893-4772

  Schools: 2 \ Teachers: 45 \ Students: 526 \ Special Ed Students: 92 \ LEP Students: 47 \ College-Bound: 64% \ Ethnic: Hispanic 31%, Caucasian 69% \ Exp: $286 (Med) \ Poverty: 17% \ Title I: $163,607 \ Special Education: $121,000 \ Bilingual Education: $5,000 \ Open-Close: 08/14 - 05/28 \

  Edwin Shoemate 1,57,288
  Tim Smith 3,91
  April Reiman 31,36,83,88*
  David Ellaway 73,295
  Dee Conroy 2
  Shannon Guardian 11,55*
  Tracie Moore 67
  Sue Reed 274*

Public Schs..Principal	Grd	Prgm	Enr/#Cls	SN	
Cobden Elem Sch 413 N Appleknocker St, Cobden 62920 Erin Wiltowski	PK-5	TV	212 15	63%	618/893-2311 Fax 618/893-4742
Cobden Jr Sr High Sch 413 N Appleknocker St, Cobden 62920 Crystal Housman	6-12	TV	314 25	59%	618/893-4031 Fax 618/893-2138

- **Dongola Unit School Dist 66** PID: 00321933   618/827-3841
  1000 High St, Dongola 62926   Fax 618/827-4641

  Schools: 1 \ Teachers: 18 \ Students: 286 \ Special Ed Students: 73 \ College-Bound: 63% \ Ethnic: Hispanic 5%, Caucasian 95% \ Exp: $178 (Low) \ Poverty: 20% \ Title I: $109,266 \ Special Education: $91,000 \ Open-Close: 08/17 - 06/04 \ DTBP: $168 (High)

  Paige Maginel 1
  Kim Johnson 4
  John Goddard 8,11,57,58,74,271,275*
  Phil Miller 67
  Joni Lewis 2*
  Preston Hall 6*
  Josh Ditto 16,73,286*

Public Schs..Principal	Grd	Prgm	Enr/#Cls	SN	
Dongola Sch 1000 High St, Dongola 62926 Salina Hillard	PK-12	T	286 50	80%	618/827-3524 Fax 618/827-4422

- **Jonesboro Cmty Cons SD 43** PID: 00321969   618/833-6651
  309 Cook Ave, Jonesboro 62952   Fax 618/833-3410

  Schools: 1 \ Teachers: 31 \ Students: 370 \ Special Ed Students: 82 \ LEP Students: 4 \ Ethnic: Asian 1%, African American 1%, Hispanic 5%, Caucasian 93% \ Exp: $159 (Low) \ Poverty: 20% \ Title I: $127,708 \ Special Education: $92,000 \ Open-Close: 08/18 - 05/21 \ DTBP: $162 (High)

  Kevin Westall 1
  Nyla Montgomery 12
  Jama Elddelman 73
  Jenny Sadler 2
  Casey Johnson 67

Public Schs..Principal	Grd	Prgm	Enr/#Cls	SN	
Jonesboro Elem Sch 309 Cook Ave, Jonesboro 62952 Thomas Starks	PK-8	T	370 23	56%	618/833-5148

- **Lick Creek School Dist 16** PID: 00321983   618/833-2545
  7355 Lick Creek Rd, Buncombe 62912   Fax 618/833-3201

  Schools: 1 \ Teachers: 12 \ Students: 150 \ Special Ed Students: 27 \ Ethnic: Asian 1%, African American 1%, Caucasian 98% \ Exp: $93 (Low) \ Poverty: 11% \ Title I: $25,820 \ Special Education: $31,000 \ Open-Close: 08/17 - 06/02

  Brent Boren 1,11,73,83
  Blayne Holshouser 67

Public Schs..Principal	Grd	Prgm	Enr/#Cls	SN	
Lick Creek Elem Sch 7355 Lick Creek Rd, Buncombe 62912 Brent Boren	PK-8	T	150 11	39%	618/833-2545

1	Superintendent	8	Curric/Instruct K-12	19	Chief Financial Officer	29	Family/Consumer Science	39	Social Studies K-12	49	English/Lang Arts Elem	59	Special Education Elem	69	Academic Assessment
2	Bus/Finance/Purchasing	9	Curric/Instruct Elem	20	Art K-12	30	Adult Education	40	Social Studies Elem	50	English/Lang Arts Sec	60	Special Education Sec	70	Research/Development
3	Buildings And Grounds	10	Curric/Instruct Sec	21	Art Elem	31	Career/Sch-to-Work K-12	41	Social Studies Sec	51	Reading K-12	61	Foreign/World Lang K-12	71	Public Information
4	Food Service	11	Federal Program	22	Art Sec	32	Career/Sch-to-Work Elem	42	Science K-12	52	Reading Elem	62	Foreign/World Lang Elem	72	Summer School
5	Transportation	12	Title I	23	Music K-12	33	Career/Sch-to-Work Sec	43	Science Elem	53	Reading Sec	63	Foreign/World Lang Sec	73	Instructional Tech
6	Athletic	13	Title V	24	Music Elem	34	Early Childhood Ed	44	Science Sec	54	Remedial Reading K-12	64	Religious Education K-12	74	Inservice Training
7	Health Services	15	Asst Superintendent	25	Music Sec	35	Health/Phys Education	45	Math K-12	55	Remedial Reading Elem	65	Religious Education Elem	75	Marketing/Distributive
		16	Instructional Media Svcs	26	Business Education	36	Guidance Services K-12	46	Math Elem	56	Remedial Reading Sec	66	Religious Education Sec	76	Info Systems
		17	Chief Operations Officer	27	Career & Tech Ed	37	Guidance Services Elem	47	Math Sec	57	Bilingual/ELL	67	School Board President	77	Psychological Assess
		18	Chief Academic Officer	28	Technology Education	38	Guidance Services Sec	48	English/Lang Arts K-12	58	Special Education K-12	68	Teacher Personnel	78	Affirmative Action

Illinois School Directory

Vermilion County

● **Shawnee Cmty Unit Sch Dist 84** PID: 00322004   618/833-5709
3365 N State Route 3, Wolf Lake 62998   Fax 618/833-4171

Schools: 2 \ **Teachers:** 24 \ **Students:** 300 \ **Special Ed Students:** 76 \ **College-Bound:** 80% \ **Ethnic:** African American 3%, Caucasian 97% \ **Exp:** $445 (High) \ **Poverty:** 29% \ **Title I:** $238,418 \ **Special Education:** $100,000 \ **Open-Close:** 08/17 - 06/04 \ **DTBP:** $174 (High)

Shelly Clover-Hill	1,83	Beth Marks	8,79*
Amy Reynolds	11*	Tim Cualls	67
Robert Hathaway	85*		

Public Schs..Principal	Grd	Prgm	Enr/#Cls	SN	
Shawnee Elem Sch	PK-5	T	162	97%	618/833-4975
3365 N State Route 3, Wolf Lake 62998			5		Fax 618/833-4977
Amy Reynolds					
Shawnee Jr Sr High Sch	5-12	T	149	97%	618/833-5307
3365 N State Route 3, Wolf Lake 62998			20		Fax 618/833-5468
Karen Schaefer					

UNION PRIVATE SCHOOLS

Private Schs..Principal	Grd	Prgm	Enr/#Cls	SN	
Shawnee Hills Chrn Academy	K-12		27		618/833-1870
110 Florsheim Dr, Anna 62906			3		
Bonnie Vines					

VERMILION COUNTY

VERMILION PUBLIC SCHOOLS

● **Armstrong Ellis SD 61** PID: 00322066   217/569-2115
3571 Gifford Ave, Armstrong 61812   Fax 217/569-2116

Schools: 1 \ **Teachers:** 11 \ **Students:** 80 \ **Special Ed Students:** 9 \ **Ethnic:** Asian 3%, Hispanic 1%, Native American: 1%, Caucasian 94% \ **Exp:** $628 (High) \ **Poverty:** 16% \ **Title I:** $47,300 \ **Special Education:** $17,000 \ **Open-Close:** 08/20 - 05/26

William Mulvaney	1,11,83	Bob Rawlings	3
Sheree Bussard	4*	James Edenburn	6,67
Carolyn Rice	12*	Merissa Wright	73
Kurt Thornsbrough	288	Brittany Hesterberg	295

Public Schs..Principal	Grd	Prgm	Enr/#Cls	SN	
Armstrong Ellis Elem Sch	PK-8		80	48%	217/569-2115
3571 Gifford Ave, Armstrong 61812			12		
Kurt Thornsbrough					

● **Armstrong Twp High SD 225** PID: 00322092   217/569-2122
30474 Smith, Armstrong 61812   Fax 217/569-2171

Schools: 1 \ **Teachers:** 17 \ **Students:** 140 \ **Special Ed Students:** 12 \ **College-Bound:** 69% \ **Ethnic:** African American 2%, Hispanic 1%, Caucasian 98% \ **Exp:** $232 (Med) \ **Poverty:** 10% \ **Title I:** $3,660 \ **Special Education:** $17,000 \ **Open-Close:** 08/19 - 05/28 \ **DTBP:** $183 (High)

William Mulvaney	1,83	Kathy Remington	2*
Bob Rawlings	3*	Jackie Davis	4*
John Neubaum	5*	Darren Loschen	6,16,73,76,288,295
Allison Bartlow	10,12,60*	Mike High	33,69*
Gordon Headrick	67		

Public Schs..Principal	Grd	Prgm	Enr/#Cls	SN	
Armstrong Twp High Sch	9-12	V	140	39%	217/569-2122
30474 Smith, Armstrong 61812			20		
Darren Loschen					

● **Bismarck-Henning Cmty SD 1** PID: 00322119   217/759-7261
17268 E 2750 North Rd, Bismarck 61814   Fax 217/759-7942

Schools: 3 \ **Teachers:** 35 \ **Students:** 859 \ **Special Ed Students:** 89 \ **LEP Students:** 4 \ **College-Bound:** 85% \ **Ethnic:** Asian 1%, African American 2%, Hispanic 6%, Caucasian 92% \ **Exp:** $264 (Med) \ **Poverty:** 16% \ **Title I:** $202,716 \ **Special Education:** $160,000 \ **Open-Close:** 08/25 - 05/21 \ **DTBP:** $195 (High) \ 🅵 🅃

Scott Watson	1	Tom Johnson	6*
Audrey Carpenter	8	Sean Click	11,58,69,296
Dave Clapp	67	Dale McCoy	73

Public Schs..Principal	Grd	Prgm	Enr/#Cls	SN	
Bhra High Sch	9-12	V	337		217/759-7291
17268 E 2750 North Rd, Bismarck 61814			28		Fax 217/759-7815
Brent Rademacher					
Bismarck Henning Elem Sch	PK-4		332	38%	217/759-7251
5 Holloway St, Bismarck 61814			16		Fax 217/759-7263
Lisa Acton					🅵 🅃
Bismarck Henning Jr High Sch	5-8		262	33%	217/759-7301
17302 E 2750 North Rd, Bismarck 61814			35		Fax 217/759-7313
Rusty Campbell					🅵 🅃

● **Danville School District 118** PID: 00322212   217/444-1000
110 E Williams St, Danville 61832   Fax 217/444-1006

Schools: 11 \ **Teachers:** 353 \ **Students:** 5,505 \ **Special Ed Students:** 876 \ **LEP Students:** 180 \ **Ethnic:** Asian 1%, African American 49%, Hispanic 10%, Caucasian 40% \ **Exp:** $237 (Med) \ **Poverty:** 34% \ **Title I:** $4,578,394 \ **Special Education:** $3,990,000 \ **Bilingual Education:** $45,000 \ **Open-Close:** 09/08 - 06/10 \ 🅵

Dr Alicia Geddis	1,83	Narcissus Rankin	2,5,80,91
Skip Truex	3	Sue Barnes	4
Mark Bacy	6*	Mary Ellen Bunton	8
John Hart	9,15,69,88,275,280,294	Dr Elizabeth Yacobi	10,15
Brandi Kuchefski	12,57,298	Julie Cox	48,280
Molly Bailey	58	William Dobbles	67
Kim Pabst	68,78,79,273	Scott Williams	73,95,295*
Heather Smith	84	Mike Orr	295

Public Schs..Principal	Grd	Prgm	Enr/#Cls	SN	
Danville High Sch	9-12	T	1,414	65%	217/444-1500
202 E Fairchild St, Danville 61832			150		Fax 217/444-1590
Tracy Cherry					

79 Student Personnel	91 Safety/Security	275 Response To Intervention	298 Grant Writer/Ptnrships	**School Programs**	**Social Media**		
80 Driver Ed/Safety	92 Magnet School	277 Remedial Math K-12	750 Chief Innovation Officer	A = Alternative Program			
81 Gifted/Talented	93 Parental Involvement	280 Literacy Coach	751 Chief of Staff	G = Adult Classes	🅵	= Facebook	
82 Video Services	95 Tech Prep Program	285 STEM	752 Social Emotional Learning	M = Magnet Program			
83 Substance Abuse Prev	97 Chief Infomation Officer	286 Digital Learning		T = Title I Schoolwide	🅃	= Twitter	
84 Erate	98 Chief Technology Officer	288 Common Core Standards	**Other School Types**	V = Career & Tech Ed Programs			
85 AIDS Education	270 Character Education	294 Accountability	Ⓐ = Alternative School				
88 Alternative/At Risk	271 Migrant Education	295 Network System	Ⓒ = Charter School	New Schools are shaded			
89 Multi-Cultural Curriculum	273 Teacher Mentor	296 Title II Programs	Ⓜ = Magnet School	New Superintendents and Principals are bold			
90 Social Work	274 Before/After Sch	297 Webmaster	Ⓨ = Year-Round School	Personnel with email addresses are underscored			

IL—231

Vermilion County

Market Data Retrieval

School	Grd	Prgm	Enr/#Cls	SN	Phone
Edison Elem Sch 2101 N Vermilion St, Danville 61832 Betsy Porter	K-5	T	267 15	78%	217/444-3350 Fax 217/444-3354
Garfield Elem Sch 1101 N Gilbert St, Danville 61832 Nicole Zaayer \ Stacie Sollars	K-5	T	300 15	82%	217/444-1750 Fax 217/444-1791
Ⓐ Kenneth D Bailey Academy 502 E Main St, Danville 61832 Mitzi Campbell	7-12		100	84%	217/477-0300 Fax 217/477-0399
Liberty Elem Sch 20 E Liberty Ln, Danville 61832 Angelique Simon	K-4	T	212 17	78%	217/444-3000 Fax 217/444-3006
Mark Denman Elem Sch 930 Colfax Dr, Danville 61832 Jennifer Richardson	K-5	T	680 30	84%	217/444-3200 Fax 217/444-3204
Meade Park Elem Sch 200 S Kansas Ave, Danville 61834 Chris Rice	K-5	T	387 22	91%	217/444-1925 Fax 217/444-1928
North Ridge Middle Sch 1619 N Jackson St, Danville 61832 Eliza Brooks	7-8	T	698 50	69%	217/444-3400 Fax 217/444-3488
Ⓜ Northeast Elem Magnet Sch Ⓨ 1330 E English St, Danville 61832 Justin Thorlton	K-5	MT	278 14	40%	217/444-3050 Fax 217/444-3080
South View Upper Elem Sch 133 E 9th St, Danville 61832 Lindsey Prunkard	5-6	T	701 45	80%	217/444-1800 Fax 217/444-1882
Southwest Elem Sch 14794 Catlin Tilton Rd, Danville 61834 Lindsey Prunkard	PK-4	T	499 25	76%	217/444-3500 Fax 217/444-3507

- **Georgetown-Ridge Farm CUSD 4** PID: 00322444 217/662-8488
  502 W Mulberry St, Georgetown 61846 Fax 217/662-3402

Schools: 3 \ **Teachers:** 69 \ **Students:** 1,010 \ **Special Ed Students:** 199 \ **LEP Students:** 5 \ **College-Bound:** 45% \ **Ethnic:** African American 2%, Hispanic 2%, Caucasian 96% \ **Exp:** $172 (Low) \ **Poverty:** 21% \ **Title I:** $425,808 \ **Special Education:** $306,000 \ **Open-Close:** 08/12 - 05/28

Jean Neal ....1,11 Amy Cavanaugh 2
Rubin Rowe ....3 Darla Attutis 4
Kevin Thomas ....6,58 Lisa Cramer 8,13,288,296,298
Michael Gragart ....67 Trent Eisenbarth 286

Public Schs..Principal	Grd	Prgm	Enr/#Cls	SN	
Georgetown-Ridge Farm High Sch 500 W Mulberry St, Georgetown 61846 Kevin Thomas	9-12	TV	285 28	57%	217/662-6716 Fax 217/662-3404
Mary Miller Junior High Sch 414 W West St, Georgetown 61846 John Tosh	6-8	T	204 16	71%	217/662-6606 Fax 217/662-6345
Pine Crest Elem Sch 505 S Kennedy Dr, Georgetown 61846 Ashley Vaughn	PK-5	T	463 20	61%	217/662-6981 Fax 217/662-3413

- **Hoopeston Area Cmty Unit SD 11** PID: 00322509 217/283-6668
  615 E Orange St, Hoopeston 60942 Fax 217/283-5431

Schools: 4 \ **Teachers:** 85 \ **Students:** 1,100 \ **Special Ed Students:** 246 \ **LEP Students:** 11 \ **College-Bound:** 57% \ **Ethnic:** African American 1%, Hispanic 17%, Caucasian 81% \ **Exp:** $481 (High) \ **Poverty:** 27% \ **Title I:** $625,142 \ **Special Education:** $681,000 \ **Open-Close:** 08/20 - 05/27 \ **DTBP:** $233 (High)

Robert Richardson ....1 Mark Eigner 2,5
Wade Clemmons ....3 Tina Samet 4*
Matthew Colston ....6* Emily Brown 8,275,288*
Suzi Root ....8,11* Dan Walder 11,57,72,271,273*
Roseellen Cornelius .... 15 Mary Johnson 31,36,77,83,88,270*
Dave McFadden .... 67 Jim Eyrich 73,295*

Public Schs..Principal	Grd	Prgm	Enr/#Cls	SN	
Hoopeston Area High Sch 615 E Orange St, Hoopeston 60942 John Klaber	9-12	T	328 40	96%	217/283-6661
Hoopeston Area Middle Sch 615 E Orange St, Hoopeston 60942 Michelle White	6-8	T	274 25	95%	217/283-6664 Fax 217/283-7943
John Greer Elem Sch 609 W Main St, Hoopeston 60942 Dan Walder	3-5	T	271 9	99%	217/283-6667 Fax 217/283-7038
Maple Elem Sch 500 S 4th St, Hoopeston 60942 Suzi Root	PK-2	T	296 18	75%	217/283-6665 Fax 217/283-5438

- **Oakwood Cmty Unit Sch Dist 76** PID: 00322638 217/446-6081
  12190 US Route 150, Oakwood 61858 Fax 217/446-6218

Schools: 3 \ **Teachers:** 63 \ **Students:** 1,000 \ **Special Ed Students:** 119 \ **LEP Students:** 4 \ **College-Bound:** 57% \ **Ethnic:** Asian 1%, African American 2%, Hispanic 6%, Caucasian 92% \ **Exp:** $380 (High) \ **Poverty:** 17% \ **Title I:** $304,420 \ **Special Education:** $232,000 \ **Open-Close:** 08/25 - 05/28

Larry Maynard ....1 Sheila Odle 2,4
John Siddens ....3 Charlotte Lunt 5
John Odle ....6 Michelle Kimbro 8,11,57,88,285,286,288*
Dawn Lee ....31,36* Lisa Acton 58
Randy Smith .... 67 Chris Richardson 73

Public Schs..Principal	Grd	Prgm	Enr/#Cls	SN	
Oakwood Grade Sch 408 S Scott St, Oakwood 61858 Nichole Lapenas	PK-6	T	518 22	44%	217/354-4221 Fax 217/354-2712
Oakwood High Sch 5870 US Route 150, Fithian 61844 Tim Lee	9-12	V	303 21	36%	217/354-2358 Fax 217/354-2603
Oakwood Junior High Sch 21600 N 900 East Rd, Danville 61834 Anne Burton	7-8	T	154 14	51%	217/443-2883 Fax 217/776-2228

- **Potomac Cmty Unit Sch Dist 10** PID: 00322652 217/987-6155
  7915 US Route 136, Potomac 61865 Fax 217/987-6663

Schools: 1 \ **Teachers:** 13 \ **Students:** 145 \ **Special Ed Students:** 26 \ **Ethnic:** African American 1%, Caucasian 99% \ **Exp:** $267 (Med) \ **Poverty:** 19% \ **Title I:** $68,072 \ **Special Education:** $47,000 \ **Open-Close:** 08/19 - 05/26

Jim Owens .... 1,11,83 Pam Boen 2
Katy Bulldock ....58,288* Vance Hambleton 67
Jim Ochs 73,286*

Public Schs..Principal	Grd	Prgm	Enr/#Cls	SN	
Potomac Elem Sch 7915 US Route 136, Potomac 61865 Candace Freeman	PK-8	T	145 13	42%	217/987-6155

1	Superintendent	8	Curric/Instruct K-12	19	Chief Financial Officer	29	Family/Consumer Science	39	Social Studies K-12	49	English/Lang Arts Elem	59	Special Education Elem	69	Academic Assessment
2	Bus/Finance/Purchasing	9	Curric/Instruct Elem	20	Art K-12	30	Adult Education	40	Social Studies Elem	50	English/Lang Arts Sec	60	Special Education Sec	70	Research/Development
3	Buildings And Grounds	10	Curric/Instruct Sec	21	Art Elem	31	Career/Sch-to-Work K-12	41	Social Studies Sec	51	Reading K-12	61	Foreign/World Lang K-12	71	Public Information
4	Food Service	11	Federal Program	22	Art Sec	32	Career/Sch-to-Work Elem	42	Science K-12	52	Reading Elem	62	Foreign/World Lang Elem	72	Summer School
5	Transportation	12	Title I	23	Music K-12	33	Career/Sch-to-Work Sec	43	Science Elem	53	Reading Sec	63	Foreign/World Lang Sec	73	Instructional Tech
6	Athletic	13	Title V	24	Music Elem	34	Early Childhood Ed	44	Science Sec	54	Remedial Reading K-12	64	Religious Education K-12	74	Inservice Training
7	Health Services	15	Asst Superintendent	25	Music Sec	35	Health/Phys Education	45	Math K-12	55	Remedial Reading Elem	65	Religious Education Elem	75	Marketing/Distributive
		16	Instructional Media Svcs	26	Business Education	36	Guidance Services K-12	46	Math Elem	56	Remedial Reading Sec	66	Religious Education Sec	76	Info Systems
		17	Chief Operations Officer	27	Career & Tech Ed	37	Guidance Services Elem	47	Math Sec	57	Bilingual/ELL	67	School Board President	77	Psychological Assess
		18	Chief Academic Officer	28	Technology Education	38	Guidance Services Sec	48	English/Lang Arts K-12	58	Special Education K-12	68	Teacher Personnel	78	Affirmative Action

Illinois School Directory — Vermilion County

- **Rossville-Alvin Cmty Unit SD 7** PID: 00322755   217/748-6666
  350 N Chicago St, Rossville 60963   Fax 217/748-6144

Schools: 1 \ **Teachers:** 18 \ **Students:** 300 \ **Special Ed Students:** 72 \
Ethnic: Hispanic 5%, Caucasian 94% \ **Exp:** $747 (High) \ **Poverty:** 17% \
Title I: $119,987 \ **Special Education:** $105,000 \ **Open-Close:** 08/24 -
06/01 \ **DTBP:** $173 (High)

Crystal Johnson 1   Denise Scharlach 2
Jake Hill 6   Alexis Heidrick 11
Heath Kendrick 11,57,73,83,288   William Ray 67

Public Schs..Principal	Grd	Prgm	Enr/#Cls	SN	
Rossville-Alvin Elem & JHS 350 N Chicago St, Rossville 60963 Crystal Johnson	PK-8	A	300 12	58%	217/748-6666

- **Salt Fork Cmty Unit SD 512** PID: 00322781   217/427-2116
  701 1/2 W Vermilion St, Catlin 61817   Fax 217/427-2117

Schools: 3 \ **Teachers:** 63 \ **Students:** 900 \ **Special Ed Students:** 141
\ **College-Bound:** 30% \ **Ethnic:** African American 1%, Hispanic 2%,
Caucasian 97% \ **Exp:** $156 (Low) \ **Poverty:** 9% \ **Title I:** $112,226 \
Special Education: $239,000 \ **Open-Close:** 08/20 - 06/04 \ **DTBP:** $185
(High)

Phillip Cox 1,83   Cindy Decker 2
Eric Free .... 3*   Robin Johnson 4,5
Dustin Dees 6   Wade Czerwonka 6
Wade Czerwonka .... 6*   Rebecca Hawkins 12*
Nina McDowell .... 16*   Terri Hoskins 16*
Darcy Sheperd .... 38,88*   Troy Chew 67
John Simmons .... 73*   Kurk Willer 73,76*
Miranda Simmons 285*

Public Schs..Principal	Grd	Prgm	Enr/#Cls	SN	
Salt Fork High Sch 701 W Vermilion St, Catlin 61817 Darin Chambliss	9-12		261 15	38%	217/427-2468
Salt Fork North Elem Sch 216 N Webster St, Catlin 61817 Eric Free	PK-5	T	257 20	20%	217/427-5421 Fax 217/427-9866
Salt Fork South Elem Jr HS 7087 N 600 East Rd, Sidell 61876 Brian Allensworth	PK-8	TV	380 50	62%	217/288-9306

- **Westville Cmty Unit Sch Dist 2** PID: 00322834   217/267-3141
  125 W Ellsworth St, Westville 61883   Fax 217/267-3144

Schools: 3 \ **Teachers:** 81 \ **Students:** 1,306 \ **Special Ed Students:** 268
\ **College-Bound:** 51% \ **Ethnic:** African American 1%, Hispanic 4%,
Caucasian 95% \ **Exp:** $193 (Low) \ **Poverty:** 22% \ **Title I:** $438,532 \
Special Education: $378,000 \ **Open-Close:** 08/19 - 06/02 \ **DTBP:** $252
(High)

Dr Seth Miller 1,11,288   Pam Dalenberg 15*
Guy Goodlove .... 27,57,270*   Sheila Owen 34*
Mike Waters .... 36,69*   Leann Gallion 67
Lisa Coburn 73*

Public Schs..Principal	Grd	Prgm	Enr/#Cls	SN	
Judith Giacoma Elem Sch 200 S Walnut, Westville 61883 Nathan Ford	PK-6	T	732 38	62%	217/267-2154 Fax 217/267-3484 📘🇹
Westville High Sch 918 N State St, Westville 61883 Guy Goodlove	9-12	TV	374 25	53%	217/267-2183 Fax 217/267-7593
Westville Junior High Sch 412 Moses Ave, Westville 61883 Jared Ellison	7-8	T	200 15	62%	217/267-2185 Fax 217/267-3621

VERMILION CATHOLIC SCHOOLS

- **Diocese of Peoria Ed Office** PID: 00313338
  Listing includes only schools located in this county. See District Index for
  location of Diocesan Offices.

Catholic Schs..Principal	Grd	Prgm	Enr/#Cls	SN	
Schlarman Academy 2112 N Vermilion St, Danville 61832 Mark Janesky	PK-12		560 15		217/442-2725 Fax 217/442-0293

VERMILION PRIVATE SCHOOLS

Private Schs..Principal	Grd	Prgm	Enr/#Cls	SN	
Danville Christian Academy 428 N Walnut St, Danville 61832 Brenda Adams	PK-12		55 5		217/442-1579 Fax 217/442-1767
Danville Lutheran Sch 1930 N Bowman Avenue Rd, Danville 61832 Kim Wright	PK-8		115 6		217/442-5036 Fax 217/442-1159
Faith Christian Academy 301 E Main St, Sidell 61876 Dr Vickie McCarty	K-12		15		217/651-4709
First Baptist Christian Sch 1211 N Vermilion St, Danville 61832 Ken Seest	PK-12		151 13		217/442-2434 Fax 217/442-8731
Middlefork Sch 15009 Catlin Tilton Rd, Danville 61834 Monica Campbell	K-12		80		217/443-8273 Fax 217/443-0217
Norte Dame De La Salette Acad 5065 Olivet Rd, Georgetown 61846 Timothy Sick	8-12		85		217/662-2127 Fax 217/662-2427

VERMILION REGIONAL CENTERS

- **Regional Office of Ed 54** PID: 01536686   217/431-2668
  200 S College St Ste B, Danville 61832   Fax 217/431-2671

Aaron Hird 1   Shari Hutson 2
Jeri Callaway 74

- **Vermilion Assoc for Special Ed** PID: 02184080   217/443-8273
  15009 Catlin Tilton Rd Ste B, Danville 61834   Fax 217/443-0217

Kristin Dunker 1   Lori Cummings 2
Sarah Imhoff 15

- **Vermilion Voc Ed Delivery Sys** PID: 04182533   217/443-8742
  2000 E Main St, Danville 61832   Fax 217/554-1674

Nick Chatterton 1

79	Student Personnel	91	Safety/Security	275	Response To Intervention	298 Grant Writer/Ptnrships
80	Driver Ed/Safety	92	Magnet School	277	Remedial Math K-12	750 Chief Innovation Officer
81	Gifted/Talented	93	Parental Involvement	280	Literacy Coach	751 Chief of Staff
82	Video Services	95	Tech Prep Program	285	STEM	752 Social Emotional Learning
83	Substance Abuse Prev	97	Chief Infomation Officer	286	Digital Learning	
84	Erate	98	Chief Technology Officer	288	Common Core Standards	**Other School Types**
85	AIDS Education	270	Character Education	294	Accountability	Ⓐ = Alternative School
88	Alternative/At Risk	271	Migrant Education	295	Network System	Ⓒ = Charter School
89	Multi-Cultural Curriculum	273	Teacher Mentor	296	Title II Programs	Ⓜ = Magnet School
90	Social Work	274	Before/After Sch	297	Webmaster	Ⓨ = Year-Round School

School Programs
A = Alternative Program
G = Adult Classes
M = Magnet Program
T = Title I Schoolwide
V = Career & Tech Ed Programs

Social Media
📘 = Facebook
🇹 = Twitter

New Schools are shaded
New Superintendents and Principals are bold
Personnel with email addresses are underscored

IL—233

Wabash County

WABASH COUNTY

WABASH PUBLIC SCHOOLS

- **Allendale Cmty Cons SD 17** PID: 00322925 — 618/299-3161
  101 N 3rd St, Allendale 62410 — Fax 618/299-2015

  Schools: 1 \ **Teachers:** 11 \ **Students:** 130 \ **Special Ed Students:** 27 \ **Ethnic:** African American 1%, Hispanic 1%, Caucasian 99% \ **Exp:** $265 (Med) \ **Poverty:** 19% \ **Title I:** $58,472 \ **Special Education:** $27,000 \ **Open-Close:** 08/12 - 05/18

  Robert Bowser 1,11,83,288
  Darlene Smith 12*
  Ryan Dougherty 35,85
  James Barger 84
  Debbie Hipsher 2
  Michele Loeffler 16,73*
  Gary Buchanan 67
  Brittany Weiss 88

Public Schs..Principal	Grd	Prgm	Enr/#Cls	SN	
Allendale Elem Sch 101 N 3rd St, Allendale 62410 Bob Bowser	PK-8	T	130 15	62%	618/299-3161

- **Wabash Cmty Unit Sch Dist 348** PID: 00322949 — 618/262-4181
  218 W 13th St, Mount Carmel 62863 — Fax 618/262-7912

  Schools: 4 \ **Teachers:** 91 \ **Students:** 1,450 \ **Special Ed Students:** 263 \ **LEP Students:** 8 \ **College-Bound:** 39% \ **Ethnic:** Asian 1%, African American 1%, Hispanic 1%, Caucasian 97% \ **Exp:** $139 (Low) \ **Poverty:** 16% \ **Title I:** $494,656 \ **Special Education:** $494,000 \ **Open-Close:** 08/13 - 05/19 \ **DTBP:** $176 (High)

  Chuck Bleyer 1
  Sharon Tombolson 5
  Micheal Brewer 8,11,271,288
  Laura Taylor 37*
  Kevin Smith 73*
  Chris Taylor 274*
  Darlene Underwood 2
  Kyle Buss 6,80*
  Regina Paddick 36,69*
  Tim Schuler 67
  Meagan Mobley 270

Public Schs..Principal	Grd	Prgm	Enr/#Cls	SN	
Mt Carmel Elem Sch 1300 N Walnut St, Mount Carmel 62863 Sheila Odom	PK-2	T	396 18	60%	618/263-3876 Fax 618/262-7189
Mt Carmel Grade Sch 1520 Poplar St, Mount Carmel 62863 Chris Taylor	3-6	T	379 18	55%	618/262-5699 Fax 618/263-9096
Mt Carmel High Sch 201 N Pear St, Mount Carmel 62863 Jake Newkirk	9-12	ATV	482	44%	618/262-5104 Fax 618/262-8781
Mt Carmel Junior High Sch 201 N Pear St, Mount Carmel 62863 Jake Newkirk	7-8	AT	234 25	54%	618/262-5104 Fax 618/262-2302

WABASH CATHOLIC SCHOOLS

- **Diocese of Belleville Ed Off** PID: 00317671
  Listing includes only schools located in this county. See District Index for location of Diocesan Offices.

Catholic Schs..Principal	Grd	Prgm	Enr/#Cls	SN	
St Mary's Sch 417 Chestnut St, Mount Carmel 62863 Cindy Brogan	PK-8		126 12		618/263-3183 Fax 618/263-3596

WARREN COUNTY

WARREN PUBLIC SCHOOLS

- **Monmouth-Roseville CUSD 238** PID: 00323058 — 309/734-4712
  105 N E St, Monmouth 61462 — Fax 309/734-4755

  Schools: 5 \ **Teachers:** 124 \ **Students:** 1,686 \ **Special Ed Students:** 236 \ **LEP Students:** 320 \ **Ethnic:** Asian 4%, African American 5%, Hispanic 29%, Caucasian 62% \ **Exp:** $324 (High) \ **Poverty:** 16% \ **Title I:** $457,660 \ **Special Education:** $452,000 \ **Bilingual Education:** $101,000 \ **Open-Close:** 08/19 - 05/21 \ **DTBP:** $174 (High)

  Edward Fletcher 1,83
  David Greenlief 3
  Barry Trone 5
  Becky Hutton 8*
  Kevin Killey 67
  Don Johnson 73
  Shelly Smith 2
  Teresa Allen 4*
  Jeremy Adolthson 6
  Amy Freitag 11,57,296,298*
  Megan Thornton 69*

Public Schs..Principal	Grd	Prgm	Enr/#Cls	SN	
Central Intermediate Sch 401 E 2nd Ave, Monmouth 61462 Becky Hutton	4-6	T	341	55%	309/734-2213 Fax 309/734-3123
Harding Primary Sch 415 E 9th Ave, Monmouth 61462 Katy Morrison	2-3	T	206 13	53%	309/734-4915 Fax 309/734-5221
Lincoln Early Childhood Sch 325 S 11th St, Monmouth 61462 Joe Pilger	PK-1	T	367 17	53%	309/734-2222 Fax 309/734-6712
Monmouth-Roseville High Sch 325 W 1st Ave, Monmouth 61462 Jeff Ewing	9-12	TV	509 25	45%	309/734-5118 Fax 309/734-2918
Monmouth-Roseville Junior HS 200 E Gossett St, Roseville 61473 Donald Farr	7-8	TV	233 30	45%	309/426-2682 Fax 309/426-2303

- **United Cmty Unit Sch Dist 304** PID: 00323151 — 309/734-9413
  1905 100th St, Monmouth 61462 — Fax 309/734-0223

  Schools: 4 \ **Teachers:** 82 \ **Students:** 950 \ **Special Ed Students:** 158 \ **LEP Students:** 3 \ **College-Bound:** 90% \ **Ethnic:** Asian 1%, African American 1%, Hispanic 5%, Caucasian 93% \ **Exp:** $180 (Low) \ **Poverty:** 14% \ **Title I:** $175,776 \ **Special Education:** $202,000 \ **Open-Close:** 08/19 - 05/25

  Jeff Whitsitt 1,11,83
  Kay Shaver 36,69*
  Roger Schurtz 73*
  Tammy Walters 5
  Dana Poole 67

Public Schs..Principal	Grd	Prgm	Enr/#Cls	SN	
United High Sch 1905 100th St, Monmouth 61462 Amy Schmitz	9-12	V	249 40	33%	309/734-9411

---

1 Superintendent	8 Curric/Instruct K-12	19 Chief Financial Officer	29 Family/Consumer Science	39 Social Studies K-12	49 English/Lang Arts Elem	59 Special Education Elem	69 Academic Assessment
2 Bus/Finance/Purchasing	9 Curric/Instruct Elem	20 Art K-12	30 Adult Education	40 Social Studies Elem	50 English/Lang Arts Sec	60 Special Education Sec	70 Research/Development
3 Buildings And Grounds	10 Curric/Instruct Sec	21 Art Elem	31 Career/Sch-to-Work K-12	41 Social Studies Sec	51 Reading K-12	61 Foreign/World Lang K-12	71 Public Information
4 Food Service	11 Federal Program	22 Art Sec	32 Career/Sch-to-Work Elem	42 Science K-12	52 Reading Elem	62 Foreign/World Lang Elem	72 Summer School
5 Transportation	12 Title I	23 Music K-12	33 Career/Sch-to-Work Sec	43 Science Elem	53 Reading Sec	63 Foreign/World Lang Sec	73 Instructional Media
6 Athletic	13 Title V	24 Music Elem	34 Early Childhood Ed	44 Science Sec	54 Remedial Reading K-12	64 Religious Education K-12	74 Inservice Training
7 Health Services	15 Asst Superintendent	25 Music Sec	35 Health/Phys Education	45 Math K-12	55 Remedial Reading Elem	65 Religious Education Elem	75 Marketing/Distributive
	16 Instructional Media Svcs	26 Business Education	36 Guidance Services K-12	46 Math Elem	56 Remedial Reading Sec	66 Religious Education Sec	76 Info Systems
	17 Chief Operations Officer	27 Career & Tech Ed	37 Guidance Services Elem	47 Math Sec	57 Bilingual/ELL	67 School Board President	77 Psychological Assess
	18 Chief Academic Officer	28 Technology Education	38 Guidance Services Sec	48 English/Lang Arts K-12	58 Special Education K-12	68 Teacher Personnel	78 Affirmative Action

Illinois School Directory

Washington County

Public Schs..Principal	Grd	Prgm	Enr/#Cls	SN
United Junior High Sch 2140 State Highway 135, Monmouth 61462 Christopher Schwarz	6-8	T	182 22	38% 309/734-8511
United North Elem Sch 411 W Hunt Ave, Alexis 61412 Maggie Wallace	PK-5	T	266 13	38% 309/482-3332 Fax 309/482-3341
United West Elem Sch 2138 State Highway 135, Monmouth 61462 Patrick Coate	PK-5	T	230 15	52% 309/734-8513 Fax 309/734-8515

WARREN CATHOLIC SCHOOLS

- **Diocese of Peoria Ed Office** PID: 00313338
  Listing includes only schools located in this county. See District Index for location of Diocesan Offices.

Catholic Schs..Principal	Grd	Prgm	Enr/#Cls	SN
Immaculate Conception Sch 115 N B St, Monmouth 61462 Randy Frakes	K-8		133 10	309/734-6037 Fax 309/734-6082

WARREN REGIONAL CENTERS

- **Delabar Cte System** PID: 04184385 309/734-7545
  105 Northeast St Ste 1, Monmouth 61462 Fax 309/734-2452

Dr Ashlee Spannagel 1,11,73

WASHINGTON COUNTY

WASHINGTON COUNTY SCHOOLS

County Schs..Principal	Grd	Prgm	Enr/#Cls	SN
Hoyleton Education Center 350 N Main St, Hoyleton 62803 Cynthia Sanders	Spec		38 7	69% 618/493-9019 Fax 618/493-7510

WASHINGTON PUBLIC SCHOOLS

- **Ashley Cmty Cons SD 15** PID: 00323230 618/485-6611
  450 N Third St, Ashley 62808 Fax 618/485-2124

Schools: 1 \ Teachers: 12 \ Students: 130 \ Special Ed Students: 21 \ LEP Students: 3 \ Ethnic: Hispanic 1%, Caucasian 99% \ Exp: $153 (Low) \ Poverty: 14% \ Title I: $41,332 \ Special Education: $35,000 \ Open-Close: 08/11 - 05/21 \ DTBP: $161 (High)

Brian Hodge .... 1,11 Stacie Schultze 4*
Jami Rollie .... 12* Jeff Stern 67
Angela Smith 84

Public Schs..Principal	Grd	Prgm	Enr/#Cls	SN
Ashley Elem Sch 450 N Third St, Ashley 62808 Brian Hodge	PK-8	T	130 9	54% 618/485-6611

- **Irvington Cmty Cons SD 11** PID: 00323278 618/249-6439
  500 Superior Street, Irvington 62848 Fax 618/249-6440

Schools: 1 \ Teachers: 5 \ Students: 60 \ Special Ed Students: 15 \ Ethnic: Asian 2%, African American 2%, Hispanic 3%, Caucasian 94% \ Exp: $246 (Med) \ Poverty: 14% \ Title I: $20,491 \ Special Education: $17,000 \ Open-Close: 08/17 - 06/01

Charles David Schulte .... 1,11,83 Summer Krunk 59
Sandra Neabuhr 67

Public Schs..Principal	Grd	Prgm	Enr/#Cls	SN
Irvington Elem Sch 500 Superior Street, Irvington 62848 David Schulte	PK-8	T	60 8	76% 618/249-6439

- **Nashville Cmty Cons SD 49** PID: 00323292 618/327-3055
  750 E Gorman St, Nashville 62263 Fax 618/327-4501

Schools: 1 \ Teachers: 39 \ Students: 585 \ Special Ed Students: 117 \ Ethnic: Asian 1%, African American 1%, Hispanic 3%, Native American: 1%, Caucasian 95% \ Exp: $211 (Med) \ Poverty: 9% \ Title I: $96,268 \ Special Education: $214,000 \ Open-Close: 08/13 - 05/25 \ DTBP: $180 (High)

Michael Brink .... 1,11,73,288 Lori McDonnough 2
Jason Finke .... 9,57,69* Charles Fairbanks 12,275*
David Engele .... 67 Annette Harper 274*

Public Schs..Principal	Grd	Prgm	Enr/#Cls	SN
Nashville Grade Sch 750 E Gorman St, Nashville 62263 Charles Fairbanks	PK-8		585 28	38% 618/327-4304 Fax 618/327-4503

- **Nashville Cmty HSD 99** PID: 00323319 618/327-8286
  1300 S Mill St, Nashville 62263 Fax 618/327-4512

Schools: 1 \ Teachers: 26 \ Students: 410 \ Special Ed Students: 76 \ LEP Students: 3 \ Ethnic: African American 1%, Hispanic 1%, Caucasian 98% \ Exp: $272 (Med) \ Poverty: 6% \ Title I: $45,972 \ Special Education: $68,000 \ Open-Close: 08/13 - 05/25 \ DTBP: $159 (High) \ 📘 🐦

Brad Turner .... 1 Tammy Roskowski 2
Paula Fark .... 4* Alicia Heggemeier 6*
Melissa Harriss .... 7,83,85 Leann White 11,275*
Paul Welte .... 16,73,295,296* Tesha Maschhoff 38,69*
Jennifer Maschhoff ...... 60* Shawn Cook 67

Public Schs..Principal	Grd	Prgm	Enr/#Cls	SN
Nashville High Sch 1300 S Mill St, Nashville 62263 Mark Begando	9-12	TV	410 40	28% 618/327-8286

Wayne County
Market Data Retrieval

- **Oakdale Cmty Cons Sch Dist 1** PID: 00323333   618/329-5292
  280 E Main St, Oakdale 62268   Fax 618/329-5545

Schools: 1 \ **Teachers:** 7 \ **Students:** 69 \ **Special Ed Students:** 12 \ **Ethnic:** Caucasian 100% \ **Exp:** $115 (Low) \ **Poverty:** 7% \ **Special Education:** $33,000 \ **Open-Close:** 08/12 - 05/14 \ **DTBP:** $185 (High)

Charles Peterson 1,11	Jayme Schoenherr 2
Mary Cotton 59*	Jeff Bergmann 67
Allison Moran 73*	

Public Schs..Principal	Grd	Prgm	Enr/#Cls	SN	
Oakdale Elem Sch 280 E Main St, Oakdale 62268 Ryan Wamser	K-8		69 4	49%	618/329-5292

- **West Washington Co Cmty SD 10** PID: 00323357   618/243-6454
  400 S Hanover St, Okawville 62271   Fax 618/243-2400

Schools: 2 \ **Teachers:** 41 \ **Students:** 544 \ **Special Ed Students:** 104 \ **LEP Students:** 8 \ **College-Bound:** 82% \ **Ethnic:** Asian 1%, African American 1%, Hispanic 3%, Caucasian 96% \ **Exp:** $180 (Low) \ **Poverty:** 8% \ **Title I:** $66,904 \ **Special Education:** $148,000 \ **Open-Close:** 08/17 - 05/21 \ **DTBP:** $187 (High)

Scott Fuhrhop 1	Melissa Leadendecker 2
Gene Brammeier 3*	Jon Kraus 6*
Leon Spinka 11,270*	Keith Senior 27,83,85,88*
Tricia Schleifer 36,83,275*	Kurt Heckert 67
Jane Ford 73,286*	

Public Schs..Principal	Grd	Prgm	Enr/#Cls	SN	
Okawville Grade Sch 400 S Hanover St, Okawville 62271 Leon Spinka	PK-6		278 16	30%	618/243-6157 Fax 618/243-9066
Okawville Jr Sr High Sch 400 S Hanover St, Okawville 62271 Keith Senior	7-12	V	266 25	31%	618/243-5201 Fax 618/243-6110

WASHINGTON CATHOLIC SCHOOLS

- **Diocese of Belleville Ed Off** PID: 00317671
  Listing includes only schools located in this county. See District Index for location of Diocesan Offices.

Catholic Schs..Principal	Grd	Prgm	Enr/#Cls	SN	
St Ann Sch 675 S Mill St, Nashville 62263 Jennifer Mason	K-8		93 9		618/327-8741 Fax 618/327-4904

WASHINGTON PRIVATE SCHOOLS

Private Schs..Principal	Grd	Prgm	Enr/#Cls	SN	
Immanuel Lutheran Sch 606 S Hanover St, Okawville 62271 Dr Dennis Fancher	PK-8		64 6		618/243-6142 Fax 618/243-6562
Trinity Lutheran Sch 155 N Main St, Hoyleton 62803 Chris Dehning	PK-8		75 5		618/493-7754

Trinity-St John Lutheran Sch   PK-8   118   618/327-8561
680 W Walnut St, Nashville 62263   8
Amy Kurtz

WAYNE COUNTY

WAYNE PUBLIC SCHOOLS

- **Fairfield Cmty High SD 225** PID: 00323515   618/842-2649
  300 W King St, Fairfield 62837   Fax 618/842-5187

Schools: 1 \ **Teachers:** 24 \ **Students:** 430 \ **Special Ed Students:** 58 \ **College-Bound:** 10% \ **Ethnic:** African American 2%, Hispanic 1%, Caucasian 97% \ **Exp:** $267 (Med) \ **Poverty:** 17% \ **Title I:** $129,574 \ **Special Education:** $103,000 \ **Open-Close:** 08/17 - 05/28 \ **DTBP:** $186 (High)

Jill Fulkerson 1,11	Rhonda Koker 2*
Jeff Heisner 3*	Stephanie Johnson 4*
Dennis Gifford 5*	Bob Wells 6*
Jala Taylor 7	Brenda Simpson 16
Lori Robson 38*	Michelle Richards 60,88*
Chris Miller 67	Marc Leighty 73,286*
Becky August 90*	

Public Schs..Principal	Grd	Prgm	Enr/#Cls	SN	
Fairfield Cmty High Sch 300 W King St, Fairfield 62837 Jill Fulkerson	9-12	AV	430 45	47%	618/842-2649

- **Fairfield Pub Sch District 112** PID: 00323486   618/842-6501
  806 N 1st St, Fairfield 62837   Fax 618/842-2932

Schools: 2 \ **Teachers:** 43 \ **Students:** 700 \ **Special Ed Students:** 157 \ **Ethnic:** Asian 1%, African American 4%, Hispanic 1%, Caucasian 94% \ **Exp:** $301 (High) \ **Poverty:** 31% \ **Title I:** $363,856 \ **Special Education:** $195,000 \ **Open-Close:** 08/17 - 05/28 \ **DTBP:** $174 (High)

Scott England 1,11	Kathy Schmitz 2
Norlyn Crandall 5	Amy Duckworth 59*
Dan Coomer 67	Rhonda Clark 73*

Public Schs..Principal	Grd	Prgm	Enr/#Cls	SN	
Center St Elem Sch 200 W Center St, Fairfield 62837 April Smith	4-8	T	323 30	63%	618/842-2679 Fax 618/842-6609
North Side Elem Sch 806 N 1st St, Fairfield 62837 Kristina Gardner	PK-3	T	346 13	43%	618/847-4341

- **Geff Cmty Cons School Dist 14** PID: 00323539   618/897-2465
  201 E Lafayette St, Geff 62842   Fax 618/897-2565

Schools: 1 \ **Teachers:** 13 \ **Students:** 92 \ **Special Ed Students:** 20 \ **Ethnic:** Hispanic 2%, Caucasian 98% \ **Exp:** $280 (Med) \ **Poverty:** 22% \ **Title I:** $38,433 \ **Special Education:** $26,000 \ **Open-Close:** 08/17 - 05/18

Jill Barger 1,11,84	Bryce Kovacichi 6,35,73

1	Superintendent	8	Curric/Instruct K-12	19	Chief Financial Officer	29	Family/Consumer Science	39	Social Studies K-12	49	English/Lang Arts Elem	59	Special Education Elem	69	Academic Assessment
2	Bus/Finance/Purchasing	9	Curric/Instruct Elem	20	Art K-12	30	Adult Education	40	Social Studies Elem	50	English/Lang Arts Sec	60	Special Education Sec	70	Research/Development
3	Buildings And Grounds	10	Curric/Instruct Sec	21	Art Elem	31	Career/Sch-to-Work K-12	41	Social Studies Sec	51	Reading K-12	61	Foreign/World Lang K-12	71	Public Information
4	Food Service	11	Federal Program	22	Art Sec	32	Career/Sch-to-Work Elem	42	Science K-12	52	Reading Elem	62	Foreign/World Lang Elem	72	Summer School
5	Transportation	12	Title I	23	Music K-12	33	Career/Sch-to-Work Sec	43	Science Elem	53	Reading Sec	63	Foreign/World Lang Sec	73	Instructional Tech
6	Athletic	13	Title V	24	Music Elem	34	Early Childhood Ed	44	Science Sec	54	Remedial Reading K-12	64	Religious Education K-12	74	Inservice Training
7	Health Services	15	Asst Superintendent	25	Music Sec	35	Health/Phys Education	45	Math K-12	55	Remedial Reading Elem	65	Religious Education Elem	75	Marketing/Distributive
		16	Instructional Media Svcs	26	Business Education	36	Guidance Services K-12	46	Math Elem	56	Remedial Reading Sec	66	Religious Education Sec	76	Info Systems
		17	Chief Operations Officer	27	Career & Tech Ed	37	Guidance Services Elem	47	Math Sec	57	Bilingual/Fl I	67	School Board President	77	Psychological Assess
		18	Chief Academic Officer	28	Technology Education	38	Guidance Services Sec	48	English/Lang Arts K-12	58	Special Education K-12	68	Teacher Personnel	78	Affirmative Action

Illinois School Directory   White County

Herb Fenton 6   Roy Keith Estheimer 67

Public Schs..Principal	Grd	Prgm	Enr/#Cls	SN	
Geff Elem Sch 201 E Lafayette St, Geff 62842 Jill Barger	K-8	T	92 9	47%	618/897-2465

● **Jasper Cmty Cons Sch Dist 17** PID: 00323553   618/842-3048
2030 County Road 1020 N, Fairfield 62837   Fax 618/842-3289

Schools: 1 \ **Teachers:** 13 \ **Students:** 185 \ **Special Ed Students:** 35 \
Ethnic: African American 1%, Hispanic 1%, Caucasian 98% \ **Exp:** $381
(High) \ **Poverty:** 21% \ **Title I:** $63,971 \ **Special Education:** $53,000 \
Open-Close: 08/14 - 05/14 \ **DTBP:** $168 (High)

Shari Berger 1,11,73,83   Eric Basnett 6*
Cindy Ellis .... 9,69*   Hannah Harrison 16,82,286
Derek Demaret 67

Public Schs..Principal	Grd	Prgm	Enr/#Cls	SN	
Jasper Elem Sch 2030 County Road 1020 N, Fairfield 62837 Dr Jon Julius	K-8	T	185 10	37%	618/842-3048

● **New Hope Cmty Cons Sch Dist 6** PID: 00323591   618/842-3296
1804 County Road 445 N, Fairfield 62837   Fax 618/847-7000

Schools: 1 \ **Teachers:** 13 \ **Students:** 180 \
Special Ed Students: 28 \ **Ethnic:** African American 1%, Native American:
1%, Caucasian 99% \ **Exp:** $291 (Med) \ **Poverty:** 13% \ **Title I:** $36,507 \
Special Education: $40,000 \ **Open-Close:** 08/10 - 05/19

Julie Harrelson 1,11   Kevin Greathouse 6*
Jason Simpson 67   Noah West 73

Public Schs..Principal	Grd	Prgm	Enr/#Cls	SN	
New Hope Elem Sch 1804 County Road 445 N, Fairfield 62837 Julie Harrelson	PK-8	T	180 9	40%	618/842-3296

● **North Wayne Cmty Unit SD 200** PID: 00323436   618/673-2151
206 Mulberry St, Cisne 62823   Fax 618/673-2152

Schools: 4 \ **Teachers:** 39 \ **Students:** 383 \ **Special Ed Students:** 71
\ **LEP Students:** 3 \ **College-Bound:** 75% \ **Ethnic:** Hispanic 1%,
Caucasian 99% \ **Exp:** $306 (High) \ **Poverty:** 14% \ **Title I:** $106,969 \
Special Education: $99,000 \ **Open-Close:** 08/17 - 05/27 \ **DTBP:** $168
(High)

Lucas Schroeder 1,11   Adam Ellis 6*
Rebecca Eskew 36,58,83,88   Sonny Smith 67
Shawn Levi 73,84,295

Public Schs..Principal	Grd	Prgm	Enr/#Cls	SN	
Cisne High Sch South Route 45, Cisne 62823 Kevin Bowen	9-12	V	118 13	53%	618/673-2154 Fax 618/673-2155
Cisne Middle Sch 206 Mulberry St, Cisne 62823 Joyce Carson	5-8	T	108 10	53%	618/673-2156 Fax 618/673-2186
Johnsonville Elem Sch Route 161, Johnsonville 62850 Janice Brashear	PK-4	T	87 6	46%	618/673-3044 Fax 618/673-3094
Mt Erie Elem Sch 300 School Dr, Mount Erie 62446 Donna Williams	K-4	T	63 5	38%	618/854-2611 Fax 618/854-2600

● **Wayne City Cmty Unit SD 100** PID: 00323618   618/895-3103
408 E Mill St, Wayne City 62895   Fax 618/895-2331

Schools: 2 \ **Teachers:** 39 \ **Students:** 530 \ **Special Ed Students:** 92
\ **College-Bound:** 76% \ **Ethnic:** African American 1%, Caucasian
99% \ **Exp:** $221 (Med) \ **Poverty:** 22% \ **Title I:** $262,642 \
Special Education: $145,000 \ **Open-Close:** 08/13 - 05/19 \ **DTBP:** $179
(High)

Myron Caudle 1,11,73   Kate Feather 2
David Garrison 3   Jake Talbert 6
Ruth Kissner .... 10,38,69,83*   Dana Smithpeters 12*
Crystal Slover .... 16*   Eric Lingafelter 27*
Beth Bowen .... 58*   Joe Coy 67
Jackie Matthews 270*

Public Schs..Principal	Grd	Prgm	Enr/#Cls	SN	
Wayne City Attendance Center 403 Mill St, Wayne City 62895 Tony Richardson	PK-8	T	382 17	50%	618/895-3103 Fax 618/952-2331
Wayne City High Sch 403 Mill St, Wayne City 62895 Eric Lingafelter	9-12	V	144 20	40%	618/895-3108 Fax 618/952-2331

WAYNE PRIVATE SCHOOLS

Private Schs..Principal	Grd	Prgm	Enr/#Cls	SN	
Orchardville Mennonite Sch 1046 County Highway 13, Keenes 62851 Gardell Strite	1-10		75 4		618/895-1327

WHITE COUNTY

WHITE PUBLIC SCHOOLS

● **Carmi-White Co School Dist 5** PID: 00323682   618/382-2341
211 W Robinson St, Carmi 62821   Fax 618/384-3207

Schools: 6 \ **Teachers:** 92 \ **Students:** 1,400 \ **Special Ed Students:** 290
\ **LEP Students:** 6 \ **College-Bound:** 74% \ **Ethnic:** Asian 1%, Hispanic
1%, Caucasian 98% \ **Exp:** $270 (Med) \ **Poverty:** 17% \ **Title I:** $474,735 \
Special Education: $470,000 \ **Open-Close:** 08/14 - 05/21 \ **DTBP:** $174
(High)

Bradley Lee 1,11   Shelia Napier 2
Randy Warrick .... 3*   Laura Goemaat 4
Bart King .... 5,10*   Kurt Simons 6
Jane Sykes 7   Dr Amy Dixon 8,57,69,74,271,285,288*
Amy Atteberry .... 10,11,34,88,275*   Jarrod Newell 10,27*
Robin Huggins .... 16,73,76,295,296,298*   Penny Gunter 38*
Amy Rice 58   Andy Accord 67
Leannette Lovell 83,270*

---

79 Student Personnel	91 Safety/Security	275 Response To Intervention	298 Grant Writer/Ptnrships	School Programs	Social Media
80 Driver Ed/Safety	92 Magnet School	277 Remedial Math K-12	750 Chief Innovation Officer	A = Alternative Program	▓ = Facebook
81 Gifted/Talented	93 Parental Involvement	280 Literacy Coach	751 Chief of Staff	G = Adult Classes	
82 Video Services	95 Tech Prep Program	285 STEM	752 Social Emotional Learning	M = Magnet Program	▓ = Twitter
83 Substance Abuse Prev	97 Chief Infomation Officer	286 Digital Learning		T = Title I Schoolwide	
84 Erate	98 Chief Technology Officer	288 Common Core Standards	Other School Types	V = Career & Tech Ed Programs	
85 AIDS Education	270 Accountability	294 Accountability	Ⓐ = Alternative School		
88 Alternative/At Risk	271 Migrant Education	295 Network System	Ⓒ = Charter School	New Schools are shaded	
89 Multi-Cultural Curriculum	273 Teacher Mentor	296 Title II Programs	Ⓜ = Magnet School	New Superintendents and Principals are bold	
90 Social Work	274 Before/After Sch	297 Webmaster	Ⓨ = Year-Round School	Personnel with email addresses are underscored	

IL—237

Whiteside County

Market Data Retrieval

Public Schs..Principal	Grd	Prgm	Enr/#Cls	SN	
Brownsville Attendance Center 1187 County Road 700 E, Carmi 62821 Kathy Price	Spec		64 7	78%	618/265-3256 Fax 618/265-3006
Carmi-White County High Sch 800 W Main St, Carmi 62821 Jarrod Newell	9-12	TV	350 30	48%	618/382-4661 Fax 618/382-2453
Carmi-White County Jr High Sch 800 W Main St, Carmi 62821 Bart King	7-8	T	187 22	61%	618/382-4661 Fax 618/382-2453
Jefferson Attendance Center 713 4th St, Carmi 62821 Dr Amy Dixon	2-3	T	227 10	66%	618/382-7016 Fax 618/382-7512
Lincoln Attendance Center 113 10th St, Carmi 62821 Dr Amy Dixon	PK-1	T	233 9	52%	618/384-3421 Fax 618/382-5138
Washington Attendance Center 205 W Main St, Carmi 62821 Amy Atteberry	4-6	T	345 10	56%	618/382-4631 Fax 618/384-2076

- **Grayville Cmty Unit Sch Dist 1** PID: 00323814 618/375-7114
  728 W North St, Grayville 62844 Fax 618/375-6521

Schools: 2 \ **Teachers:** 25 \ **Students:** 280 \ **Special Ed Students:** 63 \ **College-Bound:** 100% \ **Ethnic:** Caucasian 100% \ **Exp:** $376 (High) \ **Poverty:** 21% \ **Title I:** $111,320 \ **Special Education:** $74,000 \ **Open-Close:** 08/12 - 05/24

Julie Harlson .... 1,11,83 Maria Neeley 2
Shannon Reid ....3 Sara Putnay 4
Marc Stendeback ....6 Jennifer Neeley 7
Maranda Morris .... 12 Kathy Bishop 34
Kim Milligan ....36,69 Levi Johnson 58
Stephanie Hatcher .... 67 Pete Hall 76
Darleen Greer 752

Public Schs..Principal	Grd	Prgm	Enr/#Cls	SN	
Grayville Jr Sr High Sch 728 W North St, Grayville 62844 Julie Harrelson	7-12	TV	141 16	48%	618/375-7114 f t
Wells Elem Sch 704 W North St, Grayville 62844 Levi Johnson	PK-6	T	138 20	58%	618/375-7214 Fax 618/375-3575

- **Norris City-Omaha-Enfield SD 3** PID: 00323890 618/378-3222
  409 E 3rd St, Norris City 62869 Fax 618/378-3286

Schools: 3 \ **Teachers:** 54 \ **Students:** 675 \ **Special Ed Students:** 145 \ **College-Bound:** 69% \ **Ethnic:** Hispanic 1%, Caucasian 99% \ **Exp:** $367 (High) \ **Poverty:** 18% \ **Title I:** $218,967 \ **Special Education:** $218,000 \ **Open-Close:** 08/20 - 05/28

Matthew Vollman ....1,11 Jim Tucker 6*
Brad Wehlermann .... 10 Jill Pruitt 58*
Joe Lane .... 67 Annette Braden 69*
Kim Fuqua 83*

Public Schs..Principal	Grd	Prgm	Enr/#Cls	SN	
Booth Elem Sch 215 N 1st St, Enfield 62835 Carla Carter	PK-8		148 11	66%	618/963-2521 Fax 618/963-2716
Norris City-Omaha Elem Sch 580 US Highway 45 S, Norris City 62869 D Reavis	PK-8		378 20	39%	618/378-3212 Fax 618/378-3902
Norris City-Omaha-Enfield HS 205 E Eubanks St, Norris City 62869 Todd Haley	9-12	TV	190 20	42%	618/378-3312 Fax 618/378-3364

WHITE PRIVATE SCHOOLS

Private Schs..Principal	Grd	Prgm	Enr/#Cls	SN	
Carmi Christian Sch 907 State Route 14 W, Carmi 62821 Debbie Dolan	K-12		14		618/382-2807

WHITE REGIONAL CENTERS

- **Ohio-Wabash Valley Reg Voc Sys** PID: 04184440 618/378-2274
  800 S Division St, Norris City 62869 Fax 618/378-3058
  John Cummins 1

- **Wabash-Ohio Valley Sp Ed Dist** PID: 02182185 618/378-2131
  800 S Division St, Norris City 62869 Fax 618/378-3153
  David Kaytor .... 1,11 Brad Blades 2,15
  Jennifer Acord .... 15,74 Monica Girten 15

WHITESIDE COUNTY

WHITESIDE COUNTY SCHOOLS

County Schs..Principal	Grd	Prgm	Enr/#Cls	SN	
Whiteside Area Career Center 1608 5th Ave, Sterling 61081 Mary Stouffer	Voc	G	630 11	60%	815/626-5810 Fax 815/626-1001 f

WHITESIDE PUBLIC SCHOOLS

- **East Coloma-Nelson Cesd 20** PID: 00324088 815/625-4400
  1602 Dixon Rd, Rock Falls 61071 Fax 815/625-4624

Schools: 1 \ **Teachers:** 21 \ **Students:** 245 \ **Special Ed Students:** 47 \ **LEP Students:** 5 \ **Ethnic:** African American 3%, Hispanic 13%, Caucasian 84% \ **Exp:** $366 (High) \ **Poverty:** 15% \ **Title I:** $69,413 \ **Special Education:** $58,000 \ **Open-Close:** 08/13 - 05/18 \ **DTBP:** $42 (Low)

Christopher Lensing .... 1,11,73 Randy Hammelman 3*
Gwyn Brown .... 7* Nicole Sands 12*
Christopher Buikema 67

Public Schs..Principal	Grd	Prgm	Enr/#Cls	SN	
East Coloma-Nelson Elem Sch 1602 Dixon Rd, Rock Falls 61071 Andrew Blackert	K-8		245 19	49%	815/625-4400

---

1 Superintendent	8 Curric/Instruct K-12	19 Chief Financial Officer	29 Family/Consumer Science	39 Social Studies K-12	49 English/Lang Arts Elem	59 Special Education Elem	69 Academic Assessment
2 Bus/Finance/Purchasing	9 Curric/Instruct Elem	20 Art K-12	30 Adult Education	40 Social Studies Elem	50 English/Lang Arts Sec	60 Special Education Sec	70 Research/Development
3 Buildings And Grounds	10 Curric/Instruct Sec	21 Art Elem	31 Career/Sch-to-Work K-12	41 Social Studies Sec	51 Reading K-12	61 Foreign/World Lang K-12	71 Public Information
4 Food Service	11 Federal Program	22 Art Sec	32 Career/Sch-to-Work Elem	42 Science K-12	52 Reading Elem	62 Foreign/World Lang Elem	72 Summer School
5 Transportation	12 Title I	23 Music K-12	33 Career/Sch-to-Work Sec	43 Science Elem	53 Reading Sec	63 Foreign/World Lang Sec	73 Instructional Tech
6 Athletic	13 Title V	24 Music Elem	34 Early Childhood Ed	44 Science Sec	54 Remedial Reading K-12	64 Religious Education K-12	74 Inservice Training
7 Health Services	15 Asst Superintendent	25 Music Sec	35 Health/Phys Education	45 Math K-12	55 Remedial Reading Elem	65 Religious Education Elem	75 Marketing/Distributive
	16 Instructional Media Svcs	26 Business Education	36 Guidance Services K-12	46 Math Elem	56 Remedial Reading Sec	66 Religious Education Sec	76 Info Systems
	17 Chief Operations Officer	27 Career & Tech Ed	37 Guidance Services Elem	47 Math Sec	57 Bilingual/ELL	67 School Board President	77 Psychological Assess
	18 Chief Academic Officer	28 Technology Education	38 Guidance Services Sec	48 English/Lang Arts K-12	58 Special Education K-12	68 Teacher Personnel	78 Affirmative Action

Illinois School Directory — Whiteside County

Erie Cmty School District 1 PID: 00324105
520 5th Ave, Erie 61250
309/659-2239
Fax 309/659-2230

Schools: 3 \ **Teachers:** 68 \ **Students:** 650 \ **Special Ed Students:** 109 \ **College-Bound:** 64% \ **Ethnic:** Hispanic 4%, Caucasian 95% \ **Exp:** $484 (High) \ **Poverty:** 9% \ **Title I:** $77,071 \ **Special Education:** $256,000 \ **Open-Close:** 08/14 - 05/20 \ **DTBP:** $174 (High)

Marty Felefena	1	Michelle Misfeldt	2
Josh Vandewostine	3	Ella Bright	4*
Dave Deshane	5	Brian Howell	6*
Kali Livengood	11,51,54,296*	Barbara Proeger	16,82*
Chad Miner	67	William Patton	73
Chuck Milem	83		

Public Schs..Principal	Grd	Prgm	Enr/#Cls	SN	
Erie Elem Sch 605 6th Ave, Erie 61250 Kali Livengood	PK-4	T	266 25	25%	309/659-2239 Fax 309/659-2588
Erie High Sch 435 6th Ave, Erie 61250 Tim McConnel	9-12	V	204 14	28%	309/659-2239 Fax 309/659-2514
Erie Middle Sch 500 5th Ave, Erie 61250 Charles Milem	5-8		175 12	31%	309/659-2239 Fax 309/659-7254

Montmorency Cmty Cons SD 145 PID: 00324167
9415 Hoover Rd, Rock Falls 61071
815/625-6616
Fax 815/625-8432

Schools: 1 \ **Teachers:** 22 \ **Students:** 230 \ **Special Ed Students:** 41 \ **Ethnic:** African American 1%, Hispanic 17%, Caucasian 82% \ **Exp:** $111 (Low) \ **Poverty:** 14% \ **Title I:** $84,458 \ **Special Education:** $59,000 \ **Open-Close:** 08/19 - 05/21

Alex Moore	1	Tammie Prescott	2
Tory Escamilla	6*	Angela Howard	12*
Kim Kobbeman	35*	Joe Schueller	67
Josh Petty	73*		

Public Schs..Principal	Grd	Prgm	Enr/#Cls	SN	
Montmorency Elem Sch 9415 Hoover Rd, Rock Falls 61071 Megan Dillon	PK-8		230 25	37%	815/625-6616 Fax 815/645-8432

Morrison Cmty Unit Sch Dist 6 PID: 00324181
300 Academic Dr, Morrison 61270
815/772-2064
Fax 815/772-2531

Schools: 4 \ **Teachers:** 70 \ **Students:** 1,033 \ **Special Ed Students:** 153 \ **College-Bound:** 75% \ **Ethnic:** Asian 1%, African American 1%, Hispanic 5%, Caucasian 94% \ **Exp:** $128 (Low) \ **Poverty:** 10% \ **Title I:** $137,916 \ **Special Education:** $289,000 \ **Open-Close:** 08/20 - 05/27 \ **DTBP:** $178 (High) f t

Scott Vance	1	Kailay Hanson	2
Dean Wallace	3	Lynelle Criss	4*
Gregg Dolan	6*	Andy Harridge	9,13,83
Dwayne Shaper	16,73,295	Christine Tichler	59*
Cathleen Vegter	67	Joe Robbins	275*

Public Schs..Principal	Grd	Prgm	Enr/#Cls	SN	
Morrison High Sch 643 Genesee Ave, Morrison 61270 Cory Bielema	9-12	V	269 30	33%	815/772-4071
Morrison Junior High Sch 300 Academic Dr, Morrison 61270 Joe Robbins	6-8		239 20	40%	815/772-7264
Northside Elem Sch 520 N Genesee St, Morrison 61270 Andy Harridge	PK-2		249 13	29%	815/772-2153 Fax 815/772-4952
Southside Elem Sch 100 Academic Dr, Morrison 61270 Jeremy Keesee	3-5		247 12	41%	815/772-2183 Fax 815/772-2371

Prophetstown-Lyndon-Tampico 3 PID: 00324260
79 Grove St, Prophetstown 61277
815/537-5101
Fax 815/537-5102

Schools: 4 \ **Teachers:** 60 \ **Students:** 800 \ **Special Ed Students:** 183 \ **College-Bound:** 55% \ **Ethnic:** African American 1%, Hispanic 4%, Caucasian 95% \ **Exp:** $196 (Low) \ **Poverty:** 14% \ **Title I:** $237,477 \ **Special Education:** $274,000 \ **Open-Close:** 08/24 - 05/24 \ **DTBP:** $167 (High)

John Petzke	1,11	Geri Lundquist	4
Ginger Blasdell	5	Laura Crisp	16
Amanda Dybek	23,38,69	Angela Glassburn	23,38,69
James Melton	67		

Public Schs..Principal	Grd	Prgm	Enr/#Cls	SN	
Plt Middle Sch 38 Ferry St, Prophetstown 61277 Keith Stewart	6-8	T	162 20	58%	815/537-5084 Fax 815/438-3095
Prophetstown Elem Sch 301 W 3rd St, Prophetstown 61277 Justin Hovey	PK-5	T	157 15	54%	815/537-2345 Fax 815/537-2417
Prophetstown High Sch 310 W Riverside Dr, Prophetstown 61277 Keith Stewart	9-12	TV	212 22	48%	815/537-5084 Fax 815/537-5162
Tampico Elem Sch 304 Kimbely St, Tampico 61283 Jim Geer	PK-5	T	180 11	59%	815/438-2255 Fax 815/438-5010

River Bend Cmty School Dist 2 PID: 00324337
1110 3rd St, Fulton 61252
815/589-2711
Fax 815/589-4630

Schools: 4 \ **Teachers:** 63 \ **Students:** 900 \ **Special Ed Students:** 132 \ **College-Bound:** 51% \ **Ethnic:** Hispanic 3%, Caucasian 97% \ **Exp:** $150 (Low) \ **Poverty:** 10% \ **Title I:** $139,268 \ **Special Education:** $397,000 \ **Open-Close:** 08/19 - 05/25 \ **DTBP:** $19 (Low)

Darryl Hogue	1,11	Rachel Snyder	2
Gary Wolfe	3	Stacey Collachia	4
Dale Wiersema	5	Patrick Henrekin	6
Amy Heyvaert	16*	Neal Luker	31*
Shelby Wilkens	34	Dan Portz	67
Cheryl Piercy	73,84	Bob Gosch	270
Cheryl Piercy	295*	Emily Johnson	297

Public Schs..Principal	Grd	Prgm	Enr/#Cls	SN	
Fulton Elem Sch 1301 7th Ave, Fulton 61252 Jeff Hoese	K-5	T	407 19	37%	815/589-2911 Fax 815/589-4614
Fulton High Sch 1207 12th St, Fulton 61252 Bob Gosch	9-12		277 34	32%	815/589-3511 Fax 815/589-3412
Fulton Pre-School 1217 14th St, Fulton 61252 Elizabeth Clark	PK-PK		47 1		815/589-2309
River Bend Middle Sch 415 12th St, Fulton 61252 Kathleen Schipper	6-8	T	206 14	39%	815/589-2611 Fax 815/589-3130

---

79 Student Personnel	91 Safety/Security	275 Response To Intervention	298 Grant Writer/Ptnrships
80 Driver Ed/Safety	92 Magnet School	277 Remedial Math K-12	750 Chief Innovation Officer
81 Gifted/Talented	93 Parental Involvement	280 Literacy Coach	751 Chief of Staff
82 Video Services	95 Tech Prep Program	285 STEM	752 Social Emotional Learning
83 Substance Abuse Prev	97 Chief Infomation Officer	286 Digital Learning	
84 Erate	98 Chief Technology Officer	288 Common Core Standards	
85 AIDS Education	270 Character Education	294 Accountability	
88 Alternative/At Risk	271 Migrant Education	295 Network System	
89 Multi-Cultural Curriculum	273 Teacher Mentor	296 Title II Programs	
90 Social Work	274 Before/After Sch	297 Webmaster	

School Programs
A = Alternative Program
G = Adult Classes
M = Magnet Program
T = Title I Schoolwide
V = Career & Tech Ed Programs

Other School Types
Ⓐ = Alternative School
Ⓒ = Charter School
Ⓜ = Magnet School
Ⓨ = Year-Round School

Social Media
f = Facebook
t = Twitter

New Schools are shaded
New Superintendents and Principals are bold
Personnel with email addresses are underscored

IL-239

Whiteside County

- **Rock Falls Elem Sch Dist 13** PID: 00324416 815/626-2604
  602 4th Ave, Rock Falls 61071 Fax 815/626-2627

Schools: 4 \ **Teachers:** 68 \ **Students:** 1,050 \ **Special Ed Students:** 194 \ **LEP Students:** 51 \ **Ethnic:** Asian 1%, African American 4%, Hispanic 31%, Native American: 1%, Caucasian 65% \ **Exp:** $263 (Med) \ **Poverty:** 26% \ **Title I:** $491,948 \ **Special Education:** $291,000 \ **Open-Close:** 08/12 - 05/19 \ **DTBP:** $148 (High) \

Dan Arickx 1,11	Max Crossland 3*
Carolyn Clifton 4*	Scott Rogers 6*
Tara Kristoff 9,74*	Paula Garcia 57,271*
Troy Ebenezer 67	Steve Kelmen 73,295*
Kyle Ackman 83,270*	Rhonda Conklen 274*

Public Schs..Principal	Grd	Prgm	Enr/#Cls	SN	
Dillon Elem Sch 1901 8th Ave, Rock Falls 61071 Roy Calkins	K-2	T	275 16	71%	815/625-3356 Fax 815/625-2943
Merrill Elem Sch 600 4th Ave, Rock Falls 61071 Brody Rude	3-5	T	286 13	70%	815/625-4634 Fax 815/625-1747
Riverdale Preschool Center 3505 Prophet Rd, Rock Falls 61071 Chelese Palmer	PK-PK	T	181	80%	815/625-5280 Fax 815/625-5316
Rock Falls Middle Sch 1701 12th Ave, Rock Falls 61071 Kyle Ackman	6-8	T	284 17	65%	815/626-2626 Fax 815/626-3198

- **Rock Falls Twp High SD 301** PID: 00324466 815/625-3886
  101 12th Ave, Rock Falls 61071 Fax 815/625-3889

Schools: 1 \ **Teachers:** 40 \ **Students:** 630 \ **Special Ed Students:** 130 \ **LEP Students:** 8 \ **College-Bound:** 54% \ **Ethnic:** African American 2%, Hispanic 25%, Caucasian 73% \ **Exp:** $248 (Med) \ **Poverty:** 17% \ **Title I:** $203,995 \ **Special Education:** $131,000 \ **Open-Close:** 08/17 - 05/19 \ **DTBP:** $175 (High) \

Ron McCord 1	Lori Berogan 2*
Bryan Berogan 3*	Mike Berentes 11,69,83,273,298*
Kristina Schauff 16*	Jason Sands 33,38,79,85,88,270*
Kevin Parker 33*	Nick Velazquez 57
Merle Galrap 67	

Public Schs..Principal	Grd	Prgm	Enr/#Cls	SN	
Rock Falls Township High Sch 101 12th Ave, Rock Falls 61071 Mike Berentes	9-12	AT	630 45	51%	815/625-3886

- **Sterling Cmty Unit Sch Dist 5** PID: 00323929 815/626-5050
  410 E Le Fevre Rd, Sterling 61081 Fax 815/622-4156

Schools: 6 \ **Teachers:** 182 \ **Students:** 3,500 \ **Special Ed Students:** 670 \ **LEP Students:** 172 \ **College-Bound:** 56% \ **Ethnic:** Asian 1%, African American 3%, Hispanic 37%, Caucasian 59% \ **Exp:** $282 (Med) \ **Poverty:** 16% \ **Title I:** $913,146 \ **Special Education:** $1,100,000 \ **Bilingual Education:** $69,000 \ **Open-Close:** 08/19 - 05/28 \ **DTBP:** $198 (High) \

Dr Tad Everett 1	Tim Schwingle 2
Wayne Cherry 2	Brian Musselman 3
Jim MacNamara 4	Greg King 6*
Rebecca Haas 8,11,58,72,81*	Sara Dail 15,68,273
Heather Johnson 16*	Karina Valdez 57
Paul Sandefer 67	Matthew Fuller 76
Jon Schlemer 80*	Joe Ghibellini 84

Public Schs..Principal	Grd	Prgm	Enr/#Cls	SN	
Challand Middle Sch 1700 6th Ave, Sterling 61081 Lindsy Stumpenhorst	6-8	T	765 50	61%	815/626-3300 Fax 815/622-4173
Franklin Elem Sch 1510 E 25th St, Sterling 61081 Brooke Dir	PK-2	T	399 18	55%	815/625-5755 Fax 815/622-4187
Jefferson Elem Sch 806 E Le Fevre Rd, Sterling 61081 Heather Wittenauer	PK-2	T	436 20	67%	815/625-6402 Fax 815/622-4191
Lincoln Elem Sch 1501 E 6th St, Sterling 61081 Cindy Frank	3-5	T	340 13	70%	815/625-1449 Fax 815/622-4196
Sterling High Sch 1608 4th Ave, Sterling 61081 Jason Austin	9-12	T	1,017 70	56%	815/625-6800 Fax 815/622-4157
Washington Elem Sch 815 W Le Fevre Rd, Sterling 61081 Liz Engstrom	3-5	T	381 16	63%	815/625-2372 Fax 815/622-4199

WHITESIDE CATHOLIC SCHOOLS

- **Diocese of Rockford Ed Office** PID: 00328345
  Listing includes only schools located in this county. See District Index for location of Diocesan Offices.

Catholic Schs..Principal	Grd	Prgm	Enr/#Cls	SN	
Newman Central Catholic Sch 1101 W 23rd St, Sterling 61081 Jennifer Oetting	9-12		254 18		815/625-0500 Fax 815/625-8444
St Andrew Catholic Sch 701 11th Ave, Rock Falls 61071 Deacon Lemmer	PK-8		206 10		815/625-1456 Fax 815/625-1724
St Mary's Sch 6 W 6th St, Sterling 61081 Particia Wackenhut	PK-8		268 14		815/625-2253 Fax 815/625-8942

WHITESIDE PRIVATE SCHOOLS

Private Schs..Principal	Grd	Prgm	Enr/#Cls	SN	
Christ Lutheran Sch 2000 18th Ave, Sterling 61081 Russell Helbig	PK-8		90 10		815/625-3800 Fax 815/625-3585
Fairfield Amish Mennonite Sch RR 2, Tampico 61283 Gordon Headings	1-8		86 5		815/716-3428
Unity Christian Sch 711 10th St, Fulton 61252 Chris Pluister	PK-12		180 11		815/589-3912 Fax 815/589-4430

WHITESIDE REGIONAL CENTERS

- **Bi-County Special Ed Co-op** PID: 02229018 815/622-0858
  2317 E Lincolnway Ste A, Sterling 61081 Fax 815/622-3182

Laurie Heston 1

1	Superintendent	8	Curric/Instruct K-12	19	Chief Financial Officer	29	Family/Consumer Science	39	Social Studies K-12	49	English/Lang Arts Elem	59	Special Education Elem	69	Academic Assessment
2	Bus/Finance/Purchasing	9	Curric/Instruct Elem	20	Art K-12	30	Adult Education	40	Social Studies Elem	50	English/Lang Arts Sec	60	Special Education Sec	70	Research/Development
3	Buildings And Grounds	10	Curric/Instruct Sec	21	Art Elem	31	Career/Sch-to-Work K-12	41	Social Studies Sec	51	Reading K-12	61	Foreign/World Lang K-12	71	Public Information
4	Food Service	11	Federal Program	22	Art Sec	32	Career/Sch-to-Work Elem	42	Science K-12	52	Reading Elem	62	Foreign/World Lang Elem	72	Summer School
5	Transportation	12	Title I	23	Music K-12	33	Career/Sch-to-Work Sec	43	Science Elem	53	Reading Sec	63	Foreign/World Lang Sec	73	Instructional Tech
6	Athletic	13	Title V	24	Music Elem	34	Early Childhood Ed	44	Science Sec	54	Remedial Reading K-12	64	Religious Education K-12	74	Inservice Training
7	Health Services	15	Asst Superintendent	25	Music Sec	35	Health/Phys Education	45	Math K-12	55	Remedial Reading Elem	65	Religious Education Elem	75	Marketing/Distributive
		16	Instructional Media Svcs	26	Business Education	36	Guidance Services K-12	46	Math Elem	56	Remedial Reading Sec	66	Religious Education Sec	76	Info Systems
		17	Chief Operations Officer	27	Career & Tech Ed	37	Guidance Services Elem	47	Math Sec	57	Bilingual/ELL	67	School Board President	77	Psychological Assess
		18	Chief Academic Officer	28	Technology Education	38	Guidance Services Sec	48	English/Lang Arts K-12	58	Special Education K-12	68	Teacher Personnel	78	Affirmative Action

Illinois School Directory — Will County

- **Regional Office of Ed 47** PID: 02098209 815/625-1495
  1001 W 23rd St, Sterling 61081 Fax 815/625-1625
  Robert Sondgeroth 1   Sherrie Pistole 2
  Chris Tennyson 15   Paulett Bendixon 73,76,295

- **Whiteside Regional Voc System** PID: 04180224 815/626-5810
  1608 5th Ave, Sterling 61081 Fax 815/626-1001
  Josh Johnson 1

WILL COUNTY

WILL COUNTY SCHOOLS

County Schs..Principal	Grd	Prgm	Enr/#Cls	SN	
Joseph E Fisher Sch 1205 N Larkin Ave, Joliet 60435 Deborah Nagel	Spec		50 6	65%	815/744-8520 Fax 815/744-8525
Ⓐ Lincoln Sch 960 Royce Ave, Joliet 60432 Scott Pritchard	6-12		100		815/774-8900 Fax 815/722-3352
M P Mackay Education Center HS 516 S Cedar Rd, New Lenox 60451 Marie Goulet-Raffety	Spec	A	50 7	36%	815/463-8068 Fax 815/463-8072
Wilco Area Career Center 500 Wilco Blvd, Romeoville 60446 Bosa Goodale	Voc		350 16		815/838-6941 Fax 815/838-1163

WILL PUBLIC SCHOOLS

- **Beecher Cmty Sch Dist 200-U** PID: 00324533 708/946-2266
  538 Miller St, Beecher 60401 Fax 708/377-6849

  Schools: 3 \ **Teachers:** 66 \ **Students:** 1,100 \ **Special Ed Students:** 166 \ **LEP Students:** 36 \ **College-Bound:** 91% \ **Ethnic:** Asian 1%, African American 3%, Hispanic 19%, Caucasian 77% \ **Exp:** $242 (Med) \ **Poverty:** 6% \ **Title I:** $107,784 \ **Special Education:** $493,000 \ **Open-Close:** 08/21 - 06/02 \ **DTBP:** $231 (High)

  Bradley Cox 1,11,83   Marla Heldt 2,5
  Mike Stanula 3   Robert Ogdon 6
  Nicole Black .... 9,69,270*   Jack Gaham 10
  Vicki Ploense .... 16*   Larry Hermen 67
  Joseph Duncan 73,286

Public Schs..Principal	Grd	Prgm	Enr/#Cls	SN	
Beecher Elem Sch 629 Penfield St, Beecher 60401 Nicole Black	PK-5		442 23	29%	708/946-2202 Fax 708/946-6075
Beecher High Sch 538 Miller St, Beecher 60401 Jack Gaham	9-12	V	352 30	25%	708/946-2266 Fax 708/946-3403
Beecher Junior High Sch 101 E Church Rd, Beecher 60401 Mike Meyer	6-8		237 17	27%	708/946-3412 Fax 708/946-2763

- **Chaney-Monge School Dist 88** PID: 00324583 815/722-6673
  400 Elsie Ave, Crest Hill 60403 Fax 815/722-7814

  Schools: 1 \ **Teachers:** 30 \ **Students:** 500 \ **Special Ed Students:** 104 \ **LEP Students:** 96 \ **Ethnic:** African American 15%, Hispanic 47%, Caucasian 39% \ **Exp:** $364 (High) \ **Poverty:** 16% \ **Title I:** $139,559 \ **Special Education:** $263,000 \ **Open-Close:** 08/19 - 05/27 \ **DTBP:** $233 (High)

  Andy Siegfried 1,83   Mary Ann Egizio 2
  Larry Contos 3   Jackie Hall 9,11,69,85,270,288*
  Mary Waddell .... 16*   Antonia Galen 34,59,273
  Jason Gentile 35   Misty Kosek 37*
  Lauren Ligammari .... 57*   Drew Lopez 67
  Debbie Shields .... 73*   Leticia McCullough 271*

Public Schs..Principal	Grd	Prgm	Enr/#Cls	SN	
Chaney Monge Sch 400 Elsie Ave, Crest Hill 60403 Jackie Hall	PK-8	AT	500 20	78%	815/722-6673

- **Channahon School District 17** PID: 00324612 815/467-4315
  24920 S Sage St, Channahon 60410 Fax 815/467-4343

  Schools: 4 \ **Teachers:** 82 \ **Students:** 1,234 \ **Special Ed Students:** 142 \ **LEP Students:** 26 \ **Ethnic:** Asian 1%, African American 1%, Hispanic 13%, Caucasian 85% \ **Exp:** $263 (Med) \ **Poverty:** 11% \ **Title I:** $221,748 \ **Special Education:** $270,000 \ **Open-Close:** 08/19 - 05/27 \ **DTBP:** $246 (High)

  Nicholas Henkle 1,11,83   Michael Schroeder 2,5
  Kevin Gutzman 3   Brad Homerding 6*
  Mary Minarich .... 16,82*   Bill Roseland 59
  Bridget North 59   Joe Pope 67
  David Bergstrom 73,295

Public Schs..Principal	Grd	Prgm	Enr/#Cls	SN	
Channahon Junior High Sch 24917 W Sioux Dr, Channahon 60410 Dr Chad Uphoff	7-8		302 20	12%	815/467-4314 Fax 815/467-2188
N B Galloway Elem Sch 24805 W Roberts Rd, Channahon 60410 Dacia Cobarrubias \ Mary Kelly	PK-2		396 22	5%	815/467-4311 Fax 815/467-3093
Pioneer Path 24920 S Sage St, Channahon 60410 Erin Dooley	3-4		241 16	13%	815/467-4312 Fax 815/467-8851
Three Rivers Sch 24150 S Ford Rd, Channahon 60410 Laura DuBois	5-6		295 16	14%	815/467-4313 Fax 815/467-3089

- **Crete-Monee Cmty SD 201-U** PID: 00324636 708/367-8300
  1500 S Sangamon St, Crete 60417 Fax 708/672-2696

  Schools: 9 \ **Teachers:** 324 \ **Students:** 5,000 \ **Special Ed Students:** 855 \ **LEP Students:** 125 \ **College-Bound:** 66% \ **Ethnic:** Asian 1%, African American 63%, Hispanic 15%, Caucasian 21% \ **Exp:** $373 (High) \ **Poverty:** 15% \ **Title I:** $1,372,556 \ **Special Education:** $4,788,000 \ **Bilingual Education:** $19,000 \ **Open-Close:** 08/19 - 06/04 \ **DTBP:** $190 (High)

  Dr Kara Coglianese 1   Ken Furma 2,298
  Kenneth Surma 2,15   Keith McLean 3
  Vicente Castillo 3   Pamela Pansa 4
  Gloria O'Neill 5   Robin Tobias 6*
  Kathleen Lynenhale 7   Laura Hirsch 8,11,15,57,72,285,288,298
  Harrison Neal 15,68   Dr Rochelle Clark 15,79*

---

79 Student Personnel	91 Safety/Security	275 Response To Intervention	298 Grant Writer/Ptnrships	**School Programs**	**Social Media**		
80 Driver Ed/Safety	92 Magnet School	277 Remedial Math K-12	750 Chief Innovation Officer	A = Alternative Program			
81 Gifted/Talented	93 Parental Involvement	280 Literacy Coach	751 Chief of Staff	G = Adult Classes	= Facebook		
82 Video Services	95 Tech Prep Program	285 STEM	752 Social Emotional Learning	M = Magnet Program			
83 Substance Abuse Prev	97 Chief Infomation Officer	286 Digital Learning		T = Title I Schoolwide	= Twitter		
84 Erate	98 Chief Technology Officer	288 Common Core Standards	**Other School Types**	V = Career & Tech Ed Programs			
85 AIDS Education	270 Accountability	294 Accountability	Ⓐ = Alternative School				
88 Alternative/At Risk	271 Migrant Education	295 Network System	Ⓒ = Charter School	New Schools are shaded			
89 Multi-Cultural Curriculum	273 Teacher Mentor	296 Title II Programs	Ⓜ = Magnet School	New Superintendents and Principals are bold			
90 Social Work	274 Before/After Sch	297 Webmaster	Ⓨ = Year-Round School	Personnel with email addresses are underscored			

Will County
Market Data Retrieval

Eric Bertram 27,73,74,76,295
Ellen Belotti 58
Christina Cobbins 68
Natalie Nash 71
Kristen Rappold 83,88*
Stacey Elliott 297
Gail Bohnenstiehl 49
Nelson Albrect 67
Janet Graham 69
Krystal Schmitt 76
Michael Summa 295

Public Schs..Principal	Grd	Prgm	Enr/#Cls	SN	
ⓂBalmoral Elem Sch 1124 W New Monee Rd, Crete 60417 Janice Van Kuiken	K-5	T	457 36	76%	708/367-2500 Fax 708/672-2613
ⓂCoretta Scott King Mag Sch 1009 Blackhawk Dr, Park Forest 60484 Bryon Mane	K-6	T	331	50%	708/367-4700 Fax 708/672-2621 🅕
Crete Elem Sch 435 North St, Crete 60417 Erin Lane	K-5	T	392 40	72%	708/367-8430 Fax 708/672-2645 🅕🅣
Crete-Monee Early Learning Ctr 1500 S Sangamon St, Crete 60417 Kelly Chesta	PK-PK	T	198	53%	708/367-2770 Fax 708/672-2762
Ⓐ Crete-Monee Education Center 5154 W Main St, Monee 60449 Brian Wortel	6-12	T	40	79%	708/367-2660 Fax 708/672-2764
Crete-Monee High Sch 1515 W Exchange St, Crete 60417 Marjorie Triche	9-12	TV	1,432 61	67%	708/367-8211 Fax 708/367-0332
Crete-Monee Middle Sch 635 Olmstead Ln, University Pk 60484 Kokona Chrisos	6-8	T	1,015 48	70%	708/367-2400 Fax 708/672-2777 🅕🅣
Monee Elem Sch 25425 S Will Center Rd, Monee 60449 **Amos Vaughn**	K-5	T	435 25	60%	708/367-2600 Fax 708/534-3691
Talala Elem Sch 430 Talala St, Park Forest 60466 Kristin Elliott	K-5	T	293 14	89%	708/367-2560 Fax 708/672-2620 🅕🅣

- **Elwood Cmty Cons SD 203** PID: 00324741 815/423-5588
  409 N Chicago Ave, Elwood 60421 Fax 815/423-5808

Schools: 1 \ Teachers: 29 \ Students: 318 \ Special Ed Students: 47 \
LEP Students: 8 \ Ethnic: Asian 2%, African American 3%, Hispanic 18%,
Caucasian 78% \ Exp: $291 (Med) \ Poverty: 11% \ Title I: $72,519 \
Special Education: $64,000 \ Open-Close: 08/19 - 05/28 \ DTBP: $189
(High) \ 🅕

Cathie Pezanoski 1,11,83
Dan Bosonetta 3*
Mary Balltti 16*
Jeff Grosso 2,73,84,286*
Tonya Peterson 6,37,59,69,88,288*
Mathew Walsh 67

Public Schs..Principal	Grd	Prgm	Enr/#Cls	SN	
Elwood Cmty Cons Sch 409 N Chicago Ave, Elwood 60421 Ryan Rekruciak	PK-8		318 25	35%	815/423-5588

- **Fairmont School District 89** PID: 00324765 815/726-6318
  735 Green Garden Pl, Lockport 60441 Fax 815/726-6157

Schools: 1 \ Teachers: 25 \ Students: 350 \ Special Ed Students: 72
\ LEP Students: 61 \ Ethnic: African American 45%, Hispanic 43%,
Caucasian 12% \ Exp: $447 (High) \ Poverty: 23% \ Title I: $146,055
\ Special Education: $336,000 \ Bilingual Education: $4,000 \
Open-Close: 08/17 - 05/28 \ DTBP: $220 (High)

Dr Diane Sapella 1
Luis Spoonhour 67
Jerry Yaggy 2
Brian Chandler 73*

Public Schs..Principal	Grd	Prgm	Enr/#Cls	SN	
Fairmont Sch 735 Green Garden Pl, Lockport 60441 Tamela Daniels	PK-8	T	350 20	100%	815/726-6318

- **Frankfort School Dist 157-C** PID: 00324806 815/469-5922
  10482 Nebraska St, Frankfort 60423 Fax 815/469-8988

Schools: 3 \ Teachers: 166 \ Students: 2,521 \ Special Ed Students: 312
\ LEP Students: 31 \ College-Bound: 54% \ Ethnic: Asian 3%,
African American 6%, Hispanic 7%, Caucasian 83% \ Exp: $414 (High)
\ Poverty: 2% \ Title I: $52,410 \ Special Education: $1,397,000 \
Bilingual Education: $4,000 \ Open-Close: 08/19 - 05/27 \ DTBP: $229
(High)

Maura Zinni 1
Rodney Davis 3
Jacob Nelson 16,73,95,295
Edith Lutz 67
Kate Ambrosini 2,15
Janet McClarence 9,11,296
Jennifer Bajda 59
Shayna Cole 68,79

Public Schs..Principal	Grd	Prgm	Enr/#Cls	SN	
Chelsea Intermediate Sch 22265 S 80th Ave, Frankfort 60423 Doug Wernet	3-5		821 18	4%	815/469-2309 Fax 815/464-2043
Grand Prairie Elem Sch 10480 Nebraska St, Frankfort 60423 Kirsten Frankovich	PK-2		799 37	4%	815/469-3366 Fax 815/464-2899
Hickory Creek Middle Sch 22150 S Owens Rd, Frankfort 60423 **Tricia Dotson**	6-8		901 30	5%	815/469-4474 Fax 815/469-7930

- **Homer Cmty Cons Sch Dist 33C** PID: 00324832 708/226-7600
  15733 S Bell Rd, Homer Glen 60491 Fax 708/226-7627

Schools: 6 \ Teachers: 259 \ Students: 3,800 \ Special Ed Students: 552
\ LEP Students: 272 \ Ethnic: Asian 2%, African American 1%, Hispanic
9%, Caucasian 88% \ Exp: $322 (High) \ Poverty: 4% \ Title I: $144,550
\ Special Education: $1,688,000 \ Bilingual Education: $55,000 \
Open-Close: 08/24 - 06/03 \ DTBP: $188 (High)

Craig Schoppe 1
Thomas Akerman 3
Karen Norville 9,11,298
Renee Karalus 11,59
Christine Graefin 57
Eric Nush 73
Aleksas Kirkus 2,15
Roberts Rounsaville 5
Michael Szopinski 9,12,15,288
Michael Portwood 15,68
Deb Martin 67

Public Schs..Principal	Grd	Prgm	Enr/#Cls	SN	
Goodings Grove Sch 12914 W 143rd St, Homer Glen 60491 Mark Leipart	1-4		377 14	11%	708/226-7650 Fax 708/301-7288
Hadley Middle Sch 15731 S Bell Rd, Homer Glen 60491 Kristen Schroeder	5-6		823 26	10%	708/226-7725 Fax 708/226-7733
Homer Junior High Sch 15711 S Bell Rd, Homer Glen 60491 Troy Mitchell	7-8		906 50	9%	708/226-7800 Fax 708/226-7859
Luther J Schilling Sch 16025 S Cedar Rd, Homer Glen 60491 Candis Gasa	K-4		734 24	8%	708/226-7900 Fax 708/301-1583
William E Young Elem Sch 16240 S Cedar Rd, Homer Glen 60491 Nathan Baldwin	PK-4		465	9%	708/226-2010 Fax 815/838-6406
William J Butler Elem Sch 1900 S Farrell Rd, Lockport 60441 Dr Melissa Onesto	1-4		494 30	5%	708/226-5155 Fax 708/836-0667

1 Superintendent	8 Curric/Instruct K-12	19 Chief Financial Officer	29 Family/Consumer Science	39 Social Studies K-12	49 English/Lang Arts Elem	59 Special Education Elem	69 Academic Assessment
2 Bus/Finance/Purchasing	9 Curric/Instruct Elem	20 Art K-12	30 Adult Education	40 Social Studies Elem	50 English/Lang Arts Sec	60 Special Education Sec	70 Research/Development
3 Buildings And Grounds	10 Curric/Instruct Sec	21 Art Elem	31 Career/Sch-to-Work K-12	41 Social Studies Sec	51 Reading K-12	61 Foreign/World Lang K-12	71 Public Information
4 Food Service	11 Federal Program	22 Art Sec	32 Career/Sch-to-Work Elem	42 Science K-12	52 Reading Elem	62 Foreign/World Lang Elem	72 Summer School
5 Transportation	12 Title I	23 Music K-12	33 Career/Sch-to-Work Sec	43 Science Elem	53 Reading Sec	63 Foreign/World Lang Sec	73 Instructional Tech
6 Athletic	13 Title V	24 Music Elem	34 Early Childhood Ed	44 Science Sec	54 Remedial Reading K-12	64 Religious Education K-12	74 Inservice Training
7 Health Services	15 Asst Superintendent	25 Music Sec	35 Health/Phys Education	45 Math K-12	55 Remedial Reading Elem	65 Religious Education Elem	75 Marketing/Distributive
	16 Instructional Media Svcs	26 Business Education	36 Guidance Services K-12	46 Math Elem	56 Remedial Reading Sec	66 Religious Education Sec	76 Info Systems
	17 Chief Operations Officer	27 Career & Tech Ed	37 Guidance Services Elem	47 Math Sec	57 Bilingual/ELL	67 School Board President	77 Psychological Assess
	18 Chief Academic Officer	28 Technology Education	38 Guidance Services Sec	48 English/Lang Arts K-12	58 Special Education K-12	68 Teacher Personnel	78 Affirmative Action

Illinois School Directory — Will County

Joliet Public School Dist 86   PID: 00324856
420 N Raynor Ave, Joliet 60435
815/740-3196
Fax 815/740-5441

Schools: 21 \ **Teachers:** 674 \ **Students:** 12,000 \ **Special Ed Students:** 1,638 \ **LEP Students:** 2,888 \ **Ethnic:** African American 24%, Hispanic 65%, Caucasian 10% \ **Exp:** $451 (High) \ **Poverty:** 21% \ **Title I:** $4,022,919 \ **Special Education:** $8,768,000 \ **Bilingual Education:** $611,000 \ **Open-Close:** 08/24 - 05/28 \ **DTBP:** $243 (High) \ 🇫 🇹

Dr Theresa Rouse 1	Tamera Mitchell 2,15
Paul Dufresne 3	Tracie Suter 4
Christina Smith 5	Joel Sischo 6,35
Ankhe Bradley 9,15,69,273,296	Tricia Nagel 9
Joann Culp 11*	Natacia Campbell 15,68
Sunni McNeal 15,78,79	Adam Rusik 24
Melissa Mendoza-Thomps 34,88*	Jennifer Smith 59
Tonya Roberts 67	Sandy Zalewski 71
John Armstrong 73,76,84	Paul Dusresne 91*
Carrie Busse 275,280	Kim Kneigue 286

Public Schs..Principal	Grd	Prgm	Enr/#Cls	SN	
A O Marshall Elem Sch 319 Harwood St, Joliet 60432 Lisa Moreno	K-5	T	473 26	99%	815/727-4919 Fax 815/727-9274 🇫🇹
Dirksen Junior High Sch 203 S Midland Ave, Joliet 60436 Markisha Mitchell	6-8	T	721 25	99%	815/729-1566 Fax 815/744-2346
Edna Keith Elem Sch 400 4th Ave Ste 1, Joliet 60433 Casonya Henderson	K-5	T	328 19	98%	815/723-3409 Fax 815/740-5951
ⓜ Eisenhower Academy 406 Burke Dr, Joliet 60433 Nicole Bottigliero	1-5	T	242 11	99%	815/723-0233 Fax 815/740-5455
Farragut Elem Sch 701 Glenwood Ave, Joliet 60435 Joy Hopkins	K-5	T	663 28	99%	815/723-0394 Fax 815/740-5950
ⓜ Forest Park Individual Ed Sch 1220 California Ave, Joliet 60432 Jacob Darley	K-5	T	280 12	100%	815/723-0414 Fax 815/740-5452
Gompers Junior High Sch 1501 Copperfield Ave, Joliet 60432 Rita Sparks	6-8	TV	956 37	100%	815/727-5276 Fax 815/726-5341
Hufford Junior High Sch 1125 N Larkin Ave, Joliet 60435 Kyle Sartain	6-8	T	1,185	98%	815/725-3540 Fax 815/744-5974
Issac Singleton Elem Sch 1451 Copperfield Ave, Joliet 60432 Laura Hodge	K-5	T	580	100%	815/723-0228 Fax 815/740-5417
Lynne Thigpen Elem Sch 207 S Midland Ave, Joliet 60436 Renita Streeter	K-5	T	606 40	99%	815/741-7629 Fax 815/729-6612
M J Cunningham Elem Sch 500 Moran St, Joliet 60435 Luis Gonzalez	K-5	T	547 26	100%	815/723-0169 Fax 815/726-3040
Marycrest Early Childhood Ctr 303 Purdue Ct, Joliet 60436 Melissa Mendoza-Thomps	PK-PK		425 13	1%	815/725-1100 Fax 815/741-7632
Pershing Elem Sch 251 N Midland Ave, Joliet 60435 Vernecia Gee-Davis	K-5	T	536 24	99%	815/725-0986 Fax 815/741-7633
Sandburg Elem Sch 1100 Lilac Ln, Joliet 60435 Saundra Russell-Smith	K-5	T	410 13	99%	815/725-0281 Fax 815/741-7615
Sator Sanchez Elem Sch 1101 Harrison Ave, Joliet 60432 Maria Arroyo	K-5	T	751	100%	815/740-2810 Fax 815/740-2816
T E Culbertson Elem Sch 1521 E Washington St, Joliet 60433 Larry Tucker	K-5	T	333 16	99%	815/723-0035 Fax 815/740-5454
Taft Elem Sch 1125 Oregon St Ste A, Joliet 60435 Doriane Henderson	K-5	T	416 17	99%	815/725-2700 Fax 815/741-7635
Thomas Jefferson Elem Sch 2651 Glenwood Ave, Joliet 60435 Consuelo Ramirez	K-5	T	452 19	100%	815/725-0262 Fax 815/741-7631
ⓐ Thompson Inst Center 1020 Rowell Ave, Joliet 60433 Ann Keane	K-8	T	76 8	22%	815/740-5458 Fax 815/726-7992
Washington Junior High Sch 402 Richards St, Joliet 60433 Rolland Jasper	6-8	T	798 60	98%	815/727-5271 Fax 815/740-5451
Woodland Elem Sch 701 3rd Ave, Joliet 60433 Kimberly Gordon	K-5	T	399 23	99%	815/723-2808 Fax 815/740-2633

Joliet Twp High Sch Dist 204   PID: 00325123
300 Caterpillar Dr, Joliet 60436
815/727-6970
Fax 815/727-1277

Schools: 3 \ **Teachers:** 359 \ **Students:** 6,589 \ **Special Ed Students:** 1,041 \ **LEP Students:** 501 \ **College-Bound:** 60% \ **Ethnic:** Asian 1%, African American 21%, Hispanic 52%, Caucasian 26% \ **Exp:** $160 (Low) \ **Poverty:** 13% \ **Title I:** $1,396,143 \ **Special Education:** $4,929,000 \ **Bilingual Education:** $76,000 \ **Open-Close:** 08/19 - 05/28 \ **DTBP:** $223 (High) \ 🇫 🇹

Karla Guseman 1	Ilandus Hampton 2,15
Joe Lopez 3	Brian Furczyk 4
Brian Shaw 5,79	Dianne McDonald 7,10,44,69,85*
Brian Conant 10,12,280	Christopher McGuffey ... 10,27,30,72*
Nicole McMorris 10	Paul Oswald 10
Iman Ellis Bowen 13,16,60,271	Isabel Gloria 57
Frank Edmon 67	Chris Olson 68
Nancy Tutko-Mangun 68	Kristine Schlismann 71*
Karen Harkin 73,76	Jennifer Stansbury 88*
Thomas Casey 91	Bradley Uffelmann 295
Wendy Davis 295	

Public Schs..Principal	Grd	Prgm	Enr/#Cls	SN	
Central Joliet Twp High Sch 201 E Jefferson St, Joliet 60432 Shad Hallihan	9-12	TV	3,339	72%	815/727-6750 Fax 815/727-6824
ⓐ Pathways Academy 110 Collins St, Joliet 60432 Jennifer Stansbury	9-12	V	100 10	94%	815/727-6810 Fax 815/727-6996
West Joliet Twp High Sch 401 N Larkin Ave, Joliet 60435 Theresa Giibson	9-12	GTV	3,350	48%	815/727-6951 Fax 815/744-3070

Laraway Cmty Cons SD 70-C   PID: 00325161
1715 Rowell Ave, Joliet 60433
815/727-5115
Fax 815/727-5289

Schools: 1 \ **Teachers:** 42 \ **Students:** 427 \ **Special Ed Students:** 79 \ **LEP Students:** 74 \ **Ethnic:** African American 50%, Hispanic 43%, Caucasian 6% \ **Exp:** $4,282 (High) \ **Poverty:** 24% \ **Title I:** $162,021 \ **Special Education:** $161,000 \ **Bilingual Education:** $4,000 \ **Open-Close:** 08/19 - 06/01 \ **DTBP:** $109 (High)

Dr Joe Salmieri 1	Valerie Teegardin 2
Sherryn Knight	Cheryl Stokes 6*
Geraldine Mahalik 12,72*	Gary Knight 67
Brian Johnson 73*	Erin Ventsias 88,270,275

---

79 Student Personnel	91 Safety/Security	275 Response To Intervention	298 Grant Writer/Ptnrships	**School Programs**
80 Driver Ed/Safety	92 Magnet School	277 Remedial Math K-12	750 Chief Innovation Officer	A = Alternative Program
81 Gifted/Talented	93 Parental Involvement	280 Literacy Coach	751 Chief of Staff	G = Adult Classes
82 Video Services	95 Tech Prep Program	285 STEM	752 Social Emotional Learning	M = Magnet Program
84 Substance Abuse Prev	97 Chief Information Officer	286 Digital Learning		T = Title I Schoolwide
84 Erate	98 Chief Technology Officer	288 Common Core Standards	**Other School Types**	V = Career & Tech Ed Programs
85 AIDS Education	270 Accountability	294 Accountability	Ⓐ = Alternative School	
88 Alternative/At Risk	271 Migrant Education	295 Network System	Ⓒ = Charter School	New Schools are shaded
89 Multi-Cultural Curriculum	273 Teacher Mentor	296 Title II Programs	Ⓜ = Magnet School	New Superintendents and Principals are bold
90 Social Work	274 Before/After Sch	297 Webmaster	Ⓨ = Year-Round School	Personnel with email addresses are underscored

Social Media 🇫 = Facebook   🇹 = Twitter

Will County

Market Data Retrieval

Public Schs..Principal	Grd	Prgm	Enr/#Cls	SN	
Laraway Sch 1715 Rowell Ave, Joliet 60433 Aaron Ventsias	PK-8	V	427 30	98%	815/727-5196

● **Lincoln-Way Cmty HS Dist 210** PID: 00325197   815/462-2345
1801 E Lincoln Hwy, New Lenox 60451   Fax 815/462-2519

Schools: 3 \ Teachers: 387 \ Students: 6,811 \ Special Ed Students: 836 \ LEP Students: 36 \ College-Bound: 82% \ Ethnic: Asian 2%, African American 4%, Hispanic 11%, Caucasian 83% \ Exp: $216 (Med) \ Poverty: 2% \ Title I: $154,694 \ Special Education: $2,739,000 \ Bilingual Education: $2,000 \ Open-Close: 08/27 - 05/27 \ DTBP: $75 (Low)

Dr R Scott Tingley ... 1	Bradley Cauffman ... 2,15	
Kelly Luzzo ... 2	Rich Wilkey ... 3	
Kristin Feltz ... 4	Michael Leone ... 5*	
Dr Aimee Feehery ... 10,74	Brian Murphy ... 10,69,70,76,275*	
Cheryl Kay ... 28,73,295	Laura Erlenbaugh ... 60*	
Joseph Kirkeeng ... 67	Robert Schiffbauer ... 68	
Jen Hannon ... 71	Pat Shaughnessy ... 297	

Public Schs..Principal	Grd	Prgm	Enr/#Cls	SN	
Lincoln-Way Central High Sch 1801 E Lincoln Hwy, New Lenox 60451 Steve Provis	9-12	V	2,059	7%	815/462-2100 Fax 815/485-7648
Lincoln-Way East High Sch 201 Colorado Ave, Frankfort 60423 Dr Sharon Michalak	9-12	V	2,837	6%	815/464-4000 Fax 815/464-4132
Lincoln-Way West High Sch 21701 Gougar Rd, New Lenox 60451 Dr Monica Schmitt	9-12		1,915	8%	815/717-3500 Fax 815/717-3509

● **Lockport Twp High Sch Dist 205** PID: 00325214   815/588-8100
1323 E 7th St, Lockport 60441   Fax 815/588-8109

Schools: 2 \ Teachers: 198 \ Students: 3,890 \ Special Ed Students: 582 \ LEP Students: 73 \ College-Bound: 78% \ Ethnic: Asian 2%, African American 6%, Hispanic 20%, Caucasian 72% \ Exp: $285 (Med) \ Poverty: 5% \ Title I: $317,748 \ Special Education: $2,414,000 \ Bilingual Education: $4,000 \ Open-Close: 08/14 - 05/26 \ DTBP: $170 (High) \

Dr Robert McBride ... 1	Stefanie Croix ... 2
William Thompson ... 3,91	David Niedospial ... 5
James Pruhty ... 6*	Andrea Cobbett ... 12,50,53*
Tony Cundari ... 15,68	Todd Elkei ... 35,85*
Marissa Chovanec ... 47*	Anne Lopez ... 67
Kimberly Brehm ... 71*	Matt Dusterhoft ... 73,95*
Sue Hudders ... 83*	Ann King ... 297

Public Schs..Principal	Grd	Prgm	Enr/#Cls	SN	
Lockport Twp High Sch-Central 1222 S Jefferson St, Lockport 60441 Kerri Green	9-9		900		815/588-8200 Fax 815/588-8209
Lockport Twp High School-East 1333 E 7th St, Lockport 60441 John Greenan	10-12	V	3,000 225	16%	815/588-8300 Fax 815/588-8309

● **Manhattan School Dist 114** PID: 00325288   815/478-6093
25440 S Gougar Rd, Manhattan 60442   Fax 815/478-7660

Schools: 3 \ Teachers: 95 \ Students: 1,540 \ Special Ed Students: 257 \ LEP Students: 21 \ Ethnic: African American 1%, Hispanic 10%, Caucasian 89% \ Exp: $164 (Low) \ Poverty: 2% \ Title I: $27,050 \ Special Education: $824,000 \ Open-Close: 08/19 - 05/27

Rusty Ragon ... 1,11	David Blackman ... 3
Mike Leone ... 5	Ray Hollenbeck ... 6*
Kristen Morphew ... 9,288	Michelle Hallinghan ... 16,82
Melissa Hester ... 59	Scott Mancke ... 67
Janice Leppin ... 73	Ronald Pacheco ... 270*

Public Schs..Principal	Grd	Prgm	Enr/#Cls	SN	
Anna McDonald Elem Sch 200 2nd St, Manhattan 60442 Ryan McWilliams	3-5		484 28	2%	815/478-3310 Fax 815/478-4035
Manhattan Junior High Sch 15606 W Smith Rd, Manhattan 60442 Ronald Pacheco	6-8		504 30	4%	815/478-6090 Fax 815/478-6094
Wilson Creek Elem Sch 25440 S Gougar Rd, Manhattan 60442 Kim Maher	PK-2		552	2%	815/478-4527 Fax 815/478-6035

● **Milne-Kelvin Grove District 91** PID: 00325305   815/838-0737
808 Adams St, Lockport 60441   Fax 815/834-4339

Schools: 2 \ Teachers: 38 \ Students: 550 \ Special Ed Students: 116 \ LEP Students: 22 \ Ethnic: Asian 1%, African American 2%, Hispanic 13%, Caucasian 84% \ Exp: $583 (High) \ Poverty: 7% \ Title I: $76,254 \ Special Education: $354,000 \ Bilingual Education: $2,000 \ Open-Close: 08/31 - 05/04 \ DTBP: $240 (High)

Donna Gray ... 1	Athena Dingles ... 2
Jim Pierson ... 3*	John Jennings ... 5,11,57,83,270*
Jaime Kovil ... 12,296	Brian Kincaid ... 13,16,73,76,295*
Brian Kincaid ... 16,84	Sharon Bruemmer ... 16*
Larry Spencer ... 59*	Laura Garrett ... 67
Erin Rae ... 69,288,752	Eileen Holly ... 77,275
Lynn Krumlinde ... 79	Kathy Henderson ... 88*

Public Schs..Principal	Grd	Prgm	Enr/#Cls	SN	
Kelvin Grove Middle Sch 808 Adams St, Lockport 60441 John Jennings	4-8		372 24	33%	815/834-4339
Milne Grove Elem Sch 565 E 7th St, Lockport 60441 Jamie Koziol	PK-3		231 10	39%	815/838-6893

● **Minooka Cmty High Sch Dist 111** PID: 00294201   815/521-4311
26655 W Eames St, Channahon 60410   Fax 815/467-9733

Schools: 2 \ Teachers: 150 \ Students: 2,800 \ Special Ed Students: 310 \ LEP Students: 46 \ College-Bound: 75% \ Ethnic: Asian 1%, African American 4%, Hispanic 20%, Caucasian 75% \ Exp: $271 (Med) \ Poverty: 4% \ Title I: $86,223 \ Special Education: $889,000 \ Open-Close: 08/12 - 05/21 \ DTBP: $191 (High) \

Kenneth Lee ... 1	Don Troy ... 2
Cathy Haase ... 5	Robert Tyrell ... 6
Joe Pacetti ... 10,79,83*	John Troy ... 15,19
Marissa Welch ... 16	Sean Hackney ... 50*
Mike Brozovich ... 67	Jim Kelly ... 73,297*
Karen Soukup ... 294	

1 Superintendent	8 Curric/Instruct K-12	19 Chief Financial Officer	29 Family/Consumer Science	39 Social Studies K-12	49 English/Lang Arts Elem	59 Special Education Elem	69 Academic Assessment
2 Bus/Finance/Purchasing	9 Curric/Instruct Elem	20 Art K-12	30 Adult Education	40 Social Studies Elem	50 English/Lang Arts Sec	60 Special Education Sec	70 Research/Development
3 Buildings And Grounds	10 Curric/Instruct Sec	21 Art Elem	31 Career/Sch-to-Work K-12	41 Social Studies Sec	51 Reading K-12	61 Foreign/World Lang K-12	71 Public Information
4 Food Service	11 Federal Program	22 Art Sec	32 Career/Sch-to-Work Elem	42 Science K-12	52 Reading Elem	62 Foreign/World Lang Elem	72 Summer School
5 Transportation	12 Title I	23 Music K-12	33 Career/Sch-to-Work Sec	43 Science Elem	53 Reading Sec	63 Foreign/World Lang Sec	73 Instructional Tech
6 Athletic	13 Title V	24 Music Elem	34 Early Childhood Ed	44 Science Sec	54 Remedial Reading K-12	64 Religious Education K-12	74 Inservice Training
7 Health Services	14 Instructional Media Svcs	25 Music Sec	35 Health/Phys Education	45 Math K-12	55 Remedial Reading Elem	65 Religious Education Elem	75 Marketing/Distributive
	15 Asst Superintendent	26 Business Education	36 Guidance Services K-12	46 Math Elem	56 Remedial Reading Sec	66 Religious Education Sec	76 Info Systems
	16 Instructional Media Svcs	27 Career & Tech Ed	37 Guidance Services Elem	47 Math Sec	57 Bilingual/ELL	67 School Board President	77 Psychological Assess
	17 Chief Operations Officer	28 Technology Education	38 Guidance Services Sec	48 English/Lang Arts K-12	58 Special Education K-12	68 Teacher Personnel	78 Affirmative Action
	18 Chief Academic Officer						

Illinois School Directory — Will County

Public Schs..Principal	Grd	Prgm	Enr/#Cls	SN	
Minooka Cmty High Sch -Central 301 S Wabena Ave, Minooka 60447 Ronald Kiesewetter	11-12	AV	1,292 60	16%	815/467-2140 Fax 815/467-2431
Minooka Cmty High Sch South 26655 W Eames St, Channahon 60410 Bryan Zwemke	9-10	AV	2,800		815/521-4001 Fax 815/467-5784

● Mokena Public School Dist 159 PID: 00325331   708/342-4900
11244 Willow Crest Ln, Mokena 60448   Fax 708/479-3143

Schools: 3 \ **Teachers:** 99 \ **Students:** 1,500 \ **Special Ed Students:** 206 \ **LEP Students:** 88 \ **Ethnic:** Asian 2%, African American 3%, Hispanic 8%, Caucasian 88% \ **Exp:** $337 (High) \ **Poverty:** 3% \ **Title I:** $67,626 \ **Special Education:** $1,093,000 \ **Bilingual Education:** $1,000 \ **Open-Close:** 08/19 - 05/27 \ **DTBP:** $276 (High)

Dr Mark Cohen 1	Dr Terri Shaw 2,19	
Chris Crawford 3	Ann Lewandowski 4*	
Dr Kathleen Wilkey 9,11,15,69,83,288	Michael Everett 67	
Jacob Smith 73,84	Allison Cirone 79,298,752	

Public Schs..Principal	Grd	Prgm	Enr/#Cls	SN	
Mokena Elem Sch 11244 Willow Crest Ln, Mokena 60448 Rachel Chorley	PK-3		631 40	19%	708/342-4850 Fax 708/479-3120
Mokena Intermediate Sch 11331 195th St, Mokena 60448 David McAtee	4-5		343 19	16%	708/342-4860 Fax 708/479-3103
Mokena Junior High Sch 19815 Kirkstone Way, Mokena 60448 Michael Rolinitis	6-8		510 40	16%	708/342-4870 Fax 708/479-3122

● New Lenox School District 122 PID: 00325379   815/485-2169
102 S Cedar Rd, New Lenox 60451   Fax 815/485-2236

Schools: 12 \ **Teachers:** 283 \ **Students:** 5,300 \ **Special Ed Students:** 838 \ **LEP Students:** 22 \ **Ethnic:** Asian 1%, African American 1%, Hispanic 9%, Caucasian 88% \ **Exp:** $271 (Med) \ **Poverty:** 3% \ **Title I:** $139,478 \ **Special Education:** $2,508,000 \ **Open-Close:** 08/20 - 05/28 \ **DTBP:** $189 (High) \ 📘

Lori Motsch 1	Bob Groos 2,4,5,7,298
Jason Sterritt 3,91	Dawn Pate 5
Jim Havlin 6*	Marianne Cucci 9,12,286,288,296
Dr Peggy Manville 11,57,83	Liza Bruni 15,59,79,88,271,280,285
Heidi Morgan 16	Christa Blatt 59
Mandy Novotny 59	Rhonda Starklauf 67
Leanne Soltys 71	Andy White 73,76,295

Public Schs..Principal	Grd	Prgm	Enr/#Cls	SN	
Alex M Martino Jr High Sch 731 E Joliet Hwy, New Lenox 60451 Dr Bonnie Groen	7-8		575 34	8%	815/485-7593 Fax 815/485-9578
Arnold J Tyler Elem Sch 511 E Illinois Hwy, New Lenox 60451 Patsy Fisher	1-3		364 24	17%	815/485-2398 Fax 815/462-2570
Caroline Bentley Elem Sch 513 E Illinois Hwy, New Lenox 60451 Mary Zastro	4-6		402 24	14%	815/485-4451 Fax 815/485-7599
Cherry Hill Elem and ECC 205 Kingston Dr, New Lenox 60451 Emily Schissler	PK-PK		140 7	26%	815/462-7831 Fax 815/722-8536
Haines Elem Sch 155 Haines Ave, New Lenox 60451 Michelle Hall	1-3		383 20	13%	815/485-2115 Fax 815/462-2571
Liberty Junior High Sch 151 Lenox St, New Lenox 60451 Shane Street	7-8		637 30	12%	815/462-7951 Fax 815/462-0672
Nelson Prairie Sch 2366 Nelson Rd, New Lenox 60451 Tyler Broders	1-3		441 20	10%	815/462-2874 Fax 815/462-2881
Nelson Ridge Elem Sch 2470 Nelson Rd, New Lenox 60451 Megan Baldermann	4-6		459 19	10%	815/462-2870 Fax 815/462-2880
Oster-Oakview Sch 809 N Cedar Rd, New Lenox 60451 Theresa Baumann	4-6		500 17	13%	815/485-2125 Fax 815/462-2572
Spencer Crossing Interm Sch 1711 Spencer Rd, New Lenox 60451 Megan Calleros	4-6		459 30	8%	815/462-7997 Fax 815/462-0958
Spencer Pointe Elem Sch 1721 Spencer Rd, New Lenox 60451 Kim Gray	1-3		457 18	4%	815/462-7988 Fax 815/462-3978
Spencer Trail Kindergarten Ctr 1701 Spencer Rd, New Lenox 60451 Lori Motsch	K-K		449 11	12%	815/462-7007 Fax 815/462-0670

● Peotone Cmty Unit SD 207-U PID: 00325460   708/258-0991
212 W Wilson St, Peotone 60468   Fax 708/258-0994

Schools: 5 \ **Teachers:** 97 \ **Students:** 1,453 \ **Special Ed Students:** 274 \ **LEP Students:** 33 \ **College-Bound:** 78% \ **Ethnic:** Asian 1%, African American 1%, Hispanic 10%, Caucasian 88% \ **Exp:** $201 (Med) \ **Poverty:** 5% \ **Title I:** $139,268 \ **Special Education:** $1,113,000 \ **Open-Close:** 08/21 - 05/28 \ **DTBP:** $245 (High)

Steve Stein 1	Trevor Moore 2
Dave Osborne 3	Terry Wuske 4*
Jennifer Haag 5	Craig Fantin 6,31,83,88*
Dawn Barber 7*	Dr Charles Vitton 8,11,69,73,288,298*
Sherry Schubbe 16*	Nichole Schultz 36*
Amy Loy 57,58,271,275*	Tara Robinson 67
Shannon Anselmo 77	Dave Weissbohn 295

Public Schs..Principal	Grd	Prgm	Enr/#Cls	SN	
Peotone Early Educ Shaw Ctr 212 W Wilson St, Peotone 60468 Dr Charles Vitton	PK-PK		69		708/258-0991
Peotone Elem Sch 426 N Conrad St, Peotone 60468 Carole Zurales	K-3		340 16	25%	708/258-6955 Fax 708/258-0455
Peotone High Sch 605 W North St, Peotone 60468 Jason Spang	9-12		476 24	21%	708/258-3236 Fax 708/258-6991
Peotone Intermediate Ctr 9526 W Manhattan Monee Rd, Frankfort 60423 Joanne Obszanski	4-5		218 6	26%	815/469-5744 Fax 815/469-6086
Peotone Junior High Sch 1 Blue Devil Dr, Peotone 60468 Scott Wenzel	6-8		343 40	21%	708/258-3246 Fax 708/258-6669

● Plainfield Cons Sch Dist 202 PID: 00325525   815/577-4000
15732 S Howard St, Plainfield 60544   Fax 815/577-1067

Schools: 30 \ **Teachers:** 1,619 \ **Students:** 25,000 \ **Special Ed Students:** 4,199 \ **LEP Students:** 2,120 \ **College-Bound:** 78% \ **Ethnic:** Asian 7%, African American 11%, Hispanic 25%, Caucasian 57% \ **Exp:** $156 (Low) \ **Poverty:** 5% \ **Title I:** $2,249,456 \ **Special Education:** $16,460,000 \ **Bilingual Education:** $567,000 \ **Open-Close:** 08/31 - 06/04 \ **DTBP:** $204 (High) \ 🐦

---

79 Student Personnel	91 Safety/Security	275 Response To Intervention	298 Grant Writer/Ptnrships	**School Programs**	**Social Media**
80 Driver Ed/Safety	92 Magnet School	277 Remedial Math K-12	750 Chief Innovation Officer	A = Alternative Program	📘 = Facebook
81 Gifted/Talented	93 Parental Involvement	280 Literacy Coach	751 Chief of Staff	G = Adult Classes	🐦 = Twitter
82 Video Services	95 Tech Prep Program	285 STEM	752 Social Emotional Learning	M = Magnet Program	
83 Substance Abuse Prev	97 Chief Infomation Officer	286 Digital Learning		T = Title I Schoolwide	
84 Erate	98 Chief Technology Officer	288 Common Core Standards	**Other School Types**	V = Career & Tech Ed Programs	
85 AIDS Education	270 Character Education	294 Accountability	Ⓐ = Alternative School		
88 Alternative/At Risk	271 Migrant Education	295 Network System	Ⓒ = Charter School	New Schools are shaded	
89 Multi-Cultural Curriculum	273 Teacher Mentor	296 Title II Programs	Ⓜ = Magnet School	New Superintendents and Principals are bold	
90 Social Work	274 Before/After Sch	297 Webmaster	Ⓨ = Year-Round School	Personnel with email addresses are underscored	

Will County

Market Data Retrieval

Name	Page
Dr Lane Abrell	1
Bonnie Delange	2
Rose Kidd	2
Paul Gonzalez	3
Sandy Bressers	5
Cheril Phillips	8
Paula Sereleas	8
Dr Dan McDonnell	10
Jennifer Orlos	15,91
Jason Stanley	31,79
Ashley Meyers	58
Elizabeth Massaro	58
Roxanne Ross	58
Kevin Kirberg	67
Dr Scott Fink	68
Thomas Hernandez	71
Kathy Cecil	76
Maribeth Hampton	76
Ryan Schlott	76
Russell Moore	295
Anthony Arbogast	2,3,15,19
Dawn Bjorklund	2
Jason Oskorep	3
Steve Belcher	3
Christina Edwards	7
Dr Glenn Wood	8,15,27,74,285,288,294
Dr Tammy Sroczynski	9
Cindy Westfall	11,298
Mina Griffith	15,58,77,88,275,752
Michelle O'Shea	57
Ashley Meyers	58*
Jeni Alonzo	58
Roxanne Ross	58*
Dr Craig Brown	68
Shannon Miller	68
Margie Bonuchi	73,76,84
Lucia Testin	76
Nora Campos	76
Laura Weed	286
Ryan Boyce	297

Public Schs..Principal	Grd	Prgm	Enr/#Cls	SN		
Aux Sable Middle Sch 2001 Wildspring Pkwy, Joliet 60431 Christian Rivara	6-8		972	33%	815/439-7092 Fax 815/577-9476	
Bonnie McBeth Early Lrng Ctr 15730 S Howard St, Plainfield 60544 Kristin Brower	PK-PK		753 24	26%	815/439-4288 Fax 815/254-4315	
Central Elem Sch 23723 Getson Dr, Plainfield 60544 Jennifer Hennegan	K-5		657 25	30%	815/436-9278 Fax 815/436-8415	
Charles Reed Elem Sch 2110 Clublands Pkwy, Plainfield 60586 Curtis Hudson	K-5		531 32	34%	815/254-2160 Fax 815/254-9385	
Creekside Elem Sch 13909 S Budler Rd, Plainfield 60544 Patti Hudson	K-5		561 38	45%	815/577-4700 Fax 815/372-0607	
Crystal Lawns Elem Sch 2544 Crystal Dr, Joliet 60435 Carol Betzold	K-5		298 18	42%	815/436-9519 Fax 815/436-8433	
Drauden Point Middle Sch 1911 Drauden Rd, Plainfield 60586 Kai Freeman	6-8	V	722 60	29%	815/577-4900 Fax 815/439-9385	
Eagle Pointe Elem Sch 24562 Norwood Dr, Plainfield 60585 William Stockey	K-5		677 30	13%	815/577-4800 Fax 815/609-9403	
Elizabeth Eichelberger ES 12450 Essington Rd, Plainfield 60585 Trevor Harris	K-5		647	27%	815/577-3606 Fax 815/577-6407	
Freedom Elem Sch 11600 Heritage Meadows Dr, Plainfield 60585 Laurie Boyce	K-5		720	13%	815/254-4005 Fax 815/254-9706	
Grand Prairie Elem Sch 3100 Caton Farm Rd, Joliet 60431 Heather Whisler	K-5		611 32	38%	815/436-7000 Fax 815/436-1233	
Heritage Grove Middle Sch 12425 S Van Dyke Rd, Plainfield 60585 Danielle Cournaya	6-8	V	951 50	17%	815/439-4810 Fax 815/436-4661	
Indian Trail Middle Sch 14723 S Eastern Ave, Plainfield 60544 John Evans	6-8	V	714 25	35%	815/436-6128 Fax 815/436-7536	
Ira Jones Middle Sch 15320 W Wallin Dr, Plainfield 60544 Tom Novinski	6-8	V	898	17%	815/267-3600 Fax 815/439-7201	
John F Kennedy Middle Sch 12350 Essington Rd, Plainfield 60585 Aj Hundal	6-8	V	1,012	28%	815/439-8024 Fax 815/254-7375	
Lakewood Falls Elem Sch 14050 S Budler Rd, Plainfield 60544 Scott Winters	K-5		661 31	49%	815/439-4560 Fax 815/886-0463	
Liberty Elem Sch 1401 Essington Rd, Bolingbrook 60490 Michelle Imbordino	K-5		606 36	17%	815/609-3037 Fax 815/609-5963	
Lincoln Elem Sch 14740 Meadow Ln, Plainfield 60544 Casey Hartman	K-5		676	17%	815/577-4500 Fax 815/609-5853	
Meadow View Elem Sch 2501 Mirage Ave, Plainfield 60586 Brian Sorg	K-5		526 36	38%	815/439-4828 Fax 815/436-3747	
Ⓐ Plainfield Academy 23930 W Lockport St, Plainfield 60544 Tod Schnowske	6-12	T	169 3	43%	815/439-5521 Fax 815/439-7014	
Plainfield Central High Sch 24120 W Fort Beggs Dr, Plainfield 60544 Chris Chlebek	9-12	V	2,070	31%	815/436-3200 Fax 815/439-2882	
Plainfield East High Sch 12001 S Naperville Rd, Plainfield 60585 Joseph O'Brien	9-12		2,240	28%	815/577-0324 Fax 815/577-0979	
Plainfield North High Sch 12005 S 248th Ave, Plainfield 60585 Ross Draper	9-12	V	2,269	14%	815/609-8506 Fax 815/254-6138	
Plainfield South High Sch 7800 Caton Farm Rd, Plainfield 60586 Bob Yanello	9-12	V	2,429	27%	815/439-5555 Fax 815/436-5108	
Ridge Elem Sch 1900 Caton Ridge Dr, Plainfield 60586 Stacey Dibitetto	K-5		558 33	32%	815/577-4630 Fax 815/609-9387	
River View Elem Sch 2097 S Bronk Rd, Plainfield 60586 Tracey Markowski	K-5		643 32	29%	815/439-4840 Fax 815/436-4930	
Thomas Jefferson Elem Sch 1900 Oxford Way, Joliet 60431 **Vicky Foster**	K-5		639 24	28%	815/577-2021 Fax 815/254-6862	
Timber Ridge Middle Sch 2101 S Bronk Rd, Plainfield 60586 Constantine Kariotakis	6-8	V	1,019 50	38%	815/439-3410 Fax 815/439-3412	
Walker's Grove Elem Sch 24810 W 135th St, Plainfield 60544 Jeffery Schafermeyer	K-5		577 34	8%	815/439-2885 Fax 815/439-2883	
Wesmere Elem Sch 2001 Wesmere Pkwy, Plainfield 60586 Dr Debra Coberley	K-5		526 36	29%	815/439-3244 Fax 815/439-3413	

● **Reed-Custer Cmty Unit SD 255-U** PID: 00324569   815/458-2307
255 S Comet Dr, Braidwood 60408   Fax 815/458-4106

Schools: 3 \ Teachers: 109 \ Students: 1,476 \ Special Ed Students: 267 \ LEP Students: 25 \ College-Bound: 63% \ Ethnic: Asian 1%, African American 1%, Hispanic 8%, Caucasian 90% \ Exp: $317 (High) \ Poverty: 7% \ Title I: $174,424 \ Special Education: $643,000 \ Open-Close: 08/14 - 05/21 \ DTBP: $157 (High)

Name	Page		Name	Page
Mark Mitchell	1		Mark Hulbert	2,3,15
Terry Bennet	3		Marilyn Montana	4
Chuck Anderson	6		Christine Nelson	8,11,15
Danielle Valiente	8		Carrie Hill	58
Greg Boyer	67		Dwayne Dubbert	73,82,295
Vern Reed	91		Stacey Schott	294

Public Schs..Principal	Grd	Prgm	Enr/#Cls	SN	
Reed-Custer Elem Sch 162 S School St, Braidwood 60408 Heather Faletti	2-5	T	600 20	45%	815/458-2145 Fax 815/458-4039

1	Superintendent	8	Curric/Instruct K-12	19	Chief Financial Officer	29	Family/Consumer Science	39	Social Studies K-12	49	English/Lang Arts Elem	59	Special Education Elem	69	Academic Assessment
2	Bus/Finance/Purchasing	9	Curric/Instruct Elem	20	Art K-12	30	Adult Education	40	Social Studies Elem	50	English/Lang Arts Sec	60	Special Education Sec	70	Research/Development
3	Buildings And Grounds	10	Curric/Instruct Sec	21	Art Elem	31	Career/Sch-to-Work K-12	41	Social Studies Sec	51	Reading K-12	61	Foreign/World Lang K-12	71	Public Information
4	Food Service	11	Federal Program	22	Art Sec	32	Career/Sch-to-Work Elem	42	Science K-12	52	Reading Elem	62	Foreign/World Lang Elem	72	Summer School
5	Transportation	12	Title I	23	Music K-12	33	Career/Sch-to-Work Sec	43	Science Elem	53	Reading Sec	63	Foreign/World Lang Sec	73	Instructional Tech
6	Athletic	13	Title V	24	Music Elem	34	Early Childhood Ed	44	Science Sec	54	Remedial Reading K-12	64	Religious Education K-12	74	Inservice Training
7	Health Services	15	Asst Superintendent	25	Music Sec	35	Health/Phys Education	45	Math K-12	55	Remedial Reading Elem	65	Religious Education Elem	75	Marketing/Distributive
		16	Instructional Media Svcs	26	Business Education	36	Guidance Services K-12	46	Math Elem	56	Remedial Reading Sec	66	Religious Education Sec	76	Info Systems
		17	Chief Operations Officer	27	Career & Tech Ed	37	Guidance Services Elem	47	Math Sec	57	Bilingual/ELL	67	School Board President	77	Psychological Assess
		18	Chief Academic Officer	28	Technology Education	38	Guidance Services Sec	48	English/Lang Arts K-12	58	Special Education K-12	68	Teacher Personnel	78	Affirmative Action

Illinois School Directory — Will County

School	Grd	Prgm	Enr/#Cls	SN	Phone
Reed-Custer High Sch 249 S Comet Dr, Braidwood 60408 Tim Ricketts	9-12	TV	474 53	34%	815/458-2166 Fax 815/458-4138 f t
Reed-Custer Middle Sch 407 S Comet Dr, Braidwood 60408 Shane Trager	6-8	T	348 50	39%	815/458-2868 Fax 815/458-4118

● **Richland School Dist 88A** PID: 00325721   815/744-6166
1919 Caton Farm Rd, Crest Hill 60403   Fax 815/744-6196

Schools: 1 \ Teachers: 56 \ Students: 923 \ Special Ed Students: 133 \ LEP Students: 128 \ Ethnic: Asian 5%, African American 20%, Hispanic 39%, Caucasian 36% \ Exp: $284 (Med) \ Poverty: 13% \ Title I: $160,706 \ Special Education: $249,000 \ Bilingual Education: $29,000 \ Open-Close: 08/17 - 05/25 \ DTBP: $111 (High)

Joseph Simpkins 1,73,83   Dr Ann Del Real 2
Jeff Pristas .... 3*   Sherri Russell 6
Lori Weber .... 12*   Veda Newman 57
K Bonie 59   Stephanie Hernandez 67

Public Schs..Principal	Grd	Prgm	Enr/#Cls	SN	Phone
Richland Elem Sch 1919 Caton Farm Rd, Crest Hill 60403 J Lindsey \ J Christian	PK-8	T	923 18	47%	815/744-6166

● **Rockdale School District 84** PID: 00325745   815/725-5321
715 Meadow Ave, Rockdale 60436   Fax 815/725-3099

Schools: 1 \ Teachers: 18 \ Students: 275 \ Special Ed Students: 45 \ LEP Students: 39 \ Ethnic: African American 12%, Hispanic 50%, Caucasian 38% \ Exp: $192 (Low) \ Poverty: 18% \ Title I: $79,084 \ Special Education: $123,000 \ Bilingual Education: $16,000 \ Open-Close: 08/19 - 05/26 \ f t

Dr Paul Schrik 1,57   Chuck Puckett 3
Lori Gehrke 11   Amy Walls 16
Angie Stadler 67   Shaun Mooney 73

Public Schs..Principal	Grd	Prgm	Enr/#Cls	SN	Phone
Rockdale Elem Sch 715 Meadow Ave, Rockdale 60436 Jeffrey Peterson	PK-8	T	275 8	72%	815/725-5321

● **Summit Hill School Dist 161** PID: 00325769   815/469-9103
20100 S Spruce Dr, Frankfort 60423   Fax 815/469-0566

Schools: 6 \ Teachers: 208 \ Students: 2,800 \ Special Ed Students: 477 \ LEP Students: 139 \ Ethnic: Asian 4%, African American 7%, Hispanic 12%, Caucasian 77% \ Exp: $186 (Low) \ Poverty: 3% \ Title I: $112,428 \ Special Education: $1,737,000 \ Bilingual Education: $12,000 \ Open-Close: 08/31 - 06/04 \ DTBP: $186 (High)

Barb Rains 1   Doug Wiley 2,5
Dave Hesse 3,91   Frank Zajac 4,16
Fred Pufattl .... 6*   Leslie DeBoer 7,57,59,271,752
John Snipes 9,11,288,296,298   Rich Marron 67
Kevin Perkins 73

Public Schs..Principal	Grd	Prgm	Enr/#Cls	SN	Phone
Arbury Hills Elem Sch 19651 Beechnut Dr, Mokena 60448 Francie Boss	1-4		188 16	15%	708/479-2106 Fax 708/478-8995
Dr Julian Rogus Elem Sch 20027 S 88th Ave, Frankfort 60423 Colin Bradley	PK-4		696 19	6%	815/464-2034 Fax 815/464-2250
Frankfort Square Elem Sch 7710 W Kingston Dr, Frankfort 60423 Jason Isdonas	1-4		217 8	12%	815/469-3176 Fax 815/464-2068
Hilda Walker Interm Sch 19900 80th Ave, Tinley Park 60487 Maura Carroll	5-6		685 34	12%	815/464-2285 Fax 815/464-2160
Indian Trail Elem Sch 20912 S Frankfort Square Rd, Frankfort 60423 Dana Wright	1-4		362 16	14%	815/469-6993 Fax 815/806-8352
Summit Hill Junior High Sch 7260 W North Ave, Frankfort 60423 Laura Goebel	7-8		732 30	12%	815/469-4330 Fax 815/464-1596

● **Taft School District 90** PID: 00325800   815/838-0408
1605 S Washington St, Lockport 60441   Fax 815/838-5046

Schools: 1 \ Teachers: 20 \ Students: 300 \ Special Ed Students: 68 \ LEP Students: 18 \ Ethnic: Asian 1%, African American 2%, Hispanic 17%, Caucasian 80% \ Exp: $239 (Med) \ Poverty: 7% \ Title I: $59,910 \ Special Education: $183,000 \ Open-Close: 08/19 - 05/28 \ DTBP: $219 (High)

James Calabrese 1,11,57,73,83   Peter Howard 6*
Susan Stein 59   Tony Peloso 67

Public Schs..Principal	Grd	Prgm	Enr/#Cls	SN	Phone
Taft Sch 1605 S Washington St, Lockport 60441 Jared Reardon	PK-8	T	300 18	29%	815/838-0408

● **Troy Cmty Cons SD 30-C** PID: 00325824   815/577-6760
5800 Theodore Dr, Plainfield 60586   Fax 815/577-3795

Schools: 7 \ Teachers: 296 \ Students: 4,100 \ Special Ed Students: 562 \ LEP Students: 331 \ Ethnic: Asian 2%, African American 14%, Hispanic 32%, Caucasian 52% \ Exp: $197 (Low) \ Poverty: 6% \ Title I: $435,383 \ Special Education: $1,713,000 \ Bilingual Education: $81,000 \ Open-Close: 08/27 - 05/07 \ DTBP: $183 (High) \ f t

Dr Todd Koehl 1   Ellen Wandless 2
Ben Hettel 3   Mark Baumann 5
Meagan DeGroot .... 6*   Anne Gmazel 9
Dr Jenna Woodlawn 9,15,73,74   Dr Kristin Johnson 9,12,15,57,69,273,288
Ronald Sarver 16,76   Michelle Laird 59
Mark Griglione 67   Christine Hodge 68
Liz Boyles 76   Marc Solodky 83,88,752
Paul Keto 295

Public Schs..Principal	Grd	Prgm	Enr/#Cls	SN	Phone
Troy Heritage Trail Elem Sch 3389 Longford Dr, Joliet 60431 Brooke Allen	PK-4	T	419 24	51%	815/577-9195 Fax 815/773-2398
Troy Hofer Elem Sch 910 Vertin Blvd, Shorewood 60404 Kristin Copes	K-4		388	30%	815/577-6758 Fax 815/267-8180
Troy Middle Sch 5800 Theodore Dr, Plainfield 60586 Renee Marski	7-8		978 45	34%	815/230-9920 Fax 815/577-2867
Troy-Craughwell Elem Sch 3333 Black Rd, Joliet 60431 Kathy Barker	PK-4	T	466	46%	815/577-7313 Fax 815/729-7435

---

79 Student Personnel
80 Driver Ed/Safety
81 Gifted/Talented
82 Video Services
83 Substance Abuse Prev
84 Erate
85 AIDS Education
88 Alternative/At Risk
89 Multi-Cultural Curriculum
90 Social Work
91 Safety/Security
92 Magnet School
93 Parental Involvement
95 Tech Prep Program
97 Chief Infomation Officer
98 Chief Technology Officer
270 Character Education
271 Migrant Education
273 Teacher Mentor
274 Before/After Sch
275 Response To Intervention
277 Remedial Math K-12
280 Literacy Coach
285 STEM
286 Digital Learning
288 Common Core Standards
294 Accountability
295 Network System
296 Title II Programs
297 Webmaster
298 Grant Writer/Ptnrships
750 Chief Innovation Officer
751 Chief of Staff
752 Social Emotional Learning

School Programs
A = Alternative Program
G = Adult Classes
M = Magnet Program
T = Title I Schoolwide
V = Career & Tech Ed Programs

Other School Types
Ⓐ = Alternative School
Ⓒ = Charter School
Ⓜ = Magnet School
Ⓨ = Year-Round School

Social Media
f = Facebook
t = Twitter

New Schools are shaded
New Superintendents and Principals are bold
Personnel with email addresses are underscored

Will County

School	Grd	Prgm	Enr/#Cls	SN	Phone
Troy-Cronin Elem Sch 210 E Black Rd, Shorewood 60404 Jill Howard	PK-4	T	605 26	36%	815/577-7314 Fax 815/729-7441
Troy-Orenic Intermediate Sch 5820 Theodore Dr, Plainfield 60586 Larry Piatek	5-6		994	36%	815/577-6759 Fax 815/577-1233
Troy-Shorewood Elem Sch 210 School Rd, Shorewood 60404 Sherri Blanchette	PK-4		432 25	31%	815/577-7312 Fax 815/729-7447

- **Union School District 81** PID: 00325862   815/726-5218
  1661 Cherry Hill Rd, Joliet 60433   Fax 815/726-5056

Schools: 1 \ Teachers: 13 \ Students: 105 \ Special Ed Students: 17 \ LEP Students: 7 \ Ethnic: African American 23%, Hispanic 27%, Caucasian 49% \ Exp: $799 (High) \ Poverty: 15% \ Title I: $33,379 \ Special Education: $22,000 \ Open-Close: 08/17 - 06/04 \ DTBP: $102 (High)

Timothy Baldermann	1	Dr Richard Dombrowski	2
Dawn Pate	5	Cathy Wikert	6*
Nicole Sharkey	9*	Bill Roseland	59
Patrick Sweeney	67	William Buyerly	73

Public Schs..Principal	Grd	Prgm	Enr/#Cls	SN	Phone
Union Sch 1661 Cherry Hill Rd, Joliet 60433 Timothy Baldermann	PK-8	T	105 9	56%	815/726-5218

- **Valley View Cmty SD 365-U** PID: 00325587   815/886-2700
  801 W Normantown Rd, Romeoville 60446   Fax 815/886-7820

Schools: 20 \ Teachers: 1,155 \ Students: 18,000 \ Special Ed Students: 2,619 \ LEP Students: 2,726 \ College-Bound: 68% \ Ethnic: Asian 7%, African American 21%, Hispanic 48%, Caucasian 25% \ Exp: $126 (Low) \ Poverty: 10% \ Title I: $3,292,082 \ Special Education: $13,111,000 \ Bilingual Education: $362,000 \ Open-Close: 08/14 - 05/26 \ DTBP: $206 (High) \

Rachel Kinder	1	Gary Grizaffi	2,15
Anthony Bersani	3	Mike Lopez	3
Meghan Gibbons	4*	David Richards	5
Susan Gregory	7	Adam Hurder	9
Amanda Dykstra	9	Megan Healy	9
Rachel Dellamorte	9	Karen Flories	10
Greg Harris	11	Judie Nash	15,68
Astrid Welch	16,73,82,295	Dorletta Payton	27
Tammie Conn	27	Jacci Brown	34*
Amy Paris	39,280	Rachel Schlechter	41,50
Adriene Potilechio	42,45	Dr Jillian Tsoukalas	43,46
Christy Vehe	44,47	Ricardo Sanchez-Lopez	57
Mary Wurster	58,79	Steven Quigley	67
Brandie McCurry	68	Mike Locascio	69,76
Jim Blaney	71,93	Amy Irvin	74
Karen Hess	74	Ladonya Stanley	74
Alberto Diaz	76,91,295	Lisa Allen	79
Megan McAllister	79	Michelle Laird	79
Jason Pick	83*	Elizabeth Martinez	273
Rhonda Reinert	294	Susan Kalafut	295

Public Schs..Principal	Grd	Prgm	Enr/#Cls	SN	Phone
A Vito Martinez Middle Sch 590 Belmont Dr, Romeoville 60446 Sarah Dedonato	6-8	TV	796 70	58%	815/886-6100 Fax 815/886-7264
Bernard J Ward Elem Sch 200 Recreation Dr, Bolingbrook 60440 Kathleen Nigro	PK-5	T	437	86%	630/972-9200 Fax 630/972-9420
Beverly Skoff Elem Sch 775 W Normantown Rd, Romeoville 60446 Cheryl Lockard	K-5	T	757	67%	815/886-8384 Fax 815/886-8389
Bolingbrook High Sch 365 Raider Way, Bolingbrook 60440 Jason Pascavage	9-12	GTV	3,445 100	59%	630/759-6400 Fax 630/759-6365
Brooks Middle Sch 350 Blair Ln, Bolingbrook 60440 Dr Keith Wood	6-8	T	1,140	65%	630/759-6340 Fax 630/759-6360
Hubert Humphrey Middle Sch 777 Falcon Ridge Way, Bolingbrook 60440 Dan Laverty	6-8	TV	653 37	72%	630/972-9240 Fax 630/739-8521
Independence Elem Sch 230 S Orchard Dr, Bolingbrook 60440 Jacqueline Mitchem	K-5	T	652 27	75%	630/759-7282 Fax 630/759-6366
Irene H King Elem Sch 301 Eaton Ave, Romeoville 60446 April Vacik	PK-5	T	447 30	75%	815/886-3380 Fax 815/886-7840
Jamie McGee Elem Sch 179 Commonwealth Dr, Bolingbrook 60440 Tony Valenza	K-5	T	449 25	44%	630/759-4300 Fax 630/759-6363
Jane Addams Middle Sch 905 Lily Cache Ln, Bolingbrook 60440 Teresa Polson	6-8	TV	691 25	54%	630/759-7200 Fax 630/759-6362
John Lukancic Middle Sch 725 W Normantown Rd, Romeoville 60446 Tricia Rollerson	6-8	T	583	63%	815/886-2216 Fax 815/886-2264
John Tibbott Elem Sch 520 Gary Dr, Bolingbrook 60440 Ana Wilson	K-5	T	575 33	79%	630/739-7155 Fax 630/739-8522
Jonas Salk Elem Sch 500 King Arthur Way, Bolingbrook 60440 Alyson Ewald	K-5	T	616 25	59%	630/739-3603 Fax 630/739-8518
Kenneth L Hermasen Elem Sch 101 Wesglen Pkwy, Romeoville 60446 Loretta Furtute	K-5	T	527 28	56%	815/886-7581 Fax 815/886-5593
Oak View Elem Sch 150 N Schmidt Rd, Bolingbrook 60440 Robert Pinciak	K-5	T	564 30	74%	630/759-9300 Fax 630/759-6359
Pioneer Elem Sch 1470 Raven Dr, Bolingbrook 60490 Carmen Killingsworth	K-5	T	527 36	43%	630/771-2420 Fax 630/771-0199
Robert Hill Elem Sch 616 Dalhart Ave, Romeoville 60446 Jody Ellis	K-5	T	736	52%	815/886-4343 Fax 815/886-7299
Romeoville High Sch 100 N Independence Blvd, Romeoville 60446 Derek Kinder	9-12	GTV	1,869 60	58%	815/886-1800 Fax 815/886-3426
Valley View Early Chldhd Ctr 753 Dalhart Ave, Romeoville 60446 Jacqueline Brown	Spec	T	385 14	58%	815/886-7827 Fax 815/886-7830
Wood View Elem Sch 197 Winston Dr, Bolingbrook 60440 Jessica McCaslin	K-5	T	343 24	69%	630/739-0185 Fax 630/739-8517

- **Will Co School District 92** PID: 00325240   815/838-8031
  708 N State St, Lockport 60441   Fax 815/838-8034

Schools: 4 \ Teachers: 135 \ Students: 1,550 \ Special Ed Students: 250 \ LEP Students: 48 \ Ethnic: Asian 1%, African American 1%, Hispanic 11%, Native American: 1%, Caucasian 86% \ Exp: $328 (High) \ Poverty: 5% \ Title I: $143,325 \ Special Education: $1,081,000 \ Bilingual Education: $1,000 \ Open-Close: 08/19 - 05/27 \ DTBP: $233 (High)

Tim Arnold	1,11	Dave Blatchley	2,15

1	Superintendent	8	Curric/Instruct K-12	19	Chief Financial Officer
2	Bus/Finance/Purchasing	9	Curric/Instruct Elem	20	Art K-12
3	Buildings And Grounds	10	Curric/Instruct Sec	21	Art Elem
4	Food Service	11	Federal Program	22	Art Sec
5	Transportation	12	Title I	23	Music K-12
6	Athletic	13	Title V	24	Music Elem
7	Health Services	15	Asst Superintendent	25	Music Sec
		16	Instructional Media Svcs	26	Business Education
		17	Chief Operations Officer	27	Career & Tech Ed
		18	Chief Academic Officer	28	Technology Education
29	Family/Consumer Science	39	Social Studies K-12	49	English/Lang Arts Elem
30	Adult Education	40	Social Studies Elem	50	English/Lang Arts Sec
31	Career/Sch-to-Work K-12	41	Social Studies Sec	51	Reading K-12
32	Career/Sch-to-Work Elem	42	Science K-12	52	Reading Elem
33	Career/Sch-to-Work Sec	43	Science Elem	53	Reading Sec
34	Early Childhood Ed	44	Science Sec	54	Remedial Reading K-12
35	Health/Phys Education	45	Math K-12	55	Remedial Reading Elem
36	Guidance Services K-12	46	Math Elem	56	Remedial Reading Sec
37	Guidance Services Elem	47	Math Sec	57	Bilingual/ELL
38	Guidance Services Sec	48	English/Lang Arts K-12	58	Special Education K-12
59	Special Education Elem	69	Academic Assessment		
60	Special Education Sec	70	Research/Development		
61	Foreign/World Lang K-12	71	Public Information		
62	Foreign/World Lang Elem	72	Summer School		
63	Foreign/World Lang Sec	73	Instructional Tech		
64	Religious Education K-12	74	Inservice Training		
65	Religious Education Elem	75	Marketing/Distributive		
66	Religious Education Sec	76	Info Systems		
67	School Board President	77	Psychological Assess		
68	Teacher Personnel	78	Affirmative Action		

Illinois School Directory — Will County

Gary Moser 3	Lynn Onderisin 4
Mark Murray 6,16,82*	Kim West 15,58*
Matthew Dusterhoft 67	Greg Bolek 73
Teresa Martin 88,270*	

Public Schs..Principal	Grd	Prgm	Enr/#Cls	SN
Ludwig Elem Sch 710 N State St, Lockport 60441 Lisa Lyke	4-5		384 17	25% 815/838-8020 Fax 815/838-3226
Oak Prairie Junior High Sch 15161 S Gougar Rd, Homer Glen 60491 Sue Forcash	6-8		565 32	20% 815/836-2724 Fax 815/834-2178
Reed Elem Sch 14939 W 143rd St, Homer Glen 60491 Cathy Slee	2-3		276 16	23% 708/301-0692 Fax 708/301-6501
Walsh Elem Sch 514 MacGregor Rd, Lockport 60441 Teresa Martin	PK-1		341 24	20% 815/838-7858 Fax 815/838-3346

● **Wilmington Cmty Unit SD 209-U** PID: 00325886 815/926-1751
209U Wildcat Ct, Wilmington 60481 Fax 815/926-1692

Schools: 4 \ **Teachers:** 87 \ **Students:** 1,400 \ **Special Ed Students:** 231 \ **LEP Students:** 10 \ **College-Bound:** 66% \ **Ethnic:** Hispanic 4%, Native American: 1%, Caucasian 95% \ **Exp:** $410 (High) \ **Poverty:** 13% \ **Title I:** $251,494 \ **Special Education:** $254,000 \ **Open-Close:** 08/26 - 06/03 \ **DTBP:** $229 (High) \

Dr Matt Swick 1	Lisa Hipes 2
Jim Habing 3	Tina Brownlee 4
Brian Goff 6*	Kevin Feeney 8,11,15,57,58,69,288*
Tim Cragg 67	Mike McCormick 73,84

Public Schs..Principal	Grd	Prgm	Enr/#Cls	SN
Bruning Elem Sch 1910 Bruning Dr, Wilmington 60481 Beth Norman	PK-1	T	209 12	44% 815/926-1683 Fax 815/476-0130
Stevens Intermediate Sch 221 Ryan St, Wilmington 60481 Venita Dennis	2-5	T	354 19	43% 815/926-1689 Fax 815/476-1941
Wilmington High Sch 209 Wildcat Ct, Wilmington 60481 Scott Maupin	9-12	TV	419 38	40% 815/926-1752 Fax 815/926-1691
Wilmington Middle Sch 715 S Joliet St, Wilmington 60481 Adam Spicer	6-8	T	291 18	45% 815/926-1687 Fax 815/476-4256

WILL CATHOLIC SCHOOLS

● **Diocese of Joliet Ed Office** PID: 00325965 815/838-2181
16555 Weber Rd, Crest Hill 60403 Fax 815/838-2182

Schools: 53 \ **Students:** 17,485

Listing includes only schools located in this county. See District Index for location of Diocesan Offices.

John Belmonte SJ 1	Dr Colleen Bruckmann 8,15,69,74,273
Karen Udell 15,68	Madonna Turner 15
Ryan Purcell 64	Jonathan Pugh 67
Mary Ann Draudt 73	

Catholic Schs..Principal	Grd	Prgm	Enr/#Cls	SN
Cathedral of St Raymond Sch 608 N Raynor Ave, Joliet 60435 Marjorie Hill	PK-8		353 20	815/722-6626 Fax 815/727-4668
Holy Family Sch 600 Brookforest Ave, Shorewood 60404 Anthony Wilkinson	PK-8		300 14	815/725-8149 Fax 815/725-8649
Joliet Catholic Academy 1200 N Larkin Ave, Joliet 60435 Jeffrey Budz	9-12		939 49	815/741-0500 Fax 815/741-9530
Mother Teresa Catholic Academy 24201 S Kings Rd, Crete 60417 Annie Murray	PK-8		275 10	708/672-3093 Fax 708/367-0640
Providence Catholic Chldrn Aca 1800 W Lincoln Hwy, New Lenox 60451 Laura McErlean	PK-K		155 5	815/485-7129 Fax 815/485-5165
Providence Catholic High Sch 1800 W Lincoln Hwy, New Lenox 60451 John Harper	9-12	G	1,160 36	815/485-2136 Fax 815/485-2709
St Andrew the Apostle Sch 505 Kingston Dr, Romeoville 60446 Carol Albreski	PK-8		186 14	815/886-5953 Fax 815/293-2016
St Anthony Pre-School 7659 W Sauk Trl, Frankfort 60423 Patricia Smart	PK-K		50 8	815/469-5417 Fax 815/806-2421
St Dennis Sch 1201 S Washington St, Lockport 60441 Lisa Smith	PK-8		230 10	815/838-4494 Fax 815/838-5435
St Dominic Sch 420 E Briarcliff Rd, Bolingbrook 60440 Sr Marie Isaac	PK-8		276 12	630/739-1633 Fax 630/739-5989
St Joseph Sch 275 W North St, Manhattan 60442 Colleen Domke	PK-8		150 9	815/478-3951 Fax 815/478-7412
St Joseph Sch 529 Madison St, Lockport 60441 Lynne Scheffler	PK-8		230 10	815/838-8173 Fax 815/838-0504
St Jude Parish Sch 241 W 2nd Ave, New Lenox 60451 Kathy Winters	K-8		235 9	815/485-2549 Fax 815/485-0234
St Jude Sch 2204 McDonough St, Joliet 60436 Lucas Stangler	PK-8		165 12	815/729-0288 Fax 815/729-0344
St Mary Immaculate Sch 15629 S Route 59, Plainfield 60544 Jennifer Errthum	PK-8		553 22	815/436-3953 Fax 815/439-8045
St Mary Nativity Sch 702 N Broadway St, Joliet 60435 Dr J Chavez	PK-8		150 10	815/722-8518 Fax 815/726-4071
St Mary Sch 11409 195th St, Mokena 60448 Jeanne Wolski	K-8		305 9	708/479-3383 Fax 708/326-9331
St Paul the Apostle Sch 130 Woodlawn Ave, Joliet 60435 Colleen Brodhead	PK-8		395 18	815/725-3390 Fax 815/725-3180
St Rose Sch 626 S Kankakee St, Wilmington 60481 Nancy Schwab	PK-8		143 10	815/476-6220 Fax 815/476-5644

WILL PRIVATE SCHOOLS

Private Schs..Principal	Grd	Prgm	Enr/#Cls	SN
Calvary Christian Sch 9S200 Route 59, Naperville 60564 Emery Risdall	K-8		175 30	630/375-8600 Fax 630/375-8601

Williamson County

Market Data Retrieval

School	Grd	Prgm	Enr/#Cls	Phone
Center for Disability Services 311 S Reed St, Joliet 60436 Joni Bolek	Spec		40 7	815/744-3500 Fax 815/744-3504
Christ's Academy 114 Channahon St, Shorewood 60404 Sharon Meiergerd	PK-12	G	75 8	815/630-5376
Covenant Classical Sch 1852 95th St, Naperville 60564 Lisa Eekhoff	K-8		145	630/983-7500
Crest Hill Christian Sch 21514 W Division St, Lockport 60441 Cindy Ferguson	1-8		18 2	815/905-1544
Families of Faith Academy 24466 W Eames St, Channahon 60410 Karen Blan	PK-12		100	815/521-1381 Fax 815/467-4476
Furqaan Academy-Boilingbrook 519 E Briarcliff Rd, Bolingbrook 60440 Haiat Bousmaha	PK-8		220	630/914-5015
Heritage Christian Sch 21739 S La Grange Rd, Frankfort 60423 Keith Betry	K-12		23 8	815/464-9100
Illinois Lutheran High Sch 1610 Main St, Crete 60417 Joe Archer	7-12		157	708/672-3262 Fax 708/672-0512
Illinois Lutheran Sch 448 Cass St, Crete 60417 Jeff Falck	PK-6		150 9	708/672-5850 Fax 708/672-0353
Joliet Montessori Sch 1600 Root St, Crest Hill 60403 Heidi Geiger	PK-9		75 7	815/741-4180 Fax 815/741-9753
Midwest Chrn Mont Academy 314 E Briarcliff Rd, Bolingbrook 60440 Eileen Contos	PK-6		40	630/783-8644
Noonan Elem Academy 19131 Henry Dr, Mokena 60448 Joseph Dunn	PK-8		290 17	708/479-8988 Fax 708/479-6059
Romeoville Christian Academy 301 W Normantown Rd, Romeoville 60446 Carla Snyder \ Lee Johnson	PK-12		149 12	815/886-4850 Fax 815/886-5716
Sch Exp Arts & Lrng-Romeoville 1265 Naperville Dr Ste D, Romeoville 60446 Dave Michalski	Spec		25	630/226-0004
St Joseph Academy 403 N Hickory St Ste B, Joliet 60435 Jan Novotny	PK-8		54	815/723-4567 Fax 815/723-4581
Trinity Christian Sch 901 Shorewood Dr, Shorewood 60404 John Vugteveen	PK-8		240 17	815/577-9310 Fax 815/577-9695
Trinity Sch 1361 E Lincoln Hwy, New Lenox 60451 Joy Vrlec	Spec	G	20 4	815/463-0719 Fax 815/463-0726
Zion Lutheran Sch 540 Oak Park Ave, Beecher 60401 Joann Hess	PK-8		66 8	708/946-2272 Fax 708/946-2611

WILL REGIONAL CENTERS

- **Lincoln Way Area Special Ed** PID: 02098481   815/806-4600
  601 Willow St, Frankfort 60423   Fax 815/806-4601

  Sarah Rexroad 1   Greg Furgason 73

- **Lockport Area Special Ed Co-op** PID: 02182264   815/838-8080
  1343 E 7th St, Lockport 60441   Fax 815/838-8086

  Dr Hassan Von Schlegell 1   Kimberly McDonald 275

- **Professional Dev Alliance** PID: 04420012   815/744-8334
  2705 McDonough St, Joliet 60436   Fax 815/744-8396

  Hallie Brenczewski 1   Mary Chignoli 74

- **Southern Will Co Spec Ed Dist** PID: 02182276   815/741-7777
  1207 N Larkin Ave, Joliet 60435   Fax 815/741-7779

  Dr Bill Roseland 1   Tiffany Frey 15

- **Trees-Three Rivers EFE Sys** PID: 04182210   815/280-2990
  1215 Houbolt Rd H1019, Joliet 60431

  Brian Gordon 1,73

- **Will Co Regional Office of Edu** PID: 02098479   815/740-8360
  116 N Chicago St Ste 400, Joliet 60432   Fax 815/740-4788

  Shawn Walsh 1   Paula Earls 5
  Dr Peter Sullivan 15

WILLIAMSON COUNTY

WILLIAMSON COUNTY SCHOOLS

County Schs..Principal	Grd	Prgm	Enr/#Cls	SN	Phone
Marion Learning Center 409 S Court St, Marion 62959 Melissa Cockburn	Spec	A	22 4	79%	618/997-1533
ⓐ Project Echo 17428 Route 37, Johnston City 62951 Edwin Henriksen	8-12		15	84%	618/983-6628 Fax 618/983-6975

WILLIAMSON PUBLIC SCHOOLS

- **Carterville Cmty Unit SD 5** PID: 00326749   618/985-4826
  306 Virginia Ave, Carterville 62918   Fax 618/985-2041

  Schools: 4 \ **Teachers:** 124 \ **Students:** 2,400 \ **Special Ed Students:** 310 \ **LEP Students:** 13 \ **College-Bound:** 71% \ **Ethnic:** Asian 2%, African American 3%, Hispanic 6%, Caucasian 89% \ **Exp:** $185 (Low) \ **Poverty:** 12% \ **Title I:** $516,871 \ **Special Education:** $240,000 \ **Open-Close:** 08/11 - 05/20 \ **DTBP:** $174 (High)

  Keith Liddell 1   Stephanie McCaughan 2,84
  Bill Ren .... 3*   Jeanne Ellis 4*
  Michael Bradford 5   Brett Diel 6*
  Wendy Johnson 7   Sarah Barnstable 8,11,69,77,88,275,294*
  Jaime Hodge 58   David Scwartz 67
  Dave Baburnich 73,286,295*

Public Schs..Principal	Grd	Prgm	Enr/#Cls	SN	Phone
Carterville High Sch 1415 W Grand Ave, Carterville 62918 Todd Rogers	9-12	V	581 30	31%	618/985-2940 Fax 618/985-2741

1 Superintendent	8 Curric/Instruct K-12	19 Chief Financial Officer	29 Family/Consumer Science	39 Social Studies K-12	49 English/Lang Arts Elem	59 Special Education Elem	69 Academic Assessment
2 Bus/Finance/Purchasing	9 Curric/Instruct Elem	20 Art K-12	30 Adult Education	40 Social Studies Elem	50 English/Lang Arts Sec	60 Special Education Sec	70 Research/Development
3 Buildings And Grounds	10 Curric/Instruct Sec	21 Art Elem	31 Career/Sch-to-Work K-12	41 Social Studies Sec	51 Reading K-12	61 Foreign/World Lang K-12	71 Public Information
4 Food Service	11 Federal Program	22 Art Sec	32 Career/Sch-to-Work Elem	42 Science K-12	52 Reading Elem	62 Foreign/World Lang Elem	72 Summer School
5 Transportation	12 Title I	23 Music K-12	33 Career/Sch-to-Work Sec	43 Science Elem	53 Reading Sec	63 Foreign/World Lang Sec	73 Instructional Tech
6 Athletic	13 Title V	24 Music Elem	34 Early Childhood Ed	44 Science Sec	54 Remedial Reading K-12	64 Religious Education K-12	74 Inservice Training
7 Health Services	15 Asst Superintendent	25 Music Sec	35 Health/Phys Education	45 Math K-12	55 Remedial Reading Elem	65 Religious Education Elem	75 Marketing/Distributive
	16 Instructional Media Svcs	26 Business Education	36 Guidance Services K-12	46 Math Elem	56 Remedial Reading Sec	66 Religious Education Sec	76 Info Systems
	17 Chief Operations Officer	27 Career & Tech Ed	37 Guidance Services Elem	47 Math Sec	57 Bilingual/ELL	67 School Board President	77 Psychological Assess
	18 Chief Academic Officer	28 Technology Education	38 Guidance Services Sec	48 English/Lang Arts K-12	58 Special Education K-12	68 Teacher Personnel	78 Affirmative Action

Illinois School Directory — Williamson County

	Grd	Prgm	Enr/#Cls	SN	
Carterville Intermediate Sch 300 School St, Carterville 62918 Tom Webb	4-6	T	505 40	38%	618/985-6411 Fax 618/985-2492
Carterville Junior High Sch 816 S Division St, Carterville 62918 Jeff Hartford	7-8		328	32%	618/985-4500 Fax 618/985-3402
Tri-C Elem Sch 1405 W Grand Ave, Carterville 62918 Sarah Barnstable	PK-3	T	677 33	43%	618/985-8742 Fax 618/985-4907

● **Crab Orchard Cmty Sch Dist 3** PID: 00326804
19189 Cory Bailey St, Marion 62959
618/982-2181
Fax 618/982-2080

Schools: 1 \ **Teachers:** 29 \ **Students:** 497 \ **Special Ed Students:** 85 \ **College-Bound:** 67% \ **Ethnic:** Caucasian 100% \ **Exp:** $228 (Med) \ **Poverty:** 11% \ **Title I:** $77,663 \ **Special Education:** $76,000 \ **Open-Close:** 08/05 - 05/21

Derek Hutchins ....1,11 Ben Taylor 3,5
Keith Johns ....6* Debbie Hale 7,83,85,275*
Sy Stone ....8,273,288* Amanda Killman 12*
Tara Tanner ....12* Teresa McDonald 16,82*
Matt Troxel ....67 Jonathan Brown 69*
Tom Harrison 73,295*

Public Schs..Principal	Grd	Prgm	Enr/#Cls	SN	
Crab Orchard Sch 19189 Cory Bailey St, Marion 62959 Sy Stone	PK-12	V	497 30	43%	618/982-2181

● **Herrin Cmty School District 4** PID: 00326842
500 N 10th St, Herrin 62948
618/988-8024
Fax 618/942-6998

Schools: 4 \ **Teachers:** 152 \ **Students:** 2,300 \ **Special Ed Students:** 473 \ **LEP Students:** 18 \ **College-Bound:** 68% \ **Ethnic:** Asian 1%, African American 5%, Hispanic 2%, Caucasian 92% \ **Exp:** $164 (Low) \ **Poverty:** 18% \ **Title I:** $887,155 \ **Special Education:** $384,000 \ **Open-Close:** 08/11 - 05/26 \ **DTBP:** $175 (High)

Dr Terry Ryker ....1,84 Rachel Wright 2
Mike Lentz ....3 Andrew Anderson 6*
Cassandra Burgess 8,11,57,83,285,286,288,298 Beth Johnson
16,82*
Rebecca Lewis ....23* Stacy Linton 35,85*
Cathy Shelton ....36,69,79* David Loucks 67
Rob Wrolson 73,295*

Public Schs..Principal	Grd	Prgm	Enr/#Cls	SN	
Herrin Cmty Elem Sch 5200 Herrin Rd, Herrin 62948 **Bobbi Heuring**	2-5	T	696 27	66%	618/942-2744 Fax 618/942-5817
Herrin High Sch 700 N 10th St, Herrin 62948 Jeff Johnson	9-12	TV	767 70	52%	618/942-6606 Fax 618/942-7562
Herrin Middle Sch 700 S 14th St, Herrin 62948 Brad Heuring	6-8	T	506 40	61%	618/942-5603 Fax 618/988-8821
North Side Primary Center 601 N 17th St, Herrin 62948 Matt Viernow	PK-1	T	391 20	62%	618/942-5418 Fax 618/942-3579

● **Johnston City Cmty Unit SD 1** PID: 00326933
200 E 12th St, Johnston City 62951
618/983-8021
Fax 618/983-6034

Schools: 4 \ **Teachers:** 72 \ **Students:** 1,100 \ **Special Ed Students:** 230 \ **College-Bound:** 61% \ **Ethnic:** Hispanic 3%, Caucasian 96% \ **Exp:** $413 (High) \ **Poverty:** 18% \ **Title I:** $415,306 \ **Special Education:** $120,000 \ **Open-Close:** 08/13 - 05/21 \ **DTBP:** $173 (High)

Kathy Clark ....1,83,84 Lori Linton 2
Andria Murrah ....8,11,69,73,275,288,752* Debbie Ryker 36*
Chris Cullum 67

Public Schs..Principal	Grd	Prgm	Enr/#Cls	SN	
Jefferson Elem Sch 1108 Grand Ave, Johnston City 62951 Andria Murrah	PK-2	T	216 21	71%	618/983-7561 Fax 618/983-6556
Johnston City High Sch 1500 Jefferson Ave, Johnston City 62951 Josh Pietrantoni	9-12	TV	358 30	61%	618/983-8639 Fax 618/983-6812
Lincoln Elem Sch 20163 Corinth Rd, Pittsburg 62974 Michelle Smiley	3-4	T	158 6	70%	618/982-2130 Fax 618/982-2353
Washington Elem Mid Sch 200 E 12th St, Johnston City 62951 Josh Pietrantoni	5-8	T	318 25	60%	618/983-7581 Fax 618/983-6409

● **Marion Cmty School Dist 2** PID: 00326983
1700 W Cherry St, Marion 62959
618/993-2321
Fax 618/997-3412

Schools: 7 \ **Teachers:** 268 \ **Students:** 3,914 \ **Special Ed Students:** 752 \ **LEP Students:** 18 \ **Ethnic:** Asian 1%, African American 9%, Hispanic 3%, Caucasian 86% \ **Exp:** $272 (Med) \ **Poverty:** 21% \ **Title I:** $1,588,940 \ **Special Education:** $523,000 \ **Open-Close:** 08/24 - 05/25 \ **DTBP:** $208 (High) \ 🅵 🆃

Dr Keith Oates ....1 Kim Watson 2,19
Jeff Moake ....3,91 Kyle Hartwell 4
Amy Sanders ....11,15,288,296 Jaime Hodge 34,58,90
John Barwick ....67 Jerry Stanley 73,84,286,295

Public Schs..Principal	Grd	Prgm	Enr/#Cls	SN	
Adam Sch 15470 Lake of Egypt Rd, Creal Springs 62922 Kim Burns	PK-8	T	274 11	48%	618/996-2181 Fax 618/996-3339
Jefferson Elem Sch 700 E Boulevard St, Marion 62959 Kimberly Brave	PK-5	T	436 15	43%	618/997-5766 Fax 618/993-3287
Lincoln Elem Sch 400 Morningside Dr, Marion 62959 John Fletcher	K-5	T	538 24	56%	618/997-6063 Fax 618/997-0459
Longfellow Elem Sch 1400 W Hendrickson St, Marion 62959 Lindsay Watts	K-5	T	261 15	65%	618/993-3230 Fax 618/997-8046
Marion High Sch 1700 Wildcat Dr, Marion 62959 Joey Ohnesorge	9-12	T	1,107 80	48%	618/993-8196 Fax 618/997-8749
Marion Junior High Sch 1609 W Main St, Marion 62959 Becky Moss	6-8	T	860 42	54%	618/997-1317 Fax 618/997-0477
Washington Elem Sch 420 E Main St, Marion 62959 Tommy Colboth	K-5	T	536 34	48%	618/993-8534 Fax 618/997-0460

---

79 Student Personnel	91 Safety/Security	275 Response To Intervention	298 Grant Writer/Ptnrships
80 Driver Ed/Safety	92 Magnet School	277 Remedial Math K-12	750 Chief Innovation Officer
81 Gifted/Talented	93 Parental Involvement	280 Literacy Coach	751 Chief of Staff
82 Video Services	95 Tech Prep Program	285 STEM	752 Social Emotional Learning
83 Substance Abuse Prev	97 Chief Infomation Officer	286 Digital Learning	
84 Erate	98 Chief Technology Officer	288 Common Core Standards	**Other School Types**
85 AIDS Education	270 Character Education	294 Accountability	Ⓐ = Alternative School
88 Alternative/At Risk	271 Migrant Education	295 Network System	Ⓒ = Charter School
89 Multi-Cultural Curriculum	273 Teacher Mentor	296 Title II Programs	Ⓜ = Magnet School
90 Social Work	274 Before/After Sch	297 Webmaster	Ⓨ = Year-Round School

School Programs
A = Alternative Program
G = Adult Classes
M = Magnet Program
T = Title I Schoolwide
V = Career & Tech Ed Programs

Social Media
🅵 = Facebook
🆃 = Twitter

New Schools are shaded
New Superintendents and Principals are bold
Personnel with email addresses are underscored

IL—251

Winnebago County
Market Data Retrieval

WILLIAMSON CATHOLIC SCHOOLS

- **Diocese of Belleville Ed Off** PID: 00317671
  Listing includes only schools located in this county. See District Index for location of Diocesan Offices.

Catholic Schs..Principal	Grd	Prgm	Enr/#Cls SN	
Our Lady of Mt Carmel Sch 300 W Monroe St, Herrin 62948 Jason Swann	PK-8		296 12	618/942-4484 Fax 618/942-2864

WILLIAMSON PRIVATE SCHOOLS

Private Schs..Principal	Grd	Prgm	Enr/#Cls SN	
Agape Christian High Sch 5208 Meadowland Pkwy A, Marion 62959 Seth Knox	9-12		79	618/997-9302 Fax 618/997-9304
Marion Adventist Christian Sch 9314 Old Route 13, Marion 62959 Dell Jean Dickenson	PK-8		10 1	618/997-1430
Unity Christian Sch 100 E College St, Energy 62933 William McSparin	PK-8		211 15	618/942-3802 Fax 618/942-7228

WILLIAMSON REGIONAL CENTERS

- **Williamson Co Cte System** PID: 04184438   618/993-2138
  411 S Court St, Marion 62959   Fax 618/997-3950

  Sharon Helleny 1

- **Williamson Co Special Ed Dist** PID: 02184107   618/993-2138
  411 S Court St, Marion 62959   Fax 618/997-3950

  Jami Hodge 1   Jenny Malanowski 2
  Kathy Keel 34

WINNEBAGO COUNTY

WINNEBAGO COUNTY SCHOOLS

County Schs..Principal	Grd	Prgm	Enr/#Cls SN	
ⓐ Regional Learning Center-Star 5949 Safford Rd, Rockford 61101 Craig Pate	9-12		126	72% 815/227-8495

WINNEBAGO PUBLIC SCHOOLS

- **Durand Cmty Sch Dist 322** PID: 00327092   815/248-2171
  200 W South St, Durand 61024   Fax 815/248-2599

  > **Schools:** 4 \ **Teachers:** 52 \ **Students:** 565 \ **Special Ed Students:** 82 \
  > **LEP Students:** 3 \ **College-Bound:** 62% \ **Ethnic:** Hispanic 2%, Native American: 1%, Caucasian 96% \ **Exp:** $301 (High) \ **Poverty:** 9% \
  > **Title I:** $85,184 \ **Special Education:** $384,000 \ **Open-Close:** 08/21 - 05/26 \ **DTBP:** $184 (High)

  Kurt Alberstett 1,11   Bill Damon 2
  Chad Gassman .... 3,91*   Amy McIntosh 4
  Fred Kormoczy .... 5*   Peter Robertson 6*
  Carrie Meinert .... 7,85*   Shana Rufner 9,274,275,288
  Michael Leskowich .... 10,35,83,271*   Sue Szymanski 12*
  Audra Hill 16   Stacie Waggoner 27,31,36,69*
  Andrea Schrock 36,90   Brian Grande 67
  Nicole Richardson 73,84,295   Krista Scarols 273
  Lisa Franke 285*

Public Schs..Principal	Grd	Prgm	Enr/#Cls SN	
ⓐ Dolan Ed Ctr-Durand Cud 322 10104 Farm School Rd, Durand 61024 Mark Parent	4-12		27 10	71% 815/599-3975 Fax 815/599-3985
Durand Elem Sch 200 W South St, Durand 61024 Shana Rufener	PK-6		285 24	29% 815/248-2171 Fax 815/248-9968
Durand High Sch 200 W South St, Durand 61024 Michael Leskowich	9-12	V	186 45	22% 815/248-2171
Durand Junior High Sch 200 W South St, Durand 61024 Michael Leskowich	7-8		99 8	33% 815/248-2171

- **Harlem Unit Sch District 122** PID: 00327121   815/654-4500
  8605 N 2nd St, MacHesney Pk 61115   Fax 815/654-4600

  > **Schools:** 11 \ **Teachers:** 450 \ **Students:** 6,300 \ **Special Ed Students:** 1,135 \ **LEP Students:** 276 \ **Ethnic:** Asian 2%, African American 6%, Hispanic 14%, Caucasian 78% \ **Exp:** $300 (High) \ **Poverty:** 17% \ **Title I:** $2,233,113 \ **Special Education:** $4,587,000 \ **Bilingual Education:** $58,000 \ **Open-Close:** 08/24 - 05/27 \ **DTBP:** $191 (High)

  Dr Julie Morris 1   Gail Aldrich 2
  Mike Chandler 3   Jill Mosher 4
  Donald West 5   Rebecca Hoffmann 6
  Michelle Erb 8,11,15   Shelley Wagner 8
  Rebecca Logan 9   Scott Rollinson 15,68
  Heidi Lange 59,79,288   Sue Berogan 67
  Rachel Freeman 68   Aaron Guske 73,76,84,295

Public Schs..Principal	Grd	Prgm	Enr/#Cls SN	
Donald C Parker Early Ed Ctr 808 Harlem Rd, MacHesney Pk 61115 Amanda Hayes	PK-K	T	668 30	62% 815/654-4559 Fax 815/654-4613
Harlem High Sch 1 Huskie Cir, MacHesney Pk 61115 Ronald Yarbrough	9-12	AT	1,900 115	50% 815/654-4511 Fax 815/654-5484
Harlem Middle Sch 735 Windsor Rd, Loves Park 61111 Matthew Cascio	7-8	T	984 50	57% 815/654-4510 Fax 815/654-4540
Loves Park Elem Sch 344 Grand Ave, Loves Park 61111 Lisa Clark	1-6	T	335 26	76% 815/654-4501 Fax 815/654-4553

1 Superintendent	8 Curric/Instruct K-12	19 Chief Financial Officer	29 Family/Consumer Science	39 Social Studies K-12	49 English/Lang Arts Elem	59 Special Education Elem	69 Academic Assessment
2 Bus/Finance/Purchasing	9 Curric/Instruct Elem	20 Art K-12	30 Adult Education	40 Social Studies Elem	50 English/Lang Arts Sec	60 Special Education Sec	70 Research/Development
3 Buildings And Grounds	10 Curric/Instruct Sec	21 Art Elem	31 Career/Sch-to-Work K-12	41 Social Studies Sec	51 Reading K-12	61 Foreign/World Lang K-12	71 Public Information
4 Food Service	11 Federal Program	22 Art Sec	32 Career/Sch-to-Work Elem	42 Science K-12	52 Reading Elem	62 Foreign/World Lang Elem	72 Summer School
5 Transportation	12 Title I	23 Music K-12	33 Career/Sch-to-Work Sec	43 Science Elem	53 Reading Sec	63 Foreign/World Lang Sec	73 Instructional Tech
6 Athletic	13 Title V	24 Music Elem	34 Early Childhood Ed	44 Science Sec	54 Remedial Reading K-12	64 Religious Education K-12	74 Inservice Training
7 Health Services	15 Asst Superintendent	25 Music Sec	35 Health/Phys Education	45 Math K-12	55 Remedial Reading Elem	65 Religious Education Elem	75 Marketing/Distributive
	16 Instructional Media Svcs	26 Business Education	36 Guidance Services K-12	46 Math Elem	56 Remedial Reading Sec	66 Religious Education Sec	76 Info Systems
	17 Chief Operations Officer	27 Career & Tech Ed	37 Guidance Services Elem	47 Math Sec	57 Bilingual/ELL	67 School Board President	77 Psychological Assess
	18 Chief Academic Officer	28 Technology Education	38 Guidance Services Sec	48 English/Lang Arts K-12	58 Special Education K-12	68 Teacher Personnel	78 Affirmative Action

Illinois School Directory — Winnebago County

School	Grades	Prgm	Enr/#Cls	SN	Phone
ⓂMacHesney Elem Sch 8615 N 2nd St, MacHesney Pk 61115 Abigail Edwards	4-6	T	378 21	52%	815/654-4509 Fax 815/637-7421
Maple Elem Sch 1405 Maple Ave, Loves Park 61111 Tammy Poole	1-6	T	282 24	74%	815/654-4502 Fax 815/654-4563 ⓕⓣ
Marquette Elem Sch 8500 Victory Ln, MacHesney Pk 61115 Brock Morlan	1-3	T	300 18	60%	815/654-4503 Fax 815/654-4565
Olson Park Elem Sch 1414 Minahan Dr, MacHesney Pk 61115 Dyonna Johnson	1-6	T	288 18	36%	815/654-4504 Fax 815/654-4528
Ralston Elem Sch 710 Ralston Rd, MacHesney Pk 61115 Christy Brown	1-6	T	337 20	36%	815/654-4505 Fax 815/654-4572 ⓕⓣ
Rock Cut Elem Sch 7944 Forest Hills Rd, Loves Park 61111 Ryan Reinecke	1-6	T	432 21	60%	815/654-4506 Fax 815/654-4574
Windsor Elem Sch 935 Windsor Rd, Loves Park 61111 Melissa Yuska	1-6	T	416 27	69%	815/654-4507 Fax 815/654-4585

● **Hononegah Cmty High SD 207** PID: 00327274 815/624-5010
307 Salem St, Rockton 61072 Fax 815/624-5029

> **Schools:** 1 \ **Teachers:** 110 \ **Students:** 1,500 \ **Special Ed Students:** 218 \ **LEP Students:** 13 \ **College-Bound:** 71% \ **Ethnic:** Asian 3%, African American 2%, Hispanic 8%, Caucasian 88% \ **Exp:** $250 (Med) \ **Poverty:** 5% \ **Title I:** $158,198 \ **Special Education:** $1,066,000 \ **Open-Close:** 09/03 - 05/28 \ **DTBP:** $215 (High)

Michael Dugan 1		Justin Krueger 2	
David Berg 3		Maria Small 4*	
Steve Cofoid 6,274*		Kathy Eckmann 11,288	
Therresa Mohr 11,275		Rob Conerton 16,73,295*	
David Kurlinkus 67			

Public Schs..Principal	Grd	Prgm	Enr/#Cls	SN	
Honenegah Cmty High Sch 307 Salem St, Rockton 61072 Chad Dougherty	9-12	AV	1,500 60	19%	815/624-2070 Fax 815/624-5025

● **Kinnikinnick Cmty Cons SD 131** PID: 00327298 815/623-2837
5410 Pine Ln, Roscoe 61073 Fax 815/623-9285

> **Schools:** 4 \ **Teachers:** 105 \ **Students:** 1,750 \ **Special Ed Students:** 317 \ **LEP Students:** 24 \ **Ethnic:** Asian 2%, African American 3%, Hispanic 8%, Caucasian 88% \ **Exp:** $224 (Med) \ **Poverty:** 9% \ **Title I:** $246,086 \ **Special Education:** $666,000 \ **Open-Close:** 08/17 - 06/07 \ **DTBP:** $225 (High)

Keli Freedlund 1,11	Brett Hruby 2,84
Mimi Bannon 9,16,69,73,288	David Young 67
Lisa Yaun 79	

Public Schs..Principal	Grd	Prgm	Enr/#Cls	SN	
Kinnikinnick Sch 5410 Pine Ln, Roscoe 61073 Shaun Newmes	4-5		365 23	23%	815/623-2837 Fax 815/623-1797
Ledgewood Elem Sch 11685 S Gate Rd, Roscoe 61073 Chad Etnyre	PK-1		394 19	21%	815/623-2837 Fax 815/623-1410
Roscoe Middle Sch 6121 Elevator Rd, Roscoe 61073 Julia Cropp	6-8	T	608 24	26%	815/623-2837 Fax 815/623-7604
Stone Creek Elem Sch 11633 S Gate Rd, Roscoe 61073 Shane Caiola	2-3		386 20	22%	815/623-2837 Fax 815/623-3646

● **Pecatonica Cmty Unit SD 321** PID: 00327315 815/239-1639
1300 Main St, Pecatonica 61063 Fax 815/239-2125

> **Schools:** 3 \ **Teachers:** 64 \ **Students:** 950 \ **Special Ed Students:** 168 \ **LEP Students:** 8 \ **College-Bound:** 99% \ **Ethnic:** Asian 1%, African American 2%, Hispanic 5%, Caucasian 92% \ **Exp:** $138 (Low) \ **Poverty:** 8% \ **Title I:** $110,874 \ **Special Education:** $382,000 \ **Open-Close:** 08/24 - 05/28

William Faller 1,83	Alan Olson 3*
Connie White 4*	Sue Siemens 5*
Kevin Kunkel 6*	Heather Baker 8*
Carrie Brockway 11,296*	Tina Clark 12*
Sally Hoff 67	Jeff Bowman 73

Public Schs..Principal	Grd	Prgm	Enr/#Cls	SN	
Pecatonica Elem Sch 721 Reed St, Pecatonica 61063 Carrie Brockway	PK-4		339 16	29%	815/239-2550 Fax 815/239-1418
Pecatonica High Sch 1300 Main St, Pecatonica 61063 Todd France	9-12	V	250 30	26%	815/239-2611 Fax 815/239-9128
Pecatonica Middle Sch 1200 Main St, Pecatonica 61063 Timothy King	5-8		297 25	25%	815/239-2612 Fax 815/239-1274

● **Prairie Hill Cmty Cons SD 133** PID: 00327389 815/389-3964
6605 Prairie Hill Rd, South Beloit 61080 Fax 844/272-8107

> **Schools:** 2 \ **Teachers:** 50 \ **Students:** 743 \ **Special Ed Students:** 110 \ **LEP Students:** 8 \ **Ethnic:** Asian 2%, African American 1%, Hispanic 4%, Caucasian 92% \ **Exp:** $237 (Med) \ **Poverty:** 7% \ **Title I:** $74,367 \ **Special Education:** $302,000 \ **Open-Close:** 08/14 - 05/21 \ **DTBP:** $237 (High)

Clint Czizek 1,11,57	Andrea Fjaistad 2
Courtney Prentice 67	Mike Weeden 73*
Emily Breakfield 286	Kerry Drifcoll 288

Public Schs..Principal	Grd	Prgm	Enr/#Cls	SN	
Prairie Hill Elem Sch 14714 Willowbrook Rd, South Beloit 61080 Kevin Finnegan	PK-4		427 21	15%	815/389-3301 Fax 815/389-8582
Willowbrook Middle Sch 6605 Prairie Hill Rd, South Beloit 61080 Mike Plourde	5-8		300	16%	815/389-3957 Fax 844/272-8075

● **Rockford School District 205** PID: 00327406 815/966-3000
501 7th St, Rockford 61104 Fax 815/972-3420

> **Schools:** 46 \ **Teachers:** 1,682 \ **Students:** 28,940 \ **Special Ed Students:** 4,553 \ **LEP Students:** 4,528 \ **College-Bound:** 50% \ **Ethnic:** Asian 4%, African American 34%, Hispanic 30%, Caucasian 31% \ **Exp:** $397 (High) \ **Poverty:** 31% \ **Title I:** $21,858,911 \ **Special Education:** $20,851,000 \ **Bilingual Education:** $1,337,000 \ **Open-Close:** 09/02 - 06/08 \ **DTBP:** $239 (High) \ ⓕⓣ

Dr Ehren Jarrett 1	Dane Youngblood 2
Jamie Murray 2	Michele Sather 2
Ann Delang 3	Michael Phillips 3
Wilson Bailey 3	Renee Beauchamp 4

Code	Description	Code	Description	Code	Description	Code	Description
79	Student Personnel	91	Safety/Security	275	Response To Intervention	298	Grant Writer/Ptnrships
80	Driver Ed/Safety	92	Magnet School	277	Remedial Math K-12	750	Chief Innovation Officer
81	Gifted/Talented	93	Parental Involvement	280	Literacy Coach	751	Chief of Staff
82	Video Services	95	Tech Prep Program	285	STEM	752	Social Emotional Learning
83	Substance Abuse Prev	97	Chief Infomation Officer	286	Digital Learning		
84	Erate	98	Chief Technology Officer	288	Common Core Standards		
85	AIDS Education	270	Accountability	294	Character Education		
88	Alternative/At Risk	271	Migrant Education	295	Network System		
89	Multi-Cultural Curriculum	273	Teacher Mentor	296	Title II Programs		
90	Social Work	274	Before/After Sch	297	Webmaster		

School Programs
A = Alternative Program
G = Adult Classes
M = Magnet Program
T = Title I Schoolwide
V = Career & Tech Ed Programs

Other School Types
Ⓐ = Alternative School
Ⓒ = Charter School
Ⓜ = Magnet School
Ⓨ = Year-Round School

Social Media
ⓕ = Facebook
ⓣ = Twitter

New Schools are shaded
New Superintendents and Principals are bold
Personnel with email addresses are underscored

Winnebago County

Michael Slife 5
Joyce Turnipseed 7
Heidi Dettman 8
Dr Travis Woulfe 11,70,298
Michelle Jahr 19
Bridget French 27,31,36
Kimberly Nelson 34
Jennifer Lawrence 58
Matthew Zediker 68
Earl Dotson 71
Diana Alt 74,81
Angela Hite-Carter 79,88
Maureen Kirschmann 93
Melissa Douglas 280
Monica Bayne 297
Mat Parker 6
Ben Epperson 8
Joyann Kirschbaum 9,34
Dr Matthew Vosberg 15
Bonnie Spurling 20,23
Reid Jutras 27
Misael Nascimento 57
Kenneth Scrivano 67
Emily Beaumont 69
Susan Uram 73
Chris Taskey 76
Fred Diehl 91
Jason Barthel 97
Brooke Peterson 294

Public Schs..Principal	Grd	Prgm	Enr/#Cls	SN		
Auburn High Sch 5110 Auburn St, Rockford 61101 Jenny Keffer	9-12	TV	1,827		62%	815/966-3300 Fax 815/489-2788
Beyer Early Childhood Center 333 15th Ave, Rockford 61104 Laura Blackwell	PK-PK	T	335 187		52%	815/966-3390 Fax 815/972-3446
Brookview Elem Sch 1750 Madron Rd, Rockford 61107 Melanie Wiest	K-5	T	558 20		45%	815/229-2492 Fax 815/921-0328
C Henry Bloom Elem Sch 2912 Brendenwood Rd, Rockford 61107 Pati Strehl	K-5	T	409 18		71%	815/229-2170 Fax 815/921-0327
Cherry Valley Elem Sch 6754 Armer Dr, Rockford 61109 Carolyn Timm	K-5		640 9		49%	815/332-4938 Fax 815/972-3454
Clifford P Carlson Elem Sch 4015 Pepper Dr, Rockford 61114 Kristina Miller	K-5	T	371 14		63%	815/654-4955 Fax 815/972-3447
Conklin Elem Sch 3003 Halsted Rd, Rockford 61101 Sidney Graves	K-5	T	308 17		78%	815/654-4860 Fax 815/972-3401
Constance Lane Elem Sch 620 Gregory St, Rockford 61104 Aimee Kasper	K-5	T	567 21		91%	815/966-3380 Fax 815/921-0326
Eisenhower Middle Sch 3525 Spring Creek Rd, Rockford 61107 Jeff Carlson	6-8	T	968 60		55%	815/229-2450 Fax 815/489-2787
Ⓜ Ellis Elem Sch 222 S Central Ave, Rockford 61102 Taren Turner	K-5	T	445 70		91%	815/966-3909 Fax 815/966-3134
Fairview Early Childhood Ctr 512 Fairview Ave, Rockford 61108 Darcy Dunn	PK-PK		730 18		34%	815/227-8400 Fax 815/921-0333
Flinn Middle Sch 2525 Ohio Pkwy, Rockford 61108 Cory Schrank	6-8	TV	874 53		66%	815/229-2800 Fax 815/489-2725
Froberg Elem Sch 4555 20th St, Rockford 61109 Christina Ulferts	K-5	T	422 10		54%	815/874-2464 Fax 815/921-0329
© Galapagos Rockford CS [162] 2605 School St, Rockford 61101 Nikole Laskov	K-8	T	281		37%	815/708-7946 Fax 815/708-7966
Gifted Acad Marshall ES 4704 N Rockton Ave, Rockford 61103 Jessica Powell	1-4		391		21%	815/966-3370 Fax 815/966-3347
Gifted Acad Marshall MS 4664 N Rockton Ave, Rockford 61103 Jill Faber	5-8		471		17%	815/490-5400 Fax 815/489-2644
Gregory Elem Sch 4820 Carol Ct, Rockford 61108 Kristine Leider	K-5	T	344 13		71%	815/229-2176 Fax 815/921-0303
Guilford High Sch 5620 Spring Creek Rd, Rockford 61114 Ronald Carter	9-12	GTV	1,789 55		51%	815/654-4870 Fax 815/972-3498
Hillman Elem Sch 3701 Green Dale Dr, Rockford 61109 Carolyn Kloss	K-5	T	578 17		76%	815/229-2835 Fax 815/489-2789
© Jackson Charter Sch 315 Summit St, Rockford 61107 Shavina Baker	K-8	T	383		44%	815/316-0093 Fax 815/316-0170
Kennedy Middle Sch 520 Pierpont Ave, Rockford 61103 Treveda Redmond	6-8	TV	486 50		89%	815/654-4880 Fax 815/489-2793
Lathrop Elem Sch 2603 Clover Ave, Rockford 61102 Penny El-Azhari	K-5	T	381 19		81%	815/966-3285 Fax 815/972-3426
© Legacy Academy of Excellence 4029 Prairie Rd, Rockford 61102 Dr Barbara Forte	K-12	T	318		36%	815/961-1100 Fax 815/968-4597
Ⓜ Lewis Lemon Elem Sch 1993 Mulberry St, Rockford 61101 Christina Ulferts	K-5	T	344 24		88%	815/967-8000 Fax 815/972-3430
Lincoln Middle Sch 1500 Charles St, Rockford 61104 James Parker	6-8	TV	662 60		80%	815/229-2400 Fax 815/489-2757
Ⓜ Maria Montessori Sch 2021 Hawthorne Dr, Rockford 61107 Candice Collins	PK-3		267 15		41%	815/654-4906 Fax 815/489-2699
Maud E Johnson Elem Sch 3805 Rural St, Rockford 61107 Amber Miller	K-5	T	449 16		60%	815/229-2485 Fax 815/972-3485
Ⓜ McIntosh Elem Sch 525 N Pierpont Ave, Rockford 61101 Al Gagliano	K-5	T	348 20		88%	815/966-3275 Fax 815/489-2794
Nashold Early Childhood Center 3303 20th St, Rockford 61109 Erin Salberg	PK-PK		660 18		46%	815/229-2155 Fax 815/489-2792
Riverdahl Elem Sch 3520 Kishwaukee St, Rockford 61109 Tommy Gibbons	PK-3	T	521 30		83%	815/229-2870 Fax 815/972-3449
Rockford East High Sch 2929 Charles St, Rockford 61108 Dr Peter Verona	9-12	TV	1,807		66%	815/229-2100 Fax 815/489-2785
Ⓜ Rockford Env Science Academy 1800 Ogilby Rd, Rockford 61102 Benjamin Stover	6-8	T	1,090		76%	815/489-5509 Fax 815/489-2783
Ⓐ Rockford Innovative Lrng Ctr 1907 Kishwaukee St, Rockford 61104 Angelina Bua	9-12		250			815/977-3766
Rolling Green Elem Sch 3615 W Gate Pkwy, Rockford 61108 Holly Lyman	PK-5	T	585 40		75%	815/229-2881 Fax 815/921-0330
Ⓐ Roosevelt Cmty Education Ctr 978 Haskell Ave, Rockford 61103 Morgan Gallagher	9-12	GT	467 22		72%	815/966-3250 Fax 815/921-0332
Spring Creek Elem Sch 5222 Spring Creek Rd, Rockford 61114 Ray Owens	K-5	T	478 22		42%	815/654-4960 Fax 815/921-0331
Ⓜ Steam Academy at Haskell Ⓨ 515 Maple St, Rockford 61103 Loree Leathers	K-5	MT	301 12		86%	815/966-3355 Fax 815/967-8077
Ⓜ Summerdale Early Childhood Ctr 3320 Glenwood Ave, Rockford 61101 Jennifer Lakelman	PK-PK		500 12		55%	815/966-3280 Fax 815/972-3472
Thomas Jefferson High Sch 4145 Samuelson Rd, Rockford 61109 Donald Rundall	9-12	TV	1,719 79		69%	815/874-9536 Fax 815/921-0316

1 Superintendent	8 Curric/Instruct K-12	19 Chief Financial Officer	29 Family/Consumer Science	39 Social Studies K-12	49 English/Lang Arts Elem	59 Special Education Elem	69 Academic Assessment
2 Bus/Finance/Purchasing	9 Curric/Instruct Elem	20 Art K-12	30 Adult Education	40 Social Studies Elem	50 English/Lang Arts Sec	60 Special Education Sec	70 Research/Development
3 Buildings And Grounds	10 Curric/Instruct Sec	21 Art Elem	31 Career/Sch-to-Work K-12	41 Social Studies Sec	51 Reading K-12	61 Foreign/World Lang K-12	71 Public Information
4 Food Service	11 Federal Program	22 Art Sec	32 Career/Sch-to-Work Elem	42 Science K-12	52 Reading Elem	62 Foreign/World Lang Elem	72 Summer School
5 Transportation	12 Title I	23 Music K-12	33 Career/Sch-to-Work Sec	43 Science Elem	53 Reading Sec	63 Foreign/World Lang Sec	73 Instructional Tech
6 Athletic	13 Title V	24 Music Elem	34 Early Childhood Ed	44 Science Sec	54 Remedial Reading K-12	64 Religious Education K-12	74 Inservice Training
7 Health Services	15 Asst Superintendent	25 Music Sec	35 Health/Phys Education	45 Math K-12	55 Remedial Reading Elem	65 Religious Education Elem	75 Marketing/Distributive
	16 Instructional Media Svcs	26 Business Education	36 Guidance Services K-12	46 Math Elem	56 Remedial Reading Sec	66 Religious Education Sec	76 Info Systems
	17 Chief Operations Officer	27 Career & Tech Ed	37 Guidance Services Elem	47 Math Sec	57 Bilingual/E.l.	67 School Board President	77 Psychological Assess
	18 Chief Academic Officer	28 Technology Education	38 Guidance Services Sec	48 English/Lang Arts K-12	58 Special Education K-12	68 Teacher Personnel	78 Affirmative Action

Illinois School Directory — Winnebago County

School	Grd	Prgm	Enr/#Cls	SN	Phone
ⓂTwo-Way Language Imm-Barbour 1506 Clover Ave, Rockford 61102 James Robinette	K-8	T	754 26	75%	815/490-4100 Fax 815/489-2663
Washington Elem Sch 1421 West St, Rockford 61102 Gregory Midgett	K-5	T	462 15	83%	815/966-3740 Fax 815/972-3484
Welsh Elem Sch 2100 Huffman Blvd, Rockford 61103 Blake Hand	K-5	T	491 16	82%	815/966-3260 Fax 815/489-2674
West Middle Sch 1900 N Rockton Ave, Rockford 61103 Larry Goodrich	6-8	T	930 50	73%	815/966-3200 Fax 815/489-2770
West View Elem Sch 1720 Halsted Rd, Rockford 61103 Jake Sayre	K-5	T	493 18	72%	815/654-4945 Fax 815/972-3481
Whitehead Elem Sch 2325 Ohio Pkwy, Rockford 61108 Pam Miner	K-5	T	598 17	72%	815/229-2840 Fax 815/489-2718
Wilson Aspire Sch 520 N Pierpont Ave, Rockford 61101 Angela Rieke	Spec		25	86%	815/966-3770 Fax 815/489-2689

• **Rockton School District 140** PID: 00328151   815/624-7143
1050 E Union St, Rockton 61072   Fax 815/624-4640

Schools: 3 \ **Teachers:** 94 \ **Students:** 1,600 \ **Special Ed Students:** 236 \ **LEP Students:** 16 \ **Ethnic:** Asian 1%, African American 2%, Hispanic 8%, Caucasian 88% \ **Exp:** $170 (Low) \ **Poverty:** 9% \ **Title I:** $194,705 \ **Special Education:** $591,000 \ **Open-Close:** 08/19 - 05/27 \ **DTBP:** $224 (High)

Glenn Terry 1,57   Kim Garst 2
Tim Ehlers 3   Brenda Willey 4
Lindy Daniels 9,11,288   Michelle Anderson 12*
Katie Littlefield 67   James Hall 73

Public Schs..Principal	Grd	Prgm	Enr/#Cls	SN	
Rockton Grade Sch 1050 E Union St, Rockton 61072 Kindyl Etnyre	PK-2	T	545 25	27%	815/624-8585 Fax 815/624-1002
Stephen Mack Middle Sch 11810 Old River Rd, Rockton 61072 Autum Czizek	6-8		529 50	21%	815/624-2611 Fax 815/624-5900
Whitman Post Elem Sch 1060 E Union St, Rockton 61072 Megan Forsythe	3-5		483 21	26%	815/624-4006 Fax 815/624-2125

• **Shirland Cmty Cons SD 134** PID: 00328175   815/629-2000
8020 North St, Shirland 61079   Fax 815/629-2100

Schools: 1 \ **Teachers:** 12 \ **Students:** 111 \ **Special Ed Students:** 15 \ **LEP Students:** 3 \ **Ethnic:** Hispanic 3%, Native American: 4%, Caucasian 93% \ **Exp:** $478 (High) \ **Poverty:** 13% \ **Title I:** $31,451 \ **Special Education:** $79,000 \ **Open-Close:** 08/21 - 05/28 \ **DTBP:** $180 (High) \ 🅕

Dr John Ulferts 1,288   Catherine Sweeney 2,11
Manuel Camacho 4   Jake James 7,83,296*
Sarah Maxey ....12*   Will Holmes 12*
Amber Miller ....16*   William Diemel 67
Amber Emerson 73*

Public Schs..Principal	Grd	Prgm	Enr/#Cls	SN	
Shirland Cmty Cons Sch 8020 North St, Shirland 61079 John Ulferts	PK-8		111 10	35%	815/629-2000

• **South Beloit Cmty Sch Dist 320** PID: 00328199   815/389-3478
850 Hayes Ave, South Beloit 61080   Fax 815/389-3477

Schools: 5 \ **Teachers:** 67 \ **Students:** 960 \ **Special Ed Students:** 124 \ **LEP Students:** 68 \ **Ethnic:** Asian 1%, African American 3%, Hispanic 28%, Caucasian 68% \ **Exp:** $183 (Low) \ **Poverty:** 21% \ **Title I:** $378,591 \ **Special Education:** $613,000 \ **Open-Close:** 08/12 - 05/27 \ **DTBP:** $244 (High)

Scott Fisher 1,11   Terri Gille 2,84
Phillip Alseth 3   Don Ramballt 4*
Sam Cady 6   Josephine Ott 38,69*
Imari Hanserd 57,58,88   Scott Bonnet 67
Hailey Marshall 68   Andrew Klabunde 73
Nick Jupin 73   Rebecca Pope 83,85

Public Schs..Principal	Grd	Prgm	Enr/#Cls	SN	
Blackhawk Elem Sch 840 Blackhawk Blvd, South Beloit 61080 Mike McCoy	5-6	T	154 7	63%	815/389-4001 Fax 815/389-8811
Clark Elem Sch 464 Oak Grove Ave, South Beloit 61080 Matt Roer	PK-1	T	194 12	44%	815/389-2311 Fax 815/389-9002
Riverview Elem Sch 306 Miller St, South Beloit 61080 Tim Doherty	2-4	T	236 11	64%	815/389-1231 Fax 815/389-9067
South Beloit High Sch 245 Prairie Hill Rd, South Beloit 61080 Clint Czizek	9-12	TV	246 25	63%	815/389-9004 Fax 815/389-9268
South Beloit Jr High Sch 840 Blackhawk Blvd, South Beloit 61080 Mike McCoy	7-8	T	128 10	66%	815/389-1421 Fax 815/389-8811

• **Winnebago Cmty Unit SD 323** PID: 00328254   815/335-2456
304 E McNair Rd, Winnebago 61088   Fax 815/335-7574

Schools: 4 \ **Teachers:** 97 \ **Students:** 1,330 \ **Special Ed Students:** 218 \ **LEP Students:** 26 \ **College-Bound:** 74% \ **Ethnic:** Asian 1%, African American 4%, Hispanic 7%, Caucasian 88% \ **Exp:** $235 (Med) \ **Poverty:** 18% \ **Title I:** $467,008 \ **Special Education:** $554,000 \ **Open-Close:** 08/24 - 05/28 \ **DTBP:** $357 (High)

Dr John Schwuchow 1   Mike Prestgaard 3
Mary Ellen Droy ....4*   Michael Reinders 5
Will Hartje ....6*   Mary Skaggs 7*
Staci Thompson ....8,12,16*   Alison Behn 31*
Jennifer Brenner ....36*   Heather Baker 57
Christine Kaufman 58,77   Christopher Schoeneweisf 67
Ross Eberle 73,295

Public Schs..Principal	Grd	Prgm	Enr/#Cls	SN	
Dorothy Simon Elem Sch 309 S Benton St, Winnebago 61088 Heather Baker	PK-2		307 20	4%	815/335-2318 Fax 815/335-3127
Jean McNair Elem Sch 304 E McNair Rd, Winnebago 61088 Sean Monahan	3-5		289 13	1%	815/335-1607
Winnebago High Sch 200 E McNair Rd, Winnebago 61088 Matthew Bennett	9-12	V	465 35	1%	815/335-2336 Fax 815/335-7548
Winnebago Middle Sch 407 N Elida St, Winnebago 61088 Cathy Finley	6-8		300 30	1%	815/335-2364 Fax 815/335-1437

---

79 Student Personnel	91 Safety/Security	275 Response To Intervention	298 Grant Writer/Ptnrships
80 Driver Ed/Safety	92 Magnet School	277 Remedial Math K-12	750 Chief Innovation Officer
81 Gifted/Talented	93 Parental Involvement	280 Literacy Coach	751 Chief of Staff
82 Video Services	95 Tech Prep Program	285 STEM	752 Social Emotional Learning
83 Substance Abuse Prev	97 Chief Infomation Officer	286 Digital Learning	
84 Erate	98 Chief Technology Officer	288 Common Core Standards	**Other School Types**
85 AIDS Education	270 Character Education	294 Accountability	Ⓐ = Alternative School
88 Alternative/At Risk	271 Migrant Education	295 Network System	Ⓒ = Charter School
89 Multi-Cultural Curriculum	273 Teacher Mentor	296 Title II Programs	Ⓜ = Magnet School
90 Social Work	274 Before/After Sch	297 Webmaster	Ⓨ = Year-Round School

School Programs
A = Alternative Program
G = Adult Classes
M = Magnet Program
T = Title I Schoolwide
V = Career & Tech Ed Programs

Social Media
🅕 = Facebook
🅣 = Twitter

New Schools are shaded
New Superintendents and Principals are bold
Personnel with email addresses are underscored

Winnebago County

WINNEBAGO CATHOLIC SCHOOLS

- **Diocese of Rockford Ed Office** PID: 00328345   815/399-4300
  555 Colman Center Dr, Rockford 61108   Fax 815/399-6278

Schools: 43 \ **Students:** 11,358

Listing includes only schools located in this county. See District Index for location of Diocesan Offices.

Michael Kagan 1
Vito Defrisco 8,15,69
John Jelinek 64
Cris Mimer 2
Elizabeth Heitkamp 11,15,74

Catholic Schs..Principal	Grd	Prgm	Enr/#Cls	SN	Phone
All Saints Catholic Academy 409 N 1st St, Rockford 61107	PK-8		316 15		815/962-8515 Fax 815/962-8526
Boylan Central Cath High Sch 4000 Saint Francis Dr, Rockford 61103 Chris Rozanski	9-12		950 75		815/877-0531 Fax 815/877-2544
Holy Family Catholic Sch 4407 Highcrest Rd, Rockford 61107 Mrs Gendron	PK-8		363 18		815/398-5331 Fax 815/398-5902
St Bridget Sch 604 Clifford Ave, Loves Park 61111 Mary Toldo	PK-8		370 19		815/633-8255 Fax 815/633-5847
St Peter Catholic Sch 320 Elmwood Ave, South Beloit 61080 Erica Schwartz	PK-8		81 10		779/475-0560 Fax 779/475-0562
St Rita Catholic Elem Sch 6284 Valley Knoll Dr, Rockford 61109 Patrick Flanagan	PK-8		280 15		815/398-3466 Fax 815/398-6104

WINNEBAGO PRIVATE SCHOOLS

Private Schs..Principal	Grd	Prgm	Enr/#Cls	SN	Phone
Allegro Academy 6413 Forest Hills Rd, Rockford 61114 Jean McCormack	K-8		100		815/877-1489 Fax 815/877-4461
Alpine Academy of Rockford 5001 Forest View Ave, Rockford 61108 Robert McVinnie	PK-6		100 8		815/227-8894 Fax 815/227-8899
Alpine Christian Sch 325 N Alpine Rd, Rockford 61107 Marci Baker	K-8		40 5		815/399-0880
Ⓐ Beautiful Beginnings 118 N Main St, Rockford 61101 Latrica Saygo	6-10		20		815/703-4712
Christian Life Center Sch 5950 Spring Creek Rd, Rockford 61114 Mike Hoekstra \ Carrie Smith	PK-12	V	700		815/877-5749 Fax 815/877-4358
Concordia Lutheran Sch 7424 N 2nd St, MacHesney Pk 61115 Katy Krause	PK-5		120 6		815/633-6450 Fax 815/654-7998
Easterseals Acad-MacHesney PK 8301 Mitchell Rd, MacHesney Pk 61115 Jacque Ruch	Spec		60		815/623-4800
Keith Country Day Sch 1 Jacoby Pl, Rockford 61107 Dr Jim Norris	PK-12		300 34		815/399-8823 Fax 815/399-2470
Menta Academy Northwest 8702 N 2nd St, MacHesney Pk 61115 Rory Conran	Spec		45		815/975-3297
Montessori Private Academy 8101 Sayer Rd, Rockford 61108 Sue Haney-Bauer	PK-9		166 8		815/332-8101 Fax 815/332-8104
North Love Christian Sch 5301 E Riverside Blvd, Rockford 61114 Tony Cotelleso	K-12	V	166 13		815/877-6021 Fax 815/877-6076
Our Lady Sacred Heart Academy 3445 Elmwood Rd, Rockford 61101 Louis Bageanis	K-12		50		815/399-3021
Rockford Christian Elem Sch 220 Hemlock Ln, Rockford 61107 Matthew Nyberg	PK-5		520		815/391-8006 Fax 815/399-8280
Rockford Christian High Sch 1401 N Bell School Rd, Rockford 61107 Amycarol Bedows \ Drew Popejoy	6-12		1,200 22		815/399-3465 Fax 815/391-8004
Rockford Iqra Sch 5925 Darlene Dr, Rockford 61109 Dr Ronald Hassan	PK-12		134		815/397-6899 Fax 815/397-1681
Rockford Lutheran Academy 1711 Delcy Dr, Rockford 61107 Curtis Wudtke	PK-5		292 18		815/226-4947 Fax 815/226-4886
Rockford Lutheran High Sch 3411 N Alpine Rd, Rockford 61114 Don Gillingham	6-12		550 35		815/877-9551 Fax 815/636-4429
Spectrum Sch 4848 Turner St, Rockford 61107 Dr Mary Cunat	PK-8		96 15		815/877-1600 Fax 815/877-1685
St Paul Academy 1001 Bishop Washington Ave, Rockford 61102 Vache Fleming	PK-K		6 5		815/965-4308 Fax 815/965-8476
St Paul Lutheran Sch 811 Locust St, Rockford 61101 Bruce Volkert	PK-8		110 10		815/965-3335
Walter Lawson Children's Home 1820 Walter Lawson Dr, Loves Park 61111 Katie Johnson	Spec		50 5		815/633-6636 Fax 815/633-6387

WINNEBAGO REGIONAL CENTERS

- **Boone-Winnebago Reg Off of Ed** PID: 02098510   815/636-3060
  300 Heart Blvd, Loves Park 61111   Fax 815/636-3069

Dr Lori Fanello 1   Scott Bloomquist 15
Stephanie Putzstuck 30

- **Career Educ Assoc N Ctl IL** PID: 04182260   815/921-1651
  4151 Samuelson Rd, Rockford 61109   Fax 815/921-1669

Margie Hartfiel 1

- **Winnebago Co Special Ed Co-op** PID: 02182290   815/624-2615
  11971 Wagon Wheel Rd, Rockton 61072   Fax 815/624-8118

Sarah Moore 1

---

1 Superintendent	8 Curric/Instruct K-12	19 Chief Financial Officer	29 Family/Consumer Science	39 Social Studies K-12	49 English/Lang Arts Elem	59 Special Education Elem	69 Academic Assessment
2 Bus/Finance/Purchasing	9 Curric/Instruct Elem	20 Art K-12	30 Adult Education	40 Social Studies Elem	50 English/Lang Arts Sec	60 Special Education Sec	70 Research/Development
3 Buildings And Grounds	10 Curric/Instruct Sec	21 Art Elem	31 Career/Sch-to-Work K-12	41 Social Studies Sec	51 Reading K-12	61 Foreign/World Lang K-12	71 Public Information
4 Food Service	11 Federal Program	22 Art Sec	32 Career/Sch-to-Work Elem	42 Science K-12	52 Reading Elem	62 Foreign/World Lang Elem	72 Summer School
5 Transportation	12 Title I	23 Music K-12	33 Career/Sch-to-Work Sec	43 Science Elem	53 Reading Sec	63 Foreign/World Lang Sec	73 Instructional Tech
6 Athletic	13 Title V	24 Music Elem	34 Early Childhood Ed	44 Science Sec	54 Remedial Reading K-12	64 Religious Education K-12	74 Inservice Training
7 Health Services	15 Asst Superintendent	25 Music Sec	35 Health/Phys Education	45 Math K-12	55 Remedial Reading Elem	65 Religious Education Elem	75 Marketing/Distributive
	16 Instructional Media Svcs	26 Business Education	36 Guidance Services K-12	46 Math Elem	56 Remedial Reading Sec	66 Religious Education Sec	76 Info Systems
	17 Chief Operations Officer	27 Career & Tech Ed	37 Guidance Services Elem	47 Math Sec	57 Bilingual/ELL	67 School Board President	77 Psychological Assess
	18 Chief Academic Officer	28 Technology Education	38 Guidance Services Sec	48 English/Lang Arts K-12	58 Special Education K-12	68 Teacher Personnel	78 Affirmative Action

Illinois School Directory

Woodford County

WOODFORD PUBLIC SCHOOLS

- **El Paso-Gridley CUSD 11** PID: 00328955   309/527-4410
  97 W 5th St, El Paso 61738

Schools: 4 \ Teachers: 88 \ Students: 1,200 \ Special Ed Students: 144 \ LEP Students: 3 \ Ethnic: African American 2%, Hispanic 5%, Caucasian 93% \ Exp: $211 (Med) \ Poverty: 8% \ Title I: $152,790 \ Special Education: $540,000 \ Open-Close: 08/19 - 05/26

Name	Code
Brian Kurz	1
Jessi Sinn	2
Amber Buss	8,11,57,275,288
Randy Barth	67
Bri Herrman	2
John Carr	3
Cheryl Steber	13,16,82*
Alex DePauw	73,295*

Public Schs..Principal	Grd	Prgm	Enr/#Cls	SN	
Centennial Elem Sch 135 W 5th St, El Paso 61738 Tim Fairchild	3-4	T	181 11	38%	309/527-4435 Fax 309/527-4438 **f**
El Paso-Gridley High Sch 600 N Elm St, El Paso 61738 Brian Quam	9-12	TV	368 45	30%	309/527-4415 Fax 309/527-4411
El Paso-Gridley Jr High Sch 403 McLean St, Gridley 61744 Robby Tomlinson	5-8	TV	362 20	38%	309/747-2156 Fax 309/747-2938
Jefferson Park Elem Sch 250 W 3rd St, El Paso 61738 Kelly Throneburg	PK-2	T	313 12	33%	309/527-4405 Fax 309/527-4407

- **Eureka Cmty Unit Sch Dist 140** PID: 00328993   309/467-3737
  109 W Cruger Ave, Eureka 61530   Fax 309/467-2377

Schools: 5 \ Teachers: 102 \ Students: 1,567 \ Special Ed Students: 155 \ LEP Students: 4 \ College-Bound: 86% \ Ethnic: Asian 1%, African American 1%, Hispanic 3%, Caucasian 96% \ Exp: $190 (Low) \ Poverty: 6% \ Title I: $156,846 \ Special Education: $630,000 \ Open-Close: 08/12 - 05/28

Name	Code
Robert Bardwell	1,11,83
Stacie Bauman	4
Jason Greene	6*
Jason Bachman	36*
Tyler Breitbarth	73*
Andrew Underwood	2*
Ken Scharf	5
David Tapp	16*
Chad Leman	67
Mike Zimmerman	295*

Public Schs..Principal	Grd	Prgm	Enr/#Cls	SN	
Congerville Elem Sch 310 E Kauffman St, Congerville 61729 Randal Berardi	K-4		87 5	20%	309/448-2347 Fax 309/448-5122
Davenport Elem Sch 301 S Main St, Eureka 61530 Stephanie Brown	PK-4		424 20	29%	309/467-3012 Fax 309/467-5265
Eureka High Sch 200 W Cruger Ave, Eureka 61530 Kirk Edwards	9-12	AV	469 30	16%	309/467-2361 Fax 309/467-2648
Eureka Middle Sch 2005 S Main St, Eureka 61530 Kelly Nichols	5-8	A	480 30	24%	309/467-3771 Fax 309/467-2052

Public Schs..Principal	Grd	Prgm	Enr/#Cls	SN	
Goodfield Elem Sch 308 W Robinson St, Goodfield 61742 Randal Berardi	PK-4		90 5	16%	309/965-2362 Fax 309/965-2270

- **Fieldcrest Cmty School Dist 6** PID: 00329117   309/432-2177
  1 Dornbush Dr, Minonk 61760   Fax 309/432-3377

Schools: 4 \ Teachers: 73 \ Students: 909 \ Special Ed Students: 144 \ LEP Students: 4 \ College-Bound: 67% \ Ethnic: African American 1%, Hispanic 5%, Caucasian 94% \ Exp: $73 (Low) \ Poverty: 11% \ Title I: $170,367 \ Special Education: $545,000 \ Open-Close: 08/19 - 05/26 \ DTBP: $198 (High)

Name	Code
Dr Kari Rockwell	1,11
Ron Kreiser	3
Cindi Koudelka	8*
William Lapp	60*
Matthew Wendling	73
Rose Lutz	2
Gregg Frei	5
Nate Lorton	12
Mykin Bernardi	67

Public Schs..Principal	Grd	Prgm	Enr/#Cls	SN	
Fieldcrest High Sch 1 Dornbush Dr, Minonk 61760 William Lapp	9-12		328 27	38%	309/432-2529 Fax 309/432-2064
Fieldcrest Intermediate Sch 306 N Maple St, Toluca 61369 Jacob Wall	3-5	T	185 30	50%	815/452-2411
Fieldcrest Middle Sch 102 W Elm St, Wenona 61377 Nate Lorton	6-8		285 9	45%	815/853-4331 Fax 815/853-4786
Fieldcrest Primary Sch 523 Johnson St, Minonk 61760 Jason Chaplin	PK-2	T	160 14	53%	309/432-2838 Fax 309/432-2192

- **Germantown Hills SD 69** PID: 00329052   309/383-2121
  103 Warrior Way, Germantwn Hls 61548   Fax 309/383-2123

Schools: 2 \ Teachers: 55 \ Students: 900 \ Special Ed Students: 75 \ LEP Students: 4 \ Ethnic: Asian 1%, African American 1%, Hispanic 4%, Caucasian 94% \ Exp: $232 (Med) \ Poverty: 3% \ Title I: $30,521 \ Special Education: $376,000 \ Open-Close: 08/13 - 05/19 \ DTBP: $232 (High)

Name	Code
Dan Mair	1,11
Doug Cupples	3*
Denise Hough	5,35
Jean Wilmarth	16*
Mike Dexheimer	73*
Stacy Tellor	2
Kim Kiesewetter	4*
Kate Williams	6
Jason Hunt	67

Public Schs..Principal	Grd	Prgm	Enr/#Cls	SN	
Germantown Hills Elem Sch 103 Warrior Way, Metamora 61548 Dr Shelli Nafziger	PK-4		446 20	16%	309/383-2121 Fax 309/383-3392
Germantown Hills Middle Sch 103 Warrior Way, Metamora 61548 Kate Williams	5-8		365 22	15%	309/383-2121 Fax 309/383-4739

- **Lowpoint-Washburn CUSD 21** PID: 00329210   309/248-7522
  508 E Walnut St, Washburn 61570   Fax 309/248-7518

Schools: 3 \ Teachers: 27 \ Students: 325 \ Special Ed Students: 55 \ College-Bound: 53% \ Ethnic: African American 1%, Hispanic 2%, Caucasian 97% \ Exp: $150 (Low) \ Poverty: 11% \ Title I: $67,606 \ Special Education: $203,000 \ Open-Close: 08/17 - 05/28 \ DTBP: $193 (High)

Woodford County

Market Data Retrieval

Duane Schupp 1,84	Aaron Davis 6*
Mark Zulz 57,69,83*	Willa Warnkes-Sipp 67
Kim Krohn 73*	

Public Schs..Principal	Grd	Prgm	Enr/#Cls	SN	
Lowpoint-Washburn Elem Sch 701 N Lynn St, Washburn 61570 Duane Schupp	K-3	T	98 6	54%	309/248-7221 Fax 309/248-7906
Lowpoint-Washburn Jr Sr HS 508 E Walnut St, Washburn 61570 Mark Zulz	7-12	T	145 19	50%	309/248-7521 Fax 309/248-7410
Lowpoint-Washburn Middle Sch 508 E Walnut St, Washburn 61570 Duane Schupp	4-6		79 4		309/248-7087

- **Metamora Cmty Cons Sch Dist 1** PID: 00329076   309/367-2361
  815 E Chatham St, Metamora 61548   Fax 309/367-2364

Schools: 1 \ **Teachers:** 56 \ **Students:** 875 \ **Special Ed Students:** 90 \ **Ethnic:** Hispanic 3%, Caucasian 96% \ **Exp:** $182 (Low) \ **Poverty:** 6% \ **Title I:** $81,127 \ **Special Education:** $318,000 \ **Open-Close:** 08/19 - 05/25 \ **DTBP:** $228 (High)

Martin Payne 1,83	Lisa DeVore 2*
Mike Uzelac 3*	Karla Kiesewetter 4*
George Oplt 5	Tim Damery 9,11,69,288*
Ashley Aman 12*	Jeanne Jacobs 16*
Bob Fisher 67	Paul Weber 73,295,297*

Public Schs..Principal	Grd	Prgm	Enr/#Cls	SN	
Metamora Grade Sch 815 E Chatham St, Metamora 61548 Tim Damery	PK-8		875 33	18%	309/367-2361

- **Metamora Twp HS Dist 122** PID: 00329090   309/367-4151
  101 W Madison St, Metamora 61548   Fax 309/367-4154

Schools: 1 \ **Teachers:** 65 \ **Students:** 970 \ **Special Ed Students:** 108 \ **LEP Students:** 3 \ **Ethnic:** Asian 1%, African American 1%, Hispanic 3%, Caucasian 95% \ **Exp:** $253 (Med) \ **Poverty:** 4% \ **Title I:** $38,885 \ **Special Education:** $484,000 \ **Open-Close:** 08/13 - 05/28 \ **DTBP:** $240 (High)

Sean Olaughlin 1,57	Rhonda Danner 2,11
Kelly Kanaga 3*	Rick Frye 3*
Jared Hart 6*	Lisa Doty 7*
Jennifer Murphy 12	Bill Upp 16,73,76*
Deb Bachfischer 16,82*	Dan Ballard 26*
Garry Finch 36,69*	Dr Jennifer Jewel 38,83,752*
Melissa Heil 67	

Public Schs..Principal	Grd	Prgm	Enr/#Cls	SN	
Metamora High Sch 101 W Madison St, Metamora 61548 Ron Kiesewetter	9-12	GV	970 70	16%	309/367-4151 Fax 309/367-4351

- **Riverview Cmty Cons Sch Dist 2** PID: 00329155   309/822-8550
  1421 Spring Bay Rd, East Peoria 61611   Fax 309/822-8414

Schools: 1 \ **Teachers:** 18 \ **Students:** 232 \ **Special Ed Students:** 45 \ **LEP Students:** 3 \ **Ethnic:** Asian 1%, African American 1%, Caucasian 98% \ **Exp:** $246 (Med) \ **Poverty:** 15% \ **Title I:** $64,746 \ **Special Education:** $49,000 \ **Open-Close:** 08/17 - 05/25 \ **DTBP:** $265 (High)

Daren Lowery 1,73,83	Dianne Maxheimer 2,9*
Micheal Allen 6	Evan Ruach 67
Mark Miller 69,73,95	

Public Schs..Principal	Grd	Prgm	Enr/#Cls	SN	
Riverview Elem Sch 1421 Spring Bay Rd, East Peoria 61611 Daren Lowery	PK-8		232 20	58%	309/822-8550

- **Roanoke-Benson Cmty Unit SD 60** PID: 00329179   309/923-8921
  208 W High St, Roanoke 61561   Fax 309/923-7508

Schools: 3 \ **Teachers:** 43 \ **Students:** 500 \ **Special Ed Students:** 77 \ **College-Bound:** 83% \ **Ethnic:** African American 1%, Hispanic 2%, Caucasian 98% \ **Exp:** $209 (Med) \ **Poverty:** 6% \ **Title I:** $58,141 \ **Special Education:** $231,000 \ **Open-Close:** 08/14 - 05/20 \ **DTBP:** $174 (High)

Thomas Welsh 1,11,83	Peggy Schippert 12,51,54*
Brad Sauder 67	Nathan Foote 69*
Mike Oliveri 73*	

Public Schs..Principal	Grd	Prgm	Enr/#Cls	SN	
Roanoke-Benson High Sch 208 W High St, Roanoke 61561 Mike Tresnak	9-12	V	163 25	21%	309/923-8401 Fax 309/923-9151
Roanoke-Benson Jr High Sch 131 S Reiter St, Benson 61516 John Streit	5-8		147 8	27%	309/394-2233 Fax 309/394-2612
Sowers Elem Sch 202 W High St, Roanoke 61561 Thomas Welsh	K-4		192 10	30%	309/923-6241 Fax 309/923-7638

WOODFORD CATHOLIC SCHOOLS

- **Diocese of Peoria Ed Office** PID: 00313338
  Listing includes only schools located in this county. See District Index for location of Diocesan Offices.

Catholic Schs..Principal	Grd	Prgm	Enr/#Cls	SN	
St Mary Sch 400 W Chatham St, Metamora 61548 Rich Koehler	PK-8		174 9		309/367-2528 Fax 309/367-2169

WOODFORD PRIVATE SCHOOLS

Private Schs..Principal	Grd	Prgm	Enr/#Cls	SN	
Countryside Private Sch 775 County Rd 1700 E, Eureka 61530 Chris Leman	K-12		96		309/467-3535
Prairie Christian Sch 3 N Grant St, El Paso 61738 Doug Wettstein	K-8		44 5		309/527-4020

1 Superintendent	8 Curric/Instruct K-12	19 Chief Financial Officer	29 Family/Consumer Science	39 Social Studies K-12	49 English/Lang Arts Elem	59 Special Education Elem	69 Academic Assessment
2 Bus/Finance/Purchasing	9 Curric/Instruct Elem	20 Art K-12	30 Adult Education	40 Social Studies Elem	50 English/Lang Arts Sec	60 Special Education Sec	70 Research/Development
3 Buildings And Grounds	10 Curric/Instruct Sec	21 Art Elem	31 Career/Sch-to-Work K-12	41 Social Studies Sec	51 Reading K-12	61 Foreign/World Lang K-12	71 Public Information
4 Food Service	11 Federal Program	22 Art Sec	32 Career/Sch-to-Work Elem	42 Science K-12	52 Reading Elem	62 Foreign/World Lang Elem	72 Summer School
5 Transportation	12 Title I	23 Music K-12	33 Career/Sch-to-Work Sec	43 Science Elem	53 Reading Sec	63 Foreign/World Lang Sec	73 Instructional Tech
6 Athletic	13 Title V	24 Music Elem	34 Early Childhood Ed	44 Science Sec	54 Remedial Reading K-12	64 Religious Education K-12	74 Inservice Training
7 Health Services	14 Instructional Media Svcs	25 Music Sec	35 Health/Phys Education	45 Math K-12	55 Remedial Reading Elem	65 Religious Education Elem	75 Marketing/Distributive
	15 Asst Superintendent	26 Business Education	36 Guidance Services K-12	46 Math Elem	56 Remedial Reading Sec	66 Religious Education Sec	76 Info Systems
	16 Chief Operations Officer	27 Career & Tech Ed	37 Guidance Services Elem	47 Math Sec	57 Bilingual/ELL	67 School Board President	77 Psychological Assess
	17 Chief Academic Officer	28 Technology Education	38 Guidance Services Sec	48 English/Lang Arts K-12	58 Special Education K-12	68 Teacher Personnel	78 Affirmative Action

WOODFORD REGIONAL CENTERS

- **Central Illinois Voc Ed Co-op** PID: 04177722 309/367-2783
  101 W Madison St, Metamora 61548
  Debra Henderson 1

- **Woodford Co Special Ed Assoc** PID: 02184054 309/367-4901
  205 S Englewood Dr, Metamora 61548 Fax 309/367-4905
  Eric Scroggs .... 1 Maureen Whallen 34

Illinois School Directory

DISTRICT INDEX

SCHOOL DISTRICT	NO. OF SCHOOLS	ENROLL-MENT	COUNTY	PAGE
PUBLIC SCHOOL DISTRICTS				
A-C Central Cmty Unit SD 262	2	419	Cass	9
Abingdon-Avon Cmty Unit SD 276	4	877	Knox	139
Addison School Dist 4	9	4,000	Du Page	88
Adlai E Stevenson HSD 125	1	4,337	Lake	146
Akin Elem School Dist 91	1	80	Franklin	107
Albers Elem School Dist 63	1	200	Clinton	17
Alden-Hebron School Dist 19	2	430	McHenry	179
Allen-Otter Creek CCSD 65	1	70	La Salle	141
Allendale Cmty Cons SD 17	1	130	Wabash	234
Alsip-Hazelgrn-Oaklawn SD 126	5	1,580	Cook	20
Altamont Cmty Unit SD 10	2	700	Effingham	104
Alton Cmty School Dist 11	12	6,000	Madison	169
Alwood Cmty Unit Sch Dist 225	2	385	Henry	116
Amboy Cmty Unit Sch Dist 272	3	720	Lee	159
Anna Cmty Cons Sch Dist 37	3	695	Union	230
Anna-Jonesboro Cmty HSD 81	1	530	Union	230
Annawan Cmty Unit SD 226	2	330	Henry	116
Antioch Cmty Cons Sch Dist 34	6	2,775	Lake	146
Aptakisic-Tripp Sch Dist 102	4	2,400	Lake	146
Arbor Park School Dist 145	4	1,350	Cook	21
Arcola Cmty Unit Sch Dist 306	2	717	Douglas	87
Argenta Oreana Cmty Unit SD 1	3	800	Macon	165
Argo Cmty High School Dist 217	1	2,100	Cook	21
Arlington Hts School Dist 25	9	5,550	Cook	21
Armstrong Ellis SD 61	1	80	Vermilion	231
Armstrong Twp High SD 225	1	140	Vermilion	231
Arthur CUSD 305	4	1,140	Douglas	87
Ashley Cmty Cons SD 15	1	130	Washington	235
Ashton-Franklin Center SD 275	2	560	Lee	159
Astoria Cmty Unit Sch Dist 1	3	320	Fulton	109
Athens Cmty Unit Sch Dist 213	4	1,100	Menard	188
Atwood Heights SD 125	3	620	Cook	21
Auburn Cmty Unit Sch Dist 10	4	1,317	Sangamon	211
Aviston Elem School Dist 21	1	390	Clinton	17
Avoca School Dist 37	2	750	Cook	22
Ball Chatham Cmty Unit SD 5	6	4,500	Sangamon	211
Bannockburn Sch Dist 106	1	155	Lake	147
Barrington Cmty Unit SD 220	12	9,000	Lake	147
Bartelso School Dist 57	1	158	Clinton	17
Bartonville School Dist 66	1	300	Peoria	196
Batavia Unit School Dist 101	8	5,518	Kane	128
Beach Park Cmty Cons SD 3	5	2,106	Lake	147
Beardstown Cmty Sch Dist 15	3	1,560	Cass	9
Beecher City Cmty Unit SD 20	2	333	Effingham	104
Beecher Cmty Sch Dist 200-U	3	1,100	Will	241
Belle Valley School Dist 119	1	1,038	St Clair	217
Belleville Public Sch Dist 118	11	4,500	St Clair	217
Belleville Township HSD 201	3	4,500	St Clair	217
Bellwood School Dist 88	7	2,425	Cook	22
Belvidere Cmty Unit SD 100	10	8,500	Boone	4
Bement Cmty Unit Sch Dist 5	3	298	Piatt	202
Benjamin Sch Dist 25	2	650	Du Page	89
Bensenville Elem Sch Dist 2	3	2,350	Du Page	89
Benton Cmty Cons Sch Dist 47	2	1,150	Franklin	107
Benton Cons High Sch Dist 103	1	561	Franklin	107
Berkeley School Dist 87	6	2,600	Cook	22
Berwyn North School Dist 98	4	2,600	Cook	22
Berwyn South School Dist 100	8	3,700	Cook	23
Bethalto Cmty Unit SD 8	5	2,500	Madison	169
Bethel School Dist 82	1	170	Jefferson	122
Big Hollow School Dist 38	3	1,800	Lake	148
Bismarck-Henning Cmty SD 1	3	859	Vermilion	231
Bloom Twp High Sch Dist 206	3	3,558	Cook	23
Bloomingdale School Dist 13	3	1,390	Du Page	89
Bloomington School Dist 87	10	5,200	Mclean	185
Blue Ridge Cmty SD 18	3	700	Dewitt	87
Bluford Unit School Dist 318	1	350	Jefferson	122
Bond Co Cmty Unit Sch Dist 2	6	1,750	Bond	4
Bourbonnais Elem Sch Dist 53	5	2,400	Kankakee	134
Braceville Elem School Dist 75	1	112	Grundy	111
Bradford Cmty Unit Sch Dist 1	1	145	Stark	223
Bradley Elem School Dist 61	3	1,500	Kankakee	134
Bradley-Bourbonnais CHSD 307	1	2,100	Kankakee	134
Breese Elementary SD 12	2	630	Clinton	17
Bremen Cmty High SD 228	5	4,800	Cook	23
Brimfield Cmty Unit SD 309	2	680	Peoria	196
Brookfield-LaGrange Park SD 95	2	1,257	Cook	23
Brooklyn School Dist 188	1	161	St Clair	217
Brookwood School Dist 167	4	1,200	Cook	24
Brown Co Cmty Unit Sch Dist 1	3	750	Brown	5
Brownstown Cmty Unit SD 201	2	380	Fayette	105
Brussels Cmty Unit Sch Dist 42	2	106	Calhoun	8
Buncombe Cons School Dist 43	1	60	Johnson	127
Bunker Hill Cmty Unit SD 8	2	600	Macoupin	167
Burbank School Dist 111	8	3,400	Cook	24
Bureau Valley Cmty Unit 340	4	1,082	Bureau	6
Burnham School Dist 1545	1	180	Cook	24
Bushnell Prairie Cmty USD 170	3	630	McDonough	178
Butler School Dist 53	2	518	Du Page	89
Byron Cmty Unit SD 226	3	1,523	Ogle	194
Cahokia Unit Sch Dist 187	10	3,400	St Clair	218
Cairo School Dist 1	2	315	Alexander	3
Calhoun Cmty Unit Sch Dist 40	2	484	Calhoun	8
Calumet City School Dist 155	3	1,026	Cook	24
Calumet Public School Dist 132	3	1,200	Cook	24
Cambridge Cmty Unit SD 227	2	432	Henry	116
Canton Union School Dist 66	5	2,490	Fulton	109
Carbon Cliff Barstow SD 36	1	270	Rock Island	207
Carbondale Cmty HSD 165	1	1,000	Jackson	120
Carbondale Elem School Dist 95	4	1,560	Jackson	120
Carlinville Cmty Unit SD 1	4	1,400	Macoupin	167
Carlyle Cmty Unit Sch Dist 1	3	1,006	Clinton	17
Carmi-White Co School Dist 5	6	1,400	White	237
Carrier Mills-Stonefort SD 2	2	450	Saline	210
Carrollton Cmty Unit SD 1	2	600	Greene	111
Carterville Cmty Unit SD 5	4	2,400	Williamson	250
Carthage Elementary SD 317	2	400	Hancock	114
Cary Cmty Cons Sch Dist 26	5	2,426	McHenry	179
Casey-Westfield Cmty USD C-4	2	875	Clark	15
Cass School Dist 63	2	766	Du Page	89
Center Cass Sch Dist 66	3	1,100	Du Page	90
Central A&M Cmty Unit SD 21	5	670	Christian	14
Central City School Dist 133	1	349	Marion	174
Central Cmty High Sch Dist 71	1	615	Clinton	17
Central Cmty Unit SD 4	4	1,100	Iroquois	118
Central Cmty Unit SD 301	7	4,500	Kane	128
Central Sch Dist 51	2	1,400	Tazewell	225
Central School Dist 3	4	837	Adams	1
Central School Dist 104	2	700	St Clair	218
Central Stickney Sch Dist 110	1	384	Cook	25
Centralia City Sch Dist 135	4	1,250	Marion	174
Centralia High School Dist 200	1	900	Marion	174
Century Cmty Unit SD 100	2	369	Pulaski	204
Cerro Gordo Cmty Unit SD 100	2	490	Piatt	202
Chadwick Milledgevill CUSD 399	2	450	Carroll	8
Champaign Cmty Unit Sch Dist 4	19	10,179	Champaign	10
Chaney-Monge School Dist 88	1	500	Will	241
Channahon School Dist 17	4	1,234	Will	241
Charleston Cmty Unit SD 1	6	2,500	Coles	19
Chester Cmty Unit Sch Dist 139	2	950	Randolph	205
Chester-E Lincoln Cmty SD 61	1	300	Logan	163
Chicago Heights Elem SD 170	10	3,100	Cook	25
Chicago PSD-Ausl			Cook	25
Chicago PSD-Isp			Cook	26
Chicago PSD-Network 1			Cook	28
Chicago PSD-Network 2			Cook	29
Chicago PSD-Network 3			Cook	29
Chicago PSD-Network 4			Cook	30
Chicago PSD-Network 5			Cook	31
Chicago PSD-Network 6			Cook	31
Chicago PSD-Network 7			Cook	32
Chicago PSD-Network 8			Cook	32

School Year 2020-2021 800-333-8802 IL-Q1

DISTRICT INDEX

Market Data Retrieval

SCHOOL DISTRICT	NO. OF SCHOOLS	ENROLL-MENT	COUNTY	PAGE
Chicago PSD-Network 9			Cook	33
Chicago PSD-Network 10			Cook	33
Chicago PSD-Network 11			Cook	34
Chicago PSD-Network 12			Cook	35
Chicago PSD-Network 13			Cook	35
Chicago PSD-Network 14			Cook	36
Chicago PSD-Network 15			Cook	37
Chicago PSD-Network 16			Cook	37
Chicago PSD-Network 17			Cook	38
Chicago PSD-Options			Cook	38
Chicago Public School Dist 299	666	355,156	Cook	25
Chicago Ridge Sch Dist 127-5	3	1,476	Cook	41
Christopher Unit Sch Dist 99	2	702	Franklin	107
Cicero School Dist 99	17	12,418	Cook	42
Cissna Park Cmty Unit SD 6	1	294	Iroquois	118
Clay City Cmty Unit SD 10	3	350	Clay	16
Clinton Cmty Unit Sch Dist 15	5	1,800	Dewitt	87
Cmty Cons Sch Dist 146	5	2,500	Cook	42
Coal City Cmty Unit Sch Dist 1	5	2,151	Grundy	112
Cobden Cmty Unit Sch Dist 17	2	526	Union	230
Collinsville Cmty Sch Dist 10	13	5,000	Madison	170
Colona Cmty School Dist 190	1	400	Henry	116
Columbia Cmty Unit SD 4	4	2,000	Monroe	189
Community Cons School Dist 15	20	12,000	Cook	42
Community Cons School Dist 46	8	3,800	Lake	148
Community Cons School Dist 59	15	6,000	Cook	43
Community Cons School Dist 89	5	2,300	Du Page	90
Community Cons School Dist 93	9	3,200	Du Page	90
Community Cons School Dist 168	3	1,287	Cook	44
Community Cons School Dist 180	2	630	Du Page	90
Community Cons School Dist 181	9	3,800	Du Page	91
Community Cons School Dist 204	1	156	Perry	201
Community High School Dist 94	1	2,006	Du Page	91
Community High School Dist 99	2	5,015	Du Page	91
Community High School Dist 117	2	2,677	Lake	148
Community High School Dist 128	2	3,397	Lake	148
Community High School Dist 155	5	5,800	McHenry	179
Community High School Dist 218	5	5,400	Cook	44
Community Unit School Dist 7	3	1,250	Macoupin	167
Community Unit School Dist 16	3	939	Sangamon	211
Community Unit School Dist 200	20	12,000	Du Page	91
Community Unit School Dist 201	5	1,365	Du Page	92
Community Unit School Dist 300	27	20,985	McHenry	180
Community Unit School Dist 303	16	12,262	Kane	128
Community Unit School Dist 308	21	17,250	Kendall	137
Consolidated High Sch Dist 230	3	7,308	Cook	44
Cook County School Dist 104	5	1,800	Cook	44
Cook County School Dist 130	11	4,000	Cook	45
Cook County School Dist 154	1	225	Cook	45
Cornell Cmty Cons Sch Dist 426	1	110	Livingston	160
Coulterville Unit Sch Dist 1	1	196	Randolph	205
Country Club Hills SD 160	3	1,221	Cook	45
Cowden Herrick CUSD 3A	2	380	Shelby	216
Crab Orchard Cmty Sch Dist 3	1	497	Williamson	251
Crescent Iroquois Cmty SD 249	1	70	Iroquois	118
Creston Cmty Cons Sch Dist 161	1	88	Ogle	194
Crete-Monee Cmty SD 201-U	9	5,000	Will	241
Creve Coeur Sch Dist 76	2	600	Tazewell	226
Crystal Lake Elem District 47	12	7,500	McHenry	181
Cumberland Cmty Unit SD 77	3	1,000	Cumberland	84
Cypress School Dist 64	1	120	Johnson	127
Dakota Cmty Unit Sch Dist 201	2	750	Stephenson	224
Dallas Elem Sch Dist 327	1	193	Hancock	114
Dalzell Elem School Dist 98	1	56	Bureau	6
Damiansville School Dist 62	1	85	Clinton	17
Danville School Dist 118	11	5,505	Vermilion	231
Darien Public Sch Dist 61	3	1,400	Du Page	92
Decatur Public Schools 61	18	8,700	Macon	165
Deer Creek-Mackinaw CUSD 701	3	1,040	Tazewell	226
Deer Park Cmty Cons SD 82	1	75	La Salle	141
Deerfield Public SD 109	6	3,400	Lake	149
DeKalb Cmty Unit SD 428	12	6,600	De Kalb	84
Deland-Weldon Cmty Unit SD 57	2	200	Piatt	202
Delavan Cmty Unit Sch Dist 703	2	480	Tazewell	226
DePue Unit Sch Dist 103	1	390	Bureau	6
Des Plaines Cmty Cons SD 62	11	4,800	Cook	45
DeSoto Grade School Dist 86	1	203	Jackson	120
Diamond Lake School Dist 76	3	900	Lake	149
Dieterich Community Unit SD 30	2	550	Effingham	104
Dimmick Cmty School Dist 175	1	160	La Salle	141
Dist 50 Schools	2	700	Tazewell	226
Dixon Cmty Unit Sch Dist 170	5	2,432	Lee	160
Dolton School Dist 149	8	2,600	Cook	46
Dolton-Riverdale Sch Dist 148	10	2,183	Cook	46
Dongola Unit School Dist 66	1	286	Union	230
Donovan Cmty Unit Sch Dist 3	2	290	Iroquois	119
Downers Grove School Dist 58	13	5,000	Du Page	93
Du Quoin Cmty Unit SD 300	3	1,420	Perry	201
Dunlap Cmty Unit Sch Dist 323	8	4,500	Peoria	196
Dupage High School Dist 88	2	3,929	Du Page	93
Dupo Cmty School Dist 196	2	985	St Clair	218
Durand Cmty Sch Dist 322	4	565	Winnebago	252
Dwight Common Elem SD 232	1	450	Livingston	161
Dwight Twp High Sch Dist 230	1	221	Livingston	161
E F Lindop Elem Sch Dist 92	1	480	Cook	47
Earlville Cmty Unit Sch Dist 9	1	430	La Salle	141
East Alton Elementary SD 13	3	800	Madison	170
East Alton-Wood River SD 14	1	556	Madison	170
East Aurora School Dist 131	20	14,000	Kane	129
East Coloma-Nelson Cesd 20	1	245	Whiteside	238
East Dubuque Unit SD 119	2	672	Jo Daviess	125
East Maine School Dist 63	6	3,500	Cook	47
East Moline Public Sch Dist 37	5	2,650	Rock Island	207
East Peoria Cmty HS Dist 309	1	1,000	Tazewell	226
East Peoria Elem Sch Dist 86	7	1,500	Tazewell	226
East Prairie School Dist 73	1	505	Cook	47
East St Louis Sch Dist 189	11	5,200	St Clair	218
Eastland Cmty Unit SD 308	2	650	Carroll	8
Edgar Co Cmty Sch Dist 6	3	307	Edgar	103
Edinburg Cmty Unit Sch Dist 4	1	290	Christian	14
Edwards Co Cmty Unit SD 1	3	896	Edwards	104
Edwardsville Cmty Unit SD 7	15	7,500	Madison	170
Effingham Cmty Sch Dist 40	5	2,400	Effingham	104
Egyptian Cmty Unit Sch Dist 5	1	400	Alexander	3
El Paso-Gridley CUSD 11	4	1,200	Woodford	257
Eldorado Cmty Unit Sch Dist 4	3	1,200	Saline	210
Elementary School Dist 159	5	1,700	Cook	47
Elgin School Dist U-46	58	38,000	Kane	130
Elmhurst Cmty Unit SD 205	13	8,499	Du Page	93
Elmwood Cmty Unit Sch Dist 322	2	700	Peoria	196
Elmwood Park Cmty Unit SD 401	5	2,800	Cook	47
Elverado Cmty Unit SD 196	4	420	Jackson	120
Elwood Cmty Cons SD 203	1	318	Will	242
Emmons School Dist 33	1	300	Lake	149
Erie Cmty School Dist 1	3	650	Whiteside	239
Eswood Cmty Cons SD 269	1	68	Ogle	194
Eureka Cmty Unit Sch Dist 140	5	1,567	Woodford	257
Evanston Twp High SD 202	1	3,800	Cook	48
Evanston-Skokie Cmty CSD 65	18	8,030	Cook	48
Evergreen Park Cmty HSD 231	1	850	Cook	49
Evergreen Park Elem SD 124	5	1,900	Cook	49
Ewing Northern Cmty SD 115	1	210	Franklin	108
Fairfield Cmty High SD 225	1	430	Wayne	236
Fairfield Pub Sch Dist 112	2	700	Wayne	236
Fairmont School Dist 89	1	350	Will	242
Fairview South School Dist 72	1	722	Cook	49
Farmington Ctl Cmty SD 265	3	1,425	Peoria	197
Farrington Cmty Cons SD 99	1	58	Jefferson	122
Fenton Cmty High Sch Dist 100	1	1,433	Du Page	94
Field Cmty Cons Sch Dist 3	1	275	Jefferson	123
Fieldcrest Cmty School Dist 6	4	909	Woodford	257
Fisher Cmty Unit School Dist 1	2	601	Champaign	10
Flanagan-Cornell Unit 74 SD	1	195	Livingston	161
Flora Cmty Unit School Dist 35	3	1,396	Clay	16

Illinois School Directory — DISTRICT INDEX

SCHOOL DISTRICT	NO. OF SCHOOLS	ENROLLMENT	COUNTY	PAGE
Flossmoor School Dist 161	5	2,374	Cook	49
Ford Heights School Dist 169	2	455	Cook	49
Forest Park School Dist 91	5	861	Cook	50
Forest Ridge Sch Dist 142	4	1,650	Cook	50
Forrestville Valley CUSD 221	3	750	Ogle	194
Fox Lake School Dist 114	2	741	Lake	149
Fox River Grove Cons SD 3	2	390	McHenry	181
Frankfort Cmty Unit SD 168	4	1,650	Franklin	108
Frankfort School Dist 157-C	3	2,521	Will	242
Franklin Cmty Unit SD 1	3	290	Morgan	192
Franklin Park Pub Sch Dist 84	4	1,400	Cook	50
Freeburg Cmty Cons SD 70	2	780	St Clair	219
Freeburg Cmty High Sch Dist 77	1	675	St Clair	219
Freeport School Dist 145	10	4,000	Stephenson	224
Fremont School Dist 79	3	2,200	Lake	149
Fulton Co Cmty Unit Sch Dist 3	2	400	Fulton	109
Galatia Cmty Unit Sch Dist 1	2	364	Saline	210
Galena Unit School Dist 120	3	830	Jo Daviess	125
Galesburg Cmty Unit SD 205	8	4,500	Knox	140
Gallatin Cmty Unit Sch Dist 7	1	750	Gallatin	110
Galva Cmty Unit Sch Dist 224	2	525	Henry	117
Gardner Cmty Cons SD 72-C	1	152	Grundy	112
Gardner S Wilmington HSD 73	1	200	Grundy	112
Gavin School Dist 37	2	850	Lake	150
Geff Cmty Cons School Dist 14	1	92	Wayne	236
General George S Patton SD 133	1	268	Cook	50
Geneseo Cmty Unit Sch Dist 228	5	2,000	Henry	117
Geneva CUSD 304	10	5,808	Kane	131
Genoa-Kingston Cmty SD 424	4	1,700	De Kalb	85
Georgetown-Ridge Farm CUSD 4	3	1,010	Vermilion	232
Germantown Elem Sch Dist 60	1	250	Clinton	18
Germantown Hills SD 69	2	900	Woodford	257
Giant City Cmty Cons SD 130	1	210	Jackson	120
Gibson Cty-Melvin-Sibley CUSD5	3	1,000	Ford	106
Gifford Cmty Cons SD 188	1	183	Champaign	10
Glen Ellyn School Dist 41	5	3,549	Du Page	94
Glenbard Twp High Sch Dist 87	4	7,500	Du Page	94
Glenbrook High Sch Dist 225	2	5,102	Cook	50
Glencoe Sch Dist 35	3	1,200	Cook	51
Glenview Cmty Cons Sch Dist 34	8	4,900	Cook	51
Golf School Dist 67	2	725	Cook	51
Goreville Cmty Unit SD 1	1	565	Johnson	127
Gower School Dist 62	2	900	Du Page	94
Grand Prairie Cmty Cons SD 6	1	80	Jefferson	123
Grand Ridge CCSD 95	1	189	La Salle	141
Granite City Cmty Unit SD 9	8	5,764	Madison	171
Grant Cmty Cons Sch Dist 110	2	600	St Clair	219
Grant Cmty High Sch Dist 124	1	1,850	Lake	150
Grant Park Cmty Unit SD 6	3	475	Kankakee	135
Grass Lake School Dist 36	1	190	Lake	150
Grayslake Cmty HS Dist 127	2	3,000	Lake	150
Grayville Cmty Unit Sch Dist 1	2	280	White	238
Greenfield Cmty Unit SD 10	2	444	Greene	111
Greenview Cmty Unit SD 200	1	211	Menard	188
Griggsville-Perry Cmty SD 4	3	340	Pike	203
Gurnee School Dist 56	4	2,083	Lake	150
Hall Twp High School Dist 502	1	405	Bureau	6
Hamilton Cmty Cons SD 328	2	600	Hancock	114
Hamilton Co Cmty Unit SD 10	4	1,199	Hamilton	114
Hampton School Dist 29	1	210	Rock Island	207
Hardin Co Cmty Unit Sch Dist 1	2	500	Hardin	115
Harlem Unit Sch Dist 122	11	6,300	Winnebago	252
Harmony-Emge School Dist 175	3	800	St Clair	219
Harrisburg Cmty Unit SD 3	4	1,879	Saline	210
Harrison School Dist 36	1	404	McHenry	181
Hartsburg Emden School Dist 21	2	200	Logan	163
Harvard Cmty Unit Sch Dist 50	5	2,633	McHenry	181
Harvey Public School Dist 152	6	2,264	Cook	51
Havana Cmty Sch Dist 126	3	1,000	Mason	177
Hawthorn Cmty Cons Sch Dist 73	7	4,300	Lake	151
Hazel Crest School Dist 152-5	2	1,000	Cook	52
Henry Senachwine CUSD 5	2	580	Marshall	176
Heritage Cmty Unit Sch Dist 8	2	421	Champaign	11
Herrin Cmty School Dist 4	4	2,300	Williamson	251
Herscher Cmty School Dist 2	4	1,650	Kankakee	135
Heyworth Cmty Sch Dist 4	2	975	Mclean	185
Hiawatha Cmty Unit SD 426	2	450	De Kalb	85
High Mount Sch Dist 116	1	475	St Clair	219
Highland Cmty Sch Dist 5	6	3,000	Madison	171
Hillsboro Cmty Unit Sch Dist 3	4	1,700	Montgomery	190
Hillside School Dist 93	1	410	Cook	52
Hinckley-Big Rock Cmty SD 429	3	696	De Kalb	85
Hinsdale Twp High Sch Dist 86	2	4,000	Du Page	95
Hollis Cons School Dist 328	1	135	Peoria	197
Homer Cmty Cons Sch Dist 33C	6	3,800	Will	242
Homewood Flossmoor CHSD 233	1	2,897	Cook	52
Homewood School Dist 153	3	2,000	Cook	52
Hononegah Cmty High SD 207	1	1,500	Winnebago	253
Hoopeston Area Cmty Unit SD 11	4	1,100	Vermilion	232
Hoover-Schrum Sch Dist 157	2	850	Cook	52
Huntley Cmty School Dist 158	8	9,606	McHenry	182
Hutsonville Cmty Unit SD 1	2	324	Crawford	83
Illini Bluffs Cmty Unit SD 327	3	909	Peoria	197
Illini Central CUSD 189	4	663	Mason	177
Illini West High Sch Dist 307	1	350	Hancock	114
Illinois Vly Ctl Sch Dist 321	5	2,173	Peoria	197
Indian Creek Cmty Unit SD 425	3	740	De Kalb	85
Indian Prairie Sch Dist 204	34	27,400	Du Page	95
Indian Springs Sch Dist 109	6	2,764	Cook	52
Iroquois Co Cmty Unit SD 9	4	1,000	Iroquois	119
Iroquois West Cmty Unit SD 10	5	980	Iroquois	119
Irvington Cmty Cons SD 11	1	60	Washington	235
Itasca School Dist 10	3	1,033	Du Page	96
Iuka Community Cons Sch Dist 7	1	225	Marion	174
J Sterling Morton HSD 201	4	8,600	Cook	53
Jacksonville School Dist 117	9	3,200	Morgan	192
Jasper Cmty Cons Sch Dist 17	1	185	Wayne	237
Jasper Co Cmty Unit SD 1	4	1,278	Jasper	122
Jersey Cmty Sch Dist 100	5	2,647	Jersey	125
Johnsburg Cmty School Dist 12	4	1,800	McHenry	182
Johnston City Cmty Unit SD 1	4	1,100	Williamson	251
Joliet Public School Dist 86	21	12,000	Will	243
Joliet Twp High Sch Dist 204	3	6,589	Will	243
Jonesboro Cmty Cons SD 43	1	370	Union	230
Joppa-Maple Grove Unit SD 38	2	230	Massac	177
Kaneland Cmty Unit SD 302	7	4,560	Kane	132
Kankakee School Dist 111	11	5,200	Kankakee	135
Kansas Cmty School Dist 3	1	205	Edgar	103
Keeneyville Elem Sch Dist 20	3	1,597	Du Page	96
Kell Cons School Dist 2	1	100	Marion	174
Kenilworth School Dist 38	1	425	Cook	53
Kewanee Cmty Unit Sch Dist 229	6	2,000	Henry	117
Kildeer Countryside CCSD 96	7	3,213	Lake	151
Kings Cons School Dist 144	1	90	Ogle	194
Kinnikinnick Cmty Cons SD 131	4	1,750	Winnebago	253
Kirby School Dist 140	7	3,500	Cook	53
Knoxville Cmty Unit SD 202	3	1,068	Knox	140
Komarek School Dist 94	1	580	Cook	54
La Grange Cmty School Dist 105	5	1,300	Cook	54
La Grange Elem Sch Dist 102	6	3,100	Cook	54
La Grange-Highlands SD 106	2	850	Cook	54
La Harpe Cmty Sch Dist 347	1	209	Hancock	115
La Moille Cmty Unit SD 303	3	205	Bureau	6
La Salle Elem SD 122	2	900	La Salle	142
Ladd Cmty Cons Sch Dist 94	1	190	Bureau	6
Lake Bluff Elem Sch Dist 65	2	880	Lake	151
Lake Forest Cmty HSD 115	1	1,600	Lake	151
Lake Forest School Dist 67	5	1,660	Lake	152
Lake Park Cmty High SD 108	2	2,500	Du Page	96
Lake Villa Cmty Cons SD 41	4	2,700	Lake	152
Lake Zurich Cmty Sch Dist 95	8	5,516	Lake	152
Lansing School Dist 158	5	2,500	Cook	54
Laraway Cmty Cons SD 70-C	1	427	Will	243
LaSalle Peru Twp HSD 120	1	1,200	La Salle	142

School Year 2020-2021 — 800-333-8802 — IL-Q3

DISTRICT INDEX

SCHOOL DISTRICT	NO. OF SCHOOLS	ENROLL-MENT	COUNTY	PAGE
Lawrence Co Cmty Sch Dist 20	3	1,125	Lawrence	159
Le Roy Cmty Unit SD 2	3	775	Mclean	186
Lebanon Cmty Unit Sch Dist 9	2	540	St Clair	220
Leland Cmty Unit Sch Dist 1	1	260	La Salle	142
Lemont High Sch Dist 210	1	1,400	Cook	55
Lemont-Bromberek Sch Dist 113A	3	2,300	Cook	55
Lena-Winslow Cmty Unit SD 202	3	850	Stephenson	224
Lewistown Community Unit SD 97	2	620	Fulton	110
Lexington Cmty Sch Dist 7	3	490	Mclean	186
Leyden Cmty High Sch Dist 212	2	3,420	Cook	55
Liberty Cmty Unit Sch Dist 2	1	650	Adams	2
Libertyville Pub Sch Dist 70	5	2,258	Lake	152
Lick Creek School Dist 16	1	150	Union	230
Limestone Cmty High SD 310	2	1,000	Peoria	197
Limestone Walters CCSD 316	1	200	Peoria	198
Lincoln Cmty High Sch Dist 404	1	811	Logan	163
Lincoln Elem School Dist 27	5	1,200	Logan	163
Lincoln Elem School Dist 156	1	950	Cook	55
Lincoln-Way Cmty HS Dist 210	3	6,811	Will	244
Lincolnshre-Prairieview SD 103	3	1,832	Lake	153
Lincolnwood Sch Dist 74	3	1,200	Cook	55
Lisbon Cmty Cons Sch Dist 90	1	106	Kendall	138
Lisle Cmty Unit Sch Dist 202	3	1,450	Du Page	96
Litchfield Cmty Unit SD 12	6	1,450	Montgomery	191
Lockport Twp High Sch Dist 205	2	3,890	Will	244
Lombard Elem SD 44	8	3,100	Du Page	97
Lostant Cmty Unit Sch Dist 425	1	55	La Salle	142
Lowpoint-Washburn CUSD 21	3	325	Woodford	257
Ludlow Cons Cmty Sch Dist 142	1	57	Champaign	11
Lyons Elem School Dist 103	6	2,612	Cook	56
Lyons Twp HS Dist 204	2	4,200	Cook	56
Macomb Cmty Unit Sch Dist 185	4	2,000	McDonough	178
Madison Cmty Unit Sch Dist 12	3	700	Madison	172
Maercker School Dist 60	3	1,401	Du Page	97
Mahomet-Seymour Cmty SD 3	4	3,170	Champaign	11
Maine Twp High Sch Dist 207	3	6,322	Cook	56
Malden Cmty Cons SD 84	1	100	Bureau	7
Manhattan School Dist 114	3	1,540	Will	244
Mannheim School Dist 83	6	2,800	Cook	56
Manteno Cmty Unit Sch Dist 5	3	2,100	Kankakee	135
Marengo Cmty High Sch Dist 154	1	700	McHenry	182
Marengo Union Elem Cons SD 165	3	1,200	McHenry	182
Marion Cmty School Dist 2	7	3,914	Williamson	251
Marissa Cmty Unit Sch Dist 40	2	550	St Clair	220
Maroa Forsyth CU Sch Dist 2	3	1,215	Macon	165
Marquardt School Dist 15	5	2,491	Du Page	97
Marseilles Elem Sch Dist 150	1	550	La Salle	142
Marshall Cmty Sch Dist C-2	4	1,250	Clark	15
Martinsville Cmty Unit SD C-3	2	400	Clark	16
Mascoutah Cmty Sch Dist 19	5	4,000	St Clair	220
Massac Unit School Dist 1	7	2,100	Massac	177
Matteson Elem SD 162	7	2,700	Cook	57
Mattoon Cmty Unit Sch Dist 2	5	2,500	Coles	19
Maywood-Melrose Brdview SD 89	9	4,300	Cook	57
Mazon-Verona-Kinsman ESD 2-C	2	325	Grundy	112
McClellan Cons SD 12	1	45	Jefferson	123
McHenry Cmty Cons Sch Dist 15	8	4,300	McHenry	183
McHenry Cmty High Sch Dist 156	2	2,143	McHenry	183
McLean Co Unit Dist 5	23	13,346	Mclean	186
Medinah Elementary SD 11	3	700	Du Page	97
Mendon Cmty Unit School Dist 4	3	670	Adams	2
Mendota Cmty School Dist 289	3	1,200	La Salle	142
Mendota Twp High Sch Dist 280	1	541	La Salle	143
Mercer County SD 404	5	1,300	Mercer	189
Meredosia-Chamberburg SD 11	1	195	Morgan	192
Meridian Cmty School Dist 101	2	450	Pulaski	204
Meridian Cmty Unit Sch Dist 15	3	1,065	Macon	166
Meridian Cmty Unit SD 223	4	1,614	Ogle	194
Metamora Cmty Cons Sch Dist 1	1	875	Woodford	258
Metamora Twp HS Dist 122	1	970	Woodford	258
Midland Cmty Unit Sch Dist 7	3	720	Marshall	176
Midlothian School Dist 143	4	1,800	Cook	57
Midwest Ctl Cmty Unit SD 191	3	900	Mason	177
Milford Area Public SD 124	2	610	Iroquois	119
Millburn Cmty Cons Sch Dist 24	2	1,150	Lake	153
Miller Cmty Cons Sch Dist 210	1	158	La Salle	143
Millstadt Cmty Cons SD 160	2	800	St Clair	220
Milne-Kelvin Grove Dist 91	2	550	Will	244
Minooka Cmty Cons Sch Dist 201	7	4,400	Grundy	112
Minooka Cmty High Sch Dist 111	2	2,800	Will	244
Mokena Public School Dist 159	3	1,500	Will	245
Moline-Coal Valley SD No 40	15	7,182	Rock Island	207
Momence Cmty Unit Sch Dist 1	3	1,100	Kankakee	136
Monmouth-Roseville CUSD 238	5	1,686	Warren	234
Monroe School Dist 70	1	287	Peoria	198
Monticello Cmty Unit SD 25	5	1,600	Piatt	202
Montmorency Cmty Cons SD 145	1	230	Whiteside	239
Morris Cmty High Sch Dist 101	1	867	Grundy	113
Morris Elem School Dist 54	1	1,200	Grundy	113
Morrison Cmty Unit Sch Dist 6	4	1,033	Whiteside	239
Morrisonville Cmty Unit SD 1	2	250	Christian	14
Morton Cmty Unit Sch Dist 709	7	3,060	Tazewell	227
Morton Grove School Dist 70	1	900	Cook	58
Mt Olive Cmty Unit Sch Dist 5	2	452	Macoupin	167
Mt Prospect School Dist 57	4	2,222	Cook	58
Mt Pulaski Cmty Unit SD 23	2	530	Logan	164
Mt Vernon City Sch Dist 80	4	1,700	Jefferson	123
Mt Vernon Twp HS Dist 201	1	1,250	Jefferson	123
Mt Zion Cmty Unit Sch Dist 3	5	2,400	Macon	166
Mulberry Grove Cmty Sch Dist 1	3	400	Bond	4
Mundelein Cons High SD 120	1	2,026	Lake	153
Mundelein Elem School Dist 75	4	1,586	Lake	153
Murphysboro Cmty Unit SD 186	4	1,800	Jackson	121
N Pekin-Marquette Hts SD 102	3	512	Tazewell	227
Naperville Cmty Unit SD 203	22	17,000	Du Page	98
Nashville Cmty Cons SD 49	1	585	Washington	235
Nashville Cmty HSD 99	1	410	Washington	235
Nauvoo-Colusa CUSD 325	1	244	Hancock	115
Neoga Cmty Unit School Dist 3	2	535	Cumberland	84
Nettle Creek Cmty SD 24-C	1	91	Grundy	113
New Athens CUSD 60	1	500	St Clair	220
New Holland Middletown ESD 88	1	90	Logan	164
New Hope Cmty Cons Sch Dist 6	1	180	Wayne	237
New Lenox School Dist 122	12	5,300	Will	245
New Simpson Hill Cons SD 32	1	200	Johnson	127
New Trier Twp HS Dist 203	2	3,978	Cook	58
Newark Cmty Cons Sch Dist 66	2	239	Kendall	138
Newark Cmty High Sch Dist 18	1	170	Kendall	138
Niles Elem School Dist 71	1	600	Cook	58
Niles Twp High School Dist 219	3	4,555	Cook	58
Nippersink School Dist 2	3	1,100	McHenry	183
Nokomis Cmty Unit Sch Dist 22	2	630	Montgomery	191
Norridge School Dist 80	2	1,000	Cook	59
Norris City-Omaha-Enfield SD 3	3	675	White	238
North Boone Cmty Unit SD 200	6	1,600	Boone	5
North Chicago Cmty Unit SD 187	8	3,900	Lake	153
North Clay Cmty Unit SD 25	2	618	Clay	16
North Greene Unit Dist 3	2	875	Greene	111
North Mac Cmty Unit SD 34	3	1,150	Macoupin	168
North Palos School Dist 117	5	3,402	Cook	59
North Shore School Dist 112	10	3,800	Lake	154
North Wamac School Dist 186	1	120	Clinton	18
North Wayne Cmty Unit SD 200	4	383	Wayne	237
Northbrook Elem School Dist 27	3	1,237	Cook	59
Northbrook School Dist 28	4	1,870	Cook	59
Northbrook-Glenview SD 30	3	1,195	Cook	60
Northwestern CUSD 2	2	356	Macoupin	168
Norwood Sch Dist 63	2	475	Peoria	198
O'Fallon Cmty Cons Sch Dist 90	7	3,761	St Clair	221
O'Fallon Twp School Dist 203	2	2,400	St Clair	221
Oak Grove School Dist 68	1	900	Lake	154
Oak Grove School Dist 68	1	250	Peoria	198
Oak Lawn Cmty High SD 229	1	1,850	Cook	60
Oak Lawn-Hometown Sch Dist 123	6	3,000	Cook	60

Illinois School Directory — DISTRICT INDEX

SCHOOL DISTRICT	NO. OF SCHOOLS	ENROLLMENT	COUNTY	PAGE
Oak Park & River Forest SD 200	1	3,468	Cook	60
Oak Park Elem School Dist 97	10	6,000	Cook	60
Oakdale Cmty Cons Sch Dist 1	1	69	Washington	236
Oakland Cmty Unit Sch Dist 5	2	245	Coles	19
Oakwood Cmty Unit Sch Dist 76	3	1,000	Vermilion	232
Oblong Cmty Unit Sch Dist 4	2	565	Crawford	83
Odell Cmty Cons Sch Dist 435	1	150	Livingston	161
Odin Public School Dist 722	2	250	Marion	175
Oglesby Public Sch Dist 125	2	529	La Salle	143
Ohio Cmty Cons School Dist 17	1	113	Bureau	7
Ohio Cmty High School Dist 505	1	33	Bureau	7
Okaw Valley Cmty Unit SD 302	3	475	Moultrie	193
Olympia Cmty Unit Sch Dist 16	5	1,900	Mclean	187
Opdyke-Belle Rive Cmty CSSD 5	1	140	Jefferson	123
Orangeville Cmty Unit SD 203	1	380	Stephenson	225
Oregon Cmty Unit Sch Dist 220	3	1,461	Ogle	195
Orion Cmty Unit Sch Dist 223	3	990	Henry	117
Orland School Dist 135	10	5,201	Cook	61
Ottawa Elementary Sch Dist 141	5	1,950	La Salle	143
Ottawa Twp High School Dist 140	1	1,450	La Salle	143
Palestine Cmty Unit SD 3	2	375	Crawford	83
Palos Cmty Cons Sch Dist 118	3	2,050	Cook	61
Palos Heights School Dist 128	4	700	Cook	61
Pana Cmty Unit School Dist 8	4	1,347	Christian	14
Panhandle Cmty Unit SD 2	3	520	Montgomery	191
Paris Cmty Unit Sch Dist 4	1	480	Edgar	103
Paris Union School Dist 95	4	1,452	Edgar	103
Park Forest Chicago Hgt SD 163	6	2,000	Cook	62
Park Ridge Niles CMCSD 64	8	4,500	Cook	62
Patoka Cmty Unit SD 100	1	260	Marion	175
Paw Paw Cmty Unit SD 271	1	120	Lee	160
Pawnee Cmty Unit Sch Dist 11	2	550	Sangamon	212
Paxton-Buckley-Loda CUSD 10	3	1,300	Ford	107
Payson Cmty Unit School Dist 1	2	550	Adams	2
Pearl City Cmty Unit SD 200	1	431	Stephenson	225
Pecatonica Cmty Unit SD 321	3	950	Winnebago	253
Pekin Cmty High Sch Dist 303	1	1,821	Tazewell	227
Pekin Public School Dist 108	11	3,650	Tazewell	227
Pembroke Cmty Cons SD 259	1	200	Kankakee	136
Pennoyer School Dist 79	1	444	Cook	62
Peoria Heights Cmty SD 325	2	720	Peoria	198
Peoria Public Sch Dist 150	30	12,531	Peoria	198
Peotone Cmty Unit SD 207-U	5	1,453	Will	245
Peru Elem Sch Dist 124	2	970	La Salle	143
Pikeland Cmty Sch Dist 10	3	1,200	Pike	203
Pinckneyville Cmty High SD 101	1	415	Perry	201
Pinckneyville Sch Dist 50	2	504	Perry	201
Plainfield Cons Sch Dist 202	30	25,000	Will	245
Plano Cmty Unit Sch Dist 88	5	2,400	Kendall	138
Pleasant Hill CUSD 3	2	311	Pike	203
Pleasant Hill School Dist 69	1	230	Peoria	199
Pleasant Plains Cmty Unit SD 8	3	1,271	Sangamon	212
Pleasant Valley Sch Dist 62	2	363	Peoria	199
Pleasantdale School Dist 107	2	845	Cook	62
Polo Cmty Unit Sch Dist 222	3	603	Ogle	195
Pontiac Cmty Cons Sch Dist 429	4	1,300	Livingston	161
Pontiac Twp High School Dist 90	2	700	Livingston	161
Pontiac-Wm Holliday SD 105	2	500	St Clair	221
Pope Co Cmty Unit Sch Dist 1	2	530	Pope	203
Porta Cmty Unit Sch Dist 202	3	1,009	Menard	189
Posen-Robbins Sch Dist 143-5	5	1,452	Cook	63
Potomac Cmty Unit Sch Dist 10	1	145	Vermilion	232
Prairie Central Cmty USD 8	6	2,150	Livingston	162
Prairie Du Rocher CCSD 134	1	152	Randolph	205
Prairie Grove Cons SD 46	2	720	McHenry	183
Prairie Hill Cmty Cons SD 133	2	743	Winnebago	253
Prairie Hills Elem SD 144	8	3,000	Cook	63
Prairieview-Ogden Sch Dist 197	3	247	Champaign	11
Princeton Elem Sch Dist 115	4	1,156	Bureau	7
Princeton Twp HSD 500	1	550	Bureau	7
Princeville Cmty Unit SD 326	2	761	Peoria	200
Prophetstown-Lyndon-Tampico 3	4	800	Whiteside	239
Prospect Hts School Dist 23	4	1,500	Cook	63
Proviso Twp High Sch Dist 209	3	4,339	Cook	63
Putnam Co Cmty Unit SD 535	4	853	Putnam	204
Queen Bee School Dist 16	4	1,900	Du Page	98
Quincy School Dist 172	10	6,700	Adams	2
Raccoon Cons School Dist 1	1	240	Marion	175
Ramsey Cmty Unit Sch Dist 204	2	450	Fayette	105
Rankin Cmty School Dist 98	1	250	Tazewell	228
Rantoul City School Dist 137	5	1,750	Champaign	11
Rantoul Twp High Sch Dist 193	2	765	Champaign	12
Reavis Twp HSD 220	1	1,800	Cook	64
Red Bud Cmty Unit Sch Dist 132	2	1,000	Randolph	205
Red Hill Cmty School Dist 10	3	977	Lawrence	159
Reed-Custer Cmty Unit SD 255-U	3	1,476	Will	246
Rhodes School Dist 84 1/2	1	637	Cook	64
Rich Twp High School Dist 227	2	2,800	Cook	64
Richland Co Cmty Unit SD 1	3	2,500	Richland	206
Richland School Dist 88A	1	923	Will	247
Richmond-Burton Cmty HSD 157	1	636	McHenry	183
Ridgeland School Dist 122	5	2,300	Cook	64
Ridgeview Cmty Unit SD 19	2	600	Mclean	187
Ridgewood Cmty HSD 234	1	900	Cook	64
Riley Cmty Cons Sch Dist 18	1	267	McHenry	184
River Bend Cmty School Dist 2	4	900	Whiteside	239
River Forest Sch Dist 90	3	1,400	Cook	65
River Grove School Dist 85-5	1	750	Cook	65
River Ridge Cmty Unit SD 210	3	500	Jo Daviess	126
River Trails Sch Dist 26	4	1,600	Cook	65
Riverdale Cmty Unit SD 100	3	1,160	Rock Island	208
Riverside Public Sch Dist 96	5	1,686	Cook	65
Riverside-Brookfld Twp SD 208	1	1,630	Cook	65
Riverton Cmty Unit SD 14	3	1,443	Sangamon	212
Riverview Cmty Cons Sch Dist 2	1	232	Woodford	258
Roanoke-Benson Cmty Unit SD 60	3	500	Woodford	258
Robein Cmty School Dist 85	1	175	Tazewell	228
Robinson Cmty Unit Sch Dist 2	4	1,616	Crawford	83
Rochelle Cmty Cons SD 231	5	1,600	Ogle	195
Rochelle Twp High Sch Dist 212	1	900	Ogle	195
Rochester Cmty Unit SD 3-A	5	2,215	Sangamon	212
Rock Falls Elem Sch Dist 13	4	1,050	Whiteside	240
Rock Falls Twp High SD 301	1	630	Whiteside	240
Rock Island-Milan Sch Dist 41	14	5,800	Rock Island	208
Rockdale School Dist 84	1	275	Will	247
Rockford School Dist 205	46	28,940	Winnebago	253
Rockridge Cmty Unit SD 300	5	1,097	Rock Island	209
Rockton School Dist 140	3	1,600	Winnebago	255
Rome Cmty Cons Sch Dist 2	1	450	Jefferson	123
Rondout School Dist 72	1	140	Lake	154
Rooks Creek Cmty Cons SD 425	1	50	Livingston	162
Roselle School Dist 12	2	700	Du Page	99
Rosemont Elem Sch Dist 78	1	220	Cook	66
Rossville-Alvin Cmty Unit SD 7	1	300	Vermilion	233
Round Lake Area Co Dist 116	10	7,300	Lake	154
Rowva Cmty School Dist 208	2	600	Knox	140
Roxana Cmty Unit Sch Dist 1	4	2,000	Madison	172
Rutland Cmty Cons SD 230	1	75	La Salle	144
S Wilmington Cons Elem SD 74	1	85	Grundy	113
Salem Cmty High Sch Dist 600	1	650	Marion	175
Salem Elem Sch Dist 111	2	1,000	Marion	175
Salt Creek School Dist 48	3	550	Du Page	99
Salt Fork Cmty Unit SD 512	3	900	Vermilion	233
Sandoval Cmty Unit SD 501	2	504	Marion	175
Sandridge Sch Dist 172	1	350	Cook	66
Sandwich Cmty Unit SD 430	6	2,000	De Kalb	85
Sangamon Valley Cmty Unit SD 9	4	687	Macon	166
Saratoga Cmty Cons SD 60C	1	799	Grundy	113
Saunemin Cmty Cons SD 438	1	115	Livingston	162
Scales Mound Cmty Unit SD 211	3	265	Jo Daviess	126
Schaumburg Cmty Cons SD 54	28	15,296	Cook	66
Schiller Park School Dist 81	3	1,500	Cook	67
School Dist 45 Dupage Co	8	3,410	Du Page	99
Schuyler-Industry CUSD 5	4	1,100	Schuyler	215

School Year 2020-2021 800-333-8802 IL-Q5

DISTRICT INDEX

Market Data Retrieval

SCHOOL DISTRICT	NO. OF SCHOOLS	ENROLLMENT	COUNTY	PAGE
Scott Morgan Cmty Unit SD 2	1	231	Scott	215
Selmaville Cmty Cons SD 10	1	260	Marion	176
Seneca Cmty Cons Sch Dist 170	2	503	La Salle	144
Seneca Twp High Sch Dist 160	1	430	La Salle	144
Serena Cmty Unit School Dist 2	4	665	La Salle	144
Sesser-Valier Cmty Unit SD 196	3	700	Franklin	108
Shawnee Cmty Unit Sch Dist 84	2	300	Union	231
Shelbyville Cmty Sch Dist 4	3	1,250	Shelby	216
Sherrard Cmty Sch Dist 200	4	1,400	Mercer	189
Shiloh School Dist 1	1	380	Edgar	103
Shiloh Village Sch Dist 85	2	571	St Clair	221
Shirland Cmty Cons SD 134	1	111	Winnebago	255
Signal Hill Sch Dist 181	1	330	St Clair	221
Silvis School Dist 34	2	648	Rock Island	209
Skokie School Dist 68	5	1,700	Cook	67
Skokie School Dist 69	3	1,700	Cook	67
Skokie School Dist 73 1/2	3	1,118	Cook	67
Smithton Cmty Cons SD 130	1	568	St Clair	222
Somonauk Cmty Unit SD 432	3	800	De Kalb	86
South Beloit Cmty Sch Dist 320	5	960	Winnebago	255
South Central Cmty Unit SD 401	3	650	Marion	176
South Fork School Dist 14	2	319	Christian	14
South Holland School Dist 150	3	1,000	Cook	68
South Holland School Dist 151	4	1,753	Cook	68
South Pekin Grade Sch Dist 137	1	200	Tazewell	228
Southeastern Cmty Unit SD 337	2	450	Hancock	115
Southwestern Cmty Unit SD 9	5	1,300	Macoupin	168
Sparta Cmty School Dist 140	3	1,213	Randolph	205
Spoon River Valley Cmty SD 4	2	320	Fulton	110
Spring Garden Cmty CSD 178	2	249	Jefferson	124
Spring Lake Elem SD 606	1	60	Tazewell	228
Spring Valley Cmty Cons SD 99	1	633	Bureau	7
Springfield Pub Sch Dist 186	33	13,000	Sangamon	213
St Anne Cmty Cons Sch Dist 256	1	351	Kankakee	136
St Anne Cmty HSD 302	1	210	Kankakee	136
St Elmo Cmty Unit Sch Dist 202	2	440	Fayette	106
St George School Dist 258	1	431	Kankakee	136
St Joseph Cmty Cons SD 169	2	850	Champaign	12
St Joseph-Ogden Cmty HSD 305	1	450	Champaign	12
St Libory Cons Sch Dist 30	1	53	St Clair	222
St Rose School Dist 14-15	1	207	Clinton	18
Stark Co Cmty Unit SD 100	3	692	Stark	223
Staunton Cmty Unit Sch Dist 6	3	1,200	Macoupin	168
Steeleville Cmty Sch Dist 138	2	425	Randolph	206
Steger School Dist 194	3	1,500	Cook	68
Sterling Cmty Unit Sch Dist 5	6	3,500	Whiteside	240
Steward Elem School Dist 220	1	51	Lee	160
Stewardson-Strasburg SD 5-A	2	374	Shelby	216
Stockton Cmty Unit SD 206	3	603	Jo Daviess	126
Streator Elem School Dist 44	3	1,540	La Salle	144
Streator Twp High Sch Dist 40	1	844	La Salle	145
Sullivan Cmty Unit SD 300	3	1,100	Moultrie	193
Summersville Sch Dist 79	1	245	Jefferson	124
Summit Hill School Dist 161	6	2,800	Will	247
Sunnybrook School Dist 171	2	1,012	Cook	68
Sunset Ridge Sch Dist 29	2	480	Cook	68
Sycamore Cmty Unit SD 427	7	3,800	De Kalb	86
Taft School Dist 90	1	300	Will	247
Tamaroa Elem School Dist 5	1	82	Perry	201
Taylorville Cmty Unit SD 3	4	2,480	Christian	15
Teutopolis Cmty Unit SD 50	3	1,000	Effingham	105
Thomasboro Cmty Cons SD 130	1	150	Champaign	12
Thompsonville Cmty USD 174	2	285	Franklin	108
Thornton Fractnl Twp HSD 215	4	3,177	Cook	69
Thornton Twp High Sch Dist 205	4	4,524	Cook	69
Tolono Cmty Unit Sch Dist 7	4	1,615	Champaign	12
Tonica Cmty Cons Sch Dist 79	1	159	La Salle	145
Township High School Dist 113	2	3,616	Lake	155
Township High School Dist 211	7	12,490	Cook	69
Township High School Dist 214	10	12,000	Cook	69
Tremont Cmty Unit SD 702	3	1,000	Tazewell	228
Tri-City Cmty Unit Sch Dist 1	1	570	Sangamon	214
Tri-Point Cmty Unit SD 6J	3	395	Livingston	162
Tri-Valley Cmty School Dist 3	3	1,150	Mclean	187
Triad Cmty School Dist 2	6	4,000	Madison	172
Trico Cmty Unit Sch Dist 176	3	850	Jackson	121
Triopia Cmty Unit Sch Dist 27	2	382	Morgan	192
Troy Cmty Cons SD 30-C	7	4,100	Will	247
Tuscola Cmty Unit SD 301	3	1,000	Douglas	88
Union Ridge School Dist 86	1	675	Cook	70
Union School Dist 81	1	105	Will	248
United Cmty Unit Sch Dist 304	4	950	Warren	234
United Twp High Sch Dist 30	2	1,678	Rock Island	209
Unity Point Cmty Cons SD 140	1	610	Jackson	121
Urbana School Dist 116	10	4,175	Champaign	12
Valley View Cmty SD 365-U	20	18,000	Will	248
Valmeyer Cmty School Dist 3	1	430	Monroe	190
Vandalia Cmty Unit SD 203	4	1,490	Fayette	106
Venice Cmty Unit School Dist 3	1	80	Madison	172
Vienna High School Dist 13-3	1	360	Johnson	127
Vienna Public School Dist 55	1	410	Johnson	127
Villa Grove Cmty Unit SD 302	3	651	Douglas	88
Virginia Cmty Unit Sch Dist 64	1	320	Cass	9
Vit Cmty Unit School Dist 2	2	370	Fulton	110
Wabash Cmty Unit Sch Dist 348	4	1,450	Wabash	234
Wallace Cmty Cons Sch Dist 195	1	410	La Salle	145
Waltham Elementary SD 185	1	200	La Salle	145
Waltonville Cmty Unit SD 1	2	325	Jefferson	124
Warren Community Unit SD 205	2	400	Jo Daviess	126
Warren Twp High Sch Dist 121	2	4,049	Lake	155
Warrensburg-Latham CU SD 11	3	1,200	Macon	166
Warsaw Cmty Unit Sch Dist 316	2	444	Hancock	115
Washington Cmty HS Dist 308	1	1,406	Tazewell	229
Washington School Dist 52	2	930	Tazewell	229
Waterloo Cmty Unit Sch Dist 5	5	2,739	Monroe	190
Wauconda Cmty Unit SD 118	6	4,500	Lake	155
Waukegan Cmty Unit SD 60	24	17,000	Lake	156
Waverly Cmty Unit SD 6	2	369	Morgan	193
Wayne City Cmty Unit SD 100	2	530	Wayne	237
Wesclin Cmty Unit Sch Dist 3	4	1,375	Clinton	18
West Aurora School Dist 129	18	12,000	Kane	132
West Carroll CUSD 314	3	1,054	Carroll	8
West Central Cmty Unit SD 235	3	820	Henderson	116
West Chicago Elementary SD 33	8	4,300	Du Page	99
West Harvey-Dixmoor Pub SD 147	3	1,000	Cook	70
West Lincoln-Broadwell ESD 92	1	220	Logan	164
West Northfield Sch Dist 31	2	880	Cook	70
West Prairie Cmty Unit Dist 103	4	600	McDonough	178
West Washington Co Cmty SD 10	2	544	Washington	236
Westchester Public SD 92 1/2	3	1,250	Cook	70
Western CUSD 12	3	570	Pike	203
Western Springs Sch Dist 101	4	1,435	Cook	71
Westville Cmty Unit Sch Dist 2	3	1,306	Vermilion	233
Wethersfield Cmty Unit SD 230	2	580	Henry	117
Wheeling Cmty Cons Sch Dist 21	13	6,058	Cook	71
Whiteside School Dist 115	2	1,036	St Clair	222
Will Co School Dist 92	4	1,550	Will	248
Williamsfield Cmty Unit SD 210	1	275	Knox	140
Williamsville Cmty Unit SD 15	4	1,540	Sangamon	214
Willow Grove School Dist 46	1	165	Clinton	18
Willow Springs School Dist 108	1	359	Cook	71
Wilmette Public School Dist 39	6	3,563	Cook	71
Wilmington Cmty Unit SD 209-U	4	1,400	Will	249
Winchester Cmty Unit SD 1	2	680	Scott	215
Windsor Cmty Unit SD 1	2	300	Shelby	216
Winfield School Dist 34	2	275	Du Page	100
Winnebago Cmty Unit SD 323	4	1,330	Winnebago	255
Winnetka School Dist 36	5	1,100	Cook	72
Winthrop Harbor School Dist 1	2	542	Lake	156
Wolf Branch School Dist 113	2	720	St Clair	222
Wood Dale School Dist 7	4	1,082	Du Page	100
Wood River-Hartford Elem SD 15	3	706	Madison	172
Woodland Cmty Unit Sch Dist 5	2	540	Livingston	162
Woodland School Dist 50	5	5,700	Lake	156

Illinois School Directory — DISTRICT INDEX

SCHOOL DISTRICT	NO. OF SCHOOLS	ENROLLMENT	COUNTY	PAGE
Woodlawn Unit School Dist 209	2	503	Jefferson	124
Woodridge Elem Sch Dist 68	7	2,950	Du Page	100
Woodstock Cmty Unit SD 200	12	6,600	McHenry	184
Worth School Dist 127	4	1,087	Cook	72
Yorkville Cmty Unit SD 115	10	6,200	Kendall	139
Zeigler Royalton CUSD 188	2	370	Franklin	108
Zion Public School Dist 6	7	2,700	Lake	157
Zion-Benton Twp High SD 126	2	2,100	Lake	157

CATHOLIC DIOCESE

SCHOOL DISTRICT	NO. OF SCHOOLS	ENROLLMENT	COUNTY	PAGE
Archdiocese of Chicago Ed Off	198	75,039	Cook	72
Diocese of Belleville Ed Off	30	5,497	St Clair	222
Diocese of Joliet Ed Office	53	17,485	Will	249
Diocese of Peoria Ed Office	43	11,872	Peoria	200
Diocese of Rockford Ed Office	43	11,358	Winnebago	256
Diocese of Springfield Ed Off	44	10,260	Sangamon	214

REGIONAL CENTERS

SCHOOL DISTRICT	COUNTY	PAGE
Adams Co Special Ed Co-op	Adams	3
Aero Special Ed Co-op	Cook	82
Area 3 Learning Technology Ctr	Peoria	200
Area 5 Learning Technology Hub	Madison	174
Area 6 Learning Technology Ctr	Crawford	83
Belleville Area Sp Svc Co-op	St Clair	223
Bi-County Special Ed Co-op	Whiteside	240
Black Hawk Area Spec Ed Dist	Rock Island	210
BMP Spec Ed Co-op	Bureau	7
Boone Co Special Ed Co-op	Boone	5
Boone-Winnebago Reg Off of Ed	Winnebago	256
Career & Tech Ed Consortium	Stephenson	225
Career Development System	Cook	82
Career Educ Assoc N Ctl IL	Winnebago	256
Career Preparation Network	Cook	82
Central Illinois Rural Rvs	Jersey	125
Central Illinois Voc Ed Co-op	Woodford	259
Christian-Montgomery EFE Sys	Montgomery	191
Clay-Jaspr-Richlnd-N Wayne EFE	Clay	16
Cooperative Assn for Spec Ed	Du Page	102
Delabar Cte System	Warren	235
Des Plaines Valley EFE System	Cook	82
Dupage Area Occupational Sys	Du Page	102
Dupage Reg Office of Ed 19	Du Page	102
E St Louis Area JT Agreement	St Clair	223
East St Louis Reg Voc System	St Clair	223
Eastern Illinois Area of Sp Ed	Coles	20
Eastern Illinois EFE System	Coles	20
Echo Joint Agreement	Cook	82
EFE System 330	Champaign	13
Eisenhower Cooperative	Cook	82
Five Co Reg EFE System	Alexander	3
Ford Co Spec Ed Co-op	Ford	107
Four Rivers Spec Ed Dist	Morgan	193
Franklin-Jefferson Sp Ed Co-op	Franklin	109
Grundy Area Voc Ed System	Grundy	113
Grundy Co Special Ed Co-op	Grundy	113
Heartland Technical Academy	Macon	167
Henry-Stark Co Sp Ed Dist 801	Henry	118
Indian Valley Voc Ed System	De Kalb	86
Iroquois Spec Educ Association	Iroquois	119
Iroquois-Kankakee Reg Off Ed	Kankakee	137
Jamp Special Ed Services	Pulaski	204
Kankakee Area Reg Voc Ed Sys	Kankakee	137
Kankakee Area Special Ed Co-op	Kankakee	137
Kaskaskia Spec Ed Dist	Marion	176
Kishwaukee Ed Consortium	De Kalb	87
Knox-Warren Spec Ed Dist	Knox	141
La Grange Area Dept of Spec Ed	Cook	82
Lake County Regional of Ed	Lake	158
LaSalle-Putnam Sped Alliance	La Salle	145
Learning Tech Ctr of Illinois	Champaign	13
Lee Co Spec Ed Association	Lee	160
Leyden Area Spec Ed Co-op	Cook	82
Lincoln Way Area Special Ed	Will	250
Livingston Area EFE System	Livingston	163
Livingston Co Spec Svc Unit	Livingston	163
Lockport Area Special Ed Co-op	Will	250
Mackinaw Valley Spec Ed Assoc	Mclean	188
Macon-Piatt Roe#39	Macon	167
Macon-Piatt Spec Ed	Macon	167
Madison Co Cte System	Madison	174
Madison Co Reg 1 Spec Ed Co-op	Madison	174
Maine Twp Spec Ed Program	Cook	82
McHenry Co Reg Office of Ed 44	McHenry	185
McHenry Co Work Force Ctr	McHenry	185
McLean-DeWitt Reg Voc System	Mclean	188
Mid-State Special Education	Christian	15
Mid-Valley Special Ed Co-op	Kane	134
Monroe-Randolph Reg Off	Monroe	190
Montgomery-Carlinville Reg SE	Christian	15
Moraine Area Career System	Cook	82
Niles Twp Dept of Spec Ed #807	Cook	82
North Cook Interm Svc Center	Cook	82
North Dupage Spec Ed Co-op	Du Page	102
North Suburban Ed Reg for Voc	Cook	82
Northern Kane Co Reg Voc Sys	Kane	134
Northern Suburban Spec Ed Dist	Lake	159
Northwest Special Ed Dist	Jo Daviess	126
Northwest Suburban Sp Ed Org	Cook	82
Northwestern IL Association	De Kalb	87
NW Ed Council Stdnt Success	Cook	82
Ogle Co Educational Co-op	Ogle	196
Ohio-Wabash Valley Reg Voc Sys	White	238
Okaw Regional Voc System	Randolph	206
Peoria Co Special Ed Assoc	Peoria	200
Peoria Ed Reg Emp & Career	Peoria	200
Perandoe Special Ed Dist	Randolph	206
Philip J Rock Center & School	Du Page	102
Professional Dev Alliance	Will	250
Region 3 Spec Ed Co-op	Madison	174
Regional Office of Ed 1	Morgan	193
Regional Office of Ed 3	Fayette	106
Regional Office of Ed 8	Stephenson	225
Regional Office of Ed 9	Champaign	13
Regional Office of Ed 11	Coles	20
Regional Office of Ed 12	Richland	207
Regional Office of Ed 13	Clinton	19
Regional Office of Ed 16	De Kalb	87
Regional Office of Ed 17	Mclean	188
Regional Office of Ed 20	Saline	211
Regional Office of Ed 21	Franklin	109
Regional Office of Ed 24	Grundy	113
Regional Office of Ed 26	McDonough	179
Regional Office of Ed 28	Henry	118
Regional Office of Ed 30	Jackson	121
Regional Office of Ed 33	Knox	141
Regional Office of Ed 35	La Salle	146
Regional Office of Ed 40	Macoupin	169
Regional Office of Ed 41	Madison	174
Regional Office of Ed 47	Whiteside	241
Regional Office of Ed 48	Peoria	201
Regional Office of Ed 53	Tazewell	229
Regional Office of Ed 54	Vermilion	233
Regional Office of Ed Kane Co	Kane	134
Regional Office of Education 3	Fayette	106
Regional Office-Career Tech Ed	Sangamon	215
Rock Island Reg Off of Ed 49	Rock Island	210
Rural Champaign Co Sp Ed Co-op	Champaign	13
Sangamon Area Spec Ed Dist	Sangamon	215
Sangamon-Menard Roe #51	Sangamon	215

DISTRICT INDEX

SCHOOL DISTRICT	NO. OF SCHOOLS	ENROLLMENT	COUNTY	PAGE
School Assoc for Sp Ed-Dupage			Du Page	102
South Cook Interm Svc Center			Cook	82
South Eastern Special Ed Dist			Jasper	122
Southern Will Co Spec Ed Dist			Will	250
Southwest Cook Co Assc Spec Ed			Cook	82
Special Ed Dist of McHenry Co			McHenry	185
Special Education Dist Lake Co			Lake	159
Speed Seja 802			Cook	82
St Clair Co Regional Off of Ed			St Clair	223
Starved Rock Assoc Voc Tech Ed			La Salle	146
Tazewell Co Area EFE #320			Tazewell	229
Tazewell-Mason Sp Ed Assoc			Tazewell	229
Trees-Three Rivers EFE Sys			Will	250
Tri-Co Special Ed Association			Mclean	188
Tri-Co Special Ed JT Agreement			Jackson	122
Twin Rivers Career & Tech Ed			Crawford	83
Two Rivers Voc Ed System			Cass	9
UT Area Career Center			Rock Island	210
Valley Ed for Employment Sys			Kane	134
Vermilion Assoc for Special Ed			Vermilion	233
Vermilion Voc Ed Delivery Sys			Vermilion	233
Wabash-Ohio Valley Sp Ed Dist			White	238
West 40 Interm Serv Center 2			Cook	82
West Central IL Spec Ed Co-op			McDonough	179
Western Area Career System			Fulton	110
Western Area Career System			McDonough	179
Whiteside Regional Voc System			Whiteside	241
Will Co Regional Office of Edu			Will	250
Williamson Co Cte System			Williamson	252
Williamson Co Special Ed Dist			Williamson	252
Winnebago Co Special Ed Co-op			Winnebago	256
Woodford Co Special Ed Assoc			Woodford	259

Illinois School Directory

COUNTY INDEX

COUNTY District/City	NO. OF SCHOOLS	ENROLLMENT	PAGE
ADAMS			
Adams Co Special Ed Co-op/Quincy			3
Central School Dist 3/Camp Point	4	837	1
Liberty Cmty Unit Sch Dist 2/Liberty	1	650	2
Mendon Cmty Unit School Dist 4/Mendon	3	670	2
Payson Cmty Unit School Dist 1/Payson	2	550	2
Quincy School Dist 172/Quincy	10	6,700	2
ALEXANDER			
Cairo School Dist 1/Cairo	2	315	3
Egyptian Cmty Unit Sch Dist 5/Tamms	1	400	3
Five Co Reg EFE System/Tamms			3
BOND			
Bond Co Cmty Unit Sch Dist 2/Greenville	6	1,750	4
Mulberry Grove Cmty Sch Dist 1/Mulberry GRV	3	400	4
BOONE			
Belvidere Cmty Unit SD 100/Belvidere	10	8,500	4
Boone Co Special Ed Co-op/Belvidere			5
North Boone Cmty Unit SD 200/Poplar Grove	6	1,600	5
BROWN			
Brown Co Cmty Unit Sch Dist 1/Mt Sterling	3	750	5
BUREAU			
BMP Spec Ed Co-op/Tiskilwa			7
Bureau Valley Cmty Unit 340/Manlius	4	1,082	6
Dalzell Elem School Dist 98/Dalzell	1	56	6
DePue Unit Sch Dist 103/Depue	1	390	6
Hall Twp High School Dist 502/Spring Valley	1	405	6
La Moille Cmty Unit SD 303/La Moille	3	205	6
Ladd Cmty Cons Sch Dist 94/Ladd	1	190	6
Malden Cmty Cons SD 84/Malden	1	100	7
Ohio Cmty Cons School Dist 17/Ohio	1	113	7
Ohio Cmty High School Dist 505/Ohio	1	33	7
Princeton Elem Sch Dist 115/Princeton	4	1,156	7
Princeton Twp HSD 500/Princeton	1	550	7
Spring Valley Cmty Cons SD 99/Spring Valley	1	633	7
CALHOUN			
Brussels Cmty Unit Sch Dist 42/Brussels	2	106	8
Calhoun Cmty Unit Sch Dist 40/Hardin	2	484	8
CARROLL			
Chadwick Milledgevill CUSD 399/Chadwick	2	450	8
Eastland Cmty Unit SD 308/Lanark	2	650	8
West Carroll CUSD 314/Mount Carroll	3	1,054	8
CASS			
A-C Central Cmty Unit SD 262/Ashland	2	419	9
Beardstown Cmty Sch Dist 15/Beardstown	3	1,560	9
Two Rivers Voc Ed System/Virginia			9
Virginia Cmty Unit Sch Dist 64/Virginia	1	320	9
CHAMPAIGN			
Champaign Cmty Unit Sch Dist 4/Champaign	19	10,179	10
EFE System 330/Champaign			13
Fisher Cmty Unit School Dist 1/Fisher	2	601	10
Gifford Cmty Cons SD 188/Gifford	1	183	10
Heritage Cmty Unit Sch Dist 8/Homer	2	421	11
Learning Tech Ctr of Illinois/Champaign			13
Ludlow Cons Cmty Sch Dist 142/Ludlow	1	57	11
Mahomet-Seymour Cmty SD 3/Mahomet	4	3,170	11
Prairieview-Ogden Sch Dist 197/Royal	3	247	11
Rantoul City School Dist 137/Rantoul	5	1,750	11
Rantoul Twp High Sch Dist 193/Rantoul	2	765	12
Regional Office of Ed 9/Champaign			13
Rural Champaign Co Sp Ed Co-op/Champaign			13
St Joseph Cmty Cons SD 169/Saint Joseph	2	850	12
St Joseph-Ogden Cmty HSD 305/Saint Joseph	1	450	12
Thomasboro Cmty Cons SD 130/Thomasboro	1	150	12
Tolono Cmty Unit Sch Dist 7/Tolono	4	1,615	12
Urbana School Dist 116/Urbana	10	4,175	12
CHRISTIAN			
Central A&M Cmty Unit SD 21/Assumption	5	670	14
Edinburg Cmty Unit Sch Dist 4/Edinburg	1	290	14
Mid-State Special Education/Morrisonville			15
Montgomery-Carlinville Reg SE/Morrisonville			15
Morrisonville Cmty Unit SD 1/Morrisonville	2	250	14
Pana Cmty Unit School Dist 8/Pana	4	1,347	14
South Fork School Dist 14/Kincaid	2	319	14
Taylorville Cmty Unit Sch Dist 3/Taylorville	4	2,480	15
CLARK			
Casey-Westfield Cmty USD C-4/Casey	2	875	15
Marshall Cmty Sch Dist C-2/Marshall	4	1,250	15
Martinsville Cmty Unit SD C-3/Martinsville	2	400	16
CLAY			
Clay City Cmty Unit SD 10/Clay City	3	350	16
Clay-Jaspr-Richlnd-N Wayne EFE/Flora			16
Flora Cmty Unit School Dist 35/Flora	3	1,396	16
North Clay Cmty Unit SD 25/Louisville	2	618	16
CLINTON			
Albers Elem School Dist 63/Albers	1	200	17
Aviston Elem School Dist 21/Aviston	1	390	17
Bartelso School Dist 57/Bartelso	1	158	17
Breese Elementary SD 12/Breese	2	630	17
Carlyle Cmty Unit Sch Dist 1/Carlyle	3	1,006	17
Central Cmty High Sch Dist 71/Breese	1	615	17
Damiansville School Dist 62/Damiansville	1	85	17
Germantown Elem Sch Dist 60/Germantown	1	250	18
North Wamac School Dist 186/Centralia	1	120	18
Regional Office of Ed 13/Carlyle			19
St Rose School Dist 14-15/Saint Rose	1	207	18
Wesclin Cmty Unit Sch Dist 3/Trenton	4	1,375	18
Willow Grove School Dist 46/Centralia	1	165	18
COLES			
Charleston Cmty Unit SD 1/Charleston	6	2,500	19
Eastern Illinois Area of Sp Ed/Charleston			20
Eastern Illinois EFE System/Mattoon			20
Mattoon Cmty Unit Sch Dist 2/Mattoon	5	2,500	19
Oakland Cmty Unit Sch Dist 5/Oakland	2	245	19
Regional Office of Ed 11/Charleston			20
COOK			
Aero Special Ed Co-op/Burbank			82
Alsip-Hazelgrn-Oaklawn SD 126/Alsip	5	1,580	20
Arbor Park School Dist 145/Oak Forest	4	1,350	21
Archdiocese of Chicago Ed Off/Chicago	198	75,039	72
Argo Cmty High School Dist 217/Summit	1	2,100	21
Arlington Hts School Dist 25/Arlington HTS	9	5,550	21
Atwood Heights SD 125/Alsip	3	620	21
Avoca School Dist 37/Wilmette	2	750	22
Bellwood School Dist 88/Bellwood	7	2,425	22
Berkeley School Dist 87/Berkeley	6	2,600	22
Berwyn North School Dist 98/Berwyn	4	2,600	22
Berwyn South School Dist 100/Berwyn	8	3,700	23
Bloom Twp High Sch Dist 206/Chicago HTS	3	3,558	23
Bremen Cmty High SD 228/Midlothian	5	4,800	23
Brookfield-LaGrange Park SD 95/Brookfield	2	1,257	23
Brookwood School Dist 167/Glenwood	4	1,200	24
Burbank School Dist 111/Burbank	8	3,400	24
Burnham School Dist 1545/Burnham	1	180	24
Calumet City School Dist 155/Calumet City	3	1,026	24
Calumet Public School Dist 132/Calumet Park	3	1,200	24
Career Development System/Oak Forest			82
Career Preparation Network/Chicago HTS			82
Central Stickney Sch Dist 110/Chicago	1	384	25
Chicago Heights Elem SD 170/Chicago HTS	10	3,100	25
Chicago PSD-Ausl/Chicago			25
Chicago PSD-Isp/Chicago			26
Chicago PSD-Network 1/Chicago			28
Chicago PSD-Network 2/Chicago			29
Chicago PSD-Network 3/Chicago			29
Chicago PSD-Network 4/Chicago			30
Chicago PSD-Network 5/Chicago			31
Chicago PSD-Network 6/Chicago			31
Chicago PSD-Network 7/Chicago			32
Chicago PSD-Network 8/Chicago			32
Chicago PSD-Network 9/Chicago			33
Chicago PSD-Network 10/Chicago			33
Chicago PSD-Network 11/Chicago			34
Chicago PSD-Network 12/Chicago			35
Chicago PSD-Network 13/Chicago			35
Chicago PSD-Network 14/Chicago			36
Chicago PSD-Network 15/Chicago			37
Chicago PSD-Network 16/Chicago			37
Chicago PSD-Network 17/Chicago			38
Chicago PSD-Options/Chicago			38
Chicago Public School Dist 299/Chicago	666	355,156	25
Chicago Ridge Sch Dist 127-5/Chicago Ridge	3	1,476	41
Cicero School Dist 99/Cicero	17	12,418	42
Cmty Cons Sch Dist 146/Tinley Park	5	2,500	42
Community Cons School Dist 15/Palatine	20	12,000	42
Community Cons School Dist 59/Elk Grove Vlg	15	6,000	43
Community Cons School Dist 168/Sauk Village	3	1,287	44
Community High School Dist 218/Oak Lawn	5	5,400	44
Consolidated High Sch Dist 230/Orland Park	3	7,308	44

School Year 2020-2021   800-333-8802

COUNTY INDEX

Market Data Retrieval

COUNTY District/City	NO. OF SCHOOLS	ENROLL- MENT	PAGE
Cook County School Dist 104/Summit	5	1,800	44
Cook County School Dist 130/Blue Island	11	4,000	45
Cook County School Dist 154/Thornton	1	225	45
Country Club Hills SD 160/Cntry CLB Hls	3	1,221	45
Des Plaines Cmty Cons SD 62/Des Plaines	11	4,800	45
Des Plaines Valley EFE System/River Grove			82
Dolton School Dist 149/Calumet City	8	2,600	46
Dolton-Riverdale Sch Dist 148/Riverdale	10	2,183	46
E F Lindop Elem Sch Dist 92/Broadview	1	480	47
East Maine School Dist 63/Des Plaines	6	3,500	47
East Prairie School Dist 73/Skokie	1	505	47
Echo Joint Agreement/South Holland			82
Eisenhower Cooperative/Crestwood			82
Elementary School Dist 159/Matteson	5	1,700	47
Elmwood Park Cmty Unit SD 401/Elmwood Park	5	2,800	47
Evanston Twp High SD 202/Evanston	1	3,800	48
Evanston-Skokie Cmty CSD 65/Evanston	18	8,030	48
Evergreen Park Cmty HSD 231/Evergreen Pk	1	850	49
Evergreen Park Elem SD 124/Evergreen Pk	5	1,900	49
Fairview South School Dist 72/Skokie	1	722	49
Flossmoor School Dist 161/Chicago HTS	5	2,374	49
Ford Heights School Dist 169/Ford Heights	2	455	49
Forest Park School Dist 91/Forest Park	5	861	50
Forest Ridge Sch Dist 142/Oak Forest	4	1,650	50
Franklin Park Pub Sch Dist 84/Franklin Park	4	1,400	50
General George S Patton SD 133/Riverdale	1	268	50
Glenbrook High Sch Dist 225/Glenview	2	5,102	50
Glencoe Sch Dist 35/Glencoe	3	1,200	51
Glenview Cmty Cons Sch Dist 34/Glenview	8	4,900	51
Golf School Dist 67/Morton Grove	2	725	51
Harvey Public School Dist 152/Harvey	6	2,264	51
Hazel Crest School Dist 152-5/Hazel Crest	2	1,000	52
Hillside School Dist 93/Hillside	1	410	52
Homewood Flossmoor CHSD 233/Flossmoor	1	2,897	52
Homewood School Dist 153/Homewood	3	2,000	52
Hoover-Schrum Sch Dist 157/Calumet City	2	850	52
Indian Springs Sch Dist 109/Justice	6	2,764	52
J Sterling Morton HSD 201/Cicero	4	8,600	53
Kenilworth School Dist 38/Kenilworth	1	425	53
Kirby School Dist 140/Tinley Park	7	3,500	53
Komarek School Dist 94/N Riverside	1	580	54
La Grange Area Dept of Spec Ed/La Grange			82
La Grange Cmty School Dist 105/La Grange	5	1,300	54
La Grange Elem School Dist 102/La Grange Pk	6	3,100	54
La Grange-Highlands SD 106/La Grange	2	850	54
Lansing School Dist 158/Lansing	5	2,500	54
Lemont High Sch Dist 210/Lemont	1	1,400	55
Lemont-Bromberek Sch Dist 113A/Lemont	3	2,300	55
Leyden Area Spec Ed Co-op/Franklin Park			82
Leyden Cmty High Sch Dist 212/Franklin Park	2	3,420	55
Lincoln Elem School Dist 156/Calumet City	1	950	55
Lincolnwood Sch Dist 74/Lincolnwood	3	1,200	55
Lyons Elem School Dist 103/Lyons	6	2,612	56
Lyons Twp HS Dist 204/La Grange	2	4,200	56
Maine Twp High Sch Dist 207/Park Ridge	3	6,322	56
Maine Twp Spec Ed Program/Park Ridge			82
Mannheim School Dist 83/Franklin Park	6	2,800	56
Matteson Elem SD 162/Richton Park	7	2,700	57
Maywood-Melrose Brdview SD 89/Melrose Park	9	4,300	57
Midlothian School Dist 143/Midlothian	4	1,800	57
Moraine Area Career System/Oak Lawn			82
Morton Grove School Dist 70/Morton Grove	1	900	58
Mt Prospect School Dist 57/Mt Prospect	4	2,222	58
New Trier Twp HS Dist 203/Northfield	2	3,978	58
Niles Elem School Dist 71/Niles	1	600	58
Niles Twp Dept of Spec Ed #807/Morton Grove			82
Niles Twp High School Dist 219/Skokie	3	4,555	58
Norridge School Dist 80/Norridge	2	1,000	59
North Cook Interm Svc Center/Des Plaines			82
North Palos School Dist 117/Palos Hills	5	3,402	59
North Suburban Ed Reg for Voc/Park Ridge			82
Northbrook Elem School Dist 27/Northbrook	3	1,237	59
Northbrook School Dist 28/Northbrook	4	1,870	59
Northbrook-Glenview SD 30/Northbrook	3	1,195	60
Northwest Suburban Sp Ed Org/Mt Prospect			82
NW Ed Council Stdnt Success/Arlington HTS			82
Oak Lawn Cmty High SD 229/Oak Lawn	1	1,850	60
Oak Lawn-Hometown Sch Dist 123/Oak Lawn	6	3,000	60
Oak Park & River Forest SD 200/Oak Park	1	3,468	60
Oak Park Elem School Dist 97/Oak Park	10	6,000	60
Orland School Dist 135/Orland Park	10	5,201	61
Palos Cmty Cons Sch Dist 118/Palos Park	3	2,050	61
Palos Heights School Dist 128/Palos Heights	4	700	61
Park Forest Chicago Hgt SD 163/Park Forest	6	2,000	62

COUNTY District/City	NO. OF SCHOOLS	ENROLL- MENT	PAGE
Park Ridge Niles CMCSD 64/Park Ridge	8	4,500	62
Pennoyer School Dist 79/Norridge	1	444	62
Pleasantdale School Dist 107/Burr Ridge	2	845	62
Posen-Robbins Sch Dist 143-5/Posen	5	1,452	63
Prairie Hills Elem SD 144/Markham	8	3,000	63
Prospect Hts School Dist 23/Prospect HTS	4	1,500	63
Proviso Twp High Sch Dist 209/Forest Park	3	4,339	63
Reavis Twp HSD 220/Burbank	1	1,800	64
Rhodes School Dist 84 1/2/River Grove	1	637	64
Rich Twp High School Dist 227/Matteson	2	2,800	64
Ridgeland School Dist 122/Oak Lawn	5	2,300	64
Ridgewood Cmty HSD 234/Norridge	1	900	64
River Forest Sch Dist 90/River Forest	3	1,400	65
River Grove School Dist 85-5/River Grove	1	750	65
River Trails Sch Dist 26/Mt Prospect	4	1,600	65
Riverside Public Sch Dist 96/Riverside	5	1,686	65
Riverside-Brookfld Twp SD 208/Riverside	1	1,630	65
Rosemont Elem Sch Dist 78/Rosemont	1	220	66
Sandridge Sch Dist 172/Chicago HTS	1	350	66
Schaumburg Cmty Cons SD 54/Schaumburg	28	15,296	66
Schiller Park School Dist 81/Schiller Park	3	1,500	67
Skokie School Dist 68/Skokie	5	1,700	67
Skokie School Dist 69/Skokie	3	1,700	67
Skokie School Dist 73 1/2/Skokie	3	1,118	67
South Cook Interm Svc Center/Chicago HTS			82
South Holland School Dist 150/South Holland	3	1,000	68
South Holland School Dist 151/South Holland	4	1,753	68
Southwest Cook Co Assc Spec Ed/Oak Forest			82
Speed Seja 802/Chicago HTS			82
Steger School Dist 194/Steger	3	1,500	68
Sunnybrook School Dist 171/Lansing	2	1,012	68
Sunset Ridge Sch Dist 29/Northfield	2	480	68
Thornton Fractnl Twp HSD 215/Lansing	4	3,177	69
Thornton Twp High Sch Dist 205/South Holland	4	4,524	69
Township High School Dist 211/Palatine	7	12,490	69
Township High School Dist 214/Arlington HTS	10	12,000	69
Union Ridge School Dist 86/Harwood HTS	1	675	70
West 40 Interm Serv Center 2/Hillside			82
West Harvey-Dixmoor Pub SD 147/Harvey	3	1,000	70
West Northfield Sch Dist 31/Northbrook	2	880	70
Westchester Public SD 92 1/2/Westchester	3	1,250	70
Western Springs Sch Dist 101/Western Sprgs	4	1,435	71
Wheeling Cmty Cons Sch Dist 21/Wheeling	13	6,058	71
Willow Springs School Dist 108/Willow Spgs	1	359	71
Wilmette Public School Dist 39/Wilmette	6	3,563	71
Winnetka School Dist 36/Winnetka	5	1,100	72
Worth School Dist 127/Worth	4	1,087	72

CRAWFORD

Area 6 Learning Technology Ctr/Robinson			83
Hutsonville Cmty Unit SD 1/Hutsonville	2	324	83
Oblong Cmty Unit Sch Dist 4/Oblong	2	565	83
Palestine Cmty Unit SD 3/Palestine	2	375	83
Robinson Cmty Unit Sch Dist 2/Robinson	4	1,616	83
Twin Rivers Career & Tech Ed/Robinson			83

CUMBERLAND

Cumberland Cmty Unit SD 77/Toledo	3	1,000	84
Neoga Cmty Unit School Dist 3/Neoga	2	535	84

DE KALB

DeKalb Cmty Unit SD 428/Dekalb	12	6,600	84
Genoa-Kingston Cmty SD 424/Genoa	4	1,700	85
Hiawatha Cmty Unit SD 426/Kirkland	2	450	85
Hinckley-Big Rock Cmty SD 429/Hinckley	3	696	85
Indian Creek Cmty Unit SD 425/Shabbona	3	740	85
Indian Valley Voc Ed System/Sandwich			86
Kishwaukee Ed Consortium/Malta			87
Northwestern IL Association/Sycamore			87
Regional Office of Ed 16/Dekalb			87
Sandwich Cmty Unit SD 430/Sandwich	6	2,000	85
Somonauk Cmty Unit SD 432/Somonauk	3	800	86
Sycamore Cmty Unit SD 427/Sycamore	7	3,800	86

DEWITT

Blue Ridge Cmty SD 18/Farmer City	3	700	87
Clinton Cmty Unit Sch Dist 15/Clinton	5	1,800	87

DOUGLAS

Arcola Cmty Unit Sch Dist 306/Arcola	2	717	87
Arthur CUSD 305/Arthur	4	1,140	87
Tuscola Cmty Unit SD 301/Tuscola	3	1,000	88
Villa Grove Cmty Unit SD 302/Villa Grove	3	651	88

DU PAGE

Addison School Dist 4/Addison	9	4,000	88

Illinois School Directory

COUNTY INDEX

COUNTY / District/City	NO. OF SCHOOLS	ENROLLMENT	PAGE
Benjamin Sch Dist 25/West Chicago	2	650	89
Bensenville Elem Sch Dist 2/Bensenville	3	2,350	89
Bloomingdale School Dist 13/Bloomingdale	3	1,390	89
Butler School Dist 53/Oak Brook	2	518	89
Cass School Dist 63/Darien	2	766	89
Center Cass Sch Dist 66/Downers Grove	3	1,100	90
Community Cons School Dist 89/Glen Ellyn	5	2,300	90
Community Cons School Dist 93/Bloomingdale	9	3,200	90
Community Cons School Dist 180/Burr Ridge	2	630	90
Community Cons School Dist 181/Clarendon Hls	9	3,800	91
Community High School Dist 94/West Chicago	1	2,006	91
Community High School Dist 99/Downers Grove	2	5,015	91
Community Unit School Dist 200/Wheaton	20	12,000	91
Community Unit School Dist 201/Westmont	5	1,365	92
Cooperative Assn for Spec Ed/Glen Ellyn			102
Darien Public Sch Dist 61/Darien	3	1,400	92
Downers Grove School Dist 58/Downers Grove	13	5,000	93
Dupage Area Occupational Sys/Addison			102
Dupage High School Dist 88/Addison	2	3,929	93
Dupage Reg Office of Ed 19/Wheaton			102
Elmhurst Cmty Unit SD 205/Elmhurst	13	8,499	93
Fenton Cmty High Sch Dist 100/Bensenville	1	1,433	94
Glen Ellyn School Dist 41/Glen Ellyn	5	3,549	94
Glenbard Twp High Sch Dist 87/Glen Ellyn	4	7,500	94
Gower School Dist 62/Willowbrook	2	900	94
Hinsdale Twp High Sch Dist 86/Hinsdale	4	4,000	95
Indian Prairie Sch Dist 204/Aurora	34	27,400	95
Itasca School Dist 10/Itasca	3	1,033	96
Keeneyville Elem Sch Dist 20/Hanover Park	3	1,597	96
Lake Park Cmty High SD 108/Roselle	2	2,500	96
Lisle Cmty Unit Sch Dist 202/Lisle	3	1,450	96
Lombard Elem SD 44/Lombard	8	3,100	97
Maercker School Dist 60/Westmont	3	1,401	97
Marquardt School Dist 15/Glendale HTS	5	2,491	97
Medinah Elementary SD 11/Roselle	3	700	97
Naperville Cmty Unit SD 203/Naperville	22	17,000	98
North Dupage Spec Ed Co-op/Roselle			102
Philip J Rock Center & School/Glen Ellyn			102
Queen Bee School Dist 16/Glendale HTS	4	1,900	98
Roselle School Dist 12/Roselle	2	700	99
Salt Creek School Dist 48/Villa Park	3	550	99
School Assoc for Sp Ed-Dupage/Lisle			102
School Dist 45 Dupage Co/Villa Park	8	3,410	99
West Chicago Elementary SD 33/West Chicago	8	4,300	99
Winfield School Dist 34/Winfield	2	275	100
Wood Dale School Dist 7/Wood Dale	4	1,082	100
Woodridge Elem Sch Dist 68/Woodridge	7	2,950	100
EDGAR			
Edgar Co Cmty Sch Dist 6/Chrisman	3	307	103
Kansas Cmty School Dist 3/Kansas	1	205	103
Paris Cmty Unit Sch Dist 4/Paris	1	480	103
Paris Union School Dist 95/Paris	4	1,452	103
Shiloh School Dist 1/Hume	1	380	103
EDWARDS			
Edwards Co Cmty Unit SD 1/Albion	3	896	104
EFFINGHAM			
Altamont Cmty Unit SD 10/Altamont	2	700	104
Beecher City Cmty Unit SD 20/Beecher City	2	333	104
Dieterich Community Unit SD 30/Dieterich	2	550	104
Effingham Cmty Sch Dist 40/Effingham	5	2,400	104
Teutopolis Cmty Unit SD 50/Teutopolis	3	1,000	105
FAYETTE			
Brownstown Cmty Unit SD 201/Brownstown	2	380	105
Ramsey Cmty Unit Sch Dist 204/Ramsey	2	450	105
Regional Office of Ed 3/Vandalia			106
Regional Office of Education 3/Vandalia			106
St Elmo Cmty Unit Sch Dist 202/Saint Elmo	2	440	106
Vandalia Cmty Unit SD 203/Vandalia	4	1,490	106
FORD			
Ford Co Spec Ed Co-op/Gibson City			107
Gibson Cty-Melvin-Sibley CUSD5/Gibson City	3	1,000	106
Paxton-Buckley-Loda CUSD 10/Paxton	3	1,300	107
FRANKLIN			
Akin Elem School Dist 91/Akin	1	80	107
Benton Cmty Cons Sch Dist 47/Benton	2	1,150	107
Benton Cons High Sch Dist 103/Benton	1	561	107
Christopher Unit Sch Dist 99/Christopher	2	702	107
Ewing Northern Cmty SD 115/Ewing	1	210	108
Frankfort Cmty Unit SD 168/W Frankfort	4	1,650	108
Franklin-Jefferson Sp Ed Co-op/Benton			109
Regional Office of Ed 21/Benton			109
Sesser-Valier Cmty Unit SD 196/Sesser	3	700	108
Thompsonville Cmty USD 174/Thompsonville	2	285	108
Zeigler Royalton CUSD 188/Mulkeytown	2	370	108
FULTON			
Astoria Cmty Unit Sch Dist 1/Astoria	3	320	109
Canton Union School Dist 66/Canton	5	2,490	109
Fulton Co Cmty Unit Sch Dist 3/Cuba	2	400	109
Lewistown Community Unit SD 97/Lewistown	2	620	110
Spoon River Valley Cmty SD 4/London Mills	2	320	110
Vit Cmty Unit School Dist 2/Table Grove	2	370	110
Western Area Career System/Canton			110
GALLATIN			
Gallatin Cmty Unit Sch Dist 7/Junction	1	750	110
GREENE			
Carrollton Cmty Unit SD 1/Carrollton	2	600	111
Greenfield Cmty Unit SD 10/Greenfield	2	444	111
North Greene Unit Dist 3/White Hall	2	875	111
GRUNDY			
Braceville Elem School Dist 75/Braceville	1	112	111
Coal City Cmty Unit Sch Dist 1/Coal City	5	2,151	112
Gardner Cmty Cons SD 72-C/Gardner	1	152	112
Gardner S Wilmington HSD 73/Gardner	1	200	112
Grundy Area Voc Ed System/Morris			113
Grundy Co Special Ed Co-op/Morris			113
Mazon-Verona-Kinsman ESD 2-C/Mazon	2	325	112
Minooka Cmty Cons Sch Dist 201/Minooka	7	4,400	112
Morris Cmty High Sch Dist 101/Morris	1	867	113
Morris Elem School Dist 54/Morris	1	1,200	113
Nettle Creek Cmty SD 24-C/Morris	1	91	113
Regional Office of Ed 24/Morris			113
S Wilmington Cons Elem SD 74/S Wilmington	1	85	113
Saratoga Cmty Cons SD 60C/Morris	1	799	113
HAMILTON			
Hamilton Co Cmty Unit SD 10/Mc Leansboro	4	1,199	114
HANCOCK			
Carthage Elementary SD 317/Carthage	2	400	114
Dallas Elem Sch Dist 327/Dallas City	1	193	114
Hamilton Cmty Cons SD 328/Hamilton	2	600	114
Illini West High Sch Dist 307/Carthage	1	350	114
La Harpe Cmty Sch Dist 347/La Harpe	1	209	115
Nauvoo-Colusa CUSD 325/Nauvoo	1	244	115
Southeastern Cmty Unit SD 337/Augusta	2	450	115
Warsaw Cmty Unit Sch Dist 316/Warsaw	2	444	115
HARDIN			
Hardin Co Cmty Unit Sch Dist 1/Elizabethtown	2	500	115
HENDERSON			
West Central Cmty Unit SD 235/Biggsville	3	820	116
HENRY			
Alwood Cmty Unit Sch Dist 225/Woodhull	2	385	116
Annawan Cmty Unit SD 226/Annawan	2	330	116
Cambridge Cmty Unit SD 227/Cambridge	2	432	116
Colona Cmty School Dist 190/Colona	1	400	116
Galva Cmty Unit Sch Dist 224/Galva	2	525	117
Geneseo Cmty Unit Sch Dist 228/Geneseo	5	2,000	117
Henry-Stark Co Sp Ed Dist 801/Kewanee			118
Kewanee Cmty Unit Sch Dist 229/Kewanee	6	2,000	117
Orion Cmty Unit Sch Dist 223/Orion	3	990	117
Regional Office of Ed 28/Atkinson			118
Wethersfield Cmty Unit SD 230/Kewanee	2	580	117
IROQUOIS			
Central Cmty Unit SD 4/Ashkum	4	1,100	118
Cissna Park Cmty Unit SD 6/Cissna Park	1	294	118
Crescent Iroquois Cmty SD 249/Crescent City	1	70	118
Donovan Cmty Unit Sch Dist 3/Donovan	2	290	119
Iroquois Co Cmty Unit SD 9/Watseka	4	1,000	119
Iroquois Spec Educ Association/Gilman			119
Iroquois West Cmty Unit SD 10/Gilman	5	980	119
Milford Area Public SD 124/Milford	2	610	119
JACKSON			
Carbondale Cmty HSD 165/Carbondale	1	1,000	120
Carbondale Elem School Dist 95/Carbondale	4	1,560	120
DeSoto Grade School Dist 86/De Soto	1	203	120
Elverado Cmty Unit SD 196/Elkville	4	420	120
Giant City Cmty Cons SD 130/Carbondale	1	210	120
Murphysboro Cmty Unit SD 186/Murphysboro	4	1,800	121
Regional Office of Ed 30/Murphysboro			121

School Year 2020-2021   800-333-8802   IL-R3

COUNTY INDEX

Market Data Retrieval

COUNTY District/City	NO. OF SCHOOLS	ENROLLMENT	PAGE
Tri-Co Special Ed JT Agreement/Carbondale			122
Trico Cmty Unit Sch Dist 176/Campbell Hill	3	850	121
Unity Point Cmty Cons SD 140/Carbondale	1	610	121
JASPER			
Jasper Co Cmty Unit SD 1/Newton	4	1,278	122
South Eastern Special Ed Dist/Sainte Marie			122
JEFFERSON			
Bethel School Dist 82/Mount Vernon	1	170	122
Bluford Unit School Dist 318/Bluford	1	350	122
Farrington Cmty Cons SD 99/Bluford	1	58	122
Field Cmty Cons Sch Dist 3/Texico	1	275	123
Grand Prairie Cmty Cons SD 6/Centralia	1	80	123
McClellan Cons SD 12/Mount Vernon	1	45	123
Mt Vernon City Sch Dist 80/Mount Vernon	4	1,700	123
Mt Vernon Twp HS Dist 201/Mount Vernon	1	1,250	123
Opdyke-Belle Rive Cmty CSSD 5/Opdyke	1	140	123
Rome Cmty Cons Sch Dist 2/Dix	1	450	123
Spring Garden Cmty CSD 178/Mount Vernon	2	249	124
Summersville Sch Dist 79/Mount Vernon	1	245	124
Waltonville Cmty Unit SD 1/Waltonville	2	325	124
Woodlawn Unit School Dist 209/Woodlawn	2	503	124
JERSEY			
Central Illinois Rural Rvs/Jerseyville			125
Jersey Cmty Sch Dist 100/Jerseyville	5	2,647	125
JO DAVIESS			
East Dubuque Unit SD 119/East Dubuque	2	672	125
Galena Unit School Dist 120/Galena	3	830	125
Northwest Special Ed Dist/Elizabeth			126
River Ridge Cmty Unit SD 210/Hanover	3	500	126
Scales Mound Cmty Unit SD 211/Scales Mound	3	265	126
Stockton Cmty Unit SD 206/Stockton	3	603	126
Warren Community Unit SD 205/Warren	2	400	126
JOHNSON			
Buncombe Cons School Dist 43/Buncombe	1	60	127
Cypress School Dist 64/Cypress	1	120	127
Goreville Cmty Unit SD 1/Goreville	1	565	127
New Simpson Hill Cons SD 32/Tunnel Hill	1	200	127
Vienna High School Dist 13-3/Vienna	1	360	127
Vienna Public School Dist 55/Vienna	1	410	127
KANE			
Batavia Unit School Dist 101/Batavia	8	5,518	128
Central Cmty Unit SD 301/Burlington	7	4,500	128
Community Unit School Dist 303/Saint Charles	16	12,262	128
East Aurora School Dist 131/Aurora	20	14,000	129
Elgin School Dist U-46/Elgin	58	38,000	130
Geneva CUSD 304/Geneva	10	5,808	131
Kaneland Cmty Unit SD 302/Maple Park	7	4,560	132
Mid-Valley Special Ed Co-op/Saint Charles			134
Northern Kane Co Reg Voc Sys/Elgin			134
Regional Office of Ed Kane Co/Geneva			134
Valley Ed for Employment Sys/Sugar Grove			134
West Aurora School Dist 129/Aurora	18	12,000	132
KANKAKEE			
Bourbonnais Elem Sch Dist 53/Bourbonnais	5	2,400	134
Bradley Elem School Dist 61/Bradley	3	1,500	134
Bradley-Bourbonnais CHSD 307/Bradley	1	2,100	134
Grant Park Cmty Unit SD 6/Grant Park	3	475	135
Herscher Cmty School Dist 2/Herscher	4	1,650	135
Iroquois-Kankakee Reg Off Ed/Kankakee			137
Kankakee Area Reg Voc Ed Sys/Bourbonnais			137
Kankakee Area Special Ed Co-op/Saint Anne			137
Kankakee School Dist 111/Kankakee	11	5,200	135
Manteno Cmty Unit Sch Dist 5/Manteno	3	2,100	135
Momence Cmty Unit Sch Dist 1/Momence	3	1,100	136
Pembroke Cmty Cons SD 259/Hopkins Park	1	200	136
St Anne Cmty Cons Sch Dist 256/Saint Anne	1	351	136
St Anne Cmty HSD 302/Saint Anne	1	210	136
St George School Dist 258/Bourbonnais	1	431	136
KENDALL			
Community Unit School Dist 308/Oswego	21	17,250	137
Lisbon Cmty Cons Sch Dist 90/Newark	1	106	138
Newark Cmty Cons Sch Dist 66/Newark	2	239	138
Newark Cmty High Sch Dist 18/Newark	1	170	138
Plano Cmty Unit Sch Dist 88/Plano	5	2,400	138
Yorkville Cmty Unit SD 115/Yorkville	10	6,200	139
KNOX			
Abingdon-Avon Cmty Unit SD 276/Abingdon	4	877	139
Galesburg Cmty Unit SD 205/Galesburg	8	4,500	140

COUNTY District/City	NO. OF SCHOOLS	ENROLLMENT	PAGE
Knox-Warren Spec Ed Dist/Galesburg			141
Knoxville Cmty Unit SD 202/Knoxville	3	1,068	140
Regional Office of Ed 33/Galesburg			141
Rowva Cmty School Dist 208/Oneida	2	600	140
Williamsfield Cmty Unit SD 210/Williamsfield	1	275	140
LA SALLE			
Allen-Otter Creek CCSD 65/Ransom	1	70	141
Deer Park Cmty Cons SD 82/Ottawa	1	75	141
Dimmick Cmty School Dist 175/La Salle	1	160	141
Earlville Cmty Unit Sch Dist 9/Earlville	1	430	141
Grand Ridge CCSD 95/Grand Ridge	1	189	141
La Salle Elem SD 122/La Salle	2	900	142
LaSalle Peru Twp HSD 120/La Salle	1	1,200	142
LaSalle-Putnam Sped Alliance/Ottawa			145
Leland Cmty Unit Sch Dist 1/Leland	1	260	142
Lostant Cmty Unit Sch Dist 425/Lostant	1	55	142
Marseilles Elem Sch Dist 150/Marseilles	1	550	142
Mendota Cmty School Dist 289/Mendota	3	1,200	142
Mendota Twp High Sch Dist 280/Mendota	1	541	143
Miller Cmty Cons Sch Dist 210/Marseilles	1	158	143
Oglesby Public Sch Dist 125/Oglesby	2	529	143
Ottawa Elementary Sch Dist 141/Ottawa	5	1,950	143
Ottawa Twp High Sch Dist 140/Ottawa	1	1,450	143
Peru Elem Sch Dist 124/Peru	2	970	143
Regional Office of Ed 35/Ottawa			146
Rutland Cmty Cons SD 230/Ottawa	1	75	144
Seneca Cmty Cons Sch Dist 170/Seneca	2	503	144
Seneca Twp High Sch Dist 160/Seneca	1	430	144
Serena Cmty Unit School Dist 2/Serena	4	665	144
Starved Rock Assoc Voc Tech Ed/Peru			146
Streator Elem School Dist 44/Streator	3	1,540	144
Streator Twp High Sch Dist 40/Streator	1	844	145
Tonica Cmty Cons Sch Dist 79/Tonica	1	159	145
Wallace Cmty Cons Sch Dist 195/Ottawa	1	410	145
Waltham Elementary SD 185/Utica	1	200	145
LAKE			
Adlai E Stevenson HSD 125/Lincolnshire	1	4,337	146
Antioch Cmty Cons Sch Dist 34/Antioch	6	2,775	146
Aptakisic-Tripp Sch Dist 102/Buffalo Grove	4	2,400	146
Bannockburn Sch Dist 106/Bannockburn	1	155	147
Barrington Cmty Unit SD 220/Barrington	12	9,000	147
Beach Park Cmty Cons SD 3/Beach Park	5	2,106	147
Big Hollow School Dist 38/Ingleside	3	1,800	148
Community Cons School Dist 46/Grayslake	8	3,800	148
Community High School Dist 117/Antioch	2	2,677	148
Community High School Dist 128/Vernon Hills	2	3,397	148
Deerfield Public SD 109/Deerfield	6	3,400	149
Diamond Lake School Dist 76/Mundelein	3	900	149
Emmons School Dist 33/Antioch	1	300	149
Fox Lake School Dist 114/Spring Grove	2	741	149
Fremont School Dist 79/Mundelein	3	2,200	149
Gavin School Dist 37/Ingleside	2	850	150
Grant Cmty High Sch Dist 124/Fox Lake	1	1,850	150
Grass Lake School Dist 36/Antioch	1	190	150
Grayslake Cmty HS Dist 127/Grayslake	2	3,000	150
Gurnee School Dist 56/Gurnee	4	2,083	150
Hawthorn Cmty Cons Sch Dist 73/Vernon Hills	7	4,300	151
Kildeer Countryside CCSD 96/Buffalo Grove	7	3,213	151
Lake Bluff Elem Sch Dist 65/Lake Bluff	2	880	151
Lake County Regional of Ed/Grayslake			158
Lake Forest Cmty HSD 115/Lake Forest	1	1,600	151
Lake Forest School Dist 67/Lake Forest	5	1,660	152
Lake Villa Cmty Cons SD 41/Lake Villa	4	2,700	152
Lake Zurich Cmty Sch Dist 95/Lake Zurich	8	5,516	152
Libertyville Pub Sch Dist 70/Libertyville	5	2,258	152
Lincolnshre-Prairieview SD 103/Lincolnshire	3	1,832	153
Millburn Cmty Cons Sch Dist 24/Wadsworth	2	1,150	153
Mundelein Cons High SD 120/Mundelein	1	2,026	153
Mundelein Elem School Dist 75/Mundelein	4	1,586	153
North Chicago Cmty Unit SD 187/North Chicago	8	3,900	153
North Shore School Dist 112/Highland Park	10	3,800	154
Northern Suburban Spec Ed Dist/Highland Park			159
Oak Grove School Dist 68/Libertyville		900	154
Rondout School Dist 72/Lake Forest	1	140	154
Round Lake Area Co Dist 116/Round Lake	10	7,300	154
Special Education Dist Lake Co/Gages Lake			159
Township High School Dist 113/Highland Park	2	3,616	155
Warren Twp High Sch Dist 121/Gurnee	2	4,049	155
Wauconda Cmty Unit SD 118/Wauconda	6	4,500	155
Waukegan Cmty Unit SD 60/Waukegan	24	17,000	156
Winthrop Harbor School Dist 1/Winthrop HBR	2	542	156
Woodland School Dist 50/Gurnee	5	5,700	156
Zion Public School Dist 6/Zion	7	2,700	157

Illinois School Directory

COUNTY INDEX

COUNTY District/City	NO. OF SCHOOLS	ENROLL- MENT	PAGE
Zion-Benton Twp High SD 126/Zion	2	2,100	157
LAWRENCE			
Lawrence Co Cmty Sch Dist 20/Lawrenceville	3	1,125	159
Red Hill Cmty School Dist 10/Bridgeport	3	977	159
LEE			
Amboy Cmty Unit Sch Dist 272/Amboy	3	720	159
Ashton-Franklin Center SD 275/Ashton	2	560	159
Dixon Cmty Unit Sch Dist 170/Dixon	5	2,432	160
Lee Co Spec Ed Association/Dixon			160
Paw Paw Cmty Unit SD 271/Paw Paw	1	120	160
Steward Elem School Dist 220/Steward	1	51	160
LIVINGSTON			
Cornell Cmty Cons Sch Dist 426/Cornell	1	110	160
Dwight Common Elem SD 232/Dwight	1	450	161
Dwight Twp High Sch Dist 230/Dwight	1	221	161
Flanagan-Cornell Unit 74 SD/Flanagan	1	195	161
Livingston Area EFE System/Pontiac			163
Livingston Co Spec Svc Unit/Flanagan			163
Odell Cmty Cons Sch Dist 435/Odell	1	150	161
Pontiac Cmty Cons Sch Dist 429/Pontiac	4	1,300	161
Pontiac Twp High Sch Dist 90/Pontiac	2	700	161
Prairie Central Cmty USD 8/Fairbury	6	2,150	162
Rooks Creek Cmty Cons SD 425/Graymont	1	50	162
Saunemin Cmty Cons SD 438/Saunemin	1	115	162
Tri-Point Cmty Unit SD 6J/Kempton	3	395	162
Woodland Cmty Unit Sch Dist 5/Streator	2	540	162
LOGAN			
Chester-E Lincoln Cmty SD 61/Lincoln	1	300	163
Hartsburg Emden School Dist 21/Hartsburg	2	200	163
Lincoln Cmty High Sch Dist 404/Lincoln	1	811	163
Lincoln Elem School Dist 27/Lincoln	5	1,200	163
Mt Pulaski Cmty Unit SD 23/Mount Pulaski	2	530	164
New Holland Middletown ESD 88/Middletown	1	90	164
West Lincoln-Broadwell ESD 92/Lincoln	1	220	164
MACON			
Argenta Oreana Cmty Unit SD 1/Argenta	3	800	165
Decatur Public Schools 61/Decatur	18	8,700	165
Heartland Technical Academy/Decatur			167
Macon-Piatt Roe#39/Decatur			167
Macon-Piatt Spec Ed/Decatur			167
Maroa Forsyth CU Sch Dist 2/Forsyth	3	1,215	165
Meridian Cmty Unit Sch Dist 15/Macon	3	1,065	166
Mt Zion Cmty Unit Sch Dist 3/Mt Zion	5	2,400	166
Sangamon Valley Cmty Unit SD 9/Niantic	4	687	166
Warrensburg-Latham CU SD 11/Warrensburg	3	1,200	166
MACOUPIN			
Bunker Hill Cmty Unit SD 8/Bunker Hill	2	600	167
Carlinville Cmty Unit SD 1/Carlinville	4	1,400	167
Community Unit School Dist 7/Gillespie	3	1,250	167
Mt Olive Cmty Unit Sch Dist 5/Mount Olive	2	452	167
North Mac Cmty Unit SD 34/Girard	3	1,150	168
Northwestern CUSD 2/Palmyra	2	356	168
Regional Office of Ed 40/Carlinville			169
Southwestern Cmty Unit SD 9/Brighton	5	1,300	168
Staunton Cmty Unit Sch Dist 6/Staunton	3	1,200	168
MADISON			
Alton Cmty School Dist 11/Alton	12	6,000	169
Area 5 Learning Technology Hub/Edwardsville			174
Bethalto Cmty Unit SD 8/Bethalto	5	2,500	169
Collinsville Cmty Sch Dist 10/Collinsville	13	5,000	170
East Alton Elementary SD 13/East Alton	3	800	170
East Alton-Wood River SD 14/Wood River	1	556	170
Edwardsville Cmty Unit SD 7/Edwardsville	15	7,500	170
Granite City Cmty Unit SD 9/Granite City	8	5,764	171
Highland Cmty Sch Dist 5/Highland	6	3,000	171
Madison Cmty Unit Sch Dist 12/Madison	3	700	172
Madison Co Cte System/Edwardsville			174
Madison Co Reg 1 Spec Ed Co-op/Granite City			174
Region 3 Spec Ed Co-op/Cottage Hills			174
Regional Office of Ed 41/Edwardsville			174
Roxana Cmty Unit Sch Dist 1/Roxana	4	2,000	172
Triad Cmty School Dist 2/Troy	6	4,000	172
Venice Cmty Unit School Dist 3/Venice	1	80	172
Wood River-Hartford Elem SD 15/Wood River	3	706	172
MARION			
Central City School Dist 133/Centralia	1	349	174
Centralia City Sch Dist 135/Centralia	4	1,250	174
Centralia High School Dist 200/Centralia	1	900	174
Iuka Community Cons Sch Dist 7/Iuka	1	225	174

COUNTY District/City	NO. OF SCHOOLS	ENROLL- MENT	PAGE
Kaskaskia Spec Ed Dist/Centralia			176
Kell Cons School Dist 2/Kell	1	100	174
Odin Public School Dist 722/Odin	2	250	175
Patoka Cmty Unit SD 100/Patoka	1	260	175
Raccoon Cons School Dist 1/Centralia	1	240	175
Salem Cmty High Sch Dist 600/Salem	1	650	175
Salem Elem Sch Dist 111/Salem	2	1,000	175
Sandoval Cmty Unit SD 501/Sandoval	2	504	175
Selmaville Cmty Cons SD 10/Salem	1	260	176
South Central Cmty Unit SD 401/Kinmundy	3	650	176
MARSHALL			
Henry Senachwine CUSD 5/Henry	2	580	176
Midland Cmty Unit Sch Dist 7/Sparland	3	720	176
MASON			
Havana Cmty Sch Dist 126/Havana	3	1,000	177
Illini Central CUSD 189/Mason City	4	663	177
Midwest Ctl Cmty Unit SD 191/Manito	3	900	177
MASSAC			
Joppa-Maple Grove Unit SD 38/Joppa	2	230	177
Massac Unit School Dist 1/Metropolis	7	2,100	177
MCDONOUGH			
Bushnell Prairie Cmty USD 170/Bushnell	3	630	178
Macomb Cmty Unit Sch Dist 185/Macomb	4	2,000	178
Regional Office of Ed 26/Macomb			179
West Central IL Spec Ed Co-op/Macomb			179
West Prairie Cmty Sch Dist 103/Colchester	4	600	178
Western Area Career System/Macomb			179
MCHENRY			
Alden-Hebron School Dist 19/Hebron	2	430	179
Cary Cmty Cons Sch Dist 26/Cary	5	2,426	179
Community High School Dist 155/Crystal Lake	5	5,800	179
Community Unit School Dist 300/Algonquin	27	20,985	180
Crystal Lake Elem Distict 47/Crystal Lake	12	7,500	181
Fox River Grove Cons SD 3/Fox River GRV	2	390	181
Harrison School Dist 36/Wonder Lake	1	404	181
Harvard Cmty Unit Sch Dist 50/Harvard	5	2,633	181
Huntley Cmty School Dist 158/Algonquin	8	9,606	182
Johnsburg Cmty School Dist 12/Johnsburg	4	1,800	182
Marengo Cmty High Sch Dist 154/Marengo	1	700	182
Marengo Union Elem Cons SD 165/Marengo	3	1,200	182
McHenry Cmty Cons Sch Dist 15/McHenry	8	4,300	183
McHenry Cmty High Sch Dist 156/McHenry	2	2,143	183
McHenry Co Reg Office of Ed 44/Woodstock			185
McHenry Co Work Force Ctr/Woodstock			185
Nippersink School Dist 2/Richmond	3	1,100	183
Prairie Grove Cons SD 46/Crystal Lake	2	720	183
Richmond-Burton Cmty HSD 157/Richmond	1	636	183
Riley Cmty Cons Sch Dist 18/Marengo	1	267	184
Special Ed Dist of McHenry Co/Woodstock			185
Woodstock Cmty Unit SD 200/Woodstock	12	6,600	184
MCLEAN			
Bloomington School Dist 87/Bloomington	10	5,200	185
Heyworth Cmty Sch Dist 4/Heyworth	2	975	185
Le Roy Cmty Unit SD 2/Le Roy	3	775	186
Lexington Cmty Sch Dist 7/Lexington	3	490	186
Mackinaw Valley Spec Ed Assoc/Bloomington			188
McLean Co Unit Dist 5/Normal	23	13,346	186
McLean-DeWitt Reg Voc System/Bloomington			188
Olympia Cmty Unit Sch Dist 16/Stanford	5	1,900	187
Regional Office of Ed 17/Bloomington			188
Ridgeview Cmty Unit SD 19/Colfax	2	600	187
Tri-Co Special Ed Association/Bloomington			188
Tri-Valley Cmty School Dist 3/Downs	3	1,150	187
MENARD			
Athens Cmty Unit Sch Dist 213/Athens	4	1,100	188
Greenview Cmty Unit SD 200/Greenview	1	211	188
Porta Cmty Unit Sch Dist 202/Petersburg	3	1,009	189
MERCER			
Mercer County SD 404/Aledo	5	1,300	189
Sherrard Cmty Sch Dist 200/Sherrard	4	1,400	189
MONROE			
Columbia Cmty Unit SD 4/Columbia	4	2,000	189
Monroe-Randolph Reg Off/Waterloo			190
Valmeyer Cmty School Dist 3/Valmeyer	1	430	190
Waterloo Cmty Unit Sch Dist 5/Waterloo	5	2,739	190
MONTGOMERY			
Christian-Montgomery EFE Sys/Hillsboro			191
Hillsboro Cmty Unit Sch Dist 3/Hillsboro	4	1,700	190

School Year 2020-2021   800-333-8802

COUNTY INDEX

Market Data Retrieval

COUNTY District/City	NO. OF SCHOOLS	ENROLL-MENT	PAGE
Litchfield Cmty Unit SD 12/Litchfield	6	1,450	191
Nokomis Cmty Unit Sch Dist 22/Nokomis	2	630	191
Panhandle Cmty Unit SD 2/Raymond	3	520	191
MORGAN			
Four Rivers Spec Ed Dist/Jacksonville			193
Franklin Cmty Unit SD 1/Franklin	3	290	192
Jacksonville School Dist 117/Jacksonville	9	3,200	192
Meredosia-Chambersburg SD 11/Meredosia	1	195	192
Regional Office of Ed 1/Jacksonville			193
Triopia Cmty Unit Sch Dist 27/Concord	2	382	192
Waverly Cmty Unit SD 6/Waverly	2	369	193
MOULTRIE			
Okaw Valley Cmty Unit SD 302/Bethany	3	475	193
Sullivan Cmty Unit SD 300/Sullivan	3	1,100	193
OGLE			
Byron Cmty Unit SD 226/Byron	3	1,523	194
Creston Cmty Cons Sch Dist 161/Creston	1	88	194
Eswood Cmty Cons SD 269/Lindenwood	1	68	194
Forrestville Valley CUSD 221/Forreston	3	750	194
Kings Cons School Dist 144/Kings	1	90	194
Meridian Cmty Unit SD 223/Stillman Vly	4	1,614	194
Ogle Co Educational Co-op/Byron			196
Oregon Cmty Unit Sch Dist 220/Oregon	3	1,461	195
Polo Cmty Unit Sch Dist 222/Polo	3	603	195
Rochelle Cmty Cons SD 231/Rochelle	5	1,600	195
Rochelle Twp High Sch Dist 212/Rochelle	1	900	195
PEORIA			
Area 3 Learning Technology Ctr/Edwards			200
Bartonville School Dist 66/Bartonville	1	300	196
Brimfield Cmty Unit SD 309/Brimfield	2	680	196
Diocese of Peoria Ed Office/Peoria	43	11,872	200
Dunlap Cmty Unit Sch Dist 323/Peoria	8	4,500	196
Elmwood Cmty Unit Sch Dist 322/Elmwood	2	700	196
Farmington Ctl Cmty SD 265/Farmington	3	1,425	197
Hollis Cons School Dist 328/Peoria	1	135	197
Illini Bluffs Cmty Unit SD 327/Glasford	3	909	197
Illinois Vly Ctl Sch Dist 321/Chillicothe	5	2,173	197
Limestone Cmty High SD 310/Bartonville	2	1,000	197
Limestone Walters CCSD 316/Peoria	1	200	198
Monroe School Dist 70/Bartonville	1	287	198
Norwood Sch Dist 63/Peoria	2	475	198
Oak Grove School Dist 68/Bartonville	1	250	198
Peoria Co Special Ed Assoc/Bartonville			200
Peoria Ed Reg Emp & Career/Peoria			200
Peoria Heights Cmty SD 325/Peoria HTS	2	720	198
Peoria Public Sch Dist 150/Peoria	30	12,531	198
Pleasant Hill School Dist 69/Peoria	1	230	199
Pleasant Valley Sch Dist 62/Peoria	2	363	199
Princeville Cmty Unit SD 326/Princeville	2	761	200
Regional Office of Ed 48/Peoria			201
PERRY			
Community Cons School Dist 204/Pinckneyville	1	156	201
Du Quoin Cmty Unit SD 300/Du Quoin	3	1,420	201
Pinckneyville Cmty High SD 101/Pinckneyville	1	415	201
Pinckneyville Sch Dist 50/Pinckneyville	2	504	201
Tamaroa Elem School Dist 5/Tamaroa	1	82	201
PIATT			
Bement Cmty Unit Sch Dist 5/Bement	3	298	202
Cerro Gordo Cmty Unit SD 100/Cerro Gordo	2	490	202
Deland-Weldon Cmty Unit SD 57/De Land	2	200	202
Monticello Cmty Unit SD 25/Monticello	5	1,600	202
PIKE			
Griggsville-Perry Cmty SD 4/Griggsville	3	340	203
Pikeland Cmty Sch Dist 10/Pittsfield	3	1,200	203
Pleasant Hill CUSD 3/Pleasant Hill	2	311	203
Western CUSD 12/Barry	3	570	203
POPE			
Pope Co Cmty Unit Sch Dist 1/Golconda	2	530	203
PULASKI			
Century Cmty Unit SD 100/Ullin	2	369	204
Jamp Special Ed Services/Grand Chain			204
Meridian Cmty School Dist 101/Mounds	2	450	204
PUTNAM			
Putnam Co Cmty Unit SD 535/Granville	4	853	204
RANDOLPH			
Chester Cmty Unit Sch Dist 139/Chester	2	950	205
Coulterville Unit Sch Dist 1/Coulterville	1	196	205

COUNTY District/City	NO. OF SCHOOLS	ENROLL-MENT	PAGE
Okaw Regional Voc System/Chester			206
Perandoe Special Ed Dist/Red Bud			206
Prairie Du Rocher CCSD 134/Pr Du Rocher	1	152	205
Red Bud Cmty Unit Sch Dist 132/Red Bud	2	1,000	205
Sparta Cmty School Dist 140/Sparta	3	1,213	205
Steeleville Cmty Sch Dist 138/Steeleville	2	425	206
RICHLAND			
Regional Office of Ed 12/Olney			207
Richland Co Cmty Unit SD 1/Olney	3	2,500	206
ROCK ISLAND			
Black Hawk Area Spec Ed Dist/East Moline			210
Carbon Cliff Barstow SD 36/Silvis	1	270	207
East Moline Public Sch Dist 37/East Moline	5	2,650	207
Hampton School Dist 29/Hampton	1	210	207
Moline-Coal Valley SD No 40/Moline	15	7,182	207
Riverdale Cmty Unit SD 100/Port Byron	3	1,160	208
Rock Island Reg Off of Ed 49/Moline			210
Rock Island-Milan Sch Dist 41/Rock Island	14	5,800	208
Rockridge Cmty Unit SD 300/Taylor Ridge	5	1,097	209
Silvis School Dist 34/East Moline	2	648	209
United Twp High Sch Dist 30/East Moline	2	1,678	209
UT Area Career Center/East Moline			210
SALINE			
Carrier Mills-Stonefort SD 2/Carrier Mills	2	450	210
Eldorado Cmty Unit Sch Dist 4/Eldorado	3	1,200	210
Galatia Cmty Unit Sch Dist 1/Galatia	2	364	210
Harrisburg Cmty Unit SD 3/Harrisburg	4	1,879	210
Regional Office of Ed 20/Harrisburg			211
SANGAMON			
Auburn Cmty Unit Sch Dist 10/Auburn	4	1,317	211
Ball Chatham Cmty Unit SD 5/Chatham	6	4,500	211
Community Unit School Dist 16/New Berlin	3	939	211
Diocese of Springfield Ed Off/Springfield	44	10,260	214
Pawnee Cmty Unit Sch Dist 11/Pawnee	2	550	212
Pleasant Plains Cmty Unit SD 8/Pleasant PLNS	3	1,271	212
Regional Office-Career Tech Ed/Springfield			215
Riverton Cmty Unit SD 14/Riverton	3	1,443	212
Rochester Cmty Unit SD 3-A/Rochester	5	2,215	212
Sangamon Area Spec Ed Dist/Springfield			215
Sangamon-Menard Roe #51/Springfield			215
Springfield Pub Sch Dist 186/Springfield	33	13,000	213
Tri-City Cmty Unit Sch Dist 1/Buffalo	1	570	214
Williamsville Cmty Unit SD 15/Williamsville	4	1,540	214
SCHUYLER			
Schuyler-Industry CUSD 5/Rushville	4	1,100	215
SCOTT			
Scott Morgan Cmty Unit SD 2/Bluffs	1	231	215
Winchester Cmty Unit SD 1/Winchester	2	680	215
SHELBY			
Cowden Herrick CUSD 3A/Cowden	2	380	216
Shelbyville Cmty Sch Dist 4/Shelbyville	3	1,250	216
Stewardson-Strasburg SD 5-A/Strasburg	2	374	216
Windsor Cmty Unit SD 1/Windsor	2	300	216
ST CLAIR			
Belle Valley School Dist 119/Belleville	1	1,038	217
Belleville Area Sp Svc Co-op/Belleville			223
Belleville Public Sch Dist 118/Belleville	11	4,500	217
Belleville Township HSD 201/Belleville	3	4,500	217
Brooklyn School Dist 188/Lovejoy	1	161	217
Cahokia Unit Sch Dist 187/Cahokia	10	3,400	218
Central School Dist 104/O Fallon	2	700	218
Diocese of Belleville Ed Off/Belleville	30	5,497	222
Dupo Cmty School Dist 196/Dupo	2	985	218
E St Louis Area JT Agreement/E Saint Louis			223
East St Louis Reg Voc System/E Saint Louis			223
East St Louis Sch Dist 189/E Saint Louis	11	5,200	218
Freeburg Cmty Cons SD 70/Freeburg	2	780	219
Freeburg Cmty High Sch Dist 77/Freeburg	1	675	219
Grant Cmty Cons Sch Dist 110/Fairview HTS	2	600	219
Harmony-Emge School Dist 175/Belleville	3	800	219
High Mount Sch Dist 116/Swansea	1	475	219
Lebanon Cmty Unit Sch Dist 9/Lebanon	2	540	220
Marissa Cmty Unit Sch Dist 40/Marissa	2	550	220
Mascoutah Cmty Sch Dist 19/Mascoutah	5	4,000	220
Millstadt Cmty Cons SD 160/Millstadt	2	800	220
New Athens CUSD 60/New Athens	2	500	220
O'Fallon Cmty Cons Sch Dist 90/O Fallon	7	3,761	221
O'Fallon Twp School Dist 203/O Fallon	2	2,400	221
Pontiac-Wm Holliday SD 105/Fairview HTS	2	500	221

School Year 2020-2021

Illinois School Directory — COUNTY INDEX

COUNTY / District/City	NO. OF SCHOOLS	ENROLLMENT	PAGE
Shiloh Village Sch Dist 85/Shiloh	2	571	221
Signal Hill Sch Dist 181/Belleville	1	330	221
Smithton Cmty Cons SD 130/Smithton	1	568	222
St Clair Co Regional Off of Ed/Belleville			223
St Libory Cons Sch Dist 30/Saint Libory	1	53	222
Whiteside School Dist 115/Belleville	2	1,036	222
Wolf Branch School Dist 113/Swansea	2	720	222
STARK			
Bradford Cmty Unit Sch Dist 1/Bradford	1	145	223
Stark Co Cmty Unit SD 100/Wyoming	3	692	223
STEPHENSON			
Career & Tech Ed Consortium/Freeport			225
Dakota Cmty Unit Sch Dist 201/Dakota	2	750	224
Freeport School Dist 145/Freeport	10	4,000	224
Lena-Winslow Cmty Unit SD 202/Lena	3	850	224
Orangeville Cmty Unit SD 203/Orangeville	1	380	225
Pearl City Cmty Unit SD 200/Pearl City	1	431	225
Regional Office of Ed 8/Freeport			225
TAZEWELL			
Central Sch Dist 51/Washington	2	1,400	225
Creve Coeur Sch Dist 76/Creve Coeur	2	600	226
Deer Creek-Mackinaw CUSD 701/Mackinaw	3	1,040	226
Delavan Cmty Unit Sch Dist 703/Delavan	2	480	226
Dist 50 Schools/Washington	2	700	226
East Peoria Cmty HS Dist 309/East Peoria	1	1,000	226
East Peoria Elem Sch Dist 86/East Peoria	7	1,500	226
Morton Cmty Unit Sch Dist 709/Morton	7	3,060	227
N Pekin-Marquette Hts SD 102/Marquette HTS	3	512	227
Pekin Cmty High Sch Dist 303/Pekin	1	1,821	227
Pekin Public School Dist 108/Pekin	11	3,650	227
Rankin Cmty School Dist 98/Pekin	1	250	228
Regional Office of Ed 53/Pekin			229
Robein Cmty School Dist 85/East Peoria	1	175	228
South Pekin Grade Sch Dist 137/South Pekin	1	200	228
Spring Lake Elem SD 606/Manito	1	60	228
Tazewell Co Area EFE #320/Pekin			229
Tazewell-Mason Sp Ed Assoc/Pekin			229
Tremont Cmty Unit SD 702/Tremont	3	1,000	228
Washington Cmty HS Dist 308/Washington	1	1,406	229
Washington School Dist 52/Washington	2	930	229
UNION			
Anna Cmty Cons Sch Dist 37/Anna	3	695	230
Anna-Jonesboro Cmty HSD 81/Anna	1	530	230
Cobden Cmty Unit Sch Dist 17/Cobden	2	526	230
Dongola Unit School Dist 66/Dongola	1	286	230
Jonesboro Cmty Cons SD 43/Jonesboro	1	370	230
Lick Creek School Dist 16/Buncombe	1	150	230
Shawnee Cmty Unit Sch Dist 84/Wolf Lake	2	300	231
VERMILION			
Armstrong Ellis SD 61/Armstrong	1	80	231
Armstrong Twp High SD 225/Armstrong	1	140	231
Bismarck-Henning Cmty SD 1/Bismarck	3	859	231
Danville School Dist 118/Danville	11	5,505	231
Georgetown-Ridge Farm CUSD 4/Georgetown	3	1,010	232
Hoopeston Area Cmty Unit SD 11/Hoopeston	4	1,100	232
Oakwood Cmty Unit Sch Dist 76/Oakwood	3	1,000	232
Potomac Cmty Unit Sch Dist 10/Potomac	1	145	232
Regional Office of Ed 54/Danville			233
Rossville-Alvin Cmty Unit SD 7/Rossville	1	300	233
Salt Fork Cmty Unit SD 512/Catlin	3	900	233
Vermilion Assoc for Special Ed/Danville			233
Vermilion Voc Ed Delivery Sys/Danville			233
Westville Cmty Unit Sch Dist 2/Westville	3	1,306	233
WABASH			
Allendale Cmty Cons SD 17/Allendale	1	130	234
Wabash Cmty Unit Sch Dist 348/Mount Carmel	4	1,450	234
WARREN			
Delabar Cte System/Monmouth			235
Monmouth-Roseville CUSD 238/Monmouth	5	1,686	234
United Cmty Unit Sch Dist 304/Monmouth	4	950	234
WASHINGTON			
Ashley Cmty Cons SD 15/Ashley	1	130	235
Irvington Cmty Cons SD 11/Irvington	1	60	235
Nashville Cmty Cons SD 49/Nashville	1	585	235
Nashville Cmty HSD 99/Nashville	1	410	235
Oakdale Cmty Cons Sch Dist 1/Oakdale	1	69	236
West Washington Co Cmty SD 10/Okawville	2	544	236
WAYNE			
Fairfield Cmty High SD 225/Fairfield	1	430	236
Fairfield Pub Sch Dist 112/Fairfield	2	700	236
Geff Cmty Cons School Dist 14/Geff	1	92	236
Jasper Cmty Cons Sch Dist 17/Fairfield	1	185	237
New Hope Cmty Cons Sch Dist 6/Fairfield	1	180	237
North Wayne Cmty Unit SD 200/Cisne	4	383	237
Wayne City Cmty Unit SD 100/Wayne City	2	530	237
WHITE			
Carmi-White Co School Dist 5/Carmi	6	1,400	237
Grayville Cmty Unit Sch Dist 1/Grayville	2	280	238
Norris City-Omaha-Enfield SD 3/Norris City	3	675	238
Ohio-Wabash Valley Reg Voc Sys/Norris City			238
Wabash-Ohio Valley Sp Ed Dist/Norris City			238
WHITESIDE			
Bi-County Special Ed Co-op/Sterling			240
East Coloma-Nelson Cesd 20/Rock Falls	1	245	238
Erie Cmty School Dist 1/Erie	3	650	239
Montmorency Cmty Cons SD 145/Rock Falls	1	230	239
Morrison Cmty Unit Sch Dist 6/Morrison	4	1,033	239
Prophetstown-Lyndon-Tampico 3/Prophetstown	4	800	239
Regional Office of Ed 47/Sterling			241
River Bend Cmty School Dist 2/Fulton	4	900	239
Rock Falls Elem Sch Dist 13/Rock Falls	4	1,050	240
Rock Falls Twp High SD 301/Rock Falls	1	630	240
Sterling Cmty Unit Sch Dist 5/Sterling	6	3,500	240
Whiteside Regional Voc System/Sterling			241
WILL			
Beecher Cmty Sch Dist 200-U/Beecher	3	1,100	241
Chaney-Monge School Dist 88/Crest Hill	1	500	241
Channahon School Dist 17/Channahon	4	1,234	241
Crete-Monee Cmty SD 201-U/Crete	9	5,000	241
Diocese of Joliet Ed Office/Crest Hill	53	17,485	249
Elwood Cmty Cons SD 203/Elwood	1	318	242
Fairmont School Dist 89/Lockport	1	350	242
Frankfort School Dist 157-C/Frankfort	3	2,521	242
Homer Cmty Cons Sch Dist 33C/Homer Glen	6	3,800	242
Joliet Public School Dist 86/Joliet	21	12,000	243
Joliet Twp High Sch Dist 204/Joliet	3	6,589	243
Laraway Cmty Cons SD 70-C/Joliet	1	427	243
Lincoln Way Area Special Ed/Frankfort			250
Lincoln-Way Cmty HS Dist 210/New Lenox	3	6,811	244
Lockport Area Special Ed Co-op/Lockport			250
Lockport Twp High Sch Dist 205/Lockport	2	3,890	244
Manhattan School Dist 114/Manhattan	3	1,540	244
Milne-Kelvin Grove Dist 91/Lockport	2	550	244
Minooka Cmty High Sch Dist 111/Channahon	2	2,800	244
Mokena Public School Dist 159/Mokena	3	1,500	245
New Lenox School Dist 122/New Lenox	12	5,300	245
Peotone Cmty Unit SD 207-U/Peotone	5	1,453	245
Plainfield Cons Sch Dist 202/Plainfield	30	25,000	245
Professional Dev Alliance/Joliet			250
Reed-Custer Cmty Unit SD 255-U/Braidwood	3	1,476	246
Richland School Dist 88A/Crest Hill	1	923	247
Rockdale School Dist 84/Rockdale	1	275	247
Southern Will Co Spec Ed Dist/Joliet			250
Summit Hill School Dist 161/Frankfort	6	2,800	247
Taft School Dist 90/Lockport	1	300	247
Trees-Three Rivers EFE Sys/Joliet			250
Troy Cmty Cons SD 30-C/Plainfield	7	4,100	247
Union School Dist 81/Joliet	1	105	248
Valley View Cmty SD 365-U/Romeoville	20	18,000	248
Will Co Regional Office of Edu/Joliet			250
Will Co School Dist 92/Lockport	4	1,550	248
Wilmington Cmty Unit SD 209-U/Wilmington	4	1,400	249
WILLIAMSON			
Carterville Cmty Unit SD 5/Carterville	4	2,400	250
Crab Orchard Cmty Sch Dist 3/Marion	1	497	251
Herrin Cmty School Dist 4/Herrin	4	2,300	251
Johnston City Cmty Unit SD 1/Johnston City	4	1,100	251
Marion Cmty School Dist 2/Marion	7	3,914	251
Williamson Co Cte System/Marion			252
Williamson Co Special Ed Dist/Marion			252
WINNEBAGO			
Boone-Winnebago Reg Off of Ed/Loves Park			256
Career Educ Assoc N Ctl IL/Rockford			256
Diocese of Rockford Ed Office/Rockford	43	11,358	256
Durand Cmty Sch Dist 322/Durand	4	565	252
Harlem Unit Sch Dist 122/MacHesney Pk	11	6,300	252
Hononegah Cmty High SD 207/Rockton	1	1,500	253
Kinnikinnick Cmty Cons SD 131/Roscoe	4	1,750	253
Pecatonica Cmty Unit SD 321/Pecatonica	3	950	253

School Year 2020-2021 — 800-333-8802

COUNTY INDEX

Market Data Retrieval

COUNTY District/City	NO. OF SCHOOLS	ENROLL- MENT	PAGE
Prairie Hill Cmty Cons SD 133/South Beloit	2	743	253
Rockford School Dist 205/Rockford	46	28,940	253
Rockton School Dist 140/Rockton	3	1,600	255
Shirland Cmty Cons SD 134/Shirland	1	111	255
South Beloit Cmty Sch Dist 320/South Beloit	5	960	255
Winnebago Cmty Unit SD 323/Winnebago	4	1,330	255
Winnebago Co Special Ed Co-op/Rockton			256

WOODFORD

District/City	NO. OF SCHOOLS	ENROLL- MENT	PAGE
Central Illinois Voc Ed Co-op/Metamora			259
El Paso-Gridley CUSD 11/El Paso	4	1,200	257
Eureka Cmty Unit Sch Dist 140/Eureka	5	1,567	257
Fieldcrest Cmty School Dist 6/Minonk	4	909	257
Germantown Hills SD 69/Germantwn Hls	2	900	257
Lowpoint-Washburn CUSD 21/Washburn	3	325	257
Metamora Cmty Cons Sch Dist 1/Metamora	1	875	258
Metamora Twp HS Dist 122/Metamora	1	970	258
Riverview Cmty Cons Sch Dist 2/East Peoria	1	232	258
Roanoke-Benson Cmty Unit SD 60/Roanoke	3	500	258
Woodford Co Special Ed Assoc/Metamora			259

IL-R8   800-333-8802   **School Year 2020-2021**

Illinois School Directory

DISTRICT PERSONNEL INDEX

NAME/District	JOB FUNCTIONS	PAGE
A		
Abad, Sonia/Cicero School District 99	5	42
Abbatte, Monique/Cicero School District 99	9	42
Abcar, Rebecca/Giant City Cmty Cons SD 130	12,280	121
Abel, Julie/Litchfield Cmty Unit SD 12	67	191
Abell, Jeff/Meredosia-Chambersburg SD 11	8,288	192
Abell, Mike/O'Fallon Cmty Cons Sch Dist 90	295	221
Abernathy, Angie/Staunton Cmty Unit Sch Dist 6	4	168
Ablin, Carrie/Prairie Hills Elem SD 144	5,7,34,59,77,79,88	63
Abney-Giraldo, Jaimie/Elgin School District U-46	20,23,74	130
Abrahamson, Ryan/West Aurora School Dist 129	2	132
Abrassart, Kim/Bradley-Bourbonnais CHSD 307	4	134
Abrego, Art, Dr/Hawthorn Cmty Cons Sch Dist 73	57,296	151
Abrell, Lane, Dr/Plainfield Cons Sch Dist 202	1	246
Accord, Andy/Carmi-White Co School Dist 5	67	237
Acevedo, Annette, Dr/Elgin School District U-46	57	130
Ackerman, Jody/Career & Tech Ed Consortium	2	225
Ackerman, Josh/Triad Cmty School District 2	16,82	172
Ackermann, Eileen/River Trails Sch Dist 26	4	65
Acklin, Jim/Edgar Co Cmty Sch Dist 6	1	103
Ackman, Kyle/Rock Falls Elem Sch Dist 13	83,270	240
Acord, Jennifer/Wabash-Ohio Valley Sp Ed Dist	15,74	238
Acosta, Michelle/Barrington Cmty Unit SD 220	34	147
Acton, Elizabeth/Thomasboro Cmty Cons SD 130	752	12
Acton, Lisa/Oakwood Cmty Unit Sch Dist 76	58	232
Adair, Barry/North Clay Cmty Unit SD 25	67	16
Adams, Darren/Deer Creek-Mackinaw CUSD 701	5	226
Adams, Denean, Dr/Elementary School District 159	9,15,288	47
Adams, Frank/Pleasantdale School Dist 107	2,3,11,84,296	62
Adams, Jan/Somonauk Cmty Unit SD 432	5	86
Adams, Jeremy/Woodland Cmty Unit Sch Dist 5	67	162
Adams, Judy/Odell Cmty Cons Sch Dist 435	73,83	161
Adams, Laretta/Chicago Heights Elem SD 170	2	25
Adams, Marcy/Palestine Cmty Unit SD 3	16	83
Adams, Tammy/Patoka Cmty Unit SD 100	4	175
Adams, Wendy/Alton Cmty School District 11	68	169
Adamski, Nicole/Kings Cons School District 144	67	194
Adamski, Sandra/Crystal Lake Elem Distict 47	57	181
Adamski, Sandra/Rhodes School District 84 1/2	57	64
Adcock, Stan/Paw Paw Cmty Unit SD 271	1,11,83	160
Adden, Alice/Mt Olive Cmty Unit Sch Dist 5	73	168
Addis, James/Ottawa Elementary Sch Dist 141	73,295,297	143
Ade, Gary/Pana Cmty Unit School Dist 8	6	14
Adelman, Joe/McLean Co Unit District 5	2	186
Adkins, Amy/Byron Cmty Unit SD 226	68	194
Adkins, Christopher/Kaneland Cmty Unit SD 302	68	132
Adkins, Ray/Geneva CUSD 304	91	131
Adkins, Ryan/Yorkville Cmty Unit SD 115	16,73,295	139
Admire, Darla/Abingdon-Avon Cmty Unit SD 276	4	139
Adolthson, Jeremy/Monmouth-Roseville CUSD 238	6	234
Adrianven, Lisa/Prairie Hills Elem SD 144	57	63
Ady, William/Belvidere Cmty Unit SD 100	15,68	4
Aguirre, Samuel/Illinois Dept of Education	57	1
Agustin, Tiffany/Northwestern IL Association	76	87
Ahlemeyer, John, Dr/Maroa Forsyth CU Sch Dist 2	1	165
Ahlgrim, John, Dr/Warren Twp High Sch Dist 121	1	155
Ahsell, Katie/Community Cons School Dist 59	78,88,296	43
Aikman, Ryan/Sullivan Cmty Unit SD 300	6	193
Akerman, Thomas/Homer Cmty Cons Sch Dist 33C	3	242
Akers, Jean/Bushnell Prairie Cmty USD 170	4	178
Akers, Thomas/Cambridge Cmty Unit SD 227	1	116
Akridge-Dixon, Rebecca/Matteson Elem SD 162	59	57
Alajakis, Nicholas/Waukegan Cmty Unit SD 60	15,71,751	156
Alberico-Madl, Theresa/East Prairie School Dist 73	11,83,288	47
Albers, Amy/Delavan Cmty Unit Sch Dist 703	8,11,58,69	226
Albers, Karen/Coulterville Unit Sch Dist 1	1,11,73,84	205
Alberstett, Kurt/Durand Cmty Sch Dist 322	1,11	252
Albertini, Mark/Carbondale Cmty HSD 165	6	120
Albrecht, Bradley/River Ridge Cmty Unit SD 210	1,11	126
Albrecht, Cathleen/New Trier Twp HS District 203	67	58
Albrecht, Harold/Ohio Cmty High School Dist 505	67	7
Albrecht, Michelle/St Libory Cons Sch District 30	275	222
Albrecht, Shean/River Ridge Cmty Unit SD 210	6	126
Albrect, Nelson/Crete-Monee Cmty SD 201-U	67	242

NAME/District	JOB FUNCTIONS	PAGE
Albro, Bryan/Rondout School District 72	3	154
Aldrich, Gail/Harlem Unit Sch District 122	2	252
Aldridge, Leonard/Dupo Cmty School District 196	73,84	218
Aldrige, Kim/Red Hill Cmty School Dist 10	2	159
Alewelt, Brad/Rochester Cmty Unit SD 3-A	3	212
Alexander, Bill/Community Unit School Dist 16	67	211
Alexander, Gary/Tuscola Cmty Unit SD 301	1	88
Alexander, John/Frankfort Cmty Unit SD 168	67	108
Alexander, Marcus, Dr/Pembroke Cmty Cons SD 259	1	136
Alexander, Neil/Lincoln Cmty High Sch Dist 404	6	163
Alexander, Rodney/Proviso Twp High Sch Dist 209	67	63
Alfaro, Yadi/Woodridge Elem Sch District 68	57	100
Alfred, Mable, Dr/Elementary School District 159	1	47
Algrim, Katie/Regional Office of Ed Kane Co	74	134
Ali, Sayeed/Quincy School District 172	67	2
Allaman, Chad, Dr/District 50 Schools	1,11,83,84	226
Allan, William/Lyons Twp HS District 204	82	56
Allard, Becky/Gavin School District 37	2,3,4,5,12,73	150
Allen, Andrew/East Aurora School Dist 131	73	129
Allen, Andrew/Serena Cmty Unit School Dist 2	295	144
Allen, Andy/Serena Cmty Unit School Dist 2	16,73	144
Allen, Brett/Staunton Cmty Unit Sch Dist 6	33	168
Allen, Jeff/Oblong Cmty Unit Sch Dist 4	3	83
Allen, Kim/Franklin Cmty Unit SD 1	2	192
Allen, Lindsay/Community Unit School Dist 308	9,69,288	137
Allen, Lisa/Valley View Cmty SD 365-U	79	248
Allen, Micheal/Riverview Cmty Cons Sch Dist 2	6	258
Allen, Mike/Gibson Cty-Melvin-Sibley CUSD5	6	106
Allen, Molly/Regional Office of Ed 17	15	188
Allen, Patrick/Wallace Cmty Cons Sch Dist 195	6	145
Allen, Paula/Galatia Cmty Unit Sch Dist 1	6	210
Allen, Randy/Ball Chatham Cmty Unit SD 5	91	211
Allen, Silvia/Blue Ridge Cmty SD 18	35	87
Allen, Teresa/Monmouth-Roseville CUSD 238	4	234
Allert, Carole/Black Hawk Area Spec Ed Dist	58	210
Alli, Sam/Odin Public School Dist 722	8	175
Allison, Amy/Lake Park Cmty High SD 108	16,76	96
Allison, Chad/Illinois Vly Ctl Sch Dist 321	1	197
Allison, Rob/Community Unit School Dist 308	3	137
Allsopp, Adam/Ewing Northern Cmty SD 115	67	108
Almasi, Anthony/Norwood Sch Dist 63	83,85	198
Almendarez, Sue/Indian Springs Sch Dist 109	34,274	53
Alonzo, Jeni/Plainfield Cons School Dist 202	58	246
Alseth, Phillip/South Beloit Cmty Sch Dist 320	3	255
Alstat, Joe/Bond Co Cmty Unit Sch Dist 2	6	4
Alston, Kyle/South Holland School Dist 151	73,295	68
Alston, Ted/Polo Cmty Unit Sch Dist 222	6	195
Alt, Diana/Rockford School District 205	74,81	254
Alt, Jeff/Freeburg Cmty High Sch Dist 77	73,76,84	219
Alt, Jessica/McLean Co Unit District 5	58	186
Altenburg, Tod/Lombard Elem SD 44	68	97
Altig, Tom/Argenta Oreana Cmty Unit SD 1	73	165
Altmayer, Mark/Huntley Cmty School Dist 158	2,19	182
Alvarado, Katye/Waltham Elementary SD 185	59	145
Alvarado, Samantha/Peoria Heights Cmty SD 325	8	198
Alvarez, Abby/Plano Cmty Unit Sch Dist 88	57	138
Alvarez, Elizabeth/Chicago PSD-Network 8	15	32
Alvarez, Enid/Cook County School Dist 130	12,49,81	45
Alverado, Anna/Freeport School District 145	1	224
Alvey, Roger, Dr/Illini Bluffs Cmty Unit SD 327	1	197
Alvis, Heather/Community Cons School Dist 204	6,7	201
Amadei, Michael/Des Plaines Cmty Cons SD 62	15,68	45
Amadio, Richard/Bloom Twp High Sch Dist 206	3	23
Amadio, Tom/Chicago Heights Elem SD 170	1	25
Amador, Ashlee/Orion Cmty Unit Sch Dist 223	6	117
Aman, Ashley/Metamora Cmty Cons Sch Dist 1	12	258
Amarsaglia, Alex/Smithton Cmty Cons SD 130	73,295	222
Amato-Zech, Natalie/Community Cons School Dist 59	9,59	43
Ambroiggie, Elisabeth/Waukegan Cmty Unit SD 60	57	156
Ambrosini, Kate/Frankfort School Dist 157-C	2,15	242
Ambuehl, Ellie/La Grange Area Dept of Spec Ed	1	82
Amendt, Julie/Marengo Cmty High Sch Dist 154	11,88,275	182
Amerio, Scott/Rantoul Twp High Sch Dist 193	1	12
Amerman, Carolyn/Hiawatha Cmty Unit SD 426	5	85
Amistadi, Duane/Wood River-Hartford Elem SD 15	3,91	172
Amm, Jill/Pontiac Cmty Cons Sch Dist 429	2	161

School Year 2020-2021   800-333-8802   IL-T1

DISTRICT PERSONNEL INDEX

Market Data Retrieval

NAME/District	JOB FUNCTIONS	PAGE
Amos, Renea/Bloom Twp High Sch Dist 206	5	23
Anastacio, Lindsay/Arlington Hts School Dist 25	79	21
Anderews, Matthew/Dunlap Cmty Unit Sch Dist 323	8,69,288	196
Andersen, Arthur/Keeneyville Elem Sch Dist 20	73	96
Andersen, Mary/Darien Public Sch Dist 61	274	92
Anderson Wolf, Sarah/Huntley Cmty School Dist 158	8	182
Anderson-Maier, Brandi/Peru Elem Sch Dist 124	9	143
Anderson, Andrew/Herrin Cmty School District 4	6	251
Anderson, Brian/La Grange Elem Sch Dist 102	67	54
Anderson, Chuck/Reed-Custer Cmty Unit SD 255-U	6	246
Anderson, Denise/Effingham Cmty Sch Dist 40	4	104
Anderson, Doug/Itasca School District 10	6	96
Anderson, Erica/Edwards Co Cmty Unit SD 1	85	104
Anderson, Erin/Crystal Lake Elem District 47	40,280	181
Anderson, Joel/Henry Senachwine CUSD 5	3,5	176
Anderson, Kathy/Vienna High School Dist 13-3	57,298	127
Anderson, Keith/Morris Elem School Dist 54	6	113
Anderson, Kevin/Rosemont Elem Sch Dist 78	1	66
Anderson, Kimberly/Community Unit School Dist 201	2,5,11,296,298	92
Anderson, Marianne/Mannheim School District 83	67	56
Anderson, Mark/Batavia Unit School Dist 101	2,5,91	128
Anderson, Marsha/LaSalle Peru Twp HSD 120	4	142
Anderson, Mary/Bensenville Elem Sch Dist 2	16,73	89
Anderson, Mary Kay/Heritage Cmty Unit Sch Dist 8	58,88	11
Anderson, Megan/Rantoul Twp High Sch Dist 193	11,83,88,275,296,298	12
Anderson, Michelle/Rockton School District 140	12	255
Anderson, Patrick, Dr/Wood River-Hartford Elem SD 15	1	172
Anderson, Rachel/Eldorado Cmty Unit Sch Dist 4	36	210
Anderson, Scott/Lincolnwood Sch Dist 74	67	55
Anderson, Shannon/Momence Cmty Unit Sch Dist 1	1	136
Anderson, Sherri/Lake Park Cmty High SD 108	71	96
Anderson, Steve/Homewood Flossmoor CHSD 233	67	52
Anderson, Sue/Grant Park Cmty Unit SD 6	2	135
Anderson, Wesley/Century Cmty Unit SD 100	67	204
Anderton, Gary/Christopher Unit Sch Dist 99	67	107
Andreshak, Michael/Kirby School District 140	2,84	53
Andrews, Dan/Tri-Point Cmty Unit SD 6J	73,286	162
Andrews, Kara/Mt Vernon Twp HS District 201	27	123
Andrews, Kristen/Genoa-Kingston Cmty SD 424	67	85
Andrews, Matt/Heyworth Cmty Sch District 4	9	185
Andrews, Melanie/Mt Vernon Twp HS District 201	1	123
Andrews, Melanie/Regional Office of Ed 13	15,58	19
Andrews, Michelle/Abingdon-Avon Cmty Unit SD 276	11,296	139
Andriano, Dave/Bradley Elem School Dist 61	15	134
Andriano, David, Dr/Iroquois Co Cmty Unit SD 9	1,11,83	119
Andrievosky, Dimitri/Libertyville Pub Sch Dist 70	73,84	152
Anfuso, Elio/Komarek School District 94	3	54
Angelaccio, Don, Dr/Prospect Hts School Dist 23	1,11	63
Angelos, Catharine/Lombard Elem SD 44	34	97
Annerud, Mark/Evanston-Skokie Cmty CSD 65	295	48
Anselmo, Shannon/Peotone Cmty Unit SD 207-U	77	245
Anthony, Scott/Consolidated High Sch Dist 230	297	44
Antonacci, Jamie/Sangamon Valley Cmty Unit SD 9	79,83	166
Aper, Ashley/Chester-E Lincoln Cmty SD 61	59	163
Apgar, Eric/Round Lake Area Co Dist 116	8,15	155
Appel, Bryan/Plano Cmty Unit Sch Dist 88	3	138
Applebee, Phillip/Maroa Forsyth CU Sch Dist 2	6	165
Appleby, Mark/Reavis Twp HSD 220	3	64
Applegate, Lisa/Pekin Public School Dist 108	295	227
Applegate, Michael/Sherrard Cmty Sch Dist 200	6	189
Aqel, Ruba/Indian Springs Sch Dist 109	57	53
Arains, Elena/Woodstock Cmty Unit SD 200	2	184
Arakelian, Kimberly/Northbrook Elem School Dist 27	2,3,15	59
Arbogast, Anthony/Plainfield Cons Sch Dist 202	2,3,15,19	246
Arbogast, Anthony/Roselle School District 12	2,3,15	99
Arbuckle, Carie/Egyptian Cmty Unit Sch Dist 5	58,275,288	3
Arbuckle, Peggy/McLean-DeWitt Reg Voc System	275	188

NAME/District	JOB FUNCTIONS	PAGE
Archer, Lori/Heritage Cmty Unit Sch Dist 8	6	11
Archinbel, Ellen/Western CUSD 12	11	203
Ardeleanu, Nada/Golf School District 67	67	51
Arensdorff, Mike/Oak Park Elem School Dist 97	16,73,84	60
Arentsen, Leig-Ann/Germantown Elem Sch Dist 60	2	18
Arey, Beth/Evanston Twp High SD 202	33	48
Argyelan, Alice/Kankakee Area Reg Voc Ed Sys	15,68	137
Arickx, Dan/Rock Falls Elem Sch Dist 13	1,11	240
Arie, Kristy/Iroquois West Cmty Unit SD 10	6	119
Arkebauer, Rex/Greenview Cmty Unit SD 200	67	188
Arnold, Pam/Greenfield Cmty Unit SD 10	12	111
Armour, Angela/Mid-State Special Education	1	15
Armour, Angela/Montgomery-Carlinville Reg SE	1	15
Arms, Andrea/Central Sch Dist 51	752	225
Armstrong, Amy/Champaign Cmty Unit Sch Dist 4	67	10
Armstrong, Candace/New Simpson Hill Cons SD 32	8,38	127
Armstrong, Carmen/Harvey Public School Dist 152	91	51
Armstrong, Dan/Huntley Cmty School Dist 158	71	182
Armstrong, Jennifer/Rural Champaign Co Sp Ed Co-op	1	13
Armstrong, John/Joliet Public School Dist 86	73,76,84	243
Armstrong, Michelle/Herscher Cmty School Dist 2	5,16	135
Armstrong, Susan/Hardin Co Cmty Unit Sch Dist 1	8,57,288	115
Armstrong, Todd/Argenta Oreana Cmty Unit SD 1	67	165
Arndt, Christine/Big Hollow School District 38	12,15	148
Arnold, Angie/Pekin Public School Dist 108	16,73,82,84	227
Arnold, Danielle/Deerfield Public SD 109	9	149
Arnold, Heather/Rochester Cmty Unit SD 3-A	7	212
Arnold, Hollie/Kell Cons School District 2	69	175
Arnold, Jodi/West Central Cmty Unit SD 235	67	116
Arnold, Tim/Will Co School District 92	1,11	248
Arns, Dan/Quincy School District 172	91	2
Arreguin, Sandra, Dr/Niles Twp High School Dist 219	10,15	58
Arresola, Cindy/Echo Joint Agreement	15,68	82
Arrington, John/Thornton Twp High Sch Dist 205	27	69
Arriola, Colleen/Cicero School District 99	7,40,43	42
Arteberry, Brian/Belleville Area Sp Svc Co-op	2	223
Arthalony, Colin/A-C Central Cmty Unit SD 262	6	9
Artman, Vickie, Dr/Joppa-Maple Grove Unit SD 38	1	177
Arvanitis, Athena/New Trier Twp HS District 203	72	58
Asche, Ben/Pearl City Cmty Unit SD 200	10	225
Ascolani, Damon/Lemont-Bromberek Sch Dist 113A	67	55
Aseltine, Megan, Dr/Skokie School District 69	9,15	67
Aseltine, Sarah/Skokie School District 69	57	67
Ash, Dana/Harvey Public School Dist 152	59	51
Ashman, Randy/Urbana School District 116	3,19,27	12
Ashy, Ben/West Carroll CUSD 314	10,38	9
Ashy, Ben/West Carroll CUSD 314	10,38	9
Askew, Mandi/Donovan Cmty Unit Sch Dist 3	12	119
Aslinger, Melanie/McLean Co Unit District 5	58	186
Asmus, Janine/Leyden Cmty High Sch Dist 212	16,81,82	55
Asmus, Ryan/Gower School District 62	67	94
Asplund, John, Dr/Galesburg Cmty Unit SD 205	1	140
Atchison, Aaron/Rich Twp High School Dist 227	71	64
Atherton, Paula/Forest Park School District 91	5	50
Attaway, Justin/Skokie School District 69	2,3,4,5	67
Atteberry, Amy/Carmi-White Co School Dist 5	10,11,34,88,275	237
Attutis, Darla/Georgetown-Ridge Farm CUSD 4	4	232
Atwell, Tim/Kewanee Cmty Unit Sch Dist 229	6	117
Audisho, Christina/Lincolnwood Sch Dist 74	71	55
Aughenbaugh, Denise/Mendota Twp High Sch Dist 280	10,69,274,275	143
August, Becky/Fairfield Cmty High SD 225	90	236
Augustine, Beth/Riverside-Brookfld Twp SD 208	38	65
Augustine, Dave/Cahokia Unit Sch Dist 187	3	218
Augustyn, Julie/Community Cons School Dist 93	83,88	90
Aumiller, Elaine, Dr/Mt Prospect School Dist 57	1	58
Aurand, Michelle/Hamilton Cmty Cons SD 328	31,36,69,83	114
Austin, Kenya/Country Club Hills SD 160	2	45

1	Superintendent	16	Instructional Media Svcs	30	Adult Education	44	Science Sec
2	Bus/Finance/Purchasing	17	Chief Operations Officer	31	Career/Sch-to-Work K-12	45	Math K-12
3	Buildings And Grounds	18	Chief Academic Officer	32	Career/Sch-to-Work Elem	46	Math Elem
4	Food Service	19	Chief Financial Officer	33	Career/Sch-to-Work Sec	47	Math Sec
5	Transportation	20	Art K-12	34	Early Childhood Ed	48	English/Lang Arts K-12
6	Athletic	21	Art Elem	35	Health/Phys Education	49	English/Lang Arts Elem
7	Health Services	22	Art Sec	36	Guidance Services K-12	50	English/Lang Arts Sec
8	Curric/Instruct K-12	23	Music K-12	37	Guidance Services Elem	51	Reading K-12
9	Curric/Instruct Elem	24	Music Elem	38	Guidance Services Sec	52	Reading Elem
10	Curric/Instruct Sec	25	Music Sec	39	Social Studies K-12	53	Reading Sec
11	Federal Program	26	Business Education	40	Social Studies Elem	54	Remedial Reading K-12
12	Title I	27	Career & Tech Ed	41	Social Studies Sec	55	Remedial Reading Elem
13	Title V	28	Technology Education	42	Science K-12	56	Remedial Reading Sec
15	Asst Superintendent	29	Family/Consumer Science	43	Science Elem	57	Bilingual/ELL

58	Special Education K-12	72	Summer School	88	Alternative/At Risk	277	Remedial Math K-12
59	Special Education Elem	73	Instructional Tech	89	Multi-Cultural Curriculum	280	Literacy Coach
60	Special Education Sec	74	Inservice Training	90	Social Work	285	STEM
61	Foreign/World Lang K-12	75	Marketing/Distributive	91	Safety/Security	286	Digital Learning
62	Foreign/World Lang Elem	76	Info Systems	92	Magnet School	288	Common Core Standards
63	Foreign/World Lang Sec	77	Psychological Assess	93	Parental Involvement	294	Accountability
64	Religious Education K-12	78	Affirmative Action	95	Tech Prep Program	295	Network System
65	Religious Education Elem	79	Student Personnel	97	Chief Information Officer	296	Title II Programs
66	Religious Education Sec	80	Driver Ed/Safety	98	Chief Technology Officer	297	Webmaster
67	School Board President	81	Gifted/Talented	270	Character Education	298	Grant Writer/Ptnrships
68	Teacher Personnel	82	Video Services	271	Migrant Education	750	Chief Innovation Officer
69	Academic Assessment	83	Substance Abuse Prev	273	Teacher Mentor	751	Chief of Staff
70	Research/Development	84	Erate	274	Before/After Sch	752	Social Emotional Learning
71	Public Information	85	AIDS Education	275	Response To Intervention		

Illinois School Directory

DISTRICT PERSONNEL INDEX

NAME/District	JOB FUNCTIONS	PAGE
Avant-Bey, Tracy/Proviso Twp High Sch Dist 209	73,75,84,95,297	63
Avedano, Wilson/Rochester Cmty Unit SD 3-A	73,76,295	212
Avery, Sue/Braceville Elem School Dist 75	11,16,69,273,286,288	111
Aviles, Melissa/Earlville Cmty Unit Sch Dist 9	2	141
Awad, Mo/Park Forest Chicago Hgt SD 163	76	62
Awdziejczyk, Nancy/NW Ed Council Stdnt Success	1	82
Axelsen, Josh/Regional Office of Ed Kane Co	88	134
Ayala, Carmen, Dr/Illinois Dept of Education	1	1
Ayer, Dan/Nauvoo-Colusa CUSD 325	9,59,88,273	115
Ayer, Shaila/West Central Cmty Unit SD 235	57,58,275	116
Ayers, Jay/Community Unit School Dist 16	4	211
Azab, Carrie/Schaumburg Cmty Cons SD 54	34	66

B

NAME/District	JOB FUNCTIONS	PAGE
Babulic, Janell/Aero Special Ed Co-op	68	82
Baburnich, Dave/Carterville Cmty Unit SD 5	73,286,295	250
Bachar, Stacey/Aptakisic-Tripp Sch Dist 102	2,4,15,91	146
Bachfischer, Deb/Metamora Twp HS Dist 122	16,82	258
Bachman, Jason/Eureka Cmty Unit Sch Dist 140	36	257
Bachman, Nita/Mahomet-Seymour Cmty SD 3	7,85	11
Bachtold, Dave/Paxton-Buckley-Loda CUSD 10	3	107
Bachtold, Dawn/Paxton-Buckley-Loda CUSD 10	67	107
Backe, Maureen/McLean Co Unit District 5	9	186
Bacy, Mark/Danville School District 118	6	231
Badman, Shirley/Villa Grove Cmty Unit SD 302	2,68,84	88
Bae, Kellie/Lake Bluff Elem Sch Dist 65	9,288	151
Baele, Loren, Dr/Oak Grove School District 68	1,83	198
Baer, Erick, Dr/St Rose School District 14-15	1,11,73,83,84,288	18
Baez, Ernie/Community Cons School Dist 15	3	43
Baffoe, Kevin/Rich Twp High School Dist 227	3	64
Bagares, John/Argo Cmty High School Dist 217	10	21
Bagby, Robert/Lincoln Cmty High Sch Dist 404	83	163
Baghdassarian, Ray/Rosemont Elem Sch Dist 78	73,286	66
Bagley, Andrew/Southwestern Cmty Unit SD 9	67	168
Baglin, Gary/Stockton Cmty Unit SD 206	73	126
Bahnks, Tara/Knoxville Cmty Unit SD 202	12	140
Bahnks, Tara/Knoxville Cmty Unit SD 202	8	140
Bahr, Andrew/Cerro Gordo Cmty Unit SD 100	83,88	202
Baig, Faisal/Golf School District 67	16,73,76	51
Bailey, Christy/Auburn Cmty Unit Sch Dist 10	36,69	211
Bailey, Jacalyn/Rich Twp High School Dist 227	7,60	64
Bailey, Linda/Creve Coeur Sch Dist 76	67	226
Bailey, Molly/Danville School District 118	58	231
Bailey, Rob/Grant Park Cmty Unit SD 6	6	135
Bailey, Sharon/Madison Cmty Unit Sch Dist 12	2	172
Bailey, Teresa/Warrensburg-Latham CU SD 11	2,68	166
Bailey, Wilson/Rockford School District 205	3	253
Baima, Mary/Allen-Otter Creek CCSD 65	1,11	141
Bain, Breanna/New Simpson Hill Cons SD 32	16,82,286	127
Bainter, Brent/Lincoln Elem School Dist 27	6,72	163
Bair, Tim/Highland Cmty Sch District 5	2,5,84	171
Baird, Amy/Creve Coeur Sch Dist 76	83	226
Baird, Ben/Glencoe Sch District 35	79	51
Baird, John/Community Unit School Dist 303	3,4,5,15,91	128
Bajda, Jennifer/Frankfort School Dist 157-C	59	242
Baker, Amy/Orangeville Cmty Unit SD 203	67	225
Baker, Carol/Urbana School District 116	2,19	12
Baker, Dan/Polo Cmty Unit Sch Dist 222	73,295	195
Baker, Dan/Seneca Twp High Sch Dist 160	35	144
Baker, Diane/Gifford Cmty Cons SD 188	2	10
Baker, Ebony/Lake Park Cmty High SD 108	77,79,90	96
Baker, Heather/Pecatonica Cmty Unit SD 321	8	253
Baker, Heather/West Lincoln-Broadwell ESD 92	1,11,57,73,288	164
Baker, Heather/Winnebago Cmty Unit SD 323	57	255
Baker, Krystin/Dupo Cmty School District 196	31,36,83,85	218
Baker, Matt/LaSalle Peru Twp HSD 120	71	142
Baker, Tony/Plano Cmty Unit Sch Dist 88	1	138
Bakii, Afrim/Minooka Cmty Cons Sch Dist 201	295	112
Bala, Stephanie/Pekin Cmty High Sch Dist 303	12	227
Balayti, Deborah/Palos Cmty Cons School Dist 118	73,286	61
Bald, Rebecca/Marquardt School District 15	71	97
Baldermann, Timothy/Union School District 81	1	248
Baldridge, Dwain, Dr/Regional Office of Ed 13	27	19
Baldwin, Christine/Indian Springs Sch Dist 109	11,74,88,273,285	53
Baldwin, Christine/Indian Springs Sch Dist 109	9,11,73,74,88,273,285	53
Bales, Jennifer/Jasper Co Cmty Unit SD 1	58	122

NAME/District	JOB FUNCTIONS	PAGE
Balestri, Michael/Oglesby Public Sch Dist 125	298	143
Ballard, Cheri/Indian Creek Cmty Unit SD 425	4	85
Ballard, Dan/Metamora Twp HS Dist 122	26	258
Ballard, Jim/Edwards Co Cmty Unit SD 1	3	104
Ballard, Laura/Roxana Cmty Unit Sch Dist 1	57,58,77,275	172
Ballard, Rosanne/Kirby School District 140	5	53
Ballentine, Dajuan/E F Lindop Elem Sch Dist 92	3	47
Ballou, Justin/Whiteside School District 115	73,286,295	222
Balltti, Mary/Elwood Cmty Cons SD 203	16	242
Ban, Jennifer, Dr/Pleasantdale School Dist 107	9,15,298	62
Banas, Leslie/Komarek School District 94	6	54
Banbor, Jakub/Westchester Public SD 92 1/2	73,84,285	70
Bandy, Eric/Salem Cmty High Sch Dist 600	67	175
Baney, Rebecca/Kewanee Cmty Unit Sch Dist 229	8	117
Baney, Rebecca/Kewanee Cmty Unit Sch Dist 229	8	117
Banick, Erika/Reavis Twp HSD 220	41	64
Banks, Celia/Elgin School District U-46	280	130
Banks, Karen/Hinsdale Twp High Sch Dist 86	7	95
Banks, Paiyuan/Bourbonnais Elem Sch Dist 53	34	134
Banks, Peggy/Thornton Fractnl Twp HSD 215	4	69
Bannon, Mimi/Kinnikinnick Cmty Cons SD 131	9,16,69,73,288	253
Bannoveln, Erik/Windsor Cmty Unit SD 1	11,288	216
Banye, Jana/Palestine Cmty Unit SD 3	51,54	83
Baptist, Jan/Bellwood School District 88	2	22
Barajaz, Liz/Newark Cmty Cons Sch Dist 66	59	138
Baran Janco, Lisa/Leyden Cmty High Sch Dist 212	57	55
Barbanente, Jean/Dupage High School Dist 88	12,88	93
Barbeau, Terra/Prairie Du Rocher CCSD 134	12	205
Barber, Dawn/Peotone Cmty Unit SD 207-U	7	245
Barbic, Joe/Indian Valley Voc Ed System	1	86
Barbini, Matt/Libertyville Pub Sch Dist 70	1	152
Barble, Leslie/Unity Point Cmty Cons SD 140	13,288,296	121
Barbour, Alex, Dr/Lake Villa Cmty Cons SD 41	9,11,57,69,271,288,296,298	152
Barclay, Elisabeth/East Peoria Cmty HS Dist 309	7,85	226
Bardwell, Robert/Eureka Cmty Unit Sch Dist 140	1,11,83	257
Bargar, Megan/Community High School Dist 117	79	148
Barger, James/Allendale Cmty Cons SD 17	84	234
Barger, Jill/Geff Cmty Cons School Dist 14	1,11,84	236
Baricovich, Jon/Cook County School Dist 104	9,57,76,79,270,288,296	44
Barker, Darcie/Beardstown Cmty Sch Dist 15	16	9
Barker, Susan, Dr/Zion-Benton Twp High SD 126	60	157
Barklow, Lisa/East Dubuque Unit SD 119	2	125
Barnabas, Chris/Lincolnwood Sch Dist 74	68	55
Barnard, Leonard/Canton Union School Dist 66	67	109
Barnes, Carla/Benton Cmty Cons Sch Dist 47	84	107
Barnes, Jeff/Paris Union School District 95	36	103
Barnes, Jim/Marseilles Elem Sch Dist 150	67	142
Barnes, Marilyn/Ford Heights School Dist 169	9,11	49
Barnes, Michelle/Peoria Heights Cmty SD 325	6	198
Barnes, Michelle/Stewardson-Strasburg CUSD 5-A	12,51,54	216
Barnes, Shane/Quincy School District 172	5	2
Barnes, Sue/Danville School District 118	4	231
Barnett, Dean/Hazel Crest School Dist 152-5	67	52
Barnhart, Brian, Dr/Western Springs Sch Dist 101	1	71
Barnhart, Cindy/Wood River-Hartford Elem SD 15	59	172
Barnstable, Sarah/Carterville Cmty Unit SD 5	8,11,69,77,88,275,294	250
Baron, Sean/Peru Elem Sch Dist 124	76	143
Barr, Denise/Crystal Lake Elem Distict 47	71	181
Barr, Jen/Cahokia Unit Sch Dist 187	16,73,286	218
Barr, Wayne/Princeton Elem Sch Dist 115	3,5,91	7
Barrett, Andrew, Dr/Geneva CUSD 304	8,11,15,31,69,74,288,296	131
Barrett, Dawn/Cary Cmty Cons Sch Dist 26	9	179
Barrett, Elizabeth/Athens Cmty Unit Sch Dist 213	54	188
Barrett, Elizabeth/Athens Cmty Unit Sch Dist 213	54	188
Barrett, James/Dunlap Cmty Unit Sch Dist 323	5	196
Barrett, Tanya/Bensenville Elem Sch Dist 2	4	89
Barrick, Sara/Elmwood Park Cmty Unit SD 401	58	48
Barrie, Dan/East Maine School District 63	3,91	47
Barringer, Eric/Clinton Cmty Unit Sch Dist 15	16,73,295	87
Barrios, Eduardo/Community Cons School Dist 59	73	43
Barron, Josh/Community High School Dist 218	15	44
Barry, Aly/Shiloh School District 1	73	103
Barry, John/Franklin Park Pub Sch Dist 84	2	50
Barry, John/Rhodes School District 84 1/2	2	64
Barry, Mark/Lake Bluff Elem Sch Dist 65	67	151
Barry, Rod/Liberty Cmty Unit Sch Dist 2	67	2

School Year 2020-2021   800-333-8802   IL-T3

DISTRICT PERSONNEL INDEX

Market Data Retrieval

NAME/District	JOB FUNCTIONS	PAGE
Barry, Sean/Tremont Cmty Unit SD 702	1	228
Barschak, Dale/Smithton Cmty Cons SD 130	67	222
Bartelt, Jon, Dr/Bloomingdale School Dist 13	1	89
Barth, Randy/El Paso-Gridley CUSD 11	67	257
Barthel, Jason/Rockford School District 205	97	254
Bartlett, Tasha/Pikeland Cmty Sch Dist 10	7	203
Bartley, Shane/Quincy School District 172	3	2
Bartlow, Allison/Armstrong Twp High SD 225	10,12,60	231
Barto, Kevin/Downers Grove School Dist 58	3,91	93
Bartok, David/Eldorado Cmty Unit Sch Dist 4	67	210
Barton, Buster/Byron Cmty Unit SD 226	1,57	194
Barwick, John/Marion Cmty School Dist 2	67	251
Basa, Jacqueline/Central Stickney Sch Dist 110	67	25
Basnett, Eric/Jasper Cmty Cons Sch Dist 17	6	237
Bass, Kelly/Westchester Public SD 92 1/2	9,11,15,280,288,296,298	70
Basso, Chip/Sesser-Valier Cmty Unit SD 196	6	108
Bates, Amy/Frankfort Cmty Unit SD 168	8,36,69,88	108
Bates, Brian/Learning Tech Ctr of Illinois	73,286	13
Bates, Dave/Auburn Cmty Unit Sch Dist 10	6	211
Batka, Rich/Brookfield-LaGrange Park SD 95	3	23
Batson, James/Fenton Cmty High Sch Dist 100	73	94
Battaf, Scott/Mascoutah Cmty Sch Dist 19	6	220
Battaglia, Liz/Oak Park Elem School Dist 97	76	60
Batts, Tarra/Echo Joint Agreement	2	82
Bauer, Barry/Iroquois Co Cmty Unit SD 9	6	119
Bauer, Bruce, Dr/Dalzell Elem School Dist 98	1,83	6
Bauer, Jason/Pana Cmty Unit School Dist 8	1	14
Bauer, Tracie/O'Fallon Cmty Cons Sch Dist 90	59	221
Baughman, Jeff/Le Roy Cmty Unit SD 2	69	186
Baughman, Maggie/Le Roy Cmty Unit SD 2	34	186
Baughman, Nick/Yorkville Cmty Unit SD 115	8,11,18,34,83,270,296,298	139
Baum Gartener, Susan/Centralia City Sch Dist 135	4	174
Bauman, Anthony/Bloomington School District 87	6,35,80	185
Bauman, Barb/Freeburg Cmty Cons SD 70	67	219
Bauman, Joy/Belvidere Cmty Unit SD 100	8	4
Bauman, Stacie/Eureka Cmty Unit Sch Dist 140	4	257
Baumann, Kim/North Chicago Cmty Unit SD 187	7	153
Baumann, Mark/Troy Cmty Cons SD 30-C	5	247
Baumann, Scott/Warsaw Cmty Unit Sch Dist 316	67	115
Baumgartner, Kristie/Alton Cmty School District 11	1	169
Bavery, Brittany/Hamilton Cmty Cons SD 328	4	114
Bavis, Peter/Evanston Twp High SD 202	10,288	48
Bayer, Kim/Butler School District 53	13,37,69,77,83	89
Bayle, Ben/DeKalb Cmty Unit SD 428	73,76,98,297	84
Bayless, Julie/Princeville Cmty Unit SD 326	8,275	200
Baylor-Schmidt, Sandra/Chadwick Milledgevill CUSD 399	67	8
Bayne, Monica/Rockford School District 205	297	254
Baysinger, Stefanie/Princeville Cmty Unit SD 326	2	200
Bazile, Arleta/Posen-Robbins Sch Dist 143-5	274	63
Beach, Kara/Wheeling Cmty Cons Sch Dist 21	71	71
Beale, Deb/Riverdale Cmty Unit SD 100	4	208
Bean, Allison/Argo Cmty High School Dist 217	83	21
Bean, Ron/Speed Seja 802	67	82
Bean, Todd/Rooks Creek Cmty Cons SD 425	1,11,73,83,84	162
Bean, Tom, Dr/Libertyville Pub Sch Dist 70	68	152
Beard, Connor/Medinah Elementary SD 11	76,295	97
Beard, Noel/Jacksonville School Dist 117	67	192
Beardsley, Stacy/Evanston-Skokie Cmty CSD 65	9,15,288	48
Bearidge, Lindsey/Northwestern CUSD 2	4	168
Beasley, Brigette/Bloomington School District 87	67	185
Beauchamp, Renee/Rockford School District 205	4	253
Beaumont, Emily/Rockford School District 205	69	254
Beaupre, Jedd/St Anne Cmty Cons Sch Dist 256	67	136
Beaver, Clay/Willow Grove School Dist 46	67	18
Beaver, Tom/Forest Ridge Sch Dist 142	3	50
Beccue, Ryan/St Elmo Cmty Unit School Dist 202	6	106
Bechelli, Eric/Gavin School District 37	67	150

NAME/District	JOB FUNCTIONS	PAGE
Becherer, April/Columbia Cmty Unit SD 4	5	190
Becich, Julia/Lake Zurich Cmty Sch Dist 95	68	152
Beck, Bobby/Villa Grove Cmty Unit SD 302	9,73,76,79	88
Beck, Greg/Teutopolis Cmty Unit SD 50	83,288	105
Beck, Kurt/West Carroll CUSD 314	3	8
Beck, Michelle/Effingham Cmty Sch Dist 40	8,11,57,83,285,288,296,298	105
Beck, Robert/Streator Twp High Sch Dist 40	16,73,82,84	145
Becker, Jerry/Galva Cmty Unit Sch Dist 224	10,93,273	117
Becker, Lyn/Montgomery-Carlinville Reg SE	15	15
Becker, Melody/J Sterling Morton HSD 201	57	53
Becker, Robin/Germantown Elem Sch Dist 60	1,11,83	18
Becker, Todd/Fenton Cmty High Sch Dist 100	6,35,72	94
Beckham, Tammy/Spring Garden Cmty CSD 178	1,11	124
Beckwith, Bob/Rock Island-Milan Sch Dist 41	2,298	208
Beckwith, Tatia, Dr/Creve Coeur Sch Dist 76	9	226
Beckworth, Eric/East Peoria Elem Sch Dist 86	67	227
Bednar, Jim/Prospect Hts School Dist 23	67	63
Bednara, Brien/Grant Cmty Cons Sch Dist 110	73,295,297	219
Bednara, Brien/Grant Cmty Cons Sch Dist 110	84	219
Beedy, David/Elmhurst Cmty Unit SD 205	285	93
Beemsterboer, Timothy/Ridgeland School District 122	59,79	64
Beerheide, Thomas/Sunset Ridge Sch Dist 29	2	68
Beery, Dave/Maine Twp High Sch Dist 207	71	56
Beetz, Linda/Forrestville Valley CUSD 221	2	194
Beever, Rachel/Eastern Illinois Area of Sp Ed	2	20
Beg, Farheen/Butler School District 53	16,73,76,84,295	89
Beggs, Ted/Cypress School District 64	296	127
Begley, Nick/Deerfield Public SD 109	67	149
Behn, Alison/Winnebago Cmty Unit SD 323	31	255
Behnke, Tonya/Flora Cmty Unit School Dist 35	58	16
Behrens, Dusty/McLean Co Unit District 5	295	186
Behrouzi, Habib/Schaumburg Cmty Cons SD 54	286	66
Beiermann, Jerry/Athens Cmty Unit Sch Dist 213	5	188
Beiermann, Tom/Bethalto Cmty Unit SD 8	67	169
Beiermeister, Ali/La Grange-Highlands SD 106	9	54
Beil, Mary/Highland Cmty Sch District 5	16,82	171
Bein, Dave/Barrington Cmty Unit SD 220	2,15	147
Bein, Lori/Arlington Hts School Dist 25	1	21
Beine, Julie/Millstadt Cmty Cons SD 160	2	220
Belcher, Kurt/Patoka Cmty Unit SD 100	67	175
Belcher, Steve/Plainfield Cons Sch Dist 202	3	246
Belesiotis, Kristie/Round Lake Area Co Dist 116	68	155
Belkaoui, Hedi/Archdiocese of Chicago Ed Off	69	72
Bell, Aaron/Posen-Robbins Sch Dist 143-5	295	63
Bell, Ashlee/Riverton Cmty Unit SD 14	7	212
Bell, Christine/New Trier Twp HS District 203	91	58
Bell, Colette/Schaumburg Cmty Cons SD 54	15,21,24,35,74	66
Bell, Jerry, Dr/Peoria Public Sch Dist 150	10	198
Bell, Joshua/Bureau Valley Cmty Unit 340	73,84	6
Bell, Kevin/Rochelle Cmty Cons SD 231	2	195
Bell, Nathan/Paris Union School District 95	73	103
Bell, Robin/Delavan Cmty Unit Sch Dist 703	34	226
Bell, Tyler/Belvidere Cmty Unit SD 100	76,95,98,295	4
Bellamey, Penny/Joppa-Maple Grove Unit SD 38	31,38	177
Bellaver, Greg/Hillsboro Cmty Unit Sch Dist 3	67	191
Bellm, Debra/High Mount Sch SD 116	83,90	220
Belmont, Becky/Warren Twp High Sch Dist 121	6	155
Belmonte SJ, John/Diocese of Joliet Ed Office	1	249
Belotti, Ellen/Crete-Monee Cmty SD 201-U	58	242
Belrichard, Amy/Crystal Lake Elem Distict 47	7	181
Belt, Marge/Belle Valley School Dist 119	83	217
Beltman, Todd/Leyden Cmty High Sch Dist 212	74,95	55
Benard, Steve/Goreville Cmty Unit SD 1	67	127
Benavides, Jamie/Geneva CUSD 304	79	131
Bendele, Beth/O'Fallon Cmty Cons Sch Dist 90	16	221
Bender, Julie/Waterloo Cmty Unit Sch Dist 5	34,58	190
Bender, Matt/Oak Grove School District 68	67	198

#		#		#		#		#	
1	Superintendent	16	Instructional Media Svcs	30	Adult Education	44	Science Sec	58	Special Education K-12
2	Bus/Finance/Purchasing	17	Chief Operations Officer	31	Career/Sch-to-Work K-12	45	Math K-12	59	Special Education Elem
3	Buildings And Grounds	18	Chief Academic Officer	32	Career/Sch-to-Work Elem	46	Math Elem	60	Special Education Sec
4	Food Service	19	Chief Financial Officer	33	Career/Sch-to-Work Sec	47	Math Sec	61	Foreign/World Lang K-12
5	Transportation	20	Art K-12	34	Early Childhood Ed	48	English/Lang Arts K-12	62	Foreign/World Lang Elem
6	Athletic	21	Art Elem	35	Health/Phys Education	49	English/Lang Arts Elem	63	Foreign/World Lang Sec
7	Health Services	22	Art Sec	36	Guidance Services K-12	50	English/Lang Arts Sec	64	Religious Education K-12
8	Curric/Instruct K-12	23	Music K-12	37	Guidance Services Elem	51	Reading K-12	65	Religious Education Elem
9	Curric/Instruct Elem	24	Music Elem	38	Guidance Services Sec	52	Reading Elem	66	Religious Education Sec
10	Curric/Instruct Sec	25	Music Sec	39	Social Studies K-12	53	Reading Sec	67	School Board President
11	Federal Program	26	Business Education	40	Social Studies Elem	54	Remedial Reading K-12	68	Teacher Personnel
12	Title I	27	Career & Tech Ed	41	Social Studies Sec	55	Remedial Reading Elem	69	Academic Assessment
13	Title V	28	Technology Education	42	Science K-12	56	Remedial Reading Sec	70	Research/Development
15	Asst Superintendent	29	Family/Consumer Science	43	Science Elem	57	Bilingual/ELL	71	Public Information

#		#		#	
72	Summer School	88	Alternative/At Risk	277	Remedial Math K-12
73	Instructional Tech	89	Multi-Cultural Curriculum	280	Literacy Coach
74	Inservice Training	90	Social Work	285	STEM
75	Marketing/Distributive	91	Safety/Security	286	Digital Learning
76	Info Systems	92	Magnet School	288	Common Core Standards
77	Psychological Assess	93	Parental Involvement	294	Accountability
78	Affirmative Action	97	Tech Prep Program	295	Network System
79	Student Personnel	96	Chief Information Officer	296	Title II Programs
80	Driver Ed/Safety	98	Chief Technology Officer	297	Webmaster
81	Gifted/Talented	270	Character Education	298	Grant Writer/Ptnrships
82	Video Services	271	Migrant Education	750	Chief Innovation Officer
83	Substance Abuse Prev	273	Teacher Mentor	751	Chief of Staff
84	Before/After Sch	274	Before/After Sch	752	Social Emotional Learning
85	AIDS Education	275	Response To Intervention		

Illinois School Directory — DISTRICT PERSONNEL INDEX

NAME/District	JOB FUNCTIONS	PAGE
Bendetti, John/Community Cons School Dist 93	2,15	90
Bendixon, Paulett/Regional Office of Ed 47	73,76,295	241
Benes, Caitlin/Hiawatha Cmty Unit SD 426	57	85
Benes, Craig/Itasca School District 10	1,11	96
Benesiel, Joshua/Dieterich Community Unit SD 30	9,11,58,88,288,296	104
Benetazzo, Paul/Naperville Cmty Unit SD 203	3	98
Benford, Alyssia/Steward Elem School Dist 220	2	160
Beniaris, Margarite/Des Plaines Cmty Cons SD 62	34,79,274	45
Benjamin, Rhonda/Sandoval Cmty Unit SD 501	275	175
Benjamin, Vicky/Centralia High School Dist 200	16	174
Bennet, Terry/Reed-Custer Cmty Unit SD 255-U	3	246
Bennett, Brad/Robein Cmty School District 85	1,11,83	228
Bennett, Carol/Fremont School District 79	9,11	149
Bennett, Greg/Lewistown Community Unit SD 97	6	110
Bennett, Heather/Round Lake Area Co Dist 116	71	155
Bennett, Jason/Warren Community Unit SD 205	73,286,295	126
Bennett, Lee/Centralia High School Dist 200	6	174
Bennett, Micah/Newark Cmty Cons Sch Dist 66	83	138
Bennett, Scott/Bradley-Bourbonnais CHSD 307	76	134
Bennin, Jill/Sherrard Cmty Sch Dist 200	16	189
Benning, Karie/Streator Elem School Dist 44	88	144
Benoist, Diana/Community High School Dist 99	83	91
Benson, Heather/Lena-Winslow Cmty Unit SD 202	16	224
Benson, Nakia/Rantoul City School Dist 137	73,76,84	11
Bent, Chad/Lewistown Community Unit SD 97	73,76	110
Bentley, Chad/Limestone Walters CCSD 316	6,83,85	198
Bentlinger, Angie/Sangamon-Menard Roe #51	2	215
Benton, Kathy/Tri-City Cmty Unit Sch Dist 1	280	214
Bentsen, Sammuel/Fenton Cmty High Sch Dist 100	3,15,68	94
Benway, Darcy, Dr/O'Fallon Twp School Dist 203	1	221
Benz, Joann/Athens Cmty Unit Sch Dist 213	69,78,270	188
Beranek, Scott/E F Lindop Elem Sch Dist 92	4,294	47
Berardi, Luisa/Maywood-Melrose Brdview SD 89	71	57
Berentes, Mike/Rock Falls Twp High SD 301	11,69,83,273,298	240
Berg, Benda/Carbondale Cmty HSD 165	277	120
Berg, Beth/Elgin School District U-46	68	130
Berg, Cynthia/Bloom Twp High Sch Dist 206	7	23
Berg, David/Hononegah Cmty High SD 207	3	253
Berg, Mark/Midwest Ctl Cmty Unit SD 191	67	177
Berger, Mary/Northbrook School District 28	274	59
Berger, Shari/Jasper Cmty Cons Sch Dist 17	1,11,73,83	237
Bergeson, Erin/Rochelle Twp High Sch Dist 212	60	195
Bergin, Christine/Forrestville Valley CUSD 221	79	194
Bergman, Linda/Ludlow Cons Cmty Sch Dist 142	84	11
Bergmann, Jeff/Oak Park & River Forest SD 200	3	60
Bergmann, Jeff/Oakdale Cmty Cons Sch Dist 1	67	236
Bergogna, Diane/LaSalle Peru Twp HSD 120	2	142
Bergren, Colleen/Lyons Elem School Dist 103	79	56
Bergren, Laurel/Community Unit School Dist 303	88	128
Bergstrom, David/Channahon School District 17	73,295	241
Bergstrom, Linda/Union Ridge School Dist 86	273	70
Bergthold, Brian/Thornton Fractnl Twp HSD 215	79	69
Bergthold, Dana/Community Cons School Dist 181	11,59,79	91
Berjer, Aline/Edwards Co Cmty Unit SD 1	5	104
Berkson, Thomas/Skokie School District 73 1/2	4	67
Berlinski, Andy/Princeton Twp HSD 500	10,11,69,74	7
Bermillion, Phil/Belvidere Cmty Unit SD 100	25	4
Bernard, Elizabeth/Opdyke-Belle Rive Cmty CSSD 5	2	123
Bernardi, Mykin/Fieldcrest Cmty School Dist 6	67	257
Bernero, Michelle/Forest Park School District 91	7	50
Berogan, Bryan/Rock Falls Twp High SD 301	3	240
Berogan, Lori/Rock Falls Twp High SD 301	2	240
Berogan, Sue/Harlem Unit Sch District 122	67	252
Berry Coleman, Latoya/Collinsville Cmty Sch Dist 10	8,11,288,296,298	170
Berry, Brett/North Greene Unit Dist 3	6	111
Berry, Mark/O'Fallon Cmty Cons Sch Dist 90	91	221
Berry, Mark/O'Fallon Cmty Cons Sch Dist 90	91	221
Berry, Nicole/Rock Island-Milan Sch Dist 41	34	208
Berry, Ryan/Skokie School District 68	2,15,19	67
Berry, Sean/Tremont Unit SD 702	10	228
Bersani, Anthony/Valley View Cmty SD 365-U	3	248
Berta, Brian/Dwight Twp High Sch Dist 230	3	161
Bertels, Jill/Edwardsville Cmty Unit SD 7	67	170
Berthoux, Mary Lynn/Sesser-Valier Cmty Unit SD 196	58	108
Bertnagolli, Mike/Community Unit School Dist 7	6	167
Bertolozzi, Mark/Des Plaines Cmty Cons SD 62	2,4,15	45
Bertram, Eric/Crete-Monee Cmty SD 201-U	27,73,74,76,295	242
Bertram, Eric/St Anne Cmty HSD 302	73	136
Bertsche, Joanne/Evanston Twp High SD 202	298	48
Besgrove, Joni/Prairie Central Cmty USD 8	4	162
Besler, Paula/Maine Twp High Sch Dist 207	67	56
Beswick, Eryn/Adams Co Special Ed Co-op	58	3
Beswick, Eryn/Quincy School District 172	58	2
Betley, Marian/Cmty Cons Sch Dist 146	7	42
Betthauser, Tricia/Adlai E Stevenson HSD 125	6	146
Bettis, Brian/Scott Morgan Cmty Unit SD 2	6	215
Bettis, Kevin/Porta Cmty Unit Sch Dist 202	67	189
Bettis, Vern/Cmty Cons Sch Dist 146	28,73,76,286	42
Betts, Diane, Dr/North Cook Interm Svc Center	15	82
Betz, Emily, Dr/E F Lindop Elem Sch Dist 92	9,285	47
Betz, Erison, Dr/E F Lindop Elem Sch Dist 92	69,79,280	47
Betz, Rosemary/Beach Park Cmty Cons SD 3	12,16,57,59	147
Beu, Josh/Elgin School District U-46	3	130
Bevans, Troy/Rock Island-Milan Sch Dist 41	16,73,76,82,295	208
Beverlin, Karen/Peoria Co Special Ed Assoc	2	200
Beyers, Brad/Prairie Central Cmty USD 8	6	162
Beyers, Brian/Oak Park & River Forest SD 200	275	60
Beyers, Wilfred, Dr/Pana Cmty Unit School Dist 8	67	14
Bhardwaj, Mary/Aptakisic-Tripp Sch Dist 102	79	146
Bhatia, Karan/Elgin School District U-46	2	130
Bialk, R/Lincolnshre-Prairieview SD 103	69,73,84,295,297	153
Bialk, Robert/Elmhurst Cmty Unit SD 205	73,76,295	93
Bialobok, Jennifer/Lyons Twp HS District 204	71	56
Bianco, Kathy/Wauconda Cmty Unit SD 118	67	155
Bible, Laurie/Zion-Benton Twp High SD 126	6	157
Bickel, Chris/Leland Cmty Unit Sch Dist 1	9,83,288	142
Bickerman, Wylee/Midland Cmty Unit Sch Dist 7	12,296	176
Bickle, Alyx/Indian Creek Cmty Unit SD 425	36	85
Bicknell, Diane/New Holland Middletown ESD 88	12	164
Bien-Aime, Rodney/Union Ridge School Dist 86	73,84	70
Bierman, Jessica/Teutopolis Cmty Unit SD 50	88	105
Bierman, Paul/Tolono Cmty Unit Sch Dist 7	84,295	12
Biggerstaff, John/Hamilton Co Cmty Unit SD 10	3	114
Biggs, Corie/Palestine Cmty Unit SD 3	67	83
Biggs, Don/Carbondale Cmty HSD 165	3	120
Biggs, Kelley/Edwards Co Cmty Unit SD 1	36,69	104
Bilecki, Frank/Chicago Public School Dist 299	93	25
Billesbach, Kelli/Belvidere Cmty Unit SD 100	7	4
Billhartz, Marcia/Pontiac-Wm Holliday SD 105	12	221
Billingsley, Michelle/Wood River-Hartford Elem SD 15	2,11,68	172
Bima, Bob/Princeton Elem Sch Dist 115	12	7
Binder, Zack/Williamsfield Cmty Unit SD 210	36,69,79	140
Binegar, Stacey/Athens Cmty Unit Sch Dist 213	8,288	188
Birch, Angela/Marissa Cmty Unit Sch Dist 40	69	220
Birch, Michael/Illinois Vly Ctl Sch Dist 321	67	197
Birdsong, Jonathan/Diocese of Belleville Ed Off	1	222
Birkmeier, Shayne/Central Cmty Unit SD 301	9,69	128
Bishop, Janel/Oak Park & River Forest SD 200	35,80,83,85	60
Bishop, Janet/East Maine School District 63	71	47
Bishop, Kathy/Grayville Cmty Unit Sch Dist 1	34	238
Bittner, Marilyn/Bloom Twp High Sch Dist 206	27	23
Bivens, Dana/Vandalia Cmty Unit SD 203	58	106
Bivin, Jeff/Lake Zurich Cmty Unit Sch Dist 95	69	152
Bjorklund, Dawn/Plainfield Cons Sch Dist 202	2	246
Black, Cindy/Harrisburg Cmty Unit SD 3	11,84	210
Black, David/Norwood Sch Dist 63	1,73	198
Black, Debora/Dimmick Cmty School Dist 175	67	141
Black, Eric/Dwight Twp High Sch Dist 230	80	161
Black, Nicole/Beecher Cmty Sch Dist 200-U	9,69,270	241
Blackard, Tricia/Collinsville Cmty Sch Dist 10	27,72,75,95	170
Blackard, Tricia, Dr/Regional Office of Ed 41	15,88	174
Blackburn, David/Dixon Cmty Unit Sch Dist 170	2,5,91	160
Blackburn, Martha/O'Fallon Twp School Dist 203	60,274	221
Blackman, David/Manhattan School Dist 114	3	244
Blade, Janet/Cumberland Cmty Unit SD 77	57	84
Blade, Robert/Cumberland Cmty Unit SD 77	67	84
Blades, Brad/Wabash-Ohio Valley Sp Ed Dist	2,15	238
Blades, Michael/Zion-Benton Twp High SD 126	50,53,56	157
Blair, Brian/Pontiac Twp High Sch Dist 90	48	161
Blair, Daftan/New Trier Twp HS District 203	3	58
Blake, Antwan/Winfield School District 34	3	100
Blake, Janice/Cairo School District 1	2,19	3

DISTRICT PERSONNEL INDEX

Market Data Retrieval

NAME/District	JOB FUNCTIONS	PAGE
Blake, Jason/Community High School Dist 155	67	179
Blake, Jill/Polo Cmty Unit Sch Dist 222	16	195
Blake, Sinead/Argo Cmty High School Dist 217	15	21
Blakey, Debra/Benton Cmty Cons Sch Dist 47	9	107
Bland, Chris/Leland Cmty Unit Sch Dist 1	73,76	142
Bland, Michael/Bradley Elem School Dist 61	73,295,297	134
Blaney, Jim/Valley View Cmty SD 365-U	71,93	248
Blank, Travis/Palestine Cmty Unit SD 3	6	83
Blankenbaker, Jason/Oblong Cmty Unit Sch Dist 4	6	83
Blankenheim, Ed/West Northfield Sch Dist 31	3	70
Blankenship, Ed/Pope Co Cmty Unit Sch Dist 1	58	204
Blankenship, Jason/Southwestern Cmty Unit SD 9	73,295	168
Blankenship, Julie/Belleville Township HSD 201	7,77	217
Blankenship, Kevin/Scott Morgan Cmty Unit SD 2	1,11,288	215
Blankenship, Kevin/Winchester Cmty Unit SD 1	1,83	215
Blasdell, Ginger/Prophetstown-Lyndon-Tampico 3	5	239
Blatchley, Dave/Will Co School District 92	2,15	248
Blatchley, David/Community High School Dist 94	3	91
Blatt, Christa/New Lenox School District 122	59	245
Blechle, Jeremy/Chester Cmty Unit Sch Dist 139	6	205
Blessman, Joseph/Orion Cmty Unit Sch Dist 223	1,11	117
Bleyer, Chuck/Wabash Cmty Unit Sch Dist 348	1	234
Blickem, Cassie/Valley Ed for Employment Sys	1	134
Blickensdefer, Steve/Mt Zion Cmty Unit Sch Dist 3	3	166
Blissett, Sheleah/Country Club Hills SD 160	59,79,275	45
Blockinger, James, Dr/Gurnee School District 56	67	150
Bloemker, Don/Brownstown Cmty Unit SD 201	67	105
Bloemker, Glen/Sandwich Cmty Unit SD 430	73,76,295	86
Bloodworth, Nathan/Calhoun Cmty Unit Sch Dist 40	73	8
Bloomquist, Scott/Boone-Winnebago Reg Off of Ed	15	256
Bloyd-Hamm, Jennifer/Galesburg Cmty Unit SD 205	2,3,15	140
Blue, Jim/Paris Cmty Unit Sch Dist 4	67	103
Blumberg, Scott/Oak Grove School District 68	73,84	154
Bobek, Christopher/Woodland School District 50	15	156
Bocka, Barbara/Elmwood Park Cmty Unit SD 401	88	48
Bockhorn, Tricia/Monroe-Randolph Reg Off	2	190
Bockwoldt, Keith/Hinsdale Twp High Sch Dist 86	73,76,84,97,98,295	95
Boehne, Vaughn/Indian Creek Cmty Unit SD 425	67	85
Boehrnsen, Helen/St George School District 258	1	136
Boen, Pam/Potomac Cmty Unit Sch Dist 10	2	232
Boente, Jon/Belleville Public Sch Dist 118	2,3,5	217
Boeschen, Becky/Central Cmty High Sch Dist 71	2	17
Boever, Tracie/Grant Cmty Cons Sch Dist 110	83,270	219
Boewey, Brad/Centralia High School Dist 200	6	174
Bogart, Colleen/Minooka Cmty Cons Sch Dist 201	2	112
Bogart, Josh/Vandalia Cmty Unit SD 203	3	106
Bogert, Doug/East Alton Elementary SD 13	5	170
Bohm, Eric/Pontiac Twp High Sch Dist 90	10,12,13,88,273,288,296	161
Bohnenstiehl, Gail/Crete-Monee Cmty SD 201-U	49	242
Bohnenstiehl, Kelly/Signal Hill Sch Dist 181	1,11	221
Bohnenstiehl, Kelly/Wood River-Hartford Elem SD 15	9	172
Bohnsack, Anne/Rockridge Cmty Unit SD 300	38,83	209
Bohula, Chris/Orland School District 135	84	61
Boies, Josh/West 40 Interm Serv Center 2	73,76	82
Boike, Ryan, Dr/Belleville Public Sch Dist 118	1	217
Boland, Michele/Princeville Cmty Unit SD 326	5	200
Bolden, Brandy/Maywood-Melrose Brdview SD 89	280	57
Bolek, Greg/Will Co School District 92	73	249
Bolhous, Jayce/Community Unit School Dist 300	73,84	180
Bolin, Diane/Casey-Westfield Cmty USD C-4	83,93	15
Boll, Bonnie/Township High School Dist 214	2	69
Bolliger, Sonja/Tremont Cmty Unit SD 702	4	228
Bollow, Lisa/Community High School Dist 99	60	91
Bolton, Arlethea/Harvey Public Sch Dist 152	30	51
Boltz, Kim/Prairie Grove Cons SD 46	5	183
Bond, Ann, Dr/Peoria Public Sch Dist 150	58	198
Bonds, Andrea/Rich Twp High School Dist 227	67	64
Bonds, Jason/Fremont School District 79	67	149
Bone, Larry/Belvidere Cmty Unit SD 100	3,91	4
Bonham, Michelle/Queen Bee School District 16	9,59,88	98
Bonie, K/Richland School Dist 88A	59	247
Bonner, Colly/Illini Central CUSD 189	298	177
Bonnet, Scott/South Beloit Cmty Sch Dist 320	67	255
Bonnette, Tim/Pekin Cmty High Sch Dist 303	3	227
Bono, Shannon/River Grove School Dist 85-5	12	65
Bonomo, Jeff/Rich Twp High School Dist 227	10,69,76	64
Bontkowski, Holly/Naperville Cmty Unit SD 203	8	98
Bonuchi, Margie/Plainfield Cons Sch Dist 202	73,76,84	246
Bonuma, Tatiana, Dr/Leyden Cmty High Sch Dist 212	15	55
Boone, DeMario/Peoria Public Sch Dist 150	91	198
Boone, DeMario/Peoria Public Sch Dist 150	91	198
Boore, Melissa, Dr/Lyons Twp HS District 204	60	56
Booth, Daniel/Carbondale Elem School Dist 95	1	120
Booth, Derrick/Peoria Public Sch Dist 150	752	198
Booth, Jim/East Peoria Cmty HS Dist 309	3	226
Boozer, Shila/Springfield Pub Sch Dist 186	8,15,288	213
Boraz, Michael/Chicago PSD-Network 15	15	37
Borchert, Jim/Community Cons School Dist 180	3	90
Bordsen, Donna/Community Unit School Dist 300	5	180
Boreman, Randy/Geneseo Cmty Unit Sch Dist 228	3	117
Boren, Brent/Lick Creek School Dist 16	1,11,73,83	230
Borio, Dan/Woodland Cmty Unit Sch Dist 5	73	162
Borley, Deb/East Dubuque Unit SD 119	7	125
Bornhoeft, Liz/Hampton School District 29	67	207
Borries, Brandi/Diocese of Springfield Ed Off	1	214
Boryszewski, Kimberly, Dr/Schiller Park School Dist 81	1	67
Boscolo, Amy/Highland Cmty Sch District 5	6	171
Bosgraas, Robert/Shelbyville Cmty Sch Dist 4	67	216
Bosnich, Mellisa/Peru Elem Sch Dist 124	16,73,285	143
Bosonetta, Dan/Elwood Cmty Cons SD 203	3	242
Boss, Nichole/Monticello Cmty Unit SD 25	2	202
Boss, Rick/Central School District 3	5	1
Boston, Mitch/Williamsville Cmty Unit SD 15	73,295	214
Boswell, Jim/Bremen Cmty High SD 228	16,71,73,95,97,98	23
Boswell, Patrice/Evergreen Park Elem SD 124	274	49
Botensten, Dawn/Kankakee School District 111	4	135
Bothwell, Laura/Winfield School District 34	16,82,83,270	100
Botterbush, Karen/Alton Cmty School District 11	60	169
Botts, Rebecca/Richmond-Burton Cmty HSD 157	27	184
Boucher, Alan/Sherrard Cmty Sch Dist 200	1	189
Boudouris, JR/Rochester Cmty Unit SD 3-A	6	212
Boudreau, Jeff/Iroquois-Kankakee Reg Off Ed	73	137
Bouillon, Natalie/Wood River-Hartford Elem SD 15	69,273,275	172
Bounds, Lisa/Prairie Central Cmty USD 8	58	162
Bournes, Stephen, Dr/Rich Twp High School Dist 227	10,11,15,83,288,296	64
Bouslog, Steve/Princeton Elem Sch Dist 115	67	7
Bova, Jennifer/Des Plaines Cmty Cons SD 62	71	45
Bowcott, Diana/Norwood Sch Dist 63	4	198
Bowen, Beth/Wayne City Cmty Unit SD 100	58	237
Bowen, Jori/Community High School Dist 117	33,74	148
Bowen, Sarah/Adlai E Stevenson HSD 125	79	146
Bowen, Shaunita/Evergreen Park Cmty HSD 231	83,88	49
Bower, Mark/Harmony-Emge School Dist 175	6	219
Bowers, Anne, Dr/Woodridge Elem Sch District 68	90	100
Bowgren, Amber/Harvard Cmty Unit Sch Dist 50	57	181
Bowman, Christy/Des Plaines Cmty Cons SD 62	29,43,46	45
Bowman, Heather/Washington School Dist 52	9	229
Bowman, Jason/East Peoria Cmty HS Dist 309	6	226
Bowman, Jeff/Pecatonica Cmty Unit SD 321	73	253
Bowman, Joann/Ohio Cmty Cons School Dist 17	16	7
Bowman, Kasie/Mulberry Grove Cmty Sch Dist 1	2,16,296	4
Bowman, Kevin/Greenfield Cmty Unit SD 10	1	111
Bowman, Kevin/Northwestern CUSD 2	1,11	168
Bowman, Margie/Pope Co Cmty Unit Sch Dist 1	2	204

1 Superintendent	16 Instructional Media Svcs	30 Adult Education	44 Science Sec	58 Special Education K-12
2 Bus/Finance/Purchasing	17 Chief Operations Officer	31 Career/Sch-to-Work K-12	45 Math K-12	59 Special Education Elem
3 Buildings And Grounds	18 Chief Academic Officer	32 Career/Sch-to-Work Elem	46 Math Elem	60 Special Education Sec
4 Food Service	19 Chief Financial Officer	33 Career/Sch-to-Work Sec	47 Math Sec	61 Foreign/World Lang K-12
5 Transportation	20 Art K-12	34 Early Childhood Ed	48 English/Lang Arts K-12	62 Foreign/World Lang Elem
6 Athletic	21 Art Elem	35 Health/Phys Education	49 English/Lang Arts Elem	63 Foreign/World Lang Sec
7 Health Services	22 Art Sec	36 Guidance Services K-12	50 English/Lang Arts Sec	64 Religious Education K-12
8 Curric/Instruct K-12	23 Music K-12	37 Guidance Services Elem	51 Reading K-12	65 Religious Education Elem
9 Curric/Instruct Elem	24 Music Elem	38 Guidance Services Sec	52 Reading Elem	66 Religious Education Sec
10 Curric/Instruct Sec	25 Music Sec	39 Social Studies K-12	53 Reading Sec	67 School Board President
11 Federal Program	26 Business Education	40 Social Studies Elem	54 Remedial Reading K-12	68 Teacher Personnel
12 Title I	27 Career & Tech Ed	41 Social Studies Sec	55 Remedial Reading Elem	69 Academic Assessment
13 Title V	28 Technology Education	42 Science K-12	56 Remedial Reading Sec	70 Research/Development
15 Asst Superintendent	29 Family/Consumer Science	43 Science Elem	57 Bilingual/ELL	71 Public Information

72 Summer School	88 Alternative/At Risk	277 Remedial Math K-12
73 Instructional Tech	89 Multi-Cultural Curriculum	280 Literacy Coach
74 Inservice Training	90 Social Work	285 STEM
75 Marketing/Distributive	91 Safety/Security	286 Digital Learning
76 Info Systems	92 Magnet School	288 Common Core Standards
77 Psychological Assess	93 Parental Involvement	294 Accountability
78 Affirmative Action	95 Tech Prep Program	295 Network System
79 Student Personnel	97 Chief Information Officer	296 Title II Programs
80 Driver Ed/Safety	98 Chief Technology Officer	297 Webmaster
81 Gifted/Talented	270 Character Education	298 Grant Writer/Ptnrships
82 Video Services	271 Migrant Education	750 Chief Innovation Officer
83 Substance Abuse Prev	273 Teacher Mentor	751 Chief of Staff
84 Erate	274 Before/After Sch	752 Social Emotional Learning
85 AIDS Education	275 Response To Intervention	

Illinois School Directory

DISTRICT PERSONNEL INDEX

NAME/District	JOB FUNCTIONS	PAGE
Bowser, Robert/Allendale Cmty Cons SD 17	1,11,83,288	234
Boyce, Ryan/Plainfield Cons Sch Dist 202	297	246
Boyd, Marty/Oregon Cmty Unit Sch Dist 220	4	195
Boyer, Greg/Reed-Custer Cmty Unit SD 255-U	67	246
Boyer, Lori/Pearl City Cmty Unit SD 200	4	225
Boyer, Stephanie/Granite City Cmty Unit SD 9	58	171
Boylan, David/Mendota Twp High Sch Dist 280	77	143
Boyles, Liz/Troy Cmty Cons SD 30-C	76	247
Boyum, Lesley/Community Unit School Dist 200	295	91
Bozarth, Justin/Tuscola Cmty Unit SD 301	38,69	88
Brackett, Will/Oak Park Elem School Dist 97	295	61
Braden, Annette/Norris City-Omaha-Enfield SD 3	69	238
Bradford, Michael/Carterville Cmty Unit SD 5	5	250
Bradford, Mindy/Yorkville Cmty Unit SD 115	2,3,17	139
Bradley, Ankhe/Joliet Public School Dist 86	9,15,69,273,296	243
Bradley, Michelle/Eldorado Cmty Unit Sch Dist 4	2	210
Bradley, Vanessa/South Holland School Dist 151	71	68
Bradt, Carissa/Northwest Special Ed District	2	126
Brady, Jennifer/Community High School Dist 94	16	91
Bragg, Shirley/Lansing School Dist 158	11,69,83,88,288,294,298	54
Bramer, Judith/Community Cons School Dist 15	5	43
Bramley, Scott/Evanston Twp High SD 202	280	48
Bramley, Tom/Community Cons School Dist 15	5	43
Brammeier, Gene/West Washington Co Cmty SD 10	3	236
Brandt, Jesse/Hall Twp High School Dist 502	1,11,83	6
Brandt, Kailey/Braceville Elem School Dist 75	57,88,271,294	111
Brandt, Leticia/Cicero School District 99	69,76	42
Brandt, Sarah/St Libory Cons Sch District 30	67	222
Brannock, Chuck/Heyworth Cmty Sch District 4	67	185
Branon, Tim/Central City School Dist 133	1	174
Brant, Kathy/Schiller Park School Dist 81	9,11,71,298	67
Braun, Jan/Lewistown Community Unit SD 97	8,11,57,58,69,88	110
Braun, Nancy/McLean Co Unit District 5	58	186
Bravo, Milagros/Des Plaines Cmty Cons SD 62	57,89,271	45
Bray, Susan/La Harpe Cmty Sch Dist 347	12	115
Breakfield, Emily/Prairie Hill Cmty Cons SD 133	286	253
Breckel, Vicki/Cahokia Unit Sch Dist 187	58,77,275	218
Breen, Linda/Community Unit School Dist 300	34	180
Brehm, Kimberly/Lockport Twp High Sch Dist 205	71	244
Brehm, Mike/Ludlow Cons Cmty Sch Dist 142	73	11
Breiby, Becky/Sherrard Cmty Sch Dist 200	5	189
Breiler, Amy/Wheeling Cmty Cons Sch Dist 21	24,49	71
Breitbarth, Tyler/Eureka Cmty Unit Sch Dist 140	73	257
Breitenbucher, Karla/Bradley-Bourbonnais CHSD 307	26,75	134
Breitsprecker, Lisa/Galena Unit School Dist 120	270	125
Brem, Debbie/Harmony-Emge School Dist 175	4	219
Bremmer, Chad/Pearl City Cmty Unit SD 200	67	225
Brenczewski, Hallie/Professional Dev Alliance	1	250
Brendel, Jerry/Cooperative Assn for Spec Ed	2	102
Brennan, Jennifer/Williamsville Cmty Unit SD 15	2,68	214
Brennan, Marina/Homewood Flossmoor CHSD 233	275	52
Brenner, Jennifer/Winnebago Cmty Unit SD 323	36	255
Brenner, Sarah/Belvidere Cmty Unit SD 100	285	4
Bresnahan, Terri/Berkeley School Dist 87	1	22
Bressers, Sandy/Plainfield Cons Sch Dist 202	5	246
Bretag, Ryan/Glenbrook High Sch Dist 225	10,70	50
Brewer, Bruce/Windsor Cmty Unit SD 1	16	216
Brewer, Micheal/Wabash Cmty Unit Sch Dist 348	8,11,271,288	234
Brewer, William/Ball Chatham Cmty Unit SD 5	67	211
Brickman, Jay/Hinckley-Big Rock Cmty SD 429	8,73	85
Bridge, Robert/Cary Cmty Cons Sch Dist 26	67	179
Bridges, Dan/Naperville Cmty Unit SD 203	1	98
Bridges, Maura/Harvard Cmty Unit Sch Dist 50	27	181
Brifcani, Angelica/Community Cons School Dist 15	57	43
Briggs, Denise/Roxana Cmty Unit Sch Dist 1	35	172
Briggs, Keith/Community Cons School Dist 93	67	90
Briggs, Kim/North Clay Cmty Unit SD 25	58	16
Briggs, Mark/Roxana Cmty Unit Sch Dist 1	6	172
Bright, Ella/Erie Cmty School District 1	4	239
Bright, Lenora/Oak Grove School District 68	275	198
Brilowski, Nick/Fremont School District 79	71	149
Brimner, Cathy/Arcola Cmty Unit Sch Dist 306	58	87
Brink, Amy/Centralia High School Dist 200	7	174
Brink, Brian/Tamaroa Elem School Dist 5	1	201
Brink, Danielle/Dupage High School Dist 88	71	93
Brink, Melanie, Dr/Waltonville Cmty Unit SD 1	1	124

NAME/District	JOB FUNCTIONS	PAGE
Brink, Michael/Nashville Cmty Cons SD 49	1,11,73,288	235
Briseno, Jeanette/Berwyn South School Dist 100	57	23
Brittin, Brad/Streator Twp High Sch Dist 40	69,83	145
Britton, James/Township High School Dist 211	68	69
Broadrick, Pam/Tri-Valley Cmty School Dist 3	275	187
Brockmeyer, Donna/Grant Cmty Cons Sch Dist 110	16	219
Brockway, Carrie/Pecatonica Cmty Unit SD 321	11,296	253
Brodback, Amanda/Brussels Cmty Unit Sch Dist 42	67	8
Brodie, Blake/Fenton Cmty High Sch Dist 100	3,5	94
Broehm, Britt/Cowden Herrick CUSD 3A	288	216
Broncato, Patrick, Dr/Woodridge Elem Sch District 68	1	100
Brook, Alexandra/East Maine School District 63	67	47
Brookman, Lamanda/Mt Vernon Twp HS District 201	57,83,275,286,294	123
Brooks, Andrew/Delavan Cmty Unit Sch Dist 703	1,84	226
Brooks, Annie, Dr/Illinois Dept of Education	11	1
Brooks, Anthony/Abingdon-Avon Cmty Unit SD 276	67	139
Brooks, Anthony/Crystal Lake Elem Distict 47	59	181
Brooks, Brian/St Joseph-Ogden Cmty HSD 305	1,11	12
Brooks, Carol/Career Development System	1	82
Brooks, Carol/Illinois Dept of Education	26,31,75	1
Brooks, Hollie/Flora Cmty Unit School Dist 35	2	16
Brooks, Jeff/Chester-E Lincoln Cmty SD 61	67	163
Brooks, Kathy/Macomb Cmty Unit Sch Dist 185	4	178
Brooks, May/Illini Central CUSD 189	67	177
Brooks, Pam/Gardner S Wilmington HSD 73	67	112
Brooks, Robin/Selmaville Cmty Cons SD 10	1,11,73,83	176
Brophy, Edward/Forest Park School District 91	3,15,69	50
Broshous, Douglas/Stockton Cmty Unit SD 206	5	126
Brosseau, Heath/Indian Springs Sch Dist 109	37,59,77,85,90,275,294	53
Brosseau, Michelle/Bourbonnais Elem Sch Dist 53	52	134
Brothers, Janet/Kenilworth School District 38	85	53
Brown, Adny/Western Springs Sch Dist 101	3	71
Brown, Andrew/Bement Cmty Unit Sch Dist 5	73	202
Brown, Anita/Taylorville Cmty Unit SD 3	8,11,296	15
Brown, Bruce, Dr/North Cook Interm Svc Center	1	82
Brown, Christine/Woodland Cmty Unit Sch Dist 5	88	162
Brown, Craig, Dr/Plainfield Cons Sch Dist 202	68	246
Brown, David/General George S Patton SD 133	12,15,298	50
Brown, Dayna/McLean Co Unit District 5	71	186
Brown, Demetria/Elementary School District 159	2	47
Brown, Diana/School Dist 45 Dupage Co	79	99
Brown, Doug/Riverton Cmty Unit SD 14	3	212
Brown, Emily/Hoopeston Area Cmty Unit SD 11	8,275,288	232
Brown, Greg/Belvidere Cmty Unit SD 100	2,3,17	4
Brown, Greg/Jersey Cmty Sch Dist 100	67	125
Brown, Gwyn/East Coloma-Nelson Cesd 20	7	238
Brown, Ina/Mt Zion Cmty Unit Sch Dist 3	297	166
Brown, Jacci/Valley View Cmty SD 365-U	34	248
Brown, Jessica/Urbana School District 116	68,74	12
Brown, Jill/Milford Area Public SD 124	37	119
Brown, Jonathan/Crab Orchard Cmty Sch Dist 3	69	251
Brown, Julie, Dr/Pontiac-Wm Holliday SD 105	1,11	221
Brown, Kristen/Charleston Cmty Unit SD 1	58	19
Brown, Lisa/Murphysboro Cmty Unit SD 186	34	121
Brown, Mary/Fairview South School Dist 72	67	49
Brown, Mary Ann/Crystal Lake Elem Distict 47	2	181
Brown, Matt/Community Unit School Dist 16	3	211
Brown, Melanie/Naperville Cmty Unit SD 203	2,79	98
Brown, Melissa/Alwood Cmty Unit Sch Dist 225	67	116
Brown, Melissa/Illini Bluffs Cmty Unit SD 327	2	197
Brown, Michelle/Jersey Cmty Sch Dist 100	12,298	125
Brown, Michelle/Unity Point Cmty Cons SD 140	2	121
Brown, Paula/General George S Patton SD 133	69	50
Brown, Pete/Havana Cmty Sch District 126	3	177
Brown, Renee/Arthur CUSD 305	16,82	87
Brown, Robert/Evanston Twp High SD 202	12,17	48
Brown, Tammy/Kewanee Cmty Unit Sch Dist 229	57,271	117
Brown, Terry/Athens Cmty Unit Sch Dist 213	3	188
Brown, Virginia/North Shore School Dist 112	2	154
Brown, Zorina/East St Louis Sch Dist 189	93	218
Browne, Dana/Lemont High Sch Dist 210	38	55
Browning, Jill/Community High School Dist 99	71,297	91
Brownlee, Tina/Wilmington Cmty Unit SD 209-U	4	249
Brownlow, Merryl, Dr/Palos Heights School Dist 128	1	61
Broy, Keecia/Oak Park Elem School Dist 97	67	60
Brozovich, Mike/Minooka Cmty High Sch Dist 111	67	244

School Year 2020-2021   800-333-8802   IL-T7

DISTRICT PERSONNEL INDEX

Market Data Retrieval

NAME/District	JOB FUNCTIONS	PAGE
Brua, Julie, Dr/Gavin School District 37	1	150
Bruch, Joyce/Mt Olive Cmty Unit Sch Dist 5	2	167
Bruch, Thomas/Peoria Public Sch Dist 150	71,295	198
Bruckmann, Colleen, Dr/Diocese of Joliet Ed Office	8,15,69,74,273	249
Brue, Matt/Porta Cmty Unit Sch Dist 202	1,11	189
Brueggemann, Keith/Alton Cmty School District 11	4	169
Bruemmer, Sharon/Milne-Kelvin Grove District 91	16	244
Bruesch, John/Barrington Cmty Unit SD 220	8,15	147
Bruley, Brandi/New Holland Middletown ESD 88	1,11	164
Brumback, Jennifer/East St Louis Sch Dist 189	10,18	218
Brumball, Adam, Dr/Geneseo Cmty Unit Sch Dist 228	1,11	117
Brunelle, Roger/Naperville Cmty Unit SD 203	71,97	98
Bruner, Susan/DePue Unit Sch Dist 103	8	6
Bruni, Liza/New Lenox School District 122	15,59,79,88,271,280,285	245
Brunner, Gary/Pontiac Twp High Sch Dist 90	6	161
Brunner, Valerie/Mt Zion Cmty Unit Sch Dist 3	16	166
Brunnworth, David/Mt Olive Cmty Unit Sch Dist 5	67	168
Bruno, David/Berwyn South School Dist 100	68,69,79,88,275,294,752	23
Bruno, Robert/Glen Ellyn School District 41	67	94
Bruns, James/Iroquois Co Cmty Unit SD 9	67	119
Brusak, David/Maywood-Melrose Brdview SD 89	15,68	57
Bruscato, Mary/Elmwood Park Cmty Unit SD 401	67	48
Bruso, Erica/Community High School Dist 155	2	179
Brutton, Lori/Valmeyer Cmty School Dist 3	11,16,82	190
Bryan, Dan/Wethersfield Cmty Unit SD 230	67	117
Bryan, Eric/Hamilton Cmty Cons SD 328	9,11,88,275	114
Bryan, Jamie/Kewanee Cmty Unit Sch Dist 229	10,83,270,273	117
Bryan, Jeff/Tri-Point Cmty Unit SD 6J	1,11,83,84,288	162
Bryant, Eric/Hall Twp High School Dist 502	6	6
Bryant, Eric/La Grange Cmty School Dist 105	3	54
Bryant, Foy/Prairie Hills Elem SD 144	3	63
Bryant, Fran/Posen-Robbins Sch Dist 143-5	67	63
Bryant, Jodi/Homewood Flossmoor CHSD 233	68,71	52
Brydon, Amber/Skokie School District 73 1/2	77	67
Bryson, Kerry/Ottawa Elementary Sch Dist 141	67	143
Bubulka, Caroline/Bloomington School District 87	4	185
Bucciarelli, Christine/Ottawa Elementary Sch Dist 141	35,277,280,285,296	143
Buchanan, Barry/Seneca Twp High Sch Dist 160	3,91	144
Buchanan, Gary/Allendale Cmty Cons SD 17	67	234
Buchanan, Greg, Dr/Crystal Lake Elem Distict 47	15,68	181
Bucher, Aaron/Vit Cmty Unit School Dist 2	73,98	110
Bucher, Erin/Vit Cmty Unit School Dist 2	76	110
Buchs, Beau/River Ridge Cmty Unit SD 210	8,11,57,58,88,275,285	126
Buckley, Katie/Le Roy Cmty Unit SD 2	285	186
Budde, Mary/East Alton-Wood River SD 14	16	170
Budin, Paul/Community Cons School Dist 15	90	43
Budzynski, Christopher/Huntley Cmty School Dist 158	73,76,98,295	182
Buenik, Tom/Mundelein Cons High SD 120	38	153
Bugg, Kent, Dr/Coal City Cmty Unit Sch Dist 1	1	112
Buglio, Janet/Indian Prairie Sch Dist 204	71	95
Buie, Christy/Edwardsville Cmty Unit SD 7	7	170
Buikema, Christopher/East Coloma-Nelson Cesd 20	67	238
Bulak, Josh/Batavia Unit School Dist 101	72	128
Bulhe, Jennette/Newark Cmty High School Dist 18	2	138
Bull, Christy/Spoon River Valley Cmty SD 4	4	110
Bullard, Julie/Anna Cmty Cons Sch Dist 37	1,11	230
Bulldock, Katy/Potomac Cmty Unit Sch Dist 10	58,288	232
Bullington, Nicole/Iroquois Spec Educ Association	1	119
Bullis, Brian, Dr/Fremont School District 79	9,15	149
Bullock, Keith/Community High School Dist 99	83	91
Bultemeier, Corey/Wilmette Public School Dist 39	2	71
Bumann, Shannon/Alwood Cmty Unit Sch Dist 225	1,11	116
Bunch, Kelle/Liberty Cmty Unit Sch Dist 2	1,11,83	2
Bundy, Elisa/Community Cons School Dist 46	7	148
Buniak, Linda/Community Cons School Dist 59	9	43
Bunker, America/Silvis School District 34	7	209
Bunn, James/North Palos School Dist 117	2,11,15,76,286	59

NAME/District	JOB FUNCTIONS	PAGE
Bunton, Mary Ellen/Danville School District 118	8	231
Burbatt, Anthony/Midlothian School District 143	16,73,76,286,295	57
Burcenski, Jacob/Woodland Cmty Unit Sch Dist 5	285	162
Burchfield, Mike/Rochelle Cmty Cons SD 231	73,76,297	195
Burdette, Emory/Evergreen Park Elem SD 124	46	49
Burdi, Joseph/Bellwood School District 88	3	22
Burgener, Terry/Kaskaskia Spec Ed District	15	176
Burger, Steven/Elgin School District U-46	9,15,78	130
Burgess, Cassandra/Herrin Cmty School District 4	8,11,57,83,285,286,288,298	251
Burgess, Joe/Knoxville Cmty Unit SD 202	1,11,288	140
Burgett, Chad/Charleston Cmty Unit SD 1	2,8,15,88,294	19
Burgner, Josh/Central A&M Cmty Unit SD 21	67	14
Burgos, Maria/Cicero School District 99	9	42
Burk, Dusty/Ball Chatham Cmty Unit SD 5	6	211
Burke, Michelle/Schaumburg Cmty Cons SD 54	285	66
Burke, Robert/Woodland School District 50	3	156
Burkes, Lynn, Dr/Yorkville Cmty Unit SD 115	67	139
Burkett, Jacob/Salem Elem Sch District 111	73	175
Burkett, Jerilyn/Woodstock Cmty Unit SD 200	5	184
Burkett, John/Mt Vernon City Sch Dist 80	3	123
Burkett, Tracy/Patoka Cmty Unit SD 100	12	175
Burkhalter, Tim/Lake Forest Cmty HSD 115	6	151
Burkiewicz, Jason/Annawan Cmty Unit SD 226	80	116
Burle, Kelly/Midlothian School District 143	34,37,59,77,79,83	57
Burman, Laurel/New Trier Twp HS District 203	60	58
Burmeister, Barry/McHenry Cmty High Sch Dist 156	6	183
Burmeister, Janice/North Boone Cmty Unit SD 200	4	5
Burnett, Sara/Tri-Valley Cmty School Dist 3	12,81,296	187
Burnham, Jeremy, Dr/Proviso Twp High Sch Dist 209	57,63	63
Burnham, Lynn/Knox-Warren Spec Ed District	2	141
Burns, Carole/Bloom Twp High Sch Dist 206	13,60,77,90	23
Burns, Julie/High Mount Sch Dist 116	274	220
Burns, Merritt/Oglesby Public Sch Dist 125	16,69,85,270	143
Burns, Tim, Dr/Special Ed Dist of McHenry Co	1,11	185
Burress, Megan/Community Unit School Dist 200	58	91
Burrows, Nikki/Giant City Cmty Cons SD 130	59	121
Bush, Janet/Murphysboro Cmty Unit SD 186	2,11,19	121
Bushue, Mary/Teutopolis Cmty Unit SD 50	11	105
Busick, Ryan/Central Cmty Unit SD 4	2,19	118
Buss, Amber/El Paso-Gridley CUSD 11	8,11,57,275,288	257
Buss, Kyle/Wabash Cmty Unit Sch Dist 348	6,80	234
Bussard, Adam/Illinois Vly Ctl Sch Dist 321	2,7,15,295	197
Bussard, Sheree/Armstrong Ellis SD 61	4	231
Busse, Carrie/Joliet Public School Dist 86	275,280	243
Butcher, Jerry/Carthage Elementary SD 317	15	114
Bute, John, Dr/Prairie Grove Cons SD 46	1	183
Butler, Fred/Hillsboro Cmty Unit Sch Dist 3	3	191
Butler, Laura/Hillsboro Cmty Unit Sch Dist 3	68	191
Butler, Leslie/Polo Cmty Unit Sch Dist 222	73	195
Butler, Todd/Cumberland Cmty Unit SD 77	1,11	84
Butterbrodt, Christina/Livingston Co Spec Svc Unit	15	163
Butterbrodt, Chuck/Dwight Common Elem SD 232	73,286	161
Butterbrodt, Chuck/Dwight Twp High Sch Dist 230	76,95,295	161
Butts, John, Dr/Medinah Elementary SD 11	1	97
Buyerly, William/Union School District 81	73	248
Byczek, Julie/Antioch Cmty Cons Sch Dist 34	4	146
Byers, Angie/Effingham Cmty Sch Dist 40	67	105
Byrd, Danielle/Cook County School Dist 154	2,73	45
Byrd, Marla/Waterloo Cmty Unit Sch Dist 5	2	190
Byrd, Spencer/Serena Cmty Unit School Dist 2	1,83	144
Byrne, Joseph/Berkeley School Dist 87	28,73,76	22
Byrne, Melissa, Dr/Community Unit School Dist 303	27,36	128
Byrne, Susan/Aptakisic-Tripp Sch Dist 102	76	146
Byrns, Erin/Hoover-Schrum Sch Dist 157	3	52
Byron, Carol/La Grange Area Dept of Spec Ed	58	82

1 Superintendent	16 Instructional Media Svcs	30 Adult Education	44 Science Sec	58 Special Education K-12	72 Summer School	88 Alternative/At Risk	277 Remedial Math K-12
2 Bus/Finance/Purchasing	17 Chief Operations Officer	31 Career/Sch-to-Work K-12	45 Math K-12	59 Special Education Elem	73 Instructional Tech	89 Multi-Cultural Curriculum	280 Literacy Coach
3 Buildings And Grounds	18 Chief Academic Officer	32 Career/Sch-to-Work Elem	46 Math Elem	60 Special Education Sec	74 Inservice Training	90 Social Work	285 STEM
4 Food Service	19 Chief Financial Officer	33 Career/Sch-to-Work Sec	47 Math Sec	61 Foreign/World Lang K-12	75 Marketing/Distributive	91 Safety/Security	286 Digital Learning
5 Transportation	20 Art K-12	34 Early Childhood Ed	48 English/Lang Arts K-12	62 Foreign/World Lang Elem	76 Info Systems	92 Magnet School	288 Common Core Standards
6 Athletic	21 Art Elem	35 Health/Phys Education	49 English/Lang Arts Elem	63 Foreign/World Lang Sec	77 Psychological Assess	93 Parental Involvement	294 Accountability
7 Health Services	22 Art Sec	36 Guidance Services K-12	50 English/Lang Arts Sec	64 Religious Education K-12	78 Affirmative Action	95 Tech Prep Program	295 Network System
8 Curric/Instruct K-12	23 Music K-12	37 Guidance Services Elem	51 Reading K-12	65 Religious Education Elem	79 Student Personnel	97 Chief Infomation Officer	296 Title II Programs
9 Curric/Instruct Elem	24 Music Elem	38 Guidance Services Sec	52 Reading Elem	66 Religious Education Sec	80 Driver Ed/Safety	98 Chief Technology Officer	297 Webmaster
10 Curric/Instruct Sec	25 Music Sec	39 Social Studies K-12	53 Reading Sec	67 School Board President	81 Gifted/Talented	270 Character Education	298 Grant Writer/Ptnrships
11 Federal Program	26 Business Education	40 Social Studies Elem	54 Remedial Reading K-12	68 Teacher Personnel	82 Video Services	271 Migrant Education	750 Chief Innovation Officer
12 Title I	27 Career & Tech Ed	41 Social Studies Sec	55 Remedial Reading Elem	69 Academic Assessment	83 Substance Abuse Prev	273 Teacher Mentor	751 Chief of Staff
13 Title V	28 Technology Education	42 Science K-12	56 Remedial Reading Sec	70 Research/Development	84 Erate	274 Before/After Sch	752 Social Emotional Learning
15 Asst Superintendent	29 Family/Consumer Science	43 Science Elem	57 Bilingual/ELL	71 Public Information	85 AIDS Education	275 Response To Intervention	

IL-T8

Illinois School Directory

DISTRICT PERSONNEL INDEX

NAME/District	JOB FUNCTIONS	PAGE
C		
Caban, Judy/Calumet City School Dist 155	2	24
Cacciatore, Christina/Round Lake Area Co Dist 116	20,23	155
Cacciatore, Sarah/Oak Grove School District 68	288	154
Cadard, Jackeiyn/Downers Grove School Dist 58	34	93
Caddy, Susan/Maercker School District 60	2,3,4,5,91	97
Cadena, Fred/West Chicago Elementary SD 33	3	99
Cady, Sam/South Beloit Cmty Sch Dist 320	6	255
Caforio, Kara/Elmhurst Cmty Unit SD 205	67	93
Cahill, Carrie, Dr/Midlothian School District 143	9,11,27,57,74,273,285,288	57
Cahill, Neill/Stockton Cmty Unit SD 206	67	126
Cain, Donna/Dupage High School Dist 88	67	93
Cain, Megan/Carrier Mills-Stonefort SD 2	2	210
Calabrese, James/Taft School District 90	1,11,57,73,83	247
Calderon, Miguel/Illinois Dept of Education	68	1
Caldwell, Betrenna/Brooklyn School District 188	2,12	217
Caldwell, Jennifer/Silvis School District 34	37,59,83,85,270,752	209
Caldwell, Jim/Lincolnwood Sch Dist 74	3	55
Caldwell, Justin/Bradley-Bourbonnais CHSD 307	67	134
Caldwell, Nick/Shelbyville Cmty Sch Dist 4	38	216
Callahan, Cindy/Belle Valley School Dist 119	9	217
Callahan, Patrick/Knoxville Cmty Unit SD 202	67	140
Callaway, Jeri/Regional Office of Ed 54	74	233
Callaway, Tina/Hutsonville Cmty Unit SD 1	67	83
Callis, Eric/La Grange-Highlands SD 106	73,76	54
Calloni, Trish/Christopher Unit Sch Dist 99	4	107
Calomese, Heather/Illinois Dept of Education	58	1
Calow, Deedee/Warren Community Unit SD 205	12	126
Calrroll, Laurie/Henry Senachwine CUSD 5	4	176
Calvin, Sherri/Meridian Cmty School Dist 101	4	204
Camacho, Manuel/Shirland Cmty Cons SD 134	4	255
Camden, Kevin/Hinsdale Twp High Sch Dist 86	67	95
Camden, Shelly/Cass School District 63	67	89
Camerer, Jordan/Lena-Winslow Cmty Unit SD 202	76	224
Cameron, Rhonda/Havana Cmty Sch District 126	8,58	177
Cameron, Scott/Pawnee Cmty Unit Sch Dist 11	1,288	212
Cammiso, Lou/Naperville Cmty Unit SD 203	91	98
Cammy, Blythe/Roselle School District 12	67	99
Camp, Dan/Illinois Vly Ctl Sch Dist 321	6	197
Camp, Michael/Bloom Twp High Sch Dist 206	57	23
Campbell, Brock/Northwestern CUSD 2	67	168
Campbell, Chuck/Neoga Cmty Unit School Dist 3	67	84
Campbell, Janice/Mendota Twp High Sch Dist 280	57	143
Campbell, Jennifer/Limestone Cmty High SD 310	16,82	197
Campbell, Judith, Dr/Decatur Public Schools 61	10,73,288	165
Campbell, Lori, Dr/East Aurora School Dist 131	8,15	129
Campbell, Marcus/Evanston Twp High SD 202	15,296	48
Campbell, Michael/Bloom Twp High Sch Dist 206	88	23
Campbell, Natacia/Joliet Public School Dist 86	15,68	243
Campbell, Tim/Plano Cmty Unit Sch Dist 88	67	138
Campbell, Toya/Evanston Twp High SD 202	68,751	48
Campos, Nora/Plainfield Cons Sch Dist 202	76	246
Camps, Jordi/East Maine School District 63	2,4	47
Campwerth, Lualice/Carlyle Cmty Unit Sch Dist 1	16,273	17
Canady, Lynn/Iroquois Spec Educ Association	2	119
Canavan, Kelly/Richmond-Burton Cmty HSD 157	38,69,88,270	184
Candelario, Anna/Maywood-Melrose Brdview SD 89	59	57
Canete, Tracy/South Pekin Grade Sch Dist 137	59	228
Canfield, Celeste/Rochelle Cmty Cons SD 231	57	195
Cann, Stephanie/Granite City Cmty Unit SD 9	1	171
Canna, Debbie/Moraine Area Career System	1	82
Cannata, Sam/School Assoc for Sp Ed-Dupage	2	102
Cannon-Ruffo, Colleen/Naperville Cmty Unit SD 203	9	98
Cannon, Cathy/Brookfield-LaGrange Park SD 95	9,74,273,288,296	23
Cano, Alma/Cook County School Dist 130	34	45
Cantrell, Eric/Eldorado Cmty Unit Sch Dist 4	3	210
Cantrell, Lisa/Carbon Cliff Barstow SD 36	67	207
Cantu, Dean, Dr/Elmwood Cmty Unit Sch Dist 322	67	196
Canzoneri, Francesca/Community Unit School Dist 201	4	92
Caparelli-Ruff, Elizabeth/East Aurora School Dist 131	58,79	129
Capel, Grant/Anna Cmty Cons Sch Dist 37	67	230
Capiga, Catia/Community Unit School Dist 200	68	91
Caposey, Phillip, Dr/Meridian Cmty Unit SD 223	1	194
Capps, Shelly/Cambridge Cmty Unit SD 227	9,11,54,274,275,298	116
Cappuli, Carly/La Grange-Highlands SD 106	37	54

NAME/District	JOB FUNCTIONS	PAGE
Capranica, Kim/McHenry Cmty Cons Sch Dist 15	79	183
Caraker, Mike/Damiansville School Dist 62	67,73,286,295	18
Caravello, Joe/Evanston-Skokie Cmty CSD 65	73,82	48
Caraway, Susan/East Alton-Wood River SD 14	83	170
Carbonari, Mary/Maywood-Melrose Brdview SD 89	79	57
Card, Pam/Rhodes School District 84 1/2	5	64
Cardamone, Tom/Lake Forest School District 67	7	152
Cardenas-Lopez, Elizabeth/Evanston-Skokie Cmty CSD 65	12,280	48
Cardona, Paula/East Aurora School Dist 131	295	129
Carey-Boyd, Robin/East St Louis Sch Dist 189	58	218
Carey, Kevin/Community Unit School Dist 201	1,83	92
Carey, Maureen/Reavis Twp HSD 220	7	64
Carioscio, Mike/Oak Park & River Forest SD 200	3,17,71,97,295,297	60
Carleton, Ronald/Mannheim School District 83	3,5,91	56
Carli, David/Geneva CUSD 304	6	131
Carlin, Peter/Rock Island-Milan Sch Dist 41	23	208
Carlin, Quirino/Elmwood Park Cmty Unit SD 401	295	48
Carlson, Ashley/Iroquois West Cmty Unit SD 10	9,298	119
Carlson, Carl/Putnam Co Cmty Unit SD 535	1	204
Carlson, Jake/Zion-Benton Twp High SD 126	69,79	157
Carlson, Jason/Lisbon Cmty Cons Sch Dist 90	67	138
Carlson, Jim, Dr/Seneca Twp High Sch Dist 160	1	144
Carlson, Michael/Colona Cmty School Dist 190	11,57,69,275,298,752	116
Carlson, Mike/Colona Cmty School Dist 190	13,280,285,298,752	116
Carlson, Ryan/Bureau Valley Cmty Unit 340	73	6
Carlstrom, Phyllis/Skokie School District 68	68,71	67
Carmean, Michelle/Tonica Cmty Cons Sch Dist 79	4	145
Carmona Colon, Luz/Saratoga Cmty Cons SD 60C	57	113
Carmona, Alfonso/Chicago PSD-Network 10	15	33
Carney, Emily/LaSalle Peru Twp HSD 120	33,38,69	142
Carney, Sean/Adlai E Stevenson HSD 125	15	146
Carole, Deb/Grant Cmty High Sch Dist 124	5	150
Caron, Haley/Hiawatha Cmty Unit SD 426	752	85
Caron, William, Dr/Scales Mound Cmty Unit SD 211	1,11	126
Carpani, Mark/Community Unit School Dist 7	73,295	167
Carpenter, Audrey/Bismarck-Henning Cmty SD 1	8	231
Carpenter, Cindy/DeKalb Cmty Unit SD 428	2,84	84
Carpenter, Josh, Dr/Elgin School District U-46	8,15	130
Carpenter, Kelly/Macomb Cmty Unit Sch Dist 185	58	178
Carpenter, Kelly, Dr/Dupo Cmty School District 196	1,11,288	218
Carpenter, Terrie/North Shore School Dist 112	76	154
Carr, Craig/Jasper Co Cmty Unit SD 1	6	122
Carr, Gary/Bartonville School District 66	3	196
Carr, John/El Paso-Gridley CUSD 11	3	257
Carrasco, Jacki/Huntley Cmty School Dist 158	81	182
Carrasco, Jacqueline/Woodstock Cmty Unit SD 200	9	184
Carrera, James/Community Unit School Dist 201	84,295	92
Carretto, Trudy/Rutland Cmty Cons SD 230	12,73,270,273,275,288	144
Carrick, Chauncey/Sycamore Cmty Unit SD 427	6,83,85,270	86
Carrington, Steve/Murphysboro Cmty Unit SD 186	71,84,97	121
Carson, Clarence/Chicago Public School Dist 299	3	25
Carson, David/Belvidere Cmty Unit SD 100	15	4
Carson, Tammy/DeKalb Cmty Unit SD 428	3	84
Carsrud, Jessica/Giant City Cmty Cons SD 130	76,82	121
Cartee, Kevin/Red Bud Cmty Unit Sch Dist 132	6	205
Carter, Andy/Ramsey Cmty Unit Sch Dist 204	3	105
Carter, Charlotte/Evanston-Skokie Cmty CSD 65	274	48
Carter, Danielle/Grayslake Cmty HS District 127	10,15,68,288	150
Carter, Diane/Woodstock Cmty Unit SD 200	5	184
Carter, Jim/Peoria Heights Cmty SD 325	3	198
Carter, Josh/Gibson Cty-Melvin-Sibley CUSD5	27,31,36	106
Carter, Karen/Coulterville Unit Sch Dist 1	12	205
Carter, Shane/Edwards Co Cmty Unit SD 1	8,11,34,57,58,74,273	104
Carter, Tanya, Dr/Lansing School Dist 158	79	54
Caruso, Becky/Cicero School District 99	59	42
Caruso, Mike/Consolidated High Sch Dist 230	295	44
Carver, Kevin/Cass School District 63	5	89
Casbohm, Ronald/Township High School Dist 113	16,73,295	155
Casella, Kevin/Community Cons School Dist 93	297	90
Casey, Dave/Rochelle Cmty Cons SD 231	67	195
Casey, Lori/Woodland School District 50	1,83	156
Casey, Thomas/Joliet Twp High Sch Dist 204	91	243
Casillas, Daniel/Champaign Cmty Unit Sch Dist 4	68	10
Cass, Ladel/Belvidere Cmty Unit SD 100	5	4
Cassidy, Leo/Oak Lawn-Hometown Sch Dist 123	3,91	60
Cassidy, Maureen/McHenry Cmty Cons Sch Dist 15	57	183

DISTRICT PERSONNEL INDEX

Market Data Retrieval

NAME/District	JOB FUNCTIONS	PAGE
Castelli, Courtney, Dr/Columbia Cmty Unit SD 4	9,15,285,298	190
Castillo, Omar, Dr/Keeneyville Elem Sch Dist 20	1	96
Castillo, Robert/Dallas Elem Sch Dist 327	67	114
Castillo, Vicente/Crete-Monee Cmty SD 201-U	3	241
Castleberry, Craig/Jacksonville School Dist 117	3,11	192
Castleman, Kevin/Joppa-Maple Grove Unit SD 38	67	177
Castleman, Mike/Olympia Cmty Unit Sch Dist 16	6	187
Castro, Jose/Moline-Coal Valley SD No 40	63	207
Cater, Sue/Ohio Cmty Cons School Dist 17	7	7
Cater, Sue/Princeton Elem Sch Dist 115	7	7
Cater, Susan/Princeton Twp HSD 500	7,85	7
Cates, Daniel, Dr/Township High School Dist 211	1	69
Caudle, Myron/Wayne City Cmty Unit SD 100	1,11,73	237
Cauffman, Bradley/Lincoln-Way Cmty HS Dist 210	2,15	244
Caupert, John/Waterloo Cmty Unit Sch Dist 5	67	190
Cavallo, Louis, Dr/Forest Park School District 91	1,11,83,288	50
Cavallore, Phyllis/Archdiocese of Chicago Ed Off	18	72
Cavanaugh, Amy/Georgetown-Ridge Farm CUSD 4	2	232
Cavanaugh, Kate/Lake Forest School District 67	59	152
Cavino, Chris/Hinsdale Twp High Sch Dist 86	10,11,15,18,288,296,298	95
Cavins, Patty/O'Fallon Cmty Cons Sch Dist 90	2,12,296	221
Cawley, Andrew/Waltham Elementary SD 185	73	145
Cazalet, Katie/Dunlap Cmty Unit Sch Dist 323	6	196
Cecil, Kathy/Plainfield Cons Sch Dist 202	76	246
Cederna, Brie, Dr/Community High School Dist 117	60	148
Ceko, Jennifer/Seneca Cmty Cons Sch Dist 170	83,90	144
Center, Susan, Dr/Round Lake Area Co Dist 116	8,18	155
Centers, Luanne/Oakland Cmty Unit Sch Dist 5	4	19
Cerda, Jaime/Leyden Area Spec Ed Co-op	5	82
Cerniglia, Brian/Arlington Hts School Dist 25	67	21
Cervantes, Tianna/Galesburg Cmty Unit SD 205	67	140
Cesario, Eduardo/Waukegan Cmty Unit SD 60	8,15,18	156
Cesario, Rick/Nippersink School District 2	3	183
Chafee, Ian/Burbank School District 111	16,73	24
Chalmers, Lori/East St Louis Sch Dist 189	68	218
Chambers, Daniel/Union Ridge School Dist 86	79	70
Chambers, Dawn/South Pekin Grade Sch Dist 137	67	228
Chambers, Josh/Glenbard Twp High Sch Dist 87	15,68,79	94
Chambers, Kimberly, Dr/Adlai E Stevenson HSD 125	68	146
Chambers, Quennetta/Cahokia Unit Sch Dist 187	58	218
Chambers, Sinead/Worth School District 127	9,57,59,88,275	72
Champ, Latoya/Oak Park Elem School Dist 97	2	60
Chan, Ann/Elgin School District U-46	15,68	130
Chan, David/Evanston Twp High SD 202	16	48
Chan, Fdavid/Evanston Twp High SD 202	286	48
Chandler, Brian/Fairmont School District 89	73	242
Chandler, Mike/Harlem Unit Sch District 122	3	252
Chandler, Tara/Paxton-Buckley-Loda CUSD 10	8,16,69,74,273,288	107
Chanthasene, Tommy/Crystal Lake Elem Distict 47	295	181
Chapa, Eddie/Area 6 Learning Technology Ctr	295	83
Chapman, Carrie/McLean Co Unit District 5	58	186
Chapman, John/Alsip-Hazelgrn-Oaklawn SD 126	73,76	20
Chapman, Justin/High Mount Sch Dist 116	67	220
Chapman, Mary Jane/LaSalle-Putnam Sped Alliance	1,11	145
Chapman, Phillip/Newark Cmty High Sch Dist 18	67	138
Chapman, Seth/Community Unit School Dist 303	15,19	128
Charleston, Jeff/Cmty Cons Sch Dist 146	2,5,19	42
Charron, Brian/Waterloo Cmty Unit Sch Dist 5	1	190
Chase, Jonathan/Lake Villa Cmty Cons SD 41	73,76,295	152
Chase, Mindi/Newark Cmty High Sch Dist 18	6	138
Chastin, Danielle/South Central Cmty Unit SD 401	36,69,88	176
Chaterton, Zack/Farmington Ctl Cmty SD 265	1	197
Chatterton, Nick/Vermilion Voc Ed Delivery Sys	1	233
Chaudoin, Ginger/Lincoln Elem School Dist 27	11,57,270,271,273	163
Chavez, Tiffany/Township High School Dist 113	60	155
Cheek, Shannon/Arthur CUSD 305	1	87
Cheng, Moses, Dr/Community High School Dist 94	74,294	91
Cherney, Todd/Downers Grove School Dist 58	17	93
Cherry, Dorene/Cicero School District 99	2	42
Cherry, Wayne/Sterling Cmty Unit Sch Dist 5	2	240
Cherullo, Ernest/Cook County School Dist 130	59,79	45
Chestang, Warren/South Holland School Dist 151	3,91	68
Chew, Troy/Salt Fork Cmty Unit SD 512	67	233
Chiappetta, Jennifer/Community Cons School Dist 59	9,270	43
Chiaventone, Jamie/Thompsonville Cmty USD 174	36,79	108
Chico, Marie/Momence Cmty Unit Sch Dist 1	4	136
Chiffman, Mike, Dr/Pearl City Cmty Unit SD 200	1,11,73	225
Chignoli, Mary/Professional Dev Alliance	74	250
Childers, Jim/Beardstown Cmty Sch Dist 15	3,17	9
Chiles, Thomas, Dr/Lena-Winslow Cmty Unit SD 202	1	224
Chin, Ellie/Arlington Hts School Dist 25	16	21
Chin, Nicholas/Waukegan Cmty Unit SD 60	11	156
Chism, Michelle/East St Louis Sch Dist 189	34	218
Chisom, Sandra/Cahokia Unit Sch Dist 187	285	218
Chiswick, Wendy/Community Cons School Dist 46	79	148
Chiszar, David/Community Unit School Dist 303	69,294	128
Chiuppi, Rich/East Prairie School Dist 73	73	47
Chou, Jadine/Chicago Public School Dist 299	91	25
Chovanec, Marissa/Lockport Twp High Sch Dist 205	47	244
Chrisman, Anthony/Harrisburg Cmty Unit SD 3	3	210
Chrisman, Brent/Pearl City Cmty Unit SD 200	9,11,57,88,286,288,298	225
Chrisman, Brent/Regional Office of Ed 8	16	225
Chrismen, Brent/Pearl City Cmty Unit SD 200	9	225
Christensen, Amanda/Regional Office of Ed 16	1	87
Christensen, Cynthia/S Wilmington Cons Elem SD 74	1,11	113
Christensen, Dee/Central Cmty Unit SD 4	11	118
Christensen, Denny/Gardner Cmty Cons SD 72-C	67	112
Christensen, Michael/Hawthorn Cmty Cons Sch Dist 73	3	151
Christenson, Amber/Cornell Cmty Cons Sch Dist 426	12	161
Christian, Amy/Pana Cmty Unit School Dist 8	4	14
Christian, Gorman/Park Ridge Niles CMCSD 64	295	62
Christianson, Eric/Waukegan Cmty Unit SD 60	79	156
Christianson, Lori/Gibson Cty-Melvin-Sibley CUSD5	68	106
Christl, Patrick/Pennoyer School District 79	73	62
Christner, Lori/Carthage Elementary SD 317	59	114
Christopher, Anne/Southwestern Cmty Unit SD 9	2,11,19,294	168
Christophersen, Laurie/Emmons School District 33	67	149
Christy, Bob/Red Hill Cmty School Dist 10	67	159
Chung, Jake, Dr/Salt Creek School District 48	1,84	99
Churchill, Paula/Vit Cmty Unit School Dist 2	16,82	110
Churchman, Alan/Jersey Cmty Sch Dist 100	3,5,91	125
Ciesielski, Laurie/Princeton Twp HSD 500	2	7
Cieszykowski, Alicia/Mannheim School District 83	2,4,19,37,76,83	56
Cimaglia, Marie/Marquardt School District 15	15,68	97
Cirone, Allison/Mokena Public School Dist 159	79,298,752	245
Cisna, Barry/West Central Cmty Unit SD 235	295	116
Cissna, Jennifer/Ashton-Franklin Center SD 275	58	159
Ciszek, Paul/Nippersink School District 2	16,295	183
Cittadino, Scott/Wauconda Cmty Unit SD 118	15,16,73,76,95,295	155
Claassen, Laura/La Harpe Cmty Unit Sch Dist 347	2	115
Clancy, Claire/Alton Cmty School District 11	16	169
Clanton, Keppen/Northwestern CUSD 2	273	168
Clapp, Dave/Bismarck-Henning Cmty SD 1	67	231
Clapp, Jack/Villa Grove Cmty Unit SD 302	3	88
Clapp, Marlene/Massac Unit School District 1	4	178
Clark, Brett/Maine Twp High Sch Dist 207	71	56
Clark, Brett/Maine Twp Spec Ed Program	71	82
Clark, Cassie/Kaskaskia Spec Ed District	1	176
Clark, Cheryl/Pinckneyville Cmty High SD 101	73	201
Clark, Chris/South Fork School Dist 14	3,10,15,275,288	14
Clark, Chris/South Fork School Dist 14	1	14
Clark, Craig/Centralia City Sch Dist 135	1	174
Clark, Debbie/Cumberland Cmty Unit SD 77	12,54,275	84
Clark, Jim/Villa Grove Cmty Unit SD 302	67	88

1	Superintendent	16	Instructional Media Svcs	30	Adult Education	44	Science Sec	58	Special Education K-12
2	Bus/Finance/Purchasing	17	Chief Operations Officer	31	Career/Sch-to-Work K-12	45	Math K-12	59	Special Education Elem
3	Buildings And Grounds	18	Chief Academic Officer	32	Career/Sch-to-Work Elem	46	Math Elem	60	Special Education Sec
4	Food Service	19	Chief Financial Officer	33	Career/Sch-to-Work Sec	47	Math Sec	61	Foreign/World Lang K-12
5	Transportation	20	Art K-12	34	Early Childhood Ed	48	English/Lang Arts K-12	62	Foreign/World Lang Elem
6	Athletic	21	Art Elem	35	Health/Phys Education	49	English/Lang Arts Elem	63	Foreign/World Lang Sec
7	Health Services	22	Art Sec	36	Guidance Services K-12	50	English/Lang Arts Sec	64	Religious Education K-12
8	Curric/Instruct K-12	23	Music K-12	37	Guidance Services Elem	51	Reading K-12	65	Religious Education Elem
9	Curric/Instruct Elem	24	Music Elem	38	Guidance Services Sec	52	Reading Elem	66	Religious Education Sec
10	Curric/Instruct Sec	25	Music Sec	39	Social Studies K-12	53	Reading Sec	67	School Board President
11	Federal Program	26	Business Education	40	Social Studies Elem	54	Remedial Reading K-12	68	Teacher Personnel
12	Title I	27	Career & Tech Ed	41	Social Studies Sec	55	Remedial Reading Elem	69	Academic Assessment
13	Title V	28	Technology Education	42	Science K-12	56	Remedial Reading Sec	70	Research/Development
15	Asst Superintendent	29	Family/Consumer Science	43	Science Elem	57	Bilingual/ELL	71	Public Information

72	Summer School	88	Alternative/At Risk	277	Remedial Math K-12
73	Instructional Tech	89	Multi-Cultural Curriculum	280	Literacy Coach
74	Inservice Training	90	Social Work	285	STEM
75	Marketing/Distributive	91	Safety/Security	286	Digital Learning
76	Info Systems	92	Magnet School	288	Common Core Standards
77	Psychological Assess	93	Parental Involvement	294	Accountability
78	Affirmative Action	95	Tech Prep Program	295	Network System
79	Student Personnel	96	Chief Information Officer	296	Title II Programs
80	Driver Ed/Safety	97	Chief Technology Officer	297	Webmaster
81	Gifted/Talented	98	Character Education	298	Grant Writer/Ptnrships
82	Video Services	270	Migrant Education	750	Chief Innovation Officer
83	Substance Abuse Prev	273	Teacher Mentor	751	Chief of Staff
84	Erate	274	Before/After Sch	752	Social Emotional Learning
85	AIDS Education	275	Response To Intervention		

Illinois School Directory — District Personnel Index

NAME/District	JOB FUNCTIONS	PAGE
Clark, Kathy/Johnston City Cmty Unit SD 1	1,83,84	251
Clark, Kena/Milford Area Public SD 124	73	119
Clark, Mildred/West Harvey-Dixmoor Pub SD 147	3	70
Clark, Nancy/West Central Cmty Unit SD 235	2	116
Clark, R C/East St Louis Sch Dist 189	67	218
Clark, Rhonda/Fairfield Pub Sch District 112	73	236
Clark, Rich/Community Unit School Dist 16	3	211
Clark, Rochelle, Dr/Crete-Monee Cmty SD 201-U	15,79	241
Clark, Russ/Marissa Cmty Unit Sch Dist 40	5	220
Clark, Shannon/Rantoul City School Dist 137	3	11
Clark, Tina/Pecatonica Cmty Unit SD 321	12	253
Clarkson, Jessica/Arthur CUSD 305	58	87
Clausen, Brian/Limestone Cmty High SD 310	6	197
Clausius, Kathy/Altamont Cmty Unit SD 10	58,88	104
Clauson, Margaret/Skokie School District 69	1	67
Clay, Jason/Vandalia Cmty Unit SD 203	6	106
Clay, Scott, Dr/East Maine School District 63	1	47
Claycomb, Shannon/Brownstown Cmty Unit SD 201	16,82	105
Clayton, Deborah/Prairie Hills Elem SD 144	2	63
Clayton, Jeanne/La Harpe Cmty Sch Dist 347	5	115
Cleary, Barbi/Iuka Community Cons Sch Dist 7	2	174
Cleek, Robin/Hawthorn Cmty Cons Sch Dist 73	67	151
Clementz, Annie Rae/Illinois Dept of Education	69,294	1
Clemmons, Wade/Hoopeston Area Cmty Unit SD 11	3	232
Cleveland, Kimberly/Glenview Cmty Cons Sch Dist 34	4	51
Click, Sean/Bismarck-Henning Cmty SD 1	11,58,69,296	231
Clifton, Carolyn/Rock Falls Elem Sch Dist 13	4	240
Clifton, Janine/Iroquois Co Cmty Unit SD 9	4	119
Clifton, Tyson/St George School District 258	3	136
Cline, Kim/Keeneyville Elem Sch Dist 20	59	96
Cline, Kim/Wheeling Cmty Cons Sch Dist 21	15	71
Cline, Robert/School Dist 45 Dupage Co	2	99
Cline, Steve/Bement Cmty Unit Sch Dist 5	6,8	202
Clinton, Reggie/Two Rivers Voc Ed System	1	9
Cloat, Julia/Huntley Cmty School Dist 158	9	182
Clodi, Megan/Mt Vernon Twp HS District 201	60,77	123
Closen, John/Area 3 Learning Technology Ctr	1	200
Cloud, Denise/Tolono Cmty Unit Sch Dist 7	4	12
Clough, Lauren/DeSoto Grade School Dist 86	6,73	120
Clover-Hill, Shelly/Shawnee Cmty Unit Sch Dist 84	1,83	231
Clupimski, Theresa/Mannheim School District 83	16,286	56
Coady, Angela/Villa Grove Cmty Unit SD 302	12	88
Coady, Joanne/Central A&M Cmty Unit SD 21	58	14
Coalson, Brian/Staunton Cmty Unit Sch Dist 6	73	168
Coates, Toby/Donovan Cmty Unit Sch Dist 3	1,11	119
Coates, Toby/Wallace Cmty Cons Sch Dist 195	59,69,88,270,271,273,274	145
Coats, Chris/Illini Bluffs Cmty Unit SD 327	67	197
Coats, Clint/Scott Morgan Cmty Unit SD 2	3,5	215
Cobb-Powers, Katie/Peoria Public Sch Dist 150	34	198
Cobbett, Andrea/Lockport Twp High Sch Dist 205	12,50,53	244
Cobbins, Christina/Crete-Monee Cmty SD 201-U	68	242
Coburn, Lisa/Westville Cmty Unit Sch Dist 2	73	233
Cochran, Terry/Lawrence Co Cmty Sch Dist 20	7,35,85	159
Cochrane, Brandon/East Aurora School Dist 131	79	129
Cochrane, Dan/Community Unit School Dist 200	58	91
Cockrum, Danielle/Community Cons School Dist 15	2	42
Code, Jack/Freeport School District 145	58,79,83,85,88,271	224
Coder, Sheri/East Moline Public Sch Dist 37	9,11,15,69,275,288,296,298	207
Coe, Jason/Charleston Cmty Unit SD 1	67	19
Coers, John/New Holland Middletown ESD 88	67	164
Coffey, Barb/Lincoln Elem School Dist 27	73,84,295,297	163
Coffey, Lindsey/Bradley Elem School Dist 61	57,59,88	134
Coffey, Sarah, Dr/Western Springs Sch Dist 101	9,15,69,273,288	71
Cofoid, Steve/Hononegah Cmty High SD 207	6,274	253
Coglianese, Kara, Dr/Crete-Monee Cmty SD 201-U	1	241
Cognetti, Michelle/Moraine Area Career System	73	82
Cohen, Carie/Lake Zurich Cmty Sch Dist 95	60	152
Cohen, Cyndi/East Prairie School Dist 73	2	47
Cohen, Cyndi/Skokie School District 73 1/2	2	67
Cohen, Mark, Dr/Mokena Public School Dist 159	1	245
Cohen, Rebecca/New Trier Twp HS District 203	4	58
Cohen, Reisa/Community Cons School Dist 15	6,21,24,43,46	43
Cohenour, Dawn/Illinois Vly Ctl Sch Dist 321	73	197
Cohla, Adam/River Grove School Dist 85-5	84,286	65
Colbrese, Egan/Rock Island-Milan Sch Dist 41	15,68,90,273	208
Cole, Kathryn/Steeleville Cmty Unit Sch Dist 138	274	206
Cole, Shayna/Frankfort School Dist 157-C	68,79	242
Coleman, Amanda/Odin Public School Dist 722	38,83,88,270	175
Coleman, Brian/Cary Cmty Cons Sch Dist 26	1	179
Coleman, Mark/Prospect Hts School Dist 23	3	63
Coleman, Nancy/Fenton Cmty High Sch Dist 100	33,60	94
Coles, Daniel, Dr/Wauconda Cmty Unit SD 118	1	155
Coletta, Jeanette/Beach Park Cmty Cons SD 3	67	147
Colgan, Kathleen/J Sterling Morton HSD 201	68	53
Colgan, Stacy/Naperville Cmty Unit SD 203	90	98
Colin, Holly/North Shore School Dist 112	15,59,79,83,88	154
Colin, Holly, Dr/Mundelein Elem School Dist 75	12,34,59,88,271	153
Collachia, Stacey/River Bend Cmty School Dist 2	4	239
Collenberger, Brenda/St Joseph Cmty Cons SD 169	4	12
Collier, Jody/Spoon River Valley Cmty SD 4	8,11	110
Collier, Karen/Kell Cons School District 2	6	174
Collins, Christoher/School Dist 45 Dupage Co	9,11,15	99
Collins, David/North Chicago Cmty Unit SD 187	73	154
Collins, Jackie/Sullivan Cmty Unit SD 300	31,36,270	193
Collins, Joseph/J Sterling Morton HSD 201	35,80	53
Collins, Josh/Peoria Public Sch Dist 150	5	198
Collins, Karen/Creston Cmty Cons Sch Dist 161	2	194
Collins, Shawn/Earlville Cmty Unit Sch Dist 9	6	141
Collins, Susan/Pikeland Cmty Unit Sch Dist 10	4	203
Colmone, Chad/Tri-City Cmty Unit Sch Dist 1	1	214
Colston, Matthew/Hoopeston Area Cmty Unit SD 11	6	232
Colvolt, Becky/McHenry Cmty High Sch Dist 156	60	183
Colwell-Forck, Tracy/Pleasant Valley Sch Dist 62	1	199
Comer-Jaworski, Lyn/Township High School Dist 214	81	69
Compardo, Cj/Williamsville Cmty Unit SD 15	11,296,298	214
Conant, Brian/Joliet Twp High Sch Dist 204	10,12,280	243
Concannon, Beth, Dr/Leyden Cmty High Sch Dist 212	3,15,68	55
Condon, Edward, Dr/River Forest Sch Dist 90	1	65
Condon, Matt/Morton Grove School Dist 70	6,9,11,83,271	58
Condon, Robert/Alsip-Hazelgrn-Oaklawn SD 126	59	20
Condon, Wendy/Seneca Cmty Cons Sch Dist 170	4	144
Condron, Tim/Mattoon Cmty Unit Sch Dist 2	1	19
Conerton, Rob/Hononegah Cmty High SD 207	16,73,295	253
Conestent, John/Lemont High Sch Dist 210	80	55
Conkleign, Christine/Riley Cmty Cons Sch Dist 18	1	184
Conklen, Rhonda/Rock Falls Elem Sch Dist 13	274	240
Conklin, Wendy/Northbrook School District 28	35	59
Conkling, Mary, Dr/Lake Villa Cmty Cons SD 41	59,83	152
Conley, Tracy/Brown Co Cmty Unit Sch Dist 1	2	5
Conlin, Marci/Glen Ellyn School District 41	15,68	94
Conlon-Wasik, Kathleen/Grayslake Cmty HS District 127	67	150
Conn, Tammie/Valley View Cmty SD 365-U	27	248
Connelly, Michael, Dr/Wheeling Cmty Cons Sch Dist 21	1	71
Connelly, Michale/Martinsville Cmty Unit SD C-3	67	16
Connelly, Sean/Gavin School District 37	34,79	150
Connelly, Victoria/Sherrard Cmty Unit SD 200	57,296,298	189
Conner, Belinda/Elverado Cmty Unit SD 196	11,58,288,298	120
Conner, Rob/Glenview Cmty Cons Sch Dist 34	5	51
Conner, Vicki/Galva Cmty Unit Sch Dist 224	38,69,83	117
Connolly, Bridget/Niles Twp High School Dist 219	60,79	58
Connolly, John/Consolidated High Sch Dist 230	73,98	44
Connolly, Lori/Alsip-Hazelgrn-Oaklawn SD 126	9	20
Connolly, Sean/Zion Public School District 6	79	157
Connor, Belinda/Elverado Cmty Unit SD 196	8,11,288	120
Connor, Jack/Dwight Twp High Sch Dist 230	3	161
Connor, Seren/Carbondale Elem School Dist 95	16	120
Connors, Mike/Riverside-Brookfld Twp SD 208	73	65
Conrad, Greg/Huntley Cmty School Dist 158	295	182
Conrad, Randy/Leyden Cmty High Sch Dist 212	6	55
Conrey, Jim/Adlai E Stevenson HSD 125	71	146
Conroy, Bailey/Saunemin Cmty Cons SD 438	2	162
Conroy, Deb/Dwight Twp High Sch Dist 230	2,19	161
Conroy, Debbie/Dwight Common Elem SD 232	2,19	161
Conroy, Dee/Cobden Cmty Unit Sch Dist 17	2	230
Conroy, James/New Trier Twp HS District 203	38,270	58
Considine, Gena/Butler School District 53	12	89
Consolino, John/Iuka Community Cons Sch Dist 7	1,73,83	174
Consolino, John/Kell Cons School District 2	1	174
Contos, Larry/Chaney-Monge School Dist 88	3	241
Conway, Cheri/Fremont School District 79	2	149
Conway, Michael/Lake Villa Cmty Cons SD 41	67	152
Conwell, Jennifer/Elmhurst Cmty Unit SD 205	7	93

DISTRICT PERSONNEL INDEX

Market Data Retrieval

NAME/District	JOB FUNCTIONS	PAGE
Conwell, Kelly/Glenview Cmty Cons Sch Dist 34	295	51
Cook, Chris/Leyden Cmty High Sch Dist 212	35	55
Cook, Dan/Century Cmty Unit SD 100	16,31,73,76,295	204
Cook, Danielle/Champaign Cmty Unit Sch Dist 4	274	10
Cook, Janet/Glenbard Twp High Sch Dist 87	15,60,79,752	94
Cook, Jared/Central A&M Cmty Unit SD 21	286	14
Cook, Lawrence, Dr/Homewood Flossmoor CHSD 233	2	52
Cook, Lee/Community Unit School Dist 200	10,73,286	91
Cook, Robyn/Community Cons School Dist 15	73	43
Cook, Sharon/Woodland School District 50	68	157
Cook, Shawn/Nashville Cmty HSD 99	67	235
Cook, Travis/Hamilton Cmty Cons SD 328	6	114
Cooke, Mary/Harvard Cmty Unit Sch Dist 50	12,51,280,288	181
Cooley, Jason/Dolton-Riverdale Sch Dist 148	3	46
Cooley, Lisa/Township High School Dist 214	60	69
Coomer, Dan/Fairfield Pub Sch District 112	67	236
Coon, Casey/Regional Office of Ed 8	68	225
Cooper, Claire/Bensenville Elem Sch Dist 2	5	89
Cooper, Debbie/Wilmette Public School Dist 39	72	71
Cooper, Jacob/Posen-Robbins Sch Dist 143-5	73,84	63
Cooper, Jodi/Mt Vernon City Sch Dist 80	59	123
Cooper, Josh/Newark Cmty High Sch Dist 18	6	138
Cooper, Michael/Johnsburg Cmty School Dist 12	73,76,286	182
Cooper, Norquise/East St Louis Sch Dist 189	5	218
Cope, Lesa/Roxana Cmty Unit Sch Dist 1	34	172
Copeland, Paul/DeSoto Grade School Dist 86	67	120
Copeland, Rollie/Putnam Co Cmty Unit SD 535	67	204
Copes, Lance/Grundy Area Voc Ed System	1	113
Coplan, Kelley/West Prairie Cmty Unit Sch 103	7	178
Corbett, John, Dr/Wood Dale School Dist 7	1	100
Corbit, Nathan/Vienna Public School Dist 55	21	127
Corcoran, John/La Grange-Highlands SD 106	67	54
Corcoran, Mike/Evanston Twp High SD 202	16,73,82,98	48
Corey, Melissa/Porta Cmty Unit Sch Dist 202	58	189
Corley, Ciara/Cahokia Unit Sch Dist 187	2	218
Cormeny, Peggy/Springfield Pub Sch Dist 186	93	213
Cornale, Mike/Gardner Cmty Cons SD 72-C	2,3	112
Cornelius, Roseellen/Hoopeston Area Cmty Unit SD 11	15	232
Cornett, Jeremy/Du Quoin Cmty Unit SD 300	6	201
Cornett, Ross/Altamont Cmty Unit SD 10	16,73,286,295	104
Cornwell, Shelly/Creve Coeur Sch Dist 76	2	226
Correa, Amy/Evanston-Skokie Cmty CSD 65	57	48
Correa, Sandra/Crystal Lake Elem Distict 47	76,295	181
Corrigan, Alicia/Community Cons School Dist 15	79	43
Corrigan, Cheryl/Pontiac Cmty Cons Sch Dist 429	59,88	161
Corrigan, Roger/Pontiac Twp High Sch Dist 90	67	161
Corrigan, Timothy/Union Ridge School Dist 86	9	70
Corrington, Michael/Mannheim School District 83	9,12,69,81,280,288,296,298	56
Corriveau, Kristin/Community Unit School Dist 300	8,15	180
Corsi, Anthony/Community High School Dist 218	69	44
Cortesi, Christina/Adlai E Stevenson HSD 125	83	146
Corzine, Doug/Frankfort Cmty Unit SD 168	10,12,294,296	108
Costello, Sam/Chicago Heights Elem SD 170	67	25
Cothran, Anne, Dr/Des Plaines Valley EFE System	1	82
Cotters, Branden/Argo Cmty High School Dist 217	10,12	21
Cotton, Angela/Brooklyn School District 188	67	217
Cotton, Mary/Oakdale Cmty Cons Sch Dist 1	59	236
Couch, Kim/Manteno Cmty Unit Sch Dist 5	7	135
Coughlin, Jane/Berwyn South School Dist 100	93	23
Coughlin, Mike/Seneca Twp High Sch Dist 160	12,57,60,77,83,88,294	144
Coultas, Michael/Hamilton Cmty Cons SD 328	76	114
Coultas, Michael/Nauvoo-Colusa CUSD 325	73	115
Courter, Alta/Annawan Cmty Unit SD 226	16,82	116
Courtney, David/Edwardsville Cmty Unit SD 7	2,15,91,294	170
Courtney, Saskia/Peoria Public Sch Dist 150	5	198
Courtney, Troy/Yorkville Cmty Unit SD 115	68	139
Couson, Ira/Hardin Co Cmty Unit Sch Dist 1	83	115
Couzad, Linda/O'Fallon Twp School Dist 203	67	221
Covalt, Becky/McHenry Cmty High Sch Dist 156	60	183
Covault, Todd/Decatur Public Schools 61	2,3,17	165
Covington, Joann/N Pekin-Marquette Hts SD 102	4	227
Cowan, Eric/Mt Pulaski Cmty Unit SD 23	67	164
Cowan, Lori/Bartonville School District 66	4	196
Cowell, Terese/Lake Zurich Cmty Sch Dist 95	2	152
Cowger, David/Edwards Co Cmty Unit SD 1	1,83	104
Cox, Bradley/Beecher Cmty Sch Dist 200-U	1,11,83	241
Cox, Dan/Rochester Cmty Unit SD 3-A	1	212
Cox, Julie/Danville School District 118	48,280	231
Cox, Phillip/Salt Fork Cmty Unit SD 512	1,83	233
Cox, Rick/Eldorado Cmty Unit Sch Dist 4	11,57,69,270,273,274,296	210
Cox, Stephanie/Libertyville Pub Sch Dist 70	3	152
Coy, Joe/Wayne City Cmty Unit SD 100	67	237
Cozyra, Paige/Elmwood Park Cmty Unit SD 401	36	48
Cozza, Ron, Dr/Palos Cmty Cons Sch Dist 118	9,15,288	61
Cozzi, Anthony/River Forest Sch Dist 90	2,3,91	65
Craft, Tim/Du Quoin Cmty Unit SD 300	73	201
Cragg, Tim/Wilmington Cmty Unit SD 209-U	67	249
Craig, Anna/Goreville Cmty Unit SD 1	36,69,79	127
Craig, Jeff, Dr/West Aurora School Dist 129	1	132
Cramer, Jane/Heritage Cmty Unit Sch Dist 8	83	11
Cramer, Lisa/Georgetown-Ridge Farm CUSD 4	8,13,288,296,298	232
Cramer, Sandy/Community Cons School Dist 15	297	43
Cramer, Shelly/Central School District 3	73	1
Crandall, Norlyn/Fairfield Pub Sch District 112	5	236
Crane, Paula/Prairie Central Cmty USD 8	1	162
Cranford, Kendell/Monroe School District 70	17	198
Crank, Shain/Galatia Cmty Unit Sch Dist 1	1	210
Crater, Cheryl/Odell Cmty Cons Sch Dist 435	59	161
Craven, Jamie/Peru Elem Sch Dist 124	1,11,83	143
Crawford, Chris/Mokena Public School Dist 159	3	245
Crawford, Dennis/Bourbonnais Elem Sch Dist 53	2,3,4,84,91	134
Crawford, Paula/Homewood Flossmoor CHSD 233	80	52
Crawley, Connie/Lincoln Elem School Dist 27	4	163
Crawmer, Jacinda/Urbana School District 116	68	12
Crayne, Mike/Gallatin Cmty Unit Sch Dist 7	3	110
Creadon, Joseph/Elgin School District U-46	3	130
Crean, Pat/Lemont-Bromberek Sch Dist 113A	2,3,5	55
Creech, Mellisa/Glenbard Twp High Sch Dist 87	73	94
Creek, Cathy/Manteno Cmty Unit Sch Dist 5	8,11,69,275,285,288,296,298	136
Creek, Glenna/Grant Cmty Cons Sch Dist 110	2	219
Creel, Holly/Streator Elem School Dist 44	2,3,5,76,286,288,296,298	144
Cremascoli, Kari/Wilmette Public School Dist 39	1	71
Crespell, Anthony/Mundelein Cons High SD 120	57	153
Cretia, Rasoc/Waukegan Cmty Unit SD 60	34	156
Crider, Elizabeth/Regional Office of Ed 48	1	201
Cripps, Kevin/Iuka Community Cons Sch Dist 7	67	174
Cripps, Tammy/Ewing Northern Cmty SD 115	12	108
Crisp, Laura/Prophetstown-Lyndon-Tampico 3	16	239
Criss, Lynelle/Morrison Cmty Unit Sch Dist 6	4	239
Crist, Allen/River Ridge Cmty Unit SD 210	67	126
Crockett, Anitra/Bourbonnais Elem Sch Dist 53	7,13,37,59,79,90	134
Croix, Stefanie/Lockport Twp High Sch Dist 205	2	244
Crook, Amy/DeKalb Cmty Unit SD 428	13,57	84
Cropper, Kim/Leyden Cmty High Sch Dist 212	5	55
Cross, Mark/Cass School District 63	1	89
Cross, Ronda/Putnam Co Cmty Unit SD 535	11	204
Cross, Sandi/Elmwood Cmty Unit Sch Dist 322	752	196
Crossland, Max/Rock Falls Elem Sch Dist 13	3	240
Crotty-Kagan, Sheila/Community Unit School Dist 300	20,23	180
Crotty, Angela, Dr/Midlothian School District 143	2,5,84,298	57
Crotty, Mark/Lansing School Dist 158	2,4,5,73	54
Crouch, Tom/Kishwaukee Ed Consortium	1	87
Crouse, David/Astoria Cmty Unit Sch Dist 1	5,9	109
Crow, Lori/Meridian Cmty School Dist 101	2	204

1 Superintendent	16 Instructional Media Svcs	30 Adult Education	44 Science Sec	58 Special Education K-12	72 Summer School	88 Alternative/At Risk	277 Remedial Math K-12
2 Bus/Finance/Purchasing	17 Chief Operations Officer	31 Career/Sch-to-Work K-12	45 Math K-12	59 Special Education Elem	73 Instructional Tech	89 Multi-Cultural Curriculum	280 Literacy Coach
3 Buildings And Grounds	18 Chief Academic Officer	32 Career/Sch-to-Work Elem	46 Math Elem	60 Special Education Sec	74 Inservice Training	90 Social Work	285 STEM
4 Food Service	19 Chief Financial Officer	33 Career/Sch-to-Work Sec	47 Math Sec	61 Foreign/World Lang K-12	75 Marketing/Distributive	91 Safety/Security	286 Digital Learning
5 Transportation	20 Art K-12	34 Early Childhood Ed	48 English/Lang Arts K-12	62 Foreign/World Lang Elem	76 Info Systems	92 Magnet School	288 Common Core Standards
6 Athletic	21 Art Elem	35 Health/Phys Education	49 English/Lang Arts Elem	63 Foreign/World Lang Sec	77 Psychological Assess	93 Parental Involvement	294 Accountability
7 Health Services	22 Art Sec	36 Guidance Services K-12	50 English/Lang Arts Sec	64 Religious Education K-12	78 Affirmative Action	94 Tech Prep Program	295 Network System
8 Curric/Instruct K-12	23 Music K-12	37 Guidance Services Elem	51 Reading K-12	65 Religious Education Elem	79 Student Personnel	97 Chief Infomation Officer	296 Title II Programs
9 Curric/Instruct Elem	24 Music Elem	38 Guidance Services Sec	52 Reading Elem	66 Religious Education Sec	80 Driver Ed/Safety	98 Chief Technology Officer	297 Webmaster
10 Curric/Instruct Sec	25 Music Sec	39 Social Studies K-12	53 Reading Sec	67 School Board President	81 Gifted/Talented	270 Character Education	298 Grant Writer/Ptnrships
11 Federal Program	26 Business Education	40 Social Studies Elem	54 Remedial Reading K-12	68 Teacher Personnel	82 Video Services	271 Migrant Education	750 Chief Innovation Officer
12 Title I	27 Career & Tech Ed	41 Social Studies Sec	55 Remedial Reading Elem	69 Academic Assessment	83 Substance Abuse Prev	273 Teacher Mentor	751 Chief of Staff
13 Title V	28 Technology Education	42 Science K-12	56 Remedial Reading Sec	70 Research/Development	84 Erate	274 Before/After Sch	752 Social Emotional Learning
15 Asst Superintendent	29 Family/Consumer Science	43 Science Elem	57 Bilingual/ELL	71 Public Information	85 AIDS Education	275 Response To Intervention	

Illinois School Directory — DISTRICT PERSONNEL INDEX

NAME/District	JOB FUNCTIONS	PAGE
Crowder, Jennifer/Okaw Valley Cmty Unit SD 302	58	193
Crowe, Dan/Mundelein Cons High SD 120	73,76	153
Crowe, Dan/Mundelein Elem School Dist 75	73	153
Crowl, Zach/Knox-Warren Spec Ed District	1	141
Croy, Cathy/Clay City Cmty Unit SD 10	1	16
Cruise, Carla/Collinsville Cmty Sch Dist 10	57	170
Cruise, Linda/Cary Cmty Cons Sch Dist 26	59	179
Crum, Steve/Cahokia Unit Sch Dist 187	3	218
Crumrin, Lori/Hutsonville Cmty Unit SD 1	2	83
Cruson, David/Gallatin Cmty Unit Sch Dist 7	38	110
Crutchfield, Janice/Freeport School District 145	67	224
Cruz, Jeanette/Evanston Twp High SD 202	7	48
Cryan, Jeremy/Oak Lawn Cmty High SD 229	6	60
Cryder, Ashley/Belleville Township HSD 201	12,69,90	217
Cualls, Tim/Shawnee Cmty Unit Sch Dist 84	67	231
Cucci, Marianne/New Lenox School District 122	9,12,286,288,296	245
Cuevas, Josue/Waukegan Cmty Unit SD 60	15,76	156
Cuevas, Lori/Sunnybrook School District 171	37	68
Cuffle, Pam/Riverton Cmty Unit SD 14	67	212
Culbreth, Robin/Thompsonville Cmty USD 174	296	108
Cullen, Heather/Park Forest Chicago Hgt SD 163	76	62
Cullerton, Julie/Rosemont Elem Sch Dist 78	2	66
Cullinan, Vicky/Lake Zurich Cmty Sch Dist 95	2	152
Cullum, Chris/Johnston City Cmty Unit SD 1	67	251
Culp, Brenda/Delavan Cmty Unit Sch Dist 703	5	226
Culp, Joann/Joliet Public School Dist 86	11	243
Culver, Arthur/East St Louis Reg Voc System	1	223
Culver, Arthur/East St Louis Sch Dist 189	1	218
Cummings, Lori/Vermilion Assoc for Special Ed	2	233
Cummins, John/Ohio-Wabash Valley Reg Voc Sys	1	238
Cummins, Kara/Tri-City Cmty Unit Sch Dist 1	9,88,93	214
Cummins, Kevin/Community Unit School Dist 16	73	211
Cummins, Sandy/Maroa Forsyth CU Sch Dist 2	2	165
Cundari, Tony/Lockport Twp High Sch Dist 205	15,68	244
Cundiff, Denise/Burnham School District 1545	2,79	24
Cundiff, Denise/Burnham School District 1545	4,5	24
Cunningham, Nathaniel/Thornton Twp High Sch Dist 205	1	69
Cunningham, Ruth/Triad Cmty School District 2	4	172
Cuny, Dane/Salt Creek School District 48	67	99
Cunzeman, Eric/Griggsville-Perry Cmty SD 4	67	203
Cupples, Doug/Germantown Hills SD 69	3	257
Curless, Pam/United Twp High Sch Dist 30	5	209
Curry, Allyson/Regional Office of Ed 26	68	179
Curry, Mike/Abingdon-Avon Cmty Unit SD 276	1	139
Cushing, Ingred/LaSalle Peru Twp HSD 120	11	142
Cushing, Michael, Dr/Ottawa Twp High Sch Dist 140	1	143
Cushing, Tom/Lyons Twp HS District 204	67	56
Cusic, Cody/Eldorado Cmty Unit Sch Dist 4	5	210
Cygnar, Ann/Community Cons School Dist 15	59	43
Czerwonka, Wade/Salt Fork Cmty Unit SD 512	6	233
Czerwonka, Wade/Salt Fork Cmty Unit SD 512	6	233
Czizek, Clint/Prairie Hill Cmty Cons SD 133	1,11,57	253

D

NAME/District	JOB FUNCTIONS	PAGE
D'Alfonso, Christian/Morton Cmty Unit Sch Dist 709	275	227
D'Ambrosio, Cindy/Cooperative Assn for Spec Ed	15,74	102
D'Amore, Rico/Warren Twp High Sch Dist 121	73	155
Dabbs, Kate/Springfield Pub Sch Dist 186	34	213
Dabrowski, Matthew/Fox Lake School Dist 114	67	149
Daciuk, Irene/Berkeley School Dist 87	2	22
Dada, Moshin/Community Cons School Dist 181	2,5,19,91	91
Dahl, Tracy/Northwest Special Ed District	1	126
Dahlem, Kim/Community High School Dist 155	60,77,79,83,91	179
Dahlquist, Faith/Community Unit School Dist 308	8,15	137
Dahlstrom, Polly/Sherrard Cmty Sch Dist 200	8,11,58,273	189
Dahly, Barbra/Maywood-Melrose Brdview SD 89	9,15	57
Dahm, Bob/Millstadt Cmty Cons SD 160	67	220
Dail, Sara/Sterling Cmty Unit Sch Dist 5	15,68,273	240
Dailey, Katie/Marshall Cmty Sch Dist C-2	16,82	15
Dal Canton, Paula/Litchfield Cmty Unit SD 12	36,88	191
Dal Santo, Patricia/Regional Office of Ed Kane Co	1	134
Dale, Kevin/Rochelle Twp High Sch Dist 212	2,11	195
Dalenberg, Pam/Westville Cmty Unit Sch Dist 2	15	233
Daley, Mark/Argenta Oreana Cmty Unit SD 1	5	165
Dallacqua, Lisa/East Aurora School Dist 131	8,74	129
Dallio, Angelena/Gardner S Wilmington HSD 73	11,288	112

NAME/District	JOB FUNCTIONS	PAGE
Dalton, Beth, Dr/Kildeer Countryside CCSD 96	15,68,74,273,294	151
Dalton, Stacy/Raccoon Cons School Dist 1	2	175
Daly, Karen/River Trails Sch Dist 26	12,57	65
Daly, Karen/River Trails Sch Dist 26	12,57	65
Daly, Scott/Rockridge Cmty Unit SD 300	6	209
Damery, Tim/Metamora Cmty Cons Sch Dist 1	9,11,69,288	258
Dames, Don/Cook County School Dist 104	91	44
Damisch, Lea/Marengo Union Elem Cons SD 165	1,11	182
Damler, Megan/Paris Cmty Unit Sch Dist 4	69,88	103
Damon, Bill/Durand Cmty Sch Dist 322	2	252
Dampf, Elizabeth/Round Lake Area Co Dist 116	74	155
Dance, Tracey/Quincy School District 172	2	2
Daniel, Raquell/Princeville Cmty Unit SD 326	12	200
Daniels, Alfred/Harvey Public School Dist 152	3	51
Daniels, Amber/Pana Cmty Unit School Dist 8	752	14
Daniels, Harold/Bellwood School District 88	73,286,295	22
Daniels, Kevin/Round Lake Area Co Dist 116	67	155
Daniels, Lindy/Rockton School District 140	9,11,288	255
Daniels, Ron/Regional Office of Ed 13	1,83	19
Daniels, Suzanne/Bloomington School District 87	68	185
Dannenberg, Daniel/Kankakee School District 111	73,95	135
Danner, Kerry/Rowva Cmty School Dist 208	11,58,296	140
Danner, Rhonda/Metamora Twp HS Dist 122	2,11	258
Dare, Jill/Raccoon Cons School Dist 1	84,298	175
Dargert, Bill/Pleasant Plains Cmty Unit SD 8	2,3,19	212
Darko, Julie/East Peoria Cmty HS Dist 309	38,69,79	226
Darling, Cindy/Marquardt School District 15	73,76	97
Darling, Kathy/Cumberland Cmty Unit SD 77	2	84
Darlinger, Jennifer/Indian Creek Cmty Unit SD 425	58	85
Darnell, Jeremy/Gibson Cty-Melvin-Sibley CUSD5	1	106
Darnell, Kelly/Thompsonville Cmty USD 174	2	108
Darr, Cheryl/Southwestern Cmty Unit SD 9	4	168
Darr, Mark/Vit Cmty Unit School Dist 2	6,10,27,31,95	110
Darre, Cynthia/Rhodes School District 84 1/2	4	64
Das, Atanu/East Prairie School Dist 73	67	47
Dase, Jeff/Decatur Public Schools 61	8,15,79	165
Dasgupta, Shawn/East Peoria Cmty HS Dist 309	5	226
Dash, Brandon/Central Sch Dist 51	5	225
DaSilva, Cassio/Fairview South School Dist 72	3	49
Daso, Alan/East Moline Public Sch Dist 37	752	207
Daugherty, Doug/Lawrence Co Cmty Sch Dist 20	1,11	159
Daugherty, Jeffrey, Dr/Belleville Area Sp Svc Co-op	1	223
Daugherty, Jill/Bartelso School District 57	67	17
Daugherty, Kevin/Le Roy Cmty Unit SD 2	67	186
Dave, Shona/Winfield School District 34	83,270	100
David, Pam/Roselle School District 12	73	99
Davidsmeyer, Barbie/Jacksonville School Dist 117	57,58,79,271	192
Davidsmeyer, Matt/Pikeland Cmty Sch Dist 10	5	203
Davidson, John/North Greene Unit Dist 3	5	111
Davis-Jones, Shelly, Dr/Dolton School District 149	1	46
Davis-Smith, Lisa/Dolton-Riverdale Sch Dist 148	11	46
Davis, Aaron/Lowpoint-Washburn CUSD 21	6	258
Davis, April/Dolton School District 149	34	46
Davis, Beatrice/Evanston-Skokie Cmty CSD 65	15,68	48
Davis, Ben/Mt Zion Cmty Unit Sch Dist 3	6	166
Davis, Blondean, Dr/Matteson Elem SD 162	1	57
Davis, Doreen/Brookwood School District 167	67	24
Davis, Jackie/Armstrong Twp High SD 225	4	231
Davis, Jeanne/Lewistown Community Unit SD 97	1,83	110
Davis, Jeremy/Community High School Dist 155	2,11,15,68,91	179
Davis, Kathy/Dakota Cmty Unit Sch Dist 201	4	224
Davis, Kelton/Monroe-Randolph Reg Off	1,73	190
Davis, Kirby/Neoga Cmty Unit School Dist 3	36	84
Davis, Kristina/West Chicago Elementary SD 33	1	99
Davis, Lester/Rochelle Cmty Cons SD 231	3	195
Davis, Linda/Egyptian Cmty Unit Sch Dist 5	11,88,274,296	3
Davis, Linda/Egyptian Cmty Unit Sch Dist 5	11,69	3
Davis, Lynn/Manteno Cmty Unit Sch Dist 5	4	135
Davis, Matt/Galesburg Cmty Unit SD 205	4	140
Davis, Michelle/Creve Coeur Sch Dist 76	4	226
Davis, Patsy/Deer Creek-Mackinaw CUSD 701	4	226
Davis, Rodney/Frankfort School Dist 157-C	3	242
Davis, Ruth/Zion Public School District 6	67	157
Davis, Sharron/Prairie Hills Elem SD 144	67	63
Davis, Stephen/Lemont-Bromberek Sch Dist 113A	73,76,295,297	55
Davis, Thomas/Heritage Cmty Unit Sch Dist 8	1,11,73	11

DISTRICT PERSONNEL INDEX

NAME/District	JOB FUNCTIONS	PAGE
Davis, Tonya/Calumet City School Dist 155	67	24
Davis, Wendy/Joliet Twp High Sch Dist 204	295	243
Davison, Carol/Central School District 104	11,296	218
Davoren, Colleen/Community High School Dist 99	295	91
Dawson, Dana/Ladd Cmty Cons Sch Dist 94	16	6
Dawson, Jody/Warrensburg-Latham CU SD 11	12	166
Day, Amy/Sangamon Valley Cmty Unit SD 9	4	166
Day, Dustin/Waverly Cmty Unit SD 6	1,11	193
Day, Mary Ann/East Peoria Cmty HS Dist 309	2	226
Daymon, Jessica/Hardin Co Cmty Unit Sch Dist 1	2	115
De George, Ron/Park Ridge Niles CMCSD 64	3,5	62
De Leon, Jorge/Dupage High School Dist 88	90	93
Deadman, Bryan/Beecher City Cmty Unit SD 20	69	104
Dean, Adam/Huntley Cmty School Dist 158	91	182
Dean, Adam/Triopia Cmty Unit Sch Dist 27	1,11,83	192
Dean, Kris/Tri-Co Special Ed Association	15,58	188
Deany, Michael/Schiller Park School Dist 81	3,5	67
Dearing, Cheryl/Pontiac Cmty Cons Sch Dist 429	59	161
Dearman, Scott, Dr/Dunlap Cmty Unit Sch Dist 323	1	196
Deassuncao, Kathi Lee/Springfield Pub Sch Dist 186	30	213
Deatherage, Ken/Triad Cmty School District 2	6	172
Debaene, Matt/Moline-Coal Valley SD No 40	8,15,16,273	207
Debartalo, Tim/Bloom Twp High Sch Dist 206	4	23
Debartolo, Micheal/Wheeling Cmty Cons Sch Dist 21	2,15,19	71
Debelak, Wally/Gardner S Wilmington HSD 73	3	112
Debernardi, Brian/La Salle Elem SD 122	1	142
DeBoer, Leslie/Summit Hill School Dist 161	7,57,59,271,752	247
Debons, Mark/East Peoria Cmty HS Dist 309	4	226
Debruin, Jan/Sandridge Sch Dist 172	59,270,752	66
DeCarlo, Jaime/Mundelein Cons High SD 120	15,60,79	153
Decker, Cindy/Salt Fork Cmty Unit SD 512	2	233
Decker, Stephanie/Limestone Cmty High SD 310	69	197
Decker, Susan/Cornell Cmty Cons Sch Dist 426	16	161
Decleck, Tracy/United Twp High Sch Dist 30	2	209
Declue, Jaci/Dupo Cmty School District 196	67	218
Decman, Richard, Dr/Herscher Cmty School Dist 2	1	135
DeCock, Teri/Hampton School District 29	12	207
DeCristosaro, Romona/Evanston-Skokie Cmty CSD 65	15,34,59	48
Deens, Joni/Regional Office of Ed 26	298	179
Dees, Dustin/Salt Fork Cmty Unit SD 512	6	233
Dees, Laura/Champaign Cmty Unit Sch Dist 4	4	10
Deets, Dave/Harmony-Emge School Dist 175	1,11	219
Deets, Jill/Maywood-Melrose Brdview SD 89	280	57
Defore, Julie/Rutland Cmty Cons SD 230	69,76,295	144
Defore, Shaun/Waltham Elementary SD 185	3	145
Defries, Doris/Gibson Cty-Melvin-Sibley CUSD5	2	106
Defrisco, Vito/Diocese of Rockford Ed Office	8,15,69	256
Degnan, Judy/School Dist 45 Dupage Co	67	99
Degrave, Larry/Hardin Co Cmty Unit Sch Dist 1	73,76,286	115
DeGroot, Jodie/Scott Morgan Cmty Unit SD 2	31,36,69,83	215
DeGroot, Meagan/Troy Cmty Cons SD 30-C	6	247
DeGuzman, Rene/Community Cons School Dist 180	73,76,286,295	90
Deist, Barrett, Dr/Bethalto Cmty Unit SD 8	2,15	169
Dejarnett, Jodi/Frankfort Cmty Unit SD 168	7,58,275	108
Dejaynes, Brendon/A-C Central Cmty Unit SD 262	73	9
Del Castillo, Rocio/Huntley Cmty School Dist 158	8,11,15,78	182
Del Real, Ann, Dr/Richland School Dist 88A	2	247
Delack, Morgan/Community Cons School Dist 15	71	43
DeLaney, Andrea/Calumet Public School Dist 132	59	25
DeLaney, Leonard/Fisher Cmty Unit School Dist 1	67	10
Delang, Ann/Rockford School District 205	3	253
Delange, Bonnie/Plainfield Cons Sch Dist 202	2	246
Delano, Margaret/Kishwaukee Ed Consortium	2	87
Delapena, Bridgett/Archdiocese of Chicago Ed Off	15	72
Delawder, Scott/Area 3 Learning Technology Ctr	73,295	200
Delboccio, Dave/West Northfield Sch Dist 31	73,98,295	70
DelGado, David/Maywood-Melrose Brdview SD 89	84	57
DelGado, Gabriela/Harvey Public School Dist 152	57	51
Delgato, Guille/Bloomington School District 87	57	185
DelGrosso, Stephanie/Cook County School Dist 130	9	45
Dell, Susan/Hinckley-Big Rock Cmty SD 429	2	85
Dellamorte, Rachel/Valley View Cmty SD 365-U	9	248
Delli, Dane, Dr/Glenview Cmty Cons Sch Dist 34	1	51
Dellorto, Jessica/Plano Cmty Unit Sch Dist 88	16,82	138
DeLong, Josh/Braceville Elem School Dist 75	1	111
DeLong, Josh/Gardner S Wilmington HSD 73	1	112
DeLong, Josh/Pontiac Cmty Cons Sch Dist 429	9	161
DeLuca, Lea/West Chicago Elementary SD 33	9	99
DeLuca, Paula/Archdiocese of Chicago Ed Off	4	72
DelValle, Miguel/Chicago Public School Dist 299	67	25
Demarah, Michael/Braceville Elem School Dist 75	3	111
Demaret, Derek/Jasper Cmty Cons Sch Dist 17	67	237
Demay, James/Crescent Iroquois Cmty SD 249	6	118
Dembo, Steve/Skokie School District 69	67	67
Demler, Dave/Regional Office of Ed 26	15	179
Demonte, Tony/Wilmette Public School Dist 39	16,73	71
DeMoraes, Tyler/Saratoga Cmty Cons SD 60C	73,76,286,295	113
DeNault, Michael/Summersville Sch Dist 79	1	124
Denenberg, Adam/Des Plaines Cmty Cons SD 62	12,17,19,73,76,98,288,296	45
Deneve, Darrin/Carlinville Cmty Unit SD 1	6	167
Deneve, Heather/Carlinville Cmty Unit SD 1	2	167
Denison, Alyssa/Marengo Union Elem Cons SD 165	73	182
Denk, Richard/Ottawa Twp High Sch Dist 140	76,295	143
Dennhardt, Jason/Riverdale Cmty Unit SD 100	73	208
Denning, Amanda/Heyworth Cmty Sch District 4	12	185
Dennis, Bridgett/Fulton Co Cmty Unit Sch Dist 3	58	109
Dennis, Diana/Pontiac Twp High Sch Dist 90	4	161
Dennis, James/Streator Twp High Sch Dist 40	3	145
Dennison, Courtney/Sycamore Cmty Unit SD 427	88,274	86
Dennison, Lonnie/Stark Co Cmty Unit SD 100	5	223
Dennison, Mariah/Gallatin Cmty Unit Sch Dist 7	6	110
Depatis, Gary/Virginia Cmty Unit Sch Dist 64	1,11,83	9
DePaul, Todd/Indian Prairie Sch Dist 204	3	95
DePauw, Alex/El Paso-Gridley CUSD 11	73,295	257
Depoister, John/Manteno Cmty Unit Sch Dist 5	3,91	135
Deporter, Eric/Glen Ellyn School District 41	2,3,4,5,15	94
Deppe, Brooke/Galena Unit School Dist 120	38,69	125
DePue, Carol/Northern Kane Co Reg Voc Sys	1	134
Derango, Dean/Serena Cmty Unit School Dist 2	6	144
Derenzy, Tad/Canton Union School Dist 66	15	109
Derman, Mary/Forest Ridge Sch Dist 142	67	50
Derrick, Matt/Alton Cmty School District 11	73,76,84,286,295	169
DeRubeis, Katy/Ladd Cmty Cons Sch Dist 94	59	6
Deschepper, Douglas, Dr/Orangeville Cmty Unit SD 203	1,83	225
Desecki, Mary Ann/Schiller Park School Dist 81	67	67
Deshane, Dave/Erie Cmty School District 1	5	239
DeSimone, June/Orland School District 135	68	61
Detaeye, Todd/Moline-Coal Valley SD No 40	12,15,68,69	207
Deterding, Kim/Prairie Du Rocher CCSD 134	67	205
Detering, Brad, Dr/Salem Cmty High Sch Dist 600	1,11	175
Detering, Brett/Anna-Jonesboro Cmty HSD 81	288	230
Deters, Justin/Stewardson-Strasburg SD 5-A	8,58,288	216
Deters, Rick/New Holland Middletown ESD 88	3	164
Detloff, Eva/Barrington Cmty Unit SD 220	7	147
Dettman, Heidi/Rockford School District 205	8	254
Deuser, Michael, Dr/Chicago Public School Dist 299	23	25
Deval, Erin/Palos Cmty Cons Sch Dist 118	79,88	61
Dever, Beth/Avoca School District 37	2,3,4,5,79,84,91	22
DeVore, Lisa/Metamora Cmty Cons Sch Dist 1	2	258
Devos, Danielle/Tri-City Cmty Unit Sch Dist 1	2	214
DeWalt, Jeff/Ottawa Twp High Sch Dist 140	12	143
DeWar, Scott/Harrisburg Cmty Unit SD 3	88	210
Dewelde, Lisa/Wauconda Cmty Unit SD 118	7,15,68,74,85	155
Dewey, Kim/Kings Cons School District 144	12	194

#	Function	#	Function	#	Function	#	Function	#	Function	#	Function	#	Function
1	Superintendent	16	Instructional Media Svcs	30	Adult Education	44	Science Sec	58	Special Education K-12	72	Summer School	88	Alternative/At Risk	277	Remedial Math K-12
2	Bus/Finance/Purchasing	17	Chief Operations Officer	31	Career/Sch-to-Work K-12	45	Math K-12	59	Special Education Elem	73	Instructional Tech	89	Multi-Cultural Curriculum	280	Literacy Coach
3	Buildings And Grounds	18	Chief Academic Officer	32	Career/Sch-to-Work Elem	46	Math Elem	60	Special Education Sec	74	Inservice Training	90	Social Work	285	STEM
4	Food Service	19	Chief Financial Officer	33	Career/Sch-to-Work Sec	47	Math Sec	61	Foreign/World Lang K-12	75	Marketing/Distributive	91	Safety/Security	286	Digital Learning
5	Transportation	20	Art K-12	34	Early Childhood Ed	48	English/Lang Arts K-12	62	Foreign/World Lang Elem	76	Info Systems	92	Magnet School	288	Common Core Standards
6	Athletic	21	Art Elem	35	Health/Phys Education	49	English/Lang Arts Elem	63	Foreign/World Lang Sec	77	Psychological Assess	93	Parental Involvement	294	Accountability
7	Health Services	22	Art Sec	36	Guidance Services K-12	50	English/Lang Arts Sec	64	Religious Education K-12	78	Affirmative Action	95	Tech Prep Program	295	Network System
8	Curric/Instruct K-12	23	Music K-12	37	Guidance Services Elem	51	Reading K-12	65	Religious Education Elem	79	Student Personnel	97	Chief Information Officer	296	Title II Programs
9	Curric/Instruct Elem	24	Music Elem	38	Guidance Services Sec	52	Reading Elem	66	Religious Education Sec	80	Driver Ed/Safety	98	Chief Technology Officer	297	Webmaster
10	Curric/Instruct Sec	25	Music Sec	39	Social Studies K-12	53	Reading Sec	67	School Board President	81	Gifted/Talented	270	Character Education	298	Grant Writer/Ptnrships
11	Federal Program	26	Business Education	40	Social Studies Elem	54	Remedial Reading K-12	68	Teacher Personnel	82	Video Services	271	Migrant Education	750	Chief Innovation Officer
12	Title I	27	Career & Tech Ed	41	Social Studies Sec	55	Remedial Reading Elem	69	Academic Assessment	83	Substance Abuse Prev	273	Teacher Mentor	751	Chief of Staff
13	Title V	28	Technology Education	42	Science K-12	56	Remedial Reading Sec	70	Research/Development	84	Erate	274	Before/After Sch	752	Social Emotional Learning
15	Asst Superintendent	29	Family/Consumer Science	43	Science Elem	57	Bilingual/ELL	71	Public Information	85	AIDS Education	275	Response To Intervention		

Illinois School Directory — District Personnel Index

NAME/District	JOB FUNCTIONS	PAGE
DeWitt, Ed/Mendota Cmty School Dist 289	3	142
Dewitte, Josh/Collinsville Cmty Sch Dist 10	3,91	170
Dexheimer, Mike/Germantown Hills SD 69	73	257
Dexter, Ashley/Century Cmty Unit SD 100	8,12,69,83,85	204
Dexter, David/Century Cmty Unit SD 100	6	204
Dey, Doug/Bunker Hill Cmty Unit SD 8	3,5,91	167
Dezell, Anne/Lena-Winslow Cmty Unit SD 202	9,11,58,275	224
Dhameres, Nate/Glenbard Twp High Sch Dist 87	76	94
Diamond, Nan/School Assoc for Sp Ed-Dupage	58	102
Diaz, Alberto/Valley View Cmty SD 365-U	76,91,295	248
Diaz, Janet/Addison School District 4	274	88
Diaz, Stephanie, Dr/Community Cons School Dist 46	57	148
DiBartolo, Phillip/Chicago Public School Dist 299	71,97	25
Dick, Dianne/Calhoun Cmty Unit Sch Dist 40	4	8
Dickey, Janet/Opdyke-Belle Rive Cmty CSSD 5	59	123
Dickinson, Bridget/Community Unit School Dist 200	58	91
Dickinson, Laura/Forest Park School District 91	2	50
Dickman, Dan/Willow Springs School Dist 108	3	71
Dickson, Dave/Grant Park Cmty Unit SD 6	67	135
Diddlebock, Christopher/Monroe-Randolph Reg Off	15	190
Didier, Allison/Rantoul City School Dist 137	58	11
Diedrich, Ryan/Manteno Cmty Unit Sch Dist 5	5	135
Diefenbach, Tomi/Freeburg Cmty Cons SD 70	1	219
Diehl, Eric/Steger School Dist 194	2	68
Diehl, Fred/Rockford School District 205	91	254
Diehl, Rachael/Steger School Dist 194	4	68
Dieken, Tonya/Prairie Central Cmty USD 8	8	162
Diel, Brett/Carterville Cmty Unit SD 5	6	250
Diemel, William/Shirland Cmty Cons SD 134	67	255
Dierkx, Guy/Riverdale Cmty Unit SD 100	6	208
Dietrich, Jennifer/N Pekin-Marquette Hts SD 102	9,11	227
Dietz, Greg/Maine Twp High Sch Dist 207	15,68,70,78,273	56
Dietz, Greg/Maine Twp Spec Ed Program	15,68	82
Digangi, Melissa/Zion-Benton Twp High SD 126	10	157
Digg, Starla/Galatia Cmty Unit Sch Dist 1	4	210
Dilallo, Caitlin/Huntley Cmty School Dist 158	58	182
Dilallo, Caitlin/Komarek School District 94	59,79,85,88,275	54
Dilillo, Susan/Park Ridge Niles CMCSD 64	68	62
Dillard, Lakeshia/Iroquois Co Cmty Unit SD 9	38	119
Dilliner, Brandon/Sesser-Valier Cmty Unit SD 196	3	108
Dillman, Andy/Grant Park Cmty Unit SD 6	73	135
Dillon, Amy/Community High School Dist 128	83,88	148
Dillow, Nancy/Mazon-Verona-Kinsman ESD 2-C	1,11,83	112
Dillow, Stephanie/Carbondale Cmty HSD 165	91	120
DiMartino, Charles/Thornton Fractnl Twp HSD 215	2	69
Dimit, John/Urbana School District 116	67	12
DiNello, Tony/Mazon-Verona-Kinsman ESD 2-C	6	112
Dinger, Kathy/Bushnell Prairie Cmty USD 170	1	178
Dingles, Athena/Milne-Kelvin Grove District 91	2	244
Dinkheller, Kim/Quincy School District 172	9,11,69,73,275,286,298	2
Dioguardi, Gina/Arbor Park School District 145	59	21
Dirkmeyer, Vance/North Greene Unit Dist 3	3	111
Disney, Cheryl/Galatia Cmty Unit Sch Dist 1	73,295	210
Dite, Lori/Morris Cmty High Sch Dist 101	60	113
Ditkowsky, Ben/Barrington Cmty Unit SD 220	69,76,294	147
Ditto, Josh/Dongola Unit School Dist 66	16,73,286	230
Divenere, George/Community High School Dist 155	73,76,84,295	179
Dixon, Aaron/Carbondale Elem School Dist 95	3	120
Dixon, Amy, Dr/Carmi-White Co School Dist 5	8,57,69,74,271,285,288	237
Dixon, Rebecca/Country Club Hills SD 160	79	45
Dixon, Scott/Woodridge Elem Sch District 68	73,76,295	100
Dixon, Tim/Illinois Vly Ctl Sch Dist 321	3	197
Dixson, Ramona/Rock Island-Milan Sch Dist 41	11,31,51,54,69,72,294,298	208
Dizon, Nicole/New Trier Twp HS District 203	71	58
Doan, Mark/Effingham Cmty Sch Dist 40	1	104
Dobbelaire, Shannan/Central Sch Dist 51	2	225
Dobbles, William/Danville School District 118	67	231
Dobbs, Jeff/Bloomington School District 87	34	185
Dobbs, Michael/Ball Chatham Cmty Unit SD 5	3	211
Dobra, Christine/North Palos School Dist 117	9,13,27,69,74,83,273,288	59
Docherty, Sean/Mt Vernon Twp HS District 201	10,11,296,298	123
Dockens, Kenya/Hillside School District 93	88,90	52
Doder, Cindy/Whiteside School District 115	16	222
Doerr, Scott, Dr/Nokomis Cmty Unit Sch Dist 22	1	191
Doetch, Ashley/North Boone Cmty Unit SD 200	58	5
Doig, Lisa/Atwood Heights SD 125	11	21
Doka, Armir/DeKalb Cmty Unit SD 428	2	84
Dolan, Gregg/Morrison Cmty Unit Sch Dist 6	6	239
Dolan, Patrick/Naperville Cmty Unit SD 203	3	98
Dole, Lake/Diamond Lake School Dist 76	69,79	149
Dolehide, Debbie/Cass School District 63	2	89
Dolener, Jessica/Farrington Cmty Cons SD 99	4	122
Dolezal, Angela/Riverside Public Sch Dist 96	9,11,57,69,288	65
Doll, Adam/Bond Co Cmty Unit Sch Dist 2	3	4
Doman, Rich/Gibson Cty-Melvin-Sibley CUSD5	3	106
Dombek, Jim/Sycamore Cmty Unit SD 427	67	86
Dombrowski, Richard, Dr/Union School District 81	2	248
Domchymski, Adam/Oak Park Elem School Dist 97	295	60
Domeracki, Douglas, Dr/Community High School Dist 94	1	91
Domeracki, Ryan/Dupage High School Dist 88	2,4,5,91	93
Dominick, Brian/Cicero School District 99	3	42
Dominick, Randy/Zeigler Royalton CUSD 188	67	108
Donahue, Brenda/Marseilles Elem Sch Dist 150	1	142
Donahue, Jana/Community Cons School Dist 46	34	148
Donahue, Mark/O'Fallon Cmty Cons Sch Dist 90	24	221
Donahue, Mark/O'Fallon Cmty Cons Sch Dist 90	24	221
Donahue, Paul/Pana Cmty Unit School Dist 8	8,58	14
Donald, Luana/Rantoul Twp High Sch Dist 193	4	12
Donaldson, Amy/Auburn Cmty Unit Sch Dist 10	11,296,298	211
Donatelli, Jennifer/Naperville Cmty Unit SD 203	8	98
Donath, Tracy/Peoria Public Sch Dist 150	42,45,285	198
Donato, Jessica/Northbrook School District 28	2,4,7,275	59
Donato, Jim/Evergreen Park Cmty HSD 231	76	49
Donegan, Kate/Skokie School District 73 1/2	1	67
Donermeyer, John/Dolton-Riverdale Sch Dist 148	70	46
Donkin, R Matthew/Frankfort Cmty Unit SD 168	1,11	108
Donnan, Valerie/Special Education Dist Lake Co	1	159
Donoho, Leshelle/Maroa Forsyth CU Sch Dist 2	68	165
Donohue, Cindy/Richmond-Burton Cmty HSD 157	4	184
Donono, Kent/Farrington Cmty Cons SD 99	67	122
Donovan, Tom/Aptakisic-Tripp Sch Dist 102	73,98,295	146
Doolin, Bonnie/Forest Park School District 91	2,12	50
Dore, Cindy/Woodridge Elem Sch District 68	7,11,35,59,77,88	100
Dorm, Julie/Rowva Cmty School Dist 208	4	140
Dorner, Kay, Dr/Tuscola Cmty Unit SD 301	275	88
Dornick, Rick/Rochelle Cmty Cons SD 231	6	195
Dorothy, Coy/Warsaw Cmty Unit Sch Dist 316	6	115
Dorsam, Michael/Bradley-Bourbonnais CHSD 307	16,82	134
Doss, Jacqueline/Country Club Hills SD 160	67	45
Doss, Jerry/Thornton Twp High Sch Dist 205	15,68	69
Doster, Craig, Dr/Beach Park Cmty Cons SD 3	1	147
Dotson, Earl/Rockford School District 205	71	254
Dotson, Jeremy/Dupage Reg Office of Ed 19	2	102
Dotson, Tim/Limestone Walters CCSD 316	1,11,73	198
Dotts, Tony/Community High School Dist 99	295	91
Doty, Gordon/Red Bud Cmty Unit Sch Dist 132	3	205
Doty, Lisa/Metamora Twp HS Dist 122	7	258
Doty, Mariel/Round Lake Area Co Dist 116	57	155
Doubert, Adam/Williamsfield Cmty Unit SD 210	5	140
Doucet, Melissa/Winfield School District 34	52,73,280,285,286,288	100
Doughan, Gary/Paris Union School District 95	5	103
Doughan, Gary/Saunemin Cmty Cons SD 438	1,11	162
Dougherty, Chris, Dr/Taylorville Cmty Unit SD 3	1	15
Dougherty, Ryan/Allendale Cmty Cons SD 17	35,85	234
Doughty, Bruce/Glenbrook High School Dist 225	67	50
Doughty, Walter/Woodland School District 50	5	156
Douglas, Katie/Morton Grove School Dist 70	79	58
Douglas, Melissa/Rockford School District 205	280	254
Douglas, Paul/Champaign Cmty Unit Sch Dist 4	2	10
Douglas, Scott/Quincy School District 172	6	2
Dowden, Andrew/Oakland Cmty Unit Sch Dist 5	67	19
Dowden, Lucas/Kildeer Countryside CCSD 96	73,76,285,295	151
Downes, Mr/St Joseph Cmty Cons SD 169	5	12
Downey, Mark/Polo Cmty Unit Sch Dist 222	5	195
Downing, Jonathan/Warrensburg-Latham CU SD 11	10	166
Doyle-Perritt, Colleen/Unity Point Cmty Cons SD 140	57,271	121
Doyle, Deb/Center Cass Sch Dist 66	9	90
Doyle, Kathleen, Dr/South Cook Interm Svc Center	15	82
Doyle, Lauri/Community Unit School Dist 308	67	137
Doyle, Lisa/A-C Central Cmty Unit SD 262	12,275	9
Doyle, Natalie/Rock Island Reg Off of Ed 49	34	210
Doyle, Terica/Carbondale Cmty HSD 165	78,80	120

DISTRICT PERSONNEL INDEX

Market Data Retrieval

NAME/District	JOB FUNCTIONS	PAGE
Doyle, Tony/Rochelle Cmty Cons SD 231	9,11,15,69,88,288,298	195
Drafall, Todd/Downers Grove School Dist 58	2	93
Drake, April/Windsor Cmty Unit SD 1	58	216
Drake, Ed/Lyons Twp HS District 204	3	56
Drake, Henry/Bloom Twp High Sch Dist 206	67	23
Drake, Queen/Springfield Pub Sch Dist 186	274	213
Drake, Thomas/Warren Twp High Sch Dist 121	67	155
Drangsholt, Megan/Cook County School Dist 154	12,59,88,298	45
Draniczarek, Paul/Ridgewood Cmty HSD 234	67	64
Draudt, Mary Ann/Diocese of Joliet Ed Office	73	249
Dreher, Andrew/McHenry Cmty Cons Sch Dist 15	295	183
Dreher, Corey/Sunset Ridge Sch Dist 29	3	68
Dremel, Cathy/Batavia Unit School Dist 101	67	128
Drenthe, Jeff/West Aurora School Dist 129	295	132
Drescoll, Pam/Lemont High Sch Dist 210	67	55
Drew, Amy/Ashton-Franklin Center SD 275	36,69,83,88	159
Drew, Delene/Newark Cmty Cons Sch Dist 66	2,19	138
Drifcoll, Kerry/Prairie Hill Cmty Cons SD 133	288	253
Driscoll, Matthew/Evanston Twp High SD 202	91	48
Drobysh, Cathy/Community Cons School Dist 93	76	90
Droege, Tiffany/Belleville Township HSD 201	16	217
Droll, Carolyn/Wheeling Cmty Cons Sch Dist 21	21,35,46	71
Drombrowski, Jim/Burnham School District 1545	3	24
Droy, Mary Ellen/Winnebago Cmty Unit SD 323	4	255
Dryier, Kim, Dr/Consolidated High Sch Dist 230	11,16,27,57,88,275,294,298	44
Du Clos, Carol/North Chicago Cmty Unit SD 187	58	154
Duback, Michael/La Grange-Highlands SD 106	2	54
Dubbert, Dwayne/Reed-Custer Cmty Unit SD 255-U	73,82,295	246
Duckworth, Amy/Fairfield Pub Sch District 112	59	236
Dudek, Shannon, Dr/Morris Elem School Dist 54	1	113
Dudley, Deeanne/DePue Unit Sch Dist 103	58	6
Dudzik, John/Cook County School Dist 130	15,68	45
Duecker, Danita/Belle Valley School Dist 119	7	217
Duell, Alicia/Wheeling Cmty Cons Sch Dist 21	76	71
Duff, Jay/Mannheim School District 83	295	56
Duffin, Vanessa/Speed Seja 802	68	82
Duffy, Jenna/Northbrook School District 28	79	59
Duffy, Lynne/Wheeling Cmty Cons Sch Dist 21	34	71
DuFour, Jeffery, Dr/Joppa-Maple Grove Unit SD 38	8,13,58,69,288	177
Dufresne, Paul/Joliet Public School Dist 86	3	243
Dugan, Kathleen, Dr/Bensenville Elem Sch Dist 2	11,69,74,279,280,288,296,298	89
Dugan, Michael/Hononegah Cmty High SD 207	1	253
Dugan, Tood/Bunker Hill Cmty Unit SD 8	1,11	167
Duggan, James, Dr/Bourbonnais Elem Sch Dist 53	9,57,285,286,288,298	134
Duggan, Mike/Community Cons School Dist 181	3	91
Duginske, Jacquie/Community Unit School Dist 300	45	180
Duhig, Matthew/Community Unit School Dist 200	3	91
Duhig, Michael/Community Unit School Dist 200	3	91
Dujmovich, Linda/Marengo Cmty High Sch Dist 154	67	182
Duke, Jessie/Dupo Cmty School District 196	34	218
Duke, Melinda/Century Cmty Unit SD 100	9	204
Duke, Steve/Dupo Cmty School District 196	3,4	218
Dukes, Brian/Pontiac Cmty Cons Sch Dist 429	1	161
Duklias, Wendy/Taylorville Cmty Unit SD 3	2	15
Dulakis, Wendy/South Fork School Dist 14	2	14
Duling, Shannon/Princeville Cmty Unit SD 326	1	200
Dulle, Katie/Lemont High Sch Dist 210	7	55
Dunaway, Jeff/Bluford Unit School Dist 318	3	122
Duncan, Colin/Prairie Central Cmty USD 8	76,295	162
Duncan, Joseph/Beecher Cmty Sch Dist 200-U	73,286	241
Duncan, Kris/Edwards Co Cmty Unit SD 1	6	104
Duncan, Leslie/Western CUSD 12	58	203
Dungy, Andrea/Ewing Northern Cmty SD 115	2	108
Dunham, Emily/Sunset Ridge Sch Dist 29	12,79	68
Dunker, Kristin/Vermilion Assoc for Special Ed	1	233
Dunleavy, John/River Trails Sch Dist 26	76	65
Dunmead, Mary/Geneva CUSD 304	5	131

NAME/District	JOB FUNCTIONS	PAGE
Dunn, Brent/Jacksonville School Dist 117	5	192
Dunn, Jamie/Deland-Weldon Cmty Unit SD 57	67	202
Dunn, Julie/Iroquois Co Cmty Unit SD 9	16	119
Dunn, Kathleen/Cook County School Dist 104	2,88,752	44
Dunn, Ronda, Dr/Regional Office of Ed 30	8	121
Dunn, Shelly/EFE System 330	2	13
Dunne, Jennifer/Antioch Cmty Cons School Dist 34	59,77,79	146
Dunne, Marta/Sandwich Cmty Unit SD 430	57	85
Dunnell, Scott/Forest Park School District 91	71	50
Dunnill, Nicole/Dwight Twp High Sch Dist 230	57	161
Dunning, Kathy/Joppa-Maple Grove Unit SD 38	59	177
DuPont, Paula/Community Cons School Dist 180	67	90
Duran, Rosaura/Thornton Twp High Sch Dist 205	68	69
Durica, Deanna/Berwyn South School Dist 100	67	23
During, Blake/South Central Cmty Unit SD 401	6	176
Durlak, Karen/Grant Cmty High Sch Dist 124	288	150
Duross, Andrew/Schaumburg Cmty Cons SD 54	1	66
Durre, Heather/Flora Cmty Unit School Dist 35	73,84	16
Duskey, Deborah/Matteson Elem SD 162	59	57
Dusresne, Paul/Joliet Public School Dist 86	91	243
Dust, Rich/Thornton Fractnl Twp HSD 215	67	69
Dusterhoft, Matt/Lockport High Sch Dist 205	73,95	244
Dusterhoft, Matthew/Will Co School District 92	67	249
Dustman, Brian/Staunton Cmty Unit Sch Dist 6	3	168
Duty, Connie/Century Cmty Unit SD 100	5	204
Dvorak, Christopher/Regional Office of Ed 35	1	146
Dwaid, Matt/Rooks Creek Cmty Cons SD 425	67	162
Dwyer, Mary/Kirby School District 140	59	53
Dwyer, Michael/Consolidated High Sch Dist 230	6,35	44
Dwyer, Richard/Riverdale Cmty Unit SD 100	10,27,57	208
Dybek, Amanda/Prophetstown-Lyndon-Tampico 3	23,38,69	239
Dyer, Tim/Roxana Cmty Unit Sch Dist 1	3,91	172
Dykas, Cindy/Worth School District 127	2,4	72
Dykstra, Amanda/Valley View Cmty SD 365-U	9	248
Dykstra, Kim/Community Unit School Dist 16	16	211
Dzaillo, Michael, Dr/Mannheim School District 83	11,68,79,294	56

E

NAME/District	JOB FUNCTIONS	PAGE
Eager, Becky/Earlville Cmty Unit Sch Dist 9	11	141
Eager, Kristine/Waltham Elementary SD 185	1	145
Eagleson, Denise/Richland Co Cmty Unit SD 1	16	206
Eaker, Josh/Robein Cmty School District 85	67	228
Ealey, Amber/Tazewell-Mason Sp Ed Assoc	34	229
Ealey, Leonard/Pekin Public School Dist 108	9,11,57,83,88,271,274,288	227
Earleywine, Paige/Flora Cmty Unit School Dist 35	7	16
Earls, Paula/Will Co Regional Office of Edu	5	250
Earp, Paulette/Galesburg Cmty Unit SD 205	5	140
East, Shelley/Paris Cmty Unit Sch Dist 4	12	103
Eaton, Sheila/Sparta Cmty School Dist 140	31	205
Ebbesmeyer, Steve/Belleville Public Sch Dist 118	4	217
Ebenezer, Troy/Rock Falls Elem Sch Dist 13	67	240
Eberle, Lan, Dr/Bartonville School District 66	1	196
Eberle, Ross/Winnebago Cmty Unit SD 323	73,295	255
Ebson, Nicole/J Sterling Morton HSD 201	6	53
Eccarius, Doug/Indian Prairie Sch Dist 204	15	95
Echols, Kim, Dr/Rich Twp High School Dist 227	68,74,78,273	64
Eckberg, Matt/East Peoria Cmty HS Dist 309	67	226
Ecker, Leslie/Shiloh Village Sch Dist 85	67	221
Eckert, Ashley/Beardstown Cmty Sch Dist 15	69,83	9
Eckert, Carol/Belleville Township HSD 201	67	217
Eckle, Rhonda/Havana Cmty Sch District 126	7	177
Eckles, Elliott/Barrington Cmty Unit SD 220	3	147
Eckmann, Kathy/Hononegah Cmty High SD 207	11,288	253
Economou, Nancy/Kenilworth School District 38	83	53
Eddings, Kari/Porta Cmty Unit Sch Dist 202	2	189
Eddings, Melissa/Iuka Community Cons Sch Dist 7	11,296	174
Eddy, Bill/Ramsey Cmty Unit Sch Dist 204	6	105

#		#		#		#		#		#	
1	Superintendent	16	Instructional Media Svcs	30	Adult Education	44	Science Sec	58	Special Education K-12	72	Summer School	88	Alternative/At Risk	277	Remedial Math K-12
2	Bus/Finance/Purchasing	17	Chief Operations Officer	31	Career/Sch-to-Work K-12	45	Math K-12	59	Special Education Elem	73	Instructional Tech	89	Multi-Cultural Curriculum	280	Literacy Coach
3	Buildings And Grounds	18	Chief Academic Officer	32	Career/Sch-to-Work Elem	46	Math Elem	60	Special Education Sec	74	Inservice Training	90	Social Work	285	STEM
4	Food Service	19	Chief Financial Officer	33	Career/Sch-to-Work Sec	47	Math Sec	61	Foreign/World Lang K-12	75	Marketing/Distributive	91	Safety/Security	286	Digital Learning
5	Transportation	20	Art K-12	34	Early Childhood Ed	48	English/Lang Arts K-12	62	Foreign/World Lang Elem	76	Info Systems	92	Magnet School	288	Common Core Standards
6	Athletic	21	Art Elem	35	Health/Phys Education	49	English/Lang Arts Elem	63	Foreign/World Lang Sec	77	Psychological Assess	93	Parental Involvement	294	Accountability
7	Health Services	22	Art Sec	36	Guidance Services K-12	50	English/Lang Arts Sec	64	Religious Education K-12	78	Affirmative Action	95	Tech Prep Program	295	Network System
8	Curric/Instruct K-12	23	Music K-12	37	Guidance Services Elem	51	Reading K-12	65	Religious Education Elem	79	Student Personnel	96	Chief Information Officer	296	Title II Programs
9	Curric/Instruct Elem	24	Music Elem	38	Guidance Services Sec	52	Reading Elem	66	Religious Education Sec	80	Driver Ed/Safety	97	Chief Technology Officer	297	Webmaster
10	Curric/Instruct Sec	25	Music Sec	39	Social Studies K-12	53	Reading Sec	67	School Board President	81	Gifted/Talented	98	Character Education	298	Grant Writer/Ptnrships
11	Federal Program	26	Business Education	40	Social Studies Elem	54	Remedial Reading K-12	68	Teacher Personnel	82	Video Services	270	Migrant Education	750	Chief Innovation Officer
12	Title I	27	Career & Tech Ed	41	Social Studies Sec	55	Remedial Reading Elem	69	Academic Assessment	83	Substance Abuse Prev	273	Teacher Mentor	751	Chief of Staff
13	Title V	28	Technology Education	42	Science K-12	56	Remedial Reading Sec	70	Research/Development	84	Erate	274	Before/After Sch	752	Social Emotional Learning
15	Asst Superintendent	29	Family/Consumer Science	43	Science Elem	57	Bilingual/ELL	71	Public Information	85	AIDS Education	275	Response To Intervention		

Illinois School Directory — District Personnel Index

NAME/District	JOB FUNCTIONS	PAGE
Edelheit, Jason/Glencoe Sch District 35	2,3,11,17,19,294,296,298	51
Eden, Angela/Neoga Cmty Unit School Dist 3	4	84
Edenburn, James/Armstrong Ellis SD 61	6,67	231
Edgar, Tom, Dr/Community Cons School Dist 15	9,15,69,294	43
Edholm, Jennifer/West Prairie Cmty Sch Dist 103	11,296	178
Edison, Anthony, Dr/Posen-Robbins Sch Dist 143-5	1	63
Edler, James/Forest Park School District 91	9	50
Edman, Christopher/Lincolnwood Sch Dist 74	73,76,84	55
Edmon, Frank/Joliet Twp High Sch Dist 204	67	243
Edmonds, Christopher/Butler School District 53	67	89
Edmondson, Andy/Hardin Co Cmty Unit Sch Dist 1	1	115
Edmundson, Mark/Le Roy Cmty Unit SD 2	2	186
Edwards, Brandie/Thornton Fractnl Twp HSD 215	73,76,286	69
Edwards, Chris/Wood River-Hartford Elem SD 15	73,295,297	172
Edwards, Christina/Plainfield Cons Sch Dist 202	7	246
Edwards, Doug/Jamp Special Ed Services	1,11	204
Edwards, Ginger/Ramsey Cmty Unit Sch Dist 204	8,60,88,92	105
Edwards, Laura/Indian Valley Voc Ed System	15	86
Edwards, Michael/Taylorville Cmty Unit SD 3	58	15
Edwards, Ron/Pleasant Hill CUSD 3	1	203
Edwards, Tulicia/Oak Park Elem School Dist 97	68	60
Eeten, Erin/Hartsburg Emden School Dist 21	4	163
Egan, Len/Community High School Dist 94	79	91
Egan, Stacey/East Alton Elementary SD 13	59	170
Egan, Taylor/Geneva CUSD 304	67	131
Egerstaffer, Kim/Special Ed Dist of McHenry Co	2	185
Eggemeyer, Brian/Iroquois West Cmty Unit SD 10	73,295,297	119
Eggerding, Scott/Lyons Twp HS District 204	10,11,74,273,288,296,298	56
Eggleston, Fran/Kaneland Cmty Unit SD 302	58	132
Egizio, Mary Ann/Chaney-Monge School Dist 88	2	241
Ehlenburg, Debbie/Alden-Hebron School Dist 19	1,11	179
Ehlers, Tim/Rockton School District 140	3	255
Ehling, Barbara/Streator Elem School Dist 44	67	144
Ehrat, Sandra/Freeport School District 145	11	224
Ehrhart, Elizabeth/Forest Ridge Sch Dist 142	9,11,57,273,285,288,298	50
Ehrman, Adam/Community Unit School Dist 16	1	211
Ehrman, Adam, Dr/Bourbonnais Elem Sch Dist 53	1	134
Ehrmann, Joseph/Community Unit School Dist 300	73	180
Eichmiller, James/Downers Grove School Dist 58	73,286,297	93
Eichorst, Rose/Forest Ridge Sch Dist 142	7	50
Eidelman, Julia/Glencoe Sch District 35	16	51
Eigner, Mark/Hoopeston Area Cmty Unit SD 11	2,5	232
Eilers, John/Southeastern Cmty Unit SD 337	67	115
Eiron-Conway, Jennifer/Urbana School District 116	76	12
Eisenbarth, Trent/Georgetown-Ridge Farm CUSD 4	286	232
Ek, Paula/East Aurora School Dist 131	9	129
Ekena, Jeff/Regional Office of Ed 53	1	229
Ekhoff, Andrew/Bradley-Bourbonnais CHSD 307	73	134
Ekstrom, Erica/Community Unit School Dist 200	58	91
Elddelman, Jama/Jonesboro Cmty Cons SD 43	73	230
Elder, Nick/EFE System 330	1	13
Eldridge-Stark, Martha/North Suburban Ed Reg for Voc	1,11	82
Eldridge, Anna/Vienna Public School Dist 55	58	127
Elfering, Sara/Antioch Cmty Cons Sch Dist 34	9	146
Elias, Melanie/Lisbon Cmty Cons Sch Dist 90	1,83	138
Elimire, Cody/Murphysboro Cmty Unit SD 186	8,85	121
Eliscu, Joshua/E F Lindop Elem Sch Dist 92	73,84,286,295	47
Elkei, Todd/Lockport Twp High Sch Dist 205	35,85	244
Ellaway, David/Cobden Cmty Unit Sch Dist 17	73,295	230
Elledge, Tammy/Coal City Cmty Unit Sch Dist 1	8,69,73,297	112
Ellena, Tyler/Putnam Co Cmty Unit SD 535	31,69	204
Elliott, Angie/Le Roy Cmty Unit SD 2	35,83,85	186
Elliott, Brett/Stark Co Cmty Unit SD 100	1,11	223
Elliott, Cathy/Alton Cmty School District 11	7,58,90,752	169
Elliott, Keri/Mt Pulaski Cmty Unit SD 23	12	164
Elliott, Sherrie/Paxton-Buckley-Loda CUSD 10	4	107
Elliott, Stacey/Crete-Monee Cmty SD 201-U	297	242
Ellis Bowen, Iman/Joliet Twp High Sch Dist 204	13,16,60,271	243
Ellis, Adam/North Wayne Cmty Unit SD 200	6	237
Ellis, Carla/Oak Park Elem School Dist 97	4	60
Ellis, Cindy/Jasper Cmty Cons Sch Dist 17	9,69	237
Ellis, Deborah/Odin Public School Dist 722	288	175
Ellis, Jeanne/Carterville Cmty Unit SD 5	4	250
Ellis, Juletta/Pana Cmty Unit School Dist 8	10,69	14
Ellison, Randal/Elgin School District U-46	88	130
Elman, Dain/Gurnee School District 56	285	150

NAME/District	JOB FUNCTIONS	PAGE
Elschlager, Tina/Nauvoo-Colusa CUSD 325	16,57	115
Elser, Dawn/Central School District 104	1,288	218
Ely, Randy/Chester-E Lincoln Cmty SD 61	3	163
Elzen, Tom/Freeport School District 145	73,84,295	224
Eman, Carla/Peoria Public Sch Dist 150	2	198
Embry, John/Deer Creek-Mackinaw CUSD 701	73,286,295	226
Emerson, Amber/Shirland Cmty Cons SD 134	73	255
Emerson, Don/Tri-Point Cmty Unit SD 6J	36,69	162
Emerson, Jake/Manteno Cmty Unit Sch Dist 5	2	135
Emery, Sarah/Regional Office of Ed 20	15	211
Emmons, Gary/High Mount Sch Dist 116	3	219
Emmons, Matt/Henry Senachwine CUSD 5	6	176
Empen, Margo/Dixon Cmty Unit Sch Dist 170	1	160
Emricson, Jason/Community Unit School Dist 300	76,295	180
Encher, Scott/Brookfield-LaGrange Park SD 95	67	23
Enderess, Shawna/Pearl City Cmty Unit SD 200	12,280	225
Enderle, Paul/Oak Lawn-Hometown Sch Dist 123	1	60
Endress, Deb/Regional Office of Ed 8	8	225
Endress, Scott/Princeville Cmty Unit SD 326	57,271	200
Engel, Ami/Community Unit School Dist 300	42	180
Engel, Mike/Warren Twp High Sch Dist 121	2,3,15	155
Engelbrecht, David/Marengo Cmty High Sch Dist 154	1,73	182
Engelbrecht, Terie/Johnsburg Cmty School Dist 12	8,18,285,288	182
Engele, David/Nashville Cmty Cons SD 49	67	235
Engelland, Justin/Lake Forest School District 67	67	152
Engelman, John/Gardner S Wilmington HSD 73	6,10,88	112
Engerski, Garry/Marshall Cmty Sch Dist C-2	3,5	15
England, Scott/Fairfield Pub Sch District 112	1,11	236
Engle, Brian/Glenview Cmty Cons Sch Dist 34	16,28,73,286	51
Englehart, Luke/Yorkville Cmty Unit SD 115	6	139
Englert, Craig/Matteson Elem SD 162	2,15	57
English, Kirk/Newark Cmty High Sch Dist 18	3	138
Enstrom, Vince/Benjamin Sch District 25	67	89
Entsminger, Mary/Chicago Heights Elem SD 170	9,11,69,72,83,280,296,298	25
Epcke, Judi/Northbrook School Dist 28	73,98	59
Epley, Monte/Nokomis Cmty Unit Sch Dist 22	5	191
Epperson, Ben/Rockford School District 205	8	254
Epperson, Christina/Hamilton Co Cmty Unit SD 10	58,69	114
Epperson, Daniel/Warrensburg-Latham CU SD 11	5	166
Epperson, Ray/McLean Co Unit District 5	8,15	186
Epperson, Victor/Leland Cmty Unit Sch Dist 1	36	142
Epplin, Sarah/Centralia City Sch Dist 135	59	174
Epplin, Tammy/Community Cons School Dist 204	59	201
Erb, Michelle/Harlem Unit Sch District 122	8,11,15	252
Erbach, Colette/Waukegan Cmty Unit SD 60	6	156
Erckfritz, Cyndie/Alden-Hebron School Dist 19	5	179
Erdey, Carla/Consolidated High Sch Dist 230	71	44
Ericksen, Mary/Midlothian School District 143	7	57
Erickson, Don/Reavis Twp HSD 220	73	64
Erickson, Don/Reavis Twp HSD 220	73	64
Erickson, Renee/Township High School Dist 211	60	69
Eriksen, Stephanie/North Shore School Dist 112	7	154
Erjavec, Gerald/Hillside School District 93	43	52
Erlenbaugh, Laura/Lincoln-Way Cmty HS Dist 210	60	244
Erstad, Lyle/Lake Zurich Cmty Sch Dist 95	3	152
Ervay, Brad/Granite City Cmty Unit SD 9	76,295	171
Escamilla, Tory/Montmorency Cmty Cons SD 145	6	239
Eshenk, Gary/Berwyn North School Dist 98	73	22
Eskew, Marc/Kansas Cmty School District 3	67	103
Eskew, Rebecca/North Wayne Cmty Unit SD 200	36,58,83,88	237
Eskridge, Brad/Schuyler-Industry CUSD 5	67	215
Eskridge, Grace/Alden-Hebron School Dist 19	274	179
Esler, Maryann/Wilmette Public School Dist 39	274	71
Esposito, Linda/Worth School District 127	83	72
Ess, Theresa/South Fork School Dist 14	11,286,296	14
Essex, Lisa/Egyptian Cmty Unit Sch Dist 5	2	3
Essig, Jennifer/Washington Cmty HS Dist 308	67	229
Esslinger, Laura/Porta Cmty Unit Sch Dist 202	5	189
Esters, Stephanie/Carbondale Elem School Dist 95	71	120
Estes, Scott, Dr/East Peoria Elem Sch Dist 86	7,12,68,79,280,286,288	227
Estheimer, Roy Keith/Geff Cmty Cons School Dist 14	67	237
Etherington, Matt/Cass School District 63	297	89
Etling, Hiedi/Smithton Cmty Cons SD 130	2	222
Etnyre, Jeremy/Dunlap Cmty Unit Sch Dist 323	88	196
Eucker, Adam/Williamsville Cmty Unit SD 15	6	214
Evans, Alicia, Dr/Rich Twp High School Dist 227	2,3,5,15,91	64

DISTRICT PERSONNEL INDEX

Market Data Retrieval

NAME/District	JOB FUNCTIONS	PAGE
Evans, Brian/Bloomington School District 87	91	185
Evans, Daniel/Matteson Elem SD 162	16,73,295	57
Evans, Dawayne, Dr/Hoover-Schrum Sch Dist 157	1	52
Evans, Dwayne, Dr/Thornton Fractnl Twp HSD 215	93	69
Evans, Frank, Dr/Salt Creek School District 48	2,11	99
Evans, Renee/Tri-Co Special Ed JT Agreement	2	122
Evans, Ryan/Brookfield-LaGrange Park SD 95	83	23
Evans, Taylor/Mt Vernon Twp HS District 201	2,19	123
Evans, Tonya/Blue Ridge Cmty SD 18	4	87
Evans, Tonya/Central Cmty Unit SD 4	1,83	118
Evans, Zabrina/Chicago PSD-Options	15	38
Eveland, Rachel/Peoria Public Sch Dist 150	60	198
Everett, Michael/Mokena Public School Dist 159	67	245
Everett, Tad, Dr/Sterling Cmty Unit Sch Dist 5	1	240
Evers, Andrea, Dr/Murphysboro Cmty Unit SD 186	1	121
Eversgerd, Brad/Aviston Elem School Dist 21	67	17
Ewing, Brandon/Waukegan Cmty Unit SD 60	67	156
Ewold, Mike/Grant Park Cmty Unit SD 6	3	135
Eyre, Ramona/Bluford Unit School Dist 318	275	122
Eyrich, Jim/Hoopeston Area Cmty Unit SD 11	73,295	232

F

NAME/District	JOB FUNCTIONS	PAGE
Fabes, Lisa/Wilmette Public School Dist 39	67	71
Fabjance, Cathi/Community Cons School Dist 15	274	43
Fabris, Hope/Seneca Cmty Cons Sch Dist 170	275	144
Fagan, Kennan/Triad Cmty School District 2	2,11,16,69,73,74,76,286	172
Fager, Donna/Carbondale Cmty HSD 165	2,4,5,11,19,296	120
Fahnoe, Chris/Arlington Hts School Dist 25	73,295	21
Fairbanks, Charles/Nashville Cmty Cons SD 49	12,275	235
Fairman, Jovaughn/Komarek School District 94	73	54
Faith, Nathan/Rockridge Cmty Unit SD 300	67	209
Faith, Ryan/Zion-Benton Twp High SD 126	73,286	157
Faivre, Malloy/Hiawatha Cmty Unit SD 426	6	85
Faivre, Rich/Earlville Cmty Unit Sch Dist 9	1	141
Faletti, Charlie/La Salle Elem SD 122	67	142
Falk, Dale/Northbrook-Glenview SD 30	2,3,15	60
Falk, Pete/Herscher Cmty School Dist 2	8,11,273,288,296,298	135
Falkenbury, Karma/Whiteside School District 115	2	222
Faller, Angelia/Polo Cmty Unit Sch Dist 222	36,69	195
Faller, William/Pecatonica Cmty Unit SD 321	1,83	253
Falls, Sherry/West Carroll CUSD 314	4	8
Fanello, Lori, Dr/Boone-Winnebago Reg Off of Ed	1	256
Fansler, Mike/Mundelein Elem School Dist 75	6	153
Fantin, Craig/Peotone Cmty Unit SD 207-U	6,31,83,88	245
Fark, Paula/Nashville Cmty HSD 99	4	235
Farley, William/Community Unit School Dist 200	2,5,15,80,91	91
Farlow, Kent/Thornton Fractnl Twp HSD 215	72	69
Farmer, Jim/Mendon Cmty Unit School Dist 4	67	2
Farnsworth, Duane/Indian Creek Cmty Unit SD 425	83	85
Farnsworth, Jennifer/Ball Chatham Cmty Unit SD 5	8,15,288	211
Farquer, Tim/Williamsfield Cmty Unit SD 210	1,11	140
Farrell, Justin/Elgin School District U-46	2	130
Farris, Alicia/Highland Cmty Sch District 5	286	171
Farris, Jerry/Flanagan-Cornell Unit 74 SD	8,58	161
Farris, Jerry/Flanagan-Cornell Unit 74 SD	1,11	161
Farris, Katrina/Mattoon Cmty Unit Sch Dist 2	34	19
Fas, Laurie/Limestone Cmty High SD 310	4	197
Fatheree, Rowdy/Mt Vernon Twp HS District 201	751	123
Fatigante, Cathy/Dwight Twp High Sch Dist 230	60	161
Fatout, Suzanne/West Aurora School Dist 129	2,298	132
Faulkner, Erica/Chicago Public School Dist 299	752	25
Faulkner, Norman/North Wamac School Dist 186	67	18
Feaney, Adam/Rowva Cmty School Dist 208	10	140
Feather, Kate/Wayne City Cmty Unit SD 100	2	237
Feehery, Aimee, Dr/Lincoln-Way Cmty HS Dist 210	10,74	244
Feeley, Mike/Fenton Cmty High School Dist 100	73	94
Feeney, Kevin/Wilmington Cmty Unit SD 209-U	8,11,15,57,58,69,288	249
Feeney, Sue/Community High School Dist 218	15,60,752	44
Fehrholz, Shannon/Sangamon-Menard Roe #51	15	215
Feinstein, Amy/Golf School District 67	57	51
Feld, Adam/Edinburg Cmty Unit Sch Dist 4	6	14
Felda, Matsa/J Sterling Morton HSD 201	69,294	53
Feldheim, Kathy/Bannockburn Sch Dist 106	280	147
Feldkamp, Lynne/Tri-Point Cmty Unit SD 6J	2	162
Feldman, Jason/Antioch Cmty Cons Sch Dist 34	68	146
Feldman, John/Bartelso School District 57	28,73	17
Felefena, Marty/Erie Cmty School District 1	1	239
Feltes, Amanda/Hartsburg Emden School Dist 21	10,36,69	163
Feltgen, Carol/Batavia Unit School Dist 101	2	128
Feltz, Kristin/Lincoln-Way Cmty HS Dist 210	4	244
Fennelly, Margot/North Cook Interm Svc Center	7	82
Fenske, Emily/Oak Park Elem School Dist 97	9	60
Fenton, Herb/Geff Cmty Cons School Dist 14	6	237
Fenton, Jeff/Central Cmty Unit SD 4	6	118
Fergenson, Chad/Dakota Cmty Unit Sch Dist 201	6	224
Fergeson, Kim/Charleston Cmty Unit SD 1	68	19
Fergus, Mary/Elgin School District U-46	71	130
Ferill, Lela/Morrisonville Cmty Unit SD 1	2,19	14
Fernandez, Alex/Gavin School District 37	295	150
Ferrell, Ronald, Dr/Brooklyn School District 188	1,11,57,83,288	217
Ferrell, Ronald, Dr/Venice Cmty Unit School Dist 3	1	172
Ferrell, Sarah/Kell Cons School District 2	83	175
Ferrier, T/Mundelein Elem School Dist 75	2	153
Fessler, Arthur, Dr/Community Cons School Dist 59	1	43
Fessler, Jill/Pleasant Plains Cmty Unit SD 8	8,11,58,288,752	212
Fetcho, Jeff/Hamilton Co Cmty Unit SD 10	1,11	114
Fetcho, Lisa/Hamilton Co Cmty Unit SD 10	38	114
Fetter, Pattie/North Mac Cmty Unit SD 34	2	168
Fettig, Janet/Evergreen Park Elem SD 124	76	49
Fetzer, Meg/Regional Office of Ed Kane Co	2	134
Fetzner, Rob/Crystal Lake Elem District 47	67	181
Feucht, Jeffrey, Dr/Lake Park Cmty High SD 108	1	96
Feyerer, Jeff/Fairview South School Dist 72	2	49
Fiarito, Frank/River Trails Sch Dist 26	67	65
Ficker, Joseph/Burbank School District 111	3	24
Fickes, Brett/Thornton Twp High Sch Dist 205	10	69
Fidor, Mark/Fairview South School Dist 72	73,286	49
Fiedentop, Kelly/Donovan Cmty Unit Sch Dist 3	273	119
Fiegel, Craig, Dr/Mascoutah Cmty Sch Dist 19	1	220
Field, Debra/Blue Ridge Cmty SD 18	5	87
Field, Johnathon/Sangamon Valley Cmty Unit SD 9	8	166
Fields, Paul/Nippersink School District 2	73	183
Fields, Paul/Richmond-Burton Cmty HSD 157	73,295	184
Fields, Steve/Cary Cmty Cons Sch Dist 26	3	179
Fields, Tasia/Waukegan Cmty Unit SD 60	73	156
Fies, Michael/Thornton Fractnl Twp HSD 215	11,16,69,280,288,294,298	69
Fig, Scott/Carrier Mills-Stoneford SD 2	67	210
Figueroa, Angel/Waukegan Cmty Unit SD 60	15,68	156
File, Meg/Bond Co Cmty Unit Sch Dist 2	8,11,57,73,286,296	4
Filipiak, Keith/Lisle Cmty Unit Sch Dist 202	1	96
Fillmore, Scott/Marengo Union Elem Cons SD 165	3	182
Filyaw, Jennifer/Wesclin Cmty Unit Sch Dist 3	1,11	18
Finaldi, Gina/Lincolnshre-Prairieview SD 103	34,59,79	153
Finch, Christopher/La Grange Elem Sch Dist 102	9,11,15	54
Finch, Garry/Metamora Twp HS Dist 122	36,69	258
Finch, Janette/Sherrard Cmty Sch Dist 200	73	189
Finders, Scott/Anna-Jonesboro Cmty HSD 81	10,752	230
Findley, Julie/Oakland Cmty Unit Sch Dist 5	16	19
Fink, Angela, Dr/Marengo Cmty High Sch Dist 154	10,93	182
Fink, Scott, Dr/Plainfield Cons Sch Dist 202	68	246
Finke, Jason/Nashville Cmty Cons SD 49	9,57,69	235
Finke, John/Community Unit School Dist 16	5	211
Finke, Mike/Butler School District 53	6	89
Finkelstein, Jaime/Manteno Cmty Unit Sch Dist 5	8,69	136

1 Superintendent	16 Instructional Media Svcs	30 Adult Education	44 Science Sec	58 Special Education K-12	72 Summer School	88 Alternative/At Risk	277 Remedial Math K-12
2 Bus/Finance/Purchasing	17 Chief Operations Officer	31 Career/Sch-to-Work K-12	45 Math K-12	59 Special Education Elem	73 Instructional Tech	89 Multi-Cultural Curriculum	280 Literacy Coach
3 Buildings And Grounds	18 Chief Academic Officer	32 Career/Sch-to-Work Elem	46 Math Elem	60 Special Education Sec	74 Inservice Training	90 Social Work	285 STEM
4 Food Service	19 Chief Financial Officer	33 Career/Sch-to-Work Sec	47 Math Sec	61 Foreign/World Lang K-12	75 Marketing/Distributive	91 Safety/Security	286 Digital Learning
5 Transportation	20 Art K-12	34 Early Childhood Ed	48 English/Lang Arts K-12	62 Foreign/World Lang Elem	76 Info Systems	92 Magnet School	288 Common Core Standards
6 Athletic	21 Art Elem	35 Health/Phys Education	49 English/Lang Arts Elem	63 Foreign/World Lang Sec	77 Psychological Assess	93 Parental Involvement	294 Accountability
7 Health Services	22 Art Sec	36 Guidance Services K-12	50 English/Lang Arts Sec	64 Religious Education K-12	78 Affirmative Action	95 Tech Prep Program	295 Network System
8 Curric/Instruct K-12	23 Music K-12	37 Guidance Services Elem	51 Reading K-12	65 Religious Education Elem	79 Student Personnel	97 Chief Infomation Officer	296 Title II Programs
9 Curric/Instruct Elem	24 Music Elem	38 Guidance Services Sec	52 Reading Elem	66 Religious Education Sec	80 Driver Ed/Safety	98 Chief Technology Officer	297 Webmaster
10 Curric/Instruct Sec	25 Music Sec	39 Social Studies K-12	53 Reading Sec	67 School Board President	81 Gifted/Talented	270 Character Education	298 Grant Writer/Ptnrships
11 Federal Program	26 Business Education	40 Social Studies Elem	54 Remedial Reading K-12	68 Teacher Personnel	82 Video Services	271 Migrant Education	750 Chief Innovation Officer
12 Title I	27 Career & Tech Ed	41 Social Studies Sec	55 Remedial Reading Elem	69 Academic Assessment	83 Substance Abuse Prev	273 Teacher Mentor	751 Chief of Staff
13 Title V	28 Technology Education	42 Science K-12	56 Remedial Reading Sec	70 Research/Development	84 Erate	274 Before/After Sch	752 Social Emotional Learning
15 Asst Superintendent	29 Family/Consumer Science	43 Science Elem	57 Bilingual/ELL	71 Public Information	85 AIDS Education	275 Response To Intervention	

Illinois School Directory

DISTRICT PERSONNEL INDEX

NAME/District	JOB FUNCTIONS	PAGE
Finn, Elizabeth/Bond Co Cmty Unit Sch Dist 2	270,288	4
Fischer, Becky/Skokie School District 73 1/2	9	67
Fischer, Rita, Dr/Community High School Dist 128	10,11,15,270,288,296,298	148
Fiscus, Steven/Tuscola Cmty Unit SD 301	27,60	88
Fisher, Bob/Metamora Cmty Cons Sch Dist 1	67	258
Fisher, Catherine/Maercker School District 60	11,57,88,285,286,288,296,298	97
Fisher, Dale, Dr/Deerfield Public SD 109	15,68	149
Fisher, Jessica/Trico Cmty Unit Sch Dist 176	16	121
Fisher, Lisa/DeSoto Grade School Dist 86	59	120
Fisher, Melissa/Edwards Co Cmty Unit SD 1	4	104
Fisher, Rose/Carthage Elementary SD 317	88	114
Fisher, Scott/South Beloit Cmty Sch Dist 320	1,11	255
Fisk, Justin/Adlai E Stevenson HSD 125	57	146
Fiske, Gina/Alsip-Hazelgrn-Oaklawn SD 126	73	20
Fitton, James/Riverside Public Sch Dist 96	2,3	65
Fitzgerald, Kristin/Naperville Cmty Unit SD 203	67	98
Fitzgerald, Laura/Tolono Cmty Unit Sch Dist 7	8,11,69,296,298	12
Fitzgerald, Shelley/Heritage Cmty Unit Sch Dist 8	5	11
Fitzgerrald, Todd, Dr/Komarek School District 94	1,11	54
Fitzpatrick, Becky/Arlington Hts School Dist 25	11,16,27,69,73,285	21
Fitzpatrick, Jeff/Freeport School District 145	6	224
Fitzpatrick, Kathy/Elgin School District U-46	298	130
Fitzpatrick, Rachael/Ohio Cmty Cons School Dist 17	67	7
Fitzsimmons, Renee/Lake Forest Cmty HSD 115	10	151
Fitzsimons, Andrew/Cary Cmty Cons Sch Dist 26	73,76,295	179
Fizer, Shelly/New Athens CUSD 60	2	220
Fjaistad, Andrea/Prairie Hill Cmty Cons SD 133	2	253
Flack, Hugh/McHenry Cmty High Sch Dist 156	3	183
Fladung, Victoria/Geneva CUSD 304	295	131
Flahaven, Marlene/River Grove School Dist 85-5	67	65
Flaherty, Jessica/Lostant Cmty Unit Sch Dist 425	2	142
Flaherty, Wendy/Keeneyville Elem Sch Dist 20	2,3,5	96
Flanigan, Matthew/Mt Vernon Twp HS District 201	67	123
Flanigan, Megan/Decatur Public Schools 61	39,280	165
Flater, Jeff/Farmington Ctl Cmty SD 265	6	197
Flavin, Denise/Burbank School District 111	9,69,83,286,288	24
Fleck, Amy/Ohio Cmty High School Dist 505	83	7
Fleck, Franzy, Dr/Burbank School District 111	1	24
Fleming, Greg/Lake Zurich Cmty Sch Dist 95	3	152
Fleming, Jane/Chicago Public School Dist 299	280	25
Fleming, Joe/Zion-Benton Twp High SD 126	295	157
Fleming, Mark, Dr/Worth School District 127	1,11	72
Fleming, Penny/Community High School Dist 155	5	179
Fleming, Penny/Crystal Lake Elem Distict 47	5	181
Fleming, Rhonda/Tamaroa Elem School Dist 5	2	201
Flemming, Denise/DeKalb Cmty Unit SD 428	286	84
Fleshner, Jason/Okaw Valley Cmty Unit SD 302	3,5	193
Flesner, Travis/Rantoul Twp High Sch Dist 193	6	12
Fletcher, Edward/Monmouth-Roseville CUSD 238	1,83	234
Floore, Michael/Madison Cmty Unit Sch Dist 12	5	172
Flor, Karen/Community Cons School Dist 15	7	43
Flores, Beth, Dr/Golf School District 67	1	51
Flores, Christine/Lemont High Sch Dist 210	60	55
Flories, Karen/Valley View Cmty SD 365-U	10	248
Flott, Stephanie/Dwight Twp High School Dist 230	16,82	161
Flott, Stephanie/Prairie Central Cmty USD 8	16,82	162
Flowers, Lori/Pontiac-Wm Holliday SD 105	7	221
Flynn, Allen/Liberty Cmty Unit Sch Dist 2	3	2
Foderaro, Kerry, Dr/Cass School District 63	11,57	89
Foiles, Jesse/South Fork School Dist 14	73,295	14
Folger, Tammy/Galesburg Cmty Unit SD 205	71	140
Foltz, Michael/River Ridge Cmty Unit SD 210	288	126
Fonpanetta, Augustino/New Trier Twp HS District 203	6	58
Fontana, Sarah/Round Lake Area Co Dist 116	48,280	155
Fontanetta, Heather/Wauconda Cmty Unit SD 118	58,79	155
Fontanetta, Jeff/Roselle School District 12	6	99
Foote, Glen/East Dubuque Unit SD 119	67	125
Foote, Nathan/Roanoke-Benson Cmty Unit SD 60	69	258
Foppe, Leslie, Dr/Salem Elem Sch District 111	1,11	175
Ford-Sills, Evisha, Dr/Posen-Robbins Sch Dist 143-5	15,59,79,83,90	63
Ford, Dan/North Palos School Dist 117	3,91	59
Ford, Dan/Sandwich Cmty Unit SD 430	3	85
Ford, Dee/South Fork School Dist 14	69,88	14
Ford, Don/Centralia City Sch Dist 135	73,295	174
Ford, Jane/West Washington Co Cmty SD 10	73,286	236
Ford, Joanna/Deerfield Public SD 109	15,79	149
Ford, Rodger/Community High School Dist 218	3	44
Fore, Rich/Edwardsville Cmty Unit SD 7	3	170
Forman, Scott/Cook County School Dist 104	6,27	44
Forst, Dennis/Darien Public Sch Dist 61	2,11,19	92
Forthman, James/Pope Co Cmty Unit Sch Dist 1	6	204
Fortin, Ryan/Lansing School Dist 158	3,91	54
Fosley, Nicole/Grant Park Cmty Unit SD 6	36,69,83,85,88	135
Foster, Devetta/Posen-Robbins Sch Dist 143-5	3	63
Foster, Earnestine/Matteson Elem SD 162	15	57
Foster, Jeff/Freeburg Cmty Cons SD 70	73	219
Foster, Joel/Dimmick Cmty School Dist 175	35,83,85	141
Foster, Joni/Goreville Cmty Unit SD 1	4	127
Foster, Mallory/Cumberland Cmty Unit SD 77	58,294	84
Foster, Matthew/Waukegan Cmty Unit SD 60	46	156
Fountain, Daniella/Lemont-Bromberek Sch Dist 113A	11,68,69,275,288,294,296,298	55
Fournier, Theresa, Dr/Northbrook Elem School Dist 27	15,68,79,273	59
Foutch, Dustin, Dr/Central Cmty High Sch Dist 71	1,11,83	17
Fowler, Rachel/Moline-Coal Valley SD No 40	88	207
Fowler, Tarah/Indian Prairie Sch Dist 204	10	95
Fowlkes, Sherly/Harvey Public School Dist 152	298	51
Fox, Alex/Edwardsville Cmty Unit SD 7	6	170
Fox, April/Eastern Illinois Area of Sp Ed	15,271	20
Fox, Colleen/Stockton Cmty Unit SD 206	1	126
Fox, D Todd/Southeastern Cmty Unit SD 337	1,83	115
Fox, Jason/Effingham Cmty Sch Dist 40	2,3,15,73,76,91	104
Fox, Jennifer/Effingham Cmty Sch Dist 40	34	105
Fox, Jon/La Salle Elem SD 122	6	142
Fox, Kenneth, Dr/Chicago Public School Dist 299	7	25
Fox, Nancy/Pontiac Twp High Sch Dist 90	2	161
Fox, Roberta/DePue Unit Sch Dist 103	6	6
Fox, Scott/Palos Cmty Cons School Dist 118	76,295	61
Fox, Sherri/Harrisburg Cmty Unit SD 3	16,73	210
Foxall, Jeff/East Alton-Wood River SD 14	3,5	170
Fradkin, Cam/Genoa-Kingston Cmty SD 424	5	85
Fraiely, Tamara/Marshall Cmty Sch Dist C-2	8,36,69	15
Frake, Vasiliki/East Maine School District 63	59	47
Frakes, Melinda/West Central Cmty Unit SD 235	73,97,297	116
Fraley, Luke/Calhoun Cmty Unit Sch Dist 40	67	8
Frampton, Sheila/Regional Office of Ed 30	76	121
Francis, Sue/Odell Cmty Cons Sch Dist 435	2	161
Franck, Carolyn/Yorkville Cmty Unit SD 115	2	139
Franco, Georgette/Fox Lake School Dist 114	4	149
Francois-Bulv, Shalima/North Chicago Cmty Unit SD 187	58	154
Frangidakis, Zack/Forest Park School District 91	295	50
Frank, Michele/Marengo Union Elem Cons SD 165	5	182
Franke, Lisa/Durand Cmty Sch Dist 322	285	252
Frankford, Eric/Valmeyer Cmty School Dist 3	1,11,73	190
Frankiewicz, Laura/Kaneland Cmty Unit SD 302	58	132
Franklin, Airielle/South Holland School Dist 151	76	68
Franklin, Angelica/Champaign Cmty Unit Sch Dist 4	8	10
Franklin, Angi/Urbana School District 116	15,68,74	12
Franklin, Joe/Pekin Public School Dist 108	68,79	227
Franklin, Julie/Harrison School Dist 36	2	181
Franklin, Lindsay/Morton Cmty Unit Sch Dist 709	79	227
Franks, Jim/East Moline Public Sch Dist 37	3	207
Franks, Jim/Silvis School District 34	3	209
Franky, Dustin/Paxton-Buckley-Loda CUSD 10	11,73,295,298	107
Fransen, Kristine/Arbor Park School District 145	5	21
Frantini, Mike/Wheeling Cmty Cons Sch Dist 21	73,98,295	71
Franzen, Justin/St Joseph-Ogden Cmty HSD 305	6	12
Fraticola, Christy/Genoa-Kingston Cmty SD 424	38	85
Frattinger, Angel/Bloomingdale School Dist 13	57	89
Fray, Michaela/Quincy School District 172	8,69	2
Frazer, Kristy/Whiteside School District 115	274	222
Frazier, Karen/Pekin Public School Dist 108	67	227
Frazier, Kevin/Olympia Cmty Unit Sch Dist 16	67	187
Frazier, Leslee/Carrollton Cmty Unit SD 1	69,273	111
Frazier, Tom/Bloomington School District 87	27,30,75	185
Frazier, Tom/McLean-DeWitt Reg Voc System	1	188
Frebus-Flaman, Marion/Naperville Cmty Unit SD 203	34,48,89	98
Frech, Don/Iuka Community Cons Sch Dist 7	6	174
Frederick, Jonathon/Limestone Cmty High SD 310	16,73	197
Free, Eric/Salt Fork Cmty Unit SD 512	3	233
Freedlund, Keli/Kinnikinnick Cmty Cons SD 131	1,11	253
Freeman, David/Spoon River Valley Cmty SD 4	6	110
Freeman, Elizabeth/Community Unit School Dist 300	74	180

DISTRICT PERSONNEL INDEX

Market Data Retrieval

NAME/District	JOB FUNCTIONS	PAGE
Freeman, Elizabeth/Fremont School District 79	9,88	149
Freeman, Jennifer/Illinois Vly Ctl Sch Dist 321	57,58	197
Freeman, Kyle, Dr/Washington Cmty HS Dist 308	1	229
Freeman, Michael/McHenry Co Reg Office of Ed 44	15	185
Freeman, Rachel/Harlem Unit Sch District 122	68	252
Freewalt, Michael/Evergreen Park Elem SD 124	295	49
Freeze, Roger/Wesclin Cmty Unit Sch Dist 3	10,69,83,285	18
Fregeau, Paul, Dr/Decatur Public Schools 61	1	165
Frehner, Greg/Vienna Public School Dist 55	1,11,83	127
Frei, Gregg/Fieldcrest Cmty School Dist 6	5	257
Freise, Kyle/Batavia Unit School Dist 101	295	128
Freitag, Amy/Monmouth-Roseville CUSD 238	11,57,296,298	234
French, Bridget/Rockford School District 205	27,31,36	254
French, Casey/Virginia Cmty Unit Sch Dist 64	67	9
French, Kirtus/Porta Cmty Unit Sch Dist 202	73,295	189
Frendreis, John/Grass Lake School District 36	67	150
Frerichs, Jennifer/Rantoul City School Dist 137	15	11
Frerichs, Tim/Prairieview-Ogden Sch Dist 197	5	11
Frericks, Carol/Quincy School District 172	79	2
Frerking, Greg/Freeburg Cmty High Sch Dist 77	1,11,83,288	219
Fresen, Betsy/Kildeer Countryside CCSD 96	71	151
Fretueg, Beau, Dr/Schuyler-Industry CUSD 5	1,11	215
Fretz, Nate/Springfield Pub Sch Dist 186	2,84	213
Freundt, Chuck/Naperville Cmty Unit SD 203	9,15	98
Frey, Tiffany/Southern Will Co Spec Ed Dist	15	250
Frezza, Peter/Cook County School Dist 154	3	45
Fricano, Gino/Chicago Ridge Sch Dist 127-5	73,295	41
Frichtl, Jenny/Arcola Cmty Unit School Dist 306	2	87
Frick, Karen/Anna Cmty Cons Sch Dist 37	73	230
Frick, Sandy/Waltonville Cmty Unit SD 1	67	124
Fricke, Heather/Mt Pulaski Cmty Unit SD 23	16,73,286	164
Friday, Shelia/Elementary School District 159	298	47
Friedericks, Susan/Matteson Elem SD 162	4	57
Friedman, Janean/Emmons School District 33	1,11,288	149
Friedrich, Travis/Macon-Piatt Spec Ed	15	167
Friedricks, Ryan/Bradley-Bourbonnais CHSD 307	3	134
Fritch, Ryan/Pope Co Cmty Unit Sch Dist 1	1,11	204
Fritcher, Bill/Neoga Cmty Unit School Dist 3	1	84
Fritcher, Charles/Dieterich Community Unit SD 30	3,91	104
Fritz, David/Alton Cmty School District 11	67	169
Friziellie, Heather/Fox Lake School Dist 114	1	149
Froebe, Kent/Lincoln Elem School Dist 27	1,83	163
Froelich, Jackie/Dwight Twp High Sch Dist 230	38	161
Frole, Christine/Township High School Dist 214	4	69
Froman, Ellie/Warsaw Cmty Unit Sch Dist 316	2	115
Froman, Stephanie/Warsaw Cmty Unit Sch Dist 316	58	115
Frost, Kimberly/McHenry Cmty Cons Sch Dist 15	5	183
Frost, Lea, Dr/Park Ridge Niles CMCSD 64	79	62
Frost, Leeann/Park Ridge Niles CMCSD 64	11,59,83,88,90,270,271	62
Frost, Steve/Adlai E Stevenson HSD 125	67	146
Fruenot, Jay/St Anne Cmty Cons Sch Dist 256	16,73,76,286,295	136
Fruge, Jamie/Lincoln Elem School Dist 27	7,275	163
Fruit, Jenette/Earlville Cmty Unit Sch Dist 9	8	141
Frusher, David, Dr/Steger School Dist 194	1	68
Fry, Dan/Central Cmty Unit SD 4	3	118
Fry, Natlie/Harrisburg Cmty Unit SD 3	8,57,298	210
Fry, Sara/Scott Morgan Cmty Unit SD 2	12,280	215
Fry, Shone/East Alton-Wood River SD 14	4	170
Frye, Dianne/Dixon Cmty Unit Sch Dist 170	68	160
Frye, Richard/Grand Ridge CCSD 95	67	141
Frye, Rick/Metamora Twp HS Dist 122	3	258
Frye, Ron/Seneca Twp High Sch Dist 160	67	144
Frye, Tina/East St Louis Sch Dist 189	68	218
Fryzlewicz, Nancy/Salt Creek School District 48	68	99
Ftumpf, Andy/Winchester Cmty Unit SD 1	9	215
Fuchs, Deb/Serena Cmty School Dist 2	4	144
Fuchs, Julie-Ann, Dr/Kaneland Cmty Unit SD 302	2,15	132

NAME/District	JOB FUNCTIONS	PAGE
Fuerstenau, Greggory, Dr/Litchfield Cmty Unit SD 12	1	191
Fuhrhop, Scott/West Washington Co Cmty SD 10	1	236
Fulkerson, Ed/Macomb Cmty Unit Sch Dist 185	12,91	178
Fulkerson, Jill/Fairfield Cmty High SD 225	1,11	236
Fuller, Matt/Barrington Cmty Unit SD 220	15,73	147
Fuller, Matthew/Sterling Cmty Unit Sch Dist 5	76	240
Fuller, Rachel/Rochester Cmty Unit SD 3-A	16	212
Fullerlov, Rhyse/Sherrard Cmty Sch Dist 200	67	189
Fullerton, Lauryn/Chicago PSD-Network 17	15	38
Fulton, Jill/Herscher Cmty School Dist 2	275	135
Fulton, Latonya/East St Louis Sch Dist 189	58	218
Fults, Dave/Willow Grove School Dist 46	1,11	18
Funk, Jessica/Western CUSD 12	1,288	203
Funkhouser, Kim/Community Unit School Dist 200	2	91
Fuqua, Kim/Norris City-Omaha-Enfield SD 3	83	238
Furbee, Andy/Manteno Cmty Unit Sch Dist 5	79	136
Furbush, Mary, Dr/Cooperative Assn for Spec Ed	1	102
Furczyk, Brian/Joliet Twp High Sch Dist 204	4	243
Furgason, Greg/Lincoln Way Area Special Ed	73	250
Furgason, Greg/Speed Seja 802	73,76	82
Furlan, Tom/Grant Cmty High Sch Dist 124	73	150
Furlong, Monica/Huntley Cmty School Dist 158	59,88	182
Furma, Ken/Crete-Monee Cmty SD 201-U	2,298	241

G

Gabriel, Corey/Signal Hill Sch Dist 181	3	221
Gadow, Shawn/Oregon Cmty Unit Sch Dist 220	73,295	195
Gaerlan, Adrian/Elmhurst Cmty Unit SD 205	2	93
Gaffney, Jacklyn/Mannheim School District 83	7	56
Gagnon, Dratina/Allen-Otter Creek CCSD 65	59	141
Gaham, Jack/Beecher Cmty Sch Dist 200-U	10	241
Gainer, Bridget/Hillside School District 93	12,57,59,83,273,275	52
Gaither, Joe/Olympia Cmty Unit Sch Dist 16	3	187
Gajewski, Mary/Mt Olive Cmty Unit Sch Dist 5	16	168
Galan, Tony/Park Ridge Niles CMCSD 64	59	62
Galba, Mark/Lyons Elem School Dist 103	3	56
Gale, R Dane/Belle Valley School Dist 119	1	217
Galen, Antonia/Chaney-Monge School Dist 88	34,59,273	241
Gales, Nicole, Dr/Springfield Pub Sch Dist 186	69	213
Gall, Emily/Odell Cmty Cons Sch Dist 435	67	161
Gall, Rebecca/Hollis Cons School Dist 328	12	197
Gallaher, Kris/Brown Co Cmty Unit Sch Dist 1	73,76,84	5
Gallion, Leann/Westville Cmty Unit Sch Dist 2	67	233
Gallo, Michelle/Indian Prairie Sch Dist 204	79	95
Gallo, Nancy/North Shore School Dist 112	3	154
Gallois, Doug/Winfield School District 34	2	100
Gallois, Gretchen/Naperville Cmty Unit SD 203	68	98
Galloway, Erin/St Anne Cmty Cons Sch Dist 256	6	136
Gallt, Kelley, Dr/Lake Zurich Cmty Unit SD 95	1	152
Galrap, Merle/Rock Falls Twp High SD 301	67	240
Galt, Steve/Gallatin Cmty Unit Sch Dist 7	67	110
Galuski, Brian/Morton Grove School Dist 70	73,286	58
Galvin, Mike/Midlothian School District 143	3,91	57
Gambill, Jason/East Peoria Elem Sch Dist 86	34,57,59,77,90,271,273,275	227
Gambill, Jered/Sandoval Cmty Unit SD 501	67	175
Ganan, Brian, Dr/La Grange Cmty School Dist 105	1	54
Gandhi, Ashish/Ridgeland School District 122	73	64
Gannon, Amy/Zion Public School District 6	57	157
Gannon, Amy/Zion Public School District 6	9,11,280,285,288,296,298	157
Gannon, Andrea/Belleville Township HSD 201	30,88	217
Garcia-Sanchez, Minerva/Chicago PSD-Network 7	15	32
Garcia, Caridad/East Aurora School Dist 131	68	129
Garcia, Charles/Hoover-Schrum Sch Dist 157	67	52
Garcia, Hector, Dr/Community Cons School Dist 181	1	91
Garcia, Louis/Kaneland Cmty Unit SD 302	5	132
Garcia, Luis/Round Lake Area Co Dist 116	5	155
Garcia, Paula/Rock Falls Elem Sch Dist 13	57,271	240

#		#		#		#		#	
1	Superintendent	16	Instructional Media Svcs	30	Adult Education	44	Science Sec	58	Special Education K-12
2	Bus/Finance/Purchasing	17	Chief Operations Officer	31	Career/Sch-to-Work K-12	45	Math K-12	59	Special Education Elem
3	Buildings And Grounds	18	Chief Academic Officer	32	Career/Sch-to-Work Elem	46	Math Elem	60	Special Education Sec
4	Food Service	19	Chief Financial Officer	33	Career/Sch-to-Work Sec	47	Math Sec	61	Foreign/World Lang K-12
5	Transportation	20	Art K-12	34	Early Childhood Ed	48	English/Lang Arts K-12	62	Foreign/World Lang Elem
6	Athletic	21	Art Elem	35	Health/Phys Education	49	English/Lang Arts Elem	63	Foreign/World Lang Sec
7	Health Services	22	Art Sec	36	Guidance Services K-12	50	English/Lang Arts Sec	64	Religious Education K-12
8	Curric/Instruct K-12	23	Music K-12	37	Guidance Services Elem	51	Reading K-12	65	Religious Education Elem
9	Curric/Instruct Elem	24	Music Elem	38	Guidance Services Sec	52	Reading Elem	66	Religious Education Sec
10	Curric/Instruct Sec	25	Music Sec	39	Social Studies K-12	53	Reading Sec	67	School Board President
11	Federal Program	26	Business Education	40	Social Studies Elem	54	Remedial Reading K-12	68	Teacher Personnel
12	Title I	27	Career & Tech Ed	41	Social Studies Sec	55	Remedial Reading Elem	69	Academic Assessment
13	Title IV	28	Technology Education	42	Science K-12	56	Remedial Reading Sec	70	Research/Development
15	Asst Superintendent	29	Family/Consumer Science	43	Science Elem	57	Bilingual/ELL	71	Public Information

#		#		#	
72	Summer School	88	Alternative/At Risk	277	Remedial Math K-12
73	Instructional Tech	89	Multi-Cultural Curriculum	280	Literacy Coach
74	Inservice Training	90	Social Work	285	STEM
75	Marketing/Distributive	91	Safety/Security	286	Digital Learning
76	Info Systems	92	Magnet School	288	Common Core Standards
77	Psychological Assess	93	Parental Involvement	294	Accountability
78	Affirmative Action	95	Tech Prep Program	295	Network System
79	Student Personnel	97	Chief Information Officer	296	Title II Programs
80	Driver Ed/Safety	98	Chief Technology Officer	297	Webmaster
81	Gifted/Talented	270	Character Education	298	Grant Writer/Ptnrships
82	Video Services	271	Migrant Education	750	Chief Innovation Officer
83	Substance Abuse Prev	273	Teacher Mentor	751	Chief of Staff
84	Erate	274	Before/After Sch	752	Social Emotional Learning
85	AIDS Education	275	Response To Intervention		

IL-T20

Illinois School Directory — DISTRICT PERSONNEL INDEX

NAME/District	JOB FUNCTIONS	PAGE
Garcia, Ricardo/J Sterling Morton HSD 201	22,25	53
Gardner, Mary/Waterloo Cmty Unit Sch Dist 5	9	190
Gardner, Randy/Meridian Cmty School Dist 101	3	204
Gardner, Stephanie/Community Cons School Dist 181	76	91
Garlish, Christy/Farmington Ctl Cmty SD 265	2	197
Garlovsky, Elizabeth/Township High School Dist 113	67	155
Garnar, Cara/Sandoval Cmty Unit SD 501	2	175
Garneau, Kathy/Bannockburn Sch Dist 106	285	147
Garner, Rose/West Central Cmty Unit SD 235	4	116
Garner, Todd/Mt Zion Cmty Unit Sch Dist 3	67	166
Garnhart, Christy/Forrestville Valley CUSD 221	8	194
Garrard, Brian/St Elmo Cmty Unit Sch Dist 202	10	106
Garrett, Adam/Edwardsville Cmty Unit SD 7	31,36,58,79,81	170
Garrett, Ann/Mt Vernon Twp HS District 201	16,57,82	123
Garrett, Hannah/Alwood Cmty Unit Sch Dist 225	2,84	116
Garrett, Keisa/East St Louis Sch Dist 189	15	218
Garrett, Laura/Milne-Kelvin Grove District 91	67	244
Garrett, Sherri/Gardner S Wilmington HSD 73	2	112
Garrett, Sherry/Braceville Elem School Dist 75	2	111
Garrison, David/Wayne City Cmty Unit SD 100	3	237
Garrison, Jennifer, Dr/Vandalia Cmty Unit SD 203	1	106
Garrison, Neal/Mahomet-Seymour Cmty SD 3	36	11
Garst, Kim/Rockton School District 140	2	255
Garver, Gwen/BMP Spec Ed Co-op	1	7
Garwood, James, Dr/Skokie School District 68	1	67
Garza, Ignacio/Bellwood School District 88	57	22
Gasbarro, Armand/Marquardt School District 15	2,5,15,91	97
Gassman, Chad/Durand Cmty Unit SD 322	3,91	252
Gaston, John/Salem Elem Sch District 111	67	175
Gaston, Nic/Indian Creek Cmty Unit SD 425	5	85
Gateley, Tim/Tolono Cmty Unit Sch Dist 7	73,286	12
Gates, Shelley/Evanston Twp High SD 202	27	48
Gatinski, Diana/Streator Elem School Dist 44	7	144
Gatta, Lou/Evanston-Skokie Cmty CSD 65	5	48
Gauch, Mike/Harrisburg Cmty Unit SD 3	1	210
Gaunky, Scott/Lincolnshre-Prairieview SD 103	3	153
Gaut, Gary/Greenview Cmty Unit SD 200	5	188
Gauthier, Leah, Dr/Elmwood Park Cmty Unit SD 401	1	47
Gauthier, Lia/Elmwood Park Cmty Unit SD 401	8,11,78,90,298	47
Gavin, Kathleen, Dr/Oak Lawn-Hometown Sch Dist 123	15,285,288,298	60
Gavin, Kathy/Niles Twp Dept of Spec Ed #807	2,11	82
Gavin, Sherri/Indian Creek Cmty Unit SD 425	2	85
Gay, Evelyn/East Moline Public Sch Dist 37	5	207
Gay, James, Dr/Consolidated High Sch Dist 230	1	44
Gean, Sheryl/Valmeyer Cmty School Dist 3	274	190
Gear, Ann, Dr/Special Education Dist Lake Co	34	159
Geary, Amanda/Deland-Weldon Cmty Unit SD 57	1,11	202
Geary, Cheryl/Evanston-Skokie Cmty CSD 65	2	48
Geddeis, Karen/Glenbrook High Sch Dist 225	16,71	50
Geddis, Alicia, Dr/Danville School District 118	1,83	231
Gegenheimer, Al/Nettle Creek Cmty SD 24-C	1	113
Gehrig, Joshua/Zion-Benton Twp High SD 126	3	157
Gehrig, Marie/Beach Park Cmty Cons SD 3	81	147
Gehrig, Wileen/Warren Twp High Sch Dist 121	10,68	155
Gehrke, Lori/Rockdale School District 84	11	247
Geibel, Missy/Hinsdale Twp High Sch Dist 86	7	95
Geidner, Susan/Avoca School District 37	73	22
Geier, Jan/Community Unit School Dist 303	9,15,34	128
Geiger, Sarah/Zeigler Royalton CUSD 188	8	108
Geisd, Ryan/Spring Valley Cmty Cons SD 99	6	7
Geist, Ryan/Grant Cmty High Sch Dist 124	83,752	150
Geltmaker, Brooke/Illinois Vly Ctl Sch Dist 321	8,11,288,298	197
Genard, Kathy/Tremont Cmty Unit SD 702	69	228
Genesio, Heather/Pinckneyville Cmty High SD 101	33	201
Gentile, Jason/Chaney-Monge School Dist 88	35	241
Geocaris, Chris/Warren Twp High Sch Dist 121	10,15	155
Geocaris, Jill/Maine Twp High Sch Dist 207	30	56
Geocaris, Jill/Maine Twp Spec Ed Program	30	82
Geoffray, Connie/Carlyle Cmty Unit Sch Dist 1	4	17
Georgia, Philip/Community Cons School Dist 15	68	43
Geraci, Stephen/Burnham School District 1545	1,11,83,84	24
Geraghty, Mary/Glenview Cmty Cons Sch Dist 34	59,79,752	51
Gerard, Melissa/Franklin Cmty Unit SD 1	11	192
Gerard, Mike/Pikeland Cmty Sch Dist 10	67	203
Gerardi, Tom/Cicero School District 99	34	42
Gerardot, Meredith/Community Unit School Dist 308	88	137
Gerdes, Kyle/DeKalb Cmty Unit SD 428	79	84
Germany, Barbra/Lemont-Bromberek Sch Dist 113A	4	55
Gerth, Heather/Iroquois Co Cmty Unit SD 9	12,51,54,57,72,298	119
Gerth, Shanna/East Peoria Elem Sch Dist 86	16	227
Gervacio, Alex/Naperville Cmty Unit SD 203	69	98
Gervase, Jennifer/Evergreen Park Elem SD 124	52,280	49
Gerzi, Wes/Liberty Cmty Unit Sch Dist 2	5	2
Gesell, Daniel/Kankakee Area Reg Voc Ed Sys	2	137
Getz, Kathy/Tri-City Cmty Unit Sch Dist 1	7	214
Geyman, Melissa/North Boone Cmty Unit SD 200	2,5	5
Ghibellini, Joe/Sterling Cmty Unit Sch Dist 5	84	240
Gholson, Cindy/Cypress School District 64	58	127
Gholson, Tiffany/East St Louis Sch Dist 189	79,93,752	218
Ghosn, Jill/Indian Prairie Sch Dist 204	4	95
Giamis, Anthony/Oak Grove School District 68	67	154
Giannini, Stefanie/Marquardt School District 15	4	97
Giarrante, Anne/Geneva CUSD 304	79,88	131
Gibbons, Meghan/Valley View Cmty SD 365-U	4	248
Gibbons, Michael/Diocese of Belleville Ed Off	2	222
Gibbs, Ellen/Benton Cmty Cons Sch Dist 47	12	107
Gibson, Cariee/Round Lake Area Co Dist 116	74	155
Gibson, Elizabeth/Kankakee School District 111	34	135
Gibson, Greg/Indian Prairie Sch Dist 204	297	95
Gibson, John/Homewood School Dist 153	2	52
Gibson, Kathy/Komarek School District 94	2	54
Gielow, Larry/Red Bud Cmty Unit Sch Dist 132	67	205
Gierch, Cindy/Tazewell Co Area EFE #320	58,275	229
Giertz, Mark/Miller Cmty Cons Sch Dist 210	11,57,74,83,271,275	143
Giese, Sherry/Edwards Co Cmty Unit SD 1	2	104
Giesey, Dann/Woodland School District 50	73,295	157
Gifford, Dennis/Fairfield Cmty High SD 225	5	236
Gifford, Lisa/Peoria Public Sch Dist 150	39,280	198
Giglio-Byczek, Lisa/Bremen Cmty High SD 228	60,88	23
Giglio, Joseph/Oak Lawn Cmty High SD 229	3	60
Gilbert, Dan/Libertyville Pub Sch Dist 70	3	152
Gilbert, Dave/DePue Unit Sch Dist 103	73	6
Gilbert, Jacquese/Township High School Dist 211	12,72	69
Gilbert, Lanell/South Holland School Dist 151	67	68
Gilbert, Ronald/Beardstown Cmty Sch Dist 15	1	9
Gilbert, Vickie/DePue Unit Sch Dist 103	2	6
Gilbertson, Brandon/Seneca Cmty Cons Sch Dist 170	73,295,297	144
Gilbertson, Shane/Mazon-Verona-Kinsman ESD 2-C	67	112
Gilchrist, John/New Trier Twp HS District 203	35	58
Gilchrist, Lance/Winnetka School Dist 36	297	72
Gildart, Melinda/Chicago Public School Dist 299	2	25
Gilhooly, Kathlene/Rosemont Elem Sch Dist 78	12	66
Gill, Becky/Barrington Cmty Unit SD 220	9	147
Gill, Jamie/Diocese of Belleville Ed Off	64	222
Gill, Jennifer/Springfield Pub Sch Dist 186	1	213
Gille, Terri/South Beloit Cmty Sch Dist 320	2,84	255
Gillegos, Joel/Northbrook School District 28	3,5,91	59
Gilles, Ryan/Canton Union School Dist 66	5	109
Gillespie, Lisa/Lake Forest School District 67	76	152
Gillis, Amy/Scott Morgan Cmty Unit SD 2	4	215
Gillono, Mark/Hinsdale Twp High Sch Dist 86	2	95
Gilmore, Carl/Woodstock Cmty Unit SD 200	67	184
Gilmore, Lynn/Springfield Pub Sch Dist 186	23,48,61	213
Gilmore, Robert/Hillside School District 93	16,76,295,297	52
Gimm, Zach/Lake Zurich Cmty Unit Sch Dist 95	10	152
Giombetti, Trish/Grass Lake School District 36	73	150
Giordano, Heather/St Anne Cmty HSD 302	752	136
Giordano, Marie/Ladd Cmty Cons Sch Dist 94	67	6
Giovanini, Brian/Indian Prairie Sch Dist 204	70	95
Giovengo, Korrin/Pontiac Cmty Cons Sch Dist 429	5	161
Gipe, Tim/Sandwich Cmty Unit SD 430	6	85
Girard, Ron, Dr/Mundelein Cons High SD 120	71	153
Girodano, Heather/St Anne Cmty Cons Sch Dist 256	752	136
Girshan, Michelle/Robein Cmty School District 85	16,270	228
Girten, Monica/Wabash-Ohio Valley Sp Ed Dist	15	238
Gittleson, Traci/Ashton-Franklin Center SD 275	6	159
Given, Lori/Mt Vernon City Sch Dist 80	11,296,298	123
Gladwell, Cindy/East Peoria Elem Sch Dist 86	4	226
Glaser, Maria/Niles Elem School District 71	16	58
Glasper, Tisha/Venice Cmty Unit School Dist 3	67	172
Glassburn, Angela/Prophetstown-Lyndon-Tampico 3	23,38,69	239
Glauberman, Kelly/Glencoe School District 35	67	51

School Year 2020-2021   800-333-8802   IL-T21

DISTRICT PERSONNEL INDEX

Market Data Retrieval

NAME/District	JOB FUNCTIONS	PAGE
Glauck, Amy/Kildeer Countryside CCSD 96	11,59,88,90,271	151
Gleason, Susan/Lincoln Cmty High Sch Dist 404	67	163
Gleissner, Joe/Ashton-Franklin Center SD 275	73,98,286	159
Glenn, Nicholas/North Shore School Dist 112	71	154
Glick, Christy/Schuyler-Industry CUSD 5	58,88	215
Glickman, Lynn/Community Cons School Dist 46	1	148
Glidewell, Tammie/Bradley Elem School Dist 61	4	134
Gliwa, Alex/Woodridge Elem Sch District 68	3,91	100
Gloria, Isabel/Joliet Twp High Sch Dist 204	57	243
Glosniak, Jacqueline/Cicero School District 99	71	42
Glowacki, Heather/Wilmette Public School Dist 39	68	71
Glowacki, Lora/Columbia Cmty Unit SD 4	4	189
Glynn, Joe/Albers Elem School District 63	6	17
Gmazel, Anne/Troy Cmty Cons SD 30-C	9	247
Goacher, Jeanne/Columbia Cmty Unit SD 4	58	190
Gober, Breanna/Mascoutah Cmty Sch Dist 19	16,82	220
Goble, Jay/North Mac Cmty Unit SD 34	1,83	168
Gockel, Kevin/East Alton-Wood River SD 14	6	170
Goddard, John/Dongola Unit School Dist 66	8,11,57,58,74,271,275	230
Goddard, Sara/New Simpson Hill Cons SD 32	83,90	127
Godfrey, Kristen/Fairview South School Dist 72	16,82	49
Godier, Donnie/Prairie Du Rocher CCSD 134	3	205
Godinez, Juan/Salt Creek School District 48	3	99
Goebel, Drew/Clinton Cmty Unit Sch Dist 15	2,5,11	87
Goebel, Ed/Morrisonville Cmty Unit SD 1	67	14
Goemaat, Laura/Carmi-White Co School Dist 5	4	237
Goetz, Angela/Oak Lawn-Hometown Sch Dist 123	57	60
Goff, Brian/Wilmington Cmty Unit SD 209-U	6	249
Goff, Mary Beth/Unity Point Cmty Cons SD 140	12	121
Goff, Peter/DeKalb Cmty Unit SD 428	6	84
Goff, Peter/Kaneland Cmty Unit SD 302	6	132
Goggins, Dan/Bremen Cmty High SD 228	15,68,79,83	23
Goken, Tammy/Warren Community Unit SD 205	4	126
Gold, Bob/Big Hollow School District 38	1	148
Gold, Jason/Lyons Elem School Dist 103	273	56
Goldberg, Paul, Dr/East Prairie School Dist 73	1	47
Golding, Jeannie/Chester Cmty Unit Sch Dist 139	294	205
Goldman, Matt/Deland-Weldon Cmty Unit SD 57	5	202
Goldstein, Brad/Winnetka School Dist 36	2,3,4,5,19	72
Golwitzer, Terrie/Bradley Elem School Dist 61	67	134
Gonigam, Brett/East Peoria Cmty HS Dist 309	80	226
Gonzales, Anna/West Aurora School Dist 129	71,93	132
Gonzales, Stacey/Consolidated High Sch Dist 230	10	44
Gonzalez, Dan/Grayslake Cmty HS District 127	3	150
Gonzalez, Gus/Wood Dale School Dist 7	3	100
Gonzalez, Jennette/Ridgewood Cmty HSD 234	16	64
Gonzalez, Maribel/Community Cons School Dist 59	5	43
Gonzalez, Paul/Plainfield Cons Sch Dist 202	3	246
Gonzalez, Robert/West Aurora School Dist 129	67	132
Good, Kendra/Rantoul City School Dist 137	2	11
Goode, Sarah/Signal Hill Sch Dist 181	12	221
Goodin, Theresa/Carbondale Cmty HSD 165	12,298	120
Gooding, Mick/Central School District 3	3	1
Goodlove, Guy/Westville Cmty Unit Sch Dist 2	27,57,270	233
Goodwin, Stacy/Maroa Forsyth CU Sch Dist 2	12	165
Goodwine, Michelle/Hutsonville Cmty Unit SD 1	16,82	83
Gorchels, Lisa/DeKalb Cmty Unit SD 428	34	84
Gordan, Matt, Dr/Rankin Cmty School Dist 98	1,73	228
Gordon, Amanda/Flanagan-Cornell Unit 74 SD	83	161
Gordon, Breanna/Edwardsville Cmty Unit SD 7	4	170
Gordon, Brian/Trees-Three Rivers EFE Sys	1,73	250
Gordon, Cynthia/Schaumburg Cmty Cons SD 54	59,81	66
Gordon, Paul, Dr/Glen Ellyn School District 41	1	94
Gordon, Pete/Frankfort Cmty Unit SD 168	35	108
Gordon, Sandi/Park Forest Chicago Hgt SD 163	4,5	62
Gordon, Sean/Community Cons School Dist 93	3,91	90
Gordon, Shane/Bluford Unit School Dist 318	1,11	122

NAME/District	JOB FUNCTIONS	PAGE
Gorgal, Kevin/Moline-Coal Valley SD No 40	80	207
Gorguis, Rita/Skokie School District 69	2	67
Gorman, Don/Peoria Heights Cmty SD 325	67	198
Gorman, Jana/Community Unit School Dist 200	68	91
Gorman, Jeff/Central Cmty Unit SD 301	67	128
Gorman, Stacey/Mundelein Cons High SD 120	10	153
Gorman, Ty/Barrington Cmty Unit SD 220	73	147
Gorr, Mary, Dr/Mt Prospect School Dist 57	7,11,16,57,77,83,88,288	58
Gorson, Gary/Township High School Dist 211	73,76,98	69
Gorvett, Julie/Schaumburg Cmty Cons SD 54	9,15,35	66
Gosch, Bob/River Bend Cmty School Dist 2	270	239
Goscinski, Theresa/Freeburg Cmty Cons SD 70	83	219
Goselin, Scott/Bradley Elem School Dist 61	1	134
Gosen, Lisa/Hawthorn Cmty Cons Sch Dist 73	76	151
Goshko, Michele/Darien Public Sch Dist 61	297	92
Gosline, Molly/Adlai E Stevenson HSD 125	752	146
Gotshall, Brad/Pontiac-Wm Holliday SD 105	6,69,280,285,288	221
Gould, Kelly/Wood Dale School Dist 7	59	100
Gould, Richard/Peoria Public Sch Dist 150	91	198
Gound, Robert/Warsaw Cmty Unit Sch Dist 316	1,84	115
Gourley, Michael/Morris Cmty High Sch Dist 101	273	113
Gowen, Raymond/Gibson Cty-Melvin-Sibley CUSD5	4	106
Gradert, Guy/West Prairie Cmty Sch Dist 103	1,83	178
Grady, Susan/Community Cons School Dist 93	9,288,296,298	90
Grady, Susan/Hinsdale Twp High Sch Dist 86	72	95
Grady, William/Palos Heights School Dist 128	67	61
Graefin, Christine/Homer Cmty Cons Sch Dist 33C	57	242
Graf, Carol/Willow Springs School Dist 108	59	71
Graff, Cheryl/Regional Office of Ed 30	1	121
Gragart, Michael/Georgetown-Ridge Farm CUSD 4	67	232
Graham, Chris/St Joseph Cmty Cons SD 169	6	12
Graham, Easton/Carbondale Cmty HSD 165	74	120
Graham, Ethan/Carbondale Cmty HSD 165	10,73,286,295	120
Graham, Janet/Crete-Monee Cmty SD 201-U	69	242
Graham, Jeff/Ludlow Cons Sch Dist 142	1,83	11
Graham, Kirk/Meredosia-Chambersburg SD 11	6	192
Graham, Michelle/Richmond-Burton Cmty HSD 157	67	184
Graham, Nina/Thornton Twp High School Dist 205	67	69
Graham, Rob/Community Unit School Dist 7	3	167
Graham, Sarah/Two Rivers Voc Ed System	15	9
Graham, Susan/Sandwich Cmty Unit SD 430	5	85
Grammer, Matt/Chester-E Lincoln Cmty SD 61	73	163
Grammer, Rhonda/Triad Cmty School District 2	7	172
Grand, Daniel/Cook County School Dist 130	3	45
Grande, Brian/Durand Cmty Sch Dist 322	67	252
Grandgeorge, Traci/Marseilles Elem Sch Dist 150	11,73,295	142
Graner, Ryan/Calhoun Cmty Unit SD 40	6	8
Grap, Donna/Cary Cmty Cons School Dist 26	5	179
Gravel, R, Dr/Glenbrook High Sch Dist 225	2,15,16,73,76,295	50
Graves, Kara/Belvidere Cmty Unit SD 100	76	4
Graves, Kris/Tolono Cmty Unit Sch Dist 7	16	12
Graves, Roger/Triopia Cmty Unit Sch Dist 27	3	192
Graves, Tera/Livingston Area EFE System	1,11	163
Gray-Everett, Darlene/Dolton School District 149	67	46
Gray, Annie/Carlyle Cmty Unit Sch Dist 1	1	17
Gray, B/Community Unit School Dist 200	295	91
Gray, Chelsea/Barrington Cmty Unit SD 220	68	147
Gray, Donna/Milne-Kelvin Grove District 91	1	244
Gray, Lauren/Sunset Ridge Sch Dist 29	16	68
Gray, Steven/Princeton Twp HSD 500	3,5	7
Gray, Tracey/Belleville Public Sch Dist 118	11,83,280,285,288,296,298	217
Grayer, Toni/Posen-Robbins Sch Dist 143-5	68	63
Grayned, Ashley/Decatur Public Schools 61	11,70,74,750	165
Graziani, Anthony/Steger School Dist 194	3	68
Greathouse, Kevin/New Hope Cmty Cons Sch Dist 6	6	237
Greco-Lenzey, Brunella/School Dist 45 Dupage Co	9,69	99
Green, Christie/Waverly Cmty Unit SD 6	12	193

1 Superintendent	16 Instructional Media Svcs	30 Adult Education	44 Science Sec	58 Special Education K-12	72 Summer School	88 Alternative/At Risk	277 Remedial Math K-12
2 Bus/Finance/Purchasing	17 Chief Operations Officer	31 Career/Sch-to-Work K-12	45 Math K-12	59 Special Education Elem	73 Instructional Tech	89 Multi-Cultural Curriculum	280 Literacy Coach
3 Buildings And Grounds	18 Chief Academic Officer	32 Career/Sch-to-Work Elem	46 Math Elem	60 Special Education Sec	74 Inservice Training	90 Social Work	285 STEM
4 Food Service	19 Chief Financial Officer	33 Career/Sch-to-Work Sec	47 Math Sec	61 Foreign/World Lang K-12	75 Marketing/Distributive	91 Safety/Security	286 Digital Learning
5 Transportation	20 Art K-12	34 Early Childhood Ed	48 English/Lang Arts K-12	62 Foreign/World Lang Elem	76 Info Systems	92 Magnet School	288 Common Core Standards
6 Athletic	21 Art Elem	35 Health/Phys Education	49 English/Lang Arts Elem	63 Foreign/World Lang Sec	77 Psychological Assess	93 Parental Involvement	294 Accountability
7 Health Services	22 Art Sec	36 Guidance Services K-12	50 English/Lang Arts Sec	64 Religious Education K-12	78 Affirmative Action	95 Tech Prep Program	295 Network System
8 Curric/Instruct K-12	23 Music K-12	37 Guidance Services Elem	51 Reading K-12	65 Religious Education Elem	79 Student Personnel	97 Chief Infomation Officer	296 Title II Programs
9 Curric/Instruct Elem	24 Music Elem	38 Guidance Services Sec	52 Reading Elem	66 Religious Education Sec	80 Driver Ed/Safety	98 Chief Technology Officer	297 Webmaster
10 Curric/Instruct Sec	25 Music Sec	39 Social Studies K-12	53 Reading Sec	67 School Board President	81 Gifted/Talented	270 Character Education	298 Grant Writer/Ptnrships
11 Federal Program	26 Business Education	40 Social Studies Elem	54 Remedial Reading K-12	68 Teacher Personnel	82 Video Services	271 Migrant Education	750 Chief Innovation Officer
12 Title I	27 Career & Tech Ed	41 Social Studies Sec	55 Remedial Reading Elem	69 Academic Assessment	83 Substance Abuse Prev	273 Teacher Mentor	751 Chief of Staff
13 Title V	28 Technology Education	42 Science K-12	56 Remedial Reading Sec	70 Research/Development	84 Erate	274 Before/After Sch	752 Social Emotional Learning
15 Asst Superintendent	29 Family/Consumer Science	43 Science Elem	57 Bilingual/ELL	71 Public Information	85 AIDS Education	275 Response To Intervention	

Illinois School Directory
DISTRICT PERSONNEL INDEX

NAME/District	JOB FUNCTIONS	PAGE
Green, Christine/Lake Zurich Cmty Sch Dist 95	2	152
Green, Jonathan/Meridian Cmty School Dist 101	1,11	204
Green, Mariahh/Kell Cons School District 2	2	174
Green, Thera/Liberty Cmty Unit Sch Dist 2	60	2
Green, William/Cook County School Dist 104	67	44
Greenacre, Dawn/Sandwich Cmty Unit SD 430	88	86
Greenberg, Jessica/La Grange Elem Sch Dist 102	16	54
Greene, Brian/Career & Tech Ed Consortium	1	225
Greene, Jason/Eureka Cmty Unit Sch Dist 140	6	257
Greene, Juliann/Bensenville Elem Sch Dist 2	59	89
Greene, Tammy/Kings Cons School District 144	270	194
Greenhalge, Chris/Illini West High Sch Dist 307	73	114
Greenlee, Mike/North Boone Cmty Unit SD 200	1,11	5
Greenley, Jeremy/Egyptian Cmty Unit Sch Dist 5	67	3
Greenlief, David/Monmouth-Roseville CUSD 238	3	234
Greenwood, Latoya/East St Louis Sch Dist 189	68	218
Greenwood, Sheila/Bement Cmty Unit Sch Dist 5	1,11	202
Greer, Darleen/Grayville Cmty Unit Sch Dist 1	752	238
Greg, Abby/Mt Vernon Twp HS District 201	7	123
Gregory, Clarance/Evanston Twp High SD 202	3	48
Gregory, Debbie/Meredosia-Chambersburg SD 11	4	192
Gregory, Scott/Decatur Public Schools 61	4	165
Gregory, Susan/Valley View Cmty SD 365-U	7	248
Gregory, Todd/Lake Zurich Cmty Sch Dist 95	35,80	152
Greief, Larry/Riley Cmty Cons Sch Dist 18	3	184
Grelyak, David/Township High School Dist 211	3	69
Grescham, Missy/District 50 Schools	59	226
Gresham, Allen/Limestone Cmty High SD 310	1	197
Gresham, Annette/Central Sch Dist 51	59	225
Gresham, Annette/Washington Cmty HS Dist 308	60	229
Gress, Dennis/Westchester Public SD 92 1/2	2,3,4,5,19,84	70
Gress, Steve/Alsip-Hazelgrn-Oaklawn SD 126	2,15	20
Gressel, Rachel/Evanston Twp High SD 202	57	48
Greuter, Margorie/East Peoria Cmty HS Dist 309	1,11	226
Grey, Ben/Community Cons School Dist 59	15,286	43
Grey, Jason/Dakota Cmty Unit Sch Dist 201	1	224
Grey, Tracy/Red Hill Cmty School Dist 10	6	159
Grice, Chris/Dupage High School Dist 88	79	93
Grice, Jonathan/Adlai E Stevenson HSD 125	22,25	146
Grider, Tony/Sangamon Area Spec Ed District	73	215
Griffin, Chris/Jersey Cmty Sch Dist 100	295	125
Griffin, Don/Regional Office of Ed 13	8,16,73	19
Griffin, Jill, Dr/Bethalto Cmty Unit SD 8	1,11	169
Griffin, Joe/Bethalto Cmty Unit SD 8	296,298	169
Griffin, Lisa/Centralia High School Dist 200	38	174
Griffin, Millicent/Country Club Hills SD 160	76	45
Griffith, Mina/Plainfield Cons Sch Dist 202	15,58,77,88,275,752	246
Griglione, Mark/Troy Cmty Cons SD 30-C	67	247
Grill, John/St George School District 258	2	136
Grimm, Sue/River Trails Sch Dist 26	4	65
Grimm, Tom/Dunlap Cmty Unit Sch Dist 323	3	196
Grimsley, Rod/Gifford Cmty Cons SD 188	83	10
Grimsley, Rodney, Dr/Crescent Iroquois Cmty SD 249	1,11	118
Gripp, Chad/Bradford Cmty Unit Sch Dist 1	1,11,73	223
Grisham, Brent/Pleasant Plains Cmty Unit SD 8	6	212
Grissom, Gail/Casey-Westfield Cmty USD C-4	73	15
Grizaffi, Gary/Valley View Cmty SD 365-U	2,15	248
Grochocinski, Cynthia/North Palos School Dist 117	7,35,85	59
Grode, Christopher/Columbia Cmty Unit SD 4	1	189
Grogan, Charles/South Pekin Grade Sch Dist 137	3	228
Grohmann, Dave/Belle Valley School Dist 119	3	217
Gromm, Jennifer/Saratoga Cmty Cons SD 60C	83	113
Gronski, Tim/Geneseo Cmty Unit Sch Dist 228	2,5,12,91	117
Groody, Patrick/Community High School Dist 128	67	148
Grooms, Beth/Marshall Cmty Sch Dist C-2	12	15
Groos, Bob/New Lenox School District 122	2,4,5,7,298	245
Grosch, Michael/Leyden Cmty High Sch Dist 212	91	55
Grosclaude, Deb/Lewistown Community Unit SD 97	2	110
Grosclaude, Deb/Lewistown Community Unit SD 97	2	110
Gross, Carly/Fairview South School Dist 72	79	49
Gross, Clarence/Red Hill Cmty School Dist 10	288	159
Grossi, Robert/Kankakee School District 111	2,5,15,16,76,80,82	135
Grossman, Ilysa/Rondout School District 72	90	154
Grosso, Jeff/Elwood Cmty Cons SD 203	2,73,84,286	242
Groves, Clarance/Red Hill Cmty School Dist 10	11,296	159
Gruber, Lisa/Riley Cmty Cons Sch Dist 18	88	184
Gruhn, Janine/West Northfield Sch Dist 31	11,59,79,88,296	70
Grule, Matt/Windsor Cmty Unit SD 1	67	216
Grundke, John/Lyons Twp HS District 204	6	56
Gruper, Stasia/Crystal Lake Elem Distict 47	74	181
Grzanich, Susan, Dr/Peoria Public Sch Dist 150	298,750	198
Guardian, Shannon/Cobden Cmty Unit Sch Dist 17	11,55	230
Guarraci, Laura/Niles Elem School District 71	11,79,296	58
Guay, Steven/Central School District 104	73,286	218
Guenzler, Claudine/West Carroll CUSD 314	2	8
Guerrero, Stephanie/Sangamon Valley Cmty Unit SD 9	67	166
Guerrero, Tammy/Mendota Twp High Sch Dist 280	83,88,90	143
Guethle, Alyssa/Elverado Cmty Unit SD 196	4	120
Guiffre, Marcia/Northwest Suburban Sp Ed Org	15	82
Guile, Gina/Auburn Cmty Unit Sch Dist 10	2	211
Guilliams, Greg/Deer Creek-Mackinaw CUSD 701	3	226
Gum, Mike/Riverton Cmty Unit SD 14	2,73,84	212
Gunnell, James, Dr/Aero Special Ed Co-op	1	82
Gunter, Penny/Carmi-White Co School Dist 5	38	237
Gunthorp, Kristina/Antioch Cmty Cons Sch Dist 34	9,12,15,74,275,288,296	146
Gunty, Joe/J Sterling Morton HSD 201	12	53
Gupta, Kato/Leyden Cmty High Sch Dist 212	38	55
Gurney, Robert/Wheeling Cmty Cons Sch Dist 21	15,68	71
Guseman, Karla/Joliet Twp High School Dist 204	1	243
Guske, Aaron/Harlem Unit Sch District 122	73,76,84,295	252
Gust, Carolyn/Oak Park & River Forest SD 200	5	60
Gustis, Steven/Woodridge Elem Sch District 68	67	100
Gutierrez, Marcy/Hillsboro Cmty Unit Sch Dist 3	34,88	191
Gutierrez, Martha/Woodland School District 50	68	157
Gutierrez, Miguel/Thornton Fractnl Twp HSD 215	295	69
Gutzman, Kevin/Channahon School District 17	3	241
Gutzmer, John/Champaign Cmty Unit Sch Dist 4	73,76,84,295	10
Guyton, Arthur/Peoria Public Sch Dist 150	6	198
Guzak, Debra/Sunnybrook School District 171	88	68
Guzik, Michele/Norridge School Dist 80	9,15	59
Gwaltney, Craig/Alsip-Hazelgrn-Oaklawn SD 126	1	20

H

NAME/District	JOB FUNCTIONS	PAGE
Haag, Jennifer/Peotone Cmty Unit SD 207-U	5	245
Haan, Eric/Eastland Cmty Unit SD 308	95,295	8
Haas, Lisa/River Ridge Cmty Unit SD 210	7	126
Haas, Lloyd/River Ridge Cmty Unit SD 210	5	126
Haas, Lora/Peoria Co Special Ed Assoc	1	200
Haas, Lora/Princeville Cmty Unit SD 326	58	200
Haas, Rebecca/Sterling Cmty Unit Sch Dist 5	8,11,58,72,81	240
Haas, Terry/Whiteside School District 115	91	222
Haase, Cathy/Minooka Cmty Cons Sch Dist 201	5	112
Haase, Cathy/Minooka Cmty High Sch Dist 111	5	244
Haase, Dave/Iroquois West Cmty Unit SD 10	67	119
Habel, Joshua/Maywood-Melrose Brdview SD 89	295	57
Habing, Jim/Wilmington Cmty Unit SD 209-U	3	249
Hacke, Derek/Highland Cmty Sch District 5	8,11,57,83,88,288,296,298	171
Hacke, Kyle/Southwestern Cmty Unit SD 9	1	168
Hackett, Damon/Dunlap Cmty Unit Sch Dist 323	2,11,15,19,68,83	196
Hackett, Erin/Central Stickney Sch Dist 110	1	25
Hackett, Judith, Dr/Northwest Suburban Sp Ed Org	1	82
Hackl, Keith/Warrensburg-Latham CU SD 11	3,91	166
Hackney, Jennifer/Kell Cons School District 2	12	174
Hackney, Joel/Flora Cmty Unit School Dist 35	1,11,83	16
Hackney, Sean/Minooka Cmty High Sch Dist 111	50	244
Hackney, Sherry/Maercker School District 60	55	97
Hadjan, Jamie/Jacksonville School Dist 117	2,19	192
Hadley, Jason/Taylorville Cmty Unit SD 3	6	15
Hadley, Shane/Ramsey Cmty Unit Sch Dist 204	67	105
Haenisch, Julie/Glenbrook High Sch Dist 225	7	50
Haertling, Jennifer/Steeleville Cmty Sch Dist 138	15	206
Hafeli, Mike/Centralia City Sch Dist 135	3	174
Hafer, Sharon/Dixon Cmty Unit Sch Dist 170	7	160
Haffner, Evan/Monroe School District 70	6	198
Haffner, John/West Chicago Elementary SD 33	2	99
Hagemann, Jen/Meridian Cmty Unit SD 223	5	194
Hagene, Keith/Pinckneyville Cmty High SD 101	1	201
Hagenow, Amy/Bradley-Bourbonnais CHSD 307	7	134
Hagler, Bob/Pawnee Cmty Unit Sch Dist 11	73	212
Hagler, Bob/Pawnee Cmty Unit Sch Dist 11	73,98,286	212
Hahn, Jane/Johnsburg Cmty School Dist 12	2	182
Hahn, Ryan/Heyworth Cmty Sch District 4	73,295	185

DISTRICT PERSONNEL INDEX

Market Data Retrieval

NAME/District	JOB FUNCTIONS	PAGE
Hahn, Sandy/Marissa Cmty Unit Sch Dist 40	4	220
Hail, Joy/Diamond Lake School Dist 76	67	149
Hainds, Tammy/Mercer County SD 404	38	189
Haines, Steve/Seneca Twp High Sch Dist 160	6	144
Hajdu, Leah/Coal City Cmty Unit Sch Dist 1	76	112
Halbrook, Kylie/Morrisonville Cmty Unit SD 1	273	14
Haldeman, Kevin/Murphysboro Cmty Unit SD 186	73	121
Hale, Debbie/Crab Orchard Cmty Sch Dist 3	7,83,85,275	251
Hale, Roger/Bourbonnais Elem Sch Dist 53	16,73,76,295,297	134
Hall, Allen/Shiloh School District 1	1	103
Hall, Caleb/West Prairie Cmty Sch Dist 103	6	178
Hall, Dawn/Glenbrook High Sch Dist 225	27,95	50
Hall, Jackie/Chaney-Monge School Dist 88	9,11,69,85,270,288	241
Hall, James/Rockton School District 140	73	255
Hall, Janina/North Chicago Cmty Unit SD 187	8	153
Hall, Kristin/Paw Paw Cmty Unit SD 271	296	160
Hall, Kyla/Teutopolis Cmty Unit SD 50	36,69	105
Hall, Leona/Ladd Cmty Cons Sch Dist 94	6	6
Hall, Lindsey, Dr/Mahomet-Seymour Cmty SD 3	1	11
Hall, Pete/Grayville Cmty Unit Sch Dist 1	76	238
Hall, Preston/Dongola Unit School Dist 66	6	230
Hall, Tim/Hiawatha Cmty Unit SD 426	67	85
Hallberg, John/Community High School Dist 218	5,11,286,296,298	44
Haller, Mark/Illinois Dept of Education	4	1
Halliman, Tina, Dr/Speed Seja 802	1	82
Hallinghan, Michelle/Manhattan School Dist 114	16,82	244
Hallom, Vanessa/Posen-Robbins Sch Dist 143-5	79	63
Halls, Josh/St Joseph-Ogden Cmty HSD 305	76,295	12
Halperin, Adam/Community Cons School Dist 46	3	148
Halperin, Adam/Fremont School District 79	3	149
Halpin, Trent/Central Sch Dist 51	9	225
Halverson, Greg/Marengo Cmty High Sch Dist 154	35	182
Halverson, Joshua/Wood Dale School Dist 7	73,76,286,295	100
Halverson, Kim/Hinckley-Big Rock Cmty SD 429	6	85
Halverson, Lisa/Park Ridge Niles CMCSD 64	274	62
Halverson, Robert/West Aurora School Dist 129	298	132
Halwaphca, Mark/Carrollton Cmty Unit SD 1	1,11	111
Hambleton, Vance/Potomac Cmty Unit Sch Dist 10	67	232
Hamelin, Jan/Riverdale Cmty Unit SD 100	3	208
Hamerlinck, Tom/Orion Cmty Unit Sch Dist 223	3	117
Hamil, Phillip/Aviston Elem School Dist 21	1,11,83	17
Hamil, Phillip/Tamaroa Elem School Dist 5	11,83,288	201
Hamilton, Anna/Maine Twp Spec Ed Program	58	82
Hamilton, Doug, Dr/Matteson Elem SD 162	15	57
Hamilton, Jennifer/Ohio Cmty Cons School Dist 17	1,11	7
Hamilton, Jennifer/Ohio Cmty High School Dist 505	1,11	7
Hamilton, Jill/Pawnee Cmty Unit Sch Dist 11	2	212
Hamilton, Joe/Leyden Cmty High Sch Dist 212	80	55
Hamilton, Melanie/Frankfort Cmty Unit SD 168	34	108
Hamilton, Michelle/Steeleville Cmty Sch Dist 138	31,36,69,83,88	206
Hamilton, Quint/Zeigler Royalton CUSD 188	1,11	108
Hamilton, Scott/Tolono Cmty Unit Sch Dist 7	6	12
Hamilton, Steve/Clinton Cmty Unit Sch Dist 15	4	87
Hamilton, Tony/Lemont High Sch Dist 210	71	55
Hamm, Jane/Central School District 104	2,274	218
Hamm, Tracy/Oak Park Elem School Dist 97	59	60
Hammel, Mitch/Chester Cmty Unit Sch Dist 139	67	205
Hammelman, Randy/East Coloma-Nelson Cesd 20	3	238
Hammer, Bill/Beecher City Cmty Unit SD 20	16	104
Hammer, Geri/Peoria Public Sch Dist 150	68	198
Hammerberg, Lucy, Dr/Bannockburn Sch Dist 106	67	147
Hammil, Paige/Serena Cmty Unit School Dist 2	58	144
Hammond, Carla/Christopher Unit School Dist 99	2	107
Hammond, Christopher/Bradley-Bourbonnais CHSD 307	2	134
Hamon, Neil/Central Cmty High School Dist 71	6	17
Hamon, Terry/New Athens CUSD 60	67	220
Hampton, Ilandus/Joliet Twp High Sch Dist 204	2,15	243
Hampton, Maribeth/Plainfield Cons Sch Dist 202	76	246
Hampton, Sarit/Thornton Twp High Sch Dist 205	298	69
Hamrick, Dorothy/Bradley Elem School Dist 61	34	134
Hance, Beth/Clay City Cmty Unit SD 10	2	16
Hancock, Lonna/Queen Bee School District 16	9,285	98
Hand, Karen/High Mount Sch Dist 116	12	219
Handke, Deborah/La Grange Elem Sch Dist 102	2	54
Handy, Ginger/Windsor Cmty Unit SD 1	12	216
Haney, Becy/North Shore School Dist 112	2	154
Hanke, Katrina/Wesclin Cmty Unit Sch Dist 3	36,79	18
Hankey, Sue/River Trails Sch Dist 26	16	65
Hankins, Bree/Springfield Pub Sch Dist 186	71	213
Hankins, Monica/Le Roy Cmty Unit SD 2	4	186
Hanks, Adam/Vienna Public School Dist 55	6,275	127
Hanley, Matt/Community Cons School Dist 89	71	90
Hanlon, Jack/South Fork School Dist 14	67	14
Hanlon, Megan/Morrisonville Cmty Unit SD 1	11	14
Hanna, Rita/Bureau Valley Cmty Unit 340	2	6
Hannaford, Todd/Bethalto Cmty Unit SD 8	6	169
Hannagan, Sean/St Elmo Cmty Unit Sch Dist 202	9,12	106
Hannam, Jeff/Cambridge Cmty Unit SD 227	6,273	116
Hannel, Lisa/Pleasant Hill CUSD 3	12	203
Hannigan, Catherine/Downers Grove School Dist 58	2,4,5	93
Hannigan, Pete, Dr/Hawthorn Cmty Cons Sch Dist 73	1	151
Hannon, Jen/Lincoln-Way Cmty HS Dist 210	71	244
Hanrahan, Bob/Skokie School District 73 1/2	73	67
Hanrahan, Robert/Skokie School District 73 1/2	73	67
Hansen, Becky/Tremont Cmty Unit SD 702	11	228
Hansen, Eric/Diamond Lake School Dist 76	73,76	149
Hansen, Kelly/Barrington Cmty Unit SD 220	10,288	147
Hansen, Victoria/Bellwood School District 88	9,12,285,298	22
Hanserd, Imari/South Beloit Cmty Sch Dist 320	57,58,88	255
Hanson, Cassie/Geneseo Cmty Unit Sch Dist 228	58	117
Hanson, Kailay/Morrison Cmty Unit Sch Dist 6	2	239
Hanson, Leslie/Bloomington School District 87	7,11,36,58,77,83,90,275	185
Hanson, Maureen/La Salle Elem SD 122	7	142
Hanson, Rick/Orland School District 135	3	61
Hanson, Risa/Woodstock Cmty Unit SD 200	2,19	184
Hanson, Steve/Mendota Twp High Sch Dist 280	6,35	143
Harbach, Sarah/Warren Community Unit SD 205	16	126
Harbauer, Ken/Glen Ellyn School District 41	297	94
Harbaugh, Elizabeth/Shiloh School District 1	2,8,11,88,273,274,296	103
Harbaugh, Veronica/St Joseph-Ogden Cmty HSD 305	297	12
Harden, James, Dr/McLean Co Unit District 5	68,79	186
Harding, Calvin/Echo Joint Agreement	73	82
Harding, Gina/O'Fallon Cmty Cons Sch Dist 90	274	221
Harding, Sherry/Pekin Public School Dist 108	273	227
Hardmon, Michelle/Prairie Hills Elem SD 144	59,79	63
Hardy, Brian/Schuyler-Industry CUSD 5	73,84,286	215
Hardy, Vicki/Carthage Elementary SD 317	1,11	114
Haren, Aryan/Community High School Dist 117	74,286	148
Hargraves, Joe/Zeigler Royalton CUSD 188	3	108
Harig, Marty/Seneca Twp High Sch Dist 160	16,73,76,286,295,297	144
Haring, Amy/Princeton Elem Sch Dist 115	16	7
Haring, Kirk/Princeton Twp HSD 500	1	7
Harkin, Karen/Joliet Twp High Sch Dist 204	73,76	243
Harkin, Susan/Community Unit School Dist 300	3,5,15,17,751	180
Harkness, Joe/Elmwood Cmty Unit Sch Dist 322	3	196
Harlan, Derek/Centralia High School Dist 200	38,69,83,88	174
Harlson, Julie/Grayville Cmty Unit Sch Dist 1	1,11,83	238
Harmon, Michael/Princeville Cmty Unit SD 326	67	200
Harms, Dirk/Prairieview-Ogden Sch Dist 197	67	11
Harms, Mark/Flanagan-Cornell Unit 74 SD	67	161
Harmsen, Kim/Prairie Du Rocher CCSD 134	88,270	205
Harnacke, Linda/New Holland Middletown ESD 88	4	164
Harner, Patrick/Five Co Reg EFE System	1,11	3
Harness, Chris/Valmeyer Cmty School Dist 3	16,73,295	190

1 Superintendent	16 Instructional Media Svcs	30 Adult Education	44 Science Sec	58 Special Education K-12	72 Summer School	88 Alternative/At Risk	277 Remedial Math K-12
2 Bus/Finance/Purchasing	17 Chief Operations Officer	31 Career/Sch-to-Work K-12	45 Math K-12	59 Special Education Elem	73 Instructional Tech	89 Multi-Cultural Curriculum	280 Literacy Coach
3 Buildings And Grounds	18 Chief Academic Officer	32 Career/Sch-to-Work Elem	46 Math Elem	60 Special Education Sec	74 Inservice Training	90 Social Work	285 STEM
4 Food Service	19 Chief Financial Officer	33 Career/Sch-to-Work Sec	47 Math Sec	61 Foreign/World Lang K-12	75 Marketing/Distributive	91 Safety/Security	286 Digital Learning
5 Transportation	20 Art K-12	34 Early Childhood Ed	48 English/Lang Arts K-12	62 Foreign/World Lang Elem	76 Info Systems	92 Magnet School	288 Common Core Standards
6 Athletic	21 Art Elem	35 Health/Phys Education	49 English/Lang Arts Elem	63 Foreign/World Lang Sec	77 Psychological Assess	93 Parental Involvement	294 Accountability
7 Health Services	22 Art Sec	36 Guidance Services K-12	50 English/Lang Arts Sec	64 Religious Education K-12	78 Affirmative Action	95 Tech Prep Program	295 Network System
8 Curric/Instruct K-12	23 Music K-12	37 Guidance Services Elem	51 Reading K-12	65 Religious Education Elem	79 Student Personnel	97 Chief Innovation Officer	296 Title II Programs
9 Curric/Instruct Elem	24 Music Elem	38 Guidance Services Sec	52 Reading Elem	66 Religious Education Sec	80 Driver Ed/Safety	98 Chief Technology Officer	297 Webmaster
10 Curric/Instruct Sec	25 Music Sec	39 Social Studies K-12	53 Reading Sec	67 School Board President	81 Gifted/Talented	270 Character Education	298 Grant Writer/Ptnrships
11 Federal Program	26 Business Education	40 Social Studies Elem	54 Remedial Reading K-12	68 Teacher Personnel	82 Video Services	271 Migrant Education	750 Chief Innovation Officer
12 Title I	27 Career & Tech Ed	41 Social Studies Sec	55 Remedial Reading Elem	69 Academic Assessment	83 Substance Abuse Prev	273 Teacher Mentor	751 Chief of Staff
13 Title V	28 Technology Education	42 Science K-12	56 Remedial Reading Sec	70 Research/Development	84 Erate	274 Before/After Sch	752 Social Emotional Learning
15 Asst Superintendent	29 Family/Consumer Science	43 Science Elem	57 Bilingual/ELL	71 Public Information	85 AIDS Education	275 Response To Intervention	

IL-T24

Illinois School Directory
DISTRICT PERSONNEL INDEX

NAME/District	JOB FUNCTIONS	PAGE
Harp, Marla/Benton Cons High Sch Dist 103	10,11,288,298	107
Harper, Amber/Bureau Valley Cmty Unit 340	11,298	6
Harper, Annette/Nashville Cmty Cons SD 49	274	235
Harper, Jane/Homewood Flossmoor CHSD 233	16,82,286	52
Harper, Jason/Rochelle Cmty Cons SD 231	1	195
Harper, Jason/Rochelle Twp High Sch Dist 212	1	195
Harr, Matt/McLean Co Unit District 5	72,90	186
Harrell, Tracey/Tremont Cmty Unit SD 702	12	228
Harrell, Wendy/Silvis School District 34	2,11,84,296	209
Harrelson, Julie/New Hope Cmty Cons Sch Dist 6	1,11	237
Harres, Scott/Wolf Branch School Dist 113	1	222
Harridge, Andy/Morrison Cmty Unit Sch Dist 6	9,13,83	239
Harris, Adam/Arlington Hts School Dist 25	71,297	21
Harris, Brian, Dr/Barrington Cmty Unit SD 220	1	147
Harris, Brock/Thompsonville Cmty USD 174	1,11	108
Harris, Donald/Granite City Cmty Unit SD 9	5,57,69,71,79,275,294,298	171
Harris, Donald/Ottawa Twp High Sch Dist 140	67	143
Harris, Greg/Valley View Cmty SD 365-U	11	248
Harris, Jann/Arthur CUSD 305	11	87
Harris, Jeanette/Naperville Cmty Unit SD 203	7	98
Harris, Jeffrey/Ridgeview Cmty Unit SD 19	67	187
Harris, Karen/Community Cons School Dist 168	68	44
Harris, Kevin/Huntley School Dist 158	4	182
Harris, Kevin/McHenry Cmty Cons Sch Dist 15	4	183
Harris, Michelle/Heyworth Cmty Sch District 4	16,82	185
Harris, Pam/Northern Kane Co Reg Voc Sys	58	134
Harris, Rebecca/Lombard Elem SD 44	68	97
Harris, Rodney/Canton Union School Dist 66	3,91	109
Harris, Tonya/Illini Central CUSD 189	7	177
Harris, Twyla/Dolton School District 149	15	46
Harris, William/Dupo Cmty School District 196	27,57	218
Harrison, Hannah/Jasper Cmty Cons Sch Dist 17	16,82,286	237
Harrison, Jennifer/Illini Central CUSD 189	4	177
Harrison, Matt/Spoon River Valley Cmty SD 4	5	110
Harrison, Susan/West Northfield Sch Dist 31	71,295	70
Harrison, Tom/Christopher Unit Sch Dist 99	73,295,297	107
Harrison, Tom/Crab Orchard Cmty Sch Dist 3	73,295	251
Harriss, Melissa/Nashville Cmty HSD 99	7,83,85	235
Harrod, Lisa/Manteno Cmty Unit Sch Dist 5	1	135
Harsted, Sandy/Deer Park Cmty Cons SD 82	6,35	141
Hart, Alyssa/Dunlap Cmty Unit Sch Dist 323	57,58,79,90	196
Hart, Jared/Metamora Twp HS Dist 122	6	258
Hart, John/Danville School District 118	9,15,69,88,275,280,294	231
Hart, Justin/Mundelein Cons High SD 120	35	153
Hart, Renee/Alton Cmty School District 11	8,16,51,57,69,280,285,288	169
Hart, Rick/Pleasant Valley Sch Dist 62	11	199
Hartfiel, Margie/Career Educ Assoc N Ctl IL	1	256
Harting, Ty, Dr/Community High School Dist 218	1	44
Hartje, Will/Winnebago Cmty Unit SD 323	6	255
Hartke, Nick/Stewardson-Strasburg SD 5-A	3	216
Hartle, Keishia/Brussels Cmty Unit Sch Dist 42	6	8
Hartlieb, Annette/Regional Office of Ed 3	11,15,74	106
Hartlieb, Annette/Regional Office of Education 3	15	106
Hartman, Scott/Eastland Cmty Unit SD 308	6	8
Hartman, Tom/Forrestville Valley CUSD 221	73,84	194
Hartranft, Candice/Niles Twp Dept of Spec Ed #807	15,58	82
Hartweg, Kelli/Community High School Dist 128	60	148
Hartwell, Kyle/Marion Cmty School Dist 2	4	251
Haruska, Christopher/Round Lake Area Co Dist 116	45	155
Harvey, Arnett/Cahokia Unit Sch Dist 187	1,11	218
Harvey, Kristen/Effingham Cmty Sch Dist 40	5	104
Harvey, Richard/Rochelle Twp High Sch Dist 212	6	195
Haselhorst, Ryan/Highland Cmty Sch District 5	295	171
Haskell, Joseph/East St Louis Sch Dist 189	88	218
Hasse, Kelly/Thornton Fractnl Twp HSD 215	79	69
Hasselbring, Cade/Tri-Valley Cmty School Dist 3	3,5	187
Hassell, Kim/Patoka Cmty Unit SD 100	2	175
Hassler, Michelle/Calumet City School Dist 155	59	24
Hasten, John/Kansas Cmty School District 3	1,11,288	103
Hasting, Valerie/Four Rivers Spec Ed District	74,77	193
Hastings, Jennifer/Rural Champaign Co Sp Ed Co-op	59	13
Hastings, Kyle/Lyons Elem School Dist 103	15	56
Hastings, Scot/Morris Cmty High Sch Dist 101	67	113
Hatcher, Diane/A-C Central Cmty Unit SD 262	16	9
Hatcher, Stephanie/Grayville Cmty Unit Sch Dist 1	67	238
Hatczel, Kathy/Brookwood School District 167	9,73	24
Hatfield, Katie/Tuscola Cmty Unit SD 301	83,88	88
Hatfield, Patrick/Leyden Cmty High Sch Dist 212	2	55
Hatfield, Rebecca/Northwest Special Ed District	68	126
Hathaway, Robert/Shawnee Cmty Unit Sch Dist 84	85	231
Hatje, Joel/Riverside-Brookfld Twp SD 208	3	65
Hauck, Cindy/Okaw Valley Cmty Unit SD 302	2	193
Hauffe, Rick/Central A&M Cmty Unit SD 21	2,84	14
Haugeberg, Beth/Avoca School District 37	16,73,295,297	22
Hauger, David/Dakota Cmty Unit Sch Dist 201	3	224
Haugland, Becky/Carrollton Cmty Unit SD 1	7	111
Hauser, Danielle/Township High School Dist 211	10,11,69,74,296	69
Hausherr, Lori/Round Lake Area Co Dist 116	76	155
Hausmann, Jerry/Pleasant Hill CUSD 3	3,5	203
Havel, Tim/Freeburg Cmty Cons SD 70	3	219
Havemann, Judy/Elgin School District U-46	273	130
Havenaar, Nancy/Naperville Cmty Unit SD 203	20	98
Haverly, Joe/North Boone Cmty Unit SD 200	67	5
Havis, Mary, Dr/Berwyn South School Dist 100	1	23
Havlin, Jim/New Lenox School District 122	6	245
Hawkins, Brian/St Joseph Cmty Cons SD 169	3	12
Hawkins, Casey/Trico Cmty Unit Sch Dist 176	69	121
Hawkins, Rebecca/Salt Fork Cmty Unit SD 512	12	233
Hawkins, Walter/Crescent Iroquois Cmty SD 249	73	118
Hawley, Alison, Dr/River Forest Sch Dist 90	9,11,79,288	65
Hawley, Kent/Griggsville-Perry Cmty SD 4	1,11	203
Hawley, Rod/Odin Public School Dist 722	67	175
Hawthorne, Oscar/North Chicago Cmty Unit SD 187	11,15,16,69	154
Haye, Shannon/Center Cass Sch Dist 66	16,82	90
Hayes, Christine/Field Cmty Cons Sch Dist 3	67	123
Hayes, Darcie/Mt Zion Cmty Unit Sch Dist 3	4	166
Hayes, Jason/DePue Unit Sch Dist 103	67	6
Hayes, Jason/Massac Unit School District 1	1,11,83	177
Hayes, Linda/Salem Elem Sch District 111	4	175
Hayes, Marci/Peoria Public Sch Dist 150	59	198
Hayes, Mark/Community Unit School Dist 7	67	167
Hayes, Sean/Central A&M Cmty Unit SD 21	6	14
Hayes, Timothy/New Trier Twp HS District 203	15,79	58
Hayner, Nicole/Pontiac Twp High Sch Dist 90	35,83,85	161
Haynes, James/Rowva Cmty School Dist 208	67	140
Haynie, Susan/Kirby School District 140	297	53
Hays, Robyn/North Mac Cmty Unit SD 34	67	168
Haywood, Jessica/Regional Office of Ed 35	4	146
Hazzard, Jackie/Bourbonnais Elem Sch Dist 53	5	134
Head, Lynn/West Aurora School Dist 129	5	132
Headrick, Gordon/Armstrong Twp High SD 225	67	231
Healy, Julie/St Elmo Cmty Unit Sch Dist 202	1	106
Healy, Megan/Valley View Cmty SD 365-U	9	248
Healy, Mike/Community Unit School Dist 200	6	91
Heard, Timothy/Prairie Hills Elem SD 144	6	63
Heath, Eric/Peoria Heights Cmty SD 325	1	198
Heath, Misty/Jasper Co Cmty Unit SD 1	2	122
Heavner, Ryan/Greenview Cmty Unit SD 200	1	188
Heberling, Sarah/Tri-City Cmty Unit Sch Dist 1	31,36,57,69	214
Heck, Deann, Dr/Central A&M Cmty Unit SD 21	1,11,83	14
Heck, Travis/Tri-City Cmty Unit Sch Dist 1	67	214
Heckel, Nick/Oak Grove School District 68	5	154
Heckert, Kurt/West Washington Co Cmty SD 10	67	236
Hedlund, Laurie/Rhodes School District 84 1/2	3,16	64
Heeke, Kathryn/La Grange Cmty School Dist 105	9,280,285,288	54
Hefferan, Samia/Bloomingdale School Dist 13	34,59,271,275	89
Hefkett, Nick/Bartonville School District 66	67	196
Heggemeier, Alicia/Nashville Cmty HSD 99	6	235
Heiar, Wes/East Dubuque Unit SD 119	9,34	125
Hoid, Fred/Community Unit School Dist 300	1	180
Heidbreeder, Dale/Central Sch Dist 51	1,83	225
Heidenreich, Jody/Calhoun Cmty Unit Sch Dist 40	5	8
Heiderscheidt, John/Elgin School District U-46	91	130
Heidgen, Cara/Batavia Unit School Dist 101	38	128
Heidrick, Alexis/Rossville-Alvin Cmty Unit SD 7	11	233
Heil, James/Marissa Cmty Unit Sch Dist 40	67	220
Heil, Melissa/Metamora Twp HS Dist 122	67	258
Heing, Mary/Bureau Valley Cmty Unit 340	16	6
Heinold, Dale/Stark Co Cmty Unit SD 100	73,84	224
Heinz, Cheryl/Marengo Union Elem Cons SD 165	59,88	182
Heinz, Jarred/Pikeland Cmty Sch Dist 10	6	203
Heinz, Laurie, Dr/Community Cons School Dist 15	1	42

DISTRICT PERSONNEL INDEX

Market Data Retrieval

NAME/District	JOB FUNCTIONS	PAGE
Heinzes, Travis/Forrestville Valley CUSD 221	8	194
Heiser, Lisa/Saunemin Cmty Cons SD 438	34	162
Heisner, Jeff/Fairfield Cmty High SD 225	3	236
Heitkamp, Elizabeth/Diocese of Rockford Ed Office	11,15,74	256
Heitzman, Trudy/Illini Bluffs Cmty Unit SD 327	4	197
Helbig, Eric/Woodlawn Unit School Dist 209	1	124
Heldt, Marla/Beecher Cmty Sch Dist 200-U	2,5	241
Helfand, Stephanie/New Trier Twp HS District 203	16,76,98	58
Helfer, Jason, Dr/Illinois Dept of Education	8,15	1
Helfers, Pete/Gurnee School District 56	9,11,74,83,273,286,288,294	150
Helleny, Sharon/Williamson Co Cte System	1	252
Heller, Becky/Northbrook School District 28	81	59
Heller, Justin/Prospect Hts School Dist 23	295	63
Hellrigel, Todd/Midwest Ctl Cmty Unit SD 191	1	177
Hellrigel, Todd/Tazewell-Mason Sp Ed Assoc	67	229
Helpingstine, Dale/Selmaville Cmty Cons SD 10	67	176
Helsel, Michele/Steger School Dist 194	67	68
Helton, Mike/Goreville Cmty Unit SD 1	73	127
Helton, Scott, Dr/Dupage High School Dist 88	1	93
Henderson, Debra/Central Illinois Voc Ed Co-op	1	259
Henderson, Heath/Le Roy Cmty Unit SD 2	73,295	186
Henderson, James, Dr/Proviso Twp High Sch Dist 209	1	63
Henderson, Jason, Dr/Edwardsville Cmty Unit SD 7	1	170
Henderson, Kathy/Milne-Kelvin Grove District 91	88	244
Henderson, Mary, Dr/Roselle School District 12	1,11	99
Hendricks, Sandra/Rochester Cmty Unit SD 3-A	27,31,36,69,79	212
Hendricks, Scott/Waverly Cmty Unit SD 6	6	193
Henke, Bill/Calhoun Cmty Unit Sch Dist 40	295	8
Henke, Lon/Triad Cmty School District 2	3	172
Henkel, Amy/Ogle Co Educational Co-op	15	196
Henkel, Roger/Pontiac Twp High Sch Dist 90	5	161
Henkle, Nicholas/Channahon School District 17	1,11,83	241
Henley, Chad/Avoca School District 37	6	22
Henne, Marsha/Saratoga Cmty Cons SD 60C	2	113
Hennessy, James/Evergreen Park Elem SD 124	3	49
Henning, Brittany/East Aurora School Dist 131	69,294	129
Henning, Valerie/Illini Central CUSD 189	88	177
Henrekin, Patrick/River Bend Cmty School Dist 2	6	239
Henrichs, Emily/St Rose School District 14-15	67	18
Henricksen, Ami/Riverdale Cmty Unit SD 100	76	208
Henrikson, Andy, Dr/Mundelein Elem School Dist 75	11	153
Henry, Denise/St Clair Co Regional Off of Ed	34,58	223
Henry, Jason, Dr/Sesser-Valier Cmty Unit SD 196	1,11	108
Henry, Kerri/Sesser-Valier Cmty Unit SD 196	36	108
Henry, Leslie/Edgar Co Cmty Sch Dist 6	67	103
Henry, Megan/Wood River-Hartford Elem SD 15	7,85	172
Henry, Scotty/Meridian Cmty School Dist 101	67	204
Hensley, George/Cumberland Cmty Unit SD 77	3,91	84
Hensley, Lorylee/Vienna Public School Dist 55	73	127
Hensley, Matt/Mahomet-Seymour Cmty SD 3	6	11
Henson, Colleen/Mascoutah Cmty Unit Sch Dist 19	7	220
Henson, Jamie/Brimfield Cmty Unit SD 309	76	196
Henson, Michael/Pope Co Cmty Unit Sch Dist 1	67	204
Hepner, Michelle/Geneseo Cmty Unit Sch Dist 228	4	117
Heppard, Brenda/Morton Cmty Unit Sch Dist 709	68	227
Herak, Katie/North Shore School Dist 112	2	154
Herchenbach, Seth/Richmond-Burton Cmty HSD 157	16	184
Herdes, Kerry/South Central Cmty Unit SD 401	1,83	176
Heredia, Kristin, Dr/Ottawa Twp High School Dist 140	73	143
Hergenroeder, Nick/Waterloo Cmty Unit Sch Dist 5	73	190
Herman, Jennifer/West Aurora School Dist 129	58	132
Hermann, David/Miller Cmty Cons School Dist 210	1	143
Hermen, Larry/Beecher Cmty Sch Dist 200-U	67	241
Hermes, James/Spring Valley Cmty Cons SD 99	1	7
Hermes, Jennifer/Lake Forest Cmty HSD 115	2,3,4,5,11,15,17	151
Hermes, Jennifer/Lake Forest School District 67	2,3,4,5,17,19	152
Hernan, Elliot/Illini Central CUSD 189	5,6	177

NAME/District	JOB FUNCTIONS	PAGE
Hernandez, Eric/Chadwick Milledgevill CUSD 399	295	8
Hernandez, Pam/Lombard Elem SD 44	2,4	97
Hernandez, Rudolfo/Cicero School District 99	1	42
Hernandez, Stephanie/Richland School Dist 88A	67	247
Hernandez, Sylvia/Lincolnwood Sch Dist 74	294	55
Hernandez, Thomas/Plainfield Cons Sch Dist 202	71	246
Herndon, David/La Grange Cmty School Dist 105	67	54
Herndon, Mathew/Wood River-Hartford Elem SD 15	6	172
Herrera, Oscar/Harvey Public School Dist 152	73,84	51
Herrig, Scott/Genoa-Kingston Cmty SD 424	73,98	85
Herrin, John/Libertyville Pub Sch Dist 70	2,15	152
Herrman, Bri/El Paso-Gridley CUSD 11	2	257
Herrmann, Denise, Dr/Community Unit School Dist 303	15,18,74,294	128
Herrmann, Gina/Oak Park Elem School Dist 97	15,68,74	60
Herrmann, Scott, Dr/Bannockburn Sch Dist 106	1,83	147
Herron, Mark/Crystal Lake Elem Distict 47	3	181
Hersey, Tara/Freeport School District 145	45	224
Hertel, Paul/Des Plaines Cmty Cons SD 62	1	45
Herter, Kelly/Beardstown Cmty Sch Dist 15	2,19	9
Herz, Ken/Limestone Walters CCSD 316	67	198
Herzing, Lois/Woodlawn Unit School Dist 209	12	124
Hess, Karen/Valley View Cmty SD 365-U	74	248
Hesse, Dave/Summit Hill School Dist 161	3,91	247
Hesselberth, Kelly/St Anne Cmty Cons Sch Dist 256	34,88	136
Hester, Kristine/Fox River Grove Cons SD 3	67	181
Hester, Melissa/Manhattan School Dist 114	59	244
Hesterberg, Brittany/Armstrong Ellis SD 61	295	231
Heston, Laurie/Bi-County Special Ed Co-op	1	240
Hettel, Ben/Troy Cmty Cons SD 30-C	3	247
Hettmansberger, Mark/Odell Cmty Cons Sch Dist 435	1,11,57	161
Hetzler, Jennifer/Central School District 3	7	1
Heuer, Carl/Prairieview-Ogden Sch Dist 197	6	11
Heurich, Douglas/Northbrook Elem School Dist 27	3	59
Heuring, Mark/Whiteside School District 115	1	222
Hewervine, Lois/St Joseph Cmty Cons SD 169	67	12
Hewitt, Jeff/Triad Cmty School District 2	67	172
Hewitt, Larry, Dr/Northbrook School District 28	1	59
Hewitt, Megan/Downers Grove School Dist 58	71	93
Hewitt, Will/Waterloo Cmty Unit Sch Dist 5	3	190
Hewlin, Monty/Area 6 Learning Technology Ctr	1	83
Heyer, Ray/Franklin Park Pub Sch Dist 84	3,5	50
Heyvaert, Amy/River Bend Cmty School Dist 2	16	239
Hibbs, Christy/Athens Cmty Unit Sch Dist 213	294	188
Hichins, Lisa, Dr/Batavia Unit School Dist 101	1	128
Hickam, Matt/Du Quoin Cmty Unit SD 300	1,11,57	201
Hickaman, Katie/Murphysboro Cmty Unit SD 186	38	121
Hicklin, April/Heyworth Cmty Sch District 4	10,83,88	185
Hickman, Martin/McLean Co Unit District 5	2,295	186
Hickman, Otis/Waukegan Cmty Unit SD 60	3	156
Hicks, Karen/DeSoto Grade School Dist 86	16,286	120
Hicks, Phil/Zeigler Royalton CUSD 188	5	108
Hieronymus, Ashley/Deland-Weldon Cmty Unit SD 57	58	202
Higginbottom, Shontae/Chicago PSD-Network 5	15	31
Higgins, Emily/Schuyler-Industry CUSD 5	11	215
High, Mike/Armstrong Twp High SD 225	33,69	231
High, Patty/Iroquois-Kankakee Reg Off Ed	74	137
Highland, Kim/Ottawa Twp High Sch Dist 140	752	143
Hight, Kara/Vienna High School Dist 13-3	60,275	127
Hightower, Zipporah/Chicago PSD-Isp	15	26
Hild, Christy/Mattoon Cmty Unit Sch Dist 2	9,12,69,79,275,285,288,752	19
Hildebrand, Denise, Dr/Community Unit School Dist 308	58	137
Hildreth, Elena/Elgin School District U-46	4	130
Hiler, Joyce/Jacksonville School Dist 117	4	192
Hill, Audra/Durand Cmty Sch Dist 322	16	252
Hill, Belinda/Giant City Cmty Cons SD 130	1	121
Hill, Carrie/Reed-Custer Cmty Unit SD 255-U	58	246
Hill, Christopher/Deland-Weldon Cmty Unit SD 57	12,280	202

1	Superintendent	16	Instructional Media Svcs	30	Adult Education	44	Science Sec	58	Special Education K-12	72	Summer School
2	Bus/Finance/Purchasing	17	Chief Operations Officer	31	Career/Sch-to-Work K-12	45	Math K-12	59	Special Education Elem	73	Instructional Tech
3	Buildings And Grounds	18	Chief Academic Officer	32	Career/Sch-to-Work Elem	46	Math Elem	60	Special Education Sec	74	Inservice Training
4	Food Service	19	Chief Financial Officer	33	Career/Sch-to-Work Sec	47	Math Sec	61	Foreign/World Lang K-12	75	Marketing/Distributive
5	Transportation	20	Art K-12	34	Early Childhood Ed	48	English/Lang Arts K-12	62	Foreign/World Lang Elem	76	Info Systems
6	Athletic	21	Art Elem	35	Health/Phys Education	49	English/Lang Arts Elem	63	Foreign/World Lang Sec	77	Psychological Assess
7	Health Services	22	Art Sec	36	Guidance Services K-12	50	English/Lang Arts Sec	64	Religious Education K-12	78	Affirmative Action
8	Curric/Instruct K-12	23	Music K-12	37	Guidance Services Elem	51	Reading K-12	65	Religious Education Elem	79	Student Personnel
9	Curric/Instruct Elem	24	Music Elem	38	Guidance Services Sec	52	Reading Elem	66	Religious Education Sec	80	Driver Ed/Safety
10	Curric/Instruct Sec	25	Music Sec	39	Social Studies K-12	53	Reading Sec	67	School Board President	81	Gifted/Talented
11	Federal Program	26	Business Education	40	Social Studies Elem	54	Remedial Reading K-12	68	Teacher Personnel	82	Video Services
12	Title I	27	Career & Tech Ed	41	Social Studies Sec	55	Remedial Reading Elem	69	Academic Assessment	83	Substance Abuse Prev
13	Title V	28	Technology Education	42	Science K-12	56	Remedial Reading Sec	70	Research/Development	84	Erate
15	Asst Superintendent	29	Family/Consumer Science	43	Science Elem	57	Bilingual/ELL	71	Public Information	85	AIDS Education

88	Alternative/At Risk	277	Remedial Math K-12
89	Multi-Cultural Curriculum	280	Literacy Coach
90	Social Work	285	STEM
91	Safety/Security	286	Digital Learning
92	Magnet School	288	Common Core Standards
93	Parental Involvement	294	Accountability
95	Tech Prep Program	295	Network System
97	Chief Innovation Officer	296	Title II Programs
98	Chief Technology Officer	297	Webmaster
270	Character Education	298	Grant Writer/Ptnrships
271	Migrant Education	750	Chief Innovation Officer
273	Teacher Mentor	751	Chief of Staff
274	Before/After Sch	752	Social Emotional Learning
275	Response To Intervention		

IL-T26

Illinois School Directory

DISTRICT PERSONNEL INDEX

NAME/District	JOB FUNCTIONS	PAGE
Hill, David/Community Cons School Dist 93	1,11	90
Hill, David/Vienna High School Dist 13-3	6	127
Hill, Doug/Altamont Cmty Unit SD 10	12	104
Hill, Jake/Rossville-Alvin Cmty Unit SD 7	6	233
Hill, Jeff/Porta Cmty Unit Sch Dist 202	6	189
Hill, Jeff, Dr/Morton Cmty Unit Sch Dist 709	1	227
Hill, Jessica/Maroa Forsyth CU Sch Dist 2	90	165
Hill, Laura/Elgin School District U-46	69,294	130
Hill, Stefanie/Genoa-Kingston Cmty SD 424	8,285,288	85
Hill, Steve/Grant Cmty High Sch Dist 124	67	150
Hill, T/Belvidere Cmty Unit SD 100	23	4
Hill, Teresa, Dr/South Holland School Dist 151	1,11	68
Hill, Whitney/Ramsey Cmty Unit Sch Dist 204	25	105
Hillary, Chuck/Knoxville Cmty Unit SD 202	5	140
Hillegonds, Cary/Chicago Ridge Sch Dist 127-5	11,34,59,69,271	41
Hillen, Terry/Butler School District 53	7	89
Hillman, Brad/Indian Prairie Sch Dist 204	10,15	95
Hillman, Deanne/Decatur Public Schools 61	68,751	165
Hillman, Tracy/River Trails Sch Dist 26	298	65
Hilsabeck, Matt/Rochester Cmty Unit SD 3-A	5	212
Hilt, Jame/Mattoon Cmty Unit Sch Dist 2	58	19
Himebaugh, Greg/Deerfield Public SD 109	2,3,5,15	149
Hinderliter, Cynthia/Pekin Cmty High Sch Dist 303	16,73,76,286	227
Hines-Newell, Coletta/Arlington Hts School Dist 25	4	21
Hines-Newell, Coletta/River Trails Sch Dist 26	4	65
Hinmen, Chris/Pawnee Cmty Unit Sch Dist 11	9,11,83	212
Hinson, Melanie/Mt Pulaski Cmty Unit SD 23	273	164
Hinton Lopez, Lori, Dr/Park Ridge Niles CMCSD 64	9,15,69,74,288,296	62
Hintz, Phil/Gurnee School District 56	73,297	150
Hintz, Phillip/Barrington Cmty Unit SD 220	76	147
Hinz, Kathy, Dr/Crystal Lake Elem Disticrt 47	1	181
Hipes, Lisa/Wilmington Cmty Unit SD 209-U	2	249
Hipsher, Debbie/Allendale Cmty Cons SD 17	2	234
Hird, Aaron/Regional Office of Ed 54	1	233
Hirsch, Laura/Crete-Monee Cmty SD 201-U	8,11,15,57,72,285,288,298	241
Hirsch, Melissa, Dr/Northbrook-Glenview SD 30	11,16,57,275,288,294,296,298	60
Hitchings, Bret/Heartland Technical Academy	1	167
Hitcho, Jonathan/Kildeer Countryside CCSD 96	2,4,15	151
Hite-Carter, Angela/Rockford School District 205	79,88	254
Hixson-Rusike, Jeninne/Bellwood School District 88	68	22
Hlavacek, Jill/Naperville Cmty Unit SD 203	73	98
Hobbs, Ryan/Eldorado Cmty Unit Sch Dist 4	1,83	210
Hobbs, Tiffany/Christopher Unit Sch Dist 99	12,16,82	107
Hobrock, Jamie/Triopia Cmty Unit Sch Dist 27	16,73	192
Hoburg, Ron/Alwood Cmty Unit Sch Dist 225	3	116
Hock, Michael/Reavis Twp HSD 220	5	64
Hock, Sandra/Burbank School District 111	37,59,77,79,81,90	24
Hockensmith, Jean/School Dist 45 Dupage Co	71	99
Hodan, Joyce/Cicero School District 99	9,15	42
Hodge- Bates, Dena/Kewanee Cmty Unit Sch Dist 229	11,296,298	117
Hodge, Brian/Ashley Cmty Cons SD 15	1,11	235
Hodge, Christine/Troy Cmty Cons SD 30-C	68	247
Hodge, Jaime/Carterville Cmty Unit SD 5	58	250
Hodge, Jaime/Marion Cmty School Dist 2	34,58,90	251
Hodge, Jami/Williamson Co Special Ed Dist	1	252
Hodges, Travis/Community Cons School Dist 59	297	43
Hodges, Valerie/Harrisburg Cmty Unit SD 3	4	210
Hoefling, Kent/La Grange-Highlands SD 106	3	54
Hoeflinger, Tammy/Bensenville Elem Sch Dist 2	68	89
Hoekstra, Mike/Woodland Cmty Unit Sch Dist 5	3	162
Hoelescher, Brian/Central Sch Dist 51	11,57,69,274,275,288	225
Hoerchler, Aaron/Wesclin Cmty Unit Sch Dist 3	67	18
Hoereth, Michele/Flossmoor School District 161	67	49
Hoesman, Chad/Regional Office of Ed 40	15,74	169
Hofer, Andrew/Mercer County SD 404	6	189
Hoff, Sally/Pecatonica Cmty Unit SD 321	67	253
Hoffard, Vince/New Simpson Hill Cons SD 32	67	127
Hoffman, Angie/South Pekin Grade Sch Dist 137	4	228
Hoffman, Justin/N Pekin-Marquette Hts SD 102	3	227
Hoffman, R Alan, Dr/McHenry Cmty Cons Sch Dist 15	1	183
Hoffman, Susan/River Trails Sch Dist 26	73,295,297	65
Hoffmann, Jason/Belleville Township HSD 201	295	217
Hoffmann, Rebecca/Harlem Unit Sch District 122	6	252
Hoftender, David/Scales Mound Cmty Unit SD 211	3	126
Hogan, Camille/Arbor Park School District 145	9,12,275	21
Hogan, Kim/New Simpson Hill Cons SD 32	76	127

NAME/District	JOB FUNCTIONS	PAGE
Hogan, Mark/Mt Zion Cmty Unit Sch Dist 3	5	166
Hogan, Scott/Tri-Co Special Ed Association	1	188
Hoge, Katie/Macomb Cmty Unit Sch Dist 185	73,84	178
Hogg, Britney/Central Cmty High Sch Dist 71	13,16,82	17
Hogue, Darryl/River Bend Cmty School Dist 2	1,11	239
Hohlbauch, Jill/Arcola Cmty Unit Sch Dist 306	73	87
Hohlfeld, Lisa/Creston Cmty Cons Sch Dist 161	59	194
Hoke, Jill/Porta Cmty Unit Sch Dist 202	34	189
Holaday, Amy/Glencoe School District 35	9,57,69,74,270,273,275	51
Holbrook, Matt/Niles Elem School District 71	67	58
Holcomb, Fritz/Freeburg Cmty Cons SD 70	5	219
Holcomb, Fritz/Smithton Cmty Cons SD 130	5	222
Holder, Mark/Bellwood School District 88	1,11	22
Holfinger, Mary/Antioch Cmty Cons Sch Dist 34	5	146
Holland, Mark/Altamont Cmty Unit SD 10	5	104
Hollenbeck, Ray/Manhattan School Dist 114	6	244
Holliday, Brett/Litchfield Cmty Unit SD 12	3,4	191
Hollingsworth, Michael/Midlothian School District 143	1	57
Holloman, Heath/Vienna Public School Dist 55	3,5	127
Holloway, Rob/Gallatin Cmty Unit Sch Dist 7	16,27,73,76,295	110
Holly, Eileen/Milne-Kelvin Grove District 91	77,275	244
Holly, Kevin/Mundelein Elem School Dist 75	67	153
Holly, Kristen/Charleston Cmty Unit SD 1	15,79,298	19
Holman, Justin/Seneca Cmty Cons Sch Dist 170	6	144
Holmes, Deborah/United Twp High Sch Dist 30	33	209
Holmes, Elbert, Dr/Thornton Twp High Sch Dist 205	12	69
Holmes, Laura/Vit Cmty Unit School Dist 2	88	110
Holmes, Will/Shirland Cmty Cons SD 134	12	255
Holshouser, Blayne/Lick Creek School Dist 16	67	230
Holt, David/La Grange Elem Sch Dist 102	68,71	54
Holthaus, Troy/Maroa Forsyth CU Sch Dist 2	38,69,83	165
Holthouse, Frank/Leyden Cmty High Sch Dist 212	27	55
Holtsclaw, Amy/Athens Cmty Unit Sch Dist 213	16,82	188
Holtz, Jane/River Trails Sch Dist 26	5	65
Holtz, Rich/Richmond-Burton Cmty HSD 157	3	184
Holtzman, Kathy/Rutland Cmty Cons SD 230	271	144
Homb, Paul/Scales Mound Cmty Unit SD 211	67	126
Homerding, Brad/Channahon School District 17	6	241
Honaker, Jess/Winfield School District 34	6	100
Honza, Sarah/Giant City Cmty Cons SD 130	85	121
Hood, Laura/Goreville Cmty Unit SD 1	2	127
Hood, Melanie/East St Louis Sch Dist 189	34	218
Hook, Jim/North Palos School Dist 117	71	59
Hooper, Kevin/Queen Bee School District 16	2	98
Hooper, Laura/Huntley Cmty School Dist 158	5	182
Hoover, Jennifer/Smithton Cmty Cons SD 130	12	222
Hoover, Kathy/Pikeland Cmty Sch Dist 10	16	203
Hoover, Patrick/Aptakisic-Tripp Sch Dist 102	9,57,273	146
Hopkins, Heather, Dr/Glenview Cmty Cons Sch Dist 34	68	51
Hopkins, Kathleen/Perandoe Special Ed District	1	206
Hopkins, Kimberly/E St Louis Area JT Agreement	1	223
Hopkins, Kimberly/East St Louis Sch Dist 189	58	218
Hopkins, Scott/Southwestern Cmty Unit SD 9	69	168
Hopper, Aaron/Panhandle Cmty Unit SD 2	1,11,83	191
Hopper, Michelle/Forest Park School District 91	79	50
Hoppis, Jennifer/Serena Cmty Unit School Dist 2	38	144
Horath, Kathleen/Decatur Public Schools 61	58	165
Horath, Kathy/Macon-Piatt Spec Ed	1	167
Horazdovsky, Barb/Cook County School Dist 104	294	44
Horn, Jodi/Kings Cons School District 144	2	194
Horn, Mandy/Regional Office of Ed 21	8	109
Hornaday, Ryan/Tuscola Cmty Unit SD 301	6	88
Hornby, Joan/Mundelein Cons High SD 120	30	153
Horner, Beth/High Mount Sch Dist 116	1,73	219
Horner, Scott/Columbia Cmty Unit SD 4	6,35,80	190
Horner, Staci/Deer Park Cmty Cons SD 82	4	141
Horrell, Steve/Macomb Cmty Unit Sch Dist 185	6	178
Horton, Roxanne/Sycamore Cmty Unit SD 427	16,73,295	86
Horton, Torano/Thornton Twp High Sch Dist 205	2,15	69
Hosfeldt, Laura/Pope Co Cmty Unit Sch Dist 1	273	204
Hoskins, Terri/Salt Fork Cmty Unit SD 512	16	233
Hoss, Amy/Monticello Cmty Unit SD 25	7,31	202
Hoster, Edward/Dupage High School Dist 88	19	93
Hostetter, Darin/Marshall Cmty Sch Dist C-2	73	15
Hosty, Jennifer/Berwyn South School Dist 100	2,5	23
Houberg, Larry/Herscher Cmty School Dist 2	2,3	135

DISTRICT PERSONNEL INDEX

Market Data Retrieval

NAME/District	JOB FUNCTIONS	PAGE
Houdek, Jennifer/Kaneland Cmty Unit SD 302	297	132
Hougard, Megan/Chicago PSD-Network 16	15	37
Hough, Denise/Germantown Hills SD 69	5,35	257
House, Tristan/Benton Cons High Sch Dist 103	76	107
Houston, Eileen/Emmons School District 33	275	149
Hoversen, Mark/Glenview Cmty Cons Sch Dist 34	2	51
Howard, Angela/Montmorency Cmty Cons SD 145	12	239
Howard, Becky/Carrollton Cmty Unit SD 1	68	111
Howard, Nicole, Dr/Proviso Twp High Sch Dist 209	10,15,69,79	63
Howard, Peter/Taft School District 90	6	247
Howard, Phil/Lake Zurich Cmty Sch Dist 95	16,73,82,286,297	152
Howe, Adriana/Braceville Elem School Dist 75	12	111
Howe, Dan/O'Fallon Twp School Dist 203	73	221
Howell, Amy/Red Bud Cmty Unit Sch Dist 132	59	205
Howell, Bob/Illinois Vly Ctl Sch Dist 321	5	197
Howell, Brian/Erie Cmty School District 1	6	239
Howell, Don/Canton Union School Dist 66	73	109
Hruby, Brett/Kinnikinnick Cmty Cons SD 131	2,84	253
Hruby, Carrie/O'Fallon Cmty Cons Sch Dist 90	1,11	221
Hu, George/Lincolnwood Sch Dist 74	295	55
Hubbard, Bradford/Community High School Dist 117	15	148
Hubbard, Bradford, Dr/Antioch Cmty Cons Sch Dist 34	1	146
Hubbard, Gina/Plano Cmty Unit Sch Dist 88	73	138
Hubbard, Michael/East St Louis Sch Dist 189	91	218
Hubbard, Paula/Madison Co Reg 1 Spec Ed Co-op	1,11	174
Hubbirt, Robert, Dr/Berwyn North School Dist 98	15	22
Huber, Cole/Edgar Co Cmty Sch Dist 6	273	103
Huber, Nicole/DeKalb Cmty Unit SD 428	7	84
Huckelberry, Racheal/New Simpson Hill Cons SD 32	2	127
Hudders, Sue/Lockport Twp High Sch Dist 205	83	244
Huddleston, Thomas/Rochelle Twp High Sch Dist 212	67	195
Hudgens, Diane/Macomb Cmty Unit Sch Dist 185	2	178
Hudson, Robert, Dr/Aptakisic-Tripp Sch Dist 102	11,15,70,74	146
Huenecke, Todd, Dr/Benjamin Sch District 25	77,83	89
Hueramo, Billy/DeKalb Cmty Unit SD 428	9	84
Huff, Anne/Harrison School Dist 36	9,11,69,74,88,275,288	181
Huffaker, Paul/Prairie Hills Elem SD 144	69,74,285	63
Huggins, Robin/Carmi-White Co School Dist 5	16,73,76,295,296,298	237
Hughes, Alli/Staunton Cmty Unit Sch Dist 6	7	168
Hughes, Ana/Streator Twp High Sch Dist 40	57	145
Hughes, Bob/Consolidated High Sch Dist 230	3,91	44
Hughes, Dana/Bannockburn Sch Dist 106	57	147
Hughes, Darren/Downers Grove School Dist 58	67	93
Hughes, Jerry/Orland Cmty Unit School Dist 135	91	61
Hughes, Katharine/Winnetka School Dist 36	71	72
Hughes, Sunny/Edgar Co Cmty Sch Dist 6	2	103
Huisinga, Gary/Monticello Cmty Unit SD 25	67	202
Hulbert, Mark/Reed-Custer Cmty Unit SD 255-U	2,3,15	246
Hulbert, Rob/Field Cmty Cons Sch Dist 3	16,73,84,295	123
Hulet, Brad/Canton Union School Dist 66	6	109
Hulett, William/Hazel Crest School Dist 152-5	3	52
Hull, Robert/Alwood Cmty Unit Sch Dist 225	73,76,286	116
Huls, Travis/Gifford Cmty Cons SD 188	67	10
Hulting, Marybeth/Antioch Cmty Cons Sch Dist 34	67	146
Humbels, Eric/Schiller Park School Dist 81	73	67
Humbles, Abby, Dr/Dunlap Cmty Unit Sch Dist 323	67	196
Hume, Dewinn/Rock Island-Milan Sch Dist 41	3	208
Humes, Jeff/Odin Public School Dist 722	1,11	175
Humm, Carol/Flossmoor School District 161	9,18,296	49
Hummel, John/Harvard Cmty Unit Sch Dist 50	73,76,295	181
Hummel, Lauren/Township High School Dist 211	3,17	69
Humphrey, Gregg/Pleasant Plains Cmty Unit SD 8	67	212
Humphries, Kristin, Dr/East Moline Public Sch Dist 37	1	207
Humphry, Chad/Cambridge Cmty Unit SD 227	67	116
Hunt, Dan/Riverside Public Sch Dist 96	67	65
Hunt, Jason/Germantown Hills SD 69	67	257
Hunt, Mark/Litchfield Cmty Unit SD 12	5,79	191
Huntsman, Dave/Hiawatha Cmty Unit SD 426	3	85
Hurder, Adam/Valley View Cmty SD 365-U	9	248
Hurlburt, Thomas, Dr/Cook County School Dist 154	1	45
Hurley, Carisa/Illinois Dept of Education	34	1
Hurst, Mike/Dolton-Riverdale Sch Dist 148	273	46
Huston, John/Illini West High Sch Dist 307	67	114
Hutcherson, Lynette/General George S Patton SD 133	2	50
Hutchings, Danny/Coal City Cmty Unit Sch Dist 1	6	112
Hutchins, Derek/Crab Orchard Cmty Sch Dist 3	1,11	251
Hutchison, Jessica/Avoca School District 37	9	22
Hutson, Shari/Regional Office of Ed 54	2	233
Hutson, Teanna/Beach Park Cmty Cons SD 3	5	147
Hutton, Becky/Monmouth-Roseville CUSD 238	8	234
Hutton, Brian/Sherrard Cmty Sch Dist 200	295	189
Hutton, Brian/Sherrard Cmty Sch Dist 200	76	189
Huyett, Melydi/Polo Cmty Unit Sch Dist 222	11	195
Hyatt, Joan/Lake Zurich Cmty Sch Dist 95	7	152
Hybert, Felice/Kankakee School District 111	8,11,18,83,286,288,296,298	135
Hyde, Angie/Pawnee Cmty Unit Sch Dist 11	79	212
Hyde, Maggie/Alwood Cmty Unit Sch Dist 225	12	116
Hyde, Rhonda/Lincoln Cmty High Sch Dist 404	11	163
Hylbert, Daniel, Dr/Cissna Park Cmty Unit SD 6	1,11,83	118
Hyre, Brad/Collinsville Cmty Sch Dist 10	15,79	170

I

NAME/District	JOB FUNCTIONS	PAGE
Ibbotson, Adam/Williamsville Cmty Unit SD 15	8,12,288	214
Idowu, Oyindamola/Niles Twp High School Dist 219	73,98	58
Ignoffo, Greg/Leyden Cmty High Sch Dist 212	67	55
Igoe, Christine, Dr/Naperville Cmty Unit SD 203	15,58,79	98
Ikejiaku, Alexander, Dr/Peoria Public Sch Dist 150	15,68	198
Illum, Sandra/Momence Cmty Unit Sch Dist 1	67	136
Imberger, Kristin/Oak Park Elem School Dist 97	76	60
Imhoff, Sarah/Vermilion Assoc for Special Ed	15	233
Imig, Vince/Tremont Cmty Unit SD 702	3	228
Ing, Kristin/Ewing Northern Cmty SD 115	1,11,84	108
Ingalls, Chevi/Central School District 3	8	1
Ingente, Amy/Elgin School District U-46	45	130
Inglese, Anton/Batavia Unit School Dist 101	2,16,19,76,95	128
Ingold, Tony/East Peoria Elem Sch Dist 86	1,11	226
Ingram, Joseph/South Holland School Dist 150	6	68
Inman, Brooks/Okaw Valley Cmty Unit SD 302	6	193
Iovinelli, Jessica/Elmwood Park Cmty Unit SD 401	73	48
Iovinelli, Jessica/Grayslake Cmty HS District 127	16,28,73,295	150
Ireland, John/Oblong Cmty Unit Sch Dist 4	73,286	83
Irslinger, Bert/Nippersink School District 2	67	183
Irvin, Amy/Valley View Cmty SD 365-U	74	248
Irving, Kellen/Paw Paw Cmty Unit SD 271	6	160
Irwin, Laura/Chester-E Lincoln Cmty SD 61	1,11,73,83	163
Isaacs, Lori/Community Cons School Dist 46	7	148
Isackson, Dana/Macomb Cmty Unit Sch Dist 185	8	178
Iseda, Takumi/Evanston Twp High SD 202	71	48
Isenburg, Jamason/Tremont Cmty Unit SD 702	73,286	228
Isenhower, Jeffery/Prairieview-Ogden Sch Dist 197	1	11
Isenhower, Jeffrey/Prairieview-Ogden Sch Dist 197	8,11,16,69,73,74,288	11
Isherwood, Christina/Avoca School District 37	57	22
Isoye, Steven/Niles Twp High School Dist 219	1	58
Israel, Marla/Adlai E Stevenson HSD 125	10	146
Ivey, Karen/Calumet Public School Dist 132	67	25
Ivory-Tatum, Jennifer/Urbana School District 116	1,84	12
Izquierdo, Erami/Iroquois West Cmty Unit SD 10	57,271	119

J

NAME/District	JOB FUNCTIONS	PAGE
Jachtorowycz, Natalie/Glenview Cmty Cons Sch Dist 34	67	51
Jackson, Andrea/Urbana School District 116	8,93	12
Jackson, Cary/Dieterich Community Unit SD 30	1,73	104
Jackson, Chris/Seneca Twp High Sch Dist 160	38,69,275	144
Jackson, Coretta/Ford Heights School Dist 169	2,3,5,15,84	49

1	Superintendent	16	Instructional Media Svcs	30	Adult Education	44	Science Sec	58	Special Education K-12	72	Summer School
2	Bus/Finance/Purchasing	17	Chief Operations Officer	31	Career/Sch-to-Work K-12	45	Math K-12	59	Special Education Elem	73	Instructional Tech
3	Buildings And Grounds	18	Chief Academic Officer	32	Career/Sch-to-Work Elem	46	Math Elem	60	Special Education Sec	74	Inservice Training
4	Food Service	19	Chief Financial Officer	33	Career/Sch-to-Work Sec	47	Math Sec	61	Foreign/World Lang K-12	75	Marketing/Distributive
5	Transportation	20	Art K-12	34	Early Childhood Ed	48	English/Lang Arts K-12	62	Foreign/World Lang Elem	76	Info Systems
6	Athletic	21	Art Elem	35	Health/Phys Education	49	English/Lang Arts Elem	63	Foreign/World Lang Sec	77	Psychological Assess
7	Health Services	22	Art Sec	36	Guidance Services K-12	50	English/Lang Arts Sec	64	Religious Education K-12	78	Affirmative Action
8	Curric/Instruct K-12	23	Music K-12	37	Guidance Services Elem	51	Reading K-12	65	Religious Education Elem	79	Student Personnel
9	Curric/Instruct Elem	24	Music Elem	38	Guidance Services Sec	52	Reading Elem	66	Religious Education Sec	80	Driver Ed/Safety
10	Curric/Instruct Sec	25	Music Sec	39	Social Studies K-12	53	Reading Sec	67	School Board President	81	Gifted/Talented
11	Federal Program	26	Business Education	40	Social Studies Elem	54	Remedial Reading K-12	68	Teacher Personnel	82	Video Services
12	Title I	27	Career & Tech Ed	41	Social Studies Sec	55	Remedial Reading Elem	69	Academic Assessment	83	Substance Abuse Prev
13	Title V	28	Technology Education	42	Science K-12	56	Remedial Reading Sec	70	Research/Development	84	Erate
15	Asst Superintendent	29	Family/Consumer Science	43	Science Elem	57	Bilingual/ELL	71	Public Information	85	AIDS Education

88	Alternative/At Risk	277	Remedial Math K-12
89	Multi-Cultural Curriculum	280	Literacy Coach
90	Social Work	285	STEM
91	Safety/Security	286	Digital Learning
92	Magnet School	288	Common Core Standards
93	Parental Involvement	294	Accountability
95	Tech Prep Program	295	Network System
97	Chief Information Officer	296	Title II Programs
98	Chief Technology Officer	297	Webmaster
270	Character Education	298	Grant Writer/Ptnrships
271	Migrant Education	750	Chief Innovation Officer
273	Teacher Mentor	751	Chief of Staff
274	Before/After Sch	752	Social Emotional Learning
275	Response To Intervention		

IL-T28

Illinois School Directory

DISTRICT PERSONNEL INDEX

NAME/District	JOB FUNCTIONS	PAGE
Jackson, Curta/Ford Heights School Dist 169	4	49
Jackson, Cynthia/Massac Unit School District 1	58	178
Jackson, Gregory, Dr/Ford Heights School Dist 169	1	49
Jackson, Janice, Dr/Chicago Public School Dist 299	1	25
Jackson, Janiece, Dr/E F Lindop Elem Sch Dist 92	1,11	47
Jackson, Jeremy/Benton Cons High Sch Dist 103	295	107
Jackson, Mary/Community Cons School Dist 204	67	201
Jackson, Mary/Highland Cmty Sch District 5	27,36	171
Jackson, Michelle/Northbrook School District 28	81	59
Jackson, Tom/East Aurora School Dist 131	71	129
Jacobellis, Sharon/Barrington Cmty Unit SD 220	38,60	147
Jacobs, Amy/Thornton Twp High Sch Dist 205	2	69
Jacobs, Jeanne/Metamora Cmty Cons Sch Dist 1	16	258
Jacobs, Michele/Deer Creek-Mackinaw CUSD 701	1,11	226
Jacobsen, Denise/Orion Cmty Unit Sch Dist 223	2	117
Jacobson, Dollie/Warren Twp High Sch Dist 121	2	155
Jacobus, Hiedi/Porta Cmty Unit Sch Dist 202	83	189
Jahr, Michelle/Rockford School District 205	19	254
Jain, Darshan/Adlai E Stevenson HSD 125	47	146
Jakaitis, Tracey/Elgin School District U-46	35	130
Jakupi, Bob/Butler School District 53	3,4	89
James-Gross, Lori, Dr/Unity Point Cmty Cons SD 140	1	121
James, Bobi/La Harpe Cmty Sch Dist 347	67	115
James, Grant/La Harpe Cmty Sch Dist 347	3	115
James, Jake/Shirland Cmty Cons SD 134	7,83,296	255
James, Kim/Elmhurst Cmty Unit SD 205	59	93
James, Seth/Neoga Cmty Unit School Dist 3	58	84
Jamison, Jennifer/Gibson Cty-Melvin-Sibley CUSD5	31,36	106
Jancek, Richard, Dr/Dwight Common Elem SD 232	1	161
Jancek, Richard, Dr/Dwight Twp High Sch Dist 230	1,11,288	161
Janecke, Sarah/Warren Community Unit SD 205	88	126
Janeteas, Thomas/Leyden Cmty High Sch Dist 212	19	55
Janettas, Karen/Orland School District 135	34,59,77,88,90,275	61
Janisch, John/Indian Springs Sch Dist 109	73,295	53
Jankovics, Monika/Beach Park Cmty Cons SD 3	4	147
Jankowicz, Tom/Argo Cmty High School Dist 217	57,271	21
Jannotta, Lindsay/Batavia Unit School Dist 101	2	128
Jansen, Elizabeth/Indian Prairie Sch Dist 204	79	95
Janssen, Chris/Spoon River Valley Cmty SD 4	1,84	110
Janssen, Mark/Freeburg Cmty Cons SD 70	2,11,15	219
Janvrin, Valerie/Sangamon Valley Cmty Unit SD 9	11,88,275,285,288	166
Jarrett, Ehren, Dr/Rockford School District 205	1	253
Jarrett, Sandra/Community High School Dist 117	60	148
Jaruseski, Joe/Naperville Cmty Unit SD 203	295	98
Jasculca, Christopher/Hinsdale Twp High Sch Dist 86	71	95
Jasko, Laura/Illini Central CUSD 189	57	177
Jason, Delfaye/East St Louis Sch Dist 189	2	218
Jason, Lyndon/Heyworth Cmty Sch District 4	6	185
Jason, Lynn/Midland Cmty Unit Sch Dist 7	5	176
Jazdzewski, Margaret/Lemont High Sch Dist 210	68	55
Jazo, Daniel/Millburn Cmty Cons Sch Dist 24	6	153
Jeffers, Linda/Indian Springs Sch Dist 109	2,13,84,288,296,298,752	52
Jeffers, Robert/Worth School District 127	16,73,295	72
Jefferson, Lance/Park Forest Chicago Hgt SD 163	67	62
Jeffrey, Tiffanie, Dr/Roselle School District 12	79	99
Jelinek, John/Diocese of Rockford Ed Office	64	256
Jenkins, Barb/Belleville Public Sch Dist 118	274	217
Jenkins, David/Crystal Lake Elem Distict 47	15,73,295	181
Jenkins, Janet/Robinson Cmty Unit Sch Dist 2	16,82	83
Jenkins, Kelly/Princeville Cmty Unit SD 326	73,295	200
Jenkins, Kerry/Nauvoo-Colusa CUSD 325	4	115
Jenkins, Rebecca/Lake Forest Cmty HSD 115	15,68	151
Jenkins, Rebecca/Lake Forest School District 67	9,15,16,68,81	152
Jenkins, Roxanne/New Athens CUSD 60	57	220
Jennett, Julie/Woodstock Cmty Unit SD 200	58	184
Jennings, Angie/Waverly Cmty Unit SD 6	5	193
Jennings, Bill/St Anne Cmty HSD 302	67	136
Jennings, James/Elmwood Park Cmty Unit SD 401	2,15	47
Jennings, James/Riverdale Cmty Unit SD 100	58	208
Jennings, John/Milne-Kelvin Grove District 91	5,11,57,83,270	244
Jensen, Marilyn/Bureau Valley Cmty Unit 340	72,83,296	6
Jensen, Matt/Washington School Dist 52	73	229
Jensen, Pamela/Community Unit School Dist 303	74	128
Jerbi, Phil/Genoa-Kingston Cmty SD 424	6	85
Jerger, April/Thornton Fractnl Twp HSD 215	68	69
Jerrell, Bryce/Carrier Mills-Stonefort SD 2	1,288	210
Jessep, Fred/Auburn Cmty Unit Sch Dist 10	67	211
Jett, Christopher/S Wilmington Cons Elem SD 74	67	113
Jewel, Jennifer, Dr/Metamora Twp HS Dist 122	38,83,752	258
Jewell, Matt/Community Unit School Dist 200	9	91
Jilek, Angie/Frankfort Cmty Unit SD 168	6	108
Jilek, Julie/Northwest Suburban Sp Ed Org	2	82
Jimenez Captai, Yesenia/Round Lake Area Co Dist 116	79	155
Jimenez, Amy/Rutland Cmty Cons SD 230	67	144
Jimenez, Karla/Elgin School District U-46	93	130
Jimenez, Veronica/Community High School Dist 94	61	91
Jinkins, Ann Marie/Rochelle Twp High Sch Dist 212	16	195
Joaquin-Schube, Kristine/Skokie School District 69	59	67
Jobst, Jen/Ottawa Twp High Sch Dist 140	57	143
Jodlowski, Colleen/Chester-E Lincoln Cmty SD 61	2	163
Jodlowski, Colleen/Lincoln Elem School Dist 27	2	163
Johaness, Misty/Raccoon Cons School Dist 1	1,11,83	175
Johannsen, Curt/Woodstock Cmty Unit SD 200	2	184
Johns, Charles, Dr/Glenbrook High Sch Dist 225	1	50
Johns, Keith/Crab Orchard Cmty Sch Dist 3	6	251
Johns, Kevin/Pembroke Cmty Cons SD 259	9,15	136
Johns, Stephen, Dr/Millburn Cmty Cons Sch Dist 24	2,3,4	153
Johnson-Millon, Sarah/Hillside School District 93	2,15	52
Johnson, Amy/Central Sch Dist 51	67	225
Johnson, Amy/Summersville Sch Dist 79	6	124
Johnson, Andrew/Jasper Co Cmty Unit SD 1	1	122
Johnson, Angela/Evanston-Skokie Cmty CSD 65	30,93	48
Johnson, Annette/East Aurora School Dist 131	67	129
Johnson, Antionette/East St Louis Sch Dist 189	8,57	218
Johnson, Bambi/Community Cons School Dist 46	4,5	148
Johnson, Benjamin/Benton Cons High Sch Dist 103	1	107
Johnson, Beth/Herrin Cmty School District 4	16,82	251
Johnson, Bob/Flora Cmty Unit School Dist 35	3	16
Johnson, Brad/Ottawa Twp High Sch Dist 140	3	143
Johnson, Brian/Laraway Cmty Cons SD 70-C	73	243
Johnson, Burgandy/Braceville Elem School Dist 75	4	111
Johnson, Carl/Colona Cmty School Dist 190	1,11,288	116
Johnson, Casey/Jonesboro Cmty Cons SD 43	67	230
Johnson, Cathy/Township High School Dist 214	2,15	69
Johnson, Chad/Farmington Ctl Cmty SD 265	67	197
Johnson, Christopher/New Trier Twp HS District 203	2,3,11,15	58
Johnson, Cindy/Iroquois Spec Educ Association	2	119
Johnson, Crystal/Rossville-Alvin Cmty Unit SD 7	1	233
Johnson, Crystal/St George School District 258	59	136
Johnson, Dan/Johnsburg Cmty School Dist 12	1	182
Johnson, Don/Monmouth-Roseville CUSD 238	73	234
Johnson, Doriph/Bloom Twp High Sch Dist 206	10,12,15,296,298	23
Johnson, Doug/McLean Co Unit District 5	3,91	186
Johnson, Emily/River Bend Cmty School Dist 2	297	239
Johnson, Eric/Saunemin Cmty Cons SD 438	67	162
Johnson, Gregory/Oak Park & River Forest SD 200	10,15	60
Johnson, Heather/Crescent Iroquois Cmty SD 249	273	118
Johnson, Heather/Meridian Cmty Unit Sch Dist 15	36,69,72,88	166
Johnson, Heather/Sterling Cmty Unit Sch Dist 5	16	240
Johnson, Herald/Chicago Public School Dist 299	93	25
Johnson, Jacqueline/Community High School Dist 218	25	44
Johnson, Jacquelyn/Community Unit School Dist 300	280	180
Johnson, Jacquline/Rochelle Twp High Sch Dist 212	7	195
Johnson, Jeff/Kewanee Cmty Unit Sch Dist 229	67	117
Johnson, Jeffrey/Morris Cmty High Sch Dist 101	6	113
Johnson, Jeremiah, Dr/Community Cons School Dist 168	59,77	44
Johnson, Jesse/Freeport School District 145	71,298	224
Johnson, Jim/Morton Grove School Dist 70	3	58
Johnson, Josh/Gibson Cty-Melvin-Sibley CUSD5	67	106
Johnson, Josh/Whiteside Regional Voc System	1	241
Johnson, Kathleen/Cook County School Dist 104	59	44
Johnson, Kathy/Jasper Co Cmty Unit SD 1	8,11,57,69,275,288,298	122
Johnson, Katie/Gardner Cmty Cons SD 72-C	12	112
Johnson, Keith/Fremont School District 79	5	149
Johnson, Kim/Dongola Unit School Dist 66	4	230
Johnson, Kristin, Dr/Troy Cmty Cons SD 30-C	9,12,15,57,69,273,288	247
Johnson, Krystal/Grant Park Cmty Unit SD 6	58,273	135
Johnson, Leo/Maroa Forsyth CU Sch Dist 2	2	165
Johnson, Levi/Grayville Cmty Unit Sch Dist 1	58	238
Johnson, Marci/Illinois Dept of Education	31,81	1
Johnson, Marni/Township High School Dist 214	13,15,77,78,90,271,275,294	69

School Year 2020-2021   800-333-8802   IL-T29

DISTRICT PERSONNEL INDEX

Market Data Retrieval

NAME/District	JOB FUNCTIONS	PAGE
Johnson, Mary/Hoopeston Area Cmty Unit SD 11	31,36,77,83,88,270	232
Johnson, Matthew/Geneva CUSD 304	58	131
Johnson, Megan/Belvidere Cmty Unit SD 100	8,12,15,18,69,296	4
Johnson, Rachel/Martinsville Cmty Unit SD C-3	12	16
Johnson, Regina/Berwyn North School Dist 98	2	22
Johnson, Renee/Springfield Pub Sch Dist 186	45	213
Johnson, Richard/Twin Rivers Career & Tech Ed	1	83
Johnson, Robin/Salt Fork Cmty Unit SD 512	4,5	233
Johnson, Ron/Centralia City Sch Dist 135	67	174
Johnson, Sandy/Breese Elementary SD 12	5	17
Johnson, Shara/Stewardson-Strasburg SD 5-A	16,73,82	216
Johnson, Sheila, Dr/Niles Twp High School Dist 219	2	58
Johnson, Stephanie/Fairfield Cmty High SD 225	4	236
Johnson, Steve/Creve Coeur Sch Dist 76	1	226
Johnson, Tom/Bismarck-Henning Cmty SD 1	6	231
Johnson, Tori/Glenbard Twp High Sch Dist 87	68	94
Johnson, Wendy/Carterville Cmty Unit SD 5	7	250
Johnson, Wendy/Monroe School District 70	2	198
Johnson, William/Huntley Cmty School Dist 158	10	182
Johnston, Bill/Round Lake Area Co Dist 116	2,15,19	154
Johnston, Christine/St George School District 258	69,74,273	136
Joiner-Herrod, Carla/E F Lindop Elem Sch Dist 92	67	47
Joiner, Denise/Northwestern CUSD 2	88	168
Joiner, Keith/Giant City Cmty Cons SD 130	3	121
Jokisch, Todd/A-C Central Cmty Unit SD 262	67	9
Jolly, Kerry/Streator Elem School Dist 44	4	144
Jonas, Lindsay/Community Unit School Dist 300	12	180
Jones-Raymond, Shophia, Dr/Thornton Fractnl Twp HSD 215	1	69
Jones, April/Rantoul Twp High Sch Dist 193	7	12
Jones, Beth/Barrington Cmty Unit SD 220	15,79	147
Jones, Chad/Hollis Cons School Dist 328	1,11	197
Jones, Cheryl/Deland-Weldon Cmty Unit SD 57	2	202
Jones, Chris/Meridian Cmty Unit Sch Dist 15	67	166
Jones, Damian/Argenta Oreana Cmty Unit SD 1	1,11	165
Jones, Dan/Hinsdale Twp High Sch Dist 86	6	95
Jones, Doug/Benton Cmty Cons Sch Dist 47	6	107
Jones, Greg/Bensenville Elem Sch Dist 2	3	89
Jones, Greg/Cowden Herrick CUSD 3A	67	216
Jones, Janice/Serena Cmty Unit School Dist 2	5	144
Jones, Keith/Sesser-Valier Cmty Unit SD 196	83,85,88,270,296	108
Jones, Kevin/Lake Park Cmty High SD 108	27	96
Jones, Krystal/Oak Park & River Forest SD 200	69	60
Jones, Lisa/LaSalle Peru Twp HSD 120	752	142
Jones, Lois/Trico Cmty Unit Sch Dist 176	67	121
Jones, Mary/Momence Cmty Unit Sch Dist 1	2	136
Jones, Matt/Granite City Cmty Unit SD 9	67	171
Jones, Maureen/Community Cons School Dist 89	2,15,17	90
Jones, Michelle/West Aurora School Dist 129	73,286	132
Jones, Nicole/Amboy Cmty Unit Sch Dist 272	67	159
Jones, Rhonda/Prairie Hills Elem SD 144	4	63
Jones, Scott/Morton Cmty Unit Sch Dist 709	6	227
Jones, Tammy/Community Cons School Dist 168	67	44
Jones, Torri/Madison Cmty Unit Sch Dist 12	7	172
Jones, Vincent/Thornton Twp High Sch Dist 205	84,295	69
Jontry, Mark/Regional Office of Ed 17	1	188
Joos, Kitty/Pleasant Hill School Dist 69	2	199
Jordahl, Jane/Rantoul City School Dist 137	6	11
Jordan, Andrew/Donovan Cmty Unit Sch Dist 3	58	119
Jordan, Bonnie/Philip J Rock Center & School	1	102
Jordan, Carol/Washington Cmty HS Dist 308	7,83,85	229
Jordan, Carol/Washington Cmty HS Dist 308	7,83,85	229
Jordan, Stephanee/Moline-Coal Valley SD No 40	8,11,57	207
Joseph, Mike/Freeburg Cmty Cons SD 70	6	219
Jourdain, Ernst/Posen-Robbins Sch Dist 143-5	57	63
Jourgen, Ron/Grand Prairie Cmty Cons SD 6	67	123
Joyce, Kathleen/Marengo Cmty High Sch Dist 154	90	182
Joyce, Sean/North Palos School Dist 117	73,295	59
Judd, Kylie/Putnam Co Cmty Unit SD 535	274	204
Judge, Jeffrey/Elgin School District U-46	7	130
Judkins, Viodelda/Champaign Cmty Unit Sch Dist 4	57,271	10
Jukes, Anna/Opdyke-Belle Rive Cmty CSSD 5	12,76	123
Julius, Denise, Dr/South Holland School Dist 150	1	68
Julius, Jon/Edwards Co Cmty Unit SD 1	79	104
Juneker, Delinda/Egyptian Cmty Unit Sch Dist 5	4	3
Junna, Robert/Mannheim School District 83	73,84	56
Jupin, Nick/South Beloit Cmty Sch Dist 320	73	255
Juracka, Steve/Diamond Lake School Dist 76	9,11,15,57,68,288,296,298	149
Juris, Ken/Niles Elem School District 71	3	58
Juske, Ted/Johnsburg Cmty School Dist 12	6	182
Juskiewicz, Libby/Des Plaines Cmty Cons SD 62	57	45
Justice, Cathy/Tri-City Cmty Unit Sch Dist 1	83,270,271	214
Justiniano, Annel/Queen Bee School District 16	57	98
Jutras, Reid/Rockford School District 205	27	254

K

NAME/District	JOB FUNCTIONS	PAGE
Kabat, Sandra/Farrington Cmty Cons SD 99	1,73	122
Kaczmarek, Amie/Marquardt School District 15	34,59	97
Kaeji, Judy/Gallatin Cmty Unit Sch Dist 7	1,11	110
Kaffka, Diane/Arlington Hts School Dist 25	79	21
Kagan, Michael/Diocese of Rockford Ed Office	1	256
Kahler, Doug/Adlai E Stevenson HSD 125	76,295	146
Kahn, Jay/Lake Bluff Elem Sch Dist 65	2,5,298	151
Kahover, Gail/Northbrook Elem School Dist 27	71	59
Kain, Cathy/Wallace Cmty Cons Sch Dist 195	2	145
Kaiser, Dan/Dwight Twp High Sch Dist 230	10,88	161
Kaiser, Katherine/Harmony-Emge School Dist 175	274	219
Kalafut, Susan/Valley View Cmty SD 365-U	295	248
Kalagian, Valerie/Sullivan Cmty Unit SD 300	73	193
Kalister, Tonya/Hollis Cons School Dist 328	274	197
Kalisz, Brian/Community Cons School Dist 46	295	148
Kallal, Lisa/Calhoun Cmty Unit Sch Dist 40	273	8
Kalou, Mary/Maine Twp High Sch Dist 207	2,13,15	56
Kalou, Mary/Maine Twp Spec Ed Program	2,15	82
Kambic, Rick/Fenton Cmty High Sch Dist 100	71	94
Kaminski, Kathy/Medinah Elementary SD 11	2	97
Kamm, Carrie, Dr/Oak Park Elem School Dist 97	78	60
Kamperman, Deborah/Queen Bee School District 16	4	98
Kampmeyer, Bill/Shiloh Village Sch Dist 85	73,76	221
Kamprath, Kristen/Central School District 3	58	1
Kanaga, Kelly/Metamora Twp HS Dist 122	3	258
Kane, Elaine/Alton Cmty School District 11	12,15	169
Kania, Sharon/Ohio Cmty Cons School Dist 17	4	7
Kania, Sharon/Ohio Cmty High School Dist 505	4	7
Kann, Jim/Byron Cmty Unit SD 226	6	194
Kanne, Elizabeth/Naperville Cmty Unit SD 203	79	98
Kanobe, John/E F Lindop Elem Sch Dist 92	270	47
Kaplan, Bob/Schaumburg Cmty Cons SD 54	67	66
Kaplanes, James/Community Cons School Dist 15	91	43
Kapraun-Veach, Jennifer/Oakland Cmty Unit Sch Dist 5	6	19
Karalus, Renee/Homer Cmty Cons Sch Dist 33C	11,59	242
Karasek, Nate/Warren Twp High Sch Dist 121	72	155
Kargol, Patty/Midland Cmty Unit Sch Dist 7	2	176
Karlson, Dena/Belvidere Cmty Unit SD 100	76	4
Karmenzind, Shaun/Monroe School District 70	67	198
Karpman, Keri/Addison School District 4	59,296	88
Karraker, Brian/New Athens CUSD 60	1	220
Karsten, Rebecca/Valmeyer Cmty School Dist 3	58,69	190
Kartha, Sunith/Evanston-Skokie Cmty CSD 65	67	48
Karvelas, Bessie, Dr/Proviso Twp High Sch Dist 209	750	63
Kash, Pam/Waltonville Cmty Unit SD 1	2	124
Kashner, Alex/Eastland Cmty Unit SD 308	1,11,73,83	8
Kasprzyk, Anna/Lake Villa Cmty Cons SD 41	2	152
Kassing, Wendy/Shiloh Village Sch Dist 85	275	221
Katini, Kelli/McHenry Cmty Cons Sch Dist 15	34,59,88,275	183

#		#		#		#		#		#	
1	Superintendent	16	Instructional Media Svcs	30	Adult Education	44	Science Sec	58	Special Education K-12	72	Summer School
2	Bus/Finance/Purchasing	17	Chief Operations Officer	31	Career/Sch-to-Work K-12	45	Math K-12	59	Special Education Elem	73	Instructional Tech
3	Buildings And Grounds	18	Chief Academic Officer	32	Career/Sch-to-Work Elem	46	Math Elem	60	Special Education Sec	74	Inservice Training
4	Food Service	19	Chief Financial Officer	33	Career/Sch-to-Work Sec	47	Math Sec	61	Foreign/World Lang K-12	75	Marketing/Distributive
5	Transportation	20	Art K-12	34	Early Childhood Ed	48	English/Lang Arts K-12	62	Foreign/World Lang Elem	76	Info Systems
6	Athletic	21	Art Elem	35	Health/Phys Education	49	English/Lang Arts Elem	63	Foreign/World Lang Sec	77	Psychological Assess
7	Health Services	22	Art Sec	36	Guidance Services K-12	50	English/Lang Arts Sec	64	Religious Education K-12	78	Affirmative Action
8	Curric/Instruct K-12	23	Music K-12	37	Guidance Services Elem	51	Reading K-12	65	Religious Education Elem	79	Student Personnel
9	Curric/Instruct Elem	24	Music Elem	38	Guidance Services Sec	52	Reading Elem	66	Religious Education Sec	80	Driver Ed/Safety
10	Curric/Instruct Sec	25	Music Sec	39	Social Studies K-12	53	Reading Sec	67	School Board President	81	Gifted/Talented
11	Federal Program	26	Business Education	40	Social Studies Elem	54	Remedial Reading K-12	68	Teacher Personnel	82	Video Services
12	Title I	27	Career & Tech Ed	41	Social Studies Sec	55	Remedial Reading Elem	69	Academic Assessment	83	Substance Abuse Prev
13	Title V	28	Technology Education	42	Science K-12	56	Remedial Reading Sec	70	Research/Development	84	Erate
15	Asst Superintendent	29	Family/Consumer Science	43	Science Elem	57	Bilingual/ELL	71	Public Information	85	AIDS Education

#		#		#	
88	Alternative/At Risk	277	Remedial Math K-12		
89	Multi-Cultural Curriculum	280	Literacy Coach		
90	Social Work	285	STEM		
91	Safety/Security	286	Digital Learning		
92	Magnet School	288	Common Core Standards		
93	Parental Involvement	294	Accountability		
95	Tech Prep Program	295	Network System		
97	Chief Information Officer	296	Title II Programs		
98	Chief Technology Officer	297	Webmaster		
270	Character Education	298	Grant Writer/Ptnrships		
271	Migrant Education	750	Chief Innovation Officer		
273	Teacher Mentor	751	Chief of Staff		
274	Before/After Sch	752	Social Emotional Learning		
275	Response To Intervention				

IL-T30

Illinois School Directory — DISTRICT PERSONNEL INDEX

NAME/District	JOB FUNCTIONS	PAGE
Katzenberger, Julie/West Carroll CUSD 314	1,11	8
Katzin, David/Franklin Park Pub Sch Dist 84	1,11,83	50
Kaufhold, Ken/Niles Elem School District 71	73	58
Kaufman, Christine/Winnebago Cmty Unit SD 323	58,77	255
Kaufman, Donna/Regional Office of Ed 9	15	13
Kaufman, Nancy/Manteno Cmty Unit Sch Dist 5	68	136
Kaufmann, Brenda/Scott Morgan Cmty Unit SD 2	2	215
Kauling, Ray/Wesclin Cmty Unit Sch Dist 3	6	18
Kave, Colin/East Moline Public Sch Dist 37	4	207
Kave, Colin/Silvis School District 34	4	209
Kavelman, Trent/Lincoln Elem School Dist 27	16,82	163
Kawazoe, Yoko/Carbondale Elem School Dist 95	274	120
Kay, Cheryl/Lincoln-Way Cmty HS Dist 210	28,73,295	244
Kaye, Brian/Arlington Hts School Dist 25	15,68	21
Kaye, Holly/Keeneyville Elem Sch Dist 20	76	96
Kaye, Piedad, Dr/Mannheim School District 83	57	56
Kaytor, David/Wabash-Ohio Valley Sp Ed Dist	1,11	238
Kazmier, Penny/Barrington Cmty Unit SD 220	67	147
Kazmierczak, Tim/Benjamin Sch District 25	3	89
Kazubowski, Shane/Wethersfield Cmty Unit SD 230	1,73,83	117
Keane, Jeanne/Oak Park Elem School Dist 97	3	60
Keane, Kevin/Homewood School Dist 153	3	52
Kechan, Robert/Streator Elem School Dist 44	11	144
Keck, Roberta/Macomb Cmty Unit Sch Dist 185	77	178
Kedjidjian, Cathy/Glenview Cmty Cons Sch Dist 34	71	51
Kedrowski, Debra/Hinsdale Twp High Sch Dist 86	751	95
Kee, Richard/Egyptian Cmty Unit Sch Dist 5	3	3
Keefe, Elizabeth/Millburn Cmty Cons Sch Dist 24	11,57,59,83	153
Keefe, Tim/Smithton Cmty Cons SD 130	6	222
Keel, David, Dr/Granite City Cmty Unit SD 9	10,27,31,74,83,285	171
Keel, Kathy/Williamson Co Special Ed Dist	34	252
Keeley, Patrick/Warren Twp High Sch Dist 121	15,79	155
Keeley, Tim/Addison School District 4	2,3,17,19	88
Keenan, Elizabeth, Dr/Chicago Public School Dist 299	58	25
Keeney, Patrick/Lebanon Cmty Unit Sch Dist 9	1	220
Keenon, Jason/Kildeer Countryside CCSD 96	9	151
Keeton, Mike/Waverly Cmty Unit SD 6	67	193
Keifer, Stefanie/Sullivan Cmty Unit SD 300	90	193
Keigher, Judith/Community High School Dist 218	84	44
Keilman, Joanne/Midlothian School District 143	67	57
Keith, Jessica/Sullivan Cmty Unit SD 300	4	193
Keith, Toia/Speed Seja 802	4	82
Kekelik, Joe/Speed Seja 802	3	82
Keller, Leslie/Clay City Cmty Unit SD 10	12	16
Keller, Sally/Paris Union School District 95	2	103
Keller, Suzanne/Rochester Cmty Unit SD 3-A	8,11,286,294	212
Kellett, Matt/Evergreen Park Elem SD 124	16,73,76,297	49
Kelley, Carol, Dr/Oak Park Elem School Dist 97	1	60
Kelley, Kathleen/Columbia Cmty Unit SD 4	36	190
Kelley, Krystina/Belle Valley School Dist 119	16	217
Kelley, Mary Beth/Stark Co Cmty Unit SD 100	16	224
Kelley, Matt/Kankakee Area Reg Voc Ed Sys	1,11	137
Kellie, Lora/Rondout School District 72	7	154
Kellum, Debra/Community High School Dist 128	27,33,75	148
Kelly, Briant/Community High School Dist 128	15,68,78,273	148
Kelly, Bryan/Skokie School District 69	9	67
Kelly, Jackie/Sherrard Cmty Sch Dist 200	12	189
Kelly, Jerod/Kell Cons School District 2	3	174
Kelly, Jim/Minooka Cmty High Sch Dist 111	73,297	244
Kelly, Mary/Glencoe Sch District 35	16,82	51
Kelly, Mary/Saratoga Cmty Cons SD 60C	298	113
Kelly, Stacy/Mendota Cmty School Dist 289	12	142
Kelmel, Jim/Morrisonville Cmty Unit SD 1	3	14
Kelmen, Steve/Rock Falls Elem Sch Dist 13	73,295	240
Kelsall, Jennifer, Dr/Ridgewood Cmty HSD 234	1	64
Keltner, John/Pearl City Cmty Unit SD 200	3	225
Kelty, Dave/LaSalle Peru Twp HSD 120	16	142
Kemp, Karl/Chicago Public School Dist 299	6	25
Kemp, Ryan/Dwight Twp High Sch Dist 230	6	161
Kemper, Kreg/Hillside School District 93	6,35	52
Kendall, Bill, Dr/Bremen Cmty High SD 228	1	23
Kendall, Chris/Peoria Ed Reg Emp & Career	1	200
Kendrick, Heath/Rossville-Alvin Cmty Unit SD 7	11,57,73,83,288	233
Kendrick, Kara/Township High School Dist 214	15	69
Kendrick, Tarin/Niles Twp Dept of Spec Ed #807	1	82
Kendryna, Suzanne/Moraine Area Career System	15,95	82

NAME/District	JOB FUNCTIONS	PAGE
Kenne, John/Anna Cmty Cons Sch Dist 37	37,69	230
Kennedy, Aaron/O'Fallon Cmty Cons Sch Dist 90	24	221
Kennedy, Craig/Zion Public School District 6	295	157
Kennedy, Jake/Ridgeview Cmty Unit SD 19	6	187
Kennedy, Linda/Schuyler-Industry CUSD 5	84	215
Kennedy, Mike/McHenry Cmty High Sch Dist 156	79	183
Kennedy, Paula/Indian Creek Cmty Unit SD 425	8,12	85
Kenney, Jennifer/Coal City Cmty Unit Sch Dist 1	12	112
Kenney, Karla/Pekin Public School Dist 108	34	227
Kenny, David/Belvidere Cmty Unit SD 100	295	4
Kenser, Brad/DePue Unit Sch Dist 103	1,11,288	6
Keoster, Brian/Teutopolis Cmty Unit SD 50	2,5	105
Keown, Kevin/Marshall Cmty Sch Dist C-2	6	15
Keplar, Judy/Belleville Public Sch Dist 118	67	217
Kepley, Doug/Bement Cmty Unit Sch Dist 5	16	202
Kepple, Jason/Spoon River Valley Cmty SD 4	295	110
Kerke, Joseph/Union Ridge School Dist 86	83	70
Kern, Alesha/Ridgeview Cmty Unit SD 19	7	187
Kerr, Christian/Byron Cmty Unit SD 226	2	194
Kerr, Pam/Peoria Heights Cmty SD 325	38	198
Kerr, Sue/Elgin School District U-46	67	130
Kerr, Tim/Southeastern Cmty Unit SD 337	8,58,69,286	115
Kessey, Rachel/Prairie Grove Cons SD 46	12,79	183
Kessler, Kim/South Eastern Special Ed Dist	1	122
Kessler, Megan/Salem Cmty High Sch Dist 600	38,69,83,88	175
Kester, Kent/Joppa-Maple Grove Unit SD 38	3	177
Ketchum, Ryan/Central Cmty High Sch Dist 71	296	17
Ketner, Ronda/Dimmick Cmty School Dist 175	270	141
Keto, Paul/Troy Cmty Cons SD 30-C	295	247
Kettering, Mark/Grayslake Cmty HS District 127	60	150
Kettleborough, Gary/Mendota Twp High Sch Dist 280	5	143
Keys, Tessa/Harmony-Emge School Dist 175	67	219
Keyser, Stacy/Cumberland Cmty Unit SD 77	6	84
Khalfani, Akil/Dolton School District 149	3	46
Khelghati, Andalib/Evanston-Skokie Cmty CSD 65	15	48
Kherat, Sharon, Dr/Peoria Public Sch Dist 150	1	198
Kibitlewski, Kathy/Gurnee School District 56	16	150
Kidd, Rose/Plainfield Cons Sch Dist 202	2	246
Kiedaisch, Jennifer/Sunset Ridge Sch Dist 29	288	68
Kierznowski, Mark/East Prairie School Dist 73	2,3	47
Kiesewetter, Karla/Metamora Cmty Cons Sch Dist 1	4	258
Kiesewetter, Kim/Germantown Hills SD 69	4	257
Kiewicz, Elizabeth/Round Lake Area Co Dist 116	9	155
Kilgore, Jon/Pontiac Twp High Sch Dist 90	1,11	161
Kilinski, Brian/McHenry Cmty Cons Sch Dist 15	68	183
Killam, Kai/East Moline Public Sch Dist 37	67	207
Killam, Melissa/North Greene Unit Dist 3	58	111
Killey, Kevin/Monmouth-Roseville CUSD 238	67	234
Killman, Amanda/Crab Orchard Cmty Sch Dist 3	12	251
Kilmartin, Derek/La Salle Elem SD 122	11,34,296,298	142
Kilmer, Jennifer/Gardner S Wilmington HSD 73	38,69,270	112
Kilrea, Timothy, Dr/Lyons Twp HS District 204	1	56
Kilver, Carol, Dr/Pikeland Cmty Sch Dist 10	1	203
Kim, Julie/Township High School Dist 214	69	69
Kim, Tom/Niles Twp High School Dist 219	15,68	58
Kimbro, Bryan/Ramsey Cmty Unit Sch Dist 204	5	105
Kimbro, Michelle/Oakwood Cmty Unit Sch Dist 76	8,11,57,88,285,286,288	232
Kimbrough, Kimberly/Bloom Twp High Sch Dist 206	44	23
Kimmelman, Leah, Dr/North Shore School Dist 112	9	154
Kinane, Tom/Elmwood Park Cmty Unit SD 401	73	48
Kincaid, Brian/Milne-Kelvin Grove District 91	13,16,73,76,295	244
Kincaid, Brian/Milne-Kelvin Grove District 91	16,84	244
Kincaid, Heather/Community Unit School Dist 308	10,69,288	137
Kincaid, Heather/Community Unit School Dist 308	10,69,288	137
Kindel, Christy/Tri-City Cmty Unit Sch Dist 1	10,11,73,74,288	214
Kinder, Jean/Quincy School District 172	4	2
Kinder, Rachel/Valley View Cmty SD 365-U	1	248
Kinder, Vanessa, Dr/South Cook Interm Svc Center	1	82
King, Ann/Lockport Twp High Sch Dist 205	297	244
King, Bart/Carmi-White Co School Dist 5	5,10	237
King, Christina/Goreville Cmty Unit SD 1	58	127
King, Corey/Community Cons School Dist 59	76	43
King, Dora/North Chicago Cmty Unit SD 187	67	154
King, Greg/Sterling Cmty Unit Sch Dist 5	6	240
King, Jeff, Dr/Elgin School District U-46	3,15	130
King, Ken/Trico Cmty Unit Sch Dist 176	3	121

School Year 2020-2021 — 800-333-8802 — IL-T31

DISTRICT PERSONNEL INDEX

Market Data Retrieval

NAME/District	JOB FUNCTIONS	PAGE
King, Laurie/Riley Cmty Cons Sch Dist 18	4	184
King, Marybeth/Cicero School District 99	68	42
King, Rebecca/Porta Cmty Unit Sch Dist 202	2	189
King, Ric/Schaumburg Cmty Cons SD 54	2,15	66
Kingsfield, Jill, Dr/Community Cons School Dist 89	9,11,15,57,296,298	90
Kingsford, Cassie/Orion Cmty Unit Sch Dist 223	27	117
Kinnamon, Tricia/Hamilton Cmty Cons SD 328	58	114
Kinosky, Richard/Shiloh School District 1	6	103
Kinsall, Kevin/Community Cons School Dist 93	297	90
Kinser, Rachel/Northwestern CUSD 2	6	168
Kinshofer, Gary/McHenry Cmty High Sch Dist 156	67	183
Kirberg, Kevin/Plainfield Cons Sch Dist 202	67	246
Kirby, Jason/West Central Cmty Unit SD 235	10,69	116
Kirby, Jody/Edgar Co Cmty Sch Dist 6	16	103
Kirby, Steve/Pawnee Cmty Unit Sch Dist 11	6	212
Kirchner, Anna/Bradley Elem School Dist 61	5	134
Kirchner, Brittany/A-C Central Cmty Unit SD 262	34	9
Kirk, Mary/Community Unit School Dist 7	16	167
Kirkeeng, Joseph/Lincoln-Way Cmty HS Dist 210	67	244
Kirkley, Diane/Hollis Cons School Dist 328	2	197
Kirkpatrick, Chris/Woodstock Cmty Unit SD 200	6	184
Kirkton, Samantha/Deland-Weldon Cmty Unit SD 57	57,69,83	202
Kirkus, Aleksas/Homer Cmty Cons Sch Dist 33C	2,15	242
Kirlic, Joan/Western Springs Sch Dist 101	7,83,88	71
Kirschbaum, Joyann/Rockford School District 205	9,34	254
Kirschmann, Maureen/Rockford School District 205	93	254
Kirshner, Jarrett/Maine Twp High Sch Dist 207	6	56
Kissel, Tom/West Lincoln-Broadwell ESD 92	67	164
Kissner, Ruth/Wayne City Unit SD 100	10,38,69,83	237
Kitson, Christina/Polo Cmty Unit Sch Dist 222	2	195
Kiwiet, Janine/Darien Public Sch Dist 61	67	92
Klabunde, Andrew/South Beloit Cmty Sch Dist 320	73	255
Klaisner, Mark, Dr/West 40 Interm Serv Center 2	1	82
Klasen, Kellie/Arlington Hts School Dist 25	79	21
Klaska, Matt/Vit Cmty Unit School Dist 2	1,11,83	110
Klaus, Jon/Carlinville Cmty Unit SD 1	3	167
Klawitter, Linda/Community Unit School Dist 201	11,34,58,79,88,275	92
Kleber, Ken/Champaign Cmty Unit Sch Dist 4	68,74,273	10
Kleber, Margaret/Community Cons School Dist 181	67	91
Kleckner, Karen/Dakota Cmty Unit Sch Dist 201	67	224
Klee, William/Chicago PSD-Network 4	15	30
Klein, Gabi/Peoria Public Sch Dist 150	4	198
Klein, Kylie/Evanston-Skokie Cmty CSD 65	294	48
Klein, Lyle/Carthage Elementary SD 317	270	114
Kleinmeyer, Susan/Cicero School District 99	6,21,40,81	42
Kleist, Carrie/Monroe School District 70	275,288	198
Kleist, Robb/Ohio Cmty Cons School Dist 17	5	7
Kleist, Robb/Ohio Cmty High School Dist 505	5	7
Klesath, Kerry/Farmington Ctl Cmty SD 265	58	197
Klimczak, Susan/Park Forest Chicago Hgt SD 163	73,295	62
Klimek-Gagor, Romana/River Grove School Dist 85-5	57	65
Kline, Steve/Decatur Public Schools 61	3,91	165
Klinedinst, Courtney/Illini Bluffs Cmty Unit SD 327	69,83	197
Klinedinst, Kevin/West Prairie Cmty Sch Dist 103	3	178
Klingenburg, Glenda/Bureau Valley Cmty Unit 340	5	6
Kloess, Kelly/Dupo Cmty School District 196	16	218
Klokkenga, Kim/Dunlap Cmty Unit Sch Dist 323	38	196
Klopfleisch, Lynn/Arcola Cmty Unit School Dist 306	16	87
Kloptowski, Jolanta/Union Ridge School Dist 86	67	70
Kloss, Jim/Berwyn South School Dist 100	73,76,295,297	23
Klouse, Mark/Rochelle Twp High Sch Dist 212	3	195
Klover, Denise/Argenta Oreana Cmty Unit SD 1	16	165
Kluck, Sarah/Mt Vernon City Sch Dist 80	4	123
Kluesner, Ann/Pleasant Hill School Dist 69	12	199
Klusmeyer, Seth/Mendon Cmty Unit School Dist 4	73	2
Kman, Rita/Richland Co Cmty Unit SD 1	2	206
Knaggs, Kevin/Delavan Cmty Unit Sch Dist 703	38,83,88	226

NAME/District	JOB FUNCTIONS	PAGE
Knar, Richard/Moline-Coal Valley SD No 40	6	207
Knawa, Kathy/Flossmoor School District 161	7	49
Kneigue, Kim/Joliet Public School Dist 86	286	243
Knetsch, James/Steward Elem School Dist 220	67	160
Knier, Linda/New Trier Twp HS District 203	69,93	58
Knight, Gary/Laraway Cmty Cons SD 70-C	67	243
Knight, Meghan/Township High School Dist 214	27,285,752	69
Knight, Sherryn/Laraway Cmty Cons SD 70-C	5	243
Knipe, Trevor/Nauvoo-Colusa CUSD 325	2	115
Knittel, Rodney/Greenfield Cmty Unit SD 10	67	111
Knoblauch, Herb/Washington Cmty HS Dist 308	6	229
Knoepfel, Kevin/Paris Union School District 95	67	103
Knoll, Erin, Dr/Schaumburg Cmty Cons SD 54	15,288,752	66
Knop, Brady/West Carroll CUSD 314	10	9
Knorr, Lisa/Southeastern Cmty Unit SD 337	2,84	115
Knott, Patti/Heritage Cmty Unit Sch Dist 8	31	11
Knowles, Terry/Mt Vernon City Sch Dist 80	73,84,295	123
Knowlton, Andy/Mendota Twp High School Dist 280	3	143
Knox, Keith/N Pekin-Marquette Hts SD 102	67	227
Knox, Ryan/Athens Cmty Unit Sch Dist 213	6	188
Knuth, Josh/Warren Community Unit SD 205	8	126
Ko, David, Dr/Niles Twp High School Dist 219	67	58
Kobbeman, Kim/Montmorency Cmty Cons SD 145	35	239
Kobel, Tom/Fenton Cmty High Sch Dist 100	3,5	94
Koberna, Kristen/Granite City Cmty Unit SD 9	9,11	171
Kocanda, Trisha/Winnetka School Dist 36	1,83	72
Kociss, Keegan/Cmty Cons Sch Dist 146	71,97	42
Koehl, Todd, Dr/Troy Cmty Cons SD 30-C	1	247
Koehler, Wesley/Franklin Cmty Unit SD 1	16,73,286	192
Koehnke, Michael/Mt Vernon Twp HS District 201	69,79,88,91,288	123
Koenig, Brent/Lebanon Cmty Unit Sch Dist 9	67	220
Koenig, Jennifer/Rondout School District 72	67	154
Koepell, Matt/Clinton Cmty Unit Sch Dist 15	6	87
Koerner, Sherry/Township High School Dist 214	2	69
Koerner, Timothy/St George School District 258	297	136
Koester, Bradley/Teutopolis Cmty Unit SD 50	67	105
Koester, Keri/Gallatin Cmty Unit Sch Dist 7	58	110
Koester, Lori/Carbondale Cmty HSD 165	38,81	120
Koester, Norma/Teutopolis Cmty Unit SD 50	4	105
Koetters, Don/Payson Cmty Unit School Dist 1	3	2
Kogut, Kathleen/East Aurora School Dist 131	34	129
Kohl, Andrew/Northbrook-Glenview SD 30	73,285,286,295	60
Kohl, Mike/Bradley-Bourbonnais CHSD 307	6	134
Kohl, Steve/Woodland School District 50	73	157
Kohl, Tiffany/Bradley-Bourbonnais CHSD 307	8,11,69,288	134
Koker, Rhonda/Fairfield Cmty High SD 225	2	236
Kokla, Jessica/Newark Cmty Cons Sch Dist 66	752	138
Kolarik, Jacey/Zion-Benton Twp High SD 126	41	157
Kolitwenzew, Ramie/St Anne Cmty HSD 302	11,69,273,275,286,296,298	136
Koll, Rusty/Elmwood Cmty Unit Sch Dist 322	12,88,296,298	196
Kolodziej, Jim/Community High School Dist 99	3,91	91
Kolowski, Marcella/Monroe School District 70	4	198
Kolstad, Luann/Park Ridge Niles CMCSD 64	2	62
Koltz, Becky/Community High School Dist 94	71	91
Kolves, Lisa/Havana Cmty Sch District 126	68	177
Komitas, Theresa/Community Unit School Dist 308	71	137
Konczyk, Gretchen/Plano Cmty Unit Sch Dist 88	5	138
Kondela, David/West Northfield Sch Dist 31	285,298	70
Koning, Melissa/Lincoln Cmty Unit School Dist 404	57,60	163
Konstans, Randy/Community High School Dist 99	6	91
Koo, Josh/Glenbrook High Sch Dist 225	72	50
Koontz, Angie/Somonauk Cmty Unit SD 432	36,83	86
Koontz, Angie/Somonauk Cmty Unit SD 432	36,83	86
Koontz, Robert/Mulberry Grove Cmty Sch Dist 1	1	4
Koopman, Mark/Community High School Dist 128	3	148
Kooy, Valerie/Lansing School Dist 158	81	54
Kopsic, Jeff/Highland Cmty Sch District 5	76	171

1 Superintendent	16 Instructional Media Svcs	30 Adult Education	44 Science Sec	58 Special Education K-12	72 Summer School	88 Alternative/At Risk	277 Remedial Math K-12
2 Bus/Finance/Purchasing	17 Chief Operations Officer	31 Career/Sch-to-Work K-12	45 Math K-12	59 Special Education Elem	73 Instructional Tech	89 Multi-Cultural Curriculum	280 Literacy Coach
3 Buildings And Grounds	18 Chief Academic Officer	32 Career/Sch-to-Work Elem	46 Math Elem	60 Special Education Sec	74 Inservice Training	90 Social Work	285 STEM
4 Food Service	19 Chief Financial Officer	33 Career/Sch-to-Work Sec	47 Math Sec	61 Foreign/World Lang K-12	75 Marketing/Distributive	91 Safety/Security	286 Digital Learning
5 Transportation	20 Art K-12	34 Early Childhood Ed	48 English/Lang Arts K-12	62 Foreign/World Lang Elem	76 Info Systems	92 Magnet School	288 Common Core Standards
6 Athletic	21 Art Elem	35 Health/Phys Education	49 English/Lang Arts Elem	63 Foreign/World Lang Sec	77 Psychological Assess	94 Parental Involvement	294 Accountability
7 Health Services	22 Art Sec	36 Guidance Services K-12	50 English/Lang Arts Sec	64 Religious Education K-12	78 Affirmative Action	95 Tech Prep Program	295 Network System
8 Curric/Instruct K-12	23 Music K-12	37 Guidance Services Elem	51 Reading K-12	65 Religious Education Elem	79 Student Personnel	96 Chief Information Officer	296 Title II Programs
9 Curric/Instruct Elem	24 Music Elem	38 Guidance Services Sec	52 Reading Elem	66 Religious Education Sec	80 Driver Ed/Safety	98 Chief Technology Officer	297 Webmaster
10 Curric/Instruct Sec	25 Music Sec	39 Social Studies K-12	53 Reading Sec	67 School Board President	81 Gifted/Talented	270 Character Education	298 Grant Writer/Ptnrships
11 Federal Program	26 Business Education	40 Social Studies Elem	54 Remedial Reading K-12	68 Teacher Personnel	82 Video Services	271 Migrant Education	750 Chief Innovation Officer
12 Title I	27 Career & Tech Ed	41 Social Studies Sec	55 Remedial Reading Elem	69 Academic Assessment	83 Substance Abuse Prev	273 Teacher Mentor	751 Chief of Staff
13 Title V	28 Technology Education	42 Science K-12	56 Remedial Reading Sec	70 Research/Development	84 Erate	274 Before/After Sch	752 Social Emotional Learning
15 Asst Superintendent	29 Family/Consumer Science	43 Science Elem	57 Bilingual/ELL	71 Public Information	85 AIDS Education	275 Response to Intervention	

IL-T32

Illinois School Directory
DISTRICT PERSONNEL INDEX

NAME/District	JOB FUNCTIONS	PAGE
Kopta, Kristen, Dr/Pennoyer School District 79	1,11	62
Kormoczy, Fred/Durand Cmty Sch Dist 322	5	252
Korney, Stephan/Community High School Dist 128	72	148
Kornick, Karen/Northbrook Elem School Dist 27	7	59
Korpal, Steven/Community High School Dist 94	295	91
Korsesko, Ryan/Mercer County SD 404	12	189
Korte, Erin/Damiansville School Dist 62	2	18
Korte, Matt/Germantown Elem Sch Dist 60	67	18
Korzenlowski, Nick/Skokie School District 69	76,295	67
Kosek, Misty/Chaney-Monge School Dist 88	37	241
Koshy, Abin/East Maine School District 63	295	47
Kosirog, John/Niles Elem School District 71	1	58
Koska, Susan/United Twp High Sch Dist 30	67	209
Kosowski, Thomas/Community High School Dist 218	67	44
Koss, Fred/Tolono Cmty Unit Sch Dist 7	67	12
Kossak, Justin/Greenview Cmty Unit SD 200	73,295	188
Kostecki, Tim/Evergreen Park Elem SD 124	2	49
Kostes, Tom, Dr/North Palos School Dist 117	67	59
Kotalik, Linda, Dr/Lisle Cmty Unit Sch Dist 202	8,12,15,73	96
Koudelka, Cindi/Fieldcrest Cmty School Dist 6	8	257
Koutavas, Christopher/Hinsdale Twp High Sch Dist 86	71	95
Koutavas, Ted/Rich Twp High School Dist 227	73,95	64
Kovacichi, Bryce/Geff Cmty Cons School Dist 14	6,35,73	236
Kovack, Mark/Township High School Dist 211	15,79	69
Kovar, Michelle/Community Unit School Dist 300	2	180
Kovil, Jaime/Milne-Kelvin Grove District 91	12,296	244
Kowalczyk, Claire/Community Cons School Dist 15	15	43
Kowalczyk, Eileen/Mt Prospect School Dist 57	67	58
Kowalczyk, Ritchie/LaSalle Peru Twp HSD 120	3	142
Kowalski, Linda/Triad Cmty School District 2	57,58	172
Kowalski, Lisa/Morton Cmty Unit Sch Dist 709	2,19	227
Kozal, Daniel, Dr/Argo Cmty High School Dist 217	67	21
Kozeal, Renee/Princeton Twp HSD 500	16	7
Kozic, Dejan/Round Lake Area Co Dist 116	73,84	155
Kraemer, Julie/Hutsonville Cmty Unit SD 1	1,84	83
Kraft, Deanna/Dakota Cmty Unit Sch Dist 201	295	224
Kramarsic, Doug/Oglesby Public Sch Dist 125	67	143
Kramer, Dave/Blue Ridge Cmty SD 18	73	87
Kramer, Ryon/Delavan Cmty Unit Sch Dist 703	6	226
Kramer, Staci/Bushnell Prairie Cmty USD 170	12,296	178
Kramp, Lisa/Arlington Hts School Dist 25	79	21
Kramper, Staci/Sparta Cmty School Dist 140	6	205
Kramper, Staci/Sparta Cmty School Dist 140	6	205
Kratochvil, Tim/Pawnee Cmty Unit Sch Dist 11	10	212
Kratzer, Jeff/Princeville Cmty Unit SD 326	6	200
Kraus, Jon/West Washington Co Cmty SD 10	6	236
Krause, Amy/Pontiac Twp High Sch Dist 90	16,73,84,286,295	161
Krause, Anne/Atwood Heights SD 125	59	21
Krawczyk, Julie/Buncombe Cons School Dist 43	2	127
Krebs, Jordan/Henry Senachwine CUSD 5	36	176
Kreger, Tom/Township High School Dist 113	15,68,78	155
Krehbiel, Erica/Glen Ellyn School District 41	71	94
Kreiser, Ron/Fieldcrest Cmty School Dist 6	3	257
Kreiter, Kevin/Brimfield Cmty Unit SD 309	6	196
Kreke, Ashley/Dieterich Community Unit SD 30	69,83	104
Kreller, Katie/Community Cons School Dist 89	59,79,90	90
Kreuter, Hunter/Joppa-Maple Grove Unit SD 38	6	177
Kreutztrager, Debra/Roxana Cmty Unit Sch Dist 1	1	172
Kribbs, Shirlee/Westchester Public SD 92 1/2	5	70
Krickovich, Angela/Rantoul Twp High Sch Dist 193	2	12
Krinsky, Janice/Community Cons School Dist 59	67	43
Kristoff, Tara/Rock Falls Elem Sch Dist 13	9,74	240
Kroc, Tami/Gurnee School District 56	7,57,59,79,85,88,90,275	150
Kroeze, David, Dr/Northbrook Elem School Dist 27	1	59
Krohn, Kim/Lowpoint-Washburn CUSD 21	73	258
Krolik, James/Proviso Twp High Sch Dist 209	295	63
Krones, Mary/Township High School Dist 211	60	69
Krouse, Tambree/Edwards Co Cmty Unit SD 1	16,82	104
Kruckman, Susan/Special Education Dist Lake Co	7	159
Krueger, Justin/Hononegah Cmty High SD 207	2	253
Krueger, Karen/Community High School Dist 218	50,63	44
Krueger, Keely/Woodstock Cmty Unit SD 200	8,11,15,57,61,275,296,298	184
Krueger, Lisa/Community High School Dist 218	3	44
Krug, Jan/La Salle Elem SD 122	69,77,271	142
Krugel, Sandy/Saratoga Cmty Cons SD 60C	280,285,288,752	113
Krumlinde, Lynn/Milne-Kelvin Grove District 91	79	244

NAME/District	JOB FUNCTIONS	PAGE
Krumsieg, Tom/Wesclin Cmty Unit Sch Dist 3	3,4,5	18
Krunk, Summer/Irvington Cmty Cons SD 11	59	235
Krupinski, Tomasz/Marquardt School District 15	295	97
Krupps, Philip/Brown Co Cmty Unit Sch Dist 1	67	5
Kruse, Calvin/Orion Cmty Unit Sch Dist 223	295	117
Kuberski, Jae/Highland Cmty Sch District 5	7	171
Kuceba, Kathleen/Berkeley School Dist 87	4	22
Kuchefski, Brandi/Danville School District 118	12,57,298	231
Kuchnicki, Angie/Alton Cmty School District 11	58	169
Kucko, Mike/Addison School District 4	76	88
Kudrna, Merri Beth, Dr/Wood Dale School Dist 7	9,69	100
Kuechenberg, Dave/Community Cons School Dist 15	16,73,295	43
Kueker, Tammy/Red Bud Cmty Unit Sch Dist 132	7,85	205
Kuhar, Aprille/North Mac Cmty Unit SD 34	4	168
Kuhlman, Joseph/Scott Morgan Cmty Unit SD 2	275	215
Kuhlmann, Melissa/Carrier Mills-Stonefort SD 2	8,57,58,83	210
Kuhn, Tracy/Cary Cmty Cons Sch Dist 26	57	179
Kuhns, Shelly/Altamont Cmty Unit SD 10	67	104
Kujawa, Craig/Bethel School District 82	1	122
Kujawa, Elizabeth/Leyden Cmty High Sch Dist 212	4	55
Kukulka, Nancy/Forest Ridge Sch Dist 142	37	50
Kulenkamp, Roy/Carlinville Cmty Unit SD 1	34	167
Kunde, Wayne/Mascoutah Cmty Sch Dist 19	3	220
Kunesh, Matt/Community Cons School Dist 181	16,73,286	91
Kunkel, Kevin/Pecatonica Cmty Unit SD 321	6	253
Kunst, Carol, Dr/General George S Patton SD 133	1,11	50
Kunth, Courtney/Galesburg Cmty Unit SD 205	7	140
Kuntz, Kristy/Community Unit School Dist 200	68	91
Kuntzman, Chris/Taylorville Cmty Unit SD 3	73,285,295	15
Kunz, Brittney/Dakota Cmty Unit Sch Dist 201	2	224
Kunz, K/Wesclin Cmty Unit Sch Dist 3	73,295	18
Kunz, Karen/Belle Valley School Dist 119	67	217
Kunz, Kelly/Wesclin Cmty Unit Sch Dist 3	73,84,98,295	18
Kunz, Mike/Collinsville Cmty Sch Dist 10	16,28,82	170
Kunzer, Chris/Naperville Cmty Unit SD 203	84	98
Kupka, Nancy, Dr/Community High School Dist 99	67	91
Kurlinkus, David/Hononegah Cmty High SD 207	67	253
Kurokawa, Lynn/Golf School District 67	79	51
Kurtz, Aaron/Jasper Co Cmty Unit SD 1	73	122
Kurz, Brian/El Paso-Gridley CUSD 11	1	257
Kush, David/Homewood Flossmoor CHSD 233	294	52
Kusnerich, Chris/Alton Cmty School District 11	6	169
Kutz, Elizabeth/Oglesby Public Sch Dist 125	84	143
Kuykendall, Jim/Charleston Cmty Unit SD 1	3,91	19
Kuzniewski, Mark, Dr/Brookfield-LaGrange Park SD 95	1	23
Kweli, Sharadi/Momence Cmty Unit Sch Dist 1	73	136
Kyle, Charles, Dr/Community Unit School Dist 200	15	91
Kyne, Margaret/Union Ridge School Dist 86	2	70
Kyro, Arlene/Edwardsville Cmty Unit SD 7	5	170
Kyser, Casey/East Moline Public Sch Dist 37	2	207

L

NAME/District	JOB FUNCTIONS	PAGE
La Born, Cindy/Naperville Cmty Unit SD 203	5	98
LaBella, Frances/Flossmoor School District 161	2,15	49
LaBorn, Jim/Community Cons School Dist 181	3	91
Labuhn, Katie/Lake Forest School District 67	2	152
Lach, Michael/Township High School Dist 113	10,11,15,27,69,74,81	155
Lachel, Jennifer/Harrison School Dist 36	16,73	181
Ladd, Ann/Princeville Cmty Unit SD 326	274	200
Lagioia, Tammie/Oak Lawn-Hometown Sch Dist 123	76	60
Laidley, Tara/Mascoutah Cmty Sch Dist 19	73,286	220
Lain, Jamie/Seneca Cmty Cons Sch Dist 170	16	144
Laird, Michelle/Troy Cmty Cons SD 30-C	59	247
Laird, Michelle/Valley View Cmty SD 365-U	79	248
Laird, Scott/Athens Cmty Unit Sch Dist 213	1,11	188
Lakin, Keri/Jersey Cmty Sch Dist 100	34,58	125
Lalor, John/Alden-Hebron School Dist 19	6	179
Lamantia, Frank/Community High School Dist 218	26,27,29	44
Lamar, Alecia/West Harvey-Dixmoor Pub SD 147	73	70
Lamb, Donna/Sherrard Cmty Sch Dist 200	17,83,88,270,275,288	189
Lamb, Matt/Kings Cons School District 144	1,11	194
Lambe, Jeremy, Dr/Ottawa Elementary Sch Dist 141	7,77,752	143
Lambert, Dan/Wilmette Public School Dist 39	4	71
Lambert, Rick/Winthrop Harbor School Dist 1	67	156
Lambert, Ryan/Farmington Ctl Cmty SD 265	16,286	197
Lamberti, Valerie/Glencoe Sch District 35	11,34,37,55,59,79	51

DISTRICT PERSONNEL INDEX

Market Data Retrieval

NAME/District	JOB FUNCTIONS	PAGE
Lambesis, George/Berwyn South School Dist 100	3	23
Lamboley, Daniel/McLean Co Unit District 5	10	186
Lamboley, Mark/Peru Elem Sch Dist 124	67	143
Lamboley, Michele/Mackinaw Valley Spec Ed Assoc	1	188
Lamboley, Michelle/McLean Co Unit District 5	34,58,77,90	186
Lambrecht, Kathleen/Chicago Ridge Sch Dist 127-5	7,83,85	41
Lamczyk, Zach/Salem Cmty High Sch Dist 600	73,74,76,295	175
Lamer, Ken/Meridian Cmty Unit SD 223	3	194
Lamerti, Frank/New Trier Twp HS District 203	5	58
Lamkey, Fred/Mt Pulaski Cmty Unit SD 23	1,11,83	164
Lampe, Joe/Central Cmty High Sch Dist 71	3	17
Lampert, Joan/Bannockburn Sch Dist 106	69	147
Lamping, Mary, Dr/Round Lake Area Co Dist 116	3,17	155
Lancaster, Eric/North Mac Cmty Unit SD 34	5	168
Landeck, Lance/Oakland Cmty Unit Sch Dist 5	1,73	19
Landgraf, Brad, Dr/Millstadt Cmty Cons SD 160	1	220
Landgraf, Mitch/Mendota Twp High Sch Dist 280	38	143
Landmeier, Anna/Evanston Twp High SD 202	83	48
Landorf, Karen/Community Cons School Dist 93	70,73	90
Landreth, Larry/Patoka Cmty Unit SD 100	3	175
Landris, Kevin/Sullivan Cmty Unit SD 300	3,5	193
Landry, Dan/Grayslake Cmty HS District 127	79	150
Landry, Tracie/Grayslake Cmty HS District 127	10	150
Landstrom, Mary-Beth/Chester-E Lincoln Cmty SD 61	4	163
Lane, Becky/Pekin Cmty High Sch Dist 303	4	227
Lane, Chuck/Centralia High School Dist 200	1	174
Lane, David/Lake Forest Cmty HSD 115	67	151
Lane, Gary/Riverton Cmty Unit SD 14	5	212
Lane, Joe/Norris City-Omaha-Enfield SD 3	67	238
Lane, Lynette/Harvey Public School Dist 152	4	51
Lane, Michael/Monticello Cmty Unit SD 25	3	202
Lane, Theresa/Mt Zion Cmty Unit Sch Dist 3	5	166
Lang, Mary/Gavin School District 37	5	150
Lang, Robert, Dr/Community High School Dist 99	15,68,74,273,296	91
Lange, Heidi/Harlem Unit Sch District 122	59,79,288	252
Lange, Randy/La Grange Elem Sch Dist 102	74	54
Lange, Tim/St Libory Cons Sch District 30	6	222
Langellier, Jon/North Mac Cmty Unit SD 34	73	168
Langevin, Ed/Consolidated High Sch Dist 230	5	44
Langley, Angela/Robinson Cmty Unit Sch Dist 2	5	83
Langley, Greg/Harrisburg Cmty Unit SD 3	6	210
Langley, John/Pleasant Plains Cmty Unit SD 8	73	212
Langly, Theresa/Triopia Cmty Unit Sch Dist 27	2	192
Langman, Robert, Dr/Darien Public Sch Dist 61	1	92
Langton, John/Addison School District 4	1	88
Lanier, Mary/Deer Creek-Mackinaw CUSD 701	10,88	226
Lankton, Dean/Flanagan-Cornell Unit 74 SD	73	161
Lanni, Melanie/Round Lake Area Co Dist 116	57	155
Lannom, Rob/Anna Cmty Cons Sch Dist 37	6	230
Lannon, John/Heritage Cmty Unit Sch Dist 8	67	11
Lantz, Chris/Atwood Heights SD 125	67	21
Lantz, Tecia/Southeastern Cmty Unit SD 337	270,295	115
Lapetino, Chris/Wheeling Cmty Cons Sch Dist 21	40,43	71
LaPointe, Marcus/Elgin School District U-46	3	130
Lapp, William/Fieldcrest Cmty School Dist 6	60	257
Lara, Jennifer/O'Fallon Twp School Dist 203	16	221
Laratta, Rebecca/Gower School District 62	9,13,69,73,79,83,88,286	94
Laratta, Rebecca/Gower School District 62	286,298	94
LaReau, Justin/Donovan Cmty Unit Sch Dist 3	3	119
Lark, Philip/Beecher City Cmty Unit SD 20	1,11	104
Larkin, David/Woodlawn Unit School Dist 209	271	124
Larkin, Myra/Rankin Cmty School Dist 98	12	228
Larramore, Amy/Sparta Cmty School Dist 140	58	205
Larsen, Adam/Oregon Cmty Unit Sch Dist 220	15	195
Larsen, Deb/Maine Twp High Sch Dist 207	60,79	56
Larsen, Mark/Belleville Township HSD 201	6	217
Larson, Andrew/Tolono Cmty Unit Sch Dist 7	1,83	12

NAME/District	JOB FUNCTIONS	PAGE
Larson, Charlotte/Bellwood School District 88	59	22
Larson, David, Dr/Glenbard Twp High Sch Dist 87	1	94
Larson, Holly/Newark Cmty High Sch Dist 18	60,88	138
Larson, Jeremy, Dr/Paris Union School District 95	1	103
Larson, Jeremy, Dr/Paris Union School District 95	11	103
Larson, Jill/Brookwood School District 167	72	24
Larson, Mary/Evanston-Skokie Cmty CSD 65	7	48
Larson, Victoria, Dr/Harvard Cmty Unit Sch Dist 50	15	181
Lascelles, Anne/Winnetka School Dist 36	274	72
Lascelles, Bob/Vit Cmty Unit School Dist 2	67	110
Lascelles, Charles/Vit Cmty Unit School Dist 2	3	110
Lascola, Mike/Belvidere Cmty Unit SD 100	69,79	4
Lasher, Karen/Township High School Dist 211	2	69
Lasiewicki, Peg/Arlington Hts School Dist 25	7,34,37,57,79,90,271,275	21
Lasko, Bennett/North Shore School Dist 112	67	154
Laskowski, Amy/La Grange-Highlands SD 106	59,79	54
Lasky, Melinda/Yorkville Cmty Unit SD 115	79	139
Lasley, Carla/Grant Cmty Cons Sch Dist 110	58	219
Lasley, Carla/Grant Cmty Cons Sch Dist 110	9,11,57,67,74,88,275,288	219
Latham, Todd/Geneva CUSD 304	2	131
Latman, Robin/Flossmoor School District 161	59	49
Latourette, Carissa/Millburn Cmty Cons Sch Dist 24	67	153
Lattyak, Kelli/Bremen Cmty High SD 228	47	23
Lattz, Catherine/Ridgeland School District 122	59,79,88	64
Laudadio, Fred/McHenry Cmty Cons Sch Dist 15	9,16,73,74,285,288,295,297	183
Laudadio, Robert/Bensenville Elem Sch Dist 2	67	89
Lauderdale, Tracy/O'Fallon Cmty Cons Sch Dist 90	6	221
Lauer, Jim/Mendota Twp High Sch Dist 280	67	143
Lauer, Rachel/Marseilles Elem Sch Dist 150	2,298	142
Lauer, Ray/Smithton Cmty Cons SD 130	3	222
Laughlin, Jennifer/Skokie School District 69	280	67
Lauk, Raymond, Dr/Maywood-Melrose Brdview SD 89	2,4,5,294	57
Laurent, Monica/Whiteside School District 115	69	222
Lauria, Catherine/West Northfield Sch Dist 31	2,3,15	70
Lauritzen, Cindy/Hiawatha Cmty Unit SD 426	4	85
Lauritzen, Leslie/Lake Zurich Cmty Sch Dist 95	5	152
LaVelle, John/Consolidated High Sch Dist 230	2,15	44
LaVigueur, Jamie/Community Cons School Dist 181	71	91
Lavitola, Donna/Lake Forest Cmty HSD 115	298	151
Law, Adam/Geneva CUSD 304	15,68,273	131
Law, Bruce/Township High School Dist 113	1	155
Law, Jennifer/Lisle Cmty Unit Sch Dist 202	11,34,57,58,79,88	96
Lawinger, Sandy/Community Cons School Dist 89	7	90
Lawler, Lisa/Emmons School District 33	2,3,298	149
Lawless, Beth/Streator Elem School Dist 44	90	144
Lawrence, Aletta/Mt Vernon City Sch Dist 80	1	123
Lawrence, Jennifer/Rockford School District 205	58	254
Lawrence, Larry/Dolton-Riverdale Sch Dist 148	67	46
Lawrence, Liz/Niles Elem School District 71	69,77,88	58
Lawrence, Lynn/La Grange Elem Sch Dist 102	37,273	54
Lawrence, Reginald, Dr/Rock Island-Milan Sch Dist 41	1	208
Lawrence, Tara/Calumet City School Dist 155	296	24
Lawrence, Tawanda, Dr/Country Club Hills SD 160	9,11,73,288,296	45
Lawrence, Tawanda, Dr/Oak Park Elem School Dist 97	9,69	60
Lawry, Amanda/Central Sch Dist 51	285	225
Lawson, David/McHenry Cmty High Sch Dist 156	2,3,4,11,19	183
Lawson, Joe/Vandalia Cmty Unit SD 203	67	106
Lawson, Julious/Chicago PSD-Network 11	15	34
Lawson, Lori/Lincoln Cmty High Sch Dist 404	4	163
Layer, Barbara/Lake Park Cmty High SD 108	67	96
Layer, Cindy/Willow Springs School Dist 108	6	71
Lazar, Ryan/Gurnee School District 56	69	150
Lazarevic, Jovan/Fenton Cmty High Sch Dist 100	15	94
Lazarz, Don/Midwest Ctl Cmty Unit SD 191	6	177
Le, Dan/LaSalle Peru Twp HSD 120	6	142
Lea, Prentiss, Dr/Community High School Dist 128	1	148
Leadendecker, Melissa/West Washington Co Cmty SD 10	2	236

1 Superintendent	16 Instructional Media Svcs	30 Adult Education	44 Science Sec	58 Special Education K-12	72 Summer School	88 Alternative/At Risk	277 Remedial Math K-12
2 Bus/Finance/Purchasing	17 Chief Operations Officer	31 Career/Sch-to-Work K-12	45 Math K-12	59 Special Education Elem	73 Instructional Tech	89 Multi-Cultural Curriculum	280 Literacy Coach
3 Buildings And Grounds	18 Chief Academic Officer	32 Career/Sch-to-Work Elem	46 Math Elem	60 Special Education Sec	74 Inservice Training	90 Social Work	285 STEM
4 Food Service	19 Chief Financial Officer	33 Career/Sch-to-Work Sec	47 Math Sec	61 Foreign/World Lang K-12	75 Marketing/Distributive	91 Safety/Security	286 Digital Learning
5 Transportation	20 Art K-12	34 Early Childhood Ed	48 English/Lang Arts K-12	62 Foreign/World Lang Elem	76 Info Systems	92 Magnet School	288 Common Core Standards
6 Athletic	21 Art Elem	35 Health/Phys Education	49 English/Lang Arts Elem	63 Foreign/World Lang Sec	77 Psychological Assess	94 Parental Involvement	294 Accountability
7 Health Services	22 Art Sec	36 Guidance Services K-12	50 English/Lang Arts Sec	64 Religious Education K-12	79 Affirmative Action	95 Tech Prep Program	295 Network System
8 Curric/Instruct K-12	23 Music K-12	37 Guidance Services Elem	51 Reading K-12	65 Religious Education Elem	79 Student Personnel	97 Chief Infomation Officer	296 Title II Programs
9 Curric/Instruct Elem	24 Music Elem	38 Guidance Services Sec	52 Reading Elem	66 Religious Education Sec	80 Driver Ed/Safety	98 Chief Technology Officer	297 Webmaster
10 Curric/Instruct Sec	25 Music Sec	39 Social Studies K-12	53 Reading Sec	67 School Board President	81 Gifted/Talented	270 Character Education	298 Grant Writer/Ptnrships
11 Federal Program	26 Business Education	40 Social Studies Elem	54 Remedial Reading K-12	68 Teacher Personnel	82 Video Services	271 Migrant Education	750 Chief Innovation Officer
12 Title I	27 Career & Tech Ed	41 Social Studies Sec	55 Remedial Reading Elem	69 Academic Assessment	83 Substance Abuse Prev	273 Teacher Mentor	751 Chief of Staff
13 Title V	28 Technology Education	42 Science K-12	56 Remedial Reading Sec	70 Research/Development	84 Erate	274 Before/After Sch	752 Social Emotional Learning
15 Asst Superintendent	29 Family/Consumer Science	43 Science Elem	57 Bilingual/ELL	71 Public Information	85 AIDS Education	275 Response To Intervention	

IL-T34

Illinois School Directory — DISTRICT PERSONNEL INDEX

NAME/District	JOB FUNCTIONS	PAGE
Leahy, Christina, Dr/Central Stickney Sch Dist 110	11	25
Leak, Donna, Dr/Community Cons School Dist 168	1	44
Leali, Lisa/Kenilworth School District 38	9,18	53
Leali, Lisa, Dr/Lake Bluff Elem Sch Dist 65	1	151
Leato, Gary/Midland Cmty Unit Sch Dist 7	16,27,73,76	176
LeBaron, Scott/Alden-Hebron School Dist 19	16,73,82	179
LeBlanc, Debra, Dr/Benjamin Sch District 25	9,11,57,69,88,270,296	89
Lebrecht, Kris/Prospect Hts School Dist 23	274	63
Lebris, Elizabeth/Kenilworth School District 38	73,297	53
Lechner, Ray/DeKalb Cmty Unit SD 428	1	84
Lecrone, Chad/Richland Co Cmty Unit SD 1	15	206
Ledbetter, Nicky/Fulton Co Cmty Unit Sch Dist 3	2	109
Leden, Todd, Dr/Kaneland Cmty Unit SD 302	1	132
Lee, Amy/Plano Cmty Unit Sch Dist 88	58	138
Lee, Amy/Woodland Cmty Unit Sch Dist 5	36,69,83,270	162
Lee, Andrea/Calhoun Cmty Unit Sch Dist 40	1	8
Lee, Bradley/Carmi-White Co School Dist 5	1,11	237
Lee, Darin/Collinsville Cmty Sch Dist 10	6	170
Lee, Darrell/Prairieview-Ogden Sch Dist 197	3	11
Lee, Dawn/Oakwood Cmty Unit Sch Dist 76	31,36	232
Lee, Elizabeth/Morris Cmty High Sch Dist 101	83	113
Lee, Elizabeth/Winfield School District 34	67	100
Lee, Eric/West Harvey-Dixmoor Pub SD 147	3,91	70
Lee, Heather/Richland Co Cmty Unit SD 1	36	206
Lee, Kathy/Washington School Dist 52	274	229
Lee, Katie/Wilmette Public School Dist 39	9,11,57,69,270,273,288,298	71
Lee, Kenneth/Minooka Cmty High Sch Dist 111	1	244
Lee, Louis/Indian Prairie Sch Dist 204	15,68	95
Lee, Michelle/Dallas Elem Sch Dist 327	1	114
Lee, Michelle, Dr/La Harpe Cmty Sch Dist 347	1,11,83	115
Lee, Mike/New Trier Twp HS District 203	12	58
Lee, Norman/Newark Cmty Cons Sch Dist 66	98,286,295	138
Lee, Rusty/Jersey Cmty Sch Dist 100	295	125
Lee, Susan/Grass Lake School District 36	77	150
Leeck, Henry/Opdyke-Belle Rive Cmty CSSD 5	67	123
Leek, Dustin/Edwards Co Cmty Unit SD 1	73	104
LeFevre, Robert/Township High School Dist 211	67	69
Leffelman, Al/Tonica Cmty Cons Sch Dist 79	67	145
Legan, Jewel/Donovan Cmty Unit Sch Dist 3	73	119
Legan, Victoria/Crescent Iroquois Cmty SD 249	2,83	118
LeGare, Toni/Berwyn South School Dist 100	4	23
Legate, Michael/UT Area Career Center	28	210
Lehmann, Julie/Harvard Cmty Unit Sch Dist 50	67	181
Lehr, Mike/Champaign Cmty Unit Sch Dist 4	10,288	10
Lehtola, Jon/Rockridge Cmty Unit SD 300	73,295	209
Leibforth, Dale/Evanston Twp High SD 202	47	48
Leighty, Marc/Fairfield Cmty High SD 225	73,286	236
Leitner, Lisa/Dunlap Cmty Unit Sch Dist 323	4	196
Lekkas, Angelo/Iroquois West Cmty Unit SD 10	1	119
Lekrone, Annette/West Prairie Cmty Sch Dist 103	73,76,286,295	178
Leli, Anthony/Chicago Heights Elem SD 170	2,19	25
Leli, Phil/Chicago Heights Elem SD 170	16,73	25
Leman, Chad/Eureka Cmty Unit Sch Dist 140	67	257
Lemke, Mariann/Elmhurst Cmty Unit SD 205	70	93
Lemon, Donna/Panhandle Cmty Unit SD 2	2	191
Lemone, Laura/Chicago PSD-Network 14	15	36
LeMore, Alicia/West Harvey-Dixmoor Pub SD 147	16	70
Lenaghan, Aaron/Dupage High School Dist 88	10,73	93
Lenger, Messina/Region 3 Spec Ed Co-op	1	174
Lenihan, Stacy/Township High School Dist 211	4	69
Lensing, Christopher/East Coloma-Nelson Cesd 20	1,11,73	238
Lensing, Heidi/Carbon Cliff Barstow SD 36	16,73,275,286,288	207
Lentz, Jay/Hamilton Co Cmty Unit SD 10	4	114
Lentz, Mike/Herrin Cmty School District 4	3	251
Leonard, Ariana/Elmhurst Cmty Unit SD 205	57	93
Leonard, Dan/Cornell Cmty Cons Sch Dist 426	3	160
Leonard, Jon/Argo Cmty High School Dist 217	16	21
Leonard, Kim/Evergreen Park Elem SD 124	67	49
Leonard, Peter/Chicago Public School Dist 299	69	25
Leonard, Robert/Woodland School District 50	2	156
Leonard, Sarah/Rockridge Cmty Unit SD 300	11,296	209
Leone, Michael/Lincoln-Way Cmty HS Dist 210	5	244
Leone, Mike/Manhattan School Dist 114	5	244
Lepinski, Nancy/Fremont School District 79	2	149
Leppert, Lori, Dr/Forest Ridge Sch Dist 142	34,59,69,79	50
Leppin, Janice/Manhattan School Dist 114	73	244
Lequatte, Lorie/Regional Office of Ed 21	1	109
Lerci, Jan/Steger School Dist 194	9,57,69	68
Leroy, Chrystal, Dr/Kenilworth School District 38	1	53
Lesak, David/Lansing School Dist 158	73,295	54
Lesak, Tom/Newark Cmty High Sch Dist 18	73	138
Lesczynski, Gerald/Lincoln Elem School Dist 156	3,91	55
Leskowich, Michael/Durand Cmty SD Dist 322	10,35,83,271	252
Leslie, Cathy/Palos Heights School Dist 128	79	61
Lesniak, Margaret/Aero Special Ed Co-op	2,11	82
Lessen, Jackie/West Lincoln-Broadwell ESD 92	3,5	164
Lessen, Laurie/Hartsburg Emden School Dist 21	2	163
Lett-Foreman, Tracy, Dr/Country Club Hills SD 160	68,71,298	45
Letterle, Sunny/Cambridge Cmty Unit SD 227	280	116
Lettiere, Brett/Argo Cmty High School Dist 217	72	21
Leuenberger, John/Lena-Winslow Cmty Unit SD 202	67	224
Levendoski, Denise/Nippersink School District 2	2	183
Levendoski, Denise/Richmond-Burton Cmty HSD 157	2	184
Levi, Shawn/North Wayne Cmty Unit SD 200	73,84,295	237
Levine-Stein, Adam/Deerfield Public SD 109	73,76,295	149
Levy, Carrie/Evanston Twp High SD 202	69	48
Lewandowski, Ann/Mokena Public School Dist 159	4	245
Lewe-Brady, Marjory/West Chicago Elementary SD 33	91	99
Lewis-Williams, Kimberly/Hoover-Schrum Sch Dist 157	2,11,294,296,298	52
Lewis, Adam/Elverado Cmty Unit SD 196	73,76,84,286,752	120
Lewis, Billy/Belvidere Cmty Unit SD 100	8,11,36,69,78,79,298	4
Lewis, Cedric/Dolton School District 149	2,73,84	46
Lewis, Danielle/Regional Office of Ed 26	16,297	179
Lewis, Gary/Regional Office of Ed 9	1	13
Lewis, Joni/Dongola Unit School Dist 66	2	230
Lewis, Leigh/Triad Cmty School District 2	1	172
Lewis, Rebecca/Herrin Cmty School District 4	23	251
Lewis, Shanna/Lyons Twp HS District 204	5	56
Lewis, Shawn/Princeton Twp HSD 500	4	7
Lewis, Sophia/Naperville Cmty Unit SD 203	73	98
Ley, Brian/Havana Cmty Sch District 126	67	177
Leyden, Greg/Bloomingdale School Dist 13	3	89
Leyva-Cutler, Beatriz/Dunlap Cmty Unit Sch Dist 323	73	196
Liberatore, Matt/Township High School Dist 214	73,79	69
Lickenbrock, Shannon/Staunton Cmty Unit Sch Dist 6	38,69	168
Liddell, Keith/Carterville Cmty Unit SD 5	1	250
Lieb, Amy/Lena-Winslow Cmty Unit SD 202	2	224
Liebe, Kevin/North Shore School Dist 112	3,5,91	154
Liebig, Penni/Lebanon Cmty Unit Sch Dist 9	2	220
Ligammari, Lauren/Chaney-Monge School Dist 88	57	241
Liles, Kim/Center Cass Sch Dist 66	12,58,79,83,752	90
Lilja, Molly/North Boone Cmty Unit SD 200	288	5
Lillie, Lillie/Darien Public Sch Dist 61	4	92
Lillis, Michelle/Rock Island-Milan Sch Dist 41	6	208
Lind, Jason/Millburn Cmty Cons Sch Dist 24	1,11	153
Lind, Thomas, Dr/Nippersink School District 2	1	183
Lind, Tom/Richmond-Burton Cmty HSD 157	1	184
Lindeloof, Staci/Gibson Cty-Melvin-Sibley CUSD5	273	106
Lindem, Mark/Gurnee School District 56	2,19	150
Lindeman, Matt/Clay City Cmty Unit SD 10	3,5	16
Lindenann, Pamela/Burbank School District 111	15,68,74,91,273,275	24
Lindenmeyer, Michele, Dr/Milford Area Public SD 124	1	119
Lindenmeyer, Michele, Dr/Stewardson-Strasburg SD 5-A	11	216
Lindhorst, Alisha/Akin Elem School District 91	34	107
Lindsay, Jennifer/N Pekin-Marquette Hts SD 102	59,69	227
Lindsay, Shawn/Hollis Cons School Dist 328	73	197
Lindsey, Bethany/Brookwood School District 167	1,11	24
Lindy, Michael/Ashton-Franklin Center SD 275	1	159
Lines, Chris/Morris Elem School Dist 54	4	113
Lines, James/Deer Creek-Mackinaw CUSD 701	57,58,83,85,275,296	226
Lingafelter, Eric/Wayne City Cmty Unit SD 100	27	237
Lingo, Marcy/Lyons Twp HS District 204	4	56
Linhart, Sandy/Norwood Sch Dist 63	11	198
Link, Bill, Dr/Pekin Public School Dist 108	1	227
Link, Logan/Fulton Co Cmty Unit Sch Dist 3	38	109
Linnemann, Katrina/Lena-Winslow Cmty Unit SD 202	38,69,83,85,270	224
Linnig, Ryan/Dimmick Cmty School Dist 175	1,11	141
Linton, Cheryl/N Pekin-Marquette Hts SD 102	2	227
Linton, Lori/Johnston City Cmty Unit SD 1	2	251
Linton, Stacy/Herrin Cmty School District 4	35,85	251
Linton, Teresa/Carlyle Cmty Unit Sch Dist 1	58	17
Liparoto, Lisa/Fox River Grove Cons SD 3	7	181

DISTRICT PERSONNEL INDEX

Market Data Retrieval

NAME/District	JOB FUNCTIONS	PAGE
Lipowski, Edwin/Bremen Cmty High SD 228	72	23
Lippeth, Julie/Winthrop Harbor School Dist 1	2	156
Lippold, Karen/La Grange-Highlands SD 106	7	54
Lippoldt, Kate/Bradley-Bourbonnais CHSD 307	38	134
Lippoldt, Keith/Bensenville Elem Sch Dist 2	295	89
Liptrot, Kristine/Yorkville Cmty Unit SD 115	71	139
Lis, Chrystal/Rhodes School District 84 1/2	12	64
Lis, David/Ridgeland School District 122	67	64
Litherland, Sheri/Bureau Valley Cmty Unit 340	8,285	6
Little, Carla, Dr/Woodland School District 50	67	157
Little, Ron/Christopher Unit Sch Dist 99	3	107
Littlefair, Julie/Mt Vernon Twp HS District 201	18	123
Littlefield, Katie/Rockton School District 140	67	255
Litton, Toni/Alwood Cmty Unit Sch Dist 225	58,275	116
Livatino, Chris/Evanston Twp High SD 202	6	48
Lively, Donna/Du Quoin Cmty Unit SD 300	4	201
Livengood, Kali/Erie Cmty School District 1	11,51,54,296	239
Livingston, Dawn/Winnetka School Dist 36	67	72
Livingston, Jeff/Aptakisic-Tripp Sch Dist 102	6	146
Livingston, Thomas, Dr/Atwood Heights SD 125	1	21
Llanes, Melanie/Dolton-Riverdale Sch Dist 148	59	46
Lloyd, Melanie/Rock Island-Milan Sch Dist 41	76	208
Locascio, Daniel/Franklin Park Pub Sch Dist 84	67	50
Locascio, Mike/Valley View Cmty SD 365-U	69,76	248
Lock, Amanda/Charleston Cmty Unit SD 1	7	19
Lock, Kiersti/Hamilton Cmty Cons SD 328	2	114
Lockett, Dekietrich/East St Louis Sch Dist 189	27,31	218
Lockman, Thomas/Champaign Cmty Unit Sch Dist 4	2,19	10
Lodes, Shea/Whiteside School District 115	6	222
Lodge, Cheryl/Trico Cmty Unit Sch Dist 176	6	121
Loeffler, Michele/Allendale Cmty Cons SD 17	16,73	234
Loehr, Robert/Oak Lawn Cmty High SD 229	67	60
Loepker, Sarah/Odin Public School Dist 722	83,85,90	175
Loera, Jacqueline/East Maine School District 63	68	47
Loftin, Michael/Oak Lawn-Hometown Sch Dist 123	2,4,15	60
Lofton, Eboney/Oak Park Elem School Dist 97	9,18,69,294	60
Logan, Joanne/Mundelein Elem School Dist 75	2	153
Logan, Rebecca/Harlem Unit Sch District 122	9	252
Loghnane, Liz/Bannockburn Sch Dist 106	73	147
Logsdon, Kent/Red Bud Cmty Unit Sch Dist 132	73	205
Loiacono, Erica/Community Unit School Dist 200	71	91
Lois, Allison/North Boone Cmty Unit SD 200	12,298	5
Loizzi, Annie/Barrington Cmty Unit SD 220	297	147
Lolkema, Myra/South Holland School Dist 150	73,286,295	68
Lombard, Jessica/Huntley Cmty School Dist 158	9,15	182
Long, Courtney/Lombard Elem SD 44	67	97
Long, Geff/Mercer County SD 404	295	189
Long, Matt/Central School District 3	6	1
Long, Mindy/Cooperative Assn for Spec Ed	271	102
Long, Robert/Stewardson-Strasburg SD 5-A	5	216
Long, Tom/Galena Unit School Dist 120	67	125
Longis, Deb/Milford Area Public SD 124	7	119
Longo, Margret, Dr/Evergreen Park Elem SD 124	1	49
Lonigro, Lisa/Rhodes School District 84 1/2	7	64
Lonsdale, Bob/Wolf Branch School Dist 113	67	222
Lootens, Ryan/Silvis School District 34	6	209
Lopez, Al/Niles Twp High School Dist 219	91	58
Lopez, Anne/Lockport Twp High Sch Dist 205	67	244
Lopez, David, Dr/West Harvey-Dixmoor Pub SD 147	11,59,79	70
Lopez, Drew/Chaney-Monge School Dist 88	67	241
Lopez, Eliza/Arbor Park School District 145	57	21
Lopez, Francela/Berwyn North School Dist 98	49,57	22
Lopez, Gerardo/South Holland School Dist 150	3	68
Lopez, Joe/Joliet Twp High Sch Dist 204	3	243
Lopez, LaZaro, Dr/Township High School Dist 214	10,15,16,57,72,277,294,296	69
Lopez, Lori, Dr/Park Ridge Niles CMCSD 64	9,15	62
Lopez, Mike/Valley View Cmty SD 365-U	3	248
Lopez, Robert, Dr/Waukegan Cmty Unit SD 60	91	156
Loppnow, Jeff/Northbrook-Glenview SD 30	76	60
Lora, Danielle/Mt Pulaski Cmty Unit SD 23	9,59,88,288	164
Lorenzo, Heather/Community Cons School Dist 46	77,79	148
Lorsbach, Christie/Calhoun Cmty Unit Sch Dist 40	11,88,275,288,296	8
Lorton, Kerry/Central Illinois Rural Rvs	1	125
Lorton, Nate/Fieldcrest Cmty School Dist 6	12	257
Loschen, Darren/Armstrong Twp High SD 225	6,16,73,76,288,295	231
Lothian, Becky/Niles Twp High School Dist 219	76	58
Lott, Debbie/Athens Cmty Unit Sch Dist 213	2	188
Loucks, David/Herrin Cmty School District 4	67	251
Lough, Julie/Orion Cmty Unit Sch Dist 223	5	117
Louis, Larry/Pinckneyville Sch Dist 50	3	201
Louis, Paul/Community Cons School Dist 46	9,15,79	148
Louissaint, Roosevelt/Rich Twp High School Dist 227	295	64
Lovel, Larry/Trico Cmty Unit Sch Dist 176	1	121
Lovelace, Gloria/Spring Lake Elem SD 606	67	228
Lovelace, Jim/Ball Chatham Cmty Unit SD 5	5	211
Loveless, Abe/East St Louis Reg Voc System	73	223
Loveless, Abe/East St Louis Sch Dist 189	16,73,76,84	218
Lovell, Leannette/Carmi-White Co School Dist 5	83,270	237
Loving, Lori/Regional Office of Ed 33	15	141
Lowe, Bobbi/Hillsboro Cmty Unit Sch Dist 3	7,83,85	191
Lowe, Rc/Orion Cmty Unit Sch Dist 223	12,296	117
Lowery, Daren/Riverview Cmty Cons Sch Dist 2	1,73,83	258
Lowery, Michael/Kansas Cmty School District 3	273	103
Lowman, Debbie/Rankin Cmty School Dist 98	67	228
Lowman, Trisha/Central Cmty High School Dist 71	57,288	17
Loy, Amy/Peotone Cmty Unit SD 207-U	57,58,271,275	245
Lozano, Maria/West Aurora School Dist 129	57	132
Lubeck, Debbie/Pleasantdale School Dist 107	9,11,57,59	62
Lubelfeld, Michael, Dr/North Shore School Dist 112	1	154
Lucas, Blake/Community Unit School Dist 16	6	211
Lucas, Susan/Hall Twp High School Dist 502	38,69,88	6
Lucht, Cari/Red Bud Cmty Unit Sch Dist 132	5	205
Luchterhand, Sandy/East Dubuque Unit SD 119	11	125
Lucie, Jennifer/Warsaw Cmty Unit Sch Dist 316	11,296	115
Luckenbill, Jeanne/Mt Zion Cmty Unit Sch Dist 3	7	166
Luckert, Mari-Anne/Roxana Cmty Unit Sch Dist 1	4	172
Luckett, Denise/Gallatin Cmty Unit Sch Dist 7	2	110
Luckner, Amy/DeKalb Cmty Unit SD 428	69,70	84
Lueders, Shannon/Community Unit School Dist 308	10,69,288	137
Lueders, Shannon/Community Unit School Dist 308	10,69,288	137
Luedloff, Thomas/Community Cons School Dist 59	9,15	43
Luehmann, Joanna/Pontiac-Wm Holliday SD 105	9	221
Luehrs, Jacqueline/Forest Park School District 91	90	50
Lueke, Connie/Hamilton Co Cmty Unit SD 10	38	114
Lugge, Tiffany/O'Fallon Twp School Dist 203	38	221
Lukascy, Melanie/Waltham Elementary SD 185	288	145
Lukasik, Evan/Kenilworth School District 38	67	53
Lukemeyer, Veronica/Grant Cmty High Sch Dist 124	41,50,57	150
Luker, Neal/River Bend Cmty School Dist 2	31	239
Lum, Jaymie/Rockridge Cmty Unit SD 300	2	209
Lund, Andrew/McHenry Cmty Cons Sch Dist 15	91	183
Lund, David/Champaign Cmty Unit Sch Dist 4	3	10
Lundeen, Marty/Itasca School District 10	67	96
Lundeen, Megan/Geneseo Cmty Unit Sch Dist 228	274	117
Lundeen, Steve/DeKalb Cmty Unit SD 428	25	84
Lundquist, Geri/Prophetstown-Lyndon-Tampico 3	4	239
Lundrie, Gina/Pleasant Hill CUSD 3	2	203
Lunt, Charlotte/Oakwood Cmty Unit Sch Dist 76	5	232
Luosa, Brian/Waukegan Cmty Unit SD 60	2	156
Lusk, Frank/Flora Cmty Unit School Dist 35	5	16
Lustik, Jill/Minooka Cmty Cons Sch Dist 201	59	112
Luttrell, Jody/Maroa Forsyth CU Sch Dist 2	5	165
Lutz, Edith/Frankfort School Dist 157-C	67	242

Job Function Codes

#	Function	#	Function	#	Function	#	Function	#	Function	#	Function
1	Superintendent	16	Instructional Media Svcs	30	Adult Education	44	Science Sec	58	Special Education K-12	72	Summer School
2	Bus/Finance/Purchasing	17	Chief Operations Officer	31	Career/Sch-to-Work K-12	45	Math K-12	59	Special Education Elem	73	Instructional Tech
3	Buildings And Grounds	18	Chief Academic Officer	32	Career/Sch-to-Work Elem	46	Math Elem	60	Special Education Sec	74	Inservice Training
4	Food Service	19	Chief Financial Officer	33	Career/Sch-to-Work Sec	47	Math Sec	61	Foreign/World Lang K-12	75	Marketing/Distributive
5	Transportation	20	Art K-12	34	Early Childhood Ed	48	English/Lang Arts K-12	62	Foreign/World Lang Elem	76	Info Systems
6	Athletic	21	Art Elem	35	Health/Phys Education	49	English/Lang Arts Elem	63	Foreign/World Lang Sec	77	Psychological Assess
7	Health Services	22	Art Sec	36	Guidance Services K-12	50	English/Lang Arts Sec	64	Religious Education K-12	78	Affirmative Action
8	Curric/Instruct K-12	23	Music K-12	37	Guidance Services Elem	51	Reading K-12	65	Religious Education Elem	79	Student Personnel
9	Curric/Instruct Elem	24	Music Elem	38	Guidance Services Sec	52	Reading Elem	66	Religious Education Sec	80	Driver Ed/Safety
10	Curric/Instruct Sec	25	Music Sec	39	Social Studies K-12	53	Reading Sec	67	School Board President	81	Gifted/Talented
11	Federal Program	26	Business Education	40	Social Studies Elem	54	Remedial Reading K-12	68	Teacher Personnel	82	Video Services
12	Title I	27	Career & Tech Ed	41	Social Studies Sec	55	Remedial Reading Elem	69	Academic Assessment	83	Substance Abuse Prev
13	Title V	28	Technology Education	42	Science K-12	56	Remedial Reading Sec	70	Research/Development	84	Erate
15	Asst Superintendent	29	Family/Consumer Science	43	Science Elem	57	Bilingual/ELL	71	Public Information	85	AIDS Education

#	Function	#	Function
88	Alternative/At Risk	277	Remedial Math K-12
89	Multi-Cultural Curriculum	280	Literacy Coach
90	Social Work	285	STEM
91	Safety/Security	286	Digital Learning
92	Magnet School	288	Common Core Standards
94	Parental Involvement	294	Accountability
95	Tech Prep Program	295	Network System
97	Chief Information Officer	296	Title II Programs
98	Chief Technology Officer	297	Webmaster
270	Character Education	298	Grant Writer/Ptnrships
271	Migrant Education	750	Chief Innovation Officer
273	Teacher Mentor	751	Chief of Staff
274	Before/After Sch	752	Social Emotional Learning
275	Response To Intervention		

Illinois School Directory — DISTRICT PERSONNEL INDEX

NAME/District	JOB FUNCTIONS	PAGE
Lutz, Rose/Fieldcrest Cmty School Dist 6	2	257
Luzzo, Kelly/Lincoln-Way Cmty HS Dist 210	2	244
Lyday, John/Champaign Cmty Unit Sch Dist 4	71	10
Lyle, Juan/La Grange Elem Sch Dist 102	73,297	54
Lyle, Kim/DeKalb Cmty Unit SD 428	8,11,288,296	84
Lynch, Dennis/Hamilton Co Cmty Unit SD 10	67	114
Lynd, Eric/Pekin Cmty High Sch Dist 303	295	227
Lynde, Christine/Byron Cmty Unit SD 226	67	194
Lynenhale, Kathleen/Crete-Monee Cmty SD 201-U	7	241
Lynn, Jared/Mahomet-Seymour Cmty SD 3	84	11
Lynn, Kelly/Roselle School District 12	9,15	99
Lynne, Kelly/Roselle School District 12	9	99
Lyons, Jill/O'Fallon Cmty Cons Sch Dist 90	9	221
Lyons, Kevin/Big Hollow School District 38	67	148
Lyons, Kevin/Woodstock Cmty Unit SD 200	71	184
Lyons, Matt/Chicago Public School Dist 299	68	25

M

NAME/District	JOB FUNCTIONS	PAGE
Maas, Shelby/Mendon Cmty Unit School Dist 4	83	2
Mac, Cao/Cicero School District 99	16,71,84,97,295	42
MacChia, Joseph/Oak Lawn-Hometown Sch Dist 123	16,73,286,295	60
Maccrindle, Amy/Huntley Cmty School Dist 158	8,69	182
Machnikowski, Jan/Brookwood School District 167	4	24
MacHola, Paulina/Cary Cmty Cons Sch Dist 26	2	179
Macias, Dan/Rutland Cmty Cons SD 230	3	144
Macias, Jorge/Chicago Public School Dist 299	57,89,271	25
Macias, Laura/Elgin School District U-46	16,73,76,82,295	130
Mack, Oliver/Regional Office of Ed 48	88	201
Mack, Rodney/Community Unit School Dist 200	73,76,297	91
Macke, David/Marshall Cmty Sch Dist C-2	67	15
MacKenna, Beth/Rock Island-Milan Sch Dist 41	4	208
Macklin, Lara/Okaw Valley Cmty Unit SD 302	16,73	193
MacNamara, Jim/Sterling Cmty Unit Sch Dist 5	4	240
Madden, Sandy/Hinckley-Big Rock Cmty SD 429	12,54	85
Maddox-Reihl, Kimberly/Regional Office of Ed 17	275,298	188
Madison, Zena/Carbondale Elem School Dist 95	6	120
Madlem, Susan/Oblong Cmty Unit Sch Dist 4	2	83
Madueno, William/Pennoyer School District 79	43	62
Magdziasz, Thomas/Oak Lawn Cmty High SD 229	73	60
Maggiore, Martha/Prairie Grove Cons SD 46	9,83	183
Maginel, Paige/Dongola Unit School Dist 66	1	230
Magliano, Courtney/Community Cons School Dist 89	68	90
Magoulias, Dr/Rochester Cmty Unit SD 3-A	67	212
Magrini, Amy/Champaign Cmty Unit Sch Dist 4	5	10
MaGuire, Kim/Carlinville Cmty Unit SD 1	4	167
MaGuire, Michael/Union Ridge School Dist 86	1,11	70
Mahaffey, Monica/Berkeley School Dist 87	16	22
Mahaffy, Tim, Dr/Fox River Grove Cons SD 3	1,11	181
Mahalik, Geraldine/Laraway Cmty Cons SD 70-C	12,72	243
Maher, Lisa/Community Unit School Dist 200	2	91
Maher, Sheri/Ridgeland School District 122	9,12	64
Mahle, Gaylin/Centralia High School Dist 200	67	174
Mahon, Jessica/Chicago Public School Dist 299	285	25
Mahone, Nara/Harvard Cmty Unit Sch Dist 50	58,79	181
Mahoney, Kim/Steger School Dist 194	59	68
Mahoney, Thomas, Dr/Oregon Cmty Unit Sch Dist 220	1,11,83	195
Mahr, Bertie/Bushnell Prairie Cmty USD 170	4	178
Mair, Dan/Germantown Hills SD 69	1,11	257
Majchrowski, Erin/Morton Grove School Dist 70	2	58
Major, Dwight/Elementary School District 159	3	47
Major, John/Carbondale Elem School Dist 95	67	120
Majstorovic, Lela/Elgin School District U-46	10,15,78	130
Maki, Rita/Zion-Benton Twp High SD 126	5	157
Makula, Nino/River Grove School Dist 85-5	3	65
Malahy, Sandra/Lostant Cmty Unit Sch Dist 425	1,11,73,83,84,288	142
Malak, Tina/Lemont High Sch Dist 210	10,11,69,88,270,288	55
Malanowski, Jenny/Community Cons School Dist 204	2,84	201
Malanowski, Jenny/Williamson Co Special Ed Dist	2	252
Maldonado, Beatriz/Berwyn South School Dist 100	7,9,11,15,90,285,286,288	23
Malec, Su/Wood Dale School Dist 7	7	100
Malek, Jean/Lake Zurich Cmty Sch Dist 95	71	152
Malik, Nadia/Lyons Twp HS District 204	83	56
Malinee, Vera/Sesser-Valier Cmty Unit SD 196	2,71	108
Malinski, Beth/Westchester Public SD 92 1/2	59,88	70
Mallek, Stacey/Arlington Hts School Dist 25	2,15	21
Malley, Sue/Woodstock Cmty Unit SD 200	4	184
Mallory, James/Medinah Elementary SD 11	67	97
Malloy, John/Cmty Cons Sch Dist 146	67	42
Malmstrom, Ian/Colona Cmty School Dist 190	6	116
Malone, John/Northwestern IL Association	1,11	87
Malone, Susanna/Glenbard Twp High Sch Dist 87	12,57	94
Malusa, Kay/Pennoyer School District 79	59	62
Malusa, Michael/Pennoyer School District 79	67	62
Manahan, Colin/Bloomington School District 87	2,3,5,17,19,91	185
Mancke, Scott/Manhattan School Dist 114	67	244
Manderino, Micheal, Dr/Leyden Cmty High Sch Dist 212	10,11,69,72,288,296	55
Mandisodza, Melanie/Homewood School Dist 153	11,59,69,79	52
Mandrell, Kelly, Dr/Polo Cmty Unit Sch Dist 222	1,11,83	195
Mandujano, Rene/Belvidere Cmty Unit SD 100	57	4
Manecke, Sarah/Rowva Cmty School Dist 208	12	140
Mangan, Tim/Freeport School District 145	73	224
Mangold, Adam/Washington Cmty HS Dist 308	69	229
Manheim, Nick/Community Unit School Dist 303	67	128
Manier, Robert/Carrier Mills-Stonefort SD 2	16,73,286	210
Maniscalco, Domenico/Hinsdale Twp High Sch Dist 86	68,78	95
Manka, Tom/Dupage High School Dist 88	3	93
Manley, Jim/Dixon Cmty Unit Sch Dist 170	73	160
Manley, Leonard/Cahokia Unit Sch Dist 187	6	218
Mann, Greg/Morris Elem School Dist 54	73,84,295	113
Mann, Jessica/Northbrook School District 28	81	59
Mannen, Cathy/Tuscola Cmty Unit SD 301	67	88
Mansfield, Von, Dr/Homewood Flossmoor CHSD 233	1	52
Manter, Bob/Carrier Mills-Stonefort SD 2	298	210
Mantych, Kim/Nippersink School District 2	280	183
Manville, Peggy, Dr/New Lenox School District 122	11,57,83	245
Maples, Jon/Chicago Public School Dist 299	298	25
Maranto, Pasquale/Schiller Park School Dist 81	2	67
Marcelo, Pete/Yorkville Cmty Unit SD 115	15,58,88	139
March, Jason/Mendota Cmty School Dist 289	73,295	142
Marcinkewicz, Christine/Cass School District 63	73	89
Marcy, Ashalie/Le Roy Cmty Unit SD 2	16,82	186
Margliano, Joel/Kankakee School District 111	76	135
Mari, Lisa/Round Lake Area Co Dist 116	58	155
Marian, Sandra/Wauconda Cmty Unit SD 118	57	155
Marietta, Mat/Area 5 Learning Technology Hub	295	174
Marinello, Anthony/South Cook Interm Svc Center	8,79	82
Marino, Marilyn/North Palos School Dist 117	273	59
Markey, Paula/West Central Cmty Unit SD 235	1,11,83	116
Markovitch, Karrie/Mt Olive Cmty Unit Sch Dist 5	6	168
Marks, Beth/Shawnee Cmty Unit Sch Dist 84	8,79	231
Marks, Pam/Earlville Cmty Unit Sch Dist 9	27,36,69,83,270	141
Marks, Shelly/Homewood School Dist 153	67	52
Marky, Michelle/West Central IL Spec Ed Co-op	2	179
Marler, Barbara, Dr/Skokie School District 68	57,271	67
Marlin, Shannon/Peoria Public Sch Dist 150	79,294	198
Marlow, Chris/Central School District 3	67	1
Marlow, Jim/New Athens CUSD 60	8	220
Marotz, Kelly/Sandridge Sch Dist 172	9,69,74	66
Marquardt, Wally/Sandwich Cmty Unit SD 430	8,12,288	85
Marquith, Zac/Knoxville Cmty Unit SD 202	16,295	140
Marr, Shelly/North Palos School Dist 117	5	59
Marrero, Tammy/West 40 Interm Serv Center 2	88	82
Marron, Rich/Summit Hill School Dist 161	67	247
Mars, Norman/Harmony-Emge School Dist 175	5	219
Marsden, Karen/Galena Unit School Dist 120	2	125
Marsh, Jill/Geneva CUSD 304	42	131
Marshal, Jessica/Chicago Public School Dist 299	39	25
Marshall, Alex/Somonauk Cmty Unit SD 432	3,91	86
Marshall, Hailey/South Beloit Cmty Sch Dist 320	68	255
Marshall, Jennifer/Winnetka School Dist 36	295	72
Marshall, Karen/Dolton-Riverdale Sch Dist 148	71,73,76,286,294,295	46
Marshall, Kathy/Regional Office of Ed 28	15	118
Martel, Chad/Ball Chatham Cmty Unit SD 5	4	211
Martelli, Thomas/Kirby School District 140	67	53
Martin, Beth/Winnetka School Dist 36	11,37,59,77,79	72
Martin, Cheley/Canton Union School Dist 66	37,58,77,79	109
Martin, Christine/School Assoc for Sp Ed-Dupage	8,15,69	102
Martin, Deb/Homer Cmty Cons Sch Dist 33C	67	242
Martin, Greg/Benjamin Sch District 25	73,76	89
Martin, Joel, Dr/Park Ridge Niles CMCSD 64	15,68,273	62
Martin, Julie/Central City School Dist 133	275	174
Martin, Justin/Western CUSD 12	73,286	203

DISTRICT PERSONNEL INDEX

Market Data Retrieval

NAME/District	JOB FUNCTIONS	PAGE
Martin, Kevin/River Forest Sch Dist 90	16,73,76,295	65
Martin, Kim/Hamilton Cmty Cons SD 328	34	114
Martin, Kristi/Richmond-Burton Cmty HSD 157	6	184
Martin, Liz/Crescent Iroquois Cmty SD 249	280	118
Martin, Lori/Giant City Cmty Cons SD 130	67	121
Martin, MacKenzie/Benton Cons High Sch Dist 103	38	107
Martin, Maria/Lombard Elem SD 44	49,57	97
Martin, Mark, Dr/Brussels Cmty Unit Sch Dist 42	1,11	8
Martin, Sandra, Dr/Butler School District 53	2	89
Martin, Scott/Prairie Grove Cons SD 46	16,73	183
Martin, Sheila/Pekin Cmty High Sch Dist 303	10,11,15,69,288,296,298	227
Martin, Teresa/Will Co School District 92	88,270	249
Martinez, Diana/Rosemont Elem Sch Dist 78	57	66
Martinez, Elizabeth/Valley View Cmty SD 365-U	273	248
Martinez, Lena/Brookwood School District 167	15,59	24
Martinez, Sonia/Dupage Area Occupational Sys	2	102
Martinez, Trisha/Winfield School District 34	7	100
Martino, Peter/Community High School Dist 94	11,72,83,296,298	91
Martzluf, Cody/Illini Bluffs Cmty Unit SD 327	16,73,84	197
Martzluf, Cody/Limestone Walters CCSD 316	16	198
Marvel, Marsha/Rochester Cmty Unit SD 3-A	54	212
Marzolf, Don, Dr/Maine Twp High Sch Dist 207	11,69,280,298	56
Mascal, Amy Jo/Streator Twp High Sch Dist 40	10,11	145
Maschhoff, Jennifer/Nashville Cmty HSD 99	60	235
Maschhoff, Tesha/Nashville Cmty HSD 99	38,69	235
Mascitti, Ron/Chicago Heights Elem SD 170	3,91	25
Maselli, Anne/Archdiocese of Chicago Ed Off	71	72
Masini, Joe/Mendota Twp High Sch Dist 280	273	143
Mason-Schultz, Kathryn/Evanston-Skokie Cmty CSD 65	4	48
Mason, Graig/Cook County School Dist 130	9,45	45
Mason, Ruth/Waterloo Cmty Unit Sch Dist 5	4	190
Mason, Tracie/Lebanon Cmty Unit Sch Dist 9	7	220
Massaglia, Bobette/Astoria Cmty Unit Sch Dist 1	73,76,84,286,295	109
Massaro, Elizabeth/Plainfield Cons Sch Dist 202	58	246
Massey, Steve/Crescent Iroquois Cmty SD 249	67	118
Massie, Kelli/Clay-Jaspr-Richlnd-N Wayne EFE	1	16
Massie, Kelli/Flora Cmty Unit School Dist 35	27,31	16
Mast, Kim/Quincy School District 172	51	2
Masters, Tracy/Sesser-Valier Cmty Unit SD 196	12,31	108
Masterson, Terry/Bremen Cmty High SD 228	3,5,91	23
Masterson, Terry/Evergreen Park Cmty HSD 231	3	49
Mastey, Eric/J Sterling Morton HSD 201	27	53
Matan, Alan/Maine Twp High Sch Dist 207	57	56
Matar, Alyssa/Charleston Cmty Unit SD 1	2	19
Matcalf, Lora/Rochelle Cmty Cons SD 231	4	195
Mather, Alan/Chicago Public School Dist 299	27,36	25
Mathias, Sam/Chicago Public School Dist 299	70,750	25
Mathis, Dan/Southwestern Cmty Unit SD 9	83	168
Mathis, Mark/Fulton Co Cmty Unit Sch Dist 3	3	109
Mathison, Becky/Skokie School District 73 1/2	9,69	67
Matic, Marko/Community Cons School Dist 46	2	148
Matis, Jessica/Morton Grove School Dist 70	16	58
Matise, Joseph/Ridgeland School District 122	1	64
Matson-Dite, Elise/Archdiocese of Chicago Ed Off	68	72
Mattern, Daniel/Whiteside School District 115	3	222
Matteson, Michael/Rutland Cmty Cons SD 230	1,11,83	144
Matteson, Mike/Wallace Cmty Cons Sch Dist 195	1,11,73,83	145
Matthews, Dan/Clinton Cmty Unit Sch Dist 15	67	87
Matthews, Denise/River Forest Sch Dist 90	59	65
Matthews, Eric/Galesburg Cmty Unit Sch Dist 205	6	140
Matthews, Jackie/Illinois Dept of Education	71	1
Matthews, Jackie/Wayne City Cmty Unit SD 100	270	237
Matthewson, Clint/Farmington Ctl Cmty SD 265	73	197
Mattix-Wand, Gerry/East Alton-Wood River SD 14	73,295	170
Maturo, Karen, Dr/Hawthorn Cmty Cons Sch Dist 73	74	151
Matuszewski, Tressa/Kaneland Cmty Unit SD 302	58	132
Matzenbacker, Holly/Belleville Township HSD 201	4	217

NAME/District	JOB FUNCTIONS	PAGE
Mauck, Mary/La Salle Elem SD 122	59	142
Maunton, Josiah/Lebanon Cmty Unit Sch Dist 9	6	220
Maurer, Kevin/Knoxville Cmty Unit SD 202	3	140
Maville, Karla/Belvidere Cmty Unit SD 100	67	4
Maville, Karla/Boone Co Special Ed Co-op	67	5
Max, Jamie, Dr/West Aurora School Dist 129	10	132
Maxey, Kevin/St Elmo Cmty Unit SD 202	67	106
Maxey, Monica/Summersville Sch Dist 79	11,59,69,88,275	124
Maxey, Sarah/Shirland Cmty Cons SD 134	12	255
Maxheimer, Dianne/Riverview Cmty Cons Sch Dist 2	2,9	258
Maxwell, Brian/Somonauk Cmty Unit SD 432	73,76	86
May, Elliot/School Assoc for Sp Ed-Dupage	73	102
May, Jeremy/Zeigler Royalton CUSD 188	6	108
May, Joann/McHenry Cmty High Sch Dist 156	4	183
May, Lauren/Oak Lawn Cmty High SD 229	16	60
Mayer, Andy/Waterloo Cmty Unit Sch Dist 5	16	190
Mayer, Lee/Belleville Township HSD 201	6	217
Mayerhofer, Steven, Dr/Altamont Cmty Unit SD 10	1,11,83	104
Mayhall, Ryan/Niles Twp Dept of Spec Ed #807	76,295	82
Maynard, Kevin/Cumberland Cmty Unit SD 77	10,27	84
Maynard, Larry/Oakwood Cmty Unit Sch Dist 76	1	232
Mayoros, Mike/Community Unit School Dist 201	3	92
Mayster, Alex/Evergreen Park Elem SD 124	71	49
Mazurkiewicz, Carol/Sandridge Sch Dist 172	4	66
Mazza, Nick/Township High School Dist 214	295	69
McAbee, Maureen/Community Cons School Dist 59	9,15,57,288	43
McAdow, Brian/Woodstock Cmty Unit SD 200	15,68	184
McAllister, Megan/Valley View Cmty SD 365-U	79	248
McAnally, Lonie/Porta Cmty Unit Sch Dist 202	27	189
McAnally, Michelle/Newark Cmty High Sch Dist 18	69	138
McArdle, Lauren/Lake Zurich Cmty Sch Dist 95	15,58	152
McArthur, Bonnie/Thomasboro Cmty Cons SD 130	1,84	12
McAtee, John/Pleasantdale School Dist 107	16,98	62
McBride, Cheryl/Springfield Pub Sch Dist 186	4	213
McBride, Robert, Dr/Lockport Twp High Sch Dist 205	1	244
McBurney, Raven/A-C Central Cmty Unit SD 262	5	9
McCabe, Jim/Waltham Elementary SD 185	67	145
McCabe, Michael/Pontiac Cmty Cons Sch Dist 429	73	161
McCall, Clodagh/Lombard Elem SD 44	59,79,275	97
McCall, Valerie/Cary Cmty Cons Sch Dist 26	9,11,288	179
McCameron, Cheryl/Emmons School District 33	286	149
McCance, Sue/Fulton Co Cmty Unit Sch Dist 3	67	109
McCane, Gail/Tri-Valley Cmty School Dist 3	58	187
McCarthy, Dan/Argo Cmty High School Dist 217	38	21
McCarthy, Maria/Berwyn North School Dist 98	59	22
McCartney, Jeffrey/Winthrop Harbor School Dist 1	1,11	156
McCartney, Robert/Burbank School District 111	73,95,295,297	24
McCarty, Jeff/Nauvoo-Colusa CUSD 325	3	115
McCarty, Josh/Paris Cmty Unit Sch Dist 4	3	103
McCarty, Nicole/Bradley Elem School Dist 61	2,11	134
McCaskill, Chris/Brown Co Cmty Unit Sch Dist 1	16,82	5
McCaughan, Stephanie/Carterville Cmty Unit SD 5	2,84	250
McClain, Kelly, Dr/Bethalto Cmty Unit SD 8	68,79	169
McClain, Rebecca/Windsor Cmty Unit SD 1	2	216
McClarence, Janet/Frankfort School Dist 157-C	9,11,296	242
McClary, Liz/Emmons School District 33	16,73	149
McCleery, John/Bushnell Prairie Cmty USD 170	67	178
McClelan, Ryan/Red Bud Cmty Unit Sch Dist 132	11,296,298	205
McClellan, Craig/Joppa-Maple Grove Unit SD 38	73	177
McClelland, Rebecca/Greenfield Cmty Unit SD 10	84	111
McClendon, Sondra/Bellwood School District 88	67	22
McClenning, Wendy/Beardstown Cmty Sch Dist 15	73,76,286	9
McCleverty, Jack/Sandridge Sch Dist 172	3	66
McClintock, David/Alton Cmty School District 11	3,5,91	169
McClinton, Linda, Dr/Hazel Crest School Dist 152-5	9	52
McClinton, William, Dr/Elementary School District 159	67	47
McCloskey, Alana/Morton Grove School Dist 70	76	58

1 Superintendent	16 Instructional Media Svcs	30 Adult Education	44 Science Sec	58 Special Education K-12	72 Summer School	88 Alternative/At Risk	277 Remedial Math K-12
2 Bus/Finance/Purchasing	17 Chief Operations Officer	31 Career/Sch-to-Work K-12	45 Math K-12	59 Special Education Elem	73 Instructional Tech	89 Multi-Cultural Curriculum	280 Literacy Coach
3 Buildings And Grounds	18 Chief Academic Officer	32 Career/Sch-to-Work Elem	46 Math Elem	60 Special Education Sec	74 Inservice Training	90 Social Work	285 STEM
4 Food Service	19 Chief Financial Officer	33 Career/Sch-to-Work Sec	47 Math Sec	61 Foreign/World Lang K-12	75 Marketing/Distributive	91 Safety/Security	286 Digital Learning
5 Transportation	20 Art K-12	34 Early Childhood Ed	48 English/Lang Arts K-12	62 Foreign/World Lang Elem	76 Info Systems	92 Magnet School	288 Common Core Standards
6 Athletic	21 Art Elem	35 Health/Phys Education	49 English/Lang Arts Elem	63 Foreign/World Lang Sec	77 Psychological Assess	93 Parental Involvement	294 Accountability
7 Health Services	22 Art Sec	36 Guidance Services K-12	50 English/Lang Arts Sec	64 Religious Education K-12	78 Affirmative Action	95 Tech Prep Program	295 Network System
8 Curric/Instruct K-12	23 Music K-12	37 Guidance Services Elem	51 Reading K-12	65 Religious Education Elem	79 Student Personnel	97 Chief Information Officer	296 Title II Programs
9 Curric/Instruct Elem	24 Music Elem	38 Guidance Services Sec	52 Reading Elem	66 Religious Education Sec	80 Driver Ed/Safety	98 Chief Technology Officer	297 Webmaster
10 Curric/Instruct Sec	25 Music Sec	39 Social Studies K-12	53 Reading Sec	67 School Board President	81 Gifted/Talented	270 Character Education	298 Grant Writer/Ptnrships
11 Federal Program	26 Business Education	40 Social Studies Elem	54 Remedial Reading K-12	68 Teacher Personnel	82 Video Services	271 Migrant Education	750 Chief Innovation Officer
12 Title I	27 Career & Tech Ed	41 Social Studies Sec	55 Remedial Reading Elem	69 Academic Assessment	83 Substance Abuse Prev	273 Teacher Mentor	751 Chief of Staff
13 Title V	28 Technology Education	42 Science K-12	56 Remedial Reading Sec	70 Research/Development	84 Erate	274 Before/After Sch	752 Social Emotional Learning
15 Asst Superintendent	29 Family/Consumer Science	43 Science Elem	57 Bilingual/ELL	71 Public Information	85 AIDS Education	275 Response to Intervention	

IL-T38

Illinois School Directory — District Personnel Index

NAME/District	JOB FUNCTIONS	PAGE
McClure, Clifford/Paxton-Buckley-Loda CUSD 10	1	107
McCluskey, Dianna/Community Cons School Dist 15	2	42
McClusky, Katie/Glen Ellyn School District 41	9,15,294	94
McCollum, Tammy/Akin Elem School District 91	1,11,73,288	107
McComb, Max/Mahomet-Seymour Cmty SD 3	67	11
McConahay, Martin/Lyons Elem School Dist 103	2	56
McConnell, Anthony/Lemont-Bromberek Sch Dist 113A	1	55
McConnell, Brian/Rhodes School District 84 1/2	9,69,74,83,88,285,294	64
McConnell, Scott/Lake Zurich Cmty Sch Dist 95	67	152
McConnell, Treca/Goreville Cmty Unit SD 1	7	127
McConville, Joanna/Hall Twp High School Dist 502	10,60,271,273	6
McCord, Ron/Rock Falls Twp High SD 301	1	240
McCorde, Darrielle/J Sterling Morton HSD 201	71	53
McCormick, Jill/DeKalb Cmty Unit SD 428	24	84
McCormick, Kim/Bluford Unit School Dist 318	2	122
McCormick, Mike/Wilmington Cmty Unit SD 209-U	73,84	249
McCormick, Tammie/Astoria Cmty Unit Sch Dist 1	2	109
McCow, Donna/Creve Coeur Sch Dist 76	288	226
McCoy, Dale/Bismarck-Henning Cmty SD 1	73	231
McCoy, Jennifer/Pontiac Twp High Sch Dist 90	10,56	161
McCoy, Joe/Flora Cmty Unit School Dist 35	67	16
McCoy, Mike/Serena Cmty Unit School Dist 2	3	144
McCoy, Miriam/Elementary School District 159	57	47
McCoy, Rodney/Bethel School District 82	67	122
McCoy, Tony/Elmwood Cmty Unit Sch Dist 322	10,27,60,270,273	196
McCracken, Jay/La Moille Cmty Unit SD 303	1,11,73,83	6
McCray, Alicia/Matteson Elem SD 162	67	57
McCreery, Shane/Mundelein Cons High SD 120	68	153
McCue-Newport, Laura/Washington Cmty HS Dist 308	4	229
McCue-Newport, Laura/Washington Cmty HS Dist 308	4	229
McCulley, Matt/Big Hollow School District 38	73	148
McCulloch, Dan/Community Unit School Dist 201	6	92
McCullough, Chris/Granite City Cmty Unit SD 9	4	171
McCullough, Leticia/Chaney-Monge School Dist 88	271	241
McCurdy, Heather, Dr/Reavis Twp HSD 220	10,12,298	64
McCurdy, Joseph/Oak Lawn Cmty High SD 229	5,15	60
McCurdy, Joseph/Oak Lawn Cmty High SD 229	4	60
McCurren, Josh/Christopher Unit Sch Dist 99	6	107
McCurry, Brandie/Valley View Cmty SD 365-U	68	248
McDade, Latanya/Chicago Public School Dist 299	8,18	25
McDaniel, Michael/Brookwood School District 167	3	24
McDermott, Bob/Rochester Cmty Unit SD 3-A	2	212
McDermott, David/Moline-Coal Valley SD No 40	2,4,5,19,31	207
McDermott, Katrina/Archdiocese of Chicago Ed Off	11	72
McDermott, Kimberly/New Trier Twp HS District 203	68	58
McDermott, Lizzie/Chicago Public School Dist 299	45	25
McDermott, Patrick/Freeport School District 145	2,7,15	224
McDermott, Paul, Dr/Forest Ridge Sch Dist 142	1	50
McDonald, Dianne/Joliet Twp High Sch Dist 204	7,10,44,69,85	243
McDonald, Kimberly/Lockport Area Special Ed Co-op	275	250
McDonald, Teresa/Crab Orchard Cmty Sch Dist 3	16,82	251
McDonnell, Anne/Saratoga Cmty Cons SD 60C	67	113
McDonnell, Anne/Streator Elem School Dist 44	57	144
McDonnell, Dan, Dr/Plainfield Cons Sch Dist 202	10	246
McDonnough, Lori/Nashville Cmty Cons SD 49	2	235
McDougal, Sarah/Fenton Cmty High Sch Dist 100	38	94
McDowell, Nancy/Hillsboro Cmty Unit Sch Dist 3	2	190
McDowell, Nick/Hardin Co Cmty Unit Sch Dist 1	67	115
McDowell, Nina/Salt Fork Cmty Unit SD 512	16	233
McDowell, Shelly/McClellan Cons SD 12	288	123
McEntee, Phil/Lombard Elem SD 44	2	97
McFadden, Dave/Hoopeston Area Cmty Unit SD 11	67	232
McFadden, Emily/Community Cons School Dist 15	73	43
McFarland, Jesse/Paxton-Buckley-Loda CUSD 10	58	107
McFarland, Scott/Springfield Pub Sch Dist 186	67	213
McFarling, Jesse/Ford Co Spec Ed Co-op	1	107
McFarling, Jesse/Gibson Cty-Melvin-Sibley CUSD5	58	106
McField, Denise/Evergreen Park Elem SD 124	79	49
McGehee, Dolores/McClellan Cons SD 12	4	123
McGeough, Una/Skokie School District 68	67	67
McGhee, Lynn/Seneca Cmty Cons Sch Dist 170	9,57,69,271,273,288,294	144
McGiles, Jana/Monticello Cmty Unit SD 25	68	202
McGiles, Mike/Jacksonville School Dist 117	15,17	192
McGill, Butch/Roxana Cmty Unit Sch Dist 1	67	172
McGill, Patrick/Glenbard Twp High Sch Dist 87	10,15,285,286,288	94
McGinn, Anthony/Community Unit School Dist 300	71	180
McGinnis, Hailey/Vandalia Cmty Unit SD 203	2	106
McGinnis, Patty/New Simpson Hill Cons SD 32	59	127
McGivern, Paul/Morton Grove School Dist 70	67	58
McGlade, Julie/Chicago PSD-Network 1	15	28
McGovern, Karen/Maine Twp High Sch Dist 207	2	56
McGowan, Michael/Sunnybrook School District 171	73,295,297	68
McGownd, Wes/Bartonville School District 66	16	196
McGrath, Angela/Stark Co Cmty Unit SD 100	36,69	224
McGrath, Haley/Arthur CUSD 305	2	87
McGrath, Jill/Riverside-Brookfld Twp SD 208	63	65
McGraw, Kevin/Triad Cmty School District 2	5	172
McGreer, Mary/Mt Vernon City Sch Dist 80	9,57,69,270,280,285,288	123
McGuan, Lesley/Seneca Twp High Sch Dist 160	2	144
McGuffey, Christopher/Joliet Twp High Sch Dist 204	10,27,30,72	243
McGuffin, Mindy, Dr/School Assoc for Sp Ed-Dupage	1	102
McGuire, Jennifer/Hillside School District 93	5,7,270	52
McGuire, Susan/Marengo Cmty High Sch Dist 154	297	182
McGuire, Travis/Hinckley-Big Rock Cmty SD 429	1,288	85
McGukin, Ryan/Woodland Cmty Unit Sch Dist 5	1	162
McGurk, Nick/Streator Twp High Sch Dist 40	60	145
McHolland, James/Evanston-Skokie Cmty CSD 65	6,35	48
McHugh, Jeff/Lake Forest School District 67	9	152
McHugh, Terri/Schaumburg Cmty Cons SD 54	71	66
McIlravy, Sherry/Knox-Warren Spec Ed District	15	141
McIlvain, Tim/Learning Tech Ctr of Illinois	1	13
McIntosh, Amy/Durand Cmty Sch Dist 322	4	252
McIntyre, John/West Carroll CUSD 314	67	9
McKay, Colleen, Dr/Cook County School Dist 130	1,11	45
McKay, Curtis/Belleville Township HSD 201	295	217
McKay, James/Brown Co Cmty Unit Sch Dist 1	3	5
McKay, James/Community High School Dist 117	1,11	148
McKay, Joan/Belle Valley School Dist 119	2	217
McKee, Amanda/Rome Cmty Cons Sch Dist 2	67	123
McKee, Mandy/Carbondale Cmty HSD 165	60,280	120
McKee, Sean/Whiteside School District 115	67	222
McKenna, George/Regional Office of Ed 48	15	201
McKenna, Kevin/Effingham Cmty Sch Dist 40	84	105
McKenzie, Michael/Peoria Public Sch Dist 150	2	198
McKinley, Russell/Reavis Twp HSD 220	67	64
McKinney, Kayla/Meridian Cmty Unit SD 223	7,83,85	194
McKinney, Michelle/Meridian Cmty Unit Sch Dist 15	16	166
McKissick, Scott/Hampton School District 29	1,11,73,83	207
McKune, Michelle/Tremont Cmty Unit SD 702	58	228
McLean Miller, Natalie/Anna-Jonesboro Cmty HSD 81	83,273	230
McLean, Keith/Crete-Monee Cmty SD 201-U	3	241
McLeeren, Gayla/Benton Cons High Sch Dist 103	297	107
McLemore, Natalie/Kenilworth School District 38	6	53
McLendon, Kirston/La Salle Elem SD 122	73,76,84	142
McLeod, Leslie/Community Cons School Dist 46	297	148
McMahan, Caroline/Deer Creek-Mackinaw CUSD 701	273	226
McMahan, Joseph/Vienna Public School Dist 55	57	127
McMahan, Joseph/Vienna Public School Dist 55	57	127
McMahon, Chris/Belleville Public Sch Dist 118	16,73,76,286,295	217
McMahon, Chris/Pontiac-Wm Holliday SD 105	67	221
McMahon, Joshua/J Sterling Morton HSD 201	11,15,74,83,271,273,275	53
McMahon, Kara/Community Unit School Dist 300	8,18	180
McMaster, Linda/Sparta Cmty School Dist 140	4	205
McMath, Brian/Chester Cmty Unit Sch Dist 139	3	205
McMillan, Lindsay/Richmond-Burton Cmty HSD 157	7	184
McMillion, Nick/Illinois Vly Ctl Sch Dist 321	71	197
McMorris, Nicole/Joliet Twp High Sch Dist 204	10	243
McMullen, Deb/Elgin School District U-46	42	130
McNeal, Laurie/Franklin-Jefferson Sp Ed Co-op	2	109
McNeal, Sunni/Joliet Public School Dist 86	15,78,79	243
McNeely, Bobby/Flora Cmty Unit School Dist 35	6	16
McNelis, Suan/Putnam Co Cmty Unit SD 535	58,77	204
McNickels, Chelsea/Joppa-Maple Grove Unit SD 38	83,88	177
McOnnell, Kate/Archdiocese of Chicago Ed Off	58	72
McParland, Bob/Community High School Dist 218	71	44
McPartlin, Amy/Prospect Hts School Dist 23	2,3,4,5,19	63
McPherrin, Ryan/Community Cons School Dist 93	71	90
McPherson, Zach/Du Quoin Cmty Unit SD 300	67	201
McQueeny, Molly/Regional Office of Ed Kane Co	71	134
McQuill, Tina/Virginia Cmty Unit Sch Dist 64	90	9
McSarland, John/Richland Co Cmty Unit SD 1	4	206
McShane, Linda/La Grange Elem Sch Dist 102	69	54

DISTRICT PERSONNEL INDEX

Market Data Retrieval

NAME/District	JOB FUNCTIONS	PAGE
McSwenney, Sean/Community High School Dist 218	41	44
McTague, Ryan, Dr/McHenry Cmty High Sch Dist 156	1,11,83	183
McVey, Larry/Springfield Pub Sch Dist 186	11,296	213
McVickers, Ryan/Mt Pulaski Cmty Unit SD 23	6	164
McWhorter, Laurin/O'Fallon Cmty Cons Sch Dist 90	59	221
McWilliams, Juanita/Prairie Hills Elem SD 144	16,76,286,297	63
Meadows, Robert/Sangamon Valley Cmty Unit SD 9	1,11	166
Means, Kevin/Southwestern Cmty Unit SD 9	5	168
Meardy, Ryne/Washington Cmty HS Dist 308	3	229
Meciej, Jill/Marquardt School District 15	9	97
Medina, Araceli/Cicero School District 99	57	42
Medina, Jose/Beach Park Cmty Cons SD 3	3	147
Medina, Margarita/Atwood Heights SD 125	57	21
Meehan, Mary/Aero Special Ed Co-op	88	82
Meek, Scott/Northbrook School District 28	273	59
Meese, Michelle/Oblong Cmty Unit Sch Dist 4	9,15,288	83
Megazzini, Steve/East Aurora School Dist 131	3,15	129
Megerle, Jodi/River Trails Sch Dist 26	13,15,34,59,78,83,88,275	65
Mehaffey, Trent/Columbia Cmty Unit SD 4	84	190
Mehochko, Christopher/Regional Office of Ed 24	1	113
Mehta, Tina/Lemont High Sch Dist 210	4	55
Meidel, Melanie/Elgin School District U-46	15	130
Meighan, Duane, Dr/Country Club Hills SD 160	1	45
Meighan, Dwayne/Freeport School District 145	8,12,15,16,31,57,285	224
Meilinger, Barbara/Elmwood Park Cmty Unit SD 401	7	47
Meinert, Carrie/Durand Cmty Sch Dist 322	7,85	252
Meister-Louria, Wendy/Community High School Dist 128	57	148
Meister, Dave/Morrisonville Cmty Unit SD 1	1,73	14
Meixner, John/Regional Office of Ed 26	1	179
Mejiakrag, Miroslava/Chicago Public School Dist 299	2,19	25
Melborne, Char/Regional Office of Ed 21	73,74	109
Melinder, Amy/Woodridge Elem Sch District 68	71	100
Mellenthin, Peggy/Fenton Cmty High Sch Dist 100	90	94
Melnick, Helen/Northbrook Elem School Dist 27	67	59
Meloy, Barbara/Earlville Cmty Unit Sch Dist 9	67	141
Melton, James/Prophetstown-Lyndon-Tampico 3	67	239
Memenga, Matt/Bradley Elem School Dist 61	3	134
Mendenhall, Jenny/Riverton Cmty Unit SD 14	58	212
Mendez, Amanda/Argenta Oreana Cmty Unit SD 1	31	165
Mendoza-Thomps, Melissa/Joliet Public School Dist 86	34,88	243
Mendoza, Anthony/Lincolnshre-Prairieview SD 103	5	153
Mendoza, Daniel/Arlington Hts School Dist 25	3	21
Mendoza, Donn, Dr/Round Lake Area Co Dist 116	1	154
Mendoza, Said/Queen Bee School District 16	76	98
Meng, Chrisitne/Patoka Cmty Unit SD 100	31,36,69	175
Menhanti, Ali/Township High School Dist 113	2,15	155
Menicocci, Elena/Lincolnwood Sch Dist 74	16	55
Meno, Christine/Patoka Cmty Unit SD 100	83	175
Mentgen, DeWayne/Starved Rock Assoc Voc Tech Ed	1	146
Mentgen, Laura/Allen-Otter Creek CCSD 65	73,295	141
Mentzer, Brian/Belleville Township HSD 201	1,11	217
Merar, Peg/Warren Twp High Sch Dist 121	60	155
Merboth, Angie/Serena Cmty Unit School Dist 2	11	144
Mercier, Aaron/Regional Office of Ed 8	1	225
Meredith, Rick/Raccoon Cons School Dist 1	3	175
Merritt, Michael, Dr/Gardner Cmty Cons SD 72-C	1	112
Merriweather, Rakyah/Thornton Twp High Sch Dist 205	297	69
Mertel, Diane/La Salle Elem SD 122	2	142
Mertes, John/Rhodes School District 84 1/2	73,295,297	64
Mertz, Carolyn/East Prairie School Dist 73	35,85	47
Mertz, Ehren/Indian Creek Cmty Unit SD 425	6	85
Meske, Gloria/Fairview South School Dist 72	68	49
Messenger, Angela/Hiawatha Cmty Unit SD 426	286	85
Messersmith, Dave/Western Area Career System	1	179
Messersmith, David/Western Area Career System	1	110
Messinger, Melissa/Evanston-Skokie Cmty CSD 65	71	48
Messmer, Shawn/Maine Twp High School Dist 207	10,15,280,288	56

NAME/District	JOB FUNCTIONS	PAGE
Messmer, Shawn/Maine Twp Spec Ed Program	8,15	82
Metgtzer, Leroy/Granite City Cmty Unit SD 9	3,91	171
Metzger, Kent/Mattoon Cmty Unit Sch Dist 2	3,91	19
Meyer, Bill/Elgin School District U-46	3	130
Meyer, Brian/Anna-Jonesboro Cmty HSD 81	16,73,76,286	230
Meyer, Charles/Bond Co Cmty Unit Sch Dist 2	73	4
Meyer, Danette/Schaumburg Cmty Cons SD 54	15,68	66
Meyer, Georgina/Roselle School District 12	83,90	99
Meyer, Jacqueline/Lincoln Cmty High Sch Dist 404	56	163
Meyer, Lisa/Pontiac Twp High Sch Dist 90	38,57,69,270	161
Meyer, Mary/Palos Cmty Cons School Dist 118	5	61
Meyer, Matt/Morton Grove School Dist 70	11,15,57,288,296,298	58
Meyer, Rosemarie/Wheeling Cmty Cons Sch Dist 21	9,15	71
Meyers, Ashley/Plainfield Cons Sch Dist 202	58	246
Meyers, Ashley/Plainfield Cons Sch Dist 202	58	246
Meyers, Denise/Auburn Cmty Unit Sch Dist 10	58	211
Meyers, Doug/Career & Tech Ed Consortium	28	225
Michaels, Rachel/Pennoyer School District 79	69	62
Michalik, Debra/Maine Twp High School Dist 207	68	56
Michaud, Dawn/Galesburg Cmty Unit SD 205	58,77,90	140
Michelini, Diane/Komarek School District 94	9,69,288	54
Michelini, Glen/Wheeling Cmty Cons Sch Dist 21	3	71
Michelli, Candy/Indian Prairie Sch Dist 204	74	95
Michels, Crystal/Mt Vernon Twp HS District 201	22	123
Michels, Joe/West Carroll CUSD 314	73,295	9
Michicich, Deborah/Evergreen Park Elem SD 124	4	49
Mickey, Melissa/Adlai E Stevenson HSD 125	2	146
Middelkamp, Scott/Columbia Cmty Unit SD 4	67	190
Middendorf, Michelle/Farrington Cmty Cons SD 99	59,88	122
Middlebrook, Elizabeth/Bradley Elem School Dist 61	77	134
Middleton, Donna/Oak Park Elem School Dist 97	7,13,34,37,59,77,88,752	60
Miener, Bill/Edwardsville Cmty Unit SD 7	16,73,76,82,295	170
Migalla, Elizabeth/Winnetka School Dist 36	76	72
Mihelbergel, Adam/Bannockburn Sch Dist 106	9,11,27,88,275,288,298	147
Mikelski, Diana/Township High School Dist 211	5	69
Mikol, Kristy/Woodstock Cmty Unit SD 200	58	184
Milam, Glenda/Shiloh School District 1	16,82	103
Milberg, Nicole/Chicago PSD-Network 6	15	31
Mildice, Roxanne/Community Unit School Dist 200	2	91
Milem, Chuck/Erie Cmty School District 1	83	239
Miles, Evan/Blue Ridge Cmty SD 18	6	87
Miles, Lori/Quincy School District 172	88	2
Miles, Ryan/Community High School Dist 117	73,98	148
Mileur, Charlene/Murphysboro Cmty Unit SD 186	7	121
Milewski, Fran/Johnsburg Cmty School Dist 12	36,57,58,69,79,88	182
Milledge, Traci/La Grange Elem Sch Dist 102	59	54
Miller, Amber/Shirland Cmty Cons SD 134	16	255
Miller, Anne/Community Unit School Dist 300	67	180
Miller, April/Beach Park Cmty Cons SD 3	9	147
Miller, Betty/Polo Cmty Unit Sch Dist 222	4	195
Miller, Chris/Fairfield Cmty High SD 225	67	236
Miller, Chris/Skokie School District 69	16,73,297	67
Miller, Debbie/Community Unit School Dist 308	7	137
Miller, Eric/Glenview Cmty Cons Sch Dist 34	2,15	51
Miller, Jackie/Nippersink School District 2	59	183
Miller, Jackie, Dr/Richmond-Burton Cmty HSD 157	13,60,83	184
Miller, Jay/Adlai E Stevenson HSD 125	60	146
Miller, Jennifer/District 50 Schools	5,6	226
Miller, Jeri/Goreville Cmty Unit SD 1	8	127
Miller, Johnnetta/West Harvey-Dixmoor Pub SD 147	1	70
Miller, Justin/Benton Cmty Cons Sch Dist 47	2,11	107
Miller, Justin/Canton Union School Dist 66	80	109
Miller, Justin/Joppa-Maple Grove Unit SD 38	2	177
Miller, Katie/Collinsville Cmty Sch Dist 10	76	170
Miller, Kelly/Henry-Stark Co Sp Ed Dist 801	76	118
Miller, Ken/Community Unit School Dist 308	68	137
Miller, Kenneth/Coal City Cmty Unit Sch Dist 1	67	112

1 Superintendent	16 Instructional Media Svcs	30 Adult Education	44 Science Sec	58 Special Education K-12	72 Summer School	88 Alternative/At Risk	277 Remedial Math K-12
2 Bus/Finance/Purchasing	17 Chief Operations Officer	31 Career/Sch-to-Work K-12	45 Math K-12	59 Special Education Elem	73 Instructional Tech	89 Multi-Cultural Curriculum	280 Literacy Coach
3 Buildings And Grounds	18 Chief Academic Officer	32 Career/Sch-to-Work Elem	46 Math Elem	60 Special Education Sec	74 Inservice Training	90 Social Work	285 STEM
4 Food Service	19 Chief Financial Officer	33 Career/Sch-to-Work Sec	47 Math Sec	61 Foreign/World Lang K-12	75 Marketing/Distributive	91 Safety/Security	286 Digital Learning
5 Transportation	20 Art K-12	34 Early Childhood Ed	48 English/Lang Arts K-12	62 Foreign/World Lang Elem	76 Info Systems	92 Magnet School	288 Common Core Standards
6 Athletic	21 Art Elem	35 Health/Phys Education	49 English/Lang Arts Elem	63 Foreign/World Lang Sec	77 Psychological Assess	93 Parental Involvement	294 Accountability
7 Health Services	22 Art Sec	36 Guidance Services K-12	50 English/Lang Arts Sec	64 Religious Education K-12	78 Affirmative Action	95 Tech Prep Program	295 Network System
8 Curric/Instruct K-12	23 Music K-12	37 Guidance Services Elem	51 Reading K-12	65 Religious Education Elem	79 Student Personnel	96 Chief Infomation Officer	296 Title II Programs
9 Curric/Instruct Elem	24 Music Elem	38 Guidance Services Sec	52 Reading Elem	66 Religious Education Sec	80 Driver Ed/Safety	98 Chief Technology Officer	297 Webmaster
10 Curric/Instruct Sec	25 Music Sec	39 Social Studies K-12	53 Reading Sec	67 School Board President	81 Gifted/Talented	270 Character Education	298 Grant Writer/Ptnrships
11 Federal Program	26 Business Education	40 Social Studies Elem	54 Remedial Reading K-12	68 Teacher Personnel	83 Video Services	271 Migrant Education	750 Chief Innovation Officer
12 Title I	27 Career & Tech Ed	41 Social Studies Sec	55 Remedial Reading Elem	69 Academic Assessment	83 Substance Abuse Prev	273 Teacher Mentor	751 Chief of Staff
13 Title V	28 Technology Education	42 Science K-12	56 Remedial Reading Sec	70 Research/Development	84 Erate	274 Before/After Sch	752 Social Emotional Learning
15 Asst Superintendent	29 Family/Consumer Science	43 Science Elem	57 Bilingual/ELL	71 Public Information	85 AIDS Education	275 Response To Intervention	

IL-T40

Illinois School Directory

DISTRICT PERSONNEL INDEX

NAME/District	JOB FUNCTIONS	PAGE
Miller, Kim/Beecher City Cmty Unit SD 20	2	104
Miller, Kimberly/Indian Prairie Sch Dist 204	79	95
Miller, Kris/Iroquois Co Cmty Unit SD 9	5	119
Miller, Lisa/Cambridge Cmty Unit SD 227	36,69,83,85	116
Miller, Mara/East Peoria Elem Sch Dist 86	37	227
Miller, Mark/Delavan Cmty Unit Sch Dist 703	73,295	226
Miller, Mark/Opdyke-Belle Rive Cmty CSSD 5	1,11,73,83	123
Miller, Mark/Riverview Cmty Cons Sch Dist 2	69,73,95	258
Miller, Marla/Sherrard Cmty Sch Dist 200	2,4	189
Miller, Maureen/Bremen Cmty High SD 228	57,63	23
Miller, Maureen/Winnetka School Dist 36	16,73,84	72
Miller, Michael/Henry Senachwine CUSD 5	1,11	176
Miller, Mike/Nokomis Cmty Unit Sch Dist 22	2,73,84	191
Miller, Monica/Community Cons School Dist 168	72,76	44
Miller, Perry/Rockridge Cmty Unit SD 300	1	209
Miller, Phil/Dongola Unit School Dist 66	67	230
Miller, Rick/Fox River Grove Cons SD 3	3	181
Miller, Rob/Sandoval Cmty Unit SD 501	1,11	175
Miller, Ryan/Benton Cons High Sch Dist 103	6	107
Miller, Seth, Dr/Westville Cmty Unit Sch Dist 2	1,11,288	233
Miller, Shannon/Plainfield Cons Sch Dist 202	68	246
Miller, Shannon/United Twp High Sch Dist 30	10,11,15,69,296	209
Miller, Steve/Harvard Cmty Unit Sch Dist 50	3	181
Miller, Steve/Lake Bluff Elem Sch Dist 65	3	151
Miller, Steve/Sherrard Cmty Sch Dist 200	286,751	189
Miller, Tabatha/Staunton Cmty Unit Sch Dist 6	16,82	168
Miller, Tamara/Venice Cmty Unit School Dist 3	2	172
Miller, Tracey/Community Cons School Dist 181	18,69,294	91
Miller, Tricia/Williamsville Cmty Unit SD 15	2,5	214
Millhouse, Erika, Dr/Sunnybrook School District 171	15,34,59,69,77	68
Milligan, Kim/Grayville Cmty Unit Sch Dist 1	36,69	238
Milligan, Stephanie/Harrisburg Cmty Unit SD 3	274	210
Mills, David/Silvis School District 34	9,11,288	209
Mills, Jill/Morris Elem School Dist 54	2	113
Mills, Sofia/Central Cmty Unit SD 301	57	128
Mills, Sophia/Kaneland Cmty Unit SD 302	57	132
Milner, Harold/General George S Patton SD 133	73,76,286	50
Milt, Terry/McClellan Cons SD 12	1	123
Milton, Colin/Bremen Cmty High SD 228	41	23
Mimer, Cris/Diocese of Rockford Ed Office	2	256
Minarich, Mary/Channahon School District 17	16,82	241
Minasian, Pat/Washington School Dist 52	1	229
Minch, Stephen/Springfield Pub Sch Dist 186	73,76,295	213
Miner, Chad/Erie Cmty School District 1	67	239
Miner, Micah/Maywood-Melrose Brdview SD 89	73	57
Minestra, Kim/Evanston Twp High SD 202	4	48
Mingus, Seth/South Pekin Grade Sch Dist 137	1,83	228
Mingus, Seth/South Pekin Grade Sch Dist 137	298	228
Minion, Tara/Rantoul City School Dist 137	68,71	11
Minkus, Gail/Glen Ellyn School District 41	76	94
Minor, Felicia/Edwardsville Cmty Unit SD 7	4	170
Minor, Mark/Benton Cons High Sch Dist 103	67	107
Minor, Mary/Odin Public School Dist 722	4	175
Minsley, Joshua/Lake Zurich Cmty Sch Dist 95	69,76	152
Minter, Jami/West Prairie Cmty Sch Dist 103	69	178
Miranda, Sam/Kildeer Countryside CCSD 96	3,5,91	151
Mirenda, Pam/Central Cmty Unit SD 301	4	128
Misener, Eric/Seneca Cmty Cons Sch Dist 170	1,11	144
Misfeldt, Michelle/Erie Cmty School District 1	2	239
Misner, Brad/Egyptian Cmty Unit Sch Dist 5	1	3
Missey, Jennifer/Millstadt Cmty Cons SD 160	83,90,270	220
Mitchell, Anita/Riley Cmty Cons Sch Dist 18	67	184
Mitchell, Dale, Dr/Homewood School Dist 153	1	52
Mitchell, Dan/Miller Cmty Cons Sch Dist 210	67	143
Mitchell, Heather/Benton Cons High Sch Dist 103	10,73,84	107
Mitchell, Jamey/Massac Unit School District 1	2	177
Mitchell, Karen/Bellwood School District 88	15	22
Mitchell, Mark/Ford Heights School Dist 169	67	49
Mitchell, Mark/Reed-Custer Cmty Unit SD 255-U	1	246
Mitchell, Nalo/Springfield Pub Sch Dist 186	36	213
Mitchell, Rick/Summersville Sch Dist 79	3	124
Mitchell, Roger/St Elmo Cmty Unit Sch Dist 202	3,5	106
Mitchell, Tamera/Joliet Public School Dist 86	2,15	243
Mitchell, Tanya/Cahokia Unit Sch Dist 187	11,36,68,69,88,288,294,296	218
Mitchell, Tim/Steeleville Cmty Sch Dist 138	67	206
Mitkova, Reni/Township High School Dist 113	30,57	155
Mitsdarffer, Joan/Central A&M Cmty Unit SD 21	5	14
Mlincsek, Ken/Community High School Dist 117	3	148
Moad, John/Granite City Cmty Unit SD 9	6,35	171
Moake, Jeff/Marion Cmty School Dist 2	3,91	251
Moan, Michael, Dr/Woodstock Cmty Unit SD 200	1	184
Mobley, Meagan/Wabash Cmty Unit Sch Dist 348	270	234
Moeller, Todd/O'Fallon Twp School Dist 203	6	221
Moen, Keenan/Indian Creek Cmty Unit SD 425	73,84	85
Mogge, Patrick/Township High School Dist 214	30,71	69
Mohen, Echelle/Calumet Public School Dist 132	73,285,286	25
Mohmmad, Sami/Elmhurst Cmty Unit SD 205	295	93
Mohn, Jim/Illini Bluffs Cmty Unit SD 327	3,5	197
Mohr, Therresa/Hononegah Cmty High SD 207	11,275	253
Molbeck, Elizabeth/Marengo Cmty High Sch Dist 154	4	182
Moller, Barb/Carbon Cliff Barstow SD 36	285	207
Mollet, Janet/Fox River Grove Cons SD 3	4	181
Mollett, Marcy/Mulberry Grove Cmty Sch Dist 1	11	4
Mollett, Nathan/Mulberry Grove Cmty Sch Dist 1	67	4
Molzen, Christy/Sullivan Cmty Unit SD 300	2,19	193
Mombela, Crissy/Skokie School District 68	59,77,296,752	67
Monaco, James/J Sterling Morton HSD 201	16,50	53
Monaghan, Susan/Deerfield Public SD 109	2	149
Monak, Annie/Skokie School District 73 1/2	82	67
Mondini, Sinikka/Naperville Cmty Unit SD 203	71	98
Mondragon, Dalila/Zion-Benton Twp High SD 126	68	157
Mongan, Esther, Dr/Central Cmty Unit SD 301	11,15,68,69,88,273,288	128
Mongon, Michael/Bremen Cmty High SD 228	6	23
Monn, Kris, Dr/Minooka Cmty Cons Sch Dist 201	1	112
Monroe, Jennifer/Signal Hill Sch Dist 181	2	221
Montana, Marilyn/Reed-Custer Cmty Unit SD 255-U	4	246
Montemayor, Maria/Cook County School Dist 130	5	45
Monterroso, Julieta/South Holland School Dist 151	59	68
Montgomery, Charolette/Ball Chatham Cmty Unit SD 5	2,19,298	211
Montgomery, Dena/Marengo Union Elem Cons SD 165	5	182
Montgomery, Nyla/Jonesboro Cmty Cons SD 43	12	230
Montgomery, Shinora/Dolton-Riverdale Sch Dist 148	9,93	46
Montgomery, Tim/Benton Cons High Sch Dist 103	3	107
Moody, Rebecca/Northwestern IL Association	8	87
Moon, Mina/Glenbrook High Sch Dist 225	57	50
Mooney, Angela/West 40 Interm Serv Center 2	71	82
Mooney, Shaun/Rockdale School District 84	73	247
Moore, Alex/Montmorency Cmty Cons SD 145	1	239
Moore, Brenda/Sullivan Cmty Unit SD 300	7	193
Moore, Brian/Anna-Jonesboro Cmty HSD 81	3	230
Moore, Cheryl/Community High School Dist 94	68	91
Moore, Christine/Riley Cmty Cons Sch Dist 18	16,73,295,297	184
Moore, Cynthia/Cahokia Unit Sch Dist 187	5	218
Moore, Jackie, Dr/Oak Park & River Forest SD 200	67	60
Moore, Jason/Opdyke-Belle Rive Cmty CSSD 5	6	123
Moore, Jeff/Cook County School Dist 104	5	44
Moore, Jodi/Leland Cmty Unit Sch Dist 1	1,11	142
Moore, Kim/Pleasant Plains Cmty Unit SD 8	88	212
Moore, Kristen/Avoca School District 37	59,69,83,88,270,275,752	22
Moore, Kristen/Skokie School District 73 1/2	59	67
Moore, Lee/West Prairie Cmty Sch Dist 103	67	178
Moore, Mark/Community Unit School Dist 303	2,10,15,68	128
Moore, Michael, Dr/Posen-Robbins Sch Dist 143-5	2,16	63
Moore, Rich/River Forest Sch Dist 90	67	65
Moore, Russell/Plainfield Cons Sch Dist 202	295	246
Moore, Ryan/Carbon Cliff Barstow SD 36	3	207
Moore, Sandi/Butler School District 53	2	89
Moore, Sandy/Fisher Cmty Unit School Dist 1	5	10
Moore, Sarah/Winnebago Co Special Ed Co-op	1	256
Moore, Steve/Winchester Cmty Unit SD 1	67	215
Moore, Susan/Trico Cmty Unit Sch Dist 176	4	121
Moore, Tracie/Cobden Cmty Unit Sch Dist 17	67	230
Moore, Trevor/Peotone Cmty Unit SD 207-U	2	245
Mora, Eberto/Community Unit School Dist 300	68,78	180
Morack, Robert/Reavis Twp HSD 220	6	64
Morales, Alfred/East Aurora School Dist 131	93	129
Moran, Allison/Oakdale Cmty Cons Sch Dist 1	73	236
Moran, Becky/Round Lake Area Co Dist 116	6	155
Moran, Christina/Crystal Lake Elem District 47	9,15	181
Moran, Maureen/Western Springs Sch Dist 101	59	71
Moran, Tim/Granite City Cmty Unit SD 9	27	171
Moreno, Janet/Maywood-Melrose Brdview SD 89	2	57

DISTRICT PERSONNEL INDEX

Market Data Retrieval

NAME/District	JOB FUNCTIONS	PAGE
Moreno, Lucero/Cook County School Dist 130	2,4,15	45
Moreno, Nadia/Marengo Cmty High Sch Dist 154	57	182
Moreth, Cary/Bloomingdale School Dist 13	67	89
Morey, Valerie/Woodland School District 50	57	157
Morford, Tim/Hillsboro Cmty Unit Sch Dist 3	38	191
Morgan, Christine/Belvidere Cmty Unit SD 100	73	4
Morgan, Derek/Central School District 104	6	218
Morgan, Heidi/New Lenox School District 122	16	245
Morgan, Justin/Trico Cmty Unit Sch Dist 176	73,295	121
Morgan, Kris/Olympia Cmty Unit Sch Dist 16	11,58,88,92,298	187
Morgan, Mary/Consolidated High Sch Dist 230	4	44
Morgese, Melisa/Wheeling Cmty Cons Sch Dist 21	2	71
Morphew, Kristen/Manhattan School Dist 114	9,288	244
Morrell, Brittnie/Virginia Cmty Unit Sch Dist 64	2,298	9
Morris, Brad/North Wamac School Dist 186	1,11,83,84,288	18
Morris, Julie, Dr/Harlem Unit Sch District 122	1	252
Morris, Lauretta/Marshall Cmty Sch Dist C-2	27,84	15
Morris, Maranda/Grayville Cmty Unit Sch Dist 1	12	238
Morris, Phil/Regional Office of Ed Kane Co	73,76,295	134
Morris, Scott/School Dist 45 Dupage Co	9	99
Morris, Sharon/United Twp High Sch Dist 30	7	209
Morrisey, Joe/Kansas Cmty School District 3	80,85	103
Morrison, Brittany/Bremen Cmty High SD 228	2	23
Morrison, Cherie/Springfield Pub Sch Dist 186	10,41,44,285	213
Morrison, Jd/Morris Cmty High Sch Dist 101	73,286	113
Morrisroe, Josie/Lake Zurich Cmty Sch Dist 95	2	152
Morrissey, Crysta/Community Cons School Dist 93	15,79,752	90
Morrissey, Michelle/Stark Co Cmty Unit SD 100	4	223
Morrow, Jay, Dr/United Twp High Sch Dist 30	3	209
Morscheiser, Sarah/La Salle Elem SD 122	83,90,270,273	142
Mortensen, Daniel/Aptakisic-Tripp Sch Dist 102	3	146
Morton, Adam/Regional Office of Ed 20	34	211
Morton, Jason/Meredosia-Chambersburg SD 11	67	192
Morton, Judy/Lemont High Sch Dist 210	2	55
Morton, Steve/Princeton Twp HSD 500	16,73,286,295,297	7
Mose, Michael/Mt Zion Cmty Unit Sch Dist 3	10	166
Moser, Gary/Will Co School District 92	3	249
Moser, Mark/Des Plaines Cmty Cons SD 62	6,35	45
Moses, Sarah/DeKalb Cmty Unit SD 428	67	84
Mosher, Jill/Harlem Unit Sch District 122	4	252
Moslander, Tina/Arbor Park School District 145	67	21
Moss, Mary/La Salle Elem SD 122	4,57	142
Mostacci, Michael/Schaumburg Cmty Cons SD 54	3	66
Moten, LeBaron/Waukegan Cmty Unit SD 60	3,17	156
Motley, Ann/Kansas Cmty School District 3	2	103
Motsch, Lori/New Lenox School District 122	1	245
Motsenbocker, Pamela/Fremont School District 79	68	149
Mounce, Adam/Berwyn North School Dist 98	67	22
Mount, Jeremey/Malden Cmty Cons SD 84	67	7
Mouser, Aime/Tri-Valley Cmty School Dist 3	16	187
Mouser, David/Tri-Valley Cmty School Dist 3	1,11	187
Moy, Jean/Niles Twp High School Dist 219	68	58
Moyer, David, Dr/Elmhurst Cmty Unit SD 205	1	93
Muckensturm, Eric/Pontiac-Wm Holliday SD 105	84	221
Mudd, Amanda/Prairie Du Rocher CCSD 134	4	205
Mudd, Victoria/Red Bud Cmty Unit Sch Dist 132	60	205
Mudge, Joan/East Alton Elementary SD 13	67	170
Muehleip, Jill/Galena Unit School Dist 120	9,12	125
Mueller, Cari/East Alton-Wood River SD 14	57	170
Mueller, Christine/East Moline Public Sch Dist 37	68	207
Mueller, Kathy/Grass Lake School District 36	2	150
Mueller, Kristi/Burbank School District 111	11,296,298	24
Mueller, Kylie/Steeleville Cmty Sch Dist 138	2	206
Mueller, Mary Ellen/Niles Elem School District 71	57	58
Mueller, Michelle/Regional Office of Ed 40	1	169
Muench, Cheryl, Dr/Park Forest Chicago Hgt SD 163	9,74	62
Muerhoff, Tammy/Rock Island Reg Off of Ed 49	1	210
Muhl, Tracy/Northbrook School District 28	67	59
Mulaned, Lily/Oak Grove School District 68	34,59	154
Mulheron, Melanie/Thornton Fractnl Twp HSD 215	68	69
Mulholland, Stephanie, Dr/Steeleville Cmty Sch Dist 138	1,11	206
Mullaney, Doug/Community High School Dist 94	6	91
Muller, Elizabeth/Odell Cmty Cons Sch Dist 435	12	161
Mulligan, Thomas/Arcola Cmty Unit Sch Dist 306	1,11	87
Mullin, Michelle/Kankakee School District 111	68	135
Mullins, Colleen/Community Cons School Dist 15	12,49,52,55,280,298	43
Mullins, Jay/Byron Cmty Unit SD 226	69,72,83	194
Mullins, Sean/McLean Co Unit District 5	286	186
Mullins, Sean/Olympia Cmty Unit Sch Dist 16	73,286	187
Mulvaney, Annie/Johnsburg Cmty School Dist 12	2,11,19,84,751	182
Mulvaney, Josh/Ball Chatham Cmty Unit SD 5	73,76,295	211
Mulvaney, William/Armstrong Ellis SD 61	1,11,83	231
Mulvaney, William/Armstrong Twp High SD 225	1,83	231
Mumford, Tiffany/North Greene Unit Dist 3	2	111
Mumm, Sarah, Dr/Kaneland Cmty Unit SD 302	9,11,57,69,275,298	132
Munch, John/Community Cons School Dist 181	15,68	91
Munda, Greg/Freeport School District 145	3,91	224
Munda, Mike/Lake County Regional of Ed	15	158
Munoz Breto, Nancy/School Dist 45 Dupage Co	15,68,78,273	99
Munoz, Nancy/Calumet Public School Dist 132	68	25
Munson, Dave/Warrensburg-Latham CU SD 11	67	166
Murillo, Brenda/Speed Seja 802	2	82
Murphy, Beth/Galena Unit School Dist 120	10,16,27,81	125
Murphy, Brandon/Dupage High School Dist 88	6	93
Murphy, Brian/Lincoln-Way Cmty HS Dist 210	10,69,70,76,275	244
Murphy, Chad/Ashton-Franklin Center SD 275	67	159
Murphy, Erin, Dr/West Northfield Sch Dist 31	1	70
Murphy, Erinn/Carbondale Cmty HSD 165	69,288	120
Murphy, Gregg, Dr/Iroquois-Kankakee Reg Off Ed	1	137
Murphy, Jennifer/Metamora Twp HS Dist 122	12	258
Murphy, Jim/Grant Cmty Cons Sch Dist 110	6	219
Murphy, Joseph/Argo Cmty High School Dist 217	2	21
Murphy, Kimberly/Lake Park Cmty High SD 108	60,88	96
Murphy, Melissa/Community Unit School Dist 200	8,11,15	91
Murphy, Melissa/North Palos School Dist 117	9,13,16,69,74,83,273,288	59
Murphy, Michelle/Kell Cons School District 2	35	174
Murphy, Patrick/Mt Olive Cmty Unit Sch Dist 5	1	167
Murphy, Steve/Carbondale Cmty HSD 165	1	120
Murphy, Temple/Community High School Dist 128	73	148
Murphy, Theresa/Cass School District 63	59	89
Murphy, Trish/La Grange Cmty School Dist 105	16,73	54
Murrah, Andria/Johnston City Cmty Unit SD 1	8,11,69,73,275,288,752	251
Murray, Jamie/Rockford School District 205	2	253
Murray, Jennifer/East Alton-Wood River SD 14	67	170
Murray, Jon/Geneseo Cmty Unit Sch Dist 228	80	117
Murray, Logan/Dwight Twp High School Dist 230	73	161
Murray, Mark/Will Co School District 92	6,16,82	249
Murray, Ryan/Oak Grove School District 68	83,88	154
Murtaugh, Susan/Aptakisic-Tripp Sch Dist 102	68	146
Musa, Tim/Community Cons School Dist 93	295	90
Music, Matt/Richland Co Cmty Unit SD 1	6	206
Musselman, Brian/Sterling Cmty Unit Sch Dist 5	3	240
Mutchler, Kent, Dr/Geneva CUSD 304	1	131
Mycyk, Mary/Cicero School District 99	46	42
Myers, David/Peoria Public Sch Dist 150	3	198
Myers, Jill/Macomb Cmty Unit Sch Dist 185	67	178
Myers, Josh/Sangamon Valley Cmty Unit SD 9	6	166
Myers, Kevin/Mundelein Elem School Dist 75	1	153
Myers, Kevin, Dr/Mundelein Cons High SD 120	1	153
Myers, Nick, Dr/Schaumburg Cmty Cons SD 54	15	66
Myers, Shannon/Mt Vernon City Sch Dist 80	7	123
Myers, Tiffany/New Trier Twp HS District 203	77,90	58
Myszka, Nancy/Schiller Park School Dist 81	4	67

1 Superintendent	16 Instructional Media Svcs	30 Adult Education	44 Science Sec	58 Special Education K-12	72 Summer School	88 Alternative/At Risk	277 Remedial Math K-12
2 Bus/Finance/Purchasing	17 Chief Operations Officer	31 Career/Sch-to-Work K-12	45 Math K-12	59 Special Education Elem	73 Instructional Tech	89 Multi-Cultural Curriculum	280 Literacy Coach
3 Buildings And Grounds	18 Chief Academic Officer	32 Career/Sch-to-Work Elem	46 Math Elem	60 Special Education Sec	74 Inservice Training	90 Social Work	285 STEM
4 Food Service	19 Chief Financial Officer	33 Career/Sch-to-Work Sec	47 Math Sec	61 Foreign/World Lang K-12	75 Marketing/Distributive	91 Safety/Security	286 Digital Learning
5 Transportation	20 Art K-12	34 Early Childhood Ed	48 English/Lang Arts K-12	62 Foreign/World Lang Elem	76 Info Systems	92 Magnet School	288 Common Core Standards
6 Athletic	21 Art Elem	35 Health/Phys Education	49 English/Lang Arts Elem	63 Foreign/World Lang Sec	77 Psychological Assess	93 Parental Involvement	294 Accountability
7 Health Services	22 Art Sec	36 Guidance Services K-12	50 English/Lang Arts Sec	64 Religious Education K-12	78 Affirmative Action	94 Tech Prep Program	295 Network System
8 Curric/Instruct K-12	23 Music K-12	37 Guidance Services Elem	51 Reading K-12	65 Religious Education Elem	79 Student Personnel	97 Chief Information Officer	296 Title II Programs
9 Curric/Instruct Elem	24 Music Elem	38 Guidance Services Sec	52 Reading Elem	66 Religious Education Sec	80 Driver Ed/Safety	98 Chief Technology Officer	297 Webmaster
10 Curric/Instruct Sec	25 Music Sec	39 Social Studies K-12	53 Reading Sec	67 School Board President	81 Gifted/Talented	270 Character Education	298 Grant Writer/Ptnrships
11 Federal Program	26 Business Education	40 Social Studies Elem	54 Remedial Reading K-12	68 Teacher Personnel	82 Video Services	271 Migrant Education	750 Chief Innovation Officer
12 Title I	27 Career & Tech Ed	41 Social Studies Sec	55 Remedial Reading Elem	69 Academic Assessment	83 Substance Abuse Prev	273 Teacher Mentor	751 Chief of Staff
13 Title V	28 Technology Education	42 Science K-12	56 Remedial Reading Sec	70 Research/Development	84 Erate	274 Before/After Sch	752 Social Emotional Learning
15 Asst Superintendent	29 Family/Consumer Science	43 Science Elem	57 Bilingual/ELL	71 Public Information	85 AIDS Education	275 Response To Intervention	

Illinois School Directory

DISTRICT PERSONNEL INDEX

NAME/District	JOB FUNCTIONS	PAGE
N		
Nacke, Shelley/Community Unit School Dist 300	15,58,83,85	180
Naddeu, Jennifer/Schaumburg Cmty Cons SD 54	59	66
Nadler, Julia, Dr/Wauconda Cmty Unit SD 118	15	155
Nagel, Charles, Dr/Spring Lake Elem SD 606	1,11	228
Nagel, Stacy/Abingdon-Avon Cmty Unit SD 276	69	139
Nagel, Tricia/Joliet Public School Dist 86	9	243
Naglak, Darek/Lyons Elem School Dist 103	9	56
Nail, Dustin/Damiansville School Dist 62	1,11,288	18
Naleway, Rachel/West Aurora School Dist 129	58	132
Napier, Shelia/Carmi-White Co School Dist 5	2	237
Nascimento, Misael/Rockford School District 205	57	254
Nash, Judie/Valley View Cmty SD 365-U	15,68	248
Nash, Natalie/Crete-Monee Cmty SD 201-U	71	242
Nash, Veronica, Dr/Chicago Public School Dist 299	81,92	25
Nasinska, Krystyna/Reavis Twp HSD 220	57	64
Nason, Dave/Central Sch Dist 51	73,76,295	225
Nasshan, Kim, Dr/Lincolnwood Sch Dist 74	1	55
Nault, Jason/Waukegan Cmty Unit SD 60	294	156
Nauman, Shelley/Spring Valley Cmty Cons SD 99	270,273	7
Nauman, Shelly/Spring Valley Cmty Cons SD 99	9,59	7
Nava, Nancy/Grass Lake School District 36	91	150
Navarre, Lenell, Dr/Bloom Twp High Sch Dist 206	1,11	23
Navarre, Torie/Dolton-Riverdale Sch Dist 148	275	46
Naville, Kelly/East Alton-Wood River SD 14	7,85	170
Neabuhr, Sandra/Irvington Cmty Cons SD 11	67	235
Neahring, Marti/West Aurora School Dist 129	79,91,752	132
Neal, Harrison/Crete-Monee Cmty SD 201-U	15,68	241
Neal, Jean/Georgetown-Ridge Farm CUSD 4	1,11	232
Neal, Jenny/Evanston Twp High SD 202	57	48
Neal, M C/Urbana School District 116	73,76	12
Nealon, Elisabeth/Cicero School District 99	15,79	42
Neathery, Mekelle/Virginia Cmty Unit Sch Dist 64	8,11,285,288,296	9
Neaveill, Jodi/Cerro Gordo Cmty Unit SD 100	9,12,274	202
Nedved, Peter/Orion Cmty Unit Sch Dist 223	67	117
Neeley, Jennifer/Grayville Cmty Unit Sch Dist 1	7	238
Neeley, Maria/Grayville Cmty Unit Sch Dist 1	2	238
Neeley, Tom/Morton Cmty Unit Sch Dist 709	67	227
Neese, Kelsi/Western CUSD 12	2	203
Neff, Erin/La Harpe Cmty Sch Dist 347	16	115
Negron, David/Maywood-Melrose Brdview SD 89	1,11	57
Neibuhr, Brock/Paxton-Buckley-Loda CUSD 10	6	107
Neilon, Joe/Community High School Dist 94	286,297	91
Nelk, Tedra/Oakland Cmty Unit Sch Dist 5	90,752	19
Nell, Joanne/Spoon River Valley Cmty SD 4	58	110
Nelsen, James/Pennoyer School District 79	6,35	62
Nelson, Alonzo/East St Louis Sch Dist 189	3	218
Nelson, Angela/Fenton Cmty High School Dist 100	33	94
Nelson, Brooke/East Peoria Cmty HS Dist 309	82	226
Nelson, Catherine/Crystal Lake Elem Dist 47	2,15	181
Nelson, Christine/Reed-Custer Cmty Unit SD 255-U	8,11,15	246
Nelson, Deb/Macomb Cmty Unit Sch Dist 185	5	178
Nelson, Ernie/Skokie School District 68	3,5	67
Nelson, Greg/Waverly Cmty Unit SD 6	73,76,286	193
Nelson, Jacob/Frankfort School Dist 157-C	16,73,95,295	242
Nelson, Jim/North Dupage Spec Ed Co-op	1	102
Nelson, Julie/Henry Senachwine CUSD 5	58	176
Nelson, Kathy/Delavan Cmty Unit Sch Dist 703	16	226
Nelson, Kim/Moline-Coal Valley SD No 40	7,85	207
Nelson, Kimberly/Rockford School District 205	34	254
Nelson, Kyle/Canton Union School Dist 66	4	109
Nelson, Marie/Madison Cmty Unit Sch Dist 12	67	172
Nelson, Mark/Mattoon Cmty Unit Sch Dist 2	5	19
Nelson, Preston/Edwards Co Cmty Unit SD 1	8,288	104
Nelson, Sheila/Cairo School District 1	67	3
Nemeth, Brian/Kirby School District 140	73,98	53
Nero, Denise/River Grove School Dist 85-5	79	65
Ness, Elizabeth/Somonauk Cmty Unit SD 432	6	86
Netemeier, Michael/Central Cmty High Sch Dist 71	67	17
Nettles, Curt/Clinton Cmty Unit Sch Dist 15	1	87
Nettles, Paul/Creve Coeur Sch Dist 76	6	226
Nettleton, Kelly/School Dist 45 Dupage Co	34	99
Neubauer, Carl/Tri-Valley Cmty School Dist 3	67	187
Neubaum, John/Armstrong Twp High SD 225	5	231
Neumann, Linda/Indian Springs Sch Dist 109	4	52
Neuner, Kenneth/Mascoutah Cmty Sch Dist 19	5	220
Nevarez, Lorenzo/Ridgeland School District 122	57	64
Neville, Kristina/Tazewell-Mason Sp Ed Assoc	1	229
Nevius, Lisa/Waverly Cmty Unit SD 6	2	193
Newby, William, Dr/Grass Lake School District 36	1	150
Newell, Christine/Lyons Elem School Dist 103	88	56
Newell, David/Egyptian Cmty Unit Sch Dist 5	5	3
Newell, Jarrod/Carmi-White Co School Dist 5	10,27	237
Newendyke, Jen/Regional Office of Ed 8	15	225
Newkirk, Brad, Dr/Batavia Unit School Dist 101	8,11,18,57,69,273,288	128
Newlan, Terry/Robein Cmty School District 85	4	228
Newlin, Monte/Regional Office of Ed 12	1	207
Newman, Veda/Evergreen Park Elem SD 124	7,57,77,79	49
Newman, Veda/Richland School Dist 88A	57	247
Newsome, Nicole/Rhodes School District 84 1/2	59	64
Ney, Scott/Geneva CUSD 304	3	131
Nice, Amy/Teutopolis Cmty Unit SD 50	16	105
Nicholas, Daniel/Round Lake Area Co Dist 116	39	155
Nicholas, Doug/River Ridge Cmty Unit SD 210	73,295	126
Nichols, Brian/Oak Lawn-Hometown Sch Dist 123	67	60
Nichols, Dana/Harvey Public School Dist 152	9,68,285,288	51
Nichols, Joseph/Geneseo Cmty Unit Sch Dist 228	6	117
Nichols, Joshua/Amboy Cmty Unit Sch Dist 272	1,11	159
Nichols, Raynard/Madison Cmty Unit Sch Dist 12	73,84	172
Niebrugge, Cory/Dieterich Community Unit SD 30	67	104
Niedermeyer, Robert/J Sterling Morton HSD 201	73	53
Niedospial, David/Lockport Twp High Sch Dist 205	5	244
Niedringhause, Tiffany/O'Fallon Twp School Dist 203	11,74	221
Niehaus, Gary/Community Unit School Dist 7	5	167
Niemeier, Lori/Community Unit School Dist 16	2,11,19,296,298	211
Niemeyer, Lisa/Aviston Elem School Dist 21	273	17
Nighswander, Joe/New Simpson Hill Cons SD 32	1,84	127
Nikkila, David/Community High School Dist 117	295	148
Nikolic, Vesna/Gower School District 62	2,19	94
Nikolic, Vesna/Gower School District 62	2,19	94
Niles, Grady/O'Fallon Cmty Cons Sch Dist 90	84	221
Niles, Grady/O'Fallon Cmty Cons Sch Dist 90	73	221
Niles, Mary/Community Cons School Dist 59	46	43
Nimke, Jennifer/Lombard Elem SD 44	71	97
Nissen, Suzanne/West Chicago Elementary SD 33	79	99
Nissen, Vickie/Community Cons School Dist 59	2,15	43
Nix, Amanda/Athens Cmty Unit Sch Dist 213	4	188
Noble, Brett/Galena Unit School Dist 120	6	125
Noble, Mike/West Carroll CUSD 314	58	9
Noble, Molly/Amboy Cmty Unit Sch Dist 272	2	159
Noccio, Blair, Dr/Indian Springs Sch Dist 109	1,83	52
Nochnagel, Gary/Argo Cmty High School Dist 217	3	21
Nohelty, Kevin, Dr/Dolton-Riverdale Sch Dist 148	1	46
Noisey, Stacey/Lake Zurich Cmty Sch Dist 95	8,34,57,273	152
Nolan, Beth/Decatur Public Schools 61	67	165
Nolan, Bob/West Carroll CUSD 314	5	9
Noland, Tabatha/Unity Point Cmty Cons SD 140	16,82	121
Nolasco, Raymond/Spring Valley Cmty Cons SD 99	67	7
Nolde, Jennifer/Community High School Dist 117	2,15,298	148
Nolen, Jim/North Boone Cmty Unit SD 200	3,91	5
Nolten, Patrick/Naperville Cmty Unit SD 203	15,294	98
Nordstrom, Matt/Annawan Cmty Unit SD 226	1	116
Norman, Keith/Jersey Cmty Sch Dist 100	73,295,297	125
Norrell, Jennifer, Dr/East Aurora School Dist 131	1	129
Norris, Kathy/Carlinville Cmty Unit SD 1	67	167
Norris, Nadine/Community Unit School Dist 201	8,16,73,76,286,288,295	92
North, Bridget/Channahon School District 17	59	241
Northrup, Christine/Mahomet-Seymour Cmty SD 3	58	11
Norton, Amber/Mercer County SD 404	73	189
Norton, Kristen/Alden-Hebron School Dist 19	57,271	179
Norton, Mike/Alden-Hebron School Dist 19	67	179
Norton, Vicki/Smithton Cmty Cons SD 130	9,59,69,83,88,270	222
Norville, Karen/Homer Cmty Cons Sch Dist 33C	9,11,298	242
Norway, Amanda/Galva Cmty Unit Sch Dist 224	16,73,76,82	117
Nottke, Regina/Park Forest Chicago Hgt SD 163	15,59	62
Nottmeyer, Hope/Salem Cmty High Sch Dist 600	16,82	175
Novack, Paul/Bensenville Elem Sch Dist 2	2,19	89
Novak, Eric/Reavis Twp HSD 220	2,4,11	64
Novara, Len/Murphysboro Cmty Unit SD 186	6	121
Novotny, Cheryl/Center Cass Sch Dist 66	274	90
Novotny, Kristin/Bloomingdale School Dist 13	16	89

DISTRICT PERSONNEL INDEX

Market Data Retrieval

NAME/District	JOB FUNCTIONS	PAGE
Novotny, Mandy/New Lenox School District 122	59	245
Novotny, Rod/Downers Grove School Dist 58	295	93
Novsek, Joe/Breese Elementary SD 12	1	17
Nowakowski, Ben, Dr/Community Cons School Dist 180	2,11	90
Noyes, Douglas/Elmwood Park Cmty Unit SD 401	6,35,80,85	47
Nugent, Sean/Maercker School District 60	1,83	97
Nunez, Carlos/Hillside School District 93	73	52
Nunn, Megan/South Fork School Dist 14	4	14
Nunn, Megan/Taylorville Cmty Unit SD 3	4	15
Nunnally, Sherie/South Holland School Dist 150	67	68
Nusbaumer, Jackie/Nettle Creek Cmty SD 24-C	67	113
Nush, Eric/Homer Cmty Cons Sch Dist 33C	73	242
Nuss, Erin/Gibson Cty-Melvin-Sibley CUSD5	11,57,69,79,285,288,296,298	106
Nuss, Lisa/Community Cons School Dist 15	15,68	43
Nutt, Carol/Carbon Cliff Barstow SD 36	7	207
Nutter, Doug/Pekin Cmty High Sch Dist 303	35,80	227
Nuxoll, Trent/Mahomet-Seymour Cmty SD 3	2	11
Nyhlen, Beth/Center Cass Sch Dist 66	6	90
Nykasa, April/Bremen Cmty High SD 228	27,29	23
Nylen, Laura/Indian Prairie Sch Dist 204	286	95

O

NAME/District	JOB FUNCTIONS	PAGE
O Daniel, Jessica/Frankfort Cmty Unit SD 168	93	108
O'Brien, Kimberly/Riley Cmty Cons Sch Dist 18	13,57,59	184
O'Brien, Laurel/Glen Ellyn School District 41	79	94
O'Brien, Terry/Beach Park Cmty Cons SD 3	2	147
O'Connell, Jeff, Dr/Lake Park Cmty High SD 108	2,3,5,15,91	96
O'Connell, Peg/Berkeley School Dist 87	67	22
O'Connor, Julie/Western Springs Sch Dist 101	67	71
O'Connor, Kathleen/Kankakee School District 111	15	135
O'Connor, Patricia/Community Cons School Dist 181	2	91
O'Daniell, Brent/Genoa-Kingston Cmty SD 424	1	85
O'Day, Paul/Warsaw Cmty Unit Sch Dist 316	36,69,83	115
O'Dea, Stacy/Wauconda Cmty Unit SD 118	58	155
O'Dell, Nathan/Geneseo Cmty Unit Sch Dist 228	83,273	117
O'Donnell, Laura/Olympia Cmty Unit Sch Dist 16	1,288	187
O'Flanagan, Kayli/Miller Cmty Cons Sch Dist 210	73,295	143
O'Hara, Kim/Community Unit School Dist 308	76	137
O'Keeffe, Brian/Arbor Park School District 145	2,3,5,11,15	21
O'Leary, Mary/Prairie Grove Cons SD 46	16	183
O'Malley, Michelle/Dolton-Riverdale Sch Dist 148	4	46
O'Neil, Andrew/Champaign Cmty Unit Sch Dist 4	58	10
O'Neil, Gineen, Dr/Southwest Cook Co Assc Spec Ed	1	82
O'Neill, Dennis/Harmony-Emge School Dist 175	2	219
O'Neill, Gloria/Crete-Monee Cmty SD 201-U	5	241
O'Neill, Shannon/Barrington Cmty Unit SD 220	74	147
O'Riley, Doug/Galva Cmty Unit Sch Dist 224	1,11	117
O'Rourke, Thomas/Mt Prospect School Dist 57	68	58
O'Shea, Heide/Galena Unit School Dist 120	58	125
O'Shea, Jerome, Dr/Marquardt School District 15	1	97
O'Shea, Michelle/Plainfield Cons School Dist 202	57	246
O'Shea, Tom/Bremen Cmty High SD 228	50,53	23
O'Sullivan, Mary/J Sterling Morton HSD 201	47	53
Oates, Keith, Dr/Marion Cmty School Dist 2	1	251
Obafemi, Raphael/Evanston-Skokie Cmty CSD 65	2,3,17,19,298	48
Oberg, Dan/Community High School Dist 94	2	91
Obert, Jody/Liberty Cmty Unit Sch Dist 2	12	2
Obidi, Siania/Oak Park Elem School Dist 97	68	60
Obrill, David/Mt Prospect School Dist 57	3	58
Obsuszt, Mike/Barrington Cmty Unit SD 220	6	147
Ocenas, Dan/Antioch Cmty Cons Sch Dist 34	295	146
Ochoa, Ana, Dr/Burbank School District 111	2,4,5	24
Ochs, Jim/Potomac Cmty Unit Sch Dist 10	73,286	232
Ochs, Lauren/Mahomet-Seymour Cmty SD 3	16	11
Oconnell, Cynthia/Newark Cmty Cons Sch Dist 66	6	138
Oddo, Jacqui/Hillside School District 93	4	52
Odin, Jenn/Homewood Flossmoor CHSD 233	752	52

NAME/District	JOB FUNCTIONS	PAGE
Odle, Andy/Zeigler Royalton CUSD 188	73,76,84	108
Odle, John/Oakwood Cmty Unit Sch Dist 76	6	232
Odle, Ray/Central A&M Cmty Unit SD 21	3	14
Odle, Sheila/Oakwood Cmty Unit Sch Dist 76	2,4	232
Odonvan, Lisa/Elementary School District 159	43	47
Oeffling, Tom/Johnsburg Cmty School Dist 12	67	182
Oertle, Stephen/Roxana Cmty Unit Sch Dist 1	8,11,15,83,88,285,288,296	172
Oesterreich, Nancy/Cicero School District 99	11,52,294	42
Oeth, Rick/Sparta Cmty School Dist 140	73,76,98,286,295,297	205
Ofisher, Gary/West Harvey-Dixmoor Pub SD 147	2,84	70
Ogarek, Douglas/Ridgeland School District 122	2,3,15	64
Ogdon, Robert/Beecher Cmty Sch Dist 200-U	6	241
Ogle, Matt/Eastern Illinois Area of Sp Ed	73	20
Ogle, Nathan/Sullivan Cmty Unit SD 300	275	193
Oglesby, Susan/North Chicago Cmty Unit SD 187	4	153
Ohlson, Jeff/Princeton Twp HSD 500	6,60	7
Ohlwein, Brigid/Wheeling Cmty Cons School Dist 21	11	71
Ohnesorge, Donetta/Dieterich Community Unit SD 30	6	104
Okeefe, Maureen/Hampton School District 29	7	207
Olaughlin, Sean/Metamora Twp HS Dist 122	1,57	258
Olawumi, Tracy, Dr/Posen-Robbins Sch Dist 143-5	9,11,15,16,72	63
Olderman, Maggie/Dimmick Cmty School Dist 175	270	141
Olesen, Kyle/Community Unit School Dist 308	73,295	137
Olin, Alyssa/Newark Cmty High School Dist 18	90,752	138
Oliver, Deanna/Regional Office of Ed Kane Co	15,68,88	134
Oliver, Tracy/Naperville Cmty Unit SD 203	2	98
Oliveri, Mike/Roanoke-Benson Cmty Unit SD 60	73	258
Olivero, Kelly/Community Cons School Dist 15	280	43
Oller, Bob/Auburn Cmty Unit Sch Dist 10	3,5	211
Ololee, Kizwanda/Hoover-Schrum Sch Dist 157	57,59,271	52
Olsen, Joshua, Dr/Livingston Co Spec Svc Unit	1	163
Olson, Alan/Pecatonica Cmty Unit SD 321	3	253
Olson, Chris/Joliet Twp High Sch Dist 204	68	243
Olson, David/Sycamore Cmty Unit SD 427	71	86
Olson, Eden, Dr/Skokie School District 73 1/2	76	67
Olson, Eric, Dr/Park Ridge Niles CMCSD 64	1	62
Olson, Katharine, Dr/Northbrook Elem School Dist 27	9,15,69	59
Olson, Mary/Waukegan Cmty Unit SD 60	35	156
Olson, Melissa/Riverdale Cmty Unit SD 100	85	208
Olson, Shawn, Dr/Kirby School District 140	1	53
Olson, Steve/Community High School Dist 155	1	179
Olson, Steve/Medinah Elementary SD 11	6	97
Olson, Wesley/Bond Co Cmty Unit Sch Dist 2	1	4
Oltmanns, Dawn/Central Cmty Unit SD 4	58	118
Omalley, Paul, Dr/Butler School District 53	1,11	89
Omalley, Tom/Evergreen Park Cmty HSD 231	1	49
Ondera, Peggy/Elgin School District U-46	34,274	130
Onderisin, Lynn/Will Co School District 92	4	249
Ongena, Charlie/Beach Park Cmty Cons SD 3	73	147
Ongtengco, James/Fenton Cmty High Sch Dist 100	1	94
Ontiveros, Hector/Barrington Cmty Unit SD 220	73	147
Oosterhoff, Heather/St Anne Cmty Cons Sch Dist 256	83,270	136
Oosterhoff, Heather/St Anne Cmty HSD 302	83	136
Opels, Dan/Community Unit School Dist 300	3	180
Oplt, George/Metamora Cmty Cons Sch Dist 1	5	258
Opp, Cynthia/Tamaroa Elem School Dist 5	88	201
Oquendo, Terry/Kenilworth School District 38	85	53
Orama, Jessica/Hinsdale Twp High Sch Dist 86	3	95
Oray, Demicka/Posen-Robbins Sch Dist 143-5	295,297	63
Ordenez, Mark/Maine Twp High Sch Dist 207	16,73,76,98,286,295,297	56
Ordonez, Mark/Maine Twp Spec Ed Program	73,98	82
Ordoqui, Kelly/Bloomingdale School Dist 13	73,76,286,295	89
Orlos, Jennifer/Plainfield Cons School Dist 202	15,91	246
Orr, Mike/Danville School District 118	295	231
Orsello, Jenni/Golf School District 67	90	51
Ortega, Marsha/Gardner S Wilmington HSD 73	57	112
Ortgiesen, Mary/Meridian Cmty Unit SD 223	2	194

---

1 Superintendent	16 Instructional Media Svcs	30 Adult Education	44 Science Sec	58 Special Education K-12	72 Summer School	88 Alternative/At Risk	277 Remedial Math K-12	
2 Bus/Finance/Purchasing	17 Chief Operations Officer	31 Career/Sch-to-Work K-12	45 Math K-12	59 Special Education Elem	73 Instructional Tech	89 Multi-Cultural Curriculum	280 Literacy Coach	
3 Buildings And Grounds	18 Chief Academic Officer	32 Career/Sch-to-Work Elem	46 Math Elem	60 Special Education Sec	74 Inservice Training	90 Social Work	285 STEM	
4 Food Service	19 Chief Financial Officer	33 Career/Sch-to-Work Sec	47 Math Sec	61 Foreign/World Lang K-12	75 Marketing/Distributive	91 Safety/Security	286 Digital Learning	
5 Transportation	20 Art K-12	34 Early Childhood Ed	48 English/Lang Arts K-12	62 Foreign/World Lang Elem	76 Info Systems	92 Magnet School	288 Common Core Standards	
6 Athletic	21 Art Elem	35 Health/Phys Education	49 English/Lang Arts Elem	63 Foreign/World Lang Sec	77 Psychological Assess	93 Parental Involvement	294 Accountability	
7 Health Services	22 Art Sec	36 Guidance Services K-12	50 English/Lang Arts Sec	64 Religious Education K-12	78 Affirmative Action	94 Tech Prep Program	295 Network System	
8 Curric/Instruct K-12	23 Music K-12	37 Guidance Services Elem	51 Reading K-12	65 Religious Education Elem	79 Student Personnel	97 Chief Information Officer	296 Title II Programs	
9 Curric/Instruct Elem	24 Music Elem	38 Guidance Services Sec	52 Reading Elem	66 Religious Education Sec	80 Driver Ed/Safety	98 Chief Technology Officer	297 Webmaster	
10 Curric/Instruct Sec	25 Music Sec	39 Social Studies K-12	53 Reading Sec	67 School Board President	81 Gifted/Talented	270 Character Education	298 Grant Writer/Ptnrships	
11 Federal Program	26 Business Education	40 Social Studies Elem	54 Remedial Reading K-12	68 Teacher Personnel	82 Video Services	271 Migrant Education	750 Chief Innovation Officer	
12 Title I	27 Career & Tech Ed	41 Social Studies Sec	55 Remedial Reading Elem	69 Academic Assessment	83 Substance Abuse Prev	273 Teacher Mentor	751 Chief of Staff	
13 Title V	28 Technology Education	42 Science K-12	56 Remedial Reading Sec	70 Research/Development	84 Erate	274 Before/After Sch	752 Social Emotional Learning	
15 Asst Superintendent	29 Family/Consumer Science	43 Science Elem	57 Bilingual/ELL	71 Public Information	85 AIDS Education	275 Response To Intervention		

IL-T44

Illinois School Directory

DISTRICT PERSONNEL INDEX

NAME/District	JOB FUNCTIONS	PAGE
Ortiz, Craig/Morris Cmty High Sch Dist 101	1	113
Ortiz, Lori/Riverdale Cmty Unit SD 100	5	208
Ortiz, Marcela/La Grange Cmty School Dist 105	57	54
Orwig, Ann/Stark Co Cmty Unit SD 100	67	224
Osborne, Dave/Peotone Cmty Unit SD 207-U	3	245
Osburn, Kaine/Avoca School District 37	1	22
Oskorep, Jason/Plainfield Cons Sch Dist 202	3	246
Osland, Paul/Chicago Public School Dist 299	5	25
Oslovich, George/Woodstock Cmty Unit SD 200	10,69,73,76,84,295	184
Osman, Pauline/Williamsville Cmty Unit SD 15	4	214
Ossmon, Amanda/Earlville Cmty Unit Sch Dist 9	16,73	141
Oster, Kristen/Wesclin Cmty Unit Sch Dist 3	16,82	18
Ostermeier, Adrianne/Springfield Pub Sch Dist 186	273	213
Ostrowski, Wayne/Cass School District 63	3	89
Oswald, Paul/Joliet Twp High Sch Dist 204	10	243
Ott, Josephine/South Beloit Cmty Sch Dist 320	38,69	255
Otten, Lisa/Quincy School District 172	68	2
Otto, Christian, Dr/Libertyville Pub Sch Dist 70	59,285	152
Outven, Kathleen/Argenta Oreana Cmty Unit SD 1	752	165
Overbeck, Casey/Casey-Westfield Cmty USD C-4	67	15
Overbey, Tina/Freeburg Cmty High Sch Dist 77	752	219
Owen, Sheila/Westville Cmty Unit Sch Dist 2	34	233
Owen, Theresa/Belvidere Cmty Unit SD 100	30,58,77,88,752	4
Owen, Theresa/Boone Co Special Ed Co-op	58	5
Owens, Angie/Waltonville Cmty Unit SD 1	2	124
Owens, Danielle, Dr/Pekin Cmty High Sch Dist 303	1	227
Owens, Jeff/Marseilles Elem Sch Dist 150	6,9,69,288	142
Owens, Jim/Potomac Cmty Unit Sch Dist 10	1,11,83	232
Owens, Leslie/Lyons Twp HS District 204	38,79,88,275	56
Owens, Lynn/Lake Zurich Cmty Sch Dist 95	59	152
Owens, Scott/Woodlawn Unit School Dist 209	67	124
Owens, Suzanne/Orland School District 135	68	61
Owings, Shannon/Tri-Co Special Ed JT Agreement	68	122
Owsley, Shane/Community Unit School Dist 7	1	167
Oyman, Allie/Mt Prospect School Dist 57	76	58

P

NAME/District	JOB FUNCTIONS	PAGE
Pabst, Kim/Danville School District 118	68,78,79,273	231
Pacatte, Colleen, Dr/Gurnee School District 56	1	150
Pace, Corey/Southwestern Cmty Unit SD 9	31	168
Pace, Lauren/Maywood-Melrose Brdview SD 89	34	57
Pacelli, Sue/Community Unit School Dist 201	7,85	92
Pacetti, Joe/Minooka Cmty High Sch Dist 111	10,79,83	244
Pacheco, Ronald/Manhattan School Dist 114	270	244
Paddick, Regina/Wabash Cmty Unit Sch Dist 348	36,69	234
Padilia, Crystal/Midland Cmty Unit Sch Dist 7	9,11,274	176
Padilla, Victoria/Regional Office of Ed 17	15	188
Page, Gary/St Joseph-Ogden Cmty HSD 305	57,83,273,275,294	12
Page, Timothy/A-C Central Cmty Unit SD 262	1,11	9
Page, Vedia/Dolton School District 149	59	46
Pagoria, Kathy/Palos Cmty Cons Sch Dist 118	4	61
Palacios, Edgar/Bensenville Elem Sch Dist 2	57	89
Palagi, Patti/Community Unit School Dist 303	11,36,58,77,88,275,752	128
Palan, John, Dr/Grant Park Cmty Unit SD 6	1,11	135
Palazzo, Sam/Norridge School Dist 80	67	59
Palbicke, Patrick/Lincolnshre-Prairieview SD 103	2,15	153
Palcer, Matthew/Avoca School District 37	11	22
Palen, Cynthia/Saunemin Cmty Cons SD 438	88	162
Palese, Lisa/Mid-Valley Special Ed Co-op	1	134
Palmer, Adam/Hawthorn Cmty Cons Sch Dist 73	68,273	151
Palmer, Don/Rhodes School District 84 1/2	3	64
Palmer, Donna/Galesburg Cmty Unit SD 205	2	140
Palmer, Jake/Fisher Cmty Unit School Dist 1	6	10
Palmer, Mandy/West Prairie Cmty Sch Dist 103	4	178
Palmer, Stephanie/Norridge School Dist 80	1	59
Palmisano, Anthony, Dr/School Dist 45 Dupage Co	1,11	99
Palombit, Daniel/Community Unit School Dist 300	79	180
Palomo, Anthony/South Holland School Dist 151	57	68
Paluch, Kristina/Riley Cmty Cons Sch Dist 18	12,52	184
Paluszkiewicz, Jean/Oak Lawn Cmty High SD 229	2	60
Palzet, Dave, Dr/Pleasantdale School Dist 107	1	62
Pampuch, Sandy/Community High School Dist 94	60	91
Panopoulos, Joann/New Trier Twp HS District 203	15,58	58
Pansa, Pamela/Crete-Monee Cmty SD 201-U	4	241
Paonessa, Anne/Batavia Unit School Dist 101	12	128
Papanicolaou, Michelle/Fenton Cmty High Sch Dist 100	10,11,69,74,273,296,298	94

NAME/District	JOB FUNCTIONS	PAGE
Pappas, Dina/Park Ridge Niles CMCSD 64	285	62
Pappas, Sean/Mendota Cmty School Dist 289	67	142
Parchem, Ken/Lemont High Sch Dist 210	2	55
Paris, Amy/Valley View Cmty SD 365-U	39,280	248
Parisi, Adam/Mt Prospect School Dist 57	2,3,5,15,19	58
Parisi, Thomas/Community Unit School Dist 300	35,80	180
Park, Jayne/Streator Twp High Sch Dist 40	7	145
Parker, Alicia/Huntley Cmty School Dist 158	59	182
Parker, Jim/Granite City Cmty Unit SD 9	68,273	171
Parker, Kevin/Rock Falls Twp High SD 301	33	240
Parker, Lisa/Martinsville Cmty Unit SD C-3	31,36,69	16
Parker, Lisa, Dr/Streator Elem School Dist 44	1	144
Parker, Lynda/Oak Park & River Forest SD 200	38	60
Parker, Mat/Rockford School District 205	6	254
Parker, Tammy/Red Hill Cmty School Dist 10	73	159
Parks, Charles/Carrier Mills-Stonefort SD 2	11	210
Parks, Karen/Harrison School Dist 36	67	181
Parks, Megan/Donovan Cmty Unit Sch Dist 3	16	119
Parks, Shenthe/Chicago PSD-Network 12	15	35
Parks, Stuart/Grand Prairie Cmty Cons SD 6	1,11,73,288	123
Parmer, Staci/Community Cons School Dist 46	68	148
Parola, Troy/Mundelein Cons High SD 120	6	153
Parr, Chris/Jasper Co Cmty Unit SD 1	3,5	122
Parrillo, Tom/Ridgewood Cmty HSD 234	2,11	64
Parrish, Denny/Goreville Cmty Unit SD 1	5	127
Parrish, Doug/Freeburg Cmty High Sch Dist 77	67	219
Parson, Jeff/Wethersfield Cmty Unit SD 230	6	117
Parsons, Jason/Canton Union School Dist 66	8,11,57,69,88,271,273	109
Parsons, Shelly/Herscher Cmty School Dist 2	34,58,88	135
Partney, Bo/Dwight Common Elem SD 232	67	161
Pasbrig, Ashley/Athens Cmty Unit Sch Dist 213	58	188
Pasbrig, Ashley/Williamsville Cmty Unit SD 15	58	214
Pasco, Anne/Community Unit School Dist 300	286	180
Pasely, Scott/Bond Co Cmty Unit Sch Dist 2	58,88	4
Pasero, Brian/Chester Cmty Unit Sch Dist 139	1,11,84	205
Passman, Michael/Chicago Public School Dist 299	71	25
Patchett, Jeffery/Oblong Cmty Unit Sch Dist 4	1,11,83	83
Patchett, Mary/Oblong Cmty Unit Sch Dist 4	6	83
Pate-Hefty, Caroline/Maywood-Melrose Brdview SD 89	59,79,90	57
Pate, Craig/Hiawatha Cmty Unit SD 426	58,79,296,298	85
Pate, Dawn/New Lenox School District 122	5	245
Pate, Dawn/Union School District 81	5	248
Pater, David/Community High School Dist 94	275	91
Patrick, Frank/Willow Springs School Dist 108	1,73,288	71
Patrick, Julie/Lake Forest School District 67	76	152
Patrick, Patricia/Avoca School District 37	12	22
Pattenaude, Jim/Paris Cmty Unit Sch Dist 4	295	103
Patterson, Ericka, Dr/Park Forest Chicago Hgt SD 163	15,68	62
Patterson, Janice/Lake Forest School District 67	297	152
Patterson, Kimako, Dr/Prairie Hills Elem SD 144	1,83	63
Patterson, Michael/Malden Cmty Cons SD 84	1,11	7
Patterson, Myra/Community Cons School Dist 168	9,11,84,88,288	44
Patterson, Valerie/Community Unit School Dist 308	79	137
Patton, William/Erie Cmty School District 1	73	239
Pauley, Jason/Centralia High School Dist 200	4	174
Paulsen, Brad/Community Unit School Dist 200	67	91
Paulsen, Erin/Eastland Cmty Unit SD 308	8	8
Pavelonis, Janice/Carbondale Elem School Dist 95	9,11,57,88,288,298	120
Pavljasevic, Mark/La Grange Elem Sch Dist 102	3	54
Pavone, Luke/Elmhurst Cmty Unit SD 205	15,68	93
Pawlak, Emmie/Keeneyville Elem Sch Dist 20	9,11,69,288,296,298	96
Pawlak, Laura/Barrington Cmty Unit SD 220	59	147
Paxson, Scott/Stark Co Cmty Unit SD 100	6	223
Payne, Martin/Metamora Cmty Cons Sch Dist 1	1,83	258
Payne, Maurice/Decatur Public Schools 61	73,76,297	165
Payne, Sarah/Patoka Cmty Unit SD 100	7,59	175
Payne, Terri/Panhandle Cmty Unit SD 2	67	191
Payne, Yolanda/Hazel Crest School Dist 152-5	59,275	52
Payton, Dorletta/Valley View Cmty SD 365-U	27	248
Payton, Mark/Kaneland Cmty Unit SD 302	3,91	132
Pazden, Tom/Pennoyer School District 79	57	62
Pearce, Jeni/Stockton Cmty Unit SD 206	12	126
Pearce, Tiffany/Cahokia Unit Sch Dist 187	68	218
Pearcy, Jan/Tri-Co Special Ed JT Agreement	1	122
Pearman, Alan/Egyptian Cmty Unit Sch Dist 5	6	3
Pearson, Janet/Ottawa Twp High Sch Dist 140	2,11,19,88,296	143

School Year 2020-2021   800-333-8802   IL-T45

DISTRICT PERSONNEL INDEX

Market Data Retrieval

NAME/District	JOB FUNCTIONS	PAGE
Pearson, Jason, Dr/Community Unit School Dist 303	1	128
Pearson, Jennifer/Glenbrook High Sch Dist 225	60	50
Pearson, John, Dr/East Alton-Wood River SD 14	1	170
Pearson, Lisa/Woodstock Cmty Unit SD 200	58	184
Pease, Lisa/Bannockburn Sch Dist 106	2,79	147
Peccola, Gary/Collinsville Cmty Sch Dist 10	67	170
Peck, Shelley/Homewood School Dist 153	71	52
Peckham-Dodge, Linda/Orland School District 135	67	61
Peebles, Mike/Pleasant Hill CUSD 3	67	203
Peince, Jamie/Wesclin Cmty Unit Sch Dist 3	58	18
Pelka, Rich/Kings Cons School District 144	5,91	194
Pellegrini, Nicole/Hall Twp High School Dist 502	2	6
Pellus, Kelsey/Lemont High Sch Dist 210	90	55
Peloso, Tony/Taft School District 90	67	247
Pelsor, Amanda/Brookfield-LaGrange Park SD 95	73	23
Pelyon, Dawn/Rowva Cmty School Dist 208	88	140
Pembroke, Cinda/Leyden Area Spec Ed Co-op	2	82
Pembrook, Joe/Greenfield Cmty Unit SD 10	6	111
Pembrook, Lindsey/South Fork School Dist 14	83,294	14
Pena, Jennifer/Darien Public Sch Dist 61	16,73	92
Pence, Todd/St Joseph Cmty Cons SD 169	1,11,83,288	12
Pendleton, Darrell/St George School District 258	67	136
Penk, Nancy/Riverton Cmty Unit SD 14	38	212
Penman, Jason/Paw Paw Cmty Unit SD 271	67	160
Penman, Robert/Thornton Twp High Sch Dist 205	69,70,294	69
Pennell, Chris/Four Rivers Spec Ed District	1	193
Pennington, Paul/Elgin School District U-46	6	130
Penrod, Chris/Harrisburg Cmty Unit SD 3	67	210
Penrod, Doug/Athens Cmty Unit Sch Dist 213	67	188
Penrod, Vicki/Summersville Sch Dist 79	2	124
Pepper, Becky/Pikeland Cmty Sch Dist 10	58	203
Perce, Steve/Batavia Unit School Dist 101	15,68,751	128
Perdomo, Joshua/Community Unit School Dist 300	57,61	180
Perez, Lisa/Chicago Public School Dist 299	16	25
Perhach, Heather/Woodland Cmty Unit Sch Dist 5	16	162
Perkins, Kevin/Summit Hill School Dist 161	73	247
Perkins, Shawn/Hillsboro Cmty Unit Sch Dist 3	73	191
Perri, Kendra/Lincolnshre-Prairieview SD 103	9	153
Perrin, David, Dr/Rochelle Twp High Sch Dist 212	10,69,79,273,288	195
Perry, Daniel/Chicago PSD-Network 13	15	35
Perry, Kathy/Saratoga Cmty Cons SD 60C	1,11	113
Perry, Neal/Lombard Elem SD 44	2,15,17,19,73,98,751	97
Pershnick, Brian/Dwight Twp High Sch Dist 230	67	161
Pershnick, Coreen/Dwight Twp High Sch Dist 230	68	161
Perva, Michael/Kewanee Cmty Unit Sch Dist 229	73,286	117
Pesek, Jeffry/J Sterling Morton HSD 201	67	53
Pestana, Mario/Elgin School District U-46	57	130
Peters, Jessica/Winfield School District 34	77	100
Peters, Paul/Lexington Cmty Sch Dist 7	1,11	186
Peters, Rachelle/Fox Lake School Dist 114	6	149
Petersen, Lisa/Riverdale Cmty Unit SD 100	37	208
Petersen, Thomas/Township High School Dist 211	71,298	69
Peterson, Allison/Coal City Cmty Unit Sch Dist 1	16	112
Peterson, Brigid/Elmhurst Cmty Unit SD 205	59	93
Peterson, Brooke/Rockford School District 205	294	254
Peterson, Charles/Oakdale Cmty Cons Sch Dist 1	1,11	236
Peterson, Jacque/Rockridge Cmty Unit SD 300	16,82	209
Peterson, Jan/Woodlawn Unit School Dist 209	6	124
Peterson, Jarrod/North Boone Cmty Unit SD 200	16,286	5
Peterson, Jim/Bloomington School District 87	73,76,95,295	185
Peterson, Joan/Indian Prairie Sch Dist 204	9	95
Peterson, Jodi/Mendota Cmty School Dist 289	34,59,77	142
Peterson, Juanita/Miller Cmty Cons Sch Dist 210	6	143
Peterson, Kevin/Bradley-Bourbonnais CHSD 307	27	134
Peterson, Kimberly/Staunton Cmty Unit Sch Dist 6	67	168
Peterson, Melissa/West Prairie Cmty Unit Sch Dist 103	5	178
Peterson, Suzy/Zion Public School District 6	9	157
Peterson, Tammy/Beardstown Cmty Sch Dist 15	57,271	9
Peterson, Tonya/Elwood Cmty Cons SD 203	6,37,59,69,88,288	242
Petkunas, Frank/Iroquois-Kankakee Reg Off Ed	15	137
Petrasek, Kimberly/Mannheim School District 83	1	56
Petrella, Joe/Wood Dale School Dist 7	67	100
Petrick, Jeff/Naperville Cmty Unit SD 203	295	98
Petrie, Scott/Mercer County SD 404	1	189
Petro, Ann/Township High School Dist 214	67	69
Petroline, Dena/Bond Co Cmty Unit Sch Dist 2	2	4
Petry, Bud/Cissna Park Cmty Unit SD 6	67	118
Pettis, Erika, Dr/Sunnybrook School District 171	1	68
Petty, Beth/Richland Co Cmty Unit SD 1	16,73,295,297	206
Petty, Gretchen/Pikeland Cmty Sch Dist 10	93	203
Petty, Josh/Montmorency Cmty Cons SD 145	73	239
Petzke, John/North Shore School Dist 112	16,88,98,295	154
Petzke, John/Prophetstown-Lyndon-Tampico 3	1,11	239
Pezanoski, Cathie/Elwood Cmty Cons SD 203	1,11,83	242
Pezzuto, Nick/Chicago Heights Elem SD 170	6,68,285	25
Pfister, Megan/Newark Cmty High Sch Dist 18	57	138
Pflug, Daina/Central Cmty Unit SD 301	2	128
Pflug, Tim/North Shore School Dist 112	76	154
Phell, Bijal/Argo Cmty High School Dist 217	60	21
Phelps, Bruce/Elgin School District U-46	2	130
Phelps, Dave/Brown Co Cmty Unit Sch Dist 1	6	5
Phelps, Katelynn/Bluford Unit School Dist 318	4	122
Phiilips, Wendy/Highland Cmty Sch District 5	270	171
Phillips, Angela/Park Ridge Niles CMCSD 64	79	62
Phillips, Ashley/Lincoln Elem School Dist 27	9	163
Phillips, Cheril/Plainfield Cons Sch Dist 202	8	246
Phillips, Crystal/Unity Point Cmty Cons SD 140	274	121
Phillips, David/Galena Unit School Dist 120	3	125
Phillips, Denise/Iuka Community Cons Sch Dist 7	37	174
Phillips, Diane/Community High School Dist 128	30	148
Phillips, Greg/Hartsburg Emden School Dist 21	67	163
Phillips, Heather/Pana Cmty Unit School Dist 8	2	14
Phillips, James/Northbrook Elem School Dist 27	76	59
Phillips, James/Northbrook Elem School Dist 27	76	59
Phillips, Jerry/Meredosia-Chambersburg SD 11	3	192
Phillips, Mary/Maine Twp High Sch Dist 207	2	56
Phillips, Matt/Northwestern CUSD 2	16,73,84	168
Phillips, Michael/Rockford School District 205	3	253
Phillips, Steven/Rome Cmty Cons Sch Dist 2	1,11,73,83	123
Phillips, Vicki/Brown Co Cmty Unit Sch Dist 1	1	5
Phurman, Meg/Springfield Pub Sch Dist 186	7,57,58,271	213
Piccatto, John/Hall Twp High School Dist 502	67	6
Picciolini, Cassie/Chicago Ridge Sch Dist 127-5	4	41
Picciolini, Katheryn/Chicago Ridge Sch Dist 127-5	2	41
Pick, Jason/Valley View Cmty SD 365-U	83	248
Pickard, Katelyn/Pearl City Cmty Unit SD 200	59	225
Pickens, Tenika/Community Cons School Dist 180	59,79	90
Pickering, Lisa/Marquardt School District 15	7	97
Piehler, Theresa/Central School District 3	2	1
Piekarski, Micheline/Oak Park & River Forest SD 200	4	60
Piekarski, Vickie/McHenry Cmty High Sch Dist 156	11,27,33,57,60,88,274	183
Pieper, Dallas/Dakota Cmty Unit Sch Dist 201	5	224
Pieper, Dallas/Freeport School District 145	5	224
Pieper, Jera/Franklin-Jefferson Sp Ed Co-op	1	109
Pieper, Rose/Bushnell Prairie Cmty USD 170	2	178
Pierce, Anya/Evanston Twp High Sch 202	70	48
Pierce, Barbara/Peoria Public Sch Dist 150	71,297	198
Pierce, Lora Lee/Patoka Cmty Unit SD 100	6	175
Piercy, Cheryl/River Bend Cmty School Dist 2	295	239
Piercy, Cheryl/River Bend Cmty School Dist 2	73,84	239
Pierzon, Donna/Effingham Cmty Sch Dist 40	7	105
Pierson, Jim/Milne-Kelvin Grove District 91	3	244
Pilati, Francesca/Niles Twp Dept of Spec Ed #807	34	82
Pilip, Megan/Kaneland Cmty Unit SD 302	77	132

1	Superintendent	16	Instructional Media Svcs	30	Adult Education	44	Science Sec	58	Special Education K-12	72	Summer School
2	Bus/Finance/Purchasing	17	Chief Operations Officer	31	Career/Sch-to-Work K-12	45	Math K-12	59	Special Education Elem	73	Instructional Tech
3	Buildings And Grounds	18	Chief Academic Officer	32	Career/Sch-to-Work Elem	46	Math Elem	60	Special Education Sec	74	Inservice Training
4	Food Service	19	Chief Financial Officer	33	Career/Sch-to-Work Sec	47	Math Sec	61	Foreign/World Lang K-12	75	Marketing/Distributive
5	Transportation	20	Art K-12	34	Early Childhood Ed	48	English/Lang Arts K-12	62	Foreign/World Lang Elem	76	Info Systems
6	Athletic	21	Art Elem	35	Health/Phys Education	49	English/Lang Arts Elem	63	Foreign/World Lang Sec	77	Psychological Assess
7	Health Services	22	Art Sec	36	Guidance Services K-12	50	English/Lang Arts Sec	64	Religious Education K-12	79	Affirmative Action
8	Curric/Instruct K-12	23	Music K-12	37	Guidance Services Elem	51	Reading K-12	65	Religious Education Elem	80	Student Personnel
9	Curric/Instruct Elem	24	Music Elem	38	Guidance Services Sec	52	Reading Elem	66	Religious Education Sec	81	Driver Ed/Safety
10	Curric/Instruct Sec	25	Music Sec	39	Social Studies K-12	53	Reading Sec	67	School Board President	82	Gifted/Talented
11	Federal Program	26	Business Education	40	Social Studies Elem	54	Remedial Reading K-12	68	Teacher Personnel	83	Substance Abuse Prev
12	Title I	27	Career & Tech Ed	41	Social Studies Sec	55	Remedial Reading Elem	69	Academic Assessment	84	Erate
13	Title V	28	Technology Education	42	Science K-12	56	Remedial Reading Sec	70	Research/Development	85	AIDS Education
15	Asst Superintendent	29	Family/Consumer Science	43	Science Elem	57	Bilingual/ELL	71	Public Information		

88	Alternative/At Risk	277	Remedial Math K-12		
89	Multi-Cultural Curriculum	280	Literacy Coach		
90	Social Work	285	STEM		
91	Safety/Security	286	Digital Learning		
92	Magnet School	288	Common Core Standards		
93	Parental Involvement	294	Accountability		
95	Tech Prep Program	295	Network System		
97	Chief Information Officer	296	Title II Programs		
98	Chief Technology Officer	297	Webmaster		
270	Character Education	298	Grant Writer/Ptnrships		
271	Migrant Education	750	Chief Innovation Officer		
273	Teacher Mentor	751	Chief of Staff		
274	Before/After Sch	752	Social Emotional Learning		
275	Response To Intervention				

Illinois School Directory — DISTRICT PERSONNEL INDEX

NAME/District	JOB FUNCTIONS	PAGE
Pillen, Kate/Edgar Co Cmty Sch Dist 6	36	103
Pillen, Laurie/Rochelle Twp High Sch Dist 212	38,69	195
Pillion, Michael/Oglesby Public Sch Dist 125	1,11	143
Piltaver, Susan/Schiller Park School Dist 81	59	67
Pinkerton, Grace/Scott Morgan Cmty Unit SD 2	270	215
Pinkerton, Todd/Cornell Cmty Cons Sch Dist 426	67	161
Pinney, Mike/School Dist 45 Dupage Co	76,295	99
Pinter, Jeff/La Moille Cmty Unit SD 303	67	6
Piotrowski, Ed/Lyons Twp HS District 204	68	56
Piotrowski, Leslie/Hawthorn Cmty Cons Sch Dist 73	71	151
Piper, Andy/Northern Suburban Spec Ed Dist	15,68,74	159
Pipher, Rob/Prairie Du Rocher CCSD 134	1	205
Piraino, Tony/Cerro Gordo Cmty Unit SD 100	67	202
Pirtle, Griselda/Community Cons School Dist 59	89	43
Piscitelli, Kerri/Community High School Dist 218	60	44
Pistole, Sherrie/Regional Office of Ed 47	2	241
Pittman, Erin/Big Hollow School District 38	59	148
Pitts, Alecia/Anna-Jonesboro Cmty HSD 81	4	230
Pitts, Deborah/Prospect Hts School Dist 23	76	63
Planeta, Tracy/Grant Park Cmty Unit SD 6	5,31	135
Plascencia, Theresa/Waukegan Cmty Unit SD 60	1	156
Plater, R Mathew/Havana Cmty Sch District 126	1,11,83	177
Plath, Donna/Grass Lake School District 36	59,88,275	150
Plaza, Rebecca/Mundelein Cons High SD 120	16,82	153
Pletctsch, Debbie/Henry Senachwine CUSD 5	55	176
Plocher, Terry/Highland Cmty Sch District 5	4	171
Ploense, Vicki/Beecher Cmty Sch Dist 200-U	16	241
Plote, Janet/Leland Cmty Unit Sch Dist 1	67	142
Plumb, Brian/Riverdale Cmty Unit SD 100	67	208
Plumbo, Tharla/Ludlow Cons Cmty Sch Dist 142	67	11
Plumlee, Diane/Pinckneyville Cmty High SD 101	60	201
Plummer, Evan/Chicago Public School Dist 299	20,27	25
Plummer, Sheila/Cumberland Cmty Unit SD 77	37,83	84
Plunk, Kelly/Wauconda Cmty Unit SD 118	58	155
Plymire, Linda/Allen-Otter Creek CCSD 65	71	141
Plymire, Linda/Allen-Otter Creek CCSD 65	71	141
Pochop, Frank/Maywood-Melrose Brdview SD 89	3	57
Podgorski, Jim/Community High School Dist 155	3	179
Podjasek, Heidi, Dr/Community Unit School Dist 308	752	137
Podzimek, Shanon/Community High School Dist 155	71	179
Poe, Lisa/Aero Special Ed Co-op	34	82
Poelker, Todd/Lincoln Cmty High Sch Dist 404	10,16,69,88,273	163
Poindexter, Tara/Signal Hill Sch Dist 181	34	221
Point, Dale/Harrison School Dist 36	3	181
Polanin, Bradley/Riverton Cmty Unit SD 14	1	212
Polen, Debbie/Rhodes School District 84 1/2	71	64
Polk, Gwen/Waukegan Cmty Unit SD 60	2,15	156
Pollard, Tammy/Gifford Cmty Cons SD 188	73	10
Pollina, Michele/Northbrook-Glenview SD 30	752	60
Polowy, Dan/Central Cmty Unit SD 301	3	128
Polowy, Tameran/Princeton Twp HSD 500	38,88	7
Poloz, Shab/Arlington Hts School Dist 25	49,62	21
Polyak, Nick, Dr/Leyden Cmty High Sch Dist 212	1	55
Pomlianovich, John/North Wamac School Dist 186	73	18
Ponivas, Jason/Zion-Benton Twp High Sch Dist 126	4	157
Pontarelli, Julia/McHenry Cmty High Sch Dist 156	68	183
Poole, Bill/Jacksonville School Dist 117	16,28,73,76,84	192
Poole, Dana/United Cmty Unit Sch Dist 304	67	234
Poole, Mary/Benton Cmty Cons Sch Dist 47	4	107
Poore, Gwen/Carbondale Cmty HSD 165	72	120
Pope, Joe/Channahon School District 17	67	241
Pope, Rebecca/South Beloit Cmty Sch Dist 320	83,85	255
Pope, Royal/Pembroke Cons SD 259	3	136
Popovich, Jim/McHenry Cmty High Sch Dist 156	69	183
Popovich, Seneca/St Anne Cmty Cons Sch Dist 256	16	136
Popp, Mike, Dr/West 40 Interm Serv Center 2	15	82
Popp, Sandra/Fox Lake School Dist 114	68	149
Porche-Box, Sheloanda/Matteson Elem SD 162	59	57
Porter, Brenda/Park Forest Chicago Hgt SD 163	7	62
Porter, Jennifer/Community Unit School Dist 300	2	180
Porter, Lorraine/West Harvey-Dixmoor Pub SD 147	4	70
Porter, Randy/North Boone Cmty Unit SD 200	295	5
Porter, Thomas/Thornton Twp High Sch Dist 205	60,79	69
Portwood, Michael/Homer Cmty Cons Sch Dist 33C	15,68	242
Portz, Dan/River Bend Cmty School Dist 2	67	239
Portz, Travis/Ramsey Cmty Unit Sch Dist 204	8,11,54,58,296,298	105
Posego, John/Lisle Cmty Unit Sch Dist 202	3	96
Posey, Krystal/Stockton Cmty Unit SD 206	58	126
Posing, Gary/Homewood Flossmoor CHSD 233	16,73,295	52
Post, Pete/Indian Creek Cmty Unit SD 425	3	85
Potemp, Dolores/Momence Cmty Unit Sch Dist 1	58,79	136
Potempa, Monica/Leyden Area Spec Ed Co-op	15	82
Potilechio, Adriene/Valley View Cmty SD 365-U	42,45	248
Potratz, Maria/Mt Prospect School Dist 57	73	58
Potsic, Joann/Alsip-Hazelgrn-Oaklawn SD 126	3	20
Potsic, Mike/Central Cmty Unit SD 301	58,79	128
Potter, Brenda/River Ridge Cmty Unit SD 210	69,83	126
Potter, Teri/River Ridge Cmty Unit SD 210	4	126
Potthast, Susan/Grass Lake School District 36	90	150
Potts, Candace/Pope Co Cmty Unit Sch Dist 1	38,69,83	204
Potts, TJ/East Dubuque Unit SD 119	1,11	125
Povolish, Kyle/Carbondale Cmty HSD 165	85	120
Powell, Adam/Abingdon-Avon Cmty Unit SD 276	16	139
Powell, David/Hillsboro Cmty Unit Sch Dist 3	1	190
Powers, Beth/Community Cons School Dist 89	67	90
Powers, Cathy/Wesclin Cmty Unit Sch Dist 3	90,271,752	18
Powers, Pat/McLean Co Unit District 5	4	186
Poynter, Jared/Hiawatha Cmty Unit SD 426	1,11	85
Poynter, Jeffery/McHenry Co Work Force Ctr	1	185
Pozzi, Jyll/Dalzell Elem School Dist 98	2	6
Prabo, Kathleen/Evergreen Park Elem SD 124	9,11,69,74,288	49
Prasch, Debbie/Community Cons School Dist 181	3	91
Prather, James/Rhodes School District 84 1/2	1,11	64
Prather, Sandy/Brown Co Cmty Unit Sch Dist 1	12	5
Pray, Ryan/Deland-Weldon Cmty Unit SD 57	6	202
Preble, Kurt/Diamond Lake School Dist 76	3	149
Preis, Beth/Northbrook-Glenview SD 30	71	60
Prentice, Courtney/Prairie Hill Cmty Cons SD 133	67	253
Prentiss, Tammy/Hinsdale Twp High Sch Dist 86	1	95
Prescott, Tammie/Montmorency Cmty Cons SD 145	2	239
Presley, D/Unity Point Cmty Cons SD 140	67	121
Presley, Dan/Carlinville Cmty Unit SD 1	295	167
Presnell, Cindi/Mascoutah Cmty Sch Dist 19	8,11,57,69,81,88,273,288	220
Prestgaard, Mike/Winnebago Cmty Unit SD 323	3	255
Preston, William/Pleasant Hill School Dist 69	67	199
Preuss, Fred/Oak Park & River Forest SD 200	3	60
Pribble, Tim/Galatia Cmty Unit Sch Dist 1	67	210
Price, Carrie/Ottawa Elementary Sch Dist 141	6	143
Price, Charisse/Prairie Central Cmty USD 8	5	162
Price, Joel/Community Unit School Dist 201	67	92
Price, John/North Chicago Cmty Unit SD 187	1	153
Price, Stanley Ellis/Tri-City Cmty Unit Sch Dist 1	6	214
Price, Susan/Belleville Public Sch Dist 118	5,57,59,77,88,90,270	217
Price, Westley/Lena-Winslow Cmty Unit SD 202	752	224
Priebe, Grover/East Dubuque Unit SD 119	3	125
Priest, Tony/Cahokia Unit Sch Dist 187	91	218
Primdahl, Terry/Community Unit School Dist 303	5	128
Primus, Doug/McHenry Cmty High Sch Dist 156	73	183
Pristas, Jeff/Richland School Dist 88A	3	247
Pritchard, Michelle/Unity Point Cmty Cons SD 140	34	121
Pritzker, Phil/Wheeling Cmty Cons Sch Dist 21	67	71
Probst, Beth/Jasper Co Cmty Unit SD 1	27	122
Proeger, Barbara/Erie Cmty School District 1	16,82	239
Prola, Andrea/Butler School District 53	79	89
Prombo, Michael/Harvard Cmty Unit Sch Dist 50	2,19	181
Prost, Robert/Kirby School District 140	3	53
Prost, Timothy/Community High School Dist 218	73,76	44
Prowell, Jeffrey/Elgin School District U-46	5	130
Prucha, Jeannine/Community High School Dist 218	10,47	44
Prudencio, Amy/Carbondale Cmty HSD 165	83,90,93	120
Pruhty, James/Lockport Twp High Sch Dist 205	6	244
Pruitt-Adam, Joylynn/Oak Park & River Forest SD 200	1	60
Pruitt, Jill/Norris City-Omaha-Enfield SD 3	58	238
Prusator, Jeff/Mendota Twp High Sch Dist 280	1	143
Prusko, Kara/Township High School Dist 211	60	69
Pryor, Kim/Signal Hill Sch Dist 181	6	221
Ptacek, Steve/Jacksonville School Dist 117	1	192
Ptak, Kim, Dr/Glenbrook High Sch Dist 225	2,3,4	50
Ptashkin, Samantha/Barrington Cmty Unit SD 220	71	147
Puckett, Chuck/Rockdale School District 84	3	247
Puckett, Matt/Lincoln Cmty High Sch Dist 404	33	163
Pueyo, Limaris/Community Unit School Dist 200	51,57	91

DISTRICT PERSONNEL INDEX

Market Data Retrieval

NAME/District	JOB FUNCTIONS	PAGE
Pufattl, Fred/Summit Hill School Dist 161	6	247
Pugh, Jonathan/Diocese of Joliet Ed Office	67	249
Pugh, Mike/Salem Elem Sch District 111	3,91	175
Pullen, Cynthia/Community Cons School Dist 59	68	43
Purcell, Michael/Indian Prairie Sch Dist 204	10	95
Purcell, Ryan/Diocese of Joliet Ed Office	64	249
Pursell, Kyle/Pinckneyville Sch Dist 50	67	201
Pustelnik, Mark/United Twp High Sch Dist 30	6	209
Pustelnik, Mike/J Sterling Morton HSD 201	2	53
Putlak, Christine/Aero Special Ed Co-op	15	82
Putnam, Todd, Dr/North Dupage Spec Ed Co-op	15,58,74,275	102
Putnay, Sara/Grayville Cmty Unit Sch Dist 1	4	238
Putney, Natalie/Midwest Ctl Cmty Unit SD 191	31,38,69	177
Putzstuck, Stephanie/Boone-Winnebago Reg Off of Ed	30	256
Pygott, Andy/Meridian Cmty Unit Sch Dist 15	1,11,83	166
Pytel, Pawel/Berkeley School Dist 87	2	22

Q

NAME/District	JOB FUNCTIONS	PAGE
Quagliano, Anthony/Huntley Cmty School Dist 158	67	182
Quain, Debra/Kankakee Area Special Ed Co-op	1,11	137
Quest, Al/Amboy Cmty Unit Sch Dist 272	5	159
Quick, Joshua/Robinson Cmty Unit Sch Dist 2	1,11	83
Quigley, Steven/Valley View Cmty SD 365-U	67	248
Quijada, Moris/Kenilworth School District 38	3	53
Quillen, Terri/Schuyler-Industry CUSD 5	2	215
Quine, Cliff/Pleasant Valley Sch Dist 62	67	199
Quinn, Kevin/Mundelein Cons High SD 120	3	153
Quinonez, Katirie/Darien Public Sch Dist 61	752	92

R

NAME/District	JOB FUNCTIONS	PAGE
RA-El, Gegi/Cahokia Unit Sch Dist 187	8,280	218
Raab, Jennifer/Scales Mound Cmty Unit SD 211	12	126
Rabe, Jessica/Crescent Iroquois Cmty SD 249	4	118
Rabin, Susanna/North Shore School Dist 112	5	154
Raby, Brent, Dr/West Aurora School Dist 129	8,11,15	132
Raciti, Mark/Lincolnwood Sch Dist 74	6	55
Rackos, Marline/Rutland Cmty Cons SD 230	2	144
Raczak, Michael/Indian Prairie Sch Dist 204	67	95
Rademaker, David/Patoka Cmty Unit SD 100	1,11,288	175
Rader, Scott/Shelbyville Cmty Sch Dist 4	3,91	216
Radtke, Bill/Riverside Public Sch Dist 96	3	65
Radtke, Meghan/Community Cons School Dist 180	83,270	90
Radziejewski, Teri/Franklin Park Pub Sch Dist 84	68	50
Rae, Erin/Milne-Kelvin Grove District 91	69,288,752	244
Raflores, Alice/Glenbrook High Sch Dist 225	68	50
Ragon, Rusty/Manhattan School Dist 114	1,11	244
Rahm, James/Wesclin Cmty Unit Sch Dist 3	12	18
Rainbolt, Lori/Smithton Cmty Cons SD 130	90	222
Rains, Barb/Summit Hill School Dist 161	1	247
Rains, Jamie/Robinson Cmty Unit Sch Dist 2	58	83
Raisley, Stephen/Sandoval Cmty Unit SD 501	73	175
Raitzer, Kristin/Northbrook School District 28	9,11,16,69,280,288,296,298	59
Rajcevich, Mark/Medinah Elementary SD 11	3	97
Rakers, Nathan/Whiteside School District 115	9	222
Rakes, Sandy/Coal City Cmty Unit Sch Dist 1	58	112
Rakestraw, Linda/Indian Prairie Sch Dist 204	10,15	95
Raley, Heath/Mendota Twp High Sch Dist 280	27,33,75	143
Ramage, Michelle/Rantoul City School Dist 137	1,11	11
Ramballt, Don/South Beloit Cmty Sch Dist 320	4	255
Ramos, Eric/Adlai E Stevenson HSD 125	35	146
Ramos, Richard/Elgin School District U-46	84	130
Ramsay, Amy/Leyden Cmty High Sch Dist 212	60	55
Ramski, Julie/Archdiocese of Chicago Ed Off	34	72
Rana, Dave/Community Cons School Dist 168	3,91	44
Ranallo, Katie/Seneca Cmty Cons Sch Dist 170	59,77	144
Rancilio, Anthony/Central Cmty High Sch Dist 71	73	17
Randazzo, Jean/Marquardt School District 15	67	97

NAME/District	JOB FUNCTIONS	PAGE
Randle, Lance/Peoria Public Sch Dist 150	5	198
Rangel, Angela/Community Cons School Dist 181	68	91
Ranghausen, Dylan/Calhoun Cmty Unit Sch Dist 40	36,69	8
Rank, Kelly/Alsip-Hazelgrn-Oaklawn SD 126	59	20
Ranken, Miriah/Creston Cmty Cons Sch Dist 161	67	194
Rankin, Narcissus/Danville School District 118	2,5,80,91	231
Rappaport, Adam/Winnetka School Dist 36	3	72
Rappold, Kristen/Crete-Monee Cmty SD 201-U	83,88	242
Rasar, Mark/Skokie School District 69	9	67
Rasco, Branson/East Moline Public Sch Dist 37	16,73,76,295,297	207
Rashid, Jan, Dr/River Grove School Dist 85-5	1,11	65
Raso, Liane/Center Cass Sch Dist 66	67	90
Ratereee, Bonnie/West Harvey-Dixmoor Pub SD 147	67	70
Raterman, Diane/Knoxville Cmty Unit SD 202	4	140
Rathunde, Joanne/Millburn Cmty Cons Sch Dist 24	73,76,295	153
Ratini, Michele/Leyden Cmty High Sch Dist 212	90	55
Ratliff, Joe/Genoa-Kingston Cmty SD 424	3,36	85
Ratz, Jacob/Prairie Du Rocher CCSD 134	35,85	205
Ratzke, Betty/Antioch Cmty Cons School Dist 34	2	146
Raubach-Davis, Holly/Washington Cmty HS Dist 308	73,76,286	229
Rauch, David/Clay City Cmty Unit SD 10	67	16
Rausch, Lisa/West Aurora School Dist 129	58	132
Rawlings, Bob/Armstrong Ellis SD 61	3	231
Rawlings, Bob/Armstrong Twp High SD 225	3	231
Ray, Brandon/Staunton Cmty Unit Sch Dist 6	5	168
Ray, Paula/Meridian Cmty Unit Sch Dist 15	5	166
Ray, William/Rossville-Alvin Cmty Unit SD 7	67	233
Raya, Mira/Carbon Cliff Barstow SD 36	57	207
Rayapati, Sangeetha/Moline-Coal Valley SD No 40	67	207
Raymer, Cathy/Villa Grove Cmty Unit SD 302	4	88
Raymond, Jill/Chicago Heights Elem SD 170	15,59,752	25
Raymond, Marisa/Maywood-Melrose Brdview SD 89	4	57
Raymond, Mike/Triad Cmty School District 2	2,296	172
Razor, Lennard/Flossmoor School District 161	73,76,286,295	49
Rea, Brian/Payson Cmty Unit School Dist 1	6	2
Rea, Diana/Du Quoin Cmty Unit SD 300	9	201
Reagan, Robert/Cambridge Cmty Unit SD 227	10	116
Reale, Anne/Rantoul Twp High Sch Dist 193	67	12
Reams, Colleen/Vandalia Cmty Unit SD 203	4	106
Reavley, Catharine/Astoria Cmty Unit Sch Dist 1	83	109
Reber, Lisa/Meridian Cmty Unit SD 223	4	194
Reda, Joe/Bloom Twp High Sch Dist 206	6,80	23
Redden, Scott/Alden-Hebron School Dist 19	3	179
Redding, Kevin/Dupage High School Dist 88	38	93
Redell, Susan/Medinah Elementary SD 11	11,73,83,88,286,288,296,298	97
Redfeairn, Debbie/Centralia City Sch Dist 135	2,5	174
Redfeairn, Randy/Centralia High School Dist 200	3	174
Redfern, Troy/Staunton Cmty Unit Sch Dist 6	6	168
Redman, Caryn/Gavin School District 37	69,88	150
Redman, Patty/Wood River-Hartford Elem SD 15	4	172
Redmond, Yvonne/Calumet Public School Dist 132	2	24
Redmonte, Bev/Elmhurst Cmty Unit SD 205	71	93
Redwitz, Katie/Iroquois West Cmty Unit SD 10	31	119
Reed, Chris/Warrensburg-Latham CU SD 11	73	166
Reed, Duane/Lena-Winslow Cmty Unit SD 202	5	224
Reed, Lisa/Pope Co Cmty Unit Sch Dist 1	8,288,298	204
Reed, Mark/Galesburg Cmty Unit SD 205	8	140
Reed, Sue/Cobden Cmty Unit Sch Dist 17	274	230
Reed, Vern/Reed-Custer Cmty Unit SD 255-U	91	246
Reeder, Jessica/Sullivan Cmty Unit SD 300	11,34,57,58,72,273	193
Reedy, Bret/Warrensburg-Latham CU SD 11	6	166
Reedy, Jill/Macon-Piatt Roe#39	15	167
Reedy, Tip/Williamsville Cmty Unit SD 15	1	214
Reel, Dyllon/Earlville Cmty Unit Sch Dist 9	35,80,85	141
Reeley, Tony/Eastern Illinois Area of Sp Ed	1	20
Rees, Benjamin/Alwood Cmty Unit Sch Dist 225	6,27,57,69,83	116
Rees, Benjamin/Alwood Cmty Unit Sch Dist 225	6,27,57,69,83	116

1 Superintendent	16 Instructional Media Svcs	30 Adult Education	44 Science Sec	58 Special Education K-12	72 Summer School	88 Alternative/At Risk	277 Remedial Math K-12
2 Bus/Finance/Purchasing	17 Chief Operations Officer	31 Career/Sch-to-Work K-12	45 Math K-12	59 Special Education Elem	73 Instructional Tech	89 Multi-Cultural Curriculum	280 Literacy Coach
3 Buildings And Grounds	18 Chief Academic Officer	32 Career/Sch-to-Work Elem	46 Math Elem	60 Special Education Sec	74 Inservice Training	90 Social Work	285 STEM
4 Food Service	19 Chief Financial Officer	33 Career/Sch-to-Work Sec	47 Math Sec	61 Foreign/World Lang K-12	75 Marketing/Distributive	91 Safety/Security	286 Digital Learning
5 Transportation	20 Art K-12	34 Early Childhood Ed	48 English/Lang Arts K-12	62 Foreign/World Lang Elem	76 Info Systems	92 Magnet School	288 Common Core Standards
6 Athletic	21 Art Elem	35 Health/Phys Education	49 English/Lang Arts Elem	63 Foreign/World Lang Sec	77 Psychological Assess	94 Parental Involvement	294 Accountability
7 Health Services	22 Art Sec	36 Guidance Services K-12	50 English/Lang Arts Sec	64 Religious Education K-12	78 Affirmative Action	95 Tech Prep Program	295 Network System
8 Curric/Instruct K-12	23 Music K-12	37 Guidance Services Elem	51 Reading K-12	65 Religious Education Elem	79 Student Personnel	96 Chief Infomation Officer	296 Title II Programs
9 Curric/Instruct Elem	24 Music Elem	38 Guidance Services Sec	52 Reading Elem	66 Religious Education Sec	80 Driver Ed/Safety	97 Chief Technology Officer	297 Webmaster
10 Curric/Instruct Sec	25 Music Sec	39 Social Studies K-12	53 Reading Sec	67 School Board President	81 Gifted/Talented	270 Character Education	298 Grant Writer/Ptnrships
11 Federal Program	26 Business Education	40 Social Studies Elem	54 Remedial Reading K-12	68 Teacher Personnel	82 Video Services	271 Migrant Education	750 Chief Innovation Officer
12 Title I	27 Career & Tech Ed	41 Social Studies Sec	55 Remedial Reading Elem	69 Academic Assessment	83 Substance Abuse Prev	273 Teacher Mentor	751 Chief of Staff
13 Title V	28 Technology Education	42 Science K-12	56 Remedial Reading Sec	70 Research/Development	84 Erate	274 Before/After Sch	752 Social Emotional Learning
15 Asst Superintendent	29 Family/Consumer Science	43 Science Elem	57 Bilingual/ELL	71 Public Information	85 AIDS Education	275 Response To Intervention	

IL-T48

Illinois School Directory

DISTRICT PERSONNEL INDEX

NAME/District	JOB FUNCTIONS	PAGE
Reese, Kevin/Dolton-Riverdale Sch Dist 148	2,3	46
Reese, Steve/Yorkville Cmty Unit SD 115	295	139
Reeter, Angela/Regional Office of Education 3	8	106
Regan, Holly/Rantoul Twp High Sch Dist 193	16	12
Regnier, Jennifer/Hinsdale Twp High Sch Dist 86	38,69,90	95
Rehfeldt, Rich/Galena Unit School Dist 120	73,84,98	125
Reibel, Anthony/Adlai E Stevenson HSD 125	69	146
Reich, Beth/Grant Cmty High Sch Dist 124	2	150
Reiche, Teresa/Barrington Cmty Unit SD 220	15,68	147
Reichert, Jennifer/Peoria Heights Cmty SD 325	73	198
Reid, Craig/Moline-Coal Valley SD No 40	73,76,84	207
Reid, Jenny/Bremen Cmty High SD 228	22,25	23
Reid, John/Hawthorn Cmty Cons Sch Dist 73	84	151
Reid, Shannon/Grayville Cmty Unit Sch Dist 1	3	238
Reid, Zach/Greenview Cmty Unit SD 200	31,69,83	188
Reif, Rodney/Carrollton Cmty Unit SD 1	67	111
Reiff, Paul/Community High School Dist 128	57	148
Reifing, Bryan/Lebanon Cmty Unit Sch Dist 9	3	220
Reiley, Darrick, Dr/Monroe School District 70	1,11,73,83	198
Reilley, Lynn/Sycamore Cmty Unit SD 427	34,58,90	86
Reilly, Barry, Dr/Bloomington School District 87	1	185
Reiman, April/Cobden Cmty Unit Sch Dist 17	31,36,83,88	230
Rein, James/St Joseph-Ogden Cmty HSD 305	67	12
Rein, Terri/St Joseph-Ogden Cmty HSD 305	69	12
Rein, Tracy/West Carroll CUSD 314	9	9
Rein, Tracy/West Carroll CUSD 314	9	9
Reinders, Michael/Winnebago Cmty Unit SD 323	5	255
Reiner, Lana/Waukegan Cmty Unit SD 60	58	156
Reinert, Rhonda/Valley View Cmty SD 365-U	294	248
Reiniche, John/Bloomingdale School Dist 13	2,296	89
Reining, John/Forrestville Valley CUSD 221	67	194
Reinke, Dawn/Winfield School District 34	9,12,57,69,288,294,298	100
Reinking, Andrew, Dr/Madison Cmty Unit Sch Dist 12	1,11	172
Reis, Jill/Regional Office of Ed 1	1	193
Reis, Joyce/South Eastern Special Ed Dist	2	122
Reisberg, Darren/Illinois Dept of Education	67	1
Reiskis, Anthony/West Aurora School Dist 129	73,295	132
Reiss, Michelle/Edinburg Cmty Unit Sch Dist 4	8,69	14
Reiss, Mike/Ramsey Cmty Unit Sch Dist 204	16,73,76	105
Reithmaier, Angie/Regional Office of Ed 17	5	188
Reitz, Josh/McHenry Cmty Cons Sch Dist 15	9,11,15,69,83,273,294,296	183
Relleke, Jill/Granite City Cmty Unit SD 9	58,90	171
Remington, Kathy/Armstrong Twp High SD 225	2	231
Remington, Lacey/Vit Cmty Unit School Dist 2	58,69,77	110
Ren, Bill/Carterville Cmty Unit SD 5	3	250
Renken, Stephanie/Southwestern Cmty Unit SD 9	58	168
Renko, Jacqueline/Flossmoor School District 161	57	49
Renkosik, Doug/Huntley Cmty School Dist 158	3	182
Rennecker, Stefanie/Western CUSD 12	36,69	203
Rensing, Keith/Carlyle Cmty Unit Sch Dist 1	67	17
Renz, Melissa/Matteson Elem SD 162	68	57
Repp, Robert/Winnetka School Dist 36	295	72
Reschke, Steve/Le Roy Cmty Unit SD 2	10	186
Resler, Kristine/Bremen Cmty High SD 228	67	23
Restoff, Kathryn/Pinckneyville Cmty High SD 101	2	201
Reuter, Cindy/Community Unit School Dist 200	8	91
Revello, Julie/Northbrook Elem School Dist 27	59	59
Rexroad, Sarah/Lincoln Way Area Special Ed	1	250
Reyes, Kenneth/Leyden Cmty High Sch Dist 212	3	55
Reynold, Kristin/Odin Public School Dist 722	7	175
Reynolds, Amy/Shawnee Cmty Unit Sch Dist 84	11	231
Reynolds, Elizabeth, Dr/Calumet Public School Dist 132	1	24
Reynolds, Katie/Lincolnshire-Prairieview SD 103	9,11,15,16,57,273,288	153
Reynolds, Matt/Mt Vernon City Sch Dist 80	67	123
Reynolds, Sheri/Hillsboro Cmty Unit Sch Dist 3	274	191
Reynolds, Tim/Rowva Cmty School Dist 208	73	140
Reznicek, Curt/Franklin Cmty Unit SD 1	67	192
Rheinecker, Cory/Sparta Cmty School Dist 140	67	205
Rheingans, Curt/Creston Cmty Cons Sch Dist 161	1,84	194
Rhinehart, Kris/Lawrence Co Cmty Sch Dist 20	58	159
Rhoades, Brian/Mt Zion Cmty Unit Sch Dist 3	2,8,11,15,31,58,296,298	166
Rhoades, Jen/Athens Cmty Unit Sch Dist 213	51	188
Rhoades, Marjorie/Bushnell Prairie Cmty USD 170	79	178
Rhodes, Brenda/Polo Cmty Unit Sch Dist 222	7	195
Ribbens, Mark/Wauconda Cmty Unit SD 118	6	155
Rice-Maurer, Sue/Marengo Union Elem Cons SD 165	2	182
Rice, Amy/Carmi-White Co School Dist 5	58	237
Rice, Anita/Lincoln Elem School Dist 156	58,288	55
Rice, Anita/Lincoln Elem School Dist 156	1	55
Rice, Carolyn/Armstrong Ellis SD 61	12	231
Rice, Mike/Kaneland Cmty Unit SD 302	10	132
Rice, Patrick, Dr/Cairo School District 1	1,11,83	3
Rich, Matt, Dr/Winfield School District 34	1,11	100
Richardella, Ilsa/Community High School Dist 218	2	44
Richards, David/Valley View Cmty SD 365-U	5	248
Richards, Heather/Flanagan-Cornell Unit 74 SD	59	161
Richards, Michelle/Fairfield Cmty High SD 225	60,88	236
Richards, Randy/Heyworth Cmty Sch District 4	5	185
Richardson, Amy/Livingston Area EFE System	58	163
Richardson, Brenda/Country Club Hills SD 160	9	45
Richardson, Chris/Oakwood Cmty Unit Sch Dist 76	73	232
Richardson, Daryl/Hillside School District 93	67	52
Richardson, Diann/Urbana School District 116	79	12
Richardson, Mark/Woodlawn Unit School Dist 209	8	124
Richardson, Molly/Marshall Cmty Sch Dist C-2	2	15
Richardson, Nicole/Durand Cmty Sch Dist 322	73,84,295	252
Richardson, Robert/Hoopeston Area Cmty Unit SD 11	1	232
Richer, Rose/Nippersink School District 2	16	183
Richmond, Andy/Carbon Cliff Barstow SD 36	1,11,83	207
Richmond, Daniel/West Harvey-Dixmoor Pub SD 147	79	70
Richmond, Tim/Lake Park Cmty High SD 108	97,295	96
Richter, Adam/Lebanon Cmty Unit Sch Dist 9	73,76,84,97,98,286,295	220
Rick, Dan/Dixon Cmty Unit Sch Dist 170	8,12,15	160
Rickenberg, Amanda/Morton Cmty Unit Sch Dist 709	58	227
Ricker, David/Park Forest Chicago Hgt SD 163	2,3	62
Ricketts, Julie/West Central Cmty Unit SD 235	12,286,296	116
Rickhoff, Kurt/Albers Elem School District 63	67	17
Riddell, Jay/Midland Cmty Unit Sch Dist 7	67	176
Riddle, Meredith/Cerro Gordo Cmty Unit SD 100	16	202
Riddle, Scott/Mendon Cmty Unit School Dist 4	1	2
Rider, Jamie/Gallatin Cmty Unit Sch Dist 7	4	110
Ridlen, Kendra/Oblong Cmty Unit Sch Dist 4	58,69,752	83
Riechmann, Teena/Valmeyer Cmty School Dist 3	275	190
Riffey, Michael/North Mac Cmty Unit SD 34	3	168
Rigg, Crista/West Prairie Cmty Sch Dist 103	2,11,88	178
Rigg, Cyle/Southeastern Cmty Unit SD 337	6	115
Rigg, Jim, Dr/Archdiocese of Chicago Ed Off	1	72
Riggio, Mike/Du Quoin Cmty Unit SD 300	73,98,295	201
Rightnowar, Brian/Mt Vernon Twp HS District 201	3,17	123
Rigsby, Bo/Hampton School District 29	3	207
Riha, Cynthia/Oak Lawn-Hometown Sch Dist 123	59,275	60
Rijpma, Jorden/Galena Unit School Dist 120	57	125
Riley, Marty/Chicago Heights Elem SD 170	4,5	25
Rimzz, Dan/Putnam Co Cmty Unit SD 535	28,73	204
Ringberg, Scott/United Twp High Sch Dist 30	4	209
Riordan, Daniel, Dr/Reavis Twp HSD 220	1	64
Riordan, Michael, Dr/Oak Lawn Cmty High SD 229	1	60
Rios, Stefanie/Harrison School Dist 36	280	181
Ripley, Darren/Murphysboro Cmty Unit SD 186	17	121
Riportella, Edie/Golf School District 67	2	51
Rister, Beth, Dr/Regional Office of Ed 20	1	211
Rita, Miche'Le/Bremen Cmty High SD 228	295	23
Ritchey, John/Marshall Cmty Sch Dist C-2	8	15
Ritchie, Mindy/Galesburg Cmty Unit SD 205	752	140
Ritter, Melissa/Ramsey Cmty Unit Sch Dist 204	1,84	105
Rittman, Eric/Villa Grove Cmty Unit SD 302	16	88
Rivard, Donna/Keeneyville Elem Sch Dist 20	79	96
Rivera, Arnie/Chicago Public School Dist 299	3,17	25
Rivera, Gabrielle/Bethalto Cmty Unit SD 8	4	169
Rivera, Kristopher/Lyons Elem School Dist 103	1	56
Rivera, Rachel/Proviso Twp High Sch Dist 209	2	63
Rizzo, Joe/Alsip-Hazelgrn-Oaklawn SD 126	5	20
Road-Armel, Lee/Beecher City Cmty Unit SD 20	67	104
Roalson, Dawn/Ottawa Twp High Sch Dist 140	58	143
Roark, Jeremy/Mahomet-Seymour Cmty SD 3	5	11
Robb, Ross/Galesburg Cmty Unit SD 205	20,23	140
Robbins, Cory/Du Quoin Cmty Unit SD 300	2,3	201
Robbins, Joe/Morrison Cmty Unit Sch Dist 6	275	239
Robbins, Marsha/St Joseph Cmty Cons SD 169	2	12
Robbon, Jim/High Mount Sch Dist 116	6	219
Roberson, Aaron/East Maine School District 63	9,11,16,69,74,83,273,296	47

School Year 2020-2021   800-333-8802   IL-T49

DISTRICT PERSONNEL INDEX

Market Data Retrieval

NAME/District	JOB FUNCTIONS	PAGE
Roberts, Chris/Mattoon Cmty Unit Sch Dist 2	73,76,84,295	19
Roberts, Chris/Steward Elem School Dist 220	752	160
Roberts, Gary/Warren Community Unit SD 205	5	126
Roberts, James/Lake Park Cmty High SD 108	11,288	96
Roberts, Jim/Lake Park Cmty High SD 108	15,69	96
Roberts, Keely, Dr/Zion Public School District 6	1	157
Roberts, Keith/Darien Public Sch Dist 61	73,98,295	92
Roberts, Mick/Paris Union School District 95	6	103
Roberts, Tim/Lake Park Cmty High SD 108	298	96
Roberts, Tonya/Joliet Public School Dist 86	67	243
Robertson, Ashley/Community Cons School Dist 59	37	43
Robertson, Karen/Henry Senachwine CUSD 5	68	176
Robertson, Maria/Decatur Public Schools 61	71	165
Robertson, Peter/Durand Cmty Sch Dist 322	6	252
Robertson, William, Dr/Fremont School District 79	1	149
Robins, Angela/Pembroke Cmty Cons SD 259	4	136
Robinson, Anne/Community High School Dist 155	2	179
Robinson, Brett/Cerro Gordo Cmty Unit SD 100	1,11	202
Robinson, Elizabeth/Frankfort Cmty Unit SD 168	57	108
Robinson, Gladys/Bellwood School District 88	4	22
Robinson, Holly/Donovan Cmty Unit Sch Dist 3	8,37,69,83	119
Robinson, John/Community Unit School Dist 200	3	91
Robinson, John/Hartsburg Emden School Dist 21	73,286	163
Robinson, Kathleen, Dr/Community Cons School Dist 181	9,11,15,57,69,81	91
Robinson, Kevin/Collinsville Cmty Sch Dist 10	68	170
Robinson, Latroy/General George S Patton SD 133	67	50
Robinson, Leigh/East Alton-Wood River SD 14	10,69,74,273	170
Robinson, Sheri/Vienna Public School Dist 55	2	127
Robinson, Tara/Peotone Cmty Unit SD 207-U	67	245
Robinson, Wendell/Hardin Co Cmty Unit Sch Dist 1	11,83,274,296,298	115
Robinzine, John/Thornton Fractnl Twp HSD 215	27	69
Robison, Allison/Goreville Cmty Unit SD 1	16,82	127
Robison, Uta/Collinsville Cmty Sch Dist 10	2	170
Robson, Lori/Fairfield Cmty High SD 225	38	236
Rock, Angela/Benton Cmty Cons Sch Dist 47	7,83	107
Rockey, Billy/Mt Zion Cmty Unit Sch Dist 3	10,73,285,286,295	166
Rockrohr, Steve/Glenbrook High Sch Dist 225	6	50
Rockwell, Kari, Dr/Fieldcrest Cmty School Dist 6	1,11	257
Rodden, Dan/Tri-City Cmty Unit Sch Dist 1	5	214
Rodea, Danea/Komarek School District 94	57	54
Rodeffer, Donna/Hamilton Cmty Cons SD 328	7	114
Rodewald, Robert/Bourbonnais Elem Sch Dist 53	67	134
Rodgers, Barry/Winnetka School Dist 36	9,70	72
Rodgers, Keir/Township High School Dist 214	88	69
Rodgreguez, Jesse, Dr/Zion-Benton Twp High SD 126	1	157
Rodiguez, Astrid/Queen Bee School District 16	83	98
Rodino, Mary/Evanston Twp High SD 202	2,11,19	48
Rodriguez, Cesar/Proviso Twp High Sch Dist 209	71	63
Rodriguez, Michele/Fenton Cmty High Sch Dist 100	57,271	94
Rodriguez, Sergio/Cicero School District 99	59	42
Rodriguez, Shannon/Park Ridge Niles CMCSD 64	57	62
Rodriguez, Sylvia/Elgin School District U-46	57	130
Roeder, Janice/Rhodes School District 84 1/2	67	64
Roedl, Justin/Cumberland Cmty Unit SD 77	6	84
Roeharig, David/Creve Coeur Sch Dist 76	59	226
Roeschley, James/Waverly Cmty Unit SD 6	8,36,69	193
Rogalevich, Sophia/Big Hollow School District 38	68	148
Rogers, Chris/Unity Point Cmty Cons SD 140	73,76,286,295,297	121
Rogers, Eli/Aptakisic-Tripp Sch Dist 102	79	146
Rogers, Eric/Diamond Lake School Dist 76	2,3	149
Rogers, Janet/Harvey Public School Dist 152	67	51
Rogers, Jeanine/General George S Patton SD 133	9,69,288	50
Rogers, Jill/Martinsville Cmty Unit SD C-3	1,11,83	16
Rogers, Julie/Tri-Valley Cmty School Dist 3	4	187
Rogers, Mark/Abingdon-Avon Cmty Unit SD 276	73,295	139
Rogers, Merre/Flanagan-Cornell Unit 74 SD	12	161
Rogers, Michelle/South Fork School Dist 14	8	14

NAME/District	JOB FUNCTIONS	PAGE
Rogers, Mike/Macon-Piatt Roe#39	2	167
Rogers, Ron/Unity Point Cmty Cons SD 140	83,85	121
Rogers, Scott/Rock Falls Elem Sch Dist 13	6	240
Rogers, Zach/Belleville Township HSD 201	16,73,82	217
Rohlwing, Kurt/Round Lake Area Co Dist 116	10	155
Rohlwing, Susan/Community Unit School Dist 300	8	180
Rohlwing, Todd/Community Unit School Dist 300	91	180
Rohman, Daniel/Morton Cmty Unit Sch Dist 709	83	227
Rohr, Vince/Brownstown Cmty Unit SD 201	6	105
Rohrer, Stephen/Lincoln Elem School Dist 27	67	163
Roiland, Kenneth/Woodstock Cmty Unit SD 200	3,91	184
Rojas, Carlos/Des Plaines Cmty Cons SD 62	57	45
Rokis, Deb/Geneseo Cmty Unit Sch Dist 228	7	117
Roland, Ken/Township High School Dist 214	3	69
Rolfing, Elise/Valmeyer Cmty School Dist 3	7,83,85	190
Rollie, Jami/Ashley Cmty Cons SD 15	12	235
Rollinson, Scott/Harlem Unit Sch District 122	15,68	252
Roloff, Anne, Dr/Niles Twp High School Dist 219	10,11,57,69	58
Romadka, Ashley/Ball Chatham Cmty Unit SD 5	68	211
Romagnoli, Leslie/McLean Co Unit District 5	57	186
Romani, Jeff/Community Cons School Dist 89	73,76,295,297	90
Romano, Angelica/West Chicago Elementary SD 33	68	99
Romano, Dean/Geneva CUSD 304	2,15	131
Rominski, Brian/Prospect Hts School Dist 23	3	63
Romios, Helen/Elmhurst Cmty Unit SD 205	68	93
Ronen, Shonda/Bunker Hill Cmty Unit SD 8	8	167
Ronna, Mary/Milford Area Public SD 124	67	119
Ronquest, Christina/Learning Tech Ctr of Illinois	2,297	13
Roodhouse, James/Geneseo Cmty Unit Sch Dist 228	73,76	117
Roop, Josh/Tri-Valley Cmty School Dist 3	6	187
Root, Bud/Rantoul Twp High Sch Dist 193	27	12
Root, Darren/Auburn Cmty Unit Sch Dist 10	1	211
Root, Suzi/Hoopeston Area Cmty Unit SD 11	8,11	232
Rosado, Glend, Dr/East Aurora School Dist 131	15,79	129
Rosales, Miguel/Hoover-Schrum Sch Dist 157	16,73,76,84	52
Rosas, Sandra/Leyden Cmty High Sch Dist 212	5	55
Rose, Anna/Peoria Public Sch Dist 150	57	198
Rose, Heather/Forest Ridge Sch Dist 142	2	50
Rose, Lindsey/North Shore School Dist 112	57	154
Rose, Sarah/Deerfield Public SD 109	79	149
Rose, Sherry/Limestone Walters CCSD 316	2	198
Roseland, Bill/Channahon School District 17	59	241
Roseland, Bill/Union School Dist 81	59	248
Roseland, Bill, Dr/Southern Will Co Spec Ed Dist	1	250
Rosenberger, Patty/DeSoto Grade School Dist 86	12,288	120
Rosenblum, Laura/Indian Prairie Sch Dist 204	9,15	95
Roser, Amy/McLean Co Unit District 5	67	186
Roskowski, Tammy/Nashville Cmty HSD 99	2	235
Ross, Angeline/Salt Creek School District 48	9	99
Ross, Bob/Naperville Cmty Unit SD 203	3,17,68	98
Ross, Ellyn/Aptakisic-Tripp Sch Dist 102	67	146
Ross, Gilda/Glenbard Twp High Sch Dist 87	83,88	94
Ross, Kevin/Marshall Cmty Sch Dist C-2	1,11,83	15
Ross, Roxanne/Plainfield Cons Sch Dist 202	58	246
Ross, Roxanne/Plainfield Cons Sch Dist 202	58	246
Ross, Tom/Grant Cmty High Sch Dist 124	6	150
Ross, Valencia/Lincoln Elem School Dist 156	67	55
Rossi, Marilyn/High Mount Sch Dist 116	2	219
Rossi, Pat/Ridgewood Cmty HSD 234	3	64
Rossi, Sara/Community Cons School Dist 15	280	43
Rossman, Teri/Dimmick Cmty School Dist 175	59,71,84	141
Rossmiller, Kevin/Silvis School District 34	67	209
Rost, Elizabeth/Monticello Cmty Unit SD 25	27	202
Roth, Jim/Carlinville Cmty Unit SD 1	5	167
Roth, Kraig/Dupo Cmty School District 196	58	218
Roth, Kristine, Dr/Kirby School District 140	9,12,288	53
Rothe, Jeri/Carrollton Cmty Unit SD 1	93	111

1	Superintendent	16	Instructional Media Svcs	30	Adult Education	44	Science Sec	58	Special Education K-12	72 Summer School
2	Bus/Finance/Purchasing	17	Chief Operations Officer	31	Career/Sch-to-Work K-12	45	Math K-12	59	Special Education Elem	73 Instructional Tech
3	Buildings And Grounds	18	Chief Academic Officer	32	Career/Sch-to-Work Elem	46	Math Elem	60	Special Education Sec	74 Inservice Training
4	Food Service	19	Chief Financial Officer	33	Career/Sch-to-Work Sec	47	Math Sec	61	Foreign/World Lang K-12	75 Marketing/Distributive
5	Transportation	20	Art K-12	34	Early Childhood Ed	48	English/Lang Arts K-12	62	Foreign/World Lang Elem	76 Info Systems
6	Athletic	21	Art Elem	35	Health/Phys Education	49	English/Lang Arts Elem	63	Foreign/World Lang Sec	77 Psychological Assess
7	Health Services	22	Art Sec	36	Guidance Services K-12	50	English/Lang Arts Sec	64	Religious Education K-12	78 Affirmative Action
8	Curric/Instruct K-12	23	Music K-12	37	Guidance Services Elem	51	Reading K-12	65	Religious Education Elem	79 Student Personnel
9	Curric/Instruct Elem	24	Music Elem	38	Guidance Services Sec	52	Reading Elem	66	Religious Education Sec	80 Driver Ed/Safety
10	Curric/Instruct Sec	25	Music Sec	39	Social Studies K-12	53	Reading Sec	67	School Board President	81 Gifted/Talented
11	Federal Program	26	Business Education	40	Social Studies Elem	54	Remedial Reading K-12	68	Teacher Personnel	82 Video Services
12	Title I	27	Career & Tech Ed	41	Social Studies Sec	55	Remedial Reading Elem	69	Academic Assessment	83 Substance Abuse Prev
13	Title V	28	Technology Education	42	Science K-12	56	Remedial Reading Sec	70	Research/Development	84 Erate
15	Asst Superintendent	29	Family/Consumer Science	43	Science Elem	57	Bilingual/ELL	71	Public Information	85 AIDS Education

88 Alternative/At Risk	277 Remedial Math K-12
89 Multi-Cultural Curriculum	280 Literacy Coach
90 Social Work	285 STEM
91 Safety/Security	286 Digital Learning
92 Magnet School	288 Common Core Standards
93 Parental Involvement	294 Accountability
95 Tech Prep Program	295 Network System
97 Chief Information Officer	296 Title II Programs
98 Chief Technology Officer	297 Webmaster
270 Character Education	298 Grant Writer/Ptnrships
271 Migrant Education	750 Chief Innovation Officer
273 Teacher Mentor	751 Chief of Staff
274 Before/After Sch	752 Social Emotional Learning
275 Response To Intervention	

Illinois School Directory — DISTRICT PERSONNEL INDEX

NAME/District	JOB FUNCTIONS	PAGE
Rothrock, Tim/Okaw Valley Cmty Unit SD 302	67	193
Rotimi, Catherine/Cook County School Dist 130	57	45
Rottman, Jennifer/Chicago PSD-Network 3	15	29
Roundcount, Travis, Dr/Mt Zion Cmty Unit Sch Dist 3	1	166
Rounds, Tedd/Momence Cmty Unit Sch Dist 1	6	136
Roundtree, Jamie/Champaign Cmty Unit Sch Dist 4	9,12	10
Rounsaville, Roberts/Homer Cmty Cons Sch Dist 33C	5	242
Rouse, Theresa, Dr/Joliet Public School Dist 86	1	243
Rowe, Gary/Rock Island-Milan Sch Dist 41	67	208
Rowe, Jennifer/Indian Prairie Sch Dist 204	78	95
Rowe, Karen/Huntley Cmty School Dist 158	7	182
Rowe, Pam/Newark Cmty Cons Sch Dist 66	9,280,288	138
Rowe, Ralph/Mazon-Verona-Kinsman ESD 2-C	73	112
Rowe, Rubin/Georgetown-Ridge Farm CUSD 4	3	232
Rowe, Scott/Huntley Cmty School Dist 158	1	182
Rowells, Curt/Community High School Dist 117	6	148
Roy, Cheryl/Lemont High Sch Dist 210	2,3,91	55
Royalty, Kyan/Midwest Ctl Cmty Unit SD 191	73	177
Rozanski, Chris/Huntley Cmty School Dist 158	6	182
Ruach, Evan/Riverview Cmty Cons Sch Dist 2	67	258
Rubenstein, Kevin/Elmhurst Cmty Unit SD 205	15,79,83	93
Rubenstein, Kevin, Dr/Lake Bluff Elem Sch Dist 65	11,37,59,73,77,90,286	151
Rubio, Gail/Cook County School Dist 130	59,79	45
Rucker, Vincent/Hazel Crest School Dist 152-5	73	52
Rude, Thomas, Dr/St Libory Cons Sch District 30	1,11,84	222
Rudenga, Sarah/Flossmoor School District 161	16	49
Rudluff, Angela/Cypress School District 64	67	127
Rudolph, Jerry/North Boone Cmty Unit SD 200	73	5
Ruebush, Angie/Pikeland Cmty Sch Dist 10	11,15,74,275,296,298	203
Ruelli, Anthony/Glen Ellyn School District 41	2	94
Ruelli, Steve/Glenview Cmty Cons Sch Dist 34	3,91	51
Ruesch, Cindy, Dr/Community Unit School Dist 303	7,57,68,79,81,93	128
Ruetercox, Dawn/Consolidated High Sch Dist 230	69,76	44
Ruff, Erin/Manteno Cmty Unit Sch Dist 5	58,79	136
Rufner, Shana/Durand Cmty Sch Dist 322	9,274,275,288	252
Ruggeberg, Kathryn/Rock Island-Milan Sch Dist 41	8,11,15,285,286,288,298	208
Ruggeberg, Perky/Meridian Cmty Unit SD 223	5	194
Ruh, Kari/Batavia Unit School Dist 101	36,58,79	128
Ruhl, Jennifer/Ramsey Cmty Unit Sch Dist 204	7	105
Ruiz, Fernando/Cicero School District 99	91	42
Ruiz, Leo/Evanston-Skokie Cmty CSD 65	76	48
Ruland, Joshua, Dr/Minooka Cmty Cons Sch Dist 2019	11,15,57,69,88,288,296	112
Rummel, Nicole, Dr/Mahomet-Seymour Cmty SD 3	8,12	11
Runde, Doug/Teutopolis Cmty Unit SD 50	73,76,295	105
Runge, Matt/Pleasant Plains Cmty Unit SD 8	1	212
Runge, Rick/Murphysboro Cmty Unit SD 186	67	121
Runyon, Kirstin/Charleston Cmty Unit SD 1	16,82	19
Ruppert, Chad/Nokomis Cmty Unit Sch Dist 22	67	191
Ruscitti, Darlene, Dr/Dupage Reg Office of Ed 19	1	102
Rusik, Adam/Joliet Public School Dist 86	24	243
Russ, Angie/Salt Creek School District 48	288	99
Russeau, Rod/Community High School Dist 99	73,76,84,286,295	91
Russell, Kevin/Downers Grove School Dist 58	1	93
Russell, Lisa/Maroa Forsyth CU Sch Dist 2	4	165
Russell, Pam/Cahokia Unit Sch Dist 187	4	218
Russell, Renee/West Central Cmty Unit SD 235	16,82	116
Russell, Rusty/Limestone Cmty High SD 310	3	197
Russell, Sherri/Richland School Dist 88A	6	247
Russo, David/Lincolnwood Sch Dist 74	9,12,15	55
Russo, Janet/Community Cons School Dist 59	2	43
Russo, Scott/Community Unit School Dist 201	3	92
Rusteberg, Virginia/Valmeyer Cmty School Dist 3	67	190
Rutherford, Lori/Mt Zion Community Unit Sch Dist 3	274	166
Ruttkay, Jennifer/Lincolnwood Sch Dist 74	59	55
Ruyle, Bob/Southwestern Cmty Unit SD 9	3	168
Ryan-Toye, Martha/Riverside Public Sch Dist 96	1	65
Ryan, Kevin, Dr/North Shore School Dist 112	9,11,15,69,288	154
Ryan, Matt/Western Springs Sch Dist 101	73	71
Ryan, Mike/Community High School Dist 218	3,15,68	44
Ryan, Mike/Maercker School District 60	73	97
Ryan, Reggie/Northbrook Elem School Dist 27	73,295	59
Ryan, Terry/Northbrook School District 28	71,76	59
Ryan, Tommi Jo/Spring Garden Cmty CSD 178	6	124
Ryba, Missy/Farmington Ctl Cmty SD 265	8,11,57,58,294	197
Ryder, Denise/Limestone Cmty High SD 310	12,15	197
Ryerson, Tom/Moline-Coal Valley SD No 40	8	207
Ryker, Debbie/Johnston City Cmty Unit SD 1	36	251
Ryker, Terry, Dr/Herrin Cmty School District 4	1,84	251
Ryner, Sara/La Harpe Cmty Sch Dist 347	57,58,69,270,273,288,294	115
Rynor, Sarah/North Mac Cmty Unit SD 34	8,11	168
Rzasa, Diane/Allen-Otter Creek CCSD 65	67	141

S

NAME/District	JOB FUNCTIONS	PAGE
Saake, Gary/Community High School Dist 94	67	91
Saathoff, Tim/Central Cmty Unit SD 4	73,286	118
Sabado, Arlene/Proviso Twp High Sch Dist 209	2	63
Sabinson, Kip/Warren Community Unit SD 205	67	126
Sabo, Carolyn/Waterloo Cmty Unit Sch Dist 5	7	190
Sabourin, Jennifer/Salt Creek School District 48	79	99
Sadler, Jenny/Jonesboro Cmty Cons SD 43	2	230
Saeks, Randy/Glencoe Sch District 35	76,295	51
Sager, Barb/North Boone Cmty Unit SD 200	7	5
Sahr, Grant/Indian Prairie Sch Dist 204	8	95
Sailor, Colleen/Princeton Twp HSD 500	67	7
Saindon, Curtis/Woodridge Elem Sch District 68	2,5,15	100
Sala, Andrea, Dr/Arbor Park School District 145	1,83	21
Salazar, Basilio/Community Unit School Dist 300	8,752	180
Salazar, Demetrio/Henry Senachwine CUSD 5	73,295	176
Salem, Shadia/North Palos School Dist 117	57,89	59
Salemi, Philip/Westchester Public SD 92 1/2	1	70
Salgado, Diana/Sunnybrook School District 171	752	68
Sallee, Melissa/Mendota Twp High Sch Dist 280	29	143
Sallis, Deetra/DeKalb Cmty Unit SD 428	68	84
Sally, Paul, Dr/New Trier Twp HS District 203	1	58
Salm, Debbie/Huntley Cmty School Dist 158	2	182
Salmieri, Joe, Dr/Laraway Cmty Cons SD 70-C	1	243
Salmons, Bobbi/Central School District 3	12	1
Salus, Jordan/Lake Forest Cmty HSD 115	16,73	151
Salus, Jordan/Lake Forest Cmty HSD 115	73,98	151
Salus, Jordan/Lake Forest School District 67	73,98,295,297	152
Salzer, Nancy/Chicago Ridge Sch Dist 127-5	67	41
Samet, Tina/Hoopeston Area Cmty Unit SD 11	4	232
Samojedny, Christie, Dr/Skokie School District 68	9,11,83,273,275,285,288,298	67
Sample, Michael/Sesser-Valier Cmty Unit SD 196	8,31,73	108
Sampson, Justin/Community Cons School Dist 59	71	43
Sampson, Kate/Elmhurst Cmty Unit SD 205	71	93
Samuelian, Patty/North Shore School Dist 112	273	154
Sanburg, Neil/Grundy Co Special Ed Co-op	1,11	113
Sanchez-Lopez, Ricardo/Valley View Cmty SD 365-U	57	248
Sanchez, Melissa/Cicero School District 99	298	42
Sanchez, Mireya/Community Cons School Dist 93	57,89	90
Sanchez, Paul/West Harvey-Dixmoor Pub SD 147	9	70
Sanchez, Yesenia/North Chicago Cmty Unit SD 187	8,18,36,79	153
Sandberg, Dan/Community High School Dist 155	3	179
Sandefer, Paul/Sterling Cmty Unit Sch Dist 5	67	240
Sander, Joe, Dr/Washington Cmty HS Dist 308	2,15	229
Sanders, Amy/Marion Cmty School Dist 2	11,15,288,296	251
Sanders, Eugene/Limestone Cmty High SD 310	67	197
Sanders, George/New Trier Twp HS District 203	78	58
Sanders, Kristin/Moline-Coal Valley SD No 40	15,58,77,78,79,90	207
Sanders, Roxana/Oak Park & River Forest SD 200	68	60
Sanders, Ted/Grand Ridge CCSD 95	1	141
Sanders, Tiffany/Chicago PSD-Network 9	15	33
Sanders, Tony/Elgin School District U-46	1	130
Sanderson, Jerry/Diocese of Peoria Ed Office	15	200
Sanderson, Nicole/Wolf Branch School Dist 113	9,288	222
Sanderson, William/Evergreen Park Cmty HSD 231	15,69,79,93	49
Sandiford, Bill/Robinson Cmty Unit Sch Dist 2	67	83
Sandretto, Angela/Community Unit School Dist 7	11,34	167
Sands, Jason/Rock Falls Twp High SD 301	33,38,79,85,88,270	240
Sands, Nicole/East Coloma-Nelson Cesd 20	12	238
Sanford, Jarvis/Chicago PSD-Ausl	15	25
Sanford, Jim/Norwood Sch Dist 63	67	198
Sangroula, Laura/Des Plaines Cmty Cons SD 62	9,15	45
Sangston, Ken/Seneca Cmty Cons Sch Dist 170	67	144
Sannemin, Stephanie/Henry Senachwine CUSD 5	2	176
Santacruz, Ernesto/Cook County School Dist 130	73,286	45
Santel, Jennie/Breese Elementary SD 12	2	17
Sanz, Marcelo/Niles Twp High School Dist 219	76	58
Sapada, Ashley/Komarek School District 94	274	54
Sapella, Diane, Dr/Fairmont School District 89	1	242
Sarfaty, Susan/St Clair Co Regional Off of Ed	1,11	223

DISTRICT PERSONNEL INDEX

Market Data Retrieval

NAME/District	JOB FUNCTIONS	PAGE
Sarff, Lori/Illini Central CUSD 189	58	177
Sargeant, Jay/Community High School Dist 155	15,68	179
Sarrels, Kelly/Hinsdale Twp High School Dist 86	57	95
Sarris, Alicia/Highland Cmty Sch District 5	73	171
Sartore, Renee/Community Unit School Dist 308	57	137
Sarver, Ronald/Troy Cmty Cons SD 30-C	16,76	247
Satchwell, Mary/Maercker School District 60	67	97
Sather, Michele/Rockford School District 205	2	253
Satkiewicz, Judith/Rondout School District 72	73	154
Satorius, James/Minooka Cmty Cons Sch Dist 201	67	112
Satterwhite, Latrece, Dr/Elgin School District U-46	58,79	130
Sauber, Cody/Hiawatha Cmty Unit SD 426	73,295	85
Sauder, Brad/Roanoke-Benson Cmty Unit SD 60	67	258
Sauer, Dale/Shiloh Village Sch Dist 85	1	221
Saunders, Michael/Morton Cmty Unit Sch Dist 709	296	227
Saurez, Juan/McHenry Cmty Cons Sch Dist 15	57	183
Savage-William, Pat/Evanston Twp High SD 202	67	48
Savage, Cathy/Community Cons School Dist 59	76,295	43
Savage, Rachel, Dr/Moline-Coal Valley SD No 40	1	207
Savage, Scott/Pana Cmty Unit School Dist 8	73,295	14
Saveley, Elizabeth/North Boone Cmty Unit School Dist 200	273	5
Saverson, Adrienne/Calumet Public School Dist 132	11,57,74,83,280,288,296	24
Saviano, Tina/Glenbard Twp High Sch Dist 87	60	94
Sawyer, Doug/Belle Valley School Dist 119	73,295	217
Sax, Adam/Antioch Cmty Cons Sch Dist 34	9,11,69,73,76,270,286,294	146
Sayre, Tracie/Triopia Cmty Unit Sch Dist 27	67	192
Scaduto, Diane/Dakota Cmty Unit Sch Dist 201	7	224
Scanavino, Joe/Sangamon Valley Cmty Unit SD 9	57	166
Scarmardo, Dave/Glen Ellyn School District 41	3	94
Scarols, Krista/Durand Cmty Sch Dist 322	273	252
Scarsella, Anthony, Dr/Palos Cmty Cons Sch Dist 118	1	61
Schab, Angelica/East Maine School District 63	274	47
Schacht, Marshal/St Joseph-Ogden Cmty HSD 305	88	12
Schackmann, Sharon/Palestine Cmty Unit SD 3	58	83
Schaefer, Carla/Pekin Cmty High Sch Dist 303	2,5	227
Schaefer, Diane/Freeburg Cmty High Sch Dist 77	2	219
Schaefer, Kim/Red Bud Cmty Unit Sch Dist 132	2	205
Schaefer, Marcus/Roxana Cmty Unit Sch Dist 1	73,76,295	172
Schaeflein, Kathy/Homewood School Dist 153	9	52
Schafer, Kenton/Elverado Cmty Unit SD 196	67	120
Schafer, Steve/Illini Bluffs Cmty Unit SD 327	6	197
Schaibley, Teresa/Miller Cmty Cons Sch Dist 210	16	143
Schalk, Jennifer, Dr/Naperville Cmty Unit SD 203	8,18	98
Schall, Joe/Iroquois Co Cmty Unit SD 9	73,76	119
Schall, Leslie/Reavis Twp HSD 220	60	64
Schamberger, Joyce/Amboy Cmty Unit Sch Dist 272	12	159
Scharf, Ken/Eureka Cmty Unit Sch Dist 140	5	257
Scharlach, Denise/Rossville-Alvin Cmty Unit SD 7	2	233
Schauer, Peter/Lake Park Cmty High SD 108	6	96
Schauff, Kristina/Rock Falls Twp High SD 301	16	240
Schaver, Candy/A-C Central Cmty Unit SD 262	8,69,83,85,88,273	9
Schaver, Darrell/Springfield Pub Sch Dist 186	3,80	213
Schell, Mary/Alton Cmty School District 11	2,274	169
Scheloz, Mary Ann/Decatur Public Schools 61	11,296	165
Schenk, Bill/Antioch Cmty Cons Sch Dist 34	3,91	146
Schenk, Lindy/Astoria Cmty Unit Sch Dist 1	11,296	109
Scheri, Mark/Hall Twp High School Dist 502	3	6
Schermerhorn, Leslie/McHenry Co Reg Office of Ed 44	1	185
Scheuermann, Dave/Auburn Cmty Unit Sch Dist 10	73	211
Schierloh, Darcy/Lena-Winslow Cmty Unit SD 202	84	224
Schiess, Rhonda/Rhodes School District 84 1/2	274	64
Schiffbauer, Robert/Lincoln-Way Cmty HS Dist 210	68	244
Schiller, Jeff/West Aurora School Dist 129	3	132
Schilling, Nathon/Lansing School Dist 158	1	54
Schillinger, Katherine/Glen Ellyn School District 41	5	94
Schillo, Debbie/Evergreen Park Cmty HSD 231	10,74,273,288	49
Schillo, Deborah/Evergreen Park Cmty HSD 231	10,11	49

NAME/District	JOB FUNCTIONS	PAGE
Schilson, Kim/Illini West High Sch Dist 307	1,11	114
Schilt, Jennifer/Red Hill Cmty School Dist 10	4	159
Schippert, Peggy/Roanoke-Benson Cmty Unit SD 60	12,51,54	258
Schlechte, Bob/Stewardson-Strasburg SD 5-A	67	216
Schlechter, Rachel/Valley View Cmty SD 365-U	41,50	248
Schleifer, Tricia/West Washington Co Cmty SD 10	36,83,275	236
Schleizer, Shawn, Dr/East Maine School District 63	15,68,79	47
Schlemer, Jon/Sterling Cmty Unit Sch Dist 5	80	240
Schlemmer, Jan/Community Cons School Dist 180	7	90
Schlichter, Erika/Huntley Cmty School Dist 158	8,15,16,70,285	182
Schlinger, Helga/Lemont High Sch Dist 210	76	55
Schlismann, Kristine/Joliet Twp High Sch Dist 204	71	243
Schlott, Ryan/Plainfield Cons Sch Dist 202	76	246
Schlueter, Kathleen/Western CUSD 12	34	203
Schmedeke, Amy/Morrisonville Cmty Unit SD 1	58	14
Schmidgall, Mary/Pontiac Cmty Cons Sch Dist 429	4	161
Schmidt, Andrew/Bloom Twp High Sch Dist 206	16,73,84,95,295	23
Schmidt, Angie/Lincolnwood Sch Dist 74	4	55
Schmidt, Bob/Community High School Dist 94	73	91
Schmidt, Cj/Vandalia Cmty Unit SD 203	73	106
Schmidt, Eric/Robinson Cmty Unit Sch Dist 2	83	83
Schmidt, James/Homewood Flossmoor CHSD 233	77	52
Schmidt, Jeremy/Grant Cmty High Sch Dist 124	13,69,270,271,273,296	150
Schmidt, Jim/Plano Cmty Unit Sch Dist 88	6	138
Schmidt, Julie/Kildeer Countryside CCSD 96	1	151
Schmidt, Kristi/Marseilles Elem Sch Dist 150	12	142
Schmidt, Patricia/Community Unit School Dist 300	69,294	180
Schmidt, Robert/Batavia Unit School Dist 101	3	128
Schmidt, Sarah/Carrollton Cmty Unit SD 1	34	111
Schmidt, Sherrie/Community Unit School Dist 300	7	180
Schmidt, Steve/Itasca School District 10	73,295	96
Schmidt, Todd/Elmhurst Cmty Unit SD 205	3	93
Schmidt, William, Dr/Woodridge Elem Sch District 68	15,68,78,79,273	100
Schmieg, John/Waterloo Cmty Unit Sch Dist 5	8,11,51,286,288,296	190
Schmit, Rick/Sandwich Cmty Unit SD 430	1,11	85
Schmitt, Christine/New Trier Twp HS District 203	83	58
Schmitt, Krystal/Crete-Monee Cmty SD 201-U	76	242
Schmitt, Margo/Barrington Cmty Unit SD 220	74,81,92,274	147
Schmitt, Vanessa/Proviso Twp High Sch Dist 209	79	63
Schmittler, Dale/Edwards Co Cmty Unit SD 1	13,93	104
Schmitz, Kathy/Fairfield Pub Sch District 112	2	236
Schnable, Karen/Riley Cmty Cons Sch Dist 18	2,5	184
Schneider, Chuck/Tonica Cmty Cons Sch Dist 79	1,11	145
Schneider, Jessi/Rankin Cmty School Dist 98	6	228
Schneider, Patricia/Freeport School District 145	42,48	224
Schneider, Scott/Illini West High Sch Dist 307	16,57,69,74,83,271,273	114
Schneider, Thomas, Dr/Community Cons School Dist 180	1	90
Schneider, Valery/Silvis School District 34	5	209
Schneiderman, Jonathan/Forrestville Valley CUSD 221	8	194
Schneman, Dale/Blue Ridge Cmty SD 18	67	87
Schnider, Max/Elverado Cmty Unit SD 196	91	120
Schnieder, Kurt, Dr/Northern Suburban Spec Ed Dist	1	159
Schnoor, Meg, Dr/Community Cons School Dist 15	9,11,15,288	43
Schoby, Ashlee/Riverton Cmty Unit SD 14	7	212
Schock, Nicholas/Community High School Dist 117	76	148
Schoedel, Alisha/Hollis Cons School Dist 328	270	197
Schoell, Blair/Grant Cmty High Sch Dist 124	26,29,35,63	150
Schoellhorn, Krista/Columbia Cmty Unit SD 4	16	190
Schoeneweisf, Christopher/Winnebago Cmty Unit SD 323	67	255
Schoenfelder, Steve/Community High School Dist 117	6	148
Schoenherr, Jayme/Oakdale Cmty Cons Sch Dist 1	2	236
Schon, Jenny/Community Unit School Dist 200	68	91
School, Kristen, Dr/Mendota Cmty School Dist 289	1,11,83	142
Schoolman, Michelle/Milford Area Public SD 124	273	119
Schoonover, Geoff/Cornell Cmty Cons Sch Dist 426	1,11,73,83,288	160
Schoot, Joshua/Community Cons School Dist 181	2	91
Schoppe, Craig/Homer Cmty Cons Sch Dist 33C	1	242

1 Superintendent	16 Instructional Media Svcs	30 Adult Education	44 Science Sec	58 Special Education K-12	72 Summer School	88 Alternative/At Risk	277 Remedial Math K-12
2 Bus/Finance/Purchasing	17 Chief Operations Officer	31 Career/Sch-to-Work K-12	45 Math K-12	59 Special Education Elem	73 Instructional Tech	89 Multi-Cultural Curriculum	280 Literacy Coach
3 Buildings And Grounds	18 Chief Academic Officer	32 Career/Sch-to-Work Elem	46 Math Elem	60 Special Education Sec	74 Inservice Training	90 Social Work	285 STEM
4 Food Service	19 Chief Financial Officer	33 Career/Sch-to-Work Sec	47 Math Sec	61 Foreign/World Lang K-12	75 Marketing/Distributive	91 Safety/Security	286 Digital Learning
5 Transportation	20 Art K-12	34 Early Childhood Ed	48 English/Lang Arts K-12	62 Foreign/World Lang Elem	76 Info Systems	92 Magnet School	288 Common Core Standards
6 Athletic	21 Art Elem	35 Health/Phys Education	49 English/Lang Arts Elem	63 Foreign/World Lang Sec	77 Psychological Assess	93 Parental Involvement	294 Accountability
7 Health Services	22 Art Sec	36 Guidance Services K-12	50 English/Lang Arts Sec	64 Religious Education K-12	78 Affirmative Action	95 Tech Prep Program	295 Network System
8 Curric/Instruct K-12	23 Music K-12	37 Guidance Services Elem	51 Reading K-12	65 Religious Education Elem	79 Student Personnel	96 Chief Information Officer	296 Title II Programs
9 Curric/Instruct Elem	24 Music Elem	38 Guidance Services Sec	52 Reading Elem	66 Religious Education Sec	80 Driver Ed/Safety	97 Chief Technology Officer	297 Webmaster
10 Curric/Instruct Sec	25 Music Sec	39 Social Studies K-12	53 Reading Sec	67 School Board President	81 Gifted/Talented	270 Character Education	298 Grant Writer/Ptnrships
11 Federal Program	26 Business Education	40 Social Studies Elem	54 Remedial Reading K-12	68 Teacher Personnel	82 Video Services	271 Migrant Education	750 Chief Innovation Officer
12 Title I	27 Career & Tech Ed	41 Social Studies Sec	55 Remedial Reading Elem	69 Academic Assessment	83 Substance Abuse Prev	273 Teacher Mentor	751 Chief of Staff
13 Title V	28 Technology Education	42 Science K-12	56 Remedial Reading Sec	70 Research/Development	84 Erate	274 Before/After Sch	752 Social Emotional Learning
15 Asst Superintendent	29 Family/Consumer Science	43 Science Elem	57 Bilingual/ELL	71 Public Information	85 AIDS Education	275 Response To Intervention	

Illinois School Directory

DISTRICT PERSONNEL INDEX

NAME/District	JOB FUNCTIONS	PAGE
Schorfheide, Jeannette/Lebanon Cmty Unit Sch Dist 9	69,83,294	220
Schorsch, Carl/Ridgewood Cmty HSD 234	73,295	64
Schoth, Gene/Mt Pulaski Cmty Unit SD 23	5	164
Schott, Joshua/Community Cons School Dist 15	2	42
Schott, Stacey/Reed-Custer Cmty Unit SD 255-U	294	246
Schrader, Christan/Black Hawk Area Spec Ed Dist	1,11	210
Schraeder, Latasha/Carbondale Elem School Dist 95	79	120
Schreiber, Edmar/Bond Co Cmty Unit Sch Dist 2	67	4
Schrewe, Kristin/Roxana Cmty Unit Sch Dist 1	16	172
Schrik, Paul, Dr/Rockdale School District 84	1,57	247
Schrock, Andrea/Durand Cmty Sch Dist 322	36,90	252
Schroeder, Betsy/Ball Chatham Cmty Unit SD 5	71	211
Schroeder, Lucas/North Wayne Cmty Unit SD 200	1,11	237
Schroeder, Lynn/School Assoc for Sp Ed-Dupage	68	102
Schroeder, Michael/Channahon School District 17	2,5	241
Schroeder, Monica, Dr/North Shore School Dist 112	15,68	154
Schroeder, Shannon/Burbank School District 111	7	24
Schroen, Jenna/Odell Cmty Cons Sch Dist 435	34	161
Schubbe, Sherry/Peotone Cmty Unit SD 207-U	16	245
Schubert, Jamie/Galena Unit School Dist 120	4	125
Schubert, Jeff/McHenry Cmty Cons Sch Dist 15	2	183
Schubert, Joaquin/Skokie School District 69	59	67
Schuchman, Becky, Dr/Carlinville Cmty Unit SD 1	1	167
Schuck, Beth/Community High School Dist 94	76	91
Schueller, Joe/Montmorency Cmty Cons SD 145	67	239
Schuenke, Lisa/Jersey Cmty Sch Dist 100	2,68	125
Schuh, Dave/Crystal Lake Elem District 47	91	181
Schuler, David, Dr/Township High School Dist 214	1	69
Schuler, Jeff, Dr/Community Unit School Dist 200	1	91
Schuler, Seth/Cowden Herrick CUSD 3A	1,11,73,83	216
Schuler, Tim/Wabash Cmty Unit Sch Dist 348	67	234
Schullian, Johna/Regional Office of Ed 21	2,11	109
Schulman, Lauren/Northbrook-Glenview SD 30	59,69,79,83,88,270,280	60
Schulte, Charles David/Irvington Cmty Cons SD 11	1,11,83	235
Schulte, Stacey/Grant Cmty Cons Sch Dist 110	11	219
Schultz, Barbara/Stockton Cmty Unit SD 206	4	126
Schultz, Debi/Saratoga Cmty Cons SD 60C	7	113
Schultz, Heather/Northbrook School District 28	79	59
Schultz, Heidi/Streator Elem School Dist 44	34,37,59,69,275	144
Schultz, Joe/Donovan Cmty Unit Sch Dist 3	67	119
Schultz, Kevin/Dixon Cmty School Dist 170	3	160
Schultz, Natasha/Marengo Cmty High Sch Dist 154	69	182
Schultz, Nichole/Peotone Cmty Unit SD 207-U	36	245
Schultze, Stacie/Ashley Cmty Cons SD 15	4	235
Schulz, Ryan/Arlington Hts School Dist 25	3,5,91	21
Schumacher, Kyle, Dr/La Grange Elem Sch Dist 102	1	54
Schumer, David/McLean Co Unit District 5	73,84	186
Schupp, Duane/Lowpoint-Washburn CUSD 21	1,84	258
Schuright, Shane/Shelbyville Cmty Sch Dist 4	1,11	216
Schurman, Gina/Springfield Pub Sch Dist 186	68,79	213
Schurman, Tim/Chadwick Milledgevill CUSD 399	1,11	8
Schurtz, Roger/United Cmty Unit Sch Dist 304	73	234
Schuster, Aaron/Highland Cmty Sch District 5	67	171
Schuster, Lyndl, Dr/River Trails Sch Dist 26	2,15	65
Schutter, Eva/Morris Cmty High Sch Dist 101	57	113
Schutz, Stacy/North Greene Unit Dist 3	67	111
Schwalenberg, Geoffrey/Belleville Public Sch Dist 118	274	217
Schwalenberg, Geoss/Belleville Public Sch Dist 118	274	217
Schwamberger, George/Amboy Cmty Unit Sch Dist 272	6	159
Schwartz, Elise/Carlinville Cmty Unit SD 1	11,296	167
Schwartz, Joe/Eswood Cmty Cons SD 269	1,11,83	194
Schwartz, Lisa/Payson Cmty Unit School Dist 1	67	2
Schwartz, Scott, Dr/Deerfield Public SD 109	9,11,74,288	149
Schwartz, Tom/Johnsburg Cmty School Dist 12	3,5	182
Schwarzkopf, Todd/Herscher Cmty School Dist 2	6	135
Schwarzlose, Robert/Woodlawn Unit School Dist 209	3	124
Schweitzer, Christine/Eswood Cmty Cons SD 269	67	194
Schweitzer, Marg/Cook County School Dist 154	67	45
Schwemmer, Gabrielle/Sparta Cmty School Dist 140	1,11,83	205
Schwengel, Kenneth/Stewardson-Strasburg SD 5-A	1	216
Schwieterman, Bonnie/Lombard Elem SD 44	297	97
Schwingle, Tim/Sterling Cmty Unit Sch Dist 5	2	240
Schwuchow, John, Dr/Winnebago Cmty Unit SD 323	1	255
Scidham, Peggy/Bartonville School District 66	2	196
Sclulorffton, Tony/Township High School Dist 214	76	69
Scodro, Nadine/Palos Cmty Cons Sch Dist 118	67	61
Scofield, Michael/Zion Public School District 6	84,295	157
Scott, Allister/Community High School Dist 94	273,288	91
Scott, Christy/Bunker Hill Cmty Unit SD 8	7,85	167
Scott, Dee/Casey-Westfield Cmty USD C-4	1,11	15
Scott, Jason/Ford Heights School Dist 169	73	49
Scott, Jodi/Regional Office of Ed 33	1	141
Scott, Kenneth, Dr/Prairie Hills Elem SD 144	68	63
Scott, Linda/Carlyle Cmty Unit Sch Dist 1	2,68	17
Scott, Lori/Champaign Cmty Unit Sch Dist 4	298	10
Scott, Mark/North Greene Unit Dist 3	1	111
Scott, Michael/Prairie Central Cmty USD 8	3,91	162
Scott, Patricia/East Alton-Wood River SD 14	60	170
Scott, Shawna/Hamilton Co Cmty Unit SD 10	2,19	114
Scott, Todd/Bement Cmty Unit Sch Dist 5	67	202
Scribner, Tara/Washington School Dist 52	16,82	229
Scrivano, Kenneth/Rockford School District 205	67	254
Scroggins, Steven/Wood River-Hartford Elem SD 15	67	172
Scroggs, Eric/Woodford Co Special Ed Assoc	1	259
Scual-Bet, Stepahine/Cahokia Unit Sch Dist 187	298	218
Sculles, Kelly/Northbrook School District 28	57,752	59
Scully, Ann/Antioch Cmty Cons Sch Dist 34	7,34,57,59,79	146
Scwartz, David/Carterville Cmty Unit SD 5	67	250
Seachrist, Jennifer/Effingham Cmty Sch Dist 40	58,88	105
Seaman, Mike/Beardstown Cmty Sch Dist 15	67	9
Searl, Richard/Golf School District 67	3	51
Searle, Andrew/Mundelein Cons High SD 120	2,19	153
Seaton, Jennifer/Geneva CUSD 304	34	131
Seaton, Matthew/Streator Twp High School Dist 40	1	145
Seawall, Don/Batavia Unit School Dist 101	73,76	128
Seda, Jorge/Beach Park Cmty Cons SD 3	79	147
Sedlak, Ursula/Northbrook-Glenview SD 30	67	60
Seeley, Penny/Community Unit School Dist 7	4	167
Seelman, Amy, Dr/Pontiac-Wm Holliday SD 105	9	221
Seeman, Ben/Herscher Cmty School Dist 2	76	135
Sefcik, Cristine, Dr/Grant Cmty High Sch Dist 124	1	150
Sefton, Jessica/Brownstown Cmty Unit SD 201	35,85	105
Segal, Noreen/Wheeling Cmty Cons Sch Dist 21	57	71
Segarra, Rafael/Indian Prairie Sch Dist 204	57	95
Seger, Jessica/Mascoutah Cmty Sch Dist 19	58	220
Segersten, Margaret/Harvard Cmty Unit Sch Dist 50	8,69,296,298	181
Seggebruch, Phil/East Peoria Elem Sch Dist 86	35	227
Sego, Tom/East Peoria Elem Sch Dist 86	3	226
Segovia, Maurico/Chicago PSD-Network 2	15	29
Seibert, Brenda/Deer Creek-Mackinaw CUSD 701	2	226
Seibert, Nancy/Mascoutah Cmty Sch Dist 19	34,58,77,90	220
Seick, Colleen/Community Cons School Dist 15	73	43
Seifert, Kristine/River Trails Sch Dist 26	9,11,59,69,74,285,286,288	65
Seitzinger, Mike/Lawrence Co Cmty Sch Dist 20	67	159
Self, Rita/Henry Senachwine CUSD 5	38,83,88	176
Selix, Douglas/Elmwood Park Cmty Unit SD 401	295	48
Selk, Rebecca/Bradley Elem School Dist 61	9,273,275,285,294,296,298	134
Sellars, Miranda/East Alton Elementary SD 13	7,83	170
Selman, Lori/Marissa Cmty Unit Sch Dist 40	6	220
Seman, Matt/Williamsville Cmty Unit SD 15	67	214
Semande, Christy/Canton Union School Dist 66	16,82	109
Semenske, Anne/J Sterling Morton HSD 201	44	53
Senensky, Georiga/Morton Grove School Dist 70	4	58
Senffner, Michelle/Regional Office of Ed 24	15	113
Senica, Carol/Grundy Co Special Ed Co-op	15	113
Senior, Keith/West Washington Co Cmty SD 10	27,83,85,88	236
Senn, Derek/Skokie School District 68	16,73,286,295	67
Sennert, Michael/St Joseph Cmty Cons SD 169	9,16,73,82	12
Sensabaugh, Amber/Silvis School District 34	5,16,280	209
Sepich, Steve/District 50 Schools	3	226
Sepiol, Christina, Dr/Indian Prairie Sch Dist 204	7,15,58,79	95
Serdar, Brie/Community High School Dist 117	15	148
Sereleas, Paula/Plainfield Cons Sch Dist 202	8	246
Sergenti, Mike/East Peoria Cmty HS Dist 309	91	226
Sernus, Drew/Worth School District 127	67	72
Serratore, Tony/Consolidated High Sch Dist 230	67	44
Session, Sheryl/Meredosia-Chambersburg SD 11	11	192
Sesto, Julie/Marseilles Elem Sch Dist 150	7	142
Setaro, Fran/Chicago Ridge Sch Dist 127-5	9,12,27,88	41
Setchell, Nina/Polo Cmty Unit Sch Dist 222	752	195
Settles, Lauren/Bushnell Prairie Cmty USD 170	31,38,270	178
Seymour, Darin/Franklin Cmty Unit SD 1	3	192

DISTRICT PERSONNEL INDEX

Market Data Retrieval

NAME/District	JOB FUNCTIONS	PAGE
Shabo, Miriam/Archdiocese of Chicago Ed Off	2	72
Shackelford, Beth/O'Fallon Twp School Dist 203	2	221
Shackelford, Mike/Brownstown Cmty Unit SD 201	1,11,73	105
Shade, Jim/Pikeland Cmty Sch Dist 10	3	203
Shadel, Steve/Niles Twp High School Dist 219	285	58
Shadel, Steven/Skokie School District 69	46,280,285	67
Shaeffer, Dale/Lewistown Community Unit SD 97	67	110
Shaffer, Amanda/Midwest Ctl Cmty Unit SD 191	16	177
Shaffer, Keith/East Maine School District 63	13,27,73,95,295,297	47
Shah, Khushali/Prairie Grove Cons SD 46	67	183
Shah, Ushma, Dr/Elgin School District U-46	9,15,78	130
Shake, John/Illinois Dept of Education	76	1
Shanafelt, Ami/Central Cmty High Sch Dist 71	12	17
Shaner, Jared/Dixon Cmty Unit Sch Dist 170	6,27	160
Shannahan, Matt/Cmty Cons Sch Dist 146	3,91	42
Shannon, Amy/Saratoga Cmty Cons SD 60C	295	113
Shaper, Dwayne/Morrison Cmty Unit Sch Dist 6	16,73,295	239
Sharkey, Brett/Lombard Elem SD 44	9,18	97
Sharkey, Nicole/Union School District 81	9	248
Sharma Lewis, Bhavna, Dr/Diamond Lake School Dist 76	1	149
Sharp, Chad/Bushnell Prairie Cmty USD 170	3	178
Sharp, Donna/Bement Cmty Unit Sch Dist 5	38	202
Sharp, Lindsay/Community Unit School Dist 300	27	180
Sharp, Morgan/Steger School Dist 194	37	68
Shaughnessy, Pat/Lincoln-Way Cmty HS Dist 210	297	244
Shaver, Carolyn/Palos Cmty Cons Sch Dist 118	6	61
Shaver, Kay/United Cmty Unit Sch Dist 304	36,69	234
Shaw, Brian/Joliet Twp High Sch Dist 204	5,79	243
Shaw, Chris/Astoria Cmty Unit Sch Dist 1	67	109
Shaw, Doug/Peoria Public Sch Dist 150	67	198
Shaw, Dwaine/Annawan Cmty Unit SD 226	67	116
Shaw, Jennifer/Rochester Cmty Unit SD 3-A	58	212
Shaw, Pamela/Riverside Public Sch Dist 96	59	65
Shaw, Terri, Dr/Mokena Public School Dist 159	2,19	245
Sheckler, Josh/Hollis Cons School Dist 328	67	197
Sheehan, Daniel/Monticello Cmty Unit SD 25	6	202
Sheehan, Dayrim/Morton Cmty Unit Sch Dist 709	57	227
Sheehan, Mark/Oak Park Elem School Dist 97	2,3,4,5,15	60
Sheffey, Janice/Pearl City Cmty Unit SD 200	2	225
Sheldon, Maggie/Aero Special Ed Co-op	8,15	82
Shelton, Cassy/Central School District 104	59	218
Shelton, Cathy/Herrin Cmty School District 4	36,69,79	251
Shelton, Codjhia/Prairie Hills Elem SD 144	46	63
Shelton, Jill/Massac Unit School District 1	16	178
Shelton, Marcus/Berkeley School Dist 87	4	22
Shenefelt, Christine/Polo Cmty Unit Sch Dist 222	4	195
Shepard, Scott/Community High School Dist 155	15,79	179
Sheperd, Darcy/Salt Fork Cmty Unit SD 512	38,88	233
Shephard, Heather/Marengo Cmty High Sch Dist 154	2	182
Sherall, Mario/Mascoutah Cmty Sch Dist 19	18,280	220
Sheridan, Colleen/New Trier Twp HS District 203	7,85	58
Sheridan, Katie/Kildeer Countryside CCSD 96	9,12,49,57,69,280	151
Sheridan, Sean/Rhodes School District 84 1/2	6,35	64
Sherman, Allison/Oak Grove School District 68	1	154
Sherman, Tom/Mattoon Cmty Unit Sch Dist 2	2,15	19
Sherman, Valerie/Raccoon Cons School Dist 1	6	175
Sheventon, Jamie/Thompsonville Cmty USD 174	83	108
Shevess, Dave/High Mount Sch Dist 116	76,286	220
Shields, Debbie/Chaney-Monge School Dist 88	73	241
Shields, Emily/Cooperative Assn for Spec Ed	79	102
Shimmin, Larry/UT Area Career Center	1	210
Shimp, Tim/Yorkville Cmty Unit SD 115	1	139
Shinall, Tony/Brimfield Cmty Unit SD 309	1	196
Shinn, Michelle, Dr/Lake Forest School District 67	34,83,91,275,296	152
Shipley, Reid/Centralia High School Dist 200	10,79	174
Shippon, Matthew/Delavan Cmty Unit Sch Dist 703	67	226
Shippy, Michelle/Dakota Cmty Unit Sch Dist 201	16	224

NAME/District	JOB FUNCTIONS	PAGE
Shockey, Chris/Freeport School District 145	68,273	224
Shoemaker, Kimberly/Cypress School District 64	1,11,83	127
Shoemate, Edwin/Cobden Cmty Unit Sch Dist 17	1,57,288	230
Sholl, Joanna/La Harpe Cmty Sch Dist 347	73,286,297	115
Sholtis, Kelly/Springfield Pub Sch Dist 186	83,88,270	213
Shore, Erin/Kaneland Cmty Unit SD 302	83	132
Short, Ed/Elementary School District 159	73	47
Short, Marci/Elgin School District U-46	12,296	130
Short, Michael/Somonauk Cmty Unit SD 432	67	86
Short, Shannon/Illini West High Sch Dist 307	2	114
Shortridge, Brad/Genoa-Kingston Cmty SD 424	2,15	85
Shortsleeve, Julie/Donovan Cmty Unit Sch Dist 3	2	119
Shostachuk, Joanna/Community Cons School Dist 15	68,273	43
Shover, Inky/Western CUSD 12	67	203
Shrader, David/Sunnybrook School District 171	2,3,4,5,91	68
Shrewsbury, Stacey/Pontiac Cmty Cons Sch Dist 429	67	161
Shrode, Trisha, Dr/Elgin School District U-46	8,73	130
Shuh, Judy/Crystal Lake Elem Dist 47	76,79	181
Shulman, Lisa/Consolidated High Sch Dist 230	79	44
Shumaker, Leonard/Morton Cmty Unit Sch Dist 709	3,91	227
Shuman, Samantha/Berwyn South School Dist 100	81	23
Shumway, Tage/Southwest Cook Co Assc Spec Ed	2,11	82
Shupe, Shari/Illini West High Sch Dist 307	12	114
Shurtz, Kathy/Benton Cons High Sch Dist 103	60,88	107
Shutter, Kathryn/St Anne Cmty HSD 302	6,60,85	136
Sibley, Dionne/Silvis School District 34	280	209
Sibley, Tonisha/La Grange Elem Sch Dist 102	2,4,5,15,91	54
Sibley, Tonisha/West Harvey-Dixmoor Pub SD 147	2,4,294	70
Sickele, Margaret, Dr/Berkeley School Dist 87	9,15,83	22
Sickling, Vanessa/Century Cmty Unit SD 100	2	204
Siddens, John/Oakwood Cmty Unit Sch Dist 76	3	232
Sidor, Cyndi/Oak Park & River Forest SD 200	2	60
Siegfried, Amanda/Oak Park Elem School Dist 97	71	60
Siegfried, Andy/Chaney-Monge School Dist 88	1,83	241
Siegfried, Michael/Nauvoo-Colusa CUSD 325	67	115
Sieghan, Jen/Winnetka School Dist 36	280	72
Siegler, Tom/Bartelso School District 57	1,83,84	17
Siemens, Sue/Pecatonica Cmty Unit SD 321	5	253
Siepel, Michelle/Peoria Public Sch Dist 150	73,84,295	198
Sierra-Sanders, Alicia/Rock Island-Milan Sch Dist 41	7,58,77,79,83,88	208
Sierra, Gina/Pennoyer School District 79	288,296,298	62
Sierra, Joseph/Elmwood Park Cmty Unit SD 401	3	47
Sievers, Kate, Dr/Calhoun Cmty Unit Sch Dist 40	83	8
Sikorski, Laura/Millburn Cmty Cons Sch Dist 24	5	153
Silagi, Chris/Community Unit School Dist 200	15,34,36,77,79,83,88,90	91
Silver, Jonathan/Oak Park & River Forest SD 200	275	60
Silverman, Matt/Glenview Cmty Cons Sch Dist 34	9,11,69,74,83,271,288,296	51
Sima, Meg/Lisle Cmty Unit Sch Dist 202	67	96
Simeck, Michael/Lake Forest School District 67	1,11	152
Simeck, Mike/Lake Forest Cmty HSD 115	1	151
Simko, Karen/School Dist 45 Dupage Co	7	99
Simmons, Angela/Fulton Co Cmty Unit Sch Dist 3	1	109
Simmons, Bridgette/Posen-Robbins Sch Dist 143-5	71	63
Simmons, Dawn/River Forest Sch Dist 90	71	65
Simmons, Debbie/Rome Cmty Cons Sch Dist 2	16	123
Simmons, Dotty/Central A&M Cmty Unit SD 21	69	14
Simmons, John/Salt Fork Cmty Unit SD 512	73	233
Simmons, Karen/Genoa-Kingston Cmty SD 424	79	85
Simmons, Miranda/Salt Fork Cmty Unit SD 512	285	233
Simmons, Terrie/North Cook Interm Svc Center	2	82
Simmons, Tom/Union Ridge School Dist 86	3	70
Simms, Angela/Roxana Cmty Unit Sch Dist 1	5	172
Simms, Eric/Orland School District 135	295	61
Simms, Lucia/Madison Cmty Unit Sch Dist 12	4	172
Simon, Eric/Community Unit School Dist 308	3	137
Simon, Tracy/Lemont-Bromberek Sch Dist 113A	286	55
Simon, Victor, Dr/Gower School District 62	1	94

1 Superintendent	16 Instructional Media Svcs	30 Adult Education	44 Science Sec	58 Special Education K-12	72 Summer School	88 Alternative/At Risk	277 Remedial Math K-12
2 Bus/Finance/Purchasing	17 Chief Operations Officer	31 Career/Sch-to-Work K-12	45 Math K-12	59 Special Education Elem	73 Instructional Tech	89 Multi-Cultural Curriculum	280 Literacy Coach
3 Buildings And Grounds	18 Chief Academic Officer	32 Career/Sch-to-Work Elem	46 Math Elem	60 Special Education Sec	74 Inservice Training	90 Social Work	285 STEM
4 Food Service	19 Chief Financial Officer	33 Career/Sch-to-Work Sec	47 Math Sec	61 Foreign/World Lang K-12	75 Marketing/Distributive	91 Safety/Security	286 Digital Learning
5 Transportation	20 Art K-12	34 Early Childhood Ed	48 English/Lang Arts K-12	62 Foreign/World Lang Elem	76 Info Systems	92 Magnet School	288 Common Core Standards
6 Athletic	21 Art Elem	35 Health/Phys Education	49 English/Lang Arts Elem	63 Foreign/World Lang Sec	77 Psychological Assess	93 Parental Involvement	294 Accountability
7 Health Services	22 Art Sec	36 Guidance Services K-12	50 English/Lang Arts Sec	64 Religious Education K-12	78 Affirmative Action	95 Tech Prep Program	295 Network System
8 Curric/Instruct K-12	23 Music K-12	37 Guidance Services Elem	51 Reading K-12	65 Religious Education Elem	79 Student Personnel	96 Title II Programs	296 Title II Programs
9 Curric/Instruct Elem	24 Music Elem	38 Guidance Services Sec	52 Reading Elem	66 Religious Education Sec	80 Driver Ed/Safety	98 Chief Technology Officer	297 Webmaster
10 Curric/Instruct Sec	25 Music Sec	39 Social Studies K-12	53 Reading Sec	67 School Board President	81 Gifted/Talented	270 Character Education	298 Grant Writer/Ptnrships
11 Federal Program	26 Business Education	40 Social Studies Elem	54 Remedial Reading K-12	68 Teacher Personnel	82 Video Services	271 Migrant Education	750 Chief Innovation Officer
12 Title I	27 Career & Tech Ed	41 Social Studies Sec	55 Remedial Reading Elem	69 Academic Assessment	83 Substance Abuse Prev	273 Teacher Mentor	751 Chief of Staff
13 Title V	28 Technology Education	42 Science K-12	56 Remedial Reading Sec	70 Research/Development	84 Erate	274 Before/After Sch	752 Social Emotional Learning
15 Asst Superintendent	29 Family/Consumer Science	43 Science Elem	57 Bilingual/ELL	71 Public Information	85 AIDS Education	275 Response To Intervention	

Illinois School Directory — DISTRICT PERSONNEL INDEX

NAME/District	JOB FUNCTIONS	PAGE
Simons, Anne/Lake Forest Cmty HSD 115	4	151
Simons, Anne/Lake Forest School District 67	4	152
Simons, Kurt/Carmi-White Co School Dist 5	6	237
Simonson, Curt, Dr/Franklin Cmty Unit SD 1	1	192
Simosky, Dawn/Community Unit School Dist 308	5	137
Simov, Nick/Argo Cmty High School Dist 217	73,76,295,297	21
Simpkins, Joseph/Richland School Dist 88A	1,73,83	247
Simpson, Brenda/Fairfield Cmty High SD 225	16	236
Simpson, Chris/Richland Co Cmty Unit SD 1	1,11	206
Simpson, Dorothy/Whiteside School District 115	11,296	222
Simpson, Jason/New Hope Cmty Cons Sch Dist 6	67	237
Simpson, Kelli/Morris Cmty High Sch Dist 101	16,82	113
Simpson, Kelli/Saratoga Cmty Cons SD 60C	16	113
Simpson, Kevin/Hinsdale Twp High Sch Dist 86	91	95
Simpson, Luke/Dalzell Elem School SD 98	67	6
Simpson, Michelle/Woodland Cmty Unit Sch Dist 5	4	162
Sims, Shonette/Geneva CUSD 304	8	131
Sines, Lndsey/Windsor Cmty Unit SD 1	752	216
Singer, Laura/Northbrook Elem School Dist 27	49,52	59
Singer, Mitch/Northbrook Elem School Dist 27	59	59
Singh, Abe/Grayslake Cmty HS District 127	2,4,5,11,15	150
Singh, Abe/Hawthorn Cmty Cons Sch Dist 73	2,4,5,15	151
Sinn, Jessi/El Paso-Gridley CUSD 11	2	257
Sinnott-Snooks, Marigrace/Alsip-Hazelgrn-Oaklawn SD 126	67	20
Siore, Gina/Central Cmty Unit SD 4	36	118
Siri, Scott/Mendota Twp High Sch Dist 280	73,76,295	143
Sirianni, Darren/East Dubuque Unit SD 119	10,27,270,271,273	125
Sischo, Joel/Joliet Public School Dist 86	6,35	243
Sisil, Jessica/Palestine Cmty Unit SD 3	1,11,73,288	83
Sisul, Justin/Downers Grove School Dist 58	16,73,277,280	93
Sitkowski, Ivy/Grass Lake School District 36	12	150
Sitton, Amy/Egyptian Cmty Unit Sch Dist 5	79,270	3
Sivertsen, Rolf/Canton Union School Dist 66	1	109
Skaggs, Mary/Winnebago Cmty Unit SD 323	7	255
Skelly, Lisa/East Aurora School Dist 131	298	129
Skelton, Sean/East Alton Elementary SD 13	73	170
Skentzos, Nora/Brookfield-LaGrange Park SD 95	9,15,79	23
Skertich, Brad, Dr/Collinsville Cmty Sch Dist 10	1	170
Skibinski, Brian/Forest Ridge Sch Dist 142	71,73,97	50
Skibinski, Rick/Woodlawn Unit School Dist 209	3	124
Skibinski, Sheryl/Woodlawn Unit School Dist 209	4	124
Skic, Andy/Community Cons School Dist 59	3,91	43
Skillern, Rebecca/Pontiac-Wm Holliday SD 105	5	221
Skinkis, Kevin, Dr/Riverside-Brookfld Twp SD 208	1	65
Skinlo, Michelle/Mattoon Cmty Unit Sch Dist 2	67	19
Skinner, Amanda/Pana Cmty Unit School Dist 8	286	14
Skinner, Quillard/Lostant Cmty Unit Sch Dist 425	67	142
Skocy, Dave/Mattoon Cmty Unit Sch Dist 2	11,15,27,57,68,273,296,298	19
Skoczylas, Crystal/Indian Springs Sch Dist 109	15	53
Skog, Carol/Wood Dale School Dist 7	57	100
Skold, Kris/West Lincoln-Broadwell ESD 92	83,85	164
Skowronski, Carleen/Burbank School District 111	67	24
Skubal, Samantha/J Sterling Morton HSD 201	73,286	53
Skube, Jeanne/Grundy Area Voc Ed System	15	113
Skully, Ann/Community Cons School Dist 15	15,79,83,275	43
Slagel, Mark/Prairie Central Cmty USD 8	67	162
Slager, Allen/Arbor Park School District 145	3	21
Slager, Donald/Westchester Public SD 92 1/2	67	70
Slattery, Jason/Cook County School Dist 130	67	45
Slexter, Ryan/Sangamon Valley Cmty Unit SD 9	5	166
Slife, Michael/Rockford School District 205	5	254
Slife, Rhiannon/Vienna High School Dist 13-3	69,83,88,273	127
Sligar, Lisa/Kell Cons School District 2	16,59	174
Sloat, Mike/Central City School Dist 133	6	174
Slocomb, Paul/Signal Hill Sch Dist 181	67	221
Slover, Crystal/Wayne City Cmty Unit SD 100	16	237
Slusher, Beth/School Dist 45 Dupage Co	73,286	99
Small, Lisa/Township High School Dist 211	10,11,15,57,60,288	69
Small, Maria/Hononegah Cmty High SD 207	4	253
Smallwood, Mike/River Ridge Cmty Unit SD 210	3	126
Smargiassi, Michael/Triad Cmty School District 2	80	172
Smargiassi, Tom/Lena-Winslow Cmty Unit SD 202	6	224
Smeed, Ira/Pembroke Cmty Cons SD 259	67	136
Smeets, Adam/Indian Prairie Sch Dist 204	73,84,98	95
Smetana, Kristen/Riverside-Brookfld Twp SD 208	2,15,19,298	65
Smit, Kara/North Palos School Dist 117	28	59
Smith Peters, Randy/Harrisburg Cmty Unit SD 3	5	210
Smith, Alicia/Western CUSD 12	16	203
Smith, Alyssa/East Alton Elementary SD 13	9,12,288	170
Smith, Amy/Newark Cmty High Sch Dist 18	1	138
Smith, Angela/Ashley Cmty Cons SD 15	84	235
Smith, Angela/West Aurora School Dist 129	3,4,15	132
Smith, Brad/Adlai E Stevenson HSD 125	41	146
Smith, Brad/Granite City Cmty Unit SD 9	73,84	171
Smith, Bryan/Bradley-Bourbonnais CHSD 307	83	135
Smith, Cara/Meridian Cmty School Dist 101	79	204
Smith, Carol/Community Unit School Dist 303	71	128
Smith, Christina/Joliet Public School Dist 86	5	243
Smith, Christine/Cook County School Dist 104	69	44
Smith, Dan/Henry Senachwine CUSD 5	3	176
Smith, Dan/Moline-Coal Valley SD No 40	3,91	207
Smith, Dana, Dr/Flossmoor School District 161	1	49
Smith, Darin/Carlyle Cmty Unit Sch Dist 1	6	17
Smith, Darlene/Allendale Cmty Cons SD 17	12	234
Smith, David/Shiloh School District 1	67	103
Smith, Deanna/Stockton Cmty Unit SD 206	3	126
Smith, Ed/O'Fallon Cmty Cons Sch Dist 90	3	221
Smith, Erica/Central School District 3	1,11	1
Smith, Heather/Danville School District 118	84	231
Smith, Heather/Knoxville Cmty Unit SD 202	6	140
Smith, Jacob/Mokena Public School Dist 159	73,84	245
Smith, Janelle/Byron Cmty Unit SD 226	58	194
Smith, Jason/Coal City Cmty Unit Sch Dist 1	2	112
Smith, Jay/Gifford Cmty Cons SD 188	11,76,88,288	10
Smith, Jay/Gifford Cmty Cons SD 188	1	10
Smith, Jeff/Regional Office of Ed 16	5,15	87
Smith, Jeffrey/Township High School Dist 214	70	69
Smith, Jennifer/Joliet Public School Dist 86	59	243
Smith, Jill/Byron Cmty Unit SD 226	16	194
Smith, Jim/Evergreen Park Cmty HSD 231	73,286	49
Smith, Joe/Frankfort Cmty Unit SD 168	85	108
Smith, John/Meridian Cmty Unit SD 223	67	194
Smith, Johnny/Indian Springs Sch Dist 109	67	53
Smith, Judith/Marquardt School District 15	16	97
Smith, Kaleb/Madison Co Cte System	1,11	174
Smith, Karen/Kaneland Cmty Unit SD 302	5	132
Smith, Kari, Dr/Elmwood Park Cmty Unit SD 401	79	48
Smith, Katherine/Lyons Twp HS District 204	69,70	56
Smith, Katie/Pinckneyville Cmty High SD 101	83,88	201
Smith, Kenny/Pikeland Cmty Sch Dist 10	752	203
Smith, Kevin/Minooka Cmty Cons Sch Dist 201	3	112
Smith, Kevin/Thompsonville Cmty USD 174	67	108
Smith, Kevin/Wabash Cmty Unit Sch Dist 348	73	234
Smith, Kyle/Carrollton Cmty Unit SD 1	6	111
Smith, Marc/Carlyle Cmty Unit Sch Dist 1	73,295	17
Smith, Marcus/Community Cons School Dist 46	37	148
Smith, Marilyn/Pinckneyville Cmty High SD 101	57	201
Smith, Marilyn/Quincy School District 172	273	2
Smith, Mark/Arthur CUSD 305	286	87
Smith, Matt/Community Unit School Dist 303	73,76,295	128
Smith, Michael/Liberty Cmty Unit Sch Dist 2	76,295	2
Smith, Michael/Pikeland Cmty Sch Dist 10	84,285	203
Smith, Michael/Pikeland Cmty Sch Dist 10	73	203
Smith, Michelle/Berwyn North School Dist 98	1	22
Smith, Mike/West Aurora School Dist 129	15,68	132
Smith, Monica/Havana Cmty Sch District 126	5	177
Smith, Randall/Macomb Cmty Unit Sch Dist 185	3	178
Smith, Randy/Oakwood Cmty Unit Sch Dist 76	67	232
Smith, Renea/Mt Zion Cmty Unit Sch Dist 3	752	166
Smith, Rick/Franklin Cmty Unit SD 1	6	192
Smith, Ronda/Carrollton Cmty Unit SD 1	8	111
Smith, Sean/Gurnee School District 56	3,91	150
Smith, Shane/Stewardson-Strasburg SD 5-A	6	216
Smith, Shannon/Tuscola Cmty Unit SD 301	73	88
Smith, Shelly/Monmouth-Roseville CUSD 238	2	234
Smith, Sheri/Forrestville Valley CUSD 221	1,11	194
Smith, Sherie/Vienna Public School Dist 55	67	127
Smith, Sherri/Rochelle Twp High Sch Dist 212	5	195
Smith, Sonny/North Wayne Cmty Unit SD 200	67	237
Smith, Stephen/Benton Cmty Cons Sch Dist 47	1	107
Smith, Tim/Cobden Cmty Unit Sch Dist 17	3,91	230
Smith, Tim/Princeton Elem Sch Dist 115	1	7

School Year 2020-2021 — 800-333-8802

DISTRICT PERSONNEL INDEX

Market Data Retrieval

NAME/District	JOB FUNCTIONS	PAGE
Smith, Wesley/Chicago Ridge Sch Dist 127-5	3	41
Smith, Whitney/Vandalia Cmty Unit SD 203	5	106
Smith, Yavonnda/Urbana School District 116	8	12
Smithing, William/Riverside-Brookfld Twp SD 208	67	65
Smithpeters, Dana/Wayne City Cmty Unit SD 100	12	237
Smitt, Jason/Palos Heights School Dist 128	16,28,73	61
Smock, Craig/Morton Cmty Unit Sch Dist 709	15	227
Smolen, Lynn/Fox Lake School Dist 114	83	149
Smolinski, Erica, Dr/Niles Elem School District 71	288	58
Smolka, Matthew/Glencoe Sch District 35	16	51
Smolkovich, Cherie/Tri-Point Cmty Unit SD 6J	67	162
Snell, Ryan/Robein Cmty School District 85	35	228
Sniadecki, Trish/Naperville Cmty Unit SD 203	8	98
Snider, Kim/Forrestville Valley CUSD 221	16	194
Snider, Steven/Eastland Cmty Unit SD 308	67	8
Snipes, John/Summit Hill School Dist 161	9,11,288,296,298	247
Snodgrass, Barry/Geneseo Cmty Unit Sch Dist 228	67	117
Snowden, Sandra/Carbondale Cmty HSD 165	30,88	120
Snowden, Travis/Vit Cmty Unit School Dist 2	2,19,84	110
Snyder, Alicia/Mt Vernon City Sch Dist 80	59	123
Snyder, Anne/Stark Co Cmty Unit SD 100	8	224
Snyder, Bryan/Cicero School District 99	73	42
Snyder, Dave, Dr/Orland School District 135	9,273	61
Snyder, Emily/Donovan Cmty Unit Sch Dist 3	6	119
Snyder, Jennifer/Ridgewood Cmty HSD 234	69,83,271,273	64
Snyder, Jesse/Stockton Cmty Unit SD 206	6	126
Snyder, Kelly/Millstadt Cmty Cons SD 160	16	220
Snyder, Matthew/Macon-Piatt Roe#39	1,11	167
Snyder, Rachel/River Bend Cmty School Dist 2	2	239
Soat, Ben/Galena Unit School Dist 120	10,274	125
Sobczak, Wayne/Community High School Dist 117	67	148
Sodaro, Tom/Sandwich Cmty Unit SD 430	91	86
Sofianos, Terry/La Grange Elem Sch Dist 102	15,59	54
Sogarty, Becky/Windsor Cmty Unit SD 1	8,73,88	216
Solarz, Lourene/Rosemont Elem Sch Dist 78	16,82	66
Soldan, Jim/Evergreen Park Cmty HSD 231	6	49
Solodky, Marc/Troy Cmty Cons SD 30-C	83,88,752	247
Soltys, Leanne/New Lenox School District 122	71	245
Soluri, Suzanne/La Grange Area Dept of Spec Ed	15	82
Sommer, Brandon/Century Cmty Unit SD 100	1,11,288	204
Sommer, Chris/Diocese of Springfield Ed Off	2	214
Sommerfeld, Marcia/Glenbard Twp High Sch Dist 87	68	94
Sommers, Susan/Mascoutah Cmty Sch Dist 19	4	220
Sommerseld, Jean/Ridgeland School District 122	77	64
Sommerville, Janet/Naperville Cmty Unit SD 203	8	98
Son, Martin/Brownstown Cmty Unit SD 201	12,296	105
Sonders, Tina/Grant Cmty High Sch Dist 124	60	150
Sondgeroth, Byron/N Pekin-Marquette Hts SD 102	1	227
Sondgeroth, Robert/Lee Co Spec Ed Association	1,11	160
Sondgeroth, Robert/Regional Office of Ed 47	1	241
Sonntag, Jessica/Hinckley-Big Rock Cmty SD 429	58	85
Sons, Roger/Sandridge Sch Dist 172	67	66
Sornberger, Joe/Rowva Cmty School District 208	1	140
Sostak, Betsy/Aptakisic-Tripp Sch Dist 102	57	146
Soto, Pedro/Chicago Public School Dist 299	15,751	25
Soto, Sharon/Dwight Twp High Sch Dist 230	4	161
Soukup, Karen/Minooka Cmty High Sch Dist 111	294	244
Soukup, Susan/Community High School Dist 117	16	148
Soulders, Mark/Massac Unit School District 1	67	178
Southwell, Paul/East Moline Public Sch Dist 37	57	207
Southwell, Paul/Silvis School District 34	57	209
Souza, Aaron/Minooka Cmty Cons Sch Dist 201	73,76,295	112
Spaan, Adelcert/Sunset Ridge Sch Dist 29	67	68
Spain, Kevin/Elverado Cmty Unit SD 196	1	120
Spak, Helene/Northbrook Elem School Dist 27	274	59
Spannagel, Ashlee, Dr/Delabar Cte System	1,11,73	235
Spanos, Julia/Pekin Public School Dist 108	59	227

NAME/District	JOB FUNCTIONS	PAGE
Spapara, Jerry/Archdiocese of Chicago Ed Off	15	72
Sparber, Shana/Kaneland Cmty Unit SD 302	67	132
Sparenberg, Tom/St Anne Cmty HSD 302	3,91	136
Sparkman, Holly/Rock Island-Milan Sch Dist 41	71	208
Sparks, Rod/Oblong Cmty Unit Sch Dist 4	67	83
Sparks, Tony/LaSalle Peru Twp HSD 120	67	142
Sparlin, John, Dr/Community Unit School Dist 308	1,11	137
Spatafore, Nicole/Berkeley School Dist 87	59	22
Spaulding, Melody/Carbondale Elem School Dist 95	73	120
Spaulding, Sonya, Dr/E F Lindop Elem Sch Dist 92	12,275,288	47
Speakman, Lisa/School Dist 45 Dupage Co	57	99
Speckhart, Barb/Payson Cmty Unit School Dist 1	73	2
Spektor, Boris/New Trier Twp HS District 203	297	58
Spencer, Cheryl/Elmhurst Cmty Unit SD 205	4	93
Spencer, Cindy/Kansas Cmty School District 3	8,12,298	103
Spencer, Larry/Milne-Kelvin Grove District 91	59	244
Spencer, Terry/Momence Cmty Unit Sch Dist 1	3,91	136
Spicer, Terri/Marseilles Elem Sch Dist 150	4	142
Spiller, Jeanne/Kildeer Countryside CCSD 96	9,15,273,288,296,298,752	151
Spina, Nancy/Edwardsville Cmty Unit SD 7	15,68	170
Spinka, Leon/West Washington Co Cmty SD 10	11,270	236
Spiwak, Myron/New Trier Twp HS District 203	2	58
Spoonhour, Luis/Fairmont School District 89	67	242
Spotanski, Amy/Mt Vernon City Sch Dist 80	2	123
Sprague, Laura/Geneva CUSD 304	71	131
Sprague, Sharon/Evanston-Skokie Cmty CSD 65	34	48
Sprandel, Charles/Indian Prairie Sch Dist 204	69,70	95
Sprangers, John/North Shore School Dist 112	68	154
Springborn, Thomas/Prairie Du Rocher CCSD 134	11,73,288	205
Springborn, Tom/Monroe-Randolph Reg Off	27,30	190
Springer, Leslie/Community High School Dist 94	60	91
Springer, Tiffany/Galesburg Cmty Unit SD 205	8,11,280,285,296	140
Sproul, Ethan/Putnam Co Cmty Unit SD 535	76	204
Spurling, Bonnie/Rockford School District 205	20,23	254
Spurlock, Robbie/Eldorado Cmty Unit Sch Dist 4	4	210
Spychalski, Annetta/Lombard Elem SD 44	11,280,298	97
Sqhrurjohn, John/Township High School Dist 113	3	155
Squires, Mike/Pleasant Plains Cmty Unit SD 8	73,295	212
Sroczynski, Tammy, Dr/Plainfield Cons Sch Dist 202	9	246
Sroka, Chrys, Dr/Prospect Hts School Dist 23	59,79,88,275	63
St Clair, John/Lemont High Sch Dist 210	6	55
St John, Robert/Ridgewood Cmty HSD 234	6	64
St Pierre, Teri/Steger School Dist 194	68	68
Staab, Tiffany/Minooka Cmty Cons Sch Dist 201	59	112
Stabile, Maureen/Township High School Dist 214	298	69
Stabler, Jason/Bureau Valley Cmty Unit 340	1	6
Stacey, Carol/Sangamon Valley Cmty Unit SD 9	2	166
Stacey, Teresa/Sesser-Valier Cmty Unit SD 196	67	108
Stachacz, Brian/Lyons Twp HS District 204	2	56
Stachacz, Scott/Flossmoor School District 161	3	49
Stachowiak, Jeannie, Dr/North Palos School Dist 117	1	59
Stacy, Carrie/North Palos School Dist 117	11,15,27,59,83,90,296	59
Stadler, Angie/Rockdale School District 84	67	247
Stadlman, Carolyn/Crystal Lake Elem Distict 47	43,46,285	181
Stadt, Raymond/Community High School Dist 218	22,25,44	44
Stadtler, Kurt/Darien Public Sch Dist 61	3,5	92
Staehlin, Mark/Community High School Dist 99	2,4,5,11	91
Stafford, Jody/Vienna Public School Dist 55	4	127
Stafford, Joshua/Vienna High School Dist 13-3	16	127
Stafford, Joshua/Vienna High School Dist 13-3	1,11	127
Stafford, Tracy/Eldorado Cmty Unit Sch Dist 4	58	210
Stafford, Tyreese/Bellwood School District 88	5	22
Stahl, David/Sandwich Cmty Unit SD 430	67	85
Staker, Catherine/Alwood Cmty Unit Sch Dist 225	8,37	116
Stales, Kenneth/Hazel Crest School Dist 152-5	1	52
Staley, Jeff/Bremen Cmty High SD 228	76	23
Stallion, Angela/Lake Zurich Cmty Sch Dist 95	8,11,15,271,288,296,298	152

Code	Description	Code	Description	Code	Description	Code	Description	Code	Description	Code	Description
1	Superintendent	16	Instructional Media Svcs	30	Adult Education	44	Science Sec	58	Special Education K-12	72	Summer School
2	Bus/Finance/Purchasing	17	Chief Operations Officer	31	Career/Sch-to-Work K-12	45	Math K-12	59	Special Education Elem	73	Instructional Tech
3	Buildings And Grounds	18	Chief Academic Officer	32	Career/Sch-to-Work Elem	46	Math Elem	60	Special Education Sec	74	Inservice Training
4	Food Service	19	Chief Financial Officer	33	Career/Sch-to-Work Sec	47	Math Sec	61	Foreign/World Lang K-12	75	Marketing/Distributive
5	Transportation	20	Art K-12	34	Early Childhood Ed	48	English/Lang Arts K-12	62	Foreign/World Lang Elem	76	Info Systems
6	Athletic	21	Art Elem	35	Health/Phys Education	49	English/Lang Arts Elem	63	Foreign/World Lang Sec	77	Psychological Assess
7	Health Services	22	Art Sec	36	Guidance Services K-12	50	English/Lang Arts Sec	64	Religious Education K-12	78	Affirmative Action
8	Curric/Instruct K-12	23	Music K-12	37	Guidance Services Elem	51	Reading K-12	65	Religious Education Elem	79	Student Personnel
9	Curric/Instruct Elem	24	Music Elem	38	Guidance Services Sec	52	Reading Elem	66	Religious Education Sec	80	Driver Ed/Safety
10	Curric/Instruct Sec	25	Music Sec	39	Social Studies K-12	53	Reading Sec	67	School Board President	81	Gifted/Talented
11	Federal Program	26	Business Education	40	Social Studies Elem	54	Remedial Reading K-12	68	Teacher Personnel	82	Video Services
12	Title I	27	Career & Tech Ed	41	Social Studies Sec	55	Remedial Reading Elem	69	Academic Assessment	83	Substance Abuse Prev
13	Title V	28	Technology Education	42	Science K-12	56	Remedial Reading Sec	70	Research/Development	84	Erate
15	Asst Superintendent	29	Family/Consumer Science	43	Science Elem	57	Bilingual/ELL	71	Public Information	85	AIDS Education

Code	Description	Code	Description
88	Alternative/At Risk	277	Remedial Math K-12
89	Multi-Cultural Curriculum	280	Literacy Coach
90	Social Work	285	STEM
91	Safety/Security	286	Digital Learning
92	Magnet School	288	Common Core Standards
93	Parental Involvement	294	Accountability
95	Tech Prep Program	295	Network System
97	Chief Infomation Officer	296	Title II Programs
98	Chief Technology Officer	297	Webmaster
270	Character Education	298	Grant Writer/Ptnrships
271	Migrant Education	750	Chief Innovation Officer
273	Teacher Mentor	751	Chief of Staff
274	Before/After Sch	752	Social Emotional Learning
275	Response To Intervention		

Illinois School Directory — DISTRICT PERSONNEL INDEX

NAME/District	JOB FUNCTIONS	PAGE
Stalnecker, Lisa/St Anne Cmty Cons Sch Dist 256	2	136
Stambaugh, Jennifer/Kaneland Cmty Unit SD 302	2	132
Stambaugh, Tammy/Astoria Cmty Unit Sch Dist 1	4	109
Standerder, Zakry/Regional Office of Ed 11	15	20
Stanevicius, Rich/Kankakee School District 111	3	135
Stanford, Carlos/Brooklyn School District 188	85	217
Stanford, Paul/East Peoria Cmty HS Dist 309	16,73,76,295	226
Stanford, Trisha/Waltonville Cmty Unit SD 1	69	124
Stange, Edward, Dr/Sunset Ridge Sch Dist 29	1,11,83	68
Stanifer, Hillary/Blue Ridge Cmty SD 18	1,83	87
Stankiewicz, Stan/Wilmette Public School Dist 39	3	71
Stanley, Colene/Waltonville Cmty Unit SD 1	12	124
Stanley, Daniel/Community High School Dist 128	2,5,15	148
Stanley, Deb/Grant Park Cmty Unit SD 6	4,16	135
Stanley, Jason/Plainfield Cons Sch Dist 202	31,79	246
Stanley, Jerry/Marion Cmty School Dist 2	73,84,286,295	251
Stanley, Ladonya/Valley View Cmty SD 365-U	74	248
Stanowski, Kevin/Carlyle Cmty Unit Sch Dist 1	5	17
Stansbury, Jennifer/Joliet Twp High Sch Dist 204	88	243
Stanton, Lee/Matteson Elem SD 162	11,15,57,288	57
Stanton, Rebbeca/Heyworth Cmty Sch District 4	36,69	185
Stanton, Sammy/Christopher Unit Sch Dist 99	34	107
Stanton, William/Wauconda Cmty Unit SD 118	69	155
Stanula, Mike/Beecher Cmty Sch Dist 200-U	3	241
Staples, Donelle/Zion Public School District 6	16,71,286,295	157
Staples, Gail/Silvis School District 34	34	209
Staples, Jack/Carrollton Cmty Unit SD 1	3,5	111
Staples, Josh/Grant Cmty High Sch Dist 124	3	150
Stapleton, Rachel/New Holland Middletown ESD 88	2	164
Star, Matthew/Hamilton Cmty Cons SD 328	67	114
Starck-King, Paul/Proviso Twp High Sch Dist 209	2,15,19	63
Stark, Patty/Oakland Cmty Unit Sch Dist 5	8,11,35,69,79,83	19
Starker, Matt/Pontiac Cmty Cons Sch Dist 429	6	161
Starklauf, Rhonda/New Lenox School District 122	67	245
Starks-Turner, Felicia, Dr/Oak Park Elem School Dist 97	9,11,19,79,288,296,298	60
Starr, Karen/Community Cons School Dist 59	59	43
Starr, Rick/Central City School Dist 133	67	174
Statler, Betsy/St Anne Cmty Cons Sch Dist 256	4	136
Statler, Betsy/St Anne Cmty HSD 302	4	136
Statler, Terri/Flossmoor School District 161	68	49
Stauder, Jeff/Pana Cmty Unit School Dist 8	3,5	14
Stauder, Kent/Okaw Valley Cmty Unit SD 302	1,11	193
Stauffenberg, Mark/Manteno Cmty Unit Sch Dist 5	67	136
Stauner, Matthew/McHenry Cmty Cons Sch Dist 15	67	183
Stavropoulos, Maria/Prospect Hts School Dist 23	73,286	63
Stawick, Jeff, Dr/Cmty Cons Sch Dist 146	1	42
Stearns, Julie/Calumet Public School Dist 132	2,294	24
Steber, Cheryl/El Paso-Gridley CUSD 11	13,16,82	257
Stec, Ted/Lombard Elem SD 44	1	97
Steckel, Tammy/Roxana Cmty Unit Sch Dist 1	2,7	172
Stecken, Dan/Seneca Twp High Sch Dist 160	10,11,68	144
Steckling, Eric/Deerfield Public SD 109	71	149
Steele, Jaimee/Schuyler-Industry CUSD 5	69,77,83,752	215
Steele, Tom/Manteno Cmty Unit Sch Dist 5	73,295	136
Steelman, Trisha/Staunton Cmty Unit Sch Dist 6	2	168
Stegal, Charlie/St Anne Cmty HSD 302	1	136
Stegall, Charlie/St Anne Cmty Cons Sch Dist 256	1,11	136
Stegman, Kelsey/Leland Cmty Unit Sch Dist 1	16,82	142
Stegmann, Shirley/Chester Cmty Unit Sch Dist 139	8	205
Steider, Alan/Cambridge Cmty Unit SD 227	73,295	116
Steiger, Molly/Paxton-Buckley-Loda CUSD 10	5	107
Stein, Allison/Hawthorn Cmty Cons Sch Dist 73	9,15,69,288	151
Stein, Charles/Tamaroa Cmty Cons Sch Dist 5	67	201
Stein, Erin/River Trails Sch Dist 26	68	65
Stein, Steve/Peotone Cmty Unit SD 207-U	1	245
Stein, Susan/Taft School District 90	59	247
Steinke, Jody/Quincy School District 172	8	2
Steinke, Judy/Riverside Public Sch Dist 96	4	65
Steinmeyer, Corena/Dixon Cmty Unit Sch Dist 170	58,88	160
Steinseifer, Barb/Big Hollow School District 38	9	148
Stellern, Dennis/Oak Lawn-Hometown Sch Dist 123	295	60
Stelter, James/Bensenville Elem Sch Dist 2	1	89
Stelzer, John/Oak Park & River Forest SD 200	6	60
Stempien, Allison/Lake Forest Cmty HSD 115	68	151
Stempien, Allison/Lake Forest School District 67	68	152
Stence, Chad/Frankfort Cmty Unit SD 168	3	108

NAME/District	JOB FUNCTIONS	PAGE
Stendeback, Marc/Grayville Cmty Unit Sch Dist 1	6	238
Stephen, Jordan/East Prairie School Dist 73	70	47
Stephens, Christopher/Rosemont Elem Sch Dist 78	67	66
Stephens, Diana/Hutsonville Cmty Unit SD 1	11,54,296	83
Stephens, Jeff/Regional Office of Ed 1	7,91	193
Stephens, Richard/Burnham School District 1545	67	24
Stephenson, Joaquim/Evanston-Skokie Cmty CSD 65	752	48
Stephenson, Josh/Hinsdale Twp High Sch Dist 86	2,3,4,5,19	95
Sterling, Erin/East Maine School District 63	57	47
Stern, Jeff/Ashley Cmty Cons SD 15	67	235
Sterpin, Jenny/Lake Forest Cmty HSD 115	79	151
Sterritt, Jason/New Lenox School District 122	3,91	245
Stetz-Jackson, Gabriella/Township High School Dist 214	74	69
Stevens, Cam/Rosemont Elem Sch Dist 78	35,85	66
Stevens, Jimmy/Zeigler Royalton CUSD 188	36,69,79,83,85	108
Stevens, Karen/Washington Cmty HS Dist 308	11,69,273,288,298	229
Stevenson, Don/Evanston-Skokie Cmty CSD 65	3	48
Steward, Megan/Brussels Cmty Unit Sch Dist 42	12	8
Steward, Scott/Salem Cmty High Sch Dist 600	6	175
Stewart, Alex/Gurnee School District 56	5	150
Stewart, Brandon/Lawrence Co Cmty Sch Dist 20	73	159
Stewart, Gary/Marissa Cmty Unit Sch Dist 40	76,295	220
Stewart, Jessica/Downers Grove School Dist 58	7,35,57,77,83,88,90,271	93
Stewart, Lashawn/Momence Cmty Unit Sch Dist 1	8,11	136
Stewart, Teresa/Williamsfield Cmty Unit SD 210	67	140
Stewart, Tracey/Elgin School District U-46	23,27	130
Stice, Tami/Jacksonville School Dist 117	68	192
Stickler, Amy/Athens Cmty Unit Sch Dist 213	81	188
Stickler, Amy/Athens Cmty Unit Sch Dist 213	81	188
Stielow, Phil/Meridian Cmty Unit Sch Dist 15	73	166
Stier, Tina/Abingdon-Avon Cmty Unit SD 276	8	139
Stigge-Kaufman, Sydney/East St Louis Sch Dist 189	298	218
Still, James/Newark Cmty High Sch Dist 18	11,93,273	138
Stines, Matthew/Grant Cmty Cons Sch Dist 110	1	219
Stinger, Troy/Community High School Dist 155	3	179
Stinnett, Christine/Whiteside School District 115	59	222
Stirewalt, Gayle/Highland Cmty Sch District 5	31	171
Stirn, Todd, Dr/Central Cmty Unit SD 301	1	128
Stoettner, Janice/Career Preparation Network	1,11	82
Stoffle, Dan/Tonica Cmty Cons Sch Dist 79	3	145
Stokes, Bryon/Chicago Public School Dist 299	34	25
Stokes, Cheryl/Laraway Cmty Cons SD 70-C	6	243
Stokowski, Windy/Monticello Cmty Unit SD 25	73,84	202
Stoller, Aimee/Bureau Valley Cmty Unit 340	38	6
Stolt, Susan, Dr/Diocese of Peoria Ed Office	15	200
Stoltzenburg, Matt/Hartsburg Emden School Dist 21	6	163
Stolz, Bruce/Sangamon Valley Cmty Unit SD 9	3	166
Stolz, Lisa/Pekin Cmty High Sch Dist 303	275	227
Stone, Cameron/Iroquois West Cmty Unit SD 10	6	119
Stone, Josh/Panhandle Cmty Unit SD 2	6	191
Stone, Michael/Bradley-Bourbonnais CHSD 307	5	134
Stone, Sy/Crab Orchard Cmty Sch Dist 3	8,273,288	251
Stone, Wayne/Field Cmty Cons Sch Dist 3	1,11	123
Storaasli, Mikkel, Dr/Grayslake Cmty HS District 127	1	150
Storm, Alison/Community Unit School Dist 7	58,77	167
Storm, Alison/Staunton Cmty Unit Sch Dist 6	58	168
Stortz, Missy/Marseilles Elem Sch Dist 150	69,90,271,274,752	142
Stotz, Carrie/Avoca School District 37	73	22
Stout, Barb/Fremont School District 79	4	149
Stout, Erin/Peoria Heights Cmty SD 325	88	198
Stout, Jessica/McClellan Cons SD 12	59	123
Stovall, Hope/Rich Twp High School Dist 227	27	64
Stover, Marie/Morris Elem School Dist 54	34,59,79,88,275,285,752	113
Strader, Chad/Arcola Cmty Unit Sch Dist 306	67	87
Strande, Robert/Cass School District 63	2	89
Strang, Jay/Indian Prairie Sch Dist 204	2	95
Strange, Sherri/Martinsville Cmty Unit SD C-3	6	16
Strati, Anna/Glenbard Twp High Sch Dist 87	70	94
Stratigakes, Staci, Dr/Waukegan Cmty Unit SD 60	10	156
Strating, Julie/Lexington Cmty Sch Dist 7	9,31,58,88	186
Stratman, Julie/Regional Office of Ed 1	15	193
Stratton, Bill/Bethalto Cmty Unit SD 8	3,5,91	169
Straub, Reiley/North Dupage Spec Ed Co-op	2	102
Straub, Robert/Panhandle Cmty Unit SD 2	73,84	191
Strauman, Mike/Illini Central CUSD 189	3	177
Strauss, Rick/Wauconda Cmty Unit SD 118	5	155

DISTRICT PERSONNEL INDEX

NAME/District	JOB FUNCTIONS	PAGE
Stravos, Ramona, Dr/J Sterling Morton HSD 201	60	53
Strawn, Mark/Sangamon Area Spec Ed District	1,11	215
Streicher, Jay/Somonauk Cmty Unit SD 432	1,84	86
Streicher, Nicholas/Gurnee School District 56	6	150
Strickler, Rita/Peru Elem Sch Dist 124	84	143
Stricklin, Dwight/Lincoln Cmty High Sch Dist 404	1	163
Striedl, Sue/Naperville Cmty Unit SD 203	81	98
Strieker, Jeff/Marissa Cmty Unit Sch Dist 40	1	220
Strieter, Traci/Winthrop Harbor School Dist 1	59	156
Stringer, Sandra, Dr/Zion Public School District 6	68,78	157
Strobe-Piper, Denise/Farmington Ctl Cmty SD 265	11,296,298	197
Stroh, Terry/Skokie School District 69	43	67
Strole, Jill/Sandoval Cmty Unit SD 501	69	175
Strom, Pamela/New Trier Twp HS District 203	16	58
Strom, Taylor/Clay City Cmty Unit SD 10	69	16
Strong, Scott/St Anne Cmty Cons Sch Dist 256	9,12,57,69,79,271,273	136
Stropes, Sarah/Rockridge Cmty Unit SD 300	5	209
Strouss, Jeff/Hinckley-Big Rock Cmty SD 429	81	85
Struebing, Sarah/West Lincoln-Broadwell ESD 92	2	164
Struhs, Amy/Bushnell Prairie Cmty USD 170	69,77	178
Struif, Melissa/Greenfield Cmty Unit SD 10	36,69	111
Struna, Michael/Deer Park Cmty Cons SD 82	1,11,84	141
Stuart, Richard/Mattoon Cmty Unit Sch Dist 2	8,72	19
Stuckert, Nicole/Sycamore Cmty Unit SD 427	2,19	86
Stukenberg, Matthew/Mascoutah Cmty Sch Dist 19	67	220
Sturgeon, Matthew/Teutopolis Cmty Unit SD 50	1	105
Sturk, John/Community Unit School Dist 308	295	137
Sturz, Caryn/Cary Cmty Cons Sch Dist 26	68	179
Stutz, Paul/Morrisonville Cmty Unit SD 1	6	14
Stutzman, Pamela/Elmwood Park Cmty Unit SD 401	58	48
Styczen, Sheri/Sunset Ridge Sch Dist 29	16,73,295	68
Suarez, Oswaldo/Oak Grove School District 68	3,91	154
Suba, Mary/River Grove School Dist 85-5	4	65
Suchinski, Kevin, Dr/Hillside School District 93	1,11	52
Sudd, Debra/Brookwood School District 167	2,11	24
Sudduth, Janah/Tolono Cmty Unit Sch Dist 7	58	12
Suedbeck, Michele/Oak Park Elem School Dist 97	34	60
Suey, Kelly/Taylorville Cmty Unit SD 3	58	15
Suhre, Zack/Granite City Cmty Unit SD 9	2	171
Sulek, Virginia/Western Springs Sch Dist 101	59	71
Sullens, Chris, Dr/Kewanee Cmty Unit Sch Dist 229	1	117
Sullivan, Aaron/North Boone Cmty Unit SD 200	6	5
Sullivan, Dan, Dr/Berkeley School Dist 87	11,15,59,285,294,296,298	22
Sullivan, Kathy/Princeville Cmty Unit SD 326	16,82	200
Sullivan, Katie/Skokie School District 69	9	67
Sullivan, Laura/Eastern Illinois EFE System	1	20
Sullivan, Mickey/Regional Office of Ed 21	275	109
Sullivan, Peter, Dr/Will Co Regional Office of Edu	15	250
Sullivan, Sally/Herscher Cmty School Dist 2	67	135
Sullivan, Tara/Frankfort Cmty Unit SD 168	4,9,288,298	108
Sumer, Volkan/Tremont Cmty Unit SD 702	67	228
Summa, Michael/Crete-Monee Cmty SD 201-U	295	242
Summers, John/Vienna High School Dist 13-3	67	127
Summerville, Michael/Queen Bee School District 16	67	98
Sumner, Lonna/Brimfield Cmty Unit SD 309	7	196
Sunquist, Mike/Oak Lawn Cmty High SD 229	10,11,33,60,273	60
Surber, Kim/Peoria Heights Cmty SD 325	2	198
Surma, Kenneth/Crete-Monee Cmty SD 201-U	2,15	241
Surratt, Amanda/Triopia Cmty Unit Sch Dist 27	36,270	192
Suter, Tim/Macomb Cmty Unit Sch Dist 185	295	178
Suter, Tracie/Joliet Public School Dist 86	4	243
Sutton, Michael/Highland Cmty Sch District 5	1	171
Sutton, Nicholas/Sandridge Sch Dist 172	1	66
Suva, Julie/Proviso Twp High Sch Dist 209	76	63
Suver, Ronda/Benton Cons High Sch Dist 103	2	107
Svoboda, Sarah/Central School District 104	67	218
Swadinsky, Shanna/Elmwood Cmty Unit Sch Dist 322	4	196
Swan-Grazett, Crystal/Sandwich Cmty Unit SD 430	58	85
Swan, Ryan/Mt Vernon City Sch Dist 80	15,752	123
Swaney, Shannon/Williamsville Cmty Unit SD 15	16	214
Swanlund, Laura/Community Cons School Dist 15	70,76,77	43
Swanson, Brad/Glenbrook High Sch Dist 225	15,68,78	50
Swanson, Don/Marengo Cmty High Sch Dist 154	3	182
Swanson, Ellen, Dr/Des Plaines Cmty Cons SD 62	15	45
Swanson, Eric/Community Cons School Dist 59	3	43
Swanson, Jaylee/East Moline Public Sch Dist 37	7,34,74,77,83,88,90,271	207
Swanson, Kristin/Wilmette Public School Dist 39	13,59,79,83,88,298	71
Swanson, Lynn/Cary Cmty Cons Sch Dist 26	73	179
Swanson, Paul/Central Cmty Unit SD 4	67	118
Swarthout, Denise/Decatur Public Schools 61	71	165
Swartz, Dan/Mundelein Elem School Dist 75	9,280,285,288	153
Swartzentruber, Sarah/Milford Area Public SD 124	36,69,88	119
Sweat, Bill/Rantoul City School Dist 137	67	11
Sweeney, Catherine/Shirland Cmty Cons SD 134	2,11	255
Sweeney, Patrick/Union School District 81	67	248
Swick, Matt, Dr/Wilmington Cmty Unit SD 209-U	1	249
Swiderek, Lisa/Community High School Dist 117	4	148
Swinderman, Rachel/Edgar Co Cmty Sch Dist 6	11,54	103
Swindler, Sherri/Elmwood Cmty Unit Sch Dist 322	2	196
Swinger, Adam/Edinburg Cmty Unit Sch Dist 4	67	14
Syed, Ejaz/Des Plaines Cmty Cons SD 62	297	45
Syens, Patricia/Alden-Hebron School Dist 19	2	179
Sykes, Jane/Carmi-White Co School Dist 5	7	237
Sykes, Nanette/Schaumburg Cmty Cons SD 54	5	66
Symanski, Larry/Evergreen Park Cmty HSD 231	67	49
Szczecina, Debbie/Matteson Elem SD 162	5	57
Szczepaniak, Jim/Niles Twp High School Dist 219	16,71	58
Szczupaj, Lisa/Community Cons School Dist 15	67	43
Szejcar, Linda/Willow Springs School Dist 108	11,275	71
Szepesi, Elizabeth/Woodland School District 50	57	156
Szoke, Eric/Athens Cmty Unit Sch Dist 213	12	188
Szopinski, Michael/Homer Cmty Cons Sch Dist 33C	9,12,15,288	242
Szornik, Barbara/Dwight Common Elem SD 232	11	161
Szymanski, Sue/Durand Cmty Sch Dist 322	12	252

T

NAME/District	JOB FUNCTIONS	PAGE
Tabeek, Greg/Franklin Cmty Unit SD 1	36	192
Taboda, Maribell/Maywood-Melrose Brdview SD 89	57	57
Tae, Erica/Des Plaines Cmty Cons SD 62	57	45
Taflinger, Velvet/Macomb Cmty Unit Sch Dist 185	68	178
Tafoya, Corey, Dr/Harvard Cmty Unit Sch Dist 50	1	181
Taft, Ariane/Midwest Ctl Cmty Unit SD 191	57,58,270,271	177
Talaga, Kelly/Naperville Cmty Unit SD 203	8	98
Talbert, Jake/Wayne City Cmty Unit SD 100	6	237
Talley, Adrian, Dr/Indian Prairie Sch Dist 204	1	95
Tallman, Jonathan/Red Bud Cmty Unit Sch Dist 132	1	205
Tamcus, Scott/Queen Bee School District 16	3	98
Tamkus, Scott/Worth School District 127	3	72
Tammaro, Nikki/Elmhurst Cmty Unit SD 205	3,8,11,27,69,280,294,298	93
Tammaru, Emily, Dr/Community Cons School Dist 89	1	90
Tank, Erik/East Moline Public Sch Dist 37	295	207
Tanner, Mike/Fremont School District 79	2,3,15	149
Tanner, Tara/Crab Orchard Cmty Sch Dist 3	12	251
Tapp, David/Eureka Cmty Unit Sch Dist 140	16	257
Tarnowski, Amber/Odell Cmty Cons Sch Dist 435	16	161
Tarrantes, Erin/DeSoto Grade School Dist 86	84	120
Tarullo, Rita/Cicero School District 99	68	42
Tarver, Vicki/Glenbrook High Sch Dist 225	2	50
Tasker, Jill/Bartelso School District 57	12	17
Taskey, Chris/Rockford School District 205	76	254
Tate, Jay/Summersville Sch Dist 79	67	124
Tate, Kristin/Bethel School District 82	9	122
Tate, Lisa/Woodstock Cmty Unit SD 200	7	184

---

1 Superintendent	16 Instructional Media Svcs	30 Adult Education	44 Science Sec	58 Special Education K-12	72 Summer School	88 Alternative/At Risk	277 Remedial Math K-12
2 Bus/Finance/Purchasing	17 Chief Operations Officer	31 Career/Sch-to-Work K-12	45 Math K-12	59 Special Education Elem	73 Instructional Tech	89 Multi-Cultural Curriculum	280 Literacy Coach
3 Buildings And Grounds	18 Chief Academic Officer	32 Career/Sch-to-Work Elem	46 Math Elem	60 Special Education Sec	74 Inservice Training	90 Social Work	285 STEM
4 Food Service	19 Chief Financial Officer	33 Career/Sch-to-Work Sec	47 Math Sec	61 Foreign/World Lang K-12	75 Marketing/Distributive	91 Safety/Security	286 Digital Learning
5 Transportation	20 Art K-12	34 Early Childhood Ed	48 English/Lang Arts K-12	62 Foreign/World Lang Elem	76 Info Systems	92 Magnet School	288 Common Core Standards
6 Athletic	21 Art Elem	35 Health/Phys Education	49 English/Lang Arts Elem	63 Foreign/World Lang Sec	77 Psychological Assess	93 Parental Involvement	294 Accountability
7 Health Services	22 Art Sec	36 Guidance Services K-12	50 English/Lang Arts Sec	64 Religious Education K-12	78 Affirmative Action	95 Tech Prep Program	295 Network System
8 Curric/Instruct K-12	23 Music K-12	37 Guidance Services Elem	51 Reading K-12	65 Religious Education Elem	79 Student Personnel	96 Title II Programs	296 Title II Programs
9 Curric/Instruct Elem	24 Music Elem	38 Guidance Services Sec	52 Reading Elem	66 Religious Education Sec	80 Driver Ed/Safety	97 Chief Information Officer	297 Webmaster
10 Curric/Instruct Sec	25 Music Sec	39 Social Studies K-12	53 Reading Sec	67 School Board President	81 Gifted/Talented	98 Chief Technology Officer	298 Grant Writer/Ptnrships
11 Federal Program	26 Business Education	40 Social Studies Elem	54 Remedial Reading K-12	68 Teacher Personnel	82 Video Services	270 Character Education	750 Chief Innovation Officer
12 Title I	27 Career & Tech Ed	41 Social Studies Sec	55 Remedial Reading Elem	69 Academic Assessment	83 Substance Abuse Prev	271 Migrant Education	751 Chief of Staff
13 Title V	28 Technology Education	42 Science K-12	56 Remedial Reading Sec	70 Research/Development	84 Erate	273 Teacher Mentor	752 Social Emotional Learning
15 Asst Superintendent	29 Family/Consumer Science	43 Science Elem	57 Bilingual/ELL	71 Public Information	85 AIDS Education	274 Before/After Sch	
						275 Response To Intervention	

Market Data Retrieval

Illinois School Directory

DISTRICT PERSONNEL INDEX

NAME/District	JOB FUNCTIONS	PAGE
Tate, Steve/Bluford Unit School Dist 318	67	122
Tate, Tashara/Thornton Fractnl Twp HSD 215	79	69
Taubery, Eric/Grant Cmty High Sch Dist 124	27,44,47	150
Tauer, Gina/Hinckley-Big Rock Cmty SD 429	27,83	85
Taylor, Aaron/Charleston Cmty Unit SD 1	16,76	19
Taylor, Angela/Homewood Flossmoor CHSD 233	57,60,88	52
Taylor, Arnold/Carbondale Cmty HSD 165	57	120
Taylor, Becky/Plano Cmty Unit Sch Dist 88	4	138
Taylor, Ben/Crab Orchard Cmty Sch Dist 3	3,5	251
Taylor, Chris/Wabash Cmty Unit Sch Dist 348	274	234
Taylor, Darryl, Dr/Lincoln Elem School Dist 156	11	55
Taylor, Dawn/Carbondale Cmty HSD 165	16	120
Taylor, Jala/Fairfield Cmty High SD 225	7	236
Taylor, Jeff/Spoon River Valley Cmty SD 4	16,82	110
Taylor, Kathy/Lake Zurich Cmty Sch Dist 95	4	152
Taylor, Kyle/Colona Cmty School Dist 190	73	116
Taylor, Kyle/Orion Cmty Unit Sch Dist 223	73,76	117
Taylor, L/Proviso Twp High Sch Dist 209	3	63
Taylor, Laura/Wabash Cmty Unit Sch Dist 348	37	234
Taylor, Laura, Dr/Champaign Cmty Unit Sch Dist 4	11,15,35,83	10
Taylor, Linda/Bement Cmty Unit Sch Dist 5	285	202
Taylor, Linnay/Porta Cmty Unit Sch Dist 202	36	189
Taylor, Lisa/Heyworth Cmty Sch District 4	1	185
Taylor, Mary/Fox Lake School Dist 114	2	149
Taylor, Melissa/Belleville Township HSD 201	10,15,38,60,79,275,288	217
Taylor, Michelle/Rome Cmty Cons Sch Dist 2	55	123
Taylor, Mike/Neoga Cmty Unit School Dist 3	6	84
Taylor, Roy/North Clay Cmty Unit SD 25	6	16
Taylor, Todd/Urbana School District 116	15,54,58,79,275	12
Taylor, William/Springfield Pub Sch Dist 186	91	213
Teasley, Jeffrey/Lebanon Cmty Unit Sch Dist 9	10,275	220
Teater, Troy/Morton Cmty Unit Sch Dist 709	8,11,73,286,288,294,295	227
Tedeschi, Carol/Center Cass Sch Dist 66	2,19	90
Tedor, Maureen/Fremont School District 79	12,59,79	149
Teegardin, Valerie/Laraway Cmty Cons SD 70-C	2	243
Telford, Lisa/Odin Public School Dist 722	2	175
Tello, Victor/Berwyn South School Dist 100	5	23
Tellor, Stacy/Germantown Hills SD 69	2	257
Temple, Joshua/Riverdale Cmty Unit SD 100	1	208
Tenhouse, Krista/Liberty Cmty Unit Sch Dist 2	59	2
Tennant, Ed/Lyons Twp HS District 204	73,76	56
Tennyson, Chris/Regional Office of Ed 47	15	241
Tepper, Marc/Kildeer Countryside CCSD 96	67	151
Termunde, David/Arbor Park School District 145	73,98	21
Terneus, Leann/Warrensburg-Latham CU SD 11	4,7	166
Terranova, Shaun/Elgin School District U-46	3	130
Terrell-Smith, Nicole/Hazel Crest School Dist 152-5	2,15,84	52
Terrell, Timothy/Sunnybrook School District 171	67	68
Terry, Dallas/Carbondale Cmty HSD 165	26,27,28,29,95	120
Terry, Glenn/Rockton School District 140	1,57	255
Terry, Megan/Silvis School District 34	16	209
Terry, Melissa, Dr/Morris Elem School Dist 54	77	113
Terstriep, Erin/United Twp High Sch Dist 30	60	209
Terven, Josh/Tolono Cmty Unit Sch Dist 7	3	12
Teske, April, Dr/Anna-Jonesboro Cmty HSD 81	67	230
Teske, Shawn/Warren Community Unit SD 205	1	126
Tess, Kelly/Winnetka School Dist 36	15,74	72
Testin, Lucia/Plainfield Cons Sch Dist 202	76	246
Tetley, Phil/Prairie Central Cmty USD 8	73,84	162
Tharp, Julie/Morton Cmty Unit Sch Dist 709	5	227
Theiland, Ben/Edinburg Cmty Unit Sch Dist 4	1,288	14
Thibadeau, Brian/Northwestern CUSD 2	3,5	168
Thiele, Henry, Dr/Community High School Dist 99	1	91
Thieme, Christopher/Oak Park & River Forest SD 200	84	60
Thieme, Christopher/Oak Park & River Forest SD 200	73	60
Thierfelder, Sharon/West Aurora School Dist 129	76,295	132
Thole, Joanie/Lebanon Cmty Unit Sch Dist 9	11	220
Tholm, Andy/Community Cons School Dist 15	3	43
Thomas, Andrew/Carrollton Cmty Unit SD 1	27,73,76,286,295	111
Thomas, Angela/Pontiac Twp High Sch Dist 90	58,275	161
Thomas, Brian/Carbondale Cmty HSD 165	7,18,68,79,273,275,751	120
Thomas, Bridgette/Deer Park Cmty Cons SD 82	43,46,83,85	141
Thomas, Charo/Posen-Robbins Sch Dist 143-5	295	63
Thomas, Clarence/Maywood-Melrose Brdview SD 89	3,91	57
Thomas, Jason/Lexington Cmty Sch Dist 7	67	186
Thomas, Jennifer/Cary Cmty Cons Sch Dist 26	7,59,83,88	179

NAME/District	JOB FUNCTIONS	PAGE
Thomas, John/Harvey Public School Dist 152	1	51
Thomas, Johnnie, Dr/Rich Twp High School Dist 227	1	64
Thomas, Kevin/Georgetown-Ridge Farm CUSD 4	6,58	232
Thomas, Kevin/Homewood Flossmoor CHSD 233	27	52
Thomas, Les/Lexington Cmty Sch Dist 7	5	186
Thomas, Mary/Fenton Cmty High Sch Dist 100	2	94
Thomas, Michelle/Carbondale Cmty HSD 165	35	120
Thomas, Orlando/Champaign Cmty Unit Sch Dist 4	6,79,88,91,270,275	10
Thomas, Sandra, Dr/Country Club Hills SD 160	11,57,83	45
Thomas, Sandra, Dr/Echo Joint Agreement	1	82
Thomas, Sherri/Bloomington School District 87	15,68	185
Thomas, Steven/Woodland School District 50	9,11,16,57,69,286,288,294	156
Thomas, Taneesha/Franklin Park Pub Sch Dist 84	73,286,295	50
Thomas, Tracie/Park Ridge Niles CMCSD 64	81	62
Thomason, Rosetta/Akin Elem School District 91	2	107
Thomason, Tom/Salem Cmty High Sch Dist 600	3	175
Thompson, Amanda/Berwyn South School Dist 100	34	23
Thompson, Barbara/Fisher Cmty Unit School Dist 1	1,11,83	10
Thompson, Becky/Dallas Elem Sch Dist 327	2	114
Thompson, Greg/Pinckneyville Cmty High SD 101	67	201
Thompson, Jeniffer/Litchfield Cmty Unit SD 12	8,11,57	191
Thompson, John/Brimfield Cmty Unit SD 309	67	196
Thompson, Kyle/Regional Office of Ed 11		20
Thompson, Leslie/Egyptian Cmty Unit Sch Dist 5	73,295	3
Thompson, Mark/Fulton Co Cmty Unit Sch Dist 3	73	109
Thompson, Paul/Leyden Area Spec Ed Co-op	76	82
Thompson, Renee/Serena Cmty Unit School Dist 2	67	144
Thompson, Staci/Winnebago Cmty Unit SD 323	8,12,16	255
Thompson, William/Lockport Twp High Sch Dist 205	3,91	244
Thorns, Adam, Dr/Chicago Ridge Sch Dist 127-5	1	41
Thornsbrough, Kurt/Armstrong Ellis SD 61	288	231
Thornton, Jill/East Peoria Cmty HS Dist 309	60,90	226
Thornton, Megan/Monmouth-Roseville CUSD 238	69	234
Thornton, Rhonda/Champaign Cmty Unit Sch Dist 4	9,12,69,76,286	10
Thornton, Scott/Olympia Cmty Unit Sch Dist 16	3	187
Thorpe, Jessica/Hampton School District 29	59	207
Thorson, Michelle/Miller Cmty Cons Sch Dist 210	12	143
Thul, Denise/Cicero School District 99	49,52	42
Thurman, Jerry/Paris Union School District 95	3	103
Thurman, Lance/Springfield Pub Sch Dist 186	5	213
Thurman, Meg/Rochester Cmty Unit SD 3-A	34,57,88,275	212
Thurwanger, Tracy, Dr/Plano Cmty Unit Sch Dist 88	8,12,15,18	138
Tibbs, Mary Beth/Richmond-Burton Cmty HSD 157	5	184
Tiberend, Michele/Shiloh Village Sch Dist 85	2	221
Tiberi, Evan/Aptakisic-Tripp Sch Dist 102	295	146
Tice, Teresa/Belvidere Cmty Unit SD 100	4	4
Tichler, Christine/Morrison Cmty Unit Sch Dist 6	59	239
Ticknor, Mary/Lemont High Sch Dist 210	1	55
Tiede, Tom/Center Cass Sch Dist 66	5	90
Tileston, Brigid/Barrington Cmty Unit SD 220	20,23	147
Timm, Jennifer/Kell Cons School District 2	67	174
Timmerman, Matt/Community High School Dist 155	10,27,69,74,273,286,288,296	179
Timmermann, David/Diocese of Belleville Ed Off	15	222
Timmons, Tricia/Willow Grove School Dist 46	2	18
Tinetti, John/Skokie School District 69	3	67
Tingley, Evan/Bradley-Bourbonnais CHSD 307	79	135
Tingley, R Scott, Dr/Lincoln-Way Cmty HS Dist 210	1	244
Tippins, Alicia/Marengo Cmty High Sch Dist 154	16,82	182
Tipsord, Gary/Le Roy Cmty Unit SD 2	1,11	186
Tisch, Carrie/Cook County School Dist 130	9,15	45
Titsworth, Kelly/Mt Olive Cmty Unit Sch Dist 5	11,288	168
Titus, Jessica/Gibson Cty-Melvin-Sibley CUSD5	16	106
Tjardes, Adam/Wauconda Cmty Unit SD 118	3	155
Tjardes, Brittany/Lake Forest Cmty HSD 115	2	151
Tkachuk, Jerry/Altamont Cmty Unit SD 10	8	104
Tobias, Robin/Crete-Monee Cmty SD 201-U	6	241
Tobin, Brian/Central Cmty Unit SD 301	16,73,82,84,286,295	128
Tobin, Julie/Community Cons School Dist 93	68,273	90
Todd, Brianna/Porta Cmty Unit Sch Dist 202	7,85	189
Todoric, Mary/Community High School Dist 128	71	148
Toeben, Jamie/Breese Elementary SD 12	67	17
Toeben, Mike/Albers Elem School District 63	1,11,57,73,83,288	17
Toftoy, Matt/Newark Cmty Cons Sch Dist 66	67	138
Tokash, Tricia/Gower School District 62	57,271	94
Toland, Julie/Illini Central CUSD 189	16,82	177

DISTRICT PERSONNEL INDEX

NAME/District	JOB FUNCTIONS	PAGE
Tolbert, Cynthia/Staunton Cmty Unit Sch Dist 6	1	168
Tolczyk, George/Zion Public School District 6	2,3,19,91	157
Tolczyk, George, Dr/La Grange Cmty School Dist 105	2,11	54
Toliver, Ray/Giant City Cmty Cons SD 130	2	121
Tomazin, Tim/Community Cons School Dist 89	3,91	90
Tombolson, Sharon/Wabash Cmty Unit Sch Dist 348	5	234
Tomchuk, Joe/Schaumburg Cmty Cons SD 54	76	66
Tomlianovich, John/Centralia High School Dist 200	73	174
Tompkins, Ben/Community High School Dist 117	295	148
Tompkins, Gary/Spoon River Valley Cmty SD 4	67	110
Tompkins, Teresa/Bond Co Cmty Unit Sch Dist 2	4	4
Tomschin, Thomas/Cicero School District 99	67	42
Tondini, Don/Morris Elem School Dist 54	3	113
Tonner, Allyssa/Vienna Public School Dist 55	16,82	127
Torman, Kim/Ashton-Franklin Center SD 275	10,16	159
Torrence, Pat/Patoka Cmty Unit SD 100	16	175
Torres, Jorge/Lyons Elem School Dist 103	67	56
Torres, Michael/Skokie School District 73 1/2	3	67
Torres, Mick/Community High School Dist 128	73	148
Torres, Mike/Community High School Dist 128	16	148
Tosch, Michelle/Atwood Heights SD 125	34	21
Toschi, Jennifer/Central Stickney Sch Dist 110	69,73,288,295	25
Totheroh, Steve/Milford Area Public SD 124	10,270	119
Toulious, William/Argo Cmty High School Dist 217	1,11,288	21
Towers, Richard/Christopher Unit Sch Dist 99	1,11	107
Towery, Julie/Beardstown Cmty Sch Dist 15	4	9
Towler, Ashley/St Elmo Cmty Unit Sch Dist 202	2	106
Towne, Brian/Lyons Elem School Dist 103	68	56
Towner, Ron/Bremen Cmty High SD 228	6	23
Trach, Natalya/Maine Twp High Sch Dist 207	76	56
Tracy, Jennifer/Edinburg Cmty Unit Sch Dist 4	12	14
Tracy, Norm/Villa Grove Cmty Unit SD 302	1	88
Tragos, Peter/New Trier Twp HS District 203	8,15,74,273	58
Tragoudas, Ulli/Unity Point Cmty Cons SD 140	4	121
Traskaski, Phillip/Winthrop Harbor School Dist 1	73	156
Traub, Chad/North Clay Cmty Unit SD 25	73	16
Trausch, Heather/Community Cons School Dist 15	280	43
Travelstead, Jerry/Community Cons School Dist 204	1,11,57,288	201
Travis, Latesh/Berkeley School Dist 87	15,68	22
Traylor, Sean/Bond Co Cmty Unit Sch Dist 2	5	4
Treasure, Terry/Consolidated High Sch Dist 230	6	44
Treece, Mike/Dupo Cmty School District 196	73	218
Trejo, Gloria/West Chicago Elementary SD 33	9,280,285,288,296	99
Treto-French, Maria/Cary Cmty Cons Sch Dist 26	2,3	179
Trevino, Elisa/Waukegan Cmty Unit SD 60	68	156
Tribbett, Angie/Central Sch Dist 51	4	225
Triezenberg, Karen/Willow Springs School Dist 108	9,83,93,270,271,274	71
Trigg, Robby/Buncombe Cons School Dist 43	67	127
Trimberger, Eric/Carbondale Elem School Dist 95	2,15	120
Trimberger, Eric, Dr/Niles Twp High School Dist 219	2,3,5,15	58
Trimble, Cathy/District 50 Schools	9,69,298	226
Trimble, Lawrence/Decatur Public Schools 61	79	165
Trimble, Paige/Blue Ridge Cmty SD 18	8	87
Trimble, Susan/Robinson Cmty Unit Sch Dist 2	2	83
Tripp, Todd/Goreville Cmty Unit SD 1	6	127
Tripp, Vicki/Buncombe Cons School Dist 43	1	127
Tritle, Jean/Northwestern IL Association	68	87
Troemel, Jim/Lake Forest School District 67	6	152
Troester, Denise/Monticello Cmty Unit SD 25	5	202
Trom, Heather/Fox River Grove Cons SD 3	59,69,275	181
Tronco, Melissa/Pennoyer School District 79	12	62
Trone, Barry/Monmouth-Roseville CUSD 238	5	234
Trone, Britney/Schuyler-Industry CUSD 5	7	215
Trone, Jared/Astoria Cmty Unit Sch Dist 1	3	109
Trone, Kurt/Schuyler-Industry CUSD 5	5	215
Trone, Michael/Schuyler-Industry CUSD 5	3	215
Troxel, Matt/Crab Orchard Cmty Sch Dist 3	67	251

NAME/District	JOB FUNCTIONS	PAGE
Troy, Don/Minooka Cmty High Sch Dist 111	2	244
Troy, John/Minooka Cmty High Sch Dist 111	15,19	244
Truesdale, Timothy/J Sterling Morton HSD 201	1	53
Truex, Skip/Danville School District 118	3	231
Truitt, Shane/Mahomet-Seymour Cmty SD 3	3	11
Tsagalis, Yvonne/Dupage High School Dist 88	10,15	93
Tschantz, Kathy/Mt Pulaski Cmty Unit SD 23	2	164
Tsoukalas, Jillian, Dr/Valley View Cmty SD 365-U	43,46	248
Tucker, Alissa/Dallas Elem Sch Dist 327	9,11,16,69,88,270,298	114
Tucker, Amy/Oak Lawn Cmty High SD 229	7,85	60
Tucker, Jim/Norris City-Omaha-Enfield SD 3	6	238
Tucker, Shane/West Central Cmty Unit SD 235	6	116
Tufano, Donald/Riverside Public Sch Dist 96	16,73	65
Tufts, Tim/Steger School Dist 194	73,84,295	68
Tumtane, Jeff/Brookfield-LaGrange Park SD 95	275	23
Turek, Vivian/Bremen Cmty HSD 228	44	23
Turf, Jeanne/Warren Twp High Sch Dist 121	5,60	155
Turley, Jan/Columbia Cmty Unit SD 4	85	190
Turman, Demetra/Newark Cmty Cons Sch Dist 66	1,11,73	138
Turner, Andrew/Maine Twp High Sch Dist 207	6	56
Turner, Brad/Nashville Cmty HSD 99	1	235
Turner, Derek/Collinsville Cmty Sch Dist 10	73,95	170
Turner, Derek/Collinsville Cmty Sch Dist 10	73,84	170
Turner, Kellie/Newark Cmty Sch Dist 18	5	138
Turner, Madonna/Diocese of Joliet Ed Office	15	249
Turner, Stephen/Taylorville Cmty Unit SD 3	67	15
Turner, Toyna/Rantoul Twp High Sch Dist 193	10,60	12
Turnipseed, Joyce/Rockford School District 205	7	254
Turocy, Jenny/River Grove School Dist 85-5	6	65
Turrubiates, Julie/Lyons Elem School Dist 103	7	56
Tutko-Mangun, Nancy/Joliet Twp High Sch Dist 204	68	243
Tuttle, Brad/Jersey Cmty Sch Dist 100	1,11	125
Twaddle, Shannon/Carthage Elementary SD 317	2,5	114
Twadell, Eric, Dr/Adlai E Stevenson HSD 125	1	146
Twomey, Patrick, Dr/Macomb Cmty Unit Sch Dist 185	1,11,83	178
Tyburski, Sara/Mt Prospect School Dist 57	79,296,298,752	58
Tyler, Christi/Community Unit School Dist 308	2,19	137
Tyler, Kyra/Forest Park School District 91	67	50
Tyler, Pamela/Highland Cmty Sch District 5	58	171
Tyrell, Robert/Minooka Cmty High Sch Dist 111	6	244

U

NAME/District	JOB FUNCTIONS	PAGE
Udell, Karen/Diocese of Joliet Ed Office	15,68	249
Udstuen, Natalie/Fox Lake School Dist 114	12,288	149
Uffelmann, Bradley/Joliet Twp High Sch Dist 204	295	243
Ufkes, Brent/Carthage Elementary SD 317	67	114
Uher, Jill/Hoover-Schrum Sch Dist 157	9	52
Ukleja, Don/Fox Lake School Dist 114	3	149
Ulferts, John, Dr/Shirland Cmty Cons SD 134	1,288	255
Ullberg, Renee/Hawthorn Cmty Cons Sch Dist 73	11,59	151
Ulm, David/Maine Twp High Sch Dist 207	3,91	56
Ulm, David/Maine Twp Spec Ed Program	3	82
Ulmer, Matthew/Illinois Dept of Education	11,298	1
Ulrich, Susan/Flanagan-Cornell Unit 74 SD	4	161
Ulrich, Theresa/Glen Ellyn School District 41	62	94
Ulrich, Tim/Somonauk Cmty Unit SD 432	58,79	86
Underhill, Ed/Le Roy Cmty Unit SD 2	3	186
Underwood, Ali/Collinsville Cmty Sch Dist 10	7,34,58,77,90	170
Underwood, Andrew/Eureka Cmty Unit Sch Dist 140	2	257
Underwood, Darlene/Wabash Cmty Unit Sch Dist 348	2	234
Underwood, Gretchen/Warrensburg-Latham CU SD 11	88	166
Unger, Brian/Waterloo Cmty Unit Sch Dist 5	6	190
Upp, Bill/Metamora Twp HS Dist 122	16,73,76	258
Uram, Susan/Rockford School District 205	73	254
Urban, Maureen/Beach Park Cmty Cons SD 3	76,295	147
Urbaniak, Greg/Grant Cmty High Sch Dist 124	10,286	150
Urbanski, Renee/Community Cons School Dist 15	57,89	43

#	Job Function	#	Job Function	#	Job Function	#	Job Function	#	Job Function	#	Job Function
1	Superintendent	16	Instructional Media Svcs	30	Adult Education	44	Science Sec	58	Special Education K-12	72	Summer School
2	Bus/Finance/Purchasing	17	Chief Operations Officer	31	Career/Sch-to-Work K-12	45	Math K-12	59	Special Education Elem	73	Instructional Tech
3	Buildings And Grounds	18	Chief Academic Officer	32	Career/Sch-to-Work Elem	46	Math Elem	60	Special Education Sec	74	Inservice Training
4	Food Service	19	Chief Financial Officer	33	Career/Sch-to-Work Sec	47	Math Sec	61	Foreign/World Lang K-12	75	Marketing/Distributive
5	Transportation	20	Art K-12	34	Early Childhood Ed	48	English/Lang Arts K-12	62	Foreign/World Lang Elem	76	Info Systems
6	Athletic	21	Art Elem	35	Health/Phys Education	49	English/Lang Arts Elem	63	Foreign/World Lang Sec	77	Psychological Assess
7	Health Services	22	Art Sec	36	Guidance Services K-12	50	English/Lang Arts Sec	64	Religious Education K-12	78	Affirmative Action
8	Curric/Instruct K-12	23	Music K-12	37	Guidance Services Elem	51	Reading K-12	65	Religious Education Elem	79	Student Personnel
9	Curric/Instruct Elem	24	Music Elem	38	Guidance Services Sec	52	Reading Elem	66	Religious Education Sec	80	Driver Ed/Safety
10	Curric/Instruct Sec	25	Music Sec	39	Social Studies K-12	53	Reading Sec	67	School Board President	81	Gifted/Talented
11	Federal Program	26	Business Education	40	Social Studies Elem	54	Remedial Reading K-12	68	Teacher Personnel	82	Video Services
12	Title I	27	Career & Tech Ed	41	Social Studies Sec	55	Remedial Reading Elem	69	Academic Assessment	83	Substance Abuse Prev
13	Title V	28	Technology Education	42	Science K-12	56	Remedial Reading Sec	70	Research/Development	84	Erate
15	Asst Superintendent	29	Family/Consumer Science	43	Science Elem	57	Bilingual/ELL	71	Public Information	85	AIDS Education

#	Job Function	#	Job Function	#	Job Function
88	Alternative/At Risk	277	Remedial Math K-12		
89	Multi-Cultural Curriculum	280	Literacy Coach		
90	Social Work	285	STEM		
91	Safety/Security	286	Digital Learning		
92	Magnet School	288	Common Core Standards		
93	Parental Involvement	294	Accountability		
95	Tech Prep Program	295	Network System		
97	Chief Infomation Officer	296	Title II Programs		
98	Chief Technology Officer	297	Webmaster		
270	Character Education	298	Grant Writer/Ptnrships		
271	Migrant Education	750	Chief Innovation Officer		
273	Teacher Mentor	751	Chief of Staff		
274	Before/After Sch	752	Social Emotional Learning		
275	Response To Intervention				

Illinois School Directory — District Personnel Index

NAME/District	JOB FUNCTIONS	PAGE
Utsinger, Jeff/Stark Co Cmty Unit SD 100	10	224
Uzelac, Mike/Metamora Cmty Cons Sch Dist 1	3	258

V

NAME/District	JOB FUNCTIONS	PAGE
Vacca, Cheryl/Midlothian School District 143	34,69,270	57
Valadez, Michael/New Trier Twp HS District 203	295	58
Valdez, Eulalia/Berkeley School Dist 87	57	22
Valdez, Karina/Sterling Cmty Unit Sch Dist 5	57	240
Valek, Cheryl/Central Stickney Sch Dist 110	9,83,85,270	25
Valek, Maggie/Rhodes School District 84 1/2	93	64
Valente, Valerie/Park Forest Chicago Hgt SD 163	46	62
Valentin, Kurt, Dr/Oak Grove School District 68	2,12,298	154
Valentinas, Melissa/West Northfield Sch Dist 31	67	70
Valette, Tammy/Christopher Unit Sch Dist 99	7	107
Valiente, Danielle/Reed-Custer Cmty Unit SD 255-U	8	246
Vallace, Toby/Farmington Ctl Cmty SD 265	288	197
Valle, Glenda/Oglesby Public Sch Dist 125	73	143
Valle, Mary/Calumet City School Dist 155	3	24
Vallianatos, Carl/McHenry Cmty High Sch Dist 156	10,12,15	183
Van Fleet, Jim/Hall Twp High School Dist 502	73	6
Van Gerven, Anne/Lincolnshre-Prairieview SD 103	67	153
Van Hoose, Amy/Triad Cmty School District 2	8,12,51,288	172
Van Raiden, Audra/Community High School Dist 218	35,80	44
Van, Molly/Rock Island Reg Off of Ed 49	73,76	210
Vanaken, Ryan/Jacksonville School District 117	6	192
Vanbriesen, Tania/Byron Cmty Unit SD 226	4	194
Vance, Scott/Morrison Cmty Unit Sch Dist 6	1	239
VanCleave, Gina/Morris Elem School Dist 54	7	113
Vandemoortel, Jacob/Elgin School District U-46	39,61	130
Vandenbroek, Donna/Woodland School District 50	15,59,90	156
Vanderheydt, Jodie/Peoria Co Special Ed Assoc	31	200
Vanderleest, Linda/Geneseo Cmty Unit Sch Dist 228	270	117
Vandermey, Russ/Barrington Cmty Unit SD 220	295	147
Vanderpal, Davina/Alden-Hebron School Dist 19	8,31,36,69,83,85	179
Vanderploeg, Kent/Indian Prairie Sch Dist 204	295	95
Vanderplow, Jason/Elmhurst Cmty Unit SD 205	60	93
Vandeveer, Mike/South Central Cmty Unit SD 401	67	176
Vandevelde, John/Galva Cmty Unit Sch Dist 224	67	117
Vandeventer, Steve/Villa Grove Cmty Unit SD 302	5	88
Vandewiele, Terri, Dr/Silvis School District 34	1	209
Vandewostine, Josh/Erie Cmty School District 1	3	239
Vanduch, Margerat/Lincolnshre-Prairieview SD 103	71	153
Vanetta, Rich/Shelbyville Cmty Sch Dist 4	5	216
Vanhoorelbaeke, Kim/Fox Lake School Dist 114	82	149
VanHorn, Greg/Rantoul Twp High Sch Dist 193	73,76,286	12
VanHorn, Sarah/Benton Cmty Cons Sch Dist 47	34	107
Vanhoveln, Erik/Windsor Cmty Unit SD 1	1,83	216
Vantine, Kenneth/Bushnell Prairie Cmty USD 170	5	178
Vargas, Jesse/East Aurora School Dist 131	3	129
Varner, Kathryn/South Holland School Dist 151	9,69,74,270,271,273,288	68
Varner, Mark/Fisher Cmty Unit School Dist 1	3	10
Varughese, Neha/Sunset Ridge Sch Dist 29	57	68
Vaughn, Eddie/McClellan Cons SD 12	67	123
Vaughn, Jennifer/Bradley Elem School Dist 61	7	134
Vaughn, John/Seneca Cmty Cons Sch Dist 170	3	144
Vaughn, Kelli/Paxton-Buckley-Loda CUSD 10	6	107
Vaughn, Michelle/Central Cmty Unit SD 301	34,79	128
Vaughn, Sharon/Zeigler Royalton CUSD 188	2	108
Vaughn, Troy/Neoga Cmty Unit School Dist 3	5	84
Vazquez, Maddie/West Chicago Elementary SD 33	57	99
Veach, Jenni/Kansas Cmty School District 3	6	103
Veazey, Julia/Prairie Hills Elem SD 144	11,73,280,288,294,296,298	63
Vegter, Cathleen/Morrison Cmty Unit Sch Dist 6	67	239
Vehe, Christy/Valley View Cmty SD 365-U	44,47	248
Veihman, Justin/Palos Cmty Cons Sch Dist 118	2	61
Veile, Donna, Dr/Payson Cmty Unit School Dist 1	1,11	2
Veillon, Belinda/Nippersink School District 2	9	183
Veillon, Belinda/Richmond-Burton Cmty HSD 157	10	184
Velazquez, Gabriela/Naperville Cmty Unit SD 203	57	98
Velazquez, Nick/Rock Falls Twp High SD 301	57	240
Veldman, Kari/Clinton Cmty Unit Sch Dist 15	58	87
Velez, Maria/Downers Grove School Dist 58	76	93
Venchus, Dave/West Chicago Elementary SD 33	73	99
Venchus, Sharon/Hillside School District 93	16,82	52
Venner, Kevin/Donovan Cmty Unit Sch Dist 3	35,85	119
Ventsias, Erin/Laraway Cmty Cons SD 70-C	88,270,275	243
Venturi, Bryan/Streator Elem School Dist 44	73,295	144
Vera, Shannon/Chicago Heights Elem SD 170	57	25
Verdun, Sherri/Bethalto Cmty Unit SD 8	7	169
Verdun, Steve/Odell Cmty Cons Sch Dist 435	3	161
Vergil, Carrie/Prospect Hts School Dist 23	68	63
Verisario, Robert/Glenbard Twp High Sch Dist 87	2,3,5,15,91	94
Verkler, Dale/Iroquois Co Cmty Unit SD 9	3	119
Vermillion, Chuck/Elmwood Cmty Unit Sch Dist 322	6	196
Verner, Diane/Cary Cmty Cons Sch Dist 26	4	179
Verthein, Bradley/Hinsdale Twp High Sch Dist 86	15,79,275,752	95
Vescogni, Christie/East Peoria Elem Sch Dist 86	59	227
Vicente, Kara/Community Unit School Dist 300	8,18	180
Vichar, Frank/Riley Cmty Cons Sch Dist 18	11,288	184
Vick, Ron/Warren Community Unit SD 205	3	126
Vickers, Tom/Libertyville Pub Sch Dist 70	67	152
Victora, Jill/Marengo Union Elem Cons SD 165	37,83,85,270	182
Vieth, David/Mattoon Cmty Unit Sch Dist 2	6	19
Vieu, Scott/Berwyn North School Dist 98	3	22
Vilardo, Todd/Charleston Cmty Unit SD 1	1,11,57,83	19
Vilendrer, Michael/Des Plaines Cmty Cons SD 62	3,5	45
Vilerdal, McKenzie/Edgar Co Cmty Sch Dist 6	31,73	103
Vince, Laura/Berkeley School Dist 87	15,84	22
Vincent, Chad/Bannockburn Sch Dist 106	6	147
Vincent, Tim/Galena Unit School Dist 120	1,11	125
Violante, Kristin/Pleasantdale School Dist 107	67	62
Vipond, Chris/Community Cons School Dist 46	16,73,76	148
Vitale, Natalie/Oak Lawn-Hometown Sch Dist 123	71	60
Vitton, Charles, Dr/Peotone Cmty Unit SD 207-U	8,11,69,73,288,298	245
Vittore, Ross/Community Cons School Dist 59	68	43
Voehringer, Brad/Morton Grove School Dist 70	1	58
Vogel, Bill/Wallace Cmty Cons Sch Dist 195	67	145
Vogeler, Cynthia/Northwestern IL Association	2,298	87
Vogt, Amy/Trico Cmty Unit Sch Dist 176	11	121
Vogt, Laura/Mundelein Cons High SD 120	67	153
Vogt, Mary/Monticello Cmty Unit SD 25	48,69	202
Vohland, Natalie/South Pekin Grade Sch Dist 137	2	228
Voigts, Kristin/Community Cons School Dist 15	4	43
Voiles, Marty/Seneca Twp High Sch Dist 160	4,10,93,273	144
Voise, Nancy/Naperville Cmty SD 203	10,15	98
Volan, Gregory/North Chicago Cmty Unit SD 187	3,5	153
Voliva, Kelly/Cmty Cons Sch Dist 146	79,83,88,298,752	42
Volle, Louis/Mt Pulaski Cmty Unit SD 23	3	164
Volling, Patti/School Dist 45 Dupage Co	2,15	99
Vollman, Matthew/Norris City-Omaha-Enfield SD 3	1,11	238
Von Schlegell, Hassan, Dr/Lockport Area Special Ed Co-op	1	250
Vonderheide, Michele/Stewardson-Strasburg SD 5-A	2	216
Voorhees, Ricci/East Alton Elementary SD 13	2,17,19,298	170
Vosberg, Matthew, Dr/Rockford School District 205	15	254
Vose, Jeff/Sangamon-Menard Roe #51	1	215
Voss, Sandy/Marquardt School District 15	4	97
Voss, Sandy/Queen Bee School District 16	4	98
Vosse, Abby/Freeburg Cmty Cons SD 70	4	219
Votteler, Grace/Burbank School District 111	73	24
Vowels, Crystal/Urbana School District 116	34	12

W

NAME/District	JOB FUNCTIONS	PAGE
Waas, Christopher/Komarek School District 94	67	54
Wackerlin, Beth/Mendota Cmty School Dist 289	16,288	142
Wackerlin, Eric/Hinckley-Big Rock Cmty SD 429	67	85
Waddell, Mary/Chaney-Monge School Dist 88	16	241
Waddell, Sarah/West Aurora School Dist 129	9,285	132
Wade, Seth/Galesburg Cmty Unit SD 205	295	140
Wadell, Caleb/Elmwood Cmty Unit Sch Dist 322	73,286	196
Wadsworth, Cheryl/Antioch Cmty Cons Sch Dist 34	2,3,4,5,19	146
Waelde, Mark/Sullivan Cmty Unit SD 300	73,76,295	193
Wager, Katie/Kewanee Cmty Unit Sch Dist 229	38	117
Waggoner, Dick/Shiloh School District 1	3,5	103
Waggoner, Robert/Pinckneyville Cmty High SD 101	6	201
Waggoner, Stacie/Durand Cmty Sch Dist 322	27,31,36,69	252
Wagner, Chad, Dr/Elmwood Cmty Unit Sch Dist 322	1,11	196
Wagner, Cynthia/Hillside School District 93	9,69,288	52
Wagner, Dan/Fremont School District 79	3	149
Wagner, Fred/Hartsburg Emden School Dist 21	3	163
Wagner, Gil/West Chicago Elementary SD 33	67	99
Wagner, Julie/Mercer County SD 404	67	189
Wagner, Michelle/Waverly Cmty Unit SD 6	16	193

DISTRICT PERSONNEL INDEX

Market Data Retrieval

NAME/District	JOB FUNCTIONS	PAGE
Wagner, Nancy/River Trails Sch Dist 26	1	65
Wagner, Rachel/Bethel School District 82	73,295	122
Wagner, Scott/Pinckneyville Sch Dist 50	1,11,73,83,288	201
Wagner, Shelley/Harlem Unit Sch District 122	8	252
Wagner, Tera/Consolidated High Sch Dist 230	2	44
Wagner, Tom/Homewood Flossmoor CHSD 233	3	52
Wagnon, John/O'Fallon Cmty Cons Sch Dist 90	67	221
Wahlert, Alan/Lake Forest Cmty HSD 115	10,69	151
Wakeley, Scott, Dr/Bradley-Bourbonnais CHSD 307	1	134
Walczak, Mark/Matteson Elem SD 162	3	57
Waldau, Patricia/Elgin School District U-46	3	130
Walden, Liz/Urbana School District 116	2	12
Walder, Dan/Hoopeston Area Cmty Unit SD 11	11,57,72,271,273	232
Walder, Greg/Spring Valley Cmty Cons SD 99	73	7
Waldore, Tim/Bensenville Elem Sch Dist 2	71,297	89
Walk, Megan/Cumberland Cmty Unit SD 77	16,82	84
Walk, Regina/Wethersfield Cmty Unit SD 230	90	117
Walk, Ted/Sullivan Cmty Unit SD 300	1	193
Walker-Qualls, Gwendolyne/Oak Park & River Forest SD 200	60	60
Walker, Cathy/Gibson Cty-Melvin-Sibley CUSD5	83,88	106
Walker, Henry/Decatur Public Schools 61	5,91	165
Walker, Jakie/Red Hill Cmty School Dist 10	1,11,83	159
Walker, Kay/New Simpson Hill Cons SD 32	11,296,298	127
Walker, Kelly/Brimfield Cmty Unit SD 309	12,73	196
Walker, Mark/Morris Cmty High Sch Dist 101	3	113
Walker, Rebecca/Dallas Elem Sch Dist 327	12	114
Walker, Tanya/Bradford Cmty Unit Sch Dist 1	67	223
Walker, Thad/Meredosia-Chambersburg SD 11	1	192
Walker, Thomas/Massac Unit School District 1	73,84	178
Wall, Donna/Lemont High Sch Dist 210	73,295	55
Wall, Lisa/Glenbrook High Sch Dist 225	5	50
Wallace, Dawn/Pennoyer School District 79	2	62
Wallace, Dean/Morrison Cmty Unit Sch Dist 6	3	239
Wallace, Jason/Tuscola Cmty Unit SD 301	11,296	88
Wallace, Kenneth, Dr/Maine Twp High Sch Dist 207	1	56
Wallace, Kenneth, Dr/Maine Twp Spec Ed Program	1	82
Wallace, Mike/East Peoria Elem Sch Dist 86	6	227
Wallbaum, Bill/Franklin Cmty Unit SD 1	5	192
Waller-Gordon, Carolyn/Woodland School District 50	71	157
Waller, Steve/Urbana School District 116	6	12
Walls, Amy/Rockdale School District 84	16	247
Walls, Patricia/Rock Island-Milan Sch Dist 41	68	208
Walocha, Christopher/Belvidere Cmty Unit SD 100	285	4
Walpon, Tricia/Community Cons School Dist 168	34	44
Walrath, Beth/West Chicago Elementary SD 33	69,294	99
Walraven, Kristen/Pekin Cmty High Sch Dist 303	60	227
Walsdorf, Debra/Woodstock Cmty Unit SD 200	297	184
Walsh, Amber/New Athens CUSD 60	7,83,85	220
Walsh, Andy/Olympia Cmty Unit Sch Dist 16	4,5,79	187
Walsh, Lauren/Gardner Cmty Cons SD 72-C	16,73	112
Walsh, Mathew/Elwood Cmty Cons SD 203	67	242
Walsh, Shawn/Will Co Regional Office of Edu	1	250
Walsh, William/Hinsdale Twp High Sch Dist 86	270	95
Walston, Jeremy/Western CUSD 12	5	203
Walter, Matt/Archdiocese of Chicago Ed Off	2	72
Walter, Vickie/Aptakisic-Tripp Sch Dist 102	71	146
Walters, Andrew/Harvard Cmty Unit Sch Dist 50	6	181
Walters, Gayla/Carlinville Cmty Unit SD 1	73	167
Walters, Genevra, Dr/Kankakee School District 111	1	135
Walters, Robin/Quincy School District 172	76	2
Walters, Steve/Byron Cmty Unit SD 226	5	194
Walters, Steve/Taylorville Cmty Unit SD 3	3	15
Walters, Tammy/United Cmty Unit Sch Dist 304	5	234
Walthes, Scott/Mascoutah Cmty Sch Dist 19	295	220
Walton, Alisa/Oak Park & River Forest SD 200	275	60
Wamser, Ryan, Dr/Smithton Cmty Cons SD 130	1,84	222
Wandless, Ellen/Troy Cmty Cons SD 30-C	2	247
Wang, Catherine, Dr/Glencoe Sch District 35	1,73	51
Ward, Angela/Champaign Cmty Unit Sch Dist 4	15,36,69,74,78,81	10
Ward, Carolyn Dee/Tri-City Cmty Unit Sch Dist 1	273	214
Ward, Jim/Reavis Twp HSD 220	11	64
Ward, Josh/Pawnee Cmty Unit Sch Dist 11	67	212
Ward, Melissa/Community Cons School Dist 59	34	43
Ward, Mike/Illini Central CUSD 189	1,11	177
Ward, Tina/Evergreen Park Cmty HSD 231	16	49
Warden, Mary Jane/Park Ridge Niles CMCSD 64	73	62
Ware, Dan/Quincy School District 172	73	2
Wargin, Marcus/Oak Lawn Cmty High SD 229	69,71,72	60
Wargo, Kevin/Streator Twp High Sch Dist 40	6	145
Warke, Amy, Dr/La Grange-Highlands SD 106	1,11	54
Warlow, Chip/Le Roy Cmty Unit SD 2	3,5	186
Warnecke, Emily/East Alton Elementary SD 13	1,11	170
Warner, Andrea/Sunnybrook School District 171	7	68
Warner, Cheryl/Warrensburg-Latham CU SD 11	1,11	166
Warner, Jason/East Peoria Elem Sch Dist 86	2,15	226
Warner, Marvin/Area 5 Learning Technology Hub	1	174
Warner, Sandra/West Chicago Elementary SD 33	34	99
Warnkes-Sipp, Willa/Lowpoint-Washburn CUSD 21	67	258
Warren, Brian/Hamilton Co Cmty Unit SD 10	73,76,98,286,295	114
Warren, Brian/Riley Cmty Cons Sch Dist 18	83,85,285,286	184
Warren, Christine, Dr/Community Unit School Dist 303	8	128
Warren, Jill/Tazewell Co Area EFE #320	1	229
Warren, Marshaun, Dr/Belleville Township HSD 201	68	217
Warren, Matthew/Community Cons School Dist 15	34,88	43
Warren, Scott, Dr/Lincolnshire-Prairieview SD 103	1	153
Warren, Tyler/Bethalto Cmty Unit SD 8	73,76,95,286	169
Warren, Wanda/Zion Public School District 6	7	157
Warrenfeltz, Jennifer/Ashton-Franklin Center SD 275	9	159
Warrick, Randy/Carmi-White Co School Dist 5	3	237
Wartowski, David/Evanston-Skokie Cmty CSD 65	285	48
Washburn, James/District 50 Schools	67	226
Washington, Eric/Bremen Cmty High SD 228	6	23
Washington, Rochelle/Chicago Public School Dist 299	294	25
Waters, Mike/Westville Cmty Unit Sch Dist 2	36,69	233
Waters, Nancy/Carrollton Cmty Unit SD 1	2,298	111
Watkins, Cassandra/Harvey Public School Dist 152	2,19	51
Watkins, Mickiey/Granite City Cmty Unit SD 9	58,77,752	171
Watkins, Valerie/Maywood-Melrose Brdview SD 89	298	57
Watson-Hill, Deborah, Dr/West Harvey-Dixmoor Pub SD 147	15	70
Watson, Joanie/Decatur Public Schools 61	2	165
Watson, Kim/Marion Cmty School Dist 2	2,19	251
Watson, Rebecca/Central School District 104	37,83,88	218
Watson, Scott/Bismarck-Henning Cmty SD 1	1	231
Watt, Susan/Coulterville Unit Sch Dist 1	35,85	205
Watts, Jason/Collinsville Cmty Sch Dist 10	285	170
Watts, Jennifer/Canton Union School Dist 66	31	109
Watts, Laura/Tremont Cmty Unit SD 702	76,297	228
Watts, Traven/Spring Garden Cmty CSD 178	67	124
Waugh, Evonne, Dr/Bloomingdale School Dist 13	9,11,15,69,74,83,294,298	89
Wawczak, Pam/Wood Dale School Dist 7	5	100
Weaver, Bryan/Millstadt Cmty Cons SD 160	6	220
Weaver, Kim/Neoga Cmty Unit School Dist 3	3	84
Weaver, Lisa/Pleasant Hill School Dist 69	1	199
Weaver, Mike/Pontiac Cmty Cons Sch Dist 429	12	161
Web, Beck/Woodlawn Unit School Dist 209	7	124
Webb, Cythia/Vienna High School Dist 13-3	2	127
Webb, Lisa/Bushnell Prairie Cmty USD 170	73	178
Webb, Roy/Quincy School District 172	1	2
Webb, Steve, Dr/Goreville Cmty Unit SD 1	1	127
Webb, Tiffany/South Holland School Dist 150	9,11,15,16,69,84,288	68
Weber, Chris/Berkeley School Dist 87	295	22
Weber, Jennifer/Bethalto Cmty Unit SD 8	34,36,58,81,88,752	169
Weber, Leslie/Elmhurst Cmty Unit SD 205	8	93
Weber, Lori/Richland School Dist 88A	12	247

#		#		#		#		#		#	
1	Superintendent	16	Instructional Media Svcs	30	Adult Education	44	Science Sec	58	Special Education K-12	72	Summer School
2	Bus/Finance/Purchasing	17	Chief Operations Officer	31	Career/Sch-to-Work K-12	45	Math K-12	59	Special Education Elem	73	Instructional Tech
3	Buildings And Grounds	18	Chief Academic Officer	32	Career/Sch-to-Work Elem	46	Math Elem	60	Special Education Sec	74	Inservice Training
4	Food Service	19	Chief Financial Officer	33	Career/Sch-to-Work Sec	47	Math Sec	61	Foreign/World Lang K-12	75	Marketing/Distributive
5	Transportation	20	Art K-12	34	Early Childhood Ed	48	English/Lang Arts K-12	62	Foreign/World Lang Elem	76	Info Systems
6	Athletic	21	Art Elem	35	Health/Phys Education	49	English/Lang Arts Elem	63	Foreign/World Lang Sec	77	Psychological Assess
7	Health Services	22	Art Sec	36	Guidance Services K-12	50	English/Lang Arts Sec	64	Religious Education K-12	78	Affirmative Action
8	Curric/Instruct K-12	23	Music K-12	37	Guidance Services Elem	51	Reading K-12	65	Religious Education Elem	79	Student Personnel
9	Curric/Instruct Elem	24	Music Elem	38	Guidance Services Sec	52	Reading Elem	66	Religious Education Sec	80	Driver Ed/Safety
10	Curric/Instruct Sec	25	Music Sec	39	Social Studies K-12	53	Reading Sec	67	School Board President	81	Gifted/Talented
11	Federal Program	26	Business Education	40	Social Studies Elem	54	Remedial Reading K-12	68	Teacher Personnel	82	Video Services
12	Title I	27	Career & Tech Ed	41	Social Studies Sec	55	Remedial Reading Elem	69	Academic Assessment	83	Substance Abuse Prev
13	Title V	28	Technology Education	42	Science K-12	56	Remedial Reading Sec	70	Research/Development	84	Erate
15	Asst Superintendent	29	Family/Consumer Science	43	Science Elem	57	Bilingual/ELL	71	Public Information	85	AIDS Education

#		#	
88	Alternative/At Risk	277	Remedial Math K-12
89	Multi-Cultural Curriculum	280	Literacy Coach
90	Social Work	285	STEM
91	Safety/Security	286	Digital Learning
92	Magnet School	288	Common Core Standards
93	Parental Involvement	294	Accountability
95	Tech Prep Program	295	Network System
96	Title II Programs	296	Title II Programs
97	Chief Infomation Officer	297	Webmaster
98	Chief Technology Officer	298	Grant Writer/Ptnrships
270	Character Education	750	Chief Innovation Officer
271	Migrant Education	751	Chief of Staff
273	Teacher Mentor	752	Social Emotional Learning
274	Before/After Sch		
275	Response To Intervention		

IL-T62

Illinois School Directory

DISTRICT PERSONNEL INDEX

NAME/District	JOB FUNCTIONS	PAGE
Weber, Paul/Metamora Cmty Cons Sch Dist 1	73,295,297	258
Webster, Denise/Community Cons School Dist 59	7	43
Webster, Dionne/Urbana School District 116	31,93	12
Webster, Gary/Brooklyn School District 188	3,5	217
Webster, Kris, Dr/Sycamore Cmty Unit SD 427	8,288	86
Webster, Yancy/Polo Cmty Unit Sch Dist 222	67	195
Wece, Megan/Regional Office of Ed 30	15	121
Wedemann, Paul/Fenton Cmty High Sch Dist 100	67	94
Weed, Laura/Plainfield Cons Sch Dist 202	286	246
Weeden, Mike/Prairie Hill Cmty Cons SD 133	73	253
Weeg, Mary/Willow Springs School Dist 108	67	71
Weeks, Kathleen/Somonauk Cmty Unit SD 432	12	86
Weeks, Kelli/Rockridge Cmty Unit SD 300	4	209
Weeks, Rachael/Northbrook School District 28	81	59
Weens, Jill/Hutsonville Cmty Unit SD 1	58	83
Weer, Josh/Tremont Cmty Unit SD 702	3	228
Wegley, Brian, Dr/Northbrook-Glenview SD 30	1	60
Wegner, Linda/Dixon Cmty Unit Sch Dist 170	67	160
Wehlermann, Brad/Norris City-Omaha-Enfield SD 3	10	238
Wehrle, Karen/Lebanon Cmty Unit Sch Dist 9	5	220
Weidig, Scott/Township High School Dist 211	16,73	69
Weidman, Jim/Community Cons School Dist 46	67	148
Weidner, Laura/East Peoria Cmty HS Dist 309	90	226
Weier, Jill/Dupo Cmty School District 196	6	218
Weikle, Kristen/McLean Co Unit District 5	1	186
Weiler, Kurt/New Trier Twp HS District 203	57,271	58
Weinert, Bryan/Leyden Cmty High Sch Dist 212	73,76	55
Weinert, Donna/Worth School District 127	68	72
Weinstock, Judith/Glenbard Twp High Sch Dist 87	67	94
Weintraub, Brian/Itasca School District 10	2,3	96
Weintraub, Jonathan/Oak Park & River Forest SD 200	275	60
Weir,,Maryjo/Perandoe Special Ed District	15	206
Weir, Tom/Riverton Cmty Unit SD 14	6	212
Weishaar, Heather/Keeneyville Elem Sch Dist 20	67	96
Weiss, Bill/Wheeling Cmty Cons Sch Dist 21	3	71
Weiss, Brittany/Allendale Cmty Cons SD 17	88	234
Weiss, Eric/Collinsville Cmty Sch Dist 10	295	170
Weiss, Sharon, Dr/Diocese of Peoria Ed Office	1	200
Weissbohn, Dave/Peotone Cmty Unit SD 207-U	295	245
Welch, Angela/McHenry Cmty High Sch Dist 156	16	183
Welch, Astrid/Valley View Cmty SD 365-U	16,73,82,295	248
Welch, Danielle/Community High School Dist 94	60	91
Welch, Danielle/Mannheim School District 83	59	56
Welch, Danielle, Dr/Leyden Area Spec Ed Co-op	1	82
Welch, Marissa/Minooka Cmty High Sch Dist 111	16	244
Weld, Shannon/Lake Forest School District 67	68	152
Well, Richard/Lewistown Community Unit SD 97	15	110
Wells, April/Elgin School District U-46	81	130
Wells, Barbara/Kankakee School District 111	67	135
Wells, Bob/Fairfield Cmty High SD 225	6	236
Wells, Bryan/St George School District 258	6	136
Wells, Candace/Bradley-Bourbonnais CHSD 307	11,33,60,88,271,296	134
Wells, Jennifer/Round Lake Area Co Dist 116	752	155
Wells, La Wanna/Niles Twp High School Dist 219	68,78	58
Welsh, Kristen/Burbank School District 111	57	24
Welsh, Thomas/Roanoke-Benson Cmty Unit SD 60	1,11,83	258
Welte, Paul/Nashville Cmty HSD 99	16,73,295,296	235
Wenckowski, Eric/Township High School Dist 211	6,80	69
Wendel, Liz/West Aurora School Dist 129	69	132
Wendelin, Jay/Creve Coeur Sch Dist 76	16,73,295	226
Wendlin, Jay/N Pekin-Marquette Hts SD 102	16,73,295	227
Wendling, Matthew/Fieldcrest Cmty School Dist 6	73	257
Werden, Nancy/Staunton Cmty Unit Sch Dist 6	9,11,83,88	168
Werden, Robert/Regional Office of Ed 41	1	174
Werling, Mary/Community Cons School Dist 46	2	148
Werner, Kevin/Prairie Grove Cons SD 46	2	183
Wernetas, Tim/Sherrard Cmty Sch Dist 200	69	189
Wertheim, Greg/Galva Cmty Unit Sch Dist 224	58,77	117
Wertheim, T Greg/Henry-Stark Co Sp Ed Dist 801	1,11	118
Wertin, Abbie/Harrison School Dist 36	83	181
Wertz, Mark/Central Sch Dist 51	3	225
Weshinskey, Susan/Wood River-Hartford Elem SD 15	83,90	172
Wessel, Dave/Kishwaukee Ed Consortium	73	87
West, Donald/Harlem Unit Sch District 122	5	252
West, Kelly/St Clair Co Regional Off of Ed	74	223
West, Kim/Will Co School District 92	15,58	249

NAME/District	JOB FUNCTIONS	PAGE
West, Noah/New Hope Cmty Cons Sch Dist 6	73	237
West, Rose/Lawrence Co Cmty Sch Dist 20	12	159
West, Roy/Vienna High School Dist 13-3	3	127
Westall, Kevin/Jonesboro Cmty Cons SD 43	1	230
Westbrook, Jeff/Paw Paw Cmty Unit SD 271	73	160
Westbrook, Michelle/Pikeland Cmty Sch Dist 10	11,36,69	203
Westerdahl, Randy/Bartonville School District 66	6	196
Westerhold, Jane, Dr/Deerfield Public SD 109	1	149
Westerman, Doug/Big Hollow School District 38	5	148
Westermeyer, Gary/Scott Morgan Cmty Unit SD 2	67	215
Westfall, Cindy/Plainfield Cons Sch Dist 202	11,298	246
Westra, Kerry/Marquardt School District 15	77	97
Westrick, Chris/Taylorville Cmty Unit SD 3	3	15
Weth, Nicholas/Skokie School District 73 1/2	67	67
Wetherell, Katherine/Cumberland Cmty Unit SD 77	7	84
Wethington, Bob/Porta Cmty Unit Sch Dist 202	3	189
Wetteland, Jill/Fremont School District 79	5	149
Wetzel, Angie/Decatur Public Schools 61	7	165
Wetzel, Mark/Community Unit School Dist 300	39	180
Wexell, Candace/Henry-Stark Co Sp Ed Dist 801	68	118
Weydert, Jeff/East Dubuque Unit SD 119	5	125
Whalen, Troy, Dr/Cook County School Dist 104	1,11	44
Whallen, Maureen/Woodford Co Special Ed Assoc	34	259
Wheatley, Jim/Sherrard Cmty Sch Dist 200	3	189
Wheaton, Julia/Consolidated High Sch Dist 230	15,68,74,273	44
Wheeler, Deanna/Tolono Cmty Unit Sch Dist 7	2	12
Wheeler, Steve/Cumberland Cmty Unit SD 77	16,73,95,295	84
Whelan, Gina/Mendon Cmty Unit School Dist 4	2,84	2
Whelton, Chris/Elmhurst Cmty Unit SD 205	2,3,5,15	93
Wherley, Anthony/Illini Central CUSD 189	73,286,295	177
Wherley, Chris/Learning Tech Ctr of Illinois	76,295	13
Whicker, Ryan/Quincy School District 172	2,3,17	2
Whipple, Anne/Lake Forest School District 67	71	152
Whisler, Daniel/River Trails Sch Dist 26	3,91	65
Whiston, Tony/Creve Coeur Sch Dist 76	11	226
Whitaker, Ronell/Community High School Dist 218	50	44
Whitaker, Sherry, Dr/East St Louis Sch Dist 189	2,19	218
White, Andy/New Lenox School District 122	73,76,295	245
White, Beth/Homewood School Dist 153	73,295	52
White, Caletha/Park Forest Chicago Hgt SD 163	9,11,296,298	62
White, Cami/Heritage Cmty Unit Sch Dist 8	288	11
White, Carol/Lake Forest Cmty HSD 115	3	151
White, Carol/Lake Forest School District 67	3	152
White, Connie/Pecatonica Cmty Unit SD 321	4	253
White, Dale/Berkeley School Dist 87	3,5	22
White, Danae/Rochelle Twp High Sch Dist 212	12	195
White, Danny/Goreville Cmty Unit SD 1	3	127
White, Debbie/Northwestern CUSD 2	12,296	168
White, Diane/Community Unit School Dist 300	2	180
White, Dondelayo/Evanston Twp High SD 202	79	48
White, Jeff/Murphysboro Cmty Unit SD 186	16	121
White, Jeff/Sullivan Cmty Unit SD 300	67	193
White, Jerald/Morris Elem School Dist 54	67	113
White, Josh/Tri-Valley Cmty School Dist 3	73,295,297	187
White, Kayla/Raccoon Cons School Dist 1	67	175
White, Keri/Frankfort Cmty Unit SD 168	2	108
White, Kristi/Bushnell Prairie Cmty USD 170	7	178
White, Leann/Nashville Cmty HSD 99	11,275	235
White, Leslie/East Maine School District 63	7,35,85	47
White, Mike/Deland-Weldon Cmty Unit SD 57	3	202
White, Nita/Freeport School District 145	78	224
White, Shawn/Zion-Benton Twp High SD 126	67	157
White, Victoria/Dupo Cmty School District 196	12	218
Whitecotton, Patricia/Community Unit School Dist 300	11,298	180
Whited, Courtney/Lincolnwood Sch Dist 74	2	55
Whitehead, Erin/Eswood Cmty Cons SD 269	2	194
Whitehead, Evan/E F Lindop Elem Sch Dist 92	18,19,57,76,83,88,296,298	47
Whitehouse, Leslie/Blue Ridge Cmty SD 18	33,38,69	87
Whitehurst, Cheryl/Elmwood Cmty Unit Sch Dist 322	274	196
Whiteside, Carolyn/Putnam Co Cmty Unit SD 535	29	204
Whitlock, Doug/Griggsville-Perry Cmty SD 4	3	203
Whitlow, Michelle/Kildeer Countryside CCSD 96	2	151
Whitman, Kelly/Amboy Cmty Unit Sch Dist 272	83	159
Whitsitt, Jeff/United Cmty Unit Sch Dist 304	1,11,83	234
Whitson, Carolyn/Community Cons School Dist 59	71	43
Whittaker, Cindy, Dr/Fairview South School Dist 72	1,11,83,288	49

DISTRICT PERSONNEL INDEX

Market Data Retrieval

NAME/District	JOB FUNCTIONS	PAGE
Whittaker, Sonya, Dr/Dolton-Riverdale Sch Dist 148	6,15,68,69,288,296,298	46
Whittall, Nancy/Woodland School District 50	68	157
Whitten, Rene/Thornton Fractnl Twp HSD 215	7,57,60,77,79,81,83,88	69
Whittler, Mick/Richland Co Cmty Unit SD 1	57,58,275	206
Wickham, Jeremy/Zion Public School District 6	73	157
Wickie, Chris/Starved Rock Assoc Voc Tech Ed	2	146
Wicks, Kim/Tremont Cmty Unit SD 702	2	228
Widdersheim, Conrad/New Athens CUSD 60	273	220
Widdop, Jim/Silvis School District 34	5,88,271,275,285	209
Wiederholt, Matthew, Dr/Scales Mound Cmty Unit SD 211	8,58,288	126
Wiedhuner, Helen/Athens Cmty Unit Sch Dist 213	4	188
Wiegel, Becky/Barrington Cmty Unit SD 220	11,57,61,298	147
Wiegel, Dave/Scales Mound Cmty Unit SD 211	6	126
Wiegel, Hannah/Scales Mound Cmty Unit SD 211	16	126
Wiegel, Jason/Aero Special Ed Co-op	73,76,295	82
Wiegmann, Beth/Polo Cmty Unit Sch Dist 222	8,273	195
Wielgus, Mike/Triad Cmty School District 2	73	172
Wiemers, Brooke/Signal Hill Sch Dist 181	9,16,73,83,95,270,273	221
Wiersema, Dale/River Bend Cmty School Dist 2	5	239
Wieseman, Lacy/Bunker Hill Cmty Unit SD 8	67	167
Wiggins, Lisa/Le Roy Cmty Unit SD 2	54	186
Wikert, Cathy/Union School District 81	6	248
Wilcher, Katina/Champaign Cmty Unit Sch Dist 4	93	10
Wilcox, Lori, Dr/Aptakisic-Tripp Sch Dist 102	1	146
Wilcox, Ronnie/Kankakee School District 111	6	135
Wilcoxon, Debby/Rantoul City School Dist 137	4	11
Wild, Joel/Warren Community Unit SD 205	6	126
Wilder, Steve/Sycamore Cmty Unit SD 427	1	86
Wildermuth, Shelia/Pontiac-Wm Holliday SD 105	274	221
Wilderson, Jeff/Akin Elem School District 91	67	107
Wildman, Christopher/North Shore School Dist 112	4,11,19	154
Wildman, Patrick/Beardstown Cmty Sch Dist 15	36	9
Wiley, Beth/Arthur CUSD 305	67	87
Wiley, Cameron/River Grove School Dist 85-5	288	65
Wiley, Cara/Illinois Dept of Education	35	1
Wiley, Deborah/Vienna Public School Dist 55	83,88	127
Wiley, Doug/Summit Hill School Dist 161	2,5	247
Wiley, Leyona/West Central IL Spec Ed Co-op	1	179
Wilhite, Mike/Bond Co Cmty Unit Sch Dist 2	3	4
Wilken, Terry/Byron Cmty Unit SD 226	73,76	194
Wilken, William/Thomasboro Cmty Cons SD 130	67	12
Wilkens, Shelby/River Bend Cmty School Dist 2	34	239
Wilkerson, George/High Mount Sch Dist 116	57,69,273	219
Wilkes, Michael/Geneva CUSD 304	73,84,295,297	131
Wilkey, Kathleen, Dr/Mokena Public School Dist 159	9,11,15,69,83,288	245
Wilkey, Rich/Lincoln-Way Cmty HS Dist 210	3	244
Wilkie, Colin/Community Unit School Dist 200	3	91
Wilkins, Tara/Genoa-Kingston Cmty SD 424	16,82	85
Wilkinson, David/Lisle Cmty Unit Sch Dist 202	2	96
Wilkinson, Matthew/Zion-Benton Twp High SD 126	2,11	157
Wilks, Ashay/Community Cons School Dist 180	4	90
Wilks, Kim/Bethalto Cmty Unit SD 8	10,30,35,273,280	169
Wilks, Monica/McLean Co Unit District 5	68	186
Will, Deborah/Zion-Benton Twp High SD 126	16,82	157
Willard, Brandon/Cerro Gordo Cmty Unit SD 100	69,270	202
Willard, Jayne/Naperville Cmty Unit SD 203	8,15	98
Willax, Keith/Hardin Co Cmty Unit Sch Dist 1	3	115
Willer, Kurk/Salt Fork Cmty Unit SD 512	73,76	233
Willett, Don/Astoria Cmty Unit Sch Dist 1	1,57	109
Willey, Brenda/Rockton School District 140	4	255
Willey, Ken/Amboy Cmty Unit Sch Dist 272	3,91	159
Williams, Alice/Illini Central CUSD 189	2	177
Williams, Alicia/Waukegan Cmty Unit SD 60	4,5	156
Williams, Amanda/Freeport School District 145	4	224
Williams, Amy/LaSalle Peru Twp HSD 120	73,76,84,295	142
Williams, Ann/East Aurora School Dist 131	2,19	129
Williams, Ann, Dr/Skokie School District 73 1/2	2,19	67
Williams, Benjamin/Kankakee School District 111	79	135
Williams, Betsy/Rich Twp High School Dist 227	4	64
Williams, Cassandra/Schaumburg Cmty Cons SD 54	15,59	66
Williams, Chandra/Harvey Public School Dist 152	7	51
Williams, Corinne, Dr/Bremen Cmty High SD 228	10,11,15,69,74,270,273,288	23
Williams, Corinne, Dr/Bremen Cmty High SD 228	12	23
Williams, Dave/Addison School District 4	67	88
Williams, Derrika/Harvey Public School Dist 152	11	51
Williams, Elizabeth/Harrisburg Cmty Unit SD 3	2,19	210
Williams, Felechia/Ramsey Cmty Unit Sch Dist 204	4	105
Williams, Frank/Mascoutah Cmty Sch Dist 19	2,91	220
Williams, Frank/West Harvey-Dixmoor Pub SD 147	6	70
Williams, Greta/Proviso Twp High Sch Dist 209	69	63
Williams, Gwaine/Maywood-Melrose Brdview SD 89	67	57
Williams, Gwen/Sangamon Area Spec Ed District	2	215
Williams, Gwendolyn/Proviso Twp High Sch Dist 209	4	63
Williams, Jared/Delavan Cmty Unit Sch Dist 703	3	226
Williams, Jason/North Shore School Dist 112	9	154
Williams, Jeff/Highland Cmty Sch District 5	3,91	171
Williams, Jeff/Scales Mound Cmty Unit SD 211	4	126
Williams, Jennifer/Braceville Elem School Dist 75	67	111
Williams, Jennifer/Martinsville Cmty Unit SD C-3	16,73	16
Williams, Joseph, Dr/Queen Bee School District 16	1,11,73	98
Williams, Kate/Germantown Hills SD 69	6	257
Williams, Katie/Marshall Cmty Sch Dist C-2	58	15
Williams, Kay/Iroquois-Kankakee Reg Off Ed	2	137
Williams, Kim/Harrisburg Cmty Unit SD 3	58,752	210
Williams, Kristin/Arlington Hts School Dist 25	46,69	21
Williams, Lashanta/Rock Island-Milan Sch Dist 41	57	208
Williams, Latunja/Bloom Twp High School Dist 206	15,68,79	23
Williams, Latunja, Dr/Matteson Elem SD 162	46	57
Williams, Mike/Argenta Oreana Cmty Unit SD 1	6	165
Williams, Nikki/Harrisburg Cmty Unit SD 3	73	210
Williams, Richard/New Trier Twp HS District 203	73	58
Williams, Rossy/Kankakee School District 111	7,35	135
Williams, Scott/Danville School District 118	73,95,295	231
Williams, Scott/Fisher Cmty Unit School Dist 1	73,76	10
Williams, Scott/Mt Vernon City Sch Dist 80	6	123
Williams, Sharlyne/Community Cons School Dist 168	2,4,294	44
Williams, Susan/North Greene Unit Dist 3	83,85,90	111
Williams, Teresa, Dr/East St Louis Sch Dist 189	11	218
Williams, Timothy/Ford Heights School Dist 169	6	49
Williams, Whitman/Bannockburn Sch Dist 106	3	147
Williams, Yvonne/Matteson Elem SD 162	59	57
Williamsen, John/Lyons Elem School Dist 103	73	56
Williamsen, John/S Wilmington Cons Elem SD 74	73,295	113
Williamson, Gina/Mt Vernon Twp HS District 201	73,76,84,98,286,295	123
Williamson, John/Braceville Elem School Dist 75	73	111
Williamson, John/Braceville Elem School Dist 75	73	111
Williamson, John/Gardner S Wilmington HSD 73	73,76	112
Williamson, Roseanne, Dr/Glenbrook High Sch Dist 225	11,69,74,83,88,275,296	50
Williford, Wayne/Benton Cmty Cons Sch Dist 47	73,295	107
Willis, Chad/Indian Creek Cmty Unit SD 425	1	85
Willis, Elaine/Greenfield Cmty Unit SD 10	16,82	111
Willis, Kim/Patoka Cmty Unit SD 100	73,295	175
Willis, Mick/Peoria Public Sch Dist 150	2,19	198
Willis, Tim/Cook County School Dist 104	16,73,286,297	44
Wills, Bryan/Oregon Cmty Unit Sch Dist 220	67	195
Wills, Casey/Community Unit School Dist 16	9	211
Wills, Jillian/Gardner S Wilmington HSD 73	69,752	112
Wills, Jillian/Gardner S Wilmington HSD 73	83,752	112
Wilm, David, Dr/Wauconda Cmty Unit SD 118	8,15	155
Wilm, Paul/McHenry Cmty High Sch Dist 156	69	183
Wilmarth, Jean/Germantown Hills SD 69	16	257
Wilms, John/Schaumburg Cmty Cons SD 54	73,295	66
Wils, Chris/Hampton School District 29	6	207
Wilson, Amy/Anna-Jonesboro Cmty HSD 81	12,60	230

#									
1 Superintendent	16 Instructional Media Svcs	30 Adult Education	44 Science Sec	58 Special Education K-12	72 Summer School	88 Alternative/At Risk	277 Remedial Math K-12
2 Bus/Finance/Purchasing	17 Chief Operations Officer	31 Career/Sch-to-Work K-12	45 Math K-12	59 Special Education Elem	73 Instructional Tech	89 Multi-Cultural Curriculum	280 Literacy Coach
3 Buildings And Grounds	18 Chief Academic Officer	32 Career/Sch-to-Work Elem	46 Math Elem	60 Special Education Sec	74 Inservice Training	90 Social Work	285 STEM
4 Food Service	19 Chief Financial Officer	33 Career/Sch-to-Work Sec	47 Math Sec	61 Foreign/World Lang K-12	75 Marketing/Distributive	91 Safety/Security	286 Digital Learning
5 Transportation	20 Art K-12	34 Early Childhood Ed	48 English/Lang Arts K-12	62 Foreign/World Lang Elem	76 Info Systems	92 Magnet School	288 Common Core Standards
6 Athletic	21 Art Elem	35 Health/Phys Education	49 English/Lang Arts Elem	63 Foreign/World Lang Sec	77 Psychological Assess	93 Parental Involvement	294 Accountability
7 Health Services	22 Art Sec	36 Guidance Services K-12	50 English/Lang Arts Sec	64 Religious Education K-12	78 Affirmative Action	95 Tech Prep Program	295 Network System
8 Curric/Instruct K-12	23 Music K-12	37 Guidance Services Elem	51 Reading K-12	65 Religious Education Elem	79 Student Personnel	97 Chief Information Officer	296 Title II Programs
9 Curric/Instruct Elem	24 Music Elem	38 Guidance Services Sec	52 Reading Elem	66 Religious Education Sec	80 Driver Ed/Safety	98 Chief Technology Officer	297 Webmaster
10 Curric/Instruct Sec	25 Music Sec	39 Social Studies K-12	53 Reading Sec	67 School Board President	81 Gifted/Talented	270 Character Education	298 Grant Writer/Ptnrships
11 Federal Program	26 Business Education	40 Social Studies Elem	54 Remedial Reading K-12	68 Teacher Personnel	82 Video-Services	271 Migrant Education	750 Chief Innovation Officer
12 Title I	27 Career & Tech Ed	41 Social Studies Sec	55 Remedial Reading Elem	69 Academic Assessment	83 Substance Abuse Prev	273 Teacher Mentor	751 Chief of Staff
13 Title V	28 Technology Education	42 Science K-12	56 Remedial Reading Sec	70 Research/Development	84 Erate	274 Before/After Sch	752 Social Emotional Learning
15 Asst Superintendent	29 Family/Consumer Science	43 Science Elem	57 Bilingual/ELL	71 Public Information	85 AIDS Education	275 Response To Intervention	

Illinois School Directory

DISTRICT PERSONNEL INDEX

NAME/District	JOB FUNCTIONS	PAGE
Wilson, Brad/Benton Cmty Cons Sch Dist 47	67	107
Wilson, Chase/District 50 Schools	2	226
Wilson, Jane/Round Lake Area Co Dist 116	58	155
Wilson, Jeff/Richland Co Cmty Unit SD 1	67	206
Wilson, John/School Dist 45 Dupage Co	3	99
Wilson, Kenneth/Naperville Cmty Unit SD 203	76	98
Wilson, Linda/Speed Seja 802	34	82
Wilson, Linda/Triopia Cmty Unit Sch Dist 27	35,85	192
Wilson, Minette/Roxana Cmty Unit Sch Dist 1	7	172
Wilson, Nathaniel/DeSoto Grade School Dist 86	1,11	120
Wilson, Sandra, Dr/Peoria Public Sch Dist 150	8,15,288	198
Wilson, Todd/Rantoul Twp High Sch Dist 193	69,288	12
Wilson, Tom/District 50 Schools	73,76,295	226
Wilt, Jason/Ohio Cmty Cons School Dist 17	69,288	7
Wilt, Jason/Ohio Cmty High School Dist 505	288	7
Wilt, Lisa/Ohio Cmty High School Dist 505	73	7
Wilt, Steve/Wood Dale School Dist 7	2,11,84,298	100
Winchester, Matt/Regional Office of Ed 35	15	146
Wind, Jason/Springfield Pub Sch Dist 186	6,78,79	213
Windel, Jay/Regional Office of Ed 53	73	229
Windell, Rob/Meredosia-Chambersburg SD 11	5	192
Winemiller, Clint/Hamilton Co Cmty Unit SD 10	6	114
Wings, Susan/Harrison School Dist 36	1	181
Winkelman, Craig, Dr/Barrington Cmty Unit SD 220	3,15	147
Winkelman, Dawn/Winfield School District 34	79,88,296	100
Winter, Susan/Scales Mound Cmty Unit SD 211	31,36,69,83,752	126
Winterfield, Coleen/La Grange Cmty School Dist 105	59,83,752	54
Winters, Crissy/Colona Cmty School Dist 190	2	116
Winters, Jennie/West Northfield Sch Dist 31	9	70
Winters, Tanera/Naperville Cmty Unit SD 203	4	98
Wippman, Sarah/Northbrook School District 28	81	59
Wirt, Michelle/Carbon Cliff Barstow SD 36	4	207
Wise, Andrew, Dr/Center Cass Sch Dist 66	1	90
Wise, Lindsey/Maroa Forsyth CU Sch Dist 2	67	165
Wise, William/Rochelle Twp High Sch Dist 212	73,76	195
Wiseman, Amie/Amboy Cmty Unit Sch Dist 272	73,286	159
Wisenberger, Kevin/Lake Villa Cmty Cons SD 41	3	152
Wisnewski, Jill/Fenton Cmty High Sch Dist 100	7,85	94
Wisniewski, Terry/Hartsburg Emden School Dist 21	1,11	163
Wissinger, Miranda/Thompsonville Cmty USD 174	6	108
Witas, Cheryl/Cmty Cons Sch Dist 146	4	42
Witcofski, Erin/Minooka Cmty Cons Sch Dist 201	7	112
Witham, Cheryl/Benjamin Sch District 25	2	89
Witherby, Tina/Sparta Cmty School Dist 140	2	205
Witherspoon, Eric, Dr/Evanston Twp High SD 202	1	48
Witko, Randy/Henry Senachwine CUSD 5	67	176
Wittenauer, Amy/Amboy Cmty Unit Sch Dist 272	4,68	159
Wittenauer, Julie/Colona Cmty School Dist 190	67	116
Witter, Della/Litchfield Cmty Unit SD 12	2	191
Witting, Tom/Reavis Twp HSD 220	71,83,270	64
Witzel, Leslie/Woodlawn Unit School Dist 209	38,69,83,88	124
Witzel, Shane/Woodlawn Unit School Dist 209	6	124
Wlodarczyk, Nick/Butler School District 53	73	89
Woehlke, Paul/South Holland School Dist 151	2,3,5,15	68
Woell, Jim, Dr/Benjamin Sch District 25	1	89
Woeltje, Earl/Streator Twp High Sch Dist 40	67	145
Woestman, Daniel, Dr/Belvidere Cmty Unit SD 100	1	4
Woestman, Daniel, Dr/Boone Co Special Ed Co-op	1	5
Wojcik, Brett/Richmond-Burton Cmty HSD 157	35,85	184
Wojcik, Jenny, Dr/Rondout School District 72	1,11	154
Wojtowicz, Mike/Lake Park Cmty High Sch Dist 108	10,15,73	96
Wolcott, Greg/Woodridge Elem Sch District 68	11,57,69,83,275,288,296,298	100
Wold, Scott/Maywood-Melrose Brdview SD 89	46	57
Wolf, Deana/Heritage Cmty Unit Sch Dist 8	2	11
Wolf, Diane/Bloomington School District 87	8,11,88,285,286,288,296,298	185
Wolf, Karrie/Payson Cmty Unit School Dist 1	58	2
Wolf, Kevin/Huntley Cmty School Dist 158	60,88	182
Wolf, Lana/Annawan Cmty Unit SD 226	10,57,83,85,288	116
Wolf, Tim/Kaneland Cmty Unit SD 302	73,76	132
Wolfe, Gary/River Bend Cmty School Dist 2	3	239
Wolfe, John/Silvis School District 34	73,286,295	209
Wolfe, Karen/Regional Office of Ed 30	15	121
Wolfe, Marc/Community High School Dist 94	27	91
Wolfe, Robert/Illinois Dept of Education	2	1
Wolff, Janice/Cicero School District 99	4	42
Wolff, Michael/Cicero School District 99	5	42
Wolgan, Wendy/Cmty Cons Sch Dist 146	9,11,68,69,270,273,285	42
Woll, Angie/Wesclin Cmty Unit Sch Dist 3	88	18
Wollerman, Julie/Christian-Montgomery EFE Sys	1	191
Wollerman, Julie/Regional Office of Ed 3	1	106
Wollerman, Julie/Regional Office of Education 3	1	106
Woltman, Dave/Effingham Cmty Sch Dist 40	6	105
Woo, Jeff/Hinckley-Big Rock Cmty SD 429	73	85
Wood, Anne/Cambridge Cmty Unit SD 227	83,85	116
Wood, Connie/Hiawatha Cmty Unit SD 426	12	85
Wood, Douglas, Dr/Ball Chatham Cmty Unit SD 5	1	211
Wood, Glenn, Dr/Plainfield Cons Sch Dist 202	8,15,27,74,285,288,294	246
Wood, Joan/District 50 Schools	4	226
Wood, Mary Jo/Regional Office-Career Tech Ed	1	215
Wood, Michael/Glen Ellyn School District 41	73,84	94
Wood, Nicole, Dr/Peoria Public Sch Dist 150	9	198
Wood, Robert/Lansing School Dist 158	67	54
Wood, Roycealee/Lake County Regional of Ed	1,11	158
Woodlawn, Jenna, Dr/Troy Cmty Cons SD 30-C	9,15,73,74	247
Woodrow, Amanda/Hamilton Co Cmty Unit SD 10	16	114
Woodruff, Amanda/Community Cons School Dist 46	9,11,69,72,74,273,275,288	148
Woods, Dale/Edwards Co Cmty Unit SD 1	67	104
Woods, Lisa/Newark Cmty High Sch Dist 18	285	138
Woods, Mariba/Bloom Twp High Sch Dist 206	83	23
Woods, Scott, Dr/Rantoul City School Dist 137	57	11
Woods, Troy/Deer Park Cmty Cons SD 82	67	141
Woodward, Brian, Dr/Carbondale Cmty HSD 165	67	120
Wooley, Steve/Southwestern Cmty Unit SD 9	6	168
Woolf, Wendy/East Dubuque Unit SD 119	69,83	125
Woolfork, Jaye/Brooklyn School District 188	16,73,84	217
Woomert, Tim/Community Cons School Dist 15	76	43
Wooten, Richard/Coulterville Unit Sch Dist 1	67	205
Worrell, Glayn/Pekin Public School Dist 108	2,3,4,5,91	227
Worst, Bill/Lena-Winslow Cmty Unit SD 202	83	224
Wort, Connie/District 50 Schools	274	226
Worth, Pamela/Cass School District 63	88,93	89
Worthington, Bob/Zion-Benton Twp High SD 126	91	157
Worthington, Donald/Gibson Cty-Melvin-Sibley CUSD5	73,76	106
Worthington, Robert/Zion-Benton Twp High SD 126	91	157
Worthington, Tony/Rantoul Twp High Sch Dist 193	3,5	12
Woulfe, Travis, Dr/Rockford School District 205	11,70,298	254
Wrenn, Bill/Midland Cmty Unit Sch Dist 7	1	176
Wright, Catherine/Edwardsville Cmty Unit SD 7	8,12,34,58	170
Wright, Christine/Bethalto Cmty Unit SD 8	31	169
Wright, David/Giant City Cmty Cons SD 130	4	121
Wright, Deb/Regional Office of Ed 26	2	179
Wright, Greg/Marengo Union Elem Cons SD 165	67	182
Wright, Merissa/Armstrong Ellis SD 61	73	231
Wright, Nathan/Marengo Cmty High Sch Dist 154	6	182
Wright, Rachel/Herrin Cmty School District 4	2	251
Wright, Rob/Anna-Jonesboro Cmty HSD 81	1,11,83	230
Wright, Teresa/Marshall Cmty Sch Dist C-2	4	15
Wright, Vicky/Mattoon Cmty Unit Sch Dist 2	7	19
Wrigley, Ryan/Pekin Cmty High Sch Dist 303	67	227
Wrobel, Tracey/Community Cons School Dist 15	59	43
Wrobleski, Steven, Dr/LaSalle Peru Twp HSD 120	1	142
Wrolson, Rob/Herrin Cmty School District 4	73,295	251
Wuebbels, Rita/Wesclin Cmty Unit Sch Dist 3	7,85	18
Wuellner, Shelly/Bunker Hill Cmty Unit SD 8	4	167
Wuerger, Amelia/McHenry Cmty Cons Sch Dist 15	7,35,85	183
Wuggazer, Scott/Community High School Dist 99	15,79	91
Wuiaduch, Andrea/Community Unit School Dist 308	11,298	137
Wujek, Betsy/West Central IL Spec Ed Co-op	15,27,34,58,83,88	179
Wulczyn, Susan/Lemont-Bromberek Sch Dist 113A	34,37,57,77,79,83,88,271	55
Wunar, Lisa/Bremen Cmty High SD 228	6	23
Wunder, Diane/Midland Cmty Unit Sch Dist 7	4	176
Wurster, Brian/River Ridge Cmty Unit SD 210	285	126
Wurster, Mary/Valley View Cmty SD 365-U	58,79	248
Wuske, Terry/Peotone Cmty Unit SD 207-U	4	245
Wyant, Justin/Benton Cmty Cons Sch Dist 47	3	107
Wyatt, Travis/North Clay Cmty Unit SD 25	1,11,83	16
Wybourn, Dough/Lena-Winslow Cmty Unit SD 202	3	224
Wyckoff, Jay/Sherrard Cmty Sch Dist 200	73	189
Wyller, Tim/Community Unit School Dist 201	57	92
Wyman, Kate/Morton Cmty Unit Sch Dist 709	12,16,74	227
Wynn, Larry/Cahokia Unit Sch Dist 187	67	218

DISTRICT PERSONNEL INDEX

Market Data Retrieval

NAME/District	JOB FUNCTIONS	PAGE
Wysocki, Amy/Bethalto Cmty Unit SD 8	8,54,57,69,277,285,288	169
Wysocki, Marianne/Sunnybrook School District 171	286	68
Wysong, Cheri/Pana Cmty Unit School Dist 8	11	14

X

NAME/District	JOB FUNCTIONS	PAGE
Xagas, Lisa/Naperville Cmty Unit SD 203	79	98

Y

NAME/District	JOB FUNCTIONS	PAGE
Yacobi, Elizabeth, Dr/Danville School District 118	10,15	231
Yager, Gordan/Jasper Co Cmty Unit SD 1	67	122
Yaggy, Jerry/Fairmont School District 89	2	242
Yang, June/Prairie Hills Elem SD 144	295	63
Yarber, Laura/Mascoutah Cmty Sch Dist 19	11,298	220
Yarnall, Steve/Deer Creek-Mackinaw CUSD 701	67	226
Yasutake, Debra/East Prairie School Dist 73	59	47
Yaun, Lisa/Kinnikinnick Cmty Cons SD 131	79	253
Yean, Hannah/Rantoul Twp High Sch Dist 193	57	12
Yelnick, Brittany/Chicago Ridge Sch Dist 127-5	37	41
Yepsen, Justin/Bureau Valley Cmty Unit 340	67	6
Yoder, Brian/Flanagan-Cornell Unit 74 SD	69	161
Yoder, Jennifer/Regional Office of Ed 48	2	201
York, Emily/Mt Vernon Twp HS District 201	4	123
Young, Cynthia/Hoover-Schrum Sch Dist 157	83,88,275	52
Young, Danette/Paris Cmty Unit Sch Dist 4	1,11	103
Young, David/Kinnikinnick Cmty Cons SD 131	67	253
Young, Erik/Ridgeview Cmty Unit SD 19	1	187
Young, John/Lemont High Sch Dist 210	6	55
Young, Kent, Dr/Nauvoo-Colusa CUSD 325	1,11	115
Young, Lori/Beardstown Cmty Sch Dist 15	12,296	9
Young, Matt/Carbondale Cmty HSD 165	76,82,84,98,297	120
Young, Maurice/Bremen Cmty High SD 228	13	23
Young, Teddy/Prairie Hills Elem SD 144	3	63
Young, Zina/Tazewell-Mason Sp Ed Assoc	7	229
Youngberg, Geoffrey/Chicago Ridge Sch Dist 127-5	5	41
Youngblood, Dane/Rockford School District 205	2	253
Youngith, Janice/Benjamin Sch District 25	298	89
Youngman, Erik/Libertyville Pub Sch Dist 70	9,11,57,69,83,270,285,288	152
Yudzentis, Jayne, Dr/Downers Grove School Dist 58	15,68,74,273,751	93
Yule, Chris/Township High School Dist 214	6,68,91	69
Yurko, Joe/Hamilton Cmty Cons SD 328	1,11,57,73	114

Z

NAME/District	JOB FUNCTIONS	PAGE
Zaayenga, Tara/South Pekin Grade Sch Dist 137	12	228
Zabelin, Donald/Community High School Dist 94	30	91
Zabski, Don/Northbrook-Glenview SD 30	3,91	60
Zach, Lori/Tonica Cmty Cons Sch Dist 79	2	145
Zaehringer, Nate/Bushnell Prairie Cmty USD 170	6	178
Zagar, Stacy/Fox Lake School Dist 114	11	149
Zagorski, Sandy/Indian Springs Sch Dist 109	7	53
Zaher, Amy, Dr/Prospect Hts School Dist 23	9,11,15,57,81,273,288,298	63
Zahn, Anne/Waukegan Cmty Unit SD 60	43,81	156
Zajac, Angela/Eisenhower Cooperative	1,11	82
Zajac, Frank/Summit Hill School Dist 161	4,16	247
Zaleski, Jason/Leland Cmty Unit Sch Dist 1	2,6	142
Zalewski, Lois/McHenry Cmty Cons Sch Dist 15	298	183
Zalewski, Sandy/Joliet Public School Dist 86	71	243
Zalud, Rick/Sunnybrook School District 171	76	68
Zamora, Veronica/Naperville Cmty Unit SD 203	8	98
Zampillo, Joe/Worth School District 127	85	72
Zanocco, Megan/Boone Co Special Ed Co-op	34	5
Zapata, George/Central Stickney Sch Dist 110	3	25
Zapata, Jill/Yorkville Cmty Unit SD 115	57	139
Zarello, Paul/Bushnell Prairie Cmty USD 170	58	178
Zarembsa, Dave/Mundelein Elem School Dist 75	3	153
Zarr, Mary/Community Cons School Dist 15	74	43
Zarras, Barb/Community Cons School Dist 46	12,280	148
Zarvell, Angie/Regional Office of Ed 28	1	118
Zawaske, Sandra/Christopher Unit Sch Dist 99	83	107
Zeder, Lynn, Dr/Orland School District 135	9,11,15,57,59,69	61
Zediker, Matthew/Rockford School District 205	68	254
Zega, Deb/Odell Cmty Cons Sch Dist 435	2	161
Zehr, Adam/Huntley Cmty School Dist 158	15,68	182
Zehr, Zach/Tremont Cmty Unit SD 702	6	228
Zeko, Michelle/Ladd Cmty Cons Sch Dist 94	1,83	6
Zelek, Joseph/McHenry Cmty High Sch Dist 156	76	183
Zeleznik, Brian/Le Roy Cmty Unit SD 2	6	186
Zelinsky, Rick/Avoca School District 37	67	22
Zenhaus, Justin/Patoka Cmty Unit SD 100	8,74,273,274,275	175
Zenisek, Melanie/Arlington Hts School Dist 25	40,43	21
Zerrusen, Derrick/Charleston Cmty Unit SD 1	6	19
Zhang, Jian/Dupage High School Dist 88	295	93
Ziccardi, Gina/Community High School Dist 99	10,15,57,298	91
Zick, John/Ashton-Franklin Center SD 275	11	159
Zick, Kyle/Forrestville Valley CUSD 221	6,8	194
Zieman, Kristine/Naperville Cmty Unit SD 203	69	98
Zilm, Matt/Ogle Co Educational Co-op	1	196
Zimmer, Lynette, Dr/Lake Villa Cmty Cons SD 41	1	152
Zimmerman, Charlie/Limestone Cmty High SD 310	11,38,60,273	197
Zimmerman, Charlie/Washington School Dist 52	67	229
Zimmerman, Mike/Eureka Cmty Unit Sch Dist 140	295	257
Zimmerman, Victor, Dr/Monticello Cmty Unit SD 25	1,11	202
Zinke, Mary Jo/Amboy Cmty Unit Sch Dist 272	16	159
Zinni, Maura/Frankfort School Dist 157-C	1	242
Zipp, Marcella/Township High School Dist 214	11	69
Zires, Jose/Warren Twp High Sch Dist 121	3	155
Zoellner, Kelly/Jacksonville School Dist 117	8	192
Zola, Susan, Dr/Champaign Cmty Unit Sch Dist 4	1	10
Zoladz, Renee/New Trier Twp HS District 203	68	58
Zolecki, Tom/Indian Springs Sch Dist 109	3	52
Zomboracz, Vince/Saratoga Cmty Cons SD 60C	6	113
Zottmann, Mark/Community Cons School Dist 46	295	148
Zotto, Joe/Calumet City School Dist 155	1,11	24
Zuercher, Aaron/East Peoria Elem Sch Dist 86	73,295	227
Zugenbuehler, Lynn/Kankakee School District 111	68	135
Zulz, Mark/Lowpoint-Washburn CUSD 21	57,69,83	258
Zundell, James/J Sterling Morton HSD 201	3	53
Zurliene, TJ/Eldorado Cmty Unit Sch Dist 4	73	210
Zweeres, Joe/Saratoga Cmty Cons SD 60C	18	113
Zych, Corey/Kankakee School District 111	295	135

Code	Function	Code	Function	Code	Function	Code	Function	Code	Function	Code	Function
1	Superintendent	16	Instructional Media Svcs	30	Adult Education	44	Science Sec	58	Special Education K-12	72	Summer School
2	Bus/Finance/Purchasing	17	Chief Operations Officer	31	Career/Sch-to-Work K-12	45	Math K-12	59	Special Education Elem	73	Instructional Tech
3	Buildings And Grounds	18	Chief Academic Officer	32	Career/Sch-to-Work Elem	46	Math Elem	60	Special Education Sec	74	Inservice Training
4	Food Service	19	Chief Financial Officer	33	Career/Sch-to-Work Sec	47	Math Sec	61	Foreign/World Lang K-12	75	Marketing/Distributive
5	Transportation	20	Art K-12	34	Early Childhood Ed	48	English/Lang Arts K-12	62	Foreign/World Lang Elem	76	Info Systems
6	Athletic	21	Art Elem	35	Health/Phys Education	49	English/Lang Arts Elem	63	Foreign/World Lang Sec	77	Psychological Assess
7	Health Services	22	Art Sec	36	Guidance Services K-12	50	English/Lang Arts Sec	64	Religious Education K-12	78	Affirmative Action
8	Curric/Instruct K-12	23	Music K-12	37	Guidance Services Elem	51	Reading K-12	65	Religious Education Elem	79	Student Personnel
9	Curric/Instruct Elem	24	Music Elem	38	Guidance Services Sec	52	Reading Elem	66	Religious Education Sec	80	Driver Ed/Safety
10	Curric/Instruct Sec	25	Music Sec	39	Social Studies K-12	53	Reading Sec	67	School Board President	81	Gifted/Talented
11	Federal Program	26	Business Education	40	Social Studies Elem	54	Remedial Reading K-12	68	Teacher Personnel	82	Video Services
12	Title I	27	Career & Tech Ed	41	Social Studies Sec	55	Remedial Reading Elem	69	Academic Assessment	83	Substance Abuse Prev
13	Title V	28	Technology Education	42	Science K-12	56	Remedial Reading Sec	70	Research/Development	84	Before/After Sch
15	Asst Superintendent	29	Family/Consumer Science	43	Science Elem	57	Bilingual/ELL	71	Public Information	85	AIDS Education

Code	Function	Code	Function	Code	Function
88	Alternative/At Risk	277	Remedial Math K-12		
89	Multi-Cultural Curriculum	280	Literacy Coach		
90	Social Work	285	STEM		
91	Safety/Security	286	Digital Learning		
92	Magnet School	288	Common Core Standards		
93	Parental Involvement	294	Accountability		
95	Tech Prep Program	295	Network System		
97	Chief Innovation Officer	296	Title II Programs		
98	Chief Technology Officer	297	Webmaster		
270	Character Education	298	Grant Writer/Ptnrships		
271	Migrant Education	750	Chief Innovation Officer		
273	Teacher Mentor	751	Chief of Staff		
274	Erate	752	Social Emotional Learning		
275	Response To Intervention				

Illinois School Directory

PRINCIPAL INDEX

NAME/School	PAGE
A	
Aalfs, Jim/Barrington MS-Station Campus	147
Abbott, Jodi/Life Pointe Christian Sch	158
Abdal-Saboor, Sakinah/Brennemann Elem Sch	29
Abdallah, Hanan/Universal Sch	81
Abdul-Ahad, Zaneta/Hampton Arts Sch	34
Abell, Jeff/Meredosia-Chambersberg Sch	192
Abousweilem, Shwkar, Dr/Liberty Junior High Sch	24
Abraham, Philip/Park Junior High Sch	54
Abram, Leavelle/Leif Ericson Scholastic Acad	31
Acevedo, Antonio/Whittier Elem Sch	32
Ackerman, Allen/Saint Andrew Sch	74
Ackman, Kyle/Rock Falls Middle Sch	240
Acton, Elizabeth/Thomasboro Grade Sch	12
Acton, Lisa/Bismarck Henning Elem Sch	231
Adam, Casey/Cornerstone Academy	191
Adam, Casey/Cornerstone Academy/Christmont	190
Adam, Casey/Pana Senior High Sch	14
Adams, Brenda/Danville Christian Academy	233
Adams, Daena/Univ of Chicago CS-Woodlawn	41
Adams, Keith/Kelvyn Park High Sch	36
Adams, Marty/Hawthorn Grade Sch	175
Adams, Mike/Parkland Middle Sch	183
Adams, Rebecca/Oakland Elem Sch	146
Adams, Steve/St Gabriel Sch	75
Adams, Tammy/Campus Middle School for Girls	13
Adcock, Stan/Paw Paw Elem Sch	160
Adekunle, Folasade/Sayre Language Academy	30
Adler, Lisa/Yorkville Middle Sch	139
Adolph, Justin/Lincoln Elem Sch	195
Adreon, Scott/Dunlap High Sch	196
Adrian, Dusti/John Deere Middle Sch	208
Adrianzen, Manuel/Alfred Nobel Elem Sch	26
Aguirre, Angel/Hurley Elem Sch	34
Ahart, Kathryn/Wesley Elem Sch	89
Ahearn, Terry/Grand Ridge Cmty Cons Elem Sch	141
Aherne, Damien/Walter F Fierke Ed Center	42
Aherne, Jenny/Oak Knoll Early Childhod Ctr	179
Ahlman, Scott/Hibbard Elem Sch	29
Akason, Marissa/Acero CS-Bart De Las Casas ES [156]	38
Aksamitowski, Darcy/Roycemore Sch	80
Alaimo, Samantha/Emerson Middle Sch	62
Alba, Martha/Cooper Dual Language Academy	32
Albani, Lauren/LaSalle II Magnet Elem Sch	27
Albans, Athanasia/Fairview South Elem Sch	49
Albers, Amy/Delavan Jr Sr High Sch	226
Albers, Julie/Lincoln Elem Sch	227
Albert-Reese, Joenile, Dr/Pritzker Sch	32
Alberth, Cathy/Hannah Beardsley Middle Sch	181
Alberts, Robert/Brother Rice High Sch	72
Albreski, Carol/St Andrew the Apostle Sch	249
Albritton, Julie/Brimfield Grade Sch	196
Alcantar, Katia, Sr/Immaculate Conception Elem Sch	73
Alday, Michele/St Stanislaus Kostka Sch	76
Alderson, Paula/Olive Branch Christian Academy	3
Alegria, Laura/Oakhill Elem Sch	131
Aleman, Cyndi/Nature Ridge Elem Sch	131
Aleman, David/Otter Creek Elem Sch	131
Alexander, Debbie/Holy Family Catholic Sch	166
Alexander, Erin/Addison Early Learning Center	88
Alexander, Marsha/Garfield Elem Sch	57
Alexandru, Lucia/North Ctr-Handicap Children	80
Ali, Hussain/Horace Mann Elem Sch	61
Alimento, Corie/St Isidore Sch	101
Allar, Carolyn/John Muir Literacy Academy	66
Allen, Brad/Prairie Central High Sch	162
Allen, Brett/Staunton Elem Sch	168
Allen, Brett/Staunton High Sch	168
Allen, Brooke/Troy Heritage Trail Elem Sch	247
Allen, Chris/Northwest Elem Sch	164
Allen, Christopher/Acero CS-Zizumbo ES [156]	38
Allen, Daniel/Sullivan High Sch	193
Allen, Jim/Chiddix Junior High Sch	186
Allen, Kristin/Washington Junior High Sch	208
Allen, Lori/Zion Lutheran Sch	164
Allen, Michael/Oakton Elem Sch	48
Allen, Rick/Mid-America Preparatory Sch	216
Allen, Ryan/Univ of Chicago Lab Sch	81
Allen, Sandy/Spencer Loomis Elem Sch	152
Allensworth, Brian/Salt Fork South Elem Jr HS	233
Alli, Sam/Odin Attendance Center 9-12	175
Alli, Sam/Odin Attendance Center K-8	175
Allison, Shirley/Northwest Institute	80
Almasi, Dimitri/Elmwood Elem Sch	196
Almendarez, Sue/Player Early Childhood Center	53
Almodovar, Jorge/Meadowdale Elem Sch	180
Almodovar, Jorge/Walt Whitman Elem Sch	71
Alonzo, Elias/Instituto Hlth Sci Career Acad	39
Alsawi, Sawsan/Icci Academy	79
Alt, Rachael/South Elem Sch	181
Altamirano, Angelica/Hubbard High Sch	37
Alther, Michael/Hoffman Estates High Sch	69
Alvis, Mr/Dr Nick Osborne Primary Center	123
Alvis, Mr/J L Buford Intermediate Ed Ctr	123
Amador, Maria/Multicultural Acad Scholarship	37
Ambrose, Phil/Thurgood Marshall Lrng Center	208
Ambuehl, Chad/Roxana Junior High Sch	172
Amrhein, Jill/Jackson Middle Sch	99
Anderson-Maier, Brandi/Parkside Middle Sch	144
Anderson, Antoine/Glenbard East High Sch	94
Anderson, Brent/Murphy Junior High Sch	137
Anderson, Charles/M Clark Academy Prep Magnet HS	37
Anderson, Chris/Newport Elem Sch	147
Anderson, Cindy/Romona Elem Sch	72
Anderson, Comfort/Illinois Math & Science Acad	1
Anderson, Durrell/Bryant Elem Sch	51
Anderson, Erin/Madison Junior High Sch	98
Anderson, Felix, Dr/Blackhawk Primary Center	62
Anderson, Jason/Central Elem & Jr High Sch	117
Anderson, Jerry, Dr/Homewood Flossmoor High Sch	52
Anderson, Jillian/Park Sch	48
Anderson, Karen/J Ward Elem Sch	27
Anderson, Kate/Washington Elem Sch	47
Anderson, Kathryn/Deerfield High Sch	155
Anderson, Kim/Jerseyville East Elem Sch	125
Anderson, Kristi/Abingdon-Avon Middle Sch	139
Anderson, Kristi/Avon Elem Sch	139
Anderson, Laura/Warrensburg-Latham Elem Sch	166
Anderson, Laura, Dr/Concord Elem Sch	90
Anderson, Mary/Montessori Academy of Peace	165
Anderson, Megan/Eagle Academy	12
Anderson, Megan, Dr/DePaul Clg Prep-Gordon Campus	73
Anderson, Raquel/Da Vinci Academy	133
Anderson, Sabrina/Marcus Garvey Elem Sch	36
Anderson, Stacey/Woodland Primary Sch	157
Anderson, Tracy/Glenview Middle Sch	207
Anderson, Trisha/Bradley West Elem Sch	134
Andrews, Carly/Baker Demonstration Sch	77
Andrews, Matt/Heyworth Elem Sch	186
Andrews, Michelle/Hedding Grade Sch	139
Andrews, Renee/Trewyn K-8 Sch	199
Andrews, Shanele/Orr Academy High Sch	26
Andruch, Kelly/Kolmar Elem Sch	57
Anello, Jessica/Sch Exp Arts & Lrng-Woodstock	185
Angelos, Catharine/John Schroder ECC	97
Anglin, Sylvie/Univ of Chicago Lab Sch	81
Aniolowski, Regina/Cove Sch	78
Ankrom, Megan/Fairview Elem Sch	66
Antkiewicz, Mark/Costello Sch	56
Antonsen, Chris/Countryside Sch	13
Aponte, Marlene/Dawes Elem Sch	48
Apostoli, Karen/Wegner Elem Sch	100
Archer, Joe/Illinois Lutheran High Sch	250
Arduino, Joe/Booth Tarkington Elem Sch	71
Arias, Adriana/Nightingale Elem Sch	33
Ariola, Nancy/Oliver McCracken Middle Sch	67
Armato, Michael/St Anne Sch	160

School Year 2020-2021

PRINCIPAL INDEX

Market Data Retrieval

NAME/School	PAGE
Armbrust, Vickie/Willow Elem Sch	228
Armendariz, Mark/Lincoln Elem Sch	27
Armstrong-Belt, Cheryl/Sir Miles Davis Magnet Academy	35
Armstrong, Candace/New Simpson Hill Sch	127
Armstrong, Terrie/Glendale Elem Sch	227
Arnold, Jennifer/Field Elem Sch	123
Arnsman, Josh/Unity Middle Sch	2
Arnsman, Luke/Jefferson Primary Sch	228
Arriaga, Gerardo/Tonti Elem Sch	28
Arrigo, Mary/Noble CS-Baker Clg Prep [165]	40
Arriola-Lopez, Javier/Rachel Carson Elem Sch	28
Arroyo, Ana/Parkwood Elem Sch	131
Arroyo, Maria/Sator Sanchez Elem Sch	243
Arteaga, Guillermina/Otis P Graves Elem Sch	45
Artis, Dawn/Rivers of Life Christian Sch	173
Asaf, Karime/West Park Academy	31
Asche, Ben/Pearl City Sch	225
Asche, Ben/West Carroll High Sch	9
Ashbaugh, Brent/Rochester High Sch	212
Askew, Steven/R Brown Academy	36
Aspell, Maureen/St Petronille Sch	101
Atteberry, Amy/Washington Attendance Center	238
Auffant, Peter/Mather High Sch	36
Auge, Mr/Ivc Learning Center	197
Aughenbaugh, Denise/Mendota Twp High Sch	143
Aulisa, Gerrie/John E Albright Middle Sch	99
Austin, Jason/Sterling High Sch	240
Austria, Christopher/Plato Lrg Academy Primary [157]	41
Auth, Dave/St Malachy Sch	13
Aversa, Samantha/John Stewart Elem Sch	132
Ayer, Dan/Nauvoo-Colusa Elem Sch	115
Azab, Carrie/District 54 Early Learning Ctr	66
Azcoitia, Carlos/Mary Lou Cowlishaw Elem Sch	95
Aziz-Sims, Alahrie/Bogan Computer Tech High Sch	37

B

NAME/School	PAGE
Baal, Kathryn, Dr/Marist High Sch	73
Baalman, Maria/Evangelical Elem Sch	173
Baccheschi, Kristi/Malta Elem Sch	85
Bacci, Kristina/Gages Lake Sch	146
Bada, Bosede/Suder Montessori Magnet Sch	32
Bae, Kellie/Lake Bluff Elem Sch	151
Baer, Erick, Dr/St Rose Elem Sch	18
Baffico, Jon/St Patrick High Sch	76
Bagdasarian, Shahe/Glenbard East High Sch	94
Bagdasarian, Shahe, Dr/York Community High Sch	94
Bageanis, Louis/Our Lady Sacred Heart Academy	256
Bagger, David/Ombudsman Sch-Downers Grove	102
Bahena, Olimpia/Talcott Fine Arts Museum Acad	28
Bahnks, Chad/Knoxville High Sch	140
Bahnks, Tara/Mable Woolsey Elem Sch	140
Bailey, Leighanne/Zeigler Royalton Elem Jr HS	108
Bailey, Medina/Eagle Academy Christian Sch	78
Bailey, Stacey/Carl Sandburg Elem Sch	92
Baima, Mary/Allen Otter Creek Sch	141
Baird, Michael/Richmond Burton Cmty High Sch	184
Baird, Michele/DeSoto Grade Sch	120
Baird, Robert/St Ambrose Sch	173
Baker, Carol/George Washington Middle Sch	56
Baker, Heather/Dorothy Simon Elem Sch	255
Baker, Heather/West Lincoln-Broadwell ES	164
Baker, Jayson/Central Elem Sch	218
Baker, Marci/Alpine Christian Sch	256
Baker, Shavina/Jackson Charter Sch	254
Balaskovits, Christine/Corron Elem Sch	129
Baldassano, Brenda/St John the Baptist Sch	184
Baldermann, Jack/Westmont High Sch	92
Baldermann, Megan/Nelson Ridge Elem Sch	245
Baldermann, Timothy/Union Sch	248
Balduf, Brett/George B Carpenter Elem Sch	62
Baldwin, Nathan/William E Young Elem Sch	242
Balestri, Courtney/Putnam Co Elem Sch	204
Balestri, Michael/Lincoln Elem Sch	143
Ball, Tamika/Gage Park High Sch	37

NAME/School	PAGE
Banach, Matthew, Dr/Northwest Elem Sch	49
Baney, Rebecca/Belle Alexander Elem Sch	117
Bankester, Phil/Trinity Christian Sch	121
Bankowski, Laura/Oswego East High Sch	138
Banks, Kia/Vanderpoel Magnet Elem Sch	34
Banks, Rosalind/Lincoln Elem Sch	22
Banks, Shaymora/CICS-Washington Park ES [167]	39
Banks, Tony/Wilson Elem Sch	25
Banks, Tyneisha/Perspectives lit Math-Sci Acad [166]	41
Baratta, Kim/Proviso Area Excptnl Chldrn	20
Barber, Derek/Cambridge Sch	77
Barber, Michael/Rolling Acres Middle Sch	199
Barbic, Joe/Indian Valley Vocational Ctr	84
Barbini, Thomas/Helen Keller Jr High Sch	66
Barga, Shawanda/Country Club Hills Tech&Trade	78
Barger, Jill/Geff Elem Sch	237
Barger, Loy/Lighthouse Baptist Sch	211
Barker, Jeremiah/Galesburg Christian Sch	140
Barker, Jillian/Parkland Preparatory Academy	102
Barker, Kathy/Troy-Craughwell Elem Sch	247
Barkley, Michele/Mary Kay McNeill ELC	146
Barlow, Gary/Jacksonville Middle Sch	192
Barlow, Sheila/Powell Elem Paideia Comm Acad	35
Barnabee, Jennifer/Lincoln Elem Sch	94
Barnes, Jessica/Twin Groves Middle Sch	151
Barnstable, Sarah/Tri-C Elem Sch	251
Baron, Ananda/Zion Lutheran Sch	223
Baron, Heidi/Kellar Primary Sch	199
Barrera, Ms/CICS-Prairie	39
Barrett, Colleen/St Francis Xavier Sch	75
Barrett, Colleen/St Joseph Sch	75
Barrett, Jane/Seton Catholic Sch	209
Barrett, Kimberly/Brentwood Elem Sch	43
Barrett, Michelle/North Elem Sch	181
Barrett, Shawn/Westchester Intermediate Sch	70
Bartell, Julie/Burr Ridge Middle Sch	91
Barth, Ben/Zion Lutheran Sch	164
Bartucci, Brianna/Science Academy of Chicago	80
Basala, Rick/Sherrard Jr Sr High Sch	189
Bassett, Robert/Heritage Middle Sch	45
Baste, Khalida/Islamic Foundation Sch	102
Basurto, Tai/Dore Elem Sch	33
Battey, Robert/Grande Reserve Elem Sch	139
Bauer, Bruce, Dr/Dalzell Grade Sch	6
Bauer, Laura/Renfro Elem Sch	170
Bauerband, Nancy/Crystal Lake Montessori Sch	185
Baughman, Jeff/Le Roy Jr Sr High Sch	186
Baughman, Lucas/Emily G Johns Elem Sch	138
Baughman, Rachel/Oak Grove Elem Middle Sch	198
Baughman, Robert/Jamieson Elem Sch	29
Baumann, Theresa/Oster-Oakview Sch	245
Baumberger, Jon/Mt Olive High Sch	168
Baumgartner, Gina/River Woods Elem Sch	98
Baun, Katrina/Gurnee Christian Academy	158
Bautista, Jennifer/Orchard Place Elem Sch	46
Bawden, Meredith/Galileo Scholastic Academy	31
Baxter, Natalie/Minooka Elem Sch	112
Bay, Randy/Dakota Jr Sr High Sch	224
Bayless, Julie/Princeville Elem Sch	200
Bazile, Philip/Augustus Tolton Academy	72
Beals, Craig/Nuttall Middle Sch	83
Beam, Tracy/Marengo Cmty Middle Sch	182
Bearley, Mark/Southwestern High Sch	168
Beasley, Jessica/Learn 8 Chtr Sch-MS [164]	40
Beauford, Roger/Grant-White Elem Sch	50
Beaven, Clare/North Elem Sch	16
Becherer, April/Eagleveiw Elem Sch	190
Beck, Bobby/Villa Grove Elem Sch	88
Beck, Donna/St Luke Academy	81
Beck, Greg/Teutopolis High Sch	105
Beck, Mary/Nicholas Senn High Sch	36
Becker, Chris/Highland High Sch	171
Becker, Jerry/Galva Jr Sr High Sch	117
Becker, Robin/Germantown Elem Sch	18

Illinois School Directory — PRINCIPAL INDEX

NAME/School	PAGE
Beckham, Tammy/McClellan Elem Sch	123
Beckham, Tammy/Spring Garden Elem Sch	124
Beckley, Scott/Sparta High Sch	205
Beckley, Thomas/Chicago Jesuit Academy	77
Beckwith, Tatia, Dr/LaSalle Elem Sch	226
Bedell, Brendan/Noble CS-Rauner Clg Prep [165]	40
Bednar, Rachel/Edison Middle Sch	92
Bedows, Amycarol/Rockford Christian High Sch	256
Beebe, Stacy/Aurora Chrn Middle High Sch	133
Beekmeyer, Paul/Univ of Chicago Lab Sch	81
Beem, Robert/Woodrow Wilson Middle Sch	208
Begando, Mark/Nashville High Sch	235
Behrens, Michelle/Lord & Savior Evang Luth Sch	185
Beirne, Kevin/Montini Catholic High Sch	101
Belanger, David/Hanson Park Elem Sch	30
Belcastro, Bridget, Dr/Johnsburg Elem Sch	182
Belin, Marcus/Huntley Senior High Sch	182
Bell, Crystal/Ella Flagg Young Elem Sch	30
Bell, Jeff/Beacon Academy	77
Bell, Lawanda/Woodlawn Community Sch	33
Bell, Rashid/KIPP One Primary [163]	40
Bellamy, Andromeda/Epic Academy	39
Bellini, Nicole/Red Oak Sch	154
Bellm, Michael/Alton High Sch	169
Belobrajdic, Kristie/J E Hinchcliffe Elem Sch	221
Belville, Ryan/McAuliffe Elem Sch	30
Bemont, Kathy/Lincoln Grade Sch	83
Bending, Brett/Hampshire High Sch	180
Bendis, David/Franklin Middle Sch	92
Benedict, Chad/Mahomet-Seymour High Sch	11
Benefiel, Josh/Dieterich Elem Sch	104
Benes, Caitlin/Hiawatha Elem Sch	85
Benge, Terry/Salem4Youth Valor High Sch	163
Benhoff, Laura/New Approach Alt High Sch	105
Bennett, Brad/Robein Grade Sch	228
Bennett, Carol/Lincoln Early Learning Center	153
Bennett, Christina/Hellenic American Acad	158
Bennett, Craig/Fullerton Elem Sch	88
Bennett, Jay/Tri-Point Upper ES JHS	162
Bennett, Jon/Learn Chtr Sch-Hunter Perkins [164]	40
Bennett, Katie/Robert E Clow Elem Sch	96
Bennett, Matthew/Winnebago High Sch	255
Bennett, Thad/Christian Liberty Academy	78
Bennett, Torry/CICS-Northtown Academy [160]	39
Bennington, Marlys/Benjamin Elem Sch	186
Benson, Eric/Somonauk High Sch	86
Bentley, Maureen/St Thomas the Apostle Sch	200
Berardi, Randal/Congerville Elem Sch	257
Berardi, Randal/Goodfield Elem Sch	257
Berenson, Mitchell, Dr/Urbana High Sch	13
Berentes, Mike/Rock Falls Township High Sch	240
Berg, Dana/Bishop McNamara Cath Sch	137
Berg, Stacy/Wilder-Waite Elem Sch	196
Berg, Thomas/Hampton Elem Sch	207
Bergbreiter, Lisa/Independence Early Lrng Ctr	130
Berger, Erica/Henry Winkelman Elem Sch	70
Berger, Erica, Dr/John Middleton Elem Sch	67
Bergholtz, Jeffrey/Forest Road Elem Sch	54
Bergman, Kenton/Illinois Valley Central HS	197
Bergstrand, Gayle/Christian Hill Church Sch	78
Beringer, Curt/Lee R Foster Elem Sch	50
Berlinski, Andy/Princeton High Sch	7
Bernal, Jen/Nicholson Elem Sch	132
Bernard, Janice/Edison Elem Sch	56
Berrie, Michael/Round Lake High Sch	155
Berry, Carrie/Northeast Elem Sch	49
Berry, Clarence/Thomas Jefferson Middle Sch	156
Berry, Kathy/St Symphorosa Sch	76
Berry, Nicole/Horace Mann Early Learning Ctr	208
Bersie, Mark/St Paul Lutheran Sch	81
Bertrand, Dan, Dr/Zion Lutheran Sch	185
Bethge, Judy/Harvest Christian Academy	133
Betry, Keith/Heritage Christian Sch	250
Bettis, Beth/Greenfield High Sch	111
Betzold, Carol/Crystal Lawns Elem Sch	246
Betzolt, Susan/St Francis Borgia Sch	75
Bevard, Dustin/Parkview Middle Sch	226
Bevis, Wayne/Lindblom Math Science Academy	37
Bhatia, Maria, Dr/Sunnydale Elem Sch	131
Bhattacharyya, Ellen/KIPP Ascend Primary [163]	40
Bibb, Jenna/Stark Co Elem Sch	224
Bickel, Chris/Leland Community Sch	142
Bickel, Rich/O'Fallon Twp High Sch	221
Bickel, Rich/O'Fallon Twp HS-Milburn	221
Bickley, Melanie/Jefferson Elem Sch	84
Bickman May, Kara/Art In Motion	38
Bicknell, Mary/Noel LeVasseur Elem Sch	134
Bidlack, Lawrence/Geneva Middle School South	131
Biehl, Jackye/First Baptist Academy	223
Biela, Michael/Rickover Naval Academy	28
Bielema, Cory/Morrison High Sch	239
Bielfeldt, Kyle/Gibson City-Melvin-Sibley MS	106
Bierman, Jill/St Thomas the Apostle Sch	122
Bigane, Meg/St Giles Sch	75
Biggs, Michelle/St Matthew Sch	13
Bima, Lynette/Douglas Elem Sch	7
Binder, Zack/Williamsfield Sch	140
Binegar, Stacey/Cantrall Intermediate Sch	188
Bingaman, Donna/Greenbrier Elem Sch	21
Bingen, Chris/Jane Addams Junior High Sch	66
Bingham, Laura/Murphy Junior High Sch	137
Bione, John/Trinity Lutheran Sch	206
Bird, Meghan/Country Meadows Elem Sch	151
Birdoes, Mike/Blessed Sacrament Sch	229
Biscan, Mathew/Wheaton North High Sch	92
Bishop, Brian/New Berlin Elem Sch	212
Bishop, Lawanda/Kipling Elem Sch	27
Bixby, Sandra/Univ of Chicago Lab Sch	81
Bjork, Steve/Yorkville Intermediate Sch	139
Black, Andrea/Schmid Elem Sch	35
Black, Cheryl/Judah Christian Sch	13
Black, Nicole/Beecher Elem Sch	241
Black, Nicole/Braceville Elem Sch	111
Blackard, Tricia/Collinsville Area Voc Center	170
Blackburn, Nick/St Patrick Sch	166
Blackert, Andrew/East Coloma-Nelson Elem Sch	238
Blackley, Michelle/Daniel Wright Jr High Sch	153
Blackmer, Nathan/Lake Bluff Middle Sch	151
Blackwell, Laura/Beyer Early Childhood Center	254
Blair, Jay/Midwest Central High Sch	177
Blair, Patrick/Argenta Oreana Middle Sch	165
Blake, Jonathan/Pana Christian Academy	15
Blakely, Randy/WinGate Elem Sch	220
Blakley, Kermit/Chippewa Middle Sch	46
Blan, Karen/Families of Faith Academy	250
Blanchette, Sherri/Troy-Shorewood Elem Sch	248
Bland-Hampston, Audrey/Ryan Banks Academy	80
Bland, Craig/Jordan Elem Sch	174
Bland, Rachel/Stuart R Paddock Sch	43
Blankenship, Ed/Pope Co Elem Sch	204
Bleau, Terry/Geneva Middle School South	131
Blinstrup, Audrey/Ombudsman-South High Sch	40
Bliven, Christie/Blessed Sacrament Catholic Sch	2
Blumenshine, Emily/St Michael the Archangel Sch	145
Blumer, Thomas/Lincoln K-8 Sch	199
Bodenstab, Tracy/Whittier Elem Sch	22
Bodzioch, Paula/Mark Lund Day Sch	88
Boehm, Brett/Cowden Jr Sr High Sch	216
Boente, Jon/Franklin Sch	217
Boerger, Kary/Thomas Jefferson Primary Sch	199
Boester, Beth/Trinity Lutheran Sch	18
Bogdanic, Kelly/Central Elem Sch	164
Boger, Hugh/Scott Elem Sch	98
Boggs, Laura/St Andrew's Lutheran Sch	81
Bogott, Tricia/Verda Dierzen Early Lrng Ctr	184
Bohanek, Rob, Dr/Ridge Family Center for Lrng	44
Bohlman, Victoria/Willard Elem Sch	208
Bohm, Eric/Pontiac Township High Sch	162

School Year 2020-2021 — 800-333-8802 — IL-U3

PRINCIPAL INDEX

Market Data Retrieval

NAME/School	PAGE
Bohrer, Matthew/Lincoln-Douglas Elem Sch	224
Bolden, Michael/Addison Trail High Sch	93
Bolek, Joni/Center for Disability Services	250
Boles, John/Salem Cmty High Sch	175
Bollman Young, Jana/Red Brick Sch	205
Bolton, Doug, Dr/North Shore Academy	20
Bondy, Natalia/Fusion Academy-Lincoln Park	78
Bongle, Kerri/Adler Park Elem Sch	153
Bonilla, Luis/Eugene Field Elem Sch	71
Bonomo, Ken/Owen Elem Sch	95
Booker-Thomas, Joyce, Dr/Franklin Fine Arts Center	27
Boone, Sarah/Millikin Elem Sch	117
Booth, Karen/Guerin College Prep Sch	73
Booth, Karen/St Emily Sch	75
Booth, Robin, Dr/All Saints Academy	18
Boozer, Keneisha/Feitshans Elem Sch	213
Borchelt, Brent/Belle Aire Elem Sch	93
Borders, Kari/Douglas Prep Alternative Sch	213
Boren, Brent/Lick Creek Elem Sch	230
Boren, Maryann/Meridian Jr Sr High Sch	204
Borling, Audrey/Noble CS-UIC Clg Prep [165]	40
Borner, Julie/Union Ridge Elem Sch	70
Boros, Lauren/Noble CS-Noble Academy [165]	40
Borras, Francisco/Spry Community Links High Sch	37
Borries, Ben/Clay City High Sch	16
Borries, Ben/Clay City Junior High Sch	16
Boss, Francie/Arbury Hills Elem Sch	247
Boston, Piper/Windsor Elem Sch	21
Boswell, Edward/Orland Junior High Sch	61
Botterman, Mary, Dr/Edwin Aldrin Elem Sch	66
Bottigliero, Nicole/Eisenhower Academy	243
Bouillon, Natalie/Hartford Elem Sch	172
Bouman, Tim/Walther Lutheran High Sch	81
Bourne, Jeff/Griggsville-Perry Middle Sch	203
Bourrell, Kelly/Cardinal Joseph Bernardin ES	72
Bourrell, Kelly/St Hubert Sch	75
Bousmaha, Haiat/Furqaan Academy-Boilingbrook	250
Bousson, Jill/Acero CS-Omar Torres ES [156]	38
Boutet, Allison/Heritage Middle Sch	23
Bowen, Kevin/Cisne High Sch	237
Bowles, Julie/Chesterton Academy-Holy Family	101
Bowman, Casie/Mulberry Grove Elem Sch	4
Bowman, Heather/Lincoln Grade Sch	229
Bowman, Shannon/Medora Intermediate Sch	168
Bowser, Bob/Allendale Elem Sch	234
Bowser, Theresa/Our Lady of Lourdes Sch	166
Boxell, Kathy/Barnsdale Road Sch	54
Boyce, Laurie/Freedom Elem Sch	246
Boyd, Christine/St Mary of the Lake Sch	76
Boyd, Christine/St Thomas of Canterbury Sch	76
Brackins, Carol/Wharton Fifth Grade Center	45
Bradburn, Anthony/Roselle Middle Sch	99
Bradburn, Jonathan/Silas Willard Elem Sch	140
Bradford, Jessica/Vernon L Barkstall Elem Sch	10
Bradley, Blake/Eldorado Elem Sch	210
Bradley, Colin/Dr Julian Rogus Elem Sch	247
Bradley, Karen/Highland Elem Sch	67
Bradley, Mary/YCCS-Virtual High Sch	41
Brady, Dave/Grace Baptist Academy	214
Brady, Mary/Michael E Baum Elem Sch	165
Brady, Nicole/Cambridge Lakes Charter Sch	180
Brales, Christina/Pythagoras Childrens Academy	102
Brandes, Lori/Washington Elem Sch	131
Brandon, James/Stone Scholastic Academy	29
Brandt, Diane/Oak Grove Elem Sch	165
Brandt, Pamela/Goudy Elem Sch	27
Branon, Tim/Central City Elem Sch	174
Brasfield, Kim/Roosevelt Elem Sch	46
Brasfield, Kim/Roosevelt Junior High Sch	46
Brashear, Janice/Johnsonville Elem Sch	237
Bratten, Genie/Prather Elem Sch	171
Brau, Wayne/Visitation Catholic Sch	118
Braun, Jeff/Cuba Elem Sch	109
Braun, Jeff/Cuba Middle High Sch	109
Brauns, Gary/Greenville Junior High Sch	4
Brave, Kimberly/Jefferson Elem Sch	251
Bray, Nancy/Our Savior's Lutheran Sch	214
Brazeal, Geraldine/Christ the King Luth Sch	77
Breden, Cory/Jersey Community High Sch	125
Breeze, Jennifer/Kenneth E Neubert Elem Sch	180
Breitkreutz, Craig/Faith Lutheran Sch	158
Brekke, Erik/Miner Sch	20
Brekke, Patricia/Back of the Yards IB High Sch	26
Brennan, Stephanie/John Gates Elem Sch	129
Brennan, Stephanie/Wasco Elem Sch	129
Breo, Karin/CICS-Irving Park	39
Brett, Eileen/Wilmot Elem Sch	149
Brewer, Zeppelyn/Tri-Co Special Ed Sch	120
Brickman, Jay/Hinckley-Big Rock High Sch	85
Bridges, Jennifer/Windsor Jr Sr High Sch	216
Bridget, M, Sr/High School of St Thomas More	13
Bright, Charles/Bret Harte Elem Sch	33
Brink, Melanie/Waltonville High Sch	124
Brink, Terry, Dr/Jefferson Elem Sch	25
Brinkman, Mary/St Thomas of Villanova Sch	76
Briseno, Erik/Eisenhower Campus High Sch	44
Brito, Angela/George Washington Elem Sch	62
Brito, Angela/James G Blaine Elem Sch	30
Britton, John/St John's Lutheran Sch	119
Brizgys, Rana/Queen of Angels Sch	74
Broadwell, Deborah/Virgil Grissom Middle Sch	53
Brock, Adell/Carroll-Rosenwald Elem Sch	33
Brockschmidt, Beth/Eisenhower Elem Sch	192
Brockway, Carrie/Pecatonica Elem Sch	253
Brode-Rico, Amanda/Lake Park High Sch-East Campus	96
Broders, Tyler/Nelson Prairie Sch	245
Brodeur, Tim/Freedom Middle Sch	23
Brodhead, Colleen/St Paul the Apostle Sch	249
Brodzik, Karen/Christ Our Savior Sch	73
Brogan, Cindy/St Mary's Sch	234
Brooks, Cassandra, Dr/Learn 9 Chtr Sch-Waukegan [164]	1
Brooks, Delilah/Masters Academy	79
Brooks, Eliza/North Ridge Middle Sch	232
Brooks, Luke/Pleasant Plains High Sch	212
Brooks, Robin/Selmaville Elem Sch	176
Brower, Kristin/Bonnie McBeth Early Lrng Ctr	246
Brown, Amanda/Springfield Elem Sch	57
Brown, Anita/North Elem Sch	15
Brown, April/Program for Adaptive Lrng Sch	20
Brown, Charles/Central A & M High Sch	14
Brown, Charles/Gregory Intermediate Sch	14
Brown, Christopher/Wescott Elem Sch	60
Brown, Christy/Hilltop Elem Sch	183
Brown, Christy/Ralston Elem Sch	253
Brown, Iretha/Maya Angelou Elem Sch	51
Brown, Jacqueline/Valley View Early Chldhd Ctr	248
Brown, Jeff, Dr/Dr MLK Jr Sch-Lit/Fine Arts	48
Brown, Keith/Illini Bluffs High Sch	197
Brown, Kevin/Jerling Junior High Sch	61
Brown, Kristen/Ashmore Elem Sch	19
Brown, Levi/Clarendon Hills Middle Sch	91
Brown, Lisa/St Patrick Catholic Sch	133
Brown, Lynn/Scott Altman Primary Sch	228
Brown, Matthew/Noble CS-Johnson Clg Prep [165]	40
Brown, Mellodie/Beethoven Elem Sch	33
Brown, Michelle/Grafton Elem Sch	125
Brown, Regina/Cairo Elem Sch	3
Brown, Rufina/Parker Child Parent Center	34
Brown, Rufina/Parker Community Academy	34
Brown, Stephanie/Davenport Elem Sch	257
Brown, Stevie/Dupo Jr Sr High Sch	218
Brown, Tammy/Irving Elem Sch	117
Brown, Tiffany/Smith Elem Sch	36
Brown, Tom/Georgetowne Middle Sch	227
Brown, Vicki/South Shore Fine Arts Academy	35
Brown, Yvonne/Daniel Webster Middle Sch	156

Illinois School Directory — PRINCIPAL INDEX

NAME/School	PAGE
Broxton, Charlotte/Frazier Prospective Mag Sch	31
Broyls, Hiram/Luther Burbank Elem Sch	30
Brummel, Ann, Sr/Pope St John Paul 11 Academy S	133
Brummel, Ann, Sr/Pope St John Paul II Academy N	133
Brunaugh, Jason/Jersey Community Middle Sch	125
Bruner, Susan/Depute Unit Sch	6
Brunson, Tiffany/Forest Park Middle Sch	50
Brunson, Tiffany, Dr/Field-Stevenson Elem Sch	50
Brush, Jeremy/Parkview Junior High Sch	159
Bryan, Eric/Hamilton Elem Sch	114
Bryan, Jamie/Kewanee High Sch	117
Bryant, Bud/Cullen Elem Sch	36
Bryant, Eric/Dwight Baptist Academy	163
Bryner, Timothy/Waukegan HS Brookside	156
Bryner, Timothy/Waukegan HS-Washington	156
Bua, Angelina/Rockford Innovative Lrng Ctr	254
Bucci, Maryellen/Easterseals Academy-Tinley PK	78
Buch, Ann/Westgate Elem Sch	21
Buchanan, Priscilla/Anne Fox Elem Sch	66
Buchs, Beau/River Ridge Elem Sch	126
Buck, Bryan/Monroe Middle Sch	92
Buck, Jacob/Eisenhower Junior High Sch	92
Buckley, Christine/St Gilbert Sch	158
Buckner, Natasha/G Rogers Clark Elem Sch	27
Budd, Kelley/Lakewood Creek Elem Sch	137
Budicin, Anne/Glenwood Academy	78
Budicin, Anne/Glenwood Sch	78
Budz, Jeffrey/Joliet Catholic Academy	249
Buehler, Julie/SS Peter & Paul Sch	173
Bulak, Lisa/Benavides Steam Academy	129
Bulak, Lisa/Richmond Intermediate Sch	129
Bullock, Chantel/Rickover Junior High Sch	44
Bunker, Kyle/Garfield Elem Sch	130
Bunting, James/Glenn Raymond Sch	119
Burchell, Rick/Fox Valley Career Center	132
Buresh, Joe/Costa Catholic Academy	140
Burger, Ashley/Field Park Elem Sch	71
Burke, Brandon/John L Nash Middle Sch	118
Burke, Brandon/Ridgeview Jr Sr High Sch	187
Burke, Jeff/Benjamin Franklin Elem Sch	94
Burke, Kelly/De Lacey Family Education Ctr	180
Burke, Trisha/Ball Elem Sch	211
Burkey, Niki/Lincoln Prairie Elem Sch	180
Burkholder, Monica/Eastland Jr Sr High Sch	8
Burklund, Lee/Chicago Lighthouse Dev Center	77
Burlinski, Carol/St Isaac Jogues Sch	101
Burmeister, Janet/Concordia Lutheran Sch	214
Burnett, Emily/Arbor View Elem Sch	90
Burnett, Sara/Tri-Valley Elem Sch	187
Burnett, Sara/Tri-Valley Middle Sch	187
Burnette, Valerie/Zion Christian Sch	158
Burns, Kim/Adam Sch	251
Burns, Margaret/Sutherland Elem Sch	34
Burns, Maura/Butterfield Elem Sch	97
Burns, Melissa/St Peter Lutheran Sch	173
Burns, Merritt/Washington Junior High Sch	143
Burress, Derrick/Lake Co High Sch Tech Campus	146
Burris, Cheri/Calhoun High Sch	8
Burrough, Kay/C A Henning Elem Sch	172
Burton, Anne/Oakwood Junior High Sch	232
Burton, Maria/Lincoln Middle Sch	219
Buscemi, Kevin/Oak Ridge Elem Sch	59
Bush, Krystal/Dream Academy	130
Bush, Krystal/Larkin High Sch	130
Bush, Marcus/New Boston Elem Sch	189
Bush, Rhea/Laura Ward Elem Sch	31
Buss, Jamie/Henry Raab Elem Sch	217
Buss, Jamie/Washington Sch	217
Butala, Jeanette/Providence St Mel Sch	80
Butcher, Craig/Genoa-Kingston Middle Sch	85
Butcher, Donna/Children's House Mont Sch	133
Butler, Michael/Illinois Youth Center	1
Butler, Rhonda/Robert A Black Magnet Sch	35
Butler, Towanna/South Shore Intl Clg High Sch	38
Buttimer, Alan/Westview Elem Sch	100
Buty, Mo/Stuart G Ferst Sch	81
Buxton, Jarrod/Munhall Elem Sch	129
Buzanis, Alice/Sherwood Elem Sch	28
Bylaitis, Daniela/Inter-American Magnet Sch	30
Byndon, Samuel/Urbana Adult Education Sch	13
Byrd-Wright, Chandra/Dunne Tech Academy	36
Byrd, Marcie/Nash Elem Sch	30
Byrne, Margaret/Northwest Middle Sch	30

C

NAME/School	PAGE
Cadenas, Nora/Seward Communctn Arts Acad	33
Cady, Kristie/Bureau Valley Wyanet Elem Sch	6
Cady, Kristy/Bureau Valley Walnut Elem Sch	6
Caesar, Cheryl/Lakeview Sch	157
Caetta, Dawn/Kinzie Elem Sch	27
Cahill, Katie/St Vincent Ferrer Sch	76
Cain, Cory/Urban Prep CS-West	41
Cain, Tara/Lovett Elem Sch	30
Caiola, Shane/Stone Creek Elem Sch	253
Calderin, Aldo/Unity Junior High Sch	42
Calise, Wendy/Countryside Montessori Sch	78
Calkins, Roy/Dillon Elem Sch	240
Callaghan, Daniel/John A Bannes Elem Sch	53
Callahan, Cindy/Belle Valley Elem Sch	217
Callahan, Conrey/New Field Primary Sch	29
Callahan, Tim/Madison Elem Sch	92
Calleros, Megan/Spencer Crossing Interm Sch	245
Calloway, Karen/Kenwood Academy	38
Camerer, Mary/Washington Elem Sch	192
Camilleri, Jennifer, Dr/Strassburg Elem Sch	44
Campbell, Christy/Edgar Allan Poe Elem Sch	71
Campbell, Linda/Monroe Elem Sch	15
Campbell, Marcus/Evanston Twp High Sch	48
Campbell, Michael/Bloom Twp Alternative High Sch	23
Campbell, Mitzi/Kenneth D Bailey Academy	232
Campbell, Monica/Middlefork Sch	233
Campbell, Rusty/Bismarck Henning Jr High Sch	231
Campos, Jackie/Indian Knoll Elem Sch	99
Campos, Nelson/Miguel Juarez Middle Sch	156
Campos, Terri, Dr/Lozano Bilingual Sch	32
Canfield, Celeste/Central Elem Sch	195
Cannella, Sal/G B Swift Elem Specialty Sch	29
Cannon, Colleen/St Catherine of Siena Sch	133
Cannon, Jill/CICS-Loomis Longwood Mid HS	39
Cannon, Kristen/Riverwood Elem Sch	183
Cantrell, Wendy/Foundations Sch	223
Cantu, Manuel/St Laurence Sch	133
Canzoneri, Susan/Immaculate Conception Sch	73
Caparula, Jim/Our Lady of Grace Cath Academy	209
Cappozzo, Gabe/Kenneth Murphy Elem Sch	147
Capps, Shelly/Cambridge Cmty Elem Sch	116
Capuder, April/Gwendolyn Brooks Middle Sch	61
Cardamone, Tom/Deer Path Middle School-East	152
Cardamone, Tom/Harvard Junior High Sch	181
Carden, Kathleen/St Matthias Elem Sch	76
Carew, Jillian/Foundations College Prep CS	39
Carey, Cassy/Rochester Intermediate Sch	212
Carey, Margaret/Landmark Elem Sch	183
Carey, Wanda/Willa Cather Elem Sch	31
Carlos, Lisa/Plainfield Elem Sch	46
Carlos, Pamela/Golfview Elem Sch	180
Carlson, Ashley/Iroquois West ES-Danforth	119
Carlson, Emily/Queen of All Saints Sch	74
Carlson, Jeff/Eisenhower Middle Sch	254
Carlson, Judith/Grimes Elem Sch	34
Carlson, Michael/Colona Grade Sch	116
Carlson, Scott/Willowbrook Elem Sch	60
Carlson, Tim/Sycamore High Sch	86
Carlson, Tracy/Coal City Intermediate Sch	112
Carmody, Beth/Hubbard Woods Elem Sch	72
Caron, William, Dr/Scales Mound Elem Sch	126
Carpenter, Andy/Thomas Edison Elem Sch	67
Carpenter, Kelly/MacArthur Early Childhood Ctr	178
Carr, Amanda/Logan Junior High Sch	7

School Year 2020-2021   800-333-8802   IL-U5

PRINCIPAL INDEX

NAME/School	PAGE
Carr, Brian/Hyde Park Elem Sch	156
Carroll, Dave/Peoria Heights High Sch	198
Carroll, Maura/Hilda Walker Interm Sch	247
Carroll, Megan/Carolyn Wenz Elem Sch	103
Carson, Joyce/Cisne Middle Sch	237
Carson, Mark/Nicholson Tech Academy	34
Carter-King, Sherita/Simpson Acad for Young Women	37
Carter, Arin/John C Dunham STEM Sch	1
Carter, Carla/Booth Elem Sch	238
Carter, Donella/Gregory Elem Sch	31
Carter, Leah/Avis Huff Impact	135
Carter, Ronald/Guilford High Sch	254
Carver, Jim/Unity East Elem Sch	12
Casas, Octavio/Chicago Military Academy	38
Cascio, Matthew/Genoa-Kingston High Sch	85
Cascio, Matthew/Harlem Middle Sch	252
Casey, Nick/Okaw Area Vocational Center	106
Cass, Charlie/Central Junior High Sch	108
Castelaz, Isaac/National Teachers Academy	26
Castellano, Gina/Ridgewood High Sch	64
Castle, Laura/Acero CS-Brighton Park ES [156]	38
Castleman, Lisa/Olympia West Elem Sch	187
Cengel, Amy/Oak Terrace Elem Sch	154
Cengiz, Cafer/Horizon Sci Acad-McKinley Park [161]	1
Cervantes, Lorenzo/Lincoln Junior High Sch	67
Chalmers, Lori/Annette Harris Officer ES	218
Chambers, Sue/Cornerstone Christian Academy	188
Chambliss, Darin/Salt Fork High Sch	233
Chaplin, Jason/Fieldcrest Primary Sch	257
Chapman, Trevor/Normal Cmty High Sch	186
Chaudoin, Ginger/Washington-Monroe Elem Sch	164
Chavers, Michelle/Limestone Middle Sch	135
Chavez, J, Dr/Our Lady of Peace Sch	101
Chavez, J, Dr/St Mary Nativity Sch	249
Chelmecki, Brian/Acero CS-Major Garcia HS [156]	38
Cheng, Katherine/Armour Elem Sch	31
Cheng, Moses, Dr/Community High Sch	91
Cherry, Tracy/Danville High Sch	231
Cheshareck, Kathleen/Walnut Trails Elem Sch	112
Chesta, Kelly/Crete-Monee Early Learning Ctr	242
Chiaramonte, Jackie/SS Alphonsus & Patrick Sch	74
Chiaventone, Jamie/Thompsonville Grade Sch	108
Chiaventone, Jamie/Thompsonville High Sch	108
Chick, Dan/McClure Junior High Sch	71
Chilous, Omar/Grtr Lawndale Social Justice	37
Chinn, Chrishawn/21st Century Primary Center	62
Chinn, Chrishawn/Mohawk Primary Center	62
Chipain, George, Dr/Prussing Elem Sch	29
Chipman, Tim/South Elem Sch	192
Chisausky, Eric/Walker Elem Sch	91
Chlebek, Chris/Plainfield Central High Sch	246
Chleboun, Robert/Liberty Elem Sch	180
Choi, James/Sabio Academy	158
Chorley, Rachel/Mokena Elem Sch	245
Chrisman, Brent/Pearl City Sch	225
Chrisos, Kokona/Crete-Monee Middle Sch	242
Christensen, Cynthia/S Wilmington Grade Sch	113
Christensen, Stephanie/Hillcrest Elem Sch	207
Christenson, Audra/St Charles North High Sch	129
Christeson, Jill/Lewis & Clark Elem Sch	173
Christian, J/Richland Elem Sch	247
Christian, Jeremy/Percy Julian Middle Sch	61
Chrobak-Prince, Teresa/Hearst Elem Sch	34
Chron-Bernard, Heather/Garvy Elem Sch	28
Chvojka, Karen/Golf Middle Sch	51
Cicchelli, Kate/Bennett Day School-Flagship	77
Ciconte, Barbara/Sacred Heart Sch	74
Cieciwa, Jim/Rockland Elem Sch	153
Cigan, Chris/Learn 10 CS North Chicago [164]	154
Cimarossa, Michele/North Mac Elem Sch	168
Cinnamon, Molly, Dr/Pope John XXIII Sch	73
Cirilli, Anna/St Nicholas Cathedral Sch	76
Clabough, Pete, Dr/Smith Elem Sch	132

NAME/School	PAGE
Clanton, Keppen/Northwestern Jr Sr High Sch	168
Clapp, Adam/Lake Crest Elem Sch	19
Clapp, Adam/Monticello High Sch	202
Clapp, Adam/Oakland High Sch	19
Clark, Amanda/W S Beaupre Elem Sch	129
Clark, Cathi/Springfield Developmental Ctr	214
Clark, Chelsea/Jefferson Elem Sch	170
Clark, Chelsey/Caseyville Elem Sch	170
Clark, Deborah/Mark T Skinner West Elem Sch	27
Clark, Elizabeth/Fulton Pre-School	239
Clark, Lance/Frances Willard Elem Sch	208
Clark, Lisa/Loves Park Elem Sch	252
Clarke, James/Freedom Middle Sch	23
Clay, Karen/Illinois Elem Sch	57
Clayton, Galeta/Chicago City Day Sch	77
Clendenin, Connie/Elverado Intermediate Sch	120
Clendenin, Connie/Elverado Junior High Sch	120
Cleven, Jim/Sycamore Middle Sch	86
Clishem, Anthony, Dr/St Frances of Rome Sch	75
Clous, Allison/St John Lutheran Sch	81
Clouston, Marie/Richardson Middle Sch	34
Coady, Joanne/Kemmerer Village Sch	14
Coate, Patrick/United West Elem Sch	235
Coates, Toby/Donovan Elem Sch	119
Coats, Carrie/Central Elem Sch	150
Cobarrubias, Dacia/N B Galloway Elem Sch	241
Cobb-Powers, Katie/Valeska Hinton Early Ed Ctr	199
Cobbs, Valesta/Bond Elem Sch	34
Coberley, Debra, Dr/Wesmere Elem Sch	246
Cochran, Curtis/Calvary Baptist Academy	200
Cochran, Lisa/Word of Life Christian Sch	173
Cockburn, Melissa/Marion Learning Center	250
Cody, Laura/St Paul Sch	179
Cohen, Aaron/Telshe Yeshiva Boys Sch	81
Cohn, Amanda/Valley View Elem Sch	183
Colbert, Lori/Algonquin Pre-Kindergarten Ctr	62
Colboth, Tommy/Washington Elem Sch	251
Colby, Therese/Montessori School of Lemont	79
Cole-Jackson, Monica, Dr/Deer Creek Christian Sch	78
Coleman, Annette/Peoria High Sch	199
Coleman, Carlynda/Dunbar Elem Sch	218
Coleman, Charlotte/Kimball Middle Sch	130
Coleman, Diedre/Holmes Elem Sch	34
Coleman, Lennette, Dr/Ariel Community Academy	33
Coleman, Ray/St Monica Academy	76
Coleman, Renee/Freeport Middle Sch	224
Coleman, Ron/Trico Junior High Sch	121
Coleman, Semaj/Hoover Elem Sch	52
Collard, Tim/Faith Baptist Christian Sch	229
Collette, Terry, Dr/Hope D Wall Sch	132
Collier, Jody/Spoon River Valley Elem Sch	110
Collier, Jody/Spoon River Vly Jr Sr High Sch	110
Collins, Ben/Maine South High Sch	56
Collins, Candice/Maria Montessori Sch	254
Collins, Robert/Hawthorn Middle School North	151
Collins, S/CICS-West Belden	39
Collins, Yvette/Ellis Middle Sch	130
Columbaro, Christopher/Algonquin Lakes Elem Sch	180
Colwell-Roy, Renee/Laketown Elem Sch	213
Combs, Nikki/Lincoln Elem Sch	227
Comella, Chris/Pilgrim Lutheran Sch	80
Commare, Ben/Belvidere South Middle Sch	4
Comparini, Theresa/YCCS-Jane Addams Alt HS	41
Compere, Angie/Lundahl Middle Sch	181
Compton, Kathy/Carbondale New Sch	121
Conaway, Wendy/Owen Marsh Elem Sch	213
Condon, Matt/Park View Sch	58
Conkle, J/Metropolis Elem Sch	178
Conley, Melanie/Lincoln Elem Sch	143
Conn, Erin/Le Roy Elem Sch	186
Connell, Roderick/Montessori Children's House	173
Conrad, Sheila/Rose E Krug Elem Sch	129
Conran, Rory/Menta Academy Northwest	256

Illinois School Directory — PRINCIPAL INDEX

NAME/School	PAGE
Considine, Eileen/Columbia Explorers Academy	32
Consolino, John/Iuka Grade Sch	174
Contos, Eileen/Midwest Chrn Mont Academy	250
Converse, Susan/Woodland Elem Sch	171
Convey, Jennifer/Oak Crest Elem Sch	147
Conway, Codi/Prairie Central Elem Sch	162
Cook, Brian/Waverly High Sch	193
Cook, Danielle/Novak Academy	10
Cook, Dawn/Clay Academy	184
Cook, Jerry/Wheeling High Sch	70
Cook, Kimberly/Fieldcrest Elem Sch	63
Cook, Marty/Central Senior High Sch	1
Cooke, Fatima/Sumner Math & Science Academy	31
Cooney, Michelle/Lincoln Elem Sch	48
Cooper, Randy/Westfair Christian Academy	193
Cooper, Tara/Gillespie Middle Sch	167
Coors, Ryan/Norwood Park Elem Sch	29
Copes, Kristin/Troy Hofer Elem Sch	247
Copes, Lance/Grundy Area Voc Center	111
Cora, Brenda/Noble CS-Rowe Clark Math & Sci [165]	40
Corcoran, Joseph/Harriet Gifford Elem Sch	130
Cordina, Timothy/Nicholas A Hermes Elem Sch	129
Cordova, Shelley/Greene Elem Sch	32
Cornish, Kimberly/Still Middle Sch	96
Cornwell, Joshua/Johnsburg Junior High Sch	182
Corona, Nestor/YCCS-Aspira Antonia Pantoja HS [130]	41
Correll, John/St Joseph Sch	223
Corrigan, McKenna/St Ann Grade Sch	74
Corrough, Rachel/Forest Hills Elem Sch	71
Corzine, Doug/Frankfort Intermediate Sch	108
Cosentino, Julianne/Millennium Elem Sch	53
Cosme, James/Falconer Elem Sch	30
Costello, Lori/Waterloo High Sch	190
Costello, Timothy/Science & Arts Academy	80
Costilla, Marcelo/Reilly Elem Sch	31
Cotelleso, Tony/North Love Christian Sch	256
Cotirla, Melissa/YCCS-Innovations HS	41
Cotter, Brandon, Dr/Argo Cmty High Sch	21
Cotter, Kelly/Caledonia Elem Sch	4
Cotto, Gustavo/West Junior High Sch	217
Couch, Melissa/Clifford Crone Middle Sch	95
Coughlin, Sandra/Glenbard South High Sch	94
Countryman, Jake/McDole Elem Sch	132
Cournaya, Danielle/Heritage Grove Middle Sch	246
Covarrubias, Dustin/Willard Elem Sch	131
Cowan, Jennifer/Echo Sch	20
Cowell, Randi/New Central Elem Sch	177
Cox-Bey, Tyran/Peace Center	69
Cox, Becky/May Elem Sch	195
Cox, Chad/West Prairie High Sch	178
Cox, Chrissy/Denman Elem Sch	2
Cox, John/Central Primary Sch	225
Cox, John/Mont Sch of Peoria	200
Cox, Mark/Paris Co-op High Sch	103
Coyne-Logan, Daniel/Earl Hanson Elem Sch	208
Craft, Zachary/Highland Elem Sch	93
Craig, Angela/Turner Elem Sch	63
Craig, Anne/Maryville Jen Sch	79
Craig, Jennifer/Washington Elem Sch	92
Cramsey, Dennis, Dr/Edwardsville High School-South	171
Cramsey, Dennis, Dr/Edwardsville HS-Nelson Campus	171
Cramsey, Dennis, Dr/St Francis-Holy Ghost Sch	125
Crandall, Kip/David L Rahn Junior High Sch	195
Crank, Shain/Galatia Grade Sch	210
Craven, Pollee/Brown Co High Sch	5
Crawford, Amabel/Parker Junior High Sch	49
Crawford, Kristi/Southeast Elem Sch	86
Creech, David/Kolmar Ave Elem Sch	60
Crespo, Gina/Larsen Middle Sch	131
Cribaroo, Shannon/Mannheim Early Childhood Ctr	56
Crockett, Romian/Chalmers Elem Sch	25
Cropp, Julia/Roscoe Middle Sch	253
Croston, Robert/Jenner Academy of the Arts Sch	32
Crouse, David/Astoria Grade Sch	109
Crouse, David/Astoria Junior High Sch	109
Crow, Cynthia/Chatham Elem Sch	211
Crowder, Glennetta/Meca Christian Elem Sch	79
Crowley, Lauren/William L Thompson Elem Sch	152
Crownhart, Janet/Amboy High Sch	159
Croy, Cathy/Clay City Elem Sch	16
Crump, Karen/Jefferson Middle Sch	213
Crump, Taveras/East Aurora Extension Center	129
Cruz, Michelle/Von Steuben Middle Sch	199
Cuada, Iowa/Chicago Futabakai Japan Sch	77
Culver, Kathleen/Sarah Adams Elem Sch	152
Cummings, Kristin/Prospect Elem Sch	91
Cummins, Jay/Schaumburg Christian Sch	80
Cummins, Kara/Tri-City Sch	214
Cumpata, Karen/Dundee Highlands Elem Sch	180
Cunat, Mary, Dr/Spectrum Sch	256
Cunningham, Carla/Greenwood Elem Sch	68
Cunningham, Rachel/St Agnes Sch	214
Cupuro, Erica/Central Elem Sch	46
Curran, Kaitlin/Navajo Heights Elem Sch	62
Curry, Erin/Rutledge Hall Elem Sch	56
Curry, Patrick/Coolidge Junior High Sch	171
Curtis, Craig/Betsy Ross Elem Sch	63
Curvey, Joanne/Gilson Brown Elem Sch	169
Cushing, Ingrid/LaSalle Peru Twp High Sch	142
Cusic, Cody/Eldorado High Sch	210
Cybulski, Christopher/A B Shepard Middle Sch	149
Cyrwus, Erleah/Federico G Lorca Elem Sch	27
Czarnecki, Natalie/Medinah Intermediate Sch	97
Czizek, Autum/Stephen Mack Middle Sch	255
Czizek, Clint/South Beloit High Sch	255

D

NAME/School	PAGE
Da Costa, Martin/Winston Campus Junior High Sch	43
Dacres, Holly/Wilma G Rudolph Learning Ctr	32
Dagner, Andrew/Waltonville Grade Sch	124
Daily, Dawna/Bushnell Prairie City High Sch	178
Daily, Dawna/Bushnell Prairie City Jr HS	178
Dale, Chrissy/Fusion Academy-Evanston	78
Daley, Paula/Northbrook Sch	142
Daley, Tim/Mannheim Middle Sch	56
Daly, Karen/Euclid Elem Sch	65
Daly, Larry/St Teresa High Sch	167
Daly, Scott/Rockridge Junior High Sch	209
Daly, Stephanie/Virginia Lake Elem Sch	43
Damery, Tim/Metamora Grade Sch	258
Damon, Laura/Seventh Day Adventist Sch	145
Dandurand, Jason/Roxana Senior High Sch	172
Daniel, Tyson/CICS-Lloyd Bond	39
Daniels, Churchill/Nathan Hale Intermediate Sch	45
Daniels, Fabian/Harrison Cmty Learning Center	199
Daniels, Tamela/Fairmont Sch	242
Danielski, David/William Hammerschmidt Elem Sch	97
Dannaman, Matt/Sandoval Jr Sr High Sch	175
Danner, Kerry/Rowva Central Elem Sch	140
Darley, Jacob/Forest Park Individual Ed Sch	243
Darlington, Marissa/Nettle Creek Elem Sch	113
Darr, Mark/Vit Jr Sr High Sch	110
Dart, Scott/Westmore Elem Sch	99
Dassinger, Barton/Chavez Elem Multicultural Acad	27
Davenport, Allan/Francis Granger Middle Sch	95
Davenport, Leslie/Fox Creek Elem Sch	186
Davenport, Nicole/Camelot Sch-Bourbonnais	137
David, Wilma/Sandoval Elem Sch	33
Davidson, Amanda/Coal City Early Chldhd Center	112
Davidson, Stephen/IC Catholic Prep	100
Davidson, Tom/Washington Middle Sch	132
Davis-Dobson, Rebecca/Chicago Virtual Charter Sch [336]	39
Davis, April/Diekman Elem Sch	46
Davis, Ashley/St Mary Sch	86
Davis, Carole/Barack Obama Learning Academy	52
Davis, Chad/Moline Alt-Coolidge Campus	208
Davis, David/Kingsley Elem Sch	48
Davis, Erin/Olive-Mary Stitt Sch	21
Davis, Jill/Meridian Junior High Sch	195

PRINCIPAL INDEX

NAME/School — PAGE

Name/School	Page
Davis, Kathrina/Ridge Early Childhood Center	50
Davis, Raquel/Mt Vernon Elem Sch	36
Davis, Shauntae/St Margaret of Scotland Sch	75
Davis, Stuart/Christian Fellowship Sch	202
Davis, Tamara/Herzl Elem Sch	26
Davis, Tinishi/Manierre Elem Sch	30
Davis, Tod/Benjamin Franklin Middle Sch	213
Davis, Tonetta/Mabel O'Donnell Elem Sch	129
Davlantes, Patricia/Hawthorne Scholastic Academy	30
Davos, Georgia/Newton Bateman Elem Sch	29
Dawson, Dana/Ladd Cmty Consolidated Sch	7
Dawson, Patrick/Stratford Middle Sch	90
Day, Stacey/Mercer County High Sch	189
De Jesus, Jose/Lake Forest Academy	158
De Jong, Jennifer/Jones-Farrar IB World Sch	224
De La Sanchez, Jennifer/Whittier Elem Sch	156
De Leon, Luis/Tefft Middle Sch	131
De Los Reyes, Daniel/Darwin Elem Sch	30
Deadman, Bryan/Beecher City Jr Sr High Sch	104
Dean, Karoline/Childbridge Ctr for Education	77
Dean, Paula/St Anastasia Sch	157
Dearing, Cheryl/Champaign Early Childhood Ctr	10
Deaton, Amanda/W W Walker Elem Sch	45
Debaillie, Nathan/Orion High Sch	117
Debartlo, Erin/John Laidlaw Elem Sch	71
DeBoard, Christina/Trinity Lutheran Sch	176
Decaluwe, Scott/St Leonard Sch	75
Decanniore, Rose/Easterseals Academy-Chicago	78
Decker-Platz, Julie/Bureau Valley Jr High Elem Sch	6
Decker, Kelli/East Alton Middle Sch	170
DeConcini, Lanea/East Elem Sch	169
Dedonato, Sarah/A Vito Martinez Middle Sch	248
Deely, Maureen/Hickory Point Elem Sch	59
Deets, Dave/Harmony Intermediate Sch	219
Deets, David/Emge Junior High Sch	219
DeFeo, Anthony/Thompson Junior High Sch	138
Defore, Julie/Northwest Elem Sch	142
Degan, Cheryl/Ellsworth Elem Sch	98
Degiulio, Lauren/Moos Elem Sch	27
Dehning, Chris/Trinity Lutheran Sch	236
Dei Rossi, Slyvia/Cosmic Montessori Sch	101
Deichstetter, Lori/Krejci Academy	102
Deigan, Geoff/Prairie Crossing Charter Sch	1
Deignan, Julie/Whittier Primary Sch	199
Deininger, Heidi/Oregon High Sch	195
Del Prete, Candice/Bridgeview Elem Sch	53
Delamar, Marybeth, Dr/Benjamin Franklin Elem Sch	62
DeLaney, Andrea/Calumet Elem Sch	25
DeLaney, Jaclyn/Boone Elem Sch	29
Deletioglu, Mary/St Benedict Prep Elem Sch	74
DelGado, Carlos/Grant Primary Sch	22
DelGado, Guillermina/Bent Elem Sch	185
DelGado, Laura/Carlock Elem Sch	186
DelGado, Maureen/DeWitt Clinton Elem Sch	29
Delockery, Sheleen/Emerson Elem Sch	93
DeLuca, Lea/Leman Middle Sch	99
Deluga, Erin/Lake Zurich High Sch	152
Demar-Williams, Brenda, Dr/Earhart Elem Opt for Knwl Sch	35
Demar, Mavis/St Raphael Sch	101
Dembowski, Joseph/Bethesda Lutheran Sch	77
Deming, Kristal/Prairie Central Jr High Sch	162
Demitrowicz, Shari/Kankakee High Sch	135
Demovsky, Mike/Bartlett High Sch	130
DeMuth, Dave/Cooper Middle Sch	71
DeNault, Mike/Summersville Grade Sch	124
Dennis, Venita/Stevens Intermediate Sch	249
Denton, Kimberly/Ninos Heroes Community Academy	35
Depew, Daren/Granite City High Sch	171
Derdenger, Andrea/York Center Elem Sch	99
Dereus, Laura/Westlake Christian Academy	158
Derges, Ben/Tri-Valley High Sch	187
DeRoche, Mary/Everest Academy	78
Deron, Shaunda/Learn Chtr Sch-Excel [164]	40
Deroo, Cheryl/Glenbrook Elem Sch	130
Derricks, Jennifer/Tilton Elem Sch	195
Detering, Brett/Anna-Jonesboro High Sch	230
Deters, Justin/Stewardson-Strasburg Elem JHS	216
Detloff, Renee/Villa Montessori Sch	210
Detweiler, Eric/Frederick Sch	148
Detwiler, Margaret/St Irene Catholic Sch	101
Devens-Falk, Carol/Corkery Elem Sch	27
DeVine, Tim/Walter Payton College Prep HS	28
Devre, Renee/Deer Path Middle School-West	152
DeWar, Scott/Harrisburg High Sch	211
DeWitt, Andy/Trinity Lutheran Sch	102
Dezell, Ann/Lena-Winslow Elem Sch	224
Di Iorio, Cindi/Fusion Academy-Lake Forest	158
Di Iulio, Joey/Ridgewood Elem Sch	208
Dial, Jory/Frankfort Community High Sch	108
Diaz, Christine/Instituto-Lozano High Sch	39
Diaz, Evelia/Eli Whitney Elem Sch	32
Diaz, Jewel/Ashburn Elem Sch	33
Dibitetto, Stacey/Ridge Elem Sch	246
Dickenson, Dell Jean/Marion Adventist Christian Sch	252
Dickerson, Aaron/Unity Lutheran Chrn Elem Sch	223
Dickow, Grace/Valeo Academy	81
Didier, Josh/Paxton-Buckley-Loda Jr HS	107
Diegler-Mosley, Teresa/CS Academy Campus I	78
Diegler-Mosley, Teresa/CS Academy Campus II	78
Dietrich, Jennifer/Marquette Elem Sch	227
Dietz, Jason/Walter Sundling Jr High Sch	43
Difford, Nicole/Capron Elem Sch	5
Dilallo, Caitlin/Komarek Elem Sch	54
Dillon, Megan/Montmorency Elem Sch	239
Dillon, Noreen, Dr/St Mark Sch	200
Dillon, Trina/Ashton Franklin Jr Sr High	159
DiMarco, Andrew/St Luke Sch	75
Dimitriou, Joanne/Northwood Junior High Sch	154
DiNello, Tony/Mazon Verona Kinsman Mid Sch	112
Diol, Karrie/Robert Crown Elem Sch	155
Dion, Joey/Jacksonville High Sch	192
Dippold, Jack/St Philomena Sch	200
Dir, Brooke/Franklin Elem Sch	240
Discipio, Jacquelyn/Bryan Middle Sch	93
Dismukes, Mark/Estelle Kampmeyer Elem Sch	221
Dittmer, Tegan/Laremont Sch	146
Diveley, Steven/W M Hadley Junior High Sch	94
Divincenzo, Janice/St Alphonsus Ligouri Sch	74
Dixon, Amy, Dr/Jefferson Attendance Center	238
Dixon, Amy, Dr/Lincoln Attendance Center	238
Dixon, Jennifer/Palmer Elem Sch	29
Dixon, Mary/Dawes Elem Sch	33
Dobbins, Adrian/Eugene Field Elem Sch	29
Dobbs, Jeffrey/Dr Howard Elem Sch	10
Dobbs, Jeffrey/Sarah Raymond Early Chldhd Ctr	185
Dockery, Eric/Poe Classical Sch	36
Dockery, Monique/Westcott Elem Sch	35
Doe, Letitia/Illinois Center for Rehab & Ed	1
Doerfler, Megan/New Berlin Junior High Sch	212
Doerfler, Megan/Riverton Middle Sch	212
Doherty, Tim/Riverview Elem Sch	255
Dohman, Kara/Ardmore Elem Sch	88
Doig, Lisa/Hamlin Upper Grade Center	21
Doig, Tami/DayStar Sch	78
Dolack, Beth/St Mary of the Angels Sch	76
Dolan, Debbie/Carmi Christian Sch	238
Dolan, M/Our Lady of Humility Sch	157
Domeier, Sue/Immanuel Lutheran Sch	133
Domico, Mike/St Edward Sch	200
Dominicci, Clariza/Marvin Camras Elem Sch	30
Dominique, Kate/Wilmette Junior High Sch	72
Domke, Colleen/St Joseph Sch	249
Domovic, David/Ogden Elem Sch	37
Donald, Alison/Cornerstone Christian Sch	78
Donaldson, Amy/Auburn Elem Sch	211
Donegan, William/St Odilo Sch	76

Illinois School Directory — PRINCIPAL INDEX

NAME/School	PAGE
Donnelly, Melody/Hammitt Sch at the Baby Fold	188
Donner, Donald/Eastview Middle Sch	130
Donovan, Kathie/St Hilary Sch	75
Dooley, Erin/Pioneer Path	241
Dorethy, Bill/Unity High Sch	2
Dorken, Kevin/Lyon Elem Sch	51
Dorsey, Crystal/Higgins Community Academy	36
Doss, Artie/Lanphier High Sch	213
Dotson, Tim/Limestone Walters Elem Sch	198
Dotson, Tricia/Hickory Creek Middle Sch	242
Doughan, Gary/Saunemin Elem Sch	162
Doughan, Lisa/St Thomas Sch	13
Dougherty, Chad/Honenegah Cmty High Sch	253
Dougherty, Claudia/Holy Childhood Sch	222
Dougherty, Meghan/Columbus Manor Elem Sch	64
Dowdell, Tyrone/Wendell E Green Elem Sch	35
Downey, Casey/Stockton High Sch	126
Downey, Mark/Aplington Middle Sch	195
Downing, Jonathan/Warrensburg-Latham High Sch	166
Downs, John/North Mac Interm Mid Sch	168
Doyle, Allyn/St Sylvester Sch	76
Doyle, Ryan/Dean St Elem Sch	184
Dozier, John/Cahokia 7th Grade Center	218
Drahozal, Thomas/Morgan Park Academy	79
Drake, April/Windsor Elem Sch	216
Drake, Tiffany/Woodland Middle Sch	157
Draper, Ross/Plainfield North High Sch	246
Drayson, Marjaine/North Aurora SDA Elem Sch	133
Drayton, Danielle/Oscar Mayer Elem Sch	31
Drees, Patrick/Teutopolis Junior High Sch	105
Drew, Patrick/Carlinville High Sch	167
Driscoll, Elizabeth/St Scholastica Sch	101
Drown, Dalyn/Burr Oak Academy	25
Drown, Dalyn/Burr Oak Elem Sch	25
Drury, Mike/Chicago Christian High Sch	77
Druzinsky, Paul/Avery Coonley Sch	101
Dubinsky, Mitch/Briar Glen Elem Sch	90
DuBois, Laura/Three Rivers Sch	241
Dubose, Robin, Dr/St Paul Evanglical Luth Sch	81
Dubravec, Denise/New Trier Township High Sch	58
Ducey, John/Lovejoy Elem Sch	169
Duckett, Trent/St Johns Lutheran Sch	20
Dudley, Mark/Auburn Junior High Sch	211
Due, Julie/Mary Seat of Wisdom Sch	73
Duensing, Don/Christ Our Rock Lutheran HS	176
Duffy, Mary/Chippewa Elem Sch	61
Duffy, Mary/Indian Hill Sch	61
Duffy, Meghan/Audubon Elem Sch	30
Dugan, Bobby/Parkview Elem Sch	190
Dugan, Todd/New Holland Middletown Sch	164
Duke, Melinda/Century Elem Sch	204
Dulcamara, Paolo/Mascoutah Middle Sch	220
Duley, Travis/Paxton-Buckley-Loda High Sch	107
Dunbar, Chalese/Keller Regional Gifted Center	34
Duncan, Allen/Liberty Middle Sch	171
Duncan, Christina/Iroquois West Upper Elem Sch	119
Duncan, Julie/Haber Oaks Campus Sch	180
Dunlap, Kate/Metropolitan Preparatory Sch	79
Dunn, Darcy/Fairview Early Childhood Ctr	254
Dunn, Elizabeth/Catalyst CS-Circle Rock [159]	39
Dunn, Joseph/Noonan Elem Academy	250
Dunn, Randall/Latin School of Chicago	79
Dunson, Otis/Armstrong Int'l Studies ES	29
Dunwell, Erin/Bethany Lutheran Sch	101
DuPuis, Noelle/Hawk Hollow Elem Sch	130
Durbala, Matthew/O'Neill Middle Sch	93
Durbin, Jennifer/Illini Central High Sch	177
Durbin, Jennifer/Illini Central Middle Sch	177
Durham, Brooke/Brookport Elem Sch	178
Durham, Brooke/Unity Elem Sch	178
Durr, Michael/John Hope College Prep HS	37
Durry, Adrian/Roosevelt Middle Sch	22
Dutdut, Mike/Thayer J Hill Middle Sch	96
Duval, Doug/St Matthew Lutheran Sch	158
Dvorak, Crystal/Freeman Elem Sch	132
Dvorchak, Tracy/Naper Elem Sch	98
Dworak, Elisabeth/St Jerome Sch	75
Dwyer, Erin/Lace Elem Sch	92
Dwyer, Kevin, Dr/Roosevelt Elem Sch	62
Dwyer, Mark/Du Jardin Elem Sch	89
Dwyer, Patrick/St Malachy Sch	75
Dwyer, Richard/Riverdale Senior High Sch	208
Dye, Julie, Dr/Williamsburg Elem Sch	131

E

NAME/School	PAGE
Earnshaw, Mike/Oak Glen Elem Sch	55
Echavez, Rosario/East Lake Academy	157
Echols, Darrell, Dr/Metea Valley High Sch	95
Eckels, Stephanie/Stratton Elem Sch	10
Edelstein, Charmekia/East Elem Sch	157
Edgar, Justin/Liberty Sch	2
Edholm, Jennifer/West Prairie North Elem Sch	179
Edholm, Jennifer/West Prarie South Elem Sch	179
Edwards, Abigail/MacHesney Elem Sch	253
Edwards, Charlotte/James Avant Elem Sch	219
Edwards, Chris/Richland Co Elem Sch	206
Edwards, Derick/Clifford A Johnson Elem Sch	92
Edwards, Ginger/Ramsey High Sch	106
Edwards, James/Niles North High Sch	58
Edwards, Kirk/Eureka High Sch	257
Edwards, Ron/Pleasant Hill High Sch	203
Edwards, Sarah/Grove Elem Sch	186
Eekhoff, Lisa/Covenant Classical Sch	250
Egan, Patti/Lane Elem Sch	20
Egan, Stacey/Washington Early Childhood Ctr	170
Eggleston, Yashika/Air Force Academy High Sch	37
Ehmen, Duane/Iroquois West Middle Sch	119
Eichstaedt, Maureen/Worth Elem Sch	72
Ejma, Susan/Juliette Low Elem Sch	44
Eklund, Abbie/Lincoln Elem Sch	131
El-Azhari, Penny/Lathrop Elem Sch	254
Elagha, Hatem/Kindi Mont Academy	102
Elbert, Andy/Kipling Elem Sch	149
Elbert, Andy/Ringwood School Primary Ctr	182
Elehrman, Dee/Ombudsman Sch	102
Elias, Melanie/Lisbon Grade Sch	138
Elias, Melanie/Mazon-Verona-Kinsman Elem Sch	112
Elitzer, Marla/Ruiz Elem Sch	32
Ellerman, Jerry/Unity Elem Sch	2
Ellermeyer, Cody/Murphysboro High Sch	121
Elliot, Brad/Herscher High Sch	135
Elliott, Gus/Wethersfield Elem Sch	117
Elliott, Kristin/Talala Elem Sch	242
Elliott, Mary/St Peter Sch	133
Ellis, Caroline/Medgar Evers Elem Sch	34
Ellis, Gretta/Jackie Robinson Elem Sch	33
Ellis, Jody/Robert Hill Elem Sch	248
Ellis, Juletta/Pana Junior High Sch	14
Ellis, Mandy/Dunlap Grade Sch	196
Ellison, Jared/Westville Junior High Sch	233
Ellison, Kate/Washington Elem Sch	48
Ellison, Kim/YCCS-Progressive Leadership	41
Elllis, Chris/Parkside Elem Sch	187
Elswick, Tiffany/Alden-Hebron Elem Sch	179
Emery, Jenna/Taylor Ridge Elem Sch	209
Emken, Carly/Richwoods High Sch	199
Encarnacion, Antonette/Rivers of Life Christian Sch	173
Engelman, John/Gardner S Wilmington High Sch	112
Engle, Graydon/Country Trails Elem Sch	128
Engler, Jacob/William F Murphy Elem Sch	100
Englesman, Kathy/Sol Sch	80
English, Emily/Murrayville Woodson Elem Sch	192
English, Sarah/Early Years Program	192
Engstrom, Liz/Washington Elem Sch	240
Enriquez, Kim/Mascoutah Elem Sch	220
Entsminger, John/Jacqueline B Kennedy Elem Sch	24
Epley, Trent/Noble CS-Comer Middle Sch [165]	40
Epperson, Christina/Hamilton Co Pre-School Center	114
Epstein, Lisa/Lee Elem Sch	27

PRINCIPAL INDEX

NAME/School	PAGE
Erbach, Beth/Lakeview Elem Sch	66
Erdman, Rick/Solace Academy	80
Erickson, Andrea/Century Oaks Elem Sch	130
Ernd, Eric/Crystal Lake Central High Sch	180
Ernst, Angelica, Dr/Huff Elem Sch	130
Ernst, Scott/Epiphany Sch	73
Ernst, Zach/Hough St Elem Sch	147
Errthum, Jennifer/St Mary Immaculate Sch	249
Escamilla, Anthony/Foreman College & Career Acad	36
Eshleman, Trent/Bryce-Ash Grove Ed Center	118
Esposito, Linda/Worthwoods Elem Sch	72
Esquivel, Sonia/MacArthur Int'l Spanish Acad	66
Essa, Farah/Lake Shore Schools	79
Esser, Mary/Adm Richard E Byrd Elem Sch	43
Essex, Nathan/Auburn High Sch	211
Essig, Brad/Resurrection Lutheran Sch	133
Estes, El Roy/Cook Elem Sch	34
Estrada, Elias/Alcott Elem Sch	30
Ethel, Heather/McGaughey Elem Sch	166
Ethell, Heather/Sullivan Elem Sch	193
Etheredge, F/Aurora Central Catholic HS	133
Etheridge, Steven/Bicentennial Elem Sch	207
Etherly, Shahran/Neil Armstrong Elem Sch	47
Etnyre, Chad/Ledgewood Elem Sch	253
Etnyre, Jeremy/Hickory Grove Elem Sch	196
Etnyre, Kindyl/Rockton Grade Sch	255
Ettelbrick, Zack/Byron Middle Sch	194
Evans, Dave/Arbor Park Middle Sch	21
Evans, Jennifer/Daniel Burnham Elem Sch	42
Evans, John/Indian Trail Middle Sch	246
Evans, Pamela/John Powers Center	146
Evans, Ryan/SE Gross Middle Sch	24
Ewald, Alyson/Jonas Salk Elem Sch	248
Ewing, Br/Faith Baptist Sch	223
Ewing, Jeff/Monmouth-Roseville High Sch	234

F

NAME/School	PAGE
Faber, Jill/Gifted Acad Marshall MS	254
Fabiyi, Stephen/Metcalfe Community Academy	36
Fabrizio, S/Hawthorn Sch of Dual Language	151
Facen, Roni-Nicole/St Francis De Sales High Sch	75
Fagalde, Patti/St Luke Lutheran Sch	102
Fagan, Niall/Northridge Prep Sch	80
Fagel, Lauren, Dr/Glenbrook South High Sch	51
Fahey, Pam/Christ the King Sch	214
Fairbanks, Charles/Nashville Grade Sch	235
Fairchild, Greg/Banner Elem Sch	196
Fairchild, Tim/Centennial Elem Sch	257
Fairweather, Jeff/Bowlesburg Elem Sch	207
Faivre, Andy/Polo Cmty High Sch	195
Falck, Jeff/Illinois Lutheran Sch	250
Faletti, Heather/Reed-Custer Elem Sch	246
Falter, Dottie/Prather Elem Sch	171
Fancher, Dennis, Dr/Immanuel Lutheran Sch	236
Fancher, Kyra/Midwest Central Middle Sch	177
Fane, Julie/French STEM Academy	165
Fantuzzi, Anna Maria/Scuola Italiana Enrico Fermi	80
Farfan, Monika/Clearmont Elem Sch	43
Farr, Donald/Monmouth-Roseville Junior HS	234
Farrelly, Stephanie/Jefferson Early Chldhd Center	92
Fatheree, Rowdy/Mt Vernon High Sch	123
Faulkner, Brian/Heineman Middle Sch	182
Faust, Michaela/Richard E Byrd Elem Sch	24
Favre, Adam/Litchfield Pre-K at Sihler Sch	191
Favre, Adam/Madison Park Elem Sch	191
Faxon, Elizabeth/St Rita of Cascia Sch	133
Fearday, Greg/St Anthony of Padua High Sch	105
Fehrenbacher, Linda/Sandburg Middle Sch	94
Feiwell, Jeremy/Cardenas Elem Sch	26
Feldman, Louisa/Bethel Academy	77
Feldman, Steve/B J Hooper Elem Sch	152
Feltes, Emily/North Grand High Sch	37
Fenderson, Niki/Robertson Charter Sch	165
Fennoy, Terrien/Bernard Long Sch	172
Fenton, Andrew/Carleton W Washburne Sch	72
Fergus, Tanya/Mechanics Grove Elem Sch	153
Ferguson, Adam/St Michael Sch	101
Ferguson, Cindy/Crest Hill Christian Sch	250
Ferguson, Griselda/St Procopius Sch	76
Ferguson, Jennifer/Regional Safe Sch	141
Ferguson, Kathleen/Richard D Crosby Elem Sch	181
Ferguson, Tom/Logan Elem Sch	208
Fernandez, Leticia/Latino Youth High Sch	40
Ferrell, Jerome/McKinley Elem Jr High Sch	68
Ferrell, Jerome/McKinley Elem Sch	68
Ferrell, Ronald, Dr/Lovejoy Academy	218
Ferrell, Ronald, Dr/Venice Elem Sch	172
Feuer, Susan/Att-Ptach Special Ed Program	77
Fieber, Marrianne/DaVinci Waldorf Sch	158
Field, Johnathon/Sangamon Valley High Sch	166
Fields, Tanya/Kershaw Elem Sch	34
Figueroa, Ania/Forest Elem Sch	46
File, Meg/Early Childhood Center	4
Filipiak, Erica/Wilcox Elem Sch	213
Filippi, Rachel/Sherwood Elem Sch	154
Finan, John/Glenbrook North High Sch	51
Finch, Perry/Blackhawk Middle Sch	89
Finelli, John/Edison Park Elem Sch	28
Fink, Angela, Dr/Marengo Community High Sch	182
Fink, Kristen/Sacred Heart Sch	74
Finke, Stephanie/General Logan Attendance Ctr	121
Finkelstein, Samuel/Legal Prep Charter Academy	40
Finley, Cathy/Winnebago Middle Sch	255
Finn, Deborah/Highland Park High Sch	155
Finn, Diane/Philip J Rock Sch	1
Finnegan, Kevin/Prairie Hill Elem Sch	253
Fiscus, Steve/Tuscola High Sch	88
Fisher, Lynn/Indian Grove Elem Sch	65
Fisher, Mark/Learning House	79
Fisher, Patsy/Arnold J Tyler Elem Sch	245
Fisher, Steve/Gresham Elem Sch	26
Fiske, Gina/Early Childhood Center	20
Fitzenreider, Zak/Frank Hall Elem Sch	132
Fitzgerald, Laura/Unity Junior High Sch	12
Fitzgerald, Michael/Benjamin Middle Sch	89
Fitzpatrick, John/Locke Elem Sch	30
Flach, Robinette/Altamont Lutheran Sch	105
Flaherty, Daniel/Bridgeport Catholic Academy	72
Flanagan, Patrick/St Rita Catholic Elem Sch	256
Flanigan, Kyle/Manteno Middle Sch	136
Flatley, Paul/Prairieview Elem Sch	131
Fleming, Vache/St Paul Academy	256
Flemma, Tom/North Shore Country Day Sch	80
Fletcher, Catherine/Heritage Elem Sch	130
Fletcher, John/Lincoln Elem Sch	251
Fletcher, Karen/Camelot Theraputic Day Sch	77
Fletcher, Peter/Northridge Prep Sch	80
Fleuette, William/Apollo Elem Sch	189
Floeter, Judy/Jefferson Elem Sch	181
Flood, Tracy/Simmons Middle Sch	64
Flore-Porter, Ms/Lewis & Clark Elem Sch	169
Flores, Hamed/Madero Middle Sch	32
Floro, Adrienne/Roycemore Sch	80
Flowers, Jake/Norwood Elem Sch	198
Flowers, Latrice/Brownell Elem Sch	35
Fluga, Ben/St Paul Lutheran Sch	81
Flynn, Tom/Morton Gingerwood Elem Sch	21
Foehrkolb, Dan/Washington Middle Sch	229
Fogal, Marc/Washington Intermediate Sch	228
Fogal, Tina/Pepper Ridge Elem Sch	187
Fogarty, Brian/Park Sch	61
Foley-Acevedo, Linda/Newberry Math & Science Acad	30
Folino, Erin/St Ferdinand Sch	75
Foltz, Michael/River Ridge High Sch	126
Foltz, Michael/River Ridge Middle Sch	126
Forbes, Glenda/Camelot-Chicago Excel Roseland	39

Illinois School Directory

PRINCIPAL INDEX

NAME/School	PAGE
Forbes, Tonya/Holy Angels Sch	133
Forcash, Sue/Oak Prairie Junior High Sch	249
Ford, Lynette/Herman E Dummer Elem Sch	86
Ford, Nathan/Judith Giacoma Elem Sch	233
Forlines, Ross/Okaw Valley Middle Sch	193
Forman, Chris/Eastlawn Elem Sch	11
Forsythe, Megan/Whitman Post Elem Sch	255
Forte, Barbara, Dr/Legacy Academy of Excellence	254
Fortin, Randy/Central Middle Sch	42
Foster, Dahne/Beverly Hills Elem Sch	77
Foster, Jasen/Lebanon Elem Sch	220
Foster, Linda/Faith Christian Sch	160
Foster, Matthew/Christ Our Savior Lutheran HS	206
Foster, Sean/Central Catholic High Sch	187
Foster, Takia/Johnson Elem Sch	26
Foster, Vicky/Thomas Jefferson Elem Sch	246
Fougerol, Severine/Lycee Francais De Chicago	79
Fouks, Kathie/Achievement Ctrs-Acacia Acad	76
Fountain, Shemeka/King Middle Grade Sch	135
Fowler, Joe/Delta Learning Center	44
Fowler, Joe/Summit Learning Center	44
Fowler, Rachel/Jefferson Early Childhood Ctr	208
Fox, Brad/Stockton Middle Sch	126
Fox, Colleen/Stockton Elem Sch	126
Fox, Jennifer/Early Learning Center	105
Fox, Jon/Lincoln Junior High Sch	142
Fraas, Allison/Illinois School for the Deaf	1
Fraas, Matt/South Shores Elem Sch	165
Fraas, Matthew/Stephen Decatur Middle Sch	165
Frailey, Zachary/Beckemeyer Elem Sch	191
Frakes, Randy/Immaculate Conception Sch	235
France, Stacie/Kingsley Junior High Sch	186
France, Todd/Pecatonica High Sch	253
Francis, John/Bednarcik Junior High Sch	137
Francis, John/Genoa Elem Sch	85
Francque, Heather/St Malachy Sch	118
Frank, Cindy/Lincoln Elem Sch	240
Frank, Daniel, Dr/Francis W Parker Sch	78
Frank, Tony/Rochelle Zell Jewish High Sch	158
Frankford, Eric/Valmeyer Sch	190
Frankie, Stacie/Mark Twain Sch	169
Franklin, Carolyn/Caroline Sibley Elem Sch	46
Frankovich, Kirsten/Grand Prairie Elem Sch	242
Franks, Thomas/North Elem Sch	86
Frawley, Kristy/Holy Trinity Catholic Sch	222
Frazier, Leslee/Carrollton High Sch	111
Frazier, Tom/Bloomington Area Voc Center	185
Frederick, Christine/Pleasant Hill Elem Sch	92
Frederick, Karolyn/Fredrick Nerge Elem Sch	66
Fredericks, Juliane/Diamond Lake Sch	149
Fredericks, Juliane, Dr/West Oak Interm Sch	149
Frederickson, Cheryl/Menta Academy Hillside	79
Fredricksen, Bill/Aspen Elem Sch	151
Fredrickson, John/Beach Park Middle Sch	147
Free, Eric/Salt Fork North Elem Sch	233
Freeman, Candace/Potomac Elem Sch	232
Freeman, Kai/Drauden Point Middle Sch	246
Freeman, Maria/CICS-Loomis Longwood Mid HS	39
Freeman, Sheryl/Burnham Math & Sci Academy	35
Freeney, Sherisse/Joseph Kellman Corporate ES	31
Freeze, Roger/Wesclin Middle Sch	18
Frericks, Carol/St Dominic Sch	3
Freytas, Hctor/Riverside-Brookfield Twp HS	65
Frieden, John/Denkmann Elem Sch	208
Frieden, Jon/Pikeland Community Sch	203
Friedman, Erik/Pleasant Ridge Elem Sch	51
Friedman, Janean/Emmons Elem Sch	149
Friedman, Michelle/Henry Longfellow Elem Sch	71
Friesema, James/Belvidere North High Sch	4
Fritson, Amy, Dr/Thomas Metcalf Sch	1
Fritz-Fanning, Debra/James Shields Middle Sch	33
Froman, Brad/Warsaw High Sch	115
Fromm, Chris/Gallatin Cmty Unit Dist 7 Sch	110
Frost, Michele/Patterson Elem Sch	95
Fruit, Jenette/Earlville Cmty Unit 9 Sch	141

NAME/School	PAGE
Fry, Natalie/East Side Intermediate Sch	211
Fuhr, Lezlie/Elgin Math and Science Academy	130
Fuhr, Shannon/Prairie Central Primary East	162
Fuhrer, Lance/Neuqua Valley High Sch	95
Fuhrer, Lance, Dr/Nvhs Kathryn J Birkett Center	95
Fulkerson, Jill/Fairfield Cmty High Sch	236
Full, Andrew/Amboy Junior High Sch	159
Fults, Dave/Willow Grove Elem Sch	18
Fumagalli, Mike/Glenn Westlake Middle Sch	97
Funkenbusch, Brad/Col Isles Elem Sch	2
Furlow, Doug/Williamsville High Sch	214
Furtute, Loretta/Kenneth L Hermasen Elem Sch	248

G

NAME/School	PAGE
Gabbert, Tim/St John Lutheran Sch	13
Gabor, Clifford/Mary Lyon Sch	30
Gaffney, Elaine/St Barnabas Sch	74
Gage, Tracy/Butler Elem Sch	213
Gagliano, Al/McIntosh Elem Sch	254
Gaham, Jack/Beecher High Sch	241
Gainer, Bridget/Hillside Elem Sch	52
Gaither, Tony/Bridgeport Grade Sch	159
Gajewski, Anita/Legacy Christian Academy	223
Gale, Rdeane/Bartelso Elem Sch	17
Galfer, Erin/Marine Leadership Acad at Ames	27
Gallagher, Katherine/W S Christopher Elem Sch	33
Gallagher, Morgan/Roosevelt Cmty Education Ctr	254
Gallie, Amy/Trinity High Sch	76
Galligan, Ms/Stevenson Elem Sch	165
Gallo, Elizabeth/Byrne Elem Sch	33
Gallo, Joe/Chillicothe Jr High & Elem Ctr	197
Galyean, Kelly/Pleasant Valley Elem Sch	199
Gamble, Chris/Solomon Elem Sch	29
Gamboa, Jose/J Sterling Morton East HS	53
Ganci, Nancy/Memorial Elem Sch	15
Gannon, Andrea/Belleville Alternative Sch	217
Garard, Christopher/Gibson City-Melvin-Sibley HS	106
Garcia-Graham, Elvia/John Spry Elem Sch	32
Garcia, Heriberto/Columbus West Sch	42
Garcia, Ruth/Zapata Academy	28
Garcia, Sharon/St Francis Xavier Sch	75
Gardner, Eleanor/Westview Elem Sch	109
Gardner, Juan/Madison Jr Sr High Sch	172
Gardner, Kristina/North Side Elem Sch	236
Gardner, Mary/W J Zahnow Elem Sch	190
Gardner, Nikki/Washington Sch	181
Gardner, Tynisha/Sheila Daniels Christian Acad	158
Gargano, Dan/Sacred Heart Sch	80
Gargiulo, Rocco/Woodlands Academy Sacred Heart	158
Garnett, Deidre/Elmwood Elem Sch	157
Garrard, Brian/St Elmo Jr Sr High Sch	106
Garrett, Jeremy/Tremont Middle Sch	228
Garrison, Barbara/Brokaw Early Learning Center	137
Garstki, Larry/Roosevelt Middle Sch	65
Garza, Edward/Glenside Middle Sch	98
Garza, Ericka/Mark Twain Primary Sch	135
Gasa, Candis/Luther J Schilling Sch	242
Gaskin, Patrick/Lincoln Junior High Sch	98
Gass, Sarah, Dr/Althoff Catholic High Sch	222
Gaston, Raul/Jefferson Middle Sch	99
Gates, Sabrina/Shoesmith Elem Sch	33
Gates, Taylor-Imani/Judah Christian Sch	13
Gattuso, Thomas, Dr/YCCS-Sullivan House Alt HS	41
Gatz, Peter/Central Elem Sch	65
Gawlik, Robert/Nativity BVM Sch	73
Gay, Vincent/Noble CS-Golder Clg Prep [165]	40
Geary, Amanda/Deland-Weldon Elem Jr High Sch	202
Gee-Davis, Vernecia/Pershing Elem Sch	243
Geer, Jim/Tampico Elem Sch	239
Geiger, Heidi/Joliet Montessori Sch	250
Genandt, Lee/Willowglen Academy-Illinois	225
Gendron, Mrs/Holy Family Catholic Sch	256
Gentry, Angela/Arcola Elem Sch	87
Georgia, Phillip, Dr/W J Murphy Elem Sch	155

PRINCIPAL INDEX

NAME/School	PAGE
Geraci, Stephen/Burnham Elem Sch	24
Geraghty, Thomas/Cicero Early Childhood Center	42
Gerard, Jeff/Howard B Thomas Grade Sch	128
German, Sean/Argenta Oreana High Sch	165
Germscheid, Kathy/William M Bedell-A R C Sch	173
Gernon, Nicole/Bishop McNamara Catholic Sch	137
Gerritsen, Joanna/W C Petty Elem Sch	146
Gerth, Heather/Nettie Davis Elem Sch	119
Geverola, Latasha/DePriest Elem Sch	30
Gharashor, Narineh/Washington Irving Elem Sch	32
Gianessi, Stacie/Holy Family Parish Sch	200
Giannotta, Carlo/Grace Christian Academy	78
Giannoulis, Margo, Dr/North Elem Sch	46
Gibbons, Tommy/Riverdahl Elem Sch	254
Gibbs, Andrew/Three Oaks Elem Sch	179
Gibbs, Ellen/Benton Grade School 5-8	107
Gibbs, Ellen/Benton Grade School K-4	107
Gibson, Jacqueline/Henry W Cowherd Middle Sch	129
Gierman, Todd/Albert F Ames Elem Sch	65
Giertz, Mark/Milton Pope Elem Sch	143
Giffin, John/Vienna High Sch	127
Giggers, Donika/Little Black Pearl Art Acad	40
Giibson, Theresa/West Joliet Twp High Sch	243
Gill, Anthony/Harnew Elem Sch	64
Gillam, Kimberly/Lincoln Elem Sch	178
Gillingham, Don/Rockford Lutheran High Sch	256
Gilmartin, Laura/Holmes Elem Sch	97
Gilmore, Erin/Univ of Chicago CS-Donoghue	41
Gilmore, Kenneth/Ridgely Elem Sch	213
Ginglen, Clay/Lewistown Jr Senior High Sch	110
Gippert, Thom/Deer Path Elem Sch	179
Gipson, Andrew/N O Nelson Elem Sch	171
Girard, Lindsey/CICS-Loomis Longwood Mid HS	39
Girard, Lindsey/CICS-Loomis Primary	39
Girmscheid, Lew/Spring Hills Elem Sch	99
Given, Lori/Dr Andy Hall Early Chldhd Ctr	123
Giwa, Safurat, Dr/Pershing Humanities Mag Sch	33
Gleason, Gina/Alcuin Montessori Sch	77
Glenn, Matthew/Manteno Elem Sch & ECC	136
Glickley, Jennifer/River Trail Sch	150
Gliege, Gerald/Trinity Lutheran Sch	81
Glodich, Susan/Denning Elem Sch	108
Glover, Bernadette/Kozminski Cmty Academy	33
Glover, Mike/McHenry Middle Sch	183
Glover, Paul/Thurgood Marshall Elem Sch	22
Glowaty, Frank/SS Peter & Paul Sch	101
Gluck, William/Riverside Christian Sch	209
Gmazel, Carl/E F Kerr Middle Sch	45
Gobble, Troy/Adlai E Stevenson High Sch	146
Godfrey, Casey/Lincoln Elem Sch	65
Goebel, Laura/Summit Hill Junior High Sch	247
Goffron, Paul/Cross Evang Lutheran Sch	139
Goins, Christopher/Noble CS-Butler Clg Prep [165]	40
Gold, Jason/Fox Meadow Elem Sch	130
Gold, Jason, Dr/Komarek Elem Sch	54
Goldman, Brittany/St Bruno Sch	202
Goldman, Matt/Deland-Weldon Elem Jr High Sch	202
Goldman, Matt/Deland-Weldon High Sch	202
Goldstein, Judith/Arlyn Day Sch	158
Golliday, Sydney/John B Drake Elem Sch	33
Gomez-Munoz, Yadira/Lincoln Elem Sch	57
Gomez, Daniel/Hayt Elem Sch	29
Gomez, Gregory/Connect Christian Sch	173
Gomez, Karem/Acero CS-Octavio Paz ES [156]	38
Gonney, Aquabah/Leslie Lewis Elem Sch	26
Gonzalez, Eliza/St Ann Sch	74
Gonzalez, Luis/M J Cunningham Elem Sch	243
Gonzalez, Marin, Dr/Kanoon Magnet Sch	32
Gonzalez, Patricia/Rosa G Maddock Elem Sch	24
Gonzalez, Raquel/Horace Greeley Elem Sch	30
Goodale, Bosa/Wilco Area Career Center	241
Goodbred, Randall/Sheridan Grade Sch	144
Goode, Angie/St Norbert Sch	8
Gooding, Brad/Rushville-Industry High Sch	215
Goodlove, Guy/Westville High Sch	233
Goodman, Courtney/Eugene Field Elem Sch	62
Goodrich, Larry/West Middle Sch	255
Goodwin, Luke/Chicago Waldorf Sch	77
Gorchels, Lisa/DeKalb Early Learning Dev Ctr	84
Gordon, A, Dr/Hawthorn Sch of Dual Language	151
Gordon, Donald/Frazier Preparatory Academy [126]	39
Gordon, Donald/Univ of Chicago CS-Woodlawn	41
Gordon, Kimberly/Woodland Elem Sch	243
Gordon, Lawanda/Marya Yates Elem Sch	47
Gorgal, Gretchen/Lincoln Elem Sch	42
Gorman, Casimira/Blythe Park Elem Sch	65
Gorman, Kathleen/St John of the Cross Sch	75
Gosch, Bob/Fulton High Sch	239
Goscinski, Theresa/Freeburg Elem Sch	219
Goscinski, Theresa/Freeburg Primary Center	219
Goss, Elizabeth/Legacy Charter Sch	40
Goss, Ty/Broadmoor Junior High Sch	228
Gosselink, Wesley/Lisle Elem Sch	97
Gottlieb, Anne/YCCS-Austin Career	41
Gould, Jeff/Washington Elem Sch	160
Goulet-Raffety, Marie/M P Mackay Education Center HS	241
Gouriotis, George/Medinah Middle Sch	98
Gouriotis, John/Lake Park High Sch-West Campus	96
Gourley, Jacob/Thornton Fractional South HS	69
Gourley, Michael/Morris Cmty High Sch	113
Gowin, Bret/Egyptian Sch	3
Graber, Danielle/Whittier Sch	45
Grable, Maria/Indian Trail Elem Sch	154
Grady, Mike/Dixon High Sch	160
Grady, Senalda/Pirie Elem Fine Arts & Acadmcs	35
Graff, Stacy/Canterbury Elem Sch	181
Grafman, Amber/Jfh Educational Academy West	79
Grafton, William/Chester Grade Sch	205
Graham, Chris/St Joseph Middle Sch	12
Graham, Steven/Momence High Sch	136
Graham, Tony/Marshall Junior High Sch	16
Graham, Tyrese/Uplift Community High Sch	36
Grana, Greg/Woodlawn Middle Sch	151
Granada, Erica/Enger Sch	56
Granger, Terry/Bishop McNamara High Sch	137
Grant, Khari/Barack Obama Leadership & STEM	62
Grant, Shaun/South Elem Sch	197
Grason, Connie/Paul Revere Intermediate Sch	45
Gravel, Melanie/Wright Elem Sch	180
Graves, Christopher/LaSalle Language Academy	30
Graves, Jennifer/Steele Elem Sch	140
Graves, Seth/Pope Co High Sch	204
Graves, Sidney/Conklin Elem Sch	254
Gray, Amy/Roy Deshane Elem Sch	90
Gray, Annie/Sandoval Elem Sch	175
Gray, James/Walker Elem Sch	48
Gray, Kim/Spencer Pointe Elem Sch	245
Gray, Laura/Meadow Lane Sch	21
Gray, Lisa/SS Peter & Paul Sch	115
Gray, Stacy/McDade Classical Sch	35
Grays, Tara/Livingston Area Career Center	162
Green, Brittany/Gordon D Bush Elem Sch	219
Green, Dan/St John's Lutheran Sch	81
Green, Kerri/Lockport Twp High Sch-Central	244
Green, Matt/L E Starke Primary Sch	228
Greenacre, Dawn/Lynn G Haskin Elem Sch	86
Greenan, John/Lockport Twp High School-East	244
Greene, Glenn/Chateaux Sch	63
Greene, Joann/Helen Keller Elem Sch	53
Greenwald, Gina/Hoover Wood Elem Sch	128
Greenwood, Sheila, Dr/Bement Elem Sch	202
Greer, Heather/Pleasant Plains Middle Sch	212
Greger, Angie/Pittsfield High Sch	203
Gregoire, Lisa/Isaac Fox Elem Sch	152
Gregory, Jane/Kansas Treatment & Lrng Center	103
Gregson, David/St John Neumann Sch	173

Illinois School Directory

PRINCIPAL INDEX

NAME/School	PAGE
Gregurich, Elizabeth/Glenwood Intermediate Sch	211
Grenda, Michael/A J Katzenmaier Academy	154
Griffin, Mary/CICS-Avalon/S Shore [167]	39
Griffin, Simone/Austin College & Career Acad	37
Griffith, Carrie/Wethersfield Jr Sr High Sch	118
Griffiths, Lisa, Dr/Pope John Paul II Sch	73
Grigsby, Lisa/Glen Oaks Therapeutic Day Sch	102
Grimm, Matt/Auburn Middle Sch	211
Grinestaff, Greg/South Central Middle Sch	176
Grinston, Lillian/Vincent Gray Academy	223
Gripp, Chad/Bradford Grade Sch	223
Grishaber, Mark/Taft High Sch	36
Gritton, Gary/Calvary Baptist Christian Acad	13
Gritzmacher, Kris/St Mary Sch	158
Groce, Dan/Paririe Central Primary West	162
Grochowski, Kevin/MacArthur Middle Sch	22
Grochowski, Kevin/Sunnyside Elem Sch	22
Groen, Bonnie, Dr/Alex M Martino Jr High Sch	245
Groeneveld, Ashley/Elm Middle Sch	48
Groll, Stephen/South Fork Jr Sr High Sch	15
Groll, Steve/A-C Central Middle High Sch	9
Groom, Peter/Fenwick High Sch	73
Grosch, Jennifer/Marion Jordan Elem Sch	43
Gross, Clarence/Red Hill Jr Sr High Sch	159
Gross, Nichole/Theodore Roosevelt Elem Sch	42
Gross, Susan/Gray Elem Sch	28
Grossen, Mike/Jane Addams Elem Sch	213
Grossman, Amy/Little Fort Elem Sch	156
Grotthuss, William/Lincoln Academy	88
Groves, Jennifer, Dr/Prairie Point Elem Sch	138
Grubbs, Matt/Coventry Elem Sch	181
Gruen, Gary/Mt Zion Grade Sch	166
Grzanich, Susan/Online Learning Academy	199
Guebert, Lori/Meridian Elem Sch	166
Guehne, Alan/Red Bud High Sch	205
Guerin, Timothy/Kankakee Area Career Center	134
Guerra, Raul/Aspira Business & Finance HS [130]	38
Guillaume, Jon/Vernon Hills High Sch	148
Gunn, Nneka/Eberhart Elem Sch	27
Gunty, Ben/Noble CS-Noble Street Clg Prep [165]	40
Gurley, Michael/Camelot Tds of Naperville	101
Gustafson, John/Greenbrook Elem Sch	96
Gutierrez, Juan/Patrick Henry Elem Sch	29
Gutierrez, Marcy/Coffeen Elem Sch	191
Gutman, John/Parkview Christian Academy	139
Gutshall, Kylee/Lincoln Elem Sch	7
Guzik, Michele/John V Leigh Elem Sch	59
Guzman, Jesse/Jefferson Middle Sch	10
Guzman, Jessica/Newton Elem Sch	122

H

NAME/School	PAGE
Haack, J/Townline Elem Sch	151
Haack, Nell/Michael Collins Elem Sch	66
Haake, Julie, Dr/Twin Echo Elem Sch	170
Haarman, Kevin/Neoga Jr Sr High Sch	84
Haas, Sara/Brighton Park Elem Sch	32
Haase, Kenneth/Adlai Stevenson Elem Sch	66
Haddock, Patrick/Fox Chase Elem Sch	137
Haertling, Jennifer/Steeleville High Sch	206
Hagman, Carl/Robert Abbott Middle Sch	156
Hagstrom, Kathleen, Dr/Walt Disney Magnet Sch	28
Hailpern, Joseph/Braeside Elem Sch	154
Hainey, Evelyn/Thompsonville Christian Sch	109
Hale, Bryan, Dr/Southland College Prep Chtr HS	1
Hale, Sage/Arthur Grade Sch	88
Haley, Anthony/Camelot-Excel Southshore HS	39
Haley, Heather/Northwestern Elem Sch	168
Haley, Joe/Camelot Safe ES & HS	39
Haley, Todd/Norris City-Omaha-Enfield HS	238
Hall, Bethany/Northwood Middle Sch	184
Hall, Bonnie/Our Lady of Guadalupe Sch	73
Hall, Erin/Seventh Ave Elem Sch	54
Hall, Jackie/Chaney Monge Sch	241
Hall, Karen/Christ Lutheran Sch	121

NAME/School	PAGE
Hall, King/O'Toole Elem Sch	34
Hall, Kris/Jo Davies-Carroll Cte Academy	125
Hall, Michelle/Haines Elem Sch	245
Hall, Steve/St Paul Lutheran Sch	195
Hallihan, Shad/Central Joliet Twp High Sch	243
Hallmark, Jon/Highland Middle Sch	153
Hallums, Julie/Funston Elem Sch	30
Halverson, Lisa/Jefferson Sch	62
Hamdan, Burhan/Daarul Uloom Islamic Sch	200
Hamilton, Barbara/Hamilton Academy	133
Hamilton, Colandra/Central Park Elem Sch	57
Hamilton, Eric/Antioch Cmty High Sch	148
Hamm, Shannon/Circle Center Grade Sch	139
Hammaker, Tonya/Farragut Career Academy	37
Hammerlund, Marie/Albany Park Multicultural Acad	28
Hammond, Althea/Plamondon Elem Sch	31
Hammontree, Evan/Hyde Park Day Sch	79
Hampton, Heather/Robert Nathaniel Dett Elem Sch	32
Hampton, Kamilah/Daley Academy	32
Hamstra, Mark/Noble CS-Chicago Bulls Clg Prp [165]	40
Hand, Blake/Welsh Elem Sch	255
Haney-Bauer, Sue/Montessori Private Academy	256
Haney, Leviis, Dr/Rich Twp High Sch STEM	64
Hanfland, Karen/Beecher City Jr Sr High Sch	104
Hanford, Seth/Elgin Academy	133
Hanks, Adam/Vienna Elem Sch	127
Hannagan, Sean/St Elmo Elem Sch	106
Hannah-Reed, Tanyelle/Benjamin Mays Academy	34
Hanrahan, Robert/Ivy Hall Elem Sch	151
Hanretty, Lisa/Embers Elem Sch	78
Hansen, Allison/Acero CS-Marquez ES [156]	38
Hansen, Becky/Tremont Grade Sch	228
Hansen, Joe/West Carroll High Sch	9
Hansen, Ryan/Flanagan-Cornell Unit 74 Sch	161
Hanson, Greg/Old Orchard Junior High Sch	67
Hanson, Mari/St Clement Sch	74
Happold, Michele/Hannah Martin Elem Sch	182
Harbaugh, Elizabeth/Shiloh Community Sch	103
Harden, Stephen/Cameron Elem Sch	26
Hardmon, Michelle/Primary Learning Center	63
Hardy, Patrick, Dr/Proviso East High Sch	63
Haren, Eric/Manor Hill Elem Sch	97
Hargis, Neil/Elverado High Sch	120
Harkins, Jim/Iroquois West ES-Gilman	119
Harlan, Brian/Schaumburg High Sch	69
Harman, Stephanie/Countryside Sch	13
Harmon, Christopher/Todd Hall Elem Sch	56
Harmon, Sherry/Brownstown Elem Sch	105
Harmon, Sherry/Teutopolis Grade Sch	105
Harmon, Tammie/Wheatlands Elem Sch	138
Harner, Patrick/Five Co Reg Voc System Sch	3
Harper-Young, Kimberly/Foster Park Elem Sch	34
Harper, John/Providence Catholic High Sch	249
Harper, Staci/Delavan Elem Sch	226
Harper, Staci/Delavan Jr Sr High Sch	226
Harper, Trista/Manley Career Academy	37
Harper, Trista, Dr/Simeon Career Academy	38
Harperkelly, Holly/Hawthorn Early Childhood Ctr	71
Harr, Danel/Sheridan Elem Sch	185
Harr, Matt/NorthPoint Elem Sch	187
Harrell, Michelle/AL Raby High Sch	37
Harrelson, Julie/Grayville Jr Sr High Sch	238
Harrelson, Julie/New Hope Elem Sch	237
Harridge, Andy/Northside Elem Sch	239
Harries, Adrian/Nichols Middle Sch	48
Harrington, John/Grove Junior High Sch	43
Harris, Dayo/Village Leadership Academy	81
Harris, George/Kankakee Junior High Sch	135
Harris, Jeralyn/West Side Christian Sch	81
Harris, Kara/Greenville High Sch	4
Harris, Leonard/Nancy B Jefferson Alt High Sch	37
Harris, Madonna/Wolf Branch Elem Sch	222
Harris, Novella/Meridian Elem Sch	204
Harris, Robert/Willow Bend Elem Sch	43

PRINCIPAL INDEX

Market Data Retrieval

NAME/School	PAGE	NAME/School	PAGE
Harris, Ron/Gardner Grade Sch	112	Henley, Lauren/KIPP Ascend MS [163]	40
Harris, Suzanne/Montessori Children's House	214	Hennegan, Jennifer/Central Elem Sch	246
Harris, Trevor/Elizabeth Eichelberger ES	246	Hennemann, W Christopher/Pawnee Grade Sch	212
Hart, Eileen/Rolling Meadows High Sch	70	Henning, Dane/North Campus Alt Lrng Acad	69
Hart, Ryan/Westwood Elem Sch	184	Henning, Tempest/Peoria Hebrew Day Sch	200
Harter, Doug/Carl Sandburg Jr High Sch	43	Henriksen, Edwin/Project Echo	250
Hartford, Jeff/Carterville Junior High Sch	251	Henrikson, Martha/Oak Elem Sch	91
Hartless, Jessica/Karel Havlicek Elem Sch	22	Henry, Larita/Moving Everest Charter Sch	40
Hartman, Casey/Lincoln Elem Sch	246	Henry, Mike/Enders-Salk Elem Sch	66
Hartrich, Jamie/St Mary's Sch	188	Hensley, Brian/Pontiac Junior High Sch	161
Hasenstab, Cyndi/St James Sch	223	Hensley, Chuck/Montessori Magnet Sch-Lincoln	135
Hassan, Okab/Peck Elem Sch	27	Henson, Jerrah/Parrish Elem Sch	120
Hassan, Ronald, Dr/Rockford Iqra Sch	256	Heppner, Donata/Columbus East Sch	42
Hassel, Julie/Wentworth Intermediate Sch	24	Herb, Jeffrey/Dundee Middle Sch	180
Hasson, Katie/Rockridge High Sch	209	Hering, Jennifer/Proegler Sch	135
Hatch, Claire/Blessed Sacrament Sch	222	Hermes, Tammy/Waverly Elem Sch	193
Haug, Matthew/Prairie Knolls Middle Sch	128	Hernandez, Anita/Schubert Elem Sch	30
Haugen, Lauri/Fabyan Elem Sch	131	Hernandez, Rigo/Pickard Elem Sch	28
Haugens, Meredith/Marquardt Middle Sch	97	Herr, Nowell/Ombudsman School-Dundee	133
Haugens, Patrick/Erickson Elem Sch	89	Herrera-Vest, Angelica/Josefa Ortiz De Dominguez ES	32
Hawk, Dawn/McKay Elem Sch	34	Herrick, Devon/Hancock College Prep HS	37
Hawkins, Lance/Deer Creek-Mackinaw Interm Sch	226	**Herrick, Devon**/Ogden International HS-West	37
Hawkins, Therese/Nazareth Academy	73	Herring, Michael/Jahn Elem Sch	30
Hawkins, Tom/Churchill Junior High Sch	140	Hess, Joann/Zion Lutheran Sch	250
Hawkins, Valerie/King Elem Sch	140	Hesser, Suzi/Parkside Junior High Sch	187
Hawks, Devon/Manual Academy	199	Hester, Myron/Percy L Julian High Sch	37
Hayden, Beth/Centennial Elem Sch	61	**Hetrick, Jeff**/Goodwin Elem Sch	132
Hayes, Amanda/Donald C Parker Early Ed Ctr	252	Hetrovicz, Michelle/Big Hollow Elem Sch	148
Hayes, Craig/Roosevelt Sch	217	Hettmansberger, Mark/Odell Grade Sch	161
Hayes, James/Harvard Park Elem Sch	213	Heuer, Carl/Prairieview-Ogden Jr High Sch	11
Hayes, Jamie/Carol Mosley Braun Elem Sch	46	**Heuer, Carl**/Prairieview-Ogden South ES	11
Hayes, Julie/Parkside Elem Sch	159	**Heuring, Bobbi**/Herrin Cmty Elem Sch	251
Hayes, Laura/Massac Junior High Sch	178	Heuring, Brad/Herrin Middle Sch	251
Hayes, Margaret/St Linus Sch	75	Heyen, Nicole/Lincoln Magnet Sch	213
Haymond, Tyler/Plank Junior High Sch	138	Heyen, Patty/Hillsboro High Sch	191
Hays, Deborah/Misericordia Heart of Mercy	79	**Hickey, Anne**/Grantfork Elem Sch	171
Hays, Ellen/Amelia Carriel Junior High Sch	221	Hicklin, April/Heyworth Jr Sr High Sch	186
Hayunga, Tim/Alden-Hebron Middle High Sch	179	Hicks, Victoria/Lawrence Hall Youth Services	79
Headings, Gordon/Fairfield Amish Mennonite Sch	240	Higginbotham, Paul/Lawrenceville High Sch	159
Healy, Christa/Adams Elem Sch	163	Higgs, David/Round Lake Middle Sch	155
Healy, Stephanie/Arcadia Elem Sch	57	Hild, Christy/Riddle Elem Sch	19
Hearns, Jacqueline/Hefferan Elem Sch	27	Hiler, Courtney/Bond Elementary	14
Heckel, Nicholas/West Elem Sch	157	Hiler, Courtney/Central A & M Middle Sch	14
Heckel, Nick/Oak Grove Sch	154	**Hiles, Dan**/Dr Maude A Sanders Primary Sch	199
Hefner, Kimberly/Hollywood Elem Sch	65	Hill, Aaron/Duquoin Middle Sch	201
Heiar, Wesley/East Dubuque Elem Sch	125	Hill, Antonia/Woodgate Elem Sch	47
Heideman, Jean/Rush Day Sch	80	Hill, Belinda/Giant City Elem Sch	121
Heigert, Jeremy/J D Colt Elem Sch	191	Hill, Dawn/Taylor Elem Sch	36
Heigert, Jeremy/Russell Elem Sch	191	Hill, Deborah/Riley Early Childhood Center	52
Heilemeier, Andy/Sandwich Middle Sch	86	Hill, Doug/Altamont Grade Sch	104
Heinemann, Jonathan/St Peter Lutheran Sch	81	Hill, Jeff/Petersburg Elem Sch	189
Heinhorst, Jennifer/Flossie Wiley Elem Sch	13	Hill, Jon/Henry Senachwine High Sch	176
Heintz, Charles/Loyola Academy	73	Hill, Kellee/Tri-Point High Sch	162
Heinz, Cheryl/Grant Intermediate Sch	182	Hill, Kris/St John the Baptist Sch	206
Heinz, Julia/St Paul Lutheran Sch	81	Hill, Maria/Immaculate Cncpton St Joseph	73
Heinz, Travis/Forreston Jr Sr High Sch	194	Hill, Maria/Immaculate Cncpton-St Joseph	73
Heinzman, Brett/St Mary Sch	124	Hill, Marjorie/Cathedral of St Raymond Sch	249
Heisel, Bill/Edison Junior High Sch	228	Hill, Stefanie/Kingston Elem Sch	85
Heitzler, Dawn/Annawan Grade Sch	116	Hill, Susan/Quincy Area Christian Sch	3
Helbig, Eric/Woodlawn High Sch	124	Hill, Valeska/Cahokia High Sch	218
Helbig, Russell/Christ Lutheran Sch	240	Hillard, Salina/Dongola Sch	230
Heldt, Jessica/Wanda Kendall Elem Sch	119	Hilliard, Jennifer/Cortland Elem Sch	84
Helfand, Stephanie/Joseph Sears Sch	53	Hillman, Kristine, Dr/St Elizabeth of the Trinity	75
Heller, Mark/Plano Middle Sch	138	Hillman, Kristine, Dr/St Elizabeth Trinity Sch	75
Hellman, Michelle/Illini Central Grade Sch	177	Hillman, Laurie/Fry Elem Sch	95
Hellman, Michelle/West Campus Pre-Kindergarten	177	**Hills, Kelly**/K D Waldo Middle Sch	129
Hellmer, Anne/Esperanza Sch	78	Hiltz, Ginny/Greenbriar Elem Sch	59
Hellmer, Anne/Niles Central High Sch	58	Hinckley, Jay, Dr/Calvary Academy	214
Helmers, Denise/Neoga Elem Sch	84	Hines, Martell/Carver Elem Sch	36
Henderson, Casonya/Edna Keith Elem Sch	243	Hinton, Michael/Hoyne Elem Sch	35
Henderson, Doriane/Taft Elem Sch	243	Hiscock, Charles/West Aurora High Sch	132
Henderson, Michael/British Int'l Chicago-S Loop	77	Hiser, Rodney, Dr/Jones Elem Sch	112
Hendry, Elizabeth/Blair Early Childhood Center	33	Hitchings, Bret/Heartland Tech Acad-Eldorado	164

Illinois School Directory — PRINCIPAL INDEX

NAME/School	PAGE
Hitchings, Bret/Heartland Tech Acad-Richland	164
Hitlz, Virginia/Maria Saucedo Scholastic Acad	32
Hixon, Michele/Britten Sch	20
Hlavacs, Jason/Technology Center of Dupage	88
Ho, Bonnie/Pui Tak Christian Sch	80
Hobbs, Carl/Harvard High Sch	181
Hobbs, Linda/Notre Dame Acad-St Augustine	222
Hobbs, Linda/Notre Dame Academy-Cathedral	222
Hobin, David/Arrowhead Ranch Sch	209
Hobrock, Jamie/Triopia Grade Sch	192
Hockett, Kori/Wheaton Academy	102
Hodge, Brian/Ashley Elem Sch	235
Hodge, Dena/Neponset Grade Sch	117
Hodge, John/Irving Elem Sch	61
Hodge, Laura/Issac Singleton Elem Sch	243
Hodge, Sylvia/George W Tilton Elem Sch	31
Hodgson, Pam/Coolidge Elem Sch	54
Hoekstra, Mike/Christian Life Center Sch	256
Hoelescher, Brian/Central Intermediate Sch	225
Hoese, Jeff/Fulton Elem Sch	239
Hofer, Brian/Southwest Elem Sch	117
Hoffman, Lee/Morton Junior High Sch	227
Hoffman, Paul/Warrensburg-Latham Middle Sch	166
Hoffman, Shawn/Trinity Lutheran Sch	188
Hoffmann, Ann/Midland High Sch	176
Hoffmann, Jo Ellen/Good Shepherd Christian Acad	78
Hofmeier, Ann/Laura B Sprague Sch	153
Hogue, Carrie/Muffley Elem Sch	165
Hogue, Charles/Circle Academy	13
Hohm, Stephen/Decatur Christian Sch	167
Holland, Ashley/Heather Hill Elem Sch	49
Holland, Chala, Dr/Lake Forest High Sch	151
Holland, Lauren/G N Dieterich Elem Sch	129
Holmes, Don/Thornwood High Sch	69
Holmes, Jason/Dunlap Valley Middle Sch	196
Holt, Jayme/Franklin Preschool	19
Holtz, Liz/Oakdale Elem Sch	187
Hood, Edmund/Gurrie Middle Sch	54
Hood, Jo, Dr/McDowell Sch	27
Hood, Melanie/Vivian Adams Early Chldhd Ctr	219
Hood, Staci/Tri-County at Ward Sch	201
Hook, William/Chicago HS-Agricultural Sci	27
Hooper, Arthur/Faith Chrn Fellowship Academy	173
Hopkins, Joy/Farragut Elem Sch	243
Hopkins, Martin/O W Holmes Middle Sch	71
Horn, Brian/Century Junior High Sch	61
Horn, Liz/Sased Central Sch	211
Horn, Robert/North Mac High Sch	168
Hornberg, Kimberly/Heartland Elem Sch	131
Horne, Erin/Frances X Warde Sch-St Patrick	78
Horne, James/DeKalb High Sch	84
Horne, Justin/Timothy Christian Sch	102
Horne, Rosary/Early Childhood Center	90
Horning, Josh/Christian Life Academy	229
Horrighs, Rocky/Central Junior High Sch	217
Horton, Priscilla/James H Bowen Sch	38
Horwitz, Benjamin/Carleton W Washburne Sch	72
Hoskins, Ursula/Jacob Beidler Elem Sch	31
Hoster, Doug/Litchfield High Sch	191
Hotek, David/St Joseph High Sch	75
Houchin, Darrell/Richland Co Middle Sch	206
Houck, Darrin/Holy Cross Lutheran Sch	173
Houlihan, Amy, Dr/Campanelli Elem Sch	66
House, Collette, Dr/Cornerstone Christian Academy	86
Housman, Crystal/Cobden Jr Sr High Sch	230
Houston, Cynthia/Iyc Pere Marquette	1
Houston, Gina/St Thomas the Apostle Sch	184
Houston, Jeff/Galesburg High Sch	140
Hovey, Justin/Prophetstown Elem Sch	239
Howard, Jeff/Lisle High Sch	97
Howard, Jill/Troy-Cronin Elem Sch	248
Howard, Lucille/Hughes Elem Sch	31
Howard, William/Indiana Elem Sch	57
Howicz, Mary/White Eagle Elem Sch	96
Hoyou, Anna/Mackeben Elem Sch	182
Hubbard-Green, Sonya, Dr/Meadowview Intermediate Sch	45
Hubbird, Robert/Lincoln Elem Sch	55
Hubble, Andy/Southeast Alternative Sch	88
Huber, Cole/Chrisman High Sch	103
Huber, Cole/Chrisman-Scottland Jr High Sch	103
Hubert, Jacob/North Boone High Sch	5
Hubner, Amy/Pekin Community High Sch	227
Hudson-Barnes, Valencia/Mollison Elem Sch	33
Hudson, Curtis/Charles Reed Elem Sch	246
Hudson, Patti/Creekside Elem Sch	246
Hueber, Shelley/John Shields Elem Sch	132
Huels, Angela/Columbia Middle Sch	190
Huelsman, Gregory/Matteson Elem Sch	57
Huemmer, Robyn/Jane Stenson Elem Sch	67
Huene, Janet/Illini Bluffs Elem Sch	197
Hueramo, Billy/Little John Elem Sch	85
Huff, Anne/Harrison Elem Sch	181
Huff, Tinisa/Betsy Ross Elem Sch	50
Huffaker, Chawn/Allen Junior High Sch	6
Huffaker, Chawn/Putnam Co Primary Center	204
Huffaker, Chawn/Van Orin Grade Sch	6
Huffman, Daniel/Cumberland Elem Sch	84
Huffman, Gary/Calvary Baptist Academy	223
Huggins, Teresa/Bennett Elem Sch	35
Hughes, Mark/Monticello Middle Sch	202
Hughes, Michael/George O Barr Elem Sch	209
Hughes, Tanya/Edgewood Elem Sch	100
Huhn, Raeann/St Francis High Sch	101
Huisman, Cody/North Elem Sch	50
Hulcher, Kathy/Matheny-Withrow Elem Sch	213
Humboldt, Sarah/Salt Creek Elem Sch	44
Humphrey, Leah/Hazelgreen Elem Sch	20
Hundal, Aj/John F Kennedy Middle Sch	246
Hunt, Stacey, Dr/Brooks Middle Sch	51
Hunter, Christy/Hawthorn Elem School South	151
Hunter, Megan/Lincoln Trail Elem Sch	11
Hurd, Reiko/Springfield Learning Center	213
Hurelbrink, Eric/Meridian High Sch	166
Hurlburt, Thomas, Dr/Wolcott Sch	45
Hurley, Kristie/Jerseyville West Elem Sch	125
Hurley, Matt/Olympia North Elem Sch	187
Hutchens, April/Centerview Therapeutic Sch	77
Hutchinson, Sandy/Fernway Park Elem Sch	53
Hutchison, Jessica/Avoca West Elem Sch	22
Hutchison, Mathew/Taylorville High Sch	15
Huther, Jason/Carmel High Sch	157
Hutley, Ben/Ridgeview Elem Sch	187
Hutton, Becky/Central Intermediate Sch	234
Huyett, Melydi/Centennial Elem Sch	195
Huzenis, Christine/Northside Cath Acad-Primary	73
Huzenis, Christine/Northside Cath Academy Mid Sch	73
Hyllberg, Ken/Arnett C Lines Elem Sch	147
Hylton, Taquia/Berger-Vandenberg Elem Sch	46
Hylton, Taquia/CICS-Ralph Ellison [160]	39

I

NAME/School	PAGE
Iacobazzi, Diona/Pershing Elem Sch	23
Iacovelli, Sante/St Rita of Cascia High Sch	76
Ibbotson, Adam/Sherman Elem Sch	214
Ibrahim, Aliaa/Pennoyer Sch	62
Iddings, Scott/Leggee Elem Sch	182
Ilani, Cathryn/Einstein Academy	133
Iles-Gomez, Dawn/Hale Elem Sch	34
Illa, Luis/Drexel Elem Sch	42
Imbordino, Michelle/Liberty Elem Sch	246
Ing, Kristin/Ewing Northern Elem Sch	108
Ingalls, Chevi/Central Middle Sch	1
Inglese, Janet/Steger Intermediate Center	68
Ingram, Cordell/MacArthur High Sch	165
Ingram, Kathy/Our Lady of Tepeyac High Sch	73
Inman, Cindy/Alton Middle Sch	169
Irwin, Laura/Chester-East Lincoln Cmty ES	163
Isaac, Marie, Sr/St Dominic Sch	249
Isabelli, Gina/Western Ave Elem Sch	49

PRINCIPAL INDEX

Market Data Retrieval

NAME/School	PAGE
Isackson, Dana/Macomb Jr Sr High Sch	178
Isdonas, Jason/Frankfort Square Elem Sch	247
Isenhower, Jeff/Prairieview-Ogden North ES	11
Isenhower, John/Wesclin Senior High Sch	18
Ismail, Tammie/Aqsa Sch	77
Iturralde, Victor/Eric Solorio Academy HS	26
Ivack, Catherine/Kirk Sch	20
Ivy, Turon/Ace Amandla Charter Sch	1

J

NAME/School	PAGE
Jabbari, Christine/Rogers Elem Sch	28
Jablonski, Paula/Pactt Learning Center	80
Jackson-Ivy, Marvis/Henderson Elem Academy	34
Jackson, Amy/Sorento Elem Sch	4
Jackson, Charlena/Early Learning Center	213
Jackson, Danielle/Dr Preston L Williams Elem Sch	13
Jackson, Kelly/Highcrest Middle Sch	72
Jackson, Maureen/St Charles Borromeo Sch	133
Jackson, Mykah, Dr/Yankee Ridge Elem Sch	13
Jackson, Nichole/Hales Franciscan High Sch	73
Jackson, Phillip/Chicago Grammar Sch	77
Jackson, Sabrina, Dr/Turner-Drew Language Academy	35
Jackson, Shannae/Gwendolyn Brooks Coll Prep Aca	38
Jackson, Shawn/Hickory Bend Elem Sch	24
Jackson, Victoria/Perspectives CS-Mid Acad [166]	41
Jacob, John/Bethel Lutheran Sch	229
Jacobsen, John/Glacier Ridge Elem Sch	181
Jacobson, Lissette/Pioneer Elem Sch	99
Jacobson, Mike/H L Richards High Sch	44
Jacoby, Diane/Bible Baptist Chrn Academy	133
Jakowitsch, Todd/Lake Zurich Mid Sch N Campus	152
Jakubowski, Michael/Hope Institute Learning Acad	39
James, Cynthia/St Coletta of Illinois	81
James, Martez/Franklin Elem Sch	46
James, Mathew/Calvary Academy	77
James, William/Graymont Elem Sch	162
Jancek, Keri/Prairie Central Upper Elem Sch	162
Janecke, Andrew/Orangeville Sch	225
Janesky, Mark/Schlarman Academy	233
Janicke, Jackie/Northeast Elem Sch	49
Janisch, Ryan/North Grove Elem Sch	86
Jannakos, Protinica/St Sava Academy	81
Jansen, Tari/Depute Unit Sch	6
Janssen, Adam/Midland Middle Sch	176
Janusz, Lenayn/Big Hollow Primary Sch	148
Jaramillo, Jaime/Steinmetz Academic Center	36
Jares, Kristin/South Elem Sch	46
Jarot, Nathan/Anderson Elem Sch	128
Jasiek, Jyll/Holy Family Sch	145
Jasper, Rolland/Washington Junior High Sch	243
Jean-Baptiste, Melinda/Acero CS-Jovita Idar Elem Sch [156]	38
Jefferson, Amy/Longfellow Elem Sch	61
Jefferson, Donna/DuBois Elem Sch	213
Jefferson, Todd/Ridgeview Elem Sch	196
Jeffries, Gina/Siue East St Louis Charter Sch	219
Jemison, Terrilyn/Chicago SDA Elementary	77
Jenke, Raquel/Warren Park Elem Sch	42
Jennings, James/Riverdale Middle Sch	208
Jennings, John/Kelvin Grove Middle Sch	244
Jennings, Shellie/Hamilton Jr Sr High Sch	114
Jensen, Karrah/Cedar Ridge Elem Sch	186
Jensen, Stephanie/Andrew Cooke Magnet Elem Sch	156
Jeppson, Tom/Rutland Grade Sch	144
Jerger, Breah/Oliver Julian Kendall Elem Sch	95
Jerrell, Bryce/Carrier Mills-Stonefort ES	210
Jimenez, Jose/Hedges Elem Sch	32
Jimenez, Lourdes/Ruben Salazar Bilingual Center	28
Jirjis, Karen/Brown County Middle Sch	5
Jockisch, Brad/Bartonville Elem Sch	196
Jockisch, Lisa/Pikeland Community Sch	203
Jodlowski, Ed/Olympia High Sch	187
Johansen, Erika/Gray M Sanborn Elem Sch	43
Johansen, Kurt, Dr/South Elgin High Sch	131

NAME/School	PAGE
Johns, Kevin/Mae Jemison Elem Sch	63
Johnson-Bibbs, Monique/Medgar Evers Primary Sch	49
Johnson, Antonio/Dunlap Middle Sch	196
Johnson, Austin/North Barrington Elem Sch	147
Johnson, Brian/Alton Success Academy	169
Johnson, Christie/Education Therapy Ctr-Madison	169
Johnson, Claudia/Enos Elem Sch	213
Johnson, Crystal/Rossville-Alvin Elem & JHS	233
Johnson, Darryies/Day Treatment	199
Johnson, David/Normal West High Sch	187
Johnson, Dyonna/Olson Park Elem Sch	253
Johnson, Heather/North Elem Sch	169
Johnson, Jeff/Herrin High Sch	251
Johnson, Jennifer/Camelot School-DeKalb Campus	86
Johnson, Jessica/Manuel Perez Elem Sch	32
Johnson, Justin/Mt Zion High Sch	166
Johnson, Kathy/Sainte Marie Elem Sch	122
Johnson, Katie/Walter Lawson Children's Home	256
Johnson, Kimberly/James Hart Sch	52
Johnson, Lee/Romeoville Christian Academy	250
Johnson, Levi/Wells Elem Sch	238
Johnson, Lynor/Fox Valley Montessori Sch	133
Johnson, Mayra/Aurora Christian Elem Sch	133
Johnson, Nicole/Green Bay Early Childhood Cent	154
Johnson, Robin/Learn Chtr Sch-Romano Butler [164]	40
Johnson, Sandi/Clearview Elem Sch	156
Johnson, Steve/Highland Elem Sch	130
Johnson, Susan/Cdh Educational Center	160
Johnson, Travis/Coal City Middle Sch	112
Johnson, Vanessa/DuBois Elem Sch	36
Johnston, Christine/St George Elem Sch	136
Jokanovic, Lila/Council Oak Montessori Sch	78
Jolly, Sharla/Winfred Gerber Sch	13
Jonak, John/Westmont Junior High Sch	92
Jonas, Jennifer/Glen Hill Elem Sch	98
Jones-Riley, Kim/Mason Clark Middle Sch	219
Jones, Anetrise/Elite Scholars Steam Academy	223
Jones, Angela/St Mary's Sch	126
Jones, Carolyn/Bass Elem Sch	34
Jones, Chad/Hollis Consolidated Grade Sch	197
Jones, Chantel/Cottage Grove Upper Grade Ctr	49
Jones, Darren/Paul Revere Primary Sch	45
Jones, Don/George Washington Middle Sch	56
Jones, Donald/Algonquin Middle Sch	46
Jones, Iysha/Doolittle East Elem Sch	33
Jones, Karen/St Mary's School-Pontiac	163
Jones, Keith/Sesser-Valier Elem Sch	108
Jones, Keith/Sesser-Valier Jr High Sch	108
Jones, Kristine/Benjamin Braun Educational Ctr	20
Jones, Kristine/Project Challenge	20
Jones, Marsh, Dr/Kingswood Sch	13
Jones, Natasha/Lawndale Community Academy	31
Jones, Patrick/Viking Middle Sch	150
Jones, S/Villa Grove High Sch	88
Jones, Sara/Villa Grove Elem Sch	88
Jones, Toia/Boulder Hill Elem Sch	137
Jones, Wes/Trinity Lutheran Sch	173
Jordahl, Ann/Montessori Sch of Lake Forest	158
Jordan, Beverly, Dr/Jensen Scholastic Acad	31
Jordan, Terrance/Black Hawk Elem Sch	213
Jordon, Andrew/West Carroll Primary Sch	9
Jorgenson, Jake/Millburn Middle Sch	153
Jouglard, Sandy/St Teresa Sch	223
Joyce, Colleen/High Point Elem Sch	61
Joynt, Lawrence/Crow Island Sch	72
Juarez, Alberto/Gary Elem Sch	32
Juarez, Jasmine/Pilsen Community Academy	32
Julius, Jon, Dr/Jasper Elem Sch	237
Jung, Jill/Freeburg Cmty High Sch	219
Jurgaitis, Jason/Gavin South Junior High Sch	150
Jurs, Rebecca/Lily Lake Grade Sch	128
Justus, Teri/Deer Creek-Mackinaw Prim JHS	226

Illinois School Directory

PRINCIPAL INDEX

NAME/School	PAGE
K	
Kabat, Sandra/Farrington Elem Sch	122
Kabat, Sandra/Woodlawn Grade Sch	124
Kaese, Scott/Ivy Hill Elem Sch	21
Kahler, Kristopher/Maroa Forsyth Middle Sch	165
Kaiz, Jason/Springman Middle Sch	51
Kallieris, Jim/Washington Elem Sch	153
Kamadulski, Brian/Maryville Christian Sch	173
Kamien, Matthew/St John Lutheran Sch	81
Kampwerth, Tami, Dr/Aviston Elem Sch	17
Kane, Elsie/Peterson Elem Sch	29
Kapka, Dawn/St Anne Catholic Sch	158
Kara, Aydin/Chicago Math & Sci Academy [161]	39
Karadis, Kari, Dr/Hollywood Heights Sch	170
Karafiol, Paul/Lake View High Sch	36
Karczewski, Dana/Meadow Ridge Elem Sch	61
Kareem, Jamillah/Winnie Mandela Alt HS	81
Kargas, Barbara/Goethe Elem Sch	30
Karidis, Kari, Dr/Kreitner Elem Sch	170
Kariotakis, Constantine/Timber Ridge Middle Sch	246
Karnick, Kelley/Rotolo Middle School-Batavia	128
Karriem, Jason/Muhammad Univ of Islam	79
Kartal, Serdar/Horizon Sci Acad-Belmont [161]	1
Kartsimans, Melissa/John F Kennedy Elem Sch	67
Karvales, Bessie, Dr/Proviso Math & Science Academy	64
Kasper-Couty, Gwen/Albert Sabin Magnet Sch	31
Kasper, Aimee/Constance Lane Elem Sch	254
Kass, Miriam/Akiba Schechter Day Sch	76
Kassir, Mary/Gary Elem Sch	99
Kaszewicz, Brian/Nathan Hale Elem Sch	66
Katz, Diane/St Paul Lutheran Sch	133
Katz, Matthew/Acero CS-Rufino Tamayo ES [156]	38
Kavustuk, Nuray/Robina Lyle Elem Sch	53
Kays, Kim/Erie Elem Charter Sch	39
Kean, Justin/Gibson City-Melvin-Sibley ES	106
Keane, Ann/Thompson Inst Center	243
Keane, Sonja/St Thomas More Sch	133
Kearney, David/Lisle Junior High Sch	97
Keene, Glynis/Bloom Trail High Sch	23
Keener, Jeffery/Murphysboro Middle Sch	121
Keenley, Mary/St Theresa Sch	76
Keer, Craig/Carrie Busey Elem Sch	10
Keesee, Jeremy/Aquin Catholic Jr Sr High Sch	225
Keesee, Jeremy/Aquin Elementary	225
Keesee, Jeremy/Southside Elem Sch	239
Keffer, Jenny/Auburn High Sch	254
Kehoe, Candice/Butterfield Elem Sch	153
Kehr, Megan/Sor Juana Elem Sch	33
Keith, Dennis/Somonauk Christian Sch	86
Keller, Jill/Acero CS-Sandra Cisneros ES [156]	38
Keller, Ryan/Laverna Evans Elem Sch	221
Kelley, Matthew/Noble CS-Drw Clg Prep [165]	40
Kelly, Brandi/Sangamon Valley Middle Sch	166
Kelly, Brian/Martin L King College Prep HS	38
Kelly, Charlotte/Infant Jesus of Prague Sch	73
Kelly, Cyndie/Rosecrance Sch-G Williamson	1
Kelly, Diane/Cotton Creek Elem Sch	155
Kelly, Erin/J Sterling Morton Alt Sch	53
Kelly, Estee/Noble CS-Comer Clg Prep HS [165]	40
Kelly, Jon/Fisher Jr Sr High Sch	10
Kelly, Karla/Lincoln Elem Sch	89
Kelly, Katherine/Lions Park Sch	58
Kelly, Linda/Queen of the Universe Sch	74
Kelly, Mary/Galva Elem Sch	117
Kelly, Mary/N B Galloway Elem Sch	241
Kelly, Paul/Elk Grove High Sch	70
Kelly, Stacy/Blackstone Elem Sch	142
Kemp, Karla/Deneen Sch of Excellence	25
Kendall, Bryan/Regional Alternative Sch	185
Kendrick, Kara/The Academy at Forest View	70
Kendrick, Mike/St James Sch	75
Kendryna, Amy/Spring Trail Elem Sch	131
Kennedy, Ellen/Richards Career Academy	37
Kennedy, Michael/Frances X Warde Sch-Holy Name	78
Kennedy, Pamela/YCCS-McKinley-Lakeside HS	41
Kenner, Joyce, Dr/Whitney Young Magnet High Sch	28
Kenney, Jennifer/Coal City Elem Sch	112
Kenney, Karla/Perkin Pre-Sch Family Ed Ctr	228
Kent, Joseph/Heritage Middle Sch	68
Kepley, Doug/Bement High Sch	202
Kepley, Doug/Bement Middle Sch	202
Kern, Brian/Vandalia Junior High Sch	106
Kern, Jennifer/W W Woodbury Sch	86
Kern, Steve/Winston Churchill Elem Sch	67
Kerr, Tim/Southeastern Jr Sr High Sch	115
Kesler, Eric/Porta Central Sch	189
Ketcham, Heather/Kimes Elem Sch	144
Ketchum, Ryan/Central Community High Sch	17
Kettelkamp, K/Taylorville Junior High Sch	15
Keyser, Stacy/Cumberland Middle Sch	84
Kibelkis, David/Bremen High Sch	23
Kick, Susan, Dr/Harper Elem Sch	71
Kidd, Amber/Aspire Alternative High Sch	104
Kidd, Stephen/Gibault Catholic High Sch	190
Kiedaisch, Jennifer/Middlefork Primary Sch	68
Kieser, Vail/Kildeer Countryside Elem Sch	151
Kiesewetter, Ron/Metamora High Sch	258
Kiesewetter, Ronald/Minooka Cmty High Sch -Central	245
Kilgore, Sarah/McKinley Elem Sch	22
Killingsworth, Carmen/Pioneer Elem Sch	248
Killion, Stephen/Villa Grove Junior High Sch	88
Kilpatrick, Aaron/Parkside Primary Sch	169
Kim, Kiltae/Gunsaulus Scholastic Academy	27
Kincaid, Keith/Sandburg Elem Sch	213
Kindel, Christy/Tri-City Sch	214
Kinder, Derek/Romeoville High Sch	248
Kinel, Margaret/St Eugene Sch	75
King, Bart/Carmi-White County Jr High Sch	238
King, Cabell/Global Citizenship Exp Sch	78
King, Christina/Goreville Sch	127
King, Clyde/Arthur Ashe Elem Sch	35
King, Gail/Reavis Math & Sci Elem Sch	33
King, Jeff, Dr/Kindergarten at Pleviak	155
King, Kelly/Brook Park Elem Sch	23
King, MacQuline/Courtenay Language Arts Acad	29
King, Mr/YCCS-West	41
King, Timothy/Pecatonica Middle Sch	253
Kinne, Timothy/St Matthew Lutheran Sch	158
Kipp, Titia/Thomas J Waters Elem Sch	29
Kirby, Jason/West Central High Sch	116
Kirby, Stacy/Countryside Sch	13
Kirch, Karin/Glenbrook North High Sch	51
Kirchner, Anna/Bradley East Elem Sch	134
Kirk, Kevin/Independence Jr High Sch	61
Kirk, Paul/Roslyn Road Elem Sch	147
Kirk, Paul/St James the Apostle Sch	101
Kirkpatrick, Roy/Christopher Elem Sch	108
Kirkwood, Issac/Jack Benny Middle Sch	156
Kish, Michael/Immaculate Conception Sch	190
Kitson, Sunni/Catherine Cook Sch	77
Kittle, Erica/Drummond Elem Sch	31
Kjome, Tara/Westdale Elem Sch	57
Klaber, John/Hoopeston Area High Sch	232
Klaska, Matt/Vit Elem Sch	110
Klawitter, Linda/South Early Childhood Center	92
Kleckner, Tammy/Frassati Catholic Academy	157
Kleckner, Tammy/Frassati Catholic Academy	157
Kleifges, Jenae/Chesterbrook Academy	101
Klein, Debra/Emerson Elem Sch	92
Klein, Travis/Illini Elem Sch	219
Kleindl, Stacey/Blackhawk Elem Sch	224
Kleist, Carrie/Monroe Elem Sch	198
Klene, Scott, Dr/Olive C Martin Elem Sch	152
Kleros, Vasiliki/Fulton Elem Sch	34
Klespitz, Scott/Forest Glen Elem Sch	94
Klett, Daniel/Wauconda Cmty High Sch	155
Klich, Sheila/St Celestine Sch	74
Klimowski, Amy/Burr Elem Sch	31

School Year 2020-2021   800-333-8802   IL-U17

PRINCIPAL INDEX

NAME/School	PAGE
Klinner, Dawn/Blessed Sacrament Sch	214
Klinsky, Beth/West Elem Sch	181
Klomhaus, Laurie/Todd Early Childhood Center	132
Klosa, Serena/Ebinger Elem Sch	27
Kloss, Carolyn/Hillman Elem Sch	254
Klueppel, Amy/Bell-Graham Elem Sch	128
Klug, Zachary/Trinity Lutheran Sch	214
Knepler, Julia/Brigham Early Learning Ctr	186
Knoeppel, Mary Beth/Lincoln Elem Sch	43
Knop, Brady/West Carroll Middle Sch	9
Knowles, Bill/Warsaw Elem Sch	115
Knox, Miyoshi/Stagg Elem Sch	26
Knox, Rochonda/Libby Elem Sch	34
Knox, Seth/Agape Christian High Sch	252
Knox, Tawane/Neil Elem Sch	35
Knuckey, Dave/Longfellow Liberal Arts ES	208
Knuppel, Sarah/Pershing Early Learning Center	165
Knuth, Josh/Warren Jr Sr High Sch	126
Kobilsek, Anita/Holy Cross Sch	145
Koch, Steven, Dr/Prairie Ridge High Sch	180
Kochanowski, Nathan/Edwin A Lee Elem Sch	213
Kocher, Scott/Dieterich Jr Sr High Sch	104
Koehler, Rich/St Mary Sch	258
Koehne, Bill/Grace Lutheran Sch	78
Koenig, Dawn/Trinity Lutheran Sch	102
Koerner, Greg/Holy Cross Sch	13
Koeune, Joe/Antioch Upper Grade Sch	146
Kohl, Mark/Bradley Central Middle Sch	134
Koker, Valencia/Dewey Elem Acad of Fine Arts	26
Kolcharno, Richard/Freeport Christian Academy	225
Kolinski, Peter/Eisenhower Sch	68
Kolitwenzew, Ramie/St Anne Cmty High Sch	136
Koll, Ken/St Philip Neri Sch	76
Koll, Kenneth/Ridge Academy	80
Kolowski, Chris/P L Bolin Elem Sch	227
Kompare, Lisa/Mark Delay Sch	92
Kondrat, Susan/Madison Early Childhood Edu CT	94
Koontz, Robert/Mulberry Grove High Sch	4
Korb, Micah, Dr/Countryside Elem Sch	147
Koresko, Ryan/Mercer Co Intermediate Sch	189
Kort, Joanne/Everett Dirksen Elem Sch	66
Korte, Julie/Highland Primary Sch	171
Kos, Alison/Chauncey H Duker Sch	183
Kosina, Joe/Proviso West High Sch	64
Kosovski, Jonathan/International Prep Academy	10
Kostopouos, David/Reavis Elem Sch	55
Koulentes, Thomas/Libertyville High Sch	148
Kovalcik, Laurie/Rosemont Elem Sch	66
Kowach, Tim/Lake Co Baptist Sch	158
Kowal, Sara, Sr/Peoria Notre Dame High Sch	200
Koziol, Jamie/Milne Grove Elem Sch	244
Kraemer, Terri/Ellis Elem Sch	219
Kraft, Carmel/Vanguard Sch	70
Kramer, Candice/Sward Elem Sch	60
Kramer, Daniel/Roosevelt High Sch	36
Kramer, Kurt/Willow Creek Elem Sch	100
Kratochvil, Tim/Pawnee High Sch	212
Krause, Dan/Willowbrook High Sch	93
Krause, Jay, Dr/Metro East Lutheran High Sch	173
Krause, Katy/Concordia Lutheran Sch	256
Kreiser, Jessica/Lighted Way Assoc Sch	145
Krenz, Kel/Central Elem Sch	161
Kretzer, Laura/St Boniface Sch	173
Krielaart, Patricia/Our Lady of Tepeyac Elem Sch	73
Kroll, Anthony, Dr/Mundelein Cons High Sch	153
Krueger, Kelly/Iroquois Community Sch	46
Kruger, Jordan/Noble CS-Itw David Speer Acad [165]	40
Krugman, Michael/Whittier Elem Sch	93
Krupnack, Asher/Yeshivas Brisk Academy	82
Krupski, James/St Paul's Lutheran Sch	137
Krus, Wayne/Ingersoll Middle Sch	109
Kubelka, Scott/Raymond Ellis Elem Sch	155
Kubic, Christopher/New Tech High Zion-Benton East	157

NAME/School	PAGE
Kuchy, Jackie/North Greene Elem Sch	111
Kudelka, Jason/Fox Tech Center	133
Kuehl, Mark/Lena-Winslow High Sch	224
Kueker, Brett/Bristol Grade Sch	139
Kuhl, Lisa/Richmond Grade Sch	183
Kuhlmann, Mr/Bluffs Cmty Unit Sch	215
Kuhn, Angela/Illinois School for the Deaf	1
Kuhn, Michael/Woodruff Career & Tech Center	199
Kujath, John/Our Saviour's Lutheran Sch	158
Kujawa, Craig/Bethel Grade Sch	122
Kulenkamp, Roy/Carlinville Middle Sch	167
Kulig, Rhonda/George W Lieb Elem Sch	64
Kulik, Jeff/G Kerkstra Elem Sch	50
Kupchick, Dovid/Rabbi Oscar Fasman Yeshiva HS	80
Kurtz, Amy/Trinity-St John Lutheran Sch	236
Kurtz, Sam/Maple Sch	60
Kurtz, Samuel/Edgewood Middle Sch	154
Kurtz, Steven/Yeshiva Meor Hatorah-Boys HS	81
Kurut, Heather/Morgan Park Academy	79
Kushnir, Lena, Dr/Sager Solomon Schechter Sch	80
Kuzniewski, Frank/John Mills Elem Sch	48
Kwasny, Kate/Oakwood Elem Sch	55
Kyle, Steven/Carol Stream Elem Sch	90

L

NAME/School	PAGE
Labotka, Barbara/Cardinal Bernardin Mont Acad	72
LaCamera, Michelle/Kimball Hill Elem Sch	43
Lacost, Cheryl/Brickton Montessori Sch	77
Ladd, Elizabeth/Garden Hills Elem Sch	10
Ladd, Kyle/Shelbyville High Sch	216
Ladenburger, Stefan/Fremont Elem Sch	149
Ladenburger, Stefan/Fremont Intermediate Sch	150
Lafary, Kathy/West Central Elem Sch	116
Lafin, Lora/Westchester Primary Sch	70
LaFrance, David/Oakland Elem Sch	185
Lafranzo, Carmen/Carmel Montessori Academy	101
Lago, Joanna/Sherlock Elem Sch	42
Lahr-Well, Almeda, Dr/Lahr-Well Academy	173
Laino, Christina/Acero CS-Roberto Clemente ES [156]	38
Lake, Julie/St John the Evangelist Sch	111
Lakelman, Jennifer/Summerdale Early Childhood Ctr	254
Lakin, Kyra/Metro East Montessori Sch	173
Lamb, Bill/St Mary's of Kickapoo Sch	200
Lamb, Matt/Kings Sch	194
Lambatos, Luke, Dr/Eisenhower Elem Sch	63
Lambert, Messina/Irving Elem Sch	185
Lamm, Brian/Taylor Park Elem Sch	224
Lampley, Lyntina/Ombudsman-West High Sch	40
Landers, Joe/Wallace Elem Sch	145
Landgrave, Aaron/St John Lutheran Sch	102
Landon, Teresa/Jane Addams Elem Sch	208
Landry, Dan/Grayslake Central High Sch	150
Landskroener, Nathan/St James Lutheran Sch	3
Landstrom, Allison/Peterson Elem Sch	95
Lane, Chuck/Centralia High Sch	174
Lane, Erin/Crete Elem Sch	242
Lane, Josh/Belleville High School-East	217
Lane, Lynn/Sterling Middle Sch	199
Lane, Otis/Delta Academy	23
Langbehn, Kristie/Pablo Casals Elem Sch	26
Lange, Wendy/Penniman Elem Sch	218
Langen, Edmund/Abraham Lincoln Sch	217
Langes, Matt/Elmwood Elem Sch	98
Langford, Debra/Rogers Park Montessori Sch	80
Langietti, Melissa/Medinah Primary Sch	98
Langston, Cynthia/Lalumier Elem Sch	218
Lanham, Sarah/St John Baptist Catholic Sch	223
Lanier, Mary/Deer Creek-Mackinaw High Sch	226
Lanius, Ashley/Galatia Jr Sr High Sch	210
Lanoue, Mary/Pavilion Foundation Sch	13
Lansaw, Jeremy/Greenfield Elem Sch	111
Lanskey, Sharon/Roosevelt Elem Sch	208
Lantz, Tecia/Southeastern Elem Sch	115

Illinois School Directory

PRINCIPAL INDEX

NAME/School	PAGE
Lapenas, Nichole/Oakwood Grade Sch	232
Lapp, William/Fieldcrest High Sch	257
Laramore, Amy/Sparta Lincoln Sch	205
Lard, Melissa/Dirksen Primary Sch	228
Laredo, Lori/East Peoria Cmty High Sch	226
Larry, Cindy/Herget Middle Sch	132
Larson, Eric/Patton Elem Sch	21
Larson, Jeremy, Dr/Memorial Elem Sch	103
Larson, Jill/Brookwood Junior High Sch	24
Larson, Reggie/Alwood Elem Sch	116
Larsson, Stefan/Westfield Middle Sch	89
Lashley, Jonathan/New Life Christian Academy	200
Lasica, Sara/St Edward Sch	75
Laskov, Nikole/Galapagos Rockford CS [162]	254
Lasley, Carla/Grant Middle Sch	219
Lasswell, Stephine/East Side Elem Sch	114
Laster, Mark/Anna Junior High Sch	230
Laster, Mark/Davie Elem Sch	230
Laster, Mark/Lincoln Elem Sch	230
Latko, Brianna/St Ignatius College Prep Sch	75
Latting, Chris/Haven Middle Sch	48
Latting, Gerri/Horace Mann Sch	45
Laube, Alexander/Cove Sch	78
Laughlin, Donna/Immanuel Lutheran Sch	133
Laurent, Monica/Whiteside Middle Sch	222
Laurincik, Jennifer/Henry Clay Elem Sch	36
Laverty, Dan/Hubert Humphrey Middle Sch	248
LaVin, Ms/Gateway to Learning Sch	78
LaVin, Seth/Brentano Math & Science Acad	30
Lawler, Geralyn/St Mary of the Woods Sch	76
Lawrence, David/Lincoln Elem Sch	142
Lawrence, John/Blue Ridge High Sch	87
Lawrence, John/Swann Sch	13
Lawson, Brian/Spring Ave Elem Sch	54
Lawson, Melissa/Willow Elem Sch	52
Layne, Debbie/Westminster Christian Sch	134
Lazar, Kristina/Schramm Education Center	225
Lazarevic, Jovan/Fenton High Sch	94
Lazor, Shari/Winnebago Elem Sch	97
Lazu, Lillian/Little Village Academy	27
Leal, Francisco/Gale Math & Science Academy	29
Leamy, Sharon/SS Catherine of Siena-Lucy Sch	74
Leardi, Lisa, Dr/Springfield High Sch	213
Leathers, Loree/Steam Academy at Haskell	254
Leavitt, Karen/Bernard Zell Anshe Emet Sch	77
Leban, Greg/Westchester Middle Sch	70
Lech, Emily/Yorkville Grade Sch	139
Leckrone, Racheal/Bethalto East Primary Sch	169
Lecrone, Brian/May Watts Elem Sch	95
Lee-Diaz, Robyn/Grant Elem Sch	22
Lee, Ben/Olympia Middle Sch	187
Lee, Caitlin/St Gall Sch	75
Lee, Jim/Hope Institute Sch	214
Lee, Kenneth/KIPP One Academy [163]	40
Lee, Robert/Winston Knolls Sch	81
Lee, Terrence/Taft Primary Sch	135
Lee, Tim/Oakwood High Sch	232
Lefferson, Garrett/J W Robinson Elem Sch	56
Leggett-Gallus, Nicole/Stony Creek Elem Sch	20
Lehman, Dan/New Athens Sch	220
Lehnen, Christine/Glenwood Middle Sch	211
Leib, Tammy, Dr/Belle Valley Elem Sch	217
Leider, Kristine/Gregory Elem Sch	254
Leinweber, Fred/North Elem Sch	99
Leipart, Mark/Goodings Grove Sch	242
Leitao, Lauren/V H Nelson Elem Sch	47
Leiva, Tiffany/George Washington Elem Sch	67
Leman, Chris/Countryside Private Sch	258
Lemberger, Nicole/North Elem Sch	156
Lemenager, Andrea/Ashkum Early Literacy Center	118
Lemenager, Andrea/Chebanse Elem Sch	118
Lemenager, Tare/Onarga Academy Grand Prairie	118
Lemmer, Deacon/St Andrew Catholic Sch	240
Lemmon, Radena/Lewis & Clark Jr High Sch	173
Lempa, Dale/Calvary Christian Academy	188

NAME/School	PAGE
Leneau, Cabrina/Glenwood Elem Sch	156
Lensing, Chris/Butterworth Elem Sch	207
Lensing, Heidi/Eagle Ridge Elem Sch	207
Lentz, Jason/Algonquin Middle Sch	180
Lentz, Jay/Dahlgren Elem Sch	114
Leonard, Amy/Floyd Henson Jr High Sch	16
Leonard, Patrick/Ottawa Township High Sch	143
Leonard, Sarah/Illinois City Elem Sch	209
Leoni, Patricia/Steger Primary Center	68
Lerner, Matthew/Elmwood Elem Sch	48
Lesinski, Neil/Cary Grove Cmty High Sch	179
Leskowich, Michael/Durand High Sch	252
Leskowich, Michael/Durand Junior High Sch	252
Leslie, Jon/Emden Elem Sch	163
Leslie, Jon/Hartsburg Emden Jr Sr High Sch	163
Letourneau, Lynn/Divine Providence Sch	73
Leuschel, Kerry/Westinghouse College Prep	37
Levine, Lara/North Shore Academy	146
Levy, Cynthia, Dr/Jesse White Learning Academy	52
Lewandowski, Christina/Martin Luther King Elem Sch	13
Lewis, Ali/University Primary Sch	13
Lewis, Alicia/Bright Sch	35
Lewis, Billy/Belvidere High Sch	4
Lewis, Christopher/Rochelle Twp High Sch	195
Lewis, Cody/Effingham Junior High Sch	105
Lewis, Melissa/YCCS-Dr Pedro Albizu Campos HS	41
Liberos, Christos/Scammon Elem Sch	29
Lichipin, Leticia/Bronzeville Academy CS	39
Lidwell, Kilee/Lincoln Elem Sch	109
Liechty, Denise/Davis Primary Sch	129
Lietz, Jeana/Oak Lawn Cmty High Sch	60
Ligon, Mary Ann/Sacred Heart Sch	80
Ligue, Tim/Intrinsic School-Downtown	39
Lilja, Molly/Manchester Elem Sch	5
Lind, Beth/Koraes Sch	79
Lindsay, Jennifer/Rogers Elem Sch	227
Lindsey, J/Richland Elem Sch	247
Lingafelter, Eric/Wayne City High Sch	237
Linhart, Sandy/Norwood Primary Sch	198
Linley, Cathy/Immaculate Conception Sch	100
Linzer, Menachem/Hillel Torah N Sub Day Sch	78
Lipman, Diana/Neil Armstrong Elem Sch	67
Lira, Juan/McKinley Elem Sch	131
Lishamer, Amanda/Prairie Lake Sch	80
Liska, Scott/Southwest Elem Sch	49
Litchfield, James/Heineman Middle Sch	182
Litteken, Dennis/Mater Dei High Sch	18
Little, Ann/Morrisonville Jr Sr High Sch	14
Littlejohn, Tamara/Woodson Elem Sch	33
Littmann, Rebecca/Central Elem Sch	71
Livengood, Darlea/Woodstock North High Sch	184
Livengood, Kali/Erie Elem Sch	239
Livingston, Lucas/Cherokee Elem Sch	152
Llano, Melissa/Pietrini Elem Sch	50
Llewellyn, Hattie/New Berlin High Sch	212
Lloyd, Delores/Thomas Paine Elem Sch	13
Lobbins, Travis/Barrington MS-Prairie Campus	147
Lobdell, Andrew/Lena-Winslow Jr High Sch	224
Loch, Edwin/Reinberg Elem Sch	29
Lochhead, Tim/St Mark's Lutheran Sch	206
Lock, Aaron/Charleston High Sch	19
Lockard, Cheryl/Beverly Skoff Elem Sch	248
Lockenvitz, Jeff/Washington Elem Sch	185
Loemker, Carmen/Maryville Elem Sch	170
Loepker, Darin/Shiloh Middle Sch	221
Lofgren, Mark/Riverdale Elem Sch	208
Lofink, Mark/Zion Lutheran Sch	191
Logston, David/Humboldt Treatment & Lrng Ctr	19
Lombardi, Joseph/Father McGivney Catholic HS	173
Lombardo, Matthew/Joyce Kilmer Elem Sch	71
Long, Joshua/Southside Occupational Academy	28
Look, Jerolee/Limestone Cmty High Sch	197
Lootens, Mike/Epiphany Sch	187
Lopatka, Mike/Fairview South Elem Sch	49

PRINCIPAL INDEX

Market Data Retrieval

NAME/School	PAGE
Lopez, Claudia/Fairfield Academy	34
Lopez, Eliza/Kimberly Heights Elem Sch	21
Lopez, Maria/Laurel Hill Elem Sch	131
Lopez, Sue Ellen/Locust Elem Sch	182
Lora, Danielle/Mt Pulaski Grade Sch	164
Lorenzo, Heather/Grays Lake Early Childhood Ctr	148
Lorsbach, Christie/Calhoun Elem Sch	8
Lorton, Nate/Fieldcrest Middle Sch	257
Lorts, Becky/St Mary's Sch	8
Loschen, Darren/Armstrong Twp High Sch	231
Loth, Stephanie/Pleasant Lane Elem Sch	97
Louderman, Stacy/St Clair Co Alternative Ed Ctr	217
Lough, Marcia/Hines Primary Sch	199
Loughrige, Scott/Scullen Middle Sch	96
Louie, Laquita/Curtis Sch of Excellence	25
Louis, Allison/North Boone Middle Sch	5
Louis, Joshua/Steeple Run Elem Sch	98
Lovdahl, Sue/Lincoln Elem Sch	192
Love, Karen/St Viator High Sch	76
Love, Patrick/Alain Locke Charter Academy	38
Loversky, Tim/Wredling Middle Sch	129
Lowe, Apryl/Illinois Park Early Lrng Ctr	130
Lowe, Rc/C R Hanna Elem Sch	117
Lowe, Ryan/Pleasant Hill Elem Sch	203
Lowery, Daren/Riverview Elem Sch	258
Lowery, Elizabeth/Mary Queen of Heaven Pre-Sch	101
Lowery, Tarita/Childs Elem Sch	63
Loy, Kristi/Black Hawk Area Spec Ed Center	207
Lozdoski, Theresa/Seth Whitman Elem Sch	4
Lucas, Benetrice/Ronald McNair Elem Sch	26
Lucas, Daniel/Dirksen Elem Sch	28
Ludford, Michelle/Beaubien Elem Sch	28
Luehmann, Joanna/Pontiac Junior High Sch	221
Lugo, Jimmy/Harriet Beecher Stowe Elem Sch	31
Lukascy, Melanie/Waltham Elem Sch	145
Lukic, Manda/Beard Elem Sch	28
Lull, Mark/Maryville Elem Sch	171
Luna-Mroz, Yolanda/Decatur Classical Sch	29
Lundquist, Phil/Covenant Christian Sch	133
Lungaro, Matthew/St Agnes Sch	74
Lupo, Dominick/Lincoln Hall Middle Sch	56
Lurie, Yitzchak/Yeshiva Eitz Chaim	81
Lux, Tyler/Franklin Park Middle Sch	175
Lyke, Lisa/Ludwig Elem Sch	249
Lyman, Holly/Rolling Green Elem Sch	254
Lyman, Kate/Woodbine Elem Sch	42
Lyman, Kate/Woodrow Wilson Elem Sch	42
Lynch, Dan/Crestwood Sch	103
Lynch, Dan/Dennis Lab Sch	165
Lynch, Debbie/River Valley Sch	55
Lynch, Denise/William F Finkl Academy	32
Lynch, Katy/Meadow Glens Elem Sch	98
Lynde, Jason/El Sierra Elem Sch	93
Lynn, Robert/Charleston Middle Sch	19
Lyons, Angie/Peoria Christian Sch	200
Lyons, Latoya/William H Brown Elem Sch	32
Lyons, Tony/YCCS-Chatham Acad HS	41

M

NAME/School	PAGE
Ma, Elizabeth, Dr/Ontarioville Elem Sch	131
Maag, Dorian, Dr/Thomas Jefferson Elem Sch	208
Maaske, Matt/Knoxville Junior High Sch	140
Macek, Jennifer/Carl Sandburg Middle Sch	224
Macias, Amanda/North Greene Jr Sr High Sch	111
Maciejewski, Rhonda/Conley Elem Sch	182
MacIntyre, Kim/Naperville Christian Academy	102
Mackey, Travis/Geneseo High Sch	117
Mackin, Renee/Carl Von Linne Elem Sch	26
MacLin, Douglas/Chicago Vocational Career Acad	38
Magdaleno, Raul/Thomas Kelly College Prep	38
Magers, Tom/Broadmeadow Grade Level Sch	11
Maggiore, Martha/Prairie Grove Elem Sch	183
Maggiore, Martha/Prairie Grove Jr High Sch	183

NAME/School	PAGE
Magnafici, Matthew/Reagan Middle Sch	160
Magnuson, Katie/Skinner North Classical Sch	31
Magruder, Laura/Highlands Elem Sch	54
Maher, Kim/Wilson Creek Elem Sch	244
Mahone, Christian/South Side Elem Sch	10
Mahone, Keith/Irving Middle Sch	57
Mahoney, Angela/Eastland Elemenary Sch	8
Mahoney, Kelly/Northview Elem Sch	11
Mahr, Amy/May Whitney Elem Sch	152
Mahy, April/L J Hauser Junior High Sch	65
Majerus, Elizabeth, Dr/University Laboratory High Sch	1
Major, Jason/Dever Elem Sch	28
Maki, Angela/Melzer Elem Sch	47
Makishima, Patricia/West Leyden High Sch	55
Makowski, Denise/McCormick Elem Sch	32
Malahy, Sue/Charles A Lindbergh Middle Sch	199
Maldonado, Elisa/Autumn Creek Elem Sch	139
Malek, Bob/Joseph Academy-Des Plaines	79
Malekovic, Grace/New Horizon Christian Sch	176
Malgieri, Alysson/CICS-Washington Park ES [167]	39
Maloney, Mary, Dr/St John Brebeuf Sch	75
Maloy, Brian/Milledgeville Sch	8
Mandel, Hallel/Yeshiva Ohr Boruch	81
Mandera, Frank/Perry Elem Sch	4
Mane, Bryon/Coretta Scott King Mag Sch	242
Mann, Brian/St Peter Lutheran Sch	106
Mann, Jeremy/The Field Sch	81
Mannes, Terri/St John's Lutheran Sch	81
Manning, David/Zion Lutheran Sch	169
Manno, Ciara/Aux Sable Elem Sch	112
Mantzke, Dave/Indian Creek Elem Sch	85
Manuel, Katina/Whistler Elem Sch	36
Manwaring, Veronica/Immanuel Lutheran Sch	121
Maras, Jill/Kaneland Senior High Sch	132
Marchini, Elizabeth/Lincoln Elem Sch	4
Marcinkewicz, Christine/Cass Junior High Sch	90
Marian, Strok/Evergreen Academy Middle Sch	32
Mariano, Emily/Alessandro Volta Elem Sch	28
Marie, Cora, Sr/Childrens Center Tazwell Co	229
Marino, Karen/G Stanley Hall Elem Sch	97
Marion, Jamonica/Clissold Elem Sch	33
Marker, Erin/Kingsley Elem Sch	98
Markert, Andrea/University High Sch	1
Markey, Jason/East Leyden High Sch	55
Markoff, Jennifer/Visitation Sch	76
Markowski, Tracey/River View Elem Sch	246
Marks, Amy/Woods Creek Elem Sch	181
Markworth, Douglas/Grace Lutheran Sch	78
Marlow, Jim/New Athens Sch	220
Marotz, Kelly/Sandridge Elem Sch	66
Marquardt, Julie/Mt Zion Junior High Sch	166
Marshall, Amanda/Schiller Elem Sch	174
Marshall, Bethanie/Cissna Park Sch	118
Marski, Renee/Troy Middle Sch	247
Marten, Cheri/South Side Elem Sch	105
Marth, Stephen/Benet Academy	100
Marti, Haley/Flossmoor Hills Elem Sch	49
Martin, Christina/The Children's Sch	81
Martin, Jenny/St Andrew Sch	121
Martin, Jerry/Sonia Shankman Orthogenic Sch	80
Martin, Judy/Passow Elem Sch	50
Martin, Mark/Brussels Grade Sch	8
Martin, Meghan/Premier Academy	111
Martin, Ryan/Middletown Prairie Elem Sch	11
Martin, Stephanie/Early Learning Center	131
Martin, Susan/Washington Gifted Sch	199
Martin, Teresa/Walsh Elem Sch	249
Martin, Tom/Luther Burbank Elem Sch	24
Martinez, Efrain/Orozco Fine Arts & Sciences ES	32
Martinez, Elizabeth/Core Academy	133
Martinez, Jalitza/Olney C Allen Elem Sch	129
Martino, Marcia/Sycamore Trails Elem Sch	131
Martorano, Carol/Montessori School-Long Grove	158

IL-U20   800-333-8802   School Year 2020-2021

Illinois School Directory

PRINCIPAL INDEX

NAME/School	PAGE
Marzullo, Marcie/O'Neal Elem Sch	131
Mascal, Amy Jo/Streator Twp High Sch	145
Mason, Alene/Joplin Elem Sch	34
Mason, Emily/Noble CS-Muchin Clg Prep [165]	40
Mason, Gregory/Murray Language Academy	33
Mason, Jennifer/St Ann Sch	236
Mason, Joseph/Urban Prep CS-Englewood	41
Mason, Shannon/Shabbazz CS-Betty Shabbazz Acd [158]	1
Massey, Rhonda/Four Rivers Sp Ed Ctr-Garrison	192
Massey, Sarah/Minooka Junior High Sch	112
Mast, Greg/Arthur Christian Sch	88
Masten, Jana/Farmersville Grade Sch	191
Mastin, Emily/Franklin Primary Sch	199
Mata, Armondo/Lakeview Learning Center	79
Matanky, Leonard/Ida Crown Jewish Academy	79
Matarelli, Julie/Columbus Elem Sch	171
Mate, Kristie/Park View Elem Sch	90
Mateyka, Laurel/P H Miller Elem Sch	138
Mathews-Ndely, Michelle/CICS-Basil [167]	39
Mathis, Latrese/John Hay Community Academy	30
Mathius, Doc/Queen of Martyrs Sch	74
Matthews, Katie/Grove Ave Elem Sch	147
Matzenbacher, Lori/SS Peter & Paul Sch	190
Mau, Jill/Half Day Sch	153
Mauer, Ellen, Dr/Spaulding Sch	150
Maupin, Scott/Wilmington High Sch	249
Maurer, Meghan/Prairie View Middle Sch	53
Maurer, Terese/Lincoln Elem Sch	45
Maxwell, Chelsey/Green Bay Early Childhood Ctr	154
Maxwell, Cynthia/Sunny Hill Elem Sch	147
Maxwell, Josh/Clinton Junior High Sch	87
Maxwell, Matt/Grant Park High Sch	135
Maxwell, Matt/Grant Park Middle Sch	135
May, Carol/H R McCall Elem Sch	156
Mayhew, Robert/Good Shepherd Lutheran Sch	173
Maynard, Kevin/Cumberland High Sch	84
Mays, Shernita, Dr/Schrum Memorial Sch	52
Mayszak, Alexander/Ridgewood Elem Sch	207
Mazenis-Luzzi, Suzanne/Jungman Elem Sch	27
Mazin, Estuardo/Barry Elem Sch	26
Mazurek, Kate/KIPP Acad Chicago Austin Area [163]	39
McAllister, Gerit/Alphonsus Academy	72
McAtee, David/Mokena Intermediate Sch	245
McBride, Jac/Early Childhood Center	67
McCaffrey, Eileen/Dorn Elem Sch	59
McCann, Artis/Kennedy Elem Sch	25
McCann, Christopher/Kell Elem Sch	175
McCarry, Korrie/Cloverdale Elem Sch	90
McCarthy, Aisha/Harvard Elem Sch	26
McCarty, K/Indian Creek High Sch	85
McCarty, Vickie, Dr/Faith Christian Academy	233
McCaskill, Latonya/Sieden Prairie Elem Sch	47
McCaslin, Jessica/Wood View Elem Sch	248
McCauley, Joe/Ogden Avenue Elem Sch	54
McChristian, Tim/Duquoin High Sch	201
McClaire-Gary, Milissa/Nautilus Sch	79
McClaney, Rebecca/New Hope Academy	80
McClay, Carol/St Athanasius Sch	74
McClellan, Ryan/Red Bud Elem Sch	205
McCloskey, Jamey/Jefferson Sch	217
McCollum, Cody/Stewardson-Strasburg High Sch	216
McCollum, Eric/East Side Intermediate Sch	211
McCollum, Travis/Hamilton Co Jr Sr High Sch	114
McCollumn, Tammy/Akin Cmty Cons Elem Sch	107
McConnel, Tim/Erie High Sch	239
McConnell, Brian/Rhodes Elem Sch	64
McCormack, Jean/Allegro Academy	256
McCormick, Brendan/Good Shepherd Center	78
McCottrell, Marilyn/Fuller Elem Sch	26
McCoy, Cortez/Dyett Arts High Sch	27
McCoy, Jennifer/Lexington Cmty Jr High Sch	186
McCoy, Jennifer/Lexington High Sch	186
McCoy, Kathy/New Sullivan Elem Sch	35
McCoy, Martne/Blackberry Creek Elem Sch	132
McCoy, Mike/Blackhawk Elem Sch	255
McCoy, Mike/South Beloit Jr High Sch	255
McCoy, Tony/Elmwood Jr Sr High Sch	196
McCracken, Robyn/Quest Charter Academy	199
McCreary, Richard/New Covenent Christian Academy	79
McCree, Andrew/Ann Reid Early Childhood Ctr	98
McDavid, Maurice/Turner Elem Sch	100
McDermott, Dan/Kolb Elem Sch	64
McDermott, Scott/Wheaton-Warrenville South HS	92
McDermott, Tim/Alice Gustafson Elem Sch	128
McDonald, Matt/Westfield Elem Sch	90
McDonald, Sandee/Hendricks Elem Cmty Acad	33
McDonald, Sara/Northview Elem Sch	144
McDonald, Victoria/Robinson High Sch	83
McDonnell, Anne/Centennial Elem Sch	144
McDowell, Mark/Quincy Notre Dame High Sch	3
McDowell, Rachelle/Nokomis Jr Sr High Sch	191
McElligott, Robert/Wood Oaks Junior High Sch	59
McErlean, Laura/Providence Catholic Chldrn Aca	249
McGhee, Lynn/Seneca North Elem Sch	144
McGinn, Kathy/Queen of the Rosary Sch	74
McGovern, Anne/Hannum Elem Sch	60
McGowan, Debbie/Harrisburg Middle Sch	211
McGowen, Ryan/Staunton Junior High Sch	168
McGraw, Chris/Evans Junior High Sch	186
McGreer, Mr/Zadok Casey Middle Sch	123
McGuire, Karin/Learn Chtr Sch-Campbell [164]	40
McGuire, Mindy/Meridian Middle Sch	166
McHolland, James/Chute Middle Sch	48
McKay, Clarice/St Clare Catholic Sch	222
McKenzie, Jessica/Fox River Grove Middle Sch	181
McKinney, Andrea/Gordon Sch	63
McKinney, Dave/Havana High Sch	177
McKnight, Kristina/Ferson Creek Elem Sch	129
McLaughlin, April/Rankin Elem Sch	228
McLaughlin, Bruce/St Paul Lutheran Sch	173
McLaughlin, Holly/Ombudsman Sch-Naperville	102
McLaughlin, Joey/Lewistown Central Elem Sch	110
McLaughlin, Nick/Lostant Elem Sch	142
McLawhorn, Mrs/St Albert the Great Sch	74
McMahan, Amy/Porta Jr Sr High Sch	189
McMahon, Annette/Oak Park Elem Sch	129
McMahon, Eileen, Dr/Maine West High Sch	56
McMahon, Josh/J Sterling Morton West HS	53
McManus, Maria/STEM Magnet Academy	28
McMillin, Dennis/Farmington Central High Sch	197
McNair, Jerald/Madison Sch	68
McNally, Ann/Stock Sch	29
McNally, Noel/Vaughn Occupational High Sch	37
McNeal, Bridgette/George Washington Elem Sch	45
McNichols, Sean/Oak Lawn Hometown Middle Sch	60
McPherson, Brett/Belvidere Central Middle Sch	4
McSpadden, Charlie/Coles Elem Sch	35
McSparin, William/Unity Christian Sch	252
McVey, Mark/Schaumburg Christian Sch	80
McVinnie, Robert/Alpine Academy of Rockford	256
McWilliams, Ryan/Anna McDonald Elem Sch	244
McWilliams, Steve/Barrington High Sch	147
Meagher, Tom, Dr/SS Faith Hope & Charity Sch	74
Medina, Jacqueline/Talman Elem Sch	28
Medina, Tony/Palatine High Sch	69
Meek, Scott/Northbrook Junior High Sch	59
Meggos, Jody/Eunice Smith Elem Sch	169
Meiergerd, Sharon/Christ's Academy	250
Mekky, Nashwa/Howe Elem Sch	147
Melamed, Matthew/Park Sch	148
Melendez, Josefina/Channing Elem Sch	130
Mellott, Sarah/Rome Elem Sch	124
Melnyk, Julie/Hinckley-Big Rock Elem Sch	85
Menden, Mari Agnes, Dr/St Nicholas of Tolentine Sch	76
Mendez, Claudia/St Joseph Sch	75
Mendez, Keri/Rhodes Sch of Global Studies	48
Mendez, Nancy/James Otis Elem Sch	31
Mendez, Sarah/William Hatch Elem Sch	61
Mendoza-Thomps, Melissa/Marycrest Early Childhood Ctr	243

PRINCIPAL INDEX

NAME/School	PAGE
Mendoza, Melissa/MacArthur/Echo Sch	20
Menke, Steve/Our Lady Queen of Peace Sch	173
Menoni, Jacqueline/De Diego Community Academy	31
Mensch, Robert/Liberty Elem Sch	42
Mensik, John, Dr/Glenbard North High Sch	94
Mentgen, Dwayne/LaSalle-Peru Area Career Ctr	141
Menzer, Lydia/Chicago Academy High Sch	25
Merboth, Angie/Harding Grade Sch	144
Merrell, Lashae/Park Manor Elem Sch	35
Mershon, Michelle/St Bede Academy	145
Mertens, Rich/Belleville Twp High Sch-West	217
Merz, Nicole/Holy Angels Sch	73
Mesnard, Stacy/Vandalia Elem Sch	106
Messina, Julie/Trinity Lutheran Sch	102
Mest, Kelly/Northside College Prep HS	27
Metheney, Troy/Illinois Center for Autism	223
Metz, Trina/Beach Elem Sch	155
Metzger, Jeanette/Preschool at Early Educ Ctr	155
Meulendyke, John/Immanuel Lutheran Sch	185
Meyer, Adam/Hall High Sch	6
Meyer, Gregory/Warren Twp HS-O'Plaine Campus	155
Meyer, Jodi/Hiawatha Elem Sch	23
Meyer, Joyce/Greenwood Elem Sch	156
Meyer, Mike/Beecher Junior High Sch	241
Meyer, Missy/Chester High Sch	205
Meyer, Sheri/St James Lutheran Sch	81
Meyers, Elizabeth/Randolph Magnet Sch	35
Meziere, Traci/Anne Sullivan Elem Sch	63
Michaelsen, Eric/Lemont High Sch	55
Michalak, Sharon, Dr/Lincoln-Way East High Sch	244
Michalski, Dave/Sch Exp Arts & Lrng-Romeoville	250
Michel, Jerry/Francis Willard Elem Sch	48
Michels, Gregory/Meridian Sch	147
Michowski, Mike/Cossitt Elem Sch	54
Mickelburgh, Erika, Dr/St Paul of the Cross Sch	76
Midgett, Gregory/Washington Elem Sch	255
Miesner, Chris/Evansville Attendance Center	205
Mihelbergel, Adam/Bannockburn Elem Sch	147
Mijal, Carrie/Visitation Sch	101
Milburn, Jeff/Dakota Elem Sch	224
Milem, Charles/Erie Middle Sch	239
Miles, Lori/ABC Academy	2
Miles, Lori/Adams Co Regional Safe Sch	2
Milka, Chris/H C Storm Elem Sch	128
Millburg, Kelly/Lincoln Elem Sch	14
Miller, Adam/Wilbur Trimpe Middle Sch	169
Miller, Alexandria/South Suburban SDA Chrn Sch	80
Miller, Alicia/Southern View Elem Sch	213
Miller, Amber/Maud E Johnson Elem Sch	254
Miller, Amy/Decatur Christian Sch	167
Miller, April/Field Middle Sch	70
Miller, Brett/Herscher Intermediate Sch	135
Miller, James/Central Intermediate Sch	172
Miller, Jennifer/St Damian Sch	74
Miller, Jeri/Goreville Sch	127
Miller, Jill/Cicero East Elem Sch	42
Miller, Kathleen/Bell Elem Sch	30
Miller, Kathleen, Dr/St James Catholic Sch	5
Miller, Kristina/Clifford P Carlson Elem Sch	254
Miller, Patricia/Oglesby Elem Sch	34
Miller, Steve/Elizabeth Graham Elem Sch	213
Miller, Teresa/Minooka Primary Center	112
Miller, Toni/St Pius X Sch	101
Milleville, Rosa/Beecher City Grade Sch	104
Milligan, Courtney/Center Sch	61
Mills, Amy, Dr/Our Lady of Perpetual Help Sch	73
Mills, Bobbie/North Elem Sch	192
Mills, Jocelyn/Shabazz CS-Sizemore Acad [158]	1
Mills, Nathan/Mahomet-Seymour Jr High Sch	11
Milner, Diane/Brighton North Primary Sch	168
Milner, Diane/Shipman Elem Sch	168
Milo-Nicolasin, Natalie/Kimball Hill Elem Sch	43
Milsap, Teresa/Chicago HS for the Arts	39

NAME/School	PAGE
Milsk, Susan/Sheridan Elem Sch	152
Miner, Pam/Whitehead Elem Sch	255
Mingus, Seth/South Pekin Grade Sch	228
Minter, Gregory/Prospect High Sch	70
Miquelon, Jonathon/Clinton Elem Sch	130
Miscik, Lori/Highland Elem Sch	171
Missey, Karen/Madison Student Support Center	172
Mitchell, Brad/Timothy Christian High Sch	102
Mitchell, Brad/Timothy Christian Sch	102
Mitchell, Inez/Forrestal Elem Sch	154
Mitchell, Jara/Gallatin Cmty Unit Dist 7 Sch	110
Mitchell, John/Rice Education Center	48
Mitchell, Leslie/Gordon Gregory Middle Sch	95
Mitchell, Markisha/Dirksen Junior High Sch	243
Mitchell, Stephanie/Thomas Jefferson Elem Sch	22
Mitchell, Terry/Frohardt Elem Sch	171
Mitchell, Troy/Homer Junior High Sch	242
Mitchem, Jacqueline/Independence Elem Sch	248
Mitchem, Jeff/Lincoln Elem Sch	92
Mitchinson, Michael/Old Post Elem Sch	138
Mitera, Megan/Bert H Fulton Elem Sch	42
Mitra, Melanie/Hyde Park Day Sch	79
Modaff, Jeff/McWayne Elem Sch	128
Mody, Sunilkumar, Dr/Northlake Middle Sch	22
Moeller, Steve/St John's Lutheran Sch	133
Moes, Randy/Calvin Christian Sch	77
Mohr, Stephanie/Beck Area Career Center	205
Mojica, Fernando/Clemente Cmty Academy	37
Molina, Alberto/Goodwin Elem Sch	42
Molina, Christine/Maternity BVM Sch	73
Molinsky, Amy/Jane Addams Elem Sch	43
Molitor, Tim/Nippersink Middle Sch	183
Mollet, Ryan, Dr/Central Sch	51
Monaghan, Peter/Glenbard West High Sch	94
Monahan, Erin/St Thomas the Apostle Sch	76
Monahan, Sean/Jean McNair Elem Sch	255
Monroe, Debra/Wauconda Grade Sch	155
Monroe, Sarah/Walnut Trails Elem Sch	112
Montgomery, Ms/Highlands Elem Sch	63
Montgomery, Shinora/Early Childhood Center	46
Montgomery, Shinora/Riverdale Sch	46
Montgomery, Tiana/Albert Cassens Elem Sch	171
Montgomery, Tiana/Shiloh Village Elem Sch	221
Moody, Grace/Alcott College Prep West	30
Mooney, Terry/Christ Lutheran Sch	200
Moore-Ollie, Sherryl/Penn Elem Sch	31
Moore, Allania/Madison Elem Sch	35
Moore, Bridget/Bower Elem Sch	92
Moore, Dirk/Calvary Christian Academy	158
Moore, Dustin/Ravenswood Bapt Christian Sch	80
Moore, Justin/East St Louis Sr High Sch	219
Moore, Justin/Thornridge High Sch	69
Moore, Matt/Riverton High Sch	212
Moore, Pete/Lake Forest Country Day Sch	158
Moore, Thomas/Thresholds Young Adult Program	81
Moore, Tim/Bloomington High Sch	185
Moore, Virgil/Southwestern Middle Sch	168
Morales, Devon/YCCS-Olive Harvey Mid Clg HS	41
Morales, Veronica/Cicero West Elem Sch	42
Moran, Brian/South Elgin High Sch	131
Moran, Danielle/Hawthorne Elem Sch	92
Moredock, Bill, Dr/Little Flower Catholic Sch	214
Morehouse, Richard/St Paul Sch	163
Moreland, Matt, Dr/Pritchett Elem Sch	147
Morelli, Anthony/A-Karrasel Sch	76
Moreno, Lisa/A O Marshall Elem Sch	243
Morgan, Adrienne/Nancy Young Elem Sch	95
Morgan, Andrew/Pathways In Education-Ashburn	41
Morgan, Andrew/Pathways In Education-Avondale	41
Morgan, Andrew/Wentworth Junior High Sch	24
Morgan, Connie/South Elem Sch	16
Morgan, Jennifer/Lincoln Middle Sch	171
Morgan, Laura/Meadowview Elem Sch	148

Illinois School Directory

PRINCIPAL INDEX

NAME/School	PAGE
Morgan, Matt/Zeigler Royalton High Sch	108
Morgan, Richard/Carrier Mills-Stonefort HS	210
Morgan, Richard, Dr/Sauk Elem Sch	57
Morgan, Terry/Mt Pulaski High Sch	164
Morlan, Brock/Marquette Elem Sch	253
Morley-Hogan, Kim, Dr/Lester Crawl Primary Center	54
Morreson, Melissa/Gateway Legacy Christian Acad	173
Morrill, Steve/Thompson Middle Sch	129
Morris, Brad/North Wamac Grade Sch	18
Morris, David/Pleasant Hill Elem Sch	43
Morris, Donald/Burroughs Elem Sch	26
Morris, Sheila/Owen Scholastic Academy	34
Morrison, Jennifer/Grace Christian Sch	163
Morrison, Jim, Dr/South Middle Sch	21
Morrison, Katy/Harding Primary Sch	234
Morrison, Phil/Unity High Sch	12
Morrissey, Todd/Parkview Baptist Academy	80
Morrow, Barb/Alt Educ Ctr-Harris	165
Morrow, Gerald/Dunbar Voc Career Academy	38
Morton, Tracy/Central School Programs	130
Moscowitz, Esther/Lubavitch Girls HS of Chicago	79
Moss, Becky/Marion Junior High Sch	251
Moss, Jodie/Indian Prairie Elem Sch	181
Most, Aaron/Grace Christian Academy	137
Mostyn, Alyssa/St Ailbe Sch	74
Mota, Rachel/Mozart Elem Sch	30
Motsch, Lori/Spencer Trail Kindergarten Ctr	245
Mott, Moriah/McKinley Elem Sch	143
Mowen, J/Northside Elem Sch	117
Moy, Catherine/Haines Elem Sch	31
Mrozik, Don/John L Sipley Elem Sch	100
Muehleip, Jill/Galena Primary Sch	126
Mueller, Dawn/Marissa Jr Sr High Sch	220
Muench, Cheryl, Dr/Michelle Obama Sch Tech & Arts	62
Muench, Nicholas/Immanuel Lutheran Sch	225
Muhammad, Abdul/Douglass Academy High Sch	37
Muhammad, Ali/Corliss Early College STEM HS	38
Muhammad, Yasmeen/Nettelhorst Elem Sch	30
Mulcurnt, Denise/Ombudsman School-Crestwood	80
Mulholland, Stephanie/Steeleville Elem Sch	206
Mullaney, Joy, Dr/Immanuel Lutheran Sch	79
Mullen, Wendy/Morton Freshman Campus	53
Mullens, Nel/St Josaphat Sch	75
Muller, Nosson/Yeshivas Tiferes Tzvi Academy	82
Mullikin, Joe/Highland Elem Sch	195
Mullins, Jay/Byron High Sch	194
Mulvany, Brenda/Centralia Pre-Kindergarten Ctr	174
Munda, Michael/Lake Co Roe Alternative HS	146
Munns, Christine/Sauganash Elem Sch	28
Munos, Shawn/Jefferson Middle Sch	132
Munoz, Eve/J W Riley Elem Sch	22
Murg, Larry/Logos Christian Academy	79
Murphy, Beth/Galena High Sch	125
Murphy, Patricia/Acad St Benedict-the African	72
Murphy, Senita/N Lawndale Chtr-Christiana	40
Murphy, Senita/North Lawndale HS-Collins	40
Murphy, Tracy/Gower Middle Sch	95
Murra, Vince/Prairieview Elem Sch	148
Murrah, Andria/Jefferson Elem Sch	251
Murray, Annie/Mother Teresa Catholic Academy	249
Murray, Anthony, Dr/Kennedy Junior High Sch	98
Murray, Philip/Long Beach Elem Sch	137
Mursu, Jennifer/Fox Ridge Sch	129
Musatics, Wayne/Central Baptist Sch	173
Muting, James/St Laurence High Sch	75
Muzikowski, Ike/Chicago Hope Academy	77
Myers, Bill/Beardstown Middle High Sch	9
Myers, Debbie/Trinity Catholic Academy	145
Myers, Katherine/Great Lakes Acad Charter Sch	39
Myers, Ryan/Central Intermediate Sch	143
Myers, Scott/Hudson Elem Sch	186

N

NAME/School	PAGE
Nadrozny, Trevor/Kenwood Elem Sch	10
Nafziger, Shelli, Dr/Germantown Hills Elem Sch	257
Nagel, Chuck/Spring Lake Elem Sch	228
Nagel, Deborah/Joseph E Fisher Sch	241
Nagy, Teresa/Mahalia Jackson Elem Sch	34
Nail, Dustin/Damiansville Elem Sch	18
Nakayama, Naomi/Budlong Elem Sch	26
Nall, Kristin/Atwood-Hammond Grade Sch	88
Namlon, Emily, Dr/St Benedict Sch	74
Nanavati, Kiersten/McClellan Elem Sch	27
Nantwi, Lida/Children of Peace Sch	72
Napier, Michelle/St Richard Sch	76
Naqvi, Azra/Hadi School of Excellence	78
Narain, David/Hirsch Metro High Sch	38
Narea, Amy/Dr J Prieto Math & Sci Academy	30
Naselli, Jullanar/D H Williams Medical Prep HS	38
Nash, Maura/St John Fisher Sch	75
Nasiakos, Dana/McKenzie Elem Sch	72
Nasko, Nancy/St Pius V Sch	76
Nason, Ryanne/Carthage Middle Sch	114
Nass, Chad/Briargate Elem Sch	179
Nassr, Nancy/Ancona Sch	77
Natale, Robert/Hawthorn Middle School South	151
Nauman, Shelly/John F Kennedy Sch	7
Naumowicz, Lori/Thomas Middle Sch	21
Navarre, Michelle/Polaris Charter Academy	41
Navarro, Carmen/Mariano Azuela Elem Sch	27
Neal, Rese/Lincoln Elem Sch	70
Neathery, Mekelle/Virginia Cmty Unit 64 Sch	9
Neaveill, Jodi/Cerro Gordo Elem Sch	202
Needlman, Randy, Dr/North Park Elem Sch	80
Neely, Gayle/Ray Elem Sch	33
Negus, Jacquelyn/Quest Academy	80
Neis, Michael/St Mary Sch	133
Neitzel, Charles/Centennial High Sch	10
Nelson, Alonzo/Wyvetter Younge Alt Ctr for Ed	219
Nelson, Ashli/Seymour Jr Sr High Sch	2
Nelson, Catalina/Oakdale Elem Sch	156
Nelson, Jamikka/George Leland Elem Sch	30
Nelson, Joyce, Dr/Illinois Youth Detention Ctr	1
Nelson, Julie/Henry Senachwine Grade Sch	176
Nelson, Kimberly/Gallistel Language Academy	36
Nelson, Laura/Orion Middle Sch	117
Nelson, Maria, Sr/St Jude Sch	200
Nelson, Preston/Albion Grade Sch	104
Nelson, Preston/Edwards Co High Sch	104
Nendez, Linnet/Virginia Frank Child Dev Ctr	81
Nessner, Elizabeth/Healy Elem Sch	31
Nettleton, Kelly/Stevenson Elem Sch	99
Netzel, Anastasia/Jack London Middle Sch	71
Neuman, Sara/Bais Yaakov High Sch	77
Newberry, Dave/Lakes Community High Sch	148
Newell, Jarrod/Carmi-White County High Sch	238
Newell, Justin/Civic Memorial High Sch	169
Newkirk, Jake/Mt Carmel High Sch	234
Newkirk, Jake/Mt Carmel Junior High Sch	234
Newmes, Shaun/Kinnikinnick Sch	253
Newsome, Anna/Steuben Elem Sch	135
Newton-Duggins, Tracy/Marie Schaefer Elem Sch	221
Neylon, Kelly/Meadowview Elem Sch	100
Nicasio, Mariana/Indian Trail Elem Sch	93
Nichols, John/Graham Elem Sch	31
Nichols, Katie/Blue Ridge Interm Jr High Sch	87
Nichols, Kelly/Eureka Middle Sch	257
Nickerson, Daniel/Sr Thea Bowman Catholic Sch	222
Niebrugge, Amy/Central Grade Sch	105
Nielsen, Maureen/Sacred Heart Sch	101
Niemerg, Nick/St Michael the Archangel Sch	216
Nieminski, Bruce/Columbia Central Sch	68
Niforatos, Lisa/Fairmount Elem Sch	93
Nightingale, Jeffrey/Prairie Sch	61
Nigro, Kathleen/Bernard J Ward Elem Sch	248
Nikchevich, Ann/Naperville Christian Academy	102
Nikokavouras, Debbie/McPherson Elem Sch	29
Nikson, Patricia/Fairview Elem Sch	213

PRINCIPAL INDEX

Market Data Retrieval

NAME/School	PAGE
Nitka, David/Rondout Elem Sch	154
Nitsche, Michelle/St Cajetan Sch	74
Nitzel, Mike/Thomas Jefferson Elem Sch	208
Nobilio, Joshua/Crystal Lake South High Sch	180
Nolan, John/St Joseph Pre-School	214
Nolan, Rita/Montessori Sch of Englewood	40
Nolan, Theresa, Dr/Tinley Park High Sch	23
Nolazco, Nicole/St Barbara Elem Sch	74
Nolazco, Nicole/St Mary Sch	76
Nolen, Allison/Lutheran Assoc Sch	167
Nolen, Kent, Dr/YCCS-West Town Acad Alt HS	41
Nolting, Robert/Victor J Andrew High Sch	44
Nonnemacher, Jennifer/Fischer Middle Sch	95
Noon, Laura/Highlands Elem Sch	98
Noonan, Julie/St Philip the Apostle Sch	101
Nordstrom, Courtney/Ravinia Elem Sch	154
Nordstrom, Matt/Annawan High Sch	116
Norman, Beth/Bruning Elem Sch	249
Norman, Josh/Wilson Intermediate Sch	228
Norris, Jim, Dr/Keith Country Day Sch	256
Norris, Rodney/Midwest Central Primary Sch	177
Norton, Jeremy/Beardstown Christian Academy	9
Norton, Vicki/Smithton Elem Sch	222
Norton, Victoria/Martinsville Elem Sch	16
Norwood, Lauren/Burke Elem Sch	33
Nothnagel, Megan/Ridge Central Elem Sch	42
Nottingham, Carrie/North Prairie Junior High Sch	156
Novak, Carin/Lester Elem Sch	93
Novinski, Tom/Ira Jones Middle Sch	246
Novotny, Jan/St Joseph Academy	250
Novy, Debra/Marian Central Catholic HS	184
Novy, Kristin/Christopher House Charter Sch	39
Nowak, Julie/James B Conant High Sch	69
Nowak, Sarah/Arlene Welch Elem Sch	95
Nowinski, Jamie/St Patricia Sch	76
Noyes, Matt/Triad Middle Sch	172
Nyberg, Matthew/Rockford Christian Elem Sch	256
Nystrom, Camron/MacArthur Middle Sch	63

O

NAME/School	PAGE
O'Brien, Joseph/Plainfield East High Sch	246
O'Brien, Kate/Holy Family Catholic Academy	73
O'Brien, Michael/Cyd Lash Academy	146
O'Connell, Casey/Homestead Elem Sch	137
O'Connell, John/Sheridan Math & Science Acad	28
O'Connell, Ms/CICS-Bucktown	39
O'Connor, Amy/Barbara Vick Early Chld Center	33
O'Dell, Nathan/Geneseo Middle Sch	117
O'Hearn, Brenna/St Margaret Mary Sch	184
O'Leary, Cheryl/Edison Primary Sch	135
O'Neil, Christine/Beebe Elem Sch	98
O'Neill, Edward/New Horizon Center	80
O'Reilly, Eileen/Mother McAuley Lib Arts HS	73
O'Toole, Paul/Stevenson Elem Sch	34
O'Toole, Sharon/St Alexander Sch	74
O'Toole, Sharon/St Walter Sch	76
O'Young, Mary/Country Meadows Montessori Sch	158
Obert, Jody/Liberty Sch	2
Obert, Melissa/St Mary Sch	5
Obritzberger, Petra/German Int'l School Chicago	78
Obszanski, Joanne/Peotone Intermediate Ctr	245
Ochoa, Adriana/Leal Elem Sch	13
Ocon, Juan/Benito Juarez Cmty Academy	26
Odiotti, Michael/Cristo Rey St Martin Clg Prep	158
Odom, Sheila/Mt Carmel Elem Sch	234
Odonnell, Diana/Rupley Elem Sch	44
Oester, Cari/Glenn Elem Sch	186
Oetting, Jennifer/Newman Central Catholic Sch	240
Ogle, Greg/Calvary Baptist Academy	110
Ogle, Nathan/Sullivan Middle Sch	193
Ohnesorge, Joey/Marion High Sch	251
Oi, Lisa/St Therese Sch	76
Okamoto, Joan/Christian Heritage Academy	77
Oken, Barbara/Farnsworth Elem Sch	28
Oldham, Tina/Herrick Elem Sch	216
Oleksy, Wendy/Columbus Elem Sch	27
Olsem, Lisa/Kenyon Woods Middle Sch	130
Olsen, Eric/Amos Alonzo Stagg High Sch	44
Olsen, Kevin/J W Riley Sch	71
Olson, Erik/Hamline Elem Sch	32
Olson, Mike/Putnam Co Junior High Sch	204
Olson, Sara/Elm Elem Sch	91
Olstock, Jeffery, Dr/Crescent City Grade Sch	118
Oluewu, Khalid/Daniel Webster Elem Sch	31
Onesto, Melissa, Dr/William J Butler Elem Sch	242
Ophus, Daniel/Fairview Elem Sch	58
Opp, Cynthia/Tamaroa Elem Sch	201
Orbe-Lugo, Anamaria/Hammond Elem Sch	32
Orbe, Andres/North Elem Sch	154
Ordaz, Araceli/Maplebrook Elem Sch	98
Orozco, Susan/East Aurora ECC	129
Orr, Derrick/CICS-Wrightwood [160]	39
Orstead, Jessica/Academy South	69
Orth, John/Jack Hille Middle Sch	50
Ortiz, Rita/Bridge Elem Sch	28
Ortlund, Christine/Hunting Ridge Elem Sch	43
Orwig, J/Jefferson Elem Sch	7
Osborne, Sally/Prairie Children Pre-Sch	95
Osiecki, Nilma/St Bartholomew Sch	74
Otte, Mike/Elim Christian Sch	78
Outlaw, Ramona/Harlan Community Academy HS	38
Overstreet, Cory/Kellogg Elem Sch	34
Owens, Brandon/Dwight Grade Sch	161
Owens, Jeff/Marseilles Elem Sch	142
Owens, Kristine/St Catherine of Alexandria Sch	74
Owens, Ray/Spring Creek Elem Sch	254
Owsley, Shane/Gillespie High Sch	167
Ozimek, Sandy/Algonquin Road Elem Sch	181

P

NAME/School	PAGE
Pacheco, Erica/Aspira Haugan Middle Sch [130]	39
Pacheco, Ronald/Manhattan Junior High Sch	244
Pacourek, Michael/James Shields Elem Sch	32
Padak, Sandy/Silver Creek Elem Sch	172
Paden, Quincy/Holy Trinity High Sch	73
Padera, Shirley/Alan B Shepard Elem Sch	134
Padilla, Krystle/Mark Bills Middle Sch	199
Pae, Joyce/Chicago Academy Elem Sch	25
Page, Gary/St Joseph-Ogden High Sch	12
Page, Natalie/Sesser-Valier High Sch	108
Pagel, Mark/Prairieview Elem Sch	90
Pagel, Robert/St Paul Lutheran Sch	209
Painter, Marc/Wheaton Christian Grammar Sch	102
Pala, Keri/Mary Endres Elem Sch	184
Palcer, Matthew/Marie Murphy Middle Sch	22
Palmer, Chelese/Riverdale Preschool Center	240
Palmer, Jake/Fisher Grade Sch	10
Palmer, S/John V Leigh Elem Sch	59
Palmer, Stephanie/James Giles Sch	59
Palz, Keith/Chicago Tech Academy HS	39
Panagakis, Ekaterini/Wacker Elem Sch	28
Panczyk, Eva/St Constance Sch	74
Panozzo, John/Shabonee Sch	59
Pantges, Richard/Corpus Christi Catholic Sch	187
Panzer, Jodie/Glenbrook North High Sch	51
Papagianis, Jean/Kilmer Elem Sch	29
Papierski, Michael/Highlands Middle Sch	54
Papp, Kelly/Greenman Elem Sch	132
Paquin, Dawn/Timber Trails Elem Sch	131
Parent, Mark/Dolan Ed Ctr-Durand Cud 322	252
Parker, Amanda/St Genevieve Sch	75
Parker, Amonaquenette/Huntley Middle Sch	84
Parker, Dave/Oblong Elem Sch	83
Parker, Don, Dr/Posen Intermediate Sch	63
Parker, James/Lincoln Middle Sch	254
Parker, James/Stevenson Middle Sch	57

Illinois School Directory — PRINCIPAL INDEX

NAME/School	PAGE
Parker, Philip/Glenview New Church Sch	78
Parrott, Rob/Warren Twp HS-Almond Campus	155
Pascavage, Darren, Dr/Academy High	13
Pascavage, Jason/Bolingbrook High Sch	248
Pastere, Cara/Lincoln-Gavin Elem Sch	25
Patchett, Jeff/Oblong High Sch	83
Pate, Craig/Regional Learning Center-Star	252
Patel, Sheela/Lake Shore Academy	158
Patera, Jason/Chicago Academy for the Arts	77
Patino, Carlos/W A Johnson Elem Sch	89
Patrick, Ron/East Moline Christian Sch	209
Patsiopoulos, Konstantinos/Holden Elem Sch	27
Patten, Marianne/Onahan Elem Sch	29
Patterson, Mechelle/C F Simmons Middle Sch	129
Patterson, Michael/Malden Elem Sch	7
Patterson, Reginald/Longwood Elem Sch	24
Paulette, Nancy/Calmeca Academy	32
Pauley, Lynn/L'Abris Academy	189
Paull, Laura/Mark Twain Elem Sch	34
Paulmeyer, Maureen/Prairie Junior High Sch	20
Paulson, Patricia/Parsons Accelerated Elem Sch	165
Pautler, Steven/St Mary Sch	176
Pavek, Adrienne/H H Conrady Junior High Sch	59
Paver-Nepote, Sharon/Wagoner Elem Sch	44
Pavichevich, Anna/Amundsen High Sch	26
Pawelczyk, Chris/Zion Benton Township High Sch	157
Payne, Amina/Independence Elem Sch	20
Payne, Bonnie/Victory Christian Academy	124
Payne, Melissa/Lisle Elem Sch	97
Payne, Patricia/Coolidge Middle Sch	68
Payne, Temple/Christ the King Jesuit Prep	77
Payne, Vincent/Colin Powell Middle Sch	47
Payton, Christopher/Mades-Johnstone Center	128
Pearce, Ed/British School of Chicago	77
Pearce, Jamison/Spring Wood Middle Sch	96
Pearce, Julie/Flora Elem Sch	16
Pearce, Toby/Flora High Sch	16
Pearlstein, Leah/Cedar Lubavitch Girls Sch	77
Pechacek, Roshune/Paec Elem Sch	20
Pegg, Sandra/Millstadt Cons Sch	220
Pegg, Sandra/Millstadt Primary Center	220
Pehlke, Robin/Glenbrook North High Sch	51
Peifer, Kristina/Morton Academy	227
Peifer, Kristina/Sugar Creek Elem Sch	187
Peila, Joseph/Chappell Elem Sch	27
Pekol, Jeana/Minooka Intermediate Sch	112
Pellillo, Marco/Grant Elem Sch	25
Peloquin, Jennifer/Palos West Elem Sch	61
Pena, Ruben/Hinsdale Middle Sch	91
Pennell, Margaret/Holy Family Sch	173
Pennock, Brandi/Western Junior High Sch	203
Peoples-Brown, Terea/Emmett Till Math & Sci Academy	33
Perez, Israel/Yates Elem Sch	31
Perez, Lourdes/Washington Dual Language Acad	57
Perez, Nicholas/Pathways In Educ-Brighton Park	41
Perez, Nicholas/Pathways In Educ-Humboldt Park	41
Perkins, Carmel/William Carter Elem Sch	26
Perrott, Audrey/Near North Montessori Sch	79
Perry, Christine/Julia S Molloy Ed Center	20
Perry, Gloria/Oliver Parks 6th Grade Center	218
Perry, Terrycita/Dixon Elem Sch	35
Pestrak, Regina/St Matthew Sch	101
Peters, Joe/West Central Middle Sch	116
Peters, Matthew/Lotus Elem Sch	149
Peters, Scott/Prairieland Elem Sch	187
Peterson, Jarrod/North Boone Upper Elem Sch	5
Peterson, Jeffrey/Rockdale Elem Sch	247
Peterson, Jodi/Woodland Elem Sch	162
Peterson, Jodi/Woodland High Sch	162
Peterson, Karen/Illini Bluffs Middle Sch	197
Peterson, Shari/Downers Grove Christian Sch	101
Petmezas, George/Mill Creek Elem Sch	131
Petties, Cederrall/Earle Elem Sch	34
Pettinga, Nate/Southwest Chicago Chrn Sch	81
Peyton, Ryan/Ruth M Schneider Elem Sch	87
Pfaff, Christine/Prairie Elem Sch	151
Pfanenstiel, Laura/Evergreen Elem Sch	89
Pfeffer, Julie/Crow Island Sch	72
Pfleiger, Mark/Quincy Area Voc Tech Center	1
Phelan, Julie/Seymour Elem Sch	2
Phillips, Elroy/Success Academy	132
Phoenix, Anne/St Joseph Sch	158
Piatek, Larry/Churchill Elem Sch	137
Piatek, Larry/Troy-Orenic Intermediate Sch	248
Picchione, Michelle/St Joan of Arc Sch	101
Piedrahita, Gilberto/Jordan Community Sch	29
Pierce, Onquanette/Brookwood Middle Sch	24
Pierce, Scot/Scarlet Oak Elem Sch	21
Piet, Jean/Aero Special Education Center	20
Pietrantoni, Josh/Johnston City High Sch	251
Pietrantoni, Josh/Washington Elem Mid Sch	251
Pietroski, Christopher/Jay Stream Middle Sch	90
Pietrzak, Lindsay/Manning Elem Sch	92
Pignatiello, Bret/Liberty Intermediate Sch	134
Pike, Mariam, Dr/Wolcott Sch	81
Pilger, Joe/Lincoln Early Childhood Sch	234
Pilkington, Jon/Hubble Middle Sch	92
Pilut, Mark/Carl Sandburg Middle Sch	153
Pinciak, Robert/Oak View Elem Sch	248
Pinter, Nate/Jefferson Elem Sch	143
Piper, Christopher/Eastview Elem Sch	109
Piper, David/YCCS-Assoc House	41
Pirtle, Sherry/Alex Haley Academy	35
Pisano, Joe/Forest Park Middle Sch	50
Pitcher, Jessica/Robeson Elem Sch	10
Pittenger, Andrew/Dwight High Sch	161
Pittington, Michele/Benjamin Franklin Elem Sch	207
Pittman, Chris/Spring Grove Elem Sch	183
Piwnicki, Larry/Livingston Co Crossroads Acad	160
Piwowarski, Richard/Resurrection College Prep HS	74
Planeta, Tracy/Grant Park Elem Sch	135
Plath, Donna/Grass Lake Elem Sch	150
Plaza, Jessica/Orrington Elem Sch	48
Plenert, Denise/Pontiac Christian Sch	163
Plocher, Catherine/Burley Elem Sch	26
Plourde, Mike/Willowbrook Middle Sch	253
Pluister, Chris/Unity Christian Sch	240
Plummer, Brian/Milligan Academy Safe Sch	164
Pluskota, James/Edison Elem Sch	93
Poalson, Tracey/Youthbuild McLean Co CS	1
Podraza, Christina/Jefferson Elem Sch	94
Poelker, Todd/Lincoln Cmty High Sch	163
Poelking, Lori/Copeland Manor Elem Sch	153
Poepping, Summer/Westfield Sch	156
Pohlmann, Elizabeth/Reba O Steck Elem Sch	96
Poirot, Jennifer/Wolf Branch Middle Sch	222
Pokora, Jon, Dr/Waterbury Elem Sch	96
Pokorny Lyp, Arwen/Hinsdale South High Sch	95
Polega, Maryanne/Ascension Sch	72
Policht, Joanne/St John the Baptist Sch	101
Polk, Candace/Coram Deo Classical Sch	124
Pollack, Joel/Creekside Elem Sch	130
Pollard, Docilla/Carnegie Elem Sch	26
Pollock, Rovel/Marquette Elem Sch	26
Polson, Teresa/Jane Addams Middle Sch	248
Polt, Amy/Jtc Academy East	223
Polt, Amy/Jtc Academy West	223
Poole, Jammie/John Marshall Metro High Sch	37
Poole, Kim/Rochester Junior High Sch	212
Poole, Tammy/Maple Elem Sch	253
Pope, Jason/Bottenfield Elem Sch	10
Popejoy, Drew/Rockford Christian High Sch	256
Porch, Danielle/Caldwell Elem Acad of Math-Sci	26
Porod, Greg/St Cletus Sch	74
Porreca, Kathleen/Regina Dominican High Sch	74
Porrey, Joseph/George T Wilkins Jr High Sch	53
Porsche, Brittany/Lakewood Sch	180
Porte, Elizabeth/Unity Christian Sch	137
Porten, Raymond/Indian Hill Elem Sch	155

PRINCIPAL INDEX

NAME/School	PAGE
Porter, Adrienne/Menta Academy Chicago West	79
Porter, Betsy/Edison Elem Sch	232
Porter, Jeffrey/Mann Elem Sch	35
Porter, Sauda/Perspectives CS-Joslin [166]	41
Portillo, Rosalva/Lincoln-Irving Elem Sch	208
Portwood, Mark/Cissna Park Sch	118
Portz, Travis/Ramsey Grade Sch	106
Posey, Stephanie/Naperville North High Sch	98
Postma, John/Lansing Christian Sch	79
Potempa, Kiara/Trusting Hearts Pre-Sch & Kdgn	81
Potenza, Darlene/St Zachary Sch	76
Potter, Carol/St Joseph Sch	206
Potthoff, Marsha/McHenry West High Sch	183
Powell, Cory/Chaddock Sch	3
Powell, Debbie/St John the Baptist Sch	109
Powell, Eron/Perspectives CS-HS of Tech [166]	41
Powell, Eron/Perspectives CS-Ldrship Acad [166]	41
Powell, Jessica/Gifted Acad Marshall ES	254
Powell, Pamela/Empire Elem Sch	224
Powell, Pamela/Richton Square Sch	57
Powers, Joseph, Dr/Jones College Prep Sch	27
Powers, Kim/The Governor French Academy	223
Powley, Kaela/St John Lutheran Sch	206
Prado, Kathleen/Central Middle Sch	49
Prairie, Brad/Kankakee Trinity Academy	137
Prange, Robert/Johns Hill Magnet Sch	165
Pratl, Charlotte/St George Sch	75
Prentiss, Nicole/J B Nelson Elem Sch	128
Pressler, Michael, Dr/Maine East High Sch	56
Price, Brian/George Washington Elem Sch	208
Price, Duane/Bureau Valley High Sch	6
Price, Kathy/Brownsville Attendance Center	238
Price, Keith/North Clay Cmty High Sch	16
Price, Kim/Glen Crest Middle Sch	90
Prickett, Jeff/McHenry East High Sch	183
Prikkel, Tim/Robert Frost Elem Sch	71
Pritchard, Scott/Lincoln Sch	241
Probst, Beth/Jasper Co Junior High Sch	122
Probst, Beth/Newton Cmty High Sch	122
Profita, Natalie/Sorrick Sch	59
Prola, Andrea/Butler Junior High Sch	89
Prorok, Daniel/Liberty Elem Sch	61
Prosen, Chad/Brook Forest Elem Sch	89
Prosise, Roger/Joseph Sears Sch	53
Protz, Randy/Vandalia Cmty High Sch	106
Provis, Steve/Lincoln-Way Central High Sch	244
Prunkard, Lindsey/South View Upper Elem Sch	232
Prunkard, Lindsey/Southwest Elem Sch	232
Pruski, Christine/James R Wood Elem Sch	86
Pryce, Amanda/Lyon Magnet Elem Sch	156
Ptak, Megan/Jefferson Junior High Sch	98
Puetz, Patricia/Henking Primary Sch	51
Pugh, Nathan/Mattoon Middle Sch	19
Pulido, Alex/St Mary Sch	173
Pullum, Toyia/John Foster Dulles Elem Sch	26
Pulse, Stephanie/Summit Elem Sch	170
Purpura, Glenn/Kingswood Academy	102
Purse, Kathleen/Indian Trail Jr High Sch	88
Pusatcioglu, Heather/Piccolo Sch of Excellence	26
Pusateri, Tom/Hartgrove Academy	78
Puttin, Mike/Holy Cross Catholic Sch	133

Q

NAME/School	PAGE
Quadri, Habeeb/Mcc Acad-Morton Grove Campus	79
Quadri, Habeeb/Mcc Academy-Skokie Campus	79
Quain, Debora/Kankakee Area Co-op Day Sch	134
Qualls, Kim/Cary Junior High Sch	179
Quam, Brian/El Paso-Gridley High Sch	257
Quinlan, Bryan/Monroe Elem Sch	30
Quintana, Erma/New Life Christian Sch	80
Quintana, Hector/Salem Christian Sch	80
Quirk, Amber/Westview Hills Middle Sch	97

R

NAME/School	PAGE
Rabe, Sarah/Centennial Elem Sch	130
Racasi, Diana/Pulaski Int'l Sch of Chicago	32
Rademacher, Brent/Bhra High Sch	231
Rader, Donnell/Beasley Elem Mgnt Academic Ctr	33
Radke, Carey/Arnold W Kruse Ed Center	42
Raffel, David/Morris Grade Sch	113
Raffen, Tammy/Harbor Academy	20
Rahm, James/New Baden Elem Sch	18
Rahm, Kerrick/Beckemeyer Elem Sch	17
Rahm, Kerrick/Carlyle Grade Sch	17
Raine, Janelle/Ridge Circle Elem Sch	131
Rainey, Bryan/Carlyle Junior High Sch	17
Rakers, Jason/Pocahontas Elem Sch	4
Rakers, Nathan/Whiteside Elem Sch	222
Ramirez, Consuelo/Thomas Jefferson Elem Sch	243
Ramirez, Sergio/George Washington Elem Sch	36
Ramos, Dan/Kiefer Sch	200
Ramos, Dawn/Tilden Career Community Acad	38
Ramsey, Michele/Early Learning Center	43
Ramseyer, Dean/Light House Academy	200
Randle-Robbins, Evelyn/Arnold Mireles Academy	35
Rangel, Berenice/Academy for Global Citizenship	38
Rapacz, Kara/Sacred Heart-Griffin High Sch	214
Rapinchuk, Craig/Parkview Christian Academy	139
Rasar, Mark/Holmes Junior High Sch	43
Raspante, Christopher/Bridge View Extended Day Sch	77
Raspante, Christopher/Challenger Day Sch	77
Rassi, Nic/Cornerstone Christian Academy	188
Rath, Jennifer/Canty Elem Sch	28
Ratliff, Tony/Thornton Township High Sch	69
Ratner, Tracey/Longwood Elem Sch	95
Rawls, Shaka/Leo High Sch	73
Ray, Karren/Northside Learning Center	36
Rayburn, Terrie/Dvorak Tech Academy ES	26
Rea, Diana/Duquoin Elem Sch	201
Read, Amy/Herrick Middle Sch	93
Reagan, Robert/Cambridge Cmty Jr Sr High Sch	116
Reardon, Jared/Taft Sch	247
Reavis, D/Norris City-Omaha Elem Sch	238
Reavis, Denise/St Aloysius Catholic Sch	214
Rebolledo, Marilou/Andrew Jackson Language Acad	31
Redmond, Daniel/Durkin Park Elem Sch	34
Redmond, Treveda/	254
Reed, Bill/Athens High Sch	188
Reed, Jeff/Rochester Elem Sch 2-3	212
Reed, Jeff/Rochester Elem Sch EC-1	212
Reed, Lakita/Cuffe Math Science Tech Acad	34
Reeder, Gina/Churchville Middle Sch	93
Reedy, Kevin/North Elem Sch	191
Reedy, Kevin/St Germaine Sch	75
Rees, Ben/Alwood Jr Sr High Sch	116
Rees, Dan/Good Shepherd Lutheran Sch	229
Reeves, Brian/Columbia High Sch	190
Regul, Nancy/Parkview Elem Sch	180
Reich, Elizabeth/Serena Hills Elem Sch	49
Reichart, Kaitlin/Our Lady of Grace Sch	73
Reichert, Lanee/Unity West Elem Sch	12
Reid, Erin/Robert A Jamieson Sch	199
Reid, Tonisia/Sanders Academy of Excellence	80
Reid, Tonisia/Sanders Academy-Excellence	80
Reidy, Catherine/Mt Greenwood Elem Sch	27
Rein, Mary/Harry E Fry Elem Sch	24
Reincke, Angela/Sleepy Hollow Elem Sch	180
Reinecke, Ryan/Rock Cut Elem Sch	253
Reingruber, Kristin/Glen Oaks Elem Sch	59
Reingruber, Kristin/Monroe Elem Sch	91
Reinhardt, Michelle/Edgebrook Elem Sch	183
Reinke, Dawn/Winfield Central Sch	100
Reinke, Dawn/Winfield Primary Sch	100
Reisner, Jessica/Tarkington Sch of Excellence	26
Reiss, Michelle/Edinburg Cmty Unit Sch	14
Reith, Heidi/St John Vianney Sch	75

Illinois School Directory — PRINCIPAL INDEX

NAME/School	PAGE
Rekruciak, Ryan/Elwood Cmty Cons Sch	242
Renas, Edward/Annunciata Elem Sch	72
Renaud, Matt/Raccoon Sch	175
Renier, Mindy/Traughber Junior High Sch	138
Renth, Beth/Worden Elem Sch	171
Renzaglia-Weir, Mary Jo/Perandoe Ed Program Red Bud	205
Reschke, Steve/Le Roy Jr Sr High Sch	186
Reschke, Steve/Le Roy Preparatory Academy	186
Reuter, Jodi/St Catherine Laboure Sch	74
Revelle, Kenyatta/Iles Sch	213
Reynolds, Amy/Shawnee Elem Sch	231
Reynolds, Carrie/Maroa Forsyth Grade Sch	165
Reynolds, Geneva/South Central Cmty Service	80
Reynolds, Kim/Galesburg Christian Sch	140
Reynolds, Michael/New Life Celebration Chrn Acad	80
Reynolds, Patricia/Walsh Elem Sch	32
Reynolds, Tim/Mt Vernon Christian Sch	124
Rhee, Joseph/Northridge Prep Sch	80
Rhoades, Matt/Athens Junior High Sch	188
Rhoads, Sean/Elizabeth Ide Elem Sch	90
Ricca, Ashley/Neil A Armstrong Elem Sch	227
Rice, Chris/Meade Park Elem Sch	232
Rice, Holly/St Paul's Lutheran Sch	119
Richards, Jack/Momence Junior High Sch	136
Richardson, Brenda/Southwood Middle Sch	45
Richardson, Brenda/Zenon Sykuta Elem Sch	45
Richardson, Jennifer/Mark Denman Elem Sch	232
Richardson, Mary/Velma Thomas Early Chldhd Ctr	28
Richardson, Tony/Wayne City Attendance Center	237
Richardson, Wytress, Dr/Oakdale Christian Academy	80
Richter, James/St Charles East High Sch	129
Richter, Mark/William J Attea Middle Sch	51
Rick, Brooke/Marquette Academy-High Sch	145
Rick, Brooke/Marquette Academy-St Columba	145
Ricken, Jeremy/Peter M Gombert Elem Sch	95
Ricketts, Tim/Reed-Custer High Sch	247
Riechmann, Susanne/Scott Elem Sch	220
Riechmann, Teena/Valmeyer Sch	190
Rieger, Lisa/St Viator Sch	76
Rieke, Angela/Wilson Aspire Sch	255
Rielly, Mark/Trico High Sch	121
Riff, Tim/Oriole Park Elem Sch	29
Rigling, Cindy/Gems World Academy	78
Rincker, Cody/St Anthony of Padua Sch	105
Rincker, Kent/Trinity Lutheran Sch	216
Riordan, Ann, Dr/Christ the King Sch	73
Riordan, Timothy/Hawthorne Elem Sch	94
Rios, Aaron/Serena High Sch	144
Rios, Aaron/Serena Middle Sch	144
Ripka, Deidre/Morton High Sch	227
Risdall, Emery/Calvary Christian Sch	249
Ritchey, John/Marshall High Sch	16
Ritchey, Tracy/Anne M Jeans Elem Sch	90
Ritter, Karen/Niles West High Sch	59
Rivara, Christian/Aux Sable Middle Sch	246
Riven, Jay/Peoria Academy	200
Rivera, Edith/Schafer Elem Sch	99
Rivera, Faith/Frank C Whiteley Elem Sch	43
Rivera, Gladys/Lowell Elem Sch	31
Rivera, Stefanie/Roycemore Sch	80
Robaidek, Irene/Guardian Angel Orthodox Sch	78
Robbins, Joe/Morrison Junior High Sch	239
Robbins, Mandy/Glen Carbon Elem Sch	171
Roberts, Kari/Winola Elem Sch	189
Roberts, Kim/Blackhawk Elem Sch	97
Roberts, Kurt/Effingham High Sch	105
Roberts, Lewis/Gemini Middle Sch	47
Roberts, Regina/Sherman Elem Sch	26
Robertson, Angie/Pleasant Valley Elem Sch	199
Robertson, Bill, Dr/Creston Elem Sch	194
Robertson, Cathy/St Mary Sch	15
Robertson, Michelle/McClernand Elem Sch	213
Robinette, James/Congress Park Elem Sch	54
Robinette, James/Two-Way Language Imm-Barbour	255
Robinson, Brandi/Highland Prekindergarten	25
Robinson, Janelle/St Mary's Sch	206
Robinson, Leigh/East Alton-Wood River Cmty HS	170
Robinson, Melissa/New Horizons Alternative Sch	109
Robinson, Molly/Acero CS-Ines De La Cruz [156]	38
Robinson, Patrick/Whittier Elem Sch	61
Robinson, Ryan/Grand Prairie Elem Sch	123
Robinson, Ryan/Patoka Cmty Sch	175
Robinson, Tiffany/Lowrie Elem Sch	131
Robinzine, John/Center for Academics & Tech	69
Robison, Mr/Brimfield High Sch	196
Robles, Nelly/Sawyer Elem Sch	33
Robyn, Timmerman/Tyler Elem Sch	85
Roche, Erin/Prescott Elem Sch	31
Rodebaugh, Jeremy/Cerro Gordo Jr Sr High Sch	202
Rodewald, Gina/Gower West Elem Sch	95
Rodgers, Laura/Roosevelt Magnet Sch	199
Rodrigo, Michael/Wayne Thomas Elem Sch	154
Rodrigues, Astrid/Americana Elem Sch	98
Rodriguez, Anthony/Schurz High Sch	36
Rodriguez, Armando/C M Bardwell Elem Sch	129
Rodriguez, Armando/Sarah E Goode STEM Academy	37
Rodriguez, Diana/Nixon Elem Sch	30
Rodriguez, Gladys/John S Clark Elem Sch	156
Rodriguez, Jacqueline/Lowell Elem Sch	92
Rodriguez, Kathy/Charter Oak Primary Sch	199
Rodriguez, Sarah/Abraham Lincoln Elem Sch	94
Rodriguez, Sherri/Melrose Park Elem Sch	57
Roekle, David/Good Shepherd Lutheran Sch	102
Roer, Matt/Clark Elem Sch	255
Rogers, Brian/World Language Academy	37
Rogers, Deb/A-C Central Elem Sch	9
Rogers, Jeanine/General George Patton Elem Sch	50
Rogers, Keir/Newcomer Center	70
Rogers, Keir/River Trails Middle Sch	65
Rogers, Michelle/South Fork Elem Sch	15
Rogers, Stacey/Olympia South Elem Sch	187
Rogers, Thomas/Geneva High Sch	131
Rogers, Todd/Carterville High Sch	250
Rohlfing, Mark/Pinckneyville Jr High Sch	201
Rohlman, Connie/Founders Elem Sch	84
Rohlwing, Susan/Josephine Perry Elem Sch	180
Rojas, David/Reskin Elem Sch	97
Rojas, Rodolfo/Everett Elem Sch	32
Roketenetz, Margaret/St John Berchmans Sch	75
Rolinitis, Michael/Mokena Junior High Sch	245
Rollerson, Tricia/John Lukancic Middle Sch	248
Rollins, Glenn/Lutheran High Sch	214
Roman, Evelyn/Avondale-Logandale Sch	30
Romano, Barbara/Barrington Early Learning Ctr	147
Rombouts, Saskia/Academy for Global Citizenship	38
Ronen, Shonda/Wolf Ridge Elem Jr High Sch	167
Rongey, David/West Sch	51
Root, Suzi/Maple Elem Sch	232
Root, William/Berean Christian Sch	223
Rosales, Rocio/Nathan S Davis Elem Sch	33
Roscetti, Nick/Routt Catholic High Sch	193
Roscoe, Jim, Dr/Grayslake North High Sch	150
Rose, Sara/South Central Elem Sch	176
Rosenbery, Nancy/Washington Elem Sch	202
Rosentreter, Jill/Gillespie High Sch	167
Rosentreter, Jill/Gillespie Middle Sch	167
Ross, Antonio/Hyde Park Academy High Sch	38
Ross, Keli/Memorial Junior High Sch	55
Ross, Marilynn/Lewis Elem Sch	120
Ross, Scott/Margaret Mead Jr High Sch	66
Rossman, Teri/Dimmick Cmty Cons 175 Sch	141
Rothermel, Marie/Seth Paine Elem Sch	152
Roundtree, Jaime/B T Washington STEM Acad	10
Rouse, Nathaniel/Oak Park & River Forest HS	60
Rouse, Steven/Carver Military Academy	38
Rowe, Kaleb/Menta Academy Belleville	223
Rowe, Pam/Millbrook Junior High Sch	138
Rowe, Pam/Newark Elem Sch	138
Roy, Jocelyne/Four Winds Sch	101

PRINCIPAL INDEX

NAME/School	PAGE
Royster, Aaron/YCCS-Youth Dev Inst HS	41
Rozanski, Chris/Boylan Central Cath High Sch	256
Rua, Lissette/Wildwood IB World Magnet Sch	29
Rubin, Jody/Jeanine Schultz Mem Sch	79
Ruch, Jacque/Easterseals Acad-MacHesney PK	256
Rucinski, Brian/Thornton Fractional North HS	69
Rucker, Aaron/Ryder Math & Sci Elem Sch	35
Rucker, Tiffany/Markham Park Elem Sch	63
Rude, Brody/Merrill Elem Sch	240
Rude, Thomas, Dr/St Libory Elem Sch	222
Rudunzel, Steven/Immanuel Lutheran Sch	158
Rufener, Shana/Durand Elem Sch	252
Ruff, Mike/Andalusia Elem Sch	209
Ruiz-Villa, Anna/Devry Univ Advantage Acad HS	27
Ruiz, Joel/Glen Flora Elem Sch	156
Ruiz, Maricela/Garfield Elem Sch	25
Rumler, Guy/Hutsonville Grade Sch	83
Rundall, Donald/Thomas Jefferson High Sch	254
Rush-Taylor, Felicia/Cahokia 8th Grade Center	218
Rusk, Teresa/Peoria Co Juvenile Det Center	197
Russel, Jennifer/Lindsay Elem Sch	213
Russell-Smith, Saundra/Sandburg Elem Sch	243
Russell, Cortnye/Wolfs Crossing Elem Sch	138
Russell, Dave/Fearn Elem Sch	132
Russell, Gail/Northlawn Junior High Sch	144
Russell, Megan/Charles J Caruso Middle Sch	149
Russell, Michelle/Team Englewood Cmty Academy HS	37
Russell, Terri/Gwendolyn Brooks Elem Sch	95
Rutan, Kimberley/Madison Elem Sch	91
Ruzinok, Thomas/Westfield Community Sch	180
Ryan, Daniel/Univ of Chicago Lab Sch	81
Ryan, Garrett/Prairie View Sch	86
Ryan, Thomas/Rock Island Academy	208
Ryan, Tommi/Spring Garden Middle Sch	124
Ryba, Missy/Farmington Central Elem Sch	197
Rybarczyk, Kari/St Bede Sch	158
Ryder, Amanda/Argenta Oreana Elem Sch	165
Ryner, Sara/La Harpe Elem Sch	115
Rzepka, Michelle/Hillcrest Elem Sch	93

S

NAME/School	PAGE
Saccaro, Lynne/Most Blessed Trinity Academy	157
Sadder, Maya/Ed White Elem Career Academy	36
Saenz, Brian/West Elem Sch	169
Sagan, Jillian/Elizabeth Blackwell Elem Sch	66
Sagel, Joseph/Madison Elem Sch	160
Sago, Melissa/Gwendolyn Brooks Elem Sch	84
Salamon, Erin/Roosevelt Elem Sch	25
Salberg, Erin/Nashold Early Childhood Center	254
Sale, Ellen/KIPP Bloom College Prep [163]	40
Saleem, Ubaid/Institute of Islamic Ed	133
Salness, Suzanne/Mill Street Elem Sch	98
Salter, Romeldia/George Pullman Elem Sch	36
Salto, Luis/McKinley Educational Center	42
Salzar, Jayme/Circuit Breaker Sch	141
Samber, Eli/Arie Crown Hebrew Day Sch	77
Sams, Jesse/Midland Elem Sch	176
San-Roman, Barbara/Washington High Sch	38
Sanchez, Jaime/North River Elem Sch	29
Sanders, Cynthia/Hoyleton Education Center	235
Sanders, Dayna/CICS-Basil [167]	39
Sanders, Kiwana/Nathan Hale Middle Sch	45
Sanders, Kristi/Heritage Elem Sch	11
Sanders, Leonetta/Harper High Sch	37
Sanders, Sara/Franklin Middle Sch	10
Sanders, Trista/Moline Senior High Sch	208
Sanderson, William/Evergreen Park Cmty High Sch	49
Sandoval, Dawn/Catalyst CS-Maria [159]	39
Sandoval, Laura/Edna M Rollins Elem Sch	129
Sandretto, Angela/Ben-Gld Elem Sch	167
Sanlin, Tracie/Chicago Collegiate Charter Sch	39
Santellano, Sally/St John De LaSalle Academy	75
Santelle, Cathy/Woodview Sch	148
Santen, Patsy/St Vincent De Paul Sch	200
Santos, Melissa/All Saints Catholic Academy	100
Sarff, Mary/St Joseph Sch	229
Sartain, Kyle/Hufford Junior High Sch	243
Sasso, Larry/Thomas Jefferson Elem Sch	43
Satterlee, Nick/SS Peter & Paul Sch	184
Saucedo, Raquel/Chase Elem Sch	30
Saunders, Michael/Ward Grundy Elem Sch	227
Saunders, Ralph/Midwestern Christian Academy	79
Sauri, Judith/Edwards Elem Sch	27
Sauter, Larry/Highland Christian Academy	133
Savage, Susan/Robert Frost Elem Sch	44
Sawisch, Melissa/Kingsley Elem Sch	93
Saygo, Latrica/Beautiful Beginnings	256
Sayre, Jake/West View Elem Sch	255
Scaletta, Paul/Goodrich Elem Sch	100
Scanlan, Eileen/Cassell Elem Sch	26
Scarpino, Joe/St Mary Sch	139
Schaaf, Kelly/St Agatha Sch	222
Schacherer, Stephen/St Norbert Sch	76
Schaefer, Judy/Immanuel Lutheran Sch	5
Schaefer, Karen/Shawnee Jr Sr High Sch	231
Schaefer, McLain/Arland D Williams Elem Sch	19
Schafermeyer, Jeffery/Walker's Grove Elem Sch	246
Schafermeyer, Kathryn/Whittier Elem Sch	92
Schaffer, Lisa/Oak Crest Elem Sch	147
Schaffer, Lisa/Scott Elem Sch	57
Schamberger, Joyce/Amboy Central Elem Sch	159
Schardet, Wendy/Tri-County Christian Sch	225
Scheffler, Lynne/St Joseph Sch	249
Schelker, Amy/Rock Island Ctr Math & Science	208
Scheller, Karrie/Mt Olive Elem Jr HS	168
Schemidt, Jennifer/William Beye Elem Sch	61
Schenk, Tina/Tripp Elem Sch	147
Scherencel, Fawn/Hinsdale Adventist Academy	102
Schergen, Thomas/De La Salle Institute	73
Schipper, Kathleen/River Bend Middle Sch	239
Schissler, Emily/Cherry Hill Elem and ECC	245
Schissler, Paul/Augustin Lara Elem Acad	32
Schlicher, Holly/Thomas Dooley Elem Sch	67
Schlie, Angela/Immanuel Lutheran Sch	102
Schlueter, Kelly/Transitions Sch	3
Schluter, Kelly/Chrisman Elem Sch	103
Schmale, Travis/Breese Elem Sch	17
Schmeisser, Hal/East Prairie Elem Sch	47
Schmersahl, Lacey/Marissa Elem Sch	220
Schmid, Cj/Robert Frost Jr High Sch	67
Schmid, Keeley/Brookdale Elem Sch	95
Schmidt, Jeremy/Grant Cmty High Sch	150
Schmitt, Julie/Peru Catholic Sch	145
Schmitt, Kyle/St Francis De Sales Sch	158
Schmitt, Monica, Dr/Lincoln-Way West High Sch	244
Schmitt, Nathan/Kaneland Harter Middle Sch	132
Schmittler, Dale/West Salem Elem Sch	104
Schmitz, Amy/United High Sch	234
Schmitz, Stephanie/Edward J Tobin Elem Sch	24
Schnable, Kevin/McCarty Elem Sch	95
Schneider, Chuck/Tonica Grade Sch	145
Schneider, Dave/Mississippi Valley Chrn Sch	173
Schneider, Deitt/St John Lutheran Sch	206
Schneider, Scott/Illini West High Sch	114
Schneiderman, Jonathan/Forreston Grade Sch	194
Schneiderman, Jonathan/German Valley Grade Sch	194
Schnitzler, Roger/Manteno High Sch	136
Schnoor, Sara/Churchill Elem Sch	52
Schnowske, Tod/Plainfield Academy	246
Schooler, Bruce/St Angela Sch	74
Schooley, Jack/Wilson Elem Sch	171
Schoonover, Angela/Edison Middle Sch	10
Schoonover, Geoff/Cornell Grade Sch	161
Schorr, Diane/Joseph Academy-Melrose Park	79
Schrader, Ryan/West Elem Sch	86
Schrand, Melanie/Rooney Elem Sch	2

Illinois School Directory

PRINCIPAL INDEX

NAME/School	PAGE
Schrank, Cory/Flinn Middle Sch	254
Schrank, Dustin/Central Junior High Sch	227
Schrantz, Colleen/Josephinum Academy	73
Schreiber, Jill/Prairie View Grade Sch	128
Schroeder, Kristen/Hadley Middle Sch	242
Schroeder, Kristi/Maplewood Elem Sch	218
Schroeder, Lucas/Cristo Rey Jesuit High Sch	78
Schroff, A/C B Smith Primary Sch	228
Schuchman, Becky, Dr/Carlinville Intermediate Sch	167
Schuckman, Julie/Quincy Early Childhood	2
Schuenke, Cynthia/Early Childhood Center	169
Schulte, David/Irvington Elem Sch	235
Schultz, Julie/Reavis High Sch	64
Schulz, Robert/Shiloh Park Elem Sch	157
Schulze, Derek/Woodrow Wilson Elem Sch	227
Schumacher, Alison/Helen Huffman Elem Sch	218
Schumacher, Alison/Webster Elem Sch	170
Schumacher, Curt/Goshen Elem Sch	171
Schumacher, Heather/Barbara B Rose Elem Sch	147
Schupp, Duane/Lowpoint-Washburn Elem Sch	258
Schupp, Duane/Lowpoint-Washburn Middle Sch	258
Schurman, Robert/Ulysses S Grant Middle Sch	213
Schurman, Tim/Chadwick Elem Jr High Sch	8
Schuster, Ken/Lincolnwood Jr Sr High Sch	191
Schuster, Ken/Raymond Grade Sch	191
Schuth, Daniel, Dr/Devonshire Elem Sch	67
Schwab, Nancy/St Rose Sch	249
Schwalenberg, Geoff/Douglas Sch	217
Schwalenberg, Geoffrey/Westhaven Sch	217
Schwardt, Jennifer, Dr/Horizon Elem Sch	130
Schwartz, Cassandra/Apollo Elem Sch	47
Schwartz, Edward/South High Sch	91
Schwartz, Elise/Carlinville Primary Sch	167
Schwartz, Erica/St Peter Catholic Sch	256
Schwartz, Erik/Westminster Christian Sch	134
Schwartz, Joe/Eswood Cmty Cons Grade Sch	194
Schwartz, Nicholas/Waterloo Junior High Sch	190
Schwarz, Christopher/United Junior High Sch	235
Schwarze, Janice/North High Sch	91
Scifo, Jenna/St Paul Early Childhood Ctr	81
Scotkovsky, Catherine/St Juliana Sch	75
Scott, Gerald/Creative Communications Acad	46
Scott, Jamar/Hazel Dell Elem Sch	213
Scott, Ryan/Main Street Elem Sch	216
Scott, Shirley/Edward Ellington Elem Sch	30
Seaney, Adam/Rowva Jr Sr High Sch	140
Sebastian, Joylynn/Western Trails Elem Sch	90
Sedam, Tim/Mercer County Jr High Sch	189
Seegmiller, Steffanie/Arthur Lovington High Sch	88
Seelman, Amy, Dr/William Holliday Elem Sch	221
Seest, Ken/First Baptist Christian Sch	233
Sefcik, Jeff/Stanton Middle Sch	149
Segura, Joshua/John Jay Elem Sch	44
Seibel, Kevin/Elmwood Park Early Chldhd Ctr	48
Sell, Patrick/Mossville Jr High & Elem Sch	197
Sem, Ines/C I Johnson Elem Sch	129
Senior, Keith/Okawville Jr Sr High Sch	236
Sennhoplz, Helen/Instituto Justice Ldrshp Acad	39
Seoane, Jennifer/Lake Louise Elem Sch	43
Sepich, Dominic/Maercker Intermediate Sch	97
Seput, James/Plano High Sch	138
Serdar, Robert/George T Wilkins Elem Sch	53
Sergeant, Aneesa/Univ of Chicago CS-Nko	41
Session, Nicole/Robbie M Lightfoot ELC	156
Sessler, Akemi/Dryden Elem Sch	21
Setaro, Fran/Ridge Lawn Elem Sch	42
Sever, Carla/St Bruno Sch	74
Severson, Shane/Seneca South Elem Sch	144
Seykora, Jennifer/Meehan Elem Sch	4
Shabazz, Fareeda/Richard T Crane Med Prep HS	37
Shabazz, Rashid/Wadsworth Elem Sch	28
Shackelford, Zataya/CICS-Chicago Quest [160]	39
Shaner, Marc/Central High Sch	118
Shannon, Venus/Zion Central Middle Sch	157
Sharp, Corey/Beverly Manor Sch	226
Sharpe, Lekenya/Collins Academy	25
Shay, Kyle/Mayo Middle Sch	103
Shea, Victoria/Keystone Montessori Sch	79
Sheedy, Eileen/Our Lady of the Snows Sch	73
Sheedy, Eileen/Santa Lucia Grammar Sch	74
Sheffler, Shelly/Brown Co Elem Sch	5
Sheldon, Timothy/Ideal Elem Sch	54
Sheldon, Timothy/Southeast Elem Sch	49
Shelton-Montez, Michael/Catholic Children's Home Sch	173
Shelton, Kevin/Johnsburg High Sch	182
Shelton, Tara/South Loop Elem Sch	28
Shepard, Lori/St Francis Solanus Sch	3
Shepherd, Dave/Hillcrest Elem Sch	146
Shepherd, David/Antioch Elem Sch	146
Shepherd, Harold/Hanover Countryside Elem Sch	130
Shepherd, Jim/Schuyler-Industry Middle Sch	215
Shermak, Timothy/Oakbrook Elem Sch	100
Sherman, David, Dr/South Park Elem Sch	149
Sherrod, Daphne/Howe School of Excellence	26
Sherwin, Donald/Marquette Manor Baptist Acad	102
Shillinger, Jeff/Matherville Intermediate Sch	189
Shimmin, Larry/United Twp Area Career Center	209
Shimon, Sandra/Prosser Career Academy	37
Shipman, Doreen/St Patrick Sch	229
Shlensky, Alyssa/Mark Twain Elem Sch	71
Shoaff, Matthew/Okaw Valley High Sch	193
Shobert, Ron/Peoria Christian Sch	200
Shockley, Shannon/Nathan Hale Elem Sch	68
Shoemaker, Kimberly/Cypress Elem Sch	127
Shook, Lynn/Stevenson Elem Sch	185
Shores, South/South Shores Elem Sch	165
Short, Carolyn/Watseka Cmty High Sch	119
Shoufer, Jacie/Riverton Elem Sch	212
Shoufler, Clay/Williamsville Junior High Sch	214
Shoufler, Clay/Williamsville Middle Sch	214
Showers, Leslie/Stillman Valley High Sch	195
Shull, Laura/Project Help-Arcola	19
Shuman, Samantha/Piper Elem Sch	23
Sick, Timothy/Norte Dame De La Salette Acad	233
Sidarous, Matt/Midway Elem Sch	171
Sidarous, Matthew/Hamel Elem Sch	171
Siegellak, Jason/Washington Elem Sch	156
Siemer, Phil/Southwest Chicago Chrn Sch	81
Signatur, John/Bartlett Elem Sch	130
Signatur, John/Hodgkins Elem Sch	54
Sigrist, Lisa/Arcola Jr Sr High Sch	87
Sikich, Rosanne/Elsie Johnson Elem Sch	90
Sikora, Brad/Oak Forest High Sch	23
Silva, Roberto/Carman-Buckner Elem Sch	156
Silva, Theresa/Lincoln Elem Sch	56
Simmons-Kenser, Angela/Cuba Elem Sch	109
Simmons, Kevin/Prairie Trail Sch	150
Simms, Renee/Hillcrest High Sch	23
Simon, Angelique/Liberty Elem Sch	232
Simon, Pamela, Dr/Holy Trinity Catholic Sch	100
Simpkins, Kristin/Ardmore Elem Sch	99
Simpson, Deana/Monroe Center Elem Sch	195
Simpson, Jay/St Jacob Elem Sch	172
Simpson, John/East Aurora High Sch	129
Simpson, Nicole/YCCS-Scholastic Achievement	41
Simpson, Steve/Indian Creek Middle Sch	85
Sims, Angela/Ted Lenart Regional Gifted Ctr	28
Sims, Sharnette/Consuela B York Alt High Sch	37
Sims, Sonya/Springfield Christian Sch	214
Sims, Tyese/Bradwell School of Excellence	26
Sims, Vernita/Ft Dearborn Elem Sch	34
Simunovic, Darko/Noble CS-Mansueto High Sch [165]	40
Singleton, Patrina/Ravenswood Elem Sch	28
Sinovich, Samantha/Southbury Elem Sch	138
Sirianni, Darren/East Dubuque Junior Senior HS	125
Sisil, Jessica/Palestine Grade Sch	83
Sisson, Gordon/John Hersey High Sch	70
Skaggs, Julie/Cambridge Lakes Charter Sch	180
Skanes, Femi/Morgan Park High Sch	37

School Year 2020-2021   800-333-8802   IL-U29

PRINCIPAL INDEX

Market Data Retrieval

NAME/School	PAGE	NAME/School	PAGE
Skarzynski, Shelly/Wood Dale Junior High Sch	100	Snyder, Matt/Futures Unlimited Sch	164
Skelly, Lisa/Fred Rodgers Magnet Academy	129	Soat, Ben/Galena Middle Sch	125
Skomer, Kevin/Louise White Elem Sch	128	Sobkoviak, Michelle/Milford Grade Sch	119
Skorburg, Jared/Prairiewood Elem Sch	184	Sodaro, Tom/Sandwich Cmty High Sch	86
Skorusa, Beata/Montessori Foundations Chicago	79	Sofios, Antigoni/West Ridge Elem Sch	28
Slate, Karen/New Beginnings Learning Acad	46	Sohn, Jim/Baldwin Elem Sch	2
Slaughter, Michael/Marquette Catholic High Sch	173	Sokolowski, Donna/Dewey Elem Sch	48
Slee, Cathy/Reed Elem Sch	249	Solis, Edward/Glenbrook North High Sch	51
Small, Amy/Joseph E Hill Education Center	48	**Sollars, Stacie**/Garfield Elem Sch	232
Smart-Pennix, Loukisha/Unity Christian Academy	81	Solomon, Rachel/Churchill Elem Sch	94
Smart, Patricia/St Anthony Pre-School	249	**Solomon, Theresa**/Wild Rose Elem Sch	129
Smiley, Michelle/Lincoln Elem Sch	251	**Sommer, Kristina**/Sangamon Valley Intermed Sch	166
Smith, Alicia/Nathan Hale Primary Sch	45	Sommer, Landon/Century Jr Sr High Sch	204
Smith, Anthony/Center Educational Opportunity	169	Sommer, Landon/Maple Grove Elem Sch	177
Smith, April/Center St Elem Sch	236	Sonntag, Griffin/Pleasantdale Middle Sch	62
Smith, Augusta/Barton Elem Sch	34	Sopko, Angela, Dr/Everett Elem Sch	152
Smith, Brian/Rogers Elem Sch	190	Sorg, Brian/Meadow View Elem Sch	246
Smith, Camille/Bridge High Sch	101	**Sorrells, Josh**/Triopia Jr Sr High Sch	192
Smith, Camille/Mansion Private Sch	102	Sossong, Vince/St Mary Sch	184
Smith, Candice, Dr/Holy Family Lutheran Sch	78	Sotiroff, Mary/St Luke's Christian Academy	139
Smith, Carrie/Christian Life Center Sch	256	Southerland, Gretchen/Washington McKinley Elem Sch	25
Smith, Charles/Infinity Math Sci & Tech HS	27	Spain, Kevin/Elverado Primary Sch	120
Smith, Christine/Walsh Elem Sch	45	Spallasso, Katie/Bristol Bay Elem Sch	139
Smith, Cornelia/LeClaire Elem Sch	171	Spang, Jason/Peotone High Sch	245
Smith, Deborah/Woodrow Wilson Elem Sch	24	Sparks, Rita/Gompers Junior High Sch	243
Smith, Diana/Old St Mary's Sch	73	Sparrow, Daniel/Quincy Junior High Sch	2
Smith, Doug/Pittsfield South Elem Sch	203	Spaulding, Sonya, Dr/E F Lindop Elem Sch	47
Smith, Elizabeth/Hill Elem Sch	132	Speer, Michael/Marine Elem Sch	172
Smith, Erica/Central Junior High Sch	1	Spells, Denise/St Ethelreda Sch	75
Smith, Erin/Iroquois West High Sch	119	Spence, Monica, Dr/Kellar Middle Sch	63
Smith, Jason/Village Elem Sch	155	**Spencer-Burks, Tasia**/Hope Academy Magnet Sch	165
Smith, Jay/Gifford Grade Sch	10	Spencer, Chris/Coal City High Sch	112
Smith, Jeff/Canton Middle Sch	130	Spencer, Cindy/Kansas Sch	103
Smith, Jennifer/Willow Grove Kindergarten	151	Sperling, Andrew/Lake Forest Country Day Sch	158
Smith, Joanne/Batavia High Sch	128	Speth, Kathleen/Disney II Mag Sch-Kedvale	36
Smith, Julie/Greenwood Elem Sch	184	Speth, Kathleen/Disney II Mag Sch-Lawndale	36
Smith, Kelly/Acero CS-Victoria Soto HS [156]	38	Spicer, Adam/Wilmington Middle Sch	249
Smith, Kenndell/Prairie Hills Jr High Sch	63	Spicer, Aron/North Clay Elem Jr High Sch	16
Smith, Kiandra/Katie Harper-Wright Elem Sch	219	Spicer, Nicole/Bronzeville Classical Elem Sch	33
Smith, Kristen/Home Elem Sch	56	Spicher, Sandra/Knapp School and Yeshiva	79
Smith, Lisa/St Dennis Sch	249	Spinka, Leon/Okawville Grade Sch	236
Smith, Marcus/Grayslake Middle Sch	148	Spittell, Ellen/Bright Futures Preschool	140
Smith, Marilynn/Winston Campus Elem Sch	43	Spitz, Carrie/Noble CS-Pritzker Clg Prep [165]	40
Smith, Martina/Carpentersville Middle Sch	180	Spitz, Sandy/Christ Lutheran High Sch	119
Smith, Matt/Bunker Hill High Sch	167	Spohn, Jean/St Mary-Dixon Sch	160
Smith, Michael/Gary D Jewel Middle Sch	132	Spranger, Kenneth/Wells Elem Sch	207
Smith, Michelle/Lake In the Hills Elem Sch	180	Spreitzer, Kathleen/Hometown Elem Sch	60
Smith, Ms/Nob Hill Elem Sch	63	Spring, Jason/Galesburg High School N	140
Smith, Olivia/Schneider Elem Sch	132	Springborn, Thomas/Prairie Du Rocher Elem Sch	205
Smith, Paul/St Michael Sch	76	Springer, Robyn/Chiaravalle Montessori Sch	77
Smith, Richard/Christian Fenger Academy HS	38	**Sromek, Guy**/Husmann Elem Sch	181
Smith, Ronda/Carrollton Grade Sch	111	Stachura, Marty/Irving Elem Sch	23
Smith, Sarah/Salt Creek Primary Sch	99	Stacy, Fred/Equality Christian Center	110
Smith, Sarah/Stella May Swartz Elem Sch	99	Stallion, Angela/Ranch View Elem Sch	98
Smith, Sean/Grande Park Elem Sch	137	Stamps, Tequila/Lincoln Primary EC Center	22
Smith, Shontell/Warren Elem Sch	35	Standberry, Barbara, Dr/United Ed Cultural Acad	81
Smith, Slyvia/Giant Steps	102	Stangler, Lucas/St Jude Sch	249
Smith, Tyrone/Emerson Elem Sch	57	Stanislao, Joseph/Roy Elem Sch	57
Smith, Venus/Prairie Oak Elem Sch	22	Stansbury, Jennifer/Pathways Academy	243
Smith, Venus/Steger Primary Center	68	Stark, Brian/Coleman Elem Sch	130
Smithers, Jacob/Jordan Catholic Sch	209	Stark, Jason/Washington Elem Sch	83
Smogor, Dave/Lake Park Elem Sch	89	Stark, Julie/Montini Catholic Sch	184
Smolinski, Erica, Dr/Clarence E Culver Sch	58	Starks, Demetra, Dr/Bronzeville Scholastic Inst	38
Smuda, Lori/Willow Springs Elem Sch	71	Starks, Kenyatta, Dr/Bloom High Sch	23
Smyth, Tom/Notre Dame Sch	101	Starks, Thomas/Jonesboro Elem Sch	230
Snider, Chris/Havana Junior High Sch	177	Starwalt, Wendy/Pleasant Acres Elem Sch	11
Snider, David/Collinsville High Sch	170	Stary, Matt/Sch Exp Arts & Lrng-Lombard	102
Snider, Justin/Somonauk Middle Sch	86	Stasi, Rita/St Joseph Sch	101
Snodgrass, Mark, Br/San Miguel Sch-Back Yard	80	Staszcuk, Shane/Our Lady of Mt Carmel Acad	73
Snow, Brad/Collinsville Middle Sch	170	Stauder, Mary/Garfield Elem Sch	50
Snowden, Mike/Carthage Primary Sch	114	Stavrou, Constance/Lincoln Middle Sch	67
Snyder, Carla/Romeoville Christian Academy	250	Stayma, Jennifer/Stepping Stone Sch	158
Snyder, Joseph/Zion Lutheran Sch	173	Stazelczyk, Kim/Peckwas Preparatory Academy	80

Illinois School Directory — PRINCIPAL INDEX

NAME/School	PAGE
Steel, Trenese, Dr/Estelle Sauget Sch of Choice	218
Steele, Michael/STEM Academy	46
Steele, Michael/Veterans Memorial Middle Sch	45
Steffen, Lisa, Dr/John T MaGee Middle Sch	155
Stein, Bradley/Terrace Elem Sch	46
Steinkamp, Randy/Devonshire Elem Sch	43
Steinke, Jody/Quincy Senior High Sch	2
Stelly, Tracey/Lavizzo Elem Sch	36
Stevens, Karen/Washington High Sch	229
Stevens, Kim/Wayne Builta Elem Sch	96
Stewart, Brice/Maroa Forsyth Sr High Sch	165
Stewart, Keith/Plt Middle Sch	239
Stewart, Keith/Prophetstown High Sch	239
Stewart, Lashawn/Je-Neir Elem Sch	136
Stewart, Leatha/Zenon Sykuta Elem Sch	45
Stewart, Selene/Hoffman Elem Sch	51
Stewart, Sherry/St Bede the Venerable Sch	74
Stewart, Stacy/Belmont-Cragin Elem Sch	26
Stewart, Steve/Mary Morgan Elem Sch	194
Stich, Adam/Hitch Elem Sch	29
Stiemsma, Jennifer/Allendale Sch	158
Still, James/Newark Cmty High Sch	138
Stimac, Matt/Eastwood Elem Sch	170
Stingily, Byron/Lincoln Elem Sch	46
Stingily, Byron/Lincoln Junior High Sch	46
Stipp, Jason/Waubonsie Valley High Sch	96
Stirnaman, Kevin/Dorris Intermediate Sch	170
Stochl, Amanda/Lincoln Prairie Sch	66
Stockey, William/Eagle Pointe Elem Sch	246
Stockman, Angela/Northmoor Primary Sch	199
Stoffers, Elisabeth/Hunt Club Elem Sch	137
Stokes, Gina/Tri-Co Education Center	229
Stokes, Mary/St Christina Sch	74
Stolle, Brenda/Aspira Chtr-Early College HS [130]	39
Stoller, Danny/Wauconda Middle Sch	155
Stone, Brandon/Lovington Grade Sch	88
Stone, Diann/Judah Prep Academy	229
Stone, Sy/Crab Orchard Sch	251
Stoneberg, Stephanie, Dr/Prince of Peace Sch	157
Stoneking, Nick/Raes East	139
Stosek, Michael/Wells Community Academy HS	37
Stotts, Eric/Central Elem Sch	1
Stouffer, Mary/Whiteside Area Career Center	238
Stout, Laura/Temple Christian Academy	210
Stovail-Brown, Katina/Jesse Owens Community Academy	36
Stover, Benjamin/Rockford Env Science Academy	254
Straight, Derek/Woodland Intermediate Sch	157
Strang, Patricia/St Mary Sch	86
Strang, Stephanie/Benjamin Franklin Elem Sch	165
Strating, Julie/Lexington Grade Sch	186
Stratton, Donald/Grigsby Intermediate Sch	171
Street, Shane/Liberty Junior High Sch	245
Streeter, Renita/Lynne Thigpen Elem Sch	243
Strehl, Pati/C Henry Bloom Elem Sch	254
Streit, John/Roanoke-Benson Jr High Sch	258
Strenger, Stephanie/Walden Elem Sch	149
Strite, Gardell/Orchardville Mennonite Sch	237
Strong, Doelynn/Holmes Elem Sch	51
Strong, Scott/St Anne Elem Sch	136
Stroud, Sara/Alleman High Sch	209
Strouss, Jeff/Hinckley Big Rock Middle Sch	85
Struna, Michael/Deer Park Elem Sch	141
Stuart, Richard/Mattoon High Sch	19
Stuart, Steve, Dr/Edwardsville High Sch	171
Stumpenhorst, Lindsy/Challand Middle Sch	240
Stumpf, Andy/Winchester Elem Sch	215
Stumps, Andy/Brussels High Sch	8
Sturgill, Mary/Westmoor Elem Sch	59
Stutts, Cory/Catherine Cook Sch	77
Suchy, Jean/Emerson Elem Sch	23
Suggs, Ilethea/Glen Oak Cmty Learning Center	199
Sukenik, Ivy/Sunset Ridge Elem Sch	68
Sullivan, Jim/Casey-Westfield Jr Sr High Sch	15
Sullivan, Katie/Immaculate Cncpton St Joseph	73
Sullivan, Kellee/Edison Elem Sch	178
Sullivan, Matthew/Wendell Phillips Academy HS	26
Sullivan, Scott/Macomb Jr Sr High Sch	178
Sultana, Ather/Icc Elem Sch	79
Suminski, Paul/Lincoln Middle Sch	58
Summers, Beth/Freeport Alternative High Sch	224
Summers, Beth/Freeport High Sch	224
Summers, Danielle/Center Elem Sch	224
Sung, Jeannie/Westbrook Primary Sch	51
Sussman, Howard/Mark Twain Elem Sch	47
Sutton, Jennifer/Von Steuben Metro Science Ctr	37
Sutton, Terri/Vandalia Christian Academy	106
Sutton, Tony/Rowe Elem Charter Sch	41
Sveda, Gabe/Christopher Cmty High Sch	107
Swann, Jason/Our Lady of Mt Carmel Sch	252
Swanner, Joshua/Greeley Elem Sch	72
Swanson, Mervyn/Calvin Coolidge Middle Sch	199
Swanson, Stacey/Immaculate Conception Sch	113
Swearingen, Tyler/Tri-Valley Elem Sch	187
Sweazy, Melissa/Acero CS-Esmeralda Santiago ES [156]	38
Sweeney, Dennis, Dr/Grissom Elem Sch	27
Sweeney, Joe/Old Quarry Middle Sch	55
Sweetland, Kevin/Camelot-Excel Englewood HS	39
Swenson, Brigitte/Peace & Educ Coalition HS	27
Swilley, Shannon/Bourbonnais Upper Grade Center	134
Swingler, Eric/Greenville Elem Sch	4
Swopes, Jean, Dr/Lions Math & Science Chrn Acad	158
Swords, Nick/Westview Elem Sch	10
Sydnor, Dawn/Morrill MA & SC Speciality Sch	34
Sykes, Lisa/Camelot-Excel Southwest HS	39
Sykes, Tamikka/Learn 7 Chtr Sch-ES [164]	40
Sylvester, Stephanie/Liberty Elem Sch	131
Szcinski, Doug/Glenwood High Sch	211
Szczasny, Annette/Christa McAuliffe Sch	53
Szkapiak, George/Kennedy High Sch	37
Szklanecki, Robert/Palos East Elem Sch	61
Szoke, Eric/Cantrall Elem Sch	188
Szurek, Janan/Georgetown Elem Sch	95
Szwed, David/Lincoln Middle Sch	62
Szymczak, James/Hampshire Middle Sch	180
Szymczak, Jeffrey/Mooseheart Sch	133

T

NAME/School	PAGE
Tabernacki, Scott/Mt Carmel High Sch	73
Taff, Judy/Chicago Jewish Day Sch	77
Taher, Mohammed, Dr/College Prep School-America	101
Tallitsch, Jennifer/Lincoln Elem Sch	84
Tallon, Ellen/Peoria Heights Grade Sch	198
Tamez, Dana/Aptakisic Junior High Sch	146
Tanner, Joanne/Acero CS-Carlos Fuentes ES [156]	38
Tanney, John/Quentin Road Christian Sch	158
Tarasiuk, Julie/Albert Einstein Elem Sch	66
Taterka, Bob/Matthews Middle Sch	155
Tatum, Bryant/Canaan Academy	13
Taylor-Goode, Kimbreana/Langston Hughes Elem Sch	36
Taylor, Bill/St Agnes School Bohemia	74
Taylor, Brandon/Coulterville Unit Sch	205
Taylor, Chris/Mt Carmel Grade Sch	234
Taylor, Jason/E H Franzen Intermediate Sch	96
Taylor, Jason/Raymond Benson Primary Sch	96
Taylor, Joe/Greenbriar Elem Sch	25
Taylor, Lori/Union Sch	217
Taylor, Lowell/Steward Elem Sch	160
Teasley, Jeff/Lebanon High Sch	220
Tekampe, Brian/St Edward High Sch	133
Teller, Tobie/Hanna Sacks Bais Yaakov HS	78
Tellez, Luis/Irene Hernandez Middle Sch	32
Tennis, Donna/St Philip Lutheran Sch	81
Tennison, Brian/Lane Technical College Prep HS	36
Tenopir, Kurt/William Fremd High Sch	69
Tenuta, G/Fairview Elem Sch	186
Tenzillo, Cattie/St Robert Bellarmine Sch	76
Tepen, Russ/Litchfield Middle Sch	191
Teske, Shawn/Warren Elem Sch	126
Testone, Chris/Central High Sch	128

PRINCIPAL INDEX

Market Data Retrieval

NAME/School	PAGE	NAME/School	PAGE
Thacker, Randall/Mt Zion Intermediate Sch	166	Toman, Erik/Chicago Virtual Charter Sch [336]	39
Thein, Marianne/Jfh Educational Academy	79	Tomaszewski, Kathleen/Sacred Heart Sch	74
Theis, Al/St Gerald Sch	75	Tomblin, Russell/Moulton Middle Sch	216
Theis, Jillian/Griggsville-Perry Elem Sch	203	Tomei, Kathleen/Pleasantdale Elem Sch	62
Theis, Jillian/Griggsville-Perry High Sch	203	Tomic, Robert/O W Huth Middle Sch	57
Theisinger, Clayton/Putnam Co High Sch	204	Tomlinson, Robby/El Paso-Gridley Jr High Sch	257
Theodosopoulos, Mary/McCutcheon Elem Sch	29	Toney, Fenecia/Lorenzo R Smith Sust Tech Acad	136
Thibodeaux-Fox, Frances/Spencer Tech Academy	30	Topps, Natasha/Shoop Math-Sci Tech Elem Acad	36
Thigpen, Kelly/Burnside Scholastic Academy	35	Tornatore, Marcia, Dr/St Joan of Arc Sch	75
Thill, Dena/Lincoln Middle Sch	22	Torres, Jose/John L Marsh Elem Sch	36
Thoelke, Kate/St Paul Lutheran Sch	173	Torres, Maritza/Ahs-Passages Charter Sch	38
Thole, Rich/Princeville Jr Sr High Sch	200	Tortora, Nancy/Thomas Jefferson Elem Sch	22
Thomann, Andrew/Richland Co High Sch	206	Tortorello, Steven/Marian Catholic High Sch	73
Thomas, Chad/Sullivan High Sch	36	Toschi, Jennifer/Charles J Sahs Elem Sch	25
Thomas, Cheralyn/Ucan Academy	81	Tosh, John/Mary Miller Junior High Sch	232
Thomas, Connie/Western Barry Elem Sch	203	Toth, Jim/Schaumburg Christian Sch	80
Thomas, Connie/Western High Sch	203	Totheroh, Steve/Milford High Sch	119
Thomas, Eric/Knoxvill Ctr-Student Success	199	**Touch, Kelly**/Frank A Brodnicki Elem Sch	53
Thomas, Heidi/Field Elem Sch	93	Tovar, Rocio/Namaste Charter Sch	40
Thomas, Kevin/Georgetown-Ridge Farm High Sch	232	Towner, Robert/Fernwood Elem Sch	36
Thomas, Krystal/Elgin High Sch	130	Trager, Shane/Reed-Custer Middle Sch	247
Thomas, Kusan/Ray Graham Training Center	36	Travelstead, Jerry/Community Cons SD 204 Sch	201
Thomas, Lisa, Dr/Cairo Jr Sr High Sch	3	Travis, David/Yorkville High Sch	139
Thomas, Roxie/Whittier Elem Sch	52	Travis, David/Yorkville High School Academy	139
Thomas, Ryan/Carbondale Cmty High Sch	120	Travis, Sharrone/J N Thorp Elem Sch	35
Thomas, Sherrilyn/Bloomington Junior High Sch	185	Travlos, Jerry/Smyser Elem Sch	28
Thomas, Wade/Benton Cons Dist 103 High Sch	107	Treadwell, Cynthia/Aldridge Elem Sch	35
Thompson, Amy/Hanover Highlands Elem Sch	66	Trendel, Christine/Jackson Elem Sch	94
Thompson, Janelle/Wentworth Elem Sch	35	Tresnak, Mike/Roanoke-Benson High Sch	258
Thompson, Jay/Lloyd Elem Sch	27	Triche, Marjorie/Crete-Monee High Sch	242
Thompson, Jeff/Martinsville Jr Sr High Sch	16	Trigg, Cody/Springfield Southeast High Sch	213
Thompson, Karen/Elizabeth Morris Elem Sch	218	Tripp, Vicki/Buncombe Consolidated Sch	127
Thompson, Paul/Concordia Lutheran Sch	200	Trojan, Michelle/Intrinsic School-Belmont	39
Thompson, Veronica/Revere Elem Sch	35	Trotter, Giffen/Hester Junior High Sch	50
Thorlton, Justin/Northeast Elem Magnet Sch	232	Trowbridge, Brian/Lincoln-Douglas Elem Sch	2
Thornsbrough, Kurt/Armstrong Ellis Elem Sch	231	Trsar, Joe/Memorial Elem Sch	42
Thornton, Mary/Seton Academy	102	Truckenbrod, Mark/Currier Elem Sch	99
Thorpe, Crystal/Jefferson Elem Sch	160	Trude-Suter, Debra, Dr/Alexander Graham Bell Mont Sch	77
Throneburg, Kelly/Jefferson Park Elem Sch	257	Trujillo, Gerardo/Pasteur Elem Sch	27
Thuet, John/Lincoln Park High Sch	27	Trumblay, Peter/St Joseph Sch	133
Thurmond, Jasmine/King School of Social Justice	34	Tucker, Alissa/Dallas Elem Sch	114
Tidwell, Michelle/Our Lady Queen of Peace Sch	222	Tucker, Angela/Esmond Elem Sch	34
Tiemann, Karen/West 40 Regional Safe Sch MS	20	Tucker, Larry/T E Culbertson Elem Sch	243
Tiffany, Todd/Sumner Attendance Center	159	Tucker, Rob/Army Trail Elem Sch	88
Tighil, Moses/Ombudsman No 1 High School NW	40	Tully, Daniel/Notre Dame College Prep HS	73
Tillman, Tiffany/Melody Elem Sch	31	Tuner, Robert/Ombudsman-Chicago Roseland CSA	40
Tillmon, Taiyuan/Rosa L Parks Middle Sch	70	Tuomi, Matt/Concord Lutheran Sch	101
Timbers-Ausar, Conrad/Englewood STEM High Sch	37	Turner, Brad/Mulberry Grove Jr High Sch	4
Timbers-Auser, Conrad/Urban Prep CS-Bronzeville	41	Turner, Dana/John N Smyth Magnet Sch	32
Timm, Carolyn/Cherry Valley Elem Sch	254	Turner, Kevin/Alternative Optional Ed Ctr	156
Timmins, William/Friendship Junior High Sch	43	Turner, Tanya/Ludlow Elem Sch	11
Tinerella, Anthony/Marmion Academy	101	Turner, Taren/Ellis Elem Sch	254
Tingley, Jackie/Shabbona Elem Sch	134	Turner, Tim/Greenview Unit Sch	188
Tingwall, Allison/Curie Metropolitan High Sch	37	Turner, Vincent/Washington Middle Sch	213
Tippett, Billy/Eldorado Middle Sch	210	Turner, Walter/North Shore Adventist Academy	80
Tiritilli, Chris/St Mary of Gostyn Sch	101	Turyna, Brian, Dr/Wiesbrook Elem Sch	92
Titsworth, Travis/Hutsonville High Sch	83	Tusek, Ryan/South Primary Sch	172
Titus, Denise/Mark Twain Elem Sch	19	Tyrrell, Jennifer/Carl Sandburg High Sch	44
Tkachuk, Jerry/Altamont High Sch	104	Tyson, Kelly/Learn 6 Chtr Sch-N Chicago [164]	154
Tkachuk, Shirley/SS Cyril & Methodius Sch	74	**U**	
Tobin, Cecelia/Wheatland Academy	96		
Todd, Brandon/Lane Elem Sch	91	Uffelman, Kris/Thomas Elem Sch	120
Todd, Matthew/Carruthers Elem Sch	121	**Uhlman, Jill**/Tremont High Sch	228
Todora, Haidee/St Paul Catholic Sch	173	Ulery, Kristen/Madison Elem Sch	67
Toeben, Michael/Albers Elem Sch	17	Ulferts, Christina/Froberg Elem Sch	254
Tohme, Patrick/Meadowbrook Elem Sch	59	Ulferts, Christina/Lewis Lemon Elem Sch	254
Tolbert, Cindy/Alhambra Primary Sch	171	Ulferts, John/Shirland Cmty Cons Sch	255
Tolbert, Cindy/Grantfork Elem Sch	171	Ulm, Rob/Jefferson Elem Sch	19
Tolbert, Tonya/Roswell Mason Elem Sch	31	Ulrich, Daniel/McCleery Elem Sch	132
Toldo, Mary/St Bridget Sch	256	Underwood, Kenya/Edward E Sadlowski Elem Sch	36
Toledo, Efren/O A Thorp Scholastic Academy	27	**Underwood, Kenya**/John Fiske Elem Sch	33
Tolefree, Curtiss/Beulah Park Elem Sch	157	Unger, Camille/Edgebrook Elem Sch	28
Tolliver, Glenna/Vision Way Christian Sch	15	Uphoff, Chad, Dr/Channahon Junior High Sch	241

Illinois School Directory

PRINCIPAL INDEX

NAME/School	PAGE
Uptmor, Chris/Farmington Central Jr High Sch	197
Usauskas, Candice/St Mary Star of the Sea Sch	76
Utsinger, Jeff/Stark Co High Sch	224
Utsinger, Jeff/Stark Co Junior High Sch	224
Utterback, John/Clare Woods Academy	101

V

NAME/School	PAGE
Vacarri, Frank/Riley Community Cons Sch	184
Vacca, Cheryl/Spaulding Sch	57
Vacik, April/Irene H King Elem Sch	248
Valadez, Leticia/Komensky Elem Sch	23
Valadez, Leticia/Melrose Park Elem Sch	57
Valdez, Rosa/Haugan Elem Sch	29
Valencia, Jay/Canton High Sch	109
Valente, Kathleen/Barnard Elem Comp Math & Sci	33
Valentine, Karen/Edison Regional Gifted Center	28
Valenza, Tony/Jamie McGee Elem Sch	248
Valle, Barbara/Harry D Jacobs High Sch	180
Vallicelli, Arthur/Woodstock High Sch	184
Van Giesen, Don/Hillsboro Junior High Sch	191
Van Kuiken, Janice/Balmoral Elem Sch	242
Van Wageningen, Lisa/Hampshire Elem Sch	180
Vanausdoll, Jared/East Prairie Junior High Sch	88
Vance, Dana/St Helen Sch	75
Vance, Duane/Jerusalem Ev Luth Sch	79
Vander Burgh, Heidi/Okaw Valley Elem Sch	193
Vandeusen, Jennifer, Dr/Streamwood High Sch	131
Vandevelde, Stevie/Our Saviour Sch	193
Vanscyoc, Jamie/South Central High Sch	176
VanWinkle, Patti/Central Road Elem Sch	43
Varble, Leslie/Unity Point Elem Sch	121
Varn, Larry/Rich Twp HS Fine Arts Com	64
Varnes, Christi/Edison Junior High Sch	208
Vasquez, Jamie, Dr/Willows Academy	81
Vasquez, Yesenia/Madison Elem Sch	97
Vaughn, Amos/Monee Elem Sch	242
Vaughn, Ashley/Pine Crest Elem Sch	232
Vazquez, Stephanie/Instituto-Lozano Mastery HS	39
Veith, Aimee/Illinois Sch-Visually Impaired	1
Velazquez, Noe/Lords Park Elem Sch	131
Vena, Helena/Glen Grove Elem Sch	51
Venetico, Tony/Henry Marlowe Middle Sch	182
Venson, Sheila/YCCS-Youth Connection Ldrshp	41
Ventsias, Aaron/Laraway Sch	244
Venvertloh, Cindy/St Peter Sch	3
Verona, Peter, Dr/Rockford East High Sch	254
Veronda, Cynthia/Kennedy Middle Grade Sch	135
Veytsman, Amy/River Trails ELC at Parkview	65
Viernow, Matt/North Side Primary Center	251
Villa, Irene/Conrad Fischer Elem Sch	93
Villalobos, Cristina/Stone Elem Sch	89
Villalobos, Elvia/Early Childhood Ed Center	100
Vincent, Tim/Clinton Rosette Middle Sch	84
Vines, Bonnie/Shawnee Hills Chrn Academy	231
Virgil, Kelli/Oregon Elem Sch	195
Vitton, Charles, Dr/Peotone Early Educ Shaw Ctr	245
Vitulli, Mary/St Patrick Sch	158
Vivanco, Elizabeth/L D Brady Elem Sch	129
Vogel, Amanda/Vine Academy	102
Vogel, Jon/Washington Junior High Sch	98
Vogel, Scott/Donovan Jr Sr High Sch	119
Vogel, Scott/Towanda Elem Sch	187
Vogt, Mary/Lincoln Elem Sch	202
Voiles, Marty/Seneca Township High Sch	144
Volkert, Bruce/St Paul Lutheran Sch	256
Vonder Haar, Kristin/Westbrook Sch	58
Vondra, Amy/Hamilton Elem Sch	30
Vonschnase, Kyle, Dr/Hilltop Elem Sch	130
Vortman, Denny/Winchester High Sch	215
Vowels, Cris/Urbana Early Childhood Sch	13
Vrlec, Joy/Trinity Sch	250
Vugteveen, John/Trinity Christian Sch	250

W

NAME/School	PAGE
Wackenhut, Particia/St Mary's Sch	240
Waddell, Terri/Joppa High Sch	177
Waechtler, Paul/New Trier HS-Freshman Camp	58
Waggener, Jeff/Franklin Jr Sr High Sch	192
Waggoner, Katie/Hawthorn Elem School North	151
Wagner, Christine/Queen Bee Early Childhood Ctr	99
Wagner, Elaine/St Louis Sch	191
Wagner, Leland/Pierce Downer Elem Sch	93
Wagner, Michelle/St Joseph Grade Sch	12
Wagner, Scott/Pinckneyville Elem Sch	201
Wagrowski, Michael/Timber Ridge Sch	20
Walder, Dan/John Greer Elem Sch	232
Walder, Gregory/Alan B Shepard High Sch	44
Waldron, Rachel/St Benedict Prep Elem Sch	74
Waldrop, Tangie/Palestine High Sch	83
Walk, Kim/Mulberry Sch	188
Walker-Hood, Sharon/Frances B McCord Elem Sch	24
Walker, Dornetta/Washington Elem Sch	46
Walker, Dornetta/Washington Junior High Sch	46
Walker, Shaylon/Paec High Sch	20
Walker, Sherri/Harold Washington Elem Sch	35
Walker, Thad/Meredosia-Chambersberg Sch	192
Walker, Tina/Learn Chtr Sch-South Chicago [164]	40
Walker, Zarree/Crown Community Academy	31
Wall, Jacob/Fieldcrest Intermediate Sch	257
Wall, Jacob/Pleasant Valley Middle Sch	199
Wall, Michael/Forest View Elem Sch	43
Wallace, Maggie/United North Elem Sch	235
Wallace, R Jason/North Ward Elem Sch	88
Wallerstedt, Roberta/Park View Elem Sch	97
Walocha, Christopher/Washington Academy	4
Walsh, Heather/Poplar Grove Elem Sch	5
Walsh, John/Lake Zurich Mid Sch S Campus	152
Walsh, Ruth/Jane Addams Elem Sch	27
Walsh, Sean/Longfellow Elem Sch	92
Walsh, William/Hinsdale Central High Sch	95
Walshire, Ben/Millburn Elem Sch	153
Walter, Carie/Central Middle Sch	128
Walters, Kelly/Lyle Sch	117
Walthers, Michelle, Dr/St Christopher Sch	74
Walton, Claudette/V Blanche Graham Elem Sch	96
Wamser, Ryan/Oakdale Elem Sch	236
Wang, Michael/Fusion Academy-Oak Brook	102
Warco, Mrs/St Walter Sch	101
Ward, Becky/St Peter Sch	133
Ward, Charles/Our Lady Immaculate Academy	80
Ward, Debora/Cleveland Elem Sch	28
Ward, Mary Eileen/St Raymond Sch	76
Wardle, Jeff/Buffalo Grove High Sch	70
Wardynski, Jennifer/Annunciation BVM Sch	133
Warfield, Diane/Pathways Sch	217
Warner, Lilith/North Chicago High Sch	154
Warner, Sandra/Early Learning Center	99
Warnke, Justin/Thomas Jefferson Jr High Sch	100
Warren, Matthew/John G Conyers Learning Acad	43
Warrenfeltz, Jennifer/Ashton Franklin Ctr Elem Sch	159
Washausen, Jessica/Gardner Elem Sch	190
Washington, Marquis/CICS-Avalon/S Shore [167]	39
Wassel, Susan/New Hebron Christian Sch	83
Waszak, Britta/Henry Puffer Sch	93
Waterfield, Faith/Lettie Brown Elem Sch	227
Waterman, Brian, Dr/Lyons Twp High School North	56
Waterman, Brian, Dr/Lyons Twp High School South	56
Watkins, Shawna/Peaceful Pathways Mont Academy	139
Watson, Caitlien/West Prairie Middle Sch	178
Watson, Stephanie/Olson Elem Sch	184
Watt, Joey/El Vista Baptist Academy	200
Watts, Lindsay/Longfellow Elem Sch	251
Wawczak, John/J Covington Elem Sch	60
Wayne, Jerome/Clinton High Sch	87
Wayne, Michael/Oswego High Sch	138
Weatherly, Tonya/Ruggles Elem Sch	35
Weaver, Kelly/Alexander Leigh Center Autism	185

PRINCIPAL INDEX

Market Data Retrieval

NAME/School	PAGE
Weaver, Lisa/Pleasant Hill Elem Sch	199
Weaver, Mike/Lincoln Elem Sch	161
Webb, Tom/Carterville Intermediate Sch	251
Weber, Jennifer/Student Life Academy	19
Weber, Mira/Agassiz Elem Sch	26
Wechesler, Rana/Joan Dachs Bais Yaakov ES	79
Weder, Liz/Highland Middle Sch	171
Weedman, Brad/Abingdon-Avon High Sch	139
Weeks, Heidi/F E Peacock Middle Sch	96
Weh, Jered/Carlyle High Sch	17
Wei, Helen, Dr/Elizabeth Meyer Sch	67
Weidner, Emily/White Heath Elem Sch	202
Weinberg, Max/Lincolnwood Elem Sch	48
Weir, Betty/Skokie Sch	72
Weisberg, Abbie/Irving A Hokin Keshet High Sch	79
Weiss, Dennis/Eugene Field Elem Sch	208
Welch, Brad/Washington Elem Sch	161
Welch, David/Carroll Catholic Sch	164
Well, Richard/Lewistown Central Elem Sch	110
Wellbaum, Bethany/Sangamon Valley Primary Sch	166
Wells, Janice/St Sabina Academy	76
Wells, Marcy/Adams Co Juv Det Center Sch	1
Welsh, Katherine/Mitchell Elem Sch	31
Welsh, Thomas/Sowers Elem Sch	258
Wennerstrom, Beth/St John the Evangelist Sch	75
Wenthe, Vicki/Sacred Heart Sch	105
Wenzel, Scott/Peotone Junior High Sch	245
Wepking, Diane/St Mary Sch	173
Wepprecht, Molly/Bonfield Grade Sch	135
Wernentin, Tim/Sherrard Jr Sr High Sch	189
Werner, John, Dr/Indian Oaks Academy	137
Wernet, Doug/Chelsea Intermediate Sch	242
Wesley, Kreg/South Prairie Elem Sch	86
West, Lisa/Woodland Elem Sch East	157
West, Rebecca/Franklin Elem Sch	178
West, Rebecca/Jefferson Elem Sch	178
Westall, Kevin/Bluford Sch	122
Westerhoff, Brenda/Harrison Street Elem Sch	131
Westerhoff, Brenna/Geneva Middle School North	131
Westholm, Nils/Montessori Schoolhouse	214
Westley, Carol/Hynes Elem Sch	51
Wetherell, Amanda/Clara Peterson Elem Sch	107
Wettstein, Doug/Prairie Christian Sch	258
Wetzel, Katie/Dundee-Crown High Sch	180
Whaley, Ayana, Dr/Martin L King Elem Sch	70
Wheatley, Michael/Creekside Middle Sch	184
Wheeler, Caleb/Faith Bible Christian Acad	15
Whipple, Scott/Big Hollow Middle Sch	148
Whisler, Heather/Grand Prairie Elem Sch	246
Whitaker, Jeff/Rock Island High Sch	208
White-James, Takeshi/Avalon Park Elem Sch	26
White, Anthony/Norton Creek Elem Sch	129
White, Colleen/Cumberland Elem Sch	46
White, Corey/Heritage High Sch	11
White, Jeffery/Wells Preparatory Elem Acad	33
White, Margaret/Promise Christian Academy	80
White, Michelle/Hoopeston Area Middle Sch	232
White, Nicole/Tanner Elem Sch	35
White, Pamela/Carl Wehde Early Chldhd Sp Ed	181
White, Tabitha/O'Keeffe Elem Sch	26
White, Victoria/Bluffview Elem Sch	218
Whitten, Rena/Center for Alternative Lrng	69
Wickenhauser, Beth/Douglas Elem Sch	87
Wickenhauser, Beth/Lincoln Elem Sch	87
Widdop, Jim/Northeast Jr High Sch	209
Wiederholt, Matthew, Dr/Scales Mound Elem Sch	126
Wiederholt, Matthew, Dr/Scales Mound High Sch	126
Wiederholt, Matthew, Dr/Scales Mound Junior High Sch	126
Wiele, Sandy/Peoria Christian Sch	200
Wiemelt, Joseph, Dr/Urbana Middle Sch	13
Wiemers, Brooke/Signal Hill Elem Sch	221
Wiesbrook, William/Naperville Central High Sch	98
Wiest, Melanie/Brookview Elem Sch	254
Wieters, David/School of St Mary	157
Wiggenhorn, Tracy/Faith Lutheran Sch	173
Wight, Vic/Peter J Palombi Middle Sch	152
Wildes, Douglas/Elmwood Park High Sch	48
Wiley, Cameron/River Grove Elem Sch	65
Wilkerson, George/High Mount Elem Sch	220
Wilkes, Jim/Cornerstone Academy	78
Wilkinson, Anthony/Holy Family Sch	249
Wilkinson, Anthony/Rosary High Sch	133
Wilkinson, Stacy/Oak Ridge Sch	180
Wilks, Kim/Meadowbrook Intermediate Sch	169
Willett, Don/Astoria High Sch	109
Williams-Bonds, Carmen, Dr/Carbondale Middle Sch	120
Williams, Angela/Providence Englewood CS	41
Williams, Becky/Delores Moye Elem Sch	221
Williams, Dan/Young Adult Alternative Ctr	70
Williams, David/Illinois Central Christian Sch	229
Williams, Donna/Mt Erie Elem Sch	237
Williams, Eddie/Carl Sandburg Elem Sch	19
Williams, Frederick/Chopin Elem Sch	31
Williams, Jan/St Patrick Sch	214
Williams, Joe/Central High Sch	10
Williams, Joyce/Hazel Bland Promise Center	223
Williams, Kate/Germantown Hills Middle Sch	257
Williams, Michelle/St Elizabeth Sch	173
Williams, Muriel/Tabernacle Christian Academy	81
Williams, Patricia/Downers Grove Adventist Sch	101
Williams, Paulette/Johnnie Colemon Academy	36
Williams, Scott/Glenbrook North High Sch	51
Williams, Tawana, Dr/Faraday Elem Sch	31
Williams, Tiffany/Springfield Ball Charter Sch	213
Williams, Todd/Hamilton Elem Sch	208
Williams, Tori/Parkside Community Academy	35
Williams, Wayne/Neal Math & Science Academy	154
Willis, Michelle, Dr/Gillespie Tech Mag Cluster Sch	27
Willis, Noah/Washington Elem Sch	215
Willis, Noah/Webster Elem Sch	215
Willman, Christy/Franklin East Grade Sch	192
Willman, Christy/Franklin Elem Sch	192
Willman, Christy/Morrisonville Elem Sch	14
Wills, Heather/Lawn Manor Sch	21
Wills, Joi/Edward Fulton Jr High Sch	221
Wills, Justine/I-Kan Reg Alt Attendance Ctr	134
Wilson, Ana/John Tibbott Elem Sch	248
Wilson, Carol, Dr/Brunson Math & Sci Sch	29
Wilson, Christine/Taft Elem Sch	68
Wilson, Dione/Park Sch	46
Wilson, Heather/Eisenhower Junior High Sch	66
Wilson, Jenny/Trico Elem Sch	121
Wilson, Kashawndra/Noble CS-Hansberry Clg Prep [165]	40
Wilson, Kerry, Dr/Plum Grove Junior High Sch	43
Wilson, Linda/Independence High Sch	20
Wilson, Nathaniel/DeSoto Grade Sch	120
Wilson, Todd/Rantoul Twp High Sch	12
Wilson, Tony/Pinckneyville Community HS	201
Wilt, Jason/Ohio Cmty High Sch	7
Wilt, Jason/Ohio Community Grade Sch	7
Wiltowski, Erin/Cobden Elem Sch	230
Windhorst, Parker/Massac Co High Sch	178
Windings, Jennifer/Caledonia Christian Academy	204
Windsor, Paul/Lakeview Junior High Sch	90
Windy, Gary/Shepherd Middle Sch	143
Winger-Bryan, Angela/Kempton Elem Sch	162
Winkelman, Breanna/Trinity Lutheran Sch	9
Winkelman, Krista/Fremont Middle Sch	150
Winship, Stephanie/Project Insight Alt Sch	178
Winslow, Rodney/Triad High Sch	172
Winston, Valerie/Immanuel Christian Academy	79
Winters, Dellnora/School of Fine Arts	46
Winters, Kathy/St Jude Parish Sch	249
Winters, Scott/Lakewood Falls Elem Sch	246
Winters, Teresa/Hillcrest Elem Sch	130
Wipachit, Ferdinand/Phoenix Military Academy	28

Illinois School Directory

PRINCIPAL INDEX

NAME/School	PAGE
Wise, Peggie, Dr/Morton Sch of Excellence	26
Witges, Eric/West Side Primary Sch	211
Witt, Joel/Lutheran Assoc Sch	167
Wittenauer, Heather/Jefferson Elem Sch	240
Witzl, Tamara/Telpochcalli Elem Sch	32
Wojtylewski, Rita, Dr/Worthridge Elem Sch	72
Wold, Scott/Jane Addams Elem Sch	57
Woldt, John/St John Lutheran Sch	158
Woll, Angela/Trenton Elem Sch	18
Wollberg, Ryan/Woodland Elem Sch East	157
Wollberg, Ryan/Woodland Elem Sch West	157
Woller, Chris/Next Generation Sch	13
Wolski, Jeanne/St Mary Sch	249
Wood, Brad/Don D Shute Elem Sch	227
Wood, David/Our Lady of the Wayside Sch	73
Wood, Diane/Willard Elem Sch	65
Wood, Keith, Dr/Brooks Middle Sch	248
Wood, Maureen/Portage Park Elem Sch	29
Wood, Tracey/Gems World Academy	78
Woodring, Michelle/Lincoln Elem Sch	129
Woodrome, Brandon/Mascoutah High Sch	220
Woods, Deborah/Glenbrook North High Sch	51
Woods, Linda/Langford Academy	34
Woods, Scott, Dr/J W Eater Junior High Sch	11
Wooters, Jeff/Brownstown Jr Sr High Sch	105
Workman, Mike/Lincoln Junior High Sch	164
Worrell, Carrie/Faith Christian Sch	160
Worst, David/Spring Brook Elem Sch	96
Wortel, Brian/Crete-Monee Education Center	242
Wright, Brian, Dr/Bradley-Bourbonnais High Sch	135
Wright, Dana/Indian Trail Elem Sch	247
Wright, Kim/Danville Lutheran Sch	233
Wright, Kimberly/Roosevelt Elem Sch	57
Wright, Mathew/United Township High Sch	209
Wrobbel, Paul, Dr/Trinity Oaks Christian Academy	185
Wrzesinski, Stuart/Palos South Middle Sch	61
Wudtke, Curtis/Rockford Lutheran Academy	256
Wulbecker, Quinn/Adolph Link Elem Sch	66
Wyant, Casey/Sherrard Elem Sch	189
Wyller, Tim/C E Miller Elem Sch	92
Wyman, Kate/Jefferson Elem Sch	227
Wysong, Cheri/Washington Elem Sch	14

Y

NAME/School	PAGE
Yanello, Bob/Plainfield South High Sch	246
Yarbrough, Lisa/Mitchell Elem Sch	171
Yarbrough, Ronald/Harlem High Sch	252
Yates, Jamie/Farmingdale Elem Sch	212
Ye, Tony/Gateway Christian Academy	223
Yelaska, Bob/Heritage Lakes Elem Sch	90
Yildiz, Matt/Horizon Sci Acad SW Chicago [161]	39
Yoder, Brian/Flanagan-Cornell Unit 74 Sch	161
Yoo, Michelle/YCCS-Truman Middle Clg HS	41
York, Daryl/Brentwood Bapt Christian Acad	77
Young, Bob/Harvest Christian Academy	133
Young, David/E A Bouchet Math & Sci Acad	35
Young, Jordan/Rochelle Middle Sch	195
Young, Lori/Gard Elem Sch	9
Young, Lori/Grand Avenue Sch	9
Young, Nick/Lombard Middle Sch	140
Young, Sacha/Clinton Elem Sch	87
Young, Tron/Centralia Junior High Sch	174
Young, Tron/Joseph Arthur Middle Sch	218
Youngberg, Geoffrey/Elden D Finley Jr High Sch	42
Youtsey, Cristina/Old School Montessori	158
Yuska, Melissa/Windsor Elem Sch	253
Yutzy, Heather/Belding Elem Sch	28

Z

NAME/School	PAGE
Zaayer, Nicole/Garfield Elem Sch	232
Zabilka, Cynthia/St Daniel the Prophet Sch	74
Zahedi, Nahid/Community Christian Academy	78
Zahedi, Nahid/YCCS-Community Chrn Alt Acad	41
Zahm, Amy/Eisenhower High Sch	165
Zaimi, Lorianne/Peirce Int'l Studies ES	29
Zaiser, Josh/John L Hensey Elem Sch	226
Zallis, Brian/Prairie Elem Sch	98
Zampillo, Joe/Worth Junior High Sch	72
Zaniolo, Laura/Abraham Lincoln Elem Sch	61
Zarate, Frank, Dr/Our Lady of Charity Sch	73
Zarco, Mike/Illinois Youth-St Charles Ctr	1
Zarello, Paul/Bushnell Prairie City Elem Sch	178
Zarras, Barbara/Avon Center Elem Sch	148
Zastro, Mary/Caroline Bentley Elem Sch	245
Zayas, Jennifer/Chesak Elem Sch	182
Zbrozek, Adam/Colene Hoose Elem Sch	186
Zehnwirth, Elisa/Torah Academy	158
Zelaya, Christine, Dr/Oliver Wendell Holmes Elem Sch	61
Zelenka, Christine/John Murphy Elem Sch	29
Zeman, Mike/Centennial Elem Sch	138
Zeman, Ronald/Western Ave Elem Sch	131
Ziebler, Chelsey/Glenwood Elem Sch	211
Ziegler, Brent/La Moille High Sch	6
Zieleniewski, Craig/Gilberts Elem Sch	180
Zielke, Steve/St Peter Lutheran Sch	81
Zilinski, Tammy/Griffin Christian Sch	133
Zingler, Cassie/Hoover Math & Science Academy	66
Zonca, Mary Beth/Claremont Academy Elem Sch	33
Zonghetti, Kelly/South Sch	51
Zueck, Ms/Sacred Heart Sch	15
Zugel, Christine/Abbott Middle Sch	130
Zulz, Mark/Lowpoint-Washburn Jr Sr HS	258
Zurales, Carole/Peotone Elem Sch	245
Zurawski, Gregory/Coonley Elem Sch	29
Zurko, Adam/Wayne Elem Sch	131
Zursin, James/Eastview Elem Sch	180
Zver, Nancy/St William Sch	76
Zweeres, Joe/Saratoga Elem Sch	113
Zwemke, Bryan/Minooka Cmty High Sch South	245
Zych, Mark/Hiawatha High Sch	85

Illinois School Directory

DISTRICT & SCHOOL TELEPHONE INDEX

School/City/County DISTRICT/CITY/COUNTY	PID	TELEPHONE NUMBER	PAGE
21st Century Primary Center/University Pk/Cook	04872611	708/668-9490	62
A			
A B Shepard Middle Sch/Deerfield/Lake	00300599	847/948-0620	149
A J Katzenmaier Academy/North Chicago/Lake	00301763	847/689-6330	154
A O Marshall Elem Sch/Joliet/Will	00324868	815/727-4919	243
A Vito Martinez Middle Sch/Romeoville/Will	00325680	815/886-6100	248
A-C CENTRAL CMTY UNIT SD 262/ **ASHLAND/CASS**	00264488	217/476-8112	9
A-C Central Elem Sch/Chandlerville/Cass	00264490	217/458-2224	9
A-C Central Middle High Sch/Ashland/Cass	04014869	217/476-3313	9
A-Karrasel Sch/Chicago/Cook	02956596	773/637-1220	76
Abbott Middle Sch/Elgin/Kane	00298166	847/888-5160	130
ABC Academy/Quincy/Adams	12172158	217/228-7175	2
ABINGDON-AVON CMTY UNIT SD 276/ **ABINGDON/KNOX**	00299873	309/462-2301	139
Abingdon-Avon High Sch/Abingdon/Knox	00299914	309/462-2338	139
Abingdon-Avon Middle Sch/Avon/Knox	00293348	309/465-3621	139
Abraham Lincoln Elem Sch/Glen Ellyn/Du Page	00289804	630/790-6475	94
Abraham Lincoln Elem Sch/Oak Park/Cook	00272382	708/524-3110	61
Abraham Lincoln Sch/Belleville/St Clair	00316249	618/233-2414	217
Acad St Benedict-the African/Chicago/Cook	00286553	773/776-3316	72
Academy for Global Citizenship/Chicago/Cook	11131058	773/582-1100	38
Academy High/Champaign/Champaign	12318235	217/239-6000	13
Academy South/Hoffman Est/Cook	02223167	847/755-6640	69
Ace Amandla Charter Sch/Chicago/Cook	11131317	773/535-7150	1
Acero CS-Bart De Las Casas ES/Chicago/Cook	10021462	312/432-3224	38
Acero CS-Brighton Park ES/Chicago/Cook	11926279	312/455-5434	38
Acero CS-Carlos Fuentes ES/Chicago/Cook	10021450	773/279-9826	38
Acero CS-Esmeralda Santiago ES/Chicago/Cook	11718905	312/455-5410	38
Acero CS-Ines De La Cruz/Chicago/Cook	12259160	312/455-5440	38
Acero CS-Jovita Idar Elem Sch/Chicago/Cook	12259158	312/455-5450	38
Acero CS-Major Garcia HS/Chicago/Cook	11131216	773/579-3480	38
Acero CS-Marquez ES/Chicago/Cook	10912366	773/321-2200	38
Acero CS-Octavio Paz ES/Chicago/Cook	04801337	773/890-1054	38
Acero CS-Omar Torres ES/Chicago/Cook	11456248	773/579-3475	38
Acero CS-Roberto Clemente ES/Chicago/Cook	11822130	312/455-5425	38
Acero CS-Rufino Tamayo ES/Chicago/Cook	10009218	773/434-6355	38
Acero CS-Sandra Cisneros ES/Chicago/Cook	11548683	773/376-8830	38
Acero CS-Victoria Soto HS/Chicago/Cook	12259172	312/455-5446	38
Acero CS-Zizumbo ES/Chicago/Cook	11131228	773/579-3470	38
Achievement Ctrs-Acacia Acad/La Grange/Cook	02428410	708/579-9040	76
Adam Sch/Creal Springs/Williamson	00326995	618/996-2181	251
Adams Co Juv Det Center Sch/Quincy/Adams	04198221	217/228-0026	1
Adams Co Regional Safe Sch/Quincy/Adams	12376550	217/223-8700	2
ADAMS CO SPECIAL ED CO-OP/ **QUINCY/ADAMS**	02184171	217/223-8700	3
Adams Elem Sch/Lincoln/Logan	00304806	217/732-3253	163
Addison Early Learning Center/Addison/Du Page	12107531	630/458-3095	88
ADDISON SCH DIST 4/ADDISON/ **DU PAGE**	00288850	630/458-2500	88
Addison Trail High Sch/Addison/Du Page	00289696	630/628-3300	93
Adlai E Stevenson High Sch/Lincolnshire/Lake	00300367	847/415-4000	146
ADLAI E STEVENSON HSD 125/ **LINCOLNSHIRE/LAKE**	00300355	847/415-4000	146
Adlai Stevenson Elem Sch/Elk Grove Vlg/Cook	01340322	847/357-5200	66
Adler Park Elem Sch/Libertyville/Lake	00301452	847/362-7275	153
Adm Richard E Byrd Elem Sch/Elk Grove Vlg/Cook	00267210	847/593-4388	43
Adolph Link Elem Sch/Elk Grove Vlg/Cook	00273855	847/357-5300	66
AERO SPECIAL ED CO-OP/BURBANK/ **COOK**	03032662	708/496-3330	82
Aero Special Education Center/Burbank/Cook	04196950	708/496-3330	20
Agape Christian High Sch/Marion/Williamson	11728924	618/997-9302	252
Agassiz Elem Sch/Chicago/Cook	00278855	773/534-5725	26
Ahs-Passages Charter Sch/Chicago/Cook	04950407	773/433-3530	38
Air Force Academy High Sch/Chicago/Cook	11446619	773/535-1590	37
Akiba Schechter Day Sch/Chicago/Cook	00281670	773/493-8880	76
Akin Cmty Cons Elem Sch/Akin/Franklin	00292887	618/627-2180	107
AKIN ELEM SCH DIST 91/AKIN/ **FRANKLIN**	00292875	618/627-2180	107
AL Raby High Sch/Chicago/Cook	05341756	773/534-6755	37
Alain Locke Charter Academy/Chicago/Cook	04875704	773/265-7232	38
Alan B Shepard Elem Sch/Bourbonnais/Kankakee	10030528	815/929-4600	134
Alan B Shepard High Sch/Palos Heights/Cook	01559224	708/371-1111	44
Albany Park Multicultural Acad/Chicago/Cook	03008958	773/534-5108	28
Albers Elem Sch/Albers/Clinton	00266254	618/248-5146	17
ALBERS ELEM SCH DIST 63/ **ALBERS/CLINTON**	00266242	618/248-5146	17
Albert Cassens Elem Sch/Glen Carbon/Madison	11136632	618/655-6150	171
Albert Einstein Elem Sch/Hanover Park/Cook	00273867	630/736-2500	66
Albert F Ames Elem Sch/Riverside/Cook	00273685	708/447-0759	65
Albert J Shegog Christian Acad/Calumet City/Cook	11829621	708/574-7553	77
Albert Sabin Magnet Sch/Chicago/Cook	00280729	773/534-4490	31
Albion Grade Sch/Albion/Edwards	04023743	618/445-2327	104
Alcott College Prep West/Chicago/Cook	11446700	773/534-5970	30
Alcott Elem Sch/Chicago/Cook	00278867	773/534-5460	30
Alcuin Montessori Sch/Oak Park/Cook	01441732	708/366-1882	77
Alden-Hebron Elem Sch/Hebron/McHenry	00305288	815/648-2442	179
Alden-Hebron Middle High Sch/Hebron/McHenry	00305290	815/648-2442	179
ALDEN-HEBRON SCH DIST 19/ **HEBRON/MCHENRY**	00305276	815/648-2442	179
Aldridge Elem Sch/Chicago/Cook	00274940	773/535-5614	35
Alessandro Volta Elem Sch/Chicago/Cook	00281060	773/534-5080	28
Alex Haley Academy/Chicago/Cook	00275152	773/535-5340	35
Alex M Martino Jr High Sch/New Lenox/Will	00325434	815/485-7593	245
Alexander Graham Bell Mont Sch/Wheeling/Cook	03192705	847/850-5490	77
Alexander Leigh Center Autism/McHenry/McHenry	12468660	815/344-2522	185
Alfred Nobel Elem Sch/Chicago/Cook	00280456	773/534-4365	26
Algonquin Lakes Elem Sch/Algonquin/McHenry	05091767	847/532-7500	180
Algonquin Middle Sch/Algonquin/McHenry	00297978	847/532-7100	180
Algonquin Middle Sch/Des Plaines/Cook	00268745	847/824-1205	46
Algonquin Pre-Kindergarten Ctr/Park Forest/Cook	00272942	708/668-9202	62
Algonquin Road Elem Sch/Fox River GRV/McHenry	00305496	847/516-5101	181
Alhambra Primary Sch/Alhambra/Madison	00308929	618/488-2200	171
Alice Gustafson Elem Sch/Batavia/Kane	00297863	630/937-8000	128
All Saints Academy/Breese/Clinton	00317994	618/526-4323	18
All Saints Catholic Academy/Naperville/Du Page	11533262	630/961-6125	100
All Saints Catholic Academy/Rockford/Winnebago	00328632	815/962-8515	256
Allegro Academy/Rockford/Winnebago	11719856	815/877-1489	256
Alleman High Sch/Rock Island/Rock Island	00313352	309/786-7793	209
Allen Junior High Sch/La Moille/Bureau	00263769	815/638-2233	6
Allen Otter Creek Sch/Ransom/La Salle	00302597	815/586-4611	141
ALLEN-OTTER CREEK CCSD 65/ **RANSOM/LA SALLE**	00302585	815/586-4611	141
ALLENDALE CMTY CONS SD 17/ **ALLENDALE/WABASH**	00322925	618/299-3161	234
Allendale Elem Sch/Allendale/Wabash	00322937	618/299-3161	234
Allendale Sch/Lake Villa/Lake	01844782	847/245-6401	158
Alphonsus Academy/Chicago/Cook	00284658	773/348-4629	72
Alpine Academy of Rockford/Rockford/Winnebago	04937259	815/227-8894	256
Alpine Christian Sch/Rockford/Winnebago	01405570	815/399-0880	256
ALSIP-HAZELGRN-OAKLAWN SD 126/ **ALSIP/COOK**	00266876	708/389-1900	20
Alt Educ Ctr-Harris/Decatur/Macon	11435658	217/362-3360	165
ALTAMONT CMTY UNIT SD 10/ **ALTAMONT/EFFINGHAM**	00292148	618/483-6195	104
Altamont Grade Sch/Altamont/Effingham	01557812	618/483-5171	104
Altamont High Sch/Altamont/Effingham	00292162	618/483-6193	104
Altamont Lutheran Sch/Altamont/Effingham	01442152	618/483-6428	105
Alternative Optional Ed Ctr/Waukegan/Lake	04882874	224/303-2860	156
Althoff Catholic High Sch/Belleville/St Clair	00317683	618/235-1100	222
ALTON CMTY SCH DIST 11/ALTON/ **MADISON**	00308010	618/474-2600	169
Alton High Sch/Alton/Madison	00308022	618/474-2700	169
Alton Middle Sch/Alton/Madison	00308058	618/474-2200	169
Alton Success Academy/Alton/Madison	05092931	618/474-2203	169
ALWOOD CMTY UNIT SCH DIST 225/ **WOODHULL/HENRY**	00295061	309/334-2719	116
Alwood Elem Sch/Alpha/Henry	00295073	309/629-5011	116
Alwood Jr Sr High Sch/Woodhull/Henry	00295085	309/334-2102	116
Amboy Central Elem Sch/Amboy/Lee	00303802	815/857-3619	159

DISTRICT & SCHOOL TELEPHONE INDEX

Market Data Retrieval

School/City/County DISTRICT/CITY/COUNTY	PID	TELEPHONE NUMBER	PAGE
AMBOY CMTY UNIT SCH DIST 272/			
AMBOY/LEE	00303797	815/857-2164	159
Amboy High Sch/Amboy/Lee	00303814	815/857-3632	159
Amboy Junior High Sch/Amboy/Lee	00303826	815/857-3528	159
Amelia Carriel Junior High Sch/O Fallon/St Clair	11456341	618/622-2932	221
Americana Elem Sch/Glendale HTS/Du Page	00291132	630/260-6135	98
Amos Alonzo Stagg High Sch/Palos Hills/Cook	00272916	708/974-7400	44
Amundsen High Sch/Chicago/Cook	00278879	773/534-2320	26
Ancona Sch/Chicago/Cook	01441574	773/924-2356	77
Andalusia Elem Sch/Andalusia/Rock Island	00316043	309/793-8080	209
Anderson Elem Sch/Saint Charles/Kane	00298752	331/228-3300	128
Andrew Cooke Magnet Elem Sch/Waukegan/Lake	00302092	224/303-1700	156
Andrew Jackson Language Acad/Chicago/Cook	00277837	773/534-7000	31
Ann Reid Early Childhood Ctr/Naperville/Du Page	11552660	630/420-6899	98
ANNA CMTY CONS SCH DIST 37/			
ANNA/UNION	00321830	618/833-6812	230
Anna Junior High Sch/Anna/Union	00321842	618/833-6415	230
Anna McDonald Elem Sch/Manhattan/Will	00325290	815/478-3310	244
ANNA-JONESBORO CMTY HSD 81/			
ANNA/UNION	00321878	618/833-8421	230
Anna-Jonesboro High Sch/Anna/Union	00321880	618/833-8421	230
ANNAWAN CMTY UNIT SD 226/			
ANNAWAN/HENRY	00295102	309/935-6781	116
Annawan Grade Sch/Annawan/Henry	00295138	309/935-6623	116
Annawan High Sch/Annawan/Henry	00295114	309/935-6781	116
Anne Fox Elem Sch/Hanover Park/Cook	00273879	630/736-3500	66
Anne M Jeans Elem Sch/Willowbrook/Du Page	00290865	630/325-8186	90
Anne Sullivan Elem Sch/Prospect HTS/Cook	00273336	847/870-3865	63
Annette Harris Officer ES/E Saint Louis/St Clair	00316859	618/646-3970	218
Annunciata Elem Sch/Chicago/Cook	00283006	773/375-5711	72
Annunciation BVM Sch/Aurora/Kane	00328357	630/851-4300	133
ANTIOCH CMTY CONS SCH DIST 34/			
ANTIOCH/LAKE	00300379	847/838-8400	146
Antioch Cmty High Sch/Antioch/Lake	00300434	847/395-1421	148
Antioch Elem Sch/Antioch/Lake	00300381	847/838-8901	146
Antioch Upper Grade Sch/Antioch/Lake	00300393	847/838-8301	146
Aplington Middle Sch/Polo/Ogle	00312140	815/946-2519	195
Apollo Elem Sch/Aledo/Mercer	00310659	309/582-5350	189
Apollo Elem Sch/Des Plaines/Cook	04020038	847/827-6231	47
Aptakisic Junior High Sch/Buffalo Grove/Lake	02112295	847/353-5500	146
APTAKISIC-TRIPP SCH DIST 102/			
BUFFALO GROVE/LAKE	00300446	847/353-5650	146
Aqsa Sch/Bridgeview/Cook	03180271	708/598-2700	77
Aquin Catholic Jr Sr High Sch/Freeport/Stephenson	00328369	815/235-3154	225
Aquin Elementary/Freeport/Stephenson	00328668	815/232-6416	225
Arbor Park Middle Sch/Oak Forest/Cook	00266943	708/687-5330	21
ARBOR PARK SCH DIST 145/			
OAK FOREST/COOK	00266931	708/687-8040	21
Arbor View Elem Sch/Glen Ellyn/Du Page	00289842	630/469-5505	90
Arbury Hills Elem Sch/Mokena/Will	00325783	708/479-2106	247
Arcadia Elem Sch/Olympia FLDS/Cook	00271259	708/747-3535	57
ARCHDIOCESE OF CHICAGO ED OFF/			
CHICAGO/COOK	00282923	312/534-5200	72
ARCOLA CMTY UNIT SCH DIST 306/			
ARCOLA/DOUGLAS	00288666	217/268-4963	87
Arcola Elem Sch/Arcola/Douglas	00288678	217/268-4961	87
Arcola Jr Sr High Sch/Arcola/Douglas	00288680	217/268-4962	87
Ardmore Elem Sch/Addison/Du Page	04038906	630/458-2900	88
Ardmore Elem Sch/Villa Park/Du Page	00291273	630/516-7370	99
AREA 3 LEARNING TECHNOLOGY CTR/			
EDWARDS/PEORIA	04433198	309/680-5800	200
AREA 5 LEARNING TECHNOLOGY HUB/			
EDWARDSVILLE/MADISON	04433186	217/646-0221	174
AREA 6 LEARNING TECHNOLOGY CTR/			
ROBINSON/CRAWFORD	04433203	618/544-2719	83
ARGENTA OREANA CMTY UNIT SD 1/			
ARGENTA/MACON	00306828	217/795-2313	165
Argenta Oreana Elem Sch/Oreana/Macon	00306866	217/468-2412	165
Argenta Oreana High Sch/Argenta/Macon	00306842	217/795-4821	165
Argenta Oreana Middle Sch/Argenta/Macon	01398317	217/795-2163	165
Argo Cmty High Sch/Summit/Cook	00266993	708/728-3200	21
ARGO CMTY HIGH SCH DIST 217/			
SUMMIT/COOK	00266981	708/728-3200	21
Arie Crown Hebrew Day Sch/Skokie/Cook	00281709	847/982-9191	77
Ariel Community Academy/Chicago/Cook	04486963	773/535-1996	33
Arland D Williams Elem Sch/Mattoon/Coles	00266802	217/238-2800	19
Arlene Welch Elem Sch/Naperville/Du Page	04876394	630/428-7200	95
ARLINGTON HTS SCH DIST 25/			
ARLINGTON HTS/COOK	00267002	847/758-4900	21
Arlyn Day Sch/Highland Park/Lake	02956560	847/256-7117	158
Armour Elem Sch/Chicago/Cook	00276924	773/535-4530	31
Armstrong Ellis Elem Sch/Armstrong/Vermilion	00322078	217/569-2115	231
ARMSTRONG ELLIS SD 61/ARMSTRONG/			
VERMILION	00322066	217/569-2115	231
Armstrong Int'l Studies ES/Chicago/Cook	00279677	773/534-2150	29
Armstrong Twp High Sch/Armstrong/Vermilion	00322107	217/569-2122	231
ARMSTRONG TWP HIGH SD 225/			
ARMSTRONG/VERMILION	00322092	217/569-2122	231
Army Trail Elem Sch/Addison/Du Page	00288874	630/458-2502	88
Arnett C Lines Elem Sch/Barrington/Lake	00267507	847/381-7850	147
Arnold J Tyler Elem Sch/New Lenox/Will	02127850	815/485-2398	245
Arnold Mireles Academy/Chicago/Cook	00276352	773/535-6360	35
Arnold W Kruse Ed Center/Orland Park/Cook	00274861	708/614-4530	42
Arrowhead Ranch Sch/Coal Valley/Rock Island	00315506	309/799-7044	209
Art In Motion/Chicago/Cook	12367365	773/820-9426	38
Arthur Ashe Elem Sch/Chicago/Cook	00276481	773/535-3550	35
Arthur Christian Sch/Arthur/Douglas	01442528	217/543-2397	88
ARTHUR CUSD 305/ARTHUR/DOUGLAS	00288707	217/543-2511	87
Arthur Grade Sch/Arthur/Douglas	00288719	217/543-2109	88
Arthur Lovington High Sch/Arthur/Douglas	11821344	217/543-2146	88
Ascension Sch/Oak Park/Cook	00283032	708/386-7282	72
Ashburn Elem Sch/Chicago/Cook	05102237	773/535-7860	33
Ashkum Early Literacy Center/Ashkum/Iroquois	00295566	815/698-2212	118
ASHLEY CMTY CONS SD 15/ASHLEY/			
WASHINGTON	00323230	618/485-6611	235
Ashley Elem Sch/Ashley/Washington	00323242	618/485-6611	235
Ashmore Elem Sch/Ashmore/Coles	00266591	217/349-3000	19
Ashton Franklin Ctr Elem Sch/Franklin GRV/Lee	00304002	815/456-2325	159
Ashton Franklin Jr Sr High/Ashton/Lee	00303888	815/453-7461	159
ASHTON-FRANKLIN CENTER SD 275/			
ASHTON/LEE	00303864	815/453-7461	159
Aspen Elem Sch/Vernon Hills/Lake	04867862	847/990-4300	151
Aspira Business & Finance HS/Chicago/Cook	12109383	773/303-3559	38
Aspira Chtr-Early College HS/Chicago/Cook	10912421	773/243-1626	39
Aspira Haugan Middle Sch/Chicago/Cook	10009206	773/303-3549	39
Aspire Alternative High Sch/Effingham/Effingham	11826071	217/342-2865	104
ASTORIA CMTY UNIT SCH DIST 1/			
ASTORIA/FULTON	00293295	309/329-2156	109
Astoria Grade Sch/Astoria/Fulton	04430366	309/329-2158	109
Astoria High Sch/Astoria/Fulton	04430354	309/329-2156	109
Astoria Junior High Sch/Astoria/Fulton	00293312	309/329-2156	109
ATHENS CMTY UNIT SCH DIST 213/			
ATHENS/MENARD	00310506	217/636-8761	188
Athens High Sch/Athens/Menard	00310520	217/636-8314	188
Athens Junior High Sch/Athens/Menard	00310518	217/636-8380	188
Att-Ptach Special Ed Program/Skokie/Cook	02956637	847/675-1670	77
ATWOOD HEIGHTS SD 125/ALSIP/COOK	00267404	708/371-0080	21
Atwood-Hammond Grade Sch/Atwood/Douglas	00314277	217/578-2229	88
AUBURN CMTY UNIT SCH DIST 10/			
AUBURN/SANGAMON	00318522	217/438-6164	211
Auburn Elem Sch/Auburn/Sangamon	00318534	217/438-6916	211
Auburn High Sch/Auburn/Sangamon	00318546	217/438-6817	211
Auburn High Sch/Rockford/Winnebago	00327444	815/966-3300	254
Auburn Junior High Sch/Divernon/Sangamon	10914376	217/628-3414	211
Auburn Middle Sch/Auburn/Sangamon	00318558	217/438-6919	211
Audubon Elem Sch/Chicago/Cook	00278934	773/534-5470	30
Augustin Lara Elem Acad/Chicago/Cook	04487034	773/535-4389	32
Augustus Tolton Academy/Chicago/Cook	00285298	773/224-3811	72
Aurora Central Catholic HS/Aurora/Kane	00328371	630/907-0095	133
Aurora Christian Elem Sch/Aurora/Kane	11238979	630/892-1551	133
Aurora Chrn Middle High Sch/Aurora/Kane	11547952	630/892-1551	133
Austin College & Career Acad/Chicago/Cook	11131254	773/534-0660	37
Autumn Creek Elem Sch/Yorkville/Kendall	11455579	630/553-4048	139
Aux Sable Elem Sch/Minooka/Grundy	10022038	815/467-5301	112
Aux Sable Middle Sch/Joliet/Will	10028692	815/439-7092	246
Avalon Park Elem Sch/Chicago/Cook	00274988	773/535-6615	26
Avery Coonley Sch/Downers Grove/Du Page	00291675	630/969-0800	101
Avis Huff Impact/Kankakee/Kankakee	12309337	815/802-4400	135
Aviston Elem Sch/Aviston/Clinton	00266278	618/228-7245	17
AVISTON ELEM SCH DIST 21/			
AVISTON/CLINTON	00266266	618/228-7245	17
AVOCA SCH DIST 37/WILMETTE/COOK	00267454	847/251-3587	22
Avoca West Elem Sch/Glenview/Cook	00267480	847/724-6800	22

IL-V2 800-333-8802 School Year 2020-2021

Illinois School Directory
DISTRICT & SCHOOL TELEPHONE INDEX

School/City/County DISTRICT/CITY/COUNTY	PID	TELEPHONE NUMBER	PAGE
Avon Center Elem Sch/Round Lk Bch/Lake	00300472	847/223-3530	148
Avon Elem Sch/Avon/Knox	00293336	309/465-3851	139
Avondale-Logandale Sch/Chicago/Cook	00278984	773/534-5350	30

B

School/City/County DISTRICT/CITY/COUNTY	PID	TELEPHONE NUMBER	PAGE
B J Hooper Elem Sch/Lindenhurst/Lake	00301359	847/356-2151	152
B T Washington STEM Acad/Champaign/Champaign	00264880	217/351-3901	10
Back of the Yards IB High Sch/Chicago/Cook	11926231	773/535-7320	26
Bais Yaakov High Sch/Chicago/Cook	04332714	773/267-1494	77
Baker Demonstration Sch/Wilmette/Cook	00281993	847/425-5800	77
Baldwin Elem Sch/Quincy/Adams	00263070	217/223-0003	2
BALL CHATHAM CMTY UNIT SD 5/ CHATHAM/SANGAMON	00318560	217/483-2416	211
Ball Elem Sch/Chatham/Sangamon	00318572	217/483-2414	211
Balmoral Elem Sch/Crete/Will	00324674	708/367-2500	242
Banner Elem Sch/Dunlap/Peoria	02108036	309/243-7774	196
Bannockburn Elem Sch/Bannockburn/Lake	00300496	847/945-5900	147
BANNOCKBURN SCH DIST 106/ BANNOCKBURN/LAKE	00300484	847/945-5900	147
Barack Obama Leadership & STEM/Chicago HTS/Cook	12102725	708/668-9100	62
Barack Obama Learning Academy/Markham/Cook	12104565	708/825-2400	52
Barbara B Rose Elem Sch/S Barrington/Lake	04838196	847/844-1200	147
Barbara Vick Early Chld Center/Chicago/Cook	04875766	773/535-2671	33
Barnard Elem Comp Math & Sci/Chicago/Cook	00275009	773/535-2625	33
Barnsdale Road Sch/La Grange Pk/Cook	11180920	708/482-3003	54
BARRINGTON CMTY UNIT SD 220/ BARRINGTON/LAKE	00267492	847/381-6300	147
Barrington Early Learning Ctr/Barrington/Lake	03008063	224/770-4300	147
Barrington High Sch/Barrington/Lake	00267519	847/381-1400	147
Barrington MS-Prairie Campus/Barrington/Lake	04020076	847/304-3990	147
Barrington MS-Station Campus/Barrington/Lake	00267521	847/756-6400	147
Barry Elem Sch/Chicago/Cook	00278996	773/534-3455	26
Bartelso Elem Sch/Bartelso/Clinton	00266292	618/765-2164	17
BARTELSO SCH DIST 57/BARTELSO/CLINTON	00266280	618/765-2164	17
Bartlett Elem Sch/Bartlett/Kane	00298178	630/213-5545	130
Bartlett High Sch/Bartlett/Kane	04747573	630/372-4700	130
Barton Elem Sch/Chicago/Cook	00275011	773/535-3260	34
Bartonville Elem Sch/Bartonville/Peoria	00312255	309/697-3253	196
BARTONVILLE SCH DIST 66/ BARTONVILLE/PEORIA	00312243	309/697-3253	196
Bass Elem Sch/Chicago/Cook	00275023	773/535-3275	34
Batavia High Sch/Batavia/Kane	00297849	630/937-8600	128
BATAVIA UNIT SCH DIST 101/ BATAVIA/KANE	00297837	630/937-8800	128
Beach Elem Sch/Round Lake/Lake	00301919	847/270-9930	155
BEACH PARK CMTY CONS SD 3/ BEACH PARK/LAKE	00300501	847/599-5005	147
Beach Park Middle Sch/Beach Park/Lake	00300549	847/596-5860	147
Beacon Academy/Evanston/Cook	12178011	224/999-1177	77
Beard Elem Sch/Chicago/Cook	03008946	773/534-1228	28
Beardstown Christian Academy/Beardstown/Cass	02236944	217/323-1685	9
BEARDSTOWN CMTY SCH DIST 15/ BEARDSTOWN/CASS	00264505	217/323-3099	9
Beardstown Middle High Sch/Beardstown/Cass	00264529	217/323-3665	9
Beasley Elem Mgnt Academic Ctr/Chicago/Cook	01821663	773/535-1230	33
Beaubien Elem Sch/Chicago/Cook	00279029	773/534-3500	28
Beautiful Beginnings/Rockford/Winnebago	12374942	815/703-4712	256
Beck Area Career Center/Red Bud/Randolph	00316586	618/473-2222	205
Beckemeyer Elem Sch/Beckemeyer/Clinton	00266319	618/227-8242	17
Beckemeyer Elem Sch/Hillsboro/Montgomery	00311005	217/532-6994	191
Bednarcik Junior High Sch/Aurora/Kendall	05092137	630/636-2500	137
Beebe Elem Sch/Naperville/Du Page	00290712	630/420-6332	98
BEECHER CITY CMTY UNIT SD 20/ BEECHER CITY/EFFINGHAM	00292174	618/487-5100	104
Beecher City Grade Sch/Beecher City/Effingham	00292186	618/487-5108	104
Beecher City Jr Sr High Sch/Beecher City/Effingham	00292198	618/487-5117	104
BEECHER CMTY SCH DIST 200-U/ BEECHER/WILL	00324533	708/946-2266	241
Beecher Elem Sch/Beecher/Will	00324545	708/946-2202	241
Beecher High Sch/Beecher/Will	00324557	708/946-2266	241
Beecher Junior High Sch/Beecher/Will	05276711	708/946-3412	241
Beethoven Elem Sch/Chicago/Cook	00275073	773/535-1480	33
Belding Elem Sch/Chicago/Cook	00279043	773/534-3590	28
Bell Elem Sch/Chicago/Cook	00279055	773/534-5150	30
Bell-Graham Elem Sch/Saint Charles/Kane	04915225	331/228-2100	128
Belle Aire Elem Sch/Downers Grove/Du Page	00289335	630/719-5820	93
Belle Alexander Elem Sch/Kewanee/Henry	00295358	309/852-2449	117
Belle Valley Elem Sch/Belleville/St Clair	00316213	618/236-5200	217
BELLE VALLEY SCH DIST 119/ BELLEVILLE/ST CLAIR	00316201	618/236-5200	217
Belleville Alternative Sch/Belleville/St Clair	12315312	618/222-3723	217
BELLEVILLE AREA SP SVC CO-OP/ BELLEVILLE/ST CLAIR	02184078	618/355-4700	223
Belleville High School-East/Belleville/St Clair	00316378	618/222-3700	217
BELLEVILLE PUBLIC SCH DIST 118/ BELLEVILLE/ST CLAIR	00316237	618/233-2830	217
BELLEVILLE TOWNSHIP HSD 201/ BELLEVILLE/ST CLAIR	00316366	618/222-8241	217
Belleville Twp High Sch-West/Belleville/St Clair	00316380	618/222-7500	217
BELLWOOD SCH DIST 88/BELLWOOD/COOK	00267600	708/344-9344	22
Belmont-Cragin Elem Sch/Chicago/Cook	05102213	773/534-2900	26
Belvidere Central Middle Sch/Belvidere/Boone	05095696	815/544-0190	4
BELVIDERE CMTY UNIT SD 100/ BELVIDERE/BOONE	00263422	815/544-0301	4
Belvidere High Sch/Belvidere/Boone	00263446	815/547-6345	4
Belvidere North High Sch/Belvidere/Boone	10905210	815/544-2636	4
Belvidere South Middle Sch/Belvidere/Boone	00263434	815/544-3175	4
BEMENT CMTY UNIT SCH DIST 5/ BEMENT/PIATT	00314306	217/678-4200	202
Bement Elem Sch/Bement/Piatt	00314318	217/678-4200	202
Bement High Sch/Bement/Piatt	05097943	217/678-4200	202
Bement Middle Sch/Bement/Piatt	05097931	217/678-4200	202
Ben-Gil Elem Sch/Gillespie/Macoupin	00307705	217/839-4828	167
Benavides Steam Academy/Aurora/Kane	12038461	630/299-7560	129
Benet Academy/Lisle/Du Page	00325977	630/969-6550	100
Benito Juarez Cmty Academy/Chicago/Cook	01601059	773/534-7030	26
Benjamin Braun Educational Ctr/Oak Forest/Cook	04197083	708/687-4971	20
Benjamin Elem Sch/Bloomington/Mclean	11558286	309/557-4410	186
Benjamin Franklin Elem Sch/Decatur/Macon	00306945	217/362-3560	165
Benjamin Franklin Elem Sch/Glen Ellyn/Du Page	00289749	630/790-6480	94
Benjamin Franklin Elem Sch/Moline/Rock Island	00315518	309/743-1607	207
Benjamin Franklin Elem Sch/Park Ridge/Cook	00273104	847/318-4390	62
Benjamin Franklin Middle Sch/Springfield/Sangamon	00318962	217/787-3006	213
Benjamin Mays Academy/Chicago/Cook	02107604	773/535-3892	34
Benjamin Middle Sch/West Chicago/Du Page	00288977	630/876-7820	89
BENJAMIN SCH DIST 25/WEST CHICAGO/DU PAGE	00288965	630/876-7800	89
Bennett Day School-Flagship/Chicago/Cook	12177861	312/236-6388	77
Bennett Elem Sch/Chicago/Cook	00275085	773/535-5460	35
BENSENVILLE ELEM SCH DIST 2/ BENSENVILLE/DU PAGE	00288989	630/766-5940	89
Bent Elem Sch/Bloomington/Mclean	00306153	309/828-4315	185
BENTON CMTY CONS SCH DIST 47/ BENTON/FRANKLIN	00292899	618/439-3136	107
Benton Cons Dist 103 High Sch/Benton/Franklin	00292978	618/439-3103	107
BENTON CONS HIGH SCH DIST 103/ BENTON/FRANKLIN	00292966	618/439-3103	107
Benton Grade School 5-8/Benton/Franklin	02055788	618/438-4011	107
Benton Grade School K-4/Benton/Franklin	00292916	618/438-7181	107
Berean Christian Sch/Fairview HTS/St Clair	00317633	618/825-0609	223
Berger-Vandenberg Elem Sch/Dolton/Cook	00269036	708/841-3606	46
BERKELEY SCH DIST 87/BERKELEY/COOK	00267698	708/449-3350	22
Bernard J Ward Elem Sch/Bolingbrook/Will	00325599	630/972-9200	248
Bernard Long Sch/Madison/Madison	00309026	618/877-1712	172
Bernard Zell Anshe Emet Sch/Chicago/Cook	00281682	773/281-1858	77
Bert H Fulton Elem Sch/Tinley Park/Cook	00274847	708/614-4525	42
BERWYN NORTH SCH DIST 98/ BERWYN/COOK	00267806	708/484-6200	22
BERWYN SOUTH SCH DIST 100/ BERWYN/COOK	00267856	708/795-2300	23
BETHALTO CMTY UNIT SD 8/ BETHALTO/MADISON	00308242	618/377-7200	169

School Year 2020-2021 800-333-8802 IL-V3

DISTRICT & SCHOOL TELEPHONE INDEX

Market Data Retrieval

School/City/County DISTRICT/CITY/COUNTY	PID	TELEPHONE NUMBER	PAGE
Bethalto East Primary Sch/Bethalto/Madison	00308254	618/377-7250	169
Bethany Lutheran Sch/Naperville/Du Page	00291560	630/355-6607	101
Bethel Academy/Northlake/Cook	04295099	708/865-2855	77
Bethel Grade Sch/Mount Vernon/Jefferson	00296613	618/244-8095	122
Bethel Lutheran Sch/Morton/Tazewell	02992617	309/266-6592	229
BETHEL SCH DIST 82/MOUNT VERNON/ JEFFERSON	00296601	618/244-8095	122
Bethesda Lutheran Sch/Chicago/Cook	00281785	773/743-0800	77
Betsy Ross Elem Sch/Forest Park/Cook	00269696	708/366-7498	50
Betsy Ross Elem Sch/Prospect HTS/Cook	00273348	847/870-3868	63
Beulah Park Elem Sch/Zion/Lake	00302470	847/746-1429	157
Beverly Hills Elem Sch/Chicago/Cook	01405099	773/779-5158	77
Beverly Manor Sch/Washington/Tazewell	02043888	309/745-3921	226
Beverly Skoff Elem Sch/Romeoville/Will	10002363	815/886-8384	248
Beyer Early Childhood Center/Rockford/ Winnebago	00327470	815/966-3390	254
Bhra High Sch/Bismarck/Vermilion	00322133	217/759-7291	231
BI-COUNTY SPECIAL ED CO-OP/ STERLING/WHITESIDE	02229018	815/622-0858	240
Bible Baptist Chrn Academy/Carpentersvle/ Kane	02827622	847/428-0870	133
Bicentennial Elem Sch/Coal Valley/ Rock Island	00315544	309/431-1614	207
Big Hollow Elem Sch/Ingleside/Lake	00300563	847/740-5321	148
Big Hollow Middle Sch/Ingleside/Lake	04803309	847/740-5322	148
Big Hollow Primary Sch/Ingleside/Lake	04924525	847/740-5320	148
BIG HOLLOW SCH DIST 38/INGLESIDE/ LAKE	00300551	847/740-1490	148
Bishop McNamara Cath Sch/Bradley/Kankakee	00326359	815/933-8013	137
Bishop McNamara Catholic Sch/Bourbonnais/ Kankakee	00326103	815/933-7758	137
Bishop McNamara High Sch/Kankakee/Kankakee	00325989	815/932-7413	137
Bismarck Henning Elem Sch/Bismarck/ Vermilion	00322121	217/759-7251	231
Bismarck Henning Jr High Sch/Bismarck/ Vermilion	00322145	217/759-7301	231
BISMARCK-HENNING CMTY SD 1/ BISMARCK/VERMILION	00322119	217/759-7261	231
Black Hawk Area Spec Ed Center/East Moline/ Rock Island	01539523	309/796-2500	207
BLACK HAWK AREA SPEC ED DIST/ EAST MOLINE/ROCK ISLAND	02182226	309/796-2500	210
Black Hawk Elem Sch/Springfield/Sangamon	00318895	217/525-3195	213
Blackberry Creek Elem Sch/Elburn/Kane	05364423	630/365-1122	132
Blackhawk Elem Sch/Freeport/Stephenson	00320757	815/232-0490	224
Blackhawk Elem Sch/Glendale HTS/Du Page	01531143	630/893-5750	97
Blackhawk Elem Sch/South Beloit/Winnebago	05318981	815/389-4001	255
Blackhawk Middle Sch/Bensenville/Du Page	00288991	630/766-2601	89
Blackhawk Primary Center/Park Forest/Cook	00272978	708/668-9500	62
Blackstone Elem Sch/Mendota/La Salle	01557836	815/539-6888	142
Blair Early Childhood Center/Chicago/Cook	00277071	773/535-2076	33
Blessed Sacrament Catholic Sch/Quincy/ Adams	00319801	217/228-1477	2
Blessed Sacrament Sch/Belleville/St Clair	00317700	618/397-1111	222
Blessed Sacrament Sch/Morton/Tazewell	00313376	309/263-8442	229
Blessed Sacrament Sch/Springfield/Sangamon	00319409	217/522-7534	214
Bloom High Sch/Chicago HTS/Cook	00267959	708/755-1122	23
Bloom Trail High Sch/Chicago HTS/Cook	00267947	708/758-7000	23
Bloom Twp Alternative High Sch/Chicago HTS/ Cook	02202656	708/754-4095	23
BLOOM TWP HIGH SCH DIST 206/ CHICAGO HTS/COOK	00267935	708/755-7010	23
BLOOMINGDALE SCH DIST 13/ BLOOMINGDALE/DU PAGE	00289050	630/893-9590	89
Bloomington Area Voc Center/Bloomington/ Mclean	00306177	309/829-8671	185
Bloomington High Sch/Bloomington/Mclean	00306191	309/828-5201	185
Bloomington Junior High Sch/Bloomington/ Mclean	00306189	309/827-0086	185
BLOOMINGTON SCH DIST 87/ BLOOMINGTON/MCLEAN	00306141	309/827-6031	185
BLUE RIDGE CMTY SD 18/FARMER CITY/ DEWITT	00288563	309/928-9141	87
Blue Ridge High Sch/Farmer City/Dewitt	00288575	309/928-2622	87
Blue Ridge Interm Jr High Sch/Mansfield/ Dewitt	00288587	217/489-5201	87
Bluffs Cmty Unit Sch/Bluffs/Scott	00320226	217/754-3815	215
Bluffview Elem Sch/Dupo/St Clair	00316598	618/286-3311	218
Bluford Sch/Bluford/Jefferson	00296637	618/732-8242	122
BLUFORD UNIT SCH DIST 318/ BLUFORD/JEFFERSON	00296625	618/732-8242	122
Blythe Park Elem Sch/Riverside/Cook	00273697	708/447-2168	65
BMP SPEC ED CO-OP/TISKILWA/ BUREAU	02183907	815/646-8031	7
Bogan Computer Tech High Sch/Chicago/Cook	00276950	773/535-2180	37
Bolingbrook High Sch/Bolingbrook/Will	00325604	630/759-6400	248
BOND CO CMTY UNIT SCH DIST 2/ GREENVILLE/BOND	00263329	618/664-0170	4
Bond Elem Sch/Chicago/Cook	00275114	773/535-3480	34
Bond Elementary/Assumption/Christian	00265559	217/226-4022	14
Bonfield Grade Sch/Bonfield/Kankakee	00299110	815/933-6995	135
Bonnie McBeth Early Lrng Ctr/Plainfield/ Will	04944654	815/439-4288	246
BOONE CO SPECIAL ED CO-OP/ BELVIDERE/BOONE	02182305	815/544-9851	5
Boone Elem Sch/Chicago/Cook	00279093	773/534-2160	29
BOONE-WINNEBAGO REG OFF OF ED/ LOVES PARK/WINNEBAGO	02098510	815/636-3060	256
Booth Elem Sch/Enfield/White	00323802	618/963-2521	238
Booth Tarkington Elem Sch/Wheeling/Cook	00281527	847/520-2775	71
Bottenfield Elem Sch/Champaign/Champaign	00264725	217/351-3807	10
Boulder Hill Elem Sch/Montgomery/Kendall	00299691	630/636-2900	137
BOURBONNAIS ELEM SCH DIST 53/ BOURBONNAIS/KANKAKEE	00298958	815/929-5100	134
Bourbonnais Upper Grade Center/Bourbonnais/ Kankakee	01529229	815/929-5200	134
Bower Elem Sch/Warrenville/Du Page	00290889	630/393-9413	92
Bowlesburg Elem Sch/Silvis/Rock Island	00315398	309/792-2947	207
Boylan Central Cath High Sch/Rockford/ Winnebago	00328383	815/877-0531	256
Braceville Elem Sch/Braceville/Grundy	00294043	815/237-8040	111
BRACEVILLE ELEM SCH DIST 75/ BRACEVILLE/GRUNDY	00294031	815/237-8040	111
BRADFORD CMTY UNIT SCH DIST 1/ BRADFORD/STARK	00320563	309/897-2801	223
Bradford Grade Sch/Bradford/Stark	00320575	309/897-4611	223
Bradley Central Middle Sch/Bradley/ Kankakee	00299005	815/939-3564	134
Bradley East Elem Sch/Bradley/Kankakee	00299017	815/933-2233	134
BRADLEY ELEM SCH DIST 61/ BRADLEY/KANKAKEE	00298996	815/933-3371	134
Bradley West Elem Sch/Bradley/Kankakee	00299029	815/933-2216	134
BRADLEY-BOURBONNAIS CHSD 307/ BRADLEY/KANKAKEE	00299031	815/937-3707	134
Bradley-Bourbonnais High Sch/Bradley/ Kankakee	00299043	815/937-3707	135
Bradwell School of Excellence/Chicago/Cook	00275140	773/535-6600	26
Braeside Elem Sch/Highland Park/Lake	00301000	224/765-3400	154
Breese Elem Sch/Breese/Clinton	00266321	618/526-7128	17
BREESE ELEMENTARY SD 12/ BREESE/CLINTON	00266307	618/526-7128	17
Brehm Preparatory Sch/Carbondale/Jackson	02824060	618/457-0371	121
BREMEN CMTY HIGH SD 228/ MIDLOTHIAN/COOK	00268070	708/389-1175	23
Bremen High Sch/Midlothian/Cook	00268082	708/371-3600	23
Brennemann Elem Sch/Chicago/Cook	00279122	773/534-5766	29
Brentano Math & Science Acad/Chicago/Cook	00279134	773/534-4100	30
Brentwood Bapt Christian Acad/Des Plaines/ Cook	02189781	847/298-3399	77
Brentwood Elem Sch/Des Plaines/Cook	00267208	847/593-4401	43
Bret Harte Elem Sch/Chicago/Cook	00275798	773/535-0870	33
Briar Glen Elem Sch/Wheaton/Du Page	00289854	630/545-3300	90
Briargate Elem Sch/Cary/McHenry	00305317	224/357-5250	179
Brickton Montessori Sch/Chicago/Cook	03016515	773/714-0646	77
Bridge Elem Sch/Chicago/Cook	00279158	773/534-3718	28
Bridge High Sch/Downers Grove/Du Page	03217501	630/355-6533	101
Bridge View Extended Day Sch/Niles/Cook	04937338	847/588-2038	77
Bridgeport Catholic Academy/Chicago/Cook	00283862	773/376-6223	72
Bridgeport Grade Sch/Bridgeport/Lawrence	00303735	618/945-5721	159
Bridgeview Elem Sch/Bridgeview/Cook	00268135	708/496-8713	53
Brigham Early Learning Ctr/Bloomington/ Mclean	00306505	309/557-4411	186
Bright Futures Preschool/Galesburg/Knox	00300068	309/973-2031	140
Bright Sch/Chicago/Cook	00275164	773/535-6215	35
Brighton North Primary Sch/Brighton/ Macoupin	01550412	618/372-3813	168
Brighton Park Elem Sch/Chicago/Cook	03380926	773/535-7237	32
BRIMFIELD CMTY UNIT SD 309/ BRIMFIELD/PEORIA	00312293	309/446-3378	196
Brimfield Grade Sch/Brimfield/Peoria	00312308	309/446-3366	196
Brimfield High Sch/Brimfield/Peoria	00312310	309/446-3349	196
Bristol Bay Elem Sch/Yorkville/Kendall	11134115	630/553-5121	139
Bristol Grade Sch/Bristol/Kendall	00299811	630/553-4383	139
British Int'l Chicago-S Loop/Chicago/Cook	12114091	773/998-2472	77

Illinois School Directory

DISTRICT & SCHOOL TELEPHONE INDEX

School/City/County DISTRICT/CITY/COUNTY	PID	TELEPHONE	PAGE NUMBER
British School of Chicago/Chicago/Cook	05359997	773/506-2097	77
Britten Sch/Westchester/Cook	04196986	708/343-7500	20
Broadmeadow Grade Level Sch/Rantoul/Champaign	00265121	217/893-5405	11
Broadmoor Junior High Sch/Pekin/Tazewell	01524401	309/477-4731	228
Brokaw Early Learning Center/Oswego/Kendall	11563176	630/551-9600	137
Bronzeville Academy CS/Chicago/Cook	12259201	773/285-8040	39
Bronzeville Classical Elem Sch/Chicago/Cook	12314629	773/535-8085	33
Bronzeville Scholastic Inst/Chicago/Cook	10009127	773/535-1150	38
Brook Forest Elem Sch/Oak Brook/Du Page	00289127	630/325-6888	89
Brook Park Elem Sch/La Grange Pk/Cook	00268202	708/354-3740	23
Brookdale Elem Sch/Naperville/Du Page	02855693	630/428-6800	95
BROOKFIELD-LAGRANGE PARK SD 95/BROOKFIELD/COOK	00268197	708/485-0606	23
BROOKLYN SCH DIST 188/LOVEJOY/ST CLAIR	00316392	618/271-1014	217
Brookport Elem Sch/Brookport/Massac	01845009	618/564-2482	178
Brooks Middle Sch/Bolingbrook/Will	05343194	630/759-6340	248
Brooks Middle Sch/Harvey/Cook	02126181	708/333-6390	51
Brookview Elem Sch/Rockford/Winnebago	00327494	815/229-2492	254
Brookwood Junior High Sch/Glenwood/Cook	00268240	708/758-5252	24
Brookwood Middle Sch/Glenwood/Cook	00268238	708/758-5350	24
BROOKWOOD SCH DIST 167/GLENWOOD/COOK	00268226	708/758-5190	24
Brother Rice High Sch/Chicago/Cook	00283109	773/429-4300	72
BROWN CO CMTY UNIT SCH DIST 1/MT STERLING/BROWN	00263575	217/773-3359	5
Brown Co Elem Sch/Mt Sterling/Brown	00263599	217/773-7500	5
Brown Co High Sch/Mt Sterling/Brown	00263587	217/773-7500	5
Brown County Middle Sch/Mt Sterling/Brown	00263628	217/773-7500	5
Brownell Elem Sch/Chicago/Cook	01821687	773/535-3030	35
BROWNSTOWN CMTY UNIT SD 201/BROWNSTOWN/FAYETTE	00292459	618/427-3355	105
Brownstown Elem Sch/Brownstown/Fayette	00292461	618/427-3368	105
Brownstown Jr Sr High Sch/Brownstown/Fayette	00292473	618/427-3839	105
Brownsville Attendance Center/Carmi/White	00323709	618/265-3256	238
Bruning Elem Sch/Wilmington/Will	00325898	815/926-1683	249
Brunson Math & Sci Sch/Chicago/Cook	00279201	773/534-6025	29
BRUSSELS CMTY UNIT SCH DIST 42/BRUSSELS/CALHOUN	00264206	618/883-2131	8
Brussels Grade Sch/Brussels/Calhoun	00264220	618/883-2131	8
Brussels High Sch/Brussels/Calhoun	00264218	618/883-2131	8
Bryan Middle Sch/Elmhurst/Du Page	00289490	630/617-2350	93
Bryant Elem Sch/Harvey/Cook	00270138	708/331-1390	51
Bryce-Ash Grove Ed Center/Milford/Iroquois	04198180	815/889-4120	118
Budlong Elem Sch/Chicago/Cook	00279160	773/534-2591	26
Buffalo Grove High Sch/Buffalo Grove/Cook	00271663	847/718-4000	70
BUNCOMBE CONS SCH DIST 43/BUNCOMBE/JOHNSON	00297356	618/658-8830	127
Buncombe Consolidated Sch/Buncombe/Johnson	00297368	618/658-8830	127
BUNKER HILL CMTY UNIT SD 8/BUNKER HILL/MACOUPIN	00307585	618/585-3116	167
Bunker Hill High Sch/Bunker Hill/Macoupin	00307597	618/585-3232	167
BURBANK SCH DIST 111/BURBANK/COOK	00274471	708/496-0500	24
BUREAU VALLEY CMTY UNIT 340/MANLIUS/BUREAU	00263874	815/445-3101	6
Bureau Valley High Sch/Manlius/Bureau	00264141	815/445-4004	6
Bureau Valley Jr High Elem Sch/Manlius/Bureau	04801911	815/445-2121	6
Bureau Valley Walnut Elem Sch/Walnut/Bureau	00264103	815/379-2900	6
Bureau Valley Wyanet Elem Sch/Wyanet/Bureau	00264189	815/699-2251	6
Burke Elem Sch/Chicago/Cook	00275217	773/535-1325	33
Burley Elem Sch/Chicago/Cook	00279184	773/534-5475	26
Burnham Elem Sch/Burnham/Cook	00268276	708/862-8636	24
Burnham Math & Sci Academy/Chicago/Cook	00275229	773/535-6530	35
BURNHAM SCH DIST 1545/BURNHAM/COOK	00268264	708/862-8636	24
Burnside Scholastic Academy/Chicago/Cook	00275231	773/535-3300	35
Burr Elem Sch/Chicago/Cook	00279196	773/534-4090	31
Burr Oak Academy/Calumet Park/Cook	03389362	708/824-3090	25
Burr Oak Elem Sch/Calumet Park/Cook	00268343	708/388-8010	25
Burr Ridge Middle Sch/Burr Ridge/Du Page	00290853	630/325-5454	91
Burroughs Elem Sch/Chicago/Cook	00277033	773/535-7226	26
Bushnell Prairie City Elem Sch/Bushnell/McDonough	00305032	309/772-9464	178
Bushnell Prairie City High Sch/Bushnell/McDonough	00305018	309/772-2113	178
Bushnell Prairie City Jr HS/Bushnell/McDonough	00305020	309/772-3123	178
BUSHNELL PRAIRIE CMTY USD 170/BUSHNELL/MCDONOUGH	00305006	309/772-9461	178
Butler Elem Sch/Springfield/Sangamon	00318900	217/787-3189	213
Butler Junior High Sch/Oak Brook/Du Page	00289139	630/573-2760	89
BUTLER SCH DIST 53/OAK BROOK/DU PAGE	00289115	630/573-2887	89
Butterfield Elem Sch/Libertyville/Lake	00301464	847/362-3120	153
Butterfield Elem Sch/Lombard/Du Page	00290425	630/827-4000	97
Butterworth Elem Sch/Moline/Rock Island	00315532	309/743-1604	207
Byrne Elem Sch/Chicago/Cook	00277045	773/535-2170	33
BYRON CMTY UNIT SD 226/BYRON/OGLE	00311768	815/234-5491	194
Byron High Sch/Byron/Ogle	00311770	815/234-5491	194
Byron Middle Sch/Byron/Ogle	02043876	815/234-5491	194

C

School/City/County	PID	TELEPHONE	PAGE
C A Henning Elem Sch/Troy/Madison	03047148	618/667-5401	172
C B Smith Primary Sch/Pekin/Tazewell	00321438	309/477-4713	228
C E Miller Elem Sch/Westmont/Du Page	00291431	630/468-8300	92
C F Simmons Middle Sch/Aurora/Kane	00297502	630/299-4150	129
C Henry Bloom Elem Sch/Rockford/Winnebago	00327482	815/229-2170	254
C I Johnson Elem Sch/Aurora/Kane	00297526	630/299-5400	129
C M Bardwell Elem Sch/Aurora/Kane	00297514	630/299-5300	129
C R Hanna Elem Sch/Orion/Henry	00295437	309/526-3386	117
Cahokia 7th Grade Center/Cahokia/St Clair	11824841	618/332-3722	218
Cahokia 8th Grade Center/Cahokia/St Clair	11824853	618/332-3722	218
Cahokia High Sch/Cahokia/St Clair	00316433	618/332-3730	218
CAHOKIA UNIT SCH DIST 187/CAHOKIA/ST CLAIR	00316419	618/332-3700	218
Cairo Elem Sch/Cairo/Alexander	00263288	618/734-1027	3
Cairo Jr Sr High Sch/Cairo/Alexander	00263264	618/734-2187	3
CAIRO SCH DIST 1/CAIRO/ALEXANDER	00263238	618/734-4102	3
Caldwell Elem Acad of Math-Sci/Chicago/Cook	00275243	773/535-6300	26
Caledonia Christian Academy/Olmsted/Pulaski	11232121	618/742-8223	204
Caledonia Elem Sch/Caledonia/Boone	00263458	815/547-1977	4
CALHOUN CMTY UNIT SCH DIST 40/HARDIN/CALHOUN	00264232	618/576-2722	8
Calhoun Elem Sch/Hardin/Calhoun	00264256	618/576-2341	8
Calhoun High Sch/Hardin/Calhoun	00264244	618/576-2229	8
Calmeca Academy/Chicago/Cook	05277210	773/535-7000	32
CALUMET CITY SCH DIST 155/CALUMET CITY/COOK	00268288	708/862-7665	24
Calumet Elem Sch/Calumet Park/Cook	00268355	708/388-8820	25
CALUMET PUBLIC SCH DIST 132/CALUMET PARK/COOK	00268331	708/388-8920	24
Calvary Academy/South Holland/Cook	02956663	708/333-5471	77
Calvary Academy/Springfield/Sangamon	02087614	217/546-5987	214
Calvary Baptist Academy/Belleville/St Clair	03064067	618/234-3620	223
Calvary Baptist Academy/Canton/Fulton	03214999	309/647-3444	110
Calvary Baptist Academy/Chillicothe/Peoria	02190443	309/274-4343	200
Calvary Baptist Christian Acad/Urbana/Champaign	02824383	217/367-2262	13
Calvary Christian Academy/Lake Villa/Lake	02985286	847/356-6198	158
Calvary Christian Academy/Normal/Mclean	00306804	309/452-7912	188
Calvary Christian Sch/Naperville/Will	02209915	630/375-8600	249
Calvin Christian Sch/South Holland/Cook	00281838	708/331-5027	77
Calvin Coolidge Middle Sch/West Peoria/Peoria	00312724	309/672-6506	199
Cambridge Cmty Elem Sch/Cambridge/Henry	00295188	309/937-2028	116
Cambridge Cmty Jr Sr High Sch/Cambridge/Henry	00295190	309/937-2051	116
CAMBRIDGE CMTY UNIT SD 227/CAMBRIDGE/HENRY	00295176	309/937-2144	116
Cambridge Lakes Charter Sch/Pingree Grove/McHenry	10910136	847/464-4300	180
Cambridge Sch/Chicago/Cook	10758902	773/924-1200	77
Camelot Safe ES & HS/Chicago/Cook	11926267	773/902-2487	39
Camelot Sch-Bourbonnais/Bourbonnais/Kankakee	12106197	815/602-8200	137
Camelot School-DeKalb Campus/Genoa/De Kalb	04908492	815/787-4144	86
Camelot Tds of Naperville/Naperville/Du Page	05012278	630/355-0200	101
Camelot Therapeutic Day Sch/Mt Prospect/Cook	03180348	224/612-8338	77

DISTRICT & SCHOOL TELEPHONE INDEX

Market Data Retrieval

School/City/County DISTRICT/CITY/COUNTY	PID	TELEPHONE NUMBER	PAGE
Camelot-Chicago Excel Roseland/Chicago/Cook	11828421	773/629-8379	39
Camelot-Excel Englewood HS/Chicago/Cook	11926396	773/675-6654	39
Camelot-Excel Southshore HS/Chicago/Cook	12045268	773/902-7800	39
Camelot-Excel Southwest HS/Chicago/Cook	12045270	773/424-0721	39
Cameron Elem Sch/Chicago/Cook	00279237	773/534-4290	26
Campanelli Elem Sch/Schaumburg/Cook	00273893	847/357-5333	66
Campus Middle School for Girls/Urbana/Champaign	11226926	217/344-8279	13
Canaan Academy/Urbana/Champaign	04991009	217/367-6590	13
Canterbury Elem Sch/Crystal Lake/McHenry	00305367	815/788-5650	181
Canton High Sch/Canton/Fulton	00293362	309/647-1820	109
Canton Middle Sch/Streamwood/Kane	00298192	630/213-5525	130
CANTON UNION SCH DIST 66/ CANTON/FULTON	00293350	309/647-9411	109
Cantrall Elem Sch/Cantrall/Menard	00310532	217/487-7312	188
Cantrall Intermediate Sch/Cantrall/Menard	10005066	217/487-9082	188
Canty Elem Sch/Chicago/Cook	00279249	773/534-1238	28
Capron Elem Sch/Capron/Boone	00263525	815/569-2314	5
CARBON CLIFF BARSTOW SD 36/ SILVIS/ROCK ISLAND	00315350	309/792-2002	207
Carbondale Cmty High Sch/Carbondale/Jackson	00296106	618/457-3371	120
CARBONDALE CMTY HSD 165/ CARBONDALE/JACKSON	00296089	618/457-3371	120
CARBONDALE ELEM SCH DIST 95/ CARBONDALE/JACKSON	00295994	618/457-3591	120
Carbondale Middle Sch/Carbondale/Jackson	00296039	618/457-2174	120
Carbondale New Sch/Carbondale/Jackson	01779735	618/457-4765	121
Cardenas Elem Sch/Chicago/Cook	02107563	773/534-1465	26
Cardinal Bernardin Mont Acad/Chicago/Cook	05009972	773/975-6330	72
Cardinal Joseph Bernardin ES/Orland Hills/Cook	05219696	708/403-6525	72
CAREER & TECH ED CONSORTIUM/ FREEPORT/STEPHENSON	04180767	815/232-0709	225
CAREER DEVELOPMENT SYSTEM/ OAK FOREST/COOK	04177966	708/225-6021	82
CAREER EDUC ASSOC N CTL IL/ ROCKFORD/WINNEBAGO	04182260	815/921-1651	256
CAREER PREPARATION NETWORK/ CHICAGO HTS/COOK	04180509	708/709-7903	82
Carl Sandburg Elem Sch/Charleston/Coles	00266606	217/639-4000	19
Carl Sandburg Elem Sch/Wheaton/Du Page	00291041	630/682-2105	92
Carl Sandburg High Sch/Orland Park/Cook	00272928	708/671-3100	44
Carl Sandburg Jr High Sch/Rolling MDWS/Cook	00272667	847/963-7800	43
Carl Sandburg Middle Sch/Freeport/Stephenson	00320769	815/232-0340	224
Carl Sandburg Middle Sch/Mundelein/Lake	00301634	847/949-2707	153
Carl Von Linne Elem Sch/Chicago/Cook	00280092	773/534-5262	26
Carl Wehde Early Chldhd Sp Ed/Crystal Lake/McHenry	12035639	815/788-3100	181
Carleton W Washburne Sch/Winnetka/Cook	00281929	847/446-5892	72
CARLINVILLE CMTY UNIT SD 1/ CARLINVILLE/MACOUPIN	00307626	217/854-9823	167
Carlinville High Sch/Carlinville/Macoupin	00307638	217/854-3104	167
Carlinville Intermediate Sch/Carlinville/Macoupin	00307688	217/854-9523	167
Carlinville Middle Sch/Carlinville/Macoupin	03240663	217/854-3106	167
Carlinville Primary Sch/Carlinville/Macoupin	00307676	217/854-9849	167
Carlock Elem Sch/Carlock/Mclean	00306517	309/557-4412	186
CARLYLE CMTY UNIT SCH DIST 1/ CARLYLE/CLINTON	00266333	618/594-8283	17
Carlyle Grade Sch/Carlyle/Clinton	00266345	618/594-3766	17
Carlyle High Sch/Carlyle/Clinton	00266357	618/594-2453	17
Carlyle Junior High Sch/Carlyle/Clinton	04354671	618/594-8292	17
Carman-Buckner Elem Sch/Waukegan/Lake	00302133	224/303-1500	156
Carmel High Sch/Mundelein/Lake	00283123	847/566-3000	157
Carmel Montessori Academy/Warrenville/Du Page	02827543	630/393-2995	101
Carmi Christian Sch/Carmi/White	11229253	618/382-2807	238
CARMI-WHITE CO SCH DIST 5/ CARMI/WHITE	00323682	618/382-2341	237
Carmi-White County High Sch/Carmi/White	00323711	618/382-4661	238
Carmi-White County Jr High Sch/Carmi/White	00323747	618/382-4661	238
Carnegie Elem Sch/Chicago/Cook	00275267	773/535-0530	26
Carol Mosley Braun Elem Sch/Calumet City/Cook	04920402	708/868-9470	46
Carol Stream Elem Sch/Carol Stream/Du Page	00289153	630/588-5400	90
Caroline Bentley Elem Sch/New Lenox/Will	00325381	815/485-4451	245
Caroline Sibley Elem Sch/Calumet City/Cook	00269024	708/868-1870	46
Carolyn Wenz Elem Sch/Paris/Edgar	00292071	217/466-3140	103
Carpentersville Middle Sch/Carpentersvle/McHenry	00297992	224/484-2100	180
Carrie Busey Elem Sch/Savoy/Champaign	00264737	217/351-3811	10
Carrier Mills-Stonefort ES/Carrier Mills/Saline	00318314	618/994-2413	210
Carrier Mills-Stonefort HS/Carrier Mills/Saline	00318326	618/994-2392	210
CARRIER MILLS-STONEFORT SD 2/ CARRIER MILLS/SALINE	00318302	618/994-2392	210
Carroll Catholic Sch/Lincoln/Logan	00313388	217/732-7518	164
Carroll-Rosenwald Elem Sch/Chicago/Cook	00277057	773/535-9414	33
CARROLLTON CMTY UNIT SD 1/ CARROLLTON/GREENE	00293881	217/942-5314	111
Carrollton Grade Sch/Carrollton/Greene	00293893	217/942-6831	111
Carrollton High Sch/Carrollton/Greene	00293908	217/942-6913	111
Carruthers Elem Sch/Murphysboro/Jackson	00296273	618/687-3231	121
CARTERVILLE CMTY UNIT SD 5/ CARTERVILLE/WILLIAMSON	00326749	618/985-4826	250
Carterville High Sch/Carterville/Williamson	00326775	618/985-2940	250
Carterville Intermediate Sch/Carterville/Williamson	00326787	618/985-6411	251
Carterville Junior High Sch/Carterville/Williamson	11925366	618/985-4500	251
CARTHAGE ELEMENTARY SD 317/ CARTHAGE/HANCOCK	00294483	217/357-3922	114
Carthage Middle Sch/Carthage/Hancock	00294548	217/357-3914	114
Carthage Primary Sch/Carthage/Hancock	04804717	217/357-9202	114
Carver Elem Sch/Chicago/Cook	00275308	773/535-5674	36
Carver Military Academy/Chicago/Cook	00275293	773/535-5250	38
CARY CMTY CONS SCH DIST 26/ CARY/MCHENRY	00305305	224/357-5100	179
Cary Grove Cmty High Sch/Cary/McHenry	00305460	847/639-3825	179
Cary Junior High Sch/Cary/McHenry	00305329	224/357-5150	179
CASEY-WESTFIELD CMTY USD C-4/ CASEY/CLARK	00265896	217/932-2184	15
Casey-Westfield Jr Sr High Sch/Casey/Clark	00265901	217/932-2175	15
Caseyville Elem Sch/Caseyville/Madison	00308357	618/346-6205	170
Cass Junior High Sch/Darien/Du Page	00289206	331/481-4020	90
CASS SCH DIST 63/DARIEN/DU PAGE	00289191	630/985-2000	89
Cassell Elem Sch/Chicago/Cook	00275322	773/535-2640	26
Catalyst CS-Circle Rock/Chicago/Cook	10912445	773/945-5025	39
Catalyst CS-Maria/Chicago/Cook	11822116	773/993-1770	39
Cathedral of St Raymond Sch/Joliet/Will	00326672	815/722-6626	249
Catherine Cook Sch/Chicago/Cook	11551757	312/266-3381	77
Catholic Children's Home Sch/Alton/Madison	00319435	618/465-3594	173
Cdh Educational Center/Dixon/Lee	12369246	815/255-8866	160
Cedar Ridge Elem Sch/Bloomington/Mclean	11558274	309/557-4413	186
Centennial Elem Sch/Bartlett/Kane	03399161	630/213-5632	130
Centennial Elem Sch/El Paso/Woodford	00328967	309/527-4435	257
Centennial Elem Sch/Orland Park/Cook	03396195	708/364-3444	61
Centennial Elem Sch/Plano/Kendall	00299768	630/552-3234	138
Centennial Elem Sch/Polo/Ogle	00312114	815/946-3811	195
Centennial Elem Sch/Streator/La Salle	00303448	815/672-2747	144
Centennial High Sch/Champaign/Champaign	00264749	217/351-3951	10
CENTER CASS SCH DIST 66/ DOWNERS GROVE/DU PAGE	00289220	630/783-5000	90
Center Educational Opportunity/Troy/Madison	12163846	618/667-0633	169
Center Elem Sch/Freeport/Stephenson	00320771	815/232-0480	224
Center for Academics & Tech/Calumet City/Cook	04428686	708/585-2353	69
Center for Alternative Lrng/Calumet City/Cook	12318223	708/585-9401	69
Center for Disability Services/Joliet/Will	01780564	815/744-3500	250
Center Sch/Orland Park/Cook	01881429	708/364-3242	61
Center St Elem Sch/Fairfield/Wayne	00323498	618/842-2679	236
Centerview Therapeutic Sch/Northbrook/Cook	02956651	847/559-0110	77
Central A & M High Sch/Moweaqua/Christian	00320367	217/768-3866	14
Central A & M Middle Sch/Assumption/Christian	00265547	217/226-4241	14
CENTRAL A&M CMTY UNIT SD 21/ ASSUMPTION/CHRISTIAN	00265535	217/226-4042	14
Central Baptist Sch/Granite City/Madison	02828432	618/931-0964	173
Central Catholic High Sch/Bloomington/Mclean	00313390	309/661-7000	187
Central City Elem Sch/Centralia/Marion	00309454	618/532-9521	174
CENTRAL CITY SCH DIST 133/ CENTRALIA/MARION	00309442	618/532-9521	174

IL-V6   800-333-8802   School Year 2020-2021

Illinois School Directory
DISTRICT & SCHOOL TELEPHONE INDEX

School/City/County DISTRICT/CITY/COUNTY	PID	TELEPHONE NUMBER	PAGE
CENTRAL CMTY HIGH SCH DIST 71/ **BREESE/CLINTON**	00266395	618/526-4578	17
CENTRAL CMTY UNIT SD 4/ASHKUM/ **IROQUOIS**	00295554	815/698-2212	118
CENTRAL CMTY UNIT SD 301/ **BURLINGTON/KANE**	00297904	847/464-6005	128
Central Community High Sch/Breese/Clinton	00266400	618/526-4578	17
Central Elem & Jr High Sch/Kewanee/Henry	00295360	309/853-4290	117
Central Elem Sch/Camp Point/Adams	00262868	217/593-7795	1
Central Elem Sch/Des Plaines/Cook	00268757	847/824-1575	46
Central Elem Sch/Ingleside/Lake	00300795	847/973-3280	150
Central Elem Sch/Lincoln/Logan	00304818	217/732-3386	164
Central Elem Sch/O Fallon/St Clair	00316562	618/632-6336	218
Central Elem Sch/Plainfield/Will	00325537	815/436-9278	246
Central Elem Sch/Pontiac/Livingston	00304399	815/844-3023	161
Central Elem Sch/Riverside/Cook	00273702	708/447-1106	65
Central Elem Sch/Rochelle/Ogle	00312188	815/562-8251	195
Central Elem Sch/Wilmette/Cook	00281589	847/512-6100	71
Central Grade Sch/Effingham/Effingham	00292289	217/540-1400	105
Central High Sch/Burlington/Kane	03400332	847/464-6030	128
Central High Sch/Champaign/Champaign	00264751	217/351-3911	10
Central High Sch/Clifton/Iroquois	00295578	815/694-2321	118
CENTRAL ILLINOIS RURAL RVS/ **JERSEYVILLE/JERSEY**	04184402	618/498-5541	125
CENTRAL ILLINOIS VOC ED CO-OP/ **METAMORA/WOODFORD**	04177722	309/367-2783	259
Central Intermediate Sch/Monmouth/Warren	11702102	309/734-2213	234
Central Intermediate Sch/Ottawa/La Salle	00303151	815/433-3761	143
Central Intermediate Sch/Roxana/Madison	00309105	618/254-7594	172
Central Intermediate Sch/Washington/ Tazewell	00321000	309/444-3943	225
Central Joliet Twp High Sch/Joliet/Will	00325135	815/727-6750	243
Central Junior High Sch/Belleville/ St Clair	00316275	618/233-5377	217
Central Junior High Sch/Camp Point/Adams	11828407	217/593-7741	1
Central Junior High Sch/East Peoria/ Tazewell	00321153	309/427-5200	227
Central Junior High Sch/W Frankfort/ Franklin	00293219	618/937-2444	108
Central Middle Sch/Burlington/Kane	00297928	847/464-6000	128
Central Middle Sch/Evergreen Pk/Cook	00269531	708/424-0148	49
Central Middle Sch/Golden/Adams	03245209	217/696-4652	1
Central Middle Sch/Tinley Park/Cook	00274835	708/614-4510	42
Central Park Elem Sch/Midlothian/Cook	00271479	708/385-0045	57
Central Primary Sch/Washington/Tazewell	11456418	309/444-3580	225
Central Road Elem Sch/Rolling MDWS/Cook	00272540	847/963-5100	43
Central Sch/Glencoe/Cook	00269880	847/835-7600	51
CENTRAL SCH DIST 51/WASHINGTON/ **TAZEWELL**	00320991	309/444-3943	225
CENTRAL SCH DIST 3/CAMP POINT/ **ADAMS**	00262856	217/593-7116	1
CENTRAL SCH DIST 104/O FALLON/ **ST CLAIR**	00316550	618/632-6336	218
Central School Programs/Elgin/Kane	03249451	847/888-5340	130
Central Senior High Sch/Camp Point/Adams	00262870	217/593-7731	1
CENTRAL STICKNEY SCH DIST 110/ **CHICAGO/COOK**	00268367	708/458-1152	25
CENTRALIA CITY SCH DIST 135/ **CENTRALIA/MARION**	00309466	618/532-1907	174
Centralia High Sch/Centralia/Marion	00309583	618/532-7391	174
CENTRALIA HIGH SCH DIST 200/ **CENTRALIA/MARION**	00309571	618/532-7391	174
Centralia Junior High Sch/Centralia/Marion	01529267	618/533-7130	174
Centralia Pre-Kindergarten Ctr/Centralia/ Marion	12308981	618/533-7122	174
CENTURY CMTY UNIT SD 100/ **ULLIN/PULASKI**	00314760	618/845-3518	204
Century Elem Sch/Ullin/Pulaski	00314772	618/845-3572	204
Century Jr Sr High Sch/Ullin/Pulaski	00314784	618/845-3518	204
Century Junior High Sch/Orland Park/Cook	04454295	708/364-3500	61
Century Oaks Elem Sch/Elgin/Kane	00298207	847/888-5181	130
CERRO GORDO CMTY UNIT SD 100/ **CERRO GORDO/PIATT**	00314332	217/763-5221	202
Cerro Gordo Elem Sch/Cerro Gordo/Piatt	00314344	217/763-2551	202
Cerro Gordo Jr Sr High Sch/Cerro Gordo/ Piatt	00314356	217/763-2711	202
Chaddock Sch/Quincy/Adams	01778420	217/222-0034	3
Chadwick Elem Jr High Sch/Chadwick/Carroll	00264282	815/684-5191	8
CHADWICK MILLEDGEVILL CUSD 399/ **CHADWICK/CARROLL**	00264323	815/684-5191	8
Challand Middle Sch/Sterling/Whiteside	01170608	815/626-3300	240
Challenger Day Sch/Niles/Cook	04937340	847/588-2038	77
Chalmers Elem Sch/Chicago/Cook	00277069	773/534-1720	25
CHAMPAIGN CMTY UNIT SCH DIST 4/ **CHAMPAIGN/CHAMPAIGN**	00264713	217/351-3800	10
Champaign Early Childhood Ctr/Champaign/ Champaign	00264842	217/351-3881	10
Chaney Monge Sch/Crest Hill/Will	00324600	815/722-6673	241
CHANEY-MONGE SCH DIST 88/ **CREST HILL/WILL**	00324583	815/722-6673	241
Channahon Junior High Sch/Channahon/Will	01821819	815/467-4314	241
CHANNAHON SCH DIST 17/CHANNAHON/ **WILL**	00324612	815/467-4315	241
Channing Elem Sch/Elgin/Kane	00298219	847/888-5185	130
Chappell Elem Sch/Chicago/Cook	00279275	773/534-2390	27
Charles A Lindbergh Middle Sch/Peoria/ Peoria	00312891	309/693-4427	199
Charles J Caruso Middle Sch/Deerfield/Lake	00302353	847/945-8430	149
Charles J Sahs Elem Sch/Chicago/Cook	00268379	708/458-1152	25
Charles Reed Elem Sch/Plainfield/Will	10007894	815/254-2160	246
CHARLESTON CMTY UNIT SD 1/ **CHARLESTON/COLES**	00266589	217/639-1000	19
Charleston High Sch/Charleston/Coles	00266618	217/639-5000	19
Charleston Middle Sch/Charleston/Coles	00266620	217/639-6000	19
Charter Oak Primary Sch/Peoria/Peoria	02045824	309/693-4433	199
Chase Elem Sch/Chicago/Cook	00279287	773/534-4185	30
Chateaux Sch/Hazel Crest/Cook	00271168	708/335-9776	63
Chatham Elem Sch/Chatham/Sangamon	00318584	217/483-2411	211
Chauncey H Duker Sch/McHenry/McHenry	04940579	779/244-1100	183
Chavez Elem Multicultural Acad/Chicago/ Cook	04291330	773/535-4600	27
Chebanse Elem Sch/Chebanse/Iroquois	00295580	815/697-2642	118
Chedar Lubavitch Girls Sch/Chicago/Cook	02963953	773/465-0863	77
Chelsea Intermediate Sch/Frankfort/Will	00324818	815/469-2309	242
Cherokee Elem Sch/Lake Forest/Lake	00301256	847/234-3805	152
Cherry Hill Elem and ECC/New Lenox/Will	03249243	815/462-7831	245
Cherry Valley Elem Sch/Rockford/Winnebago	00327511	815/332-4938	254
Chesak Elem Sch/Lk In The Hls/McHenry	04914271	847/659-5700	182
CHESTER CMTY UNIT SCH DIST 139/ **CHESTER/RANDOLPH**	00314966	618/826-4509	205
Chester Grade Sch/Chester/Randolph	00314978	618/826-2354	205
Chester High Sch/Chester/Randolph	00314980	618/826-2302	205
CHESTER-E LINCOLN CMTY SD 61/ **LINCOLN/LOGAN**	00304686	217/732-4136	163
Chester-East Lincoln Cmty ES/Lincoln/Logan	00304698	217/732-4136	163
Chesterbrook Academy/Naperville/Du Page	05291864	630/527-0833	101
Chesterton Academy-Holy Family/Lisle/ Du Page	12180375	630/442-1424	101
Chiaravalle Montessori Sch/Evanston/Cook	02192001	847/864-2190	77
Chicago Academy Elem Sch/Chicago/Cook	04951671	773/534-3885	25
Chicago Academy for the Arts/Chicago/Cook	02956613	312/421-0202	77
Chicago Academy High Sch/Chicago/Cook	11822104	773/534-0146	25
Chicago Christian High Sch/Palos Heights/ Cook	00281852	708/388-7650	77
Chicago City Day Sch/Chicago/Cook	02917095	773/327-0900	77
Chicago Collegiate Charter Sch/Chicago/ Cook	11926384	773/536-9098	39
Chicago Futabakai Japan Sch/Arlington HTS/ Cook	02956558	847/590-5700	77
Chicago Grammar Sch/Chicago/Cook	12105351	312/944-5600	77
CHICAGO HEIGHTS ELEM SD 170/ **CHICAGO HTS/COOK**	00268381	708/756-4165	25
Chicago Hope Academy/Chicago/Cook	11015002	312/491-1600	77
Chicago HS for the Arts/Chicago/Cook	11446683	773/534-9710	39
Chicago HS-Agricultural Sci/Chicago/Cook	02852031	773/535-2500	27
Chicago Jesuit Academy/Chicago/Cook	10971063	773/638-6103	77
Chicago Jewish Day Sch/Chicago/Cook	05378113	773/271-2700	77
Chicago Lighthouse Dev Center/Chicago/Cook	03185697	312/666-1331	77
Chicago Math & Sci Academy/Chicago/Cook	05348596	773/761-8960	39
Chicago Military Academy/Chicago/Cook	04875728	773/534-9750	38
CHICAGO PSD-AUSL/CHICAGO/COOK	11931248	773/534-0129	25
CHICAGO PSD-ISP/CHICAGO/COOK	12232681	773/553-2568	26
CHICAGO PSD-NETWORK 1/CHICAGO/ **COOK**	11931080	773/534-1038	28
CHICAGO PSD-NETWORK 2/CHICAGO/ **COOK**	11931092	773/534-1100	29
CHICAGO PSD-NETWORK 3/CHICAGO/ **COOK**	11931107	773/534-6520	29
CHICAGO PSD-NETWORK 4/CHICAGO/ **COOK**	11931119	773/534-1035	30
CHICAGO PSD-NETWORK 5/CHICAGO/ **COOK**	11931121	773/534-6544	31
CHICAGO PSD-NETWORK 6/CHICAGO/ **COOK**	11931133	773/534-7565	31

DISTRICT & SCHOOL TELEPHONE INDEX

Market Data Retrieval

School/City/County DISTRICT/CITY/COUNTY	PID	TELEPHONE NUMBER	PAGE
CHICAGO PSD-NETWORK 7/CHICAGO/COOK	11931145	773/535-7101	32
CHICAGO PSD-NETWORK 8/CHICAGO/COOK	11931157	773/535-8211	32
CHICAGO PSD-NETWORK 9/CHICAGO/COOK	11931169	773/535-8955	33
CHICAGO PSD-NETWORK 10/CHICAGO/COOK	11931171	773/535-7543	33
CHICAGO PSD-NETWORK 11/CHICAGO/COOK	11931183	773/535-7267	34
CHICAGO PSD-NETWORK 12/CHICAGO/COOK	11931195	773/535-8975	35
CHICAGO PSD-NETWORK 13/CHICAGO/COOK	11931200	773/535-7525	35
CHICAGO PSD-NETWORK 14/CHICAGO/COOK	12313247	773/535-8193	36
CHICAGO PSD-NETWORK 15/CHICAGO/COOK	12313259	773/535-8232	37
CHICAGO PSD-NETWORK 16/CHICAGO/COOK	12313261	773/535-8240	37
CHICAGO PSD-NETWORK 17/CHICAGO/COOK	12313273	773/535-8520	38
CHICAGO PSD-OPTIONS/CHICAGO/COOK	11559424	773/553-1530	38
CHICAGO PUBLIC SCH DIST 299/CHICAGO/COOK	00274914	773/553-1000	25
CHICAGO RIDGE SCH DIST 127-5/CHICAGO RIDGE/COOK	00268513	708/636-2000	41
Chicago SDA Elementary/Chicago/Cook	01405142	773/873-3005	77
Chicago Tech Academy HS/Chicago/Cook	11446621	773/534-7755	39
Chicago Virtual Charter Sch/Chicago/Cook	10024000	773/535-6100	39
Chicago Vocational Career Acad/Chicago/Cook	00275334	773/535-7990	38
Chicago Waldorf Sch/Chicago/Cook	12108846	773/465-2662	77
Chiddix Junior High Sch/Normal/Mclean	00306529	309/557-4405	186
Childbridge Ctr for Education/Palatine/Cook	12179998	847/221-7752	77
Children of Peace Sch/Chicago/Cook	00283472	312/243-8186	72
Children's House Mont Sch/West Dundee/Kane	04314138	847/426-3570	133
Childrens Center Tazwell Co/Creve Coeur/Tazewell	02193134	309/699-6141	229
Childs Elem Sch/Robbins/Cook	00273257	708/388-7203	63
Chillicothe Jr High & Elem Ctr/Chillicothe/Peoria	01531155	309/274-6266	197
Chippewa Elem Sch/Palos Heights/Cook	00272851	708/388-7260	61
Chippewa Middle Sch/Des Plaines/Cook	00268769	847/824-1503	46
Chopin Elem Sch/Chicago/Cook	02107501	773/534-4080	31
Chrisman Elem Sch/Chrisman/Edgar	00291912	217/269-2022	103
Chrisman High Sch/Chrisman/Edgar	04933289	217/269-2823	103
Chrisman-Scottland Jr High Sch/Chrisman/Edgar	00291924	217/269-3980	103
Christ Lutheran High Sch/Buckley/Iroquois	04877623	217/394-2547	119
Christ Lutheran Sch/Jacob/Jackson	00296455	618/763-4664	121
Christ Lutheran Sch/Peoria/Peoria	00313302	309/637-1512	200
Christ Lutheran Sch/Sterling/Whiteside	02825985	815/625-3800	240
Christ Our Rock Lutheran HS/Centralia/Marion	05363728	618/226-3315	176
Christ Our Savior Lutheran HS/Evansville/Randolph	04912950	618/853-7300	206
Christ Our Savior Sch/South Holland/Cook	10015231	708/333-8173	73
Christ the King Jesuit Prep/Chicago/Cook	11421449	773/261-7505	77
Christ the King Luth Sch/Chicago/Cook	01442047	773/536-1984	77
Christ the King Sch/Chicago/Cook	00283147	773/779-3329	73
Christ the King Sch/Springfield/Sangamon	00319447	217/546-2159	214
Christ's Academy/Shorewood/Will	03219561	815/630-5376	250
Christa McAuliffe Sch/Tinley Park/Cook	03006314	708/429-4565	53
Christian Fellowship Sch/Du Quoin/Perry	02991510	618/542-6800	202
Christian Fenger Academy HS/Chicago/Cook	00275607	773/535-5430	38
Christian Heritage Academy/Northfield/Cook	02965444	847/446-5252	77
Christian Hill Church Sch/Tinley Park/Cook	02965470	708/349-7166	78
Christian Liberty Academy/Arlington HTS/Cook	02965547	847/259-4444	78
Christian Life Academy/Hopedale/Tazewell	03434527	309/449-3346	229
Christian Life Center Sch/Rockford/Winnebago	01845308	815/877-5749	256
CHRISTIAN-MONTGOMERY EFE SYS/HILLSBORO/MONTGOMERY	04184309	217/532-9591	191
Christopher Cmty High Sch/Christopher/Franklin	00293013	618/724-9461	107
Christopher Elem Sch/Christopher/Franklin	00292992	618/724-2631	108
Christopher House Charter Sch/Chicago/Cook	11926372	773/922-7500	39
CHRISTOPHER UNIT SCH DIST 99/CHRISTOPHER/FRANKLIN	00292980	618/724-9461	107
Churchill Elem Sch/Glen Ellyn/Du Page	00289751	630/790-6485	94
Churchill Elem Sch/Homewood/Cook	00270358	708/798-3424	52
Churchill Elem Sch/Oswego/Kendall	10012734	630/636-3800	137
Churchill Junior High Sch/Galesburg/Knox	00299952	309/973-2002	140
Churchville Middle Sch/Elmhurst/Du Page	00289646	630/832-8682	93
Chute Middle Sch/Evanston/Cook	00269309	847/859-8600	48
Cicero Early Childhood Center/Cicero/Cook	12309765	708/982-4500	42
Cicero East Elem Sch/Cicero/Cook	00268587	708/652-9440	42
CICERO SCH DIST 99/CICERO/COOK	00268563	708/863-4856	42
Cicero West Elem Sch/Cicero/Cook	04802109	708/780-4487	42
CICS-Avalon/S Shore/Chicago/Cook	10009191	773/721-0858	39
CICS-Basil/Chicago/Cook	05102201	773/778-9455	39
CICS-Bucktown/Chicago/Cook	03060580	773/645-3321	39
CICS-Chicago Quest/Chicago/Cook	11722580	773/565-2100	39
CICS-Irving Park/Chicago/Cook	10912419	773/433-5000	39
CICS-Lloyd Bond/Chicago/Cook	11446994	773/468-1300	39
CICS-Loomis Longwood Mid HS/Chicago/Cook	04755752	773/238-5330	39
CICS-Loomis Primary/Chicago/Cook	11131149	773/429-8955	39
CICS-Northtown Academy/Chicago/Cook	05277258	773/478-3655	39
CICS-Prairie/Chicago/Cook	04889925	773/928-0480	39
CICS-Ralph Ellison/Chicago/Cook	10029177	773/478-4434	39
CICS-Washington Park ES/Chicago/Cook	04928375	773/324-3300	39
CICS-West Belden/Chicago/Cook	05102196	773/637-9430	39
CICS-Wrightwood/Chicago/Cook	10009177	773/434-4575	39
Circle Academy/Urbana/Champaign	11231828	217/367-6923	13
Circle Center Grade Sch/Yorkville/Kendall	05356220	630/553-4388	139
Circuit Breaker Sch/Peru/La Salle	04196429	815/220-0740	141
Cisne High Sch/Cisne/Wayne	00323450	618/673-2154	237
Cisne Middle Sch/Cisne/Wayne	00323448	618/673-2156	237
CISSNA PARK CMTY UNIT SD 6/CISSNA PARK/IROQUOIS	00295619	815/457-2171	118
Cissna Park Sch/Cissna Park/Iroquois	00295633	815/457-2171	118
Civic Memorial High Sch/Bethalto/Madison	00308278	618/377-7230	169
Clara Peterson Elem Sch/Paxton/Ford	00292796	217/379-2531	107
Clare Woods Academy/Wheaton/Du Page	04935299	630/289-4221	101
Claremont Academy Elem Sch/Chicago/Cook	05348649	773/535-8110	33
Clarence E Culver Sch/Niles/Cook	00271778	847/966-9280	58
Clarendon Hills Middle Sch/Clarendon Hls/Du Page	04914506	630/861-4800	91
Clark Elem Sch/South Beloit/Winnebago	00328204	815/389-2311	255
Clay Academy/Woodstock/McHenry	03252903	815/337-2529	184
CLAY CITY CMTY UNIT SD 10/CLAY CITY/CLAY	00266137	618/676-1431	16
Clay City Elem Sch/Clay City/Clay	00266151	618/676-1431	16
Clay City High Sch/Clay City/Clay	11457539	618/676-1522	16
Clay City Junior High Sch/Clay City/Clay	11457527	618/676-1522	16
CLAY-JASPR-RICHLND-N WAYNE EFE/FLORA/CLAY	04184397	618/662-4059	16
Clearmont Elem Sch/Elk Grove Vlg/Cook	00267222	847/593-4372	43
Clearview Elem Sch/Waukegan/Lake	00302107	224/303-1600	156
Clemente Cmty Academy/Chicago/Cook	10026503	773/534-4000	37
Cleveland Elem Sch/Chicago/Cook	00279328	773/534-5130	28
Clifford A Johnson Elem Sch/Warrenville/Du Page	03326229	630/393-1787	92
Clifford Crone Middle Sch/Naperville/Du Page	04751407	630/428-5600	95
Clifford P Carlson Elem Sch/Rockford/Winnebago	00327509	815/654-4955	254
CLINTON CMTY UNIT SCH DIST 15/CLINTON/DEWITT	00288484	217/935-8321	87
Clinton Elem Sch/Clinton/Dewitt	00288537	217/935-6772	87
Clinton Elem Sch/South Elgin/Kane	00298221	847/888-7045	130
Clinton High Sch/Clinton/Dewitt	00288496	217/935-8337	87
Clinton Junior High Sch/Clinton/Dewitt	00288501	217/935-2103	87
Clinton Rosette Middle Sch/Dekalb/De Kalb	00287961	815/754-2226	84
Clissold Elem Sch/Chicago/Cook	00275358	773/535-2560	33
Cloverdale Elem Sch/Carol Stream/Du Page	04915237	630/588-5300	90
CMTY CONS SCH DIST 146/TINLEY PARK/COOK	00274823	708/614-4500	42
COAL CITY CMTY UNIT SCH DIST 1/COAL CITY/GRUNDY	00294055	815/634-2287	112
Coal City Early Chldhd Center/Coal City/Grundy	11101649	815/634-5042	112
Coal City Elem Sch/Coal City/Grundy	00294067	815/634-2334	112
Coal City High Sch/Coal City/Grundy	00294079	815/634-2396	112
Coal City Intermediate Sch/Coal City/Grundy	00294081	815/634-2182	112
Coal City Middle Sch/Coal City/Grundy	04909783	815/634-5039	112
COBDEN CMTY UNIT SCH DIST 17/COBDEN/UNION	00321892	618/893-2313	230
Cobden Elem Sch/Cobden/Union	00321919	618/893-2311	230
Cobden Jr Sr High Sch/Cobden/Union	00321921	618/893-4031	230

Illinois School Directory

DISTRICT & SCHOOL TELEPHONE INDEX

School/City/County DISTRICT/CITY/COUNTY	PID	TELEPHONE NUMBER	PAGE
Coffeen Elem Sch/Coffeen/Montgomery	00311031	217/534-2314	191
Col Isles Elem Sch/Quincy/Adams	04454001	217/222-4059	2
Coleman Elem Sch/Elgin/Kane	00298233	847/888-5190	130
Colene Hoose Elem Sch/Normal/Mclean	00306531	309/557-4414	186
Coles Elem Sch/Chicago/Cook	00275360	773/535-6550	35
Colin Powell Middle Sch/Matteson/Cook	10031390	708/283-9600	47
College Prep School-America/Lombard/Du Page	04459702	630/889-8000	101
Collins Academy/Chicago/Cook	10912316	773/534-1840	25
Collinsville Area Voc Center/Collinsville/Madison	03248512	618/343-6140	170
COLLINSVILLE CMTY SCH DIST 10/ **COLLINSVILLE/MADISON**	00308333	618/346-6350	170
Collinsville High Sch/Collinsville/Madison	00308371	618/346-6320	170
Collinsville Middle Sch/Collinsville/Madison	00308474	618/343-2100	170
COLONA CMTY SCH DIST 190/ **COLONA/HENRY**	00295205	309/792-1232	116
Colona Grade Sch/Colona/Henry	00295217	309/792-1232	116
Columbia Central Sch/Steger/Cook	00274598	708/753-4700	68
COLUMBIA CMTY UNIT SD 4/ **COLUMBIA/MONROE**	00310867	618/281-4772	189
Columbia Explorers Academy/Chicago/Cook	04951657	773/535-4050	32
Columbia High Sch/Columbia/Monroe	00310881	618/281-5001	190
Columbia Middle Sch/Columbia/Monroe	00310879	618/281-4993	190
Columbus East Sch/Cicero/Cook	00268599	708/652-6085	42
Columbus Elem Sch/Chicago/Cook	00279354	773/534-4350	27
Columbus Elem Sch/Edwardsville/Madison	00308618	618/656-5167	171
Columbus Manor Elem Sch/Oak Lawn/Cook	00272136	708/424-3481	64
Columbus West Sch/Cicero/Cook	04802111	708/780-4482	42
Community Christian Academy/Chicago/Cook	03439591	773/289-0796	78
COMMUNITY CONS SCH DIST 15/ **PALATINE/COOK**	00272514	847/963-3000	42
COMMUNITY CONS SCH DIST 46/ **GRAYSLAKE/LAKE**	00300848	847/223-3650	148
COMMUNITY CONS SCH DIST 59/ **ELK GROVE VLG/COOK**	00267193	847/593-4300	43
COMMUNITY CONS SCH DIST 89/ **GLEN ELLYN/DU PAGE**	00289830	630/469-8900	90
COMMUNITY CONS SCH DIST 93/ **BLOOMINGDALE/DU PAGE**	00289141	630/893-9393	90
COMMUNITY CONS SCH DIST 168/ **SAUK VILLAGE/COOK**	00273790	708/758-1610	44
COMMUNITY CONS SCH DIST 180/ **BURR RIDGE/DU PAGE**	00290841	630/734-6600	90
COMMUNITY CONS SCH DIST 181/ **CLARENDON HLS/DU PAGE**	00290061	630/861-4900	91
COMMUNITY CONS SCH DIST 204/ **PINCKNEYVILLE/PERRY**	00314162	618/357-2419	201
Community Cons SD 204 Sch/Pinckneyville/Perry	00314174	618/357-2419	201
Community High Sch/West Chicago/Du Page	00291558	630/876-6200	91
COMMUNITY HIGH SCH DIST 94/ **WEST CHICAGO/DU PAGE**	00291546	630/876-6200	91
COMMUNITY HIGH SCH DIST 99/ **DOWNERS GROVE/DU PAGE**	00289323	630/795-7100	91
COMMUNITY HIGH SCH DIST 117/ **ANTIOCH/LAKE**	00300422	847/395-1421	148
COMMUNITY HIGH SCH DIST 128/ **VERNON HILLS/LAKE**	00301517	847/247-4500	148
COMMUNITY HIGH SCH DIST 155/ **CRYSTAL LAKE/MCHENRY**	00305458	815/455-8500	179
COMMUNITY HIGH SCH DIST 218/ **OAK LAWN/COOK**	00282313	708/424-2000	44
COMMUNITY UNIT SCH DIST 7/ **GILLESPIE/MACOUPIN**	00307690	217/839-2464	167
COMMUNITY UNIT SCH DIST 16/ **NEW BERLIN/SANGAMON**	00318675	217/488-2040	211
COMMUNITY UNIT SCH DIST 200/ **WHEATON/DU PAGE**	00290877	630/682-2000	91
COMMUNITY UNIT SCH DIST 201/ **WESTMONT/DU PAGE**	00291429	630/468-8000	92
COMMUNITY UNIT SCH DIST 300/ **ALGONQUIN/MCHENRY**	00297966	847/551-8300	180
COMMUNITY UNIT SCH DIST 303/ **SAINT CHARLES/KANE**	00298740	331/228-2000	128
COMMUNITY UNIT SCH DIST 308/ **OSWEGO/KENDALL**	00299689	630/636-3080	137
Concord Elem Sch/Darien/Du Page	00289218	331/481-4010	90
Concord Lutheran Sch/Bensenville/Du Page	00291883	630/766-0228	101
Concordia Lutheran Sch/MacHesney Pk/Winnebago	00328307	815/633-6450	256
Concordia Lutheran Sch/Peoria/Peoria	00313314	309/691-8921	200
Concordia Lutheran Sch/Springfield/Sangamon	00319344	217/529-3309	214
Congerville Elem Sch/Congerville/Woodford	00329002	309/448-2347	257
Congress Park Elem Sch/Brookfield/Cook	00270578	708/482-2430	54
Conklin Elem Sch/Rockford/Winnebago	00327535	815/654-4860	254
Conley Elem Sch/Algonquin/McHenry	10013465	847/659-3700	182
Connect Christian Sch/South Roxana/Madison	02120967	618/254-0188	173
Conrad Fischer Elem Sch/Elmhurst/Du Page	00289658	630/832-8601	93
CONSOLIDATED HIGH SCH DIST 230/ **ORLAND PARK/COOK**	00272904	708/745-5203	44
Constance Lane Elem Sch/Rockford/Winnebago	00327793	815/966-3380	254
Consuela B York Alt High Sch/Chicago/Cook	03337826	773/535-7021	37
COOK COUNTY SCH DIST 104/ **SUMMIT/COOK**	00274641	708/458-0505	44
COOK COUNTY SCH DIST 130/ **BLUE ISLAND/COOK**	00267961	708/385-6800	45
COOK COUNTY SCH DIST 154/ **THORNTON/COOK**	00274720	708/877-5160	45
Cook Elem Sch/Chicago/Cook	00275396	773/535-3315	34
Coolidge Elem Sch/Lansing/Cook	00270712	708/474-4320	54
Coolidge Junior High Sch/Granite City/Madison	00308694	618/451-5826	171
Coolidge Middle Sch/Phoenix/Cook	00274433	708/339-5300	68
Coonley Elem Sch/Chicago/Cook	00279380	773/534-5140	29
Cooper Dual Language Academy/Chicago/Cook	00277100	773/534-7205	32
Cooper Middle Sch/Buffalo Grove/Cook	00281395	847/520-2750	71
COOPERATIVE ASSN FOR SPEC ED/ **GLEN ELLYN/DU PAGE**	02182018	630/942-5600	102
Copeland Manor Elem Sch/Libertyville/Lake	00301488	847/362-0240	153
Coram Deo Classical Sch/Mount Vernon/Jefferson	12313352	618/244-9338	124
Core Academy/Aurora/Kane	02826941	630/906-7900	133
Coretta Scott King Mag Sch/Park Forest/Will	10030205	708/367-4700	242
Corkery Elem Sch/Chicago/Cook	00277124	773/534-1650	27
Corliss Early College STEM HS/Chicago/Cook	00276857	773/535-5115	38
CORNELL CMTY CONS SCH DIST 426/ **CORNELL/LIVINGSTON**	00304131	815/358-2216	160
Cornell Grade Sch/Cornell/Livingston	00304143	815/358-2216	161
Cornerstone Academy/Chicago/Cook	04292437	312/573-8854	78
Cornerstone Academy/Nokomis/Montgomery	11722384	217/563-7600	191
Cornerstone Academy/Christmont/Nokomis/Montgomery	11435634	217/563-7600	190
Cornerstone Christian Academy/Bloomington/Mclean	05012125	309/662-9900	188
Cornerstone Christian Academy/Sycamore/De Kalb	02165814	815/895-8522	86
Cornerstone Christian Sch/Chicago HTS/Cook	04328543	708/756-3566	78
Corpus Christi Catholic Sch/Bloomington/Mclean	00313467	309/662-3712	187
Corron Elem Sch/South Elgin/Kane	05276503	331/228-6900	129
Cortland Elem Sch/Cortland/De Kalb	04038877	815/754-2360	84
Cosmic Montessori Sch/Aurora/Du Page	11905847	630/585-8881	101
Cossitt Elem Sch/La Grange/Cook	00270580	708/482-2450	54
Costa Catholic Academy/Galesburg/Knox	00313405	309/344-3151	140
Costello Sch/Lyons/Cook	04795570	708/783-4300	56
Cottage Grove Upper Grade Ctr/Ford Heights/Cook	00269062	708/758-1400	49
Cotton Creek Elem Sch/Island Lake/Lake	04362678	847/526-4700	155
Coulterville Unit Sch/Coulterville/Randolph	00315001	618/758-2881	205
COULTERVILLE UNIT SCH DIST 1/ **COULTERVILLE/RANDOLPH**	00314992	618/758-2881	205
Council Oak Montessori Sch/Blue Island/Cook	04328531	708/926-9720	78
COUNTRY CLUB HILLS SD 160/ **CNTRY CLB HLS/COOK**	00268680	708/957-6200	45
Country Club Hills Tech&Trade/Cntry CLB Hls/Cook	11828213	708/798-9542	78
Country Meadows Elem Sch/Long Grove/Lake	04870261	847/353-8600	151
Country Meadows Montessori Sch/Gurnee/Lake	03403695	847/244-9352	158
Country Trails Elem Sch/Elgin/Kane	10805074	847/717-8000	128
Countryside Elem Sch/Barrington/Lake	00267533	847/381-1162	147
Countryside Montessori Sch/Northbrook/Cook	01441861	847/498-1105	78
Countryside Private Sch/Eureka/Woodford	12380056	309/467-3535	258
Countryside Sch/Champaign/Champaign	04021123	217/355-1253	13
Courtenay Language Arts Acad/Chicago/Cook	04949513	773/534-5790	29
Cove Sch/Northbrook/Cook	01441768	847/562-2100	78
Covenant Christian Sch/Aurora/Kane	02165149	630/801-7955	133
Covenant Classical Sch/Naperville/Will	11589340	630/983-7500	250
Coventry Elem Sch/Crystal Lake/McHenry	00305381	815/788-5500	181

DISTRICT & SCHOOL TELEPHONE INDEX

Market Data Retrieval

School/City/County DISTRICT/CITY/COUNTY	PID	TELEPHONE NUMBER	PAGE
COWDEN HERRICK CUSD 3A/COWDEN/ SHELBY			
Cowden Jr Sr High Sch/Cowden/Shelby	00320288	217/783-2126	216
	00320290	217/783-2137	216
CRAB ORCHARD CMTY SCH DIST 3/ MARION/WILLIAMSON	00326804	618/982-2181	251
Crab Orchard Sch/Marion/Williamson	00326830	618/982-2181	251
Creative Communications Acad/Calumet City/Cook	00269000	708/868-7585	46
Creekside Elem Sch/Elgin/Kane	02896166	847/289-6270	130
Creekside Elem Sch/Plainfield/Will	04944630	815/577-4700	246
Creekside Middle Sch/Woodstock/McHenry	00306000	815/337-5200	184
Crescent City Grade Sch/Crescent City/Iroquois	00295657	815/683-2141	118
CRESCENT IROQUOIS CMTY SD 249/ CRESCENT CITY/IROQUOIS	00295645	815/683-2141	118
Crest Hill Christian Sch/Lockport/Will	01405532	815/905-1544	250
CRESTON CMTY CONS SCH DIST 161/ CRESTON/OGLE	00311809	815/384-3920	194
Creston Elem Sch/Creston/Ogle	00311811	815/384-3920	194
Crestwood Sch/Paris/Edgar	00292019	217/465-5391	103
Crete Elem Sch/Crete/Will	00324650	708/367-8430	242
CRETE-MONEE CMTY SD 201-U/ CRETE/WILL	00324636	708/367-8300	241
Crete-Monee Early Learning Ctr/Crete/Will	12038435	708/367-2770	242
Crete-Monee Education Center/Monee/Will	10022557	708/367-2660	242
Crete-Monee High Sch/Crete/Will	00324662	708/367-8211	242
Crete-Monee Middle Sch/University Pk/Will	00324686	708/367-2400	242
CREVE COEUR SCH DIST 76/ CREVE COEUR/TAZEWELL	00321012	309/698-3600	226
Cristo Rey Jesuit High Sch/Chicago/Cook	04486676	773/890-6800	78
Cristo Rey St Martin Clg Prep/Waukegan/Lake	05358565	224/215-9400	158
Cross Evang Lutheran Sch/Yorkville/Kendall	00299794	630/553-7861	139
Crow Island Sch/Winnetka/Cook	00281931	847/446-0353	72
Crown Community Academy/Chicago/Cook	00277150	773/534-1680	31
Crystal Lake Central High Sch/Crystal Lake/McHenry	00305472	815/459-2505	180
CRYSTAL LAKE ELEM DISTICT 47/ CRYSTAL LAKE/MCHENRY	00305355	815/788-5000	181
Crystal Lake Montessori Sch/Woodstock/McHenry	02854883	815/338-0013	185
Crystal Lake South High Sch/Crystal Lake/McHenry	01821754	815/455-3860	180
Crystal Lawns Elem Sch/Joliet/Will	00325549	815/436-9519	246
CS Academy Campus I/Chicago/Cook	12375049	773/778-0818	78
CS Academy Campus II/Chicago/Cook	12375037	312/675-8691	78
Cuba Elem Sch/Cuba/Fulton	00293489	309/785-8054	109
Cuba Middle High Sch/Cuba/Fulton	00293491	309/785-5023	109
Cuffe Math Science Tech Acad/Chicago/Cook	00276338	773/535-8250	34
Cullen Elem Sch/Chicago/Cook	00275413	773/535-5375	36
CUMBERLAND CMTY UNIT SD 77/ TOLEDO/CUMBERLAND	00287882	217/923-3132	84
Cumberland Elem Sch/Des Plaines/Cook	00268771	847/824-1451	46
Cumberland Elem Sch/Toledo/Cumberland	00287894	217/923-3132	84
Cumberland High Sch/Toledo/Cumberland	00287909	217/923-3132	84
Cumberland Middle Sch/Toledo/Cumberland	04362604	217/923-3132	84
Curie Metropolitan High Sch/Chicago/Cook	01556076	773/535-2100	37
Currier Elem Sch/West Chicago/Du Page	04284246	630/293-6600	99
Curtis Sch of Excellence/Chicago/Cook	01556131	773/535-5050	25
Cyd Lash Academy/Gages Lake/Lake	04198051	847/231-5570	146
Cypress Elem Sch/Cypress/Johnson	00297382	618/657-2525	127
CYPRESS SCH DIST 64/CYPRESS/ JOHNSON	00297370	618/657-2525	127

D

D H Williams Medical Prep HS/Chicago/Cook	10009103	773/535-1120	38
Da Vinci Academy/Elgin/Kane	04930718	847/841-7532	133
Daarul Uloom Islamic Sch/Peoria/Peoria	12365783	309/691-9089	200
Dahlgren Elem Sch/Dahlgren/Hamilton	00294433	618/736-2316	114
DAKOTA CMTY UNIT SCH DIST 201/ DAKOTA/STEPHENSON	00320707	844/632-5682	224
Dakota Elem Sch/Dakota/Stephenson	00320733	815/449-2852	224
Dakota Jr Sr High Sch/Dakota/Stephenson	00320719	815/632-5682	224
Daley Academy/Chicago/Cook	03008972	773/535-9091	32
Dallas Elem Sch/Dallas City/Hancock	00294574	217/852-3201	114
DALLAS ELEM SCH DIST 327/ DALLAS CITY/HANCOCK	00294562	217/852-3201	114
DALZELL ELEM SCH DIST 98/ DALZELL/BUREAU	00263678	815/663-8821	6
Dalzell Grade Sch/Dalzell/Bureau	00263680	815/663-8821	6
Damiansville Elem Sch/Damiansville/Clinton	00266424	618/248-5188	18
DAMIANSVILLE SCH DIST 62/ DAMIANSVILLE/CLINTON	00266412	618/248-5188	17
Daniel Burnham Elem Sch/Cicero/Cook	00268575	708/652-9577	42
Daniel Webster Elem Sch/Chicago/Cook	00281151	773/534-6925	31
Daniel Webster Middle Sch/Waukegan/Lake	00302119	224/303-2760	156
Daniel Wright Jr High Sch/Lincolnshire/Lake	00301555	847/295-1560	153
Danville Christian Academy/Danville/Vermilion	11235812	217/442-1579	233
Danville High Sch/Danville/Vermilion	00322248	217/444-1500	231
Danville Lutheran Sch/Danville/Vermilion	00322901	217/442-5036	233
DANVILLE SCH DIST 118/DANVILLE/ VERMILION	00322212	217/444-1000	231
DARIEN PUBLIC SCH DIST 61/ DARIEN/DU PAGE	00289268	630/968-7505	92
Darwin Elem Sch/Chicago/Cook	00279407	773/534-4110	30
Davenport Elem Sch/Eureka/Woodford	00329014	309/467-3012	257
David L Rahn Junior High Sch/Mount Morris/Ogle	03399367	815/732-5300	195
Davie Elem Sch/Anna/Union	00321854	618/833-6415	230
DaVinci Waldorf Sch/Wauconda/Lake	12179194	847/526-1372	158
Davis Primary Sch/Saint Charles/Kane	00298764	331/228-2200	129
Dawes Elem Sch/Chicago/Cook	00277174	773/535-2350	33
Dawes Elem Sch/Evanston/Cook	00269323	847/905-3400	48
Day Treatment/Peoria/Peoria	11450842	309/673-1898	199
DayStar Sch/Chicago/Cook	04990744	312/791-0001	78
De Diego Community Academy/Chicago/Cook	01532563	773/534-4451	31
De La Salle Institute/Chicago/Cook	00283161	312/842-7355	73
De Lacey Family Education Ctr/Carpentersvle/McHenry	03394094	224/484-2300	180
Dean St Elem Sch/Woodstock/McHenry	00306024	815/338-1133	184
Decatur Christian Sch/Forsyth/Macon	00307561	217/877-5636	167
Decatur Classical Sch/Chicago/Cook	00279744	773/534-2200	29
DECATUR PUBLIC SCHOOLS 61/ DECATUR/MACON	00306921	217/362-3000	165
Deer Creek Christian Sch/Chicago HTS/Cook	03100192	708/672-6200	78
DEER CREEK-MACKINAW CUSD 701/ MACKINAW/TAZEWELL	00321074	309/359-8965	226
Deer Creek-Mackinaw High Sch/Mackinaw/Tazewell	00321098	309/359-4421	226
Deer Creek-Mackinaw Interm Sch/Deer Creek/Tazewell	00321086	309/447-6226	226
Deer Creek-Mackinaw Prim JHS/Mackinaw/Tazewell	00321103	309/359-4321	226
DEER PARK CMTY CONS SD 82/ OTTAWA/LA SALLE	00302602	815/434-6930	141
Deer Park Elem Sch/Ottawa/La Salle	00302614	815/434-6930	141
Deer Path Elem Sch/Cary/McHenry	04803323	224/357-5350	179
Deer Path Middle School-East/Lake Forest/Lake	10756239	847/615-4470	152
Deer Path Middle School-West/Lake Forest/Lake	00301270	847/604-7400	152
Deerfield High Sch/Deerfield/Lake	00301103	224/632-3000	155
DEERFIELD PUBLIC SD 109/ DEERFIELD/LAKE	00300587	847/945-1844	149
DEKALB CMTY UNIT SD 428/ DEKALB/DE KALB	00287959	815/754-2350	84
DeKalb Early Learning Dev Ctr/Dekalb/De Kalb	12101616	815/754-2999	84
DeKalb High Sch/Dekalb/De Kalb	00287985	815/754-2100	84
DELABAR CTE SYSTEM/MONMOUTH/ WARREN	04184385	309/734-7545	235
DELAND-WELDON CMTY UNIT SD 57/ DE LAND/PIATT	00314382	217/736-2311	202
Deland-Weldon Elem Jr High Sch/Weldon/Piatt	00314394	217/736-2401	202
Deland-Weldon High Sch/De Land/Piatt	00314409	309/928-7691	202
DELAVAN CMTY UNIT SCH DIST 703/ DELAVAN/TAZEWELL	00321115	309/244-8283	226
Delavan Elem Sch/Delavan/Tazewell	00321139	309/244-8283	226
Delavan Jr Sr High Sch/Delavan/Tazewell	12169321	309/244-8285	226
Delores Moye Elem Sch/O Fallon/St Clair	05275365	618/206-2300	221
Delta Academy/Midlothian/Cook	11422015	708/389-1175	23
Delta Learning Center/Crestwood/Cook	11220702	708/371-1880	44
Deneen Sch of Excellence/Chicago/Cook	00275425	773/535-3035	25
Denkmann Elem Sch/Rock Island/Rock Island	00315867	309/793-5922	208
Denman Elem Sch/Quincy/Adams	00263044	217/222-2530	2
Denning Elem Sch/W Frankfort/Franklin	00293221	618/937-2464	108
Dennis Lab Sch/Decatur/Macon	00306971	217/362-3510	165
DePaul Clg Prep-Gordon Campus/Chicago/Cook	00283264	773/539-3600	73
DePriest Elem Sch/Chicago/Cook	00279433	773/534-6800	30

Illinois School Directory
DISTRICT & SCHOOL TELEPHONE INDEX

School/City/County DISTRICT/CITY/COUNTY	PID	TELEPHONE NUMBER	PAGE
DEPUE UNIT SCH DIST 103/			
DEPUE/BUREAU	00263692	815/447-2121	6
Depute Unit Sch/Depue/Bureau	00263707	815/447-2121	6
DES PLAINES CMTY CONS SD 62/			
DES PLAINES/COOK	00268733	847/824-1136	45
DES PLAINES VALLEY EFE SYSTEM/			
RIVER GROVE/COOK	04182600	708/779-4786	82
DeSoto Grade Sch/De Soto/Jackson	00296132	618/867-2317	120
DESOTO GRADE SCH DIST 86/			
DE SOTO/JACKSON	00296120	618/867-2317	120
Dever Elem Sch/Chicago/Cook	00279445	773/534-3090	28
Devonshire Elem Sch/Des Plaines/Cook	00267246	847/593-4398	43
Devonshire Elem Sch/Skokie/Cook	00274201	847/568-4901	67
Devry Univ Advantage Acad HS/Chicago/Cook	10000377	773/697-2216	27
Dewey Elem Acad of Fine Arts/Chicago/Cook	00277198	773/535-1666	26
Dewey Elem Sch/Evanston/Cook	00269335	847/859-8140	48
DeWitt Clinton Elem Sch/Chicago/Cook	00279330	773/534-2025	29
Diamond Lake Sch/Mundelein/Lake	03389879	847/566-6601	149
DIAMOND LAKE SCH DIST 76/			
MUNDELEIN/LAKE	00300654	847/566-9221	149
Diekman Elem Sch/Dolton/Cook	00268991	708/841-3838	46
DIETERICH COMMUNITY UNIT SD 30/			
DIETERICH/EFFINGHAM	00292215	217/925-5247	104
Dieterich Elem Sch/Dieterich/Effingham	01558608	217/925-5248	104
Dieterich Jr Sr High Sch/Dieterich/Effingham	00292227	217/925-5247	104
Dillon Elem Sch/Rock Falls/Whiteside	00324428	815/625-3356	240
Dimmick Cmty Cons 175 Sch/La Salle/La Salle	00302638	815/223-2933	141
DIMMICK CMTY SCH DIST 175/			
LA SALLE/LA SALLE	00302626	815/223-2933	141
DIOCESE OF BELLEVILLE ED OFF/			
BELLEVILLE/ST CLAIR	00317671	618/235-9601	222
DIOCESE OF JOLIET ED OFFICE/			
CREST HILL/WILL	00325965	815/838-2181	249
DIOCESE OF PEORIA ED OFFICE/			
PEORIA/PEORIA	00313338	309/671-1550	200
DIOCESE OF ROCKFORD ED OFFICE/			
ROCKFORD/WINNEBAGO	00328345	815/399-4300	256
DIOCESE OF SPRINGFIELD ED OFF/			
SPRINGFIELD/SANGAMON	00319394	217/698-8500	214
Dirksen Elem Sch/Chicago/Cook	00279457	773/534-1090	28
Dirksen Junior High Sch/Joliet/Will	00324935	815/729-1566	243
Dirksen Primary Sch/Pekin/Tazewell	00321517	309/477-4711	228
Disney II Mag Sch-Kedvale/Chicago/Cook	11131266	773/534-3750	36
Disney II Mag Sch-Lawndale/Chicago/Cook	11926243	773/534-5010	36
DISTRICT 50 SCHOOLS/WASHINGTON/			
TAZEWELL	00321713	309/745-8914	226
District 54 Early Learning Ctr/Schaumburg/Cook	12101587	847/230-1700	66
Divine Providence Sch/Westchester/Cook	00283185	708/562-2258	73
DIXON CMTY UNIT SCH DIST 170/			
DIXON/LEE	00303905	815/284-7722	160
Dixon Elem Sch/Chicago/Cook	00275437	773/535-3834	35
Dixon High Sch/Dixon/Lee	00303917	815/453-4966	160
Dolan Ed Ctr-Durand Cud 322/Durand/Winnebago	02860583	815/599-3975	252
DOLTON SCH DIST 149/CALUMET CITY/COOK	00268977	708/868-8300	46
DOLTON-RIVERDALE SCH DIST 148/			
RIVERDALE/COOK	00268874	708/841-2290	46
Don D Shute Elem Sch/East Peoria/Tazewell	00321165	309/427-5500	227
Donald C Parker Early Ed Ctr/MacHesney Pk/Winnebago	04749662	815/654-4559	252
Dongola Sch/Dongola/Union	00321945	618/827-3524	230
DONGOLA UNIT SCH DIST 66/			
DONGOLA/UNION	00321933	618/827-3841	230
DONOVAN CMTY UNIT SCH DIST 3/			
DONOVAN/IROQUOIS	00295671	815/486-7398	119
Donovan Elem Sch/Donovan/Iroquois	00295683	815/486-7321	119
Donovan Jr Sr High Sch/Donovan/Iroquois	00295695	815/486-7395	119
Doolittle East Elem Sch/Chicago/Cook	00277265	773/535-1040	33
Dore Elem Sch/Chicago/Cook	00277289	773/535-2080	33
Dorn Elem Sch/Hickory Hills/Cook	00271871	708/598-5509	59
Dorothy Simon Elem Sch/Winnebago/Winnebago	00328280	815/335-2318	255
Dorris Intermediate Sch/Collinsville/Madison	05356268	618/346-6311	170
Douglas Elem Sch/Clinton/Dewitt	00288513	217/935-2987	87
Douglas Elem Sch/Princeton/Bureau	00263965	815/875-6075	7
Douglas Prep Alternative Sch/Springfield/Sangamon	04286282	217/525-4400	213
Douglas Sch/Belleville/St Clair	00316287	618/233-2417	217
Douglass Academy High Sch/Chicago/Cook	00278960	773/534-6176	37
Downers Grove Adventist Sch/Downers Grove/Du Page	02982507	630/968-8848	101
Downers Grove Christian Sch/Downers Grove/Du Page	02827854	630/852-0832	101
DOWNERS GROVE SCH DIST 58/			
DOWNERS GROVE/DU PAGE	01844562	630/719-5800	93
Dr Andy Hall Early Chldhd Ctr/Mount Vernon/Jefferson	00296807	618/244-8087	123
Dr Howard Elem Sch/Champaign/Champaign	00264775	217/351-3866	10
Dr J Prieto Math & Sci Academy/Chicago/Cook	11454721	773/534-0210	30
Dr Julian Rogus Elem Sch/Frankfort/Will	04940488	815/464-2034	247
Dr Maude A Sanders Primary Sch/Peoria/Peoria	00313120	309/672-6571	199
Dr MLK Jr Sch-Lit/Fine Arts/Evanston/Cook	00269385	847/859-8500	48
Dr Nick Osborne Primary Center/Mount Vernon/Jefferson	00296819	618/244-8068	123
Dr Preston L Williams Elem Sch/Urbana/Champaign	00265456	217/384-3628	13
Drauden Point Middle Sch/Plainfield/Will	05070440	815/577-4900	246
Dream Academy/Elgin/Kane	03011814	847/888-5000	130
Drexel Elem Sch/Cicero/Cook	00268604	708/652-5532	42
Drummond Elem Sch/Chicago/Cook	00279471	773/534-4120	31
Dryden Elem Sch/Arlington HTS/Cook	00267026	847/398-4280	21
Du Jardin Elem Sch/Bloomingdale/Du Page	00289086	630/894-9200	89
DU QUOIN CMTY UNIT SD 300/			
DU QUOIN/PERRY	00314033	618/542-3856	201
DuBois Elem Sch/Chicago/Cook	00275451	773/535-5582	36
DuBois Elem Sch/Springfield/Sangamon	00318924	217/787-3066	213
Dunbar Elem Sch/E Saint Louis/St Clair	00316718	618/646-3840	218
Dunbar Voc Career Academy/Chicago/Cook	00277320	773/534-9000	38
Dundee Highlands Elem Sch/Dundee/McHenry	00297980	224/484-4700	180
Dundee Middle Sch/Dundee/McHenry	00298001	224/484-4500	180
Dundee-Crown High Sch/Carpentersvle/McHenry	00298063	224/484-5000	180
DUNLAP CMTY UNIT SCH DIST 323/			
PEORIA/PEORIA	00312322	309/691-3955	196
Dunlap Grade Sch/Dunlap/Peoria	00312334	309/243-7772	196
Dunlap High Sch/Dunlap/Peoria	00312346	309/243-7751	196
Dunlap Middle Sch/Dunlap/Peoria	01530280	309/243-7778	196
Dunlap Valley Middle Sch/Dunlap/Peoria	11180932	309/243-1034	196
Dunne Tech Academy/Chicago/Cook	00275504	773/535-5517	36
DUPAGE AREA OCCUPATIONAL SYS/			
ADDISON/DU PAGE	04189402	630/620-8770	102
DUPAGE HIGH SCH DIST 88/			
ADDISON/DU PAGE	00289684	630/530-3981	93
Dupage Montessori Sch/Naperville/Du Page	11228728	630/369-6899	101
DUPAGE REG OFFICE OF ED 19/			
WHEATON/DU PAGE	02097724	630/407-5800	102
DUPO CMTY SCH DIST 196/ST CLAIR	00316574	618/286-3812	218
Dupo Jr Sr High Sch/Dupo/St Clair	00316603	618/286-3214	218
Duquoin Elem Sch/Du Quoin/Perry	00314071	618/542-2646	201
Duquoin High Sch/Du Quoin/Perry	00314045	618/542-4744	201
Duquoin Middle Sch/Du Quoin/Perry	00314057	618/542-2646	201
DURAND CMTY SCH DIST 322/			
DURAND/WINNEBAGO	00327092	815/248-2171	252
Durand Elem Sch/Durand/Winnebago	00327107	815/248-2171	252
Durand High Sch/Durand/Winnebago	04449355	815/248-2171	252
Durand Junior High Sch/Durand/Winnebago	04449343	815/248-2171	252
Durkin Park Elem Sch/Chicago/Cook	05277208	773/535-2322	34
Dvorak Tech Academy ES/Chicago/Cook	00277332	773/534-1690	26
Dwight Baptist Academy/Dwight/Livingston	01779620	815/584-3182	163
DWIGHT COMMON ELEM SD 232/			
DWIGHT/LIVINGSTON	01557850	815/584-6219	161
Dwight Grade Sch/Dwight/Livingston	00304167	815/584-6220	161
Dwight High Sch/Dwight/Livingston	00304179	815/584-6200	161
DWIGHT TWP HIGH SCH DIST 230/			
DWIGHT/LIVINGSTON	00304155	815/584-6219	161
Dyett Arts High Sch/Chicago/Cook	00275530	773/535-1825	27

E

E A Bouchet Math & Sci Acad/Chicago/Cook	00275188	773/535-0501	35
E F Kerr Middle Sch/Blue Island/Cook	00267973	708/385-5959	45
E F Lindop Elem Sch/Broadview/Cook	00270918	708/345-3110	47
E F LINDOP ELEM SCH DIST 92/			
BROADVIEW/COOK	00270906	708/345-8834	47
E H Franzen Intermediate Sch/Itasca/Du Page	00290267	630/773-0100	96
E ST LOUIS AREA JT AGREEMENT/			
E SAINT LOUIS/ST CLAIR	02184042	618/646-3146	223

School Year 2020-2021   800-333-8802   IL-V11

DISTRICT & SCHOOL TELEPHONE INDEX

Market Data Retrieval

School/City/County DISTRICT/CITY/COUNTY	PID	TELEPHONE NUMBER	PAGE
Eagle Academy/Rantoul/Champaign	11421956	217/926-6002	12
Eagle Academy Christian Sch/Lansing/Cook	12379370	708/418-3000	78
Eagle Pointe Elem Sch/Plainfield/Will	05070476	815/577-4800	246
Eagle Ridge Elem Sch/Silvis/Rock Island	00315362	309/792-2002	207
Eagleveiw Elem Sch/Columbia/Monroe	11553987	618/281-4995	190
Earhart Elem Opt for Knwl Sch/Chicago/Cook	00275554	773/535-6416	35
Earl Hanson Elem Sch/Rock Island/ Rock Island	00315879	309/793-5930	208
Earle Elem Sch/Chicago/Cook	00277344	773/535-9130	34
Earlville Cmty Unit 9 Sch/Earlville/ La Salle	00302676	815/246-8361	141
EARLVILLE CMTY UNIT SCH DIST 9/ **EARLVILLE/LA SALLE**	00302664	815/246-8361	141
Early Childhood Center/Alsip/Cook	12374966	708/631-0490	20
Early Childhood Center/Alton/Madison	04937417	618/463-2166	169
Early Childhood Center/Bloomingdale/ Du Page	11927742	630/307-3750	90
Early Childhood Center/Dolton/Cook	00268939	708/841-2602	46
Early Childhood Center/Greenville/Bond	12375051	618/664-5009	4
Early Childhood Center/Skokie/Cook	04762559	847/677-4560	67
Early Childhood Ed Center/Wood Dale/ Du Page	03004574	630/694-1174	100
Early Learning Center/Effingham/Effingham	00292320	217/540-1460	105
Early Learning Center/Geneva/Kane	11925392	630/444-8700	131
Early Learning Center/Mt Prospect/Cook	12108640	847/593-4306	43
Early Learning Center/Springfield/Sangamon	04286268	217/525-3163	213
Early Learning Center/West Chicago/Du Page	10031132	630/293-6000	99
Early Years Program/Jacksonville/Morgan	11445914	217/243-2876	192
EAST ALTON ELEMENTARY SD 13/ **EAST ALTON/MADISON**	00308539	618/433-2051	170
East Alton Middle Sch/East Alton/Madison	00308541	618/433-2201	170
East Alton-Wood River Cmty HS/Wood River/ Madison	00309349	618/254-3151	170
EAST ALTON-WOOD RIVER SD 14/ **WOOD RIVER/MADISON**	00309337	618/254-3151	170
East Aurora ECC/Aurora/Kane	10028109	630/299-7460	129
East Aurora Extension Center/Aurora/Kane	12108248	630/299-3084	129
East Aurora High Sch/Aurora/Kane	00297538	630/299-8000	129
EAST AURORA SCH DIST 131/ **AURORA/KANE**	00297497	630/299-5550	129
EAST COLOMA-NELSON CESD 20/ **ROCK FALLS/WHITESIDE**	00324088	815/625-4400	238
East Coloma-Nelson Elem Sch/Rock Falls/ Whiteside	00324090	815/625-4400	238
East Dubuque Elem Sch/East Dubuque/ Jo Daviess	00297136	815/747-3188	125
East Dubuque Junior Senior HS/East Dubuque/ Jo Daviess	00297148	815/747-3188	125
EAST DUBUQUE UNIT SD 119/ **EAST DUBUQUE/JO DAVIESS**	00297124	815/747-2111	125
East Elem Sch/Alton/Madison	10031649	618/463-2130	169
East Elem Sch/Zion/Lake	00302494	847/872-5425	157
East Lake Academy/Lake Forest/Lake	11018432	847/247-0035	157
East Leyden High Sch/Franklin Park/Cook	00270839	847/451-3000	55
EAST MAINE SCH DIST 63/DES PLAINES/ **COOK**	00269098	847/299-1900	47
East Moline Christian Sch/East Moline/ Rock Island	02119279	309/796-1485	209
EAST MOLINE PUBLIC SCH DIST 37/ **EAST MOLINE/ROCK ISLAND**	00315386	309/792-2887	207
East Peoria Cmty High Sch/East Peoria/ Tazewell	00321268	309/694-8300	226
EAST PEORIA CMTY HS DIST 309/ **EAST PEORIA/TAZEWELL**	00321256	309/694-8300	226
EAST PEORIA ELEM SCH DIST 86/ **EAST PEORIA/TAZEWELL**	00321141	309/427-5100	226
East Prairie Elem Sch/Skokie/Cook	00269220	847/673-1141	47
East Prairie Junior High Sch/Tuscola/ Douglas	00288795	217/253-2828	88
EAST PRAIRIE SCH DIST 73/ **SKOKIE/COOK**	00269218	847/673-1141	47
East Side Elem Sch/Mc Leansboro/Hamilton	00294457	618/643-2328	114
East Side Intermediate Sch/Harrisburg/ Saline	02107733	618/253-7637	211
EAST ST LOUIS REG VOC SYSTEM/ **E SAINT LOUIS/ST CLAIR**	04176510	618/646-3000	223
EAST ST LOUIS SCH DIST 189/ **E SAINT LOUIS/ST CLAIR**	00316639	618/646-3000	218
East St Louis Sr High Sch/E Saint Louis/ St Clair	00316732	618/646-3700	219
EASTERN ILLINOIS AREA OF SP ED/ **CHARLESTON/COLES**	02183921	217/348-7700	20
EASTERN ILLINOIS EFE SYSTEM/ **MATTOON/COLES**	04177837	217/258-6283	20
Easterseals Acad-MacHesney PK/MacHesney Pk/ Winnebago	12319928	815/623-4800	256
Easterseals Academy-Chicago/Chicago/Cook	12319916	312/491-4110	78
Easterseals Academy-Tinley PK/Tinley Park/ Cook	11227762	708/802-9050	78
EASTLAND CMTY UNIT SD 308/ **LANARK/CARROLL**	00264294	815/493-6301	8
Eastland Elemenary Sch/Shannon/Carroll	00264309	815/864-2300	8
Eastland Jr Sr High Sch/Lanark/Carroll	00264311	815/493-6341	8
Eastlawn Elem Sch/Rantoul/Champaign	00265133	217/893-5404	11
Eastview Elem Sch/Algonquin/McHenry	00298013	847/532-7400	180
Eastview Elem Sch/Canton/Fulton	01538517	309/647-0136	109
Eastview Middle Sch/Bartlett/Kane	04365149	630/213-5550	130
Eastwood Elem Sch/East Alton/Madison	00308553	618/433-2199	170
Eberhart Elem Sch/Chicago/Cook	00277356	773/535-9190	27
Ebinger Elem Sch/Chicago/Cook	00279483	773/534-1070	27
ECHO JOINT AGREEMENT/SOUTH HOLLAND/ **COOK**	03032674	708/333-7880	82
Echo Sch/South Holland/Cook	02048216	708/596-3200	20
Ed White Elem Career Academy/Chicago/Cook	00276728	773/535-5672	36
Edgar Allan Poe Elem Sch/Arlington HTS/ Cook	00281486	847/670-3200	71
EDGAR CO CMTY SCH DIST 6/ **CHRISMAN/EDGAR**	00291900	217/269-2513	103
Edgebrook Elem Sch/Chicago/Cook	00279495	773/534-1194	28
Edgebrook Elem Sch/McHenry/McHenry	00305757	779/244-1200	183
Edgewood Elem Sch/Woodridge/Du Page	00289969	630/795-6000	100
Edgewood Middle Sch/Highland Park/Lake	00301012	224/765-3200	154
Edinburg Cmty Unit Sch/Edinburg/Christian	00265585	217/623-5603	14
EDINBURG CMTY UNIT SCH DIST 4/ **EDINBURG/CHRISTIAN**	00265561	217/623-5733	14
Edison Elem Sch/Danville/Vermilion	00322274	217/444-3350	232
Edison Elem Sch/Elmhurst/Du Page	00289505	630/834-4272	93
Edison Elem Sch/Macomb/McDonough	00305147	309/837-3993	178
Edison Elem Sch/Stickney/Cook	00270944	708/783-4400	56
Edison Junior High Sch/Pekin/Tazewell	00321452	309/477-4732	228
Edison Junior High Sch/Rock Island/ Rock Island	00315881	309/793-5920	208
Edison Middle Sch/Champaign/Champaign	00264787	217/351-3771	10
Edison Middle Sch/Wheaton/Du Page	00290906	630/682-2050	92
Edison Park Elem Sch/Chicago/Cook	11240130	773/534-0960	28
Edison Primary Sch/Kankakee/Kankakee	00299275	815/932-0621	135
Edison Regional Gifted Center/Chicago/Cook	00279017	773/534-0540	28
Edna Keith Elem Sch/Joliet/Will	00324911	815/723-3409	243
Edna M Rollins Elem Sch/Aurora/Kane	03343980	630/299-5480	129
Education Therapy Ctr-Madison/Troy/Madison	04196390	618/667-0633	169
Edward E Sadlowski Elem Sch/Chicago/Cook	12172263	773/535-8040	36
Edward Ellington Elem Sch/Chicago/Cook	00279536	773/534-6361	30
Edward Fulton Jr High Sch/O Fallon/ St Clair	00317463	618/628-0090	221
Edward J Tobin Elem Sch/Burbank/Cook	00274574	708/599-6655	24
EDWARDS CO CMTY UNIT SD 1/ **ALBION/EDWARDS**	00292095	618/445-2814	104
Edwards Co High Sch/Albion/Edwards	00292124	618/445-2327	104
Edwards Elem Sch/Chicago/Cook	00277368	773/535-4875	27
EDWARDSVILLE CMTY UNIT SD 7/ **EDWARDSVILLE/MADISON**	00308606	618/656-1182	170
Edwardsville High Sch/Edwardsville/Madison	00308632	618/656-7100	171
Edwardsville High School-South/Edwardsville/ Madison	03388916	618/692-7466	171
Edwardsville HS-Nelson Campus/Edwardsville/ Madison	12173023	618/468-5801	171
Edwin A Lee Elem Sch/Springfield/Sangamon	02106959	217/585-5828	213
Edwin Aldrin Elem Sch/Schaumburg/Cook	00273910	847/357-5400	66
EFE SYSTEM 330/CHAMPAIGN/ **CHAMPAIGN**	04180315	217/355-1382	13
EFFINGHAM CMTY SCH DIST 40/ **EFFINGHAM/EFFINGHAM**	00292265	217/540-1500	104
Effingham High Sch/Effingham/Effingham	00292306	217/540-1100	105
Effingham Junior High Sch/Effingham/ Effingham	00292277	217/540-1300	105
EGYPTIAN CMTY UNIT SCH DIST 5/ **TAMMS/ALEXANDER**	00263290	618/776-5251	3
Egyptian Sch/Tamms/Alexander	00263305	618/776-5251	3
Einstein Academy/Elgin/Kane	05256541	847/697-3836	133
Eisenhower Academy/Joliet/Will	00324909	815/723-0233	243
Eisenhower Campus High Sch/Blue Island/ Cook	00282325	708/597-6300	44
EISENHOWER COOPERATIVE/CRESTWOOD/ **COOK**	02097657	708/389-7580	82

Illinois School Directory

DISTRICT & SCHOOL TELEPHONE INDEX

School/City/County DISTRICT/CITY/COUNTY	PID	TELEPHONE NUMBER	PAGE
Eisenhower Elem Sch/Jacksonville/Morgan	00311421	217/245-5107	192
Eisenhower Elem Sch/Prospect HTS/Cook	00273350	847/870-3875	63
Eisenhower High Sch/Decatur/Macon	00306995	217/362-3100	165
Eisenhower Junior High Sch/Darien/Du Page	00289270	630/964-5200	92
Eisenhower Junior High Sch/Hoffman Est/Cook	00273922	847/357-5500	66
Eisenhower Middle Sch/Rockford/Winnebago	00327561	815/229-2450	254
Eisenhower Sch/South Holland/Cook	00274445	708/339-5900	68
EL PASO-GRIDLEY CUSD 11/EL PASO/WOODFORD	00328955	309/527-4410	257
El Paso-Gridley High Sch/El Paso/Woodford	00328979	309/527-4415	257
El Paso-Gridley Jr High Sch/Gridley/Woodford	00306361	309/747-2156	257
El Sierra Elem Sch/Downers Grove/Du Page	01878848	630/719-5825	93
El Vista Baptist Academy/Peoria/Peoria	02190455	309/692-8675	200
Elden D Finley Jr High Sch/Chicago Ridge/Cook	00268525	708/636-2005	42
ELDORADO CMTY UNIT SCH DIST 4/ELDORADO/SALINE	00318340	618/273-6394	210
Eldorado Elem Sch/Eldorado/Saline	00318376	618/273-9324	210
Eldorado High Sch/Eldorado/Saline	00318364	618/273-2881	210
Eldorado Middle Sch/Eldorado/Saline	00318405	618/273-8056	210
ELEMENTARY SCH DIST 159/MATTESON/COOK	00274158	708/720-1300	47
Elgin Academy/Elgin/Kane	00298893	847/695-0300	133
Elgin High Sch/Elgin/Kane	00298269	847/888-5100	130
Elgin Math and Science Academy/Elgin/Kane	12318194	630/883-5013	130
ELGIN SCH DIST U-46/ELGIN/KANE	00298154	847/888-5000	130
Eli Whitney Elem Sch/Chicago/Cook	00278776	773/534-1560	32
Elim Christian Sch/Crestwood/Cook	00282014	708/389-0555	78
Elite Scholars Steam Academy/Swansea/St Clair	12160480	618/726-2022	223
Elizabeth Blackwell Elem Sch/Schaumburg/Cook	02042470	847/357-5555	66
Elizabeth Eichelberger ES/Plainfield/Will	11072684	815/577-3606	246
Elizabeth Graham Elem Sch/Springfield/Sangamon	04286270	217/525-3220	213
Elizabeth Ide Elem Sch/Darien/Du Page	00289244	630/783-5200	90
Elizabeth Meyer Sch/Skokie/Cook	04303359	847/673-1223	67
Elizabeth Morris Elem Sch/Cahokia/St Clair	00316512	618/332-3718	218
Elk Grove High Sch/Elk Grove Vlg/Cook	00271675	847/718-4400	70
Ella Flagg Young Elem Sch/Chicago/Cook	00281216	773/534-6200	30
Ellis Elem Sch/Belleville/St Clair	00317176	618/538-6114	219
Ellis Elem Sch/Rockford/Winnebago	00327573	815/966-3909	254
Ellis Middle Sch/Elgin/Kane	00298271	847/888-5151	130
Ellsworth Elem Sch/Naperville/Du Page	00290724	630/420-6338	98
Elm Elem Sch/Burr Ridge/Du Page	00290073	630/861-4000	91
Elm Middle Sch/Elmwood Park/Cook	00269244	708/452-3550	48
ELMHURST CMTY UNIT SD 205/ELMHURST/DU PAGE	00289488	630/834-4530	93
ELMWOOD CMTY UNIT SCH DIST 322/ELMWOOD/PEORIA	00312360	309/742-8464	196
Elmwood Elem Sch/Elmwood/Peoria	00312384	309/742-4261	196
Elmwood Elem Sch/Elmwood Park/Cook	00269256	708/452-3558	48
Elmwood Elem Sch/Naperville/Du Page	00290736	630/420-6341	98
Elmwood Elem Sch/Zion/Lake	00302509	847/746-1491	157
Elmwood Jr Sr High Sch/Elmwood/Peoria	04290362	309/742-2851	196
ELMWOOD PARK CMTY UNIT SD 401/ELMWOOD PARK/COOK	00269232	708/452-7292	47
Elmwood Park Early Chldhd Ctr/Elmwood Park/Cook	05091858	708/583-5860	48
Elmwood Park High Sch/Elmwood Park/Cook	00269268	708/452-7272	48
Elsie Johnson Elem Sch/Hanover Park/Du Page	02178316	630/671-8800	90
ELVERADO CMTY UNIT SD 196/ELKVILLE/JACKSON	00296144	618/568-1321	120
Elverado High Sch/Elkville/Jackson	00296168	618/568-1104	120
Elverado Intermediate Sch/Vergennes/Jackson	11079254	618/684-3527	120
Elverado Junior High Sch/Vergennes/Jackson	00296170	618/684-3527	120
Elverado Primary Sch/Elkville/Jackson	00296156	618/568-1321	120
Elwood Cmty Cons Sch/Elwood/Will	00324753	815/423-5588	242
ELWOOD CMTY CONS SD 203/ELWOOD/WILL	00324741	815/423-5588	242
Embers Elem Sch/Niles/Cook	11227592	847/518-1185	78
Emden Elem Sch/Emden/Logan	00304753	217/376-3151	163
Emerson Elem Sch/Berwyn/Cook	00267868	708/795-2322	23
Emerson Elem Sch/Elmhurst/Du Page	00289529	630/834-5562	93
Emerson Elem Sch/Maywood/Cook	00271340	708/450-2002	57
Emerson Elem Sch/Wheaton/Du Page	00290918	630/682-2055	92
Emerson Middle Sch/Niles/Cook	04807604	847/318-8110	62
Emge Junior High Sch/Belleville/St Clair	00317188	618/397-6557	219
Emily G Johns Elem Sch/Plano/Kendall	10902880	630/552-9182	138
Emmett Till Math & Sci Academy/Chicago/Cook	00276118	773/535-0570	33
Emmons Elem Sch/Antioch/Lake	00300707	847/395-1105	149
EMMONS SCH DIST 33/ANTIOCH/LAKE	00300692	847/395-1105	149
Empire Elem Sch/Freeport/Stephenson	00320795	815/232-0380	224
Enders-Salk Elem Sch/Schaumburg/Cook	01529188	847/357-6400	66
Enger Sch/Franklin Park/Cook	00271091	847/455-5299	56
Englewood STEM High Sch/Chicago/Cook	12366763	773/535-3685	37
Enos Elem Sch/Springfield/Sangamon	00318948	217/525-3208	213
Epic Academy/Chicago/Cook	11454862	773/535-7930	39
Epiphany Sch/Chicago/Cook	00283214	773/762-1542	73
Epiphany Sch/Normal/Mclean	00313417	309/452-3268	187
Equality Christian Center/Equality/Gallatin	02119243	618/276-4236	110
Eric Solorio Academy HS/Chicago/Cook	11548633	773/535-9070	26
Erickson Elem Sch/Bloomingdale/Du Page	00289062	630/529-2223	89
ERIE CMTY SCH DIST 1/ERIE/WHITESIDE	00324105	309/659-2239	239
Erie Elem Charter Sch/Chicago/Cook	10009189	773/486-7161	39
Erie Elem Sch/Erie/Whiteside	00324117	309/659-2239	239
Erie High Sch/Erie/Whiteside	00324129	309/659-2239	239
Erie Middle Sch/Erie/Whiteside	00324131	309/659-2239	239
Esmond Elem Sch/Chicago/Cook	00275578	773/535-2650	34
Esperanza Sch/Chicago/Cook	01779060	312/243-6097	78
Estelle Kampmeyer Elem Sch/O Fallon/St Clair	00317437	618/632-6391	221
Estelle Sauget Sch of Choice/Cahokia/St Clair	11070686	618/332-3820	218
Eswood Cmty Cons Grade Sch/Lindenwood/Ogle	00311847	815/393-4477	194
ESWOOD CMTY CONS SD 269/LINDENWOOD/OGLE	00311823	815/393-4477	194
Euclid Elem Sch/Mt Prospect/Cook	00273609	847/259-3303	65
Eugene Field Elem Sch/Chicago/Cook	00279598	773/534-2030	29
Eugene Field Elem Sch/Park Ridge/Cook	00273099	847/318-4385	62
Eugene Field Elem Sch/Rock Island/Rock Island	00315893	309/793-5935	208
Eugene Field Elem Sch/Wheeling/Cook	00281400	847/520-2780	71
Eunice Smith Elem Sch/Alton/Madison	00308060	618/463-2077	169
EUREKA CMTY UNIT SCH DIST 140/EUREKA/WOODFORD	00328993	309/467-3737	257
Eureka High Sch/Eureka/Woodford	00329026	309/467-2361	257
Eureka Middle Sch/Eureka/Woodford	00329038	309/467-3771	257
Evangelical Elem Sch/Godfrey/Madison	02191942	618/466-1599	173
Evans Junior High Sch/Bloomington/Mclean	11715903	309/557-4406	186
Evanston Twp High Sch/Evanston/Cook	01821637	847/424-7000	48
EVANSTON TWP HIGH SD 202/EVANSTON/COOK	00269505	847/424-7000	48
EVANSTON-SKOKIE CMTY CSD 65/EVANSTON/COOK	00269282	847/859-8000	48
Evansville Attendance Center/Evansville/Randolph	00315099	618/853-4411	205
Everest Academy/Lemont/Cook	11018030	630/243-1995	78
Everett Dirksen Elem Sch/Schaumburg/Cook	03251844	847/357-5600	66
Everett Elem Sch/Chicago/Cook	00277382	773/535-4550	32
Everett Elem Sch/Lake Forest/Lake	00301282	847/234-5713	152
Evergreen Academy Middle Sch/Chicago/Cook	03340990	773/535-4836	32
Evergreen Elem Sch/Carol Stream/Du Page	01398288	630/876-7810	89
Evergreen Park Cmty High Sch/Evergreen Pk/Cook	00269593	708/424-7400	49
EVERGREEN PARK CMTY HSD 231/EVERGREEN PK/COOK	00269581	708/424-7400	49
EVERGREEN PARK ELEM SD 124/EVERGREEN PK/COOK	00269529	708/423-0950	49
EWING NORTHERN CMTY SD 115/EWING/FRANKLIN	00293025	618/629-2181	108
Ewing Northern Elem Sch/Ewing/Franklin	00293037	618/629-2181	108

F

F E Peacock Middle Sch/Itasca/Du Page	00290279	630/773-0335	96
Fabyan Elem Sch/Geneva/Kane	11457163	630/444-8600	131
Fairfield Academy/Chicago/Cook	04875742	773/535-9500	34
Fairfield Amish Mennonite Sch/Tampico/Whiteside	01843831	815/716-3428	240
Fairfield Cmty High Sch/Fairfield/Wayne	00323527	618/842-2649	236
FAIRFIELD CMTY HIGH SD 225/FAIRFIELD/WAYNE	00323515	618/842-2649	236
FAIRFIELD PUB SCH DIST 112/FAIRFIELD/WAYNE	00323486	618/842-6501	236
Fairmont Sch/Lockport/Will	00324789	815/726-6318	242
FAIRMONT SCH DIST 89/LOCKPORT/WILL	00324765	815/726-6318	242

School Year 2020-2021   800-333-8802   IL-V13

DISTRICT & SCHOOL TELEPHONE INDEX

Market Data Retrieval

School/City/County DISTRICT/CITY/COUNTY	PID	TELEPHONE NUMBER	PAGE
Fairmount Elem Sch/Downers Grove/Du Page	00289373	630/719-5830	93
Fairview Early Childhood Ctr/Rockford/Winnebago	03050183	815/227-8400	254
Fairview Elem Sch/Hoffman Est/Cook	00273946	847/357-5700	66
Fairview Elem Sch/Mt Prospect/Cook	00271584	847/394-7320	58
Fairview Elem Sch/Normal/Mclean	00306555	309/557-4415	186
Fairview Elem Sch/Springfield/Sangamon	00318950	217/525-3211	213
Fairview South Elem Sch/Skokie/Cook	00274366	847/929-1048	49
FAIRVIEW SOUTH SCH DIST 72/ SKOKIE/COOK	00274342	847/929-1048	49
Faith Baptist Christian Sch/Pekin/Tazewell	01845188	309/347-6178	229
Faith Baptist Sch/Belleville/St Clair	03214951	618/236-1044	223
Faith Bible Christian Acad/Rosamond/Christian	02112568	217/562-5054	15
Faith Christian Academy/Sidell/Vermilion	12377750	217/651-4709	233
Faith Christian Sch/Dixon/Lee	02165826	815/652-4806	160
Faith Chrn Fellowship Academy/South Roxana/Madison	03432995	618/254-9636	173
Faith Lutheran Sch/Antioch/Lake	01405271	847/395-1660	158
Faith Lutheran Sch/Godfrey/Madison	02210861	618/466-3833	173
Falconer Elem Sch/Chicago/Cook	00279550	773/534-3560	30
Families of Faith Academy/Channahon/Will	11228510	815/521-1381	250
Faraday Elem Sch/Chicago/Cook	00279562	773/534-6670	31
Farmersville Grade Sch/Farmersville/Montgomery	00311263	217/227-3306	191
Farmingdale Elem Sch/Pleasant PLNS/Sangamon	00318807	217/626-1221	212
Farmington Central Elem Sch/Farmington/Peoria	00293594	309/245-1000	197
Farmington Central High Sch/Farmington/Peoria	00293582	309/245-1000	197
Farmington Central Jr High Sch/Farmington/Peoria	00293570	309/245-1000	197
FARMINGTON CTL CMTY SD 265/ FARMINGTON/PEORIA	00293568	309/245-1000	197
Farnsworth Elem Sch/Chicago/Cook	00279574	773/534-3535	28
Farragut Career Academy/Chicago/Cook	00277394	773/534-1300	37
Farragut Elem Sch/Joliet/Will	00324959	815/723-0394	243
FARRINGTON CMTY CONS SD 99/ BLUFORD/JEFFERSON	00296663	618/755-4414	122
Farrington Elem Sch/Bluford/Jefferson	00296675	618/755-4414	122
Father McGivney Catholic HS/Glen Carbon/Madison	11818608	618/855-9010	173
Fearn Elem Sch/North Aurora/Kane	04946468	630/301-5001	132
Federico G Lorca Elem Sch/Chicago/Cook	11548621	773/534-0950	27
Feitshans Elem Sch/Springfield/Sangamon	00319112	217/525-3030	213
FENTON CMTY HIGH SCH DIST 100/ BENSENVILLE/DU PAGE	00289713	630/766-2500	94
Fenton High Sch/Bensenville/Du Page	00289725	630/766-2500	94
Fenwick High Sch/Oak Park/Cook	00283226	708/386-0127	73
Fernway Park Elem Sch/Orland Park/Cook	00270516	708/349-3810	53
Fernwood Elem Sch/Chicago/Cook	00275633	773/535-2700	36
Ferson Creek Elem Sch/Saint Charles/Kane	03240338	331/228-2300	129
FIELD CMTY CONS SCH DIST 3/ TEXICO/JEFFERSON	00296687	618/755-4611	123
Field Elem Sch/Elmhurst/Du Page	00289531	630/834-5313	93
Field Elem Sch/Texico/Jefferson	00296699	618/755-4611	123
Field Middle Sch/Northbrook/Cook	00281242	847/272-6884	70
Field Park Elem Sch/Western Sprgs/Cook	00281319	708/246-7675	71
Field-Stevenson Elem Sch/Forest Park/Cook	00269701	708/366-5703	50
FIELDCREST CMTY SCH DIST 6/ MINONK/WOODFORD	00329117	309/432-2177	257
Fieldcrest Elem Sch/Oak Forest/Cook	00271170	708/210-2872	63
Fieldcrest High Sch/Minonk/Woodford	00329143	309/432-2529	257
Fieldcrest Intermediate Sch/Toluca/Woodford	00310001	815/452-2411	257
Fieldcrest Middle Sch/Wenona/Woodford	00310037	815/853-4331	257
Fieldcrest Primary Sch/Minonk/Woodford	00329131	309/432-2838	257
First Baptist Academy/O Fallon/St Clair	11232389	618/632-6223	223
First Baptist Christian Sch/Danville/Vermilion	00322884	217/442-2434	233
Fischer Middle Sch/Aurora/Du Page	11448514	630/375-3100	95
FISHER CMTY UNIT SCH DIST 1/ FISHER/CHAMPAIGN	00264907	217/897-6125	10
Fisher Grade Sch/Fisher/Champaign	00264919	217/897-1133	10
Fisher Jr Sr High Sch/Fisher/Champaign	00264921	217/897-1225	10
FIVE CO REG EFE SYSTEM/TAMMS/ ALEXANDER	04177760	618/747-2703	3
Five Co Reg Voc System Sch/Tamms/Alexander	04197124	618/747-2703	3
Flanagan-Cornell Unit 74 Sch/Flanagan/Livingston	00304234	815/796-2233	161

School/City/County DISTRICT/CITY/COUNTY	PID	TELEPHONE NUMBER	PAGE
FLANAGAN-CORNELL UNIT 74 SD/ FLANAGAN/LIVINGSTON	00304222	815/796-2233	161
Flinn Middle Sch/Rockford/Winnebago	00327755	815/229-2800	254
FLORA CMTY UNIT SCH DIST 35/ FLORA/CLAY	00266163	618/662-2412	16
Flora Elem Sch/Flora/Clay	00266204	618/662-2014	16
Flora High Sch/Flora/Clay	00266187	618/662-8316	16
Flossie Wiley Elem Sch/Urbana/Champaign	03250113	217/384-3670	13
Flossmoor Hills Elem Sch/Flossmoor/Cook	00269610	708/647-7100	49
FLOSSMOOR SCH DIST 161/CHICAGO HTS/ COOK	00269608	708/647-7000	49
Floyd Henson Jr High Sch/Flora/Clay	00266175	618/662-8394	16
FORD CO SPEC ED CO-OP/GIBSON CITY/ FORD	10031601	217/784-5470	107
FORD HEIGHTS SCH DIST 169/ FORD HEIGHTS/COOK	00269050	708/758-1370	49
Foreman College & Career Acad/Chicago/Cook	00279615	773/534-3400	36
Forest Elem Sch/Des Plaines/Cook	00268783	847/824-1380	46
Forest Glen Elem Sch/Glen Ellyn/Du Page	00289763	630/790-6490	94
Forest Hills Elem Sch/Western Sprgs/Cook	00281321	708/246-7678	71
Forest Park Individual Ed Sch/Joliet/Will	00324961	815/723-0414	243
Forest Park Middle Sch/Forest Park/Cook	02204161	708/366-5742	50
FOREST PARK SCH DIST 91/ FOREST PARK/COOK	00269684	708/366-5700	50
FOREST RIDGE SCH DIST 142/ OAK FOREST/COOK	00269737	708/687-3334	50
Forest Road Elem Sch/La Grange Pk/Cook	00270592	708/482-2525	54
Forest View Elem Sch/Mt Prospect/Cook	00267260	847/593-4359	43
Forrestal Elem Sch/Great Lakes/Lake	00301749	847/689-6310	154
Forreston Grade Sch/Forreston/Ogle	00311873	815/938-2301	194
Forreston Jr Sr High Sch/Forreston/Ogle	00311885	815/938-2175	194
FORRESTVILLE VALLEY CUSD 221/ FORRESTON/OGLE	00311859	815/938-2036	194
Foster Park Elem Sch/Chicago/Cook	00275657	773/535-2725	34
Foundations College Prep CS/Chicago/Cook	12101654	773/298-5800	39
Foundations Sch/O Fallon/St Clair	11223431	618/975-0270	223
Founders Elem Sch/Dekalb/De Kalb	00287997	815/754-3800	84
Four Rivers Sp Ed Ctr-Garrison/Jacksonville/Morgan	04196948	217/245-7174	192
FOUR RIVERS SPEC ED DIST/ JACKSONVILLE/MORGAN	02182056	217/245-7174	193
Four Winds Sch/Warrenville/Du Page	04990641	630/836-9400	101
Fox Chase Elem Sch/Oswego/Kendall	04939556	630/636-3000	137
Fox Creek Elem Sch/Bloomington/Mclean	04944824	309/557-4416	186
FOX LAKE SCH DIST 114/SPRING GROVE/ LAKE	00300719	847/973-4114	149
Fox Meadow Elem Sch/South Elgin/Kane	04450811	847/888-7182	130
Fox Ridge Sch/Saint Charles/Kane	03240340	331/228-2400	129
FOX RIVER GROVE CONS SD 3/ FOX RIVER GRV/MCHENRY	00305484	847/516-5100	181
Fox River Grove Middle Sch/Fox River GRV/McHenry	00305501	847/516-5105	181
Fox Tech Center/Aurora/Kane	11827752	630/906-7900	133
Fox Valley Career Center/Maple Park/Kane	03248500	630/365-5113	132
Fox Valley Montessori Sch/Aurora/Kane	02825973	630/896-7557	133
Frances B McCord Elem Sch/Burbank/Cook	00274548	708/599-4411	24
Frances Willard Elem Sch/Rock Island/Rock Island	00315908	309/793-5940	208
Frances X Warde Sch-Holy Name/Chicago/Cook	00283410	312/466-0700	78
Frances X Warde Sch-St Patrick/Chicago/Cook	11239818	312/466-0700	78
Francis Granger Middle Sch/Aurora/Du Page	04032263	630/375-1010	95
Francis W Parker Sch/Chicago/Cook	00281711	773/353-3000	78
Francis Willard Elem Sch/Evanston/Cook	00269490	847/905-3600	48
Frank A Brodnicki Elem Sch/Justice/Cook	00268147	708/496-8716	53
Frank C Whiteley Elem Sch/Hoffman Est/Cook	03247623	847/963-7200	43
Frank Hall Elem Sch/Aurora/Kane	00297667	630/301-5005	132
FRANKFORT CMTY UNIT SD 168/ W FRANKFORT/FRANKLIN	00293207	618/937-2421	108
Frankfort Community High Sch/W Frankfort/Franklin	00293233	618/932-3126	108
Frankfort Intermediate Sch/W Frankfort/Franklin	00293245	618/937-1412	108
FRANKFORT SCH DIST 157-C/ FRANKFORT/WILL	00324806	815/469-5922	242
Frankfort Square Elem Sch/Frankfort/Will	00325795	815/469-3176	247
FRANKLIN CMTY UNIT SD 1/ FRANKLIN/MORGAN	00311366	217/675-2395	192
Franklin East Grade Sch/Franklin/Morgan	00311380	217/675-2334	192
Franklin Elem Sch/Dolton/Cook	00268886	708/201-2083	46
Franklin Elem Sch/Franklin/Morgan	00311378	217/675-2395	192
Franklin Elem Sch/Metropolis/Massac	00310324	618/524-2243	178

IL-V14   800-333-8802   School Year 2020-2021

Illinois School Directory
DISTRICT & SCHOOL TELEPHONE INDEX

School/City/County DISTRICT/CITY/COUNTY	PID	TELEPHONE	PAGE NUMBER
Franklin Elem Sch/Sterling/Whiteside	01170581	815/625-5755	240
Franklin Fine Arts Center/Chicago/Cook	00279627	773/534-8510	27
Franklin Jr Sr High Sch/Franklin/Morgan	00311392	217/675-2395	192
Franklin Middle Sch/Champaign/Champaign	00264799	217/351-3819	10
Franklin Middle Sch/Wheaton/Du Page	00290932	630/682-2060	92
Franklin Park Middle Sch/Salem/Marion	00309777	618/548-7704	175
FRANKLIN PARK PUB SCH DIST 84/ FRANKLIN PARK/COOK	00269787	847/455-4230	50
Franklin Preschool/Mattoon/Coles	12313003	217/238-8800	19
Franklin Primary Sch/Peoria/Peoria	00312774	309/682-2693	199
Franklin Sch/Belleville/St Clair	00316299	618/233-2413	217
FRANKLIN-JEFFERSON SP ED CO-OP/ BENTON/FRANKLIN	02182317	618/439-7231	109
Frassati Catholic Academy/Mundelein/Lake	00286723	847/223-4021	157
Frassati Catholic Academy/Wauconda/Lake	00287636	847/526-6311	157
Frazier Preparatory Academy/Chicago/Cook	10912433	773/521-1303	39
Frazier Prospective Mag Sch/Chicago/Cook	10912330	773/534-6880	31
Fred Rodgers Magnet Academy/Aurora/Kane	05274268	630/299-7175	129
Frederick Sch/Grayslake/Lake	04913679	847/543-5300	148
Fredrick Nerge Elem Sch/Roselle/Cook	01529190	847/357-5777	66
FREEBURG CMTY CONS SD 70/ FREEBURG/ST CLAIR	00317061	618/539-3188	219
Freeburg Cmty High Sch/Freeburg/St Clair	00317097	618/539-5533	219
FREEBURG CMTY HIGH SCH DIST 77/ FREEBURG/ST CLAIR	00317085	618/539-5533	219
Freeburg Elem Sch/Freeburg/St Clair	00317073	618/539-3188	219
Freeburg Primary Center/Freeburg/St Clair	10901252	618/539-3188	219
Freedom Elem Sch/Plainfield/Will	10911324	815/254-4005	246
Freedom Middle Sch/Berwyn/Cook	10004385	708/795-5800	23
Freeman Elem Sch/Aurora/Kane	00297681	630/301-5002	132
Freeport Alternative High Sch/Freeport/ Stephenson	11561441	815/233-0796	224
Freeport Christian Academy/Freeport/ Stephenson	02236889	815/235-9840	225
Freeport High Sch/Freeport/Stephenson	00320812	815/232-0400	224
Freeport Middle Sch/Freeport/Stephenson	00320800	815/232-0500	224
FREEPORT SCH DIST 145/FREEPORT/ STEPHENSON	00320745	815/232-0300	224
Fremont Elem Sch/Mundelein/Lake	04802264	847/837-0437	149
Fremont Intermediate Sch/Mundelein/Lake	10970887	847/388-3700	150
Fremont Middle Sch/Mundelein/Lake	00300757	847/566-9384	150
FREMONT SCH DIST 79/MUNDELEIN/ LAKE	00300745	847/566-0169	149
French STEM Academy/Decatur/Macon	00307119	217/362-3380	165
Friendship Junior High Sch/Des Plaines/ Cook	00267272	847/593-4350	43
Froberg Elem Sch/Rockford/Winnebago	00327626	815/874-2464	254
Frohardt Elem Sch/Granite City/Madison	00308747	618/451-5821	171
Fry Elem Sch/Naperville/Du Page	04943650	630/428-7400	95
Ft Dearborn Elem Sch/Chicago/Cook	00275669	773/535-2680	34
Fuller Elem Sch/Chicago/Cook	00277447	773/535-1687	26
Fullerton Elem Sch/Addison/Du Page	00288886	630/458-2950	88
FULTON CO CMTY UNIT SCH DIST 3/ CUBA/FULTON	00293477	309/785-5021	109
Fulton Elem Sch/Chicago/Cook	00277459	773/535-9000	34
Fulton Elem Sch/Fulton/Whiteside	00324351	815/589-2911	239
Fulton High Sch/Fulton/Whiteside	00324363	815/589-3511	239
Fulton Pre-School/Fulton/Whiteside	10001113	815/589-2309	239
Funston Elem Sch/Chicago/Cook	00279641	773/534-4125	30
Furqaan Academy-Boilingbrook/Bolingbrook/ Will	11814080	630/914-5015	250
Fusion Academy-Evanston/Evanston/Cook	12312097	847/868-8693	78
Fusion Academy-Lake Forest/Lake Forest/ Lake	12312102	847/295-4039	158
Fusion Academy-Lincoln Park/Chicago/Cook	12312126	312/763-6990	78
Fusion Academy-Oak Brook/Oak Brook/Du Page	12312138	630/368-0824	102
Futures Unlimited Sch/Decatur/Macon	04795740	217/429-1054	164

G

School/City/County	PID	TELEPHONE	PAGE
G B Swift Elem Specialty Sch/Chicago/Cook	00280951	773/534-2695	29
G Kerkstra Elem Sch/Oak Forest/Cook	00269749	708/687-2860	50
G N Dieterich Elem Sch/Aurora/Kane	00297540	630/299-8280	129
G Rogers Clark Elem Sch/Chicago/Cook	01556052	773/534-6225	27
G Stanley Hall Elem Sch/Glendale HTS/ Du Page	00290607	630/469-7720	97
Gage Park High Sch/Chicago/Cook	00277461	773/535-9230	37
Gages Lake Sch/Gages Lake/Lake	04198049	847/223-5586	146
Galapagos Rockford CS/Rockford/Winnebago	11459599	815/708-7946	254
GALATIA CMTY UNIT SCH DIST 1/ GALATIA/SALINE	00318417	618/297-4570	210
Galatia Grade Sch/Galatia/Saline	00318429	618/268-6371	210
Galatia Jr Sr High Sch/Galatia/Saline	00318431	618/297-4571	210
Gale Math & Science Academy/Chicago/Cook	00279653	773/534-2100	29
Galena High Sch/Galena/Jo Daviess	00297198	815/777-0917	125
Galena Middle Sch/Galena/Jo Daviess	00297186	815/777-2413	125
Galena Primary Sch/Galena/Jo Daviess	00297203	815/777-2200	126
GALENA UNIT SCH DIST 120/ GALENA/JO DAVIESS	00297174	815/777-3086	125
Galesburg Christian Sch/Galesburg/Knox	04879437	309/343-8008	140
GALESBURG CMTY UNIT SD 205/ GALESBURG/KNOX	00299926	309/973-2000	140
Galesburg High Sch/Galesburg/Knox	00300020	309/973-2001	140
Galesburg High School N/Galesburg/Knox	11554230	309/973-2003	140
Galileo Scholastic Academy/Chicago/Cook	03401166	773/534-7070	31
Gallatin Cmty Unit Dist 7 Sch/Junction/ Gallatin	00293790	618/272-3821	110
GALLATIN CMTY UNIT SCH DIST 7/ JUNCTION/GALLATIN	00293855	618/272-3821	110
Gallistel Language Academy/Chicago/Cook	00275671	773/535-6540	36
GALVA CMTY UNIT SCH DIST 224/ GALVA/HENRY	00295229	309/932-2108	117
Galva Elem Sch/Galva/Henry	00295243	309/932-2420	117
Galva Jr Sr High Sch/Galva/Henry	00295255	309/932-2151	117
Gard Elem Sch/Beardstown/Cass	00264555	217/323-1364	9
Garden Hills Elem Sch/Champaign/Champaign	00264804	217/351-3872	10
GARDNER CMTY CONS SD 72-C/ GARDNER/GRUNDY	00294093	815/237-2313	112
Gardner Elem Sch/Waterloo/Monroe	11563932	618/939-3060	190
Gardner Grade Sch/Gardner/Grundy	00294108	815/237-2313	112
Gardner S Wilmington High Sch/Gardner/ Grundy	00294122	815/237-2176	112
GARDNER S WILMINGTON HSD 73/ GARDNER/GRUNDY	00294110	815/237-2176	112
Garfield Elem Sch/Chicago HTS/Cook	00268393	708/756-4150	25
Garfield Elem Sch/Danville/Vermilion	00322303	217/444-1750	232
Garfield Elem Sch/Elgin/Kane	00298283	847/888-5192	130
Garfield Elem Sch/Forest Park/Cook	00269713	708/366-6945	50
Garfield Elem Sch/Maywood/Cook	00271352	708/450-2009	57
Garvy Elem Sch/Chicago/Cook	00279665	773/534-1185	28
Gary D Jewel Middle Sch/North Aurora/Kane	04810235	630/301-5010	132
Gary Elem Sch/Chicago/Cook	04487577	773/534-1455	32
Gary Elem Sch/West Chicago/Du Page	00291481	630/293-6010	99
Gateway Christian Academy/Cahokia/St Clair	10013946	618/337-1376	223
Gateway Legacy Christian Acad/Glen Carbon/ Madison	11470294	618/288-0452	173
Gateway to Learning Sch/Chicago/Cook	02827012	773/784-3200	78
GAVIN SCH DIST 37/INGLESIDE/LAKE	00300769	847/546-2916	150
Gavin South Junior High Sch/Ingleside/Lake	00300771	847/546-9336	150
GEFF CMTY CONS SCH DIST 14/ GEFF/WAYNE	00323539	618/897-2465	236
Geff Elem Sch/Geff/Wayne	00323541	618/897-2465	237
Gemini Middle Sch/Niles/Cook	00269141	847/827-1181	47
Gems World Academy/Chicago/Cook	12030835	312/809-8941	78
General George Patton Elem Sch/Riverdale/ Cook	00273180	708/841-2420	50
GENERAL GEORGE S PATTON SD 133/ RIVERDALE/COOK	00273178	708/841-3955	50
General Logan Attendance Ctr/Murphysboro/ Jackson	00296285	618/684-6061	121
GENESEO CMTY UNIT SCH DIST 228/ GENESEO/HENRY	00295279	309/945-0450	117
Geneseo High Sch/Geneseo/Henry	00295308	309/945-0399	117
Geneseo Middle Sch/Geneseo/Henry	00295281	309/945-0599	117
GENEVA CUSD 304/GENEVA/KANE	00298594	630/463-3000	131
Geneva High Sch/Geneva/Kane	00298623	630/463-3800	131
Geneva Middle School North/Geneva/Kane	10020743	630/463-3700	131
Geneva Middle School South/Geneva/Kane	00298609	630/463-3600	131
Genoa Elem Sch/Genoa/De Kalb	05270054	815/784-3742	85
GENOA-KINGSTON CMTY SD 424/ GENOA/DE KALB	00288068	815/784-6222	85
Genoa-Kingston High Sch/Genoa/De Kalb	00288094	815/784-5111	85
Genoa-Kingston Middle Sch/Genoa/De Kalb	00288082	815/784-5222	85
George B Carpenter Elem Sch/Park Ridge/ Cook	00273063	847/318-4370	62
George Leland Elem Sch/Chicago/Cook	00278910	773/534-6340	30
George O Barr Elem Sch/Silvis/Rock Island	00316122	309/792-0639	209
George Pullman Elem Sch/Chicago/Cook	00276390	773/535-5395	36
George T Wilkins Elem Sch/Justice/Cook	03247300	708/496-8708	53
George T Wilkins Jr High Sch/Justice/Cook	12368723	708/496-8708	53
George W Lieb Elem Sch/Bridgeview/Cook	00272162	708/599-1050	64
George W Tilton Elem Sch/Chicago/Cook	01556129	773/534-6746	31
George Washington Elem Sch/Alsip/Cook	03007655	708/489-3523	45
George Washington Elem Sch/Chicago/Cook	00276766	773/535-5010	36

DISTRICT & SCHOOL TELEPHONE INDEX

Market Data Retrieval

School/City/County DISTRICT/CITY/COUNTY	PID	TELEPHONE NUMBER	PAGE
George Washington Elem Sch/Moline/Rock Island	00315594	309/743-1619	208
George Washington Elem Sch/Park Ridge/Cook	00273166	847/318-4360	62
George Washington Elem Sch/Schiller Park/Cook	00274122	847/671-1922	67
George Washington Middle Sch/Lyons/Cook	00270994	708/783-4200	56
Georgetown Elem Sch/Aurora/Du Page	03051137	630/375-3456	95
GEORGETOWN-RIDGE FARM CUSD 4/GEORGETOWN/VERMILION	00322444	217/662-8488	232
Georgetown-Ridge Farm High Sch/Georgetown/Vermilion	00322468	217/662-6716	232
Georgetowne Middle Sch/Pekin/Tazewell	00321397	309/382-3456	227
German Int'l School Chicago/Chicago/Cook	12178358	773/880-8812	78
German Valley Grade Sch/German Valley/Ogle	00311897	815/362-2279	194
Germantown Elem Sch/Germantown/Clinton	00266448	618/523-4253	18
GERMANTOWN ELEM SCH DIST 60/GERMANTOWN/CLINTON	00266436	618/523-4253	18
Germantown Hills Elem Sch/Metamora/Woodford	00329064	309/383-2121	257
Germantown Hills Middle Sch/Metamora/Woodford	02110845	309/383-2121	257
GERMANTOWN HILLS SD 69/GERMANTWN HLS/WOODFORD	00329052	309/383-2121	257
GIANT CITY CMTY CONS SD 130/CARBONDALE/JACKSON	00296194	618/457-5391	120
Giant City Elem Sch/Carbondale/Jackson	00296209	618/457-5391	121
Giant Steps/Lisle/Du Page	12239615	630/864-3800	102
Gibault Catholic High Sch/Waterloo/Monroe	00317736	618/939-3883	190
Gibson City-Melvin-Sibley ES/Gibson City/Ford	00292746	217/784-4278	106
Gibson City-Melvin-Sibley HS/Gibson City/Ford	00292734	217/784-4292	106
Gibson City-Melvin-Sibley MS/Gibson City/Ford	00292772	217/784-8731	106
GIBSON CTY-MELVIN-SIBLEY CUSD5/GIBSON CITY/FORD	00292708	217/784-8296	106
GIFFORD CMTY CONS SD 188/GIFFORD/CHAMPAIGN	00264957	217/568-7733	10
Gifford Grade Sch/Gifford/Champaign	00264969	217/568-7733	10
Gifted Acad Marshall ES/Rockford/Winnebago	12177976	815/966-3370	254
Gifted Acad Marshall MS/Rockford/Winnebago	11832020	815/490-5400	254
Gilberts Elem Sch/Gilberts/McHenry	10910148	224/484-5900	180
Gillespie High Sch/Gillespie/Macoupin	00307729	217/839-2114	167
Gillespie Middle Sch/Gillespie/Macoupin	00307717	217/839-2116	167
Gillespie Tech Mag Cluster Sch/Chicago/Cook	00275695	773/535-5065	27
Gilson Brown Elem Sch/Godfrey/Madison	00308096	618/463-2175	169
Glacier Ridge Elem Sch/Crystal Lake/McHenry	04946119	815/444-4850	181
Glen Carbon Elem Sch/Glen Carbon/Madison	00308644	618/692-7460	171
Glen Crest Middle Sch/Glen Ellyn/Du Page	00289866	630/469-5220	90
GLEN ELLYN SCH DIST 41/GLEN ELLYN/DU PAGE	00289737	630/790-6400	94
Glen Flora Elem Sch/Waukegan/Lake	00302145	224/303-1800	156
Glen Grove Elem Sch/Glenview/Cook	00269933	847/998-5030	51
Glen Hill Elem Sch/Glendale HTS/Du Page	00291144	630/260-6141	98
Glen Oak Cmty Learning Center/Peoria/Peoria	00312803	309/672-6518	199
Glen Oaks Elem Sch/Hickory Hills/Cook	00271883	708/598-5711	59
Glen Oaks Therapeutic Day Sch/Glen Ellyn/Du Page	11232119	630/469-3602	102
Glenbard East High Sch/Lombard/Du Page	00289919	630/627-9250	94
Glenbard North High Sch/Carol Stream/Du Page	00289921	630/653-7000	94
Glenbard South High Sch/Glen Ellyn/Du Page	00289933	630/469-6500	94
GLENBARD TWP HIGH SCH DIST 87/GLEN ELLYN/DU PAGE	00289907	630/469-9100	94
Glenbard West High Sch/Glen Ellyn/Du Page	00289945	630/469-8600	94
Glenbrook Elem Sch/Streamwood/Kane	00298300	630/213-5555	130
GLENBROOK HIGH SCH DIST 225/GLENVIEW/COOK	00269842	847/998-6100	50
Glenbrook North High Sch/Northbrook/Cook	00269854	847/272-6400	51
Glenbrook South High Sch/Glenview/Cook	00269866	847/729-2000	51
GLENCOE SCH DIST 35/GLENCOE/COOK	00269878	847/835-7800	51
Glendale Elem Sch/East Peoria/Tazewell	00321177	309/427-5400	227
Glenn Elem Sch/Normal/Mclean	00306567	309/557-4418	186
Glenn Raymond Sch/Watseka/Iroquois	00295750	815/432-2115	119
Glenn Westlake Middle Sch/Lombard/Du Page	00290487	630/827-4500	97
Glenside Middle Sch/Glendale HTS/Du Page	00291156	630/260-6112	98
GLENVIEW CMTY CONS SCH DIST 34/GLENVIEW/COOK	00269921	847/998-5000	51
Glenview Middle Sch/East Moline/Rock Island	00315403	309/755-1919	207
Glenview New Church Sch/Glenview/Cook	02868456	847/724-0057	78
Glenwood Academy/Glenwood/Cook	01441902	708/754-0175	78
Glenwood Elem Sch/Chatham/Sangamon	11708170	217/483-6704	211
Glenwood Elem Sch/Waukegan/Lake	00302157	224/303-2010	156
Glenwood High Sch/Chatham/Sangamon	00318596	217/483-2424	211
Glenwood Intermediate Sch/Chatham/Sangamon	04949202	217/483-1183	211
Glenwood Middle Sch/Chatham/Sangamon	00318601	217/483-2481	211
Glenwood Sch/Glenwood/Cook	04990639	847/464-8200	78
Global Citizenship Exp Sch/Chicago/Cook	11564986	312/643-0991	78
Goethe Elem Sch/Chicago/Cook	00279689	773/534-4135	30
Golf Middle Sch/Morton Grove/Cook	00270035	847/965-3740	51
GOLF SCH DIST 67/MORTON GROVE/COOK	00270011	847/966-8200	51
Golfview Elem Sch/Carpentersvle/McHenry	00298037	224/484-2800	180
Gompers Junior High Sch/Joliet/Will	00324973	815/727-5276	243
Good Shepherd Center/Hazel Crest/Cook	01779101	708/957-2600	78
Good Shepherd Christian Acad/Chicago/Cook	00282404	773/342-5854	78
Good Shepherd Lutheran Sch/Collinsville/Madison	02845521	618/344-3153	173
Good Shepherd Lutheran Sch/Downers Grove/Du Page	02828391	630/852-5081	102
Good Shepherd Lutheran Sch/Pekin/Tazewell	02193110	309/347-2020	229
Goodfield Elem Sch/Goodfield/Woodford	00329040	309/965-2362	257
Goodings Grove Sch/Homer Glen/Will	01821833	708/226-7650	242
Goodrich Elem Sch/Woodridge/Du Page	00289971	630/795-6100	100
Goodwin Elem Sch/Cicero/Cook	00268616	708/652-5500	42
Goodwin Elem Sch/North Aurora/Kane	00297693	630/301-5003	132
Gordon D Bush Elem Sch/E Saint Louis/St Clair	00316952	618/646-3930	219
Gordon Gregory Middle Sch/Naperville/Du Page	03050418	630/428-6300	95
Gordon Sch/Posen/Cook	00273269	708/388-7202	63
GOREVILLE CMTY UNIT SD 1/GOREVILLE/JOHNSON	00297394	618/995-2142	127
Goreville Sch/Goreville/Johnson	00297411	618/995-2142	127
Goshen Elem Sch/Edwardsville/Madison	11136620	618/655-6250	171
Goudy Elem Sch/Chicago/Cook	00279718	773/534-2480	27
Gower Middle Sch/Burr Ridge/Du Page	00290059	630/323-8275	95
GOWER SCH DIST 62/WILLOWBROOK/DU PAGE	00290035	630/986-5383	94
Gower West Elem Sch/Willowbrook/Du Page	00290047	630/323-6446	95
Grace Baptist Academy/Springfield/Sangamon	02825947	217/522-2881	214
Grace Christian Academy/Kankakee/Kankakee	00282088	773/762-1234	78
Grace Christian Academy/Kankakee/Kankakee	00299598	815/939-4579	137
Grace Christian Sch/Pontiac/Livingston	12379253	815/419-2030	163
Grace Lutheran Sch/Chicago/Cook	00282090	773/637-2250	78
Grace Lutheran Sch/River Forest/Cook	01844328	708/366-6901	78
Grafton Elem Sch/Grafton/Jersey	00297069	618/786-3388	125
Graham Elem Sch/Chicago/Cook	00277497	773/535-1308	31
Grand Avenue Sch/Beardstown/Cass	04744416	217/323-1510	9
GRAND PRAIRIE CMTY CONS SD 6/CENTRALIA/JEFFERSON	00296704	618/249-6289	123
Grand Prairie Elem Sch/Centralia/Jefferson	00296716	618/249-6289	123
Grand Prairie Elem Sch/Frankfort/Will	04447412	815/469-3366	242
Grand Prairie Elem Sch/Joliet/Will	00325551	815/436-7000	246
GRAND RIDGE CCSD 95/GRAND RIDGE/LA SALLE	00302729	815/249-6225	141
Grand Ridge Cmty Cons Elem Sch/Grand Ridge/La Salle	00302731	815/249-6225	141
Grande Park Elem Sch/Plainfield/Kendall	10907646	630/551-9700	137
Grande Reserve Elem Sch/Yorkville/Kendall	10031467	630/553-5513	139
GRANITE CITY CMTY UNIT SD 9/GRANITE CITY/MADISON	00308682	618/451-5800	171
Granite City High Sch/Granite City/Madison	00308723	618/451-5808	171
GRANT CMTY CONS SCH DIST 110/FAIRVIEW HTS/ST CLAIR	00317102	618/398-5577	219
Grant Cmty High Sch/Fox Lake/Lake	00300812	847/587-2561	150
GRANT CMTY HIGH SCH DIST 124/FOX LAKE/LAKE	00300800	847/587-2561	150
Grant Elem Sch/Melrose Park/Cook	00267612	708/343-0410	22
Grant Elem Sch/S Chicago HTS/Cook	00268410	708/756-4156	25
Grant Intermediate Sch/Marengo/McHenry	11918234	815/568-7427	182
Grant Middle Sch/Fairview HTS/St Clair	00317138	618/397-2764	219
GRANT PARK CMTY UNIT SD 6/GRANT PARK/KANKAKEE	00299067	815/465-6013	135
Grant Park Elem Sch/Grant Park/Kankakee	00299079	815/465-2183	135
Grant Park High Sch/Grant Park/Kankakee	00299093	815/465-2181	135
Grant Park Middle Sch/Grant Park/Kankakee	03012181	815/465-2184	135
Grant Primary Sch/Stone Park/Cook	12166733	708/345-3625	22
Grant-White Elem Sch/Forest Park/Cook	00269725	708/366-5704	50

Illinois School Directory
DISTRICT & SCHOOL TELEPHONE INDEX

School/City/County DISTRICT/CITY/COUNTY	PID	TELEPHONE NUMBER	PAGE
Grantfork Elem Sch/Highland/Madison	00308931	618/675-2200	171
Grass Lake Elem Sch/Antioch/Lake	00300836	847/395-1550	150
GRASS LAKE SCH DIST 36/ANTIOCH/LAKE	00300824	847/395-1550	150
Gray Elem Sch/Chicago/Cook	00279720	773/534-3520	28
Gray M Sanborn Elem Sch/Palatine/Cook	00272655	847/963-7000	43
Graymont Elem Sch/Graymont/Livingston	00304478	815/743-5346	162
Grays Lake Early Childhood Ctr/Grayslake/Lake	11512933	847/543-6204	148
Grayslake Central High Sch/Grayslake/Lake	00300898	847/986-3300	150
GRAYSLAKE CMTY HS DIST 127/GRAYSLAKE/LAKE	00300886	847/986-3400	150
Grayslake Middle Sch/Grayslake/Lake	00300850	847/223-3680	148
Grayslake North High Sch/Grayslake/Lake	05342827	847/986-3100	150
GRAYVILLE CMTY UNIT SCH DIST 1/GRAYVILLE/WHITE	00323814	618/375-7114	238
Grayville Jr Sr High Sch/Grayville/White	00323838	618/375-7114	238
Great Lakes Acad Charter Sch/Chicago/Cook	12101630	773/530-3040	39
Greeley Elem Sch/Winnetka/Cook	00281943	847/446-6060	72
Green Bay Early Childhood Cent/North Chicago/Lake	12104412	847/775-7100	154
Green Bay Early Childhood Ctr/Highland Park/Lake	11422431	224/765-3060	154
Greenbriar Elem Sch/Chicago HTS/Cook	00268422	708/756-4159	25
Greenbriar Elem Sch/Northbrook/Cook	00272007	847/498-7950	59
Greenbrier Elem Sch/Arlington HTS/Cook	00267040	847/398-4272	21
Greenbrook Elem Sch/Hanover Park/Du Page	00290308	630/894-4544	96
Greene Elem Sch/Chicago/Cook	00278245	773/535-4560	32
GREENFIELD CMTY UNIT SD 10/GREENFIELD/GREENE	00293922	217/368-2447	111
Greenfield Elem Sch/Greenfield/Greene	00293934	217/368-2551	111
Greenfield High Sch/Greenfield/Greene	00293958	217/368-2219	111
Greenman Elem Sch/Aurora/Kane	00297708	630/301-5004	132
GREENVIEW CMTY UNIT SD 200/GREENVIEW/MENARD	00310556	217/968-2295	188
Greenview Unit Sch/Greenview/Menard	00310568	217/968-2295	188
Greenville Elem Sch/Greenville/Bond	00263331	618/664-3117	4
Greenville High Sch/Greenville/Bond	00263343	618/664-1370	4
Greenville Junior High Sch/Greenville/Bond	00263355	618/664-1226	4
Greenwood Elem Sch/South Holland/Cook	00274380	708/339-4433	68
Greenwood Elem Sch/Waukegan/Lake	00302169	224/303-2080	156
Greenwood Elem Sch/Woodstock/McHenry	00306036	815/648-2606	184
Gregory Elem Sch/Chicago/Cook	00279756	773/534-6820	31
Gregory Elem Sch/Rockford/Winnebago	00327640	815/229-2176	254
Gregory Intermediate Sch/Moweaqua/Christian	04017902	217/768-3860	14
Gresham Elem Sch/Chicago/Cook	00275748	773/535-3350	26
Griffin Christian Sch/Dundee/Kane	11224992	847/428-5413	133
GRIGGSVILLE-PERRY CMTY SD 4/GRIGGSVILLE/PIKE	00314502	217/833-2352	203
Griggsville-Perry Elem Sch/Griggsville/Pike	10020755	217/833-2352	203
Griggsville-Perry High Sch/Griggsville/Pike	00314526	217/833-2352	203
Griggsville-Perry Middle Sch/Perry/Pike	00314540	217/236-9161	203
Grigsby Intermediate Sch/Granite City/Madison	00308735	618/931-5544	171
Grimes Elem Sch/Chicago/Cook	00277514	773/535-2364	34
Grissom Elem Sch/Chicago/Cook	00275750	773/535-5380	27
Grove Ave Elem Sch/Barrington/Lake	00267545	847/381-1888	147
Grove Elem Sch/Normal/Mclean	04944836	309/557-4417	186
Grove Junior High Sch/Elk Grove Vlg/Cook	00267296	847/593-4367	43
Grtr Lawndale Social Justice/Chicago/Cook	10009086	773/535-4300	37
Grundy Area Voc Center/Morris/Grundy	01536624	815/942-4390	111
GRUNDY AREA VOC ED SYSTEM/MORRIS/GRUNDY	04338603	815/942-4390	113
GRUNDY CO SPECIAL ED CO-OP/MORRIS/GRUNDY	02183969	815/942-5780	113
Guardian Angel Orthodox Sch/Des Plaines/Cook	11733682	847/827-5510	78
Guerin College Prep Sch/River Grove/Cook	00283812	708/453-6233	73
Guilford High Sch/Rockford/Winnebago	00327664	815/654-4870	254
Gunsaulus Scholastic Academy/Chicago/Cook	00277526	773/535-7215	27
Gurnee Christian Academy/Gurnee/Lake	01844859	847/623-7773	158
GURNEE SCH DIST 56/GURNEE/LAKE	00300903	847/336-0800	150
Gurrie Middle Sch/La Grange/Cook	00270657	708/482-2720	54
Gwendolyn Brooks Coll Prep Aca/Chicago/Cook	04776653	773/535-9930	38
Gwendolyn Brooks Elem Sch/Aurora/Du Page	04364925	630/375-3200	95
Gwendolyn Brooks Elem Sch/Dekalb/De Kalb	04876576	815/754-9936	84
Gwendolyn Brooks Middle Sch/Oak Park/Cook	00272332	708/524-3050	61

H

School/City/County DISTRICT/CITY/COUNTY	PID	TELEPHONE NUMBER	PAGE
H C Storm Elem Sch/Batavia/Kane	01821704	630/937-8200	128
H H Conrady Junior High Sch/Hickory Hills/Cook	00271895	708/598-5721	59
H L Richards High Sch/Oak Lawn/Cook	00282351	708/499-2550	44
H R McCall Elem Sch/Waukegan/Lake	00302171	224/303-1760	156
Haber Oaks Campus Sch/Crystal Lake/McHenry	11129940	815/893-5300	180
Hadi School of Excellence/Schaumburg/Cook	11512581	847/891-4440	78
Hadley Middle Sch/Homer Glen/Will	03049146	708/226-7725	242
Haines Elem Sch/Chicago/Cook	00277540	773/534-9200	31
Haines Elem Sch/New Lenox/Will	00325408	815/485-2115	245
Hale Elem Sch/Chicago/Cook	00277552	773/535-2265	34
Hales Franciscan High Sch/Chicago/Cook	00283276	773/285-8400	73
Half Day Sch/Lincolnshire/Lake	04013059	847/634-6463	153
Hall High Sch/Spring Valley/Bureau	00263721	815/664-2100	6
HALL TWP HIGH SCH DIST 502/SPRING VALLEY/BUREAU	00263719	815/664-2100	6
Hamel Elem Sch/Hamel/Madison	00308670	618/692-7444	171
Hamilton Academy/West Dundee/Kane	04244612	847/695-9732	133
HAMILTON CMTY CONS SD 328/HAMILTON/HANCOCK	00294603	866/332-3880	114
HAMILTON CO CMTY UNIT SD 10/MC LEANSBORO/HAMILTON	00294419	618/643-2328	114
Hamilton Co Jr Sr High Sch/Mc Leansboro/Hamilton	02845741	618/643-2328	114
Hamilton Co Pre-School Center/Mc Leansboro/Hamilton	03004665	618/643-2328	114
Hamilton Elem Sch/Chicago/Cook	00279768	773/534-5484	30
Hamilton Elem Sch/Hamilton/Hancock	00294627	866/332-3880	114
Hamilton Elem Sch/Moline/Rock Island	00315611	309/743-1610	208
Hamilton Jr Sr High Sch/Hamilton/Hancock	00294639	866/332-3880	114
Hamlin Upper Grade Center/Alsip/Cook	00267428	708/597-1550	21
Hamline Elem Sch/Chicago/Cook	00277564	773/535-4565	32
Hammitt Sch at the Baby Fold/Normal/Mclean	02827488	309/452-1170	188
Hammond Elem Sch/Chicago/Cook	00277576	773/535-4580	32
Hampshire Elem Sch/Hampshire/McHenry	00298049	847/792-3400	180
Hampshire High Sch/Hampshire/McHenry	11079656	847/792-3500	180
Hampshire Middle Sch/Hampshire/McHenry	00298051	847/792-3200	180
Hampton Arts Sch/Chicago/Cook	04922931	773/535-4030	34
Hampton Elem Sch/Hampton/Rock Island	00315489	309/755-0693	207
HAMPTON SCH DIST 29/HAMPTON/ROCK ISLAND	00315477	309/755-0693	207
Hancock College Prep HS/Chicago/Cook	03055236	773/535-2410	37
Hanna Sacks Bais Yaakov HS/Chicago/Cook	02828339	773/338-9222	78
Hannah Beardsley Middle Sch/Crystal Lake/McHenry	04452120	815/788-5750	181
Hannah Martin Elem Sch/Lk In The Hls/McHenry	04914283	847/659-5300	182
Hannum Elem Sch/Oak Lawn/Cook	00272265	708/423-1690	60
Hanover Countryside Elem Sch/Streamwood/Kane	00298324	630/213-5560	130
Hanover Highlands Elem Sch/Hanover Park/Cook	00273958	630/736-4230	66
Hanson Park Elem Sch/Chicago/Cook	00279782	773/534-3100	30
Harbor Academy/Hillside/Cook	11935842	708/236-3250	20
HARDIN CO CMTY UNIT SCH DIST 1/ELIZABETHTOWN/HARDIN	00294914	618/287-2411	115
Hardin Co Elem Sch/Elizabethtown/Hardin	02112518	618/287-7601	115
Hardin Co Jr Sr High Sch/Elizabethtown/Hardin	04362989	618/287-2141	115
Harding Grade Sch/Earlville/La Salle	00302717	815/792-8216	144
Harding Primary Sch/Monmouth/Warren	00323084	309/734-4915	234
Harlan Community Academy HS/Chicago/Cook	00275774	773/535-5400	38
Harlem High Sch/MacHesney Pk/Winnebago	00327145	815/654-4511	252
Harlem Middle Sch/Loves Park/Winnebago	00327169	815/654-4510	252
HARLEM UNIT SCH DIST 122/MACHESNEY PK/WINNEBAGO	00327121	815/654-4500	252
Harmony Intermediate Sch/Belleville/St Clair	12104539	618/397-3747	219
HARMONY-EMGE SCH DIST 175/BELLEVILLE/ST CLAIR	00317164	618/397-8444	219
Harnew Elem Sch/Oak Lawn/Cook	00272150	708/599-7070	64
Harold Washington Elem Sch/Chicago/Cook	00276340	773/535-6225	35
Harper Elem Sch/Wilmette/Cook	00281591	847/512-6200	71
Harper High Sch/Chicago/Cook	00277590	773/535-9150	37
Harriet Beecher Stowe Elem Sch/Chicago/Cook	00280925	773/534-4175	31
Harriet Gifford Elem Sch/Elgin/Kane	00298295	847/888-5195	130
HARRISBURG CMTY UNIT SD 3/HARRISBURG/SALINE	00318443	618/253-7637	210
Harrisburg High Sch/Harrisburg/Saline	00318467	618/253-7637	211
Harrisburg Middle Sch/Harrisburg/Saline	00318493	618/253-7637	211

School Year 2020-2021 800-333-8802 IL-V17

DISTRICT & SCHOOL TELEPHONE INDEX

Market Data Retrieval

School/City/County DISTRICT/CITY/COUNTY	PID	TELEPHONE NUMBER	PAGE
Harrison Cmty Learning Center/Peoria/Peoria	00312839	309/672-6522	199
Harrison Elem Sch/Wonder Lake/McHenry	00305525	815/653-2311	181
HARRISON SCH DIST 36/WONDER LAKE/MCHENRY	00305513	815/653-2311	181
Harrison Street Elem Sch/Geneva/Kane	00298635	630/463-3300	131
Harry D Jacobs High Sch/Algonquin/McHenry	01524384	847/532-6100	180
Harry E Fry Elem Sch/Burbank/Cook	11449324	708/599-5554	24
Hartford Elem Sch/Hartford/Madison	00309284	618/254-9814	172
Hartgrove Academy/Chicago/Cook	01844158	773/413-1700	78
Hartsburg Emden Jr Sr High Sch/Hartsburg/Logan	00304777	217/642-5244	163
HARTSBURG EMDEN SCH DIST 21/HARTSBURG/LOGAN	00304741	217/642-5244	163
HARVARD CMTY UNIT SCH DIST 50/HARVARD/MCHENRY	00305537	815/943-4022	181
Harvard Elem Sch/Chicago/Cook	00275815	773/535-3045	26
Harvard High Sch/Harvard/McHenry	00305551	815/943-6461	181
Harvard Junior High Sch/Harvard/McHenry	00305563	815/943-6466	181
Harvard Park Elem Sch/Springfield/Sangamon	00318986	217/525-3214	213
Harvest Christian Academy/Elgin/Kane	10031297	847/214-3500	133
HARVEY PUBLIC SCH DIST 152/HARVEY/COOK	00270126	708/333-0300	51
Haugan Elem Sch/Chicago/Cook	00279794	773/534-5040	29
HAVANA CMTY SCH DIST 126/HAVANA/MASON	00310154	309/543-3384	177
Havana High Sch/Havana/Mason	00310166	309/543-3337	177
Havana Junior High Sch/Havana/Mason	02108086	309/543-6677	177
Haven Middle Sch/Evanston/Cook	00269347	847/859-8200	48
Hawk Hollow Elem Sch/Bartlett/Kane	05091212	630/540-7676	130
HAWTHORN CMTY CONS SCH DIST 73/VERNON HILLS/LAKE	00300939	847/990-4200	151
Hawthorn Early Childhood Ctr/Wheeling/Cook	04943129	847/465-7290	71
Hawthorn Elem School North/Vernon Hills/Lake	02880155	847/990-4500	151
Hawthorn Elem School South/Vernon Hills/Lake	01821730	847/990-4800	151
Hawthorn Grade Sch/Salem/Marion	00309765	618/548-7702	175
Hawthorn Middle School North/Vernon Hills/Lake	00300941	847/990-4400	151
Hawthorn Middle School South/Vernon Hills/Lake	01413448	847/990-4100	151
Hawthorn Sch of Dual Language/Vernon Hills/Lake	11708730	847/990-4900	151
Hawthorne Elem Sch/Elmhurst/Du Page	00289543	630/834-4541	94
Hawthorne Elem Sch/Wheaton/Du Page	00290944	630/682-2065	92
Hawthorne Scholastic Academy/Chicago/Cook	00279809	773/534-5550	30
Hayt Elem Sch/Chicago/Cook	00279823	773/534-2040	29
Hazel Bland Promise Center/E Saint Louis/St Clair	01780447	618/274-3500	223
HAZEL CREST SCH DIST 152-5/HAZEL CREST/COOK	00270217	708/335-0790	52
Hazel Dell Elem Sch/Springfield/Sangamon	00319007	217/525-3223	213
Hazelgreen Elem Sch/Alsip/Cook	00266888	708/371-5351	20
Healy Elem Sch/Chicago/Cook	00277617	773/534-9190	31
Hearst Elem Sch/Chicago/Cook	00277629	773/535-2376	34
Heartland Elem Sch/Geneva/Kane	05092890	630/463-3200	131
Heartland Tech Acad-Eldorado/Decatur/Macon	00306933	217/872-4050	164
Heartland Tech Acad-Richland/Decatur/Macon	11736438	217/872-4050	164
HEARTLAND TECHNICAL ACADEMY/DECATUR/MACON	04184373	217/872-4050	167
Heather Hill Elem Sch/Flossmoor/Cook	00269634	708/647-7200	49
Hedding Grade Sch/Abingdon/Knox	00299885	309/462-2363	139
Hedges Elem Sch/Chicago/Cook	00277631	773/535-7360	32
Hefferan Elem Sch/Chicago/Cook	00279835	773/534-6192	27
Heineman Middle Sch/Algonquin/McHenry	10008446	847/659-4300	182
Helen Huffman Elem Sch/Cahokia/St Clair	00316471	618/332-3720	218
Helen Keller Elem Sch/Tinley Park/Cook	01550321	708/532-2144	53
Helen Keller Jr High Sch/Schaumburg/Cook	04286426	847/357-6500	66
Hellenic American Acad/Deerfield/Lake	01752880	847/317-1063	158
Henderson Elem Academy/Chicago/Cook	00277643	773/535-9080	34
Hendricks Elem Cmty Acad/Chicago/Cook	00277655	773/535-1696	33
Henking Primary Sch/Glenview/Cook	00269945	847/998-5035	51
Henry Clay Elem Sch/Chicago/Cook	00275346	773/535-5600	36
Henry Longfellow Elem Sch/Buffalo Grove/Cook	00281462	847/520-2755	71
Henry Marlowe Middle Sch/Lk In The Hls/McHenry	10009646	847/659-4700	182
Henry Puffer Sch/Downers Grove/Du Page	00291118	630/968-0294	93
Henry Raab Elem Sch/Belleville/St Clair	00316304	618/234-4330	217
HENRY SENACHWINE CUSD 5/HENRY/MARSHALL	00309909	309/364-3614	176
Henry Senachwine Grade Sch/Henry/Marshall	00309894	309/364-2531	176
Henry Senachwine High Sch/Henry/Marshall	00309911	309/364-2829	176
Henry W Cowherd Middle Sch/Aurora/Kane	04011491	630/299-5900	129
Henry Winkelman Elem Sch/Glenview/Cook	00281230	847/729-5650	70
HENRY-STARK CO SP ED DIST 801/KEWANEE/HENRY	02182044	309/852-5696	118
Herget Middle Sch/Aurora/Kane	10007375	630/301-5006	132
Heritage Christian Sch/Frankfort/Will	02970798	815/464-9100	250
HERITAGE CMTY UNIT SCH DIST 8/HOMER/CHAMPAIGN	00264971	217/834-3393	11
Heritage Elem Sch/Homer/Champaign	00264983	217/896-2421	11
Heritage Elem Sch/Streamwood/Kane	00298180	630/213-5565	130
Heritage Grove Middle Sch/Plainfield/Will	04866674	815/439-4810	246
Heritage High Sch/Broadlands/Champaign	04449381	217/834-3392	11
Heritage Lakes Elem Sch/Carol Stream/Du Page	03329192	630/588-6200	90
Heritage Middle Sch/Berwyn/Cook	04866923	708/749-6110	23
Heritage Middle Sch/Lansing/Cook	00274718	708/895-0790	68
Heritage Middle Sch/Summit/Cook	04032249	708/458-7590	45
Herman E Dummer Elem Sch/Sandwich/De Kalb	05070696	815/786-8498	86
Herrick Elem Sch/Herrick/Shelby	00320305	618/428-5223	216
Herrick Middle Sch/Downers Grove/Du Page	00289385	630/719-5810	93
Herrin Cmty Elem Sch/Herrin/Williamson	00326880	618/942-2744	251
HERRIN CMTY SCH DIST 4/HERRIN/WILLIAMSON	00326842	618/988-8024	251
Herrin High Sch/Herrin/Williamson	00326878	618/942-6606	251
Herrin Middle Sch/Herrin/Williamson	04017653	618/942-5603	251
HERSCHER CMTY SCH DIST 2/HERSCHER/KANKAKEE	00299108	815/426-2162	135
Herscher High Sch/Herscher/Kankakee	00299146	815/426-2103	135
Herscher Intermediate Sch/Herscher/Kankakee	00299134	815/426-2242	135
Herzl Elem Sch/Chicago/Cook	00277693	773/534-1480	26
Hester Junior High Sch/Franklin Park/Cook	00269828	847/455-2150	50
HEYWORTH CMTY SCH DIST 4/HEYWORTH/MCLEAN	00306385	309/473-3727	185
Heyworth Elem Sch/Heyworth/Mclean	00306402	309/473-2822	186
Heyworth Jr Sr High Sch/Heyworth/Mclean	00306414	309/473-2322	186
HIAWATHA CMTY UNIT SD 426/KIRKLAND/DE KALB	00288111	815/522-6676	85
Hiawatha Elem Sch/Berwyn/Cook	00267870	708/795-2327	23
Hiawatha Elem Sch/Kirkland/De Kalb	00288123	815/522-3336	85
Hiawatha High Sch/Kirkland/De Kalb	04453198	815/522-3335	85
Hibbard Elem Sch/Chicago/Cook	00279859	773/534-5191	29
Hickory Bend Elem Sch/Glenwood/Cook	01550319	708/758-4520	24
Hickory Creek Middle Sch/Frankfort/Will	00324820	815/469-4474	242
Hickory Grove Elem Sch/Dunlap/Peoria	11825326	309/243-8711	196
Hickory Point Elem Sch/Northbrook/Cook	00271948	847/498-3830	59
Higgins Community Academy/Chicago/Cook	00275827	773/535-5625	36
High Mount Elem Sch/Swansea/St Clair	00317217	618/233-1054	220
HIGH MOUNT SCH DIST 116/SWANSEA/ST CLAIR	00317205	618/233-1054	219
High Point Elem Sch/Orland Park/Cook	00272473	708/364-4400	61
High School of St Thomas More/Champaign/Champaign	04925658	217/352-7210	13
Highcrest Middle Sch/Wilmette/Cook	04363139	847/512-6500	72
Highland Christian Academy/Elgin/Kane	02984804	847/741-5530	133
HIGHLAND CMTY SCH DIST 5/HIGHLAND/MADISON	00308917	618/654-2106	171
Highland Elem Sch/Downers Grove/Du Page	00289397	630/719-5835	93
Highland Elem Sch/Elgin/Kane	00298336	847/888-5280	130
Highland Elem Sch/Highland/Madison	02888626	618/654-2108	171
Highland Elem Sch/Skokie/Cook	00274213	847/676-5001	67
Highland Elem Sch/Stillman Vly/Ogle	00311964	815/645-8188	195
Highland High Sch/Highland/Madison	00308955	618/654-7131	171
Highland Middle Sch/Highland/Madison	00308967	618/651-8800	171
Highland Middle Sch/Libertyville/Lake	00301490	847/362-9020	153
Highland Park High Sch/Highland Park/Lake	00301115	224/765-2000	155
Highland Prekindergarten/Chicago HTS/Cook	04028054	708/756-0008	25
Highland Primary Sch/Highland/Madison	00308943	618/654-2107	171
Highlands Elem Sch/Hazel Crest/Cook	00271182	708/335-9773	63
Highlands Elem Sch/La Grange/Cook	00270281	708/579-6886	54
Highlands Elem Sch/Naperville/Du Page	00290748	630/420-6335	98
Highlands Middle Sch/La Grange/Cook	00270308	708/579-6890	54
Hilda Walker Interm Sch/Tinley Park/Will	03239092	815/464-2285	247
Hill Elem Sch/Aurora/Kane	00297772	630/301-5007	132
Hillcrest Elem Sch/Antioch/Lake	04948155	847/838-8001	146
Hillcrest Elem Sch/Downers Grove/Du Page	00289402	630/719-5840	93
Hillcrest Elem Sch/East Moline/Rock Island	00315415	309/755-7621	207
Hillcrest Elem Sch/Elgin/Kane	00298348	847/888-5282	130
Hillcrest High Sch/Cntry CLB Hls/Cook	00268094	708/799-7000	23
Hillel Torah N Sub Day Sch/Skokie/Cook	01405075	847/674-6533	78

Illinois School Directory

DISTRICT & SCHOOL TELEPHONE INDEX

School/City/County DISTRICT/CITY/COUNTY	PID	TELEPHONE NUMBER	PAGE
Hillman Elem Sch/Rockford/Winnebago	00327731	815/229-2835	254
HILLSBORO CMTY UNIT SCH DIST 3/			
HILLSBORO/MONTGOMERY	00310996	217/532-2942	190
Hillsboro High Sch/Hillsboro/Montgomery	00311055	217/532-2841	191
Hillsboro Junior High Sch/Hillsboro/Montgomery	00311067	217/532-3742	191
Hillside Elem Sch/Hillside/Cook	00270322	708/449-6490	52
HILLSIDE SCH DIST 93/HILLSIDE/COOK	00270310	708/449-7280	52
Hilltop Elem Sch/Elgin/Kane	00298582	847/289-6655	130
Hilltop Elem Sch/McHenry/McHenry	00305769	779/244-1300	183
Hinckley Big Rock Middle Sch/Big Rock/De Kalb	00288159	630/556-4180	85
HINCKLEY-BIG ROCK CMTY SD 429/HINCKLEY/DE KALB	00288147	815/286-7578	85
Hinckley-Big Rock Elem Sch/Hinckley/De Kalb	00288161	815/286-3400	85
Hinckley-Big Rock High Sch/Hinckley/De Kalb	00288173	815/286-7501	85
Hines Primary Sch/Peoria/Peoria	00312853	309/672-6525	199
Hinsdale Adventist Academy/Hinsdale/Du Page	01405219	630/323-9211	102
Hinsdale Central High Sch/Hinsdale/Du Page	00290188	630/570-8000	95
Hinsdale Middle Sch/Hinsdale/Du Page	00290085	630/861-4700	91
Hinsdale South High Sch/Darien/Du Page	00290190	630/468-4000	95
HINSDALE TWP HIGH SCH DIST 86/HINSDALE/DU PAGE	00290176	630/655-6100	95
Hirsch Metro High Sch/Chicago/Cook	00275841	773/535-3100	38
Hitch Elem Sch/Chicago/Cook	00279861	773/534-1189	29
Hodgkins Elem Sch/Hodgkins/Cook	00270669	708/482-2740	54
Hoffman Elem Sch/Glenview/Cook	00269957	847/998-5040	51
Hoffman Estates High Sch/Hoffman Est/Cook	00272734	847/755-5600	69
Holden Elem Sch/Chicago/Cook	00277734	773/535-7200	27
HOLLIS CONS SCH DIST 328/PEORIA/PEORIA	00312401	309/697-1325	197
Hollis Consolidated Grade Sch/Peoria/Peoria	00312413	309/697-1325	197
Hollywood Elem Sch/Brookfield/Cook	00273726	708/485-7630	65
Hollywood Heights Sch/Caseyville/Madison	12230683	618/343-2740	170
Holmes Elem Sch/Chicago/Cook	00277746	773/535-9025	34
Holmes Elem Sch/Clarendon Hls/Du Page	00290566	630/515-4810	97
Holmes Elem Sch/Harvey/Cook	00270164	708/333-0440	51
Holmes Junior High Sch/Mt Prospect/Cook	00267313	847/593-4390	43
Holy Angels Sch/Aurora/Kane	00328395	630/897-3613	133
Holy Angels Sch/Chicago/Cook	00283305	773/624-0727	73
Holy Childhood Sch/Mascoutah/St Clair	00317750	618/566-2922	222
Holy Cross Catholic Sch/Batavia/Kane	11219454	630/593-5290	133
Holy Cross Lutheran Sch/Collinsville/Madison	00309260	618/344-0474	173
Holy Cross Sch/Champaign/Champaign	00313429	217/356-9521	13
Holy Cross Sch/Mendota/La Salle	00313431	815/539-7003	145
Holy Family Catholic Academy/Inverness/Cook	05243269	847/907-3452	73
Holy Family Catholic Sch/Decatur/Macon	00319473	217/423-7049	166
Holy Family Catholic Sch/Rockford/Winnebago	00328424	815/398-5331	256
Holy Family Lutheran Sch/Chicago/Cook	03016008	773/265-0550	78
Holy Family Parish Sch/Peoria/Peoria	00313443	309/688-2931	200
Holy Family Sch/Granite City/Madison	00319863	618/877-5500	173
Holy Family Sch/Oglesby/La Salle	00313455	815/883-8916	145
Holy Family Sch/Shorewood/Will	00326024	815/725-8149	249
Holy Trinity Catholic Sch/Fairview HTS/St Clair	00317827	618/628-7395	222
Holy Trinity Catholic Sch/Westmont/Du Page	00326048	630/971-0184	100
Holy Trinity High Sch/Chicago/Cook	00283460	773/278-4212	73
Home Elem Sch/Stickney/Cook	00270968	708/783-4500	56
HOMER CMTY CONS SCH DIST 33C/HOMER GLEN/WILL	00324832	708/226-7600	242
Homer Junior High Sch/Homer Glen/Will	00324844	708/226-7800	242
Homestead Elem Sch/Aurora/Kendall	05092149	630/636-3100	137
Hometown Elem Sch/Hometown/Cook	00272277	708/423-7360	60
HOMEWOOD FLOSSMOOR CHSD 233/FLOSSMOOR/COOK	00270396	708/799-3000	52
Homewood Flossmoor High Sch/Flossmoor/Cook	00270401	708/799-3000	52
HOMEWOOD SCH DIST 153/HOMEWOOD/COOK	00270334	708/799-8721	52
Honenegah Cmty High Sch/Rockton/Winnebago	00327286	815/624-2070	253
HONONEGAH CMTY HIGH SD 207/ROCKTON/WINNEBAGO	00327274	815/624-5010	253
HOOPESTON AREA CMTY UNIT SD 11/HOOPESTON/VERMILION	00322509	217/283-6668	232
Hoopeston Area High Sch/Hoopeston/Vermilion	00322523	217/283-6661	232
Hoopeston Area Middle Sch/Hoopeston/Vermilion	00322535	217/283-6664	232
Hoover Elem Sch/Calumet City/Cook	00270437	708/862-4230	52
Hoover Math & Science Academy/Schaumburg/Cook	00273996	847/357-5800	66
Hoover Wood Elem Sch/Batavia/Kane	04948947	630/937-8300	128
HOOVER-SCHRUM SCH DIST 157/CALUMET CITY/COOK	00270413	708/868-7500	52
Hope Academy Magnet Sch/Decatur/Macon	10002337	217/362-3280	165
Hope D Wall Sch/Aurora/Kane	00297710	630/301-5008	132
Hope Institute Learning Acad/Chicago/Cook	11559462	773/534-7405	39
Hope Institute Sch/Springfield/Sangamon	01780473	217/953-0894	214
Horace Greeley Elem Sch/Chicago/Cook	00279732	773/534-5800	30
Horace Mann Early Learning Ctr/Rock Island/Rock Island	03050779	309/793-5928	208
Horace Mann Elem Sch/Oak Park/Cook	00272409	708/524-3085	61
Horace Mann Sch/Blue Island/Cook	00268032	708/385-2450	45
Horizon Elem Sch/Hanover Park/Kane	01540625	630/213-5570	130
Horizon Sci Acad SW Chicago/Chicago/Cook	12101642	773/498-3355	39
Horizon Sci Acad-Belmont/Schaumburg/Cook	11934812	773/237-2702	1
Horizon Sci Acad-McKinley Park/Chicago/Cook	11934800	773/247-8400	1
Hough St Elem Sch/Barrington/Lake	00267569	847/381-1108	147
Howard B Thomas Grade Sch/Burlington/Kane	00297916	847/464-6008	128
Howe Elem Sch/Beach Park/Lake	00300537	847/599-5362	147
Howe School of Excellence/Chicago/Cook	00279873	773/534-6060	26
Hoyleton Education Center/Hoyleton/Washington	04444123	618/493-9019	235
Hoyne Elem Sch/Chicago/Cook	00275877	773/535-6425	35
Hubbard High Sch/Chicago/Cook	00277784	773/535-2200	37
Hubbard Woods Elem Sch/Winnetka/Cook	00281955	847/446-0920	72
Hubble Middle Sch/Warrenville/Du Page	00291065	630/821-7900	92
Hubert Humphrey Middle Sch/Bolingbrook/Will	01821869	630/972-9240	248
Hudson Elem Sch/Hudson/Mclean	00306579	309/557-4419	186
Huff Elem Sch/Elgin/Kane	00298350	847/888-5285	130
Hufford Junior High Sch/Joliet/Will	00324985	815/725-3540	243
Hughes Elem Sch/Chicago/Cook	00277796	773/534-1762	31
Humboldt Treatment & Lrng Ctr/Humboldt/Coles	04197057	217/856-2223	19
Hunt Club Elem Sch/Oswego/Kendall	00299706	630/636-2800	137
Hunting Ridge Elem Sch/Palatine/Cook	00272552	847/963-5300	43
HUNTLEY CMTY SCH DIST 158/ALGONQUIN/MCHENRY	00305616	847/659-6158	182
Huntley Middle Sch/Dekalb/De Kalb	00288006	815/754-2241	84
Huntley Senior High Sch/Huntley/McHenry	00305630	847/659-6600	182
Hurley Elem Sch/Chicago/Cook	00277801	773/535-2068	34
Husmann Elem Sch/Crystal Lake/McHenry	00305379	815/356-3400	181
HUTSONVILLE CMTY UNIT SD 1/HUTSONVILLE/CRAWFORD	00287715	618/563-4912	83
Hutsonville Grade Sch/Hutsonville/Crawford	00287727	618/563-4812	83
Hutsonville High Sch/Hutsonville/Crawford	00287739	618/563-4913	83
Hyde Park Academy High Sch/Chicago/Cook	00275889	773/535-0880	38
Hyde Park Day Sch/Chicago/Cook	04951176	773/834-5080	79
Hyde Park Day Sch/Northfield/Cook	11232262	847/446-4152	79
Hyde Park Elem Sch/Waukegan/Lake	00302183	224/303-1970	156
Hynes Elem Sch/Morton Grove/Cook	00270047	847/965-4500	51

I

School/City/County	PID	TELEPHONE	PAGE
I-Kan Reg Alt Attendance Ctr/Kankakee/Kankakee	04800802	815/933-4918	134
IC Catholic Prep/Elmhurst/Du Page	00326062	630/530-3460	100
Icc Elem Sch/Chicago/Cook	12261371	773/267-6167	79
Icci Academy/Chicago/Cook	12103523	773/637-3755	79
Ida Crown Jewish Academy/Skokie/Cook	00282143	773/973-1450	79
Ideal Elem Sch/Countryside/Cook	00270671	708/482-2750	54
Iles Sch/Springfield/Sangamon	00319019	217/525-3226	213
ILLINI BLUFFS CMTY UNIT SD 327/GLASFORD/PEORIA	00312425	309/389-2231	197
Illini Bluffs Elem Sch/Glasford/Peoria	00312475	309/389-5025	197
Illini Bluffs High Sch/Glasford/Peoria	00312449	309/389-5681	197
Illini Bluffs Middle Sch/Glasford/Peoria	01558945	309/389-3451	197
ILLINI CENTRAL CUSD 189/MASON CITY/MASON	00310219	217/482-5180	177
Illini Central Grade Sch/Mason City/Mason	03246083	217/482-3269	177
Illini Central High Sch/Mason City/Mason	00310233	217/482-3252	177
Illini Central Middle Sch/Mason City/Mason	01844890	217/482-5180	177
Illini Elem Sch/Fairview HTS/St Clair	00317140	618/398-5552	219
Illini West High Sch/Carthage/Hancock	00294500	217/357-2136	114

School Year 2020-2021   800-333-8802   IL-V19

DISTRICT & SCHOOL TELEPHONE INDEX

Market Data Retrieval

School/City/County DISTRICT/CITY/COUNTY	PID	TELEPHONE NUMBER	PAGE
ILLINI WEST HIGH SCH DIST 307/			
CARTHAGE/HANCOCK	10915928	217/357-9607	114
Illinois Center for Autism/Fairview HTS/			
St Clair	01780459	618/398-7500	223
Illinois Center for Rehab & Ed/Chicago/			
Cook	01778509	312/433-3125	1
Illinois Central Christian Sch/Washington/			
Tazewell	11226873	309/698-2000	229
Illinois City Elem Sch/Illinois City/			
Rock Island	00316067	309/793-8040	209
ILLINOIS DEPT OF EDUCATION/			
SPRINGFIELD/SANGAMON	00262844	217/782-4321	1
Illinois Elem Sch/Park Forest/Cook	04014156	708/747-0301	57
Illinois Lutheran High Sch/Crete/Will	03182906	708/672-3262	250
Illinois Lutheran Sch/Crete/Will	01405518	708/672-5850	250
Illinois Math & Science Acad/Aurora/Kane	02981553	630/907-5000	1
Illinois Park Early Lrng Ctr/Elgin/Kane	10795314	847/289-6041	130
Illinois Sch-Visually Impaired/Jacksonville/			
Morgan	01442451	217/479-4436	1
Illinois School for the Deaf/Jacksonville/			
Morgan	02048345	217/479-4200	1
Illinois Valley Central HS/Chillicothe/			
Peoria	00312516	309/274-5481	197
ILLINOIS VLY CTL SCH DIST 321/			
CHILLICOTHE/PEORIA	00312504	309/274-5418	197
Illinois Youth Center/Harrisburg/Saline	04340450	618/252-8681	1
Illinois Youth Detention Ctr/Naperville/			
Du Page	04192734	630/983-6231	1
Illinois Youth-St Charles Ctr/Saint Charles/			
Kane	01779979	630/584-0506	1
Immaculate Cncpton St Joseph/Chicago/Cook	05231204	312/944-0304	73
Immaculate Cncpton-St Joseph/Chicago/Cook	11929544	312/944-0304	73
Immaculate Conception Elem Sch/Chicago/			
Cook	11018389	773/375-4674	73
Immaculate Conception Sch/Chicago/Cook	00283537	773/775-0545	73
Immaculate Conception Sch/Columbia/Monroe	00317798	618/281-5353	190
Immaculate Conception Sch/Elmhurst/Du Page	00326050	630/530-3490	100
Immaculate Conception Sch/Monmouth/Warren	00313479	309/734-6037	235
Immaculate Conception Sch/Morris/Grundy	00326074	815/942-4111	113
Immanuel Christian Academy/Hillside/Cook	00282387	708/562-5580	79
Immanuel Lutheran Sch/Batavia/Kane	11237717	630/406-0157	133
Immanuel Lutheran Sch/Belvidere/Boone	00263563	815/547-5346	5
Immanuel Lutheran Sch/Crystal Lake/McHenry	00306086	815/459-1444	185
Immanuel Lutheran Sch/East Dundee/Kane	04034883	847/428-1010	133
Immanuel Lutheran Sch/Elmhurst/Du Page	01844598	630/832-9302	102
Immanuel Lutheran Sch/Freeport/Stephenson	00320989	815/232-3511	225
Immanuel Lutheran Sch/Murphysboro/Jackson	00296467	618/684-3012	121
Immanuel Lutheran Sch/Okawville/Washington	00323400	618/243-6142	236
Immanuel Lutheran Sch/Palatine/Cook	00282399	847/359-1936	79
Immanuel Lutheran Sch/Waukegan/Lake	01405283	847/249-0011	158
Independence Early Lrng Ctr/Bartlett/Kane	03249463	630/213-5629	130
Independence Elem Sch/Bolingbrook/Will	01542221	630/759-7282	248
Independence Elem Sch/Chicago HTS/Cook	04339140	708/481-6103	20
Independence High Sch/Chicago HTS/Cook	04198178	708/481-6103	20
Independence Jr High Sch/Palos Heights/			
Cook	00272863	708/448-0737	61
INDIAN CREEK CMTY UNIT SD 425/			
SHABBONA/DE KALB	00288288	815/824-2197	85
Indian Creek Elem Sch/Shabbona/De Kalb	00288317	815/824-2122	85
Indian Creek High Sch/Shabbona/De Kalb	00288329	815/824-2197	85
Indian Creek Middle Sch/Waterman/De Kalb	00288460	815/264-3351	85
Indian Grove Elem Sch/Mt Prospect/Cook	00273623	847/298-1976	65
Indian Hill Elem Sch/Round Lake/Lake	00301880	847/270-9970	155
Indian Hill Sch/Palos Heights/Cook	04934594	708/597-1285	61
Indian Knoll Elem Sch/West Chicago/Du Page	00291493	630/293-6020	99
Indian Oaks Academy/Manteno/Kankakee	04360826	815/802-3700	137
Indian Prairie Elem Sch/Crystal Lake/			
McHenry	03389697	815/788-5700	181
INDIAN PRAIRIE SCH DIST 204/			
AURORA/DU PAGE	00290205	630/375-3000	95
INDIAN SPRINGS SCH DIST 109/			
JUSTICE/COOK	00268123	708/496-8700	52
Indian Trail Elem Sch/Downers Grove/			
Du Page	00289414	630/719-5845	93
Indian Trail Elem Sch/Frankfort/Will	01830353	815/469-6993	247
Indian Trail Elem Sch/Highland Park/Lake	00300989	224/765-3500	154
Indian Trail Jr High Sch/Addison/Du Page	00288898	630/458-2600	88
Indian Trail Middle Sch/Plainfield/Will	00325563	815/436-6128	246
INDIAN VALLEY VOC ED SYSTEM/			
SANDWICH/DE KALB	04338615	815/786-9873	86
Indian Valley Vocational Ctr/Sandwich/			
De Kalb	01601073	815/786-9873	84
Indiana Elem Sch/Park Forest/Cook	00271273	708/747-5300	57
Infant Jesus of Prague Sch/Flossmoor/Cook	00283604	708/799-5200	73
Infinity Math Sci & Tech HS/Chicago/Cook	10009098	773/535-4225	27
Ingersoll Middle Sch/Canton/Fulton	00293374	309/647-6951	109
Institute of Islamic Ed/Elgin/Kane	04990615	847/695-4685	133
Instituto Hlth Sci Career Acad/Chicago/			
Cook	11822166	773/890-8020	39
Instituto Justice Ldrshp Acad/Chicago/Cook	03192949	773/890-0055	39
Instituto-Lozano High Sch/Chicago/Cook	12172213	773/890-8060	39
Instituto-Lozano Mastery HS/Chicago/Cook	12172225	773/890-8060	39
Inter-American Magnet Sch/Chicago/Cook	00280341	773/534-5490	30
International Prep Academy/Champaign/			
Champaign	12038904	217/351-3995	10
Intrinsic School-Belmont/Chicago/Cook	11918521	708/887-2735	39
Intrinsic School-Downtown/Chicago/Cook	12369284	708/887-2810	39
Ira Jones Middle Sch/Plainfield/Will	05344796	815/267-3600	246
Irene H King Elem Sch/Romeoville/Will	00325654	815/886-3380	248
Irene Hernandez Middle Sch/Chicago/Cook	11454848	773/535-8850	32
IROQUOIS CO CMTY UNIT SD 9/			
WATSEKA/IROQUOIS	00295748	815/432-4931	119
Iroquois Community Sch/Des Plaines/Cook	00268795	847/824-1308	46
IROQUOIS SPEC EDUC ASSOCIATION/			
GILMAN/IROQUOIS	02097762	815/683-2662	119
IROQUOIS WEST CMTY UNIT SD 10/			
GILMAN/IROQUOIS	00295700	815/265-4642	119
Iroquois West ES-Danforth/Danforth/			
Iroquois	00295712	815/269-2230	119
Iroquois West ES-Gilman/Gilman/Iroquois	00295724	815/265-7631	119
Iroquois West High Sch/Gilman/Iroquois	00295736	815/265-4229	119
Iroquois West Middle Sch/Onarga/Iroquois	00295877	815/268-4355	119
Iroquois West Upper Elem Sch/Thawville/			
Iroquois	04010186	217/387-2291	119
IROQUOIS-KANKAKEE REG OFF ED/			
KANKAKEE/KANKAKEE	02097918	815/937-2950	137
Irving A Hokin Keshet High Sch/Skokie/Cook	11225049	773/508-5778	79
Irving Elem Sch/Berwyn/Cook	00267882	708/795-2334	23
Irving Elem Sch/Bloomington/Mclean	00306220	309/827-8091	185
Irving Elem Sch/Kewanee/Henry	00295384	309/853-3013	117
Irving Elem Sch/Oak Park/Cook	00272370	708/524-3090	61
Irving Middle Sch/Maywood/Cook	00271364	708/450-2015	57
IRVINGTON CMTY CONS SD 11/			
IRVINGTON/WASHINGTON	00323278	618/249-6439	235
Irvington Elem Sch/Irvington/Washington	00323280	618/249-6439	235
Isaac Fox Elem Sch/Lake Zurich/Lake	04034883	847/540-7020	152
Islamic Foundation Sch/Villa Park/Du Page	03432062	630/941-8800	102
Issac Singleton Elem Sch/Joliet/Will	10910318	815/723-0228	243
ITASCA SCH DIST 10/ITASCA/			
DU PAGE	00290255	630/773-1232	96
IUKA COMMUNITY CONS SCH DIST 7/			
IUKA/MARION	00309595	618/323-6233	174
Iuka Grade Sch/Iuka/Marion	00309600	618/323-6233	174
Ivc Learning Center/Chillicothe/Peoria	12306816	309/274-0001	197
Ivy Hall Elem Sch/Buffalo Grove/Lake	00301177	847/459-0022	151
Ivy Hill Elem Sch/Arlington HTS/Cook	00267052	847/398-4275	21
Iyc Pere Marquette/Grafton/Jersey	04192710	618/786-2371	1

J

J B Nelson Elem Sch/Batavia/Kane	00297899	630/937-8400	128
J Covington Elem Sch/Oak Lawn/Cook	00272239	708/423-1530	60
J D Colt Elem Sch/Litchfield/Montgomery	00311110	217/324-3565	191
J E Hinchcliffe Elem Sch/O Fallon/St Clair	00317449	618/632-8406	221
J L Buford Intermediate Ed Ctr/Mount Vernon/			
Jefferson	00296821	618/244-8064	123
J N Thorp Elem Sch/Chicago/Cook	00275891	773/535-6250	35
J Sterling Morton Alt Sch/Cicero/Cook	04917211	708/222-3080	53
J Sterling Morton East HS/Cicero/Cook	00270463	708/780-4000	53
J STERLING MORTON HSD 201/			
CICERO/COOK	00270451	708/780-2800	53
J Sterling Morton West HS/Berwyn/Cook	00270475	708/780-4100	53
J W Eater Junior High Sch/Rantoul/			
Champaign	00265145	217/893-5401	11
J W Riley Elem Sch/Northlake/Cook	00267765	708/449-3180	22
J W Riley Sch/Arlington HTS/Cook	00281498	847/670-3400	71
J W Robinson Elem Sch/Lyons/Cook	00270970	708/783-4700	56
J Ward Elem Sch/Chicago/Cook	00278572	773/534-9050	27
Jack Benny Middle Sch/Waukegan/Lake	00302195	224/303-2460	156
Jack Hille Middle Sch/Oak Forest/Cook	00269751	708/687-5550	50
Jack London Middle Sch/Wheeling/Cook	04366002	847/520-2745	71
Jackie Robinson Elem Sch/Chicago/Cook	00278284	773/535-1777	33
Jackson Charter Sch/Rockford/Winnebago	11589285	815/316-0093	254
Jackson Elem Sch/Elmhurst/Du Page	00289555	630/834-4544	94

IL-V20   800-333-8802   School Year 2020-2021

Illinois School Directory

DISTRICT & SCHOOL TELEPHONE INDEX

School/City/County DISTRICT/CITY/COUNTY	PID	TELEPHONE NUMBER	PAGE
Jackson Middle Sch/Villa Park/Du Page	00291326	630/516-7600	99
Jacksonville High Sch/Jacksonville/Morgan	00311457	217/243-4384	192
Jacksonville Middle Sch/Jacksonville/Morgan	00311524	217/243-3383	192
JACKSONVILLE SCH DIST 117/ JACKSONVILLE/MORGAN	00311407	217/243-9411	192
Jacob Beidler Elem Sch/Chicago/Cook	00279031	773/534-6811	31
Jacqueline B Kennedy Elem Sch/Burbank/Cook	00274524	708/496-0563	24
Jahn Elem Sch/Chicago/Cook	00279897	773/534-5500	30
James Avant Elem Sch/Washington Pk/St Clair	11135884	618/646-3870	219
James B Conant High Sch/Hoffman Est/Cook	00272746	847/755-3600	69
James G Blaine Elem Sch/Chicago/Cook	00279081	773/534-5750	30
James Giles Sch/Norridge/Cook	00271845	708/453-4847	59
James H Bowen Sch/Chicago/Cook	05348651	773/535-7650	38
James Hart Sch/Homewood/Cook	00270360	708/799-5544	52
James Otis Elem Sch/Chicago/Cook	00280535	773/534-7665	31
James R Wood Elem Sch/Somonauk/De Kalb	00288343	815/498-2338	86
James Shields Elem Sch/Chicago/Cook	00278582	773/535-7286	32
James Shields Middle Sch/Chicago/Cook	11828196	773/535-7115	33
Jamie McGee Elem Sch/Bolingbrook/Will	02110209	630/759-4300	248
Jamieson Elem Sch/Chicago/Cook	00279902	773/534-2395	29
JAMP SPECIAL ED SERVICES/ GRAND CHAIN/PULASKI	02183880	618/634-9800	204
Jane Addams Elem Sch/Chicago/Cook	00274938	773/535-6210	27
Jane Addams Elem Sch/Melrose Park/Cook	00271376	708/450-2023	57
Jane Addams Elem Sch/Moline/Rock Island	04013267	309/743-1601	208
Jane Addams Elem Sch/Palatine/Cook	00272526	847/963-5000	43
Jane Addams Elem Sch/Springfield/Sangamon	00319021	217/787-3144	213
Jane Addams Junior High Sch/Schaumburg/Cook	00274005	847/357-5900	66
Jane Addams Middle Sch/Bolingbrook/Will	01543770	630/759-7200	248
Jane Stenson Elem Sch/Skokie/Cook	00274249	847/676-7301	67
JASPER CMTY CONS SCH DIST 17/ FAIRFIELD/WAYNE	00323553	618/842-3048	237
JASPER CO CMTY UNIT SD 1/ NEWTON/JASPER	00296479	618/783-8459	122
Jasper Co Junior High Sch/Newton/Jasper	11709265	618/783-4202	122
Jasper Elem Sch/Fairfield/Wayne	00323565	618/842-3048	237
Jay Stream Middle Sch/Carol Stream/Du Page	00289177	630/588-5200	90
Je-Neir Elem Sch/Momence/Kankakee	00299378	815/472-6646	136
Jean McNair Elem Sch/Winnebago/Winnebago	00328278	815/335-1607	255
Jeanine Schultz Mem Sch/Park Ridge/Cook	01441873	847/696-3315	79
Jefferson Attendance Center/Carmi/White	00323723	618/382-7016	238
Jefferson Early Childhood Ctr/Moline/Rock Island	04456671	309/743-1611	208
Jefferson Early Chldhd Center/Wheaton/Du Page	04795465	630/682-2474	92
Jefferson Elem Sch/Charleston/Coles	00266632	217/639-7000	19
Jefferson Elem Sch/Chicago HTS/Cook	00268446	708/756-4162	25
Jefferson Elem Sch/Collinsville/Madison	00308400	618/346-6212	170
Jefferson Elem Sch/Dekalb/De Kalb	00288018	815/754-2263	84
Jefferson Elem Sch/Dixon/Lee	00303943	815/934-9661	160
Jefferson Elem Sch/Elmhurst/Du Page	00289567	630/834-6261	94
Jefferson Elem Sch/Harvard/McHenry	00305575	815/943-6464	181
Jefferson Elem Sch/Johnston City/Williamson	00326945	618/983-7561	251
Jefferson Elem Sch/Marion/Williamson	00327004	618/997-5766	251
Jefferson Elem Sch/Metropolis/Massac	00310348	618/524-4390	178
Jefferson Elem Sch/Morton/Tazewell	00321347	309/263-2650	227
Jefferson Elem Sch/Ottawa/La Salle	00303187	815/434-0726	143
Jefferson Elem Sch/Princeton/Bureau	00263977	815/875-4417	7
Jefferson Elem Sch/Sterling/Whiteside	01170610	815/625-6402	240
Jefferson Junior High Sch/Naperville/Du Page	00290750	630/420-6363	98
Jefferson Middle Sch/Aurora/Kane	00297722	630/301-5009	132
Jefferson Middle Sch/Champaign/Champaign	00264816	217/351-3790	10
Jefferson Middle Sch/Springfield/Sangamon	00319033	217/585-5810	213
Jefferson Middle Sch/Villa Park/Du Page	00291338	630/516-7800	99
Jefferson Park Elem Sch/El Paso/Woodford	00328981	309/527-4405	257
Jefferson Primary Sch/Pekin/Tazewell	00321488	309/477-4712	228
Jefferson Sch/Belleville/St Clair	00316316	618/233-3798	217
Jefferson Sch/Niles/Cook	04872910	847/318-5360	62
Jenner Academy of the Arts Sch/Chicago/Cook	00279914	773/534-8440	32
Jensen Scholastic Acad/Chicago/Cook	00279926	773/534-6840	31
Jerling Junior High Sch/Orland Park/Cook	02131930	708/364-3700	61
JERSEY CMTY SCH DIST 100/ JERSEYVILLE/JERSEY	00297021	618/498-5561	125
Jersey Community High Sch/Jerseyville/Jersey	00297083	618/498-5521	125
Jersey Community Middle Sch/Jerseyville/Jersey	00297071	618/498-5527	125
Jerseyville East Elem Sch/Jerseyville/Jersey	00297095	618/498-3814	125
Jerseyville West Elem Sch/Jerseyville/Jersey	00297100	618/984-4313	125
Jerusalem Ev Luth Sch/Morton Grove/Cook	01405013	847/965-4750	79
Jesse Owens Community Academy/Chicago/Cook	00275724	773/535-5475	36
Jesse White Learning Academy/Hazel Crest/Cook	12104553	708/825-2190	52
Jfh Educational Academy/Prospect HTS/Cook	11235733	847/541-5577	79
Jfh Educational Academy West/Prospect HTS/Cook	03506015	847/541-5577	79
Jo Davies-Carroll Cte Academy/Elizabeth/Jo Daviess	02229898	815/858-2203	125
Joan Dachs Bais Yaakov ES/Chicago/Cook	00281747	773/583-5329	79
John A Bannes Elem Sch/Tinley Park/Cook	00270530	708/532-6466	53
John B Drake Elem Sch/Chicago/Cook	00277318	773/534-9129	33
John C Dunham STEM Sch/Aurora/Kane	12108236	630/947-1240	1
John Deere Middle Sch/Moline/Rock Island	00315647	309/743-1622	208
John E Albright Middle Sch/Villa Park/Du Page	00291235	630/279-6160	99
John F Kennedy Elem Sch/Schiller Park/Cook	00274134	847/671-0250	67
John F Kennedy Middle Sch/Plainfield/Will	10911300	815/439-8024	246
John F Kennedy Sch/Spring Valley/Bureau	00264048	815/664-4601	7
John Fiske Elem Sch/Chicago/Cook	00275645	773/535-0990	33
John Foster Dulles Elem Sch/Chicago/Cook	00275487	773/535-0690	26
John G Conyers Learning Acad/Rolling MDWS/Cook	04428789	847/963-3400	43
John Gates Elem Sch/Aurora/Kane	00297552	630/299-5600	129
John Greer Elem Sch/Hoopeston/Vermilion	00322547	217/283-6667	232
John Hay Community Academy/Chicago/Cook	00279811	773/534-6000	30
John Hersey High Sch/Arlington HTS/Cook	00271699	847/718-4800	70
John Hope College Prep HS/Chicago/Cook	00277758	773/535-3160	37
John Jay Elem Sch/Mt Prospect/Cook	00267325	847/593-4385	44
John L Hensey Elem Sch/Washington/Tazewell	00321737	309/745-3625	226
John L Marsh Elem Sch/Chicago/Cook	00276091	773/535-6430	36
John L Nash Middle Sch/Clifton/Iroquois	00295607	815/694-2323	118
John L Sipley Elem Sch/Woodridge/Du Page	00289995	630/795-6300	100
John Laidlaw Elem Sch/Western Sprgs/Cook	00281357	708/246-7673	71
John Lukancic Middle Sch/Romeoville/Will	10030217	815/886-2216	248
John Marshall Metro High Sch/Chicago/Cook	00280195	773/534-6455	37
John Middleton Elem Sch/Skokie/Cook	00274328	847/673-1222	67
John Mills Elem Sch/Elmwood Park/Cook	00269270	708/452-3560	48
John Muir Literacy Academy/Hoffman Est/Cook	00274017	847/357-6444	66
John Murphy Elem Sch/Chicago/Cook	00280406	773/534-5223	29
John N Smyth Magnet Sch/Chicago/Cook	00278623	773/534-7180	32
John Powers Center/Vernon Hills/Lake	03469235	847/680-8320	146
John S Clark Elem Sch/Waukegan/Lake	00302212	224/303-1570	156
John Schroder ECC/Lombard/Du Page	12308967	630/827-4265	97
John Shields Elem Sch/Sugar Grove/Kane	04801076	630/466-8500	132
John Spry Elem Sch/Chicago/Cook	00278661	773/534-1700	32
John Stewart Elem Sch/Elburn/Kane	00298685	630/365-8170	132
John T MaGee Middle Sch/Round Lake/Lake	11126974	847/270-9060	155
John Tibbott Elem Sch/Bolingbrook/Will	00326516	630/739-7155	248
John V Leigh Elem Sch/Norridge/Cook	00271857	708/456-8848	59
Johnnie Colemon Academy/Chicago/Cook	04950419	773/535-3975	36
Johns Hill Magnet Sch/Decatur/Macon	00306969	217/362-3350	165
JOHNSBURG CMTY SCH DIST 12/ JOHNSBURG/MCHENRY	00305642	815/385-6916	182
Johnsburg Elem Sch/Johnsburg/McHenry	00305654	815/385-6210	182
Johnsburg High Sch/McHenry/McHenry	01821766	815/385-9233	182
Johnsburg Junior High Sch/Johnsburg/McHenry	00305666	815/385-6210	182
Johnson Elem Sch/Chicago/Cook	00277875	773/534-1829	26
Johnsonville Elem Sch/Johnsonville/Wayne	00323462	618/673-3044	237
JOHNSTON CITY CMTY UNIT SD 1/ JOHNSTON CITY/WILLIAMSON	00326933	618/983-8021	251
Johnston City High Sch/Johnston City/Williamson	00326957	618/983-8639	251
Joliet Catholic Academy/Joliet/Will	00326086	815/741-0500	249
Joliet Montessori Sch/Crest Hill/Will	01442827	815/741-4180	250
JOLIET PUBLIC SCH DIST 86/ JOLIET/WILL	00324856	815/740-3196	243
JOLIET TWP HIGH SCH DIST 204/ JOLIET/WILL	00325123	815/727-6970	243
Jonas Salk Elem Sch/Bolingbrook/Will	01543782	630/739-3603	248
Jones College Prep Sch/Chicago/Cook	00279938	773/534-8600	27
Jones Elem Sch/Joliet/Grundy	11462144	815/290-7100	112
Jones-Farrar IB World Sch/Freeport/Stephenson	04363842	815/232-0610	224

DISTRICT & SCHOOL TELEPHONE INDEX

Market Data Retrieval

School/City/County DISTRICT/CITY/COUNTY	PID	TELEPHONE NUMBER	PAGE
JONESBORO CMTY CONS SD 43/ JONESBORO/UNION	00321969	618/833-6651	230
Jonesboro Elem Sch/Jonesboro/Union	00321971	618/833-5148	230
Joplin Elem Sch/Chicago/Cook	01340334	773/535-3425	34
Joppa High Sch/Joppa/Massac	00310362	618/543-7589	177
JOPPA-MAPLE GROVE UNIT SD 38/ JOPPA/MASSAC	00310350	618/543-9023	177
Jordan Catholic Sch/Rock Island/ Rock Island	00313481	309/793-7350	209
Jordan Community Sch/Chicago/Cook	04149244	773/534-2220	29
Jordan Elem Sch/Centralia/Marion	00309533	618/533-7145	174
Josefa Ortiz De Dominguez ES/Chicago/Cook	00277473	773/534-1600	32
Joseph Academy-Des Plaines/Des Plaines/ Cook	02959940	847/803-1930	79
Joseph Academy-Melrose Park/Melrose Park/ Cook	10967397	708/345-4500	79
Joseph Arthur Middle Sch/O Fallon/St Clair	11180944	618/632-6336	218
Joseph E Fisher Sch/Joliet/Will	04196962	815/744-8520	241
Joseph E Hill Education Center/Evanston/ Cook	11922845	847/859-8300	48
Joseph Kellman Corporate ES/Chicago/Cook	03217238	773/534-6602	31
Joseph Sears Sch/Kenilworth/Cook	00270499	847/256-5006	53
Josephine Perry Elem Sch/Carpentersvle/ McHenry	00298075	224/484-5600	180
Josephinum Academy/Chicago/Cook	00283616	773/276-1261	73
Joyce Kilmer Elem Sch/Buffalo Grove/Cook	00281448	847/520-2760	71
Jtc Academy East/E Saint Louis/St Clair	12224660	618/398-2524	223
Jtc Academy West/E Saint Louis/St Clair	12224646	618/332-3630	223
Judah Christian Sch/Champaign/Champaign	11539515	217/359-1701	13
Judah Prep Academy/Mackinaw/Tazewell	04328672	309/359-4673	229
Judith Giacoma Elem Sch/Westville/ Vermilion	00322846	217/267-2154	233
Julia S Molloy Ed Center/Morton Grove/Cook	00270865	847/966-8600	20
Juliette Low Elem Sch/Arlington HTS/Cook	00267337	847/593-4383	44
Jungman Elem Sch/Chicago/Cook	00277904	773/534-7375	27

K

K D Waldo Middle Sch/Aurora/Kane	00297564	630/299-8400	129
KANELAND CMTY UNIT SD 302/ MAPLE PARK/KANE	00298661	630/365-5111	132
Kaneland Harter Middle Sch/Sugar Grove/ Kane	04801064	630/466-8400	132
Kaneland Senior High Sch/Maple Park/Kane	00298697	630/365-5100	132
Kankakee Area Career Center/Bourbonnais/ Kankakee	04197100	815/939-4971	134
Kankakee Area Co-op Day Sch/Saint Anne/ Kankakee	04198099	815/422-4151	134
KANKAKEE AREA REG VOC ED SYS/ BOURBONNAIS/KANKAKEE	04178116	815/939-4971	137
KANKAKEE AREA SPECIAL ED CO-OP/ SAINT ANNE/KANKAKEE	02182070	815/422-4151	137
Kankakee High Sch/Kankakee/Kankakee	00299299	815/933-0740	135
Kankakee Junior High Sch/Kankakee/Kankakee	00299201	815/933-0730	135
KANKAKEE SCH DIST 111/KANKAKEE/ KANKAKEE	00299160	815/802-7730	135
Kankakee Trinity Academy/Kankakee/Kankakee	02162513	815/935-8080	137
Kanoon Magnet Sch/Chicago/Cook	02107575	773/534-1736	32
KANSAS CMTY SCH DIST 3/KANSAS/ EDGAR	00291974	217/948-5174	103
Kansas Sch/Kansas/Edgar	00291998	217/948-5175	103
Kansas Treatment & Lrng Center/Kansas/ Edgar	04197045	217/948-5751	103
Karel Havlicek Elem Sch/Berwyn/Cook	00267820	708/795-2451	22
KASKASKIA SPEC ED DIST/CENTRALIA/ MARION	02183933	618/532-4721	176
Katie Harper-Wright Elem Sch/E Saint Louis/ St Clair	00316811	618/646-3860	219
KEENEYVILLE ELEM SCH DIST 20/ HANOVER PARK/DU PAGE	00290293	630/894-2250	96
Keith Country Day Sch/Rockford/Winnebago	00328319	815/399-8823	256
KELL CONS SCH DIST 2/KELL/MARION	00309612	618/822-6234	174
Kell Elem Sch/Kell/Marion	00309624	618/822-6234	175
Kellar Middle Sch/Robbins/Cook	00273271	708/388-7201	63
Kellar Primary Sch/Peoria/Peoria	00312877	309/693-4439	199
Keller Regional Gifted Center/Chicago/Cook	00276833	773/535-2636	34
Kellogg Elem Sch/Chicago/Cook	00275944	773/535-2590	34
Kelvin Grove Middle Sch/Lockport/Will	00325317	815/834-4339	244
Kelvyn Park High Sch/Chicago/Cook	00279952	773/534-4200	36
Kemmerer Village Sch/Assumption/Christian	03389001	217/226-2139	14
Kempton Elem Sch/Kempton/Livingston	00304600	815/253-6299	162

School/City/County DISTRICT/CITY/COUNTY	PID	TELEPHONE NUMBER	PAGE
KENILWORTH SCH DIST 38/KENILWORTH/ COOK	00270487	847/256-5006	53
Kennedy Elem Sch/Chicago HTS/Cook	00268458	708/756-4830	25
Kennedy High Sch/Chicago/Cook	00277928	773/535-2325	37
Kennedy Junior High Sch/Lisle/Du Page	03267075	630/420-3220	98
Kennedy Middle Grade Sch/Kankakee/Kankakee	00299213	815/933-0760	135
Kennedy Middle Sch/Rockford/Winnebago	00328084	815/654-4880	254
Kenneth D Bailey Academy/Danville/ Vermilion	12028002	217/477-0300	232
Kenneth E Neubert Elem Sch/Algonquin/ McHenry	01881431	847/532-6800	180
Kenneth L Hermasen Elem Sch/Romeoville/ Will	04945218	815/886-7581	248
Kenneth Murphy Elem Sch/Beach Park/Lake	04015693	847/599-5052	147
Kenwood Academy/Chicago/Cook	00275956	773/535-1350	38
Kenwood Elem Sch/Champaign/Champaign	00264828	217/351-3815	10
Kenyon Woods Middle Sch/South Elgin/Kane	05348376	847/289-6685	130
Kershaw Elem Sch/Chicago/Cook	00275968	773/535-3050	34
KEWANEE CMTY UNIT SCH DIST 229/ KEWANEE/HENRY	00295346	309/853-3341	117
Kewanee High Sch/Kewanee/Henry	00295396	309/853-3328	117
Keystone Montessori Sch/River Forest/Cook	04332764	708/366-1080	79
Kiefer Sch/Peoria/Peoria	02847608	309/687-7779	200
KILDEER COUNTRYSIDE CCSD 96/ BUFFALO GROVE/LAKE	00301165	847/459-4260	151
Kildeer Countryside Elem Sch/Long Grove/ Lake	01539511	847/634-3243	151
Kilmer Elem Sch/Chicago/Cook	00279976	773/534-2115	29
Kimball Hill Elem Sch/Rolling MDWS/Cook	00272564	847/963-5200	43
Kimball Middle Sch/Elgin/Kane	00298374	847/888-5290	130
Kimberly Heights Elem Sch/Tinley Park/Cook	00266955	708/532-6434	21
Kimes Elem Sch/Streator/La Salle	00303462	815/672-2496	144
Kindergarten at Pleviak/Lake Villa/Lake	04807783	847/270-9490	155
Kindi Mont Academy/Darien/Du Page	11818701	630/560-4900	102
King Elem Sch/Galesburg/Knox	00300056	309/973-2012	140
King Middle Grade Sch/Kankakee/Kankakee	00299251	815/933-0750	135
King School of Social Justice/Chicago/Cook	00275839	773/535-3875	34
KINGS CONS SCH DIST 144/ KINGS/OGLE	00311902	815/562-7191	194
Kings Sch/Kings/Ogle	00311914	815/562-7191	194
Kingsley Elem Sch/Downers Grove/Du Page	00289426	630/719-5850	93
Kingsley Elem Sch/Evanston/Cook	03393117	847/859-8400	48
Kingsley Elem Sch/Naperville/Du Page	03328722	630/420-3208	98
Kingsley Junior High Sch/Normal/Mclean	05271682	309/557-4407	186
Kingston Elem Sch/Kingston/De Kalb	00288109	815/784-5246	85
Kingswood Academy/Darien/Du Page	04826507	630/887-1411	102
Kingswood Sch/Urbana/Champaign	04328505	217/344-5540	13
KINNIKINNICK CMTY CONS SD 131/ ROSCOE/WINNEBAGO	00327298	815/623-2837	253
Kinnikinnick Sch/Roscoe/Winnebago	00327303	815/623-2837	253
Kinzie Elem Sch/Chicago/Cook	00277942	773/535-2425	27
Kipling Elem Sch/Chicago/Cook	00275970	773/535-3151	27
Kipling Elem Sch/Deerfield/Lake	00300628	847/948-5151	149
KIPP Acad Chicago Austin Area/Chicago/Cook	11823512	773/938-8553	39
KIPP Ascend MS/Chicago/Cook	05279127	773/521-4399	40
KIPP Ascend Primary/Chicago/Cook	12101628	773/522-1261	40
KIPP Bloom College Prep/Chicago/Cook	11926360	773/938-8565	40
KIPP Bloom Primary Sch/Chicago/Cook	12368163	773/938-8567	40
KIPP One Academy/Chicago/Cook	12172251	773/938-8578	40
KIPP One Primary/Chicago/Cook	12315336	773/938-8578	40
KIRBY SCH DIST 140/TINLEY PARK/ COOK	00270504	708/532-6462	53
Kirk Sch/Palatine/Cook	04198104	847/463-8500	20
KISHWAUKEE ED CONSORTIUM/ MALTA/DE KALB	04178257	815/825-2000	87
Knapp School and Yeshiva/Chicago/Cook	03192925	773/467-3900	79
KNOX-WARREN SPEC ED DIST/ GALESBURG/KNOX	02182238	309/351-7224	141
Knoxvill Ctr-Student Success/Peoria/Peoria	11450854	309/439-0000	199
KNOXVILLE CMTY UNIT SD 202/ KNOXVILLE/KNOX	00300173	309/289-2328	140
Knoxville High Sch/Knoxville/Knox	00300226	309/289-2324	140
Knoxville Junior High Sch/Knoxville/Knox	01546849	309/289-4126	140
Kolb Elem Sch/Oak Lawn/Cook	00272148	708/598-8090	64
Kolmar Ave Elem Sch/Oak Lawn/Cook	00272289	708/422-1800	60
Kolmar Elem Sch/Crestwood/Cook	00271481	708/385-6747	57
Komarek Elem Sch/N Riverside/Cook	00270554	708/447-8030	54
KOMAREK SCH DIST 94/N RIVERSIDE/ COOK	00270542	708/447-8030	54
Komensky Elem Sch/Berwyn/Cook	00267894	708/795-2342	23
Koraes Sch/Palos Hills/Cook	01844378	708/974-3402	79
Kozminski Cmty Academy/Chicago/Cook	00275994	773/535-0980	33

IL-V22 800-333-8802 School Year 2020-2021

Illinois School Directory

DISTRICT & SCHOOL TELEPHONE INDEX

School/City/County DISTRICT/CITY/COUNTY	PID	TELEPHONE NUMBER	PAGE
Kreitner Elem Sch/Collinsville/Madison	00308412	618/346-6213	170
Krejci Academy/Naperville/Du Page	01779539	630/355-6870	102

L

School/City/County DISTRICT/CITY/COUNTY	PID	TELEPHONE NUMBER	PAGE
L D Brady Elem Sch/Aurora/Kane	00297576	630/299-5425	129
L E Starke Primary Sch/Pekin/Tazewell	00321490	309/477-4714	228
L J Hauser Junior High Sch/Riverside/Cook	00273714	708/447-3896	65
L'Abris Academy/Aledo/Mercer	12375001	309/331-3784	189
LA GRANGE AREA DEPT OF SPEC ED/ **LA GRANGE/COOK**	02183531	708/354-5730	82
LA GRANGE CMTY SCH DIST 105/ **LA GRANGE/COOK**	00270645	708/482-2700	54
LA GRANGE ELEM SCH DIST 102/ **LA GRANGE PK/COOK**	00270566	708/482-2400	54
LA GRANGE-HIGHLANDS SD 106/ **LA GRANGE/COOK**	00270279	708/246-3085	54
LA HARPE CMTY SCH DIST 347/ **LA HARPE/HANCOCK**	00294653	217/659-7739	115
La Harpe Elem Sch/La Harpe/Hancock	00294689	217/659-3713	115
LA MOILLE CMTY UNIT SD 303/ **LA MOILLE/BUREAU**	00263757	815/638-2018	6
La Moille High Sch/La Moille/Bureau	00263783	815/638-2052	6
LA SALLE ELEM SD 122/LA SALLE/ **LA SALLE**	00302767	815/223-0786	142
La Salle Peru Christian Sch/La Salle/La Salle	02087767	815/223-1037	145
Lace Elem Sch/Darien/Du Page	00289309	630/968-2589	92
LADD CMTY CONS SCH DIST 94/ **LADD/BUREAU**	00263800	815/894-2363	6
Ladd Cmty Consolidated Sch/Ladd/Bureau	00263812	815/894-2363	7
Lahr-Well Academy/Edwardsville/Madison	03218373	618/288-8024	173
Lake Bluff Elem Sch/Lake Bluff/Lake	00301232	847/234-9405	151
LAKE BLUFF ELEM SCH DIST 65/ **LAKE BLUFF/LAKE**	00301191	847/234-9400	151
Lake Bluff Middle Sch/Lake Bluff/Lake	00301220	847/234-9407	151
Lake Co Baptist Sch/Waukegan/Lake	01405269	847/623-7600	158
Lake Co High Sch Tech Campus/Grayslake/Lake	02048280	847/223-6681	146
Lake Co Roe Alternative HS/Zion/Lake	10003824	847/872-1900	146
LAKE COUNTY REGIONAL OF ED/ **GRAYSLAKE/LAKE**	03062306	847/543-7833	158
Lake Crest Elem Sch/Oakland/Coles	00266852	217/346-2166	19
Lake Forest Academy/Lake Forest/Lake	00302406	847/234-3210	158
LAKE FOREST CMTY HSD 115/ **LAKE FOREST/LAKE**	00301309	847/234-3600	151
Lake Forest Country Day Sch/Lake Forest/Lake	00302418	847/234-2350	158
Lake Forest High Sch/Lake Forest/Lake	00301311	847/234-3600	151
LAKE FOREST SCH DIST 67/ **LAKE FOREST/LAKE**	00301244	847/235-9657	152
Lake In the Hills Elem Sch/Lk In The Hls/McHenry	00298099	847/532-6900	180
Lake Louise Elem Sch/Palatine/Cook	00272576	847/963-5600	43
LAKE PARK CMTY HIGH SD 108/ **ROSELLE/DU PAGE**	00290322	630/529-4500	96
Lake Park Elem Sch/Addison/Du Page	00288903	630/458-3010	89
Lake Park High Sch-East Campus/Roselle/Du Page	00290334	630/529-4500	96
Lake Park High Sch-West Campus/Roselle/Du Page	01524372	630/529-4500	96
Lake Shore Academy/Waukegan/Lake	11828093	847/599-1680	158
Lake Shore Schools/Chicago/Cook	02204941	773/561-6707	79
Lake View High Sch/Chicago/Cook	00280028	773/534-5440	36
LAKE VILLA CMTY CONS SD 41/ **LAKE VILLA/LAKE**	00301335	847/356-2385	152
LAKE ZURICH CMTY SCH DIST 95/ **LAKE ZURICH/LAKE**	00301385	847/438-2831	152
Lake Zurich High Sch/Lake Zurich/Lake	00301397	847/438-5155	152
Lake Zurich Mid Sch N Campus/Hawthorn WDS/Lake	00301402	847/719-3600	152
Lake Zurich Mid Sch S Campus/Lake Zurich/Lake	04036520	847/540-7070	152
Lakes Community High Sch/Lake Villa/Lake	05342463	847/838-7100	148
Laketown Elem Sch/Springfield/Sangamon	00319045	217/585-5819	213
Lakeview Elem Sch/Hoffman Est/Cook	00274029	847/357-6600	66
Lakeview Junior High Sch/Downers Grove/Du Page	00289256	630/985-2700	90
Lakeview Learning Center/Chicago/Cook	02956649	773/907-4400	79
Lakeview Sch/Zion/Lake	04017433	847/872-0255	157
Lakewood Creek Elem Sch/Montgomery/Kendall	05264902	630/636-3200	137
Lakewood Falls Elem Sch/Plainfield/Will	04751146	815/439-4560	246
Lakewood Sch/Carpentersvle/McHenry	03050951	224/484-2600	180
Lalumier Elem Sch/Centreville/St Clair	00316495	618/332-3713	218
Landmark Elem Sch/McHenry/McHenry	00305771	779/244-1800	183
Lane Elem Sch/Alsip/Cook	00266890	708/371-0720	20
Lane Elem Sch/Hinsdale/Du Page	00290097	630/861-4500	91
Lane Technical College Prep HS/Chicago/Cook	00280030	773/534-5400	36
Langford Academy/Chicago/Cook	00278269	773/535-9180	34
Langston Hughes Elem Sch/Chicago/Cook	00276003	773/535-5075	36
Lanphier High Sch/Springfield/Sangamon	00319057	217/525-3080	213
Lansing Christian Sch/Lansing/Cook	00282416	708/474-1700	79
LANSING SCH DIST 158/LANSING/ **COOK**	00270700	708/474-6700	54
LARAWAY CMTY CONS SD 70-C/ **JOLIET/WILL**	00325161	815/727-5115	243
Laraway Sch/Joliet/Will	00325173	815/727-5196	244
Laremont Sch/Gages Lake/Lake	02048278	847/223-8191	146
Larkin High Sch/Elgin/Kane	00298386	847/888-5200	130
Larsen Middle Sch/Elgin/Kane	00298398	847/888-5250	131
LaSalle Elem Sch/Creve Coeur/Tazewell	00321050	309/698-3605	226
LaSalle II Magnet Elem Sch/Chicago/Cook	11422429	773/534-0490	27
LaSalle Language Academy/Chicago/Cook	00280042	773/534-8470	30
LaSalle Peru Twp High Sch/La Salle/La Salle	00302858	815/223-1721	142
LASALLE PERU TWP HSD 120/ **LA SALLE/LA SALLE**	00302834	815/223-1721	142
LaSalle-Peru Area Career Ctr/Peru/La Salle	04197112	815/223-2454	141
LASALLE-PUTNAM SPED ALLIANCE/ **OTTAWA/LA SALLE**	02184092	815/433-6433	145
Lathrop Elem Sch/Rockford/Winnebago	00327781	815/966-3285	254
Latin School of Chicago/Chicago/Cook	00281814	312/582-6000	79
Latino Youth High Sch/Chicago/Cook	01752945	773/648-2130	40
Laura B Sprague Sch/Lincolnshire/Lake	00301579	847/945-6665	153
Laura Ward Elem Sch/Chicago/Cook	01556117	773/534-6440	31
Laurel Hill Elem Sch/Hanover Park/Kane	00298403	630/213-5580	131
Laverna Evans Elem Sch/O Fallon/St Clair	00317451	618/632-3335	221
Lavizzo Elem Sch/Chicago/Cook	00276687	773/535-5300	36
Lawn Manor Sch/Oak Lawn/Cook	00267430	708/423-3078	21
Lawndale Community Academy/Chicago/Cook	00277710	773/534-1635	31
LAWRENCE CO CMTY SCH DIST 20/ **LAWRENCEVILLE/LAWRENCE**	00303620	618/943-2326	159
Lawrence Hall Youth Services/Chicago/Cook	01441964	773/769-3500	79
Lawrenceville High Sch/Lawrenceville/Lawrence	00303682	618/943-3389	159
LE ROY CMTY UNIT SD 2/LE ROY/ **MCLEAN**	00306426	309/962-4211	186
Le Roy Elem Sch/Le Roy/Mclean	00306438	309/962-4771	186
Le Roy Jr Sr High Sch/Le Roy/Mclean	00306452	309/962-2911	186
Le Roy Preparatory Academy/Le Roy/Mclean	11070624	309/962-4303	186
Leal Elem Sch/Urbana/Champaign	00265420	217/384-3618	13
Learn 6 Chtr Sch-N Chicago/Great Lakes/Lake	11832018	847/377-0600	154
Learn 7 Chtr Sch-ES/Chicago/Cook	11926346	773/584-4350	40
Learn 8 Chtr Sch-MS/Chicago/Cook	11926358	773/584-4300	40
Learn 9 Chtr Sch-Waukegan/Waukegan/Lake	12110459	847/377-0690	1
Learn 10 CS North Chicago/North Chicago/Lake	12259146	847/693-5021	154
Learn Chtr Sch-Campbell/Chicago/Cook	11457735	773/826-0370	40
Learn Chtr Sch-Excel/Chicago/Cook	11131151	773/584-4399	40
Learn Chtr Sch-Hunter Perkins/Chicago/Cook	11730305	773/488-1634	40
Learn Chtr Sch-Romano Butler/Chicago/Cook	04938186	773/772-0200	40
Learn Chtr Sch-South Chicago/Chicago/Cook	11548645	773/722-8577	40
Learning House/Wheeling/Cook	11235068	847/459-8330	79
LEARNING TECH CTR OF ILLINOIS/ **CHAMPAIGN/CHAMPAIGN**	04433150	217/893-3219	13
LEBANON CMTY UNIT SCH DIST 9/ **LEBANON/ST CLAIR**	00317229	618/537-4611	220
Lebanon Elem Sch/Lebanon/St Clair	00317231	618/537-4553	220
Lebanon High Sch/Lebanon/St Clair	00317243	618/537-4423	220
LeClaire Elem Sch/Edwardsville/Madison	00308656	618/656-3825	171
Ledgewood Elem Sch/Roscoe/Winnebago	01531179	815/623-2837	253
LEE CO SPEC ED ASSOCIATION/ **DIXON/LEE**	02184119	815/284-6651	160
Lee Elem Sch/Chicago/Cook	00278489	773/535-2255	27
Lee R Foster Elem Sch/Oak Forest/Cook	00269763	708/687-4763	50
Legacy Academy of Excellence/Rockford/Winnebago	11551422	815/961-1100	254
Legacy Charter Sch/Chicago/Cook	10009256	773/542-1640	40
Legacy Christian Academy/Caseyville/St Clair	11237729	618/345-9571	223
Legal Prep Charter Academy/Chicago/Cook	11822178	773/922-7800	40
Leggee Elem Sch/Huntley/McHenry	00305628	847/659-6200	182
Leif Ericson Scholastic Acad/Chicago/Cook	00279548	773/534-6660	31

School Year 2020-2021   800-333-8802   IL-V23

DISTRICT & SCHOOL TELEPHONE INDEX

Market Data Retrieval

School/City/County DISTRICT/CITY/COUNTY	PID	TELEPHONE NUMBER	PAGE
LELAND CMTY UNIT SCH DIST 1/			
LELAND/LA SALLE	00302860	815/495-3231	142
Leland Community Sch/Leland/La Salle	00302872	815/495-3231	142
Leman Middle Sch/West Chicago/Du Page	00291534	630/293-6060	99
Lemont High Sch/Lemont/Cook	00270815	630/257-5838	55
LEMONT HIGH SCH DIST 210/			
LEMONT/COOK	00270803	630/257-5838	55
LEMONT-BROMBEREK SCH DIST 113A/			
LEMONT/COOK	00270774	630/257-2286	55
LENA-WINSLOW CMTY UNIT SD 202/			
LENA/STEPHENSON	00320874	815/369-2525	224
Lena-Winslow Elem Sch/Lena/Stephenson	00320886	815/668-0809	224
Lena-Winslow High Sch/Lena/Stephenson	00320898	815/668-0821	224
Lena-Winslow Jr High Sch/Lena/Stephenson	00320903	815/668-0818	224
Leo High Sch/Chicago/Cook	00283628	773/224-9600	73
Leslie Lewis Elem Sch/Chicago/Cook	00280078	773/534-3060	26
Lester Crawl Primary Center/Lansing/Cook	04865216	708/474-4868	54
Lester Elem Sch/Downers Grove/Du Page	00289438	630/719-5855	93
Lettie Brown Elem Sch/Morton/Tazewell	03398090	309/266-5309	227
Lewis & Clark Elem Sch/Godfrey/Madison	00308149	618/463-2177	169
Lewis & Clark Elem Sch/Wood River/Madison	00309296	618/254-4354	173
Lewis & Clark Jr High Sch/Wood River/Madison	00309301	618/254-4355	173
Lewis Elem Sch/Carbondale/Jackson	00296027	618/457-2632	120
Lewis Lemon Elem Sch/Rockford/Winnebago	04029993	815/967-8000	254
Lewistown Central Elem Sch/Lewistown/Fulton	00293647	309/547-2240	110
LEWISTOWN COMMUNITY UNIT SD 97/			
LEWISTOWN/FULTON	00293635	309/547-5826	110
Lewistown Jr Senior High Sch/Lewistown/Fulton	00293673	309/547-2288	110
Lexington Cmty Jr High Sch/Lexington/Mclean	04031831	309/365-2711	186
LEXINGTON CMTY SCH DIST 7/			
LEXINGTON/MCLEAN	00306464	309/365-4141	186
Lexington Grade Sch/Lexington/Mclean	00306488	309/365-2741	186
Lexington High Sch/Lexington/Mclean	04031829	309/365-2711	186
LEYDEN AREA SPEC ED CO-OP/			
FRANKLIN PARK/COOK	03032650	847/455-3143	82
LEYDEN CMTY HIGH SCH DIST 212/			
FRANKLIN PARK/COOK	00270827	847/451-3000	55
Libby Elem Sch/Chicago/Cook	00277992	773/535-9050	34
LIBERTY CMTY UNIT SCH DIST 2/			
LIBERTY/ADAMS	00262911	217/645-3433	2
Liberty Elem Sch/Bartlett/Kane	05091224	630/540-7680	131
Liberty Elem Sch/Bolingbrook/Will	10007909	815/609-3037	246
Liberty Elem Sch/Carpentersvle/McHenry	05091779	224/484-4800	180
Liberty Elem Sch/Cicero/Cook	04033956	708/780-4475	42
Liberty Elem Sch/Danville/Vermilion	00322315	217/444-3000	232
Liberty Elem Sch/Orland Park/Cook	01531105	708/364-3800	61
Liberty Intermediate Sch/Bourbonnais/Kankakee	00298960	815/929-5000	134
Liberty Junior High Sch/Burbank/Cook	05343089	708/952-3255	24
Liberty Junior High Sch/New Lenox/Will	05091793	815/462-7951	245
Liberty Middle Sch/Edwardsville/Madison	05264940	618/655-6800	171
Liberty Sch/Liberty/Adams	00262923	217/645-3433	2
Libertyville High Sch/Libertyville/Lake	00301531	847/327-7000	148
LIBERTYVILLE PUB SCH DIST 70/			
LIBERTYVILLE/LAKE	00301440	847/362-9695	152
Lick Creek Elem Sch/Buncombe/Union	00321995	618/833-2545	230
LICK CREEK SCH DIST 16/BUNCOMBE/			
UNION	00321983	618/833-2545	230
Life Pointe Christian Sch/Gurnee/Lake	11227554	847/662-2335	158
Light House Academy/Peoria/Peoria	11222097	309/691-3242	200
Lighted Way Assoc Sch/La Salle/La Salle	02986424	815/224-1345	145
Lighthouse Baptist Sch/Harrisburg/Saline	02826513	618/252-7579	211
Lily Lake Grade Sch/Maple Park/Kane	00297942	847/464-6011	128
Limestone Cmty High Sch/Bartonville/Peoria	00312580	309/697-6271	197
LIMESTONE CMTY HIGH SD 310/			
BARTONVILLE/PEORIA	00312578	309/697-6271	197
Limestone Middle Sch/Kankakee/Kankakee	00299158	815/933-2243	135
LIMESTONE WALTERS CCSD 316/			
PEORIA/PEORIA	00312592	309/697-3035	198
Limestone Walters Elem Sch/Peoria/Peoria	00312607	309/697-3035	198
Lincoln Academy/Roselle/Du Page	04197033	630/529-4050	88
Lincoln Attendance Center/Carmi/White	00323735	618/384-3421	238
Lincoln Cmty High Sch/Lincoln/Logan	00304870	217/732-4131	163
LINCOLN CMTY HIGH SCH 404/			
LINCOLN/LOGAN	00304868	217/732-4131	163
Lincoln Early Childhood Sch/Monmouth/Warren	00323096	309/734-2222	234
Lincoln Early Learning Center/Mundelein/Lake	12170899	847/949-2720	153
Lincoln Elem Sch/Addison/Du Page	00288915	630/458-3040	89
Lincoln Elem Sch/Anna/Union	00321866	618/833-6851	230
Lincoln Elem Sch/Bellwood/Cook	00267636	708/410-3100	22
Lincoln Elem Sch/Belvidere/Boone	00263472	815/544-2671	4
Lincoln Elem Sch/Blue Island/Cook	01827277	708/385-5370	45
Lincoln Elem Sch/Brookfield/Cook	00270982	708/783-4600	56
Lincoln Elem Sch/Calumet City/Cook	00268329	708/862-6620	55
Lincoln Elem Sch/Canton/Fulton	00293441	309/647-7594	109
Lincoln Elem Sch/Chicago/Cook	00280080	773/534-5720	27
Lincoln Elem Sch/Cicero/Cook	00268628	708/652-8889	42
Lincoln Elem Sch/Clinton/Dewitt	00288549	217/935-6383	87
Lincoln Elem Sch/Dekalb/De Kalb	00288020	815/754-2212	84
Lincoln Elem Sch/Dixmoor/Cook	00270085	708/597-4160	70
Lincoln Elem Sch/Dolton/Cook	00268915	708/201-2075	46
Lincoln Elem Sch/East Peoria/Tazewell	00321191	309/427-5450	227
Lincoln Elem Sch/Elmhurst/Du Page	00289579	630/834-4548	94
Lincoln Elem Sch/Evanston/Cook	00269361	847/905-3500	48
Lincoln Elem Sch/Hoffman Est/Kane	00298362	847/289-6639	131
Lincoln Elem Sch/Jacksonville/Morgan	00311483	217/245-8720	192
Lincoln Elem Sch/Macomb/McDonough	00305161	309/833-2095	178
Lincoln Elem Sch/Marion/Williamson	00327016	618/997-6063	251
Lincoln Elem Sch/Maywood/Cook	00271390	708/450-2036	57
Lincoln Elem Sch/Mendota/La Salle	00303034	815/538-6226	142
Lincoln Elem Sch/Monticello/Piatt	00314435	217/762-8511	202
Lincoln Elem Sch/Morton/Tazewell	00321359	309/266-6989	227
Lincoln Elem Sch/Oglesby/La Salle	00303084	815/883-8932	143
Lincoln Elem Sch/Ottawa/La Salle	00303199	815/434-1250	143
Lincoln Elem Sch/Palatine/Cook	00272588	847/963-5700	43
Lincoln Elem Sch/Pana/Christian	00265688	217/562-8500	14
Lincoln Elem Sch/Pittsburg/Williamson	00326969	618/982-2130	251
Lincoln Elem Sch/Plainfield/Will	05272325	815/577-4500	246
Lincoln Elem Sch/Pontiac/Livingston	00304416	815/844-3924	161
Lincoln Elem Sch/Princeton/Bureau	00263989	815/875-1164	7
Lincoln Elem Sch/River Forest/Cook	00273520	708/366-7340	65
Lincoln Elem Sch/Rochelle/Ogle	00312190	815/562-4520	195
Lincoln Elem Sch/Saint Charles/Kane	00298790	331/228-2500	129
Lincoln Elem Sch/Sterling/Whiteside	01170622	815/625-1449	240
Lincoln Elem Sch/Wheaton/Du Page	00290968	630/682-2075	92
LINCOLN ELEM SCH DIST 27/			
LINCOLN/LOGAN	00304789	217/732-2522	163
LINCOLN ELEM SCH DIST 156/			
CALUMET CITY/COOK	00268317	708/862-6625	55
Lincoln Grade Sch/Robinson/Crawford	00287844	618/544-3315	83
Lincoln Grade Sch/Washington/Tazewell	00321804	309/444-2326	229
Lincoln Hall Middle Sch/Lincolnwood/Cook	00270877	847/675-8240	56
Lincoln Junior High Sch/Dolton/Cook	11710927	708/201-2075	46
Lincoln Junior High Sch/La Salle/La Salle	00302793	815/223-0786	142
Lincoln Junior High Sch/Lincoln/Logan	00304832	217/732-3535	164
Lincoln Junior High Sch/Naperville/Du Page	00290762	630/420-6370	98
Lincoln Junior High Sch/Skokie/Cook	00274287	847/676-3545	67
Lincoln K-8 Sch/Peoria/Peoria	00312920	309/672-6542	199
Lincoln Magnet Sch/Springfield/Sangamon	00319071	217/525-3236	213
Lincoln Middle Sch/Berwyn/Cook	00267844	708/795-2475	22
Lincoln Middle Sch/E Saint Louis/St Clair	00316720	618/646-3770	219
Lincoln Middle Sch/Edwardsville/Madison	00308620	618/656-0485	171
Lincoln Middle Sch/Mt Prospect/Cook	00271601	847/394-7350	58
Lincoln Middle Sch/Park Ridge/Cook	00273128	847/318-4215	62
Lincoln Middle Sch/Rockford/Winnebago	00327810	815/229-2400	254
Lincoln Middle Sch/Schiller Park/Cook	00274146	847/678-2916	67
Lincoln Park High Sch/Chicago/Cook	00281125	773/534-8130	27
Lincoln Prairie Elem Sch/Lk In The Hls/McHenry	05091781	847/532-6600	180
Lincoln Prairie Sch/Hoffman Est/Cook	04870558	847/357-5955	66
Lincoln Primary EC Center/Bellwood/Cook	11421982	708/544-2815	22
Lincoln Sch/Joliet/Will	11555935	815/774-8900	241
Lincoln Trail Elem Sch/Mahomet/Champaign	00265028	217/586-2811	11
LINCOLN WAY AREA SPECIAL ED/			
FRANKFORT/WILL	02098481	815/806-4600	250
Lincoln-Douglas Elem Sch/Freeport/Stephenson	00320783	815/232-0370	224
Lincoln-Douglas Elem Sch/Quincy/Adams	00263161	217/223-8871	2
Lincoln-Gavin Elem Sch/Chicago HTS/Cook	00268404	708/756-4833	25
Lincoln-Irving Elem Sch/Moline/Rock Island	00315659	309/743-1612	208
Lincoln-Way Central High Sch/New Lenox/Will	00325202	815/462-2100	244
LINCOLN-WAY CMTY HS DIST 210/			
NEW LENOX/WILL	00325197	815/462-2345	244
Lincoln-Way East High Sch/Frankfort/Will	01550450	815/464-4000	244
Lincoln-Way West High Sch/New Lenox/Will	11456585	815/717-3500	244

Illinois School Directory — DISTRICT & SCHOOL TELEPHONE INDEX

School/City/County DISTRICT/CITY/COUNTY	PID	TELEPHONE NUMBER	PAGE
LINCOLNSHRE-PRAIRIEVIEW SD 103/ LINCOLNSHIRE/LAKE	00301543	847/295-4030	153
Lincolnwood Elem Sch/Evanston/Cook	00269373	847/859-8880	48
Lincolnwood Jr Sr High Sch/Raymond/Montgomery	00311287	217/229-4237	191
LINCOLNWOOD SCH DIST 74/ LINCOLNWOOD/COOK	00270853	847/675-8234	55
Lindblom Math Science Academy/Chicago/Cook	10009048	773/535-9300	37
Lindsay Elem Sch/Springfield/Sangamon	04914582	217/546-0200	213
Lions Math & Science Chrn Acad/Waukegan/Lake	05154149	847/360-1054	158
Lions Park Sch/Mt Prospect/Cook	00271637	847/394-7330	58
LISBON CMTY CONS SCH DIST 90/ NEWARK/KENDALL	00299627	815/736-6324	138
Lisbon Grade Sch/Newark/Kendall	00299639	815/736-6324	138
LISLE CMTY UNIT SCH DIST 202/ LISLE/DU PAGE	00290346	630/493-8000	96
Lisle Elem Sch/Lisle/Du Page	00290396	630/493-8100	97
Lisle High Sch/Lisle/Du Page	00290372	630/493-8300	97
Lisle Junior High Sch/Lisle/Du Page	00290360	630/493-8200	97
LITCHFIELD CMTY UNIT SD 12/ LITCHFIELD/MONTGOMERY	00311108	217/324-2157	191
Litchfield High Sch/Litchfield/Montgomery	00311134	217/324-3955	191
Litchfield Middle Sch/Litchfield/Montgomery	00311122	217/324-4668	191
Litchfield Pre-K at Sihler Sch/Litchfield/Montgomery	03301475	217/324-3652	191
Little Black Pearl Art Acad/Chicago/Cook	11926334	773/285-1211	40
Little Flower Catholic Sch/Springfield/Sangamon	00319497	217/529-4511	214
Little Fort Elem Sch/Waukegan/Lake	00302224	224/303-3700	156
Little John Elem Sch/Dekalb/De Kalb	00288032	815/754-2258	85
Little Village Academy/Chicago/Cook	04755697	773/534-1880	27
Livingston Area Career Center/Pontiac/Livingston	04199263	815/842-2557	162
LIVINGSTON AREA EFE SYSTEM/ PONTIAC/LIVINGSTON	04177863	815/842-2557	163
Livingston Co Crossroads Acad/Pontiac/Livingston	11435646	815/844-5749	160
LIVINGSTON CO SPEC SVC UNIT/ FLANAGAN/LIVINGSTON	02184133	815/844-7115	163
Lloyd Elem Sch/Chicago/Cook	00280107	773/534-3070	27
Locke Elem Sch/Chicago/Cook	00280119	773/534-3300	30
LOCKPORT AREA SPECIAL ED CO-OP/ LOCKPORT/WILL	02182264	815/838-8080	250
LOCKPORT TWP HIGH SCH DIST 205/ LOCKPORT/WILL	00325214	815/588-8100	244
Lockport Twp High Sch-Central/Lockport/Will	00325226	815/588-8200	244
Lockport Twp High School-East/Lockport/Will	00325238	815/588-8300	244
Locust Elem Sch/Marengo/McHenry	00305707	815/568-7632	182
Logan Elem Sch/Moline/Rock Island	00315661	309/743-1613	208
Logan Junior High Sch/Princeton/Bureau	00263991	815/875-6415	7
Logos Christian Academy/Niles/Cook	04933679	847/647-9456	79
LOMBARD ELEM SD 44/LOMBARD/DU PAGE	00290413	630/827-4400	97
Lombard Middle Sch/Galesburg/Knox	00300082	309/973-2004	140
Long Beach Elem Sch/Montgomery/Kendall	00299718	630/636-3300	137
Longfellow Elem Sch/Marion/Williamson	00327030	618/993-3230	251
Longfellow Elem Sch/Oak Park/Cook	00272394	708/524-3060	61
Longfellow Elem Sch/Wheaton/Du Page	00290970	630/682-2080	92
Longfellow Liberal Arts ES/Rock Island/Rock Island	00315960	309/793-5975	208
Longwood Elem Sch/Glenwood/Cook	00268252	708/757-2100	24
Longwood Elem Sch/Naperville/Du Page	00290231	630/428-6789	95
Lord & Savior Evang Luth Sch/Crystal Lake/McHenry	03417335	815/455-4175	185
Lords Park Elem Sch/Elgin/Kane	01540637	847/888-5360	131
Lorenzo R Smith Sust Tech Acad/Hopkins Park/Kankakee	00299433	815/944-5448	136
LOSTANT CMTY UNIT SCH DIST 425/ LOSTANT/LA SALLE	00302896	815/368-3392	142
Lostant Elem Sch/Lostant/La Salle	00302901	815/368-3392	142
Lotus Elem Sch/Spring Grove/Lake	02167109	847/973-4100	149
Louise White Elem Sch/Batavia/Kane	00297875	630/937-8500	128
Lovejoy Academy/Lovejoy/St Clair	00316407	618/271-1014	218
Lovejoy Elem Sch/Alton/Madison	02042494	618/463-2057	169
Loves Park Elem Sch/Loves Park/Winnebago	00327183	815/654-4501	252
Lovett Elem Sch/Chicago/Cook	00280133	773/534-3130	30
Lovington Grade Sch/Lovington/Douglas	00311691	217/873-4318	88
Lowell Elem Sch/Chicago/Cook	03251686	773/534-4300	31
Lowell Elem Sch/Wheaton/Du Page	00290982	630/682-2085	92
LOWPOINT-WASHBURN CUSD 21/ WASHBURN/WOODFORD	00329210	309/248-7522	257
Lowpoint-Washburn Elem Sch/Washburn/Woodford	00329258	309/248-7221	258
Lowpoint-Washburn Jr Sr HS/Washburn/Woodford	00329246	309/248-7521	258
Lowpoint-Washburn Middle Sch/Washburn/Woodford	04875417	309/248-7087	258
Lowrie Elem Sch/Elgin/Kane	00298415	847/888-5260	131
Loyola Academy/Wilmette/Cook	00283654	847/256-1100	73
Lozano Bilingual Sch/Chicago/Cook	00279990	773/534-4750	32
Lubavitch Girls HS of Chicago/Chicago/Cook	03404261	773/743-7716	79
LUDLOW CONS CMTY SCH DIST 142/ LUDLOW/CHAMPAIGN	00264995	217/396-5261	11
Ludlow Elem Sch/Ludlow/Champaign	00265004	217/396-5261	11
Ludwig Elem Sch/Lockport/Will	05091511	815/838-8020	249
Lundahl Middle Sch/Crystal Lake/McHenry	00305393	815/788-5450	181
Luther Burbank Elem Sch/Burbank/Cook	00274483	708/499-0838	24
Luther Burbank Elem Sch/Chicago/Cook	00279172	773/534-3000	30
Luther J Schilling Sch/Homer Glen/Will	01821845	708/226-7900	242
Lutheran Assoc Sch/Decatur/Macon	00307573	217/233-2001	167
Lutheran Sch/Springfield/Sangamon	02191784	217/546-6363	214
Lycee Francais De Chicago/Chicago/Cook	04990770	773/665-0066	79
Lyle Sch/Kewanee/Henry	00295413	309/853-2741	117
Lynn G Haskin Elem Sch/Sandwich/De Kalb	00288226	815/786-8812	86
Lynne Thigpen Elem Sch/Joliet/Will	05276486	815/741-7629	243
Lyon Elem Sch/Glenview/Cook	00269969	847/998-5045	51
Lyon Magnet Elem Sch/Waukegan/Lake	00302236	224/303-2300	156
LYONS ELEM SCH DIST 103/ LYONS/COOK	00270920	708/783-4100	56
Lyons Twp High School North/La Grange/Cook	00271015	708/579-6300	56
Lyons Twp High School South/Western Sprgs/Cook	00271027	708/579-6500	56
LYONS TWP HS DIST 204/LA GRANGE/COOK	00271003	708/579-6300	56

M

School/City/County DISTRICT/CITY/COUNTY	PID	TELEPHONE NUMBER	PAGE
M Clark Academy Prep Magnet HS/Chicago/Cook	00278958	773/534-6250	37
M J Cunningham Elem Sch/Joliet/Will	00324894	815/723-0169	243
M P Mackay Education Center HS/New Lenox/Will	04198128	815/463-8068	241
Mabel O'Donnell Elem Sch/Aurora/Kane	00297588	630/299-8300	129
Mable Woolsey Elem Sch/Knoxville/Knox	00300238	309/289-4134	140
MacArthur Early Childhood Ctr/Macomb/McDonough	00305185	309/833-4273	178
MacArthur High Sch/Decatur/Macon	00307107	217/362-3150	165
MacArthur Int'l Spanish Acad/Hoffman Est/Cook	00273908	847/357-6650	66
MacArthur Middle Sch/Berkeley/Cook	00267741	708/449-3185	22
MacArthur Middle Sch/Prospect HTS/Cook	00273374	847/870-3879	63
MacArthur/Echo Sch/South Holland/Cook	04197069	708/333-7812	20
MacHesney Elem Sch/MacHesney Pk/Winnebago	03389324	815/654-4509	253
Mackeben Elem Sch/Algonquin/McHenry	10013477	847/659-3400	182
MACKINAW VALLEY SPEC ED ASSOC/ BLOOMINGTON/MCLEAN	02183945	309/557-4439	188
MACOMB CMTY UNIT SCH DIST 185/ MACOMB/MCDONOUGH	00305111	309/833-4161	178
Macomb Jr Sr High Sch/Macomb/McDonough	00305197	309/833-2074	178
MACON-PIATT ROE#39/DECATUR/MACON	02098089	217/872-3721	167
MACON-PIATT SPEC ED/DECATUR/MACON	02184169	217/424-3025	167
Madero Middle Sch/Chicago/Cook	03008104	773/535-4466	32
Mades-Johnstone Center/Saint Charles/Kane	01844720	630/377-4858	128
MADISON CMTY UNIT SCH DIST 12/ MADISON/MADISON	00309014	618/877-1712	172
MADISON CO CTE SYSTEM/EDWARDSVILLE/MADISON	03032636	618/656-0415	174
MADISON CO REG 1 SPEC ED CO-OP/ GRANITE CITY/MADISON	02184030	618/451-5800	174
Madison Early Childhood Edu CT/Elmhurst/Du Page	12170708	630/617-2385	94
Madison Elem Sch/Chicago/Cook	00276065	773/535-0551	35
Madison Elem Sch/Dixon/Lee	00303931	815/934-9662	160
Madison Elem Sch/Hinsdale/Du Page	00290102	630/861-4100	91
Madison Elem Sch/Lombard/Du Page	00290451	630/827-4100	97
Madison Elem Sch/Skokie/Cook	00274299	847/675-3048	67
Madison Elem Sch/Wheaton/Du Page	00290994	630/682-2095	92
Madison Jr Sr High Sch/Madison/Madison	00309076	618/877-1712	172
Madison Junior High Sch/Naperville/Du Page	01540601	630/420-6400	98

School Year 2020-2021 — 800-333-8802 — IL-V25

DISTRICT & SCHOOL TELEPHONE INDEX

Market Data Retrieval

School/City/County DISTRICT/CITY/COUNTY	PID	TELEPHONE NUMBER	PAGE
Madison Park Elem Sch/Litchfield/Montgomery	00311146	217/324-2851	191
Madison Sch/South Holland/Cook	00274457	708/339-2117	68
Madison Student Support Center/Madison/Madison	05368194	618/877-1712	172
Mae Jemison Elem Sch/Hazel Crest/Cook	04944874	708/225-3636	63
Maercker Intermediate Sch/Westmont/Du Page	00290578	630/515-4820	97
MAERCKER SCH DIST 60/WESTMONT/DU PAGE	00290554	630/515-4840	97
Mahalia Jackson Elem Sch/Chicago/Cook	00276077	773/535-3341	34
MAHOMET-SEYMOUR CMTY SD 3/MAHOMET/CHAMPAIGN	00265016	217/586-4995	11
Mahomet-Seymour High Sch/Mahomet/Champaign	00265030	217/586-4962	11
Mahomet-Seymour Jr High Sch/Mahomet/Champaign	00265042	217/586-4415	11
Main Street Elem Sch/Shelbyville/Shelby	00320393	217/774-4731	216
Maine East High Sch/Park Ridge/Cook	00271041	847/825-4484	56
Maine South High Sch/Park Ridge/Cook	00271065	847/825-7711	56
MAINE TWP HIGH SCH DIST 207/PARK RIDGE/COOK	00271039	847/696-3600	56
MAINE TWP SPEC ED PROGRAM/PARK RIDGE/COOK	03032698	847/696-3600	82
Maine West High Sch/Des Plaines/Cook	00271077	847/827-6176	56
MALDEN CMTY CONS SD 84/MALDEN/BUREAU	00263848	815/643-2436	7
Malden Elem Sch/Malden/Bureau	00263850	815/643-2436	7
Malta Elem Sch/Malta/De Kalb	00288197	815/754-2970	85
Manchester Elem Sch/Poplar Grove/Boone	00263537	815/765-2826	5
Manhattan Junior High Sch/Manhattan/Will	04368012	815/478-6090	244
MANHATTAN SCH DIST 114/MANHATTAN/WILL	00325288	815/478-6093	244
Manierre Elem Sch/Chicago/Cook	00280169	773/534-8456	30
Manley Career Academy/Chicago/Cook	00280171	773/534-6900	37
Mann Elem Sch/Chicago/Cook	00276089	773/535-6640	35
Mannheim Early Childhood Ctr/Northlake/Cook	12033394	847/455-3611	56
Mannheim Middle Sch/Melrose Park/Cook	00271106	847/455-5020	56
MANNHEIM SCH DIST 83/FRANKLIN PARK/COOK	00271089	847/455-4413	56
Manning Elem Sch/Westmont/Du Page	00291443	630/468-8050	92
Manor Hill Elem Sch/Lombard/Du Page	00290499	630/827-4300	97
Mansion Private Sch/Naperville/Du Page	02828494	630/357-1226	102
MANTENO CMTY UNIT SCH DIST 5/MANTENO/KANKAKEE	00299316	815/928-7000	135
Manteno Elem Sch & ECC/Manteno/Kankakee	04360046	815/928-7200	136
Manteno High Sch/Manteno/Kankakee	00299354	815/928-7100	136
Manteno Middle Sch/Manteno/Kankakee	00299342	815/928-7150	136
Manual Academy/Peoria/Peoria	00312944	309/672-6600	199
Manuel Perez Elem Sch/Chicago/Cook	00277954	773/534-7650	32
Maple Elem Sch/Hoopeston/Vermilion	00322559	217/283-6665	232
Maple Elem Sch/Loves Park/Winnebago	00327195	815/654-4502	253
Maple Grove Elem Sch/Metropolis/Massac	00310386	618/543-7434	177
Maple Sch/Northbrook/Cook	00272069	847/400-8900	60
Maplebrook Elem Sch/Naperville/Du Page	00290774	630/420-6381	98
Maplewood Elem Sch/Cahokia/St Clair	00316500	618/332-3709	218
Marcus Garvey Elem Sch/Chicago/Cook	00276259	773/535-2763	36
MARENGO CMTY HIGH SCH DIST 154/MARENGO/MCHENRY	00305721	815/568-6511	182
Marengo Cmty Middle Sch/Marengo/McHenry	10003020	815/568-5720	182
Marengo Community High Sch/Marengo/McHenry	00305733	815/568-6511	182
MARENGO UNION ELEM CONS SD 165/MARENGO/MCHENRY	00305692	815/568-8323	182
Margaret Mead Jr High Sch/Elk Grove Vlg/Cook	02110194	847/357-6000	66
Maria Montessori Sch/Rockford/Winnebago	04498203	815/654-4906	254
Maria Saucedo Scholastic Acad/Chicago/Cook	00277605	773/534-1770	32
Marian Catholic High Sch/Chicago HTS/Cook	00283692	708/755-7565	73
Marian Central Catholic HS/Woodstock/McHenry	00328436	815/338-4220	184
Mariano Azuela Elem Sch/Chicago/Cook	11548669	773/535-7395	27
Marie Murphy Middle Sch/Wilmette/Cook	00267478	847/251-3617	22
Marie Schaefer Elem Sch/O Fallon/St Clair	04868165	618/632-3621	221
Marine Elem Sch/Marine/Madison	00309167	618/667-5404	172
Marine Leadership Acad at Ames/Chicago/Cook	10912328	773/534-4970	27
Marion Adventist Christian Sch/Marion/Williamson	01405544	618/997-1430	252
MARION CMTY SCH DIST 2/MARION/WILLIAMSON	00326983	618/993-2321	251
Marion High Sch/Marion/Williamson	00327066	618/993-8196	251
Marion Jordan Elem Sch/Palatine/Cook	00272590	847/963-5500	43
Marion Junior High Sch/Marion/Williamson	00327054	618/997-1317	251
Marion Learning Center/Marion/Williamson	04198233	618/997-1533	250
MARISSA CMTY UNIT SCH DIST 40/MARISSA/ST CLAIR	00317267	618/295-2313	220
Marissa Elem Sch/Marissa/St Clair	00317281	618/295-2339	220
Marissa Jr Sr High Sch/Marissa/St Clair	00317293	618/295-2393	220
Marist High Sch/Chicago/Cook	00283707	773/881-5300	73
Mark Bills Middle Sch/Peoria/Peoria	01543768	309/693-4437	199
Mark Delay Sch/Darien/Du Page	00289294	630/852-0200	92
Mark Denman Elem Sch/Danville/Vermilion	00322262	217/444-3200	232
Mark Lund Day Sch/Bloomingdale/Du Page	02825818	630/307-1882	88
Mark T Skinner West Elem Sch/Chicago/Cook	00278611	773/534-7790	27
Mark Twain Elem Sch/Charleston/Coles	00266668	217/639-8000	19
Mark Twain Elem Sch/Chicago/Cook	00278738	773/535-2290	34
Mark Twain Elem Sch/Niles/Cook	00269153	847/296-5341	47
Mark Twain Elem Sch/Wheeling/Cook	00281474	847/520-2785	71
Mark Twain Primary Sch/Kankakee/Kankakee	00299249	815/933-0722	135
Mark Twain Sch/Alton/Madison	02848585	618/463-2063	169
Markham Park Elem Sch/Markham/Cook	00271194	708/210-2869	63
Marmion Academy/Aurora/Du Page	00328448	630/897-6936	101
MAROA FORSYTH CU SCH DIST 2/FORSYTH/MACON	00307353	217/794-3488	165
Maroa Forsyth Grade Sch/Forsyth/Macon	00307365	217/877-2023	165
Maroa Forsyth Middle Sch/Maroa/Macon	04028212	217/794-5115	165
Maroa Forsyth Sr High Sch/Maroa/Macon	00307389	217/794-3463	165
Marquardt Middle Sch/Glendale HTS/Du Page	00290619	630/858-3850	97
MARQUARDT SCH DIST 15/GLENDALE HTS/DU PAGE	00290580	630/469-7615	97
Marquette Academy-High Sch/Ottawa/La Salle	00313493	815/433-0125	145
Marquette Academy-St Columba/Ottawa/La Salle	00313637	815/433-1199	145
Marquette Catholic High Sch/Alton/Madison	00319502	618/463-0580	173
Marquette Elem Sch/Chicago/Cook	00278051	773/535-9260	26
Marquette Elem Sch/MacHesney Pk/Winnebago	00327200	815/654-4503	253
Marquette Elem Sch/Pekin/Tazewell	00321402	309/382-3612	227
Marquette Manor Baptist Acad/Downers Grove/Du Page	00291728	630/964-5363	102
Marseilles Elem Sch/Marseilles/La Salle	00302951	815/795-2428	142
MARSEILLES ELEM SCH DIST 150/MARSEILLES/LA SALLE	00302925	815/795-2162	142
MARSHALL CMTY SCH DIST C-2/MARSHALL/CLARK	00265937	217/826-5912	15
Marshall High Sch/Marshall/Clark	00265949	217/826-2395	16
Marshall Junior High Sch/Marshall/Clark	00265951	217/826-2812	16
Martin L King College Prep HS/Chicago/Cook	00278063	773/535-1180	38
Martin L King Elem Sch/Dixmoor/Cook	00270097	708/385-5400	70
Martin Luther King Elem Sch/Urbana/Champaign	00265432	217/384-3675	13
MARTINSVILLE CMTY UNIT SD C-3/MARTINSVILLE/CLARK	00265999	217/382-4321	16
Martinsville Elem Sch/Martinsville/Clark	01827253	217/382-4116	16
Martinsville Jr Sr High Sch/Martinsville/Clark	00266010	217/382-4132	16
Marvin Camras Elem Sch/Chicago/Cook	11548607	773/534-2960	30
Mary Endres Elem Sch/Woodstock/McHenry	00306048	815/337-8177	184
Mary Kay McNeill ELC/Antioch/Lake	12375013	847/838-8901	146
Mary Lou Cowlishaw Elem Sch/Naperville/Du Page	04751392	630/428-6100	95
Mary Lyon Sch/Chicago/Cook	00280157	773/534-3120	30
Mary Miller Junior High Sch/Georgetown/Vermilion	00322470	217/662-6606	232
Mary Morgan Elem Sch/Byron/Ogle	00311794	815/234-5491	194
Mary Queen of Heaven Pre-Sch/Elmhurst/Du Page	11532490	630/833-9500	101
Mary Seat of Wisdom Sch/Park Ridge/Cook	00283721	847/825-2500	73
Marya Yates Elem Sch/Matteson/Cook	02130742	708/720-1800	47
Marycrest Early Childhood Ctr/Joliet/Will	01415240	815/725-1100	243
Maryville Christian Sch/Maryville/Madison	12039130	618/505-7000	173
Maryville Elem Sch/Granite City/Madison	00308785	618/931-2044	171
Maryville Elem Sch/Maryville/Madison	00308450	618/346-6262	170
Maryville Jen Sch/Des Plaines/Cook	11734404	847/390-3020	79
MASCOUTAH CMTY SCH DIST 19/MASCOUTAH/ST CLAIR	00317308	618/566-7414	220
Mascoutah Elem Sch/Mascoutah/St Clair	00317358	618/566-2152	220
Mascoutah High Sch/Mascoutah/St Clair	00317322	618/566-8523	220
Mascoutah Middle Sch/Mascoutah/St Clair	00317310	618/566-2305	220
Mason Clark Middle Sch/E Saint Louis/St Clair	00316691	618/646-3750	219
Massac Co High Sch/Metropolis/Massac	02130716	618/524-3440	178
Massac Junior High Sch/Metropolis/Massac	00310403	618/524-2645	178
MASSAC UNIT SCH DIST 1/METROPOLIS/MASSAC	00310398	618/524-9376	177
Masters Academy/Chicago/Cook	11708182	773/643-6620	79

Illinois School Directory — District & School Telephone Index

School/City/County DISTRICT/CITY/COUNTY	PID	TELEPHONE NUMBER	PAGE
Mater Dei High Sch/Breese/Clinton	00317803	618/526-7216	18
Maternity BVM Sch/Chicago/Cook	00283745	773/227-1140	73
Matheny-Withrow Elem Sch/Springfield/Sangamon	00319265	217/525-3245	213
Mather High Sch/Chicago/Cook	00280224	773/534-2350	36
Matherville Intermediate Sch/Matherville/Mercer	00310726	309/754-8244	189
Matteson Elem Sch/Matteson/Cook	00271285	708/748-0480	57
MATTESON ELEM SD 162/RICHTON PARK/COOK	00271247	708/748-0100	57
Matthews Middle Sch/Island Lake/Lake	10973619	847/526-6210	155
MATTOON CMTY UNIT SCH DIST 2/MATTOON/COLES	00266682	217/238-8850	19
Mattoon High Sch/Mattoon/Coles	00266826	217/238-7800	19
Mattoon Middle Sch/Mattoon/Coles	00266797	217/238-5800	19
Maud E Johnson Elem Sch/Rockford/Winnebago	00327779	815/229-2485	254
May Elem Sch/Rochelle/Ogle	00312205	815/562-6331	195
May Watts Elem Sch/Naperville/Du Page	03160635	630/428-6700	95
May Whitney Elem Sch/Lake Zurich/Lake	00301414	847/438-2351	152
Maya Angelou Elem Sch/Harvey/Cook	00270140	708/333-0740	51
Mayo Middle Sch/Paris/Edgar	00292045	217/466-3050	103
MAYWOOD-MELROSE BRDVIEW SD 89/MELROSE PARK/COOK	00271338	708/450-2460	57
Mazon Verona Kinsman Mid Sch/Mazon/Grundy	00294184	815/448-2127	112
Mazon-Verona-Kinsman Elem Sch/Mazon/Grundy	00294172	815/448-2471	112
MAZON-VERONA-KINSMAN ESD 2-C/MAZON/GRUNDY	00294158	815/448-2200	112
McAuliffe Elem Sch/Chicago/Cook	03401128	773/534-4400	30
Mcc Acad-Morton Grove Campus/Morton Grove/Cook	04881246	847/470-8801	79
Mcc Academy-Skokie Campus/Skokie/Cook	12374954	224/534-7638	79
McCarty Elem Sch/Aurora/Du Page	03240467	630/375-3400	95
McCleery Elem Sch/Aurora/Kane	00297758	630/301-5012	132
MCCLELLAN CONS SD 12/MOUNT VERNON/JEFFERSON	00296742	618/244-8072	123
McClellan Elem Sch/Chicago/Cook	00278128	773/535-1732	27
McClellan Elem Sch/Mount Vernon/Jefferson	00296754	618/244-8072	123
McClernand Elem Sch/Springfield/Sangamon	00319100	217/525-3247	213
McClure Junior High Sch/Western Sprgs/Cook	00281369	708/246-7590	71
McCormick Elem Sch/Chicago/Cook	00278130	773/535-7252	32
McCutcheon Elem Sch/Chicago/Cook	00280262	773/534-2680	29
McDade Classical Sch/Chicago/Cook	00276120	773/535-3669	35
McDole Elem Sch/Montgomery/Kane	10011950	630/897-1961	132
McDowell Sch/Chicago/Cook	00276132	773/535-6404	27
McGaughey Elem Sch/Mt Zion/Macon	00307420	217/864-2711	166
MCHENRY CMTY CONS SCH DIST 15/MCHENRY/MCHENRY	00305745	779/244-1000	183
MCHENRY CMTY HIGH SCH DIST 156/MCHENRY/MCHENRY	00305812	815/385-7900	183
MCHENRY CO REG OFFICE OF ED 44/WOODSTOCK/MCHENRY	02098065	815/334-4475	185
MCHENRY CO WORK FORCE CTR/WOODSTOCK/MCHENRY	04178037	815/338-7100	185
McHenry East High Sch/McHenry/McHenry	00305824	815/385-1145	183
McHenry Middle Sch/McHenry/McHenry	00305783	779/244-1600	183
McHenry West High Sch/McHenry/McHenry	00305836	815/385-7077	183
McIntosh Elem Sch/Rockford/Winnebago	00327858	815/966-3275	254
McKay Elem Sch/Chicago/Cook	00278142	773/535-9340	34
McKenzie Elem Sch/Wilmette/Cook	00281618	847/512-6300	72
McKinley Educational Center/Cicero/Cook	12472594	708/652-8890	42
McKinley Elem Jr High Sch/South Holland/Cook	01550345	708/339-8500	68
McKinley Elem Sch/Bellwood/Cook	00267650	708/410-3600	22
McKinley Elem Sch/Elgin/Kane	00298427	847/888-5262	131
McKinley Elem Sch/Ottawa/La Salle	00303204	815/433-1907	143
McKinley Elem Sch/South Holland/Cook	04487046	708/339-8500	68
MCLEAN CO UNIT DIST 5/NORMAL/MCLEAN	00306490	309/452-4476	186
MCLEAN-DEWITT REG VOC SYSTEM/BLOOMINGTON/MCLEAN	04177916	309/829-8671	188
McPherson Elem Sch/Chicago/Cook	00280274	773/534-2625	29
McWayne Elem Sch/Batavia/Kane	04037720	630/937-8100	128
Meade Park Elem Sch/Danville/Vermilion	01538567	217/444-1925	232
Meadow Glens Elem Sch/Naperville/Du Page	03245314	630/420-3200	98
Meadow Lane Sch/Merrionett Pk/Cook	00267442	708/388-6958	21
Meadow Ridge Elem Sch/Orland Park/Cook	04808476	708/364-3600	61
Meadow View Elem Sch/Plainfield/Will	04934582	815/439-4828	246
Meadowbrook Elem Sch/Northbrook/Cook	00272019	847/498-7940	59
Meadowbrook Intermediate Sch/Moro/Madison	00308307	618/377-7270	169
Meadowdale Elem Sch/Carpentersvle/McHenry	00298116	224/484-2900	180
Meadowview Elem Sch/Grayslake/Lake	04446585	847/223-3656	148
Meadowview Elem Sch/Woodridge/Du Page	00289983	630/795-6400	100
Meadowview Intermediate Sch/Cntry CLB Hls/Cook	00268692	708/957-6220	45
Meca Christian Elem Sch/Bellwood/Cook	02425975	708/547-9980	79
Mechanics Grove Elem Sch/Mundelein/Lake	00301660	847/949-2712	153
Medgar Evers Elem Sch/Chicago/Cook	00275580	773/535-2565	34
Medgar Evers Primary Sch/Ford Heights/Cook	00269074	708/758-2520	49
MEDINAH ELEMENTARY SD 11/ROSELLE/DU PAGE	00290669	630/893-3737	97
Medinah Intermediate Sch/Medinah/Du Page	00290683	630/529-6105	97
Medinah Middle Sch/Roselle/Du Page	00290671	630/893-3838	98
Medinah Primary Sch/Medinah/Du Page	00290695	630/529-9788	98
Medora Intermediate Sch/Medora/Macoupin	00307884	618/372-3813	168
Meehan Elem Sch/Belvidere/Boone	00263484	815/547-3546	4
Melody Elem Sch/Chicago/Cook	00280286	773/534-6850	31
Melrose Park Elem Sch/Melrose Park/Cook	00271405	708/450-2042	57
Melzer Elem Sch/Morton Grove/Cook	03319783	847/965-7474	47
Memorial Elem Sch/Paris/Edgar	00292057	217/466-6170	103
Memorial Elem Sch/Taylorville/Christian	00265810	217/287-7929	15
Memorial Elem Sch/Tinley Park/Cook	00274873	708/614-4535	42
Memorial Junior High Sch/Lansing/Cook	00270748	708/474-2383	55
MENDON CMTY UNIT SCH DIST 4/MENDON/ADAMS	00262947	217/936-2111	2
MENDOTA CMTY SCH DIST 289/MENDOTA/LA SALLE	00303008	815/539-7631	142
Mendota Twp High Sch/Mendota/La Salle	00302999	815/539-7446	143
MENDOTA TWP HIGH SCH DIST 280/MENDOTA/LA SALLE	00302987	815/539-7446	143
Menta Academy Belleville/Belleville/St Clair	12305941	618/230-6143	223
Menta Academy Chicago West/Chicago/Cook	11849982	773/533-9605	79
Menta Academy Hillside/Hillside/Cook	02964050	630/449-1310	79
Menta Academy Northwest/MacHesney Pk/Winnebago	12371641	815/975-3297	256
Mercer Co Intermediate Sch/Aledo/Mercer	00310673	309/582-2441	189
Mercer County High Sch/Aledo/Mercer	00310647	309/582-2223	189
Mercer County Jr High Sch/Joy/Mercer	00310805	309/584-4174	189
MERCER COUNTY SD 404/ALEDO/MERCER	00310635	309/582-2238	189
Meredosia-Chambersberg Sch/Meredosia/Morgan	00311562	217/584-1291	192
MEREDOSIA-CHAMBERSBURG SD 11/MEREDOSIA/MORGAN	00311548	217/584-1744	192
MERIDIAN CMTY SCH DIST 101/MOUNDS/PULASKI	00314796	618/342-6776	204
MERIDIAN CMTY UNIT SCH DIST 15/MACON/MACON	00306880	217/764-5269	166
MERIDIAN CMTY UNIT SD 223/STILLMAN VLY/OGLE	00311940	815/645-2230	194
Meridian Elem Sch/Blue Mound/Macon	00306892	217/692-2535	166
Meridian Elem Sch/Mounds/Pulaski	00314813	618/426-6776	204
Meridian High Sch/Macon/Macon	00307341	217/764-5233	166
Meridian Jr Sr High Sch/Mounds/Pulaski	00314825	618/342-6778	204
Meridian Junior High Sch/Stillman Vly/Ogle	00311952	815/645-2277	195
Meridian Middle Sch/Macon/Macon	00306907	217/764-3367	166
Meridian Sch/Buffalo Grove/Lake	04029723	847/955-3500	147
Merrill Elem Sch/Rock Falls/Whiteside	00324430	815/625-4634	240
METAMORA CMTY CONS SCH DIST 1/METAMORA/WOODFORD	00329076	309/367-2361	258
Metamora Grade Sch/Metamora/Woodford	00329088	309/367-2361	258
Metamora High Sch/Metamora/Woodford	00329105	309/367-4151	258
METAMORA TWP HS DIST 122/METAMORA/WOODFORD	00329090	309/367-4151	258
Metcalfe Community Academy/Chicago/Cook	02107666	773/535-5590	36
Metea Valley High Sch/Aurora/Du Page	11448526	630/375-5900	95
Metro East Lutheran High Sch/Edwardsville/Madison	01844988	618/656-0043	173
Metro East Montessori Sch/Granite City/Madison	02191930	618/931-2508	173
Metropolis Elem Sch/Metropolis/Massac	00310427	618/524-4821	178
Metropolitan Preparatory Sch/Arlington Hts/Cook	04990550	847/956-7912	79
Michael Collins Elem Sch/Schaumburg/Cook	00274031	847/357-6100	66
Michael E Baum Elem Sch/Decatur/Macon	01400582	217/362-3520	165
Michelle Obama Sch Tech & Arts/Park Forest/Cook	12102737	708/668-9600	62
Mid-America Preparatory Sch/Herrick/Shelby	11832355	618/428-5620	216
MID-STATE SPECIAL EDUCATION/MORRISONVILLE/CHRISTIAN	02183919	217/526-8121	15
MID-VALLEY SPECIAL ED CO-OP/SAINT CHARLES/KANE	02184066	331/228-4873	134
Middlefork Primary Sch/Northfield/Cook	00272100	847/881-9500	68
Middlefork Sch/Danville/Vermilion	11227449	217/443-8273	233

DISTRICT & SCHOOL TELEPHONE INDEX

Market Data Retrieval

School/City/County DISTRICT/CITY/COUNTY	PID	TELEPHONE NUMBER	PAGE
Middletown Prairie Elem Sch/Mahomet/Champaign	04236976	217/586-5833	11
MIDLAND CMTY UNIT SCH DIST 7/ SPARLAND/MARSHALL	00309923	309/469-2061	176
Midland Elem Sch/Lacon/Marshall	00309935	309/246-2775	176
Midland High Sch/Varna/Marshall	00309947	309/463-2095	176
Midland Middle Sch/Sparland/Marshall	00309973	309/469-3131	176
MIDLOTHIAN SCH DIST 143/ MIDLOTHIAN/COOK	00271467	708/388-6450	57
Midway Elem Sch/Moro/Madison	02107812	618/692-7446	171
Midwest Central High Sch/Manito/Mason	00310130	309/968-6766	177
Midwest Central Middle Sch/Green Valley/Mason	00321309	309/352-2300	177
Midwest Central Primary Sch/Manito/Mason	00310128	309/968-6464	177
Midwest Chrn Mont Academy/Bolingbrook/Will	11235513	630/783-8644	250
MIDWEST CTL CMTY UNIT SD 191/ MANITO/MASON	00310116	309/968-6868	177
Midwestern Christian Academy/Chicago/Cook	00282442	773/685-1106	79
Miguel Juarez Middle Sch/Waukegan/Lake	04455483	224/303-2660	156
MILFORD AREA PUBLIC SD 124/ MILFORD/IROQUOIS	00295839	815/889-5176	119
Milford Grade Sch/Milford/Iroquois	00295841	815/889-4174	119
Milford High Sch/Milford/Iroquois	00295827	815/889-4184	119
Mill Creek Elem Sch/Geneva/Kane	04457821	630/463-3400	131
Mill Street Elem Sch/Naperville/Du Page	00290786	630/420-6353	98
Millbrook Junior High Sch/Millbrook/Kendall	03052947	630/553-5435	138
MILLBURN CMTY CONS SCH DIST 24/ WADSWORTH/LAKE	00301608	847/356-8331	153
Millburn Elem Sch/Wadsworth/Lake	00301610	847/356-8331	153
Millburn Middle Sch/Lindenhurst/Lake	10002993	847/245-1600	153
Milledgeville Sch/Milledgeville/Carroll	00264335	815/225-7141	8
Millennium Elem Sch/Tinley Park/Cook	04867915	708/532-3150	53
MILLER CMTY CONS SCH DIST 210/ MARSEILLES/LA SALLE	00303058	815/357-8151	143
Milligan Academy Safe Sch/Decatur/Macon	11236000	217/424-3062	164
Millikin Elem Sch/Geneseo/Henry	00295310	309/945-0475	117
MILLSTADT CMTY CONS SD 160/ MILLSTADT/ST CLAIR	00317360	618/476-1803	220
Millstadt Cons Sch/Millstadt/St Clair	00317384	618/476-1681	220
Millstadt Primary Center/Millstadt/St Clair	11126699	618/476-7100	220
Milne Grove Elem Sch/Lockport/Will	00325329	815/838-6893	244
MILNE-KELVIN GROVE DIST 91/ LOCKPORT/WILL	00325305	815/838-0737	244
Milton Pope Elem Sch/Marseilles/La Salle	00303060	815/357-8151	143
Miner Sch/Arlington HTS/Cook	04027012	847/463-8400	20
MINOOKA CMTY CONS SCH DIST 201/ MINOOKA/GRUNDY	00294225	815/467-6121	112
Minooka Cmty High Sch -Central/Minooka/Will	00294213	815/467-2140	245
MINOOKA CMTY HIGH SCH DIST 111/ CHANNAHON/WILL	00294201	815/521-4311	244
Minooka Cmty High Sch South/Channahon/Will	11068205	815/521-4001	245
Minooka Elem Sch/Minooka/Grundy	00294237	815/467-2261	112
Minooka Intermediate Sch/Minooka/Grundy	04745317	815/467-4692	112
Minooka Junior High Sch/Minooka/Grundy	00294249	815/467-2136	112
Minooka Primary Center/Minooka/Grundy	11575478	815/467-3167	112
Misericordia Heart of Mercy/Chicago/Cook	02827232	773/973-6300	79
Mississippi Valley Chrn Sch/Alton/Madison	02191045	618/462-1071	173
Mitchell Elem Sch/Chicago/Cook	00280303	773/534-7655	31
Mitchell Elem Sch/Granite City/Madison	00308802	618/931-0057	171
Mohawk Primary Center/Park Forest/Cook	00273001	708/668-9300	62
Mokena Elem Sch/Mokena/Will	00325367	708/342-4850	245
Mokena Intermediate Sch/Mokena/Will	04940593	708/342-4860	245
Mokena Junior High Sch/Mokena/Will	01827332	708/342-4870	245
MOKENA PUBLIC SCH DIST 159/ MOKENA/WILL	00325331	708/342-4900	245
Moline Alt-Coolidge Campus/Moline/Rock Island	04916750	309/743-8587	208
Moline Senior High Sch/Moline/Rock Island	00315697	309/743-1624	208
MOLINE-COAL VALLEY SD NO 40/ MOLINE/ROCK ISLAND	00315491	309/743-1600	207
Mollison Elem Sch/Chicago/Cook	00278219	773/535-1804	33
MOMENCE CMTY UNIT SCH DIST 1/ MOMENCE/KANKAKEE	00299366	815/472-3501	136
Momence High Sch/Momence/Kankakee	00299380	815/472-6477	136
Momence Junior High Sch/Momence/Kankakee	00299392	815/472-4184	136
Monee Elem Sch/Monee/Will	00324703	708/367-2600	242
MONMOUTH-ROSEVILLE CUSD 238/ MONMOUTH/WARREN	00323058	309/734-4712	234
Monmouth-Roseville High Sch/Monmouth/Warren	00323101	309/734-5118	234
Monmouth-Roseville Junior HS/Roseville/Warren	00323060	309/426-2682	234
Monroe Center Elem Sch/Monroe Center/Ogle	00311976	815/393-4424	195
Monroe Elem Sch/Bartonville/Peoria	00312621	309/697-3120	198
Monroe Elem Sch/Casey/Clark	00265913	833/888-8101	15
Monroe Elem Sch/Chicago/Cook	00280315	773/534-4155	30
Monroe Elem Sch/Hinsdale/Du Page	00290126	630/861-4200	91
Monroe Middle Sch/Wheaton/Du Page	03393260	630/682-2285	92
MONROE SCH DIST 70/BARTONVILLE/PEORIA	00312619	309/697-3120	198
MONROE-RANDOLPH REG OFF/ WATERLOO/MONROE	02098170	618/939-5650	190
Mont Sch of Peoria/Peoria HTS/Peoria	03436056	309/685-8995	200
Montessori Academy of Peace/Decatur/Macon	00307030	217/362-3370	165
Montessori Children's House/Godfrey/Madison	02191837	618/467-2333	173
Montessori Children's House/Springfield/Sangamon	02191760	217/544-7702	214
Montessori Foundations Chicago/Chicago/Cook	12374980	773/254-5437	79
Montessori Magnet Sch-Lincoln/Kankakee/Kankakee	02045800	815/933-0709	135
Montessori Private Academy/Rockford/Winnebago	02854924	815/332-8101	256
Montessori Sch of Englewood/Chicago/Cook	11926322	773/535-9255	40
Montessori Sch of Lake Forest/Lake Forest/Lake	02436663	847/918-1000	158
Montessori School of Lemont/Lemont/Cook	12240365	815/834-0607	79
Montessori School-Long Grove/Long Grove/Lake	02436780	847/634-0430	158
Montessori Schoolhouse/Springfield/Sangamon	03403906	217/787-5505	214
MONTGOMERY-CARLINVILLE REG SE/ MORRISONVILLE/CHRISTIAN	10776710	217/526-8121	15
MONTICELLO CMTY UNIT SD 25/ MONTICELLO/PIATT	00314411	217/762-8511	202
Monticello High Sch/Monticello/Piatt	00314447	217/762-8511	202
Monticello Middle Sch/Monticello/Piatt	05278800	217/762-8511	202
Montini Catholic High Sch/Lombard/Du Page	00326115	630/627-6930	101
Montini Catholic Sch/McHenry/McHenry	00328450	815/385-1022	184
MONTMORENCY CMTY CONS SD 145/ ROCK FALLS/WHITESIDE	00324167	815/625-6616	239
Montmorency Elem Sch/Rock Falls/Whiteside	00324179	815/625-6616	239
Moos Elem Sch/Chicago/Cook	00280327	773/534-4340	27
Mooseheart Sch/Mooseheart/Kane	01779591	630/906-3646	133
MORAINE AREA CAREER SYSTEM/ OAK LAWN/COOK	04177992	708/422-6230	82
Morgan Park Academy/Chicago/Cook	00281979	773/881-6700	79
Morgan Park High Sch/Chicago/Cook	00276144	773/535-2550	37
Morrill MA & SC Speciality Sch/Chicago/Cook	00278233	773/535-9288	34
Morris Cmty High Sch/Morris/Grundy	00294330	815/942-1294	113
MORRIS CMTY HIGH SCH DIST 101/ MORRIS/GRUNDY	00294316	815/942-1294	113
MORRIS ELEM SCH DIST 54/ MORRIS/GRUNDY	00294251	815/942-0056	113
Morris Grade Sch/Morris/Grundy	00294263	815/942-0056	113
MORRISON CMTY UNIT SCH DIST 6/ MORRISON/WHITESIDE	00324181	815/772-2064	239
Morrison High Sch/Morrison/Whiteside	00324208	815/772-4071	239
Morrison Junior High Sch/Morrison/Whiteside	00324210	815/772-7264	239
MORRISONVILLE CMTY UNIT SD 1/ MORRISONVILLE/CHRISTIAN	00265614	217/526-4431	14
Morrisonville Elem Sch/Morrisonville/Christian	00265626	217/526-4441	14
Morrisonville Jr Sr High Sch/Morrisonville/Christian	00265638	217/526-4432	14
Morton Academy/Morton/Tazewell	12308773	309/284-8033	227
MORTON CMTY UNIT SCH DIST 709/ MORTON/TAZEWELL	00321311	309/263-2581	227
Morton Freshman Campus/Cicero/Cook	05377937	708/863-7900	53
Morton Gingerwood Elem Sch/Oak Forest/Cook	00266967	708/560-0092	21
MORTON GROVE SCH DIST 70/ MORTON GROVE/COOK	00271510	847/965-6200	58
Morton High Sch/Morton/Tazewell	00321361	309/266-7182	227
Morton Junior High Sch/Morton/Tazewell	00321373	309/266-6522	227
Morton Sch of Excellence/Chicago/Cook	00280365	773/534-6791	26
Mossville Jr High & Elem Sch/Mossville/Peoria	00312528	309/579-2328	197

Illinois School Directory
DISTRICT & SCHOOL TELEPHONE INDEX

School/City/County DISTRICT/CITY/COUNTY	PID	TELEPHONE NUMBER	PAGE
Most Blessed Trinity Academy/Waukegan/Lake	00283525	847/623-4110	157
Most Holy Redeemer Sch/Evergreen Pk/Cook	00283769	708/422-8280	73
Mother McAuley Lib Arts HS/Chicago/Cook	00283771	773/881-6500	73
Mother Teresa Catholic Academy/Crete/Will	02159126	708/672-3093	249
Moulton Middle Sch/Shelbyville/Shelby	00320408	217/774-2169	216
Moving Everest Charter Sch/Chicago/Cook	12109371	312/683-9695	40
Mozart Elem Sch/Chicago/Cook	00280389	773/534-4160	30
Mt Carmel Elem Sch/Mount Carmel/Wabash	00323008	618/263-3876	234
Mt Carmel Grade Sch/Mount Carmel/Wabash	04940842	618/262-5699	234
Mt Carmel High Sch/Chicago/Cook	00283836	773/324-1020	73
Mt Carmel High Sch/Mount Carmel/Wabash	00322987	618/262-5104	234
Mt Carmel Junior High Sch/Mount Carmel/Wabash	00322999	618/262-5104	234
Mt Erie Elem Sch/Mount Erie/Wayne	00323474	618/854-2611	237
Mt Greenwood Elem Sch/Chicago/Cook	00276170	773/535-2786	27
MT OLIVE CMTY UNIT SCH DIST 5/ MOUNT OLIVE/MACOUPIN	00307781	217/999-7831	167
Mt Olive Elem Jr HS/Mount Olive/Macoupin	01533658	217/999-4241	168
Mt Olive High Sch/Mount Olive/Macoupin	04031893	217/999-4231	168
MT PROSPECT SCH DIST 57/ MT PROSPECT/COOK	00271560	847/394-7300	58
MT PULASKI CMTY UNIT SD 23/ MOUNT PULASKI/LOGAN	00304911	217/792-7222	164
Mt Pulaski Grade Sch/Mount Pulaski/Logan	00304923	217/792-7220	164
Mt Pulaski High Sch/Mount Pulaski/Logan	00304909	217/792-3209	164
Mt Vernon Christian Sch/Mount Vernon/Jefferson	02984024	618/244-5404	124
MT VERNON CITY SCH DIST 80/ MOUNT VERNON/JEFFERSON	00296766	618/244-8080	123
Mt Vernon Elem Sch/Chicago/Cook	00276182	773/535-2825	36
Mt Vernon High Sch/Mount Vernon/Jefferson	00296869	618/244-3700	123
MT VERNON TWP HS DIST 201/ MOUNT VERNON/JEFFERSON	00296845	618/244-3700	123
MT ZION CMTY UNIT SCH DIST 3/ MT ZION/MACON	00307406	217/864-2366	166
Mt Zion Grade Sch/Mt Zion/Macon	00307432	217/864-3631	166
Mt Zion High Sch/Mt Zion/Macon	00307456	217/864-2363	166
Mt Zion Intermediate Sch/Mt Zion/Macon	00307444	217/864-2921	166
Mt Zion Junior High Sch/Mt Zion/Macon	00307468	217/864-2369	166
Muffley Elem Sch/Decatur/Macon	00307133	217/362-3340	165
Muhammad Univ of Islam/Chicago/Cook	04990897	773/643-0700	79
MULBERRY GROVE CMTY SCH DIST 1/ MULBERRY GRV/BOND	00263381	618/326-8812	4
Mulberry Grove Elem Sch/Mulberry GRV/Bond	00263393	618/326-8811	4
Mulberry Grove High Sch/Mulberry GRV/Bond	11825261	618/326-8221	4
Mulberry Grove Jr High Sch/Mulberry GRV/Bond	12167919	618/326-8221	4
Mulberry Sch/Normal/Mclean	01442334	309/862-0510	188
Multicultural Acad Scholarship/Chicago/Cook	10009074	773/535-4242	37
Mundelein Cons High Sch/Mundelein/Lake	00301696	847/949-2200	153
MUNDELEIN CONS HIGH SD 120/ MUNDELEIN/LAKE	00301684	847/949-2200	153
MUNDELEIN ELEM SCH DIST 75/ MUNDELEIN/LAKE	00301622	847/949-2700	153
Munhall Elem Sch/Saint Charles/Kane	00298817	331/228-2600	129
Murphy Junior High Sch/Plainfield/Kendall	11822893	630/608-5100	137
MURPHYSBORO CMTY UNIT SD 186/ MURPHYSBORO/JACKSON	00296261	618/684-3781	121
Murphysboro High Sch/Murphysboro/Jackson	01550383	618/687-2336	121
Murphysboro Middle Sch/Murphysboro/Jackson	00296326	618/684-3041	121
Murray Language Academy/Chicago/Cook	00276194	773/535-0585	33
Murrayville Woodson Elem Sch/Murrayville/Morgan	00311495	217/882-3121	192

N

School/City/County DISTRICT/CITY/COUNTY	PID	TELEPHONE NUMBER	PAGE
N B Galloway Elem Sch/Channahon/Will	00324624	815/467-4311	241
N Lawndale Chtr-Christiana/Chicago/Cook	04809444	773/542-1490	40
N O Nelson Elem Sch/Edwardsville/Madison	00308668	618/656-8480	171
N PEKIN-MARQUETTE HTS SD 102/ MARQUETTE HTS/TAZEWELL	00321385	309/382-2172	227
Namaste Charter Sch/Chicago/Cook	05348584	773/715-9558	40
Nancy B Jefferson Alt High Sch/Chicago/Cook	00278946	312/433-7110	37
Nancy Young Elem Sch/Aurora/Du Page	04876409	630/375-3800	95
Naper Elem Sch/Naperville/Du Page	00290798	630/420-6345	98
Naperville Central High Sch/Naperville/Du Page	00290803	630/420-6420	98
Naperville Christian Academy/Naperville/Du Page	10013647	630/637-9622	102
NAPERVILLE CMTY UNIT SD 203/ NAPERVILLE/DU PAGE	00290700	630/420-6300	98
Naperville North High Sch/Naperville/Du Page	00290815	630/420-6480	98
Nash Elem Sch/Chicago/Cook	00280418	773/534-6125	30
Nashold Early Childhood Center/Rockford/Winnebago	00327884	815/229-2155	254
NASHVILLE CMTY CONS SD 49/ NASHVILLE/WASHINGTON	00323292	618/327-3055	235
NASHVILLE CMTY HSD 99/NASHVILLE/WASHINGTON	00323319	618/327-8286	235
Nashville Grade Sch/Nashville/Washington	00323307	618/327-4304	235
Nashville High Sch/Nashville/Washington	00323321	618/327-8286	235
Nathan Hale Elem Sch/Lansing/Cook	00274706	708/895-3030	68
Nathan Hale Elem Sch/Schaumburg/Cook	00274043	847/357-6200	66
Nathan Hale Intermediate Sch/Crestwood/Cook	00268006	708/385-4690	45
Nathan Hale Middle Sch/Crestwood/Cook	01540596	708/385-6690	45
Nathan Hale Primary Sch/Crestwood/Cook	00268018	708/385-4690	45
Nathan S Davis Elem Sch/Chicago/Cook	00277162	773/535-4540	33
National Teachers Academy/Chicago/Cook	00278805	773/534-9970	26
Nativity BVM Sch/Chicago/Cook	00283850	773/476-0571	73
Nature Ridge Elem Sch/Bartlett/Kane	04868139	630/372-4647	131
Nautilus Sch/Chicago/Cook	12318259	773/462-4223	79
NAUVOO-COLUSA CUSD 325/NAUVOO/HANCOCK	00294718	217/453-6639	115
Nauvoo-Colusa Elem Sch/Nauvoo/Hancock	00294732	217/453-2231	115
Navajo Heights Elem Sch/Palos Heights/Cook	00272887	708/385-3269	62
Nazareth Academy/La Grange Pk/Cook	00283886	708/354-0061	73
Neal Math & Science Academy/North Chicago/Lake	10754310	847/689-6313	154
Near North Montessori Sch/Chicago/Cook	01559884	773/384-1434	79
Neil A Armstrong Elem Sch/East Peoria/Tazewell	00321206	309/427-5300	227
Neil Armstrong Elem Sch/Hoffman Est/Cook	00274055	847/357-6700	67
Neil Armstrong Elem Sch/Richton Park/Cook	00274160	708/481-7424	47
Neil Elem Sch/Chicago/Cook	00276211	773/535-3000	35
Nelson Prairie Sch/New Lenox/Will	00325410	815/462-2874	245
Nelson Ridge Elem Sch/New Lenox/Will	04867898	815/462-2870	245
NEOGA CMTY UNIT SCH DIST 3/ NEOGA/CUMBERLAND	00287911	217/895-2201	84
Neoga Elem Sch/Neoga/Cumberland	00287923	217/895-2200	84
Neoga Jr Sr High Sch/Neoga/Cumberland	00287935	217/775-6049	84
Neponset Grade Sch/Neponset/Henry	00263903	309/594-2306	117
Nettelhorst Elem Sch/Chicago/Cook	00280420	773/534-5810	30
Nettie Davis Elem Sch/Watseka/Iroquois	00295762	815/432-2112	119
NETTLE CREEK CMTY SD 24-C/ MORRIS/GRUNDY	00294342	815/942-0511	113
Nettle Creek Elem Sch/Morris/Grundy	00294366	815/942-0511	113
Neuqua Valley High Sch/Naperville/Du Page	04751419	630/428-6000	95
New Approach Alt High Sch/Vandalia/Fayette	12179728	618/283-9311	105
NEW ATHENS CUSD 60/NEW ATHENS/ST CLAIR	00317396	618/475-2174	220
New Athens Sch/New Athens/St Clair	00317401	618/475-2172	220
New Baden Elem Sch/New Baden/Clinton	00266515	618/588-3535	18
New Beginnings Learning Acad/South Holland/Cook	05341225	708/768-5200	46
New Berlin Elem Sch/New Berlin/Sangamon	00318704	217/488-6054	212
New Berlin High Sch/New Berlin/Sangamon	00318699	217/488-6012	212
New Berlin Junior High Sch/New Berlin/Sangamon	00318716	217/488-6012	212
New Boston Elem Sch/New Boston/Mercer	00310790	309/587-8141	189
New Central Elem Sch/Havana/Mason	00310178	309/543-2241	177
New Covenent Christian Academy/Phoenix/Cook	03192729	708/331-3661	79
New Field Primary Sch/Chicago/Cook	05278549	773/534-2760	29
New Hebron Christian Sch/Robinson/Crawford	02165888	618/544-7619	83
NEW HOLLAND MIDDLETOWN ESD 88/ MIDDLETOWN/LOGAN	00304935	217/445-2421	164
New Holland Middletown Sch/Middletown/Logan	00304959	217/445-2421	164
New Hope Academy/Arlington HTS/Cook	04954312	847/588-0463	80
NEW HOPE CMTY CONS SCH DIST 6/ FAIRFIELD/WAYNE	00323591	618/842-3296	237
New Hope Elem Sch/Fairfield/Wayne	00323606	618/842-3296	237
New Horizon Center/Chicago/Cook	01779369	773/286-6226	80
New Horizon Christian Sch/Centralia/Marion	05330446	618/533-6910	176
New Horizons Alternative Sch/Lewistown/Fulton	04196209	309/547-7323	109
NEW LENOX SCH DIST 122/NEW LENOX/WILL	00325379	815/485-2169	245
New Life Celebration Chrn Acad/Dolton/Cook	12239627	708/849-3635	80
New Life Christian Academy/Peoria/Peoria	03433028	309/637-8359	200
New Life Christian Sch/Chicago/Cook	04990861	773/637-7442	80

DISTRICT & SCHOOL TELEPHONE INDEX

Market Data Retrieval

School/City/County DISTRICT/CITY/COUNTY	PID	TELEPHONE NUMBER	PAGE
NEW SIMPSON HILL CONS SD 32/ TUNNEL HILL/JOHNSON	00297423	618/658-8536	127
New Simpson Hill Sch/Tunnel Hill/Johnson	00297447	618/658-8536	127
New Sullivan Elem Sch/Chicago/Cook	00276596	773/535-6585	35
New Tech High Zion-Benton East/Zion/Lake	11068322	847/731-9800	157
New Trier HS-Freshman Camp/Northfield/Cook	02222553	847/446-7000	58
New Trier Township High Sch/Winnetka/Cook	00271742	847/446-7000	58
NEW TRIER TWP HS DIST 203/ NORTHFIELD/COOK	00271730	847/446-7000	58
NEWARK CMTY CONS SCH DIST 66/ NEWARK/KENDALL	00299665	815/695-5143	138
Newark Cmty High Sch/Newark/Kendall	00299653	815/695-5164	138
NEWARK CMTY HIGH SCH DIST 18/ NEWARK/KENDALL	00299641	815/695-5164	138
Newark Elem Sch/Newark/Kendall	00299677	815/695-5143	138
Newberry Math & Science Acad/Chicago/Cook	00280432	773/534-8000	30
Newcomer Center/Arlington HTS/Cook	11435593	847/718-7937	70
Newman Central Catholic Sch/Sterling/Whiteside	00328486	815/625-0500	240
Newport Elem Sch/Wadsworth/Lake	00301713	847/599-5330	147
Newton Bateman Elem Sch/Chicago/Cook	00279005	773/534-5055	29
Newton Cmty High Sch/Newton/Jasper	00296510	618/783-2303	122
Newton Elem Sch/Newton/Jasper	00296522	618/783-8464	122
Next Generation Sch/Champaign/Champaign	11228285	217/356-6995	13
Nicholas A Hermes Elem Sch/Aurora/Kane	00297590	630/299-8200	129
Nicholas Senn High Sch/Chicago/Cook	00280810	773/534-2365	36
Nichols Middle Sch/Evanston/Cook	00269402	847/859-8660	48
Nicholson Elem Sch/Montgomery/Kane	00297784	630/301-5013	132
Nicholson Tech Academy/Chicago/Cook	00275047	773/535-3285	34
Nightingale Elem Sch/Chicago/Cook	00278271	773/535-9270	33
NILES ELEM SCH DIST 71/NILES/COOK	00271766	847/966-9280	58
Niles North High Sch/Skokie/Cook	00271819	847/626-2000	58
NILES TWP DEPT OF SPEC ED #807/ MORTON GROVE/COOK	05026621	847/965-9040	82
NILES TWP HIGH SCH DIST 219/ SKOKIE/COOK	00271792	847/626-3000	58
Niles West High Sch/Skokie/Cook	00271821	847/626-2500	59
Ninos Heroes Community Academy/Chicago/Cook	02129963	773/535-6694	35
Nippersink Middle Sch/Richmond/McHenry	04913277	815/678-7129	183
NIPPERSINK SCH DIST 2/RICHMOND/MCHENRY	00305886	815/678-4242	183
Nixon Elem Sch/Chicago/Cook	00280444	773/534-4375	30
Nob Hill Elem Sch/Cntry CLB Hls/Cook	00271211	708/335-9770	63
Noble CS-Baker Clg Prep/Chicago/Cook	11926308	773/535-6460	40
Noble CS-Butler Clg Prep/Chicago/Cook	11926310	773/535-5490	40
Noble CS-Chicago Bulls Clg Prp/Chicago/Cook	11446633	773/534-7599	40
Noble CS-Comer Clg Prep HS/Chicago/Cook	11131175	773/729-3969	40
Noble CS-Comer Middle Sch/Chicago/Cook	11926293	773/535-0755	40
Noble CS-Drw Clg Prep/Chicago/Cook	11822154	773/893-4500	40
Noble CS-Golder Clg Prep/Chicago/Cook	10912407	312/265-9925	40
Noble CS-Hansberry Clg Prep/Chicago/Cook	11822142	773/729-3400	40
Noble CS-Itw David Speer Acad/Chicago/Cook	12045282	773/622-7484	40
Noble CS-Johnson Clg Prep/Chicago/Cook	11559474	312/348-1888	40
Noble CS-Mansueto High Sch/Chicago/Cook	12179924	773/349-8200	40
Noble CS-Muchin Clg Prep/Chicago/Cook	11454719	312/445-4680	40
Noble CS-Noble Academy/Chicago/Cook	12045323	312/574-1527	40
Noble CS-Noble Street Clg Prep/Chicago/Cook	04875730	773/862-1449	40
Noble CS-Pritzker Clg Prep/Chicago/Cook	10021072	773/394-2848	40
Noble CS-Rauner Clg Prep/Chicago/Cook	10021084	312/226-5345	40
Noble CS-Rowe Clark Math & Sci/Chicago/Cook	10912392	773/242-2212	40
Noble CS-UIC Clg Prep/Chicago/Cook	11131163	312/768-4858	40
Noel LeVasseur Elem Sch/Bourbonnais/Kankakee	02043852	815/929-4500	134
NOKOMIS CMTY UNIT SCH DIST 22/ NOKOMIS/MONTGOMERY	00311196	217/563-7311	191
Nokomis Jr Sr High Sch/Nokomis/Montgomery	00311213	217/563-2014	191
Noonan Elem Academy/Mokena/Will	04429123	708/479-8988	250
Normal Cmty High Sch/Normal/Mclean	00306581	309/557-4401	186
Normal West High Sch/Normal/Mclean	04366753	309/557-4402	187
NORRIDGE SCH DIST 80/NORRIDGE/COOK	00271833	708/583-2068	59
Norris City-Omaha Elem Sch/Norris City/White	00323905	618/378-3212	238
Norris City-Omaha-Enfield HS/Norris City/White	00323917	618/378-3312	238
NORRIS CITY-OMAHA-ENFIELD SD 3/ NORRIS CITY/WHITE	00323890	618/378-3222	238
Norte Dame De La Salette Acad/Georgetown/Vermilion	11555753	217/662-2127	233
North Aurora SDA Elem Sch/North Aurora/Kane	01405245	630/896-5188	133
North Barrington Elem Sch/Barrington/Lake	00267571	847/381-4340	147
NORTH BOONE CMTY UNIT SD 200/ POPLAR GROVE/BOONE	00263513	815/765-3322	5
North Boone High Sch/Poplar Grove/Boone	00263549	815/765-3311	5
North Boone Middle Sch/Poplar Grove/Boone	10006412	815/765-9274	5
North Boone Upper Elem Sch/Poplar Grove/Boone	04363115	815/765-9006	5
North Campus Alt Lrng Acad/Palatine/Cook	12320240	847/755-6700	69
NORTH CHICAGO CMTY UNIT SD 187/ NORTH CHICAGO/LAKE	00301725	847/689-8150	153
North Chicago High Sch/North Chicago/Lake	00301842	847/578-7400	154
North Clay Cmty High Sch/Louisville/Clay	00266113	618/665-3394	16
NORTH CLAY CMTY UNIT SD 25/ LOUISVILLE/CLAY	00266072	618/665-3358	16
North Clay Elem Jr High Sch/Louisville/Clay	01827265	618/665-3393	16
NORTH COOK INTERM SVC CENTER/ DES PLAINES/COOK	03064689	847/824-8300	82
North Ctr-Handicap Children/Chicago/Cook	01779319	773/777-4111	80
NORTH DUPAGE SPEC ED CO-OP/ ROSELLE/DU PAGE	10031596	630/894-0490	102
North Elem Sch/Crystal Lake/McHenry	00305408	815/356-3450	181
North Elem Sch/Des Plaines/Cook	00268812	847/824-1399	46
North Elem Sch/Franklin Park/Cook	00269804	847/678-7962	50
North Elem Sch/Godfrey/Madison	00308113	618/463-2171	169
North Elem Sch/Jacksonville/Morgan	00311500	217/245-4084	192
North Elem Sch/Marshall/Clark	00265963	217/826-2355	16
North Elem Sch/Nokomis/Montgomery	00311225	217/563-8521	191
North Elem Sch/North Chicago/Lake	04747092	847/689-7345	154
North Elem Sch/Sycamore/De Kalb	00288393	815/899-8209	86
North Elem Sch/Taylorville/Christian	00265822	217/824-3315	15
North Elem Sch/Villa Park/Du Page	00291364	630/516-7790	99
North Elem Sch/Waukegan/Lake	00302248	224/303-2160	156
North Grand High Sch/Chicago/Cook	05348625	773/534-8520	37
North Greene Elem Sch/Roodhouse/Greene	00294029	217/589-4623	111
North Greene Jr Sr High Sch/White Hall/Greene	00294005	217/374-2131	111
NORTH GREENE UNIT DIST 3/ WHITE HALL/GREENE	00293960	217/374-2842	111
North Grove Elem Sch/Sycamore/De Kalb	11444817	815/899-8124	86
North High Sch/Downers Grove/Du Page	00289347	630/795-8400	91
North Lawndale HS-Collins/Chicago/Cook	10912342	773/542-6766	40
North Love Christian Sch/Rockford/Winnebago	01405556	815/877-6021	256
NORTH MAC CMTY UNIT SD 34/ GIRARD/MACOUPIN	00307743	217/627-2915	168
North Mac Elem Sch/Virden/Macoupin	00307755	217/965-5424	168
North Mac High Sch/Virden/Macoupin	00307987	217/965-4127	168
North Mac Interm Mid Sch/Girard/Macoupin	04031855	217/627-2419	168
NORTH PALOS SCH DIST 117/ PALOS HILLS/COOK	00271869	708/598-5500	59
North Park Elem Sch/Chicago/Cook	02826123	773/327-3144	80
North Prairie Junior High Sch/Winthrop HBR/Lake	04866454	847/731-3089	156
North Ridge Middle Sch/Danville/Vermilion	00322353	217/444-3400	232
North River Elem Sch/Chicago/Cook	05277260	773/534-0590	29
North Shore Academy/Highland Park/Lake	04339035	847/831-0603	146
North Shore Academy/Northbrook/Cook	04444159	847/291-7905	20
North Shore Adventist Academy/Chicago/Cook	01405116	773/769-0733	80
North Shore Country Day Sch/Winnetka/Cook	00282179	847/446-0674	80
NORTH SHORE SCH DIST 112/ HIGHLAND PARK/LAKE	00300991	224/765-3000	154
North Side Elem Sch/Fairfield/Wayne	00323503	618/847-4341	236
North Side Primary Center/Herrin/Williamson	00326919	618/942-5418	251
NORTH SUBURBAN ED REG FOR VOC/ PARK RIDGE/COOK	04184452	847/692-8023	82
North Wamac Grade Sch/Centralia/Clinton	00266541	618/532-1826	18
NORTH WAMAC SCH DIST 186/ CENTRALIA/CLINTON	00266539	618/532-1826	18
North Ward Elem Sch/Tuscola/Douglas	00288800	217/253-2712	88
NORTH WAYNE CMTY UNIT SD 200/ CISNE/WAYNE	00323436	618/673-2151	237
NORTHBROOK ELEM SCH DIST 27/ NORTHBROOK/COOK	00271924	847/498-2610	59
Northbrook Junior High Sch/Northbrook/Cook	00272021	847/498-7920	59

Illinois School Directory

DISTRICT & SCHOOL TELEPHONE INDEX

School/City/County DISTRICT/CITY/COUNTY	PID	TELEPHONE NUMBER	PAGE
Northbrook Sch/Mendota/La Salle	00303046	815/539-6237	142
NORTHBROOK SCH DIST 28/NORTHBROOK/COOK	00271986	847/498-7900	59
NORTHBROOK-GLENVIEW SD 30/NORTHBROOK/COOK	00272057	847/498-4190	60
Northeast Elem Magnet Sch/Danville/Vermilion	04453693	217/444-3050	232
Northeast Elem Sch/Evergreen Pk/Cook	00269543	708/422-6501	49
Northeast Jr High Sch/East Moline/Rock Island	00316134	309/203-1300	209
NORTHERN KANE CO REG VOC SYS/ELGIN/KANE	04178075	847/888-5000	134
NORTHERN SUBURBAN SPEC ED DIST/HIGHLAND PARK/LAKE	02123696	847/831-5100	159
Northlake Middle Sch/Northlake/Cook	00267753	708/449-3195	22
Northlawn Junior High Sch/Streator/La Salle	00303486	815/672-4558	144
Northmoor Primary Sch/Peoria/Peoria	00312968	309/692-9481	199
NorthPoint Elem Sch/Bloomington/Mclean	03048831	309/557-4420	187
Northridge Prep Sch/Niles/Cook	02162496	847/375-0600	80
Northside Cath Acad-Primary/Chicago/Cook	00285743	773/743-6277	73
Northside Cath Academy Mid Sch/Chicago/Cook	00285822	773/271-2008	73
Northside College Prep HS/Chicago/Cook	04875699	773/534-3954	27
Northside Elem Sch/Geneseo/Henry	00295322	309/945-0625	117
Northside Elem Sch/Morrison/Whiteside	00324222	815/772-2153	239
Northside Learning Center/Chicago/Cook	02176605	773/534-5180	36
Northview Elem Sch/Peru/La Salle	00303280	815/223-1111	144
Northview Elem Sch/Rantoul/Champaign	00265171	217/893-5403	11
Northwest Elem Sch/Evergreen Pk/Cook	00269555	708/425-9473	49
Northwest Elem Sch/La Salle/La Salle	00302810	815/223-0786	142
Northwest Elem Sch/Lincoln/Logan	00304844	217/732-6819	164
Northwest Institute/Chicago/Cook	03069770	773/921-2800	80
Northwest Middle Sch/Chicago/Cook	04876100	773/534-3250	30
NORTHWEST SPECIAL ED DIST/ELIZABETH/JO DAVIESS	02182082	815/599-1947	126
NORTHWEST SUBURBAN SP ED ORG/MT PROSPECT/COOK	02183555	847/463-8100	82
NORTHWESTERN CUSD 2/PALMYRA/MACOUPIN	00307834	217/436-2442	168
Northwestern Elem Sch/Palmyra/Macoupin	00307846	217/362-2210	168
NORTHWESTERN IL ASSOCIATION/SYCAMORE/DE KALB	02182094	815/895-9227	87
Northwestern Jr Sr High Sch/Palmyra/Macoupin	00307858	217/362-2210	168
Northwood Junior High Sch/Highland Park/Lake	00301139	224/765-3600	154
Northwood Middle Sch/Woodstock/McHenry	00306050	815/338-4900	184
Norton Creek Elem Sch/West Chicago/Kane	05276515	331/228-2700	129
Norwood Elem Sch/Peoria/Peoria	00312645	309/676-3523	198
Norwood Park Elem Sch/Chicago/Cook	00280468	773/534-1198	29
Norwood Primary Sch/Peoria/Peoria	00312279	309/697-6312	198
NORWOOD SCH DIST 63/PEORIA/PEORIA	00312633	309/676-3523	198
Notre Dame Acad-St Augustine/Belleville/St Clair	00317920	618/234-4958	222
Notre Dame Academy-Cathedral/Belleville/St Clair	00317712	618/233-6414	222
Notre Dame College Prep HS/Niles/Cook	00283903	847/965-2900	73
Notre Dame Sch/Clarendon Hls/Du Page	00326127	630/323-1642	101
Novak Academy/Champaign/Champaign	11071068	217/352-4328	10
Nuttall Middle Sch/Robinson/Crawford	00287856	618/544-8618	83
Nvhs Kathryn J Birkett Center/Naperville/Du Page	05272923	630/428-6000	95
NW ED COUNCIL STDNT SUCCESS/ARLINGTON HTS/COOK	04182155	847/718-6800	82

O

School/City/County	PID	TELEPHONE	PAGE
O A Thorp Scholastic Academy/Chicago/Cook	00280494	773/534-3640	27
O W Holmes Middle Sch/Wheeling/Cook	00281436	847/520-2790	71
O W Huth Middle Sch/Matteson/Cook	00271297	708/748-0470	57
O'FALLON CMTY CONS SCH DIST 90/O FALLON/ST CLAIR	00317425	618/632-3666	221
O'Fallon Twp High Sch/O Fallon/St Clair	00317487	618/632-3507	221
O'Fallon Twp HS-Milburn/O Fallon/St Clair	11456391	618/622-9647	221
O'FALLON TWP SCH DIST 203/O FALLON/ST CLAIR	00317475	618/632-3507	221
O'Keeffe Elem Sch/Chicago/Cook	00276247	773/535-0600	26
O'Neal Elem Sch/Elgin/Kane	00298491	847/888-5266	131
O'Neill Middle Sch/Downers Grove/Du Page	00289452	630/719-5815	93
O'Toole Elem Sch/Chicago/Cook	00278324	773/535-9040	34
Oak Crest Elem Sch/Beach Park/Lake	00300525	847/599-5519	147
Oak Elem Sch/Hinsdale/Du Page	00290138	630/861-4300	91
Oak Forest High Sch/Oak Forest/Cook	00268109	708/687-0500	23
Oak Glen Elem Sch/Lansing/Cook	00270750	708/474-1714	55
Oak Grove Elem Middle Sch/Bartonville/Peoria	00312671	309/697-0621	198
Oak Grove Elem Sch/Decatur/Macon	00307145	217/362-3550	165
Oak Grove Sch/Libertyville/Lake	00301866	847/367-4120	154
OAK GROVE SCH DIST 68/BARTONVILLE/PEORIA	00312657	309/697-3367	198
OAK GROVE SCH DIST 68/LIBERTYVILLE/LAKE	00301854	847/367-4120	154
Oak Knoll Early Childhod Ctr/Cary/McHenry	12318209	224/357-5550	179
Oak Lawn Cmty High Sch/Oak Lawn/Cook	00272198	708/424-5200	60
OAK LAWN CMTY HIGH SD 229/OAK LAWN/COOK	00272186	708/424-5200	60
Oak Lawn Hometown Middle Sch/Oak Lawn/Cook	00272227	708/499-6400	60
OAK LAWN-HOMETOWN SCH DIST 123/OAK LAWN/COOK	00272203	708/423-0150	60
Oak Park & River Forest HS/Oak Park/Cook	00272447	708/383-0700	60
OAK PARK & RIVER FOREST SD 200/OAK PARK/COOK	00272435	708/383-0700	60
Oak Park Elem Sch/Aurora/Kane	00297605	630/299-8250	129
OAK PARK ELEM SCH DIST 97/OAK PARK/COOK	00272318	708/524-3000	60
Oak Prairie Junior High Sch/Homer Glen/Will	00325252	815/836-2724	249
Oak Ridge Elem Sch/Palos Hills/Cook	00271900	708/598-5713	59
Oak Ridge Sch/Carpentersvle/McHenry	04838859	224/484-5800	180
Oak Terrace Elem Sch/Highwood/Lake	00301141	224/765-3100	154
Oak View Elem Sch/Bolingbrook/Will	00325630	630/759-9300	248
Oakbrook Elem Sch/Wood Dale/Du Page	00291649	630/766-6336	100
Oakdale Christian Academy/Chicago/Cook	05264809	773/779-9440	80
OAKDALE CMTY CONS SCH DIST 1/OAKDALE/WASHINGTON	00323333	618/329-5292	236
Oakdale Elem Sch/Normal/Mclean	00306608	309/557-4421	187
Oakdale Elem Sch/Oakdale/Washington	00323345	618/329-5292	236
Oakdale Elem Sch/Waukegan/Lake	01844809	224/303-1860	156
Oakhill Elem Sch/Streamwood/Kane	00298441	630/213-5585	131
OAKLAND CMTY UNIT SCH DIST 5/OAKLAND/COLES	00266840	217/346-2555	19
Oakland Elem Sch/Bloomington/Mclean	00306256	309/662-4302	185
Oakland Elem Sch/Lake Villa/Lake	00300410	847/838-8601	146
Oakland High Sch/Oakland/Coles	00266864	217/346-2118	19
Oakton Elem Sch/Evanston/Cook	00269426	847/859-8800	48
OAKWOOD CMTY UNIT SCH DIST 76/OAKWOOD/VERMILION	00322638	217/446-6081	232
Oakwood Elem Sch/Lemont/Cook	00270798	630/257-2286	55
Oakwood Grade Sch/Oakwood/Vermilion	00322626	217/354-4221	232
Oakwood High Sch/Fithian/Vermilion	00322640	217/354-2358	232
Oakwood Junior High Sch/Danville/Vermilion	00322602	217/443-2883	232
OBLONG CMTY UNIT SCH DIST 4/OBLONG/CRAWFORD	00287741	618/592-3933	83
Oblong Elem Sch/Oblong/Crawford	00287777	618/592-4225	83
Oblong High Sch/Oblong/Crawford	00287789	618/592-4235	83
ODELL CMTY CONS SCH DIST 435/ODELL/LIVINGSTON	00304313	815/998-2272	161
Odell Grade Sch/Odell/Livingston	00304325	815/998-2272	161
Odin Attendance Center 9-12/Odin/Marion	00309698	618/775-8266	175
Odin Attendance Center K-8/Odin/Marion	02055427	618/775-8266	175
ODIN PUBLIC SCH DIST 722/ODIN/MARION	00309674	618/775-8266	175
Ogden Avenue Elem Sch/La Grange/Cook	00270633	708/482-2480	54
Ogden Elem Sch/Chicago/Cook	00280482	773/534-8110	37
Ogden International HS-West/Chicago/Cook	11446578	773/534-0866	37
OGLE CO EDUCATIONAL CO-OP/BYRON/OGLE	02228997	815/234-2722	196
Oglesby Elem Sch/Chicago/Cook	00276235	773/535-3390	34
OGLESBY PUBLIC SCH DIST 125/OGLESBY/LA SALLE	00303072	815/883-9297	143
OHIO CMTY CONS SCH DIST 17/OHIO/BUREAU	00263927	815/376-4414	7
Ohio Cmty High Sch/Ohio/Bureau	00263939	815/376-4414	7
OHIO CMTY HIGH SCH DIST 505/OHIO/BUREAU	01843829	815/376-2934	7
Ohio Community Grade Sch/Ohio/Bureau	00263941	815/376-2934	7
OHIO-WABASH VALLEY REG VOC SYS/NORRIS CITY/WHITE	04184440	618/378-2274	238
Okaw Area Vocational Center/Vandalia/Fayette	00292631	618/283-5150	106
OKAW REGIONAL VOC SYSTEM/CHESTER/RANDOLPH	04184426	618/826-5471	206

School Year 2020-2021   800-333-8802   IL-V31

DISTRICT & SCHOOL TELEPHONE INDEX

School/City/County DISTRICT/CITY/COUNTY	PID	TELEPHONE NUMBER	PAGE
OKAW VALLEY CMTY UNIT SD 302/			
BETHANY/MOULTRIE			
Okaw Valley Elem Sch/Bethany/Moultrie	00311653	217/665-3232	193
Okaw Valley High Sch/Bethany/Moultrie	00311665	217/665-3541	193
Okaw Valley Middle Sch/Findlay/Moultrie	00311677	217/665-3631	193
Okawville Grade Sch/Okawville/Washington	00320343	217/756-8521	193
Okawville Jr Sr High Sch/Okawville/Washington	00323371	618/243-6157	236
	00323395	618/243-5201	236
Old Orchard Junior High Sch/Skokie/Cook	00274225	847/568-7501	67
Old Post Elem Sch/Oswego/Kendall	04747743	630/636-3400	138
Old Quarry Middle Sch/Lemont/Cook	00270786	630/257-2286	55
Old School Montessori/Grayslake/Lake	04990574	847/223-9606	158
Old St Mary's Sch/Chicago/Cook	05358589	312/386-1560	73
Olive Branch Christian Academy/Olive Branch/Alexander	11225178	618/776-6082	3
Olive C Martin Elem Sch/Lake Villa/Lake	05092199	847/245-3400	152
Olive-Mary Stitt Sch/Arlington HTS/Cook	00267090	847/398-4282	21
Oliver Julian Kendall Elem Sch/Naperville/Du Page	04807757	630/428-7100	95
Oliver McCracken Middle Sch/Skokie/Cook	00274330	847/673-1220	67
Oliver Parks 6th Grade Center/Cahokia/St Clair	00316548	618/332-3722	218
Oliver Wendell Holmes Elem Sch/Oak Park/Cook	00272368	708/524-3100	61
Olney C Allen Elem Sch/Aurora/Kane	00297617	630/299-5200	129
Olson Elem Sch/Woodstock/McHenry	10913944	815/338-0473	184
Olson Park Elem Sch/MacHesney Pk/Winnebago	04282664	815/654-4504	253
OLYMPIA CMTY UNIT SCH DIST 16/			
STANFORD/MCLEAN	00306634	309/379-6011	187
Olympia High Sch/Stanford/Mclean	00306701	309/379-5911	187
Olympia Middle Sch/Stanford/Mclean	03390854	309/379-5941	187
Olympia North Elem Sch/Danvers/Mclean	00306660	309/963-4514	187
Olympia South Elem Sch/Atlanta/Mclean	00306658	217/648-2302	187
Olympia West Elem Sch/Minier/Mclean	00306696	309/392-2671	187
Ombudsman No 1 High School NW/Chicago/Cook	11982338	708/669-7828	40
Ombudsman Sch/Bloomingdale/Du Page	04027062	630/351-9153	102
Ombudsman Sch-Downers Grove/Downers Grove/Du Page	03148376	630/629-1414	102
Ombudsman Sch-Naperville/Naperville/Du Page	03141457	630/428-9667	102
Ombudsman School-Crestwood/Crestwood/Cook	04026965	708/489-2215	80
Ombudsman School-Dundee/Elgin/Kane	04026977	847/622-0923	133
Ombudsman-Chicago Roseland CSA/Chicago/Cook	12366945	773/941-6674	40
Ombudsman-South High Sch/Chicago/Cook	12110174	773/498-5085	40
Ombudsman-West High Sch/Chicago/Cook	11982340	312/243-1550	40
Onahan Elem Sch/Chicago/Cook	00280509	773/534-1180	29
Onarga Academy Grand Prairie/Onarga/Iroquois	04800797	815/268-4001	118
Online Learning Academy/Peoria/Peoria	12375025	309/672-6790	199
Ontarioville Elem Sch/Hanover Park/Kane	00298453	630/213-5590	131
Opdyke Attendance Center/Opdyke/Jefferson	00296596	618/756-2492	123
OPDYKE-BELLE RIVE CMTY CSSD 5/			
OPDYKE/JEFFERSON	00296572	618/756-2492	123
ORANGEVILLE CMTY UNIT SD 203/			
ORANGEVILLE/STEPHENSON	00320927	815/789-4450	225
Orangeville Sch/Orangeville/Stephenson	00320939	815/789-4289	225
Orchard Place Elem Sch/Des Plaines/Cook	00268824	847/824-1255	46
Orchardville Mennonite Sch/Keenes/Wayne	02828511	618/895-1327	237
OREGON CMTY UNIT SCH DIST 220/			
OREGON/OGLE	00312035	815/732-5300	195
Oregon Elem Sch/Oregon/Ogle	00312059	815/732-2181	195
Oregon High Sch/Oregon/Ogle	00312085	815/732-5300	195
Oriole Park Elem Sch/Chicago/Cook	00280511	773/534-1201	29
ORION CMTY UNIT SCH DIST 223/			
ORION/HENRY	00295425	309/526-3388	117
Orion High Sch/Orion/Henry	00295449	309/526-3361	117
Orion Middle Sch/Orion/Henry	00295451	309/526-3392	117
Orland Junior High Sch/Orland Park/Cook	00272497	708/364-4200	61
ORLAND SCH DIST 135/ORLAND PARK/COOK	00272459	708/364-3300	61
Orozco Fine Arts & Sciences ES/Chicago/Cook	00277112	773/534-7215	32
Orr Academy High Sch/Chicago/Cook	11131242	773/534-6500	26
Orrington Elem Sch/Evanston/Cook	00269438	847/859-8780	48
Oscar Mayer Elem Sch/Chicago/Cook	00280248	773/534-5535	31
Oster-Oakview Sch/New Lenox/Will	04365943	815/485-2125	245
Oswego East High Sch/Oswego/Kendall	05341249	630/636-2200	138
Oswego High Sch/Oswego/Kendall	00299720	630/636-2000	138
Otis P Graves Elem Sch/Summit/Cook	00274665	708/458-7260	45
OTTAWA ELEMENTARY SCH DIST 141/			
OTTAWA/LA SALLE	00303149	815/433-1133	143
Ottawa Township High Sch/Ottawa/La Salle	00303137	815/433-1323	143
OTTAWA TWP HIGH SCH DIST 140/			
OTTAWA/LA SALLE	00303125	815/433-1323	143
Otter Creek Elem Sch/Elgin/Kane	05091236	847/888-6995	131
Our Lady Immaculate Academy/Oak Park/Cook	11740659	708/524-2408	80
Our Lady of Charity Sch/Cicero/Cook	00283941	708/652-0262	73
Our Lady of Grace Cath Academy/East Moline/Rock Island	00313572	309/755-9771	209
Our Lady of Grace Sch/Chicago/Cook	00283965	773/342-0170	73
Our Lady of Guadalupe Sch/Chicago/Cook	00283977	773/768-0999	73
Our Lady of Humility Sch/Beach Park/Lake	00283991	847/746-3722	157
Our Lady of Lourdes Sch/Decatur/Macon	00319526	217/877-4408	166
Our Lady of Mt Carmel Acad/Chicago/Cook	00284062	773/525-8779	73
Our Lady of Mt Carmel Sch/Herrin/Williamson	00317815	618/942-4484	252
Our Lady of Peace Sch/Darien/Du Page	00326529	630/325-9220	101
Our Lady of Perpetual Help Sch/Glenview/Cook	00284098	847/724-6990	73
Our Lady of Tepeyac Elem Sch/Chicago/Cook	03340445	773/522-0024	73
Our Lady of Tepeyac High Sch/Chicago/Cook	00285133	773/522-0023	73
Our Lady of the Snows Sch/Chicago/Cook	00284189	773/735-4810	73
Our Lady of the Wayside Sch/Arlington HTS/Cook	00284191	847/255-0050	73
Our Lady Queen of Peace Sch/Belleville/St Clair	00317839	618/234-1206	222
Our Lady Queen of Peace Sch/Bethalto/Madison	00319538	618/377-6401	173
Our Lady Sacred Heart Academy/Rockford/Winnebago	11531460	815/399-3021	256
Our Savior's Lutheran Sch/Springfield/Sangamon	00319368	217/546-4531	214
Our Saviour Sch/Jacksonville/Morgan	00319540	217/243-8621	193
Our Saviour's Lutheran Sch/Zion/Lake	01405295	847/872-5922	158
Owen Elem Sch/Naperville/Du Page	05262100	630/428-7300	95
Owen Marsh Elem Sch/Springfield/Sangamon	00319083	217/787-3173	213
Owen Scholastic Academy/Chicago/Cook	00278336	773/535-9330	34

P

School/City/County	PID	TELEPHONE NUMBER	PAGE
P H Miller Elem Sch/Plano/Kendall	00299770	630/552-8504	138
P L Bolin Elem Sch/East Peoria/Tazewell	00321218	309/427-5350	227
Pablo Casals Elem Sch/Chicago/Cook	03401130	773/534-4444	26
Pactt Learning Center/Chicago/Cook	02969971	773/338-9102	80
Paec Elem Sch/Maywood/Cook	04370297	708/338-3250	20
Paec High Sch/Maywood/Cook	04196170	708/450-1515	20
Palatine High Sch/Palatine/Cook	00272758	847/755-1600	69
PALESTINE CMTY UNIT SD 3/			
PALESTINE/CRAWFORD	00287791	618/586-2713	83
Palestine Grade Sch/Palestine/Crawford	00287806	618/586-2711	83
Palestine High Sch/Palestine/Crawford	00287818	618/586-2712	83
Palmer Elem Sch/Chicago/Cook	00280547	773/534-3704	29
PALOS CMTY CONS SCH DIST 118/			
PALOS PARK/COOK	00272784	708/448-4800	61
Palos East Elem Sch/Palos Heights/Cook	00272796	708/448-1084	61
PALOS HEIGHTS SCH DIST 128/			
PALOS HEIGHTS/COOK	00272837	708/597-9040	61
Palos South Middle Sch/Palos Park/Cook	00272813	708/448-5971	61
Palos West Elem Sch/Palos Park/Cook	00272825	708/448-6888	61
Pana Christian Academy/Pana/Christian	02824864	217/562-5893	15
PANA CMTY UNIT SCH DIST 8/			
PANA/CHRISTIAN	00265676	217/562-1500	14
Pana Junior High Sch/Pana/Christian	00265705	217/562-6500	14
Pana Senior High Sch/Pana/Christian	00265729	217/562-6600	14
PANHANDLE CMTY UNIT SD 2/			
RAYMOND/MONTGOMERY	00311251	217/229-4215	191
Paririe Central Primary West/Chenoa/Livingston	00306309	815/945-2971	162
PARIS CMTY UNIT SCH DIST 4/			
PARIS/EDGAR	00292007	217/465-5391	103
Paris Co-op High Sch/Paris/Edgar	00292069	217/466-1175	103
PARIS UNION SCH DIST 95/			
PARIS/EDGAR	00292021	217/465-8448	103
PARK FOREST CHICAGO HGT SD 163/			
PARK FOREST/COOK	00272930	708/668-9400	62
Park Junior High Sch/La Grange Pk/Cook	01398264	708/482-2500	54
Park Manor Elem Sch/Chicago/Cook	00276285	773/535-3070	35
PARK RIDGE NILES CMCSD 64/			
PARK RIDGE/COOK	00273051	847/318-4300	62
Park Sch/Evanston/Cook	00269440	847/424-2300	48
Park Sch/Orland Park/Cook	00272502	708/364-3900	61
Park Sch/Riverdale/Cook	04457780	708/849-9440	46
Park Sch/Round Lake/Lake	10902256	847/201-7010	148

Illinois School Directory
DISTRICT & SCHOOL TELEPHONE INDEX

School/City/County DISTRICT/CITY/COUNTY	PID	TELEPHONE NUMBER	PAGE
Park View Elem Sch/Glen Ellyn/Du Page	00289878	630/858-1600	90
Park View Sch/Lombard/Du Page	00290504	630/827-4040	97
Park View Sch/Morton Grove/Cook	00271546	847/965-6200	58
Parker Child Parent Center/Chicago/Cook	01532836	773/535-3853	34
Parker Community Academy/Chicago/Cook	00276297	773/535-3375	34
Parker Junior High Sch/Flossmoor/Cook	00269622	708/647-5400	49
Parkland Middle Sch/McHenry/McHenry	00305795	779/244-1700	183
Parkland Preparatory Academy/Bartlett/Du Page	12320472	630/823-8323	102
Parkside Community Academy/Chicago/Cook	00276326	773/535-0940	35
Parkside Elem Sch/Lawrenceville/Lawrence	00303644	618/943-3992	159
Parkside Elem Sch/Normal/Mclean	03048843	309/557-4422	187
Parkside Junior High Sch/Normal/Mclean	00306593	309/557-4408	187
Parkside Middle Sch/Peru/La Salle	00303307	815/223-1111	144
Parkside Primary Sch/Bethalto/Madison	00308280	618/377-4100	169
Parkview Baptist Academy/Northlake/Cook	03192676	708/562-2351	80
Parkview Christian Academy/Yorkville/Kendall	04990720	630/553-5158	139
Parkview Elem Sch/Carpentersvle/McHenry	00298130	224/484-2500	180
Parkview Elem Sch/Columbia/Monroe	03389855	618/281-4997	190
Parkview Junior High Sch/Lawrenceville/Lawrence	00303709	618/943-2327	159
Parkview Middle Sch/Creve Coeur/Tazewell	00321062	309/698-3610	226
Parkwood Elem Sch/Hanover Park/Kane	00298465	630/213-5595	131
Parrish Elem Sch/Carbondale/Jackson	00296041	618/457-5781	120
Parsons Accelerated Elem Sch/Decatur/Macon	00307171	217/362-3330	165
Passow Elem Sch/Franklin Park/Cook	00269830	847/455-6781	50
Pasteur Elem Sch/Chicago/Cook	00278362	773/535-2270	27
Pathways Academy/Joliet/Will	03396286	815/727-6810	243
Pathways In Educ-Brighton Park/Chicago/Cook	12045294	773/579-1220	41
Pathways In Educ-Humboldt Park/Chicago/Cook	12367377	773/804-8866	41
Pathways In Education-Ashburn/Chicago/Cook	11815694	773/434-6300	41
Pathways In Education-Avondale/Chicago/Cook	11926255	773/588-5007	41
Pathways Sch/Belleville/St Clair	04198063	618/355-4410	217
Patoka Cmty Sch/Patoka/Marion	00309715	618/432-5643	175
PATOKA CMTY UNIT SD 100/PATOKA/MARION	00309703	618/432-5440	175
Patrick Henry Elem Sch/Chicago/Cook	00279847	773/534-5060	29
Patterson Elem Sch/Naperville/Du Page	04032251	630/428-6500	95
Patton Elem Sch/Arlington HTS/Cook	00267117	847/398-4288	21
Paul Revere Intermediate Sch/Blue Island/Cook	04870546	708/385-4450	45
Paul Revere Primary Sch/Blue Island/Cook	00268044	708/489-3533	45
Pavilion Foundation Sch/Champaign/Champaign	11224655	217/373-1889	13
PAW PAW CMTY UNIT SD 271/PAW PAW/LEE	00303981	815/627-2841	160
Paw Paw Elem Sch/Paw Paw/Lee	00304026	815/627-2841	160
PAWNEE CMTY UNIT SCH DIST 11/PAWNEE/SANGAMON	00318766	217/625-2471	212
Pawnee Grade Sch/Pawnee/Sangamon	00318778	217/625-2231	212
Pawnee High Sch/Pawnee/Sangamon	00318780	217/625-2471	212
PAXTON-BUCKLEY-LODA CUSD 10/PAXTON/FORD	00292784	217/379-3314	107
Paxton-Buckley-Loda High Sch/Paxton/Ford	00292801	217/379-4331	107
Paxton-Buckley-Loda Jr HS/Paxton/Ford	00292813	217/379-9202	107
PAYSON CMTY UNIT SCH DIST 1/PAYSON/ADAMS	00263006	217/656-3323	2
Peace & Educ Coalition HS/Chicago/Cook	05101659	773/535-9023	27
Peace Center/Dolton/Cook	12322456	708/985-3525	69
Peaceful Pathways Mont Academy/Yorkville/Kendall	11224071	630/553-4263	139
PEARL CITY CMTY UNIT SD 200/PEARL CITY/STEPHENSON	00320953	815/443-2715	225
Pearl City Sch/Pearl City/Stephenson	00320965	815/443-2715	225
PECATONICA CMTY UNIT SD 321/PECATONICA/WINNEBAGO	00327315	815/239-1639	253
Pecatonica Elem Sch/Pecatonica/Winnebago	00327327	815/239-2550	253
Pecatonica High Sch/Pecatonica/Winnebago	00327339	815/239-2611	253
Pecatonica Middle Sch/Pecatonica/Winnebago	05342102	815/239-2612	253
Peck Elem Sch/Chicago/Cook	00278374	773/535-2450	27
Peckwas Preparatory Academy/Summit Argo/Cook	05378371	708/594-6857	80
Peirce Int'l Studies ES/Chicago/Cook	00280561	773/534-2440	29
PEKIN CMTY HIGH SCH DIST 303/PEKIN/TAZEWELL	00321579	309/347-4101	227
Pekin Community High Sch/Pekin/Tazewell	00321593	309/347-4101	227
PEKIN PUBLIC SCH DIST 108/PEKIN/TAZEWELL	00321426	309/477-4740	227
PEMBROKE CMTY CONS SD 259/HOPKINS PARK/KANKAKEE	00299419	815/944-5448	136
Penn Elem Sch/Chicago/Cook	00278386	773/534-1665	31
Penniman Elem Sch/Cahokia/St Clair	00316524	618/332-1915	218
Pennoyer Sch/Norridge/Cook	00273207	708/456-9094	62
PENNOYER SCH DIST 79/NORRIDGE/COOK	00273192	708/456-9094	62
Peoria Academy/Peoria/Peoria	05011494	309/692-7570	200
Peoria Christian Sch/Peoria/Peoria	01442578	309/686-4500	200
Peoria Co Juvenile Det Center/Peoria/Peoria	00312798	309/634-4200	197
PEORIA CO SPECIAL ED ASSOC/BARTONVILLE/PEORIA	02184121	309/697-0880	200
PEORIA ED REG EMP & CAREER/PEORIA/PEORIA	04177813	309/693-7373	200
Peoria Hebrew Day Sch/Peoria/Peoria	01405403	309/692-2821	200
PEORIA HEIGHTS CMTY SD 325/PEORIA HTS/PEORIA	00313156	309/686-8800	198
Peoria Heights Grade Sch/Peoria HTS/Peoria	00313170	309/686-8809	198
Peoria Heights High Sch/Peoria HTS/Peoria	00313194	309/686-8803	198
Peoria High Sch/Peoria/Peoria	00312970	309/672-6630	199
Peoria Notre Dame High Sch/Peoria/Peoria	00313340	309/691-8741	200
PEORIA PUBLIC SCH DIST 150/PEORIA/PEORIA	00312683	309/672-6512	198
PEOTONE CMTY UNIT SD 207-U/PEOTONE/WILL	00325460	708/258-0991	245
Peotone Early Educ Shaw Ctr/Peotone/Will	12033057	708/258-0991	245
Peotone Elem Sch/Peotone/Will	00325484	708/258-6955	245
Peotone High Sch/Peotone/Will	00325496	708/258-3236	245
Peotone Intermediate Ctr/Frankfort/Will	05070672	815/469-5744	245
Peotone Junior High Sch/Peotone/Will	00325501	708/258-3246	245
Pepper Ridge Elem Sch/Bloomington/Mclean	04287676	309/557-4423	187
Perandoe Ed Program Red Bud/Red Bud/Randolph	04934635	618/282-7228	205
PERANDOE SPECIAL ED DIST/RED BUD/RANDOLPH	02182173	618/282-6251	206
Percy Julian Middle Sch/Oak Park/Cook	00272356	708/524-3040	61
Percy L Julian High Sch/Chicago/Cook	01532757	773/535-5170	37
Perkin Pre-Sch Family Ed Ctr/Pekin/Tazewell	05096951	309/477-4730	228
Perry Elem Sch/Belvidere/Boone	00263496	815/544-9274	4
Pershing Early Learning Center/Decatur/Macon	04014259	217/362-3300	165
Pershing Elem Sch/Berwyn/Cook	00267911	708/795-2349	23
Pershing Elem Sch/Joliet/Will	00325032	815/725-0986	243
Pershing Humanities Mag Sch/Chicago/Cook	00278398	773/534-9272	33
Perspectives CS-HS of Tech/Chicago/Cook	10914572	773/358-6120	41
Perspectives CS-Joslin/Chicago/Cook	04755647	312/225-7400	41
Perspectives CS-Ldrship Acad/Chicago/Cook	10021486	773/358-6100	41
Perspectives CS-Mid Acad/Chicago/Cook	10912457	773/358-6300	41
Perspectives IIt Math-Sci Acad/Chicago/Cook	11131199	773/358-6800	41
Peru Catholic Sch/Peru/La Salle	00313687	815/224-1914	145
PERU ELEM SCH DIST 124/PERU/LA SALLE	00303266	815/223-0486	143
Peter J Palombi Middle Sch/Lake Villa/Lake	00301373	847/356-2118	152
Peter M Gombert Elem Sch/Aurora/Du Page	04811540	630/375-3700	95
Petersburg Elem Sch/Petersburg/Menard	00310582	217/632-7731	189
Peterson Elem Sch/Chicago/Cook	00280573	773/534-5070	29
Peterson Elem Sch/Naperville/Du Page	00290243	630/428-5678	95
PHILIP J ROCK CENTER & SCHOOL/GLEN ELLYN/DU PAGE	03266540	630/790-2474	102
Philip J Rock Sch/Glen Ellyn/Du Page	04939740	630/790-2474	1
Phoenix Military Academy/Chicago/Cook	05158559	773/534-7275	28
Piccolo Sch of Excellence/Chicago/Cook	00279146	773/534-4425	26
Pickard Elem Sch/Chicago/Cook	00278427	773/535-7280	28
Pierce Downer Elem Sch/Downers Grove/Du Page	01521423	630/719-5860	93
Pietrini Elem Sch/Franklin Park/Cook	00269816	847/455-7960	50
PIKELAND CMTY SCH DIST 10/PITTSFIELD/PIKE	00314576	217/285-2147	203
Pikeland Community Sch/Pittsfield/Pike	00314655	217/285-9462	203
Pilgrim Lutheran Sch/Chicago/Cook	00282519	773/477-4824	80
Pilsen Community Academy/Chicago/Cook	00277851	773/534-7675	32
PINCKNEYVILLE CMTY HIGH SD 101/PINCKNEYVILLE/PERRY	00314148	618/357-5013	201
Pinckneyville Community HS/Pinckneyville/Perry	00314150	618/357-5013	201
Pinckneyville Elem Sch/Pinckneyville/Perry	00314112	618/357-5161	201
Pinckneyville Jr High Sch/Pinckneyville/Perry	00314124	618/357-2724	201

DISTRICT & SCHOOL TELEPHONE INDEX

Market Data Retrieval

School/City/County DISTRICT/CITY/COUNTY	PID	TELEPHONE NUMBER	PAGE
PINCKNEYVILLE SCH DIST 50/			
PINCKNEYVILLE/PERRY	00314100	618/357-2724	201
Pine Crest Elem Sch/Georgetown/Vermilion	00322482	217/662-6981	232
Pioneer Elem Sch/Bolingbrook/Will	04916138	630/771-2420	248
Pioneer Elem Sch/West Chicago/Du Page	00291510	630/293-6040	99
Pioneer Path/Channahon/Will	05275482	815/467-4312	241
Piper Elem Sch/Berwyn/Cook	00267923	708/795-2364	23
Pirie Elem Fine Arts & Acadmcs/Chicago/Cook	00276376	773/535-3435	35
Pittsfield High Sch/Pittsfield/Pike	00314629	217/285-6888	203
Pittsfield South Elem Sch/Pittsfield/Pike	00314643	217/285-2431	203
Plainfield Academy/Plainfield/Will	05070452	815/439-5521	246
Plainfield Central High Sch/Plainfield/Will	00325575	815/436-3200	246
PLAINFIELD CONS SCH DIST 202/			
PLAINFIELD/WILL	00325525	815/577-4000	245
Plainfield East High Sch/Plainfield/Will	11072672	815/577-0324	246
Plainfield Elem Sch/Des Plaines/Cook	00268836	847/824-1301	46
Plainfield North High Sch/Plainfield/Will	10000652	815/609-8506	246
Plainfield South High Sch/Plainfield/Will	04944642	815/439-5555	246
Plamondon Elem Sch/Chicago/Cook	00278439	773/534-1789	31
Plank Junior High Sch/Oswego/Kendall	10023214	630/551-9400	138
PLANO CMTY UNIT SCH DIST 88/			
PLANO/KENDALL	00299744	630/552-8978	138
Plano High Sch/Plano/Kendall	00299782	630/552-3178	138
Plano Middle Sch/Plano/Kendall	04232712	630/552-3608	138
Plato Lrg Academy Primary/Chicago/Cook	11131101	773/413-3090	41
Player Early Childhood Center/Justice/Cook	00268161	708/430-8191	53
Pleasant Acres Elem Sch/Rantoul/Champaign	00265183	217/893-5402	11
PLEASANT HILL CUSD 3/PLEASANT HILL/PIKE	00314667	217/734-2311	203
Pleasant Hill Elem Sch/Palatine/Cook	00272629	847/963-5900	43
Pleasant Hill Elem Sch/Peoria/Peoria	00313211	309/637-6829	199
Pleasant Hill Elem Sch/Pleasant Hill/Pike	00314679	217/734-2311	203
Pleasant Hill Elem Sch/Winfield/Du Page	00291039	630/682-2100	92
Pleasant Hill High Sch/Pleasant Hill/Pike	00314681	217/734-2311	203
PLEASANT HILL SCH DIST 69/			
PEORIA/PEORIA	00313209	309/637-6829	199
Pleasant Lane Elem Sch/Lombard/Du Page	00290528	630/827-4640	97
PLEASANT PLAINS CMTY UNIT SD 8/			
PLEASANT PLNS/SANGAMON	00318792	217/626-1041	212
Pleasant Plains High Sch/Pleasant PLNS/Sangamon	00318821	217/626-1044	212
Pleasant Plains Middle Sch/Pleasant PLNS/Sangamon	04247731	217/626-1061	212
Pleasant Ridge Elem Sch/Glenview/Cook	00269971	847/998-5050	51
Pleasant Valley Elem Sch/Peoria/Peoria	00313235	309/673-6750	199
Pleasant Valley Middle Sch/Peoria/Peoria	05097084	309/679-0634	199
PLEASANT VALLEY SCH DIST 62/			
PEORIA/PEORIA	00313223	309/673-6750	199
Pleasantdale Elem Sch/La Grange/Cook	00273221	708/246-4700	62
Pleasantdale Middle Sch/Burr Ridge/Cook	00273233	708/246-3210	62
PLEASANTDALE SCH DIST 107/			
BURR RIDGE/COOK	00273219	708/784-2013	62
Plt Middle Sch/Prophetstown/Whiteside	00324492	815/537-5084	239
Plum Grove Junior High Sch/Rolling MDWS/Cook	00272631	847/963-7600	43
Pocahontas Elem Sch/Pocahontas/Bond	00263367	618/669-2296	4
Poe Classical Sch/Chicago/Cook	02107680	773/535-5525	36
Polaris Charter Academy/Chicago/Cook	10912378	773/534-0820	41
Polo Cmty High Sch/Polo/Ogle	00312138	815/946-3314	195
POLO CMTY UNIT SCH DIST 222/			
POLO/OGLE	00312102	815/946-3815	195
Pontiac Christian Sch/Pontiac/Livingston	02190273	815/842-1322	163
PONTIAC CMTY CONS SCH DIST 429/			
PONTIAC/LIVINGSTON	00304387	815/842-1533	161
Pontiac Junior High Sch/Fairview HTS/St Clair	00317504	618/233-6004	221
Pontiac Junior High Sch/Pontiac/Livingston	00304428	815/842-4343	161
Pontiac Township High Sch/Pontiac/Livingston	00304375	815/844-6113	162
PONTIAC TWP HIGH SCH DIST 90/			
PONTIAC/LIVINGSTON	00304351	815/844-6113	161
PONTIAC-WM HOLLIDAY SD 105/			
FAIRVIEW HTS/ST CLAIR	00317499	618/233-2320	221
POPE CO CMTY UNIT SCH DIST 1/			
GOLCONDA/POPE	00314734	618/683-2301	203
Pope Co Elem Sch/Golconda/Pope	00314758	618/683-4011	204
Pope Co High Sch/Golconda/Pope	00314746	618/683-3071	204
Pope John Paul II Sch/Chicago/Cook	00283238	773/523-6161	73
Pope John XXIII Sch/Evanston/Cook	00286888	847/475-5678	73
Pope St John Paul 11 Academy S/Aurora/Kane	00328498	630/851-4400	133
Pope St John Paul II Academy N/Aurora/Kane	00328694	630/844-3781	133
Poplar Grove Elem Sch/Poplar Grove/Boone	00263551	815/765-3113	5
Porta Central Sch/Petersburg/Menard	00310611	217/632-7781	189
PORTA CMTY UNIT SCH DIST 202/			
PETERSBURG/MENARD	00310570	217/632-3803	189
Porta Jr Sr High Sch/Petersburg/Menard	00310609	217/632-3219	189
Portage Park Elem Sch/Chicago/Cook	00280585	773/534-3576	29
Posen Intermediate Sch/Posen/Cook	00273295	708/388-7204	63
POSEN-ROBBINS SCH DIST 143-5/			
POSEN/COOK	00273245	708/388-7200	63
POTOMAC CMTY UNIT SCH DIST 10/			
POTOMAC/VERMILION	00322652	217/987-6155	232
Potomac Elem Sch/Potomac/Vermilion	00322664	217/987-6155	232
Powell Elem Paideia Comm Acad/Chicago/Cook	01532850	773/535-6650	35
PRAIRIE CENTRAL CMTY USD 8/			
FAIRBURY/LIVINGSTON	00304181	815/692-2504	162
Prairie Central Elem Sch/Fairbury/Livingston	00304210	815/692-2623	162
Prairie Central High Sch/Fairbury/Livingston	00304208	815/692-2355	162
Prairie Central Jr High Sch/Forrest/Livingston	00304260	815/657-8660	162
Prairie Central Primary East/Chatsworth/Livingston	00304090	815/635-3561	162
Prairie Central Upper Elem Sch/Forrest/Livingston	04746282	815/657-8238	162
Prairie Children Pre-Sch/Aurora/Du Page	04807745	630/375-3030	95
Prairie Christian Sch/El Paso/Woodford	11232145	309/527-4020	258
Prairie Crossing Charter Sch/Grayslake/Lake	04889901	847/543-9722	1
PRAIRIE DU ROCHER CCSD 134/			
PR DU ROCHER/RANDOLPH	00315013	618/284-3530	205
Prairie Du Rocher Elem Sch/Pr Du Rocher/Randolph	00315025	618/284-3530	205
Prairie Elem Sch/Buffalo Grove/Lake	02110912	847/634-3144	151
Prairie Elem Sch/Naperville/Du Page	00290827	630/420-6348	98
PRAIRIE GROVE CONS SD 46/			
CRYSTAL LAKE/MCHENRY	00305848	815/459-3023	183
Prairie Grove Elem Sch/Crystal Lake/McHenry	00305874	815/459-3023	183
Prairie Grove Jr High Sch/Crystal Lake/McHenry	04882862	815/459-3557	183
PRAIRIE HILL CMTY CONS SD 133/			
SOUTH BELOIT/WINNEBAGO	00327389	815/389-3964	253
Prairie Hill Elem Sch/South Beloit/Winnebago	00327391	815/389-3301	253
PRAIRIE HILLS ELEM SD 144/			
MARKHAM/COOK	00271144	708/210-2888	63
Prairie Hills Jr High Sch/Markham/Cook	00271156	708/210-2860	63
Prairie Junior High Sch/Alsip/Cook	00266917	708/371-3080	20
Prairie Knolls Middle Sch/Elgin/Kane	10805086	847/717-8100	128
Prairie Lake Sch/Elk Grove Vlg/Cook	11817018	847/593-4120	80
Prairie Oak Elem Sch/Berwyn/Cook	00267818	708/795-2442	22
Prairie Point Elem Sch/Oswego/Kendall	10012746	630/636-3600	138
Prairie Ridge High Sch/Crystal Lake/McHenry	04745563	815/479-0404	180
Prairie Sch/Orland Park/Cook	01531129	708/364-4840	61
Prairie Trail Sch/Wadsworth/Lake	00300915	847/623-4333	150
Prairie View Grade Sch/Elgin/Kane	00297954	847/464-6014	128
Prairie View Middle Sch/Tinley Park/Cook	04034821	708/532-8540	53
Prairie View Sch/Sandwich/De Kalb	00288240	815/786-8811	86
Prairieland Elem Sch/Normal/Mclean	04874932	309/557-4424	187
Prairieview Elem Sch/Bartlett/Kane	04016295	630/213-5603	131
Prairieview Elem Sch/Downers Grove/Du Page	03046479	630/783-5100	90
Prairieview Elem Sch/Grayslake/Lake	00300862	847/543-4230	148
Prairieview-Ogden Jr High Sch/Thomasboro/Champaign	00264945	217/694-4122	11
Prairieview-Ogden North ES/Royal/Champaign	00265224	217/583-3300	11
PRAIRIEVIEW-OGDEN SCH DIST 197/			
ROYAL/CHAMPAIGN	00265212	217/583-3300	11
Prairieview-Ogden South ES/Ogden/Champaign	00265080	217/582-2725	11
Prairiewood Elem Sch/Woodstock/McHenry	10804941	815/337-5300	184
Prather Elem Sch/Granite City/Madison	00308840	618/451-5823	171
Premier Academy/Morris/Grundy	11464427	815/416-0377	111
Preschool at Early Educ Ctr/Round Lake/Lake	12102799	847/270-9920	155
Prescott Elem Sch/Chicago/Cook	00280597	773/534-5505	31
Primary Learning Center/Markham/Cook	12374978	708/331-3364	63
Prince of Peace Sch/Lake Villa/Lake	00284244	847/356-6111	157
PRINCETON ELEM SCH DIST 115/			
PRINCETON/BUREAU	00263953	815/875-3162	7
Princeton High Sch/Princeton/Bureau	00264024	815/875-3308	7

Illinois School Directory

DISTRICT & SCHOOL TELEPHONE INDEX

School/City/County DISTRICT/CITY/COUNTY	PID	TELEPHONE NUMBER	PAGE
PRINCETON TWP HSD 500/PRINCETON/ **BUREAU**	00264012	815/875-3308	7
PRINCEVILLE CMTY UNIT SD 326/ **PRINCEVILLE/PEORIA**	00313259	309/385-2213	200
Princeville Elem Sch/Princeville/Peoria	00313285	309/385-4994	200
Princeville Jr Sr High Sch/Princeville/ Peoria	00313297	309/385-4660	200
Pritchett Elem Sch/Buffalo Grove/Lake	02132128	847/353-5700	147
Pritzker Sch/Chicago/Cook	00281187	773/534-4415	32
Proegler Sch/Kankakee/Kankakee	04367616	815/933-0719	135
PROFESSIONAL DEV ALLIANCE/ **JOLIET/WILL**	04420012	815/744-8334	250
Program for Adaptive Lrng Sch/Chicago HTS/ Cook	04370247	708/481-6102	20
Project Challenge/Oak Forest/Cook	04444147	708/687-4971	20
Project Echo/Johnston City/Williamson	12376299	618/983-6628	250
Project Help-Arcola/Charleston/Coles	04444202	217/345-9119	19
Project Insight Alt Sch/Macomb/McDonough	04198192	309/837-5685	178
Promise Christian Academy/Riverdale/Cook	04990926	708/201-9088	80
Prophetstown Elem Sch/Prophetstown/ Whiteside	00324313	815/537-2345	239
Prophetstown High Sch/Prophetstown/ Whiteside	00324301	815/537-5084	239
PROPHETSTOWN-LYNDON-TAMPICO 3/ **PROPHETSTOWN/WHITESIDE**	00324260	815/537-5101	239
Prospect Elem Sch/Clarendon Hls/Du Page	00290152	630/861-4400	91
Prospect High Sch/Mt Prospect/Cook	00271704	847/718-5200	70
PROSPECT HTS SCH DIST 23/ **PROSPECT HTS/COOK**	00273324	847/870-3850	63
Prosser Career Academy/Chicago/Cook	00280602	773/534-3200	37
Providence Catholic Chldrn Aca/New Lenox/ Will	04021537	815/485-7129	249
Providence Catholic High Sch/New Lenox/ Will	00326139	815/485-2136	249
Providence Englewood CS/Chicago/Cook	10021474	773/434-0202	41
Providence St Mel Sch/Chicago/Cook	02139059	773/722-4600	80
Proviso Area Excptnl Chldrn/Maywood/Cook	04196998	708/450-2129	20
Proviso East High Sch/Maywood/Cook	00273398	708/344-7000	63
Proviso Math & Science Academy/Forest Park/ Cook	10011390	708/338-4100	64
PROVISO TWP HIGH SCH DIST 209/ **FOREST PARK/COOK**	00273386	708/338-5900	63
Proviso West High Sch/Hillside/Cook	00273403	708/449-6400	64
Prussing Elem Sch/Chicago/Cook	00280614	773/534-3460	29
Pui Tak Christian Sch/Chicago/Cook	02985652	312/842-8546	80
Pulaski Int'l Sch of Chicago/Chicago/Cook	00280626	773/534-4391	32
PUTNAM CO CMTY UNIT SD 535/ **GRANVILLE/PUTNAM**	00314851	815/882-2800	204
Putnam Co Elem Sch/Hennepin/Putnam	00314875	815/882-2800	204
Putnam Co High Sch/Granville/Putnam	00314928	815/882-2800	204
Putnam Co Junior High Sch/Mc Nabb/Putnam	02845600	815/882-2800	204
Putnam Co Primary Center/Granville/Putnam	11456456	815/882-2800	204
Pythagoras Childrens Academy/Elmhurst/ Du Page	12028583	630/834-0477	102

Q

School/City/County	PID	TELEPHONE	PAGE
Queen Bee Early Childhood Ctr/Glendale HTS/ Du Page	12318182	630/344-5600	99
QUEEN BEE SCH DIST 16/**GLENDALE HTS**/ **DU PAGE**	00291120	630/260-6100	98
Queen of All Saints Sch/Chicago/Cook	00284270	773/736-0567	74
Queen of Angels Sch/Chicago/Cook	00284282	773/769-4211	74
Queen of Martyrs Sch/Chicago/Cook	00284309	708/422-1540	74
Queen of the Rosary Sch/Elk Grove Vlg/Cook	00284323	847/437-3322	74
Queen of the Universe Sch/Chicago/Cook	00284335	773/582-4266	74
Quentin Road Christian Sch/Lake Zurich/ Lake	02826094	847/438-4494	158
Quest Academy/Palatine/Cook	02956546	847/202-8035	80
Quest Charter Academy/Peoria/Peoria	11712195	309/402-0030	199
Quincy Area Christian Sch/Quincy/Adams	11235290	217/223-5698	3
Quincy Area Voc Tech Center/Quincy/Adams	02048187	217/224-3775	1
Quincy Early Childhood/Quincy/Adams	00263159	217/228-7121	2
Quincy Junior High Sch/Quincy/Adams	00263173	217/222-3073	2
Quincy Notre Dame High Sch/Quincy/Adams	01415238	217/223-2479	3
QUINCY SCH DIST 172/**QUINCY/ADAMS**	00263032	217/223-8700	2
Quincy Senior High Sch/Quincy/Adams	00263197	217/224-3770	2

R

School/City/County	PID	TELEPHONE	PAGE
R Brown Academy/Chicago/Cook	00276209	773/535-5385	36
Rabbi Oscar Fasman Yeshiva HS/Skokie/Cook	01405051	847/982-2500	80
RACCOON CONS SCH DIST 1/ **CENTRALIA/MARION**	00309727	618/532-7329	175
Raccoon Sch/Centralia/Marion	00309739	618/532-7329	175
Rachel Carson Elem Sch/Chicago/Cook	03401180	773/535-9222	28
Raes East/Galesburg/Knox	11435622	309/345-0101	139
Ralston Elem Sch/MacHesney Pk/Winnebago	00327248	815/654-4505	253
RAMSEY CMTY UNIT SCH DIST 204/ **RAMSEY/FAYETTE**	00292526	618/423-2335	105
Ramsey Grade Sch/Ramsey/Fayette	00292540	618/423-2010	106
Ramsey High Sch/Ramsey/Fayette	00292538	618/423-2333	106
Ranch View Elem Sch/Naperville/Du Page	02845789	630/420-6575	98
Randolph Magnet Sch/Chicago/Cook	02107642	773/535-9015	35
RANKIN CMTY SCH DIST 98/ **PEKIN/TAZEWELL**	00321634	309/346-3182	228
Rankin Elem Sch/Pekin/Tazewell	00321646	309/346-3182	228
RANTOUL CITY SCH DIST 137/ **RANTOUL/CHAMPAIGN**	00265119	217/893-5400	11
Rantoul Twp High Sch/Rantoul/Champaign	00265200	217/892-2151	12
RANTOUL TWP HIGH SCH DIST 193/ **RANTOUL/CHAMPAIGN**	00265195	217/892-2151	12
Ravenswood Bapt Christian Sch/Chicago/Cook	02189779	773/561-6576	80
Ravenswood Elem Sch/Chicago/Cook	00280638	773/534-5525	28
Ravinia Elem Sch/Highland Park/Lake	00301048	224/765-3700	154
Ray Elem Sch/Chicago/Cook	00276405	773/535-0970	33
Ray Graham Training Center/Chicago/Cook	00275736	773/534-9257	36
Raymond Benson Primary Sch/Itasca/Du Page	00290281	630/773-0554	96
Raymond Ellis Elem Sch/Round Lake/Lake	00301907	847/270-9900	155
Raymond Grade Sch/Raymond/Montgomery	00311299	217/229-3124	191
Reagan Middle Sch/Dixon/Lee	00303955	815/253-4966	160
Reavis Elem Sch/Lansing/Cook	00270762	708/474-8523	55
Reavis High Sch/Burbank/Cook	00273427	708/599-7200	64
Reavis Math & Sci Elem Sch/Chicago/Cook	00276417	773/535-1060	33
REAVIS TWP HSD 220/**BURBANK/COOK**	00273415	708/599-7200	64
Reba O Steck Elem Sch/Aurora/Du Page	04010394	630/375-3500	96
Red Brick Sch/Red Bud/Randolph	04934764	618/473-2222	205
RED BUD CMTY UNIT SCH DIST 132/ **RED BUD/RANDOLPH**	00315037	618/282-3507	205
Red Bud Elem Sch/Red Bud/Randolph	00315049	618/282-3858	205
Red Bud High Sch/Red Bud/Randolph	00315051	618/282-3826	205
RED HILL CMTY SCH DIST 10/ **BRIDGEPORT/LAWRENCE**	00303723	618/945-2061	159
Red Hill Jr Sr High Sch/Bridgeport/ Lawrence	00303759	618/945-2521	159
Red Oak Elem Sch/Highland Park/Lake	02043864	224/765-3750	154
Reed Elem Sch/Homer Glen/Will	04235984	708/301-0692	249
REED-CUSTER CMTY UNIT SD 255-U/ **BRAIDWOOD/WILL**	00324569	815/458-2307	246
Reed-Custer Elem Sch/Braidwood/Will	00324571	815/458-2145	246
Reed-Custer High Sch/Braidwood/Will	00325719	815/458-2166	247
Reed-Custer Middle Sch/Braidwood/Will	01821807	815/458-2868	247
Regina Dominican High Sch/Wilmette/Cook	00284361	847/256-7660	74
REGION 3 SPEC ED CO-OP/**COTTAGE HILLS**/ **MADISON**	02182068	618/462-1031	174
Regional Alternative Sch/Bloomington/ Mclean	11397044	309/828-5807	185
Regional Learning Center-Star/Rockford/ Winnebago	12225523	815/227-8495	252
REGIONAL OFFICE OF ED 1/ **JACKSONVILLE/MORGAN**	02097475	217/243-1804	193
REGIONAL OFFICE OF ED 3/ **VANDALIA/FAYETTE**	02097750	618/283-5011	106
REGIONAL OFFICE OF ED 8/ **FREEPORT/STEPHENSON**	01536650	815/599-1408	225
REGIONAL OFFICE OF ED 9/ **CHAMPAIGN/CHAMPAIGN**	02097530	217/893-3219	13
REGIONAL OFFICE OF ED 11/ **CHARLESTON/COLES**	02097580	217/348-0151	20
REGIONAL OFFICE OF ED 12/ **OLNEY/RICHLAND**	02098297	618/392-4631	207
REGIONAL OFFICE OF ED 13/ **CARLYLE/CLINTON**	02097578	618/594-2432	19
REGIONAL OFFICE OF ED 16/ **DEKALB/DE KALB**	02097695	815/217-0460	87
REGIONAL OFFICE OF ED 17/ **BLOOMINGTON/MCLEAN**	02098077	309/888-5120	188
REGIONAL OFFICE OF ED 20/ **HARRISBURG/SALINE**	02098338	618/253-5581	211
REGIONAL OFFICE OF ED 21/ **BENTON/FRANKLIN**	02097774	618/438-9711	109
REGIONAL OFFICE OF ED 24/ **MORRIS/GRUNDY**	02097815	815/941-3247	113
REGIONAL OFFICE OF ED 26/ **MACOMB/MCDONOUGH**	02098053	309/575-3226	179

DISTRICT & SCHOOL TELEPHONE INDEX

Market Data Retrieval

School/City/County DISTRICT/CITY/COUNTY	PID	TELEPHONE NUMBER	PAGE
REGIONAL OFFICE OF ED 28/			
ATKINSON/HENRY	02097839	309/936-7890	118
REGIONAL OFFICE OF ED 30/			
MURPHYSBORO/JACKSON	02097853	618/687-7290	121
REGIONAL OFFICE OF ED 33/			
GALESBURG/KNOX	02097932	309/345-3828	141
REGIONAL OFFICE OF ED 35/			
OTTAWA/LA SALLE	02098003	815/434-0780	146
REGIONAL OFFICE OF ED 40/			
CARLINVILLE/MACOUPIN	02098091	217/854-4016	169
REGIONAL OFFICE OF ED 41/			
EDWARDSVILLE/MADISON	02098106	618/296-4530	174
REGIONAL OFFICE OF ED 47/			
STERLING/WHITESIDE	02098209	815/625-1495	241
REGIONAL OFFICE OF ED 48/			
PEORIA/PEORIA	02098211	309/672-6906	201
REGIONAL OFFICE OF ED 53/			
PEKIN/TAZEWELL	02098390	309/477-2290	229
REGIONAL OFFICE OF ED 54/			
DANVILLE/VERMILION	01536686	217/431-2668	233
REGIONAL OFFICE OF ED KANE CO/			
GENEVA/KANE	02097906	630/232-5955	134
REGIONAL OFFICE OF EDUCATION 3/			
VANDALIA/FAYETTE	04177693	618/283-5011	106
REGIONAL OFFICE-CAREER TECH ED/			
SPRINGFIELD/SANGAMON	04180432	217/529-3716	215
Regional Safe Sch/Peru/La Salle	12239328	815/220-3560	141
Reilly Elem Sch/Chicago/Cook	00280640	773/534-5250	31
Reinberg Elem Sch/Chicago/Cook	00280652	773/534-3465	29
Renfro Elem Sch/Collinsville/Madison	00308436	618/346-6265	170
Reskin Elem Sch/Glendale HTS/Du Page	00290621	630/469-0612	97
Resurrection College Prep HS/Chicago/Cook	00284373	773/775-6616	74
Resurrection Lutheran Sch/Aurora/Kane	01779797	630/907-1313	133
Revere Elem Sch/Chicago/Cook	00276431	773/535-0618	35
Rhodes Elem Sch/River Grove/Cook	00273441	708/453-6813	64
Rhodes Sch of Global Studies/Skokie/Cook	00269359	847/859-8440	48
RHODES SCH DIST 84 1/2/RIVER GROVE/			
COOK	00273439	708/453-1266	64
Rice Education Center/Evanston/Cook	10022492	847/424-2450	48
Rich Twp High Sch STEM/Olympia FLDS/Cook	00273465	708/679-5600	64
RICH TWP HIGH SCH DIST 227/			
MATTESON/COOK	00273453	708/679-5800	64
Rich Twp HS Fine Arts Com/Richton Park/Cook	00273489	708/679-3000	64
Richard D Crosby Elem Sch/Harvard/McHenry	00305549	815/943-6125	181
Richard E Byrd Elem Sch/Burbank/Cook	00274495	708/499-3049	24
Richard T Crane Med Prep HS/Chicago/Cook	11926229	773/534-7600	37
Richards Career Academy/Chicago/Cook	00278491	773/535-4945	37
Richardson Middle Sch/Chicago/Cook	12179170	773/535-8640	34
RICHLAND CO CMTY UNIT SD 1/			
OLNEY/RICHLAND	00315219	618/395-2324	206
Richland Co Elem Sch/Olney/Richland	00315233	618/395-8540	206
Richland Co High Sch/Olney/Richland	00315271	618/393-2191	206
Richland Co Middle Sch/Olney/Richland	00315283	618/395-4372	206
Richland Elem Sch/Crest Hill/Will	00325733	815/744-6166	247
RICHLAND SCH DIST 88A/CREST HILL/			
WILL	00325721	815/744-6166	247
Richmond Burton Cmty High Sch/Richmond/McHenry	00305915	815/678-4525	184
Richmond Grade Sch/Richmond/McHenry	00305898	815/678-4717	183
Richmond Intermediate Sch/Saint Charles/Kane	12370219	331/228-2800	129
RICHMOND-BURTON CMTY HSD 157/			
RICHMOND/MCHENRY	00305903	815/678-4242	183
Richton Square Sch/Richton Park/Cook	10795285	708/283-2706	57
Richwoods High Sch/Peoria/Peoria	00312994	309/693-4400	199
Rickover Junior High Sch/Sauk Village/Cook	00273817	708/758-1900	44
Rickover Naval Academy/Chicago/Cook	10009165	773/534-2890	28
Riddle Elem Sch/Mattoon/Coles	00266709	217/238-3800	19
Ridge Academy/Chicago/Cook	04929458	773/233-0033	80
Ridge Central Elem Sch/Chicago Ridge/Cook	00268537	708/636-2001	42
Ridge Circle Elem Sch/Streamwood/Kane	00298489	630/213-5600	131
Ridge Early Childhood Center/Oak Forest/Cook	00269775	708/687-2964	50
Ridge Elem Sch/Plainfield/Will	05070464	815/577-4630	246
Ridge Family Center for Lrng/Elk Grove Vlg/Cook	04942321	847/593-4070	44
Ridge Lawn Elem Sch/Chicago Ridge/Cook	00268551	708/636-2002	42
RIDGELAND SCH DIST 122/OAK LAWN/			
COOK	00272124	708/599-5550	64
Ridgely Elem Sch/Springfield/Sangamon	00319124	217/525-3259	213

School/City/County DISTRICT/CITY/COUNTY	PID	TELEPHONE NUMBER	PAGE
RIDGEVIEW CMTY UNIT SD 19/			
COLFAX/MCLEAN	00306323	309/723-5111	187
Ridgeview Elem Sch/Colfax/Mclean	00306347	309/723-6531	187
Ridgeview Elem Sch/Peoria/Peoria	04939568	309/243-7717	196
Ridgeview Jr Sr High Sch/Colfax/Mclean	04354528	309/723-2951	187
RIDGEWOOD CMTY HSD 234/NORRIDGE/			
COOK	00273491	708/456-4242	64
Ridgewood Elem Sch/East Moline/Rock Island	00315453	309/755-1585	207
Ridgewood Elem Sch/Rock Island/Rock Island	00315984	309/793-5980	208
Ridgewood High Sch/Norridge/Cook	00273506	708/456-4242	64
RILEY CMTY CONS SCH DIST 18/			
MARENGO/MCHENRY	00305927	815/568-8637	184
Riley Community Cons Sch/Marengo/McHenry	00305939	815/568-8637	184
Riley Early Childhood Center/Harvey/Cook	04795439	708/210-3960	52
Ringwood School Primary Ctr/Ringwood/McHenry	00305680	815/728-0459	182
RIVER BEND CMTY SCH DIST 2/			
FULTON/WHITESIDE	00324337	815/589-2711	239
River Bend Middle Sch/Fulton/Whiteside	00324375	815/589-2611	239
RIVER FOREST SCH DIST 90/			
RIVER FOREST/COOK	00273518	708/771-8282	65
River Grove Elem Sch/River Grove/Cook	00273582	708/453-6172	65
RIVER GROVE SCH DIST 85-5/			
RIVER GROVE/COOK	00273570	708/453-6172	65
RIVER RIDGE CMTY UNIT SD 210/			
HANOVER/JO DAVIESS	00297150	815/858-9005	126
River Ridge Elem Sch/Hanover/Jo Daviess	00297162	815/858-9005	126
River Ridge High Sch/Hanover/Jo Daviess	11457864	815/858-9005	126
River Ridge Middle Sch/Hanover/Jo Daviess	11457852	815/858-9005	126
River Trail Sch/Gurnee/Lake	05303572	847/249-6253	150
River Trails ELC at Parkview/Mt Prospect/Cook	12308979	224/612-7800	65
River Trails Middle Sch/Mt Prospect/Cook	00273659	847/298-1750	65
RIVER TRAILS SCH DIST 26/			
MT PROSPECT/COOK	00273594	847/297-4120	65
River Valley Sch/Lemont/Cook	00289103	630/257-2286	55
River View Elem Sch/Plainfield/Will	04866662	815/439-4840	246
River Woods Elem Sch/Naperville/Du Page	03018733	630/420-6630	98
River's Edge Sch/Granite City/Madison	11730290	618/451-0552	173
Riverdahl Elem Sch/Rockford/Winnebago	03401659	815/229-2870	254
RIVERDALE CMTY UNIT SD 100/			
PORT BYRON/ROCK ISLAND	00315752	309/523-3184	208
Riverdale Elem Sch/Port Byron/Rock Island	00315764	309/523-3186	208
Riverdale Middle Sch/Port Byron/Rock Island	00315817	309/523-3131	208
Riverdale Preschool Center/Rock Falls/Whiteside	11817111	815/625-5280	240
Riverdale Sch/Riverdale/Cook	00268903	708/849-7153	46
Riverdale Senior High Sch/Port Byron/Rock Island	00315805	309/523-3181	208
Rivers of Life Christian Sch/Granite City/Madison	01753468	618/797-7933	173
Riverside Christian Sch/Andalusia/Rock Island	00316196	309/798-2857	209
RIVERSIDE PUBLIC SCH DIST 96/			
RIVERSIDE/COOK	00273673	708/447-5007	65
Riverside-Brookfield Twp HS/Riverside/Cook	00273740	708/442-7500	65
RIVERSIDE-BROOKFLD TWP SD 208/			
RIVERSIDE/COOK	00273738	708/442-7500	65
RIVERTON CMTY UNIT SD 14/			
RIVERTON/SANGAMON	00318728	217/629-6009	212
Riverton Elem Sch/Riverton/Sangamon	00318730	217/629-6001	212
Riverton High Sch/Riverton/Sangamon	00318742	217/629-6003	212
Riverton Middle Sch/Riverton/Sangamon	01530307	217/629-6002	212
RIVERVIEW CMTY CONS SCH DIST 2/			
EAST PEORIA/WOODFORD	00329155	309/822-8550	258
Riverview Elem Sch/East Peoria/Woodford	00329167	309/822-8550	258
Riverview Elem Sch/South Beloit/Winnebago	00328216	815/389-1231	255
Riverwood Elem Sch/McHenry/McHenry	03249293	779/244-1400	183
ROANOKE-BENSON CMTY UNIT SD 60/			
ROANOKE/WOODFORD	00329179	309/923-8921	258
Roanoke-Benson High Sch/Roanoke/Woodford	00329181	309/923-8401	258
Roanoke-Benson Jr High Sch/Benson/Woodford	00329193	309/394-2233	258
Robbie M Lightfoot ELC/Waukegan/Lake	10908779	224/303-1400	156
ROBEIN CMTY SCH DIST 85/			
EAST PEORIA/TAZEWELL	00321658	309/694-1409	228
Robein Grade Sch/East Peoria/Tazewell	00321660	309/694-1409	228
Robert A Black Magnet Sch/Chicago/Cook	00275102	773/535-6390	35
Robert A Jamieson Sch/Peoria/Peoria	01398343	309/672-6594	199
Robert Abbott Middle Sch/Waukegan/Lake	04013188	224/303-2360	156
Robert Crown Elem Sch/Wauconda/Lake	00302030	847/526-7100	155
Robert E Clow Elem Sch/Naperville/Du Page	02055776	630/428-6060	96

Illinois School Directory
DISTRICT & SCHOOL TELEPHONE INDEX

School/City/County DISTRICT/CITY/COUNTY	PID	TELEPHONE NUMBER	PAGE
Robert Frost Elem Sch/Mt Prospect/Cook	00267375	847/593-4378	44
Robert Frost Elem Sch/Mt Prospect/Cook	00281412	847/803-4815	71
Robert Frost Jr High Sch/Schaumburg/Cook	00274067	847/357-6800	67
Robert Hill Elem Sch/Romeoville/Will	00325642	815/886-4343	248
Robert Nathaniel Dett Elem Sch/Chicago/Cook	00277186	773/534-7160	32
Robertson Charter Sch/Decatur/Macon	04948806	217/428-7072	165
Robeson Elem Sch/Champaign/Champaign	00264854	217/351-3884	10
Robina Lyle Elem Sch/Bridgeview/Cook	00268173	708/496-8722	53
ROBINSON CMTY UNIT SCH DIST 2/ROBINSON/CRAWFORD	00287820	618/544-7511	83
Robinson High Sch/Robinson/Crawford	00287868	618/544-9510	83
ROCHELLE CMTY CONS SD 231/ROCHELLE/OGLE	00312176	815/562-6363	195
Rochelle Middle Sch/Rochelle/Ogle	00312217	815/562-7997	195
Rochelle Twp High Sch/Rochelle/Ogle	00312164	815/562-4161	195
ROCHELLE TWP HIGH SCH DIST 212/ROCHELLE/OGLE	00312152	815/562-4161	195
Rochelle Zell Jewish High Sch/Deerfield/Lake	10752960	847/470-6700	158
ROCHESTER CMTY UNIT SD 3-A/ROCHESTER/SANGAMON	00318845	217/498-6210	212
Rochester Elem Sch 2-3/Rochester/Sangamon	11710393	217/498-6216	212
Rochester Elem Sch EC-1/Rochester/Sangamon	00318857	217/498-9778	212
Rochester High Sch/Rochester/Sangamon	00318869	217/498-9761	212
Rochester Intermediate Sch/Rochester/Sangamon	04311801	217/498-6215	212
Rochester Junior High Sch/Rochester/Sangamon	00318871	217/498-9761	212
Rock Cut Elem Sch/Loves Park/Winnebago	00327250	815/654-4506	253
ROCK FALLS ELEM SCH DIST 13/ROCK FALLS/WHITESIDE	00324416	815/626-2604	240
Rock Falls Middle Sch/Rock Falls/Whiteside	00324442	815/626-2626	240
Rock Falls Township High Sch/Rock Falls/Whiteside	00324478	815/625-3886	240
ROCK FALLS TWP HIGH SD 301/ROCK FALLS/WHITESIDE	00324466	815/625-3886	240
Rock Island Academy/Rock Island/Rock Island	00315934	309/793-5944	208
Rock Island Ctr Math & Science/Rock Island/Rock Island	11462156	309/793-5995	208
Rock Island High Sch/Rock Island/Rock Island	00315996	309/793-5950	208
ROCK ISLAND REG OFF OF ED 49/MOLINE/ROCK ISLAND	02098302	309/736-1111	210
ROCK ISLAND-MILAN SCH DIST 41/ROCK ISLAND/ROCK ISLAND	00315831	309/793-5900	208
Rockdale Elem Sch/Rockdale/Will	00325757	815/725-5321	247
ROCKDALE SCH DIST 84/ROCKDALE/WILL	00325745	815/725-5321	247
Rockford Christian Elem Sch/Rockford/Winnebago	11420990	815/391-8006	256
Rockford Christian High Sch/Rockford/Winnebago	01405568	815/399-3465	256
Rockford East High Sch/Rockford/Winnebago	00327559	815/229-2100	254
Rockford Env Science Academy/Rockford/Winnebago	04870297	815/489-5509	254
Rockford Innovative Lrng Ctr/Rockford/Winnebago	12320513	815/977-3766	254
Rockford Iqra Sch/Rockford/Winnebago	11232286	815/397-6899	256
Rockford Lutheran Academy/Rockford/Winnebago	04320345	815/226-4947	256
Rockford Lutheran High Sch/Rockford/Winnebago	01442865	815/877-9551	256
ROCKFORD SCH DIST 205/ROCKFORD/WINNEBAGO	00327406	815/966-3000	253
Rockland Elem Sch/Libertyville/Lake	00301505	847/362-3134	153
ROCKRIDGE CMTY UNIT SD 300/TAYLOR RIDGE/ROCK ISLAND	00316031	309/793-8001	209
Rockridge High Sch/Taylor Ridge/Rock Island	00316081	309/793-8020	209
Rockridge Junior High Sch/Taylor Ridge/Rock Island	00316093	309/793-8040	209
Rockton Grade Sch/Rockton/Winnebago	00328163	815/624-8585	255
ROCKTON SCH DIST 140/ROCKTON/WINNEBAGO	00328151	815/624-7143	255
Rogers Elem Sch/Chicago/Cook	00280688	773/534-2125	28
Rogers Elem Sch/Pekin/Tazewell	00321414	309/382-3401	227
Rogers Elem Sch/Waterloo/Monroe	04015435	618/939-3454	190
Rogers Park Montessori Sch/Chicago/Cook	02432796	773/271-1700	80
Rolling Acres Middle Sch/Peoria/Peoria	00313003	309/689-1100	199
Rolling Green Elem Sch/Rockford/Winnebago	00327951	815/229-2881	254
Rolling Meadows High Sch/Rolling MDWS/Cook	00271716	847/718-5600	70
ROME CMTY CONS SCH DIST 2/DIX/JEFFERSON	00296895	618/266-7214	123
Rome Elem Sch/Dix/Jefferson	00296900	618/266-7214	124
Romeoville Christian Academy/Romeoville/Will	00325939	815/886-4850	250
Romeoville High Sch/Romeoville/Will	00325666	815/886-1800	248
Romona Elem Sch/Wilmette/Cook	00281632	847/512-6400	72
Ronald McNair Elem Sch/Chicago/Cook	01532513	773/534-8980	26
Rondout Elem Sch/Lake Forest/Lake	00301957	847/362-2021	154
RONDOUT SCH DIST 72/LAKE FOREST/LAKE	00301945	847/362-2021	154
ROOKS CREEK CMTY CONS SD 425/GRAYMONT/LIVINGSTON	00304466	815/743-5346	162
Rooney Elem Sch/Quincy/Adams	02199047	217/228-7117	2
Roosevelt Cmty Education Ctr/Rockford/Winnebago	04020351	815/966-3250	254
Roosevelt Elem Sch/Broadview/Cook	00271429	708/450-2047	57
Roosevelt Elem Sch/Chicago HTS/Cook	00268484	708/756-4836	25
Roosevelt Elem Sch/Dolton/Cook	00268941	708/201-2070	46
Roosevelt Elem Sch/Moline/Rock Island	00315702	309/743-1617	208
Roosevelt Elem Sch/Park Ridge/Cook	00273154	847/318-4235	62
Roosevelt High Sch/Chicago/Cook	00280690	773/534-5000	36
Roosevelt Junior High Sch/Dolton/Cook	12108042	708/201-2071	46
Roosevelt Magnet Sch/Peoria/Peoria	00313015	309/672-6574	199
Roosevelt Middle Sch/Bellwood/Cook	00267674	708/410-3906	22
Roosevelt Middle Sch/River Forest/Cook	00273532	708/366-9230	65
Roosevelt Sch/Belleville/St Clair	00316328	618/233-1608	217
Rosa G Maddock Elem Sch/Burbank/Cook	00274536	708/598-0515	24
Rosa L Parks Middle Sch/Dixmoor/Cook	00270102	708/371-9575	70
Rosary High Sch/Aurora/Kane	00328503	630/896-0831	133
Roscoe Middle Sch/Roscoe/Winnebago	04921585	815/623-2837	253
Rose E Krug Elem Sch/Aurora/Kane	00297629	630/299-5280	129
Rosecrance Sch-G Williamson/Rockford/Winnebago	02159267	844/711-5106	1
Roselle Middle Sch/Roselle/Du Page	00291209	630/529-1600	99
ROSELLE SCH DIST 12/ROSELLE/DU PAGE	00291170	630/529-2091	99
Rosemont Elem Sch/Rosemont/Cook	00273764	847/825-0144	66
ROSEMONT ELEM SCH DIST 78/ROSEMONT/COOK	00273752	847/825-0144	66
Roslyn Road Elem Sch/Barrington/Lake	00267583	847/381-4148	147
ROSSVILLE-ALVIN CMTY UNIT SD 7/ROSSVILLE/VERMILION	00322755	217/748-6666	233
Rossville-Alvin Elem & JHS/Rossville/Vermilion	00322767	217/748-6666	233
Roswell Mason Elem Sch/Chicago/Cook	00278087	773/534-1530	31
Rotolo Middle School-Batavia/Batavia/Kane	00297851	630/937-8700	128
ROUND LAKE AREA CO DIST 116/ROUND LAKE/LAKE	00301878	847/270-9000	154
Round Lake High Sch/Round Lake/Lake	00301921	847/270-9300	155
Round Lake Middle Sch/Round Lake/Lake	00301892	847/270-9400	155
Routt Catholic High Sch/Jacksonville/Morgan	00319552	217/243-8563	193
Rowe Elem Charter Sch/Chicago/Cook	11444245	312/445-5870	41
Rowva Central Elem Sch/Oneida/Knox	02055805	309/483-6376	140
ROWVA CMTY SCH DIST 208/ONEIDA/KNOX	00300240	309/483-3711	140
Rowva Jr Sr High Sch/Oneida/Knox	00300288	309/483-6371	140
ROXANA CMTY UNIT SCH DIST 1/ROXANA/MADISON	00309088	618/254-7544	172
Roxana Junior High Sch/Roxana/Madison	00309129	618/254-7561	172
Roxana Senior High Sch/Roxana/Madison	00309131	618/254-7551	172
Roy Deshane Elem Sch/Carol Stream/Du Page	00289189	630/588-6300	90
Roy Elem Sch/Northlake/Cook	00271118	847/451-2700	57
Roycemore Sch/Evanston/Cook	00282064	847/866-6055	80
Ruben Salazar Bilingual Center/Chicago/Cook	02107525	773/534-8310	28
Ruggles Elem Sch/Chicago/Cook	00276455	773/535-3085	35
Ruiz Elem Sch/Chicago/Cook	03336559	773/535-4825	32
Rupley Elem Sch/Elk Grove Vlg/Cook	00267387	847/593-4353	44
RURAL CHAMPAIGN CO SP ED CO-OP/CHAMPAIGN/CHAMPAIGN	02182240	217/892-8877	13
Rush Day Sch/Chicago/Cook	01844110	312/942-6627	80
Rushville-Industry High Sch/Rushville/Schuyler	00320173	217/322-4311	215
Russell Elem Sch/Litchfield/Montgomery	00311172	217/324-4034	191
Ruth M Schneider Elem Sch/Farmer City/Dewitt	00288616	309/928-2611	87
RUTLAND CMTY CONS SD 230/OTTAWA/LA SALLE	00303319	815/433-2949	144
Rutland Grade Sch/Ottawa/La Salle	00303321	815/433-2949	144

DISTRICT & SCHOOL TELEPHONE INDEX

Market Data Retrieval

School/City/County DISTRICT/CITY/COUNTY	PID	TELEPHONE NUMBER	PAGE
Rutledge Hall Elem Sch/Lincolnwood/Cook	00270889	847/675-8236	56
Ryan Banks Academy/Chicago/Cook	12318261	312/585-5883	80
Ryder Math & Sci Elem Sch/Chicago/Cook	00276467	773/535-3843	35

S

School/City/County	PID	TELEPHONE	PAGE
S WILMINGTON CONS ELEM SD 74/ S WILMINGTON/GRUNDY	00294392	815/237-2281	113
S Wilmington Grade Sch/S Wilmington/Grundy	00294407	815/237-2281	113
Sabio Academy/Buffalo Grove/Lake	05360116	847/219-8817	158
Sacred Heart Sch/Chicago/Cook	00282947	773/262-4446	80
Sacred Heart Sch/Chicago/Cook	00284426	773/768-3728	74
Sacred Heart Sch/Effingham/Effingham	00319617	217/342-4060	105
Sacred Heart Sch/Lombard/Du Page	00326141	630/629-0536	101
Sacred Heart Sch/Melrose Park/Cook	00284414	708/681-0240	74
Sacred Heart Sch/Pana/Christian	00319588	217/562-2425	15
Sacred Heart Sch/Winnetka/Cook	00284402	847/446-0005	74
Sacred Heart-Griffin High Sch/Springfield/Sangamon	00319564	217/787-1595	214
Sager Solomon Schechter Sch/Northbrook/Cook	01441847	847/498-2100	80
Saint Andrew Sch/Chicago/Cook	00284684	773/248-2500	74
Sainte Marie Elem Sch/Sainte Marie/Jasper	00296546	618/455-3219	122
Salem Christian Sch/Chicago/Cook	00281876	773/227-5580	80
Salem Cmty High Sch/Salem/Marion	00309806	618/548-0727	175
SALEM CMTY HIGH SCH DIST 600/ SALEM/MARION	00309791	618/548-0727	175
SALEM ELEM SCH DIST 111/ SALEM/MARION	00309741	618/548-7702	175
Salem Lutheran Sch/Jacksonville/Morgan	01559925	217/243-3419	193
Salem4Youth Valor High Sch/Flanagan/Livingston	12361567	815/796-4561	163
Salt Creek Elem Sch/Elk Grove Vlg/Cook	00267399	847/593-4375	44
Salt Creek Primary Sch/Elmhurst/Du Page	00291247	630/832-6122	99
SALT CREEK SCH DIST 48/VILLA PARK/DU PAGE	00291223	630/279-8400	99
SALT FORK CMTY UNIT SD 512/ CATLIN/VERMILION	00322781	217/427-2116	233
Salt Fork High Sch/Catlin/Vermilion	00322200	217/427-2468	233
Salt Fork North Elem Sch/Catlin/Vermilion	00322195	217/427-5421	233
Salt Fork South Elem Jr HS/Sidell/Vermilion	00322793	217/288-9306	233
San Miguel Sch-Back Yard/Chicago/Cook	04990756	773/890-1481	80
Sandburg Elem Sch/Joliet/Will	05100980	815/725-0281	243
Sandburg Elem Sch/Springfield/Sangamon	00319148	217/787-3112	213
Sandburg Middle Sch/Elmhurst/Du Page	00289608	630/834-4534	94
Sanders Academy of Excellence/Chicago/Cook	04999984	773/568-7240	80
Sanders Academy-Excellence/Chicago/Cook	11230446	773/568-7240	80
SANDOVAL CMTY UNIT SD 501/ SANDOVAL/MARION	00309818	618/247-3233	175
Sandoval Elem Sch/Chicago/Cook	04882886	773/535-0457	33
Sandoval Elem Sch/Sandoval/Marion	00309820	618/247-3450	175
Sandoval Jr Sr High Sch/Sandoval/Marion	00309832	618/247-3361	175
Sandridge Elem Sch/Chicago HTS/Cook	00273788	708/895-2450	66
SANDRIDGE SCH DIST 172/CHICAGO HTS/COOK	00273776	708/895-8339	66
Sandwich Cmty High Sch/Sandwich/De Kalb	00288252	815/786-2157	86
SANDWICH CMTY UNIT SD 430/ SANDWICH/DE KALB	00288214	815/786-2187	85
Sandwich Middle Sch/Sandwich/De Kalb	00288264	815/786-2138	86
SANGAMON AREA SPEC ED DIST/ SPRINGFIELD/SANGAMON	02182147	217/786-3250	215
SANGAMON VALLEY CMTY UNIT SD 9/ NIANTIC/MACON	00307482	217/668-2338	166
Sangamon Valley High Sch/Niantic/Macon	04027957	217/668-2392	166
Sangamon Valley Intermed Sch/Illiopolis/Macon	00318651	217/486-7521	166
Sangamon Valley Middle Sch/Illiopolis/Macon	00307509	217/486-2241	166
Sangamon Valley Primary Sch/Harristown/Macon	00307494	217/963-2621	166
SANGAMON-MENARD ROE #51/ SPRINGFIELD/SANGAMON	02098352	217/753-6620	215
Santa Lucia Grammar Sch/Chicago/Cook	00284488	312/326-1839	74
Sarah Adams Elem Sch/Lake Zurich/Lake	02106741	847/438-5986	152
Sarah E Goode STEM Academy/Chicago/Cook	11824607	773/535-7875	37
Sarah Raymond Early Chldhd Ctr/Bloomington/Mclean	04033504	309/827-0308	185
SARATOGA CMTY CONS SD 60C/ MORRIS/GRUNDY	00294378	815/942-2128	113
Saratoga Elem Sch/Morris/Grundy	00294380	815/942-2128	113
Sased Central Sch/Springfield/Sangamon	04198087	217/786-3250	211
Sator Sanchez Elem Sch/Joliet/Will	05276474	815/740-2810	243
Sauganash Elem Sch/Chicago/Cook	00280731	773/534-3470	28
Sauk Elem Sch/Richton Park/Cook	00271326	708/747-2660	57
SAUNEMIN CMTY CONS SD 438/ SAUNEMIN/LIVINGSTON	00304480	815/832-4421	162
Saunemin Elem Sch/Saunemin/Livingston	00304492	815/832-4421	162
Sawyer Elem Sch/Chicago/Cook	00278520	773/535-9275	33
Sayre Language Academy/Chicago/Cook	00280743	773/534-3351	30
SCALES MOUND CMTY UNIT SD 211/ SCALES MOUND/JO DAVIESS	00297241	815/845-2215	126
Scales Mound Elem Sch/Scales Mound/Jo Daviess	00297253	815/845-2215	126
Scales Mound High Sch/Scales Mound/Jo Daviess	11445782	815/845-2215	126
Scales Mound Junior High Sch/Scales Mound/Jo Daviess	11445770	815/845-2215	126
Scammon Elem Sch/Chicago/Cook	00280755	773/534-3475	29
Scarlet Oak Elem Sch/Oak Forest/Cook	00266979	708/687-5822	21
Sch Exp Arts & Lrng-Lombard/Lombard/Du Page	12467288	630/953-1222	102
Sch Exp Arts & Lrng-Romeoville/Romeoville/Will	12467290	630/226-0004	250
Sch Exp Arts & Lrng-Woodstock/Woodstock/McHenry	12234897	815/337-2005	185
Schafer Elem Sch/Lombard/Du Page	00291376	630/516-6500	99
Schaumburg Christian Sch/Schaumburg/Cook	02189793	847/885-3230	80
SCHAUMBURG CMTY CONS SD 54/ SCHAUMBURG/COOK	00273843	847/357-5000	66
Schaumburg High Sch/Schaumburg/Cook	00272760	847/755-4600	69
Schiller Elem Sch/Centralia/Marion	00309557	618/533-7140	174
SCHILLER PARK SCH DIST 81/ SCHILLER PARK/COOK	00274110	847/671-1816	67
Schlarman Academy/Danville/Vermilion	00313546	217/442-2725	233
Schmid Elem Sch/Chicago/Cook	00276508	773/535-6235	35
Schneider Elem Sch/North Aurora/Kane	00297796	630/301-5014	132
SCHOOL ASSOC FOR SP ED-DUPAGE/ LISLE/DU PAGE	02097736	630/778-4500	102
SCHOOL DIST 45 DUPAGE CO/ VILLA PARK/DU PAGE	00291261	630/516-7700	99
School of Fine Arts/Calumet City/Cook	11831997	708/868-7565	46
School of St Mary/Lake Forest/Lake	00284490	847/234-0371	157
Schramm Education Center/Pekin/Tazewell	02833401	309/346-1186	225
Schrum Memorial Sch/Calumet City/Cook	00270449	708/862-4236	52
Schubert Elem Sch/Chicago/Cook	00280793	773/534-3080	30
Schurz High Sch/Chicago/Cook	00280808	773/534-3420	36
SCHUYLER-INDUSTRY CUSD 5/ RUSHVILLE/SCHUYLER	00320135	217/322-4311	215
Schuyler-Industry Middle Sch/Rushville/Schuyler	00320185	217/322-4311	215
Science & Arts Academy/Des Plaines/Cook	04328567	847/827-7880	80
Science Academy of Chicago/Mt Prospect/Cook	11239650	847/258-5254	80
Scott Altman Primary Sch/Pekin/Tazewell	00321531	309/477-4715	228
Scott Elem Sch/Melrose Park/Cook	00271120	847/455-4818	57
Scott Elem Sch/Naperville/Du Page	01825243	630/420-6477	98
Scott Elem Sch/Scott Afb/St Clair	00317334	618/746-4738	220
SCOTT MORGAN CMTY UNIT SD 2/ BLUFFS/SCOTT	00320214	217/754-3714	215
Scullen Middle Sch/Naperville/Du Page	04938899	630/428-7000	96
Scuola Italiana Enrico Fermi/Chicago/Cook	12318273	312/971-8064	80
SE Gross Middle Sch/Brookfield/Cook	00268214	708/485-0600	24
SELMAVILLE CMTY CONS SD 10/ SALEM/MARION	00309844	618/548-2416	176
Selmaville Elem Sch/Salem/Marion	00309868	618/548-2416	176
SENECA CMTY CONS SCH DIST 170/ SENECA/LA SALLE	01557848	815/357-8744	144
Seneca North Elem Sch/Seneca/La Salle	00303345	815/357-8744	144
Seneca South Elem Sch/Seneca/La Salle	04801923	815/357-8744	144
Seneca Township High Sch/Seneca/La Salle	00303357	815/357-5000	144
SENECA TWP HIGH SCH DIST 160/ SENECA/LA SALLE	00303333	815/357-5000	144
SERENA CMTY UNIT SCH DIST 2/ SERENA/LA SALLE	01559236	815/496-2850	144
Serena High Sch/Serena/La Salle	00303383	815/496-2361	144
Serena Hills Elem Sch/Chicago HTS/Cook	00269660	708/647-7300	49
Serena Middle Sch/Serena/La Salle	00303371	815/496-9250	144
SESSER-VALIER CMTY UNIT SD 196/ SESSER/FRANKLIN	00293104	618/625-5105	108
Sesser-Valier Elem Sch/Sesser/Franklin	01844677	618/625-5105	108
Sesser-Valier High Sch/Sesser/Franklin	04364614	618/625-5105	108
Sesser-Valier Jr High Sch/Sesser/Franklin	04364602	618/625-5105	108
Seth Paine Elem Sch/Lake Zurich/Lake	00301438	847/438-2163	152

Illinois School Directory
DISTRICT & SCHOOL TELEPHONE INDEX

School/City/County DISTRICT/CITY/COUNTY	PID	TELEPHONE NUMBER	PAGE
Seth Whitman Elem Sch/Belvidere/Boone	10905208	815/544-3357	4
Seton Academy/Villa Park/Du Page	03199753	630/279-4101	102
Seton Catholic Sch/Moline/Rock Island	00313508	309/757-5500	209
Seventh Ave Elem Sch/La Grange/Cook	00270683	708/482-2730	54
Seventh Day Adventist Sch/Sheridan/La Salle	04990718	815/496-2947	145
Seward Communctn Arts Acad/Chicago/Cook	00278532	773/535-4890	33
Seymour Elem Sch/Payson/Adams	00263018	217/656-3439	2
Seymour Jr Sr High Sch/Payson/Adams	00263020	217/656-3355	2
Shabazz CS-Sizemore Acad/Chicago/Cook	04755673	773/651-1661	1
Shabazz CS-Betty Shabbazz Acd/Chicago/Cook	04812013	773/651-1221	1
Shabbona Elem Sch/Bourbonnais/Kankakee	00298984	815/929-4700	134
Shabonee Sch/Northbrook/Cook	00271962	847/498-4970	59
SHAWNEE CMTY UNIT SCH DIST 84/ **WOLF LAKE/UNION**	00322004	618/833-5709	231
Shawnee Elem Sch/Wolf Lake/Union	00322016	618/833-4975	231
Shawnee Hills Chrn Academy/Anna/Union	11232133	618/833-1870	231
Shawnee Jr Sr High Sch/Wolf Lake/Union	00322030	618/833-5307	231
Sheila Daniels Christian Acad/Waukegan/Lake	05377860	847/263-8147	158
SHELBYVILLE CMTY SCH DIST 4/ **SHELBYVILLE/SHELBY**	00320381	217/774-4626	216
Shelbyville High Sch/Shelbyville/Shelby	00320410	217/774-3926	216
Shepherd Middle Sch/Ottawa/La Salle	00303228	815/434-7925	143
Sheridan Elem Sch/Bloomington/Mclean	00306268	309/828-2359	185
Sheridan Elem Sch/Lake Forest/Lake	00301294	847/234-1160	152
Sheridan Grade Sch/Sheridan/La Salle	00303400	815/496-2002	144
Sheridan Math & Science Acad/Chicago/Cook	00278049	773/534-9120	28
Sherlock Elem Sch/Cicero/Cook	12472609	708/652-8885	42
Sherman Elem Sch/Chicago/Cook	00278568	773/535-1757	26
Sherman Elem Sch/Sherman/Sangamon	00319306	217/496-2021	214
SHERRARD CMTY SCH DIST 200/ **SHERRARD/MERCER**	00310702	309/593-4075	189
Sherrard Elem Sch/Sherrard/Mercer	00310738	309/593-2917	189
Sherrard Jr Sr High Sch/Sherrard/Mercer	01821778	309/593-2135	189
Sherwood Elem Sch/Chicago/Cook	00278570	773/535-0829	28
Sherwood Elem Sch/Highland Park/Lake	00301062	224/765-3800	154
Shiloh Community Sch/Hume/Edgar	00291950	217/887-2364	103
Shiloh Middle Sch/Shiloh/St Clair	10011388	618/632-7434	221
Shiloh Park Elem Sch/Zion/Lake	00302523	847/746-8136	157
SHILOH SCH DIST 1/HUME/EDGAR	00291948	217/887-2364	103
Shiloh Village Elem Sch/Shiloh/St Clair	00317530	618/632-7448	221
SHILOH VILLAGE SCH DIST 85/ **SHILOH/ST CLAIR**	00317528	618/632-7434	221
Shipman Elem Sch/Shipman/Macoupin	00307901	618/372-3813	168
Shirland Cmty Cons Sch/Shirland/Winnebago	00328187	815/629-2000	255
SHIRLAND CMTY CONS SD 134/ **SHIRLAND/WINNEBAGO**	00328175	815/629-2000	255
Shoesmith Elem Sch/Chicago/Cook	00276558	773/535-1765	33
Shoop Math-Sci Tech Elem Acad/Chicago/Cook	00276560	773/535-2715	36
Sieden Prairie Elem Sch/Matteson/Cook	00274184	708/720-2626	47
Signal Hill Elem Sch/Belleville/St Clair	00317554	618/397-0325	221
SIGNAL HILL SCH DIST 181/ **BELLEVILLE/ST CLAIR**	00317542	618/397-0325	221
Silas Willard Elem Sch/Galesburg/Knox	00300135	309/973-2015	140
Silver Creek Elem Sch/Troy/Madison	00309179	618/667-5403	172
SILVIS SCH DIST 34/EAST MOLINE/ **ROCK ISLAND**	00316110	309/792-9325	209
Simeon Career Academy/Chicago/Cook	00276572	773/535-3200	38
Simmons Middle Sch/Oak Lawn/Cook	00272174	708/599-8540	64
Simpson Acad for Young Women/Chicago/Cook	00278594	773/534-7812	37
Sir Miles Davis Magnet Academy/Chicago/Cook	02055128	773/535-9120	35
Siue East St Louis Charter Sch/E Saint Louis/St Clair	04889913	618/482-6912	219
Skinner North Classical Sch/Chicago/Cook	11446669	773/534-8500	31
Skokie Sch/Winnetka/Cook	04838847	847/441-1750	72
SKOKIE SCH DIST 68/SKOKIE/COOK	00274196	847/676-9000	67
SKOKIE SCH DIST 69/SKOKIE/COOK	00274251	847/675-7666	67
SKOKIE SCH DIST 73 1/2/SKOKIE/COOK	00274304	847/324-0509	67
Sleepy Hollow Elem Sch/Sleepy Hollow/McHenry	00298142	224/484-4900	180
Smith Elem Sch/Aurora/Kane	00297801	630/301-5015	132
Smith Elem Sch/Chicago/Cook	00276792	773/535-5689	36
SMITHTON CMTY CONS SD 130/ **SMITHTON/ST CLAIR**	00317566	618/233-6863	222
Smithton Elem Sch/Smithton/St Clair	00317580	618/233-6863	222
Smyser Elem Sch/Chicago/Cook	00280834	773/534-3711	28
Sol Sch/Chicago/Cook	02827256	773/252-3320	80
Solace Academy/Chicago/Cook	04990811	312/655-7000	80
Solomon Elem Sch/Chicago/Cook	00280846	773/534-5226	29
Somonauk Christian Sch/Somonauk/De Kalb	02189808	815/498-2312	86
SOMONAUK CMTY UNIT SD 432/ **SOMONAUK/DE KALB**	00288331	815/498-2315	86
Somonauk High Sch/Somonauk/De Kalb	00288367	815/498-2314	86
Somonauk Middle Sch/Somonauk/De Kalb	04939025	815/498-1866	86
Sonia Shankman Orthogenic Sch/Chicago/Cook	01441316	773/420-2900	80
Sor Juana Elem Sch/Chicago/Cook	12315178	773/535-8280	33
Sorento Elem Sch/Sorento/Bond	00263379	217/272-4111	4
Sorrick Sch/Palos Hills/Cook	04947175	708/233-8200	59
SOUTH BELOIT CMTY SCH DIST 320/ **SOUTH BELOIT/WINNEBAGO**	00328199	815/389-3478	255
South Beloit High Sch/South Beloit/Winnebago	05090579	815/389-9004	255
South Beloit Jr High Sch/South Beloit/Winnebago	00328228	815/389-1421	255
South Central Cmty Service/Chicago/Cook	03199844	773/374-2223	80
SOUTH CENTRAL CMTY UNIT SD 401/ **KINMUNDY/MARION**	00309636	618/547-3414	176
South Central Elem Sch/Kinmundy/Marion	00309650	618/547-7696	176
South Central High Sch/Farina/Marion	00292514	618/245-2222	176
South Central Middle Sch/Kinmundy/Marion	03240730	618/547-7734	176
SOUTH COOK INTERM SVC CENTER/ **CHICAGO HTS/COOK**	03064718	708/754-6600	82
South Early Childhood Center/Westmont/Du Page	12035407	630/468-8015	92
SOUTH EASTERN SPECIAL ED DIST/ **SAINTE MARIE/JASPER**	02182123	618/455-3396	122
South Elem Sch/Chillicothe/Peoria	00312566	309/274-4841	197
South Elem Sch/Crystal Lake/McHenry	00305434	815/788-5400	181
South Elem Sch/Des Plaines/Cook	00268848	847/824-1566	46
South Elem Sch/Jacksonville/Morgan	00311512	217/245-5514	192
South Elem Sch/Marshall/Clark	00265987	217/826-5411	16
South Elgin High Sch/South Elgin/Kane	10013374	847/289-3760	131
South Fork Elem Sch/Kincaid/Christian	00265602	217/237-4331	15
South Fork Jr Sr High Sch/Kincaid/Christian	00265767	217/237-4333	15
SOUTH FORK SCH DIST 14/KINCAID/ **CHRISTIAN**	00265755	217/237-4333	14
South High Sch/Downers Grove/Du Page	00289359	630/795-8500	91
SOUTH HOLLAND SCH DIST 150/ **SOUTH HOLLAND/COOK**	00274378	708/339-4240	68
SOUTH HOLLAND SCH DIST 151/ **SOUTH HOLLAND/COOK**	00274421	708/339-1516	68
South Loop Elem Sch/Chicago/Cook	03012375	773/534-8690	28
South Middle Sch/Arlington HTS/Cook	00267143	847/398-4250	21
South Park Elem Sch/Deerfield/Lake	00302339	847/945-5895	149
South Pekin Grade Sch/South Pekin/Tazewell	00321684	309/348-3695	228
SOUTH PEKIN GRADE SCH DIST 137/ **SOUTH PEKIN/TAZEWELL**	00321672	309/348-3695	228
South Prairie Elem Sch/Sycamore/De Kalb	04808842	815/899-8299	86
South Primary Sch/South Roxana/Madison	00309143	618/254-7591	172
South Sch/Glencoe/Cook	00269907	847/835-6400	51
South Shore Fine Arts Academy/Chicago/Cook	11454850	773/535-8340	35
South Shore Intl Clg High Sch/Chicago/Cook	11720075	773/535-8350	38
South Shores Elem Sch/Decatur/Macon	00307212	217/362-3320	165
South Side Elem Sch/Champaign/Champaign	03246708	217/351-3890	10
South Side Elem Sch/Effingham/Effingham	00292344	217/540-1530	105
South Suburban SDA Chrn Sch/Park Forest/Cook	01405128	708/481-8909	80
South View Upper Elem Sch/Danville/Vermilion	00322391	217/444-1800	232
Southbury Elem Sch/Oswego/Kendall	11079539	630/551-9800	138
Southeast Alternative Sch/Naperville/Du Page	03078123	630/778-4510	88
Southeast Elem Sch/Evergreen Pk/Cook	00269567	708/422-1021	49
Southeast Elem Sch/Sycamore/De Kalb	00288408	815/899-8219	86
SOUTHEASTERN CMTY UNIT SD 337/ **AUGUSTA/HANCOCK**	00294770	217/392-2172	115
Southeastern Elem Sch/Bowen/Hancock	00294768	217/842-5236	115
Southeastern Jr Sr High Sch/Augusta/Hancock	00294794	217/392-2125	115
Southern View Elem Sch/Springfield/Sangamon	00319198	217/585-5837	213
SOUTHERN WILL CO SPEC ED DIST/ **JOLIET/WILL**	02182276	815/741-7777	250
Southland College Prep Chtr HS/Richton Park/Cook	11548695	708/748-8105	1
Southside Elem Sch/Morrison/Whiteside	00324246	815/772-2183	239
Southside Occupational Academy/Chicago/Cook	03055248	773/535-9100	28
Southwest Chicago Chrn Sch/Oak Lawn/Cook	00281864	708/636-8550	81

School Year 2020-2021 — 800-333-8802 — IL-V39

DISTRICT & SCHOOL TELEPHONE INDEX

Market Data Retrieval

School/City/County DISTRICT/CITY/COUNTY	PID	TELEPHONE NUMBER	PAGE
Southwest Chicago Chrn Sch/Tinley Park/Cook	03014567	708/429-7171	81
SOUTHWEST COOK CO ASSC SPEC ED/OAK FOREST/COOK	02183608	708/687-0900	82
Southwest Elem Sch/Danville/Vermilion	00322236	217/444-3500	232
Southwest Elem Sch/Evergreen Pk/Cook	00269579	708/424-2444	49
Southwest Elem Sch/Geneseo/Henry	00295334	309/945-0699	117
SOUTHWESTERN CMTY UNIT SD 9/BRIGHTON/MACOUPIN	00307860	618/372-3813	168
Southwestern High Sch/Piasa/Macoupin	00307896	618/372-3813	168
Southwestern Middle Sch/Piasa/Macoupin	00307913	618/729-3217	168
Southwood Middle Sch/Cntry CLB Hls/Cook	00268707	708/957-6230	45
Sowers Elem Sch/Roanoke/Woodford	00329208	309/923-6241	258
SPARTA CMTY SCH DIST 140/SPARTA/RANDOLPH	00315063	618/443-5331	205
Sparta High Sch/Sparta/Randolph	00315116	618/443-4341	205
Sparta Lincoln Sch/Sparta/Randolph	00315104	618/443-5331	205
Spaulding Sch/Gurnee/Lake	00301971	847/662-3701	150
Spaulding Sch/Midlothian/Cook	04029072	708/385-4546	57
SPECIAL ED DIST OF MCHENRY CO/WOODSTOCK/MCHENRY	02182252	815/338-3622	185
SPECIAL EDUCATION DIST LAKE CO/GAGES LAKE/LAKE	02182006	847/548-8470	159
Spectrum Sch/Rockford/Winnebago	01780605	815/877-1600	256
SPEED SEJA 802/CHICAGO HTS/COOK	03266502	708/481-6100	82
Spencer Crossing Interm Sch/New Lenox/Will	10031754	815/462-7997	245
Spencer Loomis Elem Sch/Hawthorn WDS/Lake	05276709	847/719-3300	152
Spencer Pointe Elem Sch/New Lenox/Will	10031730	815/462-7988	245
Spencer Tech Academy/Chicago/Cook	00280858	773/534-6150	30
Spencer Trail Kindergarten Ctr/New Lenox/Will	10031742	815/462-7007	245
SPOON RIVER VALLEY CMTY SD 4/LONDON MILLS/FULTON	00293532	309/778-2204	110
Spoon River Valley Elem Sch/London Mills/Fulton	00293544	309/778-2207	110
Spoon River Vly Jr Sr High Sch/London Mills/Fulton	04453227	309/778-2201	110
Spring Ave Elem Sch/La Grange/Cook	00270695	708/482-2710	54
Spring Brook Elem Sch/Naperville/Du Page	03240455	630/428-6600	96
Spring Creek Elem Sch/Rockford/Winnebago	00327987	815/654-4960	254
SPRING GARDEN CMTY CSD 178/MOUNT VERNON/JEFFERSON	00296649	618/244-8070	124
Spring Garden Elem Sch/Mount Vernon/Jefferson	00296651	618/244-8070	124
Spring Garden Middle Sch/Ina/Jefferson	12375934	618/437-5361	124
Spring Grove Elem Sch/Spring Grove/McHenry	00305953	815/678-6750	183
Spring Hills Elem Sch/Roselle/Du Page	00291211	630/529-1883	99
Spring Lake Elem Sch/Manito/Tazewell	00321701	309/545-2241	228
SPRING LAKE ELEM SD 606/MANITO/TAZEWELL	00321696	309/545-2241	228
Spring Trail Elem Sch/Carol Stream/Kane	04450823	630/213-6230	131
SPRING VALLEY CMTY CONS SD 99/SPRING VALLEY/BUREAU	00264036	815/664-4242	7
Spring Wood Middle Sch/Hanover Park/Du Page	02132087	630/893-8900	96
Springfield Ball Charter Sch/Springfield/Sangamon	04811679	217/525-3275	213
Springfield Christian Sch/Springfield/Sangamon	01442683	217/698-1933	214
Springfield Developmental Ctr/Springfield/Sangamon	02826551	217/525-8271	214
Springfield Elem Sch/Midlothian/Cook	00271508	708/388-4121	57
Springfield High Sch/Springfield/Sangamon	00319150	217/525-3100	213
Springfield Learning Center/Springfield/Sangamon	*01539559	217/525-3144	213
SPRINGFIELD PUB SCH DIST 186/SPRINGFIELD/SANGAMON	00318883	217/525-3006	213
Springfield Southeast High Sch/Springfield/Sangamon	00319162	217/525-3130	213
Springman Middle Sch/Glenview/Cook	00269995	847/998-5020	51
Spry Community Links High Sch/Chicago/Cook	05277246	773/534-1997	37
Sr Thea Bowman Catholic Sch/E Saint Louis/St Clair	00318273	618/397-0316	222
SS Alphonsus & Patrick Sch/Lemont/Cook	00286955	630/783-2220	74
SS Catherine of Siena-Lucy Sch/Oak Park/Cook	00285171	708/386-5286	74
SS Cyril & Methodius Sch/Lemont/Cook	00284531	630/257-6488	74
SS Faith Hope & Charity Sch/Winnetka/Cook	00284452	847/446-0031	74
SS Peter & Paul Sch/Cary/McHenry	00328527	847/639-3041	184
SS Peter & Paul Sch/Collinsville/Madison	00319629	618/344-5450	173
SS Peter & Paul Sch/Naperville/Du Page	00326165	630/355-0113	101
SS Peter & Paul Sch/Nauvoo/Hancock	00313560	217/453-2511	115
SS Peter & Paul Sch/Waterloo/Monroe	00317853	618/939-7217	190
St Agatha Sch/New Athens/St Clair	02114700	618/475-2170	222
St Agnes Sch/Chicago HTS/Cook	00284608	708/756-2333	74
St Agnes Sch/Springfield/Sangamon	00319643	217/793-1370	214
St Agnes School Bohemia/Chicago/Cook	00283082	773/522-0143	74
St Ailbe Sch/Chicago/Cook	00284610	773/734-1386	74
St Albert the Great Sch/Burbank/Cook	00284622	708/424-7757	74
St Alexander Sch/Palos Heights/Cook	00284634	708/448-0408	74
St Aloysius Catholic Sch/Springfield/Sangamon	00319655	217/544-4553	214
St Alphonsus Ligouri Sch/Prospect HTS/Cook	00284646	847/255-5538	74
St Ambrose Sch/Godfrey/Madison	00319667	618/466-4216	173
St Anastasia Sch/Waukegan/Lake	00284672	847/623-8320	157
St Andrew Catholic Sch/Rock Falls/Whiteside	00328539	815/625-1456	240
St Andrew Sch/Murphysboro/Jackson	00317889	618/687-2013	121
St Andrew the Apostle Sch/Romeoville/Will	00326191	815/886-5953	249
St Andrew's Lutheran Sch/Park Ridge/Cook	00282557	847/823-9308	81
St Angela Sch/Chicago/Cook	00284701	773/626-2655	74
St Ann Grade Sch/Chicago/Cook	00284713	312/829-4153	74
St Ann Sch/Lansing/Cook	00284749	708/895-1661	74
St Ann Sch/Nashville/Washington	00317891	618/327-8741	236
St Anne Catholic Sch/Barrington/Lake	00284751	847/381-0311	158
ST ANNE CMTY CONS SCH DIST 256/SAINT ANNE/KANKAKEE	00299512	815/422-5022	136
St Anne Cmty High Sch/Saint Anne/Kankakee	00299548	815/427-8141	136
ST ANNE CMTY HSD 302/SAINT ANNE/KANKAKEE	00299536	815/422-5022	136
St Anne Elem Sch/Saint Anne/Kankakee	00299524	815/427-8153	136
St Anne Sch/Dixon/Lee	00328541	815/288-5619	160
St Anthony of Padua High Sch/Effingham/Effingham	00319681	217/342-6969	105
St Anthony of Padua Sch/Effingham/Effingham	00319679	217/347-0419	105
St Anthony Pre-School/Frankfort/Will	04891083	815/469-5417	249
St Athanasius Sch/Evanston/Cook	00284816	847/864-2650	74
St Barbara Elem Sch/Chicago/Cook	00284854	312/326-6243	74
St Barnabas Sch/Chicago/Cook	00284878	773/445-7711	74
St Bartholomew Sch/Chicago/Cook	00284880	773/282-9373	74
St Bede Academy/Peru/La Salle	00313596	815/223-3140	145
St Bede Sch/Ingleside/Lake	02114671	847/587-5541	158
St Bede the Venerable Sch/Chicago/Cook	00284933	773/884-2020	74
St Benedict Prep Elem Sch/Chicago/Cook	00284957	773/463-6797	74
St Benedict Sch/Blue Island/Cook	00284969	708/385-2016	74
St Boniface Sch/Edwardsville/Madison	00319710	618/656-6917	173
St Bridget Sch/Loves Park/Winnebago	00328565	815/633-8255	256
St Bruno Sch/Chicago/Cook	00285078	773/847-0697	74
St Bruno Sch/Pinckneyville/Perry	00317956	618/357-8276	202
St Cajetan Sch/Chicago/Cook	00285080	773/233-8844	74
St Catherine Laboure Sch/Glenview/Cook	00285145	847/724-2240	74
St Catherine of Alexandria Sch/Oak Lawn/Cook	00285157	708/425-5547	74
St Catherine of Siena Sch/West Dundee/Kane	00328577	847/426-4808	133
St Celestine Sch/Elmwood Park/Cook	00285183	708/453-8234	74
St Charles Borromeo Sch/Hampshire/Kane	00328589	847/683-3450	133
St Charles East High Sch/Saint Charles/Kane	00298843	331/228-4000	129
St Charles North High Sch/Saint Charles/Kane	04915213	331/228-4400	129
St Christina Sch/Chicago/Cook	00285212	773/445-2969	74
St Christopher Sch/Midlothian/Cook	00285224	708/385-8776	74
St Clair Co Alternative Ed Ctr/Belleville/St Clair	11435608	618/233-6874	217
ST CLAIR CO REGIONAL OFF OF ED/BELLEVILLE/ST CLAIR	02098314	618/825-3900	223
St Clare Catholic Sch/O Fallon/St Clair	00317982	618/632-6327	222
St Clement Sch/Chicago/Cook	00285248	773/348-8212	74
St Cletus Sch/La Grange/Cook	00285250	708/352-4820	74
St Coletta of Illinois/Tinley Park/Cook	11225300	708/342-5200	81
St Constance Sch/Chicago/Cook	00285303	773/283-2311	74
St Damian Sch/Oak Forest/Cook	00285341	708/687-4230	74
St Daniel the Prophet Sch/Chicago/Cook	00285353	773/586-1225	74
St Dennis Sch/Lockport/Will	00326232	815/838-4494	249
St Dominic Sch/Bolingbrook/Will	00326244	630/739-1633	249
St Dominic Sch/Quincy/Adams	00319746	217/224-0041	3
St Edward High Sch/Elgin/Kane	00328591	847/741-7535	133
St Edward Sch/Chicago/Cook	00285420	773/736-9133	75
St Edward Sch/Chillicothe/Peoria	00313649	309/274-2994	200
St Elizabeth of the Trinity/Chicago/Cook	00287375	773/763-7080	75
St Elizabeth Sch/Granite City/Madison	00319758	618/877-3348	173
St Elizabeth Trinity Sch/Chicago/Cook	12468880	773/763-7080	75

Illinois School Directory — District & School Telephone Index

School/City/County DISTRICT/CITY/COUNTY	PID	TELEPHONE NUMBER	PAGE
ST ELMO CMTY UNIT SCH DIST 202/ SAINT ELMO/FAYETTE	00292552	618/829-3264	106
St Elmo Elem Sch/Saint Elmo/Fayette	00292564	618/829-3263	106
St Elmo Jr Sr High Sch/Saint Elmo/Fayette	00292588	618/829-3227	106
St Emily Sch/Mt Prospect/Cook	00285456	847/296-3490	75
St Ethelreda Sch/Chicago/Cook	00285468	773/238-1757	75
St Eugene Sch/Chicago/Cook	00285470	773/763-2235	75
St Ferdinand Sch/Chicago/Cook	00285509	773/622-3022	75
St Frances of Rome Sch/Cicero/Cook	00285535	708/652-2277	75
St Francis Borgia Sch/Chicago/Cook	00285559	773/589-1000	75
St Francis De Sales High Sch/Chicago/Cook	00285573	773/731-7272	75
St Francis De Sales Sch/Lake Zurich/Lake	00285597	847/438-7921	158
St Francis High Sch/Wheaton/Du Page	00326268	630/668-5800	101
St Francis Solanus Sch/Quincy/Adams	00319760	217/222-4077	3
St Francis Xavier Sch/La Grange/Cook	00285614	708/352-2175	75
St Francis Xavier Sch/Wilmette/Cook	00285638	847/256-0644	75
St Francis-Holy Ghost Sch/Jerseyville/ Jersey	00319485	618/498-4823	125
St Gabriel Sch/Chicago/Cook	00285640	773/268-6636	75
St Gall Sch/Chicago/Cook	00285652	773/737-3454	75
St Genevieve Sch/Chicago/Cook	00285664	773/237-7131	75
St George Elem Sch/Bourbonnais/Kankakee	00299562	815/933-1503	136
St George Sch/Tinley Park/Cook	00285690	708/532-2626	75
ST GEORGE SCH DIST 258/BOURBONNAIS/ KANKAKEE	00299550	815/933-1503	136
St Gerald Sch/Oak Lawn/Cook	00285705	708/422-0121	75
St Germaine Sch/Oak Lawn/Cook	00285729	708/425-6063	75
St Gilbert Sch/Grayslake/Lake	00285755	847/223-8600	158
St Giles Sch/Oak Park/Cook	00285767	708/383-6279	75
St Helen Sch/Chicago/Cook	00285808	773/486-1055	75
St Hilary Sch/Chicago/Cook	00285834	773/561-5885	75
St Hubert Sch/Hoffman Est/Cook	00285846	847/885-7702	75
St Ignatius College Prep Sch/Chicago/Cook	00285872	312/421-5900	75
St Irene Catholic Sch/Warrenville/Du Page	00326282	630/393-9303	101
St Isaac Jogues Sch/Hinsdale/Du Page	00326294	630/323-3244	101
St Isidore Sch/Bloomingdale/Du Page	00326309	630/529-9323	101
St Jacob Elem Sch/Saint Jacob/Madison	00309193	618/644-2541	172
St James Catholic Sch/Belvidere/Boone	00328644	815/547-7633	5
St James Lutheran Sch/Chicago/Cook	00282571	773/525-4990	81
St James Lutheran Sch/Quincy/Adams	00263226	217/222-8267	3
St James Sch/Arlington HTS/Cook	00285963	224/345-7145	75
St James Sch/Millstadt/St Clair	00318027	618/476-3510	223
St James the Apostle Sch/Glen Ellyn/ Du Page	00326311	630/469-8060	101
St Jerome Sch/Chicago/Cook	00285999	312/842-7668	75
St Joan of Arc Sch/Evanston/Cook	00286022	847/679-0660	75
St Joan of Arc Sch/Lisle/Du Page	00326323	630/969-1732	101
St John Baptist Catholic Sch/Smithton/ St Clair	00318053	618/233-0581	223
St John Berchmans Sch/Chicago/Cook	00286034	773/486-1334	75
St John Brebeuf Sch/Niles/Cook	00286058	847/966-3266	75
St John De LaSalle Academy/Chicago/Cook	00286072	773/785-2331	75
St John Fisher Sch/Chicago/Cook	00286084	773/445-4737	75
St John Lutheran Sch/Champaign/Champaign	02210847	217/359-1714	13
St John Lutheran Sch/Chester/Randolph	00315166	618/826-4345	206
St John Lutheran Sch/Cntry CLB Hls/Cook	00282595	708/799-7491	81
St John Lutheran Sch/Lansing/Cook	00282624	708/895-9280	81
St John Lutheran Sch/Libertyville/Lake	01442308	847/367-1441	158
St John Lutheran Sch/Lombard/Du Page	00291754	630/629-2515	102
St John Lutheran Sch/Red Bud/Randolph	00315178	618/282-3873	206
St John Neumann Sch/Maryville/Madison	02113342	618/345-7230	173
St John of the Cross Sch/Western Sprgs/ Cook	00286101	708/246-4454	75
St John the Baptist Sch/Johnsburg/McHenry	00328656	815/385-3959	184
St John the Baptist Sch/Red Bud/Randolph	00318065	618/282-3215	206
St John the Baptist Sch/W Frankfort/ Franklin	00318041	618/937-2017	109
St John the Baptist Sch/Winfield/Du Page	00326347	630/668-2625	101
St John the Evangelist Sch/Carrollton/ Greene	00319813	217/942-6814	111
St John the Evangelist Sch/Streamwood/Cook	00286137	630/289-3040	75
St John Vianney Sch/Northlake/Cook	00286149	708/562-1466	75
St John's Lutheran Sch/Buckley/Iroquois	00295970	217/394-2422	119
St John's Lutheran Sch/Chicago/Cook	00282583	773/736-1196	81
St John's Lutheran Sch/Elgin/Kane	00298934	847/741-7633	133
St John's Lutheran Sch/La Grange/Cook	00282612	708/354-1690	81
St Johns Lutheran Sch/Mattoon/Coles	02424282	217/234-4911	20
St Josaphat Sch/Chicago/Cook	00286151	773/549-0909	75
St Joseph Academy/Joliet/Will	11722011	815/723-4567	250
ST JOSEPH CMTY CONS SD 169/ SAINT JOSEPH/CHAMPAIGN	00265236	217/469-2291	12
St Joseph Grade Sch/Saint Joseph/Champaign	00265248	217/469-2291	12
St Joseph High Sch/Westchester/Cook	00286187	708/562-4433	75
St Joseph Middle Sch/Saint Joseph/ Champaign	10022129	217/469-2334	12
St Joseph Pre-School/Chatham/Sangamon	04839877	217/483-3772	214
St Joseph Sch/Downers Grove/Du Page	00326402	630/969-4306	101
St Joseph Sch/Elgin/Kane	00328670	847/931-2804	133
St Joseph Sch/Freeburg/St Clair	00318089	618/539-3930	223
St Joseph Sch/Libertyville/Lake	00286199	847/362-0730	158
St Joseph Sch/Lockport/Will	00326385	815/838-8173	249
St Joseph Sch/Manhattan/Will	00326373	815/478-3951	249
St Joseph Sch/Olney/Richland	00318106	618/395-3081	206
St Joseph Sch/Pekin/Tazewell	00313675	309/347-7194	229
St Joseph Sch/Summit Argo/Cook	00286266	708/458-2927	75
St Joseph Sch/Wilmette/Cook	10030877	847/256-7870	75
ST JOSEPH-OGDEN CMTY HSD 305/ SAINT JOSEPH/CHAMPAIGN	00265250	217/469-2586	12
St Joseph-Ogden High Sch/Saint Joseph/ Champaign	00265262	217/469-2332	12
St Jude Parish Sch/New Lenox/Will	00326414	815/485-2549	249
St Jude Sch/Joliet/Will	00326426	815/729-0288	249
St Jude Sch/Peoria/Peoria	11716610	309/243-2493	200
St Juliana Sch/Chicago/Cook	00286319	773/631-2256	75
St Laurence High Sch/Burbank/Cook	00286383	708/458-6900	75
St Laurence Sch/Elgin/Kane	00328709	847/468-6100	133
St Leonard Sch/Berwyn/Cook	00286424	708/749-3666	75
ST LIBORY CONS SCH DIST 30/ SAINT LIBORY/ST CLAIR	00317592	618/768-4923	222
St Libory Elem Sch/Saint Libory/St Clair	00317607	618/768-4923	222
St Linus Sch/Oak Lawn/Cook	00286436	708/425-1656	75
St Louis Sch/Nokomis/Montgomery	00319851	217/563-7445	191
St Luke Academy/Chicago/Cook	00282650	773/472-3837	81
St Luke Lutheran Sch/Itasca/Du Page	00291780	630/773-0509	102
St Luke Sch/River Forest/Cook	00286486	708/366-8587	75
St Luke's Christian Academy/Montgomery/ Kendall	02435918	630/892-0310	139
St Malachy Sch/Chicago/Cook	00286498	312/733-2252	75
St Malachy Sch/Geneseo/Henry	00313728	309/944-3230	118
St Malachy Sch/Rantoul/Champaign	00313716	217/892-2011	13
St Margaret Mary Sch/Algonquin/McHenry	00328711	847/658-5313	184
St Margaret of Scotland Sch/Chicago/Cook	00286515	773/238-1088	75
St Mark Sch/Peoria/Peoria	00313730	309/676-7131	200
St Mark's Lutheran Sch/Steeleville/ Randolph	00315180	618/965-3838	206
St Mary Immaculate Sch/Plainfield/Will	00326517	815/436-3953	249
St Mary Nativity Sch/Joliet/Will	00326476	815/722-8518	249
St Mary of Gostyn Sch/Downers Grove/ Du Page	00326488	630/968-6155	101
St Mary of the Angels Sch/Chicago/Cook	00286632	773/486-0119	76
St Mary of the Lake Sch/Chicago/Cook	00286644	773/281-0018	76
St Mary of the Woods Sch/Chicago/Cook	00286656	773/763-7577	76
St Mary Sch/Alton/Madison	00319942	618/465-8523	173
St Mary Sch/Buffalo Grove/Lake	00286668	847/459-6270	158
St Mary Sch/Centralia/Marion	00318182	618/532-3473	176
St Mary Sch/Dekalb/De Kalb	00328735	815/756-7905	86
St Mary Sch/Edwardsville/Madison	00319928	618/656-1230	173
St Mary Sch/Elgin/Kane	10328761	847/695-6609	133
St Mary Sch/Metamora/Woodford	00313754	309/367-2528	258
St Mary Sch/Mokena/Will	00326531	708/479-3383	249
St Mary Sch/Mount Vernon/Jefferson	00318209	618/242-5353	124
St Mary Sch/Mt Sterling/Brown	00319899	217/773-2825	5
St Mary Sch/Plano/Kendall	00326505	630/552-3345	139
St Mary Sch/Riverside/Cook	00286694	708/442-5747	76
St Mary Sch/Sycamore/De Kalb	00328759	815/895-5215	86
St Mary Sch/Taylorville/Christian	00319916	217/824-6501	15
St Mary Sch/Woodstock/McHenry	00328802	815/338-3598	184
St Mary Star of the Sea Sch/Chicago/Cook	00286709	773/767-6160	76
St Mary's of Kickapoo Sch/Edwards/Peoria	00313766	309/691-3015	200
St Mary's Sch/Bloomington/Mclean	00313778	309/828-5954	188
St Mary's Sch/Brussels/Calhoun	00319978	618/883-2124	8
St Mary's Sch/Chester/Randolph	00318223	618/826-3120	206
St Mary's Sch/East Dubuque/Jo Daviess	00328814	815/747-3010	126
St Mary's Sch/Mount Carmel/Wabash	00318211	618/263-3183	234
St Mary's Sch/Sterling/Whiteside	00328785	815/625-2253	240
St Mary's School-Pontiac/Pontiac/ Livingston	00313807	815/844-6585	163
St Mary-Dixon Sch/Dixon/Lee	00328747	815/284-6986	160
St Matthew Lutheran Sch/Hawthorn WDS/Lake	00302573	847/438-6103	158
St Matthew Sch/Champaign/Champaign	00313845	217/359-4114	13
St Matthew Sch/Glendale HTS/Du Page	00326579	630/858-3112	101
St Matthias Elem Sch/Chicago/Cook	00286759	773/784-0999	76
St Michael Sch/Orland Park/Cook	00286802	708/349-0068	76
St Michael Sch/Wheaton/Du Page	00326567	630/665-1454	101

School Year 2020-2021 · 800-333-8802 · IL-V41

DISTRICT & SCHOOL TELEPHONE INDEX

Market Data Retrieval

School/City/County DISTRICT/CITY/COUNTY	PID	TELEPHONE NUMBER	PAGE
St Michael the Archangel Sch/Sigel/Shelby	00320018	217/844-2231	216
St Michael the Archangel Sch/Streator/La Salle	00313584	815/672-3847	145
St Monica Academy/Chicago/Cook	00286852	773/631-7880	76
St Nicholas Cathedral Sch/Chicago/Cook	00286864	773/384-7243	76
St Nicholas of Tolentine Sch/Chicago/Cook	00286876	773/735-0772	76
St Norbert Sch/Hardin/Calhoun	00320032	618/576-2514	8
St Norbert Sch/Northbrook/Cook	00286890	847/272-0051	76
St Odilo Sch/Berwyn/Cook	00286905	708/484-0755	76
St Patricia Sch/Hickory Hills/Cook	00286931	708/598-8200	76
St Patrick Catholic Sch/Saint Charles/Kane	00328838	630/338-8100	133
St Patrick High Sch/Chicago/Cook	00286943	773/282-8844	76
St Patrick Sch/Decatur/Macon	00320056	217/423-4351	166
St Patrick Sch/Springfield/Sangamon	00320044	217/523-7670	214
St Patrick Sch/Wadsworth/Lake	00286967	847/623-8446	158
St Patrick Sch/Washington/Tazewell	00313869	309/444-4345	229
St Paul Academy/Rockford/Winnebago	04990940	815/965-4308	256
St Paul Catholic Sch/Highland/Madison	00320068	618/654-7525	173
St Paul Early Childhood Ctr/Chicago/Cook	12313912	708/867-5044	81
St Paul Evanglical Luth Sch/Chicago/Cook	00282674	773/721-1438	81
St Paul Lutheran Sch/Aurora/Kane	00298946	630/896-3250	133
St Paul Lutheran Sch/Brookfield/Cook	00282662	708/485-0650	81
St Paul Lutheran Sch/Chicago/Cook	00282703	773/378-6644	81
St Paul Lutheran Sch/Moline/Rock Island	01405439	309/762-4494	209
St Paul Lutheran Sch/Mt Prospect/Cook	00282739	847/255-6733	81
St Paul Lutheran Sch/Rochelle/Ogle	00312231	815/562-6323	195
St Paul Lutheran Sch/Rockford/Winnebago	00328333	815/965-3335	256
St Paul Lutheran Sch/Troy/Madison	00309387	618/667-6314	173
St Paul Lutheran Sch/Worden/Madison	00309399	618/633-2202	173
St Paul of the Cross Sch/Park Ridge/Cook	00286981	847/825-6366	76
St Paul Sch/Macomb/McDonough	00313924	309/833-2470	179
St Paul Sch/Odell/Livingston	00313912	815/998-2194	163
St Paul the Apostle Sch/Joliet/Will	00326610	815/725-3390	249
St Paul's Lutheran Sch/Bourbonnais/Kankakee	00299603	815/932-3241	137
St Paul's Lutheran Sch/Milford/Iroquois	00295982	815/889-4209	119
St Peter Catholic Sch/South Beloit/Winnebago	00328852	779/475-0560	256
St Peter Lutheran Sch/Arlington HTS/Cook	00282765	847/253-6638	81
St Peter Lutheran Sch/Dorsey/Madison	00309404	618/888-2252	173
St Peter Lutheran Sch/Saint Peter/Fayette	00292693	618/349-8888	106
St Peter Lutheran Sch/Schaumburg/Cook	00282789	847/885-7636	81
St Peter Sch/Aurora/Kane	00328876	630/892-1283	133
St Peter Sch/Geneva/Kane	00328864	630/232-0476	133
St Peter Sch/Quincy/Adams	00320082	217/223-1120	3
St Petronille Sch/Glen Ellyn/Du Page	00326634	630/469-5041	101
St Philip Lutheran Sch/Chicago/Cook	00282791	773/561-9830	81
St Philip Neri Sch/Chicago/Cook	00287038	773/288-1138	76
St Philip the Apostle Sch/Addison/Du Page	00326646	630/543-4130	101
St Philomena Sch/Peoria/Peoria	00313936	309/685-1208	200
St Pius V Sch/Chicago/Cook	00287064	312/226-1590	76
St Pius X Sch/Lombard/Du Page	00326658	630/627-2353	101
St Procopius Sch/Chicago/Cook	00287105	312/421-5135	76
St Raphael Sch/Naperville/Du Page	00326660	630/355-1880	101
St Raymond Sch/Mt Prospect/Cook	00287129	847/253-8555	76
St Richard Sch/Chicago/Cook	00287143	773/582-8083	76
St Rita Catholic Elem Sch/Rockford/Winnebago	00328905	815/398-3466	256
St Rita of Cascia High Sch/Chicago/Cook	00287155	773/925-6600	76
St Rita of Cascia Sch/Aurora/Kane	00328890	630/892-0200	133
St Robert Bellarmine Sch/Chicago/Cook	00287179	773/725-5133	76
St Rose Elem Sch/Saint Rose/Clinton	00266462	618/526-7484	18
St Rose Sch/Wilmington/Will	00326684	815/476-6220	249
ST ROSE SCH DIST 14-15/SAINT ROSE/CLINTON	00266450	618/526-7484	18
St Sabina Academy/Chicago/Cook	00287210	773/483-5000	76
St Sava Academy/Chicago/Cook	05303807	773/714-0299	81
St Scholastica Sch/Woodridge/Du Page	00326696	630/985-2515	101
St Stanislaus Kostka Sch/Chicago/Cook	00287313	773/278-4560	76
St Sylvester Sch/Chicago/Cook	00287351	773/772-5222	76
St Symphorosa Sch/Chicago/Cook	00287363	773/585-6888	76
St Teresa High Sch/Decatur/Macon	00320094	217/875-2431	167
St Teresa Sch/Belleville/St Clair	00318297	618/235-4066	223
St Theresa Sch/Palatine/Cook	00287428	847/359-1820	76
St Therese Sch/Chicago/Cook	00287430	312/326-2837	76
St Thomas More Sch/Elgin/Kane	00328931	847/742-3959	133
St Thomas of Canterbury Sch/Chicago/Cook	00287480	773/271-8655	76
St Thomas of Villanova Sch/Palatine/Cook	00287492	847/358-2110	76
St Thomas Sch/Philo/Champaign	00313974	217/684-2309	13
St Thomas the Apostle Sch/Chicago/Cook	00287442	773/667-1142	76
St Thomas the Apostle Sch/Crystal Lake/McHenry	00328943	815/459-0496	184
St Thomas the Apostle Sch/Newton/Jasper	00320109	618/783-3517	122
St Thomas the Apostle Sch/Peoria HTS/Peoria	00313986	309/685-2533	200
St Viator High Sch/Arlington HTS/Cook	00287533	847/392-4050	76
St Viator Sch/Chicago/Cook	00287545	773/545-2173	76
St Vincent De Paul Sch/Peoria/Peoria	00314007	309/691-5012	200
St Vincent Ferrer Sch/River Forest/Cook	00287571	708/771-5905	76
St Walter Sch/Chicago/Cook	00287583	773/445-8850	76
St Walter Sch/Roselle/Du Page	00326725	630/529-1721	101
St William Sch/Chicago/Cook	00287600	773/637-5130	76
St Zachary Sch/Des Plaines/Cook	00287624	847/437-4022	76
Stagg Elem Sch/Chicago/Cook	00276584	773/535-3565	26
Stanton Middle Sch/Fox Lake/Lake	00300733	847/973-4200	149
STARK CO CMTY UNIT SD 100/WYOMING/STARK	00320616	309/695-6123	223
Stark Co Elem Sch/Wyoming/Stark	00320604	309/695-5181	224
Stark Co High Sch/Toulon/Stark	00320642	309/286-4451	224
Stark Co Junior High Sch/Toulon/Stark	00320678	309/286-3451	224
STARVED ROCK ASSOC VOC TECH ED/PERU/LA SALLE	04180195	815/223-2454	146
STAUNTON CMTY UNIT SCH DIST 6/STAUNTON/MACOUPIN	00307925	618/635-2962	168
Staunton Elem Sch/Staunton/Macoupin	00307937	618/635-3831	168
Staunton High Sch/Staunton/Macoupin	04031843	618/635-3838	168
Staunton Junior High Sch/Staunton/Macoupin	12473263	618/635-3831	168
Steam Academy at Haskell/Rockford/Winnebago	00327705	815/966-3355	254
Steele Elem Sch/Galesburg/Knox	00300147	309/973-2016	140
STEELEVILLE CMTY SCH DIST 138/STEELEVILLE/RANDOLPH	00315130	618/965-3469	206
Steeleville Elem Sch/Steeleville/Randolph	00315142	618/965-3469	206
Steeleville High Sch/Steeleville/Randolph	00315154	618/965-3432	206
Steeple Run Elem Sch/Naperville/Du Page	01540613	630/420-6385	98
Steger Intermediate Center/Steger/Cook	00274603	708/753-4200	68
Steger Primary Center/S Chicago HTS/Cook	00274639	708/753-4100	68
STEGER SCH DIST 194/STEGER/COOK	00274586	708/753-4300	68
Steinmetz Academic Center/Chicago/Cook	00280860	773/534-3030	36
Stella May Swartz Elem Sch/Oakbrook Ter/Du Page	00291259	630/834-9256	99
STEM Academy/Calumet City/Cook	11832006	708/868-7595	46
STEM Magnet Academy/Chicago/Cook	11719208	773/534-7300	28
Stephen Decatur Middle Sch/Decatur/Macon	00307200	217/362-3250	165
Stephen Mack Middle Sch/Rockton/Winnebago	01482994	815/624-2611	255
Stepping Stone Sch/Lake Villa/Lake	11236024	847/356-3334	158
STERLING CMTY UNIT SCH DIST 5/STERLING/WHITESIDE	00323929	815/626-5050	240
Sterling High Sch/Sterling/Whiteside	01170634	815/625-6800	240
Sterling Middle Sch/Peoria/Peoria	00313039	309/672-6557	199
Steuben Elem Sch/Kankakee/Kankakee	00299263	815/802-4600	135
Stevens Intermediate Sch/Wilmington/Will	00325903	815/926-1689	249
Stevenson Elem Sch/Bloomington/Mclean	00306270	309/663-2351	185
Stevenson Elem Sch/Chicago/Cook	00278673	773/535-2280	34
Stevenson Elem Sch/Decatur/Macon	00307248	217/362-3540	165
Stevenson Elem Sch/Lombard/Du Page	04363622	630/516-7780	99
Stevenson Middle Sch/Melrose Park/Cook	00271431	708/450-2053	57
Steward Elem Sch/Steward/Lee	00304076	815/396-2413	160
STEWARD ELEM SCH DIST 220/STEWARD/LEE	00304064	815/396-2413	160
Stewardson-Strasburg Elem JHS/Strasburg/Shelby	04918344	217/682-3621	216
Stewardson-Strasburg High Sch/Strasburg/Shelby	00320460	217/682-3355	216
STEWARDSON-STRASBURG SD 5-A/STRASBURG/SHELBY	00320446	217/682-3355	216
Still Middle Sch/Aurora/Du Page	04876411	630/375-3900	96
Stillman Valley High Sch/Stillman Vly/Ogle	00311988	815/645-2291	195
Stock Sch/Chicago/Cook	00280884	773/534-1215	29
STOCKTON CMTY UNIT SD 206/STOCKTON/JO DAVIESS	00297265	815/947-3391	126
Stockton Elem Sch/Stockton/Jo Daviess	00297277	815/947-3321	126
Stockton High Sch/Stockton/Jo Daviess	00297289	815/947-3323	126
Stockton Middle Sch/Stockton/Jo Daviess	04028248	815/947-3702	126
Stone Creek Elem Sch/Roscoe/Winnebago	03325017	815/623-2837	253
Stone Elem Sch/Addison/Du Page	00288941	630/628-4020	89
Stone Scholastic Academy/Chicago/Cook	00280913	773/534-2045	29
Stony Creek Elem Sch/Alsip/Cook	00266929	708/371-0220	20
Strassburg Elem Sch/Sauk Village/Cook	00273829	708/758-4754	44
Stratford Middle Sch/Bloomingdale/Du Page	03047459	630/671-4300	90
Stratton Elem Sch/Champaign/Champaign	00264763	217/373-7330	10
Streamwood High Sch/Streamwood/Kane	01827291	630/213-5500	131
STREATOR ELEM SCH DIST 44/STREATOR/LA SALLE	00303436	815/672-2926	144

Illinois School Directory

DISTRICT & SCHOOL TELEPHONE INDEX

School/City/County DISTRICT/CITY/COUNTY	PID	TELEPHONE	PAGE NUMBER
Streator Twp High Sch/Streator/La Salle	00303424	815/672-0545	145
STREATOR TWP HIGH SCH DIST 40/			
STREATOR/LA SALLE	00303412	815/672-0545	145
Stuart G Ferst Sch/Chicago/Cook	02956625	773/761-4651	81
Stuart R Paddock Sch/Palatine/Cook	00272605	847/963-5800	43
Student Life Academy/Mattoon/Coles	02109200	217/258-5286	19
Success Academy/Aurora/Kane	12101783	630/301-5000	132
Suder Montessori Magnet Sch/Chicago/Cook	10009244	773/534-7685	32
Sugar Creek Elem Sch/Normal/Mclean	00306610	309/557-4425	187
SULLIVAN CMTY UNIT SD 300/			
SULLIVAN/MOULTRIE	00311718	217/728-8341	193
Sullivan Elem Sch/Sullivan/Moultrie	00311732	217/728-2321	193
Sullivan High Sch/Chicago/Cook	00280937	773/534-2000	36
Sullivan High Sch/Sullivan/Moultrie	00311744	217/728-8311	193
Sullivan Middle Sch/Sullivan/Moultrie	00311756	217/728-8381	193
Summerdale Early Childhood Ctr/Rockford/Winnebago	00327547	815/966-3280	254
Summersville Grade Sch/Mount Vernon/Jefferson	00296924	618/244-8079	124
SUMMERSVILLE SCH DIST 79/			
MOUNT VERNON/JEFFERSON	00296912	618/244-8079	124
Summit Elem Sch/Collinsville/Madison	00308498	618/346-6222	170
Summit Hill Junior High Sch/Frankfort/Will	01395901	815/469-4330	247
SUMMIT HILL SCH DIST 161/			
FRANKFORT/WILL	00325769	815/469-9103	247
Summit Learning Center/Crestwood/Cook	04036544	708/371-1986	44
Sumner Attendance Center/Sumner/Lawrence	00303773	618/936-2412	159
Sumner Math & Science Academy/Chicago/Cook	00280949	773/534-6730	31
Sunny Hill Elem Sch/Carpentersvle/Lake	00267595	847/426-4232	147
SUNNYBROOK SCH DIST 171/			
LANSING/COOK	00274691	708/895-0750	68
Sunnydale Elem Sch/Streamwood/Kane	00298518	630/213-5610	131
Sunnyside Elem Sch/Berkeley/Cook	00267777	708/449-3170	22
Sunset Ridge Elem Sch/Northfield/Cook	00272112	847/881-9400	68
SUNSET RIDGE SCH DIST 29/			
NORTHFIELD/COOK	00272095	847/881-9400	68
Sutherland Elem Sch/Chicago/Cook	00276601	773/535-2580	34
Swann Sch/Champaign/Champaign	02956716	217/398-9270	13
Sward Elem Sch/Oak Lawn/Cook	00272306	708/423-7820	60
SYCAMORE CMTY UNIT SD 427/			
SYCAMORE/DE KALB	00288379	815/899-8100	86
Sycamore High Sch/Sycamore/De Kalb	00288410	815/899-8160	86
Sycamore Middle Sch/Sycamore/De Kalb	00288422	815/899-8170	86
Sycamore Trails Elem Sch/Bartlett/Kane	04016283	630/213-5641	131

T

School/City/County	PID	TELEPHONE	PAGE
T E Culbertson Elem Sch/Joliet/Will	00324882	815/723-0035	243
Tabernacle Christian Academy/Chicago/Cook	02087779	773/445-3007	81
Taft Elem Sch/Harvey/Cook	00274469	708/339-2710	68
Taft Elem Sch/Joliet/Will	00325070	815/725-2700	243
Taft High Sch/Chicago/Cook	00280963	773/534-1000	36
Taft Primary Sch/Kankakee/Kankakee	00299304	815/932-0811	135
Taft Sch/Lockport/Will	00325812	815/838-0408	247
TAFT SCH DIST 90/LOCKPORT/WILL	00325800	815/838-0408	247
Talala Elem Sch/Park Forest/Will	00324715	708/367-2560	242
Talcott Fine Arts Museum Acad/Chicago/Cook	00280975	773/534-7130	28
Talman Elem Sch/Chicago/Cook	05102225	773/535-7850	28
Tamaroa Elem Sch/Tamaroa/Perry	00314215	618/496-5513	201
TAMAROA ELEM SCH DIST 5/			
TAMAROA/PERRY	00314203	618/496-5513	201
Tampico Elem Sch/Tampico/Whiteside	00324507	815/438-2255	239
Tanner Elem Sch/Chicago/Cook	00276613	773/535-3870	35
Tarkington Sch of Excellence/Chicago/Cook	05277234	773/535-4700	26
Taylor Elem Sch/Chicago/Cook	00276625	773/535-6240	36
Taylor Park Elem Sch/Freeport/Stephenson	00320862	815/232-0390	224
Taylor Ridge Elem Sch/Taylor Ridge/Rock Island	00316108	309/793-8070	209
TAYLORVILLE CMTY UNIT SD 3/			
TAYLORVILLE/CHRISTIAN	00265793	217/824-4951	15
Taylorville High Sch/Taylorville/Christian	00265846	217/824-2268	15
Taylorville Junior High Sch/Taylorville/Christian	00265858	217/824-4924	15
TAZEWELL CO AREA EFE #320/			
PEKIN/TAZEWELL	04177796	309/353-5011	229
TAZEWELL-MASON SP ED ASSOC/			
PEKIN/TAZEWELL	02182159	309/347-5164	229
Team Englewood Cmty Academy HS/Chicago/Cook	11916901	773/535-3530	37
Technology Center of Dupage/Addison/Du Page	01536612	630/620-8770	88
Ted Lenart Regional Gifted Ctr/Chicago/Cook	03008116	773/535-0040	28
Tefft Middle Sch/Streamwood/Kane	00298520	630/213-5535	131
Telpochcalli Elem Sch/Chicago/Cook	04486987	773/534-1402	32
Telshe Yeshiva Boys Sch/Chicago/Cook	00282832	773/463-7738	81
Temple Christian Academy/Moline/Rock Island	02181519	309/764-1302	210
Terrace Elem Sch/Des Plaines/Cook	00268850	847/824-1501	46
TEUTOPOLIS CMTY UNIT SD 50/			
TEUTOPOLIS/EFFINGHAM	00292370	217/857-3535	105
Teutopolis Grade Sch/Teutopolis/Effingham	00292411	217/857-3232	105
Teutopolis High Sch/Teutopolis/Effingham	00292423	217/857-3139	105
Teutopolis Junior High Sch/Teutopolis/Effingham	04745745	217/857-6678	105
Thayer J Hill Middle Sch/Naperville/Du Page	02128696	630/428-6200	96
The Academy at Forest View/Arlington HTS/Cook	04011025	847/718-7772	70
The Children's Sch/Oak Park/Cook	12160492	708/484-8033	81
The Field Sch/Oak Park/Cook	12258960	708/434-5811	81
The Governor French Academy/Belleville/St Clair	02991613	618/233-7542	223
Theodore Roosevelt Elem Sch/Cicero/Cook	00268642	708/652-7833	42
Thomas Dooley Elem Sch/Schaumburg/Cook	00274081	847/357-6250	67
Thomas Edison Elem Sch/Morton Grove/Cook	00274263	847/966-6210	67
Thomas Elem Sch/Carbondale/Jackson	00296065	618/457-6226	120
Thomas J Waters Elem Sch/Chicago/Cook	00281149	773/534-5090	29
Thomas Jefferson Elem Sch/Bellwood/Cook	00267727	708/449-3165	22
Thomas Jefferson Elem Sch/Berwyn/Cook	00267832	708/795-2454	22
Thomas Jefferson Elem Sch/Hoffman Est/Cook	01550333	847/963-5400	43
Thomas Jefferson Elem Sch/Joliet/Will	00325082	815/725-0262	243
Thomas Jefferson Elem Sch/Joliet/Will	10911312	815/577-2021	246
Thomas Jefferson Elem Sch/Milan/Rock Island	00316005	309/793-5985	208
Thomas Jefferson High Sch/Rockford/Winnebago	01821871	815/874-9536	254
Thomas Jefferson Jr High Sch/Woodridge/Du Page	00290009	630/795-6700	100
Thomas Jefferson Middle Sch/Waukegan/Lake	00302262	224/303-2560	156
Thomas Jefferson Primary Sch/Peoria/Peoria	00313041	309/672-6531	199
Thomas Kelly College Prep/Chicago/Cook	00277916	773/535-4900	38
Thomas Metcalf Sch/Normal/Mclean	01559339	309/438-7621	1
Thomas Middle Sch/Arlington HTS/Cook	00267155	847/398-4260	21
Thomas Paine Elem Sch/Urbana/Champaign	00265444	217/384-3602	13
THOMASBORO CMTY CONS SD 130/			
THOMASBORO/CHAMPAIGN	00265303	217/643-3275	12
Thomasboro Grade Sch/Thomasboro/Champaign	00265315	217/643-3275	12
Thompson Inst Center/Joliet/Will	00324870	815/740-5458	243
Thompson Junior High Sch/Oswego/Kendall	01538531	630/636-2600	138
Thompson Middle Sch/Saint Charles/Kane	01539509	331/228-3100	129
Thompsonville Christian Sch/Thompsonville/Franklin	11826239	618/627-2065	109
THOMPSONVILLE CMTY USD 174/			
THOMPSONVILLE/FRANKLIN	00293166	618/627-2301	108
Thompsonville Grade Sch/Thompsonville/Franklin	11455921	618/627-2511	108
Thompsonville High Sch/Thompsonville/Franklin	00293178	618/627-2301	108
Thornridge High Sch/Dolton/Cook	00274768	708/271-4411	69
Thornton Fractional North HS/Calumet City/Cook	00274809	708/585-1000	69
Thornton Fractional South HS/Lansing/Cook	00274811	708/585-2000	69
THORNTON FRACTNL TWP HSD 215/			
LANSING/COOK	00274794	708/585-2300	69
Thornton Township High Sch/Harvey/Cook	00274782	708/225-4109	69
THORNTON TWP HIGH SCH DIST 205/			
SOUTH HOLLAND/COOK	00274756	708/225-4000	69
Thornwood High Sch/South Holland/Cook	00274770	708/339-7800	69
Three Oaks Elem Sch/Cary/McHenry	04038657	224/357-5450	179
Three Rivers Sch/Channahon/Will	04364274	815/467-4313	241
Thresholds Young Adult Program/Chicago/Cook	04990809	773/537-3280	81
Thurgood Marshall Elem Sch/Bellwood/Cook	00267662	708/544-6995	22
Thurgood Marshall Lrng Center/Rock Island/Rock Island	03245261	309/793-5924	208
Tilden Career Community Acad/Chicago/Cook	00278714	773/535-1625	38
Tilton Elem Sch/Rochelle/Ogle	00312229	815/562-6665	195
Timber Ridge Middle Sch/Plainfield/Will	04452651	815/439-3410	246
Timber Ridge Sch/Arlington HTS/Cook	04198219	847/463-8300	20
Timber Trails Elem Sch/Hoffman Est/Kane	05351804	847/289-6640	131
Timothy Christian High Sch/Elmhurst/Du Page	01844603	630/833-7575	102
Timothy Christian Sch/Elmhurst/Du Page	00291821	630/833-4717	102
Tinley Park High Sch/Tinley Park/Cook	00268111	708/532-1900	23

DISTRICT & SCHOOL TELEPHONE INDEX

Market Data Retrieval

School/City/County DISTRICT/CITY/COUNTY	PID	TELEPHONE NUMBER	PAGE
Tioga Elem Sch/Bensenville/Du Page	00289036	630/766-2602	89
Todd Early Childhood Center/Aurora/Kane	01878850	630/301-5016	132
Todd Hall Elem Sch/Lincolnwood/Cook	00270891	847/675-8235	56
TOLONO CMTY UNIT SCH DIST 7/ TOLONO/CHAMPAIGN	00265327	217/485-6510	12
TONICA CMTY CONS SCH DIST 79/ TONICA/LA SALLE	00303515	815/442-3420	145
Tonica Grade Sch/Tonica/La Salle	00303527	815/442-3420	145
Tonti Elem Sch/Chicago/Cook	00276675	773/535-9280	28
Torah Academy/Buffalo Grove/Lake	11495103	773/771-2613	158
Towanda Elem Sch/Towanda/Mclean	00306622	309/557-4426	187
Townline Elem Sch/Vernon Hills/Lake	10031558	847/990-4901	151
TOWNSHIP HIGH SCH DIST 113/ HIGHLAND PARK/LAKE	00301098	224/765-1000	155
TOWNSHIP HIGH SCH DIST 211/ PALATINE/COOK	00272722	847/755-6600	69
TOWNSHIP HIGH SCH DIST 214/ ARLINGTON HTS/COOK	00271649	847/718-7600	69
Transitions Sch/Quincy/Adams	04328490	217/223-9694	3
Traughber Junior High Sch/Oswego/Kendall	00299732	630/636-2700	138
TREES-THREE RIVERS EFE SYS/ JOLIET/WILL	04182210	815/280-2990	250
TREMONT CMTY UNIT SD 702/ TREMONT/TAZEWELL	00321751	309/925-3461	228
Tremont Grade Sch/Tremont/Tazewell	00321763	309/925-4841	228
Tremont High Sch/Tremont/Tazewell	00321775	309/925-2051	228
Tremont Middle Sch/Tremont/Tazewell	01557915	309/925-3823	228
Trenton Elem Sch/Trenton/Clinton	00266503	618/224-9411	18
Trewyn K-8 Sch/Peoria/Peoria	00313053	309/672-6500	199
Tri-C Elem Sch/Carterville/Williamson	00326751	618/985-8742	251
TRI-CITY CMTY UNIT SCH DIST 1/ BUFFALO/SANGAMON	00319277	217/364-4811	214
Tri-City Sch/Buffalo/Sangamon	01557874	217/364-4811	214
Tri-Co Education Center/Anna/Union	02198366	618/833-4541	229
TRI-CO SPECIAL ED ASSOCIATION/ BLOOMINGTON/MCLEAN	02183957	309/828-5231	188
TRI-CO SPECIAL ED JT AGREEMENT/ CARBONDALE/JACKSON	02184016	618/684-2109	122
Tri-Co Special Ed Sch/Murphysboro/Jackson	00296340	618/684-2109	120
Tri-County at Ward Sch/Du Quoin/Perry	11832941	618/542-5954	201
Tri-County Christian Sch/Freeport/Stephenson	02208325	815/233-1876	225
TRI-POINT CMTY UNIT SD 6J/ KEMPTON/LIVINGSTON	00304571	815/253-6299	162
Tri-Point High Sch/Cullom/Livingston	00304595	815/689-2110	162
Tri-Point Upper ES JHS/Piper City/Livingston	04016477	815/686-2247	162
TRI-VALLEY CMTY UNIT SCH DIST 3/ DOWNS/MCLEAN	00306775	309/378-2351	187
Tri-Valley Elem Sch/Downs/Mclean	00306787	309/378-2031	187
Tri-Valley High Sch/Downs/Mclean	00306799	309/378-2911	187
Tri-Valley Middle Sch/Downs/Mclean	04914063	309/378-3414	187
TRIAD CMTY SCH DIST 2/TROY/ MADISON	00309155	618/667-8851	172
Triad High Sch/Troy/Madison	00309208	618/667-5409	172
Triad Middle Sch/Saint Jacob/Madison	00309181	618/667-5406	172
TRICO CMTY UNIT SCH DIST 176/ CAMPBELL HILL/JACKSON	00296364	618/426-1111	121
Trico Elem Sch/Campbell Hill/Jackson	01557824	618/426-1111	121
Trico High Sch/Campbell Hill/Jackson	00296390	618/426-1111	121
Trico Junior High Sch/Campbell Hill/Jackson	00296405	618/426-1111	121
Trinity Catholic Academy/La Salle/La Salle	00313871	815/223-8523	145
Trinity Christian Sch/Carbondale/Jackson	02165761	618/529-3733	121
Trinity Christian Sch/Shorewood/Will	04990677	815/577-9310	250
Trinity High Sch/River Forest/Cook	00287650	708/771-8383	76
Trinity Lutheran Sch/Arenzville/Cass	00264658	217/997-5535	9
Trinity Lutheran Sch/Bloomington/Mclean	00306816	309/829-7513	188
Trinity Lutheran Sch/Burr Ridge/Du Page	02291833	708/839-1444	102
Trinity Lutheran Sch/Centralia/Marion	00309870	618/532-2614	176
Trinity Lutheran Sch/Edwardsville/Madison	00309416	618/656-7002	173
Trinity Lutheran Sch/Hoffman/Clinton	00266577	618/495-2246	18
Trinity Lutheran Sch/Hoyleton/Washington	00323412	618/493-7754	236
Trinity Lutheran Sch/Lombard/Du Page	00291845	630/627-5601	102
Trinity Lutheran Sch/Red Bud/Randolph	00315207	618/282-2881	206
Trinity Lutheran Sch/Roselle/Du Page	00291857	630/894-3263	102
Trinity Lutheran Sch/Springfield/Sangamon	00319382	217/787-2323	214
Trinity Lutheran Sch/Stewardson/Shelby	00320551	217/682-3881	216
Trinity Lutheran Sch/Tinley Park/Cook	00282882	708/532-3529	81
Trinity Oaks Christian Academy/Cary/McHenry	04990562	847/462-5971	185
Trinity Sch/New Lenox/Will	02858279	815/463-0719	250
Trinity-St John Lutheran Sch/Nashville/Washington	01442762	618/327-8561	236
TRIOPIA CMTY UNIT SCH DIST 27/ CONCORD/MORGAN	00311574	217/457-2283	192
Triopia Grade Sch/Concord/Morgan	00311598	217/457-2284	192
Triopia Jr Sr High Sch/Concord/Morgan	00311603	217/457-2281	192
Tripp Elem Sch/Buffalo Grove/Lake	02846446	847/955-3600	147
TROY CMTY CONS SD 30-C/PLAINFIELD/ WILL	00325824	815/577-6760	247
Troy Heritage Trail Elem Sch/Joliet/Will	04447022	815/577-9195	247
Troy Hofer Elem Sch/Shorewood/Will	11074436	815/577-6758	247
Troy Middle Sch/Plainfield/Will	00325836	815/230-9920	247
Troy-Craughwell Elem Sch/Joliet/Will	01845231	815/577-7313	247
Troy-Cronin Elem Sch/Shorewood/Will	04941664	815/577-7314	248
Troy-Orenic Intermediate Sch/Plainfield/Will	10026541	815/577-6759	248
Troy-Shorewood Elem Sch/Shorewood/Will	00325848	815/577-7312	248
Trusting Hearts Pre-Sch & Kdgn/Palos Heights/Cook	01405037	708/448-2260	81
Turner Elem Sch/Crestwood/Cook	00273300	708/388-7205	63
Turner Elem Sch/West Chicago/Du Page	00291522	630/293-6050	100
Turner-Drew Language Academy/Chicago/Cook	00275449	773/535-5720	35
TUSCOLA CMTY UNIT SD 301/ TUSCOLA/DOUGLAS	00288783	217/253-4241	88
Tuscola High Sch/Tuscola/Douglas	00288824	217/253-2377	88
Twin Echo Elem Sch/Collinsville/Madison	00308503	618/346-6227	170
Twin Groves Middle Sch/Buffalo Grove/Lake	03331339	847/821-8946	151
TWIN RIVERS CAREER & TECH ED/ ROBINSON/CRAWFORD	04184335	618/544-8664	83
TWO RIVERS VOC ED SYSTEM/ VIRGINIA/CASS	04177930	217/452-7239	9
Two-Way Language Imm-Barbour/Rockford/Winnebago	00327456	815/490-4100	255
Tyler Elem Sch/Dekalb/De Kalb	03396987	815/754-2389	85

U

Ucan Academy/Chicago/Cook	05225085	773/588-0180	81
Ulysses S Grant Middle Sch/Springfield/Sangamon	00318974	217/525-3170	213
Union Ridge Elem Sch/Harwood HTS/Cook	00274902	708/867-5822	70
UNION RIDGE SCH DIST 86/ HARWOOD HTS/COOK	00274897	708/867-5822	70
Union Sch/Belleville/St Clair	00316330	618/233-4132	217
Union Sch/Joliet/Will	00325874	815/726-5218	248
UNION SCH DIST 81/JOLIET/WILL	00325862	815/726-5218	248
UNITED CMTY UNIT SCH DIST 304/ MONMOUTH/WARREN	00323151	309/734-9413	234
United Ed Cultural Acad/Chicago/Cook	05264811	773/238-2707	81
United High Sch/Monmouth/Warren	00323175	309/734-9411	234
United Junior High Sch/Monmouth/Warren	10817120	309/734-8511	235
United North Elem Sch/Alexis/Warren	00323022	309/482-3332	235
United Township High Sch/East Moline/Rock Island	00316160	309/752-1633	209
United Twp Area Career Center/East Moline/Rock Island	04199201	309/752-1691	209
UNITED TWP HIGH SCH DIST 30/ EAST MOLINE/ROCK ISLAND	00316146	309/752-1611	209
United West Elem Sch/Monmouth/Warren	02056005	309/734-8513	235
Unity Christian Academy/South Holland/Cook	12318211	708/980-1040	81
Unity Christian Sch/Energy/Williamson	02208313	618/942-3802	252
Unity Christian Sch/Fulton/Whiteside	00324521	815/589-3912	240
Unity Christian Sch/Momence/Kankakee	02205086	815/472-3230	137
Unity East Elem Sch/Philo/Champaign	00265341	217/684-5218	12
Unity Elem Sch/Brookport/Massac	00310491	618/564-2582	178
Unity Elem Sch/Mendon/Adams	00262985	217/936-2512	2
Unity High Sch/Mendon/Adams	00262997	217/936-2116	2
Unity High Sch/Tolono/Champaign	00265389	217/485-6230	12
Unity Junior High Sch/Cicero/Cook	05265023	708/863-8229	42
Unity Junior High Sch/Tolono/Champaign	00265391	217/485-6735	12
Unity Lutheran Chrn Elem Sch/E Saint Louis/St Clair	11710379	618/874-6605	223
Unity Middle Sch/Mendon/Adams	04945581	217/936-2111	2
UNITY POINT CMTY CONS SD 140/ CARBONDALE/JACKSON	00296429	618/529-4151	121
Unity Point Elem Sch/Carbondale/Jackson	00296443	618/529-4151	121
Unity West Elem Sch/Tolono/Champaign	00265339	217/485-3918	12
Univ of Chicago CS-Donoghue/Chicago/Cook	10009268	773/285-5301	41
Univ of Chicago CS-Nko/Chicago/Cook	04812001	773/536-2399	41
Univ of Chicago CS-Woodlawn/Chicago/Cook	10029165	773/752-8101	41
Univ of Chicago Lab Sch/Chicago/Cook	00282375	773/702-9450	81
Universal Sch/Bridgeview/Cook	03341437	708/599-4100	81

Illinois School Directory
DISTRICT & SCHOOL TELEPHONE INDEX

School/City/County DISTRICT/CITY/COUNTY	PID	TELEPHONE NUMBER	PAGE
University High Sch/Normal/Mclean	02132348	309/438-8346	1
University Laboratory High Sch/Urbana/ Champaign	01404904	217/333-2870	1
University Primary Sch/Champaign/Champaign	02956766	217/333-3996	13
Uplift Community High Sch/Chicago/Cook	10009153	773/534-2875	36
Urban Prep CS-Bronzeville/Chicago/Cook	11548712	773/624-3444	41
Urban Prep CS-Englewood/Chicago/Cook	10019809	773/535-9724	41
Urban Prep CS-West/Chicago/Cook	11446566	773/534-8860	41
Urbana Adult Education Sch/Urbana/ Champaign	11449984	217/384-3530	13
Urbana Early Childhood Sch/Urbana/ Champaign	00265482	217/843-3616	13
Urbana High Sch/Urbana/Champaign	00265468	217/384-3505	13
Urbana Middle Sch/Urbana/Champaign	00265470	217/384-3685	13
URBANA SCH DIST 116/URBANA/ CHAMPAIGN	00265406	217/384-3600	12
UT AREA CAREER CENTER/EAST MOLINE/ ROCK ISLAND	04178219	309/752-1691	210

V

School/City/County DISTRICT/CITY/COUNTY	PID	TELEPHONE NUMBER	PAGE
V Blanche Graham Elem Sch/Naperville/ Du Page	04457015	630/428-6900	96
V H Nelson Elem Sch/Niles/Cook	00269189	847/965-0050	47
Valeo Academy/Hoffman Est/Cook	12113592	847/645-9300	81
Valeska Hinton Early Ed Ctr/Peoria/Peoria	04039003	309/672-6810	199
VALLEY ED FOR EMPLOYMENT SYS/ SUGAR GROVE/KANE	04182284	630/466-5736	134
VALLEY VIEW CMTY SD 365-U/ ROMEOVILLE/WILL	00325587	815/886-2700	248
Valley View Early Chldhd Ctr/Romeoville/ Will	10027648	815/886-7827	248
Valley View Elem Sch/McHenry/McHenry	00305800	779/244-1500	183
VALMEYER CMTY SCH DIST 3/ VALMEYER/MONROE	00310908	618/935-2100	190
Valmeyer Sch/Valmeyer/Monroe	00310922	618/935-2100	190
Van Orin Grade Sch/Van Orin/Bureau	00263771	815/638-3141	6
Vandalia Christian Academy/Vandalia/ Fayette	11232339	618/283-9901	106
Vandalia Cmty High Sch/Vandalia/Fayette	00292655	618/283-5155	106
VANDALIA CMTY UNIT SD 203/ VANDALIA/FAYETTE	00292590	618/283-4525	106
Vandalia Elem Sch/Vandalia/Fayette	00292629	618/283-5166	106
Vandalia Junior High Sch/Vandalia/Fayette	00292667	618/283-5151	106
Vanderpoel Magnet Elem Sch/Chicago/Cook	00276704	773/535-2690	34
Vanguard HS/Arlington HTS/Cook	04746581	847/718-7870	70
Vaughn Occupational High Sch/Chicago/Cook	00280470	773/534-3600	37
Velma Thomas Early Chldhd Ctr/Chicago/Cook	05101647	773/535-4088	28
VENICE CMTY UNIT SCH DIST 3/ VENICE/MADISON	00309222	618/274-7953	172
Venice Elem Sch/Venice/Madison	00309234	618/274-7953	172
Verda Dierzen Early Lrng Ctr/Woodstock/ McHenry	00306062	815/338-8883	184
VERMILION ASSOC FOR SPECIAL ED/ DANVILLE/VERMILION	02184080	217/443-8273	233
VERMILION VOC ED DELIVERY SYS/ DANVILLE/VERMILION	04182533	217/443-8742	233
Vernon Hills High Sch/Vernon Hills/Lake	04865539	847/932-2000	148
Vernon L Barkstall Elem Sch/Champaign/ Champaign	04803373	217/373-5580	10
Veterans Memorial Middle Sch/Blue Island/ Cook	04746995	708/385-6630	45
Victor J Andrew High Sch/Tinley Park/Cook	01538775	708/342-5800	44
Victory Christian Academy/Mount Vernon/ Jefferson	04328581	618/214-1666	124
Vienna Elem Sch/Vienna/Johnson	00297461	618/658-8286	127
Vienna High Sch/Vienna/Johnson	00297485	618/658-4461	127
VIENNA HIGH SCH DIST 13-3/ VIENNA/JOHNSON	00297473	618/658-4461	127
VIENNA PUBLIC SCH DIST 55/ VIENNA/JOHNSON	00297459	618/658-8286	127
Viking Middle Sch/Gurnee/Lake	00300927	847/336-2108	150
VILLA GROVE CMTY UNIT SD 302/ VILLA GROVE/DOUGLAS	00288836	217/832-2261	88
Villa Grove Elem Sch/Villa Grove/Douglas	00288848	217/832-2261	88
Villa Grove High Sch/Villa Grove/Douglas	11446463	217/832-2321	88
Villa Grove Junior High Sch/Villa Grove/ Douglas	11446451	217/832-2261	88
Villa Montessori Sch/Moline/Rock Island	02440858	309/764-7047	210
Village Elem Sch/Round Lake/Lake	01538555	847/270-9470	155
Village Leadership Academy/Chicago/Cook	11574527	312/675-0056	81
Vincent Gray Academy/E Saint Louis/ St Clair	02138055	618/875-7880	223
Vine Academy/Burr Ridge/Du Page	12364947	630/423-5916	102
Virgil Grissom Middle Sch/Tinley Park/Cook	01398252	708/429-3030	53
Virginia Cmty Unit 64 Sch/Virginia/Cass	00264622	217/452-3085	9
VIRGINIA CMTY UNIT SCH DIST 64/ VIRGINIA/CASS	00264608	217/452-3085	9
Virginia Frank Child Dev Ctr/Chicago/Cook	01779151	773/765-3100	81
Virginia Lake Elem Sch/Palatine/Cook	00272679	847/963-7100	43
Vision Way Christian Sch/Taylorville/ Christian	11226940	217/824-6722	15
Visitation Catholic Sch/Kewanee/Henry	00314021	309/856-7451	118
Visitation Sch/Chicago/Cook	00287686	773/373-5200	76
Visitation Sch/Elmhurst/Du Page	00326737	630/834-4931	101
VIT CMTY UNIT SCH DIST 2/ TABLE GROVE/FULTON	00293740	309/758-5138	110
Vit Elem Sch/Table Grove/Fulton	01830298	309/758-5138	110
Vit Jr Sr High Sch/Table Grove/Fulton	00293776	309/758-5136	110
Vivian Adams Early Chldhd Ctr/E Saint Louis/ St Clair	04838835	618/646-3290	219
Von Steuben Metro Science Ctr/Chicago/Cook	00281096	773/534-5100	37
Von Steuben Middle Sch/Peoria/Peoria	00313077	309/672-6561	199

W

School/City/County DISTRICT/CITY/COUNTY	PID	TELEPHONE NUMBER	PAGE
W A Johnson Elem Sch/Bensenville/Du Page	00289048	630/766-2605	89
W C Petty Elem Sch/Antioch/Lake	02108074	847/838-8101	146
W J Murphy Elem Sch/Round Lake/Lake	00301933	847/270-9950	155
W J Zahnow Elem Sch/Waterloo/Monroe	00310960	618/939-3458	190
W M Hadley Junior High Sch/Glen Ellyn/ Du Page	00289775	630/790-6450	94
W S Beaupre Elem Sch/Aurora/Kane	00297631	630/299-5390	129
W S Christopher Elem Sch/Chicago/Cook	04950421	773/535-9375	33
W W Walker Elem Sch/Bedford Park/Cook	00274689	708/458-7150	45
W W Woodbury Sch/Sandwich/De Kalb	00288276	815/786-6316	86
WABASH CMTY UNIT SCH DIST 348/ MOUNT CARMEL/WABASH	00322949	618/262-4181	234
WABASH-OHIO VALLEY SP ED DIST/ NORRIS CITY/WHITE	02182185	618/378-2131	238
Wacker Elem Sch/Chicago/Cook	00276730	773/535-2821	28
Wadsworth Elem Sch/Chicago/Cook	00276742	773/535-0730	28
Wagoner Elem Sch/Sauk Village/Cook	00273831	708/758-3322	44
Walden Elem Sch/Deerfield/Lake	00300642	847/945-9660	149
Walker Elem Sch/Clarendon Hls/Du Page	00290164	630/861-4600	91
Walker Elem Sch/Evanston/Cook	00269476	847/859-8330	48
Walker's Grove Elem Sch/Plainfield/Will	04015928	815/439-2885	246
WALLACE CMTY CONS SCH DIST 195/ OTTAWA/LA SALLE	00303565	815/433-2986	145
Wallace Elem Sch/Ottawa/La Salle	00303577	815/433-2986	145
Walnut Trails Elem Sch/Shorewood/Grundy	05341237	815/290-7400	112
Walsh Elem Sch/Chicago/Cook	00278740	773/534-7950	32
Walsh Elem Sch/Lockport/Will	00325276	815/838-7858	249
Walsh Elem Sch/Summit/Cook	00274677	708/458-7165	45
Walt Disney Magnet Sch/Chicago/Cook	00279469	773/534-5840	28
Walt Whitman Elem Sch/Wheeling/Cook	00281541	847/520-2795	71
Walter F Fierke Ed Center/Oak Forest/Cook	00274885	708/614-4520	42
Walter Lawson Children's Home/Loves Park/ Winnebago	01780643	815/633-6636	256
Walter Payton College Prep HS/Chicago/Cook	04922917	773/534-0034	28
Walter Sundling Jr High Sch/Palatine/Cook	00272617	847/963-3700	43
Waltham Elem Sch/Utica/La Salle	00303591	815/667-4417	145
WALTHAM ELEMENTARY SD 185/ UTICA/LA SALLE	00303589	815/667-4417	145
Walther Lutheran High Sch/Melrose Park/ Cook	01441782	708/344-0404	81
WALTONVILLE CMTY UNIT SD 1/ WALTONVILLE/JEFFERSON	00296936	618/279-7211	124
Waltonville Grade Sch/Waltonville/ Jefferson	00296948	618/279-7221	124
Waltonville High Sch/Waltonville/Jefferson	00296950	618/279-7211	124
Wanda Kendall Elem Sch/Watseka/Iroquois	00295786	815/432-4581	119
Ward Grundy Elem Sch/Morton/Tazewell	00321335	309/263-1421	227
WARREN COMMUNITY UNIT SD 205/ WARREN/JO DAVIESS	00297306	815/745-2653	126
Warren Elem Sch/Chicago/Cook	00276754	773/535-6625	35
Warren Elem Sch/Warren/Jo Daviess	00297332	815/745-2653	126
Warren Jr Sr High Sch/Warren/Jo Daviess	00297344	815/745-2641	126
Warren Park Elem Sch/Cicero/Cook	12168767	708/780-2299	42
WARREN TWP HIGH SCH DIST 121/ GURNEE/LAKE	00301995	847/662-1400	155
Warren Twp HS-Almond Campus/Gurnee/Lake	05279414	847/662-1400	155
Warren Twp HS-O'Plaine Campus/Gurnee/Lake	00302004	847/662-1400	155
WARRENSBURG-LATHAM CU SD 11/ WARRENSBURG/MACON	00307523	217/672-3514	166

DISTRICT & SCHOOL TELEPHONE INDEX

Market Data Retrieval

School/City/County DISTRICT/CITY/COUNTY	PID	TELEPHONE NUMBER	PAGE
Warrensburg-Latham Elem Sch/Warrensburg/Macon	00307535	217/672-3612	166
Warrensburg-Latham High Sch/Warrensburg/Macon	00307547	217/672-3612	166
Warrensburg-Latham Middle Sch/Warrensburg/Macon	11815008	217/672-3321	166
WARSAW CMTY UNIT SCH DIST 316/ **WARSAW/HANCOCK**	00294823	217/256-4282	115
Warsaw Elem Sch/Warsaw/Hancock	00294847	217/256-4614	115
Warsaw High Sch/Warsaw/Hancock	00294859	217/256-4281	115
Wasco Elem Sch/Wasco/Kane	00298855	331/228-2900	129
Washington Academy/Belvidere/Boone	00263501	815/544-3124	4
Washington Attendance Center/Carmi/White	00323761	618/382-4631	238
WASHINGTON CMTY HS DIST 308/ **WASHINGTON/TAZEWELL**	00321816	309/444-3167	229
Washington Dual Language Acad/Maywood/Cook	12032699	708/450-2065	57
Washington Early Childhood Ctr/East Alton/Madison	00308591	618/433-2001	170
Washington Elem Mid Sch/Johnston City/Williamson	02043890	618/983-7581	251
Washington Elem Sch/Bloomington/Mclean	00306282	309/829-7034	185
Washington Elem Sch/Dixon/Lee	00303979	815/934-9660	160
Washington Elem Sch/Elgin/Kane	00298544	847/888-5270	131
Washington Elem Sch/Evanston/Cook	00269488	847/905-4900	48
Washington Elem Sch/Glenview/Cook	00269191	847/965-4780	47
Washington Elem Sch/Jacksonville/Morgan	00311536	217/243-6711	192
Washington Elem Sch/Marion/Williamson	00327080	618/993-8534	251
Washington Elem Sch/Monticello/Piatt	00314459	217/762-8511	202
Washington Elem Sch/Mundelein/Lake	00301672	847/949-2714	153
Washington Elem Sch/Pana/Christian	00265743	217/562-7500	14
Washington Elem Sch/Pontiac/Livingston	00304430	815/844-3687	161
Washington Elem Sch/Riverdale/Cook	00268965	708/201-2078	46
Washington Elem Sch/Robinson/Crawford	00287870	618/544-2233	83
Washington Elem Sch/Rockford/Winnebago	00327846	815/966-3740	255
Washington Elem Sch/Rushville/Schuyler	00320197	217/322-4311	215
Washington Elem Sch/Sterling/Whiteside	01170660	815/625-2372	240
Washington Elem Sch/Waukegan/Lake	00302274	224/303-2220	156
Washington Elem Sch/Wheaton/Du Page	03247879	630/682-2222	92
Washington Gifted Sch/Peoria/Peoria	00313089	309/672-6563	199
Washington High Sch/Chicago/Cook	00276778	773/535-5725	38
Washington High Sch/Washington/Tazewell	00321828	309/444-3167	229
Washington Intermediate Sch/Pekin/Tazewell	03006338	309/477-4721	228
Washington Irving Elem Sch/Chicago/Cook	00277825	773/534-7295	32
Washington Junior High Sch/Joliet/Will	00325109	815/727-5271	243
Washington Junior High Sch/Naperville/Du Page	00290839	630/420-6390	98
Washington Junior High Sch/Oglesby/La Salle	00303096	815/883-3517	143
Washington Junior High Sch/Riverdale/Cook	12108054	708/201-2078	46
Washington Junior High Sch/Rock Island/Rock Island	00316029	309/793-5915	208
Washington McKinley Elem Sch/Chicago HTS/Cook	00268472	708/756-4841	25
Washington Middle Sch/Aurora/Kane	00297813	630/301-5017	132
Washington Middle Sch/Springfield/Sangamon	00319239	217/525-3182	213
Washington Middle Sch/Washington/Tazewell	00321799	309/444-3361	229
Washington Sch/Belleville/St Clair	00316342	618/277-2017	217
Washington Sch/Harvard/McHenry	00305587	815/943-6367	181
WASHINGTON SCH DIST 52/WASHINGTON/ **TAZEWELL**	00321787	309/444-4182	229
Washington-Monroe Elem Sch/Lincoln/Logan	00304856	217/732-4764	164
Waterbury Elem Sch/Roselle/Du Page	01557800	630/893-8180	96
WATERLOO CMTY UNIT SCH DIST 5/ **WATERLOO/MONROE**	00310934	618/939-3453	190
Waterloo High Sch/Waterloo/Monroe	00310792	618/939-3455	190
Waterloo Junior High Sch/Waterloo/Monroe	00310984	618/939-3457	190
Watseka Cmty High Sch/Watseka/Iroquois	00295798	815/432-2486	119
Waubonsie Valley High Sch/Aurora/Du Page	01398290	630/375-3300	96
Wauconda Cmty High Sch/Wauconda/Lake	00302066	847/526-6611	155
WAUCONDA CMTY UNIT SD 118/ **WAUCONDA/LAKE**	00302016	847/526-7690	155
Wauconda Grade Sch/Wauconda/Lake	00302054	847/526-6671	155
Wauconda Middle Sch/Wauconda/Lake	00302078	847/526-2122	155
WAUKEGAN CMTY UNIT SD 60/ **WAUKEGAN/LAKE**	00302080	224/303-1000	156
Waukegan HS Brookside/Waukegan/Lake	00302298	224/303-3000	156
Waukegan HS-Washington/Waukegan/Lake	04882795	224/303-3301	156
WAVERLY CMTY UNIT SD 6/WAVERLY/ **MORGAN**	00311615	217/435-8121	193
Waverly Elem Sch/Waverly/Morgan	00311627	217/435-2331	193
Waverly High Sch/Waverly/Morgan	00311639	217/435-2211	193
Wayne Builta Elem Sch/Bolingbrook/Du Page	04876382	630/226-4400	96

School/City/County DISTRICT/CITY/COUNTY	PID	TELEPHONE NUMBER	PAGE
Wayne City Attendance Center/Wayne City/Wayne	00323668	618/895-3103	237
WAYNE CITY CMTY UNIT SD 100/ **WAYNE CITY/WAYNE**	00323618	618/895-3103	237
Wayne City High Sch/Wayne City/Wayne	00323670	618/895-3108	237
Wayne Elem Sch/Wayne/Kane	00298556	630/736-7100	131
Wayne Thomas Elem Sch/Highland Park/Lake	00301153	224/765-3900	154
Webster Elem Sch/Collinsville/Madison	00308527	618/346-6301	170
Webster Elem Sch/Rushville/Schuyler	00320202	217/322-4311	215
Wegner Elem Sch/West Chicago/Du Page	04284258	630/293-6400	100
Wells Community Academy HS/Chicago/Cook	00281163	773/534-7010	37
Wells Elem Sch/East Moline/Rock Island	00315465	309/796-1251	207
Wells Elem Sch/Grayville/White	00323826	618/375-7214	238
Wells Preparatory Elem Acad/Chicago/Cook	04755659	773/535-1204	33
Welsh Elem Sch/Rockford/Winnebago	00328072	815/966-3260	255
Wendell E Green Elem Sch/Chicago/Cook	00276780	773/535-2575	35
Wendell Phillips Academy HS/Chicago/Cook	00275566	773/535-1603	26
Wentworth Elem Sch/Chicago/Cook	00276807	773/535-3394	35
Wentworth Intermediate Sch/Calumet City/Cook	04879255	708/868-7926	24
Wentworth Junior High Sch/Calumet City/Cook	00268290	708/862-0750	24
WESCLIN CMTY UNIT SCH DIST 3/ **TRENTON/CLINTON**	00266474	618/224-7583	18
Wesclin Middle Sch/Trenton/Clinton	00266527	618/224-7355	18
Wesclin Senior High Sch/Trenton/Clinton	04236914	618/224-7341	18
Wescott Elem Sch/Northbrook/Cook	00272071	847/272-4660	60
Wesley Elem Sch/Addison/Du Page	00288953	630/628-4060	89
Wesmere Elem Sch/Plainfield/Will	04452649	815/439-3244	246
WEST 40 INTERM SERV CENTER 2/ **HILLSIDE/COOK**	03064691	708/449-4284	82
West 40 Regional Safe Sch MS/Hillside/Cook	11935830	708/236-3250	20
West Aurora High Sch/Aurora/Kane	00297825	630/301-5600	132
WEST AURORA SCH DIST 129/ **AURORA/KANE**	00297643	630/301-5000	132
West Campus Pre-Kindergarten/Mason City/Mason	11433600	217/842-9846	177
WEST CARROLL CUSD 314/MOUNT CARROLL/ **CARROLL**	00264464	815/734-3374	8
West Carroll High Sch/Savanna/Carroll	00264426	815/273-7715	9
West Carroll Middle Sch/Mount Carroll/Carroll	00264373	815/244-2002	9
West Carroll Primary Sch/Savanna/Carroll	00264397	815/273-7747	9
WEST CENTRAL CMTY UNIT SD 235/ **BIGGSVILLE/HENDERSON**	00295009	309/627-2371	116
West Central Elem Sch/Biggsville/Henderson	00295011	309/627-2339	116
West Central High Sch/Biggsville/Henderson	00295059	309/627-2377	116
WEST CENTRAL IL SPEC ED CO-OP/ **MACOMB/MCDONOUGH**	02182214	309/837-3911	179
West Central Middle Sch/Stronghurst/Henderson	10001797	309/924-1681	116
WEST CHICAGO ELEMENTARY SD 33/ **WEST CHICAGO/DU PAGE**	00291479	630/293-6000	99
West Elem Sch/Alton/Madison	00308137	618/463-2134	169
West Elem Sch/Crystal Lake/McHenry	00305446	815/788-5550	181
West Elem Sch/Sycamore/De Kalb	00288434	815/899-8199	86
West Elem Sch/Zion/Lake	00302535	847/746-8222	157
WEST HARVEY-DIXMOOR PUB SD 147/ **HARVEY/COOK**	00270059	708/339-9500	70
West Joliet Twp High Sch/Joliet/Will	00325159	815/727-6951	243
West Junior High Sch/Belleville/St Clair	00316354	618/234-8200	217
West Leyden High Sch/Northlake/Cook	00270841	847/451-3122	55
West Lincoln-Broadwell ES/Lincoln/Logan	00304985	217/732-2630	164
WEST LINCOLN-BROADWELL ESD 92/ **LINCOLN/LOGAN**	00304973	217/732-2630	164
West Middle Sch/Rockford/Winnebago	04885723	815/966-3200	255
WEST NORTHFIELD SCH DIST 31/ **NORTHBROOK/COOK**	00281228	847/272-6880	70
West Oak Interm Sch/Mundelein/Lake	00300666	847/970-3544	149
West Oak Middle Sch/Mundelein/Lake	00300680	847/566-9220	149
West Park Academy/Chicago/Cook	04755611	773/534-4940	31
WEST PRAIRIE CMTY SCH DIST 103/ **COLCHESTER/MCDONOUGH**	00305068	309/776-3180	178
West Prairie High Sch/Sciota/McDonough	00305264	309/456-3750	178
West Prairie Middle Sch/Colchester/McDonough	00305082	309/776-3220	178
West Prairie North Elem Sch/Good Hope/McDonough	00305252	309/456-3920	179
West Prarie South Elem Sch/Colchester/McDonough	00305070	309/776-3790	179
West Ridge Elem Sch/Chicago/Cook	11548671	773/534-8250	28
West Salem Elem Sch/West Salem/Edwards	00292136	618/456-8881	104

Illinois School Directory

DISTRICT & SCHOOL TELEPHONE INDEX

School/City/County DISTRICT/CITY/COUNTY	PID	TELEPHONE NUMBER	PAGE
West Sch/Glencoe/Cook	03388904	847/835-6600	51
West Side Christian Sch/Chicago/Cook	01844457	773/542-0663	81
West Side Primary Sch/Harrisburg/Saline	02107745	618/253-7637	211
West View Elem Sch/Rockford/Winnebago	00328096	815/654-4945	255
WEST WASHINGTON CO CMTY SD 10/OKAWVILLE/WASHINGTON	00323357	618/243-6454	236
Westbrook Primary Sch/Glenview/Cook	00270009	847/998-5055	51
Westbrook Sch/Mt Prospect/Cook	10904993	847/394-7340	58
Westchester Intermediate Sch/Westchester/Cook	00281278	708/562-1011	70
Westchester Middle Sch/Westchester/Cook	00281292	708/450-2735	70
Westchester Primary Sch/Westchester/Cook	04282353	708/562-1509	70
WESTCHESTER PUBLIC SD 92 1/2/WESTCHESTER/COOK	00281254	708/450-2700	70
Westcott Elem Sch/Chicago/Cook	00276819	773/535-3090	35
Westdale Elem Sch/Northlake/Cook	00271132	847/455-4060	57
WESTERN AREA CAREER SYSTEM/CANTON/FULTON	04180274	309/575-3230	110
WESTERN AREA CAREER SYSTEM/MACOMB/MCDONOUGH	03266552	309/837-4821	179
Western Ave Elem Sch/Flossmoor/Cook	00269672	708/647-7400	49
Western Ave Elem Sch/Geneva/Kane	00298659	630/463-3500	131
Western Barry Elem Sch/Barry/Pike	11130248	217/335-2323	203
WESTERN CUSD 12/BARRY/PIKE	00314693	217/335-2323	203
Western High Sch/Barry/Pike	11130236	217/335-2323	203
Western Junior High Sch/Kinderhook/Pike	00314722	217/432-8324	203
WESTERN SPRINGS SCH DIST 101/WESTERN SPRGS/COOK	00281307	708/246-3700	71
Western Trails Elem Sch/Carol Stream/Du Page	02055984	630/588-6400	90
Westfair Christian Academy/Jacksonville/Morgan	01405398	217/243-7100	193
Westfield Community Sch/Algonquin/McHenry	04455653	847/532-7800	180
Westfield Elem Sch/Glen Ellyn/Du Page	00289892	630/858-2770	90
Westfield Middle Sch/Bloomingdale/Du Page	00289074	630/529-6211	89
Westfield Sch/Winthrop HBR/Lake	00302391	847/872-5438	156
Westgate Elem Sch/Arlington HTS/Cook	00267167	847/398-4292	21
Westhaven Sch/Belleville/St Clair	04746816	618/257-9201	217
Westinghouse College Prep/Chicago/Cook	11446671	773/534-6400	37
Westlake Christian Academy/Grayslake/Lake	01405300	847/548-6209	158
Westminster Christian Sch/Elgin/Kane	02087638	847/695-0310	134
Westmont High Sch/Westmont/Du Page	01530278	630/468-8100	92
Westmont Junior High Sch/Westmont/Du Page	00291467	630/468-8200	92
Westmoor Elem Sch/Northbrook/Cook	00272045	847/498-7960	59
Westmore Elem Sch/Lombard/Du Page	00291405	630/516-7500	99
Westview Elem Sch/Canton/Fulton	01538529	309/647-2111	109
Westview Elem Sch/Champaign/Champaign	00264892	217/351-3905	10
Westview Elem Sch/Wood Dale/Du Page	00291651	630/766-8040	100
Westview Hills Middle Sch/Willowbrook/Du Page	01400556	630/515-4830	97
WESTVILLE CMTY UNIT SCH DIST 2/WESTVILLE/VERMILION	00322834	217/267-3141	233
Westville High Sch/Westville/Vermilion	00322860	217/267-2183	233
Westville Junior High Sch/Westville/Vermilion	00322872	217/267-2185	233
Westwood Elem Sch/Woodstock/McHenry	04802202	815/337-8173	184
WETHERSFIELD CMTY UNIT SD 230/KEWANEE/HENRY	00295463	309/853-4860	117
Wethersfield Elem Sch/Kewanee/Henry	00295475	309/853-4800	117
Wethersfield Jr Sr High Sch/Kewanee/Henry	00295487	309/853-4205	118
Wharton Fifth Grade Center/Summit/Cook	00274653	708/458-0640	45
Wheatland Academy/Naperville/Du Page	03389154	630/375-3375	96
Wheatlands Elem Sch/Aurora/Kendall	04939544	630/636-3500	138
Wheaton Academy/West Chicago/Du Page	00291871	630/562-7500	102
Wheaton Christian Grammar Sch/Winfield/Du Page	05262186	630/668-1385	102
Wheaton North High Sch/Wheaton/Du Page	00291015	630/784-7300	92
Wheaton-Warrenville South HS/Wheaton/Du Page	00290891	630/784-7200	92
WHEELING CMTY CONS SCH DIST 21/WHEELING/COOK	00281371	847/537-8270	71
Wheeling High Sch/Wheeling/Cook	00271728	847/718-7000	70
Whistler Elem Sch/Chicago/Cook	00276821	773/535-5560	36
White Eagle Elem Sch/Naperville/Du Page	04364937	630/375-3600	96
White Heath Elem Sch/White Heath/Piatt	00314461	217/762-8511	202
Whitehead Elem Sch/Rockford/Winnebago	00328125	815/229-2840	255
Whiteside Area Career Center/Sterling/Whiteside	01170672	815/626-5810	238
Whiteside Elem Sch/Belleville/St Clair	00317621	618/239-0000	222
Whiteside Middle School/Belleville/St Clair	05100655	618/239-0000	222
WHITESIDE REGIONAL VOC SYSTEM/STERLING/WHITESIDE	04180224	815/626-5810	241
WHITESIDE SCH DIST 115/BELLEVILLE/ST CLAIR	00317619	618/239-0000	222
Whitman Post Elem Sch/Rockton/Winnebago	04360113	815/624-4006	255
Whitney Young Magnet High Sch/Chicago/Cook	01398276	773/534-7500	28
Whittier Elem Sch/Chicago/Cook	00278790	773/535-4590	32
Whittier Elem Sch/Downers Grove/Du Page	00289476	630/719-5865	93
Whittier Elem Sch/Harvey/Cook	00270205	708/331-1130	52
Whittier Elem Sch/Northlake/Cook	00267791	708/449-3175	22
Whittier Elem Sch/Oak Park/Cook	00272423	708/524-3080	61
Whittier Elem Sch/Waukegan/Lake	03398064	224/303-1900	156
Whittier Elem Sch/Wheaton/Du Page	00291077	630/682-2185	92
Whittier Primary Sch/Peoria/Peoria	00313118	309/672-6569	199
Whittier Sch/Blue Island/Cook	04943844	708/385-6170	45
Wiesbrook Elem Sch/Wheaton/Du Page	00291089	630/682-2190	92
Wilbur Trimpe Middle Sch/Bethalto/Madison	00308321	618/377-7240	169
Wilco Area Career Center/Romeoville/Will	01536703	815/838-6941	241
Wilcox Elem Sch/Springfield/Sangamon	00319253	217/525-3281	213
Wild Rose Elem Sch/Saint Charles/Kane	00298867	331/228-3000	129
Wilder-Waite Elem Sch/Peoria/Peoria	00312358	309/243-7728	196
Wildwood IB World Magnet Sch/Chicago/Cook	00281199	773/534-1188	29
WILL CO REGIONAL OFFICE OF EDU/JOLIET/WILL	02098479	815/740-8360	250
WILL CO SCH DIST 92/LOCKPORT/WILL	00325240	815/838-8031	248
Willa Cather Elem Sch/Chicago/Cook	00279263	773/534-6780	31
Willard Elem Sch/Moline/Rock Island	00315726	309/743-1620	208
Willard Elem Sch/River Forest/Cook	00273568	708/366-6740	65
Willard Elem Sch/South Elgin/Kane	00298568	847/888-5275	131
William Beye Elem Sch/Oak Park/Cook	00272320	708/524-3070	61
William Carter Elem Sch/Chicago/Cook	00275281	773/535-0860	26
William E Young Elem Sch/Homer Glen/Will	11551159	708/226-2010	242
William F Finkl Academy/Chicago/Cook	04428698	773/535-5850	32
William F Murphy Elem Sch/Woodridge/Du Page	00290023	630/795-6500	100
William Fremd High Sch/Palatine/Cook	00272772	847/755-2600	69
William H Brown Elem Sch/Chicago/Cook	00276986	773/534-7250	32
William Hammerschmidt Elem Sch/Lombard/Du Page	00290542	630/827-4200	97
William Hatch Elem Sch/Oak Park/Cook	00272344	708/524-3095	61
William Holliday Elem Sch/Fairview HTS/St Clair	00317516	618/233-7588	221
William J Attea Middle Sch/Glenview/Cook	05279153	847/486-7700	51
William J Butler Elem Sch/Lockport/Will	04940945	708/226-5155	242
William L Thompson Elem Sch/Lake Villa/Lake	04871033	847/265-2488	152
William M Bedell-A R C Sch/Wood River/Madison	02987234	618/251-2175	173
Williamsburg Elem Sch/Geneva/Kane	11074591	630/463-3100	131
WILLIAMSFIELD CMTY UNIT SD 210/WILLIAMSFIELD/KNOX	00300305	309/639-2219	140
Williamsfield Sch/Williamsfield/Knox	00300317	309/639-2216	140
WILLIAMSON CO CTE SYSTEM/MARION/WILLIAMSON	04184438	618/993-2138	252
WILLIAMSON CO SPECIAL ED DIST/MARION/WILLIAMSON	02184107	618/993-2138	252
WILLIAMSVILLE CMTY UNIT SD 15/WILLIAMSVILLE/SANGAMON	00319291	217/566-2014	214
Williamsville High Sch/Williamsville/Sangamon	00319320	217/566-3361	214
Williamsville Junior High Sch/Williamsville/Sangamon	01557886	217/566-3600	214
Williamsville Middle Sch/Williamsville/Sangamon	12031827	217/566-4070	214
Willow Bend Elem Sch/Rolling MDWS/Cook	00272681	847/963-7300	43
Willow Creek Elem Sch/Woodridge/Du Page	00290011	630/795-6600	100
Willow Elem Sch/Homewood/Cook	00270384	708/798-3720	52
Willow Elem Sch/Pekin/Tazewell	00321555	309/477-4716	228
Willow Grove Elem Sch/Centralia/Clinton	00266565	618/532-3313	18
Willow Grove Kindergarten/Buffalo Grove/Lake	00301189	847/541-3660	151
WILLOW GROVE SCH DIST 46/CENTRALIA/CLINTON	00266553	618/532-3313	18
Willow Springs Elem Sch/Willow Spgs/Cook	00281565	708/839-6828	71
WILLOW SPRINGS SCH DIST 108/WILLOW SPGS/COOK	00281553	708/839-6828	71
Willowbrook Elem Sch/Glenview/Cook	00272083	847/498-1090	60
Willowbrook High Sch/Villa Park/Du Page	00289701	630/530-3400	93
Willowbrook Middle Sch/South Beloit/Winnebago	11448318	815/389-3957	253
Willowglen Academy-Illinois/Freeport/Stephenson	11227712	815/233-6162	225
Willows Academy/Des Plaines/Cook	02156265	847/824-6900	81

School Year 2020-2021   800-333-8802   IL-V47

DISTRICT & SCHOOL TELEPHONE INDEX

Market Data Retrieval

School/City/County DISTRICT/CITY/COUNTY	PID	TELEPHONE NUMBER	PAGE
Wilma G Rudolph Learning Ctr/Chicago/Cook	01844031	773/534-7460	32
Wilmette Junior High Sch/Wilmette/Cook	00281656	847/512-6600	72
WILMETTE PUBLIC SCH DIST 39/			
WILMETTE/COOK	00281577	847/256-2450	71
WILMINGTON CMTY UNIT SD 209-U/			
WILMINGTON/WILL	00325886	815/926-1751	249
Wilmington High Sch/Wilmington/Will	00325927	815/926-1752	249
Wilmington Middle Sch/Wilmington/Will	00325915	815/926-1687	249
Wilmot Elem Sch/Deerfield/Lake	00302341	847/945-1075	149
Wilson Aspire Sch/Rockford/Winnebago	11559527	815/966-3770	255
Wilson Creek Elem Sch/Manhattan/Will	10020145	815/478-4527	244
Wilson Elem Sch/Chicago HTS/Cook	00268501	708/283-4839	25
Wilson Elem Sch/Granite City/Madison	00308905	618/451-5817	171
Wilson Intermediate Sch/Pekin/Tazewell	00321567	309/477-4722	228
WINCHESTER CMTY UNIT SD 1/			
WINCHESTER/SCOTT	00320238	217/742-3175	215
Winchester Elem Sch/Winchester/Scott	00320264	217/742-9551	215
Winchester High Sch/Winchester/Scott	00320276	217/742-3151	215
WINDSOR CMTY UNIT SD 1/WINDSOR/			
SHELBY	00320501	217/459-2636	216
Windsor Elem Sch/Arlington HTS/Cook	00267181	847/398-4297	21
Windsor Elem Sch/Loves Park/Winnebago	00327262	815/654-4507	253
Windsor Elem Sch/Windsor/Shelby	00320525	217/459-2447	216
Windsor Jr Sr High Sch/Windsor/Shelby	00320537	217/459-2636	216
Winfield Central Sch/Winfield/Du Page	00291601	630/909-4960	100
Winfield Primary Sch/Winfield/Du Page	00291596	630/909-4900	100
WINFIELD SCH DIST 34/WINFIELD/			
DU PAGE	00291584	630/909-4900	100
Winfred Gerber Sch/Urbana/Champaign	05195090	217/367-3728	13
WinGate Elem Sch/Belleville/St Clair	12115722	618/746-4802	220
WINNEBAGO CMTY UNIT SD 323/			
WINNEBAGO/WINNEBAGO	00328254	815/335-2456	255
WINNEBAGO CO SPECIAL ED CO-OP/			
ROCKTON/WINNEBAGO	02182290	815/624-2615	256
Winnebago Elem Sch/Bloomingdale/Du Page	00290633	630/351-3416	97
Winnebago High Sch/Winnebago/Winnebago	00328292	815/335-2336	255
Winnebago Middle Sch/Winnebago/Winnebago	00328266	815/335-2364	255
WINNETKA SCH DIST 36/WINNETKA/			
COOK	00281917	847/446-9400	72
Winnie Mandela Alt HS/Chicago/Cook	11723558	773/375-0529	81
Winola Elem Sch/Viola/Mercer	02045812	309/596-2114	189
Winston Campus Elem Sch/Palatine/Cook	00272693	847/963-7500	43
Winston Campus Junior High Sch/Palatine/			
Cook	11447053	847/963-7400	43
Winston Churchill Elem Sch/Schaumburg/Cook	00274108	847/357-6300	67
Winston Knolls Sch/Hoffman Est/Cook	12305343	630/283-3221	81
WINTHROP HARBOR SCH DIST 1/			
WINTHROP HBR/LAKE	00302377	847/731-3085	156
Wolcott Sch/Chicago/Cook	11916951	312/610-4900	81
Wolcott Sch/Thornton/Cook	00274744	708/877-2526	45
Wolf Branch Elem Sch/Swansea/St Clair	00317657	618/277-2100	222
Wolf Branch Middle Sch/Swansea/St Clair	05278824	618/277-2100	222
WOLF BRANCH SCH DIST 113/			
SWANSEA/ST CLAIR	00317645	618/277-2100	222
Wolf Ridge Elem Jr High Sch/Bunker Hill/			
Macoupin	00307614	618/585-4831	167
Wolfs Crossing Elem Sch/Aurora/Kendall	10012758	630/636-3700	138
Wood Dale Junior High Sch/Wood Dale/			
Du Page	00291663	630/766-6210	100
WOOD DALE SCH DIST 7/WOOD DALE/			
DU PAGE	00291625	630/595-9510	100
Wood Oaks Junior High Sch/Northbrook/Cook	00271974	847/272-1900	59
WOOD RIVER-HARTFORD ELEM SD 15/			
WOOD RIVER/MADISON	00309272	618/254-0607	172
Wood View Elem Sch/Bolingbrook/Will	00325692	630/739-0185	248
Woodbine Elem Sch/Cicero/Cook	00268678	708/652-8884	42
WOODFORD CO SPECIAL ED ASSOC/			
METAMORA/WOODFORD	02184054	309/367-4901	259
Woodgate Elem Sch/Matteson/Cook	01529205	708/720-1107	47
WOODLAND CMTY UNIT SCH DIST 5/			
STREATOR/LIVINGSTON	00304519	815/672-5974	162
Woodland Elem Sch/Edwardsville/Madison	04751110	618/692-8790	171
Woodland Elem Sch/Joliet/Will	00325111	815/723-2808	243
Woodland Elem Sch/Streator/Livingston	00304533	815/672-2909	162
Woodland Elem Sch East/Gages Lake/Lake	04746830	847/984-8800	157
Woodland Elem Sch West/Gages Lake/Lake	00302432	847/984-8900	157
Woodland High Sch/Streator/Livingston	04918007	815/672-2900	162
Woodland Intermediate Sch/Gurnee/Lake	00302444	847/596-5900	157
Woodland Middle Sch/Gurnee/Lake	00302456	847/856-3400	157
Woodland Primary Sch/Gages Lake/Lake	04018267	847/984-8700	157
WOODLAND SCH DIST 50/GURNEE/LAKE	00302420	847/596-5600	156

School/City/County DISTRICT/CITY/COUNTY	PID	TELEPHONE NUMBER	PAGE
Woodlands Academy Sacred Heart/Lake Forest/			
Lake	00287703	847/234-4300	158
Woodlawn Community Sch/Chicago/Cook	04486975	773/535-0801	33
Woodlawn Grade Sch/Woodlawn/Jefferson	00296998	618/735-2661	124
Woodlawn High Sch/Woodlawn/Jefferson	00297019	618/735-2631	124
Woodlawn Middle Sch/Long Grove/Lake	04870273	847/353-8500	151
WOODLAWN UNIT SCH DIST 209/			
WOODLAWN/JEFFERSON	00296986	618/735-2661	124
WOODRIDGE ELEM SCH DIST 68/			
WOODRIDGE/DU PAGE	00289957	217/795-6800	100
Woodrow Wilson Elem Sch/Calumet City/Cook	00268305	708/862-5166	24
Woodrow Wilson Elem Sch/Cicero/Cook	00268666	708/652-2552	42
Woodrow Wilson Elem Sch/East Peoria/			
Tazewell	00321244	309/427-5550	227
Woodrow Wilson Middle Sch/Moline/			
Rock Island	00315740	309/743-1623	208
Woodruff Career & Tech Center/Peoria/			
Peoria	11722097	309/672-6665	199
Woods Creek Elem Sch/Crystal Lake/McHenry	04752645	815/444-4800	181
Woodson Elem Sch/Chicago/Cook	00278831	773/535-1280	33
WOODSTOCK CMTY UNIT SD 200/			
WOODSTOCK/MCHENRY	00305991	815/338-8200	184
Woodstock High Sch/Woodstock/McHenry	00306074	815/338-4370	184
Woodstock North High Sch/Woodstock/McHenry	11133367	815/334-2100	184
Woodview Sch/Grayslake/Lake	03006924	847/223-3668	148
Word of Life Christian Sch/Granite City/			
Madison	11230953	618/931-3744	173
Worden Elem Sch/Worden/Madison	00309363	618/692-7442	171
World Language Academy/Chicago/Cook	10009139	773/535-4334	37
Worth Elem Sch/Worth/Cook	00282258	708/448-2801	72
Worth Junior High Sch/Worth/Cook	00282260	708/448-2803	72
WORTH SCH DIST 127/WORTH/COOK	00282246	708/448-2800	72
Worthridge Elem Sch/Worth/Cook	12165686	708/448-2800	72
Worthwoods Elem Sch/Worth/Cook	00282296	708/448-2802	72
Wredling Middle Sch/Saint Charles/Kane	04366038	331/228-3700	129
Wright Elem Sch/Hampshire/McHenry	10910150	847/683-5700	180
Wyvetter Younge Alt Ctr for Ed/E Saint Louis/			
St Clair	02176849	618/646-3760	219
Y			
Yankee Ridge Elem Sch/Urbana/Champaign	00265511	217/384-3607	13
Yates Elem Sch/Chicago/Cook	00281204	773/534-4550	31
YCCS-Aspira Antonia Pantoja HS/Chicago/			
Cook	11827623	773/486-6303	41
YCCS-Assoc House/Chicago/Cook	12172249	773/772-7170	41
YCCS-Austin Career/Chicago/Cook	11237066	773/626-6988	41
YCCS-Chatham Acad HS/Chicago/Cook	11932204	773/651-1500	41
YCCS-Community Chrn Alt Acad/Chicago/Cook	02192013	773/762-2272	41
YCCS-Dr Pedro Albizu Campos HS/Chicago/			
Cook	03068910	773/342-8022	41
YCCS-Innovations HS/Chicago/Cook	10009787	312/999-9360	41
YCCS-Jane Addams Alt HS/Chicago/Cook	10009775	312/563-1746	41
YCCS-McKinley-Lakeside HS/Chicago/Cook	04854712	312/949-5010	41
YCCS-Olive Harvey Mid Clg HS/Chicago/Cook	11435660	773/291-6518	41
YCCS-Progressive Leadership/Chicago/Cook	12259184	773/723-9631	41
YCCS-Scholastic Achievement/Chicago/Cook	01442011	773/921-1315	41
YCCS-Sullivan House Alt HS/Chicago/Cook	01442023	773/978-8680	41
YCCS-Truman Middle Clg HS/Chicago/Cook	11459721	773/907-4840	41
YCCS-Virtual High Sch/Chicago/Cook	12171245	312/429-0027	41
YCCS-West/Chicago/Cook	12171257	773/261-0994	41
YCCS-West Town Acad Alt HS/Chicago/Cook	04990768	312/563-9044	41
YCCS-Youth Connection Ldrshp/Chicago/Cook	12171269	312/225-4668	41
YCCS-Youth Dev Inst HS/Chicago/Cook	12171271	773/224-2273	41
Yeshiva Eitz Chaim/Chicago/Cook	12374992	773/455-1001	81
Yeshiva Meor Hatorah-Boys HS/Chicago/Cook	11703431	773/465-0419	81
Yeshiva Ohr Boruch/Chicago/Cook	03354082	773/262-0885	81
Yeshivas Brisk Academy/Chicago/Cook	01405063	773/274-1177	82
Yeshivas Tiferes Tzvi Academy/Chicago/Cook	01844500	773/973-6150	82
York Center Elem Sch/Lombard/Du Page	00291417	630/516-6540	99
York Community High Sch/Elmhurst/Du Page	00289622	630/617-2400	94
YORKVILLE CMTY UNIT SD 115/			
YORKVILLE/KENDALL	00299809	630/553-4382	139
Yorkville Grade Sch/Yorkville/Kendall	00299859	630/553-4390	139
Yorkville High Sch/Yorkville/Kendall	00299861	630/553-4380	139
Yorkville High School Academy/Yorkville/			
Kendall	11188427	630/553-4385	139
Yorkville Intermediate Sch/Yorkville/			
Kendall	00299835	630/553-4594	139
Yorkville Middle Sch/Yorkville/Kendall	00299823	630/553-4544	139
Young Adult Alternative Ctr/Arlington HTS/			
Cook	12225262	847/718-7877	70

Illinois School Directory

DISTRICT & SCHOOL TELEPHONE INDEX

School/City/County DISTRICT/CITY/COUNTY	PID	TELEPHONE NUMBER	PAGE
Youthbuild McLean Co CS/Normal/Mclean	11150951	309/454-3898	1
Z			
Zadok Casey Middle Sch/Mount Vernon/Jefferson	00296778	618/244-8060	123
Zapata Academy/Chicago/Cook	04486999	773/534-1390	28
ZEIGLER ROYALTON CUSD 188/MULKEYTOWN/FRANKLIN	00293257	618/596-5841	108
Zeigler Royalton Elem Jr HS/Mulkeytown/Franklin	00293271	618/596-2121	108
Zeigler Royalton High Sch/Mulkeytown/Franklin	00293283	618/596-5841	108
Zenon Sykuta Elem Sch/Cntry CLB Hls/Cook	00268721	708/957-6210	45
Zion Benton Township High Sch/Zion/Lake	00302559	847/731-9300	157
Zion Central Middle Sch/Zion/Lake	00302482	847/746-1431	157
Zion Christian Sch/Zion/Lake	02190259	847/872-4088	158
Zion Lutheran Sch/Beecher/Will	00325953	708/946-2272	250
Zion Lutheran Sch/Belleville/St Clair	00317669	618/234-0275	223
Zion Lutheran Sch/Bethalto/Madison	00309430	618/377-5507	173
Zion Lutheran Sch/Lincoln/Logan	01844914	217/732-3977	164
Zion Lutheran Sch/Litchfield/Montgomery	00311354	217/324-3166	191
Zion Lutheran Sch/Marengo/McHenry	00305989	815/568-5156	185
Zion Lutheran Sch/Mount Pulaski/Logan	00304997	217/792-5715	164
Zion Lutheran Sch/Staunton/Macoupin	00308008	618/635-3060	169
ZION PUBLIC SCH DIST 6/ZION/LAKE	00302468	847/872-5455	157
ZION-BENTON TWP HIGH SD 126/ZION/LAKE	00302547	847/731-9300	157

School Year 2020-2021   800-333-8802

Illinois School Directory

DISTRICT URL INDEX

DISTRICT	URL	PAGE
A-C Central Cmty Unit SD 262	a-ccentral.com/	9
Abingdon-Avon Cmty Unit SD 276	d276.net/	139
Addison School District 4	asd4.org/	88
Adlai E Stevenson HSD 125	d125.org/	146
Akin Elem School District 91	akin.myclassupdates.com/	107
Albers Elem School District 63	albers.k12.il.us/	17
Alden-Hebron School Dist 19	alden-hebron.org/	179
Allen-Otter Creek CCSD 65	ransomgradeschool.net/	141
Allendale Cmty Cons SD 17	allendale.wabash.k12.il.us/	234
Alsip-Hazelgrn-Oaklawn SD 126	dist126.org/	20
Altamont Cmty Unit SD 10	altamontschools.org/	104
Alton Cmty School District 11	altonschools.org/	169
Alwood Cmty Unit Sch Dist 225	sites.google.com/a/alwood.net/aw225/	116
Amboy Cmty Unit Sch Dist 272	amboy.net/	159
Anna Cmty Cons Sch Dist 37	anna37.com/	230
Anna-Jonesboro Cmty HSD 81	aj81.net/	230
Annawan Cmty Unit SD 226	annawan226.org/	116
Antioch Cmty Cons Sch Dist 34	antioch34.com/	146
Aptakisic-Tripp Sch Dist 102	d102.org/	146
Arbor Park School District 145	arbor145.org	21
Arcola Cmty Unit Sch Dist 306	arcola.k12.il.us/	87
Argenta Oreana Cmty Unit SD 1	argenta-oreana.org/	165
Argo Cmty High School Dist 217	argohs.net/	21
Arlington Hts School Dist 25	sd25.org/pages/sd25	21
Armstrong Twp High SD 225	armstrong.k12.il.us/	231
Arthur CUSD 305	cusd305.org/	87
Ashley Cmty Cons SD 15	ashleyccsd15.org/	235
Ashton-Franklin Center SD 275	afcschools.net/	159
Astoria Cmty Unit Sch Dist 1	acusd1.org/	109
Athens Cmty Unit Sch Dist 213	athens-213.org/	188
Atwood Heights SD 125	ahsd125.org/	21
Auburn Cmty Unit Sch Dist 10	auburn.k12.il.us/	211
Aviston Elem School Dist 21	avistonk-8.org/	17
Avoca School District 37	avoca37.org/	22
Ball Chatham Cmty Unit SD 5	chathamschools.org/	211
Bannockburn Sch Dist 106	bannockburnschool.org/	147
Barrington Cmty Unit SD 220	barrington220.org/	147
Bartelso School District 57	bartelsobraves.com/	17
Bartonville School District 66	bgs66.org/	196
Batavia Unit School Dist 101	bps101.net/	128
Beach Park Cmty Cons SD 3	bpd3.org/	147
Beardstown Cmty Sch Dist 15	beardstown.com	9
Beecher City Cmty Unit SD 20	bcity.efingham.k12.il.us/	104
Beecher Cmty Sch Dist 200-U	beecher200u.org/	241
Belle Valley School Dist 119	bv119.net/	217
Belleville Public Sch Dist 118	sites.google.com/a/belleville118.org/belleville-district-118/	217
Belleville Township HSD 201	bths201.org/	217
Bellwood School District 88	sd88.org/	22
Belvidere Cmty Unit SD 100	district100.com/	4
Bement Cmty Unit Sch Dist 5	bement.k12.il.us/	202
Benjamin Sch District 25	bendist25.org/	89
Bensenville Elem Sch Dist 2	bsd2.org/	89
Benton Cmty Cons Sch Dist 47	benton47.org	107
Benton Cons High Sch Dist 103	bentonhighschool.org/	107
Berkeley School Dist 87	berkeley87.org	22
Berwyn North School Dist 98	bn98.org/	22
Berwyn South School Dist 100	bsd100.org/	23
Bethalto Cmty Unit SD 8	bethalto.org	169
Bethel School District 82	bethel.roe25.com/	122
Big Hollow School District 38	bighollow.us	148
Bismarck-Henning Cmty SD 1	bismarck.k12.il.us/	231
Bloom Twp High Sch Dist 206	bloomdistrict206.org/	23
Bloomingdale School Dist 13	sd13.org/	89
Bloomington School District 87	district87.org/	185
Blue Ridge Cmty SD 18	blueridge18.org/	87
Bluford Unit School Dist 318	busd318.org/	122
Bond Co Cmty Unit Sch Dist 2	bccu2.org/	4
Bourbonnais Elem Sch Dist 53	besd53.org/	134
Braceville Elem School Dist 75	bes.grundy.k12.il.us/	111
Bradford Cmty Unit Sch Dist 1	bradfordschool.net/	223
Bradley Elem School Dist 61	bradleyschools.com/	134
Bradley-Bourbonnais CHSD 307	bbchs.org/	134
Breese Elementary SD 12	d12bobcats.org/	17

School Year 2020-2021 · 800-333-8802 · IL-W1

DISTRICT URL INDEX

Market Data Retrieval

DISTRICT	URL	PAGE
Bremen Cmty High SD 228	bhsd228.com/	23
Brimfield Cmty Unit SD 309	brimfield309.com/	196
Brookfield-LaGrange Park SD 95	d95.w-cook.k12.il.us/	23
Brooklyn School District 188	lovejoy.stclair.k12.il.us/	217
Brookwood School District 167	brookwood.s-cook.k12.il.us/	24
Brown Co Cmty Unit Sch Dist 1	bchornets.com/	5
Brownstown Cmty Unit SD 201	bcusd201.com/	105
Brussels Cmty Unit Sch Dist 42	schools.lth5.k12.il.us/brussels/	8
Buncombe Cons School Dist 43	buncombegradeschool.com/	127
Bunker Hill Cmty Unit SD 8	bhschools.org	167
Burbank School District 111	burbank.k12.il.us/	24
Bureau Valley Cmty Unit 340	bv340.org/	6
Burnham School District 1545	d1545.org/Home	24
Bushnell Prairie Cmty USD 170	bpcschools.org/	178
Butler School District 53	butler53.com/	89
Byron Cmty Unit SD 226	byron226.org	194
Cahokia Unit Sch Dist 187	cusd187-il.schoolloop.com/	218
Cairo School District 1	cairoschooldistrict1.com/	3
Calhoun Cmty Unit Sch Dist 40	calhoun40.net/	8
Calumet City School Dist 155	calumetcity155.org/	24
Calumet Public School Dist 132	sd132.org/	24
Cambridge Cmty Unit SD 227	district227.org/	116
Canton Union School Dist 66	cantonusd.org/	109
Carbon Cliff Barstow SD 36	ccb36.com/	207
Carbondale Cmty HSD 165	cchs165.jacksn.k12.il.us/	120
Carbondale Elem School Dist 95	ces95.org	120
Carlinville Cmty Unit SD 1	cusd1.com/	167
Carlyle Cmty Unit Sch Dist 1	carlyle.k12.il.us	17
Carmi-White Co School Dist 5	carmischools.org/	237
Carrollton Cmty Unit SD 1	c-hawks.net/	111
Carterville Cmty Unit SD 5	cartervillelions.org/	250
Carthage Elementary SD 317	cesd317.org/	114
Cary Cmty Cons Sch Dist 26	cary26.org/	179
Casey-Westfield Cmty USD C-4	caseywestfield.org/	15
Cass School District 63	cassd63.org/	89
Center Cass Sch Dist 66	ccsd66.org/	90
Central A&M Cmty Unit SD 21	camraiders.com/	14
Central City School Dist 133	ccs133.org	174
Central Cmty High Sch Dist 71	centralcougars.org/	17
Central Cmty Unit SD 4	clifton-u4.k12.il.us	118
Central Cmty Unit SD 301	burlington.k12.il.us	128
Central Sch Dist 51	central51.net/	225
Central School District 3	cusd3.com/	1
Central School District 104	central104.org/	218
Central Stickney Sch Dist 110	sahs.k12.il.us/	25
Centralia City Sch Dist 135	ccs135.com/	174
Centralia High School Dist 200	centraliahs.org/	174
Century Cmty Unit SD 100	centuryschool100.com/	204
Cerro Gordo Cmty Unit SD 100	cgbroncos.org/	202
Chadwick Milledgevill CUSD 399	dist399.net	8
Champaign Cmty Unit Sch Dist 4	champaignschools.org/	10
Chaney-Monge School Dist 88	chaneymonge.us/	241
Channahon School District 17	csd17.org/	241
Charleston Cmty Unit SD 1	charleston.k12.il.us/	19
Chester Cmty Unit Sch Dist 139	chester139.com/	205
Chester-E Lincoln Cmty SD 61	cel61.com/	163
Chicago Heights Elem SD 170	sd170.com/	25
Chicago Public School Dist 299	cps.edu/	25
Chicago Ridge Sch Dist 127-5	crsd1275.org/	41
Christopher Unit Sch Dist 99	cpher99.org	107
Cicero School District 99	cicd99.edu/	42
Cissna Park Cmty Unit SD 6	cissnaparkschools.org/	118
Clay City Cmty Unit SD 10	claycityschools.org/	16
Clinton Cmty Unit Sch Dist 15	cusd15.org/	87
Cmty Cons Sch Dist 146	ccsd146.k12.il.us	42
Coal City Cmty Unit Sch Dist 1	coalcityschools.org/	112
Cobden Cmty Unit Sch Dist 17	cobdenappleknockers.com/	230
Collinsville Cmty Sch Dist 10	kahoks.org/	170
Colona Cmty School Dist 190	csd190.com/	116
Columbia Cmty Unit SD 4	chseagles.com/	189
Community Cons School Dist 15	ccsd15.net/	42
Community Cons School Dist 46	d46.k12.il.us	148
Community Cons School Dist 59	ccsd59.org/	43
Community Cons School Dist 89	ccsd89.org/	90

Illinois School Directory

DISTRICT URL INDEX

DISTRICT	URL	PAGE
Community Cons School Dist 93	ccsd93.com/	90
Community Cons School Dist 168	d168.org/	44
Community Cons School Dist 180	ccsd180.org/	90
Community Cons School Dist 181	d181.org/	91
Community Cons School Dist 204	ccsd204.perry.k12.il.us/	201
Community High School Dist 94	d94.org/	91
Community High School Dist 99	csd99.org/	91
Community High School Dist 117	d117.org/	148
Community High School Dist 128	d128.org/	148
Community High School Dist 155	ww3.d155.org/pages/default.aspx?mobile=0	179
Community High School Dist 218	chsd218.org/	44
Community Unit School Dist 7	joomla.gcusd7.org/	167
Community Unit School Dist 16	pretzelpride.com/	211
Community Unit School Dist 200	cusd200.org	91
Community Unit School Dist 201	cusd201.org/#oVsUnz2QRUUF	92
Community Unit School Dist 300	d300.org/	180
Community Unit School Dist 303	d303.org/	128
Community Unit School Dist 308	sd308.org/site/default.aspx?PageID=1	137
Consolidated High Sch Dist 230	d230.org/	44
Cook County School Dist 104	sd104.schooldesk.net/	44
Cook County School Dist 130	district130.org/	45
Cook County School Dist 154	wolcottschool.com/	45
Cornell Cmty Cons Sch Dist 426	cornellgradeschool.org/	160
Coulterville Unit Sch Dist 1	coulterville1.org/index.html	205
Country Club Hills SD 160	countryclubhill.ss8.sharpschool.com/	45
Cowden Herrick CUSD 3A	cowden-herrick.k12.il.us/	216
Crab Orchard Cmty Sch Dist 3	cocusd3.org/	251
Crescent Iroquois Cmty SD 249	ccgs.k12.il.us/	118
Creston Cmty Cons Sch Dist 161	crestonschool.org	194
Crete-Monee Cmty SD 201-U	cm201u.org	241
Creve Coeur Sch Dist 76	cc76.k12.il.us/	226
Crystal Lake Elem Distict 47	d47.org/core/	181
Cumberland Cmty Unit SD 77	cumberland.k12.il.us	84
Cypress School District 64	cypressgradeschool.org/	127
Dakota Cmty Unit Sch Dist 201	dakota201.com/	224
Dallas Elem Sch Dist 327	dcbulldogs.com/	114
Dalzell Elem School Dist 98	bhsroe.org/site/?page_id=39645	6
Damiansville School Dist 62	damiansvilleelem.com/	17
Danville School District 118	danville.k12.il.us/	231
Darien Public Sch Dist 61	darien61.org/	92
Decatur Public Schools 61	dps61.org	165
Deer Creek-Mackinaw CUSD 701	deemack.org	226
Deer Park Cmty Cons SD 82	deerpark.k12.il.us/	141
Deerfield Public SD 109	dps109.org/	149
DeKalb Cmty Unit SD 428	dist428.org	84
Deland-Weldon Cmty Unit SD 57	dwschools.org/	202
Delavan Cmty Unit Sch Dist 703	delavanschools.com/	226
DePue Unit Sch Dist 103	depueschools.org/	6
Des Plaines Cmty Cons SD 62	d62.org/	45
DeSoto Grade School Dist 86	desoto86.org/	120
Diamond Lake School Dist 76	dist76.org	149
Dieterich Community Unit SD 30	dieterich.k12.il.us/	104
Dimmick Cmty School Dist 175	dimmick175.com/	141
District 50 Schools	d50schools.com/	226
Dixon Cmty Unit Sch Dist 170	dps170.org/	160
Dolton School District 149	schooldistrict149.org/	46
Dolton-Riverdale Sch Dist 148	district148.net/	46
Dongola Unit School Dist 66	dongolaschool.com/	230
Donovan Cmty Unit Sch Dist 3	donovanschools.org/	119
Downers Grove School Dist 58	dg58.org/site/default.aspx?PageID=1	93
Du Quoin Cmty Unit SD 300	duquoinschools.org/	201
Dunlap Cmty Unit Sch Dist 323	dunlapcusd.net/Pages/Splash.aspx	196
Dupage High School Dist 88	dupage88.net/	93
Dupo Cmty School District 196	dupo196.org/	218
Durand Cmty Sch Dist 322	durandbulldogs.com/	252
Dwight Common Elem SD 232	dgs.k12.il.us/	161
Dwight Twp High Sch Dist 230	dwighthigh.k12.il.us	161
E F Lindop Elem Sch Dist 92	lindop92.net/	47
Earlville Cmty Unit Sch Dist 9	earlvillecusd9.org/	141
East Alton Elementary SD 13	easd13.org/	170
East Alton-Wood River SD 14	eawr.madison.k12.il.us/	170
East Aurora School Dist 131	d131.org/	129
East Coloma-Nelson Cesd 20	ecoloma.net/	238
East Dubuque Unit SD 119	eastdbqschools.org/	125

DISTRICT URL INDEX

Market Data Retrieval

DISTRICT	URL	PAGE
East Maine School District 63	emsd63.org/	47
East Moline Public Sch Dist 37	emsd37.org	207
East Peoria Cmty HS Dist 309	ep309.org/	226
East Peoria Elem Sch Dist 86	epd86.org/	226
East Prairie School Dist 73	eps73.net/	47
East St Louis Sch Dist 189	estl189.com/	218
Eastland Cmty Unit SD 308	eastland308.com/	8
Edgar Co Cmty Sch Dist 6	chrisman.k12.il.us/	103
Edinburg Cmty Unit Sch Dist 4	ecusd4.com/	14
Edwards Co Cmty Unit SD 1	edwardscountyschools.org	104
Edwardsville Cmty Unit SD 7	ecusd7.org	170
Effingham Cmty Sch Dist 40	effingham.k12.il.us	104
Egyptian Cmty Unit Sch Dist 5	egyptianschool.com/	3
El Paso-Gridley CUSD 11	unit11.org/	257
Eldorado Cmty Unit Sch Dist 4	eldorado.k12.il.us	210
Elementary School District 159	dist159.com/	47
Elgin School District U-46	u-46.org/	130
Elmhurst Cmty Unit SD 205	elmhurst205.org/	93
Elmwood Cmty Unit Sch Dist 322	elmwood322.com/	196
Elmwood Park Cmty Unit SD 401	epcusd401.org/	47
Elverado Cmty Unit SD 196	elv196.com/	120
Elwood Cmty Cons SD 203	elwoodschool.com/	242
Emmons School District 33	emmons.lake.k12.il.us/	149
Erie Cmty School District 1	ecusd.info/	239
Eswood Cmty Cons SD 269	eswoodschool.org/	194
Eureka Cmty Unit Sch Dist 140	district140.org/	257
Evanston Twp High SD 202	eths.k12.il.us/	48
Evanston-Skokie Cmty CSD 65	district65.net/	48
Evergreen Park Cmty HSD 231	evergreenpark.org/	49
Evergreen Park Elem SD 124	d124.org/	49
Ewing Northern Cmty SD 115	ewinggradeschool.org/	108
Fairfield Cmty High SD 225	fchsmules.com/	236
Fairfield Pub Sch District 112	fairfield.d112.wayne.k12.il.us/education/district/district.php?sectionid=663	236
Fairmont School District 89	fsd89.org/	242
Fairview South School Dist 72	fairview.k12.il.us/	49
Farmington Ctl Cmty SD 265	dist265.com	197
Fenton Cmty High Sch Dist 100	fenton100.org/	94
Field Cmty Cons Sch Dist 3	fieldpanthers.com/	123
Fieldcrest Cmty School Dist 6	unit6.org/google022be64652f7be0e-html/home	257
Fisher Cmty Unit School Dist 1	district.fisherk12.com/home	10
Flanagan-Cornell Unit 74 SD	flanagan.k12.il.us/	161
Flora Cmty Unit School Dist 35	floraschools.com/	16
Flossmoor School District 161	sd161.org/	49
Ford Heights School Dist 169	fordheights169.org/	49
Forest Park School District 91	forestparkschools.org/	50
Forest Ridge Sch Dist 142	d142.org/	50
Forrestville Valley CUSD 221	fvvsd221.org/	194
Fox Lake School Dist 114	d114.org/	149
Fox River Grove Cons SD 3	dist3.org	181
Frankfort Cmty Unit SD 168	wfschools.org/	108
Frankfort School Dist 157-C	fsd157c.org/	242
Franklin Cmty Unit SD 1	franklinhigh.com/	192
Franklin Park Pub Sch Dist 84	d84.org/	50
Freeburg Cmty Cons SD 70	frg70.org/	219
Freeburg Cmty High Sch Dist 77	fchs77.org/	219
Freeport School District 145	fsd145.org/	224
Fremont School District 79	fsd79.org/	149
Fulton Co Cmty Unit Sch Dist 3	cusd3.net	109
Galatia Cmty Unit Sch Dist 1	galatiak12.org/	210
Galena Unit School Dist 120	gusd120.k12.il.us/	125
Galesburg Cmty Unit SD 205	galesburg205.org	140
Gallatin Cmty Unit Sch Dist 7	gallatincusd7.com/	110
Galva Cmty Unit Sch Dist 224	galva224.org/	117
Gardner Cmty Cons SD 72-C	ggs72.org/	112
Gardner S Wilmington HSD 73	gswhs73.org/	112
Gavin School District 37	gavin37.org/	150
General George S Patton SD 133	district133.org/default.aspx	50
Geneseo Cmty Unit Sch Dist 228	geneseoschools.org/	117
Geneva CUSD 304	geneva304.org/	131
Genoa-Kingston Cmty SD 424	gkschools.org/	85
Georgetown-Ridge Farm CUSD 4	grf.k12.il.us/	232
Germantown Elem Sch Dist 60	germantownbulldogs.org/	18
Germantown Hills SD 69	ghills.metamora.k12.il.us/	257
Giant City Cmty Cons SD 130	www2.giants.jacksn.k12.il.us	120

IL-W4 800-333-8802 School Year 2020-2021

Illinois School Directory

DISTRICT URL INDEX

DISTRICT	URL	PAGE
Gibson Cty-Melvin-Sibley CUSD5	gcmsk12.org/	106
Gifford Cmty Cons SD 188	gifford.k12.il.us/	10
Glen Ellyn School District 41	d41.org/	94
Glenbard Twp High Sch Dist 87	glenbard87.org/	94
Glenbrook High Sch Dist 225	glenbrook225.org/	50
Glencoe Sch District 35	glencoeschools.org/	51
Glenview Cmty Cons Sch Dist 34	glenview34.org/	51
Golf School District 67	golf67.net/	51
Goreville Cmty Unit SD 1	gorevilleschools.com/	127
Gower School District 62	gower62.com/	94
Grand Ridge CCSD 95	grgs95.org/	141
Granite City Cmty Unit SD 9	gcsd9.net/	171
Grant Cmty Cons Sch Dist 110	dist110.com/	219
Grant Cmty High Sch Dist 124	grant.lake.k12.il.us/	150
Grant Park Cmty Unit SD 6	grantparkdragons.org/	135
Grass Lake School District 36	gls36.org/	150
Grayslake Cmty HS District 127	d127.org/	150
Grayville Cmty Unit Sch Dist 1	grayville.white.k12.il.us/	238
Greenfield Cmty Unit SD 10	greenfieldschools.org/	111
Greenview Cmty Unit SD 200	greenviewschools.org/	188
Griggsville-Perry Cmty SD 4	griggsvilleperry.com/	203
Gurnee School District 56	d56.org/	150
Hall Twp High School Dist 502	hallhighschool.org/	6
Hamilton Cmty Cons SD 328	hhs328.com/	114
Hamilton Co Cmty Unit SD 10	unit10.com/	114
Hampton School District 29	hampton29.com/education/school/school.php?sectionid=3	207
Hardin Co Cmty Unit Sch Dist 1	hardin.k12.il.us/	115
Harlem Unit Sch District 122	harlem122.org/	252
Harmony-Emge School Dist 175	harmony175.org	219
Harrisburg Cmty Unit SD 3	hbg.saline.k12.il.us/education	210
Harrison School Dist 36	hsd36-k12-ct.schoolloop.com/	181
Hartsburg Emden School Dist 21	hartem.org/	163
Harvard Cmty Unit Sch Dist 50	cusd50.org	181
Harvey Public School Dist 152	harvey152.org	51
Havana Cmty Sch District 126	havana126.net/	177
Hawthorn Cmty Cons Sch Dist 73	hawthorn73.org/	151
Hazel Crest School Dist 152-5	sd1525.org/	52
Henry Senachwine CUSD 5	hscud5.org/	176
Heritage Cmty Unit Sch Dist 8	heritage.k12.il.us/	11
Herrin Cmty School District 4	herrinunit.org/	251
Herscher Cmty School Dist 2	hsd2.k12.il.us	135
Heyworth Cmty Sch District 4	husd4.k12.il.us/	185
Hiawatha Cmty Unit SD 426	hiawatha426.org/	85
High Mount Sch Dist 116	highmountschool.com/	219
Highland Cmty Sch District 5	highlandcusd5.org	171
Hillsboro Cmty Unit Sch Dist 3	hillsboroschools.net	190
Hinckley-Big Rock Cmty SD 429	hbr429.org/	85
Hinsdale Twp High Sch Dist 86	d86.hinsdale86.org/	95
Hollis Cons School Dist 328	hollis.peoria.k12.il.us/	197
Homer Cmty Cons Sch Dist 33C	homerschools.org/	242
Homewood Flossmoor CHSD 233	hfhs.s-cook.k12.il.us	52
Homewood School Dist 153	hsd153.org/index.asp	52
Hononegah Cmty High SD 207	hononegah.org/	253
Hoopeston Area Cmty Unit SD 11	hoopeston.k12.il.us	232
Hoover-Schrum Sch Dist 157	hsdist157.org/	52
Huntley Cmty School Dist 158	district158.org/	182
Hutsonville Cmty Unit SD 1	hutsonvilletigers.net/	83
Illini Bluffs Cmty Unit SD 327	illinibluffs.com	197
Illini Central CUSD 189	illinicentral.org/	177
Illini West High Sch Dist 307	illiniwest.org/	114
Illinois Vly Ctl Sch Dist 321	ivcschools.com/	197
Indian Creek Cmty Unit SD 425	indiancreekschools.org/	85
Indian Prairie Sch Dist 204	ipsd.org	95
Indian Springs Sch Dist 109	isd109.org/	52
Iroquois Co Cmty Unit SD 9	watseka-u9.k12.il.us/	119
Iroquois West Cmty Unit SD 10	iwest.k12.il.us/	119
Irvington Cmty Cons SD 11	irvingtongradeschool.com/index.htm	235
Itasca School District 10	itasca10.org/	96
Iuka Community Cons Sch Dist 7	iukaschool.com/	174
J Sterling Morton HSD 201	morton201.org/	53
Jacksonville School Dist 117	jsd117.org/	192
Jasper Cmty Cons Sch Dist 17	jasperpolecats.com/	237
Jasper Co Cmty Unit SD 1	cusd1.jasper.k12.il.us/	122
Jersey Cmty Sch Dist 100	jersey100.k12.il.us/	125

DISTRICT URL INDEX

Market Data Retrieval

DISTRICT	URL	PAGE
Johnsburg Cmty School Dist 12	johnsburg12.org	182
Johnston City Cmty Unit SD 1	jcindians.org/education/district/district.php?sectionid=1	251
Joliet Public School Dist 86	joliet86.org	243
Joliet Twp High Sch Dist 204	jths.org/	243
Jonesboro Cmty Cons SD 43	jonesboro43.com/	230
Joppa-Maple Grove Unit SD 38	jmg38.com/	177
Kaneland Cmty Unit SD 302	kaneland.org	132
Kankakee School District 111	k111.k12.il.us/	135
Kansas Cmty School District 3	kansas.k12.il.us/	103
Keeneyville Elem Sch Dist 20	esd20.org/	96
Kell Cons School District 2	kellgradeschool.com	174
Kenilworth School District 38	kenilworth38.org/site/default.aspx?PageID=1	53
Kewanee Cmty Unit Sch Dist 229	kcud229.org/	117
Kildeer Countryside CCSD 96	kcsd96.org/	151
Kings Cons School District 144	kings144.org/	194
Kinnikinnick Cmty Cons SD 131	kinn131.org/	253
Kirby School District 140	ksd140.org	53
Knoxville Cmty Unit SD 202	bluebullets.org/	140
Komarek School District 94	komarekschool.org/	54
La Grange Cmty School Dist 105	d105.w-cook.k12.il.us	54
La Grange Elem Sch Dist 102	dist102.k12.il.us	54
La Grange-Highlands SD 106	xbox2.district106.net/	54
La Harpe Cmty Sch Dist 347	laharpeeagles.org/	115
La Moille Cmty Unit SD 303	lamoilleschools.socs.net/	6
La Salle Elem SD 122	lasalleschools.net/	142
Ladd Cmty Cons Sch Dist 94	laddccsd94.com/	6
Lake Bluff Elem Sch Dist 65	lb65.org/	151
Lake Forest Cmty HSD 115	lfhs.org/	151
Lake Forest School District 67	lakeforestschools.org/	152
Lake Park Cmty High SD 108	lphs.org/	96
Lake Villa Cmty Cons SD 41	district41.org	152
Lake Zurich Cmty Sch Dist 95	lz95.org/	152
Lansing School Dist 158	d158.net/	54
Laraway Cmty Cons SD 70-C	laraway70c.org/	243
LaSalle Peru Twp HSD 120	lphs.net/	142
Lawrence Co Cmty Sch Dist 20	cusd20.com/	159
Le Roy Cmty Unit SD 2	leroyk12.org	186
Lebanon Cmty Unit Sch Dist 9	lcusd9.org/	220
Leland Cmty Unit Sch Dist 1	leland1.org/	142
Lemont High Sch Dist 210	lemont.k12.il.us	55
Lemont-Bromberek Sch Dist 113A	sd113a.org/	55
Lena-Winslow Cmty Unit SD 202	le-win.net/	224
Lewistown Community Unit SD 97	lewistown97.com/	110
Lexington Cmty Sch Dist 7	lexington.k12.il.us/	186
Leyden Cmty High Sch Dist 212	leyden212.org	55
Liberty Cmty Unit Sch Dist 2	libertyschool.net/	2
Libertyville Pub Sch Dist 70	d70schools.org/?sect=schools	152
Lick Creek School Dist 16	lcschool.union.k12.il.us/	230
Limestone Cmty High SD 310	limestone.k12.il.us	197
Limestone Walters CCSD 316	limestonewalters.com/	198
Lincoln Cmty High Sch Dist 404	lchsrailers.org/	163
Lincoln Elem School Dist 27	lincoln27.com/	163
Lincoln Elem School Dist 156	l156.org/	55
Lincoln-Way Cmty HS Dist 210	lw210.org/	244
Lincolnshre-Prairieview SD 103	d103.org/	153
Lincolnwood Sch Dist 74	sd74.org/home/	55
Lisbon Cmty Cons Sch Dist 90	lisbon.k12.il.us/	138
Lisle Cmty Unit Sch Dist 202	lisle202.org/	96
Litchfield Cmty Unit SD 12	lcusd12.org/	191
Lockport Twp High Sch Dist 205	lths.org/	244
Lombard Elem SD 44	sd44.org	97
Lostant Cmty Unit Sch Dist 425	lostantcomets.org/	142
Lowpoint-Washburn CUSD 21	lwdistrict21.com/Home.html	257
Lyons Elem School Dist 103	sd103.com/	56
Lyons Twp HS District 204	lths.net	56
Macomb Cmty Unit Sch Dist 185	macomb185.org/	178
Madison Cmty Unit Sch Dist 12	madisoncusd12.org/	172
Maercker School District 60	maercker.org/	97
Mahomet-Seymour Cmty SD 3	ms.k12.il.us	11
Maine Twp High Sch Dist 207	maine207.org/	56
Malden Cmty Cons SD 84	maldengradeschool.org/	7
Manhattan School Dist 114	manhattan114.org/	244
Mannheim School District 83	d83.org	56
Manteno Cmty Unit Sch Dist 5	manteno5.org/	135

Illinois School Directory

DISTRICT URL INDEX

DISTRICT	URL	PAGE
Marengo Cmty High Sch Dist 154	mchs154.org/	182
Marengo Union Elem Cons SD 165	marengo165.org/	182
Marion Cmty School Dist 2	marionunit2.org/education/district/district.php?sectionid=1	251
Marissa Cmty Unit Sch Dist 40	marissa40.org/	220
Maroa Forsyth CU Sch Dist 2	mfhs1.mfsd.k12.il.us/	165
Marquardt School District 15	d15.us/	97
Marseilles Elem Sch Dist 150	mes150.org/	142
Marshall Cmty Sch Dist C-2	marshall.k12.il.us/	15
Martinsville Cmty Unit SD C-3	martinsville.k12.il.us	16
Mascoutah Cmty Sch Dist 19	msd19.org/	220
Massac Unit School District 1	unit1.massac.org/	177
Matteson Elem SD 162	sd162.org/	57
Mattoon Cmty Unit Sch Dist 2	mattoon.k12.il.us/	19
Maywood-Melrose Brdview SD 89	maywood89.org	57
Mazon-Verona-Kinsman ESD 2-C	mvkmavericks.org/	112
McClellan Cons SD 12	mcclellan12.org/	123
McHenry Cmty Cons Sch Dist 15	d15.org	183
McHenry Cmty High Sch Dist 156	dist156.org/	183
McLean Co Unit District 5	unit5.org	186
Medinah Elementary SD 11	medinah11.org/	97
Mendon Cmty Unit School Dist 4	cusd4.com/	2
Mendota Cmty School Dist 289	m289.org/	142
Mendota Twp High Sch Dist 280	mendotahs.org	143
Mercer County SD 404	mercerschools.org	189
Meredosia-Chambersburg SD 11	mcsd11.net/	192
Meridian Cmty School Dist 101	meridian101.com/	204
Meridian Cmty Unit Sch Dist 15	meridianhawks.net/	166
Meridian Cmty Unit SD 223	meridian223.org/	194
Metamora Cmty Cons Sch Dist 1	mgs.metamora.k12.il.us/	258
Metamora Twp HS Dist 122	mths.us/	258
Midland Cmty Unit Sch Dist 7	midland-7.net/	176
Midlothian School District 143	msd143.org/index.php	57
Midwest Ctl Cmty Unit SD 191	midwestcentral.org	177
Milford Area Public SD 124	mpsk12.org/	119
Millburn Cmty Cons Sch Dist 24	millburn24.net/	153
Miller Cmty Cons Sch Dist 210	miltonpope.net/	143
Millstadt Cmty Cons SD 160	mccsd160.com/	220
Milne-Kelvin Grove District 91	d91.net/	244
Minooka Cmty Cons Sch Dist 201	min201.org/	112
Minooka Cmty High Sch Dist 111	mchs.net	244
Mokena Public School Dist 159	mokena159.org/	245
Moline-Coal Valley SD No 40	molineschools.org/	207
Momence Cmty Unit Sch Dist 1	momence.k12.il.us/	136
Monmouth-Roseville CUSD 238	mr238.org	234
Monroe School District 70	monroe70.org/	198
Monticello Cmty Unit SD 25	sages.us/	202
Montmorency Cmty Cons SD 145	mgs.whitesideroe.org/	239
Morris Cmty High Sch Dist 101	morrishs.org/	113
Morris Elem School Dist 54	morris54.org/	113
Morrison Cmty Unit Sch Dist 6	morrisonschools.org/	239
Morrisonville Cmty Unit SD 1	mohawks.net/	14
Morton Cmty Unit Sch Dist 709	morton709.org/home	227
Morton Grove School Dist 70	mgsd70.org/	58
Mt Olive Cmty Unit Sch Dist 5	mtoliveschools.org/	167
Mt Prospect School Dist 57	d57.org/	58
Mt Pulaski Cmty Unit SD 23	mtpulaski.k12.il.us/	164
Mt Vernon City Sch Dist 80	mtv80.org/	123
Mt Vernon Twp HS District 201	mvths.org/vnews/display.v/SEC/%23201%20Foundation	123
Mt Zion Cmty Unit Sch Dist 3	mtzschools.org/	166
Mulberry Grove Cmty Sch Dist 1	mgschools.com/welcome.html	4
Mundelein Cons High SD 120	d120.org/default.aspx	153
Mundelein Elem School Dist 75	district75.org/	153
Murphysboro Cmty Unit SD 186	cusd186.org/	121
N Pekin-Marquette Hts SD 102	dist102.org/	227
Naperville Cmty Unit SD 203	naperville203.org/	98
Nashville Cmty Cons SD 49	nashville49.org/ngs_main.htm	235
Nashville Cmty HSD 99	64.83.243.36/nashville/high/index.htm	235
Nauvoo-Colusa CUSD 325	nauvoo-colusa.com/	115
Neoga Cmty Unit School Dist 3	neoga.k12.il.us/	84
Nettle Creek Cmty SD 24-C	nettlecreek.org/index.php	113
New Athens CUSD 60	na60.org/	220
New Holland Middletown ESD 88	nhm88.com	164
New Hope Cmty Cons Sch Dist 6	newhopepanthers.com/	237
New Lenox School District 122	www2.nlsd122.org/c/	245

DISTRICT URL INDEX

Market Data Retrieval

DISTRICT	URL	PAGE
New Simpson Hill Cons SD 32	newsimpsonhill.com/education/school/school.php?sectionid=2	127
New Trier Twp HS District 203	newtrier.k12.il.us	58
Newark Cmty. Cons Sch Dist 66	newarkdistrict66.org/	138
Newark Cmty High Sch Dist 18	newarkhs.k12.il.us/	138
Niles Elem School District 71	culver71.net/	58
Niles Twp High School Dist 219	niles-hs.k12.il.us	58
Nippersink School District 2	nippersinkdistrict2.org/	183
Nokomis Cmty Unit Sch Dist 22	nokomis.k12.il.us/	191
Norridge School Dist 80	norridge80.org/	59
Norris City-Omaha-Enfield SD 3	ncoecusd.white.k12.il.us/	238
North Boone Cmty Unit SD 200	nbcusd.org/	5
North Chicago Cmty Unit SD 187	d187.org/	153
North Clay Cmty Unit SD 25	sites.google.com/northclayschools.com/nccusd25/district	16
North Greene Unit Dist 3	northgreene.com/	111
North Mac Cmty Unit SD 34	northmacschools.org/	168
North Palos School Dist 117	npd117.net/site/default.aspx?PageID=1	59
North Shore School Dist 112	nssd112.org/	154
North Wamac School Dist 186	northwamac.com/	18
Northbrook Elem School Dist 27	nb27.org/	59
Northbrook School District 28	ww1.northbrook28.net/	59
Northbrook-Glenview SD 30	district30.org/	60
Northwestern CUSD 2	northwestern.k12.il.us/	168
Norwood Sch Dist 63	norwood63.org	198
O'Fallon Cmty Cons Sch Dist 90	of90.net/	221
O'Fallon Twp School Dist 203	oths.k12.il.us/	221
Oak Grove School District 68	ogschool.org/	154
Oak Grove School District 68	og68.org/	198
Oak Lawn Cmty High SD 229	olchs.org/	60
Oak Lawn-Hometown Sch Dist 123	d123.org/	60
Oak Park & River Forest SD 200	oprfhs.org	60
Oak Park Elem School Dist 97	op97.org/	60
Oakdale Cmty Cons Sch Dist 1	oakdalegs.org	236
Oakland Cmty Unit Sch Dist 5	oak.k12.il.us/	19
Oakwood Cmty Unit Sch Dist 76	oakwood.k12.il.us/	232
Oblong Cmty Unit Sch Dist 4	oblongschools.net/	83
Odell Cmty Cons Sch Dist 435	odellschool.org/	161
Odin Public School Dist 722	odinpublicschools.org/	175
Oglesby Public Sch Dist 125	ops125.net	143
Ohio Cmty Cons School Dist 17	bhsroe.org/site/?page_id=39641	7
Ohio Cmty High School Dist 505	bhsroe.org/site/?page_id=39639	7
Okaw Valley Cmty Unit SD 302	okawvalley.org/	193
Olympia Cmty Unit Sch Dist 16	olympia.org/	187
Opdyke-Belle Rive Cmty CSSD 5	obr5.org/	123
Orangeville Cmty Unit SD 203	orangevillecusd.com/	225
Orion Cmty Unit Sch Dist 223	orionschools.us/	117
Orland School District 135	orland135.org/	61
Ottawa Elementary Sch Dist 141	oes141.org/	143
Ottawa Twp High Sch Dist 140	ottawahigh.com/	143
Palestine Cmty Unit SD 3	palestinecusd3.net/	83
Palos Cmty Cons Sch Dist 118	palos118.org/	61
Palos Heights School Dist 128	d128.k12.il.us/	61
Pana Cmty Unit School Dist 8	panaschools.com/	14
Panhandle Cmty Unit SD 2	panhandle.k12.il.us/	191
Paris Cmty Unit Sch Dist 4	crestwood.k12.il.us	103
Paris Union School District 95	paris95.k12.il.us/	103
Park Forest Chicago Hgt SD 163	sd163.com	62
Park Ridge Niles CMCSD 64	d64.org/	62
Patoka Cmty Unit SD 100	pcusd100.sharpschool.net/	175
Paw Paw Cmty Unit SD 271	2paws.net/lccusd/	160
Pawnee Cmty Unit Sch Dist 11	pawneeschools.com/	212
Paxton-Buckley-Loda CUSD 10	pblunit10.com/	107
Payson Cmty Unit School Dist 1	cusd1.org/	2
Pearl City Cmty Unit SD 200	pcwolves.net/	225
Pecatonica Cmty Unit SD 321	pecschools.com/district.htm	253
Pekin Cmty High Sch Dist 303	pekinhigh.net/	227
Pekin Public School Dist 108	pekin.net/Page/1	227
Pembroke Cmty Cons SD 259	pembroke.k12.il.us/	136
Pennoyer School District 79	pennoyerschool.org/	62
Peoria Heights Cmty SD 325	phcusd325.net/	198
Peoria Public Sch Dist 150	peoriapublicschools.org/	198
Peotone Cmty Unit SD 207-U	peotoneschools.org/	245
Peru Elem Sch Dist 124	perued.net	143
Pikeland Cmty Sch Dist 10	pikeland.net/	203
Pinckneyville Cmty High SD 101	pchspanthers.com/	201

Illinois School Directory

DISTRICT URL INDEX

DISTRICT	URL	PAGE
Pinckneyville Sch Dist 50	jrpanther.com/	201
Plainfield Cons Sch Dist 202	psd202.org/	245
Plano Cmty Unit Sch Dist 88	plano88.org	138
Pleasant Hill CUSD 3	phwolves.com/	203
Pleasant Hill School Dist 69	phill69.com/	199
Pleasant Plains Cmty Unit SD 8	ppcusd8.org/	212
Pleasant Valley Sch Dist 62	pv62.com/	199
Pleasantdale School Dist 107	d107.org/	62
Polo Cmty Unit Sch Dist 222	polo222.org/	195
Pontiac Cmty Cons Sch Dist 429	sites.google.com/pontiac429.org/home	161
Pontiac Twp High Sch Dist 90	pontiac.k12.il.us/	161
Pontiac-Wm Holliday SD 105	pwh105.org/	221
Pope Co Cmty Unit Sch Dist 1	popek12.org/	203
Porta Cmty Unit Sch Dist 202	porta202.org/	189
Posen-Robbins Sch Dist 143-5	prsd1435.org/	63
Potomac Cmty Unit Sch Dist 10	potomac.k12.il.us/	232
Prairie Central Cmty USD 8	prairiecentral.org/	162
Prairie Du Rocher CCSD 134	pdr134.com/	205
Prairie Grove Cons SD 46	dist46.org/	183
Prairie Hill Cmty Cons SD 133	prairiehill.org/	253
Prairie Hills Elem SD 144	phsd144.net/	63
Prairieview-Ogden Sch Dist 197	pvo.k12.il.us/	11
Princeton Elem Sch Dist 115	princeton115schools.org/	7
Princeton Twp HSD 500	phs-il.org.	7
Princeville Cmty Unit SD 326	princeville326.org/	200
Prophetstown-Lyndon-Tampico 3	plt3.org/	239
Prospect Hts School Dist 23	d23.org	63
Proviso Twp High Sch Dist 209	pths209.org/	63
Putnam Co Cmty Unit SD 535	pcschools535.org/	204
Queen Bee School District 16	queenbee16.org/	98
Quincy School District 172	qps.org	2
Raccoon Cons School Dist 1	raccoon.k12.il.us/	175
Ramsey Cmty Unit Sch Dist 204	ramsey.fayette.k12.il.us/	105
Rankin Cmty School Dist 98	rankin98.org/	228
Rantoul City School Dist 137	rcs137.org/	11
Rantoul Twp High Sch Dist 193	rths.k12.il.us/	12
Reavis Twp HSD 220	reavisd220.org/	64
Red Bud Cmty Unit Sch Dist 132	redbud132.org/	205
Red Hill Cmty School Dist 10	redhill.cusd10.org/	159
Reed-Custer Cmty Unit SD 255-U	rc255.net/	246
Rhodes School District 84 1/2	rhodes.k12.il.us	64
Rich Twp High School Dist 227	rich227.org/	64
Richland Co Cmty Unit SD 1	rccu1.net/	206
Richland School Dist 88A	d88a.org/	247
Richmond-Burton Cmty HSD 157	rbchs.com/District/1378-Untitled.html	183
Ridgeland School District 122	ridgeland122.com/	64
Ridgeview Cmty Unit SD 19	ridgeview19.org/	187
Ridgewood Cmty HSD 234	ridgenet.org	64
Riley Cmty Cons Sch Dist 18	riley18.org/	184
River Bend Cmty School Dist 2	riverbendschools.org/district/	239
River Forest Sch Dist 90	district90.org/	65
River Grove School Dist 85-5	rgsd.w-cook.k12.il.us	65
River Ridge Cmty Unit SD 210	riverridge210.org/	126
River Trails Sch Dist 26	rtsd26.org/	65
Riverdale Cmty Unit SD 100	riverdaleschools.org/	208
Riverside Public Sch Dist 96	district96.org/	65
Riverside-Brookfld Twp SD 208	rbhs.w-cook.k12.il.us	65
Riverton Cmty Unit SD 14	rivertonschools.org/	212
Riverview Cmty Cons Sch Dist 2	rgschool.com/	258
Roanoke-Benson Cmty Unit SD 60	rb60.com	258
Robein Cmty School District 85	robein.org/	228
Robinson Cmty Unit Sch Dist 2	robinsonschools.com/	83
Rochelle Cmty Cons SD 231	d231.rochelle.net/	195
Rochester Cmty Unit SD 3-A	rochester3a.net/	212
Rock Falls Elem Sch Dist 13	rfsd13.org/pages/Rock_Falls_Elementary_SD_13	240
Rock Falls Twp High SD 301	rfhs301.org/vnews/display.v/SEC/Activities	240
Rock Island-Milan Sch Dist 41	rimsd41.org/	208
Rockdale School District 84	rockdale.will.k12.il.us/	247
Rockford School District 205	www3.rps205.com/Pages/default.aspx	253
Rockridge Cmty Unit SD 300	rr300.org/	209
Rockton School District 140	rockton140.org	255
Rome Cmty Cons Sch Dist 2	rome2.net/	123
Rondout School District 72	rondout.org/	154
Rooks Creek Cmty Cons SD 425	rookscreek.k12.il.us/	162

School Year 2020-2021
800-333-8802
IL-W9

DISTRICT URL INDEX

Market Data Retrieval

DISTRICT	URL	PAGE
Roselle School District 12	sd12.k12.il.us/	99
Rosemont Elem Sch Dist 78	rosemont78.org/	66
Rossville-Alvin Cmty Unit SD 7	rossvillealvinbobcats.org/	233
Round Lake Area Co Dist 116	rlas-116.org/	154
Rowva Cmty School Dist 208	rowva.k12.il.us/	140
Roxana Cmty Unit Sch Dist 1	roxanaschools.org/	172
Rutland Cmty Cons SD 230	rutlandgs.org/	144
Salem Cmty High Sch Dist 600	salemhigh.com	175
Salem Elem Sch District 111	salem111.com	175
Salt Creek School District 48	saltcreek48.org/	99
Salt Fork Cmty Unit SD 512	saltfork.org/	233
Sandoval Cmty Unit SD 501	sandoval501.org/	175
Sandridge Sch Dist 172	d172.s-cook.k12.il.us/	66
Sandwich Cmty Unit SD 430	sandwich430.org/	85
Sangamon Valley Cmty Unit SD 9	sangamonvalley.org/	166
Saratoga Cmty Cons SD 60C	sd60c.org/pages/Saratoga_Elementary	113
Saunemin Cmty Cons SD 438	saunemin.org/	162
Scales Mound Cmty Unit SD 211	scalesmound.net	126
Schaumburg Cmty Cons SD 54	sd54.org/	66
Schiller Park School Dist 81	d81.w-cook.k12.il.us/	67
School Dist 45 Dupage Co	d45.org/	99
Schuyler-Industry CUSD 5	sid5.com/	215
Scott Morgan Cmty Unit SD 2	bluffs-school.com/	215
Selmaville Cmty Cons SD 10	selmaville.com/education/school/school.php?sectionid=3	176
Seneca Cmty Cons Sch Dist 170	sgs170.org/	144
Seneca Twp High Sch Dist 160	senecahs.org/	144
Serena Cmty Unit School Dist 2	unit2.net/	144
Sesser-Valier Cmty Unit SD 196	s-v.frnkln.k12.il.us/	108
Shawnee Cmty Unit Sch Dist 84	shawneedistrict84.com/	231
Shelbyville Cmty Sch Dist 4	shelbyville.k12.il.us/	216
Sherrard Cmty Sch Dist 200	sherrard.us/pages/Sherrard_Community_Unit_School	189
Shiloh School District 1	shiloh.k12.il.us/	103
Shiloh Village Sch Dist 85	shiloh.stclair.k12.il.us/	221
Shirland Cmty Cons SD 134	shirland134.org	255
Signal Hill Sch Dist 181	signalhill181.org/education/school/school.php?sectionid=8	221
Silvis School District 34	silvis34.org	209
Skokie School District 68	skokie68.org/	67
Skokie School District 69	sd69.org/	67
Skokie School District 73 1/2	sd735.org/education/school/school.php?sectionid=74	67
Smithton Cmty Cons SD 130	smithton.stclair.k12.il.us	222
Somonauk Cmty Unit SD 432	somonauk.net/	86
South Beloit Cmty Sch Dist 320	southbeloitschooldistrict.org/	255
South Central Cmty Unit SD 401	southcentralschools.org/	176
South Fork School Dist 14	southforkschools.com/	14
South Holland School Dist 150	sd150.org/	68
South Holland School Dist 151	shsd151.org/	68
South Pekin Grade Sch Dist 137	spgs.net/	228
Southeastern Cmty Unit SD 337	southeastern337.com/	115
Southwestern Cmty Unit SD 9	piasabirds.net	168
Sparta Cmty School Dist 140	sparta.k12.il.us/	205
Spoon River Valley Cmty SD 4	spoon-river.k12.il.us	110
Spring Garden Cmty CSD 178	springgardenhawks.org/	124
Spring Lake Elem SD 606	springlake606.org/	228
Spring Valley Cmty Cons SD 99	sv99.org/	7
Springfield Pub Sch Dist 186	sps186.org/	213
St Anne Cmty Cons Sch Dist 256	sags.k12.il.us/	136
St Anne Cmty HSD 302	sachs302.org/	136
St Elmo Cmty Unit Sch Dist 202	stelmo.org	106
St George School District 258	sg258.org/	136
St Joseph Cmty Cons SD 169	stjoe.k12.il.us/	12
St Joseph-Ogden Cmty HSD 305	sjo.k12.il.us/	12
St Libory Cons Sch District 30	stlibory30.org/	222
St Rose School District 14-15	strosedistrict14-15.com/	18
Stark Co Cmty Unit SD 100	stark100.com/	223
Staunton Cmty Unit Sch Dist 6	stauntonschools.org/index.html	168
Steeleville Cmty Sch Dist 138	steeleville138.org/	206
Steger School Dist 194	sd194.org	68
Sterling Cmty Unit Sch Dist 5	sterlingpublicschools.org/	240
Steward Elem School Dist 220	stewardschool220.org/	160
Stewardson-Strasburg SD 5-A	stew-stras.org/	216
Stockton Cmty Unit SD 206	stocktonschools.com/	126
Streator Elem School Dist 44	district.sas44.net/	144
Streator Twp High Sch Dist 40	streatorhs.org/	145
Sullivan Cmty Unit SD 300	home.sullivan.k12.il.us/	193

Illinois School Directory

DISTRICT URL INDEX

DISTRICT	URL	PAGE
Summersville Sch Dist 79	summersville79.com/	124
Summit Hill School Dist 161	summithill.org/	247
Sunnybrook School District 171	sd171.org/	68
Sunset Ridge Sch Dist 29	sunsetridge29.org/	68
Sycamore Cmty Unit SD 427	syc427.org	86
Taft School District 90	taft90.org/	247
Tamaroa Elem School Dist 5	tgs5.com/	201
Taylorville Cmty Unit SD 3	taylorvilleschools.com	15
Teutopolis Cmty Unit SD 50	teutopolisschools.org/	105
Thomasboro Cmty Cons SD 130	thomasboro.k12.il.us/	12
Thompsonville Cmty USD 174	tvilleschools.org/	108
Thornton Fractnl Twp HSD 215	tfd215.org	69
Thornton Twp High Sch Dist 205	district205.net	69
Tolono Cmty Unit Sch Dist 7	unitsevenschools.com	12
Tonica Cmty Cons Sch Dist 79	tonicagradeschool.org/	145
Township High School Dist 113	dist113.org/Pages/Default.aspx	155
Township High School Dist 211	adc.d211.org/	69
Township High School Dist 214	d214.org/	69
Tremont Cmty Unit SD 702	tremont702.net/	228
Tri-City Cmty Unit Sch Dist 1	tricityschools.org/	214
Tri-Point Cmty Unit SD 6J	tripointschools.org/	162
Tri-Valley Cmty School Dist 3	tri-valley3.org/	187
Triad Cmty School District 2	triadunit2.org/education/district/district.php?sectionid=1	172
Triopia Cmty Unit Sch Dist 27	triopiacusd27.org/	192
Troy Cmty Cons SD 30-C	troywebs.troy30c.org/	247
Tuscola Cmty Unit SD 301	tuscola.k12.il.us/	88
Union Ridge School Dist 86	urs86.k12.il.us/	70
Union School District 81	union81.com/	248
United Cmty Unit Sch Dist 304	united.k12.il.us/	234
United Twp High Sch Dist 30	uths.net/	209
Unity Point Cmty Cons SD 140	up140.org/default.aspx	121
Urbana School District 116	usd116.org/	12
Valley View Cmty SD 365-U	vvsd.org	248
Valmeyer Cmty School Dist 3	valmeyerk12.org/	190
Vandalia Cmty Unit SD 203	vcs.fayette.k12.il.us/	106
Venice Cmty Unit School Dist 3	veniceschools.org/	172
Vienna High School Dist 13-3	vhs.johnsn.k12.il.us/	127
Vienna Public School Dist 55	viennagradeschool.com/	127
Villa Grove Cmty Unit SD 302	vg302.org/education/school/school.php?sectionid=2	88
Virginia Cmty Unit Sch Dist 64	virginia64.com/	9
Vit Cmty Unit School Dist 2	sites.google.com/a/vit2.org/v-i-t-cusd-2/	110
Wabash Cmty Unit Sch Dist 348	wabash348.com/	234
Wallace Cmty Cons Sch Dist 195	wallacegs.org/	145
Waltham Elementary SD 185	wesd185.org/	145
Waltonville Cmty Unit SD 1	wcusd1.org/	124
Warren Community Unit SD 205	205warren.net/	126
Warren Twp High Sch Dist 121	d121.org/	155
Warrensburg-Latham CU SD 11	wl.k12.il.us	166
Warsaw Cmty Unit Sch Dist 316	warsawschool.com/	115
Washington Cmty HS Dist 308	wacohi.net	229
Washington School Dist 52	d52schools.com/	229
Waterloo Cmty Unit Sch Dist 5	wcusd5.net/	190
Wauconda Cmty Unit SD 118	d118.org/	155
Waukegan Cmty Unit SD 60	wps60.org/	156
Waverly Cmty Unit SD 6	waverlyscotties.com/	193
Wayne City Cmty Unit SD 100	waynecity100.org/	237
Wesclin Cmty Unit Sch Dist 3	wesclin.k12.il.us/	18
West Aurora School Dist 129	sd129.org	132
West Carroll CUSD 314	wc314.org/	8
West Central Cmty Unit SD 235	wc235.k12.il.us/	116
West Chicago Elementary SD 33	wego33.org/	99
West Harvey-Dixmoor Pub SD 147	whd147.org/	70
West Lincoln-Broadwell ESD 92	wlb92.org/	164
West Northfield Sch Dist 31	dist31.k12.il.us/	70
West Prairie Cmty Sch Dist 103	wp103.org/	178
West Washington Co Cmty SD 10	okawville-k12.org/	236
Westchester Public SD 92 1/2	sd925.org	70
Western CUSD 12	westerncusd12.org/	203
Western Springs Sch Dist 101	d101.org/htdocs/	71
Westville Cmty Unit Sch Dist 2	gowestville.org/	233
Wethersfield Cmty Unit SD 230	geese230.com/	117
Wheeling Cmty Cons Sch Dist 21	d21.k12.il.us	71
Whiteside School District 115	whiteside.stclair.k12.il.us/	222
Will Co School District 92	d92.org	248

DISTRICT URL INDEX

DISTRICT	URL	PAGE
Williamsfield Cmty Unit SD 210	billtown.org/	140
Williamsville Cmty Unit SD 15	wcusd15.org/	214
Willow Grove School Dist 46	willowgroveschool.com/	18
Willow Springs School Dist 108	willowspringsschool.org/	71
Wilmette Public School Dist 39	wilmette39.org/	71
Wilmington Cmty Unit SD 209-U	wilmington.will.k12.il.us	249
Winchester Cmty Unit SD 1	winchesterschools.net/	215
Windsor Cmty Unit SD 1	windsor.k12.il.us/	216
Winfield School District 34	winfield34.org/	100
Winnebago Cmty Unit SD 323	winnebagoschools.org/	255
Winnetka School Dist 36	www2.winnetka36.org/	72
Winthrop Harbor School Dist 1	whsd1.org/	156
Wolf Branch School Dist 113	sites.google.com/a/wbsd113.org/wolf-branch-district-113/	222
Wood Dale School Dist 7	wd7.org	100
Wood River-Hartford Elem SD 15	wrh15.org/	172
Woodland Cmty Unit Sch Dist 5	woodland5.org/	162
Woodland School District 50	dist50.net/default.aspx	156
Woodlawn Unit School Dist 209	woodlawnschools.org/	124
Woodridge Elem Sch District 68	woodridge68.org/	100
Woodstock Cmty Unit SD 200	woodstockschools.org/	184
Worth School District 127	worthschools.org/	72
Yorkville Cmty Unit SD 115	y115.org/	139
Zeigler Royalton CUSD 188	zr188.org/	108
Zion Public School District 6	zion6.com/	157
Zion-Benton Twp High SD 126	zbths.org/	157

MDR School Directory

CHARTER MANAGEMENT ORGANIZATION (CMO) INDEX

CMO No.	PID	CMO Name	Address	Phone
001	11912383	Estem Public Charter Schools	200 River Market Ave Ste 225, Little Rock AR 72201	(501) 324-9200
002	11916092	KIPP Delta Public Schools	320 Missouri, Helena AR 72342	(870) 753-9035
003	12319502	Lisa Academy Foundation	10825 Financial Centre Pkwy, Little Rock AR 72211	(501) 916-9450
004	12376823	Academies of Math & Science	2980 N Campbell Ave, Tucson AZ 85719	(520) 887-5392
005	11912826	Academy of Tucson Inc	10720 E 22nd St, Tucson AZ 85748	(520) 733-0096
006	11914305	Accelerated Learning Ctr	4105 E Shea Blvd, Phoenix AZ 85028	(602) 485-0309
007	11914288	Allen-Cochran Enterprises	1700 E Elliot Rd Ste 9, Tempe AZ 85284	(480) 632-1940
008	11914264	American Basic Schools LLC	131 E Southern Ave, Mesa AZ 85210	(480) 655-7868
009	11928033	American Leadership Acad Inc	2250 E Germann Rd Ste 14, Chandler AZ 85286	(480) 420-2101
010	11912761	Arizona Agribus&Equine Ctr Org	315 E Mulberry Dr, Phoenix AZ 85012	(602) 297-8500
011	11912759	Arizona Charter Schools	5704 E Grant Rd, Tucson AZ 85712	(520) 545-0575
012	12376835	Asu Preparatory Acad Network	PO Box 876705, Tempe AZ 85287	(602) 496-3322
013	11912723	Basis School Inc	7975 N Hayden Rd Ste B202, Scottsdale AZ 85258	(480) 289-2088
014	11914525	Benjamin Franklin Chtr Schools	690 E Warner Rd Ste 141, Gilbert AZ 85296	(480) 264-3710
015	11912668	Blueprint Education	5651 W Talavi Blvd Ste 170, Glendale AZ 85306	(602) 674-5555
016	11914226	Bright Beginnings School Inc	400 N Andersen Blvd, Chandler AZ 85224	(480) 821-1404
017	11912620	CAFA Inc	4055 E Warner Rd, Gilbert AZ 85296	(480) 635-1900
018	11913387	Career Success Schools	3816 N 27th Ave, Phoenix AZ 85017	(602) 285-5525
019	11913351	Center for Academic Success	1843 Paseo San Luis, Sierra Vista AZ 85635	(520) 458-9309
020	11914173	Compass High School Inc	PO Box 17810, Tucson AZ 85731	(520) 296-4070
021	11914159	Cornerstone Charter School Inc	7107 N Black Canyon Hwy, Phoenix AZ 85021	(602) 595-2198
022	11914147	Country Gardens Educl Svcs	6313 W Southern Ave, Laveen AZ 85339	(602) 237-3741
023	11914111	Eastpointe High School Inc	8495 E Broadway Blvd, Tucson AZ 85710	(520) 731-8180
024	11914068	Educational Impact Inc	1950 E Placita Sin Nombre, Tucson AZ 85718	(520) 296-0656
025	11914044	Eduprize Schools Inc	4567 W Roberts Rd, Queen Creek AZ 85142	(480) 888-1610
026	11912395	Espiritu Community Development	222 E Olympic Dr, Phoenix AZ 85042	(602) 243-7788
027	12378118	Fit Kids Inc Champion Schools	6991 E Camelback Rd Ste D300, Scottsdale AZ 85251	(480) 386-7071
028	11914032	GAR LLC	8253 W Thunderbird Rd Ste 105, Peoria AZ 85381	(602) 334-4104
029	11913234	Great Hearts Academies	4801 E Washington St Ste 250, Phoenix AZ 85034	(602) 438-7045
030	11913985	Heritage Academy Inc	32 S Center St, Mesa AZ 85210	(480) 969-5641
031	11914434	Humanities & Sciences Acad US	5201 N 7th St, Phoenix AZ 85014	(602) 650-1333
032	11911781	Imagine Southwest Regional	1843 W 16th Ave, Apache Jct AZ 85120	(480) 355-0502
033	11913179	Kingman Academy of Learning	3410 N Burbank St, Kingman AZ 86409	(928) 681-2400
034	11913167	Leading Edge Charter Solutions	633 E Ray Rd Ste 132, Gilbert AZ 85296	(480) 633-0414
035	11913143	Learning Matters Educl Group	4744 W Grovers Ave, Glendale AZ 85308	(602) 439-5026
036	11913959	Legacy Traditional Schools	3125 S Gilbert Rd, Chandler AZ 85286	(480) 270-5438
037	11914599	Leona Group LLC-AZ	7500 N Dreamy Draw Dr Ste 220, Phoenix AZ 85020	(602) 953-2933
038	11914381	Mgrm Pinnacle Education Inc	2224 W Southern Ave Ste 1, Tempe AZ 85282	(480) 755-8222
039	11913911	Montessori Schoolhouse Tucson	1301 E Fort Lowell Rd, Tucson AZ 85719	(520) 319-8668
040	11913923	Montessori Schools Flagstaff	2212 E Cedar Ave, Flagstaff AZ 86004	(928) 774-1600
041	12305874	Pima Prevention Partnership	1477 W Commerce Ct, Tucson AZ 85746	(520) 791-2711
042	12306309	Plc Charter Schools	2504 S 91st Ave, Tolleson AZ 85353	(623) 474-2120
043	11912101	Pointe Educational Services	10215 N 43rd Ave, Phoenix AZ 85051	(602) 843-2014
044	11913519	PPEP and Affiliates	802 E 46th St, Tucson AZ 85713	(520) 622-3553
045	11913856	Rose Management Group	3686 W Orange Grove Rd Ste 192, Tucson AZ 85741	(520) 797-4884
046	11913832	Self Development Chtr Sch Org	1709 N Greenfield Rd, Mesa AZ 85205	(480) 641-2640
047	11913337	Sequoia Schools-Edkey Inc	1460 S Horne Bldg 6, Mesa AZ 85204	(480) 461-3200
048	11912979	Skyline Education	7450 S 40th St 7500, Phoenix AZ 85042	(877) 225-2118
049	11913349	Sonoran Schools Inc	1489 W Elliot Rd Ste 103, Gilbert AZ 85233	(480) 940-5440
050	11913806	Southern Arizona Cmty Acad Inc	2470 N Tucson Blvd, Tucson AZ 85716	(520) 319-6113
051	11912929	The Charter Foundation Inc	1150 N Country Club Rd Ste 100, Tucson AZ 85716	(520) 296-1100
052	11911901	The Edge School Inc	2555 E 1st St, Tucson AZ 85716	(520) 881-1389
053	11912890	Tucson International Academy	2700 W Broadway Blvd, Tucson AZ 85745	(520) 792-3255
054	11912802	Albert Einstein Academies	3035 Ash St, San Diego CA 92102	(619) 795-1190
055	11913686	Alliance College-Ready Pub Sch	601 S Figueroa St Fl 4, Los Angeles CA 90017	(213) 943-4930
056	12305812	Alpha Public Schools	PO Box 21366, San Jose CA 95151	(408) 455-6355
057	12262961	Alta Public Schools	2410 Broadway, Huntington Pk CA 90255	(323) 923-0383
058	11912785	American Indian Model Schools	171 12th St, Oakland CA 94607	(510) 893-8701
059	12262911	Amethod Public Schools	2101 Livingston St, Oakland CA 94606	(510) 436-0172
060	12379124	Aspire Bay Area Region	1001 22nd Ave Ste 200, Oakland CA 94606	(510) 568-3101

CHARTER MANAGEMENT ORGANIZATION (CMO) INDEX

Market Data Retrieval

CMO No.	PID	CMO Name	Address	Phone
061	12379136	Aspire Central Vly Area Region	3311 Morada Ln, Stockton CA 95212	(209) 647-3047
062	12379148	Aspire Los Angeles Area Region	5901 E Slauson Ave, Los Angeles CA 90040	(323) 837-9920
063	11913648	Aspire Public Schools	1001 22nd Ave Ste 100, Oakland CA 94606	(510) 434-5000
064	11912656	Bright Star Education Group	600 S La Fayette Park Pl, Los Angeles CA 90057	(323) 954-9957
065	11913404	California Montessori Projects	5330A Gibbons Dr Ste 700, Carmichael CA 95608	(916) 971-2432
066	11913399	Camino Nuevo Charter Academy	3435 W Temple St, Los Angeles CA 90026	(213) 417-3400
067	11912709	Ceiba Public Schools	260 W Riverside Dr, Watsonville CA 95076	(831) 740-8800
068	12260028	Citizens of the World Chtr Sch	5371 Wilshire Blvd Ste 210, Los Angeles CA 90036	(323) 634-7109
069	11912565	Civicorps Schools	101 Myrtle St, Oakland CA 94607	(510) 992-7800
070	11912539	Community Learning Center Schs	1900 3rd St, Alameda CA 94501	(510) 263-9266
071	11912527	Core-Cmty Options Resources Ed	321 16th St, Marysville CA 95901	(530) 742-2786
072	12377413	Da Vinci Schools	201 N Douglas St, El Segundo CA 90245	(310) 725-5800
073	12110435	Downtown College Prep	1400 Parkmoor Ave Ste 206, San Jose CA 95126	(408) 271-8120
074	12261486	Ednovate Inc	350 S Figueroa St Ste 350, Los Angeles CA 90071	(213) 454-0599
075	11912436	Education for Change	333 Hegenberger Rd Ste 600, Oakland CA 94621	(510) 568-7936
076	11912412	Environmental Charter Schools	2625 Manhattn Bch Blvd Ste 100, Redondo Beach CA 90278	(310) 214-3408
077	11913301	Envision Education	111 Myrtle St Ste 203, Oakland CA 94607	(510) 451-2415
078	12179015	Equitas Academy Chtr Sch Inc	1700 W Pico Blvd, Los Angeles CA 90015	(213) 201-0440
079	12305824	Fenton Charter Public Schools	8928 Sunland Blvd, Sun Valley CA 91352	(818) 962-3630
080	11912357	Five Keys Charter Schools Inc	70 Oak Grove St, San Francisco CA 94107	(415) 734-3310
081	12262935	Fortune School of Education	2890 Gateway Oaks Dr Ste 100, Sacramento CA 95833	(916) 924-8633
082	11913258	Gateway Community Charters	5112 Arnold Ave Ste A, McClellan CA 95652	(916) 286-5129
083	11912319	Golden Valley Charter Schools	3585 Maple St Ste 101, Ventura CA 93003	(805) 642-3435
084	11913595	Green Dot Public Schools	1149 S Hill St Ste 600, Los Angeles CA 90015	(323) 565-1600
085	12239598	Grimmway Schools	5080 California Ave Ste 100, Bakersfield CA 93309	(661) 432-7880
086	11912280	High Desert Partnsp Acad Excel	17500 Mana Rd, Apple Valley CA 92307	(760) 946-5414
087	11913222	High Tech High	2861 Womble Rd, San Diego CA 92106	(619) 243-5000
088	11913583	ICEF Public Schools	3855 W Slauson Ave, Los Angeles CA 90043	(323) 290-6900
089	11912266	Innovative Education Managemnt	4535 Missouri Flat Rd Ste 1A, Placerville CA 95667	(800) 979-4436
090	11913375	Isana Academies	3580 Wilshire Blvd Ste 1130, Los Angeles CA 90010	(323) 291-1211
091	11913181	King-Chavez Neighborhood Schs	2260 Island Ave, San Diego CA 92102	(619) 525-7320
092	11916054	KIPP Bay Area Public Schools	1000 Broadway Ste 460, Oakland CA 94607	(510) 465-5477
093	11913571	KIPP Foundation	135 Main St Ste 1700, San Francisco CA 94105	(415) 399-1556
094	11916169	KIPP Socal Public Schools	3601 E 1st St, Los Angeles CA 90063	(213) 489-4461
095	11913155	Leadership Public Schools	99 Linden St, Oakland CA 94607	(510) 830-3780
096	12260030	Los Angeles Education Corps	3635 Atlantic Ave, Long Beach CA 90807	(562) 216-1790
097	11913557	Magnolia Ed & Research Fdn	250 E 1st St Ste 1500, Los Angeles CA 90012	(213) 628-3634
098	11912187	National Univ Academy System	1980 University Dr Ste 30, Vista CA 92083	(760) 630-4080
099	12262777	Navigator Schools	650 San Benito St Ste 230, Hollister CA 95023	(831) 217-4880
100	12361373	Olive Grove Charter Schools	2353 S Broadway, Santa Maria CA 93454	(805) 623-1111
101	11935907	Opportunities for Learning	320 N Halstead St Ste 220, Pasadena CA 91107	(888) 207-1119
102	11913052	Options for Youth Inc	320 N Halstead St Ste 280, Pasadena CA 91107	(888) 389-9992
103	12262923	Pacific Charter Institute	1401 El Camino Ave Ste 510, Sacramento CA 95815	(866) 992-9033
104	11912125	Para Los Ninos PCS	5000 Hollywood Blvd, Los Angeles CA 90027	(213) 250-4800
105	11913521	Partnerships to Uplift Cmty	1405 N San Fernando Blvd 303, Burbank CA 91504	(818) 559-7699
106	11912060	Real Journey Academies	1425 W Foothill Blvd Ste 100, Upland CA 91786	(909) 888-8458
107	11912046	Roads Education Organization	2999 Cleveland Ave Ste D, Santa Rosa CA 95403	(707) 843-4676
108	11912034	Rocketship Education	350 Twin Dolphin Dr Ste 109, Redwood City CA 94065	(877) 806-0920
109	11911872	Rocklin Academy Charter Schs	2204 Plaza Dr Ste 200, Rocklin CA 95765	(916) 778-4544
110	11912008	Semillas Sociedad Civil	4736 Huntington Dr S, Los Angeles CA 90032	(323) 352-3148
111	11911987	St Hope Public Schools	PO Box 5038, Sacramento CA 95817	(916) 649-7900
112	12101381	Summit Public Schools	780 Broadway St, Redwood City CA 94063	(650) 257-9880
113	11911925	The Accelerated School	116 E Mlk Jr Blvd, Los Angeles CA 90011	(323) 235-6343
114	12378742	The Classical Academies	157 E Valley Pkwy, Escondido CA 92025	(760) 842-8000
115	11911884	The Learner-Centered School	3325 Hacienda Way, Antioch CA 94509	(925) 755-7311
116	11911846	Tracy Learning Center	51 E Beverly Pl, Tracy CA 95376	(209) 290-0511
117	11911822	Value Schools	680 Wilshire Pl Ste 315, Los Angeles CA 90005	(213) 388-8676
118	12306244	Western Sierra Charter Schools	41267 Highway 41, Oakhurst CA 93644	(559) 642-1422
119	12262791	Ypi Charter Schools	10660 White Oak Ave B101, Granada Hills CA 91344	(818) 834-5805
120	12321684	Colorado Early College Network	4405 N Chestnut St Ste E, Colorado Spgs CO 80907	(719) 955-4685

MDR School Directory — CHARTER MANAGEMENT ORGANIZATION (CMO) INDEX

CMO No.	PID	CMO Name	Address	Phone
121	12378156	Dsst Public School Foundation	3401 Quebec St Ste 2000, Denver CO 80207	(303) 524-6324
122	12322432	Global Village Charter Collab	555 W 112th Ave, Northglenn CO 80234	(720) 353-4113
123	11916078	KIPP Colorado	1390 Lawrence St Ste 200, Denver CO 80204	(303) 934-3245
124	12305886	Rocky Mountain Prep Schools	7808 Cherry Creek Dr S, Denver CO 80231	(720) 863-8920
125	12110356	Strive Preparatory Schools	2480 W 26th Ave Ste 360B, Denver CO 80211	(720) 772-4300
126	12322626	Tatonka Education Services	10375 Park Meadows Dr Ste 230, Lone Tree CO 80124	(303) 296-6500
127	11913090	The New America Schools Netwk	925 S Niagara St Ste 140/400, Denver CO 80224	(303) 800-0058
128	11913698	Achievement First Network	370 James St Ste 404, New Haven CT 06513	(203) 773-3223
129	11915414	Jumoke Academy Inc	999 Asylum Ave Ste 200, Hartford CT 06105	(860) 216-9636
130	11913650	Aspira Educl Management Org	1220 L St NW Ste 701, Washington DC 20005	(202) 835-3600
131	11913363	Center City Public Charter Sch	900 2nd St NE Ste 221, Washington DC 20002	(202) 589-0202
132	11912591	Cesar Chavez Public Chtr Schs	3701 Hayes St NE, Washington DC 20019	(202) 547-3975
133	11912503	DC Prep	707 Edgewood St NE, Washington DC 20017	(202) 635-4590
134	11913260	Friendship Public Charter Sch	111 O St NW, Washington DC 20001	(202) 281-1700
135	11914836	KIPP DC	2600 Virginia Ave NW Ste 900, Washington DC 20037	(202) 223-4505
136	11912010	See Forever Foundation	600 Pennsylvania Ave SE, Washington DC 20003	(202) 797-8250
137	11911860	The Seed Foundation	1730 Rh Isl Ave NW Ste 1102, Washington DC 20036	(202) 785-4123
138	11914680	Academica	6340 Sunset Dr, Miami FL 33143	(305) 669-2906
139	11914549	Accelerated Learning Solutions	5850 T G Lee Blvd Ste 345, Orlando FL 32822	(888) 437-9353
140	11914496	Charter School Associates Inc	5471 N University Dr, Coral Springs FL 33067	(954) 414-5767
141	11914678	Charter Schools USA	800 Corporate Dr Ste 700, Ft Lauderdale FL 33334	(954) 202-3500
142	11912541	Cmty & Eco Dev Org Gadsden Co	20 E Washington St, Quincy FL 32351	(850) 627-7656
143	11914630	Edisonlearning Inc	1 E Broward Blvd Ste 1111, Ft Lauderdale FL 33301	(877) 890-7088
144	12261709	Forza Education Management LLC	PO Box 830, Parrish FL 34219	(727) 642-9319
145	11916420	Imagine South Florida Regional	13790 NW 4th St Ste 108, Sunrise FL 33325	(954) 870-5023
146	11916406	Imagine Southeast Regional	775 Town Center Blvd, Palm Coast FL 32164	(888) 709-8010
147	11916157	KIPP Jacksonville Schools	1440 McDuff Ave N, Jacksonville FL 32254	(904) 683-6643
148	12179651	Lake Wales Charter Schools	130 E Central Ave, Lake Wales FL 33853	(863) 679-6560
149	11913569	Lighthouse Academies	29140 Chapel Park Dr Bldg 5A, Wesley Chapel FL 33543	(800) 901-6943
150	11913947	LII Licensing Inc	6710 86th Ave N, Pinellas Park FL 33782	(727) 768-0989
151	11914379	Rader Group	101A Business Centre Dr, Miramar Beach FL 32550	(850) 650-3984
152	11913789	Superior Schools	861 N Hercules Ave, Clearwater FL 33765	(727) 799-1200
153	11916224	KIPP Metro Atlanta Schools	1445 Maynard Rd NW, Atlanta GA 30331	(404) 924-6310
154	12240195	Mountain Ed Chtr High School	1963 Tom Bell Rd, Cleveland GA 30528	(706) 219-4664
155	12259990	Gem Innovation Schools	PO Box 86, Deary ID 83823	(208) 238-1388
156	11913466	Acero Charter Schools Inc	209 W Jackson Blvd Ste 500, Chicago IL 60606	(312) 637-3900
157	11913662	American Quality Schools Corp	1315 Butterfield Rd Ste 224, Downers Grove IL 60515	(312) 226-3355
158	11912670	Betty Shabazz Intl Chtr Sch	7822 S Dobson Ave, Chicago IL 60619	(773) 651-1221
159	11912606	Catalyst Schools	6727 S California Ave, Chicago IL 60629	(773) 295-7001
160	11912553	Civitas Education Partners	1006 S Michigan Ave Ste 301, Chicago IL 60605	(312) 733-6790
161	11913636	Concept Schools	1336 Basswood Rd, Schaumburg IL 60173	(847) 824-3380
162	11912333	Galapagos Charter	3051 Rotary Rd, Rockford IL 61109	(779) 368-0852
163	11914812	KIPP Chicago	2007 S Halsted St, Chicago IL 60608	(312) 733-8108
164	12110447	Lawndale Educ & Reg Network	3021 W Carroll Ave, Chicago IL 60612	(773) 584-4399
165	11913545	Noble Network of Charter Sch	1 N State St Ste 700, Chicago IL 60602	(312) 521-5287
166	11913038	Perspectives Charter Schools	1530 S State St Ste 200, Chicago IL 60605	(312) 604-2200
167	12260016	Regeneration Schools	1816 W Garfield Blvd, Chicago IL 60609	(773) 778-9455
168	11913246	GEO Foundation	1630 N Meridian St Ste 350, Indianapolis IN 46202	(317) 536-1027
169	12315427	Goodwill Education Initiatives	1635 W Michigan St, Indianapolis IN 46222	(317) 524-4265
170	11916145	KIPP Indy Public Schools	1740 E 30th St, Indianapolis IN 46218	(317) 547-5477
171	12179027	Tindley Accelerated Schools	3960 Meadows Dr, Indianapolis IN 46205	(317) 545-1745
172	11913430	Algiers Charter School Assoc	2401 Westbend Pkwy Ste 2001, New Orleans LA 70114	(504) 302-7001
173	12115203	Collegiate Academies	2625 Thalia St, New Orleans LA 70113	(504) 503-0008
174	11930816	Crescent City Schools	3811 N Galvez St, New Orleans LA 70117	(504) 708-4136
175	11912369	Firstline Schools Inc	300 N Broad St Ste 207, New Orleans LA 70119	(504) 267-9038
176	11930725	Friends of King Schools	1617 Caffin Ave, New Orleans LA 70117	(504) 940-2243
177	12372592	Idea Public Schools S Louisana	804 Main St, Baton Rouge LA 70802	(225) 963-6539
178	12179039	Inspirenola Charter Schools	2401 Westbend Pkwy Ste 4040, New Orleans LA 70114	(504) 227-3057
179	12259213	Jcfa Charter Schools	475 Manhattan Blvd, Harvey LA 70058	(504) 410-3121
180	11916250	KIPP New Orleans Schools	1307 Oretha Castle Haley Blvd, New Orleans LA 70113	(504) 373-6269

CHARTER MANAGEMENT ORGANIZATION (CMO) INDEX

Market Data Retrieval

CMO No.	PID	CMO Name	Address	Phone
181	11912058	Renew Schools Inc	1001 Lake Forest Blvd Ste 710, New Orleans LA 70127	(504) 367-3307
182	11911913	The Choice Foundation	3201 Live Oak St, New Orleans LA 70118	(504) 861-8370
183	12110411	The Einstein Group Inc	5316 Michoud Blvd, New Orleans LA 70129	(504) 324-7450
184	11913296	Excel Academy	58 Moore St, East Boston MA 02128	(617) 874-4080
185	11916171	KIPP Massachusetts Chtr Schs	90 High Rock St, Lynn MA 01902	(781) 598-1609
186	12306086	The Community Group	190 Hampshire St Ste 2, Lawrence MA 01840	(978) 682-6628
187	12260004	Up Education Network	90 Canal St Ste 600, Boston MA 02114	(617) 307-5980
188	11913428	Baltimore Curriculum Project	2707 E Fayette St, Baltimore MD 21224	(410) 675-7000
189	11912577	City Neighbors Inc	4301 Raspe Ave, Baltimore MD 21206	(410) 325-2627
190	11914666	Connections Academy	10960 Grantchester Way Fl 3, Columbia MD 21044	(443) 529-1000
191	11916470	Imagine Mid-Atlantic Regional	4415 Nicole Dr Ste C, Lanham MD 20706	(301) 316-1802
192	11915830	KIPP Baltimore	2000 Edgewood St, Baltimore MD 21216	(410) 291-2583
193	11912228	Living Classrooms Foundation	802 S Caroline St, Baltimore MD 21231	(410) 685-0295
194	11914252	American Institutional Mgmt	5728 Schaefer Rd Ste 200, Dearborn MI 48126	(313) 624-2000
195	11914240	Bardwell Group	19800 Beech Daly Rd, Redford MI 48240	(313) 450-0642
196	11914501	Charter School Admin Services	20820 Greenfield Rd, Oak Park MI 48237	(248) 569-7787
197	11914484	Choice Schools Associates LLC	5251 Clyde Park Ave SW, Wyoming MI 49509	(616) 785-8440
198	11911858	Cornerstone Education Group	306 E 4th St, Royal Oak MI 48067	(248) 439-6228
199	11914642	CS Partners LLC	869 S Old US 23 Ste 500, Brighton MI 48114	(810) 229-5145
200	11914094	EdTec Central LLC	10 S Main St Ste 101, Mount Clemens MI 48043	(248) 582-8100
201	11914343	Education Enrichmnet Services	19236 W 11 Mile Rd, Lathrup Vlg MI 48076	(248) 905-5030
202	11914070	Education Management&Networks	27704 Franklin Rd, Southfield MI 48034	(248) 327-7673
203	11912345	Foundation for Behavioral Res	600 S Lincoln St, Augusta MI 49012	(269) 731-5796
204	11914446	Global Educational Excellence	2455 S Industrial Hwy Ste A, Ann Arbor MI 48104	(734) 369-9500
205	11914018	Hamadeh Educational Services	PO Box 1440, Dearborn MI 48121	(313) 565-0507
206	11913973	Innovative Teaching Solutions	18470 W 10 Mile Rd Ste 100, Southfield MI 48075	(248) 799-2780
207	11913961	Lakeshore Educl Management	12955 Robins Ridge Rd, Charlevoix MI 49720	(231) 547-4264
208	11916597	Leona Group LLC-Midwest	2125 University Park Dr, Okemos MI 48864	(517) 333-9030
209	11913935	MJ Management Services Inc	PO Box 1014, Flat Rock MI 48134	(734) 675-5505
210	11914575	National Heritage Academies	3850 Broadmoor Ave SE Ste 201, Grand Rapids MI 49512	(877) 223-6402
211	11913868	PrepNet LLC	3755 36th St SE Ste 250, Grand Rapids MI 49512	(616) 726-8900
212	12038734	Promise Schools	15000 Trojan St, Detroit MI 48235	(313) 964-2339
213	11914367	Romine Group LLC	7877 Stead St Ste 100, Utica MI 48317	(586) 731-5300
214	11913818	Solid Rock Management Company	3031 W Grand Blvd Ste 524, Detroit MI 48202	(313) 873-7625
215	11913753	Technical Academy Group LLC	4801 Oakman Blvd, Dearborn MI 48126	(313) 625-4700
216	11911793	Youth Visions Solutions	1450 25th St, Detroit MI 48216	(313) 558-9022
217	12262284	Harvest Network of Schools	1300 Olson Memorial Hwy, Minneapolis MN 55411	(612) 876-4105
218	12262301	Hiawatha Academies	1611 E 46th St, Minneapolis MN 55407	(612) 455-4004
219	12115033	KIPP Minnesota Public Schools	5034 Oliver Ave N, Minneapolis MN 55430	(612) 287-9700
220	12262387	MN Transitions Charter Schs	2872 26th Ave S, Minneapolis MN 55406	(612) 722-9013
221	11914355	Sabis Educational Systems	6385 Beach Rd, Eden Prairie MN 55344	(952) 918-1850
222	12261462	Confluence Academies	611 N 10th St Ste 525, Saint Louis MO 63101	(314) 588-8554
223	12115021	KIPP Kansas City	2700 E 18th St Ste 155B, Kansas City MO 64127	(816) 241-3994
224	11916303	KIPP St Louis Public Schools	1310 Papin St Ste 203, Saint Louis MO 63103	(314) 349-1388
225	12115019	KIPP Charlotte Public Schools	931 Wilann Dr, Charlotte NC 28215	(704) 537-2044
226	11916119	KIPP Enc College Prep Pub Schs	320 Pleasant Hill Rd, Gaston NC 27832	(252) 308-6932
227	12179431	Teamcfa	9935D Rea Rd Ste 167, Charlotte NC 28277	(704) 774-3038
228	12309351	The Roger Bacon Academy	3610 Thaddeus Lott Ln NE, Leland NC 28451	(910) 655-3600
229	12378924	Camden's Charter Sch Network	879 Beideman Ave, Camden NJ 08105	(856) 365-1000
230	12306593	College Achieve Ctl CS Network	365 Emerson Ave, Plainfield NJ 07062	(908) 625-1879
231	12110332	Ilearn Schools Inc	33-00 Broadway Ste 301, Fair Lawn NJ 07410	(201) 773-9140
232	11916327	KIPP New Jersey	60 Park Pl Ste 802, Newark NJ 07102	(973) 622-0905
233	11912694	Beginning with Children Fndn	217 Havemeyer St Ste 2, Brooklyn NY 11211	(212) 750-9320
234	11912644	Brighter Choice Charter Schs	250 Central Ave, Albany NY 12206	(518) 694-4100
235	11912498	Democracy Prep Public Schools	1767 Park Ave Fl 4, New York NY 10035	(212) 281-1248
236	12262894	Excellence Community Schools	2090 7th Ave Ste 605, New York NY 10027	(212) 222-5071
237	11912371	Explore Schools Inc	20 Jay St Ste 211, Brooklyn NY 11201	(718) 989-6730
238	12161604	Great Oaks Foundation	200 Broadway 3rd Fl, New York NY 10038	(917) 239-3641
239	11912292	Harlem Village Academies	15 Penn Plz Ste 15, New York NY 10001	(646) 812-9501
240	12370362	Hebrew Public Charter Schools	555 8th Ave Rm 1703, New York NY 10018	(212) 792-6234

CHARTER MANAGEMENT ORGANIZATION (CMO) INDEX

CMO No.	PID	CMO Name	Address	Phone
241	12114986	KIPP Albany Public Schools	321 Northern Blvd, Albany NY 12210	(518) 694-9494
242	11914824	KIPP NYC Public Schools	1501 Broadway Ste 1000, New York NY 10036	(212) 991-2610
243	12377906	New Visions Charter Network	205 E 42nd St Fl 4, New York NY 10017	(212) 645-5110
244	11912084	Public Prep Network Inc	192 E 151st St Frnt 1, Bronx NY 10451	(212) 346-6000
245	11912943	Success Academy Charter Schls	95 Pine St Fl 6, New York NY 10005	(646) 597-4641
246	11913478	Uncommon Schools	826 Broadway Fl 9, New York NY 10003	(212) 844-3584
247	11914563	Victory Education Partners	135 W 41st St Fl 5, New York NY 10036	(212) 786-7900
248	12179819	Accel Schools	4700 Rockside Rd Ste 345, Independence OH 44131	(216) 583-5230
249	11913416	Breakthrough Charter Schools	3615 Superior Ave E Ste 4403A, Cleveland OH 44114	(216) 456-2086
250	11912632	Buckeye on-Line School Success	119 E 5th St, E Liverpool OH 43920	(330) 385-1987
251	12106575	Carpe Diem Learning Systems	301 N Breiel Blvd Ste B, Middletown OH 45042	(513) 217-3400
252	11914654	Constellation Schools	5730 Broadview Rd, Parma OH 44134	(216) 712-7600
253	12378120	Educational Empowerment Group	1814 S Main St, Akron OH 44301	(330) 956-7203
254	12319069	Educational Solutions	1500 W 3rd Ave Ste 125, Columbus OH 43212	(614) 299-1007
255	11914460	Eschool Consultants	4480 Refugee Rd, Columbus OH 43232	(614) 322-7996
256	11916509	Imagine Ohio Regional	11518 Banning Rd, Mount Vernon OH 43050	(614) 930-1184
257	11916066	KIPP Columbus	2980 Inspire Dr, Columbus OH 43224	(614) 263-6137
258	11914393	Performance Academies LLC	2 Easton Oval Ste 525, Columbus OH 43219	(614) 512-2151
259	11913480	Summit Academy Management	2791 Mogadore Rd, Akron OH 44312	(330) 670-8470
260	12363034	United Schools Network	1469 E Main St, Columbus OH 43205	(614) 299-5284
261	12377803	Dove Public Charter Schools	9212 N Kelley Ave Ste 100, Oklahoma City OK 73131	(405) 605-0201
262	12305745	KIPP Okc Public Schools	PO Box 14128, Oklahoma City OK 73113	(405) 849-9700
263	12115069	KIPP Tulsa Public Charter Schs	1661 E Virgin St, Tulsa OK 74106	(918) 794-8652
264	12361452	Santa Fe South Public Schools	4825 S Shields Blvd, Oklahoma City OK 73129	(405) 601-5440
265	11913117	Mastery Lrng Inst-Arthur Acad	13717 SE Division St, Portland OR 97236	(503) 762-6061
266	12379045	Belmont Charter Network	1301 Belmont Ave, Philadelphia PA 19104	(215) 790-1294
267	11914185	Charter School Management Inc	419 Avenue of the States, Chester PA 19013	(610) 447-0200
268	11912448	EdSys Inc	201 Stanwix St Ste 100, Pittsburgh PA 15222	(412) 690-2489
269	11916274	KIPP Philadelphia Public Schs	5070 Parkside Ave Ste 3500D, Philadelphia PA 19131	(215) 294-8596
270	11913129	Mastery Charter Schools	5700 Wayne Ave, Philadelphia PA 19144	(215) 866-9000
271	11914408	Omnivest Properties Management	115 Pheasant Run Ste 210, Newtown PA 18940	(215) 497-8301
272	11913026	Propel Schools	3447 E Carson St Ste 200, Pittsburgh PA 15203	(412) 325-7305
273	11912888	Universal Companies Inc	800 S 15th St, Philadelphia PA 19146	(215) 732-6518
274	12312499	Charter Institute at Erskine	1201 Main St Ste 300, Columbia SC 29201	(803) 849-2464
275	12161719	Capstone Education Group	PO Box 22569, Memphis TN 38122	(901) 416-3640
276	11914628	Chancelight Behavioral Hlth-Ed	1321 Murfreesboro Pike Ste 702, Nashville TN 37217	(615) 361-4000
277	12377918	Compass Community Schools	61 N McLean Blvd, Memphis TN 38104	(901) 618-7422
278	12319629	Freedom Prep Academy Network	778 Parkrose Ave, Memphis TN 38109	(901) 881-1149
279	12038813	Gestalt Community Schools	2650 Thsnd Oaks Blvd Ste 1400, Memphis TN 38118	(901) 213-5161
280	12305850	Green Dot Pub Schs-Tennessee	4950 Fairley Rd, Memphis TN 38109	(901) 730-8160
281	12468725	Journey Community Schools LLC	802 Rozelle St, Memphis TN 38104	(901) 646-6530
282	11916200	KIPP Memphis Collegiate Schs	2670 Union Avenue Ext Ste 1100, Memphis TN 38112	(901) 452-2682
283	11916236	KIPP Nashville	123 Douglas Ave, Nashville TN 37207	(615) 226-4484
284	12038825	Lead Public Schools	2835 Brick Church Pike, Nashville TN 37207	(615) 815-1264
285	12110461	Republic Schools	3307 Brick Church Pike, Nashville TN 37207	(615) 921-6620
286	11911896	The Influence 1 Foundation	665 Madison Ave, Memphis TN 38103	(901) 526-1944
287	11912993	A Plus Charter Schools	8225 Bruton Rd, Dallas TX 75217	(214) 381-3226
288	12315738	Arrow Academy	PO Box 12207, College Sta TX 77842	(979) 703-8820
289	11913105	Baker-Ripley	PO Box 271389, Houston TX 77277	(713) 667-9400
290	11912618	Calvin Nelms Charter Schools	20625 Clay Rd, Katy TX 77449	(281) 398-8031
291	11912486	Democratic Schools Research	410 Bethel Ln, Bryan TX 77802	(979) 775-2152
292	11912450	East Waco Innovative Sch Dev	1020 Elm St Ste 100, Waco TX 76704	(254) 754-8000
293	11913325	Educational Leadership Inc	3333 Bering Dr Ste 200, Houston TX 77057	(713) 784-6345
294	12361414	Evolution Academy Charter Schs	1101 S Sherman St, Richardson TX 75081	(972) 907-3755
295	11913284	Faith Family Academy Chtr Schs	1608 Osprey Dr, Desoto TX 75115	(972) 224-4110
296	11912321	Golden Rule Schools Inc	2602 W Illinois Ave, Dallas TX 75233	(214) 333-9330
297	12160947	Great Hearts Texas	824 Broadway St Ste 101, San Antonio TX 78215	(210) 888-9475
298	11912307	Gulf Coast Council of La Raza	4129 Greenwood Dr, Corp Christi TX 78416	(361) 881-9988
299	11913624	Harmony Pub Schs-Cosmos Found	9321 W Sam Houston Pkwy S, Houston TX 77099	(713) 343-3333
300	12374772	Heritage Academy Inc	12470 Woman Hollering Rd, Schertz TX 78154	(210) 659-0329

CHARTER MANAGEMENT ORGANIZATION (CMO) INDEX

Market Data Retrieval

CMO No.	PID	CMO Name	Address	Phone
301	12371835	Idea Public Schools	2115 W Pike Blvd, Weslaco TX 78596	(956) 377-8000
302	12372554	Idea Public Schools Austin	2800 S Interstate 35 Ste 265, Austin TX 78704	(512) 822-4959
303	12372566	Idea Public Schools El Paso	813 N Kansas St Ste 100, El Paso TX 79902	(915) 201-1959
304	12372580	Idea Public Schools Tarrant	600 Bryan Ave Ste 220, Fort Worth TX 76104	(817) 885-4050
305	12372578	Idea Public Schs San Antonio	12500 San Pedro Ave Ste 500, San Antonio TX 78216	(210) 239-4250
306	11913193	Jubilee Academic Center Inc	4434 Roland Rd, San Antonio TX 78222	(210) 333-6227
307	11915828	KIPP Texas Public Schs Austin	8509 FM 969 Ste 513, Austin TX 78724	(512) 501-3643
308	11916080	KIPP Texas Public Schs Dallas	1545 S Ewing Ave, Dallas TX 75216	(972) 323-4200
309	11916133	KIPP Texas Public Schs Houston	10711 Kipp Way Dr, Houston TX 77099	(832) 328-1051
310	11916298	KIPP Texas Public Schs Sa	731 Fredericksburg Rd, San Antonio TX 78201	(210) 787-3197
311	11913131	Life School	132 E Ovilla Rd Ste 1A, Red Oak TX 75154	(469) 850-5433
312	11912163	New Frontiers Public Schools	138 Fair Ave, San Antonio TX 78223	(210) 519-3900
313	11913040	Orenda Education	2951 Williams Dr, Georgetown TX 78628	(512) 869-3020
314	11912137	Panola Charter Schools	PO Box 610, Carthage TX 75633	(903) 693-6355
315	11912096	Por Vida Inc	1135 Mission Rd, San Antonio TX 78210	(210) 532-8816
316	12113918	Priority Charter Schools	275 FM 2483, Morgans Point TX 76513	(254) 206-2013
317	11913014	Raul Yzaguirre Sch-Success Org	2950 Broadway St, Houston TX 77017	(713) 640-3700
318	12233855	Responsive Education Solutions	PO Box 292730, Lewisville TX 75029	(972) 316-3663
319	11913507	Richard Milburn Academy Inc	13003 Jones Maltsberger Rd, San Antonio TX 78247	(830) 557-6181
320	11913002	Riverwalk Education Foundation	5300 Wurzbach Rd Ste 800, San Antonio TX 78238	(210) 957-1955
321	11912981	Salvaging Teens at Risk Inc	4601 N Interstate 35, Denton TX 76207	(940) 383-6655
322	11911999	South Texas Educ Technologies	2402 E Business 83, Weslaco TX 78596	(956) 969-3092
323	11912967	Southwest Winners Foundation	1258 Austin Hwy, San Antonio TX 78209	(210) 829-8017
324	11912931	Tekoa Academy Accel Studies	327 Thomas Blvd, Port Arthur TX 77640	(409) 982-5400
325	11913674	Texans Can Academies	325 W 12th St, Dallas TX 75208	(214) 944-1985
326	11911937	Texas Center for Arts & Acad	3901 S Hulen St, Fort Worth TX 76109	(817) 766-2390
327	12378857	Trinity Basin Preparatory	2730 N State Highway 360, Grand Prairie TX 75050	(214) 946-9100
328	11912905	Trinity Charter Schools	8305 Cross Park Dr, Austin TX 78754	(512) 706-7564
329	11912955	Triumph Public High Schools	PO Box 15644, San Antonio TX 78212	(210) 227-0295
330	11911834	Two Dimensions Prep Chtr Acad	12121 Veterans Memorial Dr # 7, Houston TX 77067	(281) 227-4700
331	11913454	Uplift Education	1825 Market Ctr Blvd Ste 500, Dallas TX 75207	(469) 621-8500
332	11911810	Varnett Public School Inc	5025 S Willow Dr, Houston TX 77035	(713) 667-4051
333	11912876	Winfree Academy Charter Schs	1555 Valwood Pkwy Ste 160, Carrollton TX 75006	(972) 869-3250
334	11912864	YES Prep Public Schools	5515 South Loop E Ste B, Houston TX 77033	(713) 967-9000
335	11914616	Imagine Schools Inc	1900 Gallows Rd Ste 250, Vienna VA 22182	(703) 527-2600
336	11914604	K12 Inc	2300 Corporate Park Dr, Herndon VA 20171	(866) 283-0300
337	12305836	Green Dot Pub Schs-Washington	6020 Rainier Ave S, Seattle WA 98118	(206) 659-0956
338	12377786	Open Sky Education	20935 Swenson Dr Ste 101, Waukesha WI 53186	(262) 542-9546
339	12306000	Seeds of Health Inc	1445 S 32nd St, Milwaukee WI 53215	(414) 672-3430